American Musical Theatre

AMERICAN MUSICAL THEATRE

A Chronicle

FOURTH EDITION

GERALD BORDMAN

RICHARD NORTON

OXFORD
UNIVERSITY PRESS

OXFORD

UNIVERSITY PRESS

Oxford University Press, Inc., publishes works that further
Oxford University's objective of excellence
in research, scholarship, and education.

Oxford New York

Auckland   Cape Town   Dar es Salaam   Hong Kong   Karachi
Kuala Lumpur   Madrid   Melbourne   Mexico City   Nairobi
New Delhi   Shanghai   Taipei   Toronto

With offices in

Argentina   Austria   Brazil   Chile   Czech Republic   France   Greece
Guatemala   Hungary   Italy   Japan   Poland   Portugal   Singapore
South Korea   Switzerland   Thailand   Turkey   Ukraine   Vietnam

Copyright © 1978, 1986, 1992, 2001, 2011 by Oxford University Press, Inc.

First published in 1978 by Oxford University Press, Inc.
198 Madison Avenue, New York, New York 10016
www.oup.com

Expanded edition first published in 1986
as an Oxford University Press paperback, with corrections

Second edition first published in 1992
by Oxford University Press, Inc.

First published as a third edition in 2001
by Oxford University Press, Inc.

First published as a fourth edition in 2010
by Oxford University Press, Inc.

Oxford is a registered trademark of Oxford University Press

Library of Congress Cataloging-in-Publication Data
Bordman, Gerald Martin.
American musical theatre : a chronicle / Gerald Bordman, Richard Norton.—4th ed.
p. cm.
ISBN 978-0-19-972970-8
1. Musicals—United States—History and criticism. I. Norton, Richard, 1938–II. Title.
ML1711.B67   2011
782.1'40973—dc22   2010033708
Printed in the United States of America on acid-free paper

Contents

Foreword

THIS FOURTH EDITION brings Gerald Bordman's resourceful survey of American Musical Theatre to the close of the first decade of a new century. These are exciting times for American musical theatre, which continues to thrive and lead the world in creativity, variety and volume of new musicals produced. Whereas this volume is by necessity and definition New York-centric, musical theatre, in works both old and new, abounds in our schools, our small communities, on television and film, on computers or portable listening devices, in cars and homes, as well as in traditional stage venues.

As you review Gerry Bordman's text and my own concluding chapter, I would like to suggest several recurrent themes or trends that have only emerged with the benefit of hindsight and time. These ideas are not so much explicitly discussed, as they are reflected in the cumulative narrative.

First of all, musical theatre has now become truly global, thanks to the revolution in international travel, information technology, computers and the Internet. American musicals from *My Fair Lady* to *Hairspray* have been produced in dozens of different languages and countries. This was not always the case. In the nineteenth century, international success was principally limited to three Western European cultures: French, British and Austrian/German. France led the field with Offenbach and his peers, followed by Britain with Gilbert & Sullivan, then Germany with Strauss and Lehàr. The few American musicals that were exported typically failed, until, that is, *The Belle of New York* played in London in 1898. The two world wars severely inhibited the export of musical theatre, with a Balkanizing effect. The proliferation of *My Fair Lady* productions in Scandinavia, Russia, Israel and Japan in the 1960s expanded the potential territory for musical theatre. Only now have China and Korea begun producing American musicals with indigenous casts in local translation. It is now possible to book tickets to see *Rent* in Korea, *A Little Night Music* in Paris, *Baby* in the Philippines, *Sugar* in Bogotá and *Zorba* in Budapest.

Secondly, the role of film in relation to musical theatre has been radically redefined. Historically, following the introduction of sound in 1927, film musicals were regarded by the theatre industry as unwelcome, cheaper competition with the stage. Gradually, a symbiotic relationship evolved, whereby successful stage musicals discovered a second life on film, on which they could then play around the world and in smaller towns where stage musicals could not affordably be produced. Even lesser stage titles such as *Higher and Higher, Murder at the Vanities* or *Paint Your Wagon* are better remembered today because they were filmed, even if the films bore little semblance to the stage original. Arguably, the films of *Anna and the King of Siam* (1946) and *Pygmalion* (1938) were as instrumental in their stage musical adaptations as *The King and I* and *My Fair Lady* as were the original novel and play, respectively. Today, many a musical may be based on a successful non-musical film, then re-filmed as a musical, and perhaps even televised in a later incarnation. Indeed, stage revivals of *West Side Story, The Sound of Music* or *Grease* are often obligated to recreate the visual imagery of film or interpolate a song previously used only in a film version. Stage productions of *The Wizard of Oz, High Society,* and *Xanadu* often replicate the physical production choices, casting or vocal styles audiences expect from a film. Broadway now competes directly with film for spectacle, for intimacy and for recognizable name properties and song titles.

Thirdly, the first decade of the twenty-first century has witnessed a sad decline in the dominance of the well-crafted book musical with an original score composed for the theatre (setting aside musical theatre lions such as Stephen Sondheim, Harold Prince, and John Kander & Fred Ebb). The concomitant emergence of pop music, rock, and rhythm and blues as the dominant language of musical theatre is now undisputed. Apart from Off-Broadway and *The 101 Dalmatians Musical,* the 2009–2010 Broadway season included only two musicals with original scores composed for the theatre, *The Addams Family* and *Memphis.* However welcome the latter is as a new work, its explicit intent was to sound derivative of familiar rhythm and blues of the mid-1950s, songs you *might* have heard or *think* you could have heard on the jukebox of that era. Whether it is *Fela!*'s Afrobeat, *Come Fly Away*'s Sinatra sound, *Million Dollar Quartet*'s glimpse of early rock 'n' roll, or *American Idiot*'s contemporary punk rock sound from the band Green Day, it is increasingly likely that new musicals will be assembled from preexisting music. Producers minimize risk by giving audiences music they know; theatergoers are less interested in or perhaps less willing to absorb new and unfamiliar music. (The welcome effect of popular music's dominance of contemporary musical theatre is its ability to attract a younger audience.) And yet, a review of Bordman's early text shows that this is not nearly as recent of a phenomenon as it sounds. Ragtime, jazz and African-American music's invasion of Broadway in the early twentieth century was controversial in its day, yet ultimately won widespread acceptance. Musical theatre will always reflect each generation's evolving taste in popular music; so be it!

Lastly, once upon a time new musicals were tested or tried out in Boston, Philadelphia, Chicago, Los Angeles and other cities with loyal subscription audiences; their creators honed, pruned, cut and pasted musicals in front of working audiences, with the help of local critics. As that tryout system faded in the 1960s and 1970s for economic reasons, Michael Bennett perfected the workshop as a creative tool for new musicals with *A Chorus Line.* A less common device has been the concept album, whereby the score of *Jesus Christ Superstar, Evita, Tommy* or *American Idiot* is put up on the stage. In the last two decades, a number of alternative incubators have emerged for the development of new musicals. Regional theatres, once merely dependent upon Broadway for product, now hire resident dramaturges, host writing competitions, and recruit co-production sponsors, all with an eye to the creation of new work. Institutions such as NYMF (New York Musical Theatre Festival) and NAMT (National Alliance for Musical Theatre) are but two of many organizations with such a purpose. Lest you think from the preceding paragraph that living composers are obsolete or in eclipse, NYMF and NAMT actively endorse the creation of new work expressly written for the theatre by new bookwriters, composers and lyricists.

Let us also welcome, and not dismiss, the emergence of television's *High School Musical* in its many editions, and now the series *Glee,* which are portals to musical theatre for a younger generation. Some musical theatre enthusiasts and critics may be tempted to sneer, but the significance of attracting a new generation to musical theatre is hugely important if we are to develop new audiences, actors, writers and directors who may otherwise be drawn to film, YouTube, rock concerts, computer games, iPhones, and whatever new entertainment formats are yet to be discovered.

In closing, I would like to thank Gerald Bordman for the opportunity to continue his musical theatre history chronicle into a new century. I deeply appreciated the help and wise counsel from Grace Labatt and Brian Black at Oxford University Press, and express my deepest thanks to my friends and colleagues who have advised me, Ken Bloom, Darrel Karl, Jeffrey Dunn, Gary Schocker, Dominic McHugh, Ron Spivak and Brad Bennett.

Richard C. Norton
New York City
June 2010

Preface to the Fourth Edition

WHEN MY RENOWNED, now deceased, editor, Sheldon Meyer, and I finished the third edition of this book, we both fretted over who would be responsible for the next update a decade onward. The two of us immediately lit upon Richard Norton. Happily, Richard was able and willing. Perhaps I should say doubly happily, because I would not have been pleased to write about these last ten seasons. Richard and I, at various times, have griped about directors, choreographers, and others who seem more interested in spotlighting their own contributions than in making them blend in to achieve a unified whole. Far worse, what has happened to the music? As I've pointed out elsewhere, we do not call these entertainments "librettals," "lyricals," or "choreographals"; we call them "musicals." In the genre's heyday, when New York welcomed as many as fifty new musical comedies, operettas, and revues a year, Broadway always presented playgoers with four or five superior song-and-dance shows, *each* boasting three or four enduring melodies, sometimes more! I personally doubt if the shows itemized from the last decade will give us half a dozen such tunes altogether. And then there are the horrors of miking and amplification, which destroy the timbre of the human voice and its sense of direction.

At the same time, complaints should not be taken too seriously. They are frequently merely generational. Thus, readers are fortunate that Richard is nearly a generation younger than I. His broad, deep knowledge allows him to take a far more contemporary perspective on matters, albeit, as you'll read, not necessarily a more contented one. But readers must keep in mind the generational differences. I remember clearly how discouraged my parents and their peers were by the more pretentious mountings of the forties, fifties, and sixties. They looked back longingly on the low-minded fun of the high-kicking hits of the twenties. Even Cole Porter professed to rate the Rodgers of Rodgers and Hart above the Rodgers of Rodgers and Hammerstein. Porter may not have been totally straight-faced when he extolled Rodgers's light-hearted musical comedy ditties while dismissing his more solemn tunes for Hammerstein's "musical plays" as hymns. Hammerstein himself viciously bashed his own operettas of twenty years before in order to promote his later pretentious "musical plays."

So we can never really know what succeeding generations will think of what we like and dislike. All we can do is try to find joy across the footlights and hope that producers and authors will create more of what we do relish.

With that, I wish you goodbye and happy musical-theatre-going.

Gerald Bordman
Bala Cynwyd, Pa.
June 2010

Preface to the First Edition

I had long been aware of the need for a thorough, accurate history of the American Musical Theatre. Fine students of the field, notably Stanley Green, have published excellent works covering selected areas, but there has been no truly comprehensive work. I also became aware that young people in particular seemed unaware of the great songwriters who made those old musicals so memorable, not only someone like Vincent Youmans but even, I found to my horror, Jerome Kern!

Since there is no sense in doing things by halves, I decided to start with the first musical done in America and cover everything up to the moment the printer required the last page of typescript. So many early texts are lost, and the coverage of plays in those early years often so scant, that the seasons before 1866 are best covered in a summary—a summary that nevertheless offers a number of extended discussions and extracts from the more important or interesting musicals of the epoch.

In considering the whole range of the American Musical Theatre, these early years can be viewed as a prologue to the five great acts, four intermissions, and an epilogue that follow. Accordingly, this book has been divided into eleven chapters. The second chapter—or Act I—begins with *The Black Crook*. From there on, the book moves season by season, show by show, to cover every musical done on Broadway. Because Boston, Philadelphia, Chicago, and other cities were active in producing their own shows before World War I, the spotlight occasionally swings to light up their efforts. This is particularly true of the lively, underrated Chicago musical theatre that flourished from the turn of the century until 1914. Because three of the five acts are so long, these three have been divided into two "scenes." The division point in Act I is obvious and natural, but in Acts IV and V the choice was admittedly arbitrary. Where an opening date and theatre are not mentioned in the text they appear in parentheses directly after the show's title. When a show is mentioned later, in passing, its original opening date is provided. Similarly, in the case of revivals, when the revival date is mentioned in the text, the original opening date but not the theatre will be found immediately after the title. With a few exceptions, original opening dates are omitted from all but the first mention of importations. Speaking of importations, Continental readers may be taken aback on reading some of the plot synopses. The story outlines given in this book are those employed for the American production and in a few instances bear only the most remote resemblance to the originals. I have excluded shows that opened out of town and then closed before their anticipated Broadway openings, as there was no way to obtain accurate information on many of these shows.

Just as opening dates and theatres are given after tides, in plot synopses performers' names appear in parentheses after characters they portrayed. A number of performers changed the spelling of their names at some time during their careers, and as a rule I have employed only the best-known spelling. Thus Miss Brice will always be Fanny, and Miss Miller, Marilyn. Programs and reviews are maddeningly inconsistent in the case of a few minor names. Just how did Henry Leone, or Henri Leone, or Henry Leoni, or Henri Leoni spell his name?

Although I have recorded as many dates and names as possible, a complete listing of all statistics for every show would have doubled or tripled the length of this book. As a result, a companion volume, listing every vital fact and figure, is projected under different authorship some years from now. Readers anxious to know the names of authors not mentioned here, or who designed the shoes or served as stage manager for any show, will find the answers in that volume.

A few minor points:

Rather than burden this book with the scholarly *sic*, typographical errors have been corrected. Similarly, to avoid a plethora of quotation marks, critical comments culled from reviews have been incorporated into the text. For example, if a score is labeled mediocre or a production called lively the adjective was almost always picked from a notice to represent a consensus of the major critics.

Since few readers will want to read this book from beginning to end, but will rather "dip into" it, we have, in a handful of instances, repeated some important or interesting points.

We apologize for a few omissions. Nowhere could we find satisfactory biographical material for two major figures, William Gill and Richard Barker. In Barker's case even his alma mater, D'Oyly Carte, was unable to unearth suitable dates and background for us. And somehow, despite inquiries to all major theatre collections, not a note of music from *Adonis*, the first musical to run over 500 performances in New York, has surfaced. Nor has a copy of the libretto. But the saddest omissions of all were some 500 examples of music and lyrics we had hoped to include. Most of these were under copyright, and the cost of permissions would have inflated the price of the book beyond reason.

Among the twenty-two libraries and theatre collections consulted, special thanks must go to three. Hobart Berolzheimer, head of the Literature Department at the Free Library of Philadelphia; Mrs. Geri Duclow, librarian of its theatre collection, and her assistant, Mrs. Elaine Ebo, offered invaluable help. Manny Kean of the Kean Archives in Philadelphia provided constant and much needed advice and sheet music. Last, but certainly not least, was the professional aid provided by Paul Myers and his large, knowledgeable staff at the Theatre Collection, Library and Museum of the Performing Arts at Lincoln Center, a division of the New York Public Library. Among my many friends and associates who offered their personal assistance, particular thanks must go to Dr. Kenneth Goldstein and Stuart Tipton Cooke. To the many names unmentioned, please know you are neither unremembered nor unappreciated.

Gerald Bordman
Yellow Wood Farm
Kirk's Mills, Pa.
June 1978

Prologue

Origins to 1866

Music and drama have gone hand in hand from the beginning. Ancient Greeks and Romans sang or, at least, intoned much of their theatre. The medieval mystery plays' doggerel was often recited to an accompaniment of fife and tambour. By Elizabethan times songs in comedy, if not in tragedy, were commonplace. Shakespeare's lyrics remain familiar even if the poet might not recognize any melodies that now accompany his words. In the late 1600s Italy heard the first serious attempts to set an entire theatrical tale to music. With time these operas became the supreme achievement of the lyric stage. As the seventeenth century gave way to the eighteenth a rage for ballad operas struck England. These were dramas and comedies in which the plot was developed in dialogue rather than in recitative and in which songs were interspersed to underline the play's sentiments. In many instances melodies for these songs were not created for the entertainment but borrowed from popular airs by the librettist-lyricist, a borrowing openly acknowledged. There were, however, some original composers such as Charles Dibdin (who wrote his own librettos), Michael Arne, and William Shields who earned contemporary acclaim for their melodic efforts.

Since the rise of ballad opera coincided with the primitive beginnings of theatre in America, the first bit of musical theatre performed in the colonies was, not surprisingly, one of that genre. O. G. Sonneck, compiler of several scholarly catalogs of early American stage musicals, believed an English performer named Tony Ashton may have imported the first London ballad opera to Charleston as early as 1703. But Sonneck readily admitted to the absence of proof. Nonetheless, the first recorded performance of such a musical was in Charleston—thirty-two years later. On 8 February 1735, an advertisement in the *South Carolina Gazette* read, "On Tuesday the 18th inst. will be presented at the Courtroom the opera 'Flora, or Hob in the Well' with the Dance of the two Pierrots, and a new Pantomime entertainment, called the adventures of Harlequin Scaramouch... ."

By 1753, when Mr. and Mrs. Lewis Hallam established New York's first permanent playhouse—the New Theatre in Nassau Street—their troupe was prepared to offer not only *Flora* and the most enduring of ballad operas, John Gay's *The Beggar's Opera*, but such full-length or shorter works as *Devil to Pay*, *Damon and Phillida*, and *Virginia Unmasked*, as well as a number of harlequinades. The shorter musicals generally served as afterpieces for major mountings of now forgotten or neglected works on the order of Baker's *Tunbridge Walks*, Otway's *Venice Preserved*, and Farquhar's *The Constant Couple*. Of course they also followed performances of evergreens such as *The Beaux Stratagem* and *Romeo and Juliet* (the latter performed in David Garrick's revised version).

What was apparently our first native musical work—it advertised itself as "a new Comic Opera"—was entitled, with bittersweet appropriateness, **The Disappointment**. Announcements of its imminent premiere began to appear in Philadelphia newspapers on 6 April 1767. These notices promised local theatregoers that on 20 April the American Company—a band of traveling players who also entertained in New York and as far south as Charleston—would present the novelty at the New Theatre in Southwark (generally called simply the Southwark Theatre). But something went wrong. On 16 April a curt statement informed Philadelphians that *The Disappointment* "as it contains personal reflections, is unfit for the stage" and was being withdrawn from rehearsal. Sonneck surmises, "Evidently the parties reflected had brought pressure to bear on Mr. Douglass [head of the American Company] who could not afford to lose the good will of influential people in a city where the opposition against the theatre just then was very strong." Who the injured parties were will probably never be known. Certainly the text gives no obvious clues. Nor does it really matter, for the work, with all its faults, is adequate enough on its own. In the common practice of the time the offering had a subtitle, *The Force of Credulity*. Either name gave a reasonable hint of the plot. The curious were able to learn details of the story quickly, for in the same week that the piece was originally scheduled for production in Philadelphia the text was published in New York.

As readers discovered, *The Disappointment* had a simple plot and an even more elementary subplot. Three practical jokers—Hum, Parchment, and Quadrant—decide to gull Raccoon, "an old Debauchee," whose cowardice is exceeded only by his greed. Their plan is to allow a fraudulent letter

(purporting to reveal the location of a hidden treasure chest) to fall into the hands of Raccoon and his friends, Washball, Trushoop, and M'Snip. To make their efforts more credible the conspirators enlist the aid of Rattletrap, whom they set to "poring over the canto of Hudibras and Sydrophel in order to furnish himself with a set of hard words, which added to his knowledge in the mathematics, will sufficiently gratify him for a modern conjurer." Raccoon falls for the ruse, although in his joy he proves not as totally selfish as his teasers imagined. "Dis will make me cut de figure in life," he remarks, "and appear in de worl de proper importance; and den I'll do something for my poor ting." His "poor ting" is Moll Placket. He reiterates his promise directly to her, taking his oath to the tune of "Yankee Doodle":

> O! how joyful shall I be
> When I get de money
> I will bring it all to dee;
> O! my diddling honey!

With the "help" of Rattletrap the dupes retrieve the chest. Their joy is short-lived. Carrying it home and opening it, they find it filled with stones and recognize the trick that has been played on them. The subplot has Washball's niece, Lucy reject her uncle's offer of a substantial dowry to marry the man of his choice. She elopes with her true love, Meanwell. To express their feelings the lovers also put new lyrics to old airs. The text suggests an obviously familiar tune, which it lists solely as "My fond Shepherds etc," to furnish the melody as the young couple plight their troth:

> My dear Lucy, you ravish my heart,
> I am blest with such language as this.
> To my arms then, oh, come, we'll ne'er part
> And let's mutually seal with a kiss.

The play ends not with the humiliation of Raccoon and his friends but with Washball's acceptance of his niece's husband and with the wedding feast he provides.

Throughout the piece there are elementary but valid attempts to give characters some individuality. For example, Trushoop speaks with an Irish accent unique to him—"before" becoming "bafare"; "leave" becoming "laave"; and the "s" sound in "place" and "bliss" becoming "plashe" and "blish." Raccoon, despite his name and what a twentieth-century reader would take for a Negro accent, was seen by contemporaries as speaking English as a Frenchman might. (Shakespeare employed a similar speech for his French ladies in *Henry V*—"Oui, dat de tongues of de mans is be full of deceits.") Musically, the piece was perhaps less sophisticated. As Sonneck notes, "attempts at ensembles and choruses are exceedingly few and feeble. To improvise or to write 'accompaniments' for the 'Disappointment' cannot have been a very interesting task and we hardly regret not to know the name of the musician whose duty it was to do so." Sonneck adds that there are "only eighteen" ballads used in the work, but "the introduction of 'Yankee Doodle' is especially noteworthy, being probably the earliest reference to the tune in American literature." If the composer—or, more likely, the conductor—who was to tie together the music remains unknown, the author of the libretto and lyrics can be identified. Both the first and second editions of the musical listed his name as Andrew Barton. Scholars have questioned that attribution, crediting the work instead either to one Colonel Thomas Forrest of Germantown (an area now part of Philadelphia but then a separate village) or to John Leacock, a Philadelphia coroner. Since none of these names reappears in the history of the American Musical Theatre the matter can be dismissed as academic.

By way of a footnote, four nights after *The Disappointment* was scheduled for production, the American Company did raise the curtain on an event of historical importance. Perhaps as compensation for the earlier cancellation, the troupe mounted Thomas Godfrey's *The Prince of Parthia*, the first play written by an American to be performed professionally.

If *The Disappointment* clearly represents an American endeavor at native ballad opera, its calling itself a comic opera initiates a confusion of nomenclature that will plague our musical stage throughout its history. Only in retrospect can some of the "name-calling" be rectified, and only in retrospect could it be seen that this vernacular ballad opera deserves to be considered one of the precursors of musical comedy.

The next native work did not appear until fourteen years and one revolution later. It too served as a forerunner, but of a different genre—the spectacle or extravaganza. Francis Hopkinson called his work **The Temple of Minerva** and described it as an "oratorical entertainment." It was not a full-blown work, being given merely as part of a concert offered in Philadelphia on 11 December 1781 by the French minister in honor of George Washington. In two scenes it told how the Goddess Minerva and her High Priest unite the Genius of France and the Genius of America. Promising perpetual alliance, they end by singing a paean to General Washington. Patently descended from the masques of a century before, the form evolved in the century ahead into the set pieces and transformations for the lavish mountings of the *Black Crook* (12 September 1866) era, and in the first quarter or so of the twentieth century became the tableaux of Ziegfeldian revues. If Hopkinson's music was not borrowed, as some contend, then it may be virtually our earliest original theatre work.

There was an inkling of another great tradition of our lyric stage when **The Blockheads; or, The Fortunate Contractor** was published the next year, 1782. Its publisher called it "An opera in two acts" and claimed it was printed "As it was performed at New York." No record of any performance survives. But the text is a travesty of *The Blockade of Boston*, which General Burgoyne wrote and had performed while he occupied that city. Burlesque had come early to American boards, even though its heyday was a hundred years or more away.

On 16 April 1787 Royall Tyler became the first American to have a comedy of his own produced for American audiences. *The Contrast* was first unveiled at the John Street Theatre in New York and soon performed in Baltimore, Philadelphia, and Boston. While indisputably a straight play, it bowed to conventions of the day by including at least two songs. Early in the first act the heroine, Maria, is discovered singing a plaintive tune whose lyrics have nothing to do with the story:

The sun sets in night, and the stars shun the day;
But glory remains when their lights fade away!
Begin, ye tormentors! your threats are in vain,
For the son of Alknomook shall never complain.

In the third act, the principal comic figure, the bumptious Jonathan, following in Raccoon's footsteps, offers new lyrics to "Yankee Doodle."

The success of *The Contrast* undoubtedly led to the mounting a month later of a second Tyler work, **May Day in Town; or, New York in an Uproar.** Advertisements in New York papers announced a "comic opera in 2 acts ... . The Music compiled from the most eminent Masters. With an Overture and Accompanyments." The play was a one-performance failure. Never published, the text is lost. Nor do we know who the eminent masters might be. George O. Seilhamer, a nineteenth-century student of our stage, suggests it was "a skit on ... the much dreaded May-movings."

Three years elapsed before another domestic musical work was announced. Like *The Disappointment*, Peter Markoe's "comic opera" in two acts, **The Reconciliation; or, The Triumph of Nature** was slated to be produced in Philadelphia by the peripatetic American Company and then abruptly discarded. The reasons for the change of heart were never made known, although a reading of the work and a published critique of the period suggest the piece may have proved too stilted for even so formal an age as the eighteenth century. But the musical is interesting on several counts. First, it pioneered, at least in domestic creations, the practice of making a lyrical evening from a straight play. In this instance, Markoe chose a translation of a short German play, *Erastus*. He turned it into a full evening's entertainment by increasing the dialogue and interspersing a fair number of songs. The story, like the story of *The Disappointment*, was simple, and this time devoid of any subplot. When young Wilson makes a marriage displeasing to his father, the older man disinherits his son. For twelve years Wilson and his wife live in poverty, although somehow retaining the wherewithal to keep two servants. The elder Wilson becomes ill and, seeing death approaching, realizes how unjustly he behaved. He sets out to find his son but while seeking him is robbed of half his money. The thief turns out to be the son's servant, Simon, desperately attempting to keep his master from starving. A reconciliation follows. Perhaps more interesting is the untitled song which has survived and which offers both some idea of popular stage music of the time and an even better idea of why the text was considered "less fit for the stage than for the closet."

The year 1793 witnessed the production of two works by Raynor Taylor. Taylor was an Englishman who emigrated to America and had become an important figure on the musical scene by the turn of the century. He was instrumental in founding the Musical Fund Society in Philadelphia. His biographer notes, "As a speciality he cultivated burlesque olios or 'extravaganzas' which came dangerously near being music hall skits. He strikingly illustrates the fact that the American public of the 18th century was not horrified by secular tendencies in an organist, outside of the church walls." His 1793 efforts

included the "Mock Italian Opera, called Capocchio and Dorinna... Dressed in Character... Consisting of Recitative Airs and Duets... the whole of the music original and composed by Mr. Taylor," which was announced for presentation in Annapolis on 20 January, and his "comic burletta" **Old Woman of Eighty Three**, which was performed at the same city on 28 February. Regrettably, like much of this early music, few of Taylor's secular theatre pieces seem to have survived.

Needs Must; or, The Ballad Singers raised its curtain at the end of the same year, on 23 December. The celebrated actress Mrs. Pownall wrote the "trifle" as a vehicle for herself while she was bedridden with a broken leg. She turned to Anne Julia Hatton, a sister of Mrs. Siddons, for lyrics and some of the music.

Just over two months later Mrs. Hatton served as the librettist and lyricist for a more ambitious enterprise, when the John Street Theatre offered its public the first performance of **Tammany; or, The Indian Chief** on 3 March 1794. Mrs. Hatton's motives were not entirely artistic. By glorifying Tammany she helped promote the Tammany Society and the Antifederalist cause. Mrs. Hatton's collaborator was James Hewitt, a violinist, composer, and ultimately a highly successful music publisher. Again the plot was simple. Tammany (John Hodgkinson) loves Manana (Mrs. Hodgkinson). But the villainous Ferdinand (John Martin) abducts her. When Tammany rescues the girl, the Spaniards return and burn the two of them to death in their cabin. Some comic relief was provided by another Indian, Wegaw (W H. Prigmore). The fundamentally tragic nature of the work places it on the fringe of popular musical theatre. But it must be remembered that tragic opera had a much more general vogue in the eighteenth and nineteenth centuries than in recent years. If a few of Mrs. Hatton's lyrics had a familiar ring, there is no reason to condemn the lady. The premium the romantic era set on originality had yet to become pervasive:

> *The sun sets in night and the stars shun the day*
> *But glory unfading can never decay,*
> *You white men deceivers your smiles are in vain;*
> *The son of Alkmoonac shall ne'er wear your chain.*

With something approaching scholastic integrity, Mrs. Hatton noted this duet between Tammany and Manana was "Altered from the old Indian Song," a point Royall Tyler apparently assumed his readers took for granted when he published *The Contrast*. On her own, Mrs. Hatton was not a bad lyricist, given the traditions of the epoch. For example, Ferdinand sings:

Fury swells my aching soul,
Boils and maddens in my veins;
Fierce contending passions roll
Where Manana's image reigns.

The lines throb with life if not with poetry. How well Hewitt's music coupled with the words can only be guessed. Although many of his compositions survive, little from *Tammany* has surfaced. But if most sounds of *Tammany* are silenced forever, the mind's eye can still form a tentative picture of how the production looked to 1794 audiences, for William Dunlap left a sketchy description of the mounting in his *History of the American Theatre*. His point was that *Tammany's* scenery marked a small breakthrough in set design. Until its opening, New York sets had been culled from tired "old stock [that was] originally of the lowest grade, and had become black with age." (Dunlap records that Philadelphia scenery of the period was far superior.) Charles Ciceri, a young man who in time became New York's best scene painter and machinist, apparently made his debut with his designs for *Tammany*. Dunlap noted, "They were gaudy and unnatural, but had a brilliancy of colouring, reds and yellows being abundant." Even at this early date musicals were a feast for the eye.

The Sicilian Romance, which was offered to Philadelphians in 1795 and to New Yorkers a year later, exemplifies still another practice which would become distressingly common with time. A London success, its William Reeves score was largely jettisoned and more "American" music by its coproducer Alexander Reinagle interpolated. Reinagle's score, like Hewitt's, is apparently lost.

No work of the American Musical Theatre before *The Black Crook* (12 September 1866) has received more attention than **The Archers.** Numerous scholars have devoted extensive space to it, and Julian Mates has made it the center of his full-length study of the lyric stage of the time. Neither its quality nor its success justifies the disproportionate attention it has received. In fact, its quality is minimal. *The Archers* is competent hackwork, little more. Nor was its success exceptional. Only five performances— three in New York and two in Boston—are definitely known to have taken place, although students

surmise from various hints that another half-dozen or so representations were given in various cities.

The attention *The Archers* has won can be attributed largely to William Dunlap, who supplied both dialogue and lyrics.

> **WILLIAM DUNLAP** has long been known as "the Father of the American Stage." Born at Perth Amboy, New Jersey, on 19 February 1766, he abandoned his New York City china shop at the age of thirty and purchased a substantial interest in the old American Company. He held the position of manager until bankruptcy forced him to resign in 1805. He retired to indulge his second love, painting. Dunlap had been a pupil of Benjamin West and become a founder and vice president of the National Academy of Design. He returned to the theatre briefly in 1827. During his two theatrical stints he wrote or translated more than fifty plays. A dozen of his translations helped make August von Kotzebue almost as well known in America as he was in Germany. His other talents notwithstanding, Dunlap's major achievement may well have been his *History of the American Theatre*, published in 1832, seven years before his death.

The Archers was one of Dunlap's earliest efforts. It betrays not only something of his inexperience but also the general level of uninspired professionalism which he was never to rise above. Dunlap chose the William Tell legend as the basis for his plot. The story of Tell's struggle for Swiss freedom had great appeal for playgoers in a newly liberated land. Two years earlier, in 1794, Hewitt had composed an overture and song for another version, now lost, called *The Patriot; or, Liberty Asserted*. Dunlap's prologue proclaimed, "We tell a tale of Liberty tonight." The tale is set in Altdorf, Switzerland. Cecily (Mrs. Hodgkinson), a basket seller, enters, singing of her wares. She is followed by her sweetheart, Conrad (Lewis Hallam), who appears leading his jackass. Conrad is also a street vendor, and he, too, sings of his trade:

Here are bowls by the dozen, and spoons by the gross,
And a ladle or two in the bargain I'll toss.

But the Austrians are impressing young Swiss men into service, and a lieutenant (Joseph Jefferson, grandfather of his more famous namesake) arrives and orders Conrad seized. After a trio in which Conrad and Cecily bemoan their lot while the lieutenant sings a cynical rationale, the scene changes to Tell's home. Tell (John Hodgkinson), too, is unhappy. But his sorrow is for his whole nation. Unlike the comic pair Tell is prompted to action. He tells his wife (Mrs. Melmoth) and his young son (played as a trouser role by an ingenue, Miss Harding):

How glorious 'tis in spite of time
In spite of death, to live sublime.

By the Lake of Uri leaders of various groups of Swiss Archers meet and exhort their men. These leaders include Werner Staffach (Hallam Jr.), Walter Furst (John Johnson), and Arnold Melchthal (Joseph Tyler). Furst's daughter, Rhodolpha (Miss Broadhurst), enters. She is dressed as a huntress and surrounded by young ladies. (Did her huntresses parade in a manner later generations called an "Amazon march"?) She begs to be allowed to fight alongside the men, and her request is granted. Her motive is not entirely patriotic, for she is in love with Melchthal. The second act begins in front of the castle at Altdorf. The tyrannical Gesler (Mr. Cleveland) has ordered all the townspeople to kneel before his hat, which he has raised to the top of a pole. When Rhodolpha catches a pusillanimous burgher bowing to Gesler's orders, she makes the embarrassed villager kneel to her and to liberty instead. At a town meeting Tell exhorts the citizenry much as he had earlier incited his wife and son to action. Gesler orders Tell's execution and is deaf to the pleas of Tell's wife. Only news of the emperor's death and the uncertainty of what will follow induce the tyrant to alter his edict. Tell will be spared if he can shoot an apple off his son's head. Tell succeeds, but the treacherous Gesler fails to keep his word. Tell and his guards embark in a boat with Gesler to cross the lake. A storm churns the waters, and only Tell is able to bring the boat to safety. Jumping ashore he grabs his bow, shoots and kills Gesler, and escapes into the woods. Returned to his men, he leads the Swiss forces against Austria. In their joy, the lovers, Rhodolpha and Melchthal, sing not of their own passions but of their admiration for their leader:

Where none are lords, and none are slaves,
There look to find a Tell.

BENJAMIN CARR was an Englishman who followed in the footsteps of Hewitt, Taylor, and Reinagle, emigrating to America in 1793. Moving to Philadelphia he became an organist, composer, concert manager, and publisher. He joined Taylor in helping to found the Musical Fund Society, which long remained the prime lyric organization in Philadelphia.

The Swiss triumph. The principals join in a concerted finale extolling the virtues and rewards of bravery and liberty. Only Cecily, given practically the last word, thinks in more immediate terms:

Now war is o'er, and Conrad mine
I'll make baskets neat and fine.

The chorus ends the work by repeating the sentiments Tell had expressed moments before:

When heaven pours blessings all around
O! May mankind be grateful found.

Although publication has permitted Dunlap's text to survive, Benjamin Carr's score for the piece, like so much of this earlier music, is largely lost. Of the little that remains the best is the song Melchthal sings to Rhodolpha on learning of her determination to join the soldiers, "Why Huntress Why?"

In The American Musical Stage Before 1800 Mates suggests Charles Ciceri may have designed the sets for the mounting. If, as seems likely, his surmise is correct, it would be worth noting how Ciceri's art had matured since his work on Tammany. Edwin Duerr, in an article on Ciceri in Theatre Arts Monthly (December 1932), records, "Ciceri, and his aides, often made use of the new transparent scenery, perfected in England by de Loutherbourg in 1780. From him, also, they had learned to build up their stages with scaffolding or carpentry for such elaborate spectacles that required practicable stairways, doors, windows, mountain passes, bridges, Gothic halls, and mountain torrents. The New Yorkers probably experimented with dioramic, or moving scenery; and perhaps Dunlap and Ciceri knew side walls on their stage." Mates adds, "Ciceri also utilized artificial figures and was facile in the use of stage transformations." How many of his new skills Ciceri applied to The Archers is not known. But if tables and chairs were no longer painted on flats, for the most part scenery was still rarely architecturally conceived; flats, wings, flies, and drop curtains predominated. The Archers was first performed at the John Street Theatre on 18 April 1796, when it was advertised as "a new Dramatic Piece," but in his own history and in the published text Dunlap called the work "an opera." This was another early instance of the looseness with which musical works would be stamped throughout the history of the American Musical Theatre.

A one-performance failure of the same year was **Edwin and Angelina,** a musical version of the ballad found in Goldsmith's The Vicar of Wakefield. The libretto was by Elihu Hubbard Smith, a young doctor who died some months later of yellow fever at the age of twenty-seven. The music was by Victor Pelissier, who, with Hewitt, was long a composer and arranger for the old American Company. Slightly simplified, the plot details how the wicked Earl Ethelbert (John Martin) drives his erstwhile friend Sifrid (John Hodgkinson) into outlawry and causes Edwin (Joseph Tyler) to become a hermit. In the end both men are reunited with their loved ones: Sifrid with Emma (who never appears in the work), and Edwin with Angelina (Mrs. Hodgkinson). Ethelbert reforms. And so, grudgingly, does Sifrid's band.

Sonneck writes, "In 1797 a form of operatic entertainment was introduced in New York for which I believe the Americans to be peculiarly gifted: the melodrama." These were exaggerated and overwrought stories played out to a musical accompaniment. For the most part they were no more lyric theatre than the films and television programs of our own era that employ musical backgrounds, although a few slowly evolved into the spectacles so popular in the late nineteenth century. Surely the example Sonneck proffers as initiating the reign of melodrama does not fall legitimately into our field. The advertisement for Ariadne Abandoned by Theseus, in the Isle of Naxos called the work "a piece, in one act," adding, "Between the different passages spoken by the actors, will be Full Orchestra Music, expressive of each situation and passion. The music composed and managed by Pelissier." Although some of the music may have been in the form of songs, it seems unmistakable that the advertisement was calling the public's attention to what today we would label background music.

If the rise of the melodrama began at the end of the eighteenth century, the demise of the ballad

opera occurred simultaneously. Left for the public's pleasure were several forms of musical entertainment. Spectacles with "incidental Song" such as John Hodgkinson's **The Launch; or, Huzza for the Constitution** ("The Musick selected from the best Composers") and **Americania and Elutheria; or, A New Tale of the Genii** continued to hold sway. The latter, first done in Charleston in February 1798, was typical of the allegorical bent of so many of these works. In the piece a wood nymph demands to meet a mortal, and when a satyr brings the nymph an ignorant old hermit, the Genius of America appears and commands her domestics to teach the recluse how Elutheria, Goddess of Liberty, flew to the arms of Americania. Into these patriotic and allegorical representations a new twist was introduced at the turn of the century. As Sonneck records, "just then began the era of the American circus; and the novelty of equestrian and acrobatic feats combined with pantomimes sumptuously gotten up, like 'Bucephalus' and 'Don Juan' presented year after year."

Straight plays, too, might have a song or two for seasoning or variety. And about the same time French and Italian operas began to find their way into the playhouses. There were no auditoriums devoted solely to opera as there are today, nor was there sufficient demand or theatregoers to justify establishing such separate houses. As a result playgoers took in these early operas as part of a theatrical repertory. However alien the operas might have been, they were often the most artful, cohesive musical works available, and would remain so for nearly a century.

The early years of the nineteenth century were barren indeed for the American Musical Theatre. The paling forms of eighteenth-century lyric stage art—their life-blood fast draining away—were virtually all the musical theatre audiences had to enjoy. To some extent this dearth persisted throughout the first two-thirds of the new century, although here and there sparks of life, small promises of a renascence to come, momentarily brightened the era's candle- and gas-lit stages. In a way, this lack of creativity and productivity is puzzling, for music and musical performance were near at hand in almost every nineteenth-century playhouse. Major theatres, even those with no intention of mounting musical offerings, kept full orchestras in their pits at all times, to entertain patrons before the first curtain and between acts. Many houses kept singers and dancers on their payrolls specifically to provide audiences with entr'acte diversion. In resident companies a particularly talented member of the acting ensemble often would double in brass to perform the chore, but if such a member were not already on the payroll, one would be hired. For example, for 1853 theatre historian Odell lists Adelaide Price as "the stock *entr'acte* dancer of the [Broadway] theatre." The Broadway was then a leading home of serious drama.

For all its atrophy or apathy the musical theatre was not totally moribund. In retrospect, the first gleamings of the future become evident. The prototypes of late nineteenth-century comic opera, farce-comedy, and extravaganza, and of twentieth-century operetta, musical play, musical comedy, and revue, are all to be seen. Four types stand out.

On 3 March 1823, the Park Theatre, then the finer of New York's two playhouses, was host to a hit from England, Moncrieff's **Tom and Jerry; or, Life in London.** Jerry is Jerry Hawthorn (Mr. Cowell), a lad from the country come to London to visit his cousin, Corinthian Tom (Mr. Simpson). With Tom's friend, Bob Logic (Mr. Watkinson), the boys embark on a whirl around town. After visiting the high spots (the Burlington Arcade, Tattersal's) they become embroiled in a street melee and are hauled into court. But their adventures are not over. At a gambling house they lose their money. Fortunately, Jerry's country sweetheart, Sue (Miss Johnson), comes to take him home while Kate (Mrs. Bancker) helps restore Tom's fortune and leads him to the altar. As George Odell noted in his *Annals of the New York Stage,* "The gist of the matter is found in rapidly shifting scenes, great diversity of city types of character, and a large amount of consequent spectacle, song and dance. The dances included waltzes and quadrilles." The plot's somewhat slapdash nature allowed musical numbers and spectacular stage effects to be inserted or dropped at will. Although the era of "runs" was still several decades in the future, *Tom and Jerry* was repeated frequently for the remainder of the season. (Plays were still offered in repertory.) The show's success was attested to by the haste with which a band of Negro players produced a version, as well as by the compliment of a burlesque, *The Death of Life in London; or, Tom and Jerry's Funeral,* brought out in the summer of 1824.

Eleven years later Charles Mathews arrived at the same Park Theatre with a show he called his **Comic Annual.** Little more than a series of sketches in which Mathews introduced his audiences to a parade of city and country characters, the entertainment suggests how the loose structure of Tom and Jerry shows could be loosened further still into an incipient revue. Mathews, in what was almost a one-man show, gave patrons his version of celebrated critics discussing the poetry of Burns, Byron, Scott, and Shakespeare, told "The Old Scotch Lady's Leetle Anecdote," and portrayed Josephus Jollyfat, a Gastronomer Astronomer. Besides recounting in song the "Humors of A Country Fair" and "A Police Report," Mathews filled the evening "with Welsh, French, Scotch, Irish, Indian, Swiss, and English airs."

In the spring of 1848 three shows opened in quick succession to take New York by storm. All three centered on a young Bowery fireman called Mose ("a true specimen of one of the B'hoys"), all three bustled with characters from the high and low life of the day, and all three used Tom and Jerry frames. All three also featured the tall, well-built, ruggedly handsome Frank Chanfrau as Mose, "with his red shirt, his soap-locks [hair plastered down with soap], his 'plug' hat [a top hat], and his boots, into which the trousers were tucked at will." The first to arrive was **A Glance at New York in 1848,** to a text by B. A. Baker. In Baker's tale George Parsells (G. Clark), a "Greenhorn" from the country, comes to visit his city cousin, Harry Gordon (G.J. Arnold), and is quickly subjected to the wiles of every conceivable New York sharper. The principal sharper was Jake (W. Conover), proprietor of Loafer's Paradise. Other figures included Major Gates, a literary loafer; Mrs. Morton, president of the "Ladies' Bowling Saloon"; and six lovely members of the "saloon," who constituted a sort of primitive chorus line. Cabmen, Applewomen, and Newsboys provided local color. The show opened at the Olympic on 15 February and ran for twenty-four performances until a revised version, **A New Glance at New York,** was ready on 15 March. Additions included "luscious-voiced" Mary Taylor as Eliza Stebbens, "one of the Gals." Her inclusion allowed the development of a love interest in this primitive *Guys and Dolls,* a love interest told in the slang of the time. Liza refuses Mose's invitation to see "de wawdeville plays," but she offers him an alternative:

Liza: ... I'd rather go to Christy's. Did you ever
　　see George Christy play the bones? Ain't he
　　one of 'em?
Mose: Yes, he's some.

This prompts Liza to sing one of Christy's minstrel songs. *A New Glance* was even more successful than its parent, running fifty nights at the Olympic. Chanfrau had a third Mose saga ready at the Chatham on 17 April (it is unclear who replaced him as Mose at the Olympic). By this date excitement was such that the *Spirit of the Times* reported the police had to be called in on opening night to quell the boisterousness of the real "B'hoys" (members of rowdy gangs, composed largely of Irish immigrants), who packed the pit. Once more a country yokel, William Twill (Mr. Herbert), arrives from the country to spend a week with his city cousin, Charles Meadows (Mr. Stafford), and encounters a variety of unpleasant city types. The evening ended with Mose rescuing a child from a burning building. Sets took audiences to Chatham Square, the Chatham Theatre, the Old Dutch Church, a Soup House, City Hall, and the Catharine Fish Market. Songs included Meadows's singing of "Come Miss, Stir Your Stumps," while dances—besides jigs and a quadrille—included a "Nigger dance for eels." The show ran until mid-June. In September, Chanfrau played Mose in H. P. Grattan's *The Mysteries and Miseries of New York*, but this piece, at the National, failed.

Three years later, the celebrated W E. Burton, whose troupe was briefly the finest in New York, offered his loyal patrons a similar piece, **The World's Fair; or, London in 1851.** Beginning 15 February 1851 at his own theatre, Burton as William Waggles spent several weeks showing audiences the sights of the metropolis and introducing them to We-Peek, Lo-Po-Te, Pete Gotobed, Mrs. and Miss Smudge, Fatima, the Greek Slave, and Light of the Morning. Three more years passed before Burton ventured another such vehicle, on 11 December 1854. For **Apollo in New York** Burton mixed burlesque elements with his Tom and Jerry tour. The gods visit New York in disguise (a similar plot would be used in 1910 for *Up and Down Broadway*). Apollo (Miss McCarthy) becomes Apollini, an Italian tenor, and courts a young society belle. New Yorkers of the day recognized the courtship as a thinly veiled parody of a real romance between the singer Signor Mario and one Miss Coutt. Burton played Jupiter, come to earth as Sandy Hook, but afterwards disguised as Mrs. Partington at a Women's Rights Convention. According to the *Evening Post*, Miss McCarthy's Apollo "inclines strongly to the Know-Nothing principle in politics, and opposes foreign intervention with a good deal of force." The action moved from Sandy Hook (with Lighthouse), where the gods land and where Jupiter decides on a name, to the Staten Island ferry, to a Tavern, and finally to the women's convention. The *Evening Post* concluded the work owed its success "to localization rather

than brilliancy." In fact, its success was negligible, so Burton withdrew it after eleven nights.

On 18 August 1856, a fascinating figure entered the Tom and Jerry lists: John Brougham.

> **JOHN BROUGHAM** was born in Dublin, Ireland, on 9 May 1810. Financial problems forced him to abandon medical studies, and he made his theatrical debut at London's Tottenham Street Theatre in July 1830 in a production of *Tom and Jerry*. After acting for several seasons at Covent Garden he became manager of the Lyceum and began writing plays as well as performing. In 1843 he arrived in America, hoping to fill the place left vacant by the drowning of another great Irish star, Tyrone Power. But Power had been a brilliant, penetrating actor, while Brougham was essentially a showman. Brougham's American managerial efforts all ended in failure, but as an actor and a writer whose work ranged from farce to serious drama he was to play a major role in the American theatre for the next thirty-five years. Short, round-faced, with a high forehead and a conspicuous moustache, he soon became a beloved figure.

The entertainment Brougham offered at the Bowery transposed Moncrieff's play to America, rechristened **Life in New York; or, Tom and Jerry on a Visit.** Assigning the parts of Tom and Jerry to lesser performers (Messrs. Fisher and Dunn), Brougham appeared in a number of guises, notably Fitzgammon Bowlingreen. His redaction took audiences from Collins Wharf to Canal Street, the Astor House, and Mrs. Codfishe's ballroom (with dances and ballets choreographed by B. Yates and danced by the Henrarde Sisters). A finale at City Hall featured a fireworks display.

These vernacular Tom and Jerry romps led in time not only to the great Harrigan and Hart shows, but provided much of the impetus for both modern musical comedy and revue.

Another form that contributed significantly to both revues and musical comedies was burlesque, a more patently outlandish art that had, as we have seen, flourished sporadically even in the eighteenth century. Two figures dominated the art in the first half of the nineteenth century: James Robinson Planché and

William Mitchell. Planché began earlier and outlasted Mitchell. His work seems more "classic," less wildly impudent than Mitchell's. Because both were so prolific (Mitchell offered as many as eighty-six works in a single season!), we will offer only a sample of their art.

Planché's pieces were rarely full length. They were offered as merely one part of the elaborate bills our forefathers demanded, or at least sat through. In company with a famous drama, *The Hunchback*, Planché's "burletta" The Deep, Deep Sea was offered to patrons of the Park on 15 November 1834. The plot centered on Triton (Thomas Placide), who comes ashore in New England and announces himself to the strains of "Yankee Doodle." The entertainment presented parodies of opera arias such as "Non Piu Mesta" and "Di Tanti Palpiti," "mingled with Ride a Cock-Horse to Banbury Cross, or Oh, What a Row, What a Rumpus and a Rioting, as musical setting for the absurd quarrels of Neptune [W. H. Latham], Amphitrite [Mrs. Vernon] and Cassiope [Mrs. Archer], and the rescue of Andromeda [Mrs. Gurner] by Perseus [Mrs. S. Chapman] from the dread sea serpent." If Planché's music is forgotten, it must have enjoyed some contemporary vogue, for advertisements in the *Evening Post* informed readers, "Books containing songs of the Burletta, for sale at Box Office. Price 6 cents."

William Mitchell took over the Olympic on 9 December 1839 and for the next eleven seasons tremendously enlivened New York's theatre scene. Typical of his first season's offerings were The Roof Scrambler, a parody of Bellini's *La Sonnambula*, and The Musquitoe, a take-off of the ballerina Fanny Elssler's triumphs. The *Spirit of the Times* reported, "MITCHELL plays *Amina*, under the English, if not the more euphonious, name of *Molly Brown*. And how irresistible is the lovely *Molly*, whether in simpering gladness she engages in soft dalliance with her swain, *Swelvino* ... whether scrambling over housetops, or descending by pump-handles and water casks—or, more than all, sinking with decorous and innocent grace upon the couch of *Rodolpho*." The paper continued, "And then the musical charms of the 'Roof Scrambler'—the glad voices which mingle in the swelling chorus to hail *Swelvino*'s marriage; and the *silent* one which so eloquently describes to *Rodolpho* the mysteries of the enchanted chamber! And the grand *finale*, how mellifluously does *Molly Brown* glide from the exulting and rapturous burst of 'Ah! do not mingle' into a fitting, a joyous double shuffle!" Mitchell's own advertisements detailed scenes from *The Musquitoe*, warning, "This ballet

is founded upon the well-known properties of the Musquitoe, whose bite renders the patient exceedingly impatient, and throws him into a fit of scratching, slapping and swearing delirium." The notice further advertised, "The music had been begged, borrowed, and stolen from all sorts of Opera and Ballets, in the most impudent and free and easy style—by the Musical Director, Mr. *George Loder*."

Mitchell's second-season successes included 1940!; or, Crummles in Search of Novelty (which displayed Niblo's "a hundred years hence" and men flying routinely in balloons), and a spoof of the successful ballet *La Bayadère; or, The Maid of Cashmere*, retitled Buy-It-Dear, 'Tis Made of Cashmere. Dances for the latter included the entrance of Buy-A-Brooms, Grand Broom Dance, Procession of the Palanquin, and the Grand Trial Dance. Rarely were these pieces full length. For example, Mitchell's bills generally coupled *1940!* with *Buy-It-Dear*. As the excerpt from his advertisement to *The Musquitoe* suggests, Mitchell's fun began long before his audiences entered his house. Notices for *Billy Taylor* announced, "Produced without an Immense Expense, the entire cost being considerably under ten thousand dollars!!! The new Scenery is painted on less than 50,000 square feet of canvas, and it has not been many months in preparation!!!" Clearly, the hasty reader, glancing solely at the capitalized words, would be misinformed. But Mitchell's private ledgers are still extant, and they reveal another side of the theatre of the day. The Olympic's top price was for its dress circle—$50, the going top price for all the years before the Civil War. Balcony seats cost $25, while a place in the pit went for $12½. To allow for such prices no one but Mitchell was paid more than $25 a week.

When Planché's King Charming opened at the Broadway on 24 December 1855, it was extended the courtesy of relatively long notices by both the New York *Times* and the *Spirit of the Times* (for the most part reviews at this time were maddeningly uninformative about details of production, and these were no exception). Both papers relished Planché's story of the king (H. C. Watson), blessed with eternal youth, who grows bored after three or four centuries, so decides to take a wife. He heads for King Henpeckt's court, where the princesses quickly battle each other for his hand. A good fairy (Mme. Elizabeth Ponisi) sees to it he wins the best of the girls. The *Times* quoted one couplet as typical of Planché's wit:

A wife like this I could not live a day with
She's one to run away from, not away with.

The paper also suggested what the era looked for in the genre, noting, "Mr. Planché may be considered the father of the modern school of Burlesque. In his hands a fairy tale preserves all its delicate outline of imagination. It is, for a child, the same wonderful creation it ever was. But his labors do not end there. He has to add something for the carping appetite of mature age. Pointed jokes, smart scraps of sarcasm, quick telling local allusions; all these have to be interwoven with the original texture without impairing its delicacy." (Years later, reviewing a burlesque of *Cinderella* which opened at the Winter Garden on 9 September 1861, the *Times* by indirection implied how far the insertion of sarcasm and local allusions had been carried when it praised the work for not containing a single reference to New Jersey or to "lager-bier.")

Curiously, the *Times* gave shorter shrift to, and the *Spirit of the Times* virtually ignored, an opening at Wallack's the same evening *King Charming* premiered, an opening many scholars have come to view as far more significant in the development of the American Musical Theatre. That show was Brougham's **Pocahontas; or, The Gentle Savage.** The evening featured Charles M. Walcot as Captain John Smith, Georgina Hodson as Po-Ca-Hon-Tas, and Brougham as Pow-Ha-Tan I. Other characters, whose names give something of the flavor of the work, were Cod-Livr-Oyl, Ip-Pah-Kak, Kal-O-Mel, Kross-As-Kan-Bee, Lump-A-Sugah, and Poo-Ti-Pet. Musical numbers were largely parodies of popular songs—only Smith's comic version of a song called "Widow Machree" was singled out by critics—while dances were apparently confined to brief jigs and a clog number. The musical ran as part of ever-changing, longer bills until 23 February; it was replaced, two nights later, by a new Planché work, *Knights of the Round Table*.

Happily, the success of *Pocahontas* prompted reviewers to devote more attention to its successor a year later, this one written not by Brougham but by Walcot. Indeed, Brougham seems to have played no part in **Hiawatha; or, Ardent Spirits and Laughing Water,** either on stage or behind the scenes. Walcot naturally assumed the title role, playing, as the program noted, "a character strikingly more in the style of a School-boy than of a Long-fellow." The *Times* advised its readers, "He has interpolated jokes and puns of the most agonizing kind, and utterly regardless of historical truth makes 'Hiawatha' a critic, a censor, a satirist, a singer of comic songs, and a dancer of absurd jigs." The *Spirit of the Times*

added that there was an excellent hornpipe as well as jigs. It noted the evening was laced with "songs, choruses and concerted" passages, praising especially an "opening glee and chorus, a parody on the 'Chough and Crow' from 'Guy Mannering.'" But Walcot turned out to be far from the star of his own effort. Encomiums were lavished on a slender, sloe-eyed young lady making her New York debut, Mrs. John Wood. Her excellent singing and adroit clowning as Minnehaha soon made her a star in her own right. Kind words were also awarded to a second young woman who would become famous, although not in musicals, Mary Gannon. She portrayed Pooh-Pooh-Mammi, "an indescribably self-willed young lady." Burlesque tradition loved to dress men in women's clothes, so *Hiawatha* enlisted Mr. G. Holland to play the hero's "grandmamma," No-Go-Miss. When *Hiawatha* closed after a month's run, Mrs. Wood went into another burlesque, *Shylock; or, The Merchant of Venice Preserved*, with herself as Portia and her husband as the Jew.

The list of burlesques presented in the period just covered would fill several pages. Most likely these works, if they are extant, deserve a serious scholarly examination. But as these examples suggest, the art of burlesque was vitally alive. In time, along with the competing minstrel burlesque tradition, it led to Weber and Fields, and, even in a constricted form, to the hilarities of later revue skits.

The Negro theatre mentioned earlier and the minstrels alluded to also influenced the American musical. A playhouse catering to blacks existed in the early nineteenth century in New York, led by the first major black actor in America, James Hewlett. The level of its artistry can be garnered from descriptions of its performances of *Richard the Third* and *Othello*. In *Richard*, King Henry and the Duchess were played by the same actor, one speech began "Gib me noder Horse," and "Several fashionable songs" were added. In *Othello*, Desdemona danced a hornpipe, while Othello and Iago put aside their enmity long enough to raise their voices together in "The Rival Beauties." Odell, suggesting "the verses... look like the beginnings of negro minstrelsy," quoted one couplet: "At dancing school I next was sent, all muffled up with care,/Where I larnt to dance a minuet as graceful as a Bear!"

Few, if any, white men attended these entertainments. But interest in the Negro as a stage character was growing. This interest was heightened appreciably in 1832 when T. D. Rice "jumped" his "Jim Crow" between the acts of whatever shows were on the bills of houses at which he was appearing. Indicative of the mélange of entertainment and moods early nineteenth-century theatregoers were prepared to face in a single evening, Rice made his New York debut on 12 November between performances of two serious dramas, *The Hunchback* and *Catherine of Cleves*. Regardless of the expressive verb "jump" that immediately became associated with "Jim Crow," the dance seems to have been a shuffle, with the feet generally on the ground and upper-body movements contorted. Rice is said to have developed the routine after watching a crippled black stablehand in Louisville entertain himself. Some scholars dispute this story, especially since Rice is said to have also appropriated the Negro's tune. These scholars argue that that tune is too similar to an Irish folk tune and an English stage song. They apparently assume that because Rice is said to have derived the tune from the Negro, the melody by implication must be black in origin. In any case Rice added his own words.

> Wheel about, turn about
>   Do jes so,
> An' ebery time I wheel about
>   I jump Jim Crow.

The dance along with its music and lyrics became what Robert Toll, in his history of the minstrel show, *Blacking Up*, labeled "the first of many Afro-American dances to become a worldwide success." For years afterwards Rice appeared in shows such as *Jim Crow in London* and *The Virginia Mummy*, their advertisements often promising "he will sing his celebrated song of Jim Crow."

Although blackface artists such as Rice were precursors of minstrelsy, the minstrel show, as an entire evening's entertainment, did not take to the stage until February 1843, when Billy Whitlock, R. W Pelham, Frank Brower, and Dan Emmett, billing themselves as the Virginia Minstrels, offered an extended exhibition of the "oddities, peculiarities, eccentricities, and comicalities of that Sable Genus of Humanity." Curiously, the term "minstrels," which has ever since been linked with burnt cork amusement, was given its vogue by this group. Until its arrival most blackface performers were known as "delineators," often, more specifically, "Ethiopian delineators." The new band borrowed the last half of its name from the Tyrolese Minstrel Family, which had just toured the land to great acclaim. Although the Virginia Minstrels disbanded within a year, its success was so great that imitators

sprang up everywhere. For the most part these early minstrel groups stayed close to their home auditoriums. However, only a year after the debut of the Virginia Minstrels, a troupe known as the Ethiopian Serenaders trucked its luggage to the White House for a command performance.

While blackface seems to have originally been used in theatricals in the South and Midwest, the evening-long minstrel show that first saw the footlights in New York also saw its principal development there. Toll believes this was "because the intense competition eliminated poor performers and forced innovations." What did evolve was the first genuinely American Musical Theatre, the first great indigenous entertainment. But only in the most liberal sense of the term could a minstrel show be a work of art. As Toll noted, "It had no characterization to develop, no plot to evolve, no musical score, no set speeches, no subsidiary dialogue—indeed no fixed script at all. Each set—song, dance, joke, or skit—was a self-contained performance that strived to be the highlight of the show." The show was held together by an external framework—what today's jargon would call a format—rather than by any internal cohesion or organically dictated form. Its devil-may-care indifference to even the vaguest dramatic unities helped establish a not altogether healthy slapdash tradition in the American Musical Theatre.

The pattern that did quickly settle into place was simple. The show was divided into three parts. The first part, with its semicircle of performers flanked by comic end men Tambo and Bones and presided over by a centrally seated interlocutor, was the section that came to typify minstrelsy. Tambo and Bones received their names from the tambourine and clackers they held and which they rattled to express their approval of a song or a joke. Their comedy routines and songs were interspersed with the more serious romantic melodies rendered by the fourth principal, the balladeer. The second part of the performances was an olio. Like the opening section, it was essentially a variety bill, made less formal by the absence of the interlocutor and end men. The difference between the two parts was more of degree than of kind. Its most noteworthy feature was a "stump speech," a comic monologue. Toll quotes one that began, "Feller-fellers and oder fellers, when Joan of Ark and his broder Noah's Ark crossed de Rubicund...." The final portion of the show was an extended skit. At first these skits were simple scenes of plantation life laced with songs and dances, little more than a third type of vaudeville.

Within a decade, however, George Christy of the Christy Minstrels and his copiers supplanted scenes of life in the South with lampoons of current events or, with increasing frequency, of current plays. The sensational vogue of *Uncle Tom's Cabin* inevitably demanded spoofing, and afforded an excellent and easy transition from plantation scenes to travesties of stage plays. Under such titles as "Uncle Dad's Cabin," "Aunt Dinah's Cabin," "Life Among the Happy" (Mrs. Stowe's subtitle had been *Life Among the Lowly*), or "Happy Uncle Tom," minstrels presented a cheerily deranged version in which Uncle Tom was usually not sold down the river, in which Simon Legree often failed to appear, and in which Topsy, Eva, and all the other famous figures found ample opportunity for songs and jigs. As one lyric announced:

Oh, white folks, we'll have you to know
Dis am not de version of Mrs. Stowe;
Wid her de Darks am all unlucky
But we am de boys from Old Kentucky.

No small part of these curious inversions reflected an underlying and persistent sentiment of minstrelsy: its fundamentally anti-Negro attitude. However good-natured the kidding might be, by and large minstrel shows had little truck with abolitionist sentiment. The Civil War forced a certain change of attitude, but not a change of heart. With Reconstruction many a minstrel company briefly dropped its satirizing of stage successes to mock carpetbaggers and overambitious Negroes.

Within the pattern there was ample scope for a variety of songs, humor, and dance. Some of the most long-lived jokes in the American repertory seem to have first been tried on minstrel audiences. While no conclusive records exist, it is probable that a minstrel first asked why a chicken crossed the road and told his amazed foil the answer, "To get to the other side"; and that a fellow blackface performer first asked why a fireman wears red suspenders and informed his straightman it was "To hold up his pants." Toll points to some humor which was double-barreled, evidently to reassure patrons that it was all a masquerade as well as to provide a joke.

"'Why am I like a young widow?' a comedian asked. After the line was slowly repeated, he fired back: 'Because I do not stay long in black.'" Later, when the popularity of minstrelsy began to wane, immigrants' dialects and traits were also parodied.

Minstrel songs ranged from racial lampoons to political satire to treacly nineteenth-century sentimentality. Obviously the "coon songs" came first. Many of these, especially in the beginning, appropriated standard melodies. "Jim Crow" was not unique. A number of successful minstrels claim to have carefully studied native Negro song patterns, and to have sometimes borrowed Negro melodies and verses. But how much genuine black material audiences heard remains moot. Although political satire employed darky speech, it was clearly the product of professionals.

Of songs of a more sentimental nature, those that bear the signature of Stephen Foster are sung and loved to this day. Foster had played in minstrel shows as a young man and took readily to minstrel styles. All his songs were popular on the minstrel stage, although some, such as "Oh, Susanna!," "Old Black Joe," or "Camptown Races," were not necessarily composed with the stage in mind. But "Massa's In De Cold Cold Ground" and his masterpiece, "Old Folks At Home" ("Way Down Upon The Swanee River"), seem to have been composed at the behest of the Christy Minstrels, and the latter was first issued with E. P. Christy listed as composer. But Foster's material was the cream of the crop. More typical of the everyday melodies with which theatregoers of the era were regaled were the works of William Shakespeare Hays. While he is now all but forgotten, the remarkably prolific Hays was esteemed in his own day. "Early In De Morn'" exemplifies his work.

A few other songs from the minstrel stage have retained their popularity. For some, such as "Polly Wolly Doodle," their hold on public affection grows shakier with time. But "Dixie," which was written by Dan Emmett and introduced by him with Bryant's Minstrels on 4 April 1859, and soon employed to rally the Confederacy, has become a classic.

Most of the dancing—such as that employed with "Jim Crow" or "Essence Of Old Virginia"—derived from the same Negro shuffle that eventually led to the "buck and wing" and the "soft shoe." For the most part they were a white man's attempt to theatricalize a black man's art. But significantly the most highly praised of early minstrel dancers reversed the procedure. William Henry Lane, who performed as "Master Juba," was a Negro who based his routines on an Irish jig. From their inception, minstrel troupes composed of blacks were generally most admired for their high stepping. Here was another pattern established early on! Apart from the clowning of a great comedian on the order of Bert Williams, it would be years before anything from a Negro musical but its dances would be taken seriously.

Although the minstrel show remained popular until the turn of the century, its heyday ended with the Civil War. The new musical entertainments that erupted just after the war offered novelty, more spectacle, and, ultimately, the comfort of something that passed for a story. Leading minstrel impresarios were quick to appreciate the change of tastes. They attempted to compete by adding parades, more spectacular mountings of their own, and more non-Negro materials, and, in cases such as Francis Leon of Kelly and Leon's Minstrels, by offering female impersonations in their burlesques. But in 1883–1884, when J. H. Haverly, the last of the great minstrel impresarios, bought out New York's final survival resident troupe, the oddly named San Francisco Minstrels, the great era of blackface came to a close. Haverly increased the size of his companies, advertising forty Mastodon Minstrels, and he unveiled a scene of a "Turkish Barbaric Palace in Silver and Gold" transformed before audiences' eyes into a King's Palace. He claimed to have spent as much as $1,500 on a single costume when the whole show cost no more to produce. But his efforts were to little avail. Those who followed him— Dumont, Dockstader, and their associates—generally contented themselves with playing to elderly audiences in houses that were not always the most desirable.

While Tom and Jerry shows, burlesques, and minstrels occasionally touched on less pleasant sides of life, their approach was essentially sunny, if tongue-in-cheek. Two other forms took themselves more seriously: spectacle and opera. Ultimately spectacle joined with burlesque to evolve into the revue-extravaganzas of the early twentieth century. Technological advances and economics eventually drove it from the stage. Opera took two roads. One, uncompromising and lofty, led it away from popular stages to the confines of a few great auditoriums such as the Metropolitan Opera. The other, flexible and seeking a broader audience, abandoned recitative for dialogue, subdued its arioso flights, minimized the tragedy, and emphasized the romance of its stories. This road led straight to comic opera and operetta.

In the days before cinematographic realism and electronic trickery, scene painters and machinists vied with each other to see who could create the most startlingly lifelike effects or the most magical flights of fancy. Audiences generally accepted the results with delight and enthusiasm. Even the most serious drama (although we might scoff at it today as absurd melodrama) featured these spectacular moments. And since most theatres maintained orchestras and a small troupe of dancers, these efforts could be embellished readily with music and ballet to make them even more thrilling. One example of this sort of serious drama-cum-spectacle must suffice. On 11 January 1836, the Bowery offered Louisa Medina's **Norman Leslie**, the saga of a man falsely accused of murder and his long struggle to vindicate himself. The story took its characters and its audience to, among other places, the American Hotel on Broadway, a magnificent Ball Room, Mr. Temple's house (on fire), an Italian Palazzo and Gardens by sunset, St. Peter's, a Carnival in Rome, the Coliseum in Ruins, and a Grand Denouement. The Ball Room was the scene of quadrilles, waltzes, and gallopades; the Palazzo, of a peasant dance. At St. Peter's the hymn "Ave Maria" was sung by a large chorus. At the Carnival—where masqueraders romped as Alexander the Great, Shylock, Richard III, Hamlet, Julius Caesar, Achilles, Mahomet, and others—"sixteen ladies and gentlemen" performed a Russian dance, one Madame Trust did a Spanish dance with castanets, and a group performed a comic "Morice" Dance.

On 4 July 1828, William Niblo, who had successfully operated a popular coffee house and an entertainment park, purchased a large plot of land on the northeast corner of Broadway and Prince Street. He converted one building on the property into a theatre, naming it the Sans Souci. A year later he turned the playhouse into a concert hall and erected a large, new theatre next door. He rechristened his complex Niblo's Garden and Theatre, which his public promptly shortened to Niblo's Garden. His audiences for the most part lived so far away that the entrepreneur was forced to provide stage coach service between his far uptown establishment and the Battery. When the theatre was destroyed by fire in 1846, Niblo determined to retire, but he was persuaded instead to remain in business and erect a new house. With the city moving steadily north, the adjacent ground was soon occupied by the Metropolitan Hotel, and the theatre was entered through the hotel's lobby.

Almost from its inception Niblo's Garden regularly awed its patrons with lavish mountings of less seriously dramatic entertainments. For example, on 21 April 1841, no less an artist than Charlotte Cushman assumed the title role in Burton's **The Naiad Queen.** Neither the *Evening Post* nor the *Spirit of the Times* gave away the plot, but the latter hailed the scenery as "gorgeous in the extreme." Unfortunately, neither paper, nor the *Herald*, quoted by Odell, described the sets. Nor were the papers any more informative nearly a decade later when the house mounted Brougham's "spectacular new and original operatic drama," **Home,** in May of 1850 or the more light-hearted, fantastic **Island of Jewels** in the following month. That the latter was more comic can be judged from its cast of characters, which included such names as King Giltginger-bread the Great, Prince Prettiphello (a trouser role), and Fairy Benevolenta.

But three other spectacles have left some glimpses behind, and they are worth noting. **Faustus; or, The Demon of the Dragonfels,** which opened at the Broadway on 13 January 1851 and ran six weeks, told of the downfall of the King of Naples. Early in the story a ship is wrecked and, as the audience watches, the wreckage is transformed into Venice at Carnival, "with Gondolas passing and repassing" and with "150 persons in Grotesque and Sumptuous Costumes." The evening ended with "the intrusion of Venetians seeking redress against the base Seducer! Wizard!! Murderer!!! The Steps are Red with Blood!! Repentance comes too late. The Demon claims his own. The Palace disappears, disclosing Pandemonium! Terrific Denouement!" All this was interspersed with ballets by Mons. Schmidt that featured Adeline as principal *danseuse*, Checkini as chief grotesque dancer, and La Petite Carman.

Faustus was followed at the same house on 7 April by **The Vision of the Sun,** an Inca legend in which a maiden is sacrificially drowned in a lake. Odell found a yellowing program for the work which noted, "The waters become agitated and rise, and in their progress to the whole height of the Stage, they assume various tints, till a most Brilliant Palace rises out of the Water!"

Even the renowned actress Laura Keene was not above turning her house over to such spectacles. She had the longest run of her career when **The Seven Sisters** (based on an older German work translated as *The Seven Daughters of Satan*) began a stay of 253 performances on 26 November 1860. Promising the best of all worlds, she billed her attraction as a "Grand Operatic, Spectacular, Musical, Terpsichorean, Diabolical, Farcical Burletta." She herself portrayed Diavoline, one of the seven sisters who come from hell to see the sights of New York. Her "terpsichorean" offerings included a ballet, a Zouave drill, and a shadow dance by Polly Marshall (who played another sister, Plutella). The evening ended with a lavish transformation scene—"The Birth of the Butterfly in the Bower of the Ferns." Odell found a description of it in the New York *Express*: "Emerald light, water as clear as crystal (it was represented by looking glass), water lilies, fern leaves, revolving pillars… welded together by the genius of the scene painter [James Roberts, from the Theatre Royal, Covent Garden] in one brief and delicate vision of fairyland." Clearly, all that was lacking to turn *The Seven Sisters* into the runaway success of *The Black Crook* (12 September 1866) was the lush prosperity that the oncoming Civil War would bring, and a bevy of girls in pink tights.

Opera remained a popular entertainment, not, as in later years, confined to a single house that served as museum as much as theatre. It was, as everyone agreed, by far the most artful form in the lyric theatre. While Rossini might switch overtures and arias from opera to opera with an abandon that shocks purists today, opera remained the most conscientiously coherent lyric art form, attempting generally to integrate words and music into a meaningful whole. Of course, America, far removed from the sources, sometimes took a more freewheeling attitude, as it would in future decades with lighter importations. Both this freewheeling approach and signs of change were evident in the 1833–1834 season. The season was interesting musically in two particulars. Mrs. Joseph Wood, the celebrated English singer, made her American debut, and New York's first auditorium designed exclusively for the presentation of opera raised its curtain. Mrs. Wood arrived first. In forty-eight performances scattered from early September to the end of May, the lady offered such varied fare as *The Barber of Seville, Cinderella,* and *Robert the Devil* as well as English pieces on the order of *Love in a Village.* What artistic integrity her mountings displayed is questionable. *Robert the Devil,* for example, was not sung as Meyerbeer wrote it, but in an adaptation by Rophino Lacy. An idea of theatrical economics of the day is afforded by the grosses Mrs. Wood attained. Though her opening pulled a strong $1,679, and her eight benefits averaged $1,167, her thirty-nine regular performances achieved receipts of only about $500 apiece. Some blame for the poor showing undoubtedly belonged to the competition provided by the new Italian Opera House, at Leonard and Church streets.

Although its career was brief—to a large extent because it was erected in an out-of-the-way and unfashionable area—for much of its initial season it was society's new pet. From its opening on 18 November until it closed in financial trouble at the beginning of summer, it offered interpretations of seven operas—all, naturally, Italian. They included such now obscure works as Pacini's *Gli Arabi nelle Gallie* and Rosini's *Matilde di Shabran e Coradino.*

Within a few years English operas had a brief, pyrotechnic renaissance. Although their stories were hardly different from those of contemporary Italian and French works, something indefinably native in them allowed American audiences to feel an affinity for the works. William Michael Rooke's **Amilie,** first sung here at the Park on 15 October 1838, told a story much like that of Bellini's *La Sonnambula* and concluded with a voguish mad scene for the soprano. An especially fine singer, Jane Shirreff, was America's first Amilie. Her "I'm Over Young To Marry Yet" and another aria, "John Anderson, My Jo," were whistled much as show tunes of a later era were.

The greatest of the English composers in this new school was unquestionably Michael William Balfe. His masterpiece, **The Bohemian Girl,** was given its first American performance at the Park on 25 November 1844 and was so warmly received it held the boards until mid-December. In its libretto a Polish exile, Thaddeus, rescues a young girl, Arline, from an attacking stag. When Thaddeus and his gypsy friends are abused by Arline's noble father, they kidnap the girl and raise her as one of their own. Years later, when she is returned to her father, she refuses to marry anyone but Thaddeus. Edward Seguin and his wife sang the gypsy leader and the heroine, while one Mr. Frazer was Thaddeus. Out of this opera came one of the most popular songs of the day, long a standard in concerts, Arline's "I Dreamt That I Dwelt In Marble Halls." Balfe's **The Enchantress,** which premiered at the Chatham on 25 May 1846, was almost as popular, while other of his works were brought forth with varying success.

A third major English composer was William Vincent Wallace. His greatest work, **Maritana,** was first performed in America in Philadelphia in 1846, then two years later brought to the Bowery on 4 May 1848. Gypsies and nobles mingled in its plot much as they had in *The Bohemian Girl.* In this case the gypsy girl, Maritana, and a young noble, Don Caesar, go off to consummate their marriage despite the intrigues of Don Jose on behalf of the lascivious King of Spain. Since the Seguins did not offer the work until the last three nights of their repertory season, *Maritana's* first run was brief. But once again the man in the street was soon whistling new operatic arias—the soprano's "Scenes That Are Brightest" and the tenor's "Yes, Let Me Like A Soldier Fall." Their popularity assured frequent revivals.

Inevitably, American composers tried their own hand at similar offerings. On 27 September 1855, Niblo's Garden played host to the world premiere of **Rip Van Winkle,** an opera with a libretto by J. H. Wainright and music by George Bristow. The *Times* could only recommend it to its readers on the grounds that native opera needed support even when it was indifferently executed. The paper damned the score with faint praise, dismissing it as "pretty." Adding that it was "pervaded with a martial manner," the paper rued its lack of period flavor. Amusingly, the reviewer seemed confounded by a second act which had no basis in Irving's story, but showed instead the fantasies dreamt by the sleeping Rip. A Mr. Stretton sang the role of Rip. The opera was sung nightly until 6 October, when it entered a repertory that included *The Bohemian Girl, Maritana,* and—something of a surprise—*The Beggar's Opera.*

Since early works such as *The Archers* are probably closer in form to later comic operas and operettas than these English and American operas, the influence of these lyric pieces can be easily overrated or overlooked. Doubtless they were neither the sole nor the direct progenitors of the lighter lyric works of the late nineteenth century. But in softening the bravura, florid lines of Italian and French opera, in emphasizing and sentimentalizing romance, they helped ease theatregoers into a ready acceptance of a new form.

Although the Civil War was probably the most cataclysmic upheaval in our history, its effect on the American Musical Theatre was slight and indirect. The last wartime season, and the last season, but one, before the first great era of native musicals, 1864–1865, witnessed no major changes in the musical scene. The news of the day—the surrender at Appomattox and Lincoln's assassination—was far more dramatic than any fiction occupying the boards. The most significant theatrical events of the year were not the premieres of any new masterpieces but the long runs recorded. These runs were occasioned by New York's exploding population and, more urgently, the tremendous war-born prosperity of the Union.

The noted comedian John Sleeper Clarke had a record run of 101 performances in a repertory of his best-loved pieces; this was bettered by John E. Owens, who compiled a stay of thirty-three consecutive weeks with his own repertory, but notably with his playing of the old Yankee farmer, Solon Shingle, in *The People's Lawyer*. Neither of these extended visits meant as much to theatregoers of the time as Edwin Booth's 100-performance run in a single play, *Hamlet*. Together the three men monopolized two of New York's seven principal houses for the bulk of the season. Booth was Clarke's brother-in-law. Tragically he was also John Wilkes Booth's brother. Edwin, John, and Junius Brutus played in *Julius Caesar* on 25 November 1864. This was the night before Edwin began his run in *Hamlet*. It was the last time John appeared on the New York stage.

Musically, the theatre offered "more of more of the same." The Academy of Music at 14th Street and Union Square had long since replaced the virtually forgotten Italian Opera House. From September through May it offered New Yorkers the finest—and sometimes the latest—in German, Italian, and French operas.

Spectacle and pantomime were available to entertain younger playgoers and those seeking less high-minded diversions. Among the amazing hodgepodge of pleasantries P. T. Barnum offered at his Museum was a "musical fairy romance," **The Ring of Fate; or, Fire, Air, Earth and Water**. Beginning on 26 December 1864, Princess Eveline and Arnulph braved the elements and the supernatural on their way to the altar. It remained as the main feature on Barnum's extensive bill for a month and reappeared intermittently thereafter. At the Bowery, home of slapstick farce and roaring melodrama, a "new and gorgeous pantomime" entitled **Old Dame Trot and Her Comical Cat** headed the bill for eight weeks beginning 30 January 1865. G. L. Fox, soon to be famous as Humpty Dumpty, portrayed Sappy Saponaceous and Clown; his brother, C. K. Fox, played Antiquated Solderwell and Pantaloon; one Mons. Baptistine appeared as John Stout and Harlequin, while Mlle. Martinetti frolicked as Little Bo-Peep and Columbine. A female impersonator played Old Dame Trot to young Master Timothy's cat.

The two most prestigious minstrel houses were Bryant's and Wood's. Both opened the 1864–1865 season on 12 September. Throughout the year their bills changed to constantly spoof the rage of the moment. Bryant, for example, acknowledged Booth's triumph with a skit called "Evenings with Shakespoke," thereby competing with Wood's burlesque "Booth's Dane." The flood of actresses playing Mazeppa was mocked when Bryant appeared as Ada Leo Kate Fisher Hudson Menken Mazeppa. Bryant also doffed his hat to Owen by enacting Sole-Owen Shingle. Wood had notable success with a take-off on *The Streets of New York* and with an elaborate skit, "Petroliamania, or Oil on the Brain." Among the lesser troupes Campbell's Minstrels became Hooley and Campbell's and finally merely Hooley's. Sam Sharpley's Minstrels, advertised as "the famous Ironclads" and "the Monitors of Minstrels," made a brief appearance at the end of the season. But history would show the most significant event in minstrelsy was the opening of the San Francisco Minstrels on 8 May 1865 at 585 Broadway. The troupe—led by Charley Backus, "Billy" Bernard, "Billy" Birch, and "Dave" Wambold—came on the scene too late to be truly innovative, but in the waning years of minstrelsy it retained the highest standards of performance and production, and it went down in history, as we have mentioned, as the last great resident company in New York.

Hardly noticed at the time but of vital importance in the ensuing years was the transfer of another minstrel hall in which Sharpley's entourage had so briefly entertained to the aegis of Tony Pastor. Variety had just begun to supplant minstrels as the popular mass diversion. But it still had a low reputation. Much of the entertainment was suggestive if not lewd, and auditoriums in which it was offered saw a substantial part of their profits derive from liquor service. Pastor threw out the bars, cleaned up the entertainment, and made a point of inviting ladies to the shows. His success was too obvious to be ignored. Variety, or vaudeville as it was later called, served as training ground and sometimes as pasturage for the great names in the American Musical Theatre.

Of course a large number of the era's "straight" plays continued to have songs. Dan Bryant abandoned his blackface troupe for a time in July and August of 1865 to play a season in plays catering to an Irish-American audience, plays such as *The Irish Immigrant, The Colleen Bawn*, and *Born to Good Luck*. All the plays found places for Bryant to sing Irish or Irish-sounding ballads. Maggie Mitchell appeared in the title role with which she was identified all

Act One

Early Successes, 1866–1892

SCENE ONE

OPÉRA BOUFFE AND NATIVE ELEMENTS, 1866–1878

By the beginning of the 1866–1867 season the Civil War had been over and Reconstruction under way for almost a year and a half. Prosperity prevailed, but harmony and integrity were in short supply. This war-engendered prosperity buoyed the American theatre to no small extent and helped produce what George Odell in his *Annals of the New York Stage* labeled "A Season of Sensations." Given conditions in our native theatre at the time, no one complained if most of the sensations had something of a foreign flavor. A few—such as the American debut of the celebrated Italian actress Ristori—attested simply to the dollar's growing power to import leading talents. Other events betrayed their foreign influences less blatantly. The season's dramatic success was Joseph Jefferson in *Rip Van Winkle*, Washington Irving's tale, which had been dramatized many times before.

Jefferson, then still a rising figure on the comic stage, had himself played in several versions. This latest one—one that gave him a vehicle for the remainder of his life and became one of the best-loved stage pieces in American history—was prepared for the actor by Dion Boucicault. Although Boucicault had just spent several profitable years in the United States and with time would return to end his days here, the author was Irish born and London trained. He and Jefferson presented their new version in London for a season before bringing it to New York.

The few sensations that seemed to have no foreign connection were disasters—namely, the fiery destruction of the Winter Garden and of the New Bowery theatres. These were the fourth and fifth auditoriums to burn in Manhattan since the end of the war. It was the holocaust at the Academy of Music the previous spring that gave rise to the greatest sensation of all and to what is generally looked on as the birth of the American Musical Theatre: **The Black Crook** (12 September 1866, Niblo's).

In a way, this sensation, like Jefferson's *Rip Van Winkle* and Ristori's debut, had a foreign tinge. Legend, now disproven, says two impresarios, Henry C. Jarrett and Harry Palmer, had imported a French ballet troupe to perform *La Biche au Bois* and had booked the Academy to display its art. Suddenly without a stage, in desperation they approached William Wheatley, the manager of Niblo's Garden, hoping to obtain his house. They discovered Wheatley had committed himself to a second-rate melodramatist, Charles M. Barras, and was preparing to mount the author's piece of ersatz German romanticism. Luckily for the annals of our stage, Jarrett and Palmer's frantic cajolery induced Wheatley to merge the two offerings. The result was a five-and-a-half-hour spectacle (in many ways similar to earlier Niblo spectacles we have mentioned) which made all three men, as well as the initially reluctant Barras, comfortable for life.

Barras's story was a rather wooden variation of Carl Maria von Weber's romantic opera *Der Freischütz*. The "Arch Fiend" Zamiel (E. B. Holmes) induces Hertzog (C. H. Morton), the Black Crook, to deliver a human soul into his power each twelfth month just before midnight on New Year's Eve. Count Wolfenstein (J. W Blaisdell) has imprisoned the painter, Rudolf (spelled in many programs Rodolphe, and played originally by G. C. Boniface). Hertzog arranges for Rudolf's escape and promises to lead Rudolf to a cache of gold. The grateful Rudolf accepts, not understanding the nature of the bargain. On his way to the gold Rudolf saves the life of a dove. The dove proves to be Stalacta (Annie Kemp Bowler), the Queen of the Golden Realm. She alerts him to his dangers, takes him to fairyland, and ultimately sees to it he wins the hand of his beloved Amina (Rose Morton).

Barras probably never understood how lucky the unwanted additions were for him. His very plot was modeled on a type even then going out of vogue. His gift for characterization was minimal and his way with dialogue heavy-handed, although not exceptionally so in an age of stilted stage speech:

Rudolf: If this indeed be not a dream, tell me, bright being, you whose simple motion seems to sway the moves and passions of this Elfin Band, who art thou, and where am I.
Stalacta: I am called Stalacta, Queen of this dazzling realm, the glittering wonders that assail thine eyes are not creations of phantastic dreams, but nature's handiwork, wrought with the cunning fingers in a bounteous mood.

Not all the dialogue was so wordy. But even in fairly short speeches tricks of Victorian rhetoric prevailed. When Hertzog discovers his efforts are to prove fruitless he rails, "Foiled, tricked, crossed in the hour of my victory." The nature of the story and the demands of the large-scale spectacle allowed little play for comedy. The chief comic figure was Von Puffengruntz (J. G. Burnett), Wolfenstein's valet. Most of his laughs were gotten visually. He faints into his wife's arms, has his wig unexpectedly lifted, and receives a drubbing from his wife. What little dialogue he had ran to the order of "You snore, Madame Von Puffengruntz, you snore loud enough to split the drums of my ear and rip out the seams of my night-cap." Musically the show was a hodge-podge. Extant librettos record only two lyrics, a villagers' chorus in the first act and Stalacta's spell in the second. The villagers sang:

> *Hark, hark, hark*
> *Hark the birds with tuneful voices*
> *Vocal for our lady fair*
> *And the lips of op'ning flowers*
> *Breathe their incense in the air.*

There are, however, a number of musical cues. They indicate ballet music or melodramatic backgrounds. While much of the music, as it had been in the old ballad opera tradition, was derived from the better-known and well-loved compositions of the day, several composers contributed new melodies, notably one Thomas Baker. For the most part, the songs failed to catch the public's fancy. They were replaced at intervals all through the long run and the subsequent revivals. The only tune singled out for praise by the New York *Times* reviewer was a number he called "The Naughty Men," which was published as "You Naughty, Naughty Men" (G. Bicknell/T. Kennick). It was a simplistic ditty drifting along on an elementary ABC or A^1 A^2 A^3 pattern. The sheet music announces it was "composed for and sung by" Millie Cavendish, a young English entertainer who played Carlina, Amina's maid.

The *Times* critic noted the song was encored. But he also noted the principal ballet was "encored twice." Indeed, the ballets with girls in pink tights proved the sensation of the evening. David Costa devised the choreography, patterned in the romantic style of the day, assigning his choicest conceptions to four principal ballerinas: Marie Bonfanti, Rita Sangalli, Betty Rigl, and Rose Delval. Odell exclaimed, "The ballet, the wonderful ballet... was the thing."

The critics and the public agreed. Costa also presented a line of tall girls in carefully staged drills, proffering in these "Amazon marches" the "dance" form that most seriously rivaled classic ballet on our musical stage for forty years, until the waltzes of *The Merry Widow* (21 October 1907) swept it away.

The *Tribune* dismissed the book as "rubbish," the *Times* damned it as "trashy." But the *Times* hastily added, "No similar exhibition had been made in an American stage that we remember, certainly none where such a combination of youth, grace, beauty and élan was found... decidedly the event of this spectacular age." The *Tribune*, equally impressed, went into more detail: "Some of the most perfect and admirable pieces of scenery that have ever been exhibited upon the stage are employed in this piece." After extolling a storm scene painted by R. Smith, the paper turned its attention to the second-act finale: "A vast grotto... extending into an almost measureless perspective. Stalactites depend from the arched roof. A tranquil and lovely lake reflects the golden glories that span it like a vast sky. In every direction one sees the bright sheen or the dull richness of massy gold. Beautiful fairies, too, are herein assembled—the sprites of the Ballet, who make the scene luxuriant with their beauty." The *Black Crook* made transformation scenes (major scene changes executed while audiences watched) de rigueur for spectacle mounting. Once again the *Tribune* attempted to convey its grandeur to the paper's readers, noting the effects were devised by the Drew Brothers of London. "One by one curtains of mist ascend and drift away. Silver couches, on which the fairies loll in negligent grace, ascend and descend amid a silver rain. Columns of living splendor whirl, and dazzle as they whirl. From the clouds droop gilded chariots and the white forms of angels." Almost as an afterthought the paper noted "two bits of painting are especially remarkable," listing these as D. A. Strong's "A Wild Pass in the Hartz Mountains" and James E. Hayes's "Valley at the Foot of the Hartz Mountains."

The word "painting" is significant. Years were to pass before sets were architecturally conceived. The great scenery of this era was, with few exceptions, simply flats with perspective painted on. Unless absolutely essential to the play's action—as, say, the balcony in *Romeo and Juliet*—balconies, stairs, columns, trees, even animals and, sometimes, people, were merely oil on flat canvas. For the most part, in these decades of cheap labor, performers, not scenery, filled the stage. Moreover, as credits for *The Black Crook* demonstrate, no one man was responsible for the total integrity of the sets. Artists specialized in one type of scene and usually were allowed to design only that set which depicted their specialty. For their day, these practices worked superbly.

Odell is undoubtedly correct in stating that "the show revolutionized ballet spectacle in America." But it can seriously be questioned whether *The Black Crook* was the beginning of musical comedy in America. Textually, the early American ballad operas have as much claim. They, too, combined song, drama, and, to a lesser extent, dance into a total evening's entertainment. Nor did the more successful musicals that followed in the dozen or so years after *The Black Crook* opened seem significantly influenced by its style and tone. Rather, it was the profit the producers made on their at that time enormous investment of $50,000 and the phenomenal run of 475 performances that alerted other producers to the money to be made from such lavish productions. Another practice initiated by *The Black Crook* was the periodic revision of the production, freshening sets and costumes and introducing new material and performers. These "improvements" became known as reconstructions. The first occurred on 25 May when two new ballets, "The Bouquet" and "The Water Lily," were incorporated to display the artistry of new dancers supposedly imported from La Scala, San Carlo, and Covent Garden.

Of course there were other musical entertainments to divert theatregoers in 1866–1867. The San Francisco Minstrels opened their season on 3 September, the night of Joseph Jefferson's premiere. Three weeks later the troupe interpolated a burlesque of *The Black Crook*. The travesty so delighted audiences it was retained on the bill for most of the remaining season. While the San Francisco Minstrels had quickly established a reputation as "the most dignified, the most settled" of blackface bands, demands for their sort of entertainment held steady enough to allow a number of other organizations to flourish. In New York, Kelly and Leon's Minstrels and George Christy's company provided season-long competition. On 2 March a new playhouse, known in its first year both as Lingard's and as Wood's Theatre Comique, opened with an attempt to have the best of both worlds. It presented for its patrons' amusement "minstrels, pantomimists and ballets." Both managements failed, although in a few years the house was to know a brief period of glory.

The night after the San Francisco Minstrels opened, George L. Fox, soon to be a reigning star, began his final season at the Old Bowery, assisted by Fanny Herring, the petite darling of the gallery gods. His programs ranged from **Six Years After; or, The Ticket of Leave Man's Wife** to **Jack and Gill Went Up the Hill** to **Little Boy Blue and Hush-a-Bye Baby; or, Patty and Her Pitcher**. In this typical Fox combination of burlesque and pantomime the star assumed the roles of Disturbance Discomfiture, "alias Hush-a-Bye, a rising young gardener," and, of course, Clown. On 3 December, a burlesque-pantomime of the same order, **Tom-Tom, the Piper's Son**, began a two-week stand at the New Bowery.

At the Théâtre Français much of the season was given over to the great Italian actress Ristori, but a troupe of French actors and singers also presented a fast-changing repertory of French plays, operas, and operettas, including such Offenbach works as **Trombal-cazar** (on 2 December) and **Orphée aux Enfers** (on 17 January), without causing a stir. To be right too soon is to be wrong.

At the New York Theatre two attempts to rival *The Black Crook* were mounted with little success. On 12 December **Cendrillon**, a somewhat burlesqued version of the Cinderella story, was unveiled, with a bevy of scantily—for the time—dressed chorus girls. A rising young comedian, Mark Smith, won laughs as King Hurly Burly XIX, while a very young, soon to be famous Annie Yeamans was cast in a small supporting role. After the show was withdrawn in late January, many of the same players and dancers were seen in similar work on 29 January, **The Bird of Paradise**, which survived a mere two weeks.

The obituaries that appeared the day after BENJAMIN EDWARD WOOLF's death in Boston on 7 February 1901 give no clue as to the date of his birth, offering only the information that he was born in England and emigrated to America at a very early age. Here he apprenticed as an engraver, but left that calling to become a violinist in the orchestra his father conducted at Burton's Theatre in New York. He soon moved to Boston to himself conduct a pit band, at that city's Museum. As the Boston *Herald* noted, "He early developed the brilliant and versatile talent found so often in the race to which he belonged." His poetry was published in book

form, his art presented at leading galleries, and, between about the time of the onset of the Civil War and the mid-1890s, he wrote over thirty shows for production in Boston. Curiously, for all his musical skill and knowledge, he seems to have confined himself largely to contriving librettos. At one time or another he served as drama critic, art critic, or music critic to a succession of Boston papers, for a brief period covering drama and music for both the *Saturday Evening Gazette* and the Boston *Globe* simultaneously.

Apart from *The Black Crook* the most enduring musical of the season was **The Doctor of Alcantara**. This so-called "opéra bouffe" had its premiere four years earlier on 7 April 1862 at the Museum in Boston, Massachusetts. Its score was the work of Julius Eichberg; its libretto was by Benjamin Woolf. Eichberg figured insignificantly in the history of our musical stage, but Woolf played a more prominent role, although most of his activity was confined to Boston.

Woolf and Eichberg's piece suggests that perhaps a distinct musical genre was slowly evolving from European ballad opera, sing-spiel, or opera buffa and that with time the form would have become both sufficiently artful and native to enjoy a success equal to the vogue of a mindless spectacle such as *The Black Crook*. Just such a development did occur thirteen years later in England, when *H.M.S. Pinafore* became the rage.

For the moment, Woolf employed stale Continental motifs to assemble his story. Basically the plot revolved about two young lovers, Isabella and Carlos, who are ordered by their respective fathers, Doctor Paracelsus and Senor Balthazar, to marry mates they have never seen. None realizes that the lovers and the selected mates are one and the same. Woolf resorted to several common—and Shakespearean—ploys for comic relief and dramatic tension. At one point Carlos gains entrance to Isabella's house concealed in a basket. When the basket is thrown out a window into the river, Carlos is presumed drowned. Later Carlos is again mistaken for dead when he drinks one of the doctor's sleeping potions. Woolf's dialogue was, no doubt, spunky for its day. In one scene Isabella's mother,

Lucrezia, attempts to persuade her to accept her father's selection:

Isa: A pretty sort of gentleman he must be to have his wife selected for him.
Luc: That is an especial proof of his trust in you.
Isa: Nonsense! It is an especial proof that he is a fool. Obedience in such a case is no merit.

Eichberg's music is typified by "I Love, I Love," which Carlos sings to a baffled Lucrezia on popping out of the basket.

Three companies mounted the work successfully in New York at one time or another during the season. The American Opera offered it as part of its repertory on 13 September, at the French Theatre. Eichberg himself conducted the ensemble at the New York Theatre for two weeks beginning 3 October, while Caroline Richings included it among her bills at the French Theatre in the spring. At the New York it was followed by a week's run of the same composer's *A Night in Rome* and then by a two-week stay of an English rendering of Donizetti's opera *The Daughter of the Regiment*. In keeping with the practice of the time, the musicals were merely the main course in a theatrical feast that also included a short farce such as *Wanted, 1000 Milliners*, or *Rumti-Foo-zle* as well as diversions between the acts and sometimes between scene changes. With time the Donizetti work gravitated to the confines of opera houses, but *The Doctor of Alcantara* held its audiences' affections and was revived with some frequency in ensuing years at regular legitimate theatres.

On 2 November the Brothers Brough took over the New York Theatre with their London burlesque *Perdita*. The next musical offering was also from their shop. Irene, Jennie, and Sophie Worrell began the first of two visits on 14 January with *Camaralazman and Badoura*. These ladies, whom Odell says were "the first to give here opéra-bouffe in English," clearly possessed the diverse skills necessary to keep a mid-nineteenth-century entertainer employed. Their act included banjo solos and a cobbler's hornpipe. When their rather unattractively titled vehicle showed itself to have limited appeal, the sisters hastily converted to pantomime. Their double bill of *Cinderella* and *Aladdin* premiered on January 14 and ran a month at the Broadway. Demand was such that, after honoring commitments on the road, the sisters returned on 6 May, this time to the New York Theatre, and embarked on a two-month stay during

which *Cinderella* was coupled with any one of three works: *Aladdin, The Elves,* or *The Invisible Prince.*

Caroline Richings also began the first of her two visits on 14 January. Miss Richings's art was on a higher plane than that of the Worrells. The bills of her initial stay at the Olympic included *Maritana, The Bohemian Girl, Rose of Castile,* and the "beautiful musical drama" *The Blind Man's Daughter.* Except for *The Bohemian Girl* the works are forgotten today, although their own age viewed them with respect as exemplars of popular lyric art. When Miss Richings returned the first night in April, she added *Crown Diamonds* and the ubiquitous *Doctor of Alcantara* to her repertory.

German operas such as *Zar und Zimmermann* and *Stradella* also made the Olympic's rafters ring during a short season that began on 4 February.

The last musical offerings of the season were presented by P. T. Barnum at the Old Bowery—not to be confused with the New Bowery, which had burned. The pantomime *Jack and Gill* had a brief vogue, while *Little Boy Blue* began a successful stay on 1 April.

1867–1868

Perhaps the most surprising feature of this season was the dearth of pieces imitating *The Black Crook*. The lone work following in its path, *The White Fawn*, was mounted by *The Black Crook*'s producers and was disappointing. Its relative failure suggested the success of the first work was a little freakish. Although coming seasons did bring spectacles mounted in the *Black Crook* tradition, especially at Niblo's, only *The Black Crook* itself and *Around the World* (28 August 1875) engendered sufficient loyalties to allow for a long history of successful revivals.

On 2 September the Fifth Avenue Opera House began a promising series of burlesques of favorite plays, operas, and lighter musicals, starting with **Cinderella** and moving on to **Fra Diavolo, Shylock; or, The Merchant of Venice Preserved, Medea,** and **Ye Grand Queen Bess** (a spoof of *The Grand Duchess*). But three days after this last show opened to wonderful notices, Kelly (of Kelly and Leon) shot and killed a man in front of the theatre, business collapsed, and the theatre was shut for many months.

In any case, the attractions' popularity might not have survived after another genre, although not truly new, burst on the scene to claim theatregoers' attention. More cohesive and artistically thoughtful than the haphazard opulence of *The Black Crook,* this new genre—opéra bouffe—deserved its popularity. Despite the evident artistic integrity of the new form, American writers, for the most part, continued to produce contrived claptrap pieces that nevertheless retained the allegiance of New York theatregoers.

The musical that started the rage was Jacques Offenbach's **La Grande Duchesse de Gérolstein,** a tongue-in-cheek history of a great lady's love for a common soldier. She promotes him all the way to general before she realizes she can never win his affections away from his simple sweetheart. Paris had first heard the work only five months earlier on 12 April 1867, at the Théâtre des Variétés, with the celebrated Hortense Schneider in the lead. Its American premiere came about in a curious fashion. Ristori had returned early in September for another season at the French Theatre. But like many of the reigning stars of the time, she refused to perform every night. On one of the nights when the theatre would have been dark, 24 September, the impresario H. L. Bateman mounted *La Grande Duchesse* for Lucille Tostée. Tostée and the show "took the town by storm. 'Voici le sabre de mon père' and other airs of La Grande Duchesse were hummed, whistled, played until the ear was worn to shreds." Since New York's few theatres were generally booked ahead for most of the season, Bateman was forced to fit in performances wherever and whenever a house became available for a night or two. As a result, although the mounting achieved a "run" of 156 performances before it was withdrawn on 25 March, it did so in a happenstance repertory with Ristori and other productions. The record was impressive for the time— all the more impressive since the work was sung in French. (Hereafter, with some exceptions that should be obvious, opéra bouffe titles will be given in the language used to sing the mounting. General discussions will use the English title.)

The Devil's Auction (3 October 1867, Banvard's Opera House) was a patent attempt to capitalize on the success of *The Black Crook.* Its saga of evil versus good was similarly embellished with foreign ballerinas in an elaborate ballet, "La Fontaine de l'Amour." The spectacle lasted into December, (For further details see the discussion of the revival on 18 August 1883.)

Niblo's sequel to *The Black Crook*, **The White Fawn,** premiered on 17 January. Its fate augured ill for the future of sequels in the American Musical Theatre. James Mortimer provided the libretto, while the music was again the work of a number

of hands. The story retreated from the adult, metaphysical romanticism of Barras's plot to a lighter, fairy-tale-like world. In a sense, the story hinted at the long reign to come of librettos for adults that employed stories and motifs from childhood. The basic plot was simple. For her disobedience, Princess Graceful (Jennie De Lacey) is sealed in a dark tower by her father, King Dingdong (Mark Smith). Otherworld creatures aid her to flee into the arms of Prince Leander (Lucy Egerton). *The Black Crook*'s Germanic names gave way to comic contrivances such as King Salmon and Lord Twaddledum. At times this otherworldliness was brushed aside in the interests of topicality. The *Times* noted of the audience, "Light words inflamed them and the faintest political hint fired them. Quite a small conflict of cheering and hissing occurred during the third act over an allusion to Gen. Grant and the dialogue was not permitted to be proceeded until the General and the President received the conventional number of hurrahs." But spectacle and ballet remained the dominant attractions: "Gold, silver, silk and electricity— all the effulgence and gradation of light and color mix one with the other in the midst of an admirably arranged confusion, which probably has nowhere else been seen… fairy creatures caper about with torches on their heads which they agitate in such a manner as, notwithstanding the gracefulness of the action, makes one tremble lest they should set themselves on fire." Circus elements were fast invading Niblo's thinking. A first-act finale had children and midgets, as carpenters, masons, and other laborers, erecting the tower. Like *The Black Crook* the show was inordinately long. On opening night the fourth act did not begin until 12:05. First-nighters never saw the final grand transformation; it was discovered all too late that "eighty carpenters and twenty gasmen could not work it perfectly." *The White Fawn* was not a failure, but its run of 150 performances, coming after the year-long stay of *The Black Crook*, marked it as a major disappointment.

The minstrels who had been entertaining New Yorkers all season long brought out their biggest guns in February. The scandal-ridden Kelly and Leon's Minstrels came to life when Leon returned to the stage in "The Grand Dutch 'S'." "Mounted with a lavishness hitherto unknown in such things," the skit enjoyed the longest consecutive run in minstrelsy, 3 February to 6 June. In the cast was George Christy, now without his own troupe and making what proved to be his final Manhattan appearance. A week later the San Francisco Minstrels unveiled their most popular skit of the season, "Under the Kerosene Lamp," a take-off on Augustin Daly's popular *Under the Gaslight*. Earlier in the year they had also enjoyed some success with a travesty of Robertson's *Caste* rechristened "Caste from Memory."

Although *The Grand Duchess* inaugurated a decade-long rage for opéra bouffe, some of which are performed to this day, the season's runaway success was a native effort derived from an older British tradition. With G. L. Fox as star and librettist of **Humpty Dumpty** (10 March 1868, Olympic), American pantomime reached its peak.

GEORGE LAFAYETTE FOX was probably the first real "star" of the American Musical Theatre. He was born in Boston, most likely on 3 July 1825, although his obituary lists his birth year as 1823. Since he was "52 years, 3 months and 21 days" old when he died on 24 October 1877, the later date seems more accurate. He came from a family of "actors of a mediocre kind such as used to delight rural New England audiences but rarely appeared before city theatre goers." After his Boston debut at the age of seven in *The Hunter of the Alps*, he roamed with his family troupe until shortly before making his New York debut in 1850 in *The Demon of the Desert*. A long stint playing Gumption Cute and Deacon Perry in *Uncle Tom's Cabin* was ended so that he could try his hand at pantomime. He scored successes in *Magic Pills* and *The Devil's Doctor*, left to serve briefly in the early years of the Civil War, and returned to attract attention to himself in repertories of *Jack and the Beanstalk* and other such pantomimes. He had increasingly lengthy stands, culminating in a season long stay at the Old Bowery beginning in September of 1865. Lean, with pointed features that reflected his name, he eschewed brash comedy. Instead he drew both sympathy and laughs with performances that contained as much pathos as humor. His popularity was such that when *Humpty Dumpty* was at its height he was the highest paid actor in America. His yearly income exceeded a then-remarkable $20,000.

For Americans who have forgotten the pantomime tradition, it is important to point out how far it strayed from Mother Goose. The action of *Humpty Dumpty* begins in the "Abode of Romance" where Romance (Mrs. C. Edmonds) and Burlesque (Alice Harrison) decide to follow the antics of a group of children. The children are Humpty Dumpty (Fox), Goody Two Shoes (Emily Rigl), Goody's beau, Dan Tucker (C. K. Fox), and One Two Button My Shoe (F. Lacy). The course of the puppy-love affair between Goody and Dan does not run smoothly, complicated as it is by the suit of the Honorable Grandeur Dignity. Goody rejects him violently, toppling him backwards. When Goody and Dan are finally allowed to come together, Burlesque, in accepted pantomime fashion, turns the children into Clown, Columbine (with a twelve-inch skirt and silk tights), Pantaloon, and Harlequin (in spangled trunks and patchwork fleshings). Also in accepted pantomime fashion—especially in its American reincarnation—topical references abounded. In an allusion to the growing political graft and to the postwar inflation, the children pay a call on New York's new $100,000,000 City Hall. At one point our "manifest destiny" was acknowledged when nurses carried two babies on stage. The babies were called Alaska and St. Thomas. In others of the sixteen scenes the cast skated and demonstrated its finesse at billiards. Sets conveyed audiences from Romance's abode (by moonlight) to the Farm of Plenty, an Enchanted Garden, New York sights such as the Olympic Theatre by Night, a Candy Store, and City Hall, and, just before the Grand Transformation, to the Retreat of the Silver Sprites. As he had for both *The Black Crook* and *The White Fawn*, David Costa devised the choreography, which ranged from elaborate ballets to a simple contredanse, a country-style dance with participants ranged facing each other. As the months of the run went by, *Humpty Dumpty*, like *The Black Crook*, incorporated anything that its producers felt would appeal to playgoers. In April a champion skater, E. T. Goodrich, joined the cast, along with La Petite Ravel. By June a major "reconstruction" added a Zouave drill and bayonet combat. One new scene had three dozen people in formal dress, each carrying a shield with the name of one of the states, invite a lady named "Cuba" to join them. In the next season, the producers felt they had made enough revisions to advertise the presentation as the "second volume." These changes included ballet girls making music with wooden and straw sticks and the same young ladies dressed as men. Musically, the evening was probably even more vapid. The score, advertised as "all new," was attributed to A. Reiff, Jr., although much of his task admittedly consisted of selecting suitable airs from the standard repertory. His original material was banal and ignored in most reviews. Virtually nothing was published. It was primarily on account of the magic of Fox's cavortings that *Humpty Dumpty* recorded a first run of 483 performances and grossed $1,406,000 in New York and on its initial tour. Because Fox understood the show's appeal to children he inaugurated a series of Wednesday matinees. These proved so successful that within a few years even plays catering solely to adults began midweek afternoon performances (only *Uncle Tom's Cabin* during its 1853 run at the National had employed midweek matinees successfully before). The show was to have frequent re-mountings over the next two decades, and Fox himself played the lead 1,128 times, until his insanity caused him to be forcibly removed from the stage. Whatever its failings as a piece of artful writing, *Humpty Dumpty's* success underscored the lesson of *The Black Crook*: a vast audience awaited native lyric works tailored to the taste of the American public.

The night after H. L. Bateman withdrew *La Grande Duchesse*, he offered Tostée in a second Offenbach work **La Belle Hélène** (26 March 1868, Français). In France this retelling of the Trojan War legend disguised political barbs that were lost on American audiences. Neither critics nor theatregoers were taken with it as much as they had been with the earlier opéra bouffe. But the musical was by no means a failure, running from 26 March until 2 May. A month after it closed, Kelly and Leon's Minstrels honored it with a spoof, "La Belle L. N." Kelly, released from jail, played Paris while Leon assumed his customary drag to portray Helen. The skit was successful, but just as *La Belle Hélène* failed to equal the vogue of *La Grande Duchesse*, "La Belle L. N." fell short of the appeal of "The Grand Dutch 'S'."

For those who wanted the real thing (but in English), Sophie, Jennie, and Irene Worrell offered *Paris and Helen* and *The Grand Duchess* at the New York in April and June respectively. In May Caroline Richings returned in her older repertory, while in June a troupe from New Orleans failed to please with Offenbach's *Orphée aux Enfers* and its interpretation of *La Grande Duchesse*.

Undaunted by the disappointing showing of *La Belle Hélène* and the fiasco of the New Orleans troupe, Bateman organized the H. L. Bateman's Opera Bouffe Company and, with the folding of *The White Fawn*, presented the American premiere of Offenbach's **Barbe Bleue** (13 July 1868, Niblo's).

In this Gallic version Bluebeard is tamed by his sixth wife, the country wench Boulotte. M. Aujac and Mlle. Irma starred. Bateman's faith and determination were justified. The work was a resounding hit, running twelve weeks. *Barbe Bleue's* popularity assured the reign of opéra bouffe over the musical stage for the next several seasons. But its success did something else. The people flocking to Niblo's box office convinced many a manager that audiences would buy musical entertainments even during hot weather when they would not attend "legitimate" attractions. Within a year even Wallack's, the most august of the "legitimate" houses, offered its summer-darkened auditorium to producers of lyric pieces. The notion of the frivolous, space-filling "summer musical" was born.

1868–1869

There were changes aplenty in the new season, but none that obviously signaled major advances. The heart of the theatrical district was moving to the area between Union Square and Madison Square (14th to 23rd streets), a stretch soon to be known affectionately as "the Rialto." When the old Broadway Theatre was demolished in April of 1869, only Niblo's and the Olympic, the sites of the first two long runs in the American Musical Theatre, were left below 13th Street. Two fine, important new playhouses opened—Booth's Theatre and Pike's Opera House. Both were to have star-crossed existences, although the gutted Booth stood late into the next century as a housing for stores and lofts, while Pike's, under a series of names, became a "combination" house and a grind movie palace. Wood's Museum also opened its doors for the first time. Patterned after Barnum's, it opened every morning at eleven o'clock to exhibit its collection of oddities, a bonus of sorts for theatregoers coming to see the attractions in its auditorium at regular hours. The rapidly growing audience, with its ever-increasing purchasing power, demanded not only more auditoriums for its entertainment but more performances. Wallack's, the last holdout, capitulated and initiated Saturday matinees in line with its competitors. Meanwhile competition raced a step ahead by offering midweek matinees, which had proved so successful for *Humpty Dumpty* and would help fill the coffers of Lydia Thompson.

Musically, the French and the English dominated the season. H. L. Bateman's mounting of Offenbach's *La Grande Duchesse* with Tostée was honored with the opening night at Pike's. Before the season was finished Bateman had two companies presenting opéra bouffe on whatever stage became available. Other producers quickly followed suit. Maurice Grau struck gold at the Théâtre Français with an eleven-week run of Offenbach's melodic version of the legend of a falsely accused wife, **Geneviève de Brabant**, beginning on 22 October. He followed with almost as successful stagings of Hervé's **L'Oeil Crevé** on 11 January and Offenbach's glittering grand tour of the City of Light, **La Vie Parisienne**, on 29 March, the latter at the then astounding top of $3.00, double the customary price. New Yorkers, it seemed, could not get enough of Offenbach. His charming tale of a Peruvian street-singer, **La Périchole**, had its American premiere on 4 January. At least a dozen other examples of opéra bouffe found a place in the season's repertory. They ranged from Offenbach's still-popular *La Belle Hélène* to such now forgotten works as **Monsieur Landry, La Chanson de Fortunio, Les Bavards, Le Maître de Chapelle, Le Dragon de Villars, Le Mariage aux Lanternes** (done in English as *Married by Lanterns*), and **Le 66.** Their vogue was not lessened by the fact that they were all still being done in French.

But their vogue was challenged by something theatregoers could more readily understand: a troupe of beautiful blonde girls, often dressed seductively in tights, who clowned and crooned in English. "Small, brisk and clever" Lydia Thompson, aided by several other attractive young ladies from the British Isles, inaugurated the last of the three great musical fads of the decade: the "blonde burlesques." Their vehicle was **Ixion; or, The Man at the Wheel** (28 September 1868, Wood's Museum), an English extravaganza by F. C. Burnand. The piece had been first performed in America two years earlier in Brooklyn, but in a more straight-faced production. The new producer, Samuel Colville, retained the basic tale of a mortal man's pursuit of a goddess and of his punishment tied to a perpetually revolving wheel, but filled the production with references to contemporary and local happenings, added popular American airs and dances, and staged the whole work tongue-in-cheek. The British blondes quickly replaced the coryphées of *The Black Crook* in the hearts of Broadway's gay blades. In *Ixion* and other musical burlesques such as **The Forty Thieves** or **Sinbad**, the girls happily assumed the trouser roles that exploited their shapely limbs. When the engagement at Wood's concluded, they opened an equally profitable one

at Niblo's. The two stands carried them through the season.

Neither opéra bouffe nor blonde burlesques went unnoticed by the minstrels. Earlier spoofs such as "The Grand Dutch 'S'" had proved so rewarding that the troupes were devoting an increasing amount of time to their burlesques and less and less space to olios. Bryant's Minstrels, the San Francisco Minstrels, and Kelly and Leon all promptly inserted travesties of the latest hits in their evenings. Kelly and Leon had the biggest success with "Barber Blue," which allowed Leon, the best-known female impersonator of the time, to don a blonde wig and to kid Miss Thompson and Offenbach at the same time.

Julius Benedict's **The Lily of Killarney** (1 January 1868, Academy of Music) was a romantic opera based on Dion Boucicault's *The Colleen Bawn*. Its heroine's love for an impoverished aristocrat triumphs over all manner of mistaken identities and villainy. Along with the not dissimilar *Bohemian Girl* and *Maritana*, the piece retained the public's affection for several decades.

Apart from the minstrels, native talents for the most part ignored the musical stage. When W. H. Lingard reopened his renovated Theatre Comique on 1 February, the bill included an extended skit, **Pluto.** This burlesque extravaganza was derived from Byron's *Orpheus* by Henry B. Farnie. Its songs were by Dave Braham, whose career at the Comique would be long and glorious. The spoof allowed Alice Dunning to lighten her hair and put on tights to play Orpheus; Lingard played Pluto.

Earlier, John Brougham had offered a burlesque called **Much Ado About the Merchant of Venice** (14 October 1868, Pike's) as an afterpiece. This bit of musical fluff was received unkindly and, although revived briefly at the Fifth Avenue, was soon forgotten. But later in the season Brougham had mounted another afterpiece that bears some scrutiny. Following the premiere of his new comedy, *Better Late Than Never*, he appended a performance of a curious piece with a curious title, **The Dramatic Review for 1868** (25 January 1869, Fifth Ave.). Of course, Brougham could have no inkling of the dated annuals called revues that would flood Broadway half a century later. Nonetheless, in a small way this short collection of skits had something of the feel of the later spectacles. It opened with an allegory whose principal figures were Manhatta and Brooklyna, "the oldest of Manhatta's family, and a remarkably forward young lady... holding but ferry little intercourse with her Ma, and that she means to abridge." Other characters included New Jersia, North Rivero (a "fluent individual"), East Rivero, Public Opinion, and Captain Jinks. Succeeding skits twitted various opéras bouffes ("Bouffe à la Mode"), *Humpty Dumpty* (as "The Fox's Nest"), new theatres, and new straight plays. Effie Germon sang a song teasing the velocipede craze.

To be right too soon is to be wrong. Some years later, when the first *Passing Show* (12 May 1894) established the revue tradition in America, hardly anyone remembered Brougham's little mélange of skits and songs. Brougham himself wrote a number of longer plays interlarded at times with melody in the Tom and Jerry tour-of-a-city tradition. These plays undoubtedly helped smooth the way for Harrigan and Hart and other early vernacular musicals. But Brougham most certainly never thought of himself as a writer of musicals.

On 10 May 1869, thousands of miles west of New York, in Ogden, Utah, a golden spike driven into a rail signaled the completion of America's first transcontinental railroad connection. Although many years passed before touring companies routinely played the West Coast, long-range effects of the event—demographic changes, the opening up of California to a young movie industry—were to bear significantly on our lyric stage.

Just before the hot weather arrived, *Humpty Dumpty* took its final fall on 15 May. Three nights later, however, G. L. Fox was back with many of the same players, in a sequel called **Hiccory Diccory Dock** (18 May 1869, Olympic). Like its predecessor it reveled in the pantomime tradition. Fox once again assumed the title role and as Hiccory visited with Mrs. Jack Spratt (C. K. Fox), climbed the beanstalk with another Jack (F. Lacy), and romped with Little Red Riding Hood (Mile. A. Laurent). In the second half a transformation scene allowed Hiccory to become Clown and his cohorts to change into Pantaloon, Harlequin, Columbine, and—a rare addition—Sprite. Spectacular sets depicted a Palace of Dazzling Light, the Haunt of Fancy, and, as a finale, Hiccory's Aerial Voyage by the First Flying Velocipede. Lavish ballets, devised by David Costa, were led by Mile. Sangalli. She offered her Dance of the Lily in the Grand Ballet of Coral Nymphs. Haniola, Imre, and Bolossy Kiralfy whirled through a Magyar Czardas in the Palace scene. But the spectacle and high jinks suffered the fate of so many sequels—not unlike *The White Fawn* that had followed *The Black Crook, Hiccory Diccory Dock* was a disappointment. Fox's popularity saw to it that the evening was not a total loss. His followers came in

sufficient numbers to allow the musical to run into the first week of September. In the long haul, the evening's most important contribution was the debut of the Kiralfy brothers. Hungarian immigrants, they arrived in this country as dancers. Within a short term they became the principal producers of spectacle in New York.

The coming of summer allowed the Lauri family to mount some musical pantomimes at Wallack's. The Lauris wisely invited several of the British blondes to join them. The month-long festival included *Little Boy Blue, Mother Hubbard; or, Harlequin Little Bo-Peep*, and *Coralline; or, Sir Rupert, the Reckless*.

1869–1870

Writing in 1936, theatre historian George Odell proclaimed, "A new era in New York theatricals begins in the year 1869." He concluded his introduction to the decade of the seventies with a statement that would startle modern scholars: "Those years ... seem to me almost the very palmiest days of the drama in New York." Throughout his career Odell had little time for the lyric stage. But even if he had been more favorably inclined toward musicals, the ten seasons beginning with 1869–1870 would have afforded him small pleasure. They were years of uncertain groping for formulas, meager in their lyric offerings, stingy with their triumphs. And 1869–1870 itself was no exception. Only a fluke in the theatrical calendar allowed it to claim one of the most popular of the nineteenth century's proto-musicals.

Certainly the most obvious and baffling circumstance of the season was the abrupt and all but total disappearance of opéra bouffe from the Broadway stage—almost as if the surfeit of the preceding session precluded so much as a four-bar phrase in the new year. The Théâtre Français housed a few exceptions, mounting *La Grande Duchesse* briefly in January, *Geneviève de Brabant* for a week in February, and one performance of a double bill of *Barbe Bleue* and *Le Sourd*. And, as part of a March bill, Kelly and Leon's minstrels gave New Yorkers their first glimpse of Offenbach's one-acter **Ba-ta-clan**, in which a Chinese emperor, police official, and two citizens all reveal themselves as really Frenchmen. The piece was offered on 28 March as **Ching Chow High; or, A Cracked Piece of China.** However, the disappearance was momentary. By 1870–1871 opéra bouffe renewed its lease on theatregoers' affections.

On the other hand serious opera fared well on commercial stages all year long. The very first musical event of importance was the opening of the Carl

Rosa–C. D. Hess Company on 11 September at the Théâtre Français. The company's curtain raiser was the American premiere of Balfe's **The Puritan's Daughter**. Some may have considered it only just that opera in English was being presented at the Théâtre Français after so much opéra bouffe had been sung in French at more traditionally named playhouses. The Rosa–Hess repertory also included *The Bohemian Girl, La Sonnambula,* and *Martha.* In late October a troupe of Germans spent a week at the same house singing *Faust, Martha, The Magic Flute,* and *Robert the Devil.* Caroline Richings returned as Caroline Richings-Bernard on 15 November to offer her own season at the Grand Opera House. Her programs included many of the same works the Germans and the Rosa–Hess organization had offered, as well as *Fra Diavolo, Il Trovatore,* and *The Huguenots.* The restored Academy of Music also provided opera lovers with a season.

Virtually all the other musical offerings served up at the commercial houses were burlesques. Wood's Museum began the parade of travesties at the beginning of September. Its most notable and successful offerings were **Wip Wan Winkle**, twitting Joseph Jefferson's version then finishing its run at Booth's, and a "second company" of British blondes in *Ixion* and newer material. Since the blondes were being spoofed by minstrels and other burlesquers, they decided the height of fun might be to spoof themselves. They did so in their own version of an old hit, *The Fair One with the Golden Locks,* which they reworked as **Dora Bella, the Mill, the Mystery, the Mission, the Miss, the Minstrel and the Dyed Hair**. Alice Oates employed the same old play when she appeared for a summer season at the Olympic. Her version was called **The Fair One with the Blonde Wig**. On 13 June she brought out **The Daughter of the Regiment; or, 800 Fathers**, ostensibly a burlesque of Donizetti's opera, but one garnished with music by other composers such as Verdi and Offenbach, and spiced with specialties including Willie Edouin's take-off of Bonfanti. Richard Norton, in his research for the companion volume to this book, discovered programs indicating that on 22 August Oates offered H. B. Farnie's English version of Hervé's *Le Petit Faust* simply as **Little Faust!** Apparently overlooked by Odell and Brown in their histories and by many contemporary reviewers, this would seem to be the first New York and possibly the first American production of the work. (Kelly and Leon produced their own version a few nights later.) Lydia Thompson

herself returned from a tour of major American cities to begin a two-month stay at Niblo's Garden on 4 April. Her opening bill was **Pippin; or, King of the Gold Mines**, one of her London successes, adapted for American tastes. After a brief fling at serious melodrama, Miss Thompson and her band reverted to burlesque with revivals of *Ixion* and *The Forty Thieves.*

But the year's most successful burlesque was G. L. Fox's **Hamlet**. Fox worked together with T. C. De Leon, his collaborator on *Humpty Dumpty* and *Hiccory Diccory Dock,* to contrive what the *Times* hailed as an evening of "uproarious laughter." Edwin Booth had opened in his great *Hamlet* on 5 January and was still playing to packed houses when Fox romped onto the stage of the Olympic on 14 February. Inevitably, Fox dressed as much like Booth as possible. But not for long. Reacting to Francisco's complaint "'Tis bitter cold," Fox stopped the proceedings to don a gigantic fur hat, brightly colored woolen socks, and oversized mittens. Those intervals when Fox could not be on stage were filled with music, everything from sentimental ballads to a wild Danish cancan. The piece ran two months. But when Fox tried to follow on 18 April with a mock mounting of Booth's version of *Macbeth* he met with a poor reception. The failure of a sequel was nothing new to Fox, but this time he had the small consolation of knowing Booth's *Macbeth* also fell far short of the success of the actor's *Hamlet.*

Apart from Fox's *Hamlet,* the major hits of the year were outside the burlesque world. Both appeared rather late in the season. The financier "Big Jim" Fisk had taken over the Grand Opera House (formerly Pike's) on West 23rd Street. Slightly off the beaten path, the theatre's location made its success precarious. Fisk was determined to give its uncertain fortunes a boost. On 7 February he helped unveil the most expensive production to that date in America, a $75,000 mounting of **The Twelve Temptations**. The piece was unmistakably meant to be in the tradition of *The Black Crook.* Its story was based on the Walpurgis Night legend and adapted for the stage by Joseph C. Foster. Once again a tempter claims a lost soul, and once again the soul is rescued at the last moment. Intentionally or not, a principal figure was named Rudolph. Of course, whereas the Rudolf of *The Black Crook* had been the hero, the Rudolph (E. L. Tilton) of *The Twelve Temptations* was the villainous tempter. In the end the hero, Ulric (G. C. Boniface), is rescued not by a fairy queen but by Justice (Fanny Lovelace), Faith (Nannie Egbert),

Hope (Flora Leland), Charity (Nelly Jarman), and Purity (Marion Herbert). David Costa, the era's leading choreographer, staged the dances amid revolving temples, a fiery underworld, and the final glorious transformation. In keeping with contemporary practice, new spectacular scenes, new dances, and new artists were inserted at various times during the run. At one point a troupe of Spanish dancers was hired. All the lavishness was rewarded, and *The Twelve Temptations* ran profitably until 9 July, achieving just over 150 showings. Unfortunately, Fisk's assassination less than two years later put an end to his plans for the house and helped undermine its already shaky reputation.

But the most enduring work of the season did not appear until by normal reckoning the season was long finished, when Joseph K. Emmet opened in **Fritz, Our Cousin German** (11 July 1870, Wallack's).

Charles Gayler, the play's author, assuredly conceived of the work as a sentimental melodramatic comedy. There was no music, nor were there lyrics in his original manuscript, although places were designated for the singing of "Home, Sweet Home" and a "Guitar Song" that soon evolved into the famous "Lullaby." But Emmet was known for his fine singing voice and playing ability. A note at the beginning of the manuscript reads, "Curtain when music played once through." This suggests an overture. However, it must be remembered that in a time of cheap labor all major houses—even those devoted exclusively to straight plays—had orchestras in their pits to entertain before the show and at intermissions.

JOSEPH K. EMMET was born in St. Louis on 13 March 1841. His father died when the boy was ten and young Joseph was apprenticed to a sign painter. Joseph soon found himself making frequent visits to neighborhood theatres since his employer also painted sets for provincial playhouses. This taste of the other side of the footlights led Emmet to create a variety act as "a song and dance artist." After a brief stint on the minstrel stage Emmet returned to variety in a "Dutch" (German) act wearing a green blouse and cap and wooden shoes and singing in broken English.

Gayler's plot is complicated and covers a substantial stretch of time. Fritz (Emmet) arrives in America to seek his long-lost sister and to locate the money their father left with the girl. During the crossing he falls in love with another immigrant, Katarina (Georgia Langley). But Katarina is also sought by Colonel Crafton (Charles Fisher), whom the manuscript lists as the "leading heavy." Some years earlier Crafton had adopted an immigrant girl. Of course, the girl is Fritz's sister. Elias Grim (C. H. Rockwell), Crafton's attorney, discovers the relationship and understands that Crafton hopes to have all his adopted daughter's money. Grim demands the hand of Crafton's real daughter in return for his silence. Crafton lures Katarina away from Fritz and locks her in a house he owns, but Fritz, disguised as a washerwoman, comes to see Katarina. He alerts the girl to Crafton's plan to drug her. Katarina switches drinks on Crafton, and when he is unconscious she and Fritz flee. Grim, furious at Crafton for his refusal to give his consent, sneaks Fritz into Crafton's house to see if Crafton's adopted daughter is the woman Fritz claims she is. Fritz sings a lullaby he and his sister loved as children, and her recognition of the old song seals the identification. Later Fritz and Katarina wed. They have a child. Crafton, impoverished, attempts to kidnap the infant, but Fritz kills him. The killing occurs at a mill, where Fritz springs a trapdoor. The villain falls through, and moments later his lifeless body is seen caught in the mill wheel. Gayler's dialogue employed all the rhetoric of melodrama:

Katarina: Oh in Heaven's name forbear—take all we have—strip us of everything—but do not injure one hair of that loved darling's head.
Crafton: You plead in vain—now I will be avenged for all.

Gayler's humor was equally of his time. Fritz wins the audience's affection with his "Dutchisms." He says "foolosipher" for "philosopher" and refers to English as the "United States Language." But the bulk of the evening's comedy went to an unimportant character called Julius Snow (Mr. Kyle), listed in the manuscript as "negro—first comedian." The part was played in blackface, and a typical speech ran:

Evening parties when giben regardless of expense is a great engine of cibilization—dey open de hearts of mankind—and make dem gib de footman a dollar—when he hands de hats and de coats at de door—by de way—I must not forgit to mix up dem hats and de coats in de hall—dere are shabby persons who if dey can find dere own hats and coats for demselves—will sneak wid out gibben de footman a red cent.

While the story clearly appealed to Victorian tastes, it was Emmet's singing, playing, and acting that remained the evening's prime attraction. Songs listed in the program, and credited to Thomas Baker, included "Valking Dat Broadway Down" and "Oh, Schneider, How You Vas?" There is no reason to be certain that the half-dozen songs named were all that were offered, although they may well have been. Because playbills of the era often failed to list musical numbers, it cannot be determined exactly when Emmet's "Lullaby" became a part of the show. Although a place for it was clearly there from the start, the song was not copyrighted until 1878. Whenever it was introduced it quickly became popular, and it has remained one of the longest-lived melodies to emanate from our musical stage. This original production ran until 10 September. But for more than a decade Emmet kept busy in revivals and revisions of the work and in a series of similar pieces.

1870–1871

Perhaps the four years that elapsed between the July 1870 debut of *Fritz, Our Cousin German* and the July 1874 premiere of *Evangeline* (27 July 1874) illustrate most cogently that *The Black Crook* (12 September 1866) did not initiate a spate of creativity in the American Musical Theatre. The four years seemed desultory and aimless on the lyric stage. At best it was a time of small consolidations. In this period all three of the immediate postwar hits—*The Black Crook, Humpty Dumpty* (10 March 1868), and *Fritz*—had their first major revivals. The success of the three revivals showed that the popularity of the originals was not a season's quirk. But the revivals also illustrated how different each work was, how essentially unrelated and unconnected their styles were. *The Black Crook* was romantic, melodramatic spectacle, with its prime musical emphasis on ballet; *Humpty Dumpty* was transposed English pantomime with an element of *The Black Crook's* spectacle appended; *Fritz* was sentimental, melodramatic comedy with light songs interspersed. All three plays found imitators; the latter two were most successfully reworked by their original stars and authors.

The season of 1870–1871 offered distressingly slim pickings for lovers of the lyric stage. The schedule of opera at the Academy of Music was "the leanest in its history." Miss Richings offered three weeks of opera at Niblo's Garden, beginning 24 October. The San Francisco Minstrels got off to an early start on 29 August, but their audience petered out, and their year ended on April 1st. Their competition, both occupied with opening new auditoriums, started later. Kelly and Leon's raised its curtain on 12 September, but financial problems forced the troupe to move to Brooklyn in December. Bryant's new house near Booth's was not ready until 23 November. Once opened, Bryant outlasted his principal competitors, running happily until 7 June. Indicatively, far longer seasons were chalked up by the new variety houses, with Tony Pastor's in the lead and the Theatre Comique not far behind.

That beloved curiosity, the diminutive Lotta (Lotta Crabtree), arrived in **Heart's Ease** (12 September 1870, Niblo's). In this and the other plays in her repertory Miss Crabtree strummed her banjo, sang her simple ditties, and danced a bit. It can be argued whether or not her vehicles were in fact musicals. The fairest answer seems to be they were essentially straight plays tailored to include outlets for Lotta's abundant store of specialties. They differ from, say, Emmet's *Fritz* plays in that a man such as Emmet was primarily a singer and the songs in his vehicles were worked in with more care. Although there were exceptions, other artists rarely sang or danced in these stars' pieces, and choruses or concerted passages were unknown.

Of more conventional lyric theatre there was precious little. Most was mounted at the Grand Opera House, where a seven-and-a-half-month season of opéra bouffe ran from 26 September to 20 May. Its first night presented the New York premiere of the original French version of Hervé's **Le Petit Faust**. Although Tostée reappeared and the session saw the New York premieres of two more Offenbach works, **Les Brigands** and **Les Géorgiennes,** it was the debut on 21 December of Tostée's great rival and successor, Marie Aimée, that was the highlight of the stand.

G. L. Fox had a new pantomime ready for his followers. A happy-go-lucky mélange of Mother Goose, classical legend, and wild imagination, **Wee Willie Winkie** (5 October 1870, Olympic) let its hero meet Old Grain (George A. Beane), "The Jolly Miller on the River Dee"; Leander (R. Honeywood), "a youth of Hellespont in love with Blondette"; and Blondette

(Fannie Beane), who was the miller's daughter and "not a blonde." In twenty-two scenes Wee Willie's travels took him from a Fairy Dell to as far as China, and he participated in two elaborate transformations. The first was "The Glory of Florisette," the second—the grand finale—whisked the cast to the "Realms of Light and Beauty." The antics found Clown and Harlequin battling their own shadows, and in a minor comic "transformation" Harlequin metamorphosed into a sandwich. With music "composed and selected by Mon. F. Strebinger," the piece sang, danced, and mimed its merry way until 4 February. One interesting sidelight was the lack of apparent changes during the run. Neither programs nor newspaper announcements suggested the deletions and additions so common in the musical theatre of the time. Apparently audiences at the last performance saw much the same entertainment first-nighters had applauded. A certain sense of artistic integrity may have been creeping into the American Musical Theatre.

On 12 October the self-advertised "prince of comedy and song," M. W Fiske, opened at the Bowery in **Little Dick, the New York Bootblack,** a vehicle not unlike Lotta's or Emmet's in conception. It was withdrawn after four nights and a burlesque of *The Grand Duchess* substituted.

Jarrett and Palmer gave *The Black Crook* (12 September 1866) its first major revival on 12 December, just in time to capture the holiday trade. They captured far more, and theatregoers again flocked to Niblo's in sufficient numbers to keep the show running until 8 April (122 performances). Advertised as costing $45,000 ($15,000 for scenery alone), it featured the acrobatic Majiltons and a team of skaters, Moe and Goodrich—another early sign of how quickly circus elements were coming to dominate these extravagant mountings. Marie Bonfanti was back as prima ballerina, while one of Lydia Thompson's most beautiful girls, Pauline Markham, played Stalacta. W. T. Voegtlin, for the next decade or so one of New York's most sought-after scene painters, led the list of designers. The eye-filling depictions of "The Ravine of Zamiel" and "The Palace of Dew Drops" (this latter painted by the Drew Brothers of London) amazed audiences with "Dutch metal [imitation gold leaf], red fire, thunder and lightning, gongs, atabals and other instruments of optical and auric delectation." Unlike Fox at the Olympic, Jarrett and Palmer followed contemporary fashion by announcing frequent changes in cast and spectacle.

G. L. Fox himself attempted another burlesque on the order of his *Hamlet* travesty when he replaced *Wee Willie Winkie* with his spoof of Booth's *Richelieu.* Called **Richelieu of the Period,** its hero appropriated its star's initials, appearing as Cardinal G. L. Richelieu, a man of "obvious Cardinal Virtues." But, *Hamlet* excepted, Fox never appealed to the public at large except in more traditional pantomime. The work disappeared on 18 March.

Only one other American lyric work appeared during the entire season. After opéra bouffe left the Grand, the house attempted on 22 May to offer a successor of sorts to its popular *The Twelve Temptations* (7 February 1870), another romantic spectacle, **The Three Hunchbacks.** Its producers succeeded in luring many performers from the recently closed revival of *The Black Crook,* including prima ballerina Marie Bonfanti and the skaters Moe and Goodrich. Despite its florid Arabian Nights setting and the injection of pantomime features, the work failed to win public affection. Critics complained of the lack of integration between the main story and the pranks of Clown, Harlequin, and their crew. Changes were made, but they were unavailing. The show left after one month.

Although advertised as "a Grand, Musical and Spectacular Drama," which in the parlance of the day could have meant almost anything, the discovery of a playbill for one of the era's many theatricalizations of Bulwer-Lytton's **Paul Clifford** (12 June 1871, Niblo's), shows that this version of the tale of a gallant highwayman who learns he is of good blood, reforms, and sails for a fresh start in America had so substantial and variegated, if uncredited, a musical program that it deserves a small place in the records of our lyric theatre.

The season closed as it had opened, with opéra bouffe. But there were two important differences. The operas were housed at the renowned Wallack's and were done in English with the principal performer being, to the surprise of many, Lydia Thompson. Her repertory included the premiere of another Offenbach opera, **The Princess of Trébizonde,** on 11 September. Its plot centered on a prince caught up in a whirl of circus people. Hearing opéra bouffe in English stunned the reviewer for the *Herald.* Prudish and shortsighted, he cried:

> *Opéra bouffe* may well be said to have seen its palmiest days. The lower school of music, which it made the rage of the European capitals for the past few years, has proved, like

the intoxication of French champagne, to be only a passing exhilaration. Like champagne, too, in large doses, it has proved nauseating. Manifestly the product of the lower empire and its loose ways, this deification of the *demi-monde* has almost passed away.... It is safe to say that had a knowledge of the French language been more widespread the grossness and *equivoque* of its *dialogue* would have sooner earned for it a public condemnation.

Miss Thompson's engagement, which by today's calendar would belong to the following season, ran, with disappointing returns, from 16 August to 23 September.

1871–1872

The new season was even more lackluster than its predecessor. The New York stage's circus aspect, whose intrusion the theatre historian O. G. Sonneck had noted began three-quarters of a century before, seemed especially marked, perhaps because there were no new pieces of merit. With Kelly and Leon's gone, only Bryant and the San Francisco troupe remained as blackface regulars. They were augmented on and off throughout the theatrical year by the brief appearance of other hands. These included one black troupe, the Georgia Minstrels, who began a month's stay at Lina Edwin's Theatre at the end of the season.

Variety fared a little better. In retrospect its bills contain tantalizing previews of the future. The program of the Globe Theatre for the week of 16 October found Edward "Ned" Harrigan and Tony Hart on the bill. In the future much of their material would be unveiled at this very house. Six months later, on 15 April, the Vokes Family arrived from England with their comedy of high life below stairs, *The Belles of the Kitchen*. Interlarded with the troupe's songs and specialties, the evening was one of the biggest successes of the season. Its popularity played no small part in initiating the vogue for farce-comedy, the somewhat deceptive name for a collection of songs, dances, and other acts tied together with a loose plot. All variety houses at this time offered musical playlets, little more than skits, which nonetheless hinted at more fully fleshed vehicles to come. Unfortunately, most of these shorter offerings are lost. If enough could be found, a careful study might furnish some interesting

sidelights on the development of vernacular musical comedy.

The regular playhouses reopened in August, with Joseph K. Emmet starring in a month-long run of *Fritz, Our Cousin German* (11 July 1870). He raised his curtain at Niblo's Garden on 21 August.

One week later an ex-minstrel, G. Swayne Buckley, relit the Bowery with *On the Track*. Although Buckley played "ten instruments, sang twelve songs, and executed six dances," critics reviewed the pieces as straight melodrama. Buckley, like Lotta and Emmet, employed vehicles that defied easy classification.

Three nights later, 31 August, when the Olympic began its season, G. L. Fox was once again playing it safe with *Humpty Dumpty* (10 March 1868). His caution was rewarded. *Humpty Dumpty* added another 300 performances to its record before it closed on 11 June. During the eight-plus months that the musical remained on the boards it was twice advertised as "remodeled." First-nighters on 31 August saw the evening begin with a burlesque prologue in which the personification of Burlesque (Lulu Prior) confronted the personification of Tragedy (Annie Yeamans). These two ladies argued for supremacy before a court that included America (Flora Lee), Europe (Miss R. Melnotte), and Asia (Miss H. Naylor). The main part of the show offered a cornucopia of performers. The Kiralfys were back with lavish ballets. The Marten family performed "Tyrolean eccentricities, including a cat duo." Another band of performers was known as the Zig-Zags. A four-year-old with the stage name of Young Adonis performed a pas de deux with a two-year-old named Little Venus. On 8 January the first of the wholesale revisions took place. The burlesque prologue was changed to a two-character piece in which the Sun Spirit (played by the same lady who had impersonated Burlesque) vied with the Ice King (George Beane) to see who could conjure up the most spectacular effects. Specialties included a couple "who walk on a ceiling head downwards." The Kiralfys introduced a colorful "Warriors' Dance" in which the women, dressed as Amazons, climbed a staircase made by the men holding their shields above their heads. Similar changes occurred 1 April.

On 18 September Emmet replaced *Fritz* with **Carl, the Fiddler.** The play, like *Fritz*, was by Charles Gayler and centered on an immigrant's attempt to find a long-lost sister. The recognition scene once again came to pass when the hero sang what was in this version called "The Brother's Lullaby." Gayler was credited with writing the songs as well as the libretto. For Emmet this play initiated a series of successors to *Fritz* that were little more than minor variations on the same theme. Generally, the public proved indifferent to the changes, content with familiar figures and Emmet's fine singing. But neither the critics nor the public were especially kind to *Carl*. The *Times* was annoyed by a "dialect drama" in which the hero "wandered about the stage for three hours with a guitar strung across his back." Reviews of this nature kept theatregoers away. *Fritz* was hastily revived to alternate with *Carl* until Emmet's engagement ran its course on 30 September.

Opéra bouffe held sway at Lina Edwin's Theatre from 9 October through 3 February. With Aimée as the principal attraction, a number of works fast becoming old favorites were revived: *La Grande Duchesse, Barbe Bleue, La Périchole*. Two new offerings were added to the repertory as well, although neither gained lasting affection: Charles Lecocq's **Fleur de Thé** and Offenbach's **Le Pont des Soupirs**.

Jarrett and Palmer again revived *The Black Crook* (12 September 1866) on 18 December at Niblo's Garden, advertising with relish increasingly Barnumesque interpolations. These included a trio of Egyptian Jugglers, the St. Felix Parisienne Infant Ballet ("Children from 5 to 10 years of age dancing with the proficiency of adults"), and Professor Samwell's trained animals. The revival ran until 24 February. This was the last time the musical played on the stage where it had originally opened. On 6 May a fire left only the rear of Niblo's standing, Manhattan's ninth major theatre fire in seven years. The Niblo's Garden that rose from the ashes was a grander auditorium, despite the growing distance the years were putting between it and the main theatre area.

The season closed with the return of Lydia Thompson and her repertory of burlesque. The opening attraction at Wallack's on 15 July was *Robin Hood*, followed in August by *Blue Beard* and in September by a revival of *Ixion* coupled with *A Happy Pair*. On 21 September, the last week of her stay, Miss Thompson brought out a spoof of Sir Walter Scott's *Kenilworth*.

One extra-theatrical event of interest to theatregoers also occurred in July. A figure Broadway would soon admire for his legitimate offerings appeared briefly as a conductor of three special concerts of his orchestral pieces at the Academy of Music. He was Johann Strauss.

1872–1873

There are few seasons as intriguing as the theatrical year of 1872–1873; intriguing in its manifestations of lost possibilities for the American Musical Theatre. For in this season one of the towering figures of the nineteenth-century American stage— Augustin Daly—took a sudden interest in musicals. Daly was not only the manager of one of New York's most prestigious playhouses, but an indefatigable translator and adapter of plays, plays that were considered the last word in dramaturgy for their time. In this season, besides keeping occupied with his Fifth Avenue Theatre and his adaptations, Daly assumed temporary control of the Grand Opera House. On 26 August he inaugurated the year with a lavish mounting of Offenbach's **Le Roi Carotte**. His star in the work was John Brougham, whose Tom-and-Jerry-style slices of New York life, prototypical revues, and *Pocahontas* (24 December 1855) had taken their places as precursors of modern musicals. Despite Daly's retention of the French title, the work was offered in translation, and "Brougham played, with his Irish brogue, King Carrot, the vegetable monarch who rose out of a garden bed in a single night" to save a prince from revolution. The original was larded with political innuendo; the American interpretation presented the story more at face value. The show ran until the end of November, after which Daly had even more interesting offerings in store.

Wood's Museum attempted to present Daly with serious competition when it raised its curtain on 9 September with **Chow Chow; or A Tale of Pekin**. The extravaganza was written by the theatre's stage manager, James Barnes, and had music "arranged by W. H. Brinkworth." Based loosely and irreverently on the adventures of Byron's pirate chief in a harem, it featured Lisa Weber as Conrad and Pauline Markham as Maimounie. Characters not found in Byron included Prince Pretty Bill, Cupid, and Glowworm (Alice Atherton). Only the briefest bow was made to the subtitle when late in the last act Conrad and his friends arrived in Pekin to meet Chow Chow (a comparatively minor role played by G. C. Charles), Pig-Taili, and Sing Sing. Although the cast included several of Lydia Thompson's most popular blondes (who had made their memorable debut at this very house) and a future star such as Miss Atherton, its disappointing run lasted less than a month. Aimée opened the season at the fading Olympic on 14 October with a four-week repertory of opéra bouffe that introduced no new works. She was followed by Lydia Thompson and her blondes in their own four-week stay that gave New Yorkers a chance to see **Aladdin II** and a revival of *Kenilworth*. By 9 December Aimée was back. This time she did mount a novelty, Lecocq's tale of demi-mondaines who answer their government's call for virgins to settle an island, **Les Cents Vierges** (on 23 December). Aimée and her company remained until 11 January.

Meanwhile, at the Grand Opera House, Daly had one of his own adaptations ready on 25 November. Based loosely on *La Tour du Cadran*, a French vaudeville by H. Crémieux and H. Bocage, which sent its hero on a tour of Paris, **Round the Clock; or, New York by Dark** took its own protagonist, Roderick Killgobbin (John Brougham), on a whirl around Manhattan. Transferring the action of his adaptations to America was a common practice of Daly's. In his pursuit of Ernesta Hardacre (Emma Howson), Roderick visited a number of boutiques, the Grand Union Depot, a Liederkranz Society Ball, and Niblo's Garden during a performance of *The Black Crook* (during which Mrs. John Wood imitated the Majiltons). At one point the action was stopped for a sumptuous tableau entitled "The Daughters of Eve" depicting five thousand years of fashions in dress. The evening ended with a joyous cancan "taken from the French." The show kept the box office busy for two months. One interesting sidelight was the ruckus raised by patrons offended by an action-packed prizefight. The *Times* rushed to Daly's defense, assailing the "fastidious" who objected to some manly boxing but remained silent about the increasing violence in other shows. No one, the paper pointed out, was shot in the back, as was the case in several other plays then or recently on the stage. Collectors of theatrical trivia might note that the law firm of Ketchum and Cheatum was making what was probably its first of many appearances in the American Musical Theatre.

While *Round the Clock* took its audience to the old Niblo's, the new Niblo's Garden threw open its doors on 30 November with a ballet extravaganza in the dependable tradition of *The Black Crook*—**Leo and Lotos**. The story told how a wicked seneschal fails to keep the lovers apart. But the plot was so thin the *Times* warned audiences they must be prepared

to "derive pleasure from music, sets, and costumes" alone. Prince Leo was sung by Mlle. Diani "from the Paris Opera." Her fellow artists included Henry Collard, a dwarf famous for his imitations of great tenors, E. D. Davies, a ventriloquist, and the inevitable acrobats. The evening was "rich in marches, counter-marches and groupings of lovely Amazons." It also featured one particularly sumptuous stage picture, "The Palace of Jewels." The still popular style of mounting, and excitement over the new auditorium, helped the entertainment run until the end of March.

The irrepressible *Humpty Dumpty* (10 March 1868) returned to the Olympic for another run on 17 February. Assisting G. L. Fox with their special-ties were a harpist and violinist, a wirewalker, a pair of skaters, and ten "Bedouin Arabs." Young Adonis and Little Venus were back, a year older. With inevitable cast changes and new stage business, Fox and his company cavorted until 7 June.

The night after *Humpty Dumpty* returned, Daly presented his last production of the season with sub-stantial singing and dancing. Like *Round the Clock*, **Roughing It** was said to be based on a Parisian show, one Daly failed to identify. Although the source was Parisian, Daly again followed his customary practice of transferring the action to America. But in this instance his canvas was considerably larger than the limited tour of New York he had offered earlier. Antoinette (Mrs. John Wood), the daughter of Denis MacDuffie (Brougham), elopes with poor but social Aubrey Van Dollas (J. C. Peakes). They lead her father on a chase that takes them from Manhattan to the Rockies and then, just before the almost requisite final transformation scene, to a Chinese opium den. There Mrs. Wood had a splendid comic "death scene," recovering miraculously the moment Antoinette's father consents to her marrying Denis. At one point Mrs. Wood was honored with the flattery of impersonation, when Annie Deland portrayed her as "the queen of comedy and song." Annie Yeamans, in a few years to be Harrigan and Hart's leading lady, won applause in the cameo role of Mother Terror, an "opium crone." Sets included a very animated view of the Grand Central Depot," a transformation scene depicting the four seasons, and, most highly praised of all, Wild West stage pictures of a barroom on the plains and an Indian encampment. Western settings allowed Daly to incorporate scenes from Mark Twain and to appro-priate Twain's tide. Although the composer was listed in the program as A. Predigam, critics ignored his contribution.

The New York *Times* informed its readers: "[The evening] resembles more closely the order of plays known in Paris as revues ... . In a revue a story as slender as that of a fairy-tale, but having for personages mortals only, binds together a number of varied situations." Clearly neither Daly nor the critics could foresee the vogue for revues that would begin with *The Passing Show* (12 May 1894) twenty years later. But Daly's productions used the same formula these early revues employed, tying together specialties with a slim plot. Only the emphasis was different, and, perhaps, the fundamental approach that considered the later mountings as primarily musicals. Nor was the public quite ready. *Roughing It* was withdrawn after four weeks. Daly was to have precious little luck with his musicals until late in his career. Did he understand that he had touched the future only to step away? James T. Powers, the turn-of-the-century comedian, recorded Daly's feelings about this time: "Mr. Daly told me he was beginning to like musical comedies, as he realized that they require more talent than legitimate plays—especially the comic portion; 'for,' he said, 'in the straight plays the fun comes mostly from the pen of the author, while in musical comedies, it generally originates in the brain of the comedian.'" No doubt Powers was moved by the flattery implicit in the remark, but Daly's view held true as long as great clowns flourished.

A spectacular pantomime, **Azrael; or, The Magic Charm** (28 April 1873, Niblo's) featured James S. Maffitt as Clown, the same Maffitt who soon endeared himself to a generation of theatregoers as The Lone Fisherman in *Evangeline* (27 July 1874). A major feature of the production was the child gymnast, Lulu, advertised as "the eighth wonder of the world in 'The Wonderous Flight Through Space.' " Lulu's most sensational moment took the gymnast from an apparent standing position in one sudden bounce to a high platform, then in a triple somersault from a bar into a net. But Lulu soon embroiled the show in a minor scandal when the athlete was unmasked as a boy. *Azrael's* magic charms worked on Niblo's faithful audiences until 9 June, when the cast dropped the plot and stayed on to offer a simple variety show.

Of course, for pleasure seekers preferring minstrelsy both the San Francisco Minstrels and Bryant's Minstrels provided the expected entertainment. Bryant's troupe was augmented by Kelly and Leon. They played from 26 August to 25 June. The San Francisco Minstrels opened their season on the same night as Bryant's. But their season ended March 1. Lack of business was not the reason. They had sold their house to make way for the new Fifth Avenue Theatre; their new home was not yet ready to receive them. Although minstrelsy was slowly being strangled by variety, it was still profitable enough to think in terms of new houses. Variety also continued to expand. Tony Pastor's opened 16 September, with Harrigan and Hart on the bill, but the team soon switched to the Theatre Comique, where they would take over and rise to glory.

1873–1874

The new season was an unhappy one. The Panic of 1873 spread hard times across the land. Only the best playhouses enjoyed prosperous returns, largely because those people who still had money and work sought to forget the problems around them. During the season every major theatre gave benefits for its less fortunate neighbors.

Artistically the American Musical Theatre languished, as unproductive as the economy. Only at the very end of the year did a lone work appear to revitalize the lagging creative forces of the lyric stage. As with *Fritz, Our Cousin German* in 1869–1870, it arrived so late that by modern calculations it belonged in the next season.

Niblo's began the year with a revival of *The Black Crook* (12 September 1866). Specialty acts, increasingly important to any mounting of the piece, included the "great French caricaturist" M. Régamey, the ventriloquist E. D. Davies, the Girards in "Leg-Mania," the Female Swabian Nightingale Quartette, and the infant Vedeys (gymnast sisters) in "mid-air exploits." Undergoing the expected "reconstruction" in mid-run, it tallied over 100 additional showings before it closed on 8 December.

A nonmusical footnote enlivened the early season. On 19 August a production of **A Midsummer Night's Dream** was unveiled at the Grand Opera House. The sumptuous Victorian-style mounting included several ballets. More to our point, the evening featured G. L. Fox as Bottom and, in her New York debut, Fay Templeton, still a tot, as Puck.

Two importations got the musical season into full gear six nights later. In one, Daly presented theatregoers with Aimée in the American premiere of Lecocq's **La Fille de Madame Angot** (25 August 1873, Broadway). Its simple plot had a rather refreshing ending, when the daughter of a fishmonger realizes the man she loves is perfidious and accepts her mother's choice of a mate for her. Sung in French, it ran for three weeks to excellent business and then went into repertory with *La Grande Duchesse* and *La Périchole*.

Downtown the Olympic raised its curtain the same night on Lydia Thompson in a burlesque extravaganza ridiculing just such opéra bouffe as Aimée was singing, **Mephisto and the Four Sensations** (using much of Lecocq's score to *La Fille de Madame Angot*). In George Fawcett Rowe's text, Miss Thompson as Pluto prepared to lure Frou-Frou, Camille, Belle Hélène, and Geneviève de Brabant to the netherworld. Theatre historian Odell undoubtedly expressed the sentiments of many "high-minded" playgoers of the day when he lamented, "One might think the world would have been utterly weary of such concoctions until one remembers the persistence, in later years, of such epidemics as London Gaiety musical farces, comic opera, musical revues, etc." Miss Thompson held the stage for a month in a repertory of her new piece and her older favorites. She was succeeded on 29 September by a company offering opéra bouffe in English. Its repertory included *The Grand Duchesse* and the first translation of *Mme. Angot's Child.*

Joseph K. Emmet returned in another variation of his Fritz theme. This time his singing of a childhood lullaby helps him find not a long-lost sister, but a long-lost father. The public accepted **Max, the Merry Swiss Boy** (6 October 1873, Broadway) no more than it had accepted *Carl* (18 September 1871). The work, by Henry J. Byron, was hastily withdrawn. Emmet, guitar, dialect, and all, rushed back to the safety of *Fritz.*

Offenbach's one-acter **Monsieur Choufleuri**, in which a dinner host, his daughter, and son-in-law-to-be must masquerade as celebrated singers when the artists call in sick, was given a single-week stand as **Primadonna for a Night** (20 October 1873, Olympic). Its cast included Alice Oates, Annie Kemp Bowler, and a young W. H. Crane. A week later Daly gave *Round the Clock* (25 November 1872) a brief revival.

A spate of *Humpty Dumpty* (10 March 1868) spin-offs marked the season. The first was mounted on 25 November by Daly at the Grand Opera House. G. L. Fox and many of his loyal associates were back. But the nature of the evening was changed. It was not quite the old familiar pantomime. De-emphasis of the story created an impression of vaudeville. Daly also added an important amount of spectacle.

This allowed **Humpty Dumpty Abroad** to fall more in the category of burlesque-extravaganza or even to be considered a light-hearted version of the *Black Crook* school. The evening included much-applauded panoramas in which the children of the tale were carried from China to the North Pole to Italy. A Chinese lantern festival was hailed as "decidedly the most effective piece of stage-grouping ever seen in this city." In the "Palace of Instruments on the Isle of Harmony" the cast paraded dressed as brasses, woodwinds, cellos, and drums. Betty and Emily Rigl led the ballets, but the Martens Family's Tyroliennes, "encored four times," almost stole the show.

Gabriel Grub; or, The Story of the Goblins Who Stole the Sexton! (22 December 1873, Olympic) musicalized the famous chapter from Dickens's *Pickwick Papers* in which a soured old sexton and gravedigger is kidnapped by preternatural creatures and made to see that life can be fun. Was it a dream or not? In the stage version, unlike in the novel, it seemed clear that it was. Two major performing groups, the Majiltons (acrobats and dancers) and the Raynors (musicians adept on fiddle, banjo, and concertina), adapted and starred in the attraction, which used vaudeville turns, Amazon marches, and a host of scampering children to enliven the evening. However, despite encouraging notices, the show lingered for only thirty-four performances.

When *Humpty Dumpty Abroad* closed at the beginning of February, it was replaced on the 9th by a double bill, **Jack Harkaway at Sea** and **Humpty Dumpty at School**, with many of the same principals and a new batch of specialty acts. There was virtually no story in either piece. In *Jack* a tobacconist named Tobias Shortcut (Fox) has to impersonate a sea captain during a naval engagement; in the second part Humpty Dumpty leads his fellow pupils into mischievous stunts. The *Times* viewed the bill as a succession of "athletic performances, a ballet d'action, Tyrolean ballads, Ethiopian minstrelsy, remarkable tight-rope exercises." Odell branded the pair "a highly sublimated 'Variety' bill—it was nothing else." The producers apparently drew the same conclusion. Before long the main title for the whole evening was changed to *A Round of Pleasure*, its original subtitle. After a two-month run, during which constant revisions of the program took place, Daly and Fox separated. Fox took over management of the Broadway from Daly and moved Humpty and his friends to the house. In the last

Humpty Dumpty of the season, **Humpty Dumpty at Home,** Goody Two Shoes and Tommy Tucker pursued their on-again, off-again romance with the connivance of Humpty all during the first act. The critics agreed the story was completely forgotten in the second act, which was merely a succession of specialty acts. These included bell ringers and Reardon's Tumblericon (musical glasses). Audiences were not too pleased. The run, which began on 6 April, terminated abruptly at the beginning of May when Fox's backer withdrew his support.

While Humpty was changing costumes and vehicles a number of importations came in to offer competition. The Vokes offered their popular English extravaganza, *The Children in the Wood* (8 December 1873, Niblo's). At the Olympic the English Opéra Bouffe Troupe entertained patrons with *The Grand Duchess, The Bohemian Girl,* and *La Sonnambula.* The definition of opéra bouffe was obviously elastic. But purists could rest content when Aimée returned on 9 March for a month's engagement, singing seven of her most dependable roles.

Something pretentiously labeled **The Grand Parisian Folly** (6 April 1874, Lyceum) proved to be merely a vaudeville, with a pantomimist, bicylists, a flutist, a man of many faces, etc.

A ballet-rich version of *The Lady of the Lake* debuted at Niblo's on 25 May. But a careful reading of reviews suggests it was primarily a straight play, making an expensive bow to Niblo's tradition of musical spectacle.

Nothing more of musical interest appeared until 27 July. And even then the musical that opened at Niblo's received discouraging notices and ran a mere two weeks. But that musical was **Evangeline.** A Boston creation, it slowly found an adoring public and became one of the most frequently played, best-loved musicals of the last quarter of the nineteenth century. Billed as an extravaganza, listed on its sheet music as an opéra bouffe, it was treated by the critics as a burlesque—which it was. The New York *Times* reviewer took the occasion to damn the entire genre. Evaluating *Evangeline* as "tolerably fair," he went on to suggest the work represented the sort of theatre that required "unquestioning good-nature to take kindly to." It was a sort, he lamented, filled with "atrocious puns... [and] indifferent music," concluding, "Even Terpsichore is but a halt jade." However, the day before the work opened, this same *Times* advised its readers that *Evangeline* promised to be a considerable departure from customary

burlesque: "The music is original throughout, and the fun is brisk and piquant." In a way, both journalists were correct.

Suggested by Longfellow's poem, the libretto had the heroine (Ione Burke) and her lover Gabriel (Connie Thompson) seek each other not just in the locales of the original but in the Wild West and a wilder Africa as well. Before the lovers clasp hands in a happy ending that has no basis in Longfellow, Evangeline is also pursued by an amorous whale and cavorts with a dancing heifer. This heifer dance became one of the most popular scenes in the work, and at least one major comedian of the American Musical Theatre, Francis Wilson, spent a season of apprenticeship as half of the cow. Equally cherished by audiences was another figure not found in Longfellow, The Lone Fisherman. Taciturn to the point of not speaking a word all evening, he nonetheless intruded everywhere in the action, often straining to view through his oversized telescope a sea thousands of miles away. Although J. W. Thompson (or Thoman) originally played the role, James Maffitt soon became so identified with it that he played little else for the remainder of his career. In keeping with the burlesque tradition, Gabriel was a trouser role for a woman, and the part of the obese, clownish Catherine was given to a man (Louis Mestayer). In the latter instance another famous performer of the time, George K. Fortesque, became identified with the role, although he, like Maffitt, was not the original. The author of these shenanigans was J. Cheever Goodwin. With Goodwin we come to the first professional librettist to leave his mark on the American Musical Theatre. Unfortunately, as is the case for several early figures, precise biographical information is hard to come by.

Musically the show was equally interesting. Advertisements promised "songs, duets, trios, full chorus, etc."—in short, a complete musical scoring. But more important, all the songs were original and by one composer-lyricist, Rice.

If Rice's songs were not so memorable as to be whistled years later, they were still more than merely "indifferent." Relatively simple, sweetly melodic, appropriately theatrical, they helped impart a sense of cohesion and knowing stage craftsmanship to the evening. The heifer's dance, with its triplets and elementary syncopations, foreshadowed the style of musical composition that would in later years become associated with animated cartoon music.

J. CHEEVER GOODWIN was born into comfortable middle class surroundings in Boston about 1850. Educated at Harvard, he took employment with the Boston *Traveler* shortly after graduation. At the same time he began tinkering with an idea for a lighthearted musicalization of Longfellow. Through circumstances now unknown he met E. E. Rice, a onetime actor then a printer of advertisements. Rice was so delighted with Goodwin's plans, he abandoned printing and collaborated with Goodwin in bringing *Evangeline* onto the stage of Boston's Globe Theatre.

EDWARD E. RICE was born in Brixton, Massachusetts in 1848. Forced by poverty to find work while still a minor he joined a troupe of itinerant actors. He apparently performed all sorts of odd jobs and soon came to know well every facet of theatre. But for some reason he elected to make a career elsewhere, moving from one profession to another until just before he met Goodwin.

All season long, variety flourished. At the Theatre Comique, Harrigan and Hart presented their skit "The Mulligan Guard," initially little more than a clownish drill routine. Out of this playlet grew the Harrigan–Braham works of coming years. It was brought back off and on all season as part of a number of variety bills at the house. Pastor's flourished as well, with Harrigan and Hart even bringing "The Mulligan Guard" there for a benefit performance. Minstrels fared less happily than vaudeville. The San Francisco Minstrels, learning their new house would not be ready for the season, spent the year on the road. Bryant had the field virtually to himself. His skits included one called "Mme. Angot's Kids."

1874–1875

Once again the American Musical Theatre mirrored the national scene in general. Both remained sluggish. Revivals and importations comprised the majority of the sparse lyric offerings. In this respect the musical theatre ran counter to the quality and success of other stage offerings. The theatrical year was filled with notable performances (including Charlotte Cushman's farewell and John Drew's debut) and premieres of some of the epoch's most important plays— *The Shaughraun, The Big Bonanza, The Two Orphans,* and *Colonel Sellers.*

Maurice Grau, who later figured importantly at the Metropolitan Opera, opened the season on 24 August at the Lyceum when, in partnership with C. A. Chizzola, he starred Aimée in a repertory of opéra bouffe. The program included the American premiere of Léon Vasseur's **La Timbale d'Argent** (in which rivals for a silver bowl in a singing contest fall in love despite vows to the contrary) as well as performances of *La Princesse de Trébizonde, La Fille de Madame Angot,* and *La Périchole.* The company remained until 17 October. Many of the same opéra bouffe offerings were heard on the very same stage two weeks later. However, on this occasion they were sung in English by a troupe starring the English soprano Emily Soldene. Her program included two novelties, the American premiere of Hervé's comic tale of Merovingian intrigue and romance, **Chilpéric,** and Offenbach's **Madame L'Achiduc,** in which an archduke offers a newly wed girl his archdukedom if she will jilt her groom and marry him instead. Miss Soldene and her fellow artists kept the Lyceum lit until 2 January. Nine nights later at the Park, Chizzola and Grau brought in their own troupe, minus Aimée. Her roles were taken principally by another young French singer, Coralie Geoffroy. This return was significant primarily for the New York premiere of Lecocq's **Giroflé-Girofla,** which had premiered in Paris only the past November and which held the stage alone from 4 February to 20 March. Its story recounted the kidnapping of one of two lovely twins on the morning both girls were to be married. The troupe also gave the first New York playings of **Le Voyage en Chine** some days earlier, on 11 January. Aimée herself returned to the Lyceum on 31 March, opening with New York's first hearing of Offenbach's **La Jolie Parfumeuse,** in which a virtuous perfume salesgirl fights to maintain her purity in wicked Paris.

The Kiralfy brothers, who till now had been prominent dancers in the spectacles at Niblo's and elsewhere, turned producers to relight the same Niblo's with **The Deluge** on 7 September. Advertised as a "grand spectacular drama" but with "500 ballet and auxiliaries on stage," it was actually a musical pageant. Its source was a French drama performed in Paris some ten years earlier that related stories from the Old Testament: Adam and Eve, Cain and Abel, and the great flood.

By the time the Kiralfys had raised the curtain on their American version, the piece ran five hours, starred a "large, imposing" English lady, Julia Seaman, as Satan, and was marked by a "prodigious quantity of action ... in Pandemonium and on earth, by much dialogue, and by dances, marches and tableaux." It was also marked, at least on opening night, by mechanical problems. One reviewer chortled at "stage carpenters wrestling with ... unruly scenery and [after a mishap in the final Deluge] wading into the wings in full sight of the spectators." Despite these first-night problems, the work caught the public's fancy and ran for over two months. It was no sooner taken off the boards than the Kiralfys had a second production ready. The ambitious brothers took over management of the Grand Opera House and on 23 November mounted a revival of *The Black Crook* (12 September 1866). Once again Marie Bonfanti was on hand to lead the dancers, while the growing horde of specialists included the Benton Family (acrobats), the London Madrigal Boys, the Persian Twin Sisters, and the Vaidis children (probably the same troupe listed in the 1873 revival as the Vedeys). Significantly neither advertisements nor pre-opening announcements listed the actors who portrayed the principal figures in the story. Although this was the third revival in four seasons it demonstrated the continuing attraction of the work. The spectacle played from 23 November to 2 January.

Another spectacle in the same tradition was **Ahmed** (30 March 1875, Grand Opera), written by Mrs. Julia E. Dunn and based loosely on Washington Irving's *The Pilgrim of Love*. It was dismissed by the *Times* as "simply a vehicle for exhibiting a long series of tableaux and for introducing a number of dances." The tableaux included an elaborate grotto setting that undoubtedly recalled *The Black Crook* to many in the house, while the dancing offered "a pas de quatre by four tiny ballerine" that catered to the circus-like tone demanded by so many ticket-buyers. For all its pandering to popular taste *Ahmed* found only modest public support. It closed on 28 April. Two weeks later a revival of *The Twelve Temptations* (7 February 1870) was rushed in to keep the house open. It ran for ten nights, and with its close the Grand Opera House's season ended.

In a few short seasons the presence of Harrigan and Hart on its bills had made the Theatre Comique "the most popular 'Variety' hall in the city," temporarily eclipsing Tony Pastor's. Much of Harrigan and Hart's success stemmed from playlets Harrigan contrived, usually with a song or

two by David Braham. On 31 May Harrigan and Hart abandoned the Comique for the moment to mount a longer—although not quite full-length—play at Wallack's. Probably to satisfy their less adventuresome followers, as well as to fill out the entire evening, they offered a small variety bill with the play. But this play, **The Donovans,** was the first stop on the team's rise to fame and fortune. Its story was suggested by one of the most sensational events of the day, the kidnapping of young Charlie Ross. In Harrigan's work Michael and Norah Donovan (played by Harrigan and Hart, respectively) find the search for their missing child takes them not only around New York City but to a Kentucky plantation as well. The play ended with the rescue of the child at a railroad viaduct moments before an oncoming train might have spelled tragedy. The various locations of the tale, clearly in the school of Tom and Jerry playwriting, took its principals on a whirlwind tour. For Harrigan they had the advantage of opening up the story sufficiently to allow for the reasonable insertion of a number of additional variety acts such as the Peak Bell Ringers and Baby Bindley. If these specialties hampered any serious consideration of the adventure, no one probably cared. After all, the sight of the bereaved mother played by a man in drag hardly set a high tone.

Nat Salsbury and his Troubadours' **Patchwork** (21 July 1875, Union Square) created no stir, although it was the harbinger of those farce-comedies which would soon be the rage and lead to musical comedy. The really telling farce-comedy was its successor, but this show had fun spoofing famous actors, voguish bell ringers, and other targets. During the season, minstrelsy noted the death of Dan Bryant, the closing of his troupe, and the return of the San Francisco Minstrels in a new house.

Little footnotes enlivened the season. On 14 December the police raided the variety show at the Metropolitan Theatre to stop the cancan there. But the cancan continued. And on 20 November, Mrs. Leonowens, "late governess of the royal family of Siam," lectured at Steinway Hall, never dreaming she would eventually become the heroine of one of Broadway's most sucessful musicals, *The King and I* (29 March 1951).

1875–1876

As America prepared to celebrate its centennial, the American Musical Theatre languished. And the lyric stage was not alone in its woes. Theatre historian

George Odell noted that these were "Hard Times for the Theatres" in general. Niblo's, increasingly out-of-the-way, remained dark all season. And while Americans across the land heard more than their normal quota of facilely optimistic speeches in the course of the season, they also witnessed the horrors of the Molly Maguires and the ignominy of Custer's Last Stand.

The theatrical year was framed by opéra bouffe. Off the beaten path, **The Rose of Auvergne** made her Manhattan debut at Robinson Hall on 19 July. The Henderson and Colville company opened its season on 19 August with a reworking of *Barbe Bleue* called *Boulotte*. The piece ran until the beginning of September, when it was replaced first by *The Grand Duchess* and later by *Giroflé-Girofla*. At the same time Daly's boards played host to the Mexican Juvenile Opera Company, headed by an eight-year-old prima donna, Moron Carmen. The youngsters sang their interpretation of *The Grand Duchess* as well as Offenbach's *Robinson Crusoe*. More traditional performances began at the Lyceum (once the Théâtre Français) on 6 September when the Grau and Chizzola troupe, again starring Coralie Geoffroy, presented *Madame L'Archiduc*, *La Fille de Mme. Angot*, *Giroflé-Girofla*, *Le Canard à Trois Becs*, and *Le Petit Faust*. The season's close found the doomed Booth's housing a revival of *La Vie Parisienne* for the week of 12 June. Offenbach himself conducted the opening night, with Aimée across the footlights singing the principal role.

August also saw competing versions of **Around the World in Eighty Days**, one at the Grand Opera House (a failure, running only 16 August to 28 September) and one at the Academy of Music. (Actually, an earlier mounting was given at the unvoguish Bowery on the previous 29 March and played for a month.) Both laced their adaptations of Jules Verne with ballets, songs, and specialty acts. The mounting at the Academy on the 28th was by the Kiralfys and was the more successful of the two. In eighteen spectacular scenes it took Phileas Fogg (Owen Marlowe) from his London club room through the Suez into the interior of a "Hindoo" bungalow and to an elegant Calcutta hotel. Thereafter a "procession of Brahmins and worshippers" at "The Great Religious Festival of the Suttee" led up to a "startling" pyre and a "Grand Funeral Pageant." As if this were not enough, the "Wreck of the Henrietta" depicted "the total disappearance of the steamer under the waves." While scenes were being changed, a novel curtain—of the sort we would call a show

curtain today—formed an immense fan and concealed the movement behind it. Scene painter Matt Morgan was praised both for his inventiveness and his taste. The ballets were lauded, but so were performers in the story, notably Marlowe for his dignity and *sang-froid*. When, along with *The Black Crook* (12 September 1866), this extravaganza would prove sufficiently popular to merit regular revivals, critics would hereafter ignore actors in the tale, and devote their notices to the increasingly elaborate dances and circuslike specialties that soon came to dominate productions of *Around the World*.

One of the season's few "original" native musicals, **Humpty Dumpty in Every Clime** (25 October 1875, Booth's), gave audiences another chance to see G. L. Fox in his most beloved part. Most theatregoers could not know this was to be their last, brief chance to do so. There was virtually no plot, and the second act, in which the audience was transported around the world in eighty minutes, was branded as little more than an olio. However, the *Times* review affords an interesting picture of Fox's technique and the style of his final offering:

> [Humpty Dumpty] is sent by *Old One Two* with a letter to the nearest post office, *Clown* faces in the right direction, and then boldly marks time as though he were walking for a wager. Meanwhile the scenery moves, houses disappear, fields and a long lane are passed, and by and by the actor who has apparently travelled over a long road, reaches his goal. But just as he is depositing the letter the ever attendant *Harlequin* taps on the floor with his magic blade and, presto, the post office disappears, and where it was there stands the same house whence *Clown* set out minutes before.

This business was gone through three times. But Fox was becoming more erratic than the clown he played, in one instance attacking members of the audience for no obvious reason. On 15 November his insanity became so apparent that James Maffitt was called in to finish the performance. Fox returned and continued to act until 27 November. Committed then to an institution, he never appeared before the public again and died shortly thereafter. With him died the chief impetus for traditional pantomime in America.

At the new Eagle Theatre at Sixth Avenue between 32nd and 33rd streets, some distance above the regular theatre district, the bill for the week of

15 November included an "original and dramatic cantata." The "cantata" had music by an Englishman, Arthur Sullivan, and words by another Englishman, W. S. Gilbert. What scant attention it received was not especially favorable, and it quickly left the scene. Time forced a reconsideration of this saga of a faithless lover judged by a faithless magistrate, for the "cantata" was **Trial by Jury.**

A "Grand Christmas Pantomime" called **Nimble Nip** came in for the holiday trade. The evening featured the Worells. Sophie Worell played Prince Sweet-as-Sugar to her sister's Princess Ever-So-Fair. Neither the villainies of Blunderbore nor the temper tantrums of King Grumble-Grone stand in the way of their finding romance. Advertised attractions included "one hundred charming children" and a "fairy fountain of real water." Offering "a tolerable medley of songs and dances" and a "grand transformation scene," the show ran three weeks. It departed from the general practice of pantomime by not having the principals turn into Clown and his friends. These roles were played by minor performers.

As Odell notes: "Negro minstrelsy, once all raging, was reduced in New York, in 1875–1876, by that new 'rage'—'Variety'—to only one permanent company." Five important houses offered "that new rage" to New Yorkers. Their programs included burlesques and musical comediettas by promising young writers such as Sydney Rosenfeld.

1876–1877

There was little to distinguish this season from the preceding one—or from the one to follow. The lyric stage remained in the doldrums. The creative spurt that began almost accidentally with *The Black Crook* (12 September 1866) seemed to have exhausted itself. To aggravate matters, the horrendous Brooklyn Theatre fire on 5 December seriously affected theatre attendance for the remainder of the season, thereby coupling the artistic vacuity with economic hardship.

In the long run the most significant event of the season came at the very start, the assumption by Harrigan and Hart of management of the Theatre Comique. Their original intention seems to have been to retain it as a vaudeville house, but the popularity of sketches Harrigan inserted in the bills soon irrevocably altered their plans. Most of these skits, with names such as "Down in Dixie," "Walking for Dat Cake," "The Blue and the Grey," or "An Editor's

Troubles," were hastily, if professionally, composed and just as hastily discarded. But a few contained the nucleus for later, more extended, efforts. Out of "Old Lavender Water" came the character who was to be Harrigan's personal favorite. More important, a skit called "Centennial Marksmen; or, the International Rifle Match by the Four Picked Teams"—celebrating the multi-national shooting matches then in progress—pitted the Queen's Invincibles and the Ginger Blues against two of the most beloved creations of Harrigan's fertile imagination, The Skidmores and The Mulligan Guards. At one point Harrigan gave yet another hint of things to come when he offered a full-length play on the bill of 20 November. The play was a "romantic drama" entitled *Lascaire*, different in style from Harrigan's later works but alike in ambition.

The years of Harrigan and Hart's triumphs were just ahead. The season at hand got under way with more old-fashioned efforts, spectacles squarely in the *Black Crook* tradition. **Baba** (18 September 1876, Niblo's) had a libretto by "Arnold and Sherwood," names now lost in the ancient pages of theatrical history, and music by Max Maretzek, still remembered as an important figure of the late nineteenth-century musical scene. A number of critics singled out the marches he wrote for this piece, the *Times* insisting they were "far superior to those of most spectacles." The same reviewer bewailed that in the ten years since the premiere of *The Black Crook* an unfortunate pattern had developed emphasizing spectacle over plot. He could, with equal accuracy, have suggested spectacle had come to dominate over everything else as well, including the music. The story he felt was relegated to a secondary place told how Baba (W. H. Crane), the adopted son of the Vizier, and his young friend fall in love with two princesses. Their pursuit of the young ladies takes them to "The Grotto of the Emeralds," "The Crumbling Palace," "A Field of Mushrooms," and onto a "Magic Ship." The piece played to diminishing returns until 11 December, when the effect of the Brooklyn fire proved fatal and an audience of a mere thirty patrons had its money refunded.

The Kiralfys took over the house and mounted another spectacle, **Azurine,** on Christmas night. The story recounted the plight of "the daughter of the king of a realm in the sky ordered to spend a year on earth." But the story was plainly not the thing. The Kiralfys boasted of a cast that included "300 young ladies" and a spectacular moving panorama of the city in the sky. Only a handful of ballerinas were deemed worthy of being listed by name, an honor, as usual, not even accorded the authors of the piece. It was a two-week failure. The brothers rushed in a revival of *Around the World in Eighty Days* (28 August 1875) on 22 January, but this, too, met with little interest. Booth's relit on 14 August with an adaptation of Byron's **Sardanapalus,** replete with ballets, songs, twenty-four Negro boys, and forty-eight "extra" ladies.

For playgoers seeking more artful lyric theatre, opéra bouffe troupes came and went throughout the season. The Alice Oates Opera Company inaugurated the parade on 18 September at the Grand Opera House, singing in English their repertory of standards. A week later Aimée returned after a brief vacation. In three visits at three different houses she repeated many of her old favorites and offered New Yorkers their first opportunity to hear Lecocq's **La Petite Mariée** and Offenbach's **La Boulangère a des Écus.** Midseason, on 14 March, the Kiralfys wed opéra bouffe and extravaganza with their elaborate mounting at Booth's of Offenbach's **A Trip to the Moon,** in which King Pin and his son, Prince Caprice, take the journey to break their mundane monotony. Although it boasted of "a chorus of one hundred," tepid notices and the effects of the Brooklyn holocaust told quickly. The show closed after ten nights.

Two plays in the Tom and Jerry tradition also scored successes during the season, *Fifth Avenue* and *Life.* **Life** was Augustin Daly's adaptation and combination of two French plays, *Le Procès Veauradieux* and *Loulou.* A mélange of farce, spectacle, specialty acts, and ballet, it displeased many of Daly's more traditional customers, but nevertheless found enough of an audience to run from 27 September to 18 November. Daly's great farceur, the carrot-topped James Lewis, played a sport, Pony Mutual, and found an excuse to imitate Marie Bonfanti. His final leap was so magnificent he disappeared into the flies. This Tom and Jerry tour ended at a theatre with a set depicting fairyland on its stage. This allowed no other than Miss Bonfanti herself, as the Spirit of the Sun, and Augusta Sohlke, as the Spirit of the Snow, to dance together in an elaborate "Snow Ballet" (using music from a work New York had yet to see, Offenbach's *A Trip to the Moon*). Daly regulars in the cast included Maurice Barrymore, Georgiana Drew (Barrymore's wife, and the mother of Lionel, Ethel, and John), Charles F. Coghlan, Emily Rigl, John Brougham, and the beloved old trouper Mrs. Gilbert. **Fifth Avenue** (5 February

1877, Booth's), which had a five-week run, was more arguably a straight play, with a melodramatic plot. Richard Blake (George Rignold) wins the hand of Olive Schuyler (Maud Granger) after proving his worth by rescuing her from a shipwreck, saving her father from bankruptcy, and clearing himself of a false accusation. The shipwreck provided a challenge to the set painters; reviewers felt they met it handsomely. For all that it was a straight play, the show was larded with turns by performers from the up-and-coming vaudeville world. As "boss of all the bill-posters," Charles T. Parsloe, Jr., led a comic song and clog dance. John Wild in blackface is reported to have stopped the show, although unfortunately no critic detailed his act. Wild would go on to become one of Harrigan and Hart's favorite regulars. In his autobiography, the distinguished British actor Frederick Warde, then a member of Daly's company, recalled the equally show-stopping antics of George S. Knight. His description of Knight's turn suggests how ideas of humor change, for he applauded Knight's "wonderful acrobatic imitation of a German immigrant seized with an epileptic fit." As Odell noted in his theatre history of the time, "the songs and specialties of these clever people were encored until the perpetrators were breathless, while the principals waited in the wings for the tumult to die."

With G. L. Fox gone, a performer named Grimaldi briefly assumed the crown of pantomime. On the very stage where Fox once reigned—at the Olympic—from 12 March he and his troupe offered a month of repertory alternating between *Jack and Jill* and their version of *Humpty Dumpty.* Their mountings were coupled with olios, and when their run ended they moved over to Tony Pastor's.

Indeed, all season long variety was the most flourishing form of entertainment. Minstrelsy had dwindled to a lone stronghold, the San Francisco Minstrels, although Kelly and Leon did attempt a brief comeback late in the season at Darling's Opera House. Ironically, Darling's had long been Dan Bryant's theatre. Both variety and minstrelsy continued to spoof the hits of the season and in these skits continued to tinker with the forms of future revues and musical comedies. Odell also takes notice of some of the entertainers mentioned earlier who enlivened their more or less straight vehicles with song and dance. He remarks that Lotta's revival of **Little Nell and the Marchioness** offered "real negro serenaders" and her "unrivalled clog dance." He concludes: "Had she belonged to the 1920s, Lotta might have been drafted into the Ziegfeld Follies, the Scandals or some such froth."

Something on the order of *The Black Crook, The Wonder Child; or, The Follies of Earth, Air, and Sea* (30 April 1877, Broadway) survived only two weeks. Its story of "the sale of a poor man's beautiful daughters to three princes of the animal kingdom" served merely as a pretext for lavish ballets, elaborate scenery, and pretty girls in tights. But the cast included names soon to be prominent on musical or dramatic stages—Stella Boniface, Annie Yeamans, Jacques Kruger, and Louis Harrison.

The year ended when *Evangeline* (27 July 1874) returned on 4 June to begin a two-month run at Daly's. This run marks the real beginning of New York's affection for the piece. Eliza Weathersby sang Gabriel, while Lizzie Harold was Evangeline. As Capt. Dietrich, George S. Knight was made up to resemble the celebrated Civil War soldier General Benjamin F. Butler. Two future stars, N. C. Goodwin and Henry E. Dixey, appeared in minor roles, and during the second month of the stay George K. Fortesque donned Catherine's garments again. Looking back years later on the cast, Odell concluded that "a baker's dozen names about to be listed in the near future as the most potent to draw lovers of burlesque" graced the bill.

1877–1878

The new season resembled the calm before the storm. Musically, it was the least active season in more than half a dozen years. Lydia Thompson returned after a marked absence to open the year with a repertory of burlesques at Wallack's on 18 August. Old favorites such as *Blue Beard* appeared first. But they were soon replaced by newer works, **Oxygen; or, Prince Fritz of Virgamen** (27 August 1877) and **Robinson Crusoe** (12 September 1877). Both librettos were by H. B. Farnie, the earlier in collaboration with R. Reece. *Prince Fritz* made only passing reference to J. K. Emmet's Fritz, following instead the adventures of a student prince (Miss Thompson) and his friends. They encounter mad Dr. Ox (Horatio Saker), who has found a way to use oxygen to conquer the world. Of course, Fritz and his most important friends were trouser roles. The cast, which included Willie Edouin, Alice Atherton, and Kate Everleigh, later prompted Odell to look on it much as he had the preceding *Evangeline*'s and remark, "Almost every woman in that cast won a high place in our theatre, either in burlesque or musical comedy, or both."

Defoe would have scarcely recognized his Crusoe story. In this 1877 version the hero and Jim Cox are jilted by their sweethearts and run away to sea. A shipwreck and their sweethearts follow, as does a reconciliation, but not before a number of musical adventures overtake the principals. These include meetings with lady pirates such as Tarr, Pitch, and Rosin. For many the clowning of Willie Edouin as Friday was the evening's most memorable feature. But Friday was only one of a number of strange inhabitants of the isle on Wallack's stage. Characters such as Queen Ylang-Ylang, Jes-so, Wai-ho, O-wy-o-wy, and O-pop-i-nax also cavorted throughout the piece.

The year's most important work, Ned Harrigan's **Old Lavender,** premiered on 3 September. At this point it was not quite a full-length play but rather an extended sketch based on a shorter piece he had used earlier. Harrigan dickered with these medium-long efforts all season, bringing forth *The Rising Star, Sullivan's Christmas,* and the burlesque *A Celebrated Hard Case,* among others. All contained songs by David Braham. It was only during the week of 22 April—the last week of Harrigan and Hart's season at the Theatre Comique—that Harrigan offered a more fully fleshed version of *Old Lavender,* beginning the career of the play and the character that ever after remained his personal favorite. Harrigan's story was condemned by the *Herald* and others as old hat, but the public couldn't have cared less. Paul Cassin (F. A. Blackburn) and John Filbert (T. E. Egbert) attempt to swindle Phillip Coggswell (F. Chippendale), a banker, out of a large sum by use of fraudulent checks. To abet his machinations Cassin pretends to court Coggswell's wife, Laura (Annie Mack). When Coggswell discovers the deception he concludes his brother George, who introduced Filbert at the bank, is party to the scheme. George is a middle-aged bachelor affectionately known to his friends as Old Lavender (Harrigan). Laura and George are reduced to poverty. Phillip, too, falls on hard times. But Lavender's old mining stock proves to be valuable and when, through a warning given him by the Negro bootblack, Dick the Rat (Tony Hart), Old Lavender is able to prevent a robbery, matters end happily. Some critics also complained about florid dialogue. Lavender, for example, describing a hangover, asserts, "The density of the atmosphere, weighing upon an individual after a night of recreation, is quite sufficient to flush a goddess." None of Braham's songs from *Old Lavender* earned a high place in his canon, nor were they as urgent to the story as in later works. Hart, who generally played the principal comic role, either in blackface or in drag, here took the relatively minor role of Dick. Indeed a few performers who were soon to be pillars of the company—notably Annie Yeamans—were seen in this production in only minor parts.

Two competing companies arrived in October to offer New York a choice of opéra bouffe. Aimée came in on the 1st, singing her repertory in French. For novelty she offered the American premiere of Lecocq's **Marjolaine,** its tale of an erstwhile rake who boasts of his new bride's fidelity, based loosely on Shakespeare's *Cymbeline,* and Johann Strauss's first operetta, **La Reine Indigo,** recounting the love of the Queen's slave girl for the Queen's jester. Two weeks later the Hess Opera Company, with Emilie Melville as star, presented opera and opéra bouffe in English at the Fifth Avenue Theatre. The company returned for a second engagement, this time at the Union Square Theatre, from 21 May to 8 June.

Lydia Thompson also played a return engagement, although not at so desirable a house. Her stay at the Eagle began on 12 November with *Robinson Crusoe.* On the 21st she introduced **Piff-Paff,** playing Prince Glamour in the court of King XXXVII of Gramercie. Alice Atherton (Mrs. Edouin) as Queen Folichonne had the hit of the evening, singing "Oh, Naughty, Naughty." When the run closed on 15 December, the Edouins left the company and mounted **Babes in the Wood; or, Who Killed Cock Robin?** on 24 December. The parting clearly had been amicable, for Miss Thompson was credited with designing the costumes. More significant, William Gill, who played comic villain, was credited with collaborating in the adaptation of this Drury Lane piece with Edouin. Gill's reworking was so slapdash that the *Times* suggested he could have just as easily called the affair "Fifth Avenue, or the Cataract of the Ganges." Edouin won a solid round of applause as a female circus rider, performing on a wooden horse and unerringly caricaturing the mannerisms of circus prima donnas. One critic was prompted to compare him with G. L. Fox, noting that Edouin's style was far brasher, lacking Fox's pathos and naiveté. Before the principals were turned into Clown, Pantaloon, and their friends, doors changed places, carpetbags sprouted legs, and a transformation scene transported the cast from the arctic to the tropics. However slipshod Gill's writing was at the moment, he soon became an important librettist in the early American Musical Theatre.

Just over a week before the Edouins unveiled *Babes in the Wood,* Thomas Edison's tinkerings had reached the point where on 6 December he spoke into his primitive recording device and minutes later heard his own voice reciting "Mary Had a Little Lamb." In time, records not only helped popularize songs from the American Musical Theatre but perpetuated the very sounds of our lyric stage and its artists. Unfortunately this was a quarter of a century away, and it was the English who first recognized the value of original-cast recordings.

The night that saw Harrigan's expanded *Old Lavender,* 22 April, witnessed the return of J. K. Emmet in **The New Fritz, Our Cousin German** at the Standard. The "new" injected into the title announced the addition of several scenes and a full complement of songs. The added scenes included a prologue showing the stealing of Fritz's sister. Among the songs offered were "Oh, He Hit Me In De Nose," "Meet Me At The Garden Gate," "Sauerkraut Receipt," "She Fainted Away In My Arms," and "Oh, Don't Tickle Me." Of course none of these tunes achieved the popularity of Emmet's "Lullaby." But whether or not the "Brother's Lullaby" listed for this version was the beloved melody copyrighted in the following year or the song used years before in *Carl, the Fiddler* (18 September 1871) remains moot. As if the "new" Fritz was not enough, Emmet announced an "amended" version on 25 May, with new songs; and then on 20 June, just before ending his stay, the star advertised he was performing the "London" version.

To help boost sagging attendance at a popular drama, Niblo's tacked on a combination extravaganza-burlesque, **Nia-For-Li-Ca; or, The Halls of Montezuma** (22 April 1878, Niblo's), with characters such as Go-Ca-Chi and Tom-n-Jer-ri. Playgoers coming to see the sad tale of a persecuted Jewish maiden didn't relish having to accept such nonsense, so the piece was withdrawn after a single week.

Like Grimaldi in the preceding season, Robert Frazer attempted to claim the Fox inheritance with his production of **Humpty Dumpty's Dream** (21 May 1878, Fifth Ave.). Fraser had played Humpty in backwaters for some years and even appeared for a week in 1875–1876 at the Olympic pantomime. His new vehicle was on a double bill with a version of Dickens's *Christmas Carol* called *The Miser.* It recorded Humpty's (and Clown's) adventures in a dream world of animals and sprites. Apparently audiences were not too disturbed by the telling of a Christmas tale in spring. The pair ran until 5 June.

Minstrel shows continued to be represented by the San Francisco Minstrels, while variety theatres emerged in all parts of the city. The Olympic, converted to variety, helped give a new word for the form currency when, on 19 November, it began advertising "Genuine Vaudeville." But more important, variety or vaudeville was obviously becoming a spawning ground not merely for future stars of the musical theatre but for plotted musical theatre comedy itself. Nowhere was it more obvious than at Harrigan and Hart's. Even Tony Pastor's hinted at the coming deluge. On 8 April his bills boasted an "original operetta," *May Moving Time* (shades of Royall Tyler's *May-Day in Town* ninety years before). "Operetta," like "vaudeville," was a word just coming into playgoers' vocabularies.

SCENE TWO
H. M. S. Pinafore and the Great Transformation, 1878–1892

1878–1879

In the theatrical terms of the day, the 1878–1879 season represented a "Grand Transformation," a spectacular scene change effected before the eyes of awed spectators. The uncertain, almost fortuitous triumphs of the late sixties and early seventies gave place that year to an outpouring of lyric offerings until then inconceivable in the American Musical Theatre. Almost imperceptibly at first, the popularity of old, favored types began to decline. Pantomime found no advocate as skillful or well liked as G. L. Fox. Overly elaborate spectacle came to seem cumbersome and vulgar. Most imitators of J. K. Emmet generally offered fewer musical numbers in their evenings—straight plays with at best a song or two interpolated. Perhaps the least affected genre was burlesque. Yet even its evolution was slow. As seasons passed, it blended with vaudeville skits, Harrigan and Braham's musicals, and the freewheeling, song-studded "farce-comedies" to help create a native musical comedy.

Initially, few of the new musicals were any more artful or cohesive than musicals of the old school had been. And, given the increasing amount of competition, few enjoyed the runaway successes of *The Black Crook* (12 September 1866) or *Humpty Dumpty* (10 March 1868). But if many of the better new works failed to run as long as these old warhorses had, they nonetheless vwere usually highly profitable. Moreover, they gave their creators not only fortune, but fame. Composers and librettists before them had rarely become famous in their own right. Probably not one theatregoer in ten could say who was responsible for *The Black Crook*'s music, while Barras became a name more familiar to theatrical historians than to his own contemporaries. Fox and Emmet were remembered as performers rather than collaborators, and their partners were largely ignored. Both J. Cheever Goodwin and E. E. Rice did enjoy a certain recognition, but it came with time and with an accumulation of successes. Soon, new writers coming on the scene received more instant renown. And this burgeoning fame brought with it a sense of responsibility. When failure diminished a man's reputation as readily as it hurt his pocketbook, he became doubly careful. But the principal impetus for all the new creative change and activity, the spark for the real beginning of the American Musical Theatre, was a foreign work. The unprecedented popularity of Gilbert and Sullivan's *H. M. S. Pinafore* remains the pivotal landmark in the story of our lyric theatre. However, the English comic opera did not arrive until midseason. A few interesting pieces preceded it.

EDWARD GREEN HARRIGAN was born on 26 October 1844 in the then predominantly Irish Lower East Side of Manhattan. His father was the son of Irish immigrants who settled in Labrador as fishermen. The elder Harrigan ran away to sea, renouncing his parents' Catholic faith and becoming a determined Mason. He married the daughter of a seaman, and they settled in New York at 31 Scammel Street. Apart from a brief period in the 1850s when his father tried farming in New Jersey, young Ned was reared in the city. Ned's mother encouraged his early fascination with the theatre, but when his parents were divorced and his father married a stern Methodist, the atmosphere at home changed. At eighteen Ned left New York, winding up several years later in San Francisco. He made his first song and dance appearance there at an amateur night at Dashaway Hall, but within a short span he was well known on the bills at the city's regular variety houses. After a time, Harrigan teamed with Alex O'Brien, until the latter's heavy drinking broke up their act. Ned then joined with Sam Rickey to form a duo billed as "Noted Californian Comedians." They offered a sketch, "The Little Frauds," about a baker and a coquettish fräulein. When Rickey proved as undependable as O'Brien, Harrigan was forced to look for a new partner. He found one quickly.

Harrigan and Hart relit the Theatre Comique on 19 August, each bill offering a Harrigan playlet as a major attraction. Most of these extended sketches came and went after a week, sometimes returning a month or a season later. But on 23 September **The Mulligan Guards' Picnic** began a month's run. (There was some spelling inconsistency about some early Harrigan titles. For example, on sheet music one play was called *The Mulligan Guard Ball*. On the program, the same play was listed as *The Mulligan Guards' Ball*. For purposes of consistency in this book the latter form will be used wherever a confusion exists.) Harrigan depicted a bad day in Dan Mulligan's life. Not only does the tailor shorten Dan's trousers to the point of absurdity, but the picnic Dan had planned is disrupted by the claims of a Negro society to the picnic grounds and by a wild fight between Gustavus Lochmuller (Harry Fisher) and Tommy Fagan (William Gray). The Full Moon Union has planned a balloon ascent, singing, in "Second Degree, Full Moon Union":

> *Sail way up in a balloon*
> *It's dar you hear dem colored people*
> *Shoutin' glory in dat fiery moon.*

The fight develops because Lochmuller has mysteriously disappeared and, assuming him dead, Tommy has announced he will court his "widow." A hasty trial is held at Squire Cohog's Grocery and Court, where sassy, black Rebecca Allup (Hart) proves a hilariously hostile witness. As he would so often in ensuing years, Harrigan not only wrote the play but also acted the part Mulligan.

TONY HART was born Anthony J. Cannon to a poor Irish family in Worcester Massachusetts on 25 July 1855. The shortest

member in a large clan he became the butt of jokes and slights. His retaliations grew so out of hand he was sent to reform school. He soon ran away, coming to New York and accepting singing and dancing jobs in saloons. A brief stint with a traveling circus was followed by spells with several minstrel companies. Sometime during this period he adopted his stage name. He was only sixteen years old when he met Ned Harrigan and persuaded him that he would be an excellent replacement for Rickey. His shortness and almost femininely beautiful face made him a natural for drag roles, while his masculine approach meant his "women" tended to be raucous and combative.

At the Standard, 14 October saw the return of J. K. Emmet and his "new" *Fritz*. He, too, enjoyed a month's run. By some curious coincidence at several turning points in the history of the American Musical Theatre, producers, however unintentionally, offered something approaching a recapitulation of the past. By the year's end, three of the four major hits of the post–Civil War period were presented to playgoers for their reconsideration. Only *Humpty Dumpty* would be missing.

Harrigan had another success and another month's run beginning 25 November at the Comique with a full-length play, **The Lorgaire**. It told a story not unlike *Fritz*. The manuscript explains that "lorgaire" is Irish for detective. The sleuth in this case is Cornelius Dempsey (Harrigan) of Scotland Yard. Dempsey ascertains that Squire Ryan (Welsh Edwards) bribed a young girl switch his child with his lord's child so that his own youngster might have a better upbringing. In the course of his work Dempsey falls in love with Norah Mullahey (Lizzie Rich) and wins her hand by the final curtain. Hart played Norah's brother, Terry. Musically the show was the richest date at the Theatre Comique. David Braham wrote seven original songs and adapted three old Irish airs. The musical numbers included something rare in these Harrigan and Braham compositions: an opening chorus ("Listen To The Anvil"). More important, they included one of Braham's most popular melodies, one which years later he told an interviewer had always remained his personal favorite, "Dolly, My Crumpled Horn Cow."

A holiday revival of *Evangeline* (27 July 1874) came into Booth's from 16 December to early January. Clara Fisher was Evangeline and Nellie Larkelle was Gabriel, but more important, the production gave New Yorkers their first chance to see James S. Maffitt in the role he would always be identified with, The Lone Fisherman.

On 23 December 1878, Minnie Cummings's Drawing-Room Theatre was opened to the public. If the theatre was short-lived, its initial attraction had an even shorter life. **Manhattan Beach; or, Down Among the Breakers**—an operetta, opera, or operatic lark, depending on which advertisement one read—had music by Edward Mollenhauer and book and lyrics by Charles Barnard. Barnard based his story on a popular French work, *Niniche*, which recounted how a wily wife wins back a roving husband. The text may well have been more a translation than an adaptation, for at least one critic insisted the only thing American about the piece was a passing reference to clams at Coney Island.

Two companies brought in revivals of the preceding year's *Babes in the Wood*. The Colville Burlesque troupe opened on 23 December, like *Evangeline* in time for the holiday trade. It also revived *Robinson Crusoe* on 9 January. Rice's Surprise Party—its entourage including the Edouins, W A. Mestayer, Louis Harrison, and Henry Dixey—played three slightly separate engagements in the spring. The fluidity of pieces such as *Babes in the Wood* can be gauged by comparing the casts of characters in the various playbills. About half the figures in

the story change from production to production. The Queens of Songbirds and Tragedy disappeared after the 1877 mounting, while Dr. Bigfee, Dr. Littlepill, Dr. Callagain, and Dr. Overpaid pranced through the latest edition. Had musical numbers been listed, a similar revision would probably have been evident.

On 6 January, New Yorkers were presented with a choice of opening nights, both revivals. The Lyceum gave playgoers a second *Evangeline*. This version offered Venie Clancy and Lizzie Webster as the maid and her lover, Harry Hunter as The Lone Fisherman, and George K. Fortesque as Catherine. It ran until *H. M. S. Pinafore* preempted it in the middle of its third week. At the same time, down at the Bowery, a revival of *Baba* (18 September 1876) was mounted at an advertised cost of $50,000. It survived only a half week longer than the Lyceum's *Evangeline*. Shortly after *Baba* closed, the Bowery—an important playhouse for fifty-three years—left the English-speaking fold and began offering foreign-language mountings for the immigrants who had clustered nearby.

The week starting Monday, 13 January, marked a major turning point in the American Musical Theatre. Even if *H. M. S. Pinafore* had not had its tumultuous American premiere on Wednesday, given time, the success of **The Mulligan Guards' Ball**, which occupied the Comique from 13 January to 24 May, might well have hastened the evolution of the lyric stage. In any case it consolidated the fame of Harrigan, Hart, and Braham. Their company's halcyon days began with this production. The play was still not full length and was presented each week with a different vaudeville bill. One of these bills included George M. Cohan's father, Jerry. And like most musical works of the time the piece remained fluid, with Harrigan adding and subtracting scenes during the run. Basically it dealt with two problems confronting Dan Mulligan (Harrigan). The first of these stems from arrangements for the Mulligan Guards' Ball. Dan is especially proud of the group, which he boasts was "christened after me." But a younger element is trying to take over. Compounding matters, the hall Dan's brigade has booked for its annual ball has been booked for the identical night by a black group, the Skidmore Guards. (This was the same device Harrigan had employed in *The Mulligan Guards' Picnic*.) The blacks finally consent to use the upstairs room, while the whites remain below. In one of the most famous of all Harrigan scenes, the black revelries become so wild the floor gives way and the Skidmores come toppling down into the Mulligan party. Dan's second problem is the romance of the Mulligans' son, Tommy (Hart), and the Lochmullers' daughter, Katy (Nellie Jones). The mothers, Cordelia Mulligan (Annie Yeamans) and Bridget Lochmuller (Annie Mack), detest each other, and Dan's hackles are raised by the prospect of mixing Irish and German blood. Dan's prejudices are not completely justified since Bridget is Irish. The children decide to elope. The elopement brings the battle between Dan and Gustave Lochmuller (Harry Fisher) to a head. Like Fritz, Lochmuller was an early comic "Dutchman." At one point he warns Cordelia, "Mrs. Mulligan, don't add reputation to insult." But once the new-lyweds return, their fait accompli helps reconcile family differences.

Harrigan was excellent at characterization. The older Mulligan, like many figures Harrigan created for himself, was inclined to be garrulous, but warm and sensible. Dan's speech to Tommy asking the youngster not to forget his father's old cronies is typical:

> They wanted me to tell ye that they were pio-neers in the old guard before the war and they've saved the battle axes and russian hats and they want to march to the ball ahead of the Young Mulligans. Lave them. I owe McSweeney five and Gilmartin ten. 'Twill aise them up.

The children are more impetuous; their talk more colloquial:

Tommy: I'll tell you now how we'll fix the snap. We'll go down to Maggie's now and we'll talk it over with her about standing up with you tomorrow night.
Kitty: We can't get married at the ball.
Tommy: Hold on, let me get to the end of the story. We go to the ball together, don't we?
Kitty: Yes.
Tommy: And during intermission we'll go to Judge Walsh's home.

Harrigan's Negroes spoke a stage dialect that was probably not too far from black speech of the day, for while he employed stereotypes Harrigan always injected sympathetic notes. His Negroes may have been exaggerations, but they were not minstrel gro-tesqueries. The dialogue between Simpson Primrose

(John Wild) and Palestine Puter (Billy Gray) as they plan the Skidmore decoration is believable:

Simpson: I spect we'll have it decorated wid nice ingredients.
Puter: Oh, yes. Dar's a large chromo of Abraham Lincoln to go over de door and de floral tributes are something gorgeous.
Simpson: I understand leftenant Newlumber's Sister Ruth is gwine to stand for de Goddess of Liberty when de Skidmores march in de hall.
Puter: She'll have to stand on a flour barrel.

All these characters appeared again and again in later Mulligan episodes. Harrigan generally remem-bered their histories and kept his delineations con-sistent from play to play. Sometimes a line from one play gave a hint of a future story. For example, in *The Mulligan Guards' Ball* Cordelia notes, "I have a Silver Wedding the night after the ball," and before long *The Mulligans' Silver Wedding* entered the reper-tory. Theatregoers with an attentive ear and a good memory would also come to realize that Harrigan had favorite lines which he repeated, wittingly or not, from one show to another. One of the minor characters in the play complains the corned beef was so bad, "I've corns on me teeth from ateing it." Later figures made identical complaints. With time, Harrigan fleshed out all his better efforts, but their multi-scened construction, their debt to Tom and Jerry shows, allowed a certain looseness that left little sacred. One thing that never changed once established was Braham's hit songs. Although "The Mulligan Guard" was written in 1873 for a short vaudeville skit, it was forever after incorporated into this play and often used in other Mulligan plays. It was unquestionably the most popular and endur-ing number to come from the Harrigan and Braham partnership. But a second favorite was written spe-cifically for this production, a melody typical of the sentimental tunes found in all the Harrigan and Hart shows, "The Babies On Our Block."

Unlike *The Lorgaire*, *The Mulligan Guards' Ball* had no opening number. The first song did not come until the end of the first scene when Dan offers Cordelia's lady friends refreshment from "The Pitcher Of Beer." Obviously standard formulas had yet to be arrived at. But the evening was clearly a musical entertainment well on its way to becoming a full-fledged musical comedy.

Two nights later **H.M.S. Pinafore** burst upon New York. But New York was not the first American city to embrace the work. The active Boston theatre had grabbed that honor with its version on 25 November 1878. San Francisco was applauding it by 23 December and Philadelphia by the first week of 1879. The first New York performance took place at the Standard Theatre on 15 January, and just over a week later the Lyceum offered a competing production. Since it takes more than a week to assemble and rehearse a cast, managers clearly expected the show to be a hit. Because of the period's loose copyright laws competing companies were not unheard of. What was unheard of was the sweep that Gilbert and Sullivan's comic opera made of the New York theatre scene. By 8 February, less than four weeks after the premiere, the *Dramatic Mirror* could remark, "The constant spread of 'H. M. S. Pinafore' has led to the report that every house in New York is to do the opera within two weeks." No such monopolization came to pass. Nevertheless, on 3 May this same theatrical sheet did look back and note that at one time or another eleven major houses—Wallack's, the Fifth Avenue, the Standard, the Globe, the Olympic, Niblo's, the Lyceum, the Academy of Music, Tony Pastor's, the Germania, and the Windsor—all had played host to the piece. In its excitement, the paper overlooked a twelfth theatre, the Broadway. Some weeks as many as three companies were running simultaneously—this at a time when there were rarely more than a dozen principal houses lit in any one week. There was even an all-black troupe and a company composed solely of children. The young man who played Sir Joseph Porter in the latter was the son of a famous trouper, E. L. Davenport, and himself became a musical comedy favorite, Harry Davenport.

In W. S. Gilbert's deliriously preposterous yarn, subtitled *The Lass That Loved a Sailor*, the lass is Josephine, daughter of the *Pinafore*'s captain. She is sought in marriage by none other than "the ruler of the Queen's navee," Sir Joseph Porter, K. C. B. His account of his rise from office boy, carefully polishing "the handle of the big front door," to his current exalted position fails to move the young lady. Nor do his assurances that "love can level ranks" have any effect. Josephine remains loyal to her real love, the common sailor Ralph Rackstraw. Josephine's plight is resolved only by Buttercup, a fat, homely, jovial old woman, reduced to selling sailors "snuff and tobaccy, and excellent jacky." She confesses that many years ago she had practiced "baby-farming." To her dismay she "mixed up" two children—one patrician and one of low birth. The high-born babe

was actually Ralph, the captain was the other! Ralph is hastily made the *Pinafore*'s new commander and, allowing love to level ranks, marries Josephine. Her father, now a mere sailor, weds Buttercup, while Sir Joseph settles for a lady named Hebe.

American theatregoers were exposed to a rare, but not new, kind of musical theatre in which book, lyrics, and music combined to form an integral whole. What made the show distinctive was the literacy and wit of its words, and the artistry and almost unprecedented melodic invention of its music. W. S. Gilbert carried the absurdities of his story to the brink of acceptable extremity, while Arthur Sullivan infused old forms such as ballades, sea chanties, jigs, and octettes with such irresistibly catchy melodies that most people sang them readily and happily, unaware of the artistry behind them. Together they devised the finest patter songs (in this case Sir Joseph's history, "When I Was A Lad") the popular musical stage has ever known. Not everyone knew how to take such drollery at first hearing. The *Times* recorded: "During the first act everyone seemed more or less at sea—chorus, orchestra and soloists. The audience scarcely knew whether to accept the love-making as serious or humorous, and in consequence some very pretty passages excited general hilarity." The original American cast—which chalked up 175 performances—had Thomas Whiffen as Sir Joseph Porter, Eugene Clark as Captain Corcoran, Henri Laurent as Ralph Rackstraw, W. Davidge as Dick Deadeye, Eva Mills as Josephine, and Blanche Galton as Buttercup. Given the era's freewheeling ways, not all productions were faithful to the original. The Lyceum company, under E. E. Rice's management, gave the work a tongue-in-cheek mounting. Although lovely Lizzie Webster sang Josephine, Buttercup was George K. Fortesque. Reviews mention frequent interpolations of popular American songs. And, of course, minstrels and variety houses had a field day with satirical pieces. For example, Tony Pastor, besides offering the English work, produced a burlesque called *T. P. S. Canal Boat Pinafore*, which included characters such as Sir Joseph Lager and Dick Deadbeat. Minstrelsy remained primarily in the hands of the competent San Francisco Minstrels. They, too, joined in the fun at the expense of Gilbert and Sullivan. Their spoof was entitled "His Mud Scow Pinafore." New York, by the way, was not alone in burlesquing the *Pinafore* rage. Typically, while *H. M. S. Pinafore* was delighting patrons at Philadelphia's Broad Street Theatre, that city's 11th Street Opera House, a short walk away, was regaling its customers with *Shadboat Pinafore.*

For all the infidelities and burlesques, the extraordinary success of *H. M. S. Pinafore* alerted producers and writers to the possibilities of musicals with more coherence and artistic sensibility than heretofore. Although the days of musicals contrived almost haphazardly as stage pieces and conceived in terms of immediate theatrical values were far from over, a new approach to the American musical stage became unavoidable. Perhaps nothing ever written for our native stage surpassed the intelligence and brilliance of Gilbert and Sullivan's masterpieces, but from 1879 on Americans would at least try. Two problems presented themselves at once. As the theatre chronicler George Odell noted, "the mad rush for Pinafore caught all unprepared; a race of singing actors needed to be developed." More important, composers and writers with both talent and integrity had to appear. Happily, with time these creators and interpreters made themselves known.

One immediate result of *Pinafore's* popularity was a rush to stage other Gilbert and Sullivan works. On 21 February the Broadway raised its curtain on an earlier comic opera previously shunted aside, **The Sorcerer.** When the work failed to provide a second *Pinafore*, the house withdrew it on 8 March and hastily brought up a company of *Pinafore* from Philadelphia. But the failure hardly tarnished Gilbert and Sullivan's bright star. As one commentator suggested, even *Trial by Jury*, "which was rated rather dull when produced here three years ago, has in the light of recent events become a great work."

On 14 April at the Standard Sullivan's decade-old one-acter **Cox and Box,** written with F. C. Burnand and telling of two men who unwittingly share the same lodging, was added as a curtain raiser to *Pinafore.* It was retained on the bill for little more than a month.

A revival of *The Black Crook* (12 September 1866) opened at Niblo's on 5 March. Marie Bonfanti was once again prima ballerina. By now—thirteen years after she danced at its premiere—she must have come to look upon the work as her private annuity. One of the specialty acts assisting her was Professor Swan, billed as a "man alligator." The spectacle's return caused the *Dramatic Mirror* to suggest, "The era of the spectacle, which seemed a logical outcome of the ways, wealth and prodigality which succeeded the late war, ended abruptly with the financial crash of 1873." The statement was only partly true. Few new spectacles on the order of *The*

Black Crook followed, but *The Black Crook* itself held the boards and the hearts of theatregoers for the rest of the century. This particular revival ran until May, with a "Grand Reconstruction" announced for the final week. It closed suddenly when the manager absconded with the payroll.

For all its success, *Pinafore* could not eject opéra bouffe from the stages. All through the spring companies performing in English or French found harbor in one house or another. Besides the old standbys, they added Lecocq's **Le Petit Duc** and von Suppé's **Fatinitza** to their lists. Lecocq's piece enjoyed a vernacular production at Booth's on 17 March, and, when it left, Aimée came into the house to sing it in the original. She sang the part of a young nobleman whose plans to rescue his sweetheart from her seminary are thwarted when he is called to arms. *Fatinitza's* American premiere took place on 14 April at the Germania, a house devoted appropriately to productions in German; its debut in English occurred eight nights later at the Fifth Avenue. The displacement of French opéra bouffe by German operetta began with this piece. Now long forgotten, it remained a favorite for over a decade. Franz von Suppé has been called the German Offenbach, although his works were generally more sentimental, less laden with burlesque and political satire. But the vogue for trouser roles required *Fatinitza*, first sung in Vienna on 5 January 1876, to resort to at least one feature of burlesque—dressing a woman as a man. Cleverly, it introduced an element of triple tension by allowing its leading lady in the role of a man to have to pose as a woman. Its story told of a Russian general who falls in love with a beautiful girl, never suspecting the lady is actually one of his lieutenants, heading for a masquerade. By comic opera coincidence the lieutenant and the general's niece are sweethearts. Jeannie Winston sang the title role.

The same night New Yorkers first heard *Le Petit Due*, Philadelphians suffered through E. R. Mollenhauer and Charles Barnard's **The Wager** (18 March 1879, Park), a new farce-comedy featuring Alice Hosmer. Gentlemen at a fashionable spa bet their ladies will flirt at that evening's masked ball. The ladies overhear, so pointedly lead on the men. Seemingly a rip-off of the hit play *Pink Dominoes*, the musical closed quickly, allowing its stage to be turned over to one of the countless companies of *Pinafore* mushrooming across the country.

At the risk of briefly abandoning our chronology it might be interesting to peek at some of the other musicals Philadelphia saw during the calendar year, always remembering that Philadelphia was far from alone in mounting homegrown entertainments. Remington Fairlamb's **Valerie; or, The Treasured Tokens** (12 May 1879, Park) had been presented unsuccessfully a few seasons back at another Philadelphia house. Its revised version was no luckier, especially after the leading man stormed out in the middle of a performance. **Jumbles** (28 July 1879, Walnut St.) was another of the era's many song-and-dance–laden farce-comedies. A wife becomes jealous when she realizes her husband is falling in love with her sister, so she plots to win him back by arousing his jealousy. G. Operti and Page McCarty's **Buttons** (22 September 1879, Arch St.) was less elaborate but equally absurd and condemned as "dull." Certainly its motivations were questionable, or perhaps nonexistent. After a judge concludes his daughter isn't truly his, all the characters go out to the plains to fight Indians and heathen Chinee. A heroic captain wins the girl's hand. Matters didn't improve much, if any, with Frederick Mills's **The Mayor** (22 September 1879, Broad St.), in which a young Englishman is sent to France to help his uncle's friend usurp the throne. Disguises and complications ensue, but the young man does wind up with a very pretty lady. J. A. DeWitt's **The Royal Banquet** (17 November 1879, National) was called by its producers "a romantic spectacular opera" and by one critic "conspicuously absurd." Pirates set afire an American liner. Two ladies and a general escape on a raft, washing up on the Hazlebar Islands. The island's king is a shipwrecked American, who ordered the pirate attack so that he might have some congenial company. But when the ladies and the general are not amused, the king decrees their executions. Rescuers arrive, free the captives, and win the hands of the ladies.

Between the arrivals of *The Wager* and *Valerie* in Philadelphia, the prestigious Boston Museum unveiled its own musical, **Puss in Boots,** on 14 April. Adapted from *Le Chat Botté*, the piece mixed some original John Braham music with songs lifted from elsewhere. Its book by Fred Williams and T. R. Sullivan enlarged on the adventures of a rustic turned into a cat. A few weeks later the city gave short shrift to Fred J. Eustis and Charles F. Pidgin's **Sancho Pedro** (16 June 1879, Gaiety). The romantic nonsense featured the beautiful Sadie Martinot in trousers as the titular Pedro, with tiny, young Frank Daniels clowning as Shovel-Off.

The New York season ended in May with the return of Rice's Surprise Party and the arrival of the Salsbury Troubadours. In **The Brook** (12 May 1879, San Francisco Minstrels' Hall), the work the Salsbury troupe presented, many scholars have detected one of the origins of modern musical comedy. The piece and the company initiated a vogue for what were soon called "farce-comedies." These were plays with the merest trifle of a plot, just enough frame to provide an excuse for songs, dances, and specialties by the small band that comprised the company. In essence they were loosely justified vaudeville, differing from variety in that a performer did not merely do his or her act and disappear for the evening but rather assumed a number of guises and presented parts of his or her repertory at intervals during the show. And, of course, vaudeville rarely pretended to have a story to tell. Scholars who see in the Troubadours the seeds of later musical comedy are correct, but seeds for the twentieth-century revues were there as well. *The Brook* was subtitled *A Jolly Day at the Picnic*, a subtitle that gave away the whole plot. Three men and two women arrive at the "I-Flow-on-for-ever" brook with their picnic baskets. The picnickers bore names such as Festus Heavysides, Percy Montrose, and Blanche Sylvester. Out of their baskets came not only their meal but costumes, juggling balls, and all the other paraphernalia for their acts. For many the darling of the evening was Nellie McHenry, whose "laugh was a long ripple of merriment," cavorting as Rose Dimplecheek. Both the public and the critics agreed with the *Dramatic Mirror*, which found the evening "without plot, character, motif, or, we might almost add incident, but all the same, very funny." Soon Rice's Surprise Party, Colville's Folly, The Tourists, and a host of other bands were offering similar pieces. While Rice's troupe, which arrived a week after the Salsbury entourage, opened at the Union Square with *Babes in the Wood*, they changed to William Gill's "burlesque extravaganza," **Horrors; or, The Marajah of Zogobad,** on 28 May. Its paper-thin plot booked a young man, mistaken in the belief he has inherited a harem, on an eastbound liner. The passengers he meets provided the specialties. Willie Edouin shone as a "première danseuse" trying to perform on a ship pitching and rolling at sea. A season or two passed before the troupe officially switched to farce-comedies, although many would justifiably tag *Horrors* as a farce-comedy.

The ranks of vaudeville houses continued to swell, introducing one major new emporium, Koster and Bial's at 23rd Street and Sixth Avenue.

1879–1880

For George Odell, in his history of the New York stage, the 1879–1880 season marked the beginnings of "A Changing Theatre." Nowhere was that change more evident than on the lyric stage. If opéra bouffe repertory companies each count as a single entry, the seasons between *The Black Crook* (12 September 1866) and *H. M. S. Pinafore* (15 January 1879) averaged about eight musical mountings. Not until the 1950s was such a low figure again recorded. From the dozen or so offerings in 1878–1879 of the American Musical Theatre, the number jumped to over thirty in 1879–1880. Of course many were importations, revivals, or return engagements. Further, many American works took pride in advertising that their directors, their designers, and even their sets were from abroad. Nor was so dramatic an increase in activity matched by any similar rise in quality. It took a while before American authors and composers assimilated the aesthetic lessons Gilbert and Sullivan had offered them.

That the Mulligan plays had become a successful series was demonstrated by advertisements which called **The Mulligan Guards' Chowder** (11 August 1879, Comique) "Volume the Third." Ned Harrigan once again was Dan and Annie Yeamans, Cordelia; while Tony Hart not only played their son Tommy, but Mrs. Welcome (Rebecca) Allup as well. However, the principal plot of the evening pivoted on the behavior of two other characters, for when Walsingham McSweeny (M. Bradley) is selected as head cook of the chowder over Snuff McIntosh (Edward Burt), the explosive Snuff vows to wreck the event. His intentions are unwittingly abetted by the black Skidmores, whose Decoration Day plans call for them to celebrate on the same small piece of turf the Guards have chosen. This was the third time Harrigan had employed the device of conflicting arrangements. The blacks' march, "The Skids Are Out Today," was the hit of the show. Other songs included "Oh, Girly, Girly," "Never Take The Horseshoe From The Door," and "The Little Widow Dunn." None of Braham's songs for this piece ranked among his best. Nonetheless on 2 November the *Times* noted, "The melodies which form such an attractive part of 'The Mulligan Guard Chowder'... are played on every side. If popularity is a species of present immortality, then the composer, Mr. David Braham, should be a happy man." How curious that Harrigan and Hart were never known as Harrigan, Hart, and Braham! The actors' visibility worked to their fame. The

Chowder was served up for the hundredth time on 5 November and closed ten nights later.

Colville's organization—called for the moment the Opera Burlesque Company—brought in **The Magic Slipper** (25 August 1879, Haverly's Lyceum). The story recounted how the Baron de Boulevard's (Ed Chapman) stepdaughters—especially the wicked Clorinda (R. E. Graham, an actor)—humiliate his own daughter, Cinderella de Boulevard (Erne Roseau). Naturally Cinderella triumphs, abetted or hindered in her triumph by Prince Popette (a trouser role played by Alice Hastings), Daffydownilla, Sweetcornia, and Wheatina. The dialogue ran to lines such as "men who play polo never get married" and snatches from *Pinafore*, while the score was a similar hodgepodge. The troupe remained in town for three weeks. After a long road tour it returned with the same offering in May.

The same night that Colville's troupe opened in New York, Baltimore tried its luck with a homemade musical, W. B. Hazelton and Edward Spencer's **Electric Light** (25 August 1879, Ford's). Its hero wins his heartthrob, daughter of a comically eccentric tailor, after he is awarded a patent on an improved electric light. After a short run, the show moved on to Washington and parts west before disappearing from the record.

Maurice Grau's band of opéra bouffe interpreters began the first of three separate engagements on 1 September. Together the three stays (at the Fifth Avenue, Booth's, and the Academy of Music) added up to over four months. At first Aimée was the star, but she was soon replaced by Paola Marie, sister of an earlier opéra bouffe favorite, Irma, and sister, as well, of Bizet's original Carmen, Galli-Marie. The repertory offered nothing new. Its works were the opéra bouffe standards of the day, from *La Grande Duchesse* on.

When the Kiralfys mounted **Enchantment** (4 September 1879, Niblo's), a "grand operatic spectacle" in the *Black Crook* tradition, their advertisements promised "celebrated English singers, renowned Italian ballet premieres and extraordinary specialty features." They also offered their customarily elaborate stage effects. In this instance the effects were so complicated they caused several delays in the opening date. A number of critics questioned whether it was worth the wait. The *Times* lamented that the "silly" evening "abounds in side shows." To tie the spectacle and specialties together the work told a tale of troubled love. Andre (C. J. Campbell), a young fisherman, loves the governor's daughter,

Angeline (Jessie Greville). The governor opposes the match. The enchantress, Rayense (Mlle. Cassati), leads the lovers to the Land of the Ephemerals, the Isle of Mystery, and other unearthly places before she prevails on the girl's father to give his consent. A large segment of the public ignored the *Dramatic Mirror*'s pronouncement of the preceding year and the critics' reservations. Their way to Niblo's made easier by the new elevated railway, they flocked in sufficient number to allow *Enchantment* to offer its hundredth performance on 25 November and continue until the middle of December.

Augustin Daly remained hopeful that part of his season could be devoted to a musical presentation. His hopes suffered a setback when he mounted **Newport; or, The Swimmer, the Singer and the Cypher,** as part of a double bill on 17 September. The *Times* knowingly informed its readers that "a musical comedy it is called" and added, somewhat mysteriously, that it was the work of "an American writer living abroad." The writer remained unidentified even in the program, but was later discovered to be Olive Logan Sykes. She based her play on *Niniche,* the same source used the year before by Edward Mollenhauer in *Manhattan Beach* (12 December 1878), and used again years later by Harry B. Smith for *The Little Duchess* (14 October 1901). The woman who has to go about winning back her straying husband (Charles Leclercq) was called Mrs. Porter (Catherine Lewis). Music was by a number of composers, but one new song, sung by the wife, caught the critics' and public's fancy, surviving the show's two-week run. The song had the odd title of "Crutch And Toothpick" and twitted the dandified "dudes" of the time. Even at this early date Daly was thoughtful enough to fill his stage not just with attractive scenery, but with "a host of pretty girls."

The season's first farce-comedy troupe raised its curtain on 29 September at a theatre known briefly as Wood's Broadway—but soon to be the Bijou. Padgett and Bassett's **Bric-A-Brac** used a reception as an excuse for its jokes, specialties, and music. In keeping with general practice the songs came from everywhere, "music from 'Fatinitza,' ballads more or less familiar, some original songs." Also in keeping with the practice of these pieces the cast was small. Padgett and Bassett needed only two other performers to help them play all the parts.

If *The Brook* needed only a picnic to excuse its frivolities and *Bric-A-Brac* made do with a reception, **Across the Atlantic** (13 October 1879, Olympic) allowed its star, John A. Ransome, to portray Horace Durand, a young actor, who follows his sweetheart to Europe and there rescues her from a typical "stage villain and an unpleasant situation in which she, with her family, find themselves in Sedan [site of a famed 1870 battle in the Franco-Prussian War]." On the road to convincing his fiancée's family that marriage to an actor would not be the ultimate degradation, Horace disguises himself as a "colored" servant, a German guide, and an Irish coachman. No fewer than six other entertainers assisted Ransome and his wife (who did not play the fiancée), attesting to the swift fattening of farce-comedy rosters. Yet for all its songs, dances, and other turns the *Herald* branded it a "trashy melodrama," while the *Times* categorized it as a "drama." Drama, melodrama, farce-comedy, or prototypical musical comedy, *Across the Atlantic* steadily provided Ransome with a paycheck for nearly a decade and intermittently thereafter.

A similar, but less elaborate, mounting followed. **Hobbies** (6 October 1879, Lyceum), a farce-comedy, was commissioned by Nat Goodwin and written by Ben Woolf, the same Woolf who had provided the libretto for *The Doctor of Alcantara* (25 September 1866). Woolf was also the author of the successful play *The Mighty Dollar*. Goodwin had just organized his own farce-comedy band, Goodwin's Froliques. According to Goodwin, Woolf threw off the piece in five days but gave Goodwin and his five fellow players four years' work. Goodwin's imitations of other actors were generally the most praised specialty in the evening, although Jennie Weatherby was lauded for her bit as an old lady unwilling to accept the fact that she is no longer a languid beauty. The show represented the first peak in Goodwin's erratic, scandal-plagued career.

A few nights later Augustin Daly presented Bronson Howard's merging of Molière's *L'École des femmes* and *L'École des Maris* as **Wives** (18 October 1879, Daly's), larding it with songs and dances and embellishing it with a chorus line of twenty beauties. In its own way the show must have seemed almost full-fledged musical comedy, but apparently the amalgam was not completely satisfying. Even if it had been, to be right too soon is to be wrong. The play was not one of Daly's triumphs.

The initial revival of *H. M. S. Pinafore,* by the Juvenile Opera Co., at Wood's Broadway, occurred on 20 October, though a better *Pinafore* was not far off.

J. K. Emmet returned with a new Fritz play, **Fritz in Ireland** (3 November 1879, Park). William

Carleton's story was complicated and preposterous, leading up to the inevitable recognition scene. Baroness Hertford, feeling her husband (J. H. Rennie) has never loved her, leaves her estate to her sister, Lady Amelia (Lenore Bigelow), in case she dies before her child reaches maturity. Both she and the child do die, but the conniving Lawyer Priggins (John Mackay) persuades the baron to kidnap and substitute another child, since the baroness's sister has never seen her niece. The blackmailing Priggins attempts to force the baron to assign his wealth to him. But the baron reminds Priggins of his suspicious actions when he was sent to seek Lord Seaton's lost son in Germany. The real son was to marry Lady Amelia. Of course, Priggins wanted to prevent the wedding. He was determined to marry Amelia himself, if the inheritance did finally fall into her hands. Years pass. Fritz arrives, seeking his kidnapped sister. In dialogue almost word for word from *Fritz, Our Cousin German* (11 July 1870), the baron's "daughter" (Emily Baker) responds to Fritz's singing an old lullaby:

Louisa: Oh, how beautiful!
Fritz: Dot song make you cry.
Louisa: The melody is so soft and sad.

Reunion follows. How much melodrama and spectacle was included in these pieces can be gauged from the following note in the prologue of the manuscript:

After Priggins steals the child, Fritz discovers the theft, Priggins can make his escape on horseback pursued by Fritz, he overtakes Priggins on a dock at the waters edge, big fight Fritz knocked off dock into water, Priggins escapes in row-boat to 55 foot Yawl yacht in waiting, Fritz swims to a launch climbs in, starts engine, and races after Yawl, overhauls it, another fight, is thrown over board, Yawl makes its escape, and Fritz is rescued by fisherman.

The action is cinematographic rather than theatrical, but prefilm audiences accepted as realistic effects that today would be risible. Musically the show marked no advance over the earlier Fritz efforts, and Emmet usually incorporated his by then famous "Lullaby" in the recognition scene. New songs included "The Bells Are Ringing," "The Cuckoo Song," and "The Love Of The Shamrock."

This edition ran eight weeks and returned in May for an additional run. By this time, the shape of Emmet's future career seemed clear to him, and he was eager to convey his intentions to his audience. In the program for the Park Theatre for the week of 14 November he inserted a "Notice To Public." The notice ran, "It is Mr. EMMET'S intention to make an alteration yearly in his character of 'FRITZ,' by giving him sketches and incidents of his experience during his travels around the world, and introduce new scenes and music, making, if not an entire new drama, an entertainment not to be excelled." Possibly excluding the last value judgment, Emmet was true to his word. He was plainly astute enough to gauge accurately his audiences' tastes, and he was determined enough never to veer from his stated plans. Even after his death, his son and others would be able to thrive for a number of years by rigidly following this 1879 dictum.

The same night *Fritz in Ireland* premiered, a third farce-comedy troupe, The Tourists, settled in for a two-week visit at Haverly's Lyceum with its most successful piece, **A Pullman Palace Car**. After a first act in which a collection of socialites plan a trip west, the second and third acts take place on the train, where the travelers and assorted passersby perform their turns. Typical of how these small bands made a cast seem larger was W. A. Mestayer's switching from the role of T. Henry Slum in the first act to impersonate Richard Morgye, Faro Jack, and the Western Guerilla in the last two acts. Delightful vignettes included M. H. Watson's drunken butler, Jennie Reifferth's maiden aunt, and J. N. Long's "red-striped-shirt polo player with bogus English accent, elbows and hips thrown backward to the point of breaking." Songs included a scene from *Pinafore*, "The Old Kentucky Home," a chorus from *The Chimes of Normandy*, a serenade from *Cox and Box*, "The Skids Are Out Today" (from Harrigan and Hart), and "original with the Tourists," "Poor Cock Robin." Later programs show a markedly different collection of musical numbers, including the addition of a title song. The Tourists returned to Haverly's in their *Pullman Palace Car* on January 5 for a six-week sojourn. Rather early in their histories, the show's title and the group's name seem to have become linked as one, so the entertainment was often called *The Tourists in a Pullman Palace Car*.

A month-long revival of *Fatinitza* (14 April 1879) opened at the Standard on 17 November, competing with **The Mulligan Guards' Christmas** for first-nighters' attention. Undoubtedly the more sedate opéra bouffe drew a more stately crowd. The new work dealt with the arrival in America of Bridget Lochmuller's brother, Planxty McFudd (Welsh Edwards). To the resigned dismay of the Mulligans (Harrigan and Annie Yeamans), he courts and wins Dan's sister, Diana (Marie Gorenflo). Among the new characters Harrigan created for this play was Macaulay Jangles (Edward Burt), a slightly demented figure given to grand malapropisms. As usual Annie Mack played Bridget; Hart, Rebecca Allup; John Wild, Simpson Primrose; and Billy Gray, Palestine Puter. David Braham's songs included "The Sweet Kentucky Rose" (Hart's major song), "The Skids Are On Review," "The Mulligan Braves," and "Tu-ri-ad-i-lum, Or Santa Claus Has Come" (sung by Harrigan). If Odell is correct, Harrigan again sang "The Pitcher Of Beer" in this work. Not quite full length, *The Mulligan Guards' Christmas* was accompanied by an olio as it ran until 14 February.

Theodore Sayre's **The Strategists** (1 December 1879, Broadway) probably started life as a standard farce, this time about two brothers who espouse diametrically opposed methods for attaining the same end. The *Herald* characterized the entertainment as "'The Comedy of Errors' intensified," bolstering its assertion by noting, "There are not only two Dromios, but two sets of them." The sudden explosion of song-studded fripperies assuredly prompted the injection here of songs, dances, acrobatics, and other variety turns. At first Clinton Hall played both protagonists (or antagonists), but he eventually withdrew, and in ensuing seasons others essayed the parts.

That same night at the Fifth Avenue, Gilbert, Sullivan, and D'Oyly Carte showed Americans how they meant *H. M. S. Pinafore* to be done. They brought with them J. H. Ryley to sing Sir Joseph Porter, Hugh Talbot for Ralph, Furneaux Cook to be Dick Deadeye, and Alice Barnett as Buttercup. In a gesture of transatlantic courtesy they hired two Americans: John Cook, who performed under the name Signor Brocolini, for Captain Corcoran, and Blanche Roosevelt as Josephine. The Englishmen's crossing was not, however, purely in the name of aesthetics or altruism. Their principal reason for making the still hazardous journey was to stop the rampant pirating of their works. To this end they were determined to secure the copyright to their latest work, **The Pirates of Penzance**, by mounting it here first. They did so on New Year's Eve, 31 December 1879, again at the Fifth Avenue.

Gilbert's young hero was Frederick, whose wet-nurse, Ruth, somewhat hard of hearing, misunderstood his father's request to apprentice the boy to pilots, and apprenticed him instead to pirates. Though by his own reckoning Frederick has reached his twenty-first birthday and therefore is a free man, his mentors insist that since he was born on 29 February, his birthday comes once every four years and he is merely a five-year-old. The beautiful Mabel falls in love at first sight with Frederick, whom she labels a "Poor Wandering One." Mabel's guardian is Major-General Stanley, "the very model of a modern Major-General," who, while up on "information vegetable, animal, and mineral," knows no more of things military "than a novice in a nunnery."

A happy ending is arranged when the docile pirates yield to a band of timid police "in Queen Victoria's name." The song of the pirates, "With Cat-like Tread," soon swept the nation (with new lyrics) as "Hail, Hail, The Gang's All Here."

The cast was led by Talbot as Frederick, Ryley as Major-General Stanley, Cook as Samuel, Brocolini as Richard, and Miss Roosevelt as Mabel. If the reception of the new work by the public was disappointing—it ran only until 6 March—the Englishmen could at least leave knowing they would no longer be so easily cheated of their royalties.

In between these openings Gilbert supervised the staging of his collaboration with Frederic Clay, **Princess Toto** (13 December 1879, Standard). Its story told of a princess (Leonora Braham) who has no memory. This flaw leads her into marriage—several times in short order. Gilbert was as droll as ever, and even managed to include some twitting of popular American-Indian stories. But without superior music the piece failed.

The very next musical to open suggested American authors had the will if not the creative means to follow in Gilbert and Sullivan's paths. This "comic military opera" was New York's initial exposure to what it soon came to term derisively "the Philadelphia school"—a school Broadway saw as given to inane dialogue and banally simple music. **The First Life Guards at Brighton** had premiered on 3 November 1879 at Philadelphia's North Broad Street Theatre, and after winning generally enthusiastic notices, chalked up a two-month run before beginning its East Coast tour on 5 January 1880, at Wood's Broadway. The musical was written by J. S. Crossy and presented by his own ambitious J. S. Crossy American Comic Opera Company. In Crossy's tale Sir Charles Courtland loves a young lady who refuses to marry him because she is uncertain of her own history. Her mother had been killed in India, and she had then been separated from her father. Two down-at-the-heel rogues appear—a major (with a red nose) and a newspaperman. The reporter writes an article for Colonel Preston's local paper. This article, assailing Sir Charles's First Life Guards, leads to a duel between the colonel and Charles, and the duel in turn leads to the discovery that the colonel is the long-lost father of Charles's fiancée. Florence Ellis was the leading lady, with Eugene Clarke, Edward Connell, Charles F. Lang, and Charles Foster in principal male roles. The *Times* treated it as a "trifle," a word it often used to describe the farce-comedies, and dismissed it in a one-paragraph review as a "fiasco." Crossy kept the work on the boards for two weeks and then turned his Americans over to a presentation of *Madame Angot's Daughter*.

Evangeline (27 July 1874) returned for a brief stay at the Standard the same night the Crossy work opened. The day before its revival, the *Times* predicted hard going for it, suggesting, "[I]n these days of 'Pinafore,' burlesque will hardly kick its heels and grind out its old tunes to advantage." But *Evangeline* had developed a faithful following. It did satisfactory business during its two-week stay and came back again in May for another fortnight.

The font that *Fatinitza* had opened received replenishment on 28 January when New Yorkers were given their first opportunity to hear **The Royal Middy**, an English version of Zell and Genée's *Der Seekadet* (also spelled *Seecadet*), a tale of a gypsy girl who becomes a sailor to find her lover. Its producer was Augustin Daly, and his success with the work allowed him to gratify at one and the same time his urge to mount musicals and his penchant for German theatre. Daly awarded Catherine Lewis the title role and even utilized his rising star Ada Rehan in an ancillary role. Daly's orchestra leader, Mollenhauer, adapted the piece, retrieving in its acclaim much of the esteem he had lost the preceding year with *Manhattan Beach*. Another orchestra leader was less fortunate. Operti was ejected from Daly's, allegedly for taking notes for a rival production. Daly might have spared himself the lawsuit that followed had he known how his rivals were to fare. Daly's *Royal Middy* ran two months to excellent business; Sydney Rosenfeld's version, **The Sea Cadet**, opened 7 June at the Fifth Avenue and closed 12 June.

On 2 February playgoers had a choice of musical openings. Rice's Surprise Party brought back

Horrors (28 May 1879) for a three-week run at the Standard, while the Broadway watched Caverly's English Folly Company begin a month-long run with the burlesque *Princess Carpillona*.

A new version of *Humpty Dumpty* (10 March 1868) arrived the following night. It acknowledged the passing of time, even in the world of Mother Goose, when it pitted Humpty Dumpty Sr. against Humpty Dumpty Jr. Of course, the old favorites were present: Goody Twoshoes (Pauline Barretta), Tommy Tucker (J. F. Raymond), Old One-Two (W H. Bartholomew), as well as Old Three-Four (N. D. Jones). A stray from *The Black Crook* (12 September 1866), Stalacta, also had her moment. Humpty Senior was played by James Maffitt, who once had been called in to replace the incapacitated G. L. Fox as Humpty, on one of his vacations from the role of The Lone Fisherman. Junior was clowned by another old hand at Humpty, Robert Fraser. But the hit of the evening was a specialty act, a troupe of Spanish youngsters singing as they accompanied themselves on guitars and mandolins. The happy hodgepodge delighted New York theatregoers for eight weeks. *The Black Crook* itself was revived briefly, as a stopgap booking on the 16th at Niblo's, with one of the Kiralfys dancing Dragonfil.

The Theatre Comique's final offering of the season also bowed on 16 February. **The Mulligan Guards' Surprise** dealt with Dan's unhappiness after Cordelia (Annie Yeamans) persuades him to leave his beloved neighborhood and move to more pretentious quarters. Dan (Harrigan) embarrasses Cordelia and her family by getting roaring drunk. But Rebecca Allup (Hart) helps extricate him from his agony. The basic situation was the same Harrigan would reuse a few seasons later in what is generally considered his best work, *Cordelia's Aspirations* (5 November 1883). That Harrigan, Hart, and Braham were establishing the first ongoing traditions in the American Musical Theatre can be seen from the reviews.

In offering *The Mulligan Guards' Surprise* the first extended notice it ever gave to the Comique, the *Times* remarked that while the house's balconies were still filled with raucous fans who often interrupted the action with prolonged cheers, applause, and even comments (to which the players not infrequently responded), the ground floor was attracting an increasingly cultivated crowd. The *Times* was willing to accept partial credit for this improvement, suggesting its brief Sunday notices had helped call attention to the freshness and integrity of Harrigan and Braham's material. The paper, praising and listing Braham's songs, concluded that they "will take their places with 'Sallie Waters' and 'The Little Widow Dunn.'" The paper was a little less happy with Harrigan's writing. It saw the evening as "a superfluity of coarse fun and cheap wit, and a tiresome diffuseness of dialogue." But its criticism did not prevent it from enjoying the entertainment or allowing that the public would enjoy it even more. The public, in fact, enjoyed it for just over 100 performances, until it closed on May 15.

Years later, discussing *McAllister's Legacy*, the *Times* vividly depicted a typical Harrigan and Hart audience: "The enthusiasm began to display itself at an early stage in the proceedings. No sooner was Mr. Braham seen than he was greeted with applause and cheers. To this followed a concerted shout of 'How are you, David Braham?' When Mr. Harrigan came on the stage, which was early in the first act, he met with such a continuous round of cheers and applause that the acting had to be suspended. After the audience or a large portion had finished their shout of 'How are you, Mr. Harrigan?' he was forced to respond to the good natured greeting before the play could proceed. He said he hardly knew what to say. He had been very busy during the week and was fortunate in having a new play for them. Whether the manuscript of it should have perished in the flames which destroyed the Theatre Comique or should be handed down to future generations was for them to say. He, having said so much, could do no more than return thanks and 'curl up into Dr. McAllister'—which he did at once, amid loud applause. Mr. Hart's greeting was no less warm. He was met with 'One! two! three! How do you do, Mr. Hart?' To which he responded by placing his right hand over his heart and observing that there was too much effervescence there to express his feelings, and mat he was glad they were not compelled to leave New York for some time to come at least. Mrs. Annie Yeamans and John Wild also came in for their share of applause on appearing... . At the close of the first act Mr. Braham was presented with a valuable violin in the place of the one lost by him at the Comique fire. A lawyer of this city made the presentation speech, but although Braham was urged to reply, he wisely forbore, and let his orchestra speak for him. At this point a large number queried, in chorus, 'When was David Braham?' and responded with 'First in war, first in peace, and first in the hearts of his countrymen.' Similar remarks were also made concerning one George Washington."

Another totally native work, **Hiawatha** (21 February 1880, Standard), advertised itself as an "entirely original American operatic extravaganza." Actually it was another burlesque in the *Evangeline* tradition. Longfellow would no more have recognized this adaptation of his poem than he would have the earlier one. As before, the entertainment was largely the work of the busy E. E. Rice, this time in collaboration with Nathaniel Childs. Their story told how Romulus Smith (Henry E. Dixey) and Remus Brown (Louis Harrison) conspire with William Penn Brown (Willie Edouin) to gull Hiawatha (Alice Atherton) and Minnehaha (Marion Singer). An audience must have had to be especially alert for the librettists' puns, which probably were not as obvious to the ear as they were to the eye. At one point Penn is said to have "penn-etrated the forest, not for-rest but for plunder." The songs of *Hiawatha* were a far cry from *The Song of Hiawatha*, including as they did "Bubble, Bubble," "Indians Never Lie," and "Tea, Toast, And Kisses." Whatever flaws the writing possessed, the performance was lively. One critic grudgingly conceded the audience didn't share in his chagrin at the "brazen" foolery of Miss Atherton, and he acknowledged the growing attraction of comely chorus lines, admitting how enthusiastic theatregoers could become when "short skirts, well-displayed limbs, and not over-modest young women mingle under the searching glare of the limelight." Picturesque sets by W. T. Voegtlin, the era's leading scene painter, depicted a wigwam with a waterfall behind it, and a snowstorm. (Unlike the Kiralfys' very wet cascades, Voegtlin's falls seems to have been entirely oil on canvas.) But weaknesses of conception told. The show failed, even though the cast was studded with some of the brightest talent of the 1880s.

A revival of *The Brook* (12 May 1879) was booked into Haverly's Lyceum on 23 February for three weeks. On 8 March *Robinson Crusoe* was hurriedly restaged by Rice to supplant the failed *Hiawatha*. March and early April also saw visits by performers in plays that straddled the line between musical and straight drama. Lotta came in with her repertory, and Maggie Mitchell reappeared in her perennial *Fanchon*.

On 1 March a troupe known as the Boston Ideal Opera Company made its first New York appearance. Probably few in Niblo's that night dreamt of how successful and influential this ensemble would grow. The organization first confronted Boston with its version of *H. M. S. Pinafore* on 14 April 1879. So skillful was the production, it ran a then unheard-of nine weeks. A second operetta, *Fatinitza*, followed with equal success. This second triumph convinced the band's founder, Miss Ober, to set up a permanent troupe. Some inkling of the company's artistry can be gathered from the *Times* pronouncement that its sole offering on this visit, *Pinafore*, was "the most perfect, musically at least, that has yet been given in the City." Captain Corcoran was sung by the "celebrated oratorio singer" Myron Whitney, Adelaide Phillips was Josephine, and Mary Beebe played Buttercup. But even at this early date, the troupe included the great comic bass-baritone who would be the company's real bulwark virtually until its dissolution, its Sir Joseph, Henry Clay Barnabee.

HENRY CLAY BARNABEE was born in Portsmouth, New Hampshire, on 4 November 1833. He quit school to accept work as a dry-goods clerk, but occasional appearances in amateur theatricals, concerts, and lyceums convinced him his future lay behind the footlights. His enchanting autobiography, *My Wanderings*, describes one of the primitive musicals in which he barnstormed New England for many years. This one was first performed in his hometown on 24 and 25 May 1868: "An "operatic cantata" had its inception at this period. It was a mongrel, nondescript affair, compounded of gush, nonsense, and impossible scenery, and entitled "The Haymakers."... The work of a fanner, both in musk and in scenario. The "action" consisted of a number of chorus men, supposed to be mowing in a hay field... . The book called for two farmer's daughters, soprano and contralto, and two hired men, tenor and bass, to fall in love with them, and incidentally to engage in a series of musical mixups, such as duos, trios and quartettes... . Snipkins, a city boy gapes at the countryside and a farmer responds, "Say, I s'pose if I should go daown to Boston, I'd gawp araound same as yew do up here?" Other early musicals Barnabee toured in included Julius Eichberg's *The Two Cadis*, a tale of two rogues determined to outwit each other, and *Marmaduke Mouser*, a romp of high life below stairs that Barnabee himself adapted from a play called *Betsy Baker*. The

slightly horse-faced comedian claimed to his dying day he could not read a note of music, but his lovable villains and his sense of artistic integrity won him the respect and affection of his generation.

The last day of March saw a British double bill at the Bijou. The Bijou was the old Broadway, refurbished and renamed by John A. McCaull, a former Confederate officer and Baltimore lawyer. Under his aegis the house was soon to be a major stage for musicals, and McCaull himself would be termed "the father of comic opera in America." A group called the Opera di Camera presented two English works: **Ages Ago** by W. S. Gilbert and Frederic Clay and **Charity Begins at Home** by Bolton Rowe and Alfred Cellier. Cellier had conducted the D'Oyly Carte's New York production of *H. M. S. Pinafore* and was embarking on his own career as a comic opera composer. The double bill provided a delightful surprise, and thus started McCaull's new house off happily, running until 15 May.

A curious glimpse of the future was accorded 1880 playgoers who gathered on 9 April at Chickering Hall, normally given over to lectures and concerts. That night saw Kate Field sing, dance, mimic contemporary celebrities, and parody Italian opera in **Eyes and Ears in London,** a one-woman show of a sort that would not truly take hold until decades later. A handful of scattered performances sufficed.

The Colville Opera Burlesque returned on 3 May, offering first *The Magic Slipper* it had presented at the start of the season, then switching on 10 May to a burlesque of Verdi, *Ill Treated Il Trovatore*, which had Manrico as a trouser role (played by Eme Roseau) and threw in everything else laughable. Verdi's music was presented along with material from *Pinafore, Der Seekadet,* and the minstrel stages. The show ran a week before the troupe moved on.

The season's final hit was Franz von Suppé's **Boccaccio,** in which the poet's actual romance with the so-called Fiametta, really the Princess Maria of Naples, was given a fictitious happy ending. Jeannie Winston and Alice Hosmer sang the hero and heroine. Opening on 15 May, it consolidated the season-old vogue for middle-European operettas. *Boccaccio* ran four weeks, until hot weather withered trade.

William C. Mitchell's Pleasure Party bucked the same heat to end the theatrical year with their farce-comedy, **Our Goblins** (14 June 1880, Haverly's). Its author, William Gill, and a future star, Francis Wilson, were two of the five members of the troupe. In Gill's story Benjamin Franklin Cobb and four friends go picnicking near an old, deserted castle on the Rhine. Gill as Cobb falls asleep and dreams of the ancient revels held in the castle. Obviously, the story was only a variation of that used in the first of the farce-comedy successes, *The Brook*. As usual in these works, disparate sources were culled for the songs.

Rainbow Revels (26 July 1880, Lyceum) offered Australia's answer to the Vokeses, the Stewarts, in a "protean" (that is, lots of frenetic costume and character changes) entertainment. A quick flop, both it and its stars almost immediately disappeared from American stage annals.

On other musical stages, the San Francisco Minstrels kept the torch of blackface entertainment aflame. Some indication that even this torch sputtered now and then can be gleaned from a notice in the *Times* on 4 January advising playgoers to attend a performance, since "the patient gentlemen of the San Francisco Minstrels have discovered two new jokes, which will be utilized until further notice." Their efforts for the season included a spoof entitled "The Pirates of Sandy Hook." In the increasingly large and competitive vaudeville field, Tony Pastor, noting the success with which Harrigan and Hart were moving away, attempted to imitate the masters with playlets such as *Murphy's Wedding* and *The Parade of the Rafferty Blues*. When these failed, Pastor turned to farce-comedy. On his bill for 19 January he included *The Emigrant Train; or, Go West!* by the author of *Fritz in Ireland*, William Carleton. In the end Pastor came to the sensible realization that he was the master showman of variety. Although he later attempted innovations, he was careful never to drift too far from his basic vaudeville format.

1880–1881

The new season was much like the old. The lyric stage bustled with activity, but offered little in the way of creative novelty. Ned Harrigan and David Braham continued their Mulligan series; farce-comedies abounded; a procession of importations from France, Germany, and England graced the boards. Odell lamented, "Tourists and Troubadours and Surprise Parties, with their trifling wares, and comic opera generally were killing the taste for serious plays."

An indication of the musical theatre's new life was its busy August schedule. Seven musicals raised their curtains, while an eighth work, *Edgewood Folks*, a straight play, stopped its action at a number of points to allow its star, Sol Smith Russell, to sing his songs. One might complain that three of the shows were revivals and a fourth an enlargement of an earlier piece. None of this obviates the fact that in one month as many lyric entertainments were mounted as had been the case in entire seasons before the arrival of *H. M. S. Pinafore* (15 January 1879).

The season began with an importation. Wallack's prestigious house, nearing the end of its great career, relit on 5 August with a "Grand Pantomimic Burlesque Extravaganza" from London, **Grim Goblin**. In H. Spry and George Conquest, Sr.'s plot a princess loses a cherished keepsake and promises to wed the man who retrieves it. Conquest and his son, George Jr., were acrobats who filled the evening with their feats. One breathtaking bit was the "Wonderful Phantom Flight," which "consisted of the performer flying from floor to ceiling, where he grasped a swinging trapeze, to which a rope was thrown, and which he descended to the stage as quickly as possible." The elder Conquest was to assume a number of roles: Grim Goblin, Hick-Hac-Hoc, Prince Pigmy, and Nix, the Demon Head. Unfortunately on the very first night he broke his leg in a fall. His son, too, was injured several times. George Sr. was unable to return to the Cobweb Cave of the Grim Goblin, but his son performed, at times conspicuously bandaged. One way or another, this English mélange of childlike nonsense and spectacle held the stage until n September, when Wallack's company was ready to resume.

Farce-comedy made its initial appearance of the year four nights after *Grim Goblin*, when **Fun on the Bristol** (9 August 1880, 14th St.) began a two-week stand. The *Times* reviewer recorded that music for this version "ranges from selections from Verdi's, Donizetti's, and Bizet's operas, through Offenbach and Lecocq to popular ballads and negro minstrel jigs."

Harrigan and Hart reopened their Theatre Comique on 9 August with an enlarged but not quite full evening's version of their early success, *The Mulligan Guards' Picnic* (23 September 1878). Braham's contributions included "Sandy-Haired Mary In Our Area," "Mary Kelly's Beau," "Locked Out After Nine," "All Aboard For The M.G.R.," and "The Second Degree Full Moon Union." Accompanied by ever-changing curtain-raisers, the work ran well over 100 showings, closing 20 November.

Monday, 23 August, saw the premiere of *Edgewood Folks* as well as the return of *Fritz in Ireland* (3 November 1879), the latter at the Grand. The very next Monday witnessed three musical first nights. The peripatetic *Evangeline* (27 July 1874) replaced *Fun on the Bristol* at the 14th Street, the Kiralfys revived *Around the World* (28 August 1875) for five weeks at Niblo's, and *Dreams* made its first New York appearance at the Bijou. The *Evangeline* 1880 playgoers enjoyed was not quite the same earlier patrons had seen. A revised libretto introduced several new characters such as Peter Papyrus (Charles Groves). E. E. Rice announced he had written ten new songs for the revision. More important, the updated dialogue was by a new librettist, J. J. McNally.

Around the World unveiled a succession of spectacular sets, beginning with the arrival of a steamer—complete with whistles and steam—and culminating in a jewel-studded Oriental necropolis. One absurdity was a "teutonic Borneo brass band."

Having long worked for others, Willie Edouin broke away to form his own company of farce-comedy players. He and his wife, Alice Atherton, led the company. With Rice's recent collaborator, Nathaniel Childs, Edouin concocted a piece called **Dreams; or, Fun in a Photographic Gallery.** An old farmer and his wife are about to celebrate their sixtieth wedding anniversary. They begin to reminisce about their courting days. The aged husband soon grows tired, falls asleep, and dreams of taking his bride-to-be to a photographer's studio. (No one seemed to be bothered by the anachronism of an 1820 photograph.) A group of other customers come and go. Eventually the groom suspects the photographer of flirting with his bride, and a fight ensues. The photographer calls the police, but just as they appear the farmer awakes from his dream. Friends arrive to help celebrate the anniversary. The second act, set in the photographer's shop, contained the main business of the evening. As each customer entered to have his picture taken he would first perform his specialty. Even the husband and wife got into the spirit of things. Edouin did a turn showing all the ways to tip a hat to a lady, while Miss Atherton impersonated Buffalo Bill, George and Martha Washington, and Rip Van Winkle. Edouin and his wife each played several other characters as well as the farmer and his wife, while lanky Jacques Kruger cavorted as the photographer, Pickleback Grabiball. The costume changing must have been just short of

frantic. Looking back years later, James T. Powers, a turn-of-the-century favorite who first came to New Yorkers' attention in this piece, confirms the impression. In his autobiography he wrote, "In one scene the entire company did a specialty, making quick changes of costume for each song; the last number was patriotic, and Lotta Belton, who had an extraordinary baritone voice, sang the song; the company marked time as they stood behind her... ." If in retrospect farce-comedies seem all of a piece, critics and playgoers of the 1880s discerned distinctions. For example, the *Dramatic Mirror* compared Edouin's Sparks to Salsbury's Troubadours and found the earlier entourage closer to variety, Edouin's troupe more given to coherent burlesque. Like all farce-comedy troupes, the Sparks drew their songs from diverse sources. One, "Lardy Dah," seems to have been new and heavily applauded. Like "Crutch And Toothpick" from the preceding year, it twitted the pretensions of some dandified men-about-town:

> *He wears a penny flower in his coat, Lardy dah!*
> *And a penny paper collar round his throat, Lardy dah!*
> *In his hand a penny stick, In his mouth a quill toothpick*
> *Not a penny in his pocket, Lardy dah! Lardy dah!*
> *Not a penny in his pocket, Lardy dah!*

In its initial Broadway stay, *Dreams* ran six weeks. New Yorkers would see it again.

JOHN J. McNALLY was born in Charlestown, Massachusetts, in either 1854 or 1853 (his age was given as seventy seven when he died in March 1931). Although he earned a law degree at Harvard, he soon abandoned his practice to enter journalism, accepting a post as drama critic for the Boston *Herald.* His very first attempt at playwriting, the farce-comedy *Revels,* was an immediate success, although it reached Broadway after his reworking of *Evangeline.*

The evening of Monday, 13 September, like that of 30 August, saw three musical offerings make their bow. The 14th Street Theatre had already housed two musicals in the still young season. With the main theatre area moving steadily north it found itself increasingly out of the way and having to be content with a rapid turnover of bookings. From 13 September to 2 October it offered M. B. Leavitt's Grand English Operatic Burlesque Company in **Carmen; or, Soldiers and Seville-ians**, a London piece adapted for American tastes. New Yorkers had seen their first mounting of Bizet's five-year-old opera only the preceding season.

The other two offerings the same night had more dignity and significance. Maurice Grau's French Opera Company inaugurated its season of opéra bouffe by unveiling the first New York showing of Offenbach's nine-month-old **La Fille du Tambour-Major** at the Standard. In the opéra bouffe's story a duchess, who had once been a laundress and had been married to a painter, wants her daughter by that marriage to wed a marquis. But the daughter loves a common soldier and, with the help of her father—now a drum major in the army—marries her own choice. Paola Marie starred. She also starred in the company's other premiere, Laurent de Rillé's tale of rural love, **Babiole,** on 21 October. In the five intervening weeks several old standards were revived. A competitive version of *La Fille du Tambour-Major* played the 14th Street the week of 4 October.

Even more important was the New York visit of the Boston Ideal Opera Company at Booth's. Of course, *Pinafore* and *Fatinitza* were part of the program. However, a third offering, *The Pirates of Penzance,* served as the opening-night bill. Myron Whitney was back, this time to sing the Pirate King, and Henry Clay Barnabee portrayed Major-General Stanley. Samuel was sung by another artist who would remain loyal to the group until the end, W. H. MacDonald. Two fine performers who proved almost as steadfast were George Frothingham (as the Sergeant of Police) and Tom Karl (as Frederick). Mary Beebe was Mabel; Adelaide Phillips, Ruth. Quibblers complained that Whitney's "oratorio style" was unsuited to such comic material and that Barnabee's "little voice" probably couldn't be heard in the far reaches of the house, but few theatregoers shared their opinions. The company was respectfully received by most critics and played nearly a month.

To avoid conflicting with three other musical openings, the premiere of Alfred Cellier's London success **The Sultan of Mocha** changed its opening at the Union Square to the next night, 14 September. Considering its fate it might have been better off losing itself in the crowd. The show was withdrawn after its second week, but while it probably had no influence (unless it suggested an exotic setting for *The Mikado* to Gilbert), it was a harbinger

of a fashionable new locale for later comic operas and musical comedies. Its story told how Dolly (Leonora Braham) is sold by her greedy guardian, Captain Flint (Harry Allen), to the sultan (William Hamilton). Her dashing sailor sweetheart (Eugene Clarke) rushes in with his buddies to rescue her, and when she is kidnapped and returned to the sultan, the sailor, disguised as a pilgrim, rescues her again.

September closed with the arrival from Boston of another farce-comedy, Ben Woolf 's 'peculiarity,' **Lawn-Tennis** (20 September 1880, Abbey's Park). Its construction was peculiar indeed, for its second act was a playlet within a play. Alfred Puddifoot (Digby Bell), a dramatist, and his hosts, the Cornwallis Algernon Prouts (John Howson and Hetty Tracy), go to the all-female Man-Tamers" Club in search of material for a play. By coincidence costumes for a comic opera have been delivered to the club, so Puddifoot and the Prouts watch as the group's members perform the "operettina," called "Djack and Djill." The playlet spoofed the lyric stage of the day. King Stupidenko XIV's daughter, Djill, loves Djack despite her father's objections. The king refuses to believe his wicked seneschal when the old man reports the youngsters have been silly enough to go *up* a hill to fetch a pail of water. But the king's heart melts on learning Djill purposely tumbled down the hill so that Djack's misstep would not embarrass the young man. Neither the published text, the advertisements, nor the reviews indicate who wrote the music for the evening, but given Woolf's musical background it remains conceivable that he was at least partly to credit. The piece enjoyed a number of engagements of varying length at different houses all through the season.

The celebrated Brooklyn organist Dudley Buck attempted his hand at a native comic opera when he wrote a score to W. A. Croffut's libretto for **Deseret; or, The Saint's Difficulties** (11 October 1880, 14th St.). Its story treated a Mormon and his wives as if they were a sultan and his harem. Such levity disgusted the *Times,* which insisted Mormon polygamy deserved scorn, not comic sanction. Other papers concentrated on the piece's artistic merits. Although the *Tribune* saw it as "the first really successful American opera" and the *World* hailed it as "a veritable American Pinafore," most critics and the public at large disagreed. The work was hustled over to Brooklyn on the 25th and disappeared from theatrical history after a week's run there. *Deseret* was probably no more influential than *The Sultan of Mocha,* but like the English work it foreshadowed a theatrical fad. For the next thirty or forty years Mormons would appear on the American lyric stage solely as figures of ridicule.

The night after *Deseret* opened, Booth's housed a popularized version of Rossini's *Cinderella*, replete with specialty acts and interpolations of contemporary songs. However more high-minded critics might react, the public attended in sufficient numbers to let the piece survive until 6 November.

A revival of *Boccaccio* with Jeannie Winston at the Grand showed Americans how they might better write or treat a comic opera. But Americans went blithely on their way with farce-comedies, spectacles, and vernacular musicals. The farce-comedies came the week after the von Suppé revival when Rice's Surprise Party began a stay in a whole repertory of its pieces. The first was new. It found Edouin and his wife again working under E. E. Rice's aegis. In J. J. McNally's **Revels** (25 October 1880, 14th St.) Bon Ton George loves Maryanthus, ward of Sir Ramesgate Bramblewig. Sir Ramesgate was a pork butcher whom circumstance had made majordomo to the king of Egypt. George's brother Rufus also loves Maryandius. Rufus makes waves, but George ultimately wins his beloved. A subplot described the argumentative romance between the Bramblewigs' maid, Isis, and Calapat. Isis wants him though she admits he is "such a dorg," always chasing skirts. The work suggests how farce-comedy was borrowing from burlesque to develop more intricate stories. Its debt to burlesque was also evidenced by the fact that both George and Rufus were trouser roles. Another sign of development was that most performers played only one part in the course of the evening. Edouin was Calapat, Miss Atherton was George. But they were not the only fine performers. Rice provided them with such associates as the English star Topsy Venn and Henry E. Dixey. *Revels* further indicates the growing vogue for "Oriental" settings. The Surprise Party's repertory included a revised version of *Horrors* (28 May 1879) called *Prince Achmet*, a redoing of the failed *Hiawatha* (21 February 1880), and *Babes in the Wood*.

On 15 November the Kiralfys replaced their revival of *Around the World* with a remounting of *Enchantment* (4 September 1879), using many of the same artists they had used the previous year. The spectacle played three weeks.

Harrigan, Hart, and Braham had another hit with **The Mulligan Guards' Nominee** (22 November 1880, Comique). The title is odd since it makes no reference to the principal plot or the subplot. In the main story, Bridget Lochmuller (Annie Mack) returns from a vacation in Ireland, trailed by an officer of the law who believes she is a revolutionary. The confusion arises from the initials of her benevolent group, the Florence Nightingale Association. These initials match letter for letter those of the Fenian National Army. As a result Bridget, Cordelia (Annie Yeamans), and their friends are arrested on the Albany night-boat for "belonging to a secret order designing the capture of Canada." The subplot details Rebecca's stratagems for winning Palestine Puter (William Gray) away from the voluptuous Caroline. Like Rebecca (Hart), Caroline was played by a man (James Tierney, in both blackface and drag). The political contest between Lochmuller (Harry Fischer) and Dan (Harrigan) for Alderman-at-large took a backseat. But it did provide the most quoted line from the show. When Dan's friend McSweeny is arrested in an election brawl, Dan shouts at the policeman, "Raylease him. I'm 200 votes ahead of Lochmuller and I'll say no more." McSweeny is released. The show ran until 21 February, bolstered by such Braham numbers as "Down In Gossip Row," "Hang The Mulligan Banner Up," "A Nightcap," "Mulligan's Promises," "The Skidmore Masquerade," and the most popular of all, "The Skids Are Out Tonight," a sequel to the song success from *The Mulligan Guards' Chowder*. (For their march the "blacks" were dressed in spanking new cream-colored uniforms.)

Although minstrelsy was past its heyday, a number of bands still flourished. Several of these had come under the banner of J. H. Haverly, who also ran Niblo's and the 14th Street Theatre. As a result two minstrel troupes made rare appearances at houses normally given over to more standard fare when Haverly's Genuine Colored Minstrels played Niblo's from 6 to 18 December and Haverly's Mastodon Minstrels returned from Europe in March to further applause at the 14th Street. Since minstrel burlesque followed closely on recent successes, the same play or opera often found itself travestied a number of times in short order. The Mastodon Minstrels joined the field in spoofing *Il Trovatore*. With the well-liked Billy Emerson leading the funmakers, they called their version "Ill-True-Bad-Doer," with Emerson as Man-Wreck-Oh. The villain was Count Di-Loony (E. M. Rayne) and the heroine, played by a man, Lean-O'er-Her (Paul Vernon).

The Negro minstrels at Niblo's made way for the next-to-last musical of 1880, a revival of the preceding year's *Humpty Dumpty* (3 February 1880), with Maffitt and Fraser once again father and son. Some of their thunder was almost literally stolen from them by one of the specialty acts, a young lady named Zazel who was shot from a cannon at each performance. The show came in on 20 December, just in time for the holiday trade, and stayed until 8 January.

An importation from France closed out the year. This show was Edmond Audran's **Olivette** (correctly, *Les Noces d'Olivette*), which had its premiere at a matinee performance on 25 December. In its two and a half hours it recorded how Olivette wins her soldier-lover despite disguises, mistaken identities, kidnappings, and parental objections. An instant success, it ran five weeks at the Bijou and moved to the Fifth Avenue to continue its run. A rival troupe mounted the work at the Park on 17 January but ran only three weeks. A third company, led by Selina Dolaro and W. T. Carleton, played briefly at the Bijou beginning 19 March. The Bijou's first production affords a good example of the versatility of the period's players, for it was staged by the Comley-Barton Company, a troupe that switched with apparent ease from their farce-comedy, *Lawn-Tennis*, to this opéra bouffe. Catherine Lewis sang the title role, supported by J. C. Armand, Digby Bell, and John Howson. J. C. Duff's production at the Park offered a less attractive cast.

The Salsbury Troubadours ushered in the new year with a return engagement of *The Brook* (12 May 1879). They played the piece for two weeks beginning 3 January and then showed that they, too, were versatile by staging their version of *Widow Bedott*. This was a popular comedy of the day. The Troubadours performed it essentially as a straight play, although they could not resist interpolating a few songs.

Another straight play, partially musicalized, raised its curtain at Niblo's on 12 January. **Black Venus**, based on a piece by Adolphe Belot and advertising a collection of wild animals and three ballets (with "250 young ladies"), kept the house lit for a month. Set in Africa, the evening recounted how a slave girl wins the hand of King Morenza. Although one paper, looking at the size of the cast listed in the show's advertisements, warned readers "managerial announcements are not always to be believed," most likely the production's most ballyhooed scene did indeed have forty lady riders in a "Battle of the Amazons"—a refreshing change from the traditional march of the tall chorus girls. One intriguing question remains unanswered. Given the setting and the plot, did the performers appear in blackface?

Emma Abbott brought her opera company to the Fifth Avenue on 17 January in a repertory that ranged from *Lucia di Lammermoor* and *Faust* to *The Bohemian Girl* and *The Chimes of Normandy*. Miss Abbott sang for a fortnight and went her way. But much of her repertory was heard again at the same house from 28 February to 12 March, this time interpreted by the Max Strakosch-A. D. Hess English Opera Company. Meanwhile, on 17 January, Tony Pastor began to include a series of extended burlesques on his variety bills. The first was a take-off of Robertson's play, *School*, done as "Our School Girls." It was followed in due course by "The Pierats of Perm Yann" and "All of It." Two young ladies called themselves to audiences' attention in these burlesques. Both soon became stars on the musical stage: May Irwin and Lillian Russell. The nature of the parts they played can be gleaned from Miss Irwin's role in the Gilbert and Sullivan travesty. Her Freddy was set down as an "indentured prowler."

Since the nineteenth-century policy of opening whenever possible on Monday led to another cluster of first nights on 18 January, the American premiere of Genée's *Nisida*, called in this country **Zanina; or, The Rover of Cambaye,** was abruptly put back to the next night. Why its producer and adapter, Augustin Daly, also changed its name is lost in history. If it stemmed from some fear the name was not attractive enough, this fear may well have spilled over onto the text itself. Daly, again for reasons now lost, threw out much of Genée's music and helped give currency to a dubious practice by interpolating numerous new songs his orchestra leader, Edward Mollen-hauer, composed. One song, "In The North Sea Lived A Whale (The Torpedo And The Whale)," became the rage. At best the libretto still clung to the story of a fickle officer torn between an opera singer and an Indian princess. Laura Joyce sang the tide role. Her husband-to-be, Digby Bell, led the comedians. Daly regulars included the beloved red-headed farceur James Lewis and the radiant Ada Rehan. Daly filled the stage with real Indian Nautch dancers, magicians, and snake-charmers. Still, the work proved a disappointment and was a quick failure.

On 19 February, New Yorkers heard for the first time the popular English work **Billee Taylor.** It won American hearts and remained before the footlights on and off for several decades. When Billee is shanghaied in the middle of his wedding, his bride disguises herself as a sailor in order to look for him. Surprisingly the faithless Billee ends by marrying another girl, while his sweetheart marries his kidnapper. Presented by D'Oyly Carte in conjunction with E. E. Rice, the cast included J. H. Ryley (by this time a permanent American resident) as the kidnapper, Arnold Breedon as Billee, and Carrie Burton as his sweetheart. *Billee Taylor* introduced America to Edward Solomon, an English composer who became Lillian Russell's husband and wrote several of her musicals, the successes of which were usually attributable to Miss Russell. In America at least, Solomon never repeated the small triumph his *Billee Taylor* afforded him.

Three wholly native offerings competed for attention on 21 February. Two were making return stands: Goodwin in *Hobbies* (6 October 1879) and *The Tourists* in *A Pullman Palace Car* (3 November 1879). The third was the latest "volume" in the Mulligan series, **The Mulligans' Silver Wedding**. Harrigan's newest effort showed how careful and thoughtful he was in developing his history. Cordelia Mulligan had alluded to her impending anniversary as far back as *The Mulligan Guards' Ball* (13 January 1879), while Dan's recent victory at the polls was acknowledged by listing him as Alderman Mulligan. Unfortunately, Harrigan's growing sense of playcraft deserted him momentarily. *The Mulligans' Silver Wedding* had less plot and more vaudeville than most of its predecessors. One might almost detect the loosening influence of farce-comedy on its construction. The play centered on the Mulligans' plans for their forthcoming celebration. When a peeping Tom seems to be hovering about, a keyhole is blackened. Not one, but three black eyes are soon evident. The show's most famous scene had Cordelia attempt to kill herself by swallowing some "rat poison." The "poison" is merely whiskey Dan had falsely marked to keep it out of Rebecca's hands. When Dan is unmoved by her "death scene" Cordelia becomes doubly agonized. This very scene was later resurrected by Harrigan in *Cordelia's Aspirations* (5 November 1883), where it played to stronger effect because it fit so well into the plot. As a lyricist, however, Ned Harrigan remained observant and affectionate. His "South Fifth Avenue," sung by Tony Hart, described the changing scene and certain New Yorkers' reactions to it:

> *Oh, Dear me, Mister Puter,*
> > *Just loan me your cologne,*
> *I wish to scent my handkerchief,*
> > *Passing dis saloon.*
> *De vapor's quite distressing,*
> > *From dat Italian crew,*

> *Dis padrone emigration,*
> > *To South Fifth Avenue.*

"Wheel The Baby Out," which Harrigan sang, had a grown man unselfconsciously singing nursery rhymes in his joy at fatherhood:

> *High diddle, diddle,*
> > *The cat's in the fiddle,*
> *How are you Mister Mulligan*
> > *You'd hear the neighbors shout,*
> *The little doggy laughed*
> > *For to see such funny sport,*
> *I was always singing*
> > *When I'd wheel the baby out.*

The third, fourth, seventh, and eighth lines remained the same while the nursery jingles were altered in each of the five choruses. Once again the *Times* noted the high-class patrons Harrigan had begun to draw downstairs, although cheaper seats still lured vocal, unruly elements. Staid or raucous, the Comique's loyal followers overlooked flaws in the play and packed the house from 21 February until the end of April. Their enthusiasm was no doubt whetted by the fact that, at a top of 75, Harrigan and Hart offered the cheapest top ticket in town.

Daly, who earlier had lost quite a large sum on *Zanina*, recouped some of his losses when he mounted a second musical at his house on 5 March. **Cinderella at School** was a full-length lyric version of the same Robertson play Pastor had spoofed two months before. The music and, apparently, the book and lyrics were by Woolson Morse.

The action begins with the young ladies attending Papyrus Seminary listening to Niobe (May Fielding), a charity pupil, tell them the tale of Cinderella. An English peer, Lord Lawntennis (Charles Leclercq), arrives with his nephew, Arthur Bicycle (Harry Lacy), and Arthur's friend, Jack Polo (John Brand). The lord has come seeking a long-lost granddaughter. Suddenly a bull chases Niobe past where the men are standing, and Niobe loses her shoe in the rush. As everyone could guess from thereon, despite the machinations of the comic "head usher and chief husher," Syntax (James Lewis), charming Arthur weds Niobe. Consanguinity was blithely ignored. The chorus concludes:

> *Oh, isn't it delightful*
> *Her cup of joy is quite full.*
> > *Love's magic power*
> > *Is greater far*

Than that of Fairy grandmamma.
 Now in silks and satins
 She'll attend the matins!

With Laura Joyce, Ada Rehan, and Mrs. Gilbert assisting, the musical ran out the season.

While new forms were ineluctably taking over the musical stage, old favorites retained much of their appeal. *The Black Crook* (12 September 1866), so rusty and bedraggled in the eyes of critics, still found a ready public. The evening's Stalacta was Pauline Markham, who had come to America with Lydia Thompson and who had assumed the role of the fairy queen in the first major revival. Ballets were led by Mlles, de Rosa and Cappalini, and by Arnold Kirafly. One interesting addition was Prince Awata Katsnoshin, a magician. From 7 March to 9 April the production at Niblo's brought back happy memories for many in the house.

Jules Verne's *The Children of Captain Grant* was dramatized and set to music as **Voyagers in Southern Seas** (21 March 1881, Booth's). The production had originally been staged in its hometown by the Boston Theatre Company. But this troupe, despite the presence of Marie Bonfanti and "the Flying wonder" Ariel heading the ballets, was a far cry from the Boston Ideal entourage. Rejected as shabby and amateurish, it quickly returned home and in a short while disappeared from the theatrical picture.

March closed to the capers of W. C. Mitchell's *Pleasure Party*, once more calling to life *Our Goblins* (14 June 1880). The irrepressible Lotta went through

much of her repertory in April, while the Vokeses, who many scholars believe gave Salsbury the idea for farce-comedy, played a stand with their own old favorites, beginning with *The Belles of the Kitchen*.

In midseason the Bijou had won the race with its mounting of Audran's *Olivette*, beating the Park by three weeks. It reasserted its primacy on 5 May with its staging of a second Audran work, **La Mascotte.** Its margin of victory was less ample this time. The Park had its mounting of *The Mascot* ready four nights later. The public found that first was best. The Park Theatre's production ran only a month, while *La Mascotte* kept the Bijou lit well into August. In any case, Audran was indisputably the season's darling. Despite the Bijou's retention of the French spelling, both companies translated this tale of a country girl faithful to the shepherd she loves in the face of abductions and promises of high honors. No major names graced either cast.

Although Benjamin E. Woolf's **Photos** (9 May 1881, Grand Opera) failed to repeat the success of his earlier and not dissimilar *Hobbies* (6 October 1879), it held the boards for two seasons and allowed players such as Louis Harrison, Alice Harrison, and R. E. Graham to "provoke screams of laughter" as they aped such popular stars as Stuart Robson, Maggie Mitchell, and Sarah Bernhardt. Spoofs of contemporary ballet and "modern" art as well as a guitar solo were also worked into the all but nonexistent plot in which an early musical-comedy will required the heirs to gather at regular intervals for a family photograph. The same night saw the premiere of a new spectacle, **Castles in Spain** (9 May 1881, Niblo's Garden). After opening with a rooftop view of Madrid, the action moved to the mysterious grottoes and dells so beloved of period extravaganza to tell a story of a Spanish soldier's attempts to marry off his ambitious daughters. The star, Pauline Mark-ham, played none of these roles, instead first appearing as a loathsome witch in "eyeglasses and brown holland [a cotton or linen fabric used at the time for children's rough-wear and for windowshades]" and later being transformed into a beautiful woman in "scanty satin." Ballets included a "Minuet of the Kiss" set in Louis XV's time, with half the coryphées dressed in blue as men and the other half in pink as girls, and an extended production number depicting the changing seasons. Advertised as costing $80,000, it was waved away sneeringly by most critics and soon shuttered.

The New York premiere of von Suppé's **Donna Juanita** (16 May 1881, Fifth Ave.), whose heroine (first played in America by Jeannie Winston) must dress as a French cadet to win her lover, ran three weeks.

Nor did another costly mistake, **Elfins and Mermaids** (4 June 1881, Standard), fare better. Its utterly absurd and hopelessly convoluted story began when an English lord, long believed dead, returns to find his wife married to a reformed pirate. The work advertised itself as "a seriocomic opera," but critics dismissed it as an inane hodgepodge.

1881–1882

By the end of this new season it became clear a pattern was emerging. The lyric theatre was busy. But the business was deceptive. The bustle was created by a constant parade of revivals and importations. There were not even half a dozen original, substantial native musical works. Had Harrigan and Braham not been so productive, the record would have been sorry indeed. But the activity—foreign or rehashed—did accustom the public to a regular flow of musical theatre and did suggest how many stages could be kept lit, how many performers kept occupied, and how many cash registers kept ringing.

Harrigan and Hart opened the season on 29 August with a double novelty. One was a new play; the other was a new theatre. This "new" Theatre Comique at 728–730 Broadway had been a theatre under various names for some years. Its career had been ill-starred. Harrigan and Hart gutted the premises and installed a completely rebuilt auditorium. Not everyone was pleased by the results. One critic ruefully described the décor as "extravagant bronze and bric-a-brac style... much too gaudy." For a while at least the new house did seem to chase the jinx. To inaugurate his latest playhouse Harrigan made a sharp, surprising departure. He dropped the Mulligans and their neighbors and wrote a noticeably original part for himself, **The Major**. Roguish and flamboyant, Major Gilfeather was a far cry from steady, dependable Dan. He lived by his wits, hoodwinking even his friends when necessary. Thus, though Mrs. Pinch (Annie Mack) has given him a retainer to locate Enry Iggins (Tony Hart), the man who had eloped with her daughter, the Major has no compunctions about accepting a sum from Iggins to keep his whereabouts secret. David Braham's tunes included "The Veteran Guards' Cadets," "Clara Jenkins' Tea," and a title song. Increasing costs forced

the team to raise their top price to $1.00 a seat. The higher prices were readily accepted by Harrigan and Hart's loyal followers. Indeed, "Nothing could exceed in heartiness and friendliness the fashion in which Mr. Harrigan and other favorites of the familiar company were received, and several of the noisily hailed comedians were forced to acknowledge the public welcome in a few informal words." The piece had the longest run of any Harrigan and Hart work to date, over 150 showings.

The era's loose copyright laws and intense competition often resulted in several theatres offering their respective versions of a single piece at the same time. The first instance of this in the 1881–1882 season occurred right at the start. The Jules Verne–Adolphe d'Ennery melodrama of a patriot's suffering on the retreat from Moscow, **Michael Strogoff**, was presented at three houses in very close succession: the Tivoli's production premiered on 29 August, the Booth's staging on 31 August, and the Academy of Music's interpretation on 3 September. None was especially successful. But the spectacle at the Academy of Music was in the hands of the Kiralfys. As was their wont, they filled their evening with ballets, occasional songs, and elaborate sets. However, a reaction was clearly developing against the overwhelming stage pictures. The *Times* complained that mechanical snowfalls and waterfalls, "as a competition with nature, are somewhat ridiculous."

The popularity of Audran's *The Mascot* continued high all during the season. Its first revival appeared on 5 September. This mounting at the Bijou advertised that the work was being played "with for the first time here the composer's original orchestrations." *The Mascot* sang on happily for two months and returned, in the hands of one company or another, three more times during the season.

Le Voyage en Suisse (12 September 1881, Park) was a French musical extravaganza adapted for the London stage and produced here largely as a vehicle for a family of five acrobats, the Hanlon-Lees. One member of the family lit a cigarette as he somersaulted from the top of a stagecoach; another fell through the floor of a railway car traveling at regulation speed and slid along its bottom among the wheels. Later, the whole family turned an elegant hotel dining room into a storm of spinning plates, tureens, and food. The affair was an immediate hit. Although it moved to three different theatres, it played continuously from its opening night until the end of 1881.

Monday, 19 September, found another French work competing for attention. Offenbach's **Mme.**

Favart, recounting an imaginary romance of a real eighteenth-century prima donna, debuted at the Fifth Avenue. Its star, Catherine Lewis, had played the leading roles in *The Royal Middy* and *Olivette.* But good things did not come in threes. *Mme. Favart* was a two-week failure. When it closed, Catherine Lewis's star fell with it.

But **Patience** (22 September 1881, Standard) was a different story. For a while it seemed as if the wild triumph of *H. M. S. Pinafore* stood to be repeated. A visit by Oscar Wilde to America fanned interest in this lark about a dairymaid who must choose between a Wilde-like poet and an idyllic poet. D'Oyly Carte's largely American cast included J. H. Ryley as Bunthorne, James Barton as Grosvenor, A. Wilkinson as Murgatroyd, W. T. Carelton as Calverly Carrie Burton as Patience, Alice Burville as Angela, and Augusta Rooke as Jane. This "definitive" version ran uninterruptedly until 4 March and then for a month more continued as part of a Gilbert and Sullivan repertory. By the time it closed it had made a $100,000 profit for the Englishmen, $40,000 more than *H. M. S. Pinafore* had earned on its initial voyage. Additional sums filled the British coffers when the rights were magnanimously awarded to several other producers. While the original *Patience* was still running, E. E. Rice's Comic Opera Company brought its touring troupe into Booth's for two weeks starting 14 November, while Haverly brought his road company into his 14th Street Theatre for a fortnight commencing 6 February. After the Englishmen had sailed home, the Bijou put on the boards its own interpretation on 5 June. Although it was judged inferior as ensemble to D'Oyly Carte's, it confirmed the claim to stardom of its own Patience, Lillian Russell. Miss Russell had gotten her start at Tony Pastor's and only recently had portrayed the milkmaid in Pastor's spoof. She had been given her first principal Broadway assignment earlier in the season. With her appearance in this Gilbert and Sullivan work she began her two-decade reign as the first queen of Broadway musicals.

> **LILLIAN RUSSELL** was born in Clinton, Iowa, on 4 December 1861, the daughter of a prominent printer. Her real name was Helen (Nellie) Louise Leonard. When she was three her family moved to Chicago, where her mother soon became active in the growing women's rights movement. At sixteen Helen left her convent school to make her stage debut in Chicago in *Time Tries All.* Shortly thereafter her parents separated, and Lillian moved to New York with her mother. While studying music with Leopold Damrosch she obtained a small role in *Evangeline,* where she caught Pastor's eye. More than the leading comic opera artist of her era, she was also one of its chief ornaments—a glittering beauty with the classic, if slightly buxom, lines admired by Victorians.

The death of President Garfield cast a momentary pall over the Rialto. (The President had been shot in July, but survived until 19 September.) All Broadway shows shut the evening of his death and again the evening of his funeral. Emma Abbott and her opera company resumed the parade of lyric works on 3 October. Her bill ran from old operas such as *Lucia di Lammermoor* to new opéras bouffes such as *Olivette.* She remained at the Grand for two weeks.

The next Monday welcomed the first *Humpty Dumpty* of the season. Curiously, it was the opening attraction at Tony Pastor's new theatre on 14th Street, near Irving Place. Pastor did not begin his first season at the new house until 24 October. Why he chose not to open his own house himself and why he permitted a minor touring company of the pantomime to have the honor are puzzling. A second touring company, headed by Tony Denier, played a week at the Windsor in January. *Humpty Dumpty* (10 March 1868) was having a great fall, indeed.

The work in which Lillian Russell initially assumed a major part was Audran's **The Grand Mogul** (29 October 1881, Bijou), also known as *The Snake Charmer.* Audran's first success—mounted in Marseille in 1877—this tale of a ruler's love for the snake-charmer, Irma, was seen by New York before Paris. Selina Dolaro starred as Prince Mignapour, a part originally conceived for a tenor, while Miss Russell sang the puzzling American transcription of Irma, D'Jemma. Although Miss Russell suffered from noticeable opening-night jitters, she called attention to herself, her voice, and most of all, her beauty, and helped the opéra bouffe run until New Year's Eve.

Haverly's touring troupe, the Mastodon Minstrels, made the first of two brief appearances during the theatrical year at the 14th Street Theatre on 31 October. (They returned to the house in March.) Waning interest in minstrelsy had, as has been noted, forced Haverly to offer increasingly elaborate productions with larger and larger companies. His current band boasted over 100 performers. Among them were men like Lew Dockstader, who would attempt to keep blackface alive to the very end. Inevitably the troupe acknowledged the raging success of *Patience* with its burlesques "Thompson Street Aesthetics" and "Patient Wilde." In the latter, Leon, once of Kelly and Leon's, donned his customary drag to play Miss Patient Wilde, a young lady partial to sunflowers.

Two opéra bouffe companies were the sole lyric entries in November. H. B. Mahn's Comic Opera Company performed in English at Niblo's, while Maurice Grau's French Opera Company sang in the original language at Abbey's Park. The Mahn group's two-week stand offered *Donna Juanita, Boccaccio,* and *The Mascot.* Grau's organization also played a two-week stand, returning in April for three additional weeks at the Fifth Avenue. In those brief visits the repertory changed almost nightly, with nearly a dozen works offered. These included *La Mascotte, Les Mousquetaires au Convent, Mignon, La Fille du Tambour-Major,* and *Si J'étais Roi.*

December brought no novelties whatsoever. On the 5th, *Fritz in Ireland* (3 November 1879), with J. K. Emmet of course as the principal attraction, made the first of three seasonal visits to New York. The others came in January and April. The December visit was at the 14th Street Theatre, the others at Niblo's. Advertisements carried the seemingly inevitable announcement of Emmet's plays— "entirely rewritten." Whether Emmet or his claims of novelty were the real attraction, the show's initial three-week stay grossed $30,000, "the largest amount of money ever played to by any dramatic star in the same length of time at the prices prevailing." *Olivette* was revived in midmonth. And the day after Christmas the Vokes family brought their song-filled playlets back.

For more than a season two popular vaudevillians, Billy Barry and Hugh Fay, had been touring in a not-quite-full-length piece, **Muldoon's Picnic,** accompanied by a sizable olio. For the most part they played major variety houses, but on 9 January 1882 they came in briefly to Niblo's. The stars

impersonated two perpetually inebriated Irishmen, whose booziness befuddles their attempts to hold a picnic. The entertainment was a cross between the new farce-comedies and the shows Harrigan and Hart were presenting. Barry and Fay were skilled, popular comedians, but they were always to run a distant second to Harrigan and Hart in imagination and brilliance. Although they occasionally played legitimate stages, they remained vaudevillians at heart.

Just as Harrigan, Hart, and Braham got the season off to an excellent start, they began the new year on the right foot as well. **Squatter Sovereignty** (9 January 1882, Comique), like its predecessor, broke away from the Mulligan series. In the background of the story was the conflict between the owners of the land close to the East River and the squatters who had made their homes there. One is the Widow Nolan (Hart). She would have her daughter, Nellie (Gertie Granville), marry Terrence (M. Bradley), the son of the "astronomer" Felix McIntyre (Harrigan). But Nellie and Terrence have plans of their own. Nellie is fond of Fred Kline (James Tierney). Unfortunately, Fred's father (Harry Fisher) is one of the landowners determined to evict the squatters. When the Widow's goat gets loose, wanders over to the elder Kline's mansion, and eats his basement curtains, Kline has the goat seized. McIntyre arranges an entertainment at Kline's dinner party with his telescope, planning to break away while the guests are star-gazing and to release the Widow's animal. The matter is complicated when young Fred escorts Nellie to the dinner. He presents her under an assumed name. The older Kline, who has advertised for a bride, believes she is answering his advertisement. Matters are cleared up in time for Fred and Nellie, and Felix and the Widow, to wed. The dialogue was brisk. Its humor still leaned heavily on wordplay:

Felix: Wid the aid of that wonderful instrument,
   I could show you Uranus, Venus, Mars and
   Jew-Peter.
Widow: Has he come down?
Felix: Who?
Widow: Jew-Peter.
Felix: He never wint up.
Widow: But he did.
Felix: When?
Widow: Six months ago, for stealing an
   overcoat.

In small ways Harrigan's feeling for ethnic characters eluded him. For example, he called an Italian "Pedro." Musically there were fewer songs than usual, and they were not as well integrated. One of the best-loved numbers from the show, "Paddy Duffy's Cart," was used as the opening to the third act, where it announced Duffy's arrival. But Duffy was a very unimportant figure in the play. His arrival seemed to have been necessitated by the song rather than the other way around. Still the number and "Widow Nolan's Goat" remained popular as long as the generation that first heard them survived.

The songs helped *Squatter Sovereignty* surpass the run of *The Major*. It celebrated its 150th performance on 17 May and continued until the beginning of June. Its success meant that Harrigan and Hart had needed only two shows to keep their house lit for the entire season.

While the Theatre Comique grabbed the lion's share of attention on 9 January, at the Fifth Avenue the Comley and Barton Opera Company initiated the first of two visits during the theatrical year. With Alfred Cellier conducting, the players offered *Olivette, Mme. Favart*, and, for their final week, the first New York production of Le-cocq's *Le Jour et la Nuit*, retitled **Manola**, on 6 February. The French title gave away more of the plot, which centered on a man who has one wife by day and another by night. The company played five weeks and returned for two more in March.

A week later, on 16 January, Willie Edouin's Sparks offered *Dreams* (30 August 1880). Its two-week stand at the Bijou in January was followed by a week's engagement at the Grand in May. Edouin, his wife, and James T. Power were all back to recreate their original roles.

Dreams' first visit ended on 28 January. Two nights later the Bijou offered a new American comic opera. **L'Afrique** was by Wayman C. McCreery and W Schuyler, both newcomers. It was an amateurish botch of an evening. The *Times* referred to it as a "comic (?) opera," complaining, "[The] singing is simply torture," and exclaiming, "[W]ho ever saw coconut palms at the Cape of Good Hope!" The story related Mynheer Arent Van Zwickenboot's determined efforts to win the hand of Georgina (Marie Glover), daughter of the English Capt. Montague-Jones (Fred W Lennox). Georgina prefers Lieut. Geoffry Plantagenet Hamilton de Bracy (Philip Branson). Van Zwickenboot (Harry Standish) kidnaps the Captain and leads Zulus against the British.

Defeated, he claims he was temporarily insane. He offers half his fortune by way of apparent contrition. His apology and money are accepted:

Capt.: ... since you are now perfectly sane—as your last action has proved—why, go in peace. There will always be a seat at our mess table for you.
Mynh.: A thousand thanks, [aside] That was a pretty expensive little affair. Curse them!

FINALE

Lieut: All our dangers now are over,
    All our troubles they are past:
Capt.: [joining the hands of Lieut, and Geo.]
    Now then, take her, you deserve her,
    And may your happiness last.
Geo.: Now in peaceful pleasure living,
    May our loving never end.
Mynh.: While I know that any woman
    Shall never my heart strings rend.
Cho.: Yes, he'd better leave women alone.
Alice: [to Tops] Now my Tops, we too shall marry.
Tops: Yes, no longer must we tarry.
Cho.: Yes, we all shall now be married,
    And we'll live so happy together;
    By no storms our lives be harried,
    But all be summer weather.

                                Curtain

Despite an almost universal drubbing, the musical managed a three-week run before collapsing.

The Boston Ideal Opera, its fame and its repertory growing, paid New York another call starting on 6 February at Booth's. Not yet embarked on its attempt to promote native works, the company presented *Fatinitza, The Chimes of Normandy, The Mascot, Czar and Carpenter, Olivette, The Pirates of Penzance, H. M. S. Pinafore,* and *The Bohemian Girl*. All in a two-week visit! When the New Englanders left, Max Strakosch's Grand Italian Opera took over.

Yet another repertory company emerged a fortnight later when the Emilie Melville Opera Company settled into the Bijou for a five-week stand. Not as prodigal as some other touring troupes, it opened with a revival of *The Royal Middy*, switched on the 25th to the Manhattan premiere of Karl Millöcker's **Apajune; or, The Water Sprite** (in which mistaken identities muddle the lives of a soldier, a rustic maid, a comic nobleman, and the boardinghouse keeper who wants to marry him), and then contented itself with singing its rendering of *The Pirates of Penzance* from 13 March to 1 April.

Because the Standard Theatre was under contract to mount Edward Solomon's **Claude Duval**, the house faced the prospect of having to cut short *Patience*'s successful engagement. A compromise was reached. On Monday, 6 March, Solomon's work had its premiere. From that time until *Patience* was withdrawn at the end of the month, *Claude Duval* was sung on Monday, Tuesday, and Wednesday nights, and Wednesday matinees; Gilbert and Sullivan were left with the choice late-week evenings and Saturday matinees. When *Patience* left, *Claude Duval* continued on its own for five weeks. This tale of a romantic highwayman who saves the life of his pursuer, Charles Lorrimore, and even helps him win his lady, was beautifully mounted by W. T. Voegtlin with scenes that ended in tableaux designed after famous paintings. One had Duval and the lady, Constance, dancing a minuet alone in a field. W. T. Carleton sang Duval to L. Cadwallader's Lorrimore and Carrie Burton's Constance. J. H. Ryley and A. Wilkinson played leading comic roles. The encore mania had long been established, and on opening night at least one song, "William's Sure To Be Right," had to be sung six times.

Away from the main stem, the Windsor, a "combination" house—that is, a house booking touring attractions—offered an original comic opera on 13 March. **The Jolly Bachelors** (also called *Twelve Jolly Bachelors*) had a book by John A. Stevens and music by Edward A. Darling. It starred "pretty and vivacious" Jeannie Winston as Prince Cosmos in quest of "plump and pleasing" Amy Gordon as Princess Florida. A first-act drinking chorus gave delight "with the peculiar effect produced by the clinking of the metalic drinking cups." One week and the show was gone.

JOHN PHILIP SOUSA was born in Washington, D.C., on 6 November 1854, son of a Portuguese father and Bavarian mother. While at grammar school, he was enrolled at a private music conservatory run by John Esputa, Jr. At the age of thirteen he ran away to join a circus band. After he was returned to his parents, his father enlisted him as an apprentice musician in the U.S. Marine Band. He remained with the band for nearly seven years, all the while furthering his studies with George Felix Benkert. He then accepted work in various theatre orchestras, mostly in Philadelphia. On 1 October 1880, he was called back to become the Marine Band's fourteenth leader, a post he held until 1892.

Not every fledgling native effort tried its wings on the Rialto. For the next thirty years a number of other American theatrical centers would regularly mount home-grown presentations. Boston, Philadelphia, and especially Chicago would contribute significantly to the American Musical Theatre. On 25 March 1882, a minor premiere but important debut occurred in Washington, D.C. **The Smugglers** had a libretto by Wilson J. Vance and songs by John Philip Sousa.

Vance and Sousa had worked together in 1878 and 1879 on a comic opera that was never produced, *Katherine*. The early dates are a trifle startling, suggesting as they do that an independent tradition of comic opera might have developed even without the coming of *H. M. S. Pinafore* (15 January 1879). Yet it was *H. M. S. Pinafore* that precipitated the creation of *The Smugglers*. In 1879 Sousa had been hired to lead the orchestra for a New England tour of the Philadelphia Church Choir Company's staging of the Gilbert and Sullivan work. After a time the group added Sullivan and Burnand's *The Contrabandista* to their program, supplementing the English score with original Sousa melodies. On leaving the Philadelphia players, Sousa decided to use Burnand's story as the basis for an otherwise entirely new operetta.

In Vance's libretto a photographer named Stubbs loses his way in the Spanish mountains. He is seized by a band of smugglers and forced to marry their queen. The queen believes that her husband has died and that Stubbs fulfills a prophecy that the next king of the smugglers will be a stranger. Stubbs's protestations that he is a married man go unheeded. Love interest is provided by Violante, a kidnapped heiress held for ransom, and Enrique, her sweetheart, who has joined the band to protect her and help her escape. A happy ending for everyone comes with the arrival of the Spanish army, led by the queen's supposedly dead husband and bearing pardons for all.

The show, performed largely by amateurs, gave only a single performance in Washington. It moved to Philadelphia, where it was given five times, and then to Lancaster, Pennsylvania, for one final playing. Sousa felt his score deserved a more widespread hearing. Throughout his career he reused melodies from this show. A song called "Sighing, Ah Sighing" was heard as "Sweetheart, I'm Waiting" in *El Capitan* (30 April 1896), while "Let Us March Along" became the source of "The Lambs' March."

Another revival of *The Black Crook* (12 September 1866), advertised as the "best of the 2,387 productions of this great spectacle," appeared briefly at Niblo's starting 3 April. Dismissed as "hardly more than a variety show," the *Times* could nonetheless see it as "a last, lingering spasm of the fine old days of leg-drama, when a woman's talents lay chiefly in her heels."

On 13 April Augustin Daly sent his resident company out on tour. To keep his home box office busy he mounted a new opéra bouffe, Auguste Coedès's *Girouette*, in which King Pepin helps two pairs of lovers to the altar. Both the men and women who took the final vows were sung by young ladies. Renamed **The Weathercock,** it proved diverting enough to allow the theatre to remain open until the end of May.

The season's last touring repertory band, the C. D. Hess Acme Opera Company, closed the year at the Standard with a month's stand that began May 1. The schedule included *The Mascot, H. M. S. Pinafore, The Chimes of Normandy,* and the premiere on 8 May of Calixa Levellee's **The Widow.** A duke who would prevent his niece's marriage finally not only allows it but marries the widow who helped bring it about. The new work was a quick failure, withdrawn after four nights. (On 8 May J. W. Norcross's competing troupe offered its version of *The Mascot* with W. T. Carlton, J. H. Ryley, Pauline Hall, and Fay Templeton.)

Revivals and importations brought the season to an end. Rice's Surprise Party switched to something a bit more substantial than the farce-comedies and burlesques it had hitherto specialized in. Its ranks momentarily swelled, the group mounted a revival of *Cinderella at School* (5 March 1881) for two weeks at Booth's from 8 to 20 May.

Musical versions of *Uncle Tom's Cabin* were rife across the land. Typically, one came into Philadelphia's Chestnut Street Opera House on 22 May. Its book was by H. Wayne Ellis; its music by Cary Florio. The hoydenish Carrie Swain was starred as Topsy, while in a concession to the demand for an arioso soprano the character of Rose was added. The show toured briefly, then disappeared from the records.

Tony Pastor sometimes ventured to produce a piece that seemed to cross over not always precisely defined borders. At other times, especially in the summer, he rented his house to quasi-legitimate attractions. One such was **Venus** (5 June 1882, Tony Pastor's), "a fairy extravaganza." Its story told how several thinly disguised celebrities such as "Roscoe Conlin" and "James G. Braine" pay a visit to a damsel-dominated Venus. Some commentators thought the show was a spoof of *The Wicked World.* No one thought the show very good. In its short life it was accompanied by a slight piece, **Jumbo, the Trick Elephant.**

In Boston, the *Morning Journal's* terse review of **The Lightkeeper's Daughter** (12 June 1882, Casino) said virtually all that needed to be said about the operetta. George M. Vickers's plot was "of the old-fashioned school of melodrama, with the conventional foundling, who turns out to be a titled heiress, and the familiar villain, who on secretly learning her identity, involves her father in financial meshes in order to secure the heiress for a bride." Of course, a handsome hero comes to the rescue. Charles D. Baker's music appeared "to have been written somewhat independently of the story," while the cast and settings were only of "fair quality." The musical's life was brief.

Although Johann Strauss was a world-celebrated figure, his operettas remained virtually unknown to the American public. Some theatres catering to German audiences had staged a few of his pieces. *Die Fledermaus,* for example, was first sung in New York in 1879. But these operettas had not made their way into the major houses as had French opéra bouffe, either in English or in the original. On 29 June the Germania, a house that had once been Wallack's and was now given over to German-language productions, offered, as part of the J. W. Norcross Opera Company's program, an English translation of *Der lustige Krieg.* As **The Merry War** the work delighted playgoers willing to travel to a slightly out-of-the-way and unfashionable house. The fracas erupts after two cities both announce a famous dancer will appear at their respective opera houses on the same night. The dancer solves everything by appearing at neither. Word of mouth proved surprisingly effective, and when the mounting exhausted its booking it was immediately transferred to the Metropolitan

Concert Hall for an additional run. W. T. Carleton, Dora Wiley, Richard Golden, and a German comic, Gustav Adolfi, led the cast. All told, *The Merry War* ran seven weeks. Without fanfare the world of Strauss operetta had begun its hold on the American stage. Curiously, Strauss's masterpiece, *Die Fledermaus*, encountered little success or acclaim here until after the composer's death, when the vogue for his lesser works had subsided.

The year's last offering suggested that the American Musical Theatre had a way to go before it lost completely its circus tinge. On 31 July the New Miniature Opera Company, a Boston troupe composed solely of child performers, presented New Yorkers with its version of *Patience*. Enough New Yorkers found the version sufficiently droll to brave the heat and keep the show on the boards for five weeks.

Just off center stage, minstrelsy continued to wane and vaudeville to flourish. According to Odell, "minstrelsy had become a fountain of burlesque." The San Francisco Minstrels' programs included "Hamlet, Prince of Dunkirk" and "Patients, or Bunion-Salve's Bride." Pastor, always an innovator, attempted plotted vaudeville, again bringing his house closer to the legitimate fold. But the experiment was no more successful than his earlier tries and was soon abandoned.

1882–1883

All signs pointed to the continuing growth and health of the American Musical Theatre, even if a native element was not yet solidly evident. The lyric stage remained busy. In fact the 1882–1883 theatrical year was by far the busiest to date. Counting repertory companies as single offerings, Broadway playgoers could chose from over forty musical first nights. Admittedly, almost all were still either importations or revivals. But soon this dependence would prove to be a passing phenomenon. The onrush of lyric pieces resulted in three of New York's playhouses devoting virtually the entire season to musical offerings. More significant, for the first time a legitimate theatre was constructed as a showcase for popular musical entertainments. In its early seasons the Casino housed only importations, but its stage stood ready to receive American works. At the same time, one by one, the first great, enduring names of the American Musical Theatre came into the spotlight. If, sadly, E. E. Rice, Harrigan, Hart, and Braham mean little to anyone but scholars, the names of Lillian Russell, Fay Templeton, John

Philip Sousa, and Reginald De Koven still carry some of their first magic.

The Theatre Comique led off the season on 26 August with a type of offering new to the house. **The Blackbird** was a melodrama set in Ireland. It was closer in style to the plays performed by J. K. Emmet, and later W. J. Scanlan, Chauncey Olcott, and their ilk, than to the vernacular roughhouses Harrigan and Braham normally provided. In fact, Harrigan was not even author of the piece. A sometime member of the company, George L. Stout, received credit. And Braham's contribution was minor. Even Harrigan's fine scene painter, Charles Witham, abandoned his customary cityscapes for cascades and whirlpools in moonlight. Stout's tale followed Colonel Raymond Darcy (De Wolf Hopper) in his attempt to escape pursuers after the battle of Culloden. Displeased, the Comique's regulars withheld their patronage. *The Blackbird* was withdrawn when Harrigan and Braham had a new work ready at the end of October.

Two nights after *The Blackbird* premiered, *Billee Taylor* began the long procession of the season's revivals at the Bijou. Its stay was short. Two weeks later Lillian Russell was again singing *Patience* at the house.

The Salsbury Troubadours, led by Nate Salsbury and Nellie McHenry, brought farce-comedy back to Broadway for a week at the Windsor on 4 September and for a month's run beginning 9 April. Their piece was called **Greenroom Fun**, a title that reveals the entire plot. One character was Booth McForrest, a tribute to three tragedians—Edwin Booth, Edwin Forrest, and the now forgotten John McCullough. The first generation of farce-comedies was nearing the end of its vogue. But it was by no means exhausted, and a more mature second generation was soon to follow.

Opéra bouffe made its first appearance of the year on 11 September. Maurice Grau had organized a new company around the talents of his latest protégé, Madam Theo. His plan had been to give her the honor of opening the new Casino, but construction delays forced him to present his new star at the Fifth Avenue instead. The hasty booking revisions this change necessitated meant that for the rest of the season Madam Theo and her entourage were shunted from theatre to theatre. By the summer Grau's troupe had played five separate engagements in one New York house or another.

On 14 September, before his regular season started, Tony Pastor booked a double bill of *The*

Beautiful Galatea and *Trial by Jury* for his 14th Street house. Indifferently received and apparently ill financed, the bill shuttered without finishing out the week. Four nights later, down the block at Haverly's 14th Street Theatre, **My Sweetheart** opened as a vehicle for Minnie Palmer and R. E. Graham. Miss Palmer, "talking" her songs, was looked upon as something of a "second Lotta," while Graham, playing in German dialect, was viewed as another Emmet. *My Sweetheart*—advertised as "the difference between the love of a good, pure girl and the designs of a woman of the world"—was a straight play, adapted to the stars' requirements by William Gill. These requirements included spots for their specialties. But in the end *My Sweetheart* was no more a musical than Lotta's pieces and considerably less so than Emmet's mountings. More music was added to the work when Miss Palmer took the show to London. Cordially received there, it far surpassed its American run. After a week in New York the show was replaced by Hague's Great British Operatic Minstrels, who themselves moved on with equal speed. At the same time Tony Pastor rushed in a replacement for his disastrous opening. The Boston English Opera Company sang its version of von Suppé's *Donna Juanita* until Pastor was ready with his vaudeville bills two weeks later.

The "English" in the Boston troupe's name referred to the fact that the works they sang were translated into English. Something more exotically English followed the New Englanders two nights later at the Standard. Thanks largely to Gilbert and Sullivan, the D'Oyly Carte was London's stellar lyric troupe. But because Gilbert and Sullivan loomed so grandly in its success, the extent of Richard D'Oyly Carte's enterprise and the diversity of his presentations are often forgotten. When the company arrived for an 1882–1883 visit, its trunks and cases included costumes and sets for three works, only one of which was by its premier creators. Somewhat bravely it opened with Bucalossi's **Les Manteaux Noirs.** The reception was disappointing, and a month later the company raised the curtain on Robert Planquette's **Rip Van Winkle.** This, too, had only a modest success—perhaps the result of a $2.00 top. By the time it offered the first American performance of Gilbert and Sullivan's **Iolanthe** on 25 November, D'Oyly Carte's once glittering reputation appeared a bit tarnished. Masterpiece though it was, *Iolanthe* failed to arouse the enthusiasm *H. M. S. Pinafore* and *Patience* had engendered. Still, enough appreciative theatregoers responded to permit the comic opera

to hold the boards through the end of February. Gilbert and Sullivan's account of a fairy's tinkering with English romance and politics was superbly cast. W. T. Carleton sang Strephon; J. H. Ryley, Lord Chancellor; and Marie Jansen, Iolanthe. Curiously, if accounts in E. E. Rice's obituaries are correct, his mounting of this same work for Boston was far more successful, establishing what was then a record of nineteen weeks there. A warning to scholars about trusting critics' accuracy can be learned from reading the *Times* review, where the unidentified critic assured his readers that the show had "no plot."

The Monday after the D'Oyly Carte's arrival, 2 October, four musical offerings bowed. When one recalls that New York at this time had only thirteen principal theatres, plus a few combination houses, the figure is even more impressive. The Kiralfys resurrected *Around the World in Eighty Days* (28 August 1875), playing Niblo's for three weeks, and returning to a second house in April for an additional fortnight. Solomon's **The Vicar of Bray,** in which a vicar is comically blackmailed into allowing his daughter to marry the man of her choice, was a one-week flop at the Fifth Avenue, while the Norcross Opera Company presented two weeks of *The Merry War* at Haverly's 14th Street Theatre. The final entry among the foursome was Max Strakosch's English Opera Company, "English" again signifying works sung in translation. Its repertory at the Grand consisted of *The Bohemian Girl, Fatinitza,* and *Carmen.*

To replace the failed Solomon work, a more beloved piece of his was hurried back. The peripatetic *Billie Taylor* came to life again for a week until Madam Theo's troupe could be moved to the house.

Friend or Foe (16 October 1882, Windsor) helped make a star of a new figure, W. J. Scanlan. Scanlan, like J. K. Emmet, was known for his fine singing, and he appeared primarily in straight plays, such as this Bartley Campbell effort, generously supplied with melodies to display his talent. Scanlan's career was brief. His departure from the stage and his death resulted from paresis and its consequent insanity. In this respect his end was like that of so many of the early stars of the lyric stage—G. L. Fox, Emmet, and Tony Hart, for example. The story of *Friend or Foe* centered on Carrol Moore, an Irishman living in France. He falls in love with the daughter of the family with whom he boards. Carrol's rival for her hand is the owner of the house, who threatens to turn the family out if his suit is denied. Carrol accepts $15,000 to fight as a substitute for his rival in the Franco-Prussian War. He is caught in this subterfuge and sentenced to be shot. But his sweetheart prevails on the commanding officer and he is saved. This sort of romantic play—merely a variation of the type Emmet offered—long retained a large following. When Emmet and Scanlan were no longer available to play them, Chauncey Olcott provided similar entertainment for another generation.

Once passed over, *The Sorcerer* was revived on 17 October to capitalize on Gilbert and Sullivan's vogue and the excitement generated by the impending premiere of *Iolanthe*. Happily, it was no ordinary revival. Produced by John McCaull at his own Bijou Theatre, it was sumptuously mounted and featured Lillian Russell as Aline, John Howson as Wells, Laura Joyce as Lady Sangazure, George Olmi as Marmaduke, Digby Bell as Dr. Daly, and Charles J. Campbell as Alexis. The response kept the work before the footlights until 9 January, a run of ninety-two performances. After a four-month tour it returned for a brief run at the Casino in April.

The Casino itself, after long, costly, and heartbreaking delays, announced it was finally ready to open its doors on 21 October 1882. The house that McCaull and his partner, Rudolph Aronson, erected at 39th Street and Broadway, diagonally across from where the Metropolitan Opera House would rise one year later, was something of an oddity. It capitulated to the momentary fad for Moorish design, a surrender that quickly dated the building architecturally. Even odder was its placing its auditorium on the second floor, forcing patrons to climb at least one flight of stairs. Later the inside of the building was gutted and the orchestra brought down to street level. But McCaull and Aronson were too anxious to give Broadway its first theatre built especially for musicals. Their anxiety led to immediate, serious embarrassment—beyond, of course, the opening delays. The critics who reviewed the first attraction, Johann Strauss's **The Queen's Lace Handkerchief,** remarked disparagingly how unready the house was for patrons. A number of ticket-holders conveyed their displeasure in turn. Heating didn't work, carpets were missing, myriad little malfunctions beset the house. Fearing to lose all they had set out to achieve, McCaull and Aronson closed the theatre after one week's operation and put their production in storage. When "America's Handsomest Place of Amusement" advertised it would reopen on 30 December, its owners knew that everything was in working order. One important change of cast had taken place in the interim. Young Francis Wilson left

off playing farce-comedies to assume the comic lead and begin his rise as one of America's better musical comedy clowns. In his autobiography Wilson gave a fascinating glimpse of the movements and pacing in the staging of the times. The passage incidentally shows that even Strauss was not safe from having other men's songs inserted into his score:

> ... the baritone William T. Carleton sang an interpolated song entitled "Woman, Fair Woman," the cue to which was, "Oh, Woman, lovely Woman, what would we not do for thy sweet sake!" Having delivered himself of which he would make the conventional up-stage tour gazing most unnaturally at the muslin clouds and sky, returning to the front at the exact moment for the first note of the ballad.

The plot of the show gave the real Cervantes an imaginary romance that ended happily when he aids his imprisoned queen to escape. Strauss later used themes from this show for his "Roses from the South." Signor Perugini was the first Cervantes, replaced on the reopening by Carleton. Lilly Post was the Queen, and Mathilde Cottrelly, Cervantes' fiancée.

Theatregoers, especially devotees of the Theatre Comique, had a second shock in store for them five nights after the Casino opened. On 26 October Harrigan, Hart, and Braham had their latest effort ready. Unlike *The Blackbird*, this play had a libretto and lyrics by Harrigan himself and a fair complement of Braham tunes. But its story revolved around an ethnic group that Harrigan had previously paid scant attention to—the Jews. Harrigan assumed the title role of **Mordecai Lyons,** a Jewish pawnbroker. Lyons's daughter (Annie Mack), much against his will, has left home to become an actress. When she is "ruined" and deserted by her lover, she receives only curses from her father. But the lover discovers he has deserted Esther to court a girl who turns out to be his own daughter. Contrived reconciliations follow. By and large the critics were no happier with the new play than was the public. The *Herald* branded it unequivocally as the team's "first distinct failure." Curiosity, loyalty, and the need to prepare a replacement kept *Mordecai Lyons* going for a month.

Neither Harrigan, Hart, and Braham, opéra bouffe, nor farce-comedies could destroy the appeal of *The Black Crook* (12 September 1866) for some audiences. A touring version came in to the 14th

Street Theatre on 13 November to cater to their pleasure. But the circus element that increasingly overwhelmed the spectacle seemed particularly strong in this version. The mounting featured "Tyrolean warblers," a ventriloquist, and a trio that specialized in "grotesque eccentricities." The sideshows coupled with the spectacle, ballet, and melodrama found welcome for three weeks and then continued traipsing around the country.

Seemingly just as indestructible, the Vokes family returned with *Belles of the Kitchen* and the rest of their proto-farce-comedy repertory to delight the audiences at Niblo's from 20 November to 2 December.

Gilbert and Sullivan's *Iolanthe* premiered on 25 November; Harrigan and Braham's **McSorley's Inflation,** on 27 November. Like *Iolanthe, McSorley's Inflation* was at once a success and a disappointment. It gave Ned Harrigan and Tony Hart their most profitable run of the season, but it was a run that fell short of the best the Comique had known or was to know. The play closed on 31 March, having celebrated its hundredth performance on 19 February. Although the Mulligan gang was missing, the story of the play was more in line with the Mulligan tradition than any of the other works the Comique mounted during the year. Harrigan seems to have used "inflation" in the sense of swelling pride. Peter McSorley (Harrigan), a candidate for coroner, wants his wife, Bridget (Hart), to give up her stall at the Washington Market. He deems it unbecoming a candidate's wife. Bridget's brawny exuberance wins the day. A subsidiary plot recounted the turmoil at an African-American political convention, while other scenes raised mayhem in Chinatown (with one Chinese flying through a second-story window) and a Salvation Army office. Braham's "I Never Drink Behind The Bar," "McNally's Row Of Flats," and "The Old Feather Bed" won instant popularity. The title of another song seems forty years ahead of the times. But "The Charleston Blues" referred to a black paramilitary band like the Skidmores of the Mulligan Guards shows.

In Boston a librettist had offered $1,000 for the best score that could be set to his work. The result was Walter Gould and J. Franklin Warner's **Arctic; or, The North Pole Expedition** (27 November 1882, Windsor), a title later changed to *Influence; or, True Love Never Runs Smooth*. When Leonora, a banker's daughter, learns her fiancé, Capt. Douglass, and his ship, *Polaris*, are lost in the Arctic, she and her friends head to the rescue. But they are caught in the ice and themselves have to be rescued—by Douglass and his ship.

In New York, December brought little for lovers of the musical stage, offering only the indefatigable, aging Lotta in her standard repertory. Nor did 1883 get off to an exciting start. On New Year's night Tony Denier romped into the Windsor with a *Humpty Dumpty* (10 March 1868) that predated Lotta, while J. K. Emmet arrived at the 14th Street Theatre in something of a novelty, **Fritz Among the Gypsies.** The evening might have seemed more novel had not the plot, like virtually every one Emmet used, revolved around a recognition scene. The principal novelties and attractions of the evening turned out to be the cavortings of a "$2,500 sagacious giant dog" and a new tune which became one of Emmet's best loved, "Sweet Violets."

The play ran six weeks. Emmet, keeping the promise made years before in his programs, returned off and on during the season in various versions of his Fritz plays. For example, he performed *Fritz in England and Ireland* briefly at Niblo's and appeared in *Fritz in Ireland* later at the Cosmopolitan. Both plays were probably largely the same. Emmet rarely trod the boards of major houses anymore. Haverly's 14th Street Theatre may be viewed as a borderline house, but Niblo's was past its heyday, and the Cosmopolitan at 41st Street and Broadway was then considered far uptown. Emmet's place in the theatre of his day was clearly one shared by a number of his fellow players. Disdained by most "sophisticates," he nonetheless had such a loyal following that he could have all the bookings he chose in any but the gilt-edged houses. His type of show continued popular until the first motion pictures drew away its faithful attendants.

Solomon's second new work of the year, **Virginia; or, Ringing the Changes** (8 January 1883, Bijou), told a tale of switched babies and Mephistophelian machinations. American critics rejected it as watered-down Gilbert and Sullivan. Apart from *Billee Taylor*, Solomon was never to enjoy the same acclaim here as in London. But despite tepid notices *Virginia* played five weeks to decent business and then toured.

A revival of *The Black Venus* (12 January 1881) at Niblo's inaugurated a busy February on the 5th. "Forty secundas and coryphées, a caravan of lions, tigers, camels, zebras, horses, goats, and Nubian slaves made the actors seem very unimportant." The same night that saw the opening of *The Black Venus* offered one of the many borderline plays that filled the stages of the time. *Zara* was a romantic melo-drama written by Fred Marsden for Annie Pixley. Later in the season Marsden performed a similar service for Lotta when she returned to town in *Bob*. *Zara's* story described the unsuccessful attempt to deprive the heroine of her inheritance. Seven or eight songs were included. None was written for the show, one critic shrugging them off as "time honored chestnuts." But they suggest how musical a "straight" play of the era could seem, especially when one remembers that most legitimate theatres still maintained orchestras to play overtures and frequent background material.

One week later, 12 February, a German-language production of Millöcker's **Countess Du Barry**—depicting the rise of a callous milliner's assistant to king's favorite—was brought to the Fifth Avenue for a week. The show had originally been produced at the Thalia in the Bowery, a house catering to the large German population of New York, who still preferred to take their entertainment in their native tongue. Competing versions of Lecocq's *Le Coeur et la Main* bowed eleven nights apart. They opened in a hail of charges, countercharges, and lawsuits. McCaull got his version to the public first, opening it at his Bijou on 15 February as **Heart and Hand.** James Duff, owner of the Standard, used his mounting to replace the faltering *Iolanthe*. Duff presented his mounting as **Micaela** on 26 February. Neither production caught theatregoers' fancies, and both ran less than a month, leaving each manager to blame the other for the lack of success. In both versions a duke is reluctant to marry a princess, preferring a servant girl he has met. Of course, the girl turns out to be the princess in disguise.

Between the controversial openings, the Boston Ideal Opera Company slipped into town on what was becoming an annual visit. For the 1882–1883 season it brought with it *Fatinitza, The Musketeers, The Mascot, The Pirates of Penzance, Patience,* and *The Marriage of Figaro*.

On the 29th, the evening of *Micaela's* premiere, Thatcher, Primrose, and West's Minstrels climbed onto Niblo's stage for a week of good old-fashioned blackface.

March opened with one of the most interesting native efforts of the year, **The Dime Novel** (5 March 1883, Bijou). Called a "musical comedy," it had a book by A. C. Gunter and songs by Jesse Williams. The libretto, insisting "bad books make bad boys," spoofed the effects of reading cheap fiction. When a well-intentioned young man behaves like the heroes of pulp novels he reads, he finds himself in difficulty. Although it was well received, the public refused to respond. The show folded at the end of a single week, leaving the Bijou unexpectedly dark for some time.

Vying for attention on 5 March was a pasted-together opera company that included Henry E. Dixey and Marie Jansen. It kept the Fifth Avenue lit for nearly a month with its renditions of *Iolanthe* and *The Mascot*. After a week's respite, during which Catherine Lewis came in to sing *Olivette* and Lecocq's *Prince Conti*, it staged a week-long revival of *Cinderella at School* (5 May 1881), and then disappeared from the musical scene.

The failure of *Micaela* prompted a hasty revival of *H. M. S. Pinafore* at the Standard on 17 March, succeeded on the 26th by *Patience*.

No American played a more important role in turning farce-comedy into musical comedy than Charles H. Hoyt. Hoyt's contributions in propelling the genre from infancy into adolescence would become obvious only with time and most certainly were not obvious when Willie Edouin's Sparks romped in his earliest effort, **A Bunch of Keys** (26 March 1883, San Francisco Opera House [N.Y.]). Hoyt's story revolved around a musical-comedy will in which a deceased uncle leaves a backwater hotel to one of his nieces. To which one? The dead man's unscrupulous lawyer, Snaggs (Edouin), reads from the will: "The first drummer who is a total stranger, that shall arrive at the hotel, shall be requested to decide which of my three nieces, otherwise the Bunch of Keys, Rose, May, and Theodosia Keys, is the homeliest. And to her I bequeath my entire estate." The girls do not consider a run-down hotel worth the humiliation; but their sweethearts go to all lengths to win the prize. In the end a codicil, which Snaggs has withheld, allows for a happy ending. The show was filled with roughhouse horseplay (a frog down a character's back) and dubious humor on the order of:

> —... *the ceiling fell down completely, mashing me... my mouth is full of hair and mortar.*
> —*Very mortar-fying.*

Young James T. Powers had a field day as a hurriedly enlisted bellhop forced to run up and down the stairs at breakneck speed to tend to the hotel's clients. However gauche and inane the play seems when read today, it delighted contemporaries, playing prosperously until late June.

Harrigan, Hart, and Braham had a new work ready, The Muddy Day (2 April 1883, Comique). Mary Ann O'Leary (Hart) is a widow, courted by two mud-scow captains, Roger McNab (Harrigan) and Herman Schoonover (Harry Fisher). She decides to marry the wealthier. Her search to find out the financial status of her suitors takes her to a party on a barge, and the barge promptly sinks. At another point she even resorts to dressing as a man to learn the facts. In the end, she chooses Roger. Some of the more skittish critics were shocked by Mrs. O'Leary's entrance in only a barrel and some underwear. But most of the audience undoubtedly relished the absurdity as well as the almost Shakespearean triple-tension of a man disguised as a woman disguised as a man. Braham's tunes were not top-drawer, but they were "sung heartily" and danced "forcibly." Harrigan and Hart's large, sustained company scuffled through the proceedings until 19 May. Like so many shows during the season, The Muddy Day, while not a failure, disappointed by not achieving unmitigated success.

Leonard Graver's Cad, the Tomboy (23 April 1883, Daly's) was a borderline musical recounting the feminization of a hellion. A similar borderline instance with a similar story, Bob (14 May 1883, Fifth Ave.), gave Lotta one of her rare out-and-out failures. Its author, Fred Marsden, was also the author of a third fence-straddler, Cheek (28 May 1883, 14th St.), centering on a newspaperman who attempts to get famous people to pay him to mention them in his columns. Although Lotta was able to keep Bob alive on the road, only Cheek enjoyed a reasonably long theatrical history.

French opéra bouffe was also nearing the end of its brightest era. Even with Lillian Russell in the principal, if not the title, role, Offenbach's The Princess of Trébizonde—"the romance of a prince caught among a swirl of circus performers"—could

not accrue more than a month's stand at the Casino, beginning on 6 May. However, the impetuous Miss Russell's abrupt departure may have shortened its run more than any other thing, even though an able supporting cast included Digby Bell, John Howson, Laura Joyce, and Madeline Lucette. The Queen's Lace Handkerchief was brought in from the road to keep the Casino lit.

Boston was not alone in providing New York with occasional entertainment. On 9 May the Barton English Opera Company came from San Francisco with Balfe's twenty-five-year-old Satanella. The troupe suffered another of the disappointments so pervasive this season, departing the Standard on 19 May.

A week later Haverly brought his Mastodon Minstrels into his 14th Street Theatre for a two-week stand. The following Monday, 21 May, Rice's Surprise Party introduced one of the most popular of farce-comedies, Pop. Originally produced in San Francisco, it may well have attracted Californians partly by the glamour of its second-act setting, the salon of a great Cunard ocean liner. But its infectious fun and generally excellent songs soon found a universal welcome. Again the story line was simple. Adolphus Pop (John A. Mackay), a playwright, decides to make an ocean crossing. The people he meets provide little in the way of complications but much in the way of specialties. As his audiences expected, Mackay himself presented imitations of the best-known actors of the day, offering "encores until he was obliged to decline from sheer exhaustion." George K Fortesque danced in his elephantine fashion, while "The Dudes And The Dude Prince" presented "a number of girls marching as 'dudes'— that latest development of male fashion or folly." For a finale the cast gathered to sing a medley of songs from current comic operas.

Ludwig Englander came to Broadway's attention on 4 June, marking the start of his tenure as conductor of the Thalia Theatre. It was at the Thalia that his first work, Der Prinz Gemahl, was produced on 11 April. His librettist was Julius Hopp. Its reception was encouraging enough to prompt the company to move it to Wallack's Theatre. For the benefit of non-German-speaking patrons the program translated the title as The Prince Consort, although the work was still sung in German. When Broadway was not interested, the piece closed after two weeks. The failure nevertheless quickly provided Englander with a springboard to commercial success on the English-speaking stage.

Englander's countryman, Johann Strauss, fared more happily when the Casino brought forth its final offering of the season, **Prince Methusalem,** on 9 July. The prince of the title must win back his principality from revolutionaries before he can conclude the wedding the revolution interrupted. Her quarrel with John McCaull and Rudolph Aronson settled, Lillian Russell returned to star in the title part. The role was her second trouser role in succession, the only way a lady had at this juncture to show her shapely legs. More than any other management, the Casino was able to appreciate the possibilities of summer runs for musicals. This very first attempt of the house in its maiden season to span the summer more than paid off. *Prince Methuselem* ran into October, surviving yet another tempestuous Russell departure in September.

The Casino's first season coincided with the last full season of minstrelsy in New York. Minstrels now seemed too far removed from contemporary rhythms and complexities to remain viable. As they had in recent years, the San Francisco Minstrels relied heavily on burlesquing popular plays. *Iolanthe,* for example, reappeared as *High and Lengthy.* The play on words seems not especially funny. But comedy is one thing to one generation, another to a second. Still, there was evidence even to contemporaries that exhaustion had set in. The season ended on 24 March, significantly earlier than customary. In June, Charlie Backus, a surviving founder, died. There were rumors on the Rialto that Billy Birch, the last original member, was eager to sell the troupe and its building. Of course, the theatre was changing in less musical spheres. The theatrical center continued to move uptown. Booth's, opened seventeen years before with glimmering hope, was converted into a dry-goods store. Niblo's, now distant from the main stem, could have advertised "last years."

1883–1884

After four consecutive seasons of unprecedented activity the lyric stage slackened its pace a bit, but only a bit. Depending on how one considers certain borderline cases, approximately thirty musical mountings vied for attention, more than triple the average count before *H. M. S. Pinafore* (15 January 1879). As usual, importations and revivals constituted the bulk of the fare.

Harrigan and Hart inaugurated the season with a full-length revision of Harrigan and Braham's earlier success *The Mulligan Guards' Ball* (13 January 1879), using old material from *The Mulligan Guards' Nominee* (22 November 1880) and new Braham melodies to stretch the evening. The lessons of the preceding year had been well learned. The entire schedule of the Theatre Comique for 1883–1884 was devoted to the Mulligans. By now Harrigan and Hart's troupe was filled with beloved performers identified with specific roles. Besides the stars, favorites included Annie Yea-mans, who usually played Cordelia, and John Wild, most often cast as Simpson Primrose. No company, not even Wallack's or Daly's respected organizations, seemed to stay together so loyally nor enjoy a more devoted following. The revival of *The Mulligan Guards' Ball* held the stage from 6 August to 22 September.

The Devil's Auction, a Philadelphia production in the *Black Crook* tradition, came into the 14th Street Theatre for a two-week visit on 18 August. The show was based on a melodrama that had played the nation's theatres just after the Civil War, at the very moment *The Black Crook* (12 September 1866) became the rage. Its story recounted how Carlos (Dore Davidson), a poor shepherd, loves Madeline (Kate Girard), a farmer's daughter. Mephisto (James S. Maffitt) would help Count Fortune (W H. Bartholomew) win Madeline, but Crystaline, a good fairy, prevails. In the course of the evening spectators were transported to the Volcano of Hades and to the Golden Palace of the Pasha. Adele Cornalba led the ballets. At one point this exotic tour came to a momentary halt while the cast regaled playgoers with "The new American Singing and Dancing number, entitled 'The Wild And Wooly West.'" If the producers had hopes that popular acclaim might extend their stay, their hopes were disappointed.

Three nights after the premiere of *The Devil's Auction,* the Kiralfys relit Niblo's Garden with a Parisian importation, **Excelsior.** It, too, was of the *Black Crook* school, melodrama heavy with spectacle and ballet. Not a word was spoken in this depiction of Darkness (Ettore Coppini) defeated by Light (Mlle. Nani). The Kiralfys and Niblo's were far more alluring than their neighbors. *Excelsior* ran until 15 December.

Chicago, a great city once again after its fire, was rapidly becoming an important producing center. On 21 August, the same night *The Devil's Auction* opened, Chicago sent one of its earliest efforts for New York's inspection. S. G. Pratt's **Zenobia,** first done the preceding season in its hometown, was termed a "lyric drama" in its advertisements and "grand opera" in pre-opening synopses. Reviews suggest the latter description may have been the more accurate. Pratt's tale recounted how the proud rebel, Zenobia (Dora Hennings), is spared death when the king (E. Connell) falls in love with her daughter (Helen Wallace). Housed at the minor, out-of-the-way 23rd Street Theatre, it was condescendingly received and hastily withdrawn after its first four performances grossed a mere $129, $60, $55, and $33, respectively. Its reception, moreover, hinted at the indifference with which New York would almost always greet an arrival from the Middle West. Perhaps in this case the coldness was justified. Not a trace of the text seems to remain.

A revival of *Heart and Hand* closed in August, while September was ushered in by **Frolics of a Day** (3 September 1883, 14th St.), which starred Frank Majilton as a policeman who must keep a comic eye on some gadabouts and other big-city types. The humor and action were largely acrobatic, one critic observing, "Every man in it is knocked down with beautiful regularity aided by stuffed clubs. The oftener the man gets up the oftener he is knocked down." One week and the nonsense was gone for good.

On 10 September Maurice Grau, with Aimée once again his star, brought in the first of the season's numerous opéra bouffe troupes. Lecocq's **La Princesse des Canaries** was the curtain raiser. Its saga of a general who ousts a usurper so a princess may regain her rightful throne allowed Aimée to display "her winks and kicks and nods and smiles, and her abundance of quiet suggestiveness." By summertime, lovers of the genre had been given one or more opportunities to hear such works as *La Mascotte* and *Les Cloches de Corneville,* along with *Boccaccio* and *The Bohemian Girl.*

An importation, G. R. Sims and Frederic Clay's **The Merry Duchess,** told of a jockey who wins the hand of the Duchess of Epsom Downs. The evening featured John Nash, Selina Dolaro, and Henry E. Dixey. Dixey portrayed a comic villain, Brabazon Sykes, who connives unsuccessfully to poison the duchess's mount. This English foolery pleased audiences at the Standard from 13 September until mid-October.

September's final offering was a second Theatre Comique revival, *The Mulligan Guards' Picnic* (23 September 1878). Again the original piece had been reworked into a full evening's entertainment, by utilizing scenes from earlier Harrigan plays and new Braham tunes, in this case "Hurry, Little Children, Sunday Morning" and "Going Home With Nellie After Five." The play ran just over a month.

In Philadelphia critics and playgoers turned thumbs down on a comic opera, **Pedro, the Minstrel** (1 October 1883, Lyceum), in which the street singer is mistakenly arrested as the Duke of Valencia. A princess who has fallen in love with him engineers his release from jail. But he proves loyal to his beloved Maria.

Revivals and minstrels accounted for all of October's offerings except its last. *Fritz in Ireland* (3 November 1879) played a week at a combination house beginning 1 October, to be followed seven nights later at the same auditorium by a week's return of Rice's Surprise Parry doing *Pop* (21 May 1883). The Thatcher, Primrose, and West Minstrels arrived on the 15th for the first of three brief stands. Their later runs came in late January and late February. On 22 October competing opéra bouffe entourages raised their curtains. Grau's troupe at the Standard sang in French; the Wilbur Opera Company at the People's sang in English. Only October's closing entry was a novelty. With *Prince Methusalem* finally departed, the McCaull Opera Company at the Casino offered the New York premiere in English of Millöcker's **The Beggar Student.** The show was an instant hit, achieving a profitable run of 107 performances. In Europe it remains a repertory standard to this day. A general, rejected in his suit of a countess's daughter, dresses a poor soldier as a prince and sends him to court the girl. W. T. Carleton and Bertha Ricci sang the lovers.

When compared with busy October, November was quiet indeed. But its first offering was the high point of the season so far as native lyric pieces were concerned. On 5 November the Theatre Comique presented its first new work of the season, the work generally judged Harrigan's best, **Cordelia's Aspirations.** In a sense even this play was not new. Harrigan had employed the same basic story earlier in *The Mulligan Guards' Surprise* (16 February

1880), while he had tried out the evening's most celebrated scene in *The Mulligans' Silver Wedding* (21
February 1881). Cordelia's brother Planxty (Harry
Fisher) and her sisters come to America. They are
determined to share in Cordelia's good fortune. As
Planxty proclaims, "Cordelia's living in clover—we
must be in the field when it's ripe." Although Cordelia
(Annie Yeamans) has sailed first class on the same
ship that brought her family across and although she
had sent them all sorts of comforts to cushion their
steerage-class passage, she feels impelled to live up
to their exaggerated ideas of her wealth. She prods
Dan (Harrigan) to move to more elegant quarters
and travel in more elevated society. Planxty attempts
to get Cordelia to sign all her property over to him.
To this end he forges a woman's love letter to Dan
and arranges for Cordelia to find the letter. Driven to
distraction by Planxty's machinations and by Dan's
social gaffes, Cordelia gulps down a bottle of "Roach
Poison." Of course, the poison is merely Rebecca
Allup's cache of booze. Cordelia's death scene comes
to naught when Rebecca (Hart) confides in Dan the
real contents of the bottle. Planxty is sent packing,
and Cordelia realizes she is happier with her old
friends in her old home. Harrigan's comedy was typical of its period, full of puns and racial caricatures:

Cordelia: Many's the little luxury I sent them on
the ship—incognito.
Rebecca: No, you didn't send it dat way. You sent
me wid it.

Some humor was merely vaudeville jokes, hardly
pertinent to the story. One player remarks, "That
barkeeper—he's not fit for the counter. He's a coun-
terfit." Strange as some of the humor may now seem,
some of the pacing may well seem even stranger.
The end of Cordelia's famous drunk scene would
undoubtedly have been more abrupt had the scene
been written a generation later:

Dan: Cordelia's dying. She drank the roach poison
from the bottle.
Rebecca: She drank out of dis bottle?
Dan: Cordelia's dead.
Rebecca: Drunk.

At this point, instead of a blackout, Rebecca and
Simpson Primrose (John Wild) take the bottle,
drink from it, and launch into "Whiskey, You're The
Devil." The song finished, the curtain rose and fell on
two stage pictures—each accompanied by a reprise

of the song's chorus. None of Braham's melodies
for the evening was among his best. However, they
were serviceable. *Cordelia's Aspirations* recorded 176
showings before it closed on 5 April.

E. E. Rice suffered a quick failure with a comic
opera known variously as **Lieutenant** [or **Captain**]
Helene of the Guards (12 November 1883, Fifth
Ave.). It starred Amy Gordon, but its rising comic,
Henry E. Dixey, won laughs mimicking Henry
Irving. This time around he could do it for only a
single week; next season would be different.

November's last musical was the preceding season's *Friend or Foe* (16 October 1882), making the
first of two brief return visits. The second visit came
merely a month later. The first was at the Windsor,
the second at the Grand.

Over the summer the old Bijou had been demolished and a new house had been constructed on
its site. The new Bijou was ready to receive its first
patrons on 1 December. Again, an importation
was given the honor of opening a theatre built for
musicals. Offenbach's *Orpheus and Eurydice* (now
generally called *Orpheus in the Underworld*) was
the premiere attraction. Filled with names, such as
Amelia Summerville and Digby Bell, which became
household words to theatre-goers of the age, it ran
just over 100 performances.

Thirteen nights after the new Bijou opened,
the old Standard burned to the ground. The third
major theatre fire in a little over a year, it frightened
away a sufficient number of potential ticket-buyers
to dampen business on Broadway for the rest of
the season. To some extent the fire and the resul-
tant scare may account for the drop in the number
of musicals during 1883–1884. At the time of its
destruction the Standard had only begun to play
host to a new comic opera from England, **Estrella**.
With music by Luscombe Searelle and a libretto by
Walter Parke, the piece had raised its curtain three
nights earlier, 11 December. To watch how his bride
will react, a suspicious count disappears shortly
after their wedding. When his bride, believing
him dead, marries the young man she had wanted
in the first place, the count finds to his chagrin he
cannot reclaim her. Hubert Wilke, W. S. Rising, and
Amy Gordon sang the principal roles. The work's
reception was at best lukewarm, and when its
costumes and sets were consumed in the fire no
attempt was made to recreate them. However,
Estrella did not completely disappear. The traveling
Wilbur Opera Company added it to its repertory.
On and off for the next several years it appeared on

the company's programs at various combination houses in the city.

On Thursday, 29 November, the *Herald* sadly acknowledged, "This is the last week of the Old San Francisco Minstrels." Two nights later, 1 December 1883, minstrelsy disappeared forever as a permanent part of the New York theatre scene. But permanent companies remained elsewhere, in Philadelphia, for example. And New York would still have seasonal visits from a number of traveling companies. In fact some of the defunct troupe's performers could be seen at the People's, a combination house, on 17 December, when Haverly's American-European Consolidated Spectacular Mastodon Minstrels arrived for a week's stand.

The last of 1883's openings was **Three of a Kind** (31 December 1883, Third Ave.). The three are dry-goods clerks on a spree at a country boardinghouse. One finds romance. Nellie McHenry as Dolly Dashwood and Nate Salsbury as Jack Potts led the antics. Although the once voguish Salsbury's Troubadours was fast fading, this farce-comedy brought in profits for several more seasons.

At other combination houses, including Haverly's own in Brooklyn, J. K. Emmet could be heard in January and February of 1884 offering still another variation of his beloved Fritz stories, **Fritz, the Bohemian.** This new edition was written for Emmet by the drama critic of the Buffalo *Courier*, Thomas Kean. Kean borrowed a bit from Rip Van Winkle by having his Fritz fall into a long, deep sleep. However, this new Fritz awakens from his sleep to learn he is a prince. Emmet once more featured his dog, Rector, although Rector's value had become suddenly inflated to $4,000 and he was billed as "the largest in the world."

The prestigious Star, which had played host during the season to Henry Irving, Ellen Terry, Edwin Booth, and Helena Modjeska, among others, turned its facilities over to **Wanted, a Partner** (28 January 1884, Star). The farce-comedy centered on a theatrical agent seeking an associate to help him mount a show. In the mélange of song, dance, and other vaudeville turns, names provided some of the humor. The agent was known as Hix (Harry Bloodgood), and a rich, stage-struck investor was named after four leading New York stores or store owners, Macy Simpson Crawford Altman (R. E. Graham). Graham's big moment came when he did his version of Irving's Hamlet.

The Casino revived Strauss's *The Merry War* for a two-month run, and the Fifth Avenue presented the American premiere of **Princess Ida** a week later on 11 February. The only Gilbert and Sullivan work in three acts rather than two and the only one with a libretto entirely in blank verse, this tale of a women's seminary bent on forever keeping its doors closed to men was performed by some of the era's most skillful players. J. H. Ryley was King Gama; Cora S. Tanner, Ida; Wallace Macreery Hilarion; W. S. Rising, Cyril; Charles F. Lang, Florian; Signor Brocolini, King Hildebrand; and Genevieve Reynolds was Lady Blanche. In keeping with the common, fashionable practice of the day, an Englishman—in this instance Frank Thornton—was brought over from London's West End to stage the production. The new effort failed to recapture the appeal of some of its predecessors, achieving a modest six-week run.

In Boston, J. Preston Sweet's **Uncle Sam** (12 February 1884, Academy of Music) used lots of local color to little avail. Uncle Sam is an itinerant peddler who comes to Sleepy Hollow, Vermont, in time for a boat race. One of the rowers is David, who is enamored of Mabel, daughter of the quack Dr. Gaul, a "measles-maniac." But that does not stop David from rescuing his distressed rival. Of course, he wins Mabel's hand. A comic graveyard scene had college boys garbed as skeletons. Despite no real success in Boston, the musical took to the road, disbanding in Manchester, New Hampshire, shortly after its leading man was arrested for nonpayment of his hotel bill.

Occasionally a New York combination house would find time to book one of the oddball enterprises that touring impresarios threw together for the less demanding hinterlands. On 13 February the Cosmopolitan announced **On the Yellowstone,** a musical concoction with the rather uninviting subtitle *Realistic Scenes of the President's Trip to the National Park.* This vaudeville-cum-travelogue promised music by Operti and featured the once glamorous Pauline Markham, at this point near the end of her career. It ran a week and a half and then, apparently, toured.

March brought in a lone musical entry, a revival of Offenbach's *La Vie Parisienne,* which lasted fifty performances. In its cast was Richard Mansfield, soon to be a giant of serious dramatic acting, but then still a minor singer. In the pit conducting was Gustave Kerker, also soon to have a prominent career.

Ned Harrigan had a new story ready on 7 April, one he wryly called **Dan's Tribulations.** Did he mean to imply Dan's tribulations emanated from Cordelia's aspirations? Certainly it is Cordelia who is responsible for Dan's problems in both plays. The Mulligans have moved back downtown. Dan (Harrigan) has a grocery store, and Cordelia (Annie Yeamans), ever determined to be the lady, runs a "Frinch" academy. To avoid a foreclosure Cordelia sells the Mulligans' property to Mrs. Lochmuller (Jennie Christie) for one dollar. Almost at once Cordelia and her sometime friend have a falling-out, and for a time it seems the Mulligans will be evicted anyway. With help from their son, Tommy (Hart), matters are righted by the final curtain. In a subplot, Rebecca's husband dies, and Rebecca (also played by Hart) sells his corpse to a medical school. She decides to have the funeral at night because it is cheaper and because her cronies may not notice the absence of the corpse. However, she concludes that a corpse is necessary, so she persuades Simpson Primrose (John Wild) to act the part of the body. Since he is hiding from the police he grabs the opportunity. In the show's most hilarious scene, he also grabs the wallets of the mourners as they pass the bier. Although Hart played two wildly different roles, Harrigan spared him frantic costume changes. Rebecca appeared only in the first two acts; Tommy (weighted down with gold on his return from the West), only in the third. Another pleasing David Braham score, with songs such as "My Little Side Door," "Coming Home From Meeting," and "Cobwebs On The Wall," helped *Dan's Tribulations* run to the season's end.

H. B. Farnie, whose adaptation of *La Vie Parisienne* was still running at the Bijou, had a second translation unveiled on 14 April at the Casino. His version of Francis Chassaigne's **Falka** proved an even greater delight. It ran well into the summer, recording over 100 showings. The musical's complicated plot basically told how a girl disguises herself as her brother so that she can be abducted in his stead. Bertha Ricci, Mathilde Cottrelly, and Frank Tannehill, Jr., headed the cast.

Saratoga was the setting for **Skipped by the Light of the Moon** (14 April 1884, Fifth Ave.), apparently one of the era's best farce-comedies. The genre's rapid maturing and growing self-confidence were demonstrated by the skill and dash with which two admittedly slight situations were commingled to good effect. The principal story line concerned Felix Crackle (Louis Harrison) and Obadiah Dingle (John Gourlay), two married salesmen who decide to go to Saratoga to play it free and loose. Their wives, thinking the men are at a meeting in Connecticut, elect to use the time for a little vacation at—guess

where. The second story line concerned a pair of lovers whose parents object to their marrying. A well-meaning policeman added further comic complications.

Another send-up of contemporary theatre—this time spotlighting a decrepit touring company—was the frame on which musical numbers were hung in Graver's **The Great Scheme; or, The Dime Museum** (16 April 1884, Comedy). It was also another of those borderline cases between pure farce and farce-comedy.

Although Johann Strauss's **A Night in Venice** had been a fiasco at its Berlin premiere the preceding fall, this did not hinder its American chances. That it failed in New York, too, when it opened at Daly's on 19 April was more the result of a mediocre production than of any overriding weakness in its libretto or score. What its producer, James C. Duff, hoped would be a summer-long run terminated instead on 24 May.

A Chicago show had a much shorter run, but nevertheless was quite interesting. The action of **The Missing Link** (22 April 1884, Central Music Hall) began on a comet, "with the earth and moon in the azure distance." John Quill, a reporter from Earth, arrives, and the rest of the musical, set first in a grotto with mountains in the background, then on a tropical lawn (on a comet in space?), concerns his dealings with the coqettish Coquetina and her chorus line of girlfriends, various professors, some unhappy lovers, and the Missing Link itself (reviews didn't specify its nature). Critics bewailed the disjointed hodgepodge and the often too delicate music (such as a minuet). What the show's future might have been is moot, since, according to a trade sheet, the producer ran off with all cash on hand after the second performance.

The busy Farnie had a third adaptation ready on 6 May when his version of Offenbach's *Blue Beard* came before the footlights at the Bijou. With Jacques Kruger in the title role, it ran six weeks.

Some understanding of how sound the theatrical economics of the period were can be gathered from Broadway's willingness to mount a musical that had been a disastrous failure at its first showing. Another suggestion of this same fiscal security was offered by **Madam Piper** (12 May 1884, Wallack's). Madam Piper (Elma Delaro) is the old woman who lived in a shoe. Her husband turns out to be King Cole (John Howson). In his visits to her he discreetly disguise; himself as a miller. The king finally acknowledge; his paternity and moves his family to the palace. But neither he nor Madam Piper will permit their children to marry mates of their own choice. The youngsters take up arms to win their way. Two better-known figures of the lyric stage of the day created the work—librettist J. Cheever Goodwin and composer Woolson Morse. Their names on the playbill failed to prevent a cool reception. Shortly after the opening the *Dramatic Mirror* reported, "The Management are forcing a run for the purpose of securing prestige for the road." In his autobiography De Wolf Hopper reflected that this was a common practice of the period: "The Broadway engagement frequently was played at a loss, but what of it? Six months' losses in New York could be retrieved usually in three months on the road." *Madam Piper* ran no six months but merely five weeks; nor is there a record of how profitable its subsequent road tour was. Still, losses were the exception rather than the norm in those halcyon days.

On 19 May hefty George K. Fortesque bounced into the Fifth Avenue with a burlesque of Sardou's *Fedora*, appropriately rechristened **Well-Fed Dora**. Of course, Fortesque waddled about as Dora Roamin' Off while Hetty Tracy donned trousers to play the hero. A grab bag of songs gave the piece the texture of a farce-comedy.

Captain Mishler (26 May 1884, Comedy), another borderline musical, furthered the adventures of a clowning New York policeman as impersonated by the "Dutch" dialect vaudeville comedian Gus Williams. Two other vaudevillians, Barry and Fay, who, like Williams, jumped regularly from variety to farce to primitive musical comedy, came badly a cropper in a one-week failure with the unattractive title of **97 or 79** (2 June 1884, Third Ave.). Barry was Patrick Flynn, a member of a veterans' group which hires out its retired soldiers as messengers. Flynn is messenger #97, who is asked by Dr. Pizarro McGuire (Fay) to deliver a new watch to Mrs. McGuire and a new "washing machine" he has invented to the McGuires' laundress. Naturally Flynn gives each woman the other's item. With an irate wife hounding him, McGuire swears out a warrant for Flynn's arrest, but mistakenly lists his number as #79.

The season's final novelty was a more extended burlesque that winked at the Tom and Jerry (tour of the city) tradition and the *Black Crook's* tradition of spectacle as well. **Penny Ante; or, The Last of the Fairies** (9 June 1884, 14th St.) had book and lyrics by Jeff S. Leerburger and music by Fred J. Eustis. In Leerburger's tale a group of New Yorkers are arrested in a melee over prices at a dry-goods store. They are taken to the Tombs and from there to a fairy grotto.

The title role of Penny Ante was played in expected burlesque tradition by Charles H. Drew in drag. *Penny Ante* folded unexpectedly after two weeks and disappeared from history.

Gustave Kerker, the Bijou's conductor, in conjunction with John Donnelly, offered a repertory of opéra bouffe and light opera at the house for a month beginning 21 July. Their program included *The Chimes of Normandy, The Bohemian Girl, Fra Diavolo*, and *Maritana*. Kerker was quickly expanding his horizons and making a name for himself.

Variety continued on its prosperous path all season long, but the ever-restless Tony Pastor insisted on experimenting. Often during the year his variety bills played second fiddle momentarily to extended playlets with music: for example, *The Dude* for two weeks commencing 5 November; *Two Gay Benedicts*, which succeeded on 19 November; *Have You Seen Lilly?* on 29 November; and *The Mother Goose Party*, in time for the Christmas trade on 24 December. But most important of all, from 14 April to 3 May, Pastor's boards held a new play, *A Rag Baby*, by Charles H. Hoyt. Hoyt's first successful work, *A Bunch of Keys*, had burst on New York the preceding year, with Willie Edouin, Alice Atherton, James T. Powers, and Julian Mitchell in the cast. *A Rag Baby* featured another future star of the musical stage, Frank Daniels. Both works were straight plays, and their surviving texts give no indication of any singing. But Hoyt had apprenticed with Edouin in his first farce-comedy days, and reviews suggest that songs were indeed interpolated into both plays at the whim of the producers or the stars.

One interesting sidelight of the season was the visit of the great English favorites Henry Irving and Ellen Terry. Though their repertory was comprised wholly of straight plays, they packed houses while asking a $3.00 top. Thirty years had to pass before any Broadway musical dared charge so much.

1884–1885

Once again the season witnessed a slight slackening of musical activity. It also watched in horror as another of the epoch's endemic theatre fires destroyed the Comique. As there had been with earlier holocausts, there may have been a connection between a general drop in attendance after the fire and a falling off of production. And once more three-quarters of the entries must be classified as importations or revivals—or both. But a bright side was evident, too. In *Adonis* the season boasted one of the runaway successes of the American Musical Theatre. Moreover, historians reviewing the year may come away with a feeling that there was less slapdash in the original offerings. Americans were increasingly able to offer their countrymen evening-long musicals with plots sufficiently developed to maintain interest, and scores written with the story or, at least, the performers in mind.

Determined to keep its stage occupied for as full a year as possible, the Casino began the season with a midsummer revival of *The Little Duke* on 4 August. Its hopes were realized, and *The Little Duke* played merrily on until the beginning of October. The musical's military milieu allowed the producers to insert an Amazon march. Oddly, in this French piece sung in English, they awarded the title role to one Fraulein Januschowsky, who had been a favorite at New York's German-language theatres and who sang with a thick German accent.

Competing versions of **Sieba and the Seven Ravens** vied for first-nighters' attention on 18 August. Loose copyright laws allowed the Kiralfys to mount their version at the Star, while the Kiralfys' former home, Niblo's, brought forth its own. Based on a Hans Christian Andersen tale, both versions were translations of a dramatization popular all over Europe. Somehow the Kiralfys permitted Niblo's to outshine them. Niblo's troupe and scenery were purported to be from Vienna. (More German accents!) The house claimed to fill its stage with a chorus of 600 and a field of 110,000 perfumed roses! Perhaps theatregoers' eagerness to see how close the theatre could come to its patent exaggerations gained Niblo's a three-month run compared with the Kiralfys' two-month stay at the Star. But the Kiralfy version was published, and two quotations from the text forcefully bring to life the textures of both the work and its genre. The first reveals the basic plot; the second illustrates something of the period's staging:

> Her name was Sieba. Her mother, in a rage,
> Had cursed her seven young and gentle brothers.
> This curse gave me full power over them—
> And I transformed the seven pretty lads
> Into as many black and croaking ravens.
> The mother died of dire remorse and horror,
> While little Sieba ran after the poor birds,
> Wringing her hands in piteous lamentation,
> When night closed in, she dropped from sheer exhaustion,
> And in a lonely forest 'twas I found her.
> I gave her back her strength, and then she told me

> In trembling accents all about her woes.
> I bid her hope and pointed out a way
> To break the charm and to set free her brothers.
> I made her promise that for seven years
> She should not utter word of mouth or speech,
> And, furthermore, that she, within that time,
> Should spin and weave, in silence, seven garments,
> All in the seven colors of the rainbows,
> And of a size to clothe her seven brothers.
> If this task she accomplished, I agreed
> That she and all her brothers should be happy.

FINALE

Ruperta: Put torches to the pyre.

(*Harold sinks down in his chains.*)

The faggots are lighted. It has grown dark. The torches shed an uncertain light upon the scene.

Then are heard eight successive and very distinct strokes of a bell, accompanied by orchestra.

Sieba: (*listens intently to the strokes, then gives a shout of joy with the last stroke.*) Harold, husband! Save me!

Flourish: *Loud thunder.*

Music full and forte.

The walls sink.

At back is seen a beautiful wood (after Schwind.)

The fetters fall from Harold. His stake sinks out of sight.

He rushes to Sieba and embraces her feet. The flames go out by themselves.

Around the pyre, on ascending ground, are grouped Sieba's seven brothers in garments of the seven colors of the rainbow, mounted on splendid chargers, their swords raised as if to protect Sieba.

L. of Sieba Puck appears in splendid fairy costume with Rosalind's children in her arms.

Above this, Savanta floats as if in a cloud. In front, all kneel.

The torches are extinguished, giving place to the red light of the setting sun.

Note.—As a matter of course, the main effect depends upon quickness in producing the above.

Ruperta kneels and takes her coronet from her head, as if offering it to Savanta.

(*Music pianissimo.*)

Rosalind: (*to soft music.*) My own beloved Arthur, come to me that I may weep with joy upon your bust. (*Arthur mounts the pyre, kneels and encircles her waist.*) You, and my children, and my brothers all!

To perfect joy has turned our distress,

And nothing e'er shall cloud our happiness.
(*Music forte.*)

TRANSFORMATION

*The scene changes to a fairy paradise of gorgeous
    beauty and splendor.*
*The pyre changes to a throne, on which Ros. and
    Arthur stand in ecstatic embrace.*
*Rosalind's dress transforms into a white robe, adorned
    with jewels and flowers. A coronet sinks down upon
    her head.*
The back scene rises.
*The Fairy queen is seen in the far perspective,
    enthroned and surrounded by her court. At L. of
    her is Savanta, at whose feet, Rough crouches in
    submission. At R. Pigwidgeon with the children.*
Magic light on all.
*The persons in front have remained kneeling.
During this:*

CHORUS

Hail to the faithful
Who, for her brother
Lovingly suffered!
Sing her all hail!

Harrigan, Hart, and Braham had a new work ready
on 1 September. The Mulligans were given a rest, but
the characters that filled **Investigation** were virtually
next of kin. Bernard McKenna (Hart), a glue manufacturer with a penchant for politics, and D'Arcy
Flynn (Harrigan) seek the hand of a rich widow, Mrs.
Belinda Tuggs (Annie Yeamans). D'Arcy wins. The
broad panorama that almost any Harrigan story covered permitted the insertion of seemingly outlandish
scenes. The most famous bit in the show came when
D'Arcy and Belinda found themselves having to portray Romeo and Juliet. The vain Belinda, recalling the
English triumph of the preceding season, thinks nothing of interrupting Shakespeare's verse to ask, "Do I
look like Miss Terry?" But neither Terry nor Irving
ever suffered with a recalcitrant spotlight that refused
to do proper honor to either Flynn or Tuggs. There
is, by the way, an Elizabethan richness to the names
of many characters that fill the invariably lengthy
personae of a Harrigan play. *Investigation* included
Orion Overhoe, Oscar Onderdonk, Rev. Jonah
Woolgather, Adelaide Foglip, Alexis Canfruit, and
Gaspard Pitkins. Some critics discerned a lessening

of melodic invention in David Braham's songs. None
entered Braham's canon, although or opening night
"every piece of music had to be played three or four
times." What critics could not see was that *Investigation*
marked the beginning of the end for Harrigan, Hart,
and Braham. The play closed when its sets and
costumes were destroyed along with the Theatre
Comique two nights before Christmas. Hart's syphi-
lis-spawned problems were coming to the fore. This,
coupled with apparent recriminations over the origin
of the fire, led to a coolness between Broadway's most
celebrated pair and by the end of the season led to a
permanent split. Harrigan-Hart's opening coincided
with Jacques Kruger's return in a revival of *Dreams*
(30 August 1880) at Tony Pastor's.

Adonis opened at the Bijou on 4 September
1884. Slated by the theatre's management for a
three-month run, it succeeded beyond everyone's
expectations. When it closed on 17 April 1886,
it had compiled a record of 603 showings, far and
away the longest run in Broadway history up to that
time. The show was the work of some of the most
renowned names of the time. Written and produced
by E. E. Rice and William Gill, it catapulted Henry
E. Dixey to fame and fortune.

Dixey also accepted credit for collaboration
on the book, although most of his contribution
seems to have come from his expanding his own
part. The play's action starts when the sculptress
Talmea (Lillie Grubb) persuades the goddess Artea
(Louise V. Essing) to bring to life the statue of
Adonis (Dixey). (He comes to life first with merely
a sly wink, then with a dance on his pedestal.) Both
Talmea and her patroness, the Duchess (Jennie
Reiffarth), fall in love with the young man. So does
every girl who sees him. (Ladies in the audience also
succumbed, especially when Dixey pranced about
fetchingly in tights—a turn-about on the coryphées
and prima donnas of the day.) But he has eyes only
for a simple, if extravagantly buxom, country girl,
Rosetta (Amelia Summerville). Rosetta passes her
time "eating huckleberries all day long, and learning how to love." For all her learning she is a little
overwhelmed by Adonis' overtures, although she is
by no means at a loss for words. She replies to his
fluent advances, "I see that you can be as elegantly
phraseological as you are physically majestic, and
we rustics are unused to such bewildering conjunc-
tions!" Unfortunately, Adonis cannot escape from
his horde of pursuers, even though he resorts to
one clever disguise after another. When he realizes

the hopelessness of living the life of his choice, he returns to stone.

The disguises that Adonis assumed let him roam broadly in the burlesque tradition. Most famous of all was Dixey's spoof of Henry Irving. This bit of foolery was not confined to one brief moment but employed at length. For example, at one point, still dressed like Irving's Hamlet, Dixey played the part of an unscrupulous milkman, pumping water into his milk cans, and "in Irving's manner" informing audiences, "They tell me in the village that I sell bad milk! It may be bad water, but it can't be bad milk." Some of the burlesque may have been less broad, suggesting how close-knit was the community of theatre folk and theatregoers in the eighties. In one instance, for example, chorus girls entered four at a time, each foursome dressed in apparently familiar costumes used by chorus girls of other musicals. One reviewer was able to recognize dresses that had adorned girls in *The Merry War, Orpheus and Eurydice, The Queen's Lace Handkerchief,* and *Olivette*. Of the songs, two now forgotten numbers enjoyed wide and instant appeal: "The Susceptible Statue" and "It's English, You Know." The latter, added after the show opened and sung by Dixey while still in his Irving makeup, noted:

O the queer things we say, and the queer things we do
Are English, you know, quite English, you know.

Following the practically inevitable custom of the time, periodic changes were made in the show during its run. But Dixey remained a stalwart feature for the length of the run as well as in subsequent revivals. Her playing of Rosetta consolidated Amelia Summerville's fortunes.

Four nights later came an English burlesque, **The Corsican Brothers & Co.; or, What London Laughs At** (8 September 1884, Park), which one newspaper dismissed as "a cataclysm of weird, unearthly puns, music hall songs ... and dancing of a dark and dismal school." Even the chorus beauties, the critic complained, were not all that beautiful.

Wallack's Theatre inaugurated its season with a five-week visit by Maurice Grau's opéra bouffe ensemble, this time starring Madam Theo. When the stay was terminated, they moved for an additional week to the Bijou. Later in the season Gustave Kerker also offered a brief repertory of opéra bouffe. However, as Odell observed in his theatre history, "This form of entertainment, so popular for nearly twenty years in New York, was entering on its last stages here; Gilbert and Sullivan and Strauss and Millöcker sang the temporary eclipse of Offenbach and Lecocq and Audran." Excepting that Audran and Lecocq seem to have been permanently eclipsed in this country, the statement is just.

Revivals of both schools followed in quick order. Millöcker's *The Beggar Student* commenced a month's run at the Casino on 6 October, while Offenbach's *Orpheus and Eurydice* played a one-week fill-in at the Fifth Avenue.

Soon after Grau's troupe became ensconced in New York, Boston witnessed the premiere of the new musical spectacle **Zanita** (16 September 1884, Boston). A pastiche, whose story recounted the rivalry of a good and a bad prince for a lovely princess, it employed rhymed dialogue and music drawn from various sources. Its lavish sets and costumes and its dancing were prime attractions.

Just before *The Beggar Student* settled in, **A Parlor Match** opened a two-week visit on 22 September at Tony Pastor's. With it the short reign of the second-generation farce-comedies can be said to begin. The difference, as so often happens, was one of degree, not kind. This second generation was largely the work of Charles H. Hoyt, who was far and away the best writer of claptrap farces at the end of the century. Until *A Trip to Chinatown* (9 November 1891), songs in his plays were taken from any available source, much as the early farce-comedies had done. But Hoyt was a sturdier playwright than his predecessors. His plays, like Harrigan's later writings, were conceived as full-length works. However, Hoyt was more careful and compact, usually requiring only one set per act instead of the kaleidoscope of scenes Harrigan employed. (Of course, this may have been an inheritance from the simple settings of earlier farce-comedy.) Moreover, Hoyt eschewed ethnic material, preferring to write about native Americans familiar to most theatregoers around the country.

In his latest play Hoyt dealt with a tramp who blithely walks in and out of a house stealing merchandise, with the busy family oblivious to his presence. When he fears detection he hides in a drawer. A somewhat inebriated member of the household discovers him there. But the tramp escapes because the drunk hysterically concludes he is having delirium tremens. In the last act a spiritualist is called in to set things right. The show, featuring the team of Charles Evans and William Hoey, played a one-week return stand in April. With other casts and frequently heavily rewritten, the show toured for more than a decade, sometimes employing variant titles such as *A New Parlor Match* or *A Parlor Match up to Date*.

Time and again during these seasons Tony Pastor's stage was occupied with what may have been more primitive musical comedies. They carried such titles as *Celibacy* (6 October 1884), *Funny Valentine* (13 July 1885), *Scheming* (20 July 1885), and *The Missing Link* (6 September 1886). Most papers failed to review them or else gave them very short shrift. Even the newspapers that did often extend longer reviews, notably the *Herald,* leave an equivocal impression. These shows deserve fuller study since most likely they did, in fact, play a part in establishing patterns for future musical comedies.

On 8 November the Casino replaced *The Beggar Student* with a new work, Planquette's **Nell Gywnn,** offering Mathilde Cottrelly in the title role. But Americans did not take to this Frenchman's interpretation of an English figure. The show was a quick failure.

The Hanlons' **Fantasma; or, Funny Frolics in Fairyland** (10 November 1884, Fifth Ave.) was a "spectacular pantomime" which retained its hold on young and aging playgoers for the rest of the century. Good fairies and evil imps struggle for the possession of two youthful lovers, a contest fought in such places as a magical palace and the forbidding Arctic. In the end the principals are transformed into Columbine, Harlequin, and Clown.

A bevy of tangible English beauties, supplemented by some American ones, closed out November at the Comedy Theatre with **An Adamless Eden.** Even the orchestra players were women. Music ran from Arditi's "L'Estasi" to songs from *The Beggar Student.*

If Lilly Clay and her troupe (including Pauline Hall and Topsy Venn) hoped to repeat the stir Lydia Thompson had created in the sixties, they were disappointed. After a month's run and a modest tour many of the girls returned to England.

December proved happier. When Aimée arrived in George Jessop and William Gill's **Mam'zelle** (15 December 1884, Fifth Ave.), its plot foreshadowed the Cinderella yarns that would dominate American musical comedy thirty-five years later. Toinette Jacotot is a milliner who dreams of being a famous singer. Over objections by his prissy family, she wheedles T. Tarleton Tupper (J. O. Barrows) into wangling an audition for her at the American Café Chantant. Before long she is a star and has changed her name to Fleur de Lys. Songs ranged from excerpts from opéra bouffe to risqué Spanish and French ditties. One amusing if old-hat device had her numbers interrupted by objectors: Mrs. Tupper (Laura Wallace) from her seat in a box and Toinette's fiancé, Bob Pritchard (Frank E. Lamb), from a seat in the orchestra. Both have to be removed by ushers. The show drew good audiences, ran two weeks, toured, and returned in a couple of seasons.

A revival of *Prince Methusalem* bowed at the Casino on the 15th, while eight nights afterwards the rebuilt Standard opened its doors with von Suppé's **A Trip to Africa.** In a complicated plot Titania finds love with Antaxid while on a Nile journey. Another indication of how small and familiar the theatre was is evident from the fact that the producer of the piece, James C. Duff, was Augustin Daly's brother-in-law. Despite a lack of "names" in the cast, Duff's production enjoyed moderate business; it closed 21 February.

The old school of farce-comedy was represented by **We, Us and Co. at Mud Springs** (23 December 1884, Star). Just hours after the smoking ruins of the Comique signaled a turn in Harrigan and Hart's fortunes, William A. Mestayer and Charles Bernard presented their example of another vanishing form. They also demonstrated how complex the staging if not the plotting had grown. A party of hypochondriacs comes to Mud Springs under the care of a quack physician. Their hotel is unusual, to say the least. It is constructed atop a railroad turntable to allow all rooms some exposure to the sun. Its revolutions lead to a series of confused guests, who seem invariably to enter the wrong room at the wrong time. Many of these comings and goings are prompted by all the men patients' infatuation with the same young lady. Although Mestayer's initial visit was brief, lasting less than a month, the piece provided him and his entourage with employment for several years.

The new year was ushered in by the latest Harrigan and Braham work, **McAllister's Legacy.** By a stroke of luck, sets and costumes for the play, which was being rehearsed at the Comique when the house burned, had not yet been delivered to the theatre. Harrigan and Hart hastily booked a seeming white elephant, the Park Theatre, and opened there on 5 January 1885. Critical reception was restrained. It was as if the private tensions developing between Harrigan and Hart were evidenced in the quality of their material. But if professional aisle-sitters were reserved, Harrigan and Hart's loyal public was not. In an almost column-long notice, quoted earlier in discussing *The Mulligan Guards' Surprise* (16 February 1880), the *Times* devoted extensive space to describing the give-and-take between the performers and their steadfast patrons. *McAllister's Legacy* told a simple tale, although it was filled with the multiple scenes and song-inducing complications dear to all Harrigan creations. An old man dies and leaves some tenement property to two relatives. One is a veterinary surgeon, Dr. McAllister (Ned Harrigan). The other is rambunctious Mollie McGouldrich (Tony Hart). Mollie feels she has been given the lesser share and sets about unleashing complications. McGouldrich undoubtedly was a slight slap at the financier Jay Gould, although some programs spelled it McGoldrick. As Eddie Foy wrote in his autobiography, many Irish of the time felt Fisk was their friend and harbored grave suspicions about Gould. The name Mollie allowed Harrigan and Braham to write one of the innumerable songs of the day celebrating the name. But neither the play nor its songs caught on. Harrigan and Hart moved the work to what they hoped would be a more desirable house, the old 14th Street Theatre. The transfer failed to help business, and the show was withdrawn on 14 March.

In order not to compete with a Harrigan and Hart opening, E. E. Rice delayed the first night of **A Bottle of Ink** at the Comedy until the following evening, 6 January. Written by George H. Jessop and William Gill, the play was one of the last of the old-style farce-comedies to brave New York. Their day was over, and *A Bottle of Ink* suffered as well from being an inferior example of the genre. Jefferson Jingo (John A. Mackay) is a Wild West newspaper man, as wild as the West he covers. A number of irate figures confront him, and each confrontation invariably leads to a specialty number. One angry young man who confronts Jingo is Hermann Zwugg—played by an actor listed on the program as Jeff De Angelis. Tiny Ida Mulle sang songs from *Princess Ida*, and Maud Beverly belted out a medley of cockney music-hall ditties. Dismissed by the *Times* as a rehash of *Pop* (21 May 1883), it lingered less than a month. Despite the tremendous success of *Adonis*, Rice, like Harrigan and Hart, was approaching the end of his heyday.

January's third and final musical, a revival of Millöcker's *A pajune* (25 February 1882) on the 16th, produced by John McCaull, entertained the Casino's growing band of loyalists for two months. W. S. Rising, Mathilde Cottrelly, Francis Wilson, and Belle Archer headed the cast.

A pudgy, rubber-faced dwarf, George Bruening, stole the show in **The Kindergarten** (2 February 1885, Third Ave.), another simple-minded farce-comedy, in this instance expanded from an earlier sketch at Tony Pastor's. Obviously not all critics condemned the genre out of hand, for this one was written by Robert Griffin Morris, himself a drama critic, who had tried his skill at serious drama and would soon provide Nat Goodwin with *The Skating Rink* (23 November 1885). The show's billing confirmed how uncertain contemporary pigeonholing was. Programs called the piece a "musical farce-comedy," while some advertisements called it simply "musical comedy." Yet the idea of "musicals" still had not taken hold fully. More than one borderline or prototypical musical of the period still was reviewed as simply farce, comedy, or even drama, with only a passing acknowledgment of its musical numbers. To some extent the mediocrity of most period theatre music may have contributed to this imbalance. Certainly none of the music in *The Kindergarden* was any great shakes, and an awareness of this may have prompted subsequent advertisements to promote the show as "the funniest, most elegantly costumed and brightest combination of music, wit, action, mimicry and general attractiveness offered to the public." Until the appearance of major composers, laughs and spectacle had to predominate. Neither Bruening nor some better-known variety performers cast in supposedly more important roles stayed with the piece for long, but even with numerous cast changes the show trekked around the circuits for many seasons.

Gasparone at the Standard was February's sole major revival. The next lyrical first night occurred on 9 March when the Boston Ideal Opera Company returned after a season's absence. Included in their repertory were *Fatinitza, H. M. S. Pinafore, The*

Bohemian Girl, The Musketeers, Fra Diavolo, and *Giroflé-Girofla*—all in a brief two-week visit at the Fifth Avenue.

Monday, 16 March, presented competing first nights. The Casino put on New York's first English-speaking **Die Fledermaus,** with the rising De Wolf Hopper cast as Franke. Mark Smith played Eisenstein; Irene Perry, Prince Orlofsky; Rosalba Beecher, Rosalind; and Mathilde Cottrelly, Adele. Fine as this cast was, it could not make *Die Fledermaus* a rousing hit. Until after the turn of the century, this greatest of all Strauss operettas inexplicably failed to dazzle audiences in the same way now forgotten Strauss works did. To make employment for their company after the disappointment of *McAllister's Legacy,* Harrigan and Hart returned *The Major* (28 August 1881) to the boards.

The confusion about the right name for many of the new-style concoctions (as well as about their probable source) was also brought home by the opening of the *Times*'s review of **Over the Garden Wall** (23 March 1885, Fifth Ave.): "The evolution from sketches which used to be popular on the 'variety' stage of a style of entertainment generally termed by managers 'farcical comedy,' but having a closer relation to the vaudeville of the French stage than to English farce, and none at all to comedy, has been a curious feature of recent theatrical history." George S. Knight headed the cast as the not-altogether-sane Julius Snitz, R. E. Graham played his son, Julius, Jr., and Knight found occasion for one more of his travesties of Henry Irving. Plump George W. Monroe won laughs as a stupid Irish serving girl, Our Own Bridget. Not all the comedy found its intended mark. The *Times* also reported that some jokes about death, funerals, and religion were hissed.

Another revival of *H. M. S. Pinafore* docked at the Standard on 4 April. Sung by the same troupe that had presented *Gasparone,* it played merrily for two weeks. Two nights after the Standard opening, the Thatcher, Primrose, and West Minstrels came in for a brief stay at the Fifth Avenue.

A domestically made "comic opera," **Twins,** replaced Gilbert and Sullivan at the Standard on 20 April. It starred John A. Mackay, long the leading comedian in Rice's farce-comedies. Mackay played both the pious churchman, Dr. Titus Spinach, and his impious brother, Timothy, whose misbehavior constantly embarrasses the clergyman. Filled with tunes gathered from diverse sources, it was more a farce-comedy of the sort Mackay was known for

than the "comic opera" it claimed to be. On its opening night it competed with the second Harrigan, Hart, and Braham revival of the year, *Cordelia's Aspirations* (5 November 1883). The three-week run marked the last time Harrigan and Hart ever performed together on Broadway. They played out a short commitment in Brooklyn in June, then went their separate ways.

A happier opening took place on the next Monday, 27 April. At the Casino E. E. Rice brought in his Gaiety Opera Company with Lillian Russell as star and J. H. Ryley as its droll patter-song comedian. The vehicle was a new comic opera by Miss Russell's English husband, Edward Solomon, **Polly; or, The Pet of the Regiment.** Taking hints from both Gilbert and Sullivan and from Donizetti, its plot told how a buffoonish major general makes Polly his regiment's mascot. The show ran until 18 June. Then the same troupe closed its engagement by reviving Solomon's *Billee Taylor* for a week beginning 20 June. Miss Russell again starred.

May's first lyric offering was the month's only hit. John McCaull had split with Rudolf Aronson at the Casino. On 4 May he moved his company of players—mostly recruited from the Casino—to Wallack's, where he presented Sydney Rosenfeld's adaptation of yet another Millöcker work, *Der Feldprediger.* Retitled **The Black Hussar** for American audiences, it ran over 100 performances with Mark Smith, De Wolf Hopper, and Digby Bell as the principal comedians. The story told how a Hussar, fomenting insurrection, diverts suspicion onto a pestiferous magistrate.

Ned Harrigan, now going it alone, suffered one of the worst humiliations of his career when his **Are You Insured?** opened on 11 May at the 14th Street Theatre and folded five nights later. Actually, the play lacked not only Hart, but Harrigan himself. Had he acted in his own work, the *Herald* might not have written that the evening "gives one a higher opinion of the abilities of Hart." Harrigan's story related the problems two hustling life insurance agents, Philander Dividend (Charles Stanley) and Sarsfield Per Annum (W. H. Fitzgerald), encounter when they marry Sheriff Bouncer's roaring daughters. The critics did no more than mention the songs in passing.

Apart from Gustave Kerker's opéra bouffe troupe, the only other May arrival was J. K. Emmet, once more playing *Fritz in Ireland* (3 November 1879). The show played three weeks at an out-of-the-way house generally given over to German entertainment.

Three shows came in during June. The first two were revivals. At Niblo's the Kiralfys once more remounted *Around the World in Eighty Days* on the 1st, while *Billee Taylor* returned, as mentioned earlier, for a week. By this date revivals of *Around the World* (28 August 1875) were customarily passed over with the briefest reviews. In a one-paragraph assessment, the *Times* assured the faithful they would still find the evening replete with "bright scenery, glittering costumes, and whirling phalanxes of more or less shapely coryphées." The month's lone novelty, however, proved a resounding hit. The Zell–Genée operetta **Nanon** was produced at the Casino with Sadie Martinot, Pauline Hall, and W. T. Carleton in the leading roles in a tale of two ladies, Nanon and Ninon, in love with the same marquis. It ran from 29 June to 14 November, suggesting that the Casino had more than won the battle to keep its stage lit throughout the year.

SYDNEY ROSENFELD was long a colorful, controversial figure on the American theatrical scene. Born in Richmond, Virginia, on 26 October 1855 (or 1856), son of a prosperous merchant, he claimed to have run a Civil War blockade so that he could attend private school in New York. At fifteen he began supplying short stories to boys' magazines, and by 1874 his first play, a burlesque of *Rose Michel*, saw the footlights. Thereafter he kept busy as author, translator, producer, or director. While pursuing his various theatrical activities he still found time to write for the *Sun* and the *World* and, eventually, to become the first editor of *Puck*.

The season ended in a curious mixture of triumph and ignominy. Hoping to be the first with the best, Sydney Rosenfeld rushed in a presentation of Gilbert and Sullivan's **The Mikado** on 20 July 1885. His glee at beating out his rivals was short-lived, however. An injunction was obtained, Rosenfeld was jailed for unauthorized production, and his production disappeared after its initial showing at Union Square.

All through the season variety continued to flourish, even though many houses followed Tony Pastor in occasionally breaking their parade of vaudeville bills by introducing longer pieces. For example, on its 16 August program Koster and Bial's offered a short operetta, *Love in ye Days of Charles ye Second*. Meanwhile Hyde and Behman's became a refuge for many old minstrels, although its confused bills were anything but pure minstrelsy.

1885–1886

Moving season by season one can almost feel how long-lived were the growing pains of the American Musical Theatre. Apart from the deluge of productions that followed in the wake of *H. M. S. Pinafore* (15 January 1879), even landmark musicals left little but the record of their own success behind. Not one of the great hits of this early period established a reigning style as did, say, *The Merry Widow* (21 October 1907) or *Oklahoma!* (31 March 1943) in later years. True, *The Black Crook* (12 September 1866), *Humpty Dumpty* (10 March 1868), and the Fritz plays offered their own sequels and encouraged a number of imitations. But neither the sequels nor the imitations approached the originals in popularity. The season of 1885–1886 continued the pattern of the preceding years—a musical roster top-heavy with revivals and importations. Two English creations, *The Mikado* and *Erminie*, dominated the season. But rumblings of nascent domestic creativity were audible, even if the rumblings were first heard miles from Broadway.

The season began in earnest with the simultaneous entry of several musicals on 17 August. Millöcker's *Die Naherin*, done as **Chatter**, opened at Wallack's. This tale of a loquacious seamstress whose gabbing throws an estate into turmoil featured a droll comic performance by De Wolf Hopper as an "elderly gentleman of gallant proclivities." Mathilde Cottrelly was praised for her superb, understated clowning in the principal role. At Niblo's, Bartley Campbell's old warhorse, *Clio*, detailing the love of a duke's daughter and an artist, appeared bedecked with lavish ballets led by Adele Cornalba and tinseled with light songs. Among its spectacular effects was a palace destroyed by an earthquake. Both shows were quick, costly failures.

Actually one show came in a week before, on Monday, 10 August. This was a mounting of *The Mikado* at the People's Theatre. It ran just a week. Curiously the house was owned by Henry Miner, and one week later Miner somehow managed to reassemble the production Rosenfeld had brought in a month before, presenting it again at the Union Square. Why Miner used two different casts and, possibly, two collections of sets and costumes remains obscure. In any case, this *Mikado*, which opened concurrently with *Chatter* and *Clio*, survived a mere fortnight. Legal threats precipitated its shuttering, but the arrival at the Fifth Avenue of D'Oyly Carte's own mounting of the Gilbert and Sullivan masterpiece two nights later on 19 August undoubtedly confronted Miner with insuperable competition. The production was an immediate triumph and compiled 250 performances before it closed on 17 April. Under Richard Barker's excellent direction, this story of a Mikado's disguised son who agrees to be beheaded if he can spend a month married to the girl he loves was capitally performed by F. Federici as the Mikado; the "vest-pocket tenor" and matinee idol Courtice Pounds as Nanki-Poo; F. Billington as Pooh-Bah; George Thorne as Ko-Ko; Geraldine Ulmar as Yum-Yum; and Elsie Cameron as Katisha. Sullivan's timeless melodies were heard in his original orchestrations, not in the "alternately thin and brassy" treatment the pirated versions had offered. Songs included Nanki-Poo's showpiece, "A Wandering Minstrel," Nanki-Poo and Ko-Ko's "The Flowers That Bloom In The Spring," and Ko-Ko's "Willow, Tit-willow." Sullivan came to this country and conducted some performances in September. But the success of the work was assured without his presence.

Although short of the records accrued by a few phenomenal successes, the run was one of the longest in the New York annals up to its time. Yet it fell far short of the more than 600 performances *The Mikado* achieved in London. Oddly, Alfred Cellier's *Dorothy*, produced almost at the same time in London, markedly exceeded even that record. Down through the decades London seems to have regularly given its greatest hits far longer support than New York gave its hits. Just how much these longer runs influenced the early flowering of the English musical and how much the shorter runs on this side of the Atlantic retarded American development will probably never be known. The American "road," while highly profitable, was far more constricted than in its heyday. (The number of touring performers and companies peaked immediately after the turn of the century, just before films first lured away significant patronage.) At this time, the road could not always fully compensate for the relatively brief New York runs, despite the De Wolf Hopper comment cited earlier. Moreover England had the "provinces" to offer against our "road."

In one sense *The Mikado* had over 250 showings. D'Oyly Carte was not monopolistic. Although he fought unauthorized productions, he allowed competition to flourish—possibly in the knowledge that no one could really compete with his own style and know-how. Five nights after his own mounting premiered, D'Oyly Carte permitted James Duff to unveil his version at the Standard. Adequate but inferior, it ran three months, after which Duff moved it to Chicago, whence Rosenfeld's illicit production had come. D'Oyly Carte even permitted a touring company to visit Niblo's in March for a month, ignoring complaints that its version was filled "with local gags and very little Gilbert." A German-language version gave forth at the Thalia. And while the superior wit, melody, and coherence of *The Mikado* undoubtedly acted as a goad to challenge aspiring young American authors, the show's most immediate and most enduring influence was probably to consolidate the vogue for musical librettos with exotic, usually pseudo-Oriental, settings. Earlier *The Sultan of Mocha* (14 September 1880) and *Revels* (25 October 1880) had hinted at possibilities of just such a fashion. Things Oriental had become so modish in Victorian circles that in London Gilbert could have Bunthorne proclaim in 1881, "I do not long for all one sees/That's Japanese."

The following Monday, 31 August—almost all openings continued to be on Monday nights—Harrigan began his solo career with a revival of *Old Lavender* (3 September 1877), his own personal favorite among his plays. Harrigan again leased the old Park, refurbishing it slightly and renaming it Harrigan's Park Theatre. The play also underwent revisions while Harrigan's father-in-law, Braham, composed a number of new songs. One of these, "Ebb And Flow," was an instant bestseller. With its improvements, *Old Lavender* ran on sturdily until the end of November.

The failure of *Chatter* prompted John McCaull to offer *Die Fledermaus* at Wallack's on 14 September, using many of the principals the Casino had employed the season before. The revival lasted two weeks. When it closed, Maurice Grau brought in a season of opéra bouffe beginning 1 October, starring Mme. Anna Judic, whom Odell in his theatre history judged "perhaps the most artistic representative of the species ever seen in this country." She, alone of the French singers who graced our boards during opéra bouffe's ascendancy, was a major star in Paris, singing the premieres of numerous productions there. Her repertory included *Mlle. Nitouche, Lili,*

La Femme à Papa, Niniche, Le Grand Casimir, and *La Mascotte*. The vogue for opéra bouffe may have been waning, but in three separate engagements scattered throughout the season the company played a total of six weeks.

The Thatcher, Primrose, and West Minstrels romped into Niblo's on 5 October. It was the first of several visits this troupe and other touring minstrels would make to Manhattan during the year. These led Odell to see "the revival, in 1885–86, of the black-face art." True, there was an unusual bustle of activity. Thatcher, Primrose, and West's ensemble alone spent a total of two months in five separate stays. But their evening consisted largely of a burlesque of *Adonis* (4 September 1884), called simply *Black Adonis*. They and the troupes that played lesser, more out-of-the-way houses all deviated noticeably from the old, traditional formula, which most audiences had tired of. If the minstrels were busy they were occupied not with preserving classic forms but with establishing acceptable new entertainments. Extended burlesques and vaudeville seemed the answer.

Evangeline (27 July 1874) returned for a stay at the 14th Street Theatre beginning 7 October. In keeping with the creative fluidity of the era, the work happily announced substantial revisions. As best as can be determined these were largely cosmetic: a few new melodies, minor new scenes and dialogue, and, of course, new sets and costumes. The slim Fay Templeton was Gabriel, and the hefty Amelia Summerville, temporarily departed from *Adonis*, played Hubert. (Interestingly, her role in *Adonis* had been assumed by George K. Fortesque, playing in drag.) James Maffitt was at his post as The Lone Fisherman. Although *Evangeline* was indisputably one of the most successful and beloved works of the era, it oddly enough never had a really long run in New York. In this respect it was much like the Fritz plays and, in a few years, *Robin Hood* (28 September 1891). Its 1885–1886 run of 252 performances marked its lengthiest stay in New York.

On 2 November the Thatcher, Primrose, and West Minstrels briefly dropped their twitting of *Adonis* to poke fun at *The Mikado* instead. In their retelling it came out *The Mick-ah-do*. Later in the year they returned to perform *The Black Mikado*, which may have been the same spoof with another name. On this January visit they also reached far back to kid *Humpty Dumpty* as *Hughey Dougherty*. The burlesque reflects the continuing popularity on the road of the old pantomime, even if New York had seen the last of it. However, a careful look at minstrel programs shows the form had degenerated into little more than variety. The bill that included *The Mick-ah-do* also regaled its patrons with the boy soprano Master Witmark (later a famous music publisher) singing "Baby's Lullaby," trained dogs, drum majors' parades, and acrobats. Variety, too, was offering spoofs of *The Mikado* on the very night the minstrels presented theirs. At Koster and Bial's the travesty listed such characters as Pity Sing Sing, Yum Yum First Ward, and High Kockey (made up to resemble General Ben Butler).

Amorita followed (16 November 1885, Casino). Its heroine would have been forced to marry the wicked usurper in Florence had not his overthrow occurred moments before the final curtain. A sense of time and place was a matter of indifference to clowns of the era, so Francis Wilson won his biggest laughs nightly with a comic game of stud poker. Madeline Lucette (in the title role), Pauline Hall, and Rose Beaudet assisted. Now utterly forgotten, the operetta enjoyed a moderate three-month run.

A week later Nat Goodwin offered New Yorkers another farce-comedy, **The Skating Rink** (23 November 1885, Standard). Perhaps nothing so well reveals the attitudes and methods of farce-comedy producers as Goodwin's memoirs:

> My idea was to ascertain if any of the company had a specialty that could be injected into this porous play. It permitted all sorts of pioneering. The plot stopped at eighty thirty!... Two or three of the young ladies interpolated some of the latest New York ditties, Fanny Rice and I cribbing the See-Saw duet. I also introduced the entire act of a play called "The Marionettes," assisted by one of the [trick] skating trio, an Irish song written by a Jew, "Since Maggie Learned To Skate," and a burlesque of "Camille." I appeared as the coughing heroine!... disappearing as the dying lady on one side of the stage to return from the opposite as die Irishman in search of his daughter, Maggie.

As if all this were not enough, Goodwin adds that he inserted a number of his famous imitations and hired a man who first swallowed and then disgorged lit cigars. Obviously Goodwin knew his audiences. The piece gave him employment on and off for several years.

The same evening Goodwin opened in New York, Adam Itzel Jr., offered a new comic opera to

Baltimore. Itzel, who became known as the local John Philip Sousa, had been orchestrating and interpolating songs into Baltimore productions for some time, and lately had been director of the Academy [of Music] Opera Company. **Jack Sheppard** (23 November 1885, Academy of Music), his first full score, had a libretto by A. K. Fulton, derived from Buckstone's well-known drama about an actual, very young eighteenth-century London criminal. However, ignoring history, Itzel and Fulton gave the story a happy ending.

Both the Kiralfys and Harrigan had new works ready on 30 November. The Kiralfys fell back on the Pied Piper story for **The Ratcatcher**, filling it as was their wont with an amalgam of spectacle, ballet, and vaudeville specialties. Starring the baritone Hubert Wilke as Singold the Piper, it kept Niblo's lit for two months. (Six years later, in June of 1891, San Francisco's Tivoli offered its audiences a less expansive, somewhat more faithful version of this popular German operetta by Adolph Neuendorff and H. Italiener as **The Rat Charmer of Hamelin**.) Harrigan's **The Grip** ran only slightly longer. In Harrigan's tale two Civil War comrades, Col. Patrick Reilly (Harrigan) and Capt. Phil Clancy (Harry Fisher), promise each other that their children will wed each other and seal the promise with a grip. Years pass. Clancy announces he and his son John (H. A. Weaver, Jr.) are coming East to allow John to wed Reilly's daughter, Rosalind (Stella Boniface). But Reilly had heard the Clancys are now in bad odor. He persuades his family to behave with outlandish vulgarity. Nonetheless, John and Rosalind fall in love. By curtain time the Clancy name is cleared and everyone is happy. No outstanding Braham songs helped the evening. Nonetheless, Harrigan regulars on both sides of the footlights kept *The Grip* firmly at the Park until mid-February.

December offered two revivals of importations: *The Black Hussar* at the Star on the 12th and *Mlle. Nitouche* at the Standard on the 14th, the latter sung in English by, surprisingly, Lotta. Lotta's visit also proffered revivals of her expected repertory.

Just before 1885 moved into history **Oh! What a Night!** (28 December 1885, Grand Opera) gave Gus Williams another chance to play one of his comic German-Americans all the while it sat on the fence between old-style farce and newer farce-comedy. On the same night, up at Harlem's Theatre Comique, **Wrinkles** made its first Manhattan appearance. Like the shows at Tony Pastor's, these musicals toured the hinterlands and sometimes played second-class theatres in New York City's outlying neighborhoods but never touched base at first-class playhouses in the heart of the theatre district.

Crazy Patch (18 January 1886, Standard) hung its songs and dances on the little saga of Sybilla Tubbs (Kate Castleton), a young lady "just from boarding school" who visits a favorite old-maid aunt. However, Sybilla's supposed new sophistication leads to problems which only her real naiveté unwittingly unravels. Some of the fun also came from an escaped madman ("a pugilistic lunatic") and a pursuing doctor who, naturally, are mistaken for one another. Yet one more farce-comedy policeman contributed his share of laughs.

In England, **Jack-in-the-Box** (8 February 1886, Union Square) had been deemed by many commentators a musical. But in America most perceived it as an old-fashioned "melodrama of the extreme school." Nonetheless, since its star, Carrie Swain, sang, danced, and did some acrobatics, it clearly can be called borderline. It is discussed in some detail in the first volume of *American Theatre: A Chronicle of Comedy and Drama* on pages 234–35.

On 15 February 1886 three shows opened at once. One was Ned Harrigan's final effort for the season at the Park, **The Leather Patch**. To be rid of a shrewish wife (Annie Yeamans), McCarthy (Harrigan) decides to play dead. Before his "burial" he writes a codicil to his will, leaving everything to his son, then he places the will in a leather patch on a pair of trousers. After McCarthy's "death" Roderick McQuade (John Sparks), an undertaker, courts the Widow McCarthy. When Roderick needs a pair of trousers to bury an Indian, the widow gives him the pair with the patch. Jefferson Putnam (John Wild), a Negro graverobber, steals them. McCarthy's "ghost" eventually returns to right matters and reform his wife. The free-flowing give-and-take offered opportunities for slices of contemporary life such as a jubilant black wake and "a lively illustration of the methods of Baker-Street clothing dealers." Characters allowed their brief moment on the stage included, to name only a few, "the seedy shyster, the convivial Police Justice, the negro vagabond, the Sixth Ward gin seller." The *Times* critic rued the conspicuous advertising of a particular brand of whiskey, a commercial intrusion for which Harrigan was probably compensated, but which could be defended as another bit of realism. In its afterthoughts, several weeks later, the *Times* praised the work for presenting "as much broad humor and local color as 'The Beggar's Opera,' without a touch of the immorality of the amusing work that set London in a furor in 1725. Harrigan has found a new field as surely as John Gay did." No doubt heartfelt and well meant, the praise was a little late in the day. Again Braham produced no hits. But *The Leather Patch* was sufficiently diverting to run until May.

At the Casino first-nighters heard a more enduring work, Johann Strauss's **The Gypsy Baron**. The Casino brought over William Castle from grand opera to sing Sandor and awarded the role of Zsupan to the up-and-coming Francis Wilson. Wilson clowned in a German accent and introduced "a topical song" written by the operetta's translator, Sydney Rosenfeld. Rosenfeld at least remained faithful to the original story of a nobleman who returns from exile and falls in love with a gypsy, a young lady unaware she, too, is of noble birth. But the work enjoyed only a modest success, running until 10 May. Its three-month stay was about average for the Casino. Hindsight makes it difficult to understand how Strauss's best works—operettas like *The Gypsy Baron* and *Die Fledermaus*—achieved merely middling receptions, while lesser, virtually forgotten Strauss pieces such as *Prince Methusalem* were greater hits.

The newer, more acceptable generation of farce-comedies was represented when William Gill's **A Toy Pistol** bowed (20 February 1886, Comedy). Gill's story was a variation and elaboration on the one he had used the previous year in *A Bottle of Ink* (6 January 1885). To save his failing paper, the *Toy Pistol*, editor Isaac Roost sends himself fraudulent telegrams and disguises himself as an Italian musician, a clerk, a washerwoman, and a "Milesian Mikado." In keeping with the old practice of doubling in roles so dear to farce-comedy, one actor (D. G. Longworth) portrayed three characters with typical musical stage names of the period: Ernest Seeker, J. Lancelot Hustler, and Primrose Path. A few critics singled out such songs as "Collar Cuffs" and "I Give It Up" as praiseworthy, although everything from the show—culled, again in farce-comedy fashion, from myriad sources—has been forgotten. The reason for Gill's revisions was to create a vehicle for Tony Hart, and for most 1886 theatregoers it was Hart's name that loomed as the principal attraction. He was welcomed as effusively as he always had been when he played with Harrigan. One critic noted, "A large majority of spectators yelled with delight, others stamped their feet, hammered their canes, and clapped their hands. Floral tributes in profusion were handed to Mr. Hart." His best moment came

when, as the Irish washerwoman buying a bit of tea, he subjected the defenseless salesclerk to a long, rambling history of trials and tribulations. Unfortunately Gill's work, lacking Harrigan's verisimilitude and artistry, was patently theatrical. Hart played Broadway for five weeks and then went on tour.

We, Us and Co. (29 December 1884) returned on 8 March for a week's visit to the Standard.

The Ivy Leaf (8 March 1886, Niblo's) represented a different theatrical school, Irish romantic drama, whose handsome hero was always able to raise his lovely Irish tenor voice in song between exploits.

Another popular artist arrived in a starring vehicle one month after Hart. Lillian Russell played the title role in **Pepita; or, The Girl with the Glass Eyes** (16 March 1886, Union Square). Pepita was the daughter of the eccentric Professor Pongo, fabricator of performing automata. When his robot prima donna breaks down just before the performance of an opera, Pepita takes its place. The leading male automaton soon malfunctions, and Pepita is happy to substitute her real lover in the part. Unlike many other musical queens, Russell was always careful to surround herself with the best available talent. Professor Pongo was played by Jacques Kruger (who had written the spoof of *Patience* that made Miss Russell famous), while the young hero was played by a youthful minstrel performing for the first time on the legitimate stage: Chauncey Olcott. To Kruger fell the newly voguish "topical song," twitting the day's national and local foibles, even when they bore no relation to the plot. At least one critic recorded that Olcott's "nasal tones were inopportunely mirth provoking," although everyone was surprised when Miss Russell suddenly disclosed a violin and accompanied herself in one number. The material was by Alfred Thompson and Miss Russell's husband, Edward Solomon. Solomon was no doubt delighted when "almost all the numbers of the score were encored." *Pepita* held the stage until 22 May and enjoyed a profitable tour.

A more interesting and more successful work followed Miss Russell by two weeks. When **The Little Tycoon** opened at the Standard on 29 March, it had already been running three months in Philadelphia. The original cast was transferred to New York, while a new contingent continued the Philadelphia stand, playing there until early June and returning the next season for several shorter engagements. *The Little Tycoon* was the work of a Philadelphia socialite, Willard Spenser.

Spenser's simple plot assuredly recalled *The Bourgeois Gentleman*. General Knickerbocker (R. E. Graham) and his daughter, Violet (Carrie M. Dietrich), are returning from Europe accompanied by the fatuous nobleman whom Knickerbocker has selected to be his daughter's husband, Lord Dolphin (E. H. Van Veghten). But Violet's heart is given to Alvin (W. S. Rising). By no coincidence Alvin is on the same crossing. Lest Alvin and Violet meet, the General has his daughter locked in her cabin. Violet's lady friends obtain a passkey to free her. Furious, the General announces his daughter will wed the lord immediately upon their return to Newport. However, once home, the General receives a letter from "His Royal Highness Sham, The Great Tycoon of Japan," announcing his imminent appearance at the Knickerbocker mansion. Overwhelmed by the potentate and the "craze for everything that's Japanase" (it was, after all, the year of *The Mikado*), the General forgets his English favorite and presents his daughter to the monarch. Of course, the Tycoon is merely Alvin in disguise. Lord Dolphin's domineering mama, the Marchioness of Pullhimback, angrily hurries off with her Milquetoast son. The music, lyrics, and dialogue were simple almost to the point of being puerile. Much of the humor came from outrageous puns. The General entertains the Tycoon by singing "The Cats On Our Back Fence":

WILLARD SPENSER was born in Cooperstown, New York, apparently in 1852. Scion of a wealthy family, he attended the best private schools. After his marriage he settled in St. Davids, then an elite suburb of Philadelphia. His obituaries mention no occupation but state that he had had select schooling by the best available teachers of music he could find. Spenser came to represent to New York the figurehead of the "Philadelphia school" of musical theatre. Savagely criticized, he allowed only his first two musicals a New York hearing. On the other hand, both Philadelphia and the road gave all his musicals warm receptions as late as 1912.

Oh! the cats on our back fence!
Politicians they of sense.

Win they with cooperation,
With con-catty, ratty-oscination.

The Tycoon requests the General sing some more. Flattered, the General is soon at the monarch's beck and call:

Gen. Knickerbocker: Any other request the Great Tycoon can make I pledge myself to grant.
Lord Dolphin: Oh, ah!
Alvin: Show-im-up, tight squeak, ki-yi; Choke-imoph Tycoon yah-yah, ki-yi! Chum-yah, boo-jumsnark hop-scotch Tycoonee,—yum yum.
Gen. Knickerbocker: Yes, I understand. You have my unqualified consent, your majesty. (*To Rufus*) But what does he say?
Rufus: Great Tycoon ask for hand of General Knickerbocker's beautiful daughter.
Lord Dolphin: (*In consternation*) Oh, ah!
Gen. Knickerbocker: I swoon! How very unfortunate! My daughter's hand is promised to Lord Dolphin.
Lord Dolphin: (*Despairingly*) Oh, ah!
Gen. Knickerbocker: But hold. Never was there such a craze for everything that's Japanase. She's yours.
Lord Dolphin: (*Despairingly*) Oh, ah!

Dolphin's two monosyllables were his only sounds throughout the work. With Alvin and Violet hand in hand the company reprised the little waltz that was the most popular melody in the show, "Love Comes Like A Summer Sigh."

Originally slated for a five-week stay, *The Little Tycoon* ran until June. Although a success, it was by no means the phenomenon it had been in Philadelphia. To New York it stood as a distressing example of "the Philadelphia school," with its inane librettos, driveling dialogue, and elementary music. Critics even assailed Philadelphia for capitulating more readily to audience demands for encores. Most galling to Spenser was the charge he had borrowed the setting and many of his ideas from *The Mikado*. Spenser replied by showing he had copyrighted the musical on 24 October 1882—three years before *The Mikado's* premiere. He contended he had offered the work to a Colonel Morse, D'Oyly Carte's agent, and that Morse had retained the manuscript for several years before returning it. The best part of the production was the colorful Japanese costumes, judged equal to the handiwork of New York's costumers.

March's only other entry was yet another revival at Niblo's of *The Black Crook* (12 September 1866), adding another month's run to its history. Its additions for this revival included the Mignani family, performing the march from *Aida* on sweepers' brooms, and a "Mikado Ballet"—these in a work set in Germany.

Washington, like Philadelphia and Boston, was mounting its own productions. On 12 April a short new John Philip Sousa work, **The Queen of Hearts; or, Royalty and Roguery,** opened on a double bill with *Trial by Jury*. Sousa conducted. Edward M. Taber's libretto took as its source the Mother Goose rhyme in which the Knave of Hearts steals the Queen's tarts. All the characters were cards in the deck. The piece was not a success and was never revived after its brief three-performance run.

In San Francisco, another flop ran a half week longer. **The Medium** (19 April 1886, Tivoli) was F. W. Page's musicalization of Charles Hawtrey's popular comedy *The Private Secretary*. Complications ensue in the play after an eccentric curate is mistaken by a doddering old man for the man's nephew, and the uncle tries to turn him into a gallivanting man-about-town. At one point, the curate is also mistaken for a spiritualist. It was this last bit that was expanded in the song-and-dance version, with Page himself assuming the tide role.

W. J. Scanlan came into Niblo's on 26 April in **Shane-na-Lawn,** another of those Irish romantic dramas laced with song out of which he made a career. Shane was a clever Irish lad who clears a girl of false charges of murder and wins himself a bride. Scanlan's offering competed for attention with a new William Gill effort, **Arcadia** (26 April 1886, Bijou). Like several other librettists during the year, Gill had recourse to childhood favorites for his tale. Tom, Tom, the Piper's Son (George Richards) runs away from home, visiting the Garden of Trumpetta's Palace and Mephistopheles' Country Seat before trudging back to his own hearth. Gill wrote himself a part that allowed him to traipse in and out playing bagpipes. The show lacked a centralizing figure such as Adonis and suffered as well from a bad score. David Braham's brother John "selected and arranged" the music. The most notable number was "Hic-hiccough Hic-hiccough," its new words attached to Sullivan's "Willow, Tit-willow" from *The Mikado*. The show was a flop, closing after a three-week stand.

Four shows with varying degrees of musical seriousness opened 3 May. At Wallack's John McCaull offered the most musically cohesive of the arrivals,

Rudolph Dellinger's reworking of *Maritana* as **Don Caesar.** Bertha Ricci and Mathilde Cottrelly were featured. But critics and audiences did not take to the importation, and it was soon withdrawn. The Vokeses returned in a repertory of their song-studded farce-comedies: *In Honor Bound, My Milliner's Bill,* and *A Christmas Pantomime Rehearsal.* But the most successful "musical" was something of a curiosity. Richard Mansfield, heretofore a figure in the middle ranks of musical performers, began his career as a dramatic star with **Prince Karl.** To smooth the transition from the lyric to the dramatic stage, he inserted several tunes. The compromise pleased playgoers; the show ran through the summer at the Madison Square.

The night of 3 May also welcomed a new Charles Hoyt contrivance at the Standard, **A Tin Soldier.** It was typical of the works he was writing and producing at the time. A young couple attend a masked ball. The husband (George Boniface, Jr.) has got himself up in an array of kitchen utensils to look like a mock knight. He returns home early, and his servant, Rats, dons his master's costume. Rats runs off to the ball, where the obvious complications and confusions ensue. The ball setting allowed for the free and easy introduction of a number of vaudeville turns. As the *Dramatic Mirror* noted, the evening metamorphosed into "a sugar coated variety olio punctuating the act with charming inconsistency." One character was named after the spanking new masterpiece that was the talk of New York. To this figure, Brooklyn Bridge (Paul Arthur), fell the "inevitable topical song with verses ad libitum." Led by young James T. Powers as Rats, the performers played for two months, after which the road extended a vigorous welcome.

The following Monday, 10 May, brought in the biggest hit of the year, a show that remained popular for close to half a century. The Casino's mounting of an English work, **Erminie** (Harry Paulton/Edward Jakobowski), that had premiered only the preceding 9 November at London's Comedy Theatre, gave it its longest run—571 performances—and secured the stardom of its principal comic, Francis Wilson.

Erminie was based on a long-popular French play, *Robert Macaire.* Macaire and his cohort, Jacques Strop, were a pair of murderers who tie up a groom and steal his bride. For the heroine, her kidnapping is a blessing in disguise, freeing her from a marriage she hadn't wanted. In Paulton's retelling the menacing murderers became two harmless vagabonds, Ravennes (W. S. Daboll) and Cadeaux (Wilson). Pauline Hall played the heroine, Erminie. Daboll portrayed Ravennes as a dashing, plausible rascal, while Wilson emphasized Cadeaux's sympathetic, wistful side. Together the men won encores with "We're A Philanthropic Couple." *Erminie*'s delicate balance of the romantic and the picaresque established a model for a generation of comic operas. The show made comic rogues light-opera stereotypes, its pink ballroom set made pink as popular for rooms as *The Black Crook* (12 September 1866) had made it for tights, and its "Lullaby" ("Dear Mother, In Dreams I See Her") became one of the best-loved songs of the generation.

FRANCIS WILSON was born in Philadelphia on 7 February 1854 and made his debut at that city's historic Chestnut Street Opera House in 1878. At first he played mostly in dramas and comedies, but a prolonged stint with *Our Goblins* convinced him his future lay with musicals. His performances in early Casino shows such as *The Queen's Lace Handkerchief* and, especially, *Erminie* gave him a firm leg up in the field. He sang the role of Cadeaux from *Erminie* nearly 1,300 times. Unlike rubber-faced clowns of James T. Powers's ilk or an overwhelming hulk of a man such as De Wolf Hopper, the well-proportioned, if large-nosed, Wilson, while as acrobatic as clowns of the day had to be, relied on an exceptional grace of movement and on a more intellectual approach than his great associates. In later years, when he felt he was too old for energetic antics, he became a successful lecturer and scholarly author. He also served as founder and first president of Actors' Equity.

Lydia Thompson attempted to capitalize on the perennial appeal of nostalgia with a revival on 17 May of *Oxygen* (27 August 1877). Judging by the reception, she would have been best advised to let aging playgoers survive with their memories intact. Two weeks at the 14th Street Theatre and she was gone.

McNish, Johnson, and Slavin's Minstrels followed the successful practice of troupes such as the Thatcher, Primrose, and West entourage by concentrating on burlesque. They chose the still-running

The Little Tycoon, distorting it under the name *Little Fly Coon*. The company was rewarded with two weeks of good business.

A pair of rival translations of Audran's *Le Serment d'Amour* opened two nights apart: **The Crowing Hen** at Wallack's on 29 May and **The Bridal Trap** at the Bijou on 31 May. The latter was by the rambunctious, trouble-prone Sydney Rosenfeld. Broadway was more amused by the battle outside the houses than by the opéra bouffe itself. The Bijou and Wallack's faced each other across Broadway. Rosenfeld and his producers, Miles and Barton, put a stereopticon on the roof of the Bijou and projected insulting comments about *The Crowing Hen* on Wallack's facade. McCaull, the producer of *The Crowing Hen*, hired calcium lights to blot out the insults and then procured his own stereopticon to throw insults at the Bijou. The antics did little for the shows. *The Bridal Trap* closed on 26 June, *The Crowing Hen* two weeks later. During their short stays both told how a peasant girl wins a count despite his aunt's stratagems. McCaull's cast, featuring Bertha Ricci, Mathilde Cottrelly, Signor Perugini, and De Wolf Hopper, was by far the better of the two.

Most critics ignored a commonplace farce-comedy, **A Soap Bubble** (31 May 1886, Windsor), but it proved to have some uncommon strength, belying its name, and toured the backwaters for several seasons. Montgomery Phister's diaphanous plot twitted the manufacturing and advertising of soaps and speculation in soap stocks. (Even at this date Ivory Soap had garnered nationwide attention by a knowing advertising policy far ahead of the field.)

An even worse flop was Millöcker's **The Maid of Belleville**, which opened at the Star on 24 June and closed 7 July. Its love story was played out on a lower social level than was Audran's, for here a coy village lass settles for the sergeant of her dreams. June ended with another of the era's many comedies that sneaked a song or two into their action, *Humbug*. Then the season came to a quiet finish in July with a revival of *Falka* at Wallack's.

1886–1887

There was little reason to cheer during this season. Wallack's great company, for example, was in its last year. When it disbanded, an institution and an era passed. Musically, the year again offered little but importations and revivals. New domestic contributions were few and far between. Neither they nor the imported novelties were particularly exciting.

August was busy, despite hot weather. Minstrelsy headed the parade when Lester and Allen's troupe arrived 9 August for a fortnight. The Bijou, like the Casino, eagerly eyed the possibility of keeping open all year long. When *Humbug* closed, the theatre, on 16 August, offered its patrons a bit of summer fluff billed as a "musical comedy," **Soldiers and Sweethearts.** George Schleiffarth wrote music to Owen Westford and Susie Russell's scissors-and-paste book. Major Ashley (Westford) is worried about the irresponsible behavior of his son, Lt. Ashley (Frederick Darell). The young soldier's lady friends stage an amateur performance of *Satanella* (it occupied the entire second act) and then disguise themselves as soldiers to enter the barracks. The settings afforded an excuse for the standard Amazon march, while the newly de rigueur "topical song" was awarded to Henry V. Donnelly, who sang it with a conspicuously "Yankee twang." The show lasted three weeks, just long enough to keep the Bijou occupied until the next booking was available.

A more promising work failed even more miserably when it opened at the Standard the same night, 16 August. **The Maid and the Moonshiner** had a libretto by Charles Hoyt and music by Edward Solomon. It starred two reigning favorites of the day, Lillian Russell and Tony Hart. Few new American musicals at the time offered a more encouraging lineup. Yet everything seemed to go wrong. Atrocious notices, heat, and backstage bickering toppled the piece after a dismal two-week run. For that short time, Upton O. Dodge (Hart), a bungling assistant moonshiner, helped his boss, Bourbon Miller (John E. Brand), win the hand of Virginia (Miss Russell) from a rich plantation owner (James Radcliffe). The action moved from a steamboat landing (showing the boat arrive), to a plantation, to a still in the Blue Ridge Mountains. Hart stopped the show with a comic number, "Flag Of Truce," while Miss Russell won critical kudos for her "easygoing style." No one mentioned the name of the young man who assisted Hoyt in staging the work, Julian Mitchell. His efforts marked the beginning of a forty-year career that would make him the most prolific director in the history of the American Musical Theatre, although his value would not be appreciated until he flourished under the aegis of Weber and Fields. There is one amusing footnote to the fiasco. All Hoyt's early successes had titles beginning with the indefinite article "A." The failure of *The Maid and the Moonshiner* convinced him the indefinite article was

his lucky talisman, and for the rest of his career all his shows had titles starting with "A."

Two revivals followed. The Kiralfys threw open the doors at Niblo's on 21 August with a remounting of *Around the World in Eighty Days* (28 August 1875), while on the 23rd Ned Harrigan began his season with a brief return of *Investigation* (1 September 1884). The Kiralfys inserted the same "Mikado Ballet" they had used the preceding season in *The Black Crook*. Clearly it belonged more naturally here in an international tour.

August's final entry was an importation. John McCaull brought over Victor Roger's **Josephine Sold by Her Sisters** (30 August 1886, Wallack's) and enjoyed the profits from the French piece to mid October. A janitress's daughter becomes an opera singer, but her jealous sisters arrange for an Egyptian pasha to kidnap her under the pretense of offering her a place at the Cairo opera. Louise Parker sang Josephine, Mathilde Cottrelly was the ringleader of the sisters, and De Wolf Hopper was the pasha.

The Bijou began its new season on 13 September. From then until the end of April one man dominated its stage, Nat Goodwin. By and large his vehicles were much like *The Skating Rink* (23 November 1885), which he had offered the preceding year. In fact, *The Skating Rink* held the boards for a month beginning 26 February. But for his opener Goodwin selected a new English work, **Little Jack Sheppard.** Loie Fuller assumed the title role, finding an appropriate moment to include her flowing-skirt dance. Yet Goodwin saw to it his part of Jonathan Wild remained pivotal. He stopped the show with an interpolated "topical song," sang a spoof of sentimental ballads, and imitated the more celebrated performers then on Broadway. Critics accepted the work for the light frippery it was, although the *Times* did feel obligated to call attention to the increasing "display" of "limbs" by the chorus girls. The not quite full-length musical was played until December with one or another additional short pieces.

Our Irish Visitors (13 September 1886, Third Ave.) answered to the names of Colonel Gilhooley (Thomas Murray) and Jerry McGinnis (Mark Murphy). Actually they were not all that new to America, for they had been visiting variety stages and theatres in outlying areas for some while. On one excuse or another the visitors went to the circus, witnessed a "nigger duel," and helped with a boat race. With two of their friends they also dolled themselves up as ballerinas and offered their version of toe dancing. In between all this, supporting players intoned a "kissing song" and one gal presented a cornet solo. And if that were not enough, a trained bear (real or a costumed dancer?) danced. The potpourri proved a potent drawing card on secondary circuits for years and years.

Four nights later, on the 17th, Lew Dockstader took over the old home of the San Francisco Minstrels, renamed it after himself, and launched a whole season of traditional minstrelsy. Success prompted him to schedule future seasons. His first three were highly successful, but by the 1889–1890 season he apparently had worn out his welcome, so he relinquished the house in midterm. Now and then during his early seasons he would take a week's respite, handing over his stage to other similar groups, such as the Georgia Coloured Parlor Minstrels.

With the Bijou booked, *Adonis* (4 September 1884) played its first return engagement at the Fifth Avenue. Opening 20 September, it arrived before many loyalists expected it. Great hopes had been held that *Adonis* would repeat its American success in London, but the London reception was cool, the run brief—150 performances. Dixey and his statue lingered in New York for two weeks before embarking on a national tour. The production returned again in May, recording an additional two months at the Bijou.

Aimée suffered a three-performance embarrassment with **Marita** (28 September 1886, Union Square), which Barton Hill had translated from Victorien Sardou's vaudeville *Piccolino*, and for which the show's musical director, Theodore Bendix, wrote a handful of songs. The star portrayed a Swiss shepherdess who finds a way to lure her skirt-chasing heartthrob to the altar.

The ubiquitous Sydney Rosenfeld was librettist for a Philadelphia hit, **The Mystic Isle; or, The Law of Averages** (2 October 1886, Temple). John B. Grant composed the score. Since the law of averages means there can be few truly mystic isles, a statistician, Chickerlick, comes with his daughter to one he believes is genuinely mystic. There he hopes she can escape her impecunious suitor. But, of course, not only is the suitor there, so are oddball islanders and a botany class from a ladies' seminary, chaperoned by their teacher. In the end Chickerlick admits the island is merely the "average abode of chance and circumstance, chaos and confusion." The musical ran six weeks.

The run of *Erminie* was forced to suspend for the month of October when a previous commitment required the Casino to house **The Commodore,** an adaptation of Offenbach's *La Créole*. This story of an old seaman who would force his daughter to marry a man she doesn't like was brought over from England by the Earl of Lonsdale with an entirely English cast led by a young lady with an apparently notorious reputation, Violet Cameron, who was Lydia Thompson's niece. "One of the worst failures in the history of the Casino," there was no outcry to extend its planned stay. The commitment honored, Offenbach's work disappeared from Broadway annals, and *Erminie* resumed its run.

The following Monday, 11 October, Ned Harrigan had his first new work of the year ready for inspection. Bernard O'Reagan, a saloon-keeper (Harrigan), receives a surprise visit from his English cousin and namesake (Joseph Sparks), who has come to America to collect for the Parnell fund. The American gives the Englishman a thousand dollars. The saloon-keeper is engaged to Bedalia McNeirney (Annie Yeamans), but in a change of heart has secretly married Bedalia's daughter, Kate (Amy Lee). Suspecting as much, Bedalia "borrows" the Parnell fund money to bribe the truth from Bernard's cronies. The money gets lost—stuck to some plaster—and the efforts to recover it lead to a series of brouhahas. These take the cast to Chinatown and the Salvation Army Headquarters and cause the black leader, Silas (John Wild), to fall through a skylight and into a fire. His wife, Lulu (Dan Collyer), protests she doesn't like "roasted coon." David Bra-ham's best efforts were "The U.S. Black Marines" and "The Trumpet In The Cornfield Blows." Although **The O'Reagans** was not one of Harrigan and Braham's better efforts, it enjoyed a satisfactory run of sixteen weeks.

Kenilworth (25 October 1886, Casino) starred Violet Cameron, but this burlesque seems to have been a far cry from one of the same name her aunt Lydia Thompson had performed some fourteen years earlier. It even managed a burlesque within a burlesque, finding some way in which Scott's characters could make fun of Gilbert's *Pygmalion and Galatea*. American critics and playgoers found both the piece and its star disappointing.

The evening of 25 October also played host to a return visit of the Thatcher, Primrose, and West Minstrels. The group returned in February for a second short stay. But lovers of minstrelsy could take heart when what promised to be a new permanent blackface band settled in as Dockstader's Minstrels. Both groups continued to give increasing emphasis to the burlesque portion of the bill. For instance, Dockstader rushed in his spoof *Little Black Shepherd* just two weeks after Goodwin's opening.

November's only entries were both revivals and both by Gilbert and Sullivan. *The Mikado* bowed on 1 November, giving way three weeks later to *Princess Ida*. *Ida*, too, stayed for three weeks. Courtice Pounds, Géraldine Ulmar, and Signor Brocolini led both casts at the Fifth Avenue.

Goodwin had a new bit of foolery ready at the Bijou on 11 December. In **Turned Up**, Caraway Jones, a bibulous undertaker, with "carroty locks and goatee and a crimson nose," marries Sabina Medway (Jennie Weatherby), whom he believes to be the widow of a sea captain. But the knot is no sooner tied than Sabina's "dead" husband (C. B. Bishop) returns. The captain's chagrin is increased when an African queen appears who contends she is his wife. Jones brings about a happy ending by leaving with the Negress to run a plantation. Typical of Goodwin's business was his appearance as "a bridegroom in all his splendor." Moments later he is dunked in a river, and on emerging he fishes a cigar stub from his pocket and attempts to relight it with his waterlogged matches. The piece was by Mark Melford, with its songs borrowed from the usual variety of sources. Coupled with *Turned Up* was Goodwin's travesty of Henry Irving, *Those Bells*.

George W. Monroe's characterization of Our Own Bridget in *Over the Garden Wall* (23 March 1885) had been so successful that Scott Marble wrote **My Aunt Bridget** (6 December 1886, People's) as a new vehicle for the comedian, furthering the adventures of Bridget McVeigh. Just what those adventures were no major reviewer bothered to record. To a man they looked on the new show as little more than an entertaining vaudeville with Bridget serving as a rotund, robust, and good-humored commère. But Monroe played his part so well and picked his ever-changing lineup of supporting players so wisely that the entertainment continued to lure patrons into the early 1890s.

While Monroe had years of activity and acclaim ahead of him, poor Tony Hart's career was coming ineluctably to its tragic end. After the failure the preceding season of *A Toy Pistol* (20 February 1886) and *The Maid and the Moonshiner* (16 August 1886) early in this season, he was back as a mustachioed Con O'Grady, cavorting at the Donnybrook Fair in, appropriately, **Donnybrook** (13 December 1886, People's). *The Theatre* lamented, "He looks pale, haggard, and thin," and recalled, "Only a little while ago

he and his partner 'owned the town.' Tony was the cunningest little fellow that walked the streets." The show's brief, unhappy tour wrote "finis" to Hart's once brilliant career.

The year 1887 began in a buzz of activity. Five musicals appeared in January, led on the 3rd by yet another visit of *Evangeline* (27 July 1874). It played a single week at Niblo's, departing to make room on the 17th for an even older favorite, *The Black Crook* (12 September 1866). Featured were D'Alvini, a juggler, and an "Operetta Ballet," to music from then current or recent comic-opera hits. Stalacta wove her magic for three weeks.

Most critics ignored the revival, preferring to give their attention to **Indiana** at the Star. Its name notwithstanding, *Indiana* was basically a French work with music by Audran. Its story centered on a heroine who complicates her life by resorting to disguises in order to spy on a fiancé she has never seen. Lilly Post assumed the title role, while Digby Bell was in charge of the comedy. H. B. Farnie's adaptation was not to New York's taste. Its producer, the busy John McCaull, did not accept the judgment. Although he removed it after three weeks, he sent it touring, then brought it back for reconsideration in July. New York refused to reconsider.

For a change of pace, Goodwin dropped his brand of farce-comedies and mounted a production of *The Mascot* on 24 January. Of course, given Goodwin's school of theatre, the presentation was far less faithful to the original than other mountings of the work New York had seen. While the insertion of specialties and interpolations had become commonplace in all but the most conscientiously staged importations, Goodwin carried domestication further than most performers. He showered patrons with imitations of celebrities, topical songs, and local allusions. But his audiences loved it. *The Mascot* ran a month and had a return engagement in late March.

January closed with Harrigan's second and last new work of the season, **McNooney's Visit**. In going to pay a call on Widow Gilmartin (Annie Yeamans), McNooney (Harrigan) inadvertently exchanges carpetbags with the man seated next to him on the train. The bag contains burglar's tools. McNooney is arrested and jailed, escapes, gets into a brawl, and is arrested and jailed again. Besides bringing in another widow, Harrigan resorted to one more old favorite device: a goat. Braham, too, was content to rest on his laurels, writing only three new songs. Not even as good as *The O'Reagans*, the play was nevertheless able to sustain itself on Harrigan's loyal following for ten weeks at the Park.

At the beginning of February John McCaull granted an interview to the *Times*. His pessimistic assessment of the lyric scene embraced both sides of the footlights. He knew of no Americans who could write good music, and insisted "we haven't even an American librettist as yet." His "as yet" was mildly hopeful, but he felt no urgent need for a fine native wordsmith: "My audiences will stand any amount of gags, and topical songs. It doesn't matter in the least how bad they are. Sometimes I think the worse they are the better they are appreciated." But McCaull did feel that "the music they require, however, must be good." If nothing else, the producer saw some didactic value in the lyric stage, concluding, "[C]omic opera at the present time is far ahead of anything as a musical educator."

The irrepressible Nate Salsbury and his Troubadours practiced their fading art in a new piece, **The Humming Bird** (7 February 1887). The *Times* insisted it could have been called "The Mongoose" or "The Ibis" with equal pertinence. Its specialties took place as some New Yorkers meet by chance at Shakespeare's statue in Central Park. Three weeks and they were gone.

Lanky, beaming Sol Smith Russell was the star of **Pa** (14 February 1887, Standard), which told of a father's problems marrying off his daughters and which some reviewers treated as a musical and others as a farce with songs.

The season's most durable lyric work raised its curtain at the Fifth Avenue on 21 February. As might be expected it was an importation. And as might also be guessed, it was another in Gilbert and Sullivan's great series. **Ruddigore** (spelled *Ruddygore* in contemporary programs and advertisements) has never ranked high in the Savoyard canon. In this, history has reflected the 1887 evaluation. But even second-best Gilbert and Sullivan was notably superior in wit, melody, style, and coherence to anything else then gracing the stage. D'Oyly Carte's ensemble played this story of a young man's overcoming a fatal, familial curse only until 9 April. Principals included Courtice Pounds, George Thorne, Geraldine Ulmar, Kate Foster, and Fred Billington.

J. K. Emmet also opened on 21 February, at the Standard, and surprisingly ran just one week less than *Ruddigore*. His vehicle was his old standby, *Fritz, Our Cousin German* (11 July 1870), advertised with the seemingly inevitable "new songs" and "new scenes." The nuances of Emmet's career are probably lost forever. Still, it is curious to see him, after so many years of playing short engagements at backwater houses, once again enjoying a reasonably extended stay at a major theatre. Was there a sudden wave of nostalgia or perhaps some premonition that Emmet's days were numbered?

The next Monday, 28 February, also welcomed a pair of musicals. At the Star, *Humming Bird* was supplanted by McCaull's production of yet another importation, Rudolph Dellinger's **Lorraine,** adapted by W. J. Henderson. Perhaps rashly, McCaull had contracted for this story of Louis XIII's natural son finding romance at Louis XIV's court before its German premiere. Signor Perugini, De Wolf Hopper, Mathilde Cottrelly, and Gertrude Griswold sparked the proceedings. But their antics were not enough. The musical fared even less well than its predecessor, fading away after two weeks. Competing with it for first-nighters was the return of *The Skating Rink*, mentioned earlier.

The season's last original work arrived on 31 March. It was the closing salvo in Nat Goodwin's series of farce-comedy plays. **Big Pony; or, The Gentlemanly Savage** had a book by A. C. Wheeler and music by Edward Darling. Goodwin played an Indian—in dress suit and soft hat—whose attempts to settle some family quarrels take him not just to the Wild West but to Mexico and Spain as well. He was assisted again by Loie Fuller in her nimble skirt dances. The piece played three weeks until Goodwin decided to bring back *Little Jack Sheppard* for a week to close his stay.

By April the season was effectively finished. Ten more musicals followed. Eight were revivals. In order of their appearance they were *A Trip to Africa* on 11 April; *Cordelia's Aspirations* (5 November 1883, the only native work) on 18 April; *The Gypsy Baron* on 2 May; *The Black Hussar*, 7 May; *Gasparone*, 16 May; *Iolanthe*, 30 May; *Falka*, 31 May; and *The Beggar Student*, 25 July.

Most critics waved away **The Pyramid** (16 May 1887, Star), a comic opera that fell in with the new vogue for exotic settings—this time, ancient Egypt. The composer was Charles Puerner, who would meet a succession of failures whenever he attempted to climb out of his more comfortable station as a pit conductor. Puerner also was colibrettist, along with Caryl Florio. Their story predated by two decades the rage for plunking down Americans in exotic lands and appeared sixty years before a very similar tale served Alan Jay Lerner in *Brigadoon* (13 March 1947). In this instance, two young American explorers are examining the long-sealed tomb of Ramses XXVIII, when to their amazement Ramses and his whole court suddenly come to life. It seems they do this for a day every several centuries. One of the Americans falls in love with Ramses' daughter and the other with a friend of the princess.

The Kiralfys offered another, more alluring bit of exotica, **The Fall of Babylon,** on 25 June at an open-air amphitheatre on Staten Island, a cooling ferry ride away from Manhattan. A purported thousand performers, playing on "a stage larger than a city block, fronted by a great wall of masonry, flanked by two turreted towers," acted, chanted, and pirouetted as soldiers, royalty, commoners, and dancing girls. Odell called it "a sensation of the summer of 1887."

Away from the heart of Broadway the season saw constant activity. None of it was really important, and most of the plays seem hopelessly lost; yet it should be given a moment's notice. For example, in his history of the New York stage, Odell records the two-week engagement at a minor combination house of *The Red Fox,* "another of those frequent Irish plays of political and sentimental interest, interspersed with an occasional song." At the Oriental Theatre, once the Bowery Gardens, musicals catering to the area's Jewish audiences were beginning to be mounted. The leading composer appears to have been Joseph Lateiner, and the year's programs included his "musical drama" *Emigration to America* and his "historical operetta" *Joseph and His Brothers.* The former began with a pogrom in Balta and took those who escaped to Ellis Island, to an East Side ghetto, and to a triumphal wedding. Clearly, both the Irish and, more slowly, the Jews—two definitive influences on the American Musical Theatre—were preparing the way for the future.

1887–1888

In retrospect the 1887–1888 season seems distressingly lackluster. Yet in its own day it clearly marked an improvement over the preceding year. If no novelty as enduring as *Ruddigore* appeared, it must be remembered that *Ruddigore's* premiere was a disappointment. The event of the year was unatheatrical: the great blizzard of 12 March. It provided New Yorkers with lifelong memories far more vivid than those afforded by any musical of the day. In the theatre itself the most newsworthy occurrences were the burning of the Union Square Theatre in February and two benefits. The first of these benefits was held for Tony Hart at the Academy of Music.

Originally scheduled for 15 March, it was postponed a week by the blizzard's after-effects. On 21 May the Metropolitan Opera House was the scene of a similar gala for the great actor and impresario Lester Wallack. Both men were seriously ill and Hart by this time hopelessly insane. Neither ever again played for his public.

August gave the season a sluggish opening. The Kiralfys relit Niblo's on the 17th with their version of John Brougham's old melodrama *The Duke's Motto.* They rechristened the work **Lagardère,** filled it with ballet and spectacle, and gave the popular Maurice Barrymore the title role of a duke who disguises himself as a hunchback to achieve his ends. A gypsy ballet and a ballet based on Shakespeare's seven ages of man offered diversions from the plot. The Kiralfys were rewarded with a two-month run.

John McCaull and his comic opera company had almost as long a stay with their importation of a minor German operetta, von Suppé's **Bellman.** The fine singer-actor Hubert Wilke, Marion Manola, and two rising young comedians, De Wolf Hopper and Jefferson De Angelis, headed the cast. Wilke played the title role, a poet who loves and wins a countess. De Angelis and Harry MacDonough played two Jewish powder-makers. Jews as comic figures—often passed off as Dutchmen—would soon become stock-in-trade of musicals. But these were among the first, and the *Times* was at once appalled and amused at how much time they were allotted. Hopper cavorted as an upstart, pompous millionaire. The work ran at Wallack's from 22 August to 8 October. Its first night coincided with the return at the Star of McNish, Johnson, and Slavin's Refined Minstrels.

A quartet of musicals appeared on 12 September. The least musical, if not the least substantial, was a burlesque, **The Wily West,** in which John T. Kelly amused patrons at Harrigan's Park Theatre. Its hero, inspired by tales of Buffalo Bill, gives up a position as a dry-goods clerk and goes west. On the same night, one of the final offerings of Rice's Surprise Party, **A Circus in Town,** romped into the Bijou. The faithful John A. Mackay was in the lead. Edward Holst and Woolson Morse concocted the piece, but the work was too much of a fading school to win acceptance. Oddly enough, though, the story touched gingerly on a new, ominous social problem—labor unrest. Circus performers call a strike. One performer writes a love note to the circus owner's wife and spends the rest of the evening contriving its return after he learns his boss is insanely jealous. Nonetheless, several reviewers insisted the piece had no sustained plot. The *Times* recorded, "The music included a drinking chorus, a rather effective 'dude quartet' and a sentimental solo." The show was abruptly withdrawn in a rare midweek closing on 22 September, and a similar troupe with a similar piece, Salsbury's Troubadours in *The Humming Bird*, dutifully filled the remaining three weeks of the stand. This time around it offered Nellie McHenry's take-off of Ophelia.

The third opening, at the Standard, was important, although the play itself was minor and not especially successful. The show was a Chicago mounting, **The Arabian Nights; or, Aladdin's Wonderful Lamp.** It was a traditional burlesque-pantomime in which the hero was played as a trouser role. In this instance Loie Fuller portrayed Aladdin. The show's importance lay in its Chicago origins. The city was rapidly becoming a major production center. Under the aegis of David Henderson, the producer of the work, an era was beginning there. Henderson was determined to present musicals of the highest quality at the newly built Chicago Opera House and decided on elaborate spectacles in the English tradition as the best way to impress Chicagoans. And impressed they were! When the Imperial Burlesque Company (as Henderson initially called his troupe) opened there on 4 June 1887, lavish effects such as a widow's shanty transformed into a glittering boudoir elicited such applause that the play was forced to halt while the scene painter was called on stage for a bow. Henderson's career was to be brief, but more than any other man he probably pioneered the now virtually forgotten and dismayingly underrated school of Chicago musicals. *The Arabian Nights* ran until the end of October. Its failure to repeat its Chicago success in New York continued a sad and only occasionally broken precedent.

Characters gathered at a railroad station after some trains have been delayed provided the fun, song, and dances in Hoyt's **A Hole in the Ground** (12 September 1887, 14th St.). A "Stranger" (George Richards) who butts into everyone's business was the central figure, and his run-in with a rude Station Agent (Frank Lawton) a comic highlight. Other characters included a Deaf Lady, a Tarrier, the Lady of the Lunch Counter, several Tailor-Made Girls, a Roper-in for the Grand Union Hotel, and a Base Ball Umpire. The umpire was played by young Julian Mitchell made up to resemble a then celebrated baseball diamond figure.

The Casino's season got under way with another of the house's importations, **The Marquis.** For this American version of Paul Lacombe's *Jeanne, Jeanette et Jeanneton,* the heroines' names were changed to Mae, Marie, and Marion. The French title more accurately reflected the plot, which centered on three country girls who arrive together in Paris. One sets up a cabaret, one becomes a dancer, while the third marries into the nobility. Bertha Ricci, Isabelle Urquhart, and Sylvia Gerrish were aided in unfolding the story by Mark Smith, Courtice Pounds, Max Freeman, Henri Leoni, and James T. Powers. Despite so fine a cast of Casino favorites, the show failed to repeat the runaway success of its predecessor, *Erminie* (10 May 1886). Even so, it ran profitably from 19 September to 3 December.

September closed with the season's lone visit of an opéra bouffe company to the city. Although Maurice Grau was the producer, he no longer had a glittering star to lead his entourage. He was, moreover, presenting an art form fast losing vogue. Grau seems to have acknowledged opéra bouffe's waning popularity by including in his repertory one German operetta, *Fatinitza.* The French works included *Le Grand Mogul, Serment d'Amour, La Fille de Mme. Angot,* and *La Mascotte.* The troupe departed Wallack's after three weeks of disappointing business.

In Philadelphia, **The Smith Family; or, The Legend of Wyoming** (3 October 1887, Broad St.) enjoyed a month's run. With music by Samuel H. Speck (who also served as conductor) and libretto by E. A. Niven, it recounted two love stories. The less happy one told of Nellie, a Vassar girl and ward of Deacon Smith, who is wooed by the mercenary John Smythe. In the other, Jim Smith, a miner from the West, believes the girl he loves, Eleanor Smith, is too close a relation to court until he learns her guardian, General Smith, is not really her father. The action took place not out west but in Pennsylvania's Wyoming Valley.

With Hart gone, Ned Harrigan's creative abilities inexplicably continued to wane. He came to rely increasingly on revivals of his old favorites. To open his 1887–1888 season he brought back *The Leather Patch* (15th February 1886) for a month's run beginning 10 October.

A far more successful and an original work by E. E. Rice and John Braham opened at the Bijou on the 18th. At least, **The Corsair** was original in that it was new. A travesty of Byron's poem, it featured Amelia Summerville as Conrad. Frank David as a sub-Corsair was given the requisite topical song.

Equally requisite was an Amazon march. A trick dancing mule and a telephone that summoned with a cowbell added humorous touches. As a result, the production by Henry E. Dixey, in association with Miles and Barton, was so sumptuous and the evening so lively that patrons ignored its general critical rejection and flocked to the show for 180 performances. Dockstader's Minstrels spoofed the work as *The Coarse Hair*.

The American premiere of **Dorothy** took place on 5 November at the Standard. This comic opera by Gilbert and Sullivan's erstwhile conductor, Alfred Cellier, had outrun *The Mikado* in London. Two young English ladies condescend to act as barmaids during a harvest festival. They fall in love with two customers. One of the men, Geoffrey, prefers his newfound country wench to the girl his rich uncle demands he marry, someone named Dorothy. Circumstances lead the girls to disguise themselves as men and challenge their new beaux to duels. Of course, in the end Dorothy and one of the serving girls prove to be one and the same. The two pairs of lovers wed. Lillian Russell sang Dorothy; Agnes Stone was her conspirator-cousin. Harry Paulton, Eugene Oudin, John E. Brand, and William Hamilton were the principal males. New York foretold *Dorothy's* future reckoning by judging it pleasant but inferior. It enjoyed only modest returns, playing until 17 December.

Two nights after *Dorothy's* arrival, Harrigan brought in his second offering of the year and his second revival, *Cordelia's Aspirations* (5 November 1883). Apparently a stopgap booking, it stayed for just two weeks until Harrigan had his lone new work ready to present.

For the second time in the season a minor work of great significance raised its curtain in New York. John McCaull's company gave New Yorkers their first view of **The Begum** (21 November 1887, Fifth Ave.), thereby introducing theatregoers to two new names that would loom large in the future—Reginald De Koven and Harry B. Smith.

Smith's first libretto set the style that he would follow for the rest of his long career. The Begum of Oude has a simple way of disposing of a husband who has come to bore her. She merely makes him her General-in-Chief, declares war, and sends him off to die in battle. But when her latest spouse, Howja-Dhu, engages the enemy, he returns unobligingly victorious. She has no choice but to accept the results. Mathilde Cottrelly portrayed the Begum, and De Wolf Hopper played Howja-Dhu.

Besides Howja-Dhu, the cast of characters was filled with the absurd names so beloved by writers of the day. Hubert Wilke enacted Klahm-Chowdee; Digby Bell, Myhnt-Jhuleep; and Jefferson De Angelis, Jhustt-Naut. This journeyman effort failed to please New Yorkers (although the *Times* praised both the show and McCaull's courage in mounting an American work), but the sensible economics of the time allowed McCaull to pack the show on to Chicago, where De Koven's social standing enabled the producer to have a profitable run and recoup his costs.

REGINALD DE KOVEN was born in Middletown, Connecticut, on 3 April 1859. When he was thirteen his clergyman father moved his family to England. The young man was educated at Oxford and then went to Germany and France to pursue his musical studies. In Paris he worked under the tutelage of Léo Delibes. He returned to America, settling in Chicago. After a brief stint in business, a marriage to a wealthy girl allowed him to abandon day-to-day drudgery and concentrate on composing.

HARRY B. SMITH was born in Buffalo, New York, on 28 December 1860. His family moved to Chicago, where he began earning a living as a newspaper man. Stints as a music critic and then as a drama critic whetted his appetite for the stage. In time he became the most prolific librettist and lyricist in history. By his own estimate he wrote (alone or with collaborators) books for over 300 shows and lyrics for some 6,000 songs. He was the first American lyricist honored by the publication of an anthology of his lyrics.

Harrigan's only new work of the season, **Pete**, bowed on 22 November. When he was in partnership with Hart, he often wrote blackface roles for his associates, notably Rebecca Allup for Hart. But he rarely assumed black roles himself. Now he created and played the principal role of a faithful Negro servant. Pete is an ex-slave and the guardian of a supposedly illegitimate girl (Dan Collyer). He proves her legitimacy to enable her to receive an inheritance. In one great scene Harrigan won vociferous approval telling in pantomime how the girl's father had died in battle. David Braham's best numbers were "The Old Black Crow" and "The Old Barn Floor." Although closer than most Harrigan works to serious Victorian melodrama, the show was an immediate hit, running 170 performances before it closed on 21 April. Harrigan's still loyal following was not upset by his opening-night apology for not completely forgetting some of his Irish mannerisms.

San Francisco's William Furst (actually a Baltimore native) first came to New York's attention when he provided incidental music and some songs for an elaborately mounted dramatization of H. Rider Haggard's **She** (29 November 1887, Niblo's).

December's first entry, on the 5th, was still another in the Casino's continuing parade of importations, Lecocq's **Madelon**. Lillian Grubb, Bertha Ricci, Isabelle Urquhart, Mark Smith, James T. Powers, and Courtice Pounds (condemned by the *Herald* for his "high collar" voice) acted out this interweaving of romantic and comic liaisons, in which, for example, an innkeeper's wife plans to elope with a sausage maker. It opened on 5 December and played for just over a month.

Another San Franciscan, this time an honest-to-goodness native, Clay M. Greene, was the author of **Our Jennie** (26 December 1887, People's), which featured Jennie Yeamans. On opening night ushers were kept so busy during curtain calls scurrying to deliver bouquet after bouquet to Miss Yeamans that one critic implied that early leavers (of which there were apparently many) missed the evening's funniest part.

If the Casino remained steadfast in its dependence on importations, the Kiralfys stuck with equal tenacity to their peculiar brand of musical spectacle. They ushered in 1888 with one more of the type, **Mazulm, the Night Owl**, adapted from an old pantomime. Its cast of 300 traveled to "The Palace of Jewels" and watched a "Japanese Ballet." The mounting occupied the spacious Academy of Music from 9 January through 10 March.

Check 44; or, Tobogganing (16 January 1888, Star), billed as a "satirical, lyrical, diaphanous lampoon," seemed to some critics to backslide into the primitiveness of the earlier farce-comedy, although it had several elaborate settings and a slightly more than elementary plot. The entertainment opened in a New York City bank, where it is discovered that a dear little old lady's check—number 44, of course—has been misfiled. Somehow the search for the instrument takes everyone to a tobogganing slide in Montreal. They really needn't have gone that far, since tobogganing rinks were all the rage in New York City at the moment, with newspapers carrying ads for competing establishments. W. A. Mestayer and his wife, Theresa Vaughn, headed a company that provided three hours of "songs, dances, variety acts and horse-play of a diverting and boisterous nature." Many of the songs were old favorites, including a medley from *La Périchole*. The seemingly requisite acrobatic turn was provided by farce-comedy's umpteenth comic policeman. All this was sufficient to please less demanding playgoers for a month at the Star and on a subsequent tour.

The Boston Ideal Opera Company returned for one of their periodic visits on the 16th. The program consisted largely of works that today would be confined to grand opera houses—*The Elixir of Love*, *The Daughter of the Regiment*, *Martha*, *Carmen*, and *Fra Diavolo*. In a slightly lighter vein they also offered Firmin Bernicat's *François la Basbleu* as **Victor, the Bluestocking**. After a month at the Fifth Avenue they moved to Niblo's for a final week and then set off again for the hinterlands. Their opening night coincided with the return of *Erminie* to the Casino, where the work chalked up an additional 136 performances. Pauline Hall, Francis Wilson, and W. S. Daboll were back to recreate their original roles.

Just before the Boston company spent its week at Niblo's, the Thatcher, Primrose, and West Minstrels played a week at the house. They were the second blackface entourage to entertain there, the Progressive Minstrels, a lesser touring band, having played the house for a week in November. But minstrelsy was undeniably dying. Dockstader's Minstrels, who had attempted to follow in the path of the San Francisco Minstrels by offering New York a permanent company, threw in the towel in February and took to the road.

February's only other musicals were brief returns by the Salsbury Troubadours in *Three of a Kind* (15 February 1886) and Nat Goodwin in *Turned Up* (11 December 1886). Goodwin continued to turn up in this and his other pieces at combination houses—theatres devoted to touring plays—for the next several seasons, but Nate Salsbury was preparing to leave the theatre to run Buffalo Bill's traveling Wild West show.

March, like December, had only one musical arrival. And as in December, the piece was a work by Lecocq. A revival of *The Pearl of Pekin (Fleur de Thé)*, laced with interpolations by Gustave Kerker, was made moderately welcome, keeping the Bijou lit until the end of May.

However, a less than full-fledged musical also appeared. **Maggie the Midget** (13 March 1888, 14th St.) starred the well-liked Maggie Mitchell. As in her big hit *Fanchon*, she played a hoyden who, this time, with the help of a large Newfoundland dog, overcomes villainy to win wealth and a handsome young man. David Braham's songs were no better than the play, so Miss Mitchell quickly discarded it.

The Kiralfys had yet one more of their unique mountings at Niblo's ready on 2 April when they unveiled their version of Sardou's *La Patrie* as **Dolores**. Incongruous ballets, such as a gypsy number with the principals all in black, and "Dresdenia" with the ensemble made to resemble Dresden china, bore little or no relation to a tale of a Flemish count who is forced to take no action on his wife's infidelity lest he reveal he is a revolutionary. The mounting lasted two weeks.

Rosina Vokes also made an appearance in April. She offered the same fare her family had been regaling playgoers with for nearly two decades.

Amanuensis (23 April 1888, Dockstader's) was in two acts. The first was set in a lawyer's office, where his associates and clients provided the musical numbers. The second act took place on the roof of the lawyer's building, where the wide-open space allowed for the injection of some spectacle along with giving more room to jugglers and acrobats.

Upside Down (23 April 1888, Niblo's), which had been seen earlier at some outlying combination houses, was possibly even more retrograde. On the flimsiest of excuses it bundled together some young men who have run away to become circus roustabouts, an oddball inventor, some pretty girls, and a "trick elephant."

That same night brought in a revival of Harrigan's *Old Lavender* (3 September 1878). The public refused it the affection Harrigan bestowed on it, and Harrigan closed the play in two weeks' time, closing his season as well.

Ostensibly a spoof of the wild speculation in natural gas stocks, **Natural Gas** (1 May 1888, Fifth Ave.) soon abandoned its pretense of plot for the sake of typical farce-comedy turns. These included

a clog dancer, a blackface artist, acrobats, and a contortionist. Three men sang about the vicissitudes touring actors encounter (offering imitations of celebrated players as they moved from verse to verse). Characters largely forgotten included a penniless speculator, a malapropian Irish scrubwoman, who believes she has struck it rich, and the acrobatic policeman she loves. Jennie Yeamans, so recently in the failed *Our Jennie*, was among the better-known players.

The first musical to play the new Broadway Theatre at 41st Street arrived on 2 May. Although the theatre for years was to be one of New York's principal homes of musicals, its opening had been awarded to Fanny Davenport in *La Tosca*, Sardou's play. But the initial lyric attraction had luminaries enough, with Camille D'Arville and Lillian Russell sharing starring honors. Like *La Tosca*, **The Queen's Mate** had started its career as a Parisian hit, Lecocq's *La Princesse de Canaries*. This retitled revival was presented in an adaptation by Harry Paulton, who had collaborated on *Erminie*. Paulton also played a major role in the company. The show was a resounding hit. Except for a brief summer vacation it ran on steadily into the fall.

McCaull and his company were soon ready with another new American work. **The Lady or the Tiger?** (7 May 1888, Bijou) was based on Frank R. Stockton's short story of the same name. The new work had a book by Sydney Rosenfeld and music by Julius J. Lyons and McCaull's conductor, Adolph Nowack. In the original tale the hero and the emperor's daughter are in love, but the hero is to be fed to the lions. There are two doors in the arena. One opens to unleash the hungry lion and bring the hero instant death. The other opens to bring forth a beautiful maiden and instant marriage. In either case, the emperor's daughter will lose her beloved. She indicates which door to choose and the hero opens it. The story ended there, leaving the reader to guess what was in the princess's mind. The most celebrated change made by Rosenfeld was to let the audience see the princess's selection. It turns out to be an old hag. Although the show was coolly received by the critics, it played comfortably until the end of June. No doubt the presence in the cast of De Wolf Hopper, Jefferson De Angelis, and Mathilde Cottrelly (this time as the old crone) induced playgoers to ignore the critical verdict.

A week later the Casino displayed its summer attraction—Francis Chassaigne's **Nadjy**. The love of a margrave's nephew for his Nadjy triumphs over his emperor's command to marry a girl the monarch has kidnapped for him. Richard Barker, D'Oyly Carte's assistant, who became the era's leading transatlantic director of musicals, staged the work, with Marie Jansen in the title part and Isabelle Urquhart, Mark Smith, and James T. Powers in support. The Casino's faith in the work was justified, and the piece played merrily on until mid-October.

At the end of the month, real estate speculation provided the frame for similar antics in **Town Lots; or, A Paper City** (28 May 1888, Bijou). Its author was Herbert Hall Winslow, an Iowan then starting out on what would be a long, prolific, if not very distinguished career; its star was slim, droll Jacques Kruger.

John McCaull's band closed the season with a revival of Johann Strauss's *Prince Methusalem*. It ran for a month, and but for one instance should be no more than a passing footnote in the history of the American Musical Theatre. Sometime during the run and somewhere in the second act, De Wolf Hopper departed from the text and inserted a poem, "Casey at the Bat," by Ernest Lawrence Thayer. Just how Hopper justified the insertion of this bit of baseball lore into an operetta will probably never be known. But his reading drew insistent encores, and for the rest of his career there was hardly a performance in which Hopper was not called on to recite the piece. The interpolation vividly illustrates the freewheeling attitudes of late nineteenth-century authors and performers, and the easygoing acceptance of their audiences. In later years, when consistent stylistic tone and creative integrity came to matter more, Hopper often found the poem had to be recited at intermission or during curtain calls instead of in midperformance. Hopper, for the record, recalled the date of his first recitation as 13 May 1888—a Sunday when there was no regular performance. Even so, this would make his first reading of the piece take place during the run of *The Lady or the Tiger?* But Hopper insisted *Prince Methusalem* was the show.

All through the season combination houses offered works with musical interludes. For example, W. J. Scanlan, his career almost at its end, appeared in *The Irish Minstrel* by Fred Marsden. Scanlan, like J. K. Emmet, generally took credit for the songs in his pieces. But so responsible and good-natured a scholar as Odell alluded to persistent accusations when he wrote of them, "[E]ach purveyor was declared to have composed his most popular melody." Odell unwittingly recorded the uncertain vagaries of fame when, writing in his history of the New York theatre

in 1941, he added that both Emmet's "Lullaby" and Scanlan's "Peek-A-Boo" were still sung. He could not have reiterated the statement sixty years later.

Ninety miles south of New York a few Philadelphians were able to attend a concert performance of a musical novelty. We normally pass over such concerts, but this one holds some special interest because more than fifteen years before Chicago devoted a whole musical to the matter, and sixty-five years before Broadway, Philadelphians could assess "Paul Eaton's new baseball comic opera," **Angela; or, The Umpire's Revenge** (28 June 1888, Grand Opera). A star pitcher of a college baseball team—one reviewer stated he was named Eli Yale—joins the New York Baseball Club so that he can be near his sweetheart, Angela. But after the pitcher insults an umpire, the umpire lures the young man away from his wedding to Angela and substitutes another groom. Hero and heroine can be wed only when the substitute groom is shown to be a girl.

1888–1889

In number and in quality the preceding season had marked the lowest ebb since the onrush that followed *H. M. S. Pinafore* (15 January 1879). There was a slight upturn in the new season, but it was deceptive. There were simply more revivals or return engagements. And a small rise in quality was largely attributable to a single importation: *The Yeomen of the Guard*.

The season got off to a slow start. Only two musical offerings bowed in August; only two in September. Each month disclosed one novelty and one revival. The first new musical of the year was a Kiralfy production. But in this instance it was produced by just one of the brothers, Bolossy. His private family bickerings scarcely affected the mounting the public saw. **Mathias Sandorf** was a typical period melodrama bedecked with typical Kiralfy splendor (there was real water in the waterfall) and studded with typical Kiralfy specialty acts and ballets. In true Kiralfy fashion "the ballet took precedence of dramatic values." The story followed the perilous career of a Hungarian patriot. Condemned to death, he escapes, makes a fortune overseas, and uses his wealth to take revenge on his betrayers. Of course, as with most of the family's productions, *Mathias Sandorf* was housed at Niblo's, enjoying the theatre's shelter from 18 August through 13 October.

The two revivals followed in short order. Dellinger's *Lorraine* arrived two nights after *Mathias*

Sandorf. It played for just a fortnight and was replaced at the same house, Wallack's, by a month-long run of von Suppé's *Boccaccio.* Marion Manola, De Wolf Hopper, Jefferson De Angelis, and Annie Myers figured prominently in both, with Digby Bell joining them in the second.

Waddy Googan, Harrigan and Braham's only original effort for the season, opened on 3 September, the same night *Boccaccio* returned. Ned Harrigan's compassion for the underdogs of any racial or religious group was again asserted in his simple story. Waddy Googan (Harrigan) is a hack driver. His wife, Mary (Annie Yeamans), keeps a small restaurant. Together they see that justice is done to Bianca (Annie O'Neill), an Italian waif they have adopted, and that punishment is meted out to her harasser, Shang Wilkins (Charles Sturges). But Harrigan could put his personally generous feelings aside to record accurately the prejudices of his characters. One figure remarks, "De Irish is de wise man, de German is de fool," while another comments, "[T]he Irish can crowd the Dutch out dead or alive." Unwittingly Harrigan also demonstrated how one century's complaints and problems are repeated in the next. At one point this bit of dialogue occurs:

Mary: ... that's the garbage fleet.
Waddy: Yes and when they dump the garbage they choke the channels of our harbor.
Mary: Yes and kill all the fish.

Later Mary explodes, "Bad luck to the street gangs I say. They're like two armies fighting, when school is out." Harrigan's exceedingly large cast of characters often surpassed the resources of his good-sized company. This, plus probably the desire for a small tour de force, prompted Harrigan to play not only the title role but the minor part of Joe Cornello as well. Reviews of the era rarely mentioned the dancing in Harrigan and Braham musicals, but the *Times* noted that a tarantella stopped the show and that a march by the midnight police squad at the Second Precinct also won applause. Abetted by David Braham's pleasant melodies, *Waddy Googan* survived until 3 December.

The Star Theatre played host to a new farce-comedy, **Zig-Zag,** for two weeks beginning 1 October. The slightest of plots took patrons of a Turkish bath for a spree on Mount Olympus. Its reception was more enthusiastic than either its producers or the theatre had expected. Although the *Herald* sneered, "unutterable trash," the public disagreed. Previous

commitments forced it to be pulled when its initial booking ended, but word-of-mouth enthusiasm brought it back for two more engagements later in the season: one at Niblo's and one at the Bijou.

October's next entry was a second farce-comedy. Charles Hoyt's **A Brass Monkey** bowed at the Bijou on 15 October and compiled a run of 104 showings before it closed on 4 January. An old auctioneer named Doolittle Work (Alf M. Hampton) has always ridiculed his superstitious friends who have insisted the brass monkey he forever carries has caused the breakup of his four marriages. He dies, bequeathing his estate to his nephew, Dodge Work (Tim Murphy), on the condition the young man retain the brass monkey. When the nephew's own marriage starts to come apart he puts the monkey up for auction. The show was the first of three Hoyt works to be staged during the year. *A Tin Soldier* (5 May 1885) was revived at the 14th Street Theatre on 24 December with a cast that included the young Marie Cahill, while *A Midnight Bell* premiered at the Bijou on 5 March, offering in its cast Thomas Q. Seabrooke, who later starred in a number of musical comedies, and introducing a sixteen-year-old Maude Adams, who went on to fame in less lyric enterprises. Although a comedy, *A Midnight Bell* was a more serious attempt by Hoyt at playwriting. The specialties that Hoyt contrived to inject in his other pieces were omitted.

Since the early 1880s Charles L. Davis had been performing the part of a farmer, Alvin Joslin, in a play of the same name. As far as big-city audiences, at least at first-class houses, were concerned, he and his play couldn't compare with Denman Thompson's Josh Whitcomb. Now Davis again tested New York's reaction when he appeared in a heavily musicalized and vaudevillized sequel called **One of the Old Stock** (15 October 1888, Windsor). New York was a city where new stock was constantly rising to the top and calling the shots, but even old-line critics found Davis–Joslin crude, unsubtle, and unmoving beside Thompson's remarkable fellow Yankee.

That evening, 15 October, also witnessed Lydia Thompson's second attempt at a comeback. Like *Ixion* (28 September 1868) just twenty years before, **Penelope** resorted to classic legend for its plot. Miss Thompson was garbed as Ulysses to show her still-attractive features to best advantage. But librettist H. P. Stevens and composer Edward Solomon concocted a weak vehicle that only emphasized the passing of a once fresh art. *Penelope* folded forlornly after a single week at the Star.

The first of two happy gifts from England arrived at the Casino on the 17th. Gilbert and Sullivan's **The Yeomen of the Guard** demonstrated the continuing vitality of the English musical stage. Richard Barker directed this tale of a jester's unrequited love, with J. H. Ryley as Jack Point, George Broderick as Sir Richard, Henry Hallam as Colonel Fairfax, George Olmi as Sgt. Meryll, Charles Renwick as Leonard Meryll, Fred Solomon as Wilfred Shadbolt, Bertha Ricci as Elsie Maynard, Sylvia Gerrish as Phoebe, Isabelle Urquhart as Dame Carruthers, and Kate Uart as Kate. Perhaps because the musical touched on tragedy its reception was somewhat restrained. But it ran into January, inscribing 100 performances in the record book and winding up on the happy side of the ledger.

An older English masterpiece, *A Midsummer Night's Dream*, closed out the month at the Star. Of course it was not really a musical, but in keeping with a common practice of the day this production was prodigal in its presentation of ballet and occasional songs.

While Lew Dockstader made another effort to establish a permanent company at the auditorium that once housed the San Francisco Minstrels, he had to tinker desperately with traditional formulas to keep his box office humming. The whole month of January was devoted to a farce-comedy, *Kitty*, and when it closed the bills that followed looked very much like standard variety. The lone visit by a minstrel troupe presenting anything that resembled the old format occurred when Thatcher, Primrose, and West began a brief stay on 5 November.

Starting 12 November, Henry E. Dixey and *Adonis* (4 September 1884) paid a two-week visit to the Star just below the heart of the theatrical district that then ran from Union Square to slightly above Herald Square. The show and its star were also available to theatregoers unwilling to stray far from their home neighborhoods. For example, in May the production visited the Grand Opera House, now given over almost wholly to touring attractions. During the season this same house played most of the preceding season's hits: *The Irish Minstrel* (9 April 1888), *The Corsair* (18 October 1887), and an opéra bouffe troupe.

Just a month after Lydia Thompson's failure and the Savoyard success, England offered America a new delight. The fame of George Edwardes's London Gaiety Burlesque Theatre, of its cheery musicals, and, most of all, of its lovely dancing girls whetted appetites and stimulated advance sales at the Standard.

When **Monte Cristo, Jr.** opened on 15 November the great expectations proved a stumbling block. An uneasy sense of disappointment set in. Most of the regrets were directed toward the quality of the work itself, a travesty in doggerel verse of Dumas's tale. But the English girls, led by small, slender, husky-voiced Nellie Farren and augmented by a number of American beauties, elicited the happiest applause and began a new rage on the lyric stage. As Odell records, "[A] bevy of young and beautiful English girls introduced us to a new style of dancing in long, swishy skirts that immediately caught our fancy and started a fashion, a craze, that lasted here several years. Tights went out and the lovely skirt dancing came in." Actually, the flowing grace of this style of choreography already had been seen by Americans in the dancing of Loie Fuller. But she was a solo performer. It was the cumulative effect of an entire line of lovely young ladies in movement that so strongly impressed itself on susceptible theatregoers. The impression was reinforced when the English company replaced *Monte Cristo, Jr.* with a more acceptable piece, **Miss Esmeralda**, on 17 December. This burlesque of the Esmeralda–Captain Phoebus romance from *The Hunchback of Notre Dame* ran until 5 January when contracts took the company on tour. It returned with both shows in two other engagements during the winter and spring.

Chicago, too, was prepared to offer New York its wares. On 26 November, that city's version of the Cinderella tale traveled east after a six-month run at home. Alfred Thompson and Harry B. Smith made the adaptation, and David Henderson mounted it. In **The Crystal Slipper** Cinderella (Marguerite Fish) is a "slavey" in the castle of Baron von Anthracite (R. E. Graham). Her only friends are the Baron's valet, Yosemite, and the Baron's mouser, Thomas Cat. Of course, the good Prince Polydore von Prettiwitz (Mamie Cerbi) comes to her rescue. Although the New York run of four weeks fell far short of its home stand, the visit did call New Yorkers' attention to two rising stage clowns. Yosemite was played by Eddie Foy and the cat by George Ali. Ali, as Foy recalled in his autobiography, "spent almost his entire career inside a caricatured imitation of some animal's skin." Miss Fish added an exotic touch to the evening. Only recently arrived from Vienna, she played Cinderella with a German accent.

A December revival of *The Lorgaire* (25 November 1878) suggested that Harrigan and Braham apparently no longer had the creative drive to produce a string of new plays each season.

But it remains to Harrigan's credit as a producer that he did not attempt to fall back comfortably on one or two of his biggest hits to complete his season. Harrigan drew from the whole range of his canon. But Harrigan's audiences were not as brave, nor were they as willing to rehear anything but the best. As a result Harrigan had to make frequent changes on his posters throughout the season. His 1878 work gave way to his year-old *Pete* (22 November 1887) on 31 January and this in turn to a work from a year earlier, *The O'Reagans* (11 October 1886), on 4 March. When this failed, Harrigan endeavored to present an old acquaintance under a new name. *4-11-44*, which opened on 21 March, was merely a minor rewriting of *McNooney's Visit* (31 January 1887). Three weeks later he rushed in *The Grip* (30 November 1885). This lasted only a week, as a discouraged Harrigan abruptly terminated the season and announced he was leaving the Park.

New York types—old stock and new—were the characters in Charles Alfred Byrne's **The Kitty** (31 December 1888, Dockstader's). The action began in a corner grocery store where one figure wins a sizable kitty in a poker game, which allows him to splurge at a restaurant "that seemed to be an amalgamation of Delmonico's and a Bowery beanery," and finally led to a matrimonial agency. The Mestayers, having set aside *Check 44*, headed the cast.

January 1889 was almost entirely given over to revivals and return engagements. Both *The Queen's Mate* and *The Pearl of Pekin* paid return calls on die 7th. On the 21st the Casino brought back its production of *Nadjy* for an additional three months. And *Pete* closed out the month at the Park. One of the two new "musicals" was **Myles Aroon** by George Jessop and Horace Townsend. It was a vehicle for Scanlan, and he introduced a handful of songs into the romantic piece as was his wont. The work remained for just two weeks at the 14th Street, since Scanlan's most loyal followers took their patronage to more outlying houses.

John Wild, who had gained fame in blackface as Simpson Primrose in the Harrigan and Hart shows, came in with the other novelty, a vehicle written especially for him, **Running Wild** (21 January 1889, Star). He burnt his cork again to appear as D'Oily Float and as Joe King. For his first entrance his totally white suit was in marked contrast to his blackened face, but his loyal fans instantly recognized his jaunty walk, "that inimitable unctuous roll." Although he received a prolonged ovation on this first entrance (and responded with the expected

speech), the show was all but stolen from him by two supporting players, Harry Brinsley in the non-speaking but laugh-getting role of "The Gentleman who removes the ashes" and St. George Hussy as "the Lady as does the cleaning." Critics heard a distinctly Brahamian tinge in the ballads and marches that were sprinkled throughout the evening.

In contrast to January, February had a number of novelties and no revivals. Two openings occurred on the 11th. Bolossy Kiralfy mounted still another spectacle at Niblo's, **The Water Queen.** This saga of die Queen of the Rhine's love for a mortal lasted only three weeks. **Later On,** which debuted at the Star, fared even more unhappily, surviving a single week. On 25 February the same house brought in **Said Pasha.** Although the show had apparently been mounted independently in San Francisco, this production had originated in Philadelphia, and New York chose to view it as another horrible example of the "Philadelphia school." Sung to Richard Stahl's music, Scott Marble's story told how the Pasha (Francis Gaillard) attempts to circumnavigate the globe in record time. His daughter, Serena (Helen Dingeon), accompanies him to be with her lover, Hassen Bey (R. N. Dunbar). A Mexican (Hubert Wilke) in search of a perfect woman almost persuades Serena to change her affections. The music was undistinguished, although far more sophisticated than Spenser's. But some of Marble's dialogue could have justified New Yorkers' seeing a Philadelphia influence in the work. For example, just as one character in *The Little Tycoon* (24 March 1886) grunted his way through the story, a comic figure named Nockey (Stanley Felch) spent the evening giving every possible inflection to a single word, "why." To drive the knife home, critics found the harem of chorus girls especially unattractive. Although the production played only a fortnight, it returned after a road tour for a second Rialto engagement in April.

A February flop in San Francisco nonetheless says something about how national American theatre could be. Ion Arnold and George Morgan's **Yetiva** (25 February 1889, Tivoli) was described in its programs as a "new American opera," although, of course, it was operetta. The program also promised a "Grotesque Dance by real indians." Col. Dwight has moved from Tennessee and made a fortune in New Mexico while his daughter, Yetiva, attends school back east. When she returns for vacation, she falls in love with Dick Dudley, king of the cowboys. A jealous Mexican, Juana, tries to have Yetiva kidnapped and spreads stories that Dwight is not really Yetiva's father. But all ends happily. That the show was an immediate failure did not discourage its authors or a Philadelphia producer, for it was revised and retitled *A Trip to the Rockies*, and brought out on the other side of the continent at the historic Walnut Street Theatre on 2 September 1895. It failed again.

In New York, March reverted to the safety or necessity of revivals. All stays were brief. Harrigan's presentations aside, the month welcomed a touring company of *Evangeline* at the Star and John McCaull's production of von Suppé's *Boccaccio* at Palmer's. This latter house had been Wallack's, but with Broadway's lack of respect for the past and pandering to raging egos it had been renamed the moment Wallack died.

April was surprisingly busy. In a way it was also varied, even if much of the variety stemmed from works written years before. The openings of the 1st were illustrative. McCaull replaced *Boccaccio* at Palmer's with another importation, Czibulka's **The May Queen**. At the same time, the sturdy *Erminie* came in to Niblo's for a week. Seven nights later Harrigan's *The Grip* also began a week's stand.

Two novelties vied for attention on 22 April. One was an American operetta, **Dovetta**. Its authors were Betsy Banker and Charles Raynaud; its composer, Mrs. E. Marcy Raymond. In their story Dovetta (Fatmah Diard) was an American Indian, torn between her love for the Indian brave, Rainbow (Joseph Lynde), and Lt. Robert Brambleton (W S. Rising) of the U.S. Army. When she learns she is actually white, adopted by the chief after a raid on a settlement, she selects Robert. Some of Robert's fellow officers were Clubby and Broomy, played by Hattie Delaro and Ruby Stuart as trouser roles. Together the girls led the expected Amazon march. The work barely managed to stay alive beyond its first week at the Standard, lingering only for a few matinees. The *Times*'s treatment of the work indicates the fundamental disbelief then prevalent in many quarters in our native ability to match England's musicals. On the front page of its Sunday edition for May 21, the paper devoted a long article—with review—to the London opening of Alfred Cellier's *Doris*. In the theatre news on page 5 the paper noted tersely, almost incredulously, that *Dovetta* would open the following night and that "there is opportunity for the success of an American work and it is to be sincerely hoped that new production will be found excellent." Two days later a one-paragraph review dismissed the piece without any kind words, suggesting as a parting shot that New York could create musicals every bit as bad as Philadelphia's.

The other newcomer was an immediate hit. **Fritz in a Madhouse** gave J. K. Emmet his first new vehicle in several years. The plot was preposterously involved. Fritz is the son of the Baron von Wolfenstein (Harold Hartsell). The baron disowns the boy after he is jailed. What the baron does not know is that his son was jailed fighting in defense of a lady. Fritz loves Collie (Louise Balfe), a daughter of rich, uncouth Joe Parker (Edmund D. Lyons). Mrs. Parker (Ethel Greybrooke), a social climber, disdains her husband and his affectionate daughter. She has sent her son (C. D. Bennett) away to be educated out of reach of his father and sister's compromising influences. A letter leads Mrs. Parker to think her husband is having an affair. Fritz eventually must show her that it was her son, not her husband, who was the subject of the letter and that it was her son's attempt to abuse a lady that landed Fritz in a fight and in jail. Although the last act was set in a madhouse, the setting was only an incidental accommodation to the title. The real source of the title was a line of Fritz's in the play: "... dis world is one great madhouse—and love is de only disease worth catching." Actually the original title had been *Uncle Joe*. The emphasis and the title were changed when Emmet saw possibilities in the story. Devotees flocked to the 14th Street Theatre for seven weeks before Emmet adjourned for vacation and a planned road tour.

In Philadelphia, **King Cole II** (22 April 1889, Broad St.) seems to have been an attempt by Woolson Morse and J. Cheever Goodwin to rework their earlier *Madam Piper*, possibly for a second New York hearing. If so, nothing came of it. It received divided notices, although almost all aisle-sitters applauded the prologue, in which Mother Goose told playgoers that her subjects were unhappy and, as she turned the pages of a gigantic book which occupied the whole stage and was resplendent with glass pendants and prisms, famous Mother Goose characters—Mary Quite Contrary, Jack and Jill, and others—stepped out one by one to air their plaints. When Old King Cole rues he has no son and heir, the good lady allows him to adopt Peter Piper. The young man's misadventures as King Cole II occupied the two main acts. After three weeks, the characters all scampered back to Toyland.

The two New York novelties were followed on 29 April at the Standard by Imre Kiralfy's revival of *The Black Crook* (12 September 1866), still a dependable, albeit fading, standby. It was good for a two-week stand. Kiralfy's staging ignored a growing reaction against the old piece. The *Times* exemplified this new feeling when, in its review of *The Water Queen*, it gratuitously branded *The Black Crook* "probably the stupidest stage play ever invented."

While New Yorkers awaited late-season arrivals, San Francisco's famed musical house unveiled "a new American operetta," **The First Lieutenant** (6 May 1889, Tivoli). The creation of two writers from nearby Oakland, N. Clifford Page and Clark Wise, its long, convoluted plot retailed how Lieutenant Benson is drugged and left for drowned by Second Lieutenant Vaughn, his rival for the hand of Melanie, the governor's daughter. The ship which rescues him is seized by pirates, and Benson is sold into slavery in Morocco. There he wins the respect of the Sultan, is allowed to return home in disguise to bring Melanie and Vaughn back with him, and ultimately, on a second voyage back home, tricks Vaughn into a confession. One San Francisco reviewer was dismayed that the hero was sung by a basso instead of a tenor: "It is like substituting the modern parlor with gas turned down as the scene of wooing in place of the dear old balcony of Romeo and Juliet with the moon beaming and the silver-voiced lover having the best of odds every time."

By May, back in New York, producers and theatre owners began to be concerned about keeping their houses lit throughout the summer. For the most part the better managers and theatres were lucky in the summer of 1889, although none of their successful offerings are especially remembered a hundred or more years later. John McCaull hit the jackpot first on 8 May with his production at Palmer's of von Suppé's **Clover,** in which a reckless noble and his faithful servant rebound from bankruptcy. Von Suppé's vivacious score kept the box office busy until early October, particularly as enlivened by Miss Cottrelly, Oudin, De Angelis, and Hopper.

One night later the Casino raised its curtain on a lavish revival of Offenbach's *The Brigands*, using W S. Gilbert's translation. Lillian Russell and statuesque Isabelle Urquhart were its principal beauties and singers. Until mid-September they helped the Casino's patrons forget the heat.

The third summer-spanning success arrived four nights later. Sydney Rosenfeld's adaptation of Lecocq's *La Jolie Persane* was rechristened **The Oolah** to cast attention on the role portrayed by its star, Francis Wilson. Marie Jansen was the pretty Persian and Hubert Wilke her lover. The show had the "Oriental" setting so prevalent in musical librettos of the era and a plot about comic divorces not unlike *The Begum* (21 November 1887). When divorces for women become too easy and too frequent in old Persia the ruler decrees that before a divorced woman can remarry a man of her choice, she must marry a public servant called an oolah. Royal ladies were assigned a special oolah, Hoolagoolah. Wilson not only secured his hold on stardom with the show but introduced several lines that quickly obtained common currency. As Hoolagoolah he demanded women "think twice about divorcing once." He proudly admitted, "I have been married a hundred and fifteen times and not once deceived. I have known men who have been married but once, but who were deceived a hundred and fifteen times."

A revival of *Mazulm* (9 January 1888) appeared on the same night *The Oolah* opened. The Kiralfy mounting lasted a mere week.

An abrupt cancellation of a booking forced Niblo's to rush in a hodgepodge touring farce-comedy for a week. Critics insisted **Pat's [New] Wardrobe** (20 May 1889, Niblo's) had no plot and was merely an excuse for a collection of old and new songs, sketches, and a dancing leading man who could show off his clothing. That leading man, playing a character named Pat O'Hoolihan, was a very young Pat Rooney. Down the years he would become a beloved figure in vaudeville, revue, and musical comedy.

America's most famous touring company, The Bostonians, did not always bring their complete repertory to New York. A typical example of one of their shows never to play Broadway was **Suzette,** Oscar Weil's adaptation and musicalization of Chivot and Duru's *La Dormeuse Éveillée.* It was given a performance at San Francisco's Baldwin Theater on 31 May 1889. Suzette is a charming but incorrigible madcap: "I hate cooking and washing dishes and sewing—anything but wild oats." Her uncle, despairing of taming her, returns her to her innkeeper foster father. After she goes to sleep she is kidnapped and dressed as a man. Later she turns the tables and kidnaps the kidnappers. However, when she falls in love with the innkeeper's son, Rene, she quiets down and even helps amass the 3,000-crown dot required for the marriage.

Back in New York, a comic-opera fiasco ended the year. A week's run beginning 3 June was all that **Ardriell** could muster at the Union Square. The show was based on *La Poupée de Nuremberg* and so told the same tale as *Pepita*. Odell says the music was by J. A. Norris, writing under the pen name J. Adahm, but newspapers of the day insist Adahm was German.

1889–1890

In his theatre history, Odell judged the new theatrical year "A Very Brilliant Season." As usual, his evaluation did not take into account lyric enterprises. By and large it was another distressing season for musicals. Yet in retrospect historians can catch faint glimmers, hear tentative stirrings of better things to come.

Niblo's inaugurated the season on 17 August with one more of its gargantuan mountings, **Antiope.** Bolossy Kiralfy adapted and expanded the work from a shorter piece that had been done at London's Alhambra. He retained the story of an Amazonian queen's unrequited love for a neighboring prince. The youth prefers the queen's demure young sister, Antiope. When the queen would wrathfully destroy the lovers, a *deus ex machina* (in pink tights) sets things right. The extravaganza's main claim to fame is that it served to introduce Carmencita to New York audiences. Although the *Times* singled her out as "an agile, graceful, mercurial woman, with flashing eyes and mobile features," the dancer was apparently lost amid Niblo's swollen casts and overwhelming scenery. Not until she joined Koster and Bial's variety bill later in the year did she embark on her meteoric rise. The rest of the cast was panned, especially for its "coarse, unpleasant" singing. Spectacle included Niblo's umpteenth Amazon march and a luxurious barge that "moved forward and backward with equal facility." For all its unevenness, *Antiope* was something of a hit, running until the end of September.

Frank Tannehill, Jr.'s farce-comedy **Bric-A-Brac** held Tony Pastor's stage briefly from 17 August before Pastor's regular variety season opened. Its songs and dances were attached to the story of a millionaire who invites a group of "geniuses" to a ball. The most flamboyant genius is a writer of comic operas. A runaway balloon carries the party to Africa, where circus people, seeking animals, rescue them. Specialties included Alf Hampton's imitations, Maude Giroux's love ballads, and an unidentified "darky" whistler.

August's only other musical entry was an importation by the authors of *Erminie*, Harry Paulton and Edward Jakobowski. Called **Paola** (26 August 1889, Fifth Avenue), it totally failed to win the affection that had been showered on its predecessor. Paulton,

Louise Beaudet, and Chauncey Olcott (praised for his "light, sweet tenor") romped through the adventures of a comic coward assigned to execute a Corsican vendetta. It ran until 5 October before its producer, the J. C. Duff Opera Company, withdrew it.

McKenna's Flirtation opened at the Park on 2 September. The title and the house suggest it was a new Harrigan and Braham work, but in fact Harrigan had temporarily retired from the theatrical scene. Its plot was fairly simple, recording complications that follow fast when McKenna, a Harlem contractor, is mistakenly delivered a love note Mrs. Ryan (Marie Cahill) has meant for another man. Dramatic representations of an elevated train and of ships sailing into port embellished the story. The producers and the author, Edgar Selden, employed the practice of farce-comedies and some other, older shows by borrowing music from a number of sources, most often the variety stages. With a cast also recruited largely from vaudeville favorites of the time, notably short, stout, and red-haired William Barry (as McKenna) and tall, thin Hugh Fay (as Mr. Ryan), 104 performances were chalked up before it closed on 30 November. For Miss Cahill, her excellent notices marked the beginning of a career that would keep her a star for nearly a generation.

If *McKenna's Flirtation* depicted the more riotous side of Irish life, **The Fairy's Well** (also advertised as *The Fairies' Well*) recounted its more romantic side. The work was of that type so popular with Irish audiences of the time. Essentially a straight play, it punctuated its most dramatic moments with song. The show had been on tour for over a year. In 1888–1889 it had made several stops in Brooklyn. It arrived at the 14th Street Theatre, a house that often played host to Irish plays, on 9 September and lingered for two weeks before resuming its peregrinations. Its appearance so close to the main stem prompted the *Times* to attack the genre as a whole:

> There is not an original idea in the play, and the auditor is confronted at every turn with familiar scenes, incidents, characters and dialogue. The hero is the traditional servant in corduroy, who makes pert answers to his social superiors and sings and dances without excuse or apology in the most inappropriate places. The heroine is a peculiar young woman who is beset on the one hand by a hard-hearted mortgage holder and on the other by a villain with papers that reflect the character of her departed mother.

Carroll Johnson, long a minstrel, led the undistinguished cast. An "Irish jaunting car" was featured on stage.

More solid lyric material was heard the following Monday night when the Casino presented its first offering of the season, a revival of Offenbach's *La Fille du Tambour-Major*, translated as **The Drum Major**. The adaptation was by Max Freeman and Edgar Smith. Freeman doubled as director and Smith as a performer. Pauline Hall and James T. Powers were prominent in the cast, but even their talents could not overcome a mediocre, humorless translation and an indifferent reception that made it known pretty stage pictures were not enough. The piece had a slightly forced run of eight weeks.

Two return engagements brought September to a close, *Zig-Zag* (1 October 1888) and *The Pearl of Pekin*. Both stayed only a week.

The Seven Ages (7 October 1889, Standard) was conceived in the hope of providing Henry E. Dixey with a vehicle that might approach the success of *Adonis* (4 September 1884). Unfortunately, *The Seven Ages* suffered the fate of most sequels, falling far short of its predecessor's triumph. In fact, so many mishaps—lines muffed, long scene changes, a scene halted while a costume was changed—occurred opening night that few would have been surprised had the show been an immediate failure. But Dixey was too stalwart a professional to surrender to such happenstance misfortunes. Rehearsals and revisions quickly knocked the show into shape, and, while *The Seven Ages* never turned into a runaway hit, it nevertheless enjoyed a highly satisfactory run of 152 performances and a profitable road tour. As in *Adonis*, the curtain rose to reveal a living statue. However, instead of Dixey as a white marble Greek, playgoers beheld a supporting actor, George Howard, as a bronze Shakespeare. The statue comes to life to start Bertie Van Loo on a journey covering his entire history, taking Bertie not only back to his infant days in a baby carriage but into the future to see himself as an old man of ninety. In between Bertie cavorts as a lover, a soldier, and a justice of the peace.

Spider and Fly (14 October 1889, Comique) was something of an oddity, half spectacle, half musical comedy. It narrated what happens after two goddesses, Progressa and Anarchia (or Ignorancia), adopt two boys whose nicknames provided the show's title.

November was no more generous than October, also bringing in only two lyric works, both revivals. On the 11th W. J. Scanlan began a four-week visit in

Myles Aroon at the Star, while on the 20th the Casino quickly remounted *Erminie* to replace the faltering *Drum Major*. With Francis Wilson occupied elsewhere, the part of Cadeaux so identified with him went to James T. Powers.

Kajanka premiered at Niblo's on 2 December. "Another attempt to recapture some of the fine careless raptures of The Black Crook and its Niblo successors," the piece had an initial run of five weeks. But unlike some of its ilk which enjoyed longer first runs, *Kajanka* caught the fancy of a number of cities on the road and held up so well on its tour that it came back a year later for a second stay. The libretto, by a famous clown of the period, George D. Melville, told a straightforward tale with pantomime trappings. The wicked son of a bad fairy attempts to kidnap Kajanka (Edith Craske). Good fairies, assisted by Clown and Pantaloon, save the girl. As always, Niblo's filled the show with specialty numbers. Four young ladies in long, flying skirts performed a butterfly dance, and the Donazettis were hailed as "the best tumbling act ever seen here." Even principals doubled in brass. William Ruge, who played the wicked son, "give a remarkable exhibition as acrobat and contortionist."

For a second season in a row performers from London's Gaiety Theatre crossed the Atlantic to display their act. Their vehicle for this occasion was **Faust up to Date.** Some important cast members—notably Florence St. John, slated to play Marguerite—were too ill to perform at the opening, and their absence dampened the work's reception. But the beguiling line of Gaiety girls ("a frank display of the lower limbs") went a long way to compensate for the missing principals. The show held the stage at the Broadway for a month, beginning 10 December, toured major cities, and returned in April for a short farewell stay.

A revival of *The Brigands* (26 December 1870) ushered in the new year and the new decade on 6 January 1890. Its presence on the Casino stage was interesting for two reasons. For one, it was the second of a string of revivals the house found it necessary to resort to during the season. The year was probably the most difficult the house had endured since its opening. Few novelties of merit seemed to be available to it; indeed, few novelties of merit seemed to be available at all. Second, it was an opéra bouffe. Although newspapers of the time had long considered the opéra bouffe a waning vogue (and scholars of a later day would agree), many of the best examples of the genre still found a large audience.

What had largely disappeared was the opéra bouffe repertory company, playing different pieces each night—playing them rather faithfully and often singing them in French. These new opéra bouffe mountings reflected both management's and performers' contentment with the larger profits and comforts of long runs. They were generally staged with a freedom that disconcerted purists, adding alien interpolations and business on a scale that jolted those who knew and loved the originals.

Another jolt was in store for devotees of a kindred art form the night after *The Brigands* returned. The long-awaited American premiere of Gilbert and Sullivan's *The Gondoliers* took place at the Park on 7 January. This last of their masterpieces told a lighthearted yarn of two gondoliers whose romances are interrupted when a misunderstanding makes them kings for a day. Although it was an "authorized" production, it was so badly bungled critics shook their heads in dismay. Advance sales and some forcing allowed the mounting to run until 13 February. Then D'Oyly Carte, who had hurried over, recast and restaged the work and reopened it at Palmer's, where it ran for an additional two months. Principals in this "definitive" version included Fred Billington, Richard Temple, Richard Clarke, Kate Talby, Norah Phyllis, and Esther Palliser.

Eddie Foy, fast rising to prominence, was the source of much of the mirth at Niblo's in **Bluebeard, Jr.,** the third of David Henderson's elaborate Chicago extravaganzas to visit New York in as many years. The libretto by Clay M. Greene (to music by Fred Eustis and Richard Maddern) played loose with the famous pirate's story, centering mainly upon his marriage to Fatima. Bluebeard, or Ben Ali Barbazuli (Frank Blair), purchases Fatima (Alice Johnston) from her cynical father, O'Mahdi Benzini (Foy). Before the marriage can be consummated, the bride is rescued by her lover. Bluebeard is not put to death for the murder of his other wives. A more diabolical punishment awaits him. His slain wives are resurrected and return to the harem to torment him. The production catered to the insistent demand for spectacle with a grand ballet, "The Light of Asia," and "The Ballet of the Birds and Insects." Seventy Amazons marched "in armor that really clanked." Over 200 performers filled the stage. On its Chicago opening the preceding 11 June, the *Tribune* happily reported "the art of using electric lights to advantage was never better illustrated... the pictures by this means were toned and varied." New York critics apparently took such wonders for granted, ignoring

both the lighting and Richard Barker's lively staging. The producer and authors also kept a careful eye on the large children's audience, introducing in the "Glittering Grotto of Fantastic Fancy" Jack, the Giant Killer, Puss in Boots, the Babes in the Wood, and the Old Woman Who Lived in a Shoe. Most New Yorkers welcomed the piece, for a month starting 13 January, but meddling do-gooders from the Gerry Society prevented the children of the old lady in the shoe from performing.

On 25 January the Casino brought forth a particularly elaborate revival of *The Grand Duchess* with Lillian Russell as star. Gustave Kerker conducted. For want of better novelties to compete with, the work ran up 100 showings.

One of the biggest hits of the season, **The City Directory** (10 February 1890, Bijou), had a libretto by Paul M. Potter and music by "the old minstrel man," W. S. Mullaly. Potter's libretto was a cross between the old Tom and Jerry theme and the farce-comedies of Hoyt, with perhaps a touch of Harrigan's slices of New York life thrown in. It dealt with the confusions that ensue when a Chicago detective, John Smith (Charlie Reed), comes to New York to arrest a local crook, John Smith. Before the evening is over, nearly a dozen John Smiths are caught up in the muddle, and a tour of Manhattan has been made. The other John Smiths in the play include a businessman (John W. Jennings), an athlete (Alf Hampton), a ballet-master (Ignacio Martinetti), an actor (William Collier), a messenger boy (Joseph Jackson), an elevator operator (a new calling) (Josie Sadler), and a "bunco-steerer" (a confidence man) (William F. Mack). As the ballet-master, Martinetti was able to prance about like "a veritable jumping jack," in contrast to the more graceful dancing of Amelia Glover, then at the beginning of a brief period of celebrity. *The City Directory* compiled 152 performances, marking its hundredth showing by announcing that it had been "rejuvenated" with new sets, new bits, and new songs.

Adolph Muller's imported operetta **King's Fool** (17 February 1890, Niblo's) was a typical work of the time, with the heroine in a trouser role of a princess everyone is determined to pass off as a boy until a court jester comes to her aid. It was also a two-week failure. Its small place in the history of the American Musical Theatre has been secured solely because it marked the debut of Della Fox, who would briefly rival Lillian Russell as a prima donna.

While *The Gondoliers* slowly won a loyal following, Savoyards could see two older favorites when

The Mikado and *The Pirates of Penzance* each played a week at the Broadway in the spring. *The Mikado* opened on 31 March, *The Pirates* two weeks later. Both were touring companies making New York just another stop on their journeys.

De Wolf Hopper saw his name above the title when **Castles in the Air** premiered at the Broadway on 5 May. He was not only the star but was at least the nominal head of the De Wolf Hopper Comic Opera Company, which produced the work.

Castles in the Air had a libretto by C. A. Byrne. His story reminded the *Dramatic Mirror* of the plot for Offenbach's *Les Bavards*, although the trade paper dutifully, if unbelievingly, reported that the show's program insisted Byrne drew his idea from Cervantes' *Los Dos Habladores*, Offenbach's source. Cabolastro (Thomas Q. Seabrooke) offers the debt-ridden Bul-Bul (Marion Manola) disguise to help him elude his creditors on the condition that Bul-Bul outtalk Cabolastro's garrulous wife (Rose Leighton). Bul-Bul consents, since he loves Cabolastro's daughter, Blanche (Della Fox). Interestingly, Hopper played none of the pivotal roles, appearing instead off and on throughout the evening as a freethinking judge, Filacoudre. Most of his laughs came from his broad clowning in scenes that had little to do with the tale. One was a hilarious pantomime billiard match played—sans table, cues, or balls—with Miss Fox. Given Byrne's dialogue, Hopper's comic skills were sorely needed. Byrne's idea of humor ran to lines such as, "All old men die at an advanced age; it is only the young who have a chance to die early." The score was composed by one of the most prominent figures of the turn-of-the-century American Musical Theatre, Gustave Kerker.

WILLIAM DE WOLF HOPPER was born in New York City on 30 March 1858. Never getting beyond the equivalent of high school, he took turns trying various trades before he made his debut as an actor in 1879 in *Our Daughters*. A small legacy enabled him to turn actor-manager, but his tour failed and he soon exhausted his funds. Although he hoped to become a serious dramatic actor, he was so toweringly tall other performers were reluctant to have him in their company, where he would only dwarf them. By 1884, when he accepted a role in Sousa's *Désirée*, he

---

was resigned to confining his booming basso voice to the musical stage. Increasingly adroit performances in shows such as *The Begum* and *The Lady or the Tiger?* speedily consolidated his reputation.

Della Fox's performance in the role of Blanche skyrocketed her to fame. The swiftness of the rise, coming so soon after her debut, suggests how intimate the confines of Broadway remained. *Castles in the Air* played to satisfied audiences until 16 August, recording 105 performances.

The same evening Byrne and Kerker's piece opened, the reunited Kiralfys restored to Niblo's stage their ever-ready *Around the World in Eighty Days* (28 August 1875), still featuring the "Mikado Ballet." It lasted a month.

A rousing revival of *H. M. S. Pinafore* completed May's musical entries. Featuring Digby Bell, Chauncey Olcott, and a cast of 200, it filled the large Academy of Music from 12 to 30 May. On 2 June the same company gave the New York season its second interpretation of *The Mikado*.

Among the many musicals being mounted for local consumption elsewhere was one that premiered in Philadelphia. Frederick Wink and Herman Brunswick's **Amina; or, The Shah's Bride** (19 May 1890, Broad St.) was set in Teheran, where the old shah has just died. The new shah, unhappy that he must wed a girl he was betrothed to in infancy and has never seen, sends Mercutio, a disguised substitute, to the wedding. The bride-to-be, equally concerned, orders her maid, Amina, to stand in for her. Is there any need to tell the rest of the story? Yes, because in a surprise ending the citizens refuse to believe that Mercutio and Amina are not the real thing, so the startled couple are elevated to the throne.

Back in New York at the Casino, Chassaigne's **The Brazillian** arrived the same evening as *The Mikado*. Marie Halton, Edith Ainsworth, Grace Golden, George Olmi, and Richard F. Carroll were featured in this saga of a wily lady's maid who lands spouses for herself and her mistress after they are captured by Brazilian bandits. If the management had hoped to span the summer with the work, they were disappointed. The work received only a moderate run, closing in mid-August.

Palmer's, too, brought in a musical that seemed to have been slated for a summer run and failed.

Richard Stahl's operetta **The Sea King** was even less well attended than *The Brazilian*. Hubert Wilke, Edwin Stevens, Esther Palliser, Lena Merville, Annie Myers, and J. C. Miron could do little to save this tale of a wandering Dutch seaman who lands in Spain, finds a lady who had been waiting all her life for him, and wins her over her uncle's objections. It opened on 23 June and folded 3 August.

No better indication of the fading of minstrelsy and the telling influences of the new English shows could be offered than the fate of the old San Francisco Minstrels' Theatre, rechristened Dockstader's in recent years. Lew Dockstader himself appeared there only from October to December. The house closed at the end of 1889 only to reopen in February of 1890 as the Gaiety!

GUSTAVE KERKER was born in Herford, Germany, on 28 February 1857. He began his studies as a cellist at the age of seven and continued his musical education when his family moved to Louisville, Kentucky, three years later. As a young man he played in the city's theatre orchestras, rising soon to be a conductor. In 1879 he composed his first operetta. *Cadets*, which played briefly in the South. E. E. Rice caught a performance and offered the composer-conductor a chance to work with him. Moving to New York, he soon became the principal conductor at the Casino. On occasion he interpolated his own numbers in importations of the period both at the Casino and elsewhere, most notably in Lecocq's *The Pearl of Pekin*.

Away from the mainstream a number of proto-typical musicals played at other houses. For example, on 14 October Tony Pastor's sheltered the Burton Stanley Opera Company's *Mrs. Partington*, the text of which is apparently lost, while Wild and Collier's Comedy Theatre presented a number of song-larded farces such as *Running Wild, The Mashers*, and *A Legal Holiday*. These works, too, seemingly left no trace.

1890–1891

The number of new musicals dropped noticeably as the new decade began. But, as frequently happened,

a drop in numbers was coupled with a rise in quality. The new season and the following one brought the first great act of the American Musical Theatre to a close with several native creations which gave assurances that, even if the domestic lyric stage had not totally found itself, it was confidently on the right track.

Before New York's season got under way, Chicago played host to an elaborate new musical on 23 July. Henry E. Dixey, looking for another *Adonis* (4 September 1884), turned his attention to Washington Irving's evergreen *Rip Van Winkle*, which had been serving Joseph Jefferson as a dramatic vehicle for so many years. But Dixey's **Rip** retained little of the original story except the name of the central figure, the long nap, and a few quaint spellings. A real estate broker unable to sell his Kaatskill Mountains land for one cent an acre persuades a happy old man to promote it by a marathon snooze. Rip falls asleep, wakes up to find himself young, and sells the property for a large sum. One interesting feature of the show was its architecturally conceived sets. Old-fashioned drops were minimized. The mountain started at the footlights and climbed as it moved backstage. But the sets were more interesting than the rest of the evening. Dixey was never able to whip the show into suitable shape for a New York visit.

August's activity was testimony to the failure of the late-spring musicals to survive the summer. Palmer's, the Broadway, and the Casino all needed new midsummer attractions. Palmer's brought its offering in first, presenting **The Red Hussar** on 5 August. Its book by H. P. Stevens and score by Edward Solomon were not particularly noteworthy. But the part of Kitty Carroll, a young lady who disguises herself as a Red Hussar in order to follow her sweetheart to France, was played by Marie Tempest, making her American debut. She created what the papers love to call a "sensation" and almost single-handedly kept the box office humming until she had to return to England in mid-October.

On the 14th the Casino revived one of the earliest opéra bouffe favorites, shortening its title a bit to *Mme. Angot*. It ran concurrently with *The Red Hussar*, even closing on the same night, 11 October.

Francis Wilson completed the trio of August openings with his second starring vehicle, **The Merry Monarch** (18 August 1890, Broadway). J. Cheever Goodwin based his libretto on *L'Etoile (The Star of Fate)*. Its plot dealt with the curious fate that binds King Anso IV (Wilson) to one of his subjects.

The king selects the saucy street vendor, Lazuli (a trouser role played by Marie Jansen), to be the annual human sacrifice. His astrologer, Sirocco (Charles Plunkett), discovers Lazuli's horoscope is so tied to Anso's that if one dies the other will die. The rest of the evening is spent frantically trying to keep the reckless boy alive. Wilson, like Beatrice Lillie years later, was a master at puncturing spurious claims to dignity. His first entrance was one of the highlights of the show. Brought in on a majestic palanquin, he promptly tumbles down the steps in descending. His constant refusal to finish a thought, but rather to leave it hanging with an "and so forth and so on," not only justifies the king's name but predated the same peculiarity in a later stage ruler—the king of *The King and I* (29 March 1951). A number of the songs by Emile Chabrier and Woolson Morse became the delights of the day, notably, "When I Was A Child Of Three," "The Ostrich Song," and "Love Will Find A Way." (By July, programs at San Francisco's Tivoli Opera House were announcing that the theatre had purchased the West Coast rights to the French original and would shortly mount it under the title **The Guiding Star**, with the king portrayed by Ferris Hartman, the company's leading clown—and father of the later comic dancer, Paul.)

In his autobiography Wilson casts a further sidelight on what a grab bag of talents and materials these old shows often developed into. While in Washington, Wilson spotted two young Negro boys dancing in the street for pennies. He was so taken with their improvisations that he took them with him to New York and incorporated their routine in the show—until some killjoys of the anti–child-labor movement who had troubled *Bluebeard* a year before deprived theatregoers of a novel specialty act and the two youngsters of a legitimate income. With or without the boys *The Merry Monarch* held court until 4 October. The show was one of the many of the era directed by Richard Barker, an Englishman whose reputation for staging musicals earned him frequent transatlantic crossings.

Two nights before *The Merry Monarch* premiered, *Kajanka* (2 December 1889) returned to Niblo's. It added an additional two weeks to its record. Vying for attention with Wilson's vehicle was an extravaganza by William Gill and Robert Frazer, **Hendrik Hudson** (18 August 1890, 14th St.). With trouser roles all the rage, the title part was given to Fay Templeton.

In *Hendrik Hudson* Miss Templeton made her entrance in much talked-about bottom kid leggings,

"the newest and most artistic amplification of the Sarah Bernhardt kid gloves." Her Hendrik was a faithless husband who goes to Florida with his bevy of chorus girls. When he finds Columbus (Eva Randolph) living in retirement there, he signs the old man for appearances at the forthcoming World's Fair. Other characters were Miss Manhattan (Toma Hanlon), the Marquis Perfecto de Cubanas (Edw. G. Whalen), and Kill von Kull, editor of the *New Amsterdam Kicker* (Edwin Stevens). Miss Templeton won encores singing a topical song, "The Same Old Thing," but at least one critic felt most of her performance was "merely twaddle and tights." Miss Templeton was not yet star enough to save a generally disdained show. The producers withdrew the piece after just sixteen performances. The withdrawal did not, however, mark the end for the musical. The era's healthy theatrical economics allowed the show to be taken on the road for repairs and to be brought back for a reconsideration on 27 October at the Park. The consensus found the repairs inadequate, and *Hendrik Hudson* had its final curtain after a second fortnight.

FAY TEMPLETON was born into a theatrical family on Christmas Day 1865, in Little Rock, Arkansas. She made her first stage appearance less than four years later on 16 August 1869, as Cupid. New York first saw her in 1873 as Puck in *A Midsummer Night's Dream*. In 1880 she joined a juvenile company of *H. M. S. Pinafore*, and within a year graduated to romantic leads in musicals such as *Evangeline*, *The Mascot*, and *Billee Taylor*. For the most part she served her apprenticeship on the road. In 1886 she was featured prominently in the original London mounting of *Monte Cristo, Jr.* Her vivacity and her fetchingly throaty delivery so endeared her to her generation that not even a persistent weight problem, making her notably buxom in an era of buxom beauties, could alienate its allegiance.

In San Francisco, playgoers assessed a new musical that, like Dixey's *Rip*, never reached Broadway. **Peti, the Vagabond** (25 August 1890, Bush St.) told of a rich grocer who marries his daughter to a supposed Hungarian count, only to have the man turn out to be a spendthrift and a forger. Peti (Hubert Wilke), a seeming gypsy, helps right matters and proves to be the real count. Clay Greene wrote the libretto.

The first of the minstrel bands to play New York followed *Hendrik Hudson's* initial visit at the 14th Street Theatre. The Cleveland Minstrels featured Billy Emerson and Barney Fagan. Their format was a reversion to more traditional blackface bills, minimizing the recently expanded burlesque portion and concentrating on old, beloved songs. Their two-week stand was part of a national junket. George Thatcher had broken away from Primrose and West during the preceding year. Both in 1889–1890 and in 1890–1891 Primrose and West made several appearances in outlying combination houses, but Thatcher's troupe succeeded in getting a week's booking at the Bijou beginning 3 November. John Wild, so long the leading player of blackface roles in the Harrigan and Braham shows, costarred with Thatcher.

On the same night the Cleveland Minstrels bowed, 1 September, an importation called **The Seven Swabians** raised its curtain. But the curtain that rose was far uptown at the Harlem Opera House. This theatre was essentially a combination house, offering its stage to touring attractions and post-Broadway runs. Yet, situated as it was in an area of elegant, upper-middle-class brownstones, it was judged ideal for the sort of tryouts later reserved for Philadelphia or Boston or New Haven. *The Seven Swabians* was just this sort of tryout. Mounted with panache by the McCaull Opera Company and featuring many of the company's leading players such as Mathilde Cottrelly and Chauncey Olcott, it quickly proved to be one of those errors in judgment even the best of managements make. It never reached the heart of the Rialto. But the Harlem Opera House would soon witness a far more important and successful tryout.

September's only other entry was a curiosity, suggesting that Broadway had not yet completely shed its circus aspect. The cast of **The Pupil in Magic** consisted of a band of troupers known as The Liliputians. As the name suggests, the appealing performers were midgets, who had been playing as an ensemble for several seasons in Berlin. They ranged in age from eighteen to forty-three years, in height from twenty-eight to thirty-eight inches. The principal members were Selma Gomer, Adolf Zink, and Franz Ebert. Ebert, "a droll little fellow with a face

that is comedy in itself," quickly became the darling of both critics and public. The play was by Robert Breitenbach with music "selected and arranged" by Carl Joseph. In Breitenbach's story, Fritz (Miss Gomer), on a visit to his toymaker uncle, falls asleep and dreams he signs a bargain with Puck (Ebert) that wins him the love of every woman he encounters. Near the end, a vision of his mother searching for him fills Fritz with remorse. A transformation scene carries him back to the toymaker's shop. Spectacular dream sequences included a grand ballet depicting the wedding of Princess Lydia (Minchen Becker) to Fritz, a trip to the North Pole, and a tour of Paris. The company regaled audiences for five weeks at Niblo's, returning in December for another month at the Bijou. In between these engagements and afterwards, *The Pupil in Magic* played several of the city's combination houses and toured around the country. The Liliputians were no ninety-day wonder. Their appeal proved surprisingly long-lived. When they and their audiences tired of one vehicle they had another play ready to offer.

The only full-fledged musicals to arrive in October were an adaptation of Planquette's *Surcout*, retitled **Paul Jones**, and **Poor Jonathan**. Both opened on the 6th. *Paul Jones* starred Agnes Huntington in another of the era's many trouser roles. The piece played a month, attesting again, as did *Mme. Angot*, to the market that remained for selected opéra bouffe.

The arrival of Millöcker's *Poor Jonathan* at the Casino ended that house's string of bad luck for the time being. Lillian Russell and Jefferson De Angelis headed the cast, while Harry Macdonough and Fanny Rice helped De Angelis spark the comedy. The plot, which told how an American millionaire, deserted by his protégé, is tricked out of committing suicide by his loyal cook, was typical turn-of-the-century frippery. Yet the show was unusual in one way. It was a German operetta with an American setting. But the adapters were aghast at some scenes of the original, such as Negroes picking cotton in New York City. They quietly moved the first-act setting from Manhattan to West Point, substituting lively cadets for the cavorting blacks. Obviously there were limits to the absurdities even comic opera could tolerate. Or perhaps it was simply that absurdities were acceptable only in alien settings. In any case, *Poor Jonathan* was the biggest hit at the Casino since *Erminie*, compiling 202 performances before it was recast for a tour at the beginning of May.

The busy night of 6 October brought in another interesting work, but one that was not really a musical. *Blue Jeans* was one of the great thrillers of the age, most famous for a scene in which its hero is strapped to a treadmill moving ever closer to a menacing saw while the heroine is locked in a nearby room. But *Blue Jeans* included in its cast a number of veterans of farce-comedies and other light musical efforts, such as Jacques Kruger and Jennie Yeamans. Further, it had a number of mood-setting tunes, old and new, "composed and arranged" by the same old minstrel who had provided melodies for *The City Directory* (10 February 1890), W. S. Mullaly. The piece vividly illustrates the difficulty of drawing a clear-cut line between musicals and straight plays of the time.

At Niblo's the Casino's erstwhile performer, director, and adapter, Max Freeman, mounted **Claudius Nero** on 22 October. Based on Ernest Eckstein's romance, *Nero*, it was another of Niblo's ballet- and song-embellished spectacles (with real lions on stage). It closed unexpectedly in mid-December when its leading dancer walked out, claiming substantial unpaid back salary. After some refinancing and recasting the show moved on to the Broadway for three additional weeks.

Charles H. Hoyt enhanced his rapidly growing reputation with **A Texas Steer** (10 November 1890, Bijou). This time his hero was Maverick Brander (Tim Murphy), who gets himself elected to Congress so that his wife and daughter can visit Washington. Before the final happy curtain he has a run-in with the army (he wins) and with a clever lady blackmailer, who wangles his appearance before a hidden camera and has him plant a kiss on her cheek. This one he loses, and since the lady's claim to fame has been that Daniel Webster kissed her mother, he walks away asking, "Did it cost Daniel Webster one hundred dollars ... ?"

With farce-comedy and comic opera taking over more and more stages there was ever less room for fading spectacles of the *Black Crook* type. They were, however, hardly down and out. The Hanlons offered a lavish example to Brooklyn with **Superba** (24 November 1890, Academy of Music). Its mortal lovers are in mortal danger from the machinations of a jealous fairy with the absurd name of Wallawalla. An array of eye-catching scenery and lavish ballets diverted patrons from the story's inanities. However, Brooklyn was as close to Manhattan's theatrical heartland as this extravaganza got for several seasons.

The musical which *Claudius Nero* supplanted when it moved uptown was J. Cheever Goodwin's

second creation to appear during the season. **Pippins** (26 November 1890, Broadway) featured the mammoth Amelia Summerville as the lithe Atalanta. Of course the title came from the apples dropped to distract Atalanta during her race. The show, badly hurt by unfavorable notices, was crippled hopelessly when Miss Summerville was injured in an accident. As a result the record shows the piece ran only to 6 December before fading into oblivion.

A more successful novelty ushered in December. **Ship Ahoy** (8 December 1890, Standard) was billed as an "operatic extravaganza" with a libretto by H. Grattan Donnelly and a score by Fred Miller. A comic-opera troupe is shipwrecked on an island. The men would set up a kingdom with themselves in charge, but the ladies of the ballet, led by Mlle. Auburni Ernani (Bertha Ricci), revolt and establish their own republic. In an ending that ten years later would become a cliché, the troupe is rescued by the U.S. Navy. Because the show was a Philadelphia mounting, New York critics came down hard on it. The *Times* insisted the dialogue was traditional Philadelphia drivel, while the *Dramatic Mirror* heard Gilbert and Sullivan in every song. The trade paper cited the tune sung by Commodore Columbus Cook (Edward M. Favor) of the *U. S. S. Cuckoo* as a direct steal from a song it called "The Ruler Of The Queen's Navee" ("When I Was A Lad"). The loose plot allowed a flood of vaudeville turns to be inserted, and several critics insisted these were the mainstay of the evening.

New York usually did applaud Philadelphia productions for the excellence of their sets and costumes. *Ship Ahoy* was no exception. A stage picture of the white squadron sailing out of Chesapeake Bay won general approbation. Willard Spenser and other Philadelphians had long since learned that New York's rejection was rarely repeated on the road. After five weeks the company embarked on a tour that brought it back to several other New York theatres during the season. On its return it sought to assure patrons its songs were not cacophonously modern, but were "music with melody."

While *Ship Ahoy* was being unveiled at the Standard, the Harlem Opera House far uptown was hosting another tryout. But this show was soon to make history: Charles Hoyt's **A Trip to Chinatown**. Hoyt was a conscientious craftsman by the standards of the time. With his straight play, *A Texas Steer*, one of the joyous hits of the 1890–1891 season, he saw no reason to rush his new work downtown. Instead, he took it on the road for nearly a year. Its phenomenal New York run was part of the next season's record.

The J. C. Duff Opera Company arrived at the Broadway on 22 December to entertain holiday crowds with a repertory of Gilbert and Sullivan works: *The Pirates of Penzance, Patience*, and *Iolanthe*.

On 29 December a rejuvenated Edward Harrigan returned to the New York scene with two new attractions. The first was his new theatre, called simply Harrigan's, at 35th Street and Broadway. The second was his (and Braham's) new work, **Reilly and the Four Hundred**. "The Four Hundred" was the phrase coined by social arbiter Ward McAllister to define the limits of high society. Wiley Reilly (Harrigan), a pawnbroker, sets up his son, Ned (Harry Davenport), as a lawyer so that the young man may have entrée into this high echelon. Reilly hopes Ned will marry Emeline (Isabelle Archer), the niece of his rich fellow Irishman, Commodore Toby Tow (James Radcliffe). Ned does, and Reilly marries the commodore's sister, Lavina (Hattie Moore). But before the weddings can take place Reilly must expose Herman Smeltz (Harry Fisher), a sausage tycoon and one of the Four Hundred, as an ex-ship's butcher who had been dismissed for stealing. The plot was obviously the next step after the Mulligans' own efforts to enter society. It reflected the view of high society that, while upstart parents might not enter the charmed circle, their children could be considered. Harrigan's dialogue and characterization were as fine as ever, though occasionally Harrigan did stretch theatrical coincidence in the name of theatrical brevity. For example, the commodore's servant pawns an old ship's log that belonged to his master. It reveals Smeltz's crimes to Reilly. Reilly no sooner reads the incriminating passage than Smeltz himself walks in. Nor were the songs always well motivated. The hit of the evening was one of Braham's classics, "Maggie Murphy's Home." But Maggie, referred to as a "chippie," was a very minor figure in the play. Her brief scene consisted merely of her announcement that she will indulge in a "challenge jig" at a benefit ball. The song is sung at the opening of the next scene, Foley's benefit at Casey's Hall. Some indication of the staging of the time can be garnered from a note in the typescript at the end of the song. It reads "after each chorus, waltz. Bus[iness] of perspiration etc., after the song." An indication of how long audiences of the time could be expected to sit quietly in their seats is given at the beginning of the

same typescript where the "time of acting" is listed as "three hours." Harrigan was able to reassemble most of his old associates such as Annie Yeamans (as an Irish housekeeper) and John Wild (as an argumentative black). Newcomers included two future stars, Ada Lewis, who quickly became a favorite in "tough girl" parts, and Harry Davenport. *Reilly and the Four Hundred* gave Harrigan and Braham one of their greatest triumphs, running 202 performances.

The final musical of 1890 arrived the night after the Harrigan premiere. **The Babes in the Wood** (30 December 1890, Niblo's) was a resuscitation of the old pantomime with William A. Mestayer and George K. Fortesque as the Babes. One ludicrous moment found Fortesque, a behemoth of a man, abducted by a two-and-a-half-foot dwarf. Spectacle included a Shakespearean tableau. Despite the evening's better moments, the musical failed miserably (its scenery seized for nonpayment), ending the year on a downbeat note.

Sentimental and patriotic ballads underscored the story of another romantic Irish drama. **An Irishman's Love** (12 January 1891, Third Ave.), but once again whether this was a true musical is moot.

The game, aging Lydia Thompson (the *Times* ungallantly announced that she was fifty-five) tried again with a vehicle called **The Dazzler**. Other papers attempted to be kinder, although Miss Thompson clearly had seen her best days. The *Dramatic Mirror* noted, "Her voice is a thing of the past... but she can dance with all, or nearly all of her pristine nimbleness." When, late in the first act, she donned her old Robinson Crusoe costume, "the bald-headed contingent smiled with reminiscent satisfaction, and went out between the acts to talk over the halcyon days of their vanished youth." In the show's simple plot a wild, uncouth Irishman named Mulligan (Thomas J. Grady) somehow manages to woo and win the actress Kitty Starlight (Miss Thompson). Miss Thompson's persistence was rewarded with a modicum of success. She occupied the Park for a week beginning 19 January and the Standard for most of February, and then she came back for brief stays at other houses.

The only other new musical to appear in January was J. J. McNally's farce, **A Straight Tip** (26 January 1891, Bijou). It dealt with the inheriting of a hotel; the inheritance only settles when Dick Dasher bets on the right horse following a tip. James T. Powers was the show's star, inserting a number of songs, dances, and an imitation of Carmencita into McNally's material. One or two other specialties were also interpolated. The show also served to call attention to Peter F. Dailey in the supporting role of Jack Postsand Poole.

Minnie Palmer, never to repeat her success in *My Sweetheart* (18 September 1882), even masqueraded as a boy in **A Mile a Minute** (9 February 1891, People's). At times the scenery, particularly a moonlit view of the Thames, seemed to steal the show. However, the script's co-author, Charles Klein, shortly would move on to better things. With a popular vaudevillian replacing Miss Palmer, the show was kept touring for several seasons. No such luck blessed **The Fakir** (2 March 1891, Standard), whose fake fakir could not turn his assemblage of turns into a hit. In a small way that was surprising, since the people whom old Seth Baker (Mark Sullivan) decides to hoodwink were represented as actors, chorus girls, and other professionals. One critic complained that singers were drowned out by "blaring brass and distracting tympany."

March brought in little more than January or February, being noteworthy only for the return of W. J. Scanlan presenting a week each of *Myles Aroon* (21 January 1889) and *The Irish Minstrel* (9 April 1888) at the 14th Street Theatre, and for another of the many song-studded farce-comedies, **U and I** (23 March 1891, Standard). Its excuse for its specialties was to have John Ungerblotz (Gus Williams) and O'Donovan Innes (John T. Kelly), back from a toot, fall asleep in the apartment of a voice coach, Mlle. Vermicelli (Gertrude Zella). Miss Zella was "rapturously encored" for her kissing song, while Kelly won applause for dancing a jig and for singing (in a thick brogue). Typical of how other specialties were introduced was the appearance of the janitor to check on the apartment. He turned out to be an acrobat. At one point a group of girls entered dressed as rosebuds. *U and I* was presented by George Lederer, who would shortly make his mark as a producer of more genuinely musical enterprises.

By April, managers were clearly biding their time, awaiting the propitious moment to bring in those spring offerings they hoped would turn into "summer musicals." The lone voice raised in song belonged to Joseph Murphy, a minor player in the tradition of Emmet and Scanlan, who offered a month-long repertory at the 14th Street Theatre that included *The Kerry Gow, Shaun Rue*, and *The Donagh*.

The most successful summer entertainment not only spanned the summer but enjoyed later revivals and long held the affection of those who saw

it. **Wang** (4 May 1891, Broadway) had J. Cheever Goodwin's third libretto for the season and his second in less than a year done in collaboration with composer Woolson Morse. Its principal characters were stock favorites of the era's musicals: the grotesquely made-up clown and the hero played as a trouser role. It was set in the Orient, which had become almost the *sine qua non* of comic opera. All that Goodwin overlooked were the outrageously punning names so often given characters of the time. Wang (De Wolf Hopper) is the comic, conniving regent of Siam. While the young prince, Mataya (Delia Fox), bridles at his elder's machinations, he is more preoccupied by his romance with Gillette (Anna O'Keefe). Gillette is the eldest daughter of La Veuve Frimousse (Marion Singer), the widow of a former French consul, who has managed to secure in her custody the entire treasury of Siam. Although her daughters are so numerous they compose an entire chorus line and although she is anxious to marry them all off, she suspects that Mataya courts Gillette only in the hope of retrieving his country's money. But Mataya convinces her and her daughter of his sincerity by renouncing the throne. At this point Wang grabs the throne and the hand of the susceptible widow, taking from her hand at the same moment the precious royal coffer. Goodwin's lyrics and Morse's melodies are exemplified by two songs. "A Pretty Girl" (sung by Mataya early in the first act) juxtaposes a simple, charming tune with an equally simple lyric that turns unexpectedly cynical.

The work's principal comic number (sung near the end of the evening by Wang, Mataya, and a French Colonel) was "Ask The Man In The Moon," a song that in keeping with common practice of the time was most meaty in its verse, with only a rudimentary chorus. Also in keeping with then common practice, the song satirized contemporary affairs in New York, ignoring entirely the problems of the plot. One verse ran:

> *New York is a city of wealth,*
> *Millionaires we can count by the score;*
> *And can boast of a host*
> *Who have hundreds of thousands or more.*
> *But Grant's monument tho' isn't built—*
> *If you'd ask a subscription they'd swoon;*
> *Will the Washington Arch, be completed next March,*
> *You must ask of the man in the moon.*

When a real Siamese king visited America in the 1930s, he is said to have requested to hear songs from the show. As Wang, Hopper reached what is generally acknowledged as the pinnacle of his career. His entrance—not unlike Francis Wilson's in *The Merry Monarch* (18 August 1890)—and his extended opening monologue, even on paper, capture some flavor of the great clowning of the period. Wang first appears on an elephant "over whom a gorgeous canopy is held by six slaves."

CHORUS OF WELCOME

(At end of Chorus, Pepat [played by "tiny Alfred Klein"] endeavors to have the elephant kneel)

Pepat: Hurri gurry baloo masam!

(*Elephant declines to kneel; Pepat jabs him with pike; elephant raises trunk and trumpets. Pepat continued jabbing and elephant shows annoyance*)

Wang: Say! What are you trying to do with this elephant anyway? Make him do a song-and-dance! Are you aware that your monarch is patiently awaiting to descend?

Pepat: But he won't kneel, sire!

Wang: Won't kneel—scoundrel! In the bright lexicon of middle age there is no such word as Won't! What are you on the salary list for, anyway? Make him kneel!

(*Pepat jabs elephant again, who, with a flourish of his trunk, knocks Pepat over. Crowd manifest alarm*)

Serves you right! I wish he had broken every one of the two hundred and forty eight bones in your wretched carcass. You know as much about elephants as a black cat does of dummy whist! Hand me that fish spear up here!

(*Pepat, picking himself up, hands pike, with fear and trembling to Wang, who shouts to elephant*)

Enteuthen exelaunei parassangas dekas!

(As he jabs elephant, the latter again trumpets and stampedes about stage, crowd dodging him with screams, in great confusion; finally, with a last blast of rage, he rushes off R. 4. E., leaving Wang, who has stood up to prod him, clinging to branch of tree L. I. E., facing audience)

(*Clinging to branch, to Pepat*) Come here! come here! you moon faced concentration of imbecility! and let your monarch fall on you! Do you want me to break the royal neck?

(**Pepat** dodging Wang's legs, gets under him so the latter can rest his foot on the former's shoulders; when Wang lets go of branch, Pepat collapses with him; Fracasse hastens to assist Wang to arise. Pepat is cowering with fear, on his hands and knees)

[**Wang** launches into a song "The Regent Wang," and when it is finished he chases away the crowd and dismisses his retainers.]

(*Addressing audience*) Between ourselves, what I want to be alone for, is to think; I never can think in a crowd, and I have got enough to think about to kill a cat. When my brother, the late king, died six years ago, he left the royal coffer a howling vacuum. What in the name of Daniel Dancer he did with all the shekels he raked in during his reign, staggered me. He didn't take them with him, I'll swear, for I had a post mortem made that developed nothing except a quarrel among the surgeons. For six years I have hunted high low Jack and the game and not found a sign of them. The result has been, I have lived the life of a royal pauper. I have not been able to reign, I have only sprinkled. I have borrowed right and left; I have plastered the palace with mortgages, and worst of all in a moment of reckless extravagance, I purchased a sacred elephant from the king of Cambodia, and confound his colossal impudence, he absolutely wants to be paid for it. An embassy from that besotted monarch dunning me for the price, has stuck to me closer than a porous plaster for the last one hundred and eighty four days. I don't dare behead them for he would go to war and lick me out of my royal boots. The result is, I'm obliged to do the sneak act and play hide and seek with them all over my kingdom. Dodging them is one of the things that brings me here today. The other and far more important one, is this letter addressed to Mataya—(*taking letter from pocket*)—which is the first ray of hope which has trickled into my atmosphere of chronic, cold, black gloom. (*Reads letter*) Paris, November 17th. My dear Prince: Shortly before your royal father's death, distrusting as he did, your uncle's honesty—(*spoken*)—I would not have had my brother's suspicious nature for $17.50!—(*reads*)—He confided to me a chest, with instructions to deliver it to you upon your coronation. My hours are numbered and I shall never see Siam again; but I send you the enclosed key, and have charged Madame Frimousse with the sacred duty of seeing that the chest it unlocks reaches you on the day named. Its contents are unknown to her, as they are to me—(*speaking*) well, you can wager your saccharine existence that they won't be unknown to me long, once I interview Madame

Frimousse! (*Reads*) My sight fails—farewell;
follow in your father's footsteps and emulate
his example. (*signed*) Frimousse. (*Restoring
letter to pocket. Rising*) There can't be any doubt
about it, that chest contains the treasure I have
hunted for six long weary years! and as Mataya
hasn't got any idea of its existence, he won't lose
anything by not getting it. What does he know
about the value of money, anyway? He's got
enough to occupy his mind, smoking cigarettes
and raising a moustache; whereas let yours
truly once get his fingers on it and I'll make
things hum! Let's see! I've got the key, I hope!
(*Produces key and returns it to pocket*) That's all
right! and now to tackle the widow Frimousse
and secure the chest. (*Goes to house L. H.
and raps. Widow appears at door*) I beg your
pardon—
Widow: If you want anything to eat, you'll have to
go round to the back door! (*Slams door in his
face*)
Wang: First blood for the widow! But at the call
of time, the Siamese Chicken came up smiling!
(*Raps again at door of house, L. H.*)
Widow: (*Again appearing at door L. H.*) If you
don't go away, I'll set the dog on you! (*As she
goes to again slam door, Wang puts his foot in it
and prevents her*)
Wang: No, you don't! What do you take me for,
anyway, a book peddler or a junkman? Don't
you know a real live Regent when you see him?
Widow: Mon Dieu! Mon Dieu! Can I ever forgive
myself? (*Curtseys*)

Della Fox as Mataya, like Hopper, confirmed her
claim to stardom. Of course the show easily lasted
through the summer and then left for an extended tour.
O'Dowd's Neighbors (4 May 1891, Bijou)—"by
courtesy a farce-comedy"—presented the thinnest
of plots about goings-on in an area dominated by
Irish families. One reviewer quoted an example of
the play's humor when he reported the hero asked,
"How can I be disturbing the peace at night when I'm
playing on brass 'St. Patrick's Day In The Morning'!"
Visual gags had O'Dowd (Mark Murphy) appearing as Romeo in Elizabethan costume, but with
unsightly modern boots and a garish red wig. Songs
ranged from "'Boom, Tir-ra, Tir-ra' to Donizetti's
still admired 'Lucia' sextet."
The Casino hoped to repeat the welcome success of *Poor Jonathan* with its mounting on 7 May
of another German work, Joseph Hellmesberger's

Apollo. Divine law states that if the lady elected to
serve as Apollo's oracle during a festival is kissed,
disaster will follow. The evening was spent keeping the lady and her lover apart until the festival
finished. Although the cast included the principals
who had shone so brilliantly in the earlier production, especially Lillian Russell and Jefferson De
Angelis, it failed fully to please either critics or
playgoers. The piece, called a "burlesque operetta,"
survived only until 11 July. One telling footnote was
the presence of Gustave Kerker on the conductor's
podium. Composing American comic operas was
still an uncertain livelihood.
But Harry B. Smith was slowly and surely making
the composition of librettos pay. For Digby Bell and
the McCaull Opera Company he wrote The Tar and
the Tartar (11 May 1891, Palmer's) in collaboration
with a young Baltimore conductor-composer, Adam
Itzel, Jr. Smith resorted to an age-old motif, the disappearance of a ruler and the substitution of a commoner who resembles him. Smith acknowledged the
antiquity of his basic plot, but later proudly pointed
out that his version appeared three years before *The
Prisoner of Zenda*. Once again McCaull and Palmer's
knew the pleasure of watching a production run
comfortably through the hot weather.
Matters were equally happy for George W.
Monroe. Not willing to let go of the comic gold
mine he had discovered in Bridget McVeigh, he
impersonated her again in that rarity, a successful
sequel, Aunt Bridget's Baby (18 May 1891, Bijou).
The baby couldn't have been all that young, since
in the person of Nellie Rosebud she was applauded
for some nimble dancing, although the *World* complained she showed "more effusion than talent."
Once again critics begrudged their readers any idea
of the plot. At best one reviewer noted that the
second act took place on a yacht cruising at sea. But
then the story and even elementary logic were never
as important in this order of concoction as was
winning a quick laugh or a big hand, so when the
rotund star, with his/her poker face and gurgling
laugh, romped off into the wings a band of Castilian
Lady Troubadours was given the spotlight to do
its stuff. Despite ever-changing supporting players,
in this show Monroe found a meal ticket for three
seasons.
May's other offering was another free and easy
farce-comedy larded with songs and specialty acts,
A Knotty Affair (18 May 1891, Park) by Herbert
Hall Winslow. A newspaper's search for the source
of an anonymous tip led the cast from an editorial

office to a swank apartment to a "Kirmess" hall. The search continued nightly for just two weeks.

The season ended on 11 July with the arrival of *The Grand Duchess*, revived by the distressed Casino to fill the void left in the aftermath of *Apollo's* failure. Lillian Russell and Jefferson De Angelis were again the principals. But even this Offenbach revival fell short of expectations, running just until 22 August.

1891–1892

The preceding season's revival of *The Grand Duchess* in July was the only break in an unusually long hiatus that lasted from mid-May until August. Critics rued that what little plot a farce-comedy called **The High Roller** (3 August 1891, Bijou) contained collapsed by the end of the first act, leaving the last act an "ordinary variety show." The *Times* itemized some of the musical numbers: "It contains a decidedly revelatory dance to set things going.... Four queer young men sing amusingly, and another dance, introducing the inevitable Amazon March, leads up to a 'Tar and Tartar' chorus and the curtain."

Across the continent in San Francisco the same night welcomed another premiere. **Aquilo** (3 August 1891, Tivoli) had a book by R. C. White, a member of the cast, and music by Adolph Bauer, the house's orchestra leader. A young man, his sweetheart, and his sister head for the North Pole. There they discover a route, by way of a desert island, a dark cave illuminated by "boreal lights," and the Land of Pax, to a perpetually sunlit Eden, where they are greeted by King Candace and Queen Lucidas: "Around the world the tidings roll/A path is found from pole to pole." So gorgeous was the mounting that local play-goers ignored the absurdities and applauded the musical for three weeks.

Two traditional musicals and one traditional spectacle in the Niblo style arrived in Manhattan during the week of August 24. All three were disappointments; the first and the last to arrive, outright failures. The first was a work written by Americans but with its heart and inspiration patently in the Old World, where a handsome young noble, Marcel (Edward Webb), falls in love with a flower-girl (Mamie Smith). He courts and wins her at a Students' Ball where everyone waltzed bedecked in strikingly colorful dominoes. *Fleurette's* libretto was by one Mrs. C. Doremus and Edgar Smith; its music was by Emma R. Steiner. Miss Steiner was apparently something of a musician, for besides composing the score she conducted the orchestra.

However, her labors were to little avail. **Fleurette** (24 August 1891, Standard) lacked the requisite wit, melody, and flair for success. It closed after a single week.

The night after *Fleurette's* premiere, the Casino mounted a production of Strauss's "Oriental" **Indigo**, an operetta with a trouble-plagued history of innumerable rewritings. Troubles of a sort plagued it at the Casino, too. Most of the house's stars, performers such as Francis Wilson and Lillian Russell, had moved elsewhere. Only Jefferson De Angelis remained of its stellar roster. As a result, critics and public generally viewed the new presentation as a lackluster effort. It ran just over a month, closing on 3 October.

Niblo's spectacle, opening on the 27th, was advertised as an operetta and was called **The Khédive**. It proved another in the string of "Oriental" subjects so popular in the musicals and straight plays of the time. The son (Wallace McCreery) of an American-born Khédive of Turkey (Ferris Hartman) revolts when he cannot marry the girl (Lotta Gilman) of his choice. Both Niblo's and its distinctive mountings were nearing the end of their days; neither would linger into the new century. *The Khédive's* fate reflected the waning power of both the theatre and the genre to attract patrons. It ran a mere week and a half.

A long life awaited **Eight Bells** (7 September 1891, Union Square), which was called, variously, a "pantomime comedy" and an "acrobatic pantomime." The leading acrobats (and bell ringers) were the Byrne Brothers (John E, James A., Matthew, and Andrew), with John also credited for devising the entertainment. The *Herald*, which suggested the show's subtitle was **The Misfortunes of McGozzie**—and which found the entire evening "terrifically and calisthentically funny"—recorded that the show's high spot came in the second act when "a ship is wrecked and rolls over and over while three of its passengers scramble for dear life." The critic called the scene "as novel at it was grotesquely funny." If obituaries are correct, the show served the brothers, with occasional respites, as a vehicle for twenty years, albeit almost all that time was spent on second-class stages on the road or in outlying neighborhoods.

When *Reilly and the Four Hundred* closed just before the height of summer, Ned Harrigan concluded its appeal had hardly diminished. As a result he soon announced the show was "on vacation," not permanently shuttered. His judgment was vindicated when the work relit Harrigan's Theatre on

14 September and played an additional 100 performances before giving way to *The Last of the Hogans* in December. In the spring, shortly before Harrigan ended his 1891–1892 season, Reilly and his friends came back for still another visit, albeit a brief one of three weeks.

The night of Reilly's return in September also marked the return of W. S. Cleveland's Minstrels. Theirs was an art falling as rapidly out of vogue as Niblo's spectacles. The minstrels' single week at the Park was all the blackface entertainment the Rialto was offered during the season, at least in any semblance of the old minstrel show.

J. J. McNally's farce-comedy **Boys and Girls** (21 September 1891, Park) replaced Cleveland's troupe the following Monday. The plot revolved around a hero (James A. Sturgis) left $50,000 on the condition he spend it all. If he fails the money goes to his friends and relatives. Naturally they throw obstacles in his way. Its cast included a number of names soon to move to the top in musical comedy circles, although not always as performers, notably May Irwin (as a tough girl) and Julian Mitchell (as director). The dancer Ignacio Martinetti delighted with his graceful leaps, and the Leopolds won applause for more purely acrobatic turns. But the show was not accepted, and disappeared after a single week.

Competing with *Boys and Girls* for first-nighters was a third bit of contemporary pseudo-Orientalia, Bill Nye's **The Cadi** (21 September 1891, Union Square). Nye at least attempted something different in "Orientalia," allowing his exotica to take place in New York. A mischievous boy (Minnie Dupree) leads a Wyoming postmaster to believe he has been made Turkish consul in Manhattan. Enlivened by the cavortings of Thomas Q. Seabrooke as the postmaster and Charles Parsloe as a pigtailed, pidgin-English–speaking Chinese, the piece played until 19 December.

Two musicals opened on 28 September 1891. Both were hits and one a landmark in the history of the American Musical Theatre. The lesser of the two was **Mavourneen**, a vehicle written for W. J. Scanlan by George H. Jessop and Horace Townsend. Scanlan played Terence Dwyer, a young Irishman whose betrothed is abducted. Dwyer goes to America, becomes rich, and returns home to use his money to retrieve his girl. The show introduced the song which next to "Peek-A-Boo" is most associated with Scanlan, "Molly O!" As was his custom, Scanlan took credit for both the words and music. The show gave every indication of being a smash hit and lifting

Scanlan to new heights. But his behavior during the run grew increasingly odd and forced him to close the show on Christmas night. The following week he was committed to an insane asylum, dying of paresis (syphilis-induced insanity) seven years later. Only a month before Scanlan's removal from the stage, Tony Hart had died from the same cause.

Robin Hood (28 September 1891, Standard) was the first successful American comic opera or operetta cast in a mold that could be recognized as contemporary, or, at least, could have been so recognized while operetta held a place on the musical stage. Curiously, like several mid-nineteenth-century hits such as *Evangeline* (27 July 1874) and *Fritz, Our German Cousin* (11 July 1870), its New York stays were brief. In *Robin Hood*'s case there were two reasons for its relatively short runs. First of all, the work was produced by the Boston Ideal Opera Company, a troupe, as we have seen, based in Boston and devoted to touring the nation with its repertory. New York was simply another stop on the itinerary. Second, the company (increasingly referred to just as the Bostonians) had reservations about the piece. The troupe had long wanted to stage an American work. The preceding season it had mounted *Don Quixote* with a libretto and lyrics by Harry B. Smith and music by Reginald De Koven. The work had enjoyed only a small success but seems to have been removed from the schedule more because of backstage politics than any true failure. Nonetheless, when De Koven and Smith presented the company with a second work, the Bostonians were so unsure of its feasibility that they used costumes and settings from other productions. If Smith's memory served him well, the total expenditure for the original production was $109.50. Its enthusiastic reception prompted the management to buy new sets and costumes to the tune of $5,000. This redecked mounting was what New Yorkers saw. Since the show grossed $12,000 a week at the Standard, the investment was quickly repaid. While critics, as was then their wont, failed to describe the physical production, they were unstinting with their praise of the performance—praise often begrudged groups based outside New York. The *Times* hailed the troupe as "a genuine operetta company, equipped with voices and method." Nor was this praise meant solely for the principals, for the paper continued, "There is probably not another operetta chorus, which, after three or four minutes of dialogue, could pick up the refrain of the song, and without orchestral support, sing it in tune and in the original key."

Smith's story was reasonably faithful to the old legend. The Sheriff of Nottingham (Henry Clay Barnabee) wrongfully deprives Robert, Earl of Huntington (Tom Karl), of his lands, conferring them upon his protégé, Guy of Gisborne (Peter Lang). Guy is also awarded the hand of Maid Marian (Caroline Hamilton), the Sheriff's ward. In despair, Robert takes to outlawry. Under the name of Robin Hood he assumes leadership of a band of rather mild brigands. The treachery of one of the band members leads to Robin Hood's capture, and he is condemned to die, but only after he witnesses the marriage of Marian to Guy. At the same wedding the Sheriff plans to forcibly wed Annabel (Lea Van Dyke), the sweetheart of another of Robin Hood's band, Alan-a-Dale (Jessie Bartlett Davis). As the wedding is about to take place, Alan-a-Dale reminds his betrothed of their vows by singing "Oh, Promise Me" from his hiding place. But before the ceremony is finished, Robin Hood's loyal band—including Friar Tuck (George B. Frothingham), Little John (W. H. MacDonald), and Will Scarlet (Eugene Cowles)—comes to the rescue. They have with them a pardon from Richard the Lion-Heart, who has newly returned from the wars. Something of the tenor of Smith's piece can be gauged by the fact that he wrote the part of the Sheriff for the most beloved of the Bostonians, Barnabee, making the Sheriff into a comic, and not unlikable, villain:

(The Sheriff enters with Guy and six journeymen tinkers.)
Sheriff: Ah, here we are on the borders of Sherwood Forest, where the outlaw Robin Hood commits his fearful crimes. What is the matter with the Earl of Huntington? If you tremble like that you will shake down some of these trees. You seem to think you have got to be shaken before Robin is taken.
Guy: But I'm thinking of the desperado, Robin Hood Br-r-r (trembles).
Sheriff (imitating him): Br-r-r. What are you doing?
Guy (trembling): I am quaking at the dreaded name of Robin Hood. They say he sticks at nothing.
Sheriff: I don't care if he sticks at everything. Robin Hood never robs from the poor—sensible man; they have nothing worth taking. As journeymen tinkers we are too poor to attract his attention. Perhaps we will get a chance to capture this Robin, whoever he may be. You seem to forget that I have my eagle eye with me.
Gut: Which is your eagle eye?

Sheriff: The left—and it's a wonder. Trust to my colossal intellect, friend Guy, and we will not only bring Marian back so you can marry her, but we will hang Robin on a highly ornate and commodious gallows.

Much of the success of Robin Hood and possibly the main reason it held the stage for so long over the years was the popularity of "Oh, Promise Me." The song was not written for Robin Hood and was added only when it was felt another song was needed for Alan-a-Dale. In his memoirs Barnabee wrote, "It was taken from an old Italian melody, known and sung by every peasant in that lovely land of music. It is said it was unconsciously plagiarized by Reginald De Koven." Since De Koven remarked, in an interview several years after Robin Hood opened, that much of his music was imitative, there may be a certain truth in Barnabee's story. Strangely, the pervasive lack of confidence in the work and its authors almost kept the song out of the show. Jessie Bartlett Davis, who had been assigned the trouser role, at first refused to sing it. Only when De Koven transposed the key and made some minor revisions did she acquiesce.

The other great hit of the show was a convivial drinking song, "Brown October Ale," in which Little John led a stirring male chorus. Its vogue led to similar numbers in later operettas. The songs of the day's better comic operas were not looked on merely as catchy melodies tailored to be easily sung by the man-in-the-street. Both composers and students of the time took a more artful, considered approach. They understood the classic forms around which they wrote their melodies and sought an interesting and pertinent variety of these classic forms to fill out their musical selections. In his Standard Light Operas, George P. Upton listed a duet, a quartet, a quintet, a tantara, a waltz, and a romance among Robin Hood's numbers. Robin Hood did superb business during its strictly limited one-month run. This brisk trade encouraged the Bostonians to pay a second call later in the season for an additional five weeks. Whenever they returned thereafter, Robin Hood was almost certain to be in their repertory.

At a matinee on 1 October Rudolph Aronson offered his patrons a type of work fast fading from regular Broadway stages—grand opera. Beating out the impresario Oscar Hammerstein by a matter of hours, he gave New Yorkers their first exposure to Mascagni's Cavalleria Rusticana. The opera had had its world premiere in May of 1890 and its American premiere in Philadelphia on 9 September 1891.

Hammerstein, who believed he had sole New York rights, hauled Aronson into court, but he lost on a technicality. Legal problems out of the way, Aronson put it on a regular bill, coupled with a translation of Carl Zeller's *Der Vogelhändler*. Misunderstandings and petty jealousies keep a bird handler and his sweetheart apart and flirting with royalty until just before the final curtain. The operetta was renamed **The Tyrolean** and starred Marie Tempest. The double bill began a run at the Casino on 5 October. Mascagni's opera was dropped on 5 December, but *The Tyrolean* ran until 11 January, chalking up 100 performances.

On 5 October, two other musicals came in. One was a three-month return of Francis Wilson in *The Merry Monarch* (18 August 1890). The other was a curious pastiche that combined Thatcher's Minstrels with Rich and Harris's Comedy Company in a spoof of high society called **Tuxedo.** It was essentially a vaudeville that resulted from assorted characters, including a tough Irish upstart (Hugh Dougherty), being thrown together on the porch of a grand hotel. At one point two principals spoofed President Benjamin Harrison and ex-President Grover Cleveland—in blackface. Its opening number had been extracted from *A High Roller* (3 August 1891). The wild mélange played only a month in its original stay, but its popularity brought it back to several other houses over the season and in later years.

The quick closing of *The Khedive* had left Niblo's dark at one of the best moments of the theatrical year. Not until 12 October did the house reopen its doors. And then it played host to "one of the most dismal failures ever seen in New York." The show was **Beautiful Star,** with a libretto by William H. Day (a successful scene designer) and a score by Charles Puerner. Brutally panned, this tale from the Arabian Nights lasted a mere four nights.

Lillian Russell, until recently a glittering fixture at the Casino, returned to New York on 26 October at the head of her own company in Audran's **La Cigale.** The grasshopper of the title is a simple maiden who wins a chevalier away from a scheming duchess. For 112 performances Miss Russell delighted her admirers at the Garden Theatre, singing not only Audran's music but a number of interpolations by young Ivan Caryll, a Belgian who would soon take his place in the world of operetta.

A straight play destined for years of popularity, **Hoss and Hoss,** premiered on 2 November. But the amount of music in many straight plays of the period can be perceived by the songs thrown into the piece.

On opening night they included "Annie Laurie," the quartet from *Rigoletto*, a "kangaroo dance," and a take-off on Carmencita.

More Audran music was heard when David Belasco and Charles Frohman joined forces with Mrs. Leslie Carter to present **Miss Helyett** (3 November 1891, Star). In this American version Mrs. Carter, an "oriflamme of red hair in an incredible braid far down her back," played (and sang, although not well) a simple American girl named Verity from Verity Village, Pennsylvania, who slips while walking on a mountain path, landing helplessly and in an embarrassing position. The nice young man who rescues her discreetly disappears. Verity spends the rest of the evening seeking him out. Since Belasco, Mrs. Carter, and, at this early date, Frohman were known entirely for their straight mountings, no one need have been surprised when pre-opening announcements insisted the piece was "not a comic opera, but a quaint and amusing comedy with 'musical attachments.'" But these same announcements noted, "The orchestra has been enlarged to thirty musicians and is under the direction of William Furst. There are twenty musical numbers."

A Trip to Chinatown (9 November 1891, Madison Square) reached the heart of the New York theatre district after nearly a year on the road and became the biggest hit of the season. Nearly a quarter of a century elapsed before a straight play broke its record of 657 performances, and nearly thirty years went by before *Irene* (18 November 1919), the first musical to surpass its stay. As originally conceived, the show had a libretto and lyrics by Charles Hoyt and music by Percy Gaunt. Its plot was simple. Rashleigh Gay (Lloyd Wilson), Wilder Daly, and their lady friends plan to spend an evening at a masquerade ball. Daly's young lady is Rashleigh's sister, Tony (Lillian Barr). But Rashleigh and Tony fear their Uncle Ben (George A. Beane) will not let them out for so riotous a night on the town. So they tell him they are going on a tour of Chinatown. They have dutifully invited a widow, Mrs. Guyer (Anna Boyd), to act as chaperone. But her letter of acceptance inadvertently gets delivered to Uncle Ben. Thinking he has made a conquest of the vivacious widow, Ben allows the youngsters to go on their tour, and he goes out to meet Mrs. Guyer at the restaurant she has mentioned in her letter. Of course, the restaurant is the very one Rashleigh and Wilder have booked for their own pre-ball dinner. At the restaurant Ben becomes increasingly intoxicated while waiting for his lady to appear. Only when Mrs. Guyer and the youngsters have gone off to the ball does he learn the widow had been there all the while. His embarrassment increases when he realizes that in his rush to the tryst he had forgotten his wallet. All the principals meet at the end of the evening. Uncle Ben would chastise his wards for their deception, but they have learned of his escapade, so there is mutual forgiving. To string out the thin story Hoyt used his arsenal of farce-comedy and vaudeville tricks. For example, he employed a series of running jokes. The servant Slavin Payne (Harry Gilfoil) is forever put down when he attempts to be helpful:

Slavin: Is anything required of me?
Rashleigh: Yes. Get out!

Slavin: Anything else I can do?
Ben: Yes. Keep out!

Slavin: Any service I can perform, sir?
Ben: Yes. Leave the room!

A number of characters are almost vaudeville vignettes. The most important figure apart from the youngsters, Ben, and the widow was a hypochondriac named Welland Strong (Harry Conor). He knows that everything he loves is killing him, so he keeps a notebook to record how each rich meal or each cigar lessens his life expectancy. But Hoyt does manage to impart a certain extra dimension while maintaining his running gags and stock humor. Here is how he takes what is really a vaudeville monologue and turns it into part of the play's regular dialogue:

Ben: Have a glass of wine?
Strong: I will! Wine is harmful to me. It shortens my life. But I'll take it! (drinks)
Ben: You don't look badly, old man!
Strong: No! That's the exasperating thing about it!
Wilder: Which lung is affected, sir?
Strong: Neither as yet. But the left one probably will be by Saturday night.
Rashleigh: Do you cough much?
Strong: Not at all! That's a very serious feature. My malady is so deepseated that I can't bring the cough to the surface. But instead I feel a sensation which, in a well man would be called a thirst for liquor.
Tony: And what do the doctors say?
Strong: No two agree.

Ben: And who shall decide when doctors disagree?
Strong: Usually the coroner. Why, I had seven of them. One fool said that nothing ailed me. Do you know, the only man who really understood my case was a horse doctor! He said if I stayed in Boston I'd die in sixty days. Out here I'd live two years if I obeyed certain rules. Here's the book of rules and it tells how much I shorten my life each time I break one. That glass of wine shortened it nineteen hours.

The persistently freewheeling ways of the era's musical theatre are interestingly illustrated by surviving texts of Hoyt's libretto. In them the setting for the third act differs and the relationships among the characters vary slightly. Significantly, while Wilder Daly plays a major, balancing role in all extant texts, he appears in no programs! Musically the freewheeling is also evident. One of the show's most popular numbers was Gaunt's adaptation of an old sixteen-bar melody to new words by Hoyt, "Reuben And Cynthia." Typical of its many choruses was:

Reuben, Reuben, I've been thinking,
What a strange thing that would be,
If the streams of drinking water,
All turned salty as the sea.
Cynthia, Cynthia, I've been thinking,
You can safely take my word,
More than half the population,
Wouldn't know it had occurred.

Many of the lyrics were remarkably fresh and natural. The opening verse to "The Widow" runs:

Do you know her? Have you met her?
If so, you'll ne'er forget her—
The pretty little widow with the laughing eyes of brown.
Demure in her sobriety,
Severe in her propriety,
But the life of all society,
The jolliest thing in town.

If some of the words are no longer current usage, they were more commonplace at the turn of the century. But the best-remembered of the Hoyt-Gaunt songs is assuredly "The Bowery," sung as a reminiscence by Strong to the partying couples.

Another illustration of the era's freewheeling practices occurred when road companies were sent out.

While the first of the touring companies was in Milwaukee, Charles K. Harris's "After The Ball" was added and soon became one of the show's musical numbers wherever the show was performed. (See the discussion when *A Trip to Chinatown* returns in February 1894.) It was easy to insert and remove songs. For the most part the lead-ins were so generalized that with few exceptions, such as possibly "The Widow" or "The Chaperone," almost any song might have followed. "Reuben And Cynthia" is treated almost as a drinking song, led into simply by a universal "Drink hearty!" A simulated "coon" song, "Push Dem Clouds Away," is sung after Uncle Ben says, "I want you four young people to get 'round the piano and sing me my favorite quartette." And even though "The Widow" fits logically into the plot, the song is actually brought up by Wilder's comment, "That's a great song Billy Parker wrote and dedicated to her." In short, there was still some instinct prompting librettists to look at songs as extraneous, something to be kept formally apart. This attitude was underscored in the directions and staging. After "The Bowery" Hoyt's directions read, "exit à la militaire," while one unidentified song comes with the following directions: "Musical introduction. Tony and Flirt down C. and sing. Then the two boys join them. Then as they go up R. and L., Widow enters R.U.E. in white Chinese dress and does Chinese specialty. Then Strong, who is getting pretty drunk, down C. and sings with [W]idow, all joining in chorus and dance at finish." However loosely incorporated the musical numbers, Hoyt saw to it they were well done. Tiny young Ollie Archmere won especially large applause for her pert dances. (In February 1892 Loie Fuller joined the cast to swirl her skirts more widely than she had before, in an elaborate imitation of butterfly wings. She was replaced the following October by Bessie Clayton, a young lady whose winning manner and stunning legs soon made her a favorite at Weber and Fields.) But whatever sort of dancing momentarily halted the plot, Hoyt saw to it the evening as a whole was tautly staged. The *Times* reported the "piece gallops from start to finish."

Con McFadden (John Kernell) was **The Hustler** (23 November 1891, Bijou). Of course, in the gay nineties the term had not yet taken on quite the pejorative meaning later attached to it. In those really no more innocent days a hustler was simply a go-getter. But the scrapes Con got himself into and wangled himself out of were secondary to the turns he hustled up—a typical farce-comedy bag including a mimic and ballad singer, a toe-dancer,

a ventriloquist, and a barbershop quartet. As usual, critics pooh-poohed the whole affair, but audiences savored it for several seasons.

Carroll Johnson, like many of his Irish brethren, moved easily back and forth between minstrel entertainments and romantic melodramas that proudly wore the green. **The Gossoon** (30 November 1891, People's) naturally allowed its brave but lovesick serving lad to sing several songs.

Curiously, actors who affected a brogue were rarely called dialect comedians. That term seemed to be reserved for players impersonating foreigners speaking English. Emmet and such later, more clownish examples as Weber and Fields naturally come to mind. There were numerous other "Dutch" artists, now totally forgotten. One was Charles A. Gardner, a sometime minstrel, a composer of many of his own melodies, and, at times, a comedian on the periphery of the legitimate stage. His vehicles included **Karl, the Peddler** (15 November 1886, Theatre Comique [Harlem]), **Captain Karl** (22 August 1891, Grand Opera), and jumping ahead slightly in our chronology, **Fatherland** (1 August 1892, Union Square). This last show advertised the inclusion of a Tyrolean Quartet.

An elaborate pantomime of **Cinderella** filled the Academy of Music from just before Thanksgiving until the day after Christmas. Romping with Cinderella (Fanny Ward) and her young-lady-in-trousers prince (Bertha Ricci) were such unusual characters as The Insect Queen and Baron Stone Broke. Naturally, since this was pantomime, Clown, Pantaloon, Harlequin, and Columbine were also present.

The Last of the Hogans, Harrigan and Braham's only new work of the season, bowed on 21 December. The title throws the evening slightly out of perspective, since there were two stories running concurrently and that dealing with the Hogans was neither as important nor as entertaining as the other. Judge Dominick Murray, a "sporting" Irishman (Harrigan), is handling two cases. One concerns a will leaving a substantial fortune to "the last of the Hogans." He proves to be a bricklayer. The judge's other case concerns a group of blacks attempting to sell their church. One of the church members, Esaw Coldstream (John Wild), runs an illegal society—The Mystic Star—dedicated to exterminating Italians who charge less for shoeshines than Negroes do. During a meeting on a barge, their scow is cut loose and collides with a tug on which the judge is holding an illegal prizefight. After the yacht's bowsprit crashed through the barge's rotten timbers the curtain fell on a "capitally devised scene of comic consternation." Ada Lewis assumed several roles, appearing first as a "froway" servant and later as a hard-boiled music hall artist, while Annie Yeamans, in a noteworthy change of pace for her, portrayed a warmly sentimental spinster. The *Times*, which not long before had compared Harrigan to Gay, now compared him to Hogarth and Dickens. As theatre historian George Odell noted, audiences must have loved "a stage full of sidewalks of New York," for the show enjoyed four profitable months at the box office.

A Night at the Circus (22 December 1891, Park) was a farce-comedy starring Nellie McHenry. When some wives secretly decide to spend an evening performing with a touring circus, their husbands opt to escort some lovely ladies for a night on the town—starting at the very same circus. Madeline Milan, a seemingly drab governess, changes places with Electra, queen of the arena, exposes the marrieds, and brings about a reconciliation. The show's initial run was a month, but it made several later returns and toured for a decade.

In an era fond of dialect performers, a rarely heard dialect was a Scandinavian one. Among its most noted practitioners was Gus (sometimes Augustus) Heege. After skirting the Rialto whipping his new vehicle into shape, he finally gave Manhattanites his **Yon Yonson** (28 December 1891, Park). Its story was closer to the melodramatics and pathos favored by Emmet than to the purer comedy of many later dialect players. Yon's adventures included his saving a sweet girl from being murdered by a treacherous logger, who leaves her unconscious on a log jam and walks away to await the jam's breaking. Actually its story had sufficient substance to allow many critics to consider it simply a play with music, and its elaborate production (a moving train, a lumber camp with a log jam seen in the rear) suggested the sort of stage realism usually reserved for nonmusical plays at the time. Yet performers did include another quartet (in tobogganing costumes), acrobats, and dancers. Playgoers didn't quibble over nomenclature; they gave this first New York showing a four-week run and welcomed Gus and Yon back, right into the early years of the next century.

An even more successful musical followed in just over a week. In **The Lion Tamer** (30 December 1891, Broadway)—an American version of Lecocq's *Le Grand Casimir*—Francis Wilson found another vehicle to delight his loyal admirers. Wilson played Casimir, a timid lion tamer who also owns a failing

circus. When he feigns suicide to leave his wife debt-free, complications ensue. With most of Lecocq's music discarded, the *Times* lamented that Richard Stahl's score was "commonplace" but resignedly accepted that "no one expected him to suddenly develop the faculty for melodic inventiveness." What luster the music displayed came from John Philip Sousa's orchestrations. During the run, Marie Jansen, Wilson's leading lady, became ill and a chorus girl who was her understudy had to go on. Truth is often as amazing as fiction. This popular motif of 1920s Broadway musicals and 1930s Hollywood musicals unfolded on the very real Rialto stage of 1892. The chorus girl who called attention to herself in such storybook fashion was Lulu Glaser.

LULU GLASER was born in Allegheny City, Pennsylvania, on 2 June 1874. The buoyancy with which she threw about her long hair and displayed her attractive legs so delighted Wilson that he agreed to hire her for his chorus, even though she confessed she had had no previous professional experience. It was this same buoyancy and these same legs (which for years she displayed in light brown tights) that kept her a star for a quarter of a century.

Odell records another interesting footnote, one that demonstrates the danger of trusting to autobiographical memories. Wilson remembered the incident of the two young African-American entertainers in connection with *The Merry Monarch* (18 August 1890), but Odell lists their names and the roles they played in *The Lion Tamer* as well as details of the Gerry Society's action against them after they opened the show. Other cast changes notwithstanding, Wilson was *The Lion Tamer* for Broadway's audiences until early May.

The first three months of 1892 were occupied largely with revivals or importations. The Casino revived *Nanon* for Marie Tempest on 12 January and then tried a French novelty, Audran's **Uncle Célestin**, on 15 February. Its story centered on an effete young man who hopes to marry the daughter of a snobbish baron but who learns he will lose the inheritance left him by his uncle unless he agrees to run a common tavern. Even Jefferson De Angelis's genial clowning could not infuse enough life into the piece to please New Yorkers. It had a slightly forced run of two months. On that same 15 February Agnes Huntington appeared in Planquette's **Captain Thérèse** at the Union Square. She played a lady who must dress as a man in order to rescue her falsely imprisoned lover. A poor reception necessitated her switching to *Paul Jones* on 29 February. She played this revival for a week and then returned to the road.

A supposed American novelty came in among those openings. Actually it was merely a retooling of the previous autumn's farce-comedy *Boys and Girls*. **The New Boys and Girls** (22 February 1892, Park) elicited some of the critical remarks so common to the genre: "Even in the beginning there is but little pretense of a 'play.' Toward the close, songs, dances and imitations follow without even the time-honored 'thread of story'" Still, favorites such as Otis Harlan and blonde, buxom May Irwin (from the earlier mounting), plus six "harmoniously curved maids who sang real songs with real voices," made for a fun-filled evening.

Robin Hood's myth claimed the stage again, but this time it was the legendary hero's fellow Englishmen who created the work. **The Foresters** (17 March 1892, Daly's) was a play by Alfred Tennyson, embellished with songs and back ground music by Arthur Sullivan. It ran from mid-March until late April.

The first quarter's lone genuine American novelty was W. A. Mestayer's **Our Grab Bag** (2 March 1892, Park), a farce-comedy only slightly more cohesive than his earlier Tourists vehicle, *A Pullman Palace Car*. Sheepshead sells turpentine and kerosene as alcohol in a prohibition town. The villain, running for mayor on the prohibitionist ticket, holds Sheepshead's mortgage and threatens trouble. Thankfully, by curtain time, all the prohibitionists have reformed. The piece, with which Mestayer had been touring on and off for a year and a half, remained for two weeks, giving New Yorkers an opportunity to see two future stars, singer Andrew Mack and comedian Raymond Hitchcock.

The end of March witnessed a major success in San Francisco. **Bluff King Hal!** (28 March 1892, Tivoli) was an operetta, with a libretto by Daniel O'Connell and music by H. J. Stewart, telling how a disguised Henry VIII pursues the daughter of an innkeeper at Windsor. It was hailed as "full of grace and poetry," and such notices prompted the public to respond so enthusiastically that the work held the boards for three weeks, reputedly chalking up record grosses in doing so.

Three musicals opened in Manhattan on 18 April. Millöcker's **The Child of Fortune,** with a libretto about the love life of a bohemian photographer, began an unrewarding run at the Casino. At the 14th Street Theatre, A. C. Gunter provided the libretto for a "fantastic operetta," **Polly Middles,** for which W. W. Lowitz composed the score. Polly (Annie Pixley), a "Drury Lane soubrette," and a group of fellow tourists in 1877 Pompeii drink a potion offered them by a German scientist. Suddenly they are transported back in time to Pompeii in its gaudy heyday. The shock of Vesuvius' great eruption sends them back to 1877. Richard Barker directed. The third opening was a farce-comedy, **A Jolly Surprise,** which played briefly at the Bijou.

Another musical was scheduled to open at Philadelphia's Grand Opera House the same evening. **A Tin Napoleon** was allegedly derived by Charles T Vincent from Albin Valabrègue's *Les Aventures de Mons. Martin.* But just before the opening the composer, in a huff about artistic differences, decamped with all the music. So the piece was performed as a straight play until Richard Stahl could throw together a new score. One interesting sidelight: the stage manager was none other than James A. Herne, the rising actor and playwright.

The increasingly busy Harry B. Smith was librettist and lyricist for **Jupiter** (2 May 1892, Palmer's), in which Digby Bell starred. Its score raised Julian Edwards from the ranks of conductors into the more select circle of composers.

> JULIAN EDWARDS was born in Manchester, England, on 11 December 1855. After studying music in Edinburgh and London he accepted a post as conductor with the Carl Rosa Opera Company. J. C. Duff invited him to America to be his musical director.

Smith's tale for *Jupiter* was much like the one used decades later in *Amphitryon 38* and in the musical *Out of This World* (21 December 1950). Jupiter assumes the guise of a hard-drinking shoemaker in order to seduce the shoemaker's wife (Laura Joyce

Bell). The proprieties of the day led at least one critic to damn the show as sacrilege. Other critics had a more legitimate complaint: the show did not represent a noteworthy achievement on the part of either Smith or Edwards. However, at least one critic was so pleased with the scenery he devoted a few words to describing it—a rare practice at this time. The first act, done primarily in buff and blue, was set in a Roman square, with a triumphal arch at center stage. (On opening night Bell accidentally knocked over the arch on his first entrance.) The second act was set on "Mount Olympus among silver-lined clouds and an eccentric moon." This setting provided a background for E. Forrest Jones as Marcus Coonius to sing a medley of minstrel songs. The cast included a still relatively unknown young lady, Trixie Friganza. But it was largely Bell's antics that kept the work on the boards for two months. Ignoring his ancient Roman toga, Bell joked about poker and baseball, and sang "Annie Rooney."

The next Monday, 7 May, saw another great clown, De Wolf Hopper, return for an additional four weeks of *Wang* (4 May 1891).

The season's umpteenth Irish brogue was heard when **Sport McAllister, One of the 400** (16 May 1892, Bijou) appeared. "Sport" was actually Jeremiah McAllister (Robert Gaylor), whose success as a bettor makes him bet he can succeed in politics. Along with vaudeville turns that helped smooth Sport's way, celebrated athletes were hired now and then to boost attendance during the farce-comedy's seasons-long tours.

A "lyric-comedy" called **Elysium** (16 May 1892, Herrmann's), based on Marie Uchard's *My Uncle Barbassou*, recorded the consternation of a young man (Clement Bainbridge) on learning he is heir to his uncle's estate—a harem. A eunuch (Max Figman) provided the comedy. The hero's consternation was small compared with that of some of the critics. "Positively indecent," the *Times* wailed. The public seemed to agree, and the piece left hastily.

The abysmal failure of *Beautiful Star* left its composer, Charles Puerner, undiscouraged. He tried again on 28 May with a comic opera, **The Robber of the Rhine**. His librettist was a figure more often thought of as an actor in straight plays, Maurice Barrymore. This variation of the Robin Hood legend, peopled with gypsies and German brigands, was selected to open the new Fifth Avenue Theatre. Although it was staged by the capable Richard Barker and gave New Yorkers their first major glimpse of Hayden Coffin and Marie Dressler, the work met with a cool welcome. It ran only until the beginning of July.

June was ushered in on an unhappy note. The Broadway Theatre had hoped **King Kaliko**, a comic opera with a book by Frank Dupree and a score by Fred Solomon and R. L. Scott, would keep it lit through the summer. Edwin Stevens and Eva Davenport played the leads. Instead, the musical, which opened on the 7th, was a two-week flop. Its chief novelty was its setting, the Sandwich Islands (Hawaii)—a locale its librettist called home.

The Casino had better luck with another in its procession of importations, **The Vice Admiral**. The titular hero is a young man willed a fortune provided he marry before his twentieth birthday. The success of Millöcker's operetta made amends for the disappointment of his *The Child of Fortune*. Again, Jefferson De Angelis's clowning sparked the evening. *The Vice Admiral* sang his way into New Yorkers' hearts from 18 June until 10 September.

The Garden Theatre also found itself a summer-long attraction in its mounting on 27 June of a lavish spectacle, **Sinbad**. The "$10,000 beauty," Louise Montague, played the title role. Spectacular sets took playgoers beneath the ocean and to the Valley of Diamonds. The construction of the piece was not as careful as the construction of its sets. The dialogue was filled with puns that were considered old hat and outrageous even in an era that was tolerant of old and strained puns. Its songs were culled from numerous sources and changed at intervals during the run. But the management could only remind the musical's critics that the audiences who flocked to the house until 8 October obviously didn't share the detractors' concern.

Henry E. Dixey brought the season to a close with a series of revivals. Opening on 18 July with *The Mascot*, he later switched to *Patience, Iolanthe*, and a double bill of *Trial by Jury* and *The Sorcerer*. Dixey's company included Trixie Friganza. In the pit Julian Edwards conducted. Like Gustave Kerker before him, Edwards clearly was determined to play it safe until he was sure composing alone could bring him a dependable income. The troupe played until 1 October.

Away from the mainstream, theatregoers could attend a number of minor efforts. For example, at the Thalia the Liliputians tried out a piece called *The Dwarfs' Wedding*. Deemed unworthy of better houses, the play was soon withdrawn and a new Robert Breitenbach work substituted. At Koster and

Bial's the bill for 19 October included *Carmen up to Date*, a spoof not completely in the Gaiety tradition. At the London, another vaudeville house, McIntyre and Heath offered *Way Down South*. McIntyre and Heath were the earliest blackface act to make a mark in the legitimate theatre, although most of their career was spent in vaudeville. They were almost certainly the most enduring of blackface pairs. One of the great stories of the backstage world was their famous feud. While they acted and starred together for decades, an early disagreement led to their never speaking to each other off stage for most of their careers. Another future vaudeville great, Willy West,

was a principal in their troupe. In their extended skit, McIntyre played an old colored woman named Hannah, Heath played a "fly coon" and a poacher, and West portrayed a porter.

One sad note was the appearance of *Fritz in Ireland* (3 November, 1879) at the Grand Opera House. The title role was played by J. K. Emmet, Jr., son of its originator. The young Emmet spent a number of years touring in his father's old vehicles and in some new ones, such as Sydney Rosenfeld's *Fritz in Prosperity*. He never won the love or fortune bestowed on his father, but for a while made a respectable living from the pieces.

Intermission

Further British Influences and New Stirrings, 1892–1902

By the early nineties the great musical circus began to lose its appeal. Audiences had become jaded with more color than content. Freaks seemed less curious, clowns all of the same ilk, and spectacles appeared much like preceding spectacles. Another generation had to pass before audiences and economic conditions chased vestiges of carnival glitter and tricks from the musical stage. These vestiges survived as long as they did because a new group of brasher clowns came to tickle changing fancies, while spectacle found an outlet in a form that made its first tentative appearance at the beginning of this intermission: the revue. To a small extent vestiges still survive, attesting to the undying appeal of some theatrical extravagance and outlandishness.

All through this period future patterns quietly continued to take shape. For the first time a separation of lyric works into operetta, musical comedy, and revue could be discerned, although the pattern is clearer in retrospect than it was to critics and playgoers of the time. Musically, the stage remained under the influence of London. Two great hits,

A *Gaiety Girl* and *Florodora*, flanked the period, reasserting the hegemony won for the English musical stage by Gilbert and Sullivan. The influence of the Gaiety musicals, coupled with the vogue of American farce-comedy, led directly to modern musical comedy. Both the American and English pieces reveled in the vernacular. They dealt not with royalty or unworldly figures but with more or less everyday men and women in more or less everyday difficulties. The English pieces had style and a certain cohesion; the American works offered zest and more pertinent domestic material.

Theatrical royalty and its friends found refuge in comic opera, clothed in that genre's universally higher musical pretensions. The higher social order of its characters and its loftier musical aims were the genre's unifying traits. As often as not the form was not even accorded the courtesy of a generally accepted name. One playgoer's comic opera was another's opéra bouffe and a third's operetta. To some extent this confusion of nomenclature stemmed from the multiple sources of the American works, or, perhaps more accurately, from the blending and refashioning of these sources by American writers. The earliest Offenbachian opéra bouffe used mythological and other outlandish settings to mask sharp political commentary. Offenbach's successors brought their settings closer to contemporary France and substituted sentiment for satire. English comic opera, its standards set by Gilbert and Sullivan, generally kept its brilliantly witty and literate satire—satire more often social than specifically political—in the forefront. Its music, however artful, tended to be less arioso than either French or Viennese scores. Viennese operetta was the most carefree and playful. Its gay plots were more frivolous than preposterous. And far more so than either the French or English school, the Viennese works were determinedly contemporary. Almost every major Viennese operetta purported to take place in the very world its audience inhabited. American comic opera at this time clearly owed its main debt to Gilbert and Sullivan. But American writers, lacking Gilbert and Sullivan's genius, reduced Gilbert's great satire to buffoonery and Sullivan's magnificent melodies to tinkly pleasantries.

Acrobatic clowns and prima donnas dominated the musical stage of the period. The clowns were almost always in grotesque makeup and the prima donnas as often as not in tights, both thereby underscoring the traditions out of which they came. For most of the period their supremacy was acknowledged by having whole show companies named for them. The Francis Wilson Comic Opera Company or the De Wolf Hopper Comic Opera Company or the Alice Nielsen Comic Opera Company visited a town, as much as *Half a King* or *El Capitan* or *The Fortune Teller*. But hard times, brought on by the Panic of 1893, combined with an all too loose system of theatrical bookings, prompted a number of theatre magnates to merge their offices, forming what soon became known as "the Trust" or "the Syndicate." For better or worse this group completely changed producing and booking practices in the decade that followed. One of its initial coups was to end effectively the reign of the actor-manager, although, in fairness to the Trust, many a performer was undoubtedly thankful to be relieved of responsibility for his own ledgers.

Neither the Trust nor the stars could create the geniuses to write their material. It became evident during this intermission that Reginald De Koven was never to write a second *Robin Hood*. John Philip Sousa, in many ways a better and more theatrical

melodist, had only modest luck with his stage pieces and soon tired of them. Theatre orchestra conductors who hastily donned composers' mantles—Ludwig Englander, William Furst, Gustave Kerker, as well as one man who was not a conductor, A. Baldwin Sloane—were musicianly, competent enough to orchestrate their own works, but basically they were hacks. When Victor Herbert appeared, the public and press alike were quick to appreciate his melodic gifts, and he would set the standards for American operetta composition for nearly a quarter of a century. No librettists or lyricists of similar magnitude emerged during this era.

Mounting changed little. Most musicals still relied on flats with perspective painted on. "Well-painted" remained a conventional expression of critical praise. Architecturally conceived sets were few and far between. Nor was one man customarily responsible for all the sets of a single evening. Specialists evolved, one painting little but garden scenes, a second called in for interiors, a third known for his street scenes. Even the Casino, generally credited with the best production staff, filled its stage with people rather than scenery. (In an age of low-paid performers, casts ranged from 60 to 200.) The first use of motion pictures to advance the action appeared. But film was offered more for its novelty than for its functional advantages. Its potentials and its implications largely passed unrealized.

Outside the theatrical mainstream a phenomenon occurred that would have more significance in the long run than anything else in the period. African-American music became popular. Ragtime's origins were untheatrical. Ben Harney first brought the infectious rhythm to New York in 1896. His success, while not as dramatic as sometimes thought, was immediate. Ragtime spread with remarkable speed in the burgeoning vaudeville circuits, and before long singers were interpolating so-called "ragtime" into loosely structured farce-comedies and the new revue form. The popularity of ragtime helped briefly to revive old songs from the waning minstrel tradition. Together they were responsible for the "coon" song rage of the turn of the century.

1892–1893

Appropriately, if unwittingly, the season was one of reminiscence and recapitulation. Over half the lyric pieces presented in 1892–1893 were revivals. Off and on throughout the theatrical year the best-loved offerings from the first harvest of American musicals graced Broadway's stages. By summer New York had been given the opportunity to enjoy once more all the major native successes except *Evangeline* and *Humpty Dumpty*. New Yorkers who chanced to visit other cities at the right time could have caught these two favorites playing before packed houses across the country. They also could have caught a road company of *A Trip to Chinatown*, which began its tour on 29 August at the Harlem Opera House. The original cast, of course, continued at the Madison Square until April.

The first musical to arrive was a past favorite. One of the most recent hits, *Wang*, with De Wolf Hopper still heading the cast, returned for a month's engagement at the Broadway on 15 August (and later for a week at the same house beginning 14 November). Decker Brothers' Minstrels, a modest, traditional troupe, relit the Third Avenue on 20 August for a week's stand.

The Kid (22 August 1892, Columbus) framed its musical treats in the story of a young girl, Evangeline, and her battles with Ebenezer Newrich and his snooty daughter Emily.

A touring company of *Around the World in Eighty Days* performed for a week starting 27 August at the fading Niblo's. But the biggest and perhaps the most surprising success among the older works was the remounting of *The Black Crook* (12 September 1866) on 1 September. Its original performers and scenery had long since disappeared, and since neither programs nor reviews detail the musical numbers, probably many of the 1866 songs had been replaced. Nonetheless the new production remained faithful in spirit to the sensation of a quarter of a century earlier. The settings were lavish and, besides the actors cast for the dramatic roles, the company included a host of ballet artists, acrobats (tightrope walkers, head balancers, and others), and a contingent of French quadrille dancers. New songs included "Ta-Ra-Ra-Boom-Dee-Ay" (Henry J. Sayers). With an oddly fitting irony the show opened at the Academy of Music, whose burning in 1866 supposedly had led to the creation of the musical. Curiosity and nostalgia helped pack the auditorium for the whole season. When *The Black Crook* closed on 20 May, it had added another 306 performances to its record and had grossed an additional $375,000.

12PM (5 September 1892, Bijou) was a farce-comedy for Jennie Yeamans and was touted as a new work. But it proved to be merely a reworking or perhaps only a retitling of *Jacqueline*, which the star

had withdrawn after it failed on the road some years before. It dealt with a young lady's encounter with a ghost.

The skimpy parade of new, full-blown American musicals began on 19 September with the arrival of *Puritania* and *Candy*. **Puritania** was written by C. M. S. McLellan and Edgar Stillman Kelley for the prima donna of *Erminie*, Pauline Hall. McLellan's book described how in 1640 Elizabeth (Louise Beaudet), a Salem maiden, is condemned as a witch. She is saved by a young English earl, Vivian George Trevelyan (Miss Hall), who carries her off to England. But she goes mad from her experience and in front of King Charles (John Brand) recites a mock incantation. At that very moment an anti-Royalist conspirator, Killsen Burgess (Harry Macdonough), sets off a bomb. To the king this validates the judgment against Elizabeth. In the end Burgess turns out to be Elizabeth's father. He is pardoned; she is cleared. She and the earl wed. It was a satisfactory vehicle for Miss Hall, and it remained at the Fifth Avenue Theatre until 5 November, when it headed out into the hinterlands.

Candy, at the Union Square, was the latest in the series concocted by Robert Breitenbach for the Liliputians. It told how Sam Nollendorf (Mr. Durand) offers the hand of his daughter, Kitty (Minchen Becker), to anyone who can cure her addiction to candy. Tom Klapps (Franz Ebert), a bootblack, disguises himself as Prince Ole Hugh Ham and rids the young girl of her habit. Everyone then sails for Africa with the real prince (Mr. Kahn) to quell a revolution. They take a band of Amazons with them. Having restored the prince to his throne, they prepare to sail home on their steamer, *S. S. Microscope*. A storm shipwrecks them on a cannibal shore, but the grateful prince comes to their rescue. The first and last of the four acts ended with transformation scenes. At the Nollendorf home the guests were whisked off to "a candy palace" for a ballet; at the end the cast became part of an elaborate "Rose Festival." The musical stage could still support these theatrical freak shows, so when it became obvious that the show was settling down for a small run, one of the most popular midgets, Adolf Zink, was given "Ta-Ra-Ra-Boom-Dee-Ay" to interpolate as well as a prizefight with his fellow Liliputian, baby-faced, "tottly"-legged Ebert. The German origins of most of the people associated with the show—as well, probably, as a good share of the audience—were acknowledged when the piece was published with English and German texts side by side.

One old standby, *Squatter Sovereignty*, opened the same night as *Candy* and *Puritania*. It signaled an entire season of revivals at Harrigan's, a tacit admission that the great showman had passed his most fruitful years. Hart was dead. Dave Braham's newer songs never enjoyed the general vogue of his former melodies, and, while Ned Harrigan continued to write effective material, he was never again able to assemble it with the compelling theatricality his better offerings displayed. His later works were all to be "comparative failures."

Rudolph Aronson suggested just how pervasive the feeling of creative exhaustion was when he removed the Casino from the legitimate fold and reopened it on 26 September as a vaudeville house. Since the theatre had been given over from its inception to importations, his action hinted that the font of foreign inspiration had run as dry as the native one. Vaudeville proved unpopular at the theatre. By November comic opera once more held its stage.

On 24 September, the *Dramatic Mirror* announced that William Hoey was now singing a new song in the touring company of *A Parlor Match*. The song was "The Man Who Broke The Bank At Monte Carlo" (Fred Gilbert). The trade paper noted happily that the song "proved very funny, and aided by capital make-up, it received several encores." The song was ever after identified both with Hoey and the show. In later years, even when he was appearing in straight plays such as *The Globe Trotter*, Hoey found a way of inserting the song into his material.

A return of *The Lady or the Tiger?* was October's first musical entry, filling the bill at the Broadway between *Wang's* two engagements.

John F. Sheridan, who had won fame in Australia as a female impersonator, was starred in **Mrs. O'Brien, Esq.** (31 October 1892, Bijou). He cavorted as Bridget O'Brien, who "practices" law without benefit of a degree. But she means well.

November opened with a visit to the Garden Theatre by the Bostonians, singing their greatest hit, *Robin Hood* (28 September 1891). It cheered New York in this sluggish season from 7 November until Christmas Eve and then again from 22 May until the 1st of July, with a one-week break. For seekers of novelty, Smith and De Koven, the authors of *Robin Hood*, had a new work ready one week after the revival of their masterpiece. **The Fencing Master** (14 November 1892, Casino) gave Broadway several causes for small celebration. The show marked the return of the Casino to the legitimate realm and also marked the first American musical

ever to play the theatre. It was as well the first new lyric piece of the season to enjoy an unqualified success. But though it was American in origin it was set in the lavish palaces of fifteenth-century Milan and Venice, its scene and mood even more alien to our shores than Sherwood Forest. The play's principal figure was not its fencing master, Torquato (William Broderick), but his daughter Francesca. She is in love with Fortunio (Hubert Wilke), who would be Duke of Milan had not the spendthrift Galeazzo Visconti (Charles Hopper) usurped the throne. Unfortunately, since Francesca has been raised as a boy, Fortunio has no idea of her true sex and has found romance elsewhere. His heart is given to the Countess Filippa (Grace Golden). When the bankrupt duke sells Filippa's hand in marriage to a Venetian and orders Fortunio to escort the countess to her wedding, Fortunio plans an elopement. He reveals his plan to Francesca and she, in desperation, betrays him. Fortunio challenges her to a duel, and only when she is injured is her real nature ascertained. She takes the blame for the duel, and is imprisoned. A marchesa who loves the supposed boy and is unaware of the truth helps Francesca escape. At a masked ball Fortunio realizes he loves Francesca. The duke and his astrologer (Jerome Sykes)—two more of Smith's comic villains—are overthrown and Fortunio's rights restored. De Koven carefully filled his score with appropriate Mediterranean styles—tarantellas, barcaroles, habaneras, and maranescas—and while many of the melodies were attractive, none proved lastingly popular. Probably the best were "Ah Yes, I Love Thee" and "A Wild Bird That Singeth." With Marie Tempest starred in yet another trouser role, *The Fencing Master* delighted New York until the end of February.

November's third and final lyric piece was Harrigan's *The Mulligan Guards' Ball* (13 January 1879). It proved far and away the most popular of his four revivals, running from 30 November to 18 March.

Another of the season's new successes, **The Isle of Champagne**, followed on 5 December, although its relatively short run belies its popularity around the turn of the century. With a text by Charles Alfred Byrne and Louis Harrison and with music by W. W. Furst (long the pit leader at San Francisco's Tivoli), the musical recounted how King Pommery Sec makes his fortune when a ship is wrecked off his island. The king's domain flows with champagne, but water is unknown. The wrecked vessel has a large supply of water on board which Pommery Sec promptly commandeers. Other characters had such likely names as the Baron Heidsic and the Marquis Mumm. As an added attraction the mounting offered "stage pictures prolific in gold, silver, and silk tights." Starring Thomas Q. Seabrooke, the show played until 21 January at Hammerstein's 2,600-seat Manhattan Opera House and, after touring Harlem, Brooklyn, and points farther afield, returned on 29 May for a summer run at the elegant Fifth Avenue. With or without its original star *The Isle of Champagne* played constantly for over a decade.

Dan Daly, young Tyrone Power, and Julius Witmark, a future music publisher, were featured players in **A Society Fad** (5 December 1892, Bijou), which spoofed high-society fripperies, including money-oriented matchmaking.

At year's end three attractions opened which attested to the variety—and uncertainty—of contemporary musical stages. **If I Were You** (20 December 1892, Herrmann's) was written by William Young, at the time considered one of America's most promising serious dramatists. It was a comedy about the rocky road of young love and brought out as a vehicle for a popular comic-opera star, Marion Manola, who wanted to venture into less lyric entertainments and who played the young lady of the starry-eyed couple opposite her husband, John B. Mason, soon to be recognized as one of our finest actors. No doubt to ease the transition for Miss Manola several songs were inserted for her to sing. Just how many is open to question. "One song, the first, was quite enough," one critic complained, while another regretted that the "few songs" she sang were enough to noticeably impede the comedy's progress. Odell states that during the play's third and final week she sang "two songs." How many songs make a musical? Most likely playgoers looked upon the piece as a straight play and never kept count.

There were more, but less artful, songs, along with some swirling and kicking dancing, in **Miss Blythe of Duluth** (26 December 1892, Grand Opera), which William B. Gill wrote as a vehicle for the tireless Annie Pixley. As Bessie Blythe she freed her sister and brother-in-law from the clutches of some rapacious, bogus English nobility. The play gave promise of being one of Miss Pixley's biggest hits, but its tour was cut short by her sudden early death.

Some nine blocks downtown the Hanlons, to compete with Miss Pixley's opening, brought in *Superba* to the 14th Street Theatre, still a first-class house albeit a fading one. The extravaganza had been touring intermittently since the Hanlons initially presented it more then two years before. For the moment, in honor of the Columbian year, its fairy story was interrupted to present a series of tableaux depicting "The Wealth of the World and the Genius of America." More visits to this house and outlying combination houses followed for the rest of the century.

Audran's *La Cigale* was revived the night after Christmas at the Garden for two weeks, but the booking was clearly a stopgap until **The Mountebanks** was ready to raise its curtain on 11 January. This joining of W. S. Gilbert with Alfred Cellier, who years before had conducted some of Sullivan's scores in New York, piqued Broadway's curiosity. At least it did before the curtain went up. Even with Lillian Russell and the American-born English favorite Hayden Coffin singing the leads, the show, which detailed the complications produced by a magic philter that makes "everyone who drinks it exactly what he pretends to be," proved mildly disappointing. Nonetheless, the musical ran a month and a half, then toured. If London and New York tastes were not always the same, there were cases where, for better or worse, they did coincide. Gilbert's complaint in *The Mountebanks* that many a song has "twenty verses and each verse has a chorus" suggests that pandering to the demand for excessive encores was as prevalent in England as it was in America.

A more important event for the New York stage, if not for the American Musical Theatre, occurred two weeks later when the Empire Theatre first opened its doors at 39th Street and Broadway on 25 January 1893. With time this house became one of the most venerated in theatrical annals, occupying a niche alongside Wallack's and Daly's, and enduring far longer. Its grandeur may have given its proprietor, Charles Frohman, even more grandiose ambitions, for no sooner had the theatre opened than he was in secret consultation with a number of other theatre owners. To the extent that Frohman hoped to end the chaos in national bookings his plans were admirable. Most theatres were independently owned. A few more aggressive entrepreneurs owned a handful of houses. But anything like the transcontinental chains of later years was unknown. As a result, to book a national tour required long, elaborate correspondence with a large number of house managers. If bookings were made late or had to be changed suddenly, a company often found itself skipping its way back and forth across the country. By grouping together important theatres across the land and handling all their bookings from one office, producers could move troupes from city to city with some geographic logic. Moreover, given a long view of a season, dark weeks could be minimized. Unfortunately, the men with whom Frohman conferred—notably Abe Erlanger—were not highly ethical. Out of these talks came the infamous "Trust" or "Syndicate," a booking monopoly that shortly had marked effects on theatrical practices, including those of the American musical. Anyone refusing to bow to the dictates of the monopoly found whole cities with no available theatres.

One quirky entry was **Friend Fritz** (26 January 1893, Herrmann's), which some unsuspecting playgoers may have assumed was the latest episode in Our Cousin German's saga. Actually it was a translation of Émile Erckmann-Alexandre Chatrian's *L'Ami Fritz*, which opera-lovers were even then beginning to become familiar with in Mascagni's version. Since Marion Manola and her husband played the romantic leads, there was a good deal of music in this version, too. But none by Mascagni. Instead composer Julian Edwards and his lyricist Stanislaus Stange combined to create the songs, which Suzel, the farmer's daughter in love with a middle-aged landowner, was able to sing for a month.

San Francisco enjoyed a surprise hit with **His Majesty** (8 February 1893, Grand Opera House), which had a libretto by Peter Robinson and music by H. J. Stewart. King Cadenza got his job as ruler of Patata by answering an advertisement Patata's citizens placed in European newspapers for a monarch. He is dismayed to find his salary is a measly fifty dollars a week. To cover costs and create the necessary three acts of comic complications, Cadenza and his queen decide to take in boarders. A love interest was provided by the palace gardener, really a disguised prince, and the queen's handmaiden. With the popular Ferris Hartman cavorting as the king, the evening was so well received that it was soon moved to the Tivoli for a run.

No more musicals bowed in New York until 27 February, when André Messager's **The Basoche** replaced *The Fencing Master* at the Casino. Its plot recounted the rocky road a marriage takes after a husband and wife each suspects the other of being unfaithful. The *Basoche* of the title was a French legal fraternity. The evening proved a harsher disappointment than *The Mountebanks* and was withdrawn after two weeks. The same night saw the opening of **A Mad Bargain,** a farce-comedy filled

with names working their way to the top of the lyric stage: J. J. McNally and Julian Mitchell (its authors), James T. Powers, Peter F. Dailey, and Richard Carle. McNally's plot recounted the plight of a would-be suicide. Lacking the courage to take his own life, he persuades his cousin to arrange an "accident." When he has a change of heart, he cannot locate his cousin to stop the arrangement. His contrivances to keep out of death's way comprised much of the fun. In keeping with the farce-comedy tradition extraneous songs were interpolated.

March saw nothing but revivals. Lillian Russell began a month's run on the 3rd in *Giroflé-Girofla; The Gondoliers* was rushed in on the 16th at the Casino to fill the vacancy created by the failure of *The Basoche*; and on the 20th Harrigan returned *Cordelia's Aspirations* (5 November 1883) to the footlights.

The burlesque traditions of the seventies and early eighties had become passé, especially those based on classical models. But minstrels and variety performers, as we have seen, kept the art alive, if truncated. A harbinger of its revival appeared on 3 April when Charles Brookfield's full-length parody of *Lady Windermere's Fan,* **The Poet and the Puppets,** was unveiled at the Garden. In that it occupied the entire evening it was an even more ambitious undertaking than later Weber and Fields spoofs. It advertised itself simply as a burlesque of Oscar Wilde's play, eschewing the delicious possibilities of twitting the title as well as the story. Typical of its changes, Lady Agatha was rechristened in honor of her most indicative line. She became Lady Yesmama, and May Robson, who played the role, had little else to do except walk across the stage uttering the phrase. The "little else," however, included a take-off on Loie Fuller's skirt dance, employing a third leg. Besides characters based on Wilde's figures, audiences beheld a bard (Harry Mills), Hamlet (Max Figman), Ophelia (May Irwin), a fairy (again Miss Irwin), and an actor impersonating Wilde himself (Henry Miller as Oscar O'Flaherty Wilde). The famous men's scene was filled with minstrel jokes. The evening amused knowledgeable playgoers for nearly two months.

At the Casino, Rudolph Aronson's worst fears were being realized. His attempt at vaudeville was a failure, and now he was "having trouble finding musicals." When the revival of *The Gondoliers* drew only middling attendance, he hurried in a revival of *Adonis* on 18 April, frantically inserting the strongman Sandow as an added attraction on 12 June in a final attempt to save the house. But his maneuvers went for nought, and after he put the theatre into receivership his stockholders successfully petitioned to have him removed. More than any other incident, this vividly illustrates the plight of the musical theatre at the time and its lack of resourceful talent. Thomas Canary and George Lederer took over the management, but Lederer was quickly to outshine his associate.

The last of Harrigan's revivals, *Reilly and the 400* (29 December 1890), competed on 1 May for the attention of first-nighters with De Wolf Hopper's newest vehicle, **Panjandrum** (1 May 1893, Broadway). Written for him by the same team that had provided him with *Wang*, J. Cheever Goodwin and Woolson Morse, it fell short of its predecessor's raging popularity but even so kept the Broadway lit through the summer until 30 September. The plot was preposterous. On an island in the Philippines, Pedro (Hopper) fails as a bullfighter and thus forfeits the affection of Paquita (Della Fox). To win the girl back he agrees to help in an elopement Paquita has planned for the ward of a Spanish grandee and a coach driver. The party is captured by a savage tribe. Their king is Panjandrum. Unbeknownst to all but a few in the tribe, the king has been dead for six years. Pedro looks remarkably like him and is persuaded to take his place. He does so admirably. The *Times* rather cruelly condemned Miss Fox, "who can neither act nor sing and who is not pretty," but nevertheless felt the show would be successful, and added "Every one in town will go to see De Wolf Hopper imprison a tiger in a hogshead by tying a knot in his tail." The show followed the then still fashionable practice of making constant revisions in an effort to lure satisfied patrons back more than once, announcing a "second edition" on 28 June just before the worst summer heat was expected. In his memoirs Hopper stated the title was cynically arrived at in a determined effort to publicize his name. As he remembered, "We purposely called the play by the meaningless syllables, 'Panjandrum.' Rather than stumble over 'Panjandrum,' the public asked for seats for Hopper, as we intended they should." Although Hopper may have been unaware the syllables had taken on a meaning since Samuel Foote first employed them, this statement's real significance is to demonstrate that the play was patently not the thing; it was merely a vehicle for a star's special talents. On the very day *Panjandrum* premiered, President Cleveland pressed a button to open Chicago's year-late Columbian Exposition.

But the celebration was short-lived. On 6 May National Cordage, a speculative stock which had hit 147, collapsed, and the Panic of 1893 began.

GEORGE LEDERER was born in Wilkes-Barre, Pennsylvania, in 1861. Although he began his career as an actor, he soon tried his hand at producing, sending a play called *Florimel* on national tour. His partner in this fledgling effort was Sydney Rosenfeld, with whom he would work at the Casino.

As so often happened a half-century or so later, the season's biggest hit came virtually last. Called **1492** (15 May 1893, Palmer's), it was, like the Chicago Fair, a year late with its honors, but few cared. The work originated in Boston, where its creators, E. E. Rice and R. A. Barnet, scoured the upper echelons of vaudeville for performers. They were not so careful in seeking out a composer, settling all too easily on Carl Plueger. Walter Jones essayed the dual roles of King Ferdinand and the tramp Charlie Tatters. Richard Harlow, popular as a female impersonator, played Queen Isabella. "Specialists" included Theresa Vaughn, cast vaguely as "Fraulein," bringing over from her variety turn her singing of English and American songs (such as "Annie Rooney") in an arch-German. Like *Panjandrum*, *1492* underwent frequent alterations. Two weeks after the opening, for example, a fashion show–cum–ballet called "Six Daily Hints from Paris" was inserted. It was so well received that on 13 November of the next season "Six More Daily Hints from Paris" was added along with a dance of store-window mannequins. New York audiences applauded the show in one form or another for 354 performances.

In Philadelphia, at a house devoted primarily to vaudeville, one bill was given over largely to a not quite full-length Richard Stahl operetta, **The Merry Cobbler** (22 May 1893, Bijou), in which fairies will grant an artisan all his wishes, so long as he wears a pair of slippers they have given him and does not wear any of his own shoes. Milton Aborn had the title role.

During their late-season return to Manhattan the Bostonians offered the newest De Koven–Smith effort, **The Knickerbockers** (29 May 1893, Garden). Miles Bradford (W. H. MacDonald) comes to New Amsterdam to court the governor's daughter,

Katrina (Camille D'Arville). But because he helps a fellow Puritan escape from jail he is accused of being a spy. His friend, Hendrick (Edwin W. Hoff), persuades Miles to disguise himself as Hendrick's fiancée, Priscilla (Jessie Bartlett Davis), and to flee. The governor (Henry Clay Barnabee) gets wind of the plan and sends soldiers to arrest Miles. Instead, they arrest the protesting Priscilla. She escapes, disguising herself as a British soldier. Miles, in yet another disguise, takes service as the governor's bodyguard. But he becomes jealous of a British soldier he believes is receiving too much of Katrina's attention. Of course, the "soldier" is Priscilla. A happy ending follows. Although the *Times* hailed the work in its review headlines as "A REAL NEW YORK OPERETTA," "A Genuine American Work," and "an Event," the text of its notice was more reserved, rating the music as "cold and uninspired" and complaining that Smith ignored the possibilities of local color. The public agreed with the reservations, and after a single week the Bostonians were again singing *Robin Hood*. Interestingly, the critics, while praising old favorites such as Barnabee and Miss Davis, were most lavish in their praise of a recent addition to the troupe's roster, Miss D'Arville. The reasons why Miss D'Arville, who had shared starring honors with Lillian Russell, was content to lose herself in the relative anonymity of a traveling repertory company are lost. One answer may lie in the dearth of stellar roles available to her. But her reputation suffered not at all. Within a year her name was again above a title.

The season's final lyric offering was Robert Planquette's **The Talisman** (21 June 1893, Manhattan Opera House), which had premiered only six months before in Paris. Most critics and advance notices overlooked the plot—as did Florian Bruyas in his history of French musicals—all suggesting the feeble story line was merely an excuse for sumptuous Louis XV sets and costumes. In New York it proved an insufficient excuse. The piece folded two weeks later, and Hammerstein sold his auditorium to Koster and Bial, who moved their vaudeville up from 23rd Street.

1893–1894

While the number of musical works reaching New York in this season jumped by more than half over the figure of the preceding year—from two dozen to better than three dozen—the increase did not mean higher standards. Rather it attested to the turnover

prompted by both the generally mediocre quality of the new works and the effects of the Panic of 1893. Well above a third of the productions were revivals. A lone, small note of encouragement came from the drop in the percentage of importations. Americans were not writing very good musicals, but they were writing more of them.

All of August's entries were old favorites. *The Black Crook* (12 September 1866) returned to the scene of its 1892–1893 triumph; its cast cavorted on the stage of the Academy of Music from 14 August to 23 September. Twelve nights later *1492* relit Palmer's after a summer vacation, while a touring company of *A Night at the Circus* (21 December 1891) began a two-week stay at the Park. On the 28th, Harrigan reopened his house with a revival of *Dan's Tribulations* (7 April 1884), the first rehearing the play had received in seven years. It was greeted politely, but without real enthusiasm, by both critics and the public, inaugurating a sadly unsatisfying year for Harrigan. He kept it on the boards only until 7 October, when his sole original offering of the season was ready.

September's four lyric works were all new, or tried to be. The ambivalent arrival was **The Brand New City Directory** (5 September 1893, Bijou), a fresh mounting of the recent hit (10 February 1890) that kept the show's original frame but filled it with new specialties and dialogue. The original's three acts were compressed into two, with much of the second half devoted to a burlesque of a Faust rehearsal in which Willis Sweatnam, long of the minstrel stages, portrayed a stage manager and half-sang, half-talked a song. Rubber-faced William B. Wood brought over from variety his monologue justifying his nailing his suspenders to his shirt. Nellie Parker introduced the "latest" London successes, while Amelia Glover performed her lively dances.

"A spectacular play," **A Trip to Mars** (8 September 1893, Niblo's), opened three nights later. The mounting was a vehicle for the Liliputians, written for them, as always, by Robert Breitenbach. Its music was by Fritz Krause. The plot reveled in the preposterous science fiction of the time. Professor Heddison devises a pill that "miniaturizes" people. By way of a secret cabinet he sends his small folk to Mars. On the way back they visit the clouds and a marvelous grotto reminiscent of *The Black Crook* (12 September 1866). They return to Earth, landing on the dome of the World Building. The trip to the clouds offered a much publicized effect, advertised as "The Flying Heads," in which only the midgets' heads, with wings attached, were seen flying across on the stage. Other noteworthy moments devised by Carl Rosenberg included "The blinding glories of an electrical apotheosis, the novel beauties of a snow-bird dance," and a chariot drawn by the "smallest ponies in the world." The electrical apotheosis occurred on both sides of the footlights, for Niblo's proudly announced that the auditorium was lit by electricity.

William Gill's **The Rising Generation** (11 September 1893, Park) was a farce-comedy that tipped its hat both to the growing social standing of the Irish and to the burgeoning musical comedy. In a story larded with "rollicking music" and specialties it traced the rise of Martin McShayne from a lowly bricklayer to a successful contractor. After three weeks it headed for the road.

Hoyt loaded the dice in his **A Temperance Town** (18 September 1893, Madison Square). The good guys were the "wets," Launcelot "Mink" Jones (George Richards), the Vermont village boozer, and his buddy, Fred Oakhurst (E. F. Nagle), while the hypocritical, devious, treacherous bad guys were the "drys." Even their names were against them, such as Rev. Hardman (Richard H. Dillon), Squire Belcher (William Cullington), and the village's sanctimonious druggist, Kneeland Pray (Joseph Frankau). When it turns out Oakhurst, though badly wounded himself, had saved the life of the minister's son during the Civil War, the opposing sides are reconciled. The curtain line is Jones's: "... a man may have many a noble thought and do many a good action even if he is a rum-seller!" The farce-comedy chalked up 125 showings on its first New York visit. Although its songs and dances have long since been consigned to oblivion, *A Temperance Town* still reads well, and often as brahmin a scholar as Quinn has suggested it has "permanent worth."

The month's most eagerly awaited musical raised its curtain at the Casino on 25 September. But **The Rainmaker of Syria**, besides being an artistic disappointment, soon became embroiled in the legal battles raging around the house. Its book and lyrics were by Sydney Rosenfeld and its music, somewhat surprisingly, by Rudolph Aronson, who had been temporarily restored to his old hegemony at the theatre by court order. Rosenfeld's libretto was period exotica. The Egyptian Amosis (Mark Smith) pretends to be a rainmaker. Studying past droughts, he discerns a pattern and correctly predicts when the next rain will arrive. King Thesaurus (Harry Davenport) would award him the hand of an ugly princess, but

Amosis demurs. He prefers "King" Hatchupoo (also spelled Hatshepu) (Bertha Ricci), whom he knows to be an attractive woman in disguise. The show closed on 12 October when Rosenfeld broke his own connections with the Casino and refused to pay the cast. The incident also left Aronson once again out of office.

October was the season's busiest month, but it was not especially fruitful. **The Golden Wedding** (2 October 1893, Bijou) was a farce-comedy which reportedly had regaled Boston for five months. New York aisle-sitters turned thumbs down. Characters included an addlebrained Englishman on his first American visit, a boozy Irishman, and one Tippecanoe Tappington Bolivar. A beloved female impersonator, obese George Fortesque, performed in a gaudy red-and-green gown. The show's best song was an interpolation, the already wildly popular "After The Ball."

On the same night that *The Golden Wedding* arrived in New York, Philadelphia sat in judgment on a new musical, and its verdict was not all that favorable. The critic for the great *Public Ledger* observed of Richard Stahl's **Shing Ching** (2 October 1893, Grand Opera), "Had it preceded 'The Mikado' the impression would have been deeper." Of course, this show was set in China, not Japan. But its list of characters included the likes of Bi-Kloride, Lord High Mandarin and Executioner. And Frank Dumont's plot did revolve around possible executions since Princess Shing Ching, Daughter of the Moon, like Turandot, beheads any suitor who cannot solve three riddles she proffers him. When Wing Hi, a Tartar prince, answers all three, Shing Ching knows she has found true love. Although a few aisle-sitters were kinder, the *Public Ledger*'s man deprecated the music: "[I]t is rarely that any of it stands out either for character or originality, and the experienced listener cannot escape the notion that he has heard it all before."

Back in New York the next night, a revival of *Erminie* (10 May 1886) with Francis Wilson, Lulu Glaser, and Christie MacDonald ushered in the month and kept audiences at the Broadway delighted into December.

Harrigan's only novelty of the year was **The Woolen Stocking** (9 October 1893, Harrigan's). In his customary blend of comedy, melodrama, and sentimentality, Harrigan retailed the plight of Paddy Dempsey (Edward Mack), who saves a mine owner, is made his heir, loses the deed to the mine, and goes blind. Larry McLarney (Harrigan), a stevedore boss, retrieves the deed for Dempsey. Larry also woos and wins Widow Hickey (Annie Yeamans), a hotel-keeper. Besides Harrigan and Miss Yeamans, other regulars, such as John Wild, Joseph Sparks, and Paula Edwards, assumed roles of various importance. If the substance of Harrigan's story and the drift of Braham's songs were the same as they long had been, the added spark that had once spelled success was wanting, and the very sameness now told against the work. "Little Daughter Nell" and "The Sunny Side Of Thompson Street" enjoyed small, brief vogues, but neither entered the canon of Braham favorites. Harrigan kept the piece going until he could prepare a revival of his own best-loved work, *Old Lavender*. After *The Woolen Stocking* was withdrawn on 16 December, Harrigan promptly settled down to revise it. He brought it back on 19 February. Unfortunately the revisions changed its reception not a jot. Harrigan closed it after one week and abruptly ended his season. The early closing was another sad indication of his falling star.

A new Fritz play, **Fritz in Prosperity** (23 October 1893, Grand Opera House), like so many offerings of the period, revealed changes in the wind. Critics complained about the "Americanization" of Fritz in this latest opus of the busy Rosenfeld and also noted the virtual absence of song. *Fritz in Prosperity* was as close as any of the series came to being a pure straight play.

On 25 October Lillian Russell returned to the Casino in a musical written for her by the same team that had provided Thomas Q. Seabrooke with *The Isle of Champagne* (5 December 1892) the preceding season. Set to William Furst's music, Charles Alfred Byrne and Louis Harrison's book for **Princess Nicotine** told of the marriage of a pretty cigarette maker, Rosa (Miss Russell), to a rich tobacco planter, Chicos (Perry Averill). The local governor, Don Pedro (Digby Bell), had wanted Rosa for himself. He arranges for Chicos's arrest and goes to woo Rosa. But just in front of the honeymoon cottage he falls into a stream. Rosa rescues him. In her innocence she sets his clothes out to dry and invites him into her house. Chicos escapes, returns, and, seeing the governor's clothing outside, misconstrues the situation. Explanations follow in time for a happy ending. For her endeavors Miss Russell received a salary of $700 a week, plus half the profits. But she undoubtedly earned every penny of it, for she kept this musical of such modest achievement before the footlights for three full months. Assisting her, at considerably less pay, besides Bell, were Dan Collyer and Marie Dressler.

Another reigning musical queen brightened the Rialto the next night, when Marie Tempest arrived as star of **The Algerian** (26 October 1893, Garden). If her star twinkled a little less brightly than did Miss Russell's, her luck in having a Reginald De Koven score to sing was a hoped-for compensation. Once again in this glum season hopes were dashed. Although for many years afterwards De Koven insisted this was his favorite score, his public did not agree. Moreover, instead of assigning the book to Harry B. Smith, who had served him honorably for so long, he entrusted it to a newcomer, Glen MacDonough. MacDonough later went on to write a number of remunerative librettos, but his work for *The Algerian* betrayed his lack of experience. Not that his basic plot line was much different from the run-of-the-mill comic-opera tale. He chose the safe setting of the mysterious "Orient," supposedly basing his tale on an unnamed Alphonse Daudet novel. In Algiers the impecunious Prince of Montenegro (Joseph Herbert) establishes a fake harem to lure tourists. He hires his "wives" from the chorus of a stranded opera company. One visitor, Col. La Grange (Julius Steger), falls in love with a supposed concubine, but Celeste, the Countess of Monvel (Miss Tempest), who loves La Grange and who was once a member of the opera company, exposes the hoax. Miss Tempest and De Koven still drew well enough at the box office to keep the show in New York until mid-December.

At least one critic thought Glen MacDonough's thin thread of story for **Delmonico's at Six** (6 November 1893, Bijou) suspiciously close to Hoyt's for *A Trip to Chinatown* (9 November 1891). Remembering that Hoyt's characters never do get to Chinatown, MacDonough may have prompted the critic's comparison by remarking in his opening night speech that he gave his farce-comedy its name "because it has nothing to do with Delmonico's." (The critic suggested the name would attract patrons on the road.) Marie Jansen, fading but still popular, was starred as Trixie Hazelmere. She danced in black tights, sang songs, and shocked some watchers by imitating a tipsy lady. She also, in the plot, helped some young lovers get together. An example of period humor came when Ignacio Martinetti as Trixie's not very faithful suitor exclaims, "Can she suspect? But no! She lives in a flat; in a flat there is not room even for suspicion." Martinetti also revived one of his best-loved specialties, his send-up of a ballerina. The show's two stands at a first-class Broadway house were brief. However, it was happily enough received wherever it moved to be able to orbit in outer theatrical space for several seasons. Actually that orbit—in the rapidly expanding number of theatres being constructed in secondary neighborhood shopping areas and in smaller cities and towns—was increasingly playing host to musicals that never made it to the big time.

Julian Edwards's continuing seriousness of purpose was manifest on 22 November when his **King Rene's Daughter** joined Gounod's *Philemon and Baucis* on a double bill at Herrmann's Theatre. The two works were to have opened together a week earlier, but the illness of Eleanor Mayo, who was to sing the title role in Edwards's work, forced a week's separation in the premieres. Count Tristan (Charles Bassett) comes to King Rene's court to marry the king's daughter, Iolanthe. At the court he falls in love with a winsome blind girl who has never been told other people are not blind. Tristan demands King Rene (William Pruette) cancel the wedding so that he can marry the young lady, only to discover she is Iolanthe. The libretto was derived from Henrik Hertz's drama, which was also the source of Tchaikovsky's opera *Iolanta*. If the story was not much different from many on the boards at the same moment, the music attempted to be. It elicited a not unexpected outcry from some of the critics, the *Herald* bewailing it "wallows in Wagner." But the *Dramatic Mirror* hailed it as "musicianly and musical." The public seemed to side with the *Herald*, for the double bill was withdrawn after two weeks.

December played it safe with three revivals for the holiday crowds. The preceding season's success *The Fencing Master* (14 November 1892) returned briefly on the 11th, without, of course, Miss Tempest, who had taken *The Algerian* on the road. A week later Harrigan revived his personal favorite, *Old Lavender* (3 September 1877), for a month's run at his house.

A French work, **The Voyage of Susette,** mounted as a spectacle at the American, began a month-long engagement on 23 December.

On Christmas afternoon, **Africa** (25 December 1893, Star), a show that had initially delighted San Francisco in June and had slowly wound its way east, began the first of several very brief New York stands. Clay M. Greene, a rising San Franciscan, and the more established J. Cheever Goodwin did the libretto; Randolph Cruger, orchestra director at San Francisco's California Theatre, composed the score. The great minstrel man George Thatcher produced and starred in the work. Maurice Merrill, just

out of Harvard and eager for fame, decides to go to Africa to locate the missing Tippoo Tip. Maurice's father, Moses (all characters' names began with M), is opposed to his idea and, taking the advice of a quack, Dr. Medikus (Thatcher's role), tricks Maurice into sailing to a tropical island he owns. There, at his instructions, his employees pretend they have reached Africa and make matters so frightening for Maurice—even suggesting at one point that they will boil and eat him—that he heads back home. A wild "Hottentot" dance, with performers' scantily clad bodies blackened, was a high point of the show.

The Bostonians came to town that night, opening with their most popular piece, *Robin Hood* (28 September 1891). They offered the work until 15 January, celebrating their twelve-hundredth representation of it on 8 January. A less important but new piece also opened on Christmas night—the premiere at the Bijou of a farce-comedy with musical interpolations, **A Country Sport.** With Peter F. Dailey, May Irwin, Ada Lewis, and Richard Carle among the pranksters, the show became one of the biggest hits of the season, running until the spring. Dailey played Harry Hardy, of Jokersville-on-the-Hudson, who is left his uncle's considerable fortune on the condition he prove himself "a thoroughbred sport." With a phony preacher, Con Connelly (Carle), he heads for the Bowery's fun spots. He resists efforts to convert him to the cloth and manfully shows he is entitled to the inheritance. Dailey's high jinks included inviting the wax figure of a policeman at a dime museum to dinner (and having him accept!) and, in company with Miss Irwin, waltzing with wire dummies at a cheap clothing store.

New Year's night 1894 brought back the Liliputians in a revival of *The Pupil in Magic* (15 September 1890). The show was the last that could be called a musical ever to play Niblo's. At the end of the next season, the old house that once sheltered *The Black Crook* (12 September 1866) and *Evangeline* (10 May 1886) was demolished. Bad times coupled with the theatrical center's move northward had sealed its doom.

The Bostonians, too, were soon to pass from the scene, and no small part of their demise was their inability to find a number of strong follow-ups to *Robin Hood*. Henry Clay Barnabee and his associates were aware of their difficulty and attempted to counter it by commissioning three works that "waved the starspangled banner of native art." One of these, *The Knickerbockers* (29 May 1893), had reached

New York the preceding season. The other two were included as part of their 1893–1894 visit. **The Maid of Plymouth** (15 January 1894, Broadway) was offered first. Clay M. Greene's version of the Priscilla Alden and Miles Standish legend was set to music by Thomas P. Thorne. Their romantic adaptation was a far cry from the arch-burlesque treatment Rice had given *Evangeline*. The text was competent by the standards of the time, and the lyrics sometimes rose to a popular poetry:

> Amid the storm they sang,
> And the stars heard, and the sea
> And the sounding aisles of the dim woods rang
> With the anthem of the free.

On the other hand, Greene's Indians often spoke (and sang) in the "metre and style of 'Hiawatha.'" This led the *Times* to view both the work and the production as a travesty and to condemn its "shopworn patter." Most other papers took the work more seriously, even if they could not wax enthusiastic over it. Almost without exception, they viewed Thorne's music as serviceable, but not memorable. Eugene Cowles sang Miles; Margaret Reid, Priscilla; Edwin W. Hoff, John Alden. Barnabee played an Elder, while Jessie Bartlett Davis portrayed an Indian.

One week later—on 22 January—Harrigan replaced *Old Lavender* with a revival of *The Leather Patch* (11 February 1886), and still another week later **Prince Kam; or, A Trip to Venus** (29 January 1894, Casino) premiered. Originally mounted in Boston in September and unfavorably received, it spent the intervening months on the road attempting to whip itself into shape. Its librettists were those of *Princess Nicotine*, Byrne and Harrison, and its composer, Gustave Kerker. The title role was a trouser part for Camille D'Arville. As Prince Kam of Thibet she takes a flying machine to visit the King of Mars (William Pruette), where the prince falls in love with Venus (Fannie Johnson). Venus follows Kam back to Earth. Pruette and Miss Johnson, a vivacious blonde, stopped the show singing a song that took a jaundiced view of love, while Miss D'Arville won applause for her pyrotechnical rendition of "A Leap From The Earth To The Sky." E. E. Rice produced the evening with an éclat typical of both him and the Casino. As one satisfied critic noted, "the young ladies of the chorus were innumerable, the costumes rainbows and jewels." A month's run was followed by a tour.

The Rainmakers (29 January 1894, Park) starred Donnelly and Girard. Henry V. Donnelly shortly would move on to establish one of New York City's most popular stock companies. For the moment, though, he played Percival Airtight, who, with his partner, Phelix Bottle, runs a resort hotel hurt by a drought. Their efforts to make rain provided the frame for the evening's capers, which saw the appearance of such characters as Sendum Upp and Mrs. General Peiper Heidsieck. Charles J. Ross and Mabel Fenton found excuses to introduce spoofs of *Fedora* and *Virginius*.

February opened with one of the season's many revivals, *A Trip to Chinatown* (9 November 1891), which began a seven-week stay at the Madison Square Theatre on 12 February. In the course of its travels it had picked up one major interpolation, "After The Ball" (Charles Harris). The song was spectacularly successful. It reputedly sold five million copies. Isadore Witmark attributed to the money Harris made as his own publisher "the establishment of mushroom publishing houses financed on a shoestring." With "Reuben And Cynthia" and "The Bowery" still on the program, no American show up to this date could boast so many songs that have remained part of our active musical heritage.

The second of the Bostonians' new American works, **The Ogallalas** (12 February 1894, Broadway), claimed to be the first major musical to center on the American Indian. *Pocahontas* (24 December 1855), *Hiawatha* (25 December 1856), *Dovetta* (22 April 1889), and other works were apparently forgotten. The new piece offered a tale that must have reminded many of a section from *The Last of the Mohicans*. General Andover (Henry Clay Barnabee) is escorting a group of ladies across the prairie when they are captured by Indians. Captain Deadshot (Edgar Temple) is also captured when he attempts to rescue them. Deadshot, an Indian known as War Cloud (W. H. MacDonald), and a Mexican bandit, Cardenas (Eugene Cowles), all court one of the young ladies, Edith (Bertha Waltzinger). Edith decides on Deadshot just as the army arrives to free the prisoners. As she had in *The Maid of Plymouth*, Jessie Bartlett Davis found herself cast as an Indian. The novelty of Young E. Allison's subject was the principal attraction, along, perhaps, with the troupe's fame and quality. Henry Waller's music was nondescript. Barnabee was forced to admit, "American art languished on its native hearth." The Bostonians were able to revert to *Robin Hood* before heading out once more to the hinterlands.

On 19 February Harrigan brought back *The Woolen Stocking*. Confessing he was in trouble, Harrigan had already leased his stage to an outside attraction, so the revival was a one-week stopgap.

About Town (26 February 1894, Casino) had a somewhat unusual history. As *Der Corner Grocer aus Avenue A* it had been running as a straight play down at the Germania Theatre on 8th Street since the middle of October. Its author, Adolph Philipp, played the title role in this slice of German and Yiddish life. The evening recounted the rise of a barber (Jacques Kruger) and his move uptown to Fifth Avenue. He and his newly rich friends have more money than *savoir-faire*. The cast of characters was filled with names such as Waldorf Metropole (played with "open-mouthed imbecility" by David Warfield) and Houston Streets (W. F. Mack). Willis P. Sweatnam inserted a minstrel monologue, Amelia Glover "danced her prettiest," while sad-miened Dan Daly injected his special brand of lugubrious humor. Harriet Sterling paraded about in a "gleaming golden satin gown eliciting gasps from the audience." Although in outline *About Town* appears to have been a variation of a popular Harrigan theme, it was, essentially, another farce-comedy, "an offshoot, in form and substance, from The City Directory and other haphazard melees of riotous fun, song, and dance." But the looseness of its construction was markedly more noticeable than in most farce-comedies, and at least one critic considered it "a new kind of entertainment… a hodgepodge of music, vaudeville, and fun." In short, *About Town* was another unwitting precursor of the revue, the form the same Casino would introduce to New Yorkers later in the season. But this first dip in new waters failed to please uptown theatregoers, and the show closed after three weeks.

The evening *About Town* opened, an old part of the Fritz series, *Fritz in a Madhouse* (22 April 1889), appeared at the American. *Au courant* theatregoers had long since lost interest in the series, but J. K. Emmet, Jr., continued to trek profitably across the country and in and out of Manhattan's combination houses with one or another of his father's plays. With the arrival of *Fritz in a Madhouse*, the American entered the ranks of combination houses.

The early closing of Harrigan's season made his theatre available unexpectedly. On 5 March Pauline Hall starred in a revival of *The Princess of Trébizonde*, "modernized almost beyond recognition." The *Times* bewailed that what was "once an opéra bouffe with music by Jacques Offenbach [and a libretto filled with] Gallic wit had degenerated into an evening of cheap horse play!" leaning heavily on snide contemporary references. It added that Miss Hall was past her prime and had no business appearing in "a garment of black gauze of astonishing transparency." Better or worse, the old opéra bouffe ran out the month.

Three weeks later Lillian Russell also returned in an old French work, *Giroflé-Girofla*, filling the void left by the failure of *About Town* at the Casino. She, too, lasted a month. Miss Russell had to compete for attention on opening night with the latest Gilbert and Sullivan premiere, **Utopia, Ltd.** (26 March 1894, Broadway). Although the work has been relegated to a low place in the Savoyard hierarchy, this early example of the havoc Western culture wreaks on an idyllic South Sea world was patently superior to most of the drivel forthcoming at the time. Audiences appreciated its superiority, and the D'Oyly Carte production ran until mid-May. A cast of performers who never really made it to the top included a Mr. Peterkin as Captain Corcoran, J. J. Dallas, Kate Talby, and Clinton Elder.

1492 had moved from Palmer's to the Garden Theatre on 5 February, adding new songs to celebrate the change of house. In late March it introduced another novelty, "living pictures," or tableaux. The earliest mountings recreated such then popular works of art as Bouguereau's "Cupid and Psyche," Canova's "Diana," and Cott's "Springtime." These posed moments caught on, and before long musical after musical felt it necessary to have at least one such set piece in the show.

The Idea, an extravaganza with Fred Hallen and Joe Hart, began a three-week engagement at the Park on 9 April. Many of the characters were named after New York hotels: Hoffman Howes (Hallen), Gilsey Howes (Donald Harold). Another was named Peach Blow (Fanny Bloodgood) after the much publicized Chinese vase of the time. Still other figures had stage names typical for the era. One young lady was called May B. Quiet. The evening was a sort of primitive *Guys and Dolls* (24 November 1950). In a Tom and Jerry frame it told how a young man was saved from a life of dissipation. A transformation scene moved from a gambling house to a Salvation Army meeting.

April's only other lyric offering was an English burlesque extravaganza, *Cinderella*. It opened at the Abbey on 23 April and delighted audiences until 16 June.

May's first two musicals swelled the total of revivals. On the 7th, Henry E. Dixey romped into Palmer's for a two-week visit with *Adonis* (4 September 1884) and Chauncey Olcott began a week's run with *Mavourneen* (28 September 1891) at the 14th Street Theatre.

At the end of the same week, on Saturday, 12 May 1894, the most significant show of the season premiered at the Casino. *The Passing Show* was, in fact, a milestone, a breakaway, for it was the first American revue. When it referred to itself as such—and it didn't bandy the new term about—it spelled it "review." The *Times*, discussing the work the Sunday before it opened, put the evening in an interesting perspective—reminding theatregoers of some stage history which they might have forgotten. The paper described the show as "a kind of entertainment little known in this country, and not attempted since John Brougham's time. It is a review, in dramatic form, of the chief events of the past year—political, historical and theatrical." Of course, the *Times* could have no way of foreseeing that *The Passing Show*, unlike Brougham's efforts, which failed to produce successors, would be the real progenitor of a half-century of revues. Indeed most critics judged the work as just another entertainment, not as an essentially new theatrical form. But then the producers themselves branded the evening "a topical extravaganza" more urgently than they advertised it as a revue. One exception, the *World*, recording the evening's French antecedents and spelling "revue" accordingly, granted that "the scheme had merit" but found the execution dull. The chic French spelling had to wait for more than a decade for general acceptance. But the French spelling would have been appropriate, since George Lederer and Sydney Rosenfeld did, as the *World* reported, derive much of their inspiration for the evening from the raging Parisian vogue, and not from Brougham.

The Gallic revue, like its American cousin, was only a few steps removed from another French theatrical child, vaudeville. It had become the popular Paris theatre attraction when something was needed to replace the waning demand for opéra bouffe. Unlike vaudeville each entertainer did not make a single appearance offering material he (or she) had often written himself or had commissioned especially for his act. Instead each performer appeared off and on throughout the evening performing dialogue and songs written by librettists and composers responsible for the entire work Of course, specialties found their way into the show, particularly in the early years. To dress up the affair and make it more "legitimate," the shows were elaborately mounted.

Moreover, with virtually no exceptions, early revues were tied together with plots, however gossamer, to further a sense of legitimization. These early revues also evidenced their debt to the burlesque tradition by leaning heavily on take-offs of current stage hits.

The Passing Show was responsible for shaping the first generation of revues. Two shows Rosenfeld selected for twitting were Pinero's *The Amazons* and *Sowing the Wind*. In the Pinero piece a mother raises her daughters as boys, giving them such names as Thomasin and Noeline. Rosenfeld changed their names to Lady Tom-A-Line (Madge Lessing), Lady Dick-A-Line (Lillian Thurgate), and Harry Line (no "Lady" or "A") (Belle Stewart). In *Sowing the Wind* Lord Brabazon (Paul Arthur) attempts to wreck the reputation of his ward, Rosamond (played for the first two weeks by Adele Ritchie, thereafter by Jessie Carlisle), to prevent her marrying. Rosenfeld retained the names of the principals but changed a minor character such as Watkin to Weebit (Lucy Daly). In fact, Rosenfeld used the characters from *Sowing the Wind* to provide the slim plot for the evening. Rosamond's father (now called Brabson) and a detective (Jefferson De Angelis) he hires search the town for the girl. The performers stayed in character all evening long, interweaving the songs and dances and extraneous material with the satire. The extra material included "living pictures"; allusions to the headlines of the day in a song on the order of "Coxey's Army"; the comedy of the Tamale Brothers (they had a song, "Hot Tamales"); and the acrobatics of the Amazons. "L'Enfant Prodigue" was recast as a ballet with four Pierrots and four temptresses. In a lighter vein, "Round the Opera in Twenty Minutes" embroiled Tannhäuser, Escamillo, Pagliacci, and other notable operatic characters in a comic melee. A hit of the evening was "Old Before His Time." The construction of the song marked no advance. Its chorus was a simplistic Ludwig Englander melody that covered a single sentence, repeated once, "Yes, that is one thing, yes, that is one thing makes a man old before his time." The meat of the song remained in its verse. Although it blamed premature aging on such things as "that everlasting tariff, out of reason out of rhyme," it saved its sharpest barbs for a whole verse assailing the new school of writing and acting:

> *The modern school of acting's*
> *such a thing of pure delight,*
> *The heroine has consumption,*
> *the hero meningitis.*

The villain, yellow jaundice;
oh, his sufferings are fearful.
The scene's laid in a hospital,
to make it nice and cheerful;
And the happ'nings, tho' abnormal,
are supported by statistics.
It's a school of realism,
and endorsed by realistics;
And the audiences are wading
thro' the mire and the slime,
As they feel themselves grow old
before their time.

With a cast of 100, the show ran into August and then embarked on an extended tour.

The season ended the week after *The Passing Show* arrived when a revival of *The Mikado* began a run at the Fifth Avenue that kept the house lit the entire summer, and Thomas Q. Seabrooke opened in **Tabasco** (14 May 1894, Broadway). Originally mounted for Boston, with a book by R. A. Barnet and music by George W. Chadwick it was another of the era's virtually countless bits of pseudo-Orientalia. Hot-Ham-Head-Pasha, the Bey of Tangiers (Walter Allen), beheads any chef who fails to put enough tabasco in his food. Dennis O'Grady assumes the post of chef. His problem is made difficult by a scarcity of the seasoning, until he discovers two tramps (Robert E. Bell and Edward Smith) with a case salvaged from a shipwreck which they are peddling as hair tonic. He tries to keep the bey's palate satisfied and to woo a native girl, Lola (Elvia Cox), at one and the same time. By a series of comical contrivances, he succeeds.

The move northward that doomed Niblo's removed the Union Square as well from the legitimate fold. But the theatre was not demolished. Instead it became one of B. F. Keith's major vaudeville houses. Interestingly, when Keith reopened it he included shortened versions of Broadway musical successes as part of the bill. *Said Pasha, The Mascot, The Princess of Trébizonde,* and *The Mikado* were all offered at one time or another. But the experiment proved a disappointment, and by the middle of the season it was dropped.

1894–1895

Artistically and financially the doldrums persisted throughout the new season. The nation could not shake off the effects of the 1893 panic, nor could the American Musical Theatre rouse itself from its lethargy. New lyric pieces fell slightly in number, but a precise figure is difficult to agree on with so many offerings still falling into borderline categories. Even so, there were hints of happier seasons ahead, for those perspicacious enough to see them. *A Gaiety Girl* sailed in from London to infuse musicals with a new sense of style and tone, and to start a decade-long vogue for English musical comedy. Even more significant, Victor Herbert, the first truly enduring name in the history of our musical stage, made his initial appearance as a comic-opera composer. For those not gifted with foresight the season nevertheless offered its share of ephemeral delights. Several shows, now all but forgotten, were applauded and awarded long and profitable runs.

The season (now following the divisions in Burns Mantle's *Best Plays* series at mid-June each year) began with the arrival of **Dr. Syntax** (23 June 1894, Broadway), a rewriting of the 1881–1882 success *Cinderella at School*. Once again a waif at a boarding school lands a wealthy young man despite the machinations of the titular comic villain. A vehicle for De Wolf Hopper, it had been announced as being in the works the preceding September when disappointing grosses on the road for *Panjandrum* warned that show would not prove as long-lasting as *Wang*. Since Woolson Morse had done the original score for *Cinderella at School* as well as for *Wang* and *Panjandrum*, he was naturally called upon to make the musical revisions, while J. Cheever Goodwin, Morse and Hopper's associate in their last two outings, brought the book up-to-date. Hopper's happy relationship with his writers stemmed not only from his theatrical success but from his fidelity to the material they proffered him. He was not given to originating too much business of his own. In an 1894 interview Hopper noted, "as a general thing I am simply interpreting the libretto of Cheever Goodwin." But he could not resist confessing that he did add a line to a young lady having difficulty on a ladder, admonishing her, "Don't stutter with your feet." Text and ad-libs combined to satisfy New York audiences for 169 showings.

Boston enjoyed a huge hit with Fred Miller, Jr.'s **Davy Jones** (2 July 1894, Boston Museum). Commodore Dominick Shay (Dan Daly), a millionaire shipowner, decides to sail around the world with his many daughters (between nine and sixteen, depending on which synopsis is used) and marry them off to suitable noblemen. He makes an exception for one daughter, Rozalie, since she loves Sandy, who, as the seventh son of a seventh son, is bound to bring them all luck. He doesn't. Instead they are shipwrecked on the Isle of Nowhere, an uninhabited speck used by King Tim Turn Foo of the Hoodo Islands to cache his excess wealth. The king has the group arrested and orders the girls to marry his many sons. Rozalie is to wed It (Richard F. Carle), the heir apparent. But the U.S. Navy steams in for an eleven-o'clock rescue. The show ran most of the summer.

Across the country, San Francisco had a little hit of its own with **Dick Turpin** (9 July 1894, Tivoli). Its libretto was the work of H. Grattan Donnelly; its score by Bowness Briggs, who was listed in programs as a bachelor of music. The early eighteenth-century highwayman's legendary ride from London to New York was mentioned (though, of course, not shown) in the story. Villainous Sir Oliver Cross intends to disguise himself as Turpin in order to kidnap and forcibly marry Eleanor Mortimer. But Turpin, himself disguised as a Yorkshire farmer, and his gypsy friends get wind of the scheme and rescue the lady. They also trick Cross into wedding the gypsy queen. Although the real Turpin was executed in 1739, this "romantic comic opera," not unlike Baltimore's *Jack Sheppard* (23 November 1885), ended happily, with the revelation that Turpin was actually the master of Rookwood Hall—years before stolen from him by Cross. So the curtain falls on the joyous wedding of Eleanor and the real master of Rookwood Hall. The minor role of an innkeeper's daughter was assumed by Alice Neilson, soon to be so much more famous back east.

Meanwhile, back in the very center of eastern theatricals, no further musicals premiered until **Miss Innocence Abroad** (25 August 1894, Bijou) arrived by way of Paris and London. Miss Innocence was so naïve she was unaware of her noble birth and humbly accepted a position as a milliner. (Sweet young milliners soon became stock heroines of the musical stage.) Rose Beaudet, Melville Stewart, and Fanny Rice led the cast. New Yorkers found the evening less entertaining than the Parisian play or the London musical on which it was based, and it disappeared after thirty-three showings.

Two nights later a revised edition of *1492* (15 May 1893) opened for a brief stay prior to an extended road tour. With a roster continually in flux, this time around it offered, among other changes, an interpolation of a Strauss waltz, "Ich Liebe Dich." For the road, the show changed its title slightly and voguishly to *1492 up to Date*. Down at the 14th Street Theatre other firstnighters sat through a comedy-drama called *Coon Hollow*, a straight play nonetheless replete with songs and specialties.

The Casino began its season on 30 August with **The Little Trooper** (also called *Little Miss Trooper*). Originally a French musical with text by Raymond and Mars and music by Victor Roger, it was heavily revised by Clay Greene and William Furst to serve as Della Fox's first solo starring vehicle. Jefferson De Angelis was featured, and Richard Barker staged the evening. Barker and his principals were responsible for whatever success the show enjoyed in its sixty-eight-performance stay.

Broadway's mite of cheer increased a bit when Francis Wilson unveiled **The Devil's Deputy** (10 September 1894, Abbey's). Richard Barker was again the director. Like Hopper, Wilson cavorted to a Goodwin libretto. In this instance Goodwin based his tale on the old German belief in good devils as well as bad ones. An actor named Lorenzo (Rhys Thomas) is caught in a backstage embrace with the wife of General Karamatoff (J. C. Miron) and forced to flee, still wearing a devil's costume. He comes to a provincial inn, where he tells a band of wedding guests he is a good devil. Seeing Karamatoff approach, he convinces the groom, Melissen (Wilson), to change places with him. But Karamatoff has come merely to bring him before a princess (Adele Ritchie) for a command performance. The princess falls in love with the actor, not realizing he is someone other than the man she has sent for. Luckily, Lorenzo is able to engineer one more exchange of place with Melissen. The groom returns to his bride (Lulu Glaser), and the actor wins the princess. Although Wilson spread his jollity for seventy-two performances—still a healthy run for the time—the joy might have been greater had Wilson's original plans for the work been fulfilled. The Syndicate would soon largely destroy the importance of the actor-manager, but Wilson at this time called his own shots. The evening was his conception and his production. Wilson had first approached John Philip Sousa with Goodwin's partially finished text, hoping the March King would create the show's score. But Wilson, in his own way, was as tough in financial transactions as the Trust he so despised. He refused to allow Sousa to share in the royalties, and when Sousa then offered to compromise for a flat fee of $1,500—the equivalent of about 15 percent of just one week's gross—Wilson adamantly refused to go above $1,000. Since by his own admissions it cost no more than $25,000 to mount a comic opera, the additional cost was not excessively burdensome. Wilson turned to *Erminie's*

Edward Jakobowski, who gave him adequate if lackluster songs. No one can say how much that $500 cost the comedian. But for some reason the affair must have rankled. Wilson, intentionally or otherwise, ignored the show in his autobiography.

The theatrical economy, unhealthy by the standards of the day, was enviably sound by the criteria of another century. As a result the American Musical Theatre time and again in this period saw cities all around the nation mount their own offerings. On the same night New Yorkers first applauded *The Devil's Deputy*, Clevelanders witnessed the premiere of **By King's Command,** a comic opera by a local journalist, W. S. Rose, with a score by Edward Beach. If the production was not up to the best of the time—the reviews said the mounting needed no apology—the plot was quite typical of the nonsense so beloved by the era. Two principalities, Pam and Mirande, prepare to go to war over a land dispute. The King of France orders the argument settled by mating the respective prince and princess—who had loved each other all along but were kept apart by their feuding houses.

Humpty Dumpty still retained his theatrical allure. The night after *The Devil's Deputy* opened, Robert Breitenbach reincarnated him and his world as a playground for his Liliputians. In **Humpty Dumpty up to Date** (11 September 1894, Fifth Ave.), a wealthy wine dealer and his servant whip a fairy who has helped the merchant's daughter elope. As punishment they are turned into Humpty Dumpty and Pantaloon. "That ripened and cynical baby," Franz Ebert, played Humpty—played it, if the *Times* is correct, mostly in German. He and his fellow midgets romped with giant pigs and living tulips. Young and old were entertained for eight weeks.

One of the most important musicals in the history of the American Musical Theatre opened the following week—18 September 1894, at Daly's. Like so many early milestones in our theatrical history it was imported as well as important. **A Gaiety Girl** had a libretto by Owen Hall, lyrics by Harry Greenbank, and music by Sydney Jones. The show was not the first of the so-called "Gaiety musicals," originated in the West End by the great English producer George Edwardes. In fact, *A Gaiety Girl* did not even play his Gaiety Theatre. It had been preceded by *In Town* and was followed by *The Shop Girl* (both of which were housed for at least part of their runs at the Gaiety). *In Town* was a loosely structured affair. The looseness of its story allowed for interpolations and occasional program changes. But the success

of its contemporary story and setting pointed the way. The story of *A Gaiety Girl* was tauter and more complex, yet still broad enough to allow for specialties, additions not by the authors, and alterations. It told how a group of chorus girls from the Gaiety are shunned at an elegant party until they consent to perform. A young officer falls in love with one of the girls, but a rival for his affections plants a diamond comb in the actress's pocket and accuses her of theft. The officer helps clear her.

Curiously, most English scholars (who consider Edwardes the originator of English musical comedy or even of musical comedy as an international theatrical genre) select either *In Town* or *The Shop Girl* as the landmark work. But it was undoubtedly the year-long London run of *A Gaiety Girl* that assured the continuation and legendary status of the series. *A Gaiety Girl* combined the vernacular appeal of farce-comedy with the integrity of comic opera. Interpolated specialties were limited, songs bore a more discernible relationship to the story, and the audience could identify more easily with the characters and the situations than with the royalty and absurdities of the comic opera. Puns were minimized. The chorus line was young, svelte (by standards of the day), and graceful. All the cast dressed stylishly in the latest fashions. Both in England and America, Gaiety shows quickly set standards for clothes-conscious playgoers.

For the next ten years or so, good English musicals were always given the heartiest welcome and, far more so than the otherwise influential *H. M. S. Pinafore* (15 January 1879), the flattery of constant imitation. Not all critics were impressed. The *Times* called *A Gaiety Girl* "nondescript" and at best ranked it with the old Hoyt pieces. In America the show, with Blanche Massey and W. Louis Bradfield in the principal roles, was produced by Augustin Daly, who not many years before had pioneered in modern musical mountings.

But the latest vogue could not stifle the appeal of older traditions, and *The Black Crook* (12 September 1866) played to two weeks of good business when it came into the Grand Opera House on 24 September as part of its annual road tour. Some of the additions to this version are startling. Despite its Continental setting one production number was "The American Roll Call of Honor." "Want And Abundance" introduced social commentary in "twenty-two distinct pictures" featuring eighty performers.

The evening of 1 October brought in two entertainments that by modern lights would not fall into the musical mainstream. Comstock's Minstrels began a week's run at St. James Hall. More important, Chauncey Olcott appeared at his customary berth in the 14th Street Theatre with **The Irish Artist,** another of the sentimental melodramas that allowed him to please his followers with half a dozen songs. Scholars generally feel it was this show that firmly established Olcott as "successor to Emmet and Scanlan" in romantic Irish melodramas and determined the style of production he would be most often associated with thereafter. Olcott portrayed Maurice Cronin, who returns to his home in Wexford after a successful career in London. He finds an old buddy has turned against him and would jealously shame Cronin and his family. Critics noted Olcott was "cheered with vehemence" and "admired vociferously." Nineteenth-century audiences were apparently far less restrained than contemporary ones, and audiences for Irish plays the least restrained.

Although he usually played a staunchly Catholic native of Ireland, **CHAUNCEY OLCOTT** was born in Buffalo, New York, on 21 July 1860 and educated to the city's public schools. He made his debut at the Buffalo Academy of Music, listed on the program as a "ballad singer." His Broadway debut was opposite Lillian Russell to *Pepita*.

The text of Charles Hoyt's farce-comedy **A Milk White Flag** (8 October 1894, Hoyt's) included only four songs plus spottings for several musical drills. But Hoyt advertised it as a musical comedy, and its audiences undoubtedly looked on it as such. The story detailed the rivalry between two social clubs with fashionable military bents, a story not unlike the early Harrigan and Hart, acted out on a higher social plane. The Daly Blues have constantly outshone the Ransome Guards, and the Guards are out for vengeance. They decide to hold the biggest, gaudiest funeral the town has ever seen. All they lack is a corpse. Their problem is solved when Piggott Luce (R. A. Roberts), a shady contractor, agrees to go through with a fake burial and flee town. In fleeing town he will also escape the law and a wife who is suing him for divorce and alimony. His "death" of course upsets his widow (Isabelle Coe). If her divorce has been granted, she cannot be his heir;

if it has not been granted, she must publicly and hypocritically grieve. Hypocrisy is a small price to pay for the inheritance, but it would also interfere with her courtship by the club's "colonel" (Charles Stanley). All ends happily. The hoax is exposed and the divorce granted. The "widow" and her "colonel" agree to wed, while Piggott claims the hand of his ex-wife's best friend (Lillie Deaves). Unlike *A Trip to Chinatown*, no songs from *A Milk White Flag* set the country humming. Except for "Love's Serenade" they were either humorous or martial, or both. The verse of "Wouldn't You Like To Fondle Little Baby?" ran:

> *My Uncle Freddie bought a box of roses*
> *To send his sweetheart, a pretty Kitty Lee.*
> *In the box he put a note,*
> *And this is what he wrote:*
> *"My dearest when you wear them think of me."*
> *He left the box alone for half a minute;*
> *The roses I was mean enough to sneak,*
> *And a pair of papa's trousers I put in it.*
> *Now Uncle Fred and Kitty never speak.*

The wit in "Warriors Bold" was more succinct, vaguely Gilbertian:
> *Our thirst for blood*
> *And our love for mud*
> *Cannot be called extensive;*
> *And we don't like storms*
> *For our uniforms*
> *Are horribly expensive.*

Staged by Julian Mitchell, *A Milk White Flag* entertained New York for six months.

The English musical stage celebrated the four-hundredth anniversary of Columbus even more roundaboutly than did the American. It's **Little Christopher Columbus** (15 October 1894, Garden), for which Ivan Caryll did the London score, actually dealt with a cabin boy who turned out to be Columbus's descendant. The book was modified slightly for New York taste, with Gustave Kerker called in to supplement the original music. Shortly after the show opened, its title was contracted to *Little Christopher*. A large cast included Charles Bigelow, Harry Macdonough, Helen Bertram, Henri Leoni, and Alexander Clark. However little real homage it paid to Columbus, like *1492* it caught the public's fancy, running almost the rest of the season, then touring successfully.

More minstrelsy enlivened New York when Primose and West, combined for the moment with Dockstader's organization, raised the curtain at the

Grand Opera House on 27 October. But the merger of the two groups betrayed the fact that the heyday of the minstrels had ended.

The season's biggest hit, **Rob Roy** (29 October 1894, Herald Square), was to prove Reginald De Koven's longest New York run. Although at its debut it evoked a storm of argument over whether or not it was superior to *Robin Hood*, posterity, if it has chosen at all, has relegated it to second place. Harry B. Smith's book was confused and drifting. While Rob Roy (William Pruette) is the titular figure, the comic mayor of Perth (Richard F. Carroll) holds the piece together as much as anyone. He is another in Smith's long line of comic villains. He changes sides and costumes with every change of fortune in the Scottish and English war. He marries his daughter Janet (Juliette Cordon) first to a Scotsman and then to an Englishman, blissfully unaware that all the while she is married to Rob Roy. Concurrently, Flora MacDonald (Lizzie MacNichol) and the besieged Prince Charles (Baron Berthald) pursue their own romance. When the prince is in danger of capture Flora dons his clothes and is jailed in his stead. Rob Roy, Lochiel (W. H. McLaughlin), and their Highlanders eventually see that both Charles and Flora escape to France. Once more, none of De Koven's songs appealed to the public for long, although one of Janet's songs—probably "The Merry Miller"—was "three times encored" on opening night. But the professionalism of the piece was valued highly enough to give it a run of 253 performances in two briefly separated stays.

November's first offering was an importation, **The Queen of Brilliants** (7 November 1894, Abbey's), for which Edward Jakobowski composed the music. Lillian Russell, Hubert Wilke, and Digby Bell enacted a tale of a countess who runs away from home to join a variety troupe. Even Miss Russell's potent allure could not overcome its langours, and it left after twenty-nine showings. When it closed Miss Russell rushed into a revival of *The Grand Duchess* to fill her contracted engagement.

Less promising but far more successful, **The Brownies** tapped the children's market and ran for ninety-six performances at the out-of-the-way 14th Street Theatre beginning 12 November. In its calcium-lit never-never-land the villain, Dragonfels (G. L. Broderick), attempts to thwart the marriage of Prince Florimel (Alice Johnson), an adopted Brownie, to Princess (or Queen) Titania (Marie Louise Day). When the Brownies attempt to aid Florimel, a demon ensnares them. But they escape

and set all wrongs right. The critics of the day were especially impressed by the "dazzling" spectacle the house was able to mount, notably a first-act deluge and a second-act earthquake. Specialties included five men imitating a German band.

The South Before the War (19 November 1894, Bijou) had been touring backwaters for some time and was rushed into Broadway as a stopgap booking. It featured buck-and-wing dancing and a production number called "Waiting On The Levee." One critic deemed the singing of the black chorus "very bad" and dismissed the whole affair as "not worthy of Broadway."

Victor Herbert's name first graced a New York program when **Prince Ananias** bowed on 20 November 1894, at the Broadway Theatre. Librettist Francis Neilson's story was set in sixteenth-century France, where a band of strolling players headed by one La Fontaine (Henry Clay Barnabee) are ordered to appear before the king and amuse him or suffer the consequences. They fail, but a poet traveling with them dispels the king's depression, and they are forgiven. The poet is named Louis (W. H. MacDonald), though he is affectionately called Prince Ananias by the players. The vagabond prince's reward is the hand of the leading lady of the strollers, Idalia (Jessie Bartlett Davis). Almost to a man New York critics damned the libretto as too long and trite, but praised the music as above average. Herbert's best number was Idalia's wistfully melancholy "Amaryllis" early in Act II. The Bostonians were never to duplicate the success of *Robin Hood*, but *Prince Ananias* remained in their repertory for two years, including this New York run of fifty-five showings.

VICTOR HERBERT was born in Dublin on 1 February 1859. After his father died, when Victor was three, his mother moved to England to live with her father, Samuel Lover, a novelist of some repute. She began Herbert's musical training early, and when she remarried and moved with her new husband to Stuttgart, her son was enrolled at the local conservatory to study cello, his principal instrument for the rest of his life. While working as a cellist with the Stuttgart Opera, he fell in love with the leading soprano of the company, Theresa Förster. She accepted a contract with the Metropolitan on the stipulation that Herbert be engaged there as a cellist. She and Herbert were married shortly before they sailed. Herbert soon supplemented their income by composition and conducting, rising to the post of bandmaster with the 22nd Regiment Band. How he came to the attention of the Bostonians is uncertain, but in the summer of 1894 he and a librettist, Francis Neilson, signed a contract to provide the famed organization with a new comic opera, receiving a $500 advance and royalties of no less than 5 percent. Herbert imposed an unusual condition for an unknown, demanding that "no changes shall be made in the libretto or music" without his consent. Here was a theatrical figure with integrity! Herbert always was to insist on this clause, and the one time it was accidently omitted an absurd contretemps ensued.

In The Flams (26 November 1894, Bijou) the popular comic William F. Hoey cavorted as Marmaduke Flam, a good-hearted impostor. The play was studded with interpolated songs and living pictures.

The same night The Flams arrived, the name of another composer made its first Broadway appearance. But Alfred G. Robyn's light was to shine more dimly and briefly than Herbert's, although he was only a year younger and survived Herbert by more than a decade. In Jacinta (26 November 1894, Fifth Ave.) the St. Louis–born organist and his librettist, William Lapere, told a singularly undemocratic story, perhaps revealing the imperialist sentiments growing in an era of revived manifest destiny. Two naval officers, Miguel (Stuart Harold) and Morrelos (Signor Perugini), are condemned to die for their efforts to overthrow the Mexican republic and are spared only when the emperor's son restores the monarchy. As a reward Miguel wins Blanca (Cecile Essing) and Morrelos weds Jacinta (Louise Beaudet). Jacinta and the marching chorus won encores nightly with "A Soldier Need Not Fear." Signor Don Giovanni Perugini, who, one paper observed, "shone in... three satin and lace suits," was not an Italian. He was an American named Jack Chatterton. For a brief time he was also Lillian Russell's husband, until in a scandalous, acrimonious divorce he accused her of using his makeup

and monopolizing his mirror. Miss Russell not only won the case, she won general sympathy at a time when divorce was still customarily frowned upon. Chatterton's career was shattered.

Ned Harrigan and David Braham came a cropper with **Notoriety** (10 December 1894, Harrigan's), December's only new lyric piece, even though more than one critic felt Harrigan remained "still unrivaled in his peculiar line." The conflict between whites and blacks which Harrigan had handled so good-naturedly before again provided the basis for his plot. A black "Accident Society" sends Fred Hoffman a letter threatening to blow off his head unless he pays them $100. Because the signature reads merely "A. S." Hoffman suspects the "A" stands for anarchist. Harrigan as Barry Nolan, a retired policeman and now a barkeeper, solves the problem. Annie Yeamans was on hand to impersonate a rich New York Irish junk dealer, while Joseph Sparks gained applause as a forlorn but aggressive "female darky trance medium." Braham's songs used the stylish expressions of the day in numbers such as "The Girl That's Up To Date" and "Out On A College Rah Rah," while still finding a place for the requisite sentimentality in "The Old Neighborhood." Excellent scenery effectively evoked night in the seething Tenderloin district and the lawn of a Hudson River villa—where a comic rendering of "As You Like It" ended the evening. But the efforts were to no avail. By February, Harrigan had replaced Notoriety with a revival of The Major.

"Of plot there is very little," a reviewer observed of **The Side Show** (17 December 1894, Niblo's), but that was no serious drawback for a touring musical. This one served as a vehicle for James B. Macke, popular on vaudeville stages for his character Grimesey Me Boy, which he brought with him to the show.

There was a discernible plot in Barney Ferguson's vehicle, **Duffy's Blunders** (24 December 1894, Jacobs). At least there was in the first act, when the tailor's attempts to help his buddy, McTurk, only plunged McTurk deeper into hot water. In the second act everyone adjourned for a night out at a roof garden, allowing for a multitude of vaudeville turns.

In the farce-comedy **McFadden's Elopement** (31 December 1894, Third Ave.), bumbling Con McFadden nearly upsets his elopement with Tillie Hulick, daughter of an incompetent inventor. But all ends happily. Specialty turns (imitations), medleys of popular hits, and spoofs of other current favorites ("The Girl I Would Have Left Behind Me") were sprinkled throughout the entertainment.

Westward Ho, with a libretto by a Boston attorney, Richard Ware, and music by Benjamin Woolf, bowed at the Boston Museum on New Year's Eve. Their story recounted the adventures of Hair Trigger Hal—actually the Earl of Ravenswood in disguise—when he visits Maverick, Wyoming, a town run by women. The earl wins the mayor-elect for a bride, and the earl's brother, Sir Lionel, who follows him, wins the hand of the district attorney. The show, well received at home, never reached New York. Another show that never reached the main stem was **Off the Earth,** a musical that got only as close as Harlem and Brooklyn. A slapdash affair, it was praised largely for the clowning of Eddie Foy.

New York, like Boston, would not neglect the modern woman. On 25 January, Sydney Rosenfeld and Ludwig Englander brought their newest creation into the Bijou. This first musical of 1895 was entitled, a little prematurely, **The 20th Century Girl.** But its more than "up to date" title couldn't save it from a critical drubbing. It quickly closed. The brash Rosenfeld was not easily daunted. He rewrote his story of Percy Verance (Helen Dauvray), who sets herself up as a "girl bachelor," dresses like a man (prompting her infuriated guardian—Edwin Stevens—to dress like a woman), runs for Congress, and leads a carefree life, and reopened the show with only slightly more success in May. During both runs the press singled out A. H. Wilson for his comic yodeling in the dialect role of Professor Blinderbogen. Critics also praised the songs which the multi-talented Rosenfeld was said to have composed, calling special attention to "The Play's The Thing," "The Ambitious Magpie," and "The Antidote."

Stanislaus Stange and Julian Edwards had better luck with **Madeleine; or, The Magic Kiss,** which followed *The 20th Century Girl* into the Bijou, beginning a ten-week run on 25 February. Stange's story was another of the epoch's preposterous concoctions. On his hundredth birthday the Baron de Grimm (Aubrey Boucicault) discovers that each kiss he receives from a virgin will take twenty-five years off his life. Three kisses reduced him to seventy-five, fifty, and twenty-five. But when Madeleine (Camille D'Arville), his young bride, kisses him he fears he will be reduced to a baby. Happily hers is "The Kiss of Love" and all ends well. On this simple plot Edwards, as conscientious if not as talented a composer as Herbert, hung a number of pleasant tunes such as "Heart, Foolish Heart" and "I Would Have Told Thee Long Ago." In singing the

title role, Miss D'Arville once again saw her name above the title. Indeed, the lobby of the Bijou was ringed with flowers in honor of the occasion.

No major houses offered new musicals in March. But uptown at the Harlem Opera House, Thomas Q. Seabrooke appeared briefly beginning 4 March in a sequel to *Tabasco* called **The Grand Vizier.** Seabrooke once again played Dennis O'Grady, this time using whiskey instead of hot sauce to win love and position.

David Henderson, who made a name for himself in Chicago with his elaborate spectacles, brought in one of his biggest hits, **Aladdin, Jr.** (8 April 1895, Broadway). Not all the people on the program were strangers to New York. The libretto, for example, was by J. Cheever Goodwin. In spite of the "Jr." in the title, the plot was the one that had served pantomime so well with the usual setting in Peking, the expected villain, Abanazar (Henry Norman), and Widow Twankey (rechristened Widow Bohea) (Ada Deaves). Another character was the delicious Tu Tee Fru Tee (L. Easton). Anna Boyd played Aladdin. "An immense amount of well-painted scenery" took audiences from Peking to a magic cave to a "gilt and amber" glen, as well as a laundry, gardens, and an Egyptian palace. A jumble of songwriters added their melodies, and the show delighted youngsters of all ages for six weeks.

April's only other musical was a revival at Abbey's of Offenbach's opéra bouffe *La Périchole* with Lillian Russell as star. The engagement was a holding action while Miss Russell and Abbey's management prepared a new musical they hoped would erase the stain of their November failure.

Less delightful, apparently, was the revival of *The Bohemian Girl,* which came into the Star as part of a light opera repertory and folded after a single performance.

A "Spectacular Comic Opera," **The Viking** (9 May 1895, Palmer's), retold the adventures of Eric the Red and Leif Ericson. Its librettists admitted their plot was "largely drawn from the rosehued chambers of fancy." Eric (Bernard Dyllyn) is slated to marry Princess Njarda (Beatrice Goldie), but he prefers Thora (Grace Reals), and Njarda loves Bjohnson Bjones (Harry Dietz). The lovers get their way. The show had two strikes against it from the start. Instead of opening in the evening and charging standard prices ($1.50 top), the producers elected to have an afternoon opening at $5.00 top for charity. As a result, the premiere was poorly attended, the balconies virtually empty.

Lillian Russell's new vehicle was ready on 16 May at Abbey's. In this instance, "ready" might not have been the happiest term, for the press bewailed a patent lack of rehearsals, noting the fact that even Miss Russell at times had to be audibly prompted. The Tzigane had a book by Harry B. Smith and a score by Reginald De Koven. Miss Russell played a Russian gypsy, Vera. She loves a young officer, Kazimir (Hubert Wilke). But Kazimir's uncle commands Vera to marry Vasili (Jefferson De Angelis), a serf. Vera suspects Kazimir is behind the order. She runs away. Years later, after Napoleon's retreat from Moscow, Vera returns. She is now a lady of some wealth and position. She discovers Kazimir has remained faithful and marries him. Critics complained that the book was static and that Smith ignored the colorful possibilities of the 1812 setting much as he had the opportunities of seventeenth-century New Amsterdam in The Knickerbockers (29 May 1893). If Smith ignored possibilities, Henry E. Hoyt, a distinguished scene painter of the day, did not. His work, especially an encampment scene for which he drew startlingly lifelike horses, was showered with praise. Smith himself blamed the show's failure on the fact that ticket-buyers could not remember its name. But this was undoubtedly rationalization. They could as easily have called it the Russell show as they had Panjandrum (1 May 1893) the Hopper show. Curiously, Miss Russell's leading comedian, De Angelis, insisted in his autobiography that it became the chic thing to pronounce the title correctly. Unfortunately, it never became chic enough to help The Tzigane last out the month of June.

A touring revival of The Lily of Killarney stopped for a week at the Grand.

Gus Heege furthered the adventures of his Swedish-American hero in A Yenuine Yentleman (26 May 1895, Bijou). His hero finds his gumption, not his Swedish diploma, helps him on his road to riches. Percy Gaunt wrote the music.

Three of the four closing offerings leaned to burlesque. Two in fact were extended full-length burlesques of single shows, suggesting the popularity of the 1892–1893 travesty of Lady Windermere's Fan had prompted composers and authors into some new naughtiness. Hamlet II (27 May 1895, Herald Square) rejected one cliché of the older burlesque formula by allowing a man to play the hero. Mixing Shakespeare with contemporary slang, it offered its patrons a "Trilbyesque" Ophelia and songs such as "What's The Matter With Ham?" In

the scene with the players the strolling actors twitted nontheatrical celebrities whose notoriety had earned them places on variety bills of the day. One player confessed he was hired after he tried to jump off a bridge (Steve Brodie had appeared in variety after his escapade on the Brooklyn Bridge), another was a former prizefighter (Bob Fitzsimmons led a parade of fighters before the footlights), while the soubrette announced she had been divorced eleven times in ten years.

The busy J. Cheever Goodwin and Ludwig Englander combined their talents to interrupt the chain of burlesques with the season's last traditional comic opera, A Daughter of the Revolution (27 May 1895, Broadway). Starring Camille D'Arville, and set in 1776, it followed Marion Dunbar as she pretends to be a renegade in order to pass through enemy lines. She wins the affection of the British General Grumm (Hallen Mostyn) and his wife (Miss Sidney Worth), and then frees her lover, Captain Arthur Lee (Clinton Elder), who has been arrested as a spy. Even though Miss D'Arville was one of the leading prima donnas of her day, neither she nor the authors received the lion's share of attention. In a day when there were no films or television to provide spectacular scenes, all aspects of the theatre were called upon to satisfy the demand. Comic opera was often no exception. The first scene of the third act depicted Washington crossing the Delaware. Only loosely connected with the plot, the scene nonetheless won what little attention A Daughter of the Revolution earned. But it was not enough to tide the show over the hot weather. Curiously, like The Tzigane before it, the show was assailed as ill rehearsed.

The popular dramatization of du Maurier's Trilby (1894) inevitably found itself the subject of an extended burlesque as Thrilby (3 June 1895, Garrick). Joseph Herbert, who wrote the libretto to Charles Puerner's music, assumed the title role. Set in the studio of three privateers and then at a theatre, it turned Svengali into Spaghetti (Alexander Clark); and the rest of the characters had such names as Butter-Scotch and Madame Sans Ragene, allowing Sardou as well as du Maurier to be ribbed between songs and specialties. At one point du Maurier (A. G. Andrews) determines to eliminate Spaghetti. He succeeds in forcing the villain to climb one side of the proscenium. From an upper box Spaghetti sings a sardonic farewell. Noisy scene changes, so common in the era, prompted a gag that provoked some of the evening's biggest laughs. At the end of a scene in a laundry the lights were blacked out and the inevitable clatter ensued. But when the lights went on again, audiences saw the identical set with the identical players in their identical spots.

Both *Madame Sans Gêne* and *Trilby* were also twitted on 8 June in The Merry World, the Casino's sequel to its well-thought-of *Passing Show*. Hoping to profit from the best of both merry worlds, the house called its offering both a burlesque and, using the spelling of the day, a review. The fledgling form still used skits much longer than would eventually be the norm and utilized a theatrical tour as a slim plot. Besides spoofing straight plays of the day, the show parodied the season's musicals. In one skit Dr. Syntax's daughter Madeleine is engaged to Rob Roy. A superb cast included Dan Daly, Amelia Summerville, Virginia Earle, David Warfield, Louis Harrison, and Louis Mann. Since so many shows still opened "cold" in New York during this period, no one quibbled at *The Merry World*'s premiere if "at midnight a third of the show had not been given." (Shades of *The Black Crook*!) Edgar Smith and Nicolas Biddle wrote the dialogue, while William Furst contributed most of the songs the specialists didn't contribute themselves.

1895–1896

Little changed for the American economy or the American Musical Theatre in the new season. At least little change was apparent. But subtle, not immediately obvious, transitions were in the wind. With time what became known as Gaiety Theatre musicals—although not all were actually mounted at London's Gaiety—shamed American writers and managers into devising more thoughtful, more tasteful lyric offerings of their own. But unlike many turning points in our later musical history, no hue and cry accompanied the improvements. Reading interviews with writers and performers of this period, and following criticism of the time, one is left with an impression that by and large America was satisfied with the entertainment it created for itself. It was especially appreciative and happy when a superior piece such as *El Capitan* premiered late in the season, but it was not about to complain of the string of mediocrities that preceded or trailed this success.

The ever-active Boston stage provided New York with its only musical novelty in July when The Sphinx began what it hoped would be a summer run at the Casino on the 8th. The Near East was

to *fin-de-siècle* American musicals what Italy was to Elizabethan drama, a setting at once exotic and commonplace. Into this world the authors injected a bit of local pride when Harvard's Professor Papyrus (Edwin Stevens) discovers a woman's seminary whose pupils are preparing to elope with a band of Bedouins. They will visit the Sphinx, where each couple will be presented with a riddle. Papyrus's request to join them is disdained until his valet, Ptimmins (Tallmadge Baldwin), reveals that the professor has a book filled with answers to the puzzles. The riddler is a woman, Hathor (Marie Millard), who falls in love with Papyrus and is condemned to ask him a riddle not answered in the book. Papyrus inadvertently gives the correct reply. He and Hathor wed. The evening was sumptuously and ingeniously mounted, with Hathor's first entrance, seeming to float out of the Sphinx, particularly impressive. But the writing was not as fetching as the story, and, while the show ran four weeks in the summer heat, it was at best a modest success.

St. Louis was far from the cultural hubbub of Boston or New York but it, too, could mount its own lyric works. On 15 July its Uhrig's Garden presented a new comic opera called **Ollamus**, whose story coupled the popular theme of feminist agitation with the popular setting of never-never-land. Miss Jones, an unsuccessful candidate for the U.S. presidency, lands in Utopiana and attempts to overthrow the king, Ollamus. She uses a trick phonograph to let people believe they are eavesdropping on private conversation. Her plan is foiled, but Ollamus is forgiving.

Back in New York the new season began in earnest with the arrival of a second Boston success, **Kismet** (12 August 1895, Herald Square). Unrelated to the famous Otis Skinner vehicle, it did, however, play out its story in the same "Oriental" splendor. A Sultan decrees that the first boy born to any of his wives shall be chief of state but that all boys born thereafter must be put to death. The Princess Ramadamus (Rose Leighton) gives birth to a girl. Determined to be a power behind the throne, she announces the child is a boy and names it Kismet (Lizzie MacNichol). When her second child is in fact a male, she is forced to name it Haidee and raise it as a girl. Both children are kept in ignorance of their true sex. Kismet becomes sultan and sends for suitors to woo Haidee (Richard F. Carroll). In the end Kismet marries one of Haidee's suitors and Haidee assumes the throne. There was little comment about Gustave Kerker's undistinguished score, but several other matters disturbed the critics. The *Times* complained that Carroll, who was also the librettist, cheapened the evening by playing to the gallery. A number of critics decried what they considered unnecessarily suggestive innuendoes in the dialogue. The *Dramatic Mirror* rushed to the show's defense, arguing it was less suggestive than many. When the debate had no effect on ticket sales, the show folded after three weeks.

Three nights after the opening of *Kismet*, Alfred Cellier's London favorite, *Dorothy*, began a delayed, trouble-plagued (last-minute cast changes, costumes unready) revival at the Standard. The next night *The Merry World* was rushed back to the Casino after a disappointing Chicago stand and proved even more in demand as a cool-weather ticket than it had originally. It compiled an additional 148 performances.

Fleur-De-Lis (29 August 1895, Palmer's), a comic opera by J. Cheever Goodwin and William Furst, starred Della Fox in the title role and Jefferson De Angelis. Barker was the director. The Count Des Escarbilles (De Angelis) and the Marquis De Rosolio (Arthur Wheelan) go to war over their claims to a duchy. One of the noblemen has a daughter (Miss Fox), the other a son (Melville Stewart). The lovers manage to wangle a peace agreement despite the frequent interference of the count's uncooperative foot, which develops a nervous kick whenever he and the marquis are on the verge of reconciliation. The plot was a spoof of the dying tradition of melodrama that filled the evening with besieged castles (the hero made a thrilling forty-foot jump in the course of the evening), lost wills, and ghosts. For De Angelis his billing finally moved him from years as a featured player to stardom.

JEFFERSON DE ANGELIS was born in San Francisco on 30 November 1859. He made his first stage appearance at the age of twelve in early vaudeville at Baltimore's Odeon Theatre. In the early eighties he toured the world with his own dramatic company. But his ambition to be a serious actor, like De Wolf Hopper's, gave way to the realization that his métier lay elsewhere. New York first applauded him in *A Bottle of Ink* (6 January 1885). Increasingly important roles followed in musicals such as *The Begum*, *The Lady or the Tiger?*, *Poor Jonathan*, and *Apollo*.

The *Times*, which had recently been attacking Miss Fox in her appearances, continued its apparent hate affair when it snidely noted no improvement in her "babyish face and plump figure." But the paper, as it had in its previous criticism, leaned backward to confess it was clearly in the minority in its dislike of the star. Indeed, it was. This time, most critical complaints were leveled at Furst's latest colorless score. The same *Dramatic Mirror* that defended the librettist of *Kismet* now bewailed: "It is time that orchestral leaders of the Kerker and Furst order should cease to figure as operatic composers." Once again the public and the *Dramatic Mirror* went their separate ways. *Fleur-De-Lis* had a satisfactory run of sixty-five performances and a season-long tour.

Four musicals of one sort or another competed for attention on September 2. A return engagement of *Rob Roy* (29 October 1894) relit the Herald Square, recently vacated by *Kismet*. The Fifth Avenue offered a one-performance fiasco called **The Bathing Girl**. It told of Miss Terriberry (Grace Golden), a bathing girl, who arrives at a resort hotel where country bumpkins try to pass themselves off as potentates. She finally finds romance with J. Klingsbury Boats (William Stevens). The humor heard on that single presentation ran to the order of:

—Where is your yacht?
—Why, she's in the water, where she yacht to be!

A moonlit beach provided a suitable background for romantic scenes, while on a brighter stage "a bevy of girls in bathing costumes, costumes known only to the comic artists, twirl about."

Only slightly more successful was **The White Crook**, billed as "A Grand Spectacular Extravaganza," although it was as much commonplace vaudeville as anything. Affection remained for *The Black Crook* (12 September 1866), but the day when it could be imitated with some promise of a ready audience was long gone. The press awarded the evening at the Gaiety mere passing notice.

Among the offerings, only **Princess Bonnie** enjoyed a moderate success. Written by the same Willard Spenser who had achieved fame with *The Little Tycoon* (24 March 1886), the show had been a Philadelphia hit, running at the Chestnut Street Theatre in Spenser's hometown from 26 March to 7 July 1894. A subsequent road tour— of which the New York stay was a brief part— chalked up nearly 1,000 additional performances. *Princess Bonnie* recounted the heartwarming history of an infant rescued from a shipwreck by a Maine lighthouse keeper (F. Lennox, Jr.). Named Bonnie (Hilda Clark), she grows up and falls in love with a rich summer resident, Roy Stirling (W. M. Armstrong). But the Spanish Admiral Pomposo (J. S. Greensfelder) comes to claim her as a princess and take her to Spain. She is saved from an undesirable marriage when Shrimps (the lighthouse man) and Roy follow her to Spain and again rescue her. Philadelphia continued to mount occasional musicals of its own, even though few ever reached New York. Their reception there was generally so cool that Philadelphia, like Boston and Chicago, came to feel that a musical's provenance, not its quality, determined New York's judgment. Spenser apparently had been vocal in his conclusions, prompting the *Times* to scoff at any suggestion "some of the New York papers formed a cabal against his work because it came from Philadelphia." The *Times* insisted Spenser himself was at fault. It wrote of his music, "simplicity is its chief characteristic. A child might have written it, provided the child were not Mozart." By no means a failure—it ran forty performances at the Broadway—*Princess Bonnie* fell far short of the popularity of *The Little Tycoon*. With it, Spenser quietly retired from the New York musical stage, although he continued to write for Philadelphia productions.

A week after the rash of openings **The Chieftain** (9 September 1895, Abbey's) raised its curtain. The importation narrated the comic plight of a tourist taken prisoner by bandits whose "chieftainess" falls in love with him. In good comic-opera fashion the man's wife appears. Audiences of the time were attracted by its star, Francis Wilson, by its director, Richard Barker, and by its composer, Arthur Sullivan. But Sullivan was no longer in top form and his librettist, F. C. Burnand, no match for Gilbert. Still, the show was pleasing enough to run until early November.

May Irwin, the great "coon-shouter," interpolated a number of "coon songs" into the "farcical conceit" J. J. McNally created for her, **The Widow Jones** (16 September 1895, Bijou). The show was the first to honor her with stardom. The press was happy to note "elevation to stardom has not changed her in any respect. She is as round, as blond, as innocent looking... and as blue-eyed as ever." To underscore the event, Miss Irwin introduced what is often considered her best number, Charles E. Trevathan's "The Bully Song." Its lyrics recited in Negro dialect the singer's determined search for "dat nigger dat treated

folks so free." Miss Irwin played Beatrice Byke, who escapes her fortune-hunting suitors by running off to Maine and pretending to be the widow of a man drowned the year before. She soon finds herself saddled with the man's debts, his daughter, and, eventually, the "drowned" man himself.

Early in October combination houses such as the Grand and the 14th Street began advertising returns of the preceding season's musicals. *The Irish Artist* (1 October 1894), *Mavourneen* (28 September 1891), and the inevitable *Black Crook* (12 September 1866) all made one or more appearances. The enviable resiliency the healthy theatrical economics of the time allowed is shown by the appearance at intervals of the panned and troubled *20th Century Girl* (25 January 1895). One curiosity of the month was the American premiere of Humperdinck's opera *Hansel and Gretel* at Daly's. Anton Seidl conducted.

Gilbert, with a new partner, Osmond Carr, fared less happily than Sullivan had with Burnand. Gilbert's plot centered on a governor given to practical joking. He makes a commoner the butt of his humor, unaware the commoner is his king in disguise. **His Excellency** (14 October 1895, Broadway) was a quick failure; its rapid closing hastened by public resentment at its producers' attempt to charge $2.00 top instead of the customary $1.50.

Leonardo (21 October 1895, Garrick) also flopped in short order. Richard Mansfield, the distinguished actor and manager, produced the work, attesting once again to the fascination the early musical stage held for serious artists. A "romantic comic opera" with music by the composer of *The Maid of Plymouth* (15 January 1894), Thomas P. Thorne, it presented the historical da Vinci in an imaginary love affair. The Duke of Milan (Hobart Smock) travels to Florence to commission a statue of himself from Leonardo (George Devoll). But when the duke discovers his daughter, Beatrice (Marguerite Lemon), has become enamored of the artist, he banishes the young man. The duke encounters hard times as Leonardo's star rises. Leonardo helps restore the duke to power, and by curtain time he is granted Beatrice's hand.

One week later, Ivan Caryll's London success **The Shop Girl** (28 October 1895, Palmer's) premiered. Those English scholars who look on *The Shop Girl* as the first real musical comedy cite its relatively tight book as a principal argument. The story was simple enough, recounting the search for Bessie Brent by her late father's friend. Bessie, unaware of the wealth now hers, works happily as the shop girl of the title. Bessie's fiancé loves her as much when he learns she is an heiress as when he thought she was poor. In London, George Edwardes's production at the Gaiety broke the house record with a run of 546 performances. In New York the stay was far shorter. Another $2.00 top may have hurt business, but one English history student has suggested Britain's territorial dispute with Venezuela, deemed a violation of the Monroe Doctrine, disturbed a sufficient number of American playgoers to cut down attendance. Although new songs were advertised in celebration of the fiftieth performance, the run was terminated two weeks later. Two London originals repeated their roles for Broadway. Seymour Hicks recreated his role as Bessie's suitor, Charles. George Grossmith, Jr. (the son of the great Gilbert and Sullivan favorite) made his Rialto debut as a man-about-town, Bertie Boyd. Ethel Sydney was Bessie.

The Wizard of the Nile (4 November 1895, Casino), Victor Herbert's second comic opera, established him as a name to be reckoned with. At the same instance it secured fame and fortune for its star, Frank Daniels, long a popular figure in farce-comedy. And it also introduced Herbert to Harry B. Smith, a librettist with whom he would work so often in the future. For the second time in the season Egypt provided the setting. Moreover, Smith's plot was a variation of the story Rosenfeld had used two years before in The Rainmaker of Syria. Drought plagues the land. But a cheeky traveling magician, Kibosh, offers to bring rain. He does. Unfortunately the rain will not stop and disastrous floods ensue. The king (Walter Allen) orders Kibosh sealed in a tomb, only to discover his zealous courtiers have sealed him in as well. He is so grateful to escape alive that in his enthusiasm he pardons Kibosh. A romantic subplot depicts the fond feelings shared by Cleopatra (Dorothy Morton) and a musician, Ptarmigan (Edwin Isham). But, defying comic-opera tradition, the lovers do not wed in the end. Instead, Cleopatra settles down to await the arrival of Mark Antony. Daniels had to look to his laurels, for many a critic was captivated by "childish faced, innocent" Miss Morton, playing Cleopatra in a blond wig.

Herbert's score was less operatic than his music for Prince Ananias, but that was only in keeping with the lighter nature of the piece. All through his career Herbert endeavored to adopt his style to the nature of his libretto. There were few of the waltzes Herbert was later associated with, but much martial music—a reflection of his experience as a bandleader as well as of the story. Nonetheless, one waltz, "Star Light, Star Bright," was the hit of the show. The pleasant, simplistic melody is forgotten today because so much finer material poured from Herbert's pen in later years.

Also forgotten, sadly, is Herbert's skill as an orchestrator. Like all the more musicianly composers of his time Herbert orchestrated his own works. Although he sought primarily rich, well-balanced sound, Herbert always pursued novel instrumental effects. He hit on one of his happiest for a minor number from this piece. The accompaniment to the "Stonecutters' Song" was composed for piano and xylophone—"a glittering, chipping combination." Unlike Kerker in Kismet, Herbert contrived enough passages of pseudo-Oriental colorings to draw delighted comments from reviewers. The show ran 105 performances in New York, changing some of its initial post-Broadway bookings in order to satisfy the demand for seats. Daniels retained the role of Kibosh for two years, and when he left other lesser comedians kept the road pleased for a decade.

Behemoth, but graceful, Peter F. Dailey was starred in John J. McNally's The Night Clerk (11 November 1895, Bijou), where he portrayed Owen Moore, a night clerk not above his own night on the town. His support included the popular Jennie Yeamans and young Raymond Hitchcock. The Times noted, "There were a dozen pretty girls in tasteful gowns, some of whom could sing. Gertrude Fort sang 'Ben Bolt' acceptably with a violin obbligato, and there was the Olympia Male Quartet, with well-selected songs and a drill in Seventh Regiment uniform." The clerk stayed seven weeks at the Bijou before first heading uptown and then further away on the road.

The Merry Countess (2 November 1895, Garrick), an importation based on a French hit, Niniche, which had served as the source for Newport (15 September 1879) and would serve again for other shows later, closed abruptly in the middle of its second week. In its short stay it allowed sad-faced Dan Daly, fleeing a jealous husband, to knock over furniture, take refuge in a bathhouse whose floor promptly collapses, and then desperately try to wheel the contraption into the safety of the audience.

Fast upon the heels of A Gaiety Girl (18 September 1894), The 20th Century Girl (25 January 1895), The Bathing Girl (2 September 1895), and The Shop Girl (28 October 1895), The Bicycle

Girl wheeled into New York on 18 November. This "musical farce-comedy" was designed primarily as a touring attraction, and its brief New York stay was at the Grand, a combination house. The musical's title reflected the bicycle craze that was sweeping the nation. The story was commonplace. Grace Fordyce (Nellie McHenry) inherits the Briarwood Bicycle Company from her late father. She is courted by the so-called Baron Byke, who is actually the disguised son of the president of Briarwood's archrival. Stephen Forster, a modest young student, also seeks her hand. A bike race determines which man she shall wed, and, of course, Stephen wins. At best the evening had some fun with feminist agitation. A "new" girl sang "See The Conquering Shero," while a "new" man wore bloomers and a bonnet and carried a baby. The show treated its songs in the same commonplace fashion it handled most of its libretto. As the *Dramatic Mirror* noted, "The incidental music comprised a topical song called 'Long Ago,' with a talking chorus, a clambake song, medleys and parodies on popular songs, and many other melodious selections." But in one respect the mounting was not commonplace. The bike race was depicted by means of "Kinetoscope," an innocent glimpse of a not so innocent future. Edison's "Vitascope" would not be unveiled at Koster and Bial's until five months later, 20 April 1896.

A week after *The Bicycle Girl* bowed, another traveling farce-comedy came in from the hinterlands. In **A Happy Little Home** (25 November 1895, 14th St.), Owen Moore (plump George W. Monroe) dresses up as a girl and takes a job as an Irish housekeeper so that he may be near his sweetheart, Miss Gayfeather. He soon learns he must ward off the advances of his girl's father. The slapdash nature of farce-comedy construction was illustrated by the fact that most of the songs were in the third act. As usual they were essentially vaudeville specialties, with performers arriving at the Gayfeather house in the guise of visitors. Indeed the affair was so slapdash that the author refused to allow his name on the program. He was Charles Klein, whose greatest success was just a few months away.

Excelsior, Jr., the season's biggest success, opened on 29 November. It was a double-barreled opening, for it also allowed New Yorkers to gape for the first time at the attractions of Oscar Hammerstein's new Olympia Theatre, a house the financially reckless impresario was soon to lose. Originally conceived in Boston, *Excelsior, Jr.*'s libretto was by R. A. Barnet. Its music was largely by E. E. Rice—the last show

he helped write, although his career as producer and director had another decade to run. Additional new tunes were by several hands, including A. Baldwin Sloane. Old tunes—"of which there were many"—were also offered. Neither the program nor the press identified them. The titular hero is left a large fortune with the stipulation he must first scale a mountain as his father had done before him. He goes to Switzerland, where he meets the operator of a shooting gallery, William Tell ("whose overture is much admired"). The young man is courted by Bertha, the innkeeper, and by an elderly Venetian lady who hears him sing and believes he is serenading her. But Excelsior has eyes only for Mary Vanderbuilt Lamb, an American heiress. He climbs the mountain and wins Mary. Bertha settles for Tell, and the Venetian lady is left sadder but wiser. The title part was played as a trouser role by Fay Templeton. One critic rued Miss Templeton had "grown formidably corpulent," undoubtedly unaware the performer's contract stipulated she must remain under 150 pounds. Marie Cahill and Richard Carle used smaller parts to move toward stardom. In keeping with the fashion of the day, new songs were added at intervals. A spring announcement advised that the role of the St. Bernard had been expanded by popular request.

Charles Hoyt tripped himself up with **A Runaway Colt** (2 December 1895, American). His star was not an old theatrical trouper, but Adrian "Pop" Anson, a legend-in-his-own-time baseball player with the Chicago White Stockings. Only Hoyt called his team the "Colts," and "Pop" must show everyone that the game is on the up-and-up. A number of prizefighters were moving successfully from the ring to the stage at this time, but Anson could not follow in their tricky footsteps. The show lingered a mere three weeks. It had scarcely closed when Hoyt brought in a better one.

In an era when successful shows recouped their investments quickly and even short-lived productions often turned a small profit, the creative fever could hit small towns. On 16 December, for example, Baldwinsville, New York, mounted its own comic opera. **Next Year** took place at a college reunion. One of the grads has invented a flying machine and with three of his old buddies flies to another planet. Written by Harry P. Bigelow, who never made it to Broadway, it was a local hit. The correspondent for the village reported in the *Dramatic Mirror* that "a foot-ball chorus and a polar bear dance" were the most applauded numbers.

A musical travesty called **A Stag Party; or, A Hero in Spite of Himself** (17 December 1895, Garden) enjoyed a fortnight's run. Bill Nye and Paul Potter wrote the book; Herman Perlet, the music. Members of a gun club prepare to hunt a stag, but a neighboring landowner seizes the animal. The club decides to retrieve it and complications ensue. The large cast included a number of up-and-coming talents: Marie Dressler, Louis Harrison, Leo Ditrichstein, and John Slavin. Richard Barker staged the work.

Two more London successes arrived at the end of 1895. **An Artist's Model** (23 December 1895, Broadway), with music by Sidney Jones, won favor; **The School Girl** (30 December 1895, Bijou) did not. The artist's model jilted her poor painter to marry a rich suitor. Widowed, she is rebuffed by the artist, but eventually wins a reconciliation. The school girl wins a man her mother hoped to grab for herself. Minnie Palmer was the lucky pupil.

On 6 January 1896 there was a pair of musical openings. Another English hit, **Gentleman Joe**, seemed about to be a quick failure at the Fifth Avenue. With the law harassing its star, M. B. Curtis, a substitute had to go on opening night. The show was shuttered after ten performances. Revised, and with James T. Powers in the lead, it reopened at the end of the month and enjoyed a limited vogue. Powers, a man of many comic faces, portrayed a hack driver in league with servants cavorting while their masters are away.

But Charles Hoyt's **A Black Sheep** was a hit at Hoyt's from the start. The story line was thin. Goodrich Mudd, alias Hot Stuff (Otis Harlan), a Wild West lush, is bequeathed a fortune provided he returns to the East and marries his cousin. He is satisfied to remain where he is, so a local paper arranges a mock lynching to scare him out of town. Bessie Clayton's attractive legs and lively dances were "much admired," while Harlan won encores with "Some Things Are Better Left Unsaid." The *Times* rejoiced that songs such as Harlan's were not incorporated in the all-too-common "I'll sing you a song that will tell you all about it style." On the other hand, the *Dramatic Mirror* insisted the show's musical numbers were hardly related to the plot, sung, as they were, by members of a burlesque troupe stranded in Hot Stuff's village. But Hoyt persisted in advertising his show as "a musical comedy," and the public flocked to it for the rest of the season.

A touring show that had originated at Detroit's Whitney Opera House stopped briefly at the People's Theatre on 27 January. **Down on the Suwanee River** was a musical spectacle by R. H. Stephens. Forty of the forty-two performers in its cast were African Americans. Essentially a pageant of black history, it moved its players from Africa to a Southern plantation to Rafferty's Hall in New York, where the evening ended with a giant Cakewalk. Although *Down on the Suwanee River* played an out-of-the-way house, interest in Negro music seems to have exploded all over New York's theatrical heartland in the following month. Several times during February 1896 the *Times* carried notices such as this:

> New Negro Melodies. Flora Irwin will sing in the second act of "Gentleman Joe" at the Bijou Theatre to-night two new and original darky songs, which have been composed and written for her. They are called "Honey Does Yer Love Yer Man" and "Nigger with a White Spot on His Face."

On 16 February newspaper advertisements for Keith's Union Square Theatre announced that the next day would mark the "Debut on the High Class Vaudeville Boards of the noted Western Entertainer" Ben Harney. Harney, a white man, accompanied by his black stooge, Strap Hill, first regaled Broadway audiences with a new form of black musical composition, ragtime. Listed eleventh on a bill of fifteen acts, Harney failed to elicit so much as a simple notice from reviewers of the *Times*, the *World*, or the *Herald*. But the public was taken with the new style. Ragtime, more than any other black musical form of the era, fueled the "coon song" rage and permanently established African-American modes as the main influence on American popular song. By the end of the month Primrose and West revealed they had hired Madison Square Garden for an evening of cakewalking, with 200 dancers.

Another importation, **The Lady Slavey** (3 February 1896, Casino), was the eighth English musical of the season. Dan Daly starred. Daly played a lackadaisical sheriff ordered to seize the estate of a bankrupt Englishman. The Englishman (Henry Norman) desperately tries to marry one of his four eldest daughters (Virginia Earle), who, with the help of a flighty music hall singer (Marie Dressler), bags a wealthy young heir (Charles Dickson). The show's producer, George Lederer, followed the pattern of the day by allowing American textual revisions and musical interpolations. But Lederer went to extremes. His "Americanized" book was "practically new," and his entire score was by Gustave Kerker. Apparently, not a note of John Crook's original score was heard. The plump, bulldog-miened Miss Dressler and the tall, thin, lugubrious Daly combined their abundant talents to stop the show nightly with an acrobatic waltz, "The Human Fly."

With *Excelsior, Jr.* moved to another house, Oscar Hammerstein was able to present his own creation, **Marguerite,** at the Olympia on 10 February. Hammerstein's libretto played havoc with the Faust legend. Faust (Thomas Evans Green) becomes a painter and Marguerite (Alice Rose) his wife. Mephisto (Adolph Dahm-Peterson) appears and, with his magical dragon-headed staff, brings Faust's paintings to life. Later Faust and his wife are transported to Mephisto's summer home, "The Palace of the Flowers." If a number of the critics had unkind things to say about the book, most of the reviewers treated Hammerstein's gifts as a composer with surprising respect. Hammerstein filled the evening with appealing stage pictures. He introduced each major dance number with a voguish "living picture." These tableaux (apparently Faust's paintings) came to life to allow pretty girls to dance at the court of Louis XV, to display a Hussar march and drill as well as to permit a cancan, a peasant dance, and an Oriental dance. One special effect illuminated 1,700 electric bulbs hanging from the ceiling and from strips dangling down to the floor. But Hammerstein had been unwise to let the profitable *Excelsior, Jr.* leave his new house. The comparative failure of *Marguerite* contributed to the flamboyant Hammerstein's bankruptcy.

Robin Hood (28 September 1891) returned the same evening *Marguerite* premiered, to initiate a rash of late winter revivals. As might be expected, the production was the Bostonians' venerated interpretation, with Henry Clay Barnabee, W. H. MacDonald, Eugene Cowles, and Jessie Bartlett Davis repeating their great roles. But another name had been added to the troupe's roster, "a young Californian, to whom is entrusted the minor soprano role [of Annabel]." There was no foreseeing the damage Alice Nielsen would inflict on the company that brought her to public attention.

Only one fresh piece broke the chain of revivals. Lillian Russell suffered her third failure in two seasons when she and her handpicked company offered **The Goddess of Truth** (26 February 1896, Abbey's). The critics complained that Stanislaus Stange's retelling of the Pygmalion legend lacked

wit and that Julian Edwards's score lacked memorable melodies. Indeed, the *Times* took the opportunity to comment on the generally "barren days" for the musical theatre and even to assail Miss Russell, especially the "narrow range of her abilities as an actress." The paper professed the star was at her best only "when she poses in her ornate draperies in the revealing glare of the calcium light." The show left after a somewhat forced run of forty-five showings.

On 2 March Chauncey Olcott returned to the 14th Street Theatre in a revival of *The Irish Minstrel* (4 September 1888), inexplicably rechristened *The Minstrel of Clare.* (Did Olcott fear audiences might confuse *The Irish Minstrel* with *The Irish Artist?*) *1492* (15 May 1893) visited the Grand during the same week. To fill out her scheduled stay at Abbey's Miss Russell hastily mounted *The Little Duke* for a fortnight beginning 6 April. Another Fritz play, *Fritz in Love,* appeared on the combination circuit in April.

The year's most enduring work, **El Capitan** (20 April 1896, Broadway), had a book by Charles Klein (who in November had provided the American text for *The Merry Countess* and later in the month had disclaimed credit for *A Happy Little Home*). More important, it had a score by John Philip Sousa. Sousa and Tom Frost collaborated on the lyrics. Although in later years Sousa insisted on calling Klein's book the finest libretto America had ever produced, it was, at best, little better than average. Certainly in outline it seems barely distinguishable from myriad other contrivances of the time. A rebel band led by El Capitan is determined to overthrow Don Medigua, viceroy of Peru. But Medigua (De Wolf Hopper) captures El Capitan, secretly executes him, and assumes his place in disguise. When the rebels capture Pozzo (Charles Klein), his chamberlain, and mistake the servant for the viceroy, Medigua is at no pains to enlighten them. But Medigua's wife (Alice Hosmer) and daughter (Bertha Waltzinger), hearing of his apparent capture, set out to rescue him, assisted by the daughter's suitor, Count Hernando Verrada (Edmund Stanley). Meanwhile, Estrelda (Edna Wallace Hopper), daughter of a former viceroy, falls in love with the supposed El Capitan. To further complicate Medigua's life the Spanish Army arrives to help him against the rebels. As El Capitan he leads the rebels in circles until they are too tired to fight. His family arrives in time to explain his and Pozzo's true identities to the Spanish commander. Medigua himself has a little explaining to do to his wife regarding Estrelda. But everything ends happily. Estrelda is given to the man who loves her, Scaramba; the count wins the daughter; and Medigua and his wife once again reign over Peru. Much of Sousa's lovely score was culled by him from earlier works. "The Legend Of The Frogs" (cut before the show opened) had been "The Fable Of The Frogs" in *The Queen of Hearts*, and the lovers' beautiful "Sweetheart, I'm Waiting" was a revision of "Sighing, Ah Sighing" from *The Smugglers*. But the enduring masterpiece of the evening was El Capitan's own march, derived from "El Capitan's Song," sung by Medigua and the chorus.

The show gave its star and producer, De Wolf Hopper, "in wondrous garb and 'make-up'" as a bearded, plumed conquistador, the greatest success of his career. Its first New York run tallied 112 performances. With or without him as star it played virtually without interruption throughout the country for four years. It ran six months in London and over the years has enjoyed several notable revivals.

The year's last original work was the Casino's third annual summer "review," **In Gay New York**, which arrived on 25 May. Since revues still had to have plots, *In Gay New York* described a visit by newlyweds from Maine (how librettists loved to bring in Maine!) to New York. They visit Grand Central, the Waldorf, Coney Island, and the Casino—where they see bits from the season's most popular plays satirized. The plays twitted included *The Heart of Maryland* (in the revue's version David Warfield became entangled in the bell ropes) and Henry Irving's *Macbeth*. Besides the numerous vaudeville specialties, the evening included a "Newspaper Ballet" and an "Icicle Ballet." Virginia Earle, Madge Lessing, Julius Steger, Walter Jones, Lee Harrison, Warfield, Richard Carle, and John Slavin were part of the large cast. With dialogue by Hugh Morton and music by Gustave Kerker, the evening lasted till midnight.

Two opera companies also appeared at the end of May with traditional repertories that ranged from operetta to grand opera. But the financial climate told and by mid-August, when *In Gay New York* shut down for vacation, not a single musical was playing on Broadway. Lovers of lyric theatre or nostalgia in the New York area could, however, have taken themselves to Manhattan Beach, where a well-attended revival of *Evangeline* (27 July 1874) was advertised as "just pure and simple—NOT up to date."

1896–1897

Economically and creatively, the theatre continued to tread water. The new season brought nothing to compare in merit and durability with the preceding April's *El Capitan*. However, with the opening of Weber and Fields' Music Hall it did witness one last extended flourish of a more or less classic burlesque tradition.

The only summer entries were all-star revivals of Gilbert and Sullivan's *H. M. S. Pinafore* and *Patience* at the Herald Square. Lillian Russell, Henry E. Dixey, and W. T. Carleton headed the roster. But Miss Russell, accustomed to being the center of attention, received a rude shock, probably made doubly painful by her recent failures. Sadie Martinot caused an outpouring of gasps and comments when she appeared as Lady Angela, wearing what is reputed to have been the first strapless gown seen on the New York stage.

The main season began poignantly with a Ned Harrigan and David Braham offering. Harrigan's day had passed, and he had fallen on hard times. His theatre had been taken over by Richard Mansfield, who had rechristened it the Garrick. No Harrigan play had reached Broadway in 1895–1896. One work, *My Son Dan*, had been tried out, only to fold on the road. The mere fact that Harrigan felt the need to take a new show on the road suggested his own awareness of his faltering flair. Harrigan had always opened his new pieces confidently in New York. Coincident with the closing of *My Son Dan*, Harrigan had announced a "temporary retirement." But by 31 August Harrigan had a fresh opus ready to inaugurate the season at the Bijou. **Marty Malone** (Harrigan) is an Irish sailor who has renounced a chance to be Prince Consort of Ghoola-Ghoola and who befriends a street waif, Pauline Jordan (Pauline Train). Pauline becomes a music hall singer, then proves to be an heiress and leaves Marty to marry rich and handsome Lord John Foxwood (John Hollis). Marty finds solace with a girl attached to some Cuban revolutionaries. Harrigan's tale began in a dilapidated sailor's home in the harbor slums and ended, much as *Notoriety* had, on the lawn of a great estate, with painted yachts "sailing" in the distance. The cliché-filled tale, with perhaps a hint of Chaplin's film *City Lights*, disappointed Harrigan's faithful, even though they greeted the piece with "noisy acclaim." Nor was Braham able to come up with a truly popular song, although "Savannah Sue"—"neatly executed" by Dan Collyer, Dave Braham, Jr. and Gussie Hart (as a "darky damsel")—was much applauded, like the show itself, at the premiere. When *Marty Malone* closed, Harrigan drifted into a less publicly proclaimed retirement, returning only intermittently to the stage.

September was an unusually busy month. Ten musicals bowed. The month began inauspiciously with Ludwig Englander and Harry B. Smith's **The Caliph** (3 September 1896, Broadway). Smith professed to have based his libretto on the legend of Harun al-Rashid, but in fact it was merely another of the comic contrivances set in pseudo-Oriental splendor so dear to the time. With crime rampant in Baghdad, the caliph, Hardluck XIII (Jefferson De Angelis), is persuaded by his cynical vizier to spend some time in disguise among criminal elements so that by better understanding their methods he may more readily eradicate them. Before long the caliph himself has committed every crime in the book. His plans for reform are thwarted, however, when he is abducted by his younger brother, Brikbrak (Alfred C. Whelan). The young man will release the caliph only if he is allowed to marry Djemma (Minnie Landers)—the very girl the caliph had hoped to wed. The caliph agrees and officiates over not only the marriage of Brikbrak and Djemma but over that of his own daughter and her fiancé as well. For De Angelis the show was his first solo starring part. In a day of broad physical comedy, the press was happy to note that "as an acrobat he can hold his own with any star comedian on our stage." His funniest moment found him hopelessly entangled in a hammock. Richard Barker directed. *The Caliph* had been scheduled to run until 26 October. Poor notices and poorer attendance closed the show ahead of time, with a loss of most of its $16,000 investment.

On 5 September 1896, the three-year-old Imperial Music Hall on Broadway at 29th Street was reopened as Weber and Fields' Music Hall. Both the stage and the auditorium were small. The house held only 665 seats, and audiences watched performers do their bit on a stage a mere sixteen feet deep. At $1.50 top a sold-out performance could realize no more than $700. But backstage costs, with one exception, were low. At first costumes and sets were rented, and a stage crew of nine drew a total of $132 a week in salaries. But principals asked as much as $200 a week. Thus with actors' fees included, it cost almost $700 a performance to keep the house open. The new music hall was never to be the moneymaker standard-size musical houses were. But at the moment Weber and Fields were not eyeing long-term riches. Their experiences in variety had been artistically enriching and on occasion financially rewarding, but more often uncertain. The young clowns were looking for steady employment.

LEW FIELDS (Lewis Schanfield) was born in New York City's Bowery on 1 January 1867 to immigrant parents of modest means. JOE WEBER (whose middle name was Morris) was born a few blocks away from the Fields home just over seven months later, 11 August 1867. His parents, too, were immigrants. The boys were childhood friends. They first performed together at the age of ten, doing a "Dutch" act not very different at heart from the dialect clowning they would use the rest of their lives. They moved from amateur to professional variety, rising almost to the top before they decided to borrow money and try their hand as legitimate performers and impresarios. In their act the tall, thin Fields and the shorter, stockier Weber customarily made up with chin whiskers, dressed in gaudily checkered suits (Weber's heavily padded), and sported derbies.

The renaissance of the burlesque tradition had begun a few seasons earlier with Charles Brookfield's parody of *Lady Windermere's Fan* (3 April 1893), its rebirth coming at virtually the same moment as the birth of the revue. Both dealt in travesty, but burlesque aimed its mockery at a single principal target while the revue shot its barbs all over the map. The limitations of the burlesque tradition constrained and eventually killed it, while the revue's open flexibility allowed it to evolve and flourish for half a century. Curiously, when Weber and Fields eventually abandoned burlesque they turned to book shows, almost never to revues. The relative cohesion and discipline of their tradition dictated their futures. But the opening attraction at their new house suggested they were willing to compromise. The first part of their evening was a pure, unalloyed olio; only the second part was a sustained burlesque. This practice of a double bill obtained as long as the music hall flourished. For their first burlesque the team chose the same show so well spoofed in *In Gay New York: The Heart of Maryland*. They called their version **The Art of Maryland**. Mary Land became a cook, the creator of chicken à la Maryland. But the material was weak, missing even the obvious opportunity to have fun with Mrs. Carter's swinging on the clapper of the church bell to ensure "The bell shall not ring!" When the London hit *The Geisha* opened in September and immediately became one of the outstanding successes of the new season, Weber and Fields hastily dropped *The Art of Maryland* and substituted their first major triumph, **The Geezer.** In the burlesque, Li Hung Chang (a Chinese official with that name had visited America earlier in the year) comes seeking an American heiress as bride for his emperor. The heiress's dowry must be sufficient to pay off the indemnity demanded by Japan after the 1894–1895 war. Other characters included a tea-house keeper, Two-Hi (played by Sam Bernard), who offers all comers "one pie-cee beer mit pretzels." Occidentals were kidded as well. The famous reporter Nellie Bly became Nellie Fly; the actress May Yohe, whose marriage had made her Lady Francis Pelham Clinton Hope, found herself kidded as Ladies Faith, Hope, and Charity; the ubiquitous police commissioner, Teddy Roosevelt, gave his name to all the policemen in the cast: A. Roosevelt, B. Roosevelt, etc. The tradition of comic opera out of which *The Geisha* came was made fair game in the opening chorus, a spoof of opening choruses:

> *Hurrah! Hurrah! We laugh and sing,*
> *So loudly let the welkin ring.*
> *We must admit, though far from slow,*
> *What welkin is, we do not know.*

But musical traditions alien to comic opera and *The Geisha* also found a place. "Miss Lucy" honored the raging "coon song" vogue with lyrics Wordsworth might not have disdained for his Lucy:

> *The bees hum in the blossom vine,*
> *The birds break out in song.*
> *The sun, he say, "Ise obleeged to shine,"*
> *When Miss Lucy pass along.*

The text was by Joseph Herbert, who left Weber and Fields at the end of the season, but the music was by the composer who remained loyal to the house until his death, John Stromberg. One other change Weber and Fields introduced in their second week was an "animatograph," an early, primitive form of motion pictures. In doing so they were catering to that new fad that had begun the preceding season. Days earlier, Tony Pastor had offered his patrons a "kineopticon" and the Union Square a "cinematograph." Weber and Fields discarded their film show after a short time, preferring to satirize its flickering, jerky movements by rapidly rotating the screens in front of their calcium spots. It was the first use of a device that would soon become a commonplace.

Sidney Jones's London hit **The Geisha** opened on 9 September at Daly's. Owen Hall wrote the book; Harry Greenbank, the lyrics; and Lionel Monckton supplied additional melodies. The story told of the love of a naval officer—whose uniform would be appropriated by a decade or more of musical heroes—and a geisha at a tea house. The lovers are parted at the end, but not tragically. The Englishman weds a comely English girl, and O Mimosa San marries an Oriental. Dorothy Morton and Van Rensselaer Wheeler were featured, while one of the evening's dancers was Isadora Duncan. Because of various commitments, Daly was not able to allow *The Geisha* to run uninterruptedly. However, in a series of engagements during this season and the next it compiled over 200 performances. For reasons no longer clear it also underwent constant cast changes.

If burlesque was renascent, minstrelsy continued to wane. When the Cleveland Haverly Minstrels came to town the same night as *The Geisha*, they were relegated to the Star Theatre, once a major house but by this date a less important auditorium.

Englander and Smith had a second comic opera, **Half a King** (14 September 1896, Knickerbocker), ready a week after the *Caliph* premiere. By the lights of the time they served Francis Wilson and Lulu Glaser better than they had Jefferson De Angelis, although nothing from *Half a King* has remained popular. In this musical version of Chivot and Duru's *Le Roi de Pique*, two mountebanks, Tireschappe (Wilson) and Mistris (Peter Lang), attempt to foist the waif Pierrette (Miss Glaser) on the Duke de Chateau Margaux (J. C. Miron). They kidnap the duke's intended bride and send Pierrette in her place. But Pierrette bungles her chance and returns to her mountebanks. Wilson, like De Angelis, was praised for his "acrobatic humor," although it was generally conceded that Wilson's style was the least broad and most cerebral of the major clowns of his day. Wilson had fun with a trick donkey and delighted audiences with a topical song in which he instructed real kings of the day how to run their realms. Henry E. Hoyt painted a beautiful outdoor view of Paris, while Richard Marston contributed his painterly skills to a palace interior. Richard Barker again directed. Whatever posterity has thought of the piece, Wilson's commission kept him profitably occupied for two months in New York and the rest of the season on tour. The show was the first to play Abbey's under its new and more enduring name of the Knickerbocker.

J. Cheever Goodwin and Woolson Morse, deprived of De Wolf Hopper's talents, nevertheless managed to delight Broadway with **Lost, Strayed or Stolen** (16 September 1896, Fifth Ave.). The show was a musical version of Grange and Bernard's *Le Baptême du Petit Oscar*. A nurse gives a child about to be baptized to a soldier, and the soldier disappears. The baby's father and three godfathers go in search of the child, encountering special complications (as well as specialties) when they arrive at the apartment of Rose D'Ete (Georgia Caine), an actress who is also the soldier's mistress. The comic highlight of the evening was a scene in which Rose, as each new caller arrives, shoves his predecessor into a single, minuscule closet. One popular song, "Ootchy Kootchy," was not sung to the baby. With so many soldiers among the principals, the producers could not resist the inevitable marches and drills, but their excess elicited cries for moderation.

On 21 September Victor Herbert suffered one of the worst failures of his career when **The Gold Bug** opened at the Casino on Monday and closed the next Saturday. Although only three musical numbers were published, Herbert was not to blame for the show's failure. In fact, one number, "The Gold Bug March," is still heard occasionally. Much of the show's trouble stemmed from delaying the opening night several times. Even on that first night many costumes were not ready. A shaky performance accentuated the libretto's flatness. This book by Glen MacDonough, with whom Herbert collaborated more happily in later years, revolved around Willet Float (Max Figman), the Secretary of the Navy, and "a man with a past." The skeleton in his closet is the Indian wife he deserted. His daughter by her, Wawayanda (Molly Fuller), appears and blackmails him into abetting her romance. Characters included Lady Patty Larceny (played by young Marie Cahill), Doolittle Work (Henry Norman), and a politician called Constant Steele (Robert Fisher). For many, Miss Cahill was the delight of the evening. She assumed the part of a young woman who still pursues the perfect mate, even if she has been divorced fifteen times. Her song, "When I First Began To Marry, Years Ago," her cancan, and her cachuca with her ex-mates were all show-stoppers. Two performers not given characters to play and not even listed by name on the program were nonetheless shortly to make

an indelible mark, on the history of the American Musical Theatre: Bert Williams and George Walker.

Two other important debuts occurred when Anna Held made her first American appearance in a revival of Charles Hoyt's *A Parlor Match* (21 September 1896, Herald Square). The show's young producer, Florenz Ziegfeld, Jr., had only recently called attention to himself in Chicago.

***

FLORENZ ZIEGFELD was born in March of 1867. His father, an austere martinet, headed the Chicago Musical College, one of the city's many music schools. Ziegfeld's reaction to a heavy dose of classical music was a lifelong aversion to great musical masterpieces and an indifference to music in general. Although in later years Ziegfeld always sought out the best composers for his shows as a matter of sound business practice, his attitude toward them and their music was often infuriating and alienating. Ziegfeld fell in love with show business when Buffalo Bill and Annie Oakley came to Chicago in 1883. Ziegfeld later claimed he played hooky from school several days running to see the troupe. At twenty-two he staged a show called *The Dancing Ducks of Denmark* until the SPCA forced a closing of the attraction. (He had induced the ducks to dance by heating the bottoms of their feet.) He became secretary-treasurer of his father's school, but his spendthrift recklessness caused him to be removed quickly. When his father was made musical director for the 1893 Columbian Exposition in Chicago, young Ziegfeld was sent to secure performers. The elder Ziegfeld was appalled at the collection of jugglers, acrobats, and circus bands his son signed. On his return Ziegfeld also signed the strongman Sandow. It was as Sandow's promoter at the fair and on the tour that followed that Ziegfeld first came to the public eye. For his initial Broadway venture Ziegfeld decided to reunite the once famous comedy team of Charles Evans and William Hoey in a revival of their old favorite, the Hoyt play *A Parlor Match*. Ziegfeld and Evans went to Europe seeking new faces. In London they saw Anna Held at the Palace.

ANNA HELD professed to be a native of Paris, but records suggest she was actually born in Warsaw in 1873. Her father was a French-Jewish glove maker; her mother was Polish. Her father died when she was still a child, and she and her mother moved to London, where they found employment in the garment industry. A young admirer wangled her a job as a chorus girl. She soon moved over to the more serious Yiddish theatre, then to Dutch and Parisian music halls. When Ziegfeld and Evans saw her, Miss Held had just returned to the stage after an unhappy marriage that produced one child. Miss Held and Ziegfeld hoped to marry after the opening of *A Parlor Match*, but Anna's first husband, a Catholic, refused her a divorce. Ziegfeld and Miss Held lived together as husband and wife until their union was recognized in common law in 1904. Acknowledging that her first entrance evoked "a prolonged and sincere 'O h!'" from her audience, one critic proceeded to describe her: "Mlle. Held is not very tall; she has lots of hair, not quite black, and combed back loosely from a smooth low brow; her costume was a radiant combination of pale blue and pale salmon, heavily embroidered... . Her eyes are long, narrow, and heavily circled; her nose is Straight; her mouth perfect... . Her voice is not as charming as she is, but it will do." The diminutive coquette skyrocketed to the same glittering stardom as Weber and Fields, and Bert Williams.

In his fiscal high-flying Oscar Hammerstein foreshadowed Ziegfeld. Deep in financial difficulties, Hammerstein still found time to write both libretto and music for another comic opera, **Santa Maria** (24 September 1896, Olympia), and to unveil it at the house he was about to lose. Camille D'Arville was the star. The title had nothing to do with saints or Columbus; it was, for no special reason, the heroine's name. A gypsy informs the king of Holland that years before, while the king was away at war, his wife bore him a child, but gave it away. The king sends a trusted lieutenant in search of the child, hoping to identify it by an unusual birthmark. The lieutenant returns with a beautiful girl, who falls in love with him. The grateful king makes the two his heirs. James T. Powers provided much of the comedy as

a judge in a land where offenses against women are tried by all-female juries. The judge sees to it that his jurors are especially comely and, from a soda fountain built into his bench, squirts soda water at girls who misbehave to keep them in hand. Critics complained that the songs had as little to do with the story as did the title. But the public ignored the carping. They flocked to the theatre long enough to let the show run 100 performances and salve some of Hammerstein's wounds.

Robert Breitenbach and his composer, Carl Pleininger, closed out the month with **The Merry Tramps** (28 September 1896, Star). It was one more vehicle for the Liliputians, with the midgets performing in "colloquial German and American English" and with the program boasting the scenery was painted in Germany. In another of the period's fantastic science-fiction plots, Professor Willard (A. Durand) invents a magic machine that tells him who in all the earth is best qualified to marry his daughter, Mary (Bertha Jaeger). Willard, Mary, and a man-ape set out on a magic train and airship to test three leading prospects. Each is given a sum of money, and the one who does best with it will win. Two squander their capital. The third man, Jim (Adolf Zink), increases it. Franz Ebert, generally conceded the most beloved of the little people, assumed a number of roles, appearing "as a drunk, a lady-killer in pink coat and knee smalls, an old Jew, a frivolous woman, and Adonis taking a shower." The show played five weeks at the house and then embarked on a tour.

October's first entry was a revival of *Evangeline* (27 July 1874), with Henry E. Dixey as The Lone Fisherman and George K. Fortesque once again playing Catherine. The show featured a dozen pretty chorus girls and a grand "Amazon March." Eleven nights later, 12 October, the Casino acknowledged that farce-comedy was unmistakably evolving into musical comedy when it presented its patrons J. J. McNally's latest effort, **A Good Thing**. McNally's tale described Billy Biddall's embarrassment when his love letters to Minnie Millett (Agnes Milton) fall into her mother's hands and the old lady presumes they are meant for her. Peter F. Dailey soon to be a pillar of strength at Weber and Fields, starred as Billy. The songs were all interpolations, and the specialties included five girls in a bicycle dance. The principals took time off from the plot to burlesque grand opera, while Flora Irwin stepped front and center to introduce the latest "coon songs." But Casino patrons wanted more cohesive material. *A Good Thing* survived a mere three weeks.

Hogan's Alley (12 October 1896, People's) brought to life the denizens of a beloved comic strip. Their comic misadventures were interrupted time and again by all manner of vaudeville turns.

In spite of failures and of the slapdash nature of some of the hits, musicals, however, were voguish and profitable. When a revival of *A Night at the Circus, Brian Boru,* and *In Mexico* all raised their curtains on 19 October, half of the sixteen shows playing the main stem were musicals by standards of the time.

The extent to which shows were conceived for special audiences can be gauged when it was noted that **Brian Boru** was the first show since the days of Dion Boucicault with a totally Irish story aimed at more than the local Irish trade. And the story was indeed Irish. In glens filled with fairies and banshees, Brian Boru (Max Eugene), the Irish king, is tempted by the British princess, Elfrida (Amanda Fabris), to betray his own people. She fails, and Brian leads his forces to victory. But if Stanislaus Stange's story was Celtic, Julian Edwards's music was not. Still theatregoers of all backgrounds made the show a modest hit at the Broadway, relishing in particular the scene in which the thwarted Elfrida turns on the king:

Rude barbarian, wild uncouth!
Elfrida now to thee speaks truth—
I never loved thee—thou wert my tool;
I hate and scorn thee, poor weak fool!

Indeed, Miss Fabris "trilled with a vigor that moved the audience to wild applause." Older theatregoers could take special delight in the presence of Amelia Summerville as an "elderly baby." The once mammoth comedienne had become probably the first major celebrity to undertake a publicized, rigid diet. At least one amused critic compared the relatively slim Miss Summerville with the unromantically burly hero.

In Mexico was part of the Bostonians' repertory. The group's fortunes had begun to fail, and they were shunted off to a new but somewhat out-of-the-way house, the Murray Hill. The story was set in the Mexican War. The wounded Captain Selden (William E. Phillip) falls in love with his nurse, Marquita Mason (Hilda Mason), but Ramon Falcon (W. H. MacDonald) would force the girl to marry him by threatening to make public compromising letters her guardian had written. She is spared when a peasant named Theresa (Jessie Bartlett Davis), a girl Falcon has wronged, stabs him to death. Other Bostonian stalwarts took lesser roles, Eugene

Cowles appearing as a faithful half-breed and Henry Clay Barnabee as a "Varmount sutler" (Vermont settler). With a book by C. T. Dazey and music by Oscar Weil—who had earlier composed *Suzette* for the Bostonians—it was originally produced as *A Wartime Wedding.* The *Times,* in an interesting observation, suggested the Mexican War was a poor setting for a tale, noting that since the war had never been "cherished" by Americans it would elicit no patriotic fervor. The company's repertory nature allowed it to keep weak works on its program, often with the hope of slowly improving them. In his autobiography, Barnabee recalled that the musical "seemed to fit our organization like a glove, and yet proved an incorrigible misfit with regard to the patronizing public." The Bostonians immediately replaced the work with *The Bohemian Girl* on 26 October and finished their engagement.

Maggie Cline, the headlining Irish belter, played Mary Brady, "a womanly woman with a man's nerve," in **On Broadway** (26 October 1896, Grand Opera). She not only belted out her famous "Throw Him Down, McCloskey," but even was aided by a character of that name, who, sure enough, knocked down his and her opponents, especially the troublesome Mr. Black.

On 2 November the Casino replaced its own failure, *A Good Thing,* with **Jack and the Beanstalk,** a children's extravaganza—another genre new to the house—and was awarded with two months of good holiday business. R. A. Barnet's fable found Jack, Old Mother Hubbard's son (Madge Lessing), selling his cow with the crumpled horn to buy a beanstalk. He climbs it with Sinbad the Sailor (E. Gerard) and together they visit Cloudland, where King Cole (H. V. Donnelly), Miss Moffett (Merri Osborne), and Puss 'n Boots (Marie Godoy) live. Miss Osborne won encores with two "coon songs," one sung straight and the other rendered as an English coster might do it. The show was the first with a complete score by A. Baldwin Sloane, although a number of his songs had been heard the preceding year in *Excelsior, Jr.* (29 November 1895).

Harry B. Smith had yet another libretto ready—with another Oriental setting—for **The Mandarin** (2 November 1896, Herald Square). His mandarin (George Honey) disguises himself as Fan-Tan (G. C. Boniface, Jr.), a carpenter, in order to woo Fan-Tan's beautiful wife (Bertha Waltzinger). But the police come to arrest Fan-Tan, who has been out on a spree. Naturally they haul in the disguised mandarin despite his protests. The mandarin's cohorts then mistakenly hustle Fan-Tan to the safety of the mandarin's home and twelve wives. But when the real Fan-Tan has his saviors bring him his own wife, he falls afoul of a law permitting a man no more than a dozen mates. Only the mandarin's confession saves Fan-Tan from the block. The score was another disappointment by Reginald De Koven, who was beginning to be assailed as a once-lucky hack. De Koven, in an interview, defended himself as best he could from critical complaints that his music was increasingly derivative. He insisted all composers are "imitative" and that it was too soon to expect our still young nation to develop a fresh style of its own. Either ignorant of or ignoring the Negro influence beginning to be felt all about him, he pontificated, "[W]hat we need is music in America, not American music." *The Mandarin* departed after five weeks.

A. BALDWIN SLOANE was born in Baltimore on 28 August 1872, receiving his musical training there from various professors. An early fondness for the lyric stage made him one of the founders of Baltimore's Paint and Powder Club, a semiprofessional theatrical group, which mounted some of his fledgling efforts. Moving to New York, he began composing in accepted Tin Pan Alley style and soon found his songs being interpolated into musicals and employed by vaudevillians. Sloane's melodies were devoid of distinction, but he was genial and prolific, and quickly found increasing call for his services.

Another Irish lady, also a surefire draw, was Nellie McHenry. Her vehicle, **A Night in New York** (30 November 1896, Harlem Opera), recounted the plight of two husbands who go without their wives to a ball, only to meet their wives at the dance. Miss McHenry served as peacemaker.

The season's runaway hit was E. E. Rice's mounting of Ivan Caryll's London success *The Gay Parisienne*, retitled **The Girl from Paris** (8 December 1896, Herald Square). The libretto concerned the troubles of an austere old Englishman (Charles A. Bigelow) who returns from a Continental tour to find himself sued for breach of promise by a young French lady (Clara Lipman). The musical ran into the summer.

"The upper ten of Thompson Street and Minetta Lane have joined last night with the white-faced Eastsiders in according rapturous greeting to" **Darkest America** (21 December 1896, People's). So the *Dramatic Mirror* informed its readers when this all-black show appeared in New York. A history of blacks in America from plantation days through Reconstruction into then present times held together turns by buck-and-wing dancers, a male impersonator, a monologuist, and numerous singers. A steamboat race was depicted with "so much realism that the gallery was with difficulty restrained."

Across the continent, San Francisco's famed Tivoli annually presented a Christmas spectacle for youngsters. This year's offering was **Mother Goose,** which opened on 18 December. Edwin Stevens, who assumed the tide role, created the book and lyrics, while the music was "composed and selected" by Max Hirschfield. From his lair in the Cavern of Gloom in the Region of Despair, Rusticus, the Bad Genius, labors to wrest Jill from Jack and award her to the wicked Baron Bosche. But a good fairy, Rose, intercedes. She gives Jack a magic flageolet and tells him where to find a magic pail. Before the inevitable happy ending and the final transformation of Our Childhood Fancies, Jack's quest takes him to the village of Hey-Down-Derry, an enchanted glen, an underwater Oyster Palace—where Jack watches the march of the Mermans—and the palace of the King of Hearts.

No further musicals appeared in New York until 28 December, when another London favorite, **Dorcas** (for which *Erminie's* Harry Paulton collaborated with Edward Paulton on the book while Watty Hydes and Clement Lockname did the score), opened at the Lyric the same evening Gustave Kerker and Hugh Morton's **An American Beauty** arrived at the Casino. The London musical described how an Englishman, engaged to a girl he has never met, determines to evaluate her by visiting her in disguise. She gets wind of the ploy and pulls one of her own. The Casino's show was plainly tacked together as a vehicle for Lillian Russell and had the virtue of not trying to call itself a comic opera or anything else on its program. Miss Russell played Gabrielle Dalmont, a young lady who goes riding, forgetting it is her wedding day. Circus proprietors Bangle, Budd, and Bingle spot her and offer her employment as the circus queen. She politely rejects the offer. But she conceives the idea of giving a circus ball. The Earl of Beverly (Harold Blake) falls in love with her and disguises himself as a gardener, hoping to woo and win her without the glamour of his station. When she declines his hand, he obtains a magic flower which causes anyone inhaling its fragrance to sleep and to fall in love with the first person she sees on waking. Of course the Earl arranges that it is he whom Gabrielle sees. But the groom Gabrielle has forgotten, Prince Schwepps (Owen Westford), convinces the earl that Gabrielle has learned his identity and is bluffing. The earl leaves, only to return and win Gabrielle again. Miss Russell made her entrance at the ball on a stage elephant and lingered to watch a lineup of specialties that filled out the ballroom scene. Her followers kept ticket sales brisk until the end of February, when she took the show on the road.

A completely different sort of lady arrived at the Bijou 29 December, the night after Miss Russell's opening. May Irwin, the leading singer of "coon songs," stalked on stage in John J. McNally's newest farce-comedy, **Courted into Court.** Dottie Dimple (Miss Irwin), an actress, decides to divorce her husband, Worthington Best, Jr. (John C. Rice), when he becomes jealous of the attention his own father (Raymond Hitchcock) pays to Dottie. The Judge (Joseph M. Sparks), hoping to marry Dottie himself, insists on granting the divorce even after Dottie reconsiders and wants the case dropped. Clara Palmer, Ada Lewis, and Jacques Kruger virtually completed the cast—an all-star lineup. Although on opening night Miss Lewis as a German dancer won the loudest applause for "The Oompah," two of Miss Irwin's biggest hits came from songs added to the play: "Mister Johnson Turn Me Loose" (by the same Ben Harney who had brought ragtime to New York) and "All Coons Look Alike To Me" (Ernest Hogan).

The first new show to appear in 1897 was also a farce-comedy, Charles Hoyt's **A Contented Woman** (4 January 1897, Hoyt's). But it was unusual in that instead of culling its songs willy-nilly as was farce-comedy's wont, it seems to have had a score by a single composer, Richard Stahl. Of course Hoyt had earlier used Percy Gaunt to write whole scores for his farce-comedies, but few of his fellow farceurs copied him. Hoyt resorted to the popular motif of a woman's rebellion for his story. When Benton Holme (William H. Currie), a mayoral candidate, rudely tears off a button his wife (Caroline Miskel-Hoyt) has sewn on incorrectly, she decides to run against him on a reform ticket. With women's suffrage in the air Hoyt found a receptive audience, although the success of A Contented Woman fell short of some of his earlier hits.

The preceding season's flop *Kismet* (12 August 1895) was revived the same night A Contented

Woman premiered. It failed once again, but the mere fact it was revived further illustrates the relative freedom from critical and financial burdens this epoch's musical theatre enjoyed.

The next night, 5 January, an importation, **Shamus O'Brien,** began a two-month run at the Broadway, depicting an Irish rebel's escape.

Charles E. Blaney's **A Boy Wanted** (18 January 1897, Star) became the second farce-comedy in a row to have songs by a single composer. In this case the music was by Harry James. Blaney's story unfolded the escapades of Phoney Dice in his efforts to find a soft berth and an easy buck. But neither the music nor the play was up to Broadway standards, and the show, after a week at the Star, returned to the hinterlands for which it had been conceived.

The 14th Street Theatre, like the Star, was generally looked on as a combination house. Every now and then, however, it played host to an attraction not quite right for Broadway. More often than not these were plays designed for specific ethnic groups, usually the Irish. Just such a play opened on 25 January when Chauncey Olcott appeared in Augustus Pitou's **Sweet Inniscarra.** It called itself a romantic drama, but in keeping with Olcott's practice half a dozen songs were written for the piece. Olcott portrayed Gerald O'Carroll, who returns to Ireland from London high life to woo Kate O'Donoghue (Georgia Busby). Although Kate's father has other plans for her, love triumphs. If this, like most Olcott vehicles, was more straight play than musical, with "Sweet Inniscarra," "Kate O'Donoghue," and "The Old Fashioned Mother" it showed greater concern with the pertinence of its songs than most farce-comedies or some more pretentious efforts demonstrated. The 14th Street Theatre was often content with bookings of one week or a fortnight. *Sweet Inniscarra* remained there the rest of the season.

At Gay Coney Island, one more farce-comedy, appeared for a week beginning 1 February at a combination house, the Columbus. Mistaken identities lead its stars, the team of J. Sherrie Matthews and Harry Bulger, a merry chase around the resort. Matthews and Bulger, along with Maurice Levi, composed most of the songs.

All through this period Boston continued actively mounting local productions. The success of the Bostonians had prompted a number of groups to form there in hopes of emulating their early prosperity. One was the Boston Cadets, and for this ensemble R. A. Barnet created a variation of "Jack and the Beanstalk," calling it **Simple Simon.** In Boston the good Fairy Queen helps Simple Simon in his courtship of Curly Locks, whose heart has been turned to stone by a witch.

By 1897, English musicals had supplanted French opéra bouffe as the reigning musical mode. While French plays frequently served as the inspiration for American librettos, few new French lyric works found their way across the Atlantic. Although sung in German, *Ta Ta-To To*, opening at the Irving Place on 11 February, was an exception. The piece departed quickly. A second French importation, **La Falote** (1 March 1897, Casino) confirmed the disfavor the Gallic pieces had fallen into when it struggled through a two-week run. Its silly plot was no help. A flirtatious baroness disguises herself as a "castle-haunting spook." Even J. Cheever Goodwin's adaptation was to no avail.

Between the two debacles, Weber and Fields changed bills at their music hall. One of the current theatrical hits was Stanley Weyman's *Under the Red Robe*, a play about Cardinal Richelieu. At the music hall it became **Under the Red Globe**, and its hero was Fishglue. The action now took place in Gaily's Gambling House, which audiences of the day understood as Daly's, next door. Audiences themselves were changing at Weber and Fields. "Music Hall" had long connoted food and, more especially, drink service, during the performance. To attract a better element the team announced service would be suspended while the play was on, and shortly thereafter service was discontinued altogether. While some patrons undoubtedly rued the loss of such amenities, Weber and Fields did succeed in attracting more couples, more women, and a generally higher social stratum than customarily attended music halls. Just how successful they were, and how rapid their success, was suggested when one reviewer noted the theatre was "packed to suffocation, every seat and every inch of standing room being occupied."

The extent to which the word "musical" in the title added box office appeal was shown when one of the most popular of all American actresses, Ada Rehan, revived Charlotte Cushman's once popular vehicle, *Meg Merrilies*, calling it not a "romantic melodrama" but rather a "romantic musical play."

The last outstanding success the Bostonians were to enjoy was Victor Herbert's **The Serenade** (16 March 1897, Knickerbocker). It had been given its world premiere in Cleveland a month earlier and then had been taken to Chicago with the rest of the Bostonians' repertory while it was polished. Looking back over the musical stage years later, the greatest of the Bostonians, Henry Clay Barnabee, concluded the work was "the best American contribution to genuine comic opera—as distinguished from musical comedy, which I consider 'Robin Hood' to be—up to now revealed." Barnabee's strange classification of *Robin Hood* (28 September 1891) probably stemmed from his belief that the comic part of the villainous sheriff was the pivotal role, whereas comic elements were secondary in *The Serenade*. Herbert's scholarly and thoughtful biographer, Edward N. Waters, shares some of Barnabee's sentiments: "The score was one of the best Herbert ever did, and he never surpassed some of its concerted and dramatic numbers." The public of 1897 most certainly fell in love with Herbert's melodious songs, especially the famous serenade itself, "I Love Thee, I Adore Thee." Harry B. Smith's libretto, while not on a par with Herbert's music, sufficed. Unfortunately, Herbert was never to collaborate with a first-rate librettist.

In *The Serenade* everyone loves the ravishing Dolores (Jessie Bartlett Davis). Her guardian, the Duke of Santa Cruz (Barnabee), would keep her for himself; Alvarado (W. H. MacDonald), the dashing baritone of the Madrid Opera, courts her; and Romero (Eugene Cowles), president of the Royal Madrid Brigandage Association (he is a brigand on alternate days, a monk the rest of the time), also pines for her. Alvarado's life is complicated by Yvonne (Alice Nielsen), whom he jilted but who still loves him. The duke hides Dolores in a convent. With the strains of the serenade to guide them, Alvarado and Dolores eventually are able to rush into each other's arms. Yvonne must be content with Lopez (William E. Philip), secretary to the brigands. The show played to packed houses until 22 May when previous commitments forced the Bostonians to move on. The success of Nielsen as Yvonne encouraged her to leave the Bostonians and form her own company. Taking Cowles with her, she inflicted a wound on the Bostonians that hastened their demise. But the ambitious Miss Nielsen was to prove no more loyal to the comic-opera stage than she had been to the group that nurtured her.

Vaudeville still eyed legitimate musicals with uncertainty. Farce-comedies in particular were draining away some of the best talents from the variety stage. So it is not too surprising that vaudeville houses continued to seek ways of identifying themselves with the legitimate arena. Koster and Bial's, instead of performing miniature comic opera, tried approaching the revue format by giving a bill a title and by having a librettist and composer tie the specialties together. On

22 March they called their bill **In Gayest Manhattan; or, Around New York in Ninety Minutes.** The indefatigable Harry B. Smith wrote some lyrics and dialogue and Ludwig Englander wrote some songs. Smith's slim plot had a retired tragedian, Delsarte Flam—played by Henry E. Dixey—audition potential pupils. Somehow an excuse was discovered to allow a grand march by chorus girls dressed to represent firefighters and also to permit a glimpse of the sort of spectacle early twentieth-century extravaganzas would offer when the girls posed to form a gigantic "floral fountain." But the novelty had no noticeable appeal; no one was deceived or no one cared. In a few weeks the house quietly dropped the title.

Miss Manhattan (23 March 1897, Wallack's) was an extravaganza with a plot suspiciously like the one *Miss Philadelphia* had used in the City of Brotherly Love the year before (Broadway would see that play in the following season). Of course, William Penn gave place to Father Knickerbocker, who visits Chollie Knickerbocker in a dream to admonish the young man's spendthrift ways and who finds himself taken on a tour of the town. He is beset by bicycles, flying motor-carriages, and a cable car ("realistically depicted rounding Dead Man Curve"). At one point an up-to-date Miss Manhattan kicks off his hat. (Kicking off hats seems to have been modish in this theatrical year. Earlier, in *An American Beauty*, Lillian Russell had sung of a saucy French demimondaine who teased erring husbands by promising them "I keek off ze 'igh chapeau/Wiz ze wee little point of my toe, Papa!") Knickerbocker's progress was further halted as a women's brass band provided accompaniment for yet another Amazon drill. The cast was filled with minor names destined to remain unimportant. The score was by various hands, but the librettist was a writer new to the musical theatre—one who would remain around some while—George V. Hobart.

Whites in blackface were the attraction at Hi Henry's Minstrels, which stopped over at the Star for a week beginning 29 March 1897. "Hindoo jugglers" and a cornet player, not truly standard minstrel fare, were on their bill.

Eleven nights later Stanislaus Stange and Julian Edwards brought in their second offering of the season, **The Wedding Day** (8 April 1897, Casino). Actually it was an adaptation of Audran's *La Petite Fronde*, and in this instance Edwards merely supplemented the score. In its story a French peasant girl, a lady, and a baker combined their efforts to secure a Franco-Spanish treaty. Although it offered three top stars in the same show—a rarity at the time—it

was something of a disappointment. Jefferson De Angelis, Della Fox, and Lillian Russell combined could not earn it more than seventy-two performances, in two separate engagements.

For a few weeks Herbert had two works running simultaneously when *The Wizard of the Nile* (4 November 1895) played a popular return engagement beginning 19 April.

Miss Manhattan was in her last days when Weber and Fields offered her a mate, **Mister New York, Esquire.** The new bill, their last for the season, marked a departure from the burlesques they had rapidly made famous. They called it a "travesty" to suggest that it mocked things in general and was not built around a specific play. Audiences were not appreciative. Good businessmen that they were, Weber and Fields withdrew it and never used the term "travesty" again.

Ivan Caryll and Lionel Monckton's London hit, **The Circus Girl** (23 April 1897, Daly's), arrived as April's last offering, delighting Anglophile New York at its producer's own theatre almost as much as it had charmed the West End at Edwardes's Gaiety. James T. Powers led the funmaking, in a tale of a schoolgirl in love with a circus performer who turns out to be an heir.

Audiences at cheap-priced theatres were far less demanding than playgoers at first-class houses, yet even they had their limits. Trade sheets reported that hooting, booing, and stomping at **The Isle of Gold** (26 April 1897, Olympic) were so deafening that the musical, apparently giving its first performances anywhere, was taken off permanently at week's end. The papers did not say what the show was about.

A German musical, **At the French Ball** (3 May 1897, Bijou), also met with a cool reception. The production was "a traveling show," stopping only briefly in New York, which featured Fanny Rice ("moderation is scarcely her watchword") as a shoemaker's wife who dreams of owning a silk gown. It lingered only a month. The vogue for almost anything English was acknowledged in the columns of "The Matinee Girl," a weekly feature in the *Dramatic Mirror*. Its anonymous authoress asked, "Why is it that the English composers send us over such dainty verses and tripping airs in comparison to some of the domestic stuff we get?" The lady concluded, "I am getting to be a bit of an Anglomaniac so far as musical comedies are concerned." History has not shared her judgments. Like her male contemporaries she mistook the high style and cohesion of English offerings for genuine, overriding quality.

Having catered since late January to its Irish audience, the 14th Street Theatre apparently aimed at a different crowd when it presented **The Widow Goldstein** on 17 May. Another farce-comedy with songs from various sources, it recounted how Hettie Goldstein (Jennie Reiffarth) outtricks the sly, greedy Cyrus Russell (R. F. Cotton), thereby allowing a number of young lovers to wed. It also included, as did so many of its type, jugglers, a waiter turned magician, a "collegate" band, and other variety acts.

The Bijou replaced *At the French Ball* on 24 May with a repertory company to play old favorites such as *Erminie* and *The Chimes of Normandy* for "a summer season." A further sign hot weather was at hand was the back-to-back (and side-by-side) arrival of two revues. **A Round of Pleasure** raised its curtain at the Knickerbocker on 24 May, while **The Whirl of the Town** romped into the Casino the next night. Both, of course, had plots. Sydney Rosenfeld's, for the former, was the simpler of the two. The Duke of Marlinspike (Richard Carle) is shown around America by Welkin Ring (Jerome Sykes) and his daughters, Aurora (Marguerite Sylva) and Niobe (Marie Celeste). What the duke saw was "over 100" performers (and 200 mechanical horses in a miniature Madison Square Garden Horse Show). He witnessed a dagger dance, and "Dutch" clowning by Gus and Max Rogers. The duke reciprocated by parodying Hamlet. Ludwig Englander provided everyone with music. The show received a divided press—although its advertisements were quick to acknowledge the *Herald*'s praise of "one real round of Pleasure" in an early use of excerpts from notices in daily ads. But the criticisms apparently told. By 19 June substantial revisions had been announced, and soon ads advised, "Something New Every Night." The show lasted six weeks, closed for vacation, then reopened as *One Round of Pleasure* for a fortnight prior to touring.

Hugh Morton and Gustave Kerker's *The Whirl of the Town* at the Casino met with a happier response. Audiences were coming to look forward to the house's annual summer revue, and the house was perfecting its presentations. Morton's plot was not much different from Rosenfeld's. Bibulous, kleptomaniacal Willie Badboy (Dan Daly) steals Dimples (Madge Lessing), a mermaid, from the aquarium and takes her on a trip around New York. Pursued by her keeper (Louis Harrison), as well as by a detective (David Warfield) and the multi-disguised proprietors (John Slavin and Harry MacDonough) of a freak museum, they visit a cable car, the Rialto,

the Met (where they watch a "vaudeville"), and the Cave of Jewels off Coney Island. Typical of Morton's dialogue was the half-high Willie's response to the mermaid's urgent need for a tank. He assures her he's quite a tank himself. Mimics, jugglers, and other specialties filled the scenes. *The Whirl of the Town* far outstripped its next-door neighbor, compiling 127 showings.

While *A Round of Pleasure* was soliciting firstnighters' approval in New York, the Bostonians, out on the road, offered their faithful followers a new American comic opera. But their musical adaptation of **Rip Van Winkle** suffered the same unkind reception most of their native material was accorded. The troupe quickly dropped the piece.

The economy and generally lax quality of the year's shows were not the only things adversely affecting attendance. As early as 27 March trade journals were lamenting that "bicycle fever" was hurting theatres, and on 29 May the *Dramatic Mirror*'s Chicago correspondent bewailed, "Those bicycle legs are beginning to knock the everlasting spots out of the big downtown playhouses." By July the number of active roof gardens had dwindled by half compared with the preceding season, and few regular theatres were open.

1897–1898

The number of new musical shows dropped noticeably during the new season. The lessening vogue for farce-comedy was partly responsible. To the extent that the decline in numbers reflected the passing of these relatively haphazard concoctions it meant a step forward for coherent musical comedy writing. Unfortunately, the decline resulted more from the continued creative exhaustion of the lyric stage as a whole. Economic doldrums, the third cause of the falling off of production, ended abruptly in March when the U. S. S. *Maine* was blown up in Havana harbor. Bicycle fever speedily succumbed to war fever. A month later we were officially at war, and the economy began to hum again.

A freakish affair was the first entry of the new season. Although **Captain Cook** was billed as a "comic opera"—and did indeed have a comic-opera plot and score—it was primarily a gigantic spectacle. It was mounted not at one of the standard legitimate houses but in the huge arena of Madison Square Garden on 12 July. The premiere was attended by Queen Liliuokalani of Hawaii. The story, if it could be heard in the unmicrophoned vastness of the building, depicted Captain Cook's reception as a god when he arrived in Hawaii. The captain is awarded Princess Ia Ia. But Oponuii, who loves the princess, leads a rebellion to discredit and expel Cook. His rebellion coincides with an eruption of Mauna Loa, convincing superstitious islanders that Oponuii is opposed by the gods. But the kindly Cook assures the natives that Oponuii is a good man. He gives the princess in Marriage to the youthful rebel and sails away. Written by inexperienced hands, the show was a quick failure.

The strange creatures and spectacular scenery three mortals encounter on their way to the North Pole were the principal attractions in **Nature** (26 August 1897, Academy of Music). The leader of the expedition was Sir John Hampton (Edwin W. Hoff), a tenor, but the audience's favorite seemingly was droll Hans Schultz (Joseph Cawthorn), especially after he offered it his version of the intermezzo from *Cavalleria Rusticana*—on his concertina. Marie Bonfanti, of *The Black Crook* fame, was credited with choreographing some of the sumptuous ballets. A show to which parents could bring children on matinee days, *Nature* played seven profitable weeks at the huge auditorium.

On 30 August two more musicals appeared. **Very Little Faust and More Marguerite** raised its curtain at the same Olympia Theatre in which Hammerstein had offered his own *Marguerite* two seasons before. The new work was a French burlesque adapted for the American stage and originally presented at Manhattan Beach for a summer run prior to its Broadway sally. Broadway felt that something was lost in the sea crossing, and the show survived just twenty-four showings.

But J. J. McNally's latest farce-comedy, **The Good Mr. Best** (30 August 1897, Garrick), had an even shorter stay, just two weeks. Between the various incidental songs and specialties, McNally unfolded the confusion created when an uncle gives twins large allowances on the condition they never marry. Tom does marry—his uncle's ex-wife, in fact. But he hides both his marriage and his twin brother's death from his generous relative. When the uncle shows up Tom is forced to impersonate his late brother, Tim. He discovers his brother was even naughtier than he.

Weber and Fields' Music Hall relit on 2 September. The principal attraction was **The Glad Hand; or, Secret Servants**, which managed to twit both the Yukon Gold Rush, then at its height, and William Gillette's popular *Secret Service*. While Weber and Fields's spy waited for his all-important

dispatch a little gambling seemed in order. Only the gamblers—Sam Bernard, Peter F. Dailey, Charles J. Ross, and John Kelly—apparently flustered by the tension of the wait, got their games confused. A brouhaha ensued when one of the players threw his dice and insisted he rolled a flush. Mabel Fenton arrived on the scene to insert a spoof of the famous demimondaine Cléo de Mérode. Oddly, the material was by an Englishman, Kenneth Lee. It was his first and only effort for the house. But a far more important figure also made his debut at the theatre with the same production. Julian Mitchell took over as stager. Under his reign the productions, despite the minuscule stage, achieved an opulence and style that made them the talk of the town. His chorus line rapidly established a reputation as more eye-filling than even the Casino's. In their day his girls basked in much the renown that Ziegfeld's were to have a generation later, and it was not accidental that Ziegfeld hired Mitchell to stage his early *Follies*.

The London hit **In Town** (6 September 1897, Knickerbocker) had a libretto by Adrian Ross and James T. Tanner, and melodies by Osmond Carr. The evening proved a disappointment to New Yorkers. *In Town* is generally acknowledged as the first of George Edwardes's new style of Gaiety shows and as such is often considered the first English musical comedy. It premiered in London 15 October 1892, one day short of a year before *A Gaiety Girl's* premiere. Like its successor it opened at the Prince of Wales Theatre, but unlike *A Gaiety Girl* (which opened in New York 17 September 1894) it did eventually move to the Gaiety. Its libretto told how the out-of-pocket Captain Coddington invited all the ladies of the Ambiguity Theatre to lunch. The captain's friend, Lord Clanside, agrees to foot the bill on the condition he can join the party. A group of uninvited guests appears, and everyone moves to the Ambiguity to watch a rehearsal. Coddington woos and wins the prima donna. The looseness of the story allowed for numerous interpolations and changes. W. Louis Bradfield, who had played the male lead in *A Gaiety Girl*, was Coddington.

> **JULIAN MITCHELL**, the most prolific of all musical stagers, was born in 1854 and while still a youngster began his theatrical career as a call boy at Niblo's. He soon found himself on the other side of the footlights, dancing in an early revival of *The Black Crook*.

By the time he was twenty he was producing and dancing in his own touring productions. But a growing deafness—which became almost total with time—forced him to abandon performing. Charles Hoyt hired him to direct *The Maid and the Moonshiner* and *A Trip to Chinatown.*

Signs that the ailing Hoyt was losing his once surefire theatrical know-how were all too evident in **A Stranger in New York** (13 September 1897, Garrick). The stranger, played by droll Harry Conor, who had served Hoyt so well in *A Trip to Chinatown*, runs into some people preparing to attend a ball and is mistaken by them for an out-of-town celebrity. Hoyt's plot was thinner than his plots had been of late, but the playing, singing, and dancing put the evening over. Conor had a show-stopper in "When Someone Pulls The Strings." The comedian sang this put-down of behind-the-scenes practices all the while he toyed with a mechanical monkey on a string. Fading Amazon marches were spoofed in "Dead Broke Brigade." As usual with Hoyt, the character names were fun, this time including Haight Work and May Ketchum. The show played at the Garrick for eight weeks and subsequently toured for over a year. This was a far cry from some of Hoyt's earlier successes, but most likely still highly profitable.

If parents could have bundled their children off to *Nature*, they could just as easily have taken them to see **The Fair in Midgettown** (20 September 1897, Star). Of course the little people of Midgettown were the Liliputians, unquestionably aging but apparently as irresistible as ever. Their fair became a brightly colored, hilarious carnival, made all the more joyful with their travesty of *The Geisha*, another scene in which the midgets appeared dressed as famous historical figures (Washington, Napoleon, etc.), and by a brief, flickering look at that new wonder, the cinematograph. One critic recorded of the *Geisha* takeoff: "The chorus sang in English, the midgets in German, and the band played in the Coney Island dialect." Like *Nature* it stayed around seven weeks, then went out on tour.

Francis Wilson brought *Half a King* (14 September 1896) back for a brief engagement at the Broadway on the 20th. Another importation from London, **The French Maid** (27 September 1897, Herald Square) had the longest run of any of the season's musicals—160 performances. E. E. Rice produced and staged the work for which Walter Slaughter wrote the music and Basil Hood the libretto, whose exasperatingly complicated plot (the *Times* devoted half a column attempting to dissect it) begins when the British send a free-loading Indian prince to a French spa. Marguerite Sylva headed a cast that included Anna Robinson and Eva Davenport.

The same night *The French Maid* premiered, **McFadden's Row of Flats** began a one-week stay at the People's, a combination house normally outside the range of this history. All summer long its producers had taken large, illustrated ads in trade journals urging theatre bookers around the country to schedule it into their houses. Typically, it differed from shows designed to play the great Manhattan houses more in degree than in kind. The story, by E. W. Townsend, found Tim McFadden and Jacob Baumgartner rivals for alderman. A tie vote can be broken only by the flats' poet, Terrence McSwatt. McFadden gets Mrs. Murphy to consent to her daughter Mary Ellen's marrying McSwatt, thus winning the election. The music was largely by one Ivan L. Davis. In extending the show the courtesy of a review, the *Dramatic Mirror* singled out the songs as "pretty."

McFadden's Row of Flats was not the only 1897–1898 creation intended primarily or wholly for the hinterlands. The list of touring musicals setting out in September included *Bimbo of Bombay, In Old Madrid, Bo-Peep,* and *Darkest Africa.* None, except a heavily revised *Bo-Peep,* ever approached the Rialto, and most, apparently, left no record at all behind. A number of trade journal listings were artists' companies rather than individual shows. The De Wolf Hopper Opera Company or the Francis Wilson Opera Company played the big time. But a dozen or so lesser names, long forgotten, took smaller, generally seedier, contingents around giving one- and two-night stands.

September's last offering, **The Belle of New York** (28 September 1897, Casino), is a curious, fascinating anomaly. Another Hugh Morton and Gustave Kerker contrivance (which George Lederer not only produced, but also staged), it was greeted with middling enthusiasm and racked up a New York run of only fifty-six showings. But after its American tour it traveled to London, where Englishmen were as taken with it as Americans had been for the past several seasons with West End musicals. It played there for 674 performances, the first American musical ever to run a year or more in the West End. Long runs in Paris and Berlin followed. Both Paris and London have entertained periodic revivals. Morton's story had Violet Gray (Edna May), a fashion-conscious Salvation Army belle, mend the spendthrift ways of Harry Brown (Harry Davenport), who has been cast out by his hypocritical, "reformist" father, Ichabod (Dan Daly). The elder Brown is the president of an organization known as (depending on which text one reads) either the "Young Men's Rescue League and Anti-Cigarette Society of Cohoes" or the "Anti-Cigarette and Enjoyment League Against All Amusements." So grateful is the elder Brown that he is prepared to annul Harry's marriage to Cora Angelique (Ada Dare) and force his son to wed Violet. The Salvation Army belle realizes that Harry and Cora are genuinely in love, and that she could not earn Harry's affection, so she purposely alienates Ichabod with a risqué French ditty, "At Ze Naughty Folies Bergère (My feet zey fly up in ze air)." Before he meets his salvation, by honest labor as a soda jerk, Harry encounters a variety of clowns, including an infuriatingly polite lunatic (David Warfield). The first-act finale was set in Chinatown and began with a "showy, bizarre ballet." Kerker's music, as undistinguished as always, was nevertheless as good as he wrote and exemplified by the title number. The song was introduced by "a mixed-ale pugilist," Blinky Bill (William Cameron), to announce Violet's initial appearance—in the Chinatown scene just before the first-act curtain!

The attitudes and styles of Morton's guys and dolls in "The Anti-Cigarette League" (sung by Ichabod) or "The Purity Brigade" (Violet's principal number) contrasted strikingly with those of Frank Loesser's a half-century later:

> I hope I do not shock
> My late converted flock
> By changing to a costume that could be described
>   as snappy,
> I would not have you think
> That I would ever sink
> From my high state of piety, to anything claptrappy.

In both New York and London young Miss May rocketed to stardom in the title role.

Two productions of Audran's La Poupée came to town during the season. In both instances the story told of a monk in an impoverished monastery who learns his uncle will make the monastery rich if the monk will leave it and marry. The monk attempts to honor both his vows and his uncle by marrying a doll, but the uncle, learning of the plan, slyly substitutes a real girl. The first, and more successful, version opened 21 October with Anna Held at what until a few weeks before had been the Olympia and now, under new management, was called the Lyric. The second appeared briefly at Daly's in mid-April.

Having tired of playing Kibosh in Victor Herbert's The Wizard of the Nile (4 November 1895), Frank Daniels handed his role over to a replacement and commissioned Herbert and Harry B. Smith to write a new operetta for him. Although the first announcements insisted the show would be a sequel to the earlier show and that Daniels would again impersonate the magician, it arrived with a different tale. In The Idol's Eye (25 October 1897, Broadway), Daniels played Abel Conn, "an aeronaut who seeks and finds adventure." He finds it in India after Jamie McSnuffy (Alf C. Whelan), "the last of the McSnuffys of Castle McSnuffy," a kleptomaniac drummed out of a Highlands regiment, steals a sacred £100,000 ruby from the eye of an idol. The ruby magically makes everyone love the possessor. The ruby's mate, a stone that makes its owner hated, lies not far away in the jungle. Ned Winner (Maurice Darcy), an American novelist, is in India to court a Cuban beauty, Maraquita Tabasco (Helen Redmond). Her father (Will Danforth) insists Ned must earn £100,000 before he will consent to her marrying the young man. At this juncture Conn appears on the scene. He picks up the wrong ruby, causing the lovers to have a falling-out. The two gems change hands from moment to moment, realigning emotions faster than Abel can handle them. The show succeeded largely on the strength of the genial Daniels's clowning, including a first appearance dropping from the flies in a balloon and landing on an idol. He stopped the show—and ultimately provided the basis for a future vehicle—singing of "The Tattooed Man":

> He had designs upon himself,
> She had designs on him,
> And she loved to look at the picture book
> Which he had on ev'ry limb.

The song recounted the resourcefulness of the unfaithful "human picture gallery," concluding with one of the word-plays so beloved of the era, "You can beat a tattoo,/But you can't beat a tattooed man!" Herbert's unpretentious score marked a falling off from the richness and fine melodies of The Serenade (16 March 1897). But the critic of the Evening Post, waxing unduly ecstatic, nevertheless glimpsed the immediate future when he wrote of Herbert, "Indeed, now that Suppé is dead, Sullivan written out, and Strauss practically quiescent, he has no superior in Europe." After two months in New York the show headed out for another of Daniels's extended road tours.

McSorley's Twins (25 October 1897, Grand Opera) dealt with the problems McSorley encounters in his bid to become an alderman, especially after his daughters, Kate and Duplicate, intervene. Nat M. Wills, rising fast on vaudeville stages, brought his tramp act aboard, and room was found for a *Camille* travesty and "divaricate" dances.

The persistent popularity of romantic Irish pieces found a long-lived example in **An Irish Gentleman** (29 November 1897, 14th St.). The hero was Jack Shannon (Andrew Mack) and, stopping only long enough to pour out his heart in song at intervals, he bests a heartless villain and wins the hand of a lovely colleen who turns out, to no one's surprise but Jack's, to be an heiress. Mack's show-stoppers included "My Heart's Delight" and "An Irish Street Singer." The star toured with the show for several seasons and revived it successfully in 1904.

By November of 1897 the Trust or Syndicate had become so visible and so obnoxious in its methods that the *Dramatic Mirror* began a series of weekly supplements recounting its brutalities and adding horrified and saddened commentaries by those theatrical figures affected. It seemed at the time the new monopoly would drive its enemies from the boards and kill any show not bringing a handsome return. History recorded otherwise, but the shock of the Syndicate's initial actions still threw much of Broadway into a panic. Henry Clay Barnabee, Francis Wilson, and a number of other artists claimed the Trust brought an end to the era of the performer-manager. And it is true that within a few years musical stars no longer produced their own shows. But the healthy salaries stars were beginning to draw, coupled with their willingness to let others take the financial risks and managerial bothers, probably had more to do with the decline of the actor-manager than did any machination of Klaw, Erlanger, Frohman, and their cohorts.

May Irwin arrived with another of the song-filled comedies she was known for. Its story was reminiscent of an earlier Irwin vehicle, *Courted into Court* (26 December 1896). In **The Swell Miss Fitzwell** (15 November 1897, Bijou) she played a poor American girl who marries a French count. The count's father disinherits him. Miss Fitzwell sets up a shop, but a misunderstanding there with her spouse leads to a divorce suit. When the misunderstanding is resolved the divorce action proves infuriatingly difficult to withdraw.

November's only other musical was the first of two Philadelphia hits to reach Manhattan during the season. **1999** (15 November 1897, Casino) had been mounted at the Chestnut Street Theatre the previous April, ran out the season, and returned after a summer hiatus for a fall engagement. Called the "most complete, costly and up-to-date musical" the city had ever seen, it had book and lyrics by Herman Lee Ensign and music by Edward Hoist, two names all but unknown to Broadway. Set at a coeducational institution in a world dominated by women, it recounted the complications that ensue when the school's lady astronomer, Professor Brent (Clara Alene Jewell), invites a group of Martians to visit the earth. Professor Brent hopes to make marriages for her daughters Electra (Claresse Agnew) and Corona (Bertha Waltzinger). She succeeds, but she herself also wins the hand of the king of Mars. A subplot depicted the arrival by a flying machine of a Spanish Countess (Mathilde Cottrelly) to woo a bogus millionaire. The subplot nearly wrecked the show at its New York opening when the flying machine became stuck in its tracks and could not be made to operate. *1999* had been rushed in to fill the vacancy left by *The Belle of New York* and remained at the Casino for five weeks.

December's first offering (on the 2nd) was **Pousse Café,** Weber and Fields's replacement for *The Glad Hand.* Its subtitle, *The Worst Born,* poked fun at one of the season's great straight-play hits, David Belasco's *The First Born,* although the musical had fun at the expense of *La Poupée* and J. M. Barrie's *The Little Minister* as well. Even its scenery was contrived to resemble sets from shows that were travestied. The evening tied its burlesques together with a plot that bravely aimed its barbs at the Trust. Bierheister (Fields) and Weishaben (Sam Bernard) form a "skindecat" to cheat Weinshoppen (Weber) out of royalties from a mechanical doll he has invented. Bierheister invites Weinshoppen to sign a contract sight unseen:

Bierheister: Here is der disagreement papers.... .
 Now I von't read der commencing of der contract to you because dere are a few tings I vish to write in after you sign your name to it.

So successful had the team become in less than two seasons that they were able to raise the price of seats for the first ten rows to $2.00 without serious complaint.

Another in the decreasingly fashionable farce-comedies began a brief stay when William Gill's **My Boys** (6 December 1897, Manhattan) opened. Using music by assorted, uncredited composers, it told of Silas Plummer's plans to marry off his five sons when unbeknown to him the five boys are married. Silas (George Richards) spent much of the evening in a running gag tripping over any steps that crossed his path. Gill's dialogue ran to such repartee as

Son: Well?
Silas: You don't look it.

Another 6 December arrival, at the American, was one of the three companies of the Castle Square Opera Players, another group whose repertory ranged from comic to grand opera. They, too, played out the season. (A second contingent of the Castle Square Players was in the midst of a two-year stay in Philadelphia.)

The most successful American musical of the season bowed next. At the time, the popularity of **The Highwayman** (13 December 1897, Broadway) bolstered greatly Reginald De Koven's sagging reputation, even though it has since joined all of De Koven's scores except *Robin Hood* in obscurity. Its Harry B. Smith libretto told a tale not unlike that earlier hit. When Sir John Hawkhurst (Edwin White) ruins Dick Fitzgerald (Joseph O'Hara) at the gaming tables, Fitzgerald becomes a highwayman under the name of Captain Scarlet. He and Lady Constance (Hilda Clark) fall in love. Hawkhurst seizes a pardon meant for Fitzgerald, but Constance retrieves it from him at gunpoint. If the comic villain, the Sheriff of Nottingham, was for many the principal delight of *Robin Hood*, the equally comic, conceited constable, Foxy Quiller, stole the new comic opera. In hefty Jerome Sykes's hands he became such a popular figure that Smith and De Koven later were prompted to write a second work about him. Smith's autobiography reveals something of the caliber of the period's bit players as well as of the era's idea of humor. According to the librettist an actor was chagrined when a line of his received one of the biggest laughs of the evening each night. The line, delivered by a young sailor, read, "I would rather be Lord High Admiral of England's navy with you for a wife than a common sailor without you." The actor, chagrined or no, at least had steady employment, for *The Highwayman* ran out the season.

The few critics who took notice of **Protecto** (20 December 1897, People's) considered it a vaudeville masquerading as a spectacle. Its acrobats were said to be better than its singers and dancers.

New Yorkers failed to greet E. E. Rice's production of **The Ballet Girl** (21 December 1897, Manhattan) as enthusiastically as had provincial England. The plot described the rivalry between a fortune-hunting father and his carefree son for the affections of a ballet dancer. David Lythgoe, Louise Willis-Hepner, Allene Crater, and Thomas Ricketts helped enliven J. T. Tanner's book, Adrian Ross's lyrics, and Carl Kiefert's music.

Two more young ladies bounced in six nights later. **The Telephone Girl** (27 December 1897, Casino) was another Gustave Kerker and Hugh Morton collaboration, one New Yorkers took to more eagerly than they had the team's *Belle of New York* (28 September 1897). The show's initial run of 104 performances almost doubled the stay of the other show, and in June it returned for an additional three weeks. Estelle Coocoo (Clara Lipman), a telephone operator, is furious at the attention Beauty Fairfax (Eleanor Elton) pays to Estelle's young man. Estelle eavesdrops on phone calls between Beauty and the man who is keeping her, Colonel Goldtop (Charles Dickson). She disguises herself as Beauty's maid, gets incriminating evidence, and persuades Beauty to give up chasing her beau. Clara Lipman's husband, Louis Mann, another of the many German-dialect comedians taking over as Broadway's principal funnymen, played a telephone repairman, Hans Nix. Nix thinks nothing of making a phone call to the warden of Sing Sing to accuse him of harboring thieves. He also flustered the other principals by hiding behind a screen and squirting seltzer at them.

Miss Philadelphia premiered the same night. The musical had been done originally two seasons before at Philadelphia's Chestnut Street Opera House. It was such a success it went through two "editions" and then spent most of the 1896–1897 season on the road. It had featured one rising young comedian, William Collier, for most of its early run, but by the time it reached New York another rising young star, Joseph Cawthorn, had replaced Collier. As has been mentioned, the story was similar to the one used later by *Miss Manhattan*. William Penn returns to visit a young man called William Penn, Jr., and together with Ruth Springarden (Springarden was then a fashionable street in Philadelphia) they embark on a tour of the city. They call at the Union League, the Mint, Wanamaker's Department Store, and an inn on the Wissahickon (all actual places). Among characters they meet are Dodge Trolleys, "a rapid young man about town"; Prestissimo, an Italian street singer; and Etta Candie, "a real sweet thing." The show played briefly at one of New York's combination houses, the Star, and continued on its tour.

Charges of plagiarism flew back and forth after **The Nancy Hanks** (27 December 1897, Garden) reached Broadway in the wake of a long cross-country tour. Competing musicals accused Frank Tannehill, Jr., author of the book and the show's costar, of stealing some of their best scenes. Tannehill retorted that his show had been on the boards before the other shows had gone into rehearsal, even if it had been brought into Manhattan tardily. The author played Richard Chandos, who, with his friend, the Marquis de la Rochelle (Harry Beresford), is evicted by their landlady for nonpayment of rent. A music hall star, Pearl Dodo (Marie Jansen), lets them use her apartment while she is on tour. At one point the marquis shaves off his mustache and pretends to be a lady. When Chandos's aunt, Hetty Evergreen (Tannehill), appears unexpectedly, he tells her he is Chandos's wife. (Most audiences were aware of an actual Hetty Green, a notoriously rich miser and quite famous in her day.) "Singing and dancing 'specialties'" played "an important part" in the entertainment.

They played an even more important part in **A Hot Old Time** (27 December 1897, Grand Opera), which used a shopworn tour-of-the-city frame as plot and which starred a big name in contemporary vaudeville, Johnny Ray. One critic compared it to "a glass of beer... covered with froth."

Apart from some German operetta sung in German at the Irving Place Theatre, the only musicals of sorts to arrive in New York in January 1898 were farce-comedies.

Two once famous, now forgotten comics, Hap Ward and Harry Vokes, headed the cast of **The Governors** (3 January 1898, Hoyt's). As usual they played Percy and Harold, who for this outing run a hotel but pretend they are state governors. A lady approaches them, telling them her husband is in prison and, when they offer to see about a pardon, begging them to keep him there. The boys also own a share in a mine and, as everybody knew they would,

strike it rich just before eleven o'clock. Specialties included a quartet singing "musty songs."

A Hired Girl (10 January 1898, Star) by Charles E. Blaney slanted toward burlesque; its title role was played by James T. Kelly in drag. The role had little to do with the main story line in which Lord Green Goods is pursued by a female detective, U. Bet Gilbert. When she realizes he is innocent of the crime he has supposedly committed, she marries him. The musical side of the evening featured an old minstrel, Willis J. Sweatnam, who, in the role of Link Missing, sang many of his old minstrel favorites.

R. A. Barnet continued to work with the Cadets in Boston. On 7 February they presented his latest work (with music by E. W. Corliss) at the Tremont there. **Queen of the Ballet** marked a departure from the children's extravaganza he had done the preceding year. The story was right out of the English and burgeoning American musical comedy tradition. Conspirators deprive Jack Hardwicke (Walter S. Hawkins) of his fortune. When he retrieves it he also wins Beatrice Jerome (Sheafe C. Rose), Queen of the Jollity Ballet.

In **Who Is Who** (7 February 1898, Third Ave.) a clientless lawyer implicates his partner in fictitious crimes so that he will have someone to represent. He also courts the daughter of the show's Dutch-dialect comedian. Eight pretty chorus girls raised their voices in "The Race Track Girls," "Flirting With The Man In The Moon," and "The Dutch Saengerfest."

The rambunctious Maggie Cline found a vehicle in the loosely plotted **A Baggage Check** (14 February 1898, Star). She also found an excuse for belting out her inevitable "Throw Him Down, McCloskey."

On 15 February the Spanish blew up the American battleship *Maine* in Havana harbor. When the Primrose and West Minstrels arrived at the Grand Opera House on the 21st, they offered not only traditional minstrel numbers along with a ventriloquist and tumblers, but a saber-rattling new song, "Uncle Sam Tell Us Why You Are Waiting."

Both new musicals arriving in Manhattan in February were failures. A German operetta, **Lilli Tse** (17 February 1898, Daly's), survived thirty-five performances as curtain raiser to a straight play, while **A Normandy Wedding** (21 February 1898, Herald Square) fell three performances short of that dismal figure. The show had initially opened in the Midwest in September as *Papa Gou Gou*. Its librettists, J. Cheever Goodwin and Charles Alfred Byrne, and its composer, William Furst, spent the next five and a half months trying to whip it into shape. Thomas Q. Seabrooke had originally starred, but by the time Broadway saw the musical Richard F. Carroll had replaced him as an unprincipled old cider-maker determined to get rich and find a wealthy husband for his daughter. Based on a French play, translated as *The Goose Girl*, and filled with American slang that made no effort to retain any Gallic flavor, the musical abandoned its travels after New York rejected it.

By the time **Sinbad; or, The Maid of Balsora** (14 March 1898, American) opened, war fever had risen to new heights, so Harry B. Smith's tale of Sinbad's struggles to rescue his beloved Ninetta from the villainous smuggler, Snarleyow, not only took the characters to the good ship *Roc*, the frozen, glittering Valley of Diamonds, a cannibal island, and Sinbad's palace, but also allowed them to inspect the White Squadron. Of course, Sinbad's guardian fairy, Cupid, was no small help in these matters. Among the other figures in the story were Count Spaghetti, Salamagundi, and Maraschino. Sinbad was presented as a trouser role, but Sinbad's venal father was played by young Raymond Hitchcock, although at this early date he still received short shrift from the critics. The musical was produced by the Castle Square Opera Co., which gave no credit in its programs to any composer.

Weber and Fields introduced their final change of bill on St. Patrick's Day. One of the hits of the year was Paul M. Potter's *The Conquerors*, the story of a cynical Prussian officer's attack on a French maiden. She defends her virtue in Gallic style, throwing the wine she had been ordered to drink in the officer's face. In the new version, **The Con-Curers**, the girl is ordered to eat a pie. According to Weber and Fields's biographer, this is the earliest recorded instance of a man getting a pie in his face. One more favorite Weber and Fields trick also made its first appearance here—a statue smoking a cigar.

Another London offering, Talbot's **Monte Carlo** (21 March 1898, Herald Square), began a disappointing run on the same evening that the English hit *The Geisha* opened a return engagement at Daly's. *Monte Carlo*'s producer and director, E. E. Rice, added a number of his own songs and gave Marie Cahill some new comic material in a vain effort to enliven Sidney Carlton's (read Harry Greenbank's) original tale of gaming and romance.

One week later, on 28 March, *In Gay New York* (28 May 1896) returned to the Casino, while down at the 14th Street Theatre **Fun on the Pacific Mail**,

a farce-comedy based on *The Overland Route*, came in briefly from the hinterlands. The passengers on the transpacific steamship were largely vaudevillians displaying their specialties. They included the popular singer Maggie Cline and a more pretentious artist, Madame Alexa.

A lone new offering appeared in April. It appeared at an otherwise obscure, out-of-the-way venue; and it appeared only briefly. But **A Trip to Coontown**, which opened at the Third Avenue Theatre on 4 April, was a landmark in that it was entirely written, performed, and produced by blacks. It was the creation of two particularly talented African Americans, Bob Cole and Billy Johnson. Johnson played Jim Flimflammer, a "bunco steerer" (what today we would call a "con man") who tries to fleece old Silas Green out of a $5,000 pension, but is outsmarted by the old man. Cole played a tramp called Wayside Willie. The show created no stir on Broadway, but New Yorkers would shortly pay more respectful attention to Cole and the two Johnson brothers (Rosamond and J. W.) with whom he worked.

For the moment it gave more respectful attention to a musical that opened one week later, John Philip Sousa's **The Bride Elect** (11 April 1898, Knickerbocker). Because Charles Klein was ill, Sousa decided to write the book himself. That proved a mistake. His inferior libretto was inordinately complicated. In as simple terms as possible, the death of a pet goat leads to war between two kingdoms. King Papagallo XIII (Albert Hart) of Tiberio wins and demands the hand of Princess Minutezza (Christie MacDonald) of Capri. But Minutezza loves Papagallo's nephew, Guido (Frank Pollock), Duke of Ventroso. Minutezza arranges for a female brigand, La Pastorella (Nella Bergen), to abduct the king. Minutezza's mother, Queen Bianca (Mabella Baker), thinking Papagallo has kidnapped Minutezza, marches on La Pastorella's camp and releases the prisoners. Minutezza is allowed to marry Guido, while Papagallo settles for the widowed Bianca. The show, which had been touring profitably since December, played sixty-four performances to generally good business, until hot weather closed it. It toured again the next year.

Sousa disdained a small fortune by refusing an offer of $100,000 made by the managers of the New Haven Theatre in which it gave its world premiere for exclusive rights to the show. He also rejected an offer of $10,000 from the New York *Journal* for permission to publish "The Bride Elect March," a song based on the show's second-act finale, "Unchain The Dogs Of War." In later years Sousa is said to have considered this the best march he had ever written. First-night audiences also awarded encores to Minutezza's lullaby, "The Snow Baby."

The remainder of April was filled with revivals. Led by James T. Powers and Virginia Earle, the second company of *La Poupée* bowed at Daly's on the 15th, the same evening *The Wedding Day* began a return stay. On 25 April *The Lady Slavey* reappeared.

In San Francisco, a new musical comedy began its short life. **The Purser** (25 April 1898, Baldwin) retailed the plight of a purser on a P&O liner, who is forced to sail without his wife the day after his wedding. His wife boards incognito and is courted by several male passengers. The officer is chased by several divorcées. Naturally, by curtain time man and wife are arm in arm.

In New York, a "Chinese-Japanese opera," **The Koreans** (3 May 1898, Herald Square), was May's only original full-scale musical. It opened and closed in the same week. The plot revolved around the contrast of Oriental and Occidental cultures, a theme that was to become increasingly popular. But *The Koreans* played no part in making the motif so popular. In its tale, George Washington Tree (Richard F. Carroll) writes his proposal of marriage to Fidelia (Alice Holbrook) on his cuff, but inadvertently sends the shirt to a Chinese laundry. The laundry's owner absconds, taking all the clothing in the shop with him. George and Fidelia follow him to Korea. There George, a union organizer, organizes an ancestor worshippers' union. The show had first been mounted the previous spring in Boston, where it had been known as *The Walking Delegate*. A year's overhauling proved futile.

A more popular piece with an Oriental setting, *The Mikado*, returned the same night as the opening attraction of the American Opera Company's "summer season" at the Star. The troupe later performed *The Bohemian Girl*, *Olivette*, and *Pinafore*, among others. Taking no chances on its audiences not receiving value for money, it offered a vaudeville bill before each main presentation. On 16 May, the Royal Italian Opera came into Wallack's, bringing with it two Puccini operas, the two-year-old *La Bohème* and the first New York performance of *Manon Lescaut*.

Thomas Q. Seabrooke returned on the 18th with his dependable *The Isle of Champagne* (5 December 1892) at the Broadway, and five nights later Francis

Wilson, Henry Dixey, and Lulu Glaser revived *Erminie* (10 May 1886) at the Casino.

By rights, **A Cook's Tour at Koster and Bial's** should be dismissed as a vaudeville. But since the management again decided to give the evening a title and a "plot" some passing notice is justified. The plot had a theatrical producer, Mr. Klawlanger, take his company on a world tour. A few current plays were spoofed in between specialties. Earlier in the season the house had gone one step further, offering **Au Bain,** its own translation of a supposed French musical. (Bruyas lists no such show in his detailed history of the French musical theatre.) Adele Ritchie played a young lady who hides in the water rather than wed her cousin. In what was apparently a shocking scene for its time the calcium sputtered as the triumphant miss emerged from the water in her bathing suit at the end of the evening. The *Times*'s priggish critic could only lament archly that the parents of playgoers who enjoyed the moment "used to go to church and pray." Later in the season Ritchie again won kudos at the theater when she was featured in **Le Rêve,** beginning on 23 May. She portrayed an artist's sweetheart, who refuses to pose as Hero for his painting of Hero and Leander. A dream convinces the artist that his girl is unfaithful, but all ends happily. The libretto was by Joseph Herbert; the music by Max Gabriel.

Oscar Hammerstein also embellished his Olympia vaudeville with airs of legitimacy. On 16 May he offered **War Bubbbles,** a "patriotic extravaganza," as an afterpiece. This virtually plotless hodgepodge included trained Boston terriers playing football, a comic Yiddish military drill, and a "Spirit of '76" finale concluding with "The Star Spangled Banner." When the piece promptly folded, Hammerstein's losses caused him to lose the Olympia.

In San Francisco, localites John P. Wilson and L. G. Carpenter provided the book and Chester S. Packard the music for "A Satirical Musical Travesty," **The Poster** (23 May 1898, Tivoli). The entertainment professed to spoof the "art-poster craze." An artist—played by Edwin Stevens, who a year and a half before had been Mother Goose at the same house—loves an heiress, but her father will not consent to an engagement until the artist can sell one of his paintings for $10,000. In despair the artist smokes some hashish. His drug-induced dreams provide cues for three ballets—one of playing cards, one of magazine frontispieces, and one of up-to-date posters. He also imagines he is visited by a medieval ancestor in armor, who brandishes a sword and challenges him, "Draw! Draw!" He responds dejectedly, "Alas! I cannot draw. I am a poster artist." Of course, in the end his painting of his beloved as Aphrodite brings the requisite $10,000 at an auction rigged by his fiancée. An interesting remark concluded one review of the musical: " 'The Poster' labors under the disadvantage of local origin, and San Francisco had seldom been partial to home productions." The show had only a two-week stand.

Another show promptly followed at the same house. **An American Hero** (6 June 1898) played free and loose with the John Paul Jones legend, but the evening's show-stealer was the protean Edwin Stevens, this time as a comic old tar.

1898–1899

The Spanish-American War revitalized the national economy and gave the theatre a necessary stimulus in the process. By April the theatrical year was being hailed as "the most successful season the American theatre has ever known." If musicals shared in the general prosperity they did so somewhat indiscriminately. There was no noticeable change in the number of new lyric pieces, nor was there an appreciable difference in quality over preceding years. But two shows—*The Fortune Teller* and *The Romance of Athlone*—contained songs that remained popular long after.

The Casino monopolized the beginning of the season. Its roof opened for the summer on 18 June with a entertainment staged by E. E. Rice and titled simply **Rice's Summer Nights**. These nights were essentially vaudeville, but part of one of the bills made it a theatrical landmark. On 5 July 1898, the evening ended with an extended afterpiece called **Clorindy; or, The Origin of the Cake Walk**. The playlet had a libretto and lyrics by Paul Laurence Dunbar and music by Will Marion Cook. Its cast of forty (later reduced to thirty) was led by Ernest Hogan. All were blacks. The premiere marked the first time an all-black effort played at a major house—albeit a roof garden—patronized exclusively by whites. The piece itself was so wildly successful it remained on the bill most of the summer. Relatively short though it was, it followed the practice of longer shows by making revisions intermittently from 25 July on. Its popularity—which the *Times* called "sensational"— prompted imitations. Rice himself quickly had black material performed by others on his changing bills.

In August the main attraction at Koster and Bial's was Cole and Johnson's **Kings of Koon-dom**, with "over twenty of the Darktown contingent." At least one long-popular, if now forgotten, song, "Darktown Is Out Tonight," came from *Clorindy*'s score. But while the show represented a successful breakthrough, its artistic importance is sometimes overstated. The Cakewalk and ragtime had both been working their way into the theatrical mainstream. And, as *A Trip to Coontown* demonstrated, black artists were already venturing into full-fledged musical works. Although prejudice kept them out of the better houses, these longer shows were the real precursors of later black musicals.

When hitches developed in preparations for the Casino's annual revue, *The Telephone Girl* (27 December 1897) was called in off the road and made comfortable for a brief return stay. By 25 July the new revue was ready. **Yankee Doodle Dandy** was another Hugh Morton and Gustave Kerker collaboration. Morton modishly incorporated the anti-Spanish sentiments of the hour into his plot. Teddy Two-shoes (Edna Wallace Hopper in a trouser role) falls in love with a girl depicted in the stucco ceiling of the New York Academy of Design. The molding comes to life. She announces her name as Honoria (Madge Lessing) and declares that she was once a young Roman matron. Teddy, Honoria, and an inventor, Gideon Terwilliger (Thomas Q. Seabrooke), scour the town seeking two Spanish spies, Don Alfonso de Alcantara (J. C. Miron) and Don Pascuale de Mackerel (Richard Carle). A $10,000 reward has been offered for their capture. Honoria disguises herself as a Spanish girl to trap the villains. The chase takes everyone to a platform of the El and to Printing House Square at night (with offices lit and war bulletins being issued). A visit to the Battery prompted a "Yankee Doodle Ballet," with figures from colonial times up to the moment prancing across the scene. A collegiate ballet and a ballet in which dancers broke out of eggs in an incubator were also offered. In a salute to Teddy Roosevelt chorus girls marched as "Tough Riders." The finale took everyone to Washington, where, at the White House, they participated in the booming new rage for ragtime. A Cakewalk to "Coon Chowder Party" brought down the curtain. The show was looked upon as something of a disappointment. In keeping with the practice of the day, changes were made regularly and, given the lukewarm press, perhaps more frequently than would otherwise have been the case.

Titillating hints of prurience became evident when the *Dramatic Mirror* noted a month after the opening, "Clara Betz, an artist's model, was introduced last week in Yankee Doodle Dandy at the Casino, posing to considerable applause."

A name out of a fast receding past, Imre Kiralfy, appeared for a few nights on the program of the Madison Square Garden when he mounted a two-a-day spectacle, *Our Naval Victories*. But the event could in no way be considered a musical, and the Kiralfy name makes its last appearance in this history.

Also fading rapidly and soon to seem as distant as the old extravaganzas were the decade's farce-comedies. They were increasingly relegated to combination houses and the road. In 1898–1899 only two would play a prime house. The first farce-comedy, **In Atlantic City** (13 August 1898, Star), told for all eight performances how a prospective father-in-law goes about winning the affection of his son's bride-to-be.

The season had its first smash hit when James T. Powers clowned his way through Ivan Caryll and Lionel Monckton's London success, **A Runaway Girl** (25 August 1898, Daly's). Powers, continuing to rely heavily on the importations, played a jockey smuggler who helps the romance of a convent girl passing for a street singer.

Five evenings later **A Day and a Night in New York** (30 August 1898, Garrick) began a sixty-three-performance run. The story was simple. Marble Hart (Otis Harlan), a young prig, is brought to his senses when a trip to New York reveals that his rich, snobbish fiancée was once a showgirl. As always the scenes were larded with interpolated songs. This was one of the two farce-comedies to play a major house and also the last new Charles Hoyt work New York was ever to see. Like so many important theatrical figures of the nineteenth century (Emmet, Fox, Hart, Scanlan), Hoyt became insane. He died at the age of forty-one in November 1900.

The season's first full-fledged American hit was **The Charlatan** (5 September 1898, Knickerbocker), although its run of only forty performances may seem to belie its success. John Philip Sousa wrote the songs while recuperating from a nervous breakdown brought on by his hectic activities during the war. To ease his load, he also utilized songs from his earlier shows. Luckily, Charles Klein had recovered from the illness that kept him from helping with *The Bride Elect* and provided a better libretto than Sousa might have created on his own. From its inception the work

was designed for De Wolf Hopper and his opera company. In Klein's story Prince Boris (Edmund Stanley) must marry someone of his own station or forfeit his estate. His treacherous uncle, Gogol (Mark Price), tricks him into marrying the daughter of a travelling charlatan, Demidoff (Hopper), by passing off Demidoff's daughter (Nella Bergen) as Princess Ruchkowski. Gogol assumes that the name is fictitious. But a real Princess Ruchkowski (Adine Bouvier) appears with the Grand Duke (Arthur Cunningham). Demidoff exposes Gogol's machinations, and the Grand Duke assures everyone he will persuade the czar to allow a happy ending. In the custom of the time the show was completely booked for its road tour long before its New York premiere. Its post-Broadway journey broke record after record, grossing more than $10,000 a week in Baltimore, Washington, and Boston. It returned for an additional New York run in May.

Another hit opened three nights later, 8 September, when Weber and Fields began their third season. The opening attraction was **Hurly-Burly**. Harry B. Simth joined Edgar Smith in providing dialogue and lyrics to accompany John Stromberg's songs. Two of Stromberg's successes emerged from the score, "Emmaline" and "Dinah," the latter introduced by one of the house's great comedians, Peter F. Dailey. A pair of newcomers added their talents and glamour to the roster: Fay Templeton and David Warfield. Given his later fame as a serious actor in Belasco's plays, it is easy to forget Warfield began as a "Dutch" comedian. The main plot of the evening featured Dailey as an American theatrical agent about to take over all the regular London music halls. But his rival in love puts on free vaudeville at lesser theatres and hurts Dailey's trade. Into this Weber and Fields bring a mummy of Cleopatra they own. Warfield resuscitates the dead queen (played by Miss Templeton), and she takes them all back to ancient Egypt, where they meet such figures as Octopus Sneezer (John T. Kelly). The evening began with the customary, although somewhat shortened, olio and did not end until midnight.

The Liliputians delighted their followers in **The Golden Horseshoe** (15 September 1898, Irving Place) as they sought a treasure buried near Kalamazoo. In one act gold gave way to pink for a masquerade ball and ballet. The show ran a month.

When Klein and Sousa were creating a new vehicle for Hopper and his company, Harry B. Smith and Ludwig Englander were writing one for Francis Wilson and his group. Their effort, **The Little Corporal** (19 September 1898, Broadway), ran a month longer than *The Charlatan* in New York but shattered no records on the road. Smith's story managed to combine quaint European characters with another Egyptian setting. Honoré St. André (Denis O'Sullivan) and his valet, Petipas (Wilson), while ardent royalists, are forced to join Napoleon's Egyptian expedition as professors of science. St. André writes a lampoon on Bonaparte and is arrested. To save his master, Petipas disguises himself as Napoleon, intending "personally" to free the prisoner. While he is in the disguise, the Arabs attack and are convinced they have caught the commander. The valet and his master are sentenced to death, and the real Napoleon scornfully rejects pleas for help. Petipas effects their escape. St. André marries his loyal sweetheart, Adele (Maud Lillian Berri), and Petipas wins Adele's foster-sister, Jacqueline (Lulu Glaser). Although Americans wrote and performed the show, the pervasive English hold on our musical stage was evidenced by Wilson's proud announcements that Percy Anderson, an English water colorist, did the sets and that the English director, Richard Barker, staged the work, "as usual."

A touring extravaganza called **Wine, Women, and Song** (19 September 1898, Grand Opera House) visited New York for a week. Its story followed Rip Van Winkle's two brothers in their search for him, and its musical numbers were "composed chiefly of a series of ballets by young women in decidedly abbreviated costumes." Rip was also the subject of a burlesque mounted the same night at Koster and Bial's as part of a double bill. Preceded by an olio, **In Gotham** featured Rip (Dick Bernard) traveling through the city trying to find proof of his identity. A young lady in the cast named Eva Tanguay attracted considerable attention, as did a song by Alfred E. Aarons, "Rag Time Liz." Ragtime was sweeping the musical stage. Every loosely structured musical that could incorporate a ragtime tune did so. Even sedate comic operas were soon to capitulate.

At the end of the preceding season Sam Bernard had left Weber and Fields to try his luck as a solo star in a new musical.

Bernard's new vehicle turned out to be **The Marquis of Michigan** (21 September 1898, Bijou), for which Glen MacDonough contrived the book and Edward W. Townsend composed most of the score. It had a month-long shakedown on the road that began in Poughkeepsie (it is easy to forget that every modest-size American town had its legitimate theatre in this era). The story was the sort Bernard would spend the rest of his life making funnier than it truly was. Herman Engel, an artist, is captured by brigands. His life is spared when he tells the outlaws he is the Marquis of Michigan. He makes a marriage of convenience with Etna Vesuvius (whose temper, naturally, is always erupting). Later, believing Etna (Alice Atherton) has died, Hermann takes a second wife. A fuming Etna appears. Fortunately the Chevalier Maginnice (William Burress) discovers through hypnosis that Etna is his own long-lost wife. In a subplot Dan Collyer played a man accused of stealing a bracelet. He is acquitted thanks to a brilliant defense by an all-admiring, all-believing, female lawyer (Harriet Sterling). She is brought down to earth when the only payment he can offer is the bracelet he had denied stealing. Most critics had very kind words for Bernard, if not for the show. But some singled out A. B. Sloane's interpolations, often in mock ragtime, as above average. Audiences enjoyed the evening, for all its faults, and it stayed for six weeks before moving on.

SAM BERNARD was born in Birmingham, England, on 3 June 1863. His real name was Samuel Barnett. Brought to America as a child, he started a children's playhouse in an old barn behind his home at 72 Bayard Street in New York. His first professional appearance was at the Grand Duke's Theatre in the rough-and-tumble Five Points section. He moved swiftly up the professional ladder, playing the New York Museum and other more important variety stages before joining Weber and Fields.

The operetta that next raised its curtain displayed none of the lapses of taste so common to the time. Its great songs have survived although the inferior ragtimes inserted into most Broadway musicals of the season have passed into oblivion. The work was Victor Herbert's **The Fortune Teller** (26 September 1898, Wallack's). Out of it came "the most famous gypsy music in American operetta literature": "Romany Life" and "Gypsy Love Song."

The score "fitted the dramatic action well, and there was scarcely a number that failed to propel the play along." If there was anything to carp about it was that Harry B. Smith's latest book needed all the propelling it could get. Written for Alice Nielsen and her new opera company, it allowed the star to play the roles of two look-alikes: Musette, a gypsy fortune-teller, and Irma, an heiress studying ballet in Budapest. Musette is loved by a gypsy musician, Sandor (Eugene Cowles). Irma and a handsome Hungarian hussar, Ladislas (Frank Rushworth), are in love, but Irma is being pressed to marry the Count Berezowski (Joseph Herbert). Their similarity in looks gets both girls in trouble with their sweethearts, but in the end helps extricate Irma from the count's clutches and provide a happy ending. An up-and-coming comedian, Joseph Cawthorn, cavorted as Musette's father, while an equally fast-rising figure, Julian Mitchell, staged the work. The great songs were carefully distributed. Ladislas and an actress friend of his (Marguerite Sylva) were given the lovely waltz, "Only In The Play." As Irma, Miss Nielsen sang a coy profession of injured innocence, "Always Do As People Say You Should," then as Musette she led the chorus in the fiery "Romany Life." The comic opera's great hit, "Gypsy Love Song," fell to Sandor. Like many shows of the time, its New York engagement was looked upon merely as part of its national tour. It remained in Manhattan only five weeks before moving on its appointed rounds.

A forgotten farce-comedy, **A Sure Cure,** premiered the same night as *The Fortune Teller,* staying only a week before it, too, went to its next booking.

The American version of *L'Auberge Tohu Bohu,* a London and Paris hit, was known here as **Hotel Topsy Turvy** (3 October 1898, Herald Square). Eddie Foy, Marie Dressier, and Aubrey Boucicault presided over a tale of rival woolen-drapers whose children fall in love and, with the help of a comic count, reconcile the families. Billed as a "vaudeville operetta," it appealed to New York as well as Europe, playing twelve weeks to good houses. Its opening coincided with the arrival of yet another specialty-filled farce-comedy, John F. Byrne's **Going to the Races,** at the Grand Opera House and Haverly's Minstrels at the 14th Street Theatre. Byrne was a member of an acrobatic family and wrote the piece as a vehicle for them. He contrived a spectacular fire scene that allowed performers to leap from high windows and to form a human ladder. Haverly's contingent offered imitations by the Nicholas Sisters, Buck Shaffer, and Nellie O'Brien in "Cotton Field Frolics," as well as a mini-operetta, "The Princess of Madagascar."

A fourth musical opening the same night was the Castle Square Players productions of *Patience.* In a way the Gilbert and Sullivan work was just another of the many operas and comic operas this troupe presented week after week during the several years they remained at the American. But the cast of this mounting may give some hint of the organization's probable excellence and certainly attests to its astuteness in spotting potential talent. Murgatroyd was played by Frank Moulan, Bunthorne by Raymond Hitchcock, and Angela by Lizzie MacNichol. Both men were to become stars in their own right.

There were two Smiths in **Have You Seen Smith?** (3 October 1898, Star), John J. Smith and J. Jay Smith, but they were not the main figures in the comic misunderstandings. These misunderstandings start to pop up after I. Work Days marries A. Bleecker Knight's ex-wife, and Mr. Knight weds the former spouse of Mr. Days. As they would only in musical comedy, the newlyweds agree to share an apartment, with half of the main room serving as the Dayses' kitchen and dining room, while the remaining half becomes the Knights' parlor. Most of the more than two dozen characters in the farce figured briefly in the ensuing complications, then launched into their specialty acts.

The next Monday—10 October—provided three openings. Yet another farce-comedy, Herbert Hall Winslow's **A High Born Lady,** came in for a week at the Star. The play told how Willie Du-Much is sent to Europe by his uncle to prevent his marrying Flossie O'Shaughnessy. Flossie marries a millionaire, and when he dies she and Willie marry. The tune critics singled out for praise was one more "coon song," "The Doodle Doodle Wagon's Done Got You At Last." West's Minstrels replaced *Going to the Races* at the Grand, and the Royal Italian Opera began a brief season at the Casino, offering such works as *La Bohème* directly across the street from the Metropolitan. West's troupe advertised that it was offering "up-to-date" ballads and "witticism mostly of contemporary interest."

In **A Spring Chicken** (31 October 1898, Metropolis), its hero, having been an incubator baby, is convinced he is a chicken. He becomes uncontrollably upset whenever anyone mentions barnyards or chicken dinners (so naturally they're mentioned with theatrical frequency). After falling asleep in a real cradle, he awakes cured. Good specialty acts diverted attention from the absurdity of the plot.

May Irwin, the critic Edward A. Dithmar wrote, "is fun alive." Playgoers must have thought so, too, for they gave **Kate Kip, Buyer** (31 October 1898, Bijou) a sixteen-week run. Besides showing what a good businesswoman its heroine was, MacDonough's script had the "ample and beaming" star, as Kate, give a kidnapper his comeuppance and reunite some long-lost daughters with their mother. But plot was not the thing. Audiences came to hear Miss Irwin shout her "coon songs," tell her stories, and crack her jokes. Her hit song this time was "When You Ain't Got No Money (You Needn't Come Round)." Typical of her comic bits was her routine of telling fortunes with cards and warning that "a dark man is doing a black deed in a dark place"—only to discover a "colored janitor stealing coal."

On 3 November Weber and Fields rushed in their parody of Broadway's newest hit, *Cyrano de Bergerac*, calling it **Cyranose de Bric-a-Brac**. The *Times* praised "a troop of Gascons and gentlemen of France who for beauty and amiability have never been surpassed." Weber and Fields's chorus line was quickly gaining the reputation that it retained as long as the Music Hall thrived, and the *Times* quotation almost assuredly refers to girls dressed as men rather than to any male members of the company. Fields may have been amiable, but he was anything but attractive in his Cyranose makeup. He gave audiences a chance to see it close up by making his entrance from the rear of the house, running down the aisle to the stage. For good measure he and Weber added a lampoon of Hall Caine's *The Christian, The Heathen.* An actor impersonating Caine protested volubly from the balcony.

The Star offered another farce-comedy on 7 November. **The Finish of Mr. Fresh** dealt with a comic divorce case presided over by Judge E. Z. Mark. So little was thought of it by its producers and author that no writer was given credit for the text in the program. But the piece is not without passing historical interest, for its score was by one composer, David Braham. Undoubtedly it marked a sad decline in his once solid reputation. Braham was more at sea without his son-in-law Harrigan than Harrigan was ever at a loss without Hart. In an interview shortly after the play opened, Braham never referred to the new piece, talking only about his halcyon days at the Comique. He mentioned that all his songs were written for specific performers, not necessarily for specific dramatic situations. In a sense that should have enabled him to write well for the loosely plotted musicals still rampant. But in his years with Harrigan, years in which the same performers came back to play in show after show,

he developed a familiarity with his artists that was impossible in the newer casting system.

When the Italians left the Casino, a Viennese work, known in Sydney Rosenfeld's translation as **A Dangerous Maid**, settled in for a two-month run starting 12 November. The story told of a poor girl who dreams she has a rich lover. More interesting than the plot was a comment in the *Times* on the performance: "The managers of the Casino have a rule against the abominable encore nuisance, and last night it was bravely inforced, in spite of considerable opposition in the audience." It would be years before the nuisance would be eradicated, and even the Casino would have to make strategic retreats from time to time.

Two evenings afterwards the team of Stanislaus Stange and Julian Edwards had another comic opera ready for Jefferson De Angelis and his troupe: **The Jolly Musketeer**. Richard Barker was the director. The plot revolved around the complicated marital arrangements necessary in the class-conscious world of operetta librettos. Henri, the musketeer Count of Beaupret (De Angelis), loves a commoner, Yvette (Maud Hollins). The count's father will not allow him to marry a lowborn girl, so the Marquis de Chantilly (Van Rensselaer Wheeler), who has been condemned to die for his part in a duel, agrees to marry the girl and leave her a widowed marquise. But after the wedding the marquis is pardoned. He and Yvette realize they are in love. Henri obligingly accepts Yvette's cousin instead. The *Times*, apparently deeming comic open more high-minded and cohesive, lamented "how fast this species of entertainment is going down hill toward operetta." The critic's major complaint was that the rough-house clowning of Harry MacDonough and De Angelis had no pertinence to the plot. De Angelis was almost as great an attraction as De Wolf Hopper or Francis Wilson was, and his new show was good, if unexceptional, in its comedy, music, and staging. He kept it in New York at the Broadway for a month, then braved the hinterlands, returning for a brief stay in June.

Another father's objections to his son's marriage plans provided the springboard for the action in **The Little Host** (26 December 1898, Herald Square). Edgar Smith and Louis De Lange, who had worked together at Weber and Fields's, created the book, while W. T. Francis and Thomas Chilvers composed the music. In the story Jack Dashington's stuffy father (R. E. Graham) wants him to marry Susie Jones (Mabel Bouton). Jack (Hugh Chilvers) prefers Margery Dazzle, an actress. Margery, dressed as a man, throws a party, inviting both Susie and the elder Dashington. Their unseemly behavior forces the father to consent to Jack and Margery's marriage. Comic bits included "a waltz song by Alice Johnson, with a noiseless but violently acrobatic piano accompaniment by John Slavin," as well as a drunk who, told to take a cab home, walks into a refrigerator. Della Fox again donned trousers to assume the title role. Keeping in mind the *Times*'s comment in its review of *The Jolly Musketeer*, one suspects the term "operetta" may have fallen into disrepute for some reason during the season. In its pre-opening publicity *The Little Host* went out of its way to assure potential patrons it was a musical comedy and not an operetta. Its very plot would mark it as musical comedy, though, of course, heretofore Miss Fox had only been identified with more arioso forms. Whatever the reasons, the show, announced from the start as playing a limited run, met with only a modest reception and was soon gone.

The Star kept turning over farce-comedies like pancakes. Charles E. Blaney's **A Female Drummer** was its Christmas-week attraction. Johnstone Bennett, a female impersonator, embraced the old burlesque tradition as he played Haza Bargain, a female corset-drummer who takes her male customers out for a night on the town, then blackmails them into ordering her complete line. The former minstrel Willis P. Sweatnam again found employment in the genre, this time singing his old songs in the character of Super Stitious.

Chauncey Olcott brought his latest piece of fustian claptrap into the 14th Street Theatre on 9 January. In **A Romance of Athlone** Augustus Pitou told a more than ordinarily complicated story. Amid gypsy bands, abductions, and duels, Dick Ronyane rescues his older half-brother Francis (Dustin Farnum) from the machinations of Standish Fitzsimmons and wins the hand of Rose Manning (Olive White). Complaining about the story, the *Dramatic Mirror* added, "[W]hat the audiences wanted was not a good play, but an opportunity to hear Mr. Olcott sing." Why Olcott limited the number of songs in his plays remains puzzling. But in this instance he gave his loyal public one of his most endearing melodies—one he wrote himself— "My Wild Irish Rose." The quick turnover of shows at the 14th Street Theatre generally came to a halt whenever an Olcott vehicle arrived. *A Romance of Athlone* was no exception. The play stayed on the boards at the old house for eleven weeks.

A revival of Offenbach's *La Belle Hélène*, starring Lillian Russell and Thomas Q. Seabrooke, began a fifty-two-performance stand at the Casino on 12 January. The mounting emphasized music and spectacle, relegating the work's veiled political references and humor to secondary roles. Both the *Times* and the *Dramatic Mirror* noted with chagrin that nobody dared stop Miss Russell from breaking the Casino's no-encores rule.

A "spectacular extravaganza" with a plot as fustian as Olcott's came into the Grand on 16 January, but lasted only one week. **The Evil Eye** belonged to Evil Eye Warburg, who kidnaps Gerta after slaying her father and who is hounded to death by her acrobatic brothers, Nid and Nod. Most of its songs were adopted from music long known to its audiences.

Unable to think of a properly funny distortion, Weber and Fields offered their latest burlesque on 19 January with the same title as the show it lampooned, **Catherine.** The original play was something like Cinderella, played on a more starkly realistic level and with an unhappy ending. In the travesty Fay Templeton was the poor working girl. Rose Beaumont was her wicked sister, "trying to make herself sick by smoking cigarettes in order that Catherine may have more work to do." David Warfield was their lazy father, "sent out for a walk in the vain hope that a cable car may run over him." Peter F. Dailey impersonated a duchess, while Weber and Fields appeared as kids in "trousers-nightgowns."

January's last new entry provided another Harry B. Smith libretto. **The Three Dragoons** (30 January 1899, Broadway) had a score by Reginald De Koven. While De Koven was by no means as prolific as Smith, both were beginning to be attacked for the dreary mechanical nature of their productions. Julian Mitchell's staging helped gloss over the general mediocrity, and rotund Jerome Sykes, who had come to the public's attention as Foxy Quiller in *The Highwayman*, put a further comic sheen on the evening as Don Bambola Bambolio, king of Portugal— whose presence in the story is never really explained. The show was not a failure, but public and critics alike had now been given a new standard of musical composition by Victor Herbert, even if no really striking, original librettist had appeared to better Smith's obviously uninspired material. In his latest story, three British dragoons who save the life of an old Frenchman are left his fortune with the stipulation that his niece may pick one as a husband. Since all three have fiancées this would seem to present a problem. But one of the men, Jack (Joseph O'Mara), has loved the very girl who turns out to be the man's niece, Inez (Marguerite Lemon).

Two more farce-comedies played briefly in February. **Brown's in Town,** dotted with the voguish "coon songs," told of a mismanaged elopement, and had no character named Brown. It stayed two weeks at the Bijou, while **Johnny on the Spot** lasted a week at the out-of-the-way Columbus. No review even hinted at the plot, which centered on characters named Wood B. Conn and William Was Easy.

J. Sherrie Matthews and Harry Bulger, in their first starring roles, pleased Broadway with **By the Sad Sea Waves** (28 February 1899, Herald Square), a musical for which they wrote much of the dialogue. In their plot Palmer Coin and Boston Budge, desperate for work, present themselves as an athletic instructor and a music professor in what they believe to be a school. It is, in fact, a lunatic asylum. The staff and patients provided vaudeville turns that filled out the evening, and, along with the stars, sang "a mixture of airs from 'The Mikado' and popular 'coon' songs." Turns included "the violin playing of Josie De Witt with the soft violet calciums illuminating her shapely arms" and the ragtime piano of Edward Wayburn (later Ned Wayburn, the famous director and choreographer). Anna Held joined the cast shortly before the show closed. Bulger and Matthews—"music hall performers of the kind known technically as 'sidewalk conversationalists'"—were not destined to survive long as a team. Matthews took ill, retired, and died young, leaving Bulger to fend for himself as best he could.

Gus and Max Rogers were another comic pair whose stardom was to have a relatively short span. Just as Matthews's illness broke up his act, Gus's sudden death put an end to the brothers' partnership. But their act survived long enough to be a thorn in the side of Weber and Fields, although some critics felt it served merely as a foil to demonstrate Weber and Fields's excellence. The pair was backed by the Syndicate, apparently nettled at being parodied in *Pousee Café* (2 December 1897). Of course, the Trust was also aware of how successful Weber and Fields were, and undoubtedly hoped for a share of their ticket sales. As a result, on 2 March 1899, **A Reign of Error** was given the honor of opening the group's new Victoria Theatre—the first major theatre built on 42nd Street. How closely the Rogers Brothers' act was patterned on Weber and Fields was hinted at in the persistent legend that Tony Pastor's demented manager, Harry Kernell, had given the Rogers Brothers their start by standing at the back of the house while Weber and Fields performed, writing down every bit of business the comedians used and teaching it to the young brothers. Like the older team they always appeared as "Dutch" comedians. To their credit the Rogers Brothers never slavishly imitated the successful burlesque formula Weber and Fields had devised for their music hall. Instead they used a wispy plot, which often changed course between acts, to tie together the evening. Their earliest librettos were the work of the successful farce-comedy writer J. J. McNally In *A Reign of Error* Gus played Hans Wurst and Max was Carl Leetlewurzer. They were pursued by Dr. Dago Daggeri—described in the program as "a consistent stage villain if specialties permitted." The specialties included La Petite Adelaide's Rag-Time Toe Dancers. One comic bit offered Ada Lewis as a seasick clairvoyant, while Georgia Caine, "with her languid way of frisking," sang several songs. Maurice Levi, the show's conductor, wrote the songs, among them "I Am A Dago," "Bonnie Little Johnnie," and what had almost overnight become a requisite, the fresh Negro rhythms, "The Origin Of The Coon Song" and "I Wonder What's That Coon's Game."

Joseph M. Gaites, who, like McNally, turned eventually to musical comedy librettos, saw one of his farce-comedies, **The Air Ship,** fly briefly across the scene at a combination house in mid-March.

Parental interference reared its head once more during the season with **In Gay Paree** (20 March 1899, Casino). Adapted by Clay M. Greene from a French farce, its audiences watched Emelie Bartavel (Margaret Warren) and the boulevardier Henri Distrait (Harry Davenport) attempt a trial honeymoon to please Papa Bartavel (George Beane). During the test Henri runs off with an old flame, Louisette (Mabel Gilman), leaving Emelie free to marry the man she wanted in the first place, Theodore Lacour (Edward B. Tyler). Since the setting was Paris, the first act offered a lively cancan, but also found time for Miss Gilman to win encores with a song about letters from her "Tootsie Wootsie Woo" and for Charles Dickson as a flirtatious German, Hector Von Donnerblitz, to sing a kissing duet with Marie George. In the second act "The English dancer, Violet Holmes... turned cartwheels and did high kicking in a costume of lemon and salmon and black, and kept herself in a perpetual halo of lingerie while she was in view." Ludwig Englander provided music to Grant Stewart's lyrics. The last regular new book show of the season, the evening achieved a satisfactory run of six weeks.

Helter Skelter arrived 6 April to bring Weber and Fields's season to a close. It combined spoofs of several of the town's straight-play hits: *Lord and Lady Algy, Zaza, The Great Ruby,* and *The King's Musketeers.* Fay Templeton played a sleepwalker who mistakes David Warfield (as Detective Nosenstein) for Apollo. The mistake convinces Fields, a jewel thief, that Miss Templeton is in fact asleep. Mabel Fenton employed Mrs. Carter's mannerisms and costumes in playing Zaza. Oddball performers included a pantomimist named Gernella as a poodle. In this curious mélange space was found for Miss Templeton and Peter F. Dailey to sing John Stromberg's latest "coon songs," such as "What? Marry Dat Gal?" Thrilling was the word one critic used to describe "the Oriental and saltatorial finale, with nimble Bessie Clayton."

The last new musical to play a combination house this season was **Finnigan's 400** (10 April 1899, People's). It related the attempts of some Irish families to raise themselves socially. All the families live in Finnigan's Flats, but by evening's end they have succeeded in earning enough money to vacation at the relatively posh Hotel de Finnigan out in the country. So loose a plot permitted the easy injection of all manner of vaudeville turns.

Three extravaganzas and three revivals wrote an end to the 1898–1899 season. The most successful of the spectacles was the first to arrive, **The Man in the Moon.** It opened on 24 April at the New York Theatre (until then the Olympia Music Hall, next door to the former Olympia Theatre). Its array of then glamorous names should have assured success. Louis Harrison and Stanislaus Stange collaborated on the book, while Englander, Kerker, and De Koven were listed as composers. George Lederer, besides producing the work, followed his occasional practice of staging it. The cast included such rising young talents as Marie Dressler, Christie MacDonald, and Sam Bernard. The story was not much different from the frames used for summer revues. Willie Billion (John E. Henshaw) loves the statue of Diana atop Madison Square Garden. She (Miss MacDonald) comes to life and joins Willie on a tour of New York ending at the "Temple of Freedom" and "The Golden Halls of Columbia." They are followed everywhere they visit by an infuriated Viola Alum (Miss Dressler), attended by a violinist who expresses all her emotions for her on his violin. The evening was a veritable three-ring circus, offering, as it did, an Orchid Ballet and

a Pony Ballet as well as introducing a wild assortment of characters ranging from Sherlock Holmes (Ferris Hartman) and Conan Doyle (Bernard) to Continuous Porter (Walter Jones), Psyche, and Dewdimple. The hodgepodge delighted young and old for 192 showings.

An Arabian Girl and Forty Thieves (29 April 1899, Herald Square) was a reworking for New York of David Henderson's long-popular Chicago mounting of *Ali Baba.* Julian Mitchell staged the spectacle. In one scene real water cascaded down into a moonlit glen. The forty thieves drilled in unison, the *corps de ballet* formed a gigantic dragon, and both the chorus and ballet dancers combined for some showy calisthenics in Baghdad's public square. J. Cheever Goodwin's libretto narrated how Ali Baba defeats the forty thieves, who are in league with the corrupt police chief, Arraby Gorrah. As a reward Ali is made Caliph of Baghdad and wins the hand of Morgiana, a slave girl. Ali Baba was a trouser role in the pantomime tradition. If the young lady who played it (Dorothy Morton) caused no stir, a rising comedian did. Several reviewers singled out the clowning of Edwin Foy as Cassin D'Artagnan. Foy sat in a collapsing chair, tripped down slippery stairs, and did a comic turn with a donkey.

EDDIE FOY was born in Greenwich Village on 9 March 1856. His real family name was Fitzgerald. When he was a youngster his family decided to move to Chicago. Jim Fisk had promised them all free passage and had told them to pick up their passes on a Saturday. On the preceding Friday Edward Stokes killed Fisk. Foy's mother nonetheless sent young Edwin to see what could be done. Foy discovered that Fisk had made out the passes moments before he was shot. (Foy's determined mother later served as Mary Todd Lincoln's nurse during Mrs. Lincoln's last years.) Young Foy started his career in newsboy theatricals. He adopted his stage name when he and Jack Finnegan became a pair of acrobatic clowns. They toured Western mining towns, breaking up the act when Foy determined to return to Chicago to try the big time there. He quickly secured comic roles in Henderson's productions.

Less successful than *An Arabian Girl* was **Mother Goose** (1 May 1899, 14th St.), which folded after ten performances when its actors refused to work without pay. The show had been ill-starred from its inception. Originally mounted as *Bo-Peep*, it had failed on the road during the preceding season. Edgar Smith and Louis de Lange attempted to salvage it. Both Bo-Peep and Mother Goose figure prominently in the plot. Mother Goose (Frank Blair) escapes from her book and flees to Banbury Cross in time for Banbury Fair. There Jack Horner (Olive Redpath) and Bo-Peep (Marie Celeste) fall in love and wed.

Henry E. Dixey returned with *Adonis* (4 September 1884) on 9 May, but its day was over and Dixey could only keep it on the boards for two weeks. The same night saw *Erminie* (10 May 1886) back at the Casino. This was the third summer in a row a revival of the old musical had come to New York. Francis Wilson recreated his original role, assisted by Lillian Russell and Thomas Q. Seabrooke. There were complaints about the raggedness of the scenery, and howls that the pink ballroom was no longer pink. But fans of the old piece were happy to have it back, so well cast. It stayed a month, giving place to the season's final entry, a return on 5 June of *The Jolly Musketeer* (14 November 1898).

1899–1900

An even twenty musicals arrived on the Rialto for this end-of-the-century season: three revivals, two importations, and fifteen American originals. It would be the lowest figure for several decades. The number represented less than a fourth of the total legitimate offerings. Sadly, there was no remarkable quality to compensate for the comparatively low quantity, although by and large the productions offered the light-hearted diversion theatregoers sought.

Only one "summer" musical was introduced. **The Rounders** was unveiled 12 July as the Casino's annual hot-weather offering and proved attractive enough to linger into the fall. With Charles McLellan away in London for the English edition of *The Belle of New York*, Harry B. Smith was asked to write the book, which he adapted from the French comedy *Les Fêtards*. The philandering Marquis de Baccarat (Harry Davenport) is married to an American Quaker, Priscilla (Mabel Gilman). When she discovers the dancer Thea (Phyllis Rankin) is

her husband's mistress, Priscilla swallows her pride and her modesty, dons one of Thea's scanty costumes, and makes the Marquis sit up and take notice. Other characters included a Duke du Pay de Clam (Dan Daly), Siegfried Gotterdammerung (Joseph Cawthorn), and Maginnis Pasha (Thomas Q. Seabrooke). Besides his dialect comedy Cawthorn made an appearance playing the concertina. The sad-faced Daly won applause for his comically agile dances, while Seabrooke emphasized his Irish brogue in his search for laughs. But not all was perfect in these pre-microphone days. While most critics praised Miss Gilman's fine singing voice, several complained about her diction. Englander, who was becoming a sort of composer-in-residence, replaced Victor Roger's French score with one supposedly more in the American idiom.

No other regular musical opened until mid-September, but **The Last of the Rohans** (31 August 1899, Academy of Music), in keeping with the practice of so many Irish pieces of the time, had a number of songs for its star, Andrew Mack.

The summer doldrums ended when two shows opened simultaneously on 18 September: **Cyrano de Bergerac** and **The Rogers Brothers in Wall Street**. The musical version of *Cyrano* was the first of four new Victor Herbert scores heard in this single season. It opened at the Knickerbocker less than a year after the American premiere of Rostand's play and less than two years after its world premiere in Paris. It also followed by less than a season Weber and Fields's hilarious burlesque (3 November 1898). As a result it found itself in immediate difficulties. Because the comic opera's stars were two outstanding comedians (Francis Wilson as Cyrano, Lulu Glaser as Roxane), the singing of Herbert's music suffered. On the other hand Herbert's lovely, romantic songs were often inimical to the piece's comedy. Herbert's biographer noted audiences "never made up their minds as to whether they had seen a great play travestied or a mediocre burlesque almost ennobled." The piece was removed after twenty-eight performances, and an extended road tour had to be curtailed when the provinces also rejected it.

The Syndicate, still anxious to cut into the popularity of the independent Weber and Fields, brought **The Rogers Brothers in Wall Street** to the Victoria. The boys played the proprietors of a couple of warships in a fireworks display who ultimately peddle shares in a donkey to a promoter who is convinced he is purchasing a stake in the fabulous "Little Don Key" mine. Ada Lewis was featured in another tough-girl role, although this time her Bowery toughie was a yellow journalist. J. J. McNally's book had so little to do with Wall Street, the *Times* argued, the evening "might have been called most anything with equal propriety." The immediacy of some of McNally's lines must have delighted first-nighters and startled at least one of them. The Tammany leader, Richard Croker, attended the opening, possibly to get his mind off charges of corruption being flung at him from all sides. If so, he was thwarted, for one character remarked, "It's a dull day in the city. Richard Croker hasn't been accused of anything." One short-lived hit, "The Belle Of Murray Hill," emerged from Maurice Levi's lackluster score. Not all the music was new. Louise Gunning "warbled old Scotch songs daintily," Sousa marches and Stephen Foster songs were heard, and there was even a medley of tunes from *A Runaway Girl*. (Sousa's marches served as background for the showy drills that were de rigueur in the era's musicals.) Levi, like Stromberg at the Music Hall, doubled as conductor. *The Rogers Brothers in Wall Street* ran three months before embarking on a tour of the Syndicate's houses.

Weber and Fields did not take the new competition sitting down, and when they relit their music hall on 21 September with **Whirl-i-gig** they added a stellar attraction to the roster—Lillian Russell, the leading singing beauty of the Gilded Age. As a result seats for opening night were in such demand that the management finally determined to put them up for auction. Jesse Lewisohn paid $1,000 for two boxes, while Stanford White, William Randolph Hearst, and the scandal-ridden Mr. Croker bid as high as $750 for top locations. Ordinary orchestra seats brought $100. The comedian-entrepreneurs were not above active participation in the wild speculation that ensued, for they had just given their tiny house a costly renovation, and, even more pressing, Miss Russell's contract called for the staggering sum of $1,250 a week. The first part of the evening was the customary vaudeville, with Miss Russell attempting her first "coon" number, "When Chloe Sings Her Song." The second half was a burlesque of the French farce *The Girl from Maxim's*, which Charles Frohman had brought into the Criterion three weeks before. In the original an amoral grisette upsets a sternly conventional society. Weber and Fields, as was their wont, reversed the situation, placing a prim, innocent young lady in the midst of a gay Newport set. When objections were raised to Miss Russell appearing in bed in a low-cut gown at the opening of this burlesque, the scene was hastily restaged. But no one complained of the comedy:

Uneeda: The captain is my ideal of a hero.
Sigmund Cohenski [Warfield]:—A hero! Is dot a business? A tailor is a business, a shoemaker is a business, but a hero? Better you should marry a bookkeeper.
Uneeda: A bookkeeper? I suppose you think the pen is mightier than the sword.
Cohenski: You bet your life! Could you sign checks with a sword?

Fifi [Russell]:—You might bring me a demitasse.
Cohenski: Bring me the same, and a cup of coffee.

In December the burlesque was changed to spoof Clyde Fitch's *Barbara Frietchie* as *Barbara Fidgety*. The candidate for mayor of Frederick runs on the platform "To the victims belongs what is spoiled." He promises Weber a job as tax collector, and, as Weber described the position, "I have to go along the street and whenever I see a tack, I should collect it so the bicycles wouldn't get punctured." Still later, *Sapho* was burlesqued as *Sapolio*, but Weber and Fields had concluded Miss Russell was not a strong comedienne and confined her appearances to the opening act. *Whirl-i-gig*'s 264 performances far outstripped the Rogers Brothers' run, even with allowances for the larger house they played in. When the show went on the road Weber and Fields made such large profits that from then on they limited their Broadway stays. Although they proved just as riotous and just as popular in the big road theatres, they could never bring themselves to move to a more spacious house in New York.

Contemporaries saw **Isham's Octoroons** (2 October 1899, Third Ave.) as a vaudeville; with hindsight it was an early black revue. Skits, "ragtime dances and... coon songs" made up the bulk of the evening. In a grand half-hour-long finale the company assembled for a potpourri of "selections from popular operas." Did this mean grand opera or comic operas of the day?

The Policy Players (16 October 1899, Star) was also a black show, but a much better, more strongly knit one. The plot centered on a get-rich-quick scheme that is the brainchild of Happy Hotstuff, a cocky man-about-town. To put across his idea he enlists Dusty Cheapman, a not-as-dumb-as-he-seems gambler, newly in the money, to pass himself off among the cream of black society as a former president of Haiti. The show had the lively dancing, the gutsy singing, and the still-fresh brand of comedy that quickly came to be perceived as the signature of black shows. More important, it introduced two black entertainers to most white audiences. Happy was played by George Walker, while Dusty was the creation of Bert Williams. In fact, the parts were doubly theirs, since Walker was credited with the book and Williams with the songs. The basic types they portrayed in *The Policy Players* would be the types they would assume for the rest of their careers, though, of course, with practice the delineations became more brilliantly honed, and many would come to see Bert Williams as the finest comedian of his era. In turn-of-the-century parlance, policy players were people who bet on the numbers.

Victor Herbert's **The Singing Girl** (23 October 1899, Casino) was his second vehicle for "the piquant little star" Alice Nielsen. Stanislaus Stange's book was the sort of driveling nonsense that perpetually beset Herbert. When the Duke of Linz (Eugene Cowles) is jilted he decrees all would-be lovers must first obtain a license to woo. Youngsters caught kissing must promptly marry or be imprisoned for life. But Greta, the Singing Girl, and her Count Otto (Richie Ling) prevail on the duke to live and let live. Herbert was not able to rise above this dross, although his score was superior to anything else being played on Broadway. With Nielsen's help it sounded pleasing enough to keep the show in New York eleven weeks (with only one matinee a week) and then, coupled with a revival of *The Fortune Teller*, to tour successfully.

The ever popular May Irwin returned in her latest made-to-order vehicle, **Sister Mary** (27 October 1899, Bijou). Sister Mary is the nom de plume employed by Alicia Perm to write a sensational novel. Alicia learns that her rich aunt is so incensed by the book she has said she hopes whoever wrote it is disinherited. Alicia has her hands full keeping her authorship secret, especially when her publisher, Scribner McHarper, decides to pay her an inconvenient visit. The hippy blonde was probably Broadway's best purveyor of "coon songs," and she had four new ones to offer her fans. Appropriately enough, the dance numbers also included a cakewalk.

Three musicals raised their curtains in November. The first was a revival of the preceding season's *In Gay Paree* (20 March 1899), chalking up an additional forty-eight performances at the New York.

At Florenz Ziegfeld's urging, busy Harry B. Smith, who had done the book and lyrics for *The Rounders* and the lyrics for *Cyrano, Whirl-i-gig,* and *The Singing Girl,* did both the lyrics and the book for **Papa's Wife** (13 November 1899, Manhattan), combining plot elements from two Hervé works, *La Femme à Papa* and *Mam'zelle Nitouche.* Smith told how an innocent bride learns her husband cannot be faithful even on his honeymoon and how she sets about curing him. Reginald De Koven supplemented the original score. Ziegfeld produced the piece as a vehicle for his wife. The flamboyant Miss Held stopped the show with "I Wish I Really Weren't, But I Am" and made a sensational exit in an 1899 automobile. Most historians agree with Smith, "It was with this play that Mr. Ziegfeld first revealed himself as a connoisseur of pulchritude. There were only sixteen girls in Papa's Wife, but they were all highly decorative and in their costuming economy was not considered." The show ran 147 performances, a figure surpassed only by *Whirl-i-gig.*

The London success **A Greek Slave** (28 November 1899, Herald Square), with music by Lionel Monckton and Sidney Jones, closed out November. Its tale of a statue come to life undoubtedly brought back memories of *Adonis* (4 September 1884) to many playgoers. Kate Michelena, Hugh Chilvers, Minnie Ashley, and Albert Parr figured prominently in the cast.

A third Victor Herbert piece, **The Ameer** (4 December 1899, Wallack's), united Herbert with an old associate, the happy, clownish Frank Daniels. Although critical consensus branded the new work inferior to *The Wizard of the Nile* (4 November 1895) or *The Idol's Eye* (25 October 1897), the public responded avidly. For fifty-one performances in New York and a year and a half on the road, Daniels portrayed Iffe Khan, the Ameer of Afghanistan, who is compelled to marry a rich woman in order to pay his annual tribute to the English. His courtship of a young American is frustrated when she marries the British commanding officer, but Iffe flushes out a wealthy native woman in time for a proper curtain.

Back at lesser houses the fast-waning minstrel tradition was represented by **West's Big Minstrel Jubilee** (11 December 1899, Star). Along with the old-time songs and jokes, acts included acrobats, a xylophone soloist, a bag puncher, and a spectacular tableau representing the storming of San Juan Hill.

Three Little Lambs was a Christmas present from the Boston Cadets at the Fifth Avenue Theatre. Three crooks—David Tooke, Hungry Jim, and Phyllis Argyle—try to con Jack Hardwicke and Beatrice Jerome out of their inheritances. They get Jack drunk, forcing him to forfeit his rights to an unknown lady. Furious and ashamed, Jack joins the navy and sails for Puerto Rico. There he woos and wins Beatrice, discovering at the same time she is the unknown girl to whom he has lost his fortune. If the names of the principal characters sound familiar, theatregoers had already been introduced to them in 1898. The show was a rewriting of *The Queen of the Ballet* (5 February 1898), some of the details and settings changed to acknowledge America's pride in its newly acquired territory. With a book by R. A. Barnet, music by E. W. Corliss, and a cast of attractive, youthful performers including Marie Cahill, Adele Ritchie, and Raymond Hitchcock, it played forty-nine performances. The success of the Boston Cadets was little short of phenomenal, even if it sadly suggested that the company's tinselly theatrical artifice was more rewarding than the Bostonians' soul-searching artiness. In February the *Dramatic Mirror* noted, "Since 1892 Mr. Barnet's extravaganzas have netted $168,000 for the Cadets."

Another holiday present was offered New Year's Day, 1900, when the extravaganza **Chris and the Wonderful Lamp** opened at the Victoria. It was the only score that the march king, John Philip Sousa, ever composed for children. Its book was by Glen MacDonough, who would later collaborate with Victor Herbert on youngsters' shows. Chris Wagstaff (Edna Wallace Hopper) buys Aladdin's lamp. He removes his sweetheart Fanny (Ethel Irene Stewart) from school, and in the company of the genie (Jerome Sykes) they visit Aladdin's home, Etheria. Aladdin (Emile Beaupre) falls in love with Fanny and steals the lamp in order to keep the girl with him. But she rubs the lamp, sending herself and Chris back to Earth. Children and adults applauded the show for fifty-eight performances.

A second children's extravaganza, **Little Red Riding Hood** (8 January 1900, Casino), was imported from London. It lacked the appeal of *Chris and the Wonderful Lamp* and was withdrawn after twenty-four showings.

A production of Offenbach's *The Magic Melody* as part of a double bill at the American on 22 January proved to be merely a new translation of his *La Chanson de Fortunio*.

Fay Templeton had been conspicuously missing from the season's Weber and Fields high jinks. But when she appeared in **Broadway to Tokio** (23 January 1900, New York), she recalled her earlier appearance in *Hurly Burly* (8 September 1898) playing Cleopatra's mummy. For that show provided the germ of the new musical's plot, in which the mummy travels from New York to San Francisco and back again, and then to Japan, to search for the heart that has been removed from its wrappings. Reginald De Koven wrote some of the songs, but most of the score was by A. Baldwin Sloane. Miss Templeton's mummy cakewalked with Otis Harlan and imitated a French singer shouting a "coon song." Stage-encompassing dance numbers included a "Golden Gate Ballet" (with changing light effects) and a "Cherry Blossom Ballet." Somehow a place was found to burlesque Eleanora Duse's *Camille*. For all her imperfections the mummy had enough life left to continent-hop for eighty-eight performances. The era's changing theatrical vocabulary was made evident by a comment in the *Times* that "Max Freeman, in the technical slang of the hour, staged the piece." The newsman might also have noted that the term "manager" was giving way to "producer."

The Floor Walkers (29 January 1900, Grand Opera), starred Hap Ward and Harry Vokes in their customary tramp roles. No review gave the plot of this knock-about nonsense, but the characters' names give a sense of what was deemed fun. The tramps called themselves Lord Percy Hardup and Lord Harold Poorpay, while others sported monikers such as Mrs. Waldorf-Gastoria, Cora Fay, and Eva Ready.

Kirk La Shelle, who had collaborated with Frederick Ranken on the book of *The Ameer* (4 December 1899), alone supplied the libretto for Julian Edwards's bold score for **The Princess Chic** (12 February 1900, Casino). La Shelle's tale told how Princess Chic of Normandy (Christie MacDonald), disguised as a peasant, warns Charles the Bold (Winfield Blake) of King Louis's plans to make trouble. Charles falls in love with the maid and learns her true station in time for a happy ending. The show survived only twenty-two performances.

One day short of a month after his music was heard in *Broadway to Tokio*, a "full" if "commonplace" Sloane score was heard in **Aunt Hannah** (22 February 1900, Bijou), and he enjoyed a quick if fleeting success with the requisite "coon song," "My Tiger Lily." During the dance for this song "the calcium, shining through a painted medium, threw the shadow of a big tiger lily on stage." An unbilled soloist stopped the show with "When The Cat's Away The Mice Will Play." The plot of the "musical farce" recorded how sedate, religious Aunt Hannah (Agnes Findlay) goes on a trip, leaving her mansion in the keeping of her nephew, Jack (Frederick Hallen). Over the servants' protests, Jack decides to throw a grand party. Aunt Hannah returns unexpectedly, and Jack must desperately try to make things look like what they are not. An old flame of Hannah's is at the party and sets everything right. The show ran twenty-one performances.

Even though there were many who objected to the "questionable character" of young Richard Carle's brand of comedy, he had a large following on the road both as a performer and writer. It was solely as a writer that he was represented by the musical comedy **Mam'selle Awkins** (26 February 1900, Victoria). Carle described the plight of an impoverished noble (Will Armstrong). Secretly married, he must fend off the demands of his prime creditor to marry the daughter (Mamic Gilroy) of a rich cockney soap-manufacturer. The lord hires a number of friends and acquaintances to impersonate him in such a fashion as to drive away the girl. The score was by producer Alfred E. Aarons, with additional melodies by Herman Perlet. The mam'selle could muster only thirty-five representations.

Most papers rarely bothered to report on Koster and Bial's Music Hall, perhaps considering it more of a cabaret or else deeming it beneath review. Possibly because the house's new double bill offered a magnificent ballet (which the critics praised), the house's musical burletta, **The Regatta Girl** (14 March 1900), also was noticed. For the most part, the reviewers did not like what they saw, even though Clay M. Greene and J. Cheever Goodwin were listed among the authors. The story was not new. The hero is drugged before he can race in a regatta, so his sweetheart takes his place and wins. The scenery was praised, especially a setting in Kensington Gardens. And critics took a sympathetic view of the cast, suggesting they gave the material more than it deserved. That cast included a surprising number of celebrities or soon-to-be celebrated players. Ethel Jackson portrayed the heroine, while an aging Amelia Summerville deftly handled the comedy. Jeannie Yeamans garnered salutes as well. Among the male contingent were Giovanni Perugini (once Lillian Russell's husband and leading man), Henri Leoni, and Alexander Clark. The evening's biggest laugh may not have been intentional—or was it? When the villain's boat crashed, he got out and walked on the Thames to the shore.

Long before Florenz Ziegfeld began glorifying the American girl, the Casino Theatre was as famous for its line of beauties as was the Gaiety in London.

When a new attraction was needed for the Casino, George Lederer once more called on Harry B. Smith to provide a libretto, this time suggesting it center on one of the theatre's famous beauties. What Smith concocted and called **The Casino Girl** was not a backstage tale, but a formula book of an American in an exotic setting. Laura Lee (Mabel Gilman, now spelling her name Mabelle), a former Casino chorus girl, flees to Cairo to escape a pestering English earl (Virginia Earle). She opens a millinery store and prepares to settle down, when her pursuing earl reappears. After complications brought on by a comic Khedive (Sam Bernard) and some clownish thieves, she realizes she does indeed love the Englishman. The already time-worn plot bothered no one, nor did the hodgepodge score by a number of hands. One number, "How Actresses Are Made," won encores nightly. Knowing audiences recognized in the duet by Miss Gilman and Miss Earle veiled references to the methods Lederer employed to make Edna May a star. Although the show, which opened 19 March, was revised several times during its run, with one very substantial revision by Harry's brother Robert, audiences loved it in every form, and it ran 131 performances, toured, and even crossed the Atlantic to the West End.

The Viceroy (9 April 1900, Knickerbocker), the season's last musical, almost sneaked in, arriving as part of the Bostonians' repertory, which included *Robin Hood* and *The Serenade*. The story recounted how the pirate Tivolini (Helen Bertram), in reality the rightful viceroy, regains his patrimony from his treacherous cousin (Henry Clay Barnabee), wins the hand of Beatrice (Grace Cameron), and magnanimously offers his villainous cousin a share of the government. Harry B. Smith's dreary book was coupled with a less than sterling Victor Herbert score, although some scholars have admired Tivolini's serenade, "Hear Me."

1900–1901

The nation was looking forward to a new century and preparing for another presidential election. All of William Jennings Bryan's silver-tongued oratory would not win him the White House while his countrymen felt safe and sound with William McKinley. Twenty-eight new musicals vied for Broadway's favor—nearly a third of all the plays mounted during the season. While two chalked up far and away the longest runs of the year, theatregoers were by and large not uncritically receptive.

Although a dozen straight plays tallied 100 or more performances, apart from the two musical smashes, only two other lyric pieces achieved long runs. In retrospect some regular comedies and dramas that caught New Yorkers' fancies appear worthless, but the public taste that rejected most of the season's musicals seems unquestionable. It was a dismal season.

Two importations opened the season. The Cadet Girl (25 July 1900, Herald Square), a Parisian hit adapted by Harry B. Smith, enjoyed a forty-eight-performance run. Dan Daly, Christie MacDonald, and Adele Ritchie enlivened a complicated rigmarole about a will and a medallion. Arthur Sullivan's The Rose of Persia, with its tale of a sultan's wife who goes on the town disguised as a dancer and with most of its original London cast, opened at Daly's 6 September, but failed to find an audience.

Sullivan's comic opera made the mistake of competing with the most popular first night in town, the fall reopening of Weber and Fields. They called their 1900s nonsense Fiddle-dee-dee and filled it with a topflight cast including both Lillian Russell and Fay Templeton, as well as De Wolf Hopper, David Warfield, John T. Kelly, and Bessie Clayton. Backing the principals was another dramatically beautiful chorus line. The year's burlesque was a take-off on the preceding session's dramatization of Quo Vadis, called in comic Dutch Quo Vas Iss? In it the Emperor Zero, alarmed that the W.C.T.U. has succeeded in closing all the bars in Antium and is threatening to burn Rum, has the beautiful Lythia of the local W.C.T.U. chapter tossed to the wild borax. Her would-be rescuer, Fursus, is so weak he cannot break loose from his chain of pretzels and sausages. Several of the stars shone in small roles. Hopper appeared "as the suave and formidable Petrolius, who finds opening his veins cheaper than opening a jackpot ... Warfield as an impressive and astonishingly soiled Greek philosopher; and Fields an obstreperously Roman bad boy." In mid-October a spoof of the new season's Arizona was inserted. It caused something of a furor because the chorus girls entered dressed shabbily as travel-worn soldiers. It is often forgotten that along with the Casino the music hall had the reputation of displaying the most beautiful line in New York. In December the Arizona travesty was removed and a new second act burlesqued not one but several of the town's latest hits, including the runaway smash Florodora. Out of Fiddle-dee-dee came the two most popular songs to emerge from John Stromberg and the music hall series, "I'm A Respectable Working Girl" and "Ma Blushin' Rosie." Fay Templeton introduced both. Social reforms have blunted the urgency of the working girl's plight and relegated the former to a period piece. But a succession of great minstrels and songsters from Al Jolson to Judy Garland have kept "Ma Blushin' Rosie" something of a standard. The show ran 262 times, outdistanced only by the Florodora phenomenon.

The Monks of Malabar (14 September 1900, Knickerbocker), a comic opera with music by Ludwig Englander, ran thirty-nine performances. It was the only musical to open between Weber and Fields and their new rivals, the Rogers Brothers. The staid title belied the show's farcical carryings-on. In the book J. Cheever Goodwin created for Francis Wilson the central figure is Boolboom, a French merchant living in India. To rid himself of his shrewish wife, he goes into hiding and has broadcast the news that he has been eaten by a lion. Only too late does he discover that by Indian law his own death ordains his wife's cremation. He cannot come forth and reveal the truth, or he will be put to death for lying. In a series of disguises he manages to delay his wife's execution until they are both rescued by the French Army.

Unlike the music hall show, The Rogers Brothers in Central Park (17 September 1900, Victoria) did not open cold but tried out in the hinterlands. It arrived as a tightly knit entertainment held together by J. J. McNally's thin story of "two innocent Germans having been bunkoed into buying Central Park, Missouri, thinking it was Central Park, New York." As usual much of the humor was topical:

(1st man): This town seems to be for McKinley and Roosevelt.
(2nd man): How's that?
(1st man): There's only McKinley and Roosevelt banners on Broadway.
(2nd man): Well, what of it? Banners can't vote.
(1st man): No, but they show which way the wind blows.

Maurice Levi's music was equally simple and direct. In this edition he began a series of "Reuben" songs depicting the plight of the hapless yokel in the big city, a series apparently prompted by the continuing success of "Reuben And Cynthia" from A Trip to Chinatown (9 November 1891). Cole and J. W. Johnson interpolated "Run Brudder Possum Run." Young Richard Carle helped with both lyrics and music. But the boys on 42nd Street were no real match for Weber and Fields. They took their show back on the road after seventy-two performances at the Victoria.

The talents who had combined to make a success of *The Casino Girl* (19 March 1900) brought **The Belle of Bohemia** into the 39th Street house on 24 September. George Lederer was again the producer. The book and lyrics were by Harry B. Smith and the music by Ludwig Englander, with another assist from Harry T. MacConnell. Sam Bernard, who had scored so effectively as the Khedive, was given the pivotal, if not the title, role. His brother, Dick, supported him. Smith's story smacked of Plautus and Shakespeare. A prosperous brewer (Sam) and a humble tintype photographer (Dick) look so alike that when the brewer is jailed for the photographer's misdeeds, the bohemian must take the entrepreneur's place at an important society function. The score included the inevitable "coon songs," love songs, topical tunes, waltzes, and a lullaby, but nothing of consequence. Ballets were eschewed, allowing lively clogs and waltzes to propel the entertainment. The show's fifty-five-performance run fell far short of *The Casino Girl's* stay.

A Million Dollars (27 September 1900, New York) employed a slim plot that harked back to one used by *About Town* (26 February 1894). Once again a barber (Ignacio Martinetti) comes into sudden wealth and goes on a spending spree. Produced and written by the same team responsible for *Broadway to Tokio* (23 January 1900), it was a distinct failure. Dancing highlighted the evening. The first act featured an Amazon march known as "The Allies"; the second a "Coney Island Ballet"; while almost the whole of the third act was given over to a ballet called "The Roses" and mounted in gold, silver, and, appropriately, rose. The musical had the first of four A. Baldwin Sloane scores to be heard during the season. So rapidly was Sloane earning an unenviable reputation that the *Times* could already knowingly complain that his latest score "was not equal to his modest best." Critics would soon look back longingly to Victor Herbert's four inferior efforts of the preceding year. One reason the American lyric season was so dismal was that Herbert was preoccupied as conductor of the Pittsburgh Symphony, and it would be several years before he could be persuaded to return to the musical stage.

Five musicals premiered on Broadway in October. The first was Sidney Jones's London hit **San Toy** (1 October 1900, New York), still trafficking in the fading Oriental vogue *The Mikado* had sparked

a generation before and Jones himself had most profitably pursued in *The Geisha*. Marie Celeste sang the title role while James T. Powers served as principal comedian. In runs interrupted by booking difficulties *San Toy* totaled 168 performances.

Alfred E. Aarons wrote the score for **The Military Maid** (8 October 1900, Savoy), which George V. Hobart adapted from the French. Josephine Hall was the star, playing Fleurette D'Norville, an attractive, sought-after young lady who invites her pesky suitors—and their wives—to a dinner party. Besides the inevitable drills the title promised, the evening offered a show-stopper for Miss Hall in a song entitled "Sister Mary Has The Measles." But the drills and the song were not enough, and the show was an eight-performance fiasco.

The number of touring musical novelties held just about steady, giving no clue that the real beginnings of the oh-so-brief glory seasons for the genre were just around the corner. Following the premieres of a few borderline attractions—were they musicals or plays larded with some song-and-dance numbers?—audiences welcomed **Shooting the Chutes** (8 October 1900, Metropolis). No nonmusical would have attempted to get by with so little story. In this instance the High Flyer Opera Company, without bookings or cash, is stranded out-of-season at Bugg's Hotel, Bunco Beach. When a rich milk producer comes there in search of peace and quiet, the troupers see a chance to latch on to an angel. They entertain him with a gamut of variety turns. Neither librettists nor audiences seemed to tire of punning character names, so this show offered the likes of Robin Steele, Doolittle Wright, and Uneeda Bisquit.

Sons of Ham (15 October 1900, Star) used another tired motif more skillfully. Two young tramps ride into Denver, where they are mistaken for a pair of rich twins expected home from boarding school. They are slated to inherit a large family fortune. Even the real boys' father, Ham, cannot see these newcomers are not his sons. The tramps wallow in luxury, knowing that any moment the return of the actual twins will bring their high life crashing down. Meanwhile, their biggest problem is the knowledge that the twins are fine acrobats and that they will surely be asked to demonstrate their acrobatic abilities. The fact that one supposed twin was considerably shorter than the other gave the fun an added fillip. So did the supposedly rich boys' color—they were as black as the rest of the cast. But best of all was the clowning of Bert

Williams and George Walker in the starring roles. Critics did not sing the paeans they soon would be offering, but they were clearly delighted. They also enjoyed the songs, such as "Miss Hannah From Savannah" with its chorus "My name's Miss Hannah from Savannah,/Ahm some blueblood ob de land-ah!," and Williams's droll look at a black conjuror, "Fortune Telling Man."

Hobart was also responsible for the book of **Hodge, Podge, & Co.** (23 October 1900, Madison Square), this time adapting it from a German play, *Im Himmelshof.* Hodge, Podge, & Co. receive a cryptic letter advising that one of their employees has deserted his wife and children. The writer announces she will send her son Rudolf with further details. When one Rudolf Roastemsum appears, he is taken for the man mentioned in the letter. A series of confused identities follows. Since one act took place in the "model room" of a poster studio, a parade of "comely young women in varied and sometimes startling attire" was offered. Weber and Fields's favorite, Peter F. Dailey, was costarred with Christie MacDonald. The "plump and impertinent" Dailey appeared in a "spring suit," in a kilt, and as a toreador. He bantered with chorus girls as he danced and talked confidentially to the gallery. Miss MacDonald displayed her "pert vivacity with a mere hint of fervor" as she sang and performed. A number of composers contributed a share of the music, with John W. Bratton writing most of the score. Although it was all undistinguished, the show sang and kicked its heels gaily enough to keep audiences happy for over two months.

Another "Belle" show, **The Belle of Bridgeport** (29 October 1900, Bijou), had a cast that included the hefty "blond personification of good humor," May Irwin, still a leading "coon" singer, and Raymond Hitchcock. In Glen MacDonough's book Ariel Smith saves her father's secretary, Malcolm Crane (Bert Thayer), from a false charge of theft. With Miss Irwin to belt out the Negro-derived material in her "customary 'semi-mezzo' voice," some of the finest young black talent (Bob Cole, J. W. Johnson, and J. Rosamond Johnson) combined to help with the score. When she wasn't singing or propelling the plot Miss Irwin talked with audiences about trout-fishing and department-store methods. Reviewers failed to note whether she approved of the way great retail outlets functioned, but the press did disapprove of a certain commercialism evident in *The Belle of Bridgeport* and "more and more common" in other shows. This was the brazen advertising of

special products. In Miss Irwin's vehicle a brand of whiskey and a make of typewriter were ballyhooed.

Two nights later a burlesque of *Nell Gwynn,* called **Nell Go In** (31 October 1900, New York), was part of a triple bill (the other two acts were ballets) that began a brief stay. Even the burlesque itself ran heavily to dance, including a "skipping-rope" dance, "coon" steps by Pat Rooney and Mayme Gehrue, and a showy, lively "Bal Champêtre." A shadow pantomime was also featured. Music included opera arias ("Di quella pira" and "The Jewel Song" from *Faust*). A. Baldwin Sloane composed what new tunes were required.

Jerome Sykes had scored so memorable a success as Foxy Quiller in Reginald De Koven's comic opera *The Highwayman* (13 December 1897) that Klaw and Erlanger commissioned De Koven and Harry B. Smith to write a new musical around the character. **Foxy Quiller** (5 November 1900, Broadway), with the rotund Sykes as star, suffered the fate of most written-to-order sequels. It was a fifty-performance disappointment. A young sailor, Ned Royster (W. G. Stewart), has his money stolen by a dwarf (Adolph Zink). Abel Gudgeon (Louis Cassavant), the father of Ned's fiancée, Daphne (Grace Cameron), refuses to allow the pair to wed until the money is recovered. Foxy Quiller is called in and, always talking of himself in the third person, promises to solve the crime by "deductive, inductive, and seductive" reasoning. When he finds the money in his own valise he arrests himself and sentences himself to be shot. Luckily, the real thief confesses. For many, the thief, played with such engaging mischief by the erstwhile Liliputian, Zink, almost stole the show from Sykes.

Florodora opened one week later, 12 November, at the Casino. Although it soon became a legend, it was not an immediate success. Its critical reception was mixed, seemingly justifying the fears of all the leading managers who had rejected the show despite its London success. It was left to a new managerial team, Dunne, Ryley, and Fisher, to gamble with it on the Rialto. For the first two or three weeks, it was better than even money that they had lost their entire investment. But the sextette, "Tell Me, Pretty Maiden," became wildly popular. (Technically, a double sextette for six men and six women, it was the first major hit tune from a Broadway show not sung by any of the principals.) With the *Sun* plugging the show daily, *Florodora* eventually found an audience. Before long it was playing to absolute capacity ($10,000 a week) and turning prospective ticket buyers away. When it closed after 505 performances, it was the second musical in New York history to exceed the 500 mark. By running longer in New York than in London it had strikingly reversed the pattern of the day. The show's popularity undoubtedly launched the vogue for South Sea settings that soon replaced the Orient as a favorite of librettists. Florodora was an island in the Philippines, famous for its perfume. The island and the rights to the perfume belong to the heroine, Dolores (Fannie Johnston), but the villainous magnate, Gilfain, attempts to cheat her out of her property. Dolores and her fiancé, Frank Albercoed (Bertram Godfrey), abetted by the clownish Tweedlepunch, thwart Gilfain's plans. The part of Gilfain was first played in New York by R. E. Graham, who had created the part of General Knickerbocker in *The Little Tycoon* (24 March 1886). Tweedlepunch was played by the actor who originated the role in London. He was an old American favorite long absent from New York, Willie Edouin.

A vaudeville, **Star and Garter** (26 November 1900, Victoria), was compiled primarily as a showcase for "The Marvelous Agoust Family" of jugglers. The Agousts did not make their first appearance until the beginning of the second act, in a restaurant scene which found one of the family as the maître d'hôtel, a second as a waiter, and two others as diners. While the scene at first was deceptively serene, before long, cutlery, dishes, and food were flying across the stage. The first act featured travesties of *David Harum, The Gay Lord Quex*, and *Richard Carvel* with the mocking led by Marie Cahill, Otis Harlan, and a young American who would become the toast of London as Danilo in *The Merry Widow*: Joseph Coyne.

One of America's most popular comic strips was brought to life with the opening of **The Katzenjammer Kids** (26 November 1900, Third Ave.). Somewhere on the long pre–New York tour the plot seems to have disappeared, so what Manhattan saw was largely a series of vaudeville turns cued by the mischievous actions and flip remarks of the kids (who were, of course, played by small young adults). All the singing, dancing, and what-have-you took place in or around the Katzenjammer home, with the living room shown in the first act, the lawn in the second, and the music room in the third.

Boisterous Lulu Glaser starred in **Sweet Anne Page** (3 December 1900, Manhattan), a colorless piece set in the reign of James II of England. Anne Page runs away from a miserly uncle (Fred Frear) and the prospect of an unhappy marriage. She joins a troupe of strolling players. Anne's real love is Tom

(Arthur Donaldson), a yeoman supporting William of Orange. When William succeeds to the throne, Tom is knighted and Anne learns she is a nobleman's daughter. The musical failed to run out the month.

May Irwin returned in a farce with music, **Madge Smith, Attorney** (10 December 1900, Bijou). Among the composers credited with the songs was the increasingly ubiquitous A. Baldwin Sloane. But in a unique departure from common practice, the songs were not scattered throughout the plot. Instead they were all offered in a single extended medley.

Sloane also wrote the score for **The Giddy Throng** (24 December 1900, New York), a burlesque revue with dialogue by Sydney Rosenfeld, which opened as the principal attraction on a four-part bill. The rest of the bill included a comedy act, a ballet, and a "musical sketch" by George V. Hobart and Sloane called "After Office Hours." Revues of the day still had plots to tie their numbers together. *The Giddy Throng* was no exception. Producer Noble Rhoman (Joseph Harrington) goes looking for a hit show, but the characters from current Broadway successes get in his way. For example, David Harum (William Gould) stops the action attempting to sell Gay Lord Quex (Louis Harrison) a real horse. The cast was led by May Yohe and Harrison, a jack-of-all-trades who had supplied the books for earlier Sloane shows and for the recently staged *Madge Smith, Attorney*. Many in the audience came merely to gape at Miss Yohe, whose recent marriage had made her Lady Francis Hope. She made only two brief appearances, first wearing a yellow and white dress and laden down with what she professed to be the Hope family jewels; then in a pink gown. She sang just two songs, "Kiss Me To Sleep" and "Down By The River," in a voice which the *Times* snidely rued had once possessed three notes, but had, since her marriage, lost two of them. Up-and-coming youngsters in the cast included Emma Carus and Pat Rooney. Old-timers such as Amelia Summerville brought their years of experience. This bright array of talent helped make the show a smash hit. Its 164 performances were the fourth-longest run among the season's musicals.

A Royal Rogue (24 December 1900, Broadway) had a book by Charles Klein, who had not been active as a librettist for some time, and a score by W. T. Francis. Klein's story centered on Baptiste Ballou, who in 1792 ran a Paris restaurant and ran it into debt. Ballou is an antiroyalist cutthroat, while his daughter is a social-climbing snob who pretends her father is the Duc de Chartres. She hopes her pretense will help her win the hand of Georges Girodet (F. Newton Lind). Complications arise when the revolutionary band to which Baptiste belongs selects him to assassinate the Duc de Chartres. Jefferson De Angelis and Josephine Hall starred, and while De Angelis had an explosive first entrance—blown through a kitchen door—neither the stars nor a chorus "liberal in its display of hosiery" could breathe sufficient life into the piece. It languished for a month, then disappeared.

Nor could Marie Dressler, Jobyna Howland, or Bessie Clayton inject the needed gaiety into **Miss Prinnt** (25 December 1900, Victoria), a musical comedy with the refreshing tale of Helen Prinnt, a woman editor who determines to stir up the sleepyheads at her newspaper. She eventually marries Richmond Blackstone (Theodore Babcock), a lawyer who had fought her tactics. But George V. Hobart's development was not as fresh as his basic idea, and John Golden's music and lyrics were trite. At best an irrelevant "coon song" by Miss Dressler and the chorus at the end of the first act won four encores. The show closed at the same time as *A Royal Rogue*.

The Burgomaster arrived from Chicago on New Year's Eve, bringing with it two names new to New York: librettist-lyricist Frank Pixley and composer Gustav Luders. Together they had written *King Dodo*, but could find no one to produce it. Their second effort, **The Burgomaster** (31 December 1900, Manhattan), however, was readily accepted and proved an immediate hit. Pixley's libretto had Peter Stuyvesant (Henry E. Dixey) and his secretary, Doodle Van Kull (Knox Wilson), fall into a drunken sleep. They are awakened in 1900 when workmen come across them while digging in City Hall Park. The pair are taken on a tour of the town. Luders's score provided a gay, endearing accompaniment to the story. Its outstanding melody, "The Tale Of The Kangaroo," began a parade of Pixley–Luders "Tale" and "Message" songs and helped spread the vogue for anthropomorphic animal tunes.

New Yorkers had developed a conditioned disdain for Chicago offerings, and *The Burgomaster* was unable to override the prejudice. This aversion is surprising in this instance, given the show's New York setting. But the producers compounded their difficulties by offering a tacky mounting. The same backdrop, depicting old Dutch ships in the harbor, was used for both the 1660 and 1900 scenes. At least the press was able to find kind words for the performers,

GUSTAV LUDERS was born in Bremen, Germany, on 13 December 1865. A thoroughly trained musician, he emigrated to America in 1888, settling first in Milwaukee and then in Chicago, in time to play an active role in the musical events at the 1893 World's Fair. When a season of opera he conducted failed at the Schiller he agreed to keep the house open by writing a musical in conjunction with Harry B. Smith. Unfortunately, *Little Robinson Crusoe*, with Eddie Foy as star, didn't keep the box office humming either. Luders teamed up with Pixley, a local newspaperman.

not merely for Dixey's nimble clowning but for such stellarly played bit parts as Raymond Hitchcock's vain, loquacious actor, E. Booth Talkington. *The Burgomaster*'s stay at the Manhattan was a disheartening thirty-three performances.

The twentieth century's initial musical did not arrive at the Herald Square until 7 January. **The Girl from Up There** starred Edna May as a young lady who has lain frozen in a cloth-of-gold gown at the North Pole for 500 years and is released by a bolt of lightning to face the modern world. She must find the "Gold Cup of Olaf" within ninety days or she will die. Learning that pirates have stolen the cup, she dons tights and masquerades as a buccaneer. Hugh Morton's book was serviceable, filled with theatrically meaty roles. Harry Conor wandered in and out of the story as a disagreeable man who carries a pepper shaker in a town that forbids sneezing, while Harry Davenport staggered around as a tipsy officer. Edna Aug won applause for her "rainbow dance" as she sang "Seraphina And Her Concertina." But most significant, Morton's story allowed two young comedians, Dave Montgomery and Fred Stone, playing "a brace of pirates," to catch the public's eye and embark on one of Broadway's happiest careers. But the book was not sacrosanct. When Otis Harlan and Harry Kelly left the cast, their roles (King Flash and King Flush) were conveniently combined into one for Dan Daly. And serviceable may well be the kindest word for Gustave Kerker's score. The *Times* reflected the prevailing dissatisfaction with the run of Broadway composers (as it had earlier in its comments about Sloane) when its critic lamented, "Mr. Kerker's music is obviously andpersistentlyMr.Kerker's.Itisthesameoldmusic." Once more a fine cast of solid professionals figured importantly in lengthening the run of a show. *The Girl from Up There* missed entering the charmed circle of 100 performances by a mere four showings.

On the same night—7 January—**Garrett O'Magh** raised its curtain downtown at the 14th Street Theatre. Garrett (Chauncey Olcott) attempts to mollify an importuning young lady (Edith Barker) by eloping with her and behaving disgracefully so she will call off the marriage. But Garrett winds up falling in love. Essentially a straight play, it contained just enough songs to please Olcott's large Irish following.

The settings in **Mr. Coney's Isle** (14 January 1901, Third Ave.) took audiences from a comfortable hotel to a sanitorium, and finally to the local sporting club. There wasn't much plot in the show either. A group of assorted women come looking to retrieve unaccounted-for husbands or lovers and immediately find themselves in comic mix-ups or watching the specialty acts brought in on the flimsiest cues.

A hastily thrown-together "musical comedy," **The Night of the Fourth,** was rushed into the Victoria on 21 January to fill a two-week gap in its bookings. The show had originally been done the previous summer in San Francisco, and most of its plot seemed to have been left there. New York was offered little more than a vaudeville in which Maud Courtney sang Stephen Foster melodies, Walter Jones pranced through a comic fandango, and Harry Bulger, deprived of his former partner Sherrie Matthews, now held "sidewalk conversations with Joe Coyne." Acrobats, jugglers, and a magician filled in the gaps. No cry to extend the engagement beyond its announced limits was heard, so the show quickly disappeared.

Two nights later a rarity for the day, a Viennese operetta, was unveiled. Despite some lovely Johann Strauss music, the public was not receptive to **Vienna Life** (*Wiener Blut*) (23 January 1901, Broadway). Its story detailed how a countess is ready to end her marriage when she believes the count has taken up with a dancer. Six years would pass by before another show revived interest in the Viennese school. At that time Ethel Jackson, who played the forlorn countess, would appear more happily as a merry widow.

Another lively cast that included Clifton Crawford, Lotta Faust, Charles J. Ross, and Eva Tanguay propelled **My Lady** (11 February 1901, Victoria), an extravaganza by R. A. Barnet, with music by assorted writers, to a ninety-three-performance run.

A Boston show, originally done there as *Miladi and the Three Musketeers,* it was, as its earlier title suggests, a burlesque of Dumas's tale. The show's idea of humor was to change Porthos's name to Pork House. Showstoppers included a song sung in a moving automobile and a dance by the queen's scrubwomen.

> **GEORGE M. COHAN** was born in the proverbial trunk in Providence, Rhode Island, on either 3 or 4 July (depending on whose story you accept) in 1878, the son of two vaudeville troupers, Jerry and Nellie Cohan. Carried on stage as part of their act, he soon branched out as "Master Georgie" in an enlarged act. The act was further enlarged when his sister, Josephine, was included, and with time a fifth Cohan, George's wife, Ethel Levey, was added. George had no formal musical training. But his invaluable experience and native intelligence combined early on to produce a unique talent.

The season's most important musical opened at the Savoy on 25 February. Although the Savoy was "uptown" at 34th and Broadway, it was not considered a major house. At the time no one was aware of the show's importance: neither the critics, who were not overwhelmed, nor the public, who bought only enough seats to keep the show going thirty-two performances. If one person alone appreciated the occasion's significance he was undoubtedly the author of the "musical farce," twenty-two-year-old George M. Cohan. Cohan had fashioned his new musical from a vaudeville sketch he had written for his family act, "The Four Cohans." Vaudeville and the theatre were in Cohan's blood.

Cohan's fleshing out of the family act into **The Governor's Son** revealed both his remarkable theatrical know-how and his as yet incomplete artistic maturity. The faults, to do the critics and public justice, were most obvious. The book was a confusing narrative labyrinth. The principal plot does not involve the governor's son. Instead it relates the efforts of Bill Swift (N. J. Sullivan) to locate his runaway brother-in-law, Dicky Dickson (Will H. Sloan). He hires a detective, Martin McGovern (James H. Manning), unaware that McGovern is all the while helping

Dicky to hide. Dicky mischievously disguises himself as a detective and hires himself out to Swift under the alias Rudolf Schlitz. A second unhappy couple are the Curtises (Jerry and Nellie Cohan). When Mrs. Curtis becomes jealous of her husband's flirting with other ladies, Mr. Curtis hires the governor's son, Algy Wheelock (George M.), to flirt with his wife and to let him catch the pair at it. But Algy confuses Mrs. Curtis with Mrs. Dickson (Josie Cohan). Everything ends satisfactorily. The couples are reunited, and Algy wins the hand of Emerald Green (Ethel Levey). The dialogue was often singularly colloquial and snappy:

Swift: What'll I do if I catch him?
Dickson: Kick him in the shins.
Swift: All right, kiddo, I'm for you. You lead the
    league with me.

Too often, however, Cohan fell back on two-a-day clichés: "Oh, Mr. Brown. Come over here, dear, under the AnheuserBusch." It was, of course, his songs that gave Cohan his enduring fame. In *The Governor's Son* his flowing, vernacular lyrics were already evident:

Push me along in my pushcart
Push me along with the crowd
What a sensational feeling one feels
It beats all the airships and automobiles.
Oh, what a chance with your sweetheart
Closer and closer you shove.
If you got the "cush" get in the push
With the girl you love.

But his music, while jaunty and singable, still lacked Cohan's unique stamp. In one respect, Cohan did give audiences a glimpse of his future flag-waving when he sang "Yankee Doodle Doings." The five Cohans toured with the show for two years, while George improved his material and mulled over his second Broadway offering.

If Willard Spenser had despaired of achieving recognition or real acclaim in New York, he nonetheless remained steadfastly welcome in his home town of Philadelphia. On 15 April **Miss Bob White** premiered at the Chestnut Street Theatre there. Spenser's earlier works had told tales comfortably in the comic-opera tradition. Moving with the times, his latest libretto smacked clearly of then contemporary musical comedy. After losing a bet, two millionaires, Billy Van Million (John Slavin) and Artie Tre Billion (Raymond Hitchcock), must

live as tramps for two months. They head for a farm, followed by Clare Livingston (Ethel Jackson), an heiress. She disguises herself as a milkman, Bob White, and by the final curtain she has won Artie. Not even the onset of hot weather wilted Philadelphia's delight in the show, although, before its 136-performance run was over, outside romantic interests had forced Miss Jackson to withdraw. Her replacement was Marguerite Sylva.

Two musicals, one in April and one in May, closed out the season in New York. Lulu Glaser returned in **The Prima Donna** (17 April 1901, Herald Square), a musical farce Harry B. Smith and Aimee Lachaume designed for her, but it proved no more satisfactory than her *Sweet Anne Page* and quickly folded. Miss Glaser portrayed Angela Chumpley, the star of the Frivolity Theatre. When she marries Meyerbeer Supnoddle, her father disinherits her. She is not in the least disconcerted. An Egyptian pasha falls in love with her and invites her to Cairo. A series of the mistaken identities so rampant in the librettos of the age filled out the evening. The *Times*, noting that "the silly season" of summer musicals was at hand, could find little to praise and suggested the show was attempting to get by with only "high kicking and low dressing."

Sydney Rosenfeld and A. Baldwin Sloane had only slightly better luck with another burlesque revue, **The King's Carnival** (13 May 1901, New York), which recessed for the hot weather and resumed briefly in the fall. Some semblance of a story revolved about the mix-up of a royal baby and a commoner. The story soon disappeared, prompting Louis Harrison, as King Philip of Spain, to remark, "The plot grows thinner." With its disappearance the evening was given over to spoofs of such popular plays as *In the Palace of the King, When Knighthood Was in Flower, The Climbers,* and *Under Two Flags.* Besides Harrison the excellent assemblage of comics included Emma Carus, Harry Bulger, Marie Dressier, Amelia Summerville, and Adele Ritchie.

1901–1902

From Broadway's point of view there remained much to cheer about. Of twenty-three musicals offered only five were importations. Almost half the new lyric pieces ran over 100 performances. If, as happened in about every season of this period, the longest run by far was racked up by an English musical, that in no way gainsaid the stirrings of a native art. A number of domestic works were greeted with perhaps unjustified enthusiasm, but this very enthusiasm could not help encourage American composers and librettists on to better efforts. One further indication of the American Musical Theatre's growing success and confidence was the absence of any revivals, so often a sign of contemporary creative exhaustion.

The Strollers (24 June 1901, Knickerbocker), another Harry B. Smith–Ludwig Englander concoction, opened the season. Smith's libretto followed closely the story of an 1899 Viennese hit, *Die Landstreicher*, although it was deemed prudent to discard the score. The story followed a pair of vagabonds, husband and wife, in their social elevation after they assist in recovering a valuable necklace a prince has thoughtlessly bestowed on a dancer. The piece was tailored to the needs of Francis Wilson, who had reluctantly come to terms with the Syndicate. Wilson's wife in the production was "graceful and piquant" Irene Bentley, who shortly afterward married Smith. Eddie Foy had an important role as a comic jailer, Kamfer. Englander's new music was no better than the rejected Ziehrer material, although "A Lesson In Flirtation" and the evening's theme, "The Song Of The Strollers," enjoyed a passing popularity. With virtually no competition, the show ran through the summer.

Chicago's season began with Bert Leston Taylor and Walter H. Lewis's The Explorers (30 June 1901, Dearborn), whose action moved from Madagascar to the Windy City. S. Max Nix, a balloon explorer from the South Pole, falls in love with a magazine's picture of Mazie Fields, an Iowa Corn Festival Queen, so wires her to meet him in Chicago. The misdelivery of a letter allows a commercial traveler for a peroxide house to pretend to be the explorer and to win Mazie. After the show opened, the role of Bonaparte Hunter, who must tame a lady lion tamer, was added and helped Richard Carle on his rise to stardom.

Strictly speaking, the first attraction of the season at a cheap-priced Manhattan house did not appear on the stage of one of the standard combination theatres. As an offering possibly designed to span the hot weather, The Robber Baron was presented under the stars on 15 July at the Terrace Garden up at 58th Street and Lexington Avenue. It marked the only time this facility turned to legitimate amusement and one of the rare occasions when a full-blown musical mounting was introduced to audiences during the hottest weather other than in a regular Broadway house or roof garden. The

composer and librettist of the new comic opera were relative unknowns at the time and today are totally forgotten. However, several popular Broadway players were in the cast, most notably Hubert Wilke, and Mathilde Cottrelly. The action unfolded in sixteenth-century France, where Maurice de Grassi becomes a bandit after he is cheated out of his inheritance. Only when his estates are restored and he wins the hand of the girl he loves does he give up playing Robin Hood.

It was September 2nd before another musical offering appeared in New York, and it was the by now annual Rogers Brothers carnival that came into the Knickerbocker to get the season really under way. The plot of The Rogers Brothers in Washington told how a present meant for one lady is mistakenly given to a second young woman who keeps turning up with it at awkward times. The story line was so tenuous that McNally called the evening a "vaudeville farce." Composer-conductor Maurice Levi continued the "Reuben" series with "The Wedding Of Reuben And The Maid" (lyric by Harry B. Smith), but produced nothing outstanding. The principal attraction remained the "Dutch" clowning of Gus and Max Rogers, although a number of reviewers singled out young Nora Bayes for special praise. She and a chorus dressed as watermelons sang and danced "Watermelon Party." Pat Rooney's "grotesque dances" also came in for some notice, as did Gus A. Weinberg's imitation of De Wolf Hopper. This edition was certainly not all the brothers hoped it would be. They played a relatively short forty-nine-performance stand before taking to the road, from where they could watch Weber and Fields, who followed into New York hot on their heels, chalk up a rousing 225 performances.

Hoity-Toity, which opened 5 September, had a plot to tie together its olio portion. De Wolf Hopper arrives in Monte Carlo with six marriageable daughters, while Weber, Fields, and Sam Bernard (replacing David Warfield) played three East Side delicatessen owners who had cornered the sauerkraut market and come to the Riviera to gamble their winnings. Their encounters with the Hopper clan provided the continuity. Out of this vaudeville came one of Weber and Fields's most famous sketches: their routine on how to start a bank. As Herman Kaffekuchen and Frederich Schnitzel respectively, Fields and Bernard get Weber, in the role of Philip Sauerbraten, to put up money to open the bank. They assure him there will be no difficulties. At worst a bank inspector "comes around occasionally and overlooks the books." The jargon of high finance is explained. For example, "A joint note is a note signed by three or more people who all become unreliable for the full amount." When Sauerbraten sets himself up behind a teller's barred window, Kaffekuchen warns him if he is not careful he might spend a good many years behind bars. Kaffekuchen and Schnitzel each make a "posit" of five dollars, then each writes a check for $200. Sauerbraten pays out but then complains they are overdrawn. Each writes a second for far more, demanding the difference in cash. Before long the bank's reserves are exhausted and a run ensues. But Kaffekuchen and Schnitzel run even faster. On opening night the skit ran five minutes. By the end of the season, the boys were milking it for nearly half an hour. "The Pullman Porter's Ball" was also heard in the first act. Once again Lillian Russell, Fay Templeton, and Bessie Clayton headed the bevy of beauties. The eagerly awaited second-act burlesques this season turned inside out *The Man from Mars*, *The Girl and the Judge* (as *The Curl and the Judge*), and *Madame Du Barry* (as *Madame Du Hurry*). What virtually no one knew was that Weber's displeasure with his part in the *Man from Mars* travesty prompted him to stop speaking to Fields. While for over a year the team carefully concealed the fact, the rupture proved irreparable.

Born Eleanor Goldberg on 8 October 1880 in Joliet, Illinois, **NORA BAYES** had assumed her stage name by the age of eighteen, when she first appeared in vaudeville in Chicago. A diminutive girl with a big voice, she learned early how to "put over a song." She was briefly named the Wurzburger Girl because of her early 1902 success with "Down Where the Wurzburger Flows." Bayes married songwriter-performer Jack Norworth in 1908, the year they introduced "Shine On, Harvest Moon" in the *Ziegfeld Follies*; she later introduced George M. Cohan's "Over There" in vaudeville in 1917. Unlike many theatrical performers of her day, she had a robust recording career, comprising more than ninety recorded songs.

The day the reviews for *Hoity-Toity* appeared, the national telegraphs clicked away with more pressing, shocking news. President William McKinley

had been shot by an anarchist at the Pan-American Exposition in Buffalo, New York. The President hovered between life and death for a week but he succumbed on the 14th, and Theodore Roosevelt succeeded to the presidency. Two importations raised their curtains on the 16th. In fact, one set of curtains was the fabled golden drapery at the Metropolitan Opera House, where Alfred E. Aarons presented Ivan Caryll's **The Ladies Paradise** for twenty-four performances. The plot led a young lord and an opera singer to the altar despite objections from the groom's parents. Queenie Vassar and Templar Saxe were supported by a stellar cast that included John Hyams, Josephine Hall, Richard Carle, and Dave Lewis. Aarons apparently exhausted his limited funds in hiring his cast, for several critics professed to recognize the scenery as bought or borrowed from older shows. More Caryll music, written in conjunction with Lionel Monckton, graced **The Messenger Boy**, which began a 128-performance stay the same evening at Daly's. James T. Powers starred as a courier assigned to deliver a message from London to Cairo. Fearing interference, he adopts a number of comic disguises which prevent the senders from finding him when they have to stop delivery.

Turn-of-the-century critics often shortchanged later historians by insisting that contemporary musicals had "no pretense of plot" when the program's cast of characters belied the charge. **The Hottest Coon in Dixie** (16 September 1901, Third Ave.), a work by once recognized, now largely forgotten blacks, was a sad example. The comment that the entertainment was "a succession of specialties strung loosely together" implies as much. However, the same critic did allow that the piece "elicited enthusiastic applause."

Harry B. Smith approached Klaw and Erlanger, asking to be a coproducer of the next show he did for them. When they accepted, he set to work on **The Liberty Belles** (30 September 1901, Madison Square). In his autobiography he tells what followed:

With a crafty economy which I had never considered before I evolved a piece for which the costumes in the first act should cost nothing and those in the second very little. The scene of the first act was to be the dormitory of a girls' school, the pupils getting together for a supper party after the authorities had retired for the night. The girls were to wear nightgowns, pajamas and negligees, and the economical theory was that each would prefer to buy her own in order to look as pretty as nature would allow. The scene of the second act was to be a cooking school and the girls were to wear dainty but inexpensive frocks. The only outlay for costuming was to be for summer gowns in the last act.

I wrote the piece, lyrics and all, in three weeks. This important fact was afterward paragraphed and one friendly reviewer in Chicago said that he thought it quite remarkable till he saw the play and then he wondered what I had been doing all that time.

The cast included Lotta Faust, Harry Davenport, John Slavin, Harry Gilfoil, and twenty-one ladies—-"as pretty girls as can be found on the stage"—called in the program "Klaw and Erlanger's Troubadours." A number of composers contributed music—John Bratton, Clifton Crawford, Aimee Lachaume, Harry Von Tilzer, and A. Baldwin Sloane. But the slapdash piece pleased enough tired businessmen and their wives to run three months.

Owen Davis, at the time a master of touring melodrama, who gave no hint he one day would win a Pulitzer Prize, was the author of **Circus Day** (30 September 1901, Metropolis). Someone named George E. Nichols supplied the music. More important, Ned Wayburn, soon to be a major stager of musicals, directed. The problems besetting a circus company headed by Elephant Toots provided the thin story line on which songs and dances were hung.

Another Ludwig Englander score was heard when **The New Yorkers** (7 October 1901, Herald Square) bowed, but this time his collaborators were Glen MacDonough on the book and George V. Hobart for the lyrics. In MacDonough's adventure Upson Downes (Dan Daly) is an out-of-work New Yorker scrounging his way around Paris. When Downes hears rich De Long Green (George A. Schiller) announce plans to marry his daughter Olive Green (Virginia Earle) to a baron, Downes puts on an appropriate disguise and courts the girl. In the end a real baron appears to win Olive. Will Marion Cook contributed the expected "coon song."

An inanity called **Sweet Marie** (10 October 1901, Victoria) came and left quickly. The story centered on Marie and Adele Malonie (James and John Russell), sisters who run a bird store in France. They are engaged to two ne'er-do-wells, the meek Edward Gumpshion (Louis Montgomery) and the tricky

François Sceemere (Albert La Mar). When the boys learn the girls are to receive fortunes they rush the weddings. In the middle of the dual ceremony a man comes and reads their uncle's will. The document states that only the second sister to marry will be heir to his fortune. The first to marry will receive nothing. The contretemps that follows lets the girls see their suitors for the money-grabbers they really are. The *Times* felt the Russell Brothers, celebrated as female impersonators on the less critical two-a-day circuits, "were conspicuous by the rudeness of their methods and their cheerful innocence of the meaning of humor." Although one "W. Brown" was credited with the book and a certain "R. Jackson" with the music, the *Dramatic Mirror* correctly reported that the actual author was the show's producer, Oscar Hammerstein.

October's final premiere was **The Little Duchess** (14 October 1901, Casino), which Florenz Ziegfeld mounted for his wife, Anna Held. The apparently tireless Harry B. Smith took his book from the vaudeville-operetta *Niniche*. When the work was first performed in Paris nearly a quarter of a century earlier, the great French star Anna Judic created a sensation by appearing in a bathing suit. Miss Held also wore a bathing suit, but created no stir with it. She also "rolled her eyes and posed... in front of a divan for minutes at a time while the limelight man threw his brightest rays on her scintillating jewels." Girls in rosebud dresses adorned a pink boudoir and, in a double sextette that may have approached Judic's bit for titillation, removed their stockings. The story told how an actress masquerades as a duchess to avoid creditors. So slim a story seems unlikely to hamper an evening's fun, but when the show played a return engagement at the Grand Opera House a year later, the program included the astounding statement "Owing to the length of the performance the plot has been eliminated." In a day when musicals often meandered their leisurely way until 11:30 or midnight, such drastic pruning would seem an irresponsible slap at the piece's integrity. But indifference to a story line was commonplace even when most shows went into rehearsal with a clear tale to tell. All through the season the *Times* had reflected on the hapless plight of the libretto:

> There is a dark and mysterious plot in the play, so dark and mysterious that no one discovers it, and no one tries. (*Hoity-Toity*)

> Its plot is woefully thin. (*The Liberty Belles*)

... the three detectives who wandered aimlessly through the two acts could not have located that little bit of plot. (*The New Yorkers*)

There was not much to cheer in Reginald De Koven's score, so Ziegfeld rushed in a number of interpolations, which were only better by degree. Ziegfeld gave special care to every aspect of his mounting. When one scene called for his chorus girls to do a bit of fencing, he gave them all fencing lessons to assure a supple grace in their movements. Miss Held's allure and Ziegfeld's fine production kept the show going for over four months, breaking Lillian Russell's old house records in the process. It then embarked on an extended tour.

Unfortunately, **A Tipperary Christening** (14 October 1901, Third Ave.) was yet another touring musical with so slight a plot that it was viewed as merely a series of specialties. Its raucous Irish shenanigans were sparked by the team of Tony Kennedy and John J. Sheehan, popular figures in the period's vaudeville and burlesque houses.

November's sole main-stem arrival was the London pantomime **The Sleeping Beauty and the Beast** (4 November 1901, Broadway), which John J. McNally and J. Cheever Goodwin refitted for American tastes. It tapped the huge children's market so successfully it ran out the season.

Perhaps tissue-thin plots were the order of the night for the season's touring musicals. Certainly critics found none in **Fol-De-Rol** (4 November 1901, Third Ave.), which was perceived as a poor man's version of Weber and Fields's delightful productions. Even its name suggested as much. However, this jollity included a Biograph of McKinley's funeral. The show was produced by Howard and Emerson. Ida Emerson was a pleasant, attractive singer. Joseph E. Howard was a performer and composer who shortly would move on to write some of Chicago's biggest musical comedy hits. Both appeared in the show.

On 23 December **The Supper Club** began a forty-performance stay at the Winter Garden on the roof of the New York Theatre. Another of Sydney Rosenfeld's slapped-together confections, it offered the slim plot of an upstart millionaire taking his friends on a tour of New York. Few patrons remained for the whole tour. The roof supposedly seated 2,000 customers, yet only two small elevators were available to move playgoers up and down. As a result there was constant traffic during the performance,

while those willing to wait out the finale found they had to linger as long as an hour before they could get down to the street.

Ivan Caryll and Lionel Monckton found themselves with another hit when 1902's first show, **The Toreador** (6 January 1902, Knickerbocker), began a five-month run. Francis Wilson starred in a cast that featured Christie MacDonald, Adele Ritchie, Queenie Vassar, Maud Lambert, Melville Ellis, and Joseph Coyne. The story told how a discharged servant is driven by circumstances to challenge the bulls. He also finds himself embroiled in a mad anarchist's bomb schemes. In London the show was the last to play the beloved, original Gaiety. Broadway was no respecter of even established London hits, and an American "coon song" was worked into this English piece set in Spain.

Having played Lord Percy Hardup and Lord Harold Poorpay in last season's *The Floor Walkers*, Ward and Vokes, the famous tramp act, now called themselves Percy and Harold Negligee. In **The Head Waiters** (20 January 1902, Third Ave.) they made their first entrance jumping from a box onto the stage. Having landed on their feet, they decide to impersonate "two poor billionaire steal experts." They head for the Hotel Maybe, Cape Maybe, Perhaps County, State of Guess Where. There they encounter a rich, naïve Jew, a Casino chorus girl, an opium fiend, and a mean-faced fighter. A "very witching chorus" contributed its special eye appeal. All the characters wind up at Der Shamrock Rathskeller, where they participate in a spoof of a war play. The antics were written by Edmund Day, author of both touring melodramas and Broadway plays. Various writers provided songs.

Broadway respected Julian Edwards and warmly welcomed his musicalized version of the Dolly Varden story from Dickens's *Barnaby Rudge*—a musicalized version that also incorporated motifs and names from *The Country Girl*, Garrick's rewriting of Wycherley's *The Country Wife*. When her guardian, John Fairfax (Albert Parr), would prevent Dolly (Lulu Glaser) from marrying Capt. Belleville (Van Rensselaer Wheeler) and keep her for himself, Dolly furtively alters a letter of renunciation Fairfax has made her write and contrives to have Fairfax himself deliver the letter. There was praise all around—for Stanislaus Stange's handling of the libretto and Miss Glaser's "buoyant" characterization and "rippling laughter" in the title role. One lone sour note was the "execrable taste" displayed by the scene painter who colored a ballroom with garish purple columns and "very ugly" blue walls. But the public was happy to overlook such minor lapses, for **Dolly Varden** (27 January 1902, Herald Square) had a satisfactory run of 154 performances.

There was less satisfaction when Harry B. Smith and Reginald De Koven, undeterred by the failure of earlier sequels, revisited the forest of Arden, hoping **Maid Marian** (27 January 1902, Garden) would prove as rewarding as *Robin Hood* (22 September 1891). The piece had been commissioned, not without a certain desperation, by the Bostonians, whose best days had clearly passed and who soon would disappear forever from the American stage. Old ties and the presence of old favorites such as Henry Clay Barnabee and W. M. MacDonald were sufficient drawing cards to allow a sixty-four-performance run. Smith's plot recounted the troubles that develop after Richard the Lion-Hearted sends Robin Hood (Frank Rushworth) to the Crusades. Left alone, Marian (Grace Van Studdiford) is again assailed by the Sheriff of Nottingham (Barnabee) in the interests of Guy of Gisbourne (Will Fitzgerald). Robin Hood's friends, led by Little John (MacDonald), take Marian to join her lover. She is captured by Saracens. When Robin Hood comes to her rescue he and his band are betrayed into the Saracens' hands by the Sheriff, who has continued to pursue her. Marian and Robin Hood escape, return to England, and mete out justice to the Sheriff and his cohorts. Writing in 1902 in his *Standard Light Operas*, George P. Upton suggested the music for *Maid Marian* was of a higher order than that for *Robin Hood*, concluding it "occasionally approaches grand opera in its breadth and earnestness." Upton especially praised two second-act numbers: Alan-a-Dale's graceful "Tell Me Again, Sweetheart" and Marian and Robin's waltz, "True Love Is Not For A Day." Although none of De Koven's melodies have remained in the public's ken, the press noted that on opening night "every solo [was] encored." The reviewer for the *Dramatic Mirror* called the piece "the best work turned out by the librettist and composer since Robin Hood" and then turned his attention to a summary of the season to date. He hailed *Dolly Varden* as "the truest comic opera we have had the honor to see in many years" and called Weber and Fields's entertainments "the best burlesques that the world has ever seen." The public does not seem to have shared the critic's sentiments. It took a middle ground, rejecting such extravagant praise on the one hand while on the other hand passing over other papers' reservations.

Sydney Rosenfeld, George V. Hobart, and A. Baldwin Sloane hit a small jackpot with **The Hall of Fame** (3 February 1902, New York). When the Goddess Fame (Amelia Summerville) informs a fame-starved actor (Louis Harrison) there is no real glory until after death, the furious performer decides to play a trick. He announces he will go over Niagara Falls in a barrel. The barrel is found empty, and he is taken for dead. He immediately gains the fame that had eluded him, but when he reappears to have the last laugh he is grabbed and hauled away by Lady Oblivion (Marie Dressler). The musical's theatrical milieu prompted a rash of imitations. Dan McAvoy mimicked Dave Warfield, Frank Doane aped John Drew, and Annie Lewis gave her impression of Mrs. Fiske. Lady Oblivion sang of one man's moment of glory, describing what happens "When Charlie Plays The Slide Trombone." The show's hit tune, "My Pajama Beauty," suggests there was some sort of vogue for pajama-clad girls on the season's stages.

R. A. Barnet and H. L. Heartz had only moderate luck this time around with **Miss Simplicity** (10 February 1902, Casino), a vehicle for a happy-go-lucky clown, Frank Daniels. Daniels cavorted as a trolley car conductor, My Man Blossoms, abruptly elevated to a king's valet, and then made king for a day. Daniels raced about in a "gas-buggy," which finally exploded noisily, and he earned his encores singing "The Chesnutty Language Of Lovers." But despite the roughhouse comedy on the brightly lit, gaudily colored stage, the supporting material was not up to snuff, forcing Daniels and his company to hit the road after fifty-six showings. Interestingly, when Barnet and Heartz first mounted *Miss Simplicity* in Boston a year before, no character called Blossoms was in the cast, and the story centered on a royal romance.

Primrose and Dockstader's Minstrels competed for first-nighters with *Miss Simplicity*. Obviously aware of how provincial they had become, the entertainers let it be known that there would be no semicircle, no bones or tambourine, and no plantation set. Instead, these modern minstrels used a Mediterranean setting as background! Critics suggested the odd scenery only underscored how American the material was. This material included Dockstader monologues; twin midgets, Johnny and Willy Foley, in an old-fashioned double clog; and the Jackson Family, a troupe of dancing women.

Foxy Grandpa (17 February 1902, 14th St.) fared better. R. Melville Baker dramatized stories from the *Herald*, and Joseph Hart set the book to music. Hart also starred. The book was cracker-barrel hokum in which a Signor Bolero (Eugene Redding), "a facial artist who makes a living by looking like other people," is persuaded to substitute for Grandpa after the old man has fallen for the snares of the blackmailing Signorina Colonna (Beatrice Lieb). Grandpa outfoxes everyone for four months. For example, when some mischievous boys fill his hat with water they discover Grandpa has built a flap into the top of the hat, so the water drains out before he puts it on. Asked to test a trick "lung-testing machine," he first inhales air from a bicycle pump, then blows it into the machine with such force the contraption explodes. But perhaps the foxiest person was Hart. Reaction to his composing was so cool he never again wrote for Broadway.

Happy Hooligan (10 March 1902, Metropolis) was based on a comic-strip favorite. His slight adventures provided the cue for "a medley of songs, dances and specialties." These adventures centered on his courtship of the newly rich Bridget Moriarty. Her wealth attracts numerous other suitors, but she finally selects Happy, who, if one reviewer is to be believed, turns out to be a count in disguise. Before the all-smiles denouement, Happy is constantly hounded and pounded by a hot-tempered cop. One comic scene had a barber lathering a character by using a floor mop.

A. Baldwin Sloane composed at least some of the music for a short "musical comedietta," **The Belle of Broadway** (17 March 1902, Winter Garden). Thomas Q. Seabrooke played Hannibal Jerome, a quack inventor who persuades Mrs. George Washington Honeywell and her guests at Manhattan Beach to buy stock in his company.

The fiery Sultan Abdul Damit XXX, hearing about the wonders of the Pan-American Exposition, orders his flagship to sail to the fair, thereby providing yet another excuse for all the typical cheap-priced theatre turns. However indifferent Harry B. Marshall's book was, William Lorraine's music was praised, although at least one critic complained of the "inevitable" *Florodora*-like sextette. Lorraine went on to write music for Broadway. Yet just why **A Trip to Buffalo** (31 March 1902, New Star) sought amusement at the site of McKinley's assassination is moot.

A few of the surviving Liliputians were starred in **Weary Willie Walker** (28 April 1902, New Star). This time around their escapades with a pair of normal-sized tramps, Weary Willie and Tired Mike, were featured. These adventures took them to a New York street, a famous restaurant, and a haunted castle. The musical ended with the sort of transformation scene once so popular in nineteenth-century spectacles.

Another major disappointment was the second Barnet–Heartz offering of the season, **The Show Girl** (5 May 1902, Wallack's). The show was beset with problems from the beginning. E. W. Corliss was called in to write additional tunes and did produce the evening's most popular piece, "Psyche." D. K. Stevens provided more lyrics. Even after the opening, mere were more than the usual cast changes, and everyone associated with the show was undoubtedly relieved when it closed early in July. The show had originally been produced as *The Cap of Fortune* in Boston by the Cadets, apparently without difficulties. Ironically, it told of a troubled theatrical troupe. Stranded in Greece, the company's manager, Dionysius Lye (Frank Lalor), finds a magic cap and brings Psyche (Paula Edwards) back to Earth. She helps the troupe out of its troubles. She also aids Cecilia Gay (Marion Parker), the Show Girl, in her rocky romance. Yet for all its faults, critics found things to like in this E. E. Rice production. Many agreed with Rice that his new discovery, Lalor, was "a natural-born comedian." They also praised Miss Edwards's "wax-doll beauty" and Amorita's toe dancing. Even a military band on stage to accompany the expected drills elicited approval.

Trouble of another sort blossomed when **The Wild Rose** opened at the Knickerbocker, the same night as *The Show Girl*. The musical was by some of the same tightly knit coterie of hacks who dominated the lyric stage of the day. Harry B. Smith did the book and many of the lyrics, with George V. Hobart assisting on the rhymes. Smith's wife, Irene Bentley, appeared as the belle of a gypsy camp, rescued from an unwanted marriage by a comic hypnotist, Paracelsus Noodles (Eddie Foy). They flee to a rathskeller where German and French troops hang out together. Ludwig Englander tossed off his third score of the season, a score filled with " 'coon' rhythms [interpolations] alternating with the lilt of the Viennese waltz." Over the authors' objections and their threats of a suit, George Lederer allowed Marie Cahill, as an "aeronaut's lady friend," to interpolate "Nancy Brown," a song by the young actor-writer Clifton Crawford, who was then appearing in *Foxy Grandpa*. The *Evening Telegram* recorded, "Miss Cahill made the hit of the evening with her 'Nancy Brown' song," and the *Herald* counted six encores. Since so many other outside tunes were incorporated into the show, it is hard to determine why there was so much fuss over this one song in particular. If the whole thing was not a publicity stunt, then Smith and Englander were among the very first artists to tackle the problem head-on. Until this time only Victor Herbert, Julian Edwards, Reginald De Koven, and, apparently, John Philip Sousa had been forceful or prestigious enough to demand contracts that barred other men's songs from being inserted into their shows. But this vanguard of artistic and stylistic integrity had a long uphill fight ahead. Miss Cahill won this battle hands down, and for the rest of her career she insisted on interpolating at will. But her later foes proved more determined, and she retreated from some of her battles badly scarred. No fuss was made about the show's other hit, "The Little Gypsy Maid," an interpolation which Smith's wife sang. The song had music by Will Marion Cook and lyrics by Smith and Cecil Mack—not, as is often believed, by Paul Laurence Dunbar. For all the controversy and all its faults, the show proved entertaining enough to span the summer.

Two look-alike brothers were the stars of **Rudolph and Adolph** (5 May 1902, Metropolis). They assumed the roles of two men who are unrelated but who have the same surname, Dinkelspiel. Since even their wives cannot tell them apart, the expected misunderstandings arise. An "electric parasol dance," performed on an otherwise darkened stage, was the evening's show-stopper.

The success of *The Burgomaster* had sent managers fighting for the rights to do **King Dodo** (12 May 1902, Daly's), the Frank Pixley–Gustav Luders work they all had rejected earlier. By the time it reached New York, it had been delighting audiences in Chicago and parts west for a year. The story was just the captivating nonsense the rather appropriately named Pixley excelled at. King Dodo of Spoojuland discovers an elixir which allows him to turn the clock back thirty years. But he is forced to revert to his real age when his queen insists that she prefers him as he was. Even makeup which made the older Dodo resemble a duck would not discourage her. The king's ward and a soldier supply the love interest. Luders furnished another sweet, simple score, although an ominous warning of repetitions to come could be seen in the "Tale Of The Bumble Bee," a close parallel to the preceding year's "Tale Of The Kangaroo." New Yorkers could still not find it in their hearts to give a wholehearted welcome to a midwestern creation, but the sixty-four-performance run was not bad in light of the hot weather. With his performance as Dodo, the genial Raymond

Hitchcock secured his position as a leading musical comedy man.

> **RAYMOND HITCHCOCK** was born in Auburn, New York, on 22 October 1865. He came to the theatre at the comparatively late age of twenty-five, having tried his hand unhappily at a number of other trades, even spending Several years as a shoe clerk. The sharp-featured, lanky, raspy-voiced comedian quickly called attention to himself in *The Brigands* and *The Golden Wedding*. These appearances landed him juicy roles in several other productions, and he began to establish a reputation. Larger roles in New York and Philadelphia musicals followed.

However never-never-landish were the plots of so many of the era's musicals, they often inserted much topical material. Hitchcock was badly beaten up in Providence, supposedly by hirelings of the meat trust, for injecting the following lyrics:

> *Another King has risen up*
> *To contest the rights of Dodo.*
> *The Beef Trust's now to the front, you'll note,*
> *Much scornful of King Dodo.*
> *But its life will be a brief one,*
> *Our King's not to be by beef done;*
> *The finish will be Swift.*
> *Unless Dodo's lost the gift*
> *Of breaking through such Armour as the beef one.*

Pixley–Luders shows, like earlier David Henderson extravaganzas, were conceived and mounted for Chicago. In the following season New York would applaud a show that had been entertaining Chicagoans at the Studebaker Theatre since 11 March, *The Sultan of Sulu*. These New York runs were essentially happy afterthoughts, an extra reward for special merit. They were not the only musicals produced for Chicago, but the less successful had never ventured far from the Midwest. Probably the first really successful Chicago musical not to brave the Rialto was **The Storks**, which opened at the Dearborn Theatre on 18 May. Like most Chicago musicals up to its time it was brought in as a summer attraction to keep an otherwise dark house both lit and profitable. It more than achieved its purpose, running handsomely for seventeen weeks—a substantial run in 1902, even in New York. The piece had a score by Frederick Chapin and a book by Guy F. Steely and Richard Carle. Carle was also the star.

RICHARD CARLE, born Charles Nicholas Carleton in Somerville, Massachusetts, on 7 July 1871, spent his early years in local amateur theatricals. His New York debut was at the Bijou on 20 September 1891, in *Niobe*. He rose quickly playing important roles in *A Round of Pleasure* and *A Greek Slave*. At the same time, his name began appearing in author credits on shows such as *Mam'selle Awkins*. Shortly before *The Storks* premiered he had delighted Chicago audiences in a less successful musical, *The Explorers*, impersonating Bonaparte Hunter in his encounters with a lady lion tamer.

Carle's story for *The Storks* recounted how the magician Malzadoc turns King Bungloo into a stork to avenge an unjust imprisonment. Bungloo cannot remember the magic word necessary to turn him back into human form. Lady Violet is transformed into an owl when she attempts to tell Bungloo the word. The word (Mutabor) is accidentally dropped in time for a happy ending in which everyone is properly mated and Malzadoc renounces sorcery. Carle's reception in *The Storks* prompted him to make Chicago his base of operations as long as a separate Chicago musical theatre flourished. Indeed, the success of *The Storks* may have played a small part in inaugurating the great era of Chicago musicals, an era that coincided with a renaissance of the American Musical Theatre in New York and that for a brief moment gave promise of outlasting it.

While the season was fast drawing to a close, its biggest musical hit had yet to open. It arrived by boat from London (where it had become the first show to surpass 1,000 performances) and settled into a full year's run. George Dance's story followed Simon Pineapple and his bride on their unorthodox wedding trip in **A Chinese Honeymoon** (2 June 1902, Casino). When Simon gives a kiss to a young lady in China, he learns he must marry her, too. Since American producers who could leave well enough alone were nonexistent, several interpolations by William Jerome and Jean Schwartz were inserted. One of these, "Mr. Dooley," became as well liked as anything from the original Howard Talbot score. A superb cast included Thomas Q. Seabrooke, Amelia Stone, Edwin Stevens, Adele Ritchie, William Pruette, and Van Rensselaer Wheeler. Perhaps the most important feature about this production was the legend carried over its title in the playbills, for the show was the first musical presented by a name just being heard on Broadway: Sam S. Shubert.

The score for the season's final new lyric piece, *The Chaperons* (5 June 1902, New York), was by the music publisher Isidore Witmark. The plot Witmark set his music to was typical turn-of-the-century fluff, perhaps recalling a bit *The Prima Donna* (17 April 1901) from the preceding year, or an even earlier effort, *The Casino Girl* (9 March 1900). Adam Hogg (Harry Conor) is a Cincinnati pork curer. He is also the head of the society to suppress vice. Hearing horrible tales of decadence in Paris, he hurries there to see for himself. He falls in with an opera troupe, a sultan, and a rich American contractor. They all head to Cairo for further explorations. Witmark's tribulations, poignantly recorded in his autobiography, *From Ragtime to Swing*, discouraged him from ever trying his hand on Broadway again. His reluctance is surprising since his score was well received and the show's hit, "My Sambo," made a star of Eva Tanguay. Moreover, if his memory is correct, at least one company of the show remained on the road for five seasons, even though the New York run was a meager forty-nine performances. But Klaw and Erlanger's grip on the best houses was such they not only could demand revisions but, before they would book a piece, also demand a royalty for suggesting the revisions. Witmark complied, stopping short only when they attempted to add songs by other composers. When George Lederer, who had been brought in at the Syndicate's instance, added a tune while Witmark was on business elsewhere, Witmark took them to court, even though his legal expenses set him $3,000 out of pocket. Witmark was famous for harboring grievances. He never again spoke to Lederer, and writing of the incident at nearly forty years' remove still branded the pioneer producer "a henchman of the magnates."

The season ended, as it began, with comic opera. Only in this instance the comic operas were old. Such favorites as *Boccaccio* and *The Bohemian Girl* were offered by a touring company for a brief spring stand at the New Star in early June.

Act Two

The Emergence of American Talent, 1902–1907

The enthusiastic reactions of the *Dramatic Mirror* to the lyric stage during the preceding season were by no means universally shared. If anything they were a minority viewpoint. The *Times* was, perhaps, more representative of the prevailing consensus. But by 7 September 1902, the paper's reserve had itself slid into an extreme pessimism. An article headed "Musical Comedies' Vogue Said To Be on the Wane" recorded "the general opinion was that in the not far distant future the musical comedy and its kin will be found among the 'have beens' so far as concerns New York. Nearly all agree that the cycle is dead." As if to challenge so dire a judgment the American Musical Theatre in 1902–1903 burst brightly into a brief, tentative era of hope and achievement. The reasons for this happy, if short-lived, renaissance are not thoroughly apparent, even in retrospect. Undoubtedly President Theodore Roosevelt's forceful optimism provided some sort of indirect stimulus. America's economic picture was rosy—deceptively so, as the summer of 1903

would prove. And the simple coincidence of several brilliant young talents reaching maturity simultaneously played no small part.

Actually the changes wrought were not revolutionary. The improvements manifest were more of degree than of kind, often more hope than achievement. Here would be a small attempt at greater integrity; there a more daring breakthrough—blacks in a black-created show at a principal white house. At least two composers—George M. Cohan and Victor Herbert—showered Broadway with magnificent melodies and in so doing gave Irish writers their last glorious reign in the musical theatre. Comic opera remained arioso, sentimental, and, thanks usually to a dialect comedian, comic. Musical comedy remained boisterous, loose-jointed, and filled with specialties that generally had little or nothing to do with the matter at hand. Scenery was rarely, albeit increasingly, conceived architecturally. Painted flats predominated, and "well painted" was frequently the highest encomium awarded set designers' work. The painting was often garish and just as often clashed with equally gaudy costumes. Not scenery but casts of 60 to 100 or more filled musical stages. Marches and clogs dominated the "choreography." But here one major change did occur. If the Italian *Enciclopedia dello Spettacolo* is correct, sometime in 1903 Ned Wayburn, tiring of heavy-footed clog dances, put small metal plates on the bottom of dancers' shoes for a lighter, steelier sound accomplished with slighter, more graceful movement. Tap-dancing was born.

1902–1903

The season opened with **The Defender** (3 July 1902, Herald Square), a musical comedy detailing the machinations of a British betting syndicate, headed by the villainous soap magnate, Ivory D. Queers (Alexander Clark), to influence the outcome of the race between Sir Thomas Ceylon Teaton's yacht, *Hibernia*, and the American yacht, *Constitution*. But Jellie Canvas (Paula Edwards) and the detective Pinky Winkerton (Charles Wayne) foil the scheme. At one point the villain captures Jellie and ties her to railroad tracks, knowing an express train is on the way. The approach of the train and Jellie's rescue were depicted in a Biograph film interlude. The dialogue was turgid, even for the time ("Don't attempt to bribe me with your filthy lucre"), the jokes were labored ("Have you ever used Queers' soap?"), and the regular score insipid. Harry Davenport was Teaton, and Emma Carus also had an important role. What success the show enjoyed was due largely to one interpolation, "In The Good Old Summer Time" (Ren Shields/George Evans). The song, which had already been heard on a few vaudeville stages, was introduced in the show by Blanche Ring. It catapulted her to fame. She was heard from again—and again, and again—during the season. In years to come, when she was not busy on the two-a-day circuits, she propped up many a faltering vehicle by re-interpolating this and other numbers she soon made her own. "Mister Dooley," used successfully in *A Chinese Honeymoon*, was also interpolated in *The Defender*.

> · The daughter of James H. Ring, a comedian with the Boston Museum stock company, **BLANCHE RING** was born in Boston, Massachusetts on 24 April 1871, a

> descendant, she later claimed, of English Shakespearean actors. She debuted with · Richard Mansfield in the little comedy *A Parisian Romance* at age sixteen. Ring was known for her bright personality, penetrating singing voice and expert impersonations. She is best remembered for her renditions of "Come Josephine in My Flying Machine," "Yip-I-Addy-I-Aye," and "In the Good Old Summertime."

· July's only other entry was a revival of *The Mikado* (14 July 1902, Madison Square Roof Garden), noteworthy because its producers felt compelled to add a plotless spectacle, *Japan at Night*, to the bill. Together the two pieces rolled up seventy performances.

A busy season at cheap-priced houses began early with the arrival of Haverly's Mastodon Minstrels on 11 August at the Metropolis and Hi Henry's Minstrels on the 18th at the Star. By 1902 minstrel shows almost never were accorded first-class stages and were a far cry from the classic traditions of a bygone generation. For example, Henry's curtain rose to show "The Court of Nero," and his olio included a strongman who "tossed weights as though they were wafers and twisted iron bars like molasses candy." This act was followed by Winschermann's bears and monkeys. Virtually two-a-day.

Marie Cahill, who arrived in **Sally in Our Alley** (29 August 1902, Broadway), was very much like Blanche Ring, although she devoted far more time than Miss Ring to the legitimate stage. The ruckus over the interpolation of "Nancy Brown" in *The Wild Rose* (5 May 1902) had convinced Cahill of the usefulness of carefully selected interpolations and, as if to confirm the point, she scored the hit of the evening with "Under The Bamboo Tree" (Bob Cole). For the second time in four months she helped relegate an Englander score to a backseat. George V. Hobart's complex story reminded the *Times* of old Harrigan and Hart days with one significant modification: "[T]he typical Bowery boy has become a yid of the Dave Warfield type, and the Bowery girl his daughter." In this case the Jew is Izzy (Dan McAvoy), proprietor of the Heterogeneous Emporium. Although Izzy called his daughter Sarah, her friends felt "Sally" was more modish. So good a girl is Sally that she pretends her neighbor's baby is her own when the neighbor seems to be in trouble; she even steals some papers to help acquit a man of forgery. McAvoy gave the lively Miss Cahill able assistance, not only with his dialect clowning, but with some grotesque dancing in which he burlesqued a flamboyant conductor of the day ("If Creatori and his sort delight us/what a leader would have been St. Vitus"). It took four hours on opening night to tell the story and sing the songs, although by the end of the two-month run a reasonable amount of excess had been pruned.

MARIE CAHILL was born in Brooklyn, but the exact date of her birth has apparently been lost. She was fifty-nine when she died in late 1933, so it seems safe to assume she was born in 1874 (although Stanley Green, a trustworthy scholar, gives the date as 7 February 1870). Brought up in a strict, religious home, she was nevertheless a sufficiently iron-willed youngster to prevail on her parents to let her study voice and ballet. Later she studied acting under Frederick Warde. She made her debut in Hoyt's *A Tin Soldier*. Her strong personality rarely bent to the role assigned; instead the character she was supposed to play assumed her attributes. This same forcefulness, coupled with firm moral convictions that she retained from her girlhood, caused her, while playing rambunctious young ladies, to reject the leering humor and suggestiveness so common to such roles. Her shows were generally praised as clean. If her personality caused any problems, it was in her constant battle with composers for outstanding tunes.

The Rogers Brothers at Harvard (1 September 1902, Knickerbocker) offered another of this series' thin plotlines designed to hold together songs and vaudeville specialties. The plot had two old rakes as guardians for two young blades. With two French milliners and "two young women to whom virtue is too easy," they become "entangled in a double quadrille, in which the cry is always 'Change partners.'" Scenery, which followed the customary practice of one set for each act, portrayed upper New York City with a view of Grant's Tomb, the Eden Musée's entertainment hall, and, finally bowing to the title,

Harvard Yard. Maurice Levi's score included the latest in the Reuben series, "The Troubles Of The Reuben And The Maid"—with lyrics for this installment by the venerable J. Cheever Goodwin. But the music was flat and the jokes none too fresh. More than one critic suggested the Rogers Brothers proved how excellent Weber and Fields were.

Some of Sir Arthur Sullivan's last compositions were also heard 1 September, when **The Emerald Isle** was brought into the Herald Square by Sam S. Shubert. It was his second musical mounting. Although the story centered on the successful courtship by an Irish rebel of the daughter of Ireland's Lord Lieutenant, the star of the evening was Jefferson De Angelis in the role of a buffoonish professor. Neither the comedian nor the comic opera elicited much interest, and they quickly departed.

The first of the more regular touring musicals to appear was **Codfish Aristocracy** (1 September 1902, Metropolis), whose paper-thin plot of a couple of husbands doing up London and Paris without their wives and attempting comic escapes when the very angry wives decide to follow them served as a frame for all manner of songs, dances, and other variety acts.

King Highball (6 September 1902, New York) also had only a brief stay. Based on Rupert Hughes's *The Understudy*, it told another of the preposterous, never-never-land tales so beloved by the era. An astronomer who has been seeking to communicate with Mars finally attracts the attention of a young Martian lady. She succeeds in bringing him and his assistant to the planet, where they learn the law states if ever an Earthling arrives he shall be made king. Complications ensue when the assistant, who is an older man, claims he should become the ruler. They are both expelled and return to Earth. Frederick Bowers's score was as undistinguished as Charles Horwitz's dialogue. To impart a suitably unearthly aura chorus girls danced on a darkened stage lit only by tiny lightbulbs twinkling on the girls' dresses. The most rewarding moments of the evening probably came when its star, Marie Dressler, displayed her rambunctious brand of clowning. She played none of the figures mentioned in the summary of the plot (which, incidentally, required more than a full page of the program to outline its convoluted details); instead she walked off with comic honors as the king's "46th wife."

In **The Doings of Mrs. Dooley** (22 September 1902, Grand Opera), the lady, widow of a working man, inherits a fortune and chooses to find a place in society. What made the musical so diverting were the antics of the popular, buxom female impersonator George W. Monroe in the title part. He repeated his standard character, "a low-bred, unctuous and broadly amusing type of Irishwoman." Among the characters she encountered were Wannie Maker, a snooty, effeminate salesclerk at a swank department store (Wanamaker's was then a leading emporium), and Gloomy Gus.

A revival of *Robin Hood* (28 September 1891), with several of the original players (notably Henry Clay Barnabee and W. H. MacDonald) still singing their roles, came in on 8 September to begin a four-week stand at the Academy of Music.

Weber and Fields gave Broadway its first major hit of the season when they relit their Music Hall on 11 September with **Twirly-Whirly**. For the first time they called their evening a "musical comedy," thereby aligning themselves squarely with the forces of the future. A pall was cast over the opening by the realization that this was the last Stromberg score, for John Stromberg had committed suicide in July. But he had succeeded in composing an outstanding number for Lillian Russell—"Come Down, Ma Evenin' Star"—and, although she was too overcome by emotion on opening night to finish the song, it afterward remained identified with her. Other problems beset this star-crossed production. De Wolf Hopper and Sam Bernard had left for bigger salaries elsewhere and, most ominous of all, rumors were beginning to spread about the personal coolness between the stars, despite their efforts to keep it quiet. But on the brightly colored stage the treasured absurdities seemed as hilarious as ever. Tourists and natives in Seville can only talk about Mrs. Stockson Bond's purchase of the big, local castle, until Hanki Panki Poo (Will Archer), a monkey, distracts them with a seltzer siphon. (One successful interpolation in *The Defender* had been "Pinky Panky Poo.") The monkey's owner, McCracken, rues his lot in a number which in keeping with the Weber and Fields pattern was rather well integrated into the story, "Strike Out, McCracken." After a series of vaudeville repartees between McCracken and Winger, a vaudeville impresario, Mrs. Bond (Russell) arrives, announcing she is "The Leader Of Vanity Fair":

You must take up the fad I start
Whether it be racing or Delsarte
Though it seems hollow, still you must follow
The leader of the set called "smart."

Before she exits she advises her friends she will hold a gala that evening. She has asked all the resident nobility. Michael Schlaatz (Weber) and Meyer Ausgaaben (Fields) arrive in an airship. They are quickly invited to the party to replace some nobles who have determined to cut the American upstart. Meyer appears for the soiree pulling Mike in an automobile. Mrs. Bond is informed Hanki Panki Poo is drunk. She laments, "the life of a society star is not a path of roses. I envy the little stars up there. They can stay out every night and not lose their sparkle." And she beckons, "Come Down, Ma Evenin' Star." But Schlaatz and Ausgaaben are bored. To escape from the party and to have a little excitement at the same time they decide to set off a bomb. Meyer prepares the explosive and gives it to Mike to detonate: "I tell you it is easy. Go right up and kick it and as soon as you hear the explosion, step to one side and let it go past." The blast sends the monkey and the furniture flying. A tattered pair of comedians run across the stage as the curtain falls. Typical of the outrageous stage business Weber and Fields employed so skillfully was the trick sailor suit worn by one of the performers while talking to the pair. When he faced Weber, the side of the suit was black, as were his wig and mustache, and he spoke in a gruff, deep voice. When he turned to face Fields, he had a white suit, blond hair, and a high-pitched voice. Antics of this sort regaled audiences for 244 performances.

September's final offering was another of the numerous importations from London, Lionel Monckton's **A Country Girl** (22 September 1902, Daly's). It played four months and then toured. The respect American critics held for these English pieces can be seen by the amount of space the *Times* reviewer gave to it, especially his detailed discussion of the plot. Plots in American shows were given short shrift at best. Perhaps in the case of *A Country Girl* the attention was merited, not so much for the quality of the work as for the way some of its characters hinted at the future. Its hero, a handsome young man called Geoffrey Challoner, was a naval officer. The leading comedian appeared in the guise of the Rajah of Bhong. Come December, New York would rejoice in some homemade nonsense from Chicago featuring an American naval officer and a Sultan.

On 4 October Chicago welcomed a new show and a new theatre. The show, *Chow Chow*, would come to New York at the end of the season with a change of title; the theatre, the New Orpheon, would, of course, remain in Chicago. But it, too, would undergo a change of name and become the most important lyric house in the heyday of the Chicago musical.

Remnants of the once popular Liliputians (for the moment billed as The Royal Liliputians) were the stars of **In Posterland** (20 October 1902, Metropolis). Their adventures found them posing, then coming to life in *tableaux vivants* of well-known posters of the day and scampering in and out of an Amazon march. Although many of the songs were supposedly written for the show (by various writers), one hit was "In The Good Old Summer Time," which Blanche Ring had introduced months before on Broadway.

A less successful new musical and a less successful new theatre were unveiled in New York two weeks later when **Tommy Rot** opened the short-lived auditorium known as Mrs. Osborn's Playhouse on 21 October. The musical was paired with a Joseph Herbert parody of *Iris* called *Cryris. Tommy Rot* had an all-too-simple plot. Eric Leicester loves Phoebe Dare, but a will keeps them apart until the curtain falls. With so little story to dwell on, those critics who did not rail at what they considered an unseemly title found plenty to complain about in the weak score and crude jokes that ran to the order of "The boys at the club call one of the twins Inanimate and the other In-a-minute." Only Blanche Ring, playing a young lady with the inappropriate name of Innocence Demure, received general praise and with "The Belle Of Avenue A" added another song to her lifelong repertory. The show closed quickly, was revised, and reopened on 27 November as *Fad and Folly*. But the reworking was insufficient, and the show soon folded for good.

Another English importation, Leslie Stuart's **The Silver Slipper** (27 October 1902, Broadway), enjoyed a five-month run. A saucy young lady of Venus kicks her slipper out of Venus's orbit, so is banished to Earth. Intercourse between Venus and Earth apparently was more stageworthy than between Earth and Mars. Stuart's score was somewhat hand-me-down, clearly hoping to capitalize on his *Florodora* vogue with numbers like "Come Little Girl And Tell Me Truly." The gowns for this sextette were said to cost $3,000. Still, the biggest success of the evening was an American interpolation, "Tessie, You're The Only, Only, Only" (Will R. Anderson)—a song inexplicably adopted by the Boston National baseball team as its theme, although it had nothing to do with baseball or Boston.

The same 27 October saw Chauncey Olcott arrive at his customary harbor, the 14th Street Theatre, with still one more of his sentimental Irish melodramas, **Old Limerick Town**. Neil O'Brien loses his wealth, retrieves it, and finds love with a comely Irish lass. As usual, Olcott sang a handful of Irish-American melodies to please his roisterous and loyal brigades.

Apart from *Fad and Folly*, only a single musical appeared in November, **The Mocking Bird** (10 November 1902, Bijou), with book and lyrics by Sydney Rosenfeld and music by A. Baldwin Sloane. When the king of France fails to advise the governor of his Louisiana Territory that the land has been ceded to Spain, the local citizenry rebel, led by the "gentlemanly" pirate, Jean La Farge (Frank Doane). To signal one another the rebels whistle "Listen To The Mocking Bird." In the end they make the king sit up and take notice, and Jean wins the hand of Yvette Millet (Mabelle Gilman), the French ward of a wealthy New Orleans man whose advances she has spurned. The critics were more taken with the evening than the public was. The dialogue was certainly adequate, and Rosenfeld's lyrics were as good as were then being written—possibly a mite better. He could not always escape the inversions, imageries, and fustian rhetoric of the time, and he did produce phrases such as "When gentle night in sable mantle dressed." But he could also draw some fetching, natural pictures:

> *The bullfrogs huddle near the old bayou*
> *And they croak as in a dream;*
> *And the owls hoot grimly "To whit, to whoo!"*
> *In the fireflies' fitful gleam.*
> *And the frogs and the owls and the flies on wing*
> *Seem possess'd of a solemn fright;*
> *They are all of 'em asking the self-same thing—*
> *"What's the matter with the moon to-night?"*

Sloane's score was as good as any he ever did. Restricted, almost pinched, in range and persistently uninspired, it was nonetheless not unpleasant. On the opening night the finale for the first act, "Glorious France," stirringly sung and marched to, won the most encores. There was much public to-do over Rosenfeld's supposed rediscovering the "long lost" "Listen To The Mocking Bird." Whether the old minstrel tune had indeed been as completely forgotten as some of the advance notices suggested or whether it was simply the sort of clever publicity Rosenfeld was noted for is moot.

A black ensemble known as The Smart Set was responsible for **Southern Enchantment** (10

November 1902, Star). The action takes place in Hawaiian Swelldom, where a trusting George Washington Bullion comes searching for a long-lost sweetheart. He meets up with a con man, Grafton Smooth, and is inducted into the Order of the Royal Rooster before he finds both his girl and unexpected wealth. Ernest Hogan, the black comedian who always performed without stereotypical makeup, played Bullion and wrote much of the music, including his encore-earning "A Missionary Man." But, as was the case with *In Posterland*, not all the music was original. One song was Will Marion Cook's "My Little Gypsy Maid," which Broadway had heard in *The Wild Rose* (5 May 1902). The Smart Set company survived into the 1920s, but once these regular touring houses became film houses its shows were confined to Harlem and a handful of theatres in other cities devoted exclusively to black entertainments. As such, they received little or no attention in the white press.

Three musicals arrived in New York in December. The first was a fascinating work, at once artistically important and artistically disappointing. **When Johnny Comes Marching Home** (16 December 1902, New York) told a straightforward, if melodramatic, tale of the War Between the States. It told it with a surprising compassion for both sides and with a minimum of the buffoonery so commonplace in the period's lyric efforts. Indeed, some critics complained of a lack of humor in the piece. Kate Pemberton (Zetti Kennedy), a Southern belle, falls in love with a Union colonel, John Graham (William G. Stewart). But Kate's ardor for the Confederate cause is such that her young brother (a trouser role played by Julia Gifford) has little difficulty in persuading her to pilfer important papers from the pocket of General Allen, even though Allen's daughter (Maude Lambert) has been Kate's friend. Though Graham steps in and takes the papers, he is understanding. And in the end, when it is discovered that John is the long-lost son of Felix Graham (Albert McGuckin), on whose plantation much of the action unfolds, the youngsters are united. The excessive melodrama and farfetched turns of Stanislaus Stange's plot vitiated some of the artistic pretensions of the work. Similarly, Julian Edwards's score was the best of his not overly distinguished career, containing some above-average work. "My Own United States" was sung nightly by John to fervent applause.

Equally fervent applause greeted the stirring, military first-act finale—this one set at a Confederate Ball. Both Edwards and Stange were too much of their own

time to rise above the conventions of the day. "My Honeysuckle Girl," "Sir Frog And Mistress Toad," and "Fairyland" were all bows to the era's theatrical conventions. And while no interpolations were permitted to spoil what integrity the musical possessed, the show's producer nonetheless felt compelled to advertise it as "a spectacular military opera" and an "American spectacular comic opera." Although it ran only seventy-one performances, *When Johnny Comes Marching Home* enjoyed revivals in later years.

JOE HOWARD was born in 1867, the son of an Irish saloon keeper on New York's Lower East Side. Placed in an orphanage after his parents' death, he ran away to St. Louis. After a stint as a newsboy, he joined McNish, Johnson, and Slavin's Refined Minstrels, leaving this group to launch a vaudeville act in which he boxed with former heavyweight champion Bob Fitzsimmons. Settling in Chicago, Howard embarked on a career as a songwriter to supplement his income as a performer. He quickly scored one big hit, "Hello, Ma Baby." Two of his songs, "The Queen Of The Track" and "Coffee," had been inserted into *Chow Chow*.

Chicago's New Orpheon Theatre retained its original name for only a matter of weeks. Shortly after *Chow Chow* closed, the playhouse was rechristened the La Salle and under this name served as the flagship for the Chicago musical theatre. The renaming coincided with the opening of a new musical on 21 December. **The Paraders** had book and lyrics by Raymond Peck and music by Joe Howard. Peck shortly disappeared from the lyric scene, but Howard stayed on to become the most prolific and best of the Chicago-based composers. *The Paraders* recounted how an old cowboy, Major Ben Bluster, has a run-in with the spendthrift, foppish Baron von Blitzen. Wiener Schnitzel, a Buffalo lawyer, arrives to complicate matters, but a pretty American heiress, Melba Million, sets everything right. The Chicago *Tribune* dismissed the work as "an extended sketch," and *The Paraders* was withdrawn after a run of just over a month. But in one respect the *Tribune* admired the work and correctly predicted a future for similar musicals, if they were better written.

The paper's critic suggested, "[T]here is a place in Chicago for the more modest musical production provided it is thoroughly wholesome."

A conventional show, **The Billionaire** (29 December 1902, Daly's), met with immediate success in New York, although it was quickly forgotten after its final curtain. The run-of-the-mill songs Gustave Kerker and Harry B. Smith ground out covered the requisite range—"pretty songs, coon songs, semi-classical, sentimental, and topical ... ." Smith's plot focused on John Doe (Jerome Sykes), the richest man in the world. In Nice he meets a young American, Pansy Good (Nellie Follis), who is studying for the stage. He becomes so fond of her he builds her a theatre in New York. Later, back in France, Doe attempts to ride his own horse in a race. Since he is too fat, Pansy takes his place and wins. Smith's idea of humor, despite his years of professional success, was often no better than the amateurish material of, say, *Tommy Rot*. One character announced, "I will now sing a song written expressly for me, by an expressman," while a later bit of dialogue ran:

—You're so refined.
—I ought to be; my father used to own a refinery.

An even more successful musical opened at Wallack's on 29 December, the same night as *The Billionaire*. A Chicago musical which began a long run there at the Studebaker on 11 March 1902, it was one of the rare Chicago triumphs that New Yorkers openly embraced, and for many it has remained the exemplar of its type—the interaction of American mores, generally represented by the American Navy, and the strangely utopian ways of a far-off tropical isle. More often than not the isle was ruled over by an outlandish clown of a king, either a befuddled foreigner accidentally placed there or a curiously freethinking native. Ki-Ram (Frank Moulan) fills the bill to a tee. He is **The Sultan of Sulu**, a dot of land somewhere in the Philippines. As the curtain and the sun rise his reluctant wives gather before his hut to sing an exotic reveille. Ki-Ram's majordomo, Hadji (Fred Frear), sees to it the wives, willing or not, behave correctly before their master:

Hadji: Daily catechism. Do you love your husband?
Selina [a wife]: What is the answer?
Hadji: The answer is "I adore him."

But for all Hadji's careful preparation, Ki-Ram's day will not be just another round of insouciant bliss.

Lt. William Hardy (Templar Saxe) of the U.S. Navy appears to announce his country has bought the island and a navy contingent led by Colonel Budd (William C. Mandeville) will arrive momentarily to take over. Budd, admonishing his men, conveys the ambivalence of Yankee attitudes: "For the first time you are about to stand in the presence of royalty. Stiffen yourselves for the ordeal, and remember, no deference, for each of you is a sovereign in his own right." Ki-Ram is advised that changes will have to be made, for "the constitution follows the flag." But the Sultan sees no need for the slightest alteration. He enumerates the virtues of "The Smiling Isle" to the puzzled sailors:

We've not a single college
Where youth may get a knowledge
Of chorus girls and cigarettes, of poker and the like;
No janitors to sass us
No bell-boys to harass us
And we've never known the pleasure of a labor-
*   union strike.*

But the Americans are not impressed, especially their new judge advocate, Pamela Francis Jackson (Blanche Chapman). She is determined to put an end to the Sultan's bigamy. Ki-Ram, hoping to have things his way, woos her, insisting the world has become full of color and sweet fragrance "Since I First Met You." The stern Miss Jackson has all but melted and acquiesced when she realizes Ki-Ram simply means to add her to his harem. Her vengeance is as awful as it is swift. She decrees he must pay alimony to his wives: half his total income to each—or, as he quickly calculates, three times his total revenues. Ki-Ram begs for mercy, pleading his difficulties stem from the fact that more than the constitution follows the flag:

Ki-Ram: When the Colonel took me aside in there he said he was going to make me acquainted with one of the first blessings of civilization. He told me that the constitution and the cocktail follow the flag. Then he gave me an amber-colored beverage with a roguish little cherry nestling at the bottom. And, oh, little friend, when I felt that delicious liquid trickle down the corridors of my inmost being, all incandescent lights were turned on and all the birds began to sing.

But Miss Jackson's heart has hardened. Fortunately, word from Washington informs Colonel

Budd that the Supreme Court has declared "the constitution follows the flag on Mondays, Wednesdays and Fridays only," and since the Navy has imposed itself on an off day Ki-Ram is free to govern as he wishes. The New York *Times*, summarizing the plot, suggests Sulu and American values will prevail on alternate days. If the critic's summary is accurate, then deviation from the printed text had taken place. The show confirmed Frank Moulan as a star and enhanced the popularity of its librettist-lyricist, George Ade. But though Alfred G. Wathall's music was as good as anything on Broadway at that moment, Wathall never provided another score for the New York theatre.

Alphonse and Gaston (29 December 1902, Metropolis) was billed as a "cartoon comedy extravaganza in three whirls" and dealt with the problems an absurdly polite French pair ("You first, Alphonse." "No, you first, Gaston.") bring on themselves in a less well-mannered New York. Along with vaudeville specialties, the entertainment had a full slate of songs, including "Under The Bamboo Tree," which Marie Cahill was making famous in *Sally in Our Alley* (29 August 1902).

The first musical of 1903 did not arrive until 19 January, when a melodized Dickens, **Mr. Pickwick,** with book by Charles Klein and music by his brother, Manuel, had a thirty-two-performance stay at the Herald Square. Even the commanding presence of De Wolf Hopper, for whom Klein had written the book of *El Capitan,* could not save the day. Nor could a host of excellent supporting performances—Digby Bell (Weller), Louise Gunning (Arabella), and Marguerite Clark (Polly).

While *Mr. Pickwick's* opening was attracting attention on the main stem, the once important Star Theatre offered a week's run of **Zig-Zag Alley,** a "spectacular trick farce-comedy" whose settings included "a house that revolves vertically," a station on an imaginary subway between New York and Atlantic City, and the Atlantic City boardwalk. This last provided room for the marvelous trick bicycle act of Zeb and Zarrow. The piece dealt with the problems of mistaken identities that plague four eloping couples. Its best number was "Under The Bamboo Tree," which New Yorkers had heard earlier in *Sally in Our Alley.*

The season's biggest hit, **The Wizard of Oz** (20 January 1903, Majestic), was adapted for the stage by its creator, L. Frank Baum, with music by Paul Tietjens and A. Baldwin Sloane. Julian Mitchell staged the entertainment. Its story was not quite that of the original nor that made famous by the movie version thirty-odd years later. Long ago an Earthling arrived in Oz by balloon. He deposed King Pastoria (Gilbert Clayton) and sent him into exile back on Earth. A gigantic cyclone, which opens the show, whisks the old King back to his homeland. Caught up in the same storm are little Dorothy Gale (Anna Laughlin) of Kansas and her cow, Imogene (Edwin J. Stone). The king's girlfriend, Trixie (Paula Edwards), has also been transported by the winds to Oz. With the help of his old ally, General Riskitt (Harold Morey), the king sets about reclaiming his throne. Meanwhile Dorothy, aided by a witch and the former court poet, Dashemoff Dailey (Bessie Wynn), heads for a meeting with the wizard, who alone can send her back to her Kansas farm. On the road they encounter a Scarecrow, looking for a brain, and a Tin Man, looking for a heart. (They also encounter a lion. But in this version his part is minuscule.) Together they continue on to the wizard. Their path is not an easy one. At one point enchanted plants ensnare them, and only the witch's magic breaks the spell. In the end Pastoria captures the wizard (Bobby Gaylor). But the king, too, is reluctant to let any Earthling return, even Dorothy. Once again the witch comes to her aid, threatening to brew a worse storm than before if the king prevents the little girl's leaving.

The dialogue and the music were banal. The most popular songs were two interpolations: "Sammy" (James O'Dea/Edw. Hutchinson) and "Hurrah For Baffins Bay" (Vincent Bryan/Theodore Morse). However, the spectacle and the story intrigued not just regular playgoers, but the children's market as well. Mitchell's opening cyclone rivaled David Belasco in its realism and beauty, exposing "twenty-seven heavens and nine hells of scenery" by allowing one rapidly opening curtain after another to display the progress of the storm and the uprooting of Dorothy's house. Although advertisements for the show warned playgoers that if they were late and missed the opening cyclone they missed the most spectacular part of the evening, for many who saw the original production the most memorable moments of the evening were the carryings-on of Fred Stone and Dave Montgomery as the Scarecrow and the Tin Man. Coming after their initial success in *The Girl from up There,* it established them as stars. For the rest of their career they played similar roles in similar shows, taking what bygone times would have turned into pantomime and making it into a unique musical comedy genre. Time and again their offerings were to prove the major success of the season; and while they had a few imitators they had no rivals.

DAVE MONTGOMERY was born in St. Joseph, Missouri, on 21 April 1870. His early professional experience was in dramatic stock. Playing in Galveston in 1894 when Haverly's Minstrels came to town, he left his stock troupe to join the entourage, finding Stone in its company.

FRED STONE had been born to Valmont, Colorado, on 19 August 1873, but spent most of his childhood in Topeka, Kansas. He and his brother joined a circus in 1886. During their stint they served as roustabouts, acrobats, and clowns. Fred left to enter the legitimate theatre, where his first role proved to be Topsy in *Uncle Tom's Cabin*. He soon transferred his allegiance to the minstrel stage. Shortly after Montgomery and Stone met, Haverly disbanded his company. The two young men tried out a new act at a New Orleans saloon and quickly moved up to Chicago vaudeville. From there their progress took them to New York and London before they attempted their first legitimate musical.

In his autobiography Stone devoted much space to describing the acrobatics he used in later shows. However, much of his discussion of *The Wizard of Oz* centered on his makeup, vividly recording the grotesqueries so typical of clowns of the day. "We had worked out a makeup which in every particular resembled the illustrations of the fairy tale. I used a thick flesh grease paint which obliterated all the lines of my face, eyebrows, eyelashes, and features, and applied heavy streaks of black to accentuate the straight mouth and nose. One eyebrow was drawn low and the other high, with black circles around the eyes, one large and one small."

A great solo clown, Eddie Foy, had almost as big a success the next night with a revision of David Henderson's old Chicago hit, **Mr. Bluebeard** (21 January 1903, Knickerbocker). The revision went back to its English source to restore the part of Sister Anne for Foy. Foy had a field day with a recalcitrant bustle that seemed to have a mind of its own. The bustle persisted in wagging at embarrassing moments and often in directions exactly opposite from the way in which the rest of Foy was moving. The show's "pony" ballet with music by Jean Schwartz heightened the vogue for the diminutive chorines. But Foy's luck ran out when the show moved to Chicago, for it was during a performance of *Mr. Bluebeard* on 30 December 1903 that the disastrous Iroquois Theatre fire took place.

Raymond Peck and Joe Howard had a musical ready on 1 February to replace *The Paraders* at Chicago's La Salle Theatre. In spite of a title suggesting an American Indian setting, **Tom-Tom** followed a group of Americans to Japan as they search for a legendary jewel. Curiously, the hit song was "Ragtime Chinaman." Howard himself and Al Shean were featured prominently. But the show was no more successful than its predecessor.

Spotless Town (9 February 1903, Metropolis) allowed no one, under penalty of law, to stain or litter. Caught in the complications such an ordinance creates were Dietrich Schnitzel, Ludwig Sauerbraten, Chips Stake, Alkali Ike, Harvard Yale, and Vera Swell. So were a pair of midgets in a baby elephant costume and a dog trained to grab culprits by the seat of the pants, then hold on for dear life.

Blanche Ring returned to New York as **The Jewel of Asia** (16 February 1903, Criterion). While hers was the title role, she was not yet listed above the show's name. The official star of the evening was James T. Powers as Pierre Lerouge, an artist who is forced to become a waiter and ultimately finds himself with a harem all his own. But Zaidee, the Jewel of Asia and the wife of the minister of police, Simon Pasha (George O'Donnell), straightens everything out. There was no real show-stopper for Miss Ring in the evening as there had been in her two earlier productions. The book and lyrics (by Frederic Ranken and Harry B. Smith) and the music (by Englander) were lackluster. What shine the evening had came from its performers, who kept it on the boards until another musical was ready for Miss Ring.

Marie Cahill, for the second time in the season, followed hard on Miss Ring's heels. Cashing in on her controversial interpolation in *The Wild Rose* (5 May 1902), Miss Cahill reentered the arena as **Nancy Brown** (16 February 1902, Bijou), a marriage broker who arrives in the financially distressed land of Bally Hoo in time to furnish needed rich heiresses. The libretto was tailored to Miss Cahill's measurements by Frederic Ranken, in collaboration this time with George Broadhurst, and the otherwise unknown Henry Hadley provided a score. Since Miss Cahill was calling the shots, there were no difficulties about interpolations. She brought back "Under The Bamboo Tree" and had the dependable Cole and Johnson supply another number to add to her permanent repertory, "Congo Love Song." She kept encoring it for 104 performances.

On 18 February 1903, the New York Theatre was the scene of one of the most important events in American Musical Theatre history. In Dahomey opened. This was the first full-length musical written and played by blacks to be performed at a major Broadway house. There had been some misgivings in theatrical circles. The New York Times opened its review with the startling report, "A thundercloud has been gathering of late in the faces of the established Broadway managers. Since it was announced that Williams and Walker, with their all-negro musical comedy, 'In Dahomey,' were booked to appear at the New York Theatre, there have been times when trouble breeders foreboded a race war. But," the paper concluded with relief, "all went merrily last night." It was impossible for most reviewers to separate the show and its artists. However, when they did, by and large they reached the conclusion that the material was ordinary, even though the lyrics were by the distinguished black poet Paul Laurence Dunbar and the music by Will Marion Cook. Cook's numbers included a cake walk in which the audience by its applause determined the winning pair of dancers. The Times's man felt "the whole was well up to the not very exalted average of this kind of show," while Theatre Arts's reviewer, who had a few more days to make an evaluation, employed almost identical words: "It is about on the same level with the average Broadway show." J. A. Shipp's libretto told how a group of unscrupulous Boston blacks form the Get-the-Coin Syndicate and broadcast their ambitions to colonize Africa with down-and-out American blacks. They send the hustling Rareback Pinkerton (George Walker) to Florida to bamboozle a senile old man out of his fortune. A good-natured simpleton, Shylock Homestead (Bert Williams), accompanies Rareback. But Rareback makes the amazing discovery that Shylock is worth far more money than the doting old fool he has been assigned to cheat. Rareback fast-talks the slow-witted Shylock into

making him his trustee, and before long Rareback is strutting his way in the latest peacock clothes in the cream of Florida and Dahomey society. When the boys are made governors the natives break out in an orgy of wild African dancing. Inevitably, Rareback loses all sense of proportion and restraint, till even the tolerant Shylock rebels:

Rareback: Shylock I really must have the ten thousand dollars.
Shylock: And I say "No."
Rareback: Do you mean to say that you refuse?
Shylock: No, I don't refuse. "No" and "refuse" is two diffunt words. They don't sound alike. You don't even spell 'em alike. I say "No." N-O-E. No!!

Critics agreed "the headliners were the whole show, Williams in particular... ." In fact The Theatre went so far as to pronounce Williams "a vastly funnier man than any white comedian now on the American stage."

EGBERT WILLIAMS was born in Antigua, in the British West Indies, sometime between 1873 and 1876, but most likely on 12 November 1874. Coming to America as a young man, he soon found work as a banjo player in minstrel shows. Light-skinned, educated, and well spoken, Williams hoped to carve a niche for himself in the legitimate theatre. But the prejudices of the times precluded any such career for a black man. Williams was forced to darken his face with burnt cork and to assume the mannerisms and speech of the accepted stage "coon." While working on the West Coast he met George Walker, and the two created a vaudeville act that became popular on western circuits. With time the team moved east and began to appear in musical comedies written for the handful of theatres catering to African Americans. In Dahomey had been created originally for these same houses.

Although Williams and Walker remained a popular and successful team, disparities bred of discrimination prevented their ever achieving the sustained runs that Montgomery and Stone enjoyed. The fifty-three-performance run of *In Dahomey* can nonetheless be regarded as a triumphant breakthrough. A year later, when the show went to London, it was received with open arms and ran seven months.

Busy Izzie (16 March 1903, 58th St.) starred George Sidney, a Yiddish dialect comedian given more to quiet humor than to slapstick. The story found him running first a department store (that possesses a working elevator with a mind of its own) and then a hotel. Crossing his path are such figures as Gee Whiz (a farmer), Willie Cheat, Eddie Fication, Ophelia Pulse, and Delia Hand. One review gave examples of the show's humor. Thus a customer demands, "Don't forget to have that dress of mine ready on time," only to be told, "Busy Izzie never sells goods on time." When Izzie later dictates a long letter, his typist (typewriter in the day's jargon) needs merely a single tap of a key to put it on paper, but when he starts another letter simply with "I," the typing of the little word takes several minutes. Musical numbers could be acrobatic. After a lady finished singing "Sallie Mine," the chorus boys tossed the girls about in "whirlwheel fashion." Another dancer kicked her slipper "with the precision of an expert marksman from her foot to one of the upper proscenium boxes." Few touring musicals were as long-lived or as fluid. It often coupled a slight change in title with a slight change in plot and numerous changes in musical numbers. Some saw the variants as sequels, others as more of the same.

Raymond Peck had a third musical ready for Chicago's La Salle Theatre on 16 March, but this time he collaborated with a new composer, Robert Hood Bowers. Their **Rubes and Roses** related the complications that ensue when two "Dutch" comedians are sold a plot of land which straddles the Illinois-Indiana border. Al Shean and Dave Lewis were the principals. The show was soundly thrashed and closed quickly. *The Paraders* was rushed back in until another work could be readied.

One of the best loved turn-of-the-century musicals, **The Prince of Pilsen,** bowed on 17 March at the Broadway. In a sense there are three princes of Pilsen in the story. The first is Hans Wagner (John W. Ransome), a major Cincinnati brewer and alderman of the city's tenth ward. He goes to Nice with his daughter, Nellie (Lillian Coleman), to visit his son, Tom (Albert Parr), who is serving in the American Navy—suddenly a necessary affiliation for many musical comedy leading men. For different reasons both Hans and Tom are mistaken for Prince

Carl Otto, who has coincidentally booked into the same hotel. The real Carl Otto (Arthur Donaldson) arrives and, quickly sizing up the situation, decides he can have more fun if no one recognizes him. Hans finds time to court a rich American widow, Mrs. Madison Crocker (Helen Bertram), and Tom falls in love with a college girl, Edith (Anna Lichter). Everything is pleasant until a secret map falls into the elder Wagner's hands and he is accused of being a spy. At this point Carl Otto is forced to identify himself. But he also reveals he will marry Nellie, whom he has been courting in his disguise as a commoner. The show gave Frank Pixley and Gustav Luders their biggest hit. Two of Luders's top numbers, "The Heidelberg Stein Song" and "The Message Of The Violet," came from his fine score. Interestingly, the latter, the hit love tune, was sung not by the principal lovers but by the secondary leads, Tom and Edith. Luders supplied some novel orchestrations. Several of the choral numbers, notably the stein song, were sung without instrumental accompaniment, while when the full orchestra was playing, the percussions ("kettle drums, bass drum, snare drum, and cymbals") were given "a full evening's work" to emphasize the melodies' rhythms. One or more companies remained on the road for five consecutive seasons, and several revivals followed. It was only when, later, lustier operettas offered *The Prince of Pilsen* strong competition that its popularity faded.

Still another important piece opened down at the 14th Street on 27 April, the month's lone musical. While George M. Cohan's first musical show had not been much of a success, the popular Four Cohans had been able to keep *The Governor's Son* alive and well for over two years. Now young George took a second of his vaudeville sketches and expanded it into a full evening's entertainment, **Running for Office.** The story was simple and, as a Cohan biographer has said, "perfectly symmetrical." John Tiger (Jerry Cohan) decides to marry, even though he is in the middle of a campaign for mayor of Tigerville. He has been a widower for fifteen years, and the new Mrs. Tiger (Nellie Cohan) is a widow of an appropriate age. John has a grown, single daughter, Madeline (Josie Cohan), and his wife an eligible bachelor son, Augustus (George M. Cohan). Unfortunately the newlyweds forget to tell their children of their plans. While Madeline and Gussie are attracted to each other, they are kept apart by their innocent misconstructions of their parents' actions. Everything is explained, and both pairs are united in time to celebrate John's victory at the polls.

Cohan filled the show with neat touches. Tiger's opponent wants desperately to lose since he has bet $1,000 on John. Cohan's dialogue was racy and slangy—and this raised the hackles of a number of critics. It, too, bore some nicely humorous twists, as when John, who has run on a "Dry" ticket, says to a friend after the votes are in, "I've made a temperance town out of Tigerville. Let's go and get a drink." Cohan had not quite found himself musically, but the easy cadence of his best lyrics and the toe-tapping lilt of his better tunes were foretold in songs such as "If I Were Only Mister Morgan."

Curiously, even though Cohan's unique stylized dances became one of his trademarks, in *Running for Office* the airy dancing of Ethel Levey and the lively stepping of a chorus of "unusual sprightliness and good looks" were singled out for most praise.

The *Times* critic hinted at the excitement conveyed by the speed and brashness of Cohan's production ("Who are the four Cohans; where have they come from, why has it taken them so long to arrive?"), but Broadway was not bowled over. The show's forty-eight performances at the 14th Street Theatre were only sixteen more than *The Governor's Son* had attained.

Mickey Finn (4 May 1903, Third Ave) stepped out of the comic strips onto the stage, where he promptly became confused with a character named Michael Finn. Other characters sported stagier names: Daisy Donot, Nellie Haveakiss, and, once more, Gloomy Gus.

A claptrap affair called **The Runaways** came in to the Casino on the 11th from Chicago, with much fanfare and at a well-advertised cost of $75,000, to pique Broadway's fancy and chalk up 167 performances. According to the *World*, it was "a production that out Anna Helds David Belasco." (In time Chicago critics came to insist some local productions were better mounted than the best New York shows.) The *Times*, on the other hand, thought little of the physical production, allowing that the costumes were elaborate, but damning the scenery as "crude." The *Runaways's* story was a variant on the *Sultan of Sulu* theme. The dyspeptic General Hardtack (Alexander Clark) wins big by betting on a horse called The Runaway. With his winnings he transports the entire cast of 160 to the Island of Table d'hote, "that much overrun fictitious island of the South Pacific where musical comedy authors always rush pellmell for scenic effect." There he is promptly made king, only to discover that he must marry his predecessor's widow or die. The American

Navy, which seems to have spent much of its time behind the footlights, comes to the rescue. The cast contained a large array of specialists. For example, Walter Stanton, Jr., entertained dressed as a rooster. His clog dance caused his feathers and tail to bob animatedly. Arthur Dunn, a midget, brought a comic pickpocket act over from vaudeville. The score marked the inauspicious debut of Raymond Hubbell, a composer Broadway would hear much from and remember little of.

> **RAYMOND HUBBELL** was born 1 June 1879 in Urbana, Ohio, and moved as a young man to Chicago, first to study music and then to lead a dance orchestra. He took a job as staff composer with Charles K. Harris's organization. This show, which was known in the Windy City as *Chow Chow*, had opened the playhouse that soon became the La Salle Theatre.

La Salle Theatre played host to a new show the very night *The Runaways* opened in New York. **The Voyagers** may have consciously been chosen as a title that suggested *The Paraders*, but it represented the efforts of a single author who had not been connected with that earlier show. Frieda Pauline Cohen's story described the lengths to which a father would go to prevent what he deems an undesirable marriage for his daughter. He hires a ship for a world cruise. But his daughter's fiancé will go to equal lengths. He comes aboard in disguise. Love wins. The show had little appeal, and by late June a new show had replaced it.

On 1 June Oscar Hammerstein opened his Paradise Roof Garden for the hot-weather crowds with an extravaganza for which he claimed authorship, **Punch, Judy, and Co.** Critics insisted there was no plot to speak of and no music to praise. An all-female cast employed no dialogue; everything was sung or danced. Some suggested Hammerstein would be best advised to remain an impresario. The *Herald* described the "Stork Ballet," which it considered the hit of the evening, as follows: "Four nursemaids wheel in empty baby carriages, and after doing some high kicks fall asleep. Miss Elsa Hartung in a really frightful costume (that she must have been paid a large salary for wearing) dances in on her toes driving four storks and places a baby in each carriage." Few musicals of the era could escape march numbers, so a pretty chorus of soldiers paraded and Hoosier Zouaves staged an army drill. Trained donkeys and a trick horse assisted. Even so, the show only ran out the summer.

In New York, the season ended on 8 June as it began—with Blanche Ring (her fourth show of the year). This time she was assisted by Harry Conor of *A Trip to Chinatown* fame. The piece was called **The Blonde in Black** (8 June 1903, Knickerbocker), although it was originally to have been known as *The Gibson Girl*. The title was changed after Charles Dana Gibson and *Life* magazine threatened court action. The title really didn't matter. Gaston Roulette (Conor) uses his wife's Parisian dressmaking shop as home office for his matrimonial agency, the Domestic Fidelity Trust Co. He promises to forfeit his fee to any husband whose wife flirts within six months of marriage. Into the shop walks Flossie Featherly (Miss Ring), a vaudeville performer who has come to Paris in a black wig ostensibly to promote the Cakewalk, but really to become a great actress and play Camille. Before she is aware of what has happened, Gaston has paired her with an artist named Van Dyck Beard (Charles H. Bowers). A number of Gaston's couples meet at Van Dyck's atelier, and it takes Flossie a whole act to unravel the misunderstandings. Unfortunately, there was nothing Flossie or Miss Ring could do about Gustave Kerker's third-rate music, and for some reason no workable interpolation was found. Miss Ring did find a way to work in a spoof of *Camille*, and the chorus delighted audiences with a mock banjo serenade. No instruments were used. The boys and girls simply made sounds that mimicked strumming. The two sets allowed George Lederer to parade thirty show girls, first as dressmakers' models, then as artists' models. But these happier moments were not sufficient to save *The Blonde in Black*. Miss Ring doffed her wig for good after thirty performances. In the following season Eva Tanguay toured with the piece, under the title *The Sambo Girl*. Harry B. Smith and Gustave Kerker, who wrote the work in the first place, came up with a number of new songs for their new star.

In Chicago one more La Salle production closed the season. **Lunatics and Lovers** was so little thought of by its authors that they neglected to put their names on the credits. The story these anonymous scribes told portrayed the confusions that arise when three women, all named Nell, come to visit at a house situated next door to an insane asylum. It closed quickly, ending an undistinguished initial season for the small house.

1903–1904

The success and excitement of the preceding season prodded New York managers. As a result, the 1903–1904 season saw a substantial jump in the number of musicals: thirty-two lyric attractions appeared. But critics and public alike detected a decline in quality, and only eight new pieces ran over 100 performances. Two events outside the Broadway arena contributed to the shorter runs. The Panic of 1903, coming so soon after the nation had recovered from the 1893 crisis, deprived many theatregoers of dollars they might have passed across box office counters. The panic hit in the summer, and by August even President Roosevelt admitted it was particularly "ugly." Then in December the holocaust at Chicago's Iroquois Theatre, claiming hundreds of lives, frightened many still affluent playgoers into staying away from patently unsafe and overcrowded auditoriums. The crackdown on fire code violations that came in its wake closed a number of theatres. New York's most notable casualty was the cramped music hall in which Weber and Fields had so long regaled customers.

Because Abbey's Theatre recently had been renamed the Knickerbocker, some playgoers were quick to assume that the musical opening at the Herald Square on 15 June would be in the tradition of *A Gaiety Girl* and *The Casino Girl*. It was not. **The Knickerbocker Girl** used "Knickerbocker" in its older meaning—a resident of Manhattan. The show's libretto aspired to some novelty by taking its heroine, Mahitable Merton (Josephine Hall), to the as yet theatrically unexplored world of South America. There Mahitable helps catch the man who absconded with money from a mineral water company owned by her family. She also finds romance. The musical, with a book by George Totten Smith and music by Alfred E. Aarons, had been touring for some months. But Broadway's Brahmins felt even the weeks out of town had not whipped it into shape. *The Knickerbocker Girl* picked up her skirts and left after a mere two weeks.

Midsummer's Night Fancies (22 June 1903, Crystal Gardens), a double bill of burlesques, **The Darling of the Gallery Gods** and **The Dress Parade**, was the sole attraction to brave the height of the summer heat. A bit of everything was thrown in to make audiences forget the weather. Vaudeville turns included Pat Rooney's soft-shoe dances, Da Kolta's magic act, and music by the Hebrew Orphans' Band. Ned Wayburn devised a miniature minstrel show for seventeen girls. Dialogue in "The Minstrel Misses" ran:

Miss bones: Do you know how Anna Held feels?
Interlocutor: No. Tell us how she is feeling.
Miss bones: Well, better than Zieg-felt.

The bill managed a mere thirty showings. A farce about a show girl, *Vivian's Papas*, offered a number of songs and specialties but was, essentially, a straight play.

The season for touring musicals at combination houses got off to a capital start with **A Son of Rest** (17 August 1903, 14th St.). Its star, vaudeville's celebrated tramp, Nat M. Wills, assumed the role of Hunting Grubb. His first entrance presaged that of Chaplin in *City Lights* decades later. The scene is the front of a fancy summer hotel. A guest, feeling overheated, takes it upon herself to lower an awning. When she does, out rolls Grubb, who had been sleeping in the folds. The guest is a lady whose father has promised her millions if her husband will go to the Philippines and there steal a sacred cat for him. The husband has obliged but has been so long away that his wife has grown impatient. She hires Grubb to impersonate her husband, a second, tinier tramp is brought in to play the cat, and the threesome set out to gull the father out of his money. Two acts of complications followed. Songs ranged from the topical "Had She Only Let Me Dream An Hour More," to the expected "coon" number, "Sukey Sue," and the almost equally necessary anthem, "The Flag And The Girl I Love."

The season began in earnest when two English importations premiered. Edward German's **A Princess of Kensington** (31 August 1903, Broadway) failed to win a large audience, although it boasted James T. Powers as the star of a tale that begins when a fairy steals a banker's clothes and embarks on a masquerade. Paul Rubens's **Three Little Maids** (1 September 1903, Daly's), which followed, quickly found favor and profited from the first long run of the year—130 performances. Broadway relished the adventures of three daughters of a curate as they take on London sophisticates.

The Rogers Brothers in London (7 September 1903, Knickerbocker) arrived for an eight-week stay. Its plot revolved about a magic diamond which rewarded any owner with good luck but cast a curse on anyone holding it unlawfully. Their pursuit of the jewel took Gus and Max aboard an ocean liner (Act I), to Trafalgar Square (Act II), and finally to a Trenton, New Jersey, department store (Act III). The brothers resourcefully found excuses not merely for their "Dutch" routines, but for Negro and cockney bits as well. In most respects the production displayed the standard accouterments of the day, including dancing that was the "acme of gymnastics, but not of grace" and costumes "strikingly brilliant and variegated, but in no wise beautiful." A major change was the replacement of Maurice Levi by Max Hoffmann (this year assisted by M. Melville Ellis). Hoffman's bloodless music was hardly distinguishable from Levi's, but like his predecessor he produced one or two moderately popular tunes for each edition. "By The Sycamore Tree" received as much play as any of his melodies for *The Rogers Brothers in London* and exemplifies his output.

A number of critics found kind things to say about George Ade's book for **Peggy from Paris** (10 September 1903, Wallack's). The *Times* called it "fruitful in social satire," suggesting "the secret of its charm is the racy and unmistakably vernacular quality of the whole plot." But the reviewer regretted it was not "worked out with mature and intelligent craftsmanship." Ade's Peggy (Georgia Caine) was a young lady from Illinois (this was another Chicago show) who goes to Paris to train for a career in singing. After six years she returns as Fleureth Caramelle. She is exposed by her hayseed father (George Richards) at her Chicago debut. Flustered, she insists that her German maid (Josie Sadler) is Peggy. In the end, of course, she acknowledges her identity. Sadly, Ade once again collaborated with an inferior composer. In this case it was William Lorraine, who offered nothing better than "I Like You, Lil, For Fair." Critics praised Richards's "sincere and whimsical" interpretation of the father, adding it gave the whole evening a "grateful touch of human comedy." More typically, they also enjoyed Arthur Deagon (as a bouncer), who employed "grotesque mugging and contorted dancing." Perhaps even more typically, reviewers rued "garish and crude" sets and costumes. The show's run fell far short of *The Sultan of Sulu's* (29 December 1902).

Two nights after *Peggy* arrived in New York, her hometown welcomed a new musical at the La Salle. **The Isle of Spice** was the latest work in The *Sultan of Sulu* tradition. More important, it was the first smash hit the still young house enjoyed. In fact, *The Isle of Spice* was so successful it did something many New York shows had done before it, but no Chicago production had dared. It sent out a second company! It was this contingent, supplemented by some of the original Chicago players, that reached Broadway in the 1904–1905 season.

Blanche Ring threatened to repeat her persistence of the preceding season when she arrived in **The Jersey Lily** (14 September 1903, Victoria). For the first time her name was above the title. George V. Hobart's book cast her as an actress from Trouville who returns to her Jersey home to rearrange some other people's matrimonial plans to her own liking. It wasn't much of a story, and the dialogue was rarely more than competent. The *Times*'s man insisted the most enjoyable moments of the evening came whenever George Ali, playing the part of Miss Ring's parrot, was on stage. Miss Ring dutifully sang the drab songs Reginald De Koven provided for her and then quickly fell back on the repertory of personal favorites she was building, and on new interpolations, of which "Bedelia" (William Jerome/Jean Schwartz) was the best, achieving a sale of three million copies. But her strong vocal chords were not enough to carry so weak a show. Three weeks, and it was gone.

While most aisle-sitters saw no weakness in the annual Weber and Fields insanity for 1903–1904, labeled **Whoop-Dee-Doo**, first-nighters on 24 September apparently spread their lack of enthusiasm. *Whoop-Dee-Doo*'s 151 performances fell far short of the best runs the boys had compiled. Weber and Fields classified the evening as a "Musical Extravaganza" instead of a burlesque or a musical comedy. In another change, W. T. Francis was enlisted to replace the much mourned John Stromberg. He provided nothing of worth. Edgar Smith's plot unfolds at the Kaiser Wilhelm Bier Haus—on the Seine, in Paris. The opening chorus immediately establishes the situation:

> *Hoch! Hoch! Hoch!*
> *It would seem at a casual glance*
> *That Hoch! Hoch! Hoch!*
> *Is an odd salutation for France.*
> *A beer garden perched on the banks of the Seine*
> *Gives consistency quite a hard poke*
> *While adjacent Paree scarcely seems to agree*
> *With Hoch! Hoch! Hoch!*

The owner of this bedraggled stube, Pilsener Hofbrau (Louis Mann), does his best to unload the establishment on Michael Suppegreetz (Weber), a retired grocer, and Michael's friend, Meyer Schwartzgeezer (Fields). The complicated maneuvers that ensue require Mike and Meyer to pose as statues, one of their most famous routines. Trying to get a bite to eat during this imposture, they are forced to suspend their movements while one has a mouthful of bread and the other a chicken pierced on his sword.

Harry Von Tilzer, one of the legendary Tin Pan Alley greats, rarely bothered with Broadway. He was already an established name (with songs such as "A Bird In A Gilded Cage"). In 1902, he had opened his own music publishing house. On 5 October at the Victoria he presented his first full score in **The Fisher Maiden**. Although Tin Pan Alley had close ties with the burgeoning musical comedy form, the new show was, as its title hints, a comic opera of the old school. That Von Tilzer should associate himself with comic opera instead of musical comedy may seem surprising at first sight. But his allegiance falls into place when one realizes how quickly and totally Von Tilzer disappeared from the musical scene a few years later when newer, jazzier forms claimed musical comedy for their own. The piece had a standard comic-opera plot. Marjory Sax (Edna Bronson), the daughter of a New England innkeeper (Al H. Weston), loves Bob Bobstay, although he is almost old enough to be her father. When Sir George Gidding (Robert Lett) is advised by his doctor to witness a wedding in order to restore his health, he has someone impersonate Bobstay, while Bobstay himself is kept away by members of a secret society. Of course in the end love triumphs, when Marjory falls in love with the young impersonator. The book was as dreary and dumb as the plot outline suggests, and, though Von Tilzer's music was praised in many quarters, nothing caught the public's fancy. The show lingered on for a month, and Von Tilzer never again wrote a complete score for the New York stage.

Hefty George W. Monroe donned his usual skirts to portray another coarse, jolly Irish woman in **Widow Dooley's Dream** (5 October 1903, Grand Opera). His Mrs. Dooley—Bridget Gallagher Dooley—cooks for a rich family and also cares for her own niece, whose father is supposed to have buried a treasure somewhere on Long Island. A search for it proves futile until Indians appear to the widow in a dream to reveal the site. They apparently suggested a title change, too, for the musical soon was touring as *Our Bridget's Dreams*. The show's hit song was "Bedelia," which Blanche

Ring had introduced in *The Jersey Lily* (14 September 1903).

Just over a week later New York celebrated Victor Herbert's return to the musical theatre. Herbert had been missing from the Broadway scene for nearly three years while he served a not always serene term as conductor of the Pittsburgh Symphony. His tenure at an end, he returned with two scores in hand. The first was for **Babes in Toyland** (13 October 1903, Majestic). The show had been commissioned by Fred R. Hamlin and Julian Mitchell as a successor to their production of *The Wizard of Oz* (20 January 1903). Curiously *Babes in Toyland* was only the second show by Herbert written with a New York presentation primarily in mind. Except for his quick failure *The Gold Bug* (21 September 1996), his pieces had been created for essentially itinerant companies—although none of these troupes begrudged an extended stay in New York. But times were changing, and New York was surely if imperceptibly asserting its ultimate dominance. Yet times had not changed enough to ignore Chicago, so the show opened there at the Grand Opera House on 17 June 1903, playing through the summer and up to its premiere at the Majestic. The "Babes" were Jane (Mabel Barrison) and Alan (William Norris), who find themselves shipwrecked through the machinations of their wicked Uncle Barnaby (George W. Denham). Luckily, they are stranded in Toyland, where they meet Contrary Mary, the Widow Piper and her eldest son, Tom Tom, Jill, Bo Peep, Miss Muffett, Boy Blue, Simple Simon, and a host of other Mother Goose figures as well as tree spirits, fairies, life-sized dolls, and talking flowers. Uncle Barnaby appears to court Contrary Mary (Amy Ricard) and to further his wicked schemes with the help of the nefarious Toymaker (Dore Davidson). But Jane and Alan are aided by all their Mother Goose friends, and one by one Barnaby's tricks are foiled. Justice is finally meted out at a Toyland court.

The plot was not particularly original, and Glen MacDonough's dialogue was arch when it was not leaden. Still, the mediocrity of the libretto in no way hindered the success of the evening. The spectacle was magnificent—among the best Chicago and New York had ever seen: Barnaby's farm followed by the shipwreck and proceeding through Mary's garden, the Spider's forest, the floral palace of the Moth Queen, the Christmas Tree Grove, a street in Toyland, the Toymaker's workshop, his castle, and the Toyland Palace of Justice. In variety and opulence the mounting harked back to *The Black Crook* (12

September 1866) and *Humpty Dumpty* (10 March 1868)—a far cry from the one-set-per-act musicals increasingly common at the time. Best of all, *Babes in Toyland* had a perfect Herbert score. His biographer, Edward Waters, calls the music that underscored the shipwreck "equivalent to a symphonic poem." To excerpt all the tunes that are still cherished would be to quote from most of the score. The songs ranged from the stirring "March Of The Toys" to the patently cute "I Can't Do That Sum" (with Miss Barrison and the chorus tapping away on slates) to the sentimental "Toyland" (sung in the original by Bessie Wynn as Tom Tom). The show ran out the season, and several companies, of varying opulence, toured the country for years. The work marked the beginning of Herbert's great period as one of the masters of the American Musical Theatre.

October's last offering was a revival of *Erminie* (10 May 1886) on 19 October at the Casino. Francis Wilson was once again Cadeaux, while Marguerite Sylva sang the title role. Jessie Bartlett Davis, once a pillar of the much admired Bostonians, was featured. The musical was well received, attesting to its enduring appeal.

Two shows debuted simultaneously at the beginning of November. **The Girl from Kay's** (2 November 1903, Herald Square) was an importation from London and a smash hit. It had a score by Ivan Caryll and a book by Owen Hall. The action took place in a millinery shop where all the customers conveniently added their own vaudeville specialties to the entertainment. A misconstrued kiss created the complications, but a Mr. Hoggenheimer elicited most of the laughs. Sam Bernard and his fans found the Hoggenheimer role so congenial that it wasn't long before American authors sat down to write a further evening of his adventures.

A second well-liked comic, Frank Daniels, was the star of the competing premiere. It was designed around his talents by Harry B. Smith and Ludwig Englander. Smith "Americanized" a French farce, calling it **The Office Boy** (2 November 1903, Victoria). In his version Daniels played Noah Little, an office menial in the firm of Ketchum and Cheatum. When Noah falls in love with an office girl, he lies to her father that he is a member of the firm. Later he is confused with a famous jockey and forced to ride in a race. Daniels had a droll first entrance. Just before closing time, the offices of Ketchum and Cheatum are humming with activity—girls typing and boys busily running errands. A bell sounds and the staff leaves, wondering where Noah has disappeared to.

The office manager turns out the lights, and the office is dark and still. Burglars enter through a window. They head directly for a large safe. Failing to jimmy it, they blow it open. Out rolls a sleeping Noah. But Daniels was not the sole attraction. Louise Gunning's lovely voice and Eva Tanguay's abandoned dancing also earned encores. However bright and tuneful Englander's music was, it contained nothing that flourished outside the house. The hit of the evening was an interpolation—a fate Englander was long accustomed to. Daniels stopped the show nightly with "I'm On The Water Wagon Now" (Paul West/J. W. Bratton). But even this piece languished without Daniels's personable projection. Still, Daniels was funny enough to give the show a two-month run and a decent tour. Though theatregoers could not foresee it, *The Office Boy* was the first in a long line of musicals produced by Charles Dillingham.

"Bedelia" was encored for a third time this season in **Mrs. Delaney of Newport** (3 November 1903, Grand Opera), but then its writers, William Jerome and Jean Schwartz, were the authors of the show (with Jerome providing the book and lyrics). Like Mrs. Dooley, Mrs. Delaney was a widow, her husband having fallen into a tunnel being dug for a new subway. Her successful negligence suit against the city makes her a multimillionaire. All her newfound wealth turns her head. She chases away her daughter's suitor and her own, a Klondike prospector.

CHARLES DILLINGHAM was born in Hartford Connecticut on 30 May 1868, the son of an Episcopalian clergyman. Dillingham rejected college, preferring early employment in the field in which he hoped to make a career, journalism. A stint with a local paper was followed by positions in Washington and Chicago and, finally, with the New York *Evening Sun*. Soon after his arrival there he was made the paper's drama critic, his first real exposure to the stage. In 1896 he wrote and produced a play called *Ten P.M.* The show was a failure, but it caught the attention of Charles Frohman, who offered Dillingham a position in his organization. Dillingham accepted. For the next several years he served Frohman as a press agent and production assistant.

The daughter's fiancé returns disguised as an English lord. After he and the Klondiker save the widow from being murdered and having her jewels stolen, she comes to her senses. Occasions were discovered to allow the chorus to dress as Scottish fusiliers for a military drill and also as colorful Spanish dancers.

The Red Feather (9 November 1903, Lyric) suffered a perplexing failure. Two of the most venerated old hands in the musical field collaborated on it: Charles Klein wrote the book, and Reginald De Koven wrote the music. And that relative newcomer, Florenz Ziegfeld, mounted it with stunning panache, filling it, as one newspaper noted, with "the resonance of a chorus singing at the top of its voice, a dazzling splendor of superb costumes, and an abundance of handsome, young women." Most of its reviews would today be considered raves. But it lasted only sixty performances in New York, and while on tour, where it fetched more ecstatic notices, business was erratic but generally disappointing. Its story was elementary. The dashing Capt. Trevor (George L. Tallman) of the Romancian Army doesn't realize his sweetheart, Countess Hilda Von Draga (Grace Van Studdiford), is also the bandit known as "The Red Feather," whom he has been ordered to pursue. When the truth comes out it is accompanied by an acceptable explanation, and the lovers are free to unite. Thomas Q. Seabrooke handled the comic role of Baron Bulverstrauss. Perhaps significantly, Seabrooke's name was no longer above the title. Miss Van Studdiford, a Bostonian alumna, alone was starred. The *Times*, less enthusiastic than most papers, may have touched on the reason for its poor showing when it generalized, "[T]he name of comic opera, as well as the thing itself, has fallen into disfavor." If the reviewer was correct he was an astute and sensitive observer, for a number of shows that announced themselves as, and indeed were, comic operas had long, profitable runs in the next several years. But this does not gainsay that the term if not the genre was obsolescent. Within five years fewer and fewer pieces would assume the name, and after World War I the term was relegated to theatrical history.

In an interesting sidelight, *The Red Feather* was the first musical to play the lovely new Lyric on 42nd Street. The Shuberts built the house to alternate as home for both Richard Mansfield's dramatic company and the American School of Opera, which none other than De Koven had recently founded. Given De Koven's conservative bent, the school was obviously superannuated from the start.

Neither Mansfield nor De Koven occupied the house for long, although De Koven did have one of his last hits there. Mansfield had been given the honor of opening the house the previous month. He selected *Old Heidelberg* as the initial attraction. Of course *Old Heidelberg* will return to this history in musical form as *The Student Prince* (2 December 1924).

A second disappointment followed in short order: in this instance for Harry B. Smith, Victor Herbert, and their new star, Fritzi Scheff.

Babette (16 November 1903, Broadway) is a village letter writer in Antwerp during the days of Spanish domination. With the help of a soldier of fortune, Mondragon (Eugene Cowles), she enlists the aid of the king of France (Errol Dunbar) to overthrow the despotic rule. The critics were enraptured with the petite, volatile Miss Scheff. She was at once a fine actress and superb singer. As the *Times* recorded, "her archness and coquetry and flow of animal spirits exercise their full potency." Accolades for Herbert's music were equally warm. The *Evening Post* began by comparing Herbert favorably with Johann Strauss, concluding: "The Broadway Theatre is only a block from the Metropolitan Opera House, and lovers of good music and singing will find them not too far apart musically either." The praise was not far-fetched. Herbert was always careful to tailor his scores to the artists who were to perform them. Miss Scheff's range and skill allowed Herbert a breadth of composition often denied him. He took intelligent advantage of it. In all the shows he wrote for Miss Scheff he included at least one extended showpiece designed to display his star's talents. For *Babette* Herbert gave his heroine "Letters I Write All Day," in which she describes various letters she is called on to set down. Herbert gave each letter a melody appropriate to its content. For example, the music for the greedy landlord's correspondence was "crabbed, monotonous, harsh." Later this sort of number in *Mlle. Modiste* (25 December 1905) was to provide Miss Scheff with the greatest hit of her career. Lamentably, the book was bad. Harry B. Smith was getting an undesirable reputation, even in this era of hack librettists and tolerant critics. The *Times* was biting: "Mr. Smith is known as one of the largest manufacturers in this country of comic opera librettos, which of late years have been remarkably free from comic spirit in their conception and of wit in their dialogue, and the book of Babette has little that will tend to injure the reputation." The show ran only fifty-nine performances.

The claim that it was meant to be a limited engagement cannot hold, for even if Miss Scheff had other commitments someone would have been found to continue and then tour in the piece had the box office warranted.

FRITZI SCHEFF was born on 30 August 1879 in Vienna, where her mother, Anna Jaeger, was a prima donna at the Imperial Opera House. The youngster was educated at Hoch's Conservatory in Frankfort and then made her debut in Munich in 1898, singing the title role in Flotow's *Martha*. Her success was immediate, and shortly she was invited to sing at the Metropolitan Opera in New York. She made her first appearance there on 11 January 1901. Miss Scheff was lured from the Metropolitan Opera by *Babette*'s fledgling producer, Charles Dillingham. In fact he stole her not just from the Met but from Ziegfeld, who had sought her for *The Red Feather.*

Frederic Ranken and Gustave Kerker, utilizing an importation by the authors of *Erminie*, put together a bit of fluff entitled **Winsome Winnie** (1 December 1903, Casino). An American actress, Winnie Walker (Paula Edwards), is stranded in Montenegro. To earn return fare she agrees to pose as Marjorie Bell, Lord Poverish's ward. She is abducted by comic bandits but talks her way out of their den. With the show's labored humor ("This is a viper from the bottom of a pen. A regular pen viper in fact") and mediocre songs poor Winnie could neither talk nor sing her way into a run. She left after fifty-six representations.

On 2 December, just in time for the holiday trade, **Mother Goose** alighted at the New Amsterdam. The magnificent New Amsterdam, for over two decades the supreme musical house in New York, had opened a month earlier with a prestige production of *A Midsummer Night's Dream*. Musicals were still considered backwater affairs there, and straight-play openings were preferred. The house was the fourth to rise on 42nd Street and the first on the south side of the street. The Lyric had opened a few weeks before, the older, pioneering Victoria in 1899, and the Republic in 1900. But it was this great pseudo-Baroque masterpiece that signaled the inevitable primacy of the block. On its mahogany-paneled walls and splendid green onyx staircase were allegorical figures and ancient gods and a lush abundance of tropical plants and animals. On the vaulted ceilings Homeric heroes mingled with the tragic kings and queens of Shakespeare. *Mother Goose* boasted a smart array of young and old talent: Harry Bulger, Joseph Cawthorn (in the title role!), Clifton Crawford, Leila McIntyre, and Pat Rooney. Although it was an importation from London's Drury Lane, it was drastically revised for this side of the Atlantic, primarily by J. J. McNally. At one time or another in its 105-performance run nearly two dozen songs by native writers were interpolated. George M. Cohan provided "Always Leave 'Em Laughin' When You Say Goodbye" and "I Want To Hear A Yankee Doodle Tune," while Cole and Johnson contributed an "Evolution Of Ragtime" number.

Just one day short of a month after he offered *The Red Feather*, Ziegfeld presented **Mam'selle Napoleon** (8 December 1903, Knickerbocker) as a vehicle for his wife. Anna Held portrayed Mlle. Mars of the Comédie Française. Her affair with Napoleon (Arthur Lawrence) takes a dangerous turn when the emperor learns she has another lover, a common soldier (Frank Rushworth). But his fury relents after she is abducted and the young soldier disgraced. He allows them to go off together. By way of novelty Miss Held recited La Fontaine's fable of the lion and the mouse as a second-act curtain. She recited it in French! Ziegfeld surrounded his wife with a lavish production that included a set of an island with shimmering water in the distance, a sumptuous Opera Ball, and, at the very end, a tableau depicting Napoleon's return from Elba. The show had pleasant, if minor, music by Gustav Luders. But all its attractions could not lure enough patrons to keep it on the boards beyond forty-three performances.

Taking in stride all the criticism he was receiving for the librettos he was grinding out, Harry B. Smith once again assumed the burdens of producer when he brought in **The Girl from Dixie** (14 December 1903, Madison Square), a collection of clichés he threw together for Irene Bentley (Mrs. Smith). The story, which he claimed came to mind when he heard a restaurant orchestra applauded for playing "Dixie," was just enough to see the show through the last curtain. Kitty Calvert comes from an old, but impoverished, Maryland family. She is the apple of Lord Dunsmore's eye, but she politely rejects him.

Her own choice is a young man who believes she is an heiress. When he realizes no money will be forthcoming he makes his excuses and retreats, leaving Kitty to reconsider Dunsmore's overtures. Dunsmore was played by Frederick Gottschalk. The musical featured a beautiful chorus line, although the producers, concluding the term "show girl" had been overused, referred to them as "young women of haughty mien and proud carriage." The music, as one Chicago paper noted, was by "nearly all of the living American composers ... and several dead ones." Cole and Johnson led the credits with six contributions. Opening on 16 December, it was 1903's last New York show. It barely made it to the new year.

Just before Christmas two musicals opened an evening apart in Chicago. In a sense both were New York shows. The first was a designed-for-touring musical which came into the Great Northern, a combination house, on the 20th and stayed for the expected single week. A much longer run seemed in store for the second. **The Belle of Newport**, which replaced *The Isle of Spice* at the La Salle, was a curious piece in that it was basically a rewriting of *The Defender*, with more emphasis on Sir Thomas Teaton's courtship of Mrs. Jack Orchard (for which audiences of the time could probably read Mrs. Jack Gardner, Boston's famous art patron). It also offered several Ben Jerome songs not sung in New York. The production was staged by Gus Sohlke, son of the popular nineteenth-century ballerina Augusta Sohlke.

For the next several years Sohlke's chorus lines were to enjoy the same reputation in Chicago that the Casino's and Weber and Fields's lines enjoyed in New York. But few Chicagoans were to be entertained by *The Belle of Newport*. The Iroquois Theatre fire struck just over a week after the new musical opened. All Chicago theatres were immediately closed, and when, after rigorous inspection and reconstruction, they began to reopen in late winter poor attendance threatened to close them once more. *The Belle of Newport* was one of the casualties of these hard times.

If the old year in New York had ended with a musical set in the postbellum South, 1904's first song-and-dance entertainment was a visit to the Victoria on 4 January by Lew Dockstader's Minstrels. But the day was long gone when Bryant, Kelly and Leon, and the San Francisco Minstrels all could play full seasons in competition with the regular theatrical attractions. Dockstader paused briefly to spoof everything from Mayor McLellan to the gossip at Sherry's (by means of "magic wireless") and then returned to the road.

Three English musical comedies followed in rapid succession. Two Sidney Jones works, **My Lady Molly** and **The Medal and the Maid,** premiered on the 5th and the 11th respectively, while **An English Daisy** opened on 18 January. *My Lady Molly*, which featured the London favorite Vesta Tilley, had its heroine disguise herself as a man to be near her beau. Although James T. Powers was starred in *The Maid and the Medal*, its principal plot revolved about complications created when an heiress and a flower girl exchange places, using a medallion as a recognition token. *An English Daisy* offered a first-rate cast, including Charles A. Bigelow, Templar Saxe, Frank Lalor, Henri Leoni, Christie MacDonald, and Truly Shattuck. They sang and danced a tale of two lodgers about to be evicted for nonpayment who are allowed to remain provided one marries the landlord's homely niece. Not one of the three shows was a rousing hit, although the last two tried to ingratiate themselves by interpolating "coon songs." *The Medal and the Maid* inserted "In Zanzibar" (Will Cobb/ Gus Edwards), while *An English Daisy* used the busy Cole and Johnson's "Big Indian Chief."

While New York first-nighters applauded *The Medal and the Maid*, San Franciscans welcomed **The Beauty Shop** (11 January 1904, Fischer's), which had a book and lyrics by James C. Crawford and music by Ada Clement. A fake "beauty doctor" hires gorgeous women and handsome men to pose as examples of his skill. At least one of the gorgeous dolls and one of the handsome guys finds true love by eleven o'clock, while the quack is sent on his way. A stellar cast included Georgia O'Ramey, Kolb and Dill (who often had headed a Weber and Fields road company and who now played officers of the pretzel trust), and John Peachey, a London favorite. The musical comedy ran eight weeks.

In New York, the 18th also witnessed the opening of **Sergeant Kitty** at Daly's, with book and lyrics by R. H. Burnside and music by A. Baldwin Sloane. Kitty La Tour (Virginia Earle) loves Lucien Vallière (Albert Parr), and he loves her. But their lives become complicated in true musical comedy fashion when Henri de Morrilac (Harry Stone), who will be disinherited by his rich uncle if he marries before he is twenty-five but who is already secretly wed, passes off his own bride (Estelle Wentworth) as Lucien's. Furthermore, Kitty has a difficult aunt (Carrie E. Perkins) who insists that her niece marry.

Kitty marries Lucien by proxy so her aunt can see a marriage certificate. The book was generally branded as dull, while Sloane was fast acquiring the same dubious reputation as a composer that Smith had long since won for himself as a librettist. Kitty and chorus girls paraded around for seven weeks and then marched away.

Still one more Hibernian, **The Funny Mr. Dooley** (8 February 1904, Metropolis), put in an appearance. But critics gave this musical such short shrift that we cannot even hazard a guess about its plot or production.

Tommy Todd was also an Irishman, a jockey in love with rich Ima Mahoney. Only Ima's nose-in-the-air father won't hear of her marrying anyone so low—that is, until Tommy learns that Mr. Mahoney plans to enter a horse in a big race and he himself rides the horse to victory. That was the basic plot of **The Good Old Summer Time** (8 February 1904, 14th St.), which Ren Shields and George Evans wrote to cash in on the popularity of their 1902 song hit. However, since "Honey Boy" Evans took the role as Tommy and since he was most famous as a minstrel, an excuse was found to have him disguise himself in blackface for much of the evening. A place was also made for the expected "Dutch" dialect comedian, by having a German brewer pursue the same scarlet-clad widow courted by Mr. Mahoney. Critics agreed that the best new Shields/ Evans song was "The Sweetest Flower That Grows In Tennessee."

Hap Ward and Harry Vokes, the popular tramp act, provided the title for **A Pair of Pinks** (7 March 1904, 58th St.) when the drifters pose as Pinkerton detectives. They befriend a millionaire who is building a model prison, complete with private baths and bellhops. He appoints the pair to be the prison's wardens. Critics thought the idea was rife with possibilities, but noted that no authors or composers came forward to take the blame for its dreary development.

Another London hit, **Glittering Gloria**, unpacked its bags on 15 February at Daly's. Local allusions, American slang, and interpolations were added. Adele Ritchie was starred as an actress who finds herself in hot water after she asks a married man to price a jewel necklace for her. In spite of all the rewriting done to make it acceptable to Broadway, its stay was brief.

For some years Charley Grapewin had been touring two-a-day with an extended skit about a man coming home from a protracted binge.

The Awakening of Mr. Pipp (21 March 1904, 14th St.) appropriated the skit's title, added a first act showing the reason for the binge, played out the original skit as the whole second act, and concluded with a third act reconciling the husband and his wife. One novel bit was the musical's final curtain. "Instead of the usual 'everybody on,' with a hurrah song and dance finish," only the Pipps were on stage. To his wife's horror, Mr. Pipp uncorks a bottle of champagne and pours a glass for himself. Then he smiles, dashes the contents of the glass on the floor, and refills the glass with plain water. The couple start to walk offstage arm in arm as the curtain falls. Pipp's big song was "You'll Be Sorry In The Morning."

On the 22nd, two new musicals came in for inspection. The Tenderfoot was a Chicago musical which furthered the national celebrity of the versatile Richard Carle. Carle wrote both the book and lyrics besides starring as Professor Pettibone, who leaves the effete East to experience the more virile pleasures of the Wild West. But he experiences more than he bargained for when he is captured by Indians and almost burned at the stake. H. L. Heartz's music was pallid stuff. Still, Carle made a show-stopper out of "My Alamo Love." The Times reported the song had received "seven or eight encores" every night during its Chicago stay and sold 30,000 copies in its first ten weeks. Some of Carle's lyrics were praised. Yet for all his popularity in Chicago and on the road Carle was looked on as an easy mark by the New York critics, who found his humor too obvious and too often dependent on off-color double-entendres. For those who found Carle not to their taste, Helena Frederick offered a diversion with her hilarious impersonation of an heiress so exasperated by her husband that she dresses as a man and challenges him to a duel. "Yelling cowboys, swaggering Texans, and taciturn Indians" filled the stage. Although The Tenderfoot had run twenty weeks in Chicago, its eighty-one-performance run at the New York Theatre was as long an unbroken Broadway visit as Carle ever enjoyed during his heyday.

Another fine young comic, Raymond Hitchcock, reconfirmed his right to stardom the same night in the title role of The Yankee Consul (22 February 1904, Broadway). Hitchcock impersonated Adijah Booze, the lazy, bibulous American representative at Puerta Plata. In courting Donna Teresa (Eva Davenport) he gets himself mixed up in a marriage-for-revenge agency and a brewing Latin revolution. The revolution is stymied by Donna Teresa's daughter, who

fears its outbreak will coincide with the governor's ball. The arrival of the U.S. Navy, led by handsome Jack Morrell (Harry Fairleigh), squelches the incipient rebellion. Booze wins the Donna's hand, and Morell wins her daughter (Flora Zabelle). Although it called itself a "comic opera," The Yankee Consul was, like The Sultan of Sulu (29 December 1902), a choice example of early musical comedy. (Indeed, with its chorus girls dancing in pink tights it reminded more than one critic of still a third genre, The Black Crook [12 September 1866] and its successors.) The book was by Henry Blossom, who quickly became, as John Golden wrote, "one of the best musical-book writers that America ever developed." Alfred Robyn's music was light and often brassy, if not brash. The Times dismissed it as "bimmity-bang." "My San Domingo Maid" was the hit of the show. Robyn's was a minor light that flickered only a short while on Broadway. His last years were spent as an organist in the great motion picture palaces. The Yankee Consul ran 115 performances, the first long run for an American creation since Babes in Toyland opened in October.

HENRY BLOSSOM was born in St. Louis, Missouri, on 6 May 1866. He attended private schools, but spurned college to enter his father's insurance company. He soon turned to writing novels, left the insurance business, and entered the theatre with a dramatization of his own novel, Checkers. Most of Blossom's best work was to be with operetta, but he had little trouble making the easy transition to the lighter, brasher musical comedies.

There were no March musicals. A third great comic, Eddie Foy, opened at the Casino on 2 April with the season's biggest hit, Piff! Paff!! Pouf!!! The plot revolved around another musical-comedy will. This one prevents Augustus Melon (Joseph Miron) from inheriting his late wife's fortune until their four daughters marry—in order of age. The daughters are Nova (Mabel Hollins), Cora (Grace Cameron), Encora (Hilda Hollins), and Rose (Amelia Stone). The three oldest girls are the problems, for each attaches a condition to her falling in love. One will have only a man who's never been kissed, the second wants a man who has achieved some sort of greatness, while the third wants a man of almost impossible virtue. Luckily three men named Piffle (Templar Saxe), Paffle (John Hyams), and Pouffle (Foy) meet the bill. The fourth daughter is more than content with a pleasantly everyday newsman. Alice Fischer and R. E. Graham were prominent in Foy's large supporting cast. But Foy dominated the evening, most notably in a scene in which he was supposedly buried in the sand and then paraded around as a sand castle. The music was the first full score Jean Schwartz composed for Broadway.

JEAN SCHWARTZ was born in Budapest on 4 November 1878. His sister, a pupil of Liszt, cultivated his love of music and gave him his first lessons. The family moved to New York while Jean was still in his teens, and he was quickly put to work to earn his share of their support. Odd jobs in a cigar factory and a Turkish bath soon gave way to more congenial employment as a pianist with an orchestra at Coney Island, as a song-plugger at the Siegal-Copper department store on Sixth Avenue, and for the music publishing house of Shapiro-Bernstein. He formed a partnership with the young lyricist William Jerome, and before much time passed their tunes were being interpolated into Broadway shows. "When Mr. Shakespeare Comes To Town" was used in *Hoity-Toity* (for which Schwartz was accompanist), "Rip Van Winkle Was A Lucky Man" in *The Sleeping Beauty and the Beast*, "Mister Dooley" in *A Chinese Honeymoon*, "Hamlet Was A Melancholy Dane" in *Mr. Bluebeard*, and "Bedelia" in *The Jersey Lily*.

Jerome and Schwartz's biggest hits in the new show were Foy's comic number "The Ghost That Never Walked" (a theatrical term for being stranded in the sticks) and a production number, "Radium Dance," with chorus girls in luminescent costumes jumping luminescent ropes. The piece ran well into the next season.

De Wolf Hopper, the fourth great comedian to head a musical cast in less than two months, returned in a revival of *Wang* (4 May 1891) to close out April.

May brought three musicals, all flops. **The Man from China** (2 May 1904, Majestic) told of a family of Florida fruit-growers who hope an eccentric Chinese they have invited to be their guest will bail them out of their financial woes. They mistake an itinerant one-man band (Charles A. Bigelow) for their expected Oriental and welcome him in style. The bewildered wanderer readily agrees to lend them millions he does not have in return for their luxurious yacht. By the time he is exposed, his hosts' daughter (Vera Michelena) has fallen in love with him. "Fifty-seven Ways To Catch A Man" was the hit of the evening, sung by the show's principal comedienne, Stella Mayhew, in her role of Anastasia Giltedge. Although librettist-lyricist Paul West and composer John W. Bratton were both experienced, their drollery lacked the necessary flair to capture the warm-weather audience.

An incredibly old-fashioned, fustian piece, **A Venetian Romance** (2 May 1904, Knickerbocker), had even less allure. A renaissance Venetian girl is forced to masquerade as a boy to win the attentions of the young nobleman she loves. Even brigands cannot stand in her way. Not only was the show badly written, it displayed a disheartening lack of style and tone, filled as it was with mediocre vaudeville turns.

The season for touring shows ended on a down note. It was probably inevitable that the Liliputians (now regularly spelling their name as Lilliputians) would put Swift's Lilliputians on stage. Only this **Gulliver's Travels** (2 May 1904, Metropolis) paid little heed to Swift's story or satire. Rather, Gulliver and his tiny friends journey to meet Mother Goose, Humpty Dumpty, and other nursery figures. "Nondescript" was the adjective one reviewer employed in dismissing the entertainment.

The Southerners (23 May 1904, New York) called itself "A Musical Study in Black and White." General Preston's old slave, Uncle Daniel—played in blackface by Eddie Leonard—falls asleep to dream of thrilling events at the plantation fifty years before, in 1830. Young Leroy Preston (William Gould), after a tiff with his sweetheart, Polly Drayton (Elfie Fay), leaves the homestead to join the Navy. He gives instructions that the slaves are not to be sold to strangers—especially to the boorish Irish Turk, Brannigan Bey (Junie McCree), who lusts after the light-skinned black Parthenia (Vinie Daly). Preston would prefer to set his slaves free, but he knows society will not allow that. A repentant Polly disguises herself as a naval officer to follow Leroy. Preston returns to the plantation in time to foil Bey's maneuvers and to reconcile his differences with his sweetheart. The preceding season a cast had balked at including a black in their show (even though Negroes had acted in white variety bills and musical shows), but *The Southerners* bravely employed a whole black chorus for one scene. The awesome tension of their first appearance was caught by the *Times* critic, who reported, "When the chorus of real live coons walked in for the cake last night at the New York Theatre, mingling with the white members of the cast, there were those in the audience who trembled in their seats." The *Times*'s man seemed almost relieved to add: "[T]he negro composer of the score, Mr. Will Marion Cook... succeeded in harmonizing the racial broth as skillfully as he had harmonized the score." But Cook's music was not enough to overcome an otherwise claptrap show.

The season ended 6 June when an excellent vaudeville, entitled candidly **A Little of Everything**, opened on the New Amsterdam Roof. "Everything" ranged from Offenbach to a second chance to hear Cole and Johnson's "Evolution Of Ragtime." With a stellar cast headed by Fay Templeton and Peter F. Dailey it played merrily through the summer.

1904–1905

Three musicals opened in New York during the hot months, two in July and one near the end of August. Chicago also welcomed a new piece. **Paris by Night** premiered under the stars at the Madison Square Garden Roof on 2 July. It was a lively vaudeville with a thin tour-of-the-city story line to hold the turns together. The principal tourist was Isaac Goldstein (Ben Welsh). Something of a pennypincher, he complains that three months in Paris have cost him thirty dollars. His sightseeing allows him to meet a Russian detective (Henry Vogel), who is looking for Japanese spies, and Steve Hickley (Hugh Cameron), a Bowery tough posing as a South African millionaire. Steve prefaces a courtship by informing his girl, "I've a bunch of talk to hand out to you, Mamey." There were enough pleasant evenings and interest at the box office to keep the roof lit for fifty nights.

Guy Steely and Frederick Chapin, who, along with Richard Carle, had given Chicago *The Storks* in 1902, had another musical ready there on 4 July at the Dearborn Theatre. Benjamin Barclay, the breakfast-cereal tycoon from Battle Ax, Michigan (the great Kellogg interests were centered in Battle Creek), takes his niece, Dorothy Fairfax, on a voyage to **The Forbidden Land** of Tibet. A handsome young Englishman, Tom Wilkinson, accompanies

them. Their party is taken prisoner and told it will be released only if Wilkinson consents to marry Mina Doma, daughter of the Tibetan potentate. Kinkaboo, executive head of the Amalgamated Association of Asiatic Robbers, smuggles a machine into prison. The contraption allows the group to escape. Shortly after the musical opened, the lead article in the theatre section of the Chicago *Tribune* noted a marked decline in the quality of "light opera," blaming this decline on the rise of the comedian and the scarcity of good singers. The article failed to notice the local tradition of musical comedy that was evolving to replace the waning comic opera.

Meanwhile, Carle himself had found a new collaborator. The irrepressible comedian stopped briefly in New York to entertain his followers with **The Maid and the Mummy** (25 July 1904, New York). Its story centered on Washington Stubbs, a failed actor, and now a failing curio dealer. Given to manufacturing whatever "antique" his customer is seeking, Stubbs forces his man-of-all-work, Bolivar (Edward Garvie), to pretend he is a mummy so that Doctor Dubbins (George A. Beane), the wealthy inventor, can test an elixir on him and bring him back to life. For many, an old favorite and a new favorite stole the show. The veteran was Annie Yeamans of Harrigan and Hart fame. Her first entrance as Dubbins's flirtatious spinster sister was greeted with a "storm of applause." The newcomer was Janet Priest. She portrayed a street urchin, Mugsy, trying to be profane, but succeeding only in creating comic malapropisms. As became his custom, Carle provided the book and lyrics as well as playing the lead. R. H. Bowers wrote the humdrum music. As usual, New York was not as receptive as Chicago or the road. *The Maid and the Mummy* headed off to greener pastures after forty-two showings.

A second piece from Chicago followed, this time by way of an extended stay in Boston. On **The Isle of Spice** (23 August 1904, Majestic) Bompopka (Alexander Clark), king of Nicobar, "retires" his wives to a "Tomb of Silence" when they reach thirty-five. He is about to put away Kamorta (Mattie Martz) and marry Teresa (Blanche Buckner), a young American who has come to the island, when the U.S. Navy arrives. The sailors are greeted as sun gods, but Bompopka's awe vanishes quickly after he realizes their arrival will scuttle his marriage plans. Teresa is happy to change allegiances and marry Lt. Harold Katchall (George Fiske). The show attempted some unusual choreography. In a "limelight dance" a chorus of "the prettiest and most graceful girls that ever came eastward on the pike" dressed as witches in pantalettes and danced with brooms. Even the inevitable military drill offered some novelty—at least on opening night. Seventeen marines from the Brooklyn Navy Yard performed "hay-foot-straw-foot," earning themselves several encores. Although the book and Ben Jerome's music were condemned as "a rehash of all the nothings known to the musical stage" the show managed a ten-week stay.

R. Melville Baker and Joseph Hart's **Girls Will Be Girls** (27 August 1904, 14th St.) was the first of the season's lesser musicals, if indeed it was lesser. No one disputed that the old 14th Street sat at the very bottom of the theatre district, but even contemporaries seemed uncertain whether it had become the least important first-class house or lorded it over meaner touring theatres. Its openings sometimes were reviewed (as those in first-class theatres generally were) and sometimes ignored (the customary treatment for touring shows). Since *Girls Will Be Girls* was produced by the rising William A. Brady and starred a then famous, now forgotten vaudevillian, Al Leech, this was clearly one of the theatre's better attractions. Leech was a fine comedian who was also celebrated for his stair dance (a generation before Bill Robinson supposedly made it famous). He played Ebenezer Hezekiah Dodge, a school principal addicted to cock-fighting. His attempts to hide his birds—in a piano, in a mailbox, under his shirt—provided some of the best fun. In two-a-day Leech was often accompanied by a trio of girls known as The Rosebuds. They joined him here, chirping away to the audience's uninhibited delight. In fact, the gallery became so obstreperous in its demands for encores that Brady had to come before the footlights to plead for restraint.

England's pride in its navy had long made naval officers heroes in its plays, and lately in its musicals. Now the impressive might of America's growing naval arm was to be manifest increasingly in the American Musical Theatre. It took the Great White Fleet a week and a day to sail from the Majestic at Columbus Circle, where *The Isle of Spice* basked in a calcium sun, to 42nd Street. Its presence was required there after the Rajah of Oolong (Henri Leoni), over an imagined slight, summarily beheads **The Royal Chef** (1 September 1904, Lyric). Heinrich Lempauser (Sam Collins), a Chicago alderman on a Cook's tour, is not quite voluntarily enlisted as the dead chef's replacement by the obstinate Rajah, who refuses to accept that a Cook's tour is not a chef's tour. The navy lands to effect a rescue, and Lt. Harry Parker (John Park) falls in love with the Rajah's daughter (Amelia Stone). They override a revolution, and a happy ending ensues. The criticisms leveled at *The Isle of Spice* could have been equally well brought against *The Royal Chef*. And indeed they were—with a vengeance. For this was another Chicago offering (with another Jerome score) and a genuinely bad one all around. While Chicago and Boston had embraced the musical (giving it twenty-three- and sixteen-week runs respectively), it disappeared from New York after just seventeen performances.

At the same time the navy was securing the Lyric, the English sailed in with the season's first real hit, **The School Girl** (1 September 1904, Daly's). Leslie Stuart's score was heavily laced with domestic interpolations by at least half a dozen different songsmiths. American Edna May and English George Grossmith, Jr., enlivened this tale of a convent-trained girl's adventures in Paris for 120 showings.

Two musicals elbowed each other for attention the next Monday. Lulu Glaser arrived in a Harry B. Smith–Ludwig Englander musicalization of Charles Major's novel *When Knighthood Was in Flower*, retitled **A Madcap Princess** (5 September 1904, Knickerbocker). When King Henry (William Pruette) decrees Mary Tudor, who loves Charles Brandon (Bertram Wallis), must instead marry the king of France, Mary suspects that King Henry is bluffing. She calls his bluff and wins. The comic opera's forty-eight-performance run was not bad considering how strained the comedy was:

King Henry [*angry*]: I lack words.
Mart: You lack breath. You ought to try breathing exercises. My, aren't kings wearing high collars today... . That collar is an awful thing to get hot under.

Nor was the music of a higher order, but Miss Glaser, dressed as a page to effect an elopement, brought down the house with her blustering rendition of "A Typical Cavalier."

The princess's rivals were **The Rogers Brothers in Paris** (5 September 1904, New Amsterdam). It was a typical McNally-Hobart-Hoffman "Vaudeville Farce." The practically nonexistent story had Rudolph Kahn (Gus) and Adolph Finkeleiner (Max) go not only to Paris, but to the St. Louis World's Fair. En route they help Marjorie Keller (Josephine Cohan) win Walter Leonard (Fred Niblo) over Papa Keller's (John Conroy) objections. A high spot of the evening was an automobile race, with two real cars spinning wildly around an imaginary Place de la Concorde. As usual nothing distinguished came from the score, even though, as sung by Dorothy Hunting and George Austin Moore, "Under The Old Oak Tree" had to be "encored time after time." The boys clowned for nine weeks before embarking on a cross-country tour.

Hal Reid's **The Street Singer** opened at the American on September 12 with Florence Bindley starred. By today's standards the show would be a melodrama with musical interpolations. But in its day it was looked on as an addition to the roster of the lyric theatre. In fact, it was looked on with a certain pride. The Sunday before the show opened in Chicago the *Tribune* noted, "The play is said to contain a coherent plot of more than average effectiveness and musical numbers are introduced without serious jog to the dramatic properties." Even in 1905 the integration of book and music was a serious consideration, although perhaps more of a hope than of an achievement. The plot into which the songs were added told of Violet, a young street-singer whose father works for a rich man. The rich man has two sons, one good and one bad. Both eye Violet, but by the end of the evening the good young man has won her hand.

By rights **Mr. Wix of Wickham** (19 September 1904, Bijou)—a saga of a duke's daughter disguised as a shopgirl in Australia—should be given the shortest shrift. It was an importation and a flop. But twelve of the songs were by Jerome Kern, and, apart from a pair of interpolations in *An English Daisy*, these were the first Kern melodies Broadway heard. The music gave no real hint that Kern would become probably the finest, and certainly the most trailblazing, of all American theatre composers. At the time he was a young man of nineteen.

One other important figure debuted in *Mr. Wix of Wickham* when Julian Eltinge made his first appearance in a legitimate work as a female impersonator. If Kern and Eltinge were making inauspicious debuts, one major figure was making an equally sad farewell. *Mr. Wix of Wickham* marked the final mounting of E. E. Rice, virtually the first great producer and director (and, to a lesser extent, author) of the American Musical Theatre. Not only had he been part-author of two milestone shows, *Evangeline* (27 July 1874) and *Adonis* (4 September 1884), but he had been the first to offer audiences such future great stars as Henry E. Dixey, Lillian Russell, and Fay Templeton. Since he lived another twenty years, he at least had the satisfaction of knowing that both Kern and Eltinge would be added to his list of credits.

JEROME KERN was born in New York City on 27 January 1885 into prosperous middle-class surroundings. At different times his father ran stables, a street-sprinkling concession, and some merchandising houses. It was his mother, herself a pianist, who began Kern's musical training. When he was ten his family moved to Newark, New Jersey, so his father could run a small department store. Kern never completed high school, enrolling instead in the New York College of Music, where he studied, among other courses, theory and music harmony with Austin Pierce. At the same time he worked at a music publishing house. He himself always was to claim that he also studied briefly in Germany, although no records survive of this schooling. More important, he soon gravitated to England, where he fell in love with contemporary English musical comedy and all but abandoned intentions to write concert or parlor pieces. Whether or not he met Charles Frohman on his earliest trip to London is another matter of uncertainty, although Frohman was soon to play a major role in promoting his career. About the time of *Mr. Wix's* production Kern made yet one more major move, buying into T. B. Harms, which thereafter published all his music.

Della Fox had the briefest run of her career in **The West Point Cadet** (30 September 1904, Princess), four performances. She played the roles of a brother and sister. Their resemblance is so close she wears his uniform to elope. Miss Fox's penchant for trouser roles, the era's love of military drills, and a West Point setting all conspired to fill the stage with more march routines.

Even if theatre owners with new houses slated to host mostly musicals felt it more honorable to open their auditoriums with straight plays, the lyric stage had become prestigious enough and certainly profitable enough to begin to lure the great names from the top ranks of the musical world. October's first entry, **Love's Lottery** (3 October 1904, Broadway), was written by Stanislaus Stange and Julian Edwards as a vehicle for the distinguished Mme. Ernestine Schumann-Heink. She stepped down from the world of Wagnerian opera to portray Lina, a German laundress in 1818 England, who wins a lottery and the heart of Sergeant Bob Trivet (Wallace Brownlow) as well. Turgid pieces such as "My First True Love" were the best the serious but poorly endowed Edwards could provide for her. The prima donna was anything but austere. Several times on opening night she stopped to ask the audience, "Is my English goot?" Apparently it was adequate, even if her vehicle wasn't. After fifty performances she returned to Schubert and Schumann and Brahms.

The same night Mme. Schumann-Heink premiered, Lew Dockstader returned to Broadway. Only the first half of his entertainment was pure, old-fashioned minstrelsy. In the second half Dockstader parachuted down from the flies and launched into a series of skits and songs on New York Life. The skits twitted the slowness of Manhattan's rapid transit; the songs sang of "Seeing New York On A Rubberneck Hack."

The first American hit followed a week later with The Sho-Gun (10 October 1904, Wallack's). It marked the fourth Chicago production to debut in the still-young season. Like The Isle of Spice and The Royal Chef before it, it placed an American in an exotic society on the other side of the globe—in this instance, Korea. Both the setting and the story prompted the Times to compare it to what the reviewer referred to curiously as that "forgotten classic," The Mikado. (Apparently the Times's man had himself forgotten its successful revival just two seasons earlier.) George Ade provided the delicious book, as well as the lyrics. Ade's American is William Henry Spangle (Charles E. Evans), the "Goo-Goo" Chewing Gum King and "the man who put Ioway on the map." By his own description he was "born in Chicago and bred at the Waldorf-Astoria." He travels to Ka-Choo, Korea's imaginary capital, to persuade the Sho-Gun (Edward Martindell) to chew "Goo-Goo." But the Sho-Gun, Flai-Hai, is away on a pilgrimage, and an incipient revolution threatens to elevate Spangle into the royal seat or onto the chopping block. The difficulties in which Hanki-Panki (Thomas C. Leary), the royal astrologer; Omee-Omi (Georgia Caine), an amorous widow; and Hunni-Bun (Christie MacDonald), a princess, entangle the foreigner seem almost insurmountable until the U.S. Navy arrives to restore order and let Spangle sail away.

In an interview with the Milwaukee Sentinel during the show's tryout, Gustav Luders professed to rate this as the best of his scores. But this was undoubtedly press-agentry. He also insisted the music was thoroughly American, since he had "never heard of a Corean school of music." Moreover the Times felt throughout the evening "a little local color [was] gained by sparing use of the five-note scale." And Luders clearly did attempt something of what he knew his audience would accept as an Oriental flavor in production numbers such as "Hi-Ko, Hi-Ko" as much by choppy rhythm as by tonal color. Most of the regular songs were what his admirers had come to expect, and if Luders deceived himself into thinking they were all 100-percent Yankee no harm was done. But much of the score indeed echoed the pleasant Americana of the day. For example, Spangle courts Omee-Omi with "She's Just A Little Different From The Others That I Know."

The black musical comedy A Trip to Africa (17 October 1904, Third Ave.) had music by Dave Peyton. Its lyricist, librettist, and star was the comedian John Larkins. Larkins presented the thinnest of plots, something about an attempt to rescue a missionary from Zulus. Songs such as "I Want A Loving Man" and "Zongo, My Congo Queen" reportedly stopped the show, which one of the few critics who troubled to review it praised primarily for its zest. Larkins seems to have put the show aside for a time, then rewritten it as a vehicle for himself and Sissieretta Jones (the so-called Black Patti), and toured with it successfully in 1910.

Higgledy-Piggledy (20 October 1904, Weber Music Hall), another hit, presented Weber without Fields, for their split had come into the open, and the great clowns had gone their separate ways. Initially, Ziegfeld collaborated with Weber on the production, bringing to it his ever-increasing flair and his wife, Anna Held. Weber was probably astute in joining with Ziegfeld, for Weber was generally considered to have had less production acumen than Fields—a reputation that time did nothing to disprove. But the Ziegfelds and Weber could not get along, and when the show went on tour Weber was the sole producer and Trixie Friganza replaced Miss Held. Most of the old Weber and Fields regulars were absent, but Marie Dressler was added to the roster. The story, which was pretty much what the old team had always employed, had two rich Americans traveling in Europe with two young ladies. Adolf Schnitz (Weber), the mustard merchant, has brought along his daughter, Philopena (Miss Dressler), while Gottlieb Gesler (Harry Morris), "President of the American Swiss-Cheese Sandwich Trust," escorts a new-found friend, Mimi de Chartreuse (Miss Held).

The boys are unhappy with the "Bedecker" they have purchased. Schnitz deplores the "closefisted printing," while Gesler admits, "I read a little but it's a rotten story." Nevertheless Philopena assures them without it they would know nothing of "Versales and the Plats de Can Can, where Mary Ann Tonette was beheaded." Gesler is impressed:

Gesler: My! but ain't your daughter stuffed with education?
Schnitz: She ought to be. She served two years and six months in a very fine ladies' cemetery.

Gesler's name gets them involved in an insane William Tell dialogue, and the evening ends in the customary brawl. Neither the Ziegfelds nor Weber walked off with the most critical cheers. They were saved for Miss Dressler, notably in the song "A Great Big Girl Like Me," "an operatic chant varied by elephantine gambols." Maurice Levi, who had served the rival Rogers Brothers, did the score. It was pleasant enough for the evening but without anything memorable.

A London importation, Monckton's **The Cingalee** (24 October 1904, Daly's), offered one more story set in an exotic land, this time revealing the bittersweet romance between an Englishman and a native girl. It failed to find favor.

Billy B. Van, a favorite on vaudeville, musical comedy, and minstrel stages, was starred in George Totten Smith's **The Errand Boy** (31 October 1904, 14th St.). Van's celebrity might have suggested the musical (for which no composer received credit) was a first-class offering, but its producers were Sullivan, Harris, and Woods, major purveyors of touring melodrama, so once again the status of the 14th Street Theatre remains a puzzler. The story stranded a theatrical troupe in a New England village and was peopled with such stock characters as "the comedy sheriff always polishing that badge, the old maid, the drummer [traveling salesman], the manager of the op'ry house, and the Sunday supplement idea of a manager of a one-night stand company with his merrily trooping chorus and his gloriously dressed leading lady." Van was listed in the program as Patsy Bolivar, a character he had introduced more than a decade before in vaudeville. Regardless of the specific role assigned to him in any particular musical comedy, Patsy was described by a contemporary as the eternal "upstart office boy." To bring him to life, Van donned a tight red wig, shortish pants, and a loud gingham shirt. The evening's show-stopper was a song and dance done by chorus girls dressed as country bumpkins.

George M. Cohan returned to give the American Musical Theatre one of its unforgettable evenings. **Little Johnny Jones** (7 November 1904, Liberty) was responsible for a number of firsts for the brash young musical comedy man. It was his first show with Sam Harris, who was to be his longtime partner; his first show to play a major uptown house; his first solid hit; his first book with the flag-waving chauvinism he used so uniquely time and again thereafter; his first score to include some of his undying favorites. His father and mother were again given important parts, as was his wife, Ethel Levey. But Josephine Cohan and her husband had left to join the Rogers Brothers. A new name was on the roster, Donald Brian—a rising young singer and dancer who by some luck or other was on stage whenever important musical theatre history was made during the next decade. A few critics complained that *Little Johnny Jones* was more "musical melodrama" than "musical comedy." They were right, but they had no cause to berate Cohan, who had correctly advertised the work as a "musical play" or simply as a "play with music." The idea for the plot came to Cohan when he read of the exploits of Tod Sloan, an American jockey who rode a royal mount in the 1903 English Derby. In Cohan's theatricalization Sloan became Johnny Jones, the cocky, slangy, identical twin of his creator. Johnny comes to London to ride in the Derby. He is pursued by a whole chorus of attractive girls unconcerned by the knowledge that Johnny is engaged. He has no time to play around with them, but he is thoughtful enough to offer them a helpful hint. When they go to the races, he advises them, "Pawn your jewelry, go in hock, and play Yankee Doodle to win," adding, confidently, that he is "The Yankee Doodle Boy." But Johnny's ingratiating smiles belie troubles behind the scenes. Anthony Anstey (Jerry Cohan) is prepared to bribe Johnny to throw the race. Johnny indignantly refuses. When Johnny loses the race after all, the vindictive Anstey nonetheless spreads the word that Jones lost on purpose. When he shows up at the Southampton docks to sail away, Johnny is met by an angry crowd. His patriotic hackles up, he orders his luggage removed from the ship and prepares to remain in England to clear his good name and his country. A detective friend remains on the ship to search for evidence of the frame-up. If he finds any he will signal Johnny with a rocket from the ship. As the vessel disappears Johnny bids all his friends on board, "Give My

Regards To Broadway." In a "transformation" scene that became so famous Cohan had a mural depict it in the lobby of the theatre he later built, the stage darkened to indicate the passing of time. When the lights went up, Johnny was alone on the pier, leaning against a piling. Before long the ship appears out at sea, slowly making its way across the horizon. Just as Johnny is beginning to despair, the rocket is fired. The jubilant Johnny does a high-kicking reprise of "Give My Regards To Broadway" as the curtain falls. But Anstey's villainy is not ended. He kidnaps Johnny's girl, Goldie Gates (Miss Levey), and Johnny must trail them both to, appropriately, San Francisco, where Anstey runs a gambling house. At first he can find no trace of them in the hustle and bustle of Chinatown, and in a moment of temporary tranquility he pauses to soliloquize "Life's A Funny Proposition After All":

> Did you ever sit and ponder, sit and wonder, sit and think,
> Why we're here and what this life is all about? .
> It's a problem that has driven many brainy men to drink,
> It's the weirdest thing they've tried to figure out;
> About a thousand different theories, all the
>   scientists can show,
> But never yet have proved a reason why.
> With all we've thought, and all we're taught,
> Why all we seem to know is we're born and live a
>   while and then we die.
> Life's a very funny proposition after all,
> Imagination, jealousy, hypocrisy and all;
> Three meals a day, a whole lot to say;
> When you haven't got the coin you're always in the way.
> Ev'rybody's fighting as we wend our way along,
> Ev'ry fellow claims the other fellow's in the wrong;
> Hurried and worried until we're buried and there's
>   no curtain call,
> Life's a very funny proposition after all.

But Johnny is not one to philosophize all night. He is quickly back on the trail and soon succeeds in freeing Goldie and giving Anstey a well-earned comeuppance.

Little Johnny Jones was as fine and progressive a musical as 1904 New York had ever seen. At times, such as the "transformation" at the close of Act II, it harked back to *The Black Crook* (12 September 1866). But in most older pieces the transformation was pure spectacle. Cohan used it for a stunning dramatic climax. In giving his heroine the name Goldie Gates, Cohan was capitulating to the theatrical clichés of the time. And much of the humor, largely

in the hands of the detective (played by burly Tom Lewis as if he were on a perpetual jag), was a series of vaudeville routines. But Cohan's melodramatic yarn was carefully wrought and never lost sight of. Its dimensions were human: the characters had blood that rushed to their cheeks, and their dialogue was vibrant. And all the excellent Cohan songs—not just the classics—were a telling adjunct to the story line. Most critics were unkind. They condemned Cohan for using genuinely contemporary dialogue, though they often complained the talk in most musicals was absurdly stilted. They belittled his attempts at seriousness, while elsewhere they bewailed the frivolousness of the musical stage. Some even assailed his flag-waving as a poor substitute for the sugary confections of the English importations. The show's initial run was only fifty-two performances, but Cohan brought the work back in May for four more months, and again in November of 1905 for an additional month, giving the piece over 200 performances, or more than all but two other of the season's lyric efforts.

The same night Cohan opened in *Little Johnny Jones*, May Irwin premiered in George V. Hobart's comedy, **Mrs. Black Is Back** (7 November 1904, Bijou). The show resembled Pinero's *The Magistrate*, in which a widow lies about her age, forcing her to pretend her grown son is a toddler. Like all Miss Irwin's vehicles the piece was really a straight play. But as was her wont, Miss Irwin found room for several songs.

Down the Pike (7 November 1904, West End) featured Johnny Ray, once a favorite at San Francisco's notorious Bella Union, as an apartment-house janitor sucked into an eddy of comic trouble after several of the building's tenants and some of his acquaintances deem it necessary to disguise themselves as him. Among songs singled out for praise were "Back, Back To Baltimore" and "Snowball Sammy." Even more highly praised was the direction and choreography of Gertrude Hoffman, the encomiums providing another nail in the coffin of her claim that she was born in 1898.

With a title that must have recalled happy memories for a generation of old playgoers, **Humpty Dumpty** frolicked into New Amsterdam on 14 November. The show was not the old 1868 G. L. Fox extravaganza, but a Drury Lane pantomime adapted for domestic consumption by J. J. McNally and with a number of American songs interpolated. The most popular were by Cole and Johnson. Their "Sambo And Dinah" told of how, "Without respect to grammar... dusky lovers bill and coo." With Frank Moulan as the star the show ran through the holidays and almost up to spring.

A Manhattan touring house also unveiled a novelty the same evening. **Mrs. Mac, the Mayor** (14 November 1904, Metropolis) was William Gill's "comedy melodrama," starring the popular female impersonator George W. Monroe. Peggy MacNeill is a washerwoman who runs for mayor of Silverado on a reform ticket. After she triumphs over determined gambling and liquor interests her troubles are not ended. She foils a plot to blow up a mine she owns and even turns her tippling husband into a teetotaler. Somewhat more of a straight play than most circulating dramas, it confined its songs, dances, and specialties largely to the third of its four acts.

Harry B. Smith, his brother Robert, and composer Alfred E. Aarons had an embarrassingly quick flop with **A China Doll** (19 November 1904, Majestic). The doll was an automaton loved and lost by Pee Chee San (Helen Royston), who refuses to marry an "Americanized 'Chink'" until it is found. The production was beautifully mounted, especially a second-act set of a Chinese palace overlooking a lake and hills beyond. The palace itself was painted to resemble porcelain. Yet stage design technique was still relatively primitive, so at least one critic felt the illusion was hampered somewhat by "the glare of white lights."

Another quick flop was **The Baroness Fiddlesticks** (21 November 1904, Casino), a dreary affair in which a parvenu's chances for acceptance are jeopardized if it becomes known the baroness he is entertaining is an impostor. The score was by Emil Brugière, his only one to get a Broadway hearing. It was one of three musicals to open on 21 November.

Some of the top professionals of the day also had bad luck with their adaptation of Oliver Goldsmith's *She Stoops to Conquer*, the second of the evening's openings. Stanislaus Stange moved the setting to the Continent and changed the heroine's name to Rose Decourelles. The affair was also given a new title, **The Two Roses** (21 November 1904, Broadway). But Stange was as heavy-handed a librettist as Smith. His dialogue included jokes on the order of "Too many crooks spoil a policeman" and "Getting married is like going to a fire. They run there and walk back." Neither Ludwig Englander nor Gustave Kerker, who collaborated on the score, was capable of rising above such mediocrity. Englander, who did the bulk of the music, could do no better than saccharine dainties such as "What's A Kiss?" Significantly Fritzi

Scheff as Rose drew the loudest applause of the evening when she interpolated two arias from her operatic repertory at the end of the evening. Yet even the enchanting Miss Scheff could not save the show.

The happiest of the three first-class 21 November premieres was Frank Pixley and Gustav Luders's **Woodland** at the New York. Though it was a Chicago show, it eschewed the Oriental settings that were beginning to appear a Chicago trademark. Instead it chose a field farther removed from Western civilization, the woodland domain of the birds. All the characters were feathered creatures, though their behavior was singularly manlike. Prince Eagle loves Miss Nightingale, but the King of the Birds disapproves of the match. The Blue Jay, disgruntled for other reasons, attempts to lead a revolution. But the prince helps his father quell the uprising, so the grateful king allows his son to marry the nightingale. There were complaints about Pixley's earthbound dialogue and the team's persistence with "Message" and "Tale" songs—in this case "The Message Of Spring" and "The Tale Of The Turtle Dove." But the story was charming and refreshing, and Luders's lightweight grace engaging. The piece ran nearly three months.

The action in **Flo-Flo** (21 November 1904, West End) drifted from a garden at St. Augustine's Ponce de Leon Hotel to an offshore reef, but, as one paper noted, it "might just as well have been laid in the interior of a Chinese laundry for all the consistency used in bringing on the chorus numbers and specialties." The critic could discern no plot, though the cast of characters implied some stab was made at one, but he did note that the songs by lyricist Collin Davis and composer Howard Whitney were mediocre and that only two interpolations roused the audience. Singing those songs was the "happy, wholesome" Stella Mayhew—the young lady who portrayed Flo Floral—even then a rising "coon shouter." A few years hence she would enjoy some brief glory days on Broadway, and her show's title would be appropriated for a better or at least bigger hit.

One Chicago musical that never made it to New York was **His Highness the Bey.** Its failure to reach Broadway belies its importance, for it was the first musical written by the trio who created most of the great Chicago musicals: Will M. Hough, Frank R. Adams, and Joe Howard. Of course, Howard had already made a small name for himself, nationally as well as locally. Hough and Adams were still students at the University of Chicago. On 21 November their classmates packed a La Salle Theatre that had been drastically rebuilt on orders of the Chicago fire department. The story the collegians told began with the announcement that the Bey has fled his country in fear of an enemy attack. A new leader must be found. Who should wander innocently into the crisis but a bandmaster from Kankakee, Louie Wurtzelheimer (Al Shean). The world tour he is making with his wife comes to an abrupt halt when he is drafted into the job of Bey. The complications that follow find Louie prepared to arrest his spouse as an enemy spy. Luckily, the war stops because the papers find they haven't any more room for war news. The real Bey returns, and the reconciled Wurtzelheimers are permitted to go on their way. *His Highness the Bey* settled in to begin a three-month run, while the Hough-Adams-Howard team started work on its successor.

When Lew Fields broke with Weber, he promptly formed a new association with Fred Hamlin and Julian Mitchell. Together they established the Lew Fields Stock Company and began construction of a Lew Fields Theatre on 42nd Street. Victor Herbert was commissioned to write the scores for their mountings. Their first effort, **It Happened in Nordland,** inaugurated the new house on 5 December. It was an instant success, but it was soon to cause Herbert and the company public anguish and become a landmark case. The story was simple enough, its opening not unlike *His Highness the Bey.* The Queen of Nordland disappears rather than accept an unwelcome marriage. When the new American ambassadress, Katherine Peepfogle, turns out to be the Queen's double, she is pressed into impersonating her so that Nordland will not be embarrassed. Katherine discovers her long-lost brother, Hubert (Fields), and extricates him from all sorts of problems before the Queen returns and Katherine can resume her correct role. Mitchell and Fields had long since gained a reputation for lavish, tasteful productions. *It Happened in Nordland* was no exception. In an era when choruses of thirty, forty, or fifty girls were common, the men saw to it every girl was a beauty—"even in the last row." Lovely stage pictures were capped by a brilliant second-act carnival scene. Herbert's score was a charmer. Fittingly, it was less operatic than most of those he had done before, closer in style to his material for Frank Daniels's vehicles. The numbers were shorter and less arioso. There were fewer concerted pieces. The hit of the evening was "Absinthe Frappé." In the carnival scene Herbert inserted a

fully orchestrated version of his earlier piano work "Al Fresco."

In writing his contract for the show Herbert made a ghastly mistake. He neglected to include his customary clause prohibiting interpolations—a particularly dangerous omission when he knew Marie Cahill was to play Katherine. As early as the first night of the Harrisburg tryout, Miss Cahill added extraneous songs. Herbert fumed, but he was helpless. The animosities grew. At the very end of the New York run Herbert came for several nights to conduct in place of the ailing Max Hirschfeld. But he would only conduct his own music. Before Miss Cahill began each interpolation Herbert ostentatiously handed his baton to the concertmaster. This so unnerved Miss Cahill that during the final New York performance on Saturday, 26 April, she broke down in the middle of something called "Any 1905 Old Tree." She left the stage to regain her composure, and, while she did finish the performance, she demanded a showdown. To her dismay Fields took Herbert's side. She withdrew from the show, and the following Monday in Boston her understudy went on. Blanche Ring was eventually brought in to play Katherine. Amazingly, she ignored the implications of the earlier contretemps and insisted on adding her own interpolations. When Fields in turn fired her, the fiery Miss Ring stalked out—taking all Katherine's costumes with her. Both incidents received wide publicity. They failed to bring an end to the haphazard desecration created by willful performers. But they did announce the battle had been joined. The more conscientious of the established composers became increasingly careful to insert clauses prohibiting interpolations.

A second eighteenth-century English classic, *The School for Scandal,* was set to music by A. Baldwin Sloane as **Lady Teazle** (24 December 1904, Casino). But neither Sloane nor his librettist and lyricist could approach Sheridan's brilliance. In their version Joseph Surface's profligacy was demonstrated by his cavorting with a bevy of girls in short pink-and-white skirts, the sale of the family portraits was conducted in song and rhyme, and when Lillian Russell—their more than ample Lady Teazle—was discovered behind a screen she sought refuge in a French accent and a song that began, "I am ze dainty milliner." W. T. Carleton played Sir Peter Teazle; Clarence Handyside, Sir Oliver; and Van Rensselaer Wheeler, Charles. Yet neither Miss Russell, her fine supporting players, nor eighty-six beautiful chorus girls could help. The piece lasted only fifty-seven performances.

The musical was the first to carry above its title the announcement "The Messrs. Shubert present." The "Messrs." were Sam, Lee (for Levi), and J. (for Jacob) J. Shubert. As was the case with so many immigrants the dates and places of their birth are in question.

SAM SHUBERT was generally conceded to be the oldest, but the year of his birth is given as 1876 or 1877, a year or two after Lee's official birth date of 15 March 1875. LEE SHUBERT is known to have admitted privately that he was born several years earlier, possibly 1873. J. J. SHUBERT's official birth date is given as 15 August 1879 or 1880. The dates were apparently altered so that three brothers could claim American birth. Most likely, they were all born in Lithuania. Their father, David Szemanski, a ne'er do-well, alcoholic pack-peddler, fled czarist pogroms, taking his family as far as England and men, coming alone to America, settling in Syracuse. He brought his family over a year later. Sam and Lee began peddling papers in front of one of Syracuse's theatres. Before long Sam was inside the house, selling programs and souvenirs. Ambitious, bright, and energetic, the five-foot-tall Sam soon became assistant treasurer at a more important house and within months treasurer at a still better one. A meeting with Charles Hoyt prompted him to visit New York to purchase road rights to Hoyt's *A Stranger in New York* and *A Texas Steer*. The success of the first brought Lee into the picture, and Jake followed shortly thereafter. With profits from the plays the boys were able to take over houses in Syracuse. Rochester and Utica soon had Shubertrun theatres. At this point Sam tried to establish a mutually satisfactory arrangement with the Syndicate by sitting down with Abe Erlanger. What seemed to be an excellent deal was quickly worked out. But Erlanger reneged, a treachery the Shuberts never forgot nor forgave. Inevitably, the boys set their sights on

---

New York. In 1900 they leased the Herald Square Theatre. Soon the Casino was under their management. Their great building spree began when they erected the Lyric Theatre. When Sam was killed in a 1905 train accident, Lee took over the running of the organization the brothers had created. J. J. would remain the lesser of the survivors in the company, but it would be his love for operetta that gave the Shuberts some of their greatest hits.

However startling the number of chorus girls in *Lady Teazle* may seem to theatregoers in our less generous era, the figure was not much above the norm for musical extravaganzas at the turn of the century. The New York *World* ran an article on a survey it had conducted of the girls in *Lady Teazle*'s line. It affords insights into why even the usually niggardly Shuberts could be so prodigal. The ages of the young ladies ranged from sixteen to a discreetly omitted top. Most important, though the girls claimed they averaged only twenty weeks of employment a year, they were content to receive only eighteen dollars for each of the weeks they did grace the boards. The girls and the *World*'s article made it clear that a prominent place in an attractive chorus line was merely a means to an end. Forty-eight of the ladies acknowledged "independent means," seventy-eight boasted of their jewelry and furs, while seven even owned newfangled, expensive automobiles, and another seven were driven to the show each night in private carriages. In short, many chorus girls didn't need large salaries. They were "kept women." Of course, many young ladies (and young men) of the chorus were not kept. They were willing to survive on a relative pittance in hope of future glory and wealth. But well-provided-for chorus girls were not unique to this era or even to New York. Years earlier "Practical John" Hollingshead, the original proprietor of London's Gaiety, had posted what became a famous notice on his bulletin board—"Ladies drawing less than 25 shillings a week are politely requested not to arrive at the theatre in broughams." The notice was posted in the 1860s!

Two more former Weber and Fields names— Fay Templeton and Peter F. Dailey—invited their fans to visit them **In Newport** (26 December 1904, Liberty). Their musical told how old henpecked

Bankwell (Lee Harrison) hires detective Alert Pincherton (Dailey) to retrieve a letter he has written to a French girl (Miss Templeton) and thwart a blackmail scheme. Pincherton disguises himself as an ordinary policeman and winds up watching a rehearsal of a play filled with vaudeville acts before he can earn his pay. Joseph Coyne was featured as a "traditional English nincompoop." One well-received number employed a large segment of the chorus in a mock football game. J. J. McNally wrote the book, while Bob Cole, with both J. W. and J. Rosamond Johnson, did the songs. But for all the excellent talent something went wrong. They all packed their bags and left after just three weeks.

The same night *In Newport* opened, Fritzi Scheff reappeared. Rather than risk another failure in an untried piece, she sang a repertory of opéra bouffe, *Fatinitza, Giroflé-Girofla*, and *Boccaccio*. The old favorites retained sufficient appeal to give Miss Scheff a three-month run.

Another entry that night was described on its program as "a fantastic farcical frivolity and musical spectacle" and was given the ungrammatical and unappealing title of **Me, Him and I** (26 December 1904, West End). But it proved to have appeal galore. It had begun life as a short musical (or extended sketch) on one of the country's major burlesque circuits and has been called "the most successful book ever written for an American burlesque show." Its author was William Holcomb (or Holocombe), who, besides writing prolifically for burlesque, was reputedly the first man to demand and receive a royalty for a vaudeville sketch. Its three prosperous seasons on the Columbia wheel prompted him to expand the skit into a full-blown musical comedy. A Seattle railroad station and dock, a swank yacht called the *High Roller*, and Main Street, Dawson City, served as settings for his tale of a disguised English lord who has struck it rich in the Klondike, in pursuit of an American girl of his dreams. Although the girl's father is a snooty millionaire, m'lord elects to pass himself off as the manager of a backwater theatrical troupe. Lyricist Vincent Bryan and composer Max Hoffman, both well known on Broadway, were called in for the songs. Singing and dancing in the secondary role of Seattle Sal was none other than Gertrude Hoffman. She belted out "Harry, Harry, Won't You Marry Me" while pointing a pair of six-shooters "at the boys in the boxes." Bickel, Watson, and Wrothe retained the comic parts they had originated in the burlesque version, which initially had been called *On the Yucon*. Wrothe was Irish Con Conn;

Bickel, the German U-Kahn; and Watson, the tramp, Dusty Dawson. In the first act the men try to stow away on the yacht as it is about to leave for Alaska, but they are caught and thrown off. They steal an aeroplane (remember, this is only 1904!). However, the plane runs out of gas and ditches alongside the boat. Shortly afterwards the following dialogue ensues:

U-Kahn: Look, there's a submaroon boat underneath us.
Con Conn: What is a submaroon boat?
Dusty: Don't display your ignoramus. I'll explain. A submaroon boat is a boat that floats under the water. Consequently when it sinks, it comes to the top.

Even with material like that, the men went on to become vaudeville favorites.

Just as it had in *Flo-Flo*, the action in **His Honor, the Mayor of the Bowery** (7 January 1905, Murray Hill) moved from a public garden (this time, of course, in the Bowery, which itself had once suggested a garden) to the seashore (in this case with Coney Island in the distance). The mayor is Dennis O'Reilly (Dan McAvoy), a widower whose attempts to seek a new wife are thrown into a tizzy by his grown daughter's interference. On Broadway, McAvoy usually played small comic roles, often with a Jewish dialect. He should have been in his element here, but his jokes apparently were hopelessly stale. One reviewer reported that he had to rely "largely on his smile and his feet to win applause." A song called "The Sunbeam And The Morning Glory" was encored "fully a dozen times."

Chicago welcomed the first musical hit of the year on 9 January. And a curious one it was! **The Girl and the Bandit** was a rewritten, recast, and retitled version of a musical New York had already rejected, *A Venetian Romance*. Even Chicago theatre managers were not prepared for its reception. Forced out of one theatre by a previous booking, it moved to another house only to find it must vacate that one because of a previous booking there. In three separate runs the musical chalked up fifteen weeks. It toured the Midwest for two seasons.

Fantana (14 January 1905, Lyric), a musical with Chicago connections, quickly became the season's smash hit. Sam S. Shubert was not only its producer but its co-librettist, sharing credits with Robert B. Smith. Smith felt he had done all the work, though he admitted Shubert had given him the original story line. He finally prevailed on Shubert to acknowledge how small his contribution was. But Shubert never changed the published credits. Shubert's story related the adventures of Commodore Everett (Hubert Wilke), a retired naval officer and now successful owner of the Fantana vineyard. He proposes to take his daughter and the Japanese Ambassador to Japan to teach viniculture. But the trip seems abortive when the ambassador learns he will be beheaded if he returns. What the commodore fails to reckon with is the determination of his daughter, Fanny (Adele Ritchie), who is set on seeing her fiancé (Frank Rushworth), a lieutenant serving with the U.S. Navy in Japan. She persuades Hawkins (Jefferson De Angelis), her father's valet, to pose as the ambassador, and they all sail away. It takes the navy to save Hawkins from losing his head. Since the show's plot was the sort Chicago had been so receptive to, and since both Smith and the composer, Raymond Hubbell, had close ties to the city, Shubert wisely opened the tryout there. By the time the show reached the Lyric it was in tip-top shape, with Jefferson De Angelis's broad clowning winning the loudest applause. His disguise as the Japanese Ambassador afforded De Angelis a chance to chase a tassel on his hat about the stage. The tassel was quicker than the comedian, often swinging around from behind to slap him in the face. Two youngsters also called attention to themselves: Julia Sanderson and Douglas Fairbanks. Hubbell's tunes were trite but agreeable. The show's biggest hit, added for the New York run, was the already popular "Tammany" (Vincent Bryan/Gus Edwards). The show ran into the next season.

Two nights later Ivan Caryll's London hit **The Duchess of Dantzic** (16 January 1905, Daly's), a musical version of Sardou's *Madame Sans Gêne*, began a profitable stay.

The era's most celebrated animal impersonator, George Ali, was stealing the show as the ever loyal and amazingly resourceful Tige, pet dog of **Buster Brown** (24 January 1905, Majestic). He is no end of help to Buster (Master Gabriel) as the youngster goads his father into running for mayor and assists in shooing away his father's battle-axe mother-in-law (never mind that she's also grandma). The chorus, dressed in Scottish costumes, performed an old-time drill that brought down the house in the only big moment Tige couldn't steal. For the record, "Master" Gabriel was reputedly twenty-three years old. The cartoon-brought-to-life remained at the theatre for three months, but was far more successful

on the road—for which it had been designed—although the *Dramatic Mirror* recorded that its second week broke the house record set two years before by *The Wizard of Oz*.

A demented English lady comes to a Florida hotel at the beginning of **The Lost Boy** (30 January 1905, Murray Hill) in search of her lost son, but her dementia proves mild compared with what follows. A young man named Ruben Plumb is persuaded to claim he is the son. In rapid succession a mummy returns to life to present the boy with a magical "goo-goo," a King Go Go appears and claims that Ruben is his long-lost brother, and the entire cast is whisked away to the marvelous island of Flew Flew, where Ruben is declared king. Ruben was portrayed by tiny, rubber-faced Edward Blondell, who for many years had been touring in musicals based on the Katzenjammer Kids. He was credited with the book of the show (the songs were uncredited), but one paper noted the split personality of many such affairs with the observation "It is a farce-comedy while Mr. Blondell is on the stage and a musical comedy when the star is off and the chorus of twelve and the soloists step on." Songs given to that chorus and the soloists ranged from the comic "Chappies Of The Day" through the arioso "In The Land Of Romance" to the stirring "The Sun That Rose On Thirteen States Now Sets On Forty-Five."

George Lederer closed out January in Chicago with **Smiling Island** (a title which just may have been taken from the song in *The Sultan of Sulu*). The show opened at Hyde and Behman's on the 30th. Unfortunately, the critics could find no plot nor anything to like in the work. Its main attraction seemed to be the lavishness of the production with, as the advertisements proclaimed, "100 in cast MOSTLY GIRLS." The girls were not enough to save the show; it closed quickly.

A "Broadway chappie of today" was the hero of **How He Won Her** (20 February 1905, Murray Hill), which also displayed a quirky dichotomy of styles and themes. Since the book was credited to Joseph Le Brandt, a popular dispenser of touring melodrama, the basic plot of a young man, kicked out of college, who enters his father's brokerage and unmasks the nefarious peculations of a junior partner, was not surprising. But the young man is always accompanied by a bevy of beautiful girls, who not coincidentally constitute a chorus line, and he woos and wins his father's pretty secretary (a foreshadowing of the Cinderella plots of the early 1920s). Part of the action was set in Atlantic City, so the girls were able to cavort in bathing suits. Programs failed to say whose music they danced to.

The spelling of **Lilliputians in Sinbad** (27 February 1905, Murray Hill) could have alerted potential ticket-buyers mat something was awry since the beloved Liliputians of old usually (but not always) spelled their name without the double *l*. The program disclosed that none of the original troupe was in this cast. Six American midgets, supporting players of a more regular size, and twelve traditional chorus girls romped through a loosely plotted entertainment that featured characters sporting monikers such as Policeman Ketchemnow and President Keepemdowno.

Two shows opened in Chicago in mid-March one night apart. One was a touring show created specifically for cheap-priced theatres. It brought in its lighthearted nonsense and its songs and dances for the customary single week. The next night, the 14th, witnessed a much more important premiere when Hough-Adams-Howard's second show bowed. **The Isle of Bong Bong** was set on Lord Percy's hunting estate in the theatrically voguish Philippines. In order to court Marjory Gray, the young American secretary of his uncle, Lord Percy changes places with his valet. At the same time, the Sultan of the floating island of Bong Bong comes ashore to court the thrice-widowed Mrs. Rensselaer-Rensselaer. A wizard, a bandit, pirates, and a hungry offstage lion place obstacles in the lovers' way. Everything ends happily, with the Sultan consenting to anchor his island near civilization. The show had fun with other musicals of the era and with local figures. At one point Bong Bong's ruler speaks kindly of his "sometime neighbor," the Sultan of Sulu. In the first act Marjory sings lovingly of "My Illinois," mentioning in passing "Clark Street ticket scalpers" and the White Sox. Joe Howard took a role in the cast, but more important, the show called the attention of Chicago theatregoers to two artists who became Chicago favorites, Cecil Lean and Florence Holbrook. The musical settled into the La Salle for a comfortable run.

While these shows had been opening in Chicago, New York's musical scene had been quiet. A new musical finally arrived on 12 April 1905, but its arrival was overshadowed by the new theatre that housed it. The show was **A Yankee Circus on Mars.** The theatre was the Hippodrome. Built on Sixth Avenue between 43rd and 44th streets, it accelerated the northward movement of the theatrical district.

But its site on the east side of the avenue established an eastern boundary beyond which no other playhouse was ever raised. The Hippodrome was the largest legitimate theatre in the world. The statistics it claimed for itself were staggering. It accommodated over 5,000 customers at one time. The depth of its stage from footlights to back wall was 110 feet, while in length the stage exceeded 200 feet, nearly equal to a whole city block. The stage was lit by 5,000 incandescent lights and fifty-three calcium lights. The staff of over 1,000 required to run the house included seventy-eight electricians and twenty-two engineers. It employed a permanent ballet of 200 as well as 400 chorus girls and 100 chorus boys. The vastness of the house precluded ordinary entertainments. John Golden, who wrote words for some of the songs presented there, despaired, "[T]he Hippodrome was so big that audiences could never hear the lyrics." Nor could they hear most of the dialogue. Spectacle was all the house could properly offer and, in its heyday, all it presented. George V. Hobart wrote the "libretto" for the opening. But there was no real story line. The evening was essentially a series of circus acts and ballets that must have recalled *The Black Crook* (12 September 1866) to the oldsters in the auditorium. But it was far grander than anything Niblo's Garden or the Kiralfys could set before playgoers. Horses plunged into the theatre's giant tank; elephants pulled outsized automobiles. The piece was coupled with a "tableauxdrama" originally called *Andersonville: A Story of Wilson's Raiders*, but soon shortened merely to *The Raiders*. The horrors of the prison camp were depicted, followed by a Northerner's escape, a secret visit to the plantation of his Southern sweetheart, and a Civil War battle scene. From the beginning the Hippodrome offered spectacular scenes of carnage in which spectacle effectively served to water down blood and gore. Manuel Klein and Jean Schwartz composed the music. It took a season or two before the Hippodrome shows developed a pattern and found a niche for themselves. By that time Frederic W. Thompson and Elmer S. Dundy, who conceived the whole affair (and who also had created Luna Park in Coney Island), were bankrupt. Part of the problem was the lateness of the opening. Hot weather was just around the corner. Hippodrome shows did not hit their full stride until later producers offered them early in the fall.

The English hit **Sergeant Brue** (24 April 1905, Knickerbroker), with Frank Daniels capering about in the title role, repeated its London popularity.

Daniels played a London bobby who will come into a large inheritance if he can earn the rank of sergeant. Blanche Ring stopped the show nightly with an interpolation, "My Irish Molly O" (Jerome/Schwartz).

Sam Bernard and Hattie Williams also produced enough laughter to keep **The Rollicking Girl** (1 May 1905, Herald Square) titillating New Yorkers until autumn. Miss Williams was Iona, who runs away on the eve of her wedding and takes refuge in the house of the wigmaker, Schmaltz. She and Schmaltz have theatrical ambitions; together they go to the Royal Theatre. In the end, however, she realizes she loves her groom-in-waiting, and Schmaltz returns to his wigs. Much of the humor was the "Dutch" variety Bernard had mastered during his stay with Weber and Fields:

Schmaltz: Valk on this way and say, "My Lady, the letter has came."
Iona: I shall say come, not came.
Schmaltz: Not at all. You already want to teach the author his bizness. Now, ven the author says "came" he just wants to show that the maid don't know how it is to speak the words gramatic.

Joe Coyne, falling into a pattern that only *The Merry Widow* would rescue him from, donned a shiny baldpate wig to impersonate another English buffoon. The critics praised both Sydney Rosenfeld's book, which he adapted from *A Dangerous Maid* (12 November 1898), and W. T. Francis's score.

In **My Tom-Boy Girl** (1 May 1905, Metropolis), an orphan girl who earns pennies as a newsboy and is known as Ragged Joe discovers that she is an heiress. But Josie's newfound wealth and life of luxury on a southern plantation bring her only new woes. Her sister is kidnapped, and she must disguise herself as one of the villains to rescue the lass. The show's "librettist" was Charles E. Blaney, an even more accomplished creator of cliffhangers than Joseph Le Brandt. Once again the songwriters were cavalierly passed over, unless the otherwise unknown Wagner Crosby and Thomas Cutty who were listed as responsible for the specialties were the composer and lyricist. But none of their material was singled out for praise.

Two musicals came in to entertain Chicago in May. Both failed. William A. Brady presented "a topsy turvy in two acts" called **All Around Chicago** on 1 May at the McVickers. In a slim Tom and Jerry frame the piece offered everything from a Sherlock

Holmes travesty to a Moulin Rouge can-can. On 21 May **Kafoozelum** opened at Hyde and Behman's. Set in Turviana, a land inside the Earth, it recounted problems that develop when Earthlings arrive.

Between the two Chicago openings Philadelphia had its own premiere, a locally contrived piece not above having fun at the expense of the Mormons. F. J. Palmer wrote the book and H. M. Stanton the music for **The Wanderer** (15 May 1905, Chestnut St.). Zachary Jones, a church elder, has promised his twelve marriageable daughters—he also has thirteen unmarriageable girls—to Anthony Smith, whom he has never met. But when a tramp named Tony Smith shows up at Jones's Salt Lake home, he is mistaken for the groom until late in the last act. A touring favorite, Charles Grapewin, played Tony, while Broadway's diminutive darling, spunky Ada Lewis, took the role of Jones's spinster sister. (Guess who she marries in the end!) But the show was dismissed as feeble, so closed after its second week.

Two roof garden attractions opened in New York in June. **Lifting the Lid** (5 June 1905, New Amsterdam Roof) was little more than a vaudeville, with its entire second act devoted to scenes and songs from Gilbert and Sullivan. Still, it was pleasing enough to run until fall. **When We Were Forty-one** (12 June 1905, New York Roof) was Robert B. Smith's burlesque of Henry V. Esmond's popular *When We Were Twenty-One*, which Nat C. Goodwin had been touring around the country since 1900. It told how mad Dr. Hasler (Harry Bulger) attempts to put everyone over forty to sleep. Gus Edwards composed the necessary tunes. The piece was part of a longer bill presented for sixty-six performances.

Chicago had the last word of the season when **The Woggle Bug** appeared at the Garrick on 18 June. The work had a score by Frederick Chapin and a book by the creator of *The Wizard of Oz* (20 January 1903), L. Frank Baum. In another of his never-never-lands, the Princess Ozma is transformed into a boy named Tip. Jack Pumpkin-head, a seahorse, and the Woggle Bug himself help her to resume her rightful state. The critics praised the show, the man from the *Tribune* suggesting Chapin's score was so fine Victor Herbert had better look to his laurels. But attendance was disappointing. Too many parents remembered the holocaust at the Iroquois Theatre.

1905–1906

If Chicago had had the last word in 1904–1905, it also got the new season well under way before

New York came to life. The first musical to arrive raised the curtain of the La Salle on 12 August. Like the two Chicago shows that followed, it told of an American who is reluctantly elevated to the leadership of a foreign country. Cecil Lean was made **The Yankee Regent** of Wiener because he is the "32nd cousin—twice removed" of Princess Olive. Olive must choose between a prince and the regent, or abdicate. Naturally she chooses the handsome American. The show was not by Hough-Adams-Howard. Instead the libretto was by Charles Adelman and I. L. Blumstock; the score by Ben M. Jerome. The musical was a modest success, helping to keep the La Salle lit until Hough-Adams-Howard had a new show ready.

In New York the new season would prove to be the busiest and most remunerative ever for musicals that spent their nights touring combination houses. Figures would drop precipitously the very next year. Perhaps it was fortunate that neither playgoers nor professionals realized how little life was left in these vehicles. Before the end of the decade, theatres that now welcomed them would be given over in a few cases to vaudeville, but for the most part their stages would be dark while black-and-white images flickered on a screen at the back of the proscenium arch.

The season got off to an early, if unpromising, start with **Papa's Boy** (19 August 1905, Murray Hill), which had a book by Frank W. Lloyd and songs by Harry B. Lester. Lester doubled in brass by assuming the leading role of Dolly, a mama's boy. But by the time Professor Bluffem and Dolly's father, I. B. Crankie, are finished with him and all the comic complications have been unraveled, Dolly is heading for the altar. The only one of Lester's songs critics thought worthy of mention was a dreamy ballad, "Don't You Wish That You Were Me?"

The Rajah of Bhong came into Chicago's Great Northern on 20 August. There had been a Rajah of Bhong in *A Country Girl*, but apart from the curious coincidence of the names there appears to have been no connection between the two shows. This American piece had a libretto by William Roberts and music by Hal L. Campbell. Its story told of a New Yorker who escapes an unhappy love affair by taking a cruise. He is shipwrecked and made rajah by the natives of the island on which he is cast ashore. The next evening **The Geezer of Geck** opened at the Garrick. The show, for which Robert Adam wrote the book and Paul Schindler composed the music, echoed the plot of *His Highness the Bey*. A reluctant Julius Schmidt is made Geezer

and finds he must buy his wife back at an auction. But he spends so much money purchasing his harem that he has no cash left when his wife comes on the block.

The Broadway season opened with **The Pearl and the Pumpkin** (21 August 1905, Broadway). There is a pumpkin famine, even in Davy Jones's locker, where Bluebeard's stomach aches from a lack of pumpkin pie. A lad who knows how to grow them is turned into a pumpkin when he refuses to reveal the technique. A wild chase to a newly discovered pumpkin patch finds the Flying Dutchman, Captain Kidd, and a group of Vermont farmers among the racers. John Bratton's tunes and Paul West's lyrics were of an appropriate order. All in all, a pleasant children's show—except that it wasn't! The moralizing *Times* reflected: "The tendency of the nowadays musical comedy producers to utilize little-boy-and-girl lore is a more or less delightful departure from the Gallic flavor of the comic opera of the past." The paper saluted the change as "more wholesome." Apparently the *Times*'s man did not recall the day when the original *Humpty Dumpty* (10 March 1868) outran the most successful new opéra bouffe. The run of *The Pearl and the Pumpkin*, a modest seventy-two performances, matched neither.

Easy Dawson, which opened the next night, was looked upon by most critics as an attempt by Raymond Hitchcock to build a bridge for himself from musical comedy to straight play. There were four or five songs in the piece, by various composers—none particularly germane to the action on stage.

Two lyric pieces bowed the next Monday. Edna May was **The Catch of the Season** (28 August 1905, Daly's). This retelling of the Cinderella tale in contemporary dress had been a London hit and now became a transatlantic success, helped not only by Miss May but by three attractive Jerome Kern interpolations, "Raining," "Won't You Kiss Me Once Before I Go?," and "Edna May's Irish Song."

The popular blackface duo McIntyre and Heath sparked a musical vaudeville called **The Ham Tree** (28 August 1905, New York), which recounted the misadventures of two picaresque African Americans, Henry Jones (Heath) and his not very bright friend Alexander Hambletonian (McIntyre), after they are stranded in a small town and present themselves as a rajah and his minister in order to get free room and board. The *Times* noted the evening contained all the requisite blackface bits—the principals sitting on a trunk by a railroad track, and searching for food in a spooky, dark woods. William Jerome and Jean Schwartz's songs did little to suggest the minstrel antecedents of the piece, and the hit of the evening, "Good-bye Sweet Old Manhattan Isle," could have come from almost any show. But audiences loved *The Ham Tree*, and McIntyre and Heath were able to revive it profitably whenever another vehicle failed them or vaudeville routings were not to their liking. In this original production, a young comic juggler, W. C. Fields, won applause and good notices as Sherlock Baffles.

Miss Dolly Dollars (4 September 1905, Knickerbocker) was the first of the season's three Victor Herbert shows. It was written for Lulu Glaser. She portrayed Dorothy Gay, who is familiarly known as "Dolly Dollars," since her father is the condensed-soup tycoon, Sam Gay (Charles Bradshaw). Sam takes Dolly to the Henley regatta and to Paris, where she falls in love with the seemingly penniless Lord Burlingham (Melville Stewart). But Burlingham turns out to have enough money to save Sam when his business fortunes take an unexpectedly bad turn. If this Harry B. Smith story "offered many an opportunity for social satire of a delicious sort," Smith disappointed none of his detractors when he "ignored every possibility." Nor was Herbert's score top drawer. Even a real automobile chasing real people, dogs, and chickens about the stage was looked on as a device long since "worn threadbare." The musical stayed in Gotham less than two months and then took to the road for the rest of the theatrical year.

Gus and Max Rogers had better luck when they brought **The Rogers Brothers in Ireland** (4 September 1905, Liberty) to 42nd Street. This edition had Heinrich Punk (Gus) and Nicholas Knox (Max) go to Ireland to fetch the Blarney Stone for exhibition in America. They will use the money they make to help free Ireland. John J. McNally's plot suggested that heavy Irish theatrical patronage extended even to these "Dutch" comedians, but none of the numerous Anglophiles who served as daily reviewers at the time complained of the story line, although a number deplored the persistently inferior quality of the Rogers material. Actually, the reception accorded the latest edition was relatively kind, suggesting either the brothers were improving or the critics were growing indifferent. The sets were especially praised, particularly a well-painted view of the Lakes of Killarney. Gus and Max made one entrance in a pony cart and sang Irish folk songs in their German dialect. They also participated in a travesty of the reigning hit song of the moment, "In

The Shade Of The Old Apple Tree." Gus and Max made New Yorkers happy for 106 performances before they too embarked on a long tour.

Two touring musicals opened the first Monday in September. Both starred well-liked vaudevillians, and both listed known or soon-to-be-known writers among their credits. Billy S. Clifford, a dancer-comedian, had his name above the title in **A Jolly Baron** (4 September 1905, 14th St.), and his importance to the basic plot could be seen in the fact that he played Louie Baron. But the evening's biggest laughs were garnered by two dialect comedians, Joe Fields and Mark Wooley, who portrayed two German-Americans stuck in the glue trade. Librettist Joseph Le Brandt seems to have had great fun discarding all the clichés he regularly employed in his touring melodramas. Who wrote the lyrics was left unsaid, but they were set to music by one of Tin Pan Alley's greatest names, Harry Von Tilzer. None of the songs found much favor.

Gus Yorke and Nick Adams were two more popular dialect comedians. In **Bankers and Brokers** (4 September 1905, West End) they played Pincus and Plonsky, a pair of Jewish immigrants who become partners of a Wall Street sharper, B. Dunne Goode. This trickster is trying to marry Molly Sweet in hopes of getting his claws on stocks her father has left her. The stocks disappear, so everybody runs off to Palm Beach in search of them. There Plonsky dives into the deep, thinking they have been sunk among the fish. All he brings up is an angry alligator. But by eleven o'clock the boys have shown Molly that the right man for her is Wood B. Holmes. Along the way they right a number of other wrongs and become rich. Among the musical numbers were "My Pretty Rosebud," which was sung and danced by chorus girls dressed as roses, and "Bulls And Bears," which brought out the girls "wearing electrically lighted head dresses representing the heads of those animals." The show had a book and lyrics by George Totten Smith and Aaron Hoffman, and music by Gus Salzer, in the immediate future a sought-after Broadway orchestrator and conductor.

The Duke of Duluth (11 September 1905, Majestic) was a three-week flop. The latest in *The Sultan of Sulu* (29 December 1902) school of musical comedy transported a tramp named Darling Doolittle by submarine to the Island of Wot, where a prophet has predicted his arrival and where safety compels him to assume a number of disguises until the Navy can effect a rescue. Popular Nat M. Wills played Doolittle. Wills's costumes garnered as many hefty laughs as any of his stage business. His first appearance was in an outlandish sailor's suit. Later he paraded pompously around the stage dressed as an English gentleman—in a bright green cutaway and with his face made up to resemble Mr. Hyde. At one point Wills, wearing thick glasses, rode in on horseback and saluted Teddy Roosevelt in "Strenuous" ("Let our Teddy bite the Isthmus/He can cut through it by Christmas"). His star's popularity was great enough to convince producer-librettist George Broadhurst that the vehicle could be saved. A tour followed, but when the show returned the week of 4 December it survived only one week.

Hoffman also collaborated on the book and lyrics for **Tom, Dick and Harry** (25 September 1905, American), this time with Harry Williams. Another Tin Pan Alley lion, Egbert Van Alstyne, supplied melodies. For the title roles the briefly famous vaudeville team of "comedy musicians" Bickel, Watson, and Wrothe were enlisted to play out a saga of spies from Port O'Domingo attempting to steal a flying machine from West Point (remember, the Wright brothers had first flown only two years before). Of course, the team had flown an aeroplane in last season's *Me, Him and I*.

The Beauty Doctor (25 September 1905, 14th St.), centering on a lady in the "beautifying trade," arrived after a season-long tour of the West, which was home to its writers. New Yorkers, always protective of their own turf, were quick to spot borrowings from New York shows. Thus, the entertainment's funniest moments, a choking scene, were said to have been lifted from a recent Weber and Fields hit, while its catchiest song, "Hiram Green, Farewell," sounded suspiciously like Blanche Ring's current "Hiram Green, Good-Bye." Other applauded tunes included "My Scarecrow Coon" and "Pretty Little Maid Of Zanzibar."

Reginald De Koven was still listed on the program as proprietor of the Lyric when his **Happyland** raised the house's curtain on 2 October. The librettist was Frederic Ranken, working alone. The star was De Wolf Hopper. Hopper cavorted as King Ecstaticus of Elysia, a land where, according to the typescript, everything is in the style of Alma-Tadema. The monarch is bored to distraction by the happiness overflowing his kingdom:

> No little scandal e'er comes in
> To cheer and comfort me.
> They hand me love in wholesale lots
> And tons of ecstasy.   .

To make matters bad he orders everyone to marry. He also promises to marry his son to a neighboring potentate's daughter. But since he has no son, Ecstaticus commands his own daughter, Sylvia (Marguerite Clark), to masquerade as one. She flees. The king realizes that unhappiness can exist in Elysia and decides to let well enough alone. Once again the De Koven score was pleasant, but as juiceless as most of the theatrically accepted music of the day. Still, with little better around and with Hopper to put his delightful personal stamp on the proceedings, *Happyland* gave De Koven one of his longest New York stays—136 performances in two slightly separated runs.

After an ardent union organizer, Mike O'Donovan, inadvertently saves the head of the Monopoly Railroad from a bomb attack, he is welcomed into the homes of the elite, even if his gaucheries often cause howls of laughter. Such was the basic plot of **Breaking into Society** (2 October 1905, West End), for which Lee Arthur (known on Broadway as collaborator on several nonmusical hits) and Robert B. Smith (only recently embarked on a career as a Broadway lyricist and librettist) provided the book, while the vaudeville headliner Gus Edwards (of "School Days" fame) wrote the songs. More two-a-day luminaries, The Four Mortons, were starred. Sam Morton played Mike, Kate was his wife, Clara was his daughter, and Paul Morton portrayed the daughter's suitor. A fancy-dress ball and a society circus provided colorful settings.

The creators of *Tom, Dick and Harry* were also the authors of **The Belle of Avenue A** (9 October 1905, Grand Opera). Elfie Fay, a promising Broadway belter who never fulfilled her promise, was awarded the title role. As Maggie Burns, temporarily on the bread line, she agrees to pose as the wife of socialite George Fairfax in order to let him collect an inheritance dependent on his being married. Maggie's hotheaded beau, Spike McNeil, engages Carl Klatz and Solly Bloom to help him rescue his girl. The action traveled from the corner of Avenue A and 8th Street to a Fifth Avenue mansion and finally the mansion's garden. The show's title song was its biggest hit, but another number, "Good-a-bye, John," created a little mystery down the road.

Although the elder Emmet was long gone, the fame of Fritz endured, prodding J. J. McNally, William Jerome, and Jean Schwartz to reincarnate him for Joseph Cawthorn. Together they landed **Fritz in Tammany Hall** (16 October 1905, Herald Square). In order to split the district vote, Pat

McCann, the district leader, has Fritz nominated for alderman. To everyone's surprise Fritz wins. Nothing memorable came out of the Tin Pan Alley–like score, although Ada Lewis, in another of her tough-girl roles, won encores with "East Side Lil." Still, for six weeks the show pleased old-timers as well as playgoers too young to remember the original series.

The Sambo Girl (16 October 1905, West End) was merely a rehashing of the 1903 Broadway flop *The Blonde in Black.* The plot outline was retained, but the names of the characters were changed. More urgently, in place of Blanche Ring, Eva Tanguay was starred. She brought to the show the frazzled hairdo, the garish costumes, the gorgeous figure, the wildly fluttery movements, and the raucous, energized delivery that would skyrocket her into vaudeville's biggest attraction. She earned encores singing "The Banjo Serenade," backed by a horde of chorines dressed as little girls, and a drinking song, which she ended by pouring the contents of a champagne bottle over her head and expensive gown. But the big showstopper was an interpolation, in which she broadcast her defiance of society, shouting:

I don't care! I don't care!
What they may think of me.
I'm happy-go-lucky
Men say that I'm plucky,
So jolly and carefree.

"I Don't Care" became her signature song for the rest of her long career.

A German baron unable to prove his pedigree and an immigrant Jewish waiter combine their talents to rise in politics and society in **In New York Town** (23 October 1905, West End). The musical's comic high spot was supposedly a Chinese wedding, performed in Yiddish. As was customary in these shows, each act had its own setting. In this instance they were a Bowery concert hall, a street in Chinatown, and the Hotel Astor's roof garden. Albert Von Tilzer supplied the melodies.

John Henry, a George V. Hobart farce which had not quite made the grade with the late Dan Daly as star, was now sprinkled with musical numbers and rechristened **It's Up to You, John Henry** (23 October 1905, Grand Opera). Alliterative song titles such as "Aristocratic Annie" and "My Lonesome Little Louisiana Lady" had almost nothing to do with a story in which a man takes the place of his groom-to-be friend so that the friend will not have to confront his prospective father-in-law.

Victor Herbert, Glen MacDonough, and Julian Mitchell, who had been responsible for the music, lyrics, and libretto and the staging of *Babes in Toyland* (13 October 1903), had for some time planned a sequel. MacDonough agreed to write a story combining *Alice in Wonderland, Through the Looking Glass,* and the Grimms' "The Twelve Dancing Princesses." Initially it was called *Alice and the Eight Princesses.* The story had Alice, a street urchin who sells matches, dream she is in **Wonderland** (24 October 1905, Majestic). The princesses are mysteriously disappearing, and Alice solves the mystery. Out-of-town reviewers were scathing. The book was hastily, drastically, and ineptly revised. By the time it reached New York, Alice and all the Carroll figures had been dropped, and so had any attempt at a consistent story line. The *Times* saw it simply as "a very elaborate sort of vaudeville entertainment," while the reviewer for the *Evening Post*, praising, as did all his fellow critics, the performance of the trick horse operated by two men within the costume, suggested the horse could have written a better libretto. Nor was Herbert's score of much assistance. Some songs, such as "Jogra-free," were too reminiscent of his *Toyland* compositions, while other pleasantries remained incontestably second-string. However, audiences again proved more tolerant than the critics, and after a seventy-three-performance stay, *Wonderland* began a cross-country tour that kept box offices busy for not one but two full seasons.

Three musicals closed out October on the 30th. Marie Cahill and her interpolations romped into the Liberty with **Moonshine** while Messager's **Véronique** graced the Broadway's stage. The latter story recounted the adventures of two noble youngsters who run away from home rather than accept arranged marriages. Naturally they fall in love not knowing they are the very mates their parents had selected.

The first act of *Moonshine* was set at the Henley Regatta—a popular locale in the 1905–1906 season—where Miss Cahill portrayed another popular stage figure, the detective, or, specifically in this case, the ex–Secret Service agent who utilizes her police knowledge to save the reputation of the man she loves. In what seemed to be developing into a pattern, Cole and Johnson provided her with a hit in "The Conjure Man." Benjamin Hapgood Burt also struck paydirt for Miss Cahill with "Robinson Crusoe's Isle" The best the composer of the main score, Silvio Hein, could come up with was a pseudo "coon song," suspiciously like a watered-down version of Miss Cahill's 1902 "Under The Bamboo Tree."

SILVIO HEIN was a curious, somewhat pathetic figure on the musical scene. Hein was born in New York City on 15 March 1879. Although he came from a musical family he had no formal musical training. Entirely self taught, he confined his writing to the simplest tried and true lyric forms.

Simple Simon Simple (30 October 1905, West End) was based on a then popular cartoon. Its hero, a village pest, "clad according to the fashion plates issued by the advertising department of the Omega Oil Company," stands to inherit a fortune unless his wily relatives can get him to leave town. They sure try. In the end, Simon and his little black buddy, Mose (played of course by a white in blackface), join a circus. The actor who took the part of Mose was an acrobatic midget, "and when he stands on his head and wheels round and round he looks like an ebony top." Musical numbers included "Dear Old College Days," in which each chorus girl was garbed to represent a specific school, and "Froggie Frog," with the girls in lily-pad hats and Simon Simple "dressed as a huge great basso-profundo of the bull rushes."

Klaw and Erlanger continued their policy of importing Drury Lane's pantomime-spectacles when they ushered in **The White Cat** (2 November 1905, New Amsterdam). Harry B. Smith adapted the book, while William Jerome and Jean Schwartz added seven songs. The waning vogue for the genre and the inferior quality of the new mounting in particular gave the piece an extremely short run. Klaw and Erlanger were to heed the warning.

Another English importation fared far more happily. Ivan Caryll's **The Earl and the Girl** (4 November 1905, Casino), with genial Eddie Foy in charge, came into the Casino two nights later to begin a 148-performance run. Foy portrayed a traveling salesman (always toting two puppies he described as bloodhounds) who changes places with an earl so the earl can court a commoner. The suave Caryll's score was charming, but it never produced anything as popular as one of the many interpolations, "How'd You

Like To Spoon With Me?" The song marked the first real commercial success for young Jerome Kern. It is almost forgotten today because it was simply a better-than-average period tune, with none of the beguiling lyricism that was soon to set Kern's music apart. In the show it was sung by chorus girls on flower-strewn swings, led by Georgia Caine.

The Belle of the West (13 November 1905, Grand Opera), with book and lyrics by Harry B. Smith and music by Karl Hoschna, arrived in New York fresh from its Chicago drubbing. If most major New York newspapers ignored it, at least the *Dramatic Mirror* gave it a detailed review, informing its readers that the plot told of a Washington girl who settles down to teach unlettered miners in a Wild West town. When she falls in love with the handsomest and smoothest of her pupils, the others try to cause trouble. The hoydenish Miss Bindley sported her famous "diamond dress" and regaled on the xylophone. Frogs seemed to be in vogue this season, for one song was "The Frog And The Owl."

The Belle of the West's composer would move on to better things, and so would the author of **How Baxter Butted In** (13 November 1905, Murray Hill). Indeed, Owen Davis would go on to win a Pulitzer Prize. However, for the moment he was one of the most prolific writers of touring melodramas. It showed in his tale of a girl driven to distraction by her cruel stepfather and rescued only by a self-possessed man of the world. Since virtually all touring melodramas were jam-packed with musical specialties, this might easily be put down as one. But its light-hearted hero and the fact that it called itself a musical comedy give it a place here. That light-hearted hero, by the way, was played by a thirtyish Sidney Toler, who years later was one of filmdom's Charlie Chans.

Benton Scoops is **The Press Agent** (29 November 1905, Field's) who takes a party of chorus girls on an excursion boat with the idea of throwing a girl overboard as a stunt. But the ship is hijacked by a band of South American revolutionaries, who force the vessel and the girls to sail to Concarne. The American Navy has to rescue them. The story was a refreshing, if preposterous, variation on one of the period's most acceptable musical comedy plots. But even its star, Peter F. Dailey, couldn't surmount the tired jokes and equally fatigued William Lorraine score. Just as damaging, the *Times* noted, "The women in the cast cannot sing and the men cannot act... and the costuming is garish." The show, done originally with a different cast in Chicago as *The*

Filibuster, came in at Thanksgiving time and was gone by the New Year.

On 2 December Chicago's La Salle Theatre offered its patrons what proved to be far and away the biggest musical hit the city had ever seen. **The Umpire** was the latest Hough-Adams-Howard collaboration. Cecil Lean and Florence Holbrook were again the featured performers. Lean portrayed Johnny Nolan, an umpire who makes such an outrageous call he is forced to flee to Morocco. There, at a football game, he redeems himself. He also wins the hand of the center, when it turns out this star player is a lovely young lady named Maribel Lewton. The show established Lean as the leading musical comedy actor in Chicago and confirmed beyond any doubt the supremacy of Hough-Adams-Howard in the pecking order of Chicago's lyric stage. But the show also brought a new name to the city. On 31 October the *Tribune* noted that the La Salle had been sold to the Singer brothers, young men who had risen prominently in the Milwaukee and Minneapolis theatre worlds. It fell to one of these brothers, Mort Singer, to run the La Salle. Under his aegis the musicals at the La Salle came to enjoy a reputation for quality and success virtually unmatched in the city's annals. *The Umpire* began these triumphs by tallying more than 300 performances—a run half again as long as that earned by any 1905–1906 New York musical with the exception of the Hippodrome spectacle.

In New York, December's first musical was another Richard Carle vehicle, **The Mayor of Tokio** (4 December 1905, New York). As was his wont, Carle wrote the book and lyrics. He called on W. F. Peters for the music. Carle's fable found a comic-opera troupe, Kipper's Konsolidated Komiques, stranded in Tokio. They are mistaken for royalty, and the mayor's daughter falls in love with their leading man. The leading man's wealthy father appears on his yacht to rescue them. It was a typical Carle affair, with typically minor Peters music. Once more New Yorkers were not as enthusiastic as Chicago or the road, although one critic reported the audience "piled up encores three and four deep." The show stayed only fifty performances.

The Hippodrome began to find itself when the Shuberts were called in to take over the house. **A Society Circus**—which depicted what happens when Lady Volumnia (Rose La Harte) decides to stage an elaborate party—opened on 13 December, at the height of the season instead of toward its end. Twice-a-day performances became the rule. And the spectacle was changed at intervals during the run, much in line with the "reconstructions" of the nineteenth-century extravaganzas. Specialty acts came and went. At one time or another audiences could watch fountains of "dancing waters," the Hippodrome chorus transform itself into a huge floral bouquet, and an elaborate tribute to the newfangled flying machines (called "Motoring in Mid-Air"). Perfume was sprayed over the auditorium during the flower number. Gustav Luders joined Manuel Klein to compose the score, and Klein came up with the first of the modest hits he produced in his decade at the house, "Moon Dear." It could almost pass for a spoof of the songs of the time, though it was presented as a serious ballad. The show compiled 596 performances, far and away the longest run of the season. During their heyday Hippodrome spectacles almost invariably walked off with each year's long-run honors.

Another jumble of fairy tales, **The Babes and the Baron** (25 December 1905, Lyric), was one of three Christmas-night offerings. An English show, it was laced with interpolations by Aarons, Burt, Goetz, Hubbell, and Kern, among others. It survived forty-five performances.

A similar American piece, termed a "Fairyesque" by its creators, Frederic Ranken and A. Baldwin Sloane, bowed the same night. **The Gingerbread Man** (25 December 1905, Liberty) described how the flavorful King (Eddie Redway) of BonBonLand lives in fear of being eaten. He was once human, but was turned into gingerbread by the evil Machevavelius. Santa Claus arrives (on a sled pulled by eight chorus girls dressed as reindeer), and Mrs. Santa Claus turns up to set everything straight. The hit of the evening fell to the Gingerbread Man himself. His song, in which he longs to be a typical "John Dough," was encored half a dozen times on opening night. The musical stayed only long enough to profit from the holiday trade and went on the road. It returned later in the season for a second two-week stay.

The third Christmas-night offering was its best. It was also the biggest musical hit of the season, excepting the unique Hippodrome mounting. **Mlle. Modiste** (25 December 1905, Knickerbocker) is best remembered for its lovely Victor Herbert score and its radiant star, petite Fritzi Scheff. But no small part of its initial success must be credited to its book by Henry Blossom, generally conceded the best librettist Herbert ever worked with. Blossom's story was simple. The romance of Fifi, the charming little salesgirl at Mme. Cecile's hat shop on the Rue de la Paix, with Capt. Etienne de Bouvray

(Walter Percival) faces two obstacles. Mme. Cecile (Josephine Bartlett) expects her employee to marry her son (Leo Mars), while the Compte de St. Mar (William Pruette), Etienne's uncle, forbids his nephew to wed beneath his station. But one day a free-spirited American millionaire, Hiram Bent (Claude Gillingwater), bursts into the hat shop. At first Fifi suspects another masher:

Hiram: I'm sorry to frighten you, Mile. Modiste.
    I merely wanted to ask you a question.
Fifi: "No" is the answer.
Hiram: Then you can't tell me?
Fifi: Tell you what?
Hiram: The quickest way to the Louvre.
Fifi: The quickest way is to run.
Hiram: Now just for that I'll stay.
Fifi: Monsieur, I don't have the pleasure of your
    acquaintance.
Hiram: And you don't want to have, I guess.
Fifi: Monsieur, I am too polite to disagree with you.
Hiram: See here. There's a sign in your window
    "One Speaks English Here." I guess I'm the one.
Fifi: I "guess" you're not. You don't speak English.
    You speak American. Englishmen don't guess,
    they know.

Hiram is taken by Fifi's pert replies, and Fifi realizes Hiram's inquiries are unfeigned. Before long they have told each other their respective backgrounds. Fifi describes at length how she would perform "If I Were On The Stage." The delighted, open-handed Hiram offers to underwrite Fifi's musical studies. A year later a charity bazaar is held at the count's estate. The count is a gruff, purposeful fellow, avowing to all who will listen, "I Want What I Want When I Want It." He is overwhelmed by the singing of Mme. Bellini, and when he discovers she is none other than Fifi, the modiste, he gracefully withdraws his objections to a marriage. Etienne rushes over and kisses Fifi on the forehead. Fifi steps back:

Etienne: Oh, Fifi, have I offended you? Twas only
    on the forehead!
Fifi: Well, I'll have to call you down a little!

When Etienne grasps Fifi's meaning, he gives her a proper kiss.

Herbert's great number from the operetta was "Kiss Me Again." Herbert had written the waltz several years earlier and put it away until he could find a desirable spot for it. Over the complaints of

Miss Scheff Blossom, and producer Dillingham, he insisted it be retained as part of Fifi's first-act tour de force, "If I Were On The Stage," in which she sings in various styles to suggest the range of her dramatic characterizations. Miss Scheff remained identified with the song for the rest of her life. The count's song, "I Want What I Want When I Want It," became a bass-baritone standard for years. The rest of the score was almost as good, including as it did Etienne's "The Time And The Place And The Girl" and Fifi's "The Mascot Of The Troop," with its quotation from "La Marseillaise." *Mlle. Modiste* ran until vacation time and then resumed in September until a previous booking for another Herbert show forced it on to the road. It toured for three full seasons.

The first show of 1906 was equally important and equally good, although not nearly as successful. By the time **Forty-five Minutes from Broadway** opened at the New Amsterdam on 1 January, the nation was already singing its three great hits—"So Long Mary," "Mary's A Grand Old Name," and its title song. The "Gentleman Of The Press" are gathered at the Castleton home in New Rochelle to interview Tom Bennett (Donald Brian), Castleton's nephew, who stands to inherit a vast fortune if his uncle died, as he apparently did, intestate. Bennett announces he will be married to his actress-sweetheart, Flora Dora Dean (Lois Ewell), as soon as she arrives. The interview disappoints the townspeople who have also gathered at the house, for they had expected Castleton to leave his wealth to his long-faithful servant, Mary (Fay Templeton). Matters are made unhappier for Mary by Dan Cronin (James H. Manning), who courted her when he expected her to inherit the Castleton wealth and now makes no bones about his loss of interest in her. Bennett assures everyone, "I Want To Be A Popular Millionaire." No one is brazen enough to tell Tom that one quick jump toward popularity would be to rid himself of his wise-guy secretary, Kid Burns (Victor Moore). Kid has no false modesty, even on his first entrance:

Kid: I'm the real noise around this man's residence,
    understand? I'm the real noise. I'll make these
    rubes around here pay a little attention to me
    yet. Forty-five minutes from Broadway, Gee, it's
    got some of them towns in Texas tied to a post.

Mary arrives, depressed. Andy (Louis R. Grisel), the butler, tries to console her. Their dialogue is pure vaudeville, including a favorite of Cohan's, playing with nouns in apposition. But Cohan has learned how to make it all apply to the plot:

Andy: You know I knew your father, Mary.
Mary: You mean my mother, Mary. My father's name was Oscar.
Andy: How long have you been fond of Cronin. Mary?
Mary: It's three years now since he first told me that I loved him.
Andy: And nobody knew that you were engaged?
Mary: No, I didn't know it myself until he called it off.

Mary and Kid meet and discover that Kid's mother was also named Mary. The maid assures the secretary, "Mary's A Grand Old Name." Burns agrees. He suggests they might go out together for a night on the town. Ruefully, he suspects an evening of such fun is impossible "Forty-five Minutes from Broadway." Bennett reappears with Miss Dean and her snobbish mother (Julia Ralph). But it seems the snobbery is meant to camouflage her past, and part of that past was crooked Dan Cronin, who threatens to reveal her history. Burns witnesses this conversation but hasn't much time to think about it for he has stumbled on Castleton's will. Reading it he confirms that the heir is—as the orchestra, not Burns, announces—Mary. Mary enters with her luggage, but Burns, who is falling in love with her, persuades her to stay, although he doesn't mention the will. At a dinner party Bennett and Mrs. Dean fight over Mrs. Dean's dislike of Kid Burns. Bennett remains loyal, while growing angrier:

Bennett: And if you don't like it, you can go right straight to—
Flora: Tom!
Mrs. Dean: Let him say it! Let him say it!
Bennett: Oh, Hell.

Bennett finally agrees to keep Burns out of sight, only to have the bitchy Mrs. Dean start in on Mary. Cronin demands Mrs. Dean get him the combination of the Castleton safe. Cronin then phones Bennett, pretending to be his lawyer's secretary and insisting he return immediately to New York. Burns warns Bennett that Mrs. Dean and her daughter are up to no good, but Bennett refuses to listen and breaks with Kid. Mary and Burns agree to take a train together in the morning. In a dumb show Cronin attempts to rob the house but is foiled by

Mary. At the railroad station the crowds wait to see Cronin taken to jail. While they wait, they gossip that Mrs. Dean and Flora Dora have packed their bags and vanished. Mary arrives with her friends, who bid her "So Long Mary." Burns arrives and shows Mary the will. She concludes that Kid, like Cronin, really only wanted her inheritance. But Kid assures her he would marry her despite it. She rips up the will.

Here was Cohan at his peak. His story was good and not unbelievable; his earthy dialogue, albeit a little coy or a little vaudevillian at times, a far cry from even the better-than-average material Blossom had provided the week before in *Mlle. Modiste*. Cohan, moreover, was brazen enough to put all his songs in the first and third acts, leaving the second act for pure melodrama. In a sense this was as retrogressive as it was daring, suggesting the piece, like so many mountings of the preceding generation, was primarily a play, with songs tacked on. Even though Cohan worked the story and music together far more skillfully than most of his more slapdash predecessors, his efforts were not universally applauded. Some papers objected to a comedienne making an audience cry or to mixing melodrama and musical comedy. The *Times* saw it as "a case of oil and water." But even the *Times* grudgingly conceded there were "four or five capital songs." The initial New York run of ninety performances fell short of the Chicago tryout. It was not just Chicago-made shows New Yorkers disdained, but New York material in the homespun, forthright Chicago style. For all the exciting innovations in some domestic musicals, English and French shows, and American creations conceived in their unmistakably Continental mold, continued to receive the most serious attention and favor. It was a curious blind spot for Broadway and would continue to be so for another decade. This xenophilia failed to hurt Cohan financially. *Forty-five Minutes from Broadway* cost a mere $10,000 to produce and was in the black a few days after its New York opening.

One more or less American musical form, the rowdy "Dutch" comedian burlesque, was still well received in Manhattan. Perhaps the clowns' dialects, even in mockery, gave the requisite Continental tinge to the evening. In any case, **Twiddle-Twaddle** (1 January 1906, Weber's Music Hall), which opened the same night as *Forty-Five Minutes from Broadway*, chalked up 169 performances in two separate runs. Knowledgeable theatre buffs would immediately and correctly spot the title as more Weber and

Fields nonsense, although of course Fields had gone his own way. The main plot was also typical. A multi-millionaire sausage-maker takes his daughter to Europe to find her a titled husband. Edgar Smith's libretto was not without its Cohanesque chauvinisms: "We changed the words to that ['God Save The King'] and came pretty near making you British change your tune... . Hurray, I'm a Yankee." Broadway clearly had strong but ambivalent feelings. A highlight of the evening was Marie Dressler's travesty of a Spanish dance. She danced close to the footlights, but she stomped so hard a trick chair collapsed at the rear of the stage. The principal burlesque offered a double spoof, "The Squawman's Girl of the Golden West." Maurice Levi's score was serviceable at best.

Mr. Blarney from Ireland (1 January 1906, American) was advertised as an "Irish-American musical comedy-drama," so most playgoers had a good idea of its nature. Their impressions had to be confirmed when it was bruited about that its star, Fiske O'Hara, was being groomed as a rival to Chauncey Olcott. The hero is hardly off the boat and settled down to work in a real estate office when he must set to rights a blackmailer and other miscreants. He also is elected alderman (having apparently "secured his naturalization papers with strange celerity") and wins the girl he adores. The melodramatic material was in the experienced hands of Charles E. Blaney, while O'Hara himself took credit for the songs.

Broadway gave scant attention to **Comin' Thro' the Rye** (9 January 1906, Herald Square), on which George V. Hobart and A. Baldwin Sloane did the lion's share of the work. Hobart's plot had a Newport society queen (Alice Fisher) entertaining penniless artists in hopes of stumbling onto a genius. One of the artists (John Park) has painted a picture, "Comin' Thro' the Rye," using as a model a young girl (Georgie Kelly) whose irate father (Dan McAvoy) suddenly appears. The expected misunderstandings and a number of specialty acts rounded out the evening. To allow Dan McAvoy another "Dutch" role, the father was called Ippy Ipstein and the girl was his "long-lost" offspring. McAvoy fans no doubt recalled he had portrayed Izzy, the father of Sally in our Alley, three seasons back. The looseness of the plot allowed for some absurd theatrical *non sequiturs*. Although the first half was set in an artist's loft and the second at the Newport Casino, Nena Blake, dressed in a white cowgirl outfit, galloped on stage on a white pony to sing "My Broncho Boy." As usual Sloane's score was

never more than adequate. The show moved out after thirty-five performances.

Lew Dockstader and his minstrels returned on 15 January. Once again only about half his program was traditional blackface material—this time including Dockstader's own rendition of Bert Williams's "Nobody." The rest of the entertainment was more up-to-date material, hinging largely on satires of the New York political scene.

Racing the still newfangled automobiles had become so popular that a Vanderbilt offered a cup to the winner of one of the more important meets. The musical stage was quick to use it for plot material. A country girl, Dorothy Willetts (Dorothy would be a popular name for musical comedy racers), is sent for by her brother (Henry V. Donnelly), who has made a fortune in New York. She upsets the intrigues of Clarinda Larkspur (Edith Decker), who, in revenge, bribes the Willettses' chauffeur (Henry Bergman) to lose the race for **The Vanderbilt Cup** (16 January 1906, Broadway). But the Willettses' car wins with Dorothy and her lover (Aubrey Boucicault) behind the wheel. The show not only utilized the latest sports headlines for its story, it employed the newest theatrical gimmicks in the story's unfolding. Dorothy's trip east was shown to the audience by means of another newfangled device—moving pictures. For the race itself, two real cars were brought on stage, apparently on a treadmill, and drop after drop was raised to suggest the passage of scenery. The last drop, at the finish line, portrayed a group of shouting spectators—an addition to the large chorus that several papers felt was artificial and redundant. At the end of the race Barney Oldfield, the famous auto-racer, doffed his goggles to reveal he was one of the contestants. Since Oldfield was not listed in any of the programs, this was probably simply an opening-night stunt. Elsie Janis, a former child star, just coming into maturity, played Dorothy. She brought over from her vaudeville act a series of imitations, including Maude Adams as Peter Pan. Otis Harlan also won applause, in his case for an eccentric dance in which he accompanied himself with a "whistling obbligato." Unfortunately it fell to Miss Janis's lot to have to put over a weak score. However, her theatrical élan, Sydney Rosenfeld's book, and the superb, inventive staging made a hit of the evening.

An Irish-American, straight out of the comic strips, was featured in **Happy Hooligan's Trip Around the World** (22 January 1906, Murray Hill). Obviously a sequel to his 1902 adventures, it followed its absurd hero's itinerary and his triumph over the scheming Max Guggenheimer. A number of military drills won special applause.

If the Shuberts and their writers for *Fantana* (14 January 1905) hoped to repeat their success with **Mexicana** (29 January 1906, Lyric), they were badly disappointed. They disappointed theatregoers as well. "Book Stupid; Music Dull," read the *Times* headline. The book followed a New Yorker to Mexico, where he discovers he is the victim of a Porfirio Diaz swindle with a bogus mine called "Mexicana." He engineers a revolution. Raymond Hubbell's music had no more of a Mexican flavor than his songs for *Fantana* savored of Japan. *Mexicana*'s leading players, Thomas Q. Seabrooke and Christie MacDonald, were unable to improve matters.

"The abandon and infectious good humor that characterize every theatrical effort of the negro" was to become the chief decades-long virtue of black shows in many critics' eyes. So it was when the *Dramatic Mirror* reported on **Rufus Rastus** (29 January 1906, American). The show had a book by W. D. Hall, lyrics by Frank Williams and others, and music by Ernest Hogan and Tom Lemonier (along with Joe Jordan and H. Lawrence Freeman). Hogan, who refused to perform in stereotypical makeup but appeared in "natural blackface," portrayed the hapless Rufus who attempts to pay off a twenty-two-dollar debt by working for two dollars a week at the Ponce de Leon Hotel (remember the first-act setting of *Flo-Flo*?). Unfortunately his expenses come to more than his income, so the second act finds him serving as a doorkeeper at Madison Square Garden. His troubles multiply when he fails to collect admissions. Happily, in the last act he finds $50,000 in a cereal box. Foreshadowing Ted Lewis, Hogan was constantly stopping the action to inquire of his audience, "Is everybody happy?" For all their zest, the musical numbers were undistinguished. Among the best was "Oh, Say Wouldn't It Be A Dream," which postulated, "If coons could only rule this great United Land,/Say wouldn't it be a dream."

The Grafter (29 January 1906, Grand Opera) was actually Bill Grafter, a tramp who scrounges his way in and out of a plot in which a young man pretends to have a rich, famous uncle in order to appease his would-be mother-in-law. Grafter was played by the famous slapstick clown Hap Ward, now performing without his longtime partner, Harry Vokes. Ward wore his "Weary Willie" tramp costume throughout.

Comedy also dominated **Gay New York** (6 February 1906, Murray Hill). Herman Schultz goes out on the town for a night without his wife's knowing about it and inadvertently exchanges hats with a man named Jennings, who may be his son's future father-in-law. Schultz's attempts to retrieve the hat are monkeywrenched when three men named Jennings suddenly appear. Schultz was played by one of the era's countless dialect comedians. As if that weren't old-hat enough (pardon the pun), yet another Officer Ketchum was among the characters. The song to receive the most encores (a score of them according to one commentator) was "Blinkee Dee," sung by a comic "colored servant," performed as usual by a white man in blackface.

George Washington, Jr. (12 February 1906, Herald Square) was the first of two February musicals. When he unveiled his latest work, Cohan attacked the twisted, pervasive belittling of American virtues so evident in criticism of his plays. This was the flag-waving Cohan of *Little Johnny Jones* (7 November 1904) back in full stride. Senator Belgrave (Jerry Cohan), an Anglophile boastfully contemptuous of the country he serves, is determined that his son George (George M.) will marry Lord Rothburt's languid, arrogant daughter, Evelyn. But George loves Dolly Johnson (Ethel Levey), the niece of the straightforward Senator Hopkins (Eugene O'Rourke). They have all come to Mount Vernon to show the Ruthburts some Americana. If Dolly is a bit naïve about Washington's mores, George couldn't care less. He will be happy to educate her:

Dolly: Do the Senators get a big salary?
George: That's all according to what corporation they represent.
Dolly: There are no female politicians, are there?
George: There are lots of old ladies in the Senate.

Hopkins hears George is to marry Evelyn and warns Dolly. Dolly's coolness upsets George, and he finally breaks with his father:

George: I disown you as a father. Now what do you think of that!
Belgrave: You're a disgrace to the name of Belgrave.
George: Then take your name! I don't want your name! To hell with it! I'll take my own name!

And, taking heed of the estate on which they are standing, he then and there calls himself George

Washington, Jr. Hopkins enters and Belgrave snarls at him, "You did this." To which Hopkins replies, for a first-act curtain, "No, you're wrong, Belgrave. The man who used to live there [pointing to Mount Vernon] did this." Hopkins is still not completely satisfied that George is the right boy for Dolly. He informs George he will not give his consent until there's a monument to George Washington, Jr. But Hopkins himself is not beyond reproach. Lord Rothburt and Evelyn are frauds hired by him to embarrass Belgrave. George gets wind of the machinations in the nick of time and, despite their quarrel, warns his father. Belgrave sees the error of his ways, and when in gratitude he offers to erect a monument to his son, Hopkins consents to the marriage. The hit of the show was "You're A Grand Old Flag"—called "You're A Grand Old Rag" until the sort of patriots Cohan hated objected and he was forced to change the lyrics. The song was the first one written with a specific musical in mind to sell over a million copies of its sheet music. Dolly was also given a show-stopper, "I Was Born In Virginia." Although it was almost as good as *Forty-five Minutes from Broadway* and with its full complement of songs closer to accepted musical comedy, *George Washington, Jr.* didn't even attain the former's ninety performances. Once again the road was more welcoming to Cohan than his own beloved Broadway. Both musicals played return Broadway engagements, but neither added appreciably to the number of New York showings.

One oddity was Emerson Porter Browne's "miniature musical comedy," **Just a Joke** (12 February 1906, Madison Square), which was brought in as a curtain raiser in the futile hope of saving a weak comedy at the theatre. In it an English chambermaid, hooked on penny dreadfuls, spurns the proposal of an elevator boy whom she really loves and favors a dashing officer who woos and deserts her. She wakes up to realize she's been dreaming. Reviews made no mention of the songs.

A pretty, well-drilled chorus seemed to be the real selling point in **Lovers and Lunatics** (19 February 1906, Metropolis), which had been traipsing from one small town to another much of the season. Its slim plot told of a nephew who lies about whom he has married so as not to offend his rich uncle. The uncle lives next door to an insane asylum. Confusions arise when three women, all named Nell, come to visit at the house. Various escapees added to the confusion and, we can only hope, the fun. The *Dramatic Mirror* accused the musical

of offering no more than a "medley of slightly disguised popular airs" and identified one as from *The Isle of Spice*. All in all, the musical supplied a very downbeat ending to the season at combination houses.

The second February musical on Broadway was **Abyssinia** (20 February 1906, Majestic). It was as important as the Cohan piece, almost as well realized, yet far less popular. Assembled by the team that created *In Dahomey* (18 February 1903) for many of the same players, including the stars, Williams and Walker, it marked an obvious advance in writing and staging techniques for the group. After Rastus Johnson (George Walker) wins $15,000 in a lottery, Rastus and Jasmine Jenkins (Bert Williams) decide to visit the land of their ancestors, which they have determined was Abyssinia. (The stage Abyssinia displayed real water pouring down a waterfall in a mountain pass, and a colorful bazaar with a "property lion and camel and real asses.") Their ignorance of foreign ways leads Rastus and Jasmine into several misadventures culminating before the throne of Abyssinia's iron-fisted monarch, Menelik. They are brought there as a court of last appeal after they have "borrowed" a priceless vase. If Menelik sounds a gong three times, the "borrowers" must die; if he sounds it four times, they are pardoned. The long wait between the third and fourth gongs provided a memorable scene, at once comic and terrifying. One interesting feature of J. A. Shipp and Alex Rogers's libretto and lyrics was the way African blacks and American blacks were contrasted. Apparently Shipp and Rogers wanted to suggest that coming to America marked a falling away from grace, if not from perfection. The Africans speak the King's English. Indeed some of their dialogue and lyrics are so stilted they smack of parody:

> Soldiers of the King are we,
>   We bow to his supremacy,
> We know naught of disloyalty,
>   Hence can not spare an enemy.

On the other hand the Americans speak lines straight out of minstrelsy:

Jasmine: And you's a philosophy?
Rastus: Philosopher.
Jasmine: What's the duty of a philoso- philoso-
    (*finally add pede*).
Rastus: To look on the bright side of other people's
    troubles when you haven't any of your own.

Will Marion Cook and Williams supplied the score. No long-lived favorites emerged from it, but it represented the best black popular musical writing of the period, with native and international styles in reciprocal influences. Negro shows had to be particularly careful. No serious love interest could be included. No "suggestion" was allowed. Even Cohan's coy profanity was taboo. Notwithstanding their concern at offending a white audience's sensibilities, these fine black talents could win over only a handful of ticket-buyers. Thirty-one performances was all *Abyssinia* could attain.

Although **His Majesty** (19 March 1906, Majestic) professed to be a musicalization of *Man and Superman*, it most certainly was not. Bernard Shaw was not about to give his consent to an adaptation. And a show written around Blanche Ring's gaudy talents stood small chance of reflecting the balanced debates that comprised Shaw's scenes. What was presented on the stage of the Majestic on 19 March was a most un-Shavian concoction about an opera company killed in a railroad wreck. In Hell, its prima donna, Mrs. Brown of Chicago, finds all six of her ex-husbands. She gets her revenge on one who reneged on his alimony payments. The score, by the otherwise unheard-from Shafter Howard, offered nothing of merit, nor could Miss Ring find a first-rate interpolation to add during the brief three-week run.

Harry B. Smith, collaborating with composer Stafford Waters, had a new musical, **The Three Graces,** ready for inspection at the Chicago Opera House on 2 April. Smith's story told of three thieves' stealing clothes so they can pose as gentlemen at a Catskill hotel. The clothes contain papers that help them discover a missing heiress. Though several critics compared the plot—and the show—unfavorably to *Erminie*, it proved acceptable to many Chicagoans. The show ran into the hot weather.

Further west, in San Francisco, **Miss Timidity** (2 April 1906, Tivoli) had no such luck. It proved to be a reworking by a local man, Allan Dunn, of *Miss Helyett* (3 November 1891). His changes in the story were minor. What is puzzling is whose music was employed, since programs list no composer and the *Examiner* in its review says only "the songs and dances are new." The show enjoyed good reviews, but during its third week the great San Francisco earthquake and fire struck on 17–18 April, claiming both the musical and the popular theatre among its victims.

The front page of **The Social Whirl** (7 April 1906, Casino), a notorious scandal sheet, discloses that "J. E." was seen wining and dining the Broadway star Viola Dare (Adele Ritchie) at a discreet country inn. At least four men in her circle have those initials, and three of them are married. Each tries to throw suspicion on the others. All that really took place was that Viola took both James Ellingham (Frederic Bond) and his son Jack (Willard Curtis) in her car so that she could persuade the elder Ellingham she was a fit match for his boy. Small parts were excellently cast. Ada Lewis played yet another toughie. Charles J. Ross and Joe Coyne portrayed a father and son, with Coyne singing about a girl who plays love songs on a calliope; while Maud Raymond earned several encores with a song describing a black who has to dance whenever he hears a band play. Blanche Deyo and Mabel Fenton offered "crowd-pleasing" dances. The chorus whirled through a ballet done all in crimson, a hunting dance, and a routine in which the smaller girls impersonated bootblacks shining the taller girls' shoes. There was another Gustave Kerker score relegated to the sidelines by interpolations. The most popular were "You're Just The Girl I'm Looking For" (E. Ray Goetz) and "Old Man Manhattan" by the husband-and-wife team of James O'Dea and Anne Caldwell. They were typical vaudeville melodies, stronger fibered than the watery Kerker stuff. With so solid a cast of favorites the show ran from early April into the fall.

John Philip Sousa returned to the theatre after a six-year absence to write the score to Harry B. Smith's tale of **The Freelance** (16 April 1906, New Amsterdam). In Smith's story the Duke of Graftiana (Albert Hart) arranges for his son Florian (George Tallman) to wed Yolanda (Nella Bergen), daughter of the Emperor of Bragadocia (Felix Haney). The children balk. Yolanda flees, changing places with Griselda (Jeanette Lowrie), a goose girl, while Florian, not knowing of Yolanda's actions, switches stations with Griselda's husband, the goatherd Sigmund Lump (Joseph Cawthorn). When Sigmund discovers he is not to wed a real princess, he sighs, "Everytime I'm invited out to dinner, I always get just what I have at home." Smith's tale left Sousa uninspired. As the librettist noted, the best number in the show, the closing march "Drums Are Beating," never stirred a soul except on opening night, when Sousa himself conducted and was hailed back for six curtain calls. While the show helped secure Cawthorn stardom, even his clowning could not push it beyond thirty-five performances.

Philadelphians still enjoyed patronizing local productions, especially Willard Spenser's sporadic musicals. Spenser unveiled a new one—with an unusual setting—on 23 April at the Chestnut Street Theatre. **Rosalie** planted its principals in the midst of the Russo-Japanese War in Manchuria. Rosalie (Clara Maentz) finds time while nursing the wounded to win the hand of an American reporter (Albert Parr). The musical ran into June.

JOSEPH CAWTHORN was born in New York on 29 March 1867. He made his debut in variety at the age of four and appeared one year later with Haverly's Minstrels. Taken to England when he was nine, he spent the next four years performing a child act in British music halls. His first appearances on his return to America were also in vaudeville, but he soon moved over to legitimate musicals, appearing in *Excelsior, Jr.* (29 November 1895), *Miss Philadelphia* (27 December 1897), and *The Fortune Teller* (26 September 1898) among others.

Joe Howard, the Chicago favorite, braved New York with **The District Leader** (30 April 1906, Wallack's). His story was a down-to-earth, if melodramatic, slice of American politics. Tim Halloran, a candidate for the state senate, loves Grace Lowton, daughter of the Republican candidate for the same post. Halloran's manager, Sam Grady, betrays Tim and drugs his twin brother, Jim, in a Chinatown opium den. But Tom Cole, a newspaper man and Grace's brother, exposes Grady's scheme. Howard took credit for the book and lyrics as well as the music. The critics were impressed with none of it. But songs such as "Won't You Be My Girlie?" carry the melodic stamp and lyric directness that endeared Howard to his Chicago fans. Howard also appeared in the show, but he took none of the major roles, contenting himself instead with singing a single song while sitting placidly on a park bench. He didn't have to sit for long. He could hurry back to Chicago after an ignominious one-week run.

Politics were also the order of the day in **His Honor the Mayor** (28 May 1906, New York), the only musical to bow in May. His Honor (Clarence Harvey), it develops, is not very honorable. When it comes out that the mayor of Kankakee bought the election, he is forced to leave town. Amazingly, all

the action takes place in Paris and at a Hungarian spa. Spearheading the reform and the evening was the indefatigable Blanche Ring. Nothing from Julian Edwards's score really stopped the show, but Gus Edwards gave Miss Ring a fairly good tune in "Come Take A Skate With Me," and Will Cobb and Ren Shields offered an even better number in "Waltz Me Around Again Willie." To play safe she also revived "My Irish Molly O!" During several encores for this song she was abetted by the grotesque dancing of Harry Kelly and the unicycling of Henri French. Together they cavorted through the hot weather.

The season's final production was a loosely strung-together vaudeville called **Seeing New York** (5 June 1906, New York Roof). Cool rooftop breezes must have been as much of an attraction as the show itself. A hackneyed Sloane score and the thinnest of story lines by Joseph Hart and Clifton Crawford about another yokel on tour needed all the help they could get from the performers (including Mr. Crawford) and the weather. The other performers included the Six Proveanies in their bicycle act and Salerno, the juggler. A "policeman" chorus sang as a burglary progressed (the burglar ran off, taking one policeman's shield with him), while a chorus of red-gowned young women, supposedly standing in the wind at 23rd Street and Broadway, had their skirts ballooned by air blown from beneath the stage. As it turned out the evening had little other serious roof garden competition and made it through the summer.

1906–1907

The season got off to a lurid start. **Mamzelle Champagne** (25 June 1906, Madison Square Garden Roof) was never able to complete its first performance. During the second act Harry Thaw shot and killed the Garden's architect, Stanford White, in a dispute over Thaw's wife, the musical comedy starlet Evelyn Nesbit. The scene and some of its background were described in a letter by the librettist, Edgar Allan Woolf, to Burns Mantle:

"Mamzelle Champagne" was my Columbia varsity show, and was transported by a manager, Henry Pincus, to the open Madison Square Roof with a professional cast. Of course, when the college boys played it, with such lines as "I'm a good girl—you can't insult me," every line was a howl, but spoken by actresses the howls were missing. In addition to this calamity, the wind was blowing down Madison Ave. on the night of the opening—blowing all the dialogue with it. My mother and father were sitting in the front row, and through the remarks of the people behind them, they knew the show was dying, and that the author was in ill repute. When the three shots fired by Harry Thaw rang through the air, my mother jumped up in her chair and screamed, "My God, they've shot my son!" Although poor Pincus thought his show was ruined by the murder, the next night you couldn't get near the Garden, and the seats at the table where Stanford White sat sold at a premium.

Curiosity seekers continued to keep the otherwise vapid evening alive for sixty showings.

There were no new shows in July. And August's first interesting entry opened in Chicago at a house normally given over to blood-and-thunder melodrama. Actually, Lem B. Parker and W. R. Williams's **The Cowboy Girl** (5 August 1906, Alhambra) was "one of those sombrero and leather plots, bristling with bowie knives and jingling with spurs," but this time heavily larded with songs and dances. The musical was set in New Mexico. Its heroine, Gyp, must rout a vicious band whose headquarters are deep in a stalactite-filled cave. A large, attractive chorus line and a quartet listed as "Four Bad Men From Arizona" were highly commended. A Chicago stand was followed by a long tour.

Five musicals arrived in New York in August, and three of them were rewarded with long runs. First to arrive was the London hit **The Little Cherub** (6 August 1906, Criterion). That show's star, Hattie Williams, played a young lady who must first charm a snobbish earl before she can marry his son. Besides the regular Ivan Caryll score, Miss Williams sang songs by Marie Doro, Jerome Kern, and Jean Schwartz. She sang them 155 times in New York before repeating them in other cities.

The first solid American-made hit, **The Tourists** (25 August 1906, Daly's), had book and lyrics by R. H. Burnside and music by Gustave Kerker. Burnside's fable, a variation of the popular American-in-exotic-parts plot, was inordinately complicated. John Duke (Alfred Hickman) of Plymouth, Massachusetts, is registered as the Duke of Plymouth at the Oriental Hotel in Rangapang. He is evading his tutor, Mr. Todd (Richard Golden), and courting Dora

Blossom (Julia Sanderson), whose American father (Phil H. Ryley) is seeking a titled marriage for her. Todd somehow discovers John's whereabouts and telegraphs that he is on his way. Jambo-Ree (also called Ram-Dow, and played by Alfred Cahill) arrives. His master, Boojam, was to have married the Rajah's daughter (Vera Michelena) but, according to Jambo-Ree, Boojam has been eaten by a tiger and Jambo-Ree has decided to impersonate him. The hotel manager, recognizing Jambo-Ree as a rebel with a price on his head, drugs him and prepares to claim the reward. This suggests an escape to John. He writes Todd, claiming he has been kidnapped by Jambo-Ree and must be ransomed. A battered, road-weary Todd soon appears:

> We traveled thru France
> But I hadn't a chance
> to see it—for I had malaria.
> And while we were in Spain
> I was nearly insane
> with the grip, which I caught in Bulgaria.

Mr. Blossom offers Todd some reassurance: "You can sue the Government for keeping the roads in such bad condition and get damages." But Todd isn't interested. "I've got all the damages I want—what I need is repairs." Todd is blindfolded and led around the hotel courtyard, which he is told is the rebel's cave. After his negotiations with Jambo-Ree (actually John faking an Oriental accent), he is "returned" to the hotel. The Rajah (William Pruette) enters and falls in love with Dora, insisting he will abduct her if she will not marry him willingly. He accuses Todd, who has been gotten up in native dress, of being another rebel. Todd claims he is Boojam, only to have Boojam turn up hale and hearty. Everything is finally explained, and the lovers are allowed to go their own way:

> Todd: Jack, I want to congratulate you—this is the happiest day of your life!
> Jack [John]:—You are too previous, old man, I am not to be married until tomorrow!
> Todd: That's what I say—This is the happiest day of your life.

Kerker's music was his usual run-of-the-mill melodies with the expected love ditties, such as "It's Nice To Have A Sweetheart" and the apparently requisite paean to the Rialto, "Dear Old Broadway."

The authors also demonstrated the persistent influence of *Florodora*, when they gave "Which One Shall I Marry?" to a "double quartet." The *Times* ruefully concluded "that Gustave Kerker long ago gave up any idea of going down to fame by reason of anything he might write." But the paper, which four years before had predicted the demise of musical comedy, still found little attractive in the whole school. "A mystic maze of brilliant color, popular melody, obvious comicality, with the inevitable girls, girls, girls, ... when one has said that what more is there to tell about any of the so-called musical comedies?" "Nothing," contented theatergoers seemed to respond, as they stood in line for seats during the show's four-month run.

Marie Cahill came in two nights later as **Marrying Mary** (27 August 1906, Daly's). Although Mary Montgomery is a much-married young lady, her marriages never last more than an hour or two, when she runs away in fright. She has already married a senator, a Mormon, and a lush. At a vacation retreat she meets Ormsby Kulpepper (William Courtleigh) and his father, Henry Clay Kulpepper (Eugene Cowles), both of whom would marry her, though the elder Kulpepper heads the Anti-Divorce League. Just as she is trying to decide between the two, all her past mates appear. She finally realizes which one she really loves and promises this time to stay around for at least a week or so. On paper *Marrying Mary* would seem like the usual Cahill vehicle. Instead of a "Congo Love Song" or an "Arab Love Song" Benjamin Hapgood Burt and Silvio Hein presented her with "The Hottentot Love Song." And once again an interpolation, "He's A Cousin Of Mine" (Cecil Mack/Chris Smith and Silvio Hein), often got the biggest applause. Mary reprised the chorus whenever she was caught with the wrong man. But most of the critics, even the ones who customarily had reservations about Miss Cahill, were free with their praise. They lauded the show for its sense of tone and scale (there wasn't a big chorus line or any large, stagy numbers), and they praised Miss Cahill for playing a part instead of herself. Nonetheless the show stayed only six weeks before it headed to the profitable hinterlands. There is a tantalizing footnote to the show. One of the songs was "Is There Any One Here By The Name Of Smith?" Years later, Fritzi Scheff starred in *Pretty Mrs. Smith* (21 September 1914), using an almost identical plot, except that all her former husbands had been named Smith. Was there any connection?

A One Horse Town (27 August 1906, Yorkville) depicted the plight of a touring musical stranded in a Western settlement so small that it hasn't anything to pass for a theatre. But it does have a law stipulating any woman who arrives in town can't leave without marrying. So the local dialect comedian, called Herman Dingle for this affair, marries all the girls, stages a vaudeville show out in the open, and discovers a lost mine.

Lew Fields struck gold with an elaborate vaudeville, **About Town** (30 August 1906, Herald Square), held together by the required gossamer story line. The Duke of Slushington (Lawrence Grossmith) must choose between the saucy adventuress Fancy Frivol (Edna Wallace Hopper) and pert Gertie Gibson (Louise Dresser), who is, appropriately, a Gibson Girl. He is aided by a brash cab driver (Fields), who suddenly finds himself elevated to the presidency of the All-Night Bank. Fields gave his eye-filling chorus a variety of routines. They marched as soldiers in red and then again as cadets in gray. They sang and danced as Dutchmen, Gibson Girls (in white and blue), and nursemaids (in polka dots). At one point Fields divided the ladies of the ensemble into two groups: the first in red frocks and black stockings, the second all in blue. He then made the chorus boys choose a group. Whichever group was chosen, the other crossed the stage and began to rip off their clothes in a jealous pique. For the times, it was very naughty and revealing. Sketches, songs, and even the performers came and went during the 138-performance run. Besides Fields, entertainers included Jack Norworth, Vernon Castle, Miss Hopper, Miss Dresser, and, later, Peter F. Dailey and Blanche Ring. Though no hit song developed, the roster of credits included, at one time or another, Victor Herbert, Gus Edwards, Albert Von Tilzer, Raymond Hubbell, Gustave Kerker, and A. Baldwin Sloane. When business started to fall off, Fields harked back to his music hall days and inserted a burlesque of *The Great Divide*, which he rechristened "The Great Decide."

The Man from Now (3 September 1906, New Amsterdam) offered one of the primitive science fiction plots the age so relished. Professor Forecasta (Edward B. Martindell) invents a machine to let people see 1,000 years ahead and then concocts a potion that allows the drinker to visit the future he has seen. A visit to Gassar, a thirtieth-century women's college, discloses that women dominate the world. The men quickly return to the comfortably male-dominated 1906. This summary gives no hint that the star of the show was Harry Bulger, who ambled in and out of the action as a tramp called "Waffles." But the plot, as was so often the case, served only as an insubstantial frame on which to hang tours de force, specialties, and anything else that came to mind. For example, Helen Hale was brought on to sing "My Gasoline Maid" dressed as a motorcar. Chorus girls, as college girls, played a choreographed football game, exercised with dumbbells, and marched and countermarched "statuesquely." The show arrived in New York only after an extended road tour, during which it was known as *2905 or To-morrow Land*. But its Broadway run was brief, and the show was gone long before 1907 arrived.

When young W. C. Fields started out on his career as a comic juggler he reputedly cadged both tricks and makeup from James Harrigan, a headliner known as "The Tramp Juggler." As Fields did later, Harrigan moved on to more verbal comedy, though, of course, without Fields's success. One step in his transition was Harrigan's appearance as **Panhandle Pete** (10 September 1906, Metropolis) in a "panoramic musical comedy" based on George McManus's cartoon character. In a second hint of things to come the plot recounted how Abijah O'Grady, a "moving picture maker," lures Pete to play the hobo in a new flick by betting him that he can't stay out of trouble with the police. Sure enough, Pete's getup and begging keep the law on his tail and provide plenty of footage as he moves from a banquet at the Hotel Astor to Rector's and finally to a picnic at Claremont-on-the-Hudson. The songs and the staging of the musical numbers, the dialogue, and the characterizations were all serviceable. One example of the show's comedy was the wedding at the hotel, with Mrs. Newlywed played by an actor in drag. What made the entertainment a delight was Harrigan's juggling—most especially his juggling a large number of cigar boxes—and his seemingly ad-lib asides to his audience.

The plot of Paul Rubens's London hit *Lady Madcap*, retitled **My Lady's Maid** (20 September 1906, Casino), was something of a novelty, though at best it was merely a British variation of the sort of tale told in *His Highness the Bey* (21 November 1904) or *It Happened in Nordland* (5 December 1904). In this instance a maid is forced to impersonate her mistress when the madcap lady disappears.

The Red Mill (24 September 1906, Knickerbocker) was the smash hit of the season and remains one of the joys of the American Musical Theatre. If it was different, it was a difference of degree, not kind. Stripped to essentials, it was merely another of the many musical comedies that had fun with Americans in a foreign setting. But for 1906 audiences it also had the brilliant clowning of David Montgomery and Fred Stone, while for posterity it had a superior Henry Blossom book and an unforgettable Victor Herbert score. Con Kidder (Stone) and Kid Conner (Montgomery) are two aggressive young Americans. They've come to "do" Europe, but find the Continent has undone them. They are broke. Arriving at the little Dutch port of Katwykann-Zee, they nonetheless take lodgings at the inn on the square, within sight of an old, legendary red mill. The town is lorded over by a stern burgomaster, Jan Van Borkem (Edward Begley). He has promised his daughter Gretchen (Augusta Greenleaf) to the handsome governor of Zeeland, though both men know her heart belongs to the equally handsome sea captain, Doris Van Damm (Joseph M. Ratliff). Con flirts with the innkeeper's daughter, Tina (Ethel Johnson), hoping she will help soften the blow when he and Kid are revealed as penniless. Tina is as spunky as Con and Kid, but the three agree there is a double standard and the only way a woman can publicly vent her anger is to "Whistle It." Gretchen and Doris meet and talk together longingly of "The Isle Of Our Dreams." But the burgomaster's sister Bertha (Allene Crater), while she sympathizes with the lovers, warns Doris that Van Borkem will lock Gretchen in the mill and its terrifying history will repeat itself:

Doris: I don't believe that foolish story.
Bertha: It's true. It happened hundreds of
    years ago. King Johann locked the Princess
    Wilhelmina in this mill over night to keep her
    from the man she loved and she disappeared
    and no trace did they ever find of her.

Con and Kid dream of another island, and they recapitulate the pleasures to be found on "The Streets Of New York." Van Borkem discovers Gretchen and Doris have seen each other and fulfills Bertha's warning by locking Gretchen in the mill. Alone at night on the deck of the mill she prays "Moonbeams" will send her message of love to Doris. But Con manages to enter the mill and lowers Gretchen to freedom on a mill sail. The governor (Neal McCay) arrives at the burgomaster's house, with a bevy of beautiful admirers. Though he is engaged, he happily proclaims,

"Everyday Is Ladies' Day To Me." Nor is he above fancying another young lady in private, merely, as he tells her, "Because You're You." But Gretchen's escape forces both the burgomaster and the governor to face reality. The burgomaster gives Doris and Gretchen his reluctant consent, and the governor goes looking for more willing girls. Van Borkem's reluctance further melts when he learns Van Damm will inherit a large fortune. Con and Kid are hauled in for attempting to leave without paying, but Tina helps to get them a pardon.

The summary overlooks a number of Con and Kid's actions. The acrobatic Stone made a much-applauded first entrance seeming to fall down a two-story-high ladder. In the course of the evening Con and Kid disguise themselves as Italian musicians and as Sherlock Holmes and Watson. Herbert's music was of the lighter sort he created for pieces he considered musical comedy, rather than comic opera. As a comparison of "Dear Old Broadway" or "Good-bye Sweet Old Manhattan Isle" with "The Streets Of New York" demonstrates, Herbert could compose in a more Tin Pan Alley style and beat the Tin Pan Alley boys on their own grounds. Some mystery has surrounded a minor number that Montgomery and Stone sang as the Italian musicians, "Good-a-bye, John." It was printed with Blossom and Herbert's names, but it bears an uncanny resemblance to "Good-a-bye, John" from a touring show, *The Belle of Avenue A*, and credited to Harry Williams and Egbert Van Alstyne. Waters' thesis that Stone or Montgomery slyly hummed the tune while suggesting a type of song needed for the scene cannot hold water, for it fails to account for the identical lyric. The mystery remains. Outside the theatre *The Red Mill* can stake its claim to a famous first. With the show a success, Charles Dillingham constructed a large mill in front of the Knickerbocker, with electrically moved arms. He hung lights on the revolving parts, giving Broadway its first moving illuminated sign.

Two more Herbert scores followed. On Christmas night Weber presented himself at his own house in a double bill, **Dream City** and **The Magic Knight**. Herbert had several times spurned offers to write for the old Weber and Fields Music Hall. Some quirky personal pigeonholing led him to consider music halls beneath his dignity. But now that the partners, in going their separate ways, were producing more traditional fare in regular theatres, the composer was delighted to accommodate both of them. *Dream City* was flippantly listed in the

programs as "a dramatic 'pipe' in two puffs." It was set in "the immediate future according to current real estate advertisements." J. Billington Holmes (Otis Harlan), a fast-talking promoter, convinces Wilhelm Dinglebender (Weber) that his farm at Malaria Center, Long Island, will make the perfect site for an elaborate housing development. In a dream Dinglebender visualizes the fabulous new town and attends a performance at its new opera house. He is so disillusioned by the opera and the people he meets there that he refuses to sign the property transfer. Weber filled the evening with delightful bits of his "Dutch" clowning. In one scene he went fishing, casting into a tiny bucket. Told he can't possibly catch fish that way, he replies, "I know dots. I vass shust teaching der vorm to swim." The *Magic Knight*, a brilliant spoof on *Lohengrin*, was originally intended to have been part of the second act, the opera Dinglebender witnesses. But Weber, fearing many of his regulars had never seen an opera and would miss the satire, insisted it be given as an afterpiece. As Herbert's biographer notes, the evening "received as much critical acclaim and enthusiasm as any work Herbert ever wrote; yet none of his scores is now more forgotten and ignored." The *World* hailed the bill as "high art," and the *Tribune* blessed it as "a triumph of musical fooling." With the passing of time *Dream City* seems less awesome, however pretty. But the *Lohengrin* burlesque, in capable hands, could be hilarious. Lohengrin ("a professional rescuer of distressed maidens") arrives in a cab drawn by a swan. To his "Mein Lieber Schwan" Frederick (Ortrud's "hen-pecked uncle") can only respond, "Quack, Quack." Maurice Farkoa sang Lohengrin; Otis Harlan, Frederick; Cora Tracy, Ortrud; and Lillian Blauvelt, Elsa. Time and again Herbert took Wagnerian airs and subtly twisted them into hints of popular tunes. For all the kudos in the press, the show could only manage 102 performances, and when it took to the road Weber's fears proved well founded. Small city audiences were baffled by *The Magic Knight* and began walking out in distressing numbers. Weber quickly dropped it. When, after the first season's tour, another producing unit bought the rights for the one-night stands, Herbert was horrified to learn that the producers intended to drop all his music as too advanced for the backwaters and had commissioned Maurice Levi to create a more transparently tinkly score. Herbert sued and ultimately got the new material removed. But the show held no charms for small-town crowds and shortly folded.

Herbert's third score was composed for Frank Daniels, with whom he had worked so often in the past. In The Tattooed Man (18 February 1907, Criterion) Daniels portrayed Omar Khayam, Jr. Omar rules Persia during the Shah's frequent absences. But he has a peculiar birthmark, and it has been decreed that if ever another man appears with the same mark both men must die together. Fatima (May Vokes), rebuffed by Omar, tattoos the mark on not one but two other men, and Omar must spend the rest of the evening designing ways to avoid the inevitable. Though he does avoid losing his head, he meets a fate worse than death when the returning Shah (Herbert Waterous) orders him to marry Fatima. Daniels's broad, low comedy delighted his followers, and he could make a line such as "Early to bed and early to rise—and you never meet any prominent people" seem hilariously observant. But Daniels was not the whole show. Miss Vokes won applause for her comic wallflower, while Sallie Fisher, who had attracted attention with her dancing and singing some weeks before in The Man from Now, again won praise as Leila, "beloved of Omar, but nothing doing." When the principals were off stage, there was still "much of song and dance, grouping and marching, by girls in glittering golden gowns, delicate shell pink, yellow and brown, and rich combined tints of green and red." The score was not one of Herbert's best. Still, he was always looking for new ideas and, somewhat bravely for the era, eschewed an overture, opening instead with forty bars to set the mood for the opening in which a muezzin calls the faithful to prayers. The run was cut short when a fire at the neighboring New York Theatre resulted in water damage to the Criterion. The show was taken on the road and toured for a year and a half.

Nat M. Wills was even more famous than James Harrigan for his tramp act, although he was not a juggler. In A Lucky Dog (1 October 1906, Yorkville) he played a wanderer called Happy Holmes (shades of last year's Bankers and Brokers and countless other period shows). Happy's first entrance found him scampering up a gate post to escape an ominously growling cur. He lands smack in the middle of a plot in which he must help recover a magic, wish-granting ring, stolen by a villain from the finger of a Hindu god. His reward for accomplishing this is the discovery that he is the rich heroine's long-lost brother. Wills's big moment was the song "Beautiful Bed," in which he extolled the joys of a do-nothing life.

Both October's regular musical entries were also hits. Richard Carle put in his annual appearance, this time as star of The Spring Chicken (8 October 1906, Daly's). "Appearances" might be a more accurate word, since his 115 New York performances were divided among three separate engagements. Bessie McCoy, Blanche Deyo ("both fine dancers"), and Adele Rowland were prominently featured. In one respect The Spring Chicken marked a notable departure for Carle. Although he was credited with "Americanizing" the material, the show was originally a London hit with a book by George Grossmith, Jr., and music by Ivan Caryll and Lionel Monckton. The Englishmen in turn borrowed their story from a French farce, Coquin de Printemps. Given Carle's penchant for suggestive material, the story of a young lawyer so flirtatious that he jeopardizes his own marriage was obviously appealing to him. Inevitably Carle added his own songs, and in another change wrote some of the tunes as well as some of the lyrics. His biggest hit, to words by M. E. Rourke, was "A Lemon In The Garden Of Love."

Although he was American by birth, there was also English blood in The Rich Mr. Hoggenheimer (22 October 1906, Wallack's), which Harry B. Smith and Ludwig Englander wrote at the request of Charles Frohman. Sam Bernard had made a success of the Hoggenheimer character in Frohman's 1903 importation, The Girl from Kay's. Now a whole vehicle was created around the part. "Piggy" Hoggenheimer's plans for his son Guy's marriage to Lady Mildred are spoiled when the boy (Edwin Nicander) goes to America to study modern business methods and falls in love with a poor girl, Amy Leigh (Marion Garson). Pretending to be on assignment from the War Office, Hoggenheimer rushes to the States. Because her husband's actress friend, Flora Fair (Georgia Caine), is on the same ship, Mrs. Hoggenheimer books passage as well. In various disguises Hoggenheimer tracks down and spies on his son's fiancée and in the end approves of the marriage. He also helps Flora win the man she has her eye on, Percy Vere (Percy Ames). Bernard's best scenes came when, disguised as a cabbie, he finds he has picked up his own wife as a fare and when he revises the wording on a telegram to give it precisely the opposite meaning. Next to the Hippodrome spectacle and The Red Mill, The Rich Mr. Hoggenheimer was the biggest hit of the season. Three things accounted for the smashing success. Most of all there was Bernard's performance—considered by many the high point of his career.

Second, there was the fetching Georgia Caine as Flora. And last, there were several popular and universally praised songs—none by Englander. One was "Any Old Time At All" (Jerome/Schwartz), sung by Guy and Flora. Equally well liked were Jerome Kern's insertions. Kern had rapidly established a practice of interpolating, in Frohman importations, tunes that were as bright and fresh as anything being offered by all but the very best. Songs like Flora's "Don't You Want A Paper, Dearie?" and "Poker Love" (sung by two minor players, one, Flossie Hope, dressed as a man), so applauded and hummed when new, are forgotten today, largely because Kern himself later turned out superior material.

The same night *The Rich Mr. Hoggenheimer* opened, Chauncey Olcott debuted in **Eileen Asthore** (22 October 1906, New York). In this instance Olcott played a young man who squanders his patrimony, outwits a villain who would thwart his attempts to earn a second fortune, and ultimately wins the hand of Eileen O'Donnell. To many the story seemed merely a rehash of *Old Limerick Town* (27 October 1902). It was typical of the romantic pieces with which he enthralled his followers for many years. They were not really full-blown musicals, usually containing only four or five songs. But some of these songs became standards. None from *Eileen Asthore*.

Painting the Town (22 October 1906, Metropolis) offered further adventures of the Hogan's Alley denizens. Hogan and his buddy go off for a night on the town, without their wives. Their wives get wind of the plan and follow them. The night out included a visit to a vaudeville show (with a short ballet, apparently played straight) and to a nightclub, so there was more song and dance than plot.

Around the Clock (29 October 1906, American) also took its characters to a music hall, but in a clumsier way. Its first two acts dealt with a nephew who marries the girl he is supposed to be courting on behalf of his uncle, but since all the expected contretemps were ironed out by the second-act finale, the cast spent Act III at the vaudeville. Songs included "Playland," suspiciously reminiscent of "Toyland"; a comic topical number, "The Mighty Dollar"; and "Football At Vassar," with chorus girls dressed for the scrimmage.

Another London hit was Talbot and Rubens's **The Blue Moon** (3 November 1906, Casino). Its story told of a prince who loves a girl who loves another man. The great rubber-faced clown James T. Powers, continuing to throw his lot with imported

London works, was starred, assisted by a fine cast that included Clara Palmer, Ethel Jackson, Grace La Rue, Templar Saxe, and Phil Ryley. With the expected American additions, the musical repeated, albeit on a smaller scale, its West End success.

Still further English influences were seen in Robert B. Smith and Raymond Hubbell's **Mamselle Sallie**, which John C. Fisher produced on 26 November at the slightly out-of-the-way Grand Opera House down on 23rd Street. Several critics felt the plot was a rehash of *The Medal and the Maid* (11 January 1904), which Fisher had co-produced. In Smith's retelling, Muriel Oliver, a young student at Mme. Woodbury's seminary, and Emile Martell, a French military cadet, have both been bequeathed large fortunes in Thessaly and have been given identical lockets as recognition tokens. The lockets are lost and stolen. But Mamselle Sallie, a laundress, disguises herself as a brigand to retrieve them and to tie the marriage knot for the young heir and heiress. Robert was no better a librettist than his brother, Harry. He was capable of passing off as a joke lines such as "I can't eat peas, they roll off my knife." As was so often the case with musical comedies of this era, the lovers were not the stars. Top billing in *Mamselle Sallie* went to little John Slavin as a waiter impersonating a lawyer and brash Katie Barry as a comic hairdresser. Chorus girls, whirling across the stage in orange and black gowns, were supplemented at one point by "English Butterfly Dancers." Even a move to the more centrally located New York Theatre could not gain the show more than a three-week run. But Smith and Hubbell were strong-willed hacks, and *Mamselle Sallie* would be heard from again.

In **A Parisian Model** (27 November 1906, Broadway), which left first-nighters gaping, Florenz Ziegfeld surrounded Anna Held with a large chorus of breathtakingly beautiful girls, bedecked in gorgeous costumes and set in sumptuous mountings. He reserved for Anna some of the most elaborate gowns yet seen on the stage. The effects he and Julian Mitchell contrived were the talk of the town. In a scene set in an artist's studio the chorus girls entered in long, elegant cloaks. Stepping behind easels they dropped their cloaks, revealing their bare shoulders and legs. Sixteen of the chorus girls, led by the flamboyant Gertrude Hoffman, lay on a revolving stage, kicking their legs and ringing bells tied to their ankles. Later Miss Hoffman, dressed as a boy, danced with Miss Held. But the *pièce de résistance* was naturally given to Anna, who in one number wore a different gown for each chorus of the song she was singing—and she sang six cho-ruses. Anna played a painter's model who comes into a fortune through an old lady's will. But her artist lover, Julien (Henri Leoni), suspects her new-found wealth has other origins. Furiously jealous, he publicly courts another young lady, Violette (Truly Shattuck). But Anna wins him back by shocking him into the realization that he loves her best of all. A comic character named Silas Goldfinch (Charles A. Bigelow) appeared throughout the evening in various disguises—Paderewski, a Mexican, an old woman—trying to give money away. Although Max Hoffman wrote the score, Miss Held would use her two interpolations, "It's Delightful To Be Married," for which she is reputed to have written the lyrics to V. Scotto's music, and "I Just Can't Make My Eyes Behave" (Cobb/Edwards), for the rest of her short, tragic life.

A triple bill opened at the Hippodrome on 28 November. It consisted of a one-act circus, a three-scene melodrama called **Pioneer Days**, and a three-scene "Operatic extravaganza," **Neptune's Daughter**. The melodrama, "Belasco's Golden West, four times magnified," filled the stage with cowboys, lawmen, Indians, and, when an alarm was raised, a troop of cavalry charging on their horses. The "Operatic extravaganza" was set in a Breton coastal village where a one-legged man hobbles on and sees in a red sky the portent of a storm. The storm follows quickly, creating a shipwreck from which a child is dramatically rescued. Mermaids and Neptune arise from a golden barge to still the waters. In *Neptune's Daughter* the famous Hippodrome water tank (situ-ated between the main stage and the orchestra pit) was employed for the first time to receive a flock of bathing beauties instead of men and horses. Trick mechanical devices allowed chorus girls to dive into the tank and disappear. Manuel Klein wrote the songs for both the melodrama and *Neptune's Daughter*, producing for the latter one of the hits of the day, "Red Sky." The bill, with changes, ran 288 performances.

The procession of London hits resumed with Leslie Stuart's **The Belle of Mayfair** (3 December 1906, Daly's). Produced with a fine American cast led by Irene Bentley, Christie MacDonald, Bessie Clayton, and Valeska Suratt and with an unaccus-tomed faithfulness to the original story of a Romeo and Juliet romance that ends happily, it ran into spring.

Lew Dockstader's Minstrels displayed their wares beginning 17 December. The interlocutors and end men and all the old standbys lingered a paltry twen-ty-six performances, then headed back to the road.

Herbert's *Dream City* came in a week later.

The next night Frederic Ranken, Stanislaus Stange, and Reginald De Koven offered Broadway **The Student King** (25 December 1906, Garden). Its far-fetched romantic story had Francis (Henry Coote), a Prague University student, elected "Icing for a day." Princess Ilsa (Lina Abarbanell) falls in love with him, although she is already betrothed. Happily, Francis turns out to be the king's long-lost son. The king (Alexander Clark) abdicates in his favor, and Francis makes Ilsa his queen. De Koven provided a wearisome score that more than one critic branded "reminiscent." In just over a month the show was gone. But in that short time it gave theatregoers an opportunity to watch Miss Abarbanell, a young lady they would see much of, as well as two fine comedi-ans, Clark and Detmar Poppen. Miss Abarbanell had called attention to herself first in German-language productions of operettas at the Irving Place Theatre, then as Hansel at the Metropolitan Opera.

Although its producers described **Matilda** (31 December 1906, Lincoln Square) as "a screaming farce in three explosions," it was actually another old-fashioned, loosely plotted farce-comedy, larded with songs and other specialties. That loose plot recounted the complications which ensue after a man disguises himself as a woman, and a woman dresses up as a man. The second act was set on the deck of a yacht at anchor in New York Harbor, with the skyline painted on the backdrop. The spacious deck allowed room for larger song-and-dance numbers.

The Princess Beggar (7 January 1907, Casino) followed hard on *The Student King*'s heels, arriving as 1907's first musical show. It had a similarly absurd plot, with the sexes reversed. Prince Karl (Bertram Walks) would marry Elaine (Paula Edwards), a girl of the woods who saved his life. Empty royal cof-fers argue against this love match. Furthermore, the villainous Baron Lombardo (Stanley L. Forde) is conniving to put another family on the throne. But Elaine is discovered to be a real and rich princess, permitting a very happy ending. Paulton and Robyn had even less finesse and panache than the authors of *The Student King*. Yet *The Princess Beggar* ran exactly as long—forty performances.

Things got worse. In fact the *Times* headlined its review for **The Mimic and the Maid** (11 January 1907, Bijou), "Rock Bottom Reached." Its story of a courtship during the rehearsal of a play in a small town was simply another excuse for a number of specialty acts. In *A Parisian Model* Anna Held had sung a tune to two man-sized Teddy bears. *The Mimic and the Maid* filled the stage with small, mechanized ones. But nothing helped. Two performances, and the show was withdrawn. Even A. Baldwin Sloane, who composed whatever numbers the specialty acts did not bring with them, must have been especially embarrassed by the debacle. Prolific till now, he was not heard from again for three years.

The Girl from Broadway (14 January 1907, 14th St.) seems to have been something of a rarity, a touring musical admired most of all for its music. But then its composer was the rising young Karl Hoschna, still so relatively unknown that reviewers could not spell his name correctly. Herbert Hall Winslow, a respected Broadway craftsman, supplied the book, and the obscure Charles Noel Douglass, the lyrics. The book was not one of Winslow's better efforts, telling the tired saga of an heiress, stolen by gypsies and raised as a circus performer, restored finally to her rightful inheritance. Among the most encored songs were "It's Up To You To Do The Rest" and "Love's Language."

The Belle of London Town (28 January 1907, Lincoln Square) was also a quick flop—sixteen performances. But it received some good notices. The plot, praised as "able to stand alone," was a little different. Sir John Manners marries Belinda for her beauty, and she marries him for his money. But he loses his money at the same time Belinda comes into a large inheritance. She leaves him and becomes the belle of the town. But after a misunderstanding about some unsigned love letters actually meant for Belinda's cousin, they are reconciled. Like *Marrying Mary* at the beginning of the season, the show had no chorus. But the well-thought-out story and the novel intimacy proved no incentive to ticket-buyers. The weaknesses of Julian Edwards's score were only underlined by Stanislaus Stange's awkward titles and lyrics such as "Drink With Me The Night Away" and "I Should Have Been Offended If My Waist You Hadn't Squeezed." If the show was one of the last for the fading Camille D'Arville, it marked a step up the ladder for Orville Harrold.

Messager's **The Little Michus** (31 January 1907, Garden) failed to find favor and ran only twenty-nine performances.

A second Julian Edwards score was heard a week after his music for *The Belle of London Town*, when **The Girl and the Governor** opened 4 February at the Manhattan. It, too, received some good notices, though on this occasion the praise was for Edwards's songs and for the star, Jefferson De Angelis. The plot was simple. A foppish sixteenth-century Spanish governor in South America captures an English girl (Estelle Wentworth) and decides to marry her. She seems to acquiesce, asking only that the governor hire an English sailor to help with her chores. Of course, the sailor is her lover, and they elope. The evening failed to catch the public's fancy, and it stayed for only twenty-six performances.

Twenty-six performances were also all **The Rose of Alhambra** (4 February 1907, Majestic), which opened the same night, could muster. Based on a Washington Irving story of a girl (Agnes Caine Brown) who dwells in a town with an old aunt, it started life in Chicago, where it was not too cordially greeted. The critic for the Chicago *Record* left the theatre at 11:00 P.M., noting that a whole act remained to be played. The *Chronicle*'s man also had his watch out, recording "only two hearty laughs between 8:15 and 9:30." One of these would seem to have been a monk's reply to the accusation he was "seeking young maids to roast them alive." In reply he insisted, "No. I'm not a roaster. I'm a friar." Things had not improved much by the time the show reached New York. The music comprised the only score by Lucius Hosmer ever to be sung on Broadway.

Gustave Kerker had a second score ready for Broadway when **The White Hen** (also known as *The Girl from Vienna*) was unveiled at the Casino on 16 February. The plot recounted Hensee Blinker's difficulties after his lawyer (Ralph Herz) persuades Hensee (Louis Mann) to visit a marriage broker (Carrie E. Perkins). The lawyer's secretary (Lotta Faust) and the contracted wife (Louise Gunning) change places without Hensee's knowing it. Before long Blinker has two wives. The show delighted audiences for three months largely because of the droll clowning of Mann, Herz, and Miss Faust, as well as the lovely singing of Miss Gunning.

The Tattooed Man displayed his attractions beginning 18 February.

The season's third tramp star was Hap Ward, who had capered last year in *The Grafter*. No one took credit for the book of his new vehicle, **Not Yet, But Soon** (4 March 1907, American), but lyricist Harry Williams and composer Egbert Van Alstyne provided the songs. In truth, the book wasn't worth claiming credit for, since it did little but describe the antics of some inmates at Bughouse-on-the-Hudson. Bill Nerve, committed because he has a thing about working, spends most of his time changing places with other loonies. Characters' names included Keeper Sane, Whis Key, Will Smoke, Miss Gooden Smart, and the apparently inevitable Canne Catchem. "Someday When Dreams Come True" and "My Irish Girl" earned some of the loudest applause.

Three weeks passed before another musical appeared, and then from Chicago came one more American-in-foreign-parts story. George Washington Barker, a circus fakir stranded in Honolulu, makes a balloon ascent and lands on the Island of Inde. A Buddhist ceremony is in progress, and Barker is mistaken for **The Grand Mogul** (25 March 1907). The real Grand Mogul arrives, but Barker is rescued by a Yankee gunboat. More than the story was familiar. Frank Pixley's book and lyrics and Gustav Luders's tunes were pleasant but derivative. Furthermore, Baker was played by an old hand at this sort of thing, Frank Moulan. Moulan's balloon entrance had him crashing through a temple roof. He was forever pushing "Mrs. Mogul" out of his way in order to mingle with a chorus of beautiful girls. He and Maud Lillian Berri "encored many times" their "Nestle By My Side." After a five-week stay the show resumed its national trek.

Eleven months after the fiasco of his *District Leader* Joe Howard returned to New York with a show in which he and his wife, Mabel Barrison, starred. But **The Land of Nod** (1 April 1907, New York) was not a solo effort. It was a children's extravaganza written with the two men with whom he created most of his major lyric pieces, Frank R. Adams and Will M. Hough. It had been a Chicago success. Taking no chances, the producer had George V. Hobart "rearrange" the work for New York audiences, and for good measure, he added an operatic skit Hobart and Victor Herbert had written for a Lambs Club Gambol, "The Song Birds." But New York wasn't interested in Bonnie's visit to dreamland and her infatuation for the Jack of Hearts (a trouser role by Helen Bertram). Bonnie (Miss Barrison) is caught up in the wicked Sandman's scheme to steal everyone's heart and destroy the card castle. But Jack vanquishes the Sandman (William Burress), turning him into a bundle of rags. The humor was of the arch variety so beloved by writers of children's pieces. When a star falls at the Moon's feet, he (Howard) advises Bonnie, "Don't be frightened. That's only a little message from my wife, Rory Bory Alice. Alice is always throwing things." He opens the star and reads the message inside: "If you are not back

before morning I will go home to Mars! What do you think of a lady who uses that kind of grammar. No wonder I left." For the "swingers" of the era there was a wisecracking chorus girl (Carrie De Mar), whose offhand name-dropping must have been lost on tots in the audience. A similar girl had been used as a foil in *The Wizard of Oz*. Even with Hobart's and Herbert's names on the credits, *The Land of Nod* had little appeal.

The following Monday ushered in the London hit **The Orchid** (8 April 1907, Herald Square). In London this Ivan Caryll and Lionel Monckton musical had been awarded the honor of opening the new Gaiety Theatre. (The old Gaiety had been condemned to make way for urban redevelopment.) The story told of an explorer who stumbles on a seemingly priceless rare orchid, loses it, and finds another in a London florist shop. Eddie Foy starred in the New York version, and his supporting cast included such popular vaudevillians as Trixie Friganza and Irene Franklin. In a day of high public piety and propriety Foy nonetheless made a show-stopper of one interpolation, "He Goes To Church On Sunday" (Vincent Bryan/E. Ray Goetz):

> He goes to church on Sunday,
>> He passes round the contribution box;
> But meet him in the office on a Monday,
>> He's as crooked and as cunning as a fox,
> On Tuesday, Wednesday, Thursday, Friday, Saturday
>> He's robbing everybody that he can:
> But he goes to church on Sunday,
>> So they say that he's an honest man.

Although many of the day's musicals were written in incredible haste—often thrown off in a week or two—some of the most frivolous-seeming actually were the result of prolonged and intensive reworkings. **Fascinating Flora** (20 May 1907, Casino), which ran through the summer, fills four volumes of typescript versions. The cast of characters in this R. H. Burnside and Joseph Herbert libretto lists everyone's love interest. Gulliver Gayboy (Fred Bond)—"In love with his money"—bankrolls Flora Duval (Adele Ritchie)—"In love with America"—after she has left her husband because he is too much of a homebody. "You were the light of my life," she tells him, "but you never went out." Flora has no false modesty:

> I really think it must be fate
> That I was born to fascinate
> And so they call me Fascinating Flora.

She would become an opera star under Gayboy's aegis, but she admits she finds most operas boring and has no qualms about enlivening them by adding "anything with dash and go." Gayboy is also planning to marry his daughter to Jack Graham (Arthur Stanford)—"In love with Dolly"—unaware his child has secretly made a happy marriage of her own. Unluckily, Gayboy is flimflammed, and the shares with which he hoped to support his opera company turn out to be mere railroad timetables. Flora returns to her home-loving spouse. And Jack does marry Dolly (Ella Snyder). The score was Gustave Kerker's third of the season, a figure matched only by Ivan Caryll and Victor Herbert. But neither Kerker's music nor Hapgood Burt and Jerome Kern's interpolations were more than serviceable.

Another heiress deprived of her fortune until just before the final curtain was the subject of the season's last touring musical, **Miss Dolly Dimples** (27 May 1907, 14th St.). Her cutesy side battled with her treacly side as she offered such ditties as "Good-Bye, Old Home," "Because I'm So Shy," and the tide song. She appears to have won very few friends on the other side of the footlights.

At the very start of the season the *Times* discreetly acknowledged Cohan's incontestable vogue on 2 September 1906, when it described the returning *Little Johnny Jones* as "ever popular." To end the season Cohan brought back another of his pieces, *Running for Office*, on 3 June, revising it to suit the requirements of the New Amsterdam Roof and retitling it *The Honeymooners*. His fast pacing had often ruffled his critics, and when he made little allowance for the summer heat the *Morning Telegraph* commented snidely, "If Cohan would play fair and give his audience a chance to catch its breath it might make a few unkind remarks." But most unkind words came from the aisle-sitters. Appreciative audiences packed the house all summer.

If Chicago theatres largely have been missing from this account of the 1906–1907 season, that is not to be construed as any indication of the lack of activity. The truth is quite the opposite. The city's leading combination house, the Great Northern, was frequently lit for a week or two with traveling musicals New York never saw. Far more important were the two musicals Hough-Adams-Howard wrote for Mort Singer at the La Salle. *The Girl Question* ran longer than had *The Umpire*, while *The Time, the Place and the Girl*, by chalking up a run of over 400 performances, established a record in Chicago that went unbroken for many years. Both of these musicals braved New York in forthcoming seasons.

Intermission

Viennese Operetta and the American Retreat, 1907–1914

The seven-season period that began with the 1907–1908 theatrical year was at once rich and distressing. It would be absurd to write off an era that witnessed the creation of *Naughty Marietta, Sweethearts, The Firefly, Madame Sherry,* or *The Pink Lady* (to name five of the "domestic" masterpieces of the day), or that brought from overseas treasures such as *The Chocolate Soldier, Sari,* and, most of all, *The Merry Widow.* But the rage for these Viennese confections so overwhelmed the stages of the Western world that even the best local creations swiftly became imitative. For seven years all the best works offered by American composers were in this unmistakably arioso style that we would now brand "operetta." Those writers who could not or would not write in this gay, sweeping Central European idiom met with increasing disappointments. Native musical material was still presented regularly, but it often seemed intimidated by the cavalier elegance of the Viennese school.

Still, in a way, America was lucky. This seven-year retreat gave our young native talent time to regroup, rethink, and develop. When World War I broke out in Europe at the end of this period, our young composers and librettists were alive with fresh, original ideas. Every now and then during this intermission, hints of things to come were heard and seen. And one new form—the revue—advanced to just short of maturity.

Europe was not so fortunate. The war that gave American musical comedy writers their chance stifled the French and English musical stages, and inflicted a lingering, ultimately fatal wound on Viennese operetta.

There was a certain symmetry to this seven-year period. Its three most intriguing seasons were its first, its last, and the one that fell right in the middle, 1910–1911. Although *The Merry Widow* overwhelmed the opening session, a number of other productions bore importantly on the future of the American Musical Theatre. The last theatrical year would produce little of interest aside from three exceptional works. The season of 1910–1911 also offered three magnificently achieved works, but time and again its minor hits and failures contained fascinating hints of better things to come.

1907–1908

On 22 June, almost a year to the day after the lurid opening of *Mamzelle Champagne*, the Madison Square Garden Roof presented another summer musical, **The Maid and the Millionaire.** Its plot was a rehash of *The Billionaire* (29 December 1902). The setting was changed to a new outpost of the expanding American empire, Guam, but the story still recounted how a stagestruck tycoon helped a young actress on her way. Both the show and its first night were uneventful. The piece distracted its patrons from the summer heat and doldrums for seventy-two performances.

The **Follies of 1907** came in on 8 July. The *Follies* would soon include the name of their creator, Florenz Ziegfeld, in the title, and for a quarter of a century be a resplendent jewel of the musical theatre scene. But this first edition was relatively modest. Bankrolled by Klaw and Erlanger, Ziegfeld mounted the evening for $13,000—an unexceptional figure for its day. Although it became a national institution "glorifying the American girl," the *Follies* professed to be Continental in its tone and style. Its very title called to mind the Parisian *Folies Bergère*, and for playgoers who failed to make the connection the New York Theatre Roof was rechristened the Jardin de Paris. Ziegfeld's European wife, Anna Held, originally convinced him that something like the voguish Parisian revue might appeal to New Yorkers, although, curiously, the title may not have been derived from the French *Folies* but from a column written by the show's first librettist, Harry B. Smith. Smith's column had been called "Follies of the Day," and Smith suggested using a similar title for the show, "Follies of the Year." Since Ziegfeld had previously found good luck in titles of thirteen letters (excluding the article), he compromised with the thirteen characters of *Follies of 1907.* In his early programs, Ziegfeld acknowledged his superstition by numbering each letter and digit in the title, starting with a "1" under the *F* and climbing to a "13" under the "7." Smith, in honor of the Jamestown Exposition, named his compère and commère John Smith and Pocahontas. He described the highlights of the "libretto" in his autobiography: "Theodore Roosevelt, then at the height of his popularity, was prominent among the characters, wearing his Rough Rider uniform and displaying a spectacular array of teeth. Mr. Roosevelt was in the audience one evening

and laughed louder than anyone. In a scene at Grand Central Station, Chauncey Depew was in charge of the 'Misinformation Department.' The rival impresarios, Oscar Hammerstein and Heinrich Conried, fought an operatic duel supported by their respective companies; and in a court scene Caruso was found guilty of misdemeanor on account of his much-advertised adventure at the Central Park monkey house. Anthony Comstock, Commodore Perry, Andrew Carnegie, John D. Rockefeller, Edna May, and other celebrities were among the dramatis personae. There was just enough story to hold the scenes together, the theme being the introduction of Pocahontas and Captain John Smith to... modern life."

Fifty lovely chorines, the first in the long parade of breathtaking beauties made even more dazzling by their association with Ziegfeld, were billed as "Anna Held Girls" in an effort to convey to them some of the exotic, mischievous glamour of Ziegfeld's wife. The most famous name in the cast was Nora Bayes. Nothing of any lasting value emerged from the evening. "Budweiser's A Friend Of Mine" (Vincent Bryan/Seymour Furth) and "Handle Me With Care" (William Jerome/Jean Schwartz) were probably the most popular numbers in the show. Even more quickly forgotten were "I Think I Oughtn't Auto Anymore" (Bryan/E. Ray Goetz), "The Gibson Bathing Girls" (Paul West/Alfred Solomon), and "Bye Bye Dear Old Broadway" (Will Cobb/Gus Edwards). During the run of this first edition, performers and numbers were added or dropped in a way inconceivable today. Miss Bayes, for example, stayed with the show for only about half its run. In fact, Ziegfeld boasted in his advertisements of weekly changes. His feature for the week of 11 August was typical, offering Annabelle Whitford and her "Gibson Bathing Girls." The show was hardly better than many of the other producer-assemblages Broadway regularly accepted, especially in the hotter months. Trade papers reviewed it under "Vaudeville Acts." Ziegfeld's taste, imagination, lavish hand, and persistence would eventually turn the *Follies* into a legend. It played through the summer and toured briefly. Its profits were so large Ziegfeld determined to offer an even better edition the next year.

The first of August's six musicals came from Chicago. It was one of the best of the Will M. Hough, Frank R. Adams, and Joe Howard series—and one of the few to travel as far east as New York. It was no reflection on their quality that these musicals were never as enthusiastically welcomed on the Rialto as they were back home. They were solidly crafted.

Their librettos generally put reasonably real people in conceivable difficulties and let them talk their way out of their problems with dialogue that was easy on the ear. If some of the early, expository speeches were long and even naïve by later standards, they were so racily colloquial that the drawback was overlooked. The lyrics, too, were far superior to the run-of-the-mill of the day. Within limitations imposed by meter and rhyme, they were refreshingly natural, managing to avoid involutions, obsolescent imageries, and other contrivances of the period's hacks. Howard's music was totally American, and in its field the best being written. **The Time, the Place and the Girl** (5 August 1907, Wallack's) recounted how Tom Cunningham (George Anderson), a rich young man-about-town, and his gambling buddy, Happy Johnny Hicks (Arthur Deagon), take refuge in a sanatorium after fleeing from a nasty drunken brawl:

Johnny: You were bound to go into Glad Hand
    Murphy's gambling joint and mix in on a poker
    game. The ante was two-bits and the roof was
    the limit. I came in. They cleaned me in about
    forty-five minutes, but I wasn't exactly dirty
    when I blew in. Thursday always was my Jonah
    Day. By this time you was buyin' nothin' but
    grape and you was keepin' one eye shut so's
    not to count your money double. There was
    cheatin' goin' on in the game and when I gets
    wise and tips you off, you reaches over and
    pinches all the coin in sight, not knowin' just
    what you was doin'. The young guy opposite gets
    riled and says you're a shine sport, and sayin'
    he can lick you or any other man in Boston,
    he wades in to do it. Just as somebody douses
    the light I see you hit him over the head with a
    bottle and he drops like a shot. Then an awful
    bag of cats is stirred up and we mixes it up
    general all over the place, everybody taking a
    hand. You can guess the answer. Us sittin' in the
    middle of the street listenin' to an owl car comin'
    up the pike about half a mile away. I dunno how
    we got there but maybe we fell out of a window.
    I didn't know how bad that guy was hurt that
    you dropped with the bottle, but I thought
    we'd better leave Boston for a while, and as you
    said you wanted to come here, it was us on the
    caboose for Virginia. The mountains can't come
    too high for me.
Tom: You're a brick, Johnny,—for seeing me
    through this scrape.
Johnny: Take that noise away.

At the same sanatorium Tom discovers his childhood sweetheart, Margaret Simpson (Violet McMillan), and John whiles away the hours with the head nurse, Molly Kelly (Elene Foster). The budding romances suffer an unpleasant setback when Johnny and Tom learn the man they fought was Molly's brother. What saves the day for John and Molly, and also gives Tom the chance he needs to court Margaret, is a police-imposed quarantine when an infectious outbreak is suspected. By the time the quarantine is lifted, the lovers are set to be wed. "Thursday Is My Jonah Day" typified the colloquial flow and native humor of the Hough and Adams lyrics:

> Thursday always was my Jonah day;
>   Never struck any luck, any time,
> If it's Thursday when I pass away,
>   Then I know they'll "hand me mine."

The lines to Howard's excellent melody for "Blow The Smoke Away" are equally natural and expressive. They demonstrate the abrupt endings Hough and Adams often employed to good effect—a somewhat less difficult trick in the days before the AABA form overwhelmed popular song:

> Of course you're only dreaming,
>   Blow the smoke away,
> You know you can't win her,
>   Things don't ever go that way.
> Still you keep on dreaming,
>   Might as well, no doubt—
> Then your pipe goes out.

The best song, a melody still occasionally heard, was Howard's wistful "Waning Honeymoon."

Both "Blow The Smoke Away" and "Waning Honeymoon" were sung by minor characters and the chorus. The first was performed by Laurie Farnham (James Norval); the second by Mrs. Talbot (Harriet Burt). Even if New York's critics condemned the evening's "heavy-handed" sentimentality, they found kind things to say about various aspects of the production. Miss Burt won praise for her German-style dances, danced in a dress of bright "Spanish" red to the strains of "Dixie." The chorus imitated the sounds of horse races, wind in the trees, a motor car, and even an audience applauding (without the chorus boys and girls actually clapping their own hands). To the *Times* critic, the hotel setting seemed contrived to resemble the Orangerie at the

Hotel Astor, "with a sort of miniature natural bridge of rocks, where the musicians' balcony should be." *The Time, the Place and the Girl* stayed a month at Wallack's, a far cry from its record-breaking 400-performance run in Chicago.

The Shoo Fly Regiment (6 August 1907, Bijou) was an all-black show by Cole and Johnson, designed to entertain "an audience composed mostly of whites." It found many critics willing to praise its music, but few who could say anything good about its book. The story followed a regiment recruited from the Lincolnville Institute into the Spanish-American War. The boys' lady friends ("vermilion-cheeked colored girls in scarlet gowns") accompany them. Much to their own surprise, the young soldiers win a battle and return as heroes. One outstanding number was "Lit'l Gal," a song written for *The Cannibal King*, an earlier Cole and Johnson effort that never reached the big time. Oddly, the published lyrics are credited to Paul Laurence Dunbar, although he is not given credit elsewhere. The song, written in a relatively free-flowing AAB pattern, makes remarkable use of alternating major and minor chords. The regiment marched off after two weeks.

Two shows opened on 12 August. **The Alaskan**, at the Knickerbocker, was a twenty-nine-performance failure in New York; **The Yankee Tourist**, at the Astor, was the season's first long-run hit. Yet in history's so commonly perverse way, the flop was the more interesting of the two. The *Dramatic Mirror* rejoiced, "There is more originality, freshness and downright charm in 'The Alaskan' than in ten ordinary musicals put together. At last a new locale has been found [and] best of all the new field is our own—Alaska." Up in the Yukon, Richard Atwater has been staked in his mining operations by a New Yorker, Mr. Eaton. A letter from Eaton's daughter, Arlee (Agnes Cain Brown), announces her father's death and her intention to become Atwater's partner. She arrives, but mistakes Atwater for the mine foreman. When the mine fails she leaves, without learning who the foreman really is. But Atwater has fallen in love, and when another mine of his is successful he reveals his identity and wins Arlee for his wife. The "new locale" did indeed allow for some novel bits. The show opened with a sled pulled by twelve real huskies crossing the snow and starting a climb up a mountain. At one point the "pony" chorus appeared dressed as Eskimos. But the moment that "roused even the wilting Summer night crowd to enthusiasm" found the entire chorus dressed as totem poles while Totem Pole Pete (Edward Martindell)

led them in, appropriately, "The Totem Pole" ("My father's father was an eagle"). When, seventeen years later, critic after critic raved about a similar production number in *Rose-Marie* (2 September 1924), none of the reviewers apparently retained any recollection of *The Alaskan*'s version. Atwater was played by the show's composer, Harry Giraud. Although he and his librettists, Max Figman and Joseph Blethen (Blethen was also the lyricist), displayed a certain precocious integrity in handling their story and in refusing to allow interpolated material, their inexperience and lack of inspiration told against them. Not too many others agreed with the *Dramatic Mirror*'s man, and the authors never again tried their hand at Broadway musicals. However, like so many New York failures of the day, *The Alaskan* moved on to a successful road tour.

The *Dramatic Mirror* critic was far less taken with *The Yankee Tourist*, a piece which exposed all the weaknesses of typical turn-of-the-century musical comedy. "It is rather a shock," he observed, "to have the action of the play suddenly halted for the insertion of a more or less relevant song... but since the action does not depend on probabilities, the shock is not lasting." Nor did the reviewer think much of the music (mostly by Alfred G. Robyn) which interrupted the action. His kindest words were for the lyrics and the star, Raymond Hitchcock. Hitchcock played Copeland Schuyler, who assumes the name and role of Kirke Warren, a famous correspondent in the Greco-Turkish War of 1897. Schuyler feels the imposture is his best way to keep near his fiancée, Grace Whitney (Flora Zabelle), a nurse. Warren's pursuers—creditors, admirers—now pursue Schuyler, and Schuyler's troubles are compounded when he is captured by the Turks. The play was based on a hit of the preceding season, *The Galloper*, by a real and famous war correspondent, Richard Harding Davis. Again, the trade paper was in the minority. Still, for those who might share the paper's reservations about the integrity of the book and the quality of the music, the production offered compensations. Almost at the beginning came a spectacular effect, with a "realistic" ship sailing away from a "realistic" dock. An attractive chorus line, called "Teddy Girls" in the program, danced as ship stewardesses, Turks in baggy trousers and tasseled fezes, and soldiers performing a snappy gun drill. The limelights changed colors as Miss Zabelle (she was also Mrs. Hitchcock) and the chorus girls fluttered scarves and danced while singing "Rainbow." The public flocked to the Astor for 103 performances;

then the show went on a long tour. Just before the cross-country trek began, Wallace Beery replaced Hitchcock.

The season for touring musicals started early and for a time promised to be exceptionally busy. But careful followers of major trade journals, which almost weekly announced the conversion to films of some small-town playhouse or some big-city cheap-priced theatre, might have suspected how deceptive all the late summer and fall activity was. It was, in a way, like the feverish spurt of energy supposedly enjoyed by many terminally ill people. By the very next season the number of new touring musicals would drop staggeringly, and by the 1909–1910 season such shows would be all but a thing of the past.

According to the *Dramatic Mirror*, **The Hired Girl's Millions** (12 August 1907, Lincoln Square) was billed as a "musical melodrama," and since the book was by Charles E. Blaney there was little reason to question its touches of melodrama. The trade sheet felt it ran "a gamut from melodrama to musical comedy, pointed with vaudeville." However, since this story of a wicked landlady besieging a rich widow and an heiress starred two female impersonators, the comic Russell brothers—who donned numerous disguises in coming to the damsels' rescue—the musical and vaudeville aspects were in good hands.

Further north playgoers could attend the New York premiere of **Captain Rufus** (12 August 1907, Harlem Music Hall), which had originally been mounted in Chicago by that city's famous black troupe, the Pekin Stock Company. Their musical was set in the Philippines, where the colonel of a black regiment leaves his daughter, trusting she will be looked after by Captain Rufus, who is slated to arrive any day now, and also hoping the villainous Major Drummond will not molest her. Rufus Jones, a shipwrecked vagabond, saunters into camp and is mistaken for the captain. Humorous complications follow before the real Captain Rufus appears, routs the malefactor, puts down an insurrection, and hands over the girl to her fiancé. Much of the action was highly melodramatic, and the songs were considered poor. One exception was Jones's song, "The Great I Am With A Capital I." The role of the fiancé was taken by Charles Gilpin, in later years to be considered the finest black actor of his generation. He would be the original Emperor Jones.

One week later **The Lady from Lane's** (19 August 1907, Lyric) arrived. The *Dramatic Mirror*, once again at odds with the public response, saw

it as "the fourth attempt already this season to put musical plays on a more rational basis, where consistency of plot is made, relatively, of as much importance as songs and chorus girls." The other attempts were listed as *The Alaskan*, *The Time, the Place and the Girl*, and, with a curious inconsistency, the show the paper had panned a week earlier, *The Yankee Tourist*. The book the *Dramatic Mirror* admired watched millionaire Singleton Seabrook (Thomas Wise) pursue a forger. A woman detective, Adelaide Forster (Truly Shattuck), is also stalking the criminal. She believes Singleton to be the forger. She woos him, hoping he will drop his guard and make a slip. Then she arrests him. He clears himself, and the two realize they are in love. George Broadhurst's dialogue and Gustave Kerker's music were second-rate. *The Lady from Lane's* left after six weeks.

The Pekin Stock Company's second offering was **The Husband (?)** (19 August 1907, Harlem Music Hall), which spotlighted the misadventures of Punk Willis, an inadvertent bigamist. The show had a book and lyrics by Aubrey Lyles and Flournoy Miller, and music by Joe Jordan and James T. Brymn. Like Gilpin, Lyles, Miller, and Jordan would move on to bigger things.

Charles Frohman advertised **The Dairymaids** (26 August 1907, Criterion) as his "annual musical production," implying that musicals were uniquely festive events outside the ongoing theatrical mainstream. He might just as easily have considered the show his annual musical importation, for despite the native talent emerging around him, Frohman, with his impressive connections on both sides of the ocean, played it safe by bringing New York major London musical entertainments. More often than not he came to depend on one young American, Jerome Kern, for additional numbers to give his importations an added fillip and something of a domestic flavor. *The Dairymaids* was no exception. Kern added six songs. All were better than anything in the original, but none was outstandingly melodic. The best, "I'd Like To Meet Your Father," enjoyed a brief vogue. The story was reasonably simple. When two girls decide to pass some time at their rich aunt's model dairy farm, two young English lords disguise themselves as young ladies so they may be close to the girls. The show featured Julia Sanderson and marked the American debut of the nimble English patter artist Huntley Wright.

The Rogers Brothers in Panama (2 September 1907, Broadway), more so than any of the earlier Rogers Brothers affairs, approached what the age understood as musical comedy. In their 1907 escapade the U.S. Canal Commissioners are captured by revolutionaries. Two young men take their place and make admirals of their valets (Gus and Max). The fraudulent sailors and servants are exposed and jailed, but they drug the villainous jailor and escape to an island. The erstwhile valets ultimately return to mainland Panama and stage a bullfight. Humor remained as broad as always—and often had little to do with the story. Since Max played a character called Hugo Kisser, while Gus was known as A. Gustave Windt, several routines tinkered with puns on their names. Nor did Max Hoffman's music, despite titles such as "In Panama," "Under The Jungle Moon," and "Way Down In Colon Town," offer any local color. Although electric lights had been used on Broadway for some time, the *Times* could still note with a certain fresh joy that "in a painted bay there are painted ships... and they have real lights on them at night." Like so many other musicals of the year, the show offered Spanish dances by ladies in bright red dresses. *The Rogers Brothers in Panama* ran seventy-one performances and embarked on a national tour. The happiness of many theatergoers at the return of the brothers was shattered when Gus died suddenly. Astute show-people had always considered Gus the lesser of the pair and assumed Max would succeed on his own, but he seemed colorless without his brother. Max did not retire immediately, but the Rogers Brothers soon passed into theatrical history.

From its opening number, "Back To Old Broadway," to its lively finale, **Patsy in Politics** (2 September 1907, 14th St.) delighted playgoers with its "ginger" and its rapid-fire barrage of Joe Miller jokes. The musical's star, Billy B. Van, played the prank-loving Patsy Bolivar, who is also known as The Tabasco Kid. Patsy works at a hotel run by the politically ambitious Silas Hemlock, only to find himself running for supervisor in opposition to his boss. To Silas's surprise (but nobody else's), Patsy wins. Patsy's show-stopper was a comic ditty, "Much Obliged To You."

Politics reared its comic head again in **From Across the Pond** (7 September 1907, Circle), which purportedly was based on an unidentified Viennese and Berlin success. A story which traveled from Ellis Island to Chatham Square and finally to the Bowery related a German immigrant's campaign to become an alderman. The show was curtly dismissed, but in the following month *The Merry Widow* would stunningly revive the fortunes of Viennese musicals.

Unfortunately for comedienne Lulu Glaser, **Lola from Berlin** (16 September 1907, Liberty) was not a particularly good vehicle. J. J. McNally, who for years had contrived the Rogers Brothers' books, slapped together a stock of clichés and passed it off as a libretto. Lola, an immigrant and an heiress, is mistaken for an applicant for a maid's job. She is finally recognized and accepted into the home of John Westervelt (Dodson Mitchell), her late uncle's lawyer. When a note from Mrs. Westervelt (Florence Lester) to her lover is intercepted, Lola gamely claims she wrote the letter. This alienates her admirer, Arthur Paget (Jack Standing), but in the end everything is resolved. Jean Schwartz's wooden score was no better than McNally's book. Miss Glaser played her role in dialect, as did eight flaxen-haired chorus girls, dressed in "Gretchen" costumes. (The eight chorus boys were American college students.) Ralph Herz won some of the best laughs and applause for his delineation of a comic blackmailer. But the evening's virtues were few and far between. Thirty-five performances and Lola left town.

The Boy with the Boodle (16 September 1907, Metropolis), whose book was by the popular melodramatist Howard Hall, opens under the arches of the Williamsburg Bridge. There Skiddoo, a shoeshine boy who dabbles in the stock market, lives, works, and protects his little girlfriend, Tammany, after she has fled the notorious kidnapper, Plug Ugly. More villainy mars their lives before Tammany is revealed as an heiress and Skiddoo heads west to strike it rich in a Nevada mine.

Another collection of clichés comprised the story of **The Hurdy Gurdy Girl** (23 September 1907, Wallack's). The daughter of a rich sausage-maker is stolen by an Italian organ grinder. But the Italian's drunken wife takes the child to a foundling home and brings back another child. The sausage-maker is about to claim this second tot when the truth comes out. A small scar identifies the real girl. By coincidence, the girl's name was Lola (Bertha Mills). But more than one critic felt the most noteworthy playing of the evening came from another young lady, Adele Rowland, who, the *Times* announced, smiled, sang, danced, and talked "engagingly." In a cameo appearance, a much older lady, Annie Yeamans, the beloved Cordelia of the Harrigan and Hart shows, brought down the house in a role not much different from that of the sharp-tongued wife that had made her famous. Once again the music was as dreary as the book. One "realistic" setting, depicting dawn in Times Square, attracted some favorable comment, even if milkmen crossing the square in Buster Brown costumes elicited titters. The show's three-week run was even shorter than *Lola from Berlin*'s.

George Sidney had been touring for some time in lightly thrown-together musicals about an ambitious but naïve young Jew, Busy Izzy. His latest opened at the Yorkville on the 30th as **The Mazuma Man** but afterwards played the road as *Busy Izzy, the Mazuma Man*. Izzy Mark doesn't care about money. Nonetheless, Izzy manages to save a bank from failure, only to squander his reward.

The Girl Behind the Counter (1 October 1907, Herald Square) was a smash hit. The work was an importation thoroughly revamped by Edgar Smith for Lew Fields. Fields played Henry Schniff, who dons a series of disguises to help his stepdaughter, Winnie (May Naudain), marry American Charley Chetwyn (Joseph Ratliff) rather than her mother's choice, a titled Englishman. The basic show was solid, if unoriginal. Each night Fields garnered the biggest applause of the evening with a much-talked-about soda fountain scene in which he matched the color of his customers' sodas to the dress or tie the patron was wearing. When a difficult young man insisted his striped tie be duplicated, it was. But most likely, one song could also claim some credit for the show's eight-month run and profitable tour. The song was Paul Lincke's "The Glow Worm," inserted into the show after its opening. The song had already become popular, and Fields, pleading an old superstition against disturbing success, refused to insert the song—unless publisher Edward Marks paid him a thousand dollars to include it. Marks refused, but he offered to pay Fields if the song failed to stop the show and stimulate ticket sales. Fields agreed. As Marks wrote, "'Glow Worm' went in; Miss Naudain sang dozens of encores every evening; and I didn't have to pay."

Since revues were still not plotless at this early stage in their history, **The Gay White Way** (7 October 1907, Casino) sent an amateur detective (Jefferson De Angelis) to the Hotel Rooseveltia (Act I), an Actors' Fund Fair at the Metropolitan Opera House (Act II), and a 42nd Street restaurant (Act III) in search of the identity of a headless photograph. Before he ascertains its identity he views a collection of loosely introduced vaudeville turns. Blanche Ring had many of the evening's best moments. In a turnabout from her usual brassy delivery, she softly sang a Negro lullaby while dressed as a gamin and seated down by the footlights. She also portrayed the heroine in a travesty of *The Great Divide*.

She and De Angelis combined for a hilarious spoof of the great sawmill scene from *Blue Jeans*. While the tethered De Angelis was dragged ever closer to a spinning papier-mâché saw, Miss Ring babbled incessantly to the audience about her concern for his whereabouts. For those artists who didn't bring their own songs, Ludwig Englander provided some mediocre new tunes. Faulty as it may have been as a good revue, the good vaudeville in *The Gay White Way* was enough of a draw to keep the Casino lit for 105 performances.

With Fields performing at the Herald Square, Weber reopened the old Music Hall on 10 October without his old-time partner. The house had been substantially rebuilt as a result of the new fire laws that followed the Iroquois Theatre disaster. **Hip! Hip! Hooray!** attempted to revive Weber and Fields's old formula after a year's absence, even though, like the recent Rogers Brothers offering, it employed a bit more plot than formerly. Two German professors (Weber and Dick Bernard) attempt to introduce a new breakfast cereal, "Excited Oats," at Doolittle College and become involved in love affairs with a widow (Valeska Suratt) and a village belle (Bessie Clayton). Miss Clayton's sprightly, high-kicking dancing allowed her to display her still famous, still beautiful legs, while the stylish Miss Suratt paraded about modeling exceptionally large hats dwarfed only by her elaborate larger coiffures. (The size of her hats suggests that "Merry Widow Hats" were coming into fashion even before *The Merry Widow* opened.) The lone Weber was by no means the failure that Max Rogers had been, but without Fields an electric give-and-take was missing. The production had a forlornly short run.

Two Islands, which raised its curtain at the Circle on 14 October, proved to be a revised and recast version of *From Across the Pond*. It was perceived as improved but still not fully up to snuff.

Two shows came in on 19 October. **The Hoyden**, at the Knickerbocker, based on an unproduced English musical taken from Tristan Bernard's *La Soeur*, starred Elsie Janis. To suit Miss Janis and her American audiences, the show was altered until, as John Golden (one of its American lyricists) noted, "There was nothing left of the English composers' music or lyrics, and very little of the original book." That book described how the heroine falls in love with a man she believes has jilted her sister and whom she sets about humiliating. How unimpressed the rewriting left the public was evidenced by *The Hoyden*'s modest seven-week run.

The Top of the World, at the Majestic, was a musical extravaganza, written with an eye on the younger audience. The music was by Manuel Klein (of the Hippodrome) and by Anne Caldwell, who married the show's lyricist, James O'Dea, and who, about this time, gave up composing to write lyrics and librettos. In Mark E. Swan's book, Jack Frost (George Majeroni) is a policeman attached to Aurora Borealis (George W. Monroe), Queen of the North. Jack objects to people in the land of Illusia and turns them to ice. But Westinghouse Morse (John McVey) follows Jack around with a can of tropical atmosphere and thaws out Jack's victims. Two love stories were interwoven into the plot. In one a fairy prince loves Maida (Kathleen Clifford), a girl who must find a wishing pole; in the other Stalacta (Blanche Wayne) loves the explorer Shellman (Harry Farleigh). Typical of the show's knowing touches was a number in which five young ladies asked five real collies, "How'd You Like To Be My Bow-wow-wow?" The collies gave their answer by dancing with the girls. The show delighted young and old for twenty weeks.

So far it had been an interesting season—long on promise, short on distinction. But the promises, implicit in shows such as *The Alaskan; The Time, the Place and the Girl*; possibly even in the *Follies of 1907*, were intriguing enough to excuse the momentary absence of real merit. However, two nights after *The Top of the World* opened, another show arrived and radically changed the whole direction of the musical theatre—not just for the season, but for years to come. The show that opened at the New Amsterdam on 21 October 1907 was The Merry Widow.

Since its Viennese premiere on 30 December 1905, *Die lustige Witwe* had swept the Western world, becoming a legend in its own time. Curiously, like *H. M. S. Pinafore* in London and *Florodora* (20 November 1900) in New York, the work was not an immediate hit in Vienna. Some of its original notices were very unkind. But just as Sullivan had popularized his show's tunes at concerts, Franz Lehar saw to it his lovely melodies received constant playing. In a short time the theatre was selling out nightly, and *The Merry Widow* was on its way. Singlehandedly, it revived the moribund Viennese operetta. The show triumphed in Berlin. London welcomed it on 17 June 1907. Sensing its importance and its reception, the New York *Times* gave the production a full-page spread on the Sunday prior to its premiere. Indeed, in America its success was phenomenal. Trade sheets of the period were not as informative as they

have since become, and the records are confused and scattered. Yet within months after its premiere at the New Amsterdam, no fewer than three, and possibly as many as six, road companies were carrying its gorgeous strains across the land. Only one Viennese work had premiered in the preceding seven years. *The Merry Widow* made operetta the rage of the musical theatre. America's fondness for English musical comedies cooled appreciably. The older, more stolid comic opera and the new, struggling native musical comedy were stifled. Comic opera never recovered. The American musical had to bide its time for seven years. *The Merry Widow's* relatively cohesive book, its pervasive sense of style and tone, and, best of all, its magnificent Franz Lehar score set new standards. "The Merry Widow Waltz" ("I Love You So"), "Maxim's," and "Vilja" quickly became classics. In its excitement the *Dramatic Mirror* forgot its earlier, hopeful assessment of the lyric theatre, damning what weeks before it had praised. But this time it accurately evaluated the influence the new show would have:

> Coming at the end of an epoch of inane musical comedy—grant that it is at an end!—the operetta is twice welcome, on account of its own excellence and because it may start a new era in musical entertainment. The music is tuneful, bright and original, the humor fresh and genuine; the story clear and vigorous, and the characters exaggerated only a trifle beyond probabilities.

The "clear and vigorous" story told how Prince Danilo is ordered to court a rich widow, Sonia, lest her millions be lost to his country's treasury. Reluctant at first, he soon finds he is wooing the widow for herself and not for her money. The show made overnight stars of its two principals, Ethel Jackson and Donald Brian. Miss Jackson's star soon flickered, but Brian's remained bright for many years.

DONALD BRIAN was born in Saint John's, Newfoundland, on 17 February 1877. Handsome, with a dimpled round face and wavy hair, he made his stage debut in Lawrence, Massachusetts, in 1896. Thereafter he played in stock and toured in straight plays until he landed a small role in a touring company of *The Chaperones*. Appearances followed in *The Supper Club*, *The Belle of Broadway*, *Florodora*, *The Silver Slipper*, and *Myles Aroon*. George M. Cohan spotted the actor, who had become an excellent dancer and an adequate singer, and gave him important parts in *Forty-five Minutes from Broadway* and *Little Johnny Jones*. Brian's association with *The Merry Widow* has caused many writers to look on him as primarily a singer, although in fact his singing was secondary to his acting and dancing. Co-incidentally, London's original Danilo was Joseph Coyne, another American known more for his general stageworthiness than for any special vocal talents.

Even outside the theatrical world the musical's influence was enormous. In fashion, feathery, oversized "Merry Widow Hats" became de rigueur. Its irrepressible waltz had no small part in initiating what was quickly tagged "the dancing craze."

If Harry B. Smith's recollections are correct, there was a startling irony to its commanding vogue, for Smith contended that *The Merry Widow* was rushed into its original Viennese production when a principal's illness delayed what was to have been the Austrian mounting of a major American work, *Robin Hood* (28 September 1891). The truth of Smith's closing comment on the story was soon made clear. "Lehár's opera made a fortune for Colonel Savage, its producer. Eventually it cost American managers a number of fortunes, because, for several years afterward, they produced every German and Austrian operetta they could get, in the vain hope of finding another 'Merry Widow.'"

The third financial panic in fourteen years struck home forcefully two days after *The Merry Widow* opened when the Knickerbocker Trust Company closed its doors on 23 October. The glittering success of Lehár's piece both in New York and in its many road companies contrasted noticeably with the fiscal gloom. This contrast undoubtedly hastened the rash of importations from Vienna and the American imitations that followed.

Boston still remained a production center, and one week after *The Merry Widow* arrived, the Boston Cadet Corps brought its latest effort down to New York.

Miss Pocahontas (28 October 1907, Lyric) played havoc with a favorite bit of American folklore, turning Captain John Smith (Walter Jones) into a braggart, condemned to die or marry a withered old Indian crone. He chooses death. Pocahontas (Marie Dupuis) rescues him, though she really loves John Rolfe (George Fox). Pow-Ha-Tan (George Le Soir) was given an Irish father to fill the need for a traditional musical clown. New Yorkers didn't take to the show, and it was withdrawn after two weeks.

Despite its light-hearted title, **The Candy Kid** (28 October 1907, Yorkville) was really another melodrama-cum–musical comedy. Its hero was a Yale undergrad, Eddy Edson. His courtship of Bonnie Bosworth is threatened by Lopez, a corrupt, vicious villain from Colombia (the country, not the Ivy League rival). Eddy thwarts several kidnapping attempts. At one point, after a drugged Bonnie is carried aboard a ship, Eddy dashes to the pier and swings on the boom of a loading crane to effect a rescue. Lopez then attacks the U.S. consulate in Bogotá, but Eddy is there to finish off his opponent. Songs ranged from Eddy's crooning "Bye, Bye, Dreamy Eyes" to his rousing "Hark To The Scream Of The Eagle."

Edward German's **Tom Jones** (11 November 1907, Astor), the popular English comic opera, was November's first musical. It was followed a week later by a new American comic opera, Reginald De Koven's **The Girls of Holland** (18 November 1907, Lyric). Each new De Koven piece made it embarrassingly evident that De Koven was written out. His best new melodies were still pretty enough, but they did not survive constant repetition. The weakness of the music was emphasized by Stanislaus Stange's stodgy, silly book and lyrics. To prove the worth of his elixir and to win the love of the niece of Frau Van Biere (a brewer's widow!), Dr. Franz (Harry Fairleigh), with the help of Mephisto's female cousin, Ariella (Vera Michelena), brings to life the statue of Snowdrop (Edward M. Tavor). Snowdrop proves a nasty surprise, demanding the niece for himself. He is summarily returned to stone.

King Casey (18 November 1907, West End) starred James and Emma Ray. Ray played a decrepit bellhop and hotel fireman—that is, someone who lights fires in the grates of the guest rooms. A weary Casey complains he has lit ninety-seven that day alone. When he goes to light his ninety-eighth, the guest, Goldie Mine, mistakes him for a real fireman who once had rescued her from a major blaze. She starts to court him. Then a second Casey appears on the scene. He is the twin brother of the actual rescuer and is king of an island called Lalla Pa Zaza. He has come to court Goldie. A third Casey adds to the confusion until a happy ending is reached. Again, songs ran the gamut from the sweet "'Neath The Old Cherry Tree" to the stirring "Uncle Sam's Land."

Another week later, on 25 November, the third annual Hippodrome production appeared. Like the preceding season's Casino hit, *The Vanderbilt Cup*, **The Auto Race** cashed in on the fast-growing vogue for sporting cars. The vastness of the Hippodrome stage and its unsurpassed technical facilities allowed it to mount an even more spectacular chase than *The Vanderbilt Cup* could. For good measure, a naval battle, a ballet called "The Four Seasons," a gigantic garden party, and another Hippodrome circus were also staged. Of course, for that very reason, Hippodrome shows could never tour in anything approaching their original form. Their audiences had to come to them. Theatregoers came in droves—enough to keep the 5,000-seat house showing a profit twice a day for 312 performances.

Ernest Hogan, billed as "the unbleached American," was the star of **The Oyster Man** (25 November 1907, Yorkville), which had a book by Miller and Lyles, based on a story by Hal Reid, lyrics by Henry S. Creamer, and music by Hogan and Will Vodery. Among the musical numbers were "A Yankee Doodle Coon," "The White-Wash Brigade," and "When Buffalo Bill and His Wild West Show First Came To Baltimore." Hogan again cavorted as Rufus Rastus, but this was to be his last appearance. He died of tuberculosis early in 1908.

The first of the season's three George M. Cohan musicals, **The Talk of New York** (3 December 1907, Knickerbocker), continued the adventures of Kid Burns, with Victor Moore once again playing the Kid.

Kid Burns, rich from his racetrack winnings and his investments, falls in love with Geraldine Wilcox (Emma Littlefield). (Mary, his love in *Forty-five Minutes from Broadway* [1 January 1906], has, for theatrically imperative reasons, been forgotten.) Any talk of marriage is opposed by her brother, Joe (Jack Gardner). Joe loves Grace Palmer (Gertrude Vanderbilt), whom Kid exposes as a blackmailer. When Joe hears Grace accepting his father's money to leave him, Joe shoots her. Kid takes the weapon and the blame. On his release from jail he finds a repentant Grace and a Joe who approves of his marrying Geraldine. The book was well written, with Cohan's sharp, idiomatic dialogue. But Cohan's score

was the weakest he had done in some while. Not one standout emerged, though "When A Fellow's On The Level With A Girl That's On The Square" had some vogue. Nonetheless, *The Talk of New York* gave Cohan his first experience with a long New York run, just under twenty weeks.

VICTOR MOORE was born in Hammonton, New Jersey, on 24 February 1876. His first "theatrical" experience seems to have been at the age of ten, when he carried a banner in a local minstrel parade. Shortly thereafter his parents moved to Boston. There he obtained employment as a super in *Babes in the Wood* for $3.50 a week. A few years in stock followed. In 1902 he purchased the rights to a vaudeville skit entitled "Change Your Act, or Back to the Woods," paying $125 for it. The skit chronicled the end of a seedy, hard-luck vaudeville team, just handed their notice and heckled as they attempt to make their way through their final performance. Ignoring the injunction of the title, Moore used the skit off and on for the next twenty-five years, whenever no suitable legitimate vehicle offered itself. His partner was usually his wife, Emma Littlefield. Cohan signed Moore for *Forty five Minutes from Broadway* after watching the young comedian in this act.

Cohan brought in his second show two months to the day after *The Talk of New York*. It was a more than usually emotional opening. Cohan had long idolized Ned Harrigan of the old Harrigan and Hart shows. Harrigan had retired from the stage, and Broadway had more or less forgotten him. But Cohan had remembered and invited him to the first night. There Harrigan discovered that one of the principals of **Fifty Miles from Boston** (3 February 1908, Garrick—originally Harrigan's!) was named in his honor. Cohan's Harrigan (George Parson) loves Sadie Woodis (Edna Wallace Hopper), but she prefers Joe Westcott (Laurence Wheat), the baseball hero of Brookfield, Massachusetts. Sadie's brother, Jed (John Westley), has stolen $400 from the post office and lost it in a bet. Harrigan offers to supply Jed the money if he will persuade Joe to give up Sadie. But Sadie remains true to Joe. Just as Jed thinks he will go to jail, the post office burns down. Harrigan, realizing how ignoble his position is, gives Jed the money anyway. *Fifty Miles from Boston* was a peculiar show. Cohan himself called it a "play with music," as he had some of his earlier works, and as he had in *Forty-five Minutes from Broadway*, he distributed its songs unevenly. Its first two acts were largely songless melodrama. Most of the tunes were saved for Act III. The songs were better than those Cohan had written for *The Talk of New York*. One stopped the show—especially the first night with the old trouper in the house. "H-A-Double R-I-G-A-N" (published simply as "Harrigan") was the last song Cohan wrote for Broadway that entered into his classic canon. It was sung by James C. Marlowe. The song is rarely sung as written. Cohan's triplet over the word "double," perhaps under the influence of the very word, has long since been reduced to two notes. Despite the hit tune, the show ran only four weeks.

Cohan's third show, **The Yankee Prince** (20 April 1908, Knickerbocker), was even less successful. The title suggested the Yankee Doodle boy was succumbing to the glamour of Europe. But the story was vintage Cohan, with the Cohans themselves starred. Franklyn Fielding (Jerry), a rich Chicagoan, takes his daughter Evelyn (Josephine) to Europe in search of a titled husband. She meets and falls in love with Percy Springer (George), an American. Even though her father finds a willing earl, Evelyn marries Percy. With another hand-me-down Cohan score, the show ran only twenty-eight performances.

Raymond Hubbell and Robert B. Smith had a resounding hit with **A Knight for a Day** (16 December 1907, Wallack's). The evening was a rewrite of their twenty-four performance flop of the preceding year, *Mamelle Sallie* (26 November 1906). The plot of *A Knight for a Day* was trite enough, again making a whole evening out of an attempt to mate matching lockets and thereby inherit a fortune. The lockets fall into the wrong hands—the antagonists' and the comics'—before the finale resolves everything. John Slavin and May Vokes led the clowning, while Sallie Fisher and Percy Bronson played the romantic leads. Hubbell's score was a proper match for the libretto, pleasurable and forgettable. The mating made a fortune for all involved, for this time the show chalked up 176 performances. Its success was a commentary on the healthy theatrical economy of the era. Chicago remained an independently rewarding production center, as did some other cities. As Cohan and others showed time and again,

if Broadway failed to embrace material meant for it, there was often a highly lucrative welcome waiting on the road. But even Broadway was customarily easygoing enough to reconsider efforts it had only recently rejected. Although the $10,000 or $15,000 it cost to raise the curtain on a well-produced musical was not an inconsiderable sum when bread cost a nickel for a one-pound loaf, a good pair of shoes was $3.75, and a popular novel sold for $1.50, the few forms of competition and preunion wage scales kept weekly expenses so low that some extra effort could be repaid many times over.

Whereas most period musicals confined themselves to one setting for each act, **The Cat and the Fiddle** (16 December 1907, West End), called "a great musical trick and comic spectacle" on its program, had no fewer than twenty. Its book was by another master of touring melodrama, Lincoln J. Carter. This time he combined standard melodrama with very atypical fantasy. Demons come to earth in the form of humans to kidnap a girl who will be sacrificed in the enchanted land of Eye. A tramp penetrates a mysterious cavern in the Catskills and there releases a good fairy who has been trapped in a magic jar. She and her cat, after numerous adventures, rescue the girl.

Charles E. Blaney offered a similarly unusual mélange in his book for **The Bad Boy and His Teddy Bears** (23 December 1907, Lincoln Square). The mischievous Chips has befriended a family of brown bears—Papa, Mama, Teddy, and Flossie. They live near a hotel run by Badly Cook, whose daughter, Alice, loves one of their summer boarders. Cook invents a wonderful rain-making machine, but when he attempts to interest a rich man in his invention, the man and his son not only try to cheat him, they also try to lure Alice away. Chips and the bears send the rich folk packing. One act showed the home of the bears, who spoke only in pantomime. That home was underground and, according to one reviewer, looked very much like Peter Pan's house. The rich man's nasty son was played and danced by Harry Pilcer, who went on to have his evenings of celebrity on Broadway.

Playing the Ponies (23 December 1907, New Circle) recounted the further adventures of Pincus and Plonsky, the comic duo from *Bankers and Brokers*. In this sequel each of the pair thinks McGuiness is his long-lost child. They seek out the truth at Act I's racetrack and Act II's Luna Park. That truth turns out to be that McGuiness's father was Mr. McGuiness. The book was by Aaron Hoffman, lyrics by Edward Madden, and music by Theodore Morse (composer of "Dear Old Girl" and for a brief time the highest-paid pianist and staff writer on Tin Pan Alley).

Paul Rubens's **Miss Hook of Holland** (31 December 1907, Criterion) arrived from London to become an immediate hit, helped by Christie MacDonald in the leading role of a brewer's daughter loved by a bandmaster.

A fifth consecutive hit followed two nights later on 2 January when Weber brought **The Merry Widow Burlesque** into his theatre, getting 1908 off to a happy start. Weber used Lehar's music—with the composer's permission—and had George V. Hobart "retranslate" the original. In the new version Sonia became Fonia, and Danilo became Dandilo, while Margot, Clo-Clo, and Frou-Frou were joined by cuddly Goo-Goo. While Charles J. Ross was Dandilo and Lulu Glaser the first widow, most of the cast was recruited from old Weber and Fields stalwarts: Peter F. Dailey, Bessie Clayton, and Mabel Fenton. When Miss Glaser left the cast during the run, Blanche Ring was called in to replace her. The new widow brought with her the one song from the show to become a hit, "Yip-I-Addy-I-Ay" (Will Cobb/John H. Flynn). The burlesque ran out the season. Subsequently, after Dailey's death and the opening of two rival companies of Molnár's *The Devil* on the same night in August of 1908, Hobart rewrote the book, allowing the Devil (Walter Jones) to meddle in Dandilo and Fonia's courtship. The revised version was called *The Merry Widow and the Devil.*

Funabashi (6 January 1908, Casino) told one of the era's most popular stories—the romance of an American naval officer serving in the Orient. In this instance the officer was Jack Carter (Walter Percival), and he falls in love with a fellow American, Dolly Rivers (Vera Michelena). But Jack's father, the Secretary of War, orders him to marry Gwyndolin Hillary-Hoops (Margaret Rutledge). A family friend, Nan Livingston (Alice Fischer), persuades the Secretary to marry Gwyndolin himself, freeing Jack to marry Dolly. Unlike many earlier musical comedies of its sort, *Funabashi* neglected to utilize fully its setting. Japan figured only slightly in the story and was used primarily for background color. References to it were typically half-respectful, half-condescending. And in this era of a revived "manifest destiny" and "the big stick" it was not surprising to find one stirring martial air saluting "The Girl Behind The Man Behind The Gun." A refreshing change, noted by several of the critics, was the

absence of a grotesque comedian. Whatever the show's virtues, Broadway had become too crowded with hits, so *Funabashi* moved on after a brief stay.

January's next musical came in two weeks later. **Lonesome Town** (20 January 1908, New Circle) was a brave title in an era when musical tides were gay, or, at best, noncommittal. Its book was in the picaresque American minstrel tradition. Chico Brown (C. William Kolb) and Bakersfield Bill (Max M. Dill), two tramps, are chased into Watts by a wild bull. They encounter an old friend, Fresno Phil (Ben T. Dillon), who reports that Mr. Watts, the town's absentee landowner, is dead and has left no known will. Fresno poses as a lawyer, while Chico and Bill pretend to be Watts and his son. They are ultimately exposed and go on their way. Although there was no particularly good music to assist in putting over the material, *Lonesome Town* recorded a satisfactory run of eleven weeks.

Oscar Straus's **A Waltz Dream** (27 January 1908, Broadway) was well received and quickly caught up in the new rage for Viennese operetta, running until the warm weather. The story told of a young man's unhappy marriage to a foreign princess and of his sneaking off to listen to the music of his homeland, played by an all-girl orchestra in a park. The original leads were Magda Dahl and Edward Johnson, but they were soon replaced by Vera Michelena and Frank Rushworth. Several newspapers made much of Johnson's departure, announcing he was leaving to further his voice studies in Italy so that he might try his luck at opera. Of course, none of these papers could foresee that his luck would one day make him general manager of the Metropolitan Opera.

The Soul Kiss (28 January 1908, New York) was a vehicle for Adelaide Genee, whom Ziegfeld, the show's producer, advertised as "the world's greatest dancer." While she may not have been at the very top of her profession, she was a highly regarded, serious artist, and more than one reviewer was distressed to find her in such a commercial assemblage. The book was by Harry B. Smith, who at the time was writing the scripts for the new *Follies*. Suzette, a model, will not kiss the sculptor, Maurice (Cecil Lean). J. Lucifer Mephisto (Ralph Herz) wagers a million dollars that Suzette (Florence Holbrook) cannot keep Maurice faithful for one year. He tempts Maurice with historical and fictitious beauties—Carmen, Marguerite, and Cleopatra. Maurice falls in love with "The Dancer" (Genee), and they decide to marry. Suzette marries an American millionaire, and Mephisto goes off to the Bal Tabarin with a chorus girl.

The music, culled from various composers, but mainly by Maurice Levi, was of the same mediocre order as the book. One of the songs gave a generous plug to the reigning hit of the season, happily at another syndicate house, "Since My Mariutch Learned The Merry Widow Waltz." Ziegfeld was already making a name for himself with his lavish touch. The brilliant Bal Tabarin set won approval, as did an autumn hunting scene with real hounds and with girls in white hunting frocks. (Not even stiff hunting boots prevented Genee from dancing gracefully in the hunting ballet.) The star, glorified by Ziegfeld's production and promotion, proved a potent draw; the show ran sixteen weeks.

Two solidly American shows opened on 3 February: *Fifty Miles from Boston* and **Bandana Land**. For the latter, Ray Comstock, one of the most enlightened producers in Broadway history, brought together much of the leading Negro talent of the day. Williams and Walker were the stars. Most of the music was by Will Marion Cook, with supplemental numbers by Williams and by Chris Smith. Alex Rogers, who did most of the lyrics, combined with J. A. Shipp to write a libretto that told a typical Williams and Walker tale. Mose Blackstone (Alex Rogers) organizes a syndicate to buy Amos Simmons's farm and sell it to the street railway company, but he cannot raise all the needed cash. He learns rich Skunkton Bowser (Williams) is stranded with a small minstrel company and gets him to contribute the rest. Blackstone sells half the farm to the railway. The rest he turns into a black man's park, and he advises the railway the Negroes will make all sorts of noises and trouble unless the railway pays an exorbitant price for the remaining half. At the last minute Skunkton and his "guardian" Bud Jenkins (Walker) withdraw from the deal and handle the whole arrangement themselves. The play was good, clean fun. Williams and Walker led a show-stopping Cakewalk at the end of Act I. The lyrics, in frequently resorting to Negro dialect, were more patently racial than the music. Although one pedant was offended by black actors wearing straight-haired wigs, insisting their performances would have been "just as vigorous with kinks," the show was well received and played eleven weeks at the Majestic.

Nearly a Hero (24 February 1908, Casino) was another producer-assemblage with a number of composers providing the tunes for another inane Harry B. Smith libretto. Jabez Doolittle (Sam Edwards), in order to explain an absence from home, claims to be the unknown hero who rescued Harold Montague (Edgar Norton) from drowning. But Harold is not thankful, claiming his rescuer robbed him. He demands Doolittle's arrest. Ludwig Knoedler (Sam Bernard), who boards with the Doolittles, is jailed by mistake. By Act III everything is explained. Enlivened by a superb cast that also included Ethel Levey, Ada Lewis, Zelda Sears, and Elizabeth Brice, *Nearly a Hero* pleased sufficient crowds to run 116 performances.

On 23 March Mort Singer gave Chicagoans still another Hough-Adams-Howard hit at the La Salle, **Honeymoon Trail**. Cecil Lean and Florence Holbrook again were starred, while a figure new to the series, Ned Wayburn, directed. The action was set at a hotel in California, which had recently passed a law granting divorce after six months' residence. Yet love and marriage were at the forefront of the plot. Tightfisted, much-divorced George Mason, the canned-bean tycoon, won't hear of his daughter, Edna, marrying Perkins, the head of advertising at a rival cannery. To mollify her father Edna feigns interest in Bill Dudley, her stepmother's former husband. Dudley tricks Mason out of $50,000. Perkins gets Mason, who is usually averse to gambling, to bet him a similar sum. Perkins knows he will lose his own bet. Then Perkins arranges for the hotel manager, who is also a justice of the peace, to marry him and Edna while they pretend to say good-bye. Although some of Hough and Adams's lyrics were untypically stilted (" 'Tis here that hearts long since grown weary/of wife dearie, gain their liberty"), their dialogue was as crisp and witty as ever:

Edna: You had no business kissing me.
Perkins: It wasn't business—it was pleasure.

With the two late December entries the season for new touring musicals was effectively finished. The only other "novelty" to appear was **Busy Izzy's Boodle** (6 April 1907, West End), and that turned out to be little more than a rewriting of earlier Busy Izzy material. George Sidney was still Izzy, and the first act still concerned with his banking exploits, but the rest of the show dropped his ludicrous investments in a circus and replaced them with his troubles aboard a ship, where his courtship of an Italian beauty earns him the ire of her stilletto-wielding Italian suitor. Izzy recognizes that his love interests will have to lie elsewhere.

On 20 April New York was offered **The Flower of the Ranch**, a Chicago hit that Joe Howard wrote without his usual collaborators, Hough and Adams. It told the melodramatic tale of "Little Flower" (Mabel Barrison), whose father was killed by Toni Miguel (Ike Oliver) when she was still a baby and whose property was seized by Bob Branden (Frederick Knight). When she is grown, she is given papers for safekeeping by Jack Farnum (Howard). Branden gets Miguel to steal the papers. But when he learns of the reward offered for them, Miguel attempts to return them. Branden shoots him to thwart the return. However, Branden has an "awakening of conscience" and confesses all. Once again New Yorkers would not buy the Chicago school of musicals. *The Flower of the Ranch* lasted only two weeks at the Majestic.

Cohan's *The Yankee Prince* also opened 20 April. Five nights later, **The Merry-Go-Round,** a revue with enough of a plot to allow the evening to be called a musical comedy, came into the Circle Theatre. The plot followed another tour, this time of the sights of a country fair. A Chicago favorite, brash Mabel Hite (described as a female George M. Cohan), sang and danced a comic song describing her efforts to be a lady in Weehawken. Ignacio Martinetti earned several encores for his energetic dances. The Circle Theatre was temporarily rechristened Gus Edwards' Music Hall in honor of the show's composer. But none of Edwards's songs lasted much beyond the show's run.

The Gay Musician (18 May 1908, Wallack's) was anything but gay. He was an unknown comic opera composer, Eugene Dubois (Walter Percival), who invites a prima donna, Maude Granville (Amelia Stone), to hear his latest work, at the same time forcing his wife, Marie (Sophie Brandt), to play the part of his maid and slapping her when she makes a gaffe. She leaves him. In the second act Eugene and Maude are to be married, as are Maude's father and Marie. But Maude and Eugene quarrel, and he goes away with Marie. Although the book and the Julian Edwards score were praised, the public withheld its support. The show folded after just two and a half weeks.

The season's last musical in New York, **Mary's Lamb** (25 May 1908, New York), was based on the French farce *Mme. Mongodin.* It was a vehicle for Richard Carle, with book, lyrics, and music by Carle himself. Carle played "Leander Lamb, a martyr." Lamb is henpecked by a wife (Elita Proctor Otis) who displays a large framed knife she calls "The Shrine of Virtue." She boasts she once used it to discourage a too ardent lover. Leander accepts his wife's opinion of herself, referring to her as "My better two-thirds." The first time Mr. Lamb is caught with Sylvia Montrose (Henrietta Lee), Mrs. Lamb accepts his excuse of sleepwalking. But the second time she goes for the knife. At that moment an old schoolmate of Lamb's arrives. He turns out to be the old "ardent lover" and tells the true story of the knife. After that Mr. Lamb has the upper hand. *Mary's Lamb* was another of the many musicals adored on the road and rejected on Broadway. Carle, in shows of his own writing or by others, toured the country ceaselessly, as one of the most popular entertainers of the day. New York critics generally found his material "raw," and a torrid, if comic, dance he did in *Mary's Lamb* with a burlesque queen did nothing to let them change their minds. As a result, his Broadway runs were almost always short—although rarely as short as the two-week stand of *Mary's Lamb.*

The continuing success of the Hough-Adams-Howard musicals prompted the Singer brothers to erect a second Chicago theatre to house the shows. They opened the Princess Theatre on 1 June with the latest work of the trio, **A Stubborn Cinderella.** Its popularity meant that Hough-Adams-Howard had two hits running in Chicago at once. Although *Honeymoon Trail* never reached New York, *A Stubborn Cinderella* did. But its run there in no way matched its stay of over 300 performances in Chicago.

A San Francisco show had no such luck at a similarly named West Coast playhouse, closing after its prescheduled two-week stand. A local effort, **The King Maker** (15 June 1908, Princess) had book and lyrics by Waldemar Young, W. C. Patterson, and Race Whitney, and music by R. H. Bassett. It told how Warwick Plunger cons the gullible E. Z. Coyne into buying an imaginary island with the promise of cornering the coconut market. With the help of Red, a sailor-turned-janitor, an uninhabited island is found and everybody ends up reasonably happy.

Not all of the commercial activity was confined to the principal houses in Chicago and New York, or, indeed, the main theatres elsewhere. As American cities grew larger, the single auditorium that had sufficed in each became inadequate. By the early nineteenth century several of the biggest metropolises saw the erection of the first significant competition. In short order, the very largest of these cities had three playhouses. About the same time, however, another change could be observed. Call it the growth of class distinction, or simply the swelling of lower-class populations who could not afford higher-priced entertainments, but who demanded affordable tickets to plays catering to their less sophisticated and less demanding tastes. Hints of this disparity could be seen in the 1840s and 1850s, but the explosion of this audience and of theatres specifically welcoming them followed immediately after the Civil War. In a few instances, older first-class theatres were downgraded to accommodate changing demographics. However, as a theatregoing working class burgeoned and gave solid promise of offering steady patronage, playhouses were built in their neighborhoods. The coincidental expansion of American railroads made the task of touring shows increasingly easy and promoted the growth not only of both first-class and lower-class road companies (they were called "combinations" in this period) but also of a de facto circuit of stages readily available to popularly priced mountings. Most of the shows originated in New York, although some were produced first in Chicago and elsewhere. Brooklyn also produced its own musicals. **The Girl from Williamsburg** met with an enthusiastic reception when it opened at Payton's in May. But the day of the neighborhood musical was virtually over. By March 1908 there were 400 movie houses in New York City alone, and a good number of them had very recently been marginal legitimate theatres. The trend was national. In the 30 May issue of the *Dramatic Mirror* a large ad appeared, headlined, "Turn Your Opera House into a Moving Picture Nickelodeon This Summer." Many "summer" nickelodeons never returned to the legitimate fold.

1908–1909

1908–1909 got off to a promising start, and then collapsed, at least artistically. Commercially, there could be little complaint, for a third of the season's musicals ran over 100 performances. But this success reflected simply the musical theatre's skill in brightening the lives of the tired businessman and his wife. Aesthetic considerations were few and far between at this time in Broadway's history.

Two musicals appeared on 15 June, the traditional date for separating the seasons. One was a revue; the other was a book show. Both were smash hits. Indeed, **Three Twins,** at the Herald Square, was the season's biggest hit (excepting as usual the *sui generis* Hippodrome spectacle). The

musical was adapted by Charles Dickson from Mrs. R. Pacheco's *Incog*. Tom Stanhope (Clifton Crawford), disinherited by his father because of his love of Kate Armitage (Alice Yorke), disguises himself to resemble a photograph he has found. The photo is of Molly Sommers's sweetheart, Harry Winter (Willard Curtiss). Harry has a slightly demented twin brother. And so Molly (Bessie McCoy) is never sure which of the three twins she is dealing with. The complications are ironed out in time for Molly and Harry, and Tom and Kate, to wed. The libretto was clean and cheerful, but what really made the show was Bessie McCoy and two outstanding songs. The show, in turn, made Miss McCoy a star and made the lyricist, Otto Hauerbach, and the composer, Karl Hoschna, names to be reckoned with.

OTTO HAUERBACH (later Harbach) was born to Danish immigrant parents in Salt Lake City, Utah, on 1 August 1873. After graduation from Knox College he taught English and public speaking at Whitman College in Walla Walla, Washington. He arrived in New York in 1901 to work toward a doctorate at Columbia. Failing eyesight forced him to abandon his plans and take odd jobs, mostly in the newspaper field. He met Hoschna in 1902, and together they wrote an operetta, *The Daughter of the Desert*, that was never produced.

One of Hoschna's song hits in *Three Twins*, "The Yama Yama Man" (lyric by Collin Davis), is now nearly forgotten. It is a choice example of the benign infantilism that remained voguish all through this period. Miss McCoy introduced it in a satin clown outfit topped by a cone-shaped hat. A second hit from the show still enjoys periodic revivals— "Cuddle Up A Little Closer, Lovey Mine." Although the song is endearingly intimate, it was given an elaborate, formal staging with "A unique chorus setting representing the seven ages of lovers from infancy to old age." Theatrical effect rather than consistent tone governed musical mountings. The rest of the score was trippingly melodic. The show scored 288 performances.

KARL HOSCHNA was born in Kusch-warda in Bohemia on 16 August 1877. Leaving the Vienna Conservatory with honors, he accepted a post as an oboist in the Austrian Army band. In 1896 he emigrated to America and soon found work under Victor Herbert. An uncontrollable fear that oboe playing would affect his mind led him to accept work as a copyist with Witmark. In this job he began composing popular songs. Three operettas followed, all folding before they reached New York.

Another standard came out of Ziegfeld's **Follies of 1908**, the other premiere of the evening of 15 June. Nora Bayes introduced "Shine On, Harvest Moon," which she and her husband, Jack Norworth, wrote. A second of their numbers, "Over On The Jersey Side," teasingly condescending, suggested the show still expected to cater to a largely local audience who would understand the lyric's parochial sentiments and allusions. Both songs were interpolations. The official score was by Maurice Levi, who had written for the defunct Rogers Brothers burlesques. The most-played of his numbers was the martial "Song Of The Navy," its Harry B. Smith lyrics boasting, "Red, White, and Blue is ready for peace or war," a feeling close to the heart of a nation and its "big stick" President. How new and tentative the form was could be seen in several ways. For example, its sheet music clung to the older spelling, "review." Several years still had to pass before the French spelling was universally accepted. And the revue had a book—by Smith. This year's compère and commère were Adam and Eve. Their experiences viewing their progeny's accomplishments provided the thread that tied together the selections and production numbers. These numbers included a view of a tunnel being dug between Manhattan and New Jersey, followed by a view of the Jersey marshes, with Ziegfeld's beauties as giant mosquitoes. The girls later appeared as taxicabs whose lights glared out into the auditorium. Important political figures of the day were impersonated in a scene that re-created the Chicago convention. The show's success assured its continuance. It ran 120

performances at the Jardin de Paris, almost twice as long as the first edition. With this second mounting, the *Follies* started on the way to becoming both an institution and a legend.

On the Madison Square Garden Roof, a weak musical entitled **Ski-Hi** had a brief twenty-five-performance run beginning 20 June. Little more than another revue with the slimmest of plotlines, it took its titular hero (William Conley) to the Orient and then to Jupiter. It was the last of the summer musicals to play the roof. The house had never had particularly good luck with its selections, and the shooting of Stanford White on opening night two summers before had added notoriety to its ill fortune. Moreover, the theatre district was ineluctably moving away from Madison Square, dooming even more fortunate theatres.

If the critics were not speaking loosely when they said **The Mimic World** (9 July 1908, Casino) hadn't "even the semblance of a plot and makes no pretense of any," then the revue would have been years ahead of its time. Some thin thread to tie together the songs and sketches, however fragile, was still in order. The sketches were basically old-fashioned burlesques on the plays and players of the day (George M. Cohan, Kid Burns, Prince Danilo) interspersed with vaudeville turns. It satisfied a public seeking light summer entertainment.

Two shows opened 3 August. One was the **Cohan and Harris Minstrels**, at the New York. Cohan, the great musical comedy innovator, was also Cohan, the knowledgeable traditionalist. His love and respect for Harrigan had already been made evident, and in a few years his feeling about Weber and Fields, and their burlesque tradition, would have important effects on the American revue. Now Cohan and his partner, Sam Harris, boldly attempted to resuscitate a dying tradition. Their minstrels included George Evans, Eddie Leonard, and the great female impersonator Julian Eltinge. Because political conventions were then in the news, Evans acknowledged the applause greeting his first entrance by shouting, "I accept your nomination." Eltinge performed a Salome dance. Much of the second act was occupied by Cohan's one-act musical comedy "The Belle of the Barbers' Ball." Although the twenty-four performance run was a limited booking from the start, grosses were disappointing. Cohan and Harris were not discouraged. They promised to bring the troupe back again the next year.

The second opening on 3 August was **The Girl Question** at Wallack's. As they had the previous August, Hough, Adams, and Howard brought in another of their Chicago hits for New York's inspection. Once again their welcome was lukewarm, with critics again suggesting Chicago was too partial to melodrama and sentimentality. Con Ryan (Junie McCree), headwaiter at the restaurant where all the action takes place, loves Elsie Davis (Isabel D'Armond), the cashier, and is loved by Jo Forster (Georgie Drew Mendum), a waitress. Elsie marries Harold Sears (Jack Henderson), son of a railroad magnate. Sears senior forecloses the mortgage on the restaurant to turn it into a brokerage office. But Jo comes into an inheritance and sells her railroad stock to Sears in return for the restaurant. Con and Jo marry. *The Girl Question* had all the virtues of Hough-Adams-Howard shows: slangy dialogue; simple, natural lyrics; and good homespun melody. Still, the show stayed only a month before moving on.

In January the trio tried again with **A Stubborn Cinderella** (25 January 1909, Broadway). It was to be the closest they would come to repeating their Chicago popularity in the big town. Lady Leslie (Sallie Fisher), an amazingly unworldly young Scot, is traveling with a bodyguard through America on her way to a marriage with a Russian Grand Duke. She stops at Columbus College, where she agrees to unveil a statue. At the ceremony she meets Mac and, assuming he is the sculptor, asks him to make a statue of her. They head for California after being delayed by a landslide in Colorado. To while away the time, Mac tells her the story of Cinderella, and she decides he can be her Prince Charming, even though he has botched the statue. If the book was a bit less cohesive than their earlier efforts, Howard's songs were as good or better. The best was a melodic waltz, "When You First Kiss The Last Girl You Love." *A Stubborn Cinderella's* run of eighty-eight performances was the longest the team ever enjoyed in New York. One reason may have been the actor who played Mac. Several critics singled him out, predicting a bright future for him in musical comedy. He was John Barrymore.

August's final musical, **Algeria** (31 August 1908, Broadway), had a gorgeous, romantic Victor Herbert score and a dreadful Glen MacDonough book. The story told how the Sultana Zoradie (Ida Brooks Hunt) falls in love, sight unseen, with the poet of "Rose of the World." Three Foreign Legion deserters each claim to be the author, but each in turn is proven false. The poet is found to be a French captain, De Lome (George Leon Moore). Zoradie and De Lome wed. The libretto flipped back and forth between arch romance and slapstick. The deserters had names used over and over again for comic characters—Carrol Sweet, De Long Greene, and Van Cortlandt Park. A pair of comedians were presented as Mr. and Mrs. Billings F. Cooings. Outstanding among Herbert's melodies were two numbers that remain part of his classic canon, "Rose Of The World" and "Twilight in Barakeesh." In fact, Herbert's score was so fine more than one critic pleaded for a rewriting of the show. Frank McKee, the producer, closed the show after six weeks and sold the rights to Lew Fields, who promptly set about making revisions.

Ivan Caryll and Lionel Monckton's **The Girls of Gottenburg** (2 September 1908, Knickerbocker), a London hit, began a fourteen-week run. The production featured the winsome London favorite Gertie Millar as a girl whose disguise as an innkeeper's daughter forces almost everyone else into some disguise or other. Will R. Anderson, Harry Von Tilzer, and Jerome Kern all contributed interpolations.

Sporting Days, the annual Hippodrome spectacular, arrived on 5 September. Under the Shuberts the series had quickly settled into a pattern. Each year the mindless extravaganza had a theme, which could easily be stretched if a good song or an unrelated production number was judged worthy of inclusion. There were appropriate tunes: "Rowing," "Racing Game," and others that could fit in anywhere: "I'm Looking For A Sweetheart And I Think You'll Do." Two highly praised set pieces were a ballet, "The Land of the Birds," and a disingenuous but cruelly prophetic depiction of a 1950 air war, "The Battle in the Skies." As it would do on several occasions the Hippodrome mounted displays of carnage with such beguiling spectacle audiences were entranced rather than shocked. Enough New Yorkers and tourists stood in line for the twice-daily performances to give the house its longest run since *A Society Circus*—448 performances.

Just as Hough, Adams, and Howard seemed to have consolidated their hold on Chicago, their efforts began to flag. When **The Girl at the Helm** opened at the La Salle on 5 September, their names were missing from the credits. The new musical had a book and lyrics by Robert B. Smith and music by Raymond Hubbell. The plot recounted another racing saga. Colonel Higginson challenges Countess Von Hertz to a motorboat race. The colonel would also have his daughter Dorothy marry the young German he was hired to run his boat. (Here was another Dorothy as heroine of a racing plot!) But the Countess lures the young man away. Dorothy's real flame, Fred Stanhope, wins both the race and Dorothy. With Cecil Lean starred, *The Girl at the Helm* settled in for a five-month run.

New Kern songs were heard when **Fluffy Ruffles** (7 September 1908, Criterion) opened. J. J. McNally, at liberty with the closing of the Rogers Brothers series, based his funny, impudent book on cartoons from the *Herald*. Uncle Dave Dill (John Bunny) believes, "If a woman can do a man's work let her do it. And if she can do it as well, let her receive the same pay." He offers his nieces an even better deal—$500,000 apiece if they can learn a trade and stick to it for six weeks. His beautiful but difficult niece, Fluffy (Hattie Williams), is offered $1,000,000. Fluffy alone fails, claiming her bosses fired her because the men at work paid more attention to her than they did to their jobs. When all but Fluffy are taken to Europe as a bonus, Fluffy sneaks aboard ship as a maid. Uncle Dave would marry Mme. Shonts (Lida McMillan), but she was once married to a man named Franconi (Edward Durand), who disappeared after the wedding, and Dave himself was married to one of the Maloni twins (Mattie O'Brien). He has never been sure which, since both also ran away after the nuptials. While Dave and Mme. Shonts are chaperoning the nieces, their old spouses reappear. But Dave believes he has the situation well in hand:

Noggy [one of Fluffy's suitors]: What's the word?
Uncle: Do you want to do something useful?
Noggy: I don't want to, but I will.
Uncle: Well, look through the grounds and if you
    find a man named Franconi—
Noggy: Franconi, yes—
Uncle: Kill him. And if he has a woman with him
    named Maloni—
Noggy: Kill her too?
Uncle: Kill her twice, she's twins.

Maloni and Franconi go off together, allowing Uncle Dave and Mme. Shonts to wed. Fluffy reveals she has been a newspaper reporter for the *Herald* all along. She wins the hand of Augustus Traddles (George Grossmith, Jr.). For all its snappy dialogue

the book betrayed the haphazard construction peculiar to the time. "Willy's Got A New Girl Now" was introduced with a one-line lead, "I am having more trouble with my situation than Willy had with his girls," though Willy has not been mentioned before and is forgotten with the last bar of the song. The typescript included an "Eating Act" for the performer who played Noggy (spelled Noggie in the program and performed by Bert Leslie), commenting, "The act is very funny." And a team of specialty dancers, the Swizzle Sisters, wandered aimlessly in and out of the plot to do their bits. Much top Broadway talent was associated with the show. Charles Frohman produced it, a noteworthy change from his hitherto invariable importation. *Fluffy Ruffles* lingered six weeks, then toured.

Gus Edwards, flushed with the success of *The Merry-Go-Round*, hoped to make his renaming of the Circle Theatre after himself a permanent change. But the name didn't stick, nor did his follow-up show. **School Days** (14 September 1908, Circle), capitalizing on the title of his 1907 hit tune, described how Izzy Levy (Herman Timberg) comes to an East Side school and falls in love with a seeming waif, Nonnie (Janet Priest). When he breaks a window and is about to be arrested, she pays for the window with a half-dollar. Nonni, it develops, is an heiress. The plot left room for a cast of almost forty young, aspiring stars to show their stuff. Their stuff ranged from Gregory Kelly's imitations of Back Bay Brahmins to Joe Keno and Agnes Lynn's acrobatics. It was at heart a glorified amateur vaudeville show. Old and new songs by Edwards were not enough to help the evening beyond a four-week run, so it was hastily abbreviated into a suitable piece for the vaudeville circuit.

Mlle. Mischief (28 September 1908, Lyric), a Viennese importation, was rewritten around Lulu Glaser's talents. Miss Glaser played a brazen young girl who bets she can masquerade for twenty-four hours as a soldier at the local barracks. Her smart performance kept the show on the boards for ninety-six performances.

Frank Pixley and Gustav Luders had less success with **Marcelle** (1 October 1908, Casino), which ran eight and a half weeks. Although they called it a musical comedy, it was a comfortably traditional operetta. Indeed, one of its major failings was the apparent replaying of Pixley and Luders's earlier material. The plot was old hat even at this early date. Baron von Berghof (Jess Dandy) must produce a son or lose his estate to his nephew (Frank Rushworth).

The baron claims he has a son in Paris and sends Dumm (Henry Norman), his cellar master, there to abduct someone, neglecting to mention the victim must be a young man. Dumm brings back Marcelle (Louise Gunning), an actress, who agrees to change her dress and impersonate the fictitious son. When Marcelle and the nephew fall in love, a happy ending follows. Dialect comedians provided the evening's happiest moments. *Marcelle*'s most memorable scene occurred when the Baron and his nephew's lawyer, Herr Schwindle (Joseph Cawthorn), try to get each other drunk by spiking a punch bowl. Of course, each only pretends to drink from his own glass, taking every opportunity to empty the contents into a potted palm. Their increasingly frantic spikings and their growing amazement at the other's drinking prowess provided a crescendo of laughs, culminating as the two watch in dumb bafflement while the palm withers and dies. Luders's music, however light and lovely, seemed even more derivative than the book. Pixley didn't help matters with his lyrics—especially when the show's best number, "The Message Of The Red, Red Rose," so flagrantly echoed *The Prince of Pilsen*'s "The Message Of The Violet." Both Pixley and Luders seemed to be running dry.

Four nights later, the premiere of **The American Idea** (5 October 1908, New York) suggested that George M. Cohan, too, had taken to repeating himself. The plot, another of his chauvinistic parables, did little more than change names and settings. This time Dan Sullivan (Walter Le Roy) and Herman Budmeyer (Gilbert Gregory), rival millionaires from Brooklyn, arrive in Paris and are persuaded to find French counts for their daughters. But two Brooklyn boys, disguised as nobles, win the girls. Cohan filled the evening with snappy dances and marches and gave Trixie Friganza as Mrs. Waxtapper a show-stopper, singing and prancing to "Cohan's Pet Names." Both the words and music of Cohan's songs underlined the show's hand-me-down feeling. There was a spelling song, "F-A-M-E," not unlike *The Yankee Prince*'s "M-O-N-E-Y," *The Talk of New York*'s "M-A-Double R-I-E-D" and, of course, "H-A-Double R-I-G-A-N." Again after "Harrigan," *The American Idea* sang of "Sullivan," while the show's slated hit, "Too Long From Long Acre Square," recalled "Forty-five Minutes From Broadway" and "Fifty Miles From Boston." "Just like all the other Cohan pieces," one critic complained, but he added carefully that there was "no mistaking Mr. Cohan's knowledge of what will appeal to popular taste." Popular taste kept the show in New York for eight weeks, after which it went on a cross-country trek.

This was the season of reckoning for cheap-priced theatres and their made-for-touring entertainments. By season's end the *Dramatic Mirror* reported that seven of Manhattan's combination houses had deserted the legitimate field. The rest were expected to follow shortly. The story was the same on the road for which such plays and musicals were really mounted. A few in Manhattan had converted to homes for Yiddish plays; several others were given over to two-a-day. A pair of the most prestigious, the old 14th Street Theatre (now clearly categorized as a combination house) and the Harlem Opera House, were showing films, sometimes along with tab vaudeville shows. As a result only three new touring musicals played New York.

Morning, Noon and Night (5 October 1908, Yorkville) was the work of writers respected both on Broadway and on Tin Pan Alley. Joseph W. Herbert did the book, William Jerome the lyrics, and Jean Schwartz the music. Its cast was "almost entirely composed of well-known vaudeville recruits." Heading the list were Joe Welsh, famous as a Yiddish-dialect comedian, and the up-and-coming Al Shean, who was uncle to the still young Marx Brothers and would later be half of the beloved Gallagher and Shean duo. He, too, clowned with a Yiddish dialect. Herbert provided the slightest of stories, which started on Ellis Island and went on to recount the essentially comic problems Abraham Goldberg faced from a Bowery tough and the Black Hand (an early Mafia). Much of the material was simply an excuse for vaudeville turns and spoofs of Broadway plays. A send-up of *Salome* garnered especially loud applause.

How long a few of the surviving touring musicals could survive was suggested by the return at several houses in September of the 1904 show *Me, Him and I*.

When **The Golden Butterfly** (12 October 1908, Broadway) came into the Broadway one week after *The American Idea*, it further underscored the sad state of domestic creativity. Harry B. Smith's book was as cumbersome as it was complicated. Ilma Walden's lover, Franz (Walter Percival), goes to Paris to make his fortune as a composer. Baron von Affenkoff (Louis Harrison) tells Ilma (Grace Van Studdiford) Franz has met with instant success and has forgotten her. The baron invites her to sing the lead in his new opera, "The Golden Butterfly," if she will marry him. Franz returns and, not wanting to hinder Ilma's career, masquerades as a Russian prince. The real prince (Louis Cassavant) appears. He demands Franz be arrested as an impostor. Franz discloses why he has disguised himself, so the prince relents. The baron's opera is discovered to be a work the baron had stolen from Franz shortly after Franz had completed it. Ilma and Franz are reunited. More dismaying than Smith's dreary libretto was Reginald De Koven's colorless score. The composer, who orchestrated his own work and conducted on opening night, used Wagnerian-like brassy orchestrations that seemed designed to cover up the lack of fine melodies. There was no escaping De Koven was written out, and it was increasingly obvious by this time that, for all his popularity, he would go down as the creator of only a single masterpiece, *Robin Hood* (28 September 1891).

De Koven's popularity could take credit for one last hit he did participate in later in the season. **The Beauty Spot** (10 April 1909, Herald Square) had a libretto every bit as complicated as *The Golden Butterfly*, but less heavy-handed. It also had the well-liked Jefferson De Angelis and his company to perform. Joseph Herbert's story found General Samovar's daughter, Nadine (Marguerite Clark), engaged to Nikolas Kromeski (Frank Doane) but in love with Jacques Baccarel (George MacFarlane), an artist the general hates because of Jacques's *avant-garde* notions of painting. The general (De Angelis) is unaware that Baccarel had once painted his wife and called the picture "The Beauty Spot." Samovar is also unaware that Nikolas has returned from overseas, bringing a bride with him. Jacques and Nikolas exchange disguises, and the new Nikolas convinces the general to buy "The Beauty Spot" after some more clothing has been painted on the model. In the end Samovar is reconciled to Jacques and Nadine's marrying. Only the least bit superior to *The Golden Butterfly*, *The Beauty Spot* nonetheless gave De Koven his last run of any length—137 performances.

Smith was the librettist and lyricist for October's final entry. Neither his material nor Victor Herbert's score for **Little Nemo** (20 October 1908, New Amsterdam) was distinguished. But there remained a place for a pleasant children's entertainment, and this musical adaptation of Winsor McKay's cartoons filled the bill. Alone of the month's lyric pieces, it enjoyed a passing success, running 111 performances. Little Nemo (Master Gabriel—reputedly a thirty-one-year-old midget with the stature and voice of a ten-year-old boy) goes to Slumberland to recover the elixir of youth stolen by Dr. Pill's dancing missionary (Harry Kelly). A storm carries Nemo to a cannibal isle, where his tin soldiers fend off the hungry natives. He awakes and is told he must stay in his room because he has been naughty, but King Morpheus (W. W. Black) of Slumberland appears to conduct him on more adventures. The show was opulently mounted. A red and pink "Land of Valentine" was presided over by a bevy of lovely ladies. Snow fell and wind blew through a "weather factory," where human raindrops splashed in a merry ballet. "A Boy's Dream of the Fourth of July" offered "flowery bouquets of rockets and roman candles and brilliant fire." Chorus girls in brightly colored army uniforms marched in precision. On a lighter side, Collins and Hart displayed their comic acrobatics. Joseph Cawthorn (Dr. Pill), Billy B. Van, and Harry Kelly joined forces for a comic boasting session in which each proclaimed his success as a hunter. The animals they claimed they bagged had never been seen before, or since. One described a "Peninsula," the only bird to lay square eggs, while another spoke of a creature who lives on canned meat and thereby develops such Armour and becomes so Swift that he can only be laughed to death. One night when backstage problems forced Cawthorn to stall for time he hastily invented a water-dwelling creature and described its habits of gobbling food. Cawthorn named the animal a "Whiffenpoof." Some Yale students were captivated by the name, and when they founded a singing society in the following year they named it after Cawthorn's creature.

The Boys and Betty (2 November 1908, Wallack's) was a vehicle for the exuberant Marie Cahill. She played Betty Barbeau, who runs away to Paris to escape her selfish husband. Betty sets up shop and soon is wealthy. Her husband arrives, insisting he is entitled to half her fortune. Luckily, Betty learns he has remarried. She obtains a divorce and marries the best of the boys, Paul Gerard (Edgar Atchison-Ely). George V. Hobart's book was workmanlike, as was Silvio Hein's score. But in "Marie Cahill's Arab Love Song" Hobart and Hein succeeded in giving their star a bigger applause-getter than any of the interpolations she added as a matter of course. Miss Cahill didn't monopolize the applause. Clara Palmer was called back for bows after her bizarre Oriental dance. The scenery, too, won kudos. The bright colors of a Parisian flower shop were contrasted effectively with a snow storm outside, while the last act opened "with a realistic picture of a sudden Summer shower... [and] the breaking out of a rainbow." *The Boys and Betty* stayed seventeen weeks before it embarked on a long tour.

Another Yiddish-dialect comedian was featured in **Too Many Wives** (2 November 1908, Metropolis). Joe Morris was said to be younger and better-voiced than most such fun-makers. Nonetheless he played a none-too-young uncle who decides to visit his nephew and the nephew's family. The nephew's problem is that he has lied to his uncle. He actually has no wife and baby, so he must find them—and quickly. His problem is compounded when the first girl he asks to pretend to be his wife refuses and then, after he has enlisted a second girl, reconsiders. She turns up and announces to the uncle, who has already met phony wife number one, that she is the nephew's spouse. Songs singled out included the uncle's "My Honeysuckle Baby" (sung in a combination of black and Yiddish dialects) and an octet, "Let's Make Love."

On 21 November Chicago hailed the opening of a new theatre, the Garden. The owners of the house promised it would offer pieces to compete with the La Salle and the Princess. A new musical, **A Winning Miss**, was awarded the honor of being the house's first attraction and was advertised proudly as "Made in Chicago." Harold Atteridge created the book and lyrics, while W. F. Peters composed the score. Atteridge's yarn centered upon another yacht race. But the author took a novel approach, making all his characters caricatures of figures from popular plays of the day. Thus the heroine, Mary Willington, a sometime kleptomaniac, was drawn from the heroine of *The Thief*. The novelty of Atteridge's approach failed to entertain Chicagoans. The show was a quick flop, and the owners of the theatre, going back on their word, converted the Garden into a vaudeville house.

Miss Innocence (30 November 1908, New York) was a vehicle for Ziegfeld's wife, Anna Held. Her vehicles had quickly established a mystique and pattern of their own, so that audiences buying seats for "an Anna Held show" knew they would watch a titillatingly risqué story unfold in beautiful and elaborate mountings. (While critics praised the show's beautiful costumes and scenery, none, alas, apparently described them.) The plot was trivial. Anna has been kept in a girls' school of remarkable innocence since she was three years old. She runs away to Paris with Captain Montjoy (Lawrence d'Orsay), who promises to find her parents and does, after two acts complicated by the machinations of a bogus detective (Charles A. Bigelow). Though Ludwig Englander wrote the official score, the hit of the evening was an interpolation with a typical Held title, "I

Wonder What's The Matter With My Eyes" (Harry Williams/Egbert Van Alstyne). Another long-lived tune was in the show for a while. On 20 February 1909, long after the second edition of the *Follies* had left New York, the *Dramatic Mirror* reported: "Nora Bayes and Jack Norworth of F. Ziegfeld, Jr's. Follies of 1908 company have written another new song which was introduced in *Miss Innocence* yesterday. It bears the name 'Shine On, Harvest Moon,' and was sung by Lillian Lorraine early in the first act." A Jerome Remick advertisement in the same edition of the trade paper for music from *Miss Innocence* included the song in its list. The ad makes no mention of the *Follies*. Either memories were short (the song had first been sung in the *Follies of 1908*) or, more likely, *Miss Innocence* was looked on as a more important show. But the song played no part in the evening's success. Together Miss Held and Ziegfeld delighted audiences for 176 performances.

Victor Herbert's second operetta of the season opened on the same night as *Miss Innocence*. The **Prima Donna** (30 November 1908, Knickerbocker) starred Fritzi Scheff. But if Henry Blossom (its author), Herbert, and Miss Scheff hoped for another *Mlle. Modiste* (25 December 1905), they were rudely disappointed. Blossom's libretto was straightforward enough, without vaudeville turns or horseplay, but also without any overriding merit. An auto accident strands Mlle. Athenée (Miss Scheff), prima donna of the Paris Opera, in front of a nightclub. While waiting for repairs, she consents to sing a song written by Lt. Armand, Count de Fontenne (William Raymond). He falls in love with her and, when she repulses the advances of Captain Bordenave (William K. Harcourt), agrees to renounce his fiancée and marry Athenée.

The mediocre Herbert score was even more of a letdown than the unimaginative libretto. The evening was beautifully designed, from the vitality of soldiers and grisettes at play in Montmartre to the staid elegance of a clubhouse and lawn fete. But the principal attraction remained "Fritzi Scheff stamping her little feet and showing the real Fritzi Scheff temper (stage temper, of course); Fritzi Scheff beating a long roll on a tenor drum; Fritzi Scheff in short skirts and long." But Fritzi Scheff was not enough. The piece could muster only seventy-two performances.

R. H. Burnside and Manuel Klein, of the Hippodrome, brought in the season's second entertainment designed for children on 3 December. They brought it into the Majestic, the house that had so often in the past delighted children with trips to Oz and Toyland. Now the youngsters in the audience could join the children of Hamelin and The Pied Piper (De Wolf Hopper) in the Piper's City of Innocence. Here, with Father Time (Warren Fabian) benignly overseeing matters, everything is idyllic until the chauffeur and cook of an airship (Edward Heron and Grace Cameron) steal the pipes. Of course the pipes are found by curtain time and tranquility restored. Some of Klein's music was the same being sung nightly at the Hippodrome's *Sporting Days*. But in the easy give-and-take of the day's theatrical practices no one cared. Unfortunately not enough people cared for *The Pied Piper*, either. Its fifty-two performances fell far short of the record *Sporting Days* was compiling.

An inane work called **The Queen of the Moulin Rouge** (7 December 1908, Circle) completed a twenty-week run despite some devastating notices. Its book detailed how the Princess Marotz (Flora Parker), smarting from the indifference of her betrothed, King Sacha of Orcania (Carter De Haven), goes to Paris and wins the King's affections disguised as Queen of the Moulin Rouge. Its music was no better than its book. However, the staging was zesty and sometimes pleasantly risqué. Cancans and lively "student" dances helped impel the story, while one set allowed half a dozen chorus girls to disrobe behind a gauze curtain.

Peggy Machree (21 December 1908, Broadway) called itself a "comedy with music," although its sheet music listed sixteen songs from the score. Peggy was an alias used by Lady Margaret (Adrienne Augarde) in her love affair with young Barry Trevor (Joseph O'Mara). Years pass, and Barry, now rich and renowned, falls in love with Lady Margaret, seemingly forgetting his old flame, Peggy.

Still another musical conceived as a vehicle for its star's talents arrived as 1908's last offering. **Mr. Hamlet of Broadway** (23 December 1908, Casino) found Eddie Foy portraying Joey Wheeze, a circus performer stranded with his sassy, trained bear (James F. Cook) at an Adirondacks hotel. Joey is drafted into playing the melancholy Dane when the actor who was to take the lead telegraphs the hotel that he is ill. Joey's frightened prince soliloquizes, "To flee or not to flee." It wasn't much of a plot, even by 1908 standards, but as long as Foy was on stage his followers were happy. Some of his followers may have remembered that Foy had touched on Hamlet before, singing "Hamlet Was A Melancholy Dane" in the star-crossed *Mr. Bluebeard* (21 January 1903).

Only two musicals opened in January, both on the 25th. One was *A Stubborn Cinderella*. The second was the London hit **Kitty Grey**, at the New Amsterdam, graced by some minor Jerome Kern interpolations. *Kitty Grey* used as its source *Les Fêtards*, the same play Smith had used years before to fashion *The Rounders* (12 July 1899). In the new version Kitty Grey (Julia Sanderson) is an actress who teaches a troubled wife how to keep a husband.

February also brought in two musicals. Again one was American and one English. Both were hits, although the British piece's run of 272 performances (exactly twice as many as the American piece attained) made it the second biggest hit among the regular entries. Only *Three Twins* ran longer.

The American piece, **The Fair Co-ed** (1 February 1909, Knickerbocker), had the second Gustav Luders score to be sung in New York during the season, but it was Luders without his customary collaborator, Frank Pixley. Instead the popular humorist George Ade provided the book and lyrics. Ade set his plot in his beloved Bingham College (the locale of his play *The College Widow*). His heroine, Cynthia Bright (Elsie Janis), could have been first cousin to the earlier work's Jane. Cynthia is Bingham's only co-ed, a concession to her father's importance to the school. When her father dies suddenly, it is discovered his will stipulates Cynthia must marry a Bingham graduate. It's a worrisome clause since her fiancé, Davy Dickerson (Arthur Stanford), seems certain to flunk out. But learning of the requirement he makes a determined effort to succeed. Ade's humor more than Luders's songs gave the show its vogue. But times plays havoc on humor as much as anything else, and much of the fun seems hopelessly of the period:

Old grad: Why do you fellows make such a noise?
Boys: So people can see we're college boys.
Old grad: They could tell that by your passionate socks.

One big production number found Cynthia and the chorus girls attending a military ball dressed in naval uniforms—a foretaste of the army clothes Miss Janis would one day sport as the "Sweetheart of the A.E.F."

Havana (11 February 1909, Casino), the London Gaiety Theatre hit, with music by Leslie Stuart, offered James T. Powers, who had spent the last several years clowning in English importations, as an Englishman embroiled in a Cuban revolution.

Two Hough-Adams-Howard shows opened a week apart in Chicago. **The Prince of Tonight** premiered on 9 March, **The Golden Girl** on 16 March. *The Prince of Tonight* was greeted with disappointing notices, the first such Hough, Adams, and Howard received. The notices were probably accepted grudgingly. But Howard was to receive a further blow to his ego. His song "Her Eyes Are Blue For Yale" was reprised several times each evening, in the expectation that it would be the show's hit. It wasn't. Instead audiences encored the biggest success ever to come out of a Hough-Adams-Howard show, the titular hero's "I Wonder Who's Kissing Her Now." Only a handful of insiders knew that Howard had not written the song. He had purchased the rights to the melody from its composer, Harold Orlob. Although Howard for years took both credit and royalties from the song, Orlob eventually brought him to court and won belated recognition. In Hough and Adams's story an impecunious college student, Jim Southerland (Henry Woodruff), comes to Palm Beach as a lifeguard. He falls in love with Virginia Stuart (Georgia Caine), but the young heiress spurns him. Jim learns that the nectar from a blooming century plant can turn him into a prince for a night. He courts and wins Virginia in this guise, and manages to retain her love in the morning. The production had been announced as the "second of the Princess Theatre musical comedies," clearly indicating its producers and authors had every hope of many more shows to come. It was not a failure, but its four-month run was the shortest a Hough-Adams-Howard show had received. Apart from *The Golden Girl*, it was the last the trio would ever take credit for without others being involved.

Even *The Golden Girl*, although it was generally praised, elicited critical comments that suggested Chicagoans were beginning to tire of the shows. In his review for the Chicago *Tribune*, Burns Mantle saluted the La Salle as "first of the small musical comedy playhouses in Chicago," but, he continued, "these playhouses are directed by one management, furnished with entertainment by one firm of amusement purveyors, and patronized practically by one public." The musical itself, he concluded, was "as good as anything Hough and Adams have done, which is saying much or little, depending upon your admiration of these young men—or lack of it." Hough and Adams's story for *The Golden Girl* forced Dorothy Hale to choose between two West Point cadets—a boy who had been her childhood sweetheart and

slim, suave John Fiske. A golden girl appears in a vision and persuades Dorothy to select John. The musical ran six months; its run, too, was shorter than those awarded Hough, Adams, and Howard's biggest hits. Undoubtedly a certain sameness was telling. But the growing number of vaudeville houses and, more urgently, motion picture theatres were just as assuredly exerting an unfortunate influence. Yet the malaise was balanced by a certain pride Chicago could still take in its active theatre. On 7 March, the *Tribune* ran an article headed "Chicago Best Source For Musical Comedy." The article claimed that of 100 successful touring companies crossing America, 20 were presenting Chicago musicals. The article added, "Chicago's musical comedy output has been the most successful that had gone over the circuits this year." Even if the well-rounded figures are suspiciously vague, there can be no gainsaying that the Chicago musical theatre in the last years of its heyday was still noticeably vigorous.

For the second time in the season a comic strip provided the impetus for a new musical when **The Newlyweds and Their Baby** opened at the Majestic on 22 March. It was really a vaudeville. The substituting of a dwarf named Major Knott Much for the newlyweds' baby, Napoleon, and their subsequent search to reclaim their infant was sufficient plot on which to hang a grab bag of songs, dances, and specialty acts. Aimed at a more adult audience than *Little Nemo*, it managed a five-week stay.

The season's final touring novelty, **The Promoters** (29 March 1909, Metropolis), featured Hap Ward and dealt with the search for a missing piece of diamond jewelry. It was given very short shrift, at least in Manhattan. A sad, very downbeat ending to an interesting tradition. That tradition was clearly a world apart from the ideas and ideals of mainstream musicals. It responded to the requirements of its more lowly audiences—audiences who probably came to the theatre exhausted from a ceaseless struggle to carve a meagerly comfortable niche in a harsh world. As a result, the tradition, when compared with that which governed Broadway's approach to its better-heeled patrons, was far less romantic. It rarely looked at the long ago and far away. For the most part it played out its stories in what the plumber and his girl, leaning over the balcony, could perceive of as the world just outside the theatre, their here and now. Its few royal characters were caricatures (King Go Go and the King of Lalla Pa Zaza). Anything resembling real kings, queens, princes, and princesses was all but impossible to find. In short, it was a tradition much closer to Broadway's conception of musical comedy than to operetta. Its music, designed primarily for the era's vaudeville shouters and not for operatically trained singers, rang out in conformation. But, in catering to its special clientele, it went a step further. Note how many times the principal figure was a wily tramp, deliciously and hilariously adept at besting that very hoity-toity world the audience had spent the day confronting. It was as if the shows' writers were trying to say to their lower-echelon patrons, "Look! If someone as down and out as this tramp can make good and find happiness, you certainly have an excellent chance to do so." But perhaps even such a simplistic and essentially spurious notion became too much for cheap-priced ticket-buyers. For whatever reason—was it really only price?—they deserted with stunning quickness these entertainments for still cheaper ones.

April's first two offerings were *The Beauty Spot* and a well-received revival of the 1881 success *The Mascot*, starring Raymond Hitchcock and Flora Zabelle. The month closed with the arrival of **The Candy Shop** (27 April 1909, Knickerbocker). George V. Hobart's book recorded the adventures of Jack Sweet (Leslie Gaze) after his own father accuses him of theft. Jack and his friends go to Coney Island, where Jack obtains a job as a waiter, falls in love with Hilda Noble (Maud Fulton), who turns out to be an heiress, and clears his good name in time for a happy ending. John Golden, not yet aware his real future lay in producing, wrote the words and music (assisted quietly by Henry Blossom). One novel set depicted Coney Island "with carousels, the chutes and miniature taxicabs and motors spinning across the stage." Apart from that, nothing about the evening was out of the ordinary. It played seven weeks.

May's initial musical was a failure, although many observers thought it, or at least its score, deserved a lengthier hearing. A black show, written by Bob Cole and J. Rosamond Johnson as a showcase for their own talents and those of their friends, **The Red Moon** (3 May 1909, Majestic) told how Minnehaha (Abbie Mitchell), daughter of an Indian chief and a black woman, is taken back to the reservation by her father and then returned to her mother through the contriving of Slim Brown, a bogus lawyer, and Plunk Green, a quack doctor. Cole and Johnson played Brown and Green. Whatever the faults of the claptrap book, the songs were excellent. *The Dramatic Mirror*, often especially hard on Negro

shows, admitted, "the score is often quite ambitious and always pleasing to hear." The music publisher Edward B. Marks was even more enthusiastic, insisting in his autobiography, published in 1934 after many more all-black shows had been produced, that *The Red Moon* remained "the most tuneful colored show of the century."

The Midnight Sons (22 May 1909, Broadway), a musical by Glen MacDonough and Raymond Hubbell, was brought in by Lew Fields as a summer attraction. It proved so popular it ran into 1910. Its success had little to do with its plot. Senator Constant Noyes (George A. Schiller), as he is about to leave on an African junket, informs his four playboy sons—Tom (Harry Fisher), Dick (Fritz Williams), Harry (Denman Maley), and Jack (Joseph Ratliff)—they must find steady jobs or he will disinherit them. One becomes the proprietor of a hotel, the second manages a theatre, the third launches a shoe business with the fourth as a shoe salesman. Hubbell contributed a "whistle-able" score. But what made the show was Fields's elaborate production and a fine cast, recruited in a large part from vaudeville and headed by Blanche Ring. One of her interpolations, "I've Got Rings On My Fingers (And Bells On My Toes)" (Weston and Barnes/Maurice Scott), became the outstanding hit. Miss Ring used it as long as she performed. Vernon Castle attracted attention with his "amusing disjointed dances." Fields's imaginative staging started the moment the curtain rose. The audience in the theatre found that it was staring at another audience in another theatre, "with orchestra, balcony, gallery, and boxes filled." In fact the real audience could imagine it was sitting on a stage, for a row of footlights glared at the real patrons, while performers playing to the other audience kept their backs to the paying playgoers.

Richard Carle, with some assistance from M. E. Rourke and H. L. Heartz, brought in **The Boy and the Girl** (31 May 1909, New Amsterdam). The show was a rarity in that it was one of the few Carle shows Chicago disdained. In New York, it was a twenty-four-performance flop. In neither Chicago nor New York did the major critics give a hint of the plot. What little space they expended on the entertainment was devoted to praising Marie Dressler's roughhouse antics—again, sadly, without specifics.

The New York season's final musical was the 1909 edition of the **Follies** (14 June 1909, Jardin de Paris). Although Florenz Ziegfeld and Harry B. Smith had traveled to Europe looking for fresh ideas for the revue, they confessed they returned empty-handed. The most important addition to the series was Lillian Lorraine, whom Ziegfeld had used in *Miss Innocence* (30 November 1908) and who now became the *Follies'* first incontestable dazzler. Nora Bayes returned, and Eva Tanguay appeared briefly. No major song hits came out of this edition, even though Ziegfeld interpolated "By The Light Of The Silvery Moon" for a while. "Moving Day In Jungle Town" allowed Ziegfeld to offer the first of the many jungle spectaculars the series would offer. In the second act an airship, with Lillian Lorraine at the controls, circled over the audience. The show's most memorable production number suggested each state should present the nation with a battleship (all battleships at the time were named for states), and each chorus girl was dressed to represent a state, her hat modeled after the dreadnoughts of the day. One Philadelphia paper was so thrilled it seriously suggested the nation accept Ziegfeld's scheme as a quick and easy way to enlarge the fleet.

"Strings of Chinese lanterns on the front of the building, wee Chinese children giving out programs at the door and a sturdy odor of jos sticks in the auditorium prepared the throngs" in Boston for Reginald De Koven and Edward Paulton's **The Yankee Mandarin** (14 June 1909, Majestic). Hiram Swat, an American sailor about to be drowned for misbehavior in Foo Choo, agrees to accept $10,000 to be beheaded instead of a rich mandarin, Wot Ho. Just before the sentence is carried out, the mandarin is pardoned by the emperor. But Hiram insists he is now the mandarin, and for two acts he scampers in and out of comic hashes before learning that as the new Wot Ho he must accept the original's eight battle-axe wives. Among other characters was Mrs. Lotta Chinn (Ada Lewis), a much divorced lady whose many ex-husbands have formed an alimony club. Besides Wot Ho, Chinese characters included Sing Hi, Sing Lo, Sum How, No How, and Wun Hop. Although critics extolled the production—"an extremely picturesque representation of the port of Foo Choo with a plentitude of attractively decorated pagoda architecture and junks and a profusion of signs"—as well as the cast, disillusion about De Koven had long since set in. One commentator observed discreetly, "The music was characteristic of Mr. De Koven... so sweet as almost to suggest sugar." If the operetta, which smacks suspiciously of De Koven's earlier *The Mandarin* (2 November 1896), had been planned as a tryout and not merely a Boston attraction, then it failed.

The new season confirmed the triumph of Viennese operetta and the frustration of the American Musical Theatre. Julian Edwards exemplified this frustration. He offered three scores, including the music for the season's opener, *The Motor Girl*. Nothing he contributed to the shows was especially original or distinguished, and none of the shows was an outstanding success. Edwards, like Reginald De Koven and so many other American composers of the period, was fast falling into the ranks of writers who would be remembered for one superior show—or perhaps only one song. Oddly, the songs Edwards composed this season were far less in a comic-opera vein than most of his earlier ones. As the arioso operetta took over, Edwards turned unexpectedly to lighter forms.

The Motor Girl (15 June 1909, Lyric) hoped to find success in the same world of rich men's sporting cars that served *The Vanderbilt Cup* (16 January 1906) and *The Auto Race* (25 November 1907) so well. The show almost made it. It told how Dorothy Dare (Georgia Caine) dons her brother Arthur's clothes and wins the Paris auto race after she ascertains Arthur has been villainously detained. (Note how often racing musicals had heroines named Dorothy!) Much of the action was set in Holland, allowing Adelaide Sharp to dress as a "Deutscher maid" and lead a "German" chorus not unlike several the preceding season. Elizabeth Brice had fun as a countess whose action required her to appear in various disguises. The show's twelve-week run matched that of **The Girl and the Wizard** (27 September 1909, Casino), more a "comedy with music" than a musical comedy. Besides Edwards's tunes, audiences heard interpolations by Jerome Kern and Louis Hirsch. But what the audiences had really come to hear and see were J. Hartley Manners's story and Sam Bernard. Sam Bernard didn't disappoint his followers. Manners did. His story centered on Herman Scholz, a dealer in old gems and a confirmed bachelor, who lives only for his heir, Paul (William Rosélle). When Paul announces his determination to marry, Scholz sends him away. A man who is in debt to Scholz offers the dealer his daughter, Felicitas (Flora Parker), as a wife in the hope of erasing the debt. To his surprise, Scholz accepts. But Paul returns, rich on the royalties of a gun he has invented, and claims Murietta (Kitty Gordon), the girl he wanted in the first place. Scholz gives in, and all ends happily. In this day of loosely constructed plots no one seriously objected when the gem dealer's funniest scene had him portraying a screaming stage manager endeavoring to instruct some thick-headed actors, or if there was little excuse for Kitty Gordon's parading in beautiful gowns that exposed her famous back. Edwards's third score was for **Molly May** (8 April 1910, Hackett). The show had the thinnest of story lines. Molly May (Grace LaRue) is queen of the artist's models. A letter of hers meant for old Senator Sparks (James E. Sullivan) is mistakenly thought to be for Sparks's son-in-law, Jack Willoughby (Sydney Grant). The complications that ensue are resolved by curtain time. The *Dramatic Mirror* predicted, "The book, lyric and music will add fame to no one." It made no one rich, either, running only twenty-seven times.

On the other hand, not all Viennese pieces made the grade. **The Gay Hussars** (29 July 1909, Knickerbocker) introduced Broadway to Emmerich Kalman, a name it later embraced. The operetta's plot recounted the determination of a Hussar to win back a girl who jilted him for a wealthier older man. Although the show was produced by Henry W. Savage, who had done so well by *The Merry Widow* (21 October 1907), critics complained that the work was tackily mounted and that poor voices failed to do justice to the generally appreciated score. Qualified notices and hot weather hurt. The show barely made it through five and a half weeks.

Egbert Van Alstyne and his lyricist, Harry Williams, provided the songs for two musicals, one at either end of the season. **A Broken Idol** (16 August 1909, Herald Square), with an abysmal book by the inexperienced Hal Stephens, managed forty performances. The show had originally been mounted for Chicago. A noble Englishman hires an American to teach him American ways so he can court a Yankee. But when the peer learns the young lady has lost her money he jilts her. She marries the newsman she has wanted all along. In June, **Girlies** (13 June 1910, New Amsterdam), with a better book by the more knowing George V. Hobart, offered satisfying summer entertainment and ran eleven weeks at the New Amsterdam. Summer plots tended to be more frivolous than the plots of shows meant to run through the fall, winter, and spring seasons. But in a day when frivolity didn't condemn a show, the difference between the plots of summer and winter offerings was often a matter of imperceptible degree. The degree of difference was a bit more perceptible in *Girlies*. Dr. Speil (Joseph Cawthorn) teaches botany at Hightonia Co-ed College. He courts the

directress, who insists she will marry only a hero. Speil decides he can be that hero if he can live for a time in a suit made entirely of newspapers. With his dog, Blitzen (David Abraham), he gets himself into complications that parodied then current Broadway shows. These plays included *Madame X, The Witching Hour,* and *The Spendthrift.* "Swift and lively" dances embellished the attraction. Besides his fine dialect clowning, Cawthorn won applause for his concertina playing. The evening was helped greatly by the attractive performances of Jed Prouty, Ernest Truex, and Maude Raymond.

The same night as *A Broken Idol* opened, **The Cohan and Harris Minstrels** made their promised return. The entertainment included beloved old songs of the minstrel era such as "Down Where The Watermelons Grow" and "The Rose Of Killarney." Clog dances and "an old-fashioned breakdown" were offered as part of "Scenes from Blackville." A contingent of blackfaced soldiers marched in front of a drop depicting lighted battleships at sea. For two weeks tambourines jingled and end men joked at the New York, but this was virtually the last time a traditional minstrel show played the heartland of Broadway. The minstrel show era was over.

But blackface acts were far from finished. Two weeks later McIntyre and Heath, probably the most popular blackface duo of the day, presented their new vehicle **In Hayti** (30 August 1909, Circle). Both J. J. McNally's book and William Jerome and Jean Schwartz's songs were conventional. Heath portrayed Jasper Johnson, an ambitious wheeler-dealer, determined to make his pliable buddy Geronimo Jobbs (McIntyre) president of the island republic. The production displayed the homey, down-on-the farm ambience blackface shows customarily affected. Chorus girls dressed as roosters sang about "Chicken," while McIntyre and Heath carried two chickens on and off throughout the evening as pets. The show played seven weeks and toured.

Savage failed again with his second Viennese offering of the season, Edmund Eysler's **The Love Cure** (1 September 1909, New Amsterdam), the first of September's six musicals. Opera lovers knew a similar plot had been used in *La Traviata.* However, in the operetta the heroine is an actress, not a courtesan. Still, she disillusions her lover at his father's moving request. Eysler was no Verdi; *The Love Cure* ran less than five weeks.

The annual Hippodrome offering arrived on 4 September, and, as was so often the case with the great house's simple-minded spectacles, it tallied far more performances than any other musical during the season. Although part of the evening was devoted to a voyage *Inside the Earth* and to a *Ballet of the Jewels*, the principal portion was **A Trip to Japan.** R. H. Burnside called his extravaganza a "melodrama with music," but what little drama there was served solely as a frame for the stunning effects. These effects included a large steamship sailing out of port, a "Feast of [Japanese] Lanterns," and two waterfalls, one on each side of the stage, cascading down bathed in "prismatic lights." The story reflected the thinking of a world that viewed war as more glorious and romantic than ominous. It recounted how the Japanese hire a circus to disguise their shipments of submarines back to their homeland.

The next two Monday evenings witnessed the openings of the two Viennese operettas that, following on the phenomenal success of *The Merry Widow* (21 October 1907), established the hegemony of this mode through the next several seasons. The first of the pair was Leo Fall's **The Dollar Princess** (6 September 1909, Knickerbocker). Operettas are so much of their period they are frequently thought of as having been born old-fashioned. In their time the best were in every way the last word. *The Dollar Princess* was set in the business world of its day—the opening number saluting the modern "typewriter girls." So determined were its authors to suggest the story was as new as the century, they eschewed a Graustarkian setting, placing their taming-of-the-shrew tale in the United States. Valli Valli sang the title role, but Donald Brian garnered the best notices on the strength of his charm and his light footwork. Leo Fall's score was lovely, but it has not retained the affection of Americans in the way the second offering's songs have. That next entry was **The Chocolate Soldier** (13 September 1909, Lyric). It softened the antiwar satire of its source, Shaw's *Arms and the Man*, but its story of a warrior who prefers eating chocolates to fighting was still a refreshing change from the rampant militarism of the day. Ida Brooks Hunt and J. E. Gardner sang the romantic leads, while William Pruette supplied the comedy in his role as Popoff. Oscar Straus's marvelous songs, notably "My Hero," remain standards. Excepting the Hippodrome spectacle, the two shows were the runaway hits of the season, *The Dollar Princess* compiling 288 performances, *The Chocolate Soldier*, 296.

The next Monday ushered in the promised revision of the preceding year's *Algeria* (31 August 1908), rechristened **The Rose of Algeria** (20 September 1909, Herald Square). Frank Pollock replaced George Leon Moore as De Lome, and since the original Zoradie, Ida Brooks Hunt, and the original first comedian, William Pruette, were busy with *The Chocolate Soldier*, Lillian Herlein and Eugene Cowles assumed their roles. Youthful Anna Wheaton drew attention to herself as Mrs. Cooings. The revisions were not as drastic as many critics felt necessary. Disappointment in the absence of significant changes cut sharply into its ticket sales, as did the striking success of the other new arrivals. The work added just forty performances to its record.

The last Monday in September saw the premiere of Edwards's *The Girl and the Wizard.*.

October's only musical was **The Man Who Owns Broadway** (11 October 1909, New York), George M. Cohan's lyrical version of his own straight-play failure, *Popularity*. Although he changed the names of its main characters, Cohan retained the original story line of a brash but well-liked young actor (in this musical version, a musical comedy star) who overrides intrigue and backbiting to win a rich man's daughter. (More than one critic saw something autobiographical in the hero, Sydney Lyons.) Cohan also retained two stunning effects he had used in his original. Cohan exposed the actual brick wall at the rear of the stage to give the audience an authentic backstage feeling. Furthermore he goaded his audience into playing the make-believe audience that applauds so insistently Lyons is induced to make a curtain speech. It was a well-written, jargony book, in which Cohan was not above spoofing theatrical conventions ("My boy, the villains are never handcuffed until 11:00") and boosting his favorite song-and-dance man ("I'll stick to musical comedy as long as George Cohan will write them for me"). Cohan's lyrics were as natural and idiomatic as his dialogue, now and then disclosing the sort of impudent rhyming wit Broadway rarely heard before Ira Gershwin, Cole Porter, or Lorenz Hart. In "I'm All O.K. With K. And E." Lyons bets "two bits" that he'll "paralyze the Shuberts." Cohan's music was filled with pleasantries, lacking only that something extra that pulsated through his earlier hits. The personable Raymond Hitchcock portrayed Lyons. Hitchcock could not approach Cohan in dancing agility, but he did successfully execute a soft shoe. Cohan saw to it the chorus compensated for his absence with its lively stepping. *The Man Who Owns Broadway*, for which Cohan retained a warm spot the rest of his life, ran 128 performances and enjoyed a long tour.

Two musicals opened in Chicago in October. One, **The Kissing Girl**, was an immediate failure even though it had a book by Stanislaus Stange, lyrics by Vincent Bryan, and music by Harry Von Tilzer. A misconstrued kiss was the source of the evening's complications. The show opened on 25 October and left two weeks later. **They Loved a Lassie** opened on the 31st and fared better. The work had music by Benjamin Hapgood Burt and a book by George Arliss. In Arliss's tale two married men on a business trip find their footsteps dogged by an old flame both had once loved. Troubles arise when the men's wives appear on the scene. At the end of its run at the Whitney Opera House, the show listed its post-Chicago itinerary in its advertisements. The ads revealed the tour would take it to towns such as Burlington and Muscatine, Iowa.

The Flirting Princess premiered at Chicago's Princess Theatre on 1 November. Although the show was billed as an "Adams-Hough-Howard Musical," Harold Orlob was publicly acknowledged to have written nearly half the score. The intrusion of a fourth figure into the established trio was a major change, but it was not the only one. The *Tribune's* new drama critic, Percy Hammond, noted that the librettists had "departed from their usual formula." There was no "hefty romance... no dreams, little slang." Hammond concluded the musical was "a sort of review, but a blunt review." If the critic could be unstinting in his praise of anything about the show it was the physical production. He insisted Singer was superior to Ziegfeld. Hough and Adams's plot was, indeed, slight. Princess Klioh of Egypt (Violet Dare) comes to America for a good time. She flirts with every handsome young man she meets, but finally succumbs to the charms of Jack Stuart (Harry Pilcer). (A Virginia Stuart was the heroine of *The Prince of Tonight*.)

On 1 November there were competing openings in New York: **The Silver Star** with Adelaide Genee at the New Amsterdam; **Mr. Lode of Koal** with Bert Williams at the less centrally located Majestic. For *The Silver Star* Harry B. Smith sketched out something to pass for a plot, and a dozen hands contributed to manufacture a score. But it was Genee's dancing and Klaw and Erlanger's spectacle that drew the crowds. Genee danced in a military outfit, waving an American flag, and flitted under an iridescent grape arbor dressed as the "spirit of Champagne." The show never approached the popularity of *The Soul Kiss*, but it kept the New Amsterdam lit ten weeks.

Uptown at Columbus Circle Bert Williams, alone after paresis incapacitated George Walker,

could keep *Mr. Lode of Koal* on the boards only half as long. Its plot was the sort of delicious minstrel nonsense Williams reveled in. Mr. Lode dreams he has been shipwrecked on an island. Revolutionists have kidnapped the real king, Big Smoke (Matt Housley), and since an old island legend promises a great ruler will one day come from the sea, Mr. Lode finds himself a reluctant king. He spends most of the remaining three acts futilely renouncing his throne and planning foredoomed escapes from the island. Just before curtain time Big Smoke returns, and Mr. Lode finds freedom by casting his lot with the audience. The best Negro talents of the day provided the material—J. A. Shipp, Alex Rogers, Rosamond Johnson, and Williams himself—but they provided nothing of lasting worth. Williams was responsible for what little appeal the show had. With this show he began to develop the droll monologues he used for the rest of his career.

The London success **The Belle of Brittany** (8 November 1909, Daly's) fared no better, achieving the same forty-performance run as *Mr. Lode of Koal*. In that short while audiences watched a marquis lose his estate to a miller, only to see it come back into his family after the miller's daughter marries the marquis's son.

Lew Fields and Victor Herbert, who collaborated so successfully to make a long-run delight of *It Happened in Nordland* (5 December 1904), tried again with **Old Dutch** (22 November 1909, Herald Square). Glen MacDonough was replaced by Edgar Smith, who adapted the libretto from a German comedy, and by George V. Hobart, who created the lyrics. Ludwig "Old Dutch" Streusand (Fields) flees to the Tyrol with his daughter, Lisa (Alice Dovey), to escape the attentions heaped on him after he becomes a successful inventor. He registers under the name of Leopold Mueller. While butterfly hunting he loses his wallet, with all his money and identification. A real Leopold Mueller (John E. Henshaw) discovers it, pretends he is Streusand, and basks in reflected glory, while Ludwig and Lisa do menial chores to pay their bill. The book was competent at best and Herbert's music no better. One joyous moment came early in the first act. Liza and her love interest, Alfred (William Raymond), sang a simple duet, "U, Dearie." When they finished, two ingratiating little tots solemnly pantomimed the lovers' movements, earning more encores for their bit than did the principals for theirs. The little boy mime disappeared from stage history; the little girl mime did not. Her name was Helen Hayes.

Even Fields's fine production and clowning could not rescue the evening from the doldrums. The best that could be said for *Old Dutch* was that it gave a helping hand to a group of young performers such as Miss Dovey, Miss Hayes, and Vernon Castle.

Harry B. Smith and Raymond Hubbell suffered a humiliating failure when **The Air King** opened at Chicago's Colonial Theatre on 28 November, received scathing notices, and was promptly withdrawn. Whether the show had its eye on New York is moot. Had it succeeded it would have popularized a story much like that employed by *The Aviator* and its musicalization *Going Up!* (25 December 1917) nearly a decade later. Willy Ketchum (John Slavin) is a bellhop in Atlantic City. When a famous pilot fails to appear for a meet, Willy takes his place, although he has never flown before. Josephine Hall was featured as a character called Minerva Shine.

Exactly a month after Fields opened at the Herald Square, Weber's relit with Hough-Adams-Howard's **The Goddess of Liberty**. The date was 22 December, making it 1909's last musical. The plot recalled *A Broken Idol*. Jack Wingate (Edward Abeles), an Englishman living from hand to mouth in America, comes into a title but no money. He decides to marry a rich, social-climbing American, Hope Butterworth (Frances Demarest). After the engagement he falls in love with Hope's cousin, Phyllis Crane (May De Sousa), and she with him. He sends a telegram announcing his brother has not died and is still lord. Hope breaks the engagement, allowing Jack and Phyllis to go off together. It was another Hough-Adams-Howard Chicago hit that found no favor in New York. Manhattan critics not only panned the writing, they came down heavily on the production, assailing what they felt were bad English accents (was Chicago trying to ridicule even English accents?) and deploring a wrestling match that "wasn't even a good fake." *The Goddess of Liberty* survived twenty-nine performances.

Nora Bayes abandoned the *Follies* and returned to New York in **The Jolly Bachelors** (6 January 1910, Broadway), a musical produced by Lew Fields with book and lyrics by Glen MacDonough and music by Raymond Hubbell. The book was claptrap and Hubbell's score a pleasant mediocrity. In the play Miss Bayes became Miss Vandergould, an heiress who takes a job as a cashier in a drugstore. There she hopes to find romance among the less effete men of the middle class. When she mistakenly gives a customer the wrong medicine, she and her beau scour the town to retrieve it. Their search takes

them to a college campus (where Jack Norworth led students in a medley of college songs) and onto an ocean liner. The show's principal attractions were its fast pace and spectacular staging (including an airship sailing through the clouds), Miss Bayes, her excellent supporting cast, and one unforgettable interpolation, "Has Anybody Here Seen Kelly?" (C. W. Murphy and Will Letters). The *Times* critic also called attention to the tastefulness of the drugstore set, done in various shades of brown instead of the gaudy rainbow of colors so common to the time. The set provided an attractive backdrop as Robert L. Dailey led twenty chorus boys in Ned Wayburn's clog dance for "We'uns From Dixie" and as Stella Mayhew sang Irving Berlin's "Stop Dat Rag."

Four nights later, 10 January, **The Old Town** began a run of 171 performances at the brand-new Globe Theatre. The *Dramatic Mirror* put its finger on the reason for the show's success: "The new musical scored a decided hit due less to the librettist and the composer than to the two comedians." The librettist was George Ade, the composer was Gustav Luders; the two comedians were Dave Montgomery and Fred Stone. Montgomery and Stone played two stranded circus performers, Henry Clay Baxter (Stone) and Archibald Hawkins (Montgomery), who encounter their old sweethearts, Caroline (Flo Hengler) and Diana (Mae Hengler). The girls' upstart Aunt Ernestine (Allene Crater) would have them marry "better" people. Ernestine's consternation is compounded when she discovers Baxter's father was a pirate. The boys find the pirate's loot, but Ernestine confiscates it and has them driven out of town. In California they help the girls' uncle (Claude Gillingwater) get elected senator. He rewards them with the girls and the treasure. The typescript reveals how flexible and compliant an established writer such as Ade felt he had to be when writing a vehicle for special stars. Montgomery and Stone's first entrance was to be a song called "Electric Signs." In the spot where the song would go Ade wrote, "as many verses as needed, all describing what happens to boys reared in the country towns when they get among the electric signs. Refrain music will lend itself to dance if the two wish to dance this early in the game... ." Stone did elect to dance later in the evening, jumping in and out of a lariat as he pranced. He also displayed his agility on a tightrope. Charles Dillingham was Ziegfeld's closest rival in taste and prodigality, so *The Old Town* was magnificently mounted. A remarkably beautiful chorus line paraded before Homer Emens's "exceedingly lovely back drop... with a far reach of glowing California landscape." The smaller, livelier "ponies" danced in kilts and played bagpipes, staged a precision drill dressed in sky-blue, and marched in tri-colors as suffragettes.

The King of Cadonia (10 January 1910, Daly's) was imported from England the same night as *The Old Town* opened. It had a book by Frederick Lonsdale, who later wrote a number of good plays. His story followed a king as he goes in disguise among his people to see how they really live and what they really think of him. Marguerite Clark, William Norris, and Robert Dempster played the leads. The show boasted several Jerome Kern interpolations. But New York was not interested, and it was withdrawn after two weeks.

The Prince of Bohemia (13 January 1910, Hackett), an American original, did little better, managing only two and a half weeks. Its book was by J. Hartley Manners, who had been represented earlier by *The Girl and the Wizard*, and who, like Lonsdale, later wrote successful straight plays. The story was elementary. Dick Conyers (Andrew Mack), rejected by his sweetheart's father, follows the girl and her parents to Europe, where, disguised as an Irish servant, he eventually wins the father's approval. Christie MacDonald sang the sweetheart. The score was the first of three offered by A. Baldwin Sloane in the last half of the season. The disdain in which Sloane was held by the rest of the profession was reflected in a comment of the *Dramatic Mirror*'s reviewer: "[A] waltz number of superior texture which Mr. Baldwin Sloane presumably did not compose... stands out in bold relief against the medley of airs borrowed from Tosti and a dozen others which forms... Mr. Sloane's musical contributions." Sloane's second score was for **Tillie's Nightmare** (5 May 1910, Herald Square). Like Lew Fields's earlier productions—*About Town* (30 August 1906), *The Girl Behind the Counter* (10 January 1907), *The Midnight Sons* (22 May 1909), *The Jolly Bachelors* (6 January 1910)—it was really a high-class vaudeville, enhanced with spectacular effects and held together by a flimsy story line. In this case, Tillie Blobbs, a drudge in her mother's boardinghouse, dreams of marvelous things that could happen to her: a rich marriage, a yacht trip, an "aeroplane" ride. But it's all a dream. Out of Sloane's score came the single song that promised to give him a classic, "Heaven Will Protect The Working Girl." But the song's vogue died with the advent of better conditions for the working girl. Marie Dressler sang the song at the very beginning of the evening, accompanying herself with a comic lack of ability on the piano. She also had a hilarious scene on the yacht, tying on a jag as she attempted to assuage her seasickness with a magnum of champagne. Footwork by the "Original English Dancing Girls" enlivened the evening. Sloane's third score was heard in **The Summer Widowers** (4 June 1910, Broadway), with which Fields hoped to repeat the popularity of the preceding season's *The Midnight Sons*. He almost did. It ran through the summer into the fall. Again it was another superior vaudeville with such sensational scenes as an entire apartment house with all its apartments, on several floors, revealed at once. If *The Jolly Bachelors* had a noteworthy airship scene, *The Summer Widowers* sent miniature airplanes buzzing over the audience's heads. The show's lighter-than-air plot recorded the misunderstandings that arise when a prima donna throws an innocent party for some men whose wives are away on vacation. Fields filled the cast with favorites from *Old Dutch* and his other shows: Maude Lambert, Alice Dovey, Vernon Castle, Ada Lewis, little Helen Hayes, and Fields himself. But Sloane's score added nothing of importance to the entertainment.

The lone English offering to win favor during the season was **The Arcadians** (17 January 1910, Liberty), with its delightful Lionel Monckton and Howard Talbot score and its disarmingly fantastic story of unavailing efforts by denizens of Utopian Arcady to teach the English their ways. Frank Moulan starred. The work played through the spring.

The latest Chauncey Olcott vehicle, **Ragged Robin** (24 January 1910, Academy of Music) had a book by Rida Johnson Young and Rita Olcott, and songs from various hands. Disinherited through the trickery of his stepbrother, Robert Darcy becomes Ragged Robin. His stepbrother also weds Robert's sweetheart and squanders her family's money. Only after the stepbrother's death can Robert marry his beloved. At the same time, he learns his father has changed his will again, and he will be rich. The songs were unexceptional.

January's last musical, **The Young Turk** (31 January 1910, New York), was a four-week failure. With inane dialogue it told how a banker named Oxenham steals the sultan's jewels and then dies, leaving a will stipulating that his wife must marry his partner, Howe Swift, Sr. But Mrs. Oxenham becomes engaged to Swift's son, while her young daughter is betrothed to the senior Smith. In the end the jewels are returned and the couples paired off more appropriately. The music of Max Hoffman, who had provided many of the songs for the old Rogers Brothers burlesques, was only a notch or two above the libretto. Max, the surviving Rogers brother starred, but Maud Raymond—singing, dancing, giving imitations, and burlesquing grand-opera mannerisms—stole the show.

On 31 January Chicago's Princess Theatre raised its curtain on what proved to be the last of the musicals Hough, Adams, and Howard wrote together, **Miss Nobody from Starland**. As he had in *The Prince of Tonight* and *The Flirting Princess*, Howard permitted songs by other composers to be inserted, and when the show underwent revision during its ninth week he allowed additional interpolations. Hough and Adams's plot was as slight and loosely constructed as their last one had been. A chorus girl who dabbles in smuggling falls in with a pharmacist who is fleeing a charge of murder after he misfills a prescription. They wind up as performers in a Princess Theatre show. Bessie Wynn and Ralph Herz played the leads. *Miss Nobody from Starland* was no failure. No show by Hough, Adams, and Howard ever was. But it ran only fifteen weeks, a short run as the series went. An increasingly critical climate, competition from other shows and other art forms, and possibly some backstage quarrel wrote "finis" to the partnership.

Blanche Ring and her interpolations accounted for much of the success of **The Yankee Girl** (10 February 1910, Herald Square). Silvio Hein's music and George V. Hobart's book and lyrics had a certain professional competency, but little else. The demand for their services can be explained largely by their dependability. Both were more prolific than talented. The more demanding critics dismissed Hein much as they dismissed Sloane, "All the one-finger composers of musical comedies, since the halcyon days of Lederer, have grounds for action for petit larceny against Silvio Hein." There were equally unkind words for Hobart, "The book shares with the music the dullness of exhausted themes." Hobart's plot was slight. With the aid of her father (William Graham), his secretary, and the American consul, Jessie Gordon foils a series of villainous intrigues to deprive her father of his concession in Brilliatina. The villains include Brilliatina's President Castroaba (William Burress) and a Japanese called Oyama (Frederick Paulding). (Oyama remained a popular stage name for Japanese over the years. It was used as late as *La, La, Lucille* in 1919) Impressed by Jessie's maneuvers, the consul proposes and is accepted. Miss Ring carried the show, and three of her interpolations were extremely profitable: "I've Got Rings On My Fingers" (brought over from *The Midnight Sons*), "Nora Malone" (Junie McCree/Albert Von Tilzer), and "The Glory Of The Yankee Navy" (Kenneth Clark/John Philip Sousa). *The Yankee Girl* had a successful pre-Broadway tour. It played New York for twelve weeks, then continued a cross-country trek.

February's other musical was **Bright Eyes** (28 February 1910, New York). Chicago's favorites, Cecil Lean and Florence Holbrook, were starred. The show was a bitter disappointment for Dickson, Hauerbach, and Hoschna, who had hoped to repeat the success of *Three Twins* (15 June 1908). The book was based on Grant Stewart's 1906 flop, *Mistakes Will Happen*, in which Dickson had played the lead. Dickson related a backstage yarn of an actress and a playwright who lose their jobs when their secret marriage is exposed. The two set about finding an angel to back a new show the husband has written, only to discover their rich supporter is the puritanical head of a ladies' seminary. His carefree wife helps extricate the young couple from their entanglement. Karl Hoschna's score was pleasant, especially the title song—though several critics complained the song was overplayed. But *Bright Eyes* ran a mere forty performances, a far cry from the long run of *Three Twins*.

No musical appeared in March. But an odd history began late that month in Chicago. On the 28th a farce called **My Cinderella Girl** opened to mixed notices at the Whitney. Business was not encouraging, so librettist Harold Atteridge and composer William Frederick Peters were rushed in to convert the straight play to a musical comedy. Probably to many people's surprise, they succeeded (on 2 May) handsomely. Thus, for the second time in five years, Chicago had a well-liked musical about baseball—a musical advertised as "A Home Run Hit." From the start the story centered on the rivalry of two small colleges and their baseball teams. The young hero's father is opposed to academic sports, forcing the hero and his buddies to create several acts of complications and disguises before he can hit his bases-loaded home run (with home plate seen through the open doors of the team's training quarters) to win the game and his girl. At least one critic asked why the show was given its somewhat inappropriate title. No matter. It delighted Chicago for nearly five months.

A party of American tourists are aboard the *S. S. Pegasus* when the ship is battered by a violent storm. Neptune (Harrison Brockbank) appears and takes the Americans to Olympus, where "a very devil of a sport," Ruben Smith (John Slavin), flirts with Venus (Hazel Cox) and tries to elope with Juno (Clarice Vance). This was the plot of **A Skylark**, which followed *Bright Eyes* into the New York on 4 April. A magnificent production offered "a beauty chorus such as is rarely seen" in gorgeous gowns and a scene change in which "shimmering gold and silver suddenly dissolves to reveal melting clouds of pinks and heliotropes and blues." Although the show was courteously received, including its score by the otherwise unheard-of Frank Dossert, it failed to catch on.

Four nights later Edwards's *Molly May* began its stay.

The beloved De Wolf Hopper closed out April with a "song play" based loosely on Molière's *Un Médecin malgré lui*. Medford Griffin, once **A Matinee Idol** (28 April 1910, Daly's) but now down on his luck, comes to a boarding school expecting to be a teacher, finds the position filled, and so claims to be a physician. His first case is the headmaster's son, Dick (Joseph Santley), who is pretending to be ill to avoid being separated from his sweetheart. Griffin handles the situation sympathetically and learns his long-lost flame is Dick's aunt. The show was clean family entertainment, something De Wolf Hopper's fans knew his presence assured. Hopper now and then stopped to talk with his audience, at one point confessing to feeling strange appearing in contemporary instead of period clothes. The much-married comedian didn't have to say a word to grab the biggest laugh of the evening by simply staring in dumb amazement at a young man who asked him if he knew what true love meant. Silvio Hein's score was merely another collection of undistinguished melodies. Hopper drew enough crowds to keep Daly's lit for sixty-eight performances.

Three musicals opened in May. *Tillie's Nightmare* came on 5 May; the other two competed for attention on the 30th. **The Merry Whirl**, a musical play verging on burlesque, gave the New York Theatre its fourth dud in a row, but at the Casino an all-star revival of *The Mikado* (Fritzi Scheff was Yum-Yum; Andrew Mack, Nanki-Poo; and Jefferson De Angelis, Ko-Ko) was well received and found public support.

The Summer Widowers and *Girlies* both arrived before the middle of June to end the season.

1910–1911

All three of the season's outstanding new American hits were operettas, regardless of what their authors called them. While all three added luster to the roster of great American musicals, not one had an American-born composer: Karl Hoschna was Bohemian; Ivan Caryll a Belgian with long experience in France and England; and Victor Herbert an Irishman. Hoschna and Caryll's score sounded thoroughly Viennese, while *Naughty Marietta*, if not Viennese, was distinctly in the grand European tradition. But all through the theatrical year there were hints of more American innovations to come.

Florenz Ziegfeld's **Follies of 1910** opened the season on 20 June. The *Follies* were easing into a definitive pattern. They were also improving with each edition. Two newcomers were the major improvement this year—Fanny Brice and Bert Williams, probably the two finest performers Ziegfeld ever presented. Both had an almost incredible range, from hilarious ethnic travesty to broad human pathos. For Williams the debut signaled the acceptances of a major black artist in an important, otherwise white musical. Williams's numbers in his debut included "You're Gwine To Get Something What You Don't Expect," "That Minor Strain," and "I'll Lend You Everything I've Got Except My Wife" (Jean Havez/Harry Von Tilzer). In this last tune Williams made a generous offer to lend his audience anything he owned except his wife. After a pause he confided, "I'll make you a present of her."

Miss Brice went into dialect to introduce "Goodbye Becky Cohen" by another Follies first timer, Irving Berlin, and stopped the show with a ragtime love song, "Lovie Joe" (Will Marion Cook/Joe Jordan). She is said to have received twelve encores on opening night. A rash of encores was commonplace at the time, but for once they were undoubtedly a spontaneous joy rather than a forced nuisance. The Ziegfeld beauties were there, too. Anna Held appeared briefly as a comet. Her appearance was all the more remarkable in that she herself was far away. Ziegfeld had filmed the entire sequence. Lillian Lorraine, flanked by some of Ziegfeld's loveliest girls, all on flower-bedecked swings, won applause with "Swing Me High—Swing Me Low" (Ballard MacDonald/Victor Hollaender).

FANNY BRICE was born in the great melting pot of New York's Lower East Side on 29 October 1891, the daughter of saloon-keepers Charles and Rose Borach. Her first performances were warbling for pennies in her parents' saloon. At thirteen she won the amateur night contest at Keeney's Theatre in Brooklyn singing "When You're Not Forgotten By The Girl You Can't Forget." Three years later she was hired for the chorus of *The Talk of New York*, but she was fired by George M. Cohan while the show was still in rehearsal. Most students agree Cohan fired her because she couldn't dance, although a few writers have insisted her clownish antics cost her her job. She took work as a comic on the flourishing burlesque circuit, where Irving Berlin spotted her and gave her "Sadie Salome" to sing. It was her comic rendition of this song, sung in a Yiddish accent, that called her to Ziegfeld's attention. At this early date in her Career she spelled her first name "Fannie," but in time she changed it and thereafter retained the new spelling.

Ziegfeld may have derived a special pleasure from mounting **The Girl in the Kimono** at Chicago's Ziegfeld Theatre five nights after he had unveiled his latest *Follies* in New York. The show had lyrics by Harold Atteridge and music by Phil Schwartz. In Helen Bagg's book a bride clad only in a kimono is locked out of her suite and forced to spend the night with a bachelor neighbor. But Ziegfeld's pleasure must have been dampened by the disheartening notices. He quickly closed the production.

July's sole entry was **Up and Down Broadway** (18 July 1910, Casino), a revue that insisted on calling itself a musical comedy. There was a thin plot, since most contemporary revues had them. Apollo and the other gods have come to New York vowing to reform theatrical taste. Their janitor, Momus, tags along for laughs. In the end the gods conclude Broadway knows more about good entertainment than they do. Eddie Foy as Momus led an excellent cast which included two young composers, Irving Berlin and Ted Snyder, singing their own interpolations, "Sweet Italian Love" and "Oh, That Beautiful Rag." The principal score was by Jean Schwartz, and

from it emerged one hardy perennial, "Chinatown, My Chinatown," interpolated after the show opened to replace another Chinatown number, and sung by Ernest Hare (as a police officer) with the chorus. The show ran into the fall.

Young Deems Taylor tried his luck on Broadway, writing the score for **The Echo** (17 August 1910, Globe). He quickly learned his calling lay elsewhere. William Le Baron's plot was standard musical comedy nonsense. Kate (Bessie McCoy), head-waitress at the Echo House, loves a boarder, Reggie (Joseph Herbert, Jr.). But Reggie's rich, widowed mother (Evelyn Carrington) disapproves. Kate and Reggie catch Mama and a German soap manufacturer (John E. Hazzard) in a loving embrace and confront them with a photograph of the scene. Mama gives her consent. The show was most entertaining when it got to its feet. Dancing ranged from "old-fashioned clog to the latest Russian craze." Miss McCoy romped through a "French Fandango" and then led the "pony" chorus in a drummer routine which reminded the *Times* of her dance to "The Yama Yama Man." To bolster Taylor's fledgling score a large number of interpolations were added, including songs by Nat D. Ayer, John Golden, Karl Hoschna, and Jerome Kern. But *The Echo*, which opened on 17 August, barely made it into October.

Chicago's two leading musical houses, the Princess and the La Salle, both had new musicals ready for their patrons in August. The Princess began the season on the 21st with **The Wife Tamers.** Its libretto and lyrics were by Oliver Herford and James Clarence Harvey; its music by R. H. Bowers. The plot revolved around the illusions two wives insist on retaining about their husbands' pasts. The naughty husband is imagined to have been a saint, while the good one is perceived as having been a devil. Claudine, an attractive milliner, comes on the scene and sets the record straight. *The Wife Tamers* received generally warm notices, but for some reason Chicagoans were not attracted to it. It went down on the records as a failure. On the other hand, **The Sweetest Girl in Paris,** which opened at the La Salle on 29 August, was an immediate success with both the press and the public. Addison Burkhardt did the book, Collin Davis the lyrics, and Joe Howard the music. The sweet young miss in Paris is a girl with a nervous twitch that passes for a come-hither look. She rejects a number of Americans before accepting a waiter in a café. He turns out to be a Pittsburgh millionaire. Burkhardt's dialogue was run-of-the-mill for the day. When a lady complains, "This noisy bustle annoys me," her escort responds, "Then why don't you take it off!" But the show's star, Trixie Friganza, and the staging and famous chorus line of Gus Sohlke helped keep the show at the La Salle into the new year.

In New York August's final two musical offerings appeared at the very end of the month. On the 29th a London hit, Ivan Caryll and Lionel Monckton's **Our Miss Gibbs**, augmented with a number of Kern interpolations, began a two-month run at the Knickerbocker. Miss Gibbs was another in a long line of London shopgirls.

Madame Sherry (30 August 1910, New Amsterdam) was the first of the season's three triumphs for the American Musical Theatre. Its success more than confirmed the promise of Otto Hauerbach and Karl Hoschna's *Three Twins* (15 June 1908). For some curious reason the show was called a "French Vaudeville," even though it had a book—and a good one—as well as an irresistible score. Of course, Hauerbach based his work on Maurice Ordonneau's *Madame Sherry*. But Hauerbach made numerous changes in the story, while Hoschna's totally new score was far superior to the scores employed in London, Paris, and Brussels some years earlier. Edward Sherry's eccentric Uncle Theophilus (Ralph Herz), "a millionaire connoisseur of Greek Art," has set up his playboy nephew as head of The Sherry School of Aesthetic Dancing. Its pupils, all attired like young Isadora Duncans, are reminded of a basic rule of "aesthetic" dancing by their teacher Lulu (Frances Demarest), who is also Edward's sweetheart. She insists "Every Little Movement (Has A Meaning All Its Own)." Edward (Jack Gardner) arrives, upset that "Theophilus," on top of all his other demands, keeps insisting Edward write him about Edward's supposed family. Edward admits he is in no position to refuse:

Lulu: And your Uncle Theophilus has never suspected that he has been fooled?
Sherry: Never! In his letters he never fails to mention my dear wife Eusebia, my dear son Epaminondas and my daughter Scholastica.
Lulu: What crazy names!
Sherry: Chosen by Uncle!
Lulu: And you get money for every child that's born?
Sherry: Exactly.
Lulu: If I'd been you, I'd have had a whole family.
Sherry: It's bad enough to keep track of the two he *thinks* I've got.

Lulu: But aren't you afraid that some day your uncle may take it into his head to pay you a visit?
Sherry: No danger. For the last twenty-five years he has been digging around in the ruins of Greece for the lost arms of Venus de Milo. Seems to have been the only arms he ever really cared for.

When Leonard Gomez (John Reinhard), the son of Venezuela's president, visits the school, Lulu repeats her instructions for him. But it is obvious "Every Little Movement" begins to have new meanings for the two of them. A third arrival is Yvonne (Lina Abarbanell). She is Theophilus's niece and has come to New York fresh from a convent school. She is intrigued by the glitter of the big city and would like to partake of it all, but "Uncle Says I Mustn't, So I Won't." Still, she is not above comparing herself to "The Butterfly" about to emerge in all its finery. When Theophilus unexpectedly appears, Edward brazenly presents his housekeeper, Catherine (Elizabeth Murray), as his wife and two pupils as his children. Theophilus joyously assures them (and Lulu and Leonard) there is nothing like a wife's smile—"The Smile She Means For You." Soon Yvonne and Edward are left alone. Dancing together to the strains of "Every Little Movement," they, too, begin to fall in love. Theophilus has invited everyone to take a trip on his yacht, named for Yvonne. His motives are not completely selfless. From the start he has been skeptical of Edward's announced family. Catherine sings of a jilted bride begging for love ("Won't Someone Take Me Home"), while her real husband, Phillippe, tells Yvonne it is no good to teach a young girl the ways of the world, for when she learns them she runs off with "The Other Fellow." Tasting the good life makes Yvonne giddy, though she insists, "I'm All Right." But then Edward kisses her and she cannot deny "The Birth Of Passion." Theophilus jolts his guests with an announcement. They will not return to land until he has discovered what everyone's real relationship to everyone else is. By the time he learns, the relationships have changed from what they were when Edward first lied to him. Catherine and Phillippe admit they are married, Lulu and Leonard agree they will wed, and Theophilus happily consents to Edward's making Yvonne the true Madame Sherry.

Besides his marvelous book, Hauerbach gave Hoschna better than average lyrics. The words for "The Smile She Means For You" are remarkably similar to those of "Smiles" a few years later.

During the run comedienne Elizabeth Murray, who was praised for a drunk scene that never became offensive, was allowed to introduce several interpolations, the most famous of which was "Put Your Arms Around Me, Honey" (Junie McCree/ Albert Von Tilzer). Because the songs she replaced were the weakest in the show, the changes were for the better. By a curious coincidence, in all three of the season's major American hits the principal song was introduced early on and then repeated throughout the evening with different lyrics or in contexts that gave it novel nuances. As it was in most musicals of the era, dancing was a highlight of the production. In fact, the *Times* headed its review, "POLKA DOMINATES MADAME SHERRY—Very Little Waltzing." "Every Little Movement" was a "polka français," a term now rarely heard. The paper praised Miss Abarbanell's "exquisite" footwork, but went on to note that Dorothy Jardon, who had only a small part, was "the sensation of the evening when in the midst of a sort of Apache rag she turned herself into a human mummy—feet crossed and arms folded— and was tossed around." *Madame Sherry* ran into the spring and then toured, breaking house records in many of the cities it visited.

The Hippodrome's yearly extravaganza was unveiled on 3 September. It was actually a triple bill: *Ballet of Niagara, The Earthquake* (in which an earthquake upsets the plans of a South American general and frees the Indian girl he has kept as a slave), and the main part of the evening, **The International Cup**. The title hinted at an auto race, but with their customary generosity the Hippodrome management and R. H. Burnside gave audiences more. Roy Carewe (Ben Wainwright) does win the New York-to-Paris auto race after foiling villainy at the wireless station. A larger-than-life hero, he goes on to rescue a girl from a sinking yacht and win a yacht race as well. Manuel Klein supplied another competent score. But as always the imaginative effects were the thing. Two fully rigged yachts sailed across the stage, elephants and lions romped, and an iridescent rainbow stretched from one side of the proscenium to the other. The effects kept playgoers gaping for 333 performances.

In George Broadhurst's thirteen-year-old *What Happened to Jones*, the hero is a traveling salesman, peddling Bibles to hayseeds and playing cards to city slickers. Forced to flee an illegal prizefight in New York, he is taken home by his ringside neighbor. That man is a professor, expecting his bishop brother from Australia. Circumstances soon lead to the professor's sister-in-law mistaking Jones for the bishop and falling in love with him. More complications follow before a happy resolution. Now Broadhurst, with Augustus Barrett as composer, turned the affair into a Chicago musical, **The Girl and the Drummer** (4 September 1910, Grand Opera). Its reception was tepid, so, after a season's tour, it closed without ever reaching New York.

Walter De Leon, a young man just out of college who would go on to some very minor fame on Broadway, was the librettist, composer, and "romantic" lead in San Francisco of **The Campus** (18 September 1910, Princess), "a rah-rah musical comedy in three yells." As Bobby Short he nearly loses his collegiate sweetheart, Nellie Perkins, after a jealous rival spreads rumors that Bobby bribed a committee to give him the annual award for writing a farce. Luckily, a sagacious if comic janitor—played by producer and star Ferris Hartman—sees that truth and love prevail.

M. Louis Ganne's **Hans, The Flute Player** (20 September 1910, Manhattan Opera House) was an imported comic opera with an eye on the children's market. Its variation of the Pied Piper tale entertained audiences for ten weeks.

He Came from Milwaukee (21 September 1910, Casino) was another of those musical comedies in which an American teaches Europeans a few tricks, but since Sam Bernard played in dialect there was an implication that even a short stay in the New World gave a man sharp, new perspectives. Bernard was Herman Von Schellenvein, a successful immigrant, who persuades the Duke of Zurack to change places with him so the Duke can evade the clutches of a title-hunting American mother, Mrs. Matthew Harvey (Alice Gordon). Miss Harvey becomes engaged to the real duke in his disguise as Herman, and all ends well. Just as Bernard had, as a gem dealer in *The Girl and the Wizard* (27 September 1909), enjoyed some of his best moments impersonating an excitable stage manager, so in *He Came from Milwaukee* the ersatz duke won many of his biggest laughs by turning into a wild animal to accommodate a lady lion tamer. The score was by Ben Jerome, who had produced a Broadway score as early as 1903 and who wrote even more frequently for Chicago, and by Louis Hirsch, who until now had been represented only by intermittent interpolations. It was a pleasant score, its best numbers, such as "Love Is Like A Red, Red Rose," more suggestive of the soft, sentimental material Jerome was writing for Chicago audiences than the lilting style Hirsch soon became known for. Broadway embraced Bernard for four months.

> LOUIS HIRSCH was born in New York City on 28 November 1881. Reputed to have taught himself the piano at an amazingly early age, he studied under a number of American teachers before becoming a pupil of Rafael Joseffy at the Stern Conservatory in Berlin. His first ambition was to be a concert pianist. But the need for immediate income prompted him to turn to popular composing. He worked for Gus Edwards and for Shapiro-Bernstein, and for a time wrote and arranged music for Dockstader's Minstrels. As early as 1907 his songs were interpolated into Broadway shows such as *The Gay White Way* and *Miss Innocence*.

September's last musical, **Alma, Where Do You Live?** (26 September 1910, Weber's), purportedly a French piece, was one of the season's biggest hits, running 232 performances. Joe Weber's excellent mounting shared credit for the show's popularity with George V. Hobart's lively libretto and Jean Briquet's captivating score. The story revolved around another musical-comedy will. In this case the will requires the hero to refrain from marrying until he reaches a certain age. Just before the deadline his rivals plant the irresistible Alma in his path. A number of critics, but notably the *Times*, praised Hobart and Weber for discarding all the suggestiveness they found in the original. Kitty Gordon, John McCloskey, and Charles Bigelow led the cast.

The next evening in Chicago saw the premiere of **Teresa, Be Mine!** (27 September 1910, Chicago Opera). A quick flop, it recounted how Teresa is appointed by her South American country as ambassadress to Macedonia. There, the king and courtiers fall in love with her, but she settles for a lieutenant.

October's first musical was also an importation. Unfortunately Leo Fall's **The Girl on the Train** (3 October 1910, Globe) failed to live up to the great expectations the success of its tryout encouraged, and it was withdrawn after forty performances. In its homeland the show was called *Die geschiedene Frau* (*The Divorced Wife*). The girl on the train was

the lady the wife assumed was her husband's mistress. Vera Michelena and Melville Stewart were the principals.

Another failure came in the next night. **The Deacon and the Lady** (4 October 1910, New York) described the efforts of Jim Gruff (Fletcher Norton) and Marie Trouville (Clara Palmer) to secure a valuable Montana property from Deacon Flood (Harry Kelly). There were some kind words for what proved to be Alfred E. Aarons's last Broadway score, but most critics agreed with the *Dramatic Mirror*'s assessment that "no effort seems to have been made to associate the story and the score." For many of those who saw the piece its chief attraction was the riotous antics of a young comedian named Ed Wynn. He earned some of his biggest laughs clowning with a "trained panama hat." But his Broadway debut was short-lived. The musical lasted just two weeks.

A more established entertainer, Marie Cahill, had slightly better luck with a vehicle called **Judy Forgot** (6 October 1910, Broadway). Judy Evans is in a train wreck shortly after a big quarrel with her husband. As a result of the crash she loses both her luggage and her memory. She picks up the luggage of a Mrs. Stole (Truly Shattuck) and assumes her identity. The flabbergasted Mr. Stole (Joseph Santley) must go along with her to avoid antagonizing his rich uncle. A second accident, this time in an automobile, restores Judy's memory. There were serious reservations about the handling of the book and the quality of the music. One critic used his review to complain that American musical comedy composers were no longer "contributing anything fresh and splendid." Even the carefully drilled marching of the chorus girls as soldiers was seen to be old hat. Miss Cahill found excuses to impersonate a lady in an opera box and an ingenue misleading the press in an interview. The singing comedienne had sufficient following to rack up forty-four performances.

Yet another importation, **Madame Troubadour** (10 October 1910, Lyric), enjoyed a ten-week run. Grace La Rue and Georgia Caine were featured in the story of a scholar's wife who feels her husband cares more for medieval poetry than for her. A friend persuades her to flirt openly with another man. On the 24th, **The Girl in the Taxi** opened. It called itself a "musical play," but since it had only three songs it was really more of a straight piece.

Joe Howard had a second score ready for the Chicago season when **Lower Berth Thirteen** arrived at the Whitney Opera House on 16 October. With his score for *The Sweetest Girl in Paris* helping to keep the La Salle lit, it might have been expected that the new work would play the Princess. But the Singer brothers, dismayed by the breakup of Howard's old partnership and unable to find an available musical when *The Wife Tamers* failed, had converted the house to straight dramatic fare. Only rarely thereafter did the Princess play host to a lyric work. Collin Davis and Arthur Gillespie created the plot, which recounted the trials of a honeymoon couple on a train otherwise filled with a burlesque troupe. At one point the husband is mistaken for a horse thief. The show was only moderately successful.

Two musicals premiered in New York on the night of 7 November. **The Bachelor Belles**, at the Globe, was a final vehicle for the fading star of Adelaide Genee. It related the story of the Bachelor Belles, an organization dedicated to celibacy. But when Charles Van Rensselaer (John Park) appears, Daphne Brooks (Eva Fallon) falls in love and breaks her vows. The other ladies admit they are secretly engaged. Genee was not Daphne. She spoke not a line, and her dances had nothing to do with the plot. Nonetheless her allure was still such that the show ran a month.

The Bachelor Belles might have run even longer, but it vied for attention with four other openings, one of them **Naughty Marietta**. Though the new Herbert piece was far from being the runaway smash of the year, it was the finest show of the season. In fact, it was the American masterwork of the era. Interestingly, in a seven-year period given to an unconscious symmetry, it opened right in the middle of the epoch's central season. It was the fifteenth of the season's thirty-four musicals. Oscar Hammerstein had commissioned it as a showcase for the great singers of his troubled opera company, especially the diminutive soprano Emma Trentini. As Marietta, Miss Trentini scored the first of her two Broadway triumphs. Writing for such fine, thoroughly trained voices, Victor Herbert allowed himself a rare depth and range. His vocal lines were among his most operatic, his orchestrations far and away his most symphonic. Melodically the score was probably his most inventive and enthralling, with at least four of the songs taking their place among his finest, most popular classics. The conductor was Gaetano Merola, who later was instrumental in establishing the San Francisco Opera. The show was blessed from the start, and by the time it opened on 7 November at the New York Theatre, which Hammerstein had built and lost, and where he was now forced to display his presentation, its success

was beyond doubt. Rida Johnson Young's libretto was set in eighteenth-century Louisiana. Captain Dick (sung by another Hammerstein luminary, Orville Harrold) and his rangers arrive singing their marching song, "Tramp! Tramp! Tramp!" They are seeking the pirate Bras Prique. Marietta comes on the scene. She is a young lady of noble origin who has fled to America to escape an unhappy marriage. In the title song she mischievously describes herself as an impossibly capricious girl. She and Dick admit to a reciprocal fascination, but both profess, "It Never, Never Can Be Love." Adah (Marie Duchene), a quadroon slave belonging to Etienne Grandet (Edward Martindell), son of the Lieutenant Governor, appears. For a while Etienne has actually loved her, but his ardor has cooled. Still, Adah is hopeful. Love can rekindle, "'Neath The Southern Moon." When Adah has left, Marietta longingly recalls her own youthful passion and fire in Naples with the "Italian Street Song," providing a striking contrast between the sultry slave girl and her own volatile personality. Etienne falls in love with Marietta and agrees to deny he knows her real history:

Marietta: Oh Monsieur I am glad you persuaded me to come. How I have laughed. How enjoyed!
Etienne: I have observed you, and Mademoiselle, I apologize for having disbelieved your statement that you were not the Contessa D'Altona.
Marietta: Eh?
Etienne: I have seen in you tonight the spirit of the people. No lady highly born could have entered as you have into our rustic festivity.

Eventually Dick is brought face to face with his own true feelings for Marietta, confessing, "I'm Falling In Love With Some One." The villainous buccaneer turns out to be none other than Etienne. Marietta is impressed by Dick's police work, but for years she has promised she will give herself only to the man who can finish a mysterious melody that haunts her dreams and that she has sung snatches of throughout the evening. Dick, in the operetta's soaring finale, does just that. Both rejoice: "Ah, Sweet Mystery Of Life," at last you have been found.

A legend has long circulated that this most popular of all Herbert songs was not in the original production. The legend is false. "Ah, Sweet Mystery Of Life" was in the operetta from the beginning. What gave the story currency was the fact that no one apparently guessed how popular the song would become. It was originally listed in the program solely as "finale" and was not published as a separate song in the initial printing of the show's music. Its immediate and phenomenal success changed matters swiftly.

The show ran 136 performances, including extra matinees added to satisfy the demand for seats. Herbert's superb biographer, Edward Waters, states that the duration of the run was limited in advance by contractual commitments and that it could have remained in New York much longer.

The Girl and the Kaiser (22 November 1910, Herald Square), another importation, began an eight-week engagement with Lulu Glaser starred as a girl whose fortuitous meeting with the Kaiser allows her to save her lover from execution. George Jarno composed the principal score.

The Spring Maid (26 December 1910, Liberty), also foreign, was December's only musical. It was a smash hit, running into summer. No doubt Christie MacDonald's lovely singing of Heinrich Reinhardt's songs aided ticket sales. Although strictly speaking the show is not an important part of our record, one anecdote about it offers an enlightening insight into the age's theatrical morality on both sides of the footlights. The operetta's story related how a young lady stoops to conquer by becoming an attendant at Carlsbad Springs. According to Harry B. Smith, who adapted the show with his brother Robert, "Tom McNaughton, an English actor, was the leading comedian in 'The Spring Maid.' At rehearsal he asked to be allowed to interpolate a recitation called 'The Three Trees,' which he had given successfully in the London music halls. The recitation had absolutely nothing to do with 'The Spring Maid,' but McNaughton was so confident that it would be a hit that a way was found to introduce it. When it was rehearsed, accompanied by eccentric orchestral noises, the effect was so decidedly vaudevillian, that in order to account for its introduction in the operetta, a note was printed on the program stating that the fable of 'The Three Trees' was the legend of the original discovery of Carlsbad Springs, and the authority given for this ingenious invention was 'Richter's Folk Lore of Germany,' of which, paraphrasing *Sary Gamp's* friend *Betsy*, I may say that 'I don't believe there's no sich a book.' However, my old friend, Mr. Krehbiel [critic for the *Tribune*], referred to the note in his review and seemed to know all about the mythical historical work."

IVAN CARYLL was born Felix Tilken in Liège, Belgium, in 1861. The exact date may be still buried in some Belgian archives. He studied music both at Liège and Paris, settling in the French capital to compose operettas. However, he soon moved to England, where he helped adapt a number of French musicals to London's taste. In time he again started to compose his own works, many of which quickly graced American stages as well. The West End and Broadway both sang his songs for *The Shop Girl, The Circus Girl, A Runaway Girl, The Messenger Boy, The Toreador,* and a host of others.

Two musicals welcomed in 1911 on 2 January. **Marriage à la Carte** at the Casino had a score by Ivan Caryll, who had decided to settle permanently in the United States, and a book by C. M. S. McLellan, with whom Caryll would collaborate on his next four shows. McLellan's plot was slight. Mrs. Ponsonby de Coutts Wragge (Maria Davis) has divorced Napoleon Pettingill (Harry Conor) and is about to marry Lord Mirables (C. Morton Home) when a train wreck deposits Pettingill on her doorstep. By the end of Act III she has decided to remarry Napoleon. Caryll's score was dashing and gay, but inconsequential. *Marriage à la Carte* lasted eight weeks, closing a few days before Caryll and McClellan's second effort opened.

The show competed for first-nighters with **The Slim Princess** at the Globe. Its star, Elsie Janis, played Princess Talora, who cannot find a suitor because she is too slim. To make matters worse for her regal family her younger sister, Jeneka (Julia Frary), cannot marry until Talora does. When the Prince (Joseph C. Miron) learns that slim girls are stylish in America, he sends Talora to Washington. She falls in love and, after an initial reluctance, the Prince consents to her choice. Miss Janis, besides playing Talora, found excuses to impersonate Ethel Barrymore, Anna Held, Sarah Bernhardt, Sam Bernard, Eddie Foy, Harry Lauder, and George M. Cohan. When Miss Janis was not regaling patrons, Joseph Cawthorn was tickling their funny bones in another of his dialect roles, Louis von Schloppenhauer. According to the program, the music was by Leslie Stuart. But in his research for his

Victor Herbert biography, Edward Waters discovered that Herbert had a hand in part of the composition. None of the songs had any lasting value. The hit of the evening was "Let Me Live And Die In Dixie" (Elizabeth Brice and Charles King), a song its writers had already made popular in vaudeville and which was inserted into at least one other show during the season. *The Slim Princess* ran three months.

Planquette's **The Paradise of Mahomet** (17 January 1911, Herald Square) was adapted by the Smith brothers. In its brief stay its story described the abduction of a supposed widow by a Turkish prince. He tries to persuade her she, too, has died, and that his harem is actually Paradise. George Leon Moore and Grace Van Studdiford starred.

Chauncey Olcott's latest vehicle was Rida Johnson Young's "romantic drama" **Barry of Ballymore** (30 January 1911, Academy of Music). Tom Barry is a gamekeeper's son, who has promised to restore his mother's half-sister, Nanette (Alice Farrell), to the heritage of Bannon, in Galway, which she has been wrongfully deprived of. Nanette is the daughter, by a former wife, of Lord Bannon (George Sydenham), who seemingly has forgotten her. The lord's acknowledged daughter, Lady Mary (Edith Browing), is outraged at Tom's presumption. She is at this time courted by Sir Edward Emery (Howard Chambers). But after Tom bests Sir Edward in a duel and sings his expected four songs, he wins Lady Mary for himself and restores Nanette to her rightful place. Tom's songs included "I Love The Name Of Mary" and "Mother Machree." Legend has it that another song was added during the tour, but the play was not particularly successful, so "When Irish Eyes Are Smiling" had to wait until Olcott reused it (along with "Mother Machree") in a later show.

As February began, the *Dramatic Mirror* reported that five of the twenty-one successes running on Broadway were musicals. February's first two musicals jumped the total to seven.

Lew Fields's "summer" shows had been so successful that he decided to offer one at the height of the season. **The Hen Pecks** (4 February 1911, Broadway) told another homey story, elaborately mounted and stuffed with vaudeville turns. Henry Peck (Fields), fed up with married life, flees to Cranberry Cove. His wife, Henrietta (Lillian Lee), his son, Henderson (Stephen Maley), and his daughters, Henoria (Gertrude Quinlan) and Henella (Blossom Seeley) follow him there and ultimately effect a reconciliation. Fields filled the evening with the "realistic" touches the era so loved. A farm boasted real chickens, ducks, geese, and pigs. A person could be seen dressing behind the curtain of a farmhouse window. For laughs, Fields and others hurled "missiles" through a pneumatic tube. Frank Whitman earned encores for playing his violin while he did a knock-about dance. The show had an ordinary A. Baldwin Sloane score and a number of interpolations, including one by Jerome Kern and the same "Let Me Live And Die In Dixie" sung in *The Slim Princess*. The show ran until just about the time Fields would have been bringing in his hot-weather production.

During the run of the piece, Fields made some startling statements in an interview. They suggested, at one and the same time, a condescension toward his audience and, since he was so successful, a sensitive appraisal of it. He felt that "the public want pretty much the same old thing from year to year, but they want little changes and little surprises hitched to the old situations and lines." He attributed extremely short memories to his playgoers, concluding, "every entrance is, in effect, the actor's first appearance; because the three or four numbers intervening since his exit has made the audience forget just what he is doing." Equally surprising is his indifference to the integrity of the show itself. He announced his next show would be "the same sort" as *The Hen Pecks*, "except it has more of a story." He continued, "At least it has a story now, but I don't know what may happen to it after rehearsals begin. You see, an attraction of this kind can't get by on first rehearsal. Then the composer will complain that the numbers are not placed properly and the changes that suit him will probably interfere with the plot. Then the manager will find fault with the movement of the lyrics because they don't give him a chance to move the show girls around . . . . And so it goes. When it is all over, consistency of the narrative is a thing that was." As a parting shot, he added, "the author gets blamed for a lot of lines he was never guilty of."

In Chicago the La Salle's successor to *The Sweetest Girl in Paris* was a failure. **The Girl I Love**, which opened on 5 February, had a libretto by C. V. Kerr and R. H. Burnside (Burnside also did the lyrics) and a score by J. S. Zamecnik and H. L. Sanford. In the slight plot Billy Phibbs is sent packing by his uncle for an imagined slight. But Billy proves his worth and wins the girl he loves, Jesslyn Bard.

Paul Rubens's **The Balkan Princess** (9 February 1911, Herald Square), a London musical, ran 108 performances in New York. The title role of a princess who goes slumming was sung by Louise Gunning, but it was considered so arduous Christine Nielson replaced her for matinees.

A show possibly meant for New York, **Katie Did,** opened at the Colonial in Chicago on 18 February. W. C. Duncan and Frank Smithson based their libretto on *My Friend from India*, in which a barber impersonating an Indian prince is invited by a drunken Charlie Underholt to the Underholts' party. The show received good notices, especially Karl Hoschna's score, but for some reason it was soon withdrawn.

Victor Moore returned to Broadway in **The Happiest Night of His Life** (20 February 1911, Criterion). The book, by Junie McCree and Sydney Rosenfeld, began like one of George M. Cohan's librettos, through which Moore had so often romped. Its denouement, however, was the sort of musical comedy absurdity Cohan would never have allowed. Tom (Jack Henderson) has stolen $500 from his Uncle Harry (Phil Ryley). To get it back before Uncle Harry discovers his loss, Dick Brennan (Moore) suggests charging Harry $500 for a tour of the Manhattan underworld. The "tour" takes place at Mrs. Rickett's, where Uncle meets the ladies of the "Chicago Protective Order of Young Widows." The music was by Tin Pan Alley's Albert Von Tilzer, a writer who never developed a truly identifiable style of his own and who, for this show, was not above consciously imitating Cohan, in such songs as "Oh You Chicago, Oh You New York." The public sensed a bad imitation, and *The Happiest Night of His Life* lasted only three weeks.

An even worse hodgepodge came in two weeks later and also ran three weeks. **Jumping Jupiter** (6 March 1911, Criterion) was tailored to the talents of Richard Carle, a comedian with a large following, especially in Chicago and on the road. Carle wrote his own libretto in conjunction with Sydney Rosenfeld, who had collaborated on the Victor Moore book. Several of the songs were also credited to Carle. Robert Winthrop (Burrell Barbaretto) tires of his wife, Connie (Edna Wallace Hopper), and offers her a large check if she will leave. She tears up the check. But, unknown to Winthrop, Connie has been posing as Professor Goodwillie's wife. When the real Mrs. Goodwillie (Jessie Cardownie) and the professor (Carle) arrive, Winthrop sees another way out.

During the run of *Marriage à la Carte* Ivan Caryll granted an interview in which he presented his opinions of the American lyric stage: "American popular music overdoes ragtime, although in proper amount, syncopation is a legitimate device. This country, however, does not lack composers of merit. 'Robin Hood' is one of the best of its class. Besides De Koven you have Herbert... and Sousa... ." It was clear with what style of musical composition Caryll's sympathy lay. But, like so many of his contemporaries, he did not look on it as comic opera or operetta, for he added, "America has the best musical comedy soloists—Fritzi Scheff, Emma Trentini, and Emmy Wehlen—although the men do not outrank the English."

One young lady Caryll failed to mention was Hazel Dawn, although she was in no small measure responsible for giving Caryll and McLellan the season's biggest musical hit, when she opened in their "musical comedy," **The Pink Lady** (13 March 1911, New Amsterdam). McClellan based his libretto on *Le Satyre* by Georges Berr and Marcel Guillemand. A satyr is loose in the Forest of Compiègne, stealing hugs and kisses from comely young passers-by. He is the talk of all the customers at Le Joli Coucou, a restaurant in the park—all the customers except the narcissistic Benevol (Fred Wright, Jr.), who arrives urging the crowd to "Bring Along The Camera," since everything he does is worth a photo. Lucien Garidel (William Elliott), whose marriage to Angele (Alice Dovey) has been announced, arrives, calculating, "I'm Single For Six Weeks More." Before his wedding he will have one last fling with his old flame, Claudine (Miss Dawn). He sees nothing wrong in this, but he is taken aback when Angele appears with another man to have dinner. Angele and her escort coyly agree "Love Is Divine." A third couple, Desiree (Ida M. Adams) and Bebe (John E. Young), concur that, once you've met a girl by the Seine, it becomes almost impossible to remain true to an old love "By The Saskatchewan." Claudine arrives and Lucien introduces her to the suspicious Angele as the wife of his friend, the antiques dealer, Dondidier (Frank Lalor). Knowing that Angele will seek to verify their story, Lucien and Claudine rush to the Rue St. Honoré, where they beg the baffled Dondidier to back them. The Comtesse de Montavert (Louise Kelley) appears, but before she can transact her business she is kissed on the cheek. Though she did not see who did it, she blames Dondidier and brands him the satyr. Sides are hastily chosen in "Donny Didn't, Donny Did." Claudine, while not the satyr, admits to an ample supply of kisses in "The Kiss Waltz."

Angele and her escort, Maurice, arrive. The four youngsters insist that in France you must fight for "The Right To Love." But the police have been summoned by the Countess, and they appear, "properly copperly," to arrest Dondidier. At the Restaurant of the Satyrs, Dondidier, released, and now confessedly the satyr, contemplates his new notoriety and concludes, "I Like It!" But Angele and Claudine decide men do not really know how to court women. The girls would do it to soft lights and sweet music, the same music in fact that Claudine has more flippantly sung as "The Kiss Waltz." But the words have changed, with the suitor professing his heart sighs as he raises his eyes to "My Beautiful Lady." Angele wins back Lucien, while Claudine, a member of the demimonde, goes on her way.

The gay confectionary of a book was perfectly matched by the dainty, melodious score. Miss Dawn walked away with honors not just for her acting, singing, and dancing, but for her violin playing as well. So well balanced was the show that two of its biggest hits—"By The Saskatchewan" and "Donny Didn't, Donny Did," a brilliantly staged number—were given to minor players. In its review, the *Times* suggested that the show achieved a goal that shows of the epoch are rarely credited with, insisting that the fun and songs "developed logically out of its situations." The paper also praised Julian Mitchell's fine direction, notably the "magnificent bustle" at the end of the first act, and it enjoyed a real blonde posing on the steps in front of the restaurant. *The Pink Lady* ran well into the 1911–1912 season.

One week after *The Pink Lady's* premiere, *La Belle Paree* opened the spanking new Winter Garden on 20 March. The new theatre almost stole the show. The Shuberts had built it at Broadway between 50th and 51st streets, far uptown from most theatres of the day. It was a spacious house with a disproportionately large number of its nearly 1,600 seats on the orchestra level, assuring a handsome gross at capacity. Food and drink were served. The theatre was clearly to be the Shubert flagship. Before the main event of the evening the Shuberts unveiled Manuel Klein's one-act "Chinese" opera, *Bow Sing*. A small dose of culture was deemed desirable. The "Jumble of Jollity" that followed was little more than glorified vaudeville. It had an undistinguished score by Frank Tours and Jerome Kern, which included a song called "Paris Is A Paridise For Coons" sung late in the evening by a newcomer, Al Jolson. His big moment was so late in the overlong affair that all but one of the newspaper critics—and a fair part of

the audience—had left. But the Shuberts, with their excellent theatrical instinct, had faith in him and promptly gave him an earlier spot on the program. He proved a sensation and was an important factor in the show's 104-performance run. Jolson and the Winter Garden would be virtually inseparable for the next fifteen years.

AL JOLSON was born in Srednike, in what is now Lithuania, probably in 1886. His real name was Asa Yoelson. His father, a Jewish cantor, brought the family to America, settling in Washington, D.C., when Jolson was still a youngster. During the 1897–1898 season he ran away from home, joining Rich and Hoppe's Big Company of Fun Makers. He later worked in a circus and as a super in the 1899 Washington tryout of *Children of the Ghetto*. But his father put his foot down and forced him to remain at home for a time. This return lasted only a few months, and the teenager was soon back in vaudeville. For the next eleven years he moved among the theatrical outlets of the time, appearing now in two-a-day, now in burlesque (the older, less risqué type), and now on the stages of a waning minstrelsy.

Of course, Jolson was far from the whole show. The Hess Sisters did "whirlwind" Russian dances, Dazie toe-danced, and Yvette, like Frank Whitman earlier in the season, mixed footwork and fiddling. Kitty Gordon again displayed her celebrated back. Ragtime numbers were sparked by Stella Mayhew. In the finale, "cunning little" Mitzi Hajos delighted audiences by jumping from the stage to lead the orchestra. Shell pink and soft sea green dominated the sets, while abundant plumage, hobble skirts, and harem skirts bedecked parading show girls.

The Globe relit on 3 April for Nora Bayes and her husband, Jack Norworth, in Little Miss Fixit. Miss Bayes played Delia Wendell, who busies herself matchmaking and patching up problem marriages, and who doesn't get around to resolving her own marital difficulties until curtain time. Some small, felicitous touches pleased the critics. Miss Bayes eschewed the noisy first entrance so common at the time. Instead a lady, shielded behind a parasol, was seen sitting quietly through the first songs and opening dialogues. Only when she sedately lowered the umbrella was she discovered to be the star. Norworth and Miss Bayes appeared soaking wet for the first-act finale after supposedly suffering a canoe accident. Two other performers who delighted the critics apparently had no names. They were a pair of trained dancing dogs. On opening night there were eight songs in the show by various composers. The biggest hit of the evening was "Mister Moon-Man, Turn Off Your Light," which Bayes and Norworth wrote for themselves, apparently as a sort of sequel to their 1908 "Shine On, Harvest Moon." Nor was "Shine On, Harvest Moon" ignored—it opened the overture. In her customary fashion, Miss Bayes added and dropped interpolations during the seven-week Gotham stay and the long tour.

Two shows came into Chicago the first half of April. On the 3rd, Joe Howard offered a rewriting of his 1906 New York failure, The District Leader. As **Love and Politics** it failed again, even with Ned Wayburn's dynamic staging. On the 16th Sophie Tucker was starred in **Merry Mary**. The show received a critical drubbing, the critics looking on it as little more than a bad vaudeville. But the Tribune's man did have a few grudging encomiums for Miss Tucker's "fleshy love songs."

In New York, a vaudeville called **London Follies** (17 April 1911, Weber's) was a quick flop, as was a second show that opened the same night. **Doctor DeLuxe** (17 April 1911, Knickerbocker) bore brief witness to the incessant little symmetries of the period. Its failure coming after its author's early-season smash of Madame Sherry balanced the early failure and late-season hit of Caryll and McLellan. Karl Hoschna and Otto Hauerbach wrote the show as a vehicle for Ralph Herz, who had served them so well as Theophilus in Madame Sherry. Herz was an engaging comedian with an unusual background; born into vast wealth derived from the construction of the Suez Canal, he turned to the stage when his family lost its fortune. The plot Hauerbach threw together for him was simple, reminding some of De Wolf Hopper's A Matinee Idol (28 April 1910), seen the preceding year. John Truesdale, through mistaken identity, becomes a substitute for Dr. Melville. He prescribes nothing stronger than salt tablets and in the end marries Melville's daughter (Jeanette Childs). Whatever else its faults, the show offered some interesting staging. The evening began with a young boy (Albert Lamson) singing the show's

hoped-for hit song, "For Every Boy That's Lonely There's A Girl That's Lonely Too." So engrossed is he in his song, he fails to hear the honking of an automobile, which knocks him down. Truesdale's rushing to his aid starts the complications. Dousings seemed popular during the year, so bare-legged chorus girls, attempting to scamper up trellises, were sprayed by a gardener. In return the girls smashed all the windows in a summer cottage. One critic suggested, "Stage realism can go no further." The score, with one interpolation by Edward Laska, offered no outstanding melodies, but was invariably pleasant.

A Certain Party (24 April 1911, Wallack's) ran only three weeks although a number of commentators had kind words for its interesting book. Homer Caldwell (James Seeley), aspiring to a place on the reform ticket, finds he must ally himself with Jerry Fogarty (John T. Kelly), the ward boss. Since Caldwell's son George (Alfred Kappeler) had done a good turn for the brother of their maid Norah (Mabel Hite), Norah is asked to approach Fogarty. Sydney Finch (Harold Hartsell) tells Fogarty that years ago George signed his father's name to a gambling debt. But Norah prevails with the ward leader. The second act contained a highly praised burlesque of a political convention. The lateness of the season, the location of the house at the edge of the theatre area, and a weak score by Robert Hood Bowers stifled whatever chance the lively book had.

Another new theatre, the Follies Bergere, opened on 29 April. Located on 46th Street, just off Broadway, it was designed as a theatre-restaurant. Its first attraction was a triple bill. **Hell** opened the evening. Called "a profane burlesque," it was a loose vaudeville of gags about spinsters, nouveaux riches, promiscuous sailors, and others, presided over by the Devil and Mrs. Devil "forty-five seconds from Broadway." Temptation, a one-act ballet, and **Gaby**, a "satirical revuette" in three scenes, completed the bill. Ethel Levey, returning to Broadway after a protracted absence, played the title role, which purported to be a spoof of Gaby Deslys, a celebrated entertainer who had yet to make her Broadway debut. Her Gaby was represented as a Spanish dancer, but Arenera Duo's castanet-clicking dances stole her thunder. Show girls opened and closed the evening parading as "Beauties of All Nations."

Uptown at the Majestic on 8 May a black entertainment, **His Honor, the Barber**, became New York's last new musical of the stage year. Raspberry Snow's great ambition is to shave the President of the United States. Raspberry (S. H. Dudley) falls asleep on the White House steps, is chased away, then wins a jackpot at the races so big the President hears of it and calls him in. Just as he is about to realize his ambition, he wakes up. He is still outside the White House. Special bits included a donkey brought on stage in blue overalls. Critics always displayed mixed feelings about Negro shows; they were often viewed as *sui generis* and a world apart. The *Times* lamented the actors in *His Honor, the Barber* made "too much effort to imitate white performers," adding it was a failing common to black shows. But the most discerning critics, even when they could not completely rid themselves of racial distinctions, were careful to appreciate the change of values. The Boston *Evening Transcript*, praising the music, had even more praise for the way it was handled: "The music of ragtime is one thing when the youngsters of Broadway scream it and another when Negro voices croon it or give it really the rhythm its name implied." *His Honor, the Barber* ran only two weeks on the Rialto, but it toured successfully for several years.

Two May arrivals ended the Chicago season. **Will o' the Wisp** premiered at the Studebaker on 8 May. Alfred G. Robyn composed the score, while Walter Percival not only wrote the book but took the leading role as well. Percival played Forest Kidder, a well-meaning young man who is forever being caught in compromising positions by his sweetheart. Hough and Adams returned to the scene of earlier triumphs, the Princess, on 30 May. The score for their latest offering, **The Heartbreakers**, was by Harold Orlob and Melville Gideon. Sallie Fisher starred as the leading student in a school for brides. Both shows were received with little enthusiasm; the reviews for *The Heartbreakers* were reduced to little but passing notices when space was required for extended obituaries of W. S. Gilbert.

Back in New York the season closed with a revival of *H. M. S. Pinafore*, with a cast that included De Wolf Hopper, Marie Cahill, and Louise Gunning, and a revival of the 1902 success *A Country Girl*.

1911–1912

For the first time in its history, Broadway was to see over forty new musicals offered in a single season: forty-one or forty-two depending on how the double-bill at the Follies Bergere was counted. But this encouraging jump in numbers coincided with a disastrous slump in quality. Not one new American show of lasting merit appeared; even superior tunes were few and far between. Three of the importations

are sporadically revived on their native stages, although none was of the highest order. Throughout the year newspapers and trade journals commented forlornly on the sad state of the musical theatre. Bewailings of this sort have been perennial, but in 1911–1912 they were justified.

The season's first presentation, **The Red Rose** (22 June 1911, Bijou), set the tone for the months to come. It was at once professional and hackneyed. The Smith brothers' libretto was set in Paris, where Dick Lorrimer (Wallace McCutcheon), an art student, loves Lola (Valeska Suratt), a girl he believes to be a concierge's daughter, but who is in reality Baron Le Blanc's lost child. Dick's family is pleased when he and Lola have a falling-out, for the family want Dick to marry Daisy Plant (Lillian Graham). However, Daisy has eyes only for an Englishman. Dick and Lola are reconciled and marry just in time to thwart the Baron's plan to wed Lola to one Mr. Du Pont (Henry Bergman). Another Paris setting, another unimaginative story, and more lackluster dialogue. The brothers' lyrics were no better, nor was R. H. Bowers's score. To first-nighters, the happiest moment of the evening was the dainty Miss Graham's toe dance; they awarded her three encores. One curious sidelight may well have been the most interesting thing about the show: its costumes and sets were credited to its feminine lead, Miss Suratt. The show came in on 22 June, and for all its weaknesses played through the hot weather.

Four nights later the **Ziegfeld Follies of 1911** (26 June 1911, Jardin de Paris) opened. It was the first time the title officially included Ziegfeld's name. As if to honor the occasion he brought together a glamorous collection of old and new favorites: Bert Williams, Fanny Brice, Lillian Lorraine, Vera Maxwell, Bessie McCoy, and the Dolly Sisters—surrounding them with his increasingly legendary line of gorgeous girls. Still called "Anna Held Girls," their numbers had swollen to seventy-five. One important new addition to the roster was Leon Errol.

Maurice Levi and Raymond Hubbell produced the principal score for the new *Follies*, with Irving Berlin, Jerome Kern, James Blyler, and Sid Brown among those who provided additional melodies. By and large it was an undistinguished score, the best number being Berlin's "Woodman, Woodman, Spare That Tree"—a song perfectly atuned to Bert Williams's melancholy drollery. Its plea was not that of an alarmed nature-lover, but of a much put-upon husband fearful of losing his lone avenue of escape.

Perhaps the evening's most famous comedy skit was a routine using only Williams and Errol, recounting the plight of a small, nervous tourist (Errol) arriving at Grand Central Station in the midst of new subway construction. To help the tourist safely across the girders, the tall, stolid redcap (Williams) joins himself and his customer with a rope. As a safety measure it comes none too soon, for the wobbly Errol, too intrigued by the work going on far below him, falls off a girder marked "160 Foot Drop." Using a laborious hand-over-hand pull, Williams dutifully brings the man back up. Just before he has a secure foothold, Errol asks Williams, "Porter, have you a match?" Obligingly, Williams searches his pockets as the tourist once again plummets down. Already exhausted from his first hauling, Williams must once again begin his hand-over-hand rescue. As he brings Errol to safety for a second time, Errol politely remarks, "Never mind the match, Porter, I broke my pipe." While they stand together catching their breaths, the tourist asks the porter about his private life:

—You have a wife and family, I suppose?
—Oh yes sir; I's married and I'se got three child'un.
—Is that so? Ah, that's very commendable.
—Yes sir, so it is.
—What are the names of your children?
—Well, I names 'em out de Bible. Dar's Hannah and den dar's Samuel and de las' I names "Iwilla."
—Iwilla? I don't remember that name in the Bible.
—Sure 'tis. Don't you 'member where it say IWILLA RISE?

LEON ERROL was born in Sydney, Australia, on 3 July 1881. He planned to become a doctor and originally performed in Australian vaudeville solely to earn enough money to pay his way through school. However, he was so successful on stage he soon abandoned his earlier ambition. He played in Shakespearean repertory, clowned with a circus, and took small parts in comic opera. Eager for broader opportunities he came to San Francisco, taking a job as a singing waiter while looking for more serious employment. His singing went largely unapplauded, but his eccentric, wobbly-kneed dancing landed him a job in American vaudeville. The San Francisco earthquake prompted his move to the East. A stint as a vaudeville-pantomimist failed. To provide employment for himself he wrote a play called *The Lilies*. The play apparently never reached New York. How Ziegfeld discovered the comedian is uncertain.

The two climb to a higher girder to look for the right train. Since it hasn't arrived at the station, Williams sits down to have his lunch. He describes the simple food his wife prepares for him so temptingly that Errol approaches hastily to look at it, knocking the lunch pail off the girder in his excitement. Williams, his lunch irretrievably gone, sits slowly nodding his head, tapping his fingers, and staring at Errol. Abashed, Errol promises the porter an especially big tip—five cents. Williams accepts the nickel with patent scorn. This so unnerves Errol that he once again falls off the girder—this higher one marked "288 Foot Drop." As the rope keeps running out of the porter's hand, indicating Errol is falling farther and farther, Williams stands and stares deadpan at the audience. When the rope stops uncoiling, Williams mutters "Five Cents!," unwinds the rope from his waist and lets it fall, then, as a sort of coup de grace, hurls the tourist's luggage down at him. An explosion from the construction site follows. Williams, looking out into space, tells the audience that Errol is a victim of the blast. "There he goes, now he's near the Metropolitan Tower. If he kin only grab that little gold ball on the top ... 'um, he muffed it." He looks at the audience with obviously hypocritical compassion.

Walter Browne's morality play *Everywoman* was spoofed as "Everywife" (with Williams playing a character listed as "Nobody"), and *The Pink Lady* was burlesqued in drag. A production number called "HMS Vaudeville" included in its cast of characters Sir Glassup Pilsener and Capt. Headliner. One medley of popular American songs was sung in literal German translations, a stunt used years before in *1492* (7 August 1893). The revue played through the summer, then toured.

No shows opened in July, but three appeared in August. **The Girl of My Dreams** (15 May 1911, Criterion) had been traveling around the country since 1910, while Otto Hauerbach (assisted on the book by Wilbur Nesbit) and Karl Hoschna strove to recapture the charm and success of *Three Twins* (15 June 1908) and *Madame Sherry* (30 August 1910). They failed, largely because Hauerbach could not put the book in order. His story line was too frail, his dialogue dreary. Hauerbach apparently designed his story around a saucer-eyed innocent Quaker miss that one of his stars, Leila McIntyre, had portrayed in a vaudeville act. In Hauerbach's book this young lady, now called Lucy Medders, reforms Harry Swifton. Harry seems to relapse into his former ways when Mrs. Blazes is found in his room. But he was only helping her after his car had knocked her down. If the story was trite, the staging was hackneyed. Some way was found to allow the "pony" chorus to stage yet one more drill as red-cheeked soldiers with snare drums. At another point the girls played follow-the-leader as they romped through "some pretty stiff gymnastic paces." Despite the presence of John Hyams and Miss McIntyre in a large, well-chosen cast, the musical ran only forty performances. The short run was doubly sad. First, Hoschna's score, as the title song suggests, was quite good, even if too many tunes had treacly titles such as "Dr. Tinkle Tinker" and "Oooh! Maybe He's A Robber!" Second, it proved to be his last score Hoschna would hear performed. He died not quite five months later, 23 December 1911. He was only thirty-four years old and still at the height of his creative powers.

On 19 August Henry Harris and Jesse Lasky made one last attempt to keep alive their dinner-theatre, the Follies Bergère. A revue called **Hello, Paris** (to which, on 22 September, they appended, a short musical, *A La Broadway*) had some interesting staging by Ned Wayburn, songs by J. Rosamond Johnson, and the popular Harry Pilcer as the featured principal. But Harris and Lasky still could not sell their entertainments to the public. When *Hello, Paris* was withdrawn at the end of the month, they transformed the house into a regular legitimate auditorium, staidly renaming it the Fulton.

August's last entry was **The Siren** (28 August 1911, Knickerbocker), Leo Fall's attractive operetta, which Harry B. Smith translated from Stein and Willner's original. The story centered on a lovely young lady employed by the police to prove a handsome young marquis is writing satiric letters about the government. Donald Brian was starred, with up-and-coming Julia Sanderson as his leading lady, and Frank Moulan providing laughs. Charles Frohman gave it an elegant production, embellishing the score

with Kern interpolations. It became the first show of the season to have an appreciable run.

But the longest run of the season's musicals was, as indeed it was season after season, the Hippodrome's annual pageant—for 1911 called **Around the World.** The show came in on 2 September and with its unique two-a-day policy chalked up 445 performances. A skimpy plot about an eccentric millionaire who purchases a diamond against the warning of a mysterious Swami, finds the jewel stolen, and searches the world over to recover it provided all the excuse necessary for a succession of spectacular scenes. These sets included the lawn of a Hudson River mansion, a yacht plowing through the water, and a grand finale with the theatre's huge tank in the foreground "backed by a grotto of mammoth rocks, over which rises a golden barge, on which a number of beautiful women are grouped. As the changing lights begin to play, the rocks at the rear of the stage become transparent, and in them are seen some exquisitely posed and draped groups of living statuary." Manuel Klein's likable, if forgettable, score was exemplified by "It's A Long Lane That Has No Turning."

JULIA SANDERSON (née Julia Sackett) was born into a family of actors in Springfield, Massachusetts, on 20 August 1887. As a child she played small roles with a Philadelphia stock company Tiny, round-faced, and bright-eyed, she made her New York debut at fifteen as a chorus girl in *A Chinese Honeymoon*. In the following year she graduated from the chorus of *Winsome Winnie* to the show's lead. Roles in *Wang, Fantana, The Tourists*, and *The Dairymaids* followed. Like so many great performers of the era, she spent part of her apprenticeship doing a stint in London musicals. When she returned to New York to play a girl with a brogue in *The Arcadians*, her excellent notices helped earn her the feminine lead in *The Siren*.

Although its halcyon days as a production center for musicals were ending, Chicago was still far from inactive. One of its biggest hits arrived at the La Salle on 3 September, **Louisiana Lou.** Addison

Burkhardt and Frederick Donaghey created the book and lyrics, and Ben Jerome provided the score. The show starred Alexander Carr and featured Bernard Granville and Sophie Tucker (demoted from the preceding season's star billing). In her autobiography, Miss Tucker regarded the show as a forerunner of *Abie's Irish Rose*. Jacob Ladoffski (Carr), a rich New Orleans Jew, adopts a waif and raises her as his daughter Lou. A cheery man-about-town, Nixon Holmes (Granville), would marry her. (The *Tribune* couldn't resist advising its readers to translate the gay blade's name as "Nix-on-homes.") But Jacob has planned to marry Lou to Jack Konkarney, the son of a friendly Irish political boss. With the help of Lou's "chaperon," Jennie Wimp (Miss Tucker), love wins the day. Both Miss Tucker and Carr had show-stoppers. Carr won applause with the sentimental "My Rose Of The Ghetto," while Miss Tucker brought down the house each night with a foot-stomping spoof of underworld dancing, "The Puritan Prance." *Louisiana Lou* played joyously on at the La Salle well into the new year.

Bothwell Browne, a female impersonator from the vaudeville circuits, looked to cash in on Julian Eltinge's legitimate vogue with a vehicle entitled **Miss Jack** (4 September 1911, Herald Square). Jack Hayward visits a girls' seminary to see his sweetheart and finds he must disguise himself as one of the girls to avoid some awkward situations. The book was so clumsily constructed that what little plot there was had been done away with by the end of the second act, leaving the whole third act to a series of Browne's vaudeville specialties, particularly his "Egyptian" dances. Two weeks and *Miss Jack* departed.

One reason for its swift exit may have been that Julian Eltinge himself arrived a week later in **The Fascinating Widow** (11 September 1911, Liberty). Eltinge was probably the greatest of our female impersonators. His "women" were never offensive burlesques, never the blatant drag queens that Bert Savoy and his followers foisted on their audiences. Taste and restraint marked every Eltinge impersonation. In *The Fascinating Widow* Eltinge played Hal Blake, Margaret Leffingwell's suitor. When Oswald Wenworth (Cyril Chadwick), an effeminate fop, forces his attentions on Margaret (Winona Winter), Hal attacks him. To avoid repercussions Hal disguises himself as a "Mrs. Monte" and hides in a girls' dormitory. He is compelled to silence the Reverend Watts (Charles W. Butler) and Detective Bulger (James E. Sullivan) with compromising photographs after they discover Mrs. Monte smoking a pipe. He allows Wentworth to court him and then exposes him as a two-timer. *The Theatre* assured its readers, "The comedy is more consistent in *The Fascinating Widow* than is usual in musical plays." And there were kind words for Kerry Mills's lilting score. The show failed to equal the success it had enjoyed in Chicago and on the road, but its seven-week run was still considered satisfactory.

There seems to have been little that was satisfactory about **When Sweet Sixteen** (14 September 1911, Daly's). The show was ill-fated from the start. Originally announced in 1908 as "a song play" called *Victoria*, then renamed *Sweet Sixteen*, the show was at one time or another optioned by several producers, one of whom, Lew Fields, even saw it through five weeks of rehearsal before dropping it in discouragement. Harry J. Everall and Samuel H. Wallach (operating as the Ever-Wall Co.) finally brought it to New York after a long road tour that might have been a total disaster but for a cordial reception and successful run in Chicago. There Percy Hammond noted the "Sweet Sixteen" of the title "must come from [the sixteen numbers in Victor] Herbert's score, since there was no other excuse for it." In George V. Hobart's book *nouveau-riche* Mrs. Hammond (Josie Intropidi), to secure herself a place in society, demands that her daughter, Victoria (Harriet Standon), marry the Laird of Loch Lomond. Mr. Hammond (Frank Belcher) wants Victoria to marry his old friend, Jefferson Todd (William Norris). Victoria seemingly goes along with her father—for she loves Todd's secretary, Stanley Morton (Roy Purviance). Stanley and Victoria win the day, and Todd settles for Mrs. Hammond's manicurist. Hammond hinted at the mediocrity of the libretto when later in his review he added, "Theatregoers, it seems, care not who composes the book of musical comedy so long as Victor Herbert writes the music." How like a grab bag of clichés the book was can be seen in the *Dramatic Mirror's* praise, "Josie Intropidi was a joy. Her 'nigger' laugh with the accompanying facial, manual and physical play, and her mimic trombone solo... and her drum major jugglery, were the funniest things in the play." Even Herbert was not above throwing in anything that might help the show catch on. At the Hammonds' party in the second act the company sang an extended medley of Herbert favorites, ranging as a far back as *The Wizard of the Nile* (4 November, 1895). Unfortunately, nothing could save their star-crossed evening. *When Sweet Sixteen* ran a mere twelve performances. Among Herbert's works only

The Gold Bug (21 September 1896) had a shorter New York run.

Herbert had a more disheartening failure one month later when his fourth vehicle for Fritzi Scheff, **The Duchess** (16 October 1911, Lyric), managed to survive only twenty-four performances. Like *When Sweet Sixteen*, the show had a long pre-Broadway tour the preceding season and a history of name changes, including *The Rose Shop, Rosita, Mlle. Rosita,* and *Mlle. Boutoniére.* It told how foppish Count de Paravante (John E. Hazzard) wants to marry Rose, a florist's daughter, but is proscribed from marrying anyone below a marquise. So Rose agrees to wed an unknown marquis who is leaving for Africa, divorce him, and marry the count. But Rose and Phillipe (George Anderson), the marquis, fall in love, and the count is sent on his way. While the critics divided sharply on the merits of the book, most were in accord in rating Herbert's score pleasant but not outstanding. Its best number was a simple waltz, "Cupid, Tell Me Why." In the course of the evening Miss Scheff changed from the short skirts of the flower girl to the long gown of the marquise to a final appearance in a white riding habit. The set for this last scene was contrived to resemble an English hunting print, with "green turf, russet boles of trees, and huntsmen in hunting pink, to say nothing of huntresses in habits of brown and Lincoln green." On opening night Miss Scheff urgently pleaded for patronage, but when it was not forthcoming, the show was hastily returned to the road. There Miss Scheff's temperament created further problems, forcing the musical to close. Herbert was so annoyed that he never again wrote a musical for her.

Three nights after the premiere of *The Duchess*, a third Herbert opus appeared. It was his only successful work of the season. Even though a previous booking forced **The Enchantress** (19 October 1911, New York) to close after only seventy-two performances, it spent three richly rewarding years on post-Broadway tour. Its book by Fred de Gresac (actually Mrs. Victor Maurel, wife of the great French baritone) was unalloyed Graustark. Only Graustark was now called Zergovia, whose minister of war, Ozir (Arthur Forrest), persuades the prima donna, Vivien Savary (Kitty Gordon), to seduce Prince Ivan (Hal Forde). If Ivan marries a commoner, he must abdicate, and Ozir will then govern the country. Vivien succeeds, but falling in love with Ivan, she forces Ozir to give her the abdication papers, which she destroys. A timely discovery that Vivien has royal blood solves any remaining problem. The critics were happy with the book. They were happy with the star, Miss Gordon (an Englishwoman more famous for her beautiful back than her beautiful voice). They were happier with the sumptuous mounting (the production cost $60,000, although in keeping with a still common practice of the day it had only one set for each act). But they were happiest with Herbert's appropriately enchanting score. They especially praised two of the lovers' duets, "Rose, Lucky Rose" and "One Word From You," Vivien and Ozir's "All Your Own Am I (Champagne Song)," and the show's loveliest melody, sung by Vivien on her first entrance, "The Land Of My Own Romance," a song still sometimes revived. While the music sounds to us like a typical Herbert score, Herbert himself issued the startling statement, "I believe that one reason why 'The Enchantress' has had so huge a success in New York, and wherever it has played, is that I determined, when I started its composition, to disregard absolutely every foreign impulse and to write in a frank, free American style." The critics agreed. The *Dramatic Mirror* felt the score "typifies American popular music, so far as we can be said to have any type. At least, it is far removed from the sprightly brilliance of the recent Viennese inundation." The *Herald* attempted something of a balance, insisting, "He has written waltzes that would be applauded, even in Vienna, and in addition he has snappy, truly American, dashing march numbers and some graceful dances." In one respect Herbert was unerringly prophetic when he added, "American musical taste has developed to a point where it demands something that is native." His judgment would be vindicated three years later.

Five other shows appeared in the period between the openings of *When Sweet Sixteen* and *The Enchantress*. A Viennese operetta, **The Kiss Waltz** (18 September 1911, Casino), with more Kern interpolations, began an eleven-week run. A fine cast led by Robert Warwick, Eva Davenport, William Pruette, and Adele Rowland played out the tale of a young Italian composer—creator of "The Kiss Waltz"—who precipitates complications by courting one lady to divert attention from a second, more fervent courtship.

One week later, George M. Cohan had a resounding hit with **The Little Millionaire** (25 September 1911, Cohan). But if Cohan had managed to win over the public, he still had very few critics in his corner. *Theatre Magazine* blasted it as "the usual Cohan music salad ... hackneyed nonsense." The *Dramatic*

Mirror labeled it "A Cohan show. Everybody in the United States... will understand what that means." Certainly the equivocal statement was fairer to the show than was the magazine's "hackneyed." True, Cohan resorted to many by now familiar patterns— the racy, slangy dialogue; the jingoism; the intra-theatrical devices. But by the same token Cohan was tirelessly innovative. For example, he assigned the show's hit love song—"Oh, You Wonderful Girl"— to the villain's buddy. Like *Forty-five Minutes from Broadway* (1 January 1906), the three-act musical farce had not a single song in its middle act. Sadly, the plot was trite. Henry Spooner (Jerry Cohan) and his son Robert (George) are both to be married in order to fulfill the conditions of the late Mrs. Spooner's will. Bill Costigan (Tom Lewis) and his crony, Roscoe Handover (Sidney Jarvis), unsuccessfully oppose Robert's marriage to Goldie Gray (Lila Rhodes). Henry marries Goldie's aunt, Mrs. Prescott (Nellie Cohan). Just as sad as the trite plot was Cohan's failure to introduce an outstanding song. The score was gay, but not memorable. Cohan compensated by filling the evening with lively dancing. Some, like a flag-waving military drill, were commonplaces both for the time and for Cohan. But he also created several happily "zippy" routines for himself. Most of all he staged the finale—the wedding ceremony—as a "capital pantomime dance." The best man tripped on, followed by the bridesmaids. Then came the bride and groom, "toeing it to the altar." Last, but not least, the jauntily stepping minister appeared. The knot tied, the ensemble celebrated with fervent footwork as the curtain fell. New Yorkers flocked to the Cohan Theatre for 192 performances, making *The Little Millionaire* the biggest American musical hit of the season (always excepting the Hippodrome show).

On 27 September the Shuberts presented **The Revue of Revues** at the Winter Garden. It was a hodgepodge significant only in that it marked the American debut of Gaby Deslys. Her principal moment came in an extended dance-skit, "Les Débuts de Chicine," in which she portrayed a little Parisian waif willing to sell herself for stardom. Frank Tinney, in blackface, won many of the best notices for a long comic monologue. Also on the bill was a "Japanese Operetta."

Lew Fields's summer shows—*The Midnight Sons* (22 May 1909), *The Summer Widowers* (4 June 1910), and the regular season's *The Hen Pecks* (4 February 1911) that grew out of that series— were so successful it was inevitable that a new

production would be mounted for 1911–1912. **The Never Homes** (5 October 1911, Broadway) had fun with the raging feminist movement. Lilydale has been taken over by its women. Young Jimmy Louder (Will Archie), neglected by his political mother, sets fire to his house. Since the fire-women are busy redecorating the firehouse, they have no time to respond to the alarm. "Besides it's sort of damp today, and it wouldn't be good for the horses to go out." All Lilydale burns down. The women are hauled into court, where they are placed in the custody of their children. The men resume running the city. *The Never Homes*'s burlesque antecedents were honored by having hefty George W. Monroe play the mayoress. The music by Raymond Hubbell and A. Baldwin Sloane was mediocre, although "There's A Girl In Havana," encored until everybody in the house learned the tune, enjoyed some contemporary fame. The song was sung in the show by Jimmy and his little girlfriend, Fannie Hicks—a role assumed by the young girl Fields had favored since she made her debut in his production of *Old Dutch* (22 November 1909), Helen Hayes. While the sheet music credited others with its authorship, Irving Berlin is now known to have written the number. The drill work which so often in this period substituted for choreography was well received. But the most striking feature of the evening, as it was in Fields's earlier offerings, was the stunning staging. A real fire engine, its siren howling, darted across the stage. In the first-act finale, Lilydale burned in a stylized fire of gigantic tinsel ribbons waving in red and orange light. When the show ran ninety-two performances, far fewer than its predecessors, Fields's sensitive antennae should have warned him against continuing the series. Still, two more similar musicals followed. Both were quick failures.

The Duchess followed on the 16th. A cheaply produced version of Franz Lehar's fine **Gypsy Love** opened the next evening at the Globe, but bad reviews deprived it of a run. Marguerite Sylva was starred as Zorika, a wealthy young lady who dreams of marrying the gypsy half-brother of her fiancé but, in a bittersweet ending, marries her fiancé after all. On the 19th, *The Enchantress* premiered.

Four nights later Lionel Monckton's delightful London musical **The Quaker Girl** (23 October 1911, Park) won New York's heart and was awarded the longest run of the season (again ignoring the Hippodrome)—240 performances. *The Quaker Girl*'s story flattered audiences in this country by allowing Prudence, its heroine, to be wooed and won by Tony, the dashing American diplomat who had taught her what fun high life can be. Before the final happy ending, Prudence is rejected by her fellow Quakers for drinking champagne and insulted by a jealous actress. Ina Claire and Clifton Crawford were the leads.

November's first entry, Lew Fields's mounting of *The Wife Hunters* (2 November 1911, Herald Square), was a reworking of *Three Million Dollars*, which had toured at length the year before but never reached New York. The reworking was no help. A dreary book and weak score sank *The Wife Hunters* after only thirty-six performances. Its main plot revolved about Reginald Ogden Brace's efforts to find a wife. Bruce (John Park) discovers that the daughter of his business rival would suit him perfectly. In a comic subplot Emma Carus as Mrs. Homer Van Pelt proves her many prosperous marriages have only enhanced her allure to the wife hunters. Some novel staging had hedges and parts of a log cabin descend from the flies, to be assembled by the chorus as it sang "Mammy Jinny."

About this time a musical version of a beloved comic strip, **Mutt and Jeff**, made some brief appearances at outlying theatres such as the Grand Opera House. In this mounting Mutt and Jeff take a trip to South America and help quell a revolution in Nicadoria. They become rich after Jeff, as a jockey, wins a big race. With their wealth, they help a young man defeat the chewing-gum trust which would seize his chicle plantation, and they briefly take turns as president of the republic. The show received pleasant notices but never braved the main stem. In 1912–1913 six companies played one-night stands in small cities and neighborhood houses. Sequels followed, but they too carefully confined their routes to the hinterlands. Still, in 1914–1915 five companies of *Mutt and Jeff in Mexico* were on tour.

The Red Widow (6 November 1911, Astor), like so many of the season's musicals, came to New York only after an extensive tour that began the preceding season. Its story had Colonel Cicero Hannibal Butts (Raymond Hitchcock), a Yonkers corset-maker, allowing Anna Varvara (Sophie Bernard), would-be assassin of the czar, to use his wife's passport to cross into Russia. The real Mrs. Butts is arrested, and only when Anna falls in love with Captain Basil Romanoff (Theodore Martin) of the Imperial Bodyguard and renounces her old ways are the Buttses' problems solved. The book never took itself too seriously, and it was helped immeasurably by the personable Raymond Hitchcock. He made a marvelously

comic first entrance onto a stunningly conceived set. It depicted the foyer of a London theatre. Doors leading to the various levels were slightly ajar, and through them one could see a performance on stage. Hitchcock arrived nattily dressed as a playgoer, but immediately dropped the story line to acknowledge his audience's applause with "fifty-nine varieties of smiles and smirks"—a take-off on the falsely humble gratitude of celebrities not unlike a spoof Beatrice Lillie would offer in *High Spirits* (7 April 1964) a half-century later. The music, while commonplace, was unfailingly pleasing. The convenience of the Astor also stimulated sales. *The Red Widow* ran 128 performances.

About the time the show was premiering, the November issue of *The Theatre* appeared. It noted, "There was one period, not so very remote, when it seemed as if popular interest in comic opera and musical comedy was on the wane. Not so now. 'The Merry Widow' started a renascence." In its review of *The Red Widow* in its December issue, the magazine reiterated its conclusions: "The standard of musical comedy has been so raised of late that it has to be a very good show indeed to hold its own on Broadway." The review felt the new show didn't come up to the mark. Its opinion didn't affect the box office, but its generalizations suggested the increasingly thoughtful attention being given the musical stage. Although the magazine was correct in appreciating the higher senses of style and tone *The Merry Widow* (21 October 1907) displayed for all who were ready to learn, it ignored the immediate debilitating effect it produced on native creativity. Not all publications were quite so insensitive to this point.

The Three Romeos (13 November 1911, Globe) detailed the efforts of Dick Dawson (Alfred Kappeler), Bertie Montague (Edward Alfino), and Jack Willoughby (Fritz Williams) to find wives, when, for example, Jack loves Rosie Bellamy (Vivian Rushmore), but Rosie loves Bertie. R. H. Burnside (of the Hippodrome) was responsible for the book and lyrics, while Raymond Hubbell (later of the Hippodrome) did the music. Everything about the show was mediocre, and it lasted only fifty-six performances.

Vera Violetta, which the Shuberts brought into the Winter Garden on 20 November, was the major offering on a three-part bill. A brief vaudeville preceded it, and *Undine*, a one-act vehicle by Manuel Klein for the swimmer-showgirl Annette Kellerman, comprised the remaining item. As far as *Vera Violetta* was concerned, Harold Atteridge and Leonard Liebling were only minimally faithful to Louis Stein's original. The story recounted the hot water a professor's wife finds herself in after she flirts with the husband of the professor's old flame. Neither woman was Vera Violetta; that was the name of the professor's wife's irresistible perfume and of a waltz sung in its honor. Much of Edmund Eysler's music also gave way to domestic interpolations. The Shuberts breathed a sigh of relief when Gaby Deslys not only knew her lines but enunciated with something approaching clarity. Her difficulties with English had caused problems almost nightly in *The Revue of Revues*. She and Harry Pilcer stopped the show each evening with "The Gaby Glide," for which Louis Hirsch composed the air and Pilcer provided the words. José Collins also had a show-stopper in "Ta-Ra-Ra-Boom-Der-E." The song had been made famous by her mother, Lottie Collins. Opening night, the young Miss Collins's nerves were so on edge, she couldn't remember the lyric, so the conductor had to prompt her audibly. But the center of attention was Al Jolson. He portrayed a blackface waiter who burst into song at the slightest excuse. In *Vera Violetta* Jolson confirmed that the unique incandescence with which he had lit up the same house in *La Belle Paree* was no one-shot freak. The repeated encores he was called on to sing with "Rum Tum Tiddle" (Edward Madden/Jean Schwartz) and George M. Cohan's "That Haunting Melody" were the prelude to fifteen years as Broadway's biggest drawing card. With Jolson leading the way *Vera Violetta* recorded 112 showings.

Two importations followed. Henri Bereny's **Little Boy Blue** (27 November 1911, Lyric) was a twenty-two week success; Leslie Stuart's **Peggy** (7 December 1911, Casino), a quick failure. In the former a barmaid hears that a Scottish lord is seeking his lost heir, so she dresses up as a boy and stakes her claim. Gertrude Bryan played the barmaid, with Otis Harlan and Maude Odell sparking the comedy. Peggy also is a poor girl—a manicurist at a fashionable London hotel—who stumbles into marriage with a high-born Englishman. Renée Kelly, Farren Souter, and Harry Fisher played leading roles.

The critics found more to admire in **Betsy** (11 December 1911, Herald Square) than did the public, who bought tickets in such small numbers the show was withdrawn after four weeks. Admittedly the plotline had been used before. Its story seemed a rewrite of *The Duchess* with a suggestion or two from *The Little Millionaire*, although it was actually based on an older play, Kitty Chambers's 1909 failure, *An American Widow*. By the terms of her husband's will, the widowed Mrs. Killigrew (Grace La Rue) will lose her inheritance if she remarries anyone but an American. She marries Jasper Mallory (Robert Dempster), intending to divorce him and marry a titled Englishman (Alfred Deery). But she falls in love with Jasper and sends the earl on his way. What most pleased reviewers was the sense of tone and balance the evening evidenced, "a little play with music when it is needed … and dancing when something in the action can be better expressed in that way." Such virtues were too subtle to have general appeal.

Reginald De Koven once more tried and failed, this time with **The Wedding Trip** (25 December 1911, Knickerbocker). His music was not unlikable, but forever missed that indefinable extra touch that would allow it to soar above the ordinary. On opening night only one song—Aza's "Soldier's Song"—earned three encores. De Gresac and Smith, who had worked together with Herbert on *The Enchantress*, could not overcome the drawbacks in the score. In fact, without Herbert's melodic genius to gloss over the shortcomings, the book and lyrics seemed more leadenly Graustarkian than de Gresac and Smith's earlier effort. Fritzi (Christine Nielson) no sooner marries Felix (John McCloskey) than he must take the place of his twin brother, François, who has deserted the army. All of Francois's old flames pursue Felix, but he remains faithful. When he reveals the substitution he is condemned to be shot, until a kiss by the Gypsy, Aza (Dorothy Jardon), melts his stern commanding officer. *The Wedding Trip* was 1911's final musical. It barely survived into the new year.

Nor did 1912 get off to an auspicious start. Its first night saw Jean Gilbert's **Modest Suzanne** at the Liberty. The importation about a young lady from Tours who works her way up in Paris could not make it through the month.

But the tide turned one week later, when Eddie Foy romped in with **Over the River** (8 January 1912, Globe). Although it was based on Souchet's 1897 hit, *The Man from Mexico*, little of the story was retained. The plot concerned the problems of a man who must serve time in jail. Too ashamed to confess the truth to his wife, he pretends he is going on a trip to Mexico. His spouse's charity work leads her to his cell. Essentially a glorified vaudeville by the time Dillingham and Ziegfeld mounted it, with Maud Lambert and Lillian Lorraine prominent among the performers, it advertised "Real Cabaret on Stage" and did somehow contrive to set much of the action at Louis Martin's (read Sherry's). On opening night Fritzi Scheff and Geraldine Farrar were discovered among the on-stage patrons, and thereafter actresses impersonating The Red Widow and The Pink Lady were seated conspicuously among the guests. Much of the evening was given to dancing that ranged from "Turkey Trot to Tango." Specialty dancers, "The Marvelous Millers," "whirl and whirl and whirl," while composer Jean Schwartz played the piano as Lillian Lorraine and the chorus pranced through his "Chop Stick Rag." The show delighted seekers of good, light entertainment for four months, then toured.

Two more shows arrived in January. Both opened on the 22nd, and both closed after three weeks. One was an American version of Berte's *Kreolenblut*, called **The Rose of Panama** at Daly's. In the American retelling a Central American president prefers his romance to his position, so arranges for a coup to oust him. The other was a homegrown piece at the New York entitled **The Pearl Maiden.** Its story was a model of a type just going out of style. Pinkerton Kerr (Jefferson De Angelis), U.S. Consul on Mona Island, sells the Sharpe brothers (Charles J. Stine and Richard Taber) a bogus pearl bed in exchange for a yacht on which he hopes to flee with Nadine (Flora Zabelle), the pearl maiden. In the end the Sharpes are forgiving. The critics complained that the plot, tattered to begin with, was pushed beyond recognition by all sorts of extraneous additions. Their kindest words were reserved for Harry Auracher's music. None of it proved enduring. A decade passed before the composer, his name Americanized to Archer, had his lone smash success.

Rida Johnson Young's **Macushla** (5 February 1912, Grand Opera) gave Chauncey Olcott another popular touring attraction. Olcott's Sir Brian Fitzgerald inherits a debt-ridden estate. But that does not stop several English women from trying to gain his affection. Only after his horse, Macushla, wins a big purse in a race does he realize the love of his life is his lodge-keeper's daughter, Patricia (Gail Kane). As usual, his small selection of songs had to be encored.

For many the most emotional event of the season was Weber and Fields's Jubilee on 8 February, reuniting the long-estranged clowns in a bill not unlike their lovingly remembered annuals. Their old, tiny music hall was gone, so the reunion was staged at the larger Broadway ten blocks north. Besides the stars, most of the old crew was present—William Collier, John T. Kelly, Frankie Bailey, Fay Templeton, and

the still entrancing Lillian Russell. Missing were the witty, congenial Peter F. Dailey, dead three years since, and David Warfield, by 1912 Belasco's top dramatic actor and playing to packed houses in *The Return of Peter Grimm*. Warfield rushed through his evening's performance and made a tear-filled surprise appearance toward the end of the opening night. The evening was given a typically nonsensical Weber and Fields monicker, **Hokey-pokey.** In the slight plot, millionaire Jeremiah McCann (Kelly) brings his daughter (Helena Collier Garrick) to Paris to finish her education. Michael Dillpickle (Weber) and Meyer Bockheister (Fields) are there to provide complications. One routine found Meyer and Mike about to enter a bar with only a nickel between them. Meyer arranges with Mike to demur when he asks if Mike wants anything, but every time they go to order Mike forgets and requests a nickel cigar. Meyer keeps dragging Mike out to explain the plan and Mike keeps forgetting. Lillian Russell made her first appearance of the evening in a bejeweled pink gown to revive "Come Down, Ma Evenin' Star." The year's sensational hit comedy, *Bunty Pulls the Strings,* was selected for the burlesque and distorted, although not beyond recognition, as *Bunty, Bulls and Strings.* The entire overture was devoted to a John Stromberg medley. More old Stromberg tunes were sung in the course of the evening, supplemented by new tunes from A. Baldwin Sloane and W. T. Francis. The show was joyously received and had a profitable three-month run. It held out hope that a great tradition had not permanently disappeared.

Heuberger's exquisite **The Opera Ball** (12 February 1912, Liberty) was February's only musical. While Sydney Rosenfeld and Clare Kummer, both clever redactors, provided the American version of the libretto, miscastings and a generally slipshod mounting confined the run to four weeks. Marie Cahill made a wild knock-about farce out of the principal role of a captivating widow determined to flirt with all the men at the ball. Harry Conor abetted her in her antics. It was funny, but wrong.

As soon as *Vera Violetta* closed, the Shuberts rushed Jolson, now obviously their top ticket-seller, into another Winter Garden bill on 5 March. Opening the three-part evening was *A Night with the Pierrots.* A gigantic ramp led from the rear of the house to the stage, and the cast, mostly in white masks, made its entrance running from the back to the footlights. A similar entrance had been used two months before in Max Reinhardt's *Sumurun,* so one of the first businesses of the evening was a ragtime burlesque of that wordless play. The burlesque included a "Ragtime Sextet" (based on *Lucia di Lammermoor*) with Jolson and José Collins among the singers, and ended with Blossom Seeley inviting the rest of the cast to join in one by one, "Toddling The Todolo." The evening concluded with a pretentious "operatic mimodrama," *Sesostra*. In between, the main part of the evening was **Whirl of Society**. The show had a thread of a plot centering on a party that Mrs. Dean (Stella Mayhew) throws. As Mrs. Dean's blackface servant, Gus, Jolson made his first appearance as a character he would portray for most of his stage career. But despite its modest story line, *Whirl of Society* was basically a revue. Louis Hirsch's score and what became Jolson's inevitable interpolations were lively enough, but none became standards. While superb entertainers filled the cast, everyone knew who was the star. The same month *Whirl of Society* opened, *Variety* proclaimed, "The Shuberts may run the Winter Garden, but Al Jolson owns it." He most certainly owned it the next four months.

An importation, Felix Albini's **Baron Trenck** (11 March 1912, Casino) lasted five weeks. The baron is a daredevil soldier in the wars between Maria Teresa and Frederick the Great. He is ordered by the Empress to find a wife. The operetta was followed three nights later by the first of a batch of revivals which suggested both the inadequacy of the new domestic offerings and beginnings of an awareness of the possibilities of an American musical repertory. The initial revival was Cohan's six-year-old *Forty-five Minutes from Broadway* (1 January 1906). The same *Dramatic Mirror* which earlier had dismissed *The Little Millionaire* with condescending evasions warmly embraced the musical, rejoicing it had "stood the test of revival so staunchly," adding, "It was good to hear the old songs again... for they belong to a very popular class of musical Americana."

Five new musicals, brought in with an eye to the warm weather business, followed. **The Man from Cook's,** which opened on 25 March, had more Raymond Hubbell music, coupled this time to a Henry Blossom libretto. In it Prince Victor (Walter Percival) disguises himself as a Cook's agent to woo Marjorie Benton (Stella Hoban). Marjorie is betrothed to Lord Baffington, whom she has never seen, so Victor persuades Toto Soulard (Fred Walton) to impersonate the Lord, insult Marjorie's mother and allow Victor to come to her rescue. When the real Baffington (Leslie Kenyon) appears,

Victor employs a second friend to impersonate an equally offensive Marjorie. Victor and Marjorie wed. What possibilities the book may have had in proper hands will never be known. By the time the musical reached New York, it had been largely displaced by a spate of interpolated specialties. These included a mandolin and guitar band and a long-legged, eccentric dancer, Eleanor Pendleton. It was this very sort of irresponsible slapdash that the *Dramatic Mirror* discussed a week later in an article examining how seriously film competition was hurting musical comedy. The problem was not the excellence of the new movies but the tired material and tacky productions presented to the public: "The jokes are pretty musty; the stage Dutchman, Irishman and Jew have been used too long to be funny; the rag-time songs go stale with repetition, and so it is that this form of amusement is being backed off the boards in much the same fashion that melodramas were relegated to the junkpile." It also blamed composers like Hubbell, who poured out "trite forms of thrashed over melodies which run current in the decadent musical comedies on Broadway." The trade paper further complained, "orchestras now consist, in most cities, of one or two violins, a viola, a flute, a clarinet, a cornet, a trombone, a piano, a double bass and a vast array of instruments of percussion. The sounds... are inexpressibly disagreeable."

Another plot got lost in **A Winsome Widow** (11 April 1912, Moulin Rouge), a revision of Charles Hoyt's once popular *A Trip to Chinatown* (9 November 1891). It, too, became little more than a series of vaudeville turns although, curiously, the part of Wilder Daly, eliminated in the original, was restored. What raised it above the level of ordinary hot-weather fare was Ziegfeld's impeccable flair. The production was gorgeous. One number drew particular praise. Set in an ice palace, it had the Ziegfeld beauties skate in the bright sunlight, through the sunset, and finally out into a moonlit auditorium. Hubbell offered his second score in just over two weeks. It was another pastiche of trifling pleasantries. Several equally trifling, equally pleasant interpolations came from John Golden, Jerome Kern, Nat D. Ayer, Jean Schwartz, and a few minor names. One of these, "Be My Little Baby Bumble Bee" (Stanley Murphy/Henry I. Marshall), has retained sufficient appeal to enjoy occasional revivals. Ziegfeld filled the cast with sparkling, young talent: Emmy Wehlen, the Dolly Sisters, Elizabeth Brice, Charles King (who played the resurrected Daly), Frank Tinney, and Leon Errol. Mae West attracted the critics' attention for the first time. The show ran into September.

Four nights later Karl Hoschna's last score was introduced posthumously in **The Wall Street Girl** (15 April 1912, Cohan). It was a good score and gave the show's star, Blanche Ring, a song she would use for the rest of her career, "I Want A Regular Man." Ayer, Schwartz, and several others filled in the gaps Hoschna had left, but their material was patently inferior to Hoschna's. Miss Ring played Jamina Greene, a Wall Street "brokeress," who saves her father from financial ruin with the profits she earns from her half-interest in a controversial Nevada mine. She marries her partner, Dexter Barton (W. P. Carleton). Again, there was bright, up-and-coming talent in the supporting roles, with acclaim going to Charles Winninger and, especially, Will Rogers. His lariat act ("It's a pretty knot, is it not?"), surprisingly appropriate to the plot, stopped the show. Margaret Mayo and Edgar Selwyn's book was more than competent. But the show was not a resounding hit, lasting only seven weeks.

Two importations followed in short order. **The Rose Maid** arrived at the Globe on 22 April. When his debts are called in just before his wedding, a duke finds himself deserted by his friends and even his bride-to-be. Only a little flower girl remains loyal. A third-rate piece, beautifully done, it was a hit, running twenty-two weeks. The show's strong band of comedians joined Edward Gallagher and Al Shean for the first time. **Two Little Brides** (23 April 1912, Casino) played sixty-three times. In a way, the evening was more a domestic than a foreign creation, since the original score was entirely discarded and a new one by Gustave Kerker (his last for Broadway) substituted. Similarly only the outline of the original story was retained. It provided a vehicle for James T. Powers. As Polycarp Ivanovitch, he and a friend are caught talking with two students at a ladies' seminary. A local law decrees that under such circumstances the men must marry the girls.

The same night *The Rose Maid* premiered in New York, Philadelphia welcomed what proved to be Willard Spenser's last musical. **The Wild Goose** of the show at that city's Lyric Theatre was actually Princess Violet (Ethel Jackson). Her unconventional behavior while exiled in America earned her the nickname. But when it came to romance she proved conventional indeed, choosing Dick (David Reese), a handsome yachtsman, over Turnips (Will Philbrick), a cornball farmer. Although *The Wild Goose* was not nearly as successful as Spenser's

earlier efforts, running only one month, it sent Philadelphians out of the theatre singing "Moon! Moon! Mooney Spooney Moon!" and a waltz played as a motif throughout the evening, "Your Dream Love."

In May the parade of revivals began in earnest. William Brady and the Shuberts presented an all-star cast (De Wolf Hopper, Christine Nielson, and Eugene Cowles) in *Patience* on 6 May. The same night *Robin Hood* relit the New Amsterdam. Its cast included one old Bostonian, George Frothingham. *Robin Hood* ran two months; *Patience* ran one month. The shorter run reflected no lack of popularity. Rather Brady had meanwhile prepared *The Pirates of Penzance*, with much the same cast. It opened at the Casino on 3 June and, like *Patience*, had a limited engagement.

Only one new show appeared during this time, **Mama's Baby Boy** (25 May 1912, Broadway). Junie McCree adapted it from David Edwyn and George Fletcher's *Ma's New Husband*, which, in turn, was little more than a hasty rehash of Pinero's *The Magistrate*. To effect a second marriage, a woman lies about her age and, as a result, must deny her full-grown son. He poses as a cook. This imposture allowed a second-act "kitchen cabaret" in which the cast performed their vaudeville specialties. On opening night Lew Dockstader and Elizabeth Murray made guest appearances in this scene, and Al Jolson hurried down from the Winter Garden to sing songs from *Whirl of Society*. But a brief Jolson appearance was not enough to save a dismal evening. The show lasted one week.

The season brought to light the growing malaise in the world of musical comedy. At times this was manifest by a clear demand for new standards; at times by a confusion of standards. In a long article on the front page of its 29 May issue, the *Dramatic Mirror* attempted to analyze the problem. Although it missed completely the debilitating effects of our reliance on Vienna, and betrayed a certain illogicality, it nonetheless put a finger on some salient points:

"One lesson stands out with amazing clearness as a result of the season's record in musical comedy. Up to the brilliant revivals at the close of the season only two, possibly three, productions of this class can be set down as genuine Broadway successes, although one or two others were forced into respectable runs.

"The interesting point is that not a single operetta or musical comedy of the real Viennese style has amounted to much—possibly excepting the last one to be produced [*The Rose Maid*]. Further, the success of the musical entertainments appears to have been in inverse ratio to the tampering and rearrangements to which they had been subjected by the American managers. Simplicity of effect, studied, perhaps, has hit the public fancy, as a natural reaction from garish ostentation.

"Beyond this, demand for eccentric comedy has largely been converted into a demand for adequate singing. The failure of the operetta [Gypsy Love] that had far and away the best score among the new productions is ascribed by every commentator to the superlatively inane comedy injected into it for the benefit of American patrons.

"If producers are as eager to learn from experiment as they assert, we ought to have a season of really artistic musical comedies next year. Simple, straightforward plot, capable singers, light, tasteful comedy and easy romance are the elements that have won favor lately. Long may they flourish!"

1912–1913

The poor showing of the 1911–1912 season made producers doubly cautious. As a result they brought in fewer offerings (only two dozen new Americans mountings and eight new importations), but many of the pieces they did present showed a marked improvement in quality. They also relied heavily on revivals. *H. M. S. Pinafore* and *The Mikado* concluded the string of Gilbert and Sullivan revivals the Shuberts and William A. Brady had begun at the end of the preceding year. Athough each was given only two performances, both were enthusiastically received by the press and the public, and both were returned for brief runs in the spring, when *Iolanthe* was performed as well.

The Shuberts offered the season's first new musical on 22 July, *The Passing Show of 1912*. Apart from its title, it bore no connection with the *Passing Show* (12 May 1894) George Lederer had produced at the Casino eighteen years before. But Broadway's smart money knew of another connection. The Shuberts were consummate businessmen. The risks of innovation were normally too prohibitive for them, but they were quick to follow trends and capitalize on them. They could not ignore the growing success and fame of the *Follies*. Nor, given their vindictive natures, could they forgive Ziegfeld's close ties with Klaw and Erlanger. Apart from this rivalry, a summer annual could assure the success of their flagship, the Winter Garden, while Jolson was on vacation. One lucky break helped in the series'

inauguration. *A Winsome Widow* was so successful at the Moulin Rouge that Ziegfeld decided to leave it there for the summer and delay a new *Follies* until the fall. For the moment, then, the Shuberts had the field to themselves. *The Passing Show of 1912* was in two parts. The first was a "mime-dramatic ballet," "The Ballet of 1830." Mounted originally at London's Alhambra, it told of love among Paris artists. It wasn't particularly high-toned, but it had fun pretending it was. The real fun, the meat of the evening, came in the second part. From its inception *The Passing Show* remained closer to the old Weber and Fields tradition than the *Follies* did. Like the *Follies*—and like Weber and Fields, although it is often forgotten—there was always a line of beautiful girls in attractive, sometimes provocative, costumes. There were elegant sets, too, notably an ocean liner, a harem scene (filled with bathing girls), and an elaborate ragtime wedding scene. But unlike Ziegfeld's revues, the comedy in *The Passing Show* time and again came from burlesquing current shows. It was not the sustained spoof of a single Broadway hit in Weber and Fields's manner, but shorter parodies, of a sort later revues employed until they faded from the theatre scene. For their initial edition the brothers assembled an impressive array of young talent: Charlotte Greenwood (and her sometime partner, Sidney Grant), Anna Wheaton, Trixie Friganza, Jobyna Howland, Harry Fox, and Eugene and Willie Howard.

WILLIE and EUGENE HOWARD were born in Germany, sons of a Jewish cantor. Their real family name was Levkowitz. The elder Levkowitzes emigrated from Germany in 1887, when Willie, the younger of the brothers, was a year old. Willie made his debut in vaudeville thirteen years later as a boy soprano. For a short while he was a song-plugger for Witmark. His entry into the legitimate theatre was to have been in an Anna Held show, but his voice changed while the show was in rehearsal and he was fired. In 1903 he joined his brother, always the better singer and thereafter usually the straight-man, in a vaudeville act. But the shorter, sad-faced Willie was always recognized as the better of the two.

When the cast of *The Passing Show* was not mocking *Bought and Paid For, Bunty Pulls the Strings, Officer 666, The Quaker Girl,* and *The Return of Peter Grimm,* it was singing songs from Louis Hirsch's score or interpolations by Earl Carroll, Harry Orlob, and Irving Berlin. A run of 136 performances was more than enough to convince the Shuberts their new entry could be a bona-fide annual.

As if to suggest there was some curious, inarticulated influence between the Shuberts and Weber and Fields, Lew Fields styled his latest entry "A Jumble of Jollification" (much as the first Winter Garden attraction had been called "A Jumble of Jollity"). The musical's title, **Hanky-Panky** (5 August 1912, Broadway), connected it squarely with the old music hall tradition. But instead of Weber and Fields sparking the fun, Bobby North and Weber and Fields's old rival, Max Rogers, clowned as Herman Bierheister and Wilhelm Rausmitt in a series of misadventures that included another attempt—as in *Hurly-Burly* (8 September 1898)—to resuscitate Cleopatra's mummy. A. Baldwin Sloane's score was never more than satisfactory. Interpolations included Irving Berlin's "Opera Burlesque," "Oh, You Circus Day" (Edith Maida Lessing/Jimmy Monaco), and the already popular "On The Mississippi" (Ballard MacDonald/Harry Carroll). The show ran three months.

The Girl from Montmartre opened at the Criterion the same night as *Hanky-Panky.* Harry B. Smith adapted it from *The Girl from Maxim's,* cutting it to fit the talents of Richard Carle and Hattie Williams. Carle as Dr. Pepyton initiates a series of comic misconstructions by allowing a show girl (Miss Williams) to sleep in his bed. Jerome Kern and Henry Bereny supplied it with a pleasing, inconsequential score, the best number of which was Kern's "Don't Turn My Picture To The Wall." At least one song from *The Arcadians* ("Half Past Two") was also added. The show ran eight weeks and toured.

Chicago's most popular musical comedy performers, Cecil Lean and Florence Holbrook, co-starred in a new musical at that city's Ziegfeld Theatre on 11 August. Apparently unable to find satisfactory material elsewhere, Lean himself wrote the show. **The Military Girl** had a simple plot, virtually identical to one Hough and Adams employed for *The Golden Girl* (16 March 1909). Its heroine, Ione Field, must choose between two cadets; a rich, fat one her parents favor and a poor, thin young man. Naturally by curtain time she selects "Slim." If Lean was not much of a librettist he was even less of a composer.

He prudently supplemented his own material with songs from *Florodora* (12 November 1900) and several George M. Cohan shows. Lean and Holbrook were popular enough to win the show a modest run for all its weaknesses.

Die Fledermaus, disguised as **The Merry Countess,** began a four-month run in New York on 20 August. Besides praising the show, several critics commented happily on its steadfast refusal to allow encores. The incessant repetition of hit tunes, or of songs producers hoped would become hits, had long been a recurring irritant, and, unfortunately, the practice continued.

Two shows competed to close out August on the 31st. At the old Academy of Music a thrown-together musical called **The Girl from Brighton** ran until almost midnight. It pranced through its turns forty-nine times. At the Hippodrome **Under Many Flags** began a 445-performance run. Its frame-plot followed the flight of Captain Alan Strong from the White House lawn around the world. It filled the vast stage with the canals and tulip fields of Holland, Far Eastern temples, and a gigantic silver fountain. Manuel Klein's score had a somewhat greater contemporary vogue than Hippodrome scores customarily enjoyed, but nothing survived this short-lived popularity.

The Girl at the Gate, the biggest hit of Chicago's season, opened at the La Salle on 1 September. Its success was such that while the first company was enjoying a six-month run, a second troupe was sent out to entertain the rest of the Midwest. Neither contingent ever got closer to New York than Philadelphia. The show's bucolic title was deceptive. Its story was one of treachery and international intrigue. Will M. Hough and Frederick Donaghey's book was set in the installations surrounding the new Panama Canal. Normal Beane was expelled from West Point after he covered up the cheating of Tiffany Price, the brother of his sweetheart, Madelaine. Tiffany becomes the captain of the Engineers in Panama while Normal roams the world in disgrace. The two meet again just as Tiffany carelessly allows a beautiful Japanese spy—a young lady he believes loves him—to steal the plans for the canal's fortifications. Beane retrieves the plans, restores everyone's good name, and marries Madelaine. The show's dialogue betrayed many of the prejudices of the day:

Stawl: They're bright alright but they don't remain
    servants! There's only one thing worse than a
    Jap!

Tiffany: What's that?
Stawl: Another Jap.

At one point the stage directions call for a Japanese to be "Cringingly humble." Much of the dialogue fell back on old vaudeville material:

Guest: Where is that half portion of chicken I
ordered?
Coyne: We're waiting for someone to order the
other half. We can't kill half a bird.

The lovers' dialogue was often discouragingly stilted:

Normal: Miss Price, I'm compelled to ask a favor.
I'm sure you'll grant it.
Madelaine: A man with nothing to lose is always an
optimist.
Normal: I know that I couldn't present you with
a drink of water in the Sahara Desert; but what
I've got to ask is not to benefit me.

Ben Jerome's score was serviceable. *The Girl at the Gate* was virtually the last major musical written with Chicago in mind. A half-dozen or so appeared each season for the next few years, and every year one or two were considered good enough to bring east. But most had very brief runs. Their failures dissuaded producers from considering Chicago as an independent production center.

A number of "made-in-Chicago" shows played that city's Colonial Theatre during the 1912–1913 season. They were burlesques almost in the Weber and Fields tradition. For example, *Madame X* was mounted as *Madame Excuse Me*. It was followed by *The Merry Widow Remarried*.

Clifton Crawford wrote some of the songs for **My Best Girl** (12 September 1912, Park), in which he starred in New York. Its plot was reminiscent of *The Wedding Trip* (25 December 1911). Richard Venderfleet takes the place of an army deserter, serves the deserter's time, and finds a girl. The army background gave a certain legitimacy to the chorus's snappy military drills, while Crawford provided some interesting contrasts with his delightfully languid solos. Both the book and the score offered slim pickings, but Crawford was enough of an attraction to keep the show playing eight weeks.

On 16 September **The Count of Luxembourg** made its debut at the New Amsterdam, the same house at which *The Merry Widow* once had waltzed.

The Count of Luxembourg was the first of three Franz Lehar operettas rushed in during the 1912–1913 season. The operetta was the sole success of the trio. Its tale of a marriage of convenience that becomes a marriage of love was studded with memorable melodies, notably the waltz translated as "Say Not Love Is A Dream." Ann Swinburne and George L. Moore sang the lovers, while Frank Moulan clowned. **Eva,** famous only for a single waltz, followed at the same theatre on 30 December. It was poorly received and lingered only three weeks. The evening featured Sallie Fisher as an apprentice in a glass factory, wooed and won by the factory's young heir. **The Man with Three Wives** opened at the new Weber and Fields Theatre on 23 January and fared just a bit better.

The season's longest regular run was 248 performances; the show was **Oh! Oh! Delphine** (30 September 1912, Knickerbocker), C. M. S. McLellan's adaptation of the French farce *Villa Primrose*, with music by Ivan Caryll. Posterity has not concurred with the contemporary judgment of the show, which hailed it as a worthy successor to the team's *The Pink Lady* (13 March 1911). The plot was much the same French froth; but it was beguilingly handled, with a tongue-in-cheek naughtiness. The action was set in Brest, at a hotel where reserve officers on their yearly tour of duty house their wives and mistresses. Victor Jobileau (Scott Welsh) arrives with so many girls he is suspected of being "the Mormon of the house." Victor is separated from his wife, Delphine (Grace Edmond). Their friends Alphonse (Frank McIntyre) and Simone Bouchette (Stella Hoban) have fallen out of love. While Bouchette has brought along a Persian girl as mistress, the four principals agree to change partners. When rich Uncle Noel (George A. Beane) appears, they are forced to resume their original pairing, lest he disinherit them. They find they like this old way best, after all. The book was filled with "cute" touches. Delphine takes her parrot wherever she goes. The parrot is forever speaking out the show's title as a warning to his lady—even injecting it into the title song. When Bouchette attempts to pass off the Persian, Bimboula (Octavia Broske), as his wife, he warns the French commander, "She speaks no English." McLellan's lyrics were often droll. Early in the evening Victor, an artist by profession, tells philistines that ladies supply his afflatus. He employs so arcane a word, he sings, "to scare 'em," adding the dolts construe it as "Latin for harem." If the book was as well written as *The Pink Lady*, the evening nonetheless lacked two magical ingredients of the earlier hit: Hazel Dawn and a great waltz. The best Caryll could do this time around was "The Venus Waltz." In the hopes of establishing it as another "My Beautiful Lady," it was played, as one critic rued, "ad nauseum." (How swiftly the lesson of *The Merry Countess* was forgotten!) But it was patently inferior.

Tantalizing Tommy (1 October 1912, Criterion), based on *La Petite Chocolatière (The Richest Girl)*, told of a rich candy-manufacturer's daughter who learns she cannot buy love. The musical, with melodies by Hugo Felix, starred Elizabeth Brice. Despite some good notices, it floundered after thirty-one performances.

The following night another musical destined for quick oblivion came from the opposite direction. **The Charity Girl** (2 October 1912, Globe) had opened in Chicago in July and promptly created a furor. It created an uproar, of somewhat smaller proportions, in New York. There were some who thought the story was not fit for musical treatment, relating, as it did, the story of a young heiress (Marie Flynn) who gives up her comforts to do charity work in the slums. But the story was treated frivolously, in the musical comedy fashion of the day, so that many of young Rosemary's adventures revolved around a comic clairvoyant (Ralph Herz). Some idea of the show's general attitude can be gauged from the joyously syncopated song and dance Blossom Seeley and Henry Fink did as "The Ghetto Glide." Victor Hollaender's score would have been unexceptional, but for a single number. And to that number not only many critics but the police in both Chicago and New York took strenuous exception. Although the period still flaunted its rugged individualism and ill-concealed contempt for people on the dole, its moral hypocrisy demanded an outcry against any lady of the streets who would sing "I'd Rather Be A Chippie Than A Charity Bum." But the song's notoriety was not sufficient to make an otherwise somewhat feeble show into a hit. *The Charity Girl* ran two and a half weeks.

Edmund Eysler's **The Woman Haters** (7 October 1912, Astor) quickly closed. During its brief stay it followed the downfall of a German major who quarrels with a widow he is about to marry, swears off all women, and forms a woman haters' club. The widow has a club that holds its meetings at the same restaurant.

Two weeks later, on the 21st, the long-delayed **Ziegfeld Follies of 1912** appeared at the Moulin Rouge. It is remembered today largely for one interpolation, "Row, Row, Row" (William Jerome/ Jimmy Monaco), sung by Lillian Lorraine. But first-nighters found much more to applaud. Foremost were the beautiful girls, lavishly bedecked. The *Times* reported that in "The Palace Of Beauties," "The audience gasped… at the first figure to enter—a harlequin in complete attire of black lace." Venus, Carmen, and Joan of Arc followed. A finale in a circus tent had the "pony" chorus racing around the ring in tarlatan ballet dresses, while Lillian Lorraine, representing the 20th-century Girl, paraded in a lemon-colored dress with a flaming orange cape and a black headpiece. Leon Errol and Bert Williams again led the clowns. Williams introduced three sorrowfully comic songs, "My Landlady," "You're On The Right Road But You're Going The Wrong Way," and "Blackberrying Today." He combined with Errol in a hilarious taxicab number. The broken-down hack was one Williams reportedly found and bought from a Central Park driver. In the skit he played a forlorn cabbie caught between his impatient, nervous customer (Errol) and a stage horse that sat down, crossed its legs, and refused to budge. Bernard Granville came over from the Shuberts to sing the straight tunes. The *Follies* were not, as some detractors have claimed, ponderous, slow-moving affairs whose comic numbers were inserted to allow the girls to change costumes. Harry B. Smith, who bid farewell to the show with this edition, observed:

> "The Follies of 1912" began in what was then a rather novel fashion. Before the curtain rose, people in the audience started an argument, the subject of the dispute concerning the kind of entertainment those present expected and preferred. The disputants were actors in the cast placed in various parts of the auditorium. Harry Watson was a gallery god vociferously demanding the sort of show he liked. Charles Judels was a Frenchman who from his orchestra seat decried all American theatricals.

Next to *Oh! Oh! Delphine* **The Lady of the Slipper** (28 October 1912, Globe) had the longest run of any regular American musical of the season: 232 performances. Oddly, although it gave Victor Herbert one of the longest Broadway stays of his career, it remains among his least remembered works. The fault was not Herbert's, for the score, while not one of his best, was delightful. The musical's fame and fortunes have ebbed because it was created as a vehicle for its stars, and without them the heavy-handed libretto might bring down the whole enterprise. When Charles Dillingham first announced his plans, he boasted the show would have one of the greatest all-star casts in history. Inevitably, temperaments clashed; both Joseph Cawthorn and Irene Castle withdrew during rehearsals. Vernon Castle left shortly after the New York opening. But Elsie Janis, Dave Montgomery, and Fred Stone alone would have been enough to ensure its success. It was another of those wide-eyed, innocent drolleries they and their public reveled in. This time, as the title suggests, they cavorted with Cinderella (Miss Janis). Montgomery played Punks, and Stone played Spooks, two characters, as the program stated, "from the cornfield"—a cornfield all their fans knew was situated not far from Oz. Both employed much the same makeup they had used a decade before. Together the boys helped Cinderella get to the ball. They saw to it Crown Prince Maximilian (Douglas Stevenson) put the shoe on her foot in time to save his throne. In her fetchingly candid autobiography Miss Janis confessed the stars "were the least fitted to sing Victor Herbert's music. Fortunately, we could always go into our dance, and we did!" How Herbert solved his stars' problems can be seen in the two-part harmony of "A Little Girl At Home." For Cinderella he wrote a simple repetitive line, almost a monotone, allowing the better-voiced Prince to carry the engaging melody. Since much of Herbert's most beautiful writing was for descriptive sections and for the ballet numbers, no other song attained the popularity of "A Little Girl At Home." Dillingham gave the work a sumptuous mounting that included a chariot with six ponies to race Cinderella to the palace.

Probably the season's most noteworthy failure was an antiwar comic opera with a score by Walter Damrosch. Entitled The Dove of Peace (4 November 1912, Broadway), it was a fiasco, removed from the stage after a meager two weeks. Most of the blame lay with the book, which had an intriguing, if complicated, story, but which handled its material ineptly and leadenly. The story, much simplified, ran as follows: Shy Willie Perkins's grandmother (apparently something of a witch or demi-god) states in her will that if Willie (Frank Pollock) is kissed before he is twenty-five universal peace will encompass the world. But Willie is so afraid of women, he runs away to Guam, and the Spanish–American War breaks out as a result. In Guam, Terrance Donnybrook (Arthur Deagon), the peace commissioner, persuades Willie at the

last moment to kiss Hildegarde Tyler (Alice Yorke). When he does, everyone lays down his arms. Not unexpectedly peace proves stultifying. "What! No more parades, brass bands, tall soldiers with brass buttons and all that sort of thing? Nay, Nay." Conveniently, a clause in the grandmother's will is interpreted to mean only men won't fight. Suffragettes see their opportunity and seize the Senate from its sleeping members. Only then is it realized that, since Willie was on Guam when he was kissed, the time difference hid the fact that he had actually passed his twenty-fifth birthday. Everyone avidly returns to battle. Damrosch's score was strikingly superior to the book. Critic after critic lavished kudos on it. Even so, Damrosch must bear some of the blame for the show's quick failure. He was not unrealistic. He tried to write a commercial score, but his artistry was inimical to Broadway requirements. As the Herald observed, the "music is too ambitious for the 'tired businessman' who wants his to tinkle merrily." For example, although the chorus of the title song began with an especially pleasant melody, it quickly developed into a more complicated and hardly "catchy" theme. The verse, too, was a more artful than attractive lead-in to the chorus. The production was praised for exceptionally fine singing by both principals and chorus, and for the excellent symphonic sounds emanating from the orchestra pit. Nor was the evening without its livelier moments. Deagon and Jessie Bradbury were reported as "convulsing the audience" with their dance for "The Caveman and the Cavewoman." It is doubtful if any European powers ever heard of the show. They were too busy preparing for the war to come.

Another interesting failure entered just over a week after the first showing of The Dove of Peace. For nearly a decade Jerome Kern had been adding attractive interpolations to several musicals each season. Now the Shuberts, who had called on him to do a substantial part of the music for the first Winter Garden production, allowed him to compose the whole score for a lyric version of Rida Johnson Young's 1911 flop, Next, rechristened for the musical stage The Red Petticoat (13 November 1912, Daly's). While hindsight allows us to hear hints of the future Kern in some of his songs for the evening, the score was undistinguished. It received a fittingly polite reception, but no more. One passing comment in the Times review suggests a degree of artistry was expected and appreciated—a sort of artistry discounted or taken for granted today. In remarking on the presentation of one song, "Since

The Days Of Grandmamma," the paper made a point to praise a felicitous "flute and clarinet obbligato" in the orchestration. Miss Johnson did the book. As she had the year before, she told of Sophie Brush's adventures as a woman barber in a rough and tumble mining town. Sophie (Helen Lowell) delighted the *Dramatic Mirror*: "For a musical comedy the heroine of *The Red Petticoat* is a most decided novelty. She is dressed to look her homeliest; she is an old maid and a combatively amatory one." The trade sheet recorded how pleased first-nighters were when Sophie changed her make-up and dress, and won her man. But there were limits to the *Mirror's* tolerance of novelty, and it insisted archly that Nevada was "the last place in the world to furnish local color for a musical play." However, most critics agreed with its appraisal: "an unconventional musical comedy which will not especially amuse or bore." Enough ticket-buyers appeared at the box office to keep *The Red Petticoat* alive for sixty-one performances.

In their own small ways Damrosch and Kern's pieces were daring, hinting at the depth and breadth of many later Broadway musicals. **The Gypsy** (14 November 1912, Park), which opened the night after *The Red Petticoat*, looked unabashedly backward. Its story reminded playgoers of the ten-twenty-thirty melodramas that silent movies had done to death. Several commentators looked on it as a watered-down *Il Trovatore*, for it detailed the mix-up of children at a gypsy camp. In the last act the handsome young gypsy chief is proven to be the long-lost heir to the baronial hall painted on the act's backdrop. The piece was removed after twelve showings. What especially disheartened many writers was the obvious deterioration it revealed in the talents of both Frank Pixley and Gustav Luders. Their days of inventiveness and success were receding fast. No one was more disheartened than Pixley. He retired from the stage to devote his few remaining years to writing for silent pictures. He died, at fifty-two, on 31 December 1919.

(From) Broadway to Paris, a revue built primarily around the abilities of the audacious Gertrude Hoffman, arrived at the Winter Garden on 20 November. Miss Hoffman's appearances disclosed her in a variety of styles and moods "from Aubrey Beardsley poster effects, deep-shadowed, Carmen-lipped and auburn-hued, to a sunlit figure, flesh tinted and flaunting a mass of golden hair." Her skimpy costumes and wriggling dances kept the evening on the boards for ten weeks.

November's fifth musical turned out to be the last of the great Weber and Fields burlesques. On the 21st, it opened the new Weber and Fields Music Hall, which the Shuberts had built on 44th Street, and followed the comedians' traditional two-part pattern. The first part was **Roly Poly,** a vaudeville tied together with a weak plot in which Tanzman (Fields) and Schmaltz (Weber) take the waters at Raatenbad. Bijou Fitzsimmons (Marie Dressier) pursues Schmaltz, and he is forced to play dead to escape. The act ended with the colossal Miss Dressler collapsing on tall, thin Fields. Besides the great clowns, the star-studded cast included Nora Bayes, who sang "When It's Apple Blossom Time In Normandy" (Mellor, Gifford, and Trevor), Bessie Clayton, Jack Norworth, and Frank Daniels. Miss Clayton received special kudos for her "art dance." The *corps de ballet* was also praised, especially for a "stunning stage picture," with the *corps* divided into three groups—one in white, one in green, and one in scarlet. A Weber and Fields show meant a gorgeous chorus line—and *Roly Poly,* happily, proved no exception. For their second-act travesty they presented, with not too straight faces, **Without the Law.** The characters in what had once been Bayard Veiller's gripping thriller *Within the Law* were instantly recognizable to knowledgeable theatregoers. Inspector Burke became Inspector Bunk, with Weber under the greasepaint, while Fields transformed the forger Joe Garson into Joke Arson. Again the public and critics rejoiced. But things were not well backstage. The principals were all aging, and the infamous feud was still smoldering. An eight-year hiatus had deprived the company of the chance to recruit younger talent gradually and carefully. Moreover Weber, and particularly Fields, had found easier, more lucrative opportunities elsewhere. The seven-and-a-half-week run was the only time Weber and Fields played together at the theatre named for them. Indeed, it was the last time the great comics played together for New York audiences. Shortly after the house opened the Shuberts hastily changed its name to the 44th Street Theatre.

One sign that all was not well between Weber and Fields could have been read nine nights later when Fields alone offered New York **The Sun Dodgers** (30 November 1912, Broadway). Fields apparently loved night people. *The Sun Dodgers,* like *The Midnight Sons* (22 May 1909), dealt with a society that rarely awoke before the crack of noon. Mrs. Honoria O'Day (George W. Monroe) would cater to these night owls by turning her farm into a lively resort, but her nephew, with the help of Praline Nutleigh (Bessie Wynn), wangles the land for a homestead. As always Fields gave the evening a superb mounting. The *Dramatic Mirror* called the chorus line the most beautiful Broadway had seen in years and praised the effects Fields achieved at one point by having the girls dance with tiny electric bulbs on their caps and shoes. But most New Yorkers found better entertainment elsewhere, so Fields removed this "Fanfare of Frivolity" after just twenty-nine showings.

The Firefly (2 December 1912, Lyric) was the season's most endearing and most enduring musical. Behind it lay a revealing tale of backstage sensitivities. When Victor Herbert signed to write what ultimately became *Naughty Marietta* for Hammerstein's company, and notably Emma Trentini, he agreed to follow it with a second work, if the first enjoyed sufficient success. In the beginning there were good feelings all around. But as the tour of *Marietta* progressed, repetition and fatigue eroded much of the good will. Trentini grew increasingly difficult. During the first week of April 1912 a gala performance was scheduled, in honor of the twenty-fifth anniversary of Oscar Hammerstein's first theatre. It was to take place at the West End Theatre in Harlem, and Herbert was persuaded to conduct. From all accounts it was a superb performance—until Herbert signaled Trentini to encore "Italian Street Song." When she refused, Herbert thought she misunderstood his movements. He signaled again and, seeing Miss Trentini looking directly at him, motioned the orchestra to begin. Trentini walked obstinately off into the wings, and Herbert, in a fury, stalked out. The next day he announced he would never again write so much as a note for his erstwhile star. Since *Naughty Marietta* was about to close and the new show had been promised to the public, a desperate search began for Herbert's replacement. With insight and courage Hammerstein turned to a young immigrant—Rudolf Friml.

RUDOLF FRIML was born in Prague on 7 December 1879. Something of a child prodigy, he had his first composition, a "barcarolle," published when he was only ten years old. Friends and relatives combined to send

him to the Prague Conservatory, at that time flourishing under Antonin Dvořák. Soon he was accompanying the young violinist Jan Kubelik. Both with Kubelik and alone as a concert pianist, he made several tours of the United States, settling here in 1906. When Hammerstein approached him, apparently at the suggestion of Max Dreyfus and Rudolph Schirmer, he had begun to make a small reputation as a composer of light concert pieces. But his ability to write a commercial, theatrical score was untested.

The score Friml provided for *The Firefly* fully justified Hammerstein's gamble. It was one of Broadway's great scores, a worthy sequel to *Naughty Marietta*. Although it was thoroughly European in its sound, it was composed for a story, like *Naughty Marietta*'s, set in America. Unlike the earlier piece, it was not an America of a distant, romantic day, but rather of much the same world its audiences stepped out into on leaving the theatre. At a pier at the foot of 23rd Street the Van Dare yacht is preparing to sail for Bermuda. Geraldine Van Dare (Audrey Maple), the owner's niece, arrives with her fiancé, Jack Travers (Craig Campbell). They are quarreling. Geraldine, snobbish and bitchy, insists she has witnessed a flirtation between Jack and a little Italian street singer. After the two have boarded, the waif, Nina Corelli (Miss Trentini), appears. She spots an old friend in Suzette (Ruby Norton), Geraldine's maid. Prodded by Suzette she admits she did indeed wink at Jack, but, after all, what does it matter if "Love Is Like A Firefly." Her light-heartedness is a cover. At home her drunken guardian beats her. She would like to escape, and when she hears the yacht is heading for Bermuda, she inquires if Bermuda is farther away than Coney Island. Assured it is, she begs to come aboard. Suzette points out that the jealous Geraldine would never allow it, so Nina rushes home and changes into her brother's clothes. She returns, and with disarming naïveté she tells Suzette she is now Antonio Columbo, a neighborhood pickpocket. Tony sings a love song, "Giannina Mia." Another passenger, the musician Franz (Henry Vogel), believes this is the voice he has been seeking for his choir. He begs the Van Dares to allow the "boy" to accompany them. There is some reluctance. But Nina, seeing Corelli approach, runs aboard as the gangplank is raised. At the Van Dares' Bermuda estate everyone has fallen in love with the boy, except Geraldine, whom the boy reminds of the street singer. And the disguised Nina has fallen in love with Jack. She is overjoyed when she is offered a job by Jack:

Jack: How would you like to be my valet, Tony?
Nina [As Tony]: What is valet?
Franz: You have to take care of Jack's clothes and help dress him.
Nina: Dress him? He's old enough to dress himself! I don't think I do for that job.
Jack: Why not?
Nina: I'm not that kind of a boy.

Geraldine, feeling more and more isolated, sulks. Jack's uncle, John Thurston (Melville Stewart), alone offers her "Sympathy." But a thief is loose, and when the police connect the robbery with a pickpocket, Antonio Columbo, known to be on the island, Nina is forced to drop her masquerade. Amid the general consternation Franz agrees to adopt the waif, and the two go off together. The last act takes place in the Van Dare home in New York. Three years have passed. While Jack has been away his romance with Geraldine has cooled. But he comes to her house on a courtesy call just as Franz returns with his charge. Only now she is no longer Nina Corelli. Under Franz's careful tutelage she has become Giannina, a great prima donna. Jack realizes it is she he loves, and Giannina confesses she has never stopped loving him.

The characters were well drawn, if sometimes two-dimensional. For the most part, Otto Hauerbach's dialogue was satisfactory, despite occasional infelicities. Hauerbach's way with dialect suggested he did not have the most carefully attuned ear. Nina says of her early encounter with Geraldine, "She looks as if she would keel me when I smile at the young gen'man." Now and then the writing could be surprisingly stilted. The tongue-lashed little immigrant responds, "How dare you thus revile me?"

Apart from Trentini, what made the show were Friml's melodies, and with Trentini's lovely soprano so long silent, it remains Friml's score that keeps the piece alive. Rich and diverse, the music stays fresh with repeated hearing. Three of its best-loved pieces indicate its range from the lushly arioso "Giannina Mia" to the tender "Sympathy" to the bubbly "Love Is Like A Firefly."

If the comment in the *Times* review of *The Red Petticoat* about some of the orchestration disclosed a happily thoughtful side of the American Musical Theatre of this era, another comment in the *Times* review of *The Firefly* exposed a more debatable facet—the persistent demand for and granting of encores. (After all, a dispute over an encore resulted in Friml writing *The Firefly*'s score instead of Herbert.) While the *Times* and other papers had long railed against the practice, in the case of the new work the paper could note, "for once it was possible to be patient with the encore fiends."

For various reasons, nine of the season's musicals ran as long as or longer than *The Firefly*. Its 120 performances coincidentally equaled the run of Lehar's *The Count of Luxembourg*, the best of the new imports. And they alone remain unquestionably stageable today.

Two musicals came in for Chicago's inspection one night apart just before Christmas. **Frivolous Geraldine** opened at the Olympic on 22 December; **Exceeding the Speed Limit** at Cohan's Grand Opera House on the 23rd. Both were set in Paris; both were failures. *Frivolous Geraldine* told of a young lady who must choose between an "apache" and an American who is under a cloud of suspicion. She clears the American's name and marries him. The musical's book was by Theodore Stempfel; its songs were by Herbert Stothart and Joe Howard. The *Tribune*, complaining Howard's music was increasingly derivative, remarked nastily, "He cares not who writes his songs, so long as he remembers them." The show at the Opera House was a French work with music by Antony Mars, adapted as a vehicle for Carter De Haven and Elizabeth Murray.

In New York three more musicals offered themselves for approval in December. **Miss Princess** (23 December 1912, Park), more American-made Graustark, lasted two weeks. Its star, Lina Abarbanell, played Princess Polonia, who political considerations have decreed must marry Prince Alexis (Henri Leoni), though she loves a common soldier, Capt. Merton Raleigh (Robert Warwick). Her problems are solved when Alexis elopes with an actress. A way was somehow found in Graustark for two "Texas Tommy" dancers to rouse the audience "to a high pitch of enthusiasm."

Franz Lehar's *Eva* premiered on 30 December. The same night, Sam Bernard came into the Lyric with **All for the Ladies,** which for more than three months added to Broadway's merriment, even if the show made no significant contribution to Broadway's art. Bernard played Leon von Laubenheimer, a dress designer, whose comic machinations save the house of Clemente and Panturel from the financial rocks. The couturier's studio allowed a dozen or so beautiful show girls to model gowns of such high fashion that the audience audibly gasped. In keeping with so many American musical comedies, its setting was European. Its American music, by Alfred G. Robyn, was commonplace. But Robyn and his librettist, Henry Blossom, seemed to think Europe gave the songs an added cachet. The juxtaposition had worked for Robyn in *The Yankee Consul* (22 February 1904) and *A Yankee Tourist* (12 August 1907); it worked again with *All for the Ladies.*

Nearly a month passed before another musical arrived. **Somewhere Else** (20 January 1913, Broadway) was an eight-performance failure with shakingly tragic consequences. The show had the second Gustav Luders score of the season, but following the breakup of his partnership with Frank Pixley, Luders worked with a new librettist, Avery Hopwood. In later years Hopwood became a playwright of some renown, but the book for this "musical fantasy" represented one of his first public efforts and underscored his inexperience. The story line struck many critics as a bad example of a type that had flourished a decade or more before and, while still not totally out of style, was rapidly losing its freshness and appeal. To escape a nagging stepdaughter, widowed Billy Getaway (Taylor Holmes) of New York sails his yacht to the land of Somewhere Else. He and the queen (Cecil Cunningham) of Somewhere Else fall in love. But his stepdaughter, Hepzibah (Catherine Hayes), having stowed away on the boat, appears, bent on trouble. Since Billy has told the queen his only daughter was still an infant, he has Hepzibah hypnotized and made to believe she is three years old. He builds her a monstrous perambulator to reinforce the delusion. An accidental handclap brings the girl to reality, but love wins out not merely for Billy and the queen, but also for Hepzibah and the queen's step-uncle. The faults of the libretto were aggravated by the weakness of the score. Luders, who had just turned forty-eight, was either written out or in a prolonged slump, which one will never be known. Two days after the scathing reviews appeared, Luders was found dead, officially of "cerebral apoplexy." Broadway scuttlebutt rejected this explanation, preferring to believe the composer, who had harbored the highest hopes for his last piece, succumbed to the shock and distress brought on by its failure. The appraisals of his output in his obituaries were not flattering. The *Dramatic Mirror* wrote, "Mr. Luders' work was variable and not especially inspired, much of it suggesting familiar strains from many well known sources." Such harsh judgments were unfair. True, Luders did not grow with experience, as many gifted composers did. From the beginning the range of his best work was restricted. His was a small, sweet, clear voice. When it sang a felicitous melody, it sang enchantingly.

The night of Luders's death Lehar's *The Man with Three Wives* (23 January 1913, Weber and Fields) began a fifty-two-performance run. Four evenings later, Chauncey Olcott opened in **The Isle o' Dreams** (27 January 1913, Grand Opera House). It was a typical Olcott vehicle, more a romantic melodrama than a musical. It attracted a typical Olcott audience—an audience not unlike those once loyal to Harrigan and Hart. It was predominantly Irish, if a bit more refined than patrons of the 1880s. One reviewer reported, "the audience very soon became a prominent feature of the performance, insisting on manifesting its pleasure after almost every line, as is the joyful custom with Mr. Olcott's regular clientele, and fairly going mad after he sang a song. As a result it was within one or two minutes of 11 o'clock when the curtain went up on the fourth and last act." Set in 1799 at the time of Napoleon's threatened invasion of Ireland, *The Isle o' Dreams* followed the adventures and love affair of Ivor Kelway. Kelway is mistaken for a French spy. Much of the action took place in the pub run by his foster mother (Jennie Lamont) on a small island off the Irish coast. Both the pub and the islet were called The Isle o' Dreams. Out of Ernest R. Ball's numbers for the evening came two of the most popular songs the American stage has ever produced, "When Irish Eyes Are Smiling" and "Mother Machree," both, of course, sung by Olcott. Although *The Isle o' Dreams* played a mere thirty-two performances at the Grand Opera House, it toured big cities and small towns across the country for years.

Only two musicals arrived in February. Both were hits. The first was a London success, Paul Rubens's **The Sunshine Girl** (3 February 1913, Knickerbocker), graced in Frohman's American production by the beguiling Julia Sanderson, as a young lady prevented by another stage will from marrying the man of her choice. Irene and Vernon Castle—who had come to America's attention in 1912 after their success in Paris—won applause with their graceful ballroom dancing, although the biggest show-stopper was a tango Castle performed with Miss Sanderson. The Castles' popularity coupled with the new tangos and ragtime dances gave birth

to the phenomenon known as "the dancing craze."
Miss Sanderson made "Honeymoon Lane," an interpolation by Jerome Kern, one of the evening's hits.
Joseph Cawthorn provided the comedy. The show
ran into the warm weather.

Equally successful was The Honeymoon Express
(6 February 1913, Winter Garden), a rapid-paced
"farce with music" that starred Al Jolson and Gaby
Deslys. Miss Deslys wore a series of striking gowns,
from a simple black-and-white affair for her entrance
to a wildly bespangled dress for a flashy dance with
Harry Pilcer. Dixon and Doyle did several turns,
and dependable Ada Lewis portrayed another of her
tough ladies. The cast included two up-and-coming
youngsters, Harry Fox and Fanny Brice. The score
was undistinguished, but Jolson's delivery was so
sensational few noticed. No Jolson standards came
out of the score, although "You Made Me Love You"
(Joe McCarthy/Jimmy Monaco), which Jolson
sang to the last, was sometimes interpolated. Later
Jolson stopped the show when he added "Who
Paid The Rent For Mrs. Rip Van Winkle?" (Alfred
Bryan/Fred Fisher). Apart from Jolson the hit of the
evening was a spectacular stage effect that reunited
the parted honeymooners Henri Dubonet (Ernest
Glendinning) and Yvonne (Miss Deslys) in time for
the finale. It depicted a race between a train and an
auto "from the first faint glimmer of distant lights
way up on the mountain side, through the devious
turns of the road and down to the valleys, on to
the level stretch, into tunnels and out of them, and
finally, right down to the footlights with a rush and
a roar."

Before March's first entry premiered, an interesting article appeared in the Dramatic Mirror. It was
an interview with Gustave Kerker, in the first decade
of the century one of Broadway's most popular and
prolific composers, who, with one brief exception,
had not been heard from since 1907—the year of
The Merry Widow. His comments illuminated both
the endemic public confusions and his personal bitterness. He began by saying he wanted to talk about
"light operas (musical comedies we call them now)."
If a musician like Kerker did not distinguish between
the two forms, who could expect the public to be
clear in its mind? "Ever since The Merry Widow,"
Kerker continued, "managers have simply fallen all
over themselves in their efforts to acquire operettas,
written by Viennese composers." But it soon became
apparent his real objection was not to this. After
all, Kerker himself was German and could write—
though without any great flair—in the Viennese

manner. His real animosity was directed at producers for their lack of respect toward composers. He
rued the lack of respect for the integrity of score and
then, in a seeming about-face, he decried the lack of
recognition afforded interpolators: "There is a certain musical comedy playing in town now that has
the name of a famous Viennese composer in letters
of fire on the outside of the theatre. As a matter of
fact there are three numbers by this composer in the
entire score of eighteen numbers." Kerker looked
back longingly to the days when "the author had the
principal voice in the interpretation of the piece."
There was a certain justice in Kerker's remarks. But
he naturally overlooked the fact that some of the dis-
respect had been earned. It was understandable for
producers inundated with hack material to attempt
to improve their shows by any means available. But
producers recognized and respected quality. There
was little or no tampering with the work of Ivan
Caryll or Karl Hoschna or Victor Herbert.

March's first entry presented coincidentally
the music of another composer long absent from
Broadway. The American Maid (3 March 1913,
Broadway) had a score by John Philip Sousa, some
of which he lifted from his unproduced 1893 work
The Glass Blowers. The plot, too, was a reworking
of the old book by the original librettist, Leonard
Liebling. Silas Pompton, a glass manufacturer, wants
his daughter Geraldine (Louise Gunning) to marry
a duke (Charles Brown), but Geraldine prefers Jack
Bartlett (John Park). Some "modernisms" crept in.
The hero of the 1913 version distinguishes himself
in Spanish-American War combat, shown on motion
pictures while old Sousa marches were played. The
public was not receptive. The show was withdrawn
after two weeks, and without any ado Sousa bid a
final farewell to the Broadway scene, except for scattered songs and appearances. The old Broadway
Theatre, converting to a movie house, also left the
legitimate arena.

A vaudeville called Marie Dressler's All Star
Gambols frolicked for a week beginning 10 March
on the new stage meant for Weber and Fields. Charles
E. Evans brought over his playlet "It's up to You" from
the two-a-day circuits. After Robert Drouet and Mme.
Yorska presented a truncated version of Camille,
Miss Dressler and Jefferson De Angelis offered their
mock version. De Angelis and Miss Dressler led the
ensemble in "The Evolution Of Dancing." When the
show left, New York saw the start of the spring parade
of revivals that for a few seasons threatened to supplant the traditional "summer musicals." Between late

March and late May six old-timers were brought back for runs of varying length: *The Beggar Student, The Geisha, The Mikado, H. M. S. Pinafore, Iolanthe,* and *Mlle. Modiste.*

In Chicago, aisle-sitters dismissed Ashley Miller's trite book and Joseph Carl Briel's "tuneless" music for **The Seventh Chord** (30 March 1913, Illinois). ("Ugly music is not any more welcome than Cubist art," one critic pontificated.) In a skylit boardinghouse garret, a young southerner, with only three dollars in his pocket, awaits the first performance of his new opera. But on opening night the prima donna, offered a luxurious trip to Europe, deserts the company. Luckily, the boardinghouse chambermaid, who secretly loves the composer, has learned the part. She goes on and triumphs. When the deserter returns repentent she is not made welcome. A subtext of Christian Science was seen by some in the story, and one review reported that no less than Gustave Kerker was musical director.

For many decades Westerners and Midwesterners talked about a Los Angeles musical that critics rejected and that the records show was not hugely successful, **The Tik-Tok Man of Oz** (30 March 1913, Morosco). Its producer, Oliver Morosco, lavished a then noteworthy $40,000 on this mounting with music by Louis F. Gottschalk and a book by Oz's creator, L. Frank Baum. And, in fairness, most critics praised the beauty of its settings and costumes. What they objected to was the dullness and derivativeness of the book. When it reached Chicago, one reviewer lamented that it was "almost letter for letter, scene for scene, spectacle for spectacle and chorus girl for chorus girl" a copy of *The Wizard of Oz.* Thus, instead of opening with a tornado, the extravaganza opened with a storm at sea and a "nice deep blue shipwreck with lots of thunder"; instead of Dorothy and Toto, her pet dog, there was Betsy Bobbin and Hank, her pet mule. Among the other characters were the Shaggy Man; the Magnet Girl; King Ruggedo, the Metal Monarch; Queen Ann So Forth of Oogaboo; and Polychrome, the Rainbow's Daughter. Reviews suggested that the Tik-Tok Man was an approximation of the earlier Scarecrow, and that Ruggedo, in whose underground throne room the final act takes place, was this piece's answer to the Wizard.

One exceptional amateur production deserves notice. **The Lady of Luzon** opened for a week's run at Pittsburgh's Alvin Theatre on 2 April. It advertised itself as "made-in-Pittsburgh," and the Pittsburgh *Dispatch* recorded, "No amateur production was ever given on a more elaborate scale." The boast may well have been true, for the Pittsburgh Athletic Association spent $20,000 on the production. Only the most sumptuous Broadway mountings of the day equaled that figure. Like *The Girl at the Gate,* the show reflected America's concern with "the Yellow Peril." Brigado Faustino Guillermo would force Olivia Benicia, the lady of Luzon, to marry Lt. Monroe of the Army Engineer Corps. Guillermo is fond of Monroe's mother, and together they hope to wrest Olivia's land from her. But Olivia loves Rosendo Montijo. Montijo is an inventor, and Guillermo's treachery includes a plan to sell the design of a gun Montijo has invented to a Japanese spy. An American newspaperman, Warren Phyxit, arrives to set matters straight. The athletic association hired R. H. Burnside to direct the production, but it relied on local talent to write the show. Alfred W. Birdsall created the book. A local newspaperman, Marcus C. Connelly, provided lyrics for Zoel Parenteau's music. The *Dispatch* was especially happy with Parenteau's "style of his own," adding he "juggled harmony and counterpoint with daring." Parenteau was to go on to receive similar praise on Broadway, only to fade away. But for Marc Connelly the show inaugurated a distinguished career.

Only three new musicals opened in New York in the final months of the season. **The Purple Road** (7 April 1913, Liberty) told the bittersweet story of Wanda (Valli Valli), who comes with a petition to Napoleon (Harrison Brockbank) while he is in Austria. He is charmed by her and, disguised as a captain, woos her. The romance continues years later in Paris, but from an overheard conversation, Wanda realizes who her lover is and leaves. In an epilogue gaily attired rustics celebrate Napoleon's downfall while Wanda, clothed in black, sings a contrapuntal lament. The score by Heinrich Reinhardt and William Frederick Peters was gay and supple. Its best waltz, "The Mysterious Kiss," gave Peters, who ended his days as an organist in the New York movie palaces, his only theatrical hit.

The Smith brothers adapted Oscar Straus's **My Little Friend** (19 May 1913, New Amsterdam) for New World audiences, but somehow missed its Continental appeal. The story recounted how a poor count and a rich upstart try to force their children to wed. Fred Walton, Crawford Kent, William Pruette, Harry MacDonough, and Maude Gray were featured. The operetta lingered just three weeks.

Lew Fields kept the tradition of "summer" musicals alive when he brought in **All Aboard** on

5 June. Ironically it played the Roof Garden at the 44th Street Theatre, once the Weber and Fields. Fields became Jan Van Haan, a sailor down on his luck, who goes to sleep on the dock and dreams of enough vaudeville turns to fill out the evening. In the prologue and in a suffragette skit Fields walked a narrow line between pathos and farce—a technique used by many great clowns, but rarely by Fields. George Monroe, in a woman's wig and a man's trousers, hewed a more steadfast comic line in the same skit. Dancing ranged from neat little duets by the De Havens to a livelier pirate dance by Ralph Riggs and Kathryn Witchie to a chorus going through the paces of "Monkey Doodle" with real monkeys. A first-act finale ended with a Wild West shooting spree. The entertainment played through the summer months, folding just before the first cooler weather arrived.

1913–1914

The new season witnessed a further drop in the number of musical productions and, aside from three works of lasting appeal, it proffered virtually nothing of artistic or historic importance. One of the three jewels was an importation. In keeping with the chance symmetry of this seven-year period, this final season's importation established the reputation of the second of the two masters of Vienna's last golden age, Emmerich Kalman, just as the first had rocketed Franz Lehar to fame. Once more the major American hits, Victor Herbert's *Sweethearts* and Rudolf Friml's *High Jinks*, were operettas with a distinctly European bias. Indeed, in terms of native creativity, it was a doleful twelve months. Of the thirty-four musical entries, thirteen were foreign, two were revivals of older works, eight were revues, and only eleven were newly minted American book musicals.

The year began on 16 June with **The Ziegfeld Follies of 1913,** the first *Follies* to play the magnificent New Amsterdam, where, with rare exceptions, all the remaining editions were unveiled. It was not one of the better *Follies*. But Ziegfeld's taste and imagination saw to it that it was superior to any other revue the season offered. The dimple-kneed dancer Ann Pennington began her long association with the show. Songwriters Gene Buck and Dave Stamper also appeared in the credits for the first time. Both remained with Ziegfeld until his death. And Frank Tinney joined rubber-legged Leon Errol to enliven the comic department. Errol's "Turkish Trot" (a take-off on the turkey trot, a dance rage of

the day) was the show's big hit. Errol's pants kept falling down as he taught the entire cast the steps. Eventually the whole cast joined in, including a stage horse. Musically, the show was weak. José Collins made a short-lived hit out of the florid "Isle d'Amour" (Earl Carroll/Leo Edwards). But the main Raymond Hubbell and Stamper score was so pallid, Ziegfeld quickly bought the rights to several already popular tunes—"A Little Love, A Little Kiss," "Peg O' My Heart," and "Rebecca Of Sunnybrook Farm"—for Miss Collins to sing. Cubist painters and after-hours shenanigans at Rector's (a famous restaurant of the day) came in for spoofing as well, while the suffragette movement was ridiculed—in ragtime. The show's finale was a spectacular salute to the newly opened Panama Canal.

The Passing Show of 1913 followed on 24 July at the Winter Garden. The "cultural" addendum of the preceding season was dropped and the entire evening devoted to more traditional revue material. As it usually would, *The Passing Show* remained closer to the old burlesque tradition than did most of the other revue-extravaganzas, relying heavily for its comedy on satires of contemporary Broadway hits. *The Sunshine Girl, Within the Law, Broadway Jones, Oh! Oh! Delphine,* even the eight-year-old *Wizard of Oz,* were made fun of. *Peg o' My Heart,* besides being parodied, provided the slender story line that was still a requirement for revues of the day. Peg sails to America to learn the turkey trot. She spends the evening seeing the town under the tutelage of a comic couple and falls in love with Broadway Jones. Jean Schwartz replaced Louis Hirsch as composer, but not a single hit came from his pen—nor from the numerous interpolations. The cast included a number of young performers heading for bigger and better things: Charlotte Greenwood, Charles and Mollie King, and John Charles Thomas. Ned Wayburn again staged the evening, finishing with a number that had the line of girls parading up and down the steps before the U.S. Capitol. A more important piece of mounting was a runway projected out into the auditorium. By bringing the chorus beauties within arm's reach of the audience, the Shuberts helped change the nature of the chorus line. But this was not fully appreciated until the next edition.

On 26 July the Chicago *Tribune* ran an article that reflected on the Chicago musical scene. It recorded that Marc Klaw had announced European musicals were better than American shows. More important, it noted that Mort Singer had just returned from

Vienna, where he had secured the rights to two operettas. Singer, too, had apparently despaired of finding good local material any more.

Philip Bartholomae and Silvio Hein built "a musical comedy of youth" around the talents of the no-longer-quite-juvenile Joseph Santley. They called it **When Dreams Come True** (18 August 1913, Lyric). The dreams that came true were those of immigrants who saw America as a promised land, as well as Kean Hedges's dream of marrying his sweetheart, Beth (Marie Flynn). Comedy was provided by May Vokes and Amelia Summerville, the latter as a middle-aged dowager. A good dancing chorus was displayed in "The OK Two-Step" and held up to the critics' ridicule in a pointless finale with everyone imitating horses and jockeys. The evening was well crafted, if unexceptional. It had a comfortable run of eight weeks.

The biggest "made-in-Chicago" hit of the season arrived at the La Salle on 24 August and seemed to confirm the pronouncements of decline the *Tribune* had made public the preceding month, for **A Trip to Washington** was Henry Blossom and Ben Jerome's musicalization of Hoyt's *A Texas Steer* (10 November 1890), a show that had had music from its inception. The show ran to the end of November. A month later a musical called **September Morn** came into the La Salle, was panned, and quickly shuttered. In September also, Joe Howard had a fast flop with a revue called **Broadway Honeymoon**, while Joe Hyams and Leila McIntyre suffered the same fate with a sequel to *The Girl of My Dreams*, **When Love Is Young**. Slowly, without fanfare, the once thriving Chicago musical theatre was fading away.

The Doll Girl (25 August 1913, Globe) was the first of the year's many importations. Leo Fall's music was supplemented with a rash of interpolations, mostly by Jerome Kern. Some of these Kern pieces, such as "If We Were On Our Honeymoon" and "Will It All End In Smoke?," manifested his growing inventiveness, even if they were not memorably melodic. To suit the needs of the stars, Richard Carle and Hattie Williams, Harry B. Smith made substantial revisions in his adaptation of a story in which a marquis jealously pursues the little tobacconist his nephew hopes to marry. Some critics complained, but the public applauded for eleven weeks.

Critics and public alike embraced Philipp and Briquet's **Adele** (28 August 1913, Longacre). Georgia Caine, Natalie Alt, and Hal Forde interpreted the tale of a French girl in love with the son of her father's business rival. Although the piece is now neglected and practically forgotten, and its provenance suspect, it proved to be one of the most successful of the season's many musicals, running 196 performances.

The annual Hippodrome extravaganza premiered on 30 August. In an era of burgeoning national achievement and joyous flag-waving it was entitled simply **America**. Its frame-plot, reminiscent of Chicago's *The Girl at the Gate* (1 September 1912), told how plans to fortify our new Panama Canal are stolen and how Lt. Forsythe chases the thieves through a series of spectacular scenes that included a gigantic East Side fire. The chase was interrupted at times to present vignettes from American history. Manuel Klein's music was dull, but the public that flocked to see these extraordinary mountings remained generally indifferent to their scores. Still, despite good notices, *America* compiled only 360 performances, a sharp drop from preceding years.

A second Leo Fall operetta followed. It defied common practice by retaining its German tide, **Lieber Augustin** (3 September 1913, Casino). If this was a gimmick, meant to lure sophisticates, it failed. Augustin, a music teacher, helps a Thessalian princess after her father is bankrupted by a comic villain, Prince Nikola. The show played less than five weeks. It had better luck on the road when its star, De Wolf Hopper, persuaded the Shuberts to retitle it *Miss Caprice*. Nonetheless, as far as American audiences were concerned, Fall was fast on his way to becoming another one-show composer. And that show—*The Dollar Princess*—was not quite top drawer.

One truly top-drawer work, Herbert's **Sweethearts,** arrived at the New Amsterdam five nights later, 8 September. Herbert wrote the score with Christie MacDonald in mind. Her fine voice allowed him to write with a breadth and depth often denied him. The show's magnificent title song (its best number) had a range just short of two octaves. The heroine and the chorus sang this description of idealized love and lovers. The diversity and richness of the other numbers were awesome, running from the radiant sanctity of "The Angelus," sung by the romantic leads, to the beguiling fluff of "Pretty As A Picture," sung by a minor figure and the chorus. One critic exclaimed, "It is scarcely possible to enumerate the 'gems' of this work for the mere reason that practically every number could qualify as such." The critic for the *Tribune* agreed, adding a point that applied to most Herbert works and a few others in this musicianly era: "That he has written it con amore is proved by the delicate care he has bestowed upon his orchestration, which at times rises to the level of grand opera." The day of composer-orchestrated scores was rapidly waning. Unfortunately, Fred de Gresac and Harry B. Smith's book and Robert B. Smith's lyrics were musty. Many a commentator felt so fine a score deserved better writing, and the stodgy libretto may have helped shorten the run. Several inferior pieces stayed on the boards longer during the season.

Programs of the period often gave synopses of the plot. *Sweethearts*'s program coupled its synopsis with its cast listings. It read, with slight emendations: "The story of the opera is founded on the adventures of Princess Jeanne, daughter of King René of Naples, who reigned in the fifteenth century. Time has been changed to the present, and the locale to the ancient city of Bruges, to which the little princess is carried for safety in time of war, and is given the name Sylvia (Christie MacDonald). As an infant she is found in the tulip garden one morning by Dame Paula (Ethel Du Fre Houston), who conducts the Laundry of the White Geese, and who is known as 'Mother Goose.' Sylvia is brought up as the daughter of Paula, although the latter has six daughters of her own... . Mikel Mikeloviz (Tom McNaughton)... disguised as a monk, left Sylvia when an infant in Dame Paula's care. Knowing that Sylvia is the Crown Princess of the little Kingdom of Zilania, Mikel is conspiring to restore her to the throne, which is about to be offered to Franz, the heir presumptive (Thomas Conkey), who, in traveling incognito, has fallen in love with Sylvia and who finds a rival in Lieutenant Karl (Edwin Wilson), a military Lothario, betrothed to Sylvia. Mikel's plans are endangered by the schemes of [three villains. Furthermore] Liane, a milliner (Hazel Kirke), has sought temporary employment in the Laundry of the White Geese, and is mistaken by Mikel... for the lost Princess." Of course it all ends happily with Franz and Sylvia marrying and swearing to rule together. The show played 136 performances and then resumed a national tour that had begun in March of 1913. Thirty-four years later a superb revival, sparked by the antics of Bobby Clark, nearly doubled the run of the original.

A revival of Reginald De Koven's *Rob Roy* (29 October 1894), featuring Jefferson De Angelis, opened seven nights after *Sweethearts* and lingered two weeks.

Despite its European origins, Victor Jacobi's **The Marriage Market** (22 September 1913, Knickerbocker) was set rather fancifully in San Francisco, where, at an auction sale for brides, two girls offer themselves as a lark, and are bought by a cowboy and an English lord. Donald Brian was starred. The evening proved to be of more than passing interest because of one of Jerome Kern's interpolations, a lively two-step called "You're Here And I'm Here," that was added either late in the stay or, more likely, during the post-Broadway tour. In his *American Popular Song*, Alec Wilder singles out the song for special attention, noting, "It obviously seeks a native point of view, and though it hasn't the curious quality that makes for comparative permanence (the standard song), it is worthy of mention as another bar sawed away from the cage of imported culture." A simple tune, "a series of imitations of the initial phrase, the principal characteristic of which is a pronounced syncopation at the end of the third, seventh, nineteenth, and twenty-third measures," it gave Kern his biggest hit to date. Full-page advertisements for this "world-beater" extolled it as the "song hit of six different $2.00 a seat musical comedies." In his autobiography, Harry B. Smith names one of these shows as *The Laughing Husband*, stating it was for this show the song was actually written. *The Laughing Husband* came in much later and was less successful than *The Marriage Market*, so it remains the latter with which the song is generally associated. That a second bar may have been sawed away may be read in the *Dramatic Mirror*'s joyful remark, "At last we have the cowboy in comic opera [even if the comic opera is] a musical comedy by two Germans, to music made in Germany." The show had a modest success, running ten weeks and touring.

The revival of De Koven's *Rob Roy* was followed a month later by a new De Koven work, **Her Little Highness** (13 October 1913, Liberty). Based on *Such a Little Queen* by Channing Pollock (the co-librettist), it told how a revolution interrupts the betrothal ceremonies of King Stephen (Wilmuth Merkyl) of Bosnia and Queen Anna of Herzegovina, forcing them to flee to New York. There they are helped by Adolph Lauman (Willard Louis), who has plans for marrying his own daughter to the king. Stephen works in a department store until he is summoned back to Bosnia. The summons demands that he return alone, and he complies, but before long he prevails upon his people to accept Anna. Anna was played by a rising figure on the musical stage, Mitzi Hajos. Possibly because much of the action was set in America, the show offered an "exhilarating and effective display of the latest things in dance... the tango, trot, waltz, and Brazilian." Of course, given the freewheeling ways of the day, even a European setting would probably have furnished some excuse for a similar succession. The book was mediocre, and the score once more displayed De Koven's debility. The piece ran a mere two weeks. When it closed, De Koven faced up to the loss of his creativity and discreetly retired from the popular stage, closing a career that had begun a quarter of a century earlier when *The Begum* was first sung in November of 1888.

A Glimpse of the Great White Way (27 October 1913, 44th St.), a vaudeville, coupled with a one-act "comedy with music," "The Modiste Shop," eked out a single week's run on a two-a-day policy, although it had a sound Lew Fields production and Sam Bernard heading the cast. Actually "The Modiste Shop" was a cut-down version of Bernard's earlier vehicle *All for the Ladies*, shortened to about three-quarters of an hour. Frances Demarest as Miss Manhattan acted as hostess for the vaudeville, introducing such acts as "The Human Spider," a contortionist who performed on a gigantic web that filled the proscenium; the Schwartz Brothers in a mirror dance in which one brother seemed to be miming into an invisible mirror while the other brother became his reflection; and a *Carmen* ballet.

Oh, I Say! (30 October 1913, Casino) offered Jerome Kern's second complete score and a book based on a French bedroom farce. The actress Sidonie's maid, Claudine (Clara Palmer), in the mistaken belief her mistress has embarked on an extended trip, sublets Sidonie's apartment to a young couple on their honeymoon. Complications inevitably ensue when it becomes known the groom (Charles Meakins) was Sidonie's lover and when the bride's father engages Sidonie (Cecil Cunningham) to give the newlyweds a special performance. It was typical of the light, comic fluff so beloved by the era. It was well handled, but in no way out of the ordinary. Kern wrote a thoroughly pleasing, varied score, running the gamut from rag ("Katydid") to waltz ("Each Pearl A Thought") to polka ("I Know And She Knows") to tango ("I Can't Forget Your Eyes") to love song ("A Wifie Of Your Own"). All the score lacked was the truly outstanding number that could have pulled the rest together and somehow imparted a little extra melody to every other song in the show. One interesting musical sidelight was "the effective use of saxophones in the orchestration at a time when the saxophone had not yet begun to dominate popular musical scoring." Although the saxophone was a European invention, it would be American street music that gave it its first importance. But the avant-garde sounds emanating from the pit were not enough to carry the show beyond sixty-eight performances.

The Pleasure Seekers, another "Jumble of Jollification," danced into the Winter Garden on 3 November. It was a well-mounted revue of otherwise little merit, although one interpolation, "He'd Have To Get Under—Get Out And Get Under" (Grant Clarke and Edgar Leslie/Maurice Abrahams), was brought over by Bobby North from his vaudeville act and has endured. North and Harry Cooper played two businessmen who decide to give friends sailing for Europe a sendoff, and then decide to sail with them. The action moved from an elaborate re-creation of the new Ritz-Carlton Hotel to a finale that had the cast tobogganing down a Swiss mountain and throwing cotton snowballs at the audience. Max Rogers and Dorothy Jardon had one of the evening's high spots, singing a medley of old songs.

In 1911 a musical called *My Friend from Dixie* toured briefly. It garnered little attention, though it was reported to have been a crowd-pleaser. It was the work of a performer named J. Leubrie Hill, whom *Variety* later called a black George M. Cohan. Shortly afterwards ill health forced Hill into a brief retirement. He reemerged in 1913, with what apparently was a thoroughly rewritten *My Friend from Dixie*, now called **My Friend from Kentucky** (3 November 1913, Lafayette). Early on he christened the group he had assembled the Darktown Follies. Word of mouth spread quickly, so the musical soon was playing to an ever-increasing "sprinkling of whites," happy to journey to Harlem for the promised treat. Hill's basic story was already an old standby for black musicals—a sharper conning a gullible rich man. In this instance, the sharper was Kentuckian Bill Simmons (Will Brown). Jim Jackson Lee (Julius Glenn) was the sucker whom Simmons prevails on to mortgage the Lee homestead, flee his battle-axe wife, Mandy (Hill), assume the moniker Booker T. Lee, and run for president of the Colored Men's Business League. Simmons introduces Lee as a very eligible bachelor, and Lee is all too eager to use his new-found freedom to court the luscious Lucinda Langtree (Alice Ramsey). Then Mandy and her furious father, Jasper Green (Sam Gaines), arrive and quickly have a humbled Jim Jackson Lee return to the straight and narrow. White critics coming belatedly to the Lafayette published excitedly enthusiastic notices, praising especially the lively production numbers. These reviews caught Ziegfeld's attention.

He hurried uptown and immediately bought three of the evening's most applauded songs for his next *Follies*. The haunting "Rock Me In The Cradle Of Love" and the joyous "At The Ball, That's All" were given major niches, while "Night Time Is The Right Time" was incorporated into a larger number. But for Ziegfeld, and seemingly for most other playgoers, the musical was no longer *My Friend from Kentucky*. Instead it became known as **The Darktown Follies**. So successful was it that subsequent editions were launched under the newer name.

These black shows continued well into the twenties but rarely attracted much patronage from mainstream playgoers. For them only one place meant American Musical Theatre at its best, and that was Broadway. And Broadway justified their sentiments for decades onwards. Sadly, Hill was not around to participate. He died in 1916.

One of the season's biggest hits followed a week later when the curtain went up on **The Little Café** (10 November 1913, New Amsterdam). Although called a musical comedy, the C. M. S. McLellan–Ivan Caryll piece by today's lights would be another operetta. The star was Hazel Dawn, who had served the pair so well in *The Pink Lady* (13 March 1911). McLellan used yet another French farce as his source, this time Tristan Bernard's *Le Petit Café*. The plot told how Albert Loriflan (John E. Young) had for years been able to idle away his time "at the uncertain favor of a lord." When the lord turns against Albert he is forced to scratch out a living as a waiter—and a very bad waiter at that—in the Little Café. He is nearly tricked out of an inheritance, but ultimately settles down with Yvonne (Alma Francis), one of the many young ladies he had been courting. Surprisingly, Miss Dawn did not play Yvonne, but rather, as she had in *The Pink Lady*, another demimondaine. As such, the mores of the day demanded she be rejected in the end. Her character was called Gaby Gaufrette, a not altogether complimentary bow to Gaby Deslys. Originally it had been a small part, but it was enlarged and provided with a love interest when Miss Dawn was cast. A large measure of the show's popularity was attributable to the star, for the book was uneven, especially as a result of the rewriting necessary to expand Miss Dawn's part, and the score was run-of-the-mill. Its most popular tunes were "Thy Mouth Is A Rose," sung by Gaby and the chorus, and "Just Because It's You," sung by Gaby, Albert, and the chorus.

Victor Herbert's **The Madcap Duchess** (11 November 1913, Globe) gave every indication of surpassing the box office figures of both the Caryll operetta and Herbert's own September success, *Sweethearts*. Added to Herbert's renown was the fame of the co-librettist, Justin Huntly McCarthy, one of the most popular romantic novelists of the day. In fact, the new musical was a theatricalization of McCarthy's 1908 best-seller, *Seraphica*. Selected for the title role was Ann Swinburne, a rising leading lady who had scored triumphs in *The Count of Luxembourg* and the revival of *Robin Hood*. From its out-of-town opening to the morning-after reviews in New York, the piece was showered with praise, particularly Herbert's score. But theatregoers would not buy it, not in New York nor on the road. It would be unfair to blame the librettists. By now both critics and audiences had come to expect no more than an unobtrusive competency in librettos for Herbert's musicals. *The Madcap Duchess* was no exception. The book was stolid, but in no way seriously objectionable. It related how Seraphina (a one-letter change for the sake of euphony), the madcap, teen-aged Duchess of Bapaume (Miss Swinburne), assumed various disguises in her unconventional but determined courtship of Renaud, Prince of St. Pol (Glenn Hall). Unfortunately for Seraphina, Renaud is passionately in love with Stephanie, the Marquise of Phalaris (Josephine Whittell). Renaud's ardor has provoked the Duke of Orleans (Francis K. Lieb), then Regent of France, to ban the young suitor from Paris on pain of imprisonment. To see Stephanie, Renaud masquerades as a strolling player at Watteau's Versailles theatre. Seraphina appears as a young man, a serving maid, and a player, and in the end convinces Renaud that she would be the better mate for him. Critics found the show remarkable in several ways. The settings captured the light, airy grace of Watteau. Even more commendable in many eyes was the show's stringent adherence to a sense of time. Not a single anachronistic tango or turkey trot marred the period flavor. The show's failure and subsequent obscurity can only be blamed on Herbert's musicianly score. In his pursuit of art Herbert lost track of memorable melody. Edward Waters, in his biography, praises the score, but his descriptions betray the problem—"well-turned phrases," "unusual degree of dignity." He calls "Far Up The Hill" "a conversational duet," continuing, "The conversation in gavottelike phrases gives way to a strict two-part canon in the octave (eight measures) which in turn yields to eight more measures of part singing, four independent parts over an ostinato bass. So much musical science in such a short piece was probably lost on the audience....." And there was the nub of the difficulty!

November's last entry was an importation, an English pantomime, **Hop o' My Thumb**, adapted for American tastes by Sydney Rosenfeld and Manuel Klein, and brought into the Manhattan Opera House on the 26th in time to capture the pre-Christmas children's trade. Hop saves his brothers and sisters from being lost in the woods by scattering crumbs to trace their path. He also restores King Mnemonica's memory by giving him a pair of seven-league boots that allow the king to visit the land of Lost Memories. De Wolf Hopper starred, his exceptional height contrasting to the Hop of the diminutive sixty-pound English actress Iris Hawkins.

The season's biggest hit—excepting, as usual, the Hippodrome's attraction—arrived on 10 December at the Lyric. In a sense, it, too, was just right for the season. A "musical jollity" (no "jumble" here) with the appropriately frivolous title of **High Jinks**, it delighted its audiences into the summer. For those ticket-buyers who might hesitate to pay out good money for anything as loose as a "jollity," the producers were happy to refer to the piece as a "musical farce" or a "musical comedy." Its story (based on Leo Ditrichstein's 1905 hit, *Before and After*) was so slight and so padded with vaudeville turns that nobody quibbled over what terms advertisements branded the result with. Dr. Gaston Thorne (Robert Pitkin), a Parisian nerve specialist, obtains a drug-like perfume which produces the giddiest consequences when a little is sprayed near the ear. It also produces some Act I complications for the courtship of Dick Wayne (Burrell Barbaretto) and Sylvia Dale (Mana Zucca) which are not resolved until moments before the final curtain. However its own day saw it, *High Jinks* was yet another of those many pieces we would unhesitatingly call "operetta." Coming a year and a week after his brilliant debut with *The Firefly* (2 December 1912), *High Jinks* elevated Rudolf Friml into the forefront of Broadway composers. It remains one of his finest scores. In keeping with the libretto his musical numbers have a little lighter texture than his songs for Emma Trentini, and they have not achieved quite the lasting fame that some of *The Firefly's* songs enjoy. But they remain familiar enough. The hit of the evening, sung by Dick, so perfectly captured the spirit of the piece that it is often mistakenly thought of as the title song, although its actual title is "Something Seems Tingle-Ingleing." Friml filled the rest of the score with everything from exquisite waltzes such as Sylvia's "Love's Own Kiss" to the seductive syncopation of "Jim," sung by the soubrette, Adelaide. Since his contemporaries saw the piece as musical comedy, Friml apparently made no strenuous objection to an interpolation. Elizabeth Murray, who had performed so ably as the comedienne in *Madame Sherry* (30 August 1910), took the song "All Aboard For Dixie" (Jack Yellen/ George L. Cobb) and made it into one of the reigning hits of the day. It was the only number some critics singled out, and it became popular enough for Victor to include it as one of the "Gems" on its recording of the show's music.

A pair of musicals and a curious variety bill arrived on 29 December. The "all-star" variety bill included a dramatic playlet, Japanese jugglers, and Anna Held in a miniature comic opera, "Mlle. Baby." Held had brought her variety entertainment into the Casino for the holiday week. At one point during the comic opera, Miss Held's shadow was seen dressing, then the curtain rose partway to allow playgoers to watch her completing her toilette—a bit one grumpy critic condemned as "hardly proper for public exhibition." Of the pair of musicals, one was a German musical comedy called **The Girl on the Film** at the 44th Street. A cast imported from George Edwardes's Gaiety romped through the adventures of a general's daughter who runs away to work in films. The show ran eight weeks. A more interesting American piece, **Iole**, ran only three at the Longacre. It attempted to have much the same fun with Elbert Hubbard that *Patience* had with Oscar Wilde. Hubbard was a fascinating, if minor, figure on the late nineteenth- and early twentieth-century American literary scene. A successful businessman, he retired at thirty-five to devote his time to writing and publishing. He founded the Roycroft Press and brought out several "artistic" magazines. His most famous work was *A Message to Garcia*. Robert W. Chambers had originally written the satire as a novel and, with Ben Teal, adapted it for the stage. William Peters wrote the music. In the Chambers-Teal libretto Clarence Guilford (Frank Lalor) is a poet who has raised his eight daughters in sylvan isolation. The property is owned by George Wayne (Carl Gantvoort). (Note again how names have a vogue. Dick Wayne was the lover in *High Jinks*.) Wayne arrives to dispossess the Guilford clan, but falls in love with one of the daughters, Iole (Fern Rogers). Iole is engaged to marry a cubist painter, Lionel Frawley (Steward Baird), and he moves the family to his house. Coincidentally, Wayne also owns Frawley's house. As the weddings of all eight daughters are about to take place, Wayne, disguised as an organ-grinder, and seven of his friends, in similar disguises, invade the house and win the girls. Guilford, Frawley, and the other bohemians are given Wayne's wooded estate to retire to. There were kudos all around for the book and for some superior lyrics, although the writing was not as deliriously Gilbertian as some more enthusiastic reviewers suggested. There was no praise for the score that gave Sullivan no competition whatsoever. Unfortunately the weak music and perhaps too esoteric book hurt what chances the piece otherwise might have had.

The Whirl of the World opened at the Winter Garden on 10 January. It was 1914's first musical and by way of a New Year's gift offered Broadway a new composer—Sigmund Romberg. No one was overwhelmed by Romberg's first score, for Romberg was not as fortunate as Friml in his debut. *The Whirl of the World* was a lively, elaborate Winter Garden revue with a fine cast that included the Howard Brothers, Ralph Herz, Bernard Granville, Lillian Lorraine, and one Dolly sister, Rosie. The show was advertised as the "dernier cri in dance craze," and, fittingly, Herz opened the evening with a long song mocking all the dance rages from the Castle Walk to the Zulu Hop, with a bow to a few probably apocryphal steps such as the Rheumatism Dip. Dancing was clearly the strong point of the evening, ranging from a Maxixe performed by Lester Sheehan and Miss Dolly to Serge Litavkin and a *corps de ballet* in "Harlequin and the Bluebird." Herz played a marquis who bets Jack Phillips (Granville) that he can't win thirty girls in thirty days, getting each to sign her name in his little red book as proof. The story excused not only the dancing, but all sorts of outlandish comedy. Willie Howard presented a series of imitations and combined with his brother, Eugene, to spoof grand opera. Much of their humor no longer seems funny. For example, when Eugene asked Willie, "What is worse than having the earache and the toothache at the same time?" Willie's reply was "Rheumatism and St. Vitus." The evening also offered one more spectacle of a ship sailing away from a pier. Clearly, the skits and musical numbers were an ocean away from the old-world charm and grace that brought out the best in Romberg. It would be a while before Romberg would find himself or, perhaps more accurately, Broadway would find Romberg. Nonetheless, while no memorable song was forthcoming, the music was pleasant enough, and with so many increasingly popular young performers to lure in trade, the show ran twenty weeks.

SIGMUND ROMBERG was born 29 July 1887 in the Hungarian village of Nagy Kaniza. He began studying the violin as a young boy, but as he grew older planned to give up music for a career in engineering. However, he soon decided one career need not exclude the other. While furthering his engineering studies in Vienna he obtained a position as assistant manager at the Theater-an-der-Wien, the city's leading house for operetta. Finally realizing where his future lay, he moved first to London and then to New York. He accepted work as a pianist and soon became the orchestra leader at one of New York's leading restaurants, Bustanoby's. A few of his early songs were published by Joseph W. Stern, and these came to the attention of J. J. Shubert.

Another German musical comedy, The Queen of the Movies (12 January 1914, Globe), caused some to confuse it with the earlier importation *The Girl on the Film*. But it was in every way superior to its predecessor, and it ran three months. Its story had the attempts of a mad professor (Frank Moulan) to form a league for the suppression of movies thwarted when a clever actress (Valli Valli) maneuvers to compromise him. Among its lesser attractions was an added Irving Berlin tune, "Follow The Crowd."

The next evening brought in Emmerich Kalman's early Viennese masterpiece, Sari (*Der Zigeunerprimas*) (13 January 1914, Liberty). In its story of gypsy passions, an old violin virtuoso and his young son both love the same woman. Sari, the old man's daughter and the young man's sister, resolves the problem and wins herself a mate at the same time. Her performance and singing of the title role gained petite Mitzi Hajos stardom, a stardom she clung to for years, even after she shortened her professional name simply to Mitzi. The operetta's success and fame went far to compensate Kalman for his lamentable failure five years before with *The Gay Hussars*. His waltzes from *Sari* remain light concert favorites.

A third importation, The Laughing Husband (2 February 1914, Knickerbocker), based its libretto on another musical comedy misunderstanding, this time when a husband threatens to divorce his novelist wife after misconstruing her meeting with a notorious count. If the show has any hold on our attention it must be solely as the show for which Jerome Kern wrote "You're Here And I'm Here," sung and danced by Venita Fitzhugh and Nigel Barrie.

Blanche Ring opened the same night in a specially tailored vehicle, **When Claudia Smiles** (2 February 1914, 39th St.). She played Claudia Rogers, who divorces her husband, Johnny (Harry Hilliard), to further her career as an actress. The twists in the plot come from an innocent letter she sends one of her new suitors. His misreading of the letter breaks up a marriage and sends a man to jail. But before the evening is over Claudia sets everything right and winds up back in Johnny's arms. To bolster the weaker new numbers from various pens, Miss Ring interspersed some of her old favorites, such as "Bedelia" and "I've Got Rings On My Fingers." All in all it was sufficient to please her following for seven weeks in New York, plus the inevitable tour.

The Midnight Girl, an importation from France, was February's third and final musical offering. Set in Paris, the plot depicted the romance of a cabaret singer and a man she mistakes for a famous senator. It had music by Briquet and Philipp and arrived at the 44th Street Theatre just as their earlier success, *Adele*, left for the road. While *The Midnight Girl* never matched *Adele's* popularity, it nevertheless ran 104 performances with George MacFarlane, Eva Fallon, and Margaret Romaine in principal roles.

A second girl, **The Crinoline Girl**, opened at the Knickerbocker on 16 March, and since Julian Eltinge was the star there were doubting Thomases ready to assure you that the crinoline girl was no girl at all. The doubters were wrong. Richard Ainsley (Charles P. Morrison), hoping to discourage Tom Hale (Eltinge) from marrying his daughter Dorothy (Helen Luttrell), insists Tom must first earn $10,000 by his own wits. At the same time, Ainsley is also offering a $25,000 reward for the capture of a jewel thief, the Crinoline Girl (Edna Whistler), and her accomplices. Tom captures the Crinoline Girl, dresses like her to nab her accomplices, and wins Dorothy. The music was by the popular Tin Pan Alley songwriter Percy Wenrich, who wrote "Moonlight Bay," "Put On Your Old Gray Bonnet," and, in this same 1914, "You Wore A Tulip And I Wore A Big Red Rose." No comparable hit emerged from *The Crinoline Girl*, and what success the musical had must be credited to Eltinge. In New York at least that success was scant. Revealingly, the *Times* noted that Eltinge had always been more welcome

on the lucrative road. In a poignant curtain speech on opening night Eltinge expressed his hope that New York would hereafter be more receptive. His hopes were never realized, although he was looked on fondly and with respect.

More importations followed. **The Maid of Athens** (18 March 1914, New Amsterdam), with a Franz Lehar score, lasted less than three weeks. In its American version it made its hero an American naval officer, who helps a princess break up a bandit ring. The bandit king turns out to be her brother. Elbert Fretwell, Albert Pellaton, Cecil Cunningham, and Leila Hughes led the cast. **The Belle of Bond Street** (30 March 1914, Shubert), an updated version of *The Girl from Kay's* (2 November 1903), ran only a little longer, in spite of an excellent cast headed by Sam Bernard (from the original) and Gaby Deslys. In the tolerant fashion of the period the show included "Who Paid The Rent For Mrs. Rip Van Winkle?," which Al Jolson had introduced in *The Honeymoon Express* and which he was still singing on its cross-country tour.

On 9 April a colossal mounting of *H. M. S. Pinafore* began an eighty-nine-performance run at the Hippodrome. The house made no exception to its two-a-day policy for Gilbert and Sullivan, but did allow separate casts for evenings and matinees. The night-time crowds were treated to Fay Templeton as Little Buttercup.

Four nights later the last two American book musicals of this chapter arrived simultaneously. They exemplified the American musical comedy just before its great emancipation. They were musical, and they were comic. What remains moot is how American they were. Both were set in Europe, though in both American ingenuity overcomes foreign obstacles. Both had their share of waltzes and tangos, though this undoubtedly struck no one as unusual or alien. As so often happened, the more daring of the two was the less successful. It was a musical that began with a point of view as well as a plot. **The Red Canary** (13 April 1914, Lyric) escapes from its cage in Paris and disturbs the lives of all who see it, until a cool-headed American, Hunter Upjohn (T. Roy Barnes), captures it and restores it to its cage. The point the book tried to make, however naïvely, was that color and emotion are inseparable. The canary's hot coloring excited feelings and led to irrational behavior. The point was not labored, and musical comedy clichés prevailed. For many the best thing about the evening was Harold Orlob's score, his first on Broadway. A few critics predicted a bright future for him, and, indeed, he was represented regularly for more than a decade thereafter. But his was a long career without an iota of distinction. What hardly anyone knew was that his one great number, "I Wonder Who's Kissing Her Now?," was enhancing the fame of Joe Howard—to whom he had signed away the rights. *The Red Canary* survived a mere two weeks. ·

The Beauty Shop (13 April 1914, Astor) was more successful, even if its plot was creaky. Dr. Arbutus Budd is about to lose his beauty shop when he receives word from Corsica that he is an heir. But in Corsica his inheritance turns out to be an old revolver with which he is expected to continue an ancient vendetta. More diplomatic than brave, he offers to marry his enemy's daughter. When she turns out to be ugly he employs his beauty ointments, and the results so please the girl's father he drops the feud and gives Budd the money to save his shop. The book, by the same team who had written *Her Little Highness* earlier in the season, was claptrap, held together by its capable star, Raymond Hitchcock. Its score was largely by Charles Gebest, with a few interpolations by Silvio Hein. It was pleasant on the ear, but quickly forgettable, filled with sweet nothings of the day. The popular Hitchcock spent much of the second intermission, at least on opening night, chatting from the stage with the audience. He won a hearty round of applause for his tango with Marion Sunshine. On her own, Miss Sunshine performed some vibrant Spanish dances. Fifty gorgeous girls rested the eyes of tired businessmen.

After years of silence, Ludwig Englander's music was heard again when **Madam Moselle** (23 May 1914, Shubert) began a nine-performance run. The music, his last for Broadway, was undistinguished. Englander died soon afterwards. The plot, adapted by Edward Paulton from a French farce, told how both Nina and her mother love young Fred Corson. Ralph Herz, Josie Intropidi, and Diane O'Aubrey were featured. The only noteworthy thing about the evening was its intimacy. There was no male chorus and only eight girls in the ensemble.

Two spectacle revues—the only American genre to develop in this period—brought both the season and the period itself to an end. The **Ziegfeld Follies of 1914** premiered at the New Amsterdam 1 June; **The Passing Show of 1914** relit the Winter Garden nine nights later. The *Follies* was the last before the truly great editions, but, along with the edition which had opened the season, it was better than anything else of its kind on Broadway.

Bert Williams provided the high spot singing "Darktown Poker Club" and following it with his singlehanded card game. He was the only player, and his free hand became a hilariously dexterous computer. This skit generally has been considered his finest moment. Ed Wynn—in the first of his two *Follies* appearances—augmented the comic department. Errol danced an exaggerated tango with Stella Chatelaine. Errol, in fact, staged the evening after Ziegfeld battled with Julian Mitchell. Ann Pennington danced a buck-and-wing. A Palm Beach dance contest served as a finale for an evening that had begun in Hades with Vera Michelena as the Devil. The beauties and principals, marching as soldiers, presented a stirring first-act finale that concluded with "The Star Spangled Banner" and perhaps unwittingly foreshadowed a mood that World War I would make pervasive. No song from the score and no interpolation enjoyed more than a passing popularity.

Sigmund Romberg's score for the Shuberts (with Harry Carroll's four interpolations) was of the same modest order. Numerous take-offs on current hits confirmed that *The Passing Show* still held closer to the old burlesque tradition than did the *Follies*, although spectacle and show girls were not forgotten. Notable in the cast were Lillian Lorraine, José Collins, T. Roy Barnes, and Bernard Granville. Marilyn Miller made her first appearance in a legitimate New York show, although, curiously, her imitation of Julian Eltinge elicited more comment than her beauty or dancing. One reason for this puzzling oversight may have been the attention gained by the show girls. Indeed, the real importance of the edition was the success of its line of slim chorus girls. The thinner queens of the new silent movies and the proximity that the new Winter Garden ramp offered conspired to end forever the reign of more buxom beauties. Not only was the new glamour paraded on the ramp, a first-act finale had them floating in an airship. In another spectacular scene for "The Sloping Path" they danced their way up into the flies.

Chicago had one late-season opening, **The Elopers** (17 June 1914, Comedy). A lively, humorous, and colorful entertainment, with music by Hugo Frey, lyrics by Frederick Herendeen, and book by Arthur Gillespie and George E. Stoddard, the show had several reviewers hoping it would restore the fast-fading élan of Chicago musical comedy. Its basic setup was ordinary enough—"the usual girls' academy, the usual chaperon, the usual traveling salesman and the inevitable hotel." A highly praised score included the fetchingly syncopated "Every Road" ("sung and danced by John Frank, the chorus and a pretty blond ballerina"), the ragtime "That Tango Band," and a sweet waltz, "Over The Sea." But for all the encomiums, the musical fell far short of the success many expected for it.

And so seven lean years of native creativity came to an end, though they were not without interest or influence. The sweepingly gorgeous Viennese material accustomed Broadway to superior craftsmanship (sometimes badly manhandled in the adaptation) as well as to memorably melodic scores. As long as Vienna and the rest of Europe offered enough of this fine artistry, it was difficult for Americans to compete, especially when they persisted in their obsolescent ways. Significantly, the few composers who did succeed in writing masterpieces for our national stages—Victor Herbert, Karl Hoschna, Rudolf Friml—were immigrants whose music was clearly stamped "European." The "native American" music employed on Broadway during this period changed little—primarily marches, two-steps, and simple domestic waltzes. And while commercial ragtime numbers were interpolated in many American works, and often, jarringly, into foreign operettas and musical comedies, no major composer appeared capable of expanding the form into an exciting, cohesive score. It was beginning to seem that ragtime would pass on without leaving more than a superficial mark on the American Musical Theatre and that no other indisputably native musical form would emerge to replace it or the Viennese style.

The composers with the most native accent were confined to writing occasional tunes for revues—a form not wholly American in its origins but at this time displaying the healthiest American growth. Irving Berlin was the best of the lot. An exception was Jerome Kern, who by and large ignored revues, inserting his compositions in Viennese and London musicals. These shows, consciously or otherwise, modified his Americanisms, allowing his style to coalesce into a unique lyric language.

Even librettists felt the malaise. During an interview in the *Dramatic Mirror* just as this period was drawing to a close, Edgar Smith described the contemporary American musical as "a hybrid type… built upon no sure foundation of story or plot and constructed of a varied assortment of elements which cannot be expected to assimilate." American musicals for the most part, he lamented, were put together when a producer had several songs by one or more composers and possibly a star. But he prophesied that this sort of show would "fall of its own weight. From the ruins let us hope that a saner and better structure may be built." His hopes were realized with extraordinary speed.

Act Three

The Birth of the Modern Musical, 1914–1921

The seasons from mid-1914 to mid-1921 were possibly the most exciting in the history of the American Musical Theatre. These seven years saw the birth of the American Musical as it was to be known for at least the next half-century. They witnessed, as well, its astonishingly rapid maturity. From 1915 on, few years passed without one or more offerings of such enduring merit that they could not be included unhesitatingly in a permanent repertory. The great periods ahead produced more shows of higher quality, but never before or since was the joyous thrill of discovery and first achievement so pervasive.

There were two principal reasons for this sudden, glittering outpouring. The first was a disenchantment with Europe and things European; the second was our own new self-awareness and with it the onset of a genuine self-confidence.

In 1907 *The Merry Widow* had waltzed across America, cavalierly elbowing aside the bright promise of George M. Cohan, Hough–Adams–Howard, and other young native talents. A frantic rush of immigrants followed—rose maids, chocolate

soldiers, dollar princesses—until an inevitable surfeit set in.

Circumstances outside the theatre contrived to hasten and deepen this rejection. A catastrophe such as the sinking of the unsinkable *Titanic* in 1912 pointed to the end of Europe's seeming invincibility. Increasingly heated rivalries between the Great Powers set one national group against another, until finally the assassinations at Sarajevo in June 1914 led inevitably to a general European war. In the United States anti-German sentiment surfaced at theatre box offices and eventually extended to a palpable distaste for even the most harmless Austro-Hungarian operetta.

The old order on Broadway, most of it Central European in origin, passed on just before this sentiment erupted. Karl Hoschna (only thirty-four years old) died in 1911, Gustav Luders (just forty-nine years old) in 1913, and Ludwig Englander (at fifty-six) in 1914. Gustave Kerker was in virtual retirement.

Happily for the American theatre, a group of young, highly talented composers was waiting, almost literally, in the wings. Talent was not the only thing they displayed. Equally important was the new musical language they spoke. It was a new American idiom—most often a patois called "ragtime."

Ragtime's origins in Sedalia, Missouri, and elsewhere in the Midwest and South were untheatrical. Ben Harney first brought the new rhythm to New York in 1896. His success was immediate. Ragtime spread with remarkable speed through the expanding vaudeville circuits, and before long singers were interpolating so-called "ragtime" into musical comedies and revues. In 1911 Irving Berlin's "Alexander's Ragtime Band" gave the form its widest, wildest vogue.

As its vogue crested, however, ragtime dried up at its sources. Pure, classical ragtime is generally considered to have faded away by 1917, the year of the death of its most celebrated master, Scott Joplin. Claiming ragtime's place was a freer, harder, more insistent music, emanating from the same black elements that had once nurtured rag. The new music was, of course, jazz. Its pushier, seemingly chaotic sound offended many. Its Negro origins further hindered easy acceptance at a time of hardening anti-Negro sentiment, and the crucial improvisatory nature of pure jazz prevented carefully prewritten commercial materials from being anything but a pallid reflection of the original article.

Moreover, the term "jazz," like "rag" before it, spread more swiftly than did a clear understanding of its meaning. To many, jazz meant simply "fast," or "noisy," or "cacophonous"—or merely "new." It was not surprising that one critic saw nothing contradictory when he called the songs in *Love Birds* "jazz rags" (they were neither). Many scores that critics hastily labeled "jazz" during this period sound today as sedate as Victorian tea-dance melodies—devoid not just of improvisation, but of the distinctive chordings, rhythms, and patterns that helped define the style. Several years passed before there was a more universal enlightenment and acceptance. A few young composers, notably Jerome Kern, rarely employed black styles, but wrote with a new clean-cut line that was unmistakably Yankee, whatever its influences.

Both new composers and older ones combined in 1914 to form ASCAP—the American Society of Composers, Authors, and Publishers. The original impulse behind the move was to halt the endemic evasion of royalty payment. ASCAP's start was rocky, and it would take the seven-year span of this chapter before it consolidated its gains. Once it was established, regular payments to members allowed

them an artistic independence that challenged the producer's hegemony in controlling the musical idiom in shows.

The American Musical Theatre was not alone in its renaissance. The arts all across the nation were awakening. Harriet Monroe founded her *Poetry* magazine in 1912, bringing into household use names like E. A. Robinson, T. S. Eliot, and Robert Frost. In 1914 Edgar Lee Masters published his *Spoon River Anthology*. Novels were announced by new authors such as Sinclair Lewis and Willa Cather. Frank Crowninshield took over *Vanity Fair* in 1913, and a year later, H. L. Mencken and George Jean Nathan assumed the editorship of *The Smart Set*. The 1913 Armory Show alerted Americans to the power of modern painting. The Little Theatre Movement sprang up. Out of it came the Provincetown Playhouse and Eugene O'Neill, and the Washington Square Players who gave birth to the Theatre Guild. It was a heady era for the arts.

1914–1915

The European war was less than three weeks old when the season's first musical arrived. **The Dancing Duchess** (20 August 1914, Casino) moved through two worlds—the frenetic, contemporary world of the dancing craze and the carefree, war-free world of a suddenly bygone Vienna and Budapest. The Duchess of Darmia (Laura Hamilton) runs away when the Duke bans all modern dancing. Under the name Celestine she becomes the rage of Vienna's Trocadero. The repentant Duke unmasks her in Budapest, where she and her men friends have gone to enter a tango contest. Both the show's dialogue and songs were turgid. In addition it was unable to make the best of its two worlds. Its American authors, working freely from a Continental original, made a few token bows to the musical modes of the day, especially in "The Tango Breakfast," its first number, and "The Ragtime Whirl," its last. For many of the dances and the greater part of the evening's lightest capers the producers hired John Hyams and Leila McIntyre, two performers more popular on the road and in vaudeville, where Miss McIntyre's Quaker act was a headliner. Hyams and Miss McIntyre imbued *The Dancing Duchess* with a bit of vitality and a touch of modernity. But most of it was ersatz operetta, persisting in the delusion "Everybody's Happy In Vienna." Devastated by even the most lenient critics, the Duchess left the scene in two weeks' time.

The Girl from Utah (24 August 1914, Knickerbocker) was one of four shows of the 1914–1915 season that must be considered milestones in our musical theatre's history. Oddly enough, this Charles Frohman production was an importation. With a book by James T. Tanner, lyrics by Adrian Ross and Percy Greenbank, and a score by Paul Rubens and Sidney Jones, it had enjoyed a long London run with the American Ina Claire in the name role. Its plot made it a natural for Broadway. Una Trance (Julia Sanderson) of Utah arrives in London to escape an objectionable Mormon marriage. At Rumpelmeyer's she meets an actor, Sandy Blair (Donald Brian); a ludicrous butcher named Trimpel (Joseph Cawthorn) of Brixton Rest; and, to her dismay, her pursuing Mormon. The Mormon forces Una to go with him to Brixton Rest, but she leaves a trail for Blair and Trimpel to follow. At the Arts Ball (decorated in an Indian motif, with the Taj Mahal at the rear), the Mormon finally agrees that Sandy would be the better match for Una and decides to return home alone. Frohman astutely realized that, notwithstanding the excellence of the book, the show needed better songs than Rubens and Jones had provided. In what proved to be one last, inspired gesture he hired Jerome Kern to write additional numbers. Kern had interpolated tunes in Frohman's London shows for some years, possibly before New York heard its first Kern melodies. Thereafter, Kern songs had been added to numerous Frohman productions on both sides of the Atlantic. But never before were the songs of such significance. Kern's interpolations not only made the show a smash hit, they established Kern as a master of light, lyrical composition.

Kern and Frohman apparently felt that, in view of the international cataclysm, the show's story might seem unduly frivolous and old-fashioned. To assure the acceptance of its theatricality they framed the whole evening in one of Kern's most exquisitely fey melodies, "The Land Of 'Let's Pretend.'" The show's three stars—Miss Sanderson, Brian, and Cawthorn—stepped out of character at the beginning and end of the story to sing Harry B. Smith's stilted but workable lyrics for the song, lyrics inviting audiences to "find folly a good friend." Six other Kern songs were added to the main story, most in the second half—the affectionate "We'll Take Care Of You All," the willowy "Alice In Wonderland," two vivacious fox-trots, "Same Sort Of Girl" and "You Never Can Tell" (in the pattern of the preceding season's "You're Here And I'm Here"), the foot-stomping "Why Don't They Dance The Polka Anymore?," and the hit of the show, "They Didn't Believe Me." A long line of musicians and scholars has devoted prolonged analysis to this magnificent melody. In his *American Popular Song*, Alec Wilder took nearly two pages to discuss it. He called the melodic line "as natural as walking," although "its form is not conventional even by the standards of the time." In his opinion the controversial triplet coupled with the words "cert-'n-ly am" was not a concession to the lyricist's needs, and Wilder rightly observed it is usually sung "'and I'm cert-'n-ly,' making of the 'n the second note of the triplet." In the show the song was given first to Una, although its lyrics were really more suitable for a man; more often than not a man sings it today. It remains one of Kern's finest achievements. For fifty years after it was written, until the rock-and-roll sound came to dominate popular music, there was not a time when it could not have seemed absolutely up-to-date.

Because Brian was fortunate enough to star in so many of the most melodic shows of the era, it is often forgotten that he was more of a dancer than a singer. But in these gay old song-and-dance shows, where dance and song entertained equally, most performers had to be doubly skillful. No one was surprised at Brian's lively polka or snappy tap routines, nor was there any amazement when Miss Sanderson joined him, notably at the costume-ball finale, to glide gracefully arm in arm across the stage.

In the freewheeling ways of the day, other songs were interpolated into the score. Initially these included two of Herman Finck's English hits, "Gilbert The Filbert" and "Florrie The Flapper" (both with lyrics by Arthur Wimperis), as well as "At Our Tango Tea" (Worton David and Bert Lee) and "The Girl In The Clogs And Shawl" (Harry Castling and C. W. Murphy). A few less discerning critics singled these out for praise and ignored Kern's pieces. At some time during its tour "Balling The Jack" (Chris Smith and James Reese Europe) was inserted. And when *The Girl from Utah* announced a return engagement in the summer of 1915 it was noted that three new songs, none by Kern, were part of the score—"Molly Dear, It's You I'm After," "If I Can't Be Captain, I Don't Want To Play," and "Grown Up Children."

The annual Hippodrome show followed on 5 September. It ran 229 performances. This was not a bad run considering the size of the house, but it was the least successful of the eighteen extravaganzas mounted there. Its forbidding, if timely, title, **Wars of the World,** may have discouraged potential patrons, even though the wars it presented included "The War of Sport" (with Harvard winning a regatta) and "The War of Pleasure" (an Italian carnival where the fun-makers sang in the best Tin Pan Alley style of "Baby Eyes"). Even in the more serious "Wars for Religion" or "War of Brother against Brother," multi-colored spectacle all but denied any horror. Other problems contributed to the slow box office. Over the years, a sameness had crept into the presentations and the novelty of their grandeur had worn thin. Worse, in the last season or two the movies had begun to provide spectacle beyond the facilities of even the Hippodrome's vast stage. Finally, by November it was obvious that the public, fascinated by the war but disturbed by the economic uncertainties it threatened, was staying away from theatres everywhere. The Shuberts announced they were withdrawing from the productions. A new producer had to be found.

Miss Daisy (9 September 1914, Shubert) survived less than a month. Philip Bartholomae's story told of Daisy Hollister's taking a job as a maid in the Swiggets' home in order to attract their guest, the Duke of Tormina (Joseph Lertora). Daisy (Florence Mackie) wins the Duke, and her brother (Donald MacDonald) wins Miss Swigget (Anna Wheaton). As usual, Silvio Hein's music was "agreeable without being distinctive."

A more interesting failure followed. **Pretty Mrs. Smith** (21 September 1914, Casino) is about to be divorced from her third husband—all three have been named Smith. She goes to Palm Beach for rest and soul-searching. Instead, she finds all three Messrs. Smith there—a particularly nasty shock since she had believed the first two were dead. After some indecisive flirting she is reconciled with number three. Although the glamorous and popular Fritzi Scheff was starred, she found the show stolen from her by Charlotte Greenwood, a tall, slender, young girl with beautiful eyes and with long legs that seemed not to have any joints as the youngster did splits and unbelievable "flat footed" kicks. Miss Greenwood's "Long, Lean, Lanky Letty" was so well received that the show's producer, Oliver Morosco (for whom she had worked in other West Coast musicals), revised the show and retitled it *Long-Legged Letty*. It was the first of a series of musical comedies written around the comedienne's unique talents. "Letty" shows kept her busy on and off for a dozen years. *Pretty Mrs. Smith*, with Letitia

Proudfoot removed, was made into a silent movie, Fritzi Scheff repeating her Broadway role.

A Winter Garden revue—billed as a musical spectacle—appeared on 10 October. While it was called **Dancing Around,** its main attraction was the singing of Al Jolson. Unhappily, neither the Sigmund Romberg and Harry Carroll score nor Jolson's interpolations had special merit. "It's A Long, Long Way To Tipperary" (Jack Judge and Harry Williams) was inserted briefly but never became associated with either Jolson or the show. Jolson's informality, projected so irresistibly across the footlights, was captured on his recording of another of the show's interpolations, "Sister Susie's Sewing Shirts For Soldiers." Jolson sang the song, then had a member of the audience sing it with him. Finally he reached out to the other patrons, cajoling, "Now folks you've all heard the song a couple times. I think we oughta all sing it together." Jolson also clowned in the evening's skits. He wiped away his blackface to play a mincing designer in a parody of *My Lady's Dress*, a play that shared the same opening night as *Dancing Around*. He also became the entire staff of a hectically undermanned Hotel Lavender. For spectacle the Shuberts offered a locomotive race and a gavotte performed in a setting out of Watteau. The revue was not yet free of the notion that some sort of story line was necessary. But in this case, as the *Dramatic Mirror* observed, "The plot, which concerned the search of a British army officer [Bernard Granville] for a prima donna [Cecil Cunningham] wearing a crescent of court plaster on her back, dropped into oblivion about half-past nine o'clock, and never again emerged." For all its inadequacies, *Dancing Around* ran 145 performances.

In the season's biggest success, **Chin-Chin** (20 October 1914, Globe), Dave Montgomery and Fred Stone once again led the way to their unique never-never-land where the playthings of childhood come back to life in a strangely contemporary world. At a Peking toyshop tin soldiers and painted dolls sing to each other of their love, and the ways of the world in which history's heroes have hearts of gold—though they add that sometimes less than the whole truth is told. In a land such as this there is no reason not to meet Aladdin (Douglas Stevenson) and his aunt, Widow Twankey (Zelma Rawlston), who possesses "a golden lamp that looks like brass—perfectly straight, except where it's crooked, short the tall way, and tall the short way, with a little round knob on the top." The villainous Abanazar (Charles T. Aldrich), the toyshop's owner and Aladdin's employer, wants to buy the lamp and sell it to a rich American, Cornelius Bond (R. E. Graham). Bond's daughter Violet (Helen Falconer) falls in love with Aladdin, and he, in turn, falls in love with the "Yankee princess." But Bond will not hear of his daughter marrying anyone who is not a "bultibillionaire." Luckily, two Chinese mannequins, Chin Hop Hi (Stone) and Chin Hop Lo (Montgomery), who are also slaves of the lamp, bring the lamp to Aladdin. With two rubs Aladdin is rich and lastingly assured of Violet's love. The first-act curtain falls while "Ev'ry chink goes just as dippy as a coon from Mis-si-si-pi" to the "Ragtime Temple Bells." But Abanazar manages to obtain the lamp and transports them all to a circus in Holland and a park in Paris where Hi, disguised as a ventriloquist (whose most common response is "Very Good, Eddie"), a gendarme, Paderewski, Mlle. Falloffski, and Lo, masquerading as another gendarme, a widow, a coolie, and a clown, always turn up and finally put things right.

Ching [the coolie]: Now you can go.
Abanazar: Why?
Ching: Because you are the villain and we can't finish the story with you here!
Abanazar: And you can't start without me, so I will be here tomorrow night at eight-thirty. Matinees at two-fifteen.

One reviewer intimated that Hi and Lo's ultimate reward was to be turned white.

Older playgoers—or younger ones familiar with still-lively English traditions—quickly recognized the source of the evening's drolleries: the children's pantomimes once so popular in America and even now a holiday favorite in England. Abanazar, the Widow Twankey, and several minor characters had appeared regularly in British retellings of the Aladdin story since the eighteenth century and, conceivably, even earlier.

Ivan Caryll's score and Anne Caldwell's lyrics were pleasant. Not all of the lyrics were Caldwell's. Aladdin's amazement at finding the love of his life, "Goodbye Girls, I'm Through" (with words by John Golden), was popular in its day. Hi and Lo's two original numbers, "A Chinese Honeymoon" and "Ragtime Temple Bells," had lyrics by Bryan/Williams and James O'Dea, respectively. Nor was all the music by Caryll. During the run three other songs were given to the stars, "Bally Mooney" (Terence Lowry), "Go Gar Sig Gong-Jue," and

the already popular "It's A Long, Long Way To Tipperary."

Because Montgomery and Stone shows were so suitable for children, they benefited from an extra-large audience. Yet, as we have shown, critics never thought they patronized their audiences and so considered their vehicles adult entertainment. References in *Chin-Chin* to the dancing craze, bridge, futurists, and cloisonné imply a knowing crowd. But something in Montgomery and Stone's style, now irretrievably lost, must have assisted in conveying a truly universal appeal. When a brutal box office slump hit in what should have been the height of the season, *Chin-Chin* alone of all Broadway shows continued to sell out.

George V. Hobart, the popular librettist, wrote *Experience*, for which Silvio Hein composed a few songs and Max Bendix proved background music. One of the hits of the year, it was not, however, a true musical. It was followed by **The Lilac Domino** (28 October 1914, 44th St.), a European dud by the Franco-Belgian composer Charles Cuvillier. Three young men have lost so heavily at cards they agree one must wed an heiress wealthy enough to keep them all in chips. The heiress was played by Eleanor Painter. America's heartfelt sympathy for Belgium's plight was not reflected at the box office, and the operetta had a modest three-month run.

First-nighters had a choice of two musicals on 2 November, **Papa's Darling** and **The Only Girl**. *Papa's Darling* was based on the French comedy *Le Fils Surnaturel* by Grenet d'Ancourt and Maurice Vaucaire. The young lady of the title does not exist. She is the fictitious daughter of a village professor (Frank Lalor), who uses her as an excuse for his Parisian flings. It was another Harry B. Smith adaptation (he had done *The Lilac Domino*, too), with Smith also supplying lyrics for the second Caryll score to be heard in two weeks. In his autobiography Smith wrote, "In telling the plot to Klaw and Erlanger, Caryll laughed more than any audience that ever attended the play. If we could have had him in the audience instead of in the conductor's chair, we might have had a success." *Papa's Darling* was a five-week failure at the New Amsterdam.

However, the small, unlucky 39th Street Theatre had one of its few successes with *The Only Girl*. Henry Blossom, working from Frank Mandel's *Our Wives*, retained the original's intimacy by keeping to two simple sets and a relatively small cast. Four bachelors—Alan "Kim" Kimbrough (Thurston Hall), Sylvester "Corksey" Martin (Richard

Bartlett), John "Fresh" Ayre (Jed Prouty), and Andrew "Bunkie" McMurray (Ernest Torrence)—determine to stay single. Kim, in whose apartment the action takes place, hears someone in a neighboring flat play a beautiful love theme. The composer, Ruth (Wilda Bennett), proves to be as beautiful as her music, and Kim, who is a librettist, proposes they work together. Strictly business. "We both hate things sentimental. We are two machines. That's all!" Six weeks later Corksey, Fresh, and Bunkie have lapsed into matrimony. The three couples sing and dance a happy sextette, "Connubial Bliss," while off stage Ruth is heard singing her love theme. The men have second thoughts several hours later when their wives refuse to let them leave for a night on the town. But even their warning, "When You're Wearing The Ball And Chain," cannot save Kim. Ruth pleads, "You're The Only One For Me," and Kim is beyond resisting.

The love theme, which is initially heard (apart from the overture) off stage early in the first act and then is sung by Ruth moments later as "When You're Away," was one of Victor Herbert's most beguiling melodies. But the whole score, while far from Herbert's best, was above Broadway's average. Blossom's lyrics, fustian in the more serious numbers ("Ah! When in sweet raptures of love you enfold me"), could be refreshingly colloquial in the lighter tunes ("She said, 'Dear, What do I hear? That ev'ry pretty little skirt within a mile you try to flirt with! I just won't stand for it! See!'"). These lighter tunes were given to Patsy La Montrose (Adele Rowland), the one important character besides the eight lovers. Her numbers were used to inject a contemporary immediacy into the show. Her first song, "The More I See Of Others, Dear, The Better I Like You," had an almost equally long subtitle, "An Imitation Of The Present Day Ragtime Song." Actually it was a standard Herbert melody cleverly set on top of a rag-like base. Patsy and Kim sing the militaristic "Here's To The Land We Love, Boys," which acknowledged the three-month-old war and warned we would fight if we had to. In the last act she took the producers of the day to task in the delightful "You Have To Have A Part To Make A Hit." Assigning the comedienne biting or down-to-earth lyrics and more stylish music was a common practice of the time. It reflected the epoch's more decorous proprieties. But it often gave romantic leads an unworldly wholesomeness, sometimes even an irritatingly saccharine innocence.

It was rare, before the twenties, to help create more fully dimensional characters by carefully distributing assignments of various types of songs.

An unsuccessful importation, **Suzi** (3 November 1914, Casino) starred José Collins in the title role, supported by a large company. It depicted the love of an opera star for a hussar.

Although **The Heart of Paddy Whack** (23 November 1914, Grand Opera) was berthed at the sort of lower-class auditorium customarily accorded to Chauncey Olcott and his touring attractions, this one sported some startling credentials. The "Irish Drama" was from the pen of the rising young American playwright Rachel Crothers. Its songs were by Ernest R. Ball, with one having a lyric by the black poet Paul Laurence Dunbar. Henry Miller directed the play and produced it in conjunction with George M. Cohan and Sam Harris. Yet for all the celebrated names, the evening was not seen as being of a higher order (except in the mounting) than earlier Olcott pieces. And, once again, Olcott's song-warbling hero struggled through three acts, set in 1830 Ireland, to win his beloved Mona from the machinations of a persistent villain. Critics noted Olcott's strange opening-night curtain speech, in which he jestingly saluted a gentleman sitting in a stage box as his "hated rival." That rival was John McCormack.

Herbert's second entry of the season was **The Debutante** (7 December 1914, Knickerbocker). A company of 100, including a "pony" chorus dressed nattily as middies, struggled to make *The Debutante* frolicsome. The book was by Harry B. Smith, so its readers fairly well knew what the *Dramatic Mirror* meant when it suggested, "It does not soar above the level of a Smith libretto, and does not fall below it." Smith's debutante, Elaine (Hazel Dawn), the daughter of Sir Francis Vane, is engaged to a rich young American, Philip Frazer (Wilmuth Merkyl). But Philip loves Irma (Zoe Barnett). Elaine arranges with the Marquis de Frontenac (Stewart Baird) to make Philip notice the Marquis's attentions to her. Later, at a ball, she outshines Irma, and Philip is won over. Harry's brother Robert wrote the lyrics. Herbert's music, praised by many of the critics, was not his most inspired. Reviewers singled out Philip and Elaine's "The Golden Age" and "The Love Of The Lorelei," as well as the Marquis's "All For The Sake Of A Girl." Even with Miss Dawn as star, *The Debutante* lasted only six weeks.

Besides the show's weaknesses and the economic plight of the theatre, a third circumstance possibly shortened the operetta's run. It opened one night ahead of the season's most ballyhooed show, Irving Berlin's **Watch Your Step** (8 December 1914, New Amsterdam).

The twenty-six-year-old Berlin had quickly caught on to the advantages of astute public relations. In a well-spaced series of interviews, both before the show opened and during its run, Berlin insisted his great ambition was to write a "ragtime opera." Ragtime to Berlin was simply syncopation, and while syncopation had always existed, American rag was distinguished by a "more graceful rhythm." Berlin, a musical illiterate, undoubtedly understood that composing an opera—even a ragtime opera—required more than his great melodic and rhythmic gifts would ever allow. But not since George M. Cohan's works, a decade before, had there been quite so determined an effort to produce an entire score using only native musical speech. Even the earlier Negro musicals, which, consciously or not, offered ragtime in their numbers, preferred to imitate foreign styles. The *Evening Sun*, with an appreciative sense of occasion, concluded the "work is ephemeral as art, but is permanent as a landmark."

Ballyhoo or no, the score was inventive and effervescent. Although only one of its songs became a Berlin standard, and that only after forty years of neglect, the entire score deserves study. The overture itself, wrapping a medley of the best numbers around the exhilarating "Syncopated Walk," promptly raised the highest expectations. The show's dancing emphasis was established in the cute but inane opening—one of the score's few weak spots—when the chorus complains it can't work all day if it's been dancing all night. The nation was in the throes of "the dancing craze," and the nation's stellar ballroom dancers, Irene and Vernon Castle, led the cast. The first regular number of the show, sung by its ingenue, Ernesta (Sallie Fisher), was a waltz—a seemingly most unragtime tempo. But if, as Berlin proposed, ragtime was merely syncopation, then he had written a startlingly raglike waltz, "What Is Love?" "I'm A Dancing Teacher Now" had Vernon Castle kidding the dancing school explosion. It was followed by "The Minstrel Parade," "Let's Go Around The Town," and "They Always Follow Me Around." Irene Castle, who alone was not given a character to play and appeared on the program simply as Mrs. Vernon Castle, next had what was really the title song, though it was published and listed as "Show Us How To Do The Fox Trot." It was an irresistible invitation to the dance. "When I Discovered You," a fast-stepping love duet, was followed by the show's theme, "The Syncopated Walk." Berlin employed it as a frame for the overture, as the first act's principal production number and finale, as an entr'acte, and as the grand finale. Its lyric, proclaiming "ever since the dancing craze, Ev'rybody has a syncopated walk," suggested how thoroughly the new fad had spread. The second act centered upon the Metropolitan Opera, building to the musical's major production number, an "Opera Melody," ragging the most popular arias. This brings the Ghost of Verdi stalking to the old house, where he clashes with the modern boys and girls. The last entr'acte repeated "Settle Down In A One Horse," sung in the second act, and promptly followed with an orchestral piece called "Homecoming." Ernesta protests she is tired of the new music and begs to hear a "Simple Melody," while Algy in counterpoint insists he wants to listen to rag. (This is the song that was rediscovered after forty years and now is considered a great Berlin standard.) Rag triumphed with everyone ending the show again doing a "Syncopated Walk."

As usual, Berlin was his own lyricist. The dialogue was by the indefatigable Harry B. Smith—his fourth libretto in just over a month. But in this case it was moot if there was in fact a libretto. Smith himself, in the program and on the vocal score, accepted the credit "Book (if any)," and several aisle-sitters stated the show had no plot. Actually there was the thinnest of story lines. Jabez Hardacre bequeaths a legacy to any male relative who has never loved, been engaged, or married. The effort to determine which of Jabez's two male survivors better fits the description provides the continuity. The cast of characters included such minor figures as Willie Steele, "a tango lawyer," Silas Flint, "a maxixe lawyer," and Estelle, "a hesitating typewriter." Estelle was played by a statuesque beauty Ziegfeld glorified, Justine Johnstone. Curiously, the ingenue's unusual full name, Ernesta Hardacre, was not new to Broadway. Augustin Daly had included a character by that name in his proto-revue, *Round the Clock* (25 November 1872), a generation before. With "revues" still insisting on stories to hold them together and "musical comedies" still accepting the most meager excuses for plots, *Watch Your Step* demonstrates the confusion between the genres at the time: the theatrical sheets of the day discussing the "Rush of Revues" included the show (as well, sometimes, as *Chin-Chin*) in their articles. Robert Baral, in 1962, accepted it as a revue in his study of the genre. But before the month was out, another show began putting an end to the confusion thin plots created.

Dillingham's sumptuous mounting featured an elaborate, if necessarily scaled-down, re-creation of the old Metropolitan, with patrons in evening clothes filling both lower-level boxes and the Diamond Horseshoe, and a simulated production on the "Met's" stage. Besides those already mentioned, performers included Elizabeth Murray and Charles King.

Christmas week brought in three musicals **Tonight's the Night** (24 December 1914, Shubert) was an English creation about love in not so high society. On the 25th, **Lady Luxury** at the Casino vied for attention with **Hello, Broadway** at the Astor. *Lady Luxury* starred the beautiful comedienne Ina Claire as Eloise Van Cuyler, the long-repressed ward of her uncle (Harry Conor). She comes of age fifteen minutes after the curtain goes up and throws a big party. Naturally the party allowed the evening to be stuffed with specialty acts. Francis Bryan and Emilie Lea as a pair or high-kicking Russian dancers won the greatest applause. At the end of the evening the guardian reappears from a secret panel behind which he has been watching the giddy cavortings.

Lady Luxury was a quick, insignificant failure; *Hello, Broadway* was an innovative George M. Cohan revue. It had a satisfactory run and a brief tour. But it was a far more important work than its modest success suggests. Cohan discarded the heavyweight opulence of the *Follies* and the Winter Garden shows. Instead he looked back to the Weber and Fields tradition of burlesque, out of which his costar, William Collier, came. All the skits satirized American institutions, although the emphasis was on the New York stage. To speed the action, sets were changed while audiences watched. Jurors and witnesses grabbed parts of a courtroom scene and ran off stage with them as players brought on the props they would require for the spoof of *My Lady's Dress* that followed. The pacing was quick by Ziegfeld or Shubert standards, even if sketches were longer than in later, still faster-paced revues. Nor was the later clear-cut separation of skits and musical numbers always evident. Numbers utilized the auditorium as well as the stage. "Down By The Erie Canal" was first sung by Louise Dresser and a chorus shaking tambourines. A boy in the gallery took up the song, followed by an old man in a box. Then the curtains parted to disclose "ladies and gentlemen dressed in heavy, purple velvet, rowing Venetian gondolas along a green-ribbon Erie Canal." If the music included an "Old Fashioned Cake Walk" it also had a "Jesse James Glide" and a "Barnum and Bailey Rag." The first-act finale was a generous Cohan tribute to his younger competitor, Berlin. Although the rapidly churning musical world soon left Cohan sadly behind, at least at this point Cohan embraced the changes. He offered a list of composers and shows that he proclaimed were "all through." His list included the Merry Widow and "Mr." Sousa. In another way Cohan helped establish the modern revue. He liberated it from any pretense of plot. Several performers remained in character throughout the evening, but they served essentially as extended compères. In the show's most famous bit, a hat box, purporting to contain a plot, was carried on stage at intervals. At the end three players meet:

Mccluskey: Ah Ha! The hat box. Now to reveal the plot of the play. (Opens the box) Empty!
Babbit: What became of the plot?
George: There never was a plot.

From "plot (if any)" to "there never was a plot" in less than a month's time! Modern revue had arrived. Certainly theatregoers thought so, and they were obviously happy about it. Two weeks after *Hello, Broadway* appeared the *Dramatic Mirror*, under the heading "More Revues Coming," noted, "The revue, which for the last two years has been the most popular form of musical entertainment in London and Paris, is invading New York with the force and dispatch of the German Army... . The musical revue seems to be what the public wants, judging from the attendance at 'Watch Your Step' and 'Hello, Broadway'" At the same time, on the front page of its 16 January 1915 issue, *Variety* published Cohan's hope that "the permanent policy of the Astor Theatre in the future will be for 'revues' along the lines of the old Weber and Fields music hall." Cohan added that the cast of *Hello, Broadway* might serve "as the nucleus of a stock company there."

After the Christmas rush, no musicals came to New York until 25 January 1915. That night's arrival at the Knickerbocker proved an especially poignant failure. **Ninety in the Shade** was set in the Philippines, where Willoughby Parker (Richard Carle) has settled down to enjoy his reputation as a ladies' man. What the ladies don't know is that Willoughby is engaged to Polly Bainbridge (Marie Cahill). Her unexpected appearance produces immediate complications which are resolved only when Bob Mandrake (Edward Martindell), a smuggler, woos and wins Polly, leaving Parker to pursue a lady known as "The Hot Tamale" (Jean Newcombe). Although some critics complained that Guy Bolton's book belonged to an obsolescent school, they nonetheless found much to praise in it and in Jerome Kern's lovely score. But there was a feeling that Miss Cahill and Carle were perhaps a bit too old for the principal roles. Except to tie wedding knots for secondary characters who would otherwise be left at loose ends, Broadway musicals were not yet prepared to deal with love interests beyond a young boy's meeting a young girl. Miss Cahill, whose dismissal from *It Happened in Nordland* (5 December 1904) had taught her nothing, aggravated matters by insisting on her own interpolations, however inappropriate and jolting they might be. Kern was still not quite famous enough to protest effectively. The musical's incongruities, coupled with the generally bad business conditions, kept patronage down, and *Ninety in the Shade* closed abruptly and ignominiously when its unpaid actors refused to perform. Since the production was a low-budget affair, employing only eight chorus girls and eight chorus boys, the failure was doubly humiliating. For Carle and Cahill it was the virtual end of musical stardom.

In the issue of the *Dramatic Mirror* that detailed the closing, another column advised, "A radical change of policy is impending at the Princess Theatre... F. Ray Comstock, manager of the Princess, has announced that in the near future he will present there a musical comedy, the book of which has been adapted from an English original." The adaptation was by *Ninety in the Shade*'s librettist, Bolton, and the songs were assigned to its composer, Kern. No one could foresee that Comstock, Bolton, and Kern were about to make American Musical Theatre history.

> **GUY BOLTON** was born in Broxbourne, Hertfordshire, England, on 23 November 1884. His parents were American, and his father a celebrated engineer. Young Bolton studied architecture at the Atelier Masquery in New York. Later he helped design the Soldiers' and Sailors' Monument on Riverside Drive. His first attempts at playwriting went unproduced or folded out of town, but in 1914 his farce *The Rule of Three* realized a modest success. This same year saw some of his writings published in *The Smart Set* and also witnessed his first meeting with Jerome Kern.

Maid in America, the next Winter Garden revue, opened 18 February and played up to the growing patriotic fervor the European war was stimulating. Its cast of characters included a "Made-in-America French Actress" and a "Made-in-America English Lord." And while a cast of characters suggests a book, the Shuberts followed the trend and credited Atteridge solely and honestly with "Song Cues." Unfortunately Sigmund Romberg and Harry Carroll's songs were again commonplace. But the show had the customary Winter Garden glitter, unusual staging (the chorus girls flashed lights at the men in the audience as they sang of their search for "Someone's Heart"), and enough names—such as Nora Bayes, Charles Ross, Harry Fox—to give it a respectable run.

At a faded playhouse further downtown, Fiske O'Hara came in with a typical Irish music-melodrama of the epoch, **Jack's Romance** (22 February 1915, Grand Opera). As a long-lost heir falsely accused of being a highwayman, O'Hara lifted his tenor voice in occasional song. Also typical of this sort of piece was its one-week stand as part of a cross-country tour.

A fourteen-week run was recorded by an importation, **The Peasant Girl** (2 March 1915, 44th St.), which starred Emma Trentini and for which Rudolf Friml wrote additional melodies. Miss Trentini played another waif who rises to heights in the opera world. She had to fight for her laurels this time, since Clifton Crawford's lithe dancing and gay comedy almost stole the show. It was the first of two March entries. The second, **Fads and Fancies** (8 March 1915, Knickerbocker), by Glen MacDonough and Raymond Hubbell, survived for six weeks. The show was a lavish vaudeville tied together with a thin plot in which Professor Glum (Frank Moulan) enlists the aid of two detectives, Chase Clews (Tom McNaughton) and Hawkshaw Holmes (John Miller). Specialty acts included an Italian monologue by Leo Carrillo (as Giovanni Gasolini) and a black-face dialogue about beating the insurance companies conducted by Conroy and Lemaire.

In mid-April, William Brady mounted a repertory of Gilbert and Sullivan favorites: *The Yeomen of the Guard, The Mikado, The Sorcerer, Trial by Jury, H. M. S. Pinafore,* and *Iolanthe.* Brady offered the additional lure of two beloved clowns, De Wolf Hopper and Digby Bell.

Conceived by Elizabeth Marbury as a showcase for young playwrights and their one-act plays, the Princess Theatre was the smallest house in New York, seating only 299 people. Its location on the south side of West 39th Street, across from Maxine Elliott's jewel box auditorium, put it at the very edge of the theatrical map. When it announced a "radical change of policy" in March, it had been operating under its old policy for less than two years—the theatre opened on 14 March 1913. Not too surprisingly, the short plays had failed to attract sufficient audiences. Miss Marbury, an agent, and Comstock, the theatre's head, desperately needed another type of entertainment. They had commissioned Bolton and Kern to revise Paul Rubens's *Mr. Popple of Ippleton* for Broadway tastes. A private reading of the revisions proved disastrous, so they decided to limit their expenditures and produce the show as frugally as possible at the Princess. They gave their authors a freer hand but insisted that because of the house's limited capacity, there could be only one set for each act, few costume changes, and as small a cast as possible. A budget limit of $7,500 was set. The show was retitled **Nobody Home.** A pre-opening brochure promised the "Smartest musical offering of the New York season." Making virtues out of necessities, it continued. "It is said of 'Nobody Home' that there is a real story and a real plot, which does not get lost during the course of the entertainment ... this particular offering seems especially appropriate to an intimate playhouse of the character of the Princess." A cleverly coordinated campaign before the 20 April premiere spread the word that something new was afoot.

The first act is set in the Hotel Blitz (New York's Ritz-Carlton, affectionately known as "the Ritz," was almost as new as the Princess, having opened in 1907). Vernon Popple (George Anderson) is in love with Violet (Alice Dovey), but before they can marry he must obtain the consent of her snobbish, domineering aunt (Maude Odell) and her aunt's ludicrous Italian husband (Charles Judels). The chances of the aunt's acquiescing are slim, for Vernon is a "society dancer" and has been seen around town with the Winter Garden star, Tony Miller (Adele Rowland). Vernon's Dundrearyish brother, Freddy (Lawrence Grossmith), arrives and unwittingly amuses Miss Miller. She discovers he has no place to stay and lets him use the apartment she has just purchased. She will not be inconvenienced, for she is about to take her show on tour and had planned to sublet the apartment anyway. The second act moves to the apartment, in and out of which a foppish decorator keeps running as he applies last-minute touches. Vernon arrives to visit his brother; Violet arrives to find Vernon; the aunt and uncle arrive to consider subletting; and Tony arrives to precipitate the confusion. When the inevitable mistaken relationships are explained, Vernon and Violet can marry. Surprisingly, Tony announces she will marry Freddy if he will have her. He will.

The writing was not always the most felicitous. There were lines that seem incredibly stilted, even for the period:

Vernon: I hope I shan't offend you if I say you are the loveliest thing my eyes have ever rested on?

Some of the humor was outrageous:

Aunt: Do you feel like a pot roast?
Uncle: I don't know how a pot roast feels.

And some not funny at all:

Uncle: I want to be sure that in case of fire nothing happens to me.

Hotel manager: Excuse me. I am sure you have made a mistake. You mean that nothing should happen to your wife.
Uncle: No. I don't make mistakes. I mean me.

Some of the other writing seems hasty and clumsy. The uncle, an inveterate skirt-chaser, realizes he was wrong to bring his wife with him to New York. He sings his regrets, "You Don't Take A Sandwich To A Banquet," after this leadin:

Uncle: Where did you say they [his and his wife's rooms] were?
Clerk: In opposite wings.
Uncle: That's the nearest I ever got to a chicken.

Similarly, late in the second act the stage is momentarily empty, and the typescript reads "(Dance Specialty)."

Kern's music, while not as consistently fine as his songs for *The Girl from Utah*, was still excellent—although Kern did not write as much of the score as the cover of the sheet music or the title page of the program would suggest. "Beautiful, Beautiful Bed" was by C. W. Murphy and Dan Lipton. The sandwich song was by Worton David and J. P. Long. The celebrated black bandmaster James Reese Europe and his associate Ford T. Dabney provided the chorus of "At That San Francisco Fair" (Kern added an introduction). Otto Motzan composed the "Nobody Home Cake Walk." Motzan collaborated with Kern on "The Chaplin Walk" and "Any Old Night." Kern's outstanding numbers were "In Arcady"—sung in the show by a minor character—Vernon and Violet's "Another Little Girl" (both with Herbert Reynolds lyrics), Tony's "The Magic Melody," and Vernon and Violet's "You Know and I Know" (the two with Schuyler Greene words). The roster of songs changed occasionally and inexplicably. Neither "The Chaplin Walk" nor "You Know And I Know" was listed on the program of the road company that played Philadelphia in the 1915–1916 season.

Although the critics were entertained, the pre-opening publicity seemed to have backfired. "What was supposed to be a reformation of musical farce took place last night in the delightful little auditorium of the Princess Theatre," the *Sun* observed, concluding, "very little... could have been called important from any point of view." The show ran 135 performances—enough to induce Marbury and Comstock to try again with a second Bolton-Kern effort.

MARILYN MILLER, the daughter of vaudevillians, was born in Evansville, Indiana, on 1 September 1898. She made her debut with her mother and stepfather in an act known as the Columbian Trio in 1904. Later in an expanded act called the Five Columbians she toured the world for nearly ten years. Lee Shubert discovered her while she was dancing at London's Lotus Club and promptly signed the petite, blonde dancer with a face of Dresden doll beauty for *The Passing Show of 1914*. By then she had long dropped her real name, Mary Ellen or Marylynn Reynolds. It was Florenz Ziegfeld who persuaded her to drop the *n* and adopt the simpler spelling.

More Kern music was heard in **A Modern Eve** (3 May 1915, Casino), a German musical that was first "Americanized" for Chicago and further revised for New York. The story told how a wife's indiscreet action almost cost her husband his business.

On 7 May the horror of the *Lusitania* sinking was brought home to Broadway with the loss of its pre-eminent producer, Charles Frohman, and of one of its earliest librettists, Charles Klein.

The season's last production was **The Passing Show of 1915** (29 May 1915, Winter Garden), considered by many the best edition of the series. Marilyn Miller, who was to reign over musical comedy for the next two decades, stole the show and began her quick climb to the top. She highlighted the first-act finale, a lavish "Spring Ballet," and showed her versatility by dressing up as Clifton Crawford to imitate his taps and shuffles. The Howard brothers mocked Shakespeare, George du Maurier's novel *Trilby*, and the ill-starred matinee idol Lou Tellegen (as Lou Tellegram). Willie Howard as Charlie Chaplin cavorted with Miss Miller's Mary Pickford. Most of the other skits also dealt with theatrical people and current shows, but, like so many 1915 entries, for additional inspiration it looked to the San Francisco fair ("Panama-Pacific Drag") and the hula rage ("My Hula Maid"). This hula fad, part of the dancing craze, had a side benefit for chorus lines, allowing an "easy, lush, exotic carnality" somehow less vulnerable to prudish condemnation than Latin or European choreography. Like *Nobody Home* and *Hello, Broadway*, the revue looked back a bit in time with a cakewalk number.

Only twenty-three musicals opened in the 1914–1915 season, the lowest figure since 1901–1902. But the small total belied the importance of the more significant shows. *The Girl from Utah*, *Watch Your Step*, *Nobody Home*, and *Hello, Broadway* marked historic beginnings for the American musical. They established not just new, major names but, more urgent, the validity of American styles and ideas. The *Dramatic Mirror*, cantankerous, wrong-headed, and moribund, pleaded in May of 1915 for a new school of Gilbert and Sullivan operetta, blind to the miracle it had just witnessed. From 1914 on, there was a slow but essentially uninterrupted evolution of our musical style—an evolution governed almost entirely by domestic conditions. In the ensuing years Vienna, Paris, Berlin, and particularly London looked increasingly to New York for their shows or at least for their material and ideas. For the better part of the twentieth century America dominated the musical theatre.

1915–1916

The aura of superiority that emanated from the Winter Garden was short-lived. On 21 June, **The Ziegfeld Follies of 1915** came into the New Amsterdam and affirmed beyond any doubt Ziegfeld's preeminence in the field of elaborate revues. What overwhelmed the critics and audiences at this and subsequent productions was, sadly for posterity, the breathtaking but ephemeral settings of Joseph Urban.

Ziegfeld sought Urban out after admiring his scenery for Edward Sheldon's failure, *Garden of Paradise*. Instead of the more or less haphazard mélange of sets, painted in a thoughtless pastiche of gaudy colors, long accepted even in better New York productions, Urban carefully designed and colored each mounting with the flow of the entire production in mind. The 1915 edition played with shades of blue, a favorite of both Urban and Ziegfeld. The show's opening, with its simulated underwater effects, and the "Gates of Elysium" flanked by waterspouting elephants elicited the greatest enthusiasm. Reviewer after reviewer was unstinting in his praise.

JOSEPH URBAN was born in Vienna on 26 May 1872. He graduated from the Art Academy and from the Polytechnicum, where he was a pupil of Baron Carl Hassauer, who designed Vienna's Hofburg Theatre and Palais Lützow. After winning medals at several international expositions of the day, Urban was selected to design a palace for Count Esterhazy and the Czar Bridge over the Neva. He first came to America in 1901 to create an Austrian Pavilion for the 1904 St. Louis fair. The Boston Opera Company brought him back to mount several of their productions. A fine illustrator as well as an architect, the busy Urban found time to provide attractive drawings for numerous children's books.

This edition added W. C. Fields to the program and, for the first time, allowed the heretofore silent juggler to juggle lines as well. The skits included his quickly-to-be-famous billiard scene, turning the game into a frenetic tennis match as he became his own opponent. From the audience Ed Wynn directed a movie in which Bernard Granville and Mae Murray played the lovers and Leon Errol an inept villain. Bert Williams clowned as a put-upon house boy. George White, Carl Randall, and all the unforgettably beautiful girls, headed by Ina Claire and Ann Pennington, were in the superlative roster.

A rival producer to Florenz Ziegfeld, **GEORGE WHITE** was born George Weitz on Manhattan's Lower East Side in 1890. He earned his stripes in vaudeville dancing alongside Ben Ryan before making his Broadway debut in *The Echo* (1910), followed by featured roles in *The Pleasure Seekers* and *The Midnight Girl*. White learned from Ziegfeld during his appearance in the *Follies of 1915*—his twenty-year-running *George White's Scandals*, which he produced and directed four years later, was largely modeled on the *Follies* style. *Scandals* and its various iterations were primarily distinguishable from the languorous *Follies* by a faster pacing. White advanced the early careers of George Gershwin and the songwriting team of Buddy DeSylva, Lew Brown and Ray Henderson.

The score's best numbers were by Louis Hirsch. "Hold Me In Your Loving Arms" was the romantic hit when sung by Helen Rook and the chorus, while "A Girl For Each Month In The Year"—sung by Granville as part of a larger "Silver Forest" number—gave a theme to the expected parade of young ladies. But Hirsch's top tune was "Hello, Frisco!," celebrating not so much the San Francisco fair as the inauguration of transcontinental phone service. Miss Claire and Granville sang the song. A less escapist reference to the news of the day was a spectacular red, white, and blue production number, "America," with the principals representing the armed forces and one of Ziegfeld's loveliest girls, Justine Johnstone, bedecked as "Columbia." Granville welcomed "a hundred thousand refugees" with "We'll Build A Little Home In The U.S.A."

Sigmund Romberg songs were featured in the next two shows to arrive in the summer of 1915. **Hands Up** (22 July 1915, 44th St.) was a typically thrown-together Shubert hodgepodge. Calling itself—coyly, but uncertainly—a "musico-comico-filmo-melo-drama," it presented a number of younger Broadway talents, with Will Rogers receiving the loudest applause. E. Ray Goetz collaborated with Romberg on the music, but neither offered anything exceptional. A composer new to Broadway, Cole Porter, interpolated one song, "Esmerelda."

The type of music Romberg had to supply for **The Blue Paradise** (5 August 1915, Casino) was clearly more congenial to his Hungarian background, and the results were far more memorable. A Viennese creation, it told of a young European who leaves his sweetheart to make his fortune in America and returns to realize she is merely a shrew. It ran out the season. Only the Hippodrome spectacle had a longer run. The musical's book was adapted by Edgar Smith. Eight of Edmund Eysler's original songs were retained. Two songs were by Leo Edwards, and one

Cecil Lean rag was included. But it was the eight new Romberg melodies, particularly the lovely "Auf Wiedersehn," which were hummed by departing playgoers. For reasons only the Shuberts could explain, they failed to grasp the excellence of their staff composer when given suitable material. Two more seasons passed before Romberg properly established himself, and even then the Shuberts, usually so quick to capitalize on a good thing, almost let him slip away. If *The Blue Paradise* failed to assure Romberg's future, it handsomely paved one young lady's way to success. Although Cecil Lean and Cleo Mayfield were the best-known names in the cast, Vivienne Segal walked away with the loudest plaudits. Luckily for Miss Segal the lone song she was assigned was her duet with Lean to close Act I—"Auf Wiedersehn."

VIVIENNE SEGAL was born in Philadelphia on 19 April 1897. Her father was a well-to-do physician who sent his daughter to private schools and gave her private tutors. His generous support of cultural and theatrical enterprises allowed Miss Segal to start at the top. She made her debut in 1914, in Philadelphia, singing the title role in *Carmen*, and followed with Siebel in *Faust*. Her father helped underwrite the cost of *The Blue Paradise*. She was engaged to replace the original, unsatisfactory fiancée-turned-shrew.

One reason the Shuberts may have ignored Romberg's potential was increasing tensions the European war was producing, and the early evidence of anti–Austro-Hungarian feelings. But the *Dramatic Mirror* suggested that the war was not an unmitigated curse. In a 28 July article, "Comic Opera in the War," the paper thought fine musical subjects would come out of the holocaust: "The field for comic opera will be as expansive as the great deep out of which it will be born." This myopic, traditional publication failed to see that the side effects of the war would give us—indeed already were giving us—our new musical forms. The very term "comic opera" would be relegated to the shelves of history.

The next musical entry, **The Girl Who Smiles** (9 August 1915, Lyric), had a passing success and continued, for those who wanted to believe it, the illusion that the war was not really changing much. But **Cousin Lucy,** which arrived on 29 August at the Cohan and was one of those borderline pieces between a straight play and a musical, underscored the changes. The play's author was Charles Klein, who had gone down on the *Lusitania,* and one of its three Jerome Kern numbers, "Society," had some remarkable blues-like chords coloring the song's burthen.

Two Is Company (22 September 1915, Lyric), a second musical by the team that wrote *The Girl Who Smiles,* was a quick failure. The next night, at the magnificent, ill-fated Century Theatre—built too far out of the way, on Central Park, to realize its builders' ambition to see it Manhattan's leading temple of drama—Ned Wayburn produced an elaborate revue, **Town Topics.** It was a lushly ornate mounting and gave its audience a certain value for its money, running, as it did, almost to midnight. But it could not compete with the more famous spectacles playing at more centrally situated houses. It lasted nine weeks and left nothing behind but its own statistics. For comedy the fast-rising Will Rogers appeared in evening dress to deliver his monologues, producing his lariat from his top hat. Spectacle included a ballet of the seasons, performed on a revolving stage. Mannequins in an elegant dress shop came to life to provide the expected parade of beauties.

Far more successful and enduring was **The Princess Pat,** which John Cort presented on 29 September at his small playhouse on 48th Street. In the style of so many musicals of the day, it had three acts, with only one set for each. Although the names of its characters were Continental, its whole story unfolded on Long Island. Patrice O'Connor (Eleanor Painter) is an Irish beauty married to Prince Antonio di Montaldo (Joseph R. Lertora). Though she loves her husband deeply, she flirts with old Anthony Schmalz (Al Shean) to save her friend Grace Holbrook (Eva Fallon) from marrying him— and also to make the prince a trifle jealous. She pretends to elope; she and Schmalz are arrested; and the truth is out. Pat returns to the prince, and Grace finds a more suitable partner in Tony Schmalz, Jr. (Robert Ober). The critics were, for the most part, quite pleased with the show. Perhaps because the show was called a comic opera, the *Dramatic Mirror* permitted itself to wax especially ecstatic. It found Henry Blossom's libretto "a great improvement over the run of recent books." "In fact," it concluded, "the

Blossom characters might really have existed." The lyrics, as Blossom's were wont, could be light and natural in the more frivolous numbers, but stiff and involuted in the serious pieces. The show's triumph was its Victor Herbert score. At least two numbers, "Love Is The Best Of All" (sung by Pat directly after her first-act entrance) and "Neapolitan Love Song" (sung by the prince early in Act II), have found places in the canon of Herbert standards. Miss Painter was one of the many multi-talented actresses who graced the lyric stage of her generation. In later years she enjoyed modest success in a number of straight plays. In *Princess Pat* audiences enjoyed her singing as well as the delightful bonus of her graceful waltzing.

When the open-handed Dillingham took over the Hippodrome from the penny-pinching Shuberts, he renovated the entire theatre, gave the ushers smart new uniforms, printed handsome new programs, and rethought the whole production setup. Spectacle remained. The house was built for it and could not survive without it. But "personalities" were brought in. However tiny they might seem to those in the last row of the balcony, they nonetheless had their allure. R. H. Burnside was now completely responsible for assembling the company and providing what dialogue was deemed necessary. For the music, Dillingham replaced Manuel Klein, a hack, with Raymond Hubbell, another hack. Isadore Witmark, the music publisher, has written, "on account of its size, the Hippodrome was hardly the place in which to introduce song successes." Perhaps Dillingham reasoned along similar lines. But though Klein's melodies enjoyed some modest popularity and Hubbell wrote "Poor Butterfly," the one still popular song to emerge from these extravaganzas, the fallacy of this theory, and the loss to the Hippodrome, were not shown until twenty years later, when a great composer, Richard Rodgers, filled the huge house with memorable music.

Dillingham unveiled his initial presentation on 30 September. The first big name to appear was John Philip Sousa. Besides Sousa's band, theatregoers watched skiers "slide down the mountain side and leap a seemingly impassable chasm," the wedding of Jack and Jill, and New York by night from a rooftop. Patriotic bunting was unfurled, and along with Hubbell's "For The Honor Of The Flag," Marc Connelly and Zoel Parenteau offered "My Land, My Flag," the hit song from their Pittsburgh show, *The Lady of Luzon* (2 April 1913). Dillingham, who had produced the preceding season's two major smashes,

Watch Your Step and *Chin-Chin*, had Seymour Brown write a production number advertising the latter, then on tour. Whatever the show's shortcomings, it became the most successful Hippodrome spectacle up to its day and justified its cheery title, **Hip-Hip Hooray.**

Miss Information (5 October 1915, Cohan) was billed as a comedy with music, although its sheet music called it "a little comedy with a little music." Many critics ignored its music, even if Elsie Janis, its star, was customarily considered a songstress. Its book described how Mrs. Calwalder (Annie Esmond) has her son Jack (Howard Estabrook) hide her jewelry so she can enjoy the publicity a theft will bring. The plan misfires, and the jewels are stolen by a gang of crooks. A telephone girl, Dot from Nowhere (Miss Janis), in a series of disguises, solves every-thing and wins Jack. The music the critics ignored was by Jerome Kern. Most of it was not particularly good, but one tune, "Some Sort Of Somebody," was whisked away and reused several months later, at which time it was not overlooked. An interpolation, "Two Big Eyes," marked the second Cole Porter song heard on a Broadway stage.

Alone at Last (14 October 1915, Shubert), by Franz Lehar, ran until the spring. Its biggest hit, however, was the uproarious "Some Little Bug Is Going To Find You" (Benjamin Hapgood Burt and Roy Atwell/Silvio Hein), an American look at the germ menace. For the moment, with this and *The Blue Paradise*, the Central Powers forces were beat-ing the Allies in the battle of the importations.

A World of Pleasure, which also premiered on the 14th, was a predictable Winter Garden show. It had only the thread of a plot. Rich Tony Van-Schuyler (Clifton Crawford) courts an heiress (Venita Fitzhugh) and wins her at 11:30. The plot did little more than offer situations for vaudeville turns and production numbers the public came to see. Romberg's score was the pleasantly workaday mate-rial he had offered before *The Blue Paradise*, and many of the critics regretted his reversion to this patently crass style, typified by "I Could Go Home With A Girlie Like You." Only one interpolation outlived the show, "Pretty Baby" (Gus Kahn/Tony Jackson and Egbert Van Alstyne), also worked into a second Shubert show at the Winter Garden the following season.

Black shows, though still confined largely to Harlem and black districts in other cities, were increasingly drawing white interest, as *Variety*'s long and often effusive review of **Darkydom** (25 October 1915, Lafayette) demonstrated. Will Marion Cook wrote the music; Henry S. Creamer, the lyrics; and Henry Troy, the book. Its stars were Flournoy Miller and Aubrey Lyles, who played two hoboes, Steve Jenkins and Sam Peck (names both would reemploy in later shows). When the president of a large rail-road learns the two hoboes have stolen a ride on his special train, he orders the train shunted to a siding. The move staves off disaster, since an unlisted freight train was barreling toward the special and now passes by safely. So instead of having the men, who have fled, arrested, the president attempts to have his valet (played by Troy) present them with a $500 reward. The hoboes, thinking the valet is a police-man, jump from hideaway to hideaway, while two other tramps try to take credit. Of course, all ends happily. The scenery and costumes weren't much, but the trade paper singled out for praise such songs as the lively rag "Scay-A-Da-Mooch" and the rousing first-act finale, "Live And Die In Dixieland."

Around the Map (1 November 1915, New Amsterdam) provided an interesting case of missed opportunities. It advertised itself as "a musical globe trot," implying it was the latest in stylish revues. Essentially, it was. But the story that tied its various turns together told a curiously unpleasant tale. The dressmaker Impikoff (William Norris), to win the hand of Madame Kapinski (Hazel Cox), bets her he can turn the ugly sockmender, Jacqueline "Tootsi" Bonheur (Else Adler), into a great beauty and make the Count de Gai (Robert Pitkin) fall in love with her. Madame agrees to marry him if he succeeds. The count gets wind of the machinations and wagers he will be able to reject "Tootsi," no matter how attrac-tive she becomes. Kapinski brings a rival for the count's affections into the picture. But Impikoff, in various disguises, prevails. Several critics saw in this plot the possibilities for a tough, sardonic musical comedy. But the book minimized the vicious, cyni-cal undertones of the story, casting aside the chance to introduce a fresh approach to librettos. The lyrics were better, hinting at the mordant possibilities. "Here Comes Tootsi" may sound like the name of a hearty rag, and for all its use of minor key, its chorus is not unlike the welcome of "Hello, Dolly!" But its poignant verse is the wail of a lonely, gauche waif, the butt of inevitable cruelties. Herman Finck's music, unvaryingly routine, seemed totally unaware of the dark possibilities in the lyrics and dialogue. The show's attractions were enhanced by striking Urban sets that transported the audience to Berlin's Unter den Linden, a Wagnerian Dream Garden, a

Japanese Jockey Club, the San Francisco Exposition, and a finale done brazenly in torrid crimson, depicting the "Red Hot Stove Cabaret."

Almost two months elapsed between the arrival of *Around the Map* and the next new musicals. Then in Christmas week three shows came in—two on the 23rd and one on the 25th. All three were smash hits. They constituted the first such cluster of successful openings in the history of American musicals. In their quality, their diversity, and their striking acceptance they attested to the coming of age of an American art form.

Admittedly the first of these looked backward—or at least overseas. **Katinka** (23 December 1915, 44th St.) was first and simply a Continental operetta. But immigrant composers had settled here and been accepted before, and now Rudolf Friml, fulfilling the promise of *The Firefly* and *High Jinks* with another enchantingly melodic score, became a lasting part of the Broadway scene. For the next fifteen years, as long as unabashedly European musical styles remained salable to New York, he vied with Romberg for honors in the field, although his masterworks came in a four-year period that lay ten years away. Out of a sense of duty, Katinka (May Naudain) has married Boris Strogoff (Count Lorrie Grimaldi), the Russian ambassador to Austria. Her real love is Ivan Dimitri (Samuel Ash), an attaché. Ivan's American friend Thaddeus Hopper (Franklin Arcade) helps Katinka escape and hides her in his house. When Mrs. Hopper (Adele Rowland) becomes suspicious and angry, Hopper pays Arif Bey (Edward Durand) to conceal Katinka in his harem. By error Mrs. Hopper is placed in the harem. At a Viennese café the principals are all gathered. When a lady named Olga (Edith Decker) announces she is Boris's lawful wife, a happy ending follows. The story, however preposterous, was professionally handled. The music was gorgeous. "Allah's Holiday" (one of Olga's three second-act numbers) swiftly established itself as a classic. "'Tis The End," "Rackety Coo," and the beautifully arioso "My Paradise" were all far above Broadway's norm. The public responded wholeheartedly, and *Katinka* ran seven months.

The same night the incontestably American **Very Good Eddie** opened at the Princess. Some early announcements proclaimed it as the Marbury-Comstock Company's "annual Princess Theatre production." Just as *Katinka* confirmed the promise of *The Firefly* and *High Jinks*, *Very Good Eddie* even more emphatically and more importantly fulfilled the promise of *Nobody Home*. The Hudson

River Day Line's *Catskill* stops for fifteen minutes at Poughkeepsie. Dick Rivers (Oscar Shaw) comes aboard. He has fallen in love with Elsie Lilly (Ann Orr), Madame Matroppo's pupil. To be alone with Elsie he begs Madame Matroppo (Ada Lewis) to let him interview the girl for a magazine article. She agrees. Elsie is not easily wooed. She has known Rivers and suggests he is always in love with "Some Sort Of Somebody." Newlyweds Eddie and Georgina Kettle (Ernest Truex and Helen Raymond) board the boat. It is obvious from her incessant barking of commands that Georgina is determined to wear the pants in the family—though little Eddie's trousers are probably several sizes too small for her. They are followed by two more honeymooners, Percy and Elsie Darling (John Willard and Alice Dovey). The Darlings and the Kettles meet, and Eddie and Percy turn out to be old schoolmates. All four rejoice, "Isn't It Great To Be Married?" Georgina and Percy leave the boat—the one to send a telegram, the other to find some missing baggage—and the vessel sails without them. Eddie and Elsie, alone, discover they haven't even enough money for one meal. Rivers appears, and Eddie, who knows him, is forced to pretend Elsie is his bride. Rivers lends Eddie the money he will need. He also tells Eddie that Eddie's old flame Elsie Lilly is on the boat. Eddie and his "Mrs." sit down not just to dinner but to cocktails as well. Rivers returns and introduces Madame Matroppo to "Mr. and Mrs. Kettle." On top of his martinis, Eddie orders champagne for everyone. They celebrate with "Wedding Bells Are Calling Me."

At the Rip Van Winkle Inn, Rivers and Elsie Lilly dream of the joys "On The Shore At Le Lei Wi." Eddie and his Elsie, increasingly nervous at their masquerade, now discover there won't be a return boat—or a train—until the next day. There is nothing for them to do but remain overnight. To the astonishment of the desk clerk, they request separate rooms. Once they have signed the register, Eddie carefully spills ink over it to conceal his presence. Rivers is as puzzled as anybody by Eddie's behavior, insisting he'd act differently "If I Find The Girl." (The typescript gives five encores for this.) Madame Matroppo catches Eddie slinking off to eat dinner alone and orders him back upstairs to dine with his "wife." Eddie regrets he is so small he must wear a "Size Thirteen Collar." Georgina and Percy arrive but, with the register ruined, cannot be sure they have come to the right hotel. Madame Matroppo, who can never remember names correctly, assures them the only honeymooners are named "Fish."

Since it is late, they also take two rooms and head for bed. Georgina, learning that Darling's wife is named Elsie, goes upstairs with the uneasy feeling she is the same Elsie that Eddie loved long ago. A mouse scares Elsie Darling out of her room, and when she knocks on Eddie's door he comforts her, advising her to be as brave as the "Babes In The Wood." The next morning Percy and Georgina meet Rivers, who tells them Eddie Kettle and his wife are at the inn. But it is a changed Eddie who comes downstairs. He has learned how to handle himself, and when he orders Georgina to sit down, she does.

Guy Bolton and Philip Bartholomae's book was based on Bartholomae's *Over Night* (earlier announcements credited only Bartholomae with the book and Schuyler Greene with the lyrics). It was a tightly written book. The strained humor and awkward gaps of *Nobody Home* were gone. The fun flowed directly from the legitimate characterizations. On boarding, Georgina noisily issues commands about baggage and tips:

Steward: Say, boss.
Mr. Kettle [Eddie]: Are you speaking to me?
Steward: I was speaking to *her*.

But Georgina's pushiness masks her naïveté:

Mrs. Kettle: So this is the Hudson, is it? When do we get out of sight of land?
Mr. Kettle: This is a river.

There is a clever running gag on Madame Matroppo's inability to remember Rivers's name. It comes out as "Lake" or "Brooks" and ultimately is made to bear on the story when she also confuses the Kettles' name. In *Nobody Home* the title was used several times in the dialogue. In *Very Good Eddie, Oh Boy!*, and *Oh, Lady! Lady!!* Bolton used the titles for curtain lines. In this case, when Eddie, in his newfound strength, orders Georgina to sit down, the delighted clerk shouts admiringly, "Very Good, Eddie." The title came from Fred Stone's popular line in *Chin-Chin*.

Once again, accomplished as the book was, the music was better. The songs, even when not written for the show, seemed to fit naturally into place in the story. The down-to-earth nature of the characters allowed a refreshing distribution of songs. The cynical Rivers was given the optimistic "If I Find The Girl"; he and Elsie Lilly sing romantically of far-off Hawaii. But the closest thing to a pure love song, the show's hit "Babes In The Wood" (for which Kern collaborated with Greene on the lyrics), was given to two honeymooners who are not married to each other and who go their separate ways at the end of the evening. For many who saw the original its most precious memory was Ernest Truex's singing of "Size Thirteen Collar." To list the other excellent tunes would be to list almost the entire program. It is interesting how good and how surprisingly appropriate the lyrics by diverse hands proved—"Old Bill Baker" (Ring Lardner), "Some Sort of Somebody" (Elsie Janis), "Wedding Bells Are Calling Me" (H. B. Smith), "If I Find The Girl" (John E. Hazzard and Herbert Reynolds), "I'd Like To Have A Million In The Bank" and "On The Shore At Le Lei Wi" (both Reynolds). But Kern and Bolton were not content, and for their next Princess show they recruited a friend who brilliantly complemented and augmented them.

Very Good Eddie ran just under a year and toured to big profits. More than any other piece it formed the mold out of which poured a half-century of American musical comedy. Its people were everyday people—neither cartooned clowns nor cardboard lovers. Its situations were plausible—however unlikely. Its easily singable songs helped the story flow but were lovely and natural away from the stage.

The last of the Christmas week triumvirate was the Dillingham production of Irving Berlin's **Stop! Look! Listen!** (25 December 1915, Globe). This time Harry B. Smith did have a recognizable plot, and a well-written one at that. When Owen Coyne's leading lady, Mary Singer (Justine Johnstone), marries Gideon Gay (Frank Lalor) and leaves for a honeymoon in Japan, Violette (Marion Sunshine) steps forward and offers to perform the lead. The chorus girl is laughed away. Coyne's authors give him three months to find a suitable star. Together they set out around the world seeking her. They finally hire an actress who impresses them as the heroine of a "ragtime melodrama" that is the second-act finale. By the end of the third act Coyne (Harland Dixon) is convinced he has seen the girl somewhere before. Of course, she is Violette, who has been coached by Abel Connor (Harry Fox), a man who saw promise in her all the time. Her curtain line to Coyne is "And I lived right next door to your theatre." The fun was broader than in *Very Good Eddie*. The girls in the show had names such as Iona Carr, Gladys Canby, and Nora Marks. A philanthropist called Van Courtland Parke (Joseph Santley) tells the audience, "I'm looking for poor and deserving children to whom I can do some good with my money.

Little girls over eighteen preferred: no objection to good lookers." Gideon and Abel meet in the Pacific:

Gideon: Do you understand Sandwich?
Connor: Do I? All the dialects—ham, tongue—all of 'em.

At one point Coyne expresses what must have remained many customers' philosophy of an evening well spent: "I have to find some new way to undress the chorus... costumes make the show. Leave me my ponies and my clotheshorses, and musical comedy will still go on!" The theatrical setting allowed some celebrated turns to be inserted. Dixon combined with his partner, James Doyle, for comic bits and dances, while Gaby Deslys and Harry Pilcer performed ballroom specialties and ragtime stepping.

Again the music was the most durable feature of the show. Two of Berlin's best came out of this score, "The Girl On The Magazine Cover" and "I Love A Piano" (played on six pianos). Harry Fox introduced both songs. Berlin was constantly experimenting. While concerted pieces were by no means new, Berlin's contemporary American musical forms made them seem innovative. The opening was rhymed dialogue set to ragtime (using rhymes such as "nervous" and "observe us" Berlin reemployed in *Mr. President*, his last musical fifty years later).

The rest of the songs were not as well integrated into the piece as were Kern's songs at the Princess, but the music was solidly diverting, up-to-the-minute, and American all the way.

Romberg's incidental songs for *Ruggles of Red Gap*, which arrived the same night as *Stop! Look! Listen!*, were not nearly as interesting as Kern's for *Cousin Lucy* and *Miss Information*. More than either of these, the Harrison Rhodes play was straight comedy rather than musical. In any case, it was a quick flop.

January's only new musical was **Sybil** (10 January 1916, Liberty), an importation in which a prima donna poses as a duchess to save her beloved hussar. It reunited the three stars of *The Girl from Utah* (24 August 1914)—Julia Sanderson, Donald Brian, and Joseph Cawthorn. They helped it to run for 168 performances.

George M. Cohan attempted to keep his promise of a permanent revue at the Astor when he brought in **The Cohan Revue of 1916** on 9 February. But the Weber and Fields of *Hello, Broadway* (25 December 1914), William Collier, and Cohan himself were missing, and only John Hendricks's name was in both cast lists. Nonetheless, the show's sharp burlesque of the prominent people and creations of the time did continue the tradition Cohan so admired. War fervor, professional fundamentalism, and Shaw's *Major Barbara* were all spoofed when Andrew Overdraft kills the bartending evangelist Billy Holliday after Holliday opposes arming our troops. The takeoff of the season's sensational *Common Clay* was the show's high spot. In Cleves Kinkead's drama a reformed slut is brutally tongue-lashed by an unforgiving judge, who then discovers the girl is his daughter. In Cohan's court the swearing-in was on a telephone book and the witness appealed for help to 42nd Street's gods, "K and E." and "Jake and Lee." The girl's name turns out to be not Clay, but Mud. And Judge Oliver Mud is her father:

Judge: Is there a scar on your left hand ear?
Jane: Yes, on my left hand ear, you can see it right here.
Judge: My dear!
Jane: What?
Jjudge: I'm here.
Jane: Who?
Judge: Your dad.
Jane: You're mad.
Mother: No. No, it's so, I can tell by the sty on his left hand eye. Oliver!
Judge: Maud!

Jane and her lawyer, Steve, listen as Oliver and Maud Mud also remember their little boy who disappeared:

Judge: I'll find him sure as sin—I can tell him by the scar on his left hand chin.
Steve: Excuse me, please, if I butt in—but I've got a scar on my left hand chin.
Jane: Where?
Steve: There!
Jane: Is it true—it is you?
Steve: Sister!
Jane: Brother!
Mother: Father!
Judge: Mother!

Even more than in *Stop! Look! Listen!* much of the dialogue was rhymed and much of the rhyme set to a ragtime beat.

Cohan's songs, none distinguished, included the inevitable (for Cohan especially) Irish number, a necessary (for 1915–1916) San Francisco tune, a generous tribute to Ziegfeld, and a song, "Julia, Donald And Joe," which, in the fashion of that more leisurely era, had five long verses and choruses ready should audiences demand them. There was a patriotic "Young America" and, in an apparent change of heart, "Sousa Melodies." Better economic conditions and the beginning of a series momentum allowed this edition to outrun *Hello, Broadway.*

Michael Freedland, in his biography of the great jazz singer, correctly stated **Robinson Crusoe, Jr.** (17 February 1916, Winter Garden) "was the nearest Jolson had yet come to a show with a real plot," but his governing phrase lay in his subordinate clause, "although from opening night on, it was quite plain that the story was not going to interfere with his domination on stage." The "real plot" told how Hiram Westbury, exhausted from chasing movie-makers off his Long Island estate, falls asleep and dreams he is Robinson Crusoe, Jr. His chauffeur Gus (Al Jolson) becomes his Friday. They have a series of slapdash adventures with pirates and with a Spanish dancer. Trees come alive and sway to the music. Gus-Friday-Jolson has comic scenes with a goat and a crocodile, and at one point masquerades as Fatima. In these Winter Garden mountings, Sigmund Romberg's score was insignificant, and was pushed further and further aside as Jolson played with his interpolations. There were Negro spirituals, a Stephen Foster song, and, among the newer comings and goings, three tunes which Jolson used the rest of his life—"Where The Black-eyed Susans Grow" (Dave Redford/Richard Whiting), "Yaka Hula Hickey Dula" (E. Ray Goetz, Joe Young, and Pete Wendling), and "Where Did Robinson Crusoe Go With Friday On Saturday Night?" (Sam M. Lewis and Joe Young/George W. Meyer).

Anne Caldwell used the outline of another Austro-Hungarian operetta as the start of her book for **Pom-Pom** (28 February 1916, Cohan). Her story centered on another prima donna, this time one who is kidnapped and lives for a while as a pickpocket. Hugo Felix provided the score. With Mitzi Hajos, recently of *Sari*, as its star, it held the public's affection for four months, then toured.

There were two March entries: one at the very beginning of the month, the other at the end. **The Road to Mandalay** (1 March 1916, Park) had music by Oreste Vessella. Though he is now forgotten, Vessella was then a popular bandmaster. He had tried before to write for Broadway, and, although

his music had won praise from the tryout critics, book trouble prevented it from being heard in New York. This time his luck was little better. Twenty-one performances, and *The Road to Mandalay* was withdrawn. The show wasn't set in Mandalay, nor did the region have anything to do with it. Kipling's cry "come you back" provided the germ of the off-again, on-again love affair of Lt. Jack Poindexter (Frank Pollock) and Lily Montgomery (Leola Lucy). Bad luck plagued even Vessella's opening night. Miss Lucy, hurt shortly before in an accident, played the heroine from a wheelchair.

The other March entry failed to run even as long as *The Road to Mandalay*. But **See America First** (28 March 1916, Maxine Elliott) was historically far more important. For its less than two full weeks of life a New York program carried a new credit—score by Cole Porter.

See America First was advertised as "a comic opera." Produced by the enterprising Elizabeth Marbury at the Maxine Elliott, across the street from the Princess, it had Senator Higgens (Sam Edwards) leaving the effete East so his daughter can find a red-blooded American husband in the West. However, Polly Higgens (Dorothie Bigelow) has fallen in love with an Englishman, Cecil, Duke of Pendragon (John Goldsworthy). By coincidence they meet again while Cecil is vacationing as a cowboy. Polly and Cecil, and Senator Higgens and Polly's head-mistress, Sarah (Clara Palmer), are paired at the final curtain. The show lacked professional polish. But even the unyielding *Dramatic Mirror* could see that Porter and his coauthor, T. Lawrason Riggs, showed "promise of writing something wholly meritorious." Riggs rejected the theatre in favor of the church. And even Porter temporarily fled, leaving behind only one minor gem, "I've A Shooting Box In Scotland." One of the principals was another young man, Clifton Webb.

COLE PORTER was born into great wealth in Peru, Indiana, on 9 June 1891. His mother, to whom he was closely attached until her death just a few years before his own, began his musical training at an early age. By the time he was eleven he had published his musical writings. Sent to Yale to prepare to study law, he spent much of his time composing music for collegiate shows, for the glee club, and merely for the entertainment of his classmates. His football songs "Bull Dog" and "Eli" remain in use to this day in New Haven. By the time he reached Harvard Law School he knew composing was to be his life. Despite family objections he transferred to the School of Music. Broadway first heard his tunes earlier in the season when *Hands Up* and *Miss Information* each presented Porter interpolations.

April's only arrival was also a quick failure. An arid book, a lackluster score, and yet another Parisian setting left the critics and playgoers indifferent to **Come to Bohemia** (27 April 1916, Maxine Elliott). One critic did suggest, "A glorious opportunity awaits a librettist with a keen sense of the ironic in the pseudo-Bohemianism of Greenwich Village." It was shamefully long before producers and authors took the hint.

Two May musicals, neither particularly successful, were nonetheless interesting. They suggest "nostalgia" has a perennial pull. **Molly O'** (20 May 1916, Cort) was the American wife (Katherine Galloway) of Count Walter von Walden (Albert Parr), who leaves her because she makes him feel bought. He goes to Vienna. At an art students' auction there he pays $20,000 for a mysterious model. The unveiling reveals the model is Molly, who has pursued the Count because she genuinely loves him. Now he has "bought" her, thereby giving their marriage some sort of reasonable equilibrium. The show, for which the inexhaustible Smith brothers did the book and lyrics, lasted only five and a half weeks. What intrigued a few ticket-buyers was the title, which harked back to a decade before, when Blanche Ring interpolated "My Irish Molly O" in *Sergeant Brue* (24 April 1905), when a younger Jerome Kern wrote "Molly O'Halleron" as "Edna May's Irish Song" for *The Catch of the Season* (28 August 1905), and when Eddie Foy was singing the virtues of his Molly in *Mr. Hamlet of Broadway* (23 December 1908). (Older playgoers with longer memories undoubtedly recalled W. J. Scanlan's "Molly O." in *Mavourneen* [28 September 1891].) Ten years is as long or as short a time as circumstances dictate. But to the discerning playgoers of 1916 the last two seasons made 1905 seem light-years away.

The other May production, **Step This Way** (29 May 1916, Shubert), helped reinforce this sense of change. A revised version of Lew Fields's beloved *The Girl Behind the Counter* (1 October 1907), with new songs by E. Ray Goetz and Bert Grant (plus Berlin's painfully funny "I've Got A Sweet Tooth Bothering Me") and with Lew Fields himself again as star, it attracted audiences for eleven hot summer weeks.

The season ended as it began, with a new edition of **The Ziegfeld Follies** (12 June 1916, New Amsterdam). Pince-nezed Ned Wayburn, who had impressed Ziegfeld with his short-lived *Town Topics*, began a seven-year stint as stager. Urban was back, his mountings dazzling as ever. Lucille (Lady Duff Gordon) created the girls' gowns. Will Rogers was added to the growing roster of regulars. The 1916 edition had a Shakespearean theme. Bert Williams spoofed Othello; Bernard Granville and Ina Claire were Romeo and Juliet. Urban's sphinx for Antony and Cleopatra elicited awed approval. Spoofing other fields, Fanny Brice appeared in a tutu to sing about "Nijinsky" and his ballet, which Miss Brice, of course, pronounced "belly." Miss Claire mimicked Geraldine Farrar, Jane Cowl, and Irene Castle. The war inevitably made its way into the revue with Urban's North Sea naval battle. No song as popular as the previous year's "Hello, Frisco!" emerged, but Louis Hirsch, Jerome Kern, and Irving Berlin joined the dependable Dave Stamper to provide a solid, diversified score. Kern's "Have A Heart" was the best number, despite its weak ending. His "When The Lights Are Low" and Hirsch's nostalgic "Bachelor Days" were also attractive and popular.

There were twenty-seven musicals in 1915–1916, up just four from the preceding year. But the excellence and maturity of its best shows—particularly *Very Good Eddie*—mark it as a banner year in the history of the American Musical Theatre.

1916–1917

The 1916–1917 season saw a small increase in the number of musicals and a slightly more discernible drop in quality, although the season did produce the first indisputable masterpiece of our modern lyric stage. But tumultuous events here and abroad claimed prime attention. At home an urgent presidential election drew near. As the first shows of the new season were finishing their rehearsals and beginning their tryouts, the Republicans met in Chicago and nominated Charles Evans Hughes to run on a platform of avowed neutrality, a notable victory for the German-American element of the party. Five days later, 15 June, the Democrats renominated President Wilson. Pacifist sentiment was strong, and the party rallied (ironic in the light of events) to the cry, "He kept us out of war." The close results were dramatic—with Hughes going to bed on election night believing he had defeated Wilson. Yet despite pleas for peace, the awful truth remained, there was probably no way of staving off American intervention. The sickening carnage was making both sides desperate, the Central Powers fatally so. On 1 March the President gave the Associated Press the infamous Zimmermann telegram, which disclosed that the German ambassador in Washington was offering American territory to Mexico. On 18 March U-boats sank three American ships without warning and with a high loss of life. On 7 April we were at war.

A fourth of the musicals to open were importations from the belligerents—one from France, one from England, the rest from Vienna. The French and English shows were reasonably faithful to their originals, and failed or succeeded on their own merits. But the others encountered growing resistance. Two days after the Zimmermann telegram was made public, the *Dramatic Mirror* acknowledged that since the opening of the season there had been a "reaction in the theatrical world against Viennese musical plays" which, as a result, had to be "so largely Americanized ... that they lost most of their Viennese atmosphere." The two works the article mentioned as most drastically revised, *Miss Springtime* and *Her Soldier Boy*, were the only genuinely successful of the Austro-Hungarian arrivals, though *Flora Bella* had a modest run.

As usual, one of the annual extravaganzas opened the season. This year it was **The Passing Show's** turn on 22 June. The success of Cohan's revues and the excitement on front pages of the dailies convinced the Shuberts that more topicality would pay. Hughes, Wilson, the warmongering Teddy Roosevelt, and Pancho Villa were all satirized. When Roosevelt boasted that if he were still in the White House the war would be over, Wilson replied, "Over here!" Ed Wynn, lured from the *Follies*, sparked the clowns. Audiences first caught sight of him sitting in a box, shouting, "The show's terrible!" Inviting himself on stage, he proceeded to improve matters. A patriotic spectacle number offered an effective twist for an old device. Whereas races had been depicted with horses running on a treadmill that moved from one side of the stage to the other, a treadmill moving front to back allowed a troop of

horses and their riders to simulate a cavalry charge. Musically, the show had more than its customary fleeting interest. One song from this edition remains popular. It was the interpolation "Pretty Baby" (Gus Kahn/Tony Jackson and Egbert Van Alstyne), which the Shuberts had also inserted into *A World of Pleasure*. The main Romberg–Motzan score was neither better nor worse than the other scores Romberg and his associates churned out two or three times a year for these Winter Garden productions, but one of its otherwise ordinary numbers, "The Making Of A Girl," coupled Romberg's name with one new to Broadway—George Gershwin.

GEORGE GERSHWIN (Jacob Gershvin) was not quite eighteen when the show opened. He was born in Brooklyn on 26 September 1898. His love of music came very early, and his childhood friendship with his classmate, the violinist Max Rosen, reinforced the love. When the Gershwins purchased a piano so his older brother Ira could learn to play a musical instrument, it was young George, then twelve, who monopolized it. Two years later, in 1912, he began lessons with the man who most influenced his musical life, Charles Hambitzer, a composer and pianist of broad and enlightened musical tastes. From Hambitzer, George received a thorough classical training. Gershwin was aware of the native musical ferment around him, but he found most popular compositions trite. At the wedding of an aunt he heard an orchestra play several tunes that captured his attention. They were soaringly superior to the run-of-the-mill numbers bands of the day offered. When he discovered that all the songs were from the same Broadway show, he was determined to write musical comedy material, and set about studying the works of the songs' composer. The musical was *The Girl from Utah* (24 August 1914), and the songs were Jerome Kern's interpolations. Kern remained a Gershwin idol, although their music rarely followed similar paths.

The first August entry was **Yvette** (10 August 1916, 39th St.), of which no trace seems to survive. If the notices are to be believed, it must have been atrocious, with its leading lady screeching off key. The public obviously read and accepted the reviews, for *Yvette* could muster only four performances.

Broadway and Buttermilk (15 August 1916, Maxine Elliott) was a Blanche Ring vehicle that toured as *Jane O'Day of Broadway*. Neither title gave away the story line. Mary Denby's spoiled daughter, Ruth, loves wastrel Franklyn Abbot. Jane O'Day, calling herself Madame Nadine, shows Franklyn is really decent and responsible. She brings Ruth down to earth and even finds a mate for Mother Denby. The songs, which included old Blanche Ring favorites, were by various hands. Like several of the preceding year's offerings this was more a "comedy with songs," as the program stated, than a musical comedy.

The season's first importation was **The Girl from Brazil** (30 August 1916, 44th St.). Sigmund Romberg supplemented the score with songs in the best Winter Garden mode, but even they weren't good enough to keep the show on the boards beyond October.

The Big Show at the Hippodrome opened on 31 August. For the audiences that came to see it during its 425 performances, the main attraction was almost certainly the great ballerina Anna Pavlova, dancing an abbreviated version of Tchaikovsky's "Sleeping Beauty" (with Leon Bakst scenery). Charlotte skated on ice, elephants played ball, and the ensemble participated in a gigantic minstrel show. The edition also contained the one song to become a popular standard out of all the music the Shuberts and Dillingham introduced at the house. "Poor Butterfly" was, moreover, the prolific Raymond Hubbell's single claim to lasting fame. Its lyrics were by John Golden, who in a few years became one of New York's most successful and best-loved producers. This lament for Madame Butterfly was written when Dillingham thought he had secured the services of a then famous Japanese soprano, Tamaki Miura. The arrangements fell through. On opening night a Chinese-American vaudevillian introduced the song, but she was so bad she was hastily replaced.

The earliest September offerings were both imports. **Pierrot the Prodigal** (6 September 1916, Booth) was a French pantomime with music, retelling the Prodigal Son tale. It ran twenty weeks. But neither Lina Abarbanell, Charles Cuvillier and Milton Schwarzwald's delightful music, nor a more than adequate book could propel **Flora Bella** (11 September 1916, Casino) beyond fifteen weeks. Abarbanell played a princess who poses as her nonexistent twin sister to rekindle her husband's ardor.

The next September entry was **The Amber Empress** (19 September 1916, Globe). Although it lasted only forty-five performances, it was in many ways an interesting show. "The Amber Empress" is the name of a movie a group of Americans are filming in Italy. The company runs out of money and the Americans are stranded in Europe. Luckily, rich Percival Hopkins (Frank Lalor) comes to the rescue. The author of the libretto was Marc Connelly in his first Broadway effort, but the wit and compassion that distinguished his later writings were well hidden in this instance, and the pastiche of jokes that passed for a book help cut short the show's chances. This was especially sad since the show also marked the debut of Zoel Parenteau, a composer with a uniquely expressive melodic gift and with whom Connelly had collaborated in amateur productions. Several critics hailed Parenteau as a major discovery, and he was compared to Rudolf Friml and Victor Herbert, even if his musical line was far more contemporary than theirs. It was closer, if anything, to Jerome Kern's best style. Parenteau only did one other full score, and once again he was unsuccessful. Later he wrote two songs for Belasco's *Kiki* and then disappeared from the musical comedy scene.

For a second time in less than a month two importations arrived back to back. Both were given choice houses, but only the first, **Miss Springtime** (25 September 1916, New Amsterdam), chalked up a run. Looked at today the libretto seems hardly "Americanized." Its story is pure Old World. Rudolfo Marta, Pilota's sole claim to fame, refuses to return to the village for a festival in his honor. Robin gets Varady to pose as Marta. Rosita is under Marta's spell, though she has never met him. Paul, who loves Rosita, must expose the impostor to bring Rosita back into his arms. "Americanization" seems to have consisted solely of offhand references to things American, such as Robin's remark to Varady, "Oh, you Mormon you. Maybe I didn't let you in for a nice soft job, when I hired you to play Marta." In no way was Emmerich Kalman's score Americanized. It was not of an order with his best, but it was still delightful and hummable. The show's hit was its opening number, "Throw Me A Rose," and it was used effectively throughout the evening. Three Kern songs were used. Gorgeously mounted by Joseph Urban and excellently cast (its feminine lead was Sari Petrass, prima donna of Budapest's Kiraly Theatre), it attracted audiences into the spring. However, *Miss*

Springtime's happiest claim to fame was its introducing Americans to a new lyricist, P. G. Wodehouse.

Paul Rubens's **Betty** (3 October 1916, Globe), the story of a serving girl who marries an earl, was less fortunate. Even with Raymond Hitchcock, Ivy Sawyer, and Joseph Santley as principals, it survived only eight weeks.

PELHAM GRENVILLE WODEHOUSE was born at Guildford, Surrey, England, on 15 October 1881. He was educated at Dulwich College and planned on entering the financial world, but soon turned to writing. Some of his very first lyrics were set to music by a young American come to write songs for Charles Frohman's London shows— Kern, of course. Their first success saluted a then famous politician, "Mr. Chamberlain." From 1903 to 1909 Wodehouse served as a columnist on the London *Globe*. A year after he left the post, the first of his Psmith novels, *Psmith in the City*, was published. The popularity of these books earned him a trip to America, where he wrote articles for the *Saturday Evening Post* and served as drama critic for *Vanity Fair*. While covering the opening of *Very Good Eddie*, his old collaborator, Kern, approached him about working together again.

If Betty failed to win favor, Letty succeeded. Letty, of course, meant loose-jointed, high-kicking Charlotte Greenwood, who had rocketed to fame as Letitia Proudfoot in *Pretty Mrs. Smith* (21 September 1914). Now Morosco brought her back in **So Long, Letty** (23 October 1916, Shubert), with Letty as one of two wives who agree to change partners. They quickly realize they are no happier with their new spouses than they were with the old ones. After a week they are back with their original mates. The score was by Earl Carroll, who, like John Golden, soon gave up writing for producing. The title song was the show's best number. The run of ninety-six performances is deceptive. *So Long, Letty* opened in 1915, starting, as did all Letty shows, in Morosco's home base of California. By the time it reached New York, Carroll had rewritten much of the score, adding one more hit, "When You Hear

Jackson Moan On His Saxophone." After the show left Broadway and resumed its tour, additional numbers were added as late as 1917 by young composers such as Harry Tierney and Walter Donaldson. Although not one of the Letty shows played much time on Broadway, their long tours amounted to longer runs than most shows achieved. They were remembered with a particular affection by the generation that saw them.

When Ray Comstock insisted that the next Princess Theatre show should be an updated, fully musicalized version of Charles Hoyt's *A Milk White Flag* (8 October 1894), his regulars—Jerome Kern and Guy Bolton—and newly signed P. G. Wodehouse disagreed. They argued the show could never have the charm they deemed so fundamental to the theatre's earlier hits. Comstock refused to heed their warnings and signed John Golden, John Hazzard, and Anne Caldwell to do the modernization. The result was **Go to It** (24 October 1916, Princess). Although a solid cast led by Emma Janvier, Percival Knight, and Will Deming did their best to spark the old tale of a fake funeral and its effects on several romances, one critic assailed the evening as "deadly dull." After three weeks Comstock took the play on the road, where its reception was no better. He promptly announced that Kern, Bolton, and Wodehouse were working full speed on a new musical.

On 26 October, **The Show of Wonders** gave the Shuberts and the Winter Garden one more successful extravaganza. Although the score, mostly by Romberg, was weaker than usual, the production was lavish and the cast strong. Walter C. Kelly (brother of George and uncle of Grace) moved over from vaudeville to do his already popular "A Virginia Court Room"; McIntyre and Health did their blackface routines, and Willie and Eugene Howard their dialect bits. Willie also impersonated a sour elevator operator at the Giltmore Hotel with Eugene as his pretentiously dapper passenger. Willie's imitations included Jack Norworth, while Eugene did a turn on a "ukalale." Dancers included sharp little Sammy White and, best of all, Marilyn Miller, who shone in an exotic "Burmese Ballet" that opened the second act.

New York's two finest producers of musicals, Charles Dillingham and Florenz Ziegfeld, combined their impressive talents to mount an opulent revue at the Century Theatre on 6 November and called it, appropriately, **The Century Girl.** A star-studded cast featured Hazel Dawn, Leon Errol, Elsie Janis, and Van and Schenck. Urban outdid himself creating breathtaking sets—including a staircase that became Ziegfeld's trademark. Apparently the two top producers reasoned they needed two top composers. Irving Berlin and Victor Herbert were recruited to collaborate on the score. In a witty musical scene an actor portraying Herbert played "Kiss Me Again" while an actor pretending to be Berlin offered a ragtime countermelody. The approaching war clouds prompted "When Uncle Sam Is Ruler Of The Sea" and "Uncle Sam's Children." Unfortunately none of the songs represented the composers at their best. The show left nothing except its own legend. But it unwittingly participated in the demise of tradition—a tradition growing out of the fame, if not the legend, of certain theatres. For many years musical comedy houses, especially those which offered shows famous for their beautiful chorus lines, sooner or later found themselves in the title of successful attractions—*A Gaiety Girl, The Casino Girl. The Century Girl* was the last, at least for American musicals. New movie palaces rising across the land quickly seized the fame and affection legitimate auditoriums sometimes had gained.

On 29 November the Shuberts brought Ziegfeld's ex-wife, Anna Held, to the Casino in **Follow Me**. Based on a German show, discreetly un-mentioned, it credited Romberg with the score, even though most of the songs were by Harry Tierney. These included one final Held success, "Oh, I Want To Be Good But My Eyes Won't Let Me." The single tune still revived was not sung by Miss Held, but by Henry Lewis. It was "Oh Johnny, Oh Johnny, Oh!" (Ed Rose/Abe Olman). Because the plot centered on the romance of Clair La Tour, star of Paris's Theatre Varieties, the Shuberts had a ready-made excuse to bring on a procession of "Junoesque show girls" and vaudeville turns such as the dancing Cansinos.

December, which usually offered a batch of musicals, brought in only one in 1916, **Her Soldier Boy** (6 December 1916, Astor). Its success held out hope that Kalman, who had written the music for September's *Miss Springtime* and who, with Romberg, wrote the new show's score, somehow might ride above international animosities. As the title suggested the musical dealt with the war head on. It was the first to do so, although not without a romantic bent. It told how a soldier (John Charles Thomas) pretends to be his dead buddy so the buddy's family will be spared the painful truth. There is a doubly happy ending, for the soldier marries the buddy's sister (Beth Lydy) and the supposedly dead boy (Frank Ridge) turns up among the missing.

Neither Romberg's nor Kalman's music caught on, anymore than did interpolations by Clifton Crawford or the show's conductor, Augustus Barrett. But another insert, the English war song "Pack Up Your Troubles In Your Old Kit Bag And Smile, Smile, Smile" (George Asaf/Felix Powell), outlived both the show and the war. The song was rousingly delivered by Adele Rowland, playing the pal of a comic reporter. In turn, the reporter was played by Clifton Crawford, who several times won hearty rounds of applause soft-shoeing "drowsily."

The new year brought a happy upturn in the quality of its new musicals. Regrettably the public did not always respond. Jerome Kern, who, except for a few interpolations in the *Follies* and *Miss Springtime*, had not been heard from since 1915, wrote the scores for both January entries. The year 1917 was Kern's most prolific. He had a third score ready in February and two more in the fall. **Have a Heart** (11 January 1917, Liberty) was not a hit, although it deserved to be. Originally slated for the Princess, it had a good Guy Bolton–P. G. Wodehouse book, marvelous Wodehouse lyrics, and ingratiating Kern music. The plot was frivolous, but frivolity was a musical comedy tradition and, in the worrisome days of early 1917, not unwelcome. Besides, in the hands of Bolton and Wodehouse the frivolity was literate and witty. Rutherford "Rudy" Schoonmaker (Thurston Hall) and his wife, Peggy (Eileen Van Biene), decide to elope on the eve of their divorce. They hide away at a seaside resort, but their plans for a second honeymoon run into all sorts of complications, especially in the form of Dolly Barbizon (Louise Dresser), Schoonmaker's former shopgirl and now a movie star. Schoonmaker's trusted elevator boy, Henry (Billy B. Van), arrives to save the day. Wodehouse's lyrics could be literate and witty, too, as in "They All Look Alike." Or they could have just the right touch of sentimentality—as in "Honeymoon Inn," with which Rudy persuades Peggy to elope, telling her they'll survive "on bread and cheese and kisses," and insisting "this is the thing to do." Most of all, Kern's music was a delight. The song hit—sung by several minor characters—was "You Said Something," direct and memorable. But the most remarkable number was a forgotten gem, Rudy and Peggy's "And I Am All Alone." Clearly Kern and the producer wanted it to be the real hit, for it was long featured as a sample on the back of much of Kern's other sheet music. Its harmonics were striking for the day, but even more fascinating was its beautiful emotional development building up to a pause and a last melancholy phrase. Kern experimented all through this imaginative score.

Considering the number of favorable reviews *Have a Heart* received, its poor showing is a puzzle. Perhaps some confusion was created by using for its title the title of the still new and popular Kern song from the *Follies*. Whatever the reason, failure and obscurity were undeserved.

Four nights later Kern's second show premiered. **Love o' Mike** (15 January 1917, Shubert) had a book by Thomas Sydney and lyrics by Harry B. Smith. "Thomas Sydney" was a pseudonym for the real librettists, Augustus Thomas, Jr., and Harry's son, Sydney. Their plot was inane. The girls at Mrs. Marvin's house party all fall in love with Lord Michael Kildare (Lawrence Grossmith), but he has eyes only for Vivian (Vivian Wessell). The fun at the party is marred when the butler (a sometime second-story man) steals one young lady's money. Then, for reasons never explained, Mike takes credit for rescuing some people from a local tenement fire. His bravery further mars the fun of the men—as they watch their girls' adulation of Mike go out of control. With the butler (George Hassell) the boys plot a phony rescue to counter Mike's heroics. But the two-faced butler tells Mike and the girls of their plans. The dialogue was as inane as the story, often sounding like a satire on itself. Kildare discusses a genuine war wound with his man, Stafford:

Stafford: Wounded arm troubling?
Kildare: Just a bit. Soon be as right as rain.
Stafford: Have a drink, old scout.
Kildare: Thanks, help yourself.

The lyrics, perhaps under the spell of Kern's magic, were above Smith's norm. His idea of how a European might write the lyrics for a "coon song" is still amusing: he told of a girl named Susquehanna who lives in Dixie on the banks of the Catskill. But the best lyric was by Herbert Reynolds, and it was for the best song of the show, "It Wasn't My Fault." As with most Kern scores there was hardly a weak number in the show. Good dancing helped put over the songs. The dancing ranged from the suave routines of Quentin Todd to the exuberant stepping of Gloria Goodwin and Clifton Webb. While the better *Have a Heart* flopped, *Love o' Mike* ran six months.

A few days after *Love o' Mike* opened, the major Broadway producers were asked to comment on the season's musicals. Their remarks suggested their opinions were governed more by their account of

books than by any overriding vision. John Cort, who had only middling luck with the operetta *Flora Bella*, insisted the season was "strictly a musical comedy one," but Lee Shubert, his coffers piled high with profits from *The Passing Show, Show of Wonders, Follow Me, Her Soldier Boy*, and now *Love o' Mike*, stressed its quality rather than its type and unequivocally hailed 1916–1917 as "the best musical comedy season of recent years."

The same team that brought *So Long, Letty* from California in October brought a second show east in early February. **Canary Cottage** (5 February 1917, Morosco) had even less plot than *Love o' Mike*. At another house party, a group of men are entertaining "young ladies" when the men's wives and sweethearts arrive. By curtain time everyone is properly paired. Although several of the critics were unusually sharp in their denunciations, branding the evening "vulgar" and "low," and although none of Earl Carroll's score was more than superficially pleasing, *Canary Cottage* had a respectable stay.

You're in Love (6 February 1917, Casino) was more successful. Just as *Canary Cottage*'s plot bore some resemblance to *Love o' Mike*, so *You're in Love*, portraying another troubled honeymoon, recalled *Have a Heart*. In this case the young couple had to contend with a busybody aunt-in-law. The book by Otto Hauerbach and Edward Clark was conventional. Much of the success was due to Rudolf Friml's fetching score, particularly the show's title song. If the music is no longer familiar, Friml himself is to blame. His great scores have overshadowed this charming, inconsequential material. But the show also was given an imaginative mounting. The second act was set on a realistically recreated ship. The heroine (Marie Flynn) was a sleepwalker, and her nightly rambles took her onto a cargo boom. As soon as she was on it, the boom swung dramatically out over the audience. At the opening one uninhibited first-nighter removed her pink slipper and tickled her feet as she walked over him.

Oh, Boy! opened at the Princess two weeks later, on 20 February. The critics and public immediately knew they were witnessing a consummate triumph. The *Times* rejoiced, "You might call this as good as they make them if it were not palpably much better," while the *Sun* exulted, "If there be such things as masterpieces of musical comedy, one reached the Princess last night." Along with a sense of achievement came a sense of occasion. It was realized that the Princess Theatre and its bandbox shows were establishing an important American tradition.

Like *Very Good Eddie* (23 December 1915), *Oh, Boy!* had fun with mistaken relationships. It began at George Budd's apartment when Briggs (Carl Lyle), his valet, answers the door to accept a telegram. While Briggs is at the door, George's playboy friend, Jim (Hal Forde), and Jim's girls enter through the window, looking for George (Tom Powers). Not finding him in the living room, they disappear into the rest of the apartment to search for him. George arrives with his new bride, Lou Ellen (Marie Carroll). They are madly in love with each other and can't imagine how they muddled through when "You Never Knew About Me." The telegram is from Aunt Penelope (Edna May Oliver), George's Quaker guardian. She has learned he is contemplating marriage and is coming to talk to him. George fears she will cut off his allowance if she discovers he is already married. Lou Ellen decides it might be prudent for her to go home until Aunt Penelope leaves. She will do whatever George suggests, since she wants only to be "An Old-Fashioned Wife." Their cry, as George escorts her out, "Just Think ... parted like this on our bridal night," could have come from the Kettles or the Darlings. Jim returns. Jackie (Anna Wheaton), a buxom, attractive young lady in handsome evening dress, arrives, as Jim and friends did earlier, through the window. She is fleeing from a policeman whom she hit in the eye during a rumpus that began when an old gentleman known as Tootles persisted in giving her lingering looks at the Cherrytree Inn. Jim tells her he is enchanted to meet "A Pal Like You." He persuades Jackie to stay, and to claim she is Mrs. Budd if anyone comes. Meanwhile he will find Tootles. Jackie puts on Lou Ellen's pajamas just as George returns. She explains her predicament in the nick of time, for the policeman she hit is knocking at the door. George shows the policeman the wedding license, and the officer allows he has made a mistake. Before he departs he admires her pajamas, and "Mrs. Budd" offers to obtain the pattern for him. With the policeman gone, Jackie prepares to leave. But it has started to rain, and she and George agree she will have to stay. "Till The Clouds Roll By." Judge Carter, Lou Ellen's father, drops in to meet his new son-in-law, but George hurries him out while Jackie hides in the bedroom. Lou Ellen and her mother arrive. When they confront Jackie, George introduces her as his Aunt Penelope. Lou Ellen had imagined a different sort of aunt. But her surprise is nothing compared to Jackie's when Judge Carter reappears. Jackie sees that the judge is Tootles. At the Meadow Country Club Jim and Jackie dream of "Nesting Time In Flatbush." Jackie must continue her masquerade as Aunt Penelope, but she is not above ordering a couple of stiff drinks:

Jackie: Hast thou been enjoying thyself?
Lou Ellen: Not a bit. Mother won't let me speak to George.
Jackie: What have they got against the gink?
Lou Ellen: Gink?
Jackie: (George pokes Jackie) A Quaker word ... poor lad I should say...
Policeman: How about the pajama pattern?
George: It's coming ... it's coming.
Lou Ellen: Pajama pattern?
Jackie: Thee shall have it, good man, I promise thee.
Policeman: How's that?
Jackie: I will even give thy good wife mine if thee will only beat it.

The real Aunt Penelope arrives, and the policeman points out George and "his wife" to her. Before she can protest, she is served a spiked lemonade Jackie has ordered. In no time she is tipsy and forgiving.

The book was fast moving, its characters were well drawn, and its humor, as the excerpt indicates, flowed logically from the characters and situations. Song assignments proved how stunningly Bolton and Wodehouse had advanced. The wryly comic "You Never Knew About Me" was given to the principal lovers, while the cozy "Nesting Time In Flatbush" was sung by the comic leads, and the show's top tune, "Till The Clouds Roll By," was sung by the hero and the comedienne. Wodehouse's lyrics were little short of miraculous. Again they were literate and natural, with a precisely right balance of wit and sentiment. Lou Ellen laments not knowing George when they were children:

> I was often kissed 'neath the mistletoe
> By small boys excited with tea.
> If I'd known that you existed,
> I'd have scratch'd them and resisted, Dear!

But as usual it was Jerome Kern's music that capped the evening. Once more there was hardly a weak number. The show was done as *Oh, Joy!* in England. More than almost any other important American musical, *Oh, Boy!* has slipped undeservedly into limbo.

Another fine musical arrived one month later. But though **Eileen** (19 March 1917, Shubert) had one of Victor Herbert's finest scores and remained Herbert's personal favorite among all his works, it ran only eight weeks. Its ill-timed opening undoubtedly hurt, coming as it did one day after U-boats had sunk the *City of Memphis*, the *Illinois*, and the *Vigilancia*, and our ultimate, headlong plunge into war had begun. The reviewers' raves were overlooked in the headlines' compelling excitement. Moreover, war was the theme of the operetta, and even romanticized war is terrifying on the brink of real battle. Barry O'Day (Walter Scanlan), an Irish revolutionist, is about to be arrested for treason when his high-born sweetheart, Eileen Mulvaney (Grace Breen), disguised as a maid, helps him escape. He is recaptured and is on the verge of being shot when a pardon arrives. The book was well written but in no way exceptional. On the other hand the score had a magnificent Irish flavor, and three Herbert classics have come out of it: "The Irish Have A Great Day To-night," "Thine Alone," and the title song.

It was almost the end of April before another musical opened—the season's second **Passing Show** (26 April 1917, Winter Garden), coming in far ahead of its customary time. Its single memento, reflecting the new war fervor, was "Goodbye Broadway, Hello France!" (C. Francis Reisner, Benny Davis/Billy Bashette). De Wolf Hopper and Jefferson De Angelis, both stars of a bygone day, joined the ranks, to compete for laughs with Chic Sale and Ray Dooley. The consensus was that the comedy was weak. Spectacle included a harem scene featuring not only girls but soft, flickering lights reflected in tiny mirrors. As one slightly-weary-of-it-all critic noted, the girls themselves were "seriously affected by the new custom of dressing chorus girls, if at all, in things that are not so much gowns as structures." The "things" included fans, drinks, and fully set tables. In the finale the girls became college students at the Yale Bowl. Clowns, beauties, and a basic Sigmund Romberg score all combined to keep the show at the Winter Garden into the fall.

His Little Widows (30 April 1917, 44th St.) was another instance of critics and public going opposite ways. Favorably received, it played only nine weeks. William Schroeder's lame score did nothing to help the show win favor. However, its story was just the sort of fluff ticket-seekers looking for distraction should have flocked to. Jack Grayson's Mormon uncle dies. To inherit his uncle's fortune Jack (Robert Emmett Keane) must marry the dead man's eleven wives. The least desirable widow begins to pursue him. But he succeeds in avoiding all except

the loveliest of the group. The show was filled with vaudeville turns. Frank Lalor repeated bits he had performed in *The Pink Lady*, Carter De Haven sang and did a soft shoe, but a jazzy quartet, the Haley Sisters, won the biggest round of applause, largely thanks to one of its girls. She had a "voice like a moose" and performed acrobatic dances on a par with Fred Stone and Charlotte Greenwood.

Two revivals, Reginald De Koven's *The Highwayman* (13 December 1897) and Julian Edwards's *When Johnny Comes Marching Home* (16 December 1902), were the only openings in May. Both were quickly gone, although the Edwards work's six-week run was not a bad showing. It opened at the New Amsterdam, and when it had to make way for the *Follies* was still considered strong enough to be moved to the Manhattan Opera House for three more weeks. Curiously, De Koven's work had a far better, more celebrated cast that included John Charles Thomas and Jefferson De Angelis.

June ended the season with a pair of revues. The first was Raymond Hitchcock's **Hitchy-Koo** (7 June 1917, Cohan and Harris). In an interview, Hitchcock, who had heretofore worked primarily with book shows, observed, "Restlessness of American life has brought a demand for speed and the quality best described as 'Zippiness' in stage productions, and the revue is the type of entertainment in which these qualities are best expressed." He predicted the demise of the book musical, "in which the naval lieutenant rescued the irritatingly ingenuous heroine from an impossible situation, while the chief comedian acted as a sort of deus ex machina." Hitchcock was correct in sensing the faster pace that Broadway audiences sought. Shows that went on till 11:30 or 11:45 became rarer with each season. But he was wrong in thinking only the revue cleared the path for fast action. He brought to his own production some of the new pace, as well as a feeling for personal intimacy unknown till then. Like George M. Cohan and Will Rogers he made fun of even the most sacrosanct figures— Billy Sunday being dismissed as "the P. T. Barnum of the hymnbook." Hitchcock was careful to surround himself with other sterling talent. In this edition he employed Leon Errol, the baby-talking Frances White, Grace La Rue, and Irene Bordoni. Errol garnered more than his fair share of laughs, not merely for his expected drunk act, but for his routine as a cockney waiter defending his pet lobster. Spectacle included a first-act finale in which couples walked out of wedding-album pictures. Each couple took the audience back a generation further and sang or danced an appropriate period piece. E. Ray Goetz, who coproduced the evening, did most of the songs. As happened so many times, an interpolation was the hit of the show. "I May Be Gone For A Long, Long Time" (Lew Brown/Albert Von Tilzer) sang another war song to a now accepting nation. Some of Goetz's songs were actually better, but none so good as to demand rehearing. The show delighted audiences for seven months, and three more editions followed.

The Ziegfeld Follies of 1917 (12 June 1917, New Amsterdam), which closed the season, had an all-star cast—Fanny Brice, Will Rogers, W. C. Fields, Bert Williams, and, for the first time, Eddie Cantor. The stunning Dolores became the center of all eyes in a ravishing "Episode in Chiffon." Fields revived his billiard scene, calling the shots so unerringly that the *Times* wondered how he could do it night after night. Rogers twirled his rope in time with his hilarious anecdotes, which were taking on an increasingly political slant. He found Congress strange, noting, "A man gets up to speak and says nothing. Nobody listens. Then everybody disagrees." Fanny Brice vamped as an Egyptian odalisque. Cantor, in blackface, played the college-educated son of a porter (Williams), intolerant of his father's illiteracy. But he really called attention to himself singing "That's The Kind Of Baby For Me." (Alfred Harrison and Jack Egan). Again in blackface as he sang, he rolled his eyes and jumped up and down, clapping his hands and excitedly waving a handkerchief.

As always Joseph Urban created magical effects on stage and off. He presented a stunning rooftop view of New York and a scene of Lower Manhattan flanked by "fruit festooned" parapets. A set simulating Chinese lacquer had fifty Ziegfeld beauties scampering up and down red and gold ladders against a black background. Girls as flowers sprang from trap doors, and an opalescent curtain of beads parted to reveal Venuses in a gigantic bubble. A Ben Ali Haggin tableau portrayed Paul Revere riding a white horse (on a treadmill). When an actor impersonating President Wilson came to review girls dressed in red, white, and blue, the orchestra began "The Star Spangled Banner," and, as the audience rose, a tremendous flag unfurled to cover the ceiling. Raymond Hubbell and Dave Stamper's music was pleasantly adequate. Besides the necessary parade numbers such as "In The Beautiful Garden Of Girls," it included the topical "I'll Be Somewhere In France" and, somewhat bafflingly, a number advertising a forthcoming show that was not Ziegfled's, *Chu Chin Chow*. Victor Herbert wrote a "patriotic finale," "Can't You Hear Our Country Calling?" But Ziegfled could not find a top-flight interpolation. Still, Ziegfeld's touch was so sure and Ziegfeld's name so potent the show played fifteen weeks to good houses and then toured.

It was altogether a good season. Not one of the best, but one that did leave behind a number of good tunes, from *Eileen, Have a Heart, Love o' Mike,* and, most of all, *Oh, Boy!*

1917–1918

War-born prosperity and an urge to escape the daily unpleasantness of the news stimulated box office sales. As a result thirty-eight musicals were offered on Broadway—almost half again as many as the old season had seen. With theatre construction halted for the duration, a temporary theatre shortage developed. Shows that would have normally been allowed a few extra weeks to find an audience or to add a small sum to their profits were hurried off onto the road or to Cain's fabled warehouse. Therefore, despite the huge jump in the number of new musicals, there was no increase in the number playing over 100 performances—fourteen both years. However, there was a marked improvement in quality, of which perspicacious writers and audiences were gratefully aware.

At the beginning of the season there must have been playgoers who wondered if a musical could

---

EDDIE CANTOR was born on New York's Lower East Side 31 January 1892. His name was Isidore Itzkowitz or Iskowitz. His family was musical, with his father often earning money as a violinist. When young Isidore was fourteen he won first prize at an amateur night at Miner's Bowery. A year later he made his vaudeville debut at the Clinton Music Hall, and thereafter alternated between two-a-day and jobs as a singing waiter. His first legitimate appearance was in London, in a revue called *Not Likely*. A young lady named Beatrice Lillie was also in the cast. After playing a while in English music halls, he returned to America, where he was cast for a role in *Canary Cottage*.

make its way to New York without something in it by Sigmund Romberg. No fewer than six of the preceding season's scores were in large or small part by him. This dependence on an apparent hack undoubtedly perplexed more demanding ticket-buyers. Apart from the few winning melodies he inserted into *The Blue Paradise*, his songs were never more than what his kindest critics labeled "tinkly." Now another outpouring of lilting mediocrity seemed in store. The first two announcements for the coming season listed Romberg's name among the credits, and the Shuberts admitted he would be composing for several more unspecified productions. The season's opener did nothing to enhance Romberg's reputation. **My Lady's Glove** (18 June 1917, Lyric), for which he wrote some additional music, was an importation using the old folklore motif of the Fair Unknown for its story. Oscar Straus had composed the original score. Anti-German sentiment, coupled with the show's banality, made it one of the fastest flops of the year. It was gone after sixteen performances. Quite possibly the Shuberts suspected they might have trouble with the work. To fend off resentment they changed the scene to France, had chorus girls distribute free chocolates as they sang "Oo, Buy Some Candy, Sir," and gave the leads to Vivienne Segal and Charles Purcell. When the show nonetheless folded abruptly they hustled Purcell into their very next show.

The fate of Romberg's second entry was markedly different. Romberg had threatened to leave the Shuberts if more congenial material to work with was not found. J. J. Shubert, fearing to lose Romberg's services, brought a Viennese story to Rida Johnson Young with instructions to turn it into a piece for which Romberg could write an entire score in his own style. Mrs. Young, assisted by Cyrus Wood, reset the story to span over sixty years of New York life. So adroit was Mrs. Young's "Americanization" and, as the Shuberts had learned with *My Lady's Glove*, so virulent the anti-German emotions, that the source of the story (*Wie Einst im Mai*) was never mentioned on the work's programs or sheet music. The book, though its dialogue was occasionally stiff, had great appeal. **Maytime** (16 August 1917, Shubert), in 1840 New York, was not only a time for resuming outdoor work, it was a time for love. A group of apprentices, led by youthful and handsome Richard Wayne (Charles Purcell), are busy on sundry jobs at Colonel Van Zandt's home in Washington Square. The colonel's daughter, Ottillie (Peggy Wood), is engaged to

her cousin Claude (Douglas J. Wood), but she has fallen in love with Richard, and Richard with her. Alone together they dream of a life "In Our Little Home, Sweet Home." Neighbors and friends arrive, along with a gypsy band, and Ottillie leaves Richard to help as hostess. When the crowd is gone, Ottillie and Richard meet again. Richard's father, once well-to-do, had lost his money and to repay some of his debts had given Van Zandt the deed for the Wayne house. As Richard and Ottillie are talking, the deed falls from the Colonel's window. Thinking it an unimportant piece of paper, Richard writes a love poem on it and they bury it in the garden, asking each other if they will always remember this day in May. They are interrupted by Claude and the Colonel (Carl Stall):

Claude: What's this? How dare you?
Richard: What business is it of yours?
Claude: My affianced bride in the arms of a low apprentice!
Ottillie: I'm nothing of the kind. I'll never marry you! I love Dick!
Colonel: What's this? What is all this?
Claude: This fellow, this dependent—she was in his arms!
Dick: Yes, in my arms, where I intend to keep her!
Colonel: You forget yourself, Dick! Let my daughter go at once!
Dick: She loves me, Sir!
Colonel: You are discharged. Take your things and leave at once!
Ottillie: No! No! Father!
Dick: You may send me away sir, but I'll come back; and when I do it will be to claim her!
Colonel: Begone! Out of my sight!

Fifteen years later, in Mme. Delphine's Night Club, the rage of New York is "Jump Jim Crow," "a dance that's rather shocking." By chance Ottillie, now married to Claude, and Richard meet there. They admit they still love each other and confess their loneliness on "The Road To Paradise." A quarter of a century later Claude dies, leaving Ottillie penniless. Her house and its contents are put up for auction. Richard, now wealthy, comes to the auction and buys the property back for Ottillie. About thirty more years pass. Richard and Ottillie are both dead; Ottillie's granddaughter and namesake (Miss Wood) has converted the parlor into a dress shop. Dicky Wayne (Purcell), Richard's grandson, appears to court the young lady. The love story comes full circle, but with a happy ending when the old deed is unearthed and its value appreciated.

Several devices were used to tie the epochs together. William Norris, playing Ottillie's carefree brother Matthew, lived long enough to appear in all four acts, marrying a different heiress in each of the first three acts and, as a very ancient dodderer, flirting gamely with chorus girls in the last. In the first act the lovers plant a young apple tree. The tree is shown blooming in the second, dying in the third, and dead in the fourth. "Will You Remember?" was employed as a leitmotif throughout.

Maytime was the year's overwhelming hit. Its bittersweet tale and exquisite songs struck some responsive chord in troops embarking for overseas. Among departing soldiers it quickly became the ticket most requested. A legend quickly arose which asserted the demand for tickets was so great a second company had to be opened across the street from the original, but careful research by Stanley Green has shown this story to have no basis in fact. More important than its immediate success was *Maytime*'s keeping the vogue for operetta alive during the height of the war. Equally significant was the vindication of Romberg's gifts. Although he still had to battle the Shuberts for proper material, his ordeal as a staff writer was virtually behind him. America's last great composer of classical operetta had come to the fore.

The score was among Romberg's best. While clearly not 100 percent American—except possibly for the ragtime songs that give contemporary flavor to the fourth act—the score was not flagrantly Viennese. Romberg was now a Hungarian-American, and even his waltzes would show a certain intangible softening away from the sweep of the pure Continental style. "Will You Remember?" was, more than "Auf Wiedersehn," Romberg's first real classic.

Cheer Up arrived on 23 August at the Hippodrome. Even though the costly spring offensives were several months away, the news was nevertheless unsettling. A happy title and Dillingham's masterful showmanship packed the big house for 456 performances, even if Raymond Hubbell's score was routine. Spectacles included horses diving into the theatre's tank, a full-sized locomotive filled with hoboes, and a cornfield turned into a field of poppies.

Another hit, the third, bounced in six nights later. **Leave It to Jane** (28 August 1917, Longacre) was based on George Ade's *The College Widow*, a comedy that had opened at the old Garden Theatre the night after Jerome Kern's first Broadway effort, *Mr. Wix of Wickham*, premiered (19 September 1904). It is interesting to speculate whether Kern, to celebrate his first New York production or to console himself after its dreadful reviews, had attended the first night. In any case, he combined with Bolton and Wodehouse to write what was essentially another Princess Theatre show, although the continuing popularity of *Oh, Boy!* at the small house and other commitments brought the new work to a bigger uptown auditorium. Ade's plot was faithfully retained. Jane (Edith Hallor), the college widow, is the daughter of President Witherspoon of "Good Old Atwater." While her philosophy is "Wait Till Tomorrow," students all know that if there is a serious problem, the answer is to "Leave It To Jane." A serious problem quickly develops for the football-mad school. Billy Bolton (Robert G. Pitkin), a super athlete, threatens to play for archrival Bingham. Jane is recruited to lure Billy to Atwater with her "Siren's Song." She succeeds, and Billy agrees to play for Atwater under an assumed name. "The Sun Shines Brighter" for almost everyone after the victory—everyone except Billy, who feels he may have been duped. But Jane and the sirens and the crickets who warn "be glad while you may" prove irresistible. Billy wins Jane as well as the game. Much of the comedy was provided by Oscar Shaw as Stubby and Georgia O'Ramey as Flora. Miss O'Ramey mugged, let herself be hurled through the air, and stopped the show with her comic Egyptian dance for "Cleopatterer."

Bolton's solid book and Wodehouse's free-flowing lyrics were enhanced by Kern's exuberant score. "The Crickets Are Calling" and "The Siren's Song" are Kern at his winsome best, and many a show would have been grateful for so catchy a title song. When *Leave It to Jane* was revived at a house no bigger than the Princess in 1959, it ran for two years, testifying to its ageless charm.

September's initial offering was a Chicago success hoping to make good in the East. It failed. The silly plot of **Good Night, Paul** (3 September 1917, Hudson) had eccentric Uncle Paul (Frank Lalor) visiting the home of an unmarried nephew (Ralph Herz). The nephew lives with his business partner and the partner's wife (Burrell Barbaretto and Elizabeth Murray). The youngsters are on the verge of bankruptcy. Uncle Paul agrees to make them solvent again if the bachelor nephew changes places with his married partner. Along with the claptrap book came a third-rate score. Paul and his family left town after five weeks.

Two pleasant operettas followed in short order. Both were well received, and both missed being successful, possibly because the public associated them with Vienna. The first was **Rambler Rose** (10 September 1917, Empire), with a book by Harry B. Smith and songs by Victor Jacobi (by 1917 an American citizen). The rose of the story is Rosamond Lee (Julia Sanderson), an American girl who is the niece, ward, and pupil of Lady Cloverdale (Kate Sergeantson). Lady Cloverdale runs an ultramodern girls' school where books are frowned upon and the curriculum includes makeup, smoking, ragtime, and "a special course in talking at the opera." Bashful Joseph Guppy (Joseph Cawthorn) loves Rosamond, but she has eyes only for the handsome art teacher, Gerald Morgan (John Goldsworthy). When he leaves the school to return to Paris, Rosamond follows him, and he is forced to put her up at his apartment. Guppy arrives in hot pursuit. His motives are not entirely pure, for if he fails to marry before his next birthday his rich uncle will disinherit him. Guppy prevails on Gerald's friend, Marcel (Stewart Baird), to help in a ruse. Marcel is to create a statue and allow Guppy to present it as his own masterwork. Guppy hopes the money and prestige from its sale will win Rosamond. Marcel, of course, does not realize Guppy wants to marry Rosamond. The millionaire who buys the statue turns out to be Guppy's rich uncle. The uncle not only takes home the statue, he woos and wins Gerald's old flame, leaving Gerald and Rosamond free to wed. Guppy goes "back to bashfulness, it's cheaper." The plot and the dialogue contained not a hint of the war. It seemed just the sort of escapist diversion an audience would crave. But even Miss Sanderson and Cawthorn could not keep the musical on the boards beyond nine weeks.

Ten weeks was all **The Riviera Girl** (24 September 1917, New Amsterdam), which arrived seven nights later, could achieve. Here was a show that did begin life in Vienna, as Emmerich Kalman's *Czardasfürstin*. Guy Bolton created a not quite completely fresh book for New York, telling of the love of a count (Louis Cassavant) for a vaudeville singer (Wilda Bennett), and Jerome Kern wrote some new songs, including the popular, lively "Bungalow in Quogue." This song elicited amused comments from a critic who wondered if the European characters singing it had ever heard of Long Island, let alone Quogue. Gorgeous Urban

settings "all keyed to the velvet, impenetrable blue of a Mediterranean sky" were "of monumental stateliness and a rich simplicity in color." Urban allowed the costumes to provide the variety and punctuation. All the fine American additions, coupled with Kalman's lovely score, could not save the show. Not even Kalman, it turned out, could overcome international enmity.

When Edward Clark's comedy *Coat Tales* had but a thirty-two-performance run in 1916 some reviewers suggested it would have been better as a musical. Arthur Hammerstein, who produced the play, took their advice and brought it back as **Furs and Frills** (9 October 1917, Casino), with a Clark book, Clark lyrics, and Silvio Hein music. The critics wondered about the soundness of their own advice. However, those who liked it compared it to "those 'operettas intimes' with which the Princess Theatre of late years has been restoring the lost art of Gilbert and Sullivan." The story could have easily come from Bolton instead of Clark. The extravagant Mrs. Macey (Beatrice Allen) brings home a $5,000 fur coat, but before she tells her husband of the purchase, her scapegrace brother steals it and pawns it. Mr. Macey (George Anderson) unwittingly reclaims it and, not knowing its history, gives it to his partner's wife. The fur flies. If Clark was almost a Bolton, Hein was woefully short of being a Kern. A weak-voiced chorus attempted to gloss over its inadequacies by playing violins in one number. The show ran exactly as long as its source—thirty-two performances.

After the death in the spring of his partner, Dave Montgomery, Fred Stone determined to continue alone. His first solo venture confirmed that he needed no help to pack an enthralled house. **Jack o' Lantern** (16 October 1917, Globe), created by much the same team that had written and produced *Chin-Chin* for him—Ivan Caryll, Anne Caldwell, R. H. Burnside, and Charles Dillingham—once again placed Stone in his unique world halfway between reality and toyland. This time it was called Appledale Farm and run by mean, old Uncle George (Oscar Ragland), who stands to inherit a lot of money should anything happen to his young wards. He hires a man to kill them. Since he has never seen the man, he arranges for a password to identify him. When John Obadiah Lantern, who is called Jack o' Lantern because he is light in the head, inadvertently mentions the password, he is mistaken for the would-be-assassin. Catching on to the uncle's wicked plans, Jack kidnaps the children. But not without a chase: "Jack jumps off [the] haywagon, landing on the end of the see saw, which is at the side of the haywagon. As he lands he throws a policeman, who has been standing on the other end of the see saw, up in the air. The policeman does a somersault—landing on the top of the haywagon." Although Jack has proclaimed, "I'm a socialist—Got nothing and believe in sharing it with everybody," he takes the children to his mansion, where a staff attends to their wishes. From there they are transported to a "Cave of Dreams," in which all sorts of adventures befall. At one point they are in the army and Jack is the mail censor. He "censors" six letters, all in the same fashion:

> JACK: This letter must be from a married man (*reading:*
> "My mother-in-law is a kind woman. She sent me a bottle of Old Crow." (*musing*
> That doesn't sound natural—(*drawing pencil thro' part of letter*
> That's better. (*reading*
> My mother-in-law is an Old Crow.

Jack and the children finish at an Ice Palace, where Jack, dressed as Charlotte Russe, puts on a skating show. Uncle George inexplicably mends his ways in the last lines of the show, and everybody is happy.

Caryll's score was melodic and carefree. The appropriately bucolic "(Won't You) Wait Till The Cows Come Home?" remained a favorite long after Urban's magnificent sets had disappeared and Stone himself had departed to yet another world.

But while Alan Dale in the *Sun* professed to see *Jack o' Lantern* setting "a standard for the musical show," by and large it was Urban, whose "continued presence in the Broadway theatre endows it with a splendor it has never before possessed," and the inimitable Stone who were responsible for the box office bonanza. Urban did not design all the sets. Some were by Homer Emens and Ernest Albert. Still, Urban's scenery received all the praise, especially an apple orchard, stylized like drawings in a child's book, and a pink, pale green, white, and silver candyland peopled with a chorus of "gayly colored barber poles of candy, tooth-some jujubes, and lingering, delectable all-day-suckers." When Stone finished his extensive tour with the piece, Doyle and Dixon took it out to the one-night stands, using the original version written before Montgomery's death.

Doing Our Bit came into the Winter Garden on 18 October. It had the requisite patriotic trimmings, including a troopship number in which the entire chorus, men and women, was dressed as soldiers. It had Ed Wynn, Frank Tinney, and even former heavyweight boxing champion James J. Corbett. It had a score of no special interest by Romberg and Herman Timberg. It also had a warning from critics that the day of the slapdash extravaganza was waning, the *World* lambasting it as "bankrupt in talent" and "threadbare," while the *Evening Post*, affecting a blasé boredom, concluded, "the new Winter Garden show is very like all the other Winter Garden shows, though experienced first-nighters were able to note certain differences in costume detail." It had, lastly, a satisfactory run of 130 performances.

Four nights later, F. Ray Comstock and his associates, who had been instrumental in establishing the vogue for the Princess Theatre's small-scaled shows, went to the other extreme by importing the spectacular London rage **Chu Chin Chow** (22 October 1917, Manhattan Opera House). It lavishly recounted Abu Hassan's exotic and fatal machinations while disguised as the Chinese merchant, Chu Chin Chow, at Kasim Baba's palace. Kasim's brother is the famous Ali Baba, and the forty thieves figure prominently in the evening's intrigue. The extravaganza broke all London records for longevity, and its record was not surpassed for decades. The American production had a stellar cast. Tyrone Power (the fine, old dramatic actor) was Abu Hassan, and the seemingly forgotten Henry Dixey was Ali Baba, while Tessa Kosta and Florence Reed played the female leads. *Chu Chin Chow's* American reception was disappointing, although its run of 208 performances at the large Manhattan Opera House was by no means negligible.

An importation inaugurated November's offerings. It was a Havana revue, **The Land of Joy** (1 November 1917, Park). In a book rewritten for New York, audiences watched a group of Americans take a tour to Spain. The show's composer, Joaquin Valverde, was hailed as a Spanish Victor Herbert, while the set designers, the Tarazona Brothers, were compared favorably with Urban. A dancer named L'Argentina stopped the show with a heel dance, a table dance, and an impassioned tango. However, before the show finished an eleven-week run she was replaced by another dancer, Violeta.

On paper **Miss 1917** (5 November 1917, Century) was one of those shows that had almost everything. Conceived by Dillingham and Ziegfeld as a successor to *The Century Girl*, it had music by Herbert and Kern, lyrics and sketches by P. G. Wodehouse, splendid Urban sets, and a cast of old and new favorites including Lew Fields, Bessie McCoy Davis, Van and Schenck, Brice and King, Irene Castle, Bert Savoy, and Vivienne Segal. Its failure is even more astonishing when the generally rave reviews are considered. But the Century was out of the way, and the material, however good, represented no one's best—although the lovely "The Land Where The Good Songs Go" (originally composed for *Oh, Boy!*) was used by Hollywood nearly thirty years later in its supposedly biographical movie on Kern. One false legend connected with the song and the show makes a telling comment on the still vaudeville-like free-wheeling that went into assembling these revues. Kern's number was used to introduce a medley of old favorites, particularly with Bessie McCoy returning to sing them after a protracted absence. Vivienne Segal was also to sing an older tune. Kern wanted her to do "They Didn't Believe Me," but Dillingham and Herbert reached farther back for "Kiss Me Again," and Miss Segal sided with them. Kern, depending on who tells the story, never forgave her and never spoke to her again. If the story has any truth at all, it is certainly not in any enduring anger on Kern's part. When *Miss 1917* folded after six weeks, Kern rushed Miss Segal into the starring role of his very next show. While *Miss 1917* remained on the boards, Irene Castle waltzed in a blue, moonlit dreamland. Miss Davis introduced "I'm The Old Man In The Moon" and revived "The Yama Yama Man." Fields clowned as a farmer who raises pickles in a spoof of *Turn to the Right*. Urban employed his revolving stage to depict a grove of trees losing their leaves as autumn gives way to winter.

The next opening also witnessed the return of an old favorite, Alice Nielsen, who found fame in the earliest Victor Herbert operettas at the end of the nineteenth century and then left the light opera stage for grand opera. She returned to sing the principal role in **Kitty Darlin'** (7 November 1917, Casino), the Otto Harbach–Rudolf Friml adaptation of David Belasco's *Sweet Kitty Bellairs*. The book was "violently faithful to the original," rehearsing how Kitty, the flirtatious young lady from Bath, decides to play coquette with Lord Verney Kitty hides under his bed at the sound of feminine footsteps. It is Lady Standish, who also hides when voices are heard

approaching. The room is about to be searched when Kitty comes out of hiding, thereby halting the search and sparing Lady Standish. The book, however faithful, was uninspired. Critics seemed more fascinated by the change in the spelling of the librettist's name. "Up to last night he was Otto Hauerbach," the *World* noted. The old spelling was a war casualty. But neither a new spelling nor an old favorite could save *Kitty Darlin'* from a quick death.

Victor Herbert's **Her Regiment** (12 November 1917, Broadhurst) fared little better. Although it had pleasant music and the popular Donald Brian as star, it survived only forty performances. Again critics were more than kind. Possibly the public was kept away in the mistaken assumption the military title announced a war story. The show, in fact, told a romantic tale, set in Normandy just before the war erupted. Love and disguise, not hate and battle, were the themes. André de Courcy (Brian), a wealthy aristocrat, pretends to be a common soldier. Estelle Durvernay (Audrey Maple), another wealthy aristocrat, pretends to be a lady's maid. The maid and the soldier fall in love. As always, Brian's graceful dancing was as much of an attraction as his singing, or more of one. His second-act ballroom turn with Cissie Sewell won special plaudits. Frank Moulan was also on hand to provide comic relief.

Odds and Ends of 1917 (19 November 1917, Bijou) was another intimate revue. One of its producers, Jack Norworth, preferred the word "chummy," and this drew amused comment. Critics compared the evening to *Hitchy-Koo*. Its idea of humor was a first-act finale honoring famous couples of history: Anthony and Cleopatra, Elizabeth and Essex, and the Smith Brothers of cough-drop fame. The music was ordinary. One song, "Fancy You Fancying Me," received considerable advance buildup. Its mediocrity left playgoers shaking their heads. But uneven as *Odds and Ends* was, it managed a four-month stay.

The Franz Lehar operetta which followed was the fastest flop of the season. **The Star Gazer** (26 November 1917, Plymouth) was withdrawn after only eight performances. More than merely bad Lehar, it was an Austro-Hungarian composition. Its fiasco finally drove home a lesson to Broadway's producers. No more Viennese operettas were attempted until the Armistice was several months old. As they had with *My Lady's Glove*, the Shuberts attempted to avoid possible disaster by switching the setting from Austria, this time to 1830 New England. They attempted to economize by eliminating any chorus.

John Charles Thomas was the star, but on opening night an understudy had to replace the original leading lady. Her fine acting and singing catapulted Carolyn Thomson into the limelight.

Over the Top was designed as a vehicle for the ravishing Justine Johnstone. It was originally called *Oh, Justine!* Brought in on 1 December to the 44th Street Roof, it was a miniature Winter Garden revue, and that meant another largely Romberg score. The show purported to be Miss Johnstone's dream of a trip to visit her lover (Colin Campbell). T. Roy Barnes made intermittent appearances as "The Plot" to create problems and then arbitrarily resolve them. Between spectacles such as "The Land of Frocks and Frills" and a German trench attacked by American planes, specialties enlivened the proceedings. Harry and Emma Sharrock were droll mind readers, announcing inscriptions on watches, masonic badges, and Yiddish coins belonging to the audience. A pair of brightly agile young dancers made an appealing debut—Fred and Adele Astaire.

The Grass Widow (3 December 1917, Liberty) was, in view of the casualty lists appearing in the papers, perhaps a bit thoughtless as a title. Based on Bisson and St. Albin's *The Yellow Peril*, it described how the hot-headed Denise (Natalie Alt), angered at the seeming slights of Jacques, Count of Cluny (Howard Marsh), marries Anatol Pivert (George Marion), an old restaurateur. Jacques enters as the ceremony is ending and carries Denise away to Paris. Anatol follows them, but young love wins the day. It was a clean show, with a good cast, but it failed to catch on. In the hopes of surviving until an audience could be found, it took the unusual step of moving from the standard-size Liberty Theatre on 42nd Street to the small Princess three blocks south. The hoped-for business never materialized, and after a total of six weeks the show was closed. For Louis Hirsch, its composer, it was the first of three major scores he would offer in a single season and the only unsuccessful one.

Hirsch's next complete score was heard three weeks later, on Christmas night, when **Going Up** flew into the same Liberty Theatre. The show was based on James Montgomery's *The Aviator*, a well-thought-of comedy that had failed to meet expectations. This time both Hirsch and Montgomery (who collaborated with Otto Harbach on the book) knew the outcome was different. While the braggart who was its central character is universal, there was something apple pie American about *Going Up*'s hero. Robert Street (Frank Craven) writes a best-seller

on flying and boasts of his aeronautic skills. Actually he has never been in a plane. Street is challenged to an air race, and he must win the race to win the girl he loves, Grace Douglas (Edith Day). He wins. The book was laughter all the way, and the jaunty score was topped by a title number which promised to leave the ground any minute and by a universally praised dance number, "Tickle Toe." One show-stopping effect was Street's flying through the night air in a full-scale biplane late in the second act.

Hirsch's score for **The Rainbow Girl** (1 April 1918, New Amsterdam) was even better. A few critics, like the gentleman from the *American*, disagreed. But then on balance he was willing to allow "Excepting for 'The Chocolate Soldier' and 'The Only Girl' there has seldom been a musical comedy with a more interesting story." His fellow reviewers were less rash, contenting themselves with "tells a simple story simply" or falling back on "a real plot." The story was based on Jerome K. Jerome's *The New Lady Bantok*. What no critic noted was that each libretto for which Hirsch wrote the music honored a different one of the Allies. *The Grass Widow* was set in France; *Going Up*, in the USA. On 1 April, *The Rainbow Girl* took audiences to England, where Mollie Murdock (Beth Lydy), "The Rainbow Girl" of the Frivolity Theatre in London, marries Robert Dudley (Harry Benham), unaware he is Lord Wetherell. Arriving at his ancestral estate, she receives a second shock, for she is related to all his serving staff. Mollie, it seems, had run away from a serving-class family to try her luck on stage. Love levels ranks, and everyone joins the marriage celebration. Hirsch provided another vibrant title song. "I'll Think Of You" had a droll, tongue-in-cheek poignancy. It was sung in the show by the second leads, Harry Delf and Lenora Novasio. Despite rave reviews, *The Rainbow Girl* ran twenty weeks, considerably less than the all-American *Going Up*. Its late arrival and all the fine competition hurt. It remains among the season's very best newcomers.

Three other shows opened in December between *The Grass Widow* and *Going Up*. A second Valverde revue, **A Night in Spain** on 6 December at the Century Roof, failed to equal even the limited success of his *The Land of Joy*, even though Raymond Hitchcock served as compère.

Flo-Flo (20 December 1917, Cort) had a solid if elementary book, which enmeshed Flo-Flo (Vera Michelena), daughter of a bankrupt social climber, and a pseudo-Spanish nobleman (George Renavent). It also had another listenable, forgettable

Silvio Hein score. Its 220-performance run was the longest any Hein show managed. Isadore Witmark referred to Hein as "gentle and revered," insisting he wrote "Songs the whole nation sang." It sang none for long. "The Small Town Girl" and "Good Bye Happy Days" typify his output and suggest the perpetually likable quality of even Broadway's minor creations during this period. The evening was largely a succession of vaudeville turns. Thomas Handers and Arthur Mills juggled as they danced, while Oscar Figman and Leon Leonard indulged in Yiddish banter. Since the first act was set in a lingerie shop chorus girls weren't weighed down with clothes; but the second act—a wedding rehearsal—allowed them to parade in lavish gowns.

For **Words and Music** (24 December 1917, Fulton) Richard Carle was on hand with some slightly off-color jokes and a running gag that had him breaking dishes all night long. If anyone believed the program, the words were by William Shakespeare and the music by Ludwig Beethoven (no "von"), two names not heretofore familiar to the revue field. But since Raymond Hitchcock and E. Ray Goetz were the evening's producers, more knowledgeable playgoers suspected they had lent a helping hand. Their help was not enough to keep the show alive more than three weeks.

December's final show, **The Cohan Revue of 1918**, followed *Going Up* by a week, opening at the New Amsterdam as part of the New Year's Eve festivities. Even though Cohan asked Berlin to write the songs with him, something went wrong. The score was dreary, and the skits lacked the originality, snap, and wit of Cohan's earlier revues. His 1916 skit "Common Clay" had already become a minor classic. Critics generally lamented a decline in quality, although many singled out "Polly of the Follies," which managed to spoof at one and the same time the *Follies*, Belasco ("My name is not Dave Morosco, but Oliver Belasco"), and his *Polly with a Past*. Imitations proved a high spot of the evening with Charles Winninger aping Leo Ditrichstein and Nora Bayes mimicking Ina Claire and Florence Reed. Cohan was not given to sulking over failures and would probably have bounced back in a year or two with a new edition. But the animosities that grew out of the 1919 actors' strike, when Cohan sided with the producers and theatre owners, put an end to his dreams of establishing another Weber and Fields tradition.

Almost a month elapsed before 1918's first musical danced across the boards. **Girl o' Mine**

premiered at the little Bijou on 28 January. Its book was by Philip Bartholomae, who had collaborated on the initial Princess smash, *Very Good Eddie* (23 December 1915). And the book was quite good. Betty (Dorothy Dickson) comes to Paris seeking an uncle she has never met. She is assisted in her search by a prizefighter and his wife who have opened an American bar after running out of money on their honeymoon. All Elizabeth Marbury and the Shuberts, who produced the show, lacked was a second Jerome Kern. Frank Tours did the weak score. Its weakness contributed to the show's short run. Miss Dickson, who in a few years went on to become a London favorite, was praised for her captivatingly airy dances, while Frank Fay and Marie Nordstrom won kudos for their singing of satiric songs.

Kern himself may have contributed to *Girl o' Mine*'s failure when four nights later on 1 February he gave New York and the Princess another lyrical hit, **Oh, Lady! Lady!!** As prolific at this time as Hirsch and Romberg, but infinitely more inventive, Kern produced three scores in four months. *Oh, Lady! Lady!!* is best remembered as the show that did not include "Bill." How the song's elimination affected our musical history will never be known, but it did not alter the show's charm or success. The *Times* called it "virtually flawless," and many other critics, with a growing sense of occasion, compared it gleefully to the earlier Princess shows, especially "the enduring Oh, Boy!" As Willoughby "Bill" Finch (Carl Randall) and Mollie Farrington (Vivienne Segal) are about to be married, Willoughby is confronted by Fanny Weld (Florence Shirley), who claims to be his boyhood friend. She is really the girl-friend of Willoughby's man, Spike (Edward Abeles), a reformed criminal, and she is after the Farrington jewels. She steals them, but Spike extricates his master from the embarrassing and suspicious situation by recovering the jewels. Mollie is free to marry her Bill. The only song from the show to remain steadfastly favored is the discarded "Bill." Originally it was placed at the beginning of the first act when Mollie attempts to explain her infatuation to her mystified mother. Even after it was dropped, the first-act finale retained several bars of it. Kern, who was particularly fond of the song, kept trying to find a place for it in later musicals. Marilyn Miller tried it and rejected it for *Sally*. Ten years passed before it received recognition. Most of the remaining songs still await recognition. Tops in the superb score are Mollie's sly "Not Yet," her haunting "When The Ships Come Home," the gay title song that Bill and the chorus girls sang, and the lush but strangely disconnected chorus number "Moon Song." In keeping with the practice of the day, almost every song was accompanied by a dance, and the principals, notably Randall, were praised for their light footwork. Even Miss Segal was singled out for her elegant waltzing. The show's second-act set, depicting a Greenwich Village rooftop, also elicited kind comments.

Directly after the show opened, Bolton in an interview discussed "The Improvement in Musical Comedy Standards." The librettist insisted, "Our musical comedies... depend as much upon plot and the development of their characters for success as upon their music, and because they deal with subjects and peoples near to the audiences." Two points were stressed. First, "In the development of our plot... we endeavor to make everything count. Every line, funny or serious, is supposed to help the plot continue to hold." Second, "if the songs are going to count at all in any plot, the plot has to build more or less around, or at least, with them." Similar statements were forthcoming at the start of each great era of the American Musical Theatre. At this early day these standards were not a little utopian. For years after, good scores kept weak librettos on the boards long after they deserved to be forgotten. But this in no way gain-says Bolton. His foresight, his high aims, and his skills almost singlehandedly pioneered the modern book show.

Kern's two other scores were for **Toot-Toot!** (11 March 1918, Cohan) and **Rock-a-Bye Baby** (22 May 1918, Astor). Although *Toot-Toot!*, based on Rupert Hughes's 1911 hit, *Excuse Me*, was a forty-performance failure, one tune had a tremendous vogue. Ironically, it was not by Kern. "The Last Long Mile" was a hastily inserted soldiers' marching song by Emil Breitenfeld that served as a stirring first-act finale. A war song was not out of place in a plot that described how Lt. Harry Malloy (Donald MacDonald), on receiving his orders, decides to marry Marjorie Newton (Louise Allen) at once. Since no minister can be located, they chance finding one on the train taking Malloy to his base. There is a young minister on board with his wife; however, the plot requires that he conceal his identity. His calling is discovered in time for a happy ending. The book was good enough, but Kern's score, with the exception of "If," was below his standard. However, their vivacious singing of "If" launched both Louise Groody and Billy (later William) Kent on their way to prominence. Several critics mentioned that the costume designer had an easy time of it, since all the

men were in khaki. The women's costumes and the sets were largely ignored in the reviews.

If on one hand *Rock-a-Bye Baby*, based on Margaret Mayo's *Baby Mine*, had a varied, tuneful score, it also had a serious problem. Its authors, Miss Mayo and Edgar Allan Woolf, had not read Bolton's interview. The *Times*, which reflected the prevailing sentiment, thought "the adaptor selected too good a farce to work upon... too good a tale to stand idly by while the principals and the friends of the principals sing pleasant little melodies which have nothing to do with the case." Typically, the joyful "There's No Better Use For Time Than Kissing" was sung by "persons totally unconnected with the plot, who just happen to enter the lady's boudoir." The lady in question is Zoie Hardy (Edna Hibbard), who is stranded at the Rock-a-Bye Baby Inn when a new auto she is test-driving with Mr. Jenks (Walter Jones) breaks down. Business brings her husband (Frank Morgan) to the inn, and he misconstrues the situation. To reclaim her husband Zoie announces she is about to have a baby. Helpful Mr. Jenks sets out to find a baby and brings back three. When their parents come to take the babies home, everything is explained, and Mr. Hardy, realizing the lengths his wife will go to keep him, is mollified. The "pasted hit or miss" songs were luminous, the best having a loving, nurserylike warmth. The slapdash nature of construction was disclosed further when Dorothy Dickson was rushed in to dance. She was not even assigned a character part, but apparently appeared solely as herself. (However, later programs call her character Dorothy Manners.) Oblivious to the show's faults, one first-nighter wrote, "I don't know any musical comedy that has appealed to me more." The praise, not intended for publication, was recorded in his diary by twenty-one-year-old Ira Gershwin. If more people had been as pleased, *Rock-a-Bye Baby* would have played longer than eleven weeks.

The Love Mill (7 February 1918, 48th St.), which opened six nights after *Oh, Lady! Lady!!*, came from Chicago. The mill operated at the Mt. Vernon, New York, home of Mrs. Thompson (Jeanette Lowrie), a matron living a high life on a low income. She is determined to marry off her three daughters. All of them give her problems, especially fat Millie (Carrie McManus), whom she forces to drink vinegar to lose weight. By curtain time she has found mates for all three. Earl Carroll's book and lyrics and Alfred Francis's score left much to be desired. *The Love Mill* employed only eight chorus girls and cutely assigned them names, from Laura to Lauretta, whose first letters spelled the title. As sometimes happens, the reviews of a failure are more fascinating than the show itself. Several critics took the opportunity to discuss musicals in general and the season in particular. The often curmudgeonly *Dramatic Mirror* concluded it was in the middle of "a season in which the musical productions have attained a higher standard than in recent years." But then the sheet was in the minority praising the show. Heywood Broun, panning the show in the *Tribune*, reported, "The show begins with a song called 'opening chorus,' which is led by six 'Tennis Boys,' armed with three-ounce racquets. After they have committed a few foot-faults there is a joke about Haig and Haig, and presently the fat comedienne says: 'I could live on onions alone,' only to meet the response: 'If you do, you will.' The leader of Tennis Boys, by the way, is down on the programme as Joe Miller." In broader terms Broun posed a question that could still be asked, "Why is it that the book of 'The Love Mill,' like most musical comedies, is full of cynicism about marriage while the lyrics by the identical author approach the self-same institution with reverence, truth and sweetness?"

Sinbad appeared on 14 February. It was the quintessential Jolson show. The story opened at a Long Island dog show, but soon found itself in exotic settings—Cabin of the Good Ship Whale, Grotto of the Valley of Diamonds, Island of Eternal Youth. Romberg's score was no different from any other score he had supplied for the Winter Garden. Only Jolson's interpolations remain, including three of his most popular songs— "Rock-A-Bye Your Baby With A Dixie Melody" (Joe Young, Sam Lewis, and Jean Schwartz), "My Mammy" (Irving Caesar/Walter Donaldson), and "Swanee" (Irving Caesar/George Gershwin). "My Mammy" was introduced late in the run, and "Swanee," which made Gershwin famous overnight, was not brought in until the road tour was under way. The Shuberts had installed a ramp from the stage far out into the audience, and Jolson, in blackface and white gloves, and down on one knee, generally sang "Mammy" and other selected tunes within arm's reach of his admirers. "Hello, Central, Give Me No Man's Land" (also by Young, Lewis, and Schwartz) was popular at the time, as was "Chloe," which Jolson is purported to have worked on with Buddy DeSylva.

Zoel Parenteau made a second attempt to succeed on Broadway with his music for **Follow the Girl** (2 March 1918, 44th St. Roof). Henry Blossom supplied the book and lyrics. The action took place at a Maine summer hotel, where Mrs. Niles (Jobyna Howland) attempts to find a wealthy husband for her daughter, Gladys (Eileen Van Biene). Gladys needs no help. She finds Alfred Vanderveer (Harry Fender) on her own. One line in the dialogue tickled a number of critics, who reported that Walter Catlett, spying Jobyna Howland in a low-backed gown, announced he would follow "the trail of the lonesome spine." The war presented a problem for the German dialect comedian, who now had to be clearly identified as Swiss. As in *The Love Mill*, the chorus made its first appearance in tennis clothes. One of the girls seemed outstanding, and before long she had a solo. Her name was Dorothy Godfrey, a contortionist. But the book was not very good, and some of Parenteau's best music, such as "Don't Lose Your Way," was from the preceding season's *The Amber Princess*. Parenteau, except for his two songs in *Kiki*, spent the rest of his life—he died in 1972—working as musical director in various American cities.

One of the most affectionately remembered of shows, **Oh, Look!** opened the intimate Vanderbilt Theatre on 7 March. It was based on another James Montgomery farce, *Ready Money*. Long Island, which seemed to be the only proper locale for smart, intimate plots, is the site of the Welch estate, where a smart, intimate weekend is in progress. Should anyone doubt young Welch's credentials he was quickly, if stiffly, disabused:

Welch: You know my father's very wealthy.
Turner: Yes.
Welch: I'll get all that someday, but I want to be a
success by my own endeavor. He's done everything for me. He gives me all the money I want
and more. See here—a check for $10,000—a
present from my father.

But it develops that Welch (Clarence Nordstrom) is not to be the protagonist. Stephen Baird (Harry Fox), a young man on the verge of bankruptcy, commands our attention. His friend, Jackson Ives (Frederick Burton), provides him with money until Baird's gold mine can begin to produce. The new money brings an assortment of new friends. But they all desert him when the money is found to be counterfeit. Only his girl, Grace Tyler (Louise Cox), remains loyal. Luckily the mine proves a bonanza. Stephen and Grace sing the final duet knowing they will be genuinely rich.

Harry Carroll's music, with one exception, was of the same crude order as the book. The evening's big production number, repeated as the finale, was "Typical Topical Tunes." "Topical" was suitably alliterative, but meaningless. Night after night the handsome Fox stopped the show with "I'm Always Chasing Rainbows," adapted from Chopin's "Fantasy Impromptu." Though the musical could not satisfactorily fill even the new bandbox playhouse for more than sixty-seven performances, it was revamped for the road with the Dolly Sisters as stars and played to packed houses around the country.

Advertised as "a costless, castless, careless revue," **Let's Go** (9 March 1918, Fulton) lived up to its billing. It lurked around for three weeks and went away, but not before singing longingly of "The Land Of Yesterday" and looking with a jaundiced eye on an army run by women.

Toot-Toot! and *The Rainbow Girl* followed.

Fancy Free (11 April 1918, Astor) was a serviceable romp, set in Palm Beach, where there is a mix-up about who is married to whom. "The songs," the *Globe* reflected, "have very little to do with it, being more or less irrelevant." What was relevant was one young lady who stole the show and the notices. Broun, expressing himself with his customary felicity, summed up the general feeling: "Fancy Free gets up on its toes early in the evening and stays there. The ten best toes belong to Marilynn Miller."

Two all-male shows followed—all-male because they were written, staged, and performed by men in uniform. Both drew huge grosses in their very limited engagements. The first was the work of the Army's 27th Division, from Spartanburg, South Carolina. Only a lone then-recognized name— Hugh Stanislaus Stange—was featured, as one of the composers, among credits for **You Know Me, Al!** (11 April 1918, Lexington). In his colleagues' tale, three young men, Al "Livewire" Carleton, Bill "Brightlights" McGraw, and Tom "Reddycash" Brush, need to raise money to send Al's father to a health resort. To this end they pounce on a rich, retired merchant, Amos Bronson (played by Harry Gribble, the only other figure from the evening to make a name for himself in the theatre), who believes wine, women, and song are the cure for all ills. The men restore an old home, call it a hotel, and try to convince Amos that with his money it can be a spiffy new spa. Amos's daughter sees through the scheme, but when she falls in love with Al, she drops her objections. A singing chorus of twelve "girls" and twelve men, plus seven male dancers (done up as bellboys), helped put over the tunes.

Good-Bye, Bill (22 April 1918, 44th St. Roof) was neither as well constructed nor as thumpingly staged as *You Know Me, Al!* Apparently written and played entirely by men from the U.S. Ambulance Service, it depicted various aspects of army life, loosely enough strung together to allow for frequent insertions of two-a-day turns. The first act showed recruitment in New York City, and the second, training near Allentown, Pennsylvania, while the third and final act was set "in a forest spot somewhere 'over there' nine months from today." Since this last act showed Yanks capturing the Kaiser in an old beer cellar, that meant the authors were a month tardy in ending the war. But for all its faults and erroneous prognostication, the show offered at least one song that was a real rouser. The first act concluded with a Private Charles Hamp and the chorus, eight of whom were "female" nurses, singing "Buy A Bond." They sang it so stirringly that New York first-nighters bought a then whopping $17,000 worth on the spot. (The soldiers also peddled sheet music in the lobby, all proceeds going to the service.) And a trade sheet reported that the production had broken the house record at Philadelphia's old Forrest Theatre during its single-week tryout there.

Young, comely Fay Bainter, was responsible for what success **The Kiss Burglar** (9 May 1918, Cohan) enjoyed. The "burglar" (Armand Kalisz) indeed steals only a kiss when he finds himself in the boudoir of a grand duchess while fleeing from a dishonest but titled gambler. The war forces the duchess to take refuge in America. For a second time, the young man, who is American, finds himself in her apartment. When he steals his second kiss they both realize they are in love. Glen MacDonough's book and Raymond Hubbell's music were never much more than competent. Nonetheless the show chalked up 100 performances and then toured.

Biff! Bang! (30 May 1918, Century) was a vaudeville mounted by sailors from the Pelham Naval Training Station and brought in as a curiosity for two weeks. Among its "stevedore" show girls was Lew Fields's son, Joe.

With the coming of June it was time for the summer revues. **Hitchy-Koo of 1918** (6 June 1918, Globe) led off. Hitchcock informed his audience the evening was "drammed jammed with hokum and jazz." The material, mostly by MacDonough and Hubbell, was no better than what they had offered in *The Kiss Burglar.* Hubbell's music contained nothing of the promised "jazz." But the cast was strong enough to put any mediocrity across. Besides Hitchcock it included Leon Errol, Irene Bordoni, and Florence O'Denishawn. Baby-talking Ray Dooley replaced the last year's baby-talking Frances White. It stayed nine weeks and it, too, went on tour.

1918–1919

As the new season opened, the war news became less bleak. The submarine offensive, probably the greatest remaining threat, was obviously collapsing. Its diminution allowed 600,000 American troops to be transported safely to France in May, June, and July. It was increasingly apparent the war would be over soon. The feeling of imminent victory brought into the open cries for change in all aspects of American life. Suffragettes, prohibitionists, League of Nation supporters, isolationists, and Ku Klux Klansmen made public their disparate plans for a postwar world. For the country as a whole what loomed beyond the armistice remained a large, unarticulated question. This malaise of uncertainties and adjustments affected Broadway as well. Though the public packed the theatres in search of escape (and more than half the season's musicals ran over 100 performances), no truly first-rate show was presented and no smash hit of *Maytime*'s proportion emerged. The names of the season's musicals are at best only vaguely familiar. But the season was far from uninteresting. The quality of the preceding seasons often masked their creative turmoil. Now the ferment stood revealed.

The Ziegfeld Follies of 1918 (18 June 1918, New Amsterdam), which inaugurated the season, subtly and unwittingly exposed the new uncertainties, although those who didn't wish to see them were not compelled to leave the theatre concerned. Joseph Urban's sets were as luxurious as ever (particularly a gigantic re-creation of a miniature bonsai with cherry tree and bridge); the girls and their gowns, resplendent. Will Rogers, Eddie Cantor, W. C. Fields, and Ann Pennington headed the cast. Rogers joked about American politics and the Irish demand for home rule, but also appeared in musical numbers, lassoing Ann Pennington as she danced, and strutting in white tie and tails with Lillian Lorraine. Cantor, without blackface for the first time, appeared as a client in a patent attorney's office and as an enlistee taking a physical. He returned to burnt cork to sing "But—After The Ball Was Over!" Fields put aside his billiard green to wreak havoc on a putting green. Marilyn Miller—a name new to Ziegfeld's ranks—won many of the raves, while one

of the first girls ever glorified by Ziegfeld, the beautiful but star-crossed Lillian Lorraine, performed for the last time in a *Follies*. Louis Hirsch and Dave Stamper, who composed most of the score (with Gene Buck for lyricist), also seemed to look both ways at once. They gave their songs up-to-the-minute titles, but their music was in a dated style. Stamper provided one of the big production numbers, "I Want To Jazz Dance" (virtually the earliest use of the term in a Broadway song), while Hirsch composed a second production number, "When I Hear A Syncopated Tune." But Stamper's "jazz" caught none of the newer rhythms that soon pushed the old syncopation aside. It was not even the transitional shimmy. Both songs were simple commercial ragtime. The war prompted tunes such as "I'm Gonna Pin A Medal On The Girl I Left Behind" and "You Keep Sending 'Em Over And We'll Keep Knocking 'Em Down." Since the show ended its Broadway run just as the war ended, the program was revamped for the peacetime tour.

While over the years the Ziegfeld extravaganzas produced better songs than the Shubert Winter Garden revues. **The Passing Show of 1918** (25 July 1918, Winter Garden), in the day's topsyturvy way, came up with the season's biggest hit, "Smiles" (J. Will Callahan and Lee S. Roberts). The main Romberg and Jean Schwartz score reflected the same ambivalence as the *Follies* program, ranging from "The Galli-Curci Rag" to "Trombone Jazz." "Jazz" here meant the transitional "shimmy." Frank Fay, backed by a line of baby-talking chorus girls, hit paydirt with "My Baby-Talk Lady!," so the Shuberts rushed in a second "Baby" (Gus Kahn and Egbert Van Alstine). A lavish "Birdland" number included the young Astaires singing and dancing dressed as chickens.

Late last season several semiprofessional musicals written by and featuring soldiers or sailors had won applause in short engagements. The sailors' offering had played the huge Century. On August 19 a somewhat less hastily thrown-together revue, this time by soldiers from Camp Upton, opened at the same house. It ran thirty-two performances and most likely would have passed as quickly into obscurity had it not been for one thing. Irving Berlin wrote the score. Called **Yip Yip Yaphank**, it presented pictures of rookie life in its songs and sketches, including a burlesque of a *Follies* visit to the camp. It even offered a boxing match by world lightweight champion Benny Leonard, then an instructor at Upton. But the show was raised to a prominent place in our musical history by its tunes—particularly the second most popular of World War I songs, "Oh, How I Hate To Get Up In The Morning." Berlin himself sang the song, playing a private who has been asked to get up sometime before noon to attend the morning roll call. A second fine number, "Mandy," was not immediately popular, but Ziegfeld, catching the show, grabbed it for his next *Follies*. Berlin unintentionally demonstrated how much the war had gnawed away at audiences' acceptance of excessive sentimentality. "I Can Always Find A Little Sunshine In The Y.M.C.A." was laughed off the stage for lines such as "You can picture me at the close of the day," which asked "mother darling" not to worry, in a letter being written in the Y.M.C.A.

George Broadhurst, hoping to create a hit for his Broadhurst Theatre, wrote his own book and lyrics for his 20 August presentation, **He Didn't Want To Do It**. The critics wished he hadn't. The dismal book revolved about a scheme whereby some fake emeralds are stolen so insurance can be collected. Silvio Hein wrote the score, which was not much better than the libretto. In three weeks' time the Broadhurst was looking for a new tenant.

If Dillingham's Hippodrome extravaganza didn't have **Everything** as its title proclaimed on 22 August, it had enough to thrill audiences for 461 performances. There were songs by John Philip Sousa and Irving Berlin, among others. De Wolf Hopper was the star. Berlin's numbers included "The Circus Is Coming To Town." Hopper was announced as John Jingling, and a circus spectacle followed. Even though the critics were all favorable, most notices were unusually brief, a sign that Hippodrome annuals—like Winter Garden productions—were taken less seriously than they once had been.

The circus was also a prominent part of **Head Over Heels** (29 August 1918, Cohan). Edgar Allan Woolf and Jerome Kern wrote it as a vehicle for petite Mitzi, basing it on Lee Arthur's dramatization of Nalbro Bartley's *Shadows*. Mitzi played a European acrobat who falls in love with an American. She follows him to New York, and, when she realizes he can never be faithful, she settles for his business partner. Because she was no gymnast, Mitzi's acrobatics were "performed" off stage and recounted to audiences in the manner of classic Greek and French drama. Woolf's book was hackneyed, and although Kern was incapable of writing a bad score, this was among his least interesting. Mitzi carried the show for 100 performances.

Kern had a better score, but not much better success, at the end of the season, when he did **She's a Good Fellow** (5 May 1919, Globe) with Anne Caldwell. Her book must have reminded Kern of his shows with female impersonator Julian Eltinge. Young Robert McLane (Joseph Santley) has married Jacqueline Fay (Ivy Sawyer) against the wishes of her guardian. Since she is under age she is taken back to school. Before he can convince her guardians he is worthy of Jacqueline, Robert spends a substantial part of the evening disguised as a Spanish lady. In the first act Santley sported a black dress and black wig; in the second his wig and dress were red. At one point in the story, Olin Howland as a country bumpkin and Santley, still in drag, did a show-stopping burlesque of the era's high-kicking dances. The Duncan Sisters somehow found a place to insert their vaudeville songs and dances. The book was gay and the score catchy. The show's hit, "The First Rose Of Summer," was given an added boost when John McCormack recorded it. Unfortunately, the show never recovered from the actors' strike.

Fiddlers Three (3 September 1918, Cort) ran eleven weeks in the face of generally indifferent notices, which wrote off the piece as "old-fashioned" and "Absolutely Victorian." The fiddlers were violin makers in Cremona. A young lady (Tavie Belge) arrives just as a contest to see who can make the best violin is about to take place. She wins the youngest and handsomest of the craftsmen (Thomas Conkey). The principals found the show stolen from them by the lively Louise Groody as she "smiled and moved and rollicked her way into the audience's heart." Her fast-stepping dances with Hal Skelly received much of the evening's loudest applause.

A major disappointment for many was the quick failure of **The Maid of the Mountains** (11 September 1918, Casino), which José Collins, once of the *Follies*, was then singing for 1,352 performances in London. The maid, Teresa (Sidonie Espero), and her mountain brigands had no appeal to New Yorkers. The Broadway run fell 1,315 showings short of the musical's London mark.

The Girl Behind the Gun (16 September 1918, New Amsterdam) was a suitably martial title for a nation still at war. But the title had little to do with the show's plot. Playwright Robert Lambrissac (Donald Brian), on leave from Paris, visits his godmother instead of his wife. This pleases the godmother (Ada Meade), who would make her husband jealous, but it angers Robert's wife (Wilda Bennett), and she begins to flirt with a colonel. The critics raved about

Guy Bolton and P. G. Wodehouse's book, but could muster little enthusiasm for Ivan Caryll's score. But with Miss Bennett's lovely voice and Brian's dancing to make the songs seem better than they were, ticket-buyers ignored the flaws, and the girl was shouldering her gun long after the war was over.

A bad show once more prompted interesting reviews when the critics sat down to write about **Some Night** (23 September 1918, Harris). Charles Darnton of the *Evening World* shrugged off the evening as "A bad dream." Other recent achievements allowed him to conclude that, despite duds, "New York sets the pace for musical comedy. London is no longer in the running, Vienna is on its last legs and Paris has lagged behind the procession for years... ." As recently as four years earlier, no critic could conceived of this pronouncement. No one could foresee that the statement would hold true for a half-century. *Some Night*, which ran only three weeks, told how Dorothy Wayne (Roma June) "steals" money which is rightfully hers from her tight-fisted guardian. She goes to stay with John Hardy (Louis Simon), a rich young man. All ends well.

Fortunately for Rida Johnson Young and Rudolf Friml, ticket-buyers didn't confuse **Sometime** (4 October 1918, Shubert) with *Some Night. Sometime* was one of the biggest hits of the season. The great 1918 flu epidemic was raging, and one critic praised the show as "catchy as the grip and likely to last longer." It lasted into the summer heat. Why it was so enthusiastically received is not easy to see. The novelty of the book, which was one of the earliest uses of flashback, may have intrigued audiences. Enid Vaughn (Francine Larrimore) has caught her fiancé, Henry (Harrison Brockbank), in a compromising situation and has refused to see him for five years. The scene flashes back to depict the incident that caused the split, and then proceeds to move between the present and the past. In the end it develops that a vamp named Mayme using "Theda Bara tricks" had planned the incident. Henry is shown to be innocent. Enid and Henry are reunited. Mayme, left without "a single soul to vamp," pleads, "If the boob can walk, He don't have to talk: Send me any kind of man." Mayme was played by Mae West. Ed Wynn was the star (he also wrote some of the lyrics), and much of *Sometime's* popularity probably must be attributed to him. Popping in and out on the feeblest excuses in his character of Loney, he won laughs with his lisping delivery of lines such as "What is a man to do in wartime when he can't make both ends meat?—Make one end vegetables!"

Friml's music was charming enough, but between *Katinka* and *Rose-Marie* his songs had no real distinction. At times he seemed to be repeating himself and others. "The Tune You Can't Forget" has been forgotten, largely because it sounded too much like his own hit from *High Jinks*, Kern's "Little Tune, Go Away," and Hirsch's "Tickle Toe."

Friml's second October show was **Glorianna** (28 October 1918, Liberty). It was October's lone failure, although not by much. It missed by only four nights the 100-performance mark, which at this period often indicated a return on investment. Based on Catherine Chisholm Cushing's 1913 *Widow by Proxy*, a title which revealed much of the plot, it found Glorianna Grey (Eleanor Painter) pretending she is a widow to help a friend (Dorothy South) obtain the legacy of the friend's husband. When the husband (Joseph Lertora) turns up alive, there is momentary confusion, but everything is quickly straightened out. Once more Friml's music was pleasant, but it offered nothing memorable. Even the presence of Miss Painter could not edge the show over the 100 mark. Indeed, she may have been partly responsible for the musical's poor New York record. Some critics, while praising her fine singing, suggested she was too sedate. Memories of the rambunctious May Irwin in the original straight play were still vivid and dear to many. When Fritzi Scheff replaced Miss Painter for the tour, results were happier.

Late in March, Friml's third and final offering of the season, **Tumble In** (24 March 1919, Selwyn), made it over the 100-performance line. It might have run longer but for the Equity strike. Retaining the flimsy story line of its source, Mary Roberts Rinehart and Avery Hopwood's 1909 smash, *Seven Days*, it made a whole evening out of a house party quarantined for a week. Friml's music was on a level with his other two scores; nothing from *Tumble In* has gone into his standard canon. But the evening's inadequacies were not wholly creative. They were conceptual as well. The *Globe*'s review affirmed that however far American musicals had recently advanced, there was room for improvement: "To weave the songs into a musical affair has never been an art of proportions, and it is done here in the approved and without reason fashion. That they seem less of interruptions indicates only that the story, as such, didn't particularly matter." In staging and dancing, the show was more imaginative and lively. Good shimmying sparked the stepping, while one novel scene had all the principals hanging precariously over the edge of a roof as they sang "Won't You Help Me Out?"

Apart from the Hippodrome show, the season's longest run for a musical was achieved by an importation, **The Better 'Ole**. Based on Bruce Bairnsfather's cartoon and starring Charles Colburn, it opened on 19 October at the small, out-of-the-way Greenwich Village Theatre; yet not even the Armistice, which came three weeks after its opening and destroyed its immediacy, affected its popularity. Its success was so great that in a month it was playing to packed houses at the larger, uptown Cort. While the program credited Herman Darewski and Percival Knight with the score, most of the tunes were established favorites brought in to fill out the evening. Its story probably needed filling out. "Old Bill" captures a spy's plans to trap a French regiment by blowing up a bridge after the regiment has crossed. Bill blows up the bridge before they can cross. His action is misunderstood, and he is arrested. But after explaining his reasons he is vindicated.

Ladies First (24 October 1918, Broadhurst) gave Broadway three musical hits in a row. The musical looked to the growing woman's suffrage movement for its story. Betty Burt, at the instigation of "Aunt Jim" (Florence Morrison), an old suffragette, runs for mayor of her small town against her sweetheart, Benny (Irving Fisher). She really cares for Benny and doesn't mind when she loses. The deep-voiced, full-bosomed Miss Morrison was abetted in her comedy by William Kent, who played her small, brow-beaten husband. The show was based on Hoyt's *A Contented Woman* and produced as a vehicle for Nora Bayes. Its score was by A. Baldwin Sloane, who had not been heard from in five years, and the book was by Harry B. Smith, who had. Coincidentally, two reviewers struck on the same gimmick to convey their boredom with the librettist's style. Both the *Times* and the *Dramatic Mirror* referred to the adaptation as "harrybsmithed." One interpolation, "Just Like A Gypsy" (which Nora Bayes purportedly wrote with Seymour B. Simons), remained one of her favorites. Two early Gershwin numbers were introduced, "Some Wonderful Sort Of Someone" (lyrics by Schuyler Greene) and "The Real American Folk Song," for which Ira wrote the words. The latter was not inserted until the post-Broadway tour. Other numbers came and went as circumstances suggested. And circumstances must have suggested changes with some frequency. A random comparison of programs for the week of 21 April 1919 (at the Riviera in upper Manhattan) and for the week of 13 November 1919 (at the Saxon Auditorium in Toledo) discloses only two songs in common.

Friml's *Glorianna* followed *Ladies First* and was October's last show.

A second show with a Smith libretto soon came in for appraisal. Even though **The Canary** (4 November 1918, Globe) ran 152 performances, Smith considered it a failure. His recounting of the show's inception reveals his heavy-handed style and his hack willingness. "Caryll's purchase of French farces were not always good bargains. A year or two before the composer's death, Charles Dillingham sent for me and said, 'I want you to get right to work on the funniest farce I ever heard.' Chuckling and trying to keep from laughing, he informed me that the story concerned a comedy character who accidently swallowed a diamond. The humor, it appeared, consisted in the pursuit of the comedian to recover the jewel. My own risible faculties were not violently jarred by this brilliant comic idea and my comment was that it seemed rather physiological in its humor." Caryll must have come around to Smith's view and lost interest. Less than half the completed score was his. Others, including Irving Berlin, Jerome Kern, and Harry Tierney, filled in. But inspiration failed, and no one produced a top-flight number. Julia Sanderson and Joseph Cawthorn were starred, but critics distributed praise to many supporting players. Harland Dixon and James Doyle were liked for their grotsque dances in their roles as two crooks, while homely, hefty Maude

Eburne waddled hilariously around the stage in pursuit of Cawthorn.

Little Simplicity (4 November 1918, Astor) opened the same night as *The Canary*. Its story line was as simple as its heroine, Veronique (Carolyn Thomson), an Algerian flower girl who falls in love with an American (Carl Gantvoort), loses him, and five years later at the Y.M.C.A rediscovers and wins him. She also won 112 performances.

One week later the war was over. And two weeks after that yet another all-soldier musical appeared. Several reviewers thought **Good Luck, Sam!** (25 November 1918, Lexington) was the best of its kind. None of the 300 amateurs or aspiring professionals from Camp Merritt, New Jersey, who comprised the writers, performers, musicians, or stagehands went on to theatrical renown, but billings did concede that the whole entertainment had been "Big Brothered" by George M. Cohan. A slightly melodramatic story in which Private Sam Esterbrook is brought to trial for alienating the affections of an officer's girlfriend framed the evening. Typical of the spoofing was the court-martial scene in which the presiding judge practiced his golf putting while evidence was being given. A second-act setting in a guardhouse allowed for the addition of several extraneous vaudeville specialties. On opening night, Geraldine Farrar was persuaded to leave her stage box and come on stage to sing "Mighty Lak A Rose." Later, as with earlier soldier shows, doughboys sold sheet music in the lobby. Originally booked for just two weeks, the musical ran a month.

The great Princess Theatre shows had all opened while the war was raging. On 27 November, with peace not three weeks old, a new Princess musical appeared, **Oh, My Dear!** It had another likable Bolton book in which an assortment of New York oddities descend on Dr. Rockett's Health Farm, although not for the good doctor's ministrations. There is boozy Broadway Willie (Roy Atwell) fleeing his alimony-hungry ex-wife; handsome young Bruce Allenby (Joseph Santley), of Allenby Umbrellas, fleeing trust busters; and a bevy of road-company chorus girls stranded when their show folded. The girls are old friends of Willie and hope he will lend them train fare home. A Rolls-Royce drives up. Willie fears it is his ex and runs away. But it is only Mrs. Rockett (Georgia Caine). She is angry because earlier in the day she saw Dr. Rockett (Frederick Graham) downtown, holding an umbrella for a pretty young lady, and she has put the worst possible construction

on it. Seeing him surrounded by chorus girls only increases her wrath. The doctor insists they are all looking for Willie, but with Willie gone he could have a difficult time proving it. So Bruce is made to pretend he is Willie. This might have quieted Mrs. Rockett had not Willie's ex suddenly arrived. Not only can she not recognize her supposed husband, but both the doctor and his spouse realize she is the lady for whom he held the umbrella. By curtain time everything is explained, and Bruce wins the hand of the Rocketts' lovely daughter, Hilda (Ivy Sawyer). Wodehouse's lyrics were equally funny. Wodehouse made Willie's delirium tremens hilarious and colorful with pink and green spiders "fox-trotting over the floor." Wodehouse also played with variant forms of "father" in "Ask Daddy," finally rhyming "dadda" with "had a." However, there was one major change. For several reasons Jerome Kern had left the series. Louis Hirsch was called in to do the music, but his score was so obviously deficient that for the first time since *Nobody Home* interpolations were permitted. They were by Jean Schwartz, and they were no help at all. The critics were satisfied, although almost to a man they agreed it was not one of the better evenings at the small house. The *Sun* could not see the sad implications of its seemingly kind remark, "The Princess Theatre is by way of becoming an historical institution." *Oh, My Dear!* ran a respectable six months and sent out two touring companies. But it was appreciated that without Kern, or someone of Kern's caliber, there was no point in continuing, for there could be no totally achieved piece. And so the most important series in the history of the American Musical Theatre was finished. It was just four and a half years old and (if one includes *Have a Heart* and *Leave It to Jane*) had produced just seven shows.

A month passed before another musical opened. Then, on 23 December, three arrived on the same night. **Atta Boy** at the Lexington was another all-soldier show. Captain Frank Tinney headed the performers, who mocked army life and often dressed as women, as their counterparts had in earlier service shows. Coming nearly two months after the war had ended, its time had clearly passed. Three weeks and it was gone.

The other two openings were *Listen, Lester* at the Knickerbocker and *Somebody's Sweetheart* at the Central. Both were hits. **Listen, Lester** even managed to survive the August Equity strike and continue into fall. Set in a Florida hotel, where Lester Lite (Hansford Wilson) works, it told of Colonel

Dodge's attempts to retrieve embarrassing letters he had written to a lady with the unlikely name of Arbutus Quilty (Gertrude Vanderbilt). Billy Penn (Johnny Dooley) and Lester help retrieve them. Then the colonel (Eddie Garvie) is free to marry Tillie Mumm (Ada Lewis). The love interest, Mary Dodge (Ada Mae Weeks) and Jack Griffin (Clifton Webb), can also marry. The book was incessantly flippant:

Lester: Good Afternoon.
Arbutus: I can't help that. I want a room and bath.
Lester: I can give you the room, lady.
Arbutus: What exposure?
Lester: None, if you pull down the shades.

Harold Orlob's music was equally vapid. Playing with the title, the headlines of reviews warned "Not Much For Listeners" or "More Dancing Than Listening." One critic felt the show would have been happier called "Dance, Mary." He was probably right. Webb and Miss Weeks glided gracefully across the boards, while Dooley and Wilson combined for more grotesque stepping. The chorus tapped and kicked in unison.

The gypsy Zaida (Nonette) was **Somebody's Sweetheart**. But whose? Harry Edwards (Walter Scanlan) is about to wed Helen Williams (Eva Fallon), daughter of the U.S. Consul at Seville. Harry had once loved Zaida, and to avoid awkwardness at the wedding he claims her old lover was his best man, Sam Benton (William Kent). Since Sam loves Helen's sister Bessie (Louise Allen), he has to do some fast explaining. Kent's antics were a highlight of the evening, notably at the wedding, where he determines to be a very inconspicuous best man, hiding behind taller ushers and peeking out from a bridal train under which he has crept. Still another pleasant but forgettable score and more good dancing, especially by Veronica, an "oriental dancer with occidental restraint," kept the show on the boards until the summer.

Many critics hailed the plot of **The Melting of Molly** (30 December 1918, Broadhurst). As in Maria Thompson Davies's novel of the same name, Molly Carter (Isabelle Lowe) has grown fat waiting for her diplomat lover, Albert, to marry her. He cables from London that he will return in three months and insists she wear a particularly "Dear Old Gown" as her wedding dress. With the help of Dr. Moore (Charles Purcell) she reduces enough to fit into it. But when Albert enters, he is so fat she decides to marry Dr. Moore instead. Romberg's

score was unattractive. His "Jazz, How I Love To Hear It" and "Jazz All Your Troubles Away" betrayed how uncomfortable he was outside his natural style. The new, harder jazz coming in was far more inimical to him than even the gentler ragtime. The show was taken off after eleven weeks, although "Dear Old Gown" had a second chance under peculiar circumstances several years later.

No musicals arrived in January. More important matters preoccupied the nation. On 29 January 1919, the Secretary of State announced that, with the ratification by a thirty-sixth state on 16 January, Prohibition was to be the law of the land. The last legal drink would go down the hatch a second or so before the year ended. Broadway's immediate response was a rash of interpolated songs and gags. Nora Bayes, for example, added "Prohibition Blues" (Ring Lardner and Miss Bayes) to her touring *Ladies First*. But these changes were superficial. More lasting influences could not be foretold.

A Victor Herbert show opened the new year. **The Velvet Lady** (3 February 1919, New Amsterdam) ran seventeen weeks and left us one of Herbert's most endearing songs, "Life And Love." The rest of his score was not on the same level, and one critic saw the piece as "preeminently a dancing show"—a comment unheard of when Herbert was writing the music. Henry Blossom's book, based on a Frederick Jackson farce, unfolded without enough laughs to suit many in the audience. George Howell (Ray Raymond) must go to Boston to retrieve embarrassing letters that his sister's fiancé, Ned Pembroke (Alfred Gerrard), once wrote to a nightclub singer, the Velvet Lady (Fay Marbe). Coming back the train is wrecked, and George mistakenly picks up a bag containing stolen jewels. His bride (Marie Flynn) discovers the jewels and jumps to the wrong conclusion. But the Velvet Lady appears to explain everything. Since the Velvet Lady didn't appear until the last fifteen minutes, she was clearly not the center of attraction, but then neither were the lovers. For most critics the evening's happiest moments came from Georgia O'Ramey as the Howells' maid, Susie. Her vivacious clowning and even more vivacious dancing compensated for many a lesser moment.

Good Morning, Judge (6 February 1919, Shubert), an English show with music by Monckton and Talbot, boasted two George Gershwin interpolations, "I Was So Young" and "There's More To The Kiss Than XXX." The word "boasted" is not premature. A week or so earlier Jolson, touring in *Sinbad*, had introduced "Swanee." It was so sensationally received it was recorded the same weekend. It made Gershwin a name to be reckoned with.

On 12 February Sigmund Romberg and Jean Schwartz were back at the Winter Garden with what sounded like a Jolson vehicle but wasn't, **Monte Cristo, Jr.** A young man named Monte, who has just read the Dumas book, falls asleep and dreams he and his friends are characters from the novel. Done tongue-in-cheek, with a flock of vaudeville turns thrown in, it was the antithesis of the romance on which Romberg thrived. The score was typical of his Winter Garden material. Well mounted, and with names like Charles Purcell, Ralph Herz, and Chic Sale to draw the patrons, the extravaganza compiled a fine 254 performances.

Even more antiromantic was **The Royal Vagabond** (17 February 1919, Cohan and Harris), which George M. Cohan had written from a faltering operetta, *Cherry Blossoms*. In this "Cohanized Opera Comique," Stephan (Frederick Santley), Crown Prince of Bargravia, is assigned to subdue a revolutionary movement. When he falls in love with Anitza (Tessa Kosta), an innkeeper's daughter, he is converted to the revolution and becomes its leader. He triumphs—buying off his mother's troops— and a new era dawns for Bargravia. The lyrics of the opening chorus set the tone, with the villagers singing "tra la la" because "In every comic opera it's got to be sung." And the dialogue continued the fun:

Prince: Doesn't that sound like a horseman
    approaching?
Tutor: Not exactly. But it's a good effect.

Anselm Goetzl's score was correctly "Schmalzy," but Cohan and Irving Berlin threw in additional tunes to spark the gaiety. The rising Dorothy Dickson enlivened the evening and called further attention to herself with her airy dancing in the small role of Charlotte.

Both *Monte Cristo, Jr.* and *The Royal Vagabond* revealed a growing reaction to the fustian melodrama and operetta of a passing age. In a few years Sigmund Romberg helped revive the vogue, but only briefly. But for Cohan, who first led the way to modern American musical comedy, then pioneered in the modern revue, *The Royal Vagabond* could only be a one-time lark. What his future contributions would have been will never be known. More than anyone else he was thrown off balance by the divisions and enmities arising out of the actors' strike.

Friml's *Tumble In* followed.

Take It from Me (31 March 1919, 44th St.) arrived a week later with a cute idea. Tom Eggett (Jack McGowan) inherits a department store and has a good time ruining it rather than let it fall into the hands of a scheming director. Unfortunately, the book by cartoonist Will B. Johnstone was clumsily written. Nor could the public find the "breath of freshness" in the Will R. Anderson score that made music publisher Isidore Witmark single it out years later as one of his favorites. The evening was filled with vaudeville turns, such as an old man in a comic roller-skating bit.

Come Along (8 April 1919, Nora Bayes) came along at least a year too late. Its story of a nurse (Regina Richards) who goes to France and finds she must care for her wounded lover (Paul Frawley) had lost its appeal. The evening's problems were exacerbated by the drabness of its costumes, with all the men in khaki and most of the women in Red Cross or Salvation Army uniforms. A comic secondary plot attempted to redress matters. Private Barker (Allen Kearns) has a falling-out with his childhood friend (Charles Stanton) when that friend, now a lieutenant, attempts to pull rank. A sly mess sergeant (Harry Tighe) resolves matters. All the principals find themselves at the Statue of Liberty in time for a finale. Nothing in *Come Along*'s score could overcome the public's antipathy to more war stories. The musical survived for six weeks.

Two nights after Jerome Kern's *She's a Good Fellow* lit up the Globe on 5 May, the lights were turned on again at the Princess. But again Kern's name was not on the marquee. **Toot Sweet** had music by Richard Whiting, who had made his reputation with "It's Tulip Time In Holland," "Mammy's Little Coal Black Rose," and "Where The Black-Eyed Susans Grow"—the last used by Jolson in *Robinson Crusoe, Jr.* (17 February 1916). This was his first complete score. The music failed not only on its own but because its lyrics, like the show's sketches, were war-oriented—reflecting the revue's beginnings as an overseas troop entertainment. Much of the evening was a show within a show, a vaudeville presented to a "doughboy" chorus. Will Morrissey served as compère, introducing singers, mimics, comics, and a highly praised team of eccentric dancers, Miller and Ward.

Kern was credited with one interpolation in **The Lady in Red** (12 May 1919, Lyric). The musical dealt with the love of an artist and his dream girl, and their relations with a comic soap manufacturer. (The *Times* noted that in these modern, antiseptic days soap makers had replaced turn-of-the-century pickle kings.) But the show needed more than a Kern tune to save it. It stayed forty-eight performances.

La, La, Lucille (26 May 1919, Henry Miller) was the first complete Broadway score by George Gershwin. Yet though "Swanee" was by now a top hit, the critics gave Gershwin no special attention. Burns Mantle noted in the *Evening Mail*, "of the recent musical plays, La, La, Lucille is much the best." But he was looking at the show as a whole. He picked out "Tee-Oodle-Um-Bum-Bo" for praise, mentioning without further comment that Gershwin was the show's composer. The *Times* viewed the musical as "the incarnation of jazz"—a form to which Gershwin would be forever tied—but failed to mention Gershwin at all. The *Globe*, in a puzzling comment, felt, "The songs by a new young composer, George Gershwin, are tuneful if in many instances negative, but they retard the action." The action begins with a chorus line of bill collectors attempting to get John Smith (Jack Hazzard), a young dentist, to pay his overdue accounts. A lawyer arrives advising John his Aunt Roberta has died and willed him two million dollars, provided he divorce his wife, Lucille (Janet Velie). The aunt objects to the marriage, for Lucille comes from a family of jugglers. Since John won't lose the money if he remarries Lucille, they decide to get the divorce and re-wed. John takes their janitress, Fanny (Eleanor Daniels), who will act as co-respondent, to a hotel. Before they can be properly "caught," Fanny's husband, unaware of the plan, comes after his wife. A honeymoon couple in the next room get dragged into the melee when John hides Fanny and insists the young bride is the co-respondent. Everything is resolved when the "dead" aunt enters and reveals she has only been testing John and Lucille. She feels they have passed the test. The show's dialogue also passed the test—but just barely. The lawyer, Blackwood (J. Clarence Harvey), convinces Lucille and John to go through with the staged hotel scene. Once Blackwood gets Lucille and John to agree, they must convince Fanny to play along:

Fanny: ... if I risk it all, it'll have to cost you something.
Lucille: Of course! We're quite willing to pay— anything within reason.
Blackwood: How much do you want?
Fanny: Well—there's my reputation—and the risk I run with Oyama [her husband]—and the chances I take with him.

Lucille: Chances?
Fanny: I've got to figger, ma'am, in case anything should go wrong!
John: Nothing will go wrong.
Fanny: I couldn't do it for less than—$5.

Arthur Jackson and Buddy DeSylva's lyrics were not as brilliant as George's brother Ira later provided for him, but they were acceptable. And though no song from *La, La, Lucille* has entered the canon of Gershwin classics, they are very attractive. Listening to "The Best Of Everything" and "Nobody But You" one can still hear Kern's influence on the young New Yorker, but unmistakable Gershwin touches are there as well. Like so many of the season's musicals, *La La Lucille* became a casualty of the Equity strike.

A week after *La, La, Lucille*'s debut, another new name—one Gershwin would long be associated with—made its first Broadway appearance. The **Scandals of 1919** danced into the Liberty. Dancing was the word for it, as it was for many of the season's musicals. George White—who would not add his name to the title until later—was born George Weitz on the East Side and worked his way from a Bowery hoofer to a *Ziegfeld Follies* spot. With his *Follies* associate, Ann Pennington, he paced the stepping for the first edition. Their shimmying and tapping earned them encores, but while they were catching their breath other dancers, particularly a contortionist named La Sylphe, kept audiences occupied. The music by Richard Whiting (recently of *Toot Sweet*) and the lyrics of Arthur Jackson (of the competing *La, La, Lucille*) were pedestrian. White learned his lesson quickly. Future *Scandals* had some of the best songs ever to come out of Broadway's revues. Sketches by Jackson and White himself also left something to be desired. Skits spoofed bedroom farces, courtroom dramas, overcrowded hotels, and, with Prohibition just around the corner, life on a rum-running houseboat. But if the comedy too frequently misfired, the beautiful girls and giddy dancing caught New York's fancy. Another great revue series was launched.

The season's last musical, **A Lonely Romeo** (10 June 1919, Shubert) was a vehicle for Lew Fields, utilizing a book by Fields himself in partnership with Harry B. Smith. Harry's brother Robert supplied the lyrics for Malvin Franklin's and Robert Hood Bower's melodies. A light summer entertainment, it watched Augustus Tripper, a hatter by day and a "cabaret fiend" by night, get in and out of trouble when his wife discovers where he spends his evenings. There were two interpolations. One was "I Guess I'm More Like Mother Than Like Father" (Richard Egan/Richard Whiting). The second was added just before the actors' strike closed the show. Called "Any Old Place With You," it confronted Broadway playgoers with two more new names—Lorenz Hart and Richard Rodgers. Those with an alert ear might well have caught Rodgers's promise in his pleasant melody, but Hart was already more fulfilling than promising. In the song he brazenly rhymed "Virginia" with "Abyssinia" and went on to proclaim, "I'd go to hell for ya, Or Philadelphia." For all the brief display of Hart's wit and for all Fields's clowning, most critics considered the evening, as they did so many musicals, a dancing entertainment. The first-act finale brought the entire cast on, a few at a time, in a rousing crescendo of ensemble dance that had Fields himself doing flipflops as the curtain fell.

1918–1919 was qualitatively the leanest season in this period. Coming after three high-flying seasons it may seem leaner than it was. But it pointed to new directions and saw Broadway settle, not always comfortably, into the track it rolled on for the next four or five decades. It was the first season anything approaching commercial jazz played a prominent part on the musical stage, and while jazz was not yet always clearly defined or understood, the most progressive of the season's new lyric pieces mirrored its excited tempos and steely texture, pronouncing the future of American musical comedy. Only seven out-and-out revues appeared—a similar foreshadowing, but this time auguring decline and demise. Ridicule of old-world operettas gave voice to a growing intellectual rejection of the form—although, as we have noted, it was to have one brief, luminous renaissance.

1919–1920

Florenz Ziegfeld gave the season the grandest possible start. **The Ziegfeld Follies of 1919** (16 June 1919, New Amsterdam) is generally regarded as the high point of the series. Certainly the press thought so. The *American* headed its review, "1919 'Follies' Surpasses All Others." The *Herald*'s banner echoed the sentiment: "Thirteenth 'Ziegfeld Follies' Eclipses Predecessors in Beauty, Color and Action." Ultimate laurels were awarded by the *Evening Sun*: "Ziegfeld Outziegfelds Ziegfeld." From this edition came the consummate girlie revue song, Irving Berlin's "A Pretty Girl Is Like A Melody," which the greatest of revue tenors, John Steel, sang, as Ziegfeld beauties promenaded by, representing the "Barcarolle," "Elegy," "Humoresque," and other semiclassics. Berlin also gave Bert Williams his wry Prohibition protest, "You Cannot Make Your Shimmy Shake On Tea." For Eddie Cantor he composed "You'd Be Surprised," so successful a song it was soon being sung in other shows. In the first-act finale, "The Follies Minstrels," Williams and Cantor combined to sing another Berlin number, "I Want To See A Minstrel Show." As part of the same scene, Van and Schenck popularized "Mandy," which Ziegfeld had taken over from *Yip Yip Yaphank* (19 August 1918). Ray Dooley impersonated Mandy, while Marilyn Miller appeared as George Primrose. Two songs not by Berlin also had a brief vogue—"Tulip Time" (Gene Buck/Dave Stamper) and "My Baby's Arms" (Joseph McCarthy/Harry Tierney). Cantor had the best comedy of the evening as a nervous patient at "The Osteopath's Office." For Williams and Marilyn Miller, this edition marked their last *Follies* appearances. Joseph Urban's sets, particularly his harem scene, and his flower-filled urns for Miss Miller's "Sweet Sixteen" number, elicited the customary gasps of approval.

The Shubert Gaieties of 1919 (17 July 1919, 44th Street) gave the season its second revue. Its best number was "You'd Be Surprised," which was being better done at the New Amsterdam. Besides Henry Lewis, who sang it, the evening offered Gilda Gray, the shimmy queen. A quickly thrown-together affair, it was able to reassemble hastily after the actors' strike (with George Jessel replacing Henry Lewis). It ran until superior entertainment came along.

Down in the modern-day Bohemia below Washington Square, John Murray Anderson put together a new revue initially entitled *Greenwich Village Nights* but quickly changed to **Greenwich Village Follies** (15 July 1919, Greenwich Village Theatre). Ziegfeld was not pleased, but, since a "Follies" had been produced in New York before he launched his own series, he had no legal recourse. The new annual, and it became just that, gave him serious competition. "Next to Ziegfeld," Robert Baral notes in his study, *Revue*, "these revues were the most exciting annuals on Broadway." Anderson combined with Philip Bartholomae to do the sketches and lyrics. For the first score he tapped A. Baldwin Sloane. This was Sloane's second show after a protracted absence, but his work was as pallid as for *Ladies First*. One song, "I Want A Daddy Who Will Rock Me To Sleep," had a fleeting success, but as so often happened to Sloane an interpolation outshined all of his material. Ted Lewis intro-duced "When My Baby Smiles At Me" (Andrew Sterline, Ted Lewis, and Bill Munro) and retained it as his theme song throughout his long career. Like Ziegfeld's uptown revue, Greenwich Village could not ignore Prohibition. Bessie McCoy Davis ridiculed the upcoming nonsense with "I'm The Hostess Of A Bum Cabaret." Memorable produc-tion numbers included one with the cast as mari-onettes, a Javanese scene, and a stage strewn with red roses. After six weeks in which favorable word of mouth confirmed the critics' judgments, the show was moved uptown.

Oh, What a Girl! opened across the street from the *Gaieties* at the Shubert on 28 July. The exclama-tion came from both Jack Rushton (Sam Ash) and his uncle, Deacon Amos Titmouse (Harry Kelly), who love Margot Merrivale (Hazel Kirke), a caba-ret singer. Jack wins Margot only after exposing his uncle's philandering. The best song in the show was an interpolation—Irving Berlin's "You'd Be Surprised."

A week after *Oh, What a Girl!* opened, the Actors' Equity strike began. Actors, tired of years of abuses—being stranded out of town, poor pay, no rehearsal pay—demanded recognition and certain concessions. Producers refused. On 7 August the actors closed twelve shows. One by one additional houses went dark. On 13 August Eddie Cantor, Ray Dooley, John Steel, and Van and Schenck refused to perform, so the *Follies* shut down. By 21 August, twenty-four productions in New York alone had been halted. The *Greenwich Village Follies*, non-Eq-uity, was one of the few attractions to keep going. It cleaned up. Caught in the middle was George M. Cohan. Both an actor and a producer, he tried at first to be conciliatory, only to meet with vilification from the union. The response embittered him and turned him actively against the union. Many better-established actors ignored Equity and formed the Actors Fidelity League, a group more sympathetic to the producers. But numbers, not quality, told.

Only a single musical production opened during the strike. The Hippodrome, with its gift for cheery but ironic titles, brought in **Happy Days** on 23 August. Another typical Hippodrome extravaganza, it had no artistic distinction. One set was done almost entirely in gold, and another took audiences to Fairyland, while a third, like a set in the *Greenwich Village Follies*, filled the stage with roses. Acrobats, jugglers, ballerinas, and trained animals cavorted on the gigantic stage. But *Happy Days* earned itself

a dubious place in theatrical history, for, when its cast walked out on the 28th in sympathy with other Broadway performers, producers decided to recog-nize the union and end the five-week strike. One immediate effect of the strike was an increase in the cost of production and a consequent rise in ticket prices. The war and its aftermath had brought about a small inflation. But it had not seriously affected Broadway or its patrons. *The Ziegfeld Follies* had cost $88,000 to mount in 1917 (when an average musical cost $20,000 to $30,000). One year later, the *Follies* cost $120,000, and the new edition, brought in just before the actors' demands were met, represented a $170,000 investment. Ticket prices had risen accordingly. The 1917 top of $2.00 had given way to $3.00 in 1918 and $3.50 in 1919. Of course few other shows dealt in what seemed at the time astronomical figures. And a good part of the *Follies'* higher costs reflected Ziegfeld's increas-ingly extravagant demands. If an ordinary Broadway musical could no longer be put on for $20,000, the figure was not too much higher. Nonetheless during the new season almost all musicals raised their best seats to $2.50 or $3.00. The $1.50 to $2.00 top which had prevailed virtually since the Civil War was gone forever.

The strike had canceled rehearsals and try-outs for sixty shows. As a result, no new musical appeared until 23 September—with one interest-ing exception. That oddity was **Peek-A-Boo** (11 August 1919, Central) and it had not been meant for Broadway. In 1919 burlesque had yet to deteriorate into the tawdry strip shows of later decades. The two great burlesque circuits still specialized in rough-and-tumble musical comedies (filled, of course, with eye-catching chorus girls), which served as a training ground for many of our great comedi-ans. In late May the Columbia Wheel (the Eastern circuit) had premiered *Peek-A-Boo* at its New York flagship house, slating it for a summer-long run. It depicted the hilarious complications that ensue when a roustabout circus sets up next door to a staid Maine health farm. One review observed, "There is a personable chorus and the usual many special-ties—trapeze artists, a cyclist, a colored jazz band, and others." Those others included no fewer than three comics headed for stardom: Joe Cook, who apparently had left the show before it crossed Times Square, and Bobby Clark and Paul McCullough as a pair of tramps sporting the monikers Count Rolling Stone No Moss and Duke Few Clothes. Perhaps out of a misguided snobbery, Broadway playgoers would not accept the entertainment, so it was withdrawn after two weeks.

In **See Saw** (23 September 1919, Cohan), Cynthia Meyrick (Dorothea McKaye) must choose between English Lord Harrowby (Charlie Brown) and American Richard Minot (Frank Carter). Minot is the Lloyd's of London American agent, and Lord Harrowby has insured with Lloyd's against Cynthia's refusal. The book was adequate, but Louis Hirsch's score failed to provide the necessary uplift. Several reviewers mentioned the many encores for "When Two Hearts Discover" (a dozen repeats according to the *World*), but the consensus found the music "reminiscent." *See Saw* ran eleven weeks.

Roly-Boly Eyes (25 September 1919, Knickerbocker) did slightly better. A showcase for Eddie Leonard's blackface talents, it ran 100 performances. Leonard played Billy Emerson, who runs away from home after being wrongly accused of a crime and joins a minstrel troupe. He later returns home, is vindicated, and extols his loyal sweetheart (Queenie Smith) as "Ida, Sweet As Apple Cider." The song, which later became an Eddie Cantor standby, was written by Leonard. The minstrel troupe was never shown, although it might have made the show more colorful and lively. Instead all the action was set in the garden and on the sleeping porch of Ida's home.

Hitchy-Koo, 1919 appeared at the Liberty on 6 October. As always, Raymond Hitchcock served as the genial, slightly cracker-barrel, compère. Florence O'Denishawn performed her elegant, balletlike dances. For novelty, two American Indians, Chief Eagle Horse, and Princess White Deer, sang and danced. "Old Fashioned Garden," a sentimental ballad from the revue, was an instant success. The song hardly suggested the sophisticated material the world came to expect from its author, Cole Porter. But that might have been there too had not Hitchcock cut "That Black And White Baby Of Mine." The show's limited success discouraged Porter, and it was another five years before a new Cole Porter score was heard on a Broadway stage.

Hello, Alexander (7 October 1919, 4th St.), a reworking for McIntyre and Heath of *The Ham Tree*, came in the following night and stayed seven weeks. Between minstrel numbers Alexander (McIntyre), induced by Henry Clay Jones (Heath) to leave a good job, pretends he is an important dignitary. A costume ball allowed for a gaudy, peppy finale, filled with typical vaudeville turns.

A second show opened the same night. It was **Apple Blossoms** (7 October 1919, Globe), one of the season's commercial and creative triumphs. Its success was especially noteworthy in view of problems it imposed on itself. *Apple Blossoms* was an undisguised operetta, a form that, except for *Maytime* (16 August 1917), seemed to have lost broad appeal and, as the preceding season had shown, was fair game for parody. Moreover, half the score of the new piece was by Fritz Kreisler, an Austrian and the leading violin virtuoso of his generation. No Austro-Hungarian works had braved New York since *The Star Gazer* (26 November 1917) was so ignominiously hustled away during the war. The show confirmed what *Maytime* had suggested: that, given a truly fine operetta, there would still be a vast public clamoring for seats. It also demonstrated how rapidly war-born animosities had faded. But there were other problems. Was the show in three acts or a prologue and two acts? The working typescripts had it both ways, while the published program, which lists a prologue and two acts, contradicted the published text, which divided the evening into three acts. The problem is the length and richness of the prologue, or, if you will, the shortness of the first act. It takes too long to set up the basic situation. The hero does not make his appearance until well into the second act; this may have been a compelling reason for calling it Act I. Conversely, the denouement is too swift to be fully justified. Nancy Dodge (Wilda Bennett) thinks she loves Dickie Stewart (Percival Knight), the wastrel brother of her classmate, Polly, but her Uncle George (Harrison Brockbank) insists she marry Philip Campbell (John Charles Thomas). Philip is in love with a young widow, Anne Merton (Florence Shirley). Philip and Nancy capitulate and are married, but they agree that each is free to go his or her own way. They resume their old flirtations, but in the confusion of a masked ball discover they really love each other. Dickie and Anne, old flames, leave hand in hand. Even if there were faults of proportion, William Le Baron's characters and dialogue were far above operetta standards. Dickie has marvelously witty and suitable lines. He complains that at Nancy's school, "they won't let you see a girl in her room even if she isn't studying," and after the wedding confesses to the bride, "I was afraid you might think that when you were married I would want to break our engagement." Nancy, obviously determined to block out her marriage, returns from the ceremony alone:

Julie [the maid]: But where is Mr. Campbell?
Nancy: Who?

Julie: Your husband.

Nancy: Oh—Oh—isn't he here?—I guess I jumped into the wrong car, or else he did—or perhaps he isn't coming—I don't know—My brain is in a whirl anyway.

Julie: And this is your wedding day. Oh, Miss Nancy, it ain't right—you're starting out where most of them finish.

Philip is equally well drawn. He enters with the rousing if slightly Merry Widow–like "Little Girls, Goodbye," but he is no cardboard ladies' man. He is alert and humorous. He quickly realizes Dickie is Nancy's boyfriend and naughtily contrives an awkward meeting for them. But as good as the libretto was, the show might have been lackluster without its scintillating score. Embarrassingly for Kreisler, who garnered most of the pre-opening attention, it was Victor Jacobi who wrote the hit, "You Are Free," a duet for Nancy and Philip. The song had oddly Victorian lyrics for its twentieth-century message. Jacobi was responsible as well for "Little Girls, Goodbye." Time helped redress the imbalance. Nancy's first-act waltz, "Who Can Tell," which Kreisler composed, was given new lyrics and new life in 1936 as "Stars In Your Eyes." Besides two top singers, Thomas and Miss Bennett, the show featured two personable young dancers, Fred and Adele Astaire. The *Times* alerted readers to watch for "the vastly entertaining dances by the two Adaires [sic], in particular for the incredibly nimble and lackadaisical Adaire named Fred. He is one of those extraordinary persons whose senses of rhythm and humor have all been mixed up, whose very muscles, of which he seems to have an extra supply, are downright facetious." One of their dances was done to Kreisler's "Tambourin Chinois"; the other—to Jacobi's music—began when Fred playfully retrieved a ball of yarn Adele had dropped. Although the paper was careless in its spelling, it was also perspicacious. All during the twenties Adele was awarded the lion's share of praise for the team. Not until Fred was forced to perform alone did most critics and audiences fully appreciate his brilliance. *Apple Blossoms* had the added allure of three sumptuous Urban sets, re-creating a garden at a girls' school, an elegant Fifth Avenue study, and a spacious ballroom. The operetta played into May, then toured successfully.

Another hit, **The Little Whopper** (13 October 1919, Casino), followed. To facilitate her elopement, Kitty Wentworth tells her school proprietress she is going to Philadelphia to meet family friends.

She winds up in the wrong hotel room, and as one complication piles on top another, fib piles on fib. Rudolf Friml's score was second-rate, but adequate. It leaned, as Friml's next score did, toward contemporary musical comedy and away from Friml's native bent. With Vivienne Segal as star, the show ran over six months. An omen of things to come might have seen in the source of the book, *Miss George Washington, Jr.*—a silent screenplay!

Nothing but Love (14 October 1919, Lyric) was a quick flop about a young man (Andrew Tombes) who can't remember rescuing his sweetheart (Ruby Norton) until an understanding doctor (Donald Meek) jolts his recollections. The musical was sandwiched in between the procession of hits which continued with **The Passing Show of 1919** (23 October 1919, Winter Garden). The Shubert mentality could not compete with Ziegfeld or Anderson's taste. J. J.'s inevitable response was to bring on more girls. It was an answer that pleased many a tired businessman, who probably left the theatre humming the show's hit, one more interpolation, "I'm Forever Blowing Bubbles" (Jean Kenbrovin and John W. Kellette). The revue offered the Avon Comedy Four doing their famous skit, "The Doctor's Office," which the group's two long-lived survivors, Smith and Dale, continued to play for years as a wisecracking duel between a doctor and a patient. The rest of the cast—none with the big names Ziegfeld so generously paid for—included Olga Cook (later of *Blossom Time*), Walter Woolf (later of *Countess Maritza*), James Barton, Charles Winninger, and Mary Eaton: youthful and talented performers who soon left for bigger salaries which the increasingly tight-fisted Shuberts refused to pay.

Buddies (27 October 1919, Selwyn) was another hit. Just as Kreisler's reception indicated the end of ill feelings, so *Buddies* meant war stories, of a sort, were acceptable once more. Actually the story unfolds in Normandy a few days after the Armistice. A group of soldiers are billeted with Madame Benoit (Camile Dalberg) and her daughter Julie (Peggy Wood). One doughboy, Babe (Roland Young), falls in love with Julie but is too shy to court her. Fond of Babe and hoping to make him jealous enough to speak up, Julie flirts with his buddy, Sonnie (Donald Brian). Her ruse works. The music (including one song partially by Cole Porter) was flavorless, the lyrics drab. But in singing, "There is a world of fairy tales, wherein we love to dwell," or, "Good-bye, trenches; Farewell, Frenchies," they commented perceptively on the mental frame of the audiences.

One stage picture elicited special praise. The soldiers were housed in an old French barn. When taps was sounded from an offstage village, the soldiers crawl into bed, candles are extinguished and the silent barn lit only by moonlight. Such sentimental, rustic touches appeared throughout the evening. That the show was so fondly remembered was probably to the credit of its stars, Brian, Young, and Miss Wood. Brian's lithe stepping and Miss Wood's lovely singing (despite the *Times* insisting her voice was "unruly") undoubtedly were taken for granted. But some theatregoers may have been startled by Young's "manneristic and talented" dances.

With four hits in five tries, it was too much to expect the run of success to continue. Two other musicals opened the same night as *Buddies*; both closed in five weeks' time. **Fifty-Fifty, Ltd.** (27 October 1919, Comedy) turned William Gillette's *All the Comforts of Home* into a jazzy vaudeville. The old plot of a home rented to a collection of boarders was a natural, since all the guests could and did have specialty acts. Even the chorus, which apparently slept en masse in the attic, was said to be from the "Midnight Scrambles." Herbert Corthell walked away with the evening's honors for his portrayal of a henpecked husband.

In October 27th's third opening, the trio responsible for *Listen, Lester* tried to repeat its success at the same Cort Theatre with **Just a Minute**, proffering an even sillier book and weaker score than *Listen, Lester* got by on. For its composer, Harry Orlob, it was his second fast flop of the year. He had composed the slightly better music for *Nothing but Love*. In five years' time Orlob wrote five scores without a single hit tune. Although his work was the grossest hack writing, he was still enough in demand to be asked to write two more scores in the twenties. Sadly, it took thirty-odd years for him to receive credit for his lone great melody, "I Wonder Who's Kissing Her Now?," attributed to Joe Howard when it was sung in *The Prince of Tonight* (9 march 1909). What little *Just a Minute* had to recommend it came largely from its bare-legged dancing chorus, whose sprightly synchronized steps won several rounds of applause.

The Little Blue Devil (3 November 1919, Central) was also a flop, even though it had any number of good things going for it. It had two Ziegfeld favorites, Bernard Granville and Lillian Lorraine, as stars; a likable Harry Carroll score; and Clyde Fitch's *The Blue Mouse* as source. Harold Atteridge's adaptation may not have been the most cerebral, but the story was no more farfetched than many of the librettos attracting applause. Augustus Rollett passes off Paulette Divine, the Little Blue Devil, as his wife in order to win a promotion from his roving-eyed boss. He wins the promotion, but he's left with a lot of explaining to do to the real Mrs. Rollett.

It was 11 November before Sigmund Romberg's name appeared on a season's program, and when it did Romberg was listed as coproducer as well as composer. After *Maytime* the Shuberts continued to press Romberg to grind out Winter Garden scores, offering no attractive libretto to compensate. In despair, Romberg broke with them and established a producing company with Max Wilner. For their first production, **The Magic Melody,** Romberg picked the predictably bittersweet type of tale he always was to favor. Beppo Corsini, his opera rejected, his wife seemingly unfaithful, leaves home, taking his young son with him. Twenty years later, Beppo is long dead and his son has become a handsome captain. He is reunited with his long-lost mother when he sings excerpts from his father's opera. His mother is able to prove she was never untrue to Beppo, making the reunion a happy one. The dialogue and the lyrics were stodgy, and, considering all the show must have meant to Romberg, the score was annoyingly weak and derivative. The show's best number, a pleasant waltz called "Once Upon A Time," unwisely began, "Once upon a time in May, How can you forget, dear?" This echo of *Maytime* (16 August 1917) was reinforced by that show's star, Charles Purcell, playing both Beppo and his son, just as he had played both Richard and his grandson in 1917. The rest of the score sounded sometimes like Jerome Kern, sometimes like Irving Berlin, and most often like more Winter Garden dross. The show ran 143 performances at the Shubert, but was generally recorded as a failure.

Irene (18 November 1919, Vanderbilt) immediately became the season's runaway hit. It showed the work of the Princess pioneers had not been in vain. A believable plot told about believable people who sang lovely songs brought naturally into the story. If this time there was more sentimentality than wit, no one cared. It remains one of the most cherished of American musicals. Irene O'Dare (Edith Day), a poor shopgirl, is sent on an errand to the Marshalls' Long Island estate. The Marshalls' son, Donald (Walter Regan), promptly falls in love with her and finds her a job as a model in a couturier's shop run by a gentleman known as Madam Lucy (Bobbie Watson). When Irene walks off with everyone's heart at J. P. Bowden's party, both Mrs. O'Dare (Dorothy

Walters) and Mrs. Marshall (Florence Hills) put aside their prejudices, allowing Donald and Irene to marry. The solid book moved tellingly back and forth between the rags of the O'Dares' tenement and the riches of the Long Island estate. A set depicting a fire escape outside the O'Dares' flat became one of the most celebrated of the day. The show's great hit, "Alice Blue Gown," was Irene's first number; it effectively won over any audience. The remaining tunes were almost as good, especially the infectious title song and the joyous "The Last Part Of Every Party." They were incorporated for the first time into a successful Cinderella formula that was employed by musical after musical until, like Irene's gown, it wilted. Wisely, the best of the imitations never used the little cheat Joseph McCarthy and Harry Tierney resorted to, sneaking in a Chopin theme for Irene's "Castle Of Dreams." One may have been necessary to prop up a weak *Oh, Look!* score, but Tierney's material for *Irene* could have stood on its own feet. A 1973 revival, while successful, made so many changes it hardly deserved to retain the name.

Charlotte Greenwood and her Letitia Proudfoot came back to New York in **Linger Longer Letty** (20 November 1919, Fulton). A paper-thin plot portrayed Letty as her family's ugly duckling who finds love and happiness with a neighbor, Jim (Olin Howland). No one cared that there was barely enough plot to make it to 11:00 P.M. Miss Greenwood kicked high, joined Howland for several eccentric dance duets, and sang "Oh, By Jingo," so all was right with the world. But Broadway was never Letty's first home. She lingered only nine weeks and returned to the long road before her.

When F. Ray Comstock, Guy Bolton, and P. G. Wodehouse delivered another Kern-less musical, they suffered another flop, at least as far as Broadway was concerned. **The Rose of China** (25 November 1919, Lyric) had music by the Hotel Ritz's fashionable orchestra leader, Armand Vecsey. He did his house no credit. The story, which in outline does not sound like the expected Bolton material, has Tommy Telford (Oscar Shaw) forced to marry Ling Tao (Jane Richardson) when he becomes the first man to see her with her face exposed. Since he loves her, his only problem is disposing of his American fiancée, Grace (Cynthia Perot), and her grim-visaged mother (Edna May Oliver). Bolton had trouble cutting this simple story down to size. On opening night there was still one whole act to come at 11:00 P.M. At least Wodehouse could take a little heart in the *Times* calling his rhyming of "Los Angeles" and

"man jealous" "probably the greatest single achievement of its kind this season." Six weeks and *The Rose of China* moved to Chicago, where it was an "instantaneous smash," retasting the tremendous popularity it had enjoyed on its pre-Broadway tryout.

A second F. Ray Comstock and Morris Gest production was more successful. **Aphrodite** (24 November 1919, Century) was a Hippodrome-like spectacle whose book, never properly credited, and handful of songs took second place to its pageantry. The famous ballet choreographer Michel Fokine did the dances.

Five musicals opened in December. **Elsie Janis and Her Gang** (1 December 1919, Cohan) led the parade. Miss Janis had spent the war months entertaining the troops at the front lines. To the doughboys she had become "The Sweetheart of the AEF." Dressed in smart military uniforms or at least sporting a soldier's helmet, she offered Broadway the sketches and specialty acts she had put together for France. Eva Le Gallienne, who later won fame in more serious enterprises, had a small part. The Gang remained in New York seven weeks as part of a national tour.

R. H. Burnside and Raymond Hubbell, who had been creating the colossal entertainments at the Hippodrome, did a turnabout and brought their **Miss Millions** into the petite Punch and Judy Theatre on 9 December. It employed the rags-to-riches plot that was to overrun Broadway musicals in the wake of *Irene*. Jack Honeydew's uncle (Rayley Holmes) suspects Jack's fiancée, the teashop waitress Mary Hope (Valli Valli), of loving Jack (Vinton Freedley) less than she loves Jack's money. The uncle arranges for Mary to believe she has come into a large inheritance and that Jack has lost all his wealth. Mary remains true until she learns she is being used. She runs away to a farm in New Jersey, where Jack pursues her and wins her back. Without the Hippodrome's pyrotechnics to divert theatregoers' attention from the hack material, *Miss Millions*'s weaknesses were all too visible. Even at its tiny playhouse, six weeks was all the show could hold on.

Monsieur Beaucaire (11 December 1919, New Amsterdam) was an Allied effort that enjoyed a five-month run. Based on a short story by American Booth Tarkington, with a score by French André Messager and libretto and lyrics by English Adrian Ross, it had been a European success before coming to America. The plot told of the adventures of the Duc d'Orleans (Marion Greene), disguised as Beaucaire, a barber in Bam, England.

Above the classic splendor of *Aphrodite*, **Morris Gest's Midnight Whirl** (27 December 1919, Century Roof) gave late-nighters more up-to-date diversion. Gershwin's music was pleasant, but his best song, "Poppyland," was no more typical of his style than "Old Fashioned Garden" had been of Cole Porter's. Bernard Granville and Bessie McCoy Davis headed the cast.

Just before the teens slipped away, **Angel Face** (29 December 1919, Knickerbocker) appeared. Even though Victor Herbert and the Smith brothers belonged squarely in the era that was fast receding, they tried to be as modern as possible. Harry B. Smith's plot grew out of the latest medical rage, Voronoff's contention that monkey gland grafts could rejuvenate the old and feeble. But Smith had learned little from the Princess Theatre shows. His book was weak and turgid. A vial is left carelessly at Tom Larkin and Arthur Griffin's bachelor apartment. The elixir's effect on various people who sample it in the course of three acts provided the evening's fun. Between specialty turns such as Jack Donahue's supple tap and soft-shoe routines, angel-faced Betty (Marguerite Zender) wangles Arthur (Tyler Brooke) away from her older sister, Vera (Minerva Grey), while Tom (John E. Young)—who is also composer of the successful musical comedy "The Lemon Girl"—woos and wins Tessie (Emilie Lea). Brother Robert's lyrics tugged at both worlds with lines such as "Ere the world is awake, You and I will take an aeroplane." Herbert, also trying to keep in the swing of things, wrote fewer waltzes. But, with one exception, his tunes were inferior. The exception was "I Might Be Your 'Once-in-a-While,'" its light, easy grace catching the more gentle charm of a passing day. It remains a Herbert standard. The song alone was not sufficient to save the show. *Angel Face* smiled for only fifty-seven performances, then a booking jam forced it to leave while it still had respectable grosses.

A less interesting but more successful Herbert show followed a little over a month later. **My Golden Girl** (2 February 1920, Nora Bayes) had a hand-me-down Herbert score and a book by Frederic Arnold Kummer that seemed like a rewrite of *Apple Blossoms*. Peggy and Arthur Mitchell (Marie Caroll and Victor Morely) have each found extramarital love interests. They agree to a divorce. But they soon realize they still love each other. For all its lack of originality, *My Golden Girl* ran three months, helped by the cavorting of Edna May Oliver as yet another battle-axe mother, and Ned Sparks as a young, sourpuss lawyer.

The new year was five days old when **Always You** arrived at the Central. It was the first Broadway musical to have a book and lyrics by Oscar Hammerstein II. Because of his famous name, Hammerstein's contributions received closer scrutiny than they might have otherwise. Some critics were happier with his lyrics than with his book. But by and large they were gratified to find a genuine new talent in the family. Hammerstein wrote of Bruce Nash (Walter Scanlan), who wavers between the girl he fell in love with while serving in France (Helen Ford) and his American sweetheart (Julia Kelety). As in *The Rose of China*, the American girl loses. For the umpteenth time many critics saved their happiest encomiums for the show's peppy chorus and the specialty dancing, in this case by Cortez and Peggy. Kind words were also reserved for the genial clowning of Ralph Herz and of Edouard Ciannelli, the latter of whom went on to become one of Hollywood's most sought-after villains.

> **OSCAR HAMMERSTEIN II** was born in New York on 12 July 1895. His grandfather, the first Oscar, was a leading impresario whose Manhattan Opera House briefly rivaled the Metropolitan. His uncle was a leading Broadway producer, and his father was manager of the Victoria Theatre. Young Hammerstein attended Columbia where he wrote and acted in varsity shows. He took a degree in law but quickly forsook it for the stage when his uncle made him assistant manager for *You're in Love*. After a drama he wrote folded hastily out of town he turned his hand to musicals:

Frivolities of 1920 (8 January 1920, 44th St.), a revue of no merit, came and went quickly. During its brief stay, Henry Lewis and Irene Delroy sang and joked about celebrated sites from the old Waldorf's Peacock Alley to the sands of Araby.

As You Were (27 January 1920, Central) sent Sam Bernard (with peace once more a "German" comedian) as Wolfie Wafflestein back through the ages to prove to him that the great beauties of history were every bit as impossible as his wife. With Irene Bordoni as the wife and beauties, and Clifton Webb as all her lovers, this Paris original repeated its European success. Although it called itself a revue—

and Baral treats it as such—it had sufficient plot and consistent characterization to qualify as a musical comedy. Herman Darewski and E. Ray Goetz's tunes were unimaginative. But for 143 performances Miss Bordoni made sure you didn't notice.

A superb all-American entry competed with Herbert's *My Golden Girl* for attention. Charles Dillingham offered Anne Caldwell and Jerome Kern's **The Night Boat** (2 February 1920, Liberty), a lively romp about Bob White (John E. Hazzard), who pretends to be the captain of a Hudson River boat to Albany so that he can have a fling away from home. When Mrs. Maxim (Ada Lewis), his mother-in-law, becomes suspicious and decides to sail with him, White wangles the uniform of the captain, who luckily is named Robert White (Ernest Torrence). But his luck doesn't hold out. Some hastily contrived explanations bring a reluctant forgiving— and a promise to behave. There was as much fun in the music as in the book. The fast-stepping "Whose Baby Are You?" and the evening's hit, "Left All Alone Again Blues," topped a score filled with gay, woefully neglected melodies. Once again, as they had in *Fiddlers Three*, Louise Groody and Hal Skelly stole the show from its principals. Their infectious charm and exuberant singing and dancing, especially in a reprise of "Whose Baby Are You?," were highlights of the evening.

February's only other musical was a vanity production by Herman Timberg of his own material, unveiled on the 23rd. He called his revue **Tick-Tack-Toe** and tried to entertain with "Hoppy Poppy Girl," "Chinese-American Rag," and "Take Me Back To Philadelphia, Pa." With songs like that it was fortunate to record thirty-two performances at the tiny Princess. Actually reviews for *Tick-Tack-Toe* were not bad—the critic for the *World* professing to enjoy and understand the differences that separated the "jazz, rag and shimmy" numbers in the score. More interesting than the show itself or its notices was Timberg's determination to tour it. Theatrical economics remained such that this was not only feasible but common. After all, *Irene*, which cost $41,000 to bring in and grossed less than $20,000 a week at capacity, had paid off its entire nut and banked $20,000 surplus after just six weeks at the small Vanderbilt. It quickly sent out four more companies. There was such a demand for plays to fill houses across the country that during 1919–1920 there were still on tour two companies each of *Oh, Boy!* (20 February 1917), *Oh, Lady! Lady!!* (1 February 1918), and the previous year's disappointing *Oh,*

My Dear (27 November 1918). *Listen, Lester* (23 December 1918) continued to have three troupes dancing across the land, and Fritzi Scheff was still singing *Glorianna* (28 October 1918). These were only a few of the older vehicles still touring. But even musicals that failed on Broadway, such as *The Rose of China*, made huge profits on subsequent road tours. *Frivolities of 1920* betook itself to Philadelphia and points south after its quick demise in New York. *Gaieties of 1920, Hello Alexander, Hitchy-Koo,* and *Always You* were all listed by *Variety* as recent Broadway flops that paid off handsomely on the road. So it was not too unreasonable for Timberg to try to salvage both his investment and his good name. He hired Sophie Tucker to star and reopened in Far Rockaway on 24 April. But even the hinterlands would not buy the revue, and after a few weeks Timberg threw in the towel.

March had two new offerings. Both ran eleven weeks. The first probably deserved no more; the second surely should have enjoyed a longer stay. **Look Who's Here** (2 March 1920, 44th St.) starred Cleo Mayfield and Cecil Lean, both then at the height of their popularity. It had another tinkly Silvio Hein score and an adequate Frank Mandel libretto about a number of husbands and wives who meet at the same hotel when they are all supposed to be elsewhere. In every way it was run-of-the-mill, and Broadway treated it accordingly.

In his study of revues, Robert Baral calls **What's in a Name?** (19 March 1920, Maxine Elliott) "a brilliant gem… way ahead of its time." He adds, "This revue is credited with spearheading the parade of artistic musicals which came on Broadway right after World War I's Broadway renaissance." It is clear, however, from his discussion and from contemporary notices that what awed and moved playgoers was not the show's sketches or music but the glowingly beautiful sets and costumes of a young artist, James Reynolds. Carefully restrained color combinations, scenery projected delicately on screens, and subtle, gradual changes of sets evoked delighted bravos. Joseph Urban had a rival. The show's most famous setting—dancers in eighteenth-century clothes posing like Dresden china figurines on a gigantic music box—looks ludicrous on the show's sheet music, a parody of a girls' school amateur production. But for its time—before the more substantial sets of the cinema and television—it was a pace-setter.

A totally different sort of revue followed. **The Ed Wynn Carnival** (5 April 1920, New Amsterdam) was built around its star's talents. If the scenery and costumes were not a matter of indifference, no one lost sleep over them. The music, to use a future Wynn title, was a grab bag. Wynn wrote some of it himself; one interpolation was by George Gershwin, the rest by various hands. It was all undistinguished. Even the dancing chorus was dismissed as substandard. Wynn's unique, zany clowning—with his ridiculous clothes, preposterous inventions, and lispy, somewhat effeminate delivery—were the hilarious be-all and end-all of the evening. Wynn demonstrated an absurd lightning calculator, fouled up a violin solo, and deposited cigar ashes in the pit's piano. In their laughter most people forgot that Wynn was producing his own show because the established producing fraternity would not forgive him for being a leader in the Equity strike.

Two other musicals opened the same night as the *Carnival*. The Shuberts mounted a revival of *Florodora* at the Century, stirring enough happy memories to keep the sextette singing into the hot weather. Its statistics underscored the inflationary pattern on Broadway. The original, twenty years earlier, had grossed $10,000 a week at capacity. The revival needed over $16,000 to break even—and capacity at the large Century was $35,000. There were some complaints, notably from Alexander Woollcott in the *Times*, that the book had been unnecessarily refurbished with topical jokes and that songs not from the original, but from the musical's era, were added to supplement the original melodies. Eleanor Painter, Christie MacDonald, George Hassell, and the rising young Walter Woolf were featured.

"A comedy with music," **Three Showers** (5 April 1920, Harris), completed the evening's arrivals. William Cary Duncan's book was based on an old adage that, if you make a wish on a day with three showers, your wish will come true. Roberta Lee "Bob" White (Anna Wheaton) wishes for Peter Fitzhugh (Paul Frawley) and gets him. The show conveyed Broadway's idea of 1920 rusticity in a number that found Miss Wheaton dressed as a "farmerette" in pink-and-white checked trousers and a bright red sash, and had her pushed around the stage in a wheelbarrow. The score by two blacks, Turner Layton and Henry Creamer, was lively, but not memorable. *Three Showers* departed after six weeks.

Catherine Chisholm Cushing's *Kitty MacKaye* had been one of the hits of the 1913–1914 season. She converted it into a musical with Hugo Felix

providing the music. As **Lassie** the show came into the Nora Bayes on 6 April, giving New Yorkers four new musicals in two successive nights. The story remained the same: Kitty MacKaye (Tessa Kosta) was abandoned as a baby in Scotland in the 1840s. Now grown, she is returned to her wealthy London family. She falls in love with her half-brother (Roland Bottomley) and, knowing she cannot marry him, returns to her poor Scottish home. He comes after her, and when she discovers that as an infant she was substituted for a child who had died, they arrange to wed. Besides lauding the fine singing of the beautiful Miss Kosta, critics recommended the flowing footwork of Carl Hyson and Dorothy Dickson. For Miss Dickson, *Lassie* marked her last American appearance before sailing for London, where in the following year her interpretation of Marilyn Miller's role as *Sally* made her a reigning West End favorite. Although some critics and theatregoers considered *Lassie* one of the top musicals of the season, not enough agreed to make it a major success. It did run through the summer and attempted a post-Broadway tour but was closed when it proved "too high class for popular trade."

All the appeal and skill of Charles Dillingham and Frank Craven couldn't make a hit of **The Girl from Home** (3 May 1920, Globe), a musical version of Richard Harding Davis's *The Dictator*. Craven himself played the old William Collier role of Brook Travers, who flees New York, believing he will be arrested for punching a cab driver, and lands in mythical San Manana in time for the latest revolution. He further complicates his own life by pretending to be the American consul and calling in the American navy. In the end his boyish derring-do wins him Lucy Sheridan (Gladys Caldwell). It was precisely the sort of cracker-barrel fun Craven excelled at. One refreshing novelty was nine of its chorus girls, garbed as nuns, singing "Nine Little Missionaries." But its late arrival and another feeble Silvio Hein score deprived *The Girl from Home* of the popularity it might otherwise have won. The backstage bickering between Craven and the producer over what improvements were required hastened its closing.

On the other hand, a melodic, vivacious score augmented by a strong book and a clever production gave **Honey Girl** (3 May 1920, Cohan and Harris) a well-earned reward. Like *Lassie* and *The Girl from Home*, it used an old play for a start, in this case, Henry Blossom's *Checkers*. And like the horses and races it so amusingly dealt with, *Honey Girl* got off to an uncertain start. Originally produced as *What's the Odds* with the book adapted by Edgar Allan Woolf (who had worked on a silent movie version the same year), it was taken over by Sam Harris, who put in a new version of the book—this time by Edward Clark—and remounted and rechristened the piece. All he wisely retained was Albert Von Tilzer's marvelous score, with its less than marvelous Neville Fleeson lyrics. "Checkers" is the nickname given David Graham (Lynne Overman), a young man unable to stay away from racetracks. He falls in love with Honey Parker (Edna Bates), daughter of Parkertown's banker. But Honey's father (Dodson Mitchell) will not hear of their marrying until Checkers is worth $25,000. Checkers leaves to make his fortune, first promising Honey he will never again go near a horse race. When he spots a nag named "Honey Girl" running at odds of twenty-five to one, he pledges his fiancée's ring and puts a thousand dollars on the horse to win. Of course, the horse wins, and Checkers wins Honey. The book was exceptionally well written, and the songs, for the most part, in no way held up the action. The lovely "Close To Your Heart" was the standout, but it was by no means unique. Von Tilzer composed a fine, old-fashioned waltz, "I'm Losing My Heart To Someone"; two jaunty, up-to-the-minute fox-trots, the one appropriately exclaiming "I Love To Fox Trot," the other "Small Town Girl." As was often still the case, these two more voguish melodies were sung in the show by the principal comedienne, Honey's friend, Lucy (Louise Meyers), leaving the sweeter sentiments to the lovers. There was also an irresistible chorus number in the galloping "Racing Blues." The production was elaborate. A race was run on stage, with horses on a treadmill. For no good reason other than to insert a spectacle, a lovely Bluebird Ballet was added. *Honey Girl* ran well into the next season. Its neglect is saddening, and probably can be attributed to the small name Von Tilzer created for himself in the theatre. Interestingly, the Fleeson–Von Tilzer classic, "I'll Be With You In Apple Blossom Time," written in the same year, remains a barbershop quartet favorite.

The season's last musical comedy, **Betty Be Good** (4 May 1920, Casino) advertised itself as "a smart comedy with smart music." Unfortunately, it wasn't smart enough. Supposedly based on "a French vaudeville by Scribe," the plot seemed little more than a twist on the preceding season's *Somebody's Sweetheart*, with a hint of *Nobody Home* (20 April 1915) for good measure. Betty Lee

(Josephine Whittell), whom the title admonished without the fashionable exclamation point, is a touring actress who sublets her New York apartment to a man she doesn't know. At the Bon Ton Hotel in Lenox, Massachusetts, she meets her old flame, Sam Kirby (Frank Crumit). He is about to be married, but he lies to Betty, claiming he is merely the best man. The real best man is the unknown renter of Betty's flat, and he has given it to Sam and his bride for their honeymoon. When Betty returns unexpectedly, the inevitable musical comedy complications set in. Although Harry B. Smith was coming under increasing attack for the obsolescent "Joe Miller" joke material that he palmed off as librettos, his book of *Betty Be Good* suggested he didn't care. His lyrics were a little fresher. In "I'd Like To Take You Away" Smith tried, not successfully, to have the words of the chorus comprise a dialogue. But Smith was just as easily content to title a principal love song "Keep The Love Lamps Burning In The Windows Of Your Eyes." Hugo Riesenfeld, the composer, also tried to escape commonplace patterns in songs such as "Same Old Stars, Same Old Moon," where the show's chorus sang a counterpart to Sam's main theme. It was evident he lacked the melodic gift to create another "Simple Melody."

The **Scandals of 1920** (7 June 1920, Globe), the first of the annual revues to arrive, announced the coming of summer and closed the theatrical year. Dancing once again dominated George White's show, but this time Ann Pennington and White had Gershwin music to tap, soft-shoe, and shimmy to. The score was not strikingly good. Critics and historians have lauded "Idle Dreams," but the truth is the great Gershwin still lay ahead. One song, "Tum On And Tiss Me," points to the baby-talk craze, which seems to have been not so much an urge to revert to infantile ways as a reaction against the last generation's persistent retention of childhood themes (best exemplified by Fred Stone's appeal). Even the show's comedy routines on Prohibition (set in an airship), profiteering, and politics suggested the new decade would have a tougher outlook on things.

The old decade was patently over, and with it went several eras—a wartime era, a ragtime era, an era of easy grace and elegance. New ideas and new standards were noisily on the way. There was a new music called jazz; there was a new optimism tempered by a light, tongue-in-cheek cynicism. They would make the seemingly modern approaches and still contemporary music of the season's best shows—*Apple Blossoms, Irene, The Night Boat,* or *Honey Girl*—seem abruptly dated to faddists. Even George Gershwin's early "Swanee" would be put down as not real jazz. Nonetheless, the songs and the shows have remained viable and loved.

1920-1921

At four in the morning of 26 August 1920, Tennessee's ratification of the Nineteenth Amendment was delivered to the Secretary of State. Women would shortly have the vote. Broadway could only guess at the vast implications. Undeniably, it would bring changes, but not overnight. Certainly they would not be as rapid as the changes brought by ASCAP's and Equity's newfound strengths, both of which were bent toward immediate and meaningful theatrical reforms. Broadway's first reaction was its typical reaction to such upheavals—interpolated jokes and songs.

Broadway admittedly wasn't too concerned with social significance. Broadway was booming. New theatres were opening in every direction to offer stages for the explosion of new productions. Almost fifty new musicals vied for patronage in the 1920–1921 season, up 10 percent from the preceding year, and more than double the number presented at the beginning of the period.

The very first offering, **The Ziegfeld Follies of 1920** (22 June 1920, New Amsterdam) affirmed the forthcoming constitutional amendment would bring no swift alterations. Ziegfeld continued to "glorify" the American girl. Of course rows of ravishing young ladies were only a part of his evening. They posed and paraded before more sumptuous Joseph Urban décor, while John Steel sang top-flight Irving Berlin songs such as "Tell Me, Little Gypsy" and "The Girls Of My Dreams." Ben Ali Haggin framed the girls in a lush Venetian tableau for Victor Herbert's "The Love Boat." Harry Tierney and others contributed additional songs. For comedy, W. C. Fields (with baby-talking Ray Dooley to assist) attempted to repair "The Family Ford." Fanny Brice had three riotous showstoppers, "I'm A Vamp From East Broadway" (Berlin, with Bert Kalmar and Harry Ruby), "I Was A Florodora Baby" (Ballard MacDonald and Harry Carroll), and "I'm An Indian" (Blanche Merrill/Leo Edwards). Moran and Mack clowned in blackface, while Van and Schenck delighted with their high-styled duets. Young Jack Donahue advanced his dancing fame. Ziegfeld built the year's finale around his *Midnight*

Frolic, the cabaret-cum-revue playing upstairs on the New Amsterdam's roof.

Two more summer revues followed. **Cinderella on Broadway,** which opened on 24 June, was a typical Winter Garden show. It originally was to have been *The Passing Show of 1920.* But the Shuberts were conscious of a growing indifference to their annuals, although officially they professed fear that out-of-towners who kept the box office busy might somehow confuse the new edition with several older ones still trekking from city to city. The brothers announced their new show would be known as *Rip Van Winkle, Jr.*—a title that picked up another Winter Garden tradition. Just before the opening the title was inexplicably changed. The frame of Cinderella's search for Prince Charming demonstrated war-nurtured cynicisms had not completely routed an older, benign infantilism. Harold Atteridge continued to provide sketches and lyrics, while Al Goodman, later a distinguished orchestra leader, and Bert Grant replaced Sigmund Romberg as composer. There was less of Vienna and ragtime in their music, but it offered nothing outstanding. No then important names were in the cast, although Al Shean and Georgie Price soon became well known. Cinderella searched for her prince eight times a week until well into the fall.

Buzzin' Around (6 July 1920, Casino), a mediocre vaudeville, lingered less than three weeks. Magic acts, jugglers, a Chinese wedding spectacle, and a travesty of *The Mikado* were performed by a cast that included Elizabeth Brice and the evening's coproducer and director, Will Morrissey.

The Girl in the Spotlight (12 July 1920, Knickerbocker) was the season's first book musical. It played seven weeks. The backstage story was produced by an old theatrical hand, George Lederer, and set to music by another old hand, Victor Herbert. This time their experience failed them, even though the book by "Richard Bruce" (actually two more old hands, the Smith brothers) was competent enough. In it Frank Marvin (Ben Forbes), a composer, lives at the boardinghouse where Molly Shannon (Mary Milburn) works. Hearing him rehearse his compositions, she learns them by heart. When the leading lady of Marvin's opera refuses to perform, Molly goes on in her place. She becomes a star and Mrs. Marvin. The backstage settings led to a number of specialty turns. Hal Skelly appeared briefly as a dance director, Watchem Tripp, to perform his own eccentric routines. Johnny Dooley also displayed some fancy footwork. The last act included an elaborate garden set, supposedly a scene from the opera in which Molly sang. For Lederer, *The Girl in the Spotlight* represented the last of his nearly two-score productions that had begun with *Princess Nicotine* (24 October 1893) and included the first indisputable revue, *The Passing Show* (12 May 1894). Coincidentally, his erstwhile rival at the Casino, Rudolf Aronson, had died in February. Lederer himself survived in retirement until 1938.

If Ziegfeld could plug his *Midnight Frolics* in his *Follies*, the Shuberts could go him one better. On 12 July, the same night *The Girl in the Spotlight* premiered downtown at the old Knickerbocker, they opened two revues uptown at the Century. **The Century Revue** had a regular curtain. When it was over the audience could remain to see **The Midnight Rounders** on the theatre's roof. Like the *Midnight Frolics*, it was really a cabaret. *The Century Revue* displayed its line of beauties in bottles, while *The Midnight Rounders* showered them with roses. Many of the principals of the earlier show followed audiences upstairs: Walter Woolf, Madelon La Verre, Green and Blyer, and Vivian Oakland.

Silks and Satins (15 July 1920, Cohan) added one more revue to the growing tally. After fifty-three performances, it was also added to the season's list of failures. In that short while it offered theatregoers another rose number, took them into China, rejoiced at "That Colored Jazzboray," and made fun of *Macbeth*.

Poor Little Ritz Girl (28 July 1920, Central) was produced by Lew Fields, who in 1918–1919 had given Richard Rodgers and Lorenz Hart a chance to interpolate one song in his *A Lonely Romeo*. Now he let them write a whole score. But the youthful songwriters were stunned on attending the opening to find some of the songs weren't theirs. No one had told them eight of their numbers had been dropped during the tryout and replaced by Sigmund Romberg and Alex Gerber music. They were left to draw what consolation they could from the more discerning critics, who singled out their songs to praise. How values were changing was seen in the *Globe's* Kenneth MacGowan's saluting their work as "hard, brisk tunes." George Campbell's libretto made *Poor Little Ritz Girl* the third book show in a row about theatre people. It was a variation of *Betty Be Good's* (4 May 1920) apartment problem. Annie Farrell (Florence Webber), a chorus girl rehearsing "Poor Little Ritz Girl" at the Frivolity Theatre, subleases rich, handsome William Pembroke's Riverside Drive apartment. Pembroke (Charles Purcell), a bachelor,

had not intended for the apartment to be sublet and returns to use it himself. Annie persuades him to let her remain until the show opens. Pembroke agrees to take a room at his club until then. By opening night they have fallen in love. It was not the best of books, although it had a good cast to gloss over its weak spots. Andrew Tombes and Lulu McConnell provided many of the evening's laughs. By putting its sets on rollers and changing them rapidly in full view of the audience, *Poor Little Ritz Girl* gave the audiences a glimpse of advanced technique. The show ran 119 performances—not enough to make Rodgers and Hart the talk of the town. Five years had to pass before New Yorkers took proper notice of the talented team.

August's first entry, on the 9th, was the Hippodrome's annual spectacle. The title, **Good Times,** was again ironic in light of the economic and artistic problems just ahead. To standard Raymond Hubbell tunes, the public that flocked to the big house was whisked away to "The Valley Of Dreams," "Colorland," and "The Wedding Of The Dancing Doll." *Good Times* amassed 456 performances.

Tickle Me (17 August 1920, Selwyn) was the first of two shows presented during the season by Arthur Hammerstein that had book and lyrics by Otto Harbach, Oscar Hammerstein II, and Frank Mandel, and music by Herbert Stothart. The second, *Jimmie,* was the better of the two.

Tickle Me was a vehicle for Frank Tinney, who played the part of Frank Tinney. When the stage Tinney writes a scenario that Poisson Pictures believes to be a masterpiece, a backer is found to send the company on location in Tibet. In "The Veil Of Mystery" and "The Bower Of Temptation" all variety of musical comedy complications await the budding genius. By the time the company is homeward bound on the S. S. Tickle Me, even a love interest is happily resolved. The best of Stothart's score was "If A Wish Could Make It So." When the swirling, kicking chorus or dance specialists such as Olga and Mishka, and Frances Grant and Ted Wing, were not delaying the plot, Tinney resorted to his old practice of stopping the action to chat with his audience. His personal following helped keep *Tickle Me* running for six months.

Its tauter book and superior score should have helped **Jimmie** (17 November 1920, Apollo) match that run, but the show lasted only seventy-one performances. The best of the baby-talkers, Frances White, was the star, impersonating Jimmie, the long-lost daughter of Jacob Blum (Ben Welch).

Vincenzo Carlotti (Paul Porcasi), knowing Jimmie stands to inherit vast wealth, tries to substitute his own daughter for her, but his ruse fails. Jimmie and Jacob are reunited, and Jimmie is assured of her fortune. Meanwhile, she will more than earn her keep as a cabaret star. Stothart's score was the best he ever did for Broadway. Unfortunately, it was too little, too late. *Mary* had opened a month earlier, and the overwhelming success of "The Love Nest" momentarily stifled any chance for the show's hoped-for hit to become popular. "Cute Little Two By Four," while outclassed by Louis Hirsch's ballad, was still catchy and memorable. The lovely, wispy "Baby Dreams" also seemed a bit frayed, recalling earlier Kern pieces. But the happy-go-lucky title song and the jaunty "Rickety Crickety" both received some passing attention.

The new **Greenwich Village Follies of 1920** (30 August 1920, Greenwich Village) was quickly so much in demand it was rushed uptown. Opulent James Reynolds sets and complementary Robert Locher costumes transported audiences to fourteenth-century Russia, an Oriental perfumerie, and an Empire-style carnival. Bert Savoy, who had replaced the more subtle Julian Eltinge as New York's reigning female impersonator, swished about, spoofing the real beauties of the more traditional numbers. Phil Baker accompanied his comic monologues with his accordion playing. The songs, mostly A. Baldwin Sloane's customarily humdrum material, were handled by Frank Crumit and by Howard Marsh, who soon gained recognition in *Blossom Time* and went on to sing the leads in *The Student Prince* and *Show Boat*. *The Greenwich Village Follies* was always to have a blind spot—or a deaf ear—in the song department. But it had enough other attractions to run twenty-four weeks before touring.

August's last arrival was **The Sweetheart Shop** (31 August 1920, Knickerbocker). It had enjoyed an unprecedented engagement in Chicago. In April *Variety*'s Chicago man noted that not since *Madame Sherry* had "A musical premiere been such an instantaneous, unanimous and vigorous success." By the end of May he called the show "the biggest musical comedy money-maker in America." But on Broadway it was a seven-week failure. Anne Caldwell's book, depicting the romance of Natalie Blythe (Helen Ford) and an artist, Julian Lorimer (Joseph Lertora), was dismissed as "infantile" and Hugo Felix's score as little better. The show remains of interest because one of the Gershwin interpolations, "Waiting For

The Sun To Come Out," was the first published coupling of George's music with his brother Ira's lyrics. Still unknown and not wanting to ride George's coattails, Ira took his other brother's and his sister's first names and called himself Arthur Francis. The lines to "Waiting For The Sun To Come Out" gave no hint of the clever, manipulating word-master Ira shortly became. But George's music distinctly sounded his new note.

Born on 6 December 1896, **IRA GERSHWIN** (Israel Gershvin) was the oldest of the Gershwin children, two years older than George. The shy scholar of the family, Ira took occasional courses at City College but never earned a degree. His first piece, a satire entitled "The Shrine," was accepted by *The Smart Set*. He served a brief stint as a vaudeville critic on *The Clipper*. By this time he had turned his hand to lyrics.

Little Miss Charity (2 September 1920, Belmont) had a cute twist for the rags-to-riches theme. It made Angel Butterfield (Juanita Fletcher), its heroine, rich—so rich she advertises for help in giving away her wealth. Three shady characters—"Dickey" Foster (Frederick Raymond, Jr.), "Fingers" Clay (Frank Moulan), and Amy Shirley (Marjorie Gateson)—appear, intending to trick Angel out of her fortune. But Angel's enthusiasm for her plan to build a model village to accommodate poor rent-strikers wins them over. By reforming and by marrying Angel, "Dickey," the hero, goes from poverty to riches. Edward Clark's dialogue was on a par with his popular *Honey Girl* libretto. But the score was weak. And the cast's only two names—the fading Moulan and Miss Gateson—were not sufficient draws. *Little Miss Charity* threw in the towel after nine weeks.

Four nights later the long-heralded Efrem Zimbalist musical opened. Zimbalist, a distinguished violinist, had read Joseph Herbert's *The Scourge of the Sea*, a satire on the old Spanish romantic drama, and thought it would make an excellent operetta. The piece opened with a long, rhymed prologue, outlining the play, recited by the vagabond, El Remandodo. As the vagabond tells it, Pedro and Serafin both love Manuela. Manuela picks Pedro. But necessity drives Pedro into piracy, and Serafin uses this treacherously to win away Manuela. Pedro is caught and con-scripted as punishment while Manuela is compelled to accept Serafin. Herbert, and probably Zimbalist, did not expect the story to be taken seriously. The producers wouldn't take the text at all. Somewhere between the show's inception and the show's arrival at the Casino, they threw away the old text. Herbert produced a new libretto based on *Les Surprises de Divorce*. By the time the highminded *Scourge of the Sea* settled down on 39th Street, it had become the simpleminded **Honeydew** (6 September 1920, Casino). The basic plot told of complications that arise when the father-in-law of a newly remarried man takes the man's first wife for his own bride. Honeydew's appropriately simpleminded hero, Henry Honeydew—the name had also been used in *Miss Millions* (9 December 1919)—composes cantatas on the lovelife of insects. His father-in-law, a prominent exterminator, convinces him to turn one motif into a pop tune, "The June Bug," which can be used by termite-killers as a premium. Hal Forde clowned in the tide role. The critics praised the show, extolling Zimbalist's music. "Sunshine Of Love," a waltz, and "Drop Me A Line," a foxtrot, are good examples of Zimbalist's style. Although the show was one of the year's biggest hits, the truth is that the music was little better than the book. Had it not come to town with Zimbalist's name attached to it, critics probably would have given it far less attention and praise. Zimbalist may have realized this, or he may have been disgusted with the whole affair. Whatever his reasons, he never again wrote a score for the musical theatre. And the rumor, cur-rent at the opening of *Honeydew*, that Misha Elman would follow Kreisler and Zimbalist in writing for Broadway never materialized.

On 17 September *Variety* reported that business on the road had started off poorly. Figures all across the country were disappointing. But for the moment Broadway trade was still satisfactory.

On the 24th, putting ill feelings aside, George M. Cohan gamely announced he intended to con-tinue his revue series. Moreover, he had succeeded in reuniting Weber and Fields, and they would star in the new edition. The reunion never took place, and the new Cohan revue never went into rehearsal. Whether the falling-out of the great comedians was beyond repair will never be known. For publication, Cohan explained that he could not secure female principals of the caliber of his two old masters.

Pitter Patter (28 September 1920, Longacre) was a musical version of William Collier and Grant Stewart's 1906 *Caught in the Rain*. The musical retelling stayed fourteen weeks. As he did fourteen years before, Dick Crawford (William Kent), a dis-inherited scion, takes work as a soda jerk, falls in love with Muriel Mason (Jane Richardson), fights the villain in a downpour, and saves Mr. Mason (Hugh Chilvers) from financial ruin. The adaptation was by Will M. Hough (who had spent most of his career writing musicals for Chicago). William Friedlander did the music, and the two collaborated on the lyrics. Although most of the action took place in Colorado, one song honored "Baghdad On The Subway," but a finale moved the action to Cuba, allowing the cast occasion for "Jazzing Up In Havana."

George Le Maire lured Eddie Cantor and Bert Williams away from Ziegfeld and presented them on 29 September at the Shuberts' Winter Garden. He called his offering **Broadway Brevities of 1920**, hinting it was the beginning of yet one more series. Although he employed two of the greatest enter-tainers of the day, and the music included three George Gershwin interpolations and one Irving Berlin song, Le Maire could not quite put the thing together. Cantor and Williams helped keep the revue alive thirteen weeks. Cantor for the moment had left Ziegfeld, both still clinging bitterly to their positions about the Equity strike. Hoping to effect a reconciliation, Cantor had made a surprise appear-ance in the *Follies* during its first week, but left insist-ing Ziegfeld would not give him suitable material. In the 1919 *Follies* Cantor did a popular skit called "The Osteopath's Office." With minimal alteration it appeared in the *Brevities* as "The Dentist's Office." Ziegfeld sued and won. The sketch was dropped. Two fine Williams numbers came out of this eve-ning, "The Moon Shines On the Moonshine" (Francis De Witt/Robert Hood Bowers) and "I Want To Know Where Tosti Went (When He Said Goodbye)" (Chris Smith). No one could guess that this would be Williams's last important New York appearance. Eighteen months later he caught cold while on tour, and within a few days he was dead—only forty-nine years old.

F. Ray Comstock and Morris Gest, looking to repeat their preceding year's success of *Aphrodite*, brought **Mecca** into the Century on 4 October with elaborate fanfares. Its authors were English, and much was made of its being offered to Broadway before London saw it. It was another Arabian Nights tale, extravagantly mounted. Fokine choreographed. It pleased the Hippodrome–Radio City Music Hall mentality, and ran five months.

The Corts and Orlob having gone their separate ways, James Hanley was called in to provide the score for the Corts' next show, **Jim Jam Jems** (4 October 1920, Cort). The show's music was no better than in the earlier Cort-Orlob shows, and neither was the book. Cyrus Ward (Stanley Forde) keeps his niece, June (Ada May Weeks), carefully away from all society, but Johnny Case (Frank Fay), a newspaper reporter hoping to sniff out a scandal, takes her on the town. Luckily Cort hired a band of brilliant young comedians—Joe E. Miller, Joe E. Brown, Ned Sparks, and Fay. Together they made the book seem funnier than it was. Miss Weeks's attractive dancing also helped. *Jim Jam Jems* ran 105 performances and toured, changing its name to *Hello, Lester!* to capitalize on *Listen, Lester's* popularity.

For all the changes the war had produced there was still plenty of room for old-time innocence and humor. The frame of *Cinderella on Broadway* had suggested as much. Fred Stone proved it hands down when he came in with **Tip Top** (5 October 1920, Globe) and ran out the season. His success was all the more remarkable in view of the show's weaknesses. Anne Caldwell and R. H. Burnside's book was several notches below the material they had provided for *Jack o' Lantern* and *Chin-Chin*. It so lacked direction, the meager story line often got lost. Some critics looked on the evening as a revue. It almost was. The curtain rose on the trial of Miss Puff (Helen Rich), a cat, presided over by Judge Tiger (Oscar Ragland). Miss Puff had been a fairy, but she had been turned into a cat for failing to tie wedding knots for Alice (Gladys Caldwell) and Dick (Scott Welsh) and Jinia (Teresa Valerio) and Tip Top. Alice is the daughter of Jonas Barker (Ragland), a shopkeeper, and Dick, her boyfriend, is an employee. Jinia is the girl who sweeps the shop, while Tip Top is its not very handyman. An explosion propels Tip Top on stage. Sitting up, he notices a lady in the shop. Apologetically he explains:

Tip Top: I put in one raisin too many.
Adele: What on earth were you doing?
Tip Top: Making the hard liquor to put in the soft drink.
Adele: I'd like to know you better—Who are you?
Tip Top: I'm Tip Top.
Adele: I didn't say how are you, I said, who are you?
Tip Top: I'm Tip Top.
Adele: I'm glad you are—but what's your name?
Tip Top: Tip Top—it used to be Tipton Topping, but things go so fast nowadays, folks ain't got time to say it, so they call me Tip Top.

A shyster lawyer, I. Skinnem (Gus Minton), visits the store and informs Barker that Dick has inherited $5,000,000. The two conspire to keep Dick from learning about his wealth, concealing the letter Skinnem should have delivered. They hope to find a way to share the money themselves. But Tip Top discovers the letter and shows it to Dick. The résumé makes the plot seem more important than it effectively was. It was frequently sidetracked by the specialties of Stone and the Duncan Sisters (who portrayed the Terrible Twins, Bad and Worse). Stone disguised himself at one time or another as a fortune teller, a burglar, and a cigar store Indian. He fell off a horse and "walked" on his shoulder and ear. He also danced with tiny Violet Zell "clinging to his insteps." The Duncan Sisters sang and danced demurely, while sixteen "London Palace Girls," directed by John Tiller, displayed their precision movements. Six saxophonists known as the Brown Brothers played and clowned, with much clowning by a particularly lugubrious brother. The authors were aware how slipshod the writing was. The finale harked back to *Hello, Broadway* (25 December 1914):

Barker: What on earth have you fellows been searching for?
Sharpe: We've been looking for the plot of the show.
Smart: And we can't find a sign of it.
Dick: Here it is. (*points to Tip Top*)
Tip Top: Ain't I awful.

Another weakness was Ivan Caryll's score, which offered nothing as good as "Wait Till The Cows Come Home." Two interpolations for the Duncan Sisters enjoyed the most success—"Humming" (Louis Breau and Ray Henderson) and "Feather Your Nest" (Kendis and Brockman, and Howard Johnson).

A second Caryll score was played six nights later in **Kissing Time** (11 October 1920, Lyric). While Caryll's songs sang of "Mimi Jazz" and "Keep A Fox Trot For Me," his heart clearly belonged to an earlier day and his melodies were no longer strikingly memorable. George V. Hobart's book was based on a French-style comedy by Adolf Phillip and Edward A. Paulton. Robert Perronet (Paul Frawley) has Clarice (Edith Taliaferro) pose as his wife when his employer tells him only married men rise in business. The employer falls in love with Clarice, and so does Robert. Robert wins when it develops Clarice is the girl his family has planned for him to marry. The show ran nine weeks.

When **Mary** (18 October 1920, Knickerbocker) opened in Washington the preceding spring it had been *The House That Jack Built*. But with George M. Cohan at the helm no one was too startled by the change of title. One of the best loved and best remembered of the decade's shows, it was not as great a Broadway success as it is commonly supposed. Five of the season's musicals ran longer, including the more or less forgotten *Good Times, Honeydew*, and *Tip Top*. Undoubtedly its long pre-Broadway tour and its four road companies (one of which was on the boards before the main company reached New York) cut into sales at the Knickerbocker. But its critical reception by the New York press didn't help. The consensus was that the book bogged down too often. Though it was no leap forward in libretto writing, its central position was, luckily for the twenties, ahead of its time. The authors could not foresee the blight trailers and mobile homes would cause someday. Still, Jack Keene (Jack McGowan) is convinced he can make a fortune with Gaston Marceau's suggestion that he build "portable houses" to sell for $1,300 apiece. Madeline (Florrie Millership), a divorcée with eyes for Jack, and Tommy (Alfred Gerrard), a playboy, with eyes for Madeline, look at the model and reject it, even though they concede "That Might Have Satisfied Grandma." But Jack finds support from his mother's secretary, Mary (Janet Velie). Both recall wistfully "That Farm Out In Kansas." Tommy proposes to Madeline, promising to do "Anything You Want To Do, Dear." But Madeline is not prepared to say yes. Gaston (Charles Judels) enters. He claims to be an incorrigible womanizer, falling in love "Every Time I Meet A Lady." He, too, falls for Madeline. To get his mind off the situation, Tommy offers to teach the neighborhood girls how to "Tom Tom Toddle." When he and his companions dance off onto the veranda, Jack and Mary find themselves alone. It is obvious to everyone but Jack that Mary is in love with him. He thoughtlessly adds to her unhappiness when he caressingly details his plans for "The Love Nest" that will make him rich and fails to find room for her there. He announces he is going to Kansas to start building the houses. Six months later Mary is courted on every side, but she spurns all the young men's attentions. Finally, misinterpreting a suggestion of Mrs. Keene's, she consents to marry Gaston. Jack returns. Oil has been found on his land, and he will soon be rich. He realizes he loves Mary, but

assumes the realization has come too late. However, Mrs. Keene (Georgia Caine), who has determined to marry Gaston herself, prevails on Mary to break her engagement. Tom and Madeline, assuring everyone, "We'll Have A Wonderful Party," announce they will marry. Mary and Jack join the other couples in proclaiming, "Better than a palace with a gilded dome is a love nest you can call home." What made the show was Louis Hirsch's finest score and Cohan's staging. Anytime the book faltered Cohan sent his dancers spinning and tapping across the stage. Because of the show's long tryout its hit song, "The Love Nest," preceded it into town. By the time *Mary* opened the tune had swept the country. But it was merely the top number in a scintillating score. Legend has it the title song was meant to be the show's hit. During the tryout it was moved to several spots in an attempt to promote it. It ended, amusingly, with Mary herself singing it to the men's chorus as the plaint of a too much wooed young lady. The other songs included all the types that a 1920 musical hereafter could be expected to have and that were ridiculed so accurately years later in such musicals as *Lend an Ear* (16 December 1948) and *The Boy Friend* (30 September 1954). There was a dance number, "Tom Tom Toddle"; a chorus of celebration, "We'll Have A Wonderful Party"; an exchange of emotions, "Anything You Want To Do, Dear" (with a lyric that promised whenever Madeline is blue, Tom would feel melancholy, too; whenever she feels like feeling gay "all you have to do is say, dear, that you'd like to have me happy and snappy for you"). The show made its audiences happy for 219 performances.

Raymond Hitchcock and Julia Sanderson led the cast of **Hitchy-Koo 1920** (19 October 1920, New Amsterdam), which also included a young singer, Grace Moore. It was almost aggressively old-fashioned, extolling "the little New York we used to know." Jerome Kern's music was strangely elementary and drab. The titles gave away the mood— "Chick! Chick! Chick!," "Ding Dong It's Kissing Time," "Buggy Riding," and "The Old Town." The public applauded for two months, then the show went on the road.

Joseph Cawthorn, Edna May Oliver, Oscar Shaw, Joseph Santley, and Ivy Sawyer—an all-star lineup— couldn't save **The Half Moon** (1 November 1920, Liberty). William Le Baron's plot was almost too simple. It was riches-to-riches. Rich Henry Hobson (Cawthorn) threatens to disinherit his son, Charlie (Santley), when he falls in love with a rich, seemingly snobbish Boston Brahmin. But Miss Bolton

(Miss Sawyer) turns out not to be a snob, so papa Hobson relents. Le Baron's lyrics may have alienated an important part of the audience. For Hobson asks what the matter is with women now: "They're crazy to vote, but don't know how." Victor Jacobi's music was dull. Six weeks, and *The Half Moon* sailed away.

In one respect Hobson was wrong. Only 35 percent of the newly enfranchised women bothered to vote. Their ballots seemingly made no difference. Warren Gamaliel Harding was elected to replace Wilson with a majority of over seven million votes. His total was double that of his opponent, James Cox. One politician concluded, "It wasn't a landslide, it was an earthquake." Broadway felt a few tremors of its own. The theatre was no longer booming. On election week *Variety* recorded that some Broadway shows had begun to lower ticket prices. Nonetheless the onslaught of musicals continued.

Alice Delysia, the rage of London and Paris, brought in her Continental hit **Afgar** (8 November 1920, Central), and for five months theatregoers bought tickets to watch Miss Delysia form a union for harem odalisques and provide a husband for every girl. The European score was supplemented by James Monaco's "Caresses" and several McCarthy and Tierney tunes, the best of which was "Why Don't You?"

Jimmie, the musical by Harbach, Hammerstein, Mandel, and Stothart followed.

Impoverished British aristocrats who opened their castles to the public after World War II would sympathize with Countess Antonia–Celestina–Elizabeth–Selana–Wilhelmina of Pardove (alias Lady Billy) who poses as her gardener's son when she shows tourists her palace. John Smith (Boyd Marshall), visiting Pardove, suggests the "young man" go to America as a boy soprano. Lady Billy falls in love with Smith and takes his advice. Ultimately, she abandons her trouser role and marries John. Zelda Sears, who wrote the book, was a Jill of several trades. An actress and a director as well, she wrote a number of solidly professional librettos, but almost always to inferior music. **Lady Billy** (14 December 1920, Liberty) was no exception. Harold Levey's score was leaden. But the show's star, Mitzi, had enough following to allow the musical to run out the season.

Sally (21 December 1920, New Amsterdam), one of the most magical of all American musicals, was the year's biggest hit, running 570 performances. The *World* called it "nothing less than idealized musical comedy." The show had everything. As producer,

it had Florenz Ziegfeld, who knew "a little more than any of his competitors the secret of bringing beauty to his stage." It had Joseph Urban mountings. It had Leon Errol and Walter Catlett for comedy. It had the entrancing Marilyn Miller as Sally. (With this show she became Broadway's undisputed queen of musical comedy.) It had a fine Guy Bolton book. It had ballet music by Victor Herbert. And most of all it had an incandescent Jerome Kern score. The *Times* was not alone in suggesting Ziegfeld wanted his people to "put together a pretty little piece after the pattern and in the modest manner of 'Irene!'" They did better, though the resemblances were there. Wealthy Mrs. Ten Broek (played in the original by Ziegfeld's magnificent mannequin, Dolores) brings a group of poor girls looking for work to the Elm Tree Alley Inn in Greenwich Village. A dishwasher is needed, so Sally is selected. A fellow employee is "Connie," the exiled Duke Constantine of Czechogovinia (Errol). Blair Farquar (Irving Fisher), scion of the Long Island Farquars, arrives to book a party. He is captivated by Sally and urges her never to be dismayed but rather to "Look For The Silver Lining." Sally dances for joy, further impressing Blair and Connie. Connie, as Duke, is to attend a gala at the Farquars.' A theatrical agent, Otis Hooper (Catlett), who was to supply the principal entertainment for the soirée arrives and confesses his prima ballerina has backed out. Hooper also has noticed Sally dance and decides to pass her off as his leading lady. At the gala Sally is nervous, insisting to the guests she is just a "Wild Rose." Blair and Sally, whom Blair at first fails to recognize, recall the happiness of their first encounter, "Whip-poor-will." When she teases Blair, he angrily berates her. Thoroughly nonplused she drops her disguise. Otis, however, promptly produces a silver lining by disclosing he has arranged for Sally to dance in the *Ziegfeld Follies*. She triumphs in the Butterfly Ballet. Hooper and his girlfriend; Connie and Mrs. Ten Broek; and Sally and Blair all head for the Little Church Around the Corner for a triple nuptial.

The resemblances to *Irene* were somewhat coincidental. Wodehouse and Bolton had planned a Princess Theatre show with a working title, *The Little Thing*, about a girl who dreams of stardom as she washes dishes. Ziegfeld was quick to see the possibilities of a part for Marilyn Miller and a chance to promote the *Follies* in a musical just as he had plugged his cabaret in the *Follies*. Commitments kept Wodehouse from helping with the rewrite. Bolton did the job alone. Though Leon Errol was costarred, his part of Connie was a last-minute addition. Ziegfeld had promised George M. Cohan that Errol would be free for Cohan's revue. When Cohan's show failed to materialize, Ziegfeld, appreciating Errol's value as both a comedian and a director, had the role hastily inserted.

Curiously, much of the score, brilliant as it was, was not written for the show. Sally's opener, "You Can't Keep A Good Girl Down," and the closing "The Church Around The Corner" had been blocked out for *The Little Thing*. Two of the best songs, "Whip-poor-will" and "Look For The Silver Lining," were brought over from a fiasco called *Zip Goes a Million*. "The Lorelei" had been dropped from a Kern-Caldwell show. "Bill," discarded from *Oh, Lady! Lady!*, would have been in it if Kern had had his way, but he had to agree Miss Miller's voice could not properly project it. Of the show's better numbers, only the pulsating opening and the haunting "Wild Rose" were composed with *Sally* in mind. If Urban had little leeway with the finale at the Church Around the Corner, he could give freer rein to his imagination in designing the Elm Tree Inn, a Long Island garden, and backstage settings, while no restraints, but his good taste bridled his ideas for the Butterfly Ballet. The show was revived in 1948 at the height of Broadway's serious pretensions. Brought in as the hot weather approached, without Ziegfeld or Urban or Miller, it had no chance at all.

Nora Bayes returned to please the loyal Bayes following for three months with **Her Family Tree** (27 December 1920, Lyric). It reminded many of *As You Were* (27 January 1920). The action begins "at a party at the home of Nora Bayes, overlooking New Jersey, but not overlooking it altogether." A ouija board and a crystal ball hurtle the hostess and her guests back through the ages to see if Miss Bayes "might have been a goldfish or a bluebird, or a bluefish or a Goldberg." Knowledgeable theatregoers remembered that Miss Bayes's real name was Dora Goldberg.

Just before the year faded away, the Shuberts produced **The Passing Show of 1921** (29 December 1920, Winter Garden). They had skipped a 1920 edition—an ominous indication in itself—and then brought their customary summer attraction in at the dead of winter, a further sign all was not what it once had been for the big annuals. Little effort was made to buck the advances of the *Follies*. Instead, the 1921 edition was a throwback to the Shuberts' very first version. Willie and Eugene Howard were brought back for comedy, most of which burlesqued current Broadway offerings. Just as a good part of the 1912

version had been devoted to "The Ballet of 1830," so "Dream Fantasies" occupied much of the new edition's second act. Jean Schwartz's score was weak, but "My Sunny Tennessee" (Bert Kalmar and Harry Ruby) received some play. Although cast changes were frequent (Marie Dressier opened but did not remain long), the show was enough in demand to keep the Winter Garden lit for six months.

1921 arrived and with it the promise of the soon-to-be inaugurated Harding of a return to "normalcy." An agricultural depression had darkened 1920 for farmers, and now it was spreading throughout the whole nation. Broadway was not to like "normalcy."

But the year began pleasantly with a well-received revival of *Erminie* (10 May 1886). The old show, January's only musical, proved still viable when it opened at the Park on the 3rd. Old-timers could rejoice that Francis Wilson was still around to re-create his original role of Cadeaux, while De Wolf Hopper played Ravennes.

The Shuberts and Ziegfeld brought more cabaret entertainments to town at the beginning of February. It was soon obvious that Prohibition was hurting these roof "dinner-theatres." Their days were numbered, and the numbers were few indeed. Thanks largely to Eddie Cantor, normally a Ziegfeld star, the Shuberts had a modest success, but Ziegfeld, Urban, and a cast that included Oscar Shaw, Anna Wheaton, the Fairbanks Twins, and the pianist Edythe Baker could not make a go of their evening.

February also saw two regular musicals appear. Both were a little old-fashioned, but the more backward of the two was the more popular. Mignon Latour, **The Rose Girl** (Mabel Withee), flees to Paris to escape having to marry a plant foreman. Victor, the Marquis de la Roche (Charles Purcell), runs after her, woos her, and wins her. The music was as unoriginal and unimaginative as the plot. Nonetheless the show, which opened on the 11th, played fourteen weeks at the spanking new Ambassador Theatre, aided by the light-hearted performing of Marjorie Gateson and some light-footed gypsy dancing.

Lew Fields and Mollie King could not make a go of **Blue Eyes** (21 February 1921, Casino). The beautiful eyes belong to Dorothy Manners (Miss King), who knocks down a struggling writer, Bobby Brett (Ray Raymond), with her automobile. When she visits him while he is convalescing, they fall in love. Both pretend to high stations in life, but in the end both are content simply to have each other. As had happened with *The Rose Girl* and many other shows, the clowning of a secondary performer—this time the dependable Andrew Tombes as Bobby's studio mate—and lively dancing won many of the best notices.

Sigmund Romberg had less luck with **Love Birds** (15 March 1921, Apollo) than with *The Magic Melody* (11 November 1919). Edgar Allan Woolf's book recounted how Allene Charteris (Elizabeth Hines), forbidden to marry Hal Sterling (Barrett Greenwood), and refusing to marry her parents' selection, runs away to the Emir Duckin's Persian harem, where Hal comes to rescue her. Although Romberg again coproduced the show and assuredly picked the story himself, he received no inspiration from it. The score could have been transferred to a Winter Garden revue without anyone's noticing. The show garnered 105 performances. Its failure was the last straw for Wilner and Romberg. They had not succeeded with either Romberg's own musicals or with straight plays they had produced. For the time being Romberg was forced to swallow his pride and return to the Shubert fold as a staff writer. When the show left New York it was not sent to Cain's Warehouse; instead Pat Rooney and Marian Bent, who had played secondary roles that allowed them to bring their popular soft-shoe and light comic routines from vaudeville, bought the rights to the show, rewrote it to emphasize their parts, and toured it with a modicum of success.

The Right Girl (15 March 1921, Times Square) opened the same night as *Love Birds* and played a week less. The Right Girl was Dera Darcy (Carolyn Thomson) who loves a gilded youth, Henry Watkins (Robert Woolsey), even when he loses his money, and keeps on loving him when he becomes rich once more. The score was by Percy Wenrich, whose Broadway material never rivaled his Tin Pan Alley successes.

It's Up to You (24 March 1921, Casino) used songs by the Hippodrome's late Manuel Klein to fill out a skimpy and dull J. L. McManus score. It also used some devices *Mary* and *Blue Eyes* had employed to fill out its plot. Ned (Charles King) and Dick (Douglas Leavitt) pretend to be rich in order to win Mrs. Van Lando Hollistar's consent to marry her daughters, Harriet (Betty Pierce) and Ethel (Ruth Mary Lockwood). A wild real estate scheme makes them genuinely rich in time for the curtain. Each of the three acts was given a name—"Laying the Foundation," "Building," and "The House Warming." But audiences weren't amused. *It's Up to You* collapsed after three weeks.

Rudolf Friml had a flop with April's only musical, **June Love,** which followed *Mary* into the Knickerbocker on the 25th. June Love (Else Adler) is a pretty widow determined to make Jack Garrison (W. B. Davidson) her next husband. He thinks she is married, and only when he discovers she is not does he propose. Friml's score, about his worst, was so dreary only four songs were published.

Although the season was growing late, two more big hits were to come. On 3 May one of them was welcomed at the Cohan, Abe Erlanger's production of **Two Little Girls in Blue.** The little girls were the Sartoris twins, Dolly and Polly (played in the show by the Fairbanks Twins), who would like to sail to India to claim an inheritance. Since they have only enough money for one passage, they take turns making appearances on deck and in the public rooms. When the girls fall in love with Robert Barker (Oscar Shaw) and Jerry Lloyd (Fred Santley), the confusion is compounded, since the men, unaware they are courting twins, often pursue the wrong girl. By the end of the voyage, the girls and their men are engaged, and the extra fare taken care of. The best numbers were by Vincent Youmans, his first Broadway musical; and all the lyrics were by Ira Gershwin (still writing as Arthur Francis), his first complete show. George Gershwin had obtained jobs for both of them, and the two managed to come up with solid material, even though the director, Ned Wayburn, would only tell them the type of song he wanted with no details of how it would fit into the story. As David Ewen quotes Ira, "Obviously to Wayburn neither the play nor the numbers were the thing—only tempo mattered."

VINCENT YOUMANS was born in New York on 27 September 1898—one day after George Gershwin—into a family of well-to-do hat-store owners. Educated at private schools and given piano lessons from boyhood, he rejected an engineering career his family had planned for him and took a job on Wall Street. His nine-to-five routine permitted him to spend his evenings composing. In World War I he served at the Great Lakes Naval Station, where the bandleader encouraged the young sailor. One piece he wrote at the time was featured by John Philip Sousa.

After the war Youmans tucked it away, to use it a decade later as "Hallelujah." More than any of his contemporaries Youmans made constant reuse of a limited number of melodies. A song that failed in one show was revised for a later show. As a result, the body of published songs he left behind is startlingly small.

Two Youmans numbers were the cream of the score, "Dolly" (sung in the show by the men to whichever girl they were pursuing at the moment) and the titillating "Oh Me! Oh My!" (a duet for Robert and Dolly). Ira's lyrics, freer than his earlier material, were still not vintage Gershwin. But the music—angular, simple, repetitive phrases with changing harmonies—was pure Youmans. *Two Little Girls in Blue* played through the summer and went on tour.

All the publicity the soldier-composer Gitz Rice received during the war was little help when he and B. C. Hilliam—of *Buddies* (27 October 1919)—combined to write a score to go with Hilliam and L. A. Browne's trite book for **Princess Virtue** (4 May 1921, Central). The story described Liane Damerest's search for happiness in Paris. Liane (Tessa Kosta) finds it with Bruce Crawford (Bradford Kirkbride), her childhood sweetheart from back home. Two meager weeks was all the show managed.

Biff! Bing! Bang! (9 May 1921, Ambassador), a soldier revue that had been prepared for Canadian troops overseas, came in as part of a cross-country tour. Like every other service show before it, it leaned heavily on burlesques of army life and on routines with soldiers dressed as girls.

The same night saw **Phoebe of Quality Street** (9 May 1921, Shubert), a musical version of the James Barrie play. Barrie's charm proved elusive. The *Evening Post* lamented the musical "lacks action—and Quality." It was quickly withdrawn.

Oscar Straus's **The Last Waltz** (10 May 1921, Century) danced in with its libretto adapted to give it an American naval officer as hero. Its score assured its success. Walter Woolf and Eleanor Painter starred.

On 19 May, the Southern Light Opera Company brought its homegrown operetta version of **The Three Musketeers** to the Manhattan Opera House, where it failed to elicit any interest.

Nor was there much interest at first in **Shuffle Along** (23 May 1921, 63rd St.). The show had been put together after a chance meeting in Philadelphia by two black teams, Noble Sissle and Eubie Blake (for lyrics and music) and Flournoy Miller and Aubrey Lyles (for libretto). An angel was found and a limited amount of money made available. For costumes they purchased clothes from a folded show (*Roly-Boly Eyes*). The scenery was minimal. By hook or crook the company managed a series of one-night stands in New Jersey and Pennsylvania, always a step or two ahead of foreclosure, until it was felt the show was ready for New York. Although blacks had performed on Broadway and all-Negro shows had played in principal houses, in some respects there was more discrimination since the war. All the show could book was a dilapidated theatre, far from the main Broadway crowds. First-nighters were probably reminded by the plot of old Williams and Walker, and Cole and Johnson, shows. Steve Jenkins (Miller) and Sam Peck (Lyles), partners in a Jimtown grocery store, are rivals for the mayoralty—though each has assured the other he will be the winner's chief of police. Jenkins, helped by a sharper of a campaign manager, wins. True to his word, he appoints Peck chief of police. But Peck soon realizes he has nothing to do, and the two fall out. Their corruption and inefficiency, topped off now by their noisy squabbling, are too much even for lackadaisical Jimtown. Harry Walton (Roger Matthews) announces he is a reform candidate, and every citizen responds, "I'm Just Wild About Harry." Jenkins and Peck are given the boot. The book represented no step forward for the musical theatre, but the music certainly did. Blake's was a foot-stomping score. Its rhythms provoked an orgy of giddy dancing that had audiences shouting for more tap routines, soft-shoes, buck-and-wings, and precision numbers. The hit, of course, was "I'm Just Wild About Harry." Originally conceived as a waltz, it was much more at home as a fast-moving fox-trot. Romberg and Friml tried the same trick for several years, but so innate was the waltz to their thinking that nothing productive resulted. But for Blake the waltz was alien, and his native rhythms, just coming to be understood by the more advanced critics and public, offered the more logical frame for his melodies. Though "I'm Just Wild About Harry" alone is remembered, the score was first class all the way. Whether in a stunning, ahead-of-its-time love ballad like "Love Will Find A Way" (sung by Matthews and Lottie Gee as his girl, Jesse) or in the racy festivity of "Bandana Days" (essentially a chorus number), Blake's melodic gift and taste were unfailing. The brighter critics hailed the show, and the public slowly began to find its way uptown. Then midnight performances were added on Wednesdays. Theatre and society people caught these late shows and spread the word. Suddenly *Shuffle Along* was a smash. By the time it was through it had reached 504 performances on Broadway alone. The show launched a flock of great names—Florence Mills, Josephine Baker, Hall Johnson. Singlehandedly, *Shuffle Along* made black shows voguish, or at least acceptable. A 1951–1952 "revival" with new music and a different plot lasted half a week.

Three more revues followed. Fanchon and Marco, a dancing team, brought **Sunkist** (23 May 1921, Globe) from California. It had fun with the movies and the whole Hollywood scene, but it failed to please the public as much as it delighted the critics.

On the other hand, **Snapshots of 1921** (2 June 1921, Selwyn)—with Nora Bayes, Lew Fields, De Wolf Hopper, Lulu McConnell, and Gilda Gray—gave the public just the high-class vaudeville it sought. Songs saluted reigning hits. One proclaimed, "Every Girlie Wants To Be A Sally," while "Irene Rosensteen" noted, "My little Yiddle, Irene [doesn't] live in a palace/or wear blue gowns of Alice." E. Ray Goetz and George Gershwin combined to look back "On The Brim Of Her Old-fashioned Bonnet" and ahead with a "Futuristic Melody." A spectacle number advertised "Beautiful Feathers Make Beautiful Birds." *Snapshots* played six weeks.

The Broadway Whirl (8 June 1921, Times Square) and **The Whirl of New York** (13 June 1921, Winter Garden) were the last shows of the theatrical year. Their titles may have created some confusion, and neither show did a land-office business. *The Broadway Whirl*, a revue, had old and new favorites contributing bits and pieces. Richard Carle (no longer quite the star he once was), Blanche Ring (still big box office), and Charles Winninger (on the way up) headed the cast. Harry Tierney composed

most of the music. *The Whirl of New York* was "an expanded version" of *The Belle of New York* (28 September 1897). Expansion consisted of updating ("Sherrie's Tiffin Shop" replaced "Smyler's" just as the real Sherry's had outlasted Byler's), new interpolations by Al Goodman and Lew Pollack, and a series of vaudeville turns.

It was a memorable season.

In fact, it was a memorable seven years. While Europe warred, while old idols fell and new gods arose, Broadway danced merrily to an eloquent group of pipers. In seven years these masters of the American Musical Theatre had shaped the new American musical. It was a musical endearingly simple, honest, and direct. It told a believable story about everyday people. Its songs fitted in smoothly on stage and almost hummed themselves outside the theatre. Of course there were still composers and singers of the old arioso school. And there were still producers and directors of another old school willing to throw in anything as long as it worked—and mood and logic be hanged. But Broadway remained expansive enough to accommodate these schools as well.

Yet, without warning, something went awry. Not only had the country slipped into an economic depression, it seemed stymied emotionally and intellectually as well. "Normalcy" looked like a euphemism for stagnation. Postwar exhaustion and a concurrent ferment of changing values left audiences uncertain what to applaud. It was as if just at this point the great pipers asked to be paid in the very applause and understanding Broadway could not give. The pipers had nowhere else to ply their trade. But, unrewarded, they played an indifferent tune.

Broadway took three years to find itself, to sweep out the cobwebs and rearrange its house. Almost paralleling the Wilson and Harding administrations, seven years of feast gave way to three seasons of relative famine.

Intermission

The Cinderella Era, 1921–1924

A baffling and abrupt creative slump began at the opening of the 1921–1922 season and was over just as suddenly with the onset of the 1924–1925 theatrical year. Reasons for previous spurts of creativity and for previous declines—financial panics, booms, wars, migrations—were more or less apparent. None adequately explained these three years of treading water. World War I had receded far enough into the past not to matter any longer (though audiences had tired of war stories), and the postwar recession was not especially severe. Theatregoers remained, ethnically and socially, the same pleasure-seekers who had been lining up at box office for the last decade. Those who had abandoned live theatre for movies had done so some years back, and sound would not come to movies to lure away more patrons until the twenties were almost over. Radio, while growing rapidly, could not present similar competition, and was, in any case, more likely to take away audiences from films than from the living theatre.

An upheaval in musical fashions might be part of the explanation. Commercial ragtime was dying; commercial jazz had not yet found itself—nor, as we shall see, had most critics yet found jazz. But the musical theatre was never completely dependent on any one lyric language, so the transition could hardly have been convulsive. True, Reginald De Koven, representing more traditional composition, had died a year before, but he had long ceased to be an active or important figure. Ivan Caryll and Gustave Kerker, both written out, were to die in 1921 and 1923, respectively; while Victor Herbert, his creativity not quite exhausted, as *Orange Blossoms* was to show, would die in May 1924. Regrettably, two younger composers, Victor Jacobi and Louis Hirsch, were also dead by the time these three years had passed—Jacobi almost at the start and Hirsch two weeks before Herbert. But Jerome Kern, Irving Berlin, Rudolf Friml, and Sigmund Romberg, all in their mid-thirties to early forties, could be expected to continue providing the fine material Broadway was growing accustomed to. Best of all, exciting newcomers were appearing from every corner.

Yet something clearly went wrong. Perhaps Elizabeth Marbury had foreseen the problem in a 1917 interview. At that time she suggested that Kern, who then had five successful musicals competing against each other, would no longer be fresh or original in five or six years. Happily, Kern and other leading contemporaries had resiliencies beyond Miss Marbury's furthest hopes. But it did seem that these writers, practically to a man, had stopped to catch their breath.

The best material offered the public for the next three years would be for the most part from an occasional importation, or, more likely, from a revue—a form less dependent on sustained creativity. Since 1919 "the deluge of revues" had overwhelmed Broadway. Indeed, revues seemed all our musical stage cared about. It was, though, the last hurrah of extravagant revues.

One point ought to be made before examining these three seasons. Most critics reacted favorably to almost every musical put before them. Even Alexander Woollcott, Percy Hammond, and Alan Dale, probably the best and toughest of the lot, were easily seduced. In fact, Woollcott confessed to a double standard that judged musical offerings with a conscious leniency. Considering the tone of many reviews, there should have been more smash hits. But a close reading of these columns shows that quite often critics were careful to separate the immediate entertainment value of a piece from any lasting artistic merit. Time and again praise was actually bestowed on the interpreters or, just as often, on other ephemeral aspects of a production—scenery, costumes, or choreography.

1921-1922

Appropriately, in this last hurrah for the spectacular revue, The Ziegfeld Follies of 1921 (21 June 1921, Globe) opened the season. Many a critic, insisting the Follies were still improving every year, hailed this edition the "Best of them All." It was an expensive production—the first to cost Ziegfeld over a quarter of a million dollars. By the standards of the day, when an ordinary musical could still be sumptuously mounted for $50,000, it was a mammoth sum. But Joseph Urban's sets and the costumes of James Reynolds—new to the Follies—justified the outlay. Two stage pictures were especially praised. One portrayed a twelfth-century Persian court in which Florence O'Denishawn was seen as a dancing odalisque. For the other, the entire cast assembled at the opening of the second act to recreate the royal gardens of Versailles in all their splendor. As always, the parade of beautiful girls was enthralling and the comics (in this edition Raymond Hitchcock, W. C. Fields, Ray Dooley, and Fanny Brice) as funny as ever. Charles O'Donnell attempted to tune a recalcitrant piano. Miss Brice and Miss Dooley exchanged blows in one of the era's funnier prizefight skits. Fields introduced "The Professor," a character and a skit he would go on to develop later in vaudeville. But the comic highlight of the evening was "the Barrymores" in Camille. Since the Barrymores were busy elsewhere, their understudies assumed their roles for the entire run. Miss Brice graciously took on the title role, K'meel, "a bad woman but ... awfully good company." Hitchcock played her father, and Fields became her lover. Only in its songs did the Follies of 1921 betray any falling off of standards. Though Herbert and Friml joined Gene Buck and Dave Stamper to compose the score, the only durable numbers were two interpolations: "Second Hand Rose" (Grant Clarke/James Hanley) and the French "Mon Homme" (Channing Pollock/Maurice Yvain). Both were introduced by Fanny Brice, the latter as "My Man." Both injected a note of poignancy and suggested a facet of Miss Brice's talent not obvious before. Both, moreover, were basically intimate numbers that could have been performed to advantage in scaled-down productions at smaller theatres. It was a point not immediately understood. Unwittingly, Ziegfeld was foretelling the future.

George White's Scandals (11 July 1921, Liberty) opened less than a month later. For the second year in a row George Gershwin wrote the score. While Gershwin's unique idiom was clearly heard, none of his songs was exceptional. Nonetheless "South Sea Isles" and "Drifting Along With The Tide" were singled out for some praise. Both were optioned by Charles Cochran for London. White and agile Ann Pennington led the dancers, assisted this year by Lester Allen's clownish stepping. Comedy took a back seat to spectacle, song, and dance. Skits in the Scandals customarily were shorter and more broadly comic than those in the Follies. Some of the better 1921 sketches recounted the story of Samson and Delilah in slapstick pantomime, covered the mock divorce of Sillyman vs. Sillyman, and had fun with Trotsky's discomfort in the czarist luxury of the Winter Palace. Though the Scandals were looked on as snappier and more up-to-date than the Follies, they had yet to win the older show's extensive audience. While the Follies ran four months (and could have run longer) at the large Globe, the *Scandals* had virtually exhausted its lure when it closed at the smaller Liberty after a three-month stay.

One of the season's two hugely successful American musical comedies, **Tangerine** (9 August 1921, Casino), told of three men who have been jailed for not paying alimony. A brawl lands their friend, Dick Owens (Frank Crumit), in the same jail, where he is visited by the girl he loves, Shirley Dalton (Julia Sanderson). To aggravate a bad time for Dick, Shirley has decided not to marry him until his jailed comrades are once more happily back with their former wives. Dick transports them all to the South Sea isle of Tangerine, where an expatriate American, King Home-Brew (John E. Hazzard), rules a society in which women do all the work. The men soon rebel at sitting home, and the girls quickly appreciate the drudgery of the men's world. The marriages are mended; Dick and Shirley are united. Only the poor king is excluded from the happy ending. He loses his entire chorus line of wives.

Although the critics obviously enjoyed the evening, many of them noted it was a reversion to a far earlier kind of show. The *Globe* remarked that it "reminds you of *King Dodo* without a twinge of regret," while the *Times*, lauding the work as "high above the musical comedy average," added it "savors just a bit of the early Frank Moulan period." The book was indeed good, for it was by Guy Bolton and Philip Bartholomae, two Princess Theatre librettists in top form. There was no opening number. The curtain rose on a funny, expository jail scene, and from there on the action never faltered. The closest it came to joke-book writing was in scenes with the king. Yet even here the dialogue was appropriate and amusing:

King: [*crawling out of his hut in the morning*] All night I dreamed I was talking to my first wife.
Clarence: Oh, no, your majesty—for hours and hours you didn't utter a sound.
King: That's the time she was talking to me. Clarence how do I look?
Clarence: You look great.
King: That's strange. I feel terrible. How's the wife this morning?
Girls: Very well, thank you.
King: I see you have your new shredded wheat dresses on … . It's tough for the moths and great for the mosquitos. Does the wife kiss me this morning?
Girls: Of course we do.

King: Attention. Position. Present mouths. Osculate. That's very refreshing. Now how do I look Clarence?
Clarence: Terrible.
King: That's funny. I feel great.

Had the score been as good as the book, *Tangerine* would have been an outstanding show. The hit tune, "Sweet Lady" (an interpolation with music by David Zoob and Frank Crumit), and the best of Carlo and Sanders's regular score, "Listen To Me"—both sung by the lovers—depended heavily on successions of semitones. They were pleasant but forgettable. The rest of the tunes were, at best, tinkly.

A third revue, **The Mimic World** (15 August 1921, Century Roof), came and went quickly. The musical was one of the few during the season to receive genuinely bad notices. An ill-omened affair from its inception, it suffered a major blow when its star walked out on the opening. James Barton, then appearing in another show, was called in for double duty, a possibility since *The Mimic World* was performed after the regular theatres had let out. Heavyweight boxer Jack Dempsey's arrival just after the show started overshadowed anything on stage, and the applause was so persistent Dempsey was called before the footlights to say a few words. The rest of the evening was an anticlimax.

Sonny (16 August 1921, Cort) recited much the same story *Her Soldier Boy* (6 December 1916) had told five years earlier. A look-alike takes the place of a dead war buddy to spare the dead man's family anguish. The victim's mother (Emma Dunn) in this instance is blind, and she brings about a happy ending when she reveals the impostor as a long-lost twin brother. Both brothers were played by Ernest Glendinning except at a hospital encounter in which the dying man was so swathed in bandages a second actor could easily portray him. The show, considered by some as a sequel to *Buddies*, was poorly timed. The public had put the war out of its mind and seemed determined not to have it brought back. Even the highly praised drama *The Hero*, which opened less than a month later, had to be withdrawn for lack of patronage after eighty performances. *Sonny*'s farfetched ending, besides weakening any claim to seriousness the "melody play" may have made, undoubtedly also hurt its acceptance.

Put and Take (23 August 1921, Town Hall) was a harbinger of often hastily assembled black revues soon to be rushed into New York in *Shuffle Along*'s wake. Perhaps not coincidentally one of the work's authors (and performers) was Irving C. Miller, brother of the hit show's Flournoy. Critics had praise for several of the entertainment's comedians, but their loudest applause was for its "simple pep"—a salutation that would be echoed time and again in later notices of black song-and-dance treats. The musical ran one month.

The last August musical was the **Greenwich Village Follies.** This year it didn't play the Village at all. Instead, it opened on 31 August at the large Shubert Theatre, just off Broadway. A number of critics rued a loss of intimacy, but the show was a hit, leaving behind the series' most memorable tune, "Three O'clock In The Morning"—a waltz by an Englishwoman, Dorothy Terris, and Julian Robeldo, used as the finale. The song was first sung and then danced to in front of a simple blue set. Restrained use of color marked the evening. Robert Locher employed only black and white for a handsome number that had overtones of the decadence of Aubrey Beardsley. The number began with two performers dressed as black peacocks. Alone on the stage at first, they were soon part of an opulent art nouveau tableau. Throughout the evening Venetian blinds were used in place of stage curtains, allowing imaginative lighting effects. Much of this edition's comedy was placed in the hands of a team brought over from vaudeville, Brown and Watts. Their rowdy slapstick was at its best in "A Dying Duck in a Thunderstorm." James Watts soon disappeared from the theatrical scene, but big-mouthed Joe E. Brown went on to lifelong popularity. Ted Lewis and his small jazz band provided the music, some of which was sung by the vaudeville favorite Irene Franklin, and some by Al Herman, a blackface singer who never quite made it to the top.

The annual Hippodrome spectacle, **Get Together,** opened on 3 September with a "motion picture prelude." Significantly, the Hippodrome had been given over to motion pictures all summer. The main attraction of the evening was the dancing of ballet choreographer Fokine and his wife, Fokina. For this mounting he created an extended, serious ballet, *The Thunderbird.* Critics admired Fokine's dancing, but many felt his choreography was imitative, a pale reflection of the dynamism of his own work for Stravinsky's *The Firebird.* Another "ballet," done on ice, ended the evening. Its star was the famous skater Charlotte, who had appeared years before at the Hippodrome and whom Fred Stone had spoofed in *Jack o' Lantern* (16 October 1917). Between ballets elephants roamed the stage. Bulldogs and Jocko, the crow, did their juggling acts.

On 5 September, Henry Savage revived *The Merry Widow* (21 October 1907) at the Knickerbocker. Lydia Lipkowska and Reginald Pasch sang Sonia and Danilo, while Jefferson De Angelis provided the comedy. The opening of the original production fourteen years before had inaugurated a new chapter in the American Musical Theatre—an unhappy one for native American art. The 1921 opening came at the start of another disappointing period. But this time *The Merry Widow* was not to blame. The revival's opening passed without any extraordinary notice.

On 22 September, Broadway saw for the first time a new, exquisitely beautiful theatre, the Music Box, and the initial edition of a new revue series. **The Music Box Revue 1921–1922.** The two were the creations of Irving Berlin (working with George M. Cohan's old partner, Sam Harris). The shows were opulent, but the smallness of the house did not demand broad clowning nor strong musical projection, and so allowed for some intellectualization of the sketches and a softer-toned immediacy between singer and audience. A more relaxed, urbane style became possible. As a result the *Music Box Revues* helped build a bridge between the openhanded lavishness of the *Follies*-type revue and the more thoughtful intimacy of the revues of the thirties. Berlin's first score was good, including as it did the song that would become the series's theme, "Say It With Music." The number, given a relatively simple mounting, was sung by Wilda Bennett and Paul Frawley. On the other hand the Brox Sisters' clarion call of "Everybody Step" summoned the entire chorus to a floor-shaking stomp. This very sort of dancing and the sillier aspects of the still raging dancing craze—absurdities such as dancing marathons—were joshed when Sam Bernard and Rene Riano came front and center with "They Call It Dancing." Their contortions and pratfalls were nothing, however, compared with the knot Miss Riano twisted herself into while singing "I'm A Dumbbell." The revue cost $187,613, with much of that money lavished on three production numbers. In "Dining Out" chorus beauties appeared as the food and the place settings of a regal banquet. In "Eight Notes" eight of the loveliest ladies became the notes of the scale and accompanied Berlin himself on stage. While Miss Bennett sang "The Legend Of The Pearls," girls bedecked in radiant pearls paraded against a black velvet background. Apart from the comedy in some of the musical numbers, humor was the weak point of the evening. William Collier wandered in and out as a part-time compère noting, when laughs didn't come in expected places, that the show might have to be retitled "The Harris and Berlin Worries of 1922." A few critics singled out Florence Moore's lampoon of bedroom farces as the best skit of the evening. Since at its premiere the show ran from 8:25 to midnight, a number of the lesser comic pieces were quickly dropped. Berlin was a perfectionist. Later editions of the series would have some of the best comedy to come out of revues.

The season's biggest hit, **Blossom Time** (29 September 1921, Ambassador), was one of two shows of the theatrical year to run over 500 performances. Both were importations. *Blossom Time* purported to be a musical biography of Franz Schubert, employing the composer's melodies as the source of its songs. Originally a Viennese work with musical adaptations by Heinrich Berté, *Das Dreimäderlhaus*, it was an instant international success. London knew it as *Lilac Time*; Paris as *Chanson d'Amour*. The American version was drastically rewritten by Dorothy Donnelly and Sigmund Romberg. Romberg discarded most of Berté's adaptations, selecting different Schubert themes and reworking them more facilely and more theatrically than Berté had done with his choices. The evening's hit was "Song Of Love," taken from the *Unfinished Symphony*'s first movement. Two exceptionally fine singers, Bertram Peacock and Olga Cook, played Schubert and his beloved Mitzi. But it fell to another excellent vocalist, Howard Marsh, to stop the show with Schubert's "Serenade." Alone of the season's shows the operetta was revived and toured constantly over the next quarter of a century, in increasingly cheap productions, until "a road company of *Blossom Time*" became synonymous with the shabbiest theatrical commercialism.

The next entry, **The O'Brien Girl** (3 October 1921, Liberty), typified the hand-me-down nature of this interval's hits. It told the rags-to-riches story of Humphrey Drexel's sweet little Irish stenographer, Alice O'Brien (Elisabeth Hines), who receives an $800 windfall and decides to spend it all on one giddy vacation in the Adirondacks. Unfortunately, Mr. Drexel (Robinson Newbold) and his jealous wife (Georgia Caine) happen to be staying at the same hotel. But love, in the person of rich and handsome Larry Patten (Truman Stanley), is a hotel guest, too. By the evening's end Alice and Larry have decided the hotel might serve as well for a honeymoon as for a vacation. For the most part critics endorsed the show, though these same critics

looked back longingly to successes of preceding seasons. The plot recalled *Irene* (18 November 1919) and *Sally* (21 December 1920), while the Hirsch-Harbach-Mandel-Cohan team responsible for the evening suggested *Mary* (18 October 1920). These three musicals were mentioned not only in many reviews of *The O'Brien Girl*, but in notices of musical after musical for the next three years—notices which generally conceded the new shows were diverting but insisted they fell short of the quality that was making the older productions legends in their own day. While several critics mentioned "Learn To Smile" as the outstanding song, the consensus was that the score was not as fetching as earlier Hirsch scores. No song approached his preceding year's "Love Nest" in popularity or durability.

If Cohan and his authors failed to create another *Mary*, at least they enjoyed a modest success. Charles Dillingham was not so fortunate. For **The Love Letter** (4 October 1921, Globe), he reunited William Le Baron and Victor Jacobi, who, with Fritz Kreisler, had given him *Apple Blossoms* (7 October 1919). He also brought back one of the principals, the strong-voiced baritone, John Charles Thomas, and two young dancers who had received brilliant notices in minor roles—Fred and Adele Astaire. Though Le Baron had Molnar's *The Phantom Rival* to work from, though Dillingham bedecked the piece with sets and costumes reflecting the baroque splendor of Middle Europe, and though the critics, with the exception of the scathing *Sun*, were not unkind, the show lasted a mere four weeks. By changing the plot from the heroine's need to pick between husband and lover to a need simply to pick a husband, Le Baron may have made his tale seem trivial. Still, he was writing in an era when triviality in musicals was no offense. In his reworking, Madame Chariot (Katherine Stewart) selects a rich but unattractive man to marry her daughter, Miriam (Carolyn Thomson). Miriam takes refuge in fantasies in which her former suitor, Philip Delma (Thomas), returns to court her as a dashing soldier, a glamorous statesman, and a romantic artist. The flesh-and-blood Philip appears. He is a mundane businessman, but successful enough to permit Madame Charlot to reconsider her choice. One highly praised Joseph Urban set was a ballroom done all in maroon (as were the men's uniforms). Because the ballroom was seen in a dream, Urban subtly and humorously distorted chandeliers, chairs, and other features of the set. Possibly Jacobi's peculiar score was partly to blame for the short run. The musical's most touted number, "My Heart Beats For You," was almost an Irish air, belonging more to a Chauncey Olcott or a Cohan production than to an operetta set in Hungary. While the rest of the songs were more of the order Jacobi's admirers might expect, none proved another "You Are Free." Jacobi died a few weeks after the show folded. He was only thirty-seven years old and, like Gustav Luders before him, was said to have died from the shock of his show's failure.

Bombo disappointed no one—at least no one who knew and loved Al Jolson extravaganzas. The production, which premiered 6 October, was housed in a new theatre the Shuberts had built just below Central Park and had named for Jolson. There was the merest hint of a plot, with Jolson playing his black-face servant-boy Gus—this time as Bombo, serving none other than Christopher Columbus. The official Romberg score was unimportant. The hits were the interpolations. In *Bombo*, Jolson introduced three of his greatest songs—"April Showers" (B. G. DeSylva/Louis Silvers), "Toot, Toot, Tootsie!" (Gus Kahn, Ernie Erdman, Dan Russo), and "California, Here I Come" (DeSylva, Jolson/Joseph Meyer). These interpolations illustrate the freewheeling ways still current at the time. "California, Here I Come" was not added until the show left New York and went on tour. "April Showers," which grabbed most of the opening-night applause, was, as one critic noted, not even on the program. Another critic begrudged the expenditures the Shuberts lavished on the sets and costumes, insisting the money would have been better spent on a superior supporting cast. But he also revealed why, in a way, even sumptuous sets were unnecessary when Jolson was on stage. Jolson, he reported, "sang with his old-time knee-slapping, breast-beating, eye-rolling ardor, sang with a faith that moved mountains and audiences. You should have heard them cheer."

Love Dreams (10 October 1921, Times Square), with a book by Anne Nichols, who later in the season would find fame and wealth with *Abie's Irish Rose*, was a quick failure. It remains of interest, if at all, because it exemplifies the pitiful groping for new musical forms or new names to dress old forms in. It called itself a "Melody Drama," which the *Daily News* interpreted for its readers as "plusquam-perfect musical comedy." The *Globe* accepted only the first half of the author's new coinage, referring to it as a "melody play." The *Journal*, taking the leftover half, made it into a "musical drama." Renee d'Albret (Vera Michelena) is a musical comedy star whose notoriety is largely the work of her press agent. She allows herself her scandalous reputation because she supports an ailing sister with the extra money it brings. Renee becomes engaged to Larry Pell (Tom Powers), but gives him up when she realizes he prefers her sister. Her goodness is rewarded when Larry's brother, Dr. Duncan Pell (Orrin Johnson), cures her sister and falls in love with Renee. If the book attempted a more serious, somewhat soap opera–like story, Werner Janssen's music clearly looked backward. Today *Love Dreams* would unquestionably be labeled "operetta."

Harry Lauder, the tiny, kilted Scot, who was long conceded to be one of vaudeville's giants, was notorious for fighting for every possible penny. Apparently convinced heading his own two-a-day company would be more profitable than appearing at the Palace, all throughout the twenties he visited New York with his troupe and played at houses considerably larger than the venerated shrine of vaudeville. He starred in his own bill at the Lexington on 17 October 1921, then returned in 1922, 1924, 1926, and 1928.

Good Morning, Dearie (1 November 1921, Globe) remains, with the equally successful *Tangerine*, the best of the season's plotted shows. Its superiority to *Tangerine* lies in its lovely Jerome Kern music. Because it once more told of a modern-day Cinderella, critics were again drawn back to *Sally* and *Irene*. But so beguiling were the songs and so solid the book that the critics, this time, were kind in their comparisons. The story was not unusual. Society's Billy Van Cortlandt (Oscar Shaw) is engaged to Ruby Manners (Peggy Kurton), but he has fallen in love with a couturiere's assistant he has seen from the window of his tailor's. The girl in question, Rose-Marie (Louise Groody), had once been the pet of a crook, Chesty Costello (Harland Dixon)—an attachment she would dearly like to forget. Chesty, just out of prison, hopes to steal Mrs. Greyson Parks's jewels while Mrs. Parks is busy with a large party, but Billy and Rose-Marie foil the robbery and let Chesty escape on condition that he give up his old girl friend. Ruby finds a fiancé in Bill's cousin George (John Price Jones), leaving Billy and Rose-Marie free to head for Niagara Falls. The dialogue was probably meant to sound tough and to titillate a 1921 audience. Madame Bompard (Ada Lewis), Rose-Marie's employer, has written to warn the girl Chesty was free. Rose-Marie has misplaced the note and fears someone who knows Chesty will find it and show it to him:

Rose-Marie: Gee, remember what you wrote on it?

Mme B.: Not exactly.

Rose-Marie: You wrote "Costello's time is up and he's coming out—you oughter get a pal with weight behind his wallop to put the big brute to sleep."

Mme B.: My very words.

Rose-Marie: Gee, if Chesty ever got hold of that—I'd get a wallop with his weight behind it.

Later, when Chesty senses Rose-Marie is not happy to see him, he threatens her, "You better be glad—or you'll be sorry." What might make *Good Morning, Dearie* dated now are its racial attitudes and its often impossible lyrics. "Chink" and "Wop" are used unconcernedly throughout the dialogue. In fact, one of the directions in the typescript reads, "*Steve enters as Chink Waiter.*" Sadly, some of Kern's most engaging melodic phrases are wasted on lyrics such as "with your true love happy may you be." Only "Ka-lu-a" has remained a standard, though the two-part harmony of "Blue Danube Blues" made it a big hit in its day. But "Didn't You Believe?" (sung by Billy and the girls' chorus), Chesty and Rose-Marie's "Way Down Town," and the title song (sung by Rose-Marie and the men's chorus) have been undeservedly neglected, while "My Lady's Dress," cut, unfortunately, during tryout, would reward study as an example of Kern's musicianship.

Though Ed Wynn announced at the start of **The Perfect Fool** (7 November 1921, Cohan) that there was a plot about a newly married man who falls in love with a second woman, no one took the news seriously. It was simply one of the great Wynn-dominated revues—featuring his outlandish costumes and his absurd inventions. His master stroke this time around was a "non-eye-destroying spoon for ice tea." The spoon bent over the rim of the glass whenever the drink was raised. Wynn allowed a bit of Ziegfeld-like spectacle to entertain the audience while he changed costumes. In one scene chorus girls became typing-bars on a larger-than-life typewriter.

Ziegfeld's Midnight Frolic, with several of his *Follies* stars, came in on 17 November and kept the New Amsterdam Roof busy all winter. All during the heyday of roof gardens Ziegfeld's shows on the New Amsterdam roof were style-setters. Ziegfeld often used the entertainments to try out new performers or to allow his *Follies* stars to test fresh material. But these roof shows were more nearly vaudeville or cabaret than legitimate theatre.

Suzette (24 November 1921, Princess), a musical of no distinction whatsoever, struggled through four performances. Suzette (Marie Astrova) is a Montmartre flower girl who captivates the American millionaire Paul Huntley (James R. Marshall) and wins a proposal of marriage from him after she hastily pinch-hits for a temperamental prima donna. A somewhat ghoulish importation, the Spanish music drama **The Wildcat** (26 November 1921, Park), had only a slightly better reception, though its somber, driving plot approached the more serious musical plays of later years. A second foreign show—a revival of *The Chocolate Soldier* (13 September 1909)—followed, and closed out the year at the Century. The fine-voiced Tessa Kosta and Donald Brian starred, while Detmar Poppen provided the comedy.

Ain't It the Truth (19 December 1921, Manhattan Grand Opera), a "propaganda" musical staged by an organization called World War Veterans to broadcast their jobless plight, was given a one-week booking, sparsely attended. The former doughboys gloated that a haughty captain, who had assured them of work after the war, was run down and killed by a truck while seeking employment. The closing number had a singer pleading for any sort of work as the rest of the cast lined up behind him.

To open 1922, Tom and Will B. Johnstone continued their futile search for success with **Up in the Clouds** (9 January 1922, Lyric), a musical with a motion picture background. The Hollywood movie star Jean Jones (Grace Moore) returns east to expose J. Herbert Blake's disreputable school, which has been using her name without permission, and to encourage a war hero, Archie Dawson (Hal Van Rensselaer), with his patriotic screenwriting ambitions. Archie and Jean end by singing love duets.

The second musical of 1922 was an inferior Rudolf Friml piece, **The Blue Kitten** (13 January 1922, Selwyn). It managed a modest run. *The Blue Kitten* must have reminded many patrons of *The Little Café* (10 November 1913). It, too, was adopted from a French farce, in this case *Le Chasseur de Chez Maxim's*. In both *The Blue Kitten* and *The Little Café*, a waiter who comes into an inheritance was a central figure. The newly rich Theodore Vanderpop's problem is to make his daughter's fiancé, a former patron, believe Vanderpop is not his old waiter. As in *The Little Whopper* (13 October 1919), Friml seems to have been trying to speak with an American vocabulary. But his European accent betrayed him. Although "Cutie" and "Smoke Rings," probably the best numbers in the show, were written in 4/4 and

"Cutie" called for a "slow fox trot time," the world of the waltz was not too distant to go unheard. In this instance Friml did not even have *Whopper*'s American setting to help him. A number of fading performers—Joseph Cawthorn (Vanderpop), Lillian Lorraine—could not help, either.

Elsie Janis and Her Gang (16 January 1922, Gaiety) came in for two months as a vaudeville-cum-revue. Miss Janis had learned while entertaining troops in France that she didn't need scenery to win applause. Ahead of her time, she used only the barest drapes and props. But Alexander Woollcott in the *Times* felt she went too far. Her curtains seemed to him like old blankets Miss Janis had sewn together herself. Nonetheless the material was good, and Woollcott suggested her rendition of "Mon Homme" was the equal of Fanny Brice's singing it as "My Man." Other performers were handed equally worthy bits. Arriving as it did in the middle of the postwar recession, "The Bonus Blues" stopped the show. It was sung by a group of ex-soldiers in the waiting room of an employment office.

In their reviews of Marjolaine (24 January 1922, Broadhurst), several critics suggested that the show on which it was based, *Pomander Walk*, practically begged at its inception to be made into a musical. They lavished an intriguing amount of affection on Louis Parker's now all-but-forgotten play. The story told of Marjolaine Lachesnais's (Peggy Wood) troubled romance with Lieutenant Jack Sayle (Irving Beebe). The difficulty stems from Jack's father having jilted Marjolaine's mother years before. There is a doubly happy ending. The young lovers are united, and the parents, both widowed, resume their old romance. Unfortunately, the music was assigned to a hack, Hugo Felix, so that despite an indulgent reception and Peggy Wood's drawing power, *Marjolaine* ran only seventeen weeks. Burns Mantle, writing in the *Evening Mail*, offered an interesting sidelight. His complaint of unnecessary encores acknowledged that all the editorializing and campaigning against a surfeit of reprises were still not universally heeded.

An English revue, Pins and Needles (1 February 1922, Shubert), failed to cause a stir. But a revue conceived in Russia, revived in Paris, and brought to the 49th Street Theatre three days after *Pins and Needles* proved a sensation. It was Chauve Souris, and its "Parade Of The Wooden Soldiers" remains a delight. Because few of its performers spoke English, the show was largely a succession of beautifully staged songs and pantomimes. Its creator, spherical, sly Nikita Balieff, acted as compère, explaining in drolly

broken English whatever he thought audiences might not otherwise understand. His delightful little monologues helped propel the show to a run of over 500 performances. *Chauve Souris* was another of the faster-paced, more intimate revues sounding the death knell for the ponderous Ziegfeldian offerings. All during the 1920s it returned to Broadway in "revised" editions that nevertheless retained the best original material.

Two nights later, 6 February, The Blushing Bride and Frank Fay's Fables competed for the attention of the critics. Fay's was a revue of no special interest apart from the personalities of some of its performers—dependable old hands such as Bernard Granville and Fay himself (as droll and sly a compère as Balieff). It lasted thirty-two showings at the Park. On the other hand, *The Blushing Bride* at the Astor was generally well received and even its inferior Romberg score praised. But its plot, really an excuse for a series of specialty acts, was described by the *Tribune* as "a tinge of vaudeville, a shade of revue, a color of burlesque, a hue of musical comedy, a suggestion of concert." Lulu Love is a chorus girl turned hat-check girl at Paul Kominski's cabaret. Colley Collins, her suitor, hires himself out as a public chaperon whose presence disguises the fact that the couple he is with should not be together. Between assignments, propositions, and vaudeville turns Lulu and Colley pursue their courtship. Cecil Lean and Cleo Mayfield, always more popular on the road than in Manhattan, were the principals.

Although it was only late February, the excitement of the season was fast draining away. Nevertheless, For Goodness Sake (20 February 1922, Lyric) sent ecstatic critics running to their typewriters. Many of them found nice things to say about the show, but their joyous kudos were for the Astaires, who, according to the *Evening Telegram*, elicited "storm after storm of applause."

FRED and ADELE ASTAIRE were born in Omaha, Nebraska; Adele in 1898, Fred just under a year later on 10 May 1899. Their family name was Austerlitz. Adele was enrolled in Chambers's Dancing Academy in 1902. The family moved east and, after Fred received lessons from his sister, Fred and Adele obtained work on the Keith vaudeville circuit in 1906. A year later they enjoyed further private tutelage from Ned Wayburn. The young Astaires worked steadily in vaudeville for ten years, leaving it to make their legitimate debut in *Over the Top* (1 December 1917). Though his later solo career would make him far more famous than his sister, Fred was generally looked on as the lesser of the two during the early years of their partnership. Both had what can loosely be called "style" or "class." They danced with a remarkable grace and ease, creating routines that were not only inventive but often enhanced with a subtle wit. One of their most famous bits was first displayed in *For Goodness Sake*. For a number called "Upside Down," British-born choreographer Edward "Teddy" Royce had the Astaires run around the stage like circus horses in the ring. Fred and Adele described ever widening arcs until, before their audiences realized it, they had danced themselves off the stage. As Fred Astaire's biographer, Michael Freedland, notes, "It sounds simple, almost childish. But it established an Astaire trademark." Neither Fred nor Adele had a noteworthy voice, but both, nonetheless, could "put over" a song.

It was solely because of the Astaires that *For Goodness Sake* played fourteen weeks. Except for two pleasant, if unexceptional, George Gershwin songs, the music was as ordinary as the book. In the latter, Vivian Reynolds (Marjorie Gateson) sees her husband remove a cinder from a pretty young girl's eye. She misunderstands the action and places the worst construction on it. Vengefully, she plans a fling of her own. To win back his wife's attention, Perry Reynolds (John E. Hazzard) decides to disappear and make his disappearance seem like suicide. Vivian overhears his plot and confounds her husband with her indifference to his supposed death. By curtain time the misunderstandings are resolved. Not only are the Reynoldses hand in hand, but so are the secondary lovers, Teddy Lawrence and Susan Hayden, the parts the Astaires played.

The same night welcomed the arrival of *The French Doll* (20 February 1922, Lyceum), which A. E. Thomas derived from Paul Armont and Marcel Gerbidon's *Jeunes Filles des Palaces*. Its story recorded how Georgina (Irene Bordoni) is ordered by her family to find and marry a millionaire. She finds the millionaire, but she marries a nice, not especially wealthy, young man. Several songs were added for the petite star to warble, one of which was George Gershwin and Buddy DeSylva's "Do It Again."

Leo Fall's **The Rose of Stamboul** (7 March 1922, Century), with Romberg interpolations, had a three-month run. More than one critic compared Romberg's raggy additions and Fall's original material and asked why the new ones were included. The critical assault on inappropriate interpolations continued as unavailing as the critical attack on excessive encores. Tessa Kosta starred as a pasha's daughter in love with a poet, but ordered to marry a man whose name she does not recognize. The poet and the stranger prove one and the same.

Guy Bolton, forever fascinated with the workings of thieves, almost had a hit in **The Hotel Mouse** (13 March 1922, Shubert), adapting the story from a French farce. The thief in this instance is the gamin, baby-talking Mauricette (Frances White). When she makes the mistake of trying to rob Wally Gordon's suite, Wally (Taylor Holmes) shields her from the police, reforms her, and then marries her. The score was lame and probably responsible for the show's disappointing eleven-week run. It was Ivan Caryll's last work. He had died in November, not living to see his piece performed.

Just Because (22 March 1922, Earl Carroll) ran only half as long as *The Hotel Mouse* despite the presence in its cast of such fine talents as Frank Moulan and Queenie Smith. It described how a young lady pretends to be an orphan so that she can win a proposal of marriage from the director of an orphan asylum.

Charlotte Greenwood was even less lucky with a musical version of Charles Klein's *Maggie Pepper*. Of course, Miss Greenwood altered the character's first name to Letty. Her Letty begins life as a change clerk in Colby's department store. Letty's ambition arouses the ire of her supervisor, who fires her. Letty tells her woes to a stranger, who turns out to be Mr. Colby (Ray Raymond). He appoints her a buyer. Her success wins her a promotion and the love of Mr. Colby. The reviews, which called the show "unmusical comedy" and "nursery stuff," were among the harshest of the season. Even Miss Greenwood's eccentric, loose-jointed dances couldn't override the glaring inadequacies. Morosco quickly sent **Letty Pepper** (10 April 1922, Vanderbilt) to the safety of the hinterlands.

Make It Snappy, a Winter Garden revue starring Eddie Cantor instead of Jolson, opened 13 April and was virtually the last bright spot of the dying year. Cantor performed one of his most famous comedy parts—Max, the Tailor, a little man harassed by a customer who insists he wants a coat with a belt in the back. The belt the exasperated Cantor finally gave his customer was not the one the customer had in mind. Cantor also played a taxi driver and an all too timid candidate for the police academy. No Cantor standards emerged from the show, but his distinctive style of presenting songs—skipping back and forth, his hands gyrating, his eyes rolling—made the numbers festive if not memorable. When Cantor was off stage the vacuum was filled by a band of tumblers (Eight Blue Devils), the Cleveland Bonner Ballet, and chorus spectacles such as one with all the girls dressed to look like pink roses.

R. H. Burnside and "De Wolf Hopper's Funmakers" put together a revue they called **Some Party** (15 April 1922, Jolson's). The funmakers, both before the footlights and behind the scenes, were old-timers. The *Times* critic exaggerated only slightly when he observed, "the three leading comedians were in show business when Lillian Russell was a babe in arms." He referred to Hopper, Jefferson De Angelis, and Lew Dockstader. Silvio Hein, Percy Wenrich, and Gustave Kerker composed what new music the show required. The revue's simple mounting was a conscious protest against the increasingly elaborate spectacles cascading onto Broadway. The *Times* continued, "not in ten years has a revue been put forward in this pampered city with quite so stern and fine a Puritan disregard for mere good looks." In this sense the simple production was as avant-garde as it was retrogressive. The show advertised a "chorus of genuine debutantes," which probably meant nothing more than that most of the chorus girls were making their Broadway debuts. The revue's idea of humor was a parody of Mascagni operas, its heroine christened "Rustic Anna." This slow, gentle humor of another era was, unfortunately, no longer welcome.

Go Easy, Mabel (8 May 1922, Longacre), an amateurish botch of a musical comedy, came and disappeared in less time than *Some Party*. Its three acts unfolded the complications that ensue when Ted and Mabel Sparks (Will J. Deming and Estelle Winwood), bored with their marriage, try some extramarital flirting. Their flings convince them of the worth of their own marriage.

The last musical comedy of the season was **Red Pepper** (29 May 1922, Shubert), a McIntyre and Heath vehicle, with the two blackface comedians in their typical routines. The Red Pepper of the title was a racing horse whose career moves the action with little motivation, other than the desire for a change of scenery, from Havana to Arizona to Georgia. Following the horse, hoping to get rich quick from his winnings, are Jimpson Weed (Heath) and his hard-luck buddy, Juniper Berry (McIntyre). The show enjoyed only a modest success, but one of its appraisals contained a fascinating example of how unprepared even professional critics were for the latest changes in musical fashion. The *Post*, commenting on the show, exclaimed: "[T]here's nothing in the piece that is real music. Jazz, yes. Any amount of it, but jazz isn't music. Not by a long shot." Music or jazz, the score by Albert Gumble and Owen Murphy followed the scenery to oblivion.

The Ziegfeld Follies of 1922 (5 June 1922, New Amsterdam) opened a little earlier than customary, so that Broadway had the unusual appearance of two editions within the same season. This 1922 production is generally looked on as the last great edition, although most of the big names had left. Only Will Rogers remained, with Gilda Gray and Mary Eaton contributing their glamour. Miss Gray did her inevitable wriggling shimmy, while Miss Eaton, whom Ziegfeld hoped to groom as a second Marilyn Miller, danced more aesthetically. The spectacle was magnificent. Two of the most memorable sets were conceived for Fokine ballets. "Farlanjandio" unfolded in a Sicilian gypsy encampment; "Frolicking Gods" in a museum where Greek statues come to life. But this was the year in which Ziegfeld introduced his famous slogan, "Glorifying the American Girl," and he reserved the two most eye-filling mountings for his line of beauties. In "Lace Land" the ladies paraded before lace draperies coated with luminous paint. The first-act finale had the girls on a golden staircase, marching through golden gates. Ring Lardner was credited with the sketches and lyrics; Victor Herbert, Louis Hirsch, and Dave Stamper provided the basic score. But if any tune from the version remains popular it is the comic "Mr. Gallagher And Mr. Shean," which the clowns claimed they wrote themselves. Their brand of smiling humor is out of vogue today. For example, Shean describes a game played on the links. People knock a ball with a stick while a caddie "thinks and thinks." Shean guesses the game is croquet, but Gallagher assures him it's lawn tennis. After the second-act finale Ziegfeld introduced a novel curtain call. The curtain rose on a set simulating the New Amsterdam's stage door. The performers came past one by one waving to the audience as they seemingly left the theatre. The 1922 show ran for 541 performances, a record for the series. The run was helped slightly by a huge revamping in June of 1923, when Rogers left, while Eddie Cantor, Ilsa Marvenga, and Ann Pennington were brought in.

The popular Raymond Hitchcock, tiring of *Hitchy-Koo*, ended the season with a revue called **Pinwheel** (also called *Pinwheel Revel*). Like *Elsie Janis and Her Gang*, the show used little scenery, although this time it was attractively done. Like *Chauve Souris*, much of it was in pantomime. Surprisingly, since Hitchcock was in charge, there was little comedy in the show. It was an evening of dance, but not the ballroom-derived dancing filling most shows. The celebrated choreographer Michio Itow offered instead Japanese, Hindu, Spanish, Gypsy, and Greek dances, mostly to music of such masters as Brahms and Debussy. The little humor in the evening came from the two compères, Frank Fay and Hitchcock. *Pinwheel* (15 June 1922, Earl Carroll) was the seventeenth revue out of thirty-seven musical productions. The statistic is revealing in itself, and its represents the high-water mark in the popularity of the genre. Ephemeral revues so engulfed the year that only one below-average American book show, two at most, remain to represent the season. The next season saw a sharp drop in the proportion of revues to traditional musicals. In 1923–1924 the number rose again, but it was a last gasp.

1922-1923

Burns Mantle, in his annual year book of *Best Plays*, wrote that 1922–1923 was "the first theatrical season in a generation that has not been described as 'the worst in years.'" Of course, Mantle was speaking of the season as a whole, taking into account new American plays (*Icebound, You and I, The Fool, The Old Soak*), importations (*R.U.R., Loyalties*), revivals (*Romeo and Juliet, Hamlet*), and such special events as the Moscow Art Theatre's visit. He makes no mention of the musical scene, and for good reason. It was bleak. The 1922–1923 season conceivably represents the worst twelve months for the musical theatre in the seasons between the early teens and the middle thirties. An appallingly high number of offerings tried brazenly to cash in on the popularity of older hits, but their material was not only derivative, it was usually lackluster, often banal. Little more

than half a dozen songs from all the forty-one shows that opened during the season have survived as standards, a depressing figure in view of many great shows, before and since, that each produced four or five memorable songs. Of the major book shows, the best score was coupled with a weak libretto, while better books had pedestrian scores.

Strut Miss Lizzie (19 June 1922, Times Square) began the season. It was the first of many black revues hoping to follow in *Shuffle Along*'s glory. Its authors, Henry Creamer and Turner Layton, opened the show by phoning each other from opposite sides of the stage. What followed purported to be their affectionate recollections of gay times they had enjoyed. They joined forces at the end of the evening for a bit in the style of Van and Schenck, with composer Layton at the piano and lyricist Creamer standing alongside. The *Times* had serious reservations about the evening, concluding it was "happiest when its people sing and dance." The high-stepping dancing was described, not unkindly, as "raucous." *Strut Miss Lizzie* folded after four weeks.

The more conventional **Spice of 1922** (6 July 1922, Winter Garden) ran just over twice as long. The two shows were connected in a curious fashion. *Spice of 1922* introduced an American classic, "Way Down Yonder In New Orleans" (Henry Creamer/ Turner Layton). The song was an interpolation, used after it was discarded from the Creamer-Layton score for *Strut Miss Lizzie*. George Gershwin was also represented by a song, "Yankee Doodle Blues," with lyrics by Irving Caesar and Buddy DeSylva. One show-stopper was "An Old-Fashioned Cake Walk," with the entire ensemble dressed in bright reds. Nudity crept into the spectacle, although there was little complaint about the scene, set as it was in an artist's studio and done in silhouette. But some critics suggested the producer was testing the limits of public tolerance in the "Garden of Eden" number. The show's idea of comedy was a travesty of *Tosca*.

Sue, Dear (10 July 1922, Times Square), the season's first book musical, ran through the hot weather, only to succumb to a rash of more popular shows brought in during late August and early September. Its Cinderella plot recounted how Suzanne Milliken (Olga Steck), a salesgirl in a jewelry store, is hired to impersonate a bride who has telegraphed that she will be unable to attend her own wedding. Sue does not conquer the groom, but captivates and wins Phillip (Bradford Kirkbride), a heretofore woman-hating publisher.

A second black entry, **Plantation Revue** (17 July 1922, 48th St.), fared little better than *Strut Miss Lizzie* despite the presence in the cast of composer Shelton Brooks (who wrote no music for the piece), the captivating Florence Mills, and Will Vodery. Only a small part of the evening used plantation settings. New Orleans and New York were also depicted—as they had been in *Strut Miss Lizzie*. But the name did invite the public to another evening of spirited black dancing—buck-and-wing, lively tap routines, and cakewalks.

Guy Bolton, working with young Oscar Hammerstein II, provided the book for the "musigirl" comedy **Daffy Dill** (22 August 1922, Apollo), for which Hammerstein also supplied lyrics to the Herbert Stothart score. The show teetered dangerously on the brink of vaudeville, but its star, Frank Tinney, kept it going nine weeks. Tinney played himself, performing his standard routines in each of the twelve scenes. At one time or another he appeared as a Chinese magician, a coachman, and a black porter. Now and then he would halt the action and, with an "air of stuttering impromptu," talk to the orchestra leader. What little plot *Daffy Dill* possessed told yet another Cinderella story in which poor Lucy Brown (Irene Olsen) gains the love of rich Kenneth Hobson (Guy Robertson).

George White's Scandals of 1922 and **The Gingham Girl** opened on the same night, 28 August. Though the *Scandals* ran only eleven weeks at the Globe while *The Gingham Girl* ran out the season at the Earl Carroll, the *Scandals* was of more interest, for it had songs by George Gershwin, including his early and remarkable "I'll Build A Stairway To Paradise." The song served as the first-act finale, and White gave it a brilliant setting that presaged the art deco rage about to burst on the scene. While a Paul Whiteman orchestra played in the pit, girls dressed in black patent leather marched up a shimmering white staircase. The second act originally opened with Gershwin's *Blue Monday Blues*, a twenty-five-minute tragic jazz opera, to a text by Buddy DeSylva. Commercial considerations hustled the opera away after opening night, but it was ultimately revised and presented in concert as *135th St.* White was undoubtedly wrong to consider using the piece in a "tired-businessman's" entertainment such as *Scandals*. That he included it in the first place hints at the creative ferment on Broadway. Regrettably these daring ventures often were perceived merely as new dissonances, new stridencies. The show opened with a Garden of Eden number apparently less offensive

to critics than that in *Spice of 1922*. One can only guess at the feelings of Whiteman's fine jazz musicians as they accompanied the scene—playing "In The Shade Of The Old Apple Tree." For this edition White succeeded in luring W. C. Fields away from Ziegfeld. Fields appeared in a skit satirizing primitive radio and in a bit about baseball. He wrote the latter himself. But the consensus was that the material was far from Fields's best.

Its homey title suggests how different *The Gingham Girl* was. Once more critics were reminded of not-long-gone shows, *Irene* coming to mind most often. But if the critics had reservations, they willingly laid them aside. The *World* praised *The Gingham Girl*'s "book of simple charm," concluding it would have a long run, "if there is a place left on Broadway for a musical comedy of sweetness." There was. John Cousins (Eddie Buzzell) leaves Crossville Corners, New Hampshire, and his gingham-garbed girl, Mary Thompson (Helen Ford), to make his way in New York. Mary, afraid to lose him, follows. She sets herself up in the cookie business, and, when John tires of chasing chorus girls, she is waiting for him with a money-making enterprise. The music by Albert Von Tilzer and the lyrics by Neville Fleeson seemed inferior to their lilting *Honey Girl* work. But the hit of the score, "Just As Long As You Have Me," was bucolically appropriate, an excellent example of all but the most advanced writing of the day.

Molly Darling (1 September 1922, Liberty) just missed being a hit. It was interesting on two accounts. First, the story told of a good melody that failed to win public favor until it was played as jazz; and second, important action took place at a radio station. The new music and the new medium were becoming commonplaces, and Broadway would not ignore them, as the *Scandals* had already demonstrated. The young man who helped the heroine reap her $75,000 jackpot for her song was played by an up-and-coming dancer, Jack Donahue.

If *Molly Darling* offered a glimpse of the future, **Better Times**, an ironic title, all things considered, opened at the Hippodrome the next night to present one final souvenir of a special past. This was the eighteenth and last of the mammoth theatre's extravaganzas. Little had changed from the opening production. In one number the chorus formed a gigantic fan. Another number was done entirely in silhouette. A ballet with the huge ensemble all in white was danced against a black background. A second "ballet" was performed by twenty horses.

The elephants were back, as was Jocko, the juggling crow. The evening ended with the house's bathing beauties disappearing into its famous tank. Although *Better Times* ran as long as its predecessors, no producer could be found to continue the mountings when Charles Dillingham bowed out. Gorgeous, but inane, the Hippodrome productions were lumbering theatrical dinosaurs, whose day was coming to a close. What demand there was for such spectacles would be met by stage shows accompanying motion pictures at great movie palaces—or by movies themselves. The greatest of all these accompanying stage presentations would be offered years later by the Radio City Music Hall, a few blocks north of the Hippodrome site.

In the most blatant of all attempts to capitalize on the afterglow of recent seasons, the ever-opportunistic Shuberts presented **Sally, Irene and Mary** (4 September 1922, Casino). The show had begun life as a satirical Eddie Dowling sketch in Winter Garden vaudeville. Dowling soon expanded it and brought it back to New York as a three-and-a-half-hour mélange of satire and sentiment, mostly sentiment. Sally (Jean Brown), Irene (Kitty Flynn), and Mary (Edna Morn) are growing up in a tenement district. So is Jimmie Dugan (Dowling). They are visited by their rich landlady, Mrs. Jones (Winifred Harris), and her son Rodman (Hal Van Rensselaer). Years pass. Mary has been courted successfully by Rodman. But Jimmie Dugan is on his way up politically, and at the last moment he talks Mary into marrying him instead. They go off to be wed at the same time as Sally and Irene and their beaux. Vestiges of Dowling's original spoof remained. Irene was Irene O'Dare, and the opening tenement scene reminded many of the older show's famous set. Mary's last line was "They're waiting for us at the Little Church Around the Corner"—an unmistakable allusion to *Sally*. In between was a long-winded, humorless book interspersed with a hodgepodge of songs—including "Dear Old Gown" from *The Melting of Molly* (30 December 1918). Though critics ignored the score and some had serious reservations about the book and the casting, the public bought tickets, and the musical ran into June.

A moderately successful revue, **A Fantastic Fricasee**, opened at the Greenwich Village Theatre on 11 September, one night before the *Greenwich Village Follies* opened at the Shubert. The smallness of the Village house allowed the show to employ marionettes to good effect, notably in a scene in which Orlando Furioso slays a dragon. There was a soldier ballet a bit too reminiscent of "The Parade of the Wooden Soldiers." A number of critics singled out the lyrics of Robert Edwards and foresaw a bright future for the writer. Edwards's lyrics were indeed witty, at least as far as excerpts from reviews suggest. For example, he winked at "Greenwich Village flappers in their dirty batik wrappers," thereby putting on record how little Bohemia changes. Although Edwards did not go far, one young singer in the show did. She was Jeanette MacDonald.

Audiences arriving at the Shubert for the **Greenwich Village Follies** were confronted by a startling show curtain. The drop was painted by the distinguished American artist Reginald Marsh. A panoramic mural on canvas, it depicted dozens of Village celebrities going about their business. Knowledgeable playgoers could identify Sinclair Lewis, Eugene O'Neill, Zelda Fitzgerald, and a host of other figures, most now forgotten. One important addition was made to the series. John Murray Anderson introduced the first of the "Ballet Ballads" that would remain a feature of succeeding editions. His initial offering was based on Oscar Wilde's poem "The Nightingale and the Rose," sung to a melody by Louis Hirsch, then danced to Chopin airs. The edition also marked the return of Bert Savoy, the successor to Julian Eltinge's mantle—or stole—as Broadway's reigning female impersonator. The two men were worlds apart in style. Whereas Eltinge was elegant and discreet, Savoy swished and leered his way across a stage. Robert Baral in his history of the genre, *Revue*, contends that Mae West's exaggerated mannerisms were derived from Savoy's flamboyant technique and that her famous "Come up and see me sometime" reflects Savoy's "You musssst come over!" Savoy was abetted by his partner Jay Brennan, to whom he passed on all the latest scuttlebutt about a scandalous friend named Margie. Savoy's reign was brief. He was killed by lightning just after the show closed. When audiences were not laughing at Savoy and Brennan they would be amused by skits, such as the one parodying Eugene O'Neill's stark tragedies. John Hazzard milked laughs from a spoof of sentimental old ballads, "Goodbye To Dear Alaska." Hirsch's regular score was unexceptional. The two most popular songs of the evening were interpolations. Yvonne George offered her version of "Mon Homme" to compete with Fanny Brice's "My Man" and Elsie Janis's rendition of the original, while Ted Lewis and his band made a small hit out of "Georgette" (Lew Brown/Ray Henderson).

Orange Blossoms, the last Victor Herbert show done in his lifetime, opened on 19 September at the Fulton. The libretto was by Fred de Gresac (Mrs. Victor Maurel), one of Herbert's favorite collaborators, and was based on the play *La Passerelle*, which she had coauthored. Her plot was a variant of *Betsy* (11 December 1911) and Victor Herbert's *The Duchess* (16 October 1911). In de Gresac's story, Kitty agrees to marry and divorce Baron Roger Belmont in order to override a clause in his aunt's will which disinherits him if he first marries a Brazilian dancer, Helene de Vasquez. Kitty makes the marriage so pleasant the Baron decides to forget about the dancer. It was not one of Herbert's best scores. Some of the songs—"The Lonely Nest," "A Dream Of Orange Blossoms"—appeared to be waltz themes wrenched into 4/4 time. Herbert had the same problem that Rudolf Friml had. How Herbert resolved it was seen after his death in his music for *The Dream Girl* (20 August 1924). But with "A Kiss In The Dark" he left behind one final waltz classic. The song was sung in the show by Kitty, not to Roger, but to her handsome godfather, Brossac, the lawyer responsible for the arrangement between Kitty and the Baron. The original Irene, Edith Day, starred as Kitty. Her husband, Pat Somerset, played Brossac, while Robert Michaels was Roger.

The next night **The Passing Show of 1922** came to the Winter Garden, its gift to posterity one Gus Kahn–Walter Donaldson interpolation, "Carolina In The Morning." The song was introduced by the Howard Brothers, who also sang "My Coal Black Mammy." Fred Allen was a newcomer to the series. His dry humor and gravelly voice were displayed in an extended monologue, "The Old Joke Cemetery." Ethel Shutta brought down the house in a musical spoof of Eugene O'Neill's *The Hairy Ape*.

Emmerich Kalman's lovely *Die Bajadere* was brought to New York as **The Yankee Princess** (2 October 1922, Knickerbocker) and failed despite the presence of Vivienne Segal in the title role of the American actress who wins the love of an Indian rajah. But on the same night, another importation was a solid hit at the Ambassador. **The Lady in Ermine** had American interpolations by Al Goodman and one number, the show's hit, "When Hearts Are Young," by Sigmund Romberg. The story told of a conqueror (Walter Woolf) conquered by the lady (Wilda Bennett) of the castle in which he is billeted. Three nights later a Russian vaudeville called **Revue Russe** came into the Booth. Unfavorably compared to *Chauve Souris*, it beat a hasty retreat.

A vehicle for Nora Bayes called **Queen o'Hearts** (10 October 1922, Cohan) allowed the youthful Oscar Hammerstein II to continue his apprenticeship. Miss Bayes played Elizabeth Bennett, the head of a matrimonial agency, whose efforts to marry off her sister nearly come to nothing when the drunken antics of a friend's husband are misconstrued by the sister's suitor. While Lewis Gensler wrote the body of the score, Miss Bayes followed her customary practice of interpolating a number of other songs, some of which she wrote herself. The *Times* review is indicative of the tolerance of the day. Though the critic saw it as "a thoroughly conventional musical comedy, equipped with a story whose complications manage to be even sillier than those things usually are," he nonetheless recommended the show as enjoyable. The public didn't concur. Thirty-nine performances were all Miss Bayes could achieve.

The second edition of **The Music Box Revue 1922–1923** (23 October 1922, Music Box) came next, bringing with it a pair of riotous comedians all but new to Broadway, Clark and McCullough. Abetting Clark and McCullough in dispensing the evening's nonsense was wide-eyed, long-legged Charlotte Greenwood. The best comic bit of the evening fell to her. This was a humorous staging of Berlin's "Pack Up Your Sins (And Go To The Devil)" with Miss Greenwood in the devil's scarlet sending jazz musicians of the moment to their just damnation. Performers impersonating Gilda Gray, Ted Lewis, and others were hurtled into a steaming abyss. The greatest of the revue tenors, Irish-brogued John Steel, was given the hit of the evening—the song that for years afterwards Irving Berlin insisted was his personal favorite, "Lady Of The Evening." Steel sang the song in front of a simple setting of moonlit rooftops. The show's spectacle numbers were superb, if not always original. Twice in one evening the show used a similar device: In "Diamond Horseshoe" the train of Grace LaRue's Thais costume grew until it covered the stage, and as Miss LaRue sang "Crinoline Days," a stage elevator rifted her higher and higher, while her hoop-skirt extended until it almost touched both sides of the proscenium. Hassard Short's setting for "Porcelain Maid" was perhaps more dazzlingly lavish than delicate, but his finale was more dazzling yet. Done all in gold, it played upon the audience's perception of depth. Each time it seemed the rear wall of the stage had been reached another curtain parted to reveal more people and more of the set.

BOBBY CLARK was born in the rectory of the First Episcopal Church of Springfield, Ohio, on 16 July 1888. His grandfather was the church's sexton, and Clark's first public performances were as a member of the church choir. At the age of four he met a neighbor, eight-year-old PAUL McCULLOUGH, and the two began a friendship and partnership that endured until McCullough's suicide. The boys taught themselves tumbling and bugling, and McCullough later often used a toy bugle as part of their routine. They toured as a teenage minstrel act, switching briefly to circus clowning after their minstrel show folded and stranded them in Florida. In 1912 they entered vaudeville. They made a very brief, largely ignored, debut on Broadway in 1919 when Peek-A-Boo was rushed in from a burlesque circuit during the actors' strike. Three years later they made their legitimate debut in a London revue, Chuckles of 1922. When it closed they came back to America to appear in the Music Box entertainment McCullough, slightly taller than Clark, mustached, and pudgy-faced, was the stooge of the act, who vacillated between childish glee and puerile pouting. The livelier Clark scampered across the stage wearing a passionate leer and painted-on eyeglasses, his hands forever occupied with his stubby cane and his usually burnt-out cigar.

Springtime of Youth (26 October 1922, Broadhurst), adapted from the German, was October's last entry. Its story was the Enoch Arden legend. In this version, set in 1812 New Hampshire, Arden was called Roger Hathaway (George MacFarlane), and the heroine, Priscilla Alden (Olga Steck). In his autobiography Harry B. Smith claimed credit for the adaptation, although the program and sheet music omitted his name. He wrote: "The most remarkable thing about this operetta was that the critics urged the public to hear it and the public obstinately refused to take the expert advice." Smith missed the point that the growing trend to reset European musicals in American surroundings often created absurd inconsistencies of tone. In this case, imagine an 1812 New Englander singing florid Viennese waltzes. Sometimes the public was

apparently more sensitive to such incongruities than were the critics.

Up She Goes (6 November 1922, Playhouse) was hailed as a delight, and this time the public did respond. The Telegram rejoiced, "One of the best musical shows seen in this city in many moons," and to drive its point home continued, "It is better than Irene." Since the songs were by Irene's Joseph McCarthy and Harry Tierney, the comparison was not farfetched. But the music, while pleasant, had no standouts. At best, "Journey's End" was hummable in the "Love Nest"–"Cottage Small" tradition. The book was better. Frank Craven adapted it from his own Too Many Cooks, and it still reads entertainingly. Of course, Craven's Cooks were not chefs but members of the Cook family, whose unsolicited visits and advice nearly wreck the plans Alice Cook (Gloria Foy) and Albert Bennett (Donald Brian) have to marry and to build a bungalow. Playgoers watched as act by act the house took shape.

One of the season's saddest and most instructive failures opened on 7 November, the night after Up She Goes. Though it played the minuscule Punch and Judy Theatre, The 49ers survived only two weeks. Its title stemmed not from its authors' expectations of striking gold, but simply from the fact that the theatre was on 49th Street. The authors, all on their way to renown, were largely from the Algonquin's Round Table. George S. Kaufman and Marc Connelly were apparently the prime movers, with Ring Lardner, Heywood Broun, Franklin P. Adams, and Robert Benchley assisting. What they attempted was a revue that eschewed spectacle and vaudeville vulgarity. Some of the best of the old burlesque tradition was kept, though the evening was more intimate, more literate, and more bitingly witty. Benchley and Dorothy Parker ridiculed fustian historical dramas. Their imaginary playwright got some chronology confused, forcing Richelieu, Queen Victoria, and Robert E. Lee to mix uncomfortably. Kaufman constructed a glimpse of American home life with dialogue borrowed almost entirely from advertising slogans of the day. Broun rewrote Hans Christian Andersen's "The King's New Suit of Clothes," giving it a Pirandello-ish bent by suggesting pretense becomes reality. When the royal tailor is exposed and condemned, he hangs himself with an invisible sash. Adams's contribution turned the routine of business into a musical comedy—product loses customer, product wins customer. "The Love Call" ridiculed contemporary operettas. As Burns Mantle noted, "the multitude sniffed and would have none of it." *The 49ers* went the way of *Blue Monday Blues,* without the consolation of revival.

If these up-and-coming writers were too advanced for their public, one old-timer was not. George M. Cohan saw his **Little Nellie Kelly** (13 November 1922, Liberty) run out the season. The critics, though they couldn't agree on what made the play entertaining, agreed it was an evening well spent. Cohan told another of the homey Irish stories he had come to depend on, this time coupled with a satire on the mystery plays so popular at the moment. Nellie (Elizabeth Hines), daughter of Police Captain Kelly (Arthur Deagon), works at Devere's Department Store. To court her, the wealthy Jack Lloyd (Barrett Greenwood) throws a party for all the Devere girls at his aunt's mansion. Jerry Conroy (Charles King), another suitor, crashes the party; and when the aunt's jewels disappear, he is suspected. Eventually he is cleared, and Nellie decides she prefers his simple, wisecracking Irish ways to Jack's world. In the glittering twenties, when prosperity made material acquisitions more readily obtainable and clever advertising made them universally desired, Cohan often held to the earlier American dream that love outweighed riches. Curiously, the same philosophy would seem to apply at the close of Eddie Dowling's *Sally, Irene and Mary*—a departure from the ending of all three shows he was spoofing. Writing, as both Irishmen were, for heavily Irish or working-class audiences, they were undoubtedly responding to some hard-nosed inner reality these playgoers retained. But Cohan's dialogue was spunky, and his music, while not up to the best of his early masterpieces, was better than anything he had done in years. The song "Nellie Kelly, I Love You" came near to becoming standard, and "You Remind Me Of My Mother" is still sung occasionally.

In **Liza** (27 November 1922, Daly's) the critics discovered what many felt was a worthwhile successor to *Shuffle Along* (23 May 1921). Audiences were transported back to Jimtown, where an effort is being made to erect a monument to the town's deceased mayor. The town's dandies grow rich pocketing the funds. There was much praise for Maceo Pinkard's music. But, as had become the custom in reviewing black shows, the highest praise was reserved for the dancing. Words like "joyous," "zesty," "vital" filled the morning-after columns. Yet *Liza,* while enjoying a twenty-one-week run, never approached *Shuffle Along*'s raging popularity, and Pinkard's score is totally forgotten. For all his luck

outside the theatre—and he composed such standards as "Sweet Georgia Brown"—Pinkard never found success on Broadway.

The night after *Liza* opened uptown, **The Bunch and Judy** arrived at the Globe in the heart of Times Square. With the freshly acclaimed Astaires, now virtual stars, singing and dancing Jerome Kern's latest score, the run of only sixty-three performances was plainly disappointing. But Kern's lovely score contained no exceptional melody, and the book was a mess. The *Call* looked on the show simply as a "succession of variety acts." The *Times* complained, "Caldwell's play attempts nothing like [a plot]," and rationalized, "It is the scenario of the scheme—stage, moorland and cabaret." What little plot there was told of a musical comedy star who deserts the stage to marry a Scottish lord, curiously foreshadowing Adele Astaire's own decision ten years later. But in the case of Judy Jordan, she is snubbed by Lord Kinlock's friends and returns to America to make a happier second marriage with her former leading man, Gerald Lane.

Gershwin's name appeared briefly on the programs of the Bayes Theatre, where **Our Nell** (4 December 1922, Bayes), a burlesque its creators referred to as a "musical mellowdrayma," languished for five weeks. Its plot had Nell pursued by a city slicker and saved by a wholesome country boy.

The Clinging Vine was Henry Savage's Christmas gift to Broadway at the Knickerbocker. It probably would have been received more gratefully if its score had been as good as its Zelda Sears's book. The *Times* extolled it for "a novel plot and a most appealing character," and the *American,* calling it "a capital story," felt it exemplified the best in "musical comedy—or, if you prefer it, the play with music which should be rational, humorous, simple and, if possible witty... . It should be of today and the more so the better." The show related the adventures of Antoinette Allen, a young lady who runs the family paint business in Omaha. When she visits her Connecticut grandmother, the old woman forces her to play "the clinging vine" to win a husband. She not only wins a slew of suitors, but she bests them in a real estate deal. Then she announces she has had a fiancé waiting for her back home all the while and, money in hand, leaves for Omaha. With Peggy Wood as Antoinette, the show ran nearly six months despite its weak score.

Glory (25 December 1922, Vanderbilt), a James Montgomery musical comedy for which his old *Irene* partners, Joseph McCarthy and Harry Tierney, were called in to provide part of the score, was a quick failure. The "Glory" of the title was another young lady (Patti Harrold) who goes from rags to riches. She is the daughter of the village ne'er-do-well, Abner Moore (Peter Lang). When William Harriman (Walter Regan), a villager who has made good in the big town, returns for a visit he falls in love with Glory, helps her win a popularity contest, and marries her. Some of the critics, tiring of the theme even faster than the public, were abrasive in their inevitable comparisons.

Lady Butterfly (22 January 1923, Globe) used the old device of a luggage mix-up for its thin plot. Albert Hopper, a clownish wastrel, discovering he has mistakenly acquired the suitcase and papers of Enid Crawford's expected groom, decides to pretend he is the partner-to-be, whom Enid has never seen. Florenz Ames and Marjorie Gateson, two excellent performers, headed the cast. Werner Janssen wrote the score. However, most critics passed over the book and music, viewing the evening as a dancing show, praising soft-shoe and ballroom routines as well as some comic tap-dancing. They felt much the same way about a more appropriately titled piece, The Dancing Girl. The musical, which premiered on 24 January, was a typical Winter Garden revue, strung together with a vestigal plot of a ship-to-shore romance in which first-class passenger Bruce Chattfield falls in love with a steerage-class dancer, Anna. The evening's best dancing was provided by Trini, with her heel-clicking Spanish numbers. But the variety of passengers allowed almost any sort of vaudeville to be inserted. Benny Leonard, a real boxing champion, fought mock bouts, while Marie Dressler came on late in the evening to twit the season's biggest straight-play hit, the Somerset Maugham story that John Colton and Clemence Randolph had turned into Rain. Both shows found audiences, and both chalked up three-month runs.

Caroline (31 January 1923, Ambassador), the melodic Kunneke operetta Der Vetter aus Dingsda, was reset in Civil War Virginia for American theatre-goers and had a fair stay with Tessa Kosta in the title role, while an inept Sun Showers (5 February 1923, Astor) managed five weeks. Its plot pictured the attempt by a poet and a prizefighter to help a band of schoolteachers win a raise. The "Sun Showers" of the title was the name of one of the poet's works.

The Evening Mail, singing a now familiar refrain, lamented the season's biggest hit, Wildflower (7 February 1923, Casino), was not as good as Irene (18 November 1919). The Times man regretted

the book was "never funny, and now and then a little dull," but he lost his head over the music and approached good old-fashioned raving. "The most tuneful score that Rudolf Friml has written," he began, following with a whole paragraph of ardent praise in which "Bambalina" was singled out. He opened his next paragraph reiterating his kudos for Friml. His embarrassment must have been acute when he learned Friml wrote not one note of the score. The error was not entirely absurd. Half the music was written by Herbert Stothart, who had worked with Friml and whose compositions had an operetta-ish flavor. Furthermore, "Bambalina" could remind a hearer of, say, "Something Seems Tingle-Ingleing." In his study of our popular songs, Alec Wilder argues it has no distinctively American sound to it.

In any case, it was the songs by the composer of "Bambalina," Vincent Youmans, that made the show and established him as a major figure. The promise of Two Little Girls in Blue (3 May 1921) was fulfilled, and his simple linear phrasing with changing harmony became a rapidly identifiable musical trademark. The critics who lambasted the libretto were not unjust. Though the experienced Otto Harbach worked with the increasingly active Oscar Hammerstein on it, it was a lamebrain affair—the sort that continued to give musical comedy books a bad name for years to come. Fiery Nina Benedetto (Edith Day) is willed a small fortune, provided she can keep her temper for six months. In spite of all sorts of nasty provocations from her cousin Bianca (Evelyn Cavanaugh), she succeeds, winning not only her inheritance but her lover Guido (Guy Robertson) as well. Several years after the show closed, Hammerstein attempted to rationalize the use of the story. His rationalization was not especially convincing, but it did suggest that, regardless of the name Hammerstein would give to his style of writing, he was, at heart, a fabricator of operetta. Hammerstein wrote, "Wildflower was a 'feeler,' a timid attempt to bring back the operetta, but still keeping enough of Cinderella and her dancing chorus to compromise with the public who demanded those elements." Hammerstein wrote these words after the opening of Rose-Marie (2 September 1924). By that time he was already searching for a term to replace the unstylish "operetta." He decided on "musical play," a name often employed for operettas ashamed of their genre. For Edith Day, Wildflower was her last major Broadway appearance. She left to become one of London's favorite musical stars.

Go-Go (12 March 1923, Daly's), a musical comedy based on a confusion of twins, had a competent book and a competent score, with one slightly better than average number, "Rosetime And You." The twins are Isabel and Florabell Parker (both played by Josephine Stevens). During the war Jack Locksmith (Bernard Granville) met Isabel, who was a nurse in France. Setting out to find her again, Jack stumbles on Florence, a singer at "The Pink Poodle." But Isabel turns up in time for a happy ending. It was another in the line of solid but undistinguished shows that John Cort kept giving New York, of which Listen, Lester (23 December 1918) remained the best received.

Jack and Jill (22 March 1923, Globe) was another revue with musical comedy pretensions. The nouveau-riche Mrs. Malone (Georgia O'Ramey) buys a chair made of wood from the cherry tree George Washington chopped down. Anyone sitting in the chair is compelled to tell the truth. The confessions help Jill Malone (Virginia O'Brien) win Jack Andrews (Donald MacDonald) rather than the man her mother would have her marry, Jimmy Eustace. The show came in with the spring and lasted out the season thanks largely to the dancing of stylish Clifton Webb as Jimmy and the more unrestrained Ann Pennington as Jimmy's "pal," Gloria Wayne.

Neither Carlo and Sanders (of Tangerine) nor Sissle and Blake (of Shuffle Along) could save Elsie (2 April 1923, Vanderbilt). And Friml, who really did write this score, could do no more the next night for Cinders (3 April 1923, Dresden). Both shows employed the period's favorite story. Elsie unfolded the trials of a young actress in winning the acceptance of Harry Hammond's rich, snobbish family. Their ideas are far behind the times, and they do not take easily to a girl or her friends who proclaim "Everybody's Struttin' Now" and who are thrilled by "Thunderstorm Jazz." The plot was loose enough to allow for a number of vaudeville specialties. Harry was portrayed by Vinton Freedley, who soon found more congenial employment as one of Broadway's leading producers. Cinders, as its title suggests, took the obvious course in this era of rags-to-riches plots by simply retelling the Cinderella story in a modern setting. Cinders (Nancy Welford) is a waif who was discovered in an ash can and who has grown up dreaming of being a jazz-age Cinderella. Assigned to deliver a gown to a rich Mrs. Horatio Winthrop, she appropriates the dress and takes herself to a charity ball. There she meets Mrs. Winthrop's son, John (Walter Regan), and the two fall in love. Cinders is accused of stealing jewels at the party, but clears herself in time for a happy finale.

The critics simply shrugged their shoulders at How Come? (16 April 1923, Apollo). Another attempt at copying Shuffle Along (23 May 1921), it was billed as "a girly musical darkomedy." Its high-stepping black dancing was tied together with a shoestring plot in which Rastus Skunton Lime (Eddie Hunter) endeavors to embezzle funds from the Mobile Chicken Trust Corporation. The evening's best comic scene was Rastus's attempted jail break. Concluding subtlety would fail, he makes his attempt as noisy and visible as possible, only to discover the jailer is deaf and virtually blind.

Dew Drop Inn (17 May 1923, Astor), with Friml interpolations, was praised largely for James Barton's clowning, including Barton's famous drunk act. A tenuous plot revolved around a young heir's determination to make good on his own and on his fiancée's refusal to leave him for a bribe of $20,000.

Adrienne (28 May 1923, Cohan) similarly had to rely on its principals to overcome an undistinguished Albert Von Tilzer score and a plot that harked back to Marie Cahill's heyday. It used the perennially popular motif of a jewel robbery, or at least an attempted theft, as the basis for its story. Adrienne Grey believes in reincarnation. A band of jewel thieves persuades her to wear her precious stones and they lure her to a temple with the story that she will meet the spirit of a prince who loved her in a former life. Her present-day lover gets wind of the plot and helps foil the gang. Vivienne Segal played the title role, while Billy B. Van and Marie Cahill's onetime costar, Richard Carle, led the comedians.

Just as booking quirks in 1921–1922 produced two editions of the Ziegfeld Follies in one season, 1922–1923 presented two Passing Shows. The 1923 edition, which opened at the Winter Garden on 14 June, betrayed a distressing slippage in quality: no good songs and feeble comedy. These weaknesses were doubly sad because the handsome, full-voiced Walter Woolf was on hand to sing and young George Jessel replaced the Howards as master of comedy. Jessel wrote his own monologues and a skit, "Upper Box at a French Comedy." Spectacle and largely undressed girls were all that maintained the old standards. In one scene three gigantic chandeliers were formed by the ladies of the chorus. The girls also came on stage in costumes suggesting the popular bestsellers of the day, two of which were The Beautiful and Damned and just plain Damned. The show ended the season on an appropriately commonplace note.

The big revue made a comeback in 1923–1924. Twelve of the season's first nineteen musical offerings were revues of one sort or another, and, somewhat surprisingly, eight achieved some degree of success. Of course, four were time-tested series that now claimed a certain loyal clientele and had established so broad a national name for themselves that they were a likely choice for tourists. If *The Passing Show*, which technically ended the previous season, is included, all the major annuals were accounted for. This year even Burns Mantle could not ignore the general musical decline. Judging the general season better than the last, he attributed part of its superiority to "fewer of those musical entertainments of which kindly disposed reviewers are wont to write that the librettos were terrible but the music good."

Even the music was not that good in the season's first entry, **George White's Scandals of 1923** (18 June 1923, Globe). Baral in his study, *Revue*, rightly gives the show short shrift, noting merely that, while Gershwin's score "sounded bright in overture, no real hit emerged. The whole show was several grades lower than the preceding edition." Winnie Lightner attempted to put over the songs. Tom Patricola danced, played the ukulele, and acted in a travesty of *Romeo and Juliet*. Lester Allen clowned in his acrobatic dances. White arranged his girls in rows one atop the other to create a "living curtain"; he paraded them bedecked as rare jewels and turned them all into roses. Good or bad, its public supported the revue for twenty-one weeks.

One interesting book show interrupted the procession of revues. **Helen of Troy, New York** (19 June 1923, Selwyn) had a George S. Kaufman and Marc Connelly libretto, and Bert Kalmar and Harry Ruby songs. The score was the team's first, and they were not yet in full stride. Aisle-sitters found it no more than "so-so" (*Tribune*), "fairly good" (*World*), or "well-made" (*Times*). Again, not a single hit tune emerged. But the very same critics greeted the book with huzzahs: the *Tribune* hailed it as "a bright travesty," and the *World*, welcoming "the business satire of *To The Ladies* into the musical comedy field," added prophetically that Kaufman and Connelly had determined "a musical show should be taught new tricks." The story told of Helen McGuffey (Helen Ford)—even here there would be a poor Irish heroine—who loses her stenographer's job at a collar factory when the president learns his son loves the office girl.

She invents an improved, softer collar, which she sells to a rival house. Her former company is forced to merge, and she wins the heir apparent. However stale the plotline, the mordant Kaufman and Connelly wit distinguished the show. For example, the head of the vast manufacturing enterprise can never remember his own collar size. He has to refer sheepishly to his notebook to find it. There were even some very private jokes only a handful of the audience might really understand. One character was a mincing male model who posed for the collar ads. Insiders knew he was drawn after a model used by J. C. Leyendecker, the man who created the famous Arrow collar drawings.

Kaufman and Connelly came from somewhat similar backgrounds.

> **GEORGE S. KAUFMAN** was born in Pittsburgh on 16 November 1889. Because his parents had lost a son shortly before George was born, George was given a pampered upbringing, kept away from games and sports that might prove harmful. He became an avid reader. He entered the newspaper field, obtaining work with the Washington *Star*. Fired by the paper's owner when he discovered George was a Jew, he moved to New York and got a job with the *Evening Mail*. In 1915 he became drama critic for the *Tribune* and shortly thereafter for the *Times*. He gave up criticism to handle the paper's theatrical news and to try his own hand at playwriting. His first effort folded out of town.

> **MARC CONNELLY** was born just over a year after Kaufman, on 13 December 1890, in McKeesport, a steel town not far from Pittsburgh. He, too, took quickly to journalism, first locally and after 1916 in New York. While still in Pittsburgh he wrote the lyrics for a local 1913 production, *The Lady of Luzon*. His first professional theatrical plunge was helping to revise the libretto of *Erminie* for the 1921 revival. That same year he teamed with Kaufman to write *Dulcy*, a smash hit. One year later the pair had a second hit on their hands, *To the Ladies*.

July and August brought three more revues. Only the Earl Carroll **Vanities of 1923** (5 July 1923, Earl Carroll) succeeded. It was a new series, bankrolled by a Texas oilman, that would be produced erratically over the next decade. It was more interested in its girls than in what they wore—a hint sensationalism might stimulate ticket sales. Less clothing also meant less expense, and higher costs were helping to bring down the curtain on the older series. But the *Vanities'* songs and sketches were never of a high order. Nothing of permanent value was presented in any of its editions. The 1923 version opened with "The Birth of a New Revue," in which the loveliest girls were brought forth to represent the *Follies,* the *Scandals,* and the other annuals. The last girl to appear represented the *Vanities.* The first-act finale put each girl in a different fur, with the radiant Peggy Hopkins Joyce promenading in chinchilla. The inevitable staircase was also present, but Carroll found a novel use for it. Renoff (of Renoff and Renova) finished his dance by dramatically plunging down all the steps. More dainty toe dancing was performed by petite Gertie Lemmon. Bernard Granville was on hand to sing the songs, but they were undistinguished and bore titles typical of this genre, "Girls Were Made For Dancing," "A Girl Is Like Sunshine," and "My Cretonne Girl." The comedy was largely in the hands of Joe Cook, who brought his "One Man Vaudeville" over from the two-a-day circuits.

A trio of old hands on stage and behind the scenes—Arnold Daly, Harry B. Smith, Ted Snyder— tried and failed with **Fashions of 1924** (18 July 1923, Lyceum). The critics looked on it as an elaborate, poorly assembled fashion show. Nor was its comedy original or good, falling back on overworked bits such as a comic prizefight skit.

The Newcomers (8 August 1923, Ambassador) attempted unsuccessfully an idea Leonard Sillman would revive with happier results eleven years later—a revue assembled as a showcase for new talent. To some extent *The Newcomers* was a vanity production. Will Morrisey wrote the work, produced it, and served as its compère. He perched himself down by the footlights to introduce each act and provided some commentary. The acts were largely vaudevillian, including a male impersonator and a ventriloquist.

The season's biggest hit, **Little Jessie James,** opened at the modest-sized Longacre on 15 August. The critics, while not unhappy, showed no special enthusiasm. Mantle awarded it only passing mention in his review of the year. That old theatrical

shibboleth "the audience show" apparently applied here. *Little Jessie James* was not a western. All the action takes place in an apartment overlooking Central Park, where Jessie Jamieson (Nan Halperin) pursues Paul Revere (Jay Velie) and does not let bedroom-farce misunderstandings prevent her winning him. Miriam Hopkins and Allen Kearns called attention to themselves in supporting roles. "I Love You" was the most successful song to come out of a musical during the season, and its great vogue undoubtedly lengthened the box office lines. Harry Archer's score—played in the theatre by a Paul Whiteman band—was otherwise mediocre, and Archer never again had so solid a hit. A further aid in lengthening the show's run was its low initial and operating costs. There was only one set, and at a time when forty or more people comprised an ordinary chorus, *Little Jessie James* frugally employed only eight chorus girls. A 1953–1954 revival foundered quickly.

The Shuberts, always quick to sense and follow trends, established a Carroll-like revue, **Artists and Models** (20 August 1923, Shubert), just as years earlier they had offered *The Passing Show* to compete with Ziegfeld. Even more than the *Vanities,* the new series depended on nudity to entice theatregoers. Like the *Vanities* it appeared erratically and left nothing to posterity. Frank Fay, considered by many the drollest of compères, performed the task in this edition.

A late August arrival, **Little Miss Bluebeard** (28 August 1923, Lyceum), though listed on its sheet music as a "gay song-play," was a comedy for which E. Ray Goetz and George Gershwin wrote a handful of tunes for Irene Bordoni. It straddled the fence between straight play and musical.

Poppy (3 September 1923, Apollo) was one more rags-to-riches tale. Two of its songs, "What Do You Do Sundays, Mary?" and "Alibi Baby" (Howard Dietz/Arthur Samuels), were well received and had a contemporary popularity. Madge Kennedy, playing the title role of the circus waif who discovers she's an heiress, collected handsome notices. But the main attraction of *Poppy* was W. C. Fields as Eustace McGargle, the girl's preposterously unconventional guardian. The show ran the whole season.

Two more annuals followed: *The Greenwich Village Follies* ("Strong on beauty, but somewhat dull otherwise") and *The Music Box Revue.* The **Greenwich Village Follies** (20 September 1923, Winter Garden) displayed another Reginald Marsh show curtain, this time depicting an old, turn-of-the-century village. Lavish production numbers included "Moonlight Kisses" (in which great ladies of legend and history passed briefly across the stage) and a Spanish fiesta number designed by James Reynolds in the style of a Velázquez painting. There were two "Ballet Ballads." The first, based on Poe's "The Raven," was a dud and quickly withdrawn. But "The Garden of Kama," telling a tragic tale of love in India, was praised. Martha Graham danced both in the latter and in the fiesta scene, dances far removed from the modern dance style she later popularized. A new female impersonator, Karyl Norman, was called in to replace the late Bert Savoy. Norman's style was closer to the dignified Julian Eltinge's than to the rowdy Savoy's. Tom Howard presented his country bumpkin humor. The diminutive twosome of Sammy White and Eva Puck offered their brand of light comedy and dancing. The show's principal weakness was its score.

The score of **The Music Box Revue 1923–1924**, which premiered on 22 September, also proved so weak that Irving Berlin hurriedly interpolated his own "What'll I Do?," which was not written for the show. Another song, "An Orange Grove In California," was given a striking mounting. The song was first sung by John Steel and Grace Moore (whom Berlin had given "What'll I Do?") walking together in an orange grove. Slowly the grove melted away into a kaleidoscope of shimmering orange lights and the audience found itself sprayed with orange perfume. A silver and gold mesh curtain, reputed to have cost $50,000, was featured in another scene. Two extraordinary sketches for this edition have managed to survive and enjoy lives of their own. The first was Benchley's "Treasurer's Report"; the second, Kaufman's hilarious masterpiece, "If Men Played Cards as Women Do." Benchley purported to be an officer of a choral society and was offering its members his latest accounting. With embarrassed little coughs and tugs at his collar he acknowledged gaps and discrepancies. But after all, other pressing matters—such as his sister's wedding—necessitated his omitting a month here and there. In the Kaufman sketch four men (played in the show by Joseph Santley, Hugh Cameron, Solly Ward, and Phil Baker) sit down to a friendly game of bridge. John, the host, and Bob, the first player to arrive, gush over a new hatband on Bob's year-old Knox. The two men talk cattily about George, only to do a smiling about-face when George appears. Their backbiting then shifts to absent friends. The fourth player, Marc, stops the game briefly to preen himself, placing a pocket mirror on the card table,

shaving a rough spot on his carefully examined chin, and slicking down his hair with two military brushes. The skit ends with the startling revelation that one of the men's friends, somebody named Sid, will become a father in April—though he only married in January! In its original performance the skit's humor was heightened by the players eschewing all traces of effeminacy. The skit was played as Kaufman demanded, "in forthright and manly fashion."

Charles Dillingham assembled a superb cast for **Nifties of 1923** (25 September 1923, Fulton). The producer poured most of his money into this cast, giving the evening a tasteful but relatively simple mounting. Some critics viewed it as little more than stylish vaudeville. With Ziegfeld now advertising that he was glorifying the American Girl, *Nifties* boasted in turn that it was "glorifying clean American humor." The material was written by the show's stars, Sam Bernard and William Collier. They appeared together as quarreling neighbors in a skit called "Keep Off the Grass." Curiously, none of the other performers were given star billing or even mentioned in the regular advertisements, though many had recently been top names. Hazel Dawn played her violin and gave her interpretation of Jeanne Eagles in *Rain*. Frank Crumit lead the Elm City Four in barbershop favorites. Others in the excellent company were Van and Schenk, Florence Ames, Ray Dooley, Helen Broderick, the toe-dancing Lina Basquette, and the Twelve Tiller Girls, precision dancers. If Dillingham contemplated another series, he arrived on the scene with it much too late in the day, and a number of his best names were also beyond their brightest years.

Zelda Sears and Harold Levey could not recreate their success of *The Clinging Vine* (25 December 1922) in **The Magic Ring** (10 October 1923, Liberty). The show was a vehicle for Mitzi. She played a ragamuffin organ-grinder whose discovery of a magic ring brings her wealth and romance. In short, the musical was another rags-to-riches tale, with Oriental trappings. It ran ninety-six performances, almost reaching that 100 mark, which in the twenties suggested a probable return on investment.

Three nights later Arthur Hammerstein at the Century Roof failed with an imported English entertainment he rechristened **Hammerstein's 9 O'clock Revue**. But an Americanized English musical with a prizefight theme, **Battling Buttler** (8 October 1923, Selwyn), delighted both the critics and its audiences. The *Times* rejoiced, "musical comedies are really getting better."

They grew worse abruptly with **Ginger** (16 October 1923, Daly's), a Harold Orlob offering that couldn't manage five full weeks. Originally titled *Take a Chance*, it spent the evening searching for someone to test a new-style parachute. The dialogue was the *Listen, Lester* (23 December 1918) variety:

—Are you a reactionary?
—I haven't been examined yet.
—Well, do you like conventions?
—I've only attended one.

Even **The Ziegfeld Follies of 1923** (20 October 1923, New Amsterdam) was obviously a step down. Ziegfeld's stars were fast leaving him for book shows, vaudeville, and movies. Of his greatest performers, only Fanny Brice remained, and she was so displeased with the weak material given her that she, too, bid adieu to the revue when this edition closed. James Reynolds also left after this production, but unlike Miss Brice, he went out with a flourish. He set "The Legend Of The Drums" in Napoleonic times and ended the scene with a spectacular effect that simulated the burning of captured war drums. Another dazzling bit was a "Maid of Gold" number, for which the exotic dancer Muriel Stryker painted her body with special gold paint. Costumes were designed by the rage of fashionable Paris, Erté, and the scene set to music by Rudolf Friml. It did not remain in the show for long—at least not in its original form. The dancer's physician warned her that the paint would endanger her life. A gold lamé dress replaced the gold paint. As a rule, the *Follies* no longer elicited composers' best works. However, "Chansonette," a Friml melody from his background music for the show, was made into "The Donkey Serenade" a dozen or so years later. Audiences at the show went home singing "Take, Oh Take Those Lips Away" (Joseph McCarthy/Harry Tierney). Though it fell far short of the best McCarthy and Tierney songs, Ziegfeld marshaled his best forces for the number. The song was sung by the boyishly handsome Brooke Johns, whom Ziegfeld hoped to groom as John Steel's replacement, much as he hoped to find a second Marilyn Miller in Mary Eaton. Johns lacked the radiant Irish tenor of Steel, but he could play the banjo and he had no drinking problem. Unfortunately, he was no actor, and with revues fading there would be little room for him in book shows. The lips Johns bid be taken away were

the cupid bows of Ann Pennington. Paul Whiteman's orchestra accompanied the performers. Because rising costs discouraged Ziegfeld from taking the show on the road, it was able to remain in New York as long as the public wanted it. Before it closed it compiled an unusually long run for a *Follies*, 233 performances.

Some real life jumped back into the season with **Runnin' Wild** (29 October 1923, Colonial), the closest any black musical comedy of the era came to repeating *Shuffle Along*'s success. It presented the usual flimsy plot principaled by the sharper and dolt that Bert Williams and George Walker had established as a formula for Negro shows almost a quarter of century before, and that Flournoy Miller and Aubrey Lyles had perpetuated with *Shuffle Along* (23 May 1921). Miller and Lyles were the show's librettists and were also back on stage to portray Steve Jenkins and Sam Peck again. Naturally the setting was once more Jimtown. Sam and Steve jump their board bill but return to Jimtown disguised as mediums. Typical of the humor was Sam's blaming their bad business luck on "de ducks." His elaboration on his analysis shows he "de ducks" ten dollars for everything he can get away with. There were the customary racial comedy scenes; for example, the timid Negro confronted with a ghost. But what the public really enjoyed was what the *Tribune* termed "rhythm... and risible dental display." Virtually all the reviewers, employing such words as "dark" and "dusky," still implied these shows were not to be considered in the theatrical mainstream, but something *sui generis*. It may not be coincidental that the most successful of these were usually presented either at the Colonial or at Daly's, both north of 57th Street and away from the center of the theatrical district. But in this instance the critics turned out to be remarkably myopic, for there was one number in the show, a dance, that ultimately expressed and symbolized the whole gaudy era about to explode. It pronounced the beat for the "lost generation" and liberated the whole jazz movement. The dance song was, of course, "The Charleston." The dance typified the black-inspired high-stepping of the era. It was gawky, zesty, and, obviously, irresistible.

Just as Jerome Kern's *The Bunch and Judy* (28 November 1922) at the Globe followed *Liza*'s uptown opening, so Kern's **Stepping Stones** at the same house on 6 November brought the critics back downtown after *Runnin' Wild*. What interested the reviewers and the public was the debut as star of Dorothy Stone, Fred's daughter, and much publicity was given to her name being put up in lights alongside his while the first-night audience was applauding her. Kern also came in for high praise. And his score was beautiful. The virtually forgotten "Once In A Blue Moon" and "In Love With Love" rank with all but his greatest melodies. However, this musicalized version of Little Red Riding Hood, in which Rougette Hood (Dorothy Stone) is pursued by the villainous Otto De Wolfe (Oscar Ragland) and is rescued "in song dance and acrobatic comedy by one Peter Plug" (Fred Stone), demanded specialized lyrics that undoubtedly kept some of the melodies from general currency. Rougette, her mother (Allene Stone), and the girls' chorus sang "Little Red Riding Hood." Plug sang and danced to "Pie," while Rougette and Prince Silvio (Roy Hoyer) sang the love songs.

Topics of 1923 (20 November 1923, Broadhurst) was a revue written by many old Winter Garden hands for the ballyhooed Alice Delysia, who had come to Broadway two years before in *Afgar*. Neither Miss Delysia nor the show found favor. A few critics praised the gowns, and the *Times* noted that an acrobatic dancer, Nat Nazzaro, gathered more applause than the star. The revue headed quickly for Cain's warehouse, and the star returned to Europe.

Two nights later, 22 November, the group that had presented *Go-Go* (12 April 1923) the preceding season with a modicum of success tried again with **Sharlee** at Daly's. Sharlee Saunders (Juliette Day) is a nightclub singer aching to find love and a home in the country. She succeeds, but nobody on the other side of the footlights seemed to care. The show was gone before the new year arrived.

On the 27th, Dillingham brought in a French musical, *Ta Bouche*, with a score by Maurice Yvain, who composed "Mon Homme." Called **One Kiss** here, the show ran ninety-five performances at the Fulton. The story told how young love triumphs over parental objections. The cast of *One Kiss* was a remarkable roster of old and new favorites—Ada Lewis, John E. Hazzard, Louise Groody, Oscar Shaw, and John Price Jones. Dillingham, like Ziegfeld, never did things by halves.

Three memorable and noteworthy musicals closed 1923. The first two arrived on Christmas, the third on New Year's Eve. The Christmas presents were **Mary Jane McKane** at the new Imperial and **The Rise of Rosie O'Reilly** at the Liberty. The credits for *Mary Jane McKane* read almost like those of *Wildflower*, only Otto Harbach had given place to William Cary Duncan. The plot was old hat. Mary (Mary Hay), another poor Irish secretary, loses her job when her boss's son, Andrew Dunn, Jr. (Stanley Ridges), shows interest in her. She returns in a drab disguise and later goes into business with the son when his father fires him. By eleven o'clock she is Mary Dunn, with even the elder Dunn approving. To a man the critics could find nothing exciting in the plot, or in the music. The *Times* critic did, however, give Vincent Youmans proper credit this time. At most, the show was adjudged professional and diverting, while the real praise was awarded its star, Miss Hay. It ran 151 performances. In some of his better numbers—"Toodle-oo," "Flannel Petticoat Gal"—Youmans's peculiar technique of small repeated phrases varied harmonically was again immediately identifiable. Since the sale of the show's sheet music was small and complete score recordings (at least in America) were twenty years in the future, Youmans was able to put two of the show's songs away for reuse: a waltz called "My Boy And I" and "Come On And Pet Me." With new lyrics and with the former's waltz tempo dropped, they would reemerge in *No, No, Nanette* (16 September 1925) and *Hit the Deck!* (25 April 1927) respectively.

The critics did not have to reach back three or four years to find a musical to compare with *The Rise of Rosie O'Reilly*. Though most of them greeted George M. Cohan's new work affectionately, it was simply too much like *Little Nellie Kelly* (13 November 1922). *The Theatre* observed: "Rosie O'Reilly looked like all her little sisters who have gone before." Rosie (Virginia O'Brien), who sells flowers beneath the Brooklyn Bridge, meets Bob Morgan (Jack McGowan), a wealthy man-about-town. They fall in love, but Bob is disinherited and goes to work at a florist's. Eventually the elder Morgan relents. Bob and Rosie are married, though Rosie clearly would have taken Bob even if he had never been restored to his fortune. This could represent a compromise with the Cinderella ending Cohan had heretofore avoided. But nothing else was markedly different, and the score was several notches below Cohan's compositions in *Nellie Kelly*. The show ran eleven weeks before it went on tour. Cohan began slipping back to the short New York runs and long national tours of his early shows. But in his youth he had been a pathmaker, bursting with enthralling melody. By the twenties he was old-fashioned, able to compose little more than hand-me-down tunes, which often seemed an inferior rehash of his older songs.

Ziegfeld celebrated New Year's Eve by offering Broadway **Kid Boots** at the Earl Carroll, with Eddie Cantor as star and Mary Eaton as the principal beauty. William Anthony McGuire and Otto Harbach did the book, which had fun with the popular craze for golf, a sport formerly restricted to the upper classes, and bootlegging. Cantor, in whiteface for most of the show, played a less than honest caddy who sells crooked balls and booze. The plot thickens when the club champion, his friend, inadvertently uses one of the balls to play the match of the year. A romantic subplot gave the show's costar, Mary Eaton, several chances to do her light, breezy dances. George Olsen and his jazz orchestra were on hand to play the new Joseph McCarthy–Harry Tierney score, but even Cantor could not put over the mediocre music. Only an interpolation, Harry Akst's "Dinah," caught on. "Dinah," Cantor, Miss Eaton, and the Ziegfeld magic kept *Kid Boots* going for months.

One of the finest of all revues, **Charlot's Revue** (9 January 1924, Times Square) came from London. And it came as a revelation to American theatregoers. In a way (and a number of critics saw this) comparison with American shows was unfair, for André Charlot had culled his material from several of his London successes. The evening could have been called "The Best from Chariot's Revues." But this in no way gainsaid the quality of its material or the talent of its performers. Charlot made the evening seem to move at a lightning-like pace by flying in the face of Broadway practice and steadfastly refusing to allow encores. The show made the American reputation of three great English performers. The first and least was suave Jack Buchanan, a performer equally adept at singing, dancing, and light comedy. Though the show revealed Gertrude Lawrence's gift for putting across a song (and she sang the show's hit, "Limehouse Blues"), it gave her little opportunity to display her comic and acting abilities. Most of all, the show brought America Beatrice Lillie, England's greatest comedienne.

In one number Miss Lillie played an aging soubrette clinging desperately to the songs of her youth. But her greatest moment came in "March With Me," in which she attempted to lead a cadre, only to move left when they moved right, hopelessly scrambling ranks and creating further chaos by trying to set things in order. Miss Lillie would reduce an audience to nearly helpless laughter by some bit of absurdity and then devastate it completely by glowering at it in outrage for laughing at

her in the first place. *Charlot's Revue* helped point the way to the more intimate, literate, and fast-paced revues that later dominated Broadway. In after years the show would be looked back on as a milestone. Yet it is necessary to remember that the show did not start an immediate rush to a new style. It took several years before this newer type of revue caught on.

Though her career kept her largely in London or New York. **BEATRICE LILLIE** was born in Toronto, Canada, on 29 May 1894. She made her debut at the Chatham Music Hall in 1914. A stint in vaudeville quickly gave way to increasingly important appearances in London revues with snappy titles such as *Samples, Some, Cheep, Tabs,* and *A to Z.* In 1919 she interrupted this chain of revues to take the principal comedienne's role (Jackie) in the London version of the Princess Theatre hit *Oh, Boy!,* known on the West End as *Oh, Joy!*

Lollipop (21 January 1924, Knickerbocker) holds a quirky interest. It was Vincent Youmans's first complete score, to a book by Zelda Sears, who had been supplying strong librettos to limp composers. This time the situation was reversed. Miss Sears let Youmans down with a book the *Times* dismissed as "weakly Cinderella-ish." Laura "Lollipop" Lamb (Ada May Weeks), an orphan, is adopted by the well-to-do Mrs. Garrity (Miss Sears). Laura clears herself of the charge she has stolen her benefactor's purse, finds love, and ultimately throws a big costume ball. The score was not at all bad, including as it did the still familiar "Tie A Little String Around Your Finger" as well as "Take A Little One Step," which Youmans would reuse in *No, No, Nanette* (16 September 1925). *Lollipop* ran 152 performances, one more than *Mary Jane McKane.*

George Gershwin was also on the eve of finding himself, having left the *Scandals* to concentrate on book shows. He pleased the critics on the same 21 January with **Sweet Little Devil** (one of the last shows to play the desirable Astor before it became a movie house), but his songs have long since been pushed aside by greater Gershwin works that followed. The critics disagreed on the merits of the book. The *World* extolled the "novel plot," while the *Post* complained, "the plot is almost completely missing." As Frank Mandel and Laurence Schwab conceived it, *Sweet Little Devil* related Tom Nesbitt's (Irving Beebe) astonishment when Joyce West (Marjorie Gateson), the sweet *Follies* beauty he has been corresponding with, proves a callous money-grabber. It develops her roommate, the little devil Virginia Culpepper (Constance Binney), has really been doing the corresponding. Tom settles for Virginia and a life in Peru. It was, in fact, a good contemporary book, catching the smart talk of the times: "He's so mad about me," Joyce gloats, "I could kick him in the nose, and he'd say it's being done this season." *Sweet Little Devil* enjoyed a fair run of fifteen weeks.

Moonlight (30 January 1924, Longacre), a highly touted show, with music by Con Conrad and a book by William Le Baron based on his own farce, *I Love You*, had an eighteen-week stay. Like many of the period's musicals, it was a one-set, basically intimate piece—a comedy with music, although in this instance sixteen songs were published. Several of them, for example, "On Such A Night," are still pleasantly hummable. They exemplify the constant melodic appeal of even the second-string songs of the period. Conrad was a fine composer, though his best work, notably "Margie" and "Memory Lane," was done outside the theatre. No poor girl makes good in *Moonlight*. Jimmie Farnsworth (Louis Simon) bets George Van Horne (Glen Dale) that given the proper setting anyone will fall in love. He wins his bet, but only after some unexpected matches are untangled. *Moonlight*, like *Lollipop* and *Sweet Little Devil*, ran up to the warm weather.

In mid-February Eleanor Painter, most famous as Herbert's Princess Pat, came back to sing Carlo and Sanders's score for **The Chiffon Girl** (19 February 1924, Lyric). The plot was operetta with a jazz-age twist. It may have recalled *Suzette* (24 November 1921) to the few who saw that flop. A beautiful Italian fruit vendor is sent to Italy to study voice. She returns four years later a great prima donna. However, she does not marry her benefactor but her old boyfriend—now a bootlegger. The Carlo-Sanders score was no better than any of their other efforts. Nonetheless, *The Chiffon Girl* ran three months.

No musical arrived on Broadway for the next month and a half. With hot evenings approaching, the Shuberts broke the lull by offering **Vogues of 1924** (27 March 1924, Shubert). It had a fine cast and ran into the summer. Some of its numbers may have reminded playgoers of *Nifties of 1924*. Where Hazel Dawn had played her violin in the earlier show, Odette Myrtil played hers in the new entertainment. Miss Dawn had twitted *Rain*'s Sadie Thompson; so did the new show. But *Vogues* did it with a vengeance, with six Sadies and six Rev. Davidsons singing a *Florodora*-like sextette. Jimmy Savo and Fred Allen also accounted for much of the laughter. The best bit of the evening fell to Allen, in a monologue not too far removed from Benchley's "Treasurer's Report." Allen took it upon himself to teach the audience his brand of algebra, insisting, "Let X equal my father's signature."

Paradise Alley (31 March 1924, Casino), a musical with a *Sally*-like plot, had a brief spring stay. It recorded the rise of Bonnie Brown (Helen Shipman) from an alley urchin to the rage of London's musical comedy stage. Courted by a number of Englishmen, she rejects them all for Jack Harriman (Charles Derickson), an American boxer.

Sitting Pretty came on 8 April to remain until July. But *Sitting Pretty* should have run longer. Though done at the Fulton, a bandbox house just off Times Square, it was a Princess Theatre show. F. Ray Comstock and Morris Gest were once again the producers. More important, Guy Bolton, P. G. Wodehouse, and Jerome Kern were again the authors. Following the old pattern of two acts with one set for each, it portrayed the troubles of Horace (Dwight Frye), a small-time crook (how Bolton loved crooks!) who has been robbing rich men's homes. His plan to rob the Penningtons is thwarted when he falls in love with May Tolliver (Gertrude Bryan) at the Penningtons' house. May and her sister Dixie (Queenie Smith) reform Horace. Dixie's reward is the Pennington heir (Rudolf Cameron). The critics, recognizing its provenance, were delighted. The *Sun* called it "a charming and likeable sequel to the miniature musical comedies… at the Princess before the war." Kern received most of the laurels, though very kind words were also saved for Wodehouse's marvelous lyrics. Some critics had a reservation or two about the book, Percy Hammond in the *Tribune* going so far as to suggest, cantankerously and shortsightedly, that Bolton would find more rewarding employment in "smart revues" than in "the mawkish vapidities of musical comedy." The book, however, is still eminently playable, and the Kern-Wodehouse songs exquisite. The lovely title song, sung by Harold and Dixie, seems a full ten years ahead of its time in its chromatics. More of their own epoch, "A Year From

Today," "The Enchanted Train," and "All You Need Is A Girl" (all three sung by May and Bill Pennington) are graceful gems, well worth replaying, while Wodehouse's "Bongo On The Congo" lyrics (sung by Horace and his cronies) would probably stop a show even today. In the Congo, he assured playgoers, they present a visitor with a dozen wives when he arrives. A man with fewer than two dozen wives is considered a bachelor.

The evening of 5 May augured to be an interesting one at the Jolson, where a musical version of *Peg o' My Heart*, only slightly rechristened **Peg o' My Dreams**, opened. As she had in the original, Margaret O'Connell (Suzanne Keener) wins the hand of Sir Gerald (Roy Royston), who loves her even though she is an heiress. But Hugo Felix's score was even drearier than his *Marjolaine* (24 January 1922) material, and, with no Laurette Taylor or Peggy Wood to help, the show barely survived the month.

Another Cinderella version entered the arena as **Plain Jane** (12 May 1924, New Amsterdam). Jane Lee (Lorraine Manville), another tenement waif, enters her rag doll in a contest. She fails to win, but the son of the doll manufacturer who sponsored the contest falls in love with her. He has an argument with his father over Jane, quits his job, and wins enough money in a prizefight to set himself and Jane up in a competitive company. A superbly staged fight scene seems to have been its main claim to fame, for the book was drab, and the music of Tom Johnstone, who seemed to be eyeing A. Baldwin Sloane's dubious mantle, was merely the music of Tom Johnstone.

Another Johnstone score was heard on Broadway exactly a week later. It was heard, that is, if the constant laughter that filled the house didn't mercifully drown it out. For the show was **I'll Say She Is!** (19 May 1924, Casino) one of the hits of the season and the main stem's introduction to the Marx Brothers. *I'll Say She Is!* billed itself as a musical comedy revue, acknowledging the tenuous thread of a story line Will B. Johnstone created for the boys and at the same time accepting the havoc the boys wreaked on the plot. In Johnstone's original typescript the brothers are introduced applying one by one at a talent agency. Each brother offers his idea of how Gallagher and Shean's act should be revised. The action begins when the boys meet a young lady known on the program and in the script solely as Beauty (Carlotta Miles). The show's title was probably a contraction of the popular exclamation, "I'll

say she's a beauty." Carlotta Miles underwent a similar contraction to Lotta Miles. Both contractions undoubtedly seemed titillatingly suggestive to the period. Beauty was a young woman desperately determined to "search for a thrill." Her search takes her to a Chinatown opium den, where she is accused of murder. Groucho advises her, "You are charged with murder and if you are convicted you will be charged with electricity." Nor can he offer her much hope:

Groucho: You are going to be convicted of murder.
Beauty: What makes you so confident?
Groucho: I'm going to be your lawyer.

The trial approaches mayhem, with Chico, for example, trying to inveigle the judge into a poker game. After she is acquitted, Beauty attempts to continue her search for a thrill by allowing herself to be hypnotized. Her trance sends her back to Napoleon's times, where she is transformed into Josephine. Groucho appears as a mustached Napoleon and dismisses the courtiers, "Begone peasants! Take French leave." He tells Josephine he must go to meet his Waterloo, but he assures her, "I shall not fight until I see the whites of their eggs. That's a good yolk." He departs, pretending not to notice his brothers, who, as Josephine's lovers, are hiding conspicuously under tables and chairs. Chico performed some of his nimble piano playing, and Harpo followed with his tour de force on the harp as part of the Napoleon scene. The evening continued in a similar vein until eleven o'clock. At one point Groucho appeared as Cinderella, despite his mustache and (at least in the show's publicity stills) a pipe. The public and the critics were overwhelmed by the team's wild nonsense. Indeed, they soon became something of a cult. Apart from the clowning the hit of the evening was a French-style apache dance done by D'Andrea and Walters in the opium den scene.

The births of the four **MARX BROTHERS** who composed the act during its legitimate career spanned fourteen years. **LEONARD (CHICO)** was born in New York on 26 March 1887(?). **ADOLPH (HARPO)** was born mere on 21 November 1888(?). **JULIUS (GROUCHO)** followed on 2 October 1890(?), while **HERBERT (ZEPPO)** arrived nearly eleven years later, 25 February 1901. A fifth brother, **MILTON**, appeared with them briefly during their early vaudeville days, using the name **GUMMO**. The brothers belonged to a theatrical family. Their maternal grandparents had been performers in Germany; their maternal uncle was Al Shean of Gallagher and Shean. From the beginning they were encouraged in their own theatrical ambitions by their mother Minnie, who in time came to personify the pushy, conniving parent determined that her talented offspring would reach the top of the show business ladder. Years after her death, she was made the comic heroine of a Broadway musical, *Minnie's Boys* (26 March 1970). In varying combinations (often in association with outsiders) the boys appeared in a number of vaudeville acts, beginning in 1909 with one called The Three Nightingales. The acts blended singing, simple dance steps, and broad comedy. In 1912 Minnie persuaded her brother Al to write an extended skit for Gummo, Groucho, Harpo, and several other performers. Shean wrote a schoolroom sketch on the order of those made popular by Gus Edwards. The skit was called "Fun in Hi Skool." Groucho played the professor. One of his pupils was played by his Aunt Hannah, and sometimes even by his mother. Beginning in 1915, the brothers played top vaudeville in a forty-five-minute musical, "Home Again," written and staged for them by Shean and using songs, such as "Sweet Kentucky Lady," plucked from Broadway shows or Tin Pan Alley. The boys early on established the characterizations they would employ for the rest of their careers. Chico became the high-strung, fast-dealing Sicilian immigrant. Harpo, forever mute, scampered across the stage in a red wig and battered hat gleefully chasing girls and pilfering everything in sight. Out of his oversized topcoat came any absurdity the action required. The smart-aleck Groucho dressed more often than not in an ill-fitting morning suit. He walked with a deep-kneed crouch, flourished his cigar, and displayed a painted-on box mustache with boxy eyebrows to match. Zeppo, the youngest and handsomest, played straightman.

Four revues, opening on three successive May nights, all but brought the season to a close. **Innocent Eyes** (20 May 1924, Winter Garden) was mounted to showcase the famous French cabaret entertainer Mistinguett. It was a major disappointment. Mistinguett made her entrance in a dress trailed by a twelve-foot train of ostrich feathers. In her most applauded scene she portrayed a French maid sold by her callous father to a brutish Parisian apache. He throws her in the river (out of which she emerges dripping wet). She kills him and runs off with the barge man she loves. Cleo Mayfield and Cecil Lean headed the supporting cast. Unfortunately, Mistinguett had no better luck than Delysia, and she too was soon aboard an eastbound liner.

The Grand Street Follies quickly proved the most forward-looking of the new revue series, relying for effect solely on the skill of its small band of entertainers and the wit of its writers, and in a way accomplished what *The 49ers* failed to do. These *Follies* came to New Yorkers' attention under peculiar circumstances. Situated at 466 Grand Street, far from the bustling theatre district, the Neighborhood Playhouse had for several years offered a group of loyal subscribers a program of classic and popular drama. It had promised its followers that for its final presentation during the 1921–1922 season it would unveil some yet untried work. When the selection committee rejected all the efforts submitted for consideration it was decided to close the season with an intimate revue that would burlesque reigning Broadway successes of the day. The first edition of *The Grand Street Follies*, which the program branded "A low brow show for high grade morons," premiered with two subscription performances on 13 and 14 June 1922 and then played three additional non-subscription performances. The curtain rose on a skit called, appropriately, "In the Beginning," depicting the world's earliest drama critic, Adam Stale, and his wife, Eve, and from there went on to twit theatrical luminaries such as Doris Keane, Laurette Taylor, David Belasco, and John Barrymore. For this first edition the music was credited to "Great Composers, arranged mostly by Lily M. Hyland," though special note was made that Albert Carroll wrote his own words and music for "Personality." From the series' inception, Carroll and Dorothy Sands were the *Follies'* comic pillars. Their cavorting allowed audiences to overlook indifferent music that was to be characteristic of the series. After a season's hiatus, *The Grand Street Follies* went public with its second edition on 20 May 1924. As with the earlier mounting the entertainment concentrated on spoofing plays and players, especially shows the company had staged during the year such as *Blanco Posnet* and *The Player Queen*. Carroll walked away with the heartiest applause for his mimicry of John Barrymore, Elsie Janis, and Jeanne Eagels.

Round the Town (21 May 1924. Century Roof), an almost instant dropout, took its title from a column one of its writers, S. Jay Kaufman, wrote for the New York *Telegram*. Most of its contributors were newsmen, with Kaufman and Herman Mankiewicz providing the bulk of the material. The show's most talked-about skit, however, was by George S. Kaufman and Marc Connelly, who offered a tongue-in-cheek version of their own play, *Beggar on Horseback*. Naturally the title was changed slightly to "Beggars off Horseback."

Keep Kool's (22 May 1924, Morosco) title reflected the popular slogan of the presidential campaign getting under way, "Keep Cool with Coolidge!" But if its title was the last word, the cast consisted not of top stars but of names on the way up (Charles King) or on the way down (Hazel Dawn). The revue was advertised as "a musical revelation in 24 scenes," but the best it could reveal was a modestly funny skit showing how Eugene O'Neill, Avery Hopwood, and George M. Cohan would have handled the same basic story.

A dimwit affair called **Flossie** (3 June 1924, Lyric) arrived to give the season and the period the dreariest possible curtain. For her uncle's benefit Flossie (Doris Duncan) pretends to be married to Archie (Sydney Grant). Archie hadn't time to tell his fiancée, Bessie (Alice Cavanaugh), of the ruse, and she arrives to misconstrue Archie's behavior. Explanations follow, allowing Archie and Bessie, and Flossie and Chummy, to go off happily hand in hand.

Three seasons, 120 musicals, and so little to show for it. But as suddenly as the dreariness began, it ended. The American Musical Theatre was at the threshold of one of its great epochs.

Act Four

The Golden Age of the American Musical, 1924–1937

The national rage for jazz polarized the musical stage. From this period on, America's lyric works were, with rare exceptions outside of revues, clearly either up-to-date musical comedies or operettas from an older tradition. Supported by a muscle-flexing ASCAP, composers increasingly demanded and won the right to be responsible for whole scores, to do what a later generation would call "their own thing." As a result they no longer felt compelled to distort their natural idioms or to compromise them. The disturbing hodgepodge of styles that had so often debased the musical integrity of past shows vanished seemingly overnight. Coupled with this clarification of theatrical forms was a standardization of popular musical forms. The dominance of the AABA pattern in popular music began during this same period. The thirty-two-bar song became the accepted musical housing. It took a principal eight-bar melody, repeated it, inserted a secondary eight-bar melody known as a bridge, and then concluded by returning to the original eight-bar theme. Not all songs employed the pattern, nor certainly did all composers. Most of the better songwriters

were frequently willing to explore other possibilities. But the formula did free composers from at least one concern—the shape of their songs, even though at the same time it imprisoned them in a repetitive convention. By the same token, this very convention provided a challenge, demanding of songwriters that they conceive eight-bar phrases of sufficient originality and strength to sustain constant replaying.

The new breed of composers rose to the challenge handsomely. Significantly, two of the supreme mediocrities of the old school passed from the scene about this time. A. Baldwin Sloane tried to retire in 1921 and died, still young, in 1925; Raymond Hubbell composed his last score in 1928, though he survived through a quarter of a century in retirement. The onslaught of great new talent was too much for such hacks. And onslaught it was. The most notable achievement of the following thirteen-season period, 1924–1925 to 1936–1937, was the enthralling outpouring of magnificent melody. In the number and greatness of its scores no other era approaches it. In its musical comedies its superb songs were often accompanied by the most brilliant lyrics the

American Musical Theatre has ever known. Three men in particular—Ira Gershwin, Lorenz Hart, and Cole Porter—gave a new, unique sophistication to their rhymes. In his own way each made as original and lasting a contribution to his art as W. S. Gilbert had done, and yet almost all their most exciting work was done in this single period. Only in librettos was there little innovation. But the best of the librettists, and there were a number of them, exhibited such solidly professional craftsmanship that it was often easy to overlook their lack of inspiration.

In terms of "acts" this period shares with the second and fifth acts a division into two "scenes." The first five seasons, roughly paralleling Coolidge's term, were the happiest and most fruitful. Then 1929 brought the Depression and the first real competition from Hollywood musicals. Those who didn't abandon Broadway and rush west found themselves confronting a changed world and a changed audience. Alert and able, they quickly altered subtly, but perceptibly, their own ways of writing. There was no revolution in the musical theatre, but there was an undeniable change of tone.

SCENE ONE

Songwriters' Shows as Pure Entertainment, 1924–1929

1924–1925

Things were looking up all across the nation in the summer of 1924, and with Coolidge obviously about to be elected in November there was little reason for concern and some good reason to relax. As he did so frequently, Florenz Ziegfeld presented the first offering to please the tired businessman. *The Ziegfeld Follies of 1924* (24 June 1924, New Amsterdam) compiled 401 performances, the second longest run any of Ziegfeld's revues ever enjoyed. Yet it was not a critical or artistic success. Oddly, many aficionados remember it best for the beautiful cover Albert Vargas created for its sheet music, a single smiling brunette invitingly fingering a necklace. When the show opened, it included Will Rogers and Ann Pennington (both in their final *Follies*) as well as Vivienne Segal. It also displayed a line of precision dancers, the Tiller Girls. To keep things humming at the box office, Ziegfeld announced seasonally revised "editions," bringing in W. C. Fields, Ray Dooley, and Ethel Shutta for the "winter" and "spring" lineups. Miss Shutta did

her bit in between her chores in *Louie the 14th*; a police escort helped clear her path from theatre to theatre. One of the numbers Miss Shutta belted out was "Eddie, Be Good." She sang it to twenty-four Ziegfeld beauties, all made up to resemble Eddie Cantor. Harry Tierney score's had no memorable numbers, though "Adoring You" received some play. Nor was there any superior material in the supplementary songs by Raymond Hubbell, Dave Stamper, James Hanley, or Victor Herbert (who had died the previous May while working on his melodies for the show). Herbert's music provided the background for a major production number in which Peggy Fears portrayed a sleeping prince surrounded by wooden soldiers—an obvious reference to the wooden soldiers of *Chauve Souris* (4 February 1922). Even George Olsen and his band could not make the tunes sound better than they were. Fields's entry into the show was prompted by the out-of-town failure of a vehicle Ziegfeld had mounted for him, *The Comic Supplement*. Two of the skits from this fiasco were salvaged for the *Follies*. In one Fields was frustrated in his attempt to take a short nap; in the other he was set upon by his nagging wife. Apart from the number in which Miss Fears played the sleeping prince, the evening's most lauded spectacle was probably its finale, "Fine Feathers Make Fine Birds," with Ziegfeld's girls bedecked in more than their customary allotment of feathers. Interestingly, a number with a similar title had been offered in *Snapshots of 1921* (2 June 1921). The major restructurings and recastings that occurred in October, and then again in March and early summer of 1925, have led to a problem for theatrical historians. Did these last two reworkings actually constitute a 1925 edition of the revue? In any case, this *Follies* was the first of the season's many revues. Their number was impressive, but, as the season will show, their vogue was indisputably waning.

George White's Scandals of 1924 (30 June 1924, Apollo) was far less successful than the *Follies*, running 192 times. However, it left behind one Gershwin classic, rich in new jazz-age harmonies, "Somebody Loves Me." A cozy, intimate song, it was nevertheless given the gimmicky staging that was a White trademark. As she sang it, Winnie Lightner found herself wooed by past and contemporary heroes—Mark Anthony, Romeo, Harold Lloyd, and William S. Hart. Gershwin was earning $125 a week, plus royalties from the show. When he asked White for a raise, White demurred, so Gershwin left the series. Many of the revue's musical numbers incorporated burlesques. Will Mahoney spoofed Jolson's rendition of "My Mammy," while Lester Allen and Tom Patricola kidded Ann Pennington and Brooke Johns, with Allen's knees conspicuously dimpled for the occasion. The skits were at times as gimmicky as the musical staging. In one sketch the dialogue consisted solely of variously delivered "Ahs." Allen and Miss Lightner were the principals in a comic take-off of *Abie's Irish Rose*. White's spectacles for this edition included a number in which his girls formed parts of larger-than-life handbags.

The season's first book musical, **Marjorie** (11 August 1924, Shubert), detailed how brash, young Marjorie Daw (the evening was originally given her full name) passes off her brother's play as her own and persuades Brian Valcourt (Roy Royston) to produce it. Marjorie (Elizabeth Hines) also persuades Brian she would make an ideal wife for him. A large group of well-known and unknown artists all had a hand in the show, with the result that it had no distinctive style. The *Sun* complained it was "like a hundred others in the same pattern." Anything went. Much of the critics' praise was awarded to the show's comedians, Andrew Tombes (who played a curiously taciturn press agent) and Skeet Gallagher (as Marjorie's brash playwriting brother). The dances ranged from a flapper chorus doing the Charleston to the eccentric stepping of Edward Hopper. Hopper appeared briefly as a bellhop in the second act with a routine utilizing the luggage he was carrying. *Marjorie* was no triumph, but it kept a theatre lit into 1925.

Two lesser-known songwriters, Bert Kalmar and Harry Ruby, soon to be much more famous, provided the tunes for Aaron Hoffman's book to **No Other Girl** (13 August 1924, Morosco). It was a lamebrain affair about the efforts of Ananias Jones (Eddie Buzzell) to build an advertisement-lined concrete highway to Quakertown so that his fellow citizens can learn what's happening in the big, wonderful world out yonder. With the encouragement of steadfast Hope Franklin (Helen Ford) he prevails by curtain time. A number of critics applauded the pathos Eddie Buzzell managed to mix with his customary sassiness; but for at least one reviewer the best part of the evening was the oversized model of the highway with its billboards that was lugged on stage. The Kalmar-Ruby score was not memorably melodic. If much of the music had a contemporary jazz sound, one number steadfastly insisted, "I Would Rather Dance A Waltz." *No Other Girl* survived seven weeks.

Victor Herbert's last score was presented posthumously in **The Dream Girl** (20 August 1924, Ambassador). Not one of his best accomplishments, it was nonetheless pleasant and in its title song offered one final addition to Herbert's canon. The song served as Herbert's answer to changing fashions. Though several critics all too hastily branded it a waltz, it was actually a thoroughly up-to-date fox-trot. With Herbert unable to supply last-minute changes, the Shuberts discreetly added uncredited Sigmund Romberg interpolations. Rida Johnson Young and Harold Atteridge based their libretto on *The Road to Yesterday*, a 1906 play by Beulah Marie Dix and Evelyn Greenleaf Sutherland. Elspeth, fatigued from a day of hunting for antiques, falls asleep and dreams she is in the fifteenth century. She is kidnapped by a handsome ruffian. When she awakes she realizes the ruffian was Jack Warren, who has been posing as a bandit for her painter-friend, Will Levison. She and Jack decide that since they have loved each other for 500 years they might as well marry. The story toyed with the possibilities of reincarnation, allowing everyone Elspeth met in one century to behave similarly in another. But it was solely a romantic touch, not a philosophic exploration. Much of the comedy was in the hands of Billy Van. Van managed to sneak a radio into the fifteenth century and collected laughs with lines such as "The trouble in the Garden of Eden was not caused by an apple; it was caused by a green pair." Fay Bainter brought her wistful charm to the role of Elspeth. Her voice was pleasant, but small. It fell to a better singer, the handsome Walter Woolf, to play Jack and to sing the title song. *The Dream Girl* ran fifteen weeks, then toured.

The season's first fiasco, **Bye, Bye, Barbara** (25 August 1924, National), lasted a bare two weeks. It recorded the devices and disguises the Great Karloff, a balloonist and parachutist, must use to escape his alimony-seeking ex-wife, as well as Barbara Palmer's (Janet Velie) need to procure $50,000 for her actor-lover so her father will consent to their marriage. The dialogue ran to such drivel as:

Paulette [Lillian Fitzgerald]: Are you a Russian?
Karloff [Jack Hazzard]: Yes, I'm rushin' to get away.

The plot fell to pieces in the second half, and the evening was reduced to a series of specialty acts. For Carlo and Sanders it represented another futile effort to repeat their success in *Tangerine* (9 August 1921).

Golf, a favorite pastime of the era, and a rich boy's making good on his own, a favorite theme of the period, were combined with moderately happy results in **Top-Hole** (1 September 1924, Fulton). When the young golfer-playboy Robert Corcoran (Ernest Glendinning) is ordered out of the house by his father, Judge Corcoran (Walter Walker), and told not to return until he can earn $1,000 on his own, he becomes a golf instructor and wins a tournament with the encouragement of loyal Marcia Willoughby (Clare Stratton). The show kept its weekly running costs down by employing a chorus line far fewer in numbers than was the practice of the era. There were only twelve girls. However, they made up in quality what they lacked in ranks. The *Times* joyously reported they harked back to "a real Weber and Fields dancing chorus." Inviting audiences to "Dance Your Way To Paradise," they made the low-budget musical frisky enough to keep the small Fulton occupied for 104 performances.

Though **The Chocolate Dandies** (1 September 1924, Colonial) was lavishly mounted, excellently cast, polished by six months on the road, and well received, it failed to give Noble Sissle and Eubie Blake another *Shuffle Along* (23 May 1921). In their study of the songwriters, Robert Kimball and William Bolcom attribute the failure to the production's "unnecessary extravagance." Figures do indeed suggest they are right. Salaries alone were double those of *Shuffle Along*: $7,500 a week against $3,700. The relative opulence and slickness of the production disconcerted a number of critics. *Shuffle Along's* hand-me-down simplicity inadvertently had set a standard by which the twenties insisted on judging black musicals. Time and again critics—and not only in New York—seemed to resent a black musical that strove to emulate costly white mountings. Ashton Stevens's comment in the Chicago *Herald and Examiner* typified this sentiment. Stevens bemoaned, "the show seems to suffer from too much white man." Blake felt the score was his best, telling Kimball and Bolcom, "there is nothing in *Shuffle Along* anywhere near the melodies of 'Dixie Moon' or 'Jassamine Lane.'" Most critics preferred "The Slave Of Love." The show was originally known as *In Bamville*. Kimball and Bolcom explain "Bamville" as "a Negro folk expression" for a place name roughly equivalent to "Podunk." Mose Washington (Lew Payton), who owns a racehorse named Dumb Luck, falls asleep before the race and dreams his horse has won him a small fortune. He becomes president of Bamville's bank, only to have a run on the

bank start. He wakes up to discover Dumb Luck has not won. The big money has gone to Dan Jackson's Rarin'-to-Go, and with his winnings Dan (Ivan H. Browning) has also won the hand of Angeline Brown (Lottie Gee). The race was shown on stage, using three horses on a treadmill. But nothing would rekindle the interest theatregoers had shown for *Shuffle Along*. *The Chocolate Dandies* recorded a disappointing ninety-six performances.

Rose-Marie (2 September 1924, Imperial) was not only the biggest hit of the season, it was the biggest grosser of the decade. In fact, nothing surpassed its multi-million-dollar take until *Oklahoma!*, over twenty years later. The story was a variant of the plot of *Naughty Marietta* (7 November 1910), a tale that would be used again for *Rio Rita* (2 February 1927). A heroine, in a romantic North American setting, wins her love (who is usually associated with a colorful arm of the law) only after exposing a villain not immediately obvious to the characters in the play. Rose-Marie La Flamme (Mary Ellis) is a singer at Lady Jane's, a small hotel in the splendor of the Canadian Rockies. She loves Jim Kenyon (Dennis King). But Ed Hawley (Frank Greene), whose love for Rose-Marie is in no way reciprocated, throws suspicion on Jim for the murder of Black Eagle (Arthur Ludwig). Jim had come to Black Eagle's cabin after Black Eagle had accused him of taking gold off Black Eagle's land. Kenyon brought with him maps that showed he was working his own property, not the Indian's. But when Kenyon arrived at the cabin only Black Eagle's wife, Wanda (Pearl Regay) seemed to be present. Actually Hawley was there, too, but hearing Kenyon's approach, he had been hidden by Wanda, who loves him. Black Eagle returned after Kenyon had departed and discovered Hawley and his wife embracing. He started to throttle Hawley, whereupon Wanda stabbed him. Convinced that her beloved Jim is a murderer, Rose-Marie reluctantly agrees to marry Hawley. The comic but clever trader, Hard-Boiled Herman (William Kent), wheedles the truth from Wanda, allowing Sergeant Malone (Arthur Deagon) of the Mounties to make the proper arrest. Rose-Marie and Jim are reunited in the woods, where he has been hiding. The book, by Otto Harbach and Oscar Hammerstein II, was never dull, but never exceptional. Its attempt to convey an Indian accent was no more farfetched than Harbach's attempt to convey an Italian accent in his first collaboration with Friml, *The Firefly* (2 February 1912). The part-Indian Rose-Marie's first line is "I am take sleigh ride with Jeem." But the development in the dialogue is reasonably fresh and colloquial. Here is Herman attempting to force a confession from Wanda:

Herman: Going so soon?
Wanda: You don't think I stay to see Hawley marry another woman, do you?
Herman: Well, it's your own fault.
Wanda: How you mean my own fault?
Herman: Rose-Marie wouldn't be marrying him if you'd kept your promise to Jim.
Wanda: I no promise nothing.
Herman: You said you'd tell who killed Black Eagle.

The principal reason for the operetta's success was its great Friml score (with supplementary material by Herbert Stothart). It was not only glowingly melodic, it was refreshingly different. It suggested how far the Viennese tradition could be "Americanized." The musical line of the title song (sung, of course, by Jim) employed shorter phrases than was Friml's, wont, reflecting the easy lilt of American speech. Clearly bandleaders and arrangers of the time thought so, emphasizing its immediacy by giving a tango effect—then the rage—to the ninth to fourteenth bars. The unusual chromatics of Rose-Marie and Jim's "Indian Love Call," while not truly Indian, were an ocean away from Vienna. The song of "The Mounties" was a rouser for Malone and his officers that recalled *Naughty Marietta*'s "Tramp, Tramp, Tramp" and that started a vogue for such crowd-stirrers in succeeding operettas. All three of the show's biggest hits came—virtually together— early in the first act, where they did little to advance the action but effectively delineated the characters of Rose-Marie, Jim, and Sergeant Malone. The incessant beat in "Totem Tom Tom," while again not legitimately Indian, undoubtedly conveyed redskin images to the audience. This number was given the show's most memorable staging. Row after row of chorus girls dressed as totem poles marched and danced to the song's compelling beat. A few playgoers or critics probably recalled a similar show-stopping staging in *The Alaskan* (12 August 1907). Only the "Door Of Her Dreams" had an unmistakable Austro–Hungarian flavor. Friml had great hopes for it, insisting it be given a striking production number and seeing it was placed first in the sheet music listings. But the public failed to respond. It was Friml's tragedy that he could never be completely objective and gauge the temper of the times. This fading ultimately removed him from the Broadway scene.

The songs were not listed separately in the program. In what may have been an early example of Hammerstein's pretensions a program note read, "The musical numbers of this play are such an integral part of the action that we do not think we should list them as separate episodes." This was no more true than it had been of a dozen fine shows before. It announced a high ambition rather than a practical achievement. Writing in *Theater Magazine* in May 1925, when *Rose-Marie* was still the reigning hit on Broadway, Hammerstein attempted further to rationalize and intellectualize the show's triumphant success. Ignoring Friml's contributions, he suggested, "the revolution in musical comedy which *Rose-Marie* has wrought was not accidental. It was a carefully directed attack at the Cinderella show in favor of operatic musical comedy." Moving from the specific to the general, he continued, "The history of musical comedy has passed through a variety of phases, but the type that persists, that shows the signs of ultimate victory, is the operetta—the musical play with music and plot welded together in skillful cohesion." At the end of his article he asked, "Is there a form of musical play tucked away somewhere… which could attain the heights of grand opera and still keep sufficiently human to be entertaining?" He himself later provided an answer, though by that time he would be loath to admit the direct descent of his "musical play" from operetta. The show's original Rose-Marie, Mary Ellis, was brought over from the Metropolitan Opera. She found nightly performances taxing, and her Broadway career was short, though she did become a popular London star in the thirties. On the other hand, Dennis King discovered in Jim the sort of role that would keep him busy for the rest of the decade, and it launched his career as one of Broadway's great leading men.

DENNIS KING was born in Coventry, England, on 2 November 1897. He began his apprenticeship as a call boy with the Birmingham Repertory. He soon worked his way to the stage, at which time he dropped his family name of Pratt and adopted his mother's maiden name. By the late teens King was playing important roles in everything from Sophocles to Shakespeare to Somerset Maugham. His London debut was in André

Messager's *Monsieur Beaucaire* in 1919. Two years later the Barrymores brought him to New York for *Clair de Lune*. Jane Cowl brought him back to America in 1923 to play Mercutio to her Juliet. *Rose-Marie* taught King that musicals would give him steadier employment and bigger salaries, but he always took pride that he had been an accomplished actor first, a singer second.

Mounted with a "prodigal magnificence" and gorgeously sung, *Rose-Marie* ran 557 performances. Four road companies satisfied the demand for seats across the country. In London the musical was even more triumphant than in New York, with 851 showings. It established a Paris long-run record of 1,250 showings and played successfully in Berlin, Stockholm, and Moscow.

With **The Passing Show of 1924** (3 September 1924, Winter Garden), the waning series called it a day. Only the 1922 edition had a shorter run. James Barton and Lulu McConnell led the comedians through the inevitable skits about Prohibition, flappers, Coolidge, gangsters, and mahjongg. Indeed some felt there was too much Barton. In two of his better pieces he played a lost Paul Revere and a more contemporary citizen learning the art of getting into a phone booth gracefully. The chorus line, cut by the economizing Shuberts to forty-five, arranged itself in row above row to compose the expected living curtain. It also celebrated the beauties of "A Beaded Bag." Dances included a number that could almost be called an Irish Charleston, "Dublinola." However, nothing from Sigmund Romberg and Jean Schwartz's score became popular outside the theatre. The show was a mediocrity, gone after ninety-three performances.

Ninety-three performances was also the total achieved by **Be Yourself** (3 September 1924, Harris), for which George S. Kaufman and Marc Connelly created the book. In its original version, it represented Kaufman and Connelly's first collaboration. The pair had written it in 1917 as *Miss Moonshine*, a vehicle for Irene Franklin. When no production was forthcoming, the script was shelved. The revised book had music by Lewis Gensler and Milton Schwarzwald. Ira Gershwin supplied some of the lyrics (as did Kaufman and Connelly). A Hatfield-McCoy feud—this time between the

Brennans and the McLeans—comes to a boil when Matt McLean (Jack Donahue) innocently trespasses on Brennan property in the Tennessee mountains. Kaufman and Connelly reduced the feud to a collegiate rivalry with team letters awarded for every opponent shot. Intentionally or not, the production also spoofed the spectacles of the day, when the rising Queenie Smith sauntered on stage garbed as "The Spirit of Bituminous Coal." Georgia Caine, who years earlier helped make Jerome Kern's first Broadway songs popular, was now cast as Grandma Brennan, and William Collier, another star of an earlier era, directed.

Three revues followed in fast succession. **Earl Carroll's Vanities** (10 September 1924, Music Box)—Carroll added his name to the title with this edition—proclaimed it was "exalting the human form." Everyone understood Carroll meant the female form. Carroll ingeniously circumvented the rule that nudes must not move by placing one undressed young lady on a giant pendulum. However, he prudently minimized the chance of an outcry by having her swing back and forth behind an only partially revealing lace curtain. Little else was properly displayed. The clowns, headed by Joe Cook, had only second-rate material. Cook's best skit was one he had done in vaudeville, "The Electrical Factory." It afforded Cook an opportunity to display Rube Goldberg–type inventions. The singers, led by Sophie Tucker, fared no better. Miss Tucker put across a few rags with slightly off-color lyrics. She hit her peak, literally at least, when she appeared as the "High Priestess of Pep" atop a "Pyramid of Dance." Luckily for Carroll his girls were alluring enough to revitalize the tired businessman for 133 showings.

The **Greenwich Village Follies of 1924** and **Hassard Short's Ritz Revue** opened back to back. The *Follies* (16 September 1924. Shubert) had one Cole Porter tune, "I'm In Love Again," which enjoyed a vogue twenty years later. But no song proved a hit at the time, and the alarmed producers rushed in additional ditties by Owen Murphy and Jay Gorney. The new tunes had no more success than the original ones. The stars of the show were the flamboyant Dolly Sisters, who probably did not belong in the relatively intellectualized atmosphere of the series. One number they did was "The Dollies and the Collies," in which the girls' movements were mimicked by trained dogs. The edition's "Ballet Ballad" was based on Oscar Wilde's tale "The Happy Prince." Many of the critics singled out the blackface team of Moran and Mack for special praise.

Heywood Broun even quoted his favorite bit from their material. His excerpt suggests how transient are ideas of humor. Moran advised Mack that he had bought a pig for four dollars in April and sold it for four dollars in August. Mack pointed out that Moran hadn't made any money on the deal. After a deliberative pause Moran replied, "Yes, we found that out." With Vincent Lopez and his orchestra supplying the evening's music, the show lingered for 127 performances before heading for its national tour. Substantial cast changes were made for the road, and Rodgers and Hart's "Manhattan" and "Sentimental Me" were apparently added. Thus, an exceptional amount of the material New York first-nighters saw had been eliminated. The show on the road ran only until eleven o'clock; on opening night in New York the first act didn't end until eleven.

By contrast, the *Ritz Revue* (17 September 1924, Ritz) was beautifully paced and programmed from the onset. Hassard Short's evening promised to begin a new series, but didn't. Raymond Hitchcock, who had abandoned his own series, was costarred with Charlotte Greenwood. Hitchcock had little to do but serve as compère. The best comic material was handed to Miss Greenwood. "Her Morning Bath" found the lanky comedienne prevented from bathing by visits of friends, clothiers, and the neighborhood iceman. When the iceman dropped his block of ice, Miss Greenwood was able to perform an abbreviated, comic version of her famous double-jointed dance as she attempted to avoid the broken ice. Short's spectacles were excellent. In "The Red Ladies," scarlet women of the past—from Salome to Camille—paraded across the stage, while "Crystal Wedding Day" lit the stage with translucent shimmerings. The music, all ordinary, was by almost a dozen different hands. Short's evening was attractive enough to keep the bandbox Ritz lit for 109 performances.

One more book show interrupted the parade of revues. **Dear Sir** (23 September 1924, Times Square) had a libretto by Edgar Selwyn and music by Jerome Kern. It also had lyrics by a newcomer, Howard Dietz. Dietz's contributions were not all that promising, including as they did lines such as "Marriages that never fade/Always are in heaven made." Some of the lyrics from unpublished numbers were better. "If I Could Lead A Merry Mormon Life" offered first rate comedy, asserting bigamy and polygamy could "make a pig o' me." "A Houseboat On The Harlem," stuck in the muck, exposed some peculiar horrors of urban life with grace and wit. Dietz could

not have received much inspiration from the Selwyn libretto. Laddie Munn (Oscar Shaw), a man-about-town, is publicly rebuffed at Sherry's by Dorothy Fair (Genevieve Tobin). At a Park Avenue charity auction he wins her services for one week. By the time the week is over he has won her affection and her hand. Dietz could find no more excitement in Kern's score than he could in the libretto. Kern's music fell lightly on the ear, but it was far less attractive than his unappreciated *Sitting Pretty* music. The show was withdrawn after an embarrassing two weeks.

The Grab Bag (6 October 1924, Globe) was another delightful bit of Ed Wynn lunacy. Its score was culled from various sources, with Wynn himself taking credit for several of the tunes. Though Janet Velie sang and Marion Fairbanks (half of the Fairbanks Twins) danced, the evening was dominated by the great, lisping clown. Wynn made his entrance wearing a ludicrous travesty of a homburg and a kilt. He announced that a Russian Octette would sing Cossack folksongs, beginning with "He Eats French Dressing Every Night So He Can Wake Up Oily In The Morning." Another song he promised was "She Might Have Been A School Teacher, But She Hadn't Any Class." Among his inventions was a typewriter-like contraption for eating corn, allowing the diner's hands to stay cool and clean.

Nudity—even if the nudes had to hold statuesque poses—was the lure that kept the Shuberts' **Artists and Models of 1924** (15 October 1924, Astor) on the boards for nearly eight months. The brothers resorted to an antiquated practice by framing the evening with a thin story. Perhaps more accurately, the show began with a plot that took an innocent young lady from her New Hampshire home to explore the wonders of Greenwich Village. The plot quickly disappeared in a welter of spectacle and specialities, "a dazzling succession of golds and blacks and grays... rose numbers, color numbers, jazz numbers." A visit to an Italian restaurant in the Village suddenly evolved into a colorful panorama of "Mediterranean Nights." The scene gave Trini an opportunity to perform her fiery Spanish dances. Closer to home came high-stepping Charlestons and a number that proclaimed, "I Love To Dance When I Hear A March." As was the case with *The Passing Show*, the score (by Sigmund Romberg and Fred Coots) gave audiences nothing to take home. Weakest of all was the show's lame, anemic comedy.

Dixie to Broadway (29 October 1924, Broadhurst), a black revue, is remembered wistfully as enchanting Florence Mills's last major New York appearance before her untimely death. Her singing, dancing, and "native grotesqueries" stopped the show in "Jungle Nights in Dixieland." The black performers gave imitations of white favorites such as George M. Cohan, Gallagher and Shean, and Eva Tanguay. *Chauve Souris* (4 February 1922) was saluted with a march of black wooden soldiers. Typical of the evening's humor was the comedian who refused a ten-dollar bill, claiming, "That's tainted money! 'Tain't yours and 'tain't mine." The expected black vitality kept the show on the boards eight weeks.

Ziegfeld brought in a musical version of Clare Kummer's hit of eight seasons back *Good Gracious, Annabelle*. It was produced as a vehicle for his current wife, Billie Burke. Since Miss Kummer off and on had interpolated songs in musicals, it was not surprising that she wrote a number of the tunes for this musicalization, rechristened **Annie Dear** (4 November 1924, Times Square). But Ziegfeld was never content to do things by halves. Sigmund Romberg and Harry Tierney were called in to embellish the score. Miss Kummer's libretto remained faithful to her original story. Annie Leigh has run away from her rough, bearded western groom (Marion Green) on the day of the wedding and taken a job as a servant on the Long Island estate of the bibulous copper magnate, George Wimbleton (Ernest Truex). When her groom appears, minus his beard, she fails to recognize him, so he has time to ingratiate himself and effect a reconciliation. The lavish garden setting of the last act gave Ziegfeld an excuse to stop the story while he treated his customers to a "brilliant, luxurious" ballet, "Little Boy Blue's Search for the Crock of Gold at the End of the Rainbow." Miss Burke became the little boy. The ballet, at first only in blues and grays, recounted the boy's meeting Cloud, Moon, Rain, Wind, and other figures as he seeks the crock of gold. Only at the end did the stage blaze forth in an appropriate rainbow of colors. But Ziegfeld's traditional largess was wasted on *Annie Dear*. The music was inferior, and the fights between Ziegfeld, who wanted to make more changes, and Miss Kummer, who wanted to restore the original material Ziegfeld had cut, finally so exasperated the producer he threw up his hands and closed the show after 103 performances.

Miss Kummer had an even more unhappy experience when she provided the American adaptation of Leo Fall's **Mme. Pompadour** (11 November 1924, Martin Beck). The rage for Viennese operetta was long over. *Mme. Pompadour*, which told of

a romance that blossoms when its heroine (Wilda Bennett) goes slumming incognito, opened a week after *Annie Dear* and was long departed before *Annie Dear* terminated its own short run.

Another team that had reaped success a season or so back tried again and met with disappointment, though not with failure. Harlan Thompson and Harry Archer of *Little Jessie James* (15 August 1923) offered what they termed "a smart musical farce," **My Girl** (24 November 1924, Vanderbilt). The story told of the Whites (Jane Taylor and Russell Mack) throwing a fancy, if dry, party in order to win acceptance at the Rainbow Club. A bootlegger, desperately trying to hide his illegal stock, mixes his more potent drinks with the innocent stuff the Whites are serving. The complications that follow are resolved happily when the Whites win the desired acceptance. Nothing from the evening approached the popularity of *Little Jessie James*'s "I Love You." Still, because of tunes on the order of "You And I," "all the feet in the auditorium were set tapping." The six-month run was not unrewarding, but it was a far cry from the authors' earlier bonanza.

A fourth lady entered the theatrical scene the next night. **The Magnolia Lady** (25 November 1924, Shubert) was a musical version of A. E. Thomas and Alice Duer Miller's 1916 hit, *Come Out of the Kitchen*. The score was by Harold Levey. But Levey had split with Zelda Sears, collaborating instead with another popular woman—librettist and lyricist Anne Caldwell. Her book was set at The Magnolias, the Ravenel mansion in Virginia horse country. The Ravenels have come upon hard times. To help pay for their father's surgery they rent their estate to an Englishman, Kenneth Craig (Ralph Forbes). When to their surprise he insists on white servants they agree to fill the positions. Before the final curtain Craig has fallen in love with and proposed to Lily-Lou Ravenel (Ruth Chatterton). The show required more urgent surgery than did Mr. Ravenel (Skeet Gallagher). Miss Caldwell could no more inspire Levey to write vital, exciting music than could Miss Sears. Some potential customers may have been put off by the casting of Forbes and Miss Chatterton, better known for their work in straight plays. One critic felt the leading lady's small, sweet voice was "a shade studied." Whatever the reason, *The Magnolia Lady* folded after six weeks.

The distaff side was also featured in the titles of two of the three musicals that raised their curtains on the same night, 1 December. The book of one was a throwback to the poor-Irish-girl-makes-good plots of the preceding period. Society's polished Roger Utley (Nathaniel Wagner) loves April Daly (Tessa Kosta), the daughter of an uncouth upstart, Patrick Daly (Harry Allen). He calls her his **Princess April** (1 December 1924, Ambassador). But Roger's snobbish sister, Kathryn (Audrey Maple), objects to their marrying. Only when April gallantly claims to own a beaded bag found in a compromising situation, a bag everyone knows really belongs to Kathryn, does Roger's sister fall in line. More than one critic complained that Miss Kosta's lovely, clarion voice was wasted on Carlo and Sanders's tinny musical comedy jingles. The unoriginal book, weak score, and unfortunate miscasting all contributed to making *Princess April* a three-week flop.

The girl in the second title was unnamed, but she was admonished **Lady, Be Good!** (1 December 1924, Liberty). Though it was not the biggest smash of the season, it may well have been its most important musical. For with this show the rhythms, tensions, and color of stage jazz were defined; the gutsy Negro creation was given a cerebral white reinterpretation. Gershwin had demonstrated the grammar of the style in "Somebody Loves Me" and a few other, earlier, songs. Now he supplied an entire, consistent score in the idiom. Coupled with his brother Ira's fresh, colloquial, and often sassy lyrics, it introduced a new tone to the American musical stage. It was an abrupt contrast to the arioso style of operetta. These songs could almost be spoken; indeed, they often were. It may have been this the *Times* meant when it predicted the show had "a number of tunes the unmusical… will find hard to get rid of." Attempting to get to the essentials of this style, Alec Wilder in his *American Popular Song* has suggested, "The melody should be spare, containing a minimal number of notes, and the harmony should be similarly uncluttered, almost skeletal." To Wilder four songs from the show were intriguing enough to deserve special attention—"Fascinating Rhythm," "Little Jazz Bird," "The Man I Love" (dropped from the show during its tryout), and the title song. He describes "Oh, Lady, Be Good!" as "a strict A-A-B-A song, very spare in its use of harmony and without syncopation," insisting, "Its special trademark is the quarter note triple." The unusual beat of "Fascinating Rhythm" made it an immediate attention grabber. Not all the songs were so patently "jazzy." One of the loveliest and most popular tunes from the piece was the simple, echoing "So Am I." The pianistic texture

of Gershwin's music was underscored by his use of the dual pianists Arden and Ohman as a prominent part of the pit band.

The story was not especially complicated. When Dick Trevor (Fred Astaire) rebuffs Josephine Vanderwater (Jayne Auburn), she has Dick and his sister, Susie (Adele Astaire), evicted from the house she owns. Brother and sister set up housekeeping on the sidewalk, hanging their "God Bless Our Home" sign on the lamppost. A passerby named Jack Robinson (Alan Edwards) has such a torn suit that Susie momentarily forgets her own problems and mends Jack's tattered jacket. "Watty" Watkins (Walter Catlett), a clownish, garrulous lawyer who in good musical comedy fashion represents both the impecunious Trevors and the rich Vanderwaters, attempts to effect a reconciliation at the Vanderwaters' party. His fee is oddball. Watty has been threatened by a Mexican whose sister has been jailed for biting a man's ear. The Mexican insists Watty arrange his sister's release so she can collect the estate of her late husband. If Watty succeeds, the Mexican will pay him $100,000. Watty prevails on Susie to impersonate the Mexican's sister and help collect the money. Susie agrees only when she realizes that the money will help get Josephine off Dick's back. It develops that the Mexican lady's husband is not dead. He is, in fact, the very Jack Robinson whose clothes Susie sewed. He proves that the Mexican marriage was forced and illegal, convinces his uncle, who had disinherited him, that he is worthwhile, and purposes to Susie. Aided by Jack's restored fortune, Dick gives Josephine the boot and is free to marry the girl he truly loves, Shirley Vernon (Kathlene Martyn). Contemporary critics and later commentators, such as Robert Kimball and Alfred Simon, dismissed the book as a collection of "shopworn musical-comedy formulas." Perhaps Guy Bolton and Fred Thompson's outline was just that. But Bolton was too sure and witty a librettist; he rarely released anything that was not at least a notch or two above the run-of-the-mill. Not all of the dialogue was on a high, cerebral plane:

Jack: I'm just a poor hobo!
Susie: Then I must be in Hoboken.

But much of it was slangy, with a clipped, natural sound, and with a casual use of expletive a step or two removed from the underlined or coy employment such expletives had heretofore generally suffered.

At the Vanderwater party two minor figures engage in the following colloquy:

Daisey: And you said you wanted me to help you reform.

Bertie: I do—Duckie—I do. But I don't want to reform too darned fast. It might make you lose interest if there wasn't something about me for you to pick on.

The lead-in to "The Half Of It, Dearie, Blues" runs:

Dick: I'm so gosh darn blue.

Shirley: Blue? Why?

Dick: Because you're going to marry someone else and I've got to marry someone else, and oh it's hell!

Not all the songs had quite so well motivated lead-ins. Old formulas still applied here as well as to some of the jokes. Cliff (Ukulele Ike) Edwards's walking on the stage in the middle of an argument between Susie and Dick was all the cue given for "Fascinating Rhythm"; and the poignancy of "So Am I" was lessened when it was sung by Susie and Jack parting until they meet the next day for breakfast. The title song was a bit more cleverly and unusually placed. It is not sung by Dick or Jack to his girl, but by Watty as an inducement to Susie to cooperate in the masquerade. Ira Gershwin's lyrics displayed something of the same ambivalence. The Vanderwater soiree begins with the chorus singing "Oh, What A Lovely Party," the sort of song and conventional lyrics heard in show after show during the era. But the innovative, distinctive Ira Gershwin was also present, and not merely in the outstanding tunes of the evening. He opened the second act with a lyric that had recourse to the old inversions and stilted rhetoric, but he made them painless and contemporary by his diversionary, startling rhymes such as "adjectives are spilt more" and "Biltmore." No critic of the day fully sensed the importance of *Lady, Be Good!*, though some, such as the man on the *World*, hailed it as the "best musical in town." What praise the show received was largely for its immediate values as entertainment. Gershwin's music was lauded, but most of the applause went to the Astaires and to Norman Bel Geddes' brightly colored, slightly stylized sets, stylizations reflecting the growing popularity of art deco. One critic felt Bel Geddes went on a "well-earned spree after the penitential severity of [Max Reinhardt's] 'The Miracle.'" Color, comedy,

melody, and the Astaires kept *Lady, Be Good!* in New York for 330 performances.

The third 1 December opening signaled the end of another revue series. The Music Box Revue 1924–1925 reverted to what for these big extravaganzas had become an obsolescent tradition by having a compère for the evening—in this case Rip Van Winkle awakened from one more long sleep. What he heard was a hand-me-down Irving Berlin score into which Berlin felt it necessary to inject his already popular "All Alone." Grace Moore and Oscar Shaw, spotlit and holding telephones, sang the song from opposite sides of an otherwise dark stage. Miss Moore also sang "Call Of The South" and "Rock-a-bye Baby." Clark and McCullough and Fanny Brice provided the laughs. In her "Don't Send Me Back (To Petrograd)" she pleaded, "I'll even wash the sheets for the Ku Klux Klan, but don't send me back." She donned one of her favorite costumes, a tutu, for "I Want To Be A Ballet Dancer," done with Bobby Clark. It wasn't Miss Brice's fault if she looked silly in the outfit or if, in her Russian-Yiddish accent, she made "ballet dancer" sound like "belly dancer." Miss Brice and Clark also had fun playing Adam and Eve. Clark became a boxer in one of the era's many prizefight skits, "The Kid's First and Last Fight." He and McCullough appeared as "A Couple of Senseless Censors." The production numbers sped the audience to Tokyo, to old New York, and to Alice's Wonderland, shaded them beneath a gigantic weeping willow, and even sprayed them with perfume as was done in 1923. John Murray Anderson and James Reynolds designed the spectacles. The evening survived 186 showings, but Berlin and his partner Sam H. Harris read the temper of times and turned the Music Box over to general bookings.

One night after this trio appeared, The Student Prince (2 December 1924, Jolson) was sung for the first time in New York. Dorothy Donnelly took her story from *Old Heidelberg*, a play in which Richard Mansfield had appeared for years on end. In fact, this musical version was originally announced with the fuller title of *The Student Prince in Heidelberg*. It retold its old tale quite faithfully. Prince Karl Franz (Howard Marsh) is about to leave for Heidelberg with his tutor Dr. Engel (Greek Evans). Engel looks back on his own student life as his "Golden Days," assuring the prince, "we remember them all else above." They arrive incognito at the Inn of the Three Golden Apples. There they find their wish for anonymity abetted by the clownish Lutz (George Hassell), who has been dropping hints all over the place that he is the important person the students and beer girls have been waiting for. The "Students' Marching Song" heralds the arrival of the prince's future classmates. They join in a "Drinking Song," saluting in particular their favorite waitress, Kathie (Ilse Marvenga). The prince's presence is finally acknowledged, and he is invited to join the Saxon Corps. He accepts. Kathie and Karl Franz fall in love at first sight, and they swear eternal allegiance "Deep In My Heart, Dear." The prince further swears his eternal vow in an impassioned "Serenade." But Karl Franz's grandfather, the king, is taken ill, and not expected to live. Karl must return home. For important reasons of state, he must also marry Princess Margaret (Roberta Beatty), though both candidly admit their loves lie elsewhere. Margaret and her Captain Tarnitz (John Coast) ruefully wish the world were only for "Just We Two," while the prince in turn laments that he will see his beloved Kathie "Nevermore." But echoes of the past are too strong, and Karl returns to Heidelberg for one farewell with Kathie. Realizing they must go their own ways, they again promise that deep in their hearts they will remember their love forever.

Sigmund Romberg's score for this bittersweet story was his finest achievement. It was finally obvious to everyone, even the Shuberts, that Romberg was no hack. The music was Viennese-American: more sentimental and strong-fibered than Austro-Hungarian material but less grandly sweeping and less saccharine. The success of the show was phenomenal. Its original run was 608 performances, and in its heyday it required nine companies to satisfy the nationwide demand for seats. It toured virtually without cessation for a quarter of a century, until a road company of *The Student Prince*, like a road company of *Blossom Time*, became synonymous with theatrical shabbiness. Amazingly, there almost was no *Student Prince*. The Shuberts were aghast at what they considered Romberg's operatic music, appalled at the unhappy ending, and utterly bewildered by Romberg's demand for a large, strong-voiced male chorus rather than a long line of feminine beauties. They threatened to throw out both Romberg and his score. Luckily, Romberg and his lawyer won the day. The Shuberts profited from the lesson not just by watching their coffers fill. The reception awarded the fine male ensemble (thirty-six men in the original production) prompted them to insert similar groups into many of the operettas they later mounted, and these male choruses became almost a Shubert trademark.

Four musicals came in at the end of the month. The Duncan Sisters arrived in a musical version of *Uncle Tom's Cabin* called **Topsy and Eva** (23 December 1924, Harris). The sisters claimed to have written all their songs themselves. They also sang them, with Vivian in golden curls and Rosetta in blackface and pigtails. The songs presented the same sentimental, idealized picture of the old South Al Jolson and Eddie Cantor often portrayed. These new numbers included "Moon Am Shinin,'" "The Land Of Long Ago," and the hit of the show, "Rememb'ring." The sisters, aided by the appeal of the old story and new songs, kept the show in town for twenty weeks. However, this was less than half of the forty-three weeks the musical had compiled earlier in Chicago.

Betty Lee (25 December 1924, 44th St.) was only slightly less successful, playing fourteen weeks. A musical version of Paul Armstrong and Rex Beach's 1909 *Going Some*, it recounted the adventures of Wallingford Speed (Hal Skelly) and Lawrence Glass (Joe E. Brown), who arrive broke at the Chapin estate and, hearing a famous racer and his trainer are expected, pretend to be the pair. A race is arranged, and Speed is threatened with dire consequences if he loses. Cheered on by Betty Lee (Gloria Foy), he manages to win. The show offered posthumously the last Louis Hirsch songs Broadway would hear. Con Conrad filled in the gaps Hirsch had left. But no superior melodies emerged, though the songs were bouncy enough to spark the evening. Skelly and Brown as the two impostors had a large share in the show's popularity. Many who remember the wide-mouthed, impish-looking Brown only as a comedian will be surprised to learn that a number of reviewers praised him not only for his fun-making but for several "eccentric dances," including the mock soft-shoe routine he performed in the course of the evening.

A revival of Gilbert and Sullivan's *Patience* began a three-month stay at the Provincetown Playhouse beginning 29 December. On the same night, another Russian revue hoping to equal the rage of *Chauve Souris* appeared at the Frolic. Called either **Seeniaya Ptitza** or **The Blue Bird**, it drew middling attendance for eight weeks.

The first musical for 1925 was **Big Boy**, with which Jolson returned to the Winter Garden on 7 January. Once again Jolson was Gus, and this time Gus was a stable boy at the Bedfords. For years he had ridden the Bedford entry in the Derby, but a group of sharpers connive to replace Gus with a famous English jockey. Their plan is foiled, and Gus wins the Derby riding Big Boy. The show used the same device musicals such as *Honey Girl* and *The Chocolate Dandies* had already employed to good effect: the race was run with real horses moving on treadmills. Percy Hammond in the *Herald Tribune* exclaimed the race in *Big Boy* made "'Ben Hur' look like a country affair." Apart from such gimmicks, the evening was a claptrap affair, and many a night Jolson repeated his old trick of dismissing the cast midway through the performance and singing for the audience the rest of the evening. Some of the songs he introduced in *Big Boy* became Jolson standards and perennial favorites: "California, Here I Come" (actually first sung during the road tour of the 1921 *Bombo*) and "Keep Smiling At Trouble" (Jolson, DeSylva/Lewis Gensler). At one point he tested "If You Knew Susie," but dropped it and gave it to Eddie Cantor. The show should have been a smash hit with a long run, but after six weeks Jolson became too ill to continue. The scenery was stored in the hope of reviving the show when Jolson recovered.

When the Shuberts imported **The Love Song** (13 January 1925, Century), Edward Kunneke's operetta based on the life and music of Offenbach, the brothers expected another *Blossom Time*. Instead the new work moved on after just four months.

Charles Dillingham, John Cort, and Martin Beck combined forces to mount an A. Baldwin Sloane operetta, **China Rose** (19 January 1925, Martin Beck). It detailed the efforts of Cha Ming (J. Harold Murray), the Prince of Manchuria, to win the virgin, Ro See (Olga Steck). He sends a pair of ludicrous muddlers to escort her to the palace, then disguises himself as a bandit on the road. His persistence prevails, and the diffident Ro See is won over. The show had sumptuous settings. It also offered some unusual dancing. In one "Chinese" dance the leading artist startled many in the audience by bending backwards until her head touched the floor. *China Rose* opened 19 January. Just over a month later Sloane, who had attempted to return from retirement with this show, died at the age of fifty-two. His last score marked no advance over his first, or any of the many he composed in between. *China Rose* played for three months before fading.

Elsie Janis romped in with a revue called **Puzzles of 1925** (2 February 1925, Fulton). She mounted the show as austerely as she had *Elsie Janis and Her Gang* (1 December 1919). She even took credit for several of the songs, including one with the fetching title "Do-I-Or-Don't-I Blues." For most of the

evening Miss Janis acted as commère to a parade of knockabout comics, ballroom dancers, and other vaudeville acts. Only just before the final curtain did she herself come front and center to sing many of the songs she had sung for the troops in France and to imitate Lenore Ulric, Bea Lillie, and John Barrymore. Her popularity was still broad enough to keep the show on the boards fourteen weeks.

Aging, and surrounded by cleverer competitors, Harry B. Smith was less and less active. He had worked on *The Love Song*, and now, with Karl Hajos adapting Tschaikowsky melodies for him, Smith fashioned the book and lyrics for an operetta he called **Natja** (16 February 1925, Knickerbocker). Because Prince Potemkin (George Reimherr) does not fairly represent her Crimean homeland, Natja (Madeline Collins) disguises herself as a young man to win the ear of Catherine the Great and get justice for her neighbors. She also wins Lt. Vladimir Strogonoff (Warren Proctor). It was typical Smith hackwork, and the public would not buy it. The show was hurried away after four weeks.

If *Natja* presented an obsolescent form of operetta, **Sky High** (2 March 1925, Shubert) was clearly a throwback to the old producer-assemblages. The Shuberts put it all together as a vehicle for Willie Howard (with Willie's brother and erstwhile partner, Eugene, listed as coproducer). Using a Berlin and West End success (*Whirled into Happiness*) for a start, they planted the sad-faced, put-upon Willie as Sammy Myers at the Majestic Music Hall in London. There he gives up his befuddling job as an attendant to become a valet. But his master is a fake, passing himself off as a lord to make a good marriage. Sammy innocently bungles into exposing his master. The original piece was first translated by Harry Graham, then "adapted" by Harold Atteridge. At least a dozen writers helped on the songs. A Victor Herbert song, "Give Your Heart In June," was advertised as "His Last Waltz." Howard won applause not only for his clowning but for his dead-on-target imitation of Al Jolson. If he received little assistance from a tired book and score, he was able to leave the stage at intervals knowing the show's excellent dancers were ready to delight with their kicks and taps. The well-liked Howard helped keep the show going into the summer.

Another great comedian, Leon Errol, opened the following night, 3 March, in **Louie the 14th**. For the occasion, Florenz Ziegfeld and Joseph Urban completely refurbished the old Majestic, by then called the Cosmopolitan. Errol played Louie Ketchup, an army cook with the AEF who elects to remain in France. When rich Paul Trapman (J. W. Doyle) discovers there will be thirteen at the table for his grand dinner, he hastily enlists Louie as a fourteenth guest. Louie's gaucheries provide the fun and complications. Inevitably, since Errol and Louie were one and the same, a drunk scene ensued. There was, the *World* insisted, "nothing more comical than his old act of falling down horribly and humilitively every so often." The show was elaborately mounted by Ziegfeld. The dinner was served on a real gold dinner service that had once belonged to the Russian imperial family and now was the property of the Ziegfelds. A chef in the wings prepared a real meal. Unhappily, Romberg's score was a major letdown after the richness and depth of *The Student Prince.* The show's berth up at the somewhat distant Columbus Circle may have hurt attendance. *Louie the 14th* ran until it could begin a fall tour, but the tour was cut short when Errol was hurt in an accident.

George McManus's popular comic strip *Bringing Up Father* provided the inspiration and title for a musical version (6 April 1925, Lyric) of the battles between the stern-eyed Maggie, rolling pin in hand, and the dapper, henpecked Jiggs. A series of **Bringing Up Father** shows had been popular in the hinterlands for nearly a decade. They included *Bringing Up Father in Florida, Bringing Up Father on Broadway, Bringing Up Father in Ireland* (shades of Emmet's Fritz!), and *Bringing Up Father at the Seashore.* This particular production was rushed in from the road to fill a vacant theatre. In this version Maggie follows a fleeing Jiggs from Ireland to a yacht headed for Spain. The story was halted frequently for vaudeville specialties. One performer, Mary Marlowe, did a series of imitations early in the evening and came on later to perform a "Leg-mania Dance." Neither the music nor the comedy was inspired enough to attract Maggie and Jiggs's followers away from their papers. The show lasted three weeks.

Princess Ida and *The Mikado* were revived two days apart at theatres directly across the street from one another. Unlike the simple staging of *Patience* earlier in the season, both shows were given relatively elaborate productions and both had important artists in their casts, most notably Tessa Kosta as Ida; *The Mikado* was the more successful of the two newcomers. Three Gilbert and Sullivan revivals in a matter of months attested to a reawakening interest in the great English masters.

Two other musicals vied with *Princess Ida* for opening-nighters. **Tell Me More** (13 April 1925,

Gaiety) gave Broadway its second Gershwin score to a book show in five months. Just as Romberg's material for *Louie the 14th* disappointed after his work for *The Student Prince,* Gershwin's score was a letdown after *Lady, Be Good!* No Gershwin standards emerged. Nor was the book particularly strong. Its straightforward story of Kenneth Dennison's (Alexander Gray) courting of Peggy Van De Leur (Phyllis Cleveland) at a masked ball in New York and a vacation retreat in New Hampshire barely had enough twists to see it through to eleven o'clock. At one point Peggy poses as a shopgirl to test the seemingly snobbish Kenneth's ardor. Lou Holtz's clowning concealed many of the dull spots. He played poor Monty Sipkin, the beau of the comic subplot's rich Jane Wallace (Esther Howard). Besides performing his low dialect comedy Holtz was allowed to add one of his own songs just before the final curtain, a number he had been doing in vaudeville, "Oh, So La Mi." But even more of the dull spots were glossed over by the favorite cure-all of 1920s musical comedy—dancing. Sammy Lee's chorus girls were described as "comely, tireless and thoroughly expert in all the acrobatics to which modern dancing has come to bend the knee." They brought down the house with their high-stepping to Gershwin's "Kickin' The Clouds Away." As if so agile a line were not enough, three specialty dancers—Dorothy Wilson, Mary Jane, and Vivian Glenn—were seen to "reduce to absurdity the doctrine of speed, and particularly of touching the back of the head with the toes." *Tell Me More* was light and bubbly enough to register 100 performances. Interestingly, its original title was to have been *My Fair Lady,* but that was dropped as not sufficiently commercial.

Mercenary Mary (13 April 1925, Longacre), which rounded out the trio of openings, had a plot reminiscent of an earlier Gershwin show, *La, La, Lucille* (26 May 1919), though it was actually based on Herbert Hall Winslow and Emil Nyitray's 1923 farce, *What's Your Wife Doing?* Chris and Mary Skinner (Louis Simon and Winnie Baldwin) have married over the objections of Chris' grandfather. They fear he will disinherit them. So they decide to stage a divorce, get back in the will, and then quietly remarry. Chris's friend, Jerry (Allen Kearns), agrees for a fee to play co-respondent in his apartment. Mary is so nervous she drinks too much and almost spoils everything, but the uncle relents and all ends well. William B. Friedlander, who coauthored the book with Isabel Leighton and staged the piece, collaborated with Con Conrad on the songs. Their "Honey, I'm In Love With You" exemplifies the lesser tunes that filled the more commonplace musicals of the season. While a band known as the Jazz Ambassadors played the score, a "star and garter" chorus kicked its shapely, well-exposed legs in unison, and "Nellie Breen's amazing twinkling toes [touched] the ground only for the sake of bouncing off it." When New York proved indifferent, the show was hustled off to London, where it enjoyed a huge success.

The first half of June delivered three new musicals. **Lucky Sambo** (6 June 1925, Colonial), produced, as so many black shows had to be, at a somewhat déclassé house, watched Rufus Johnson (Joe Boyd) and Sambo Jenkins (Tim Moore) tricked into a dubious oil-drilling scheme by Jim Nightengale (Clarence Robinson). But the tricksters are themselves duped, and Rufus and Sambo do strike oil. It was all—book, lyrics, and music—by Porter Grainger and Fred Johnson. The critics responded to their efforts the way they responded to all black shows of the period. One reviewer wrote, "These negro musical shows vary in titles and principals but they all have one glorious feature in common—a genuine and spontaneous hilarity which can't be surpassed by the most elaborate troupe on the other side of the cotton line." Grainger and Johnson knowingly included all the stereotypes the critics and public expected. The show opened in front of Aunt Jemima's cabin, where the chorus demonstrated "the violent convulsions of the Charleston." The chorus also sang spiritual-like songs such as "I'm Comin' Home." Bit parts included a slow-moving, bug-eyed, comic porter.

On 17 May the "Junior members" of the Theatre Guild staged a matinee and evening performance of a revue they had completed to help purchase tapestries for the new theatre the Guild was building. Because the performances were to be at the Garrick, the evening was christened **The Garrick Gaieties.** The revue was small-scaled, relying for its appeal on its wit, its melody, and the skill of its young performers. Since these youngsters included Romney Brent, Sterling Holloway, and Philip Loeb, the skills were impressive. The critics hailed the skits, which bit the hand they were trying to feed by satirizing such Guild productions as *The Guardsman* and *They Knew What They Wanted* (rephrased by the players as "They Didn't Know What They Were Getting"). In "The Theatre Guild Enters Heaven," Brent appeared as St. Peter, rendering judgment on the acceptability

of the heroines in recent Guild plays. The sole political spoof was "Mr. and Mrs.," in which the Coolidges' idea of an enjoyable evening was seen to be listening silently to the radio and going to sleep by ten. The Scopes "Monkey Trail" was staged with a jury in monkey suits. The three musketeers, New York's police, and subway manners were all twitted. The evening's lone bow to "spectacle" was the opening of the second act. "Rancho Mexicana" was danced by Rose Rolando in a multi-colored set designed by her husband, the distinguished artist Miguel Covarrubias. Music for the scene was by their friend Tatanacho. As far as the rest of the production went, one critic estimated it included "about $3 worth of scenery." The most lasting part of the evening proved to be the songs, seven of which were written by Richard Rodgers and Larry Hart.

Hart's almost pyrotechnical ingenuity was revealed in the lyrics to their opening song, "Gilding The Guild." While hailing competitors like the Neighborhood Playhouse that "shine below the Macy-Gimbel line" he welcomed the greater variety and daring of the Guild, which one night served "a mild dish of folklore quaintly childish" and then turned "Oscar Wildish" the next evening. And together Rodgers and Hart made unforgettable words and music with "Manhattan." The song was sung by sad-voiced, tousled-haired Holloway and pert June Cochrane. Its mounting was the utmost in simplicity. Holloway and Miss Cochrane sang on an undecorated stage before the plain show curtain. Rodgers and Hart's main contribution was meant to be the first-act finale—their "jazz opera" "The Joy Spreader." The opera told of a salesgirl and a clerk (Betty Starbuck and Brent) accidentally locked overnight in a department store. The next morning the puritanical owner refuses to believe they were not up to some mischief. The "opera" suffered the same fate as Gershwin's "Blue Monday Blues" in the George White *Scandals* (28 August 1922). It was hastily dropped. But its removal left space for a new Rodgers and Hart song, "Sentimental Me," which Holloway and Miss Cochrane were awarded for the excellent rendition of "Manhattan." After a few additional special performances, the show became the regular attraction at the Garrick on 8 June and compiled an impressive 211 performances before it was through. *The Garrick Gaieties*, as much as *Charlot's Revue* (9 January 1924), announced that small, literate revues were the wave of the future and that the death knell of the great extravaganzas was tolling for all to hear.

Kosher Kitty Kelly (15 June 1925, Times Square), with music by Leon De Costa, hoped to attract the same Irish and Jewish elements that had long been a strong bulwark to the New York theatre and were at that very moment helping *Abie's Irish Rose* achieve the longest run until that time in Broadway's history. It failed, though it took a tack most Irish and Jews probably liked better than the mixed marriage of Anne Nichols's farce. Kitty Kelly (Helen Shipman) dates Morris Rosen (Basil Loughrane), but she finally selects Patrick O'Reilly (Fred Santley), while Morris seems happy with Rosie Feinbaum (Beatrice Allen).

1925–1926

There was a slight, unimportant drop in the number of new musicals during 1925–1926, but no slackening of excitement or of quality. However, a real if not apparent drop in the number of revues occurred, though booking quirks brought two editions of the *George White's Scandals* and *The Grand Street Follies*.

The season opened and closed with **The Grand Street Follies**. The series' spotlight remained focused on its bright travesties and impersonations, minimizing any musical originality. The earlier of the season's two editions (18 June 1925, Neighborhood Playhouse) offered a skit called "They Knew What They Wanted Under the Elms." The set recalled Robert Edmond Jones's multi-storied set for O'Neill's play. A different Broadway hit was burlesqued in each of the four rooms. Actually almost all the show's material related to recent Broadway seasons. *The Guardsman* was spoofed, with Lynn Fontanne's role assumed by the company's master impersonator, Albert Carroll. *Abie's Irish Rose* was transformed into an Italian opera. "L'Irlandesa Rose dell'Abie," while the tough-talking (for the era) *What Price Glory?* was cleansed and daintified, its foul-mouthed Sergeant Quirk "fragrant and fairy-like in lavender pyjamas."

Gilbert's Engaged (18 June 1925, 52nd St.), a freakish affair, was a musical version of W. S. Gilbert's old play *Engaged*. It utilized songs of the play's era with new words and occasional new melodies by Brian Hooker. The show met with little success and did nothing but momentarily interrupt the progression of summer revues.

The **Scandals** returned four nights later with a 1925 edition (22 June 1925, Apollo). Its cast included Harry Fox, Helen Morgan, and Tom Patricola. Strumming on his ukulele and backed by sixty of George White's fast-stepping chorus girls, Patricola provided the night's show-stoppers in his Charleston-like dances. Albertina Rasch Girls, "supremely charming and unmechanically graceful," provided more ballet-like moments. One of the evening's capital numbers was White's good-humored bow to his competitor, Irving Berlin. Gordon

Dooley impersonated the composer-producer. As he lamented he was all alone, White's beauties flitted around him "twining in and out over his body." With Gershwin gone, White hired Buddy DeSylva, Lew Brown, and Ray Henderson to do the score. Though they soon established one of the nation's best song mills, the team's efforts for this edition were unavailing. Their initial offerings are well represented by "What A World This Would Be." Neither the public nor White was unduly disturbed by the music's lack of distinction. Theatregoers flocked to the *Scandals* for 171 performances, and White signed the boys for the 1926 version.

Both **Artists and Models** (24 June 1925, Winter Garden) and **Earl Carroll Vanities** (6 July 1925, Earl Carroll) had even less of merit to offer than did the *Scandals*. Both featured their celebrated nudes. And both had quickly garnered such large regular followings that each ran out the entire season despite all the critical harrumphs. The girls were not the only attraction in *Artists and Models*. Phil Baker played the concertina while his stooge, Sid Silvers, planted in a stage box, harassed him. When Silvers complained, "I have no home," Baker, playing merrily on, promised, "I'll dig you one." "Jazz à la Russe" demonstrated how American music might be handled in *Chauve Souris*. A dance called "The Promenade Walk" was awarded "eight honestly earned encores." Hawaiian dancing was featured in "Poi Ball." Later the hula dancers became flappers, doing a fast-stepping Charleston. The Grace Hoffman Girls performed precision dancing that equaled the best the Tiller Girls were doing elsewhere. A ballet entitled "The Lily Pool" had two sets of dancers, one set pretending to be the reflection of the other. Unfortunately, Sigmund Romberg and Fred Coots's songs once again sent few playgoers whistling out of the playhouse.

For his *Vanities*, Carroll extended the stage around the front of the orchestra pit and placed tables on the extension to give a cabaret effect. He was so generous in filling his offering that at midnight the show was still not in sight of its finale. Carroll's spectacles included a bird ballet and a color ballet, while his dancers stomped as they spelled out "C-H-A-R-L-E-S-T-O-N." Comedy interludes between the lavish production numbers were generally in the hands of Ted Healy.

J. Fred Coots, who did some of the music for *Artists and Models*, did most of the score for **June Days** (6 August 1925, Astor), a musical version of Alice Duer Miller and Robert Milton's *The Charm School*. Cyrus Wood's book tampered only lightly with the original story of a young man, Austin Bevins (Roy Royston), who inherits a girls' school, decides that the only important thing to teach is charm, and is himself charmed into marriage by one of his students, Miss Curtis (Millie James). Jerome Kern had written incidental songs for the original play. His sweet, flowing style was undoubtedly correct for the tone of the piece, though his music was not among his best. Coots's music for "Why Is Love?," "Remembering You," and the title tune was more obviously a product of Tin Pan Alley. Much of the evening's comedy came from Jay C. Flippen. Performing in blackface, he played a gardener whose lady friend is so cheap she tries to send a night letter during an eclipse. The tired businessman, for whom the era insisted this sort of musical was often written, was no doubt pleased when a dormitory scene allowed chorus girls to wear noticeably sheer pajamas. The show found a limited audience and stayed eleven weeks.

Still more Coots music was heard twelve nights later when the Shuberts, with Rufus La Maire, assembled a revue called **Gay Paree** (18 August 1925, Shubert). Not a single song dealt with Paris or France, and the comedy rarely touched on either. Most of the comedy fell to Chic Sale. He offered a series of monologues, vignettes of characters from an imaginary Hickville. These home-folks included a weak-minded farm boy a deacon, and a tottering Civil War veteran. In one skit Sales helped educate Winnie Lightner:

Sales: Do you know why Peggy Hopkins Joyce
    didn't marry Santa Claus?
Lightner: No.
Sales: She didn't marry Santa Claus because there
    is no Santa Claus.

Lavish production numbers had the chorus beauties parading in "Glory of Morning Sunshine" and "Venetian Nights." A tableau called "Dixie" celebrated sentimentalized plantation days. Dancing girls shimmied to "Florida Mammy," singing as they danced, "My old-fashioned Mammy owns half of Miami." Shenanigans of this sort kept ticket sales brisk for six months.

August's last musical was the return of *Big Boy*. With Al Jolson in better health the show chalked up another 120 performances before taking to the road.

Clyde Fitch's 1901 success, *Captain Jinks of the Horse Marines*, which had launched Ethel Barrymore on her road to stardom, was brought up to date and set to music by Frank Mandel and Laurence Schwab (libretto), B. G. DeSylva (lyrics), and Lewis E. Gensler and Stephen Jones (tunes). It once again recounted the tempestuous romance of Capt. Robert Jinks (J. Harold Murray) and Suzanne Trentoni (Louise Brown), formerly of Trenton, New Jersey, and now a world-famous dancer. The updating made no effort at elaboration. The production retained the single sets used in each act: A New York pier in Act I (allowing Trentoni to make a sweeping entrance down a gangplank), and a town-house drawing room in the second act. One addition to the musical was the role of a comic hack-driver, written in to afford Joe E. Brown another chance to display his rowdy comedy and eccentric dances. Unfortunately, his material was not top quality, forcing Brown to mug where words failed him. Another good Sammy Lee chorus diverted attention with its snappy dancing. The songs were nondescript. But with its title shortened to simply **Captain Jinks** (8 September 1925, Martin Beck), the musical still found enough favor to last twenty-one weeks.

Wednesday, 16 September 1925, began what may have been the most remarkable seven days in the history of the American Musical Theatre. *No, No, Nanette* opened on that evening, followed by *Dearest Enemy* on 18 September, *The Vagabond Kind* on the 21st, and *Sunny* on the 22nd. If *Rose-Marie* was the biggest musical success of this era, **No, No, Nanette** was the most successful musical comedy. Its relatively short Broadway run of 321 performances is generally attributed to the fact that the show had already run a year in Chicago and had sent out road companies in advance of its New York opening. Oddly, the show almost died aborning at its Detroit premiere, and only its producer's determination kept it alive. No sooner had the discouraging Detroit reviews appeared than H. H. Frazee set about completely recasting his production. He also goaded his songwriters for new material. Two of the additions they gave him proved to be the hits of the show: "Tea For Two" and "I Want To Be Happy." *No, No, Nanette*'s story was typical 1920 frippery, a musical version of *His Lady Friends*, in which Clifton Crawford had starred and for which he wrote incidental songs in 1919. Nanette (Louise Groody) is the unconventional flapper ward of Jimmy Smith (Charles Winninger). Smith, a prosperous publisher of Bibles, is himself not a little unconventional. He has a weakness for sharing some of his wealth with pretty young ladies whose careers need financial encouragement. But he is more open-handed than open-minded—at least where Nanette is concerned, even though he has told her he won't be happy until he knows she is happy too. Nor is Nanette's boyfriend Tom (Jack Barker) completely in sympathy with Nanette's free ways. And to add to everyone's problems there is the sporting Billy Early (Wellington Cross), Jimmy's lawyer and good friend. Misunderstandings come to a head in Atlantic City. At first even Tom's glowing picture of a love nest where he and Nanette won't have it known they own a telephone fails to help matters. Mrs. Smith arrives, disposes of her husband's lady friends, puts Jimmy in his place, and sees that Tom and Nanette are paired and that a good deal more of Mr. Smith's generosity will thereafter be directed toward her. Vincent Youmans's score was his best, catchy and endearing for all his stylistic limitations. Several of the songs were brought over in one form or another from earlier shows. "Take A Little One-Step" was taken whole from *Lollipop*, while the title song was a clever rewriting of "My Boy And I" from *Mary Jane McKane*. "I Want To Be Happy" and "Tea For Two," the belatedly added hits, were numbers of striking simplicity. The open sentimentality of "Tea For Two," coupled with the easy directness of both its main theme and an almost identical bridge, made the song the most popular of all American standards for years afterwards. The original production was tasteful and essentially intimate. The living room set of the third act, for example, displayed homey wicker furniture, and the second-act lawn was a cozy, flower-strewn, trellised retreat. While *No, No, Nanette* played the large Globe Theatre in New York, many of the houses it booked on the road were among the smallest in their respective cities. The show was revived in an overblown production, but with a fair degree of faithfulness, in 1971. It was a smash all over again.

The subtlety, inventiveness, and sophistication of **Dearest Enemy** (18 September 1925, Knickerbocker) stood in direct contrast to the slap-on-the-back obviousness of *No, No, Nanette*. The primary colorings of Youmans's music and of Irving Caesar and Otto Harbach's lyrics gave way to the nuances and offbeat shadings of Rodgers and Hart's material. It was practically impossible not to predict the next note or turn of phrase in *Nanette*'s songs. *Dearest Enemy*'s tunes titillated their audience with delicious and unexpected surprises. Moreover, in their range the melodies occasionally touched briefly on arioso effects. "Here In My Arms" stretches to an octave and fifth in the nineteenth bar of its chorus, still pleasantly and easily singable, but a departure from the tightly knit melodies of most popular musical comedy songs. Both "Here In My Arms" and "Bye And Bye" were shortly hummed everywhere and were still popular half a century later. With his lyrics for this show Hart made public once and for all his unique, bittersweet cynicism. It was a view of the world he retained, only slightly altered, to the end of his career, and it gave his body of rhymes a philosophic backbone not found in any other major lyricist's. Shouting "War Is War," his ladies rejoice in the collapse of morality, "Hurray, we're going to be compromised!" The same change of climate was conveyed more quietly and suavely in "I Beg Your Pardon," in which the hero begged to kiss a heroine so "divinely radiant" as long as her "lady aunt" was not around to see.

In rhymes that harked back to *Patience* and *Iolanthe*, Hart captured the polite but insistent sexual give-and-take of the show's eighteenth-century subject matter. The contrast between the soft expressions and determined feelings was one that Hart would often return to with good-natured, knowing amusement. It is easy to see why the quality of the songs led the *Times* to compare the material to Gilbert and Sullivan and why more than one critic commented favorably on the operatic excellence of the work. Herbert Fields wrote the libretto.

HERBERT FIELDS was born in New York City on 26 July 1897. He was the son of Lew Fields and the brother of Dorothy Fields. After leaving Columbia, he tried his luck at acting, often appearing in dialect roles not very different from those his father had performed. He early on became friends with Rodgers and Hart, and they helped persuade him to try his hand at writing. Together the three wrote a musical, *Winkle Town*, for which they could find no producer. But Lew Fields did mount a straight play the trio wrote. *The Melody Man* told of an old immigrant's dismay on hearing his serious music played as jazz. After Rodgers and Hart inserted a few of their earliest songs, the play was offered as the work of Herbert Richard Lorenz. Not even fine acting by Lew Fields and a young actor named Fredric March could save the evening. Shortly after the show folded the boys turned their efforts to *Dearest Enemy*.

If the book was not on a par with the music, it was still better than average. Fields along with Rodgers and Hart got his inspiration from a plaque they stumbled upon on 37th Street. It read,

> [General] Howe, with Clinton, Tryon, and a few others, went to the house of Robert Murray, on Murray Hill, for refreshment and rest. With pleasant conversation and a profusion of cake and wine, the good Whig lady detained the gallant Britons almost two hours. Quite long enough for the bulk of Putnam's division of four thousand men to leave the city and escape to the heights of Harlem by Bloomingdale Road, with the loss of only a few soldiers.

That was the plot, though in sound and contemporary fashion Fields added some musical comedy touches. He inserted a love interest between Mrs. Murray's niece, Betsy Burke (Helen Ford), and Capt. Sir John Copeland (Charles Purcell). In keeping with the vogue he made Betsy an Irish leading lady. And at a time when in the first gleanings of sexual freedom nudes were being seen on stage, Fields allowed her to make her entrance in nothing but a barrel. The established producers all rejected the work. Only when *The Garrick Gaieties* had made Rodgers and Hart names to be reckoned with did George Ford gamble with it—and then only because his wife, Helen, was starred as Betsy. Helen, in fact, obtained the backer who made the production possible. Actually the show did not have to cost much since, like *No, No, Nanette* and so many other shows of the day, it used just three sets—one for each act. *Dearest Enemy* ran out the New York season, but on the road it was far less profitable than *Nanette*.

The Vagabond King (21 September 1925, Casino) swept theatregoers into the world of pure operetta. Rudolf Friml dropped the unusual chordings and rhythms that gave a suggestion of American flavor to *Rose-Marie*. His score was full-blooded and glowingly, throbbingly romantic, as befitted a musical version of Justin Huntly McCarthy's *If I Were King*. Its original production had made a star of E. H. Sothern in 1901, the same year *Captain Jinks of the Horse Marines* catapulted Ethel Barrymore to fame. For 511 performances Louis XI (Max Figman) again made the irresistibly smooth-tongued poet and scoundrel François Villon (Dennis King) "king for a day." In that one day he must woo and win Katherine de Vaucelles (Carolyn Thomson) or lose his head. He serves his king better than his king serves him. Villon rouses the Parisian rabble and routs the Burgundians—thereby saving Louis's kingdom. When Hugette (Jane Carroll), a prostitute who had hoped to marry Villon, realizes that she stands in the way of his advancement, she commits suicide. Louis in turn realizes none of his citizens would make so great a sacrifice for him and allows the poet and Katherine to wed. W. H. Post and Brian Hooker's dialogue and Hooker's lyrics were journeyman. Happily, the score was the best Friml ever wrote. It varied from the moving beauty of its love songs—Villon and Katherine's "Only A Rose" and Katherine's "Some Day"—to the poignant "Hugette Waltz," to Villon and Katherine's tremulous "Love Me To-Night," to Hugette's torrid but heartbreaking "Love For Sale," to Villon's rousing "Song Of The Vagabonds"—the last two numbers sung with the chorus. Surprisingly, though the show confirmed Dennis King's claim to stardom, his swashbuckling playing and fine singing were almost taken for granted. The lush mounting practically stole the evening. The production was as rich and overflowing as the music. In many notices James Reynolds's sets were accorded as much praise as Friml's score. Louis XI's medieval Paris was depicted "ablaze with autumn coloring."

The blaze of fall colors gave way to a "riot" of every conceivable hue in **Sunny** (22 September 1925, New Amsterdam). Its curtain rose on an extravagantly colorful circus set filled with freaks, snake charmers, barkers, and roustabouts. As the evening progressed, the circus was supplanted by a brilliant hunting scene (probably with autumn colors and certainly with bright red riding habits), an ocean liner, and an elegant ballroom (with George Olsen's jazz musicians on stage to supplement the pit orchestra). *Sunny* happily reunited Marilyn Miller and Jerome Kern. But they were only the most prominent names in a splendid array of talent. This time Charles Dillingham, the closest thing to a rival Ziegfeld had, mounted the piece. Miss Miller's co-players included Jack Donahue, Clifton Webb, Cliff "Ukulele Ike" Edwards, Mary Hay, and the fading Joseph Cawthorn. Otto Harbach and Oscar Hammerstein II, who had collaborated so handsomely on *Rose-Marie*, combined their efforts for book and lyrics. (*Sunny* was the first Hammerstein and Kern collaboration.) Theatrical imperatives made absurd demands on the writers. Edwards's contract called for him to do his speciality between precisely 10:00 and 10:15 each night. But somehow they threw everything together in a workable if uninspired plot. Basically it dealt with the romance between Sunny Peters (Miss Miller) and Tom Warren (Paul Frawley). Sunny is a circus rider come to perform in England, while Tom is an American visiting there. When Tom has to return to the States, Sunny finds she lacks the funds to follow him. She stows away instead. She is caught and has to marry Tom's best friend, Jim Denning (Donahue), to avoid the brig. Their plans call for them to get a divorce as soon as they land. And, sure enough, by curtain time Sunny and Tom are arm in arm. The ending was so last-minute that in London, where Tom was assigned to a less important player, Sunny was given to Jim merely by changing the final lines.

Kern's music was a delight: flowing, graceful, and imaginative. It was worlds beyond the simplistic jinglings, however catchy, of so many of the day's musical comedies. Even minor numbers were noteworthy. "Sunshine" has a curiously flexible melody and drive of a sort that would not be disturbed by the rhythmic distortion of later orchestral fashions. The touching "D'ye Love Me?" was equally pliant, played both as a waltz and as a fox-trot in the show. The lilting title song became an immediate hit, its fine melody coupled with such colloquial yet inventive lines as "Smiling all the while, Tomboy/where'd you get your smile from, boy?" Lines such as these were probably the brainchild of the fast-developing Hammerstein. The lyrics to the show's runaway hit, "Who?," were known to be his, and Kern often insisted the success of the song was the result of Hammerstein's coupling the sustained opening note of the chorus—sustained for two and a quarter measures and repeated five times—with the word "who." In "Two Little Bluebirds" Webb and Miss Hay provided the evening's best eccentric dancing. Still, it was Marilyn Miller's light tap-dancing and graceful ballet-like pirouettes the public came to see. Miss Miller's voice was not big—and there were occasional complaints she could not be heard in the far reaches of the house. But her airy footwork her beauty, and her indefinable magnetism were more than enough compensation. The show was the most popular ticket of the season and afterwards on the road. But unlike *Nanette*, which reaped profits from several companies, *Sunny* was felt to need the presence of its stars.

Harlan Thompson and Harry Archer, still hoping to write a second *Little Jessie James* (15 August 1923), offered the public their latest collaboration, **Merry, Merry** (24 September 1925, Vanderbilt). Another backstage yarn, it traced the history of Eve Walters (Marie Saxon) from her arrival in New York, an innocent young lady with plans to be a chorus girl, to her acceptance of everyday Adam Winslow (Harry Puck) as her husband and her abandonment of her theatrical ambitions. What changes Eve's thinking is the greedy, dishonest attempt of her roommate and fellow chorine, Sadi La Salle (Sacha Beaumont), to extort money from a stage-door Johnny. Thompson and Archer may have suspected from the start that *Merry, Merry* lacked the appeal of *Little Jessie James*. In any case, they dropped the single-set simplicity of their earlier work, moving the action from a subway to an apartment to the stage of the very Vanderbilt where the show played. Though the sets lacked the magnificence of those in *The Vagabond King* or *Sunny*, they did apparently divert audiences from the musical's lack of distinction. *Merry, Merry* had a satisfactory five-month run.

Tom Johnstone's forlorn quest for Broadway acclaim continued with his score for **When You Smile** (5 October 1925, National). But his score was as drab as a Johnstone score was expected to be. Nor did the book help matters. The title gave no clue to the plot, a musical revamping of the 1923 play *Extra*. John W. King (John Maurice Sullivan), the publisher, decides to wreck his film weekly, "The Movie News," so that he may buy its outstanding stock at a bargain price. King can think of no better way to wreck it than to put his ne'er-do-well son, Wally (Ray Raymond), in charge. But Wally and his drunken buddy, Larry Patton (Jack Whiting), turn the sheet into a gold mine. King's only consolation is that he has gained a daughter-in-law in June Willard (Carol Joyce). *When You Smile* was a quick flop.

Another quick flop was a production of **Polly**, John Gay's sequel to *The Beggar's Opera*. The show was produced on 10 October at the Cherry Lane Playhouse, far from Broadway, with an unexceptional cast. An even quicker closing befell **Holka Polka** (also known as *Spring in Autumn*) (14 October 1925, Lyric), an importation that starred Orville Harrold (the aging leading man of *Naughty Marietta*) and his daughter Patti. They played father and daughter in the show, with papa leading his daughter into a happy marriage.

Charles Dillingham followed with a second Jerome Kern musical, **The City Chap** (26 October 1925, Liberty), a musical version of Winchell Smith's *The Fortune Hunter*. James Montgomery devised the book, and Anne Caldwell handled the lyrics. Their story had down-and-out Nat Duncan (Skeet

Gallagher) arrive in the small town of Radford to court a rich man's daughter. But a visit to Graham's drugstore changes his plans. He falls in love with Betty Graham (Phyllis Cleveland) and gives up seeking the pot of gold. Kern's score was weak; so weak only three songs were published. Its best number, "No One Knows," was a reversion to the plain but charming two-steps he offered in the teens. Minor roles were filled by Betty Compton (Mayor Jimmy Walker's mistress), Irene Dunne, and George Raft. Raft did a brief tap dance in one scene. *The City Chap* was a nine-week disappointment. It was the fourth and final October musical: all failures.

Artistically, November showed little improvement, though several of its entries rolled up appreciable runs for the time. Two musicals arrived hand in hand on 2 November. **Florida Girl** at the Lyric had a comic-thriller plot. Unknown to Daphne (Vivienne Segal), smuggled diamonds have been hidden in her shoe. The shoe is stolen off her foot as she detrains in Coral Gables. For the rest of the evening Daphne, her boyfriend, Henry (Irving Beebe), the smugglers, and the police race to recover the shoe. Milton Suskind's sole Broadway score was commonplace and failed to find a public, though it touched all the popular topics of the day: the Florida land boom ("Oranges"), campus capers ("The Collegians"), and the contemporary dance rage ("Chinky China Charleston"). Earl Carroll as producer brought all his notorious talents to "bare" on the piece. The costumes he gave his chorus girls were described as "diaphanous," though in one number they dressed as sailors wearing blue taffeta silk coats, navy caps, and tight-fitting bell-bottom trousers. Some of the comedy was in the hands of the Ritz Brothers as three clowning gangsters—Aristotle, Plato, and Socrates. Like so many comics of the era, they were also agile dancers, and their dance routines earned them as much commendation as their comedy. Another comic who doubled as an eccentric dancer was Lester Allen. He played the part of a detective, resorting to disguises much like those the famous Prohibition agents Izzy and Moe were using at the time to grab bootleggers and headlines. The show employed at least one intriguing sight gag—a black toupee that turned white when its wearer was frightened. Unfortunately, nothing seemed to help. *Florida Girl* had to be withdrawn after five weeks.

Sigmund Romberg and the Shuberts undoubtedly hoped to match Friml's record of two smash hits in two consecutive seasons by following *The*

Student Prince with **Princess Flavia** (2 November 1925, Century), a lyric recounting of Anthony Hope's *The Prisoner of Zenda*. Instead, as it had with Kern and Gershwin, triumph gave way to failure—or something close to it. Romberg and the Shuberts overlooked the bold departures *The Vagabond King* had shown from *Rose-Marie* in story and musical style. Everything about *Princess Flavia*, including the royal rank in the title, seemed purposefully to recall *The Student Prince*. The plot again told of unfulfilled love. On a visit to Zenda, Rudolph Rassendyl (Harry Welchman) is mistaken for Rudolf, Crown Prince of Ruritania. When the real prince becomes incapacitated, Rassendyl is prevailed to act as a substitute at the coronation. Princess Flavia (Evelyn Herbert) falls in love with him and he with her. But they both understand such a match would be impolitic. As Karl Franz and Kathie did before them, Rassendyl and Flavia go their separate ways. To underscore the similarities, much of the music seemed almost a parody. The hit of the evening was meant to be "I Dare Not Love You." It was an extended waltz number with several melodies in the manner of "Deep In My Heart, Dear" leading up to a principal theme that was all but a parody of the same song. Romberg and his producers had learned nothing from the imitative *Melody*'s failure to recapture the appeal of *Maytime*. At best Romberg had taught the Shuberts the advantages of filling the stage with fine singers. Several critics applauded the large male chorus—the same sort of chorus Romberg had fought to get for *The Student Prince*. Harry Welchman moved on to become one of London's most popular leading men. Most important, Evelyn Herbert was finally allotted her place in the sun. It is generally conceded that Miss Herbert had the finest voice of any of the 1920s' major prima donnas. Broadway often welcomed volume before refinement. Miss Herbert's voice was big, but it was also warm and superbly modulated. *Princess Flavia* managed to run nineteen weeks before moving to Chicago.

Naughty Cinderella (9 November 1925, Lyceum), billed in its program as "a farce" and on its sheet music as "a song-farce," was really a straight play with incidental songs for its star, Irene Bordoni. Miss Bordoni played the role of an attractive French girl who wins her sweetheart away from the married woman he dotes on.

The following night saw the arrival of **Charlot's Revue of 1926** (10 November 1925, Selwyn). The new material included a popular American interpolation, "A Cup Of Coffee, A Sandwich And You" (Billy Rose, Al Dubin/Joseph Meyer). Three things that hadn't changed were its top performers, Beatrice Lillie, Gertrude Lawrence, and Jack Buchanan. They brightened Broadway for 138 additional performances.

Arthur Richman's *Not So Long Ago* was turned into an operetta for the Shuberts by Clifford Grey and Edward Kunneke. Like a *Princess Flavia* it seemed determined to echo past hits. The Shuberts, possibly still recalling the huge success they enjoyed with *Maytime* during the war years, called the evening **Mayflowers** (24 November 1925, Forrest). The title had really no pertinence to the plot. When the little seamstress, Elsie Dover (Ivy Sawyer), pretends to have a lover, her father demands the boy's name. Nonplused, she can only think of the name of her employer's son, Billy Ballard (Joseph Santley). Mr. Dover confronts Billy. Billy grasps the situation and plays along. Before he knows it, he has fallen genuinely in love with Elsie. Kunneke's music had a Continental flavor. J. Fred Coots interpolated a number of songs with a more American style. In another echo, the lyric of one tune, "Mayflowers, I love you," probably reminded some theatregoers of the opening lyric to "Wildflower." The musical barely made it into the New Year. In its failure it exemplifies the shows of the period that received generally favorable notices from tolerant critics but were shunned by a less tolerant public. The word that pervaded the morning-after notices was "charm." At least one reviewer singled out the "bustled chorus" as a relief from the skimpily clad lines of many "up-to-date" book shows.

Carlo and Sanders had another score ready for **Oh! Oh! Oh! Nurse** (7 December 1925, Cosmopolitan). Marion Gay (Rebekah Cauble) is a nurse who can inherit her aunt's estate only after she buries her first husband. She loves Dr. Sidney Killmore (John Price Jones) too much to kill him, so he persuades I. Dye (Don Barclay), a patient of Killmore's who is supposedly dying, to become a groom before he expires. But the marriage ceremony proves tonic, and I. Dye recovers overnight. Only then is it revealed the aunt's will is a bad joke. There were many who thought the whole evening a bad joke. The chorus numbers were stupefyingly inane. At one point "the line of girls simulate a train with red and white lights"—this in a hospital corridor. Patients and nurses alike gathered for another presentation with candles in hand. *Oh! Oh! Oh! Nurse* managed thirty-two showings. For Carlo and Sanders it should have been a lesson. But Broadway was to hear from them several more times, with similar results.

Jokes of a different sort regaled the audience at the Lyric the night after *Oh! Oh! Oh! Nurse* opened. The occasion was the premiere of **The Cocoanuts** (8 December 1925, Lyric), two-and-a-half hours of nonsense Irving Berlin and George S. Kaufman (aided, without public credit, by Morrie Ryskind) provided for the Marx Brothers. Perhaps two-and-a-half hours is an understatement. Opening night in New York the show was far from over at 11:30. Kaufman's book had fun at the expense of the Florida real estate boom, with Groucho as a rapacious, unethical Florida hotel owner and real estate developer, Henry W. Schlemmer. He was abetted in his schemes by Willie the Wop (Chico), Silent Sam (Harpo), and to a lesser extent by Jamison (Zeppo). Complications rear their comic head when Harvey Yates (Henry Whittemore) and Penelope Martyn (Janet Velie) steal the jewels of a rich hotel guest, Mrs. Potter (played by Groucho's incomparable foil, Margaret Dumont). The thieves throw suspicion on Robert Adams (Jack Barker), the fiancé of Mrs. Potter's niece, Polly (Mabel Withee). With the brothers' help Adams is cleared by the end of the last act. How much of what finally appeared on stage was Kaufman and how much Marxian adlibs remains moot. Almost every critic excerpted an absurdity or two for his readers. Alexander Woollcott was tickled by Groucho's announcement, "The next number on the program will be a piccolo solo which we will omit." Percy Hammond enjoyed Groucho's praise of a young lady's eyes that shone "like the pants of a blue serge suit," and Chico's identifying a blueprint as an oyster. All during the run the brothers added and dropped stage business. One night Harpo decided to throw Groucho off balance. In the middle of one of Groucho's scenes a chorus girl ran across the stage followed by a leering, horn-honking Harpo. Groucho refused to be disconcerted. He remarked, "The nine-twenty's right on time," and resumed the regular action. It was generally conceded that the evening was not as zany as *I'll Say She Is* (19 May 1924), but given such a feast of wild hilarity no one complained. Most critics were indifferent to Berlin's score, and the public seemed to agree with them. This indifference is lamentable because song after song was engaging and lilting. Berlin caught the period's infectious free-flowing gaiety in numbers like "Florida By The Sea," "Lucky Boy," "A Little Bungalow," and "The Monkey Doodle-Doo." If they didn't stop the show, they at least propelled it

happily from scene to scene. Substantial additions and changes during the summer were introduced. The show ran into the following season, then moved out to spread its laughter around the country.

The night before Christmas the latest edition of the **Greenwich Village Follies** premiered at the 46th Street Theatre. The edition's most lauded number was "Lady of the Snow." Jack Frost and human snowballs and snowflakes filled the stage, only to "melt" at the end of the scene. Chorus girls also appeared as flowerpots and as an apple pie. Florence Moore was in charge of the comedy. Recent hits such as *The Vortex* and *Cradle Switchers* were spoofed. But the consensus deemed the material inferior. Kendall Capps did soft-shoe routines, while Myrio supplied gymnastic ballet. No song hits developed, and it was acknowledged the series had run its course. Though it played 180 performances, the 1925 edition was the last in the regular series, excepting one attempt at resuscitation in 1928.

By contrast, **The Earl Carroll Vanities** (28 December 1925, Earl Carroll) seemed to be thriving. This fourth edition enlarged on earlier suggestions of cabaret, extending the apron far out into the auditorium, placing the orchestra on the side, and inviting theatregoers to dance on the new forestage before the show and during intermissions. Carroll's all but naked girls remained a prime attraction (Dorothy Knapp was billed as "the most beautiful girl in the world"), and settings as always were lush. Music and comedy were less applauded, albeit Joe Cook delighted audiences with his explanation of why he would not imitate four Hawaiians. However, several months into the run stories spread about one of Carroll's beauties taking a champagne bath during a backstage party, and this led to the producer's serving a four-month jail term.

The producers (Alex A. Aarons and Vinton Freedley) and writers (Guy Bolton and Fred Thompson) of *Lady, Be Good!* (1 December 1924) repeated with a second hit, **Tip-Toes** (28 December 1925, Liberty). It had another of the Florida settings so popular at the time. And it had a plot as simple as it was simple-minded. "The Three K's" are a vaudeville trio stranded in Palm Beach. Al and Hen (Andrew Tombes and Harry Watson, Jr.), the two men in the group, are the brother and uncle of its girl, "Tip-Toes" (Queenie Smith). They wangle a thousand dollars from one of Tip-Toes many admirers, dress her in style, and set her on the trail of Steve Burton (Allen Kearns), the glue magnate. By the end of the evening Tip-Toes and Steve have fallen in love. With *Tip-Toes* Ira Gershwin's lyric writing hit full stride. He could be outrageous, as in "These Charming People" (the title, by the way, of a Michael Arlen comedy then on Broadway), where he coupled "million dollars blokes pass" with "faux pas." Or delightfully witty, as in the same song when he told of a Mr. Smythe-Smythe who was childless until twenty-seven children appeared for the reading of the will. Or, in phrases at once clipped and flowing from "That Certain Feeling," uncloyingly sentimental. Nor was it too hard to fall in love with—or to—George Gershwin's music for the heroine's "Looking For A Boy." The words and melodies went together impeccably. And when the entire cast stamped its feet and blared its trombones to "Sweet And Low-Down," the audience stomped along. Mounted in stylishly art-deco fashion, *Tip-Toes* played merrily for 192 performances.

By the Way (28 December 1925, Gaiety), a London revue, arrived, bringing with it such bright young people as Jack Hulburt and Cicely Courtneidge. Miss Courtneidge dressed for the occasion in white tie, top hat, and tails. Though the material was branded less original than Chariot's, *By the Way* found a receptive public for five months.

Gershwin's name was on another marquee two nights after the opening of *Tip-Toes*. Some New Yorkers, seeing it there, may have done a double take, for **Song of the Flame** (30 December 1925, 44th St.), listed as a "romantic opera," was unalloyed, flamboyant operetta. Actually Gershwin only composed a part of the score. An old operetta hand, Herbert Stothart, supplied the rest. But it is generally acknowledged that the stirring title song, the best number in the show, was Gershwin's. It suggests an unusual coupling of his clipped, clean-cut musical line with central European harmonies. Harbach and Hammerstein, having moved deftly from operetta to musical comedy, moved back again to do both the book and lyrics. Their plot recalled *The Red Feather* (9 November 1903). Though she is a noble, Aniuta (Tessa Kosta) incites the peasants of Russia to revolt against oppression. She is known as "The Flame" because of the scarlet dress she wears. Prince Volodyn (Guy Robertson) falls in love with her, not suspecting her double identity. After the revolution they meet again in Paris, where they accept each other for what they truly are. The producer, Arthur Hammerstein, wisely refused to rely solely on his principals to put over the material. An extralarge orchestra gave unusual body to the accompaniments, while on stage a "Russian Art Choir" added

its voices to the regular chorus. Nor was spectacle ignored. A symbolic ballet recorded the change of Russian seasons, beginning all in wintry white and blossoming in full color as spring arrived. At an elegant palace festooned with Slavic motifs a wardrobe master removed bejeweled gown after bejeweled gown out of a seemingly bottomless trunk, and a tsarist fashion parade ensued. Hammerstein's skill and largess were awarded with a run of over six months.

Having done so well at the box office with *Gay Paree* earlier in the season, the Shuberts packaged another revue and called it **A Night in Paris** (6 January 1926, Casino de Paris), 1926's first musical. They filled the show with bright low-paid youngsters on the way up and with serviceable J. Fred Coots songs. Norma Terris sang some of the songs. Jack Pearl amused with his German dialect comedy. Gertrude Hoffman Girls danced and paraded as African savages, flowers, powder puffs and lipsticks, and gold and silver coins. The evening had the empty glitter of so many Shubert assemblages. But the Shuberts knew what the public wanted, at least that not unsizable section of the public they considered theirs. And they were right. *A Night in Paris* ran through the season. It was the sixth successive commercial hit. Not one ran less than five months.

Hello, Lola (12 January 1926, Eltinge) brought the winning streak to an abrupt halt. A musical version of Booth Tarkington's *Seventeen*, it faithfully retold the familiar story of the troubled puppy-love affair between baby-talking Lola Pratt (Edythe Baker) and Willie Baxter (Richard Keene). Willie steals his father's dress suit to impress his young lady. Dorothy Donnelly's book was competent but not good enough to overcome William Kernell's flaccid score.

Tin Pan Alley's popular Walter Donaldson collaborated with Joseph Meyer on the tunes for **Sweetheart Time** (19 January 1926, Imperial), but failed to come up with anything to equal the songs he was writing outside the theatre. A run-of-the-mill Harry B. Smith libretto (based on William Collier's *Never Say Die*) may have stifled his inspiration. It was not a little like *Oh! Oh! Oh! Nurse*. Violet Stevenson (Mary Milburn), desperate for money, is about to marry Lord Raybrook (Fred Leslie) for his. Dion Woodbury (Eddie Buzzell) appears and, falling in love with Violet, suggests she marry him instead. He tells her he is rich and dying. He promises that he will leave immediately after the wedding, and within a year she will be advised she has become a wealthy widow. She accepts. But a year later Dion returns in the pink. Violet's realization that she loves him allows for a conveniently happy ending. Smith's humor had not changed much over the years. He had one character command, "Bring me a book on livers by Bacon!" Collier staged the piece, including such stunts as a cocktail song in which the cast rattled cocktail shakers in time with the music. The hit of the evening was an interpolation by Jay Gorney, "A Girl In Your Arms." Far from top drawer, the show nevertheless thrived on a booming Broadway for 143 performances.

But even the good times could not save The Matinee Girl (1 February 1926, Forrest) from a three-week debacle. Its plot reminded some of The Firefly (2 December 1912). "Bubbles" Peters (Olga Steck) disguises herself as a cabin boy on the yacht of matinee idol Jack Sterling (James Hamilton). They sail for Cuba. When they disembark, she reveals her masquerade. Before long Jack is won over. The score by Frank Grey was no better than the one he had written for Sue Dear (10 July 1922). Nor was the show's humor better than that of Sweetheart Time, one character promising, "When we cross the Gulf Stream, I'll wear my golf suit."

Bunk of 1926 (16 February 1926, Heckscher) was another of the many one-shot revues that began to appear in the wake of the dying annuals. Housed first far uptown, it moved to the centrally located Broadhurst late in April. Gene Lockhart, who later became a much-loved movie actor, wrote most of it and was its principal entertainer. A caustic critic in the Telegram recalled that Lockhart had recently performed the part of a feeble-minded boy in Sun-Up and suggested that Lockhart was still under the role's influence when he created the revue. Typical of the show's skits was a travesty of English drawing-room drama, "Good Old Smill, or Faithful to the End." For all its lack of brilliance, the show was sufficiently frothy and diverting to last fourteen weeks.

In August, Zelda Sears had written and produced a quick flop called A Lucky Break. It was withdrawn after twenty-three performances. But Walter De Leon took the story and with Miss Sears's erstwhile collaborator, Harold Levey, and with Owen Murphy, turned it into a musical. As was so frequently the case, their title had little to do with the plot. Rainbow Rose (16 March 1926, Forrest) merely combined two voguish titular words. Sears and De Leon told of John Brace's returning home after twenty years' absence. In the interval Bruce (Jack Squire) has become wealthy. But wanting to

separate his real from his fair-weather friends, he suggests he has lost his fortune. He finds almost everyone is a true friend, especially one young lady, Rose Haven (Shirley Sherman). Undistinguished music joined to a play that hadn't been satisfactory in the first place told against the show. Only the show's excellent dancing received general commendation. Rainbow Rose lasted just a little longer than its source.

But practically everyone embraced the next night's arrival, The Girl Friend (17 March 1926, Vanderbilt). Its creators were the trio responsible for Dearest Enemy (18 September 1925): Herbert Fields, Lorenz Hart, and Richard Rodgers. After the success of their first work they had little trouble in persuading Lew Fields to be their producer. And the authors knew this time Fields would not resort to interpolations, as he had with Poor Little Ritz Girl (27 July 1920). The plot was thin and trite, written around the talents of the diminutive dancers Sammy White and Eva Puck. It recounted how Leonard Silver (White) trains for a bicycle race by hitching his wheel to a churn in the backyard of his family's dairy farm. His coach is his sweetheart, Mollie Farrell (Miss Puck), the daughter of a professional cyclist. After a shady promoter picks Silver for a big race, gamblers attempt to keep him out of it. As if these troubles are not enough, aristocratic Wynn Spencer (Evelyn Cavanaugh) attempts to woo him away from his betrothed. But Leonard wins both the race and Mollie. Whatever the weaknesses in the story line, Fields told it amusingly. Some of the jokes clearly showed their vaudeville origins, but Fields had obviously selected the least outrageous and the most literate to transpose to the legitimate stage. When a guest at the Spencer party learns Leonard has hurt his ankle he inquires with due concern, "Is it broken?"

Leonard: I says to the doctor, I says, "It ain't broken, doctor."
Guest: And what did the doctor say?
Leonard: You mustn't say ain't.

Rodgers's score had two knockouts, the title song and "The Blue Room," both sung by the romantic leads. The Charleston rhythm of the first made it as danceable as it was singable. Hart's seemingly inexhaustible stock of striking word plays is perhaps even more apparent in the too often neglected verse, where, for example, a boy proclaims he wants to keep "steady company" with a girl who'll let him "bump a knee" in the Charleston. But "The Blue Room" has remained the enduring hit which Alec Wilder in his book on American popular song calls "the first wholly distinctive Rodgers song," adding that it "is a strong, uncluttered, direct statement. In it is the first instance of a Rodgers stylistic device which he continues to use throughout his career, that of returning to a series of notes, usually two, while building a design with other notes." It is an endearing love song, enhanced by Hart's seemingly simple rhymes. Several critics placed a third song on a par with the show's two hits. "The Damsel Who Done All The Dirt" was a comic number, given to Miss Puck as a solo. When *The Girl Friend* failed to catch on at first, Rodgers and Hart waived their royalties to keep the work on the boards. Their sacrifice was justified. Word of mouth was favorable, and soon the show was selling out. Broadway supported *The Girl Friend* for nine months. It was beginning to look as if Broadway had found logical successors to the Princess Theatre's triumvirate.

April brought revivals of *H. M. S. Pinafore* and *Iolanthe. Pinafore* lured Fay Templeton out of retirement to play Buttercup. John Hazzard impersonated Sir Joseph Porter, while the fine tenor Tom Burke was Ralph. The resurgence of interest in Gilbert and Sullivan prompted Winthrop Ames to begin a policy of annual revivals with his mounting of *Iolanthe. Iolanthe*'s sixty-six performances were ten more than *Pinafore* achieved. Nonetheless Ames felt encouraged and determined to stick to his announced plans.

Another one-shot revue, **Bad Habits of 1926** (30 April 1926, Greenwich Village), tried to bury the Charleston prematurely and also to ridicule operetta into oblivion in "The Student Robin Hood of Pilsen." *The 49ers* (7 November 1922) had introduced a spoof of operettas, and, ten nights after *Bad Habits* opened, *The Garrick Gaieties* would offer another. Unfortunately just about every attempt at humor in *Bad Habits* misfired. The show received some of the worst notices of the year. It was *Bad Habits* itself which hurried on to oblivion after one of the shortest runs of the season, nineteen performances.

Three musicals arrived in May. **Kitty's Kisses** (6 May 1926, Playhouse) told a complicated story of Kitty Brown's losing a handbag with all her money in it. Kitty (Dorothy Dilley) is refused a room at the Hotel Wendel, only to be rushed upstairs moments later when she is mistaken for a woman who has rented the bridal suite. The next morning she learns she has shared the suite with a man, Mr. Dennison (Mark Smith), whose wife is looking for an excuse to divorce him. The wife's lawyer appears. He turns out to be a young man she met on the train the previous morning. His name is Robert Mason (John Boles); he has found Kitty's handbag and has fallen in love with her. The show was in competent hands. Philip Bartholomae and Otto Harbach did the book, Gus Kahn the lyrics, and Con Conrad the music. If it wasn't one of the season's more inspired evenings, it was still light-hearted fun. Brooks Atkinson, just then beginning his distinguished career as the *Times* drama critic, put his finger on the source of this gaiety, confirming how necessary dancing was to the era's musicals. Atkinson noted, "the chief distinction of *Kitty's Kisses* is the rough-and-tumble of dancing men and women, individually and in chorus, at a pace that exhilarates while it kills. As soon as the first curtain goes up the chorus begins dancing ecstatically between the railroad tracks, and from then on it glides, pops, swoops, careens, and Charlestons through hotel lobbies, bedrooms, and gardens indiscriminately." Even the leading lady, Atkinson observed, "dances on the tips of her toes upon the slightest occasion."

The 10th of May brought the first of five revues that wound up the theatrical year, **The Garrick Gaieties of 1926**. The show had many of the same principals as the first editions; it also had much of the same format. It spoofed the current Guild offerings (*Arms and the Man, Androcles and the Lion*) and made fun of the other arts. Ballet as done by the great Nijinsky was given rough treatment in "L'Après-midi d'un Papillon." The sporting world was cut down to size in a transvestite tennis match (Romney Brent becoming Helen Wills; Edith Meiser, Bill Tilden). Even the musical theatre of the day was parodied in "Rose of Arizona," which David Ewen later labeled "the grandmother of *Little Mary Sunshine.*" Operettas had come under attack earlier; ten days before, *Bad Habits* had parodied them. Rodgers and Hart's spoof seemed directed not at the older comic opera or Viennese schools so much as at *Rose-Marie* and its antecedent, *Naughty Marietta.* Its heroine Gloria Van Dyke loves Capt. Allan Sterling, chief of police of Rose Raisa, Arizona, but her father wants her to wed Gerald Slades. The bandit, Caramba, kidnaps Gloria, but Allan rescues her just as her father is about to pay the ransom. Like *Little Mary Sunshine* years later, "Rose of Arizona" was not especially scrupulous in sticking to a single target.

It went to a number of places in search of mirth. The old *Sally* tradition was gently mocked in "It May Rain," assuring audiences that it would probably rain "when the sun stops shining" and "when the sky is gray." Even opera, or at least one of the great prima donnas of the day, was appropriated to give the setting its outlandish name. But much of the spoof was unerringly on its mark. Still, the fun was harmless, and operetta emerged unscathed. Rodgers and Hart must have had a good laugh when in the very next season *Rio Rita* (2 February 1927) delighted Broadway. The show's authors, Harry Tierney and Joseph McCarthy, rather than be put off by the ridicule of its genre, seem to have complacently borrowed from the spoof. In "Back To Nature" Rodgers and Hart extolled the "Hootin', scootin' land of Arizona"; *Rio Rita* had its Texas Rangers salute "rootin' pals, hootin' pals, scootin' pals, shootin' pals." Happily, Rodgers and Hart had a worthy successor to "Manhattan," in "Mountain Greenery" with its aggressive but irresistible repetition of its first three notes. Sterling Holloway again had the honor of introducing a hit—this time with Bobbie Perkins, since June Cochrane had a small role in *The Girl Friend*. Though this *Gaieties* had nearly a half-year run, the budding series was also discontinued, with only one later attempt to revive it.

Great Temptations, another Shubert revue, came into the Winter Garden on 18 May. The cast was filled with rising and falling stars: Hazel Dawn, Miller and Lyles, J. C. Flippen, and Jack Benny. As usual Harold Atteridge was responsible for whatever dialogue the performers themselves did not provide. Maurice Rubens did the music. He was a hack who would provide a number of Broadway scores in the last half of the twenties without ever offering a single outstanding tune. One interpolation from *Great Temptations*, however, has remained popular for over fifty years: José Padilla's "Valencia." Miss Dawn introduced the song. She also participated in a burlesque of *The Shanghai Gesture*. She was assisted by Billy Van, who announced, "I like Chinese brothels because Chinese broth is so good." Miller and Lyles proved to their own satisfaction that thirteen is one-seventh of twenty-eight. Jack Benny boasted he had driven from Atlantic City to New York in four hours and five subpoenas. The Foster Girls toe-danced, and the chorus compared 1925 flappers to the ladies in Koster and Bial's 1896 line.

More Maurice Rubens music was heard in a second Shubert revue, **The Merry World** (8 June 1926, Imperial). J. Fred Coots and a number of lesser-known figures also contributed. The show was an importation from London, dismissed by one critic as "something between Chariot and Messrs. Ringling."

The second **Scandals** of the season (14 June 1926, Apollo) was vastly superior to the edition that George White had presented late the previous June. In fact, it was at one and the same time the most successful and the best of the entire series. Its run of 424 performances almost doubled the series' second longest stay. A healthy economy accounted for part of its longevity, but most of the evening's success must be attributed to its merits. The cast was the finest White had ever assembled. Ann Pennington led the dancers, Eugene and Willie Howard headed the clowns, and Harry Richman and Frances Williams were in charge of the songs. Tom Patricola was back. The McCarthy Sisters also returned, and were joined by the Fairbanks Twins at the forefront of the eye-filling chorus line. The chic Erté conceived the costumes. But the sensation of the evening was DeSylva, Brown, and Henderson's songs, undoubtedly the finest score to come out of any of the great annuals. The trio more than justified White's faith in them and silenced skeptics who could not forget their lackluster efforts in the preceding edition.

The show's songs were as diverse as they were memorable. They perfectly exemplified the range of the period's popular writing. There was an ingratiating love song, "The Girl Is You And The Boy Is Me" (sung by Harry Richman and Frances Williams), and a rousingly joyous "Lucky Day" (sung by Richman and the chorus). The team also created the most popular of all variations on the Charleston with their "Black Bottom"—danced wildly by Miss Penington. But the most durable hit was "The Birth Of The Blues," rich with the most advanced popular harmonies. By later standards, the song was over-mounted in the show. It would seem to need little except a piano, a good singer, and a spotlight. But the twenties and White would tolerate no such austerity. There was the inevitable revue staircase flanked for this number by chorus girls dressed as angels. As Richman sang the song, a battle raged between contemporary blues and the classics. The McCarthy Sisters wore gowns suggesting "The Memphis Blues" and "The St. Louis Blues," while the Fairbanks Twins opposed them in costumes symbolizing Schubert and Schumann songs. In the still fashionable practice of the day, a number of the songs were tied closely to the subjects in the skits. For example, the song "David And Lenore" was part of a skit twitting David Belasco and his reigning star Lenore Ulric. Another skit found Otto Kahn and J. P. Morgan sitting down to examine the financial scene. Irving Berlin's marriage to Ellin Mackay was the subject of "A Western Union." The title reminded audiences that Miss Mackay's father, who vigorously opposed the marriage, headed large telegraph interests.

George Gard DeSylva (better known as "BUDDY" or B. G. DeSYLVA) was born in New York City on 27 January 1895. His father had been a vaudevillian but gave up the theatre to raise a family. An early attempt by the DeSylvas to make a child performer of George was thwarted by his grandfather. While a student at the University of Southern California, Buddy helped with college shows, earned extra money by playing ukulele in a Hawaiian band, and, most significant, began writing lyrics. His lyrics came to the attention of Al Jolson, who had them set to music and used some of them in *Sinbad* (14 February 1918). In short order DeSylva was writing words for Gershwin, Herbert, and Kern. His rhymes were used in *La, La, Lucille* (26 May 1919), *Sally* (21 December 1920), *Bombo* (6 October 1921), and *Orange Blossoms* (19 September 1922), as well as in several revues.

LEW BROWN was born Louis Brownstein in Odessa, Russia, on 10 December 1893. His family settled in New Haven, then moved to New York. After quitting high school he found work with Albert Von Tilzer. Two of his earliest hits were "I May Be Gone For A Long, Long Time" (*Hitchy-Koo of 1917*) and "Oh, By Jingo" (*Linger Longer Letty*). In 1922 he wrote words to Henderson's music for "Georgette" (*Greenwich Village Follies*).

RAY HENDERSON—né Raymond Brost—was the composer of the group. He was burn on 1 December 1896 in Buffalo, where his mother, herself an excellent pianist, supervised his early musical training. He later enrolled in the Chicago Conservatory of Music His ambitions to be a serious musician soon succumbed to the enticements of jazz. He played the piano briefly in vaudeville and then became a song-plugger for Leo Feist. Before long he transferred his allegiances to Shapiro-Bernstein, where Louis Bernstein introduced him to Brown.

The next night **The Grand Street Follies** (15 June 1926, Neighborhood) wrapped up the season. Like the *Scandals*, it was the second edition in what was technically the same season. The series' most talented principals, Albert Carroll and Dorothy Sands, were on hand again with their impersonations and their satire. Carroll impersonated the famous clown Toto and Joseph Santley. Miss Sands starred in the show's take-off of *The Shanghai Gesture*, appearing not as Mother Goddam but as Mother Goshdarn. Modern theatrical design and interpretation were mocked in a new version of *Uncle Tom's Cabin*, offered "in a constructivist setting—an example of sympathetic elastic theatre." As the virtuous characters of the piece died, an Otis elevator took them to heaven, where angels greeted them with handshakes. Not letting go of a good thing, the company also presented *Jack and Jill* as the Theatre Guild, in its symbolic phase, might have done it. Musically the evening offered nothing approaching the brilliance of the new *Scandals* or *Gaieties*. But there were two interesting names among the composing credits. A few of the songs were by Randall Thompson, who shortly went on to headier musical heights. Further melodies bore the signature of Arthur Schwartz.

1926–1927

Forty-eight new musicals came before the footlights in the 1926–1927 season. High quality, coupled with the continuing national prosperity, pushed almost half beyond the 100-performance mark. In fact, thirteen ran over 200 or 300 showings, while *The Desert Song* and *Rio Rita* each played nearly 500 times. As expected the summer entries were primarily revues. Six appeared at the beginning of the season; three more opened as the warm weather returned. However, only three revues competed with the book musicals that arrived in the fall and winter. Four of the early revues were in varying degrees successful, though their overall achievements were disappointing.

The first of these should have been the *Ziegfeld Follies of 1926*, but it wasn't. The new revue was created to open a new theatre Florenz Ziegfeld and Joseph Urban helped build in Palm Beach. Though the popularity of the annuals continued to wane, and though for one reason or another Ziegfeld announced at intervals he was abandoning the *Follies*, he still hoped to open the new house with another edition of his great series. Legal entanglements, stemming from a dispute with Abe Erlanger, dealt him a bitter blow. Erlanger had bankrolled the first *Follies* and retained an important piece of the revue. Ziegfeld found himself enjoined from using the name he had made famous. As a result, the new show was premiered with the obviously temporary but not inappropriate title *Ziegfeld's Palm Beach Girl*. The name didn't last. On the way to New York it became **Ziegfeld's American Revue** (24 June 1926, Globe). Ziegfeld mounted it with his customary flair. A large ball made up of glittering mirrors opened to reveal a lavishly befeathered dancer. More feathers were in evidence later when a line of chorus girls, supposedly just out of the ocean, entered in feathered headpieces that reached the floor and were meant to suggest foam. Though a number of the chorus girls, such as Paulette Goddard, went on to fame, it was not a truly first-rate cast. Charles King was no longer youthful, James Barton, though fine, was no match for a Fields or a Williams. Still, Barton and Ray Dooley had two riotously funny skits. In a railroad car that stretched across the stage Barton appeared as a battered conductor desperately trying to wheedle a ticket from Miss Dooley in her role of an "incorrigibly cute" brat. Barton chased Miss Dooley over seats, passengers, and luggage from one side of the stage to the other. Later Barton played a stern, slave-driving Latin lover, slashing a whip as he sang, while Miss Dooley meekly and worshipfully attempted a fandango. Among the female principals Claire Luce and Peggy Fears were the beauties. For music Ziegfeld called on both Rudolf Friml and James F. Hanley. It was Hanley who came up with a winner. "No Foolin'" quickly became so popular Ziegfeld made the song title the

show title. It was a jaunty theme perfectly in tune with the time. Buck's closing line was a cute play on the expression's other meaning, "after we're wed—No Foolin'." Unfortunately this was Buck's last association with Ziegfeld. The show's run was a discouraging 108 performances. Even more disheartening to Ziegfeld must have been the pasted-together affair touring backwaters as the *Ziegfeld Follies*. A bottom-rung producer named George Wintz had managed to secure the rights to the name, and, though he also managed to secure the services of Ruth St. Denis and Ted Shawn, leading modern dance exponents, he surrounded them by an evening "closer to Minsky's" than to Ziegfeld. Ziegfeld persisted in the courts, and by the time his show reached Chicago he was able to rechristen the evening once more and at last offer it as the *Ziegfeld Follies of 1926*.

An all-black revue, **My Magnolia** (12 July 1926, Mansfield), managed to get closer to the heart of Times Square than many Negro shows of the era. But even the convenience of the Mansfield could not help it. It opened on a Thursday night and closed the following Saturday. The evening's bright spot was an ensemble that "performed Charlestons, taps, and other convolutions with frenzied expertness." For the luckless C. Luckyeth Roberts it was apparently the last straw. The score was his third in three years to be given short shrift. He disappeared from the Broadway scene.

Another minor figure, Leon De Costa, had better, if no more deserved, luck with his score for **The Blonde Sinner** (14 July 1926, Cort). He received royalties on his run-of-the-mill score for the twenty-two weeks it played New York, plus its time on tour. The story was fitting for its July opening. The Hemmingworths (Ralph Bunker and Enid Markey) rent a Long Island summer home that is well beyond their means. To balance their budget they take in boarders. But before long Mrs. Hemmingworth is accused of being a co-respondent in a divorce. The show was really a straight play with the boarders performing "three or four specialties in each act." So intimate was the mounting that only four girls—all blondes—comprised the chorus that performed the requisite Charlestons. A small part of the musical's popularity may have derived from its being the only book musical in a rash of revues. Four more revues appeared in short order.

Bare Facts of 1926 (16 July 1926, Triangle) opened at midnight two evenings later, its tide hinting at the tenor of much of its material. It offered one of the decade's many jungle numbers, done this time in silhouette while a lady recited Vachel Lindsay's "The Congo." For comedy the show kidded reigning hits of the day such as *Lulu Belle* and *The Great God Brown*. In another skit Chopin, Liszt, and Mendelssohn complained Tin Pan Alley was stealing all their best melodies. The revue provided nothing of merit, but it did provide the sort of entertainment that segments of the theatregoing public would pay for. They paid for 107 performances.

A more interesting evening premiered at the tiny Belmont Theatre ten nights later, 26 July. Called **Americana,** it touched lightly on then current foibles and fashions in its skits and in songs such as "Riverside Bus," "Kosher Kleagle," and "That Lost Barber Shop Chord." This last was a pleasant if not top-drawer number by the Gershwins that several critics nevertheless singled out as a high point of the evening. Ira also put some of his stylish verbal shorthand to a tune by Phil Charig. The result was "Sunny Disposish." Actually, while almost all of the show was intelligently assembled, nothing was outstanding or durable. No small part of *Americana's* success—and it ran 224 performances—was a result of the effectiveness of some bright young talent in their truly intimate surroundings. Charles Butterworth went on to become a well-known screen and radio figure, especially as a shy, defenseless gentleman. Butterworth had the best moment of the evening, delivering a halting, painful after-dinner speech to a group of Rotarians. His listeners, seated in elegant, high-backed chairs on both sides of him, failed to respond to anything he said. They couldn't. They were all dummies. Helen Morgan sang while sitting on the top of an upright piano. It is said that Jerome Kern recalled her plaintive rendition of "Nobody Wants Me" (Morrie Ryskind/Henry Souvaine) when he was casting about for a Julie for *Show Boat*. And Mayor Jimmy Walker's inamorata, Betty Compton, shortly made the front pages of the "Tabloid Papers" the show sang about. Two more editions of *Americana* followed in later years.

A pair of minor songsmiths, Gitz Rice and Werner Janssen, did most of the music for **Nic Nax of 1926** (2 August 1926, Cort). Rice was also one of the performers, as was the sketch writer, Roger Gray. Songs saluted the obviously growing Negro influence in both popular music and dance with "Everything Is High Yellow Now," but none of the contributions was striking or memorable. The show was condemned as "amateurish." It was also obviously trouble-plagued. Its opening had to be delayed several times. On the first night nearly a third of the numbers mentioned on the program were not included. Lights failed; scenery could not be gotten in place. Only the fancy footwork of Nat Nazzaro was acclaimed. However, the *Times* notice did suggest that the increasing number of shows was taxing Broadway's resources when it observed, "Half of the chorus is, by count, fairly good looking. This is a high average." Rice faded from the scene, and Janssen, the son of a famous New York restaurateur, successfully set his sights higher in the musical field. He wrote one more score three years later, then confined himself to serious composing and conducting.

With the great annuals dying, Earl Carroll momentarily found himself with less serious revue competition than he had had before. Given so open a market, he brazenly charged $100 a ticket for opening-night orchestra seats. In return he was prodigal with his entertainment. The show was only three-quarters over by eleven o'clock. Carroll even festooned his auditorium with Spanish decorations to give the suggestion of an Iberian fiesta. Although he enlisted some fresh song-writing talent, nothing distinguished emerged from his latest **Vanities** (24 August 1926, Carroll). His comic lineup included Moran and Mack, Smith and Dale, and Julius Tannen. Moran and Mack delighted theatergoers with an argument over a dog's paternity and with an attempt to break out of jail. Smith and Dale played two firemen who answer calls only when the whim strikes them—shades of *The Never Homes* (5 October 1911). Spectacles included a sumptuous Russian scene, a number using mosaic glass and sparkling mirrors, and a set composed largely of ladders. But Carroll's scantily clad girls remained the major lure. With their help this edition compiled 154 performances.

The arrival of book musicals began in earnest after Labor Day. Raymond Peck and Percy Wenrich, who had not been wildly successful with *The Right Girl* (15 March 1921), nonetheless tried again with **Castles in the Air** (6 September 1926, Selwyn). Theatrical acclaim continued to elude Wenrich, one of Tin Pan Alley's most prolific and famous composers. Peck's book was neither novel nor exceptional. His humor ran to one-liners such as "Perhaps there's a Methodist in my madness" and to repartee on the order of:

—Are you traveling incognito?
—No, in a Ford.

The musical was a Chicago production that had been running for nearly a year in that city when the company was split, with some staying with the original troupe and others assisting in the road unit. For New York, Vivienne Segal, J. Harold Murray, and Bernard Granville were added to the cast. In *Castles in the Air* two college graduates, Monty Blair (Granville) and John Brown (Murray), arrive at Evelyn's 21 Club, an exclusive Westchester resort they have mistaken for an inn. They quickly catch on, and Monty introduces John as a Latvian prince. Evelyn (Miss Segal) is something of a social climber, so her uncle Philip decides to teach her a lesson by taking her and her friends to Latvia, intending to expose John. The plan backfires when it is learned that John is indeed a prince. Chicago hits rarely repeated their Chicago runs on Broadway. *Castles in the Air* was no exception. Nonetheless, its five-month stay put the show squarely in the hit column.

A summer-long tryout in Philadelphia had allowed "Cross Your Heart," the hit of **Queen High** (8 September 1926, Ambassador), to sweep New York far in advance of the show's arrival. But Broadway welcomed the story, too, especially with Charles Ruggles's clowning. T. Boggs Johns (Ruggles) and George Nettleton (Frank McIntyre), partners in the Eureka Novelty Co., have fallen out. They decide a poker game will determine who runs the business. The loser, moreover, must serve as the winner's butler. Johns loses. His gaucheries as a servant worsen the rifts between the old friends, but their children, Richard Johns (Clarence Nordstrom) and Polly Nettleton (Mary Lawlor), fall in love and help bring about a reconciliation. Laurence Schwab, the producer, collaborated with Buddy DeSylva on the book, while DeSylva also did the lyrics for Lewis Gensler's score. Though "Cross Your Heart"—sung by Polly and Richard—was far and away the most popular tune, the whole score had an infectious, rippling gaiety. It included a salute to Anita Loos's popular book *Gentlemen Prefer Blondes* (a stage version opened twenty nights after *Queen High*) as well as unnecessary interpolations by James Hanley. *Queen High* ran just short of 400 performances. It was the first in a series of musicals from this season that are remembered today largely for one outstanding song in each.

The old warrior Harry B. Smith made his first appearance on the season's credits as adapter of **Naughty Riquette** (13 September 1926, Cosmopolitan), which the Shuberts imported and mounted for the aging Mitzi. Smith's story of a telephone operator whose marriage of convenience develops into a love match elicited neither loud applause nor unhappy head-shaking. It ran eleven weeks.

But five nights later Smith and the Shuberts again combined forces, this time with stunning success. **Countess Maritza** (18 September 1926, Shubert) remains Emmerich Kalman's masterpiece, an unsurpassed example of the poignant Hungarian side of Austro-Hungarian operetta. For this story of an aristocratic lady reluctant to love her handsome caretaker lest he prove a fortune hunter, Kalman composed sweeping waltzes, whirling czardas, and his most beloved song, "Play Gypsies—Dance Gypsies," sung by Walter Woolf in the Broadway production. Once again the Shuberts tampered with their material. Al Goodman and Sigmund Romberg were called in to interpolate. But the interpolations were overwhelmed by the rich, high colorings of Kalman's melodies. Even the lackluster dialogue and lyrics Smith offered could not hurt. Happily, the Shuberts gave the work a fine cast headed by Woolf, Yvonne D'Arle, Odette Myrtil, Carl Randall, and George Hassell. *Countess Maritza* ran out the season.

The Ramblers (20 September 1926, Lyric), too, ran out the season. A musical romp by Harry Ruby and Bert Kalmar (with Guy Bolton assisting them on the libretto), it starred the uproarious Bobby Clark and Paul McCullough as a roving spiritualist medium, Professor Cunningham, and his patsy, Sparrow. They stumble on a unit filming a movie in Tia Juana for the Fanny Furst Film Company and help rescue its heroine, Ruth Chester (Marie Saxon), when she is kidnapped by the villainous Black Pedro (William E. Browning). For Clark (with his painted-on glasses and his cocky cigar) and McCullough it was the first time they saw their names above the title. But their antics proved they deserved their stardom. Somewhat surprisingly, the funniest scene of the evening fell not to Clark but to McCullough. When he is persuaded to play the heavy in Ruth's movie, his makeup turns him into Black Pedro's double. Black Pedro appears on the set, and a chase ensues, filled with Keystone Cops confusion. Though the entire score of *The Ramblers* was bouncy and melodic, it is remembered, like *Queen High*'s, for one song, "All Alone Monday," sung by the romantic leads, Miss Saxon and Jack Whiting.

The same night, 20 September, **Honeymoon Lane** raised its curtain down Broadway at the Knickerbocker. It was the third musical in a row to play through the season, and like *The Ramblers* and *Queen High*, it, too, left one noteworthy tune behind. Eddie Dowling and James F. Hanley's book, lyrics, and music suggested once again George M. Cohan's slant on the poor-Irish-secretary-makes-good motif was a pathblazer. Dowling, of course, had employed a similar theme in Sally, *Irene and Mary*. Tim Murphy (Dowling) buys a cottage on romantically named Honeymoon Lane in unromantic Canningville, Pennsylvania. Tim hopes he will soon place his bride-to-be, Mary Brown (Pauline Mason), in the cottage's kitchen. Tim and Mary both work at the W. H. Kleinze Pickle Factory, and young Ted Kleinze (Al Sexton) induces Mary to try her luck on Broadway. Tim pursues her to New York, where it seems he will have a hard time competing with the big town's enticements. Their experience turns out to be a bad dream, and Tim takes Mary's hand as they walk down the lane. There was nothing original or particularly brilliant about Dowling and Hanley's material. Dowling always tended to be a bit heavy-handed and obvious. Still, a large public, substantially Irish, remained receptive to this pleasant escapism. Furthermore, Dowling and Hanley contrived another popular "love nest" song with "The Little White House (At The End Of Honeymoon Lane)" that Dowling sang in the show. A second song, "Half A Moon (Is Better Than No Moon)" had a passing vogue. When the homey, vine-covered exterior of Mary's house and the relatively somber colors of the pickle factory gave way to the theatre scenes that comprised the second act, the show erupted in a kaleidoscope of colors. But as the colors broke out, the book broke down. Most 1920s book musicals stopped their action now and then for an irrelevant specialty. But when a story moved characters into a theatre, no 1920s producer could resist a spate of vaudeville turns. In *Honeymoon Lane* these specialties included the "exquisite" dancing of Florence O'Denishawn (who played herself) and the Broadway debut of a "coon-shouting 'blues' singer," Kate Smith (who played Tiny Little—a name that did anything but describe the expansive Miss Smith).

September's last musical broke the string of successes. Ironically called **Happy Go Lucky** (30 September 1926, Liberty), it told how the family and friends of curmudgeony Chester Chapin (Taylor Holmes) attempt to change him with kindness. They do, until he catches on to their scheme. He almost reverts to his old ways, but he finally admits being agreeable is nicer. Most of the score was by Lucien Denni, his sole Broadway effort.

But there were several interpolations by the ubiquitous Hanley. Playgoers who saw the show during its 52 performances may have pondered the sad fickleness of theatrical fame. Lina Abarbanell, who years earlier had captured New York's heart in *Madame Sherry* (30 August 1910), played what was a secondary role, although she did sing three songs.

Another failure followed. But **Deep River** (4 October 1926, Imperial) was a far more important work, a "native opera" lost in a Broadway jungle of slap-stick clowns, high-kicking choruses, and snappy jazz tunes. Arthur Hopkins, one of New York's most daring producers, yet a name rarely associated with the musical theatre, presented the work. The book and lyrics were by Laurence Stallings, a generally serious playwright best remembered as co-author of *What Price Glory?* Stallings placed his story in 1835 New Orleans, days before Mr. Hercule's Quadroon Ball. At the ball the elite Creole men of the area pick the most attractive dancers and set them up as mistresses. An aged quadroon, Octavie (Rose McClendon), who is a sort of duenna to the younger girls, warns them. "Unless you catch your true love at your first quadroon ball, you will never know true love at all." Brusard (Luis Aberni), one of the leading Creoles, has his eye on Mugette (Lottice Howell), an especially beautiful quadroon. He is anxious to find a new girl, since just the previous night he threw his unfaithful mistress out, after administering a public whipping to her lover. Brusard is a dangerous man, responsible for more than mere whippings. As one character notes, "dat charm of his… it has killed three men." Two visiting Kentuckians, Colonel Streatfeld (Frederick Burton) and his brother Hazard (Roberto Ardelli), also are attracted to Mugette. When the colonel insults Brusard, a duel ensues. The colonel is killed. Mugette runs off to a voodoo séance in the Place Congo, praying to her dark spirits for Hazard's love. But Hazard, too, finds himself obliged to fight a duel with Brusard; this time Brusard is fatally wounded. Hazard cannot remain in New Orleans and, unable to take Mugette home with him, leaves the stunned girl in Octavie's hands. Mugette must dance at the ball knowing she will never find a satisfactory suitor.

Deep River had no compromising humorous intervals. The brooding story moved inexorably to its tragic end. The second act, at the voodoo ceremony, had virtually no dialogue; the building tensions of the rites, performed to a choral background, propelled the story. Some of the dialogue in the surrounding acts contained pompous passages, but these merely reflected the more formal, Latinate speech of nineteenth-century Louisiana. Southern settings, Negro life, and the relations between the black and white worlds provided all or part of the plot of many of the earliest innovative musicals: *When Johnny Comes Marching Home* (16 December 1902), this work, *Show Boat* (12 December 1927) in the next season, and eventually *Porgy and Bess* (10 October 1935). The score represented Franke Harling's sole Broadway effort. Harling was a fascinating minor figure, striving for fame in both the popular and more serious worlds of music. The year before *Deep River* was produced, the Chicago Opera had staged his full-length version of Keats's "The Eve of St. Agnes" entitled *A Light from St. Agnes*. Several years later, the man in the street might well have been whistling Harling's melody for "Beyond The Blue Horizon." For *Deep River* Harling persuaded Hopkins to hire a thirty-piece orchestra—oversized by Broadway standards of the day. He also prevailed on the producer to employ Jules Bledsoe, the black who walked away with the evening's singing honors. Bledsoe had only a minor role, and his songs served more to create atmosphere than to advance the story. Harling's music was beautiful and, like the book, reasonably uncompromising. But the show was ahead of its time. Even *Show Boat*, a year later, bowed to commercial imperatives. *Deep River* ran only four weeks. Burns Mantle, decrying the loss of such "a lovely thing," ruefully observed "the opera-going public would not come down to it, nor could the theatre public rise to it."

It is worthwhile quoting Mantle's summary of the plot of the season's next musical, **Criss Cross** (12 October 1926, Globe). "Christopher Cross, being a resourceful aviator, manages to help Captain Carleton save Dolly Day from the designing schemes of Benani, who would rob her of her birthright and a considerable fortune." Mantle makes it sound like the outline of a more or less routine musical comedy. He neglects to mention that the evening began in the "Town Hollow in Fable-land" and proceeded to the south of France, Algiers, a bazaar, "The Jar of Ali Baba," and a palace garden, then ended in "The Diamond Palace." The first and last settings in particular would tell musical comedy fans of the era that this was not quite another routine affair, but a trip to the special world of Fred Stone. Stone, of course, was Cross; his daughter, Dorothy, followed her auspicious debut in *Stepping Stones* (6 November 1923) by playing Dolly Day. Though it was a quarter of a

century since the acrobatic Stone first somersaulted onto the Broadway stage, the intervening years had apparently done little to diminish his energies. He did a tumbling act, burlesqued a harem dance, performed with a two-man stage camel, and for a finale arrived on a flying trapeze to rescue Dolly. When he and his cast were not having fun with Otto Harbach and Anne Caldwell's dialogue, they were delighting their patrons with Jerome Kern's latest tunes. The songs were not on a par with Kern's music to *Sally* or *Sunny*, but they were a discernible improvement over *The City Chap*. The best was probably "You Will—Won't You?" Stone's fantasy world allowed James Reynolds to splash his sets with an unaccustomed gaudiness. The show was not the top hit of the year, as old Stone vehicles often had been in the past, but it ran profitably for six months, then toured.

A Shubert-imported operetta, **Katja** (18 October 1926, 44th St.), began a four-month run telling one more tale of a princess who stoops to conquer her conqueror. The inevitable Shubert interpolations included songs by a name new to Manhattan, Vernon Duke.

Rudolf Friml suffered his second disappointment of the still young season when he and his associates from *Rose-Marie* (2 September 1924), Otto Harbach and Oscar Hammerstein II, offered **The Wild Rose** (20 October 1926, Martin Beck). It tallied a meager sixty-one showings. The story line was relatively uncluttered. American Monty Travers (Joseph Santley) breaks the bank at Monte Carlo, so he and his beloved Princess Elise of Borovina (Desiree Ellinger) can outwit the capitalistic oil promoters and bolshevist malcontents who beset Elise's father. One love song, "We'll Have A Kingdom," received some play, but nothing entered the Friml canon of standards. The show seemed to be one of those ill-starred affairs plagued with troubles from beginning to end. Lew Fields was to have been its principal comedian, but just before opening night he took ill, and William Collier was rushed in at the last minute. Arthur Hammerstein hired Joseph Urban to do the sets, but Urban's efforts for this production displeased his usually overwhelmed admirers. Most critics dismissed the sets with faint praise, while the *World* stated bluntly that only the opening of the second act (a palace scene) revealed Urban's customary taste and imagination.

Oh, Kay! (8 November 1926, Imperial) joined the wordsmiths of the Princess Theatre shows, Guy Bolton and P. G. Wodehouse, to the steely jazz idiom of the Gershwin brothers. Puzzlingly, when Ira took sick during the writing of the show, Howard Dietz, not Wodehouse, lent a helping hand. According to Dietz, this was done at George's insistence, so that Ira would be able to receive as much credit as possible. The new combination clicked beautifully. The incomparable Victor Moore contributed his unique, tough wistfulness. In the hands of Broadway's newest star, Gertrude Lawrence, the material took on an added glow.

The story had a good time with Prohibition and bootlegging. An impoverished Duke (Gerald Oliver Smith) has turned to rum-running to keep in pocket money. With the help of his sister, Kay (Miss Lawrence), and a sometime butler, "Shorty" McGee (Moore), he caches his stock on the Long Island estate of a young playboy, Jimmy Winter (Oscar Shaw). This is normally no problem, for Winter is frequently away. But when Winter returns unexpectedly, their scheme is jeopardized. Fortunately, the susceptible Winter falls in love with Kay, a girl he had once rescued from drowning. He helps them guy the revenue boys and renounces all his previous marital commitments—and they were legion—to marry Kay. The dialogue was charming, typified by a much quoted line, "Don't criticize a bootlegger's English if his Scotch is all right." But the show's greatest joy was the superb hit-filled Gershwin score. At least four Gershwin standards were first sung in *Oh, Kay!*: "Maybe," "Do, Do, Do" (both sung by Miss Lawrence and Shaw), "Clap Yo' Hands" (a revival-type number sung by the cast), and "Someone To Watch Over Me." The staging of this last song was memorable. Kay is pretending to be a maid. She has put on an apron and cap. Left alone on stage, she huddles in the corner of a sofa and croons her plaint to a doll. (The doll had been purchased by George Gershwin for Miss Lawrence during the Philadelphia tryout.) Since the rest of the tunes were almost as good, departing playgoers had a wide choice of melodies to whistle. *Oh, Kay!* had an eight-month run.

GERTRUDE LAWRENCE (née Gertrud Klasen) was born in London on 4 July 1898. Convent-educated, she moved out into the world as a child dancer in a 1908 Christmas pantomime. To advance her career she studied acting and elocution with Italia Conti

and dancing with Mme. Espinosa. At Mme. Espinosa's she began a lifelong friendship with another young pupil, Noël Coward. Miss Lawrence first came to America with the original *Chariot's Revue*. Like her co-performer in that entertainment, Bea Lillie, Miss Lawrence's pre-Broadway appearances were in London revues such as *Cheep, Tabs, Buzz-Buzz, A to Z,* and *Rats.* So seductive were her fragile elegance and beauty that most composers and audiences overlooked a slight off-tone in her singing.

The next night the Shuberts delivered "the new 1926 edition" of **Gay Paree** (9 November 1926, Winter Garden), threatening to initiate a new annual. A number of the original cast were back, as were some of the old songs and sketches. But there was substantial fresh material as well. In "The Gold Plaque" Helen Wehrle posed covered with burnished gold. Chic Sale portrayed an announcer at a church social and, on an unaccustomed serious note, read "Lincolniana." Muckraking Ida Tarbell was herself raked over. Though the show again proved popular, registering 175 performances, the Shuberts quietly let the series die with this second version.

Harry Archer and Harlan Thompson made one last attempt to repeat the success of their *Little Jessie James* (15 August 1923). But Archer's score for **Twinkle Twinkle** (16 November 1926, Liberty) was so weak Bert Kalmar and Harry Ruby were called in for additional numbers. Harlan Thompson's libretto watched Hollywood's Alice James (Ona Munson) give up her lucrative movie career to settle as an anonymous waitress in Pleasantville, Kansas. She falls in love with Richard Grey (Alan Edwards). A comic detective, "Peachy" Robinson (Joe E. Brown), appears and, between laughs, almost scuttles Alice's matrimonial plans by revealing who she is. The show was excellently mounted with ultra-realistic sets, notably the first scene, which showed a private railroad car. A garden set in the second act sported a real tree. Still, if one reason for the show's twenty-one-week run can be singled out, it would probably be Brown's cutting-up. The *World*, for example, professed to be awed by "Joe E. Brown doing incredible things with a 1926–1927 mouth like a subway kiosk." His humor was brash. Asked if some oysters are fresh, he retorted, "They're almost impertinent!"

Sacha Guitry and Reynaldo Hahn's comedy with music, **Mozart,** received two New York mountings during the season. The first, in English, starred Irene Bordoni and appeared at the Music Box on 22 November; the second, with Guitry and Yvonne Printemps, was done in French at the 46th Street Theatre for five weeks beginning 27 December.

On the same night that Bordoni came before the footlights, a group calling itself the French-American Opéra Comique began a six-week stand at Jolson's in classic French opéra bouffe—mostly in French. Programs included *Giroflé-Girofla, La Mascotte, Les Cloches de Corneville, La Fille de Madame Angot,* and *La Périchole.* At least one of the operettas, *Giroflé-Girofla,* was also offered in English with such respected performers as Jefferson De Angelis and Bertram Peacock in the cast.

From 1921 to 1926 a Berber chieftain named Abd-el-Krim amazed the world with his battles against the Spanish and French in the Riff revolt. Only when the French succeeded in bribing some of his tribes and he was confronted with the prospect of Moroccans slaying Moroccans did he surrender. He was sent into exile. Out of this front-page news came one of the most romantic and beloved of all operettas, **The Desert Song** (30 November 1926, Casino). Its co-producer, Frank Mandel, collaborated with Otto Harbach and Oscar Hammerstein on the book, and Sigmund Romberg supplied the ravishing score. For reasons that can only be guessed at, they made their hero a Frenchman, who, costumed in flaming red, with a red mask hiding his face, leads the Moroccan Riffs against his fellow French. His dress has given him his name, the Red Shadow (Robert Halliday). He travels with impunity between the two camps. At the French garrison he is Pierre Birabeau, the dim-witted son of the commanding general. Pierre loves Margot Bonvalet (Vivienne Segal) and in his swashbuckling disguise brazenly abducts her to the Riff encampment. But a treacherous maiden betrays the Red Shadow's hiding place. General Birabeau (Edmund Elton) arrives, challenging the Riff leader to a duel. Rather than fight his own father, the disguised Pierre lays down his sword. The chagrined Riffs strip him of leadership, and he walks off into the desert. The French pursue him, but find only Pierre, and assume he has slain the outlaw. News of the Red Shadow's death stuns Margot, for she has fallen in love with her kidnapper. But while her back is turned Pierre dons his mask. The two swear to be eternally true, heartened by the prospect of a Riff–French reconciliation.

Romberg's lushly melodic score was the triumph of the evening. From the stirring "Riff Song" in the opening scene to the haunting title song (with which the Red Shadow invited Margot to come away with him) to the rapturous "One Alone," which the lovers reprise as a finale, it was filled with rich, unforgettable melodies. In its contemporaneity *The Desert Song* was firmly in the tradition of the great Viennese operettas. Romberg took full advantage of the 1926 setting. Side by side with the arioso melodies given to Halliday and Miss Segal were up-to-the-minute pieces such as "It," which Eddie Buzzell danced and clowned through. "It" made knowing references to Clara Bow, Elinor Glyn, and other voguish figures of the day. *The Desert Song* compiled 471 performances, just short of the season's long run of *Rio Rita.*

In his review of *The Desert Song,* Richard Watts, Jr., writing in the *Herald Tribune,* observed snidely, "the lyrics gave indication that W. S. Gilbert had lived and died in vain." As if to prove the point, a revival of *The Pirates of Penzance* headed December's entries. The production was the second in a series of Gilbert and Sullivan mountings Winthrop Ames began with *Iolanthe* in the preceding year and which he hoped to make an annual affair. It chalked up an encouraging 128 performances, double the stay of its predecessor.

Oh, Please! (17 December 1926, Fulton) had a Vincent Youmans score and a book by Otto Harbach and Anne Caldwell based on a French farce by Hennequin and Veber. Three top comic talents—Beatrice Lillie, Charles Winninger, and Helen Broderick—headed the cast. Charles Purcell helped with the singing. The story detailed the troubles that plague Nicodemus Bliss (Winninger), who is suspected by his wife, Emma (Miss Broderick), of flirting with an actress named Lily Valli (Miss Lillie). For all the talents involved the show failed to catch fire. It had a disappointing New York run and not much better luck elsewhere. Part of the problem was that Miss Lillie seemed conspicuously ill at ease in her straight, romantic scenes with Purcell. But her comic moments remained delicious. At one point she lampooned modern Broadway musicals, playing not only the principals but the chorus and audience as well. She wrapped herself in a convenient tablecloth to sing the lugubrious "Love Me," assuming all sorts of preposterous attitudes, trying all the chairs and sofas in the room and peeking behind screens. As her own audience she applauded so wildly she forced herself to take bow after bow. One Youmans song from the piece has survived, the lively "I Know

That You Know," sung by Miss Lillie and Purcell. It was another of the readily identifiable Youmans pieces with a simple repeated series of notes saved from monotony by the insistent chord changes.

Rodgers and Hart, and their librettist, Herbert Fields, scored another hit with **Peggy-Ann** (27 December 1926, Vanderbilt). Old-timers who didn't read their programs carefully may have had a feeling of *déjà vu*. For the show was a reworking of Marie Dressler's musical vehicle *Tillie's Nightmare* (5 May 1910). The story was essentially the same, with the names changed. Tillie became Peggy-Ann (Helen Ford), a boarding-house drudge who dreams of partaking in the exciting worlds beyond her reach and wakes up to confront the fact that her pleasures are, indeed, only a dream. But while the story was the same, the tone was drastically altered. The broad, rough-and-tumble music hall fun of the earlier show gave way to finely turned words and music and to a plot that incorporated the latest Freudian thinking about dreams. Fields had fun with the meaningful distortions of the night: animals spoke, people had pink hair, small objects grew to outlandish size. Nocturnal embarrassments crop up when Peggy-Ann arrives at her wedding practically undressed. At one point, recalling Cohan's spoof of *Common Clay*, Peggy-Ann is required to take an oath on the telephone book. Fields was as daring in his construction as in his content. There was no raucous musical opening, nor any songs until the story was well under way. And the finale was a quiet dance on a dim stage. Though *Tillie's Nightmare* had given Sloane his one more or less durable hit in "Heaven Will Protect The Working Girl," no Rodgers and Hart classics emerged from *Peggy-Ann*. Nonetheless their words and music kept the show moving for 333 performances.

The night after *Peggy-Ann* opened, Rodgers and Hart had a second set of songs ready for **Betsy** (28 December 1926, New Amsterdam). It was the first time in a while the pair had not worked with Herbert Fields, and they must have quickly come to regret it. Their producer, Ziegfeld, hated the show from the beginning, according to his biographer. Nonetheless, the *Times* insisted he mounted it with his "customary opulence and unimpeachable taste." At heart it was a vehicle for the popular vaudevillian Belle Baker. In Irving Caesar and David Freeman's book she played a girl whose Jewish mother will not let her other children marry until Betsy has found a husband. When her brothers corral a pigeon-fancier named Archie (Allen Kearns), he imprudently falls in love with Betsy's younger sister. But Betsy is able to win him over. The book had none of the sophistication or relative subtlety of *Peggy-Ann*. It did, however, offer a hilarious new monicker when Al Shean (once of Gallagher and Shean) appeared as Stonewall Moscowitz. The quick failure of the piece—it ran just thirty-nine times—dragged down with it one of Rodgers and Hart's best tunes, a bittersweet gem, "This Funny World," that has only lately been revived. In his book on American popular song Alec Wilder gives it appreciable space, concluding: "It could easily have been written in a minor key. But Rodgers achieves his atmosphere of loneliness within the confines of a major scale. And this couldn't have been easy." Even in their less subtle shows Rodgers and Hart maintained their independent, high standards.

Miss Baker also introduced Irving Berlin's "Blue Skies," which the program stated was "specially written" for her. Ziegfeld's "unimpeachable taste" didn't stop him from injecting a number of extraneous specialties. The morning-after notices recorded that the biggest applause of the evening was garnered not by Miss Baker, but by Borrah Minnevitch and his Harmonica Orchestra. (Their antics while they played later caused the troupe to be renamed the Harmonica Rascals.) They added another famous name to the credits, for their principal number was an abbreviated version of Gershwin's "Rhapsody In Blue."

The first musical of 1927 reunited Guy Bolton, P. G. Wodehouse, and Armand Vecsey, who had pleased the road, if not New York, eight years earlier with *The Rose of China* (25 November 1919). Classified as "a musical romance" with a plot reminiscent of Edward Sheldon's old play *Romance*, it gave the real Jenny Lind a fictitious, star-crossed love affair with Capt. Rex Gurnee (Glen Dale) of West Point. Much to Barnum's relief Jenny concludes her way of life would hinder the captain's army career. Not only Barnum (Tom Wise) and Lind but Robert E. Lee and Cornelius Vanderbilt were brought back to life on the Jolson's stage. (Both Lee and Vanderbilt were portrayed by the same actor, Victor Bozardt.) Out of a less distant past Eleanor Painter, beyond her prime, but still beautiful, returned to star as Jenny. It was all competent; no more. Some critics were unhappy with Stanley Lupino's anachronistic jokes about radio, near beer, and flappers—a device Billy Van had used in *The Dream Girl* (20 August 1924). Called **The Nightingale** (3 January 1927, Jolson), the musical left after twelve weeks.

Creoles, quadroons, and New Orleans reappeared one evening later in **The Lace Petticoat** (4 January 1927, Forrest). But its approach was far more traditional than *Deep River's*. A rich Creole, Raymond de la Lange (Gerald Moore), coveting the beautiful Renita (Vivian Hart) and jealous of her open affection for Paul Joscelyn (Tom Burke), tells the girl she is a quadroon. Renita is tempted to run away, but the truth comes out in time to bring the lovers together for the Mardi Gras. All the hands responsible for the work were relatively inexperienced, and it is telling that one of the composers had also to be the show's producer. No one thought much of the effort, and it was withdrawn after two weeks.

Earl Carroll called the sixth version of his **Vanities** (4 January 1927, Earl Carroll) his "international edition." Many of the skits, songs, and performers had been seen or sung in some of Chariot's London revues. Best of the lot was a spoof of Grand Guignol, "in which the gruesome and horrendous happenings are halted at every climax" so that the players could burst into jolly song and dance. Regular New York performers included Julius Tannen and Moran and Mack. The show stayed around for nineteen weeks.

Piggy, which arrived on 11 January to open the new Royale Theatre, was a jazzed-up version of *The Rich Mr. Hoggenheimer* (22 October 1906). The story line remained, and, most happily, Sam Bernard was back in the title role. Monocled and blustering, Bernard had fun turning "minister plenipotentiary" into "minister in a penitentiary." The abbreviated, informal title characterizes the changes that were made. Ludwig Englander songs such as "Five O'clock Tea," "Be Demure," and "Cupid's Auction Sale" were replaced by Cliff Friend tunes (to Lew Brown lyrics), with up-to-date titles such as "It's Easy To Say Hello" and "Oh, Baby." But the adapters lacked the imagination, skill, and panache that Fields, Rodgers, and Hart had brought to their reworking working of *Tillie's Nightmare*. Though the show was mounted with brilliantly colored sets and costumes, and often brought to life by forty dancers of the "clippety, cloppity school of hoppers," Bernard's skill and popularity really kept it going eleven weeks. Sadly, just after the show closed, Bernard died.

Bye, Bye Bonnie (13 January 1927, Ritz) also harked back, but not as far. The show was another of the poor-Irish-secretary-makes-good line that had so dominated Broadway just a few seasons before. Bonnie Quinlin (Dorothy Burgess) is the secretary to Noah Shrivell (Louis Simon) of Shrivell Soft Soap. When teetotaling Mr. Shrivell is sent to jail for buying booze for his customers, Bonnie not only spearheads the maneuvers to free him but helps elect him to Congress on an anti-Prohibition platform. In one of the few twists in the plot she does not marry Shrivell but her old flame, the newly prosperous Ted Williams (Rudolf Cameron). The show was beset by problems. Fritzi Scheff and Frances White were to have been the stars, but both dropped out during the tryout. Albert Von Tilzer's score was tinkly, though below the quality of *Honey Girl* (3 May 1920) and *The Gingham Girl* (28 August 1922). At least one critic objected strenuously to the many "unmerited encores," particularly those taken by the specialties inserted into the show. The critic cited as notable offenders the Tampico Tappers, a dance troupe that performed the appropriately titled "Tampico Tap." A footnote should probably record that the co-librettist was the same Louis Simon who played Shrivell. Faults and virtues, the show ran four months.

In January Leon Errol came in as the main attraction of **Yours Truly** (25 January 1927, Shubert). The plot was more than usually silly and complicated. A group of crooks hope to obtain a large sum of money from sweet Mary Stillwell's rich father. Shuffling Bill (Jack Squires) would seem to be among the wickedest of the lot, but he proves to be a detective, and he keeps both Mary (Marion Harris) and her father from harm. The *Herald Tribune* hailed Errol as "the inebriate deluxe." His role of Truly had little to do with the plot, but gave him several drunk scenes. The best was his flailing attempt to get out of a taxi. When the story and Errol were not occupying the audience, its attention was given to another band of Tiller Girls, who "wind themselves up into rhythmic knots, fall on their backs without spoiling the formation, rise again just as skillfully, kick and swing, and continue their gymnastics." Raymond Hubbell's music sounded distinctly dated; "Somebody Else," for example, falling on the ear as a not very creative retinkering of Victor Herbert's "I Might Be Your Once In A While." But Errol and good times kept *Yours Truly* going through 129 showings.

The season's most heralded musical opening took place on 2 February 1927. It was a double-barreled event. Not only was the season's biggest musical hit unveiled, but the finest musical playhouse ever constructed in America was revealed to the public. The theatre was the Ziegfeld; the show was **Rio Rita**. Bankrolled by William Randolph Hearst, the Joseph Urban–designed house was a masterpiece of art deco. The auditorium was egg shaped. Seated in a gold-upholstered orchestra seat a spectator could feel engulfed by the burnished colors of Urban's stylized mural, which swept without interruptions or sharp corners from one side of the house to the other. There were no boxes to destroy the simplicity of design. The proscenium was austere. It was gold with subtle bas-relief interrupted only by a door on either side. No mouldings or other frills cluttered the arch. The lobbies and even the lavatories were spacious beyond anything New York had seen.

The show that Ziegfeld elected to open the house was a somewhat backward-looking swashbuckler. Though it was branded a musical comedy and its creators (Guy Bolton and Fred Thompson on the book, Harry Tierney and Joe McCarthy for the songs) were identified with light-hearted contemporary pieces, the show was in reality an operetta. Certainly Tierney had never before written so full-blooded and romantic a score. *Rio Rita*'s story line and its songs put it squarely in the tradition of *Naughty Marietta* (7 November 1910) and *Rose-Marie* (2 September 1924). The Texas Rangers are hunting a notorious bandit known only as the Kinkajou. The rangers are lead by a handsome hulk of a man, Jim (J. Harold Murray). Jim loves Rio Rita (Ethelind Terry), but General Esteban (Vincent Serrano), who also loves her, persuades Rita that Jim courts her because he believes her brother is the man they are looking for. Only when Jim arrests Esteban as the real villain can he and Rita hope for happiness. The comedy was provided by Bert Wheeler and Robert Woolsey, making their first appearance as a team. The book was well crafted; the music was something more. All the standard song types of the genre were present and happily inspired. There was the two-fisted men's chorus, "The Rangers' Song," the caressing waltz, "If You're In Love, You'll Waltz," the direct appeal of the title song, and the production dance number, "The Kinkajou." For many, however, the glory of the evening was Ziegfeld's breathtaking production. The *American* observed, "Urban sublimates scenery" with an art "unblemished by vulgarity." According to the *Times*, Urban brought to the Ziegfeld's stage the "limitless space of the Mexican outdoors and the evening warmth of a patio; and fine tapestries [woven with Indian designs, stylized cacti and motifs from Spanish shawls—all glowing with rhythmic color patterns] that masked the stage during scene changes." Ziegfeld filled empty spaces with 100 of his most beautiful women (counting the toe-dancing Albertina Rasch Girls). In the first act Ziegfeld, Urban, and Miss Rasch moved away from both the story and the rich colorings to present a

ballet done entirely in black and white. Its beauty and elegance compensated for its inappropriateness in an essentially swashbuckling evening. *Rio Rita* ran over a year, closing one week short of reaching the 500-performance mark.

A string of flops followed. The first was a near miss. **Judy** (7 February 1927, Royale) was a musical version of the 1924 farce *Judy Drops In*. It featured Queenie Smith, late of *Tip-Toes*, and Charles Purcell, who had left *Oh, Please!* A single set was employed for the whole evening, giving the musical the intimacy of a straight play. Having been locked out of her home by a mean stepfather, Judy is taken into the bachelor digs of a group of young men in Greenwich Village. It is all quite innocent, and Judy is carefully watched over by Mrs. Maguire (Lida Kane), the janitress. The score was by Charles Rosoff, another in the long line of aspiring composers who reached the big time once and then disappeared from the scene.

Edmund Joseph was also a member of this forlorn group. He did most of the score for a three-week failure, **Polly of Hollywood** (21 February 1927, Cohan). Will Morrissey contributed a bit of the music, as well as all the book, the lyrics, and the staging. The slight story had Polly (Midge Miller) try her luck in the movies and in the movie colony only to decide she prefers small-town ways.

A revue entitled **The New Yorkers** (10 March 1927, Edith Totten) achieved a short run. The title had been used before, in 1901, and would shortly be used again. Edgar Fairchild and Charles M. Schwab wrote half the score, the remaining half being supplied by Arthur Schwartz. Schwartz's great period lay just ahead, and nothing outstanding appeared at the moment. Much of the show's humor misfired. Typical was a late-in-the-day spoof of *Chauve Souris* (4 February 1922) entitled "Café Habima." A skit meant to mock the health faddist Bernarr MacFadden was more salacious than funny. It portrayed the celebrity in a brightly striped bathing suit as he interviewed potential secretaries simply by taking chest measurements. When the revue could not sustain its theme of life in Manhattan ("brown stone fronts that were famous once," etc.), it thought nothing of bringing on Benn Trivers and his harmonica for an interlude of "Song Of India."

Lucky (22 March 1927, New Amsterdam) was a major disappointment. It was created by the combined talents of Otto Harbach, Jerome Kern, Bert Kalmar, and Harry Ruby. The capable Charles Dillingham produced it. He mounted it with a multi-set lavishness. One scene depicted "jade temples and henna ships against the ardent blues of an Indian sea." Mary Eaton, Skeet Gallagher, Ivy Sawyer, Joseph Santley, Walter Catlett, and Ruby Keeler led the impressive cast, while Paul Whiteman and his orchestra made a brief late-evening appearance on stage. But the pieces would not come together properly. The story told how Jack Mansfield (Santley) opens the eyes of the innocent pearl diver, Lucky (Miss Eaton), to the treacheries of her supposed father. Its best number was a Kalmar and Ruby contribution, the toe-tapping "Dancing The Devil Away." All the good efforts could not induce ticket purchasers to stop by the New Amsterdam box office. *Lucky* departed after seventy-one showings.

Two openings vied for attention on 28 March; both closed on the same night seven weeks later. **Rufus Le Maire's Affairs** was the first attraction at the new Majestic Theatre on 44th Street. It was a revue with a solid cast including Charlotte Greenwood, Ted Lewis, Peggy Fears, and John Price Jones. Miss Greenwood regaled audiences with her high-kicking dances and played Lorelei Lee in a burlesque of *Gentlemen Prefer Blondes*. Lewis, wearing his battered top hat and singing with his tongue-in-cheek melancholy, led his jazz band through "Land Of Broken Dreams" and "The Prisoner's Song." Albertina Rasch rounded up another bevy of toe-dancers and put them through their paces. The revue even had something approaching a song hit in "I Can't Get Over A Girl Like You (Loving A Boy Like Me)." Its composer, Martin Broones, became still another name in the growing list of writers with only a single Broadway score to their credit.

Sigmund Romberg was anything but a one-shot composer, while Harry B. Smith had long since lost count of the shows for which he provided the book and lyrics. But neither had better luck than Broones when they offered **Cherry Blossoms** (28 March 1927, 44th St.), their musical version of Benrimo and Harrison Rhodes's *The Willow Tree*. It was a cross between *Madame Butterfly* and *Pygmalion*, with the bittersweet ending so dear to Romberg. On a world tour to forget an unhappy love affair, Ned Hamilton arrives in Japan. At a curio shop he buys a statue of a maiden carved from the heart of a willow tree. According to legend, if the soul of a woman caught in a mirror is placed before the image, the statue will come to life. When Ned follows these instructions, the canny curio salesman replaces the statue with the beautiful and quite real Yo-San. The two fall in love, but when Yo-San learns that Ned

still has a girlfriend at home, she concludes that the races will not mix and that Ned will be happier with his American sweetheart. She behaves disloyally in public so that he can have an excuse for leaving her. Years later Ned returns to Japan. He learns Yo-San is dead, but their daughter has grown to become the image of her mother. Romberg's score was anemic and Smith's lyrics cumbersomely out-to-date. The show was sumptuously mounted, the willow-filled garden of its second act winning critical kudos. Costumes were stylized, listed curiously as "French variations" of traditional Chinese dress. Neither Howard Marsh (the original Student Prince) nor Desiree Ellinger (who a year before had dramatically flown from Boston to replace an ailing Mary Ellis in *Rose-Marie*) could infuse any life into the work.

Almost a month passed before another musical appeared. Like the two shows that came immediately before it, **Lady Do** (18 April 1927, Liberty) ran just seven weeks. Billed as "a surprising musical comedy," it offered little anyone familiar with Julian Eltinge's female impersonation shows could not predict. Its plot told how Buddy Rose (Karyl Norman) follows Dorothy Walthal (Nancy Welford) from Paris to her family's Long Island estate to woo and wed her. In the process he frequently has to disguise himself as a girl. For Abel Baer *Lady Do* was his lone Broadway score. His songs, such as the title tune, characterized the minor writing of the day.

A second double opening occurred on 25 April when *Hit the Deck!* and *The Circus Princess* both premiered. Together they broke the chain of failures. **The Circus Princess**, at the Winter Garden, was a Shubert importation, the last of Emmerich Kalman's great operetta successes. Oddly its plot centered upon a disinherited prince who joins a circus. The princess was merely the girl he marries.

Hit the Deck! (25 April 1927, Belasco) was produced by Lew Fields. His son, Herbert, wrote the book, and Vincent Youmans did the score. Louise Groody, Youmans's original Nanette, played Loulou, the owner of a Newport coffee house. She falls in love with Bilge (Charles King), one of the many sailors who patronize her eatery whenever they're in port. But Bilge is reluctant to consider marriage. So Loulou takes a small fortune she has come into and follows Bilge, attempting to change his mind. She follows him all the way to China. When she finally seems to have won her point, Bilge discovers she is wealthy. He demurs. Loulou wins this round by agreeing to sign away her money to their first child. The musical offered a variety of dancing—precision chorus work, black bottoms, Charlestons, and a "knee-twisting" solo ballet by Madeline Cameron. No small factor, however, in *Hit the Deck!*'s 352-performance run was Youmans's effervescent score. Two Youmans classics came out of it, "Hallelujah" ("strutted rather than sung" by Stella Mayhew) and "Sometimes I'm Happy" (Bilge and Loulou's love song). Neither of these hits was written for the show. "Hallelujah" had been composed in Youmans's World War I navy days, while "Sometimes I'm Happy" was first written as "Come On And Pet Me" for *Mary Jane McKane* (25 December 1923). Recourse to old materials was a perennial trick of all composers, but especially of Youmans. Curiously, his great hits to come were generally written for the shows or films they were a part of. And though several of these were as durable as anything he wrote earlier, as far as Broadway was concerned, Youmans was never again to work them into a hit show.

The second shortest musical run of the season, eight performances, was the lot of **The Seventh Heart** (2 May 1927, Mayfair), an amateurish botch of a musical comedy. A vanity production (reputedly paid for by the loving sons of the authoress), it prompted one critic to suggest shows of its ilk should not be allowed in professional houses. It was followed on the next evening by another of the Shubert "A Night In" revue series, **A Night in Spain** (3 May 1927, 44th St.). As usual Harold Atteridge provided the sketches. Jean Schwartz did the music. Because the vogue for Spanish material was at its height, the show constantly resorted to Spanish themes in numbers such as "My Rose Of Spain" and "A Spanish Shawl." But it also encompassed broader horizons, moving on to "Argentina" and dancing to an "International Vamp." Inevitably it returned home for the Charleston of "Hot Hot Honey." For comedy Phil Baker and his stooge in the box, Sid Silvers, continued to trade insults. Ted and Betty Healy added to the merriment, while petite, baby-voiced Helen Kane, not yet a full-fledged star, helped sing the songs. The bright youngsters sparked the show for seven months.

A voice out of the past, Robert Hood Bowers returned to Broadway after an absence of sixteen years with his score for **Oh, Ernest!** (9 May 1927, Royale). It was a musical version of Wilde's *The Importance of Being Ernest*, which needed no music, especially Bowers's mundane material. The show clung desperately to much of the original dialogue, but resolved everything in the second-act garden without ever moving everyone into the manor house, as Wilde had done for his third act. *Oh, Ernest!* left after seven weeks.

The White Sister, an opera, was performed at the old Wallack's on 17 May. Its place in this record is questionable. Based on a Marion Crawford novel, it was set to music by Clement Giglio. It related the dilemma of a girl who has taken her vows after hearing of her sweetheart's death and now discovers he is alive and still in love with her. She chooses to remain in the nunnery.

The Grand Street Follies brought in a new edition to the Neighborhood Theatre on 19 May. This time the music was by a newcomer, Max Ewing. There was nothing noteworthy about his songs, but the series was never particularly strong in its musical department. The cavorting of Albert Carroll, Dorothy Sands, and the rest of the regulars promoted the annual trek of loyalists to the small, downtown house. Carroll impersonated Mrs. Fiske and both Ethel and John Barrymore, while Miss Sands masqueraded as Jane Cowl and Laura Hope Crews. The evening's funniest skit, "Hurray for Us," found "Cautious Cal" Coolidge giving away no information at a collegiate press conference. This year's version chalked up a 148-performance run.

Two Gilbert and Sullivan companies opened three days apart, bringing *Ruddigore* into the Cosmopolitan on the 20th and *Patience* into the Masque on the 23rd. The revivals further attested to the sudden, new interest in Savoyard musicals.

In **Tales of Rigo** (30 May 1927, Lyric), an operetta passing itself off somewhat pretentiously as a "music drama," Zita (Mira Nirska) is a member of Rigo's camp of gypsies. When she falls in love with a rich society figure, Ralph Clark (Warren Sterling), she is told that he is really her half brother. She is about to leave when she learns her informant was mistaken. The score was by another one-timer, Ben Schwartz.

A promising combination of rising young theatrical luminaries and popular oldsters had a middling success with a summer revue, **Merry-Go-Round** (31 May 1927, Klaw). It was the eighth May musical (not counting *The White Sister*). Newer faces included the authors, Morrie Ryskind and Howard Dietz on the words and sketches, and Henry Souvaine and Jay Gorney for the music. Youngsters in the cast included Philip Loeb, Leonard Sillman, and Libby Holman. William Collier and Marie Cahill led the veterans. Collier stepped in at the last moment (as he had the year before in *The Wild Rose*). His entry was so late that, according to one reviewer, he wasn't even mentioned in the program. The comedy twitted querulous customs officials, added a third story (and towel service) to New York's double-decker buses, and followed the ambulance-chasing of four lawyers named Moskowitz, Gogeloch, Babblekroit, and Svonk. Walter Kuhn, soon to be recognized as a distinguished American artist, created not the sets but the ballets and pantomimes. However, Miss Holman made the hit of the show singing Gorney's "Hogan's Alley." *Merry-Go-Round* ran until the fall.

Namiko-San (6 June 1927, Selwyn) was a short-lived curiosity. It was presented as part of a double bill. Act I was a collection of dances with music by such variegated figures as Bizet, Strauss, Edgar Stillman Kelley (of *Puritana* fame), and the set designer. The second act was a "Japanese Love Drama with Music," allegedly derived by one Leo Duran from an old Japanese drama and set to new music by Aldo Franchetti. No less than Sessue Hayakawa was said to have supervised the mounting. Ignored by most critics and the public, it disappeared after two weeks.

Talk About Girls (14 June 1927, Waldorf) finished the season. It was a lyric version of a vehicle John Hunter Booth had written for James Gleason, *Like a King*. The plot utilized a theme that in one variation or another had been tried unsuccessfully in several shows the preceding season: *The City Chap, Rainbow Rose, A Lucky Break*. The story had Philip Alsen (Russell Mack) returning to his hometown of Lower Falls, Massachusetts, in the middle of a town celebration. Since he arrives in a Rolls-Royce, it is presumed he is rich, and he is hailed as a local hero. The truth is Philip is down-and-out and the car belongs to a chance acquaintance. Luckily, he puts through a major deal for a local power plant before he can be exposed. He also wins the hand of Sue Weston (Jane Taylor). The Rolls was the real thing, pushed, not driven, on from the wings. Its funereal chauffeur was played by Andrew Tombes, who grabbed most of the evening's laughs and many of the critics' commendations. Stephen Jones—who had done most of the music for *Poppy* (3 September 1923)—and Harold Orlob contributed the music. A tired score, a mediocre book, and the heat conspired to close the show after just thirteen showings. It was an unfitting end to a generally superb year.

1927–1928

The musical theatre, growing more exciting and more productive for three consecutive seasons,

peaked in 1927–1928. The number of new lyric pieces reached an all-time high: fifty-one according to the theatre chronicler Burns Mantle, fifty-three by *Variety*'s count. Neither figure was ever approached again. The quality of the works was equally astounding; the hits included *Good News, My Maryland, A Connecticut Yankee, The Three Musketeers, Blackbirds of 1928, Rosalie, Funny Face,* and *Show Boat.* The musical stage was not alone in the magnificence of its outpouring. Among the plays Broadway hailed in this halcyon year were *Marco Millions, Strange Interlude, The Royal Family, Porgy, Paris Bound, Behold the Bridegroom, Burlesque, Coquette,* and *The Trial of Mary Dugan.* In fact, though the musical theatre had never been healthier, artistically or commercially, its share of Broadway openings was somewhat smaller than before or since. A record 270 plays (Mantle's figure; *Variety* lists 264) reached New York. This meant just 20 percent of the new attractions were musicals, compared with 28 percent a quarter of a century before (twenty-seven out of ninety-eight plays in 1902–1903); nearly 30 percent in 1960–1961 (fifteen out of forty-eight productions); and just under 60 percent (twenty-six out of forty-five) in 1998–1999.

Of the eleven musicals to open in late June, July, and August, eight were revues. But, with the exception of a rather unusual edition of the *Ziegfeld Follies,* the old annuals were missing. Three of the summer shows were black. Indeed, the 1927–1928 season marks the first year in which a number of both straight plays and musicals were filled with blacks. **Bottomland** opened the season on 27 June down at the tiny Princess Theatre. May Mandy Lee (Eva Taylor) is an ambitious and starry-eyed resident of Bottomland, a Negro slum. Hearing that her old friend, Sally (Olive Otiz), has met with success in New York, she decides to follow in her steps. But when she finds Sally disillusioned and alcoholic in a Harlem cabaret she returns home. It was a thrown-together piece written and produced by Clarence Williams, who tripled in brass by playing the piano in the theatre's orchestra. Performers whose specialties could not be worked into the plot as part of their character were simply listed as speciality acts. Catering to the white public's idea of Bottomland residents, the evening peopled its slum and Harlem with names such as Rastus, Shiftless Sam, and Mammy Chloe. At least in pandering to white expectations Williams knew what he was doing. But when he attempted some "white" ballet and ballroom dancing he brought down the ire of the critics. The *Times* assailed the evening's "slavish imitation of Caucasian song and dance," while the *Post* expounded at length, "To what avail is negro musical comedy entertainment if it puts behind it all the racial naiveté, the lugubrious humor, the vital rhythm of its own natural self, and proceeds to ape the mincing manners of Caucasian carnivals. Pickaninnies are not ladies of ensemble." Perhaps because of such notices the public wouldn't buy the piece, and it left after less than three weeks.

Bare Facts of 1927 (29 June 1927, Triangle) attracted much the same crowd the 1926 version did, but in smaller numbers. Several critics could see little difference in the two versions.

The Shuberts attempted to capitalize on the notoriety of the Wales Padlock Act, which allowed New York's district attorney to close for a year any theatre offering salacious plays. They called their offering **Padlocks of 1927** (5 July 1927, Shubert). A few ticket-buyers may have been titillated by the title, but most came to see Texas Guinan, the great nightclub hostess of the twenties, famous for greeting her patrons as "suckers." There was little she would not do for effect, and in *Padlocks* her antics included riding a horse around the stage. When she spotted celebrities in her audience, she departed from her text to adlib a few well-chosen barbs at them, and on opening night she even inveigled a censor to come on stage to tell a clean joke. Some fine, young talent assisted the flamboyant Texan—Lillian Roth, J. C. Flippen, and George Raft (then a hoofer). Billy Rose wrote most of the lyrics to music by an assortment of minor composers. Thanks mainly to Miss Guinan, the show ran out the summer.

Two black revues followed: **Africana** (11 July 1927, Daly) and **Rang Tang** (12 July 1927, Royale). Neither Donald Heywood's nor Ford Dabney's scores produced anything that became a major hit, though both contained the sort of incisively rhythmic tunes people came to enjoy in black musicals: "Everybody Shout," "Africana Stomp," "In Monkeyland," and "The Cake Walk Strut." *Africana* was in remarkable trim for opening night. It was long since over by eleven. While it bubbled along it turned its spotlight on an important new entertainer, Ethel Waters. Performers of this era often had to double in brass. The vibrant Miss Waters was no exception. Though she is best remembered for her singing and, late in her career, for her surprisingly warm dramatic acting, a number of reviewers were especially taken by her eccentric, loose-limbed dancing.

The *Times* was sufficiently impressed with her stepping to hail her as a "dusky Charlotte Greenwood." The *Times* also fell into line by giving special praise to the dancing in *Rang Tang*. "First rate dancing is a concomitant of all negro shows," it proclaimed for anyone who by this time didn't know what was expected of black revues. The paper waxed ecstatic about the jungle choreography of "Monkeyland." Another number that pleased the critics found the entire chorus strumming banjos as they danced. But the paper did imply that, like *Bottomland*, the show foolishly attempted to imitate white practices—in this case by dividing its ensemble into show girls, ponies, and ballet dancers. *Rang Tang* was the more successful of the two. Helped by the presence of Miller and Lyles (of *Shuffle* Along), it sneaked past the 100-performance barrier.

A lamebrain affair called **Kiss Me** (18 July 1927, Lyric) lasted thirty-two showings. It told how Tom Warren (Ralph Whitehead) pretends to marry Doris Dodo (Desiree Ellinger) in order to enter Prince Hussein's (Joseph Macaulay) harem and paint the prince's favorite. Inevitably Tom and Doris's mock marriage turns into the real thing.

August's first offering was **Allez-Oop** (2 August 1927, Earl Carroll), a revue with an excellent cast headed by Victor Moore and Charles Butterworth. Moore participated in a spoof of silent movies, while Butterworth drew applause with a variation of his already famous Rotary speech from the last season's *Americana*. The similarity was underscored by the fact that both speeches had been written by the man responsible for the bulk of the material in this and the earlier revue, J. P. McEvoy. Many found the evening most entertaining when "50 Dancing, Dashing Alley-Oopers" went ape "Doin' The Gorilla." All in all, the mixture of song, dance, and comedy was good enough for a fifteen-week stay.

Another revue, arriving from Greenwich Village, **The Manhatters** (3 August 1927, Selwyn) survived for eight and a half weeks without offering anything of special merit. Though it was a white musical, its big production number offered playgoers the era's umpteenth jungle dance. One skit belittled the self-important pomp of the ushers at the great movie palaces. The imaginary theatre in the skit saluted two of New York's great new auditoriums by calling itself the Roxymount. An offhand remark in a review of the shows hints at the overall quality frequently displayed by so many of these offerings that began in the Village. Observing that the evening often lacked a firm touch and professional competence, the critic insisted such failings made it seem "like most 'intimate' revues with similar geneses."

To give The Ziegfeld Follies of 1927 (16 August 1927, New Amsterdam) its customary opulence, Ziegfeld spent $289,000, a staggering sum for a show at the time. Joseph Urban accounted for a substantial part of the expenditures, creating a show curtain composed of Ziegfeld's beauties, a lush jungle scene alive with human-sized cobras, tigers, and flamingos, a bamboo forest, and a rainbow of colored lights. A live ostrich with a bejeweled collar carried Claire Luce across the jungle setting. And as the Brox sisters sang "It's Up To The Band," the curtains opened to reveal nineteen young ladies called The Ingenues dressed in white and playing on a collection of white pianos and other instruments, while the regular Ziegfeld beauties made music with kazoos. In one major respect this edition was a departure for the producer. A single star, Eddie Cantor, dominated the proceedings. "In blackface again after Kid Boots, clapping his white [gloved] hands and strutting breathlessly across the stage," he sang three Irving Berlin songs and interpolated a "revival" of the not very old Walter Donaldson favorite, "My Blue Heaven." Cantor also impersonated flamboyant Mayor Jimmy Walker, a pet shop owner with a forlorn mutt to sell, and a New York taxi driver. In a skit not unlike the tailor routine he had performed for the Shuberts in Make It Snappy (13 April 1922), Cantor became so exasperated with a customer in a hat shop he crowned the man with a straw hat. Asked in another scene why he changed his name from Levy to Ginsburg, he responded that back home in Mississippi levees were being blown up. Ziegfeld's reliance on Cantor proved the show's undoing. Cantor felt he deserved more for shouldering so much of the evening, and when Ziegfeld didn't agree, Cantor announced he was too exhausted to continue. Ziegfeld was forced to close the still-booming revue after 167 performances. The producer hauled his reluctant star before Equity, and Equity sided with Ziegfeld. But that was small consolation. Besides his three songs for Cantor, Berlin wrote most of the songs Cantor didn't sing. Unfortunately Berlin was in a low period. No great tunes were heard, though Ruth Etting did her best with "Shaking The Blues Away."

A la Carte (17 August 1927, Martin Beck), the last of the summer revues, came in the night after the Follies, and left shortly thereafter. Its sole claim to distinction was skits by the Pulitzer Prize playwright George Kelly, who took a jaundiced view of women's golfing manners, Atlantic City hotels, and backstage gossip.

A la Carte was followed two nights later by the last of the hot-weather book musicals, which fared no better. Called Footlights (19 August 1927, Lyric), it told how George Weston (J. Kent Thurber) is bamboozled into backing a Broadway musical by Jacob Perlstein (Louis Sorin) and Violet Wilding (Ruth White), a burlesque star. George loses his $20,000, but he falls in love with Hazel Deane (Ellalee Ruby), who has a small part in the show. He takes her back with him to his hometown. The original score was by Harry Denny, but by opening night it was laden with interpolations. For about half the evening the story was halted while second-rate specialties ("the crudest form of burlesque," "cheap vaudeville") attempted to divert the audience. Footlights's backstage plot made such interpolations almost inevitable, if it didn't excuse their dire lack of quality. At one point in the show Jacob Perlstein was heard to bemoan, "Such a terrible flop I never saw in my life." The critics shook their heads in sad agreement.

Three weeks went by before another musical arrived. Ballard Macdonald was the only figure of even small note associated with The Band Box Follies (5 September 1927, Daly's), which closed at the end of its first week. It tried without success to poke fun at such tired subjects as Greenwich Village, silent films, seedy hotels, and Henry VIII. Songs bore such deadly titles as "Ola In Her Gondola" and "Sh Sh Shirley."

The season began in earnest and in style with Good News (6 September 1927, 46th St.). Good News was probably the quintessential musical comedy of the "era of wonderful nonsense." The decade's jazzy sounds, its assertive, explosive beat, its sophomoric high jinks were joyously mirrored in a hilarious, melody-packed evening. To emphasize the show's collegiate background, the ushers of the theatre wore collegiate jerseys, while George Olsen and his band, themselves exemplars of the twenties, shouted college cheers as they ran down the aisle and into the orchestra pit. Above them, on stage, the scene depicted Tait College. Tait, like Leave It to Jane's Atwater, is football-mad. But Tom Marlowe (John Price Jones), the team's star, may not play if he can't pass his astronomy exam. Luckily, Tait is coeducational, and one of the prettiest of the coeds, Connie Lane (Mary Lawlor), tutors Tom sufficiently so that he manages to get through. Connie has fallen in love with Tom but believes he's engaged to Patricia Bingham—a name out of Leave It to Jane

(28 August 1917). Tom almost loses the game with a fumble, but the clownish Bobby Randall (Gus Shy) recovers, saving the game, Tait, and Tom. When Connie learns that Tom is not committed to Patricia (Shirley Vernon), she and Tom freely acknowledge their feelings for one another. The hilarity of the book and the exuberance of the production were matched, exceeded in fact, by the brilliance of DeSylva, Brown, and Henderson's tunes. Five songs became standards: "Lucky In Love," "Just Imagine," "The Best Things In Life Are Free," the title song, and "The Varsity Drag." This final number accounted for the last popular variation to appear in the period's Charleston craze. While the principal romantic leads were given the love songs, "Good News" and "The Varsity Drag" were assigned to a young lady who portrayed the secondary comic role of Flo, high-kicking, doll-faced Zelma O'Neal. Mirth and music combined to keep *Good News* alive for 557 performances in New York alone.

My Maryland (12 September 1927, Jolson) came to town after a record-breaking forty-week Philadelphia tryout. Its music was by Sigmund Romberg; its book and lyrics by Dorothy Donnelly, who had worked with Romberg on *Blossom Time* (29 September 1921) and *The Student Prince* (2 December 1924). *My Maryland* proved her last successful effort, for she died shortly after the show opened. The operetta was a romantic reworking of the Barbara Frietchie legend, based on a Clyde Fitch play, which had transformed Miss Frietchie into a young, beautiful woman caught in the sundering hatreds of the Civil War. Barbara (Evelyn Herbert) is courted by Confederate Jack Negly (Warren Hull) and Yankee Captain Trumbull (Nathaniel Wagner). When she chooses Trumbull and defends the American flag, Negly's colonel father (Louis Cassavant) would have her shot, but Stonewall Jackson (Arthur Cunningham), impressed by her youthful bravery, saves her. Romberg provided another masterful score. Negly courted Barbara with the pleading "Won't You Marry Me?"; Trumbull countered with "Silver Moon"; Barbara touched heartstrings with a prayer for guidance to her "Mother"; and the entire cast joined in the stirring "Your Land And My Land." Not everyone was enthralled with *My Maryland*'s libretto, and some critics expressed reservations about Civil War uniforms that looked suspiciously Middle European. (Had the frugal Shuberts simply refurbished costumes from an earlier failure?) But praise was almost universally accorded the singing of "the large

and inevitable Shubert male chorus" and, most of all, the era's finest soprano, Miss Herbert. Critics' kudos, coupled with prosperous times, allowed *My Maryland* to repeat its Philadelphia success and to run through the season.

A one-week flop opened the same night as *My Maryland*. Half a Widow (12 September 1927, Waldorf) reached back ten years to World War I for its story. Bob Everett (Halfred Young), convinced he will be killed in the fighting, marries Babette (Gertrude Lang), a French girl he is fond of. As his widow she will be financially secure for life and can marry the Frenchman her father has selected for her. But when Everett returns unscathed, Babette chooses to remain his wife. Like so many weaker shows of the era, it fell back on vaudeville specialties whenever its authors ran out of conversation. In *Half a Widow* a team of grotesque acrobats, "Three Must-Get-Theirs," and a troupe of Spanish dancers won the biggest applause. The Spaniards tangoed and clicked their heels. All the excuse needed to bring them on stage was one character's observing that a Red Cross nurse reminded him of a girl he had met in Spain. The music was by yet another of the numerous one-score composers, Shep Camp, with one interpolation by Geoffrey O'Hara, who had written "K-K-K-Katy" back when the war was real, and who took a small part in the play.

A revival of *The Mikado* found a fair-sized audience. The revival was the third in the series Winthrop Ames was turning into an annual event. Later in the season *Iolanthe* and *The Pirates of Penzance* were brought back, and the three comic operas played briefly in repertory.

The ranks of one-score writers were enlarged by a woman named Ida Hoyt Chamberlain, whose Enchanted Isle (19 September 1927, Lyric) failed to impart its magic to either the critics or the public. Miss Chamberlain also did the book and lyrics. Her story recounted a troubled love affair between an eastern society figure and a rugged forest ranger. Even the sleazy Count Romeo De Spagino cannot keep them apart for long. The *Sun* dismissed the writing as "doggerel" and complained that no one associated with the show understood that some lively dancing might have dispelled the evening's languors. The critic recorded with some amazement that one chorus number consisted solely of deathly still girls slowly nodding their heads.

Five hit shows opened on the night of 26 September. Three were straight plays: Somerset Maugham's *The Letter* (with Katharine Cornell),

The Shannons of Broadway, and *Jimmie's Women*. The musical successes were *Manhattan Mary* and *The Merry Malones*. **Manhattan Mary** was an Ed Wynn vehicle, more carefully plotted than usual. George White produced it and collaborated on the book. DeSylva, Brown, and Henderson came up with their second full score in three weeks. Wynn played Crickets, a waiter who helps Mary Brennan (Ona Munson) get a job in the *Scandals* after her mother's bad investments force her family to give up their restaurant in Greenwich Village. Verisimilitude was achieved by housing the show at the Apollo, where the *Scandals* generally played; by George White portraying himself on stage; and by Harry Oldridge's fine impersonation of New York's leading stage-door Johnny, Mayor Jimmy Walker. At one point in rehearsals, when White felt overwhelmed by book problems—exacerbated by Wynn's inability to project narrative dialogue—he considered converting the evening into a 1927 *Scandals*. Most likely Wynn would have been just as content. His best bits had no real connection with the unfolding story. For example, he cast aside the plot to tell the audience about his uncle. His uncle had once been mayor. Well, not exactly mayor. More like a friend of the mayor. Anyway the mayor had given him a good job in City Hall. In City Hall? Actually outside. By the time he was finished Wynn had confessed that his uncle had been a street cleaner. When White started to hoof in the last act, Wynn ran down into the pit, shooed away the conductor, and began frenetically leading the musicians. Scene-stealer that he was, at the end of the number Wynn asked the audience, "Wasn't I good?" But for all Wynn's extraneous antics, the libretto proved to be quite serviceable by the standards of the day. The disappointment of the evening was the music. But it was too much to ask the writers to repeat the richness of *Good News* regularly. Actually, the score was not bad. It was hummable and rhythmic, but not memorable. The show's good points overrode its weaknesses, and the musical delighted New Yorkers for eight months.

George M. Cohan's **The Merry Malones** (26 September 1927) ran almost as long: six months. A. L. Erlanger honored the great song-and-dance man by allowing *The Merry Malones* to open a new house Erlanger named after himself. Cohan's story used a motif from the preceding season's *Hit the Deck!* and from Cohan's own *Forty-five Minutes from Broadway* (1 January 1906). Rich Joe Westcott (Alan Edwards) must find a way of disinheriting himself, or Molly Malone (Polly Walker) won't have him. He finds

a way, but his father cannily maneuvers Molly into accepting the money. The show contained all the expected Cohan devices: the intratheatrical comments kidding the show itself; a mystery subplot; and Cohan's inevitable detective. Cohan was, as his biographer suggested, on a treadmill. But it was a pleasant treadmill, made to seem less workaday by superb mounting. One set was a painstakingly realistic recreation of a New York subway car, complete with all the latest advertisements. The chorus, seated boy-girl, boy-girl, occupied the entire length of the car with a few, center stage, as straphangers. The boys were as colorfully garbed as the girls, wearing brightly hued, checked berets and matching vests. No doubt audiences were unaware, as possibly Cohan was himself, that his performance as Molly's father would be the last time he would ever sing and dance in one of his own musicals.

Two musicals opened on 3 October. **Sidewalks of New York**, at the Knickerbocker, was by Eddie Dowling and James Hanley, the team responsible for the preceding year's *Honeymoon Lane*. Its 112-performance run was respectable, but far short of *Honeymoon Lane*'s. The plot told how Mickey O'Brien (Dick Keene) wins a $25,000 prize for a tenement design, based on a layout his friend Gertie (Ray Dooley) has dreamed of. When the philanthropist who gives the prize decides to adopt Mickey, it seems Gertie will lose him, but she doesn't. Because the action spanned several years, Miss Dooley was afforded a rare, if somewhat contrived, opportunity to display acting dimensions her followers might not have known she possessed. She began the evening playing her familiar shrill, obstreperous *enfant terrible*. By the final curtain she had evolved into a warm, affectionate young lady, capable of eliciting moments of pathos from her viewers. Some of the bit players were of special interest. Smith and Dale discovered ways to include parts of their vaudeville act, while Ruby Keeler led a long line of attractive tap-dancers. Elizabeth Murray, who had been featured in *Madame Sherry* and other pre–World War I hits, was Mickey's mother. But producer Charles Dillingham went even farther back in theatrical history to reintroduce "Three Old Timers": Barney Fagan, the old minstrel who wrote "My Gal's A High Born Lady"; James Thornton, the vaudevillian-composer of "When You Were Sweet Sixteen"; and Josephine Sabel, who years before helped make a hit of "Hot Time In The Old Town Tonight."

Yes, Yes, Yvette (3 October 1927, Harris) came in the same night from Chicago. Its producer,

H. H. Frazee, had hoped it would follow in the footsteps of his earlier *No, No, Nanette* (16 September 1925). The new piece had been a modest hit in Chicago; it became a quick flop in New York. Its book was based on James Montgomery's 1916 farce, *Nothing but the Truth.* At a Washington's Birthday celebration its hero, Richard Bennett, bets $30,000 that he can tell the truth for twenty-four hours regardless of costs. The costs turn out to be high indeed. He almost loses his fiancée, Yvette, and nearly wrecks his own business. The book was good, but Frazee failed to enlist Youmans or another major composer for the songs. *Nanette's* lyricist, Irving Caesar, tried his hand at composing, abetted by Phil Charig and Ben Jerome. The best song, Caesar's "I'm A Little Bit Fonder Of You," couldn't compare with *Nanette's* better numbers. Charles Winninger was back, as Yvette's father; the Mask and Wig's attractive graduate, Jack Whiting, was Bennett; and Yvette was sung by Jeanette MacDonald. Winninger stopped the show singing a comic paternal lament, "Woe Is Me." With no microphones to distort or deceive, most critics insisted Whiting and Miss MacDonald were better as dancers than as singers. The *Times* politely added that was the way things ought to be in "an up-to-date musical." Sammy Lee's chorus provided more up-to-date hoofing, winning accolades for its interpretation of the Black Bottom.

Sigmund Romberg had two more operettas ready for October. Both failed. The more humiliating fiasco was the first, **My Princess** (6 October 1927, Shubert). Written with his *My Maryland* partner, Dorothy Donnelly, who based her libretto on an Edward Sheldon play, it told of the attempt by a social-climbing oil heiress (Hope Hampton) to break into society by palming off a poor Italian immigrant (Leonard Ceeley) as her princely husband. She makes the mistake of marrying him, and, when her endeavors at moving up in society fail, he forces her to live with him in his Little Italy tenement. She grows to love him. In the true, undemocratic fashion of operetta, he turns out to be a real prince. No one accused the Shuberts of stinting on this production. Indeed a lack of restraint marked every aspect. Miss Hampton overacted, resorting to that school of emoting that expresses grief by pressing a fist against the forehead. A Cherry Street block party prompted a bit of "savage" Italian folk dancing, while Amerique and Neville found a spot in the last scene for a "flaming tango." Everyone seemed carried away. As the *Times* noted, "Written for the liveliest sort of expression, the music is played by an unthrottled orchestra,

sung in full voice by a chorus of healthy fellows and danced by a troupe of Albertina Rasch girls with an expert hop, skip, and jump."

At the end of the month, Romberg had only slightly better luck with **The Love Call** (24 October 1927, Majestic). Edward Locke adapted it from one of the Shubert's first straight-play hits, Augustus Thomas's *Arizona*. Some papers, such as the *Sun*, wondered out loud whether it was really necessary to keep turning old straight-play favorites into musicals. Looking into his crystal ball, the paper's critic predicted that in the 1950s young Oscar Hammerstein IV would be turning Somerset Maugham's *The Letter* into a lyric evening and advertising it as "A Musical Play of Magic Malay." But Malay and 1950 were worlds away from old Arizona. As they did in 1900, Lieutenant Denton (John Barker) and his Rangers rescue trapped ranchers from an attempted Indian massacre, precipitated by the villainous Captain Hodgman (Richard Lee). Through all the terror a romance flourishes between Lena Keller (Jane Egbert) and Tony Mustano (Joseph Macaulay). Though Romberg and the Shuberts enjoyed their greatest triumphs when they struck out into relatively fresh territory, they persisted in trying to imitate their own and others' successes. The very title of the piece harked back to *Rose-Marie*, while the "Ranger's Song" aped a title employed so happily the year before in *Rio Rita*. But the song's lyrics minimized the camaraderie of Joseph McCarthy's words, recalling instead the determined warnings in *Rose-Marie's* "The Mounties"! Smith urged, "Horse thieves run, for a chance you've none." The operetta's principal love song, "I Live, I Die For You," contained pomposities so typical of Harry B. Smith such as "Awake, from dreams arise."

A more important opening occurred 6 October 1927, the same night *My Princess* premiered. *The Jazz Singer*, the first full-length movie in which the human voice was heard, had its first public showing to wild ballyhoo. No one can calculate the effects it and the sound movies that followed had on the American Musical Theatre. But after 6 October the eyes of every Broadway artist were turned westward. Before long, many great names and a larger number of the second-stringers were riding the tracks, bound for Hollywood.

Four nights after *My Princess* opened, Mary Eaton and Oscar Shaw raised the curtain on **The 5 O'clock Girl** (10 October 1927, 44th St.). It had a thin plot, reminiscent of the poor-little-girl-makes-good stories. Every day at five Patricia Brown (Miss Eaton) leaves her job at the Snow Flake Cleaners' Shop and calls a young man whose number she has come across. He turns out to be wealthy Gerald Brooks (Shaw). When they finally meet, she is forced to play the rich society girl. Her ruse is exposed, but with the help of Gerald's valet, Hudgins (Louis John Bartels), who loves Patricia's co-worker, Susan Snow (Pert Kelton), a happy ending is manipulated. The show was written and produced by the team who had offered *The Ramblers* (20 September 1926). The book was by Guy Bolton (joined this time by Fred Thompson). Their humor generally eschewed the puns employed by the era's hack librettists. Instead they drew laughs from situations implicit in the text or in the social structure of the day:

Hudgins: When we get married we'll go and live with your parents.
Susan: It can't be done.
Hudgins: Why not?
Susan: Because they're still living with their folks.

The songs were by Bert Kalmar and Harry Ruby. As they had for their earlier work, the songwriters came up with one top-flight number, "Thinking Of You," sung by Eaton and Shaw. Norman Bel Geddes designed the show's *avant-garde* sets, modernistic fantasies that established just the right tone for this "fairy tale in modern dress."

Three failures, including Romberg's *The Love Call*, followed. **White Lights** (11 October 1927, Ritz) was another backstage story, embellished with a mediocre J. Fred Coots score. It lasted less than a month. Each night for that short spell a society girl named Polly Page (Gertrude Lang)—how many Pollys there were in this era!—triumphed over parental objections and managerial villainy to achieve stardom as a nightclub performer and to win the love of Danny Miles (Sam Ash). The plot was largely an excuse for variety turns; seven of the show's sixteen numbers were listed merely as "specialties." Unsophisticated playgoers may have found some novelty in the actors' walking up and down the theatre aisles during rehearsal scenes, but even less knowing tourists must have winced at one-liners such as "You may have been bred in old Kentucky, but you're only a crumb here."

A musical version of A. E. Thomas's *Just Suppose*, **Just Fancy** (11 October 1927, Casino) recounted in flashback the bittersweet love affair between Edward, the Prince of Wales (Joseph Santley), and Linda Lee Stafford, an American girl (Ivy Sawyer).

Linda was not as fortunate as a later American lady; Linda's Edward preferred his throne. Curiously, while Santley played both the youthful prince in the main story and the aging king in the frame, Miss Sawyer portrayed only young Linda. The distinguished, beloved old actress Mrs. Thomas Whiffen came out of retirement to play the gray-haired Linda. Raymond Hitchcock, once a star of the first magnitude, was reduced to a single appearance as a dinner speaker during a reception for the prince. Mme. Marguerite attempted to recreate the Spanish dances Chiquita had performed in Niblo's heyday— the era of the main story. For audiences requiring more modern stepping, the Chester Hale Girls did a polo ballet. Joseph Meyer and Phil Chang's score, with Leo Robin's lyrics, was never more than competent. Only the somewhat tattered popularity of its stars kept *Just Fancy* on the boards for ten weeks.

All six of November's new musicals were hits, even if some were not so successful as their creators had hoped. Rodgers and Hart and Herbert Fields were in top form when they unveiled A **Connecticut Yankee** (3 November 1927, Vanderbilt). They had fun adapting Mark Twain's story, and their New York audiences had even more fun watching their version for a full year. At his bachelor supper Martin (William Gaxton) flirts with Alice Carter (Constance Carpenter) to the chagrin of his bride-to-be, Fay Morgan (Nana Bryant). In a jealous pique Fay breaks a champagne bottle over his head, knocking him out. The unconscious Martin dreams he is back in Camelot, where his bachelor friends are fellow knights of the Round Table, Fay Morgan is metamorphosed into Morgan Le Fay, and Alice appears as Alisande La Carteloise. The courtiers are convinced the stranger is dangerous. They prepare to burn him at the stake. But Martin conveniently recalls his astronomic history and correctly predicts an eclipse of the sun. The awed knights release him. In gratitude Martin proceeds to modernize Camelot. Telephones, radios, and every conceivable modern device suddenly grace King Arthur's court. All might have been well had not Morgan Le Fay been bent on making trouble. Martin only escapes by waking from his dream. Back at the Hartford hotel he reconsiders his marriage plans, deciding to marry the girl he really loves. Two Rodgers classics came out of the show: "Thou Swell" and "My Heart Stood Still." The latter had first been used in the 1927 London revue *One Dam Thing After Another*. Rodgers and Hart had to buy the rights back from a London producer. Hart's lyrics were brilliant. Two of the best songs in the show, "On A Desert Island With Thee" and "I Feel At Home With You," were given to a second pair of lovers, Evelyn La Belle-Ans (June Cochrane) and Galahad (Jack Thompson). They agreed they deserved each other because they were not particularly bright. The show was mounted with gaudy, witty sets and costumes by John F. Hawkins, Jr. His Camelot became a land of "topless, tottering towers of the expressionist pattern. Towers of many color... ." In fact, there were too many colors for some, leading the *World* to complain of the production's "seed-catalog floridity." Busby Berkeley's dancers won their share of accolades as their routines sent them prancing over tables, over sofas, over anything between them and the other side of the stage. An interesting revival was offered in the 1943–1944 season.

The Shuberts introduced their latest edition of **Artists and Models** (15 November 1927, Winter Garden) and were satisfied to see it run nineteen weeks. Probably the majority of ticket buyers came to see the "100–Winter Garden Girls–100" (there were also 25 chorus boys). When the girls weren't forming a bracelet of nudes or posing in a living tableau of Reins [sic] Cathedral, other entertainers had their chance. Jack Pearl told dialect stories about his experiences as a deck hand on a submarine or of playing hooky from correspondence school. Florence Moore played an unsmiling, strong-armed nurse. In a more lyric vein, Ted Lewis led his little band of musicians and sang his cheerily forlorn songs. While the run was profitable, it was noticeably shorter than the earlier editions. The Shuberts put the series to bed for a number of years.

Another musical gem opened on 22 November, **Funny Face.** For its producers, Alex Aarons and Vinton Freedley, it was a doubly proud moment. They brought their show into their brand-new Alvin Theatre, the name derived by combining the initial syllables of their first names. Fred Thompson and Robert Benchley had originally written the book, when the show was called *Smarty.* But Benchley was roasted for offering the same stolen-jewels plot he had so often ridiculed in his capacity as critic for *Life.* Benchley withdrew and was replaced by Paul Gerard Smith. The Gershwins, who created the songs, and their producers reemployed favorite performers from their earlier shows: Fred and Adele Astaire, Victor Moore, and Allen Kearns. Moore was brought in at the eleventh hour in a hastily devised role. Even with Benchley gone, the stolen-jewels story remained. Jimmie Reeve (Astaire) is Frankie's unbending guardian. He has locked her pearls in his

safe and adamantly insists they will remain there. Frankie (Miss Astaire) cajoles her boyfriend, Peter Thurston (Kearns), to help her steal them. But they are not alone in their desire to put their hands on the jewels. Two comic burglars, Herbert (Moore) and Dugsie (William Kent), are also after them. Of course Frankie wins, winning Peter in the bargain. The haste with which Thompson and Smith wrote in Moore's part may have explained their frequent recourse to the very sort of puns Thompson had generally avoided in *The 5 O'clock Girl.* The puns were particularly noticeable in Moore's material:

Dugsie: I'm an artist. I etch.
Herbert: Then why don't you scratch yourself?

Even in their settings the librettists tinkered with verbal inflations. Atlantic City's Traymore Hotel became the Paymore, while the Million Dollar Pier grew into the Two Million Dollar Pier. (The settings themselves were attractive but unexceptional.) The top Gershwin tune, made even more memorable by Ira's clever shorthand, was " 'S Wonderful," sung by the lovers. Ira's lyrics for "The Babbitt And The Bromide"—a last-minute addition—were singled out for anthologizing years later. The song's verse recounted the scattered meetings over the years of two bourgeois, "sub-sti-an-tial men," played by the Astaires. Its chorus detailed a collection of driveling, unvarying commonplaces that comprised their conversations—"Hello! How are You? Howza Folks? What's New?" Not even their final meeting in heaven inspired any change of clichés. Their dance for the number allowed the Astaires a chance to offer their celebrated "runaround" step just before the final curtain. One show-stopping number provided Fred Astaire with what became a virtual trademark in later years. For "High Hat" he donned a tuxedo and, with his hands in his pockets, tapped away while a chorus of two dozen men in black tie echoed his stamping feet. Other memorable Gershwin songs were the title song (sung by the Astaires), "He Loves And She Loves" (sung by the lovers), and "My One And Only" (sung and tap-danced by Astaire, Gertrude McDonald, and Betty Compton).

Another show opened the same night as *Funny Face.* **Take the Air** (22 November 1927, Waldorf) has long been forgotten. But it was almost as successful in its day as the Gershwin work. It ran 206 performances, despite an almost nonexistent plot and a commonplace score. Gene Buck, now split from Ziegfeld, produced the show and co-authored it with Anne Caldwell. Another old *Follies* regular, Dave Stamper, did the score. The story related how Carmela Cortez (Trini) flies all the way from Spain to the Texas-Mexican border to help Happy Hokum (Will Mahoney) court Lillian Bond (Dorothy Dilley). Carmela plans a little smuggling on the side. She also helps Captain Haliday (Greek Evans) of the U.S. Army Aviation Border Patrol. Then they all fly to the Bond estate at Sands Point, Long Island, to celebrate the Hokum-Bond nuptials. Trini and Mahoney turned the affair into another dancing evening, though the dancing was a far cry from the elegant grace the Astaires brought to *Funny Face.* Trini emphasized her exotic Spanish routines, while Mahoney did "taps with the force of a pile driver," punctuated with comic pratfalls.

The popular Harry Delmar assembled an excellent group of performers for **Delmar's Revels** (28 November 1927, Shubert): Frank Fay, Winnie Lightner, Patsy Kelly, and one name not yet famous, Bert Lahr. The comedians clowned in a burlesque of English manners and spoofed theatrical groups such as the Provincetown Players and the Theatre Guild in "The Straganota Players." Critic after critic showered praise on one spectacular number, a "deepwater" ballet, "Under the Sea," in which the dancers glided along as jellyfish, octopuses, and other creatures of the ocean depths. Miss Lightner sang "I Love A Man In Uniform," while the Chester Hale Girls danced in precision. The revue had music by a number of composers. Delmar's hodgepodge was pleasant enough to run fourteen weeks.

A third new musical house opened on 30 November. The new theatre was Hammerstein's, built by Arthur Hammerstein in memory of his father, the first Oscar. Its opening attraction, **Golden Dawn**, was something of a family affair. Arthur produced it; Oscar II was co-librettist, and Reginald Hammerstein co-director. Otto Harbach again collaborated with Oscar on the book, while Emmerich Kalman, Herbert Stothart, and Robert Stolz created the music. Somewhat pretentiously they labeled their effort a "music drama." It was an odd piece to open a new American musical house, an operetta with a distinctly Viennese flavor set in Africa with white members of the cast in blackface seriously portraying blacks. A blonde native beauty named Dawn (Louise Hunter) has been reared to believe she is an African princess. She meets Steve Allen (Paul Gregory), who is being held as a prisoner of war by the German colonials. They fall in love. The heartless black overseer, Shep Keyes's (Robert

Chisholm), would keep them apart and keep Dawn for himself. To bring this about he engineers her "marriage" to the tribal god. A drought destroys the village's crops, prompting a native uprising. When Dawn still rebuffs Keyes's advances, Keyes turns the revolt against Dawn by persuading his fellow Africans she is to blame for their troubles. Her problems end only after the chief confesses Dawn is actually a white woman. Kalman's score was by no means his best, but Robert Chisholm as Keyes electrified audiences with his singing of "The Whip." A hint that something was amiss came in the reviews. Though the *Daily Mirror* lauded Joseph Urban's sets as "breathtaking," most of the other critics didn't even mention them. The show had a profitable run of 184 performances, but it was a disappointing, though prophetic, opener for the ill-fated house.

Frank Grey had tried and failed to win Broadway acclaim with *Sue Dear* (10 July 1922) and *The Matinee Girl* (1 February 1926). He made a third effort with his score for **Happy** (5 December 1927, Earl Carroll). When he failed this third time he called it quits. With its collegiate background and affirmative tide, *Happy* seemed to be trying to become another *Good News.* Fortune rather than football was the theme. Siggy Sigler (Percy Helton) must earn $100,000 on his own to inherit his family wealth. With his classmates' help, he does. He, in turn, helps untangle three love affairs, the most important of which finds Jack Gaynor (Fred Santley) writing love lyrics to Lorelei Lynn (Madeleine Fairbanks). As was the case with so many musicals of the period, the show was best when it was on its feet. Long-legged Gene Collins and Bill Brown won encores with their eccentric dancing, while the chorus started hands clapping with a rousing second-act tap dance done to the music of Carleton Kelsey's jazz band.

Eleven new shows opened on the night of 26 December. **The White Eagle**, at the Casino, was the lone musical in the batch. A lyric version of Edwin Milton Royle's *The Squaw Man* (a 1905 hit and a famous early movie), it had book and lyrics by Brian Hooker and W. H. Post, and music by Rudolf Friml. The old story was faithfully retained. When the Earl of Kerhill (Fred Tilden) steals money from his regiment, his brother James (Allen Prior) publicly takes the blame, then flees to America. Under the name Jim Carson he becomes a successful rancher and marries an Indian girl called Silverwing (Marion Keeler). On his brother's death he stands to inherit the title. But Silverwing feels her presence will hinder him and kills herself. The old play, like

Arizona earlier in the season, seemed ready-made for a thumping, romantic operetta. (Its Indian heroine may have led Friml to hope he was working on another *Rose-Marie*.) But like *The Love Call*, it was a quick flop. In this case it was a pity, for it dragged down with it one of Friml's loveliest melodies, "Give Me One Hour"—although the atrociously clumsy Hooker lyrics might have killed the song in any case. Some critics complained that the bright colors used in the sets and costumes were not correct for Indian motifs, while others could see no use in inserting a dream ballet with "cornflower-blue and gold shepherdesses." But there was general approval for the rousing "War Dance" that ended the show.

Only two plays came in the following night, 27 December. But one was Philip Barry's literate and knowing comedy *Paris Bound*; the other was *Show Boat*. **Show Boat**, at the Ziegfeld, was the outstanding commercial success and artistic triumph of the 1927–1928 season, and it has survived as one of the masterpieces of our lyric stage. Based on Edna Ferber's novel—for which, thinking it unsuitable for a musical show, she gave her very reluctant consent—it had book and lyrics by Oscar Hammerstein II and music by Jerome Kern. For Kern and, arguably, for Hammerstein it remained the high point of their careers.

In the 1880s, the heyday of the traveling showboats, the *Cotton Blossom* docks in Natchez. The townsfolk welcome it, hailing it by name. Cap'n Andy (Charles Winninger) appears to greet the crowds and tell them of all the marvelous attractions he has for them. The enticements include the sultry Julie La Verne (Helen Morgan). The captain is assisted by his wife, Parthy Ann (Edna May Oliver), and their daughter, Magnolia (Norma Terris). In the crowd is a dashing river-boat gambler, Gaylord Ravenal (Howard Marsh). He falls in love with Magnolia at first sight, and she with him. They cannot admit their feelings, but profess a willingness to "Make Believe." Their reverie is shattered when the sheriff warns Ravenal his likes are not wanted in town and he would be wise to move on. Magnolia encounters Joe (Jules Bledsoe), a black workhand on the levee. She presses him for information about Gaylord, but if he knows anything he is loath to reveal it. He suggests if anyone can give her answers it would be "Ol' Man River." On the *Cotton Blossom* Julie laments that for all his faults she "Can't Help Lovin' Dat Man" of hers, Steve (Charles Ellis). But when Magnolia tells her she, too, has found a man, Julie warns her to be cautious. The sheriff arrives. He informs the showboat that Julie is part Negro, and, since Steve is white, they are guilty of miscegenation. Steve cuts Julie's finger and sucks in some of her blood, claiming that makes his blood part Negro, too. But Steve and Julie leave the ship to spare the others any problems. Magnolia is assigned Julie's parts. Seeing his chance to get out of town and also to be with Magnolia, Gaylord volunteers to assume Steve's duties. Before long Magnolia and Gaylord tell each other. "You Are Love" and agree to marry.

Time passes. It is 1893, and the Chicago World's Fair is in progress. Gaylord and Magnolia visit the exposition. Joyful and amazed that their love is still so strong, they ask one another, "Why Do I Love You?" Secretly Gaylord has continued to gamble, and his debts become so great he deserts Magnolia, leaving her with a young daughter. Magnolia learns the manager of the Trocadero is having trouble with his alcoholic singer and wants a replacement. The boozy songstress is none other than Julie, and just before Magnolia's arrival she rehearses her evening's number, "Bill." Magnolia does not recognize Julie, but Julie recognizes her and, understanding Magnolia's plight, sacrifices what is left of her own faltering career by walking out on the nightclub so that Magnolia can have her job. After an awkward start, Magnolia makes a hit, singing Charles K. Harris's "After The Ball." But she realizes this cannot be a life for her and is easily persuaded to return to the *Cotton Blossom*. More years pass. By the 1920s Magnolia's daughter, Kim, is a young lady. An old man appears at the entrance to the showboat. He is, of course, Gaylord Ravenal. He spots Magnolia, also aged. But he insists to her, "You Are Love," as always. They head hand in hand into the ship.

Hammerstein's changes from the original Ferber story are intriguing. A slew of minor figures inevitably were dropped. Julie's ultimate degradation as a lady of the streets went unmentioned. Though at the end of the novel many of the principals were dead or had drifted far away, Hammerstein contrived to reunite all of them except Julie. His ending may have been less realistic than Miss Ferber's, but it did tie together the loose ends of the history in a theatrically happy fashion. Furthermore, Hammerstein managed to create a heroine whose character develops and matures; he also confronted black-white relations head-on.

Ziegfeld mounted the piece with his usual lavishness and taste. Joseph Urban's settings were among the finest he had ever done. Neither the imaginative stylizations he devised for the *Follies*, nor the

Graustarkian baroque of his designs for some operettas, *Show Boat*'s sets filled the stage with a colorful, slightly heightened *verismo*. The opening of the first act was a bustling levee enlivened by the arrival of Cap'n Andy's floating auditorium. Later Urban revealed the auditorium itself, its main floor and balconies crowded with spectators engrossed in the drama playing on the boat's stage. The opening of the second act brought back the splendor of the 1893 Chicago fair. John Harkrider's costumes matched Urban's sets for flair and color. Ziegfeld's cast was near perfection, though only Helen Morgan went on to real stardom. (Indeed, Howard Marsh's career began to fade after *Show Boat*. While Bledsoe helped make "Ol' Man River" an instant classic, he quickly faded from the scene.) The show was not the sort usually associated with the producer, but then the show was not the sort Broadway had ever seen before. For Ziegfeld the show may have brought back a swell of memories, recalling the same 1893 World's Fair where he first came to the public's attention.

For 1927 audiences, apart from whatever memories it evoked, it presented possibly the most important breakthrough in the history of our musical stage. Neither a Viennese operetta nor an American musical comedy, it was the first real "musical play": a lyric piece with a relatively serious romantic story about essentially everyday people set to music neither as clipped as typical musical comedy writing nor as fully arioso as operetta, although leaning toward the latter. It could be called American operetta, if only "operetta" could lose its pejorative connotations. Once again the matter of integration arises. Given the exigencies of the commercial theatre the aim of a subtle, seemingly inevitable blend of dialogue, song, and dance is a probably unattainable goal, at least in its purest form. But if inevitability is replaced by reasonableness a number of our best shows certainly attain it. And *Show Boat* is high among the best. Though "Bill" was written for a Princess Theatre show ten years earlier and though "After The Ball" was an extraneous piece incorporated for period effect, everything seemed comfortably in place. A number of the splendid musicals from the 1927–1928 season have been given important revivals at different times. None so often nor so gratifyingly as *Show Boat*.

The final musical of 1927 opened two nights after *Show Boat*. **Lovely Lady** (29 December 1927, Harris) used the French farce *Dejeuner de Soleil* as its source. It had a score by Harold Levey and Dave Stamper. The plot recounted how a young lady named Folly Watteau (Edna Leedom) induces Paul de Morlaix (Guy Robertson) to pretend he is her husband. Before long the pretense becomes reality. Much of the show's dancing was performed by yet another group of Chester Hale Girls. The sameness of the "precision and counter-point routines" in musical after musical finally drove the *Times* to urge, "there must be other dance patterns." Like Stamper's *Take the Air* earlier in the season, *Lovely Lady* was a small hit, running twenty-one weeks. And, like *Take the Air*, it left nothing memorable behind. For both Stamper and Levey, who had long been secondary figures on the Broadway scene, the musical represented their last major effort to play New York.

The first new musical of 1928, **She's My Baby** (3 January 1928, Globe) was one of those surprising failures that on paper seems to have everything. Bert Kalmar and Harry Ruby took a vacation from songwriting to provide the book, leaving the music and lyrics to Rodgers and Hart. The cast included Beatrice Lillie, Clifton Webb, Jack Whiting, and Irene Dunne. The story had the comfortable feel of an old hat. In a way it was a reversal of *Lovely Lady*'s plot. Bob Martin (Whiting) must pretend he's married and a father so that he can borrow several hundred thousand dollars from his uncle. He selects his maid, Tillie (Miss Lillie), to play his wife, and they borrow the neighbors' baby. Rodgers failed to come up with a top tune, and Hart, experimenting with the limits of colloquialism in lyrics, momentarily became too colloquial and not sufficiently bright or witty. For example, Hart purposely injected the pointless, all too ubiquitous "I mean" in sentence after sentence of "You're What I Need." It was Miss Lillie who was largely to credit for the show's surviving nine weeks. Her Tillie ate nothing but vegetables with Vitaphones, and when Webb proposed, "Let us ensconce ourselves upon the sofa," her reply was a terse, "No, I prefer to sit down." She stopped the show singing "A Baby's Best Friend Is His Mother." Webb and Ula Sharon also had a much-applauded number, "A Little House In Soho." As they sang, the house of their dreams took shape behind them, and when it was ready, chorus girls dressed as flowers provided it with an instant garden. Eight Tiller Girls—called for this occasion "Lillie Cocktails"—performed the expected precision stepping.

For **Rosalie** (10 January 1928, New Amsterdam), Ziegfeld corralled an impressive array of talent. Guy Bolton and William Anthony McGuire wrote the book; P. G. Wodehouse and Ira Gershwin wrote the words for George Gershwin and Sigmund Romberg's music. The queen of musical comedy found herself playing a princess. The *World* described her entrance. Violins tremble; trumpets blare: "Fifty beautiful girls in simple peasant costumes of satin and chiffon rush pell-mell onto the stage, all squealing simple peasant outcries of "Here she comes!" Fifty hussars in a fatigue uniform of ivory white and tomato bisque march on in a column of fours and kneel to express an emotion too strong for words. The lights swing to the gateway at the back and settle there. The house holds its breath. And on walks Marilyn Miller." Princess Rosalie falls in love with a West Pointer, Lieutenant Richard Fay (Oliver McLennan). He pulls a Lindbergh, flying the Atlantic to be with her; then she and her family reciprocate by visiting America. But Rosalie cannot marry a commoner unless her father abdicates. He does just that, joining the ex-kings of Portugal, Bulgaria, Prussia, Greece, Bavaria, and Turkey in celebration. Frank Morgan was the comic king. Romberg produced no standouts, but Gershwin gave the show a solid hit, "Oh, Gee! Oh, Joy!" Another fine Gershwin number, "How Long Has This Been Going On?," discarded during the *Funny Face* tryout, was used but failed to cause a stir. The title song associated with the piece was not in the stage version but was supplied later by Cole Porter for the movie version. A Ziegfeld production meant Urban sets. *Rosalie* was no exception. His opening set was all in brown: a brown arch framing a brown village rising to a bluish-brown sea. Several scenes were played against a scarlet and silver show curtain. Urban's lavish ballroom in the finale gave Miss Miller perfect surroundings for an elegant ballet. *Rosalie* danced on for ten months.

A cheerily titled flop, **The Optimists** (30 January 1928, Casino de Paris), was something of a vanity production. Its producer, composer, and star was Melville Gideon. An American ragtime pianist who had long lived in England, Gideon had first offered the entertainment as *The Co-Optimists* to London, where it had played in ever-changing editions for five years. The revue did have some good people in its cast, especially Luella Gear and the young dancer who would one day be Hollywood's Rosalie, Eleanor Powell. Its idea of humor was a "Song Of The Vulgar Boatman."

January's last musical, **The Madcap** (31 January 1928, Royale), just made it over the 100-performance mark—103. The piece was adapted from a French farce with a plot not unlike *The Magistrate*, except that the sex of the protagonist has been changed.

Claire Valmont (Ethel Intropodi), hoping to wheedle a proposal of marriage from Lord Clarence Steeple (Sydney Greenstreet), claims she is only twenty-nine. This presents a problem for her twenty-year-old daughter, Chibi, who must now admit to only twelve years. In turn, the lie complicates Chibi's romance with Lord Clarence's son, Harry (Harry Puck). Third-act confessions clear up everything. Arthur Treacher had a minor role, but the star of the evening was Mitzi, no longer young, and fading as an attraction. She was egregiously miscast as Chibi. The music was by Maurice Rubens, who contributed a number of Broadway scores in the late twenties: six between 1926 and 1929. His style was typical of the crisp, bouncy writing of the day, but he never produced anything memorable. His catchiest tune in *The Madcap* was "Odle-De-O," to Clifford Grey's nonsense lyric evoking the old yodeling songs.

Sunny Days (8 February 1928, Imperial) was another musical based on a French farce and, like *The Madcap*, just made it across the 100-performance line. Leon Dorsay (Frank McIntyre) tires of his young mistress, Ginette (Jeanette MacDonald), and decides to devote his time to his wife. However, his childless wife has another plan. She has decided to adopt a young girl and, of course, selects Ginette. But Ginette finally prefers a more mature liaison with Paul Morel (Carl Randall). It was the sort of plot Ivan Caryll and his generation decorated with trippingly appropriate music. In fact, an old-timer, Jean Schwartz, did the score. But the music was dishearteningly lackluster and a little out of date. Schwartz joined the composers who were abandoning Broadway for greener pastures elsewhere. To a large extent the show relied on its comedy and its dancing to attract pleasure-seekers. The blimp-like McIntyre milked laughs with a pair of ill-fitting trousers, while Billy Van stumbled through a drunk scene shouting, "Pa-leese, pa-leese." The *Times*, resigned to its inability to change dancing styles, noted "choruses of 'Sunny Days' buck and wing and cavort and stamp and clap their hands in unison." A glimmer of respect shown through the critic's report on *Sunny Days*'s "Premier Dancer," Charlotte Ayre. According to the reviewer, to impress audiences she "pivots on tiptoe and steps out in the fast tango of the music and hurdles across the stage with Carl Randall."

One of the season's biggest musical hits opened the next night. **Rain or Shine** (9 February 1928, Cohan) had a brash, undistinguished book by James Gleason and Maurice Marks, and commonplace if serviceable songs by Jack Yellen (lyrics) and Milton Ager and Owen Murphy (music). Its prime attraction was Joe Cook, who had been working his way to stardom in vaudeville and the *Vanities*. Cook played Smiley Johnson, who finds himself in charge of the Wheeler Circus, since Mary Wheeler (Nancy Welford), the show's young heiress, spends her time chasing a handsome roustabout, Jack Wayne (Warren Hull). Johnson thwarts the machinations of Jesse Dalton (Joe Lyons), who would take the show away from Mary. When the star of the show refuses to perform, Smiley takes his place, becoming almost a one-man circus. Cook juggled Indian clubs, performed a knife-throwing act, pranced on a high wire, and walked on a ball. Even a banjo-strumming leopard couldn't steal the star's thunder. Cook also found time to unveil some of his Rube Goldberg–like inventions. One enabled him to make music from the opposite side of the stage. A whirling saw approached a man holding a siphon. The man became so frightened he squirted the siphon, startling a second man standing in the crank of a Ferris wheel. Each carriage of the wheel held a violinist, and, as the wheel revolved, the freely swung violin bows hit a third man, on a pedestal, holding a hammer. The hammer struck an iron ring. Violà, music!

Rain or Shine competed with **Parisiana** (9 February 1928, Edyth Totten) for the attention of first-nighters. *Parisiana*, a mediocre revue, disappeared after twenty-eight performances.

Keep Shufflin' (27 February 1928, Daly's) was an attempt by Flournoy Miller and Aubrey Lyles to reconstruct the exciting Jimtown of *Shuffle Along* (23 May 1921). Miller and Lyles were again Steve Jenkins and Sam Peck. They form the Equal Got League and plan to promote their new equality by blowing up the local bank and redistributing the cash. (The nonsense of one era becomes the horror of another.) Of course, the boys intend to see that they are a bit more equal than others. As they had been earlier, they were up at Daly's out-of-the-way house. Eubie Blake was gone from the pit. In his place, at one piano, was Thomas "Fats" Waller, who composed the score along with Jimmy Johnson (at the other piano) and Clarence Todd. Henry Creamer and Andy Razaf set words to the tunes. The show's best number was a Razaf and Waller song, "Willow Tree," a blues tune they labeled "a musical misery." *Keep Shufflin's* reviews were the sort white critics had been writing for black musicals ever since *Shuffle Along*. Black dancing remained the yardstick

by which such evenings were rated. In the case of *Keep Shufflin'* at least one paper thought the dancing went overboard. The *World* observed that the chorus "danced with such ardor and such grotesquerie last night as to knock the show out of drawing." Not all critics were so taken. For the *Herald Tribune* the show was not Negro enough, and only "delightfully un-Nordic" touches such as the "beaming pianist" redeemed the evening. Indeed Waller must have been far more enjoyable to watch than much of the action on stage, for a number of other critics marked him out for attention. Considering the stiff competition *Keep Shufflin'* found and the show's distance from the heart of the theatre district, its run of 104 performances was not too disappointing. Obviously it nevertheless fell far short of *Shuffle Along*.

The Three Musketeers (13 March 1928, Lyric) was a musical version of Alexandre Dumas's story, adapted for the stage by William Anthony McGuire and set to music by Rudolf Friml. P. G. Wodehouse and Clifford Grey supplied the lyrics. D'Artagnan (Dennis King) comes to Paris, where he soon joins the happy band of Athos (Douglass R. Dumbrille), Porthos (Detmar Poppen), and Aramis (Joseph Macaulay). He falls in love with Constance Bonacieux (Vivienne Segal). When the Duke of Buckingham (John Clarke) accepts the French queen's love token, D'Artagnan and his companions steal off to England to recover it before its loss embarrasses the queen. For the third time in a row Dennis King found success singing Friml's glorious music. For Ziegfeld it was his third hit of the season. He was coming increasingly to depend on William Anthony McGuire as a replacement for the departed Gene Buck, and McGuire staged the work as well as taking responsibility for the libretto. But Friml's score proved the evening's most durable offering. Not quite on a par with *Rose-Marie* (2 September 1924) or *The Vagabond King* (20 September 1925), it still was a richly textured, varied, and melodic achievement. Four songs stood out: "Ma Belle," "My Sword And I," "Your Eyes," and "March Of The Musketeers."

"Unfailing Urban" once more provided Ziegfeld with eye-filing sets. The stage was framed in a Gothic-arched proscenium displaying the king's and the cardinal's escutcheons and bordered in gilt with grotesque figures. The show curtain was flat-tinted and thin-lined to resemble the drawings in primitive illuminations (a slight anachronism). The Tuileries were seen through a great circle of shrubbery; a city on a hill was silhouetted in burnt-red and buff; the queen's pavilion glistened in white, blue, and crystal. John Harkrider's plumed, multi-colored costumes added to the luster of the production. Sixteen Tiller Girls somehow found a way to do their precision movements in old France, while the Albertina Rasch Girls offered ballet-like dances. All the excellences combined to make the musical a success—but not an overwhelming success. The show ran 318 performances, a substantial falling away from the runs of Friml's other hits. But tastes were changing, and new attitudes were soon to dominate the musical world. Though Friml continued to write, *The Three Musketeers* was to be his last success.

The Beggar's Opera (28 March 1928, 48th St.), with contemporary music added, failed to find an audience.

The **Greenwich Village Follies** returned on 9 April, signaling that the warm weather and the end of the season were both near. Oddly (and significantly), when it opened it was the only revue on Broadway. The cast was high in talent: Dr. Rockwell, Benny Fields, Bobby Watson, Grace La Rue, and Blossom Seeley. Unfortunately their material was hackneyed. Travesties on plays such as *The Command to Love*, *The Trial of Mary Dugan*, and *The Silent House* all seemed to miss the mark. And too many patrons had already seen Rockwell in vaudeville, using a banana stalk to illustrate the spinal column in his anatomy lesson. Grace La Rue, in a sequined gown, won applause with "Every Little Heart That's Lonely." Sixteen more Chester Hale Girls competed for encores with Ralph Reader Girls. In short, the evening was overdone. At best, Broadway heard what was probably its first taste of calypso in this edition. Blame for a slackening in quality most likely lies with the Shuberts, who were now calling the shots. They brought the show into their Winter Garden; their dependable Harold Atteridge did most of the sketches, while Ray Perkins and Maurice Rubens did the songs. Though it ran a satisfactory 155 performances, the Shuberts were astute enough to realize the day of the annual, like the day of the operetta, was ending. When the final curtain fell on this edition, the *Greenwich Village Follies* became part of history.

Rodgers and Hart and Herbert Fields had their second hit of the season when they introduced **Present Arms** (26 April 1928, Mansfield). Charles King, who had been the shy but demanding sailor in *Hit the Deck!*, was transformed into a tough, uncouth marine, Chick Evans. He is anything but shy in his courtship of Lady Delphine (Flora Le Breton).

Fearing he will lose her to a rich German, Ludwig Von Richter (Anthony Knilling), he promotes himself to the rank of captain. When his imposture is exposed, he loses both his job and his would-be bride. But his heroism in a yacht disaster restores both his rank and esteem. In some respects the musical side of the show was peculiar. Though the piece was set in Hawaii, the songs that might have supplied local color—"Hawaii," "Kohala Welcome," and to a lesser extent "Blue Ocean Blues"—were not played until the very end. And the hit of the show, "You Took Advantage Of Me," was not given to the principals. The Rodgers-Hart-Fields team was seldom anything less than daring. The song was sung in the show by Joyce Barber and Busby Berkeley. Berkeley, doing double duty, created the evening's dances as well. His routines had his dancers off their feet so often one critic dubbed them "aerial formations." *Present Arms* fell short of repeating *A Connecticut Yankee's* success, but it ran through the summer. Rodgers attributes part of the short run to the show's similarity—including its star—to *Hit the Deck!* (25 April 1927).

Though it contained one of the best and most enduring jazz numbers of the epoch, **Here's Howe** (1 May 1928, Broadhurst) was not a hit. It was produced by Alex A. Aarons and Vinton Freedley, who had brought so much of the best Gershwin to New York. They employed their *Funny Face* librettists (Paul Gerard Smith and Fred Thompson) to flesh out a rather venturesome, freethinking story with a novel twist on the old poor-secretary-makes-good theme. Joyce Baxter (Irene Delroy) is a stenographer at the

Tredwell Motor Company, where her boyfriend, Billy Howe (Allen Kearns), works as a mechanic. In their spare time they dream together of building a combination tearoom and gas station on the Boston Post Road. But her boss offers Joyce a trip around the world, ostensibly as his secretary. When Joyce demurs, Billy insists she not give up so rare an opportunity. Billy and Joyce meet months later in Havana, where Billy has become rich by gambling. But easy come, easy go. The finale finds the two of them standing on the Boston Post Road, poor again, but hopeful. Roger Wolfe Kahn, son of the banker and Metropolitan Opera benefactor Otto Kahn, wrote the score with Joseph Meyer. Irving Caesar did the lyrics. One tune that stopped the show nightly was the best in a livelier than average score, "Crazy Rhythm." It was sung by Ben Bernie, Peggy Chamberlain, and June O'Dea. The song wasn't expected to be the show's hit. Hopes ran higher for a song called "Imagination," a number played again and again throughout the evening. Much of the music was played on stage by Bernie and his orchestra. And Bernie, "bending his knees and waving his violin to keep time [while he] patters innocuously," walked away with some of the best notices. One dance novelty elicited bravos. Miss Chamberlain and Ross Hines reversed roles in their apache number, with Miss Chamberlain throwing Hines roughly around the stage. But all its attractions were not enough to push *Here's Howe* past the July heat.

This was one season that never slackened. On 9 May another smash hit came in at the Liberty. The show was **Blackbirds of 1928**, an all-white creation for an all-black cast. The songwriters were new to Broadway. Dorothy Fields did the lyrics, and Jimmy McHugh composed the music. Together they put a lot of old-timers to shame.

The McHugh-Fields score was filled with riches. Two songs—"I Can't Give You Anything But Love" and "Diga Diga Doo"—have both retained their popularity. "I Can't Give You Anything But Love" (originally called "I Can't Give You Anything But Love, Lindy") was sung first by Aida Ward and then by Lois Deppe and Adelaide Hall. Miss Hall belted out "Diga Diga Doo" in another 1920 jungle setting. In this case the setting was not elaborate, for the *Times* noted, "As to production [the revue] is nearly nil, drapes constituting the principal stage dress. "Blackbirds" depends on its players and numbers." The player and number that drew the most applause seems to have been Bill Robinson, snazzily stepping his way through "Doin' The New Low-Down."

Amazingly, it was his only solo in the show. Sketches were routine for the black shows of the day. One more imaginative skit presented a black version of Elinor Glyn's *It*. Wisely, these comic moments were held down. They took a back seat whenever the orchestra began to play. In New York the orchestra found itself playing the score 518 times. A decade elapsed before another revue ran as long.

JIMMY McHUGH was eleven years older than Miss Fields, having been born in Boston on 10 July 1894. His mother was his first piano teacher. Preferring the practical experience offered as rehearsal pianist for the Boston Opera Company, he turned down a scholarship that would have allowed him to attend the New England Conservatory. He supplemented his income by serving as a Boston song-plugger for Irving Berlin's publishing house. Moving on to New York, he composed songs for the famous Harlem nightclub of the day, the Cotton Club. His first hit, "When My Sugar Walks Down The Street," came from one of the nightspot's revues.

The season ended with the latest edition of **The Grand Street Follies** (28 May 1928, Booth). Albert Carroll, Dorothy Sands, and Marc Loebell were back to head a cast that included a young dancer named James Cagney. As always impersonations and spoofs of current Broadway plays highlighted these *Follies*. Carroll fell back on two standbys, Ethel Barrymore and Mrs. Fiske. Miss Sands was a bit more original, impersonating Mae West as she might have done Juliet in a Max Reinhardt version on the steps of the New York Public Library. The famous scene in *Strange Interlude*, in which Nina sits down at a table with all the men in her life, was re-created in "The Strange Inner Feud" when Columbia sits down at a table with Calvin (Coolidge), Al (Smith), and Herbert (Lehman). *Coquette* was done as a miniature musical comedy. A pleasant, unexceptional show, it compiled 155 showings.

1928–1929

Burns Mantle bewailed that "the legitimate theatre came a cropper" in the "rotten season" of 1928–1929.

The season was not really all that bad, although in retrospect there was clearly a tapering off. If the fall presidential elections diverted some energies, more important forces also exerted a debilitating influence. Inevitably the rush of screen musicals that began in earnest in 1929, coupled with the first rumblings of the approaching economic debacle, had unnerving, enduring effects. Moreover, tastes in musicals were changing. Somehow this time playwrights and songsters were not thrown off balance, as they had been before, by earlier upheavals. In fact a number of the better creative talents took bold, innovative strides, though the failure of *Chee-Chee, Treasure Girl,* and, to a lesser extent, *Rainbow,* taught them painful lessons about the public tolerance of novelty. However, there was a noticeable drop in the number of new musicals, from over fifty to just over forty—a drop of 20 percent. The drop was far sharper than the drop in straight plays. The high quality that pervaded preceding seasons was also in shorter supply. As a result the number of long runs dropped. Four musicals from the magnificent 1927–1928 season had run over a year; one from the new season did, *The New Moon. Hold Everything* ran exactly a year, and *Follow Thru* chalked up fifty weeks.

A Baltimore revival of *Patience* opened the season on 25 June. It ran three weeks, as did the season's first new musical, **Say When** (26 June 1928, Morosco). The show was co-produced by Elizabeth Marbury, who had been so instrumental in initiating the Princess Theatre series a dozen years back. She advertised it as "an intimate musical comedy," sensing correctly the reaction to overblown, gaudy productions of the day. Theatrical intimacy would soon be the thing in musical productions. All that Miss Marbury misjudged was the quality of her offering. It recounted problems Diana Wynne (Dorothy Fitsgibbons) brings on herself when in a moment of weakness she accepts Count Scippio Varelli's (Joseph Lertora) proposal. She finally worms her way out of her predicament and into the arms of her real fiancé, Gregory Farnham (Bartlett Simmons). Calvin Brown based his libretto on Amelie Rives and Gilbert Emery's *Love in a Mist.* For music Miss Marbury culled songs from various writers. One tune, "Cheerio," boasted lyrics ("You'll find smiling worthwhile") by the mayor of New York, Jimmy Walker. Assignments and settings for some of the songs were so curious as to raise eyebrows. "Cheerio," for example, was given to the fiery count, while the Oriental-sounding "In My Love Boat" was sung under the magnolias of a southern garden.

July and August each had only one new musical; both were the latest editions of the surviving annuals, and both ran six months. **George White's Scandals** (2 July 1928, Apollo) had a stellar cast: the Howard Brothers, Harry Richman, Tom Patricola, Ann Pennington, and Frances Williams. The hoofers still monopolized much of the attention. The *Times* saluted Miss Pennington as the "most petite of the shake and quiver dancers" and even lauded Patricola, though it couldn't resist a slight dig at his "elephantine grace." This edition also had the last score DeSylva, Brown, and Henderson created for the series. A pale shadow of their great material for the previous edition, its opening number proclaimed correctly "Not As Good As Last Year." "I'm On The Crest Of A Wave" and "American Tune" received some play, though "Pickin' Cotton," which its authors hoped would be another "Black Bottom," got nowhere. The sketches, serviceable at best, attacked such obvious targets as Prohibition and *Strange Interlude.* One skit had all the citizens of gangster-infested Chicago wearing bulletproof clothing and armed to the teeth. A spoof of the newfangled talking movies hid actors behind a screen to shout out the dialogue. When they lose their places, the handsome matinee idol is heard to speak with a squeaky voice, while the glamorous heroine has suddenly turned baritone.

The Earl Carroll Vanities (6 August 1928, Earl Carroll) had a better than average cast for the series. W. C. Fields, Ray Dooley, and Joe Frisco were the top bananas, while Lillian Roth belted out the songs. The scantiest-clad chorus girls on the main stem were a big draw as always. Though over a dozen lyricists and tunesmiths combined their talents to fill out the score, nothing worth mentioning emerged. But Carroll's customers never expected much in the music department. Even the titles stayed comfortably in the expected girlie-show patterns—"Say It With Girls," "Getting The Beautiful Girls," "Pretty Girl," and "Painting A Vanities' Girl." The rainbow of colors that exploded over this last number gave way to more restraint in the revue's most highly praised moment, a stage bathed entirely in blue for "Blue Shadows." If Carroll's customers cared little for the music he offered, a number of them were probably even indifferent to the great clowns. Almost all the best comic material fell to Fields—or at least he made it seem so. Fields impersonated Dr. Pain, the dentist; a progression of railroad officials in "The Caledonian Express"; and Brigham Young about to take on a chorus line of brides in "The Mormon's Prayers."

Good Boy (5 September 1928, Hammerstein) opened the post–Labor Day rush of musicals. Its title may have been meant to recall the preceding year's smash opener, *Good News*. The show's surprisingly cynical libretto by Otto Harbach, Oscar Hammerstein II, and Henry Meyers was certainly as solid. But its score, by the curious combination of Herbert Stothart, Bert Kalmar, and Harry Ruby, was patently inferior. Its one memorable number was made a hit by the unique, squeaky delivery of the "boop-boop-a-doop" girl, Helen Kane—"I Wanna Be Loved By You." Miss Kane's part of Pansy McManus was not a central figure in the show. The principal character was Walter Meakin, who comes with his brother, Cicero, from their Arkansas home to try their luck in New York. Walter meets an attractive chorus girl, Betty Summers, and she wangles him a job as a chorus boy. But the ambitious Betty soon decides Walter is going no place and leaves him for the stage manager. Only when Walter starts to reap a fortune from a doll he has devised does Betty return. For many critics Arthur Hammerstein's imaginative mounting was the best part of the evening. The sights and sounds of New York were vividly recreated, climaxing in a first-act finale in which an apartment opened up to reveal a balcony with a breathtaking panorama of Central Park's skyline. Besides Miss Kane the better-known players included Eddie Buzzell as Walter, Charles Butterworth as Cicero, Barbara Newberry as Betty, and Dan Healy as the tap-dancing Bobby D'Arnell. The show's eight-month run was a happier affair for the Hammersteins and their new theatre than *Golden Dawn* had been, but the runaway hit the family had dreamed of for its house was always to elude it.

The Shuberts continued their futile search for another *Blossom Time* (29 September 1921), bringing in **White Lilacs** (10 September 1928, Shubert), a fictionalized biography of Chopin that had met with some success in Europe. Perhaps dreaming of the very bonanza *Blossom Time* remained for them, the brothers gave the importation a loving mounting. For the interior of a chateau, they painstakingly re-created Fragonard paintings for all the walls. The cast was as carefully selected as the designs. Guy Robertson and Odette Myrtil portrayed Chopin and George Sand, while a name from a fast receding past, De Wolf Hopper, handled the main comedy. In Harry B. Smith's version *White Lilacs* ran eighteen weeks.

What had originally been *Un Bon Garçon*, a French piece with music by Maurice Yvain, came in on 15 September as **Luckee Girl** (15 September 1928, Casino). It was another Shubert importation, and by the time it raised its curtain in New York only three or four of Yvain's songs remained. A staff of writers provided the interpolations. But nothing they added could prod the show beyond ten weeks. *Luckee Girl*'s sole claim to fame may be that it provided Irene Dunne with her first leading role on Broadway. She impersonated a saucy French lady, Arlette, who determinedly wins her heartthrob away from the girl he was slated to marry.

Cross My Heart (17 September 1928, Knickerbocker) survived only eight weeks. Daniel Kusell's book provided a variation on Molière. The upstart Mrs. T. Montgomery Gobble (Lulu McConnell) is determined her daughter, Elsie (Doris Eaton), will marry a title. So Elsie's real love, Charlie Graham (Bobby Watson), goes to the Slave Ship Café in Greenwich Village and hires a distressed Maharajah to go through a ridiculous ceremony. Mrs. Gobble is brought to her limited senses, and the lovers do marry. A subplot followed the romance of Sally Blake (Mary Lawlor) and Richard Todd (Harry Evans). The Harry Tierney–Joe McCarthy score was their last for Broadway. The best they could come up with was "Right Out Of Heaven," which faltered after an attractive start. If the dancing of "The Ten Little Tappers" (all girls) never faltered, neither did it win any wild applause. When *Cross My Heart* closed, Tierney joined the exodus to Hollywood. But his scores there were unsuccessful, and when he attempted to write shows again none ever got past a tryout.

The New Moon (19 September 1928, Imperial) was the only show of the season to run over 500 performances. Yet only an act of faith got it to Broadway. Though its original tryout was not disastrous, the show was quickly closed. Both the producers, Frank Mandel and Laurence Schwab, and the writers, Oscar Hammerstein II (with Mandel) and composer Sigmund Romberg felt they had the makings of a better work. The show was rewritten, recast, and reopened. The major additions were in Romberg's score. All but one of the show's hits were introduced during these revisions. The plot remained involved and farfetched. Robert Misson (Robert Halliday), a French nobleman turned revolutionary, is hiding in New Orleans in the guise of a servant to a rich shipowner, Monsieur Beaunoir (Pacie Ripple). Robert falls in love with Beaunoir's daughter, Marianne (Evelyn Herbert). Beaunoir's ship, *The New Moon*, under

Captain Paul Duval (Edward Nell, Jr.) arrives, bringing as a passenger the Vicomte Ribaud (Max Figman). Ribaud has been charged by the king with finding Misson and returning him to France. At a tavern Robert's friend Phillippe (William O'Neal) cautions him that, while love steals in, "Softly, As In A Morning Sunrise," its vows are always betrayed. But Robert ignores the warning. Given a band of "Stouthearted Men" both liberty and love will triumph. Back at Beaunoir's Marianne prepares for a ball. She acknowledges, "To be really in the fashion today, You must have a dozen beaux in your sway," but insists her dream is to have just one man. And for that man she saves her "One Kiss." Robert and Marianne admit their longing for each other, "Wanting You." But Duval, who has fallen in love with Marianne, recognizes Robert and has him seized. The vicious Ribaud tells Robert that Marianne betrayed him. Robert is to be returned home on *The New Moon*. Feigning a desire to be with Duval, Marianne sails with the ship. To her dismay Robert will have nothing to do with her. She pleads, "Lover, Come Back To Me." But Robert is mainly interested in stirring up a mutiny. He succeeds. The crew lands on an island, where they set up a free government. A ship brings news of the French Revolution. At the same time, Robert learns of Marianne's innocence.

Of the great songs in the revised show, only "Stouthearted Men" was in the original version (called in the program "Shoulder To Shoulder"), though the delightful production number "Try Her Out At Dances" was also included from the start. Apart from Romberg's melodious material, the glory of the original production was its singing. (The sets were sumptuous, but unexceptional.) Either at Romberg's insistence or because they had profited from the Shuberts' experiences, Mandel and Schwab enlisted a large, fine-voiced male chorus. Miss Herbert's supremely beautiful notes glorified Romberg's music to the farthest reaches of the auditorium. While Romberg was to remain an active writer, apart from a freakish affair nearly two decades later, *The New Moon* was his last great hit. The day of the Viennese-American operetta was over. Its incredibly melodious heyday encompassed a mere five seasons. They were the same five seasons that saw the coming of age of the sassy, cynical jazz musical comedy.

It was just such a sassy, cynical jazz musical comedy the daring trio of Rodgers, Hart, and Fields offered with **Chee-Chee** (25 September 1928, Mansfield). In his autobiography Richard Rodgers complains, "There was an appalling monotony of subject matter in even the best musical shows of the twenties." His complaint cannot apply to *Chee-Chee*. Its setting was one operetta had appropriated as its almost exclusive domain in recent years: an exotic Oriental court. No occidentals arrive to set up a comic contrast, as they did in the turn-of-the-century musical comedies. The story (based on Charles Petit's novel *The Son of the Grand Eunuch*) told of the successful attempt of Li-Pi Tchou (William Williams) to inherit his father's position as Grand Eunuch without paying the usual price. He and his wife, Chee-Chee (Helen Ford), suffer banishment in a forest before they reach their happy ending by arranging for a friend first to kidnap and then substitute for the surgeon. They play dominoes while the operation is supposedly in progress.

Rodgers and Hart attempted to integrate the songs firmly into the story. In fact, there were only six full-fledged songs in the show. In a purposeful effort to keep the story moving, the other musical "numbers" ranged from sixteen bars (the chorus of an ordinary song contains thirty-two) down to an almost unheard-of four bars. A program note similar to one *Rose-Marie* (2 September 1924) had offered was inserted into *Chee-Chee*'s playbill: "The musical numbers, some of them very short, are so interwoven with the story that it would be confusing for the audience to peruse a complete list." In a way Rodgers and Hart were too successful, for the public could take none of the songs out of the theatre. Hart's lyrics were as brilliant as ever, and Rodgers's melodies gave a clearer foretaste of the even more subtle musical lines and chromatics he would employ in the thirties. Rodgers was not above a few erudite, almost private, jokes in the score. He was delighted when a handful of the audience each night recognized the bars from Tchaikovsky's *Nutcracker Suite* inserted into the march with which Li-Pi-Tchou is led off to his supposed emasculation. Herbert Fields's beloved father, Lew, mounted the show with opulence and, perhaps, wit. Certainly a few critics were amused at the girls' Chinese dresses that seemed more like multi-colored pajamas and at the Chinese warriors in Tartar uniforms brandishing harmless little tin swords. Unfortunately, *Chee-Chee*, lacking Rodgers, Hart, and Fields's customary theatricality, could not find a public. It departed after four weeks.

October witnessed the end of another tradition when Broadway's first great song-and-dance man, George M. Cohan, brought in his last musical comedy. **Billie** (1 October 1928, Erlanger) was a musical version of Cohan's own 1912 play, *Broadway Jones*. Once again Jackson Jones's secretary, Billie (Cohan's favorite leading lady, Polly Walker), talks him out of merging his chewing-gum factory with bigger interests and thus keeps him independent. To override the musical's obviously hand-me-down nature, Cohan filled the evening with superb dancing. Everybody danced. Cohan even allowed his villain to win the audience's affection with some amusingly eccentric dance routines. Despite the diverting footwork, most critics commented on how old-fashioned Cohan's evening was. The days when Cohan was looked on as a noisy upstart were long gone, and critics generally found some kind things to say. Good notices or no, the public would not come. At least not in the numbers it once did to a Cohan work. *Billie* ran for just 112 performances. Cohan came to admit his musicals were relics of a gentler age. As his biographer McCabe said, "the Cohanic musical play had no chance to remain in a world whose innocence and optimisms it no longer mirrored." There was something poignantly existential in the song Cohan hoped be the hit of the show. "Where Were You—Where Was I?" had the subtitle "Exactly Where We Are." The title song had Billie describing how much she loved her name, even though her parents had given her a boy's name, after her father.

Paris (8 October 1928, Music Box) was as succinct, sophisticated, and naughty as its title and star could make it. Its star, Irene Bordini, was wickedly abetted in her plot to entertain by Cole Porter, who provided most of the songs. His style and wit finally became evident to the world at large with his first characteristic hit, "Let's Do It." The slight story followed Miss Bordoni as Vivienne Roland, a worldly, freethinking young lady, in her pursuit of Andrew Sabot (Eric Kalkhurst), scion of the proper New England Sabots. She gets her man. The whole affair was playfully intimate, confined to a single set (a lavish hotel suite) and with no regular chorus. However, space was found in the suite for Irving Aaronson and his ten jazz musicians, the Commanders. Since the men not only played their instruments but sang and danced as well, they constituted an ad hoc chorus. A harbinger of the chic musicals Porter and his followers would hereafter provide, *Paris* ran for six months.

Two other musicals opened the same night as *Paris*. Neither *Just a Minute* nor *Ups-a-Daisy* was as snappy as their titles, and both were soon gone. Harry Archer did most of the music, his last Broadway score, for **Just a Minute** (8 October 1928,

Ambassador). Little more than a vaudeville tied together with a flimsy story, it told of two songwriters who persuade one of their girlfriends to date a Broadway producer so the girl can interest him in the composers' songs. The plan backfires when the producer and the girl take a genuine liking to each other. *Just a Minute*'s show-business background allowed the entertainment to be filled with specialty dancers: Walker and Thompson, the Ebony Steppers, and sixteen Russell Markert Girls. They danced to the music of the pretentious-sounding pit band, Count Berni Vici and his Symphonic Girls, and to the jazzy on-stage playing of Peek-a-boo Jimmie and his band.

Lewis Gensler, still searching for another *Queen High* (8 September 1926), did the songs for **Ups-a-Daisy** (8 October 1928, Shubert). He had more of a story to work with. Ethel Billings (Luella Gear), annoyed at her husband's pretensions, demands he and his friends go mountain-climbing in the Alps to prove he really wrote a book on the subject. Of course, Billings isn't the real author. Young Roy Lindbrooke (Roy Royston) is. By the end of their adventure Billings (William Kent) is reasonably deflated, and the Billings's niece, Polly (Marie Saxon), is engaged to Roy. Even two top comedians, Miss Gear and Kent, couldn't put the material across, though they were assisted by another up-and-coming comic, Bob Hope, who played the butler, Screeves.

If DeSylva, Brown, and Henderson had disappointed their admirers with their indifferent score for the *Scandals*, they partially compensated by providing better than average scores for two of the season's book musicals. Their music for these shows was not as hit-packed as their *Good News* (6 September 1927) or *Scandals of 1926* (14 June 1926) material, but each show provided at least one knockout number. And apart from *The New Moon*, the two musicals were the major hits of the year. Knockout is perhaps a more appropriate word for the first of the two, **Hold Everything** (10 October 1928, Broadhurst), which unfolded a tale of the world of prizefighting. The sport had exploded as one of the rages of the theatrical year. Two straight plays, *Ringside* and *The Big Fight*, had already appeared, although without much success. In the new musical, "Sonny Jim" Brooks (Jack Whiting), a welterweight contender, loves Sue Burke (Ona Munson). She leaves in a huff when he refuses to think seriously about a charity boxing exhibition. Her temper is not improved when she watches flashy Norine Lloyd

(Betty Compton) try to fill her shoes. But when Brooks's opponent slaps Sue, Brooks gets fighting mad. The show had a fine cast that also included Victor Moore. However, it was Bert Lahr as the punch-drunk Gink Schiner who walked away with the best notices. Lahr staggered around the stage, crinkling his face, crossing his eyes, and gargling a nasal outcry something like "gnong, gnong, gnong." Demonstrating his ring prowess he landed a knock-out punch—on his own jaw. The morning after the opening he found himself a star.

```
BERT LAHR was born in New York City
on 13 August 1895. His given name was
Irving Lahrheim. He entered show business
at the age of fifteen. Lahr gained his experi-
ence in both burlesque and vaudeville, ini-
tially as a single and then as a team with his
first wife. Broadway applauded him briefly in
Delmar's Revels. But Hold Everything repre-
sented his big break.
```

The score for the musical included a clever twist on a title song, this one warning "Don't Hold Everything." Only one tune from the show remains alive, displaying DeSylva, Brown, and Henderson's razzle-dazzle at its best: "You're The Cream In My Coffee" (sung by Whiting).

Three Cheers (15 October 1928, Globe) had been created by the faithful R. H. Burnside and Anne Caldwell as a vehicle for the seemingly timeless Fred Stone and his daughter, Dorothy. But time did begin to catch up with Stone, who was too ill to consider a Broadway effort. Will Rogers was called in as a replacement, changing the tenor of the antics slightly. Stone's acrobatic comedy gave way to Rogers's more verbal wit. Into King Pompanola's serene wonderland of Itza a Hollywood movie crew descends for background shots. The usual misunderstandings occur, but at least Princess Sylvia has time for a romance with the director, Harry Vance (Alan Edwards). If the end of the trail was ineluctably approaching for Stone, it arrived abruptly for Raymond Hubbell. A prolific if uninspired composer of the prewar era, he saw his music becoming hopelessly out of date. Hubbell, though still reasonably young, retired to Florida, where he

lived another twenty-five years. DeSylva, Brown, and Henderson were called in for additional, more contemporary tunes, and Miss Caldwell put new words to some of Leslie Sarony's English melodies. Even with its modest score, Three Cheers was attractive enough to run six months.

Had Stone been in Three Cheers, his smiling, innocent fun would have made a sharp contrast to the leering and brash clowning of the Marx Brothers in Animal Crackers (23 October 1928, 44th St.). Everything—the George S. Kaufman–Morrie Ryskind book, the Bert Kalmar–Harry Ruby songs—took a back seat to the clowning of Zeppo, Harpo, Chico, and, maddest of all, Groucho. The action took place on the estate of Mrs. Rittenhouse, played by the brothers' matchless straight lady, Margaret Dumont. A picture is stolen, and Mrs. Rittenhouse's honored guest, the famous explorer, Captain Spalding (Groucho), sets out to retrieve it. The humor at times was so outlandish that someone who had never seen the Marx Brothers in action would wonder if it was humor at all:

Spalding: Say, I used to know a fellow that looked exactly like you by the name of Emanuel Ravelli. Are you his brother?
Ravelli [Chico]: I am Emanuel Ravelli.
Spalding: You're Emanuel Ravelli.
Ravelli: I am Emanuel Ravelli.
Spalding: Well, no wonder you look like him. But, I still insist there's a resemblance.

Groucho spoofed the "asides" of Strange Interlude and used another famous play of the era for one of his outrageous puns. Asked if he had seen a habeas corpus, he replied, "No, but I've seen Habeas Irish Rose." Groucho's first entrance—on a litter borne by native bearers and with his joining the chorus to sing "Hooray For Captain Spalding"—became a classic, the song itself forever after associated with him. The nonsense kept Broadway laughing just short of six months and then set out to tickle the nation.

In Black Scandals (26 October 1928, Totten) Rastus (Stewart Hampton) and Henry (Clarence Nance) rub a magical lamp and find themselves whisked off to Asuwere. This instant failure was "so naïvely and disarmingly amateurish that it forestalls any sort of professional criticism." Even its songs were not original, borrowed instead from other shows or from Tin Pan Alley.

An attempt to resuscitate Americana (30 October 1928, Fields'), the well-thought-of revue from 1926–1927, met with instant failure. Roger Wolfe Kahn wrote most of the music, and his orchestra was in the pit. But as far as Broadway was concerned, Kahn was destined to be a one-hit-song ("Crazy Rhythm") composer. The cast had two curiosities. The Gershwins' only sister, Frances, tried her wings as a singer, and the aging Rosamond Johnson, so prominent in earlier black musicals, returned. Indeed one novelty was the show's use of two choruses, the first white, the second black. The revue seemed to go to the same pump for its skits that the *Scandals* had primed. Like the *Scandals* it satirized talking movies, gangster-ridden Chicago (whose last honest policeman hides in a kindergarten), and *Strange Interlude* (satirizing the easy O'Neill target seemed the rage of the season). In *Americana*'s version the play was accelerated by having all the players on roller skates. One original number reflected the new law that required the city's taxi drivers to hang their pictures in their cabs. The cast sang "Remember The Face Of Your Driver," peeking through the holes in a curtain composed of oversized identification cards.

Richard Myers tried for a third time to offer Broadway an acceptable score. His "Rah!! Rah!! Rah!!" collegiate musical **Hello Yourself** (30 October 1928, Casino) ran eleven weeks, helped no doubt by the presence of Fred Waring and his popular singing group, The Pennsylvanians. The score was filled with typical period pleasantries— "He-Man," "You've Got A Way With You," and "I Want The World To Know." The book succeeded in combining two popular stage worlds, with some of the action set in the theatre as well as in academia. Bobby Short (Al Sexton) is expelled from Westley University. A happy ending follows only after the president's niece, Dale Hartley (Ruth Sennott), arranges for her producer-father to mount a play Bobby has written.

November's first musical was an importation, Noël Coward's witty, melodic revue, **This Year of Grace** (7 November 1928, Selwyn). A good deal of the grace, and fun, came from Coward himself in the cast and from the incomparable Bea Lillie. Out of the show came three Coward classics—"A Room With A View," "Dance, Little Lady," and "World Weary." This last song was sung by Miss Lillie, sitting on a stool, munching an apple.

The Gershwins and their loyal producers found themselves with a decided failure on their hands after **Treasure Girl** (8 November 1928, Alvin) opened. Looking back, Ira was inclined to blame the book,

suggesting it made its star, Gertrude Lawrence, so bitchy and grasping that it poisoned the whole evening. Miss Lawrence played the clothes-conscious, money-hungry Ann Wainwright, who is not above stepping on the toes of her would-be fiancé, Neil Forrester (Paul Frawley), to get at the $100,000 treasure Mortimer Grimes (Ferris Hartman) has hidden for his "Pirate's Party" treasure hunt. Neil brings Ann to earth when they are stranded on an island. He swims to shore, leaving her deserted. Room was found in the show for more light-hearted diversions. Clifton Webb and Mary Hay again charmed with their eccentric dancing, while Walter Catlett grabbed a reasonable number of laughs with his brash humor. The show was beautifully mounted, its show curtain welcoming audiences with an explosion of brightly colored, stylized tropical flowers. It should have set the tone for the whole evening, but, alas, it didn't. The failure of the show dragged down with it some of Ira's best lyrics and some of George's most vivacious music. Ira, for example, came up with clever, telling rhymes such as "A B C" and "incompatibility" for "I Don't Think I'll Fall In Love Today." George's striking melody for "Feeling I'm Falling" also got lost in the wreckage. One song that became a Gershwin standard, "I've Got A Crush On You," was introduced by Clifton Webb and Mary Hay.

An equally interesting and offbeat show, **Rainbow** (21 November 1928, Gallo), suffered an even worse failure. Called "a romantic musical play," it attempted to portray seriously a bit of bygone Americana, embellishing it with songs that strove to combine lean jazz with arioso passages. Surprisingly, the composer was Vincent Youmans. Not so surprisingly, the librettists were Laurence Stallings, who had tried something similar before with *Deep River* (4 October 1926) and failed, and Oscar Hammerstein II, who had tried something similar with *Show Boat* (27 December 1927) and triumphed. Their story was set during the Gold Rush of 1849. Having killed a man in a fight over a woman, Captain Stanton (Allan Prior) poses as a parson in the rough-and-tumble army of the time. He falls in love with Virginia Brown (Louise Brown), the daughter of his colonel, marrying and supporting her in some style by gambling winnings. The ubiquitous Lotta (Libby Holman) persists in trying to win him away from his bride. In the end he is cleared of wrongdoing and restored to his regular post.

There are some intriguing parallels with the *Show Boat* story. Stanton, like Ravenal, is given to gambling. Charles Ruggles played Nasty, a muleteer as colorful in his own way as Cap'n Andy. And Libby Holman's role of Lotta was not unlike Julie. Youmans produced a startlingly virile, melodic score, noticeably less angular than was his custom. In his study of American popular song Alec Wilder claims the best song in the show, "The One Girl," failed largely because lyrics such as "cheers me when I go out to fight, boys" were uncommercial. But the words fall comfortably into place when the whole song is sung. The melody does resemble Rodgers's "Blue Room," but remains original enough to stand on its own. Lotta was given a fine torch song, "I Want A Man," and Hammerstein created some of his drollest lyrics for "I Like You As You Are." *Chee-Chee* and *Treasure Girl* had failed because they went a little too far within the accepted forms of the day, but *Rainbow* failed to a large extent because it was ahead of its time. Nonetheless a number of the best critics praised the show, calling it "gorgeously different," "stirring," and "absorbing." Only the sort of score Kern gave *Show Boat* could, possibly, have made it palatable to its own age. A disastrous opening night, plagued with mechanical failures, also hurt.

December's initial offering was a five-week failure. The Shuberts called it "a comedy with music," though its songs had operetta overtones. Jeanette MacDonald played the title role of **Angela** (3 December 1928, Ambassador)—her full name was Princess Alestine Victorine Angela—and she was the daughter of Arcacia's King Louis VII (Eric Blore). For reasons of state her father insists she marry a prince. But Angela has her heart set on Count Bernadine (Roy Hoyer). Fortunately the count turns out to be a prince as well. Everything about the show seemed wrong. The *Times* noted condescendingly, "It strove to create comedy by putting a tall man and a short man together and letting a superannuated detective in a uniform cape snoop across the stage." The stilted dialogue ran to lines such as "Hearts are not fashioned of clay." Complaints were registered about the tired routines of the Chester Hale Girls. The *World* lamented even the lighting effects were "abominably done."

One of the season's best-remembered hits came in when Eddie Cantor and Florenz Ziegfeld reconciled their differences once again and together made **Whoopee** (4 December 1928, New Amsterdam). The still dependable William Anthony McGuire adapted it from Owen Davis's *The Nervous Wreck*; Walter Donaldson provided the score. Donaldson was one of Tin Pan Alley's most successful composers, but his only other score for Broadway, a partial

one at that, had been for *Sweetheart Time* (9 January 1926). Before he realizes what's happening to him, Henry Williams (Cantor), a shy hypochondriac, is induced to elope with Sally Morgan (Frances Upton). As far as Sally is concerned, the elopement is simply a delaying action. She is being pressed to marry the local sheriff, Bob Wells (Jack Rutherford), while her only heart-throb is Wanenis (Paul Gregory), apparently a half-breed Indian. The sheriff pursues the elopers to an Indian reservation, where it is revealed that Wanenis has no Indian blood. But Henry is not abandoned; his faithful nurse, Mary (Ethel Shutta), is ready to take over where Sally left off. The book's strong, well-motivated story is especially remarkable when it is realized how much of the writing was done with particular performers and not the plot in mind. For example, though Cantor played a seemingly white Anglo-Saxon Protestant, he could indulge in the following dialogue:

Wanenis: I studied the ways of your race—I went to your schools!
Henry: An Indian in a Hebrew school? Tell me, how did you get along?

But nowhere is the nature of construction more apparent than in the role performed by the show's featured player, Ruth Etting. She played a movie star called Leslie Daws. The role has no function in the plot. It simply gave Miss Etting a name. As often as not she merely came on stage to sing a song without the smallest lead-in, then walked off. All the characterization she was awarded suggested several times that she loved an irresponsible tough guy who failed to reciprocate her affections. The man never appears. Cantor had one of his all-time favorites in "Makin' Whoopee," in which he warns of the dangers of married life. But the show also had a standout ballad, "Love Me Or Leave Me," sung not by Sally but by Ruth Etting in her role of Leslie Daws. (The song would forever be identified with her. When her biography was filmed nearly a quarter-century later, the song became the title of the film.) Donaldson's score was superior all the way through, but he was not oriented toward the theatre and never again did another score. *Whoopee*'s Wild West locale thrilled Ziegfeld. No doubt he recalled all the times he played hooky as a boy to watch Buffalo Bill's entourage. Ziegfeld bedecked his beauties in feathers luxurious beyond an Indian's most colorful fantasies, and then he brought the girls on stage riding real horses. (He also hired a real cow for further verisimilitude.)

He gave Joseph Urban free rein, and Urban created a series of brilliant sets, notably a recreation in reds and rusts of the Grand Canyon. The show ran into the 1929–1930 season, when financial reverses forced Ziegfeld to sell the rights to Sam Goldwyn, who promptly closed the piece so that he could make a movie version with Cantor.

With *The New Moon* turning them away at the box office, it was not yet obvious that the old-school operetta had seen its day. The Shuberts probably helped disguise the change in taste when they brought in a very second-rate piece and saw it run twenty-one weeks. **The Red Robe** (25 December 1928, Shubert) was a swashbuckler laid in Cardinal Richelieu's France. Gil de Berault (Walter Woolf) is relieved by the cardinal (Jose Ruben) of serving a prison sentence for dueling. In gratitude de Berault agrees to capture the cardinal's enemy, Henri, Count de Cocheforet (S. Herbert Bragiotti). But the Count has a beautiful daughter, and, seeing her, de Berault allows the Count to escape. Jean Gilbert's songs for this American work differed not at all from his European material, and Harry B. Smith's lyrics were of a predictable quality. Their best number was "You And I Are Passersby." Walter Woolf, who had acquitted himself so well in *Countess Maritza*, walked off with most of the best notices. The evening's heroine was played by Helen Gilliland. A contingent of Chester Hale Girls danced in split-second precision, most notably in a show-stopping drum dance.

Houseboat on the Styx (25 December 1928, Liberty) told of some famous ladies of legend and history, such as Queen Elizabeth (Blanche Ring), who crash a stag party given by some equally prominent men on a houseboat on Hell's river. To its credit the show had a sumptuous mounting and good cast. Its demerits included another dreary Carlo and Sanders collection of songs. It also featured more Chester Hale Girls.

The Fields family joined forces with Jimmy McHugh and came up with a six-month hit, **Hello Daddy** (26 December 1928, Fields'). Herbert Fields wrote the book, sister Dorothy wrote the lyrics, and Lew Fields starred and produced the show. For years three old friends—Henry Block (Fields), Anthony Bennett (Wilfred Clark), and Edward Hauser (George Hassell)—have been paying the same young lady support for what each has been told is his child. The racket is no sooner exposed than the young man appears. He turns out to be something of an idiot. But he also turns out to be as fraudulent as his mother's claims. The hit of the show was

a comedy number, "In A Great Big Way," sung by the not-very-bright Noel (Billy Taylor) to a fiancée (Betty Starbuck) with an equally low IQ. It was a hilariously lugubrious description of love among the lower mental orders. A subplot romance between Connie Block (Mary Lawlor), Henry's daughter, and Lawrence Tucker (Allen Kearns) allowed for standard love ballads. Herbert Fields based his libretto on *The High Cost of Loving* and filled it with the sort of one-liners his father had always employed, especially word plays such as "a wolf in cheap clothing." McHugh's score was effective and entertaining in the theatre but seemed made of less solid stuff in the light of day. The show was 1928's last musical.

The first musical of the new year arrived two weeks later. **Deep Harlem** (7 January 1929, Biltmore) opened on Monday and folded on Saturday. It was a Negro revue with a tenuous story line holding the material together. The evening began in the Kingdom of the Cushites. A black tribe, they are defeated in war and sent into slavery. From there the story followed the slaves' descendants from a southern plantation to 1929 Harlem. Everything about the show seemed wrong. What the *Times* called "an abundance of flappy canvas scenery," the *Post* viewed as a *Grand Street Follies* spoof of *Aïda*. Even the dancing was spanked—unheard of for a black show. The day after the show closed, the *Herald Tribune* ran a long article prompted by its dismay with both the show's failure and with New York critics. The paper felt the show was striving to be a little different from other black entertainments. The article went on to suggest New York would never let black shows be different, that all the local critics would permit in a black musical was "meaningless whirling and fizzing with 'pep.'" Unfortunately the idea that black musicals should be allowed into the mainstream and should then be judged by the same standards was some years too advanced. *Deep Harlem* was written by and filled with largely unknown names who remained unknown after the show closed.

Polly (8 January 1929, Lyric) did better. It ran two weeks. A musical version of the 1917 hit *Polly with a Past*, it was put together by a number of experienced hands, including Guy Bolton, Irving Caesar, and Arthur Hammerstein. The story recounted how Polly Shannon (June) agrees to impersonate a French actress and flirt with Southampton's Rex Van Zile (John Hundley) in order to make Myrtle Grant (Lucy Monroe) take an interest in Rex. Of course, Polly also loves Rex, and she gets him by the final curtain. Though yet another attractive English leading lady, June, was prominently featured, the bright spot of the evening was the clowning of Fred Allen as the gravel-voiced, wisecracking reporter for the backwater *Sag Harbour Bee*. Apart from Allen, the show was as commonplace as its Phil Charig music, which always seemed to be a note or two away from the correct melody.

The next night brought one of the season's smash hits. Having struck paydirt with a musical about one sport—prizefighting—DeSylva, Brown, and Henderson (with Laurence Schwab, one of their producers, as co-librettist) went after a second sport, golfing, and came back with a winner. **Follow Thru** (9 January 1929, 46th St.) punningly called itself "a musical slice of country club life." Its main plot followed the rivalry between Lora Moore (Irene Delroy) and Ruth Van Horn (Madeline Cameron) for the Bound Brook Country Club's women's championship and for handsome Jerry Downs (John Barker) as well. Lora wins both. But much of the fun and drive of the show came from a subplot in which a determined Angie Howard (Zelma O'Neal) pursues the shy, slightly odd Jack Martin (Jack Haley), son of a chain store executive. Jack tries to teach a friend the game, only to throw his hands up in exasperation: "The trouble with your game is that you stand too close to the ball—after you've hit it." Later Jack and his friend invade the ladies' dressing room in the guise of plumbers. Jerry Downs had the musical's best ballad, "My Lucky Star," while he and Laura sang "You Wouldn't Fool Me, Would You?" But Jack and Angie had the real show-stopper, a perfect swatch of early 1929 esprit, "Button Up Your Overcoat." The evening was filled with superb, lively dancing not only by a thoroughly drilled chorus but by a young lady in the very minor role of Molly, Eleanor Powell. Her scintillating tap numbers earned her several encores every night. Though it was only early January, *Follow Thru* proved to be the season's last major hit but one.

Ned Wayburn's Gambols (15 January 1929, Knickerbocker) was a minor revue that lasted a mere thirty-one performances but at least gave Libby Holman another step up toward stardom. Her sultry-voiced renditions of "Salt Of My Tears" and "Mothers O' Men" won her applause and good notices. Most of the other good notices were reserved for the show's dances—and the entertainment was largely occupied with choreography of one sort or other. Gypsy dances, Oriental dances, and Indian dances filled the stage. At one point "two nearly nude gentlemen tossed a nearly nude lady

back and forth in the air for several minutes." Some of the best stepping was in the show's tap routines (the *Enciclopedia Dello Spettacolo* credits Wayburn with originating the tap as opposed to the older clog dance). The *Gambols'* totally forgotten score was by another of the many one-timers, Walter G. Samuels, but Arthur Schwartz, who would soon work so closely with Miss Holman, took credit for two interpolations.

Two more musicals arrived to round out the month. Jeanette MacDonald continued to move from the lead in one flop to the lead in another. In the prologue of **Boom Boom** (28 January 1929, Casino), one of the pointlessly alliterative titles the decade adored, Jean has a brief shipboard romance with Tony Smith (Stanley Ridges). Later she marries Worthington Smith (Frank McIntyre), a man much older than herself and, it develops, Tony's father. But the marriage is annulled so that she can make a more suitable marriage with Tony. Miss MacDonald had worked with McIntyre the year before in *Sunny Days* (8 February 1928). The hefty comedian was once again cast as a dirty old man, one who had just spent six months in the hospital. A friend solicitously asks if the long stay meant he was "pretty sick." To which McIntyre replied, "No. Pretty nurse." More comedy was provided by Henry Welsh as a head waiter. His suggestion of soup declined, he tells his customer, "Well, it's soup to you." The dancing was more varied. Jack Donahue and John Boyle each provided a contingent of fast-stepping girls (one band known as the "Lightning Dancers"). Kendall Capps entertained with his stunt dancing, while Cortez and Peggy danced a Spanish number. This musical version of Louis Verneuil's *Mlle. Ma Mère* had another nondescript score by Werner Jannsen, his last Broadway effort before he left for the more rewarding fields of serious composing and conducting.

In December a musicalized version of one Owen Davis play had become *Whoopee*. The last day of January saw Eddie Buzzell adapt Davis's *Easy Come, Easy Go* for his own uses. He called it **Lady Fingers** (31 January 1929, Vanderbilt), and it had a score by Joseph Meyer. Buzzell played a sociable bank robber, Jim Bailey, who, in gratitude to rich, dashing, but innocent Dick Tain (John Price Jones) for nursing him through a fever, involves Tain in his latest heist. They are forced to hide out at Dr. Jasper's Health Farm, where they encounter Mortimer Quayle (Herbert Waterous), the very banker they have just robbed. Since Dick comes from a prominent family and since he and Hope Quayle (Louise Brown) are in love, there is really very little problem setting everything right. Buzzell was no Cantor, but he was clever enough and funny enough to keep audiences coming and the show going for 132 performances.

In a startling departure for him, Earl Carroll tried his hand at operetta. Carroll worked on the book, as well as producing and staging **Fioretta** (5 February 1929, Earl Carroll). The show was so clean several critics sat up and took notice. But they also noted the desperately old-fashioned story. The wicked Duke of Venice plans to marry Fioretta (Dorothy Knapp) to the outlawed Count Di Rovani (George Houston), slay Rovani, and have the girl to himself. But with her father's help, Fioretta and the Count escape. The show had a vapid score by George Bagby and G. Romilli, featuring numbers such as "Dream Boat." Carroll's name and particular flair helped keep the show on the boards for weeks, as did the clowning of two former Ziegfeld regulars, Leon Errol (as an inebriated gondolier) and Fanny Brice (as a courtier with a ghetto accent). Carroll humored Errol's famous penchant for falling down drunk by dressing the comedian in a suit of armor, giving him a crate full of oranges to tote, and then sending him flying down a grand staircase. Errol had another drunk scene in which he jumped onto a table to give a slurred, confused after-dinner speech, concluding by falling into his listeners' laps. Miss Brice took advantage of *Fioretta*'s Italian setting to twit the overblown mannerisms of grand-opera singers and then stopped the show singing "Old Wicked Willage Of Wenice." When the story was not unfolding or the clowns cavorting, Carroll brought in "acres and battalions of girls... in spangles, trailing skirts and ostrich plumes." He even inserted a dance—which at least one critic branded as tasteless—that found the Duke's dead ancestors stepping lively in their tomb. The show could probably have run longer than 111 performances had not Carroll quarreled with his backer. The dispute revealed that the money for the show had come from a rich aunt of composer Bagby.

Pleasure Bound (18 February 1929, Majestic), a Shubert revue that was almost pure vaudeville, nevertheless had a seventeen-week run. The show had begun life as a musical version of *Potash and Perlmutter* called *Well, Well, Well*. By the time it reached Broadway the plot had been jettisoned. The dutiful Harold Atteridge provided the dialogue, while a number of writers contributed the songs. One of the composers was featured in the show, the comedian-accordionist Phil Baker. Baker had a new stooge harassing him from an upper box,

John Muldowney. Muldowney complained he was leg weary, not from standing, but from watching the long line of Busby Berkeley high-kickers. More clowning came from "excitable" Jack Pearl. Pearl's guttural German dialect burlesque caused the *Times* to sit back and realize that such dialect comedy had "almost vanished from the legitimate stage." The heyday of Weber and Fields, Sam Bernard, and their ilk was part of an ever more distant history. Pearl performed in various guises, appearing, for example, as a dress designer and later as an orchestra leader. Besides her Spanish dances, Pepita tip-toed across a

> **ARTHUR SCHWARTZ** was born in Brooklyn on 25 November 1900. Though he was destined to be a lawyer and had no formal musical education, he composed songs from a very early date. While working for his bachelor's degree at New York University, he wrote several football songs. He continued his academic studies, obtaining a master's in literature at Columbia and then taking up law. He was admitted to the bar in 1924. His law practice was still active and successful when his first songs were heard in small downtown revues.

> **HOWARD DIETZ** was born in New York City on 8 September 1896. While attending Columbia at the same time as Hart and Hammerstein, he contributed light verse and comic pieces to the college publications, to Don Marquis's column, and to Franklin P. Adams's popular "The Conning Tower" in the *World*. After serving in the navy during World War I, he began a brief but prosperous career as an advertising executive. He brought himself to Hollywood's attention when he created the roaring lion trademark for Goldwyn Pictures and in 1924 became advertising director for the young MGM. But his duties failed to keep him from lyric writing. He had written the lyrics for "Alibi Baby," which was interpolated into *Poppy* (3 September 1923). With *Dear Sir* (23 September 1924) Dietz became a full-fledged wordsmith.

line of band boxes. Aileen Stanley did her best to put across inconsequential music, such as a Baker and Maurice Rubens tune, "Just Suppose," with lyrics by Sid Silvers and Joe Jaffe.

A novelty, **Trois Jeunes Filles Nues,** a musical comedy from Paris given entirely in French, opened on 4 March at Jolson's. It launched a forty-performance parade of similar French delights: **Passionement, Comte Obligado, Ta Bouche, Un Bon Garçon,** and **Pas sur la Bouche.**

Spring Is Here (11 March 1929, Alvin) arrived a few days prematurely. For Owen Davis it must have seemed like his special season. First, two of his older works had been turned into musicals, then, with *Spring Is Here,* an original Owen Davis libretto was unveiled. It was not remarkably original. Davis derived the story from his own play *Shot-Gun Wedding,* which had never reached New York. Betty Braley (Lillian Taiz) thinks she loves Stacy Haydon (John Hundley), and only when their elopement is foiled by her father does she come to understand she was meant for Terry Clayton. If she hadn't seen the light, her sister, Mary Jane (Inez Courtney), would have been happy to become Mrs. Clayton. The Rodgers and Hart score was a dandy. To 1929 audiences it may have even sounded vaguely like a Gershwin score, since the orchestra featured Gershwin's favorite duo pianists, Victor Arden and Phil Ohman. But an oddity developed during rehearsals when Glenn Hunter was cast as Terry. Though a fine actor, he had no singing voice at all. The evening's best love songs had to be shared by Betty and her losing suitor, Stacy. Rarely has a young man been given such a lovely melody as "With A Song In My Heart" and not won the girl. "Baby's Awake Now" had lyrics showing Hart's cynical charm. Once again Rodgers and Hart's willingness to be a little different probably cost them trade. The show left before the spring did, a disappointing 104 performances to its account.

Another premature title announced **Music in May** (1 April 1929, Casino). It was another Shubert importation, substantially revised and with virtually a new score by Maurice Rubens. Its story told how Prince Stephan falls in love with a simple village girl, Vita. But it seems there is no way he can marry a commoner. So he hits on the ingenious scheme of first making Vita a baroness and then marrying her. The show ran ten weeks.

A black revue called **Messin' Around** (22 April 1929, Hudson) advertised itself as "a musical novelty," but neither the public nor the critics found it

novel—or entertaining. A thin plotline followed two comedians to a southern carnival and back to a Harlem nightclub. One of the turns featured a boxing match between two girls. The girls went at their business with abandon, clouting each other so lustily they brought down the house. However, at least two other bits also started hands clapping. One was a stunt dance performed by Bamboo McCarver on roller skates; the other a wild African strut by Cora La Redd. These bright spots weren't enough to save the evening. Richard Watts, Jr., writing in the *Herald Tribune,* alluded to the double standard his paper had complained critics used in reviewing black shows. He noted that *Messin' Around* would have been "inexcusable if white" and therefore insisted it wasn't really any better because it was black. The revue folded after four weeks.

On the other hand theatregoers found novelty, entertainment, and no little theatrical art in April's last lyric offering, a revue known as **The Little Show** (30 April 1929, Music Box). A number of names became famous with the show. The song-writing team of Arthur Schwartz and Howard Dietz came to the public's attention with this, their first joint effort.

Schwartz and Dietz's best number in *The Little Show* was "I Guess I'll Have To Change My Plan."

CLIFTON WEBB was born in Indianapolis, Indiana, on 9 November 1896 and christened Webb Parmalee Hollenbeck. While still an infant his stagestruck, domineering mother took him to New York and saw to it he made his debut at the age of three in *The Brownies.* He was enrolled in dancing school and at seven in Malcolm Douglas's Children's Theatre. In his early teens Webb's interests grew more elevated. Art lessons led to a one man show of his paintings in 1914, while instruction with Victor Maurel earned him roles in provincial grand opera. His first legitimate roles were small parts in *The Purple Road* (7 April 1913) and *See America First* (28 March 1916). Within a few years he was prominently featured in such musicals as *Listen, Lester!* (23 December 1918) and *Sunny* (21 September 1925). Tall, slim, dapper, and suave, Webb was often mistaken for an Englishman.

Schwartz had originally written the melody to early Lorenz Hart lyrics and entitled the tune "I Love To Lie Awake In Bed." Even with Dietz's superior lines, the song was not an immediate hit. It only became popular and entered the standard repertory when it was brought back from England several years after the show had closed. The songs that appealed most to the patrons were not by Schwartz, and only one had Dietz lyrics. "Can't We Be Friends?" was written by the New York banker James Warburg, under the name Paul James, and his wife, Kay Swift. And a stunning applause-getter, "Moanin' Low," had music by Ralph Rainger. The show also made stars of Clifton Webb, Libby Holman, and Fred Allen. The debonair Webb had been prominent in musicals for over a decade but had never until The Little Show secured a firm hold on the top rung of the profession.

Miss Holman's rise was far more meteoric, starting with Merry-Go-Round (31 May 1927) and including two flops in the current season. Fred Allen, like Webb, had been around a while but without ever achieving prominence. His stardom in the revue came practically out of nowhere. Ably assisting were such fine talents as Romney Brent, Bettina Hall, and Portland Hoffa (Mrs. Allen). Webb introduced "I Guess I'll Have To Change My Plan." Miss Holman sang "Can't We Be Friends?" The two combined for a rough-house staging of "Moanin' Low." The best of the sketches was a George S. Kaufman gem. "The Still Alarm" found two men (Romney Brent and Clifton Webb) in a burning hotel calmly debating the proper dress to wear on a fire escape. The firemen (Fred Allen and Harold Moffet) arrive. They are deferential and as unconcerned as the guests. One firefighter has even brought his violin (he never gets a chance to practice at home). In the end, "The Second Fireman takes Center of stage, with all the manner of a concert violinist. He goes into "Keep The Home Fires Burning." Bob, Ed [the two guests], and First Fireman wipe brow as curtain falls slowly." Nonsense of this sort, beautifully done, kept the show running for ten months.

The Grand Street Follies (1 May 1929, Booth), one of the very series that prompted intimate revues such as The Little Show, brought in a final edition the evening after The Little Show's premiere. The faithful regulars were on stage again. Albert Carroll impersonated Harpo Marx, Bea Lillie, Constance Collier, and the first Queen Elizabeth, while Dorothy Sands appeared as Lenore Ulric and Irene Bordoni. The sketches mixed history and show business. The siege of Troy was restaged as Belasco might have done it;

the Marx Brothers landed on Plymouth Rock; and Paul Revere's ride was chronicled by the sassy, irreverent reporters from The Front Page. Arthur Schwartz had more songs ready to contribute to the score. But Schwartz's best efforts were being played in The Little Show at the Music Box across the street, and the old standby performers had worn out their material and, perhaps, their welcome. The Sun observed that, while the evening often "brightened in anticipation," the hopes were never fulfilled. Substantial revisions in July failed to turn the corner.

Pansy (14 May 1929, Belmont), a Negro collegiate musical, could manage only three performances at the tiny Belmont Theatre, though blues singer Bessie Smith, famous but not yet legendary, made an appearance as herself. The college setting was almost incidental; what skimpy plot there was related how Pansy Green (Pearl McCormack) won the hand of Bob (Billy Andrews), though her father, Ulysses Grant Green (Speedy Wilson), preferred she marry Bill (Alfred Chester), the "Proposition Kid." Pansy's composer, Maceo Pinkard, had not been heard from with a full score since Liza (27 November 1922). He got his score played this time by producing the show on his own. But the normally kind Brooks Atkinson branded it "the worst show of all time." Several critics recorded that the audience hissed the performers.

To close the season, the Shuberts brought the last of their "A Night in" series, A Night in Venice (21 May 1929, Shubert). Ted Healy led the comedians, even wrestling a trained bear for laughs. Two acrobatic sailors did somersaults, and a xylophone ensemble made tinkly music. One more contingent of Chester Hale Girls competed with sixteen Allen K. Forster Girls. Tableaux whisked audiences to a moonlit Paris and a snow-covered Venice. The score was mostly by Maurice Rubens, though several others chipped in. Vincent Youmans salvaged "The One Girl" from Rainbow, but it still failed to click. Shubert's know-how rather than any overriding merit kept the show's not too demanding customers pleased into the fall.

SCENE TWO

Depression and "Talkies"— Broadway's Answer, 1929–1937

1929–1930

The onslaught of film musicals jolted Broadway, and the October stock market crash gave the American

Musical Theatre a further blow. The musical stage recovered, but it was never the same. The wildly extroverted jazz and florid romance of the twenties gave way to both the subdued, introspective material and strident muckraking of the early thirties. The great annuals were dead, though a few straggling editions came forth at irregular intervals. Viennese-American operetta was also gone. True, Noël Coward's superb *Bitter Sweet* had its American premiere in this season, but it failed to find a large public. On the other hand, in a seeming effort to cling to the past a rash of revivals was mounted with surprising success. In the midst of such change and uncertainty enough momentum and enough talent remained on Broadway to allow this great act to continue. But in theatrical terms the 1929–1930 season represents the lowering of the curtain or of the lights to effect a scene change. The remainder of the act was played in a different setting.

For the second year in a row the number of new musicals dropped precipitously, to thirty-two—the lowest figure in eleven seasons. And nine of these came in the summer, before the main season had gotten under way. A Negro nightclub revue, revised for Broadway, opened the season. **Hot Chocolate** (20 June 1929, Hudson) was principally by Andy Razaf and Fats Waller. The two had come to Broadway's attention two years before with their work for *Keep Shufflin'* (27 February 1928). Their material for their new offering was even better, including, as it did, the enduring "Ain't Misbehavin'." The plaintive undertones of the song hint at the stylings of much of the music that would come out of Broadway for the next few years. A young orchestra member was Louis Armstrong, who was called from the pit to present a trumpet solo. For Armstrong it was the beginning of forty years at the top of his profession. Skits made fun of traffic in Harlem, photographing a prizefighter, and an animal wedding. Young ladies of the chorus were listed in the program as "Hot Chocolate Drops" and chorus boys as "Bon Bon Buddies," suggesting either that the verse to "The Black Bottom" had given currency to some new expressions or that both shows were recording fashionable clichés of the day. *Hot Chocolate* caught on quickly and ran over six months.

Two flops followed. Will Morrissey and Jimmy Duffy were largely responsible for a revue called **Keep It Clean** (24 June 1929, Selwyn). They wrote much of it and were the featured players, and Morrissey helped stage it. He also opened the show walking on stage in a battered top hat and launching

into a long monologue filled with backstage references understood only by the initiated. Duffy offered an off-color song about the Lindbergh-Morrow marriage. Their helpers included Midge Miller, giving an impersonation of Bea Lillie, and Douglas Stanbury, solemnly singing of "Marching Home." Such efforts earned them only sixteen performances.

A Negro book musical, **Bamboola** (26 June 1929, Royale), told of the attempts to take a home-grown show to New York. Dancing was the highlight of the show, as it was for most black musicals. A salute to Bill Robinson found twenty of the show's top hoofers mimicking Robinson's famous routine tapping his way up and down a staircase. The evening's funniest sketch portrayed a Harlem rent party. Rigidly preconceived notions of what a black entertainment should be inevitably led one critic or another to see unwarranted attempts to imitate white musicals. The *Evening Journal* reflected the continuing insistence of most New York reviewers that black revues should be distinctively black in their vitality, tackiness, and naïveté. The paper proclaimed, "the Negro IS funny. He's very funny when he's allowed to be funny in his own way." This band of Negroes had their own way for a mere four weeks.

The season's biggest musical hit was **Earl Carroll's Sketch Book** (1 July 1929, Earl Carroll). There was no edition of the *Vanities* this season, but a number of critics suggested the *Sketch Book* was merely the *Vanities* by another name. Having taken Leon Errol and Fanny Brice away from Ziegfeld for *Fioretta*, Carroll advertised noisily that Eddie Cantor was now in his corner. And Cantor did contribute some sketches. But anyone coming to see Cantor saw only a brief sound film in which Cantor and Carroll dickered over Cantor's price. Since Ziegfeld gave Cantor a gold watch, Carroll gives him a grandfather clock. Performers in the flesh were led by Will Mahoney, with William Demarest and Patsy Kelly assisting. The funniest skit of the evening had Miss Kelly trying to take a bath while her bathroom suddenly has more traffic than Times Square. How many in the audience remembered Charlotte Greenwood's taking "Her Morning Bath" in *The Ritz Revue* (17 September 1924)? Movies were not the only technical device used. The show opened with a partly raised curtain revealing a line of beautiful "Legs, Legs, Legs," but when the curtain was fully raised it was shown the legs were merely the legs of phonographs. Jay Gorney did much of the score, with E. Y. Harburg writing the lyrics. Billy Rose, Harry and Charles Tobias, Benny Davis, Ted Snyder, and Vincent Rose all lent a hand without creating any long-lasting melodies. On the strength of its comedy and its production numbers the show ran fifty weeks.

> Born to Russian-Jewish immigrant parents on Manhattan's Lower East Side on 8 April 1896 as Isidore Hochberg, **E. Y. HARBURG** displayed an early talent for wordplay and a fascination with light verse. An enduring friendship with Ira Gershwin, formed during high school, may have informed Harburg's decision to pursue a career as a lyricist for theatre and film. Harburg, a lifelong advocate for social justice and democratic causes, was blacklisted in Hollywood from 1951-61. He is especially remembered for lyrics to songs in the film *The Wizard of Oz* as well as the popular songs "It's Only a Paper Moon" and "Brother, Can You Spare a Dime?"

Ziegfeld was less successful, though he assembled a magnificent lineup for **Show Girl** (2 July 1929, Ziegfeld). He had William Anthony McGuire adapt J. P. McEvoy's novel and hired George Gershwin to set it to music. His cast featured Ruby Keeler in the lead; Clayton, Jackson, and Durante: Eddie Foy, Jr.; Harriet Hoctor; and, playing the music, Duke Ellington. *Show Girl* was, in a way, a jazzy version of *Sally* (21 December 1920). Like *Sally* it followed a pretty unknown in her climb to Ziegfeld stardom. In keeping with its jazzier tone, Dixie Dugan was a harder, pushier young lady. But she makes it. Eddie Foy, Jr., was a salesman whose cigarette lighter kept exploding and whose gifts triggered alarms when they were opened. Jimmy Durante played a property man. He supplied his own songs, probably much to Gershwin's relief, since Ziegfeld had given Gershwin only two weeks to write a score. Ira Gershwin was also relieved when Ziegfeld asked if he would allow Gus Kahn to aid with the lyrics. The two-week deadline was no more attractive to Ira than to George. But the best lyrics were unmistakably Ira's. The incorrigible, wide-eyed hypocrisy of a young-lady-about-town is unerringly and hilariously captured in "I Must Be Home By Twelve O'clock." At three A.M.

she is still protesting she must be home by midnight. But the hit that has so long outlived the show was "Liza." Written for a second-act minstrel number with "one hundred beautiful girls seated on steps that cover the entire stage," it was to be led by Ruby Keeler. In one of Broadway's most famous incidents, Al Jolson appeared on several nights singing the song from the audience to calm Miss Keeler, who had just become Mrs. Jolson. The show also included a sumptuously mounted and blazingly choreographed ballet by Albertina Rasch to music from Gershwin's "An American In Paris." But for all its attractions the show seemed heavy and slow. Miss Keeler left before *Show Girl* ran its course of in performances.

Busby Berkeley helped stage **Broadway Nights** (15 July 1929, 44th St.), a revue that included Dr. Rockwell, Laura Lee, and Odette Myrtil in its cast. Rockwell delivered a hilarious lecture in which he proved to his own satisfaction that popcorn causes dandruff. Maurice Rubens did most of the score (his last major appearance on New York programs), and old Edgar Smith devised most of the sketches. King, King, and King offered some hot tap-dancing. Chorus girls danced through a routine bouncing rubber balls. When they finished they hurled the balls out into the auditorium. Later they assembled to form a train, prompting the *Times* to hail the "Big Railroad Year" in musicals. Not all the music was by Rubens—Johann Strauss and Rimsky-Korsakov provided backgrounds for ballets. But the material couldn't strike a responsive chord in theatregoers. Five weeks and it was gone.

A month went by before another musical—another revue—arrived. It, too, had an imposing array of talent and failed. **Murray Anderson's Almanac** (14 August 1929, Erlanger)—Anderson had dropped the John from his name, at least as far as this title was concerned—had sketches by Noël Coward, Rube Goldberg, and Peter Arno, among others. Its songs were by Milton Ager and Henry Sullivan. The evening used the frame-device of thumbing through a magazine to survey the past, present, and future. Young Jimmy Savo and no-longer-young Trixie Friganza were starred. Reginald Marsh created the show curtain. But something went wrong. Oscar Wilde's "The Young King," performed as a ballet ballad of the sort Anderson had used in the *Greenwich Village Follies*, went largely unapplauded. Skits that made fun of everything from Whistler's mother to the latest talking pictures weren't sufficiently amusing, and most of the score was no more than serviceable. The sole surviving melody, sung strangely enough as a spoof of sentimental duets by the two stars, was "I May Be Wrong."

A Noble Rogue (19 August 1929, Gansevoort), a one-week disaster, was an operetta describing the romance of a New Orleans belle, Virginia Mulford (Marguerite Zender), and the dashing buccaneer, Jean Lafitte (Robert Rhodes). Performed at a small Greenwich Village theatre, the musical was lambasted as "stupefying" and "deadening"—a work devoid of flair, wit, or melody.

Flair, wit, and melody were abundantly evident in Broadway's next lyric entry. Oscar Hammerstein II and Jerome Kern combined to write "a musical romance of the gay nineties," centering their story on a role built for Helen Morgan. (Kern and Hammerstein even indulged in private jokes with Miss Morgan, naming one character after her mother.) They called their show **Sweet Adeline** (3 September 1929, Hammerstein). The title, of course, harked back to a song and a singer of the turn of the century. But the musical's Addie Schmidt was no great opera star. She sang her songs in her father's Hoboken beer garden in the days of the Spanish-American War. Hers is an unhappy life. She loves Tom Martin (Max Hoffman, Jr.), but loses him to her sister, Nellie (Caryl Bergman). She leaves Hoboken and starts her rise to Broadway stardom in a Bowery theatre. Her climb is helped by James Day (Robert Chisholm), and, in time, she falls in love with him. Comedy relief was provided by Charles Butterworth in the role of Ruppert Day, a hick drama-lover. His outlandish awe at the rehearsal of a cheap burlesque show became the hilarious highlight of the performance. The Kern score was not as rich, diversified, or hit-filled as *Show Boat*, but it was unfailingly lovely. It included one remarkable concerted number for the principal men, "A Girl Is On Your Mind," that used blues colorings for its languid soliloquies.

If the score had a fault it may be that the songs assigned to Miss Morgan all dwelled on the same poignant note of hope and despair. But she made hits of them, especially "Why Was I Born?" This song and another tearful ballad, "Here Am I," were ever after identified with her; in the show she also sang "'Twas Not So Long Ago" (reprised by the chorus at the end of the show) and "Don't Ever Leave Me." In a novel departure, Kern's songs were not played in the overture. Instead, to create some period verisimilitude, the overture consisted of a medley of songs from the 1890s. To speed the action

within the play itself, no encores were allowed. *Sweet Adeline* was presented by Arthur Hammerstein and staged by Reginald at their family theatre. It immediately began playing to standees. At first it seemed as if it would run as long as *Show Boat*, but the stock market crash brought a sickening halt to its ticket sales, and by April it was gone. All shows were hurt by the slump, but brainlessly cheery affairs like *Earl Carroll's Sketch Book* seemed a little less damaged than pieces with serious pretensions such as *Sweet Adeline* or *Bitter Sweet*.

Kern granted an interview to the *Times* shortly after *Sweet Adeline* opened. The interview was largely a paean of praise for Oscar Hammerstein, whom the composer hailed as the "ideal collaborator." Kern was especially delighted with what he saw as Hammerstein's daring and realism. He mentioned especially a drunk scene written for Miss Morgan, noting it was not one of the era's overdone comic bits but a serious attempt to portray an unfortunate weakness in a heroine. Years later Richard Rodgers was to applaud the same virtues in Hammerstein. How curious and revealing that two of the American Musical Theatre's greatest composers—two men who had worked with brilliantly literate and witty lyricists—clearly preferred their more solemn, sentimental associate.

Like *Show Girl* and *Sweet Adeline*, **The Street Singer** (17 September 1929, Shubert) recorded the rise of a young lady to stardom. But not in a Ziegfeld show or even an ordinary Broadway musical. Set in Paris, it recorded how suave, rich George (Guy Robertson) helps an attractive flower girl (Queenie Smith) to become a shining light of the Folies Bergère. He almost loses her in the process, but they end happily in each other's arms. The music and lyrics were by a number of minor figures, but all of it was pleasant, if determinedly backward-glancing. It had all the standard types of the better second-string twenties shows: for example, a rippling waltz in "You Might Have Known I Loved You" and a lively dance creation in "Jumping Jimminy." Because Busby Berkeley was co-producer (with the Shuberts), the mounting was assured of fine dancing. Yet, oddly enough, Berkeley and Miss Smith, both proponents of flashy tapping, scored the evening's biggest hit with a charming ballet set in the Folies greenroom. No doubt most theatregoers were unaware Miss Smith began her career as a ballerina at the Metropolitan Opera. *The Street Singer* helped keep troubled minds diverted for six months, but nothing from it was strong enough to survive.

A revue originally put together at the Cape Cod Playhouse and appropriately called The Cape Cod Follies (18 September 1929, Bijou) arrived fresh from its summer success. The New Englanders sang hymns to hooked rugs, cranberries, and Puritans (they insisted the Puritans really landed at Cape Cod). They also offered Broadway's umpteenth travesty of Eugene O'Neill. Peter Joray won the highest commendations for his impersonation of Queen Victoria, while six Cape Cod Belles elicited somewhat quieter applause with their tap-dancing. The revue looked a lot less fresh far from home, so it packed its bags and headed back north after thirty performances.

The Shuberts decided to revive Victor Herbert's *Sweethearts*. It was a decision stemming from their need to occupy the Jolson Theatre for a few weeks. But the reception was so overwhelming that before the theatrical year was through they had revived *Mlle. Modiste, Naughty Marietta, The Fortune Teller, Robin Hood, The Merry Widow, Babes in Toyland, The Prince of Pilsen, The Chocolate Soldier, The Count of Luxembourg,* and *The Serenade*. Fritzi Scheff sang *Mlle. Modiste*, while Tessa Kosta, Olga Steck, Ilse Marvenga, Al Shean, and Greek Evans appeared in one or more mountings. The eleven shows kept the Jolson lit for seven months.

George White's Scandals of 1929 (23 September 1929, Apollo) was the only one of the major old annuals to make an appearance during the year. It wasn't very good. White himself wrote some of the songs as well as creating some of the sketches and dancing in the show. Cliff Friend and Irving Caesar helped with the songs. Besides White the cast included Eugene and Willie Howard and Frances Williams. The show opened with a number honoring the dancers and dances of the earlier *Scandals*, culminating in a rousing black bottom. Later on the Abbott Specialty Dancers did some fancy stepping and Marietta did a contortion dance. In the comedy routines Willie Howard was driven to mayhem by a radio that talked back to him. Spectacles included a "Parade of All Nations" and a finale set at the Café Lido in Paris, which allowed the chorus girls and other members of the cast to disappear into a tank not unlike the one the old Hippodrome once boasted. There were enough loyal fans to keep the show at the Apollo for twenty weeks, but when it departed it left nothing permanent behind.

Vincent Youmans had made his name with bright, contemporary musical comedies. Now, for the second time in a row, he met failure with a rough, romantic bit of old Americana. Youmans produced the show himself, thereby aggravating his loss. Great Day (17 October 1929, Cosmopolitan) was set in the ever popular New Orleans of long ago. The Randolph Plantation is located just outside the town. Pretty Emma Lou Randolph (Mayo Methot) is forced to sell it to the shifty Carlos Zarega (John Haynes). Her circumstances are so reduced that she is forced to go to work for Zarega. But a young engineer, Jim Brent (Allan Prior), comes along, disposes of Zarega by hurling him into the river, and restores the old homestead to Emma Lou, who consents to become Mrs. Brent. The story was a little looser and less well wrought than *Rainbow* (21 November 1928). Its looseness allowed Miller and Lyles to caper through some of comedy bits and Walter C. Kelly, famous for his judge role in vaudeville, to play a not too dissimilar judge here. But if William Cary Duncan and John Wells were not as adept as Stallings and Hammerstein had been in *Rainbow*, Youmans was in top form. Three of his finest numbers survived the grueling four-month tryout: Emma Lou's "More Than You Know," "Without A Song," and "Great Day"—the last two sung by Lijah (baritone Lois Deppe) and the plantation hands. But all the hirings and firings that Youmans as producer resorted to during the out-of-town ordeal could not shape the musical into something salable. Moreover, twelve days after the show opened the economic world collapsed. *Great Day* folded after just thirty-six performances.

Delighted with the success of their Jolson Theatre revivals, the Shuberts brought an elaborate version of *Die Fledermaus* to town. They called this revival A Wonderful Night (31 October 1929, Majestic) and brought it in two days after the Wall Street crash. The show had been done in 1912 as *The Merry Countess* and would be done again under different titles in the 1930s and 1940s. The part of Max was played by Archie Leach, who later changed his name to Cary Grant. An indestructible perennial, the show racked up 125 performances.

The finest, most cohesive work of the season, Noël Coward's Bitter Sweet (5 November 1929, Ziegfeld), was given a typically thorough and elaborate Ziegfeld mounting. In Coward's flashback tale a grandmother recalls her own marriage for love to help her granddaughter decide which young man to marry. The great English favorite Evelyn Laye (star of the original London productions of *Mary* and *The New Moon*) helped acquaint Americans with one of Coward's masterpieces, "I'll See You Again." But the times were against *Bitter Sweet*, and its New York run of twenty weeks fell far short of its earlier London success.

Six nights later, Rodgers and Hart, assisted by John McGowan and Paul Gerard Smith on the book, saw their **Heads Up** (11 November 1929, Alvin) begin a modest run of 144 showings. The musical had originally been called *Me for You* and had sported a libretto by Owen Davis, in which the heroine threw over a district attorney to marry a lawbreaker and in which Victor Moore played a not very comic villain. Such unpleasant changes were too much for tryout audiences. Perhaps Rodgers and Hart also recalled the bad luck that pursued the Gershwins when they gave Gertrude Lawrence a nasty disposition in *Treasure Girl* (8 November 1928). Using the same cast and scenery, the new story had fun with rum-running. Since Victor Moore was the principal fun-maker, a number of theatregoers found themselves recalling Moore and a similar plot in another Gershwin-Lawrence opus. *Oh, Kay!* (8 November 1926). Lieutenant Jack Mason (Jack Whiting) of the Coast Guard is convinced Mrs. Trumbell's yacht, *Silver Lady*, is rum-running. He's right; but Mrs. Trumbell (Janet Velie) is innocent. Her own captain (Robert Gleckler) is doing it on the side, without her consent. The captain burns the yacht rather than let its telltale cargo fall into government hands. But Jack is not left empty-handed. He wins Mrs. Trumbell's daughter, Mary (Barbara Newberry). Rodgers, like Kern, was virtually incapable of writing a bad score, but *Heads Up* contributed little to the standard Rodgers canon. Though a number of singers and musicians have singled out "A Ship Without A Sail" for praise, only "Why Do You Suppose?" still enjoys something approaching popularity.

While the public began to allow more masterful, serious pieces to languish, it still embraced good, light-hearted musical comedies. Two of them came in during the last week of November. The first, **Sons o' Guns** (26 November 1929, Imperial), imposed a slight handicap on itself by taking up a war theme. But it did so with such a frivolous, devil-may-care pose that no one minded. Its story was slightly reminiscent of one of the most popular musical hits of "the great war," *The Better 'Ole* (19 October 1918). Playboy Jimmy Canfield (Jack Donahue) finds himself in the army, with his former valet, Hobson (William Frawley), as his top sergeant. Things go from bad to worse for the bumbling Jim, culminating with his arrest for spying. But Jimmy escapes, bumbles

into some heroic acts, and wins a pretty French miss, Yvonne (Lily Damita). Miss Damita, who had made her name in Hollywood, surprised Broadway with her talent and vitality. No one was surprised by Donahue's likable human comedy, and even less by his supple 'ankle and knee gyrations.' Albertina Rasch girls provided ballet-like chorus numbers. A particularly attractive feature of the evening was Joseph Urban's magnificent scenery, recreating a huge Arc de Triomphe, a French village, and a red, white, and blue victory ball. The score was the last Broadway offering for another of the better second-level composers of the day, J. Fred Coots. Coots's top numbers in *Sons o' Guns* were "Why?" and "Cross Your Fingers." A run of 295 performances gave *Sons o' Guns* the third longest stay of any 1929–1930 musical.

Fifty Million Frenchmen (27 November 1929, Lyric) was almost as popular. Like *Sons o' Guns*, it had a playboy for its central figure. And, like that show, it was set in France. Only this time the setting was gay, up-to-the-minute Paris. The impetuous Peter Forbes (William Gaxton) falls in love with Looloo Carroll (Genevieve Tobin) on first sight. He bets his friend Michael Cummins (Jack Thompson) $25,000 that he can win Looloo without flaunting his money. Taking a job as a guide he pursues his new heartthrob and wins her away from the Grand Duke Ivan Ivanovitch of Russia (Mannart Kippen), whom Looloo's social-climbing parents had slated for her. His performance as Peter sealed Gaxton's reputation and established him as a top impersonator of suave but tough-fibered leading men.

In supporting roles, Evelyn Hoey, as May De Vere, brought down the house singing "Find Me A Primitive Man"; Helen Broderick was an American tourist, Violet Hildegarde, buying copies of James Joyce's *Ulysses* to send home to the kids; while Thurston Hall, who had played romantic leads in musicals like *The Only Girl* (2 November 1914), was now old enough to assume the minor role of Looloo's father. The show boasted impressive sets by Norman Bel Geddes. They turned out to be too large to fit on the stage, so the show's out-of-town opening had to be delayed while they were cut down to size. Even in reduced versions Bel Geddes' Ritz Bar, American Express Office, and Eiffel Tower were stunners. The show's dances included one more number done all in black and white. Best of all, the show had a good Cole Porter score, coupled with some of his most brilliant lyrics. Since refrains had to be simple his best lines were often in the verse; one rhymes "sacrifices," "Isis," and "vices," while a second joined "day," "play," "straight away," and "croupier." Besides Peter's "I Worship You" and May's "I'm Unlucky At Gambling," from which these excerpts are taken, the Porter flair was evident in "Where Would You Get Your Coat?" and "Tale Of An Oyster" (both sung by Violet). But the public, however much it laughed at Porter's wit in the theatre, went out into the night singing "You've Got That Thing," sung by Michael and Joyce (Betty Compton), and Peter and Looloo's "You Do Something To Me." For all the evening's attractions the critics were not overwhelmed. Irving Berlin, who was originally to have produced the show, took out a large ad praising it. In a short time word of mouth built the piece into a hit.

WILLIAM GAXTON was born in San Francisco on 2 December 1893. His Italian parents named him Arturo Gaxiola. A stint at Boone's Military Academy instilled in him the manly bearing he brought to all his roles. After furthering his education at the University of California he entered vaudeville, first in a song-and-patter act with Anna Laughlin and subsequently as a single in a skit called "A Regular Business Man." He appeared briefly in *The Music Box Revue* in 1922, men took to the road in *Betty Lee, All for You,* and *Miss Happiness.* His first important Broadway appearance was as Martin in the 1927 hit *A Connecticut Yankee* (3 November 1927).

A musical that no word of mouth could save opened the same night. **The Silver Swan** (27 November 1929, Martin Beck) told of Capt. Richard Von Orten's switch in allegiance from Hortense (Alice MacKenzie), leading lady at the opera, to Gabrielle (Vivian Hart), a new bit player. Not even the machinations of Princess Von Auen (Lina Abarbanell) can win Van Orten (Edward Nell, Jr.) away afterwards. The score was dreary, and not even another old-time star, Miss Abarbanell in the relatively minor role of the Princess, could breathe life into the piece.

Top Speed (25 December 1929, 46th St.) arrived a season or so too late. Its tale of flashy, carefree high life was the sort the twenties adored. But with the stock market crash just two months old the show was not a very welcome Christmas present. At a posh resort in the Thousand Islands two impecunious broker's

clerks, Gerry Brooks (Paul Frawley) and Elmer Peters (Lester Allen), pose as millionaires to court two very rich young ladies, Babs Green and Virginia Rollins (Irene Delroy). When Gerry is caught fishing at the fish hatchery they are almost exposed. By the time the truth does come out, love makes everyone indifferent. The show was written and produced by Guy Bolton, Bert Kalmar, and Harry Ruby. Not only were they ill-timed, they were none in top form. Indeed the best form of the evening seems to have been displayed by the exuberant girl who stole the show as Babs, Ginger Rogers. *Top Speed*'s dancers clearly took heed of the show's title. The *World* recorded that the "chorus beats out its rhythms in an increasing crescendo of high spirits." Two or three years earlier such snappiness would have probably been rewarded by a run of more than thirteen weeks.

The same night, **Woof, Woof** (25 December 1929, Royale) came in to begin a six-week stay. It was another retelling of the season's favorite plot: a poor girl's rise to stardom. This time the ending was not unlike *Merry, Merry* (24 September 1925). Susie Yates (Louise Brown) has her chance for the big time if she will become the mistress of the popular bandleader, Tommy Clair (Jack Squires). With fame and fortune so close at hand, she has second thoughts. She decides she prefers the small time with loving Monty Fleming (Al Sexton), a dancer. Their future is made easier when they win big on a dog race. Even Leonide Massine's staging—which included two whippets racing on a treadmill—failed to interest most playgoers.

More Cole Porter music, including his evergreen "What Is This Thing Called Love?" (sung by Frances Shelley and danced by Tilly Losch and others), was heard in an English revue, **Wake Up and Dream** (30 December 1929, Selwyn). An attractive cast including European favorites Jack Buchanan, Jessie Matthews, and Miss Losch brought in ticket-buyers for eighteen weeks.

There were no saving graces in **Ginger Snaps** (31 December 1929, Belmont), a black revue in which even the dancing, so often the mainstay of the period's black shows, was condemned. After a week the show was relegated to the history books.

The season's most innovative musical, **Strike Up the Band**, opened at the Times Square on 14 January 1930—the first musical of the new year and, more significant, the first of the thirties. The Gershwins and George S. Kaufman had originally written it and watched it die during a 1927 Philadelphia tryout. At that time it was an uncompromising satire on war, big business, and international politics. It was the very sort of thing Gilbert and Sullivan might have contrived had they been children of the jazz age. In the original version the Swiss protest an American tariff on their cheese. An American cheese manufacturer, Horace J. Fletcher, suggests the United States go to war over the matter. He will finance the battle so long as it goes down in the history books as the Horace J. Fletcher Memorial War. However, when his daughter's fiancé, Jim Townsend, threatens to expose Fletcher's use of Grade B milk in his products, Fletcher does an abrupt about-face, becoming an ardent pacifist. Unfortunately, his change of heart comes too late; the war fever is uncontrollable. After Fletcher is discovered wearing a Swiss watch, he himself comes under suspicion. The war delights everyone, including Swiss hotel owners who house idle American troops at inflated rates. The conflict ends when secret Swiss yodeling signals are decoded. But the war has been such fun that when a tariff is imposed on caviar, the United States and Russia gaily prepare to fight matters out. This first *Strike Up the Band* met with a refreshingly enthusiastic critical reception, but the public refused to respond. It preferred the farcical fripperies and pseudo-serious romance of the twenties' lyric stage. But in the troubled world of 1930 there seemed some hope that the musical's biting edge might prove tonic, especially if the worst of the bite were removed.

For the new version, Morrie Ryskind revised and softened the original book. The story became a dream, from which Fletcher awakes thoroughly reformed. Even the basic Swiss cheese was changed to more frivolous Swiss chocolate. George Gershwin's score introduced a number of songs that quickly became standards: "Soon," "Strike Up The Band!," and "I've Got A Crush On You." "Strike Up The Band!," the first-act finale, was sung by Townsend and the company.

Some of the best material was in comic numbers such as "A Typical Self-Made American," in which Colonel Holmes (patterned after Colonel House of the Wilson administration) tells how he got to the top. Ira's American counterpart to Sir Joseph Porter boasts, "I made mother my ideal, and never watched the clock." In its pertinence and impertinence, in its willingness to face important social issues, *Strike Up the Band* broadcast a new era in stage musicals. And though its score had the electric drive and energy of all Gershwin compositions it broke with the elementary staccato rhythms that had pervaded the preceding decade. Considering its daring and the

bad times, its six-month run was acceptable. There are two interesting sidelights to the show. George had tried to use "The Man I Love" in the score. The song was to him what "Bill" had been to Kern. But Gershwin was never to find the right show for it as Kern did for his song. Bobby Clark played Colonel Holmes to Dudley Clements's Fletcher. Paul McCullough clowned as Holmes's sidekick Gideon, while Margaret Schilling and Jerry Goff handled the romantic leads. And the sad parade of passing luminaries continued. The once popular star Blanche Ring had a small part.

If *Strike Up the Band* provided a glimpse of the American Musical Theatre to come, the next two offerings gave Broadway a chance to reflect on long-gone glories. Mitzi, about to write "finis" to her career, returned briefly in a revival of the show that had made her a star sixteen years before, *Sari* (13 January 1914). An even more popular and beloved figure of this earlier era followed in Mitzi's footsteps. Fred Stone was sufficiently recovered from the effects of an air crash to return to Broadway. Along with his wife (now listed simply as Mrs. Fred Stone) and his daughter Dorothy, he introduced for public approval another daughter, Paula. For years Stone's shows had been reigning hits of the seasons in which they were produced, and if by some chance they turned out not to be the number-one hit, they were invariably close to it. Now Stone was to suffer a Broadway affliction he had never been bothered by, failure. In **Ripples** (11 February 1930, New Amsterdam) Stone played Rip Van Winkle, the great-great-grandson of the original. Stone, for all his age and injuries, made another of his dramatic, acrobatic entrances flying through a barn door (horses' hoofprints on his coattails) and landing in a tulip bed. Rip is the town ne'er-do-well, a liar and a drunk. When he wakes from a drunken binge he finds himself surrounded by dwarfs. They turn out to be bootleggers, running from a comic state policeman, Corporal Jack Sterling (Eddie Foy Jr.). Rip hopes his daughter, Ripples (Dorothy Stone), will marry Jack; but Ripples prefers rich Richard Willoughby (Charles Collins) and lands him. Charles Dillingham was once again Stone's producer; but he enlisted the support of a new roster of writers: William Anthony McGuire for the book, Irving Caesar and John Graham for the lyrics, and Oscar Levant and Albert Sirmay for the music. Caesar revived "I'm A Little Bit Fonder Of You" from *Yes, Yes, Yvette*. Jerome Kern and Fred Coots each interpolated a song, as did the newly celebrated team of Arthur Schwartz and Howard Dietz. With John Tiller dead, his assistant Mary Read trained a new group of Mary Read Tiller Girls to dance in unison and counterpoint. But neither the star, his writers, nor his supporting cast could recapture the elusive magic that had served Stone for so long. The show left after a disheartening seven weeks.

Another flop opened the same night, the **9:15 Revue** (11 February 1930, Cohan). It lasted only one week. Though it had songs by the Gershwins, Rudolf Friml, Vincent Youmans, and Roger Wolfe Kahn, its most attractive numbers were by relative newcomers. The Warburgs, writing as Paul James and Kay Swift, offered "Up Among The Chimney Pots," while Ted Koehler set words to Harold Arlen's music and came up with a tune that remains popular long after the evening has been forgotten, "Get Happy." The song was introduced in the first-act finale by Ruth Etting. A Victor Herbert waltz, "The World Of Dreams," was danced in a Degas-like setting. For comedy Anita Loos wrote a modern-day version of *East Lynne*, while Paul Gerard Smith drew a picture of a Chicago gangster very much not the boss in his own home. And for variety the popular magician Fred Keating entertained with his deceptions. When the show closed abruptly, most of the performers found themselves out of work with little prospect of new employment. But Ruth Etting, lucky for once in her unhappy life, found herself hustled into the very next musical to reach Broadway.

Since Ziegfeld employed more experienced or dependable hands for this Ed Wynn vehicle, **Simple Simon** (18 February 1930, Ziegfeld), the results were happier than those Dillingham had produced for Stone. Wynn and Guy Bolton tailored the book to the comedian's special talents, while Rodgers and Hart created the songs. Joseph Urban's magnificent sets took everyone from Coney Island to King Cole's Palace and even up to the clouds. Oddly the book employed the very sort of story Stone had always done so well. Simon is a newspaper vendor who refuses to read the bad news of the day. He spends his time on fairy tales. When he's not reading them, he dreams about them—of course with himself figuring prominently in their stories. Brandishing a sword as big as himself, Simon rescues Cinderella. He wheels around making music on a piano built onto a bicycle. Lost with a picnic basket in a lovely Urban forest, he exults, "I love the woodth! Ah, how I love the woodth!" He loves them even after

a giant frog appears (a frog played by contortionist William J. Ferry). Wynn and the frog share the picnic. No Wynn opus was complete without his absurd inventions. In *Simple Simon* he brought forth a mousetrap with no entrance so the poor little mice couldn't be hurt. Ziegfeld played havoc with the score. He cavalierly discarded "Dancing On The Ceiling" during the tryout, though it would have allowed him an imaginative production number. "Send For Me," rewritten from *Chee-Chee's* "I Must Love You," was the show's most popular ballad. But it was Ruth Etting's singing of "Ten Cents A Dance" that proved the musical highlight of the show. In gratitude Ziegfeld revived "Love Me Or Leave Me," the song Miss Etting had sung in his *Whoopee* (2 December 1928), and inserted it in the show though it impinged on Rodgers and Hart's material.

The International Revue (25 February 1930, Majestic) cost over $200,000 to mount, a high figure at the time, and offered a seemingly irresistible lineup of talents. The cast included Gertrude Lawrence, Harry Richman, Jack Pearl, Anton Dolin, and the much-publicized dancer Argentinita. The Spanish lady bombed so badly she was out of the cast after the first week. The songs were by Dorothy Fields and Jimmy McHugh. They were a melodic match for their fine work in *The Blackbirds* two seasons before. The best tunes from the striking score were "Exactly Like You" and "On The Sunny Side Of The Street" (both introduced by Richman). Lew Leslie, the show's producer, gave the show a lavish if not particularly tasteful mounting. An elaborate Montmartre set served as a background for a "Russianized" apache dance. The dance began when its heroine jumped from a second-story window to escape her violent lover. Not only people but a dog, a donkey, and a goat crowded the scene. Reviews of the show were devastating. The *World* called it "long [the second act began at eleven o'clock] and dirty and dull," while the more tactful *Times* complained the "humor is anatomical." Because most of *The International Revue's* material was not up to its music, the excellent cast seemed at times conspicuously empty-handed. The show ran twelve weeks.

In the late twenties Charles Lindbergh, Amelia Earhart, Admiral Byrd, and other gutsy fliers had made exciting headlines out of their flying escapades. They made it imperative that Broadway take up flying, too. George White presented what became DeSylva, Brown, and Henderson's last New York show when he opened **Flying High** (3 March 1930, Apollo). It was the biggest musical comedy hit of the season, surpassed in longevity only by *Earl Carroll's Sketch Book*. Yet if Broadway legend can be believed, the book, apart from a vague outline, was not written until rehearsals began. In reality there were two loosely connected stories. One told of a love affair that grows between lonely Eileen Cassidy (Grace Brinkley) and a flashy mail pilot, Tod Addison (Oscar Shaw), after Addison parachutes down on her New York City roof. The other told how Addison's mechanic, "Rusty" Krause (Bert Lahr), establishes an all-time endurance record in the air simply because he cannot figure how to land a plane. There were a few innovative touches in the book. The show opened quietly with Eileen on the roof; chorus girls came in much later. But the consensus was that *Flying High* was a conventional, somewhat old-style musical made hilarious by Lahr's antics. The show's most famous scene was a physical given to Rusty. He pours scotch into the specimen vial and when asked his nationality replies, with a unique consistency, "Scotch, by absorption." DeSylva, Brown, and Henderson's score was a letdown. The trio's musical style was still firmly rooted in the twenties. Kate Smith's driving rendition made a show-stopper out of "Red Hot Chicago," though if any tune from the show has endured it is probably "Thank Your Father," sung by the romantic leads.

Maurice Chevalier, Eleanor Powell, and Duke Ellington and his Cotton Club orchestra each were given a full act to entertain in, in what was essentially a vaudeville that Charles Dillingham mounted at the Fulton on 30 March. The evening was mounted with little but draperies, virtually all Dillingham the first major producer hit by the Depression—could afford.

Moss Hart and Dorothy Heyward provided a rather curious story for **Jonica** (7 April 1930, Craig). Jonica (Nell Roy) leaves her convent school to attend a friend's wedding. On the train she meets some Broadway types also going to the wedding, and at the wedding she meets her old flame, Don Milan (Jerry Norris). Complications set in when a gun the young heroine is carrying for self-protection accidentally discharges. Happily Jonica's wild bullet does no harm. Don and Jonica conclude they were fated for each other. It was not the sort of piece capable of making either of its librettists as famous as they would later become. Nor was Joseph Meyer's stolid score a help. *Jonica* left New York just five weeks after her arrival. Hart in after years insisted the work, which he had adapted at the urging of the producer from Mrs. Heyward's unproduced *Have a Good Time, Jonica*, was later completely rewritten by a third, anonymous hand.

The Shuberts brought in a European operetta called **Three Little Girls** (14 April 1930, Shubert). It told a story not unlike *Maytime* (16 August 1917) of a love thwarted in one generation fulfilled by the lovers' descendants a generation or two later. Beate-Marie (Natalie Hall) and Hendrik (Charles Hedley) would marry, but Beate-Marie is forced to marry the Count von Rambow (John Goldsworthy) instead. The same fate seems about to befall Beate-Marie's daughter and Hendrik's son, but love prevails. Though the whole evening belonged to a dying tradition, it appealed to enough old-timers to run 104 performances.

One brief, oddball entry was **Kilpatrick's Old-Time Minstrels** (19 April 1930, Royale), a full-fledged minstrel entertainment of the sort Broadway hadn't seen for decades. The interlocutor, the end men, the sentimental old songs were all back. Only the compelling magic of yesteryear was missing. Tambourines and bones were quickly packed away, and the great old minstrel tradition went back into hibernation.

With traditional vaudeville venues fast disappearing, Harry Lauder again had recourse to a legitimate house for his latest bill—advertised as his "sixth annual farewell tour." The house was Jolson's, and the opening date the 21st. Such old two-a-day standbys as acrobats, dancers, and cartoonists filled the earlier part of the bill. Then Lauder, in his kilts and sporrans and plaids, regaled his followers with much of his beloved repertory.

No musicals appeared in May, but two arrived the first week in June. One was a third and final edition of **The Garrick Gaieties** (4 June 1930, Guild). Sterling Holloway and Philip Loeb of the original version were back; Albert Carroll moved over from the defunct *Grand Street Follies*; and some of the mirth was provided by a winsome young lady with the unlikely name of Imogene Coca. Unfortunately, Rodgers and Hart did not compose the songs. They were missed. None of the new songs captured the public's fancy the way "Mountain Greenery" or "Manhattan" had. But the new songs did at least give a leg up to several promising composers and lyricists. E. Y. Harburg and Vernon Duke had three songs on the program, the best of which, "I Am Only Human After All," had Ira Gershwin as co-lyricist. Harburg collaborated with Richard Myers in a song whose lyrics mimicked the unique patois of columnist Walter Winchell, "Ankle Up The Altar With Me." Marc Blitzstein contributed music for another burlesque of operetta. Johnny Mercer supplied words for "Out Of Breath (And Scared To Death Of You)." Happily, the skits were as incisive and hilarious as before. Plays such as *The Last Mile* and *Strange Interlude* were spoofed, with several of the Theatre Guild's most dependable playwrights—O'Neill, Molnar, and Shaw—getting mixed up in the proceedings. The ex–police commissioner, Grover Whalen, had just returnd to his job at Wanamaker's Department Store. This, coupled with the announced Wanamaker policy of taking anything back, provided meat for an uproarious sketch with the dapper Whalen referred to as "the gardenia of the law." To a chorus of thanksgiving in the background Whalen institutes traffic controls and the latest police methods at the staid, old store. The show ran through the summer, and just before it left on its tour a revised version, incorporating gems from the earlier editions, was placed on the boards. "Rose of Arizona," for example, replaced the Blitzstein travesty.

JOHNNY MERCER, born 18 November 1909 in Savannah, Georgia, developed an early ear for African-American musical styles, mastering the music's rhythm, slang, and easy-going charm. Known principally as a lyricist and singer, Mercer collaborated with composers Hoagy Carmichael, Harry Warren, Rube Bloom, Jerome Kern, Robert Emmet Dolan and Andre Previn, sometimes writing his own music. Mercer, a co-founder of Capitol Records, enjoyed greater success in film and popular music than in theatre, and is today best known for "On the Atchison, Topeka and the Santa Fe," "Lazybones," "Jeepers Creepers," and "Come Rain or Come Shine."

Prohibition still seemed material for mirth to the authors of the black musical **Change Your Luck**

(6 June 1930, Cohan). Broadway didn't agree. Nor did it see much original in the typical Negro stage names of the day—Hot Stuff Jackson, Romeo Green, Rat Row Sadie, or the almost inevitable Charleston Sam. And the lyricist wore threadbare the device of dropping the *g* to indicate a vowel change—"Ain't Puttin' Over Nothin,'" "Waistin' Away," "Percolatin'," and "Travelin'." So Evergreen Peppers (Leigh Whipper), the bootlegging undertaker, packed his equipment and stole away after a mere two weeks.

The season's last show started life in London as a book musical called *Dear Love*. By the time the Shuberts were finished revamping it, it arrived in New York as **Artists and Models** (10 June 1930, Majestic): the last in that dull series. Spectacle numbers paraded the girls as beauties of the past (Cleopatra, Thais), as guests in diaphanous gowns at a nobleman's wedding, and most appropriately for this revue, as models in an artist's studio. The Rath Brothers' acrobatic dances contrasted with the graceful toe-dancing of a small *corps de ballet*. Aileen Stanley and Phil Baker led the cast. Baker was again harassed by Mr. Muldowney. Regrettably, Baker's humor was not only often unfunny, but just as often smutty. The Shuberts withdrew the piece after seven weeks.

1930–1931

The theatrical year was sometimes brilliant; more often sad, even tragic. The number of original musicals continued to drop, though the decline was not as sharp as it had been in the last two sessions. Changes in theatregoers' tastes were also becoming evident. Yet once again the swings were not always too pronounced. While operetta was so moribund as to be for all practical purposes dead, the more intimate, thoughtful revue was obviously here to stay for a while. Uncertain which way to turn, lighter book musicals looked both backward and forward—some hits offering the latest in innovations and sophistication; some remaining contentedly lamebrain and irresponsible.

One surprising but incontestable change was a hardening of critical standards. Musicals were suddenly deprived of the easygoing, favored treatment they had so long received. Whether critics were concerned lest readers waste hard-to-come-by dollars or whether they felt that they had to be more critical to retain their own jobs is difficult to judge. But the old-time tolerance vanished forever.

Much of the sadness was felt as Broadway bid adieu to a number of artists who had served it long and well. A few, like J. J. McNally and Sydney Rosenfeld, had been inactive for so many years that their importance to an earlier theatrical world was not universally appreciated. A number of performers, luminaries of earlier nights far gone, took their final bows as well, some heading hopefully to Hollywood, some retiring, some dying. More tragic was the plight of the producers. All the great theatrical empires fell. Men such as Arthur Hammerstein and Charles Dillingham fell first, never again to know the power and glamour that had been theirs. During the following season even the Shuberts submitted to the bankruptcy courts—although their action was questioned by some. They quickly retrieved all their important houses, and, though they thereafter operated on a smaller scale, they actually owned a larger percentage of working theatres than ever before.

The season's opener was a disaster. **Mystery Moon** (23 June 1930, Royale) had one performance. The libretto dealt with the plight of a musical comedy road company when it books a Portal, North Dakota, theatre run by a gang of dope peddlers. One of the young ladies is even abducted by the son of the theatre owner. The songs were by the persistent Carlo and Sanders. Stanley Green, in his delightful survey of the decade's musicals, suggests one reason for the show's short run was the team's lyrics, filled with drivel such as "smother me with kisses, for it's all O.K." Seventeen years passed before Carlo and Sanders recovered sufficiently to try again.

On 1 July, changing times and crisis conditions allowed Earl Carroll to bring his 1930 **Vanities** into the New Amsterdam, once the flagship of his old Erlanger opposition. Jimmy Savo, Jack Benny, and Patsy Kelly were among the clowns. The show had trouble with the police. A swimming scene, with large mirrors revealing the action in a stage tank, had a man chasing several girls and catching one just as the lights went out. But more objectionable was a show girl's fan dance and the coarseness of some of the sketches. In one skit that really raised eyebrows Jimmy Savo played a window-dresser changing mannequins' clothes. Carroll made the requested changes. No records suggest the police objected to the first-act finale, which made a prolonged, colorful protest against Prohibition. Though E. Y. Harburg, Harold Arlen, Burton Lane, and Jay Gorney put words and music together for the show, the songs

were undistinguished. Ray Noble's "Good Night, Sweetheart," not written for the evening, was interpolated for a time. With ticket sales hyped by all the publicity the police gave the show, Carroll was able to keep this edition of the *Vanities* on the boards into the first weeks of 1931.

Broadway and bad luck continued to go hand-in-hand for Percy Wenrich, the popular Tin Pan Alley figure. Wenrich wrote the songs for a revue called **Who Cares?** (8 July 1930, 46th St.). It was a dangerous title, and the unemployed actors at the Lambs Club who put the piece together got their answer swiftly. The show left after one month. Yet not all the entertainment deserved brusque dismissal. One riotous skit, "What's Wrong with the Theatre," compared a patron's reception at a film palace and at a legitimate house. At the cinema four nattily dressed ushers welcome him rapturously, carry him to his seat, serve him tea and biscuits, and even do handstands for him until the movie begins. At the legitimate house the same patron is snarled at, ignored, shoved and robbed. In a remarkable glimpse into the future, "So This Is Television" broadcast the Dumbell Department Store Hour. Less imaginative was still one more New York dig at criminal Chicago—with society dolled up in its furs, gowns, and guns. There was also a maudlin war scene, dancing condemned as "undistinguished," and songs written off as "dismal."

A black revue managed a slightly longer stay. **Hot Rhythm** (21 August 1930, Times Square) lingered eight and a half weeks on 42nd Street. Attempting to pass itself off alternately as "A Sepia-Tinted Little Show" and "The Little Black Show," *Hot Rhythm* was nothing but a pastiche of typical black show material of the day—"rent party scenes, jungle scenes... even a beauty parade." The prison sketch that figured in so many black revues was a "lamentable burlesque of *The Last Mile*," the melodrama that had skyrocketed Spencer Tracy to fame. Whatever merit the show may have had must have been crammed into its opening numbers. The *Sun* noted that the first half-hour was the best, while the *World* admonished its readers, "leave at nine." Even with a Eubie Blake interpolation to bolster Donald Heywood and Porter Grainger's score, the show failed to generate much excitement. Soon after *Hot Rhythm* closed, the Times Square Theatre was converted into a movie house, and the inexorable decline of New York's greatest theatrical street began.

Hot Rhythm might not have been so anxious to associate itself with *The Little Show* if it had seen what The Second Little Show (2 September 1930, Royale) was to offer. The show's producers had unwisely decided not to rehire the stars of the first edition. According to Howard Dietz, they "wanted the title The Little Show to be the star." As a result Schwartz and Dietz found they were writing the songs for two revues, The Second Little Show and a revue for the players from the first version. Their best material went into the latter. An interpolation by Herman Hupfeld, "Sing Something Simple," was the outstanding number of The Second Little Show. The principal entertainer was Al Trahan, a vaudevillian famous for his comic piano playing (he played his piano in the show, too). Trahan had the title role in the evening's only good sketch, "The Guest." This miniature Marc Connelly gem had first appeared as a small piece in The New Yorker. Connelly's guest made the mistake of checking into a modern hotel, where all the service is governed by pushbuttons. By some horrendous error the buttons have been miswired. Mayhem ensues. The guest's breakfast is pressed, and his suit served sunny side up. Other sketches were humdrum, and the cast patently inferior. The Second Little Show called it a run after eight weeks.

The two masters of Viennese–American operetta, Rudolf Friml and Sigmund Romberg, brought in their latest efforts back to back. Friml's piece was a fiasco. Luana (17 September 1930, Hammerstein) was a $200,000 musical version of Richard Walton Tully's The Bird of Paradise. Written originally as a film musical, it was adapted for the stage when its filming was scrapped. Its producer, Arthur Hammerstein, perhaps sensing the drift away from operetta, billed it as a musical play. But a number of operettas had done that before, so no one was deceived. Luana (Ruth Altman) is a South Sea Island princess who renounces her prerogatives to marry an American, Paul Wilson (Joseph Macaulay). When Wilson deserts her, she commits suicide by jumping into a volcano. Neither Howard Emmett Rogers, who did the adaptation, nor J. Keirn Brennan, who wrote the lyrics, was especially clever or original. Worse, Friml's score lacked the color and fire—and the memorable melodies—that this story called for and that he had so often injected into his earlier works. Hammerstein withdrew the show after twenty-one performances.

Romberg and the Shuberts had somewhat better luck with their "musical play," Nina Rosa (20 September 1930, Majestic). First of all they had Otto Harbach to do the libretto and Irving Caesar for the lyrics. Second, they had Florenz Ziegfeld's ravishing Rio Rita, Ethelind Terry, for their lead. The story was set in the Peruvian Andes, where Jack Haines (Guy Robertson), a mining engineer, falls in love with Nina Rosa and has to fight to win her away from the hate-filled Pablo (Leonard Ceeley). Romberg's score was pretty, but a little thin-blooded. Still, it was a sufficiently pleasant evening to run 137 performances and to be accounted a modest success. In 1932 the show enjoyed a long vogue in Paris.

Three nights later Broadway applauded a solid hit, titled appropriately Fine and Dandy (23 September 1930, Erlanger). With the passage of time its most laudable asset would seem to be its vivacious Kay Swift score (with lyrics by Paul James), her only complete score ever sung in New York. The title song was one of the first public pronouncements of facile optimism that became so prevalent in the Depression. There was also an exquisite romantic ballad, "Can This Be Love?" But the principal attraction for most of its 1930 audience was unquestionably Joe Cook's clowning. Cook was several comedians rolled into one. He was almost as acrobatic as Fred Stone (in Fine and Dandy he impersonated a whole team of German acrobats); he could juggle as comically as W. C. Fields (this time Cook juggled cigarettes); his crazy Rube Goldberg inventions put him in a class with Ed Wynn (one contraption punctured balloons, cracked nuts, and punched people at the same time), while Cook's dialogue often ranked with that of the Marx Brothers. Compare the excerpt from Animal Crackers (23 October 1928) with this Fine and Dandy routine:

Joe: Are you his mother?
Mrs. Pordyce: No.
Joe: His father?
Mrs. Fordtce: No.
Joe: Well, then, how are you related to him?
Mrs. Fordyce: I'm not related to him at all.
Joe: Neither am I. Now there's a coincidence.

Joe is Joe Squibb, an employee of the Fordyce Drop Forge and Tool Company, and Mrs. Fordyce (Dora Maughan) is the founder's widow and heir. The old gal finds Joe attractive enough to promote him to general manager. Joe is not above courting her a bit to get the post. He also courts pretty young Nancy Ellis (Alice Boulden). That leaves him little time for his wife and children. A prime attraction, apart from

Cook's clowning, was the vivacious tap-dancing of Eleanor Powell.

Performers were also a main attraction at October's first show, **Brown Buddies** (7 October 1930, Liberty), a Negro musical comedy that featured Bill Robinson and his unique stepping, as well as the singing of Adelaide Hall. The story followed Sam Wilson and his girlfriends from East St. Louis to the front in World War I and home again. Unfortunately Joe Jordan's score, with interpolations by Porter Grainger and Victor Young, was not on a par with Bojangles's tapping or Miss Hall's singing. Nonetheless the evening achieved 111 showings; not bad, all things considered.

On 13 October Evelyn Herbert, Robert Halliday, George Grossmith, and Victor Moore combined their talents in vain to put across **Princess Charming** (13 October 1930, Imperial), an imported operetta bedecked in sumptuous Urban sets. The story told of a princess who prefers a sea captain to a king.

The season's best musical and biggest hit opened the next night. For the Gershwins, **Girl Crazy** (14 October 1930, Alvin) represented a retreat from the adventuresome *Strike Up the Band*. It was strictly a formula show. But it had an electrifying Gershwin score sung, in part, by an electrifying singing discovery. The newcomer was Ethel Merman, soon to be Broadway's leading musical comedy star. In *Girl Crazy* her brassy delivery stopped the show with "Sam and Delilah" and "I Got Rhythm." But she was not the only fine talent in the cast. There was the popular leading man Allen Kearns, the rising Ginger Rogers, and the always funny Willie Howard. Howard was a last-minute substitution for Bert Lahr, still busy with *Flying High*. There were also a number of as yet unrecognized talents in the pit: Benny Goodman, Gene Krupa, and Glenn Miller. In Guy Bolton and John McGowan's book a New York playboy, Danny Churchill (Kearns), is sent by his father to Custerville, Arizona, where there are supposedly no nightclubs, no gambling casinos, and no women. Danny's way of getting there is unusual. He hires Gieber Goldfarb's taxi to take him. But Danny is not one to sit around like some of the locals biding his time. He transforms a dude ranch into a club with a gaming room and lots of girls. He even succeeds in making a sheriff of Goldfarb (Howard), who talks to the Indians in Yiddish. Danny also succeeds in finding a wife in the town postmistress, Molly Gray (Miss Rogers). Miss Merman was Kate Fothergill, the daughter

of the town's saloon keeper, played in the show by another funny man, William Kent. Gershwin's masterful score included half a dozen standards. Besides "I Got Rhythm," "Sam And Delilah," and "Bidin' My Time" there were "But Not For Me," "Boy! What Love Has Done To Me!," and "Could You Use Me?" From the musical version of *East Is West*, which Ziegfeld dropped to do *Show Girl* (2 August 1929), Gershwin brought over "Embraceable You." *Girl Crazy* ran out the season.

ETHEL MERMAN (née Zimmerman) belted out her first notes in Astoria, New York on 16 January 1908. Her background was untheatrical, and her first paychecks were earned as a stenographer. She began singing in small nightclubs in 1928. One year later she appeared in vaudeville with Clayton, Jackson, and Durante. Freedley discovered her singing on a bill at the Brooklyn Paramount. Hers was a style in direct contrast with her real predecessor, Marilyn Miller. Miss Miller was a dancer, Miss Merman was not; Miss Miller had a dainty, fine-featured beauty, Miss Merman could be termed handsome; Miss Miller had a small voice, Miss Merman had a bigger one. In fact, it was her "big voice" which was usually mentioned as her chief asset. Actually there were a number of singers with bigger and better voices. What Miss Merman really had was impeccable diction and superb projection. In a sense she was closer to the Blanche Rings and Marie Cahills of an earlier era.

So did a revue which opened the following night. **Three's a Crowd** (15 October 1930, Selwyn) reunited the stars of *The Little Show* (Fred Allen, Clifton Webb, and Libby Holman) with its songwriters (Arthur Schwartz and Howard Dietz). Burton Lane, Vernon Duke, Phil Charig, and others interpolated their songs. Max Gordon, the producer, added a song already popular in England, "Body And Soul," with music by Johnny Green and words by Edward Heyman, Robert Sour, and Frank Eyton. This number and Schwartz and Dietz's

"Something To Remember You By" were the evening's hits. Curiously, the melody of "Something To Remember You By" was also first made public in England, where it was a fast fox-trot, "I Have No Words," in *Little Tommy Tucker*. Its tempo was slowed for the new lyrics, and Libby Holman introduced it as well as "Body And Soul." These songs helped establish the long, brooding musical line that grew so popular in the thirties. Social protest crept into the program with "Yaller," which bemoaned the plight of a mulatto, unloved by the white world. The show began with a bedroom skit in which a wife's lover hides under the bed when the husband returns unexpectedly. But the skit was halted by Fred Allen, who promised there would be nothing of that sort in the entertainment. The promise wasn't kept. In a later skit Clifton Webb was interrupted in his bath by Tamara Geva, who recognizes him only when he pulls out the plug and she peers over the rim. The show's comic high spot was an Allen monologue—written by Corey Ford—in which Allen played a Byrd-like explorer lecturing on his experiences at the pole. He suggested the nation's unemployment could be solved by shoveling away all the snow at the pole. He inadvertently reinforces his argument when he attempts to show slides. All that appears on the screen is white snow. Albertina Rasch, Broadway's leading choreographer at the time, staged the ballets. The lighting was especially innovative, discarding the use of footlights and hanging additional lights from the balcony. For his technical departures, Hassard Short received an award from General Electric.

The 1930 edition of **Lew Leslie's Blackbirds** (22 October 1930, Royale) advertised itself as "the world's funniest and fastest revue" dedicated to "Glorifying the American Negro." It was so elaborate a production that Leslie attached a program warning: "subject to change owing to magnitude of production." Exactly how American blacks were glorified by another eye-popping jungle number is debatable. "Mozambique" offered seventeen scantily dressed girls (in brightly colored wigs and sporting luxurious feather tails) stomping against a gaudy, stylized setting filled with lush tropical plants and native carvings. If some of the carvings the American girls danced in front of seemed more Micronesian than African, hadn't Lew Leslie been the producer of *The International Revue*? Perhaps he was momentarily confused. Leslie assembled a fine cast including Ethel Waters, Flournoy Miller

(appearing without Lyles), and Buck and Bubbles. The show spoofed the Broadway hit *Green Pastures*, smiling Aunt Jemima's imaginary marital troubles, and black honeymoons. Whereas the score for the 1928 version had been by whites, blacks did the songs for the new edition. Most of the music was by Eubie Blake and most of the lyrics by Andy Razaf. Blake provided a musicianly score with numbers such as "Memories Of You," "You're Lucky To Me," and "That Lindy Hop." But nothing caught fire as the tunes from the earlier edition had—though "Memories Of You" slowly developed into a standard. This song, with its span of an octave and a fifth, was written especially for Minto Cato to introduce in the show. Her unusual range allowed her to sing it with ease. Latecomers, however, may have missed it, for Miss Cato sang it at the end of the opening scene, sitting in front of a slave's cabin, wearing an 1850 dress and a bandanna. The show left after seven weeks.

Lew Fields joined the ranks of revue producers with **The Vanderbilt Revue** (5 November 1930, Vanderbilt). A number of the brightest young talents of the day contributed material: Dorothy Fields, Jimmy McHugh, E. Y. Harburg, and Kenyon Nicholson. Husky-voiced Lulu McConnell was in charge of most of the evening's comedy. She portrayed a dowager searching in not so quiet desperation for a gigolo, a meddling tourist at customs, and a gabber who ruins "A Quiet Game of Bridge." The morning-after notices were not kind, and the public stayed away. Fields closed the show at the end of its second week. Ruefully concluding he no longer understood changing tastes, Fields announced he was retiring. Unlike so many Broadway figures, he was true to his word. One more theatrical giant was gone from the scene.

The Vanderbilt Revue's thirteen performances were five more than an operetta entitled **The Well of Romance** (7 November 1930, Craig) received. The book for the operetta was by the witty Preston Sturges, flush with the profits from his *Strictly Dishonorable*. Reading the story or the character names one wonders if Sturges wasn't having a private joke—at his own expense, since he obviously never collected royalties. The Princess of Magnesia is ordered to marry the Baron von Sprudelwasser (Max Figman), though everyone knows he is something of a villain. The Princess is told to drink from a well whose waters induce undying love. She drinks, but so does a poet who is there at the same moment.

They fall helplessly in love, and only when the poet turns out to be a king is there a happy ending. Norma Terris and Howard Marsh, the Magnolia and Ravenal of *Show Boat*, were the Princess and the poet, while Lina Abarbanell had a secondary role. The music was by H. Maurice Jacquet.

Ten days later the Shuberts brought in **Hello, Paris** (15 November 1930, Shubert), a loosely plotted musical comedy based on Homer Cray's novel *They Had to See Paris*. Filled as it was with specialties, it had something of the flavor of an old Shubert revue. One erstwhile star of the Shuberts' own Winter Garden revues, Chic Sale, played the lead. Sale was Pike Peters, an Oklahoman, newly rich on oil, who takes his family on the grand tour. Whenever an excuse offered itself, Sale went into a cracker-barrel monologue about guzzling, tobacco-chewing, or seasickness. More than one critic felt Sale had long since lost his audience appeal. Brooks Atkinson in the *Times* speculated that Sale's problem was his lack of real perception or depth. All his characterizations were "external portraits" relying more on costume (such as steel-rimmed glasses) and makeup than on any profound insights. Sale wasn't helped by Edgar Smith's adaptation or Russell Tarbox and Michael Cleary's score, both commonplace. *Hello, Paris* said good-bye after thirty-three showings.

Two nights later Billy Rose, a songwriter turned producer, offered **Sweet and Low** (17 November 1930, 46th St.). The cast included George Jessel, James Barton, Arthur Treacher, and Rose's wife, Fanny Brice. Miss Brice and Jessel were featured in the evening's best skit, "Strictly Unbearable," a spoof of the preceding season's *Strictly Dishonorable*. Some of the songs were at a level to make even Earl Carroll wince: "When A Pansy Was A Flower," "Ten Minutes In Bed." But Rose was co-lyricist on two clean, melodic Harry Warren numbers that have survived. With Ira Gershwin he wrote "Cheerful Little Earful," and with Mort Dixon he provided rhymes for "Would You Like To Take A Walk?" Rose also collaborated with Charlotte Kent to put words to Louis Alter's "Overnight." Two songs kidded the growing Latin vogue. Both were listed slyly under "Customary Spanish Number." *Sweet and Low* played 184 performances.

Smiles (18 November 1930, Ziegfeld) ran just half as long. But on paper it was the sort of show that should have been a smash. It had a book by William Anthony McGuire from a story suggested by Noël Coward. It had a Vincent Youmans score. The stars were Marilyn Miller and Fred and Adele Astaire. Ziegfeld produced it with magnificent Joseph Urban settings that depicted a 1918 French Village and 1930 Paris and New York. (Critics were beginning to take Urban for granted. Only the Brooklyn *Eagle* gave his sets more than passing notice.) The story told of a French waif adopted by three American doughboys during the war and afterwards brought to America. She grows up to be an attractive young lady, joins the Salvation Army, flirts with high society, and finally decides to marry one of the soldiers who adopted her. Book trouble developed early. Perhaps Coward had given the plot to someone else to develop because he foresaw the difficulties of a successful dramatization. Worse, McGuire was becoming an alcoholic. His drinking and arguments became insufferable to Ziegfeld, who replaced him with a battery of writers, including Ring Lardner, though McGuire retained sole public credit. There were excellent scenes. The Astaires as society's Bob and Dot Hastings had fun trying to mix a complicated cocktail for a party at their Southampton home. Fred Astaire brought down the house with his dancing to Youmans's "Say, Young Man Of Manhattan." Tapping away dressed in top hat, white tie, and tails, he shot down a long line of similarly dressed chorus boys with his walking stick. But the succession of scenes never created a satisfactory theatrical tension. Youmans's score was solidly crafted. Still, the one Youmans classic to come from *Smiles*, "Time On My Hands," didn't become popular until long after the show closed. Like so many of the best of the early sophisticated melodies from the era, it received its first real attention in England. In the show it was sung by the heroine and Dick (Paul Gregory), one of the young men who adopt her.

On the other hand, the brittle, bitter sophistication of **The New Yorkers** (8 December 1930, Broadway) had an immediate appeal. Like Morrie Ryskind the year before, Herbert Fields softened the harshness of his attitudes a bit by making his whole tale a dream in which Alice Wentworth falls in love with the murderous bootlegger, Al Spanish. Miss Wentworth is from Park Avenue, where, in the show's most famous line, "bad women walk good dogs." The Avenue is an altogether unpleasant place. Alice's father, Dr. Wentworth, is not above flaunting his mistress, Lola McGee, in front of his wife.

But then, Mrs. Wentworth makes no bones about her gigolo. Together this crowd heads for Miami, where Al finally runs afoul of the law, not for his illegal booze or his numerous killings, but for parking too close to a fire hydrant. The show was superbly cast. Hope Williams was Alice, Charles King was Al, Ann Pennington was Lola, Richard Carle was Dr. Wentworth, and Marie Cahill was Mrs. Wentworth. For Carle and Miss Cahill the evening marked their Broadway farewells. Jimmy Durante and Fred Waring and his Pennsylvanians were also prominent. Durante, as another gangster, had a hilarious first-act finale, singing one of his own songs, "Wood," and cluttering up the stage with every conceivable wood product. Apart from Durante's material and a few of Waring's songs, the score was by Cole Porter. His best song of the evening wasn't heard for years on radio, because his words to "Love For Sale" were considered a little too wicked for general broadcasting. It was sung in the show by a minor figure, May (Kathryn Crawford), assisted by "The Three Girl Friends." More publicly witty Porter material was heard in songs such as "The Great Indoors," sung by another girl relatively unimportant to the main plot, Mona Low (Frances Williams), and the ensemble. "Let's Fly Away" (sung by Mona and Al) has since become a standard, while "I Happen To Like New York," sung by a comic hood, Mildew (Oscar Ragland), remains almost the epitome of songs praising Manhattan. At $5.50 top in the huge Broadway Theatre, *The New Yorkers* should have been a goldmine. But three days after the show opened the Bank of the United States closed and we were in the depths of the Depression. Price cuts and salary cuts were to no avail. The show closed after twenty weeks of a forced, unprofitable run.

The second revival of *Babes in Toyland* in two years played a month during the Christmas season. The Shuberts took the occasion to announce their hope that this or some other children's favorite would be mounted every year thereafter as the theatre's holiday gift to the youngsters.

Arthur Hammerstein's bad luck pursued him and the losses from his production of **Ballyhoo** (22 December 1930, Hammerstein) drove him to bankruptcy and cost him his beloved theatre. The show was a vehicle for W. C. Fields, who as Q. Q. Quale promotes a "bunion derby" to help unemployed actors get from New York to Hollywood. In Arizona he runs into his inevitable troubles with the law. He flimflams his way out of his difficulties and manages to get his crew to the Colossal Studios in California. After a grand entrance riding a steam calliope, Fields juggled cigar boxes (Cook had merely juggled cigarettes earlier in the season), played a big bass viol (patting it affectionately to make it respond), and lost his temper trying to repair a miniature car, much as he had years before repairing his Ford. Fields's opportunistic morality came to the fore when he changed his mind about robbing a man he discovers is armed—"A thing like that wouldn't be honest." When Hammerstein failed, Fields attempted unsuccessfully to run the show as a cooperative venture with the others in the cast. Unfortunately the book was lame, and Louis Alter's score (part of which had lyrics by Oscar Hammerstein) had nothing to match his "Overnight" from *Sweet and Low*. Fields took Q. Q. Quale's hint and went west, never to return to Broadway.

The year's last show was a German importation, **Meet My Sister** (30 December 1930, Shubert)—another operetta about a noble lady who stoops to conquer. Thanks to Benatsky's gay music and the cavorting of Walter Slezak, the Shubert production ran twenty-one weeks.

January 1931 saw only one new musical presented. Good times or bad, college musicals retained their vogue. Even a mediocre one like **You Said It** (19 January 1931, 46th St.) offered enough fun to run twenty-one weeks. Not centering on football, as most college musicals had, Jack Yellen and Sid Silvers's libretto recounted how ambitious, immoral Pinkie Pincus (Lou Holtz) spends his freshman year organizing a series of rackets at Kenton College. Everything from the laundry to the commissary comes under his control. But Pinkie, being a musical comedy hero, has a heart of gold. When pretty Helen Holloway (Mary Lawlor), the dean's daughter, tries her hand at a little harmless bootlegging, Pinkie steals the evidence which could wreck her budding romance. If Holtz was overage for his part, his followers didn't care. Holtz's dialect bits and cocky comedy appealed to a large number of New York theatergoers. They seemed particularly taken with his Jewish burlesque of a "la-de-dah" Englishman. *You Said It* allowed theatregoers to hear Harold Arlen's first full score.

Broadway was not overwhelmed by this first effort. The most impressive number in *You Said It*, one that Alec Wilder gives special attention to in reviewing Arlen's work, was "Sweet And Hot," "a truly swinging song." It was sung in the show with a fetching Slavic accent by Lyda Roberti.

Ever since their original successes, *The Student Prince* and *Blossom Time* had been on the road. In most major American cities their visits had become (and for years remained) annual affairs. Now, with the Depression creating more and more empty theatres in New York, the Shuberts brought both works in off the road to keep Manhattan houses lit. *The Student Prince* arrived at the Majestic on 29 January and stayed five weeks. Just before it closed, *Blossom Time* returned to the Ambassador, the house where it had originally played, and chalked up an additional three and a half weeks. Neither production offered major names in the cast.

Rodgers and Hart reunited with Herbert Fields for **America's Sweetheart** (10 February 1931, Broadhurst). When Geraldine March (Harriette Lake) becomes the rage of the silent movies, she seems to lose interest in her old beau, Michael Perry (Jack Whiting). Michael continues as a struggling actor. But the talkies reveal that Geraldine has a lisp, and her star fades. At the same time, Michael's popularity skyrockets. Forgivingly, he escorts Geraldine to the premiere of his latest movie, at Grauman's Chinese Theatre. Fields's wit punctured the crassness and ignorance of much of Hollywood's top echelons. In a variation of his famous line from *The New Yorkers*, he referred to Hollywood as a place where good plays are turned into bad movies. The score was not prime Rodgers and Hart, but it was pleasant. "I've Got Five Dollars," a proposal of marriage commenting acidly on Depression conditions, was

the most sung number from the piece. A few years after *America's Sweetheart* ended its seventeen-week run, Miss Lake moved on to Hollywood, where the studio bigwigs changed her name to Ann Sothern.

Though composer Lewis Gensler had Russel Crouse, Oscar Hammerstein II, and Morrie Ryskind for librettists, he and his associates seemed unable to whip **The Gang's All Here** (18 February 1931, Imperial) into shape. Several critics suggested the musical was so loose-jointed it should have been a revue. A war between rival gangs of bootleggers in Atlantic City provided the impetus for the story. Baby Face Martini (Jack McCauley) enlists Dr. Indian Ike Kelley (Ted Healy) to help push Horace Winterbottom (Tom Howard) out of his control of the resort's rackets. But Ike has a daughter, Peggy (Ruth Tester), and Horace, a son, Hector (John Gallaudet). They fall in love, befuddling all of Baby Face's carefully laid plans. One song had the title "By Special Permission Of The Copyright Owners I Love You." Special permission was only required for three weeks.

Perhaps its authors thought a name like **The Venetian Glass Nephew** (23 February 1931, Vanderbilt) would intrigue. They were wrong. The title scared away patrons, and the show folded after one week. Terming it "a light opera" didn't help sales either. And the story based on an Elinor Wylie novel was odd, to say the least. It was a romantic fantasy, far out of date. Cardinal Bon (Dodd Mehan), wanting a nephew, persuades the magician, Chevalier de Chastelneuf (George Houston), to make him one of Venetian glass. Rosabla (Mary Silveira) falls in love with the statue and has herself turned into porcelain so she can remain with it.

On March 17 Al Jolson returned briefly from his newfound home in Hollywood to star in **The Wonder Bar**. The show was an unusual affair for Jolson, accustomed as he was to having vehicles tailored to his special talents. *Wunderbar* had been a German hit that also enjoyed a long London run. The Shuberts converted the Nora Bayes (the roof theatre atop the 44th Street) into a cabaret, while on its open stage Jolson portrayed Monsieur Al, the proprietor of a similar establishment in Paris known as The Wonder Bar. Paris was not exactly a novel place for Jolson, who had opened the Winter Garden in *La Belle Paree* (20 March 1911) singing "Paris Is A Paridise For Coons." But now Jolson played it straight, and in whiteface. He was anything but his old clownish Gus as he attempted a deal with the thieving, philandering male partner of his star dance act. Most of the original Robert Katscher score was retained, though Jolson took credit for several interpolations. But none of the numbers became Jolson classics, and there was something incongruous about the great Mammy singer crooning "Ma Mère." Even with Patsy Kelly, Arthur Treacher, Rex O'Malley, and Trini to assist, Jolson could not draw the expected crowds. The show ran less than ten weeks, after which Jolson packed his bags to return to movieland.

April saw no musicals appear; but May was sufficiently active to compensate. The first two musicals entered together on 4 May. One was a revival of *The Mikado* at the Erlanger, with the all but forgotten Frank Moulan as Ko-Ko and Howard Marsh as Nanki-Poo. A Civic Light Opera mounting, it inaugurated a series of Gilbert and Sullivan presentations. *H. M. S. Pinafore* sailed in on 18 May. Howard Marsh was again the principal tenor, and another old-timer, Fay Templeton, returned to sing a role she had done so often, Buttercup. Like *The Mikado*, *Pinafore* stayed two weeks. *The Gondoliers* and *Patience* followed, both with Marsh and Moulan, but without Miss Templeton.

Having suffered a costly failure in October with his lavish *Blackbirds*, Lew Leslie mounted a budget-conscious entertainment he christened **Rhapsody in Black** (4 May 1931, Harris). There was no chorus, and no fancy scenery. There were also no comedy numbers. It was a sort of singing vaudeville led by Ethel Waters and the Cecil Mack Choir. But the new songs the show relied on—including one by Fields and McHugh—were workaday. Better old numbers included "St. Louis Blues" and the Hebrew "Eli, Eli." Only *Rhapsody in Black*'s austere economies allowed it to continue for ten weeks.

Next came **Billy Rose's Crazy Quilt** (19 May 1931, 44th St.), using much of the material that had served *Sweet and Low* so well all season. Fanny Brice was back, of course. And she had a new "Rose" number to add to her repertory, "Rest Room Rose," by Rodgers and Hart. But the hit of the new edition was a song she sang (in top hat and tails) with her new costars, Ted Healy and Phil Baker, "I Found A Million Dollar Baby (In A Five-And-Ten Cent Store)." With Miss Brice's clowning and Baker's sassing everyone in sight, the evening provided light fun for ten weeks.

Noël Coward, S. J. Perelman, Marc Connelly, and Burton Lane were a few of the names that graced the credits of **The Third Little Show** (1 June 1931, Music Box), but it was one of its stars, Beatrice Lillie

(the other star was Ernest Truex), who was largely responsible for what success the show enjoyed. Miss Lillie, sporting a pith helmet and sitting in a rickshaw, introduced America to Coward's "Mad Dogs And Englishmen" and advised her audiences "There Are Fairies At The Bottom Of My Garden" (Rose Fyleman/Liza Lehmann). Walter O'Keefe treated patrons to Herman Hupfeld's "When Yuba Plays The Rhumba On The Tuba," and two older musical comedy favorites, Constance Carpenter and Carl Randall, sang "You Forgot Your Gloves" (Edward Eliscu/Ned Lehak). But most theatregoers forgot the melodies as soon as the evening was over. Miss Lillie's finest comic moment was her takeoff of the celebrated monologuist Rum Draper—a performer given to appearing alone in the simplest clothes on stages set only with bare draperies. Miss Lillie introduced herself and instructed her listeners, "In this little sketch I want you to imagine far too much." When the show closed after 136 performances, its producers decided to end the series.

If the season had begun disastrously, it ended gloriously when **The Band Wagon** opened on 3 June. Arthur Schwartz and Howard Dietz, who had been so vital to the success of the first *Little Show*, gave *The Band Wagon* what is probably the greatest of all revue scores. Perhaps only the 1926 *Scandals* (14 June 1926) and *This Is the Army* (4 July 1942) were so filled with brilliant melodies. Out of this single evening came the jaunty "I Love Louisa," the effervescent "New Sun In The Sky" (singing of the hope so necessary to a dismal time), the lovely "High And Low," and, most of all, the incomparable "Dancing In The Dark." This show tune, perhaps more than any other, established the longer, more thoughtful musical line of many of the thirties' best songs. The sketches were entirely by Dietz and Kaufman (who had also contributed to *The Little Show*). They had the curtain up when the audience entered—a device used earlier in the season at *The Wonder Bar*. As Dietz tells it:

> On stage the company took seats—a reflection, as if in a mirror, of the audience arriving. The ushers on stage wore costumes identical to the ushers in the aisles below ... as the lights were dimming, the company sang in strict unison "It Better Be Good."

Dietz's lyrics, though never on a par with Porter's or Wodehouse's best, were often witty and colloquial. In the show's most lauded sketch, "The Pride of the Claghornes," an aristocratic old southern family's pride is shattered and the marriage of the daughter jeopardized when it is discovered she is still a virgin. The staging was remarkably inventive. "Dancing In The Dark" was sung by John Barker as Tilly Losch danced on raked, mirrored floors with constantly changing lighting. Revolving stages were used imaginatively by the show's designer, Albert Johnson. As a beggar at a stage door dreams of the beautiful ballerina (Miss Losch) the stage swings around, and he performs with her in the ballet. The dance done, he is back at his lonely post outside the house. A Parisian park revolved as children played "Hoops." And in the evening's most memorable set, a Bavarian merry-go-round turned as the cast sang "I Love Louisa." Hassard Short was responsible for much of the physical brilliance of the show, and Albertina Rasch for its stunning dances. The Astaires, Tilly Losch, Helen Broderick, and Frank Morgan starred. The variety of roles each star took is a testimony to their versatility and professionalism. Fred Astaire, for example, was a French brat in "Hoops," the beggar, the suitor of Miss Claghorne, an accordion player and dancer in "Sweet Music (To Worry The Wolf Away)," and a dapper man-about-town for "New Sun In The Sky." Welcomed by virtually all the critics, the show ran 260 performances at the New Amsterdam—good for the times. But when the show closed, Adele Astaire's career ended with it. Leaving to marry, she also left her brother to perform alone.

1931–1932

Times were dismal; it was the nadir of the Depression. On Broadway many of the best talents were preparing to leave for Hollywood, if they were not already there. For those who remained, especially the great old-line producers, enforced idleness or bankruptcy loomed. Producers who had lived from production to production, men like Florenz Ziegfeld, Charles Dillingham, and Arthur Hammerstein, were the hardest hit. But even the massive Shubert empire was tottering. Nonetheless, for the first time in several years the drop in the number of new musicals was slight. If the new theatrical session lacked the overall quality of the last few seasons, it nonetheless witnessed the presentation of several musical gems.

The first lyric offering to arrive was *The Pirates of Penzance*. The production was the latest in a series the Civic Light Opera had begun the preceding

season. *Iolanthe, Ruddigore,* and returns of *Pinafore* and *The Mikado* followed. When attendance waned, the company mounted a revival of *The Merry Widow,* bringing back Donald Brian to recreate the role of Danilo that had made him famous a quarter of a century before. An all-star staging of *The Chocolate Soldier* was offered next with Vivienne Segal, Charles Purcell, and Detmar Poppen in the leads. Growing more daring, the troupe presented Jones's *The Geisha* and Planquette's *The Chimes of Normandy.* Before the company left early in 1932 *Naughty Marietta, The Firefly,* and *Robin Hood,* among others, joined the repertory.

The season really opened on 1 July, as seasons, regularly had a decade or so back, with **The Ziegfeld Follies.** The 1931 edition would be the last Ziegfeld himself would ever mount. The show was not at the New Amsterdam, busy with the more up-to-date *The Band Wagon* and soon to be given over to films, but at Ziegfeld's own, equally magnificent house. Like the early *Follies,* it used a theme to tie its sketches together: this time a weighing of the old and the new. Gene Buck and Dave Stamper returned to the Ziegfeld fold and created "Broadway Reverie," a threnody insisting, "It's not the place it used to be." Ruth Etting impersonated Nora Bayes and revived "Shine On, Harvest Moon," the first hit to come from a *Follies.* Harry Richman and Jack Pearl mimicked past greats who had never played the *Follies* and sang songs no *Follies* ever heard. Richman was Al Jolson crooning "You Made Me Love You," while Pearl did Sam Bernard's "Who Paid The Rent For Mrs. Rip Van Winkle When Rip Van Winkle Was Away?" (a song Jolson also sang). Old, elegant Rector's was compared with a speakeasy then on its site. Returning to the world of 1931 Ruth Etting sang a sleazy cabaret girl's "Cigarettes, Cigars!"; Richman offered the expected call for optimism with "Help Yourself To Happiness" (both by the show's principal songwriters, Harry Revel and Mack Gordon), while Helen Morgan bemoaned the plight of Noël Coward's "Half-Caste Woman." "Do The New York" had everyone join in the requisite high-stepping. Ziegfeld's girls were as beautiful as ever, and Joseph Urban's sets dramatic and gorgeous. For a South Sea number Ziegfeld imported a big-breasted dancer he had seen in Robert Flaherty's film *Tabu.* The girl, called only Reri, could not really sing or dance and soon left the show. A lavish jungle scene employed large papier-mâché elephants, while another spectacular set celebrated the opening of the Empire State Building as the world's tallest structure. The *Follies* ran only 165 performances, but the Depression was not solely responsible for the relatively short run. Elaborate annuals had begun to seem dated even in the affluent heyday of the twenties. A faster pace of life, as reflected in other entertainments, and an undeniable, if not general, rising of intellectual standards in musicals foredoomed them.

Heywood Broun, the celebrated newspaper columnist, produced a revue called **Shoot the Works** (21 July 1931, Cohan) to make employment for over 100 of his actor friends. Its list of credits was as imposing as Ziegfeld's list, including as it did Broun, Dorothy Parker, Nunnally Johnson, Dorothy Fields, Ira Gershwin, and Irving Berlin. But in contrast to the expensive *Follies* the show was brought in on a shoestring budget of $6,000. There were no big names in the cast, though George Murphy and Imogene Coca would go on to stardom. The *Times* suggested the work's artlessness was its saving grace. It began on a bare stage with a chorus being "selected" and ended with Broun telling the critics what to write in their reviews; he even supplied the headline, "A Swell Show." In between the acts ran from Al Norman's fancy tap-dancing "in the Hal Le Roy manner" to Harry Hirschfield's cartooning. But the material proved indifferent, and in the summer heat the show never got off the ground.

The 278-performance run of the latest **Earl Carroll Vanities** (27 August 1931, Earl Carroll) far outshone the great Ziegfeld's *Follies*. Part of the show's attraction was the new, art deco Earl Carroll Theatre—an advanced, streamlined house seating 3,000 spectators. Instead of a box office cubbyhole, the lobby boasted a modern counter manned by tuxedoed ticket-vendors; free checking and free soft drinks were available. Regretfully, it soon became evident the house was too large for live entertainment, and within a few years the premises became a Woolworth's. The 1931 *Vanities* featured vaudeville's Will Mahoney, tough William Demarest, and Lillian Roth. The best numbers in the show had been heard elsewhere before. They included Ravel's "Bolero" (which provided the background for another mindless parade of beautiful, befeathered girls) and Ray Noble's "Good Night, Sweetheart." A major production number was "Parasols on Parade" with Carroll's lovely showgirls appearing as Parasol Rose et Noir, Parasol sans Gene, and even Parasol Pistachio. Most critics were unkind, especially toward the evening's limp comedy. Considering the poor quality of the material, the hard times, and the critical drubbing,

the *Vanities*'s run was remarkable. Carroll clearly had a loyal following.

For Oscar Hammerstein II, its co-librettist, the season's first new book musical, **Free for All** (8 September 1931, Manhattan), must have been a doubly painful experience. The show was a fifteen-performance dud and played at a theatre until recently the Hammerstein. Schwab and Hammerstein's story was a little like *Girl Crazy* (14 October 1930). When Steve Potter (Jack Haley), a rich man's son, gets mixed up in radical politics, his father sends him out west to run the family copper mine and stay out of trouble. Love and success follow in a place fittingly called "New Leaf Corners." The score was by Richard Whiting, another creative Tin Pan Alley figure who never seemed able to do his best work for the theatre. Benny Goodman's band (with Glenn Miller one of its musicians) played the melodies. The show, like several of the season's musicals, employed no chorus, though it is moot whether fiscal or esthetic considerations prevailed in this case.

The Thomashefskys, well respected in the fading Yiddish theatre, tried their luck with a Yiddish-style musical comedy presented in the best Broadway vernacular. **The Singing Rabbi** (10 September 1931, Selwyn) told of the rise of the Sheindels. Three sons have left their widowed mother in Galicia and made their way to separate parts of the world. When one son, Gidalia (Boris Thomashefsky), makes good in New York he persuades his mother and two brothers to emigrate. The show had run for many months downtown in the Yiddish theatre district and had apparently exhausted its potential audience. It failed to run a full week in its new version. When it closed at the Selwyn, the house went over to motion pictures, adding to the disheartening change on 42nd Street. Between new Minsky burlesques and grind movies the street was patently finished as the heart of the legitimate theatre.

A third of the old annuals made an appearance when George **White's Scandals** opened on 14 September at one of the remaining 42nd Street houses, White's favored Apollo. One sign of the changing times was that Joseph Urban did the sets for this *Follies* rival. As he had for Ziegfeld's production, he designed a set to welcome the Empire State Building. As they had the preceding season, the critics gave Urban far less attention than they once had showered on him. While the Brooklyn *Eagle* acknowledged Urban had conceived "pretty sets here and there," most critics, like Gilbert Gabriel in the *American*, were content to note in passing "the scenery is Urban's." Willie and Eugene Howard were in charge of the laughs. Together they did their famous "Pay the Two Dollars" skit, in which a lawyer's insistence his client not pay a two-dollar fine leads to higher and higher courts and bigger and bigger penalties. The diminutive Willie also appeared as a fearsome big-game hunter. Having announced he bagged a lion, he then confessed, "I bagged him and I bagged him—but he wouldn't go away." The songs were danced by Ray Bolger and sung by Rudy Vallee, Everett Marshall, and Ethel Merman. With Buddy DeSylva in Hollywood, White's once great trio of songwriters was reduced to the twosome of Lew Brown for the lyrics and Ray Henderson for the music. But their excellent showing suggested DeSylva was not missed. Miss Merman sang the hit of the evening, another bit of Depression philosophy, "Life Is Just A Bowl Of Cherries." Marshall in blackface led the first act finale. It was not quite a typical blackface number. There was growing concern, especially among the liberal elements who comprised so large a part of show business, about how blacks were being treated in America. It had been hinted at earlier in numbers such as "Yaller" in *Three's a Crowd* (15 October 1930). Brown was explicit. In "That's Why Darkies Were Born" he said they were the folk who "had to laugh at trouble" and "be contented with any old thing." Marshall also sang one of the best numbers, "The Thrill Is Gone," while Vallee sang two popular tunes, "This Is The Mrs." and (with Merman) "My Song." Easily the best of the better-known revues to come out during the season, the show was rewarded with a six-month run.

An all-black revue that opened the next night was another one-week flop. Its title, **Fast and Furious** (15 September 1931, New Yorker), was not only inaccurate, it was somewhat out of date. As Brooks Atkinson noted in the *Times*, "grinning toothsome exuberance" was no longer enough to save a show. To its credit the revue tried to move away from the stereotyped dancing black shows had offered ever since *Shuffle Along*. Cuban and Oriental dances found niches alongside a number honoring a new dance craze, "Rhumbatism." In its comedy the entertainment was less original, falling back on a courtroom scene and on a boxing match between two girls not unlike that recently performed in *Messin' Around* (22 April 1929). Most of the music was by Harry Revel, who had contributed the lion's share of the *Follies* score, but J. Rosamond Johnson and Joe Jordan were also credited with tunes.

One of 42nd Street's remaining theatres, the Liberty, housed another black show, **Singin' the Blues** (16 September 1931, Liberty). This was "a negro-melodrama" by the sometime librettist Jack McGowan. It did not have a score as such, but Eubie Blake led an orchestra that played popular tunes of the day and "incidental" songs by Dorothy Fields and Jimmy McHugh. The busy musical comedy choreographer Sammy Lee staged a number of dances. Negro specialty acts larded the story.

Nikki (29 September 1931, Martin Beck) was based on a character created by John Monk Saunders, who worked her way from his short stories into a novel and then a film. In this musical version Nikki (Fay Wray) is the friend of three young members of the lost generation, all once aviators and all now at loose ends in Paris. Their boozy, brawling existence kills all of them before the final curtain in Lisbon, leaving Nikki to go off with a newfound friend. The show was not tightly knit, and a number of specialty acts (ballroom dancers, tap dancers) were easily inserted. But the story was all wrong for the time, and Phil Charig's flat score, his last for some time, offered no inducement to attend. The show collapsed after five weeks.

The Shuberts' plodding Harold Atteridge adapted Frances Goodrich and Albert Hackett's *Up Pops the Devil* for musical purposes. The show was called **Everybody's Welcome** (13 October 1931, Shubert) and had music by Sammy Fain. Its story told of a young unmarried couple in Greenwich Village. Steve (Oscar Shaw) is a writer whose creative inspiration has run dry, so Ann (Harriette Lake) volunteers to find a job while Steve does the housework. Steve rebels until he discovers Ann is going to have a baby. Besides Shaw and Miss Lake, the cast featured Frances Williams and Ann Pennington. Miss Williams sang what eventually became a "standard" song, while Miss Pennington danced with her customary abandon and attempted some clowning. At the end of the story the cast all went to the Roxy (called Proxy's in the show) for a spectacular production number that twitted the stage and screen offerings at the film palace. Jimmy Dorsey led the pit band. One of the tunes they played asked the question, "Is Rhythm Necessary?" Fain remained one of several talented composers who never seemed to do things right on Broadway; his great successes all came after he left for Hollywood. But one Herman Hupfeld interpolation is still popular, though its real vogue came from the movie *Casablanca* years later: "As Time Goes By." Heavily discounted tickets permitted *Everybody's Welcome* to chalk up 139 performances.

The disappointing run of *Sweet Adeline* probably nipped in the bud the development of a new style of American musical play. When Jerome Kern returned to New York, it was not with Oscar Hammerstein II but in collaboration with Otto Harbach. They called **The Cat and the Fiddle** (15 October 1931, Globe) "a musical love story." Actually it was closer in style and flavor to European operettas of the day, but with its musical lines toned down to American tastes. They were apparently Kern's real tastes, too, for he had always pursued something of a lone course, composing in an unusual, unique blend of American and Continental sounds. Kern's score, filled with memorable melodies, was exceptionally rich and complete. It had recitatives and sung continuities; even regular numbers were led into with special care. The Continental aspects of Kern's writing were underscored by the play's Brussels setting. His modernity was reinforced by making the setting contemporary. A young composer named Victor Florescu (George Metaxa) has written an opera called "The Passionate Pilgrim." Victor is admired by another young composer, an American girl, Shirley Sheridan (Bettina Hall). But any love for her on his part is cooled when he suspects she would interpolate her material into his work. Happily, it is all a mistake. His brother had heard Shirley, who lives next door to Victor (shades of *The Only Girl*), playing one of her own tunes and thought the melody attractive. As it turns out, Victor has more trouble with the opera's prima donna, Odette (Odette Myrtil), than with Shirley. By the end of the evening Victor and Shirley are indeed deeply in love. There was again virtually no chorus, and the musical background of the play implies this was an economy measure rationalized. But the small cast was select. Interestingly, the musician hero was given none of the unforgettable melodies that helped the show to its 395-performance run. "The Night Was Made For Love" and "She Didn't Say 'Yes'" were introduced by a strolling guitarist, Pompineau (George Meader), promoting the romance. Shirley joined Pompineau in the latter—both songs follow directly after the opening—and late in the last act Shirley alone sang the tearful "Try To Forget."

Although many aisle-sitters remained kindly disposed toward tiny, moon-faced, rubicund Nikita Balieff, they clearly had tired of the numerous editions of his long-touring revue. So his latest edition, **New Chauve Souris** (21 October 1931, Ambassador), which included a long ballet based on a Pushkin story as well as a spoof of opéra bouffe, was regretfully chastised and soon disappeared.

If two weeks back Kern again braved new territory, the usually daring Hammerstein reverted to well-covered ground when he supplied the book and lyrics for a new Sigmund Romberg operetta, **East Wind** (27 October 1931, Manhattan). About the only original thing in the show was its specific locale, Saigon. But its love affair between a French girl and a French boy could just as readily have been set in Paris. Claudette Fortier (Charlotte Lansing) marries Rene Beauvais (William Williams), who quickly deserts her. But Rene's brother, Paul (J. Harold Murray), has long loved Claudette. He seeks her out and marries her. Like Rudolf Friml's music for *Luana* (with its similar setting), there was a sad lifelessness to Romberg's songs. While panning the musical itself, a number of critics found kind words for the production, especially Donald Oenslager's "racy, realistic sets," which the *Times* termed "Indo-Chinese baroque." The best of these scenes was for the first-act finale—a Saigon waterfront that exploded into a mass of lush tropical colors when a flower boat arrived. Charles LeMaire's costumes ran heavily to gold. A Hawaiian dancer, Ahi, earned loud applause for a hula she performed, even though she was supposed to represent a Chinese girl in Southeast Asia. When the show folded after twenty-three performances, its producers, Frank Mandel and Laurence Schwab, dissolved their partnership. Together they had brought to New York some of the twenties' best musicals, among them *The Desert Song, The New Moon, Queen High,* and *Good News.*

Another Ed Wynn carnival, **The Laugh Parade** (2 November 1931, Imperial), brought the perfect fool back to Broadway on 2 November with a grab bag of sketches and songs. The show had almost been a disaster. Its tryout had gone so badly and its advance sale had been so small that Wynn gave away seats on the first few nights to dispel the contagious gloom of an empty house. Happily he and his material were so good that the show quickly caught on. He had his customary zany inventions, including a miniature bed to catch bedbugs and a hat with a removable brim that allowed its wearer to tip it in the winter without risking a cold. Juggling with several balls at one time, he came up with one of his most often quoted lines when he instructed the orchestra leader to "play something in a jugular vein." Harry

Warren followed up on his successful songs for *Sweet and Low* (17 November 1930) and *Crazy Quilt* (19 May 1931) with two solid hits, "Ooh, That Kiss" and "You're My Everything." The growing strain on Broadway as a result of competition from newer sources of entertainment was poignantly manifested during the run of *The Laugh Parade*. So that Wynn could broadcast his weekly Texaco *Fire Chief* series, Tuesday night performances were omitted.

Here Goes the Bride (3 November 1931, 46th St.) was produced by the well-known cartoonist and theatrical dabbler Peter Arno. He also wrote the book, which, up to a point, reflected the beginnings of a more universal acceptance of divorce. June and Tony Doyle (Victoria—later Vicki—Cummings and Paul Frawley) have fallen out of love. They take their new loves with them to Reno while they get a divorce. They also take two riotous valets. The valets were played by Clark and McCullough. Actually Clark was Doyle's valet, B. Hives, and McCullough was the valet's valet. But neither the comics nor composers, Johnny Green and Richard Myers, could inject the necessary vitality into the piece. Only Arno's imaginative sets won universal praise. He brought some of his graphic humor and style over from *The New Yorker* to create with "fetching craziness" (Brooklyn *Eagle*) "grotesque and nervous rooms" (the *Times*) at once "bold and witty" (the *American*). Arno's show curtain was a blown-up scandal sheet that actually served to set the exposition in motion. But such delicious sets couldn't save the show. One week, and it was gone.

An oddity had a slightly longer run—eighteen playings. **Jack and the Beanstalk** (21 December 1931, 44th St.) was "a fairy opera for the childlike" that was encouraged to move to Broadway following several performances at Juilliard. Pooh-poohed as "extraordinarily dull," it did at least give Manhattan theatregoers an early opportunity to see a soon-to-be leading man, Ray Middleton—here cavorting as the wicked Giant.

The adventures of *Shuffle Along*'s Steve Jenkins and Sam Peck were continued in **Sugar Hill** (25 December 1931, Forrest). This time the boys got themselves involved in Harlem bootlegging. The show's plot twists were ominous and ugly. This, plus the use of a single set depicting the front of a Harlem brownstone, led several critics to view it as a musicalized, black *Street Scene*. Gyp Penrose (Broadway Jones), a gangster attempting to kill a rival, kills a little girl instead. Peck, playing detective, sets up his girlfriend, Cleo (Edna Moten), as a decoy and lures Gyp into a trap. In a further similarity to *Street Scene* a number of minor plots were woven into the main story. But there was no consistency of tone, and musical comedy trappings were legion. Penrose, for example, led the chorus in "Hot Harlem." Flournoy Miller and Aubrey Lyles again played their beloved comic pair, but they did not write most of their material; nor did they have anyone of the caliber of Eubie Blake or Fats Waller do the score. Though one of the songs was honest enough to express a sentiment dear to all the Jenkinses and Pecks in Harlem, "I Don't Want Any Labor In My Job," it said little to the few theatregoers who sat through the eleven performances and then shuffled on out.

But the following evening, 26 December 1931, witnessed the arrival at the Music Box of one of the greatest of all American musicals: **Of Thee I Sing**. The title seems an obvious one considering the plot, but there may have been something in the Zeitgeist of the time, now forgotten, that prompted it. *Here Goes the Bride* also used "My Country, 'Tis Of Thee" as a source for the title of what it hoped would be its song hit, "My Sweetheart, 'Tis Of Thee." The new show took a barbed, witty look at American political institutions. It was never malicious and never stooped to personal attacks, though some critics felt the principal character was made to look and sound a little like New York's troubled Mayor Walker. If so, it was probably a trick of director George S. Kaufman, for co-librettist George S. Kaufman was above such pettiness.

The show opens with a campaign parade. Signs the marchers carry display an un-American political candor: "Turn the Reformers Out," "Vote for Prosperity and See What You Get," "A Vote for Wintergreen Is a Vote for Wintergreen." As they parade they chant "Wintergreen For President." The scene changes to a hotel bedroom where party bigwigs are assembled. Two things are bothering them: their campaign is not proceeding as smoothly as they hoped, and not one of them can recall the name of the vice-presidential candidate. There's a minor added irritant. A man named Throttle-something-or-other keeps phoning the room. The distinguished newspaper tycoon, Matthew Arnold Fulton (Dudley Clements), tries to reassure his associates, "The people of this country demand John P. Wintergreen for President, and they're going to get him whether they like it or not." The caller appears, shyly announcing he is Alexander Throttlebottom (Victor Moore), their candidate for the vice-presidency. (Precisely who wrote what in the libretto will never be known. But it is likely Morrie Ryskind gave the principal characters their names. A major figure in *The Gang's All Here* [18 February 1931], on which he collaborated in the preceding season, was Horace Winterbottom.) The politicians all welcome their new candidate, though they are still not certain they can remember his name. But Throttlebottom comes bringing bad news. He wants to resign; the thought that her son is Vice President might prove too shameful for his mother to bear. He is talked out of quitting just as Wintergreen (William Gaxton) arrives. Wintergreen also can't remember who his running mate is, but he's more concerned with ominous reports from the grass roots. These reports all agree Wintergreen needs an issue. Fulton asks a chambermaid who happens into the room what she cares about most. When she replies that apart from money it's love, the committee has its platform. Wintergreen will run on love! To strengthen his chances the party will hold a beauty contest in Atlantic City to select a Mrs. Wintergreen for the President to love. At the seashore the contestants sing of their import to the nation, explaining one of them will be "Mrs. Prexy" (if she's "sexy"). The photographers become the girls' allies, asserting the girls have nothing to worry about, even if they lose, "Because, Because, Because… I could fall for you myself." To his colleagues' dismay, Wintergreen is not so ready to fall. He confides to Mary Turner (Lois Moran), who is acting as secretary for the contest, his fears that when he leaves the White House he'll discover his bride can't even cook. Mary suggests any girl can learn to cook. She adds she can "bake the best darned corn muffins you ever ate"— corn muffins that have no corn in them. Wintergreen is impressed. He's especially fond of corn muffins. The judges announce their decision. The winner is a loquacious southern belle, Diana Devereaux (Grace Brinkley). But Wintergreen demurs. He has decided he will marry Mary, and her muffins. Miss Devereaux stalks off demanding justice, while Mary and Wintergreen head for New York. Outside Madison Square Garden the excitement mounts, and the youngsters in the crowd agree, "Love Is Sweeping The Country." Inside the Garden speeches are interrupted by commercial messages on the loudspeaker. In the turmoil, a still unrecognized Throttlebottom barely misses being ejected from the hall. As election night begins returns are flashed on a screen. The photographs, interspersed with unrelated pictures and items, show that Wintergreen voted at least twice and that he won in Landslide, Nebraska, by 12,538 to 1 and lost in Rome, Italy, with 0 votes to Mussolini's 828,638. Wintergreen appears, thrilling the crowd by singing his campaign song, "Of Thee I Sing." But Diana arrives at the inauguration, halting the proceedings with her demand for a fair deal. For the moment she is unsuccessful. The scene switches to the White House, where a guided tour is passing through. One of the tourists is Alexander Throttlebottom. The White House guide can't tell him who the Vice President is or where the Vice President lives, but thumbing through his guides' manual he learns the Vice President is supposed to preside over the Senate. Throttlebottom decides that's better than nothing and rushes to the Capitol. The President and Mrs. Wintergreen share the oval office, with the first lady in charge of domestic and household matters. The atmosphere is tense because a movement sympathetic to Miss Devereaux is growing around the nation. Wintergreen shrugs it off, insisting "Who Cares?" The French obviously care. They send their ambassador (Florenz Ames) to the White House to protest, since a dishonor to Miss Devereaux is a dishonor to the whole French nation. Miss Devereaux, it seems, is "the illegitimate daughter of an illegitimate son of an illegitimate nephew of Napoleon!" Talk of impeachment spreads, worrying party bosses who still can't recall the name of the Vice President. But it is this very Throttlebottom who must now preside over the impeachment. He calls the roll of the Senate, rhyming those states that will rhyme and excusing the rest. All that saves Wintergreen is the news that he will soon be a father. The Senators rejoice, "Posterity is just around the corner." The French demand the baby or war. But after the Supreme Court announces that the President's wife has had twins, a solution is found. Wintergreen points out that, according to the constitution, "When the President of The United States is unable to fulfill his duties, his obligations are assumed by—" by the Vice President, of course! Gleefully clapping his hands, Throttlebottom walks away with Miss Devereaux.

Like *The Cat and the Fiddle, Of Thee I Sing* had extended passages of rhymed recitative and continuity. The tone was naturally and fittingly different, but these recitatives further signaled an advance in the musical stage's ambitions. There is, however, a slight tendency to exaggerate the importance of this advance. Many old comic operas had long passages of rhymed dialogue set to music. But in both new musicals the passages were more frequent and more thoughtfully wrought, with more important melodic lines than in most of the older works.

For its authors—the Gershwins, Kaufman, and Ryskind—the show marked the perfecting of ideas first tried in *Strike Up the Band*. To their amazement their efforts earned them the first Pulitzer Prize ever awarded to a musical. Ironically, since the award was a literary one, George was excluded. *Of Thee I Sing* also became the first musical published as a hardback book. The show's inherent brilliance, the critical kudos, and the award all contrived to give it a run of 441 performances. Gaxton and Moore proved so excellent a team that they were called on to do several shows together afterwards. Moreover, despite the Depression, a road company toured with Oscar Shaw and Donald Meek in the Gaxton and Moore parts. By coincidence that 11 January revival of *The Gondoliers* mentioned earlier gave a number of people who were calling the Gershwins the jazz Gilbert and Sullivan a chance for comparison.

Queenie Smith opened in the first new musical of 1932, **A Little Racketeer** (18 January 1932, 44th St.), after a disastrous tryout which witnessed several changes in composers, principals, and director. But nothing helped. Miss Smith played Dixie, a street urchin who pretends to fall asleep in fashionable cars hoping their owners out of pity will give her a few dollars. When handsome young Dick Barrison (John Garrick) finds her in his car, he takes her to his apartment. Learning of her little racket and of her ambition to become a mobster, he pretends to be a society burglar. They soon fall in love, and Dixie is assured of a big car all her own. Even with a supporting cast that included Carl Randall, William Kent, and Barbara Newberry, the show could muster only forty-eight performances.

Vincent Youmans called his musical version of *Smilin' Through* **Through the Years** (28 January 1932, Manhattan). Youmans had been moving away from the staccato playfulness of his earlier songs ever since *Rainbow* (21 November 1928). With his new show he also moved away from the *Show Boat* (27 December 1927) or *Rainbow* variety of still unacceptable musical play (though "musical play" is precisely what he called *Through The Years*), leaning surprisingly toward Kern-like operetta. Several times in his last active years, Youmans seemed to follow the trails blazed by Kern. The romantic story leaped back and forth across the decades. In its forty-five-year time span and in its use of its principals in dual roles, the show recalled operettas such as *Maytime* (16 August 1917) and, coincidentally or not, was set

in the same periods. By what may have been a further coincidence, both shows had principals surnamed Wayne. In 1914 Kathleen and Kenneth announce their plans to marry. But Kathleen's guardian, John Carteret (Reginald Owen), objects. He cannot forgive Kenneth's uncle, Jeremiah Wayne, for killing John's bride-to-be, Moonyeen, forty years earlier. John's thoughts send him back to those days; in his reveries Moonyeen convinces him to let the young lovers have their way. Natalie Hall played Kathleen and Moonyeen, while Michael Bartlett was both Kenneth and Jeremiah. Two Youmans classics came out of the show, though they were not universally appreciated at first hearing: Moonyeen's "Through The Years" and John's "Drums In My Heart." By and large the critics were unkind—to some extent because of their preconceived notions of a Youmans score. Nor was there an immediate public response. As a result the production was withdrawn after two and a half weeks.

On 9 February Charles Dillingham presented Maurice Chevalier at the Fulton in a one-man show, singing popular French and American songs.

If the critics were unhappy with Youmans, they were delighted with Irving Berlin. He had been in a rut for several years and only now showed signs of coming out of it. His excellent score for **Face the Music** (17 February 1932, New Amsterdam) not only suggested his uninspired period was over but nicely illustrated a major Berlin characteristic. His songs for the show are as unlike his 1920 music as his 1920 work was from his 1910 style. More than any other major American composer, Berlin's music mirrored the age in which it was written. Much of his greatness was his remarkable ability to adapt to and excel in the prevailing styles of any period. The longer lines, subtle, plaintive chordings, and more subdued gaiety of the thirties are all evident in his *Face the Music* score. The show's hits, the glibly optimistic "Let's Have Another Cup Of Coffee" and the haunting "Soft Lights And Sweet Music," are standards, but they are exemplary period pieces as well. To many the show itself seemed a localized *Of Thee I Sing*. The fact that Sam Harris produced both and that George S. Kaufman directed the two undoubtedly served to underscore the similarities. But the cohesive intermixing of book and music so successful in *Of Thee I Sing* was missing here. Berlin's songs fit nicely into the story, yet they remained individual numbers that gained or lost nothing outside the theatre. Nor was Berlin's wit as literate or as rapierlike as Ira's. The essential warmth of both his lyrics and his melodies contrasted sharply with Moss Hart's biting satirical barbs.

MOSS HART was born in New York on 24 October 1904 and was educated in its public schools. While Hart was working for Augustus Pitou, the producer mounted the young writer's melodrama. *The Holdup Man.* But the show folded on the road. Besides his job with Pitou he worked on theatricals at Jewish resorts. His comedy *Once in a Lifetime,* put into shape for Broadway by George S. Kaufman, was an immediate hit, establishing Hart as a name to be reckoned with. The libretto for *Face the Music* was his second experience in the lyric theatre. His first, *Jonica* (7 April 1930) had been a quick failure.

In Hart's story Broadway producer Hal Reisman (Andrew Tombes) enters the Automat, where the Astors and Vanderbilts have taken to eating during the Depression (it was here in the Automat that the aristocrats in morning suits and evening gowns sang "Let's Have Another Cup Of Coffee"). Reisman comes hoping to find a backer for his new show. In walks bejeweled and befurred Mrs. Martin Van Buren Meshbesher (Mary Boland). She is "lousy with money," though her money is a little newer than that of the aristocrats around her. Her husband is a policeman, and the source of their wealth is graft. But her husband and his fellow officers will be happy to have their money laundered in a musical show. With the Meshbesher cash Reisman puts on a Ziegfeldian "Rhinestones of 1932." The show is an apparent flop. However, the police and city hall have come under investigation (as indeed Tammany and Mayor Walker had), and the boys need all the money they can get. Mrs. Meshbesher barges into the investigation astride a papier-mâché elephant that could have been left over from the last *Ziegfeld Follies.* Matters take a turn for the better after the policemen persuade Reisman to add some titillating smut to their revue. The cast of *Face the Music* was fine, although it lacked the inspired assignments of *Of Thee I Sing.* Hassard Short designed the evening, again making stunning use of mirrors, and Albertina Rasch was in charge of the choreography. *Face the*

Music was not the smash hit its quality deserved, but it ran a satisfactory 165 performances.

The Shuberts had another fiasco when they brought in a German operetta, *Hotel Stadt-Lemberg,* under the title **Marching By** (3 March 1932, 46th St.). The old warhorse Harry B. Smith was responsible for most of the adaptation, while Mack Gordon and Harry Revel interpolated a number of songs not completely in keeping with the play's period. For Smith, who in fifty active years had made himself the most prolific librettist and lyricist Broadway was ever to know, the evening represented a disheartening farewell. His days of glory, which began far back with *The Begum* (21 November 1888), were long gone; his years of retirement were to be unrewardingly few.

The ailing Florenz Ziegfeld suffered a major disappointment with a musical labeled **Hot-Cha** (8 March 1932, Ziegfeld). The creators of *Face the Music* must have had a private laugh when they discovered that the money for the show came largely from two gangsters, Waxey Gordon and Dutch Schultz, who had tried to force Ziegfeld to call it leeringly *Laid in Mexico* (Ziegfeld reluctantly retained it as a subtitle). But Lew Brown got back, in part, with a couplet that kidded the more advanced shows of the season, referring to them as "Park Avenue librettos by children of the ghettos," though Brown had been a ghetto child himself. The libretto, which Brown wrote with Ray Henderson and Mark Hellinger, was anything but Park Avenue. It was really a loosely strung-together piece designed to provide a vehicle for Bert Lahr, ignoring to some extent the fact that Ziegfeld originally conceived the evening as a showcase for Lahr's glamorous costar, Lupe Velez. Lahr played Alky Schmidt, a speakeasy waiter, who finds himself in Mexico after he flees a raid on the nightclub. A promoter picks him up and advertises him as a great bullfighter. Bullfighting loses. Lahr's hilarious mannerisms—his nervous repetition to make a point, his crossing his eyes, his nasal "gnong, gnong, gnong"—helped cover the weaknesses in the book. So did Joseph Urban's "superlatively beautiful," "shimmering" sets. The *Times* advised its readers they would especially enjoy "public squares under a vast empyrean, and for a finale... a Ziegfeld fiesta." Brown and Henderson's songs included no standouts, but "You Can Make A Bed Of Roses" (which may have sounded like a remake of their "Life Is Just A Bowl Of Cherries") had a pleasing tune with a surprising turn of musical phrase. Faced with so much stronger competition, the show was lucky to survive for fifteen weeks.

April's lone American musical was a Negro revue patently attempting to cash in on the fame of the *Blackbirds*. Critics complained that the show's dancing lacked the "traditional abandon" and that the sketches resorted to such tired war-horses as Harlem rent parties and prison skits. A wary, dollar-conscious public wasn't fooled, and **Blackberries of 1932** (4 April 1932, Liberty) beat a retreat after three weeks.

A Russian revue, **The Blue Bird** (21 April 1932, Cort), was offered by Sol Hurok. Its reception was icy, and it tallied even fewer shows than had the black revue.

One-week flops were not uncommon in the Depression. **There You Are** joined the list by opening at the Cohan 16 May and closing 21 May. It told a *Rio Rita*–like story without that beloved show's singable melodies or magnificent settings. Carolita (Ilse Marvenga) agrees to marry the cynical Governor Jose Gomez (Joseph Lertora) rather than see her true love, Lloyd Emerson (Roy Cropper), jailed as the bandit, El Diable. The real El Diable (Hyman Adler), a south-of-the-border Robin Hood, appears. He gives the governor his comeuppance and unites the lovers.

Three nights later, 19 May, Ziegfeld returned *Show Boat* (27 December 1927) to New York, bringing it into the Casino. But the Casino was not the famous old musical house. It had been demolished in 1930. The new Casino had only recently been the Earl Carroll. When Carroll's financial problems deprived him of his house, Ziegfeld grabbed it and rather cruelly obliterated every reference to Carroll in the building. Yet Ziegfeld's vindictive pleasure was short-lived. He died just two months after the opening: 22 July 1932. However, *Show Boat* was a huge success, with all the original principals except Howard Marsh and Jules Bledsoe returning. Dennis King and Paul Robeson replaced them.

Two revues finished the season. A black show, unattractively called **Yeah Man** (26 May 1932, Park Lane), managed four performances at the end of May despite notices that branded it as "uncommonly bad" and "a new low." For comedy it attempted to find humor in an insane asylum. Marcus Slayter's Sixteen Black Hurricanes danced their way from a Mississippi levee at the opening of the show to a closing scene in Harlem.

Frank Morgan, most recently of *The Band Wagon* (3 June 1931), starred in **Hey Nonny Nonny!** (6 June 1932, Shubert)—a catchphrase he used throughout his career. A good part of the material was off-color. There was a song about a "Nude Ranch" and an examination of what might happen if Minsky the girlie-burlesque king, took over the Metropolitan Opera as he had 42nd Street. The suggestive material proved no lure, apparently refuting the worldly-wise police of *Face the Music*, and the show closed quickly.

1932–1933

In a way, the death of Florenz Ziegfeld at the very beginning of the season—before the first musical offering arrived—was the most significant milestone of the theatrical year. Creative talents and responsible producers would continue to appear in the American Musical Theatre, but none would be (or ever had been before) so active for so long a time and none would ever possess Ziegfeld's expensive tastes or elegant panache. His death ended an era; he left a void that was never to be completely filled. To no small extent, commercial considerations have protected his uniqueness. In Ziegfeld's heyday the living theatre had been unchallenged and supreme. In his very last years sound movies came to offer more to please the eye than the richest Ziegfeld extravaganza could hope to match. They forced a new microphoned style of singing and therefore of song that was essentially inimical to the stage.

Successes such as the incisively satiric *Of Thee I Sing* (26 December 1931) and the romantically American *Show Boat* (27 December 1927) should have suggested to both writers and producers that the lyric stage could still create forms able to keep it reasonably competitive and alive. Instead, running scared, Broadway would not prove really venturesome (with few notable exceptions) until good times returned. Luckily, enough great talent was left in New York so that the next few seasons proffered a good deal of ongoing excellence, if on a smaller scale.

Two months elapsed before the arrival of 1932–1933's first show, **Chamberlain Brown's Scrap Book** (1 August 1932, Ambassador). Brown was a notoriously shifty theatrical agent, now trying to make work for many of his out-of-work clients. He branded his production "twenty-one acts of ace vaudeville," and, indeed, it was offered on a two-a-day basis. His players looked back nostalgically at the heyday of operetta, gave scenes from Shakespeare, and spoofed *East Lynne*, community theatre, and radio. Rejected by the critics, the bill called it a run after one week.

Next, Fred Stone and his daughter Dorothy raised the curtain on their **Smiling Faces** (30 August 1932, Shubert). The basic plot was the old one of a girl who marries one man to attain sufficient social standing to marry a second and then decides she prefers the first man. The story had been used before in *Betty* (11 December 1911), *The Duchess* (16 October 1911), and *Orange Blossoms* (19 September 1922). In *Smiling Faces* the girl was motion picture actress Peggy Post, on Long Island to make a movie. The director of the picture group is Monument Spleen, a sometimes cantankerous, sometimes elfish old man. Such a tale was even more in the real world than Stone's previous *Ripples*, with its hints of Rip Van Winkle, had been. Certainly it was not the make-believe land in which Stone had always thrived. Moreover, Stone's age and illnesses had made him less able to perform the nonsensical acrobatics his fans so adored. The show came to Broadway after a lengthy, not always successful, road tour. Fred's other daughter, Paula, had been the original Peggy and was replaced by her older sister for New York. But Gotham was even less receptive than the rest of the country. The show stayed only four weeks. It was the second failure in a row for Stone, who had known only the most tremendous success heretofore. Sensing the changing times, this once beloved comedian quietly retired from the musical stage. Mack Gordon and Harry Revel created the songs. They were the last of the many fine songwriters Stone employed; unlike the others, they failed to come up with hits.

Ballyhoo of 1932 (6 September 1932, 44th St.) had no connection with W. C. Fields's vehicle of two years before. It was produced by Norman Anthony and his associates. Anthony was the editor of the popular magazine *Ballyhoo* and meant the show to be an in-the-flesh version of its barbed pages. On stage most of the barbs were hurled by Willie and Eugene Howard and, in his first important Broadway assignment, by Bob Hope. They were assisted by Lulu McConnell and Paul Hartman. Spoofs assailed Greta Garbo (as Margreta Garbitch), revolutionaries (with Howard crying "Rewolt"), and Negro evangelists (with Willie in blackface). However, the evening's comic high point was the Howard version of the *Rigoletto* quartet with little Willie's eyes

glued on the bosom of the prima donna. Even the serious numbers by E. Y. Harburg and Lewis E. Gensler were sometimes pricked with a pin. The torchy "Thrill Me" ended when the man being sung to lit up a sign advertising Ex-Lax. For Gensler the show was the final chapter in his Broadway career, remembered today solely for "Cross Your Heart" from *Queen High* (8 September 1926). Yet, though none of his songs from this show became standards, they were included in the general critical praise for the evening. Regrettably the public response was halfhearted, and the show compiled a middling ninety-five showings.

Labor Day week usually saw the first of the September musicals, but in this troubled season it was the middle of the month before a new offering appeared. **Flying Colors** (15 September 1932, Imperial) was "the fourth generation" in the revue series that had begun with *The Little Show* (20 April 1929) and then sired *Three's a Crowd* (15 October 1930) and *The Band Wagon* (3 June 1931). A number of critics and scholars have pointed out how the series was settling into an imitative pattern, especially in its songs by Arthur Schwartz and Howard Dietz. "Alone Together" was not unlike the brooding "Dancing In The Dark," the Germanisms of "Meine Kleine Akrobat" were an extension of those in "I Love Louisa," and the requisite Depression hopefulness was doled out by the delightful "A Shine On Your Shoes" instead of "Sweet Music." This last number, sung by Monette Moore, was danced in the show by Buddy and Vilma Ebsen to Larry Adler's harmonica accompaniment. Perhaps the most original melody in the evening was "Louisiana Hayride," a joyous recreation of old Negro gospel songs with lyrics in fitting Negro dialect. Started by Clifton Webb and Tamara Geva but then sung by the whole ensemble, it served as the show's rousing first-act finale.

Dietz himself considered "Fatal Fascination" one of the better numbers. It was a song in which a man responds with spoken comments as his girl tells him of his mysterious appeal to her. His replies are actually reveries of his past life and seem directed at some inner reflections rather than his girl's remarks. Another number, "Smokin' Reefers," described the influence of marijuana in Harlem. Sketches made fun of friends and relatives seeing someone off to Europe and of an accommodating hotel catering to clients driven to suicide by the Depression. The rooms on the top floor cost more. Webb (retained from *The Little Show* and *Three's a Crowd*) and Patsy Kelly were the solicitous hotel-keepers, while Charles

Butterworth was the guest. Just as Fred Allen's riotous explorer monologue was the comic high point of *Three's a Crowd*, so Butterworth's delivery of "Harvey Woofter's Five Point Plan" was the most-praised bit of fun in *Flying Colors*. To obtain shorter working hours Harvey would allow each hour only forty minutes. "Everything would be reduced in proportion. The minute would be forty seconds, a second would go in a jiffy, and the jiffy would hardly be worth mentioning." The dollar would be strengthened by renaming it, and since so many European currencies like the Frank and the Mark are named, according to Harvey, after men, he suggests renaming the dollar the Harvey. Agnes de Mille did the original choreography, but disputes with the show's producer, Max Gordon, and its librettist, Dietz, forced her to turn over her assignment to Albertina Rasch. Webb and Tamara Geva (also from *Three's a Crowd*) were given some of the best choreography of the evening, particularly an elegant, sinuous dance for "Alone Together." They danced on a specially devised stage that slowly receded into the darkness. The stage was the creation of Norman Bel Geddes, whose "crisp, modernistic" settings were no small part of the show's critical success or of its high cost—$125,000 Depression dollars. When attendance at $4.40 top proved disappointing, the best seats were reduced to $2.20. As a result the show made only the barest profit on its 188-performance run.

A "Vaudeville revue" that had Sam Bernard II as one of its authors and producers opened under the title **Belmont Varieties** (28 September 1932, Belmont). So much was thrown together so hastily that on opening night the show played far too long. A ballet based on a Degas painting drew some kind notices, but most of the bill was minor specialty acts. For example, Lilyan Astaire (Sam Bernard's niece) impersonated Bert Lahr and Bea Lillie, and Ray Benson entertained with feats of magic. The revue closed after one week then reopened at the end of October, first as the *Cosmo Varieties* and then as the *Manhattan Varieties*. The rapid name changes were unavailing, and the show shortly disappeared.

The more famous **Earl Carroll Vanities** (27 September 1932, Broadway) was a more streamlined edition than his earlier annuals, noteworthy for the imaginative staging of young Vincente Minnelli. Besides more traditional effects—such as girls representing a garden of gardenias or a locomotive or embellishing a luminous Maypole—Minnelli had the girls in glass tubes that lit up to display a variety of color and design. The cast included Helen Broderick, Harriet Hoctor, and young Milton Berle. Berle's funniest moment came when he played a coarse gangster who finds his wife entertaining a cultured Englishman in her bedroom. Round, red-faced little Will Fyffe amused audiences with his droll Scottish monologues. The evening offered an especially fine Harold Arlen melody that went largely unnoticed by critics, who applauded such forgotten songs as "Love You Are My Inspiration" (Ted Koehler/Andre Renaud), "My Darling" (Ed Hyman/ Richard Myers), and "Along Came Love" (Charles and Henry Tobias). Arlen's "I Gotta Right To Sing The Blues," with lyrics by Ted Koehler, sung by Lillian Shade, remains popular to this day. For all its improvements—and the show was a slightly better than average edition—theatregoers indicated their indifference by staying away. The show closed after eighty-seven performances, effectively ending the series, though one tentative effort was made to revive it eight years later.

A more interesting, sadder failure was the third and last in J. P. McEvoy's **Americana** (5 October 1932, Shubert) series. Musically it introduced the song which for many became the theme of the Depression era, "Brother Can You Spare A Dime?" (E. Y. Harburg/Jay Gorney). Rex Weber, a comedian, sang the number straight. Harburg and Gorney also contributed the attractive "Five Minutes Of Spring," while Harburg and Vernon Duke combined to write a rather bitter farewell to Jimmy Walker, "Let Me Match My Private Life With Yours," using Walker's tart statement "I can match my private life with any man's" as a start. Harold Arlen, Herman Hupfeld, Johnny Mercer, and Burton Lane all supplied words or music as well. But for many the show's allure was its dancing by the Charles Weidman Dancers and the Doris Humphrey Dance Group. José Limon was in the former company. Their modern dance material included a stylized prizefight and a Shaker meeting. One oddity for a show with this title was the inclusion of Alfredo Rode's Tzigane Orchestra—playing Viennese waltzes. The comedy was weak or old hat or both. Skits made fun of movie moguls, breadline racketeers, and Walker (an easy, pathetic target at this date). Albert Carroll, long a mainstay of die *Grand Street Follies*, could find nothing more novel to do than an impersonation of Lynn Fontanne, a great actress he had mimicked often before. But modern dance was apparently either too somber or too advanced for Broadway's pleasure-seekers and *Americana*'s comedy too lame. The show survived less than ten weeks.

Tell Her the Truth (28 October 1932, Cort) was the second attempt in five years to convert the 1916 hit *Nothing but the Truth* into a successful musical. It was less skillful and less enduring than *Yes, Yes, Yvette* (3 October 1927), managing to run only a week and a half, though the show had been a hit in England.

While the perennially pessimistic Burns Mantle insisted there were "precious few" outstanding musicals during the 1932–1933 season, there were three major book shows and two revues that had both merit and success. Several other shows had merit or at least interest but failed to generate any popular response. It was not a bad showing, considering the times. The hit book musical that prompted Mantle's lament was **Music in the Air** (8 November 1932, Alvin). Jerome Kern reunited with Oscar Hammerstein II for an evening that was closer in spirit to his previous collaboration with Otto Harbach, *The Cat and the Fiddle* (15 October 1931), than to the works Kern and Hammerstein had written together. As in *The Cat and the Fiddle*, the setting was present-day Europe rather than bygone America. And again the story used the musical world as its milieu. In Edendorf, a small Bavarian village, the old music teacher, Dr. Walther Lessing (Al Shean), has worked with young Karl Reder (Walter Slezak) to write a song called "I've Told Ev'ry Little Star." They decide to go to Munich to have it published. Accompanying them are Karl's sweetheart, Sieglinde (Katherine Carrington), and the Edendorf Walking Club. The distance does not deter them any more than does the chance that "There's A Hill Beyond A Hill." In Munich Karl finds himself pursued by the prima donna Frieda Hatzfeld (Natalie Hall), while the composer Bruno Mahler (Tulio Carminati) is so taken with Sieglinde he writes an operetta for her and includes a part for "A man about my age and wicked like me." He is put out when she prefers to play on a swing rather than listen to his new waltz, "One More Dance." But Sieglinde is happiest "When The Spring Is In The Air." She cannot bring herself to be a thorough professional, even when Bruno insists that she is his inspiration and that no matter what song he writes, "The Song Is You." The villagers prefer their sleepy hamlet to the dubious charms of the big city. Sieglinde and all the others return to Edendorf agreeing "We Belong Together."

The show contained some of Hammerstein's most felicitous writing. But it also betrayed evidences of his recurring pretensions. In this case every scene of the "musical adventure" was given the name of a musical style or device, starting with "Leit Motif" and running from "Etude" through "Nocturne" and "Caprice" to "Rondo." Joseph Urban designed the sets. Critical reaction to them suggested Urban was slipping, or else standards were either changing or becoming more demanding. While Robert Garland writing in the *World-Telegram* extolled the "lovely Urban mountains," Richard Lockridge of the *Post* felt "Joseph Urban's settings are pretty and not much more." Most critics kept their opinions to themselves by not even mentioning the sets. Primarily it was Kern's captivating score that accounted for the run of over seven months.

The morning of the reviews the front pages of all the papers announced that Franklin D. Roosevelt had been elected president.

Grace Moore proved the drawing card for a revival of Millöcker's *The DuBarry* in which Howard Marsh was her leading man. The show ran eighty-seven performances. This represented two more weeks than the run achieved by **George White's Music Hall Varieties** (22 November 1932, Casino). Financial difficulties prevented White from mounting a lavish *Scandals*. The stripped-down, retitled revue was his answer. White followed Carroll and Ziegfeld into the huge Casino in the hope that at $2.20 top playgoers would flock to the house. They didn't. Some of the material was old, like the Howards' "Pay the Two Dollars" skit. Bert Lahr was refreshingly restrained in his lampoon of Clifton Webb, whom he caricatured as Clifton Duckfeet. Several of the best numbers were songs Harold Arlen had written for the Cotton Club, the popular Negro nightspot. One of these was the first-act finale, "I Love A Parade," which Harry Richman sang. Eleanor Powell's scintillating tap routines added to the audience's enjoyment.

All three of the season's hit book musicals arrived in November. *Music in the Air* opened the month, while *Take a Chance* and *Gay Divorce* came in three nights apart at its end. The success of **Take a Chance** (22 November 1932, Apollo) was a surprise. It had begun life in September as a one-week flop in Pittsburgh called *Humpty Dumpty*. But co-producer Laurence Schwab had closed at least one other show on the road (*The New Moon*), rewritten it, and watched it become a smash (19 September 1928). With his associate Buddy DeSylva, he again gambled on revisions and won. *Humpty Dumpty*'s original story of an attempt to produce a revue satirizing events in American history was retained with a love interest built around it. Kenneth Raleigh (Jack

Whiting), a handsome Harvard graduate, decides to produce the revue. His backers include two not very honest young men, Duke Stanley (Jack Haley) and Louie Webb (Sid Silvers), and their attractive, honest girl friend, Toni Ray (June Knight). Kenneth falls in love with Toni, but when he realizes Duke and Louie have not been forthright in their dealings he suspects Toni is party to their schemes. Toni helps iron out everything and goes on to star in the revue. Oddly enough the star of the show, Ethel Merman, played the relatively minor role of Wanda Brill, but she dominated the evening by the force of her personality and the fact that she had all the hit songs to sing. The original score had been by Richard Whiting and Nacio Herb Brown, with Vincent Youmans called in for interpolations. To a chorus line of girls dressed as sailors, Miss Merman wailed a dirge for a departed bordello operator, "Eadie Was A Lady," with Jack Haley she offered, "You're An Old Smoothie," and from the Youmans contributions she stopped the show with another Depression uplifter, "Rise 'N' Shine." Youmans's songs were his last efforts on Broadway. For most of his final years he was too ill to compose. Stanley Green, in his study of 1930s musicals, offers the interesting note that a song called "Poppy Smoke" was to have been in the show but was dropped when "Smokin' Reefers" got to Broadway first in *Flying Colors*. The show played through the season but suffered a major change in tone just before it folded when the zany team of Olsen and Johnson, who had bought an interest, took over the parts of Duke and Louie.

Gay Divorce (29 November 1932, Barrymore) also got off to an uncertain start. The critics didn't care for it. They were uncomfortable watching Fred without Adele Astaire. She had always been considered the major partner. But Astaire, excellently supported by Claire Luce, Luella Gear, Eric Blore, and Eric Rhodes, quickly proved he could go it alone. The show's hit tune, written to stay within his very limited range, soon became the nation's number-one hit. Cole Porter said he was inspired to write "Night And Day" after hearing Mohammedan calls to prayer in Morocco and that the "drip, drip, drip" of the verse was suggested by a comment of a hostess annoyed by the sounds coming from a broken eaves spout. The show abounded in comic numbers. A song about cynical social-climbing, "Mister And Missus Fitch," stemmed from a series of hoax letters Porter and his friends had written to a paper and signed with the names of various members of the imaginary Fitch family. Blore, the perfect waiter, bemoaned, "What Will Become Of Our England?" while Miss Gear detailed amusingly the reasons "I Still Love The Red, White And Blue." The story on which these songs were hung was little better than a French bedroom farce. Mimi Pratt (Miss Luce) seeks to give her husband grounds for divorce by letting herself be caught with a paid co-respondent. Guy (Astaire), who has fallen in love with her, substitutes for the co-respondent and pesters Mimi into loving him. The sophisticated, intimate nature of the story was mirrored in the elegant, intimate sets Jo Mielziner created for the production. Eschewing the plethora of sets most Depression musicals offered (probably in hopes of competing with films), *Gay Divorce* reverted to the old practice of one set for each act. The first act unfolded in a hotel lobby; the second in Mimi's suite. True, there was a prologue that took place in Guy's home and a brief scene in a hotel corridor in Act II—but they were minor excrescences. The show witnessed another Broadway farewell. With *Gay Divorce* Fred Astaire bid the legitimate theatre a permanent good-bye.

A number of great clowns who remained loyal to the musical stage to the end of their careers romped in a week later with **Walk a Little Faster** (7 December 1932, St. James). Beatrice Lillie appeared in an S. J. Perelman sketch "Scamp of the Campus" (as a 1906 coed with the unlikely name of Penelope Goldfarb); as Frisco Fanny, a Gold Rush queen; and as a French "Chantootsy." In one of her most famous bits, after making a staid announcement dressed in a conservative evening gown, she picked up her skirt and roller-skated off stage. In another Perelman skit Bobby Clark played the Russian dictator, Josef Stalin. He also played a sourdough to Miss Lillie's Fanny. Clark's longtime partner Paul McCullough remained his complacent stooge. The songs for the show were Vernon Duke's first complete Broadway score, although his songs had been interpolated into other productions and he had written *The Yellow Mask* for London.

Out of *Walk a Little Faster* came Duke's classic "April In Paris." In his study of American popular song, Alec Wilder unashamedly calls it "a perfect theatre song" and uses a page and a half to analyze it. The song caused no stir among either the critics or first-nighters—possibly because Evelyn Hoey, who sang it, was suffering from laryngitis. It became another of the many songs that achieved fame only after the show it was written for had long closed (as did "I Gotta Right To Sing The Blues" in this same season). But even the show's minor, forgotten numbers such as "Where Have We Met Before?" have an appealing sweetness. Coming in directly behind two strong competitors and so close to *Music in the Air*, the new revue found its ticket sales were hurt. It left after sixteen weeks.

VERNON DUKE was born Vladimir Dukelsky in Pskov, Russia, on 10 October 1903. Something of a child prodigy, he composed a full ballet score at the age of eight. He studied under Reinhold Glière at the Kiev Conservatory, but was forced to flee Russia during the revolution. He eventually emigrated to America, where he met George Gershwin, who encouraged him to write popular music. Unable to support himself with his popular compositions, he returned to Europe and to serious music, but he soon found himself in London writing show tunes.

An unusual importation won general applause and ran almost eighteen weeks, but that was a healthy stand for an evening devoted largely to marionettes. **Il Teatro Piccoli di Vittorio Podreca** (22 December 1932, Lyric) did offer some typical variety acts at its start (such as Chinese acrobats). However, its four-foot puppets were indubitably its stars. In the *Times*, Atkinson called their clowning "acting in caricature," adding, "these dolls that have steamed here from Rome are clearly unrivaled by any of ours." A high point was a puppet pianist: "He can turn his pages of music in the heat of a brilliant roulade. He can toss his coat-tails back over the bench. And, best of all, he can peer at singers with the most subtly malicious cock of his head."

Shuffle Along of 1932 (26 December 1932, Mansfield) was 1932's last regular musical. It reunited the three surviving creators of the original show, after Aubrey Lyles's death. Flournoy Miller was again Steve Jenkins of Jimtown, now trying to get rich quick with U-Eat-Em Molasses. A northern slicker and his Harlem cutie attempt to fleece Jenkins and Jimtown, but fail. Eubie Blake and Noble Sissle combined to write a totally new score, but nothing from it caught the public's fancy. Possibly because the evening was set in Jimtown instead of Harlem

and had none of the violent undertones of *Sugar Hill*, the critics, almost to a man, reverted to the customary appraisal of a Negro show, minimizing the value of the book and expending most of their time and praise on the dancing. The hard times of 1932 demanded something more. Even with a meager chorus of fourteen low-paid tappers, *Shuffle Along of 1932* could not make it past its seventeenth performance. Shortened into a "tab show" to accompany motion pictures, bad luck would not let it alone. The survivors were stranded in Los Angeles.

On 27 December 1932, the night after the new *Shuffle Along* debuted, Radio City Music Hall opened its doors. Conceived as a mammoth vaudeville house, it was soon converted to a policy of first-run motion pictures coupled with elaborate, mindless spectacles of a kind once so popular at the long-darkened Hippodrome down the street.

The first show of 1933, **Pardon My English** (20 January 1933, Majestic), was another of those musicals that looked infallible on paper. Instead it was the first in a dismaying parade of flops that continued until September—one of the most disastrous stretches in the history of the American Musical Theatre. *Pardon My English* had a book by Herbert Fields and songs by the Gershwins. It was produced by the usually lucky Alex Aarons and Vinton Freedley. Troubles began at the beginning. Aarons had intended to mount the show alone, but skyrocketing costs compelled him to call in Freedley. The extended tryout was traumatic. New writers and new directors were engaged, the original star (Jack Buchanan) left, and a muddle ensued. What New York finally saw was a disjointed book in which Jack Pearl (the famous prevaricating Baron Munchausen) played a Dresden police commissioner who arrests a couple of innocent Americans, mistaking them for crooks. He also discovers his daughter is in love with a suave thief. Down the drain with the show went several lovely Gershwin numbers, including "Isn't It A Pity?," "Lorelei," and "My Cousin In Milwaukee." The show's German setting was disturbing to many regular theatregoers. Shortly before the show opened, Hitler had assumed power in Germany, and the night *Pardon My English* closed, Berlin's Reichstag burned.

At the end of their careers almost all the producers of the annual girl shows turned to operetta at a time when its day was clearly done. Florenz Ziegfeld had mounted *Bitter Sweet* (5 November 1929). Earl Carroll had tried *Fioretta* (6 February 1929), and of course the Shuberts continued a policy that was as old as their revues. Now George White tried his hand at it, bringing in Sigmund Romberg's **Melody** (14 February 1933, Casino). He hired Joseph Urban for the sets and assembled a stellar cast including Evelyn Herbert, Everett Marshall, Walter Woolf, and Hal Skelly. Edward Childs Carpenter's libretto told essentially another of the bitterweet, generation-bridging love stories Romberg was inordinately fond of but used successfully only in *Maytime* (16 August 1917). A number of theatregoers undoubtedly recalled a similar Romberg piece with a similar title, *The Magic Melody* (11 November 1919). Andree De Nemours (Miss Herbert) is forced to marry the Vicompte De Laurier (George Houston) instead of her Tristan (Marshall). Tristan is killed in battle. Years later Andree's granddaughter, Paula (Miss Herbert), marries George Richards (Walter Woolf), the nephew of Tristan's friend. The story does not quite come full circle and somehow seems wanting because of this. In a like manner, Romberg's songs were reminiscent and pleasant, but lacked some final touch. Surprisingly some of New York's toughest and most up-to-date critics welcomed *Melody* as a nostalgic escape from 1933's harsh realities. One thing they did not welcome was Urban's set. Almost to a man the critics merely mentioned them in passing or ignored them totally. This neglect was especially sad, for Urban's work for *Melody* was his last for Broadway. *Melody* witnessed another departure. Expenses at the large Casino, which coupled with a relative indifference on the part of the New York playgoers had doomed the show, doomed the theatre as well. When the operetta closed after its seventy-ninth showing, the virtually brand-new Casino disappeared from the legitimate fold.

The closest this dismal period came to having a hit was **Strike Me Pink** (4 March 1933, Majestic), which Lew Brown and Ray Henderson wrote and produced. It agonized through a bedeviled tryout, much like those several other of the season's shows endured. Its ultimate reception fell somewhere between the eventual success of *Take a Chance* and the glum failure of *Pardon My English*. A number of the problems on the road were caused by Waxey Gordon, one of the two underworld figures who had so pestered Ziegfeld in his effort to save *Hot-Cha* (8 March 1932). Gordon had originally bankrolled *Strike Me Pink* when it was known as *Forward March* and slated to be a liberal-oriented revue showcasing new talent. When the road was cold to its charms, Gordon pumped money into it and used his influence to pressure Brown and Henderson

into hiring names. By the time it reached New York Lupe Velez and Jimmy Durante were a bigger lure than the show itself. Much of the more strident left-wing material had been discarded, though "Home To Harlem" attempted to elicit some sympathy for a black criminal's longing for New York. The song was sung against Henry Dreyfuss's moving cyclorama that depicted episodes in the black man's progress—a cotton-field cabin, a prison chain gang, a Harlem nightclub. None of the show's tunes surged to the top of the popularity lists, but three songs, all somewhat more subdued than Henderson's material of old, enjoyed a contemporary vogue: "Let's Call It A Day," "It's Great To Be Alive," (taken over from *Hot-Cha*), and the title song. Durante made his first entrance down the theatre's aisle, fighting with an usher for the right to go on stage. Once behind the footlights he and Miss Velez had fun in a skit in which they both portrayed "children of nature" frolicking in Central Park. Late in the evening he reminisced about his cabaret days with Clayton and Jackson—both of whom joined in to sing their old songs, at least on opening night. Other entertainers included Hal Le Roy (who walked off with some of the best notices for his fancy tap-dancing), Eddie Garr (who did a hilarious impersonation of Ed Wynn), and mannish Hope Williams (who seemed to be looking for something to do).

April's two musicals were both fast flops, and the contrasts between the two are revealing. **Hummin' Sam** (8 April 1933, New Yorker) reached back to Charles Dazey's once-popular old melodrama *In Old Kentucky* as a source for its plot. An even older tradition was revived by having the principal male part played by a woman as a "trouser role." Once again a jockey (Gertrude "Baby" Cox) is torn between winning the Kentucky Derby to please his sweetheart (Madeline Belt) or losing to enrich himself and some crooked hangers-on. The horse and love win. *Hummin' Sam* was designed as pure, entertaining hokum. Murderously reviewed, the black musical never got past its first night.

Bertolt Brecht and Kurt Weill's **The Threepenny Opera** (13 April 1933, Empire) reached still farther back to John Gay's eighteenth-century *The Beggar's Opera* and turned it into a radical comment on modern life. Although the critics were only slightly less unreceptive, they seemingly enjoyed their first exposure to Kurt Weill's unique musical style. Gilbert Gabriel of the *American* called the book "a dreary enigma"; John Mason Brown of the *Evening Post* labeled it "appallingly stupid"; while Richard

Lockridge of the morning *Post*, responding to its political colorings, assailed it as "sugar-coated communism." The show was put away after a week and a half to await a more welcoming day.

Like Weill and Brecht, Voltaire—had he still been alive—would have had to await a more welcoming Broadway reception. Charles Weidman's version of **Candide** (15 May 1933, Booth), billed as "a new form of drama," was perceived rather as "a mixture of ballet d'action, dance recital, Broadway revue and little-theatre morality play." It tarried only one week.

No other shows arrived in May, and the season concluded with a single June entry. **Tattle Tales** (1 June 1933, Broadhurst) had begun life as a Hollywood revue assembled by the witty compère Frank Fay. It had moved across the country after its Hollywood run, and for New York, Fay's wife, Barbara Stanwyck, rejoined the show. Fay made his first appearance dressed as Louis XIV. Serving as master of ceremonies (the voguish nightclubs of the twenties saw to it that the term replaced the older "compère"), Fay announced he had appointed Ray Mayer to be the evening's "Official Mr. 'Eh Eh.'" Mayer was to come out from the wings and say "Eh Eh" whenever the going got dull. Miss Stanwyck appeared in two scenes adapted from her current motion pictures, *The Miracle Woman* and *Ladies of Leisure*. *Tattle Tales* had suffered through a troubled career even in Los Angeles, with both Fay and Miss Stanwyck out of the cast at times for various reasons, it offered New York nothing it had not seen better done, and, with the hottest summer recorded until then beginning to make itself noticed, the show discreetly departed after a month.

1933–1934

For the first time since the beginning of the century the number of new musicals dropped below twenty. In fact the number dropped all the way to thirteen (though there were nearly a dozen revivals as well). Only twice in the ensuing twelve years would the count of new lyric pieces ever reach twenty.

In certain respects the 1933–1934 season could be looked on as the conclusion of this long, brilliant act. Certainly it witnessed the sad but definite end of several of the most promising trends in the musical theatre. On the other hand it also gave quick, inviting glimpses of the future. Promising new faces were beheld in a show of the same name and elsewhere, though many of them soon left for more lucrative

situations in Hollywood. But the three seasons that followed 1933–1934 saw several fine, traditional musicals by loyal old hands, and so the curtain will not come down on this act for a while.

Only one new piece braved the hot weather. **Shady Lady** (5 July 1933, Shubert) told of Richard Brandt's attempt to paint murals for the "Shady Lady" nightclub using an ex-reformatory girl, Millie Mack, as a model. She is cold and cynical, but Richard's natural warmth melts her reserve. Richard was played by Charles Purcell, and Millie, surprisingly, by the former squeaker of baby talk Helen Kane. Both the nightclub, never shown, and Millie were suggested by the real-life Texas Guinan, and, should anyone miss the connection, one song was "Hiya, Sucker," an unmistakable reference to Texas's famous greeting. But the heat and the show's mediocrity soon told. *Shady Lady* lasted four weeks.

Milton Aborn continued the revivals his Civic Light Opera had been offering the last few seasons, bringing in *The Bohemian Girl, The Pirates of Penzance,* and *The Yeomen of the Guard.*

With the era of the great annuals over, Earl Carroll thought he had discovered a way to have his cake and eat it too. He combined with Rufus King to write a book musical about a **Murder at the Vanities** (8 September 1933, New Amsterdam). Both Florenz Ziegfeld and George White had presented book shows in which their great revues were a part of the story. In *Sally* (21 December 1920) and *Manhattan Mary* (26 September 1927), the heroine rose to become a part of the *Follies* or the *Scandals* in the last act. But Carroll seemingly went one better. All the action took place during a performance of the *Vanities*, allowing Carroll to stage numbers from a typical *Vanities* production and, in effect, producing a virtual new edition tied together by the story of a chorus girl who is murdered by the wardrobe mistress so that her daughter can be a replacement. Special production numbers included a fan scene "with four rows of blonde chorus girls tossing uneasily to languorous rhythms." The opening scene was done entirely in yellow. Not all of the show was lavish or imaginative. Carroll apparently ran into difficulty with the designers' union while the entertainment was being put together. When his staff deserted him, he settled for performing several of the scenes against simple "sable hangings." At least nine songsmiths worked on the score. They included Victor Young, Herman Hupfeld, Richard Myers, and Johnny Green. Green, with Edward Heyman, came up with a characteristic ballad of the period, "Weep No More My Baby." In a small way Carroll got back at Ziegfeld for erasing his name from his new theatre. Carroll brought the show into Ziegfeld's old berth, the gorgeous New Amsterdam, where it played just over six months.

Like *Murder at the Vanities*, **Hold Your Horses** (25 September 1933, Winter Garden) had a host of composers and lyricists working on the score, and like the Carroll piece no real hit emerged. But then *Hold Your Horses* itself was no hit. Joe Cook starred as another Joe, Broadway Joe, the driver of an old horse-driven cab. In typical Cook fashion the cab was loaded with wildly devised conveniences, including a kitchenette, a bath, and an elevator. Crooked politicians nominate Joe for mayor so that the apparent opposition, whom they actually favor will be a shoo-in. But Joe campaigns for his opponent, costing his hapless foe so many votes Joe wins. As mayor, Joe vetoes a projected subway construction to assure his fellow hack drivers a livelihood. The sets took old-timers back to Rector's, Nigger Mikes's, and the original Casino Theatre. Diamond Jim Brady, Lillian Russell, and Anna Held paraded across the stage. But oldsters who remembered that era were not generally attuned to Cook's roughhouse clowning, and younger theatregoers asked for something more than just Joe Cook. In the face of such general dissatisfaction *Hold Your Horses* was lucky to survive eleven weeks.

Sketches for **As Thousands Cheer** (30 September 1933, Music Box) were by Moss Hart, its songs by Irving Berlin. It gave its authors a melody-filled, laugh-laden successor to their *Face the Music*. The cast included Clifton Webb, Helen Broderick, Ethel Waters, and Marilyn Miller in her last stage appearance before her untimely death. Using the clever device of having each scene preceded by an appropriate newspaper headline, its skits sent their barbs far and wide: the Hoovers leaving the White House, with the President giving his cabinet a Bronx cheer; John D. Rockefeller refusing to accept Radio City as a birthday gift; commercials interrupting the singing during a Metropolitan Opera broadcast; a hotel staff falling under the influence of Noël Coward; and a Supreme Court decision that says musicals cannot end with reprises, resulting in a new number, "Not For All The Rice In China," as a finale. Berlin filled the score with top tunes. Besides "Supper Time," an African-American woman's lament for her lynched husband, and "Harlem On My Mind," in which a Josephine Baker type of expatriate longs for her old home (her lips start to whisper "Mon Cheri," but her heart keeps singing "Hi-di-ho"), Ethel Waters introduced the sizzling "Heat Wave." Marilyn Miller and Clifton Webb stepped out of a sepia-tinted photo in the rotogravure section to enjoy the "Easter Parade." Berlin had written this song during World War I, when its lyric began "Smile and show your dimple." The show was a triumph, running a year and making a handsome profit—a rarity during Depression days.

In what was becoming a once-a-decade attempt to offer *Die Fledermaus* to Broadway in a new guise, **Champagne, Sec** (14 October 1933, Morosco) was uncorked with Peggy Wood as Rosalinde and Kitty Carlisle as Prince Orlofsky. The evening revived a happier Vienna for 113 performances.

For one brief moment, 1933–1934 looked to be producer Sam Harris's season, but he was in for a major disappointment. At the end of September he had acquitted himself handsomely with *As Thousands Cheer*. Near the end of October he brought in a sequel to *Of Thee I Sing* (26 December 1931) called **Let 'Em Eat Cake** (21 October 1933, Imperial). Like *Of Thee I Sing*, it had a libretto by George S. Kaufman and Morrie Ryskind, and songs by the Gershwins. It also offered Victor Moore, William Gaxton, and Lois Moran recreating the same characters they had portrayed two years before. A number of minor characters were also back, while Florenz Ames retired as the French Ambassador to play General Snookfield. But the horrors of the Depression and of the fascist movements in Italy and Germany had thrown both the authors and the audience slightly off balance. The smiling satire of the original gave way to what the *Times*'s Brooks Atkinson termed a "bitter, hysterical mood." Wintergreen and Throttlebottom in their bid for reelection have been defeated by John P. Tweedledee. Taking their cues from fascist powers, Wintergreen and his fellow politicians, abetted by the muddled pundits of Union Square, decide to overthrow the government:

Wintergreen: Italy—black shirts! Germany—
    brown shirts! America—blue shirts! By God, if
    the American people want a revolution we can
    give it to them! We've got the shirts for it!
Fulton: He's right!
Wintergreen: You bet I'm right! Do you know
    what we'll do? We'll put a Maryblue shirt on
    every man in the country! And we'll guarantee a
    revolution or your money back.

The army, promised all the war debts, quickly takes his side. Finally it is agreed that any still festering differences will be settled by a baseball game between the Supreme Court and members of the League of Nations. Throttlebottom is made the umpire. His decisions prove controversial. In fact, Throttlebottom's calls are so unpopular that he is sentenced to the guillotine. But Mary, who had earlier provided all the blue shirts, now unites the women of America, and a happy ending prevails. Ira Gershwin, writing years later, may have touched on a second reason for the show's failure: its targets were too widespread. "If *Strike Up the Band* was a satire on War, and *Of Thee I Sing* one on Politics, *Let 'Em Eat Cake* was a satire on Practically Everything." Still, there were felicitous touches. For example, the "Maryblue" shirts recalled not just the fascist dress but the Alice blue of an earlier White House. And Ira's lyrics were brilliant. Brother George's music again was used not just for songs, but in long, clever extended passages. Only one tune became popular, the Wintergreens' "Mine," in which one melody is set in counterpoint against another.

Perhaps there was a third problem as well. *Let 'Em Eat Cake* came too soon. *Of Thee I Sing* played through an election year, and the authors might have been wiser to wait until the next election made the new show's material more immediate. The elapsed time also might have served to moderate some of its excesses. As it was, the show had little appeal. It left after less than twelve full weeks. It was the last work approaching musical comedy that George Gershwin composed for the stage. Though he was yet to give Broadway his masterful *Porgy and Bess* (10 October 1935), he died before he could return to his more traditional stage material. With him apparently died the impetus to develop this style of satirical musical. Only Frank Loesser and Abe Burrows, twenty years later, succeeded at something in any way similar.

Jerome Kern was also approaching the end of his Broadway career. No other composer in the history of the American Musical Theatre ever associated himself with so many innovative works. His Princess Theatre shows had helped define and establish the basic American musical comedy form; *Show Boat* (27 December 1927) had pioneered the American musical play; and his recent shows had pointed the way toward full-fledged American operetta. With **Roberta** (18 November 1933. New Amsterdam) he stepped back in the direction of more traditional musical comedy, though his basic melodic line remained more florid and romantic than most writers' in the field. Kern's great score for *Roberta* may have saved the show. Though Max Gordon gave it

an eye-filling presentation (its $115,000 cost was about average for the better musical mountings of the era) and cast it superbly, Otto Harbach provided a book and lyrics that were disappointingly turgid. Harbach based his story on Alice Duer Miller's novel *Gowns by Roberta*. Except for a prologue set in the States, all the action took place in contemporary Paris. It was a background not too far removed from Harbach's setting for *The Cat and the Fiddle* (15 October 1931). Unfortunately, he bungled it. John Kent (Ray Middleton), an all-American fullback at Haverhill College, learns he has inherited a dress shop run by his Aunt Minnie (Fay Templeton). But the shop is in Paris, where his aunt trades under the name of Roberta. Her assistant is a young lady named Stephanie (Tamara), and John proposes that she run the shop as his partner. She agrees. A budding romance between the two almost comes to naught when Sophie (Helen Gray), John's old college flame, appears. But he knows that Sophie has run off once before and suspects she'd do it again. Only as they are about to be married does Stephanie reveal she is a Russian princess. The ending suggests some of the ineptitudes in the libretto. Revelations of royal blood were stock conclusions in the operettas of previous decades. But with the heroine having no hope of returning to Russia as a princess, the revelation is meaningless and gratuitous.

Bob Hope provided most of *Roberta*'s few comic moments. Happily, Carl Robinson, the set designer, and Kiviette, the costumer, working under Hassard Short's supervision, created a mounting of such visual beauty that many of the libretto's languors were handsomely glossed over. Quite naturally a fashion show, "Shadows of Silver," provided the evening's spectacular highlight. While an on-stage band played appropriate music, the ten gentlemen of the chorus and a handful of the twenty-eight chorus girls sat stylishly accoutered as buyers. Before them the remaining chorus girls paraded in elegant but simple gowns, the seven most expensive shimmeringly spangled with sequins. José Limon created a stunning dance for the seven mannequins. *Roberta*'s other major dance number was a wedding scene, which found "supple, Polish-accented, blond" Lyda Roberti and her bridesmaids cavorting in the evening's most uninhibited number. One striking set represented an American bar in Paris. The bar's rear wall was composed of a thousand real bottles neatly aligned on shelves. Miss Templeton had only one number to sing, but it was Kern's lovely "Yesterdays." The sensuous score also included "The Touch Of

Your Hand," "You're Devastating," and the incomparable "Smoke Gets In Your Eyes." Tamara accompanied herself on a guitar while singing this favorite in the American bar. The songs became popular though Kern continued to be daring and innovative (witness the curiously truncated structure of "The Touch Of Your Hand") and though Harbach affixed arcane and almost unsingable lyrics such as "So I chaffed them and I gaily laughed." With the songs stimulating box office sales, *Roberta* ran nine months. During the show's New York stand *Fortune* magazine gave a fascinating breakdown on the production's financial picture. *Roberta*'s weekly nut was $20,000. At $3.30 for the best seats the weekly capacity gross would be $29,000. Had the show played consistently to full houses, it would have paid off its backers in three months. But the faults of the evening and tepid notices prevented the show from ever reaching the top figure. Nonetheless, with only *Murder at the Vanities* and *As Thousands Cheer* (both at $4.40 top) offering *Roberta* serious competition, *Fortune* predicted the show would be in the black by the time it closed. Unfortunately for Broadway, Kern found the California sunshine congenial and except for one brief return spent the rest of his life writing for Hollywood.

Lew Leslie persisted in trying to recapture the élan and popularity of his original **Blackbirds** (9 May 1928), and even when his 1933 edition (2 December 1933, Apollo) folded after three weeks he refused to abandon his efforts. Several hands provided the songs, whose musical styles were adapted to the sounds of the day but whose lyrics still clung to the expected material of the old Negro shows ("Doin' The Shim Sham," "Great Gettin' Up Mornin'"). The best thing about the short-lived revue was Bill Robinson's joyous tap-dancing.

As the old year disappeared, one thing seemed fairly certain: there would be no more Prohibition jokes on Broadway. Prohibition was gone. Utah had cast the decisive vote. Whiskey and wine could flow again.

There was no wine but plenty of women and song in 1934's first musical. More happily there was also lots of delicious comedy. **The Ziegfeld Follies** opened 4 January, bankrolled by the Shuberts and playing their Winter Garden. Mrs. Florenz Ziegfeld was billed as producer, but Billie Burke's only real interest in the show was the possible profits that might help pay her late husband's debts. The show lacked the Ziegfeld look. With both Ziegfeld and Urban gone, that was inevitable. The Brooklyn *Eagle*

complained the show was "too carelessly arranged to be Ziegfeld's"; the *American* acquiesced, finding the spectacle "not up to original snuff." In the *Times* Brooks Atkinson rued that "Ziegfeld Follies" had become a mere trade name. He lamented that the new mounting "lacks the grandee's unifying touch" and went on to slam specific scenes as "tawdry." Only one number done all in ivory and gold elicited some grudging praise from him. Still, the new *Follies* had enough glitter and frills to make a passable imitation. It also had three durable song hits, more than most of the old *Follies* ever had in a single edition. From the regular Vernon Duke score (with E. Y. Harburg lyrics) came "What Is There To Say?," while two interpolations. "The Last Round-Up" (Billy Hill) and "Wagon Wheels" (Hill and Peter De Rose), gave an unexpected western flavor to the show. Willie Howard and Fanny Brice sparked the clowning. Miss Brice mocked Aimee Semple McPherson in "Soul-Saving Sadie"; harked back to another of her Sadies, "Sadie Salome," when she did "Countess Dubinsky" ("now she strips for Minsky"); and spoofed nudists in "Sunshine Sarah." She also introduced the character of Baby Snooks, the precocious, troublesome brat, whom she would play for years on radio. In her debut the not always truthful Snooks listened skeptically to the story of Washington and the cherry tree. With Howard, Miss Brice did a parody of the hit *Sailor Beware*. Howard did a hilarious reprise of "The Last Round-Up" with a Yiddish accent. The diminutive comedian was also both the outgoing and incoming presidents in a Cuban revolution, proclaiming a New Raw Deal. Jane Froman sang Duke's number, while Everett Marshall sang the interpolations. Marshall further sounded an increasingly fashionable note of social protest with "To The Beat Of My Heart" (Harburg/Samuel Pokrass) when, to a background of dying soldiers, he asked, "why, why, why did we die, die, die in vain?" All in all a solid evening's entertainment, this Ziegfeldless *Follies* ran nearly six months.

Old theatregoers may well have been reminded by **All the King's Horses** (30 January 1934, Shubert) of a musical that predated the first *Follies*. The new show told a story not unlike Victor Herbert's *It Happened in Nordland* (5 December 1904). If playgoers had long forgotten Herbert's piece, the obituaries of Marie Cahill in August must have brought memories of it rushing back. Of course, the plot was also reminiscent of Sigmund Romberg's *Princess Flavia* (2 November 1925). *All the King's Horses* called itself "a romantic musical comedy," but its story and the flavor of its music prompted several critics to call it an operetta. When it is discovered that the famous movie star, Donald McArthur (Guy Robertson), looks enough like King Rudolf of Langenstein to be his double, Rudolf persuades Donald to take his place while he goes to Paris for a fling. Donald's passionate crooning on the radio during a speech to "his" subjects brings the long-estranged Queen Erna (Nancy McCord) eagerly back to his side. They, too, have a fling until the real Rudolf returns and Donald heads back to Hollywood. The score by Edward Horan (his only Broadway effort) was no match for the delightful old Herbert melodies. But the farfetched story and simple music had an appealing remoteness to many harassed playgoers, and they gave the show a passable run.

Four Saints in Three Acts (20 February 1934, 44th St.) was the most talked-about musical of the season, but far from its most popular. Of course, controversy and its librettist, Gertrude Stein, went hand in hand. Miss Stein often professed to be more interested in the sounds of words than in their sense, and there were few indeed who could make head or tail of her "story." As best as could be determined it dealt principally with two saints, St. Ignatius Loyola and St. Theresa of Avila, as well as with Teresa's male alter ego. There were random scenes from the saints' lives but no development. The first act took place in Avila and presented a pageant of incidents from Teresa's history. The second act, "Might It Be Mountains If It Were Not Barcelona," seemed to have even less point. In the third act St. Ignatius sees the Holy Ghost and disciplines his disciples. In the fourth act (to be expected of Miss Stein after she announced only three) a choir recapitulates the saintliness of the saints. The absurdities were underscored by having all the Spaniards played by African Americans and by the extensive use of cellophane for the sets. Miss Stein in a characteristic tautology referred to the work as "An opera to be sung." And indeed it was Virgil Thomson's precious but beautiful music that was the evening's chief delight. It had a simple, folk-like quality and drew its inspiration strongly from the church hymns of Thomson's southern background. But the piece was obviously not part of any ongoing Broadway tradition and patently unlikely to initiate one. All that survives in common currency are a few of Miss Stein's curious rhymes: "Pigeons on the grass alas" and "When this you see remember me."

Leonard Sillman's **New Faces** (15 March 1934, Fulton) was far more traditional and successful, and yet somehow innovative. Sillman achieved what Brown and Henderson had hoped to do with *Forward March* before it became *Strike Me Pink* (4 March 1933), or what earlier shows such as *The Newcomers* (8 August 1923) had attempted unavailingly. The revue was a showcase for aspiring stars. Though the entertainment had first seen the footlights as *Low and Behold* at the Pasadena Playhouse, Broadway had watched some of the performers before—in chorus lines or walk-ons, but never in any significant assignments. Now in light-hearted skits and pleasant but undistinguished songs they could be seen and heard to advantage. Only two, Imogene Coca and Henry Fonda, went to the top of the acting world, though Sillman and Nancy Hamilton made their marks as producers. The best of the material was by Miss Hamilton. In "The Disney Influence" she suggested how three current hits—*Ah! Wilderness, The Green Bay Tree*, and *Tobacco Road*—might seem in the hands of the Three Little Pigs. She herself performed a parody of Katharine Hepburn in *The Little Woman*. Imogene Coca spent most of the evening in a large topcoat, at one point sauntering across the stage in it, carrying a small feather and announcing she was doing her fan dance. The tunes were collected from a number of sources. None was top-drawer, though "Lamplight" (James Shelton) and "My Last Affair" (Haven Johnson) enjoyed a momentary vogue. The show carried Charles Dillingham's name as producer for the last time. But it was purely a courtesy. Dillingham was destitute and dying. Elsie Janis, another old name, sometimes associated with Dillingham, was credited as director. For her, too, it was a farewell to the New York stage.

S. M. Chartok revived a series of Gilbert and Sullivan works in April: *The Mikado, The Pirates of Penzance, H. M. S. Pinafore, Trial by Jury*, and *Iolanthe*. In May Charles Purcell and Donald Brian revived *The Chocolate Soldier* in an effort to make work for themselves, and the Shuberts brought back *Bitter Sweet* (with Evelyn Herbert and Allan Jones), hoping to find the audience it missed in 1929. The brothers also mounted a revival of *The Only Girl* (2 November 1914). The revival had originated on the West Coast and, in what was to become a dismaying practice in later revivals, indiscriminately culled popular Herbert favorites from his other shows and used them in place of weaker numbers from the original score.

Another operetta calling itself "a romantic musical comedy" closed the season. **Caviar** (7 June 1934, Forrest) was a twenty-performance dud. Its story was similar to *The Count of Luxembourg*, in which a couple are joined together sight unseen in a marriage of convenience and then fall in love with each other not knowing they are already married. In *Caviar* the lovers are Elena (Nanette Guilford), an American opera singer, and Dmitri (George Houston), an impoverished Russian prince. They woo in Venice and wed in Constantinople. The score was by another one-time composer, Harden Church.

One hardly traditional offering did follow the season's last regular musical. A cast reputedly largely of Africans, along with four musicians sounding away on drums and more exotic jungle instruments, performed Asadata Dafora's **Kyukunkor** [The Witch Woman] (10 June 1934, Little), a dance drama that recounted a Sierra Leone courtship and marriage. Having moved around several venues which later would be considered Off Broadway, the production enjoyed sixty-five performances on Broadway proper.

1934–1935

For the first time in years there was a rise in the number of new musicals offered to Broadway. But the increase was slight, reflecting perhaps the small turnaround in the economy. As so often happened when the number of shows rose, the quality dropped. Only one new show could be called superior, though several others maintained a reasonably high level. Nothing startlingly original appeared; if anything, it was a season when the musical theatre kept looking back over its shoulder to a happier past.

The season's very first show inaugurated this regressive tendency. While it called itself **Gypsy Blonde** (25 June 1934, Lyric), it was admittedly merely an updated version of *The Bohemian Girl*. Balfe's score was retained faithfully, but the original story was reset in contemporary Westchester. The heroine (Isabel Henderson) is lured by the gypsies away from her wealthy home and the prospects of an uninteresting marriage. In the gypsy camp she falls in love with an escaped ex-convict (George Trabert). Inevitably the modern setting and the modern dialogue clashed with the century-old melodies. The show left after three weeks.

No more new musicals appeared until the end of August, when three premiered in swift succession. **Keep Moving** (23 August 1934, Forrest) was a mediocre revue by and with relative unknowns. The biggest "name" on the roster was crotchety Tom Howard, who warned audiences not to laugh or

applaud lest they wake the critics. Singer's Midgets gave a third dimension to all the celebrated Walt Disney cartoon characters. And Clyde Hagan evoked enough laughs and clapping to wake reviewers with his take-off of a fast-talking carnival pitchman selling potato peelers. His peelings may have even landed on a critic if the reviewer happened to be in the first row. But such shenanigans were not enough to please an increasingly demanding Broadway. The unknowns remained unknown when the show left two and a half weeks after it arrived.

But four nights later a band of top professionals, all in good form, presented Broadway with a first-class revue, **Life Begins at 8:40** (27 August 1934. Winter Garden). John Murray Anderson, James Reynolds, and Albert Johnson presided over the spectacle. Harold Arlen wrote music to words by E. Y. Harburg and Ira Gershwin. Bert Lahr, Luella Gear, Ray Bolger, and Frances Williams headed the excellent cast.

RAYMOND WALLACE BOLGER was born in Dorchester, Massachusetts, on 10 January 1904. He made his first public appearance at the age of eighteen in a serious dance recital, but quickly moved over to the vaudeville circuits. Broadway first saw the "nimble, rubber-legged" dancer in *The Merry World*. More vaudeville followed until Bolger returned to Broadway for *Heads Up* and *George White's Scandals*.

The show had originally been conceived as another edition of the *Ziegfeld Follies*, and early announcements suggested the entire evening would be done daringly all in white. The title and the color scheme were changed—the former to reflect Walter Pitkin's best-seller, *Life Begins at Forty*—but the changes in no way lessened the show's attraction. Lahr performed his stage Englishman, a suicidal Frenchman, a gullible Wall Street client, and a pompous tea-concert singer gushing at the "utter, utter, utter loveliness of things" and getting as a reward a pie in his face. Miss Gear sang of "My Paramount-Publix-Roxy Rose" and bewailed that, though she dutifully bought everything in the all-promising ads, "I Couldn't Hold My Man." The rhumba beat that had begun to come to the nation's attention with "Siboney" came to Broadway with the curiously titled "Shoein' The Mare." Ray Bolger and Dixie Dunbar boosted each other's ego with "You're A Builder-Upper." Bolger also offered his interpretation of the Max Baer–Primo Camera fight, and took his work home in "The Window Dresser Goes To Bed." All the principals reassembled for the finale, "Life Begins at City Hall," in which the new mayor, Fiorello La Guardia (Lahr), awaits the arrival of Eleanor Roosevelt (Gear) to launch a gondola to Staten Island. Ex-Mayor Walker and his wife (Bolger and Williams) are found to be stowaways in the boat. Beautiful show girls twirled as untamed Cubans and posed as Doric columns and spring flowers. Even when they were still, they were in motion, for Albert Johnson placed his handsome sets on a revolving stage that turned to change scenes or because whim moved the director. John Mason Brown, writing in the *Evening Post*, complained this sort of "lazy susan" staging was so overdone it gave him vertigo. Audiences apparently disagreed. Life and fun began at 8:40 for seven months.

Saluta (28 August 1934, Imperial) was advertised as a "musical comedy satire," professing to continue where *Let 'Em Eat Cake* (21 October 1933) left off. But its authors were virtually talentless, and the only noticeable similarity was that both aimed to have fun at Mussolini's black shirts. *Saluta* went a step further, impersonating Il Duce on stage. Milton Berle played the leading role of "Windy" Walker, an "M. C." at a sleazy New York nightspot who is persuaded by his gangster cohorts to sail to Italy and stage an opera in competition with the fascists' official productions. A rich American (Dudley Clements) adds his funds to the enterprise after he is promised his daughter Elinore (Ann Barrie) will be the prima donna. Il Duce represses the whole operation, but his anger does not extend to Windy or Elinore and her boyfriend. The Americans sail gaily back on the *Rex*. The score was Frank D'Armond's lone New York exposure. Some of his lyrics were by his star, Berle. But Berle was not enough to override his writers' faults, and *Saluta* quickly disappeared.

The D'Oyly Carte Company came from London on 3 September for a fifteen-week engagement that offered ten Gilbert and Sullivan masterpieces as well as *Cox and Box*. The visit was the troupe's first in fifty years—when it had come offering New York its original mountings. The resurgence of interest that Winthrop Ames and others had sparked in the Savoyard comic operas during the late twenties made the company doubly welcome.

A spectacularly mounted operetta, **The Great Waltz** (22 September 1934, Center), proved so surprising a success it was forced to close while still profitable because a road trip had been booked before the extent of its popularity could be accurately judged. Hassard Short had suggested the show to Max Gordon after Short had produced a similar piece called *Waltzes from Vienna* in London. *Waltzes* in turn had been based on a Viennese hit. Both shows presented fictitious biographies of the Johann Strausses, father and son, and both used Strauss melodies for their songs. Moss Hart wrote the American libretto. It was not typical Hart, but it was typical operetta. In Hart's version the elder Strauss (H. Reeves-Smith) refuses to allow his son's music to be played. Countess Olga (Marie Burke) contrives to keep the father from the Dommayer's Garden's opening, thereby allowing the younger Strauss (Guy Robertson) to lead the band in his own melodies. The melodies were known and liked, but the principal attraction of *The Great Waltz* was undoubtedly its elaborate production. Mounted at the huge Center Theatre in the Rockefeller complex, it placed nearly 200 performers on the large, mechanically advanced stage. The settings and costumes had cost nearly $250,000, only one of few such expenditures between the heyday of Ziegfeld and the arrival of Mike Todd. In the evening's most magnificent moment Dommayer's Garden was transformed while the audience watched into a gigantic, sumptuous ballroom, with the entire orchestra of fifty raised from the pit in front of the stage to a balcony at the rear of the set. For some it called to mind the old Hippodrome extravaganzas that had played a few blocks down Sixth Avenue.

A vaudeville-revue, **Continental Varieties** (3 October 1934, Little), cast entirely with European talent such as Lucienne Boyer and Nikita Balieff (late of *Chauve Souris*), began a ten-week stay. Balieff served as master of ceremonies. Miss Boyer sang her Parisian hits such as "Parlez-moi d'Amour." Vincente Escudero stamped out Spanish dances, and a magician named De Roze poured all manner of drinks from a single pitcher. The entertainment was presented by Arch Selwyn and Harold B. Franklin. At the other end of the month—23 October—these same gentlemen imported Noël Coward's **Conversation Piece**, housing it at the 44th Street Theatre, next door to the Little. Pierre Fresnay and Yvonne Printemps were starred. The show was about the love of a guardian and his ward, and not to the public's taste, but it left behind it one of Coward's loveliest songs, "I'll Follow My Secret Heart."

Composer Ray Henderson and librettist Jack McGowan combined to produce their own musical **Say When** (8 November 1934, Imperial). With Buddy DeSylva in Hollywood and Lew Brown striking out on his own, Henderson worked with lyricist Ted Koehler on the songs. McGowan's story began on a transatlantic liner where two entertainers, Bob Breese (Harry Richman) and Jimmy Blake (Bob Hope), fall in with Betty and Jane Palmer (Betty Dell and Linda Watkins), the daughters of a rich banker. Romances quickly blossom. But the girls' father opposes having show people in the family. Only when Bob and Jimmy discover Mr. Palmer (Taylor Holmes) is having an affair are they able to obtain the family's blessing. The show opened to rave notices. But the public proved bafflingly fickle, and the show ran just ten weeks, despite singable Henderson ditties such as "Don't Tell Me It's Bad."

Anything Goes (21 November 1934, Alvin), the season's biggest musical hit, was more than just the runaway smash of the year. More, too, than merely a well-wrought, hilarious show, filled with unforgettable melodies and sophisticated lyrics, it was "the quintessential musical comedy of the thirties." If it was not as original or cohesive as, say, *Of Thee I Sing* (26 December 1931) or *Porgy and Bess* (10 October 1935), it never pretended to aim as high. Designed to be pure entertainment, and never losing sight of its intention, it succeeded sterlingly. That it seemed all of a piece and not the slapdash assemblage its title suggested undoubtedly amazed those who knew its history. For the show was already in rehearsal with a Guy Bolton and P. G. Wodehouse libretto that recounted the adventures of a group of shipwrecked passengers when the cruise liner *Morro Castle* burned off Asbury Park, killing 125. A new story had to be worked around the songs, sets, and principals. With both Bolton and Wodehouse unavailable, producer Vinton Freedley introduced the show's director, Howard Lindsay, to Russel Crouse, a Theatre Guild press agent, and prevailed on them to supply the new book. It was the beginning of one of the most profitable collaborations in theatrical records.

The story the neophytes concocted remained on the high seas for most of the evening, although it opened at a New York bar where the hostess, Reno Sweeney (Ethel Merman), a former evangelist, confesses she gets a kick out of Billy Crocker (William Gaxton). Reno is about to sail for England on the same ship as Hope Harcourt (Bettina Hall), the young lady Crocker fancies. Crocker goes to see Hope off, and on the spur of the moment decides to stow away so that he can remain with her. He is forced to adopt a number of disguises, at one point even clipping a dog for its hair. He finally wangles a legitimate ticket and a not quite legitimate passport from the Reverend Dr. Moon (Victor Moore), a wistful bit of a man who has been branded "Public Enemy #13." With a reverend and an erstwhile evangelist aboard, the captain distracts his Depression clientele with a rousing revival meeting. Even Reno is so moved she belts out a paean to the archangel Gabriel. But for Crocker the distraction can only be momentary. When the ship lands, his beloved Hope will marry Sir Evelyn Oakleigh (Leslie Barrie). It is to be a marriage of convenience, but it is made suddenly unnecessary when Hope's business is sold for a handsome sum. Hope and Crocker go off together, while Sir Evelyn turns his attention to Reno. A cable from Washington announces that Moon has been adjudged harmless and is no longer wanted. His ambition to rise to "Public Enemy #1" frustrated, Moon departs after adding his name to the anti-Hooverites.

HOWARD LINDSAY was born in Waterford, New York, on 29 March 1889. His family moved to Boston, where he attended Boston Latin School and Harvard. Slated for the ministry, he abandoned his studies and enrolled in the American Academy of Dramatic Arts. After graduation he was active as a performer and director in vaudeville, burlesque, and silent films as well as the legitimate stage.

RUSSEL CROUSE was Lindsay's junior by four years, having been born in Findlay, Ohio, on 20 February 1893. After graduating from Toledo's public school system he spent his early years to journalism. His first acting job came in 1928 in an appropriate play, *Gentlemen of the Press*. His name first appeared as a co-librettist when *The Gang's All Here* (18 February 1931) premiered, Lindsay and Crouse's long, successful career included *Life with Father*, which held the record as the longest-running show in Broadway's history when it closed and whose 3,224 performances make it still the longest-running straight play of the New York stage.

Donald Oenslager's stylishly contemporary sets included a triple-tiered view of the liner's decks, allowing an excellent exposure for bathing-suited chorus girls as they tapped away to Cole Porter's tunes. Though its scenery, tone, and allusions made *Anything Goes* up-to-the-minute, its refusal to allow its demimonde heroine to win her man hints that the same morality that governed *The Pink Lady* (13 March 1911) and its day still obtained. But Porter's songs betrayed no such qualms. Melodically, they ran the gamut of the period's most popular tunes: from the revival fervor of "Blow, Gabriel, Blow," to the Latin undercurrents of the sultry "All Through The Night" (sung by Billy to Hope) and "I Get A Kick Out Of You," to the jumpy "You're The Top" (in which Billy and Reno flattered each other in catalogue fashion), to Reno's hard-riding title song. The songs Ethel Merman sang would forever after be closely associated with her. Lyrically, the songs displayed Porter's erudite wit (in "You're The Top" he paired "Russia" with "Roxy usher") and civilized perspective on romance. Horrors in the news forced Porter, as well as his librettists, to make changes. Before the Lindbergh kidnapping "You're The Top" included a line that went "I shouldn't care for those nights in the air / That the fair Mrs. Lindbergh goes through." But for all the changes, the score was Porter's best up to the time and, except for *Kiss Me, Kate*, one he never again matched.

Donald Heywood's all-black operetta, **Africana,** premiered at the Venice on 26 November. Heywood had written a score for a revue with the same name that ran for nine weeks in the summer of 1927. In 1932 his music for *Blackberries* failed to survive the show's three-week run. Heywood, something of a scholar, went to Africa to study native composition before setting his own story to music. His plot recounted the return of King Yafouba's eldest son, Prince Soyonga, from school at Oxford. Soyanga is filled with ideas for reform and modernization, but goes too far when he falls in love with a maiden who is taboo because she is half white. Heywood himself conducted the opening. During the performance he was attacked by a man who claimed Heywood had stolen his melodies. The man was removed and the performance finished. The *Times, Daily News, Sun,* and *World-Telegram* all remarked that the attack was the most theatrically satisfying part of the evening. *Africana* folded after three performances, but Heywood remained on the Broadway scene.

By Broadway's crassest commercial test **Revenge with Music** (28 November 1934, New Amsterdam)

was not a hit, retrieving a paltry $45,000 of its original $120,000 investment. But it left behind some of Arthur Schwartz's more beguiling melodies, including "You And The Night And The Music" and "If There Is Someone Lovelier Than You." Still, this first effort by Schwartz and Dietz at a book show never quite came together. Dietz lays part of the blame on Libby Holman, who costarred with Georges Metaxa and Charles Winninger. He contends that singing lessons had both spoiled the natural sultriness of her voice and ruined her enunciation. This may be true. But another problem could also be that Dietz considered the work an operetta. Admittedly its simple story and setting lent itself to the genre. In Spain, provincial governor Don Emilio (Winninger) attempts unsuccessfully to woo away Maria (Miss Holman) on her wedding night. In revenge Maria's husband, Carlos (Metaxa), has a fleeting romance with Don Emilio's wife, Isabella (Ilka Chase), wooing her, as he has his wife, by insisting if there is someone lovelier he doesn't know her. While, ten years before, Rudolf Friml or Sigmund Romberg might have filled just such a tale with rich, arioso passages, Schwartz was of a different school. True, his melodic line was longer and more graceful than that of most of his competitors, but his chromatics were strictly of the decade and his range within a song carefully restricted. At best he approached Jerome Kern in Kern's latest efforts to recreate the obsolete operetta in modern, native terms. If Dietz's book was at least adequate, his lyrics were disappointingly uneven. Within Maria and Carlos's "You And The Night And The Music" he could poetically capture a mood and incorporate a startling, yet fitting, metaphor ("Our hearts will be throbbing guitars"), while elsewhere sounding as hackneyed as Harry B. Smith at his worst ("Make the most of time ere it has flown"). Seventeen colorful Spanish settings passed from one to another quickly on the season's second major revolving stage. This time no one seemed to become dizzy. Not coincidentally, the sets were the work of the same artist who had earlier mounted his spectacle on a turning platform, Albert Johnson. Even with a critical drubbing, *Revenge with Music* managed to survive for twenty weeks.

Given the declining number of live playhouses and the relative health of films, the conversion of the Hollywood Theatre from motion pictures to a legitimate auditorium must have seemed at once puzzling and heartening. The show honored to open the theatre in its new form on 13 December was **Calling All Stars.** Lew Brown did the lyrics and a number of the sketches. Harry Akst did the music. Even the title of their "I'd Like To Dunk You In My Coffee" suggests a certain comedown from the days when Brown created "You're The Cream In My Coffee" with Buddy DeSylva and Ray Henderson. Moreover Brown's continued insertion of left-wing pleas assuredly offended many in the audience. In "Straw Hat In The Rain" Brown addressed the "high hat" as "high and dry hat." For a lavish production number the producers could devise nothing more original than another jungle dance. Lou Holtz and Phil Baker handled the comedy, which the *Times* condemned as "dressing room jokes and smug obscenities." Holtz kidded late arrivals and offered his audience three kinds of gin—nitrogen, oxygen, and hydrogen. Later he ran up into a box to play stooge to Baker. While Baker made music on his concertina, he and Holtz traded insults. Everett Marshall, Jack Whiting, and Gertrude Niesen did what they could with Akst's inferior melodies.

A second December revue fared even less well. Leonard Sillman compiled it, using some of the talent (especially Imogene Coca) from *New Faces* (15 March 1934). But **Fools Rush In** (25 December 1934, Playhouse) rushed out before anyone knew it was there. In its short stay it celebrated the birth of the Dionne quintuplets and recorded an imaginary meeting between Mrs. Roosevelt and Mrs. Hoover. It also sang tunes by Will Irwin and Richard Lewine that few remembered outside the theatre.

Two more musicals arrived together on 27 December. One was an eleven-performance fiasco, the other a twenty-week disappointment. The twenty-week run was all **Thumbs Up** could muster at the St. James, though it was gorgeously mounted by John Murray Anderson, James Reynolds, and Raoul Pène Du Bois; riotously performed by Clark and McCullough, Ray Dooley, and others; and blessed as "the birthplace of two important songs." James Hanley assured his admirers he had not lost his touch and could adapt to the smoother rhythms of the thirties with "Zing! Went The Strings Of My Heart!" (sung and danced by Hal Le Roy and Eunice Healey), while Vernon Duke added "Autumn In New York" to his portfolio of classics. This was sung by J. Harold Murray before a background of moving screens showing pictures of Manhattan. Arthur Schwartz contributed several numbers, but none to equal the show's hits or his own best tunes from *Revenge with Music*. The comedy offered Miss Dooley climbing a human pyramid in "My Arab Complex" and Clark as a microphone-hogging

judge at a broadcast trial. Spectacles presented a bit of Currier and Ives Americana in the opening and, since Eddie Dowling was producer as well as co-star, an elaborate Irish number, "Eileen Avourneen."

The dud that opened the same night was an operetta with a book by Brian Hooker and Russell Janney based on a novel and play by Justin Huntly McCarthy. To that extent it resembled *The Vagabond King* (20 September 1925). Its story was just as swashbuckling, recounting the exploits of Flynn O'Flynn (George Houston) during the wars between William of Orange and James II in which O'Flynn still finds time to court and win Lady Benedetta (Lucy Monroe). However, the music for **The O'Flynn** (27 December 1934, Broadway) was not by Friml, but by Franklin Hauser. It lacked the high-colored romance and imperishable melodies that Friml had provided.

By chance, Rudolf Friml was the composer for the very next lyric attraction. **Music Hath Charms** (29 December 1934, Majestic) opened two nights later, the fourth musical of the week and the last of 1934. It was also the last new Friml score Broadway was to hear. The show had begun on the road some months before under a different name and filled with bright hope. At that time the hoardings proclaimed, "Messrs Shubert Have The Honor Of Presenting Maria Jeritza in the Rudolf Friml operetta 'Annina.'" Playing opposite the great opera star and receiving meager publicity was the rising young Allan Jones. But it soon became obvious the show was not another Friml masterpiece. Miss Jeritza was replaced by Natalie Hall, and young Jones by the older Robert Halliday. Once again an operetta told a story of similar loves in separate generations, though in *Music Hath Charms* the story leaps back over a century and a half as Maria, Marchese Del Monte Nee Di Orsano, reluctantly changes her mind about her American suitor after her grandfather narrates the love story of her great-grandmother. Miss Hall played the heroines of both epochs just as she had done in *Three Little Girls* (14 April 1930). There may have been a certain charm in Friml's music, but it was pale in comparison to his scores of the teens and twenties. The show was sumptuously if garishly mounted. For some critics its chief attraction was its excellent dancing—not dancing of the kind common on Broadway, but gavottes, polkas, and tarantellas.

Four performances were the lot of an unlikely importation, **The Land of Bells** [Il Paese dei Campanelli] (9 May 1935, Majestic). This Italian operetta told of village bells which sound every time a wife kisses someone she shouldn't be kissing. The villagers are informed that if no one kisses anyone else in town for twenty-four hours, the bells will thereafter be discreet. Despite the arrival of a chorus-load of handsome young men, the women restrain themselves for a whole day.

Discounting the Italian visitors, the plight of the Depression's musical stage was brought home by the great gap of time between the December crush of new offerings and the appearance of the next musical. Five months elapsed—January through May—before **Parade** (20 May 1935, Guild) arrived. It was the first of only ten musicals to open in 1935. And though several of these shows ran six months or more, not a single one repaid its investment. By Broadway commercial terms the year was a washout. *Parade* was a blatantly leftist tract that featured Jimmy Savo. Its much-discussed opening had the police ignoring radio reports of violent crimes but rushing to break up a parade of poor people. It saw fascists in every government seat and villains in every executive office. Not surprisingly the score was brassier and more martial than most, and the closest thing to the expected love song exclaimed, "I'm All Washed Up With Love" (Albert Silverman/ Kay Swift). Marc Blitzstein and Will Irwin contributed interpolations to what was primarily a Jerome Moross score. Bad reviews and word of mouth closed the show after five weeks.

Earl Carroll displayed his latest **Sketch Book** (4 June 1935, Winter Garden) to close out the season. With cries for social significance in the air, Carroll labeled his production a "Hysterical Historical Revue" and broadcast that it presented a chorus girl's perception of American history. This "Lorelei Lee" of the footlights had some strange ideas of the past. For her the Mexican War was a torrid dance done by a gaudily dressed line of "Gringolettes." Great figures from Washington to Lincoln to Bea Lillie were lampooned, with Charlotte Arren's take-off of Jenny Lind winning the most applause. Somehow reason was found to bring in an act of juggling animals, an eye-filling production number in honor of Carroll's (as well as Ziegfeld and Urban's) favorite color, "A Blue Paradise," and Mlle. Nirska's butterfly dance, with its billowing silks shimmering in soft pink lights. Cheerful, bustling Ken Murray, a cigar hanging from his mouth, presided. The music was undistinguished although obviously in touch with the times in songs such as "Let's Swing It." However absurd the whole conglomeration seems many years

later, the revue attracted enough patrons to record 207 performances.

1935–1936

The usually dissatisfied Burns Mantle had a brief change of heart while reviewing the 1935–1936 season. "It is quite generally admitted," he rejoiced, "that this theatrical season has been the most exciting and most satisfying of any New York has enjoyed since... the crash of '29." It would be hard to gainsay a year that gave the stage *Jubilee, On Your Toes, Jumbo, At Home Abroad,* and *Porgy and Bess,* or that poured into the repertory of long-lived favorites the fine songs 1935–1936 first sang. But it must also be remembered that, at least as far as the musical stage was concerned, only twelve new creations appeared (*Variety* listed fourteen by including two vaudeville bills). This represented a meager 10 percent of the season's productions, the smallest portion since musicals became a regular part of the New York theatrical scene in the late nineteenth century. To add insult to injury, only a single musical, *On Your Toes,* realized a decent profit. Seven of the shows were revues. A mere five were book musicals. Of these one relied heavily on spectacle, and one was virtually an opera, while a third marked a return to old-fashioned operetta. Only two were standard, contemporary pieces.

Three nights before the first new musical arrived, one major event took place in American popular music that found Broadway reacting with a somewhat surprising indifference. Most students agree that "the swing era" officially opened with the wild acclaim Benny Goodman's band received on 21 August 1935, at the Palomar Ballroom in Los Angeles. Though "swing" tunes and arrangements had already infiltrated the American Musical Theatre—witness "Let's Swing It" in Earl Carroll's *Sketch Book* (4 April 1935)—Broadway never responded with the enthusiasm or imagination it had brought to ragtime and jazz. At least two reasons probably account for this cool reception. Swing was, to no small extent, unmelodic and untheatrical. Its insistent, driving rhythms and strictly coordinated ensemble sounds were designed for what became known as "the big bands." The seeming improvisation, individuality, and intimacy of jazz were shunted aside. Though jazz, of course, originated far from theatrical footlights, its personal qualities allowed it to be adapted, however impurely, to theatrical purposes. But swing without its big bands was not as malleable, and big bands would have been lost in theatre orchestra pits. (To their credit, swing band recordings often helped popularize the era's show tunes.) Yet, even if swing had been more readily transferable, there is some cause to doubt its welcome would have been much heartier. Broadway was growing old. The word "youngster" seems slightly out of place in 1935 theatrical terms. Bright juveniles were still appearing on the stage each season, but with rare exceptions New York had become for them merely a way station on the road to Hollywood. Though no precise statistics exist, it is safe to suggest that the average age of Broadway's principal creators and stars was markedly higher than it had been twenty or forty years before.

A series of Gilbert and Sullivan revivals opened at the Adelphi on 15 July and ran until early September. The troupe returned in April for a second stand. Its slate included *The Mikado*, *The Pirates of Penzance*, *The Yeomen of the Guard*, *The Gondoliers*, *Trial by Jury*, and *H. M. S. Pinafore*. Howard Marsh, Bertram Peacock (the Schubert of the original *Blossom Time*), and Margaret Daum were the principal singers, while New York's original 1902 Sultan of Sulu, Frank Moulan, played the main comic role.

It was an unhappy year for the great funny men of old. Two of the earliest clowns of the musical stage died in the fall: De Wolf Hopper in September and Francis Wilson in October. In March of 1936 Paul McCullough committed suicide. The more conventional Cecil Lean died in July; Will Rogers was killed in a plane crash in August.

The end of August saw the season's first new work, a revue asking its patrons to **Smile at Me** (23 August 1935, Fulton). They didn't—not at a begrimed parody of *Tobacco Road* called "Tobacco Juice," not at a slipshod South Sea Island ballet, nor at the feverish hosting and clowning of Jack Osterman. The revue was quickly gone, taking with it Gerald Dolin's only Broadway score.

The procession of unprofitable "hits" began with **At Home Abroad** (19 September 1935, Winter Garden). Reverting to a favorite device of the earlier revues, the show used a tenuous story line to connect songs and sketches. In this case it relived the world cruise of Otis and Henrietta Hatrick. The natives they met in various countries kept bearing remarkable resemblances to Beatrice Lillie, Ethel Waters, and Eleanor Powell, not to mention Reginald Gardiner and Eddie Foy, Jr. Miss Lillie was a geisha girl (insisting, "It's better with your shoes off"), a Russian ballerina, the wife of an alpine guide,

and an English lady trying to make a simple purchase of "a dozen double damask dinner napkins." Miss Powell was a high-hatted, toe-tapping Eton boy and a Samoan beauty. A torchy lament, subtly leavened with humor, "Thief In The Night," fell to Miss Waters's capable voice. She also reigned as "The Hottentot Potentate," giving her subjects the benefit of her years in Harlem: both her "hotcha" and her "Je ne sais quoitcha." Actually, neither Howard Dietz's lyrics nor Arthur Schwartz's music was on a par with their best. Besides choreographing such fine dance interludes as "Farewell, My Lovely" and "Love Is A Dancing Thing," Paul Haakon brought the house down each night portraying the matador in a bullfight ballet. Vincente Minnelli created a magnificent gilt baroque setting for the show's finale and earlier in the evening won approval with a papier-mâché Matterhorn in a paper snowstorm. For the most part Minnelli's cheerful palette dripped with light colors. Thanks largely to Minnelli and the performers *At Home Abroad* survived six months.

Since **Porgy and Bess** (10 October 1935, Alvin), the season's masterpiece, called itself, honestly and accurately, "An American Folk Opera," it may seem surprising to find it at a commercial Broadway house. But the truth is it had no place else to go. New York offered no institution to compare with Vienna's Volksoper or Paris's Opéra Comique. There was nothing for the Gershwins and their associates to do but raise the artistic standards of the Great White Way. Though Norman Nadel in his *Pictorial History of the Theatre Guild* suggests a different version, it is generally agreed that Gershwin became interested in making an opera of DuBose Heyward's novel *Porgy* soon after its publication in 1925. His plans were thwarted when he learned Heyward and his wife Dorothy had signed to do a dramatization of the work for the Theatre Guild. It became part of the Guild's magnificent 1927–1928 season. Afterwards, ignoring Gershwin, the Guild began seeking someone to make a light musical of the piece as a vehicle for Al Jolson. Their prime candidate was Jerome Kern. But Heyward, reminded of Gershwin's more serious ambitions, held out. He prevailed on Gershwin to spend time both in Charleston's Cabbage Row slum and on Folly Beach off the Carolina coast studying Negroes and their music firsthand. Later Heyward and Gershwin continued to develop their project by mail, bringing Ira into the picture at the same time. In a virtually unheard-of move at this late date, Gershwin orchestrated all of the score himself.

At the end of a hot summer day a Catfish Row mother (Abbie Mitchell) attempts to lull her baby to sleep with "Summertime." When she fails, the child's father (Edward Matthews) tries by singing cynically of a widespread and earthy sentiment, "A Woman Is A Sometime Thing." The baby finally falls asleep, but the courtyard of the slum is dangerously awake. Its men are drinking and gambling away their small hoards of cash. Porgy (Todd Duncan), a cripple who rides around in a goat cart, enters. The men tease Porgy about his love for Crown's girl, Bess (Anne Brown). Unconvincingly, Porgy denies any interest in her. The women who are standing nearby applaud Porgy's disclaimer, for they hold with Serena (Ruby Elzy), "That gal Bess ain't fit for Gawd fearin' ladies to 'sociate with." But Serena is more troubled by her husband Robbins's gambling with the others, especially with Crown (Warren Coleman). Her fears are justified, for when the men get to quarreling Crown kills Robbins (Henry Davis). At the funeral the neighbors take up a collection as Serena wails, "My Man's Gone Now." With Crown having fled to avoid jail, Porgy can be more open in his sentiments about Bess. He is happy in his small world, unashamed to cry, "'I Got Plenty O' Nuttin.'"

Porgy has gotten the unethical but accommodating lawyer Frazier to arrange to divorce Crown and Bess. The matter out of the way, he then joyfully announces, "Bess, You Is My Woman Now." They join the restless slum folk in heading for a picnic. By chance, the island on which the picnic is held turns out to be the very place Crown is hiding. He appears long enough to warn Bess that she is still his. Before long he will be back to claim her. The festivities are enlivened by Sportin' Life (John W. Bubbles), a drug peddler, who gives his own version of things biblical, insisting, "It Ain't Necessarily So." Back in Catfish Row, Bess sings, "I Loves You, Porgy." Crown then appears, and in a fight with Porgy, he is killed when Porgy turns Crown's own knife on him. The police come and take Porgy to jail. Sportin' Life, seeing a chance for a fling, tells Bess that Porgy will never be set free. He lets her try some of his drugs, and she soon agrees to accompany him since "There's A Boat Dat's Leavin' Soon For New York." When Porgy is released he returns with a new dress for Bess. With pained reluctance the neighbors tell him what has happened. Porgy is undaunted. Though he has no idea where New York is, he sets out in his goat cart to go there and find Bess, crying, "I'm On My Way."

The opera was mounted with a stunning realism, most notably in the grim, pathetic courtyard where so much of the action takes place. It was staged and performed with scenes of haunting fervor—the depthless grief of the deaths, the electrifying terror of blacks caught in a ramshackle house during a hurricane, or the innocent, uninhibited gaiety of a picnic. The major New York newspapers sent both their drama and music critics to the opening. The drama critics were far more enthusiastic than the music commentators. Unfortunately, only a small audience was willing to listen to other people's woes in the Depression. As a result, the original production ran just 124 performances and, even with a Guild-sponsored post-Broadway tour, failed to retrieve its $50,000 investment. There was a wistful footnote to this original production. The small part of the lawyer was played by J. Rosamond Johnson, who a generation earlier had himself tried with little success to advance the cause of both black performers in general and the musical stage as a whole. Most sadly of all, this masterpiece marked the last major writing by George Gershwin for that same musical stage.

Two nights after the opening of *Porgy and Bess*, a third excellent but unprofitable musical appeared. **Jubilee** (12 October 1935, Imperial) was a conventional book musical—one of only two the season brought forth. Stories of the British royal family's Silver Jubilee gave Moss Hart and Cole Porter the suggestion for the show. Together they took a leisurely world cruise with their friends while working on it. The result was light-hearted, escapist fun. Another royal family is about to celebrate its jubilee. But the King (Melville Cooper) and Queen (Mary Boland) and their children are fed up with their constrained if luxurious life. When a left-wing outbreak led by a rebellious nephew prompts their advisers to order them into seclusion they decide to have a fling as commoners instead. The Queen flirts briefly with Charles Rausmiller (Mark Plant), the ape man Mowgli of the movies (a take-off on Johnny Weissmuller's Tarzan). Her daughter (Margaret Adams) has a brief romance with a celebrated writer (Derek Williams), while the Prince (Charles Walters) takes the famous dancer Karen O'Kane (June Knight) to the Café Martinique, where they "Begin The Beguine." As for the King, he can spend all his waking hours playing his beloved parlor games. Of course, they are finally recognized and forced to return to a more regal life.

By and large the critics enjoyed the show, though they had some reservations about the music. Apparently so did Porter, his producers, and his publishers.

When the songs were first issued, two that became Porter classics were not included, "Begin The Beguine" and "Just One Of Those Things" (also sung by Karen and the Prince). In fact it was several years before the latter achieved its ultimate popularity. Another Porter classic, "Why Shouldn't I?," was sung by the Princess. The show's high level of sophistication as well as its large number of private jokes and allusions undoubtedly hurt at the box office. The majority of the show's audience was not intrigued by references to George Gershwin's inevitable playing of his own music at posh parties or to Clifton Webb's domineering mother. When the popular Miss Boland left to return to Hollywood, ticket sales slumped to the point where the show had to be withdrawn after just twenty-one weeks.

The **Provincetown Follies** arrived on 3 November to begin a two-month stay at the small, out-of-the-way Provincetown Playhouse in Greenwich Village. For all its Village origins the revue spoke with a markedly British accent. Its master of ceremonies was a favorite of London and Paris nightspots, Barry Oliver, while many of the evening's loudest laughs were grabbed by Cyril Smith, especially with his monologue about a cockney lion tamer. Beatrice Kay won some good notices for her burlesque of a torch singer. The dances were staged by John Tiller's protégé, Mary Read. Dave Stamper, who had provided so many of the songs for the *Ziegfeld Follies* in their heyday, contributed several of the tunes, while two unknowns, Frederick Herendeen and Sylvan Green, rushed in a timely "Poor Porgy." Only "Red Sails In The Sunset" (Jimmy Kennedy/Hugh Williams) caught the public's fancy.

The old Hippodrome was returned to the legitimate fold for one last time when Billy Rose mounted his noisily ballyhooed production of **Jumbo** on 16 November. Actually it was not quite the Hippodrome its regulars might have remembered, for Rose made substantial renovations to house his production properly. The orchestra level was gutted and rearranged to make it resemble a circus tent. This prompted a few skeptical playgoers to remark that the original auditorium seemed more than adequate for the opening spectacles at the turn of the century, the first two of which had circus themes. After extended rehearsals and numerous delays in the announced opening, the show was brought in at the staggering cost of $340,000. Ben Hecht and Charles MacArthur's book was sufficiently loose to allow for a large number of circus acts. In fact, Actors' Equity declared the work a circus instead of a musical. Two circus proprietors, Matthew Mulligan (W. J. McCarthy) and John A.

Considine (Arthur Sinclair), have long been at loggerheads. They are not made any happier when Matt Jr. (Donald Novis) falls in love with Considine's daughter, Mickey (Gloria Grafton). Considine's drinking problem grows worse, and he faces bankruptcy until his press agent, Claudius B. Bowers, burns down Considine's house, allowing him to collect the insurance. In the end the lovers succeed in bringing the rival fathers together amicably. The songs were by Rodgers and Hart, their first for the theatre since 1931. It gave the lie to the Broadway superstition that great songs could not come out of the Hippodrome. Three Rodgers and Hart classics emerged: Mickey and Matt's driving waltz, "The Most Beautiful Girl In The World"; the wispy "Little Girl Blue" (the first-act finale, in which Mickey dreams she is a child again, being entertained by circus folk); and the lovers' assertive "My Romance."

The show's star was Jimmy Durante, playing the resourceful Bowers. But for many theatregoers the main attraction was the spectacle. Paul Whiteman, after making his entrance on a large white horse, led his orchestra, while hundreds of animals, acrobats, clowns, and other circus stand-bys cavorted in the great old house. Unfortunately not enough theatregoers were attracted. Although the show ran over seven months, its gigantic initial outlay and its abnormally high weekly running costs prevented it from recouping more than about half of its investment.

May Wine (5 December 1935, St. James), another operetta calling itself a musical play, had a book by Frank Mandel, based on Eric von Stroheim and Wallace Smith's novel *The Happy Alienist*. The show's music was by Sigmund Romberg, its lyrics by Oscar Hammerstein II. In an attempt to fall in with more or less recent fashions the musical omitted the chorus. And the curtain rose without an overture or an opening number, to give the impression of an intimate straight play. It also, as the title of its source hints, used a very twentieth-century figure as the center of its nineteenth-century plot. The cynical Baron Kuno (Walter Woolf King) encourages Marie, the Baroness Von Schlewitz (Nancy McCord), to accept the proposal of Professor Johann Volk (Walter Slezak), a psychoanalyst. He hopes to blackmail the professor. But after the wedding Marie finds herself falling in love with Johann. Johann learns of Marie's original intentions and, not knowing of her new feelings, determines to kill her. Luckily he misses, shooting merely the dummy he had made and to which the shy Johann had confessed the depths of his ardor. Mandel's libretto was claptrap.

But Romberg's score, while lightweight, was appealing. Out of it came his only show hit of the decade, "I Built A Dream One Day." For Romberg, 1935 was a relatively good year. His "When I Grow Too Old To Dream" from the movie *The Night Is Young* was even more popular than his song hit from *May Wine*. But these were the last successes he would enjoy until *Up in Central Park* (27 January 1945).

The old Hippodrome relit, a Romberg operetta running six months—the past seemed to be reasserting itself. As if to underline the return to the good old days, **George White's Scandals of 1936** (25 December 1935, New Amsterdam) came in one week before the new year of its title. Willie and Eugene Howard were on hand with Bert Lahr to head the comic section. Rudy Vallee sang the best tunes. A dance team known as Sam, Ted, and Ray did the fastest stepping. Much of the material was old hat. The Howards got their *Rigoletto* costumes out of the mothballs, and Willie went on to teach still more French lessons. Bert Lahr played a renowned cook who managed to throw even his wig in his soup. Ray Henderson again composed the songs, using still another new lyricist, Jack Yellen. But the fire had gone out of Henderson, as had the gift for readily hummable tunes. The songs often had pleasant phrases, but in the end seemed to go nowhere. Henderson joined the swelling ranks who were abandoning Broadway. He returned only once, in the early forties. And the current edition joined the growing ranks of musicals that couldn't realize a return on their investment, though in the case of the *Scandals* its 110-performance run probably precluded that anyway.

A revue which had managed to eke out ten weeks in 1934 returned in a new edition, **Continental Varieties of 1936** (26 December 1935, Masque), but this time remained for only its pre-booked nine performances.

On 1 January 1936, the musical stage mourned the loss of the man who will probably never be surpassed as its most prolific librettist and lyricist. Harry B. Smith died at the age of seventy-five. He was credited with writing, in part or alone, the books for over 300 shows and the words for over 6,000 songs. But it would take an acute, and possibly imaginative, observer to see any progression from his stilted if competent early writing to his stilted if competent final pieces. Yet in his own day he was thought of highly enough to be the first American lyricist to have his words published without the music in a hardback book.

The new year got off to an unpromising start with a five-performance fiasco called **The Illustrator's Show** (22 January 1936, 48th St.). The show had called itself to the public's attention when police raided and closed it while it was being performed uptown earlier in the year. It was originally presented by the Society of Illustrators more to put their own works before the public than as a showcase for theatrical talent. Several famous artists of the period made personal appearances. Almost without exception the critics pounced on Otto Soglow, who impersonated "The Little King" he had drawn for *The New Yorker* and for syndication. The reviewers took strong exception to the off-color sketch in which Soglow placed his lovable, rotund monarch. Two of the most successful figures of a later Broadway had a hand in the evening. Most of the lyrics were by Frank Loesser, who quickly displayed his penchant for offbeat verbal rhythms in "Bang—The Bell Rang!" while Frederick Loewe, in collaboration with Earle Crooker, inserted "A Waltz Was Born In Vienna."

As she had been in 1933, Mrs. Florenz Ziegfeld was listed as the producer of the latest edition of The **Ziegfeld Follies** (30 January 1936, Winter Garden), and as they had been in 1933, the Shuberts were the real producers. Vernon Duke and Ira Gershwin were again the songsmiths, John Murray Anderson was once more in charge of the staging, and Fanny Brice returned to lead the list of funny people in the show. But there were new, added performers. Bob Hope had important bits, including the show's hit tune. Gertrude Niesen was on hand to sing the more sultry numbers. Eve Arden provided more restrained comic moments, and Judy Canova offered more lowbrow fun, when Miss Brice was off stage. The almost legendary Josephine Baker came home from Paris to parade her talents. Miss Brice had a field day kidding her own classic "My Man" in "He Hasn't A Thing Except Me," desperately tried to reclaim a winning sweepstakes ticket she has inadvertently given away, and played Baby Snooks in Hollywood and on "Major Bones's" amateur hour. Miss Niesen and Miss Baker shared a big production number, "Island In The West Indies," which suggested that melodically and lyrically these spectacle numbers had not advanced much in a quarter of a century. But Hope and Miss Arden dramatized the evolution of the love ballad when they sang "I Can't Get Started."

The cynical flippancy of the staging underscored the changes. Hope sang the song to Miss Arden and, when she finally responded, walked away indifferently.

The most important new name on the program was George Balanchine, who worked with Robert Alton on the dances. His sensual choreography for "Five A.M." gave audiences a hint of his future prowess, a power he more decidedly displayed in his next assignment, two months later. The extent to which the show depended on Fanny Brice was made apparent to Broadway when her illness forced the show to close after 115 performances. Everything was stashed away until the fall, when she was well enough to return. But by that time all her associates had found work elsewhere, and a new cast was assembled headed by Bobby Clark in his first solo appearance.

GEORGE BALANCHINE (Gyorgi Balanchivadze) was born in St. Petersburg, Russia, on 9 January 1904. As a boy he trained at the Russian Imperial School. In the late twenties he worked with Diaghilev and in the early thirties with Colonel de Basil. Coming to New York in 1934 he founded, with Lincoln Kirstein, the School of American Ballet.

Murder in the Old Red Barn (1 February 1936, American Music Hall) was a spoof of nineteenth-century melodrama larded with later popular songs ("The Music Goes Round And Round," "Happy Days Are Here Again") and extraneous nonsense. Made surprisingly welcome, it initiated a series of similar entertainments at the same house over the next several seasons.

In a year laden with noteworthy theatrical deaths, none diminished the glitter of Broadway as much as the passing of Marilyn Miller on 7 April.

The book for the season's biggest hit, **On Your Toes** (11 April 1936, Imperial), was primarily by George Abbott, with help from Rodgers and Hart, who had thought up the plot in the first place. Its story was complicated and not always well motivated, but serviceable. Junior Dolan is the son of old vaudevillians who have educated him beyond his desires. He has become a professor of music, though he would prefer to be a simple hoofer. Dolan helps a struggling Russian ballet company restore its sagging finances by mounting a jazz ballet and even takes the lead himself when the head male dancer fails to appear. He then realizes his love for the prima

ballerina is as absurd as his parents' plan for him had been. He settles for simple Frankie Frayne (Doris Carson), his old flame who saved his life by warning him that gangsters, mistaking him for the original dancer, were out to kill him. Two triumphs were the principal reasons for the show's success. The first was the lovely Rodgers and Hart material coupled with Rodgers's impressive music for the ballet "Slaughter on Tenth Avenue." After being away for so long, this was their second fine achievement in a matter of months. They gave every promise of recapturing their incredible fecundity. The most-played song from the show was unquestionably Junior and Frankie's caressing "There's A Small Hotel," written originally for *Jumbo*. But the tunes ranged from the jaunty title song—sung by Junior, Frankie, and Sydney Cohen (David Morris)—to Frankie and Sydney's sweetly forlorn "Glad To Be Unhappy." Hart's comic lines were never better than in his hilarious roasting of the excesses of the rich (supper clubs where people are close as sardines in a can), "Too Good For The Average Man," sung by snobbish Peggy Porterfield (Luella Gear) and the equally snobbish émigré, Sergei Alexandrovitch (Monty Woolley). The main theme from the "Slaughter on Tenth Avenue" ballet became one of the few wordless excerpts from the Broadway stage to achieve independent vogue. The second great asset was, obviously, George Balanchine's superb ballets, brilliantly danced by the show's Junior Dolan, Ray Bolger, and Tamara Geva.

GEORGE ABBOTT was born in Forestville, New York, on 25 January 1887. His formal education included time at the Kearney Military Academy, the University of Rochester, and George Pierce Baker's famous 47 Workshop at Harvard. Abbott's early years in the theatre were spent acting in plays such as *Dulcy, Hell-Bent fer Heaven*, and *Processional*. In the mid-twenties he turned to writing and directing plays, first fast-moving melodramas and later even faster-moving farces. Among the plays on which he served as collaborator, director, or both were *Broadway, Chicago, Twentieth Century, Boy Meets Girl, Room Service*, and *Three Men on a Horse*. He assisted

John Murray Anderson with the direction of Jumbo, his first musical. Abbott's background in fast-moving plays (and probably his military school training) led him to place his unique stamp on those musicals he worked with. His direction was almost always to be marked by a special tautness and lively pacing.

The first ballet, "Princess Zenobia," was a satire on classic offerings. Bolger danced the part of a blackface native, discovering too late that he had forgotten to paint the rest of his body. But it was the second-act ballet, "Slaughter on Tenth Avenue," that was the high point of the evening. It took place in a sleazy West Side bar, where a hoofer pays the owner to let him spend some time with the stripper. The owner becomes jealous and shoots the girl, and the hoofer shoots him. The ballet was worked in loosely to the plot both front and back by first having Junior substitute for the male lead and then having the gangsters aim at him thinking he is the same absconding dancer. The connection was clever but hardly more germane than, say, the late Marilyn Miller's butterfly dance in *Sally* (21 December 1920), which convinced her admirers that she should be in the *Follies*. Truly integrated dance, where the ballet takes over and advances the story when the actors leave off, had to wait for *Oklahoma!* (31 March 1943) or, if that is ruled out because it was merely a dream, the opening pantomime of *Carousel* (19 April 1945). Innovation had not been popular on Broadway in recent seasons. But the originality and daring of *On Your Toes*—aided by Abbott's brisk staging—was clothed in such colorful raiment, audiences cheered for nearly ten months.

Two vaudevilles, **Broadway Sho-Window** (12 April 1936, Broadway) and **Summer Wives** (13 April 1936, Mansfield), the latter with a slim plot, both failed. The first was assembled by Gus Edwards.

Another "sho-window," **New Faces of 1936** (19 May 1936, Vanderbilt), arrived five weeks later on May 19 to close the season. This time Broadway was more receptive. Not all the faces were new. Imogene Coca was back, seemingly in the same coat she had worn all through the first edition. She also played a Cinderella who begged her fairy godmother to let her be a stripper. Mrs. Roosevelt and Mrs. Hoover were kidded again, as were the Girl Scouts. Dorothy

Parker, an easy target, was knocked in "Lottie Of The Literati" with the snide couplet, "No matter who said it, Dorothy Parker gets credit." Musically the evening was uneventful. Its best numbers were probably "My Last Affair" (Haven Johnson) and "You'd Better Go Now" (Bickely Reichner/Irvin Graham). When business fell, two anything-but-new faces, the Duncan Sisters, were rushed in with some of their material from *Topsy and Eva*. But old faces or new, the show drew crowds for only six months.

1936–1937

No new musicals appeared between the arrival of *New Faces of 1936* at the end of May and the opening of **The White Horse Inn** on 1 October. But the D'Oyly Carte played twenty weeks beginning 20 August. *The White Horse Inn* was adapted from Ralph Benatzky's melodious Berlin operetta *Im Weissen Rossl*. Mounted at the mammoth Center Theatre with even greater opulence than *The Great Waltz*, it ran 223 performances. William Gaxton, Kitty Carlisle, and Robert Halliday were the stars—though it is doubtful if anyone could see their features or even hear them clearly from the back of the balcony.

At the end of the month—on 29 October—three more stars, Jimmy Durante, Ethel Merman, and Bob Hope could be better seen and heard at the more sensibly sized Alvin. Their vehicle, **Red, Hot and Blue!**, was written and produced by the team that created the preceding season's *Anything Goes:* Cole Porter for the songs, Howard Lindsay and Russel Crouse for the book, and Vinton Freedley behind the scenes. Originally it had been designed for all three stars of *Anything Goes*. But Gaxton preferred the offer he received for *The White Horse Inn*, and Moore was busy elsewhere. Perhaps because they had Gaxton and Moore in mind at first, the librettists came up with a story that reminded many in the audience of *Of Thee I Sing* (26 December 1931). In both cases the hero's mate is to be chosen in a contest, in both the hero rejects the winner, in both the White House is a prominent setting, and in both the Supreme Court's decision is significant. "Nails" O'Reilly Duquesne (Miss Merman), a new millionairess, decides to hold a lottery for charity. Even the Senate buys tickets, hoping to make a dent in the national debt. The winner will be the person who discovers the whereabouts of Bob Hale's childhood sweetheart. She shouldn't be too hard to find, for she carries a distinctive mark. As a child she sat on a hot waffle iron, and the imprint is still there. To assist in the search, "Nails" arranges the parole of several inmates at the swank Lark's Nest Prison. The leader of the parolees, "Policy" Pinkle (Durante), resents his release, since he has risen to captain of the prison polo team. The girl is found, but Hale (Hope) can't understand what he once saw in her. However, he is not obligated to marry her, since the Supreme Court declares that any lottery benefiting the American people is unconstitutional. Bob jumps at the chance to marry "Nails." The book, however entertaining, lacked the sharpness and tonal consistency so evident in *Of Thee I Sing*. Porter's songs, while excellent, were far more conventional than the Gershwin brothers' material. The most widely played song was "It's De-Lovely," which, in its stage version, had Bob and Nails recount a romance from the lovers' first encounter to their grown son's social success. Porter's literate wit leavened the pain of the young lady "Down In The Depths" on the ninetieth floor— another song since associated with Merman. The melody of Nails's vivacious "Ridin' High" became popular, even if the words didn't. An equally lively title song received some attention, but the lovely, minor-keyed "Good-bye, Little Dream; Good-bye" was dropped during the tryout. The comic numbers were superb. In "A Little Skipper From Heaven Above" Durante told his surprised cohorts, "I'm about to become a mother," and in a spoof on country music, "The Ozarks Are Callin' Me Home," he noted that while he was busy in the kitchen fryin' chicken, he could hear Paw givin' Maw her daily lickin'. For all its merits the show was a disappointment at the box office, compiling a good, but in no way overwhelming, 183 performances.

The first of three November openings was Sigmund Romberg and Otto Harbach's operetta— they called it "a musical romance"—**Forbidden Melody** (2 November 1936, New Amsterdam). Romberg and his associates were apparently not concerned that the public would confuse the title with Romberg's earlier failures, *Melody* (14 February 1933) and *The Magic Melody* (11 November 1919). Their lack of concern was justified. The show was bad enough to flop on its own. Rumor gave out that the story had been based on an actual incident in the life of King Carol of Roumania. In Bucharest Gregor Fiorescu (Carl Brisson) is photographed in a hotel room with the wife (Ruth Weston) of a prominent politician, Colonel Geza (Arthur Vinton). To avoid difficulties he persuades an actress friend to claim it was really she with whom he was meeting. But

when Gregor finds himself falling in love with Elene (Ruby Mercer), he also finds he has a jealous and vengeful Mme. Geza on his hands. Romberg's music was pretty, but as out of date as Harbach's lyrics. Even the slightly more contemporary sound of "You Are All I've Wanted" lacked an additional something extra to put it across. When the show closed at the end of the month, the New Amsterdam Theatre, in which it had played, went over to movies. The magnificent theatre had been the last holdout on 42nd Street. With its changeover, a glittering era, actually gone for five years, was unmistakably over.

On 3 November Roosevelt was elected to a second term, thereby assuring at least the temporary continuation of state-supported theatre projects and an increasingly left-wing tone to their presentation. This new slant was bound to spill over into more commercial enterprises.

KURT WEILL was born in Dessau, Germany, on 2 March 1900. After some early musical training at the hands of his parents, he studied at the Berlin High School of Music and privately under Ferrucio Busoni. An advocate of the Zeitkunst school, he began composing operas larded with styles borrowed from contemporary popular music, especially those employing American jazz idioms. His early operas, generally well received by German operagoers, included *Der Protagonist* and *Royal Palace*. He soon joined forces with the leftish Bertolt Brecht to create two outstanding successes for the popular German theatre of the time, *Die Dreigroschenoper* and *Aufstieg und Fall der Stadt Mahogonny*. But Nazi persecution drove Weill, his wife Lotta Lenya, and Brecht to Paris. A short while later the Weills accompanied Max Reinhardt and Franz Werfel to America to assist in a mounting of *The Eternal Road*.

As if to underscore this irresistible drift, the leftish Group Theatre mounted Paul Green's play with music, **Johnny Johnson** (19 November 1936, 44th St.). The songs and background music were by Kurt Weill, a refugee whose only other Broadway exposure had come with an unsuccessful adaption of his German *Die Dreigroschenoper*.

Green's somewhat confused parable ventured into fantasy and almost into allegory as it followed the history of a benign, pacifist stonecutter (Russell Collins)—the play opens with the dedication of his monument to Peace—as he is inexorably sucked into World War I, is wounded, momentarily disrupts the war by spraying the Allied High Command with laughing gas, is committed to a mental institution, where he and his fellow inmates assume the mantles of world statesmen and establish the League of World Republics, is finally released, and goes home to peddle nonmartial toys to a war-happy village. Weill's music gained little popular currency, but it displayed the quick, nervous lines and sardonic harmonies that would become his trademark. Though the left-wing writers insisted they spoke for the masses, the masses had long since abandoned the theatre. So stark, if touching, an antiwar piece could muster only sixty-eight performances.

Like *Johnny Johnson*, Noël Coward's **Tonight at 8:30** (19 December 1936, National) was a play with music, or, more accurately, nine one-act plays, three of which had songs. "Red Peppers," for example, depicted the battle between a small-time vaudeville act and the bandleader. The show, with Coward and Gertrude Lawrence in the leads, repeated its London success.

Three failures had not discouraged Donald Heywood from trying his luck again. Writing the book and songs, co-directing the production, and conducting the orchestra, Heywood was unable to achieve more than six performances for his **Black Rhythm** (24 November 1936, Comedy). Heywood's story was a backstage yarn recounting the efforts of a young hopeful named Jenny (Jeni Le Gon) to break into the big time. For the most part the evening consisted of a series of speciality acts—such as a plantation hilly-billy band that made music with combs, jugs, and washboards. At the opening of his last show Heywood had been assaulted by an irate patron. At the opening of *Black Rhythm* two stink bombs exploded in the theatre. Since there was apparently no racial prejudice behind either incident, Heywood took the hint and finally gave up trying to please Broadway.

December's only other musical was the revue **The Show Is On** (25 December 1936, Winter Garden). It was the last show of 1936. It was also the last of the bright, brittle, tune-filled escapist revues that Americans had thrown together so knowingly since the late twenties. More good revues would follow, but they invariably seemed somewhat wanting in one

department or another, especially in their music. For *The Show Is On* the music was "mostly by" Vernon Duke with lyrics "mostly by" Ted Fetter. But their songs were not as catchy as the show's charming hit "Little Old Lady" (Hoagy Carmichael and Stanley Adams), sung and danced by Mitzi Mayfair and Charles Walters. Carmichael was one of the most popular songwriters of the thirties, creating one of the era's great standards, "StarDust." But he never found time until 1940 to sit down and compose an entire score. The Gershwin brothers contributed an uncharacteristic salute to the Viennese waltz in "By Strauss" (sung by Gracie Barrie and Robert Shafer, while Mitzi Mayfair danced), their last offering to Broadway. Rodgers and Hart wrote "Rhythm," in which Bea Lillie devastated the singers of the day, and, for a time, resuscitated "I've Got Five Dollars"—originally from *America's Sweetheart* (10 February 1931). Harburg and Arlen threw in "Josephine Waters" and Bert Lahr's show-stopper "Song Of The Woodman." And Herman Hupfeld gave Miss Lillie a riotous take-off on all the old "moon" numbers, "Buy Yourself A Balloon," in which Miss Lillie swung out over the audience while sitting on a stage moon and threw garters at the men in the house.

The show, like its predecessor, *At Home Abroad*, used a theme to tie its material together. This theme was an old and natural favorite, show business. Reginald Gardiner was Shakespeare rewriting his material to suit twentieth-century tastes; Bert Lahr played a Hollywood idol sent to lure away a Baltimore matron from a king who would give up his throne for her; and Miss Lillie as a great lady of the theatre attended "The Reading Of The Play," which, when she is told it "is about a man and a woman," she cavalierly rejects for "too much plot." Both John Gielgud and Leslie Howard were offering Hamlets to New York. In the show's most hilarious bit Gardiner played Gielgud playing Hamlet while Miss Lillie was a noisy latecomer. When Gardiner-Gielgud offered to buy her a ticket to Howard's Hamlet if she will only leave, Miss Lillie declined, saying Howard paid for her ticket to Gielgud. The show was lavishly and tastefully staged by Vincente Minnelli. His production numbers included "Parade Night," filled with the "soft, nostalgic coloring of bygone days." Another critic saluted Minnelli's "subtle, witty" designs. The show remained on into the hot weather.

In his survey of 1930s musicals, Stanley Green is quite right when he says of 1937, "More sharply than did any other year, it pitted the old versus the new."

Just how decisive the result was remained uncertain at the time. It was 23 January before the first musical hit of 1937 arrived. **Naughty Naught ('00)** was produced by the Krimsky brothers at their American Music Hall. Jerrold Krimsky, writing as John Van Antwerp, supplied the book, while Ted Fetter set words to Richard Lewine's music. The American Musical Hall was a name new to Broadway. It had been a church. Now the Krimsky brothers converted it into as genuine a replica of the old Rialto musical halls as the time and safety codes would allow. The *double entendre* of the show's title fetchingly caught the period flavor. The story dealt with a turn-of-the-century regatta in which the villainous P. De Quincy Devereux (Alexander Clark) attempts to undermine Yale's great stroke, Frank Plover (Bartlett Robinson), by plying him with spiked lemonades and having a lady of questionable repute vamp him in front of his betrothed. Virtue triumphs. Though the music didn't try too hard to have appropriate period flavor, the show pleased its happily guzzling patrons for the rest of the season and inaugurated a short, insignificant series.

A more genuine turn-of-the-century sound was evoked in **Frederika** (4 February 1937, Imperial), but not tongue-in-check. The Messrs. Shubert presented Dennis King, Helen Gleason, and Ernest Truex in Franz Lehar's 1928 hit. Its story told of a foredoomed love affair between the poet Goethe and the beautiful Frederika. While the sets and costumes were eighteenth century, the music was typical Lehar. Though the book was adequate and the music pleasant, the show was not strong enough to overcome changing tastes, the poor economy, and an undercurrent of resentment against Lehar, who had tacitly embraced the new Nazi regime. In that respect the situation was not unlike the reaction Lehar had encountered twenty years before during World War I. The show closed after twelve weeks.

Two and a half months went by before the next musical, **Babes in Arms** (14 April 1937, Shubert), appeared. But it represented a complete turnabout from the musicals that preceded it. It sang out with a youthful, contemporary vitality. It was in its own way a sort of "new faces," filled with young, relatively unknown performers. Its story was simple. To avoid being sent to a work farm, the children of traveling vaudevillians pool their talents to present a show called "Lee Calhoun's Follies." The show fails, at least financially, and the kids are hustled off to the farm. They are rescued when a French aviator, on a transatlantic flight, makes an emergency landing on the field and befriends them. The show within a show allowed for ample displays of the performers' diverse talents. And great talents many of them were! Out of this show came Alfred Drake, Mitzi Green, Ray Heatherton, Robert Rounseville, Dan Dailey, and Wynn Murray. The flexible nature of the story allowed for a dream ballet in which the would-be stars meet the magical names of Hollywood. George Balanchine did the choreography, and Rodgers and Hart created their own book. But it was their songs that were quickly recognized as the show's finest, most enduring feature. Four Rodgers and Hart standards were first heard in *Babes in Arms*. They ranged from the offbeat, romantic opening "Where Or When" (sung by Miss Green and Heatherton) to the flashy, witty "The Lady Is A Tramp" to the wistful "My Funny Valentine" (the last two both sung by Miss Green) to the vibrant "Johnny One Note" (sung by Miss Murray). "My Funny Valentine" illustrates Hart's resourcefulness. Though the song is especially popular around Valentine's Day with lyrics that could pass for a bemused holiday paean, in the show it was sung to a boy named Valentine. As with most Rodgers and Hart scores, even the lesser-known songs had style and melody. The rousing title song and the mockingly cynical "I Wish I Were In Love Again" (sung by Grace McDonald and Rolly Pickert) typify the unfailingly intelligent blend of words and music. Produced for a mere $55,000, the show ran nine months and became a gold mine.

Two May musicals, both flops, ended the season. **Orchids Preferred** (11 May 1937, Imperial) told how two bar girls persuade the innocent Marion Brown (Vicki Cummings) to join their racket. But she manages to fall in love with her first supposed victim, Richard Hope (John Donaldson). When her friends see how serious the romance is becoming, they tell Richard of their trade. Marion tries to run away, but Richard, understanding her better nature, runs after her. In the emergency exit of the posh Waldmore Hotel they agree to be Mr. and Mrs. The songs were by Dave Stamper and Frederick Herendeen, who had turned out the score for the previous season's *Provincetown Follies*. Their bad luck still held. One week and the show folded.

Sea Legs (18 May 1937, Mansfield) did a little better. It ran two weeks. Based on the play *The Cat Came Back*, it had a book and lyrics by Arthur Swanstrom and music by Michael H. Cleary. The evening was mounted as a vehicle for Dorothy Stone and her husband, Charles Collins. It was one of the few musicals written since the twenties

Intermission

Broadway's Response to the Swing Era, 1937–1942

By the summer of 1937 the swing era was at its peak. The jazz era, which had reigned through the gay, gaudy years of the twenties and, with a subdued, modified tone, continued through the somber years of the early thirties, had drifted incontestably into history. George Gershwin's death on 11 July 1937 underscored its passing. In theatrical terms, Gershwin had been the most articulate and memorable of the modernists, the personification of his high-kicking epoch. No similar figure emerged to give comparable theatrical definition to swing. To some extent this was predictable, because swing, as has been noted, was a less theatrical musical idiom than jazz or ragtime had been, and because, as an expression of popular musical speech, it was more likely to be appropriated by and developed in Hollywood than on a stage catering to an increasingly older audience. Unfortunately Broadway's most gifted melodists, men such as Richard Rodgers, Irving Berlin, and Cole Porter, while complaining about the harsh treatment their songs received at the hands of swing arrangers, actually abetted the trend toward exaggeratedly rhythmic presentation by falling into creative slumps during this period. Good songs were fewer; songs that proved lastingly popular, fewer still. National and international turmoil—the persistent Depression, the Nazi terror, the onset of World War II—undoubtedly had a debilitating influence. Librettists as well as composers were affected. Books became trite, satire less bitingly satiric, romance less flamboyantly romantic. Only toward the end of this five-year lull did two daringly pioneering works present genuine possibilities. Yet, as it turned out, neither pointed precisely in the direction that ultimately led the American Musical Theatre out of its doldrums.

1937–1938

This intermission opened with an eerie, uncomfortable season. The Depression, which had seemed to be lifting, suddenly took a turn for the worse, and the number of shows produced on Broadway fell to the lowest figure in thirty years. Almost defiantly, the number of new musicals rose slightly. Yet even here a feeling of uneasy change prevailed. Productions came from unaccustomed sources. The WPA Federal Theatre Project mounted several. The Mercury Theatre, a repertory company heretofore devoted to the classics, helped stage one of the most controversial, and a labor union offered what became the long-run hit of the year. These organizations naturally influenced the tenor of the pieces. Social and political outlook became as important as entertainment value. Harsh, provocative words claimed priority over sweet, singable melodies. A malaise affected even the more conventional commercial productions. There were few outstanding songs, and most of those were subdued ballads. Lyricists and librettists fared a bit better, but two of the biggest hits of the season, for all their success, represented unhappy matings of stars and authors.

The Federal Theatre Project opened the season in the middle of summer with a black musical comedy, **Swing It** (22 July 1937, Adelphi). Its story line followed the down-at-the-heels crew and entertainers of a rickety Mississippi showboat in their effort to find a better lot in Harlem. The show was really "a potpourri of minstrelsy, singing, dancing, mugging, clowning, spirituals, jazz, swing, tapping and the carrying of Harlem's throaty torch." Henry Jines and James Green sparked the comedy, playing two characters with Tweedledum-Tweedledee names, Rusty and Dusty. Herbie Brown's dancing waiter served up flashy tap routines between courses. Romantic interests, so carefully muted in early Negro shows, crept in, allowing Sherman Dickson and Frances Everett to smooth their path to the altar with "Ain't We Got Love." Although the strongly rhythmic, sometimes antimelodic, sounds of swing were coming to dominate the world of popular music, Eubie Blake's score was "muted, more pastel in color." His biographers attribute this to his catching the spirit of his new partner, Milton Reddie. But a look at the season's musicals will show he was in the spirit of the times as well. When neither the show nor the new Blake style appealed to the public, *Swing It* left after nine weeks.

Seeking a successor to *The Great Waltz* and *The White Horse Inn* for their behemoth Center Theatre, the Rockefellers commissioned a musical about colonial Williamsburg, which the family had begun to restore. Called **Virginia,** the show opened on 2 September. It was overwhelmed by the house. The Center, like the Hippodrome or the Earl Carroll, was adequate for spectacle, but intimate spoken dialogue and the low-ranged, croonable melodies of the American musical were lost in its vastness. With proper spectacle the more broad-stroked, highly colored Viennese operetta could pass, but it was really the spectacle that counted. From the American repertory only a musical play on the order of *Show Boat* (27 December 1927) might have made a success. Apparently this is what the Rockefellers had in mind. Their choice of Laurence Stallings as librettist was enlightened, if a bit risky. Stallings was a gifted, intelligent playwright who nonetheless had only one real success to his credit, his collaboration with Maxwell Anderson on *What Price Glory?* His two produced efforts at musical books, *Deep River* (4 October 1926) and *Rainbow* (21 November 1928), had failed as much because they were ahead of their time as for any other reason. Stallings hit upon a story for *Virginia* that had the necessary sweep and pageantry required by the house, but something went wrong. Even while the work was in rehearsal Owen Davis was called in to sharpen it. When Fortesque (Gene Lockhart) of Drury Lane comes to America in 1775 with a company of London actors, he also brings with him a letter for General Washington. The loyalists attempt to prevent the letter's delivery, but Fortesque quietly passes it to his leading lady, Sylvia Laurence (Anne Booth), who in turn passes it on to Colonel Richard Fairfax (Ronald Graham), her American admirer. Although the British seize Fairfax, he manages to get the letter through.

In selecting Arthur Schwartz to write the songs, the management made a major error. Schwartz had a long, romantic musical line, much like Jerome Kern's at his most intimate, but he was not given to the more full-bodied melodies the large house required. His martial title song approached what was needed, but the better numbers—and he composed a fine score—were small-scaled and tender. Radio, not the show, made a hit of "You And I Know" (sung by Sylvia and Richard). Three other Schwartz songs—"An Old Flame Never Dies" (Sylvia's solo), "If You Were Someone Else" (Richard's solo), and "Good-bye, Jonah" (sung and tapped by Buck and Bubbles)—can still be heard on rare occasions. Albert Stillman's slightly fustian lyrics were more in keeping with the show's requirements than with Schwartz's music. *Virginia,* like *Swing It,* ran sixty performances.

The WPA again headed the credits as producer when **A Hero Is Born** followed *Swing It* into the Adelphi on 1 October. In spite of its stirringly militant title, a type of title so beloved by the age, the musical told an innocent, childlike tale. At his christening Prince Prigio of Pantouflia (Ben Starkie) is lavishly favored by the fairies. His mother (Margaret Wycherly) has no time for such unworldly creatures and their equally unworldly gifts, so the presents are never shown to the young boy. He grows up to be an intellectual snob. One day he stumbles on the long-hidden treasures. He finds a magic cap that makes its wearer invisible, one that grants its wearer any wish, a magic carpet, and a host of other wonders. Aided by these marvels he also finds a becoming modesty and a beautiful princess, Rosalind (Drue Leyton). This surprisingly apolitical book was adapted from an Andrew Lang fairy tale by Theresa Helburn, of the faltering Theatre Guild. A. Lehman Engel, who, simply as Lehman Engel, soon became the musical theatre's leading conductor, wrote the score. The show was mounted with "circus dimensions," its scenes filled not just with a cast of nearly 100 but with "props and magic machines" of every sort. But the public was not attracted. In part the show's problem was that it was not sufficiently political for the loyal hardcore of the WPA audience, while WPA productions were automatically anathema to a large group who might have found this piece enchanting.

Broadway has generally believed that if at first you do succeed, try and try again. Certainly the Krimskys and their associates (Ted Fetter and Richard Lewine) held to the dictum. Fast on the vogue of *Naughty Naught* ('00), they relit their American Musical Hall on 9 October with **The Fireman's Flame**. It was another first-class spoof of bygone melodramas, and it, too, could have been called *A Hero Is Born*. The Red Heart Hose Boys cannot see the heroic qualities in Harry Howard (Ben Cutler). Rejected by the brigade, he joins the less desirable Bluebird Hose Company. His rescue of the rich Adolphus Vanderpool (Philip Bourneuf) and his foster daughter Daphne (Cynthia Rogers) reflects unfavorably on the Red Heart Boys. They try to besmirch Harry's good name, coupling it with the scarlet Vera Violet (Grace Coppin). But the grateful Vanderpool foils the nefarious machinations. Harry turns out to be Vanderpool's son. By curtain time Daphne is slated to be Harry's wife and Harry is made fire chief. The songs sometimes mocked the speech patterns of the earlier days ("Do My Eyes Deceive Me?"), sometimes accepted their declarative directness ("It's A Lovely Night On The Hudson River"), and sometimes wryly combined the old and the new ("Doin' The Waltz"). "Do My Eyes Deceive Me?" and "It's A Lovely Night On The

Hudson River" were love songs sung by Harry and Daphne, while Vera was awarded "Doin' The Waltz." Both the exaggerated gestures of the performers and such devices as simulated gas lamps for footlights affected proper nineteenth-century stage conventions. Theatergoers found it hard to resist such good fun. *The Fireman's Flame* surpassed the run of *Naughty Naught '00*, playing 204 performances.

The American Musical Theatre came back to the world of 1937 with its next two musicals. Nonetheless, in treating their own unhappy times these shows were poles apart. **I'd Rather Be Right** (2 November 1937, Alvin) was a warmhearted jab at the Roosevelt administration. Presidents had been portrayed on the musical stage before, especially in revue skits. But *I'd Rather Be Right* made Roosevelt the first incumbent President to become the central figure of a book musical. Since George S. Kaufman and Moss Hart wrote the book, expectations were high. And the humor in the show was every bit as biting and to the point as the fun-making in *Of Thee I Sing* (26 December 1931) or *Face the Music* (17 February 1932). Unfortunately, the book turned out to be a collection of witty lines without any interesting turns of plot. The locale is Central Park in New York and the time the Fourth of July. Peggy Jones (Joy Hodges) and Phil Barker (Austin Marshall) would like to marry but feel they must wait for a pay raise that will come only when Roosevelt balances the budget. Phil falls asleep in the park and dreams he meets Roosevelt (George M. Cohan). The President proves sympathetic to Phil's problem and sets out immediately to see what he can do to aid the lovers. But every suggestion—taxing government property, hundred-dollar postage stamps—is rejected on some ground or other. And the idea that the treasury should hire pickpockets to relieve the nation of its money painlessly is thwarted by a vengeful Supreme Court, still smarting from Roosevelt's attempt the previous January to "pack" it with additional members. Roosevelt resorts to a fireside speech, begging American women to eschew cosmetics for a year and donate the savings to the government. The women are not receptive. FDR's presidential rival, Alf Landon (Joseph Allen), reduced to a White House butler, is no help. Neither is Eleanor Roosevelt, who is away on a trip and unable to get back for Phil's dream. In the end Roosevelt suggests the youngsters ought to marry anyway. It's the right thing to do, and Roosevelt would rather be right than President. The lovers agree. Almost all the important political figures of the day except

Eleanor Roosevelt were impersonated, while dozens of prominent Americans from Walter Lippmann to John L. Lewis came in for jibes. The dialogue was rib-tickling, such as the uproarious bit between the Postmaster General and the President:

Farley: This fellow is Chairman of the Fourth Assembly District in Seattle. He wants to be Collector of the Port of New York.
Roosevelt: But we've got a Collector of the Port of New York.
Farley: Not in Seattle.

Many of the best laughs fell to Farley. In discussing the postal rates he suggests all letters be required to carry airmail stamps, even if they are only being sent from the Bronx to Brooklyn. Roosevelt professes to be shocked:

Roosevelt: No, no, Jim. That wouldn't be honest.
Farley: Oh! I thought you were talking about taxes.

Later, after Roosevelt proposes to dispose of national encumbrances, Farley inquires, "Do we need Baltimore?" In some respects the show had an old musical comedy flavor. Touches of vaudeville were interspersed throughout the evening. When Roosevelt asks to see the Wagner Act, the act turns out to be not a law but a pair of acrobats. And as soon as a crowd assembles, a Federal Theatre troupe rushes in to sing "Spring In Vienna." The show, like *Sea Legs* a few months earlier, was one of the last to use a single set for the entire evening. (When FDR needed someplace to deliver a fireside chat, a fire place was wheeled on stage.)

The most endearing touch of an older era was the show's star, George M. Cohan. It was a perfect role in many ways for the great showman. He could be brash, vital, chauvinistic, and preachy. Regrettably, there were problems for him and his audience. First of all, Cohan hated Roosevelt. At one point during the Boston tryout he inserted his own anti-Roosevelt lyrics until Rodgers and Hart read him the riot act. But even more urgently, Rodgers let Cohan down. The score was one of Rodgers's weakest. Furthermore, Rodgers's subtle, contemporary style was not only alien to Cohan, it was anathema. Behind the scenes Cohan referred to his songwriters as Gilbert and Sullivan—and he didn't mean the comparison to be complimentary. Even if he were right about Rodgers's music, Cohan was blind to the merits of Hart's lyrics—the equal of Ira Gershwin's

for *Of Thee I Sing*. The cabinet enters and sings a chorus that belies their subsequent quarreling. They insist they are such a "homogeneous cabinet," unable to be told apart, that you'd swear that they had toured with Rupert D'Oyly Carte. Each secretary follows with a personal plaint. The lone woman in the entourage, Frances Perkins (Bijou Fernandez), the Secretary of Labor, remarks that she barely has time to powder her nose. She adds that for all the good she achieves, she might as well resign and go on powdering her nose. Even in the lyrics much of the fun continued to center on Farley. In "Off The Record" Roosevelt recounts their first meeting, recalling Farley talked until Roosevelt was in such a stupor that Farley had no trouble selling him the works of James Fenimore Cooper. Regrettably, except for Peggy and Phil's love song, "Have You Met Miss Jones?," Rodgers's melodies, while filled with interesting, sophisticated phrases, never added up to memorable tunes. Although *I'd Rather Be Right* enjoyed a healthy advance sale, business was further helped by the amazing, if poignant, fact that, for the first three and a half weeks of its nine-month run, only one other musical was competing with it on Broadway—another Rodgers and Hart hit, *Babes in Arms*.

There were virtually no advance sales for **Pins and Needles.** No advertisements were placed in the major dailies, and in return no major critic attended the show's opening night. Sponsored by the International Ladies' Garment Workers Union, the evening was unveiled on 27 November at what once had been the Princess Theatre and now was given the more aggressive name the Labor Stage. The cast was recruited entirely from the rank and file of union members—cutters, weavers, machinists. So small were the union's expectations that initially only weekend performances were scheduled, thereby allowing the cast to do their regular work from Monday through Friday. The aggressive new name for the house reflected the aggressive, if honest, tone of the revue. Its most famous number insisted: "Sing Me A Song With Social Significance," adding that unless the song is "packed with social fact" no love will follow. This sort of militancy led to some regrettable extremism—with the unionists seeing fascists and other villains in every person who deigned to disagree with them, much as many right-wingers of the day saw anarchists and Communists in every member of the opposing camp. One dance number was the vitriolic "Doin' The Reactionary" ("Close your eyes to where you're bound"), a far cry from the insouciant "Doin' The Waltz" being sung uptown. In so charged an atmosphere even love became a distorted image of the group's social and political thinking, with, for example, extramarital flirting branded as "scabbing." Undoubtedly the polarization of political stances created in the ferment of the Depression and New Deal endeavors to deal with it were accurately, if unfortunately, reflected.

Happily, the show found time to leave such cares behind. In a song that may have reminded inveterate theatergoers of Luella Gear's plaint "I Couldn't Hold My Man" in *Life Begins at 8:40* (27 August 1934), a young dressmaker named Millie Weitz rued that for all her dutiful adherence to advertising injunctions, "Nobody Makes A Pass At Me." International wrongdoing was chided in "Four Little Angels Of Peace." The number presented Hitler attempting to justify the Austrian Anschluss, Mussolini excusing his invasion of Ethiopia, an unidentified Japanese rationalizing the attack on China, and, somewhat unfairly, Anthony Eden singing of supposed English injustice to South Africa, India, and Ireland. The revue's low budget kept *Pins and Needles* going for 1,108 performances—first at the 299-seat Labor Stage, later at the 849-seat Windsor. While in no way gainsaying the show's incontestable popularity, it should be remembered that even the Windsor was only about half the size of the average Broadway musical house. Had *Pins and Needles* been presented with a professional cast in a theatre of average size, its run might well have been markedly shorter.

Curiously, the show's long run helped perpetuate itself. Fans could and did make repeated visits, since sketches and musical numbers were constantly changed to keep abreast of national and international developments. For example, even before Munich Eden was replaced by a figure more deserving of ridicule, Neville Chamberlain. When the Daughters of the American Revolution refused the African-American singer Marian Anderson permission to give a concert in their Washington auditorium, a spoof of *The Hot Mikado* (23 March 1939) and *The Swing Mikado* (1 March 1939) suddenly found three little maids singing, "Three little DARs are we/Full to the brim with bigotry." During the show's long run it also underwent several minor title changes, being called at one time or another *New Pins and Needles, Pins and Needles of 1938*, and *Pins and Needles of 1939*. Perhaps the show's most enduring legacy was its gift to Broadway of a new composer-lyricist, Harold Rome.

HAROLD ROME was born in Hartford, Connecticut, on 27 May 1908. He attended Trinity College and Yale, receiving his B.A. from the latter in 1929 and a degree in architecture in 1934. Unable to find work in his chosen profession, he turned to writing music. Rome had studied piano as a boy and helped pay his own way through college by playing in jazz bands and the Yale orchestra. He came to the attention of the International Ladies' Garment Workers Union while he was writing revues for a summer camp in the Adirondacks.

If Cohan had been ill at ease with the songs Rodgers and Hart had written for him, Ed Wynn was equally uncomfortable with E. Y. Harburg, Howard Lindsay, and Russel Crouse's book for **Hooray for What!** (1 December 1937, Winter Garden). By stages he turned what had begun as a satire of the armaments race into another lunatic carnival. Gone by the time the show reached New York was the taut, hard-driving book, much of Agnes de Mille's antiwar ballet, and a number of the original leads. Wynn had to dominate his shows. But he wisely allowed enough of the story and malicious fun to remain to satisfy both the critics and his loyal following.

Chuckles is a zany scientist who invents a gas to kill appleworms. When the world powers discover it kills humans with equal efficacy, they trip over one another trying to steal it. Chuckles is invited to the League of Nations. At the Grand Hotel de l'Espionage one Mata Hari type copies his formula with the aid of a mirror, thereby getting it backwards and producing a laughing gas. The show was filled with Wynn witticisms, delivered with his exaggerated lisp: "Generally speaking diplomats are generally speaking"; "The trouble with Europe is Italy's in Ethiopia, Japan's in China, Russia's in Spain—nobody's home"; "Don't you fellows know that if you miss two more payments, America will own the last war outright?" E. Y. Harburg and Harold Arlen's score was less vulnerable to Wynn's revision than the book. The songs were pleasant, if not particularly distinguished; certainly not in keeping with the high satiric aim of the original libretto. Its best numbers were "Down With Love," "I've Gone Romantic On You," and "God's Country." The last included the rather startling phrase "every man is his own dicta-tor." June Clyde, Vivian Vance, Jack Whiting, and the fine dancer Paul Haakon were featured. Whiting introduced all three of the songs mentioned, accom-panied by Miss Vance in "I've Gone Romantic On You" and by Miss Vance and Miss Clyde in "Down With Love." Despite the havoc Wynn created, *Hooray for What!* ran for six months.

Looking back after forty years on **Between the Devil** (22 December 1937, Imperial) its librett-tist and lyricist, Howard Dietz, concluded it was "almost a good show," failing primarily because he "didn't make it hilarious enough." He is probably too harsh on himself. This kind of drawing-room musical comedy, really old French bedroom farce streamlined for modern consumption, was nearing the end of its vogue. Brooks Atkinson of the *Times* begrudged having to sit through the sort of "imbecil-ities that were risqué in 1917, piquant in 1927, and only a pain in the first and second acts today … ." In Dietz's plot Peter Anthony (Jack Buchanan), believing his first wife dead in a shipwreck, remar-ries. He no sooner settles in with the second Mrs. Anthony (Evelyn Laye) than his first wife (Adele Dixon) reappears. In a novel departure, the ending was left up to the audience. During the show's tryout Anthony was aware his first wife was still alive when he married for the second time. Howls of outrage and threats to close the show for indecency forced Dietz to modify the libretto. However troublesome the play proved for Dietz, for Arthur Schwartz it was a return to the more intimate surroundings in which he belonged. Another Schwartz standard, "I See Your Face Before Me" (sung first by Miss Laye, later by Miss Dixon and Buchanan), came from the show. It used effectively a device Schwartz gener-ally ignored, the repeated note. Even "By Myself" (a Buchanan solo), another fine and unusual number from the show, restricted itself to a limited range but came up with a richly textured melody, helped by Schwartz's striking harmonies. Dietz's lyrics were not quite equal to his partner's music. Dietz was a fine lyricist but not really on a level with the best. His lines invariably seem to lack that exquisite choice of word or phrase that would make them masterful. For example, there is something a trifle contrived in the fourth line of "I See Your Face Before Me" ("You are my only theme"). The lyrics for "Triplets," of which he is especially fond, and which was sung as an incidental number in the show by a specialty act, are not particularly smart or witty. ("She admits Lane Bryant thought they were measuring a giant"

is the description of the woman pregnant with the triplets.) They clearly need a clever production to put them over. With so many lines delivered in Buchanan's and the ladies' English accents, the evening must have sounded especially high-hat to playgoers who saw any of *Between the Devil*'s ninety-three performances.

If the story of *Between the Devil* appeared to be going out of fashion, all of **Three Waltzes** (25 December 1937, Majestic) was a museum piece. Perhaps the fact that the Shuberts were the pro-ducers of both shows had something to do with this eagerness to retrace theatrical steps. (Even Ed Wynn's emasculating the satire in their production of *Hooray for What!* probably struck them as no more than a regression to the old star-dominated assemblages that had once kept their box offices busy.) *Three Waltzes* was an adaptation of a Viennese hit, *Drei Wälzer*, using melodies from three com-posers (Johann Strauss Sr., Johann Strauss Jr., and Oscar Straus) to tell in three acts three love stories of three related generations. It would be convenient to add that the show ran three months, but it ran closer to four. It might have run even longer had it been given a more extravagant mounting at the Center. At the Majestic it looked dowdy and old hat, despite the youthful charm of Kitty Carlisle and Michael Bartlett and the fine supporting acting of Glenn Anders.

Had the activity in 1938's first week been indica-tive, the new year would have seen a happy revital-izing of the musical theatre. Three musical evenings premiered, one on 3 January and two on the 4th. One of these was actually a repertory of seven-teenth- and eighteenth-century English operas that included works by Purcell and Arne. More pertinent to 1938 America was **The Cradle Will Rock**. It had a bizarre history. It had been dropped as a WPA project in Washington and was about to be done in New York in June, with John Houseman in charge, when an injunction prevented the actors from per-forming. Houseman and Orson Welles hired the empty Venice Theatre and marched the cast and patrons twenty blocks north. Since the musicians' union would not go along with the arrangement, the show's creator, Marc Blitzstein, played his score from a piano on stage. The actors, to overcome the technicality of the injunction, bought tickets, sat with the audience and performed from their seats. The play was repeated nineteen times at the Venice, then at the Mercury on Sunday nights, and finally began a regular run at the Windsor on 3 January.

It was a hate-warped tract which sadly saw everything in black and white. Steeltown is run by Mr. Mister (Will Geer) and his family for the benefit of Mr. Mister and his family—and a few selected cohorts. Forthright Larry Foreman (Howard da Silva) organizes the workers at a steel plant to fight for union recognition. Prostitutes such as Moll (Olive Stanton) support the union cause. Blitzstein's songs were skillfully wrought, but as strident and cantankerous as the plot. The show drew few of the regular musical theatregoers (a number of better dressed first-nighters walked out early in Act I), but with $1.65 the top price at the tiny Windsor it attracted enough patrons to run 108 performances.

Blitzstein probably never meant his songs to have popular currency. But Sammy Fain, who wrote many of the tunes for **Right This Way** (4 January 1938, 46th St.), did. Considering that both "I Can Dream, Can't I?" and "I'll Be Seeing You" were from this score, the show's run was dismayingly short: fifteen performances. The short run is even more puzzling when it is remembered that the stars were Guy Robertson, Tamara (who introduced both of the show's best songs), and, in his Broadway debut, Joe E. Lewis. Blanche Ring also had a small part. A little of the surprise at the short run disappears on reading the book. The story is not especially novel or complex. Jeff Doane (Robertson) and Mimi Chester (Tamara) have been living happily without the benefit of clergy in Paris. When Jeff's newspaper reassigns him to America, he insists they must marry to accommodate back-home mores. But wedded life is not wedded bliss, and Mimi soon returns to her Paris apartment. Jeff follows, and so does a reconciliation. For most critics the evening belonged to Lewis. He introduced much of his nightclub patter and cared so little for the integrity of the piece that on several occasions he parodied the show's songs after they had been sung. Small as her part was, Miss Ring pleased her old fans by inserting "I've Got Rings On My Fingers."

One out-of-the-mainstream and very short-lived (five performances) failure was a Federal Theatre Project revue, **Showing Off** (1 February 1938, 49th St.). Eubie Blake, Milton Reddie, and Matt Shelvey wrote the songs. Harking back to the earliest revues, the show had a thin plot, beginning at a theatrical casting agency. There each performer or group (acrobats, clowns, tap dancers, and so on) came and did their stuff in vaudeville style. Then the whole cast assembled to conclude the evening with a short minstrel show.

One month passed before the next musical was unveiled, and it, too, had an ignominiously short run. **Who's Who** (1 March 1938, Hudson) ran just twenty-three performances, and the recriminations over who was to blame may have been more entertaining than the revue itself. Leonard Sillman assembled it and named the famous party-giver Elsa Maxwell as producer in return for her promised financial assistance and her plush first-night crowd. The financial assistance was never forthcoming; the first-night crowd arrived late and talked all through the show. But New York critics had long learned to pay no heed to the rudeness of the first-nighters. Nevertheless, they were not impressed with the revue. It was patently more sophisticated than Sillman's earlier efforts—if sophistication means elegant dress and talk about society's interests. Its skits included a turnabout on all the left-wing rantings in the WPA and the Group Theatre. "Forgive Us Odets" had the rich planning a revolt. Sillman's favorite, Imogene Coca, performed a whole Billy Rose saturnalia singlehandedly in the austere style of *Our Town*. A popular burlesque knockabout clown, Rags Ragland, with several of his teeth conspicuously missing, appeared in a sentimental travesty of small-time burlesque and as a performer attempting to entertain from a raft during a storm at sea. Musically, Sillman's shows were always weak, and *Who's Who* was no exception. To make matters worse the dancing was dismissed as "graceless," the singing as "voiceless."

The last two musicals of the season didn't arrive until May, but the first of these was **I Married an Angel** (11 May 1938, Shubert). Another suave, literate Rodgers and Hart contribution to the betterment of the American Musical Theatre, it had originally, like *On Your Toes* (29 November 1936), been envisioned for the screen. Based on a Hungarian play by John Vaszary the story had as its hero a banker and ladies' man, Willie Palaffi (Dennis King). Willie's bank is in trouble, and so is his courtship of a "Benny Goodman jitterbug," Anna (Audrey Christie). In a rash moment Willie breaks off his affair and swears to marry no one but an angel. When the gods wish to punish us they answer our prayers, and an angel (Vera Zorina) flies into Willie's rooms. He marries her and promptly clips her wings. But the gods above are snickering. Her open, angelic ways cause endless embarrassment until Willie's sister, the Countess Palaffi (Vivienne Segal), indoctrinates her brother's angel in the ways of the world. A vengeful Anna spreads tales about the bank's problems. But Willie's backer, Harry Szigetti (Walter Slezak), arrives to save the day. Even his arrival would have been too late had not the Countess again stepped in to help. She bribes the cab drivers who are bringing the creditors to drive so slowly that the creditors appear only after Harry and Willie have come to terms. Two distinguished Rodgers standards were first sung in the show: the title song and "Spring Is Here" (a different number from the title song for their 1929 show). Miss Segal joined King to sing the latter. But the songs, in a sense, were only one manifestation of the excellent, innovative material Rodgers and Hart created for the show. The partners also adapted the book, but Hart's drinking was becoming a problem, so Joshua Logan was called in to assist. There were two musical interludes—one in each act—in which the dialogue was rhymed and sung; and two ballets, again one in each act. The interludes were "The Modiste," in which the angel is fitted for her wardrobe, and "Angel Without Wings." The first-act ballet was straightforward, a "Honeymoon Ballet." But the second, like "The Princess Zenobia" in *On Your Toes*, was satiric. "At the Roxy Music Hall" gaily mocked both the size of the house and its lavish stage productions. Balanchine allowed Miss Segal and Miss Christie to represent the entire long line of Rockettes. Miss Zorina slithered out of a green cheesecloth sea to dance with a "headless" partner, while Slezak romped about with elephantine grace as an underwater monster. In an accompanying song, Hart was at his mischievous best. He described a typical spectacle (where acrobats performing on their "digits" seem as small as "midgets") and the audience reaction in the balcony ("so high you get the fidgets"). Who cares if "Any week you go, it's the same old show." In their autobiographies, both Rodgers and Logan looked back with special affection and amusement on the number. Rodgers could still not remember how so lavish a salute to a New York institution found its way into a musical set in Hungary. Logan added that the number provided "an astounding lesson for me. When you have no reason for putting something in a musical show, then for Christ's sake, don't give a reason. Just do it." Another novel feature was the rhymed dialogue with musical background that led into several of the songs. When the principals discuss going to the Music Hall, each has a comment. These were not verses in the customary sense, but pertinent dialogue metamorphosing into lyrics. Operatic ambitions continued to creep into musical comedy. Neither the show's novel departures nor its inconsistencies

alarmed patrons. *I Married an Angel* kept Broadway applauding for ten months.

The season's closing show was an importation from London. **The Two Bouquets** (31 May 1938, Windsor) had enjoyed a nine-month run at that city's minuscule Ambassador. Now, at the not much larger house where *The Cradle Will Rock* had recently been brandishing its sword, it met with a cool reception. In spite of a cast that included Viola Roche, Leo G. Carroll, Enid Markey, Robert Chisholm, and the not yet famous Alfred Drake and Patricia Morison (as two of the four principal lovers whose lives are complicated when flowers are delivered to the wrong recipients), the show lasted only seven weeks. Nosegays in the summer were even less alluring than bile in the cold weather.

1938–1939

Over the unproductive summer the turmoil of the preceding season subsided. In its aftermath Broadway quickly reverted to more conventional ways. But the ferment had taken its toll. The American Musical Theatre seemed pallid and limp, virtually exhausted. Even though the number of new musicals increased ever so slightly, there seemed to be only two completely achieved shows, just two works in which literate, witty dialogue, fine, memorable melodies, and choice casting and careful production joined forces. And one of these works was an importation. Several other pieces had bright moments and a good song or two, but not enough to add up to a totally satisfactory evening. The hit of the season was not in any of these categories. It was a freakish, coarse-grained, raucous affair out of the theatrical mainstream.

The season began with three shows that opened during the week of 18 September. Ruefully they demonstrated the near bankruptcy of creativity. **You Never Know** (21 September 1938, Winter Garden) led off. Like *Between the Devil* (22 December 1937), it was another dated drawing-room musical comedy. Once a play by Siegfried Geyer (Gertrude Lawrence and Leslie Howard had performed it as *Candle Light* in a 1929 P. G. Wodehouse translation), it had been transformed into a Viennese musical, *Bei Kerzenlicht*. In the story the Baron Ferdinand de Romer (Rex O'Malley) exchanges places with his man, Gaston (Clifton Webb), so that he may more conveniently woo Mme. Henri Baltin (Libby Holman). Maria (Lupe Velez), Mme. Baltin's maid, takes to wearing her mistress's clothing, and before long a second romance ensues between her and Gaston, whom she mistakes for the baron. The Shuberts retained only two of the original songs, entrusting most of the new material to Cole Porter. Porter was recovering from a riding accident which had cost him the use of one leg. It had been a long, painful recovery, and undoubtedly deprived Porter of more than just physical strength. His score was in no way up to snuff. Porter himself in later years generally referred to *You Never Know* as his worst show. Porter's way with words suffered less than his music. The lyrics for the show's best ballad, "At Long Last Love" (sung by Gaston), were good, and the rhymes for the cheerful number Gaston and Maria sang, "From Alpha To Omega," even better. A still better example of his wit and clever in-rhyming came in "What Shall I Do?" where Maria must decide between two heartthrobs. Confessing her "itch to," she rues she can't choose "which to hitch to." To aggravate the show's shortcomings, what could have been a saving intimacy was discarded in favor of a lavish production at the huge Winter Garden. Some of the action was moved to a nightclub, where Shubert show girls paraded lumberingly and battalions of dancers tapped and whirled away. These big production numbers inflated the musical's running costs and helped close it after just seventy-eight performances.

On the other hand **Hellzapoppin** (22 September 1938, 46th St.) was rushed into the highly suitable Winter Garden when the Porter piece folded, and it remained there till it ended its run of 1,404 performances. When *Hellzapoppin* closed it held the long-run record for a musical on Broadway. Like the equally long-running *Pins and Needles* (27 November 1937), it frequently added and dropped material. At one point, near the end of its run, it even changed its title slightly to *The New Hellzapoppin*. But unlike *Pins and Needles* its humor was zany, happy, and irrelevant. Olsen and Johnson, two old-time vaudevillians who had never made the big time, sparked the antics. A filmed sequence that opened the evening offered praise for the revue from Hitler (speaking with a Yiddish accent), Mussolini (ranting in a Negro dialect), and Roosevelt (talking gibberish). "Workmen" lumbered through the rows of seats with large ladders, forcing patrons to get up and out of their way; in the middle of the performance a woman screamed she had left her baby at the Automat and rushed out of the theatre. A man walked up and down the aisles attempting to give a lady a plant she had ordered; the plant grew bigger with each appearance, and by the end of the evening departing crowds could see the man sitting in the lobby with a small tree and still forlornly calling out the lady's name. Sirens, firecrackers, and guns were going off incessantly. In a show such as this there was little use for good music. Sammy Fain and Charles Tobias did journeymen's labor but came up with no winners. The show's deliriously puerile escapism was called to the nation's attention by the influential columnist Walter Winchell. After the fence-straddling reviews of the show he never missed a chance to plug it in his columns or on his radio show. He often took credit for making the show the great bonanza it turned out to be. No one disputed him.

Sing Out the News (24 September 1938, Music Box) had no such benefactor. And though it enjoyed better reviews than *Hellzapoppin* it ran only 105 performances. It represented an interesting merging of the talents of the liberal George S. Kaufman and Moss Hart with the leftish Harold Rome and Charles Friedman. Kaufman and Hart assumed the sketch-writing chores Friedman had originally been slated for, leaving Friedman solely with credit for conceiving and directing the show. The fun was still at the expense of the successful, but, being successes themselves, Kaufman and Hart knew how to temper their wit. The show's best skit was at once a deft parody of *I Married an Angel* and a dig at the GOP. In "I Married a Republican" the leaders of the party despair of finding a candidate when a male angel (played by the revue's drollest clown, Hiram Sherman) flies in through a window. They select him to oppose Roosevelt. To their horror he is all for the New Deal, but they persuade him to their point of view, causing him to lose his wings in the changeabout. In other skits Roosevelt was blamed for the weather; a young boy trying to reconcile groups of rich and poor children was arrested for disturbing the peace; and a Hollywood epic about Marie Antoinette was disrupted when the movie mogul realized the picture ended with an effective revolution. A congressional minstrel show closed the first act. The evening's ballet showed peace cruelly manhandled by the world's diplomats.

Happily, success had also come to Harold Rome, and the difference was obvious in his songs. For example, "My Heart Is Unemployed" (sung in the show by Mary Jane Walsh and Michael Loring) mixed romance and the economic picture much as "One Big Union For Two" had, but its tone was noticeably cheerier. And "Franklin D. Roosevelt Jones," the show's rousing hit, celebrating the birth of a black baby into a world of hope, became a national hit. (The song—sung in the show by Rex

Ingram and the chorus—in its sheet music is called simply "F.D.R. Jones.")

Knights of Song (17 October 1938, 51st St.) gave Arthur Sullivan (John Moore) a fictitious romance with a married American (Natalie Hall). She mediates his battles with Gilbert (Nigel Bruce) and helps him win the favor of Queen Victoria (Molly Pearson). Famous figures who paraded across the stage included the Prince of Wales (Monty Woolley), Oscar Wilde (Robert Chrisholm), and George Bernard Shaw (Winston O'Keefe). Though Laurence Schwab produced the mounting and Oscar Hammerstein staged it, the piece was written by relatively untested hands. Much the best parts of the evening were the beloved old songs Gilbert and Sullivan wrote for the English musical stage. But they could not keep the show on the boards beyond its second week.

One of the most beloved of all American show standards, "September Song," came out of the next musical to premiere, **Knickerbocker Holiday** (19 October 1938, Barrymore). It was sung in the show by the much-admired Walter Huston, making an unusual appearance on the lyric stage. As a result the evening often has been looked back on in an afterglow of longing and affection. Its admirers forget that the show was neither a financial nor a critical success. (Many forget as well that Huston was considered in some quarters too likable to be a believable villain.) Despite its low initial cost it was never able to recoup its investment during its twenty-one week run. And despite its festive title and charming, offbeat setting, it was a rather heavy-handed antifascist tract that, wittingly or no, also protested growing governmental interference from Washington.

The lyrics and libretto were by one of the most distinguished and high-principled American playwrights, Maxwell Anderson. His play begins in 1809 with Washington Irving (Ray Middleton) deciding to write a history of old New York. Irving extricates himself from his own day and enters seventeenth-century New Amsterdam, commenting on the action, sometimes participating in it, and in the end becoming a sort of *deus ex machina* to give his tale a happy ending. In Irving's old town the council awaits the arrival of a new governor, Peter Stuyvesant. The council is made up of the best names in the village— Vanderbilt, Van Cortlandt, De Peyster, and, among others, Roosevelt. But this Roosevelt speaks not in the cultured tones of a fireside chat but with the pronounced "Dutch" accent that had only recently been the stock in trade of certain stage comedians: "I

vould not be silent! I vould vant to know who done something!" The council does indeed need to know "who done something," for it is hanging day and the council has no one to hang. Arbitrarily, the councilmen select an independent-minded, troublesome knife-sharpener, Brom Broeck (Richard Kollmar). He is condemned on the exaggerated charge that he forgot to get a license. Brom, who loves Tina (Jeanne Madden), the daughter of councilman Tienhoven (Mark Smith), prefers to live. He is temporarily saved from the gallows by the arrival of Stuyvesant (Huston). But it is a mixed blessing, for Tina's father offers his daughter in marriage to the new governor, and Stuyvesant, liking the girl and understanding he is in the autumn of days, suggests they brook no delay. Stuyvesant's methods are high-handed and dictatorial. After the governor abolishes all the freedoms the town had enjoyed, even the councilmen mourn the loss of "Our Ancient Liberties." When Brom protests he is jailed. Just as Tina and Stuyvesant's wedding is about to take place, Indians attack. Brom escapes from jail, joins the fighting, and becomes its hero. When Brom accuses the governor of conspiring with the Indians, Stuyvesant reimposes the sentence of hanging. Irving steps into the picture and reminds the governor he must think of how posterity will remember him. Stuyvesant prefers a good name in history and lets the lovers go off together. Stuyvesant asks Irving if he could be considered an American:

Stuyvesant: Maybe I could qualify. I was never able to take orders.
Irving: That's how you tell an American!

Much of Kurt Weill's music for Anderson's book and lyrics was not at all traditional Broadway material. Weill's score was free in form, shaped within the requirements of the scene and lyrics, but too sprawling to be extracted and given a separate life. Moreover, even in expressive numbers such as "It Never Was Anywhere You," use of Dutch constructions in the principal lyric hindered easy acceptance. However, "September Song" was written in the customary AABA pattern and within the limited range of Huston's voice.

Knickerbocker Holiday was one of two October offerings. The second was the Krimskys' **The Girl from Wyoming** (29 October 1938, American Music Hall), with Ted Fetter and Richard Lewine again writing the songs. But good luck did not come a third time. The novelty of their musical hall spoofs had worn thin. In a *Whoopee* (4 December 1928) or *Girl Crazy* (14 October 1930) sort of tale, Harvard's dapper Ben Longwood (Philip Huston) heads west for freedom and refreshment. Instead his life is complicated by all the wrong western types. He is spared in the end thanks to the charm of the young lady of the title (June Walker). Longwood best expressed his feelings in "Stay East, Young Man." When attendance faltered, the Krimskys brought *Naughty Naught ('00)* (23 January 1937) back in repertory with the new piece, but it failed to revive flagging interest in the ersatz beer hall.

The second Cole Porter score of the season was heard in **Leave It to Me** (9 November 1938, Imperial). It suggested that following his accident Porter was having a serious problem marshaling his musical forces, although his gift for lyrics remained intact. His best ballad was "Get Out Of Town," sung by Tamara in the show. It employed the elementary device of a repeated note, but its torrid lyric gave it a welcome bite. The show's biggest hit was "My Heart Belongs To Daddy," which had no real relevance to the plot but which nonetheless rocketed Mary Martin to stardom. (She sang it wrapped in furs, sitting on a trunk at a Siberian whistle-stop and slowly doffing her garments.)

MARY MARTIN was born in Weatherfond, Texas, on 1 December 1913, and made her stage debut at the age of five, singing at a Firemen's Ball. She came to Broadway following a brief fling singing in nightclubs and the breakup of her first marriage. Radiating wholesomeness, she could employ her small, clear soprano to deliver a straight, sentimental ballad. But she just as magically could bring to her numbers a fragile wispiness or a coy impishness. It was the latter which helped her first make her mark on Broadway.

In his lyric for the song Porter had more fun with the word "daddy" than anyone since P. G. Wodehouse in *Oh, My Dear* (27 November 1918). Porter rhymed "Daddy" with everything from "caddie" to "finnan haddie," and then turned "daddy" into a series of "dada-das." Having presented a not too faithful young lady, Porter offered the other side

of the coin, more or less, with "Most Gentlemen Don't Like Love" (sung by Sophie Tucker and the chorus), insisting "they just like to kick it around."

The plot on which these love and anti-love songs were hung concerned the adventures of meek, domestic Alonzo "Stinky" Goodhue (Victor Moore), who is made ambassador to Russia after his ambitious wife (Sophie Tucker) contributes generously to Roosevelt's reelection campaign. To get himself recalled, Alonzo kicks the Nazi ambassador and shoots a political figure in Red Square (hitting a counterrevolutionary by mistake). Somehow all his mischief rebounds to his credit. Only when he begins to enjoy his work and proposes a plan for world peace do the great powers become up in arms. In a romantic subplot, Moore's partner, William Gaxton, played a brash newspaperman, working for a publisher who had coveted the ambassadorial post, and attempting to embarrass Goodhue. Tamara played Gaxton's girl, Colette. Sam and Bella Spewack adapted the story from their own play, *Clear All Wires*. Their libretto lacked the slashing satire of recent thirties shows, and its targets appeared increasingly riddled, at least on stage. Since America and, in particular, its large liberal segments were still on good terms with Russia, *Leave It to Me*'s first-act finale was set in Red Square. The Communist anthem, "The Internationale," was sung, and a friendly Joe Stalin (Walter Armin) condescended to do a little dance. By the time the show embarked on a national tour during the next season, Stalin and Hitler had signed their pact. Stalin was eliminated as a character in the show, and a warning was added to the program insisting the evening bore no relation to current events.

The season's best musical, though not its biggest hit, was November's other entry. George Abbott took Shakespeare's *Comedy of Errors*, modernized Shakespeare's dialogue, and handed it over to Rodgers and Hart for words and music. The three came up with a joyous romp, **The Boys from Syracuse** (23 November 1938, Alvin). The play retained the story of the twin Antipholuses, separated by accident shortly after birth, and their twin servants, both named Dromio. The confusions that arise when the pair from Syracuse find themselves in Ephesus, where the other master and servant reside, are only straightened out when their father appears with his explanation. In an inspired bit of casting, Teddy Hart (Larry's brother) and Jimmy Savo were assigned the parts of the two Dromios. Not only did the two diminutive comedians impart the same air of boyish innocence and pathos, but they looked so much alike they could almost have passed for twins. The evening's most famous moment fell to Savo. When a seeress pronounced, "The venom clamours of a jealous woman poisons more deadly than a mad dog's tooth"—the only line Abbott retained from the original play—Savo jumped from the wings and joyously cried, "Shakespeare!" Eddie Albert and Ronald Graham portrayed the two Antipholuses. Rodgers provided a rich, varied score, and Hart, giving no sign of his drinking problems, wrote brilliantly appropriate lyrics. Both the fetching, bittersweet waltz, "Falling In Love With Love," sung by Adriana (Muriel Angelus) and the effervescent "This Can't Be Love"—introduced by Antipholus (Albert) and Luciana (Marcy Wescott)—became immensely popular. But Hart (and Rodgers) was equally adept in the scathingly comic "What Can You Do With A Man?" ("He eats me out of house and home/But doesn't like my cooking!"), which Dromio and Luce (Wynn Murray) sang, and the moodily poetic "You Have Cast Your Shadow On The Sea," assigned to Luciana and the first Antipholus. There were also the lovely ballads, "The Shortest Day Of The Year," sung by the second Antipholus (Graham), and "Sing For Your Supper," a women's trio (Luce, Adriana, and Luciana) that nightly stopped the show. *The Boys from Syracuse* brought the ancient world alive for seven months. A fine, if minor, off-Broadway revival in 1963 confirmed that the show had lost none of its sparkle.

Two new musicals appeared in December, and both were quick flops. **Great Lady** (1 December 1938, Majestic) told an incredibly complicated plot that kept jumping back and forth in time between the French Revolution and 1939, and back and forth in place between France and America. Based loosely on the story of Eliza Bowen, a girl of somewhat dubious reputation who had several love affairs and marriages ending with her marriage in middle age to the seventy-eight-year-old Aaron Burr, it starred three gracious ladies of an earlier musical stage: Norma Terris (as Eliza), Irene Bordoni, and Helen Ford. When it folded after twenty performances, it took with it the first full Broadway score by young Frederick Loewe.

A revival of *Blossom Time* was brought in from the road where it had been touring, virtually without a halt, since its first traveling company had been sent out seventeen years before. Everett Marshall was its Schubert, a role he continued to sing until he closed his career.

At a long-disused roof theater, **Policy Kings** (30 December 1938, Nora Bayes), eked out four performances. The black musical recounted attempts by a Harlem DA to quash the local numbers racket.

The last year of the decade began with importations. The D'Oyly Carte arrived on 5 January for a brief season of Gilbert and Sullivan. The Savoyards were followed by **Set to Music** (18 January 1939, Music Box), a revue Noël Coward designed around the talents of Beatrice Lillie. Most of its material came from his London production *Words and Music*, but he culled songs from other of his shows and wrote new numbers as well. As far as American audiences were concerned, *Set to Music* was their introduction to "Mad About The Boy," "The Party's Over Now," and "The Stately Homes Of England," only the first sung by Miss Lillie. It played for 129 showings.

The first new American offering of 1939 was not unveiled until February. It, too, was a revue. And it, too, was aimed at the knowing, well-heeled crowds that supported Coward. **One for the Money** (4 February 1939, Booth) was conceived, produced, and, except for the music, written by Nancy Hamilton. Miss Hamilton was no newcomer to revues. She had been a significant factor in the success of the early Leonard Sillman revues. Like Sillman she appeared relatively indifferent to the music in her productions. At least no more major songs ever emerged from her shows than did from Sillman's. Certainly Morgan Lewis's songs were not the talk of the town. Miss Hamilton's emphasis was on her skits, and even more on her bright, young performers. In her cast, besides herself, were Brenda Forbes, Philip Bourneuf, Ruth Matteson, Keenan Wynn, Gene Kelly, and Alfred Drake. The mood of the show was quickly established when a handsome-looking family in proper evening attire was served champagne by their maid and announced, "We think that right is right and wrong is left." Drake was assigned one of the evening's most delicious bits—an affectionate dig at Orson Welles. Drake's Welles boasted he knew Shakespeare backward at two, forward at three, and personally at four. The show playfully teased modern art, Wagner, Eleanor Roosevelt, and parlor games of the idle rich. The rich were apparently neither idle enough nor rich enough to support the show for very long, but a satisfactory run of 132 performances determined Miss Hamilton to try again.

The following week brought in two shows. Both were disappointments. Ethel Merman and Jimmy Durante were partnered again, this time in **Stars in Your Eyes** (9 February 1939, Majestic).

The show had a book by J. P. McEvoy. It had music by Arthur Schwartz, but Schwartz was working with a new lyricist, Dorothy Fields. So glittering an array of talent gave every promise of bringing in a hit. But troubles began early on. The musical had originally been intended as a satire on leftist influence in Hollywood, but the producer concluded the line had been overplayed. As a result much of McEvoy's original plot was left behind in rehearsals and on the road. What survived was largely a trite love story. The great Hollywood star, Jeanette Adair (Miss Merman), loves John Blake (originally a leftist screenwriter), but John (Richard Carlson) loves Tata (Tamara Toumanova). Jeanette's pursuit of John is abetted, and sometimes complicated, by the movie-studio idea man and troubleshooter, Bill (Durante). (In the original script Bill was a union organizer.) Jeanette gets her man. On top of the book trouble, the score was not among Schwartz's best, and the hit of the evening, "It's All Yours," was made not on the strength of the song, but on Miss Merman and Durante's horseplay. Each tried to throw the other off balance with outrageous ad-libs and anything else that came to mind. It was to its stars and Joshua Logan's fluid direction that the show owed its run of 127 performances.

Lew Leslie tried for a fifth time to recapture the magic of the original *Blackbirds* (9 June 1928) with **Blackbirds of 1939** (11 February 1939, Hudson). A number of first-rate writers helped with the material: Johnny Mercer, Mitchell Parish, and Sammy Fain. Ferde Grofé did the orchestrations and J. Rosamond Johnson the vocal arrangements. "When A Blackbird Is Blue" (Parish/Fain) led into a choral version of Gershwin's "Rhapsody In Blue." Ralph Brown provided the evening's best dancing, dressed up as a pirate king. For comedy the revue milked laughs from a Harlem bridge game. But even with promising newcomers such as Lena Horne to present the songs, the evening found no takers. It closed after nine performances. For Leslie it was the last straw. He never again attempted a *Blackbirds*. Actually, although no one could realize it at the time, his original *Blackbirds* was the last in the brief, select line of jazzy Negro revues that had begun with what was really a book show, *Shuffle Along* (23 May 1921). Leslie himself was responsible for mounting half the black shows of the thirties. They were all either flops or barely successful.

Two freakish Negro shows followed; both were jazz versions of *The Mikado*. The first to arrive was **The Swing Mikado** (1 March 1939, New Yorker).

It had been the sensational success of the Federal Theatre in Chicago, compiling a remarkable run of twenty-two weeks. Mike Todd had offered to bring it to New York, and when his overtures were rebuffed he mounted his own, more lavish version with Bill Robinson in the title role and called it **The Hot Mikado** (23 March 1939, Broadhurst). While the cast of the Federal Theatre production performed in costumes and sets that resembled Africa far more than old Japan, Todd's performers went a step farther from the original. Robinson strutted in a gold suit and gold shoes, with a gold derby and gold cane. Todd's chorus girls tapped away bedecked nattily in slacks on a stage filled with stylized, modern decor. For a brief time in May the two Mikados played across the street from each other. Neither was a runaway success on Broadway. The Chicago original ran eighty-six performances; Todd's one less. But Todd astutely avoided losing money on his production by moving in lock stock, and barrel to the World's Fair in Flushing.

Between these two competitors, Frank Fay brought an uneven vaudeville bill into the 44th Street on the 2nd. Among the highlights, besides Fay himself, were Elsie Janis with her songs and imitations (including Will Rogers), Smith and Dale, Eva Le Gallienne and Richard Waring in the balcony scene from *Romeo and Juliet*, and Chester Hale's precision dancers in a white-feather routine.

Mexicana (21 April 1939, 46th St.) was a colorful but not especially exciting extravaganza which the Mexican government had initially presented at the World's Fair. There, its banjo virtuosos, folk dances, and other numbers seemed more worthwhile than in Broadway's harsher light.

The Federal Theatre, about to be disbanded, produced the penultimate show of the theatrical year, **Sing for Your Supper** (24 April 1939, Adelphi). By and large it reserved its satire for foreign matters, particularly the Nazi takeover of Austria. "The Blue Danube" under Hitler's glowering watch was transformed into the goose-stepping "Horst Wessellied." Sketches had fun at the expense of naval war games, the *Cradle Will Rock* school of sceneryless opera, and New York's official greeter, Grover Whalen. On the domestic front the show's songs took a far more optimistic view, as their titles suggest: "Oh, Boy Can We Deduct," "Bonnie Banks," and "Lucky." One uplifting ensemble number celebrated the news that "Papa's Got A Job." Papa was fortunate, since he was about to be evicted for not paying his rent. The enthusiasm of his neighbors congregating in an alley canopied with fully hung clotheslines was so moving that Brooks Atkinson in the *Times* hailed the scene as "modern theatre at its best." But in the long haul the evening's most successful number was its finale, called in the show "The Ballad Of Uncle Sam," and led by Gordon Clarke and the chorus. It was an extended, discursive paean by Earl Robinson to lyrics by John Latouche. The word poem extolled the richness and diversity of America in a hymn of hope for the future. When the war broke out, the song was redone by Paul Robeson as "Ballad For Americans" and proved a popular instrument of wholesome propaganda.

Not for the first time after a regular season had closed, an oddity came in to write a second finish to the theatrical year. On this occasion a group called the American Lyric Theatre brought out a double bill consisting of a Virgil Thomson ballet and Douglas Moore's operatic version of Stephen Vincent Benét's famous work **The Devil and Daniel Webster** (18 May 1939, Martin Beck). Its story told how Webster (Lansing Hatfield) goes to court to save his neighbor (John Hurney), who has sold his soul to the Devil (George Rasely). Fritz Reiner con-ducted, Robert Edmond Jones designed the sets, and John Houseman directed. Four nights later the group presented **Susanna, Don't You Cry**, which employed a dull, paper-thin plot as an excuse for an evening of Stephen Foster songs. Bettina Hall, Robert Chisholm, and the Hall Johnson Choir put over the beloved melodies. Each mounting was given five times.

1939-1940

The New York World's Fair provided a timely diversion for New Yorkers and visitors during the summer months of the new season. Unfortunately, the exposition's slightly unworldly euphoria was shattered in September when many of the exhibiting nations found themselves engulfed in the opening battles of World War II, just a month over twenty-five years since the guns that initiated World War I had fired away. Broadway's first response was not surprising. It ignored the war. For the musical theatre, keeping the conflict at arm's length was easier than it had been at the outbreak of World War I. At that time, the musical stage depended heavily on Vienna and to a lesser extent on London and Paris for much of its entertainments. But the Great War had made Broadway self-sufficient. It was a self-sufficiency the American Musical Theatre never afterwards lost. The new war

made itself felt in two ways. For one, there was a draining away of young talent to serve in the forces, thereby further thinning theatrical ranks already depleted by Hollywood. But this came later. The initial reaction was to change the emphasis of the librettos. Real war was the topic of the day, and real war was no joking matter. Topicality largely disappeared from the books of new Broadway musicals.

For the most part the new offerings remained steadfastly contemporary, but with equal purpose they carefully eschewed the political, economic, and social implications in the headlines. Left-wing propagandizing suffered the severest setback, especially during the period of Soviet-Nazi détente. Some residual philosophizing was tolerated partly in the spirit of a necessary patriotic ecumenism and partly because so many of both the audience and the creators held to their liberal views. In time—after two or three seasons passed by—a new interest and a new style of musical appeared. It inaugurated a major new chapter in the history of the lyric theatre.

The season opened when the Shuberts in association with Olsen and Johnson presented **The Streets of Paris** (19 June 1939, Broadhurst). The producing credits warned what sort of revue Broadway could expect. Two old New York favorites were in the cast: Luella Gear and Bobby Clark. But the roster of performers also included a number of not-so-well-known names soon to become more familiar on the Broadway stage or elsewhere: Bud Abbott, Lou Costello, Carmen Miranda, Jean Sablon, Ramon Vinay, and Gower Champion. There was little, apart from Sablon and one or two other artists, that was truly French, though Jimmy McHugh's songs sang of "Rendezvous Time In Paree," "Thanks For The Francs," and the titular "The Streets Of Paris." Harold Rome contributed one number with a Gallic reference, "The French Have A Word For It." Miss Miranda, decked out in an outlandish headdress, offered the show's hit in the first-act finale when she pointed not across the Atlantic but below the border in "The South American Way." It caught the Latin flavor that was sweeping the country. One of the show's few allusions to current international problems was the satiric dance number "Doin' The Chamberlain." Mustached, somber-suited chorus boys stepped out gingerly with their umbrellas. More typical of the show's humor were the Clark and the Abbott and Costello sketches. One of Clark's routines had him playing four characters in the same sketch—its belly laughs coming not so much from its lines as from Clark's increasingly frantic costume changes. Costello mistook a mental institution for a hotel and didn't seem to notice his error even when a swami who asked him if he wanted his palm read dabbed Costello's hand with red paint. One sign of the improving economic picture was the show's ability to hike its price from $3.30 to $4.40 as soon as success was determined.

Europe's turmoil was brought home the night after *The Streets of Paris* premiered when **From Vienna** (20 June 1939, Music Box), a revue by and with refugees from Hitler's persecutions, presented its wares. The group of Austrians and Germans were talented, but not attuned to Broadway. They lingered through the summer.

July's only entry was the season's first book musical, **Yokel Boy** (6 July 1939, Majestic). Lew Brown, who produced and directed the piece, was responsible for its story and shared credit for its tunes with Charles Tobias and Sam H. Stept. The first-act finale, "Uncle Sam's Lullaby," injected a bit of vestigial topicality into the evening, assuring the audience that we were strong enough to protect ourselves if war broke out. An entire chorus marching determinedly in soldiers' uniforms seemed to Brooks Atkinson "like the thumping epics of '17." Otherwise, Brown's plot appeared to be merely a variation on the story of *America's Sweetheart* (10 February 1931). Elmer Whipple (Buddy Ebsen), the son of a once-famous dancer, and Mary Hawkins (Lois January) have been fond of each other since childhood. When a chance to become a Hollywood star takes Mary away from her Lexington, Massachusetts, farm, Elmer follows her. Mary's career fails to live up to its initial promise, but by a fluke Elmer gets a part and becomes an overnight success. Success brings him no happiness, especially as he watches a budding romance between Mary and a matinee idol. His persistence and charm finally scotch the romance. Mary and Elmer decide they prefer a New England farm to the glamour of Hollywood. Judy Canova added to the merriment with her hillbilly rendition of three songs only loosely connected with the plot: "Catherine The Great," "Time For Jukin,'" "Comes Love." In August changes were made to tighten the narrative and bolster the humdrum score. "The Beer Barrel Polka" (Brown/Jaromir Vejvoda) was interpolated in the process. But a lion's share of credit for *Yokel Boy*'s six-month run had to be given to its principal entertainers, plus a young comic in a minor role who made critics take note, Phil Silvers.

George White's Scandals of 1939–1940 (28 August 1939, Alvin) proved to be the last in the series. The tradition of the great annuals had long since withered away; their fervor, excitement, and grandeur were only memories. But this farewell edition was not without its high moments. Ann Miller capably filled the shoes once worn by Ann Pennington. Ray Middleton was as good a singer as the *Scandals* had ever employed, although he left the cast shortly after the opening. And Ella Logan was a lively heir to the tradition of Frances Williams. The Howard Brothers, the Three Stooges, and Ben Blue were more than capable of handling comedy. Some of their original comic material was so off-color it brought down the wrath of Boston censors and was eliminated. The World's Fair was kidded, with Willie and Eugene playing Sam Trylon and Max Perisphere; unions were spoofed when a union husband was prevented from kissing his nonunion wife; Willie Howard played a French poodle "saluting" a German dachshund in a slightly vulgar but popular joke. There was even a skit about a machine that allows viewers to watch people in another room for a small price. Willie Howard used it to spy on his wife. The machine was called "Tell-u-vision." The Three Stooges splattered each other in a free-for-all pie-throwing melee, while Ben Blue provided more subtle humor with his airy pantomimes. Sammy Fain's score (with Jack Yellen lyrics) was pert and attractive. The songsmiths took account of the craze for Latin rhythms in "The Mexiconga" but came up with their best number in a hedonistic bit, of the sort that had been voguish in the now-receding Depression, "Are You Havin' Any Fun?" (sung in her Scottish brogue by Miss Logan, dressed as a sailor and accompanied by a chorus brandishing lyrics on their hats). It was a score that ranked with all but the very best of the old *Scandals* scores. The "Mexiconga" number, filled with swirling senoritas led by Ann Miller dancing against a flamboyant south-of-the-border setting, and a South Sea hula spectacle offered touches on the old-time lavishness, while a first-act finale wistfully recalled a happier past by saluting the great show tunes of the twenties. Yet for all its goodies, *The Scandals* could only run up a record of 120 showings.

The only new musical to arrive during September was **The Straw Hat Revue** (29 September 1939, Ambassador). As its name announced, it had been a summer-circuit attraction and was brought to the big town for a mere $8,000. The show threw stones at a corpse by mocking operettas with "The Grand Chandelier" and kidded the best number of *The Streets of Paris* with "Soused American Way" (in which Imogene Coca impersonated Carmen Miranda). No hits emerged from Sylvia Fine and James Shelton's songs, but a number of young talents besides Miss Coca continued their climb to the top: Danny Kaye, Alfred Drake, and Jerome Robbins. What looked so fresh in the Pennsylvania mountains seemed less attractive in an aging, ugly Broadway house. The show lasted ten weeks.

In the middle of October Rodgers and Hart came up with another hit, if not another gem. **Too Many Girls** (18 October 1939, Imperial) restored collegiate life and football to the musical stage, where Pottawatomie College joined the league that included Bingham and Tait. In some ways it was a backward institution, playing its football games on Friday because it didn't know any better. But it was far ahead of its time in insisting that freshman coeds wear beanies colored to let the boys know whether or not the girls were virgins. When Harvey Casey sends his sometimes wild daughter Consuelo (Marcy Wescott) there, he discreetly sends four football players as bodyguards. She falls in love with one of them, Clint Kelley (Richard Kollmar), only to discover his real job on the day of the big game with Texas Gentile. Consuelo announces she is heading back east immediately. Since Clint and his associates must remain with her, they will not be able to play. Common sense and love prevail for the happy ending. Two of the other fullbacks were Eddie Bracken, who provided much of the light-hearted comedy, and Hal Le Roy, who did more fancy stepping on the boards than on the grid. The solidly professional George Marion, Jr., book provided cues for an equally professional score. Like almost everyone else during the season, Rodgers and Hart fell into the Latin beat with "All Dressed Up (Spic and Spanish)" and more obviously with "She Could Shake The Maracas." The Latin numbers were sparked by the fourth fullback, Desi Arnaz. (These Latin influences probably provided excuses for Jo Mielziner's sun-splashed sets and Raoul Péne du Bois's colorful costumes, both of which sometimes smacked more of old Mexico than of New Mexico.) In "I Like To Recognize The Tune" Rodgers and Hart protested against "the musical distortions then so much a part of pop music because of the swing-band influence." Hart had a lyric field day with "Give It Back To The Indians." On those occasions when Hart was too drunk to write, Rodgers was forced to supply his own words. He proved he was a match for his irresponsible partner. Rodgers's lyrics for the opening number found the football players lamenting they

were no longer Saturday's heroes when the season is finished: "Spring is the winter of our discontent." But only once did Rodgers and Hart hit upon the magical mixture of words and music that make a standard. "I Didn't Know What Time It Was" has aged far less than the lovers (Consuelo and Clint) who sang it.

One seemingly timeless song is all that **Very Warm for May** (17 November 1939, Alvin) also left behind. The show promised to be one of the major hits of the season, reuniting Jerome Kern, Oscar Hammerstein II, and Max Gordon. Its disastrously short run of fifty-nine performances was generally attributed to a lifeless, laughless book. Whether Hammerstein was to blame, or whether the onus belonged on the revisions Gordon and his director, Vincente Minnelli, demanded during the tryout will never be known. But as the *Times*'s Brooks Atkinson concluded, the libretto presented on the first night made "a singularly haphazard appreciation of Mr. Kern's music almost a challenge." The story was not unlike *Babes in Arms* (14 April 1937). May Graham (Grace McDonald) is the daughter of an old theatrical family. They want her to go to college, but she prefers to continue the family's stage tradition. When she runs away to take a job at Winnie's Barn, a summer theatre, they chase after her. But May lands a part in the musical Ogdon Quiller's Progressive Playshop is mounting at the theatre, and she also lands Winnie Spofford's son (Richard Quine). Hammerstein's lyrics were uneven, often inferior; but they disclosed that at this early date, three years before he began working with Richard Rodgers, the style and mannerisms of his final years were coming to the fore. "May Tells All," in which May describes an imaginary elopement, revealed his penchant for American hyperbole (Hammerstein would use "world famous" to better effect in *South Pacific*), his perennial discomfort with in-rhyming, his heavy-handed verbal wit ("squirt" coupled with "Detroit"), his repetition (four "alls" in eight lines, and only the last two "alls" necessary or well employed), and his striving for simple, honest poetic images ("a moon, all misty and gray"). Although Hammerstein's lyrics were not among his best, most critics and the public rose to the challenge of appreciating Kern's lovely score. "All The Things You Are" became an immediate Kern classic, even though Kern himself is said to have felt its key and tempo changes would militate against success. The song, used in the show as part of the play within the play, was as sweet and thoughtfully conceived in its verse as in its chorus (or, as Kern always insisted, burthen). It was sung by Carroll (Hollace Shaw) and several members of the Progressive Players. The rest of the score, including the enchanting "Heaven In My Arms," was excellent, although it went with the scenery to Cain's warehouse.

The failure of *Very Warm for May* was doubly sad. Besides depriving most of the score of a chance to be heard, it closed the Broadway career of Kern on an unhappy note. Kern returned to Hollywood. He continued to produce fine songs for films. In 1945 he came back to New York to write additional material for a revival of *Show Boat* (27 December 1927) and to begin work on a new show. But he died suddenly before any real progress had been made on the new piece.

In a small footnote, Donald Brian was one of the principals, May's father. He had played the leads in *The Merry Widow* (21 October 1907) and *The Girl from Utah* (24 August 1914), thereby participating in the opening of two important acts in the American Musical Theatre. Now he closed his career at the same time as Kern. Others in the cast included Jack Whiting and Eve Arden (as Winnie).

The success of the jazzed *Mikados* (1 and 23 March 1939) and *The Boys from Syracuse* (23 November 1938) prompted the mammoth Center Theatre to mount a similar enterprise on 29 November in hopes of reviving its faltering fortunes. *A Midsummer Night's Dream* was reset in 1890 Louisiana and retitled **Swingin' the Dream.** Jimmy Van Heusen's score was sung by a predominantly black cast that included the famous jazz trumpeter Louis Armstrong as Bottom, Butterfly McQueen as Puck, and Jackie "Moms" Mabley as Quince. One minor standard, "Darn That Dream," came from the show. Settings based on Walt Disney drawings gave the production a curious cartoonlike air. Benny Goodman and his Sextet added a stylish note to the jitterbugging and ballad singing. But the lindy hop and other modern touches, such as Puck drugging the lovers by using a flit gun, dispelled the Shakespearean magic. The show was a sumptuous thirteen-performance fiasco. Its failure prompted the Rockefellers to look for some other form of entertainment to keep the house open.

December's first musical was **DuBarry Was a Lady** (6 December 1939, 46th St.). Like several other major hits of the decade, it was originally developed with the films in mind and turned into a stage piece only after it had been rejected by Hollywood. The female lead was said to have been tailored at first for Mae West, but by the time it was slated for Broadway Ethel Merman had signed to head the cast and, as a result, Cole Porter agreed to create the songs, continuing his successful partnership with Broadway's leading musical comedy star. Bert Lahr was Miss Merman's associate and actually had the pivotal role.

The story begins in New York's Club Petite, where Louis Blore (Lahr) is a washroom attendant and May Daley (Miss Merman) graces the floor show. Blore nurtures a forlorn crush on Miss Daley. When he wins $75,000 in the Irish Sweepstakes, he sees his opportunity to pursue the romance openly. But May loves a married newspaper columnist, Alex Barton (Ronald Graham). To break up the romance Blore decides to slip Alex knockout drops. By mistake he drinks the potion himself. Unconscious, he dreams he is Louis XV and May is Madame DuBarry, "mistress in name only." Just as he is about to consummate his love affair, the dim-witted dauphin shoots an arrow into his derriere. Blore awakens to realize the hopelessness of his passion. He gives Alex enough money to procure a divorce, pays the rest to the government in taxes, and resumes cleaning washbasins. The Buddy DeSylva–Herbert Fields book was a noisy, guffaw-filled caper, but Porter's music was not his best. Like almost every other major composer working on Broadway, Porter found himself in something of a creative slump. Only one minor standard appeared in the show, Alex and May's ballad "Do I Love You?," with its poignantly undertoned melody and deceptively natural lyric. Most of the score was lively, if not memorable. "Katie Went To Haiti" benefited from a lavish nightclub setting in which Ethel Merman was assisted by a line of chorus girls decked out in Caribbean styles and toting baskets of fruit on their heads. "Well, Did You Evah?" introduced Betty Grable to Broadway. And the hillbilly-like "Friendship" ("a perfect blendship") allowed Louis and May to part amicably. If the nightclub setting excused the insertion of songs with no bearing on the plot, the eighteenth-century milieu of the dream permitted Porter to set his smart, off-color rhymes to a stately gavotte for Louis and May, "But In The Morning, No." Indeed, it was Porter's unfailing gift for superior lyrics and outrageous couplets that continued to lift him through his musical doldrums. Raoul Pène du Bois's sets and costumes depicted both the eighteenth and twentieth centuries with a flamboyant elegance. *DuBarry Was a Lady* was the last full-length musical of the decade and ran almost to the close of 1940.

Christmas night at the Broadway saw one more musical entry, an abbreviated French vaudeville that called itself rather unfairly **Folies Bergère.** It was short enough to be performed twice nightly as well as on matinees. A limited audience, some undoubtedly lured by the deceptive title, kept it running for 121 showings.

A borderline musical, a folk play about a black Paul Bunyan, was 1940's first entry. **John Henry** (10 January 1940, 44th St.) was written by Roark Bradford, with melodies by Jacques Wolfe, but as far as Broadway was concerned its only virtue was the acting and, more important, the singing of its star, Paul Robeson. His John Henry was said to be able to build singlehandedly a whole railroad in a day or a great river dam in an evening. However, when the girl he loves, Julie Anne (Ruby Elzy), gives a river gambler the dinner John Henry was looking forward to and when a newfangled machine can load a boat faster than he can, he dies of a broken heart.

Like the *Scandals* earlier in the season, **The Earl Carroll Vanities** (13 January 1940, St. James) came in for one last visit. Carroll had moved his show to his Hollywood dinner theatre, where it had thrived for several years. On 13 January 1940, he braved Broadway with inferior material and, apart from his line of beautiful girls, a mediocre cast—all in a form Broadway had tired of. Jerry Lester, the edition's principal comic, burlesqued burlesque dancing. Ygor and Tanya performed a more serious adagio, while the Four Hot Shots stepped lively in "Harlem style." "Professor" Lamberti offered musical interludes on his xylophone. Carroll, once given to imaginative mountings, discovered his scenery was rejected this time as an "antique model." After twenty-five performances the company headed back west. If it left anything of value behind it was the brief popularity of the Latin beat in "I Want My Mama" (Albert Stillman/Jararaca and Vicente Paiva). However, Carroll did leave behind another legacy, one that has had irreparable effects on the American Musical Theatre. In a disastrous innovation, the producer brought microphones onto the legitimate stage. Responsible critics such as Richard Watts, Jr., and Brooks Atkinson quickly called him to account, but their far-sighted, high-principled outcries were to go largely unheeded.

There still remained some demand for small, bright revues; Nancy Hamilton proved that when she brought in a successor to her *One for the Money*. No one was very surprised when the entertainment was called **Two for the Show** (8 February 1940,

Booth). It affected the same debonair stance as the first edition, although it moderated its former anti-left militancy. Alfred Drake, Keenan Wynn, and Brenda Forbes were retained from the original cast. They were joined by Betty Hutton, Richard Haydn, and a number of other lively youngsters. Miss Hutton stopped the show with a wild jitterbug routine. But the musical hit of the evening was "How High The Moon"—the only enduring song to come from the Morgan Lewis tunes for the series. Its intriguing passage from G major through ten other major and minor chords before it returned to G made the song the delight of a generation of progressive jazz artists. The song was sung by Alfred Drake and Frances Comstock against the background of a wartime blackout in London.

The next show was also a revue. **Reunion in New York** (21 February 1940, Little) was created and performed by many of the same refugees who had offered *From Vienna* earlier in the season. In fact, it used much of the first evening's material. The revision was hardly more successful than the original, lasting eleven weeks.

No musicals opened in March, but April brought in the second Rodgers and Hart offering in less than six months. **Higher and Higher** (4 April 1940, Shubert) was an even less satisfying work than *Too Many Girls*. In contrast to the October entry, it was a relatively quick flop. Initially not a single top-drawer Rodgers melody emerged, although in later years singers such as Mabel Mercer and Frank Sinatra turned "It Never Entered My Mind" into a standard. Alec Wilder in his *American Popular Song* speaks highly of "Ev'ry Sunday Afternoon" and comments in amazed tones on the contrast between its romantic melodic line and the brusque colloquialisms of Hart's lyrics, such as "Were you that dumb? She loves the bum."

The Gladys Hurlbut–Joshua Logan book was a contrived affair relating how a group of servants, threatened with unemployment in the face of their master's bankruptcy, combined efforts to marry one of their number to a rich man. Originally written with Vera Zorina in mind, it was rashly and, according to Rodgers, fatally changed when she was not available to star in it. Marta Eggerth was enlisted as a replacement. The Hungarian actress was a fine singer, but she was no dancer, and, more important, she lacked Miss Zorina's slightly exotic glamour. She and her excellent associates (Jack Haley, Robert Chisholm, and Shirley Ross) must have been aghast when the evening's biggest applause was won by a trained seal.

As Rodgers ruefully concluded, "If a trained seal steals your show, you don't have a show."

The Shuberts brought in a talent-packed revue, **Keep Off the Grass** (23 May 1940, Broadhurst)—among the performers, Jimmy Durante, Ray Bolger, José Limon, Larry Adler, Jane Froman, and Ilka Chase. Jimmy McHugh wrote the score. Balanchine did the choreography. The show was a forty-four-performance dud. Howard Dietz had been called in during the tryout, but left after a battle with the explosive Lee Shubert. Other show doctors came and went, but the sketches and songs were too weak for mere hasty repairs. Durante tried his best to garner laughs as an uncouth man-about-town in top hat, white tie, and tails. Virginia O'Brien succeeded a little better with her deadpan, motionless rendition of a wild jitterbug number. Hapless Ilka Chase tried to make something funny out of a monologue on lovemaking among fish. Bolger portrayed a superannuated jitterbug and later displayed a more serious side to his art in a "Raffles Ballet."

Like Kern, Irving Berlin had been away mining gold in the hills of Hollywood. He returned to Broadway at the end of May to provide songs for **Louisiana Purchase** (28 May 1940, Imperial). His score was a far cry from the musicianly, exquisite melodies of *Very Warm for May*, but he was luckier than Kern in his associates. Thanks to a good book by Morrie Ryskind and a stellar cast, the show was the biggest hit of the season. On the surface Ryskind's book seemed topical, a commentary on the recently assassinated Huey Long and the Long family's domination of Louisiana politics. But the material was only lightly satiric, getting most of its laughs from the antics of Victor Moore and stock musical comedy blackouts. Moore was cast as Senator Oliver P. Loganberry, who is sent to investigate the high-handed, corrupt power of the Louisiana Purchase Company. Its attorney, Jim Taylor (William Gaxton), attempts to compromise the Senator with the sultry Marina Van Linden (Vera Zorina) and with the more coquettish Madame Bordelaise (Irene Bordoni). But Loganberry comes through unscathed. Like so many great composers' scores during the year, Berlin's music was far from his best. It had variety, leaning toward the era's most popular beat in "Latins Know How" (sung with Gallic know-how by Mme. Bordelaise), then turning from a Negro spiritual in "The Lord Done Fixed Up My Soul" to the lively title song (sung by beautiful, young Carol Bruce, in the small role of Beatrice, and a male chorus). Marina and Loganberry helped get another fine song, "You're Lonely And I'm Lonely," off to a proper start. At the time the show was running, "It's A Lovely Day Tomorrow" (also sung by Mme. Bordelaise) received considerable play, but it never found a secure niche in Berlin's canon. Nonetheless, the show ran well over a year.

The season's last musical gave the Shuberts their second major flop in two weeks. It must have irritated the brothers to see Buddy DeSylva, with whom they could rarely work harmoniously, producing the season's two biggest hits: *DuBarry Was a Lady* and *Louisiana Purchase*. The new Shubert moneyloser was called **Walk with Music** (4 June 1940, Barrymore), although it had begun life as *Three After Three*. The original title had to do not with time but with three New Hampshire farm girls—Pamela (Kitty Carlisle), Rhoda (Mitzi Green), and Carrie Gibson (Betty Lawford)—who set out for Palm Beach to marry into wealth. Their plan is to let Pamela pose as a rich girl while Rhoda pretends to be her maid and Carrie acts as chaperone. But Pamela fouls up the plan by falling in love with a poor boy, Wing D'Hautville (Jack Whiting). Luckily, rich Steve Harrington (Art Jarrett) falls in love with Rhoda, and by the time the girls arrive in Havana, Carrie has hooked Henry Trowbridge (Lee Sullivan), a nightclub owner. The nightclub scenes allowed the Shuberts to fall back on a device they so often used to mask a show's dullness: parades of beautiful, outlandishly garbed show girls. Such parades had often saved shows in the happier twenties, but by 1940 they were obsolete and ineffective. Guy Bolton worked with Parke Levy and Alan Lipscott on the book, while Johnny Mercer wrote lyrics for Hoagy Carmichael's songs. The show encountered difficulties from the moment it opened on the road. Two of the three original Gibson girls—Simone Simon and Mary Brian—were replaced by Miss Carlisle and Miss Lawford. The Shuberts threw interpolations into the score and just as quickly threw them out. By the time the show arrived at the Ethel Barrymore the score was wholly Carmichael's again. Some of his music was inventive. "The Rhumba Jumps" had a pronounced Latin beat in its verse and a solid, swinging chorus. Only "Way Back In 1939 A.D." enjoyed some appeal, but not enough to save the show.

1940–1941

This was a strange season. All its musical openings were packed together between the middle of September and the end of January. The number of new lyric shows plunged, and for the most part what did appear was mediocre to blatantly horrendous. But the season also brought forth two of the most innovative musicals of the American stage. Both were well received and successful. These two gems aside, theatregoers' attention was often more readily diverted by the news of the war and the impassioned election campaign, with Roosevelt running for an unprecedented third term, as well as by other pleasures.

Hold On to Your Hats, the season's first new musical, waited until 11 September to raise its curtain at the Shubert. It also raised high hopes for the season, for the show brought with it the long-absent Al Jolson, once Broadway's reigning musical star. Jolson had made a second career in pictures, but when his star began to fade in Hollywood he was persuaded to try a new Broadway vehicle. His new show reflected changes that had taken place since Jolson had left the stage. Guy Bolton, Matty Brooks, and Eddie Davis's book was more cohesive than the old librettos Jolson had been accustomed to. Nor was the score studded with interpolations. All *Hold On to Your Hats*'s songs were by Burton Lane, with E. Y. Harburg lyrics. And in a third departure from tradition Jolson was not the only star. Martha Raye, Jack Whiting, and Bert Gordon all had their names above the title with Jolson's. The implications were that the aging Jolson needed all the help he could get and that, even if this were not so, the days of a vehicle tailored to the demands of a single all-powerful performer were waning. Nonetheless, as he had in his heyday, Jolson still toyed with his material and sometimes discarded it altogether to talk directly to his audience. Jolson played "The Lone Rider," a popular radio cowboy, and obviously a take-off on the Lone Ranger. He finds listeners can't separate the actor from the character, and he is called upon to pursue a real-life villain, Fernando (Arnold Moss). Lane's score was good workaday material with one outstanding number, "There's A Great Day Coming Mañana." Miss Raye, grinning from ear to ear, helped make the evening cheery with her raucous singing of "Life Was Pie For The Pioneer" and "She Came, She Saw, She Cancanned," while Bert Gordon (the "Mad Russian" on Eddie Cantor's radio program) added to the merriment by playing Concho (read "Tonto") with his Russian accent. Everything conspired to make a hit of the evening, except that Jolson was unhappy in New York, claiming he could no longer stand the cold weather. The show closed after twenty weeks, although it could have run at least several more months.

The Lyric Opera Company, an American group, arrived on the 30th and spent three weeks offering Gilbert and Sullivan works. *The Gondoliers, The Mikado, Trial by Jury,* and *The Pirates of Penzance* were mounted—without exceptional staging, important names, or D'Oyly Carte authenticity.

On the next night Ed Wynn brought in **Boys and Girls Together** (1 October 1940, Broadhurst). Since he himself produced it and since it was a revue with no plot to hamper his loose-jointed antics, Wynn was able to dominate the evening, as was his wont, with his customary puns, inventions, and "one crack-brained costume after another." In a memorable scene Wynn entered paddling a boat; he put his oars aside to check his road map, and, satisfied he was where he wanted to be, called for an anchor—which promptly dropped from the flies. Wynn also got himself enmeshed in the acrobatic efforts of the La Varres. The more he attempted to untangle the knot, the more he found himself locked in. Distinguished talents such as choreographer Albertina Rasch and composer Sammy Fain were employed, but it was Wynn who kept audiences coming for 191 performances.

Another outrageous clown, who like Wynn was famous for his nonsensical inventions, arrived nine days later. Joe Cook was ostensibly the star of **It Happens on Ice** (10 October 1940, Center). For the occasion he carted cartloads of his wacky inventions onto the ice. But in truth the show was little more than another attempt to make the Center Theatre a legitimate playhouse. Over the summer the house had been rebuilt so that the stage could accommodate ice-skating spectacles, of which this was to be the first. Vernon Duke was among those called in to compose the score, but neither he nor his collaborators were particularly inspired. It soon became evident that the spectacle was sufficient. Attempts to pass for more legitimate attractions were abandoned, and the house embarked on a decade of successful ice extravaganzas. Norman Bel Geddes designed shimmering silver sets for this production, combining with Leon Leonidoff to mount eye-filling scenes such as "The Legend of the Lake."

A musical fantasy concocted by Lynn Root proved much more inspiring to Duke, and he came up with a solid score for **Cabin in the Sky** (25 October 1940, Martin Beck). Root's libretto drew a charming, unworldly picture of the Negro South. Devout Petunia Jackson (Ethel Waters) prays to the Good Lord that he spare the life of her no-good husband, "Little Joe" (Dooley Wilson). The Good Lord agrees, giving Joe six months in which to redeem himself. The Lord's General (Todd Duncan) is sent to assist, but from the nether regions comes Lucifer, Jr. (Rex Ingram), just as determined to claim what he believes is his. It looks as if Joe will succeed, but he gets into an argument with Petunia at John Henry's Café and shoots her. When they arrive at the Pearly Gates the Good Lord's stern heart melts at the entreaties of the ever-forgiving Petunia, and Little Joe is admitted along with her. Duke's tunes ranged from the jivey up-to-the-minute "Boogy-Woogy" to the wry "Honey In The Honeycomb." With his title song and "Taking A Chance On Love," Duke composed his last Broadway melodies to have popular appeal. Miss Waters's affectionate rendering of "Taking A Chance On Love" was a highlight of the show and of her career. In after years Duke looked back on *Cabin in the Sky* as his "all-time high." J. Rosamond Johnson, besides taking a small role, trained the singing chorus. Katherine Dunham led her dancers through their slithering paces, assisted in the choreography by George Balanchine. Wisely, everyone involved in the show rejected the easy excesses and crassness so many musicals resorted to. Certainly they avoided turning the evening into a black minstrel show. Throughout the production a tasteful restraint, a sense of what was appropriate to the story, was maintained. This rare display of integrity made *Cabin in the Sky* an attractive enough evening to keep ticket-buyers coming for twenty weeks.

A brainless revue called 'Tis Of Thee (26 October 1940, Maxine Elliott) opened and closed the next night. Like the earlier *Straw Hat Revue* (29 September 1939), the show was a product of the summer camps. The cast was damned as "untalented," their material as "poor." At best a pair of ballroom dancers, Cappella and Beatrice, and a comic, George Lloyd, who offered "turns in Neurasthenia," elicited some good notices. However, Lloyd and the dancers were professionals brought in to bolster the sagging entertainment.

The busy month ended more festively when Buddy DeSylva, Herbert Fields, Cole Porter, and Ethel Merman again combined their awesome talents to put across Panama Hattie (30 October 1940, 46th St.)—a smash hit, but not a very good show. It was the sort of splashy, sassy affair that in this interim period substituted for generally better material. Still, the improving economic picture helped it become the first book show since the twenties to run over 500 performances. Hattie Maloney (Miss Merman)—obviously first cousin to May Daley of *DuBarry Was a Lady*—is a bar girl in the Panama Canal Zone, where she meets Nick Bullett (James Dunn), scion of an old Philadelphia family. When Nick proposes marriage, she agrees, provided Nick's young daughter by his first wife accepts her. At first little Geraldine (Jean Carroll) is difficult, but by the end of the evening she and Hattie agree "Let's Be Buddies." For many, Miss Merman's duet with little Miss Carroll—a remarkably touching, sentimental digression for Porter—became the high spot of *Panama Hattie*. Much of the evening's best comedy came from the knockabout antics of three girl-seeking sailors, Pat Harrington, Frank Hyers, and, most of all, Rags Ragland. For the craftsman-like book Porter supplied what was at best a competent collection of tunes. Only one number from the show achieved anything more than passing popularity, "Make It Another Old Fashioned, Please." Again Porter's lyrics outclassed his melodies. "I'm Throwing A Ball Tonight" became the latest in his growing portfolio of "laundry list" tunes whose rhymes were essentially lists of people or places hilariously juxtaposed. His fresh uses of clichés, clever in-rhymes, and brazen inversions were displayed in top form in the verse to Hattie's "I've Still Got My Health," where "alabaster," "Missus Astor," and "oil castor" were rhymed. As he had for *DuBarry Was a Lady*, Raoul Pêne du Bois created colorfully flamboyant costumes and scenery that often made the evening seem better than it really was.

No new musicals opened in November, while the lone early December offering was a "one-man" show. This kind of presentation was not so commonplace as it would be a few years down the road, when the deaths of both vaudeville (already a fact) and revue (not yet obvious), plus an economic crunch, would foster it. And this one-man show, Mum's the Word (5 December 1940, Belmont), actually had four men: its star, Jimmy Savo; Hiram Sherman, who served as a sort of compère; a pianist; and a silent stooge. Savo, a diminuative, soulful eyed clown, performed a number of his older two-a-day skits—such as a hospital orderly called upon to perform emergency surgery—and sang several ditties, especially his famous plea to his river to stay away from his door. Apparently playgoers had seen it all too often, so a week and a half and he was gone.

Two more traditional musicals raised their curtains on Christmas night. Meet the People (25 December 1940, Mansfield) had originally been produced on the West Coast one year earlier, then wended its way across the country. Some of its creators, like composer Jay Gorney and skit writer Edward Eliscu, had once been minor figures on Broadway. Others were new to the living theatre. In some respects their work was in tune with the latest fads, with, for example, the Latin beat of "In Chi Chi Castenango" (also listed as "In Chichicastenango"). In others, such as "Union Label," it displayed a certain fading left-wing militancy. One comic song, designed to devastate the sentimental paeans Jolson and Cantor once sang to Dixie, brought Eddie Johnson and Jack Albertson on stage to sing about "The Same Old South." Dorothy Roberts and Ted Arkin whirled to a snappy jitterbug. Sad-faced Jack Gilford delivered a monologue on the joys and pains of being a movie fan at a double feature—with trailers. Making her debut was an attractive young lady listed in the program as Nanette Fabares. In later years she made a slight change in the spelling of her last name and went on to become one of Broadway's brightest leading ladies. The revue was generally fast paced and professional but also unexceptional. It found enough of an audience to run twenty weeks. It might have run even longer if it had not elected to compete for opening-night attention with *Pal Joey*.

Pal Joey (25 December 1940, Barrymore) was something different—a cynical, snarling, yet sentimentally lyrical examination of bought love. Gigolos were not new to the musical stage. Until now they had been secondary figures, French comic characters, or coy mentionables in a Cole Porter lyric. But here in *Pal Joey* was a musical with a hollow, self-serving, two-timing little twerp as its hero and an equally self-serving, hard, past-her-prime matron as his vis-à-vis. There were almost certainly no writers of significance on Broadway in 1940 but Rodgers and Hart who would have attempted to put something of this sort into musical form, and assuredly no one else who could have pulled it off so handsomely. The evening had its genesis in John O'Hara stories from the *New Yorker*, and O'Hara carefully adapted his own pieces. His literate, adult book follows the rise of a cheap, handsome nightclub hoofer named Joey Evans (Gene Kelly). Joey is at the beginning of a romance with a sweet, relatively innocent girl named Linda English (Leila Ernst). His line is smooth and irresistible, as he announces, "I Could Write A Book" telling of how she would "walk and whisper and look." But he soon finds it to his advantage to court Vera Simpson (Vivienne Segal), a much older and knowing lady-about-town. While she is not inexperienced at the game, she professes to be overwhelmed; not merely wild, beguiled, and turned into a simpering whimpering child, but completely "Bewitched," bothered, and bewildered. In return for Joey's favors, Vera sets him up in a posh apartment and even helps him open his own night club, Chez Joey. But Joey's fundamental selfishness soon begins to tell on Vera. Matters come to a head in Joey's apartment, where Linda discloses that she has overheard a plan to blackmail Vera by threatening to tell Vera's husband of her relation with Joey. Vera assumes this is Linda's way of scaring her out of the picture. But Linda assures Vera her ardor for Joey has cooled; in her own simple way she has seen through him. And Linda's new perceptions help Vera clarify hers. Each woman begs the other, "Take Him"; one refusing to "put a price on him," the other offering no more encouragement than "Pajamas look nice on him." Joey, realizing he has lost everything, walks off into the night. On the street he meets another young lady who, he tells her, could inspire him to write a book.

Because so much of the action took place in nightclubs it was all too easy for Rodgers and Hart to insert several extraneous cabaret numbers, songs such as "That Terrific Rainbow" and "The Flower Garden Of My Heart." But in Joey's similar numbers, such as "You Musn't Kick It Around," "Plant You Now, Dig You Later," and "Do It The Hard Way," the songs skillfully reflected the attitudes of the principals in seemingly incidental ditties. At one point Hart had devastating fun with the intellectual pretensions of the famous burlesque stripper Gypsy Rose Lee. In "Zip" his stripper (Jean Casto), as she relieves herself of her garments, bemoans that Walter Lippmann wasn't brilliant today and wonders if Saroyan will ever write a great play, but puzzles over the identity of someone named Sally Rand. Yet *Pal Joey*'s meatiest songs were those sung by Vera, Joey, and Linda, bearing directly on the plot. Here more than anywhere else in their career Rodgers and Hart's songs are a unique, curiously satisfying blend of Rodgers's warm lyricism and Hart's street urchin toughness. The juxtaposition of words and music in "Bewitched" and "Take Him" are characteristic. The evolution of stage dialogue is vividly illustrated by comparing the tinselly toughness of the scene between Rose-Marie and Mme. Bompard in *Good Morning, Dearie* (1 November 1921), written not quite twenty years earlier, with the steely, contained cruelty of a typical scene between Joey and Vera. At the end of the play, disturbed by the blackmail attempt and tired of Joey, Vera decides to break the relationship. She cuts short Joey's braggadocio.

Vera: Some other time, Beauty. Right now I have some questions to bother you with. How are you fixed, financially?

Joey: I got rid of a lot of dough, recently. Why? You want some back?

Vera: No, but I've been thinking. What if I were called away to California, or dropped dead, or something—would you be all right? I mean, for instance, would you eat?

Joey: Honey Sug, somehow, I always eat. But what's on your mind?

Vera: Well, I think I'm going to be called away to California, or maybe drop dead.

Joey: Come on, say it. This is the brush-off. Those punks gave you a scare, and you're walking out.

Vera: A slightly brutal though accurate way of putting it. You can keep the club … .

Joey foolishly turns petulant and nasty:

Vera: I have a temper, Beauty, and I want to say a few things before I lose it.

Joey: Lose it. It's all you got left to lose.

Vera's reply to this vicious retort is to call the bank and close Joey's private account. Even though Kelly's smiling warmth mitigated some of Joey's harshness, not every critic could stomach so honest an approach. In a question to which he would revise his answer a dozen years later, Brooks Atkinson in the *Times* asked, "can you draw sweet water from a foul well?" Several of his fellow aisle-sitters answered firmly "no." On the other hand, critics such as Wolcott Gibbs in *The New Yorker* hailed the musical for putting "three-dimensional" human beings on the musical stage. The public was not discouraged by the critics' divisions, and *Pal Joey* ran 374 performances. When it was revived in 1952, a changed moral climate and more relaxed theatre standards made it wildly successful.

Leonard Sillman put together another revue, called **All in Fun,** opened it at the Majestic Friday, 27 December, and closed it Saturday, 28 December. From the moment of his first entrance dressed in a white sailor suit and tapping joyously away, Bill Robinson was the bright spot of the evening. Later he donned top hat, white tie, and tails for another show-stopper. Brooks Atkinson insisted, "even when he is standing still you feel he is dancing." Sillman's favorite comedienne, Imogene Coca, was back, but she was handed some of the show's weakest material. The Latin beat of "Macumba" failed to scintillate, as did the drolleries of "April In Harrisburg" (an ur–"Boston Beguine" that spoofed the then popular "April In Paris").

Marc Blitzstein's **No for an Answer** (5 January 1941, Mecca Temple) was given equally short shrift by the public. There was no hue and cry to go beyond the initially slated three performances. A shoestring mounting, without scenery and with the composer himself alone at the piano, it told the kind of story to be expected from Blitzstein and his Communist buddies. When saintly workers at a summer resort decide to unionize at season's end they are thwarted and their leader murdered by fascistic police and greedy businessmen.

The Shuberts had no better luck with a Robert Stolz operetta based on the 1930 hit *Tonight or Never.* **Night of Love** (7 January 1941, Hudson) retained the story of a frigid prima donna (Helen Gleason) who finally finds love with a handsome but vaguely identified young man. The man (John Lodge) turns out to be a scout for the Metropolitan Opera. With the vogue of operetta at its nadir, the piece was able to survive just one week.

It looked at first as if one week was all **Crazy with the Heat** (14 January 1941, 44th St.) would last. Although the cast included old favorites Willie Howard (without his brother), Luella Gear, and Carl Randall (back in front of an audience after years of creating the dances for Broadway musicals), the revue posted its closing notice immediately after opening. However, Ed Sullivan, the newspaper columnist, liked it enough to attempt to save it. He enlisted Lew Brown to enliven the staging, added a number of South American–type singers and some first-class dancers, and reopened the show after a brief hiatus. Miss Gear, besides acting as "M.C.," smoked three cigars simultaneously in an effort to draw laughs. Willie Howard, trapped in sketches "with pointless dialogue and flat endings," encased his bony legs in tights to portray a ballet master. Informed he had killed a relative, he asked, "What have I done? Murdered my own fish and blood." One more attractive number was a serious ballet set in Toulouse-Lautrec's Paris. But the material still was not really strong enough to afford a fully entertaining evening. *Crazy with the Heat* ran an additional ninety-two performances before folding.

Although the calendar indicated that the season was little more than half over, 23 January at the Alvin witnessed the last musical premiere of the season. But it was the most imaginative, intelligent and cohesive work of the theatrical year—**Lady in**

the Dark. Dreams had long been employed as a theatrical device, but their psychoanalytic implications had been largely ignored. There had been occasional jokes, and *Peggy Ann* (27 December 1926) flirted with the matter, but it took Moss Hart to write a libretto bearing down squarely and seriously on the subject. His dialogue was far more literate than that of the run-of-the-mill Broadway musical book. His characters not only spoke grammatically correct and complete sentences, they often spoke complete paragraphs. Yet his touch was so light, stylish, and sure that he dispelled the artificiality and turgidness of the old comic-opera librettos— where years before characters also spoke whole paragraphs. A leavening influence was undoubtedly Kurt Weill's now gossamer, now brittle score and Ira Gershwin's clever, tonically jolting lyrics. Hart's plot was slight. His central figure was austere, severely tailored Liza Elliott (Gertrude Lawrence), editor of a successful fashion magazine. Although she has fought her way to the top in a man's world, she recognizes she is sufficiently unhappy to warrant a visit to a psychoanalyst's office. She has been bothered by "confused, fantastic dreams. I knew the people— they were the people I see every day—and yet they were not the people I knew at all." Primarily "They" were four men: Kendall Nesbitt (Bert Lytell), her married lover and benefactor, the man instrumental in helping her rise to her position; Randy Curtis (Victor Mature), a glamorous, shallow Hollywood idol; Randall Paxton (Danny Kaye), the magazine's photographer; and, most important of all although she fails to realize it, Charlie Johnson (Macdonald Carey), her crusty, unbowed advertising manager. In her dreams she has heard wisps of a melody that haunt her, but that she cannot identify. The four dreams she relates to her psychoanalyst finally bring her to understand that her childhood rejection by her father and his prediction she would never possess her mother's beauty have shaped her every adult move. She breaks with Kendall, rejects Curtis and Paxton, and, singing the nursery song she at last remembers, dances off with Charlie. With one exception all the work's songs were offered in the dream sequences. These were elaborate, extended production numbers that moved from one facet of a dream to another on four revolving stages. In the "Glamour Dream," done mostly in Ziegfeldian blues, Liza sees herself as "The World's Inamorata" until a portrait presented to her limns the real Liza. A "Wedding Dream" also ends unhappily when Charlie in the guise of the minister asks if anyone can

show cause why he shouldn't proceed and the chorus responds, "This woman knows she does not love this man." A gaudy "Circus Dream" finds Liza accepting the fact that, like a lady named Jenny, she has brought problems on herself by making up her mind. Full enlightenment (and the denouement) comes in the brief "Childhood Dream." Weill's most memorable melody was saved appropriately for the song that haunts Liza, "My Ship." Elsewhere his pleasant tunes often played second fiddle to Gershwin's ingenious lyrics. Gershwin's readily identifiable shorthand was heard in songs such as "One Life To Live," where he announced "gloom can jump in the riv'!" For Danny Kaye he composed the least relevant song of the work, a terrifying, tongue-twisting list of Russian composers headed by "Tschaikowsky." Many of Gershwin's drollest lines were given to Liza in the saga of "Jenny," the story of a determined young lady whose plans always backfire. Fine writing, superb casting— especially the authority and grace Miss Lawrence brought to Liza—and brilliant mounting helped Liza and her ship to sail smoothly for 467 performances.

Neither *Lady in the Dark* nor *Pal Joey* seemed to have much effect on the American Musical Theatre other than to fill the coffers at their respective houses. When both shows closed, their influence seemed nil. It would be years later, looking back, that they would be recognized as isolated beacons in an otherwise dark period illuminating ways to the future. Broadway quickly returned to the easier *Panama Hattie* type of musical.

1941-1942

The year was dominated by the war, which in the middle of the season engulfed America. Daily recountings of battlefront horrors and agonies turned theatregoers away from more serious, innovative efforts. Light, escapist material was not merely acceptable, it was encouraged. Even among straight plays, comedies such as *Blithe Spirit, Junior Miss*, and *Jason* and thrillers such as *Angel Street* and *Uncle Harry* were far more in demand than plays with timely, thoughtful statements. The exciting possibilities of *Pal Joey* and *Lady in the Dark* were shunted aside. The public wanted conventional musicals, and, to paraphrase *Of Thee I Sing* (26 December 1931), it got them, whether it liked them or not. By and large it didn't, for the season's musicals were not only conventional, they were uninspired or insipid.

The first new show of the season arrived at the Barrymore on 1 October, over eight months after the last musical premiere. With **Best Foot Forward** Winsocki joined Pottawatomie, Tait, and Bingham in the ranks of imaginary stage schools. Readers can deduce what they choose from the fact that the older schools had Anglo-Saxon names, the later colleges Indian ones. The visit to Winsocki, unlike the earlier trips, occurs not at the height of the football craze, but at prom time. As a lark Bud Hooper (Gil Stratton, Jr.) invites the Hollywood starlet Gale Joy (Rosemary Lane) to be his prom date, never seriously expecting her to accept. However, Gale's press agent, Jack Haggerty (Marty May), sees excellent promotional possibilities in the stunt and gets Gale to accept. Bud's girlfriend, Helen Schlesinger (Maureen Cannon), is so furious that she rips off part of Gale's gown, signaling a wild tearing and stripping session in which Helen's classmates claw for souvenirs. Avoiding scandal, Gale agrees to return quietly to Hollywood while Bud and Helen are reunited. The book was by John Cecil Holm, the music by Hugh Martin and Ralph Blane. Only one song became nationally popular, "Buckle Down Winsocki." When the war broke out the song had a second vogue with revised lyrics, as "Buckle Down Buck Private." Both Martin and Blane did most of their best work in Hollywood (including *Meet Me in St. Louis* three years later). Martin did the words and music for several later Broadway shows, but his clever way with words served him better than his facile melodic gifts. The show's ten-month run started a number of bright young performers on the road to stardom, especially Nancy Walker, the most original and consistently hilarious comedienne since Beatrice Lillie. She played Winsocki's ever-available, ever-rejected "Blind Date" and won applause delivering the wistfully worldly-wise "A Little Joint With A Juke Box." Even when the material occasionally let the cast down, George Abbott's lively staging glossed over its flaws.

A lamebrained piece called **Viva O'Brien** (9 October 1941, Majestic) managed to survive for twenty performances. It followed a band of J. Forster Adams's cocktail party guests on a colorful tour of Mexico and their search for a legendary wishing stone. The show employed a nine-foot-deep swimming pool that allowed a diving scene just before the finale. More water was splashed on the stage from an elaborate waterfall, part of a jungle scene that necessitated a ritual dance calling to mind the jungle numbers of the twenties spectacles. Since Chester Hale was the choreographer as well as one of the producers, he saw to it his chorus girls also did some high stepping.

Things improved when **Let's Face It** (29 October 1941, Imperial) premiered. Thanks to Herbert and Dorothy Fields's adaptation of the 1925 comedy *Cradle Snatchers* and to Cole Porter's songs, the evening was tightly professional. Thanks to the clowning of Danny Kaye it was sometimes uproarious. But the truth is that *Let's Face It* depended on its creators' know-how to put it across. It was, for all this know-how, a second-rate show. Cole Porter's melodic genius continued to elude him, although his unfailingly excellent lyrics continued to pull him through. Songs such as "Farming," "Let's Not Talk About Love," "Ace In The Hole," and "Ev'rything I Love" represented lesser achievements. Perhaps sensing this, he even allowed interpolations, with Kaye's wife, Sylvia Fine, writing much of Kaye's material. Kaye stopped the show, as he had *Lady in the Dark*, with a "jabberwocky of song, dance, illustration, and double-talk" called "Melody In Four F." The Fieldses' story, in keeping with the period's contemporary but not topical bent, made the three gigolos of the original show three young soldiers. They are recruited by three wives, who have become convinced their husbands are cheating on them. The husbands' unexpected return could have proved embarrassing had not the husbands coincidentally taken up with the soldiers' girls. Feigned outrage, preposterous excuses, and some brazen half-truths offer everyone a way out. Harry Horner, the set designer, had an easy time turning farms and country estates into bright-colored sets. John Harkrider, the costume designer, wasn't so lucky. Most of his men had to be dressed in drab khakis. To compensate he gave his fashionable ladies exaggeratedly hued and contrived wardrobes. Besides Kaye the cast included Eve Arden, Vivian Vance, Mary Jane Walsh, Benny Baker, and, in a small role, Nanette Fabray (formerly Fabares). They sparkled gaily enough to allow theatregoers to overlook the lackluster music. Aside from the sui generis *Sons o'Fun*, *Let's Face It* became the long-run winner of the season, compiling 547 performances. Its run was as much an indication of the new war-born prosperity as of any overriding merit.

A group of old Broadway and vaudeville favorites pooled their talents and prestige to mount **High Kickers** (31 October 1941, Broadhurst); George Jessel conceived the work. He wrote the book in collaboration with his songwriters, Bert Kalmar and Harry Ruby, and he costarred with his old pal Sophie Tucker. Carl Randall did the suitably old-fashioned dances. The prologue was set in 1910 at Piner's

Burlesque, where George M. Krause (Jessel) and his "High Kickers" troupe are appearing. Young George Jr. (Dick Monahan), is with the company. But the action quickly advances to 1941. George Sr. is dead, and his son (now played by Jessel) is running the company. The troupe is arrested in Chamberville, Ohio. They are released when Sophie Tucker, who is traveling with them, reminds the mayor his wife once had been a member of the troupe. Miss Tucker, playing herself, was undoubtedly meant to give the piece a certain verisimilitude. But the librettists also resorted to distortions (Piner's for what was most likely meant to be Miner's) and in-jokes (one character was S. Kaufman Hart). Besides the confused approach the authors were burdened by a lack of anything fresh to say. In another reversion to old-fashioned ways, specialty acts and parading show girls were enlisted to liven the proceedings. The score was Ruby and Kalmar's last for Broadway, but it was merely a feeble echo of their earlier vitality. Still, the old names had a following, so the show recorded a twenty-two-week run.

The spurt of October openings was followed by a void in the November calendar. But on 1 December at the Winter Garden the Shuberts reunited with Olsen and Johnson to provide Broadway with a successor to their zany *Hellzapoppin*. **Sons o' Fun** repeated the same formula (or lack of it) of outrageous nonsense. Patrons were intentionally escorted to the wrong seats, and those unlucky enough to have bought boxes had to reach them by climbing ladders. Once the show began, audience members were invited on stage to participate, and chorus girls came down the aisles to dance with theatregoers. The few formal skits burlesqued *Panama Hattie* and *Charlie's Aunt* and, in a brush with topicality, included a madcap version of the army's basic training. Ella Logan and Carmen Miranda were in charge of interpreting the Sammy Fain and Will Irwin songs (with lyrics mostly by Jack Yellen). Miss Logan sang "Happy In Love" and "It's A New Kind Of Thing," while Miss Miranda handled the Latin items such as "Thank You, South America." War clouds prompted the insertion of patriot pieces such as "It's A Mighty Fine Country We Have Here." The tunes weren't much; they were there because the show was a musical and because even zaniness must rest. It was Olsen and Johnson's unique brand of comic mayhem that pleased New Yorkers and their guests for two years.

Sunny River (4 December 1941, St. James) was set along the banks of the old man river that its librettist, Oscar Hammerstein II, had dealt with so poetically before. But the story was not actually a bit of Americana. Instead, it was a tale of foredoomed love that could as easily have been set in the Hungary of its composer, Sigmund Romberg. Indeed it was the very sort of story that Romberg loved best but that, apart from *Maytime* (16 August 1917) and *The Student Prince* (2 December 1924), had never inspired his most memorable compositions. In this instance a young café singer, Marie Sauvinet (Muriel Angelus), falls in love with the highborn Jean Gervais (Robert Lawrence). When she is told that Jean has long been in love with Cecilie Marshall (Helen Claire), she runs away to Paris, returning years later as a great prima donna. Once again romance blossoms between Marie and Jean, but once again Jean's obvious affection for Cecilie causes Marie to leave. It was a pedestrian book with equally pedestrian, if sweet, music. *Sunny River* folded after five weeks.

Three days later, 7 December 1941, Japan bombed Pearl Harbor, and the United States was caught up in World War II.

The first musical to arrive in wartime New York was **Banjo Eyes** (25 December 1941, Hollywood). It made a hasty concession to the situation when during its Philadelphia tryout it inserted the uplifting "We Did It Before (We'll Do It Again)" (Charles Tobias and Cliff Friend). But aside from this token flag-waving, it was a gaudy, escapist musical version of John Cecil Holm and George Abbott's *Three Men on a Horse*. Neither Holm (who had done the book for *Best Foot Forward*) nor Abbott participated in the adaptation, which was by Joe Quillan and Izzy Elinson, two radio script writers, for the show's star, Eddie Cantor. Holm and Abbott's original piece was so well constructed that no damage was done. The songs were by Vernon Duke, with lyrics by John Latouche and Harold Adamson. But the real attraction of the show and its principal prop was Cantor, in his first Broadway appearance since *Whoopee*. Cantor played Erwin Trowbridge, a greeting card salesman, who talks to horses in his dreams. This might not be so unusual if the horses didn't give him tips that always win. Of course, there's a catch. The horses insist Trowbridge never bet money on the races. A gang of crooks hears of his phenomenal pickings and attempts to make him work for them. But when they force him to put money on a race, his dream horses suddenly refuse to reveal anything. Duke's score, like most of the season's scores, was serviceable without being exceptional. Apart from the rousing interpolation, the hit of the evening was "We're Having A Baby (My Baby And Me)," which

Trowbridge and his wife sang. Somehow it never became a Cantor standby, although it was the last good number Cantor introduced on the Broadway stage. Late in the evening Cantor dropped his role of Erwin and came on in blackface to bring down the house with an extended medley of his old favorites. Cantor, like Jolson before him, had become enamored of the milder California weather. When the winter rigors proved too much for him, *Banjo Eyes* was forced to close in its sixteenth week, even though it was still going strong.

More Vernon Duke music and more John Latouche lyrics were heard two weeks later when **The Lady Comes Across** (9 January 1942, 44th St.) arrived as the first musical of 1942. The show had Fred Thompson, an old hand at librettos, collaborating with Dawn Powell on the book. George Balanchine created the choreography, while the suave Romney Brent directed a cast that included Evelyn Wyckoff, Joe E. Lewis, Mischa Auer, Wynn Murray, Ronald Graham, and Gower Champion. The impressive roster of talent belied the show's sometimes slapdash nature. For example, it reemployed the scenery left behind by *She Had to Say Yes*, a musical that had failed to reach Broadway the preceding season. The plot, however timely, seemed frail enough even to its authors to impel them to use the frame device of a dream. The sleeping heroine (Miss Wyckoff) sees herself meeting an FBI agent, and together they capture a spy operating a Fifth Avenue dress shop. The evening's weaknesses became apparent to its original stars, Ray Bolger and Jessie Matthews, both of whom resigned their roles before the show opened. Their foresight didn't deprive them of much work. *The Lady Comes Across* folded after a humiliating run of three performances.

On 21 January the Boston Comic Opera and the Jooss Ballet Dance Theatre combined their resources to bring in a curious repertory of modern dance and Gilbert and Sullivan operettas. For example, *H. M. S. Pinafore* was on a double bill with a ballet, *The Green Table*. In *The Mikado*, which was presented along with two ballets—*The Big City* and *A Ball in Old Vienna*—the producers felt compelled to change "gentlemen of Japan" to "gangsters of Japan." The public came anyway.

The next night Cheryl Crawford revived Gershwin's *Porgy and Bess* at the Majestic with many of the original principals (notably Todd Duncan, Anne Brown, and J. Rosamond Johnson). Time had popularized the great Gershwin melodies from the work, allowing audiences to accept it as an old friend instead of a forbiddingly daring and serious new effort. The resurgent prosperity also helped sell tickets. To ensure its acceptability to a larger audience, Miss Crawford wrenched the work more into the Broadway mainstream by removing recitative passages and by shortening it through the elimination of several musical numbers. Her tactics worked. With this production, which ran thirty-five weeks in New York and toured successfully, *Porgy and Bess* comfortably became a welcome classic of the American Musical Theatre.

A semiprofessional revue originally mounted in the fall as *V for Victory* was polished for Broadway by Alexander Cohen and presented on 11 February as **Of V We Sing** (11 February 1942, Concert). Its performers included names that would soon make a bigger mark in the theatre: Betty Garrett, Phil Leeds, and Curt Conway. The show dug for laughs at the expense of unions, the Brooklyn Dodgers, and Mother's Day ("Don't kill your mother on Mother's Day"). Excellent jitterbugging highlighted the evening. The songsmiths didn't fare so well, but they offered a range of suitable patriotic material—"You Can't Fool The People," "Red, Whites And Blues," a title song, and, returning to Flatbush, the "Brooklyn Cantata."

With so many younger performers being drafted and with the public clamoring for diverting entertainment, Clifford C. Fischer, a nightclub impresario, who had given Broadway the illegitimate *Folies Bergère* (25 December 1939), convinced the Shuberts that vaudeville and old vaudevillians would help light their dark theatres. Their first offering, **Priorities of '42** (12 March 1942, 46th St.) seemed to vindicate Fischer. Willie Howard, Lou Holtz, Phil Baker, Paul Draper, and Hazel Scott were the headliners. To a great extent the performers used their own material. There were no sketches. For the most part simple draperies and old drops from the Shubert warehouse provided backgrounds. With $1.00 top at matinees and $2.00 at night, the response at the 46th Street Theatre was so hearty that in a little over a month a second assemblage was offered two blocks south. **Keep 'Em Laughing** (24 April 1942, 44th St.) presented William Gaxton and Victor Moore, Hildegarde, Paul and Grace Hartman, Jack Cole and his dancers, and a young Zero Mostel. While most critics thought this an even more impressive and diverting bill than the first, it failed to receive the same attention. After seventy-seven times, it was revised and retitled **Top-Notchers** (29 May 1942, 44th St.). Gaxton and Moore were gone, as well as Hildegarde, but Gracie Fields was an attractive addition. Nonetheless the bill refused to catch on. After a further forty-eight showings the affair was dropped.

In the meantime Ed Sullivan and Noble Sissle quickly brought together a company of black artists including Sissle's associate of yore, Flournoy Miller. They hoped to offer Broadway a black *Priorities*. But it was becoming manifest that the first Fischer-Schubert bill was a freak success. **Harlem Cavalcade** (1 May 1942, Ritz) quickly departed.

The season's last new show, **By Jupiter** (3 June 1942, Shubert), was its best. In Broadway's heyday the slapped-together, frivolous "summer musical" had been an annual event. But *By Jupiter*, though it was light-hearted, was not lightweight. This lyric version of Katharine Hepburn's 1932 vehicle, *The Warrior's Husband*, was a firmly constructed, intelligently wrought, adult musical comedy. It was also, sadly, Rodgers and Hart's final collaboration. Hart's drinking and instability were becoming too much for Rodgers, and Rodgers discreetly made overtures elsewhere. In a sense the overtures came none too soon, for Hart died, only forty-seven, in November 1943. But the public knew none of this. All it saw was a glittering, melodic romp set in ancient Pontus. Queen Hippolyta (Benay Venuta) and her women rule over their milksop husbands, a hegemony they will hold as long as Hippolyta can wear her magic, strength-endowing girdle. A band of Greeks led by Theseus (Ronald Graham) and Hercules (Ralph Dumke) invade Pontus, hoping to capture the girdle and restore the men to their rightful place. Where their swords fail, their sexual wiles conquer. King Sapiens (Ray Bolger) assumes the throne his wife has held, and Theseus is rewarded with Hippolyta's attractive sister, Antiope (Constance Moore). The score was musicianly and finely nuanced, but only one number immediately caught the fancy of the public outside the theatre. The man in the street who whistled or sang Bolger's number "Ev'rything I've Got" was most likely unaware that the cheerful, clever commercial lyrics were matched on stage by the snarling, barbed rhymes of Hippolyta and Sapiens's duet. With time, Theseus's "Wait Till You See Her" joined the ranks of Rodgers and Hart classics. However, in the theatre, Bolger's biggest show-stopper was a minor number, "Nobody's Heart." Young Bolger was partnered in his hilarious yet affectionate dance for the song with sixty-year-old Bertha Belmore. Curiously, Miss Belmore had played the same role (Sapiens's mother) in *The Warrior's Husband. By Jupiter* ran well over a year and might have run longer had not Bolger left to entertain the troops overseas.

Act Five

The American Musical as a Conscious Art Form, 1942–1965

The fifth act in this history of the American Musical Theatre was long, approximately as long as the first, three-quarters of a century before. Like that opening act it was not consistently exciting. But if at times a whole season passed without producing an outstanding addition to the repertory, the masterworks of this era were such towering achievements that they more than compensated for dry spells.

Both the beginning and the end of the era found America at war. The act began when, for the United States, World War II was a year old. In theatrical terms the great conflict was relatively insignificant. The coming of World War I had instantly liberated the American Musical Theatre from Viennese thralldom; 1914 exposed the ferment overflowing behind the scenes and the brilliant group of young American composers, lyricists, and librettists who were waiting to display their talents. On the other hand 1942 found most young talent either in Hollywood or fighting the war. Equally discouraging, new movements in American music were far less vital, if indeed concerted new movements existed

at all. The coming fire had to be sparked by older Broadway hands—one of whom, Irving Berlin, had been instrumental in the earlier resurgence. Because they were older, because they had seen that the "war to end all wars" ended nothing, because they had suffered through the Depression, these writers and composers had become less optimistic, less flashy. They led the American Musical Theatre into a more sober, sentimental era. While war-born prosperity gave the theatre a momentarily healthy glow, it was the escapist turnback to real or exaggerated joys of a bygone Americana that became the war's impressive and lasting contribution to the lyric stage. Curiously, the last of the three wars, the Vietnam War, at the close of the epoch, forcefully affected the musical scene. The inflation it engendered, coupled with the competitive drain from richer media, hurtled theatrical economics into a frightening purgatory. Nor did national unrest that developed help the theatre in any way.

Variety records that 320 new musicals premiered during this twenty-three-year period, compared

with 426 that opened in the thirteen years of the preceding act and 139 that appeared in the seven years
of Act III. The strikingly long runs attained by the
masterworks of this final era were largely deserved,
but they should not cause the works to be overrated.
The lessening of competition within the theatre and
the dwindling number of road companies concentrated attention on the best shows during their New
York runs. If an accurate count could be made of all
the theatregoers who saw, say, *The Merry Widow* (21
October 1907) or *Rose-Marie* (2 September 1924) in
their original productions and touring companies, it
would most likely demonstrate they represented an
equal, possibly greater, proportion of the population
than did the theatregoers who flocked to *Kiss Me,
Kate* (30 December 1948) or *South Pacific* (7 April
1949). On their own terms, the older shows were
every bit as good as the new ones. Melodically they
were often more tuneful and offered a greater range
of musical languages, from George Gershwin's steely
American jazz to Rudolf Friml's full-blooded Austro-
Hungarian romanticism. By comparison the new
act sometimes seemed musically constrained and
monotonous. Nonetheless, between *Oklahoma!* (31
March 1943) and *Fiddler on the Roof* (22 September
1964), the American Musical Theatre witnessed a
sustained seriousness of approach unknown before
on the lyric stage. It achieved this with a remarkably
small number of inspired creators.

SCENE ONE

Americana Amid a New
Seriousness, 1942–1951

1942–1943

The war news had been bad all during the preceding
season. It continued unpleasant off and on during
the new theatrical year, but there were indications
that the tide was turning in favor of the Allies.
Since the war was far away and promised to stay far
away, Broadway could look happily on a side benefit. Business was booming. Of eighty offerings presented in Manhattan, twenty-four could be classified
as musicals—an abnormally high percentage. Yet the
figure was deceptive. The ice show that was clearly
becoming an annual and a Yiddish-English musical
belonged outside Broadway's mainstream. Seven
were revivals. Even among the remaining eighteen
presentations eleven were revues, and most of these
were vaudeville-assemblages of the sort that began

the past season with *Priorities* (12 March 1942).
There were only five new book musicals, and only
two of these were hits.

The season began without promise. Ed Wynn
brought in the first of the vaudeville assemblages,
Laugh, Town, Laugh (22 June 1942, Alvin). Wynn's
outrageous inventions and preposterous costumes
were laid away, and the great comedian was reduced
to serving as an amiable master of ceremonies—so
amiable that, at least on opening night, he ambled
among the audience during intermission, talking
with playgoers and the bandleader, Emil Coleman.
Wynn was slightly handicapped. Una, a donkey
in a trained animal act, had kicked him during a
rehearsal, breaking his hand. Turns included Smith
and Dale in their ancient "Dr. Kronkeit" routine,
Senor Wences's sleight-of-mouth ventriloquism,
and Jane Froman singing popular songs of the day.
For all the talent, the pastiche didn't even make it
through July. It would take Broadway producers the
rest of the season to realize these cheaply gathered-
together affairs were really not to theatregoers'
likings.

The Chocolate Soldier, Oscar Straus's 1909
operetta, had even harder going despite a fine cast
headed by Allan Jones, Helen Gleason, and Detmar
Poppen, and sought no extension of its original
three-week engagement. The new type of musical
play that came into vogue this season made such
lovely old operettas subject to particularly vehement scorn. But this was something the producers,
who brought the offering into Carnegie Hall instead
of a regular house, could not foresee. They offered
a second revival in Carnegie Hall on 15 July. Their
production of *The Merry Widow*, with Wilbur Evans
and Miss Gleason, ran thirty-nine times. It was followed on 18 August by their revival of *The New Moon*
(19 September 1928), with Evans and Ruby Mercer,
which, like *The Chocolate Soldier*, gave twenty-four
performances.

The night after the Straus revival the season's
first hit arrived, a "burlesque revue" called **Star and
Garter** (24 June 1942, Music Box). It was a Mike
Todd production that to some degree capitalized
on the closing of New York's burlesque houses after
the once-great burlesque tradition had degenerated
into a tawdry strip show. The doyenne of the burlesque wheel, the beautiful, intellectual Gypsy Rose
Lee, led a parade of well-proportioned ladies that
also included Georgia Sothern. Miss Lee's costar
was Bobby Clark. In his first chance for solid clowning in several years, he portrayed a spitball-hurling

judge, repeated his "Robert the Roué" from *The Streets of Paris* (19 June 1939), and played a modern-day Falstaff in "That Merry Wife of Windsor." Musical credits listed Irving Berlin, Harold Rome, and Harold Arlen among others, but their songs were culled from their already standard material. The newer tunes were thoroughly mediocre. But New Yorkers, who during Prohibition had obligingly drunk their whiskey in teacups, for a year and a half gleefully flocked to enjoy their burlesque at the elegant little Music Box.

Stars on Ice, billed simply as an ice-skating revue, began its long run at the Center on 2 July. Its incidental songs had music by Paul McGrane, Paul Van Loane, and Irvin Graham, and lyrics by Albert Stillman. Their titles—"Little Jack Frost," "The World Waltzes"—conveyed an idea of the production numbers they accompanied. However, in "Juke Box Saturday Night" the spectacle had the sole hit to emerge from the series. The song was a surefire boogie, a popular form customarily ignored by more conventional Broadway musicals. Its inclusion in *Stars on Ice* reflected the different audience the show was appealing to. Broadway's aging, more self-contained regular theatregoers no longer capitulated to the latest musical fads. What few boogie-woogie numbers were included in more traditional shows were there almost incidentally, to produce a contemporary flavor rather than a hit song.

The first of the season's two major hits opened two nights after *Stars on Ice.* **This Is the Army** patriotically selected 4 July as its premiere date. It ran only 113 performances at the large Broadway Theatre, but every performance was sold out to the limit of standees. The show was conceived and its songs written by a theatrical figure listed in its program as "Sgt. Irving Berlin (1917)." The erstwhile sergeant was a member of the cast as well, stopping the show nightly with his singing of a number he had performed in *Yip Yip Yaphank* (19 August 1918) almost a quarter of a century before: "Oh, How I Hate To Get Up In The Morning." Berlin and a handful of the old show's veterans, all dressed in 1917 uniforms, performed the number much as they had twenty-five years before. *Yip Yip Yaphank's* "Mandy" was also revived. The rest of the score was new. In fact it covered an exemplary range of then contemporary song styles. There were three crowd-stirrers, "American Eagles" ("America's strong just as long as they fly"), "With My Head In The Clouds" ("How I yearn to return to the one I love on the ground"), and the title song (technically, "This Is The Army, Mr. Jones"). Two poignantly expressive ballads, "I'm Getting Tired So I Can Sleep" ("I want to dream so I can be with you"), sung by Stuart Churchill in the barracks scene, and the show's hit, "I Left My Heart At The Stage Door Canteen," sung by Earl Oxford, recorded a soldier's loneliness far from home. "That's What The Well-Dressed Man In Harlem Will Wear" caught the snappy African-American musical idiom of the day. There was nothing innovative this time about Berlin's music. The day when Berlin led the popular avant-garde was long over. Though a few critics, such as Richard Watts, Jr., in the *Herald Tribune,* hailed the revue as "a great and historic show," the importance of *This Is the Army's* score was generally overlooked. It was a hit-packed, unforgettably melodic work that roused the American Musical Theatre from its lethargy. For the first time in years patrons could leave the theatre with a number of melodies to whistle or hum. The show was given an eye-filling mounting (soldiers across the giant wing of a plane) and a vigorous staging. An all-soldier cast included at one time or another Ezra Stone, Burl Ives, Gary Merrill, Julie Oshins, and Joe Cook, Jr. In the celebrated Stage Door Canteen number that opened the second act young Cook impersonated his more famous father, while other men appeared as Gypsy Rose Lee, Jane Cowl, Lynn Fontanne, Alfred Lunt, and Noël Coward. There were sketches by James McColl, but they were relatively insignificant. The show toured until late 1945, its great score announcing throughout the land that Broadway was bursting with song again.

All in all, it was a singularly busy summer—the busiest the American Musical Theatre had enjoyed in many a season—and a justifiably hopeful augury.

All three of September's offerings were vaudeville assemblages. The first and least successful was **New Priorities of 1943** (15 September 1942, 46th St.) by the same Clifford C. Fischer who had begun the short-lived fad. Despite the presence of Harry Richman, Bert Wheeler, Hank Ladd, Henny Youngman, and Carol Bruce, it recorded only fifty-four showings. On the other hand, **Show Time** (16 September 1942, Broadhurst), which opened the next night, ran through the season. Its main attractions were George Jessel and Jack Haley in old routines, Ella Logan singing her songs, and the ballroom dancing of the De Marcos. The Shuberts hoped to resuscitate the dying vogue and cash in on the success of *Star and Garter* as well by calling **Wine, Women and Song** (28 September 1942, Ambassador) a "revue-vaudeville-burlesque show."

There is no record of the Shuberts giving away wine, but they offered music and girls performing "quivers, bumps and lethargic strip tease." Margie Hart led the strippers. Jimmy Savo headed the comic department, winning applause for his rendition of "River, Stay Away From My Door." Unfortunately Savo and Miss Hart were not in a class with Bobby Clark and Gypsy Rose Lee. At sixteen performances a week the show lasted seven weeks.

Let Freedom Sing (5 October 1942, Longacre) was a more traditionally shaped revue. Harold Rome's songs were fittingly patriotic—"It's Fun To Be Free," "I Did It For Defense," "Be Calm," "Little Miss Victory Jones," and "Johnny Is A Hoarder." Numerous interpolations followed along the same line. Ostensibly, Mitzi Green, fresh from Hollywood, was the principal performer. She lent her husky voice to Rome's "The Lady Is A WAC" and Marc Blitzstein's "Fraught," besides portraying a young lady stood up by her soldier sweetheart. But Betty Garrett won even more acclaim singing Rome's lively Latin melody, "Give Us A Viva," and his jivey "History Eight To The Bar." Comedy was in the hands of Berni Gould and Phil Leeds. Together they fought battles as armchair strategists and confused everyone with their directions to Gramercy Square. Little of the material was meritorious. The show waved its flag for one week and departed.

A loosely structured musical comedy, **Count Me In** (8 October 1942, Barrymore), fared only slightly better, achieving a sixty-one-performance run. Originally mounted at Catholic University, its authors included Nancy Hamilton and a young man destined for fame as a fine critic, Walter Kerr. Their thin story recorded the attempts of Father (Charles Butterworth) to do at least as much for the war effort as Mother (Luella Gear) and the children. He succeeds when he sells phony maps to Japanese spies. So slapdash was the show, a number of critics were reminded of the worst contrivances of earlier decades. For much of its entertainment it relied on specialty acts such as the Rhythmaires and the Ross Sisters. Like so many of the old pastiches it was best when it was on its feet. Hal Le Roy supplied some glittering tap routines, while Gower and Jeanne swirled in more elegant ballroom numbers. Gower, of course, was Gower Champion. The urbane John Mason Brown, reviewing the show for the *World-Telegram*, could not resist insisting "count me out."

On 12 October the old Jolson Theatre, lately the Venice, was renamed the Molly Picon and raised its curtain on a musical biography of the celebrated star of the Yiddish Theatre. With Miss Picon playing herself, **Oy Is Dus a Leben!** recounted her rise from her early experiences at Philadelphia's Arch Street Theatre in 1912, to her marriage to Jacob Kalich and her trips in Europe to improve her art and her Yiddish, to her climb to stardom. Joseph Rumshinsky, who provided scores for Yiddish musicals on Second Avenue and thereabouts, created appropriate songs. Miss Picon's loyal following had her relive her life 139 times.

A loud, jivey musical that paid little heed to the warring world outside opened two nights later. George Abbott produced, directed, and co-authored the book with George Marion, Jr. Johnny Green returned from a long stay in Hollywood to write the score. **Beat the Band** (14 October 1942, 46th St.) told how Querida (Susan Miller) comes to New York to find her godfather. But her godfather's apartment had been sublet to a popular bandleader, Damon Dillingham (Jack Whiting). Misunderstandings and detectives complicate a budding romance between the two until a happy ending ensues in the boiler room of the Savoy-Perkins Hotel. Though Marion's titles make Green's songs sound lively—"Let's Comb Beaches," "I'm Physical, You're Cultured," "The Steam Is On The Beam," "Keep It Casual," "Break It Up"—the music was a far cry from the memorably sultry beauty of some of Green's earlier numbers. After eight weeks Abbott admitted he had erred and withdrew the show.

The most baffling revival in years came next. The Hough-Adams-Howard Chicago hit *The Time, the Place and the Girl* (5 August 1907) was pulled from the shelf and given a renewed life on 21 October at the Mansfield with slightly rewritten book and lyrics. The fascinating old piece had never been welcome in New York when it was fresh and contemporary, though it had established a Chicago long-run record in its day. A program note advised audiences: "The authors have not attempted to make it into a modern musical comedy. While all the padding and all of the bromides of the gas-lit era have been deleted the play is, nevertheless, presented as of that period ... ." A popular burlesque comedian, "Red" Marshall, and pert Vicki Cummings sparked the performers. Joe Howard even made an appearance as himself. Their labors were to no avail. New York again dismissed *The Time, the Place and the Girl* with a condescending wave of the hand.

But another old work was made most welcome. *Die Fledermaus* returned in what continued to be an unintentional pattern of once-a-decade revivals.

As *The Merry Countess* it attempted to cash in on the vogue of *The Merry Widow* and succeeded in running for 135 performances in 1912. As *A Wonderful Night* it played for 125 showings in 1929. And as *Champagne, Sec* it chalked up 113 performances in 1933. Now as **Rosalinda** (28 October 1942, 44th St.) it ran for a whopping 521 times, with Dorothy Sarnoff in the title role and the amusing refugee Oscar Karlweis as Prince Orlofsky. An authentic *Mitteleuropa* flair was imparted by several other distinguished exiles. Gottfried Reinhardt was on hand to see that some of the touches his father, Max, had used in a 1929 Berlin revival were recreated. In the orchestra pit, the famous composer Erich Wolfgang Korngold conducted.

Two weeks after the unsuccessful revival of Joe Howard's old musical and a week after Strauss's operetta settled in for a long run, George M. Cohan died, on 7 November 1942. Cohan, more than any other man, had sparked the second great act in the American Musical Theatre. Howard had been a rival who generally kept a safe distance in Chicago. But the heirs of Strauss had driven Cohan's style of art from the stage. Cohan never fully recovered from the changes they wrought, and it is doubtful if he would have appreciated the renaissance about to dawn.

Still another old musical piece followed. In a way finding it in a Broadway house was as surprising and unlikely as the revival of the Hough-Adams-Howard show, for **Once Over Lightly** (19 November 1942, Alvin) was simply an "Americanized" version of Rossini's *The Barber of Seville*. Broadway felt Rossini was better served at the Met, and the show lasted less than one full week.

Just before Christmas, Leonard Sillman presented another edition of his erratic **New Faces** (22 December 1942, Ritz). Mr. Sillman, a far from new face, appeared in the show besides serving as both producer and director. John Lund also doubled in brass, writing the show's skits and cavorting nightly behind the footlights. Irwin Corey and Alice Pearce were cast members who went on to make names for themselves. Curiously, the performer who pleased critics the most faded from the theatre scene. Tony Farrar was a dancing pantomimist who won loud cheers and considerable space in the morning-after notices for his imitation of Fanny Brice imitating Paul Draper and for a dance depicting a bullfighter who has lost his glasses. Skits included "Quiet Zone," set in a shirt hospital where doctors and nurses solemnly operate on cuffs, collars, and seams, and a piece making fun of tourists at the Radio City

Music Hall. Orson Welles was shot down in "Welles of Loneliness," while Hamlet was made to suffer the slings and arrows of outrageous recapitulation in Corey's monologue. The material itself was not particularly memorable, and the 1942 (called 1943 in the title) edition's run of ninety-four performances was the shortest in the series to date.

Eddie Cantor, George Jessel, Walter Winchell, the Marx Brothers, Georgie Price, and Hildegarde all appeared in **You'll See Stars** (29 December 1942, Maxine Elliott). Only it wasn't the real-life greats audiences saw; rather, young actors impersonating them, for *You'll See Stars* purported to be a retelling of Gus Edwards's career as a star-maker. The show had been conceived by Herman Timberg, who had written songs for the Shuberts in the halcyon days of the late teens and twenties, and who at that time had tried unsuccessfully to enter the producing ranks. The music was credited to another name out of the past, Leo Edwards. But the show was tackily put together; it played at the out-of-the-way Maxine Elliott; and, most damaging of all, it was assailed by Gus Edwards himself as inaccurate and unauthorized. It beat a retreat after four showings.

The season's first truly successful book musical was more commercial than artistic. **Something for the Boys** (7 January 1943, Alvin) was a splashy Mike Todd mounting that once again had Ethel Merman singing Cole Porter songs. Herbert Fields, who had collaborated with Buddy DeSylva on the two preceding Merman–Porter shows, did the book with his sister Dorothy. Their story was a rambling affair—contemporary but not truly topical—that begins when three cousins learn they have jointly inherited a large Texas ranch. Chiquita Hart (Paula Laurence) is a nightclub entertainer; Harry Hart (Allen Jenkins), a sidewalk pitchman; and Blossom Hart, the central figure, a chorus girl turned defense worker. Their new ranch house turns out to be as ramshackle as the plot. Worse, the Army has appropriated the building for maneuvers, since it lies close to an army base. Blossom promptly falls for the officer in charge, Sergeant Rocky Fulton (Bill Johnson). When the Army moves out, Blossom and her cousins renovate the house and open it up to servicemen's wives. Just when things seem rosy, Blossom's rival for Rocky's attentions, Melanie Walker (Frances Mercer), tells the commanding officer that the girls are loose women, and when he makes a surprise visit circumstances suggest the accusation is just. Blossom's house becomes off limits. Out of a blue sky Blossom discovers that carborundum in her fillings allows her to be a human radio. After she proves her efficacy by using her built-in communications system to save a distressed plane, all is forgiven, and Blossom and Rocky are paired. Though Cole Porter's tunes sounded bright in the theatre, especially when Miss Merman was belting them out, they represented the weakest body of songs Porter had composed for any show, except, perhaps, *You Never Know*. Todd tried to familiarize audiences with them by the novel stunt of allowing chorus boys to sing some from the orchestra pit during the overture. "Could It Be You?" and "Hey, Good Lookin'" were the best numbers of the evening, while Miss Merman and Miss Laurence brought down the house with a comic plaint of two squaws married to the same brave, "By The Mississinewah." Miss Merman, Todd's lavish, garish production, and the generally good times kept the show on the boards for over a year.

February saw the eleven-performance run of **For Your Pleasure** (5 February 1943, Mansfield), a "dance vaudeville" featuring the self-advertised "Lunts of the Dancing World," Veloz and Yolanda.

Only one musical appeared in March, and that on the very last day. But it was one of the milestones of the American Musical Theatre: **Oklahoma!** (31 March 1943, St. James). The show changed fashions in musicals for two decades. It rejected the topical and even the contemporary and instead embraced a sentimental look at bygone Americana. For the most part it also rejected wit and patently polished sophistication for a certain earnestness and directness. It was, in a way, a reversion to the standards of long-departed comic opera. Of course the new school's settings were generally native, characters mostly everyday people, the music less arioso and occasionally reflective of modern chromatics and dissonances. But the more light-hearted fun of American musical comedies or even of Viennese operettas was discarded with a certain trumpeted contempt.

It is hard to say if Rodgers and Hammerstein consciously planned so dramatic a turnabout, although they clearly understood they were attempting something uncommon. The fact that they opened in tryout with the title *Away We Go* suggests they were not espousing a revolution. However, praise accorded the show and its phenomenal success tended to concentrate attention on the changes that made *Oklahoma!* unique rather than on its place in an ongoing tradition. Its innovations were so ballyhooed that they came to dominate the thinking not only of Rodgers and Hammerstein in their future

works but of the creators and critics of the American Musical Theatre as a whole.

The curtain rises to reveal Laurey's farm. Aunt Eller (Betty Garde) is alone, churning. From the distance comes the sound of a young man's voice; he apostrophizes, "Oh, What A Beautiful Mornin'." The singing young man is Curly (Alfred Drake), and he has come to court Laurey (Joan Roberts), although he won't admit as much at first, since he and Laurey have been quarreling. Laurey pays no attention to him when she enters, but Curly is soon describing the joys of accompanying him to the box social in "The Surrey With The Fringe On Top." Laurey's excitement wanes perceptibly when Curly admits he doesn't own any such wonderful carriage. Will Parker (Lee Dixon) arrives extolling up-to-date pleasures in "Kansas City" and especially happy that fifty dollars he won there in a steer-roping contest will allow him to meet Mr. Carnes's conditions for marrying Carnes's daughter, Ado Annie (Celeste Holm). Curly returns and asks Aunt Eller if there is anybody else Laurey is seriously interested in. Aunt Eller names a few of the more attractive young men of the area and then reluctantly adds Jud Fry (Howard da Silva), their farm hand, to the list. To Curly, Jud is a "bullet-colored, growly man" and not to be trusted. Curly is dismayed to learn that Laurey has in fact consented to allow Jud to drive her to the social. Ado Annie arrives. She is torn between her desire to marry the exotic Persian peddler, Ali Hakim (Joseph Buloff), whom she believes has proposed to her, and her equally strong urge to marry Will Parker, who has finally met her father's requirements. She would be happy to accept both. Indeed there is no boy she would not be happy to accept, for as she herself acknowledges, "I Cain't Say No." Although Laurey has not considered that she might hurt Curly by accepting Jud's invitation, she is put out when she learns Curly will take a pretty lass named Gertie to the party. She poutingly protests that "Many A New Day" will dawn before she lets a man upset her. Ado Annie reappears, with her father and his shotgun. When old man Carnes (Ralph Riggs) learns that Ali invited Ado Annie to a hotel he suggests, shotgun pointing at the peddler, that there had better be a proposal of marriage. Ali agrees. He can do little else except bemoan "It's A Scandal! It's A Outrage!" Curly reminds Laurey that people are talking about them, and Laurey replies that in that case the wisest thing for her to do is to be seen with Jud. She suggests Curly not display his obvious admiration for her, since if he does, "People Will Say We're In Love." Curly visits Jud in the hovel of a smokehouse where he lives. He warns Jud to let Laurey alone, but his advice is so indirect that at first Jud does not comprehend. Curly's trick is to tell the loveless Jud how many girls would mourn if for one reason or another news got around that "Pore Jud Is Daid." But when Jud finally realizes what Curly is actually saying he grows surly and menacing. After Curly leaves he decries his lonely life and his "Lonely Room." Laurey's girlfriends are puzzled that Laurey would prefer Jud to Curly. She herself would like to have the answer to her choice come "Out Of My Dreams." As soon as the girls depart she does indeed drift off into a dream. In "The Dream Ballet" Laurey sees herself about to be married to Curly when Jud appears. In a fight Jud knocks Curly unconscious and carries off Laurey. She awakens from the dream with her fear of Jud brought home to her. She goes off silently with him as the curtain falls. At the box social there is general agreement "The Farmer And The Cowman" should be friends. But there is little friendship between Curly and Jud as they bid for Laurey's box supper. Jud offers all the money he has in the world, and Curly is forced to sell his gun and horse to outbid Jud. Jud stalks off. Relations are happier between Ado and Will, who have set the date for their marriage, though Will warns Ado Annie it's got to be "All Er Nothin'." Annie agrees, but says it's all for Will and nothing for her. Still, she finds she can accept his terms—on her terms. As the party continues, Jud dances Laurey around to the back porch. His advances rejected, he leaves her, but not without some threats. Curly appears to comfort her, and they agree to marry. The wedding crowd exults in the beauty and richness of "Oklahoma," which is soon to be a state. Just as the ceremonies begin, Jud appears, and in a fight Curly kills Jud with Jud's own knife. (Much as Porgy had killed Crown in *Porgy and Bess*.) Luckily, the local judge is present. He holds a quick trial and acquits Curly. The happy couple ride off in a surrey with a fringe. It is, indeed, a beautiful morning.

Hammerstein's libretto was based on Lynn Riggs's 1931 play, *Green Grow the Lilacs*. Hammerstein was faithful to its essentials and to many of its details, even lifting stretches of dialogue. The changes Hammerstein made are enlightening. In the original Curly was allowed to marry but detained for his trial. The decision was never announced, though given the circumstances there was little doubt of what it would be. And the original Ado Annie was left without a promise of marriage. Hammerstein created the character of Will Parker from a remark of Curly's to the villain of Riggs's play, Jeeter. In short

Hammerstein was largely tying up loose ends and expanding comic scenes. But he made one unfortunate change. In the smokehouse confrontation, "Pore Jud Is Daid" and Jud's bawling reaction to the song came perilously close to a lesser order of stage comedy. It is a scene that falls apart in all but the most professional hands. Hammerstein's lyrics were straightforward. His use of repetition, which became an increasing Hammerstein trait, could be justified in this instance since it nicely mirrored the repetition of folk lyrics used in Riggs's original. But some of Hammerstein's attempts at poetry or at least at romantic statement sounded, even in this early collaboration with Rodgers, distressingly like the fustian nonsense of Harry B. Smith and his era— "Out of your dreams and into his arms you long to fly." Nonetheless, for the most part, Hammerstein's lyrics for *Oklahoma!* had an affecting simplicity.

Rodgers's music marked a change from the suave, brash musical lines he had turned out when he was working with Hart. In its directness and apparent flatness was hidden a sophistication as knowing and intelligent as his earlier works. It is sometimes hard to realize that "Oh, What A Beautiful Mornin'" is a waltz. The melody of "The Surrey With The Fringe On Top" unerringly captures the clippety-clop of a horse pulling the vehicle. Rodgers's long-sustained opening note of his title song coupled with the driving melody that follows was one of the freshest inventions of the sort since "Who?" And the impeccable mating of words and music in "People Will Say We're In Love" justifiably made it the most popular song of the year. Much ballyhoo ensued over how well the songs and plot were integrated. They were. But such integration was neither unique nor original. Hammerstein in *Rose-Marie* (2 September 1924) and Rodgers in *Chee-Chee* (25 September 1928) had professed to offer similarly integrated works. In the teens Guy Bolton had suggested the later Princess Theatre shows aimed for something close to a natural meshing of songs and story. Even in the nineteenth century integration was sought after and sometimes achieved in better comic operas. But if the ballyhoo was overdone, that in no way gainsaid the excellent totality of *Oklahoma!* The show's musical director, Jay Blackton, appreciating the work's nature, discarded the common musical comedy practice of having the entire chorus sing only songs' melodies. Instead, he reverted to the tradition of operetta and comic opera by dividing his singers and assigning them various parts, not always the principal melodic line. Lemuel Ayers's scenery, essentially realistic sets placed before slightly stylized backdrops, captured the feeling of wide-open spaces and of homey goodness.

Virtually every critic sang the show's praises, even if few could foresee its stunning effect on the musicals to follow. Howard Barnes, writing in the *Herald Tribune*, labeled it "superb," while PM's Louis Kronenberger thought it offered "just enough to add something special to Broadway's musical life." In the *Times*, Lewis Nichols attempted to assess *Oklahoma!*'s nature as well as its worth. He concluded accurately, "Possibly in addition to being called a musical play, 'Oklahoma!' could be called a folk operetta; whatever it is, it is very good." *Oklahoma!* became more than the hit of the season. Mounted for just over $75,000, its multi-million-dollar gross allowed it to surpass *Rose-Marie's* long-held record. Its 2,248 performances in New York and the record-breaking runs of its road companies gave it one of the largest audiences in American musical history. Some of its records were later surpassed, but *Oklahoma!*'s importance in opening a new era in the American Musical Theatre will never be challenged.

The darkly handsome **ALFRED DRAKE** was born Alfredo Capurro in New York City on 7 October 1914. After studying voice with Clytie Mundy, he made his debut in 1935 as a chorus boy in Gilbert and Sullivan operettas. A stint in Atlantic City with the Steel Pier Opera Company followed. Drake understudied William Gaxton in *White Horse Inn* and then increasingly called attention to his fine baritone and his natural acting gifts in *Babes in Arms, The Two Bouquets, One for the Money,* and *Two for the Show.*

Several young artists were catapulted to fame by *Oklahoma!*, notably Celeste Holm, Alfred Drake, and Agnes de Mille. Much of Miss Holm's later career was largely outside the American Musical Theatre, but Drake and Miss de Mille went on to become significant luminaries on our lyric stage.

A vestige of an earlier era opened the night after *Oklahoma!* Kronenberger headed his *PM* review, "A Famous Name Is Taken in Vain," and he went on to report a possibly imaginary conversation in the lobby before the show began. According to the critic, Moss Hart gushed, "Who'd have thought that we'd see another Follies?" only to have Lillian Hellman respond, "What makes you think

we will?" It was moot if they did. What was called **The Ziegfeld Follies of 1943** (1 April 1943, Winter Garden) featured Milton Berle, Ilona Massey, Arthur Treacher, Sue Ryan, and Jack Cole among the performers. There wasn't even the pretense of Mrs. Florenz Ziegfeld's association; the Shuberts were the principal producers. Much of the score was by Ray Henderson, his last for Broadway. But apart from his nervous "Hold That Smile," no song managed to get any attention. Burton Rascoe in the *World-Telegram* condemned the music as "raucous and unrhythmical; it is largely scored for percussion instruments." Far more shocking was Rascoe's remark that the "scenery looks as though it came from Cain's storehouse without much retouching." Nor could the critics find many kind words for the comedy. After sneaking on stage as part of a line of kicking chorus boys, Milton Berle treated the show as something of his personal property, interrupting other acts whenever the whim prompted. His best bit may have been his role as J. Pierswift Armour, a butcher flanked by tommy-gun-toting bodyguards, who draws his war-scarce steaks from a safe-deposit box. Arthur Treacher played a butler in several skits, one of which was a spoof of *Private Lives* that degenerated into *Hellzapoppin* mayhem. Much of what praise the critics could dole out was reserved for Cole's dances—his jivey "Wedding of the Solid Sender" and his arcane "Hindu Serenade." Despite the critics' carping, the show chalked up 553 performances—a longer stay than any of Ziegfeld's annuals ever enjoyed.

A revival of a show of Ziegfeld's era closed the season. The Shuberts brought in a road company of *The Student Prince* (2 December 1924) from the backwaters. Though Everett Marshall and Ann Pennington were in the cast, the mounting displayed the famed Shubert shabbiness at its worst. Moreover, with *Oklahoma!* all the rage, Romberg's old warhorse was dismissed by faddists as beyond reclaim. Nonetheless, *The Student Prince* ran, with some forcing, through the summer and achieved 153 performances.

AGNES DE MILLE was a member of a notable theatrical family. Her grandfather was the famous nineteenth-century playwright Henry de Mille; her uncle was also a playwright, but more justly renowned

---

as Hollywood's great epic-maker, Cecil B. DeMille. Miss de Mille was born on 18 September 1905 in New York City. She graduated from UCLA cum laude. Her early ballet instruction and experience came with a large number of major and minor figures, of whom Anthony Tudor was the name most familiar to the general public. She appeared as a dancer in the 1928 edition of the *Greenwich Village Follies*. Her first theatrical choreography was for London shows—*Nymph Errant* and *Why Not Tonight?* Stints as choreographer for *Hooray for What!* (1 December 1937) and *Swingin' the Dream* (24 November 1939) brought her more heartache than fame. Less than six months before *Oklahoma!* opened, her ballet *Rodeo*, to Aaron Copland's music, had been first presented by the Ballet Russe de Monte Carlo. Its cowboy tunes and square dances made it an immediate hit and prepared the way for the *Oklahoma!* dances. Her abilities to express moods and feelings, rather than to devise formally traditional exercises, made her eminently suitable for the new sort of storied dancing that her ballets for *Oklahoma!* made the rage.

1943–1944

Although it became obvious soon after *Oklahoma!* opened that a new era was under way, it took time for the show's effects to be manifest. Broadway could not react as quickly as it once did. Its great creative talents were getting old, many were elsewhere, and huge taxation on success militated against more prolific writers creating two or three shows a year as they once had done. While awaiting the renaissance, Broadway spent most of the season fervently recalling old glories. Yet one exceptional and one very hopeful work pranced into town.

The season began with a number of determinedly old-fashioned works. The very first effort, **Early to Bed** (17 June 1943, Broadhurst), was a moderately good example of the gaudy, contemporary musical comedies that had entertained Broadway the past few seasons. It was spiced with a touch of the modern burlesque that *Star and Garter* (24 June 1942) had shown could be so profitable. Set largely in and around a Martinique bordello,

"The Angry Pigeon," run by a former schoolmarm named Madame Rowena (Muriel Angelus), it recounted the adventures that ensue when a famous bullfighter, El Magnifico (Richard Kollmar), and his son (George Zoritch) come to visit. El Magnifico remembers Rowena from her school days. The stay is complicated by the arrival of a track team that hopes to use the place for a training quarters. Almost everybody, it seems, is blind to the real business of the house. *Early to Bed*'s score was by Fats Waller, with lyrics by George Marion, Jr. Both the melodies and the lyrics tended to be flaccid. Only one comic song, a tribute to "The Ladies Who Sing With The Band," proved a show-stopper when Mary Small, Jane Deering, Jane Kean, and Miss Angelus joined forces to sing it. To compensate for the lackluster score, George Jenkins filled the stage with "prismatic and opalescent" colors, while to minimize the drag of the sluggard, double-entendre-packed book Jenkins kept his scenery in motion all evening long. The *Post*'s Wilella Waldorf announced the scenery was "the biggest hit of the show." The bawdy yarn appealed to a large segment of the theatregoing crowd, and *Early to Bed* ran out the season.

Of an even older school was *The Vagabond King* (20 September 1925), which arrived at the end of June with John Brownlee singing Dennis King's role. It failed to find the market the preceding season's revival of *The Student Prince* apparently had satisfied and closed after seven weeks.

However, a lavish revival of *The Merry Widow* (21 October 1907) reached back still farther, to the days of the second Viennese school's glory, and with a fine cast headed by Marta Eggerth, Jan Kiepura, and Melville Cooper played into the spring. Just as one distinguished refugee composer had led the orchestra for the previous season's *Rosalinda*, so another, Robert Stolz, conducted for *The Merry Widow*. Sitting prominently in the first-night audience on 4 August at the Majestic was the Sonia of the principal 1907 road company, Lina Abarbanell.

Still another old name appeared on 12 August at the Royale when **Chauve Souris 1943** premiered. "The Parade Of The Wooden Soldiers" was back, as were several other minor songs from the original. With Balieff gone, Leon Greanin served as master of ceremonies. A number of critics professed to be delighted that Greanin was more articulate than his predecessor. Contemporary additions included a duet between a Russian sniper and an American WAC. For all its revisions the show had long since worn out its welcome. It lasted less than two weeks.

The success of *The Student Prince* prompted the Shuberts to pull *Blossom Time* (29 September 1921) from the road as well, but New York would not support three operettas simultaneously, and after six weeks the show returned to its perennial touring. Opening as it did on 4 September, it failed to provide a sparkling or original send-off for the main fall season.

Laugh Time (8 September 1943, Shubert) didn't help matters when it premiered four nights later. The vaudeville was the third in a series of West Coast productions, the first of which, *Show Time* (16 September 1942), had enjoyed a long run on Broadway the preceding season. Its sequel, *Big Time*, never made it to New York. *Laugh Time*'s 126 performances fell between its predecessors in drawing power. To many it should have stayed longer, for its bill included such attractive entertainers as Ethel Waters, Frank Fay, Bert Wheeler, and Buck and Bubbles.

Nor could attractive old favorites save **My Dear Public** (9 September 1943, 46th St.), which some critics looked on as a revue and some as a book musical. To the latter its construction resembled many of the musicals of two and three decades before when a weak plot served as an excuse for a number of specialty acts. Other critics suggested it marked a return to the revue that employed a thin story line to hold it together. Book musical or revue, its slim plot told how Daphne Short (Ethel Shutta), with the connivance of the swishy Byron Burns (Eric Brotherson), persuades her husband, Barney (Willie Howard), the zipper king, to back a musical in which she has been promised the role of a harem queen. The resulting auditions and rehearsals occupied much of the evening and gave specialty acts their moment. Typical of the specialties was Al Kelly's celebrated double-talk routine. Howard revived his old revolutionary soapbox speech, varying it for the occasion by mixing a Scottish burr with his Yiddish. In "If You Want To Deal with Russia" he solved a major international problem. The credits did not distinguish between lyricists and composers. Irving Caesar, Sam Lerner, and Gerald Marks were lumped together as the songsmiths, perhaps in the hope that it would offer a small refuge from specific blame. The songs were quite bad. Caesar was also the producer and colibrettist. Even Howard and Miss Shutta couldn't overcome such material.

An admitted revue, which did indeed have a thin story line, came in three nights later. The plot of **Bright Lights of 1944** (16 September 1943,

Forrest) was almost identical to the plot that had served *My Dear Public* so inadequately—only this time two Sardi waiters decide to put on the show. Smith and Dale played the would-be producers. Somehow they found a way of running through their "Dr. Kronkeit" skit in case theatregoers had missed it the year before in *Laugh, Town, Laugh* or in any of its other numerous reincarnations. The talent they auditioned included James Barton and Frances Williams. Barton also resorted to a turn theatregoers must have come to know by heart, his drunk act. As a bonus, he added a spoof of a character he had successfully portrayed for several years, Jeeter Lester of *Tobacco Road*. Miss Williams offered a straightforward rendition of "Frankie And Johnny." The new songs the cast sang were by Jerry Livingston. But they didn't sing them for long. *Bright Lights of 1944* closed after four performances, still sixteen weeks away from the year in its title.

A more offbeat, successful entertainment followed two days after *Bright Lights*, when Sol Hurok presented Katherine Dunham and her dancers in **A Tropical Revue** (19 September 1943, Martin Beck). An evening of sizzlingly brilliant black choreography and interpretation, the show gave audiences a taste of African-American rhythms the world over in numbers such as "Darktown Strutters' Ball," "Rhumba Suite," "Rites de Passage," "Br'er Rabbit," "Woman With A Cigar," and "Bahiana." The revue stayed two months, toured profitably, and returned the following season.

Harold Orlob was yet another old-timer, but one whose name had long been missing from Broadway credits. He had hung on tenaciously in the teens, twenties, and thirties without ever surpassing the limited success of *Listen, Lester* (23 December 1918). Now, after changing waves of style had left him far behind, he attempted a musical farce of the old school, even to reemploying the custom of a single set for the whole evening. Orlob wrote both book and music for **Hairpin Harmony** (1 October 1943, National). His plot described Howard Swift's search for a radio program to push his baby food. He settles on an all-girl orchestra with a baby-talking announcer. Devastated by the critics, the show collapsed after three performances, and Orlob bid a final farewell to the musical stage.

By this time theatregoers understandably could have begun to wonder if *Oklahoma!* (31 March 1943), instead of signaling an advance, had driven Broadway into a headlong retreat. But **One Touch** of Venus (7 October 1943, Imperial) cast away any doubts. Superficially it was just another of the recent musical comedies with an innocuous plot and a contemporary setting. It bore a discernible resemblance to *I Married an Angel* (11 May 1938). Of course, the story of an unnatural or preternatural figure enjoying a brief mortality had been popular in the American Musical Theatre as far back as *Adonis* (4 September 1884). What elevated *One Touch of Venus* above recent run-of-the-mill offerings and placed it firmly in the advance guard was its intelligence and cohesiveness. S. J. Perelman and Ogden Nash based their plot on F. Anstey's *The Tinted Venus*. Their new musical told its tale with an unfailing sense of style and literate wit, never stopping to introduce extraneous bits of froth nor stooping to inject currently voguish elements of stripper burlesque. In keeping with the classic elegance of its heroine, its story was attractively simple. Whitelaw Savory (John Boles) has unearthed a long-lost statue of Venus of Anatolia and puts it on display at his museum. One early visitor to the museum is Rodney Hatch (Kenny Baker), a rather naive young barber about to become engaged. Determined to prove that his fiancée's hand has a Hellenic grace, Rodney places the engagement ring he is taking to her on the statue's finger. By some feat of magic the marble is turned to life in a blinding flash. The living, breathing Venus (Mary Martin) relishes her new existence. Almost at once she sets about winning Rodney away from his mother-dominated sweetheart, Gloria (Ruth Bond). Venus has virtually ensnared Rodney when a dream warns her of the excruciatingly humdrum life she will lead in bourgeois Ozone Heights. She realizes that once a goddess, always a goddess. In another blinding flash she is transformed back into stone. The forlorn Rodney is left standing alone in the museum. A young lady enters. Her appearance is so remarkably like the statue's that she might very well pass for Venus's country cousin:

Girl: Oh—excuse me. Can you tell me where I register for the Art Course?

Rodney: (*Looks at the statue—then at the Girl*) Why—sure... Where do you come from?

Girl: Ozone Heights.

Rodney: Do you like it there?

Girl: I wouldn't think of living any place else.

Rodney: My name is Rodney Hatch.

Girl: Mine is...

Rodney: (*Going quickly to her*) You don't have to tell me. I know.

Nash's lyrics in *One Touch of Venus* rank with the best ever created by P. G. Wodehouse, Lorenz Hart, Cole Porter, or Ira Gershwin. His romantic lines flowed easily and naturally, yet remained incontestably warm. But, as might be expected from Nash, his comic lines were even better. Hatch, Savory, and two other men seek to analyze "The Trouble With Women" and conclude, "The trouble with women is men." Much of the best material fell to Savory's secretary, played in the original by lean, angular, wry Paula Laurence. In the title song she notes that Venus, a goddess in a world dominated by gods, had only to open her bodice to equalize the odds. Later she consoles Savory by assuring him that, like so many of the "Very, Very, Very" rich, "You huddle with your memoirs, and boy! what memoirs them was." Kurt Weill's score was lovely and appropriate, if largely unexceptional. Although at the time the show opened much publicity was given to a song Mary Martin sang from a chair pulled close to the footlights, "That's Him," the only song to win enduring popularity has been Rodney and Venus's "Speak Low," an almost Porter-ish beguine that echoed the popular Latin rhythms of the day. Two triumphs of the original production were Anges de Mille's ballets. The first, "Forty Minutes for Lunch," wittily depicted Venus tasting her newfound freedom in the mindless hustle and bustle of noon hour at Rockefeller Center. The ex-goddess flirts with a sailor and cavorts in a shop window. The second-act "dream ballet," "Venus in Ozone Heights," was more like a pagan rite. The ballets coming just a season after *Oklahoma!* confirmed that Agnes de Mille had replaced George Balanchine as Broadway's leading choreographer. The dream ballet, less fortunately, suggested that such pieces from there on were de rigueur in fully realized musicals. One attractive young ballerina emerged from the evening, Sono Osato. The designer, Mainbocher, devised lovely Grecian draperies and gowns for Miss Martin. Everything on the stage of the Imperial fell together with such impeccable style that *One Touch of Venus* had 567 performances before it went on tour.

The movement to advance the art of the musical theatre took some giant steps backwards when **Artists and Models** (5 November 1943, Broadway) returned after a thirteen-year lapse. Nightclub impresario Lou Walters brought the show in and determined its tone. Walters employed only fifteen show girls, a far cry from the forty to sixty Ziegfeld and his rivals regularly presented. To open the show the girls paraded about as bottles of perfume, advertising then popular essences such as Velvet Night, Bridal Blush, and My Sin. The revue's idea of contemporary humor was revealed in songs such as "Swing Low, Sweet Harriet," done as part of a minstrel show entitled "Way Up North in Dixieland." The cast featured Jane Froman and the rising Jackie Gleason. But their material was thin and the public indifferent.

A partnership that would eventually be one of the glories of the American Musical Theatre began inauspiciously with **What's Up?** (11 November 1943, National). It marked the second public collaboration of Alan Jay Lerner and Frederick Loewe (with Arthur Pierson assisting on the book). Loewe struck up a partnership with Lerner when Loewe presented him with a joint commission from producer Henry Duffy to write the musical *The Life of the Party*. The story was an interesting reversal of the old *Sultan of Sulu* (29 December 1902) type plot—and one wonders why no one tried it when that sort of theme was all the rage. Instead of Americans visiting a potentate in some exotic land, the bigwig comes to the States. (Reflecting the growth of modern technology, the Air Force, not the once ubiquitous Navy, is involved.) But the plane carrying the Rawa of Tanglinia crashes at Miss Langley's School for Girls, allowing everyone to have a seemingly naughty, but actually harmless, good time. Jimmy Savo forsook his customary baggy trousers to play the Rawa in a snappy morning suit, supplemented by a "lorgnette" and a fez. Balanchine, working with a smaller than usual *corps de ballet*, probably found himself compelled to insert a voguish "dream ballet." But he used the opportunity to give Savo one of the evening's most delightful moments with the forlorn little comedian pursuing an Amazonian ballerina. Yet something about the nature of the book was so irresistibly old-fashioned that the best dancing of the evening came not in the new-fangled ballets but in Don Weissmuller's show-stopping tap routines. Boris Aronson housed the entertainment in scenery with a Valentine-card frilliness. Lerner and Loewe's songs, while bright, were not overwhelming, while the book revealed that Lerner had a lot to learn about writing librettos. His story was largely humorless and ill proportioned. *What's Up?* survived eight weeks.

ALAN JAY LERNER was born in New York on 31 August 1918. His family owned the Lerner Shops, a chain specializing to popular-priced women's wear. Lerner's early education was at select private schools in England and at home, after which he took a bachelor of science degree at Harvard. While there he helped write material for two Hasty Pudding shows. Lerner had settled down to write radio scripts when his meeting with Loewe redirected his energies into the legitimate theatre.

FREDERICK LOEWE was born into a theatrical family in Berlin, Germany, on 10 June 1901. His father played Prince Danilo in the original Berlin production of *The Merry Widow*. A child prodigy on the piano, Frederick became the youngest soloist ever to appear with the Berlin Philharmonic. Two of his early instructors were also famous composers, Ferruccio Busoni and Eugene d'Albert. Early Loewe songs were heard in *Petticoat Fever* (a straight play starring Dennis King) and the *Illustrators' Show* (22 January 1936). His first score was for a failure, *Great Lady* (1 December 1938). Loewe met Lerner when he was looking for someone to revise *Great Lady* for a 1942 Detroit production.

A revival of *A Connecticut Yankee* (3 November 1927) began a disappointing run of 135 performances at the Martin Beck on 17 November. Vivienne Segal as Morgan Le Fay and Dick Foran as Martin sang the leads. The prologue was brought up-to-date, making Martin a navy lieutenant. But the original body of the story was faithfully retained. Rodgers and Hart added several new numbers. The brilliant lyrics for Morgan Le Fay's catalogue of murders in "To Keep My Love Alive" demonstrated that Hart, for all his problems, had lost not a jot of his genius:

Sir Roger played the harp; I cussed the thing.
I crowned him with his harp to bust the thing.
And now he plays where harps are just the thing.

But these were the last new Hart lyrics Broadway would ever hear. Five nights after the opening, Lorenz Hart was dead.

Moss Hart's play about air force life, *Winged Victory*, included a number of songs, mostly by David Rose. But the piece was essentially a straight play-chronicle.

Oscar Hammerstein tried something novel when he jazzed up *Carmen* for an all-black cast. **Carmen Jones** (2 December 1943, Broadway) became a worker in a parachute factory, and similar changes brought everything up-to-date, although Mérimée's story and Bizet's score were retained. However, song titles now ran to "Beat Out Dat Rhythm On A Drum." Since the principal roles remained uncompromisingly strenuous, singers alternated in main roles. Both Muriel Smith and Muriel Rahn sang the title part. A patently more serious effort than the thirties' tinkering with *The Mikado, Carmen Jones* ran a surprising 503 performances, helped extensively by producer Billy Rose's astute publicity. It was the last musical offering of 1943.

A month and a half passed before another musical arrived. The preceding season Vernon Duke and Howard Dietz had done tunes for a Mary Martin musical, *Dancing in the Streets*, which folded on its tryout. Their luck with **Jackpot** (13 January 1944, Alvin) wasn't much better. The show struggled along for sixty-nine performances before throwing in the towel. Duke's music wasn't to blame, for he came up with lively, instantly hummable songs such as "Sugarfoot." In fact neither Dietz's lyrics nor Guy Bolton, Sidney Sheldon, and Ben Roberts's book was truly culpable. Rather the era of purposefulness on the musical stage was at hand, so *Jackpot* was harshly received. Its innocuous, old-fashioned plot told how Sally Madison (Nanette Fabray) is put up as first prize in a bond-selling rally. Three marines— Hank Trimble (Allan Jones), Jerry Finch (Jerry Lester), and Winkie Cotter (Benny Baker)—win her with lucky 7777777. But since they can't share her affections Jerry and Winkie settle for Nancy Parker (Mary Wickes) and WAC Sgt. Maguire (Betty Garrett).

Equally old-fashioned but eagerly welcomed was **Mexican Hayride** (28 January 1944, Winter Garden). Mike Todd gave it the most lavish, expensive mounting a musical had had in years, adding more than a touch of burlesque. Herbert and Dorothy Fields wrote the book and Cole Porter the songs. Bobby Clark was the show's roustabout star, portraying Joe Bascom, a fugitive from American justice. His hayride begins when an American girl bullfighter, Montana (June Havoc), throws him the bull's ear. When he catches it, tradition makes him the guest of the Mexican government. This gives him time to establish an illegal lottery with a newfound crony, Lombo Campos (George Givot). The Mexican government tracks them down and informs the American chargé d'affaires, David Winthrop (Wilbur Evans). Winthrop has been fond of Montana, but now suspects she is in league with Bascom. To prove her innocence she goes with Winthrop to the flower-strewn, floating gardens at Xochimilco, where American tourists spend Sunday reading the comics and where Joe and Lombo are posing as mariachi players. Realizing the law is on their scent, Joe and Lombo flee, reappearing soon after as tortilla vendors. But their plight is hopeless. The crooks are turned over to their respective governments, while Winthrop and Montana proceed with their wedding plans. The Fieldses' book was serviceable and in the hands of so many fine funmakers exceptionally diverting. Todd, as he had learned to do in *Star and Garter* (24 June 1942), provided an attractive chorus line whose costumes offered tantalizing glimpses as they moved about. But for many the best news of the evening was the Cole Porter score. It was not a great one. But it gave an unmistakable indication that he was coming out of his doldrums. The hit of the evening was another beguine, "I Love You" (sung by David). But other memorable pieces were the jolly "laundry list" of Montana's "There Must Be Someone For Me," the passionate "Carlotta"—sung by a minor character, Lolita (Corinna Mura), with the ensemble—and Montana, Joe, and Lombo's comic "Count Your Blessings." *Mexican Hayride* was added to the list of 1943–1944 shows that ran more than a year (481 performances).

R. H. Burnside, who several decades before had mounted the Hippodrome extravaganzas, brought a Gilbert and Sullivan repertory into the small Ambassador for a total of fifty-four performances. The bill included *The Mikado, Trial by Jury, H. M. S. Pinafore, Cox and Box, The Pirates of Penzance, The Gondoliers, Iolanthe, Patience, Ruddigore,* and *The Yeomen of the Guard.*

Another smash hit, **Follow the Girls** (8 April 1944, Century), was one more in the dying line of rowdy, modern musicals that were sometimes called "glorified burlesque." The popular nightclub star Gertrude Niesen did in fact play Bubbles La Marr, a burlesque queen who takes over a servicemen's canteen as her contribution to the war effort. This inadvertently excludes her 4-F suitor, Goofy Gale (Jackie Gleason), who is obliged to steal a Wave's uniform to gain entrance. Dependable Guy Bolton and Fred Thompson combined with Eddie Davis to create the book, while Phil Charig did the music, assisted by Dan Shapiro and Milton Pascal on the words. The suggestive words to one song, "I Wanna Get Married," allowed Miss Niesen to stop the show nightly. Like several musicals of the season, it used its plot as a frame for vaudeville specialties such as the dancing of the Di Gatanos. With its eye-filling chorus line and entertaining specialties *Follow the Girls* ran over two years, far longer than the merits of its basic material justified. No doubt soldiers using New York as a major leave town or embarkation point eagerly sought out this sort of girlie show, thereby lengthening its run.

There was little merit to **Allah Be Praised!** (20 April 1944, Adelphi) and even less public interest. The show, with a book and lyrics by George Marion, Jr., and music by Don Walker and Baldwin Bergersen, told a confused tale of the search for a missing American in the postwar harems of Sultanbad. The American, Tex O'Carroll (Edward Roecker), is discovered to be none other than the Sultan. The show sought laughs from the same device employed earlier in *What's Up?*, by pitting little Joey Faye against tall Jayne Manners. One imaginative bit that went down with all the claptrap was Jack Cole's ballet depicting a softball game in slow motion. During its tryout Ned Sparks had brought down the house reliving in song his pleasant stay at Dannemora prison, but by the time the show got to New York Sparks had left the cast, though the song remained. At least it remained as long as the lavish show stayed, but that was a mere two and a half weeks.

A modern version of Offenbach's *La Belle Hélène* was offered on 24 April as **Helen Goes to Troy** (24 April 1944, Alvin). The show, like *Rosalinda* before it, was based on an earlier Max Reinhardt staging. Erich Wolfgang Korngold was again on hand to conduct, but this time he was also credited with adapting the music and adding a few minor songs of his own. He was not above using other Offenbach material, such as the "Barcarolle" from *The Tales of Hoffmann*, to stimulate interest. Jarmila Novotna, William Home, and Ernest Truex were featured, although Miss Novotna (of the Metropolitan Opera) and Home didn't sing at matinees. Despite generally favorable notices, the public wouldn't come; the show died with the hot weather.

Harem sets returned in **Dream with Music** (18 May 1944, Majestic). Since the author of *Allah Be Praised* was George Marion, Jr., and the producer of the new entry Richard Kollmar, there is the possibility they had discussed some sort of Arabian Nights theme when they had worked together on *Early to Bed*. Perhaps both came to wish they had dropped the matter, for *Dream with Music* survived only a week longer than *Allah Be Praised*. Dorothy Kilgallen, Sidney Sheldon, and Ben Roberts's book recounted the adventures of a soap-opera authoress, Dinah (Vera Zorina), when she dreams she is Scheherazade. Clay Warnick's music and Edward Eager's lyrics were livelier and more imaginative than *Allah's*. Some critics found amusement in the show's use of one old song not by Warnick: a genie's appearance was underscored by "Jeannie With The Light Brown Hair." By the time *Dream with Music* arrived, dream ballets had become requisite. Balanchine dutifully provided one, though his heart and his art were clearly not in it. As one reviewer noted, Ronald Graham as Aladdin "clomps around in oversized wedgies, while Miss [Joy] Hodges is generally buried in a group of not too seductively undressed chorines."

In the nineteenth century opera had been close to a commonplace in regular Broadway houses, but in recent decades it had been limited to the Metropolitan and a few other special auditoriums. So it is probably worth noting that two performances of Pergolesi's *The Maid as Mistress* (*La Serva Padrona*) and Wolf-Ferrari's *The Secret of Suzanne* were mounted at the Alvin on 14 and 21 May. Meanwhile at the New York City Center, where a great new opera company was in the making, a revival of *The New Moon* (19 September 1928) was displayed from 17 May until 24 June. Dorothy Kirsten and Earl Wrightson sang the leads.

The season ended drearily with yet another vaudeville, **Take a Bow** (15 June 1944, Broadhurst). The evening gave New Yorkers a last chance to see at least one of the Marx Brothers, Chico. Dressed in his familiar green hat and coat, he made his first entrance from a box trying to coax a neighbor to laugh. Before his last appearance, playing the piano in the orchestra pit, he revived a poker game routine from *Cocoanuts* (8 December 1925). Others on the bill included Pat Rooney, in his popular soft-shoe routine, and "Think-a-Drink" Hoffman, magically pouring a variety of concoctions from a single pitcher. The vaudeville bubble had long since burst, so *Take a Bow* bowed out after a mere twelve showings.

Outside the theatre it was a tumultuous year. Roosevelt was elected to the only fourth term in American history and shortly after taking office became the eighth American president to die in office. The war with Germany ended 7 May, and the war with Japan just weeks after the theatrical season closed. And a good theatrical season it was! Both on stage and at the box office it outshone any session in years. The diversity of the straight-play successes can be gauged by the mention merely of *Harvey*, *The Glass Menagerie*, *Anna Lucasta*, *Ten Little Indians*, and *Soldier's Wife*, as well as a number of useful dramatizations of popular books. The American Musical Theatre proved equally diverse, equally rich, and equally successful.

Hats Off to Ice (22 June 1944, Center), the annual "icetravaganza," with songs by James Littlefield and John Fortis, got the season off to a flying start. It ran through all of 1944–1945 and then through all of 1945–1946. Songs such as "Isle Of The Midnight Rainbow" and "Headin' West" suggest the nature of the spectacle.

The first conventional musical appeared two months later. Song of Norway (21 August 1944, Imperial) was a fictionalized, romanticized stage biography of Edvard Grieg using his music as the source of its songs. An unabashed operetta, it continued the tradition most successfully represented by *Blossom Time* (29 September 1921). Grieg (Lawrence Brooks) is lured away from his Nina (Helena Bliss) and from his beloved mountains and fiords by the dashing prima donna, Louisa Giovanni (Irra Petina). She takes him to Italy with her. But the voices of Nina and his dead friend Rikard (Robert Shafer) and the voice of Norway itself are too strong to ignore. Grieg returns home. The libretto and lyrics were adequate, if at times a bit stilted or heavily showy. What made Edwin Lester's West Coast production a two-year favorite in New York was lovely Grieg music, fine mounting, and superb singing. At a time when the war and Hollywood had deprived the stage of its better voices, *Song of Norway* offered the radiant singing not only of its principals but of such minor players as the aged Ivy Scott. Unfortunately, this brief renaissance of operetta ended quickly, and these artists never again had as fine an opportunity to display their voices. The hit of the evening was "Strange Music" (sung by Grieg and Nina), with its principal theme taken from Grieg's "Wedding Day in Troldhaugen."

Star Time (12 September 1944, Majestic), another in the waning series of inexpensive and quickly assembled vaudevilles, stayed for 120 showings. Lou Holtz, Benny Fields, and the De Marcos led the bill.

A third musical that ran through two seasons was Bloomer Girl (5 October 1944, Shubert). Its advance notices hinted that it was another *Oklahoma!* (31 March 1943). It, too, used a bit of early Americana for its story; it, too, had Agnes de Mille ballets; and it, too, offered *Oklahoma!*'s unforgettable Ado Annie, Celeste Holm, in the lead role, along with the hit of *Oklahoma!*'s ballet, Joan McCracken, as its principal dancer. What first-nighters saw and heard instead was an attractively mounted production (by *Oklahoma!*'s Lemuel Ayers and Miles White) of a superficial and somewhat silly, if entertaining, book and a singable, though not well-sung, score by Harold Arlen (with E. Y. Harburg lyrics). *Bloomer Girl* had little of *Oklahoma!*'s seriousness of purpose or artistic cohesiveness. However, it did contribute one additional element to the new musical vogue. In going back to "the good old days" it resuscitated historical figures. This device intrigued librettists frequently during the rest of the season, and often thereafter. Set during the Civil War, the story recounted the rebellion of Evelina Applegate (Miss Holm), daughter of a Cicero Falls, New York, hoopskirt manufacturer. Not only does she refuse to marry the man her father has in mind for her, but she actively supports the campaign of her aunt, Dolly Bloomer (Margaret Douglass), to replace her father's profitable hoop-skirts with the more comfortable garment that soon carried her aunt's name. Evelina's independence is manifest in more dangerous ways, for, while she is an abolitionist, she falls in love and ultimately consents to wed a Southern slaveholder, Jeff Calhoun (David Brooks). Miss de Mille's Civil War ballet did not really have much pertinence to the plot, although it did to the period of the piece. With World War II still raging, it also had a certain thinly disguised timeliness. It poignantly depicted the grief of wives and mothers whose loved ones will never return. None of Arlen's fine songs became standards, though Evelina and Jeff's duet "Right As The Rain" is still occasionally heard. But three songs stood out in the evening. Besides "Right As The Rain," a beautiful, intense ballad that eschews the easy AABA formula, there was Jeff's happy, curiously rhythmed "Evelina" and the impassioned, tuneful plea for racial understanding, "The Eagle And Me," sung by black Pompey (Dooley Wilson) and a mixed chorus.

For the next musical offering R. H. Burnside reached back even beyond the years when he was an active theatrical figure to revive Reginald De Koven's *Robin Hood* (28 September 1891) at the Adelphi on 7 November. But New Yorkers preferred the nineteenth century as seen through twentieth-century eyes to the nineteenth century's view of the past. Two weeks and the old comic opera was gone. One week later the City Center brought back *The Gypsy Baron* for eleven performances, following it with brief revivals of *La Vie Parisienne* in January and *Carmen Jones* (2 May 1945) in May.

A musical version of Jeanne Eagles's great hit, *Rain*, was planned around the talents of Ethel Merman. But Miss Merman and the authors became disenchanted with each other during rehearsals (when Miss Merman demanded that her husband provide lyrics), so June Havoc was called in to play the title role in **Sadie Thompson** (16 November 1944, Alvin). The shock of the original version had long since worn away, leaving Howard Dietz and Rouben Mamoulian with a rather harsh story that didn't lend itself to conventional musical treatment. Sadie was still the sharp-tongued lady of the streets exposing the hypocrisy of the Reverend Davidson (Lansing Hatfield) on sultry Pago Pago. Unfortunately, Vernon Duke's pleasant melodies and Dietz's commonplace lyrics lacked the bite and drive that might have moved the story forward. Sadie was almost apologetic as she sang "The Love I Long For" ("I've no right to demand"). More than one reviewer felt the physical production outshone the text and cast. Boris Aronson drenched the stage in realistic rain and dramatically flew Trader Joe's Hotel up into the flies so that he could reveal a lush jungle set. Dismayingly, the jungle set was largely an excuse for the sort of orgiastic, pagan dance that had gone out of fashion with the old extravaganzas. The dance only served to underline the musical's debt to the 1920s and, given the inclination of the forties to treat almost anything from the twenties as hopelessly outdated, helped foredoom the show.

Broadway turned a deaf ear when a new operetta, **Rhapsody** (22 November 1944, Century), appealed for patronage. The music Broadway refused to heed was by Fritz Kreisler, who twenty-five years before had written half the score for fondly remembered *Apple Blossoms* (7 October 1919). Kreisler even worked old favorites such as "Caprice Viennois" and "The Old Refrain" into his new score. The book, which dealt with court intrigues in the Vienna

of Francis I (George Young) and Maria Theresa (Annamary Dickey) and which included a comic Casanova (Eddie Mayehoff), was by the relatively unknown Leonard Louis Levinson and Arnold Sundgaard. The authors attempted a pure old-school piece and thereby undoubtedly engineered their own downfall. New Yorkers might flock to a sumptuous revival of a genuine masterwork such as *The Merry Widow* or clamor for tickets to old forms resuscitated with modern amenities such as *Song of Norway* or, later in the season, *Up in Central Park*. But an uncompromising, and admittedly somewhat weak, effort to exhibit the style of a bygone era met with no approval.

Three revues followed. They were as unlike one another as Broadway could imagine. The first was the most conventional. **The Seven Lively Arts** (7 December 1944, Ziegfeld) had been given the extensive ballyhoo that attended any Billy Rose production. Pre-opening publicity boasted of its Cole Porter songs, its Igor Stravinsky ballet music, its sketches and monologues by, among others, Moss Hart, George S. Kaufman, and Ben Hecht. At carefully selected intervals announcements added names to a cast that ultimately included Beatrice Lillie, Bert Lahr, Benny Goodman, Alicia Markova, Anton Dolin, Doc Rockwell, Albert Carroll, and Dolores Gray. For many the most joyous news was that Rose had purchased the magnificent Ziegfeld and was returning it to the legitimate fold after a dozen years as a grind movie house. But the advance cheering backfired. *The Seven Lively Arts* disappointed both critics and public. Cole Porter had one bittersweet ballad, sung by Nan Wynn, that has remained popular, "Ev'ry Time We Say Goodbye." But Stravinsky's music, "Scènes de Ballet," and the Dolin–Markova dances seemed too arty to Gotham playgoers and too condescending to serious critics. The comic material was especially weak. Bert Lahr had no good numbers, although Miss Lillie got some laughs with a tropical dance routine subtitled "Let's End The Beguine," as an English lady attempting to talk like an American soldier, and as a ballet fan who wants to buy a seat but can't remember the name of the ballet and so dances the piece for the startled ticket seller. Benny Goodman led his combo in some swing renditions. Show girls—only twelve—paraded in front of not especially attractive Norman Bel Geddes sets. But for all its advertised lavishness and despite its huge (for the time) advance sale of over $350,000, word about the show spread quickly, and it closed after just over twenty weeks.

Olsen and Johnson offered the third of their loony vehicles, **Laffing Room Only** (23 December 1944, Winter Garden). It was filled with much of the same demented zaniness that had made their earlier shows so popular. But the novelty had worn off, and, further, the comedians were competing in the richest musical season Broadway had enjoyed in years. As a result *Laffing Room Only* closed after 233 performances—a good run but far from the lengthy stays of *Sons o' Fun* (1 December 1941) or *Hellzapoppin* (22 September 1938). The show left behind one song, not particularly popular at the inception, which later became a favorite on radio, the hillbilly take-off that Pat Brewster sang, "Feudin' and Fightin'" (Al Dubin/Burton Lane).

More hillbilly music was heard four nights after the opening of *Laffing Room Only* when the Theatre Guild brought in **Sing Out Sweet Land** (27 December 1944, International), a "Salute to American Folk and Popular Music" compiled by Walter Kerr. Alfred Drake and Burl Ives led the singing of native American tunes from the first Puritan days to World War II. For all the new interest in Americana and folklore, the show proved a bit esoteric for commercial purposes. It played thirteen weeks.

The next night saw the opening of another of the season's long-run hits, **On the Town** (28 December 1944, Adelphi). The musical comedy had a score by the young darling of the serious music world, Leonard Bernstein. Its book, by Betty Comden and Adolph Green, was derived from Jerome Robbins's popular ballet *Fancy Free*. Robbins remained to attend to the new ballets the evening required. His two free-wheeling, concerted ballets "Miss Turnstiles" and "Gaby in the Playground of the Rich" were not only lively in themselves but forcefully propelled the story.

JEROME ROBBINS was born in New York on 11 October 1918. His real patronymic was Rabinowitz. In 1940 Robbins joined the Ballet Theatre as a dancer, and in the following year called attention to himself in Agnes de Mille's *Three Virgins and a Devil*. Important roles in *Petrouchka* and *Pillar of Fire* followed. But it was his initial creative effort, *Fancy Free*, in 1944 that firmly established his reputation.

LEONARD BERNSTEIN was born in Lawrence, Massachusetts, on 25 August 1918. While still in grade school he began studying piano under Helen Coates. At Harvard he pursued his studies under Heinrich Gebhard and Walter Piston. After leaving college, he enrolled at the Curtis Institute in Philadelphia to study conducting under Fritz Reiner. In time he became the protégé of Serge Koussevitsky. He called himself to public attention dramatically when he substituted for an indisposed Bruno Walter at a concert of the New York Philharmonic on 13 November 1943.

Though **BETTY COMDEN** and **ADOLPH GREEN** have proved the most durable writing team in the American Musical Theatre, their paths crossed long before the opening of *On the Town*. Indeed their histories are strikingly parallel. Both were born in New York City in 1915—Miss Comden on 3 May, Green on 2 December. They attended New York University together, and both were active in collegiate theatre. In the thirties they were part of a nightclub act, the Revuers, that also included young Judy Holliday.

When Robbins was not keeping the players in motion, George Abbott kept them less literally on their toes. Three sailors embark on a twenty-four-hour leave in New York. They are the romantic Gaby (John Battles), the clownish Ozzie (Green), and the more earthbound Chip (Cris Alexander). On the subway Gaby falls in love with a picture of the month's "Miss Turnstiles" (Sono Osato), and the three pals set out to find her. In a search that takes them as far uptown as the Museum of Natural History and as far out of Manhattan as Coney Island, Chip and Ozzie find romance of a sort, respectively, in Hildy (Nancy Walker), a cab driver, and Claire de Loon (Miss Comden), an anthropology student. Hildy, besides hacking it, proudly announces, "I Can Cook, Too," though her strenuous labors in the kitchen achieve nothing more than a peeled banana.

With a dinosaur casting an empty eye on them, Claire and Ozzie confess, "I Get Carried Away." It remains for Gaby to find "Miss Turnstiles" himself. And he does. Bernstein's score was intelligent, lively, and uncompromisingly contemporary. At times it suggested the path Gershwin might have pursued had he lived. But the songs lacked the sweet melodic catchiness that Gershwin so often presented. Still, Gaby's love ballad, "Lucky To Be Me," is heard intermittently, while the opening measures of the sailors' trio, "New York, New York," are often used as a background or lead-in for scenes of Manhattan.

Gershwin's name came up again with the arrival of 1945's first musical, for part of the score was by George's brother Arthur. The show's story sent a navy lieutenant, Anthony Caufield (Arthur Maxwell), back to sixteenth-century Venice and China to establish his virility. Once he does, he wins the hand of the attractive Ghisella. Hollywood's attractive Carole Landis as Ghisella and Sue Ryan as the saucy Licetta were the pillars of the production. Miss Ryan stopped the show with a Will Morrissey interpolation, "Brooklyn, U.S.A." Noël Coward had recently made some disparaging remarks about soldiers from Flatbush, and Miss Ryan assured the audience that a nicely flowered grave awaited the Englishman in the borough. The musical's title was **A Lady Says Yes** (10 January 1945, Broadhurst), but the public responded with a firm no. The Shuberts kept it on the boards eleven weeks before calling it quits.

January's other musical was a smash hit. **Up in Central Park** (27 January 1945, Century) was a colorful Mike Todd production with a book by Herbert and Dorothy Fields and a score by Sigmund Romberg—his first success in years. Actually both the book and songs were several steps removed from what their authors had once produced—steps down. The brittle, innovative Herbert Fields of the twenties had given way to a librettist willing to write hackneyed, fustian dialogue for a shallow, melodramatic plot. Romberg's tinkly melodies rarely had more than a fragile appeal. Though it called itself a "musical play," it was like so many "musical plays" of ten and twenty years before, essentially an operetta, cleverly minimizing the fact by emphasizing the voguish Americana of its setting, its plot, and its "Currier and Ives Ballet." The ballet, an exquisitely wrought skating scene in Central Park choreographed by Helen Tamaris, was the high point of the evening. The Fieldses' book recounted the exposure and wrecking of the notorious Tweed political clan

by the dogged efforts of a New York *Times* reporter, John Matthews (Wilbur Evans). His rewards include the hand of Rosie Moore (Maureen Cannon), the daughter of one of the politicians he attacked. But this marriage takes place only after Rosie annuls a marriage made in pique because of John's attacks on her father. Fortunately for John, Rosie had married a married man. Although Romberg generally avoided the three-quarter time so identified with operetta, his songs were strictly of the genre. A thumping "The Big Back Yard" (Central Park) recalled his earlier marches, while the delicate and sweet "April Snow" reminded oldsters of songs such as "In Our Little Home Sweet Home" from *Maytime* (16 August 1917). The hit of the evening was Romberg's attempt to combine the contemporary ballad with his arioso style. The result was John and Rosie's interesting, if overblown, love song, "Close As Pages In A Book."

There were no musicals in February. March's lone entry was a failure, albeit a fascinating failure that probably deserved a better hearing. Ira Gershwin and Edwin Justus Mayer adapted Mr. Mayer's 1924 hit *The Firebrand*, calling it **The Firebrand of Florence** (22 March 1945, Alvin) and embellishing it was a rich Kurt Weill score. The plot remained the same. Benvenuto Cellini (Earl Wrightson) wins the hand of Angela (Beverly Tyler) after convincing his Duke (Melville Cooper) that he had no share in a conspiracy. Though Max Gordon bestowed a thoughtfully lavish mounting on the work, it folded after forty-three performances.

For many, Rodgers and Hammerstein's **Carousel** (19 April 1945, Majestic) was the season's triumph. For others, it was the beginning of an era of pretentious solemnity in the American Musical Theatre, an era that attempted to replace the marquee with a steeple. *Carousel* was adapted from Ferenc Molnar's 1921 success *Liliom*. Hammerstein transposed the story to 1873 New England, where Billy Bigelow (John Raitt) is a hard, mean carnival barker at an amusement park carousel. In Agnes de Mille's ballet-pantomime which opened the work and which was her first show ballet that truly moved the plot forward, Billy spots the lovely Julie Jordan (Jan Clayton) and proposes a rendezvous, while Billy's employer, Mrs. Muffin (Jean Casto), watches gloweringly. Julie is attracted to the handsome barker, but she is nonetheless uncertain. Finally she acquiesces. Julie conveys her uncertainty to her friend, Carrie Pipperidge (Jean Darling). Carrie responds, "You're A Queer One, Julie Jordan," and goes on to tell Julie of her ambitious hopes when she weds "Mister Snow." When Billy appears, he is discovered to be unexpectedly shy. He can only talk of his feelings by indirection, letting Julie know how he would act "If I Loved You." By the time "June Is Bustin' Out All Over," Julie and Billy are married. With spring everyone and everything seems to be in love. Carrie and Mr. Snow (Eric Mattson) contemplate a glowingly sentimental evening "When The Children Are Asleep." Only the villainous Jigger Craigin (Murvyn Vye) fails to share the happy reveries. The sailor complains in "Blow High, Blow Low" that he is misunderstood. Billy learns he is about to be a father. At first he is dismayed, but his second thoughts are different. If the child is a boy he will make him into a barker like himself—"Of course, it takes talent to do that well"; if it is a girl, well, he will steal and even die to see that she is supported properly. Carrie warns Julie of the company Billy is keeping, especially Jigger. But Julie can only reply, "What's The Use Of Wond'rin.'" To get money for the expected child Jigger and Billy stage a holdup, and Billy kills himself when he realizes he will be caught. Julie is comforted by Nettie Fowler (Christine Johnson), who assures her, "You'll Never Walk Alone." In purgatory, Billy demands to be judged by "The Highest Judge Of All," and he is allowed to return to earth to redeem himself and see his now-grown daughter (Bambi Linn). He sees her snubbed on the beach, and when she refuses to accept a star he has pilfered he vents his fury on himself and the others by slapping her. For this he is returned to purgatory. But he has lingered long enough to witness his daughter's graduation and understand the hope for a future without him both she and Julie hold.

An archetypal Broadway leading man with a distinctive baritone voice, **JOHN RAITT** was born 19 January 1917 in Santa Ana, California. He was chosen from the chorus of the Los Angeles Civic Light Opera to take over the role of Curly in *Oklahoma!* from Alfred Drake, launching a long theatrical career that in addition to *Carousel*, included a starring role in the original Broadway production of *The Pajama Game*.

The evening had beautifully evocative sets by Jo Mielziner and costumes by Miles White that knowingly recreated a nineteenth-century New England fishing village. Theatregoers heard better singing than in any show except *Song of Norway*. But the greatness of the evening lay in Richard Rodgers's impressively deep and varied music. Rodgers himself considered his score "more satisfying than any I've ever written"—doubly satisfying because he was aware both Gershwin and Puccini rejected the opportunity to bring *Liliom* onto the lyric stage. Eschewing an overture, the show opened with some startling dissonances in the "Carousel Waltz"—a trick Rodgers hereafter moved from his ballet music to his regular songs—but swiftly proceeded to the thoughtful, elongated musical lines of such diverse hits as "If I Loved You" and "June Is Bustin' Out All Over." Although the show had more music and less spoken dialogue than any lyric offering in years, including an eight-minute soliloquy by Billy, there was no such pretentious announcement as in *Rose-Marie* (2 September 1924) or *Chee-Chee* (25 September 1928). Songs were listed on the program by title. What few complaints there were about the evening were generally directed at Hammerstein. Both his lyrics and his dialogue were thoroughly professional, but a certain sententiousness was creeping in. In retrospect, hints of the heavy-handed repetition and preachiness of some of his later offerings are easily discerned. His solemnity and sentimentality, coupled with Rodgers's broader new style, suggest that what the new American musical play really had suddenly become was the mid-twentieth-century native answer to the Continental operetta, the same answer Hammerstein and Kern had hit upon with *Show Boat*, but never properly pursued. If this is true, it might also partially explain the appeal of operettas and operettas disguised as musical plays running so successfully at the time on Broadway. But operettas or no, drawbacks or no, the totality mesmerized most audiences into overlooking the faults.

April, like February, brought in no new shows. But three musicals were ushered in during the last two weeks of May. The first was **Blue Holiday** (21 May 1945, Belasco), an African-American variety show starring Ethel Waters, the Hall Johnson Choir, and the Katherine Dunham dancers. Duke Ellington and E. Y. Harburg were among those who supplied interpolations to bolster Al Moritz's uninteresting music. But the performers were not strong enough to fight both their lackluster material and the strong competition around them. The show left after one week.

Then, just as two jazz *Mikados* had appeared almost back to back during the 1939–1940 season, two musicals derived from *H. M. S. Pinafore* came in a week apart to close out the month. But, unlike the earlier duplication which, since one show had consciously copied the other, produced two similar pieces, the new shows took quite different tacks. About all they had in common, other than their source, was that they were both flops.

The first to arrive was **Memphis Bound!** (24 May 1945, Broadway). It wrapped its excerpts from Gilbert and Sullivan's work in a sentimental bit of nineteenth-century Americana. A contingent of black performers boards the *Calliboga Queen* bound for Memphis. The boat hits a sandbar, and the actors start a performance of *Pinafore* to earn money to pay for the ship's release. But the performers are jailed for not having a license. A trial and acquittal follow. Besides using much of *Pinafore*'s material, the show offered extensive excerpts from *Trial by Jury*, since, as one performer noted, "'Trial by Jury' is always on the same program with 'Pinafore.'" Don Walker and Clay Warnick's songs, when not lifted intact, still utilized *Pinafore* melodies with original, if consciously old-fashioned, words. For example, "The Nightingale, The Moon And I" recalled the "tale" songs of Pixley and Luders, and other allegorical ditties of their contemporaries. Of course, the production's "boogie-woogie accents" were new to Gilbert and Sullivan. As was so often the case with earlier black shows, dancing was its forte. In this case the dancing was especially good, with sixty-seven-year-old Bill Robinson tapping his way up and down flights of stairs, spelled by the more sinewy soft-shoe routines of a lavender-garbed Avon Long. But the fine stepping was no lure in a season of such strong competition. *Memphis Bound!* folded after thirty-six showings.

Hollywood Pinafore (31 May 1945, Alvin), with William Gaxton and Victor Moore as its stars, outran its rival by only seventeen performances. Its approach was precisely the opposite of *Memphis Bound!* It was contemporary and satirical, with George S. Kaufman providing the book and lyrics for his former *Of Thee I Sing* associates. In Kaufman's new version Joseph W. Porter (Moore) lords it over the Pinafore Studios in Hollywood, where the hack writers, led by Ralph Rackstraw (Gilbert Russell), dress in prison stripes and Dick Live-Eye (Gaxton) is an agent interested solely in his percentage.

Recognizable Hollywood names such as Louhedda Hopsons (a combination of the two leading gossip columnists, Hedda Hopper and Louella Parsons, played by Shirley Booth) rubbed elbows with the original Gilbertian figures. Some of Kaufman's material was superb. His version of Buttercup's song contained delicious references to the Orson Welles–Rita Hayworth marriage and to Welles's feud with William Randolph Hearst that followed the release of *Citizen Kane*. They were as witty as Gilbert's allusions to the figures of his day and also caught the unctuousness of then contemporary columnists (revealing why Kaufman's character was sometimes called Butter Up):

> *Poor Rita's divorcin' that awful man Orson*
> *(I'm making that up to please Hearst);*
> *And Alice Faye may be expecting a baby*
> *· A year from next October first.*

Even the dialogue reflected a certain Gilbertian formality:

Ralph: For you will be my father-in-law, and in accordance with an old studio custom I now sign you for *twice* your old salary or twenty times what you are worth.

Regrettably, too many of Kaufman's darts apparently missed their mark. Max Gordon gave the show an excellent mounting, including an Anthony Tudor ballet depicting the rise of a Hollywood starlet. Called "Success Story," it used melodies from a number of Sullivan works, but none from *Pinafore*. Viola Essen danced the central figure. The ballet was highly praised, even though it ran against the satiric intent of the rest of the evening. Like *Memphis Bound!*, *Hollywood Pinafore* was not sufficiently strong in all its points to compete with better offerings occupying so many Broadway stages. It succumbed to its inadequacies and the heat.

Concert Varieties (1 June 1945, Ziegfeld) was another vaudeville, assembled this time by Billy Rose when he realized *Seven Lively Arts* would not make it through the spring. It was better than most, but still not strong enough to buck the competition and the heat. Deems Taylor served as master of ceremonies, announcing such acts as Imogene Coca in a demonstration of how to wear fur coats, Zero Mostel giving a political speech, and Eddie Mayehoff mimicking famous actors. The Salici Puppets offered a variety show within a variety show, while Jerome Robbins created a ballet, "Interplay," to Morton Gould's music. When *Concert Varieties* closed, it ended the string of vaudevilles that had kept theatres lit intermittently over the preceding three seasons.

1945-1946

More or less inevitably, both the number of shows and their quality fell slightly in the first postwar season. The astonishing number of long runs held over from the preceding year deprived incoming musicals of choice houses. Few of the theatres converted to movies or radio had owners who would willingly reconvert them to legitimate offerings. The vast adjustments demanded by the change from war to peace threw both writers and their audiences off balance, so that just as a pattern seemed discernible something happened to make it seem no pattern at all.

Two operettas began the season. Neither seemed anxious to be considered an operetta, though one did acknowledge it on its sheet music—in very small type. **Marinka** (18 July 1945, Winter Garden) came first. George Marion, Jr., and Karl Farkas's book was the latest in the countless retellings of the Mayerling mystery. The score was by Emmerich Kalman, of recent years a refugee in America. Kalman apparently made some efforts to compose in contemporary modes. Because "Cab Song" suggested "The Surrey With The Fringe On Top," a few playgoers waggishly branded the show a Viennese *Oklahoma!* (31 March 1943). But most of Kalman's score retained his old three-quarter-time sweep, even if melodies such as "One Last Love Song" were not transparently Middle European. Comparison with *Oklahoma!* was unavoidable with Joan Roberts (the original Laurey) playing the title role and Harry Stockwell (Curly in a road company) as Crown Prince Rudolph. Neither of these attractive youngsters garnered the kudos won by Luba Malina for her performance as the Archduke's discarded mistress. A veteran of the Mayerling era, Ethel Levey, appeared briefly in the cameo role of Madame Sacher, doyenne of Vienna's famous hotel. Critics also praised the peasant costumes Mary Grant designed for Albertina Rasch's lively Hungarian dances. If the evening seemed largely old hat, it was nonetheless pleasant enough to earn a modest run of twenty-one weeks.

Mr. Strauss Goes to Boston (6 September 1945, Century) followed nearly two months later. It told of the Waltz King's (George Rigaud) visit to Boston in 1872, of his flirtation with Mrs. Brook Whitney (Virginia MacWatters), and of Frau Strauss's (Ruth Matteson) winning him back with the aid of President Grant (Norman Roland). The plot was reminiscent of the still-popular *Song of Norway* (21 August 1944), while the Strauss family had been on stage before in *The Great Waltz* (22 September 1934). Besides the fine singing and spectacle these earlier mountings had offered, both used the cherished melodies of the composers they depicted. *Mr. Strauss Goes to Boston* relied instead on a lame score by Robert Stolz. Stolz had been a popular Viennese figure and, like Kalman, was a refugee, but he had never enjoyed an extended vogue on this side of the Atlantic. His new score was no help. Though Miss MacWatters's glittering coloratura interpretation of the "Laughing Waltz" brought down the house and though several critics were heartily amused by Strauss's worshipful admirers screaming and swooning much as bobby-soxers were doing for Frank Sinatra, these better moments could not compensate for a general inadequacy. The show folded after a week and a half.

At the end of the month **Carib Song** (27 September 1945, Adelphi) attempted to provide a vehicle for Katherine Dunham and her dancers. It told a serious, tragic story of an unfaithful woman, her fisherman lover, and her husband's revenge. There was an element of pretension in the attempted universality of the characters. They were not given names but were identified simply as "The Woman," "The Fisherman," "The Husband" or "The Boy Possessed by a Snake." Nor was the setting more specific than a "Small West Indian Village." The dancing was excellent, while Jo Mielziner's sets and Motley's costumes seemed appropriately lush. The cast of top black entertainers included Avon Long as the villain. But the book was indifferent, Baldwin Bergersen's score not much better, and the whole affair stranded at a never popular, out-of-the-way theatre. *Carib Song* languished for thirty-six performances.

On 6 October two more operettas appeared. One was a revival of *The Gypsy Baron* as part of the City Center opera season. The other, **Polonaise** (6 October 1945, Alvin), recounted Kosciuszko's experience both in the American Revolution and in an uprising he finds when he returns to Poland. He also finds time to woo the lovely Marisha. The story jumped back and forth between the United States and Poland, injecting a slightly confused, frenetic tone into the telling. The music was attractive and familiar. It was all by Chopin, adapted with lyrics by John Latouche. Chopin's polonaises became the source of the show's ballet music. The evening received a critical drubbing, and much of the head-shaking was prompted by Jan Kiepura's atrocious acting. Robert Garland headed his *Journal American* notice "Ham and Eggerth." But Kiepura and Marta Eggerth (Mrs. Kiepura) had won a host of admirers in their recent revival of *The Merry Widow*. This loyal following helped *Polonaise* achieve 113 performances, despite the critical rejection.

On the other hand, critical kudos and long lines at the box office greeted *The Red Mill* (24 September 1906) after its 16 October bow at the Ziegfeld. Herbert and his generation had considered the work a musical comedy, but the increasing simplicity and shortened musical phrases of modern melodies—plus the musical's age—caused most commentators to look on it as operetta. Paula Stone, the daughter of its original costar Fred Stone, was co-producer. And Stone's more celebrated daughter, Dorothy, was in the cast as Tina, along with Michael O'Shea (Con), Eddie Foy, Jr. (Kid), and Odette Myrtil (Madame La Fleur, a name not in the original). There were some minor, harmless revisions, mostly to keep the dialogue from sounding dated. A few new lyrics were added, some characters were also added, and some character roles were expanded, while Gretchen's lover was now Captain Hendrik Van Damm instead of Captain Doris Van Damm. But for the most part, the story, score, and tone of the original were faithfully retained and lovingly revived. The show ran 531 performances, falling just twenty-seven performances short of doubling the 1906–1907 run. A long, highly successful tour followed.

November was active and uneven. Its first premiere was a dim-witted affair called **The Girl from Nantucket** (8 November 1945, Adelphi), which struggled through a twelve-performance stay. Walella Waldorf, writing in the *Post*, summed up the critical consensus when she noted, "It lacks everything." The book depicted the confusion that ensued when a house painter is mistakenly selected to create a mural at a museum. The score was by Jacques Belasco, his only big-time effort.

More talented, more experienced hands collaborated to create **Are You With It?** (10 November 1945, Century). They succeeded, almost in spite of themselves. Sam Perrin and George Blazer's book was adapted from George Malcolm-Smith's novel *Slightly Imperfect*. It told the kind of story that set the show several years behind the times. Wilbur Haskins (Johnny Downs) is fired from his insurance company job after he misplaces a decimal point. A carnival barker known as Goldie (Lew

Parker) persuades him to join the carnival. Wilbur is a nervous, literal, serious-minded young man who unself-consciously orders a glass of milk at Joe's Bar Room. After he falls in love with Vivian Reilly (Joan Roberts), he calms down. The show's idea of humor was to have a character in one train compartment misconstrue instructions for taking a photograph ("move over," "get it all in") being offered in the next compartment. One clever, if appropriately obsolete, device was the use of silhouettes to open the show. An entire boardinghouse was seen getting out of bed and getting dressed and ready for work. The suggestive glimpses of nudity led into a song packed with double-entendres, "Five Minutes More In Bed," with which a minor character, Marge (Jane Dulo), and a fast-stepping ensemble launched the evening. The score was the last one Harry Revel produced for Broadway. Although his Hollywood hits included "Did You Ever See A Dream Walking?," the best he could do for New York was a song such as "Here I Go Again." With no other good, fresh shows in sight, *Are You With It?* got off to a flying start and ran through the season.

In his review of the next musical to open, Louis Kronenberger of *PM* noted that "Most musicals this season have been exercises in torture." In a small way, the new arrival improved matters. **The Day Before Spring** (22 November 1945, National) was an innovative, melodic musical that didn't quite work and didn't quite make it. It reunited Alan Jay Lerner and Frederick Loewe, of *What's Up?* (11 November 1943), and furthered what soon became one of the most fruitful of lyric partnerships. Although Lerner approached his book thoughtfully and maturely, his story, at least in outline, could, like the plot of *Are You With It?*, have been the plot of a 1920s musical. Moreover, in execution Lerner still manifested a clumsy, heavy hand. The Peter Townsends return to Harrison University for their tenth reunion. There Katherine Townsend falls in love again with Alex Maitland and decides to run away with him as she had tried to a decade before. Their car broke down then and breaks down again on this second elopement. But all is forgiven, or at least understood. To tell some of the story Lerner allowed Anthony Tudor to conceive a ballet for each of the principal characters, retelling significant incidents from different points of view. The device, which seemed clever on paper, proved repetitious and tedious on stage. The happiest aspect of *The Day Before Spring* was its wide-ranging, infectious collection of songs: the sober considerations of the title song and "You

Haven't Changed At All," the bubbly gaiety of "I Love You This Morning," the simple joys of "A Jug Of Wine" (a loaf of bread, and "thou, baby"), and the then still popular Latin undercurrents of "God's Green World." The show had a first-rate cast headed by Hollywood's Irene Manning as Katherine and Broadway's Bill Johnson as Alex. But the show's faults ultimately told, and it closed after twenty-one weeks.

Betty Comden and Adolph Green, who had worked so profitably with Leonard Bernstein on the thoroughly contemporary *On the Town* (28 December 1944), now sat down with Morton Gould to produce a brash and not altogether feeling or faithful look at the bygone twenties. That the era was completely out of fashion at the moment didn't help the show's reception. Somehow even the title **Billion Dollar Baby** (21 December 1945, Alvin) suggested World War II figures rather than the millions the twenties talked about. And the songs were completely contemporary, with only the tiniest hints of the real tempos and chromatics of the earlier period. The plot recorded the desperate rise of pushy calculating Maribelle Jones (Joan McCracken), who ditches her sweet boyfriend for a dangerous gangster on the run, soon finds herself attending a lavish gangster funeral, and finally settles for a rich tycoon just before the 1929 crash. The show touched on all the favorite stereotypes of the era: the underworld, the bull market, and the great annuals (here called the "Jollities"). Much of the action took place around "Chez Georgia," where the twenties' wild hostess, Texas Guinan, lived again in Mitzi Green's impersonation of Georgia Motley. It was ersatz twenties in a day that rejected even the real thing. Still, with little real new competition in sight, *Billion Dollar Baby* was able to hold on for nearly seven months.

But in fact, there was something from the twenties the forties could embrace, and that was *Show Boat* (27 December 1927). Hammerstein gave it a sumptuous revival at the Ziegfeld on 5 January 1946. Both critics and theatregoers rejoiced. The revival confirmed what had, since *Oklahoma!* (31 March 1943) and *Carousel* (19 April 1945), seemed likely: that, fifteen years ahead of its time, Show Boat had determined the basic form and inaugurated the era of great American musical plays. With a fine cast headed by Jan Clayton (Magnolia), Charles Fredericks (Ravenal), Kenneth Spencer (Joe), and Carol Bruce (Julie), the revival played for a full year. Joy at the success of the revival was

tempered somewhat by the sudden death of Jerome Kern two months before, on 11 November 1945. He had come to New York to aid in the production and to write the songs for a new musical Rodgers and Hammerstein were to produce for him. For this revival he provided Broadway with one final song, "Nobody Else But Me."

Show Boat excepted, as far as the rest of the twenties, the public wanted little of it. A good revival of *The Desert Song* (30 November 1926) at the City Center three nights after *Show Boat* caused no great stir, although Walter Cassel was present to bring his fine voice to the part of The Red Shadow. One night after the opening of *The Desert Song* Bobby Clark tried unsuccessfully to make a modern musical comedy of Molière's *Le Bourgeois Gentilhomme*, **The Would-Be Gentleman** (9 January 1946, Booth), using Lully's music.

A popular star of the twenties, Eddie Cantor, returned to Broadway on 21 January, but only as a producer. In keeping with the current fascination for Americana, he presented a musical built around the adventures of **Nellie Bly** (21 January 1946, Adelphi). When the *World* assigns Miss Bly (Joy Hodges) the task of beating Phileas Fogg's fictitious eighty-day circumnavigation of the globe, the *Herald* hires Phineas T. Fogarty (Victor Moore) to thwart her. Frank Jordan (William Gaxton), the *Herald's* managing editor, decides to accompany Fogarty. Miss Bly not only makes good, she makes Jordan fall in love with her. The book was by the relatively inexperienced Joseph Quillan, but the tunes were in the hands of the competent Johnny Burke (words) and James Van Heusen (music). The dances were snappy, if patently old-fashioned; the best were tapped out by an all-male specialty act, The Debonairs. Besides the stars, Benay Venuta was on hand with a capital performance as an aging "toughie," Battle Annie. But the mixture failed to jell. *Nellie Bly* gave up in far less time than it took its heroine to make her trip.

Having returned to Broadway two seasons before in the brilliant *One Touch of Venus* (7 October 1943), Mary Martin heightened her reputation by appearing in a fine, offbeat "love story with music," **Lute Song** (6 February 1946, Plymouth). Based on a fourteenth-century Chinese play, *Pi-Pa-Ki*, by a writer known either as Kao-Tong-Kia or Tse-Tching, it had been worked into an American play in the late twenties by the distinguished dramatist Sidney Howard and Will Irwin. It could find no commercial takers for a number of years. The producer, Michael Meyerberg, engaged Raymond Scott to provide the songs. As the prologue announces, "It is a venerable tale of the time when the gods walked upon earth and wrought their magic in the sight of men." The scholarly Tsai-Yong (Yul Brynner) has refused to take the examinations at court, preferring to remain at home with his beautiful wife. But she and his parents prevail on him to go. His wife comforts him with her vow to remain loyal: "Mountain High—Valley Low." He does so well in the examinations he is appointed Chief Magistrate. As a result he is forced to marry the daughter of Prince Nieou Chi. His attempts to communicate with his family are blocked. His mother and father die of starvation, and his wife is reduced to beggary. She treks across the country and appears at his house. The Princess recognizes her. Sympathetic and knowing, she arranges for the wife to be reunited with her pining husband. Even the harsh Prince is touched by their obvious love and agrees to annul the second marriage: "What the Voice of Jade has ordained, the Voice of Jade may revoke." If Ward Morehouse in the *Sun* found Robert Edmond Jones's designs filled with "unearthly beauty," in the *Times* Lewis Nichols went so far as to insist, "Mr. Jones' settings, costumes and lighting are the heroes of the evening." Jones achieved many of his effects through stylization and simplicity, often relying on shadings of a single hue to color a set. Unfortunately, *Lute Song* was too esoteric for mass appeal. Even at an intimate theatre, it ran only 142 times.

A lavish, brassy, conventional musical comedy followed a week later. In **The Duchess Misbehaves** (13 February 1946, Adelphi), Woonsocket faints and dreams he is Goya cavorting with the Duchess of Alba. Jackie Gleason started in the part of Woonsocket but, realizing how hopeless the show was, left during the tryout. Joey Faye and Audrey Christie performed the main parts during all of the show's five New York performances.

Nancy Hamilton resurrected her intermittent revue series when **Three to Make Ready** followed the duchess into the Adelphi on 7 March. The cast featured Brenda Forbes, Gordon MacRae, Harold Lang, Bibi Osterwald, Meg Mundy, Carleton Carpenter, and Arthur Godfrey—almost all names on the way up. But its star was Ray Bolger, and his dancing brightened an otherwise ordinary evening. "The Old Soft Shoe," Bolger's solo in straw hat, striped blazer, white pants, and cane, stopped the show. Bolger also displayed his comic talents in such skits as "Kenosha Canoe," a spoof on the new-style musical play, purporting to show how Rodgers and

Hammerstein might adapt Dreiser's *An American Tragedy*. Morgan Lewis was back to write the songs with Miss Hamilton, but songs, on the order of "A Lovely, Lazy Kind Of Day" had little power outside the theatre.

St. Louis Woman (30 March 1946, Martin Beck) was another interesting show that failed to make a big splash. It told of the loves of Delia Green (Ruby Hill), a leading black beauty in turn-of-the-century St. Louis. Actually there was little reason for the show to be set in the period, but the suggestion of another slice of Americana didn't hurt among the faddists. Delia is fickle. She's Bigelow Brown's girl until the jockey, Little Augie (Harold Nicholas), has a winning streak that makes him the talk of the town. The vengeful Brown (Rex Ingram) beats Della, and Augie in turn promises to even the score. But before he can, Brown is shot by a woman he rejected. He curses Augie. Unnerved, the jockey starts losing races, and when he does he loses Della. But when his good luck returns Della is back to help him celebrate. The book by Countee Cullen and Arna Bontemps, from Bontemps's novel *God Sends Sunday*, left something to be desired. But the score by two solid professionals, Harold Arlen and Johnny Mercer, often helped it through the weak spots. Arlen created one of his classics for this show, Augie and Della's "Come Rain Or Come Shine," and Mercer gave Pearl Bailey, in a comic-relief role, show-stopping lyrics for "Legalize My Name." Harold Nicholas and his brother Fayard did the show's brightest hoofing. Rouben Mamoulian gave the evening a dramatic staging. His crowd scenes at the end of each act reminded playgoers of his stunning ensembles for *Porgy and Bess*. The first-act finale was a rousing cakewalk; the second act concluded with a funeral, while the last curtain fell on a mob watching a race from the wrong side of the fence.

Just as the City Center mounted *The Gypsy Baron* at the same time *Polonaise* was being presented, and then brought back *The Desert Song* when Hammerstein was offering Show *Boat*, its revival of an older black show, *Carmen Jones* (2 December 1943), followed *St. Louis Woman* by one week.

Call Me Mister (18 April 1946, National) was the first original musical of the season that could be unhesitatingly labeled a smash hit. It had fun with the mustering-out process and with its not always kind looks back at army life. Its ex-soldiers imagined the problems Paul Revere might have had, had he tried to procure his horse through modern army red tape; they discerned Noël Coward influences in the Air

Force; and in "South Wind" they depicted the snail's progress in enlightening three Southern senators. The veterans also stopped for a reverent moment of respect to their former commander-in-chief with "Face On A Dime." But the runaway hit of the show had little to do with the armed forces. Betty Garrett as a canteen hostess, exhausted from the rhumbas and congas her partners danced, pleaded, "South America, Take It Away!" Although the song was the only number in Harold Rome's score to achieve national prominence, it helped *Call Me Mister* to a run of over 700 performances.

On 12 May the City Center Opera added *The Pirates of Penzance* to its repertory.

Four nights later, the biggest hit of the season arrived. **Annie Get Your Gun** (16 May 1946, Imperial) was the Rodgers and Hammerstein production that Jerome Kern had been slated to write the songs for. With Kern's death, Irving Berlin was called in and during the short interval between then and the rehearsals composed what was immediately recognized as his greatest score. Like most of the shows of the day, *Annie Get Your Gun* was set in nineteenth-century America. But it made no pretense of being a serious musical or advancing the art of the "musical play." *Annie* set out solely to entertain. It entertained so well because it was far more artful than some of its more aggressively noble competitors. And it entertained so well it ran 1,147 performances in New York; a road company had Mary Martin as star, and the show was a four-year smash in London. Annie Oakley (Ethel Merman) is a poor but happy country girl—happy to proclaim "I Got The Sun In The Morning." She and her family have made do on native intelligence, "Doin' What Comes Natur'lly." Her sharpshooting soon makes her the rage of Buffalo Bill's Wild West Show. Sharpshooting is her life, but being of a susceptible age she finds herself falling in love with her costar Frank Butler (Ray Middleton). But Butler's ideal for "The Girl That I Marry" is a far different woman from the tough, outspoken Annie. Annie can only despair, "You Can't Get A Man With A Gun." But she has one consolation: she is a member of the greatest profession on earth. She and her cohorts agree, "There's No Business Like Show Business." And to top it all off she's initiated into an Indian tribe and can exult, "I'm An Indian, Too." She and Frank agree at least partway about romance: "They Say It's Wonderful." But Frank is especially jealous of Annie's superior marksmanship. He is well aware of her advantage, though he maintains a brave front

as they argue, "Anything You Can Do (I Can Do Better)." Only on one point is it a draw—neither can bake a pie! They remain at odds until Chief Sitting Bull (Harry Bellaver) takes Annie aside and makes her realize that only by intentionally, but discreetly, losing a match to Frank can she win him. She does just that. The Herbert and Dorothy Fields book was well crafted. The exposition was particularly fine, quickly drawing principal characters amusingly, yet poignantly. Annie first appears shooting a bird that turns out to be a decoration on a lady's hat. The incident occurs in front of a small-town hostelry that Annie hopes to supply with game so she can support her young sisters and brothers. Annie presents the proprietor with another example of her shootings:

Annie: Look it over, Mister. Look it over keerful.
  Lift up his wings. See? No buckshot in that bird.
  Jes' one little hole in his head.
Wilson: Mighty pretty shooting!
Annie: Mighty pretty eatin', too. Fer evvy one I get
  ye, ye gotta give me two nickels and a dime.
Wilson: Can't hurt to try them. I'll take two dozen.
Annie: How many is that?
Wilson: Twenty-four.
Annie: [*to her brothers and sisters*] Who do we
  know kin count up to twenty-four?

Fine as the Fieldses' libretto was, Berlin's songs really raised *Annie* to its heights. They ranged from the solid ballad melody of "They Say It's Wonderful" to the openhanded joy of "I Got The Sun In The Morning." "There's No Business Like Show Business" has become something of a professional anthem in the years since its debut. Rodgers and Hammerstein gave the show a stunning staging. And Ethel Merman established herself beyond any recall as the leading musical comedy star of her generation. Ray Middleton, who had been struggling on the sidelines since *Roberta*, was a virile, believable Frank.

No one thought that Orson Welles was anyone but Orson Welles when he arrived two weeks later to close the season as the villainous Dick Fix with his adaptation of Jules Verne's novel, the title abbreviated to **Around the World** (31 May 1946, Adelphi). Welles appeared in all sorts of disguises and even performed a magic show. He filled the stage with circus performers and animals and staged a miniature train wreck. Cole Porter provided the words and music, which were generally mediocre. His one good number, "Should I Tell You I Love You?," sung by Mary Healey, was lost in the mayhem. The critics were unkind, but the show ran seventy-five performances and might have made a modest go of it had not its late arrival forced it into the hot weather. In the August heat the show's scenery joined the ashes of *Nellie Bly*.

1946–1947

It was a curious season. Fine dramas and comedies were abundant and diversified. Better straight plays included *The Iceman Cometh, All My Sons, Joan of Lorraine, Another Part of the Forest, Years Ago, John Loves Mary, Present Laughter,* and *Happy Birthday.* Up at Columbus Circle, the American Repertory Theatre emerged to offer the bright, if short-lived, hope of a permanent dramatic company. As far as musicals were concerned, the season saw the new, more sober, intellectualized approach to lyric theatre settle in comfortably. A superficial survey of the season's musicals might suggest "sober" was an ill-chosen word. All through the theatrical year, angels, fairies, leprechauns, and evil spirits reveled in song and dance. The season's most successful lyric work was set in a miraculous village. Happily, the quality of the fantasy was noteworthy. In the best works, it was employed with intelligence, imagination, a respect for tone, and a sense of style. It made a concerted attempt to replace Americana as the reigning vogue. When it failed or petered out, the *Show Boat–Oklahoma!* school was assured a prolonged hegemony. But for this single season attempts to confront hard-nosed reality, regardless of approach, met with disappointment. The commercial debacle of the most seriously considered, genuinely artful of the season's musicals warned Broadway of the public's still-limited tolerance, even for these new "musical plays." The count of new musicals held relatively steady, but it wasn't until the very end of 1946 that the first interesting new piece appeared. The first smash hit of the season didn't arrive until January 1947.

The perennial ice revue opened the season. The latest edition was called **Icetime** (20 June 1946, Center). It introduced its audience to Mary, Mary, Quite Contrary, Old King Cole, and the Candy Fairy as well as taking it to Sherwood Forest and back to the Good Old Days. Faithful followers of the series rewarded it by flocking to Sixth Avenue for a full year.

Icetime's only summer competition was **Tidbits of 1946** (8 July 1946, Plymouth), a revue which a number of young professionals derived from a

Youth Theatre revue. Their cast was more experienced, a number of them refugees from the preceding season's failures. For example, The Debonairs escaped the wreckage of *Nellie Bly* to dance again, while Joey Faye, without his misbehaving duchess, brought over his "Flugle Street" number from vaudeville. Joseph Marais and Miranda's South American rhythms contrasted with Muriel Gaines's black songs. However, nothing was original or inviting enough to buck the heat, so the revue folded after one week.

Two months elapsed before the main season began with **Yours Is My Heart** (5 September 1946, Shubert). This American version of Lehar's last major operetta, *The Land of Smiles*, brought prewar Vienna's great matinee idol, Richard Tauber, to the New York stage to recreate the story of a Chinese prince's foredoomed romance with a Paris opera star. Tauber was no longer in his prime, and when throat trouble began to plague him the show was forced to close after only a month's run.

A second operetta followed twelve nights later. **Gypsy Lady** (17 September 1946, Century) was a pastiche of Victor Herbert melodies from five of his earliest works—primarily *The Fortune Teller* (26 September 1898) and *The Serenade* (16 March 1897)—set to a new book by Henry Myers. Myers's story was a half-serious, half-tongue-in-cheek reconstruction of a typical turn-of-the-century comic-opera plot. André (Gilbert Russell), the marquis of Roncevalle, proposes to Musetta (Helena Bliss), a gypsy princess, believing she was a princess royal in disguise. She is also beloved by the dashing Alvarado (John Tyers) and a strong, strapping gypsy, Sandor (George Britton), each of whom has an appropriate song with which to beguile her. In the end, blood proves stronger than wine. The show was originally done on the West Coast by Edwin Lester's excellent organization, the same group that had brought *Song of Norway* (21 August 1944) east two seasons before. It was given a sumptuous production, fine comedians (headed by Jack Goode), and superb singers. But Broadway had succumbed to its adulation of the new musical plays, and *Gypsy Lady* was patently old-fashioned—a conspicuously vulnerable target. Unkindly received, it left after ten weeks.

October's only musical was the unlikely revival of *Naughty Naught ('00)*, a novelty first offered New York 23 January 1937. But what had seemed good, harmless fun ten years back no longer appealed. The show came to naught, with only seventeen performances.

November's two musical offerings were both disappointments. Much had been hoped for from Max Gordon's production of **Park Avenue** (4 November 1946, Shubert). After all, it had a book by Nunnally Johnson (so successful in Hollywood) and George S. Kaufman, lyrics by Ira Gershwin, and music by Arthur Schwartz. The story centered upon Mrs. Sybil Bennett (Leonora Corbett), a New York socialite. She is the sort of charity worker who during the past war had busied herself with gathering "Bundles for Britain" and, now that the war is over, heads a group trying to get the bundles back. However, her real passion seems to be darting in and out of marriages—so many marriages she cannot keep the facts and figures straight. Sybil's confused family tree almost discourages a gentlemanly young Southerner, Ned Scott (Ray McDonald), from marrying her daughter, Madge (Martha Stewart). To everyone's dismay, the book proved heavy-handed, relatively humorless, and without enough plot twists to sustain it for two and a half hours; Schwartz's music sounded humdrum. The quality of the show's lyrics may be judged by the absence of a single excerpt in Kimball and Simon's fascinating collection of Gershwin material, though in his *Lyrics on Several Occasions* Ira included five examples that show flashes of his former pyrotechnics—at least on paper. *Park Avenue* made a brave nine-week bid for business. When it took its leave of Broadway, so did Ira Gershwin. Old age, death, and Hollywood continued depleting the ranks of those who had made the last great era so bright and fun-loving.

Katherine Dunham and her fine Negro ensemble thought they had a successor to *A Tropical Revue* with a second entertainment based on black dancing from around the world, **Bal Nègre** 7 November 1946, Belasco). Broadway didn't agree, at least not in sufficient numbers to keep the show running beyond two months.

The ever-popular Cinderella story was the basis of **If the Shoe Fits** (5 December 1946, Century), which tried to combine a sometimes off-color musical comedy book (the godmother became Cinderella's sporty rival) with all the primary colors of childhood. The result, in the "Fabulous Kingdom of Nicely," was often more a clash than a blend. Ingenious sets that popped out like the illustrations in some children's books were one uniquely attractive feature. Lacking the excellent casting and tinkly tunes of *The Lady of the Slipper* (28 October 1912), the show, booked way uptown, could find no audience.

Nor could **Toplitzky of Notre Dame** (26 December 1946, Century), which was quickly rushed into the same house three weeks later. The angels so admire Toplitzky's (J. Edward Bromberg) non-sectarian passion for Notre Dame's football team they send a fellow angel (Warde Donovan), who was a former football star, down to Toplitzky's Tarvern and allow the angel to help Notre Dame beat Army. When the angel, christened Angelo, falls in love with Toplitzky's daughter, his cohorts above also allow him to stay on earth happily ever after. Although both the Irish and the Jews were staunch theatregoers and the musical obviously hoped to draw support from both groups, neither appeared especially interested. When the show folded it took with it some pleasant Sammy Fain music (with words by George Marion, Jr.) such as "Love Is A Random Thing."

On the same night that *Toplitzky* opened, **Beggar's Holiday** (26 December 1946, Broadway), John Latouche and Duke Ellington's updating of *The Beggar's Opera*, premiered. In the new version Macheath became an American gangster. With the leading role played by Alfred Drake, so recently *Oklahoma!*'s Curly, the audience could muse over whether the stage gangster wasn't simply a nasty first cousin to the stage cowboy. Latouche retained the strange amalgam of the original: its viciousness, its cynicism, and its likability. It was an eminently theatrical combination. Regrettably, the tone would prove inimical to the subtle, untheatrical harmonies of Ellington's essentially intimate music. Much of Latouche's sting and Ellington's intimacy was lost in the cavernous auditorium of the large, inconvenient Broadway Theatre. As far as the public was concerned, the whole piece didn't quite come off. It survived a far from satisfactory fourteen weeks.

Bloomer Girl returned for a brief, popular-priced stay at the burgeoning City Center on 6 January 1947. (In May the Center also revived *Up in Central Park*.) But the year's first new musical waited until three nights later to raise its curtain. **Street Scene** (9 January 1947, Adelphi) was a faithful, largely uncompromising adaptation by Elmer Rice of his 1929 dramatic hit. The poet Langston Hughes composed the lyrics, and Kurt Weill created the score. Rice retained his original story, which dealt principally with the short-lived, star-crossed romance of Sam Kaplan (Brian Sullivan) and Rose Maurrant (Anne Jeffreys), and with the fatal consequences of the infidelity of Rose's mother (Polyna Stoska). These stark, poignant themes were played out on a single set depicting a seedy row of brownstones and with a number of character vignettes as a *basso ostinato*. Characters included Sam's Communist father, the impoverished, improvident Mrs. Hildebrand and her children who are about to be dispossessed, a happy Italian music teacher and his German wife, and the screams of a woman in delivery. The honesty and power of the book came as no surprise, but the excellence of Hughes's lyrics undoubtedly startled those Broadway types unfamiliar with him. The naturalness and directness of his lines were close to the ideal Hammerstein had been crusading for. Only when he attempted to revive the old "Love Nest" motif did Hughes go astray. In grasping for fresh images he overreached. The simple home for two was carried off in flights of fancy. Weill's score reflected his propensity for jittery, abbreviated musical lines and for startling, noncommercial harmonies. The music was thoughtful and appropriate, but not readily salable. Only the atypical "Moon-Faced, Starry-Eyed," sung and danced by two minor characters, Mae (Sheila Bond) and Dick (Danny Daniels), received some attention outside the theatre. *Street Scene's* fundamental somberness discouraged all but the most dedicated playgoers. The Shuberts aggravated matters, as was their wont, by giving the offbeat evening an off-the-beat theatre. *Street Scene* compiled only a modest run of 148 performances, though it soon drifted into the repertory of the New York City Opera.

The next evening a splendidly theatrical musical danced and sang its way onto the stage at the convenient 46th Street Theatre. **Finian's Rainbow** (10 January 1947, 46th St.) succeeded where *If the Shoe Fits* and *Toplitzky of Notre Dame* had failed, by making fantasy a popular alternative to the rage for Americana. No doubt this unworldliness represented as much an escape from postwar turmoil as did flight to an earlier era. But period costumes were easy to design, while workable fantasy proved tricky to sustain. As a result the vogue for fantasy persisted for just one season, although attempts to keep it alive continued with markedly less success for several ensuing seasons. Superficially, *Finian's Rainbow* resembled the early and mid-thirties musicals in its left-wing leanings as well as in its somewhat topical and satirical bent. But its politics was tempered by wit, melody, and, most of all, a fundamentally sunny, compassionate disposition toward even those it was laughing at. On the other hand, its more or less unhappy, sentimental ending suggested a certain earnestness of purpose that seemed quite contemporary.

Finian McLonergan (Albert Sharpe) arrives in America from Glocca Morra, Ireland, with his daughter, Sharon (Ella Logan), and with a crock of gold he has stolen from the leprechauns. He hopes to plant the gold at Fort Knox and watch it grow. He is pursued by Og (David Wayne), a mischievous leprechaun. They find themselves in Rainbow Valley, Missitucky, where Sharon falls in love with handsome Will Mahoney (Donald Richards). Their romance is complicated by Og, who has fallen for Sharon. Og is particularly nervous because he seems to become more and more a mortal with each passing day. But he still retains enough magic to turn the Negro-hating, xenophobic Senator Billboard Rawkins white after Sharon has inadvertently turned him black by making a wish in the presence of the crock Rawkins (Robert Pitkin), a parody of Mississippi's very real Senator Bilbo and Representative John Rankin, complains, "My whole family's been havin' trouble with immigrants ever since we *came* to this country." Og also gives the power of speech to mute Susan Mahoney (Anita Alvarez), a young lady who finds expression in dance. When Og realizes the futility of his passion for Sharon, he settles for Susan, admitting, "When I'm not near the girl I love, I love the girl I'm near." Will happily discovers that Sharon is willing to settle down with him. Sharon confess that Finian has no pot of gold and that his beloved Glocca Morra exists only in his mind. But it remains a lovely place nonetheless, and as her father heads off to continue his futile wanderings alone, she expresses the hope, "[M]ay we meet in Glocca Morra some fine day."

E. Y. Harburg and Fred Saidy's lyrics were a delight. To Og they gave an inventive speech and two delicious songs, "Something Sort Of Grandish" and "When I'm Not Near The Girl I Love." His heart was "in a pickle" and "not too partickle." A black trio singing "The Begat" could note that when the begetting got under par they gave birth to the ladies of the DAR. There were zesty Burton Lane love songs such as Woody's "If This Isn't Love"; romantic reveries such as Sharon's "Look To The Rainbow." However, the hit of the evening—the biggest hit to come from Broadway during the season—was "How Are Things In Glocca Morra?" That it was sung in the show by Scottish Miss Logan and that the stream it mentioned would have had to cover half of Ireland to touch all the towns it supposedly lapped bothered no one. The show ran out the rest of the season and all through the following one.

While Broadway gladly capitulated to fantasy all season long, only once did it allow itself the pleasure of nostalgia. The producers who had so successfully resuscitated *The Red Mill* closed January with a second Victor Herbert revival, *Sweethearts* (8 September 1913), at the Shubert. Herbert's score was faithfully retained, as was most of the original libretto, although again the dialogue was heavily doctored. The principal change was the enlargement of the part of Mikel Mikeloviz, to serve as a vehicle for the show's star, Bobby Clark. Clark fought battles with his shortened cane, while he and his cigar wreaked havoc on Zilania's laundry. The integrity of the show was in no way compromised, but its hilarity was enhanced inestimably. Mark Dawson, Gloria Story, and Robert Shackleton sang the romantic leads.

No musicals appeared in February, but three arrived in the space of four nights in March. The first was merely a one-man show, but the one man was Maurice Chevalier, and even if his actions during the war had cast a shadow on his good name, his reputation as an entertainer was unsullied. He packed the small Henry Miller for forty-six performances.

A fine revival of Oscar Straus's 1909 hit, *The Chocolate Soldier*, bowed two nights later, 12 March. Despite the excellent singing of Frances McCann as Nadina and the presence of the genial Hollywood clown Billy Gilbert and his catalogue of sneezes as Popoff, the public failed to respond. Once again part of the problem may have been that the evening was housed at the out-of-the-way Century, across from Central Park. A second part of the problem was that respect for old operettas was at its nadir, while a third reason was undoubtedly that one operetta had already bucked the disdain and captured the market, thanks as much to Bobby Clark's drawing power as to its own merits.

But the almost equally inconvenient Ziegfeld welcomed the season's biggest hit the next evening. Like *Finian's Rainbow*, **Brigadoon** (13 March 1947, Ziegfeld) told an unworldly tale. An offstage chorus set the scene, describing how two hunters lost their way one night on a murky brae. The hunters were two postwar Americans, Tommy Albright (David Brooks) and Jeff Douglass (George Keane). Something eerie pervades the woods in which they are lost—"Something," as Tommy says, "about this forest that gives me the feeling of being in a cathedral." Suddenly distant voices are heard, singing of a valley filled with love. Just as suddenly Tommy and Jeff see a village they hadn't noticed moments before. They arrive in the quaint village in the midst of a fair. In fact it is a sort of double celebration, for

two of the villagers, Jean MacLaren (Virginia Bosler) and Charlie Dalrymple (Lee Sullivan), are shortly to be married. Jean's older sister, Fiona (Marion Bell), should have married first, but Fiona has not found the right man and insists she is willing to spend her remaining days "Waitin' For My Dearie." Jeff is quickly taken in hand by the brash Meg Brockie (Pamela Britton), while Tommy and Fiona strike up a friendship. Charlie arrives. He "used to be a rovin' lad" but promises hereafter "I'll Go Home With Bonnie Jean." Tommy offers to go walking with Fiona through "The Heather On The Hill," but a storm prevents them. Meanwhile Meg has lured Jeff to a shed, where she confesses how many men have been "The Love Of My Life." Unfortunately she had not been the love of theirs. Still, she is willing to try again. At the MacLaren house Charlie arrives to sign the family Bible, and, although he knows tradition prohibits him from seeing his bride until the wedding, he begs Jean, "Come To Me, Bend To Me." Tommy, who has left an unhappy love affair in New York, is exhilarated by the charming Fiona. He feels "Almost Like Being In Love." But he is also a bit troubled. Brigadoon and the villagers are odd. They have refused to accept American money; they have never heard of telephones. When he discovers that Charlie has signed the Bible with the date "1746," he can no longer restrain himself. He demands Fiona tell him why Brigadoon is so odd. She takes him to the village schoolmaster, Mr. Lundie (William Hansen), who reveals that their minister was disturbed by encroaching outside influences and so took himself off one night to a hill beyond the town:

> There in the hush of a sleepin' world, he asked God that night to make Brigadoon an' all the people in it vanish into the Highland mist. Vanish, but not for always. It would all return jus' as it was for one day every hundred years. The people would go on leadin' their customary lives; but each day when they awakened it would be a hundred years later. An' when we awoke the next day, it was a hundred years later.

There is a catch, Mr. Lundie adds. None of the villagers may leave or the spell will be broken. But that is precisely what seems about to happen, for the churlish Harry Beaton (James Mitchell), who had hoped to marry Jean himself, threatens to depart and destroy the miracle. In a forest chase Harry is killed when Tommy inadvertently trips him.

Although Tommy feels he will be lost without Fiona and tells her of his love in "There But For You Go I" and "From This Day On," he is so upset by the killing he determines to return to New York. There his nagging girlfriend makes life unbearable. Before long Tommy and Jeff are again seated in the Scottish woods, with Tommy wondering if there is some way to make Brigadoon reappear. Once more they hear the townspeople singing of Brigadoon, and Mr. Lundie appears. As he leads Tommy away he remarks, "[W]hen ye love someone deeply anythin' is possible."

Although the show established Alan Jay Lerner and Frederick Loewe in the front ranks of the American Musical Theatre, it was not faultless. The second act sagged a bit and had a jarring change of tone in the New York scene. Moreover, the involutions of "There But For You Go I" and the pretentious solemnity of "From This Day On" were too heavy for so light and romantic a piece. But the freshness of the setting and the story counterbalanced some of the shortcomings. In having the hero kill the villain and in the rich Agnes de Mille chase-ballet, it successfully subscribed to the new stage conventions of the day. What's more, its Ado Annie–like Meg reminded some of Oklahoma! (31 March 1943). The lovely score helped popularize the work. "The Heather On The Hill" and "Almost Like Being In Love" were instant commercial hits, while Al Jolson, on his radio appearances, gave "Come To Me, Bend To Me" national recognition.

The new fashion in musical plays militated against the old collegiate musical. Nonetheless George Abbott courageously brought in **Barefoot Boy with Cheek** (3 April 1947, Martin Beck). The gag-filled Max Shulman libretto—on a par with his best-selling comic novels—described the riotous attempts of Yetta Samovar (Nancy Walker), a campus "pink," to convert all of the University of Minnesota (and especially the Alpha Cholera Fraternity) to her political thinking. She would also like to win the heart of Asa Hearthrug (Billy Redfield), but loses him to Clothilde Pfefferkorn (Ellen Hanley). Precisely why Shulman set such oddball people with oddball names on a legitimate campus is uncertain. But the brilliant clowning of Nancy Walker kept such questions from being explored. The show's glaring weakness was its songs, Sidney Lippman's only Broadway score. The fun on stage would have been enough to secure *Barefoot Boy with Cheek* a respectable run five or six

years earlier. But changing tastes and the summer heat took their toll.

NANCY WALKER was born into a theatrical family in Philadelphia on to May 1921 and christened Anna Myrtle Swoyer. Her father was a vaudevillian who used the stage name Dewey Barto. Trained at the Professional Children's School in New York, the comedienne made her debut in *Best Foot Forward*. Following a brief stint in films, she returned to Broadway in *On the Town*. Short and cynical-miened, Miss Walker excelled at wisecracking overreachers whose pretensions are quickly punctured. One critic observed that, whenever she struck an attitude, the attitude struck back.

A double bill of contemporary operas got off to an uncertain start but soon met with astonishing success. Gian Carlo Menotti's **The Telephone** and **The Medium** (1 May 1947, Barrymore) were intimate pieces ideally suited to a small legitimate playhouse. They were written in a musical idiom that was at once contemporary and readily acceptable. Although the writing was popular by serious standards, it was serious by popular measurement. Menotti kept studiously away from avant-garde composition. Moreover he told two good stories. *The Telephone* was little more than an old vaudeville sketch with only two singers. When the constant ringing of Lucy's phone prevents Ben (Frank Rogier) from proposing, he leaves, goes to a pay phone, and proposes to Lucy (Marilyn Cotlow) from there. *The Medium* recounted the last agonies of the charlatan Madam Flora (Marie Powers). She goes mad and determines to kill the evil spirit she believes has beset her. Instead she accidentally kills her deaf-mute assistant. None of the arias enjoyed a commercial vogue. But good notices, good word of mouth, and the appeal of something different allowed the bill to achieve 212 showings.

The season ended, as it began, with a new ice show. Actually much of **Icetime of 1948** (28 May 1947, Center) was held over from the previous edition. No one cared. Like its predecessor it ran a full year.

There were half a dozen highly entertaining musicals to cheer theatregoers during the season, even if all were flawed, none truly first-class. Every one of these hits gave the man in the street a song he liked to whistle; some even produced two hit songs. Yet there was an inadequacy about the scores. The hit tunes, like the shows they came from, were not the best their creators had offered. Constant propagandizing about the artfulness of the new musical play did, nonetheless, have certain interesting effects. By and large, even in the lightest popular musical comedies some additional effort was made to relate songs to plot, to give a feeling of cohesiveness and a pervasive unity of tone. However, the most obvious influence of the school of *Show Boat* and *Oklahoma!* was the setting of more and more pieces in an earlier America.

The season's first offering confirmed the vogue. **Louisiana Lady** (2 June 1947, Century) was a four-performance fiasco with a score by Monte Carlo and Alma Sanders. Carlo and Sanders had been absent from the New York scene since they suffered an even worse debacle with the single-performance run of their *Mystery Moon* (23 June 1930). They had spent most of the twenties trying to repeat the success of their *Tangerine* (9 August 1921), apparently forgetting that show owed most of its popularity to its star and an interpolation. The failure of *Louisiana Lady* may well have brought such painful truths home to them, for they never again wrote for Broadway. "When You Are Close To Me" typified the dullness of their last work. A musical version of Samuel Shipman and Kenneth Perkins's 1927 *Creoles*, *Louisiana Lady*'s setting resembled that of *Early to Bed* (17 June 1943). Convent-trained Marie-Louise (Edith Fellows) leaves Miss Browne's Finishing School to visit her mother, Madame Corday (Monica Moore), who runs a fashionable bordello in 1830 New Orleans. Madame Corday had been forced into the trade by the villainous Merluche (George Baxter), but she and her girls and customers go to great lengths to make her house seem like a home to Marie-Louise. Merluche appears, hoping to court Marie-Louise, and her life takes an ominous turn until she is rescued by a good-natured pirate.

Four months passed between the opening of *Louisiana Lady* and the premiere of the next lyric piece, **Music in My Heart** (2 October 1947, Adelphi). This "romantic musical play" was another operetta in the *Blossom Time* (29 September 1921) tradition, this time using Tchaikovsky melodies to embellish a story of his purported romance with the French singer Désirée Artot. The show made its concession to the new ballet rage right at the start, opening with a comparatively classic-style ballet entitled "The Storm," but apart from setting the mood of old St. Petersburg it had little relation to the story. A fine cast headed by Robert Carroll (Tchaikovsky), Martha Wright (Désirée), Vivienne Segal, and Charles Fredericks was the evening's pillar of strength, supporting it through its four-month run.

Under the Counter (3 October 1947, Shubert), an importation from London, could generate no interest and folded after twenty-seven showings despite the presence in the cast of Cicely Courtneidge (as a black-marketeering actress) and Wilfrid Hyde-White.

The season's biggest musical hit, **High Button Shoes** (9 October 1947, Century), dressed its conventional musical comedy book in modish period costumes. It allowed its bungling, small-time con man, Harrison Floy (Phil Silvers), to return to 1913 New Brunswick, New Jersey, and be greeted by his innocent old neighbors as an up-and-coming tycoon. He and his crony, Mr. Pontdue (Joey Faye), are embraced with special warmth by the Longstreets (Jack McCauley and Nanette Fabray). Harrison switches from selling not-quite-right automobiles to selling land. But when the townspeople discover the land is useless swamp, Floy is forced to flee. He takes the money, Pontdue, and Mrs. Longstreet's sister, Fran (Lois Lee), to Atlantic City. A wild Keystone Kop chase ensues. Fran returns to New Brunswick and to her boyfriend, the Rutgers football player, Hubert Ogglethorpe (Mark Dawson). Floy also reappears, promising to make amends. To get enough ready cash, he bets on Princeton in the forthcoming game with Rutgers, tries to get Rutgers's team to throw the match, and when Rutgers wins finds himself on the run again. The book, which Stephen Longstreet based on his semiautobiographical novel, *The Sisters Liked Them Handsome*, was not especially witty, but Phil Silvers's rough-and-tumble clowning kept audiences laughing. Miss Fabray and Jack McCauley stopped the show twice with Jule Styne's best melodies, the foot-stomping polka "Papa, Won't You Dance With Me?" and the sentimental soft-shoe "I Still Get Jealous."

Good as Styne's score was, the highlight of the evening was Jerome Robbins's uproarious Mack Sennett Ballet, in which Floy and Pontdue are chased by the villagers, bathers, Keystone Kops, and a bear. The chase ends in a jumbled pyramid of bodies capped by a flag-waving cop.

What promised to be an even bigger hit opened the next evening. **Allegro** (10 October 1947, Majestic) was Rodgers and Hammerstein's third collaboration, and the first which Hammerstein did not adapt from an older work. Instead of revising an existing, tightly knit plot, Hammerstein composed a loose, rambling chronicle recounting the life of an ordinary upper-middle-class professional. He planted a Greek-like chorus at the side of the stage to set the scenes and comment on the action. The chorus's costumes announce it is again the turn of the century—1905 in fact. The singers inform their listeners that the woman in the bed is Joseph Taylor's wife, Marjorie. Marjorie (Annamary Dickey) has just given birth to a son, Joe Jr. Joe's father (William Ching) already has plans for him to be a doctor, but Marjorie refuses to think so far ahead. Grandma assures them both that time will handle the child in its own way. We start out "foolishly small," but we're soon adult; Grandma (Muriel O'Malley) has seen it happen before, and she knows it will happen again. When Joe takes his first step the chorus exhorts him to move first one foot out, then the other foot, first foot, second foot,

first foot, second foot. Now the chorus exults that the whole world belongs to Joe. Time passes. Joe (John Battles) is ready for college. He is still a little shy and naïve with girls, but everything will come naturally in due course. After all, Dr. Taylor assures his wife, "A Fellow Needs A Girl." Joe overhears and thinks to himself, "They're funny when they're by themselves—not like a mother and a father. A fellow and a girl—like Jenny and me—almost." And all the while he is away at school he remains faithful to Jenny (Roberta Jonay), writing her, "You Are Never Away." Jenny is not completely happy waiting for Joe to get his feet on the ground, and her ambitious father is no help. Meanwhile, at school Joe halfheartedly courts other girls. His line to them in his flings is to insist they hardly know each other "So Far." In the end Jenny waits, and when Joe finishes college they marry. The chorus chants repeated good wishes to the couple. More time passes. It is the Depression, and Jenny's father has lost his business. Life is hard for a small-town doctor, and Jenny would push Joe on to bigger things. He finally acquiesces, though he knows it will sadden his parents. Joe is successful in Chicago, almost too successful. Social and professional pressures mount. To the despair of his nurse Emily (Lisa Kirk), Joe is blind to Jenny's cheating on him. Affectionately Emily complains, "The Gentleman Is A Dope." Just as he is about to accept an important new appointment, Joe finally learns that Jenny is unfaithful. Voices from his past sing out to him, and Joe declines the new post to return to his small town. Although the characterizations were reasonably good, the book and lyrics were assertively sentimental, rarely humorous, and filled with the drabness and repetition of everyday speech. Agnes de Mille was again Rodgers and Hammerstein's choreographer, but the rambling story failed to inspire any fine ballet. "So Far" and "A Fellow Needs A Girl" did become independently popular, and their success played no small part in the 315-performance run of *Allegro*.

On 30 October Edith Piaf brought a Continental vaudeville into the Playhouse for forty-four showings. After her premiere, over a month elapsed before the next musical appeared. **Caribbean Carnival** (5 December 1947, International) was a black revue filled with the lusty, exotic rhythms of Africa and Latin America. Pearl Primus paced the dancers. But Katherine Dunham had demonstrated that Broadway would rarely support an entire evening of such relentless vitality. The show survived for only eleven performances.

Six nights later a more conventional intimate revue met with immediate acclaim and inaugurated a spate of relatively successful examples of this once-popular type. For a brief time it looked as if revues might stage a comeback. But television's fast-paced, star-studded variety shows soon overwhelmed these more modest entertainments, whose quality, in any case, fell below the great offerings of bygone seasons. **Angel in the Wings** (11 December 1947, Coronet) featured the dancing and clowning of Paul and Grace Hartman, the droll monologues of Hank Ladd, and the singing of Elaine Stritch. The Hartmans, who had been seen primarily in vaudeville and nightclubs, made themselves at home in the intimate Coronet. Their sketches included a hilarious cooking demonstration in which a husband grew increasingly queasy as his wife detailed each step for frying snails in yogurt. Ladd wore a rowboat as he toured the St. Lawrence looking for Florence, whom he had lost on one of the Thousand Islands. Miss Stritch had the hit of the evening in "Civilization," in which she renounced the uncertain joys of the modern world and insisted, "Bongo, Bongo, Bongo, I don't want to leave the Congo." The song had not been written for the show, but was hastily added when it became a runaway success on the air. Its authors were the men who had written most of the songs, Carl Sigman and Bob Hilliard.

The daughter of devout Catholics, **ELAINE STRITCH** was born 2 February 1926 in Detroit, Michigan. Although schooled in drama at the New School for Social Research in New York, Stritch discovered a talent for comedy and a distinctive belting singing voice, which later matured into a smoky rasp.

A revival of *The Cradle Will Rock* (16 June 1937) played briefly over the holidays. The critics were not as harsh on the work as many of them once had been. Nevertheless, good times and the Christmas spirit made Marc Blitzstein's "angry, theatrical prank" seem especially dated. A fine cast led by Alfred Drake performed earnestly, but to no avail.

The year ended with the first postwar visit of the D'Oyly Carte Opera Company, who embarked on an eighteen-week stay 29 December, proffering such old favorites as *The Mikado, Trial by Jury, The* *Pirates of Penzance, Iolanthe, Cox and Box, H. M. S. Pinafore, The Gondoliers, The Yeomen of the Guard,* and *Patience.*

The first musical of 1948 was the season's second revue hit. **Make Mine Manhattan** (15 January 1948, Broadhurst) had sketches and lyrics by Arnold B. Horwitt and music by Richard Lewine, whose only other complete scores had been written for the Krimskys' American Music Hall pieces in the thirties. One pleasant, unexceptional number, an urban hoedown that served as the first-act finale, "Saturday Night In Central Park," enjoyed a passing vogue. But the evening's principal joys were its comedians, Joshua Shelley, David Burns, and Sid Caesar. In "Subway Song" Shelley sang a hilarious plaint of a young man who lives at one end of the subway system and whose girl lives at the other end. The marshmallowy dishes and bird-size portions served by restaurants such as Schrafft's were spoofed in "Traft's," where you can eat all night and not affect your appetite. In the show's best sketch Sid Caesar played a cocky, Wasp-named Hollywood director, come to make a film in New York. He assures the mayor that once the film is released New York will become world famous. But most of his time is spent arguing with a bystander (Burns) who would tell him how to shoot the film. The director doesn't get angry until the man makes a suggestion about the gloves a performer is wearing. At that point the director not only loses his temper, he loses his English accent as well, for if there's one thing he really knows it's the glove business. Theatregoers remembered that at least one major Hollywood mogul had once been a glovemaker. Colorfully mounted by Hassard Short, well sung, peppily danced, and superbly clowned, *Make Mine Manhattan* ran over a year.

A brassy, contemporary musical called **Look, Ma, I'm Dancin'** (29 January 1948, Adelphi) bounced in next. Jerome Robbins and George Abbott had conceived the evening as a vehicle for Nancy Walker. Miss Walker played Lily Malloy, a brewery heiress, who underwrites a ballet company, travels with it, and ultimately dances with it and modernizes it. Jerome Lawrence and Robert E. Lee's dialogue was commonplace and Hugh Martin's score facile. One song did slip away to earn some national prominence, "Shauny O'Shay," sung in the show by two lesser characters, Wotan (Don Liberto) and Snow White (Virginia Gorski). Most of the other songs were jivey and momentarily clever, but not memorable. What lifted the show above its material was

Abbott and Robbins's fast-paced staging, Robbins's dances (with Harold Lang in the main parts), and Miss Walker's inspired lunacy. At the end of the first-act finale Miss Walker fought off a stage full of dancers, grabbing a floral arrangement that an usher had brought down the aisle. She felt she was entitled to it, since she had paid for it and sent it to herself. Miss Walker and her troupe danced merrily on for just short of six months.

Beginning 20 February Gertrude Lawrence and Graham Payn sang those songs featured in Noël Coward's *Tonight at 8:30*, which was revived for a short stay, while nine nights later Maurice Chevalier returned for a second consecutive season with a one-man show.

March and April went by without producing any new musicals until the very last week of April. A black musical vaudeville starring Billie Holiday and called, appropriately, **Holiday on Broadway** (27 April 1948, Mansfield) came first. The star was gowned in scarlet, with white flowers in her hair and at her waist, and sported golden gloves. Among the leading lady's numbers were such old favorites as "Easy To Love" and "I Cover The Waterfront." Pyrotechnical drumming by Cozy Cole also won kudos.

Three nights later the season's third major revue, **Inside U.S.A.** (30 April 1948, Century), raised its curtain. The show was the most elaborate of the three and, on paper, promised to be the most exciting. John Gunther's best-seller of the same name had provided the inspiration. Beatrice Lillie and Jack Haley were returning to Broadway to be its stars, and with them came the feline dancer Valerie Bettis, handsome, strong-voiced John Tyers, and the bumptious Hoosier monologist Herb Shriner. Moss Hart, Arnold Auerbach, and Arnold B. Horwitt (of *Make Mine Manhattan*) wrote the sketches, while Howard Dietz and Arthur Schwartz were reunited to provide the songs. It became apparent as soon as the show began its tryout that its material fell short of everyone's high hopes. The lone hit to emerge from the score was the somewhat stiff, overblown "Haunted Heart," sung in the show by Tyers. Actually the lighter numbers were better. In a laundry-list song Haley enumerated, sometimes seriously, sometimes not, the main attraction of each state, concluding "Rhode Island Is Famous For You," while in the first-act finale, "First Prize At The Fair" (which Dietz considered the best song in the show), the whole cast sang of a boy who lost all the contests but nevertheless won a girl's affection. Haley and Miss Lillie

as two Indians adamantly informed palefaces, "We Won't Take It Back." Haley taught waiters how to be rude to customers, while Miss Lillie played a bitch whose snide, throwaway remarks ruin an actress's first night (she also used the actress's hairbrush to clean her shoes). The comedienne became a gay Mardi Gras participant ("cherchez la femme they were playing / I was the femme they were cherchezing") and the leader of a choral group singing an ode to Pittsburgh (where smoke gets in your eyes). Miss Bettis danced the part of a Chicago gun moll. If *Inside U.S.A.* was a disappointment, the quality of competitive revues was no better, so the show was able to run a year.

One outside event which conceivably prevented more tunes for the show from becoming popular was the ASCAP strike. Composers and lyricists withdrew radio and recording privileges until their demands for better terms were met. As a result the airwaves—long the principal method of popularizing a song—played largely uncopyrighted music, so new shows whose music was written after the strike began went temporarily or permanently unrecorded. *Inside U.S.A.* recorded its "original cast" album just before the deadline. But since it had to be produced in advance of the opening it was in the unique position of including a song cut during its tryout.

Three musicals closed out the season during the start of May. Another contemporary collegiate musical attempted to buck the trend and failed. **Hold It!** (5 May 1948, National) was the work of several young, unseasoned musical hands and showed it. The claptrap book was by Matt Brooks and Art Arthur. Their escapade began when a picture of Bobby Manville (Johnny Downs), dressed as a girl for his part in a Mask and Pudding show, is submitted to a Hollywood beauty contest. Naturally, Bobby wins and has to spend the rest of the evening explaining away his victory. In the end, his girl, Jessica (Jet McDonald), goes to Hollywood in his stead. Sam Lerner did journeyman lyrics for Gerald Marks's pleasant, inconsequential tunes, the best of which was "Always You."

The following night, 6 May, a masterwork by some old, experienced hands was revived at the Martin Beck, but by 1948 the twenties and its shows were considered frivolous and obsolete. In fact it was probably this very season, just before *Lend an Ear* (16 December 1948) came to make theatregoers reconsider, that the disdain for the era of wonderful nonsense was at its most rampant. As a result *Sally* (21 December 1920) would have probably failed under all but the most miraculous circumstances. Bambi Linn and Willie Howard were good in the roles Marilyn Miller and Leon Errol had originated, but they could not perform wonders. Worse, the producers hurt the integrity of the show by "modernizing" the book (though retaining the essentials of the original story) and by interpolating songs from other Kern shows. This new *Sally* ran a mere thirty-six times compared to 570 performances for Ziegfeld's production.

The Experimental Theatre, operating at the old Maxine Elliott, presented a triple bill on 9 May under the title **Ballet Ballads.** It was so well received it was rushed up to the Music Box. All three one-act plays had music by Jerome Moross and lyrics by John Latouche; each had a different choreographer. In each show a singer and a dancer shared the principal roles. *Susanna and the Elders* depicted the legend as retold by a parson at a revival meeting. *Willie the Weeper* was essentially a two-character piece (considering the singer and dancer who played Willie as one), in which Willie runs the gamut of drug-induced moods in his "Untidy Mind." Two songs, "Willie, The Weeper" and "Cocaine Lil," provided the idea for the sequence. *The Eccentricities of Davy Crockett* sang and danced a series of Davy's tall tales: his marriage to a mermaid, his saving his country from Halley's comet. The excitement generated by the opening and the fine reviews dissipated with the summer heat. *Ballet Ballads* folded on 10 July, providing a slightly downbeat ending for the season.

1948–1949

This was one of the greatest seasons in Broadway history. Just why so many fine shows appeared so suddenly was baffling, but Broadway was too grateful to ask questions. Although *Variety* listed only seventy-six productions, the quality and diversity of the season made it the best since the heyday of the 1920s. John Chapman, selecting the ten top works for the *Burns Mantle Best Plays* series, awarded places to *Death of a Salesman; Anne of the Thousand Days; The Madwoman of Chaillot; Detective Story; Edward, My Son; Life with Mother; Goodbye, My Fancy; Light Up the Sky; The Silver Whistle;* and *Two Blind Mice.* He could find no room for two of the American Musical Theatre's masterpieces, *Kiss Me, Kate* and *South Pacific,* not to mention other innovative, gorgeously melodic works that abounded in this theatrical year.

The season began inauspiciously on 3 June with an inept musical version of the Ichabod Crane legend called **Sleepy Hollow.** It came into the St. James, which had been occupied happily for six years with *Oklahoma!* The house found itself looking for a new tenant after just a week and a half.

The annual ice revue, **Howdy, Mr. Ice!** (24 June 1948, Center), had songs by Al Stillman and Alan Moran, but they were no different from the numbers Littlefield and Fortis had composed for the earlier ice shows. The public couldn't have cared less. It came to see the shimmering spectacle and got it. The skaters took the audience to Trinidad, to an African safari, and to the Himalayas, and introduced it to Little Bo-Peep. Patrons kept the box office happy for 406 performances.

September brought a rerun of the 1946 revival of *Show Boat,* this time at the City Center's popular prices. The same low prices prevailed when the house revived *The Medium* and *The Telephone* in December and *Carousel* in late January.

Comedian Morey Amsterdam led the bill in a revue named **Hilarities** (9 September 1948, Adelphi). The evening was little more than glorified vaudeville, although much of Amsterdam's humor would have been too bawdy for B. F. Keith. Other acts included Al Kelly in his time-tested double-talk routine and the popular radio and nightclub singer Connie Stevens. Ballroom dancers and acrobats helped fill the bill. No one found it very satisfying; *Hilarities* lasted less than two weeks.

A far more stylish, traditional revue opened six nights later. **Small Wonder** (15 September 1948, Coronet) featured a number of entertainers who would shortly receive prominence: Tom Ewell, Alice Pearce, Jack Cassidy, Mary McCarty, and Joan Diener. Some of its sketch material was by George Axelrod (who would soon write Ewell's big hit, *The Seven Year Itch*), and the dances were by Gower Champion. Unfortunately the producer went for his music to Albert Selden and to Baldwin Bergersen, who had a record of failures to his discredit and with this show departed from the Broadway scene. Their contributions were lackluster. Their best number brought Mary McCarty on stage in a cloche and a betasseled dress to sing with tongue-in-cheek longing of the "Flaming Youth" of the twenties. The song was a harbinger of a revival of interest in the decade which *Lend an Ear* shortly would stimulate. In a fetching monologue Ewell demonstrated the superiority of the Model T Ford to the human body (perhaps unconsciously furthering affection for the twenties). The talented youngsters kept the show running for 134 performances and might have had a greater success had not the higher prices postwar production costs forced on the show necessitated a relatively steep ticket charge, and had not so much better competition come along demanding its share of that dollar.

Rising production costs were such that the next two musicals lost $650,000 between them—a frightful sum for its day. There was little sympathy for the losses incurred by **Heaven on Earth** (16 September 1948, New Century), a dim-witted, banal, and unmelodic affair that ran twelve performances. It tried to be another *Finian's Rainbow*, but lacked that show's redeeming charms. James Aloysius McCarthy (Peter Lind Hayes), a Central Park horse-hack driver, befriends a young couple who are so poor they live in a tree. With the help of a pixy named Friday (Dorothy Jarnac), he sets them up in a model house. The outraged, blustering builder (David Burns) has the whole gang arrested, but McCarthy's imitation of Hollywood stars convinces the builder to let the nuts go. The score was by Jay Gorney, who was almost at the end of his career. John Murray Anderson directed it (with an uncredited assist from Eddie Dowling), and Raoul Pène du Bois designed the sets and costumes. For many, du Bois's sets were the saving grace of the evening, notably in a magnificent recreation of Central Park and in a comic, push-button-bedeviled "Hutton Home of Tomorrow." His efforts were futile; the show seemed beyond anyone's help.

Far more deserving of hearing was **Magdalena** (20 September 1948, Ziegfeld), a production by Edwin Lester's California-based group that had offered *Song of Norway* and *Gypsy Lady*. Unfortunately, all that most New Yorkers heard were arguments over the show's merit. It was indisputably the most controversial musical in several seasons. Those who admired it praised its intense, colorful score by Heitor Villa-Lobos, the distinguished Brazilian composer, its Ziegfeld-like opulence (at the Ziegfeld, appropriately), and its cast of fine singers. Its detractors decried its stolid book, the lack of obvious commercial appeal in the score, and the seemingly unnecessary lushness of its staging. The musical's principal story, set in the tropical richness of Colombia, recounted the efforts of simple, devout Maria (Dorothy Sarnoff) to convert her cocky, bus-driving fiancé, Pedro (John Raitt), to Christianity. A subplot described a revolt in an emerald mine, a general (Hugo Haas) sent to restore order, and the mistress (Irra Petina) he brings along.

Villa-Lobos made no concessions to popular taste, discarding the conventional AABA formula in favor of free-flowing melodies. Robert Wright and George Forrest saddled the songs with too strivingly poetic lyrics. For example, the title song, saluting the great river, announced the river's "mother is the snow" and her "love is the sea." The public hesitated, then decided to wait for more surefire entertainment. *Magdalena* closed after eleven weeks.

The public did not have long to wait for a more patently commercial offering. **Love Life** (7 October 1948, 46th St.) fell easily into the consciously artful patterns now in vogue. It was innovative and purposeful. Like the preceding season's *Allegro* (10 October 1947), it was essentially a chronicle, but it added an element of fantasy or allegory by following the vicissitudes of a single marriage through 150 years of American history. Instead of a Greek chorus to propel and comment on the action, simulated vaudeville turns performed "on one" between meatier scenes. The couple in question are Sam and Susan Cooper. In 1791 they are reasonably happily married, with two attractive children. As they move from 1821 to 1857 to 1890 the stresses and strain of staying together begin to tell. By the 1920s cynicism and infidelity are apparent. The second act is set entirely in the present, and the marriage is on the rocks. But a stylized minstrel show offers hope that things can be set right again. The show's philosophy was summed up in a song which kept arguing, "That's good economics, but awful bad for love." If Alan Jay Lerner's libretto was as uneven as it was loose-jointed, the show had several compelling assets. Nanette Fabray and Ray Middleton, both in top form, were the stars. And the score—not by Lerner's customary partner, Loewe, but by Kurt Weill—was delightful. The prolonged ASCAP strike deprived it of some of its deserved recognition. Still, the Coopers' caressing "Here I'll Stay" and Susan's jaunty "Green-Up Time" enjoyed some circulation, despite Lerner's still occasionally uneasy lyrics. The show displayed gaudy scenery and had the requisite ballets. Both were good, although unexceptional. The mixed critical reaction to *Love Life*'s novelty, the waning appeal of fantasy, and the stunning competition that appeared all through the season took their toll. *Love Life*'s 252-performance run would have seemed excellent ten or twenty years before, yet in a day of rising costs it meant a disappointment.

Where's Charley? (11 October 1948, St. James), a musical version of *Charley's Aunt*, was noticeably more conventional than *Love Life*. George Abbott provided the serviceable, if surprisingly leisurely, adaptation and directed the show as well. George Balanchine devised the choreography. The critics, while receptive, were not overwhelmed, and the show got off to, at best, a respectable start. There was little indication that it would run over two years. Three virtues most likely contributed to its surprising durability. Most conspicuous was its star, Ray Bolger, in the best role he ever had. His transvestite clowning was innocent good fun, and his soft-shoe routines (one performed partly atop a piano) enchanting. He was supported by a sterling cast that included Byron Palmer (Jack Chesney), Doretta Morrow (Kitty Verdun), and Allyn Ann McLerie (Amy Pettigue). Second, word soon spread that *Where's Charley?* was not only good fun; it was good clean fun. As a result the show began to profit from a youth market that Broadway had rarely tapped in recent years. With time Frank Loesser's brilliant score overrode the obstacles of the ASCAP strike. One fine ensemble number, "The New Ashmolean Marching Society And Students' Conservatory Band," showed fresh, tongue-in-cheek iconoclasm, just as offbeat counterpoints in Charlie and Amy's duet "Make A Miracle" similarly announced the arrival of an exciting new talent. Jack and Kitty's love song, "My Darling, My Darling," became one of the season's most popular ballads. In the long run, "Once In Love With Amy" has proved the enduring favorite. It was a second-act show-stopper which Bolger put over, alone in front of the show curtain, with his droll delivery and incomparable dancing. When the song became generally known, Bolger cajoled his audiences into singing along.

October's last musical was a Sigmund Romberg operetta with another of his beloved plots of thwarted love. **My Romance** (19 October 1948, Shubert) was a musical version of Edward Sheldon's 1913 hit, *Romance*. To the most likable melodies Romberg had written in a long while—they were far more in his natural style than his songs for *Up in Central Park*—the great prima donna Cavallini once again fell in love with Reverend Armstrong, and once again ran off to a life of song and celibacy rather than hinder his chances for advancement in the church. The principal roles were superbly sung by the dashing Lawrence Brooks and the ravishingly beautiful Anne Jeffreys. The Shuberts gave *My Romance* a surprisingly loving and careful mounting. In keeping with an old operetta tradition, each of the three acts employed only a single set. But reaction against the favorite forms of an earlier era was at its height. Not only did the public and critics fail to respond, but rumors were circulated suggesting one of the Shubert brothers had actually composed some of the melodies attributed to Romberg. Romberg and the Shuberts had worked together for nearly forty years, but by a sad coincidence *My Romance* was the last Romberg score heard in his lifetime and the last show to carry the banner "The Messrs Shubert present." The musical struggled through an unhappy run of three months.

A joyous, uninhibitedly old-fashioned musical followed and met with a livelier reception, thanks to a brightly colored Mike Todd production, the sidesplitting antics of Bobby Clark, and, to a lesser extent because of the ASCAP strike, a superior Jimmy McHugh score. Coming in an election year the show's plot could be considered topical, though it was set four years in the future, just after the 1952 election. **As the Girls Go** (13 November 1948, Winter Garden) imagined what would happen with the election of the first woman President, Lucille Thompson Wellington (Irene Rich). But though the show occasionally touched on politics and changes a woman would bring about (there are now Secret

Service Women attending her), it was largely a bur-lesque romp in which her husband, Waldo (Clark), the First Gentleman, cavorts with all the beauti-ful, scantily clad girls in sight, and helps and hin-ders his son Kenny's (Bill Callahan) romance with Kathy Robinson (Betty Jane Watson). One of its biggest laughs came from a topical sight gag when Waldo, sitting in a barber's chair, was asked if a visi-tor who has always wanted to see the inside of the White House might look at the room. When the visitor arrived he proved to be an actor impersonat-ing Thomas Dewey, who had just suffered the most stunning upset in American history in his second bid for election. More than any other musical score of the season Jimmy McHugh's excellent tunes (with lively Harold Adamson lyrics) were caught up in and hurt by the ASCAP strike. By the time the strike was settled and recordings could come out again, there were newer and equally good or better songs for art-ists to work with. McHugh's material was the best he had done since the original *Blackbirds* (9 May 1928). It went from solid ballads such as Kenny's "You Say The Nicest Things, Baby" and his "I Got Lucky In The Rain" to the lusty title song, sung by Clark and the chorus. Clark also helped put over a show-stopping comic number in "It Takes A Woman To Take A Man." Adamson and McHugh even gave a hint of things to come with "Rock, Rock, Rock!" In another way the show forewarned of an ominous turn. It cost $340,000 to mount, forcing Todd to ask a then unheard-of $7.20 top price. Though it ran nearly a year, it failed to pay off. The years of a kind Broadway economy were gone.

A consistently funny revue that had originated in Pittsburgh, **Lend an Ear** (16 December 1948, National), made stars of Yvonne Adair, Gene Nelson, William Eythe, and, most of all, a tower-ing amazon of a girl with big, wide-open eyes, Carol Channing. The show aimed its darts at every kind of absurdity and always struck dead-center. Two prominent celebrities who live by what columnists say about them are forced to book the next plane when they read they are going on vacation. When a second newspaper announces they are expecting a baby, they have to take a later flight. An opera was performed without its music. But the highlight of the evening was a devastating spoof of a 1926-style musical comedy. It was, according to the compère, the real thing, since "The Gladiola Girl" had sent out a number of road companies and one of them had never come back. Now that road company, its performers not looking a day older than when they

began, had been located and was offered as the first-act finale. The songs included all the requisite types that were once a stock-in-trade of musical comedy—"Where Is The She For Me?," "In Our Teeny Little Weeny Nest," and "Doin' The Old Yahoo Step." The parody was riotous, but some-how also managed to convey the fun and zest of the old shows. Its success marked the beginning of a turnabout in feelings toward shows of the preced-ing generation. Interestingly, in this American bur-lesque the boy and girl are both poor but pretend to be rich. When the British travesty *The Boy Friend* (30 September 1954) arrived several years later, the lovers were lordly but pretending to be poor. Gower Champion staged the dancing. The show's only weak spot was its commonplace score, typified by "Who Hit Me?" Audiences lent an ear to its mirth, and the revue ran a year on its gales of laughter.

On 29 December, Benjamin Britten's opera **The Rape of Lucretia** came to the Ziegfeld. In the days before operetta or musical comedy as we know it, operas were often performed at regular Broadway houses as well as at the opera house of the period. But with grand opera largely a museum piece and with commercial audiences attuned to lighter enter-tainment, operas rarely trod the legitimate boards anymore. Menotti operas had been notable excep-tions, but Britten's work was not welcomed by Broadway.

Some of the wildest welcomes of the season were extended to the next evening's opening, **Kiss Me, Kate** (30 December 1948, New Century). This musical, built around Shakespeare's *The Taming of the Shrew*, was Cole Porter's masterwork, although the excellent libretto of Bella and Samuel Spewack played a large part in its success. So, for that matter, did co-producer Lemuel Ayers's gay sets and an impec-cable cast led by Alfred Drake, Patricia Morison, Lisa Kirk, and Harold Lang. The action begins on the stage of Ford's Theatre in Baltimore, where Fred Graham (Drake) has just finished a run-through of his musical production of *The Taming of the Shrew*. Opening night is only hours away and nerves are on edge. Fred is feuding with his costar and ex-wife, Lilli Vanessi (Miss Morison), while Lois Lane (Miss Kirk) is unhappy about the progress of her romance with her fellow player, Bill Calhoun (Lang). Lilli's maid, Hattie (Annabelle Hill), has seen it all before and knows what it's like, "Another Op'nin', Another Show." When Bill appears, he confesses to Lois he has been gambling. Not only has he lost all his money, he has signed Graham's name to an IOU.

All Lois can ask is "Why Can't You Behave?" Meanwhile in Lilli's dressing room Fred and Lilli are fighting over each other's supposed rudeness. They are both still in love with each other, but neither will admit it. Lilli, in fact, has gone so far as to become engaged to Harrison Howell (Denis Green), a wealthy, influential Washington figure:

Lilli: Did I show you the star sapphire Harrison
    sent me? It was his mother's engagement ring.
Fred: His mother must have worn it on her big toe.
Lilli: And now it's mine!
Fred: Congratulations!
Lilli: Do you know what day this is, Fred? Our
    anniversary, and you forgot.
Fred: What anniversary?
Lilli: The first anniversary of our divorce.

This sets them reminiscing, and they remember their first show together, an impossible operetta in which they were both part of the chorus. There was a waltz in it, "Wunderbar," and they find themselves singing and dancing the song. Two surprisingly benevolent-looking gunmen enter Fred's dressing room. They have come to collect on his IOU. Fred cannot recall signing any. The men are understanding. They will give him time to refresh his memory and come back later. In Lilli's dressing room she is presented with flowers, which she recognizes as her wedding bouquet. Joyful that Fred has not forgotten, she confesses privately she remains "So In Love" with him. But Fred had meant the flowers for Lois. He arrives in time to prevent Lilli from reading the card but not from stashing it away in her costume. The play within a play begins. In "We Open In Venice" Katharine, Petruchio, Bianca, and Lucentio (Lilli, Fred, Lois, and Bill) proclaim they are merely strolling players, not film stars like Louis B. Mayer's. Their itinerary takes them from Venice around the map of Italy and back to Venice. Petruchio arrives to seek the hand of Katharine, knowing full well her reputation. She in no way hides her feeling, insisting, "I Hate Men." Petruchio woos her with "Were Thine That Special Face." But Katharine is not moved. Lilli, however, is. She has had a moment to pull out the card and read it. She and Fred use the roughhouse action of the play to indulge in a real slugging match, ending with Fred's giving her a solid spanking. Off stage Lilli announces she is leaving the show at once. Fred seems unable to force her to stay, until the hoods return. Seeing his chance, he acknowledges the baffling IOU, but tells the gunmen he will have

to renege if Lilli walks out and the show closes. Lilli stays, at gunpoint. During intermission the actors and their dressers head for the alley to escape the heat. Some of them would like to go off on dates tonight, but they recognize it's "Too Darn Hot," even for that. Back on stage, all is not going well for Petruchio, and he sighs, "Where Is The Life That Late I Led?" He longs for the women in his past. Harrison Howell appears in answer to an urgent distress call from Lilli. Before he can see her, he meets Lois. It seems they have met before, although at that time he told her his name was Harold:

Lois: Harold, don't you remember? In front of the
    Harvard Club. I had something in my eye, and
    you took me to Atlantic City to take it out?

But Lois understands the situation and promises to be discreet. Bill, on the other hand, has overheard and wonders aloud what kind of girl he's going with. Lois reassures him that she's "Always True To You In My Fashion." Harrison tells Lilli he will take her away from all this hubbub and indignity. As he details their future life together, it becomes clear he will take her so far away from everything she will die of boredom. When he falls asleep in the midst of drawing his picture of the future, Lilli and Fred sneak out. They meet the gunmen, who tell them their boss has been done away with and the IOU is no longer binding. Before they leave, the hoods, confessing they have become fascinated by the bard, urge, "Brush Up Your Shakespeare." They suggest if you quote "Othella" your girl "will think you're a helluva fella." The performance resumes. Katharine admits, "I Am Ashamed That Women Are So Simple," and bids all women be humble, upon which Petruchio happily bids her, "Kiss Me, Kate."

In *Kiss Me, Kate* the ideals that musical plays had been striving for were triumphantly realized. Here was a book with remarkably lifelike, believable protagonists, with every character having a sensible and important bearing on the plot, with every song perfectly related to the action and more often than not advancing it. Here were lyrics and dialogue that never cheapened themselves for effect, that remained literate and witty or touching throughout. The day after the show opened, long lines formed at the out-of-the-way Century (then called New Century), and the show romped merrily through 1,070 performances.

Two revues appeared in January 1949. Both missed the mark, even if both had runs that a decade or two before would have been considered satisfactory. **Along Fifth Avenue** (13 January 1949, Broadhurst) enlisted the aid of Nancy Walker, Jackie Gleason, Carol Bruce, Hank Ladd, and several other excellent featured performers, then failed to give any of them first-class material. Miss Walker had one of the better comic numbers, which allowed her to tell Sigmund Freud where to go, "If This Is Glamour!"; and Carol Bruce was assigned the most memorable of Gordon Jenkins's ballads, "The Best Time Of Day." But the rest of Jenkins's songs—and Jenkins was a leading arranger and composer of "semiclassic" pieces—were run-of-the-mill. The cast did the best it could, and its best was good enough to keep the show on the boards into the summer.

Paul and Grace Hartman scuttled the intimacy which had been so meaningful a part of their success with *Angel in the Wings* and helped Anthony Brady Farrell fill his large converted motion picture theatre with an elaborate, cumbersome revue, **All for Love** (22 January 1949, Mark Hellinger). Max Shulman was listed as "editor" of the sketches, but he could come up with nothing funnier than the skit in which the stars brought to life two gigantic mannequins that graced a large Times Square advertisement at the time. Nothing in the musical department approached the songs for the Hartmans' first show. Farrell forced the run in hopes the revue would catch on. When it didn't, he withdrew it after 141 performances.

The season's most eagerly awaited musical was virtually its last. **South Pacific** (7 April 1949, Majestic) was based on two of the stories from James A. Michener's Pulitzer Prize–winning book, *Tales of the South Pacific*. The book was adapted by Oscar Hammerstein II and Joshua Logan, while Hammerstein supplied lyrics for Richard Rodgers's music. The stars were Mary Martin and the Metropolitan Opera's great basso, Ezio Pinza. Despite the general disappointment with Rodgers and Hammerstein's previous musical, *Allegro* (10 October 1947), the new show opened to the largest advance sale in Broadway history, and despite some easily assailable shortcomings, it proved a glorious musical romance and was received with open arms. Logan and Hammerstein based their material on "Our Heroine," which told of the romance of Emile de Becque and an American nurse, Nellie Forbush, and on "Fo' Dolla," which recounted the love affair between an American lieutenant and a native girl. The two tales were tied together by having de Becque and the lieutenant undertake a wartime mission together. As the curtain rises, de Becque's two Eurasian children are singing a French children's ditty. De Becque (Pinza) is preparing to entertain an American nurse he has met and taken a liking to, although they are obviously worlds apart in more ways than nationality. Nellie (Miss Martin) describes herself as "A Cockeyed Optimist." She is optimistic even though she is still single and not getting any younger. But de Becque knows she has no reason for concern; she will meet her man "Some Enchanted Evening." For the boys who are fighting the war, things are not as simple nor as promising. Yet, at times the war doesn't seem as bothersome as the absence of the girls they have left at home. Jokingly, they pin their affection on an elderly, rough-talking harridan from a neighboring island, "Bloody Mary." Such playfulness doesn't assuage their real loneliness, and they are forced to admit, "There Is Nothin' Like a Dame." Bloody Mary (Juanita Hall) would like to marry her daughter, Liat (Betta St. John), to one of the Americans, especially Lt. Joseph Cable (William Tabbert). To entice the boys she extols the mysterious magic of her island home, "Bali Ha'i." For the moment a more urgent matter demands attention. A secret base must be established on a nearby enemy-held island. Cable is to lead the attempt, but he would like de Becque, who has lived on the island for years, to assist. De Becque demurs. He is growing fond of Nellie and would prefer to be with her. But Nellie is uncertain. In her shower she sings, "I'm Gonna Wash That Man Right Outa My Hair." However, a brief meeting with de Becque changes her thoughts completely, and she acknowledges her revised feelings, rejoicing she's in love with "A Wonderful Guy." With the mission postponed, Cable finds time to meet Liat. When the language barrier makes conversation all but impossible, he conveys his emotions in song, telling Liat, who can comprehend the gist of his statements, that she is "Younger Than Springtime." Racial and national differences emerge when Bloody Mary presses the two young lovers to pursue their affair. Cable confesses he could not marry an Asian. Bloody Mary stalks off in a fury, taking Liat with her. Cable is shaken. He receives a further jolt when he overhears Nellie explain to Emile why she cannot continue to see him:

Nellie: It means that I can't marry you. Do you
    understand? I can't marry you.

Emile: Nellie—Because of my children?

Nellie: Not because of your children. They're sweet.

Emile: It is their Polynesian mother then—their mother and I.

Nellie: ... Yes. I can't help it. It isn't as if I could give you a good reason. There is no reason. This is emotional. This is something that is born in me.

Cable concludes prejudices are not natural, "You've Got To Be Carefully Taught." Emile takes it all more philosophically, ruing in "This Nearly Was Mine" the paradise that has slipped through his fingers. With Nellie apparently out of his life, de Becque agrees to participate in the mission. Cable is killed. But on returning Emile finds Nellie has reconsidered. They sit down to discuss their future as the little French ditty that opened the evening closes it.

The faults in the evening were obvious, and, by and large, they were Hammerstein's. While he invented such felicitous phrases as "corny as Kansas in August," which enjoyed universal acclaim, many of the lyrics strove too hard, resulting in an affected simplicity. There was more than the usual repetition of lines. To some extent Hammerstein's old argument for the integrity of the whole suffered some setbacks when it was learned that "Younger Than Springtime" had been written for *Allegro* and interpolated in the new work, where, it must be admitted, it fit quite well. Nor was there really a place or need in a romantic work for the preaching of "Carefully Taught." Hammerstein's preachments got the show into trouble when it toured the South. It could also be argued that *South Pacific*, more than the earlier Rodgers and Hammerstein pieces, demonstrated that the new genre really represented the natural contemporary American evolution of the older European operetta. Although almost all the characters were Americans, three principals were not. And the setting was distinctly exotic. The rousing men's choruses were the best that had been offered since the days of Teutonic drinking songs, while the tremendously popular "A Wonderful Guy," with its beat repeated and emphasized, suggested much the same style. Because most popular singers could not properly handle the fully arioso melodies of the older works, Rodgers had to temper his love songs. Yet here and there a suggestion of the older melodic line remained evident. None of this detracts from the overriding excellence of the work.

There were two unforgettable performances in the show. Pinza brought to de Becque a manly yet graceful authority. If his great basso voice was no longer equal to Mozart, it was nevertheless far and away superior to anything else heard on Broadway. His falsetto high note at the end of "Some Enchanted Evening" brought storms of applause. Miss Martin's Nellie was apple-pie American, yet she kept Nellie's prejudices from seeming mean or parochial. The zest with which she imbued Nellie was mirrored in Logan's fluid staging and Jo Mielziner's clever deployment of sets, which allowed each scene to blend into the next without any pause.

Rodgers's richly textured, enthrallingly melodic songs made the show's score the most popular in years. Several million copies of its sheet music were sold. One technological development increased substantially the raging popularity of both the work and its music. *South Pacific*'s arrival more or less coincided with the advent of LP records, allowing buyers to take home on a single disc an original cast singing virtually all of a show's songs. *South Pacific*'s album has been described as a "blockbuster." Actually Americans had been buying original-cast albums with some regularity ever since Decca's *Oklahoma!* Moreover, the English—so often leading the way in the musical theatre—had been dutifully putting original London casts on record since the turn of the century. This resulted in the odd situation of a number of great American musicals recorded for posterity not in their homeland with their original Broadway casts, but in England with West End players. But all these older 78s were breakable and cumbersome. The new plastic 33s opened a whole new prospect of easy preservation and easier listening.

The show ran just short of 2,000 performances in New York while its road company and London company played long runs as well. When, in the following season, the Pulitzer Prize judges could find no play of outstanding merit, they resorted to a technicality in their calendar and awarded the prize to *South Pacific*. It was only the second musical to win the award.

The very last offering of the season was **Howdy, Mr. Ice of 1950** (26 May 1949, Center). One spectacle number was done all in pink. A red, white, and blue number saluted "The Forty-Eight States," while a gaudy set took spectators to jazzy New Orleans. The show proved to be the very last offering of the Center Theatre as well. Although the show ran 430 performances, increasing costs were making it less attractive to its producers and the house. The series was discontinued and the auditorium converted into additional offices for Rockefeller Center.

1949–1950

Only an incorrigible optimist of Nellie Forbush's stripe could have hoped for another season as brilliant as the preceding one. In the twenties such a hope might have been reasonable, but, as the theatre entered the fifties, sustained achievement was too much to expect. Production costs were soaring, and chances to recoup these higher costs were hurt by increasing competition, especially from television. Once a viewer had paid for his set, he could sit comfortably at home and watch a variety of entertainments at virtually no expense. Moreover, television and movies continued to drain away talent from the living theatre, especially vital, young talent with new styles and fresh approaches. The remaining talent continued to be beset by higher taxes on their success, discouraging the creativity of an earlier day.

Still, the season was interesting. There were three fascinating attempts to nudge the American Musical Theatre into the realm of higher art. None was fully realized artistically, and all three proved commercial disappointments. Indeed, there was only one solid box office hit, and that was a patently old-fashioned musical comedy glossed over with some modern sounds.

On 1 July, having played free and loose with playhouses in New York and across the country during earlier entertainments, Olsen and Johnson brought their latest bit of mayhem, **Funzapoppin,** into the huge Madison Square Garden. At a $2.50 top their noisy, vulgar "outhouse humor" pleased the pair's loyalists for thirty-one performances. One not-so-loyal reviewer noted, "*South Pacific*" costs more, but it's a better show.

The traditional season opened with a Spanish revue, **Cabalgata** (7 July 1949, Broadway), that arrived in Manhattan after an extensive tour of Latin America. Its material was culled largely from the folk songs and dances of Spain. With the growing interest in folklore of all sorts, the show was able to run to the beginning of September.

The season's opener should have been **Miss Liberty** (15 July 1949, Imperial), which was scheduled to open patriotically on 4 July, three nights before *Cabalgata*. It had been announced months earlier and gave every promise of becoming another bright light in the glowing Broadway scene. Its score was by Irving Berlin, whose *This Is the Army* (4 July

1942) had opened on an earlier Fourth of July. Its book was by two of America's most intelligent and resourceful playwrights, Robert Sherwood and Moss Hart. The cast included the popular Eddie Albert, as well as two of the most promising young ladies available: Mary McCarty, a comedienne who had called attention to herself in *Small Wonder* (15 September 1948); and *Where's Charley?*'s (11 October 1948) fine ballerina, Allyn McLerie. The musical built a fictitious romance around the presentation of the Statue of Liberty to America by France. A circulation war between Bennett's *Herald* and Pulitzer's *World* provided further color. Horace Miller (Albert) is a bungling newspaper photographer who is fired from his job after he takes the wrong photographs at the ceremony where Pulitzer presents a check for the base of "The Most Expensive Statue In The World." Horace decides he is "A Little Fish In A Big Pond" who would do better at home. His girlfriend, Maisie Dell (Miss McCarty), suggests he go to France instead and find the model for the statue. Horace agrees, but when he arrives in Paris he mistakes another model, Monique Dupont (Miss McLerie), for the one Bartholdi actually used. He befriends her by suggesting, "Let's Take An Old-Fashioned Walk." Back in the States, Maisie makes plans for the sweet domesticity of "Homework," unaware Horace is finding Monique increasingly attractive. He attempts to overcome the language barrier by professing there is "Just One Way To Say I Love You." Maisie persuades Bennett to underwrite a tour for Monique. Only when Monique arrives in New York to unexpected fanfare and hoopla does she perceive there has been a mistake. When she tells Horace and Maisie, they decide they must bluff it through. Bartholdi arrives, and the error is in danger of being exposed. Bennett would have Horace, Maisie, and Monique arrested, but Pulitzer proves more understanding. He bails Horace out of jail and offers him a job. At the dedication of the statue, all the voices are raised in song, singing a musical hymn based on Emma Lazarus's poem that began, "Give Me Your Tired, Your Poor."

Berlin's score moved from one pleasantry to another, including a lovely production waltz, "Paris Wakes Up And Smiles." The veteran Ethel Griffies stopped the show nightly with her raffish "Only For Americans," which argued, "[T]he price that's more is only for Americans from the U.S.A." But the public embraced none of the songs and, worse, perceived the book as seriously flawed. It was surprisingly humorless and heavy-handed, and, most surprisingly of all, clumsy. The characters of both leading women were sympathetically drawn, and yet, with only one hero, one girl had to be left out in the cold. That the girl turned out to be the American homebody seemed particularly unpalatable to many in the audience. When *Miss Liberty* finally made its delayed opening on 15 July, expressions of disappointment were universal. Only its large advance sale, coupled with a lack of competition, allowed it to run until April.

A good many New Yorkers also may have had great expectations for Ken Murray's **Blackouts of 1949** (6 September 1949, Ziegfeld). It had run for years at the El Capitan in Hollywood and looked forward to a reasonably long New York stay. But what the Coast had viewed as good, not always clean, fun Broadway frowned on as cheap, hackneyed vaudeville. Besides a standard assortment of turns that included ballroom dancers, knockabout clowns, and a monologist (who impersonated all the characters in his retelling of *Oliver Twist*), Murray presented a small band of show girls he labeled "glamourlovelies." Some not so young or shapely "elderlovelies" revived old songs such as "Silver Threads Among The Gold" and "Put On Your Old Gray Bonnet." Murray even staged a Tarzan jungle fantasy reminiscent of the twenties' jungle scenes. When Broadway showed its disdain, the show headed back west after fifty-one performances.

S. M. Chartock met with a similar disappointment when he attempted to establish a permanent Gilbert and Sullivan repertory company on this side of the Atlantic. Although the four shows—*The Mikado, The Pirates of Penzance, Trial by Jury,* and *H. M. S. Pinafore*—were tastefully mounted and beautifully sung, the critics bewailed the absence of a proper flair and style. Mr. Chartock withdrew his players after three fruitless weeks.

Touch and Go (13 October 1949, Broadhurst) was a pleasant revue that had first seen the footlights at Catholic University in Washington, D.C. The show had attractive music by Jay Gorney, especially the plaintive ballad "Things Will Be All Right (In A Hundred Years)," and the ingratiatingly childlike "Funny Old Little Old World." Lyrics and sketches were by the husband-and-wife team of Walter and Jean Kerr. Mrs. Kerr went on to write several successful comedies, and Mr. Kerr became New York's leading drama critic. Their efforts in the revue were generally frothy and fun, culminating in an uproarious spoof of the haggard, bedraggled heroines so voguish at the moment on the screen. Three

supposed queens of the silver screen, dressed like skid-row derelicts, proclaimed the secret to success was to "Be A Mess." In "Great Dane a-Comin'" *Hamlet* was staged as a Rodgers and Hammerstein musical, with real Rodgers melodies sung to revised lyrics on the order of "You're A Queer One, Dear Ophelia." A Tennessee Williams–style Cinderella, hidden from the prince by her wicked stepsisters, disclosed her whereabouts by flushing a toilet. Unfortunately, the resurgence in the popularity of the revue form had begun to wane. *Touch and Go* compiled a not altogether satisfactory run of 176 performances.

The last two nights of October witnessed the unveiling of two of the most daring, uncompromising musicals of the season. **Lost in the Stars** (30 October 1949, Music Box) was a musical version of Alan Paton's poetic and popular novel *Cry, the Beloved Country,* adapted for the stage by the distinguished playwright Maxwell Anderson, with music by Kurt Weill. Together they told and sang a tragic tale. A black South African preacher, Stephen Kumalo (Todd Duncan), and his wife, Grace (Gertrude Jeanette), grow concerned when they receive no letters from their son, Absalom (Julian Mayfield), who has gone to Johannesburg. They decide to go to the big city to seek him out. But they cannot find him, for Absalom is living with his pregnant girlfriend and keeping bad company in a rough part of town. To get money for himself and his girl, Absalom participates in a holdup and kills young, white, liberal Arthur Jarvis. Alone with the news that his son has been arrested, the minister broods on our insignificance and unhappiness, on his realization that we are all "Lost In The Stars." The preacher returns to Johannesburg to see his son. He also meets Absalom's girl, Irina (Inez Matthews). When he overhears her singing "Stay Well," his sympathies for her are enlisted. He agrees to marry them in prison. In the courtroom Absalom's confederates lie about their own guilt and are acquitted. Absalom will not lie, and he is sentenced to be hanged. The minister takes Irina with him back to the village. A quarter of an hour before Absalom is to die, James Jarvis (Leslie Banks) appears at the minister's house. He has not approved his son's liberal racial views, but he is not without compassion. He, too, has lost a son and can understand Stephen's feelings. Moreover he was touched by Absalom's rigid honesty in court:

Stephen: You think well of my son?
Jarvis: I tried not to. But you and I have never had
    to face what Absalom faced there. A man can

hardly do better than he did when he stood before the judge. Stay in Ndotsheni, Stephen, stay with those who cried out to you in the chapel. You have something to give them that nobody else can give them. And you can be proud of Absalom.

Stephen: And he is forgiven, and I am forgiven?
Jarvis: Let us forgive each other.
Stephen: Umnumzana-umnumzana!
Jarvis: Let us be neighbors. Let us be friends.

Unfortunately the show had its problems. Much of the action or commentary on it was provided by a Greek-like chorus, very like the one employed in *Allegro* (10 October 1947). This gave a static quality to what should have been a compelling drive. The florid richness of South African speech as conveyed by both Paton and Anderson sometimes seemed unnatural and stilted. Furthermore, there was the unyielding starkness of the story itself. All argued against commercial acceptance, and while *Lost in the Stars* ran until 1 July it was not considered a commercial success. There are three footnotes. The title song, which fit so beautifully into the work, was actually written several years before. And Weill returned to a practice that had been largely neglected on Broadway for forty years or so: He orchestrated his own work. Sadly, it was the last new Weill work heard on Broadway. He died suddenly during the run of the show, on 3 April.

An even more uncompromising musical opened the following night. **Regina** (31 October 1949, 46th St.) was an operatic rendering of Lillian Hellman's saga of interfamily struggle, *The Little Foxes.* Both the libretto and the score were by Marc Blitzstein. A superb cast featured Brenda Lewis (Birdie), Jane Pickens (Regina), George Lipton (Ben), Russell Nype (Leo), Priscilla Gillette (Alexandra), and William Warfield (Cal). As they had for *Porgy and Bess,* many newspapers sent both their drama and music critics to opening night. By and large the music critics found more to enjoy than the drama critics. To some extent this judgment was vindicated. The show struggled along for fifty-six performances. It was later added to the repertory of the New York City Opera and enjoyed a limited popularity. Had the piece been better, it might have had a longer, possibly even a successful, Broadway run. Its failure was not a reflection on the limits of acceptance so much as a reflection of *Regina's* own inadequacies. Curiously, *Lost in the Stars* also found its way into the New York City Opera's repertory, but its long

stretches of dialogue were better served in the intimacy of a legitimate playhouse. Its failure to survive—as a highly praised revival revealed—again was due largely to its own shortcomings.

Anthony Brady Farrell, still determined to mount a success at his Mark Hellinger, brought in **Texas, Li'l Darlin'** (25 November 1949, Hellinger) just before Thanksgiving. He lured Kenny Delmar, who hit the height of his popularity as the blustering Senator Claghorn on Fred Allen's radio show, to star, and got the popular musician Robert Emmett Dolan to set Johnny Mercer's words to song. John Whedon and Sam Moore did the book. Their story followed the adventures of Hominy Smith, a psalm-singing, grassroots Texas politician whose cushy berth is jeopardized by a crusading veteran and who looks at the possibility of kicking himself upstairs to the presidency. It was a conventional evening—too conventional for many. Oddly enough its one song to achieve even a passing popularity had an unconventional sixteen-bar chorus and depended for much of its interest, as so many songs had two generations back, on the lyrics of its verse. The song was a revival-meeting hymn called "The Big Movie Show In The Sky."

The season's runaway hit was 1949's last musical. It, too, was conventional, but it was conventional with a flair. **Gentlemen Prefer Blondes** (8 December 1949, Ziegfeld) was a musical version of Anita Loos's best-selling novel of more than two decades earlier. The twenties had started to come back into vogue with the affectionate travesty "The Gladiola Girl" in the preceding year's *Lend an Ear.* Two of the principals from that revue were signed for the leading female roles. Carol Channing attained a stardom she was never to lose as Lorelei Lee, and Yvonne Adair played her friend Dorothy Shaw.

Lorelei leaves her doting button manufacturer, Gus Esmond (Jack McCauley), to sail for Europe with Dorothy. Dorothy finds a stable love affair with Philadelphia's stuffy Henry Spoffbrd (Eric Brotherson). Meanwhile Lorelei's coquetry wangles a tiara from the dithering Sir Francis Beekman (Rex Evans) and gets her into romantic complications with a zipper mogul, Josephus Gage (George S. Irving). Gus learns of all her playing around and is about to throw her over, but Lorelei is resourceful enough not only to go on to a successful nightclub act but to win back Gus's affection. From the opening scene recording the wildly festive mayhem as the *Ile de France* is about to sail from the French Line pier, through the scenes depicting the high spots of

Paris, to a glittering finale at the Central Park Casino, the show was splashily mounted, which helped conceal the mediocrity of the book. Jule Styne's music was brasher and colder than his *High Button Shoes* score. He did not attempt to recapture faithfully the tones and beats of the twenties, but rather to hint at them in a thoroughly contemporary collection of songs. The show's hit ballad, "Bye, Bye, Baby," sung by Gus, quietly underscored an essentially lively melody with a touch of nostalgia. The real hits of the evening were Lorelei's two comic numbers. Lorelei recounted her rise from humble beginnings into the lap of luxury as "A Little Girl From Little Rock." As she noted, in New York, unlike Arkansas, the man a girl calls daddy ain't her "paw." She expressed her philosophy in "Diamonds Are A Girl's Best Friend," concluding that even in old age when a woman is bent over or plagued with stiff knees, she can still "stand straight at Tiffany's." Miss Channing's Lorelei was a far cry from the diminutive, shy-seeming girl of Miss Loos's book, but no one cared. She regaled audiences at the Ziegfeld for 740 performances.

CAROL CHANNING was born in Seattle, Washington, on 31 January 1921. Her early Broadway appearances included *No for an Answer* and *Proof Through the Night.* She served as Eve Arden's understudy in *Let's Face It.* A statuesque, wide-eyed blonde with a voice that could change abruptly from a babyish squeak to a baritone growl, Miss Channing's wildly gyrating flapper chorus girl in *Lend an Ear* assured her a special niche in Broadway's pantheon.

January 1950 brought in three musicals, all flops. The first was the most offbeat and had the shortest run. **Happy as Larry** (6 January 1950, Coronet) starred Burgess Meredith as an Irish tailor who is allowed to return to his grandfather's time to learn which of his grandfather's two wives was really the better one. *Heaven on Earth* (16 September 1948) had suggested that *Finian's Rainbow* (10 January 1947) had exhausted the demand for whimsical Irish tales. *Happy as Larry* confirmed it. It was gone after just three showings.

Two revues attested to the waning interest in that genre, though both were admittedly inferior, and neither would have probably been more than a modest success a few seasons back. **Alive and Kicking** (17 January 1950, Winter Garden) was fittingly strong in the dance department. Jack Cole devised the choreography, and his young dancers included two names soon to be celebrated, Bobby Van and Gwen Verdon. Cole's bizarrely conceived ballets, eclectically mixing classical, African, Hindu, and other movements, were "Abou Ben Adhem," "Calypso Celebration," "Propinquity," and "Cole Scuttle Blues." Cole himself was the principal dancer, performing with an "unearthly fire and flickering motion—his fingers dance as wildly as his feet." For comedy, Jack Gilford gave up cigarettes only to spend his day inhaling his neighbors' smoke; David Burns became a grandiloquent speaker at a literary lunch; while Leonore Lonergan made free with her tears and her handkerchief in a spoof of Edith Piaf. The skits by popular writers and comedians such as Henry Morgan, Jerome Chodorov, and Joseph Stein, like the songs by such composers as Sammy Fain and Harold Rome, were lackluster and readily forgettable. The show ran eight weeks.

Dance Me a Song (20 January 1950, Royale) could not survive even that long. While it, too, offered some fine dancing by Joan McCracken and Bob Fosse, it was neither its dances nor its songs that won most critics' kudos. The drily humorous monologues of shy Wally Cox stole the show. Cox dissected the not very bright mind of a soda jerk and documented the history of a hopelessly inept juvenile delinquent. Unfortunately, he was not well enough known to prop up the evening singlehandedly.

The faltering Theatre Guild and Anthony Brady Farrell tried to change their luck with a musical version of an old Guild success, *The Pursuit of Happiness.* The original play had been written by two of the Guild's top executives, Lawrence Langner and Armina Marshall. Herbert and Dorothy Fields and Rouben Mamoulian collaborated on the adaptation. As she had in the straight-play version, Jo Kirkland (Nanette Fabray) dons trousers and takes up arms after she is driven from her home by redcoats during the Revolution. She even uncovers a spy. By the end of the evening, she and a Hessian named Franz (Georges Guétary), who was originally thought to be the spy, are fondly embracing. Miss Fields did the lyrics for the songs by Morton Gould, a respected arranger and composer in other fields. The book was cumbersome, and Miss Fields's straight lyrics often startlingly naïve and inept. She saluted the entrance of Washington with "Mr. Washington, Uncle George," and allowed Franz to suggest, in what was meant to be the evening's hit love song, that all he wanted in life was "A Cow And A Plow And A Frau." (Guétary's French accent broke through as incongruously as Ella Logan's Scottish burr had in *Finian's Rainbow*.) Nanette Fabray was able to enhance the lilt of "That's My Fella," a song not unlike *South Pacific*'s "A Wonderful Guy." What little real success the evening enjoyed came from Pearl Bailey's clowning as a servant named Connecticut and her singing of two songs. She expressed her outlook on life in general with some felicitous Fields rhymes in "Nothin' For Nothin'" and stopped the show with her feelings on romance in "There Must Be Somethin' Better Than Love" (where she wondered out loud, even if there was, would anyone want it). Even with its attractive cast and a Guild subscription to bolster its early weeks, **Arms and the Girl** (2 February 1950, 46th St.) was added to the list of the season's failures after a 134-performance try.

The cold war in all its brutality was brought home by Gian Carlo Menotti in his opera **The Consul** (15 March 1950, Barrymore). Although none of its music had popular appeal outside the theatre and although its tale was rank topical melodrama, it was the most cohesive, fully achieved of the season's more serious offerings, and the most successful. It narrated Magda Sorel's attempt to get visas that would allow her persecuted family to flee from an unnamed Iron Curtain Country. Thwarted by red tape, she commits suicide. The evening was superbly sung by a cast of fine artists, several of whom went on to renown at the Metropolitan, the New York City Opera, or Broadway. These included Cornell MacNeil, Patricia Neway (Magda), Marie Powers, Gloria Lane, and George Jongeyans, who soon changed his name to George Gaynes. *The Consul* was voted the best musical of the season by the New York drama critics and ran eight months.

A weak musical that tried to make a whole evening out of a single joke premiered eight nights later. Vivienne Segal and Stuart Erwin were the stars of **Great to Be Alive** (23 March 1950, Winter Garden), which featured a fine cast including Bambi Linn, Rod Alexander, Valerie Bettis, and Mark Dawson. The plot told of how Mrs. Leslie Butterfield buys an old mansion from Woodrow Twigg. Woodrow has lived there happily among ghosts who will show themselves and will speak only to virgins. The ghosts— who danced the evening's ballets—and Woodrow

are on the best of terms. He and Mrs. Butterfield strike up a friendship. By the end of the evening Woodrow can no longer see or hear the ghosts. The material, by inexperienced writers, was humdrum; the cast was helpless, and the musical left after fifty-two showings.

Katherine Dunham brought a titleless dance revue into the Broadway Theatre on 19 April under Sol Hurok's aegis and pleased her admirers for thirty-seven performances.

The first revival of James Barrie's *Peter Pan* in more than a score of years delighted young and old at the Imperial, starting on the 24th. Jean Arthur and screen villain Boris Karloff made a joyful Peter and Captain Hook. Although Leonard Bernstein was lauded for his incidental music and new songs (including lyrics), critics did not suggest his writing turned the old favorite into an honest-to-goodness musical. The production ran ten months.

The season's last new revue was another Paul and Grace Hartman creation. The Hartmans came before the footlights at the opening to explain the title, **Tickets Please** (27 April 1950, Coronet). It seems they hadn't been able to devise what they felt would be an appealing name. When they attended a performance of *South Pacific*, they heard a crush of people in the lobby crying, "Tickets, please," and decided since the expression seemed to be on everyone's tongue it would make a voguish title. They also decided that if they insulted the critics, the aisle-sitters would be too embarrassed to pan the show. So they promptly insulted the newsmen and proceeded confidently with the rest of the entertainment. The Hartmans had wisely returned to the intimacy of *Angel in the Wings* (11 December 1947). Insults or no, their drollery was appealing, and the show ran until Thanksgiving. Its success suggested that an occasional revue, even one such as this with no music of any merit, could find an audience.

May came in hand in hand with a popular-priced return of *Brigadoon* at the City Center.

The season ended with the failure of another interesting attempt at something novel, a musical version of Goldoni's **The Liar** (18 May 1950, Broadhurst). Alfred Drake collaborated on the book and staged the evening, with an excellent ensemble that included William Eythe, Joshua Shelly, Russell Collins, Paula Laurence, and Melville Cooper. Lelio (Eythe) is an amorous sixteenth-century rake whose romances have forced him to flee from Rome to Venice. There he leads the Venetians to believe he is the King of Sicily. His lies and loves keep him in hot water all night. John Mundy did the music, and the co-librettist, Edward Eager, did the lyrics. The elements wouldn't hold together, and *The Liar* folded on 27 May.

1950–1951

So many good musicals opened during the 1950–1951 season, Broadway couldn't handle the crush. With rising prices and alternate sources of diversion, potential patrons became increasingly choosy. To a large extent they chose wisely. The most fully realized shows were the biggest hits. On the other hand, several better-than-average shows, while still faulty, were not able to run long enough to pay off their investments. The season also seemed to suggest that the appeal of Americana had dwindled. The one good show to turn back the clock to an earlier America was one of the better works that failed. For an instant the season may have also suggested that the revue had more life in it than local Cassandras would believe, although the Cassandras turned out to be right. Revues were moribund, even if Americana was not. One further point of interest was ominous in its implications. All the better shows were by older figures. The youngest, Frank Loesser, had just turned forty.

The very first show of the season, **Michael Todd's Peep Show** (28 June 1950, Winter Garden), was the revue that won the longest run. It was a confused affair. At times it was lavish in its mountings, at times tawdry. Strippers were headed by a long-legged New Orleans favorite, Christine. Skits made no pretense at high-minded wit or satire; they were strictly gag-filled pieces brought over from the dying burlesque wheels. Most of the clowns who performed them were drafted from the same circuits. They included such nonlegitimate comics as "Peanuts" Mann, "Bozo" Snyder, and "Red" Marshall. For his songs Todd went to Sammy Fain, Jule Styne, Harold Rome, and the King of Thailand. The King's contribution was "Blue Night," but the only song to appeal to the public was Styne's "Stay With The Happy People." After the opening, Todd was forced to modify some striptease and off-color material, but he was still correct in thinking there would be an audience for even such mildly censored shenanigans.

The musical theatre jumped from the ridiculous to the serious with a revival at the Arena (where the audience surrounded the performers) of Menotti's double bill *The Medium* and *The Telephone* (1 May 1947). The works proved as effective in the new

house as on a proscenium stage, and they added no performances to their record.

No musicals arrived in August or September, but two came in a week apart in the first half of October. **Pardon Our French** (5 October 1950, Broadway) was another Olsen and Johnson revue, graced with music by the distinguished Victor Young. Regrettably, Young's melodic gifts eluded him for the moment. The public had had enough of Olsen and Johnson's peculiar brand of zaniness, although the whole evening aimed a bit higher than their earlier efforts. The comedians went so far as to let a ballet, "Venezia and Her Three Lovers," finish without a comic interruption. Theatregoers were not interested, and the show was withdrawn after 100 performances.

One reason the public may not have been all that interested was the imminent opening of **Call Me Madam** (12 October 1950, Imperial). News from the tryout indicated that Irving Berlin had come up with another smash score for Ethel Merman and that Howard Lindsay and Russel Crouse had given her a first-class libretto. In a way *Call Me Madam* was a reversion to the topical musicals of the thirties, for it was no secret that its heroine was patterned after Perle Mesta, the Washington hostess. President Truman had appointed Mrs. Mesta minister to Luxembourg. Nonetheless, Lindsay and Crouse insisted in the program that the show was "laid in two mythical countries. One is called Lichtenburg, the other is the United States of America." In Washington, Sally Adams has just been appointed ambassador, largely, as she confesses, because she is "The Hostess With The Mostes' On The Ball." Otherwise, her credentials are meager. She is amazed, for example, that the landscape is not the same color as it is on the map. Even her efforts at a simple curtsey are ludicrous. Such gaucheries fail to faze her, for she knows she has large sums of money to distribute, and she's not above donating them freely once she falls in love with Lichtenburg's prime minister, Cosmo Constantin (Paul Lukas). Of course, she will not buy his affections, since she subscribes to that old-fashioned idea of "Marrying For Love." Hers is not the only romance blossoming. Although he doesn't realize it, her handsome, Ivy League assistant, Kenneth Gibson (Russell Nype), has fallen for Lichtenburg's Princess Maria (Galina Talva). After watching the natives dance "The Ocarina," he tentatively conveys his feeling by suggesting, since "It's A Lovely Day Today," the princess and he might work together on whatever she has planned. The course of these lovers will not run smoothly if the opposition, led by Sebastian Sebastian (Henry Lascoe), has its way. When the machinations of the other side seem to wreck Cosmo and Sally's ambitions as well as their romance, Sally stalwartly tells Cosmo she wants only what's best for him—and she is convinced she would be "The Best Thing For You." She also has to hold Kenneth's hand, for he is displaying symptoms he doesn't understand, but which she recognizes. "You're Just In Love," she counsels. The opposition succeeds in wangling Sally's recall, but not before everything else has turned out happily for both pairs of lovers. Out-of-town praises were echoed when *Call Me Madam* opened in New York. "You're Just In Love" received four or five encores a night, a thing long unheard of in the more reserved atmosphere of the postwar theatre. It was a two-part song patterned after "Simple Melody" from *Watch Your Step* (8 December 1914). This old-timer had recently enjoyed a successful revival beyond its original popularity thanks to a recording by Bing Crosby and his son Gary. Several of Berlin's other songs were almost as much in demand. One number, "They Like Ike," became popular until the networks banned it when Eisenhower became a serious candidate for President. The Republicans played it often during the 1952 campaign, and it became as popular a campaign song as any written in the century. The show ran a year and a half, then toured.

November's first arrival, **The Barrier** (2 November 1950, Broadhurst), was a four-performance flop. Many critics viewed this work, with book and lyrics by Langston Hughes (who based his writing on his earlier play *Mulatto*) and music by Jan Meyerowitz as opera, a conclusion perhaps underscored by its star, the great baritone Lawrence Tibbett. Repeating the 1935 drama, when a Georgia plantation owner, Col. Norwood (Tibbett), attempts to discipline his half-breed son (Wilton Clary), who is putting on "white airs," the young man strangles his father. He then commits suicide before a lynch mob can reach him.

November had only one other musical, but it was a far bigger success than even *Call Me Madam*. It was, in fact, one of the masterworks of the American Musical Theatre. **Guys and Dolls** (24 November 1950, 46th St.) was a sassy, irreverent love poem of lowlife in New York. Jo Swerling and Abe Burrows's book was based on stories and characters of Damon Runyon, particularly "The Idyll of Miss Sarah Brown."

ABE BURROWS (Abram Borowitz) was born in New York City on 18 December 1910 (six months after the birth of *Guys and Dolls's* composer). Before entering the entertainment field he had studied to be a doctor and an accountant and had spent several years in selling. Burrows received his apprenticeship as a summer entertainer in the Catskills. He was a successful writer of radio scripts for over a decade and was perhaps even better known as an author and performer of unusual party songs, such as "The Girl With The Three Blue Eyes."

Frank Loesser created the songs, and George S. Kaufman staged the piece. The principals were either unknown when the show opened or at best moderately celebrated: Sam Levene, Robert Alda, Vivian Blaine, and Isabel Bigley. At least for a few seasons thereafter they could all write their own meal tickets. The show opens with a ballet depicting the hustle and bustle of Manhattan's netherworld: pickpockets, hookers, sandwich men, and packaged tourists. Three scruffy horseplayers arrive and in a "Fugue For Tinhorns" argue their selections. A Salvation Army Mission band appears, lead by Sister Sarah (Miss Bigley), a sinfully beautiful young girl. She exhorts those who would listen (and there are few) to "Follow The Fold," promising, "Put down the bottle and we'll say no more." One of the horseplayers wonders out loud "why a refined doll like her is mixed up in the Mission dodge," and meets with the response, "Maybe she owns a piece of the Mission." Nathan Detroit (Levene) enters. He runs a crap game, but because of a breaking police scandal (and by convenient coincidence New York was having one of its periodic police scandals when *Guys and Dolls* opened) cops have been cracking down. Nathan bemoans to his would-be players, "I'm having terrible trouble. Everybody's scared on account of that lousy Brannigan." When he discovers he has made his pronouncement within earshot of the detective he is quick to explain to him, "I hope you didn't think I was talking about you. There are other lousy Brannigans." Nathan tells his friends he is trying to find one thousand dollars to rent the Biltmore Garage. One way or another he will come up with a place for "The Oldest Established"—"the oldest established permanent floating crap game in New York." He is especially anxious to resume when he learns Sky Masterson (Alda) is in town. Young, handsome Sky is the highest player of all. Knowing Sky's betting proclivities, Nathan determines to bet Sky a thousand on a sure thing. But Sky, when he appears, tells Nathan of a warning Sky's father once gave—bet on a sure thing and "You are going to wind up with an earful of cider." They get to talking about girls. Sky scoffs at Nathan for his loyalty to his girlfriend, Adelaide (Miss Blaine). To Sky, "all dolls are the same." Nathan wants to know why Sky hasn't a girl of his own, and Sky counters he can pick them up wherever he goes, even in Havana, where he is headed. "Not real high-class dolls," Nathan counters. When Sky boasts he can have any doll he goes after, Nathan gleefully bets him a thousand dollars he's wrong. The bet seems irresistible to Sky. He accepts. Just then the Mission band is heard, and when it appears Nathan demands that Sky take Sister Sarah to Havana. All Sky can reply is, "Cider!" In the Mission Sky promises to deliver Sarah "one dozen genuine sinners" if she will have dinner with him. She seems ready to accept until he tells her the meal is in Havana. Gamblers, she announces, are not her cup of tea. Sky snarlingly remarks she wants a breakfast-eating Brooks Brothers type. But Sarah is unmoved. She responds that when her love comes along, "I'll Know." When Sky kisses her he is rewarded with a slap. He leaves, offering to return "in case you want to take a crack at the other cheek." At the Hot Box nightclub, Nathan's Adelaide and the Hot Box Farmerettes are entertaining the customers with an appropriate yokelish song, "A Bushel And A Peck." When the show is over, and Nathan and Adelaide are alone, Adelaide reveals she has not been able to admit to her mother that she and Nathan have been engaged fourteen years. During that period she has written her mother that they have been married, and at intervals has announced the births of five children. The deception is telling on Adelaide. She has developed a chronic cold, and her doctor has given her a book to explain the illness. She reads from it:

The average unmarried female, basically insecure
Due to some frustration, may react
With psychosomatic symptoms, difficult to endure,
Affecting the upper respiratory tract.
In other words, just from waiting around
For the plain little band of gold,
A person can develop a cold.

The crapshooters are concerned not only about their game but about the effects the battle of the sexes, of the "Guys And Dolls," will have on it. Sky learns that General Matilda B. Cartwright is going to close the Mission for lack of attendance. When he repeats his offer of a dozen sinners to the general, she is so enthusiastic Sarah can do nothing but go along. The Mission band marches through, and when Nathan, who has remarked on Sky's absence, notices Sarah is not in the group he collapses on a crapshooter's shoulder.

Masterson and Sarah have indeed gone to Havana, and Sarah has had enough disguised drinks to proclaim she would go "ding, dong," "If I Were A Bell." By four in the morning they are back in Manhattan. Sky confesses this is "My Time Of Day." The two also confess, "I've Never Been In Love Before." Just then the police arrive and the gangsters pour out of the Mission. The belief that she's been duped throws cold water on Sarah's newfound feelings. On a lonely street beside an open manhole Sarah stops to rest with an old Mission helper. She would forget Sky, but the old man (Pat Rooney) isn't sure that's really the wisest thing for her. He tells her, "More I Can Not Wish You" than that she find her own true love that day. Sky appears to remind her he will keep his part of the bargain. He will have twelve sinners at that evening's meeting. When she rebuffs him, his thoughts turn to the crap game. Nathan has found an outlandish spot for it—down in the manhole! Masterson arrives at the game and, begging "Luck Be A Lady" tonight, rolls the dice. The results become evident when twelve forlorn gamblers are seen slinking toward the Mission. As the gamblers settle down for the service, Brannigan crashes in. He is made to sit and join the others. Nicely-Nicely (Stubby Kaye), one of the gamblers, is asked for his confession. He responds with a rousing revivalist anthem, "Sit Down, You're Rocking The Boat," relating his crapshooting on the way to the Pearly Gates. Brannigan then appeals to Sarah to testify to what she saw the previous night, but Sarah has undergone another change of heart and insists she saw nothing. With Brannigan out of the way, Nathan allows that he, too, has made a bet and lost. As a result he must take a certain young lady on a long-postponed trip. Sarah and Adelaide meet and discover they share the same philosophy, "Marry The Man Today"—and change him later. Sky appears in a Mission uniform, announcing he and Sarah are married. Nathan has a fit of sneezing. Its implications do not go unnoticed by Adelaide.

The most popular song from the show was "A Bushel And A Peck," one of the two nightclub numbers that had the least pertinence to the plot. "If I Were A Bell" and "I've Never Been In Love Before" both profited from some passing attention. But the score was not the work's principal forte. *Guys and Dolls's* strength was the wit and appropriateness of its lyrics, which fit so neatly into the mirth and movement of the book. This "Fable of Broadway" offered a tonal and structural cohesion rare in the annals of the American Musical Theatre. *Guys and Dolls*—sparked initially by Levene's and Miss Blaine's deliriously droll performances—ran just short of three years.

A "musical novelty" was the first of December's three lyric offerings. **Let's Make an Opera** (13 December 1950, Golden) had book and lyrics by Eric Crozier and music by Benjamin Britten. It asked its audience to participate as a group of children and their teachers created an opera about a chimneysweep who gets stuck in a chimney and has to be rescued from a wicked master. It was the sort of entertainment that two generations before would have been brought in precisely at this holiday season to profit from what was at that time a dependable children's market. The market had long since withered away, so the show was taken from the boards after five performances.

A big, bustling revue, **Bless You All** (14 December 1950, Hellinger) offered three fine comedians, Jules Munshin, Mary McCarty, and Pearl Bailey; a graceful dancer, Valerie Bettis; and the handsome leading singer of *Where's Charley?* (11 October 1948), Byron Palmer. All it lacked was the material to allow its fine talent to shine. It travestied *Peter Pan* and spoofed the Tennessee Williams–Carson McCullers school of writing in a sketch, "Southern Fried Chekhov," and in a song, "Don't Wanna Write About The South." In "Little Things (Meant So Much To Me)" Miss McCarty explained how her husband's daily insults and jibes had finally driven her to murder. The most interesting bit was the first-act finale, which suggested that someday political campaigns would be conducted largely on television and showed the programming used in the candidacy of Joe Gabriel Blow (Munshin). (Washington and Lincoln give testimonials as if they were advertising soap.) It was not half so funny or horrific as real televised campaigns a few years later.

December's last musical was **Out of This World** (21 December 1950, New Century). It reunited Cole Porter with the producers and designers of *Kiss Me, Kate* (30 December 1948). Porter composed a lovely score; co-producer Lemuel Ayers designed some of the most spacious and eye-filling settings Broadway had seen—settings that gave Mt. Olympus a star-spangled grandeur the ancient gods might have envied. Porter and his producers arrived at one inspired piece of casting, bringing Charlotte Greenwood out of retirement to play the goddess Juno. In most years that might have been enough to make a go of it. But as fine new musicals continued to arrive, *Out of This World*, stranded far uptown, found it was surviving largely on its advance sale. When business dropped at the beginning of spring, it was forced to close, a twenty-week failure. Indeed, there were things not right enough about the evening. Dwight Taylor and Reginald Lawrence's book, similar to the Jean Giraudoux–S. N. Behrman success *Amphitryon 38*, could not recapture the airy grace and sophisticated wit of the comedy. Nor was all of the casting ideal. The basic story remained. Jupiter (George Jongeyans) falls in love with a newly wed mortal, Helen (Priscilla Gillette), and sends Mercury (William Redfield) to earth to arrange a tryst. In the musical, unlike the play, the mortals live in modern-day Greece, and when Juno rushes to earth to pursue her husband, she comes into confrontation with a harmlessly snarling gangster, Niki Skolianos (David Burns). In the end, having had a successful fling, Jupiter goes back to Olympus with his spouse, and the earthly Helen is left to resume her more mundane marriage. Porter's score was diverse and melodic but inevitably met with unkind comparisons to his *Kiss Me, Kate* material. Ironically the song that has proven the most popular, "From This Moment On," was cut during the Philadelphia tryout. Admittedly Helen's beguine, "I Am Loved," sounded too much like a revision of *Kate's* "So In Love," but Porter's gifts and versatility were ingratiatingly displayed. Jupiter's opening number, "I, Jupiter," contained some of Porter's most impish rhymes, such as "sassy air" and "brassiere." In one of Porter's most endearing ballads Mercury begged the audience to "Use Your Imagination." The rest of the score ranged from Juno and Niki's exhilarating "Climb Up The Mountain" to Helen's lilting "Where, Oh Where," and Jupiter's lush, suave "Hark To The Song Of The Night," which demonstrated Porter's ability to make an obsolete expression such as "Hark" seem at home in a contemporary setting. However, for most theatregoers the triumph of the evening was the joyous cavorting of Charlotte Greenwood. Forty years after her first Broadway appearance she still retained her regal bearing, the glow in her eyes, and her incredible loose-jointed, high-kicking eccentric dances. She brought down the house nightly singing and dancing a fetching Porter ditty, "Nobody's Chasing Me."

No new musicals opened in January of 1951, but on the 29th the D'Oyly Carte began a four-week visit presenting the most popular of the Gilbert and Sullivan repertory.

Something called **Jotham Valley** (6 February 1951, 48th St.) told of how a feud between two brothers wreaks havoc on their small community. Written and presented by the Moral Rearmament movement, it was dismissed as an amateur botch by those critics who deigned to notice it.

On 19 February, the same night the D'Oyly Carte began a one week-run of *Cox and Box* and *The Pirates of Penzance*, a revue called **Razzle Dazzle** opened at the theatre-in-the-round Arena. It was scheduled for an unlimited run but lasted no longer than the final D'Oyly Carte presentation. Besides the novelty of a revue with the audience surrounding the cast, the piece attempted a sketch that continued on and off throughout the evening. It was a travesty on the popular movie *All About Eve* and featured the droll little comedienne Dorothy Greener. But the diminutive Miss Greener's herculean efforts were insufficient to keep the show alive.

Another outstanding entry, **The King and I** (29 March 1951, St. James) was based on Margaret Langdon's novel *Anna and the King of Siam*, which had already been made into a successful movie. Rodgers and Hammerstein had cautiously moved away from the Americana they had made the rage. In their previous offering, *South Pacific* (7 April 1949), they had placed their Americans on an exotic island. Now, though they once again rushed back to the nineteenth century they had ignored in *South Pacific* and just missed touching in *Allegro* (10 October 1947), they set all their action in the colorful but alien world of Siam, peopling most of their cast of characters with Siamese natives. Actually, their breakaway wasn't total, for they seized on an incident in the novel to excuse a lengthy ballet based on *Uncle Tom's Cabin*. But essentially the evening represented a distinct change in color and tone. To some extent this change was probably the inspiration of the show's star, Gertrude Lawrence, who brought the story to Rodgers and Hammerstein and asked them to create a vehicle for her. The show was the only one they ever devised around the talents of a specific performer. Hammerstein faithfully

held to the story of Anna Leonowens's arrival at the court of the Siamese king to teach his children and of her making the king her most important pupil. A nervous Anna debarks in Siam in the 1860s, but she openly confesses her fears, acknowledging that to bury them, "I Whistle A Happy Tune." One of the king's concubines, Tuptim (Doretta Morrow), accepts him as "My Lord And Master," although in secret she loves the handsome Lun Tha (Larry Douglas). Anna compassionately greets all the hopeful sweethearts, "Hello, Young Lovers." The king (Yul Brynner), however, is less tolerant and understanding. Anna's ways and Anna's teachings alternately amuse and exasperate him. They are, in fact, "A Puzzlement." But there is no denying Anna's flair with the youngsters of the royal family, and she tells them she enjoys "Getting To Know You." Sadly, this light-heartedness is denied Tuptim and Lun Tha, who lament, "We Kiss In A Shadow." When the king's unpredictable tantrums disrupt the court and her teachings, the infuriated Anna asks, "Shall I Tell You What I Think Of You?" and before the king can answer does tell him. But his head wife, Lady Thiang (Dorothy Sarnoff), begs Anna's forbearance. The king can be cruel at times, while at other times he will do or say "Something Wonderful." He displays his cruelty when he discovers the furtive affair between Tuptim and Lun Tha. Before they are dragged to their deaths each lover laments "I Have Dreamed" in vain. Even if she cannot bring them back to life, Anna does ultimately prevail on the king to establish a more humane rule. They grow closer together. When Anna asks the king, "Shall We Dance?" he accepts. But the king is fatally stricken. On his deathbed he implores his son to follow the wisdom Anna has attempted to impart.

The long evening, patently sentimental and at times archly humorous, was made even longer by the ballet "The Small House Of Uncle Thomas," an attempt by the Siamese to interpret Harriet Beecher Stowe's novel. But if Hammerstein and choreographer Jerome Robbins sometimes were long-winded, they were still too professional to let the show become insufferable. Moreover, the show was stunningly mounted in glittering golden Oriental sets by Jo Mielziner. Gertrude Lawrence, who contracted first hepatitis, then cancer, during the run and died, was an impeccable Anna, and Yul Brynner was catapulted to stardom for his imperious, physical performance as the king. More than anything else, Rodgers's soaringly beautiful score gave the evening its glow. For his fine singers he was able to write as much arioso music as the market would tolerate, while for Miss Lawrence he wrote gay, simple, appealingly sentimental melodies. Half a dozen songs from the show quickly became standards. (One of these, "Getting To Know You," was originally from *South Pacific*, where "Younger Than Springtime" replaced it.) The show ran 1,246 performances, forty-six more than *Guys and Dolls*, just as the romantic *South Pacific* outran the witty *Kiss Me, Kate*. It could be argued that the forty-six-performance difference was insignificant, but it must also be remembered that *The King and I* played in a larger house and had a higher break-even figure to maintain. It would seem to confirm, even if only in a small way, that the American public continued to prefer the sentimentality of the operetta tradition to the best wit of the musical comedy form.

April's two musicals opened one night apart in the middle of the month. **Make a Wish** (18 April 1951, Winter Garden) was a musical version of Ferenc Molnar's *The Good Fairy*. It had songs by Hugh Martin and a book by Preston Sturges (whom Abe Burrows assisted without public credit when the show received bad notices in its Philadelphia tryout). The evening depicted the adventures of Janette (Nanette Fabray), a French orphan on a tour of Paris, who breaks away from her group to visit a Paris not included in guided tours. Courted by a middle-aged millionaire, Marius (Melville Cooper), she ultimately settles for a penniless young artist, Paul (Stephen Douglass). A secondary love interest allowed Helen Gallagher and Harold Lang to bring Gower Champion's challenging choreography to life. Once again an impressive array of fine talent was unable to save weak material, so *Make a Wish* was withdrawn after 103 performances.

An even sadder failure was **A Tree Grows in Brooklyn** (19 April 1951, Alvin), for it was a funny, melodic entertainment, marvelously cast, opulently mounted, and greeted with generally favorable notices. It even managed to run 270 performances, but since it was unable to repay its original investment, it ended on the debit side of the ledger. As its title revealed, it was based on Betty Smith's phenomenal best-seller. Miss Smith collaborated with George Abbott to produce a libretto that retained the basic story and flavor of her book, while Dorothy Fields and Arthur Schwartz combined to create fitting and beautiful songs. To some extent the show may have suffered because a movie version of the novel had already been released (although the same situation clearly left *The King and I* unaffected) and because

the vogue for Americana may have been overplayed. The piece's underlying, inevitable melancholy may also have told against it. Primarily, it suffered because of the tremendous competition it had to buck at a time when the theatre could no longer support so many good attractions. *A Tree Grows in Brooklyn* brought to life again the star-crossed love of Katie (Marcia Van Dyke) for the ne'er-do-well Johnny Nolan (Johnny Johnston). Johnny could swear, "I'm Like A New Broom," and promise, "I'll Buy You A Star," but he was too unstable to keep a job or even his sobriety. This didn't stop Katie from imploring, "Make The Man Love Me," in hopes that her love would somehow reform him. This tragic love story was played out against the background of the equally unsuccessful love life of the wistfully comic Aunt Cissy (Shirley Booth), who years ago unwittingly entered into a bigamous marriage. She nonetheless longs for her faithless husband until one day he suddenly reappears and she sees him with new eyes. Although the music was probably the most beguiling Schwartz had written since *The Band Wagon*, the score never really became popular. Schwartz's tunes covered a wide variety of styles, from the rollicking polka of Katie's "Look Who's Dancing," to the bittersweet lilt of Cissy's "Love Is The Reason," to the perfect period flavor of the chorus's waltz, "If You Haven't Got A Sweetheart," to a thoroughly contemporary yet in no way inappropriate ballad such as "Make The Man Love Me." Dorothy Fields's lyrics were her best in a long while, too. Words, music, and star met in a perfect match when Shirley Booth stopped the show with reminiscences of her departed spouse, "He Had Refinement" ("He never came down to dinner without his shirt was on"). Miss Booth, who had spent most of her career as a wisecracking comedienne, had shown unsuspected dramatic abilities the preceding season in *Come Back, Little Sheba*. The role of Cissy allowed her to parade both sides of her remarkable talent to great advantage.

An offbeat musical with a libretto by the team that did *Finian's Rainbow* (10 January 1947), E. Y. Harburg and Fred Saidy, had been a smash hit in its Philadelphia tryout, but the New York reviewers were as critical as those in Philadelphia had been enthusiastic. Both sets of critics were probably extreme. **Flahooley** (14 May 1951, Broadhurst) had an ear-pleasing score and a clever idea for a book. It was delightfully staged with a capital cast that starred Barbara Cook, Jerome Courtland, Ernest Truex, Yma Sumac, and the Baird puppets. The basic idea of the book dealt with the unprecedented sales generated by a laughing doll on a market glutted with dolls that cry. Unfortunately, the book got out of hand. Miss Sumac had a voice with an abnormal range, and her three songs with no lyrics and no real relevance to the story bogged down the action. Moreover a subplot of Arab intrigue had to be created to justify bringing her on stage. A genie not unlike the leprechaun of *Finian's Rainbow* was also involved, and given a pleasant song, "The Springtime Cometh," that reminded too many people of the superior "Something Sort Of Grandish" from the earlier show. At the height of the McCarthy era the librettists added still another turn to the story by having a shrill, reactionary group, the Capsul-anti, attack the unheard-of happiness the new doll is spreading. Big business was also satirized. All through the evening B. G. Bigelow (Truex), head of the vast B. G. Bigelow, Inc., rails against the unethical practices of his competitor, A.E.I.O.U. (and sometimes Y. and W.) Schwartz, only to discover that he owns his competition. Along the way, the charming original concept got buried. Buried with the show were Sammy Fain's gay, childlike melodies and romantic ballads including the title song, "Here's To Your Illusions," "Who Says There Is No Santa Claus?," "He's Only Wonderful," and "The World Is Your Balloon"—all of which, except the title song, were sung by Miss Cook and Courtland. The show folded after eight weeks. A revised version called *Jollyanna*, starring Bobby Clark, was later presented on the West Coast. But it, too, missed the requisite innocence and failed.

The season ended on 29 May when *Oklahoma!* cheered Broadway with a return engagement. No major names were featured.

SCENE TWO

Increasing Problems—Lowering Standards, 1951–1965

1951–1952

Had some of the preceding season's shows, such as *Out of This World* and *A Tree Grows in Brooklyn*, waited until the 1951–1952 season to make their appearance, they would have met little serious competition. The American Musical Theatre sank to an abysmal state. Only nine new musicals were offered. This was the lowest figure since well back into the nineteenth century, and this was out of a total of seventy-two plays. What's more, two of these were Yiddish-American revues not usually seen in regular legitimate houses. Furthermore not a single one of the five new book shows realized a return on its investment. Four revivals and one return engagement swelled the lyric total a bit. Yet even here only one of the shows was a success.

The season opened on 13 June with **Courtin' Time** (13 June 1951, National), a musical version of Eden Phillpotts's play *The Farmer's Wife*. The show had encountered star problems on its tryout. Its original star, Lloyd Nolan, was replaced by the show's director, Alfred Drake. Drake chose not to wear two hats, and Joe E. Brown was called in to assume the lead. Brown tempered his usually broad style to play Samuel Rillings, a middle-aged, widowed Maine farmer in the late 1890s. The story of Rillings's up-and-down courtship of his housekeeper, Araminta (Billie Worth), made a charming rustic idyll. Its songs by Jack Lawrence and Don Walker matched the tenor of its book. They were simple and unassuming, typified by "Heart In Hand," which a repentant Samuel sang to Araminta as the show's quiet finale. Unfortunately this bit of relatively gentle Americana had more charm than staying power.

Seventeen (21 June 1951, Broadhurst) advanced the calendar by a decade to 1907 Indianapolis, where once again Willie Baxter (Kenneth Nelson) suffered all the pangs of his puppy-love romance with Lola Pratt (Ann Crowley), just as he had since Booth Tarkington's novel first appeared. The adaptation was by Sally Benson, famous primarily for her *New Yorker* tales that became *Junior Miss*. The music was by Walter Kent, the lyrics by Kim Gannon. The show, like *Courtin' Time*, had period charm. *Seventeen* proved more attractive at the box office, playing until November. Its music was a little less rustic, tinged with Broadway sounds. "I Could Get Married Today," a verseless number, was popular in the show but never made its mark outside the theatre, although "Summertime Is Summertime" was heard occasionally.

July's only entry was a lavish summer revue, **Two on the Aisle** (19 July 1951, Hellinger), starring Bert Lahr and Dolores Gray. Lahr played a riotous bit as Lefty Hogan, a celebrated but brainless baseball player who can't comprehend that he's being interviewed for a children's program and insists on talking about his booze and his broads. He also plays a hilariously short-sighted Central Park street sweeper who idiotically fills his trash bag with $100 bills rather than lose a small award for collecting the most trash. Miss Gray had the best of Jule Styne's songs in "Give A Little, Get A Little" love and "If You Hadn't, But You Did." The two stars played a pair of vaude-villians who could see hardly any difference between their old act and the nonsense on the stage of the Metropolitan Opera. The show was a far cry from the tasteful, witty, and melodic revues Lahr and his great fellow comedians had done in the thirties. For want of serious competition *Two on the Aisle*, with some forcing, was able to play 281 performances.

The two Jewish revues opened five nights apart in September. **Bagels and Yox** (12 September 1951, Holiday) achieved a run of 208 performances, while **Borscht Capades** (17 September 1951, Royale) lasted ninety-nine showings. "Yox" was a theatrical term for laughs, and the title was, of course, a play on the familiar Jewish coupling of bagels and lox (smoked salmon).

October's only musical, on the 8th, was a loving, opulent revival of Kern and Hammerstein's *Music in the Air* (8 November 1932). The show was given a star-filled cast that included Charles Winninger (Dr. Lessing), Dennis King (Bruno), Jane Pickens (Frieda), and Conrad Nagel (Ernst). Because anti-German feelings still ran strong in many quarters, the producers changed the scene to Switzerland. But the thoughtful attention devoted to it failed to elicit a favorable response from playgoers. Lack of business forced its withdrawal after seven weeks at the Ziegfeld.

Phil Silvers and his band of supporting come-dians were the principal inducement to see **Top Banana** (1 November 1951, Winter Garden). Silvers's character of Jerry Biffle was reputedly mod-eled on Milton Berle, the most successful of early television clowns. The noisy, imperial Biffle is told by his sponsors to establish a love interest on his pro-gram. He hires Sally Peters (Judy Lynn), and before long a real love affair develops between her and Cliff Lane (Lindy Doherty). Biffle also falls in love with Sally, but when he realizes where her heart lies he helps her with uncharacteristic selflessness to get her man. Hy Kraft's book and Johnny Mercer's songs were brassy and serviceable. The highlight of the evening remained Silvers and his cohorts running through their old vaudeville and burlesque routines, such as a man carrying a large carton announcing he's taking a case to court, then reappearing with a ladder announcing he's taking the case to a higher court. Alarmingly, the fun was all on stage. The box office told a very unfunny story. *Top Banana* ran almost a year—350 performances—without being

able to pay off its initial investment. It was another ominous hint of things to come.

A rollicking, boom-or-bust Gold Rush musi-cal, **Paint Your Wagon** opened at the Shubert on 12 November. When gold is found on land owned by Ben Rumson (James Barton), his acreage soon becomes a prosperous mining town. Ben's daughter Jennifer (Olga San Juan) falls in love with one of the miners, Julio Valveras (Tony Bavaar). But Rumson's newly acquired wealth gives him grand ideas for Jennifer, and she is sent to a school back east. In time the gold runs out, and the town becomes deserted. Ben would pick up his stakes and move on, but dies before he can leave. However, Jennifer returns to resume her love affair with Julio, and they plan to turn the town into an irrigated farming community. Alan Jay Lerner's somewhat rambling chronicle told against the forcefulness of the rest of the show, but his lyrics and Frederick Loewe's music were color-ful and memorable. Ben was given two soft, pathetic numbers—"I Still See Elisa," in which he recalls his dead wife, and "Wand'rin' Star," which he sings just before he dies. The chorus had the rousing title song and the stirring "They Call The Wind Maria." But the outstanding song of the evening was given to Julio. It was a beguine-like ballad, "I Talk To The Trees" (with imagery much like "I've Told Ev'ry Little Star" from *Music in the Air*). Like *Top Banana, Paint Your Wagon* enjoyed a relatively long run—289 perfor-mances. And like *Top Banana*, it lost money.

The once-popular month of December, with its large contingent of holiday theatregoers, saw no new musicals arrive. It was 3 January 1952, just after the holiday crush, when the season's biggest hit opened at the Broadhurst. But the show was not a new one, it was *Pal Joey* (25 December 1940). A highly success-ful revival of its hit song, "Bewitched," had recently swept the country and made it one of the best-known popular songs of the day. A superb LP recording of the entire score further whetted interest. Postwar attitudes made *Pal Joey*'s cynical, hard-nosed story less unnerving to many. With Vivienne Segal recre-ating her original role as Vera and with Harold Lang in the title role, the musical received better reviews and more patronage than the 1940 production, playing 542 performances before embarking on an extended tour. Curiously, a return of *Kiss Me, Kate* (30 December 1948) at popular prices found no takers and folded after a single week.

Celtic magic again hoped to weave its spell over Broadway in **Three Wishes for Jamie** (21 March 1952, Hellinger). Charles O'Neal and Abe Burrows wrote the book; Ralph Blane, the songs. Just before the turn of the century Jamie McRuin (John Raitt) is granted three wishes by a fairy. He wishes to travel, to marry, and to have a son. The first two wishes are speedily granted. Jamie sails from Ireland to Georgia and there marries Maeve Harrigan (Anne Jeffreys). When Maeve is discovered to be barren, the McRuins must adopt a boy to make the third wish come true. But the boy proves a mute until one day a miracle allows him to speak—in Gaelic. *Jamie's* whimsy and sentimentality were too treacly for New Yorkers—some, like Brooks Atkinson of the *Times*, condemned it as outdated operetta—and the show survived less than three months.

A revival of *Four Saints in Three Acts* (20 February 1934) at the huge Broadway Theatre on 16 April was sourly received and folded quickly.

Two revivals opened in May. Both also failed. Ever since its initial production, *Of Thee I Sing* (26 December 1931) had remained popular with amateur and stock groups, particularly as elections approached. George S. Kaufman had tried to convince Morrie Ryskind to work with him on a revival for 1948, but Ryskind, who had swung far to the right politically, refused. For reasons Kaufman was never sure of, Ryskind changed his answer when Kaufman solicited his assistance four years later. With the brash, well-liked Hollywood comedian Jack Carson as Wintergreen and Paul Hartman as Throttlebottom, the revival opened 5 May at the Ziegfeld. There were various schools of thought as to what went wrong. Many felt the stars lacked the panache of William Gaxton and Victor Moore; others resented the changed tempos used for some of the Gershwin score; some contended the new jokes used to update the book (kidding the perennial hopeful Harold Stassen and President Truman's flamboyant shirts) were glaringly inferior to the older material; and more than a few critics simply felt the piece had dated itself. There was a certain amount of truth in all these charges, but the show remained viable enough and the production sufficiently professional to deserve more than the seventy-two hearings it received.

On 8 May at the Broadway, a revival of *Shuffle Along* (23 May 1921) fared far worse; it was moot whether it could be considered a revival. All that was left of the original were two songs ("I'm Just Wild About Harry" and "Love Will Find A Way"), a much older Flournoy Miller on stage, and the title. Miller, with Paul Gerard Smith, had written a totally new book detailing the adventures of a troop

of black soldiers in Italy at the end of World War II and on their return home. Complications arise after WAC Sgt. Lucy Duke (Dolores Martin) is mistakenly informed her former husband, Longitude Lane (Miller), has been killed in action. She begins a second romance with Capt. Harry Gaillard (Napoleon Reed). Longitude suddenly reappears. At a USO performance Longitude decides to remain in the Army and sail away. The book was badly written, almost on a par with the claptrap librettos of older black shows. George Jean Nathan, the hellion critic who had so loved the original that he saw it five times, wrote in the *Journal-American*,

> Even if some of the original stuff might now seem a bit old-fashioned, it would not seem nearly as old-hat as the substitutions involving a sand-dance, which goes back to 1895, a succession of senescent, gooey music hall ballads... a 1904 vaudeville act in which a comedian on a mountain-top accidentally drops over the edge his sole remaining provisions, and a scene in a dressmaking salon with its parade of models which was already obsolete when Clara Lipman introduced it into a show at the old Herald Square Theatre....

Variety complained more succinctly, "The yarn opens as a musical comedy, presently turns into operetta, and ends as revue." Although Eubie Blake received credit for the whole new score, he later publicly disowned most of the tunes. It was a thoroughly botched affair, mercifully removed after four showings.

The season's final offering was the only new work to have both a long run and realize a profit. **New Faces of 1952** (16 May 1952, Royale) was the best in the intermittent series—and would remain so. While none of the young talent ever reached the heights of fame or enjoyed the enduring popularity of Henry Fonda, an alumnus of the 1934 edition, the show started more bright entertainers on the road to success than any earlier version had. Among the fresh faces were Eartha Kitt, Alice Ghostley, Carol Lawrence, Robert Clary, Ronny Graham, and Paul Lynde. The show had diverting sketches and pleasant songs, one of which, "Love Is A Simple Thing" (June Carroll/Arthur Siegel), sung (together with a Charles Addams variation) by virtually all the players, enjoyed a certain vogue. Better skits included Paul Lynde's monologue—with Lynde hobbling on crutches describing the trip to Africa won by him and his "late" wife, and Ronny Graham's send-up of Truman Capote. But the revue's high spots were its comic lyrics. "Lizzie Borden" kept insisting, "Oh, you can't chop your poppa up in Massachusetts." Slinky, feline Eartha Kitt made herself comfortable all over a couch as she confessed her irresistible charms had finally made life "Monotonous" (Carroll/Siegel), although traffic will stop for her, stock prices drop for her, and Truman play bop for her. A dowdy, schoolmarmish Alice Ghostley bewailed her frustrating search for romance in "The Boston Beguine" (Sheldon M. Harnick). In her Boston the "Casbah" is an Irish Bar, the underground headquarters of the DAR. She and her unnamed lover fall asleep before they can make love. It was good fun from beginning to end, and New Yorkers applauded the revue for 365 showings.

1952–1953

A pattern seemed to be emerging on Broadway of alternate seasons of feast and famine. Although *Variety* listed eleven new musicals, it appeared to have obtained its figure by including a one-woman show and at least one revival. Of conventional new lyric pieces there were once again only nine. To the extent that all, or all but one, were undisguised musical comedies or revues, untouched by the artful pretensions of the still-fashionable "musical play," they happily reverted to a convention that had lately been in no small disrepute. They made no claim to edification or catharsis, although the best, in their insouciant gaiety, were as exhilaratingly cathartic as good musical comedy fun had always been to the tired businessman. Producers were exhilarated, too. Half the new musicals made a profit for their backers.

The season began with one of the most ballyhooed affairs in recent memory. Joshua Logan, Arthur Kober, and Harold Rome had collaborated to create a lyric version of Kober's old hit *Having Wonderful Time*. They used another postcard cliché for their new title, **Wish You Were Here** (25 June 1952, Imperial). For their musical picture of life at a Jewish summer camp they went so far as to build a real swimming pool into the theatre's stage. This, coupled with the rest of the production's elaborateness, reflected the American Musical Theatre's feeling it had to compete with the new wide-screen and stereophonic sound of the movies and the obvious attractions of home television. All the season's shows but one were mammothly mounted. In the case of *Wish You Were Here*, the extensive

stage requirements precluded a customary road tryout and ultimately precluded a workable post-Broadway tour. Previews were substituted for an out-of-town break-in, and devastatingly unfavorable word of mouth began to spread as soon as they were inaugurated. The opening was delayed several times, and revisions followed fast and furiously. When the show finally opened, most critics shrugged it off as not worth all the time and effort that had gone into it. Luckily, the delays had given Eddie Fisher's recording of the title song time to become a national best-seller, and with the song cleverly repeating the title ten times in its chorus *Wish You Were Here* received inestimable publicity. The song, plus a huge advance sale, gave the public time to make up its mind. When it decided it liked the show, the musical was able to chalk up a year-and-a-half run and thumb its nose at its detractors.

As the original had in the 1930s, the story revolved around the romance of Teddy Stern (Patricia Marand) and Chick Miller (Jack Cassidy). Teddy throws over old Herman Fabricant (Harry Clark), whom she has been seeing, when Chick, a young man of her own age, comes into her life. But Camp Karefree's clownish social director, Itchy (Sidney Armus), unwittingly leads Chick to believe that Teddy has spent the night with a garment-district lothario named Pinky Harris (Paul Valentine) who specializes in selling "genuine copies of Paris originals." For a moment the romance seems over. However, Teddy is able to clear her name, so everything ends contentedly. The score was Rome's first for a book musical. His lyrics were surprisingly free of the political slant he had heretofore shown; his melodies were memorable and diverse. Itchy had two comedy numbers, "Social Director" and "Don Jose Of Far Rockaway." Even the heavy, Pinky, was allowed to lead a lilting, old-fashioned waltz, "Summer Afternoon." But Chick had the standout title ballad and an equally lovely second ballad, "Where Did The Night Go?," that somehow got lost in the attention devoted to the title song.

No musicals arrived between the opening of *Wish You Were Here* and the premiere of **An Evening with Beatrice Lillie** (2 October 1952, Booth). Reginald Gardiner and a few minor entertainers assisted Miss Lillie and manned the stage while she changed costumes. Most of the material was from the great revues Miss Lillie had starred in years before. Nobody minded. Broadway was not producing that kind of marvelous revue anymore, so any way to get the hilarious comedienne on stage was acceptable.

As she had before, Miss Lillie destroyed a star's opening night and punctured a singer's "Come Into The Garden, Maud." Miss Lillie regaled her fans and any innocents who happened to wander into the theatre until the end of May.

The New York City Opera presented *The Consul* during its fall season, beginning on 8 November, and in the spring returned the Menotti opus along with *Regina* and *Die Fledermaus.*

The season's worst musical and one of its biggest failures appeared twelve nights later. Like the preceding season's *Shuffle Along*, **Buttrio Square** (14 October 1952, New Century) sought its fun in the confrontation of American soldiers with Italian villagers. Billy Gilbert, sneezing at every turn, starred in the show, for which he shared partial blame for the book. It was gone after seven performances.

S. M. Chartock once again tried to establish an American company devoted to Gilbert and Sullivan. He even succeeded in luring away Martyn Green from his longtime home at the D'Oyly Carte. But Green's performances only served to underscore the lack of style elsewhere in the cast. Time might have smoothed matters, but Chartock's funds were limited, and so, therefore, was his time. He opened with *The Mikado* on 20 October, followed with *The Pirates of Penzance* and the double bill of *Trial by Jury* and *H. M. S. Pinafore.* When *Iolanthe* failed to enchant, the engagement was terminated after only four weeks.

Aida was reset in the Confederacy and retitled **My Darlin' Aida** (27 October 1952, Winter Garden). The pharaoh became General Farrow, Radamès was rechristened Raymond Demarest, and somehow Amneris wound up as Jessica. "Celeste Aida" evolved into the title song, and "Ritorna Vincitor!" resounded as "March On For Tennessee." Since virtually all of Verdi's difficult score was retained, evenings and matinees featured different principals. The main cast offered Elaine Malbin as Aida, William Olvis as Raymond, Dorothy Sarnoff as Jessica, and Kenneth Schon as Farrow. It was all well intentioned, but a bit ponderous and silly. Nevertheless, it found enough curiosity-seekers to survive eleven weeks.

The most notable thing about **Two's Company** (15 December 1952, Alvin) was that it marked the return of Bette Davis to Broadway—and in the most unlikely of vehicles, a musical revue. Miss Davis was not a complete stranger to the world of song and dance. She had introduced "They're Either Too Young Or Too Old" in a wartime film. But her métier had been more serious drama. Perhaps she was attracted by the original conception of *Two's Company*, which promised to present a vis-à-vis chronicle of romance and its problems down the ages. However, its authors (Peter De Vries and Charles Sherman on the sketches, Ogden Nash on the lyrics, and Vernon Duke on the music) concluded so tight a program was constricting and probably unworkable. By the time the revue premiered, it had dwindled into a conventional mediocrity, with Miss Davis assailing such easy marks as Sadie Thompson. Miss Davis got considerable attention, but Hiram Sherman and David Burns drew most of the applause. Sherman had a droll monologue about an owner of a Frank Lloyd Wright home that blends so completely into the landscape he has never been able to find it, while Burns played a W. C. Fields–style comedian desperately trying to prevent a child star from stealing a scene. Nash and Duke's songs were especially disappointing. The show depended on its advance sale and theatre parties to run ninety performances.

On 18 January 1953 Danny Kaye came into the Palace with his troupe of "international" vaudevillians and regaled fans for 128 performances.

Three musicals arrived in February. The first was **Hazel Flagg** (11 February 1953, Hellinger). It had a clever idea, several talented hands to flesh it out, and a fine cast to give it life. Yet on stage it seemed to have difficulty moving, or even breathing. Hazel is a backwater Vermont girl who is believed to be dying of radium poisoning. A magazine gets hold of her story and brings her to New York, where she is the center of attention. She finds time to fall in love with sophisticated Wallace Cook. When it is learned that she is really in the pink of health New York loses interest, but Wallace loves her all the same. Hazel was vigorously sung and danced by Helen Gallagher. Thomas Mitchell, Jack Whiting, Benay Venuta, and John Howard (Wallace) filled the top supporting roles. Ben Hecht provided the book, which he based on the film *Nothing Sacred*, while Bob Hilliard wrote words for Jule Styne's melodies. Styne's score was good. Whiting, as a Jimmy Walker–style mayor, had a fine soft-shoe number in "Every Street's A Boulevard In Old New York," and another dancer, Sheree North, received her first real Broadway acclaim in a lively bump-and-grind number that had nothing to do with the plot, but was inserted as a diversion in the mayor's testimonial for Hazel, "Salomee." The public seemed to prefer Wallace's slightly overblown ballad, "How Do You Speak To An Angel?" The show had one of the dream ballets that had become a cliché since *Oklahoma!* (31 March 1943). There were enough attractions in the show to keep it on the boards for 190 performances—not long enough to pay back its investors.

A week later a musical version of James Barrie's *What Every Woman Knows* appeared. The story of how Maggie Wylie (Betty Paul) manipulates the fortunes and love life of John Shand (Keith Andes) was faithfully retold, although **Maggie** (18 February 1953, National) lacked the charm the play so wisely talked about. Its music was commonplace, and it, too, felt it needed a dream ballet. *Maggie* lasted half a week.

No other musical of the season was greeted as effusively as February's final presentation. **Wonderful Town** (25 February 1953, Winter Garden) was a musical rendition of Joseph Fields and Jerome Chodorov's *My Sister Eileen*, which in turn was based on Ruth McKenny's semiauto-biographical stories for *The New Yorker*. Fields and Chodorov adapted the book themselves. The lyrics were created by Betty Comden and Adolph Green, whose fertile comic talents first delighted theatrego-ers in *On the Town* (26 December 1944). Their col-laborator in that hit, the glamorous composer and conductor Leonard Bernstein, once again did the music. The even more glamorous Rosalind Russell came back to Broadway to play Ruth, a role she had done in the songless movie version of the play.

A tour guide shows gawking out-of-towners the all-too-staged sights of "Christopher Street" in Greenwich Village. When the tour moves on, Ruth and her sister, Eileen (Edith Adams), appear, look-ing for lodging. They have come from Ohio to make good in the big time: Ruth as a writer and Eileen as an actress. A Village urchin grabs Ruth's typewriter, but he is stopped by Appopolous (Henry Lascoe), who forces him to relinquish the machine. Ruth can easily identify it. The letter *W* is missing. It fell off after she wrote her thesis on Walt Whitman. Appopolous offers to rent them a basement apart-ment, and before the girls can refuse he has taken the first month's rent. The room is small, dirty, and dilapidated. Worse, it is shaken periodically by blasts from nearby subway construction. Together the girls wonder "why, oh, why, oh" they left "Ohio." While Eileen quickly finds dates, Ruth forlornly admits that in the mating game she is a born loser. In fact she has come up with "One Hundred Easy Ways" to lose a man, pointing out that if she shows a man where his grammar errs, a girl can mark her towels with "Hers" and "Hers." Ruth takes her stories to the

"Manhattan" magazine, but an editor, Robert Baker (George Gaynes), advises her to go home. After she leaves he thumbs through her manuscripts. They are a mélange of other more famous writers' styles. Several of them come to life before his eyes with Ruth as the principal figure. He decides the stories are awful, but that perhaps Ruth has talent. When he attempts to tell Ruth this later at her flat, she becomes angry and exits in a huff, leaving Baker to muse over his dream of "A Quiet Girl." Life waxes anything but quiet for Ruth when Eileen gets Ruth an assignment to interview some Brazilian sailors at the Brooklyn Navy Yard. She would like to get their opinions on America, but all they want to do is dance the "Conga!" In the ensuing melee Eileen manages to slug a policeman and is arrested. The Irish policeman takes a fancy to Eileen, insisting over her protestations she is Irish, too. The brawl makes the papers and gets the girls dispossessed. To add insult to injury, Baker appears to tell Ruth that his editor liked her stories even less than he did. Yet there are silver linings. Baker has fallen in love with Ruth and promises to get her published. The public-ity has also brought an offer of a job in a nightclub. The evening ends at the Village Vortex, with Ruth and Eileen singing a gloriously cacophonous tribute to life in New York, "Wrong Note Rag."

The show was clever and knowing. Bernstein's score was a technical tour de force that ran the gamut from straight ballads to parodies of 1930 swing, but it was all facile. Because it worked faultlessly on stage, the show ran over 500 performances, but out of the theatre the public never embraced the songs as they did the material from the next new musical.

Before that show arrived a superb remounting of *Porgy and Bess* (10 October 1935), designed to tour internationally, illuminated the Ziegfeld for nine months. One of the singers who alternated in the role of Bess was Leontyne Price, who later went on to become one of grand opera's prima donnas. Cab Calloway sang "Sportin' Life." This production had scored a rousing success in Russia before its New York opening.

Can-Can (7 May 1953, Shubert) was the first of two May musicals, both of which opened to divided, largely discouraging notices and both of which estab-lished themselves as hits. Abe Burrows's libretto for the show was conventional musical comedy frippery. Two stories ran concurrently. In one a handsome young judge, Aristide Forestier (Peter Cookson), is sent to investigate reports of scandalous cancan dancing at a Montmartre café. After he falls in love with both the dance and the café's owner, La Mome Pistache (Lilo), he helps legalize the dance and, of course, marries Pistache. In a comic subplot one of the dancers, Claudine (Gwen Verdon), is pursued by both Boris (Hans Conried), a sculptor, and Hilaire (Erik Rhodes), an art critic. Their rivalry leads the critic to denounce the sculptor's work, and that leads to a hilarious rooftop duel. Lilo, the French star, was given top billing; but Miss Verdon won the lion's share of applause with her exuberant dancing. What made the show the runaway hit of the season—and after an uncertain start it went on to run for 892 times—was Cole Porter's initially unappreciated score. Except for *Anything Goes* and *Kiss Me, Kate*, Porter scores were time and again dismissed as below his previous standard. *Can-Can*'s score was no exception. It seemed at first as if Aristide's "I Am In Love" was meant to be the hit of the show. But the song was a derivative beguine. One by one Pistache's songs from the musical rose in public esteem: the sad " Allez-Vous-En, Go Away," a flowing "C'est Magnifique," the vivacious title song, and, the biggest hit of all, the haunting "I Love Paris" (sung on the same rooftop, now starlit). After the show closed Aristide's "It's All Right With Me" also became nationally known, giving the evening five new Porter standards.

Three weeks after the Porter show raised its curtain, Rodgers and Hammerstein presented what is generally considered their least satisfactory musical, Me and Juliet (28 May 1953, Majestic). The faults, as usual, were Hammerstein's. His libretto, like his libretto for *Allegro*, was created out of whole cloth and not adapted from a tested work. It had a more self-contained plot than *Allegro*, but the plot was contrived and exaggerated. Exaggeration and contrivance have long been the stock-in-trade of musical comedy, but, given Hammerstein's quest for more purposeful and artful musical theatre, they made his story seem particularly retrogressive and inappropriately inept. The plot purported to be a slice of backstage life—a familiar setting. In his autobiography, Rodgers insisted that he and Hammerstein were determined to depart from expected twists: "One of our aims was to avoid all the clichés usually found in backstage stories. Though the plot focused on various people associated with a stage musical, we established the fact at the beginning that the show within a show was a success. The backer didn't pull out, the star didn't quit and the chorus girl didn't take over. We simply used the production as the framework for a love story, though of course we did take advantage

of the theme to reveal some aspects of the world of the theatre."

Like *Can-Can, Me and Juliet* actually told two stories at once. The main tale followed the romance of Jeanie (Isabel Bigley), a chorus girl in a musical named "Me and Juliet," with Larry (Bill Hayes), an assistant stage manager. Larry's jealous rival, an electrician, Bob (Mark Dawson), will not even stop at attempted murder to keep from losing Jeanie. He cuts a spotlight that falls from the flies, but fortunately misses its mark. A comic subplot featured a dancer not unlike *Can-Can*'s Claudine. Betty (Joan McCracken) loves the stage manager, Mac (Ray Walston), but Mac has always refused to socialize with the casts of shows he works on. The problem is solved by having Mac change shows. Hammerstein's lyrics were perhaps more revealing than his book. In the show's opening Jeanie confesses she awakes every day convinced in her heart it will be "a very special day." Not only was the sentiment treacly, but it disclosed his penchant for unpoetic words such as "special." Later in the same song he coupled "munch" with "hunch." His attempts at clever rhymes lacked grace and ease. A song sung by Arthur Maxwell as the lead in the show within the show had the ungainly title "Marriage Type Love." In "The Big Black Giant" Hammerstein self-consciously seemed to reach for a phrase that would describe audiences the way "Ol' Man River" had anthropomorphized the Mississippi. Again it was cumbersome and contrived, missing the simple dignity of "Ol' Man River." Jeannie and Larry's ballad "No Other Love" became the hit of the show, although it had already enjoyed a minor vogue as a theme from Rodgers's score for the film *Victory at Sea*. The faults of the show were minimized by its professionalism. With their names still a potent drawing card, Rodgers and Hammerstein were able to turn a profit on the show's 358-performance run.

1953–1954

The American Musical Theatre continued on its roller coaster of alternating up-and-down seasons. New shows dropped in number and quality during the theatrical year. Only nine new musicals premiered on Broadway, but if three "one-man" shows are excluded, the figure dropped still farther to a mere six (plus two superior off-Broadway mountings).

No shows came in at the very beginning of the season, hoping to span the summer. Of course, two big musicals had arrived in May. The first lyric offering of the season did not appear before the footlights until 31 August, and that was a popular-priced revival of *Oklahoma!* (31 March 1943) at the City Center. Florence Henderson was its Laurey; Barbara Cook, its Ado Annie.

Anna Russell's Little Show (7 September 1953, Vanderbilt) was a little show, indeed. In fact it was simply a one-woman show (with a few other entertainers helping when Miss Russell had to change her costume or catch her breath). Miss Russell's sarcastic attacks hit such prime targets as the old Shubert operettas with "The Prince of Philadelphia," and she went on to analyze "The Decline and Fall of the Popular Song." Her fans supported her loyally at the tiny house for two weeks.

Carnival in Flanders (8 September 1953, New Century) was a ponderous affair. Preston Sturges's Hollywood luck had again eluded him. He adapted his book from the 1936 film *La Kermesse Héroïque*. The setting was novel: seventeenth-century Flanders; but the plot and dialogue were ordinary. When the Spanish Duke d'Olvereas (John Raitt) invades the Flemish village of Flacksenburg, the terrified mayor (Roy Roberts) plays dead. This allows the duke and the mayor's supposed widow (Dolores Gray) to have a brief romance before the Spaniards move on. A leaden ballet completely bogged down the action at one point. Lyricist James Van Heusen and composer Johnny Burke were co-producers as well. Their idea of a hit tune was the awkwardly titled "The Very Necessary You" or the modestly popular "Here's That Rainy Day." *Carnival in Flanders* folded the same week it opened.

At Home with Ethel Waters (22 September 1953, 48th St.) welcomed its guests for twenty-three sessions. Miss Waters and her pianist had the stage to themselves. She sang numbers she had introduced in past hits and a collection of old favorites, but little new material.

The only "one-man" show actually to star a man, **Comedy in Music** (2 October 1953, Golden), found Victor Borge accompanying himself on the piano. His verbal and pianistic wit regaled audiences at the bandbox Golden not just through the season but all through the next season and into 1956.

On the 9th and 10th respectively, the New York City Opera brought out *Regina* and *Die Fledermaus*.

The second conventional musical did not arrive until December. **Kismet** (3 December 1953, Ziegfeld) was a resounding hit, and probably would have been so even if there had been competition; but having the field to itself didn't hurt. The show

was not especially original. It was a musical version of Edward Knoblock's 1911 romantic hokum of the same name and used Alexsandr Borodin melodies for its songs. Robert Wright and George Forrest supplied lyrics, as they had for Grieg's music in *Song of Norway* (21 August 1944). Both productions had originated on the West Coast with Edwin Lester's fine company. Lester mounted the work with Oriental splendor (bustling Arabian Nights bazaars, moonlit gardens, muezzins crying from minarets) and hired Alfred Drake to recreate Otis Skinner's old role of Hajj. He becomes emir for a day and marries his daughter, Marsinah (Doretta Morrow), to the caliph (Richard Kiley). Drake dominated the evening with his fine singing and bravura acting. But it was to the caliph and to Marsinah that the hit of the evening, "Stranger In Paradise," fell. It was based on Borodin's *Polovtsian Dances*. Marsinah also sang the lovely "Baubles, Bangles And Beads" from a Borodin string quartet. Drake cavorted in such glittering showpieces as "Rhymes Have I" and "Gesticulate." And he framed the evening with the sentiments of "Sands Of Time," assuring audiences only lovers know all that there is to know. If the lyrics and dialogue had an old-fashioned ring to them, they were nonetheless precisely apposite for such gaudy Edwardian claptrap. *Kismet* led its audiences happily into its world of make-believe for 583 performances.

One week later **John Murray Anderson's Almanac** (10 December 1953, Imperial) opened. Anderson had been one of the most innovative figures behind the great extravaganzas of the twenties and shared a large part of the credit for the success of the *Greenwich Village Follies*. He had mounted another *Almanac* in 1929. Skyrocketing costs prevented his making this new edition as lavish as those of bygone days, but it was nonetheless as eye-filling and tasteful an evening as Broadway had seen in many a year. One unique lighting arrangement had slowly revolving lights set in a quilted harlequin pattern. Two rising songwriters, Richard Adler and Jerry Ross, did most of the songs, while the witty Jean Kerr contributed a number of the sketches. For his cast Anderson recruited the popular calypso singer Harry Belafonte, the droll monologist Orson Bean, and a personable singer, Polly Bergen. However, two great clowns were the mainstay of the evening: Hermione Gingold in her American debut and Billy De Wolfe. Miss Gingold announced she was particularly impressed on sailing into New York harbor to see the gigantic statue of Judith Anderson;

she performed as an old harridan of a cellist grateful for any instrument between her legs, and did a number, "Which Witch?" (Allan Melville/Charles Zwar), which left the audience wondering which witch was which. Teamed with De Wolfe in drag, she played a tippling old lady going for a visit to an aunt in Ceylon. The highlight of the evening was "Dinner for One," in which Miss Gingold portrayed a senescent grand dame whose butler—De Wolfe—has set the table to include spaces for four long-dead admirers. The butler then proceeded from chair to chair proposing toasts, getting increasingly drunk as he clattered dishes with each change of course, and when the meal was finished escorted Madam to her room. Anderson revived one of the ballet ballads from the *Greenwich Village Follies*, "The Nightingale and the Rose," mounting it with a shimmering beauty all in white, silver, and pearl gray. Neither the old songs nor the new were particularly distinguished. The best was probably the calypso, "Hold 'Em Joe," composed and sung by Belafonte. The show ran 229 performances, not enough, sadly, to reimburse its backers. Its failure marked the closing chapter in Anderson's illustrious career.

Three years after Sigmund Romberg's death, his last Broadway score was heard in **The Girl in Pink Tights** (5 March 1954, Hellinger). Herbert Fields and Jerome Chodorov based their book on the actual events that allegedly resulted in the creation of *The Black Crook* (12 September 1866), but then peopled their plot with fictitious characters. Lotta Leslie (Brenda Lewis) is concerned that all the attention being paid to a French ballet troupe scheduled to open at the Academy of Music will dampen interest in her production of Clyde Hallam's new play, "Dick, The Renegade." She wonders how she will be able to compete with all the girls in pink tights performing a few blocks from her Niblo's Garden. But a love affair soon springs up between her playwright (David Atkinson) and the most alluring of the ballerinas, Lisette Gervais (Jeanmaire). Moreover the manager of the French troupe, Maestro Gallo (Charles Goldner), expresses more than a passing interest in Lotta. During a rehearsal the Academy catches fire, and Clyde rushes over to rescue the trapped Lisette. The house and all the costumes and scenery are destroyed. Lotta suggests the ballet be made a part of Hallam's melodrama. An argument over whether Lisette's dances or Hallam's story is more important sunders the lovers. They are reconciled when the new mounting, now called "The Black Crook," proves a wild success. Romberg strove, as he had

in *Up in Central Park* (27 January 1945), to write in a contemporary style. Unfortunately his native idiom fell somewhere between the styles of 1866 and 1954. The best he could produce was a languid ballad, "Lost In Loveliness." The show's biggest attraction was the dancing of petite Jeanmaire in her legitimate stage debut. But her art and her reputation were insufficient to prolong the run beyond fifteen weeks.

On 10 March at the small Theatre de Lys in Greenwich Village the Brecht–Weill masterpiece **The Threepenny Opera** was revived for a limited engagement. The revival was offered in a biting new translation by Marc Blitzstein. Lotte Lenya, Weill's widow, recreated her original role of Jenny. The show had not been successful when it was first done in New York in 1933, and there seemed little chance for more than a modest run. It played until 30 May, when it was withdrawn after ninety-six performances. Persistent calls for its return, especially from the *Times*'s Brooks Atkinson, who ended a number of his reviews with a cry to restore the work, encouraged it to reopen at the de Lys on 20 September 1955. An aid to its success was Louis Armstrong's wildly popular recording of "Moritat," in Blitzstein's version called "Mack The Knife." Before it closed, the musical had added an additional 2,611 performances to its record. Although its vogue had no immediate influence on main-stem musicals, a decade or so later *Cabaret* and *Chicago* both proclaimed their debt to its style and form.

The week-old *Girl in Pink Tights* was called to mind the night after *The Threepenny Opera* first returned, when a fresh, imaginative musical began performances not far from the sites of Niblo's Garden and the old Academy. The Phoenix Theatre on Second Avenue and 12th Street invited New Yorkers to partake of **The Golden Apple** beginning 11 March. They came in such large numbers after reading the rave reviews that the show was hurriedly transferred uptown on 20 April. The musical—almost devoid of dialogue, and propelled by its fetchingly evocative songs and dances—was a retelling of *The Iliad* and *The Odyssey* in a turn-of-the-century America. Angel's Roost is a small town in Washington where, according to the townsfolks, "Nothing ever happens." The biggest events of the year are Ulysses' return from the Spanish-American War and the county fair. Unexpected happenings at the fair do give the citizens something to gossip about. A traveling salesman named Paris (Jonathan Lucas) arrives in a balloon and so beguiles Sheriff Menelaus's wife, Helen (Kaye

Ballard), that she runs off with him to Rhododendron. Ulysses (Stephen Douglass) and his neighbors go in pursuit. Hector (Jack Whiting), Rhododendron's mayor, engineers all sorts of delays and temptations for the boys, until Ulysses outclasses Paris in a boxing match. After more delays en route home, the soldiers return to Angel's Roost, where Ulysses finds Penelope (Priscilla Gillette) waiting faithfully.

John Latouche provided adroit, clever lyrics, while Jerome Moross's music at one and the same time managed to be thoroughly contemporary yet convey the flavor of an earlier era. Some of their material had little relation to Homer's stories, such as the show's most popular ballad, Helen's languorous "Lazy Afternoon," or the mayor's soft-shoe (which gave Whiting a routine not unlike the one he employed so divertingly in *Hazel Flagg*). But the snares in *The Odyssey* offered Latouche and Moross ample opportunity for delicious fun, and they took intelligent advantage of it. Scylla and Charybdis (Dean Michener and Whiting) became unethical stockbrokers, singing a parody of Gallagher and Shean's famous number. The sirens, metamorphosed into a burlesque nightclub act, spoofed ersatz South Sea Island songs by the "Goona-Goona" lagoon, while the intercession of the gods became the meddling of scientists in a lively rag, "Doomed, Doomed, Doomed." Daring and inventiveness were rewarded when the critics bestowed their prize for the best musical of the season on *The Golden Apple*. Yet, although the show cost only $75,000 to mount, the move uptown did not prove popular, and when the summer heat hurt business, the musical was taken off the boards at a loss.

The collaborators of *A Tree Grows in Brooklyn* (19 April 1951) reunited to try again with **By the Beautiful Sea** (8 April 1954, Majestic), a musical set in the same era as their earlier work but with a happier, more showy plot. Their star, Shirley Booth, rejoined them to enliven the festivities. Miss Booth played Lottie Gibson, an old vaudevillian who now runs a boardinghouse in Coney Island. She caters to theatrical trade. When Dennis Emery (Wilbur Evans) comes to stay, she promptly falls in love with him. But Emery's ex-wife and his daughter are also among the boarders. Not until she can win the daughter's affection can she win Emery. The plot reminded some of *Panama Hattie* (30 October 1940) clothed in popular period costumes. The show also fell back on that curious but apparently comforting ploy of having the title take on an extra significance in the story. In this case "By The

Beautiful Sea" is the name Lottie gives her boardinghouse. Arthur Schwartz's music was inferior to his fine score for *A Tree Grows in Brooklyn*. The show's best moment came when Miss Booth revived "In The Good Old Summertime" as half of a two-part number, with a lively Schwartz countermelody for the chorus to sing. Dorothy Fields invented at least one blunt, startling couplet in Dennis's love song, "Alone Too Long," with Dennis confessing he wants to kiss Lottie but he's scared. Like *A Tree Grows in Brooklyn*, *By the Beautiful Sea* was able to achieve a passable run of 270 showings, thanks largely to Miss Booth's magnetism. But like its predecessor, it was a commercial failure.

May brought revivals of *Show Boat* (27 December 1927) and *Die Fledermaus* into the City Center. *Show Boat*'s cast included Laurel Hurley (Magnolia), Robert Rounseville (Gaylord), Helena Bliss (Julie), Burl Ives (Captain Andy), Marjorie Gateson (Parthy Ann), and Laurence Winters (Joe). Strauss's operetta featured Gloria Lind, Adelaide Bishop, John Tyers, Donald Gramm, and Jack Russell.

Sandwiched between the City Center's two openings was the premiere of **The Pajama Game** (13 May 1954, St. James). If it was noisy, coarse-grained, and leftish, it was also melodic and comic—an increasingly rare phenomenon among musical comedies. George Abbott and Richard Bissell hammered out the book from Bissell's novel *7½ Cents*. When Hines (Eddie Foy Jr.), a time-study expert at the Sleep-Tite Pajama Factory, tries to speed up machines, Babe Williams (Janis Paige), head of the union grievance committee, comes to the factory's superintendent, Sid Sorokin (John Raitt), with a demand for an increase of seven and a half cents. Sid is new on the job and takes an instant liking to Babe, but when he tries to date her she refuses, since they are on opposite sides of the bargaining table. After the workers try a slowdown, Sid threatens to fire all of them. In anger Babe kicks a machine and disrupts the whole plant. She alone is fired. Since Sid is still in love with her, he determines to see if the employees can't get their raise. He invites Gladys (Carol Haney), the bookkeeper, to have drinks with him at an obscure nightspot called Hernando's Hideaway, ignoring the fact that Gladys is Hines's girlfriend. When she's drunk, Sid wangles the key to the safe. An examination of the ledgers shows him the company already had added the seven and a half cents into their costs. Sid confronts the president and wins the workers their raise. Naturally he also wins his girl.

The book was obviously lopsided and unfair to business, but its attitude could be overlooked thanks to the sunny clowning of a topnotch cast. The choreography established the reputation of both Bob Fosse and his leading dancer, Carol Haney. In his dance for "Steam Heat," Fosse employed the device that would become his trademark: startling, offbeat, close-knit posturings. He allowed his performers to dance with snapping fingers and clicking tongues as well as with their feet. The best thing in the show, its clever, memorable songs, firmly established the team of Richard Adler and Jerry Ross. Two outstanding numbers emerged: "Hey There," Sid's love ballad whose main theme sounded a little like Mozart in revised tempo, and "Hernando's Hideaway," an irresistible travesty of the sexy Latin tangos that had so long been popular. George Abbott gave the song a memorable staging, beginning it in total darkness, then, following the lyrics' instructions to "light a match," illuminating the stage only with small flickering fires. The catchy, colloquial lyrics of "Hey There" excused any mild plagiarism. Adler and Ross awarded Foy two superior comic numbers, "I'll Never Be Jealous Again," in which his actions belied his oath, and "Think Of The Time I Save," in which he recounted his minute-saving devices. The show ran two and a half years. Happily no one could foresee how tragically foreshortened the careers of both Ross and Miss Haney would be.

ROBERT LOUIS FOSSE was born in Chicago on 23 June 1927. His early career was spent dancing in Broadway shows such as *Call Me Mister* and *Make Mine Manhattan* (both during their national tours) and *Dance Me a Song*. He also appeared as a dancer in films. More than any other choreographer Fosse became responsible for making the dance director a central figure in many Broadway musicals, so that it would often come to seem the show was conceived to serve as a vehicle for choreographic conceptions. This, however, did not become evident until later.

1954–1955

The inexplicable swing of good and bad seasons continued. When the pattern held, the new theatrical year proved a banner session. Distressingly, as several of the earlier seasons rich in quality had demonstrated, Broadway could no longer handle many fine musicals. Several musicals failed which in a lesser season or in a former era would have almost certainly made the grade. Not only was the quality unusually high, but the number of musicals took a noticeable jump. There were a dozen new book shows and twenty or twenty-one lyric works, depending on how *Mrs. Patterson* was listed.

The lone June entry was a return of *Carousel* (19 April 1945) at the customary popular prices of the New York City Center. With no other musical openings all summer long to divert theatregoers' attention, the show ran well into August. The revival was strongest in its female leads, with Barbara Cook as Carrie, Jo Sullivan as Julie, and Bambi Linn back to dance the daughter.

More than a decade before country music became a national craze, a "hillbilly" revue offered the sound to knowing New Yorkers. Scenery was simple, skits omitted; only the folk music mattered. The lineup of popular figures from the field included stalwarts such as Lester Flatt and Earl Scruggs. But **Hayride** (13 September 1954, 48th St.) discovered to its sorrow that knowing New Yorkers were few and far between, so few in fact that the show was withdrawn after three weeks.

September also saw the curtain rise on a "New Musical Comedy of the 1920s." Sandy Wilson's **The Boy Friend** (30 September 1954, Royale) was a full-length travesty of the gay, unpretentious confections of the jazz age, carefully and accurately burlesquing the simplistic plot lines, the formula songs (the Charleston number, the dream of a love nest, the exchange of vows, etc.), and the stylized staging of the period. But while it was careful and accurate, it was also affectionate. Those who had sat through the original *No, No, Nanette* (16 September 1925) or *The Girl Friend* (17 March 1926) or *Mary* (15 October 1920) could now laugh at the excesses and clichés, while still experiencing a warm twinge of nostalgia. The story told how a lordly young English boy and an aristocratic young English lady each pretend to a lowly station to win the other's hand. The situation was precisely the reverse of an earlier American spoof, "The Gladiola Girl" in *Lend an Ear* (16 December 1948), in which two poor youngsters pretend to be rich. The aristocratic young lady of the evening was played on Broadway by a young lady with a face of porcelain perfection, a crystal-clear voice, and exact diction: Julie Andrews. *The Boy*

Friend was an importation from London, where it went on to establish a long-run record. It established no records at all in New York, but it provided delight through the season.

JULIE ANDREWS (née Julia Elizabeth Wells) was born 1 October 1935 in Walton-on-Thames, Great Britain. Her child's clear soprano voice won admirers by the time she was ten, leading to an early career in British pantomimes, variety, radio and television. She was a sensation singing "Je suis Titania" by Ambroise Thomas twice nightly in the British revue *Starlight Roof* in 1947. Just shy of her nineteenth birthday, she came to New York to debut as Polly in *The Boy Friend*.

More briefly, the New York City Opera delighted subscribers with *Die Fledermaus* on 3 September and *Show Boat* on the 28th.

The night after the Strauss operetta returned, Libby Holman brought in her one-woman show, **Blues, Ballads and Sin-Songs** (4 October 1954, Bijou). Miss Holman had been absent for some while from Broadway. Time had apparently not been kind to either her artistry or her drawing power, so the show folded after twelve representations.

Nor did most critics feel time had been kind to *On Your Toes* (11 April 1936), Rodgers and Hart's memorable hit. It opened in a fine production on 11 October and managed an eight-week run. Bobby Van danced Ray Bolger's part, while Vera Zorina assumed the role Tamara Geva had created. By and large the critics could still praise the "Slaughter on Tenth Avenue" ballet and Rodgers and Hart's songs, but the claptrap of the book seemed to them to belong to a discarded school. With interesting new musicals coming along at a fast clip, the public didn't bother to find out for itself if the critics were right or wrong.

One of the new musicals was **Peter Pan** (20 October 1954, Winter Garden), a lyric version of James Barrie's play. It was staged with inventive wit by Jerome Robbins and performed with rare style and panache by Mary Martin as Peter and Cyril Ritchard as Captain Hook. When Peter with the magical word "Indians" gets the Darling children to fly to Never Never Land, they flew giddily out of their nursery and virtually over the audience. No doubt, too, only this Peter could make the wicked father-figure of Captain Hook cry, "Misericordia." The show originated with Edwin Lester's California organization. When it opened on the West Coast, the music was by Mark (Moose) Charlap and the lyrics by Carolyn Leigh. While they wrote two of Peter's most joyous numbers, "I've Gotta Crow" and "I'm Flying," neither song gave promise of being a hit outside the theatre. Jule Styne was invited to write additional music to new Comden and Green lyrics. Most of their material proved more clever than memorable, but they did create one lovely ballad in "Toyland" style, "Never Never Land," as well as "Captain Hook's Waltz," which Ritchard sang with lugubrious hypocrisy, protesting he was merely "Mrs. Hook's little baby boy." The nineteen-week run of the piece was disappointing, and normally would have meant an unprofitable run. But Lester's California subscriptions, plus a lucrative sale of the whole production to television, allowed the production to make a profit. The taping of *Peter Pan*'s second television showing gives future audiences an unusual chance to see an original Broadway cast performing more or less as it did in the theatre.

Although *The Boy Friend, On Your Toes*, and *Peter Pan* all represented some measure of disappointment at the box office, their producers had the consolation that they were mounted with intelligence and taste. It remained for an overwritten, overproduced piece to become the first runaway hit of the season. **Fanny** (4 November 1954, Majestic) was a musical version of Marcel Pagnol's cinematic trilogy, *Marius, Fanny*, and *César*. The new piece attempted to cover in one evening much the same ground the three films had covered. With equal shortsightedness in the face of the restricting limitations of a Broadway stage, it attempted to show a fully rigged ship sailing the stage and offer elaborate undersea and circus ballets. Although the distinguished playwright S. N. Behrman collaborated with Joshua Logan on the book, the intimacy and warmth of the original screen masterpieces were lost. Only the story remained. César, the owner of a small waterfront café in Marseilles, hopes his son Marius will wed the young, pretty Fanny, settle down, and take over the business. But Marius prefers the sea. He sails away, leaving Fanny pregnant but unwed. Frightened, Fanny consents to become the wife of a kind, elderly sailmaker, Panisse. Panisse is even prepared to change the name of his small firm to "Panisse and Son," although he knows the child is not his. Years later Marius returns, and both he and Fanny would willingly resume their romance. But César roughly intervenes so that the good-hearted Panisse will not be hurt. Although Panisse hires a whole circus for Césario's twelfth birthday, the boy is more interested in meeting Marius, about whom he has heard so much over the years. He finds him working in a garage in Toulon and tells of his desire to go to sea. Marius discourages him, insisting he must return to his parents. Césario returns to find Panisse dying. Even on his deathbed Panisse can think only of his adopted boy. He begs Fanny to wed Marius so that Césario can grow up in a loving household.

Harold Rome's score pulled out all the sentimental stops. Songs such as "Never Too Late For Love," "Why Be Afraid To Dance?," "Love Is A Very Light Thing," "Other Hands, Other Hearts," and "Be Kind To Your Parents" employed the same unabashed directness of expression and feeling that Oscar Hammerstein regularly offered his public. Rome's most successful number was his title song, sung by Marius. As he had with "Wish You Were Here," he managed to repeat the title so often it acted as a sort of advertisement for the play. With Ezio Pinza as César and Walter Slezak as Panisse in the starring roles and with Florence Henderson and William Tabbert featured, *Fanny* embarked on a run that lasted for over two years. In retrospect, *Fanny* may well be remembered as the debut of the most important producer of the era, David Merrick.

The critical, if not commercial, success of *The Golden Apple* (11 March 1954) prompted the experimental Phoenix Theatre to attempt two more musicals during the season. Both were well received, but, learning from the fiasco of the preceding spring, the company rejected thoughts of moving uptown. The first of the two musicals—presented on 23 November—was the more offbeat, a "Ballad in Three Acts" called **Sandhog**. Written by Earl Robinson and Waldo Salt and based on Theodore Dreiser's short story "St. Columba and the River," it was a singularly stark, cohesive work which repeated several of its musical passages at intervals throughout the evening in a leitmotif fashion uncommon to Broadway. The story chronicled the career of Johnny O'Sullivan (Jack Cassidy), who gets a job as a sandhog digging tunnels under the river, marries his sweetheart Katie (Betty Oakes), leaves the job after several of his friends are killed in an accident, then returns to the work and is miraculously spared

when he is blown to safety in a second mishap. With the prosperity and complacency of the Eisenhower years settling in, the show's slightly thirtyish tone and attitude seemed somewhat out of date, but in no way compromised its integrity.

> **DAVID MERRICK** was born David Margulois in St. Louis on 27 November 1911. He studied to be a lawyer, but found the lure of the theatre irresistible and, after a brief but thorough apprenticeship, boldly entered producing ranks.

Mrs. Patterson (1 December 1954, National) recounted the conflicting dream lives of a black girl who at times wants to be a sedate, rich, white woman and at other times a dark hellion. She finally accepts reality. Although Eartha Kitt had made her name as a singer and though she sang six of the seven numbers James Shelton wrote for the show, the piece was generally looked on as a straight play. It was in fact one of those borderline affairs more common thirty or forty years before. The music came not from a pit band, but rather was amplified from recordings. In any case it was not a success, although it ran 101 performances.

A musical called **Hit the Trail** opened at the Hellinger the following night, 2 December, and closed two nights later. Its plot depicted the plight of a prima donna, Lucy Vernay (Irra Petina), whose troupe is stranded in nineteenth-century Nevada, and who must choose between a crook (Paul Valentine) and a banker (Robert Wright). The score was Frederico Valerio's sole Broadway effort. Even such fine singers as Miss Petina and Wright couldn't help it. It was unquestionably the one musical of the season that didn't even deserve a production.

The last week in December brought two of the season's most unusual and interesting works. Both failed. On the 27th, Gian Carlo Menotti offered his latest opera, **The Saint of Bleecker Street**, at the Broadway. Menotti's tale recounted the incestuous passion of Michèle for his devout little sister, Annina. When the voluptuous Desideria (Gloria Lane) opens Michele's eyes to the true nature of his feelings, he kills her. Annina takes the veil. David Poleri and Davis Cunningham alternated in the role of Michele, while Virginia Copeland and Gabrielle Ruggiero spelled each other as Annina. Musically, the opera was neither venturesome nor deep, but it was, as all of Menotti's pieces of this period were, unstintingly theatrical. At its own level it had a rare consistency of style and tone. But opera's appeal to regular Broadway playgoers was still limited. Menotti's novelty had worn off, so the best the new work could achieve was ninety-two performances: a remarkable figure for an opera but a certain indication of indifference and failure in the commercial theatre.

House of Flowers (30 December 1954, Alvin), with book and lyrics by Truman Capote, also had an uncommon consistency of style and tone, even if it was worlds away from the drab, urban harshness of Menotti's opera. Some viewers felt the uniformity of tone subtly deteriorated into simple monotony. Whether the show's boosters or detractors were correct, it was amazing that the show had any noteworthy tone at all. It had been plagued during its tryout by some of the most vicious backstage fighting Broadway had heard about in years. One thing that remained gratefully unaffected was the exquisite pastel delicacy of Oliver Messel's poetically imaginative costumes and sets. They depicted life on an unidentified West Indies isle. In this unworldly paradise a very earthy trade war has broken out between two brothels. One is run by Madame Tango (Juanita Hall). The other, "The House of Flowers," is run by the appropriately named Madame Fleur (Pearl Bailey), and filled with young ladies named after blossoms. When a group of sailors introduces an epidemic of mumps in the establishment, Madame Fleur is in desperate straits. She is not above selling one of her girls, Ottilie (professionally known as Violet), to a rich merchant. When Ottilie (Diahann Carroll) protests she intends to marry her own sweetheart, Royal (Rawn Spearman), Madame Fleur arranges to have Royal kidnapped. He escapes in time to prevent Ottilie's marriage. Madame Fleur emerges triumphant when Madame Tango's girls sail on a world cruise. Another part of the show that remained happily above backstage strife was Harold Arlen's luminous score. It was as exquisite and poetic as the settings, able to turn from the sunlit airiness of "Two Ladies In De Shade Of De Banana Tree"—a calypso number sung by Gladiola (Ada Moore) and Pansy (Enid Mosier)—to the subtly modulated languors of Ottilie's "A Sleepin' Bee" and the title song, sung by Royal and Ottilie. An intangible gossamer grace rendered the show somehow unwatchable.

When an off-Broadway revival attempted to recreate the original conception some years later, it met with no success.

Yet **Plain and Fancy** (27 January 1955, Hellinger), which arrived as 1955's first musical show and which also eschewed all the easy theatrical tricks, managed to provide an eminently satisfying evening. Even its setting was novel: the Amish country near Lancaster, Pennsylvania. Two wordly-wise New Yorkers, Ruth Winters (Shirl Conway) and Dan King (Richard Derr), come to the area to sell a farm Dan has inherited. He believes he has a customer in Papa Yoder (Stefan Schnabel). Yoder's daughter, Katie (Gloria Marlowe), has been picked to marry Ezra Reber (Douglas Fletcher Rodgers). Ezra has accepted the arrangement casually. One wife in his eyes is as good or as bad as another, so, "Why Not Katie?" Katie also stoically accepts her father's plans. Just before the wedding her old love, Peter (David Daniels), Ezra's brother, returns, and before long both wish they could be "Young And Foolish" again. The Yoders, however, will have none of this. Peter has left the community—a grievous sin among Amish. As Yoder explains to Dan, "Plain We Live." The Amish way of life is simple and clear-cut. Peter has become an outsider to be shunned. When the Yoders' barn burns down, the neighbors all help raise a new one. Peter somehow feels he has brought on the problem and determines to leave. Before he can go, Ezra gets drunk at a carnival, and only Peter's quick action minimizes the disgrace. Papa Yoder reconsiders his opinion of Peter, and Peter reconsiders his plans to leave. About the same time that Peter and Katie announce they will wed, Dan and Ruth come to the same decision. The book was by Joseph Stein and William Glickman; Albert Hague and Arnold B. Horwitt wrote the music and lyrics respectively. The show took a sympathetic look at the stern philosophy and the often hard existence of the Amish. It made an unexpected applause-getting scene out of an Amish barn-raising. Only in the "Carnival Ballet" did it employ for any length the accepted and expected Broadway musical devices. *Plain and Fancy*'s willingness to pioneer was rewarded. "Young And Foolish" became one of the most popular songs of the year, and the show had a run of 461 performances.

Silk Stockings (24 February 1955, Imperial) arrived a month later. It, too, had the potential for being an offbeat musical. But in an extended tryout, marked by as many battles and revisions as *House of Flowers* had suffered, it was turned into a slick formula musical. Luckily the old hands working on the show were some of the top professionals in the business, and they made the old formula work well enough to give *Silk Stockings* a run of 478 performances. The piece was a lyric version of a popular 1939 movie, *Ninotchka*. At the musical's world premiere its book was a joint effort of George S. Kaufman and Leueen MacGrath. By the time it arrived in New York, Abe Burrows had contributed a substantial rewriting. Kaufman had also been the original director, and though he insisted that credit be dropped he allowed his name to remain as co-author of the libretto. The story that Garbo had brought to the screen remained reasonably intact. Steve Canfield (Don Ameche), an American theatrical agent, has made him such attractive offers that Peter Boroff (Philip Sterling), a Russian composer famous for his "Ode to a Tractor," decides to stay in the West. The Communists send the unsmiling disciplinarian Ninotchka (Hildegarde Neff) to retrieve him. Steve makes Paris so attractive for the pretty girl that the Russians must in turn send a whole delegation to bring her back. She returns to Russia, only to have Steve pursue her there. Together they return to the West. A secondary plot that only touched on the principal tale had Janice Dayton (Gretchen Wyler), a Hollywood glamour queen, in Paris to make a movie.

The "Cold War" was going full blast, providing ready-made targets. A leading best-seller in the shaky hierarchy of the Kremlin is "Who's Still Who," while a Soviet official who is advised Prokofiev is dead comments, "I didn't even know he was arrested." A superb cast acted and sang surrounded by colorful Jo Mielziner sets. Yet for many the primary appeal of the show was Cole Porter's score. Although its songs never became as standard as his previous *Can-Can* score, they were melodic and varied. The most popular was probably Steve's racy "All Of You." Porter created another solid beguine in Steve's title song and a rippling number in Steve and Ninotchka's "As On Through The Seasons We Sail." Nor did his way with words fail him. "Paris Loves Lovers" at first seemed like a pleasant reworking in reverse of "I Love Paris," but before Porter was through Ninotchka interrupted Steve's picture with fitting communistic replies. The subplot allowed him to have fun at the expense of the wide screens and new sound equipment motion picture palaces had introduced with a song given to Janice, on glorious Technicolor, breathtaking CinemaScope, and "Stereophonic Sound." Both *Can-Can* (7 May 1953)

and *Silk Stockings* were set in Paris, as were Porter's first two successes, *Paris* (8 October 1928) and *Fifty Million Frenchmen* (27 November 1929). Since his new show sadly turned out to be his last, it meant he had come full circle. While Porter was as urbane and civilized as the City of Light he so loved, his most identifiable songs were written in a South American beat derived from the African jungles, often with minor key melodies he himself termed "Jewish," and his lyrics were so carefully nuanced and so often knowingly topical they defied translation or even a sea-crossing. Porter's stylish songs were unique products of the proverbial but not always successful American melting pot.

On 28 February, Ben Bagley brought the first of his **Shoestring Revues** into the tiny President, an "off-Broadway" house in the heart of the theatrical district. These low-budget productions were among the most consistently witty Broadway ever knew. "In Bed with the Reader's Digest" devastated that magazine's saccharine innocuities. "Medea in Disneyland" reduced Greek tragedy to a puerile animated confection. The shows were filled with deliciously comic songs, such as Sheldon Harnick's "Garbage." Only in their failure to produce durable standards did the *Shoestring Revues* prove disappointing. But the shows nurtured an amazing number of future stars: Dody Goodman, Beatrice Arthur, Chita Rivera, Arte Johnson, and one great comedienne who failed to reach the top, Dorothy Greener.

Another low-budget "diversion in song and dance" called **3 for Tonight** (6 April 1955, Plymouth) presented Marge and Gower Champion, Harry Belafonte, and Hiram Sherman in a refreshingly odd-ball revue that mingled old and new material. None of the new songs made an impression, but the playgoers could leave the theatre whistling such old favorites as "Shine On Harvest Moon" and "When The Saints Go Marching In." Though *3 for Tonight* ran only eighty-five performances, its minimal initial cost allowed it to make money.

Ankles Aweigh (18 April 1955, Hellinger), a raucous, rowdy musical comedy of the old school, sailed in next. By the standards of an earlier era everything was shipshape. The musical had a gag-filled, far-fetched, but workable book; an eye-appealing chorus line; unashamedly old-fashioned tap-dancing; coarse, funny comedians; and a hammock-load of songs. That the demand for such diverting claptrap had not yet died was evident from the twenty-two-week-stay *Ankles Aweigh* enjoyed. In the days to which it harked back, a similar run almost assuredly would have spelled success, but in 1955 the musical closed without returning its investment. The Guy Bolton–Eddie Davis book described the honeymoon of a Hollywood starlet and a navy flier interrupted in all sorts of exotic Mediterranean settings by the demands of her studio and navy top brass. Jane Kean and Mark Dawson as the lovers were assisted by Jane's sister Betty, Lew Parker, Gabriel Dell, and Thelma Carpenter. Sammy Fain's spunky score ranged from the jaunty "Walk Like A Sailor" to a competent ballad, "Nothing At All"—whose Dan Shapiro lyrics reflected the hyperbolic imagery Hammerstein had popularized in *Oklahoma!* (31 March 1943).

A more modish evening premiered the following night. **All in One** (9 April 1955, Playhouse) was a triple bill that included a staging of Leonard Bernstein's one-act opera, *Trouble in Tahiti*. Although the bill also offered a Tennessee Williams play and a dance program by Paul Draper, the public was unresponsive.

The next night brought a popular-price return of *Guys and Dolls* (24 November 1950). Walter Matthau was Nathan, while Helen Gallagher played Adelaide. *South Pacific* (7 April 1949), followed at City Center on 4 May, while *Finian's Rainbow* (10 January 1947) ended the Center's season on 18 May with Will Mahoney as Finian and Miss Gallagher as Sharon.

April's last musical appeared on the 23rd. It was the second of the Phoenix Theatre's two lyric offerings. If it struck a number of critics as a surprisingly conventional piece for the unconventional house to mount, it struck even more critics as a hilarious evening in the theatre. The show was a revue entitled, succinctly, **Phoenix '55**. In the teens or the twenties such a title would have hinted at the beginning of a revue series. But everyone knew the success of *Phoenix '55* rested solely on one performer. So it is doubtful that there was any intention of making the show an annual affair. The performer was Nancy Walker, and she was almost singlehandedly responsible for making the material seem hysterically funny. When she was off stage, particularly when the show's lackluster songs were being sung, the evening sagged. The high spot of the entertainment came when Miss Walker burlesqued the jerky, undisciplined method school of acting, then the rage of the theatre. Miss Walker almost literally chewed the scenery as she reacted to her own emotions—which told her to walk over sofas and actors, and generally

create mayhem. Because the show was the Phoenix's final offering of the season, the Phoenix decided to extend the run after the initial engagement had been played. As a result the show ran until hot weather at the end of July depleted its audience.

Considering the popularity of football in collegiate musicals, and of sports such as golf, prizefighting, and horseracing in other musical shows, it is startling to realize that until 1955 no New York musical had ever successfully dealt with the most American of sports, baseball. Most New Yorkers were no doubt unaware Chicago had made a hit of *The Umpire* (2 December 1905) just after the turn of the century. The oversight was joyously rectified when **Damn Yankees** (5 May 1955, 46th St.) hit a metaphoric grand slam. In a couple of ways its timing was perfect. The baseball season had just begun, and the Yankees, who are the inadvertent villains of the piece, were nearing the end of the great epoch that was the starting point for the plot. The story was not new to the more literate baseball fans. George Abbott and Douglass Wallop adapted their libretto from Wallop's best-seller, *The Year the Yankees Lost the Pennant*, which had wickedly combined the nation's chagrin at the seeming hopelessness of outclassing the great New York team with the wishful possibilities of the Faust legend. No one is more chagrined than middle-aged Joe Boyd (Robert Shafer) as he sits in his living room watching his beloved Senators take another beating. When he suggests he would sell his soul to see Washington win, a man named Applegate (Ray Walston) appears miraculously at his side and obligingly agrees to accept Joe's soul in exchange for making the Washington Senators world champions. In a flash paunchy Joe Boyd becomes strapping Joe Hardy (Stephen Douglass). Van Buren (Russ Brown), the Senators' manager, is urgently telling his down-trodden team that all they need to turn the tide is "Heart." The players know better. They need something more, something like "Shoeless Joe From Hannibal, Mo." Joe proves to be just the needed tonic, inaugurating an unprecedented winning streak. Unfortunately, Joe is lonely for his wife (Shannon Bolin). He rents a room in his own home, but his wife, of course, doesn't recognize the handsome, youthful man she sees before her. Applegate, fearing Joe's homing instincts will queer the deal, enlists the support of Lola (Gwen Verdon), a hag who has sold her soul to become a beautiful woman. Lola appears in the locker room and warns the protesting Joe not to resist her charms, for

"Whatever Lola Wants," Lola gets. Eventually Joe's longing for his wife grows too strong for him to fight.

Redhead **GWEN VERDON** was born in Culver City, California, on 13 January 1926. Her mother was a dancer. Miss Verdon studied with Jack Cole and, after making her debut in *Bonanza Bound*, which folded in tryout, worked with Cole as assistant choreographer for both *Magdalena* and *Alive and Kicking*. She danced with Cole in the latter Her dancing in *Can-Can* called her to Broadway's attention. *Damn Yankees* also called attention to her gaminlike, teasing charm.

He reneges on his deal and goes home to watch the Senators start another losing streak.

Adler and Ross's score was inventive and clever, but in some respects uncomfortably close to their material for *Pajama Game*. "Whatever Lola Wants," like "Hernando's Hideaway," was a mock tango; the soft-shoe style of Applegate's "Those Were The Good Old Days" recalled "I'll Never Be Jealous Again"; "Who's Got The Pain?," though it used a different rhythm, seemed a first cousin to "Steam Heat." But "Heart," if cornball, was fresh, and some of the minor numbers such as "Near To You" and Joe and Lola's farewell, "Two Lost Souls," displayed promising originality. Unfortunately, which direction Adler and Ross would have taken will never be known. Jerry Ross died shortly after the show opened, and Adler, after some weak solo attempts, disappeared for years from the Broadway scene. *Damn Yankees* played for over a thousand performances and had a road company headed by Bobby Clark in his last important assignment.

The season's last show was a musical version of yet another old film favorite, the Janet Gaynor and Charles Farrell silent-film classic *Seventh Heaven*. But in some way the magic of the movie's obvious sentimentality was lost in transferring the story from the screen. Although Ricardo Montalban made a suitable Chico and Gloria DeHaven was an attractive Diane, the story of the girl who remains faithful to her street cleaner, even after he is blinded in the war, seemed contrived and maudlin. Stella Unger's lyrics ran to such clichés as "Where Is That Someone For

Me?" (almost a spoof of a 1920s title) and to such trite bits as "A 'Miss You' Kiss." Victor Young's score seemed commonplace. Only in Diane and Chico's "Sun At My Window, Love At My Door" did Young come up with a catchy melody and Miss Unger provide reasonably unembarrassing lyrics. They were not enough to buck both the heat and the competition. **Seventh Heaven** (26 May 1955, ANTA) survived just over one month.

1955–1956

Did the 1955–1956 season continue the pattern of alternate feast and famine? Statistically it would appear so. The number of new lyric pieces fell to a discouraging eight: three revues and five book shows. City Center revivals and a pair of one-man shows fattened the figure slightly, as did a visit by the D'Oyly Carte. Equally discouraging, only two of the commercial ventures made profits. It would be impossible to imagine a more depressing year in the history of the American Musical Theatre, except for one thing: One of the two hits was *My Fair Lady*.

However, *My Fair Lady*, and what little else was interesting, didn't arrive until late in the season. The early months were horrendous. A brightly mounted but vacuous revue, **Almost Crazy** (20 June 1955, Longacre), opened the season. Much of its material was by the persistent, if uninspired, James Shelton, while a fine comedienne, Portia Nelson, contributed several numbers that suggested she belonged on stage rather than behind the scenes. The show got the season off to a doubly disheartening beginning by insisting in its curtain raiser, "Everything's Gonna Be Much Worse Next Year." Luckily not too many patrons had a chance to take such Cassandric utterings to heart, for *Almost Crazy* was carted away after two weeks.

A second revue, **Catch a Star!** (6 September 1955. Plymouth), fared only a mite better, running three weeks. Its songs were by Sammy Fain, a composer of pleasant melodies that never seemed to make the grade on Broadway; by Phil Charig, a voice out of the past; and by Jerry Bock, a voice soon to be heard more assertively. The evening's sketches were the joint effort of Danny and Neil Simon, the latter, of course, going on to become one of Broadway's top comic playwrights. The Simons parodied a Tennessee Williams play in "Room for Rent" and spoofed *Marty*, a popular film about a homely, ordinary New Yorker, in *Arty*.

On the 27th of the month the D'Oyly Carte began a season of eight Gilbert and Sullivan works that continued until Thanksgiving. The operettas presented were *Iolanthe, The Mikado, The Yeomen of the Guard, The Pirates of Penzance, Princess Ida, Trial by Jury, H. M. S. Pinafore,* and *Ruddigore.*

That same evening at the Ziegfeld, which was in the process of being converted into a television studio, Fred Waring presented his heavily microphoned troupe of singers for a brief stay. Their "bistro entertainment" was called **Hear! Hear!**

The next evening the popular French boulevardier Maurice Chevalier began a six-week stint with his one-man show. He was followed by the season's other solo effort, **Joyce Grenfell Requests the Pleasure** (10 October 1955, Bijou). Strictly speaking, Miss Grenfell's was not a solo performance. She had three artists assist her in some of her numbers and entertain while she changed gowns. Nonetheless her fans came to see Miss Grenfell, and she amused them for sixty-five performances with her droll lyrics set to Richard Addinsell's music.

November brought the season's first two book musicals. Both glittered with promise, and both failed. **The Vamp** (10 November 1955, Winter Garden) starred Carol Channing, who had had such glorious fun with the roaring twenties and now proposed to have an even more lavish spree in the good old days ten years or so earlier. Miss Channing played Flora Weems, a hardworking farm girl from the Bronx, who rises to fame as an incongruously gigantic, hilariously wide-eyed siren in the early movie studios of New York and Hollywood. Sadly, the airy wit John Latouche had displayed in *The Golden Apple* deserted him. His lyrics and dialogue (co-authored with Sam Locke) were heavy-handed and obvious, while James Mundy's score contained nothing memorable. Even the sumptuous mounting (especially in sets parodying the biblical scenery of early movies) seemed to bog down in its own opulence. The show closed while the rest of Broadway was celebrating New Year's Eve.

Before the month's second book musical arrived, **Katherine Dunham and Her Company** (22 November 1955, Broadway) regaled theatregoers with another of her globe-trotting dance programs. This one traveled through Brazil, Argentina, Mexico, Africa, and black North America.

Opera's Helen Traubel costarred with Bill Johnson in Rodgers and Hammerstein's latest musical, **Pipe Dream** (30 November 1955, Shubert), a lyric version of John Steinbeck's *Sweet Thursday.*

When a pretty vagrant named Suzy (Judy Tyler) is arrested for stealing food, a good-natured brothel-keeper, Fauna (Miss Traubel), extricates her from the mess and offers her a home. She soon falls in love with an impoverished marine biologist, Doc (Johnson). Doc is so poor he can't even afford the microscope his work requires, so the raffish stumblebums of the neighborhood, men to whom Doc has always been unpatronizingly friendly, stage a rigged lottery. After Doc and Suzy quarrel and Suzy says she will never again see Doc—unless, of course, he needs her—one of the men breaks Doc's arm while Doc is sleeping so that Suzy can tend it. Hammerstein's expected sentimentality was evident in songs such as Suzy's "Everybody's Got A Home But Me" and Doc's "The Man I Used To Be," and even Rodgers's attractive melodies were not up to his best. Only one song pleased the public at large, the lovers' "All At Once You Love Her," sung as the first-act finale. Miss Traubel, hefty and regal, seemed uncomfortably cast, and while she had the lively "Sweet Thursday" to sing, her most satisfying moment may well have been her lovely second-act reprise of "All At Once You Love Her." Although *Pipe Dream* ran through the season, it failed to repay its investors. The economic outlook in the theatre was growing increasingly grim. One highly praised, six-character, single-set straight comedy, *Fallen Angels,* also ran seven months without being able to recoup reasonable initial costs.

No further musicals appeared until **My Fair Lady** (15 March 1956) broke a history of failures that had beset the Mark Hellinger and went on to establish a Broadway long-run record. The musical was based on George Bernard Shaw's *Pygmalion.* Lerner and Loewe's adaptation was uncommonly faithful, and even when it deviated from the original it did so with unerring intelligence, taste, and style. As it did in the Shaw play, the evening opens just after a performance at Covent Garden, where elegantly dressed operagoers mingle with the area's lowlife. One of the denizens of the place warns a besmudged flower-seller, Eliza Doolittle (Julie Andrews), that a gentleman is taking notes of everything she says. She begins to bawl, and the gentleman tries to comfort her by his assurance he is not a policeman. He also tells her she is from Lisson Grove. She is amazed—and defensive. Eliza swears the place wasn't fit to be a pigsty, and that here she earns a bare living legitimately. The gentleman turns out to be Professor Henry Higgins (Rex Harrison), a philologist and phonetician. His attentions are soon diverted by another gentleman who proves to be Colonel Pickering (Robert Coote), author of "Spoken Sanskrit." To his new-found colleague Higgins complains, "Why can't the English teach their children how to speak?" Higgins offhandedly remarks that he could take an unedu-cated waif like the flower-seller and make her into a lady by improving her speech. He invites Pickering to move in with him, giving the colonel his address. After throwing some coins in Eliza's basket, they hurry off. Eliza would like to be a lady and dreams of its comforts, sighing, "Wouldn't It Be Loverly?" Eliza's father (Stanley Holloway) is thrown out of a pub for want of money. He decides to ask his daugh-ter to stand him and his friends a round of drinks. Under normal conditions Eliza would have prob-ably rebuffed him, but, flush with the coins Higgins has given her and with his hint she might someday be a lady, she gives her father enough to treat himself and his friends. With a knowing wink the appropri-ately named Doolittle remarks to his cronies, "With a little bit of luck, someone else'll do the blinkin' work!" At Higgins's house Pickering has settled in when a visitor is announced—none other than Eliza come to take Higgins up on his suggestion that he can turn her into a lady. Higgins is appalled, but an amused Pickering presses Higgins to try, so Eliza is carted off by Higgins's housekeeper to be bathed and properly clothed. Higgins is slightly unnerved. He protests, "I'm An Ordinary Man" enjoying soli-tude and warns:

> But let a woman in your life
>   And you are up against the wall!
> Make a plan and you will find
>   She has something else in mind;
> And so rather than do either
>   You do something else that neither
> Likes at all.

After a visit from Doolittle that Higgins sees as a form of blackmail, the professor embarks on a rigorous training program for Eliza, determined to restore her "H"s to their proper place and make her vowel sounds more musical and correct. His persistence drives Eliza into a rage, and she warns Higgins, "Just You Wait." At the same time, Higgins's persistence is rewarded, and, after a seem-ingly endless struggle, Higgins and Pickering cel-ebrate Eliza's correct pronunciation of "The Rain In Spain" with a giddy fandangoing, tangoing revel. The elated Eliza exults, "I Could Have Danced All Night."

REX (Reginald Carey) HARRISON was born 5 March 1908 in Huyton, Lancashire, Great Britain. His earliest stage appearance was with the Liverpool Repertory Theatre in September 1924, which led to a distin-guished West End career in light comedy and a film career beginning in 1930. His 1936 New York stage debut as Tubbs Barrow in *Sweet Aloes* was a personal favorite. Prior to his career-defining role as Henry Higgins in *My Fair Lady*, Harrison's only previous musical theatre credentials were provincial UK tours of *For the Love of Mike* and *Mother of Pearl*.

At the Ascot enclosure lords and ladies watch the races with a carefully regulated excitement, excite-ment with as much life in it as a formal gavotte. Higgins and Pickering have determined to risk a public presentation of their pupil. Eliza's dic-tion proves perfect, even when she reveals to their horror, "Gin was mother's milk." Her grammar and startling pronouncements entrance Freddie Eynsford-Hill (John Michael King), who promptly falls in love with her and thereafter spends an inordi-nate amount of his time "On The Street Where You Live." At an Embassy Ball Higgins brazenly dances Eliza into the arms of a Hungarian named Karpathy, who has publicly professed to spot impostors unfail-ingly. It becomes obvious from the congratulations Higgins and Pickering exchange when they return home that Karpathy was soundly gulled. Higgins and Pickering each tell the other, "You Did It," ignoring any part Eliza may have played in her own education. This prompts Eliza to leave the house. On the street she meets Freddie, who has contin-ued to mope about, and when Freddie spills out his feelings, she insists, "Show Me." The empty-headed Freddie fails to comprehend or act decisively. She hits him with her suitcase and goes on her way, but she finds she is unrecognized and out of place in her old haunts, until she meets her father. Doolittle is bitter at Higgins. The money Higgins presented him has delivered him "into the hands of middle-class morality." In short, he is about to be married. But before he succumbs he will have one last old-fash-ioned toot. While urging his cronies to "pull out the stopper" and make his final drink "a whopper," he begs, "Get Me To The Church On Time." Deserted by Eliza, the baffled and hurt Higgins sings a "Hymn To Him," inquiring "why can't a woman be more like a man," then, more specifically, why can't a woman be more like him and Pickering, and finally why a woman can't be just like he himself is. Eliza, meanwhile, visits Henry's mother (Cathleen Nesbitt), seeking advice. But Higgins barges in:

Higgins: Get up and come home and don't be a
  fool! You've caused me enough trouble for one
  morning!
Mrs. Higgins: Very nicely put, indeed, Henry. No
  woman could resist such an invitation.
Higgins: You mean I'm to put on my Sunday manners for this thing I created out of the squashed
  cabbage leaves of Covent Garden?
Mrs. Higgins: Yes, dear, that is precisely what I mean.
Higgins: I'll see her damned first.

But Eliza will not be subservient. She informs the startled Higgins that art, music, Keats, and the rain in Spain will all survive "Without You." Higgins storms out. He is furious. Still, he must wistfully acknowledge, "I've Grown Accustomed To Her Face." Alone in his study he replays primitive recordings he made while working on Eliza's speech. Eliza enters quietly. Her return is a tacit admission of her feelings and her situation. Although Higgins is joyous, all he can think to ask is "Where the devil are my slippers?"

This ending, which Shaw had allowed for a movie version, was the principal deviation from the original play. To Lerner's literate, civilized book and lyrics, Loewe appended a score that, while never inventive, was graceful and melodic. If it seemed at times derivative, the need to keep period flavor was more to blame than any failing on the composer's part. To many these period costumes and songs echoing an earlier era argued that *My Fair Lady* was a modern-day operetta, underscoring how the modern musical play was really a continuation of an older tradition.

The original production added more praiseworthy elements. The nonpareil cast was headed by Rex Harrison, who made a definitive Higgins, and Julie Andrews, who fulfilled the promise of *The Boy Friend* with her superlative performance as Eliza. The rest of the fine cast sparkled under Moss Hart's scintillating direction. Oliver Smith designed magnificent sets (most notably an Ascot conceived in black, gray, and white), and Cecil Beaton came over from England to create ravishing period costumes. Companies of the show established records in major cities all over the world. The New York company alone entertained patrons for 2,717 performances, or over six years.

One interesting sidelight was CBS-Columbia's sizable investment in the original production in order to secure recording rights. The gamble proved doubly rewarding, for not only did the show turn out to be a gold mine, but the original-cast LP became the biggest-selling show album in history until that time.

Despise its period settings and the necessary period flavor of its score, *My Fair Lady* unquestionably represented the glorious fruition of the contemporary school of musical plays with its aim of cohesiveness and tonal integrity. How ironic then that the very next musical to arrive—one week after Lerner and Loewe's masterpiece—was contemporary in setting and contemporary in sound, yet was a clear throwback to the slapdash vehicles of bygone years. The evening was meant to introduce a popular black nightclub entertainer, Sammy Davis, Jr., to the legitimate stage. **Mr. Wonderful** (22 March 1956, Broadway) told an unusually simple, straightforward tale. Charlie Welch is a small-time performer whose fiancée, Ethel (Olga James), and whose white friend, Fred Campbell (Jack Carter), both believe he belongs at the top of his profession. They persuade him to try his act at the Palm Club in Miami Beach. He does, and achieves great success. Most of the second act was merely an onstage repeat of the act Davis, his father, and his uncle had played to applause as the Will Mastin Trio. Jerry Bock, Larry Holofcener, and George Weiss's score added two new standards to the repertory.

Curiously the hit of the evening was sung not by Davis but by Miss James. It was the title song. Davis's big hit was a solid swing number, "Too Close For Comfort." Although Davis and the hit songs kept customers corning to the large Broadway Theatre for nearly a year (383 performances), theatrical economics left the show in the red.

JERRY BOCK was born in New Haven, Connecticut, on 23 November 1928, but moved at the age of two to New York City. His musical education began early and culminated with his majoring in music at the University of Wisconsin. He wrote for college musicals, television, and films before his songs were heard on Broadway for the first time earlier in the season in *Catch a Star*.

A spring season of revivals at the City Center offered *The King and I* (29 March 1951) with Zachary Scott and Jan Clayton on 18 April, followed by *Kiss Me, Kate* (30 December 1948) with Kitty Carlisle on 9 May, and *Carmen Jones* (2 December 1943) on 31 May.

The season's second commercial success was **The Most Happy Fella** (3 May 1956, Imperial). Critics divided sharply on how great an artistic success it was, but even those unhappy with the results unhesitatingly gave it top marks for sincerity. *The Most Happy Fella* was a musical adaptation of Sidney Howard's hit of the 1924–1925 season, *They Knew What They Wanted*—and it was the work of one man, Frank Loesser. While there were over forty musical numbers and while the spoken dialogue was kept to a minimum, Loesser refused to brand the work an opera or even a musical play, preferring to consider it an "extended musical comedy." His designation was honest, but it pointed to the great flaw in the work that its detractors harped on. For, although Loesser wrote the piece singlehandedly, he seemed unable or unwilling to imbue it with a consistent style and tone. Some of its passages were floridly arioso; some recalled the inventive, up-to-the-minute idioms he had employed in *Guys and Dolls*, while others were out-and-out musical comedy turns. The show retained the original drama's division into three acts—rare in modern musicals. As in Howard's play an aging vintner in the Napa Valley, Tony (Robert Weede), is attracted to a young lady he sees working in a San Francisco restaurant. In a letter he asks the girl to send him her photograph. She responds, asking for his photograph in return. But Tony, fearful of her cutting off the correspondence abruptly, sends her a photograph of his young, handsome hired hand, Joe (Art Lund). The girl, Rosabella (Jo Sullivan), arrives at the ranch and greets Joe warmly. Joe quickly disabuses her. She is ready to make a hasty retreat when word arrives that Tony has been injured in an accident while on his way to meet her. Touched by the sight of the injured man, she agrees to remain, and before much time elapses they are married. But this does not prevent a brief, impassioned love affair between Rosabella and Joe. To make his wife more at home, Tony invites her best friend, Cleo (Susan Johnson), to stay on the farm. Cleo quickly becomes involved with another hired hand, Herman (Shorty Long), and their relationship offers a light-hearted counterpoint to Tony and Rosabella's story. After Rosabella discovers she is pregnant, she decides to leave rather than hurt Tony with an admission of infidelity. When Tony tries to stop her, the truth comes out. At first Tony is livid, threatening to kill Joe. With time to reflect, he realizes that both he and Rosabella will only return to separate lonelinesses. He offers to accept the child as his own, and Rosabella, deeply moved, agrees.

The story was dangerously sentimental, but Loesser adroitly managed to underplay its most maudlin aspects. In singing Tony, Weede became the season's second major opera star to try Broadway. The most operatic of the passages fell to him. Rosabella had more conventional ballads, such as the beautiful "Somebody, Somewhere." However, an all-but-nameless male quartet was given one of the show's two major hits, "Standing On The Corner," while Cleo, Herman, and the chorus attacked the rousing second hit, a tribute to Dallas called "Big 'D.'" Despite its flaws, the evening's surefire professionalism and general excellence told. To varying degrees, it pleased and sometimes annoyed theatregoers for a year and a half.

The season's final new offering was another Phoenix Theatre revue on 22 May. It was a far cry from the preceding season's *Phoenix '55*, with its broad clowning by Nancy Walker. The new offering was called **The Littlest Revue**, a name that was probably meant to evoke echoes of the suave, intimate *Little Shows* of a quarter of a century before. A galaxy of the theatre's bright names made contributions to one department or another: Ogden Nash, Vernon Duke, John Latouche, Lee Adams, and Charles Strouse, among others. Skits had fun with old-timers who haunted the recently demolished Brevoort Hotel, off-Broadway plays, toilets, diets, and Noël Coward, while songs ran the gamut from love ballads to "Second Avenue And 12th Street Rag" (Nash/Duke) to an untraditional "Summer Is A-Comin' In" (Latouche/Duke). The material was performed by some equally bright talent that included Joel Grey, Tammy Grimes, and Charlotte Rae—all names on the way up. While the show developed a coterie of staunch admirers, they had little chance to see it in the flesh. The revue opened on 22 May and by 17 June gave its final performance.

No doubt the main reason a group of advocates could develop to sing the real or imagined virtues of so quick a flop was the practice of issuing original-cast recordings for almost every musical to reach Broadway. As mentioned earlier this practice began in America only with *Oklahoma!*, though England had been doing it, and benefiting, since the 1900s. Not only did the practice keep alive material that might otherwise have been forgotten—or used to better advantage in a later, more successful show—but on occasion, as with *Pal Joey*, it actually precipitated a major revival. Unfortunately, by the seventies the economics of the record industry put a stop to the issuance of original-cast records except for a handful of runaway hits.

1956-1957

The season was intriguing, unorthodox, and ultimately frustrating. Among composers, all the surviving old masters were absent, and only two of the better young songwriters were represented—Jule Styne and Leonard Bernstein. Not unpredictably, they offered the year's best scores. A few dependable names appeared among libretto credits: Lindsay and Crouse, Comden and Green, and George Abbott. One surprising new name was Lillian Hellman, heretofore celebrated for her stark dramas. Yet old hands and newcomers alike failed to find quite the right approach to their stories. Most of the season's musicals relied heavily on the drawing power of their female stars. Perhaps the most fascinating aspect of the season's crop was the unlikely source material nearly every show resorted to: Al Capp's comic strip, *Li'l Abner*, Voltaire's *Candide*, Don Marquis's *archy and mehitabel*, and Eugene O'Neill's *Anna Christie*. Most of these works were untheatrical, and those, like the O'Neill drama, which were fine theatre were nonetheless fundamentally unsuited for light musical treatment. They were exciting challenges, irresistible to a musical theatre that craved novelty and a certain degree of artistic daring. But for the time being they proved at once mountable physically and insurmountable aesthetically.

The season opened with a seemingly obvious possibility for adaptation, a musical version of James Hilton's novel *Lost Horizon*. Hilton collaborated with Jerome Lawrence and Robert E. Lee, two popular playwrights, on the book, and Harry Warren returned to Broadway after a long, successful sojourn in Hollywood to create the score. An exceptionally strong cast was recruited: Dennis King, Jack Cassidy, Martyn Green, Harold Lang, Carol Lawrence, and Alice Ghostley. Hilton's romantic tale of a group of harried Westerners whose plane crashes in the hidden Utopia of **Shangri-La** (13 June 1956, Winter Garden) was relived. A few are so taken with the mysterious land they elect never to return home. Somehow a tale and setting that in the mind's eye took on a unique magic seemed cumbersome and

contrived in the flesh. A specially built stage of translucent plastic, lit from below, apparently to suggest a landscape covered with glistening snow, managed only to underscore the evening's contrived nature. Warren's music was particularly disappointing. *Shangri-La* survived for just two and a half weeks.

The principal attraction of the latest in the on-again, off-again series **New Faces of '56** (14 June 1956, Barrymore) was the finest female impersonator Broadway had seen since the days of Julian Eltinge and Bert Savoy. So clever was T. C. Jones that many in the audience were unaware the performer was a male until he took off his wig and revealed his bald head during the curtain calls. His best sketch was an easy but riotous spoof of a grand *Follies* production number. Other skits satirized the popular Japanese films of the time and the successful American motion picture about violence in high schools, *The Blackboard Jungle*. The opening skit, which knocked the United Nations, was by Neil Simon and his brother, Dan. The humor was not always surefire, and the songs, in the unfortunate tradition of the series, were largely time-wasters. One attractive young lady, largely unnoticed at the time, went on to distinguish herself on the London stage, Maggie Smith. Although *New Faces of '56* ran over six months, it became one of many longer runs of the era to close in the red.

Apart from the New York City Opera's September presentations of *Orpheus in the Underworld* and the seemingly inevitable *Die Fledermaus*, nearly five months passed before another musical offering appeared. A lady named Iva Kitchell attempted a one-woman revue entitled **That Girl at the Bijou** (9 November 1956, Bijou). Her program progressed alphabetically, running from "Bacchanale (As Seen at the Opera)"—with Saint-Saëns music—to "Ze Ballet" with music by Ponchielli. Most of the material in between had music by her pianist, Harvey Brown. But even at the smallest remaining regular Broadway house, Miss Kitchell could only attract enough interest for eleven performances.

When **Li'l Abner** (15 November 1956, St. James) bounced in, the denizens of Dogpatch came to life behind the footlights. As she had for so many years on the daily comic page, Daisy Mae (Edith Adams) prepared to catch her beloved Li'l Abner (Peter Palmer) in the annual Sadie Hawkins Day chase. She is all the more determined this year because Earthquake McGoon (Bern Hoffman) has his eye on her and because Abner will also be pursued by the voluptuous Appassionata Von Climax (Tina Louise). Daisy is abetted, and now and then hindered, by such other notable Dogpatch characters as Mammy and Pappy Yokum, General Bullmoose, Senator Jack S. Phogbound, Mayor Dawgmeat, Marryin' Sam, and Evil Eye Fleagle. Their lives are further complicated after the government, declaring Dogpatch the most useless piece of real estate in the USA, decides to test an atom bomb there. The village is spared when a plaque, in which Abe Lincoln declares Dogpatch a national shrine, is uncovered as the townspeople prepare to remove a statue of Dogpatch's founder. The book could not always sustain the humor of Al Capp's cartoon, but it was serviceable. The evening burst into a foot-stomping exuberance whenever Michael Kidd set his chorus dancing to Gene de Paul's lively melodies. With Johnny Mercer as his lyricist, de Paul wrote one ballad that enjoyed a modest acclaim, Abner and Daisy Mae's "Namely You." With the help of Marryin' Sam (Stubby Kaye) and the Dogpatch community, they told of the founder of Dogpatch, a latter-day Duke of Plaza-Toro, "Jubilation T. Cornpone."

It had been many years since comic strips had provided material for a Broadway musical. Authors had apparently assumed readers of "the funnies" had left the theatre for cheaper, less intellectual entertainments. *Li'l Abner* shot that theory full of holes, running happily for just short of 700 performances.

An English revue, **Cranks** (26 November 1956, Bijou), was the brainchild of John Cranko, who later became the distinguished head of the Stuttgart Ballet. He incorporated no real skits and no songs of any matter. Instead, he offered a highly stylized evening whose "self-conscious posturings less suggested a revue than the religious rites of the Stanislavsky methodists." It left after forty showings. With it went one young performer, Anthony Newley, soon to have, his brief moment upon the New York musical stage.

November's last show was **Bells Are Ringing** (29 November 1956, Shubert), a conventional musical that in many ways was the most satisfying show of the season. Much of its charm derived from its authors' awareness that it was conventional and that nothing would be gained by pretension and overreaching. The rest of its charm came from Judy Holliday, who costarred with Sydney Chaplin. Betty Comden and Adolph Green—who had started their careers in a nightclub act with Miss Holliday—supplied book and lyrics. Their story was one of only two during the season drawn entirely from its writers' fertile imaginations and not from an older play or novel.

Growing demand for telephone-answering services provided the background of the story. Ella Peterson (Miss Holliday) works for "Susanswerphone." She is a pleasant, well-meaning girl, with confused proprieties. Her sense of dignity requires she put on her lipstick before answering the phone, but it in no way prevents her from eavesdropping on conversations or meddling in the lives of her customers. One customer who receives her special attention is Jeff Moss (Chaplin), an aspiring playwright. After Ella overhears a particularly nasty call with a producer, she rushes over to Jeff's apartment and coaxes him into rewriting his material. In no time the two are in love. But Ella's life is complicated by another customer, Sandor (Eddie Lawrence), who allows her to take orders for what are ostensibly records. Actually an order for three dozen of Beethoven's Fifth is a bet on the third horse in the fifth race at Belmont. The police enter the picture, and for a while Jeff and Ella's romance seems headed for the rocks, but just when Ella is set to pack and return home, Jeff comes back to her. Jule Styne's score, like Comden and Green's book, was comfortably old hat. The hit of the evening was the lovers' simple ballad that relied on an essentially two-note melody, "Just In Time." Somewhat more expansive was the poignant "The Party's Over," which Ella sings when she believes she has lost Jeff. Comden and Green's clever lyrics abounded in songs such as "Drop That Name" (a dig at social-climbing partygoers) and the expository opening, "It's A Perfect Relationship." Styne's melodies ranged from the contemporary sounds of the same opening to the nostalgic rag at the closing, "I'm Going Back." *Bells Are Ringing* delighted audiences for over two years.

Candide (1 December 1956, Martin Beck) was the season's most interesting failure. At least it seemed a failure to everyone at the time, including its librettist, Lillian Hellman, who claims it was the beginning of her disenchantment with the theatre. Since it marked her first efforts for the musical stage, she deferred to suggestions of her collaborators when changes were required in the book, although her instincts insisted her projected alterations were right and theirs wrong. Her instincts indeed may have been correct, for the show that was played at the Martin Beck suffered from a clumsy, uncertain, heavy-handed book. Miss Hellman could not, however, have been accused of tampering with the story line. Young Candide (Robert Rounseville) is again tutored by an ever-optimistic Pangloss (Max Adrian), who assures him everything is for the best in this best of all possible worlds. He even encourages

Candide's marriage to Cunegonde (Barbara Cook), for all the problems it will bring. In the middle of the marriage ceremony war between Westphalia and Hesse intervenes, and Cunegonde is carried off. Candide's troubles have begun. He reaches Lisbon in time for the great earthquake. There the Inquisition apparently kills Pangloss. Moving on to Paris, Candide discovers Cunegonde living in kept luxury, determined to "Glitter And Be Gay." Candide, Cunegonde, and an Old Lady (Irra Petina) they have met are carried off on a slave ship to South America. In Buenos Aires the governor proposes to make Cunegonde his mistress, and with the help of the "easily assimilated" Old Lady he convinces Candide to seek his fortune elsewhere. Candide heads for Eldorado, where he does, in fact, find a fortune. Returning to claim Cunegonde, he learns she has fled. The ship in which he sets out after her sinks, so the despairing Candide makes his way to Venice. He discovers the Old Lady working as a shill in a gambling house. She, too, is less confident and tinged with bitterness. Candide discovers Cunegonde reduced to a scrubwoman. He returns with her to Westphalia, where, to his amazement, he encounters the supposedly dead Pangloss. But Candide can no longer subscribe to the philosopher's all-accepting view of life. He and Cunegonde retire to live quietly and to make their garden grow. The show's lyrics were from the pens of three brilliant rhymers—John Latouche (who died, at the age of thirty-eight, shortly before the show opened), the Pulitzer Prize–winning poet Richard Wilbur, and Dorothy Parker. At best these lyrics were brittle and witty; at times they labored under the slight burden of the artificiality and formality of the story's period, and now and then they lapsed into Broadway trickery. For them Bernstein created a pyrotechnic, eclectic score that moved from stately eighteenth-century forms to modern tangos and jazz. The most popular, durable bit of his work turned out to be the overture, whose theme has become familiar to concertgoers. The flaws in the evening and even its unconventional successes told against the work. It played seventy-three performances and was put away until a revised production two decades later presented it with such overall flair that the public could no longer resist its charms.

Happy Hunting (6 December 1956, Majestic) was the season's second old-fashioned musical comedy, with the season's second original book to come to Broadway. Just as Lindsay and Crouse had used Harry Truman's appointment of Perle Mesta as the starting point for *Call Me Madam*, they contrived another story for Ethel Merman out of Grace Kelly's marriage to Prince Rainier of Monaco. Miss Merman played a wealthy, pushy Main Line matron, Liz Livingstone, who is so angry at not being invited to the wedding that she determines to marry her daughter, Beth (Virginia Gibson), to someone even more imposing. She sets her sights on the Duke of Granada (Fernando Lamas), a Hapsburg. In her own way she is as naive as Sally Adams was. When she hears Rainier referred to as "His Grace," she inquires, "Is his name Grace, too?" The Duke is captivated by her naïveté; Liz finds that she, and not her daughter, is being wooed. Beth is left with the pleasant young man she wanted in the first place, Sanford Stewart (Gordon Polk). Liz has one last laugh. She learns the duke's name is Jaime and is amused to contemplate the Main Line's reaction when, given the correct pronunciation, they learn she is Mrs. Jaime Hapsburg. The book was adequate, but Miss Merman was left without any first-class songs to belt out in Matt Dubey and Harold Karr's material. The show's best numbers were two country-style tunes, "Mutual Admiration Society" and "If'n." Both enjoyed momentary replayings, but neither became a Merman standard. Miss Merman, in fact, did not even sing "If'n" in the show. One cleverly staged song was "A New-Fangled Tango," sung by a chorus crammed onto a minuscule dance floor and unable to do little more than move its fingers. Miss Merman kept the show on the boards for a full year, but most of the time to far-from-full houses, and when *Happy Hunting* closed it went down in the books as one of her rare commercial failures.

After November and December's outpouring of new musicals subsided, no more new lyric pieces danced across the boards until March, when a new edition of **The Ziegfeld Follies** (1 March 1957, Winter Garden) appeared. It was advertised as a Golden Jubilee edition, fifty years after the unveiling of the initial *Follies*. Most critics felt it was an insult rather than a tribute. Much of its material and physical production had been salvaged from an edition of the *Follies* with Tallulah Bankhead that had folded during its tryout the preceding season. Sets and costumes were skimpy, unimaginative, and shabby. Worse, there were a mere eight girls (on some nights only six) to recall Ziegfeld's breathtaking line of beauties. The show had a fine cast that included Harold Lang and Carol Lawrence (both free after the *Shangri-La* debacle) and wasted the talents of a great clown, Billy De Wolfe. He did the best he could with a take-off of the writhing rock-and-roll star Elvis Presley and participated in a not very funny spoof of *My Fair Lady*. Only Beatrice Lillie had some passable material. She played a Charles Addams character at a fine restaurant in "Milady Dines Alone," kidded the Japanese craze in "Kabuki Lil," and played an airline stewardess who is forever singing "I've Got A Feeling I'm Falling" in "High and Flighty." She, too, took part in "My Late, Late Lady," singing, "I Had A Bath Last Night." The music was so indifferent no original-cast album was released. Miss Lillie's art and Ziegfeld's name kept the show alive into June.

The New York City Center began a somewhat more venturesome than usual series of spring revivals on 13 March with *The Beggar's Opera*, giving New Yorkers a chance to compare the original with the Weill-Brecht *Threepenny Opera* still playing in the Village. Jack Cassidy acted Macheath, and Shirley Jones was Polly. *Brigadoon* followed on 27 March, with Helen Gallagher and Robert Rounseville among the principals. *The Merry Widow* with Marta Eggerth and Jan Kiepura graced the boards on 10 April, and *South Pacific* on 24 April. Robert Wright and Mindy Carson were featured. The season closed with *The Pajama Game* in May.

Shinbone Alley (13 April 1957, Broadway) demonstrated once more that magic created in the mind's eye is easily destroyed by flesh-and-blood actors on a spotlit stage. In Don Marquis's *archy and mehitabel* stories, archy is a cockroach who writes free verse by throwing himself onto the keys of a typewriter. Since he can't hold down two keys at once, all his writing is in lower-case letters. Mehitabel is a friendly neighborhood cat. The producers hired Eartha Kitt, who had often been described as "feline," to portray mehitabel. But the adjective became almost meaningless in the face of human forms and sounds. Eddie Bracken, a fading Hollywood comedian who played archy, bore no resemblance to any known cockroach. What little story there was described archy's persistent, unrequited passion for mehitabel. He remains loyal even when she is lured away and made pregnant by Big Bill (George S. Irving), a tough tomcat. This almost plotless play was by Joe Darion and Mel Brooks (Brooks later went on to Hollywood acclaim). Darion also provided lyrics to George Kleinsinger's music. Together they devised some cute, if not memorable, songs. But all in all *Shinbone Alley* lacked the stuff of which hits are made, and what pleasures it offered were lost in the vastness of the large Broadway Theatre. It packed its trunks after forty-nine performances.

The Phoenix Theatre dispensed with the end-of-season revues it had offered the two preceding sessions and instead offered a loosely structured musical based on Mark Twain's Mississippi River stories. All the old favorites were present: Huckleberry Finn, Tom Sawyer, Aunt Polly, Becky Thatcher, and Injun Joe. But they, too, seemed more lovable and somehow more believable on the pages of a book. **Livin' the Life** (27 April 1957) sang its unpretentious songs for twenty-five showings and folded.

The season's final musical was in many ways its most distressing. **New Girl in Town** (14 May 1957. 46th St.) was a lyric adaptation of Eugene O'Neill's somber *Anna Christie*. If this drama was ever material for musicalization—and that is questionable—it was probably only workable in the hands of, say, Rodgers and Hammerstein or Frank Loesser or Leonard Bernstein. As it developed, though, it was George Abbott who was responsible for the transition. With the assistance of Bob Merrill, who had written a number of light, Hit Parade tunes, he turned it into a noisy, explosive musical comedy. By changing its setting from the days just after World War I to the turn of the century, he also turned it into another of this period's colorful costume pieces. The stark human drama was made to play second fiddle to splashy colors and wild dancing. However, the story line remained largely untouched. Anna, a prostitute recovering from a siege of tuberculosis, seeks a haven with her seafaring father, Chris (Cameron Prud'homme). Chris is ignorant of Anna's recent past. While she is staying with her father, she falls in love with another seaman, Mat (George Wallace). Her idyll is shattered when Mat learns of her old trade and deserts her. But he later returns, convinced Anna is willing to turn over a new leaf. Abbott wrote a workmanlike book, and Merrill filled the evening with facile, often percussive, melodies. The principal attractions of *New Girl in Town* were its lively Bob Fosse dances, with Gwen Verdon as Anna leading the fancy stepping, and the offhand comedy of Thelma Ritter in the role of Chris's companion, Marthy. Miss Ritter had a show-stopping number called "Flings" in which she insisted flings have to be "flung by the young." O'Neill's ghost may have winced, but audiences, beguiled by the stars' performances and unable to find better competition elsewhexre, kept the show in business for over a year.

1957–1958

Two of the period's finest musicals were the season's outstanding successes. Although they were strikingly different, both suggested that artistry and integrity were neither lacking nor unwelcome in the commercial theatre. If only one show boasted an abundance of the singable melodies that had enhanced the shows of earlier eras or the better Rodgers offerings of their own time, both boasted a unique appreciation of style and tone—and good enough songs. The rest of the season's musicals, however, were even less rewarding musically, and none had anything approaching the unity of feeling of the best pieces. Nonetheless almost all the other musicals had something attractive to offer—usually memorable performances—and the public that couldn't buy tickets for *West Side Story* or *The Music Man* was generally able to find some consolation on stages elsewhere.

The black poet Langston Hughes was responsible for the book and lyrics of **Simply Heavenly** (20 August 1957, Playhouse), a work that moved to the main stem after its off-Broadway success. A light-hearted, affectionate look at a small group of Harlem characters, it was a far cry from the stark, poetic material Hughes had contributed to *Street Scene* (9 January 1947). Simple (Melvin Stewart) is a likable bungler who has lost his first wife and his job to better men. He is torn between the wholesome Joyce (Marilyn Berry) and the brazenly sensual Zarita (Anna English). For a number of critics the highlight of the evening was the hero's recounting of his dream to be the first Negro to lead white Mississippians into battle. Hughes's material dominated David Martin's weak score, giving the impression the work was a play with music rather than a musical comedy. The public response to black plays was still unpredictable. Despite generally encouraging notices, theatregoers stayed away. *Simply Heavenly* closed 12 October.

September's first offering was even less successful, closing the same night as *Simply Heavenly*. **Mask and Gown** (10 September 1957, Golden) was a revue written around the talents of T. C. Jones. Jones had been the most celebrated discovery in Leonard Sillman's most recent *New Faces*, and Sillman thanked him by mounting the new show. A brief look at theatre history could have warned the producer he was heading for rocky waters. Even in their heyday, female impersonators such as Julian Eltinge and Bert Savoy never attempted one-artist shows. Eltinge appeared in book musicals that carefully explained how he came to have to dress as a woman. Others in the cast had substantial time to offer respites from what was essentially a single joke.

Savoy never attempted to rationalize his transvestite act but performed in large-scale revues that provided a variety of other distractions during the evening. Jones appeared with only four other performers, presenting uneven material by several *New Faces* authors. Jones's lame bits satirized television, Ruby Keeler–style movies, Shakespeare, and T. C. Jones. Had the material been better, there still would have been good reason to question the show's chances of success. The season would show the day of the clown was over on Broadway—at least for the foreseeable future. It was, sadly, for T. C. Jones.

The night after *Mask and Gown* premiered, *Carousel* (19 April 1945) was revived briefly at the City Center. Barbara Cook and Howard Keel played the leads, while Victor Moore came out of retirement to portray the Starkeeper. *Annie Get Your Gun* followed in February, and Nancy Walker brought her special comedy to *Wonderful Town* (25 February 1952), while *Oklahoma!* (31 March 1943) closed the Center's season in March.

West Side Story (26 September 1957, Winter Garden), as originally conceived by Jerome Robbins, was to have retold the Romeo and Juliet legend in terms of young Irish and Jewish lovers. However, Robbins and Leonard Bernstein—who was called in to do the music—decided the Irish–Jewish theme had been run dry on Broadway and, in any case, had diminishing contemporary validity. On the other hand the influx of Puerto Ricans onto the New York scene offered a group given to high passion and violence, the very meat of Shakespeare's story. Their gang wars suggested a likely substitute for family feuds. To oppose the Spanish-speaking gang, Arthur Laurents, the librettist, assembled "an anthology of what is called American" and christened the rival group the Jets. The Puerto Ricans became the Sharks. The Jets, boastful and contemptuous of the immigrants, have decided to challenge the Sharks to a street fight, a rumble. They have Riff (Mickey Calin) ask Tony (Larry Kert) to be present. Tony was a founder of the group, but he has become puzzlingly peaceable and drifted away. Riff reminds Tony of his old allegiance and of how menacing the newcomers are. Tony agrees reluctantly, falling in with the peculiar patter of the group:

Tony: What time?
Riff: Ten?
Tony: Ten it is.
Riff: Womb to tomb!

Tony: Sperm to worm! And I'll live to regret this.
Riff: Who knows? Maybe what you're waitin' for'll be twitchin' at the dance!

Suddenly Tony finds himself excited, for "Something's Coming." Meanwhile, in a bridal shop, Anita (Chita Rivera), the sweetheart of the Sharks' leader, Bernardo (Ken Le Roy), is converting Maria's communion dress into a gown for the dance. Maria (Carol Lawrence) is Bernardo's sister, and he has brought her from Puerto Rico hoping she will marry his friend Chino (Jamie Sanchez). At the dance Riff challenges Bernardo, and the groups agree to the battle. Tony and Maria spot each other and fall in love instantly. Tony can only apostrophize on his new flame, "Maria." Together Tony and Maria ignore the terror building around them in "Tonight." Most of the Puerto Ricans are nervously elated over the coming hassle, but they are confident and determined to embrace the chrome-plated comforts of "America," despite the homesick reminiscences of one of the girls, Rosalia (Marilyn Cooper). A name-calling session is interrupted by a policeman, who orders the Puerto Ricans to disperse:

Clear out, Spics. Sure; it's a free country and I ain't got the right. But it's a country with laws; and I can find the right. I got the badge, you got the skin. It's tough all over. Beat it!

But the fracas is merely delayed. When it does begin and when Tony attempts to halt it, he succeeds only in distracting his own friend Riff long enough to allow Bernardo to fatally stab him. In a fury Tony kills Bernardo with Riff's knife. While all this is going on, Maria is at home singing to herself coquettishly, "I Feel Pretty." Chino appears with the news. Before Maria's feelings have time to take form, Tony arrives, and her love for him overrides her hatred for her brother's killer. He promises to take her away; in a dream ballet ("Somewhere") the battle is reenacted, but this time the lovers are not allowed to meet. The dream turns into a nightmare, but Tony and Maria flee, seeking haven in lovemaking. The gangs, meanwhile, are concerned with their inevitable encounter with the law and, singing "Gee, Officer Krupke!," they mockingly imagine how they will handle themselves. Anita savagely taunts Maria for remaining faithful to Tony, but she is prevailed upon to deliver Maria's message for Tony to the Jets. Unfortunately the Jets so cruelly revile her that she is driven to claim Chino has shot and killed

Maria. On hearing this Tony goes after Chino, but Chino shoots him just as Tony discovers that Maria is not dead after all. Somewhat ashamed, the Jets and the Sharks jointly remove Tony's body as Maria follows them.

The evening emphasized the jangling noise, the sordidness, and the roughness of tenement life, confining its lyricism to the mere facts of the love story and to the passion of much of Bernstein's score. It also offered a dream ballet as a concession to the still voguish form. And, of course, it let its Juliet live. But none of these deviations or compromises affected the integrity of the work, which remained cohesive and overpowering. At times some theatregoers found the reflections of street language too overpowering. Even though the lyrics were printed as "If the spit hits the fan" and "Every last buggin' gang on the whole buggin' street!" they were conveniently distorted—intentionally or not—by theatrical projection. Of course it could be argued that the use of derogatory epithets such as "wop" and "spic" represented a more socially conscious and artistically responsible employment than their careless usage in the musicals of thirty and forty years before. The old usage implied an indifference or even an acceptance of such demeaning expressions. More explosive language had long been infiltrating the theatre. It had even spread to the once-staid London stage. *Look Back in Anger*, the prime example of the work of that city's new school of "Angry Young Men," opened five nights after *West Side Story*. The musical's lyrics were the first Broadway musical-play credits for Stephen Sondheim.

STEPHEN SONDHEIM was born on 22 March 1930 and educated at Williams College. He then studied music in New York with Milton Babbitt. Dropping his musical interests temporarily, Sondheim collaborated on scripts for television's *Topper* series, but returned to the musical field to write background music for the Broadway play *Girls of Summer*.

For many the most electrifying parts of the evening were—unfortunately for future generations—Robbins's tense, vibrant dances, especially the rumble. But everything was in top working order. *West Side Story* ran 981 performances in its hometown (in two slightly separated runs of 732 and 249 performances). It compiled an even greater 1,040 performances in London. Her portrayal of the original Anita launched Chita Rivera on her road to stardom.

CHITA RIVERA was born in Washington, D.C., on 23 January 1933 and christened Dolores Conchita del Rivero. After training at the American School of Ballet, she appeared as Conchita del Rivero in *Guys and Dolls* and was in the road company of *Call Me Madam*, as well as in *Can-Can*. She altered her name when she became a featured dancer in a *Shoestring Revue*.

The first of October's two new musicals brought the hilarious Nancy Walker back to Broadway in **Copper and Brass** (17 October 1957, Martin Beck). Miss Walker played the hopelessly jinxed policewoman Katey O'Shea. When she marches in a police parade all the other policemen somehow march in the opposite direction (shades of Bea Lillie's "March With Me"), and when she stoops to pick up a paper she has dropped in the Holland Tunnel (where she has been assigned as punishment) she creates a massive chain crash. Off duty, Katey becomes hopelessly trapped in the depths of a modernistic chair. Miss Walker's antics skillfully concealed the mediocrity of David Craig and David Baker's material. But as T. C. Jones had demonstrated earlier, the vogue for broad-styled, visual fun-makers had waned. For all her riotous rampaging, she could not attract sufficient patronage. *Copper and Brass* ran just over one month.

Before the next new opus premiered, the New York City Opera once more resurrected *Die Fledermaus* and *The Merry Widow* during its fall season. (Come spring, the company sang three newer works: *Trouble in Tahiti, Lost in the Stars*, and *Regina*.)

The movies' svelte Lena Horne proved a big enough box office lure to help **Jamaica** (31 October 1957, Imperial) to a run of well over a year. *Jamaica* succeeded by presenting in primary colors something *House of Flowers* (30 December 1954) had unsuccessfully attempted with pastels. Again the composer was Harold Arlen, but the librettists were the librettists of *Finian's Rainbow* (10 January 1947) and *Flahooley* (14 May 1951), E. Y. Harburg and Fred Saidy. They

found themselves on a tropical, relatively apolitical paradise called Pigeon's Island, off Jamaica's coast. There a poor, handsome fisherman, Koli (Ricardo Montalban), loves the beautiful Savannah (Miss Horne). But Savannah spends her hours dreaming of living in New York. A hustling dude, Joe Nashua (Joe Adams), has come to the island to exploit pearl-diving possibilities in its shark-infested waters. Savannah sees in him an all-expenses-paid trip to the big city. However, when Koli saves the life of Savannah's little brother during a hurricane, she comes to face reality and accepts her island suitor. She visits New York only in a dream ballet.

Although Arlen's music was obviously commercial, it was also less inspired and melodic than his *House of Flowers* score. Some numbers such as "Monkey In The Mango Tree" seemed like hand-me-downs. A number of critics preferred the comic songs "Push De Button" (Savannah's song spoofing a life with modern conveniences) and "Napoleon" (in which she sings how the great names of the past are exploited by commercial products). No critic recalled Arlen and Harburg had first used "Napoleon's A Pastry" in *Hooray for What!* (1 December 1937). Perhaps the best of Aden's ballads was Savannah's "Cocoanut Sweet." Since Miss Horne was the attraction and since she was featured in eleven of the twenty-one numbers (including reprises), most customers left satisfied. *Jamaica* was the second hit in David Merrick's burgeoning career.

A carefree lark called **Rumple** (6 November 1957, Alvin) had a novel plot. Unless cartoonist Nelson Crandal can recapture some of his original inspiration within forty-eight hours, his comic strip "Rumple" will be discontinued and his beloved little figure consigned to Oblivia, a sort of Valhalla for cartoon figures. At one point Rumple is allowed to visit Oblivia and consort briefly in a comic ballet with The Yellow Kid and other old-timers. The whole show had a happy, old-time flavor to it, including Ernest G. Schweikert's soft-shoe numbers, such as "In Times Like These." It also had Eddie Foy, Jr., in the title role and Stephen Douglass as Crandal. But its writers were all inexperienced, and producers Paula Stone and Mike Sloan, who had worked with Foy on their successful revival of *The Red Mill*, couldn't assemble everything with the necessary style. *Rumple* headed for Oblivia after forty-five showings.

But another musical with a happy, old-time flavor to it did succeed in putting its components together with a flair. In fact the homey artistry of

The Music Man (19 December 1957, Majestic) made it the biggest hit of the season. It couldn't have been more different from the season's other hit, *West Side Story*. Whereas the Bernstein–Sondheim opus tried to look at the harsh side of contemporary life with something approaching twenty-twenty vision, *The Music Man* gladly donned rose-colored glasses for a glimpse of 1912 America.

A group of traveling salesmen conduct a conversation in time with the rhythm of the train taking them to River City, Iowa. One of them is con man Harold Hill, who makes his living selling band instruments and then disappearing with the money before the instruments or his promised lessons can be delivered. His ploy is complicated in River City by Marian Paroo, "Marian, The Librarian," who has a sharp eye for swindlers. When Hill makes the mistake of claiming he was a member of the 1905 class of Gary University, she is prepared to expose him by quoting an article in "the Indiana State Educational Journal" showing the school had not yet been founded in 1905. Only the touching glee with which her young brother and her fellow townspeople await the Wells Fargo wagon that will deliver the instruments persuades her to rip out and destroy the incriminating page. Harold is forced to stay and teach the children how to play their instruments, although he cannot read a note of music. The interval allows him to fall in love with Marian, whom he had begun to court solely as a strategic maneuver. At last the band is ready for its first public appearance. The results are horrendous, but to the doting parents the ensuing cacophony sounds like angelic harmony.

One reason for the show's pervasive unity of style and tone was that it was the work of one man, Meredith Willson. Willson was born in Iowa and grew up there in the period about which he was now writing. He left to study music in New York did occasional composing, and for years was a popular orchestra leader on radio.

To a large degree, Willson captured the feeling of the time faithfully, working over his materials with imagination and resourcefulness. The show's big hit was the rousing march "Seventy-six Trombones," in which Hill pictures the rewards in having a school band. Willson used the same melody for Marian's attractive, lullaby-like love song, "Goodnight, My Someone." He also employed the clever device of using a barbershop quartet to comment on the action, with songs that allowed strong period flavor, such as the lovely "Lida Rose." He gave Harold a modern-day patter song in "Trouble." The only

jarring lapse in musical fidelity was the show's most popular love song, "Till There Was You," sung by the romantic leads, which had a distinctly late thirties or early forties sound. Robert Preston made a persuasive Harold, while Barbara Cook was a comely Marian. Significantly, this show, not *West Side Story*, walked away with all the seasonal awards. The public agreed. They kept the New York company on the boards for 1,375 performances.

A boxing musical, **The Body Beautiful** (23 January 1958, Broadway), was knocked out after just sixty showings. It had a book by Joseph Stein and Will Glickman, lyrics by Sheldon Harnick and music by Jerry Bock.

Stein and Glickman's story traced the efforts of Dave (Jack Warden), a failing boxer's manager, to make a champion out of a handsome graduate, Bob (Steve Forrest). At first the attempt seems hopeless, but when Bob starts to win he grows so egotistical he virtually wrecks his romance with Ann (Mindy Carson) and leaves everybody wishing a loss would bring him back to earth. It was all noisy and undistinguished. But its creators were intelligent men who would profit from their mistakes and proceed to better things.

Oh, Captain (4 February 1958, Alvin), a musicalized stage version of the highly popular Alec Guinness film *The Captain's Paradise*, kept the saga of Capt. Henry St. James, who has a reserved British wife in one port and a voluptuous foreign mistress in another. But instead of sailing back and forth across the Strait of Gibraltar as he did in the film, St. James cruises the English Channel and his romance unfolds in Paris. In this version Henry finally settles for dutiful monogamy. What *Oh, Captain* lost in transition was the film's light insouciance. The humor suddenly seemed heavy and contrived, and the songs were no help. One trick the show used several times was to repeat the Jay Livingston and Ray Evans songs with varying lyrics. For example, "Life Does A Man A Favor" was sung three times: once by the St. Jameses when they extol life's "simple joys," then by the captain and his crew when life "leads him down to the sea," and finally by St. James when "it puts him in Paree." Although Tony Randall, an intelligent actor, led a fine company that included the ballerina Alexandra Danilova, there was little they could do to save so uninspired an adaptation. It ran 192 showings, folding with a loss.

The worst fiasco of the season, **Portofino** (21 February 1958, Adelphi), like *Buttrio Square* (14 October 1952), went in search of fun in a confrontation of American tourists and Italian villagers. It didn't seem to find any and left after three performances.

International Soiree (12 March 1958, Bijou) was essentially a small vaudeville whose entire second half was devoted to the deep-voiced if nasal French chanteuse Patachou.

Three musicals, of sorts, came in during April. The first, **Say, Darling** (3 April 1958, ANTA), was a play based on a book about making a musical out of another book and had enough new music of its own to allow it to join the musical ranks. Richard Bissell collaborated on the story (from his own novel *Say, Darling*), with Abe Burrows and Marian Bissell. Bissell's novel recounted the backstage adventures of turning *7½ Cents* into *The Pajama Game*. Names were changed to protect the guilty, but the tough director, the cerebral, gesticulating young producer, and the fading star were all reasonably recognizable. The show had a pleasant Jule Styne score and serviceable Comden and Green lyrics. It also had a remarkably funny performance by Robert Morse. Morse played Ted Snow, the young producer. Some cognoscenti read Hal Prince for Ted Snow.

Impish **ROBERT MORSE** was born in Boston, Massachusetts, on 18 May 1931. After leaving the Navy he took work warming up television-studio audiences. His comic capers landed him in Hollywood, where he was awarded a part in *The Proud and the Profane*. Tyrone Guthrie brought him to New York for a principal role in Thornton Wilder's 1955 hit, *The Matchmaker*.

While the show was too choppy to be a good straight play and too spiritless to be a good musical, it played for nearly ten months, but it often played to barely profitable houses and was still in the red when it closed.

On 7 April Joyce Grenfell began a three-week run with her one-woman show that included numbers by Richard Addinsell and Donald Swann, with Gershwin medleys while Miss Grenfell was changing costumes.

The season's last lyric entertainment was a "Musical Salmagundi" that included comedian Mort Sahl, a dancer, Anneliese Widman, and a group labeled simply "The Folk Singers." Although the next election year was far off, the evening bore the untimely title **The Next President** (9 April 1958, Bijou) and provided each act with a socially significant label. The first act was "The Status Quo," while the second was the more awkward "A Brand New Attitude with the Same Old Prejudices." One of the Folk Singers' numbers was "The Chorus of Collective Conscience," but it fell largely to Sahl to deliver the leftish-slanted political satire in adaptations of his nightclub free-association monologues. This was the era of Eisenhower complacency, and not too many New Yorkers were willing to listen. The show was withdrawn after thirteen performances.

1958–1959

The 1958–1959 theatrical year marked the seventeenth season of this last great act. The era had run more than two-thirds of its course and gave signs of waning. The new season did bring in one of the towering masterpieces of the period, but except for that one show—*Gypsy*—it was a season of continual disappointment. Only two other regular American musicals proved commercial successes, while a third showed great staying power if no profit. Although not without their attractions, all three owed some of their popularity to lack of solid competition.

Goldilocks (11 October 1958, Lunt-Fontanne) inaugurated the season, ending a half-year in which no musicals appeared. The show had a book by Walter and Jean Kerr, who had provided most of the material some years before for *Touch and Go* (13 October 1949), and who had both found more congenial niches than the world of musical comedy. The music was by Leroy Anderson, a well-known arranger and composer of light, "semiclassical" instrumental works. The Kerrs went in search of their fun to the same source *The Vamp* (10 November 1955) had mined—the silent movie industry—and, although the famous mordant wit of the Kerrs was often evident, they too came back almost empty-handed. They kept their story closer to home, setting it in the 1913 movie colony at Fort Lee, New Jersey. The principal plot concerned the love–hate clashes between Maggie Harris (Elaine Stritch), a sharp-tongued musical comedy actress, and a vain, financially strapped young movie mogul, Max Grady (Don Ameche). They express their feelings early on in "No One'll Ever Love You [like you do]." Max keeps the infuriated Maggie working overtime on extra scenes because he has been warned he will get no further financing after his picture is finished. By the time shooting ends he has enough footage for several flicks. Of course, by the final curtain their associates have witnessed the taming of the two. Maggie has even decided to marry Max instead of socialite George Randolph Brown (Russell Nype), to whom she had been engaged. George finds solace in offering his coat to sweet, simple Lois (Pat Stanley), a girl who had been pursuing Max. Funny bits of dialogue characterized the Kerr humor. When Max's backer, growling that Max's financial statements are inadequate, spots Lois wandering aimlessly about the sets, he remarks, "I have the feeling I've come face to face with Miscellaneous Expenses." Anderson's score was gay and airily evocative of the epoch, especially such dance numbers as "The Pussy Foot" and "The Town House Maxixe," for which Agnes de Mille provided show-stopping routines. Settings were sumptuous and sunny. Unfortunately, despite flashes of wit, the book was heavy-handed, and Anderson's score lacked an outstanding love ballad. *Goldilocks* could find only a limited public, enough to keep it on the boards twenty weeks.

The New York City Opera's fall schedule included two beloved old operettas, *Die Fledermaus* and *The Merry Widow*, while the more venturesome spring season offered *Street Scene, The Devil and Daniel Webster, Regina,* and, curiously, the very next show to open—and quickly fold—at a regular theater.

David Merrick, who was quickly becoming the most active, exciting, and responsible producer on Broadway, combined forces with the National Broadcasting Company to bring Menotti's television opera **Maria Golovin** (5 November 1958, Martin Beck), to the stage. Like most Menotti librettos the story was simple. Maria Golovin's husband is a prisoner-of-war. A young, blind boy, Donato (Richard Cross), falls in love with her. When she refuses to desert her husband and marry him, Donato attempts to kill her. Donato's mother (Patricia Neway) tells him where to aim, at the same time motioning Maria (Franca Duval) to flee. Donato is led to believe Maria is dead and is taken away by his mother. Menotti's appeal had dwindled among rank-and-file theatregoers, and his latest work did not translate effectively from one medium to another. It closed after five performances.

One of the brightest revues Broadway had seen in years arrived on 11 November, with Merrick again one of the producers. Its origins were anything but ordinary. **La Plume de Ma Tante** (11 November 1958, Royale) began life as a Parisian hit and then moved on to a long London run before crossing the Atlantic. Theatregoers with little or no French had no cause for concern. The show's creator, Robert Dhery, acted as compère and offered laconic, amusing comments on the skits. The skits themselves were virtually silent, relying on a series of impeccably paced sight gags for most of the laughs. The evening's high point was a first-act finale in which four monks enter to a sedate "Frère Jacques" and begin to pull at bell ropes. The music grows faster and more pronouncedly rhythmic. By the curtain the monks are swinging on the ropes and kicking wildly. In its universality *La Plume de Ma Tante* was a latter-day *Chauve Souris* (4 April 1922), and, like its predecessor, it had little influence on revues that followed it. But its Frenchmen had a home to return to and, unlike the Russian émigrés' production, when its long run was through it said farewell for once and for all.

Rodgers and Hammerstein had a solid commercial success in **Flower Drum Song** (1 December 1958, St. James). It was a musical comedy on the order of their *Me and Juliet* (28 May 1953) and *Pipe Dream* (30 November 1955), sprinkled with just enough Oriental incense to remind theatregoers of *The King and I* (29 March 1951). Oscar Hammerstein and Joseph Fields's libretto was based on C. Y. Lee's novel and set in San Francisco's Chinatown. Its story followed Sammy Fong's uncertain journey to the altar. Sammy (Larry Blyden) loves a nightclub hostess, Linda Low (Pat Suzuki), but he is contractually obligated to marry Mei Li (Miyoshi Umeki). By arranging a marriage between Wang Ta (Ed Kenny) and Mei Li, Sammy hopes to break the arrangement and free himself. Since Wang Ta also has eyes only for Linda, Sammy invites the senior Wangs to Linda's nightclub, knowing they will be so appalled by Linda's striptease they will never consent to their son's marrying her. Wang Ta also begins to doubt his feeling for Linda, but Mei Li has seen his jacket at the apartment of her seamstress friend, Helen Chao (Arabella Hong), and has drawn the wrong conclusion. To complicate matters the Three Family Association, which regulates much of Chinatown life, insists Sammy and Mei Li's wedding take place promptly. Seemingly too late, Wang Ta confesses to Mei Li he has fallen in love with her. The wedding begins, but when the bride removes her veil she is discovered to be Linda. Mei Li and Wang Ta are free to pursue their own romance. The show was given a lavish production, and Gene Kelly, so long in Hollywood, returned to create the staging, but not the choreography. Yet a Rodgers and Hammerstein work depended on Rodgers and Hammerstein, and neither disappointed their public. Hammerstein's book and lyrics were filled with the distinctive sentimentality and distinctive simplicity his admirers adored, and with his almost unfailing professional know-how, while Rodgers's music was the best he had done since *The King and I*. It ran the gamut from the soft, flowing poetry of Wang Ta's "You Are Beautiful" to the stronger plaints of Helen's "Love, Look Away" to the joyous exuberance of Linda's "Grant Avenue" and "I Enjoy Being A Girl."

Feuer and Martin broke their string of successes (*Where's Charley?, Guys and Dolls, Can-Can, Silk Stockings*) with a fifty-six-performance dud called **Whoop-Up** (22 December 1958, Shubert). Although it was set on a modern-day Indian reservation, it was at a loss to capitalize on its rather novel setting. Glenda (Susan Johnson) runs a bar, half of which sits on the reservation. She loves Joe Champlain (Ralph Young), but Joe prefers Billie Mae Littlehorse (Asia). Glenda gets Joe in her debt by accepting parts of his automobile as payment for his drinks. By the end of the evening she not only has Joe's car, she has Joe. Moose Charlap's music was as undistinguished as the book.

The following night **A Party with Betty Comden and Adolph Green** (23 December 1958, Golden) was brought to the intimate Golden from off-Broadway. The evening was spent singing songs from all their Broadway shows, Hollywood films, and even the nightclub act in which they got their start. Enough patrons thought it as pleasant a party as any around to keep it on the boards for eighty-two showings. With its minimal budget, that was sufficient to let it return a reasonable profit.

1959's first musical, **Redhead** (5 February 1959, 46th St.), was a vehicle for Gwen Verdon. Her previous musical, *New Girl in Town*, had resorted to O'Neill's *Anna Christie* for its unlikely source. An equally untoward source offered the starting point for *Redhead*'s plot: the murders of Jack the Ripper. The book by Herbert and Dorothy Fields, Sidney Sheldon, and David Shaw made no attempt at historical accuracy. Rather, it developed its plot around the search for a killer of actresses at the turn of the century. Essie Whimple (Miss Verdon) works for her aunt in the Simpson Sisters' Waxworks. She meets handsome Tom Baxter (Richard Kiley), who had performed with a lady partner in a strongman act until his partner was murdered. After Essie helps in a performance, it becomes apparent that she is being stalked by the same killer, and there is evidence to throw suspicion on red-bearded Sir Charles Willingham (Patrick Horgan). The killer turns out to be a fellow entertainer, George Poppett (Leonard Stone), who has been able to disguise himself as Sir Charles. Their common interest and terror throw Essie and Tom together, and by the time Poppett is carted off to jail they have fallen in love. The book was serviceable, as was Albert Hague's score, but nothing more. The evening's strength lay in Miss Verdon's charm and her brilliant dancing to Bob Fosse's imaginative choreography, notably in "Pick-Pocket Tango" and "The Uncle Sam Rag." The show also served to further Kiley's path to stardom.

The show received several awards as the best musical of the season, largely because the season's only truly fine musical, *Gypsy*, opened after the balloting deadlines. Still, as a first-class dance show *Redhead* earned its run of over a year. In retrospect *Redhead* can also be seen as something of a breakaway show, more or less initiating the trend that Fosse would promote to make the choreographer so central a creative figure that his dances could be viewed as the crux of the evening.

RICHARD KILEY was born in Chicago on 31 March 1922. He studied at Loyola University and Barnum Dramatic School, and did a stint as a navy aerial gunner before calling theatregoers' attention to himself as Stanley Kowalski in a road company of *A Streetcar Named Desire*. Small roles in films followed until Broadway took notice of his singing as the caliph in *Kismet*.

The City Center low-priced ticket season began on 10 February with *The Most Happy Fella* (3 May 1956), with Art Lund again singing Joe, and proceeded to *Say, Darling* (3 April 1958), still with Robert Morse, on the 25th and *Lute Song* (6 February 1946) on 12 March. Dolly Haas assumed Mary Martin's role.

Just before *Lute Song* was heard, the commercial theatre offered a musical version of Sean O'Casey's *Juno and the Paycock*, with its title abbreviated to **Juno** (9 March 1959, Winter Garden). The music and lyrics were by Marc Blitzstein, the adaptation by Joseph Stein. Although Shirley Booth played the title role, she was given little solid comedy, while Melvyn Douglas, her costar, in the role of Jack Boyle, and Jack MacGowran as Joxer also found the comic elements in their characters minimized. The new version emphasized O'Casey's melodrama rather than his luminous, redeeming humor. It dealt principally with Juno's heartbreaks: the false hope of an inheritance; the death of her rebel son, Johnny (Tommy Rall); and her abandoning Jack to find a better world elsewhere with her daughter, Mary (Monte Amundsen). To make matters even more difficult for itself, the show was unable fully to integrate its songs, though the opening number, "We're Alive," dramatically punctured its dogged optimism with the shooting of a young rebel. Assailed by a generally unkind reception, *Juno* closed after just two weeks.

Although **First Impressions** (19 March 1959, Alvin) was little better, it ran longer. A musical version of Jane Austen's *Pride and Prejudice*, it took its title from Miss Austen's original title for her book. The story of the Bennett family, and particularly of Elizabeth Bennett's romance with Fitzwilliam Darcy, was retold as faithfully as time and physical limitations permitted. Regrettably, in their effort to achieve the leisurely elegance of the book and its era, the authors could do no better than to evoke the woodenness and stiff formality of the time at its worst. The titles of the songs ran to "A Perfect Evening," "The Heart Has Won The Game," "Wasn't It A Simply Lovely Wedding?," and "Love Will Find Out The Way." Only the appeal of Polly Bergen (Elizabeth), Hermione Gingold (Mrs. Bennett), and Farley Granger (Darcy) can account for the twelve-week run of the show.

David Merrick brought in another musical destined for a long run. Yet while **Destry Rides Again** (23 April 1959, Imperial), a lyric adaptation of the popular Marlene Dietrich and James Stewart film, ran for more than a year, it was a financial failure. Part of its failure may be attributed to the fact that it lacked tone, wit, and melody. It made do with noise and color and whatever else professional know-how could throw on stage. Like its movie antecedent, it was set in that persistently beloved piece of Americana, the Wild West, more specifically, in Bottleneck at the turn of the century, where young Destry, the son of an almost legendary lawman, is enlisted to break the murderous, corrupt stranglehold Kent's gang has on the town. The townsfolk are chagrined to discover their new defender is a shy, mild-spoken man, reluctant to employ violence. Kent (Scott Brady) sets his own girl, Frenchy, to seduce Destry, but she fails. Destry is determined to destroy Kent and his killers by lawful means, but when he brings a federal judge to try the murderer of the previous sheriff a gun battle ensues and Destry is forced to shoot it out. At one point Destry's life is saved by Frenchy, who has grown to admire him. With the gang destroyed, Destry is willing to settle down and enjoy the good life with Frenchy. He also persuades the town to set aside its arms and live peacefully. While Harold Rome composed the score, no superior popular hits emerged. The show's strong points were the performances of its stars— Andy Griffith and Dolores Gray—and the superb Michael Kidd choreography. His dance in which three of Kent's gang slash the air with their bullwhips was one of the most stunning in an era of fine dancing.

Once upon a Mattress (11 May 1959, Phoenix) offered a more innocent order of merriment. It was essentially the princess-and-the-pea story set to music, telling of the comical fairy-tale courtship of Princess Winnifred (Carol Burnett) by Prince Dauntless (Joe Bova). Before Winnifred is allowed to marry Dauntless, Queen Agravain (Jane White) makes her swim a moat, work as a chambermaid, and, of course, sleep on a pile of mattresses under which is hidden a single pea. A more straightforward romance between the dashing Sir Harry (Allen Case) and the comely Lady Larken (Anne Jones) serves as a counterpoint. The book was light and droll. Dauntless loses his heart to Winnifred on hearing her sing "The Swamps Of Home." Asked by the prince if he can call her "Winnie," she replies her friends call her "Fred." The music was by Richard Rodgers's daughter, Mary. It was skillful and musicianly, but never memorable. For Miss Burnett and her scatterbrained comedy, the show was a major stop on the road to television celebrity.

The following night a new musical called The Nervous Set (12 May 1959, Henry Miller's) transported theatregoers back to contemporary New York. Written by a group of unknown, inexperienced hands, and originally mounted in their hometown of St. Louis, it was coolly received and hastily whisked away. The plot described the problem marriage of Brad (Richard Hayes), the staid, nervous publisher of "Nerves" magazine, and his "beatnik" wife, Jan (Tani Seitz). They compromise rather than have two nervous breakdowns.

The season's best musical was its last. **Gypsy** (21 May 1959, Broadway) was based on the memoirs of Gypsy Rose Lee. It had a book by Arthur Laurents, lyrics by Stephen Sondheim (who had worked with Laurents on *West Side Story*), and music by Jule Styne. David Merrick and Leland Hayward were co-producers. Although the story told of Miss Lee's start in burlesque, she was not the central figure. The evening was dominated by the presence of her mother, Rose (Ethel Merman), the quintessential pushy stage-mother, who is not above threatening "Uncle Jocko" that she will report his talent contests are rigged if her daughter Baby June (Jacqueline Mayro) isn't given a satisfactory spot. All her daughter has is a cute little ditty to sing, which begs "Let Me Entertain You." Rose's father isn't smiling. He resents her always being away with the children. But Rose has only contempt for "Some People," stay-at-homes. Rose, June, and June's younger sister, Louise (Karen Moore), leave home to continue their search for fame and fortune. At one tryout Rose meets Herbie (Jack Klugman), who sells candy to vaudeville houses and who tells her that he has noticed her before, waiting outside a manager's office: "You looked like a pioneer woman without a frontier." They take an immediate liking to each other, and Rose is quick to suggest how alike they are. They are both strangers in the same town, and doesn't that make it a "Small World." Before long Herbie has agreed to join the act and be its agent. To flickering lights and to the tune of "Let Me Entertain You," June and Louise grow up before the audience's eyes. But "talkies" and the Depression have come, and they are hurting both vaudeville and Rose's daughters' chances. Even Herbie wants to leave to try something where he can have an opportunity to make more money. Naturally, Rose won't hear of it, insisting "You'll Never Get Away From Me." She wins, and the tour resumes. As the years wear on, June and Louise (now played by Lane Bradbury and Sandra Church) become disenchanted with living

out of a trunk. They wish their mother would marry so they could settle into a house. They themselves are older, and marriage, if they want it, cannot be far off. In fact there is a pleasant young man in the group named Tulsa (Paul Wallace) who has his eye on June. In the guise of describing a soft-shoe act he is developing, Tulsa hints of his affection in "All I Need Is The Girl." Before long June and Tulsa have eloped. At first Rose is livid. It was June for whom she sacrificed everything. When she is calmer she remembers she has another daughter, and in a flash her ambitions for Louise grow boundless. Once again "Everything's Coming Up Roses." She tells Louise not to be frightened: "You got Herbie for brains; we got you for talent; and you both got me—to yell at." They'll be "Together Wherever We Go." But vaudeville is dead, and Louise is forced to perform in burlesque. Herbie, concluding he is of no further use, leaves as unobtrusively as anyone can walk out of Rose's life. Initially, Louise has little success. She is too prim. When she realizes that burlesque is the only world in which she can succeed, she discards her inhibitions and performs with style and gusto. After a fellow stripper, Tessie (Maria Karnilova), blares out a trumpet solo to show "You Gotta Have A Gimmick," Louise realizes her own genteelness is her "gimmick." Her success is phenomenal and takes her to the very top, to Minsky's. With nothing further to strive for, Rose becomes introspective. In an extended soliloquy she concludes everything she did was not for her girls but for herself. Awareness, if it cannot bring joy, brings a certain serenity and a small ability to laugh at oneself. She walks off, confiding to Louise:

Rose: You know, I had a dream last night. It was a big poster of a mother and daughter—you know, like the cover of that ladies' magazine.
Louise: Yes, Mother?
Rose: Only it was you and me wearing exactly the same gown. It was for an ad for Minsky—and the headline said: MADAM ROSE—AND HER DAUGHTER, GYPSY!

The show offered a plethora of attractions. There was a fine production with Ethel Merman giving the most marvelously bravura performance of her career. Her electric personality made the abrasive, almost unpleasant Rose seem a little lovable. As things developed, it was to be Miss Merman's last major new role. But the show itself was something of a marvel. It was pure musical comedy, filled with all the old musical comedy tricks: burlesque routines, striptease, soft-shoe dances, rousing choruses, and love songs. Yet *Gypsy* was clearly something more, something superior. Its book—although it was a chronicle covering a number of years—was taut and relentless, with Robbins's brilliant staging underscoring its cohesiveness and flow. It was packed with laughs, yet few were trite gags. The humor realized the dream of several generations of librettists, stemming naturally, almost inevitably, from situations and characters. And the amazingly brilliant, yet unfailingly colloquial, lyrics propelled the action and deepened the characterizations. They established that Sondheim was, with Lerner, the heir to the earlier masters in the field, all now dead or retired. Most of all, there was Styne's score, the last important traditional musical comedy (as opposed to musical play) score to be heard on Broadway. It was vibrant and melodic. "Small World," "You'll Never Get Away From Me," "Everything's Coming Up Roses," and "Together Wherever We Go" all entered the ranks of standards.

1959–1960

The musical shows offered in the preceding seasons had been distressingly few. With the new theatrical year the American Musical Theatre experienced the beginning of a numerically small, but proportionately not insignificant, rise in new lyric offerings. Until the early years of the 1980s the number of new musicals remained in the teens (except for two isolated seasons) and once even reached twenty.

1959–1960 introduced a steady parade of highly entertaining musicals. None was as fully achieved as the masterpieces of preceding sessions, but with few exceptions the new shows had much to recommend them. Not all met with success, but most near-misses could console themselves with having offered value for money.

The season began modestly with **The Billy Barnes Revue** (4 August 1959, Golden). Barnes wrote the music and lyrics, while Bob Rodgers created the sketches. The small cast featured bright, young unknowns. In its spoof of "The Thirties" it was about ten years ahead of the nostalgic vogue for the period. Everything was pleasant, but nothing was outstanding. The show survived until stronger attractions began to appear.

The popular French entertainer Yves Montand brought his one-man show, with his songs and his microphone, in to start the fall season. More than one critic suggested his act would be better if shortened and put in a nightclub.

Once again, the New York City Opera's selections, both in its fall and spring seasons, included musicals first done on Broadway: *Die Fledermaus, Street Scene, The Mikado, The Merry Widow, The Cradle Will Rock,* and *The Consul.*

The season's first new book musical was an amateurish dud. **Happy Town** (7 October 1959, 54th St.) tried to make an evening out of a single joke—a Texas town without a millionaire. Several big spenders try unsuccessfully to buy the place, named Back-A-Heap. Produced with Texas oil money, it was laughed off the stage after five performances.

England sent Broadway the year's first hit, a delightful two-man show, **At the Drop of a Hat** (8 October 1959, Golden). Its authors were its performers. Michael Flanders delivered his material from his wheelchair, while his partner, Donald Swann, sat at a piano and sang his droll, Edward Learish songs. Together they ran out the season.

In 1957 Bob Merrill had provided the score for a musical version of Eugene O'Neill's *Anna Christie.* For this still young season he went to a second O'Neill play, one that was a more likely candidate for musical treatment, *Ah, Wilderness!* With Joseph Stein and Robert Russell working on the libretto, they came up with **Take Me Along** (22 October 1959, Shubert), a work that faithfully retained the small-town hominess and comic glow of the original. O'Neill had already set their story in the turn-of-the-century America so cherished by the musicals of this period. The place is Centerville, Connecticut. And the home around which the story revolves is that of Nat Miller (Walter Pidgeon), the town's newspaper editor. Nat's boozy brother-in-law, Sid (Jackie Gleason), is in the throes of a courtship with Nat's spinster sister, Lily (Eileen Herlie). And Nat's adolescent son, Richard (Robert Morse), is having a puppy-love affair with Muriel Macomber (Susan Luckey). The affair is broken off when Muriel's father learns that Richard writes poetry and reads scandalous writers such as Wilde and Ibsen. In his despair Richard imitates his uncle by going on a jag (he also visits a whorehouse). The drinking leads to a dream ballet in which he is pursued by Salome and other characters from his reading. When Richard ascertains that Muriel was forced by her father to break off their friendship, he leaves for college promising he will always love her. Sid also makes a promise: to stay away from the bottle if Lily will marry him. She accepts. Merrill again demonstrated his ability to write songs that were pleasing but were rarely strong enough to catch and hold the public's fancy. Nat had a poignant number, "Staying Young," in which he first argues that everyone is growing older except him, and in a second-act reprise wistfully confesses he is growing older too. Sid vividly described the consequences of too much drinking in "Little Green Snake." The show's best number was its title song, with its lilting old-fashioned tune. It was sung by Nat and Sid, then repeated as the finale. Though *Take Me Along* gave Gleason the best role of his career, one that fit him to a tee, and though it ran over a year, it went into the books as another long-run show that never realized a return on its investment.

Some of Broadway's most competent writers joined forces with several of the theatre's greatest clowns to offer a revue called **The Girls Against the Boys** (2 November 1959, Alvin). Richard Lewine and Albert Hague wrote the music; Arnold B. Horwitt provided the sketches and lyrics. Nancy Walker and Bert Lahr headed the cast. In "Rich Butterfly" Miss Walker played a Japanese war bride, grovelingly subservient until she learns the ways of American wives, at which point she changes her ways with a vengeance. Lahr portrayed an aging stage-door Johnny seeking an "Old-Fashioned Girl." The chorus girls who leave the theatre are all tough, hard-mouthed, and in slacks. The only bit of femininity Lahr can find is a swishy young chorus boy. The show was uneven. Its musical numbers were particularly weak. With great clowns no longer a sufficient attraction in themselves, the revue was forced to suspend after just sixteen showings.

The season's biggest hit arrived two weeks later. **The Sound of Music** (16 November 1959, Lunt-Fontanne) was a lyrical stage version of Maria Augusta Trapp's biographical *The Trapp Family Singers*. Howard Lindsay and Russel Crouse collaborated on the book, while Rodgers and Hammerstein provided the songs. The time is 1938; the place, Austria. When Maria (Mary Martin), a postulant, is deemed unprepared for convent life, she is sent to act as a governess for the children of a stern, widowed naval officer, Captain Georg von Trapp (Theodore Bikel). Her warm, sympathetic treatment of the children contrasts with their father's inflexible authoritarianism. The captain leaves for Vienna and reappears with a fiancée. On his return he is surprised and delighted that Maria has been teaching the children how to sing. Maria, fearing she is falling in love with the captain, flees to the refuge of the convent. The abbess, however, sends her back.

Georg and his fiancée find their attitudes about the Nazis unreconcilable, and agree to part. For all his authoritarianism Georg is fervently opposed to the new government. When it orders him to report for naval duty, he, his children, and Maria all escape to Switzerland. The show's plot was not unlike *The King and I*—a governess sent to work with the children of a strict, imperious father. Furthermore, the show's Austrian setting reminded many of something that *The King and I* had strongly suggested, namely that Rodgers and Hammerstein's shows exemplified the natural American evolution of operetta, even if its creators strongly rejected the argument. The sentiment, romance, and seeming seriousness of the old form remained. Only ranks and vocal ranges were reduced to comply with the more egalitarian spirit and technical limitations of the day. Not since *The King and I* had Rodgers found a story so inspiring. At least half a dozen of the songs from this score have become Rodgers standards: the opening title song, "My Favorite Things," and "Do-Re-Mi,"—all sung by Maria; "Climb Ev'ry Mountain" (closing each act); "Sixteen Going On Seventeen"; and "Edelweiss." The show opened to an advance sale of over two million dollars, ran for more than three years, toured extensively, and was well received overseas. Oscar Hammerstein's death, shortly after the show opened, meant *The Sound of Music* marked the end of the most lucrative partnership in the history of the American Musical Theatre. The film version six years later, with Julie Andrews in the lead role, was the leading-grossing musical of all time, which showed the great continued appeal of the story.

Far down in Manhattan a new show opened two nights after *The Sound of Music*, professing to spoof the old order of operettas from which the contemporary musical plays were descended. The curtain for **Little Mary Sunshine** (18 November 1959, Orpheum) rises on the Colorado Inn, high in the Rocky Mountains. Singing their song, "The Forest Rangers" appear and to her coy embarrassment proclaim their affection for "Little Mary Sunshine," the inn's proprietress. Mary (Eileen Brennan) has missed a mortgage payment on the inn and may be evicted. But she is undaunted, always able to "Look For A Sky Of Blue." The Rangers' Captain Jim (William Graham) reveals he is searching for a villainous Indian, Yellow Feather (Ray James). When the inn is visited by a great European opera star, Mme. Ernestine (Elizabeth Parrish), who lovingly recalls her own favorite hideaway, "In Izzsenschnooken On The Lovely Essenzook Zee," the romantic mood prompts Mary and Jim to admit their love for each other (and their home state) in the "Colorado Love Call." Two youngsters, Corporal Billy (John McMartin) and Nancy Twinkle (Elmarie Wendel), are also attracted to each other and agree they could be loyal, if only "Once In A Blue Moon." A big affair is held, "Such A Merry Party" that no one could possibly be unhappy. But danger, in the person of Yellow Feather, lurks not far away. Nancy dampens Billy's ardor slightly by confessing she is "Naughty, Naughty Nancy." There is momentary confusion when Billy dresses up as Yellow Feather. But the real villain is caught. The good Indians, who own the inn, give the deed to Mary, and Jim ponders the joys of marriage in Colorado. The show was absurdly funny, blessed with two adroit performances by Eileen Brennan and John McMartin. But for all the kudos it received and all the success it enjoyed—and it ran nearly three years at its small Second Avenue house—it missed the consistent satire of *The Boy Friend* (30 September 1954) or the earlier, shorter "Rose of Arizona" in *Garrick Gaieties* (10 May 1926) and "The Gladiola Girl" in *Lend an Ear* (16 December 1948). Sandy Wilson's show had kept its sights on one type of twenties musical—the modern, lean, jazzy musical comedy such as *No, No, Nanette* (16 September 1925). Rick Besoyan in *Little Mary Sunshine* drew laughs by attacking all the genres of the era. The show most quickly called to mind the operetta school of *Rose-Marie* (2 September 1924), *Naughty Marietta* (7 November 1910), and *Rio Rita* (2 February 1927), but also harked back to Jerome Kern's commercial hits of the period ("Look For The Silver Lining" from *Sally* [21 December 1920]) and Kern's more Continental pieces of a decade later ("In Egern On The Tegern See" from *Music in the Air* [8 November 1932]). From the early twenties musical comedies it culled numbers such as the party song that sounded joyously like "We'll Have A Wonderful Party" from *Mary* (18 October 1920) and "The Best Part of Every Party" from *Irene* (18 November 1919).

A flamboyant, eminently theatrical figure from the very era whose plays Besoyan was burlesquing was the subject of the next musical to appear. And when, later in the season, **Fiorello!** (23 November 1959, Broadhurst) was awarded the Pulitzer Prize it brought back to mind another musical of that era, the first to win the award, *Of Thee I Sing* (26 December 1931). Comparisons suggested that newer did not mean better, even if George Abbott and Jerome Weidman's book, Jerry Bock's score,

and Sheldon Harnick's lyrics were no mean achievement. The deliciously preposterous fictions of the earlier work were absent, as was the consistent tone that the fictions allowed and that its authors successfully maintained. To some extent the facts of Fiorello La Guardia's career dictated the broad swings back and forth from nostalgia to muckraking to satire to sentimentality. The show opened with an irresistible bit of nostalgia by showing the famous newsreels of La Guardia's reading comic strips to the children of New York during a newspaper strike. An offhand remark of his about the corrupt politicians who governed the city when he was a young lawyer takes the show back to 1914. His secretary, Marie (Patricia Wilson), who quite obviously loves him, and the rest of his staff are awed to be working for a man so clearly "On The Side Of The Angels." When Marie's friend, Dora (Pat Stanley), tells Fiorello (Tom Bosely) that the leader of their strike, Thea (Ellen Hanley), has been arrested on a trumped-up charge of soliciting, La Guardia personally berates the corrupt policeman, Floyd (Mark Dawson), who made the arrest. But La Guardia is not above associating with Ben Marino (Howard da Silva), the Republican ward leader who agrees to run him in his district against the Tammany candidate. Ben's enthusiasm is only halfhearted. He and his cronies divide their passion equally between "Politics And Poker." La Guardia takes to the streets in his campaign, impressing on those who will listen, "The Name's La Guardia." His background allows him to repeat the message in Italian and Yiddish as well. It's a message people understand. When the results are in, the boys at Marino's clubhouse are staggered to discover "The Bum Won." Meanwhile Floyd and Dora have become close, and Floyd has begun to climb the Tammany ladder. Dora starts to drift away from Thea, who is being courted by Fiorello. To the caressing melody of "'Til Tomorrow," he proposes to her before sailing off to war. Thea dies in the middle of La Guardia's next campaign. At the same time, the excess of the Walker administration catch up with it during the Seabury investigation— excesses that have given Floyd and Dora a lavish penthouse. Ben and some of his regulars enjoy the discomfort of their opponents and the unmistakable ridiculousness of their opponents' replies in court, when the Tammany men insist their wealth came from savings in a "Little Tin Box." Seabury has selected La Guardia to run on a Fusion ticket. Fiorello delays accepting only enough to warn: "And if I should decide to run again, I want all you politicians to know that my chief qualification for Mayor of this great city is my monumental ingratitude." He then fires his longtime secretary, Marie, explaining, "I can't court a girl who's working for me." Together they prepare for the forthcoming campaign.

Saratoga (7 December 1959, Winter Garden) opened, filled with promise, and closed, a major disappointment, ten weeks later. In proper hands there was no reason why Edna Ferber's colorful period piece about New Orleans and Saratoga in the 1880s could not have made as rich a musical as had her *Show Boat* (27 December 1927). But the fine talents that labored on the new adaptation were distressingly uninspired. Morton Da Costa kept the basic story of Clio Dulaine (Carol Lawrence) and Clint Maroon (Howard Keel), two fortune hunters who join forces to make their way in the world and end up caring about each other. Clio is motivated by society's disdain for her illegitimacy, while Clint is determined to avenge the railroad's stealing of his family's land. He eventually beats the railroad men at their own game. The plot seemingly became entangled in the elaborate moving stage and complicated scenery of the show. Harold Arlen's score, with Johnny Mercer lyrics, was not strong enough to break loose and soar on its own.

Unlike *Saratoga*, **Beg, Borrow or Steal** (10 February 1960, Martin Beck) promised little and delivered less. Few were disappointed when it left after five performances. The show starred a number of Hollywood and Broadway names who had seen their best days and was written for them by creators untried on Broadway. The story dealt with those bohemians the decade referred to as "beatniks." Clara (Betty Garrett) and Pistol (Eddie Bracken) are sister and brother. They live together in The Pad and run a health-food store. Pistol and his friend, Rafe (Larry Parks), also run a beatnik meeting place, The Pit. They keep alive by the skin of their teeth. Clara must choose romantically between Rafe and a seeming "square," Junior (Biff McGuire). She chooses Junior, who proves to be Rex All, the beatnik poet laureate. Given the growing association between beatniks and drugs, naming the poet after a drugstore chain was one of the evening's few felicitous touches.

Frank Loesser's **Greenwillow** (8 March 1960, Alvin) was probably the major disappointment of the season, though many serious students feel it deserves a rehearing. An idyll of bygone rural America, based on B. J. Chute's novel, it centered its attention on young Gideon Briggs. Gideon (Anthony Perkins) refuses to court his girl, Dome (Ellen McCown), because he fears he has inherited the family wanderlust. Love conquers fear. Loesser's book was so idyllic it ultimately came to seem untheatrical, and his songs, while often clever, sounded surprisingly thin. There were interesting touches such as the contrapuntal sermons of Reverend Birdsong (Cecil Kellaway) and Reverend Lapp (William Chapman), the one extolling a God of Love, the other warning of a God of Wrath. But the show's principal number, "The Music Of Home," overreached melodically without any reason and without the necessary backbone to support itself. Thanks largely to an excellent advance sale *Greenwillow* was able to survive three months.

The last major hit of the season, and its most unexpected success, followed five weeks later. **Bye Bye Birdie** (14 April 1960, Beck) was a fresh, unpretentious, funny, and melodic show that kidded the flourishing rock-and-roll rage and its wriggling superstar, Elvis Presley. If the singing sensation Conrad Birdie (Dick Gautier) is drafted, his agent, Albert Peterson (Dick Van Dyke), will lose his commissions and not have enough money to marry Rose Grant (Chita Rivera). This would be a sad state of affairs for everyone except Albert's loving mother (Kay Medford), who practically collapses at even the thought of his marrying and finds herself at death's door when Rose is mentioned specifically. But Rose has a scheme. They will write a song called "One Last Kiss," which Birdie will sing to a carefully selected typical teenage admirer. If the song clicks, they can live off the royalties until Birdie is discharged. The girl selected is Kim MacAfee (Susan Watson), and the whole entourage heads for Kim's hometown of Sweet Apple. Conrad is given a room in the MacAfee house and before long has come between Kim and her loyal beau, Hugo Peabody (Michael J. Pollard). When Mrs. Peterson's tantrums threaten to come between Albert and Rose, Rose and Hugo go out on a bender, and before long an intoxicated Rose is disrupting a staid, small-town Shriners' meeting. A wild "Shriners' Ballet" ensues. Luckily for Hugo, Kim grows weary of Conrad's egotistical, overbearing ways even before he leaves for the Army. She and Hugo, and Albert and Rose, are soon hand in hand again. The score with music by Charles Strouse and lyrics by Lee Adams was as delightful as the book. However, it contained little pure rock and roll. Conrad, Kim, and the teenagers had the hit of the show, "A Lot Of Livin' To Do."

Albert had the toe-tapping "Put On A Happy Face" and the love ballad, "Baby, Talk To Me." The town's elders sang a Charleston melody in which they gave vent to their dismay with the younger generation, "Kids," asking why the children can't be like *they* were, "Perfect, in every way!" The show enhanced the growing reputation of Chita Rivera and helped propel Dick Van Dyke, Paul Lynde (as the harassed Mr. MacAfee), Pollard, and Miss Medford on to bigger things. In rocking, rolling, and wriggling for a joyous year and a half on Broadway it also gave a major leg-up to its librettist, Michael Stewart.

> **MICHAEL STEWART RUBIN** was born in New York City on 1 August 1929. Educated at Yale, he was awarded a Master of Arts there in 1953. He served an apprentice-ship writing sketches for such off-Broadway revues as *Razzle Dazzle, The Shoestring Revue,* and *The Littlest Revue,* as well as working on Sid Caesar's television show.

Hermione Gingold's bad luck pursued her when she arrived in a revue, **From A to Z** (20 April 1960, Plymouth). Names soon to be famous in the the-atre contributed songs and sketches: Jerry Herman, Woody Allen. But to no avail. The show folded after twenty showings. Its big first-act finale was a travesty on *The Sound of Music,* rechristened "The Sound of Schmaltz," in which International Nannies, Ltd., sends Alice Cadwallader-Smith, a governess given to singing as she swings in a Central Park hammock, to assist in rearing the children of Baron von Klaptrap.

On 27 April, when *West Side Story* returned to begin the second engagement already mentioned, the City Center resumed its annual series of revivals, although this year there would be only two. It was a hint that increasing costs were shortly to sound the death knell of these low-priced presentations. *Finian's Rainbow,* with Bobby Howes and Jeannie Carson, was first, followed by *The King and I,* with Farley Granger and Barbara Cook, on 11 May.

In between the two revivals the season's last orig-inal on-Broadway musical appeared. **Christine** (28 April 1960, 46th St.) was not unlike *The King and I* (29 March 1951) in that it recounted the love story between a Western lady and an Eastern gentleman.

In this case the woman is Lady Christine FitzSimons (Maureen O'Hara) of Ireland, and the man is her widowed son-in-law, Dr. Rashil Singh (Morley Meredith). The doctor settles for a native beauty, Sita Roy (Janet Pavek), after Christine decides too many disparities separate Rashil's and her worlds. Sammy Fain provided the music. But famed novelist turned librettist Pearl Buck lacked the theatrical know-how of Oscar Hammerstein, and Fain's innocuous score was a far cry from the rich beauties Rodgers had offered. Even the lovely and gracious Miss O'Hara could not save the piece.

On 3 May 1960, **The Fantasticks** premiered at the minuscule Sullivan Street Playhouse in Greenwich Village for an unprecedented run of 42 years, and 17,162 performances. After a four year hiatus, it re-opened uptown at Fiftieth Street and Broadway under new management where it is still playing. Not many critics were overjoyed, and in the early weeks business was so slow that the backers looked certain to lose their meager $16,500 investment. But a small band of devotees plugged it, and it went on to win the Vernon Rice Award for the best off-Broadway show of the season. Attendance picked up, and when "Try To Remember" inched its way into national popularity the success of the show was assured. The Narrator (Jerry Orbach) sings the song, which opens the show and sets the bittersweet mood. He explains that the parents of The Boy called Matt (Kenneth Nelson) and The Girl called Luisa (Rita Gardner) have built a wall between their homes on the theory that the best way to bring lovers together is to make it seem they are to be kept apart. The parents go so far as to hire a bandit (played by The Narrator) to attempt, and purposely be foiled in, a rape of The Girl. But the "Rape Ballet" is followed by the young-sters' discovery of their parents' devices. The Boy and The Girl quickly fall out and go their separate ways. Eventually they return, disillusioned with the world, and embrace. The Narrator comments lacon-ically, "Without a hurt the heart is hollow." The show had originally been a one-act musical play suggested by Rostand's *Les Romanesques.* Composer Harvey Schmidt and author Tom Jones expanded it into a full-length work at the request of Lore Noto, who then produced it. None of the rest of Schmidt's score became as popular as "Try To Remember," although The Girl's "Much More" and the youngsters' "Soon It's Gonna Rain" enjoyed brief vogues when Barbra Streisand recorded them. The show did maintain a tone—an odd mixture of poignancy and whimsy. But Schmidt and Jones were never able to recreate it or move on successfully to other achievements either off Broadway or on. In this respect fortune was far less kind to them than it was to their original Narrator, Jerry Orbach.

1960–1961

Just as it was becoming obvious that the latest act was nearing its end, the man most responsible for its shape and tenor passed on. Oscar Hammerstein II died on 23 August 1960, before the season's first new musical appeared. As early as *Rose-Marie* (2 September 1924), he had attempted tentative breaks with the traditions of the American Musical Theatre. With the successful *Show Boat* (27 December 1927) and the unsuccessful *Rainbow* (21 November 1928), both still in the twenties, he had pioneered in the form which, with *Oklahoma!* (31 March 1943), established the master mold for more than two decades of lyric-theatre writing. His death, coming in a second season of good but uninspired musicals, underscored the waning of the renaissance he had so strongly influenced.

Not one of the three September offerings was a wholly New York affair, and only one was unequivocally American. The experimental Phoenix Theatre on Second Avenue opened the season with a Stratford, Ontario, production of *H. M. S. Pinafore* by the inventive English director Tyrone Guthrie. The intention of both Stratford's Shakespearean Festival and Mr. Guthrie was to mount a Gilbert and Sullivan piece without recourse to accepted D'Oyly Carte staging. Critics disagreed as to how genuinely fresh Guthrie's conceptions were. Enough Savoyards flocked to the downtown house to give the work a fifty-five-performance run. But after the production closed most directors assigned to revive *H. M. S. Pinafore* hurried back to traditional prompt books. That more conservative approach could be seen at month's end (the Phoenix mounting had opened on the 7th) when the New York City Opera presented *The Mikado* on the 30th and *The Pirates of Penzance* on 6 October. And again, when early in the new year, commencing on 17 January 1962, the City Center lit productions of all three of the above shows as well as *The Gondoliers*.

September also brought a California revue, **Vintage '60** (12 September 1960, Atkinson). A few New York names such as Sheldon Harnick, Fred Ebb, and David Baker added material in hopes of strengthening it for a more demanding Broadway. Since 1960 was an election year, a first-act finale

mocked a national political convention, honored by a visit from a man named Richard Nixon. But Broadway continued to prefer foreign and local wines to the western ones, and *Vintage '60* survived only a single week. It was David Merrick's first musical offering of the season.

FRED EBB was born 8 April 1928 in New York City. After receiving a bachelor's degree from New York University (1955) and a master's from Columbia University (1957), Ebb moonlighted as a lyricist of novelty songs and ballads, working with composers Paul Klein, Phil Springer, Norman L. Martin, and Norman Leyden with modest success. He placed a few songs in the revues *Ziegfeld Follies of 1958* and *Put It in Writing*, and on television's *That Was the Week That Was*.

His second production recompensed him for the failure of his first. He unveiled his importation from France (by way of England), **Irma La Douce** (29 September 1960, Plymouth). A saucy, galloping musical about a "poule" and her "mec," it ran well into the next season. Elizabeth Seal and Keith Michell repeated their London successes in the lead roles. Merrick was to have an amazingly busy year, one that established him indisputably as the major producer of the era. The next two shows to arrive on Broadway were his importations of two straight plays, *A Taste of Honey* and *Becket*. They were among the best plays and biggest hits of the season.

Another huge success was **An Evening with Mike Nichols and Elaine May** (8 October 1960, Golden). The two young comedians, alone on stage, satirized everything from PTA meetings to Tennessee Williams drama (where their hero is falsely accused of not being a homosexual). Perhaps because musicals or plays to display their brilliant talents were hard to come by, the pair soon largely abandoned performing and turned to writing, directing, and producing.

Stanley Holloway, who had been kept busy for several years as Doolittle in *My Fair Lady* (15 March 1956), returned to appear alone in his one-man show, **Laughs and Other Events** (10 October 1960, Barrymore). The other events included selections from Holloway's British music hall days. Unfortunately they weren't sufficiently appealing to Americans to keep the evening on the boards beyond its initial week.

The first big, new American book musical, **Tenderloin** (17 October 1960, 46th St.), had a libretto by Jerome Weidman and George Abbott, lyrics by Sheldon Harnick, and music by Jerry Bock—the team that created the preceding season's winning *Fiorello!* They took as their source a novel by Samuel Hopkins Adams based loosely on the attempts of the Reverend Mr. Parkhurst to clean up the old Tenderloin district near West 23rd Street. But what the librettists ended with was far more fiction than fact. Their Reverend Brock would eradicate his era's corruption with the help of a handsome young scandal-sheet reporter who is also a part-time singer at one of the area's roughest bars. Brock is unaware that Tommy (Ron Husmann), his supposed associate, is in cahoots with a dishonest policeman, Lieutenant Schmidt (Ralph Dunn). The two frame Brock with doctored photographs. But in court Tommy, who has been converted by a choir girl named Laura (Wynne Miller), admits the truth. A cleanup of the area begins. Brock does not remain to witness the change. He moves his crusade on to Detroit. Though *Tenderloin* was able to enlist the noted Shakespearean and Shavian actor Maurice Evans for the part of Brock, it had little else in the way of novelty to present. The plot had obvious parallels with *Fiorello!*'s, but the age it depicted, "the latter part of the 19th century," was not as flamboyant or as theatrically colorful as La Guardia's times, and the priggish, sometimes comically naive, minister no match for "The Little Flower." Bock's score was filled with pleasantries that delighted in the theatre but found no lasting popularity on the outside. Most notable were Tommy's sentimental "Artificial Flowers" and Brock's hilariously innocent interpretation of Tenderloin notions about "Good Clean Fun." *Tenderloin* ran over six months, yet closed a commercial failure.

If Bock and his collaborators were drifting away from historical figures, Meredith Willson latched on to a fascinating character who had become a legend in her own lifetime, **The Unsinkable Molly Brown** (3 November 1960, Winter Garden). Luckily for Willson her heyday encompassed the most popular period of the era, the turn of the century to 1912. At the beginning Molly is an impoverished but spunky tomboy, determined one day to be rich and grand. But when she moves from Missouri to Colorado she

meets an equally impoverished and spunky young miner, Johnny "Leadville" Brown, falls headlong in love, and marries him. Her dreams seem to come true when Johnny presents her with $300,000 he receives from selling a claim. Her joy is short-lived, for she hides the money in an oven and forgetfully burns it. The forgiving Johnny soon brings her a second fortune, and they move to Denver. Snubbed by Denver society, they head for Europe, where her wealth and her gaucheries make her the darling of the moment. She returns to Denver to have her revenge, but her gala party is wrecked by the unexpected appearance of the Browns' old mining buddies. Johnny insists on staying in Colorado, but Molly flees to Europe. She is courted by an attractive prince but, lonely for Johnny, sails to rejoin him. Her ship is the *Titanic* and when it sinks she proves one of the heroines of the disaster. Her heroism makes her acceptable to society. Willson did only the songs for *The Unsinkable Molly Brown*. The book was by Richard Morris. This may partly explain why the new work lacked something of the stylish consistency and cohesiveness of *The Music Man*. Its bent toward the commercial was undoubtedly furthered by its co-producers, the Theatre Guild. This once-daring organization, in its death throes as a responsible artistic force, had become crassly, even desperately, conscious of the box office. Yet if the show was less artful then Willson's first work, it remained rattling good theatre. Two of Willson's most durable melodies emerged from the evening, Molly's forceful "I Ain't Down Yet" and Johnny's tender love ballad, "I'll Never Say No." The show was lavishly mounted, with scenes, depicting the sinking of the *Titanic* and Molly in her lifeboat, that recalled the elaborate stage effects of prefilm days. Tammy Grimes and the strong-voiced Harve Presnell headed the cast and helped the show to achieve a 532-performance run.

A week after the opening John F. Kennedy defeated Richard M. Nixon for the presidency. Kennedy's inauguration four months later ushered in a brief era during which the arts were embraced and made welcome by the First Family.

The season's most eagerly awaited musical, **Camelot** (3 December 1960, Majestic), was Lerner and Loewe's first Broadway effort since their triumphant *My Fair Lady* (15 March 1956). Based on T. H. White's popular novel *The Once and Future King*, it continued the team's wanderings through British terrains and centuries by recalling the sunlight and shadow of Arthurian legend that lies on the other side of the Celtic mists, not far from Brigadoon. Just before his marriage to Guenevere, whom he has not met, a nervous, shy Arthur imagines what his people are thinking. He can hear them ask, "I Wonder What The King Is Doing Tonight?" He would like to tell them he is "wishing he were in Scotland fishing tonight." But the appearance of an attractive young maiden sends him scurrying for a hiding spot. She is Guenevere, and she, too, is nervous about the forthcoming marriage. She fears she has missed "The Simple Joys Of Maidenhood" she has read about in romances. "Shall kith not kill their kin for me?" she inquires. Arthur reveals himself, but not his identity. He tells her he has heard some wicked stories about the king, but that Camelot is not a bad place. After the wedding Arthur begins consolidating the Round Table. One of his knights is the dashing Lancelot (Robert Goulet), who falls in love with Guenevere almost at first sight and leaves Camelot rather than stir up trouble. But he cannot remain away and returns to court her furtively. In the show's hit number, "If Ever I Would Leave You," he lists the qualities of the passing seasons to see if any could induce him to leave, and concludes none could. When the villainous Mordred (Roddy McDowell) exposes the romance, the lovers are condemned. They escape to France, where Arthur pursues them. Arthur meets them before going into a battle with the French that may cost his life. He is forgiving, but only when a youngster begs to be made a member of the Round Table can he catch even a glimmer of hope that Camelot's "one brief shining moment" can be revived.

After President John Kennedy's death, Lerner's lyric about "one brief shining moment" became synonymous with the high noon of Kennedy's administration.

The comparisons that the critics made to *My Fair Lady* were largely unkind and somewhat unfair. Nonetheless, they were inevitable. Not only had Lerner and Loewe written the work, but *My Fair Lady*'s costar (Julie Andrews); principal featured player (Robert Coote); and director (Moss Hart) were back, as well as its designer (Oliver Smith), choreographer, and conductor. Parenthetically, the show's trouble-plagued tryout is sometimes held responsible for Hart's fatal heart attack a year later. Once again Miss Andrews was co-starred with a noted English dramatic actor, this time Richard Burton. Even the hyperbolic sweep of Lancelot's love song reminded many of "On The Street Where You Live." To some extent it could be argued that *Camelot* attempted to impose the biting realistic wit

of *My Fair Lady* on the magical fantasy of *Brigadoon*. It became especially disconcerting when Mordred was made into a comic villain. But for all its faults, *Camelot* was a fine evening's entertainment gorgeously set and dressed in medieval splendor. Its advance sale of over three million dollars gave audiences time to spread a generally favorable word of mouth after the shock of the initial disappointment. Before it had run its course *Camelot* played over two years in Manhattan, toured, and enjoyed international celebrity as well.

Two weeks later audiences were back in 1912. It was not the homey, small-town 1912 of so many recent shows but the rough-and-tumble good old days of the early oil booms. And the **Wildcat** (16 December 1960, Alvin) to end all wildcats was television's beloved Lucille Ball. She played Wildcat Jackson, who arrives in Centavo City with her crippled sister Jane (Paula Stewart). Wildcat bluffs the townspeople into believing she has drilling rights and persuades Joe Dynamite (Keith Andes) to be her foreman. Only then does she actually purchase oil leases from a comic recluse, Sookie (Don Tomkins). When Joe becomes discouraged with the prospects on her land and threatens to quit, she has him arrested on trumped-up charges and put in her custody. After further digging proves futile and all her crew seem ready to quit, Wildcat throws a stick of dynamite into a well and comes up with a spectacular gusher. She also wins Joe for a husband. It was not much of a book, although it was written by an accomplished playwright, N. Richard Nash. For most theatergoers the only inducement to see the show was Miss Ball. In June, when she tired of playing it, the show had to fold before it could retrieve its investment. While *Wildcat* was running, its showstopper was a hoedown routine with Wildcat and Sookie called "What Takes My Fancy," but a second lively number, Wildcat's commanding march, "Hey, Look Me Over," later developed into a standard. The rest of the score, with music by Cy Coleman and lyrics by Carolyn Leigh, ran from the cloyingly cute "Tippy Tippy Toes" to the mawkish "That's What I Want For Janie" to the pretentious "Tall Hope," a choral number that closed the first act.

The season's only sustained attempt at dealing with the contemporary scene, **Do Re Mi** (26 December 1960, St. James) closed out 1960. Garson Kanin's libretto was not much better than *Wildcat*'s book. It, too, depended primarily on its clowns for its strength. Fortunately its producer, David Merrick, hired two of the best: Phil Silvers and Nancy Walker. They played a husband and wife, Hubert and Kay Cram, who occasionally are in the money when one of Hubie's pie-in-the-sky schemes momentarily works. When they visit the Casacabana and their table is shoved farther and farther into the rear of the nightclub, the humiliation drives Hubie to attempt to become a big shot in the jukebox business. He kids himself, "It's Legitimate," even though he knows his associates have been racketeers. Before long the big boys muscle in, but Hubie is swimming in money. Kay concludes the old days of middle-class struggle were a more joyous "Adventure." When she complains of Hubie's underworld cronies and he responds that they help pay for the elegant dress she has on, she takes off the dress. After a while, Hubie is over his head and finally forced out. Kay is content, but Hubie is planning his next conquest. A love interest was provided by Tilda Mullen (Nancy Dussault), a waitress Hubie helps make a singing star, and the polished John Henry Wheeler (John Reardon). The show's best production number, "What's New At The Zoo," fell to Tilda. John was given the musical's hit love ballad, "Make Someone Happy": Jule Styne wrote the music, and Comden and Green the lyrics. Its stars were more loyal to *Do Re Mi* than Miss Ball was to *Wildcat*, and it ran 400 performances. Nevertheless, theatrical economics were responsible for its closing in the loss column.

The first musical of 1961 was billed as a revue, but it was little more than a one-woman show. The one woman in this case was the towering Carol Charming, given breathers by comedian Jules Munshin and Les Quat' Jeudis. Miss Channing's **Show Girl** (12 January 1961, O'Neill) had no connection with Ziegfeld's 1929 production. However, one high spot was a comparison of the musical shows of Ziegfeld's era with the musicals of her own day. With the new era coming to an end and with its clichés falling into perspective, Miss Channing took advantage of a unique opportunity for comic juxtaposition. Culling songs from the "Gladiola Girl" spoof that had rocketed her to fame in *Lend an Ear* (16 December 1948), she compared three of them with similarly placed numbers from imaginary contemporary shows. The opening number of "Gladiola," "Join Us In A Little Cup Of Tea," was contrasted with "This Is A Darned Fine Funeral," and the 1920s-style love song, "In Our Teeny Little Weeny Nest (For Two)," gave way to "Love Is A Sickness," while the high-kicking "Yahoo" step was replaced by a balletic "Switchblade Bess." Although

the show ran only three months, a low budget and successful road tour helped it show a profit.

Preston Sturges's acclaimed *Hail, the Conquering Hero* was made into a musical by Larry Gelbart, Moose Charlap, and Norman Gimbel. They contracted the title to **The Conquering Hero** (16 January 1961, ANTA) but kept the essentials of the movie's story, in which a recruit (Tom Poston), discharged after a month's service because of his allergies, is mistaken for a war hero. The picture had been done during World War II and delighted with its zany hilarity. By 1961 both timeliness and zaniness were missing. One week was the length of the new show's welcome.

Only the least bit less unsuccessful was **13 Daughters** (2 March 1961, 54th St.), whose main attraction in a year of notable scenery and scenic effects was George Jenkins's colorful Hawaiian settings. Don Ameche found himself playing a turn-of-the-century Chinese paterfamilias in Hawaii who cannot marry off his twelve younger daughters until he finds a suitable husband for his eldest. In addition, to complicate his life further, a family curse says his daughters mustn't marry at all. Ameche strove with such lines as "A bird in the hand is worth two in the bushel," but he didn't have to struggle for long.

E. Y. Harburg, Fred Saidy, and Henry Myers took Aristophanes' ancient Greek comedy *Lysistrata*, set it to Offenbach's nineteenth-century French music, gave the principal, if not the title, role to the best of all British fop portrayers, Cyril Ritchard, and came up with a new Broadway musical, **The Happiest Girl in the World** (3 April 1961, Martin Beck). It was charming, but not charming enough to survive long.

The City Center presented four revivals in its annual spring season. For 1961 it began on 12 April with *Show Boat* (27 December 1927) with Jo Sullivan, Robert Rounseville, and Joe E. Brown, and continued on 26 April with *South Pacific* (7 April 1949), *Porgy and Bess* (10 October 1935) on 17 May, and *Pal Joey* (25 December 1940) on 31 May, with Bob Fosse and Carol Bruce as the principals.

Twice before, with his musical versions of *Anna Christie* and *Ah, Wilderness!*, Bob Merrill had demonstrated his willingness to compose scores for challenging adaptations. His derring-do was again displayed when he offered a new work in association with librettist Michael Stewart and producer David Merrick. What was so unusual about **Carnival** (13 April 1961, Imperial) was that it was based on a recent and tremendously popular motion picture,

Lili, whose own score had produced at least one standard. The entire film score was discarded. But the essential story remained. Lili, an orphan, appears at a small European carnival seeking a friend of her dead father and, she hopes, the offer of a home. She is taken in hand by the carnival folk. At first she becomes enamored of the show's magician, Marco the Magnificent (James Mitchell), but she soon realizes her true future lies with the lame, misanthropic puppeteer Paul Berthalet (Jerry Orbach). She brings out his repressed warmth and goodness, and love ensues. The show lacked the fey enchantments of the film, but had virtues of its own, especially Gower Champion's vital staging. No curtain was used, and the performers often employed aisles for entrances and exits, sometimes even for part of the show. Champion's vital choreography was as exciting as his staging, culminating in the rousing ensemble dancing for "Grand Imperial Cirque De Paris," with virtually the entire cast swinging arm-in-arm around the stage. Champion found himself in the peculiar position of having to give virtually no dancing to his Lili, even though one of the film's delights had been Leslie Caron's dancing. The star of the show was Anna Maria Alberghetti, a singer, so the burden of providing her with material fell to Merrill. His songs (not only for Lili) kept a seemingly conscious distance in time and place. Their titles often appeared to have come from musicals of fifty years earlier—"Fairyland," "Sword, Rose And Cape," "Tanz Mit Mir," and "Yum Ticky." But he did manage to create a "Theme From 'Carnival'" that became almost as popular as the movie's "Hi Lili, Hi Lo." It was played all through the show and finally sung by Lili and Paul's puppets as the first-act finale. It received national attention under the more workable title of "Love Makes The World Go Round." *Carnival* walked away with most of the season's awards and ran over 700 performances, to the profit˙ of all concerned.

Regular first-class houses rarely turned their stages over to written-for-children musicals, but for a short time, beginning on 26 April, an hour-long **Young Abe Lincoln** frolicked on the Eugene O'Neill's stage after receiving thumbs-up notices from those few who reviewed it.

Donnybrook! (18 May 1961, 46th St.), the season's final musical, was, like *Carnival,* based on a film, John Ford's *The Quiet Man.* It was adapted by Robert E. McEnroe, who years before had written one successful play, *The Silver Whistle,* and had songs by Johnny Burke. The story again recounted the trials and tribulations of John Enright (Art Lund), a prizefighter who retires from the ring to Ireland after one of his punches kills an opponent. His hopes to marry Ellen Danaher (Joan Fagan) are dashed when Ellen's brother Will (Philip Bosco) refuses to give her a dowry unless John first fights him. John, fearing he might inadvertently kill Will, demurs. Since Ellen will not marry without her dowry, John has no choice but to fight. *Donnybrook!,* like *The Conquering Hero* and unlike *Carnival,* could not find the secret to moving successfully from one medium to another. Despite some good singing by Lund and some capital clowning by Susan Johnson and Eddie Foy, Jr., it languished for sixty-eight performances before calling it a run.

In one respect the season ended as it began, with the death of a notable figure. Joe Howard had never approached Oscar Hammerstein's importance on Broadway, and indeed he had rarely approached Broadway. He belonged to a time much earlier than Hammerstein's, when Broadway was not the sole production center for the American Musical Theatre. In a day when Chicago was almost as important, Howard was indisputably the best of the Chicago composers. He died at the age of ninety-three, on stage, performing. But his creative days had long since passed, and his very era seemed irretrievably far away.

1961–1962

The new season was the busiest in a dozen years and, like several recent sessions, was packed with good shows whose possibilities were never fully realized. In several ways the season gave further indication of the waning of an era, while at the same time it demonstrated that the period's high artistic principles would not be readily discarded. Almost all the season's musicals were steadfastly set in the present day; none looked back to the America of a half-century or so before. Sentimentality took several severe knockings, and even romance was often either relegated to a subservient role or given an unhappy denouement. Although dancing remained generally excellent, there were fewer of the kinds of ballet that had become commonplace since *Oklahoma!,* especially "dream ballets." A number of the musicals dealt head-on with growing racial problems or with life among one important section of theatergoers, the Jews. This, plus their modern settings, gave the season's shows a thirtyish air. Appearances, however, did not bear close scrutiny. The biting social commentary of the more purposeful Depression-era musicals was missing, while the cardboard figures and caricatures of that period's lighter pieces gave way to the more lifelike men and women the modern musical play had led audiences to expect.

A lone summer entry was **The Billy Barnes People** (13 June 1961, Royale). Barnes and his collaborator Bob Rodgers, had managed to span the summer two seasons back with the *Billy Barnes Revue*. This time their appeal, or their luck, ran out, and the show survived less than a week, taking with it skits on the order of its *Camelot* travesty, "Damn-Alot."

A Chicago revue, **From the Second City** (26 September 1961, Royale), was unusual in that it was a series of clever sketches with almost no music interjected. Most of the material was topical. A new Germany was seen as so eager to reject its recent past that it was determinedly burning Nazi books and seeking a "final solution" to the Nazi problem. A news broadcast, plucked magically from four years in the future, summed up the early achievements of America's latest President. The minimum wage has been reduced to a sensible pittance; Social Security begins at ninety-five, provided disability can be proved; and the work week has been extended to a productive sixty hours. "So much," the announcer concludes, "for the first hundred days of the Goldwater administration." New Yorkers didn't accept the revue as wholeheartedly as Chicagoans had, but in its eleven-week run it helped further the careers of such bright, young talents as Barbara Harris and Alan Arkin.

Sail Away (3 October 1961, Broadhurst) was also unusual, but in a different way. It was the work of England's idolized Noël Coward, but it was presented on Broadway before London was allowed to see it. New Yorkers were not overwhelmed by the courtesy. Less than vintage Coward, this tale of a harassed cruise hostess (Elaine Stritch) on a Cunard Mediterranean voyage left port after twenty-one weeks. It was the first musical in a busy October.

On the 8th the New York City Opera offered subscribers *The Mikado*, and one week afterwards, *Pinafore*. (In late March the City Center's own artists did both of these along with *Iolanthe* and *The Gondoliers*.)

Given the size of the Jewish segment of Broadway's playgoers and its concern with Israel, it was surprising no musical had used an Israeli setting before. Curiously, although **Milk and Honey** (10 October 1961, Beck) ran nearly a year and a half (without showing a profit), only one other major musical later used the same setting. The principal figures in *Milk and Honey* were not Israelis but American Jews in Israel as tourists. Phil is a middle-aged businessman, separated from his wife. His daughter Barbara (Lanna Saunders) and son-in-law David (Tommy Rail) live in a kibbutz. Phil meets an attractive American, Ruth, and they quickly grow fond of each other. When Phil reveals he is still married their idyll seems ended. Watching a joyous Yemenite wedding convinces Ruth that she should at least give the liaison a try, but her qualms persist, and she soon flees to Tel Aviv. Phil pursues her, but when she agrees to return he develops qualms. Ruth decides to go back to America and to wait until Phil gets his divorce. An undercurrent of unhappiness pervades Barbara and David's relationship, too, because Barbara is homesick for the United States and David accepts the probability of having to leave his beloved fatherland to please his wife. The only completely happy romance in the show was that of the central comic figure, a "yenta" named Clara Weiss who comes to Israel specifically to find a husband and succeeds in capturing an appropriately docile "nebbish," Mr. Horowitz. The score was the first by Jerry Herman to be heard on Broadway. It was a superb amalgam of Jewish colorings and rhythms within accepted theatrical forms. The show's hit was Phil and Ruth's warmly inviting "Shalom," which virtually framed the evening. The rest of the songs moved from the irresistible beat of the "Independence Day Hora" to the stirring title song, sung by David and the chorus, to David's poignant cry of "I Will Follow You," to Ruth and Phil's slightly arioso "There's No Reason In The World," to their lively "That Was Yesterday." Although Herman was destined to have an even greater success, none of his future scores was as melodically inventive or memorable. Two fine singers, formerly of the opera, Mimi Benzell and Robert Weede, played Ruth and Phil, while Second Avenue's popular Molly Picon was Clara.

JERRY HERMAN was born in New York City on 10 July 1933. He studied music from early childhood and majored in drama at the University of Miami. Three of his musicals— *I Feel Wonderful, Nightcap,* and *Parade*—were done off-Broadway before *Milk and Honey* made the big time. He also trained by writing special material for performers such as Tallulah Bankhead, Jane Froman, and Hermione Gingold. One of his songs was heard in Miss Gingold's revue, *From A to Z.*

Television's lackadaisical George Gobel bowed in a new musical version of *Three Men on a Horse*, now dubbed **Let It Ride!** (12 October 1961, O'Neill). An earlier musicalization had appeared twenty years before as *Banjo Eyes* (25 December 1941) with Eddie Cantor. Cantor had been able to keep an essentially weak vehicle going single-handedly. Gobel's version was no worse, but Gobel lacked the theatrical know-how and, surprisingly, the drawing power to keep the show alive. The high moment of the evening was a comic number called "Just An Honest Mistake," which ended, "Mr. Nixon said 'Let's Debate.'" But it was insufficient to overcome duller moments or competition.

Competition became intense two nights later. **How to Succeed in Business Without Really Trying** (14 October 1961, 46th St.) was based on Shepherd Mead's book of the same name; it was an unromantic, but not unaffectionate, satire that reunited many of the team responsible for *Guys and Dolls* (24 November 1950). Feuer and Martin were once again the producers. Abe Burrows collaborated on the libretto (with Jack Weinstock and Willie Gilbert), and composer Frank Loesser abandoned his more operatic ambitions to return to the world of pure musical comedy. The show even played the same 46th Street Theatre where *Guys and Dolls* had run. The story followed the rise of the disarmingly opportunistic J. Pierrepont Finch (Robert Morse) from window-washer to chairman of the board of World Wide Wickets Company. He does it by coolly following the precepts of Mead's book, which he pulls from his pocket and reads at necessary intervals. Mead extols the virtues of "education and intelligence and ability" but reminds his readers that "thousands have reached the top without any of these qualities." So Finch discards his work clothes and heads for the personnel office of World Wide Wickets. In his rush he literally bumps into the company's president, J. B. Biggley (Rudy Vallee), and in his ignorance is unmoved by Biggley's scolding. His indifference to Biggley catches the eye and

heart of one of the company's prettiest secretaries, Rosemary Pilkington (Bonnie Scott). She escorts him to the office of the personnel director, Mr. Bratt (Paul Reed):

Bratt: We're not hiring anyone today.
Finch: Well, I was just speaking to Mr. Biggley...
Bratt: J. B. Biggley himself? You were speaking to him?
Finch: Yes, sir. I just bumped into him.
Bratt: Ah, is he a friend of yours?
Finch: Sir, I don't think a man should trade on friendship to get a job.

This timely evasion gets Finch a position in the mail room working alongside Biggley's obnoxious nephew, Bud Frump (Charles Nelson Reilly). Although Finch is unaware of it, it also deepens the affections of Rosemary, who would be "Happy To Keep His Dinner Warm" while he wangles his way up in the world. And while his fellow employees waste time at a "Coffee Break," Finch determines to move above the mail room. He cannot take the executive mail in to Biggley—that's Frump's job. So Finch arranges to pass Biggley's secretary accidentally in the corridor. Pretending he doesn't know who she is, he offers her a flower. When she reveals her position he professes astonishment— and delight—to learn she's not the ogre Frump had described. Twimble (Sammy Smith), head of the mail room, tells Finch he will go far if he only does everything "The Company Way." Finch comprehends quickly. He refuses Twimble's post now that Twimble is to retire, insisting it rightfully belongs to Frump. Finch's knowing diplomacy is rewarded with an even better position and with Frump's jealous enmity. The personnel manager is given a buxom beauty, Hedy La Rue (Virginia Martin), to place in a secretarial slot, and he warns his men, "A Secretary Is Not A Toy." Miss La Rue is Biggley's current mistress. Biggley has another secret. He loves to knit. And Biggley, a graduate of "Grand Old Ivy," is a loyal Groundhog. Finch is able to turn Biggley's pleasures to his advantage. When the not too bright Miss La Rue is assigned to Finch and presents herself as his "assignation," he reads Mead's precept: "The smaller her abilities, the bigger her protector," and correctly surmises who is protecting Hedy. He hastily offers her to the libidinous Mr. Gatch, the director of Plans and Systems, and in no time at all he has replaced the transferred Mr. Gatch. He also leads Biggley to believe he is a Groundhog and is promoted to the

686 • ACT FIVE

head of advertising when he reveals the current head was once a Chipmunk, the Groundhogs' detested rivals. As head of advertising he must come up with a stupendous idea. Frump suggests a television treasure hunt, knowing his uncle has already rejected the plan. Miss La Rue unwittingly saves the day for Finch. Ignoring Biggley's plaint that he cannot live without "Love From A Heart Of Gold," Miss La Rue threatens to leave unless she is given a better job. When Finch suggests the young lady be made the national Treasure Girl, the grateful Biggley revises his feelings about the program. In the men's washroom the confident Finch sings a love song—to himself. Seeing in the mirror "the cool clear eyes of a seeker of wisdom and truth," he assures his reflection, "I Believe In You." Unfortunately Biggley confides to Hedy that the treasure is hidden in World Wide Wickets' offices, and Hedy reveals the hiding place on the television show. The next morning the offices are a wreck. The chairman of the board, Wally Womper (Sammy Smith), appears, out for blood. But when he learns Finch began, like he did, as a window-washer, he is mollified. Womper does not fire Biggley, but he does take Miss La Rue for his wife, and he retires, appointing Finch in his place. Finch, secure at the top, now has time to consider romance. He agrees to take the chairmanship if Rosemary has no objections:

Rosemary: Darling, I don't care if you work in the mail room, or you're chairman of the board, or you're President of the United States, I love you.
Finch: Say that again.
Rosemary: I love you.
Finch: No, before that.

Just before the final curtain Frump is seen washing windows with one hand and reading *How to Succeed* with the other.

The show's superb comedy was made even funnier by impeccable casting. Vallee, a singing idol in the twenties and early thirties, revealed a droll, deadpan delivery. Morse's gap-toothed smile and deceptively boyish appearance somehow made his double-dealing as lovable as it was hilarious. Reilly's pouting Frump was virtually a caricature of a nineteenth-century villain. Loesser's score was, for the most part, not hummably melodic. It was strongest when it was satiric. But "I Believe In You," removed from its riotously outlandish situation in the play, gradually received general and long-lasting

acceptance. Sadly, it was Loesser's last work. He died at the age of fifty-nine of cancer on 28 July 1969. He lived long enough to see *How to Succeed in Business Without Really Trying* become the American Musical Theatre's fourth Pulitzer Prize winner, and also to see it tally a run of 1,416 performances.

Kwamina (23 October 1961, 54th St.) survived for a mere thirty-two performances, but it was interesting in several respects. Its songs were by Richard Adler, in his first solo effort after the death of his partner, Jerry Ross. The book was by Robert Alan Arthur, a playwright whose works had met with respect, if not success. Their story recounted the love of a white woman for a black man in a newly freed West African country. The white girl is an attractive lady named Eve (Sally Ann Howes), and her lover is a Western-trained doctor known as both Peter and Kwamina (Terry Carter). The country's internal struggle between Western enlightenment and African superstition exacerbates an inherently difficult romance. In the end, the pair prudently decide to go their separate ways. The story and the music were a far cry from the boisterous mirth of Adler's previous shows, and neither he nor Arthur could find quite the right treatment for their pioneering, difficult theme. Nor could Agnes de Mille's vibrant African dances—notably a wedding ritual that opened the second act—save the show.

Yves Montand returned the next night with a one-man program of his songs and pleased his followers for fifty-five performances.

Two elaborate, promising musicals premiered in November, and both failed. **Kean** (2 November 1961, Broadway) was given a sumptuous mounting, enlivened by another of Alfred Drake's dependably bravura performances in the title role. The songs were by Robert Wright and George Forrest, who had heretofore contented themselves with setting words to the melodies of classical composers (Grieg's in *Song of Norway*, Borodin's in *Kismet*). The book by the untried Peter Stone was based on a Jean-Paul Sartre play that itself had been inspired by an earlier Alexandre Dumas drama. All three told of Kean's struggle to be accepted as something more than a great actor. But the material was clumsily handled and the music second-rate. It was the only show during the season resorting to the nineteenth century for its background. But *Kean* went back to the first half of the century, a period generally ignored by librettists. A respectable advance sale and Alfred Drake's name allowed the work to play for three months.

The Gay Life (18 November 1961, Shubert) did look back to the turn of the century, but it was a turn-of-the-century Vienna. The evening was based on Arthur Schnitzler's *The Affairs of Anatol*, and the libretto was devised by Fay and Michael Kanin. Both had enjoyed success in Hollywood, while Mrs. Kanin was affectionately remembered on Broadway for her comedy *Goodbye, My Fancy*. To raise expectations even higher, Arthur Schwartz and Howard Dietz were reunited for the songs. The plot recounted the relinquishing of determined bachelor and man-about-town Anatol von Huber's (Walter Chiari) tenaciously held independence for the arms of the equally determined Liesl Brandel (Barbara Cook). The evening began drolly when Mac (Jules Munshin), Liesl's brother and Anatol's best friend, awakes the sleeping hero to determine why he is not at his own wedding. The remainder of the history is a flashback. A number of musicologists have hailed Schwartz's score as one of his masterpieces. In his study of American popular song, Alec Wilder gives extensive space to three of the show's numbers: "Why Go Anywhere At All?," sung by a minor character, Liesl's "Something You Never Had Before," and the evening's touching close, Anatol's "For The First Time." But most of the critics and the public, overcome by the current rage, rock and roll, didn't hear its beauties or subtleties—or, if they did, rejected the patently reminiscent melodic lines. Only the simple, slightly stretched melodic line of "Magic Moment" enjoyed any general appeal. Actually neither the book nor the score was very theatrical. Still, Dietz placed most of the blame for the show's failure on its leading man, who, he said, with some understatement, "couldn't act, dance, sing, or speak English, which was a handicap." The show ran only slightly longer than *Kean*, 113 performances.

December's only musical plunked theatregoers back in contemporary New York. Producer David Merrick presented the latest in the Comden-Green-Styne paeans to ordinary, if slightly kooky, Manhattanites. **Subways Are for Sleeping** (27 December 1961, St. James) described the rocky course of two love affairs. Tom Bailey (Sydney Chaplin) is a good-looking, polished, professional ne'er-do-well, so out-of-pocket he sleeps in the subway. But he is attractive enough to win the heart of a moderately successful fashion magazine writer, Angie McKay (Carol Lawrence), when she is sent to interview him. Martha Vail (Phyllis Newman) is a beauty contest winner (Miss Watermelon and Miss Southern Comfort) who has lost all her clothing and

will lose her apartment if her landlord succeeds in evicting her. She spends most of her day wrapped in a towel and many of her evenings being courted on the phone by Charlie Smith (Orson Bean). Smith is another full-time ne'er-do-well, so poor he attempts to make local calls collect. Not much really happens, although Tom does get temporary employment as a Santa Claus. In the end Tom and Angie agree to write a book while Charlie and Martha start a coffee-vending service. The show's best numbers followed each other in the second act. In its comic highlight Charlie confesses to Martha, "I Just Can't Wait" ("till I see you with your clothes on"). Angie and Tom settle for a carpe diem philosophy in "Comes Once In A Lifetime." The indifferent notices the show received led to one of the American Musical Theatre's most hilarious and celebrated contretemps. Merrick found seven New Yorkers whose names were identical with those of the seven daily newspaper critics and who were willing to give his show enthusiastic praise. He then took a large advertisement in the *Herald Tribune* listing the names and quotations. To avoid legal problems he also printed a small photograph alongside each name. There were howls of outrage and laughter. The publicity helped the show run six months, not sufficiently long, however, to put it in the black.

The first musical of 1962, **A Family Affair** (27 January 1962, Rose) had a book by James and William Goldman, both of whom later went on to Hollywood and Broadway success, and music by John Kander. Essentially, it was an extended Jewish joke. Sally Nathan (Rita Gardner) and Gerry Siegel (Larry Kert) would like to marry, and there is really nothing to stand in their way, except Gerry's doting parents (Morris Carnovsky and Eileen Heckart) and Sally's outrageous guardian (Shelley Berman). Once upon a time it might have seemed funny as a short, furiously paced farce. Songs broke the momentum, and the respite gave audiences time to realize the joke was over before the show was. Fine performances couldn't push the musical beyond eight weeks.

Composer **JOHN KANDER**, born 18 March 1927 in Kansas City, Missouri, studied classical music at Columbia University under Douglas Moore and Jack Beeson. He took jobs as pianist for a tour of *An Evening with Beatrice*

Lillie, rehearsal pianist for *The Amazing Adele*, and musical director for a short-lived Off-Broadway revival of *Conversation Piece*. A breakthrough opportunity arose when Kander, working as a replacement rehearsal pianist for *West Side Story*, was nominated by *Story*'s stage manager to play auditions for *Gypsy*. From there he was hired to create dance arrangements for *Gypsy* and *Irma La Douce*, launching a long, prolific career.

The young performers in **New Faces of 1962** (1 February 1962, Alvin) naturally had none of the experience enjoyed by the older performers in *A Family Affair*. Their material was disappointing. Limp skits and weak songs touched on everything from basic education to marital infidelity. A gnawing suspicion whispered that these new faces were not quite as bright as some of the neophytes in earlier editions. The show quit after twenty-eight showings.

A second composer whose partner had recently died offered both words and music for his songs on 15 March. Unlike Adler, Richard Rodgers was a supreme melodist, and he had written his own lyrics on a few earlier occasions. Like Adler he chose an established playwright for his librettist, although Samuel Taylor had a more successful history than Robert Alan Arthur. Taylor, like Arthur, created an original story, and, coincidentally one that also dealt with an interracial romance. Experience and ability told, and the Rodgers–Taylor offering, **No Strings** (15 March 1962, 54th St.), survived both an uneven critical reception and an out-of-the-way theatre to become a long-run hit. David Jordan is an American writer from Maine who has spent the six years since winning a Pulitzer Prize having a good time in Paris. He meets a glamorous black model, Barbara Woodruff, at a photographer's studio. They take an instant liking to one another and are shortly enjoying the attractions of Paris together. Their budding love affair is abruptly terminated when David discovers Barbara has a wealthy, middle-aged admirer. The separation is not long-lasting, and the two are soon together again. They go off to Honfleur, where David hopes to resume his writing career. Inspiration refuses to come. David concludes he must return to Maine if he is to be creative once more. He offers

to take Barbara, but she reminds him of the prejudice they would encounter, and of the freedom and income she would leave behind. Although they promise to meet at some future date, they leave each other knowing they will probably never see each other again.

The show was given an imaginative staging with a minimum of movable scenery that suggested a photographer's props, but it was stylishly done and beautifully costumed. An orchestra played from behind the scenes and sometimes on stage instead of in the pit and, in keeping with the title, contained no strings. The show was framed in a poignant melody, "The Sweetest Sounds," which Barbara and David sing from opposite sides of the stage before they meet and again as they go their separate ways. Most of the other love ballads in the show had the same flavor, but Rodgers's seemingly limitless melodic gifts kept them enticingly varied: "Nobody Told Me," "Look No Further," and the title song. Early in the show Barbara is given a driving, cynical number which nonetheless managed to also sound romantic, "Loads Of Love." Critics suggested that Rodgers as a lyricist was a happy combination of the best of Hammerstein and Hart. Nevertheless, Rodgers thereafter left the lyric-writing chores to others. The show was faultlessly cast with Diahann Carroll as the all-too-worldly, forlorn Barbara and Richard Kiley as the urbane David.

College life and football returned to the Broadway stage with **All American** (19 March 1962, Winter Garden) four nights after *No Strings* arrived. It had music by Charles Strouse and lyrics by Lee Adams, whose work was every bit as good as the material they had produced for *Bye Bye Birdie* (14 April 1960). And in Ray Bolger they had a beguiling dancer and comedian. But the book by Mel Brooks, who later went on to become one of Hollywood's most creative figures, was inept and ultimately dragged the rest of the evening down with it. An immigrant, Professor Fodorski (Bolger), comes to Southern Baptist Institute of Technology, where he promptly catches the eye of the dean, Elizabeth Hawkes-Bullock (Eileen Herlie). His curious charm even inspires his football team to unaccustomed victory and catapults the professor to national attention. Fame brings headaches. Would-be exploiters arrive; peace and privacy are destroyed; and the engineering career of SBIT's star fullback, Ed Bricker (Ron Husmann), seems jeopardized by his preoccupation with his Saturday-afternoon success. To restore tranquility and proportion, Fodorski purposely loses the season's big game by keeping Bricker on the bench. But Fodorski does win the dean, and Ed wins pretty Susan Thompson (Anita Gillette). Two numbers in the charming Strouse–Adams score outlived the show: Fodorski's light, tripping soft-shoe, "If I Were You," and the nostalgic, Irish-tinted "Once Upon A Time," which Fodorski and the dean sing early in the show and which the dean twice reprises. SBIT closed for good about the same time most schools were finishing their semesters.

David Merrick had another musical ready for New York's inspection three nights after *All American* premiered, making for three major openings in just over a week. **I Can Get It for You Wholesale** (22 March 1962, Shubert) was adapted by Jerome Weidman from his own novel, with songs by Harold Rome. The musical was set in the thirties, but it made little appeal to the nostalgic. It took a hard-boiled look at the cutthroat world of New York's garment district. Even Harold Rome, who rose to prominence with his music for Depression revues, eschewed most sounds of the era and most of its propagandizing. As a result, for all its token bows to the thirties, *I Can Get It for You Wholesale* projected itself as a contemporary piece with a dateless story. It seemed to many a sort of *How to Succeed in Business Without Really Trying* (14 October 1961) stripped of that show's wit and sunny disposition. Harry Bogen (Elliott Gould) is cold, pushy, and determined—determined to rise to the top by whatever means are required. He starts as a small-time strikebreaker, moves into the garment business with a few partners, and then shoves them out of his way. He ignores the pleas of his good-hearted mother (Lillian Roth) and his adoring girlfriend and neighbor, Ruthie Rivkin (Marilyn Cooper), to act ethically. He would even ditch Ruthie for a cheap, flamboyant nightclub performer, Martha Mills (Sheree North). When, after all his machinations, he ends up a bankrupt, only his mother and Ruthie are there to console him. The ending did not necessarily imply that simplicity and goodness were the best rewards but only that Harry was neither ruthless nor cunning enough to attain his goals.

No standards emerged from Rome's serviceable, unimaginative score, but one number stopped the show nightly. It was the comic lament of a much-put-upon secretary, "Miss Marmelstein." The young lady whose delivery of the song brought down the house was a nineteen-year-old newcomer, Barbara Streisand. Enough cloak-and-suiters used the musical as a busman's holiday to keep it playing for nine

months, although it never brought Merrick's backers a profit.

For its spring semester, the New York City Opera brought out *The Consul* and *Porgy and Bess* on 28 and 31 March respectively.

The season took a breather in April, then four shows opened in May to end the season. The first was only the third of the year's new musicals ultimately to show a profit. **A Funny Thing Happened on the Way to the Forum** (8 May 1962, Alvin) had a book by Burt Shevelove and Larry Gelbart purportedly based on plays of Plautus. Accordingly, the scenery and costumes were more or less Roman, and so were the names of the characters. But what the musical really represented was a hilarious mixture of burlesque and outrageous comedy, the closest thing the American Musical Theatre could expect to an evening with the Marx Brothers, without the Marx Brothers. The story told of an attempt by the slave Pseudolus (Zero Mostel) to win his freedom by procuring the beautiful, if vapid, courtesan Philia (Preshy Marker) for his master, Hero (Brian Davies). His efforts are hindered by dashing Miles Gloriosus (Ronald Holgate), who has purchased Philia from Lycus (John Carradine), a dealer in courtesans, and by Hero's father, Senex (David Burns), who has his own plans for the girl. So Pseudolus first spreads the word that Philia is a carrier of plague and then announces that she has died. A mock funeral turns into a mad chase. When Miles learns he is Philia's brother, he gives her to Hero, and Pseudolus is granted his freedom. The show's humor leaned heavily on double-entendres and outlandish jokes. When Pseudolus is told a wine is "from the year one" he asks if that was a good year for wine. A eunuch is admonished, "Don't you lower your voice at me!"

The songs not only had lyrics by Stephen Sondheim, they had music by him as well. His tunes—from the opening "Comedy Tonight" to the finale—were light and easy on the ear, with a distinct hint of Rodgers and Hart. One of them, "Lovely," has remained popular. Yet it was Sondheim's masterful way with words that was most telling. The lovesick Hero in "Love, I Hear" wakes "too weak to walk." Pseudolus promises that in his gratitude for being made "Free," "I'll be so conscientious I may vote twice," while Senex suggests "Everybody Ought To Have A Maid." Later Senex and Hero find it outrageously "Impossible" that the other could be in love. Some of Broadway's funniest comedians assisted in the antics, with Zero Mostel leading a contingent that also boasted Jack Gilford as a farcically hysterical Hysterium. The show rocked Broadway with laughter for over two years.

A number of great singers had left opera for Broadway when their careers had begun to flag. But it was almost unheard of for a prominent opera star to assume a Broadway role when still at the height of his powers. Cesare Siepi ventured just that when he appeared in **Bravo Giovanni** (19 May 1962, Broadhurst). Handsome, with a fine voice and more than competent acting ability, he might have found a permanent home for himself in the legitimate stage had he chosen a better vehicle to initiate his new career. Regrettably, the new show, which was based on Howard Shaw's novel *The Crime of Giovanni Venturi*, managed to tell a not uninteresting story uninterestingly. Giovanni Venturi's simple restaurant is hit hard when Signor Bellardi (George S. Irving) opens a branch of his fast-food chain, Uriti, down the street. The new eatery offers cut-price minestrone, tortoni, and chicken chow mein. Its espresso spews forth from a bust of Dante. In desperation Giovanni and his girlfriend, Miranda (Michele Lee), decide to dig a tunnel from their kitchen into Uriti's and steal Uriti's food. The digging unearths an Etruscan tomb and threatens to expose their plan. But in the end the tunnel is so successful Giovanni contemplates opening restaurants next to other Uritis. Even more disappointing than the book was the score. "Ah! Comminare" enjoyed a passing vogue, but by and large the score left Siepi without a palpably enchanting number and with little to show off his fine style and range. In two engagements, broken by a summer vacation, the show compiled a total of seventy-six performances. When it passed into history, Siepi returned to the more steady employment offered by Mozart and Verdi.

The City Center season of revivals began later than usual and lapped over into the following season. The 1962 offerings were *Can-Can* (7 May 1953) on 16 May with the French singer Geneviève, *Brigadoon* (13 March 1947) on 30 May with Peter Palmer and Sally Ann Howes, and, technically in 1962–1963, *Fiorello!* (23 November 1959) on 13 June.

1962–1963

Statistically at least, the American Musical Theatre suffered a dismal year. When importations, revivals, and one-man shows were set aside, only six new offerings remained: five book shows and one revue. Not one of these was a commercial success. Their failure was not a fair reflection of their merit.

Two were worthwhile, and a third was a minor, generally unappreciated, gem. Nonetheless English works gave the real excitement and backbone to the season—something London musicals had not done since the beginning of the century.

After the opening of the City Center's *Fiorello!* on 13 June, the theatrical calendar showed nothing of interest until 2 October when **Eddie Fisher at the Winter Garden** bowed. It was as much vaudeville as a one-man show, opening with Gordon Jenkins's brief showpiece "The Broadway Zoo," followed by black comedian Dick Gregory and dancer Juliet Prowse. The star had the second act to himself.

The first of three major English hits premiered the next night. **Stop the World—I Want to Get Off** (3 October 1962, Shubert) was the work of Leslie Bricusse and Anthony Newley. Mr. Newley was starred in the role of Littlechap. As the character's name suggests, the piece was an allegory, played out on a single circuslike set. If the allegory was obviously shallow, the evening as a whole was imaginative, lively, colorful, and melodic. The show's finale, "What Kind Of Fool Am I?," became one of the most popular tunes of the year.

On the 10th the New York City Opera reinserted *The Mikado* into its programs and, nine nights later, *The Merry Widow*.

In 1950 Howard Lindsay, Russel Crouse, and Irving Berlin had made Broadway a happier, more song-filled part of town with their light-hearted political charade *Call Me Madam* (12 October 1950). It had fun with the world of ambassadorial diplomacy. Now the trio decided to throw their hats in the ring again, and this time set out to reach the very top. They reached it politically, if not artistically. **Mr. President** (20 October 1962, St. James) was a solid bit of professional craftsmanship that disappointed largely because something more had been hoped for. A prologue warns the audience not to read any real-life figures into the characters they are about to see. President Stephen Decatur Henderson and his family are all and none of the White House's recent or current occupants. The stage White House is the scene of a lively ball, where sophisticated crowds are all reveling in the dance that was sweeping America in the early sixties, the twist. When the President and his wife appear, the First Lady suggests, "Let's Go Back To The Waltz." The guests comply until the pair leave, then, as one, the whole party goes back to the twist. In the morning, the President has more serious problems to contend with. An invitation to visit Russia is canceled while he is flying there.

He determines to land at Moscow, even though it is a breach of protocol. Only a few workmen are present when he arrives. His humiliation costs him the next election. While his wife, Nell, is happy to be back home, Stephen is not. Nonetheless, he turns down a seat in the Senate when compromising conditions are attached. Henderson eventually realizes his love of his country is primary and returns to government at the behest of the new President. The warning of the prologue should have been heeded. Canceling of the Russian tour inevitably recalled Eisenhower's predicament after the U-2 incident, while in their youthful good looks and vigor the Hendersons unmistakably suggested the Kennedys. Furthermore, the President's spunkiness and the Hendersons' apparent hominess brought Harry and Bess Truman to mind. As always, Berlin filled his score with pleasing melodies and easy, homey, sentiments. Titles such as the Hendersons' "In Our Hideaway," "Meat And Potatoes," sung by two Secret Service men, Pat (Jack Haskell) and Charles (Stanley Greger), "Pigtails And Freckles," sung by Miss Henderson (Anita Gillette) and her Secret Service man, Pat, Mrs. Henderson's "Glad To Be Home," and Henderson's "This Is A Great Country" convey the tone. In the last-named song Berlin struck upon one of his typically felicitous phrases, asking, if patriotic statements are flag waving, "Do you know of a better flag to wave?" For the aging composer *Mr. President* was his last musical in this history. It sounded some eerie echoes of his very first score, *Watch Your Step* (8 December 1914), just short of a half-century before. Berlin repeated some uncommon rhymes such as "service" with "nervous," and just as in "What Is Love?" he had managed to introduce some startling ragtime effects into a simple waltz, so in "Let's Go Back To The Waltz" he introduced some unexpected harmonic changes into a bit of forthright nostalgia. The principal difference between the scores was that none of the songs from the new show won wide public acceptance. Nor did the show itself. Glowing performances by Nanette Fabray and Robert Ryan as the First Lady and the President notwithstanding, *Mr. President* ran just eight months.

Bamboche (22 October 1962, 54th St.), said to be Haitian Creole for "get-together to have a good time," was the title of Katherine Dunham's latest dance program. Actually her evening once again roamed the globe, starting in Morocco, then moving on to Brazil, Haiti, and black Africa, and concluding, as she had in 1955, with a variety of African-American dances, among them the Charleston and a grand-finale cakewalk.

A trend had been developing toward songless revues. The preceding seasons had witnessed shows such as *A Thurber Carnival* and *From the Second City*, which had the requisite sketches but for all practical purposes no singing and dancing. On 27 October London offered what may have been the most brilliant of these, **Beyond the Fringe** (27 October 1962, Golden), a collection of monologues, dialogues, and skits written by its four performers, all recently out of university. It is hard to gauge to what extent the movement toward integrated songs and the vogue for theatrically effective, but not especially memorable, melodies prompted the revues to drop isolated numbers. The revue would seem to have been the logical refuge for stray good tunes. But apart from Dudley Moore's brief moments at the piano, *Beyond the Fringe* followed the new vogue by rarely raising its voice in song.

November's first new musical took a ready-made subject and botched it. Izzy Einstein and Moe Smith were undoubtedly the most flamboyant and theatrical of the twenties' Prohibition agents. Their resourceful disguises and ruses made them popular at a time when there were few people less popular than speakeasy raiders. But their story was told in **Nowhere to Go but Up** (10 November 1962, Winter Garden) by two inexperienced writers, James Lipton on the book and lyrics, and Sol Berkowitz for the music. Theirs was not an inept job—the title song was one of the liveliest and catchiest tunes of the year—but the show demanded the sort of zaniness its performers couldn't provide. Tom Bosley impersonated Izzy, while Martin Balsam played Moe. The musical lasted one week.

On 13 November the D'Oyly Carte began a thirty-two-performance run at the City Center, presenting *The Mikado, The Gondoliers, The Pirates of Penzance, Trial by Jury, H. M. S. Pinafore*, and *Iolanthe*.

Hopes were as high for **Little Me** (17 November 1962, Lunt-Fontanne) as they had been for *Mr. President*. It was not that the book was by Neil Simon, then thought of only as the author of *Come Blow Your Horn*, nor that the songs were by *Wildcat's* Cy Coleman and Carolyn Leigh. A small flurry of anticipation might have been attributed to the show's source, Patrick Dennis's best-seller. What created the lines at the box office before the reviews were out was the presence of Sid Caesar as star. He had not frolicked through a Broadway show since

Make Mine Manhattan (15 January 1948), and in the interval had become one of television's top celebrities. Simon's libretto retained Dennis's account of the rise of Belle Poitrine (née Schlumpfort) from a waif on the wrong side of the tracks in Venezuela, Illinois, to fame and wealth. In her teens she sets her sights on Noble Eggleston, who lives on the right side of the tracks, but whose mother puts an abrupt end to her ambitions. Biding her time, Belle finally succeeds in landing a rich, eighty-year-old skinflint, Mr. Pinchley. When he dies under suspicious circumstances, she is tried for murder and acquitted. The notoriety of the trial brings her a vaudeville offer and a romance with Val du Val, who modestly considers himself the world's greatest entertainer. Further romances follow with myopic Fred Poitrine, Prince Cherney of Rozenzweig, and the imperious film director Otto Schnitzler. Each romance in some unexpected way advances both Belle's career and fortune. Although it would appear that Belle (Virginia Martin) was the central figure, Caesar was the star by virtue of his assuming the roles of all the lovers, from the sixteen-year-old Eggleston to the decrepit Pinchley. While the score produced no songs that enjoyed much acclaim outside the theatre at the time, it was bright and more than adequate. Since then, the lively "I've Got Your Number," sung in the show by Belle's old admirer (Swen Swenson), has gained some currency.

The season's biggest hit, a third London importation, opened at the Imperial 6 January 1963, after an extensive national tour. **Oliver!** was Lionel Bart's musicalization of Dickens's *Oliver Twist*. It drove critics to expressions such as "jolly bad show" and "popperetta," but the public found it unfailingly appealing. Two standards emerged from the score, the gripping ballad "As Long As He Needs Me" and the romping "Consider Yourself (At Home)." Excellent performances by Clive Revill and Georgia Brown, plus Sean Kenny's strikingly evocative skeletonized sets and costumes enhanced the performance.

Maurice Chevalier delighted his supporters for a month at the Ziegfeld, where he opened his one-man show on 28 January. Two nights after Chevalier appeared, the City Center initiated an uncustomary winter season, presenting *Brigadoon* (13 March 1947) on 30 January with Russell Nype, Peter Palmer, and Sally Ann Howes, *Wonderful Town* (25 February 1952) on 13 February, with Kaye Ballard, and *Oklahoma!* (31 March 1943) on 27 February, with Palmer as Curly. The opening of *Oklahoma!* coincided with the arrival of Jack Benny at the

Ziegfeld in a vaudeville that also offered singer Jane Morgan and a number of other acts. Unlike Eddie Fisher, earlier in the season, Benny and Miss Morgan performed intermittently all through the evening. Danny Kaye and his vaudeville troupe followed Benny into the Ziegfeld on 10 April.

Tovarich (18 March 1963, Broadway), Jacques Deval and Robert E. Sherwood's 1936–1937 hit, came back to the stage as a musical on 18 March. Once again Prince Mikail Alexandrovitch Ouratieff (Jean Pierre Aumont) and his wife, the Grand Duchess Tatiana Petrona (Vivien Leigh), have fled Soviet Russia with four billion francs. But they are broke, since the money belongs to the Czar and they intend to hold it for his heirs until the monarchy is restored. They take jobs as a butler and maid with an American family in Paris. But two Soviet agents trail them and ultimately wrest the fortune from them. Since they have grown fond of their American employers, and their employers, who have learned their real identities, remain fond of them, they decide to retain their positions. The adaptation was by untried hands and betrayed their inexperience and lack of inspiration, though some of the music was pleasantly melodic. In a move rare in mid-twentieth-century book musicals, at least one extraneous number was interpolated to help the proceedings. But what little real help the show received came from its star, Miss Leigh.

For ten days beginning 11 April Bil and Cora Baird's Marionette Theater performed two matinees daily at the Biltmore of a double bill that included a "marionette play with music," **A Man in the Moon.** Jerry Bock and Sheldon Harnick wrote songs for a story telling of an earth-boy, a moon-maiden, and a jewel thief.

Another colorful figure out of the past became the subject of a musical biography in **Sophie** (15 April 1963, Winter Garden). Sophie, of course, was Sophie Tucker, the last "Red Hot Mama." William Morris, Marcus Loew, Julian Mitchell, and Nora Bayes were all brought back to life to reenact their famous contretemps with the volatile "coon singer," and Miss Tucker (Libi Staiger) was even given a fling and romance with handsome Frank Westphal (Art Lund). The story tried to cover too much of Miss Tucker's history. It became diffuse and meandering, while the songs by Steve Allen, a well-known television entertainer, were a pale imitation of the lusty originals of Miss Tucker's day. Like the history of Izzy and Moe, which had played the same house, *Sophie* lasted just one week.

Four nights later Judy Holliday came a cropper in a musical about the Peace Corps, **Hot Spot** (19 April 1963, Majestic). The story presented a rather startling reversion to the *Sultan of Sulu* (29 December 1902) school of scenarios. The eager, incompetent Sally Hopwinder (Miss Holliday) is sent by the Peace Corps to D'Hum. She convinces the Nadir of D'Hum to proclaim a Communist threat so that more American money will be forthcoming. In various disguises she helps and hinders her own plan. Sally also has a love affair with the handsome American consul, Gabriel Snapper (Joseph Campanella). The book gave evidence of being all too hastily contrived, while Mary Rodgers's score bore even sadder witness to her lack of her father's great melodic gifts. Miss Holliday braved the odds for a little over a month before calling it quits.

As happened with some frequency in this period, the season's last new American book musical was its best, even if this time its origin and its tone weren't totally American. **She Loves Me** (23 April 1963, O'Neill) began life years before as Miklos Laszlo's *Parfumerie* and then became a fondly remembered film, *The Shop Around the Corner*. In the skillful, tasteful adaption by Joe Masteroff, who did the book, and by Jerry Bock and Sheldon Harnick, who did the songs, it was turned into the closest thing Broadway had seen to Jerome Kern's Continental confections, *Music in the Air* and *The Cat and the Fiddle*. It was set in the very era of the Kern works, the early thirties, and in the same Mitteleuropa ambiance. Maraczek's Parfumerie in Budapest is not thriving, and Maraczek is at a loss to know how he will sell a new shipment of music boxes. A young lady, Amalia Balash (Barbara Cook), appears, looking for work. He attempts to turn her away, but when she picks up a music box and sells it to the very first customer to enter the shop, he relents and hires her. Her fellow employees include a dashing philanderer, Steven Kodaly (Jack Cassidy), and shy, soft-spoken Georg Nowack (Daniel Massey). Georg is nervous because that evening he will meet for the first time a girl with whom he has been corresponding and whom he knows only as "Dear Friend." Amalia is also writing to a "Dear Friend" she has never seen. Of course, they are writing to each other. Their visions of their fellow writers are far more glamorous than the reality, but when Georg arrives at the rendezvous and realizes who his "Dear Friend" is, he keeps the secret from Amalia, claiming his presence is coincidental. Georg's front is doubly brave, for

Maraczek, suspecting him of being his wife's lover, has quarreled with him and accepted his resignation. However, a letter informs Maraczek that Kodaly is the lover. Maraczek's attempted suicide is thwarted by an employee. The bullet only wounds him. He makes up with Georg and takes him back. When Amalia reports in sick, Georg arrives at her apartment. Her initial reaction is to accuse him of snooping, to see if she were really ill. But when he presents her with a gift of ice cream and fabricates a tale about a bald-headed man who followed him after their rendezvous to question him on his relation with Amalia, she begins to lose interest in her "Dear Friend" and fall in love with Georg. Georg senses the change and is elated, for he has fallen in love with her. At a Christmas party in the shop Amalia drops a package she has meant for a friend. It is a music box. Georg confesses he too likes music boxes, and the conversation takes on a special warmth. Both admit their feelings for each other, and, after Georg quotes excerpts from her letters to "Dear Friend," Amalia realizes she has found a dear friend indeed.

The song, "Dear Friend," one of the loveliest in the work, was used throughout the evening, but never attained any independent popularity. Only the title song enjoyed anything approaching a lasting vogue. But all of the score was attractive and appropriate. The score was so long that it required two LP records. Many of the songs were conversational in tone; all furthered the plot. Set pieces accounted for the changing of the seasons (the action ran from summer to Christmas) or offered charming, incisive character vignettes that cannot readily be excerpted, but that consistently conveyed a uniform tone and style, deftly suggesting the period of the piece while remaining contemporary in their structure and harmony. Neither the dialogue nor the lyrics, taken out of context, were exceptional but they, too, maintained the integrity of the work. The show was beautifully mounted and excellently cast. Yet for all its virtues *She Loves Me* closed with a loss after a nine-month run.

The City Center's regular spring season began on 15 May with additional performances of *Oklahoma!* (31 March 1943), with many principals held over from the preceding year, followed by *Pal Joey* (25 December 1940) with Bob Fosse and Viveca Lindfors on 29 May. As it had the preceding year the series ran into the new season.

A revue called **The Beast in Me** (16 May 1963, Plymouth) brought the old season to a close. It was based on James Thurber's *Fables for Our Times*, and almost all the characters portrayed in the sketches and songs were animals. James Costigan made, the adaptation, and Don Elliot composed the music. Some of Broadway's brightest young talent was featured: Allyn Ann McLerie, Kaye Ballard, Richard Hayes, and Bert Convy, as well as Mr. Costigan. But, as it had with *Shinbone Alley* (13 April 1957), Broadway found the idea of actors in sheep's clothing too cloyingly cute. The show folded after four showings.

1963–1964

The disastrous 1962–1963 season should have discouraged producers and writers, but it didn't. Its hit shows, even though they came from England, had reaped tremendous profits. National origins ignored, statistics had disclosed that one out of five musicals returned its investment, compared to one out of twelve straight plays. So the American Musical Theatre bounced back with fervor in the new theatrical year.

After *The King and I* (29 March 1951) concluded the City Center openings on 12 June, the musical stage took a respite until the last day of September. **The Student Gypsy; or The Prince of Liederkranz** (30 September 1963, 54th St.) was, as its title suggests, a travesty on the old Graustarkian operettas. It told of a not particularly attractive girl, Merry May Glockenspiel (Eileen Brennan), who becomes the belle of a gypsy camp and is courted by Rudolph von Schlump (Don Stewart), a prince in disguise. Their road to the altar is booby-trapped by a villainous gypsy queen, but they surmount every obstacle. The satire was the work of Rick Besoyan, and its concentration on one genre served as a tacit admission that his earlier *Little Mary Sunshine*, for all its mirth, had not always been on target. *The Student Gypsy* had another sterling performance by the erstwhile Mary Sunshine, Miss Brennan, and some deliriously melodic spoofs of the Romberg-Friml-Herbert tradition. However, older musicals had long been the butt of burlesque, and *The Boy Friend* (30 September 1954) and *Little Mary Sunshine* (19 November 1959) had apparently exhausted the market for full-length take-offs. Poor attendance forced it to be withdrawn after a two-week stay.

Meredith Willson's deteriorating flair was disclosed in **Here's Love** (3 October 1963, Shubert), his third musical to reach Broadway. As he had with his first effort, *The Music Man*, Willson created the book, lyrics, and music. His task was made somewhat easier for him since he based his new show on the successful 1947 film *Miracle on 34th Street*. The real Kris Kringle (Laurence Naismith) is hired by Macy's after its regular Santa Claus goes on a binge. Kris's goodness and honesty throw the holiday's shabby commercialism into such turmoil that the United States government hauls him into court. Santa Claus and the true spirit of Christmas prevail. In the process, little Susan Walker (Valerie Lee), who has steadfastly believed in Kris Kringle, finds a new father for herself and a husband for her divorced mother (Janis Paige) in Fred Gailey (Craig Stevens), after Fred defends Santa Claus at his trial. If Willson's artistry had deserted him, his solid professional know-how had not. Everything about the show was appealing, if insistently forgettable. The delightful story lured theatregoers into the Shubert for the rest of the season, and then some.

Up on 55th Street, the New York City Opera, still performing at the City Center, included *The Mikado* and *The Merry Widow* in its fall bills, along with a glorified minstrel show, **Gentlemen, Be Seated,** on 10 October. Jerome Moross wrote the music for the evening, Edward Eager the lyrics, while the pair combined to write the book. Long before the term "politically correct" had obtained common currency, this sanitized or color-drained (depending on your bent) entertainment sang and told of a liberal's-eye view of the Old South. Some stellar names were on stage: Dick Shawn as the Interlocutor, Avon Long as Tambo, Alice Ghostley in a variety of parts, and Paul Draper as Mr. Taps.

According to its lyricist, Howard Dietz, **Jennie** (17 October 1963, Majestic) had begun life as a musical comedy about a small-town gymnastics instructress. Somewhere along the line Mary Martin, who was to be its star, objected to the slightly off-color humor of the material. Everything was jettisoned, and a new story based on Marguerite Courtney's biography of Laurette Taylor was substituted. Miss Taylor became Jennie Malone; her first husband, Charles Taylor, became James O'Connor. O'Connor (George Wallace), a small-time theatrical promoter, is promiscuous, drunken, distrustful, and cruel. Jennie tolerates him as long as she can, finally leaving him for a more engaging and considerate English playwright, Christopher Lawrence Cromwell (Robin Bailey), who clearly stood for J. Hartley Manners. The book's best moments were spoofs of turn-of-the-century melodramas, which opened and closed the show. Whether the sudden changes or mere exasperation left Arthur Schwartz and Dietz bereft of inspiration will never be known. But their songs fell far below their best work. Miss Martin learned to her dismay that she was not the powerful drawing card she had believed. Although one early week established a short-lived record gross of $92,000, she and her wholesome show packed their bags after eighty-two showings.

110 in the Shade (24 October 1963, Broadhurst) rather daringly combined the rough-hewn talents of playwright N. Richard Nash with the more delicate artistry of *The Fantasticks*'s song-writers, lyricist Tom Jones and composer Harvey Schmidt. Nash based the work on his own well-received play *The Rainmaker*. Lizzie Curry (Inga Swenson) is on the way to becoming a spinster. She is not ugly, but she is plain and shy. To add to her family's woes, the western state is in the middle of a devastating drought. If there seems to be no hope for Lizzie, there is at least a slim chance of rain, for a glib, self-assured young man named Bill Starbuck (Robert Horton) appears at the Curry farm and offers to produce rain for a cash payment of $100. Lizzie warns her father and brother that Starbuck is a fraud, but in their desperation they accept his offer. In the time he claims it will take him to work his miracle he dispels Lizzie's antagonisms, and she finds herself in love. Starbuck confesses that he is a fake, but Lizzie no longer cares. She even discourages another would-be suitor, the sheriff, File (Stephen Douglass), from arresting Starbuck for taking money under false pretenses. To Starbuck's amazement, as much as anyone else's, rain comes just when he said it would. Taking advantage of the lucky break he heads out of town, leaving a more confident and hopeful Lizzie to be courted by the sheriff. The songs Schmidt and Jones wrote for *110 in the Shade* were scarcely replayed outside the theatre, but they were effective in the show. Lizzie's first number was the poignant "Love, Don't Turn Away," but she could show a comic side in "Raunchy" when, with patent hypocrisy, she denies her fascination with sex. To some extent they helped put the show's emphasis on her instead of the rainmaker. The show was good theatre and might have run more than the ten months it did, had some stronger competition not come along.

Black poet Langston Hughes continued to be fascinated with the theatre, even if the theatre persistently refused to reciprocate. He presented his adaptation of his own novel **Tambourines to Glory** (2 November 1963, Little), which told of two women who established a gospel-singing church in Harlem. Essie Belle Johnson (Rosetta Le Noire) is genuinely devout; Laura Wright Reed (Hilda Simms) is more opportunistic. After she is involved in a killing, Laura repents and mends her grasping ways. Classic Negro spirituals were used, as well as additional material by Jobe Huntley that dovetailed harmoniously with the old favorites. The public, however, showed little interest.

The Golden Age (18 November 1963, Lyceum), which advertised itself as "An entertainment in the words and music of the Elizabethan Age," was November's other musical offering. The anthology proved too arcane for Broadway and left after one week.

On 22 November President Kennedy was assassinated in Dallas, sending the nation into shock and mourning. The somber mood did not help the opening of Noël Coward's **The Girl Who Came to Supper** (8 December 1963, Broadway), and the show needed all the help it could get. This musical version of Terence Rattigan's play *The Sleeping Prince* retold the twenty-four-hour fling of Mary Morgan (Florence Henderson), an American chorus girl in England, and the Grand Duke Charles (Jose Ferrer), Prince Regent of Carpathia, who comes to London for the coronation of George V. Mary is more interested in candlelight suppers and protestations of love than in real love, but it is with genuine regret that the grand duke says good-bye. The passing of time at the candlelight dinner was cleverly suggested by trick candles that sank deeper into their holders. The effect was possibly the most memorable bit of the show. Even though Ferrer and Miss Henderson performed valiantly, it was hefty Tessie O'Shea who had the only show-stopper, a gay music hall number called "London Is A Little Bit Of All Right." There had been one good comic song in the show during its tryout, a sardonic commentary on assassinations, "Long Live The King (If He Can)," but it was hastily pulled after Kennedy's murder.

On 26 December, a small Irish revue, **Double Dublin**, followed *Tambourines to Glory* into the intimate Little Theatre, but survived only four showings.

By mid-January of 1964 the country was beginning to recover from its grief and willing to embrace some delightful escapism. With perfect timing David Merrick offered New York what swiftly became the biggest musical hit in years, **Hello, Dolly!** (16 January 1964, St. James). The show was in no way innovative and made not the slightest pretense to artistic merit. But it was mounted and staged in rare high style (attractive sliding panels with views of old New York entertained viewers between scenes), was faultlessly cast, and in its title song presented the most popular melody to come out of a Broadway musical in many seasons. A lyric version of Thornton Wilder's hit *The Matchmaker*, it was adapted by Michael Stewart and set to music by Jerry Herman. The scene is New York in the 1890s. Dolly Levi's various business cards list her as available for, among other things, "Financial Consultation, Instruction in the Guitar and Mandolin... and Varicose Veins Reduced," but her preoccupation at the moment is "Social Introductions." She states it more succinctly, "I meddle." It is the affairs of Horace Vandergelder (David Burns) in which she is currently meddling. She describes Horace as "half-a-millionaire... that means he's got at least sixty thousand cash." She has suggested one of two women for his next wife, Irene Molloy (Eileen Brennan), the owner of a hat shop, or the rich Ernestina Money (Mary Jo Catlett). Both are decoys. Privately, Dolly has decided to capture Horace for herself. At the same time, she is conniving to allow Vandergelder's daughter to wed. Dolly is a widow given to communicating aloud with her dead husband, Ephraim. When she asks Ephraim for a sign that he approves of her designs, she is met with a disappointing silence. Dolly persists, leaving Ephraim with the request, "Sometime today!" Vandergelder is about to head from Yonkers to Manhattan to make his choice. He has two shop helpers, Barnaby (Jerry Dodge) and Cornelius (Charles Nelson Reilly), and he elevates the latter from "impertinent fool to chief clerk" in his absence. But Barnaby and Cornelius have their own plans for a day and night on Broadway, so they explode some cans of tomatoes in order to have an excuse to close the store. In Manhattan they spot Vandergelder coming down the street and take refuge in the nearest boutique. By coincidence they seek shelter in Irene Molloy's shop, Vandergelder's own destination. Only Dolly's fast talking saves the day. Dolly had arranged for Mr. Vandergelder to take Ernestina to the Harmonia Gardens Restaurant for dinner. She reserves another table for herself, pleading for some marital bliss and financial security "Before the Parade Passes By." In still another coincidence Barnaby and Cornelius are wangled into taking Mrs. Molloy and her assistant there. When Dolly, an old favorite at the Harmonia Gardens, arrives, service halts while the entire staff, trays in hand, sing her their "Hello, Dolly!" Before

long she has lured an annoyed Vandergelder away from Miss Money:

Vandergelder: That's the trouble with you, Dolly. Always putting your nose into other people's affairs. Anybody who married you would get as nervous as a cat.

Dolly: What? What's that you're saying?

Vandergelder: I said anybody who married you would...

Dolly: Horace Vandergelder, get that idea right out of your head this minute. I'm surprised that you even mentioned such a thing. Understand once and for all that I have no intention of marrying you!

Vandergelder: I didn't mean that!

Dolly: You've been hinting around at such a thing for some time, but from now on put such ideas right out of your head! Horace Vandergelder, you go your way (*She points with her left hand to the left.*) and I'll go mine. (*She points with her right hand also to the left!*)

When the floor show discloses that the young man courting Horace's daughter is a singer and that Horace's own daughter is in the chorus, pandemonium breaks loose, and everyone is hauled into court. Dolly's pleas move the judge to tears, so charges are dismissed. Even Horace recognizes there is no point in resisting Dolly. In admitting defeat, he uses a favorite expression of Dolly's late spouse. Dolly, thanking Ephraim for the sign, consents to marry Horace.

Jerry Herman's score was neither as inventive nor as melodic as his material for *Milk and Honey*, but the title song proved as persistent and as irresistible as Dolly herself and, with a tremendous boost from Louis Armstrong's recording, swept the nation. In the show Dolly and her greeters came down ramps on both sides of the proscenium to sing it within arm's reach of audiences. That the score was not particularly original was borne out when a lawsuit against Herman by Mack David and Paramount-Famous Music Company, claiming the title song was plagiarized from a 1948 tune, "Sunflower," was won by the plaintiffs. One other number, "It Only Takes A Moment," a love ballad, sung somewhat surprisingly by Cornelius in the court scene, also became popular with time. Carol Charming as Dolly had the best role of her career. When she decided to tour with the show, a number of celebrities replaced her on Broadway, including Ginger Rogers, Ethel

Merman, and Pearl Bailey (in an all-black cast). Mary Martin originated the part in London. The show ran for 2,844 performances, a new long-run record for a musical, but one it was to hold only briefly.

Paris's darling of the twenties, Josephine Baker, returned briefly on 4 February in what was essentially a one-woman show, although she was assisted by several other artists. Miss Baker sang a large repertory of French songs, as well as "Make Believe," "Hello, Young Lovers," and "April In Paris." The Aviv Dancers, the Larl Becham Trio, and Geoffrey Holder performed the evening's footwork. In two slightly separated engagements she entertained both those who had fond memories of her and a younger set to whom she was a curiosity.

A less acceptable curiosity opened two nights after Miss Baker's return. At various periods French, English, and Viennese musicals have been the rage of the musical stage, but in light lyric entertainments Broadway has never thought twice about Italy. Italian lyric pieces appeared regularly on Broadway stages only in the eighteenth century, when operas were often mounted in legitimate theatres. The musical **Rugantino** (6 February 1964, Hellinger) had enjoyed an astonishing success in its native land, and Alfred Drake "adapted" it for Broadway. It was brought over with an Italian cast, but, apart from the novelty of the whole affair, Broadway found little of interest in it. The Italians were soon packing for the trip home.

The failure of **Foxy** (16 February 1964, Ziegfeld), a musical version of Ben Jonson's *Volpone* reset in the Klondike gold rush, was sad for a number of reasons. First of all, because it was a good show. It had a rousing score by Robert Emmett Dolan that included one ballad, "Talk To Me, Baby," whose popularity survived the production. It was sung in the show by the romantic lead, Ben (John Davidson). Moreover, it had an uproarious performance by Bert Lahr in the title role. Lahr's antics included quite literally climbing the theatre's gold proscenium. Sadly, it was Lahr's last appearance before his death.

Budd and Stuart Schulberg adapted the former's novel What Makes Sammy Run? (27 February 1964, 54th St.) for the musical stage. With songs by Ervin Drake and with the popular nightclub singer Steve Lawrence as star, it settled down for a run beginning 27 February. Although the novel was twenty-three years old and although Hollywood was no longer the unassailable giant it had been, the story was still valid. It was to the motion picture industry what *I Can Get It for You Wholesale* (22 March 1962) had

been to the garment trade. Sammy Glick rises in the newspaper world by stealing other men's material. A movie script he writes gets him a job in Hollywood, where the famous producer Sidney Fineman (Arny Freeman) takes him under his wing, and where he earns the affection of a thoughtful, undemanding secretary, Kit Sargent (Sally Ann Howes). But in his greed to reach the top he throws Kit over for Laurette Harrington (Bernice Massi), daughter of the studio's chairman of the board, and pushes Fineman out of his job, after which Fineman commits suicide. He even ignores Laurette's flagrant infidelities once they are married, since his only concern is getting to the top. The score by Drake, who had written such Hollywood successes as "Tico, Tico," gave Lawrence the chance to introduce several hits, especially "My Hometown." Kit sang "A Room Without Windows." But when the public learned that Lawrence, apparently tired of playing Sammy, frequently missed performances, attendance fell and the show closed. Even though it ran 540 performances, it was added to the disheartening list of shows that failed to return their original investment.

The City Center's operetta series, starting on 10 March, regaled playgoers with six of the more popular Gilbert and Sullivan gems as well as with Offenbach's *La Vie Parisienne*.

The next new musical to arrive may have also recalled *I Can Get It for You Wholesale* (22 March 1962), for it starred Barbra Streisand, who had called herself to Broadway's attention as Miss Marmelstein. The **Funny Girl** (26 March 1964, Winter Garden) of the title was Fanny Brice, and the evening retraced the great comedienne's rise from burlesque to *Ziegfeld Follies* stardom, her trouble-plagued marriage to the crooked Nicky Arnstein (Sydney Chaplin), and her decision to devote her energies to her career after their marriage broke up. No attempt was made to use songs Miss Brice had made famous, but Jule Styne wrote several in the period idiom, notably "Sadie, Sadie," that were serviceable. His best numbers, however, made no concession to period flavor. "Don't Rain On My Parade," a song strikingly like *Hello Dolly!'s* "Before The Parade Passes By" in both style and sentiment, closed both acts with its fervent plea not to have more obstacles thrown in one's path. The evening's outstanding hit, "People," expressed the recurring loneliness and unhappiness in the life of a performer dedicated to making others laugh. The book by Isobel Lennart was adequate but unexceptional. Even the production could be faulted, especially in scenes purportedly depicting the *Ziegfeld Follies*. Their skimpiness demonstrated the price a modern economy was exacting for the mere suggestion of the opulence of a half-century before. Happily, Miss Streisand overrode any objections or carping. She proved that she alone among performers of her generation could match Fanny Brice's gifts for hilarity and pathos. Typical of her funnier moments was a first-act travesty of a spectacular Ziegfeld number. As a tenor sang "His Love Makes Me Beautiful" the gorgeous chorus girls, decked out in sumptuous bridal gowns, moved regally down a Ziegfeldian staircase. Miss Brice appeared as the final bride. If love had not made her as beautiful as the other girls, it had given her a singular advantage. She was pregnant. The nonplused tenor attempted to proceed with the song as Fanny first coyly tried to hide her embarrassment, then openly advertised her condition. Her comic responses also wreaked havoc with Nick's seduction number, "You Are Woman." Performances of *Funny Girl* without her have shown the work to be sufficiently well crafted to make a pleasant entertainment, but not the electrifying evening into which she transformed it. Next to *Hello, Dolly!, Funny Girl* was the biggest hit of the season.

April was a busy month for musicals, at least by modern standards. **Anyone Can Whistle** (4 April 1964, Majestic) had an out-of-the-ordinary plot (perhaps, in its fake miracle, a little like *110 in the Shade*). A small town has only one industry, a company that manufactures an item that never wears out. For lack of reorders the plant closes. To create a tourist market the town creates a fake miracle—water pumped to seemingly flow out of rock. The tourists come in droves. But the plan is jeopardized when the local mental institution, The Cookie Jar, brings forty-nine patients to the rock for a cure. The hoax is exposed, but not before Nurse Fay Apple (Lee Remick) and Dr. J. Bowden Hapgood (Harry Guardino) fall in love. Angela Lansbury also starred. The book by playwright Arthur Laurents seemed diffuse and ineffective. Stephen Sondheim's music and lyrics were fresh and original, but, somehow, they often didn't convey that impression in the theatre. Received with generally unkind notices, the show departed after nine showings.

No musical during the season was more literate or had a more consistent sense of style and tone than **High Spirits** (7 April 1964, Alvin), a lyric adaptation of Noël Coward's wartime hit *Blithe Spirit*. The book and music were not by Coward, but by Hugh Martin and Timothy Gray. As she had twenty years

before, the irrepressible and slightly irresponsible spiritualist, Madam Arcati (Beatrice Lillie), disrupts Charles Condomine's happy second marriage by bringing his first wife, Elvira (Tammy Grimes), back from the dead. Elvira is determined to have one last fling, and she does—flying over a posh party on the roof of a London hotel to the consternation of Charles's present wife, Ruth (Louise Troy), and to the not unamused consternation of Charles (Edward Woodward) himself. If the show had a fault, it was the lack of an outstanding tune to make it compellingly attractive to theatregoers at large. Without a "Hello, Dolly!" or a "People," it could not expect to compete for tourist trade after the smaller, solid body of knowledgeable and regular theatregoers had been exhausted. If the show had an overriding virtue—and it had—it was the brilliant clowning of Miss Lillie as the spiritualist. She arrived for her first entrance on a bicycle, removed the clips that kept her skirts in place, and turned them into bracelets, glowering at the audience when it had the presumption to laugh. But the supreme moment of the evening was a series of curtain calls she took early in the second act after a song called "Talking To You." Every parting of the curtains revealed her in another of the positions assumed by great stars in answer to applause, an uproarious mockery of curtsies and bravura gestures. Miss Lillie's stylish madness went hand in glove, as it had often before, with Coward's stylish impudence. The show ran nearly a year—375 performances—but suffered the fate of so many long runs of the era, ending its run still a financial failure.

The night after *High Spirits* breezed in, 8 April, the City Center unveiled its spring season of revivals. *West Side Story* (26 September 1957) was the first, succeeded by *Porgy and Bess* (10 October 1935) on 6 May and *My Fair Lady* (15 March 1956) on 20 May. In this last mounting Russell Nype sang Freddy and Reginald Gardiner was Doolittle.

April's last musical was a quick flop. Even with the popular Sam Levene as its star, **Café Crown** (17 April 1964, Martin Beck) could muster only three performances. Levene played Hymie, a busboy in a restaurant. Hymie's theatrical ambition and his backing of a Broadway play were the theme of the show. The action took place in the thirties, a period that seemed ready to replace the turn of the century in librettists' affection.

It was the era chosen for the background of the season's final musical, **Fade Out—Fade In** (26 May 1964, Hellinger). In fact, the show's opening number was "The Thirties." And, like *What Makes Sammy Run?*, it was set in Hollywood, in the film capital's heyday. The story was simple, one that Hollywood itself employed numerous times during the thirties. An unpromising chorus girl is accidentally given the starring part in a new motion picture. When the mistake is discovered, heads roll and the film is securely stashed away in a vault. But Rudolf (Dick Patterson), the nephew of the studio's top man, takes a liking to the girl, Hope Springfield (Carol Burnett), and arranges for a preview. The movie is a success, Hope is a star, and she and Rudolf go off hand in hand. Unlike *What Makes Sammy Run?*, whose characters were merely Hollywood stereotypes, *Fade Out—Fade In* offered cameo impersonations of great film stars of the thirties, while its delineation of the studio head, Lionel Z. Governor (Lou Jacobi), clearly pointed a wicked finger at Louis B. Mayer. Governor shared Mayer's notorious eye for starlets and his grudging nepotism. The characterization was drolly exaggerated, with Governor requiring a full-time psychiatrist at his side and with his hatred of his fourth nephew so great he can no longer say "four." Jack Cassidy was featured as a suave Hollywood leading man. Like Steve Lawrence in *What Makes Sammy Run?*, Miss Burnett became unhappy with the show, and, when no other comedienne could be recruited the show closed after 271 performances, divided into two runs separated by a three-month hiatus. To some extent Miss Burnett's displeasure was justified, for though Comden and Green did the book, Jule Styne the music (his second score of the season), and George Abbott the staging, it represented far from their best efforts. Even changes made in the book and new songs added during the three-month vacation failed to help. For her fans, Miss Burnett's funniest moment was probably her spoof of Shirley Temple.

1964–1965

This was the last season in the great era of "musical plays." One lone show earned the season its place in the act, for otherwise it was a dismal year. More than twenty years had elapsed since *Oklahoma!* (31 March 1943) had set new standards for the American Musical Theatre. *Oklahoma!* had endowed the lyric stage with a new seriousness of purpose, a new sense of cohesiveness and tonal integrity. It had made turn-of-the-century America and its homey sentimentalities stylish. In doing so it had broken long-run and financial records, some of which had remained unassailed for decades. Higher production costs and admission fees, coupled with the shrinking of legitimate-theatre offerings and the concentration on major successes of any given season, eventually allowed a few other shows to surpass *Oklahoma!*'s figures. The sole masterwork of the final season, *Fiddler on the Roof*, was alien to its great predecessors in its choices of theme and setting, but in its tenor—its seriousness, its artistry—it was not an unfitting finale. And like *Oklahoma!* it closed holding the long-run record for the American Musical Theatre.

The season began with an unusual importation, the Parisian tourist mecca, the **Folies Bergère** (2 June 1964, Broadway). Besides bringing its famous showgirls, it arrived carting fifteen tons of scenery and 1,200 costumes. The day of nudes moving across the stage had not yet come to Broadway, so one of the main attractions of the Parisian revue had to be somewhat modified. Nonetheless there were still complaints and disputes about the scantiness of some of the costumes. It was not a first-rate mounting, but the show's renown and its near nudity helped it to run until November 14.

On 6 July the New York State Theatre at the new Lincoln Center welcomed its first legitimate attraction. Plans called for the Music Theatre of Lincoln Center to revive popular Broadway musicals at reduced prices in the pattern of the City Center. The result, although it could not be foreseen at the time, was to kill the City Center series and thus, when the Music Theatre proved economically unfeasible, leave New Yorkers without a program of low-priced revivals. Richard Rodgers was the president and producing director of the new group, and he selected his own *The King and I* (29 March 1951), with Risë Stevens and Darren McGavin, for the premiere presentation. *The Merry Widow* (27 October 1907), with Patrice Munsel and Bob Wright, followed on 17 August. The operetta, which fifty-seven years before had brought to a close one era and inaugurated another, displayed a curious faculty for reappearing whenever new acts began or ended. In fact the show was also in the New York City Opera's fall schedule along with *Die Fledermaus*. And in its spring series the company presented *Porgy and Bess*, *Die Dreigroschenoper*, and *The Saint of Bleecker Street*.

From Czechoslovakia came **Laterna Magika** (3 August 1964, Carnegie Hall), a performance of Offenbach's *Tales of Hoffmann* combining live action and motion pictures. Another foreign company, this time from Austria, brought in a revival of **Wiener Blut** (11 September 1964, Lunt-Fontanne).

The work had been slightly tampered with, including some waltzes Strauss never wrote for it. But it was the first revival of the piece since the turn of the century. Although *The Merry Widow* grossed $98,000 one week, the receptions accorded to the Lehar, Offenbach, and Strauss works suggested that, while an era was coming to an end, it would not be the old operetta that would initiate the new rage.

Fiddler on the Roof (22 September 1964, Imperial) was the season's biggest hit and the last of the great masterworks of the era. Based on Sholom Aleichem's stories, it had a book by Joseph Stein, lyrics by Sheldon Harnick, and music by Jerry Bock. Although the adaptation was faithful to the essentials of Aleichem's tales, it eschewed, of necessity, some of their Yiddish parochialism, without denying their Jewishness. By emphasizing ongoing problems of family bonds and religious interaction against a backdrop of disintegrating social order, the authors gave the work a universality that allowed the evening to transcend what might have otherwise been an appeal limited largely to the sizable Jewish segment of playgoers.

The time is 1905. But no carefree, color-strewn turn-of-the-century American small town is revealed as the curtain rises. Instead, audiences see a somber, dilapidated shtetl, a Jewish community, in the Russian village of Anatevka. The scene is the exterior of the house of the community's pious dairyman, Tevye (Zero Mostel). A fiddler is playing on the roof. Tevye addresses the audience:

A fiddler on the roof. Sounds crazy, no? But in our little village of Anatevka, you might say every one of us is a fiddler of the roof, trying to scratch out a pleasant, simple tune without breaking his neck. It isn't easy. You may ask, why do we stay here if it's so dangerous? We stay because Anatevka is our home. And how do we keep our balance? That I can tell you in a word—tradition!

The villagers enter and join Tevye in singing of "Tradition," the familial hierarchy that maintains the Jews' strength. Their strength must be maintained in the face of not just local bigotries, but of officially fostered governmental onslaughts as well. When a villager asks the rabbi if there is a proper blessing for the Tsar, the rabbi replies, "Of course. May God bless and keep the Tsar—far away from us!" Tevye has five daughters, three of whom are of marriageable age, so Tevye and his wife, Golde (Maria Karnilova), have employed Yente (Beatrice Arthur), the village matchmaker, to find a mate for their eldest, Tzeitel (Joanna Merlin). The younger girls implore her—"Matchmaker, Matchmaker"—to find mates for them, too. Meanwhile Tevye goes about his business. He comes home exhausted at nights and contemplates a better life, "If I Were A Rich Man." But bad news from elsewhere suggests riches alone would not help. Jews are being evicted from other villages. Closer to home, affairs take a momentarily happier turn. Lazar (Michael Granger), the elderly, relatively well-to-do butcher, has asked for Tzeitel's hand. When Tevye consents, he and Lazar celebrate with a toast "To Life" ("L'Chaim"). But their joy is brief. Two problems arise. A constable warns Tevye to expect trouble in Anatevka. And Tzeitel will not accept Lazar as a husband, preferring the young tailor, Motel (Austin Pendleton). Tevye decides not to go against Tzteitel's wishes. At the wedding Tevye and Golde remember when their children were babies and in "Sunrise, Sunset" remark on how swiftly time has passed. Once more, though, joy is brief. The wedding is disrupted and the community vandalized by the pogrom of which the constable had warned. Tevye's second daughter, Hodel (Julia Migenes), has fallen in love with the community's intellectual and radical, Perchik (Bert Convy). At first Tevye is opposed to this marriage, too, because the youngsters talk of love, and Tevye cannot see what love has to do with arranging a marriage. Reluctantly, he acknowledges old ways are disappearing, conceding, "our old ways were new once." Unfortunately Perchik is arrested and shipped to Siberia for his dangerous antigovernment notions. Hodel elects to follow him, even if she must go "Far From The Home I Love." Perhaps the hardest blow of all for Tevye comes when he learns his third daughter, Chava (Tanya Everett), wants to marry a Christian. This time he remains adamant in his opposition, and when Chava and her fiancé, Fydka (Joe Ponazecki), elope, Tevye brokenheartedly declares, "Chava is dead to us!" Chava is hardly gone when the constable returns bringing news the community has long feared. The Jews must leave Anatevka. Tevye and his family make plans to join their Uncle Abram in America, while the rest of the Jews attempt to plan their own destinies. As they leave, they sing of their beloved "Anatevka" and wonder where else the Sabbath could be so sweet. The fiddler is seen playing on the roof. Tevye beckons to him, and, tucking his violin under his arm, he joins the exodus.

The book was unabashedly sentimental, but the insistent cruelties of the story made its sentimentality believable and palpable. Bock's melodic score captured both the vitality and pathos of traditional Jewish song and projected them in undeniably popular molds. Jerome Robbins's direction was at once forceful and compassionate, while Boris Aronson's sets were moodily evocative. Mostel's performance—his dialogues with God, his tragicomic rendition of "If I Were a Rich Man," his comic business—amounted to a titanic tour de force. Yet Mostel's several replacements as well as Tevyes in the road and international companies proved the work to be so powerful that it did not depend on a star. The show closed on 2 July 1972, after 3,242 performances—the longest run in the history of the American Musical Theatre up to its day.

If the age-old problem of anti-Semitism had been poignantly portrayed in *Fiddler on the Roof*, an even more ancient lust for battle was satirized in an English importation, **Oh, What a Lovely War!** (30 September 1964, Broadhurst). As generals bungled and horrendous casualty figures soared, a chorus sang the lilting, insouciant tunes of World War I. The show's finale was the soldier's version of Jerome Kern's 1914 hit from *The Girl from Utah*, "They Didn't Believe Me." The wartime lyrics had been composed by a then unknown Cole Porter. Once more it seemed as if subconsciously Broadway wanted to recapitulate the history of the American Musical. Just as *The Merry Widow* harked back to the opening of one era, so "They Didn't Believe me" sounded the opening notes of the succeeding period. But neither the gay songs nor the antiwar sentiments of *Oh, What a Lovely War!* attracted the public at large. The show closed after a disappointing three-and-a-half-month run.

A second British importation, the revue **Cambridge Circus** (6 October 1964, Plymouth), seemed doomed to an even shorter run. However, after twenty-three performances at the Plymouth, it was moved downtown to a tiny off-Broadway house, where in two editions—spoofing everything from Handel to the BBC—it found an audience until spring.

Two big book musicals arrived a week apart in the last half of October. **Golden Boy** (20 October 1964, Majestic) was a musical version of Clifford Odets's 1938 hit. Odets himself had begun the adaptation, but when he died in 1963, another playwright, William Gibson, agreed to finish the assignment. Because blacks had generally replaced the

white minorities who had comprised the principal fighters of the thirties, the hero was changed to an African-American. And because the blacks generally lacked the pervasive cultural heritage and cultural interests of the Italians depicted in the original play, Joe Bonaparte's central dilemma between his love of the violin and his ambitions as a prizefighter was muted. The new black Joe was a young Negro determined to get rich quick. And, of course, his name was no longer Bonaparte. Slyly Odets or Gibson had rechristened him Joe Wellington. Joe fights his way to the top only to discover his sluttish girlfriend, Lorna Moon (Paula Wayne), is having an affair with his manager, Tom Moody (Kenneth Tobey). Upset, he takes off on a wild ride and is killed in a car crash. The show's opening was postponed several times to allow Gibson to give some backbone to the plot, whose heart had been cut out. If he succeeded in making the libretto stronger than the score, it was simply because the Lee Adams–Charles Strouse tunes were so lackluster. The best-received song in the show was a production number, "Don't Forget 127th Street," in which Joe tells his young admirers not to be ashamed of their Harlem home. Donald McKayle's highly praised choreography included a fast-paced boxing match. The show ran 569 performances, thanks primarily to the box office lure of its star, Sammy Davis, Jr.

The well-liked Robert Preston proved to be a less potent draw, but then his vehicle, **Ben Franklin in Paris** (27 October 1964, Lunt-Fontanne), was not even as strong as *Golden Boy*. The patriotic old ladies' man gets Louis XVI to recognize America and rekindles the passion of a bygone love with the Countess Diane de Vobrillac (Ulla Sallert). He also abets his grandson's romance with a pretty young revolutionary, Janine Nicolet (Susan Watson). The evening's most spectacular moment occurred when Franklin took off in a large balloon. In spite of a trite book and mediocre score, Preston kept the show on the boards for six months.

November was busy. A new edition of Victor Borge's one-man show, called **Comedy in Music Opus 2** (9 November 1964, Golden), led the parade of November offerings. The next evening witnessed the opening of the short-lived—two weeks—**Something More!** (10 November 1964, O'Neill), a musical version of Gerald Green's *Portofino P.T.A.* The book, interspersed with Sammy Fain songs, followed novelist Bill Weems (Arthur Hill) and his family from their unsatisfactory life in suburban Mineola to the vaunted freedom and pleasures of

Italy. Included was one scene in which the Italians danced "The Watusi," a briefly voguish American step purportedly suggested by an African tribal celebration. Audiences found such intercontinental diversion an unsatisfactory hodgepodge.

The D'Oyly Carte Opera Company began a five-week stay at the City Center on 17 November, offering *Iolanthe, Trial by Jury, H. M. S Pinafore, The Pirates of Penzance, The Mikado,* and *Ruddigore.* (In the spring, beginning 15 April, the City Center unveiled its own Savoyard troupe doing *Pinafore, Patience, The Mikado, The Pirates of Penzance,* and *The Yeomen of the Guard.*) Four nights later, **Zizi,** a "French musical hall dance revue" which starred, appropriately, Zizi Jeanmaire, replaced the *Folies Bergère* at the Broadway Theatre and compiled forty-nine showings.

In the days of Gilbert and Sullivan and the French music hall, musicals about gypsies had been commonplace. But they were usually operettas, set in the Austro-Hungarian empire. **Bajour** (23 November 1964, Shubert) was a gypsy musical with a difference: It was a contemporary musical comedy set in present-day New York. When Johnny Dembo (Herschel Bernardi) and his gypsy family decamp in New York, Lt. MacNiall (Robert Burr) persuades his distant cousin, the anthropologist Emily Kirsten (Nancy Dussault), to "study" the tribe and report its movements to him. He learns Dembo's main ambition is to marry his son, Steve (Gus Trikonis), to Anyanka (Chita Rivera), daughter of Newark's gypsy king. Anyanka must prove her worth by pulling a successful swindle (a bajour). She succeeds, at the expense of Emily's widowed mother and with Emily's unwitting help. *Bajour* was another of the many musicals of the season that offered no more than a serviceable book and a weak plot, and that, as a result, depended for its strength on its star performer. In the case of *Bajour* that star was Miss Rivera, and her driving performance and fiery dancing as Anyanka gave the evening the muscle it required to run out the season.

December's only new musical, **I Had a Ball** (15 December 1964, Martin Beck), dealt with an equally raffish figure, Garside, a Coney Island swami. When, after a concentrated look into his crystal ball, he decides to act as a matchmaker, his couplings turn out to be all wrong. He pairs Brooks (Steven Roland), a loan shark, with Jeannie (Karen Morrow), who runs a Ferris wheel, and attempts to unite Sam the Shpieler (Richard Kiley), a pitchman, with Addie (Luba Lisa), a hustler known as

"Miss Under-the-Boardwalk." With time Jeannie and Sam discover they are a suitable couple. Once again a weak book and limp score were propped up by a star's performance. Comedian Buddy Hackett portrayed the swami and, in the greatest of the old clown tradition, improvised much of his material every night. He, too, kept his show before the footlights for the rest of the season.

The popular-priced revivals at the City Center continued with a mounting of *Brigadoon,* with Peter Palmer, 23 December. Another series of popular-priced revivals at the City Center began on 26 April with *Guys and Dolls.* Alan King, Jerry Orbach, Sheila MacRae, and Anita Gillette headed the cast. *Kiss Me Kate,* with Patricia Morison and Bob Wright, followed on 12 May and two more offerings arrived at the start of the 1965–1966 season.

It was 6 February 1965 before another new musical opened. With **Kelly** (6 February 1965, Broadhurst) the season reached its nadir. A leaden, dimwitted affair whose hero, Hop Kelly (Don Francks), was based loosely on Steve Brodie, supposedly the first man to leap from the Brooklyn Bridge, it lasted a single performance. When it folded, *Kelly* took with it $650,000 of its investors' money, a sum beyond Brodie's wildest dreams.

Costs continued to skyrocket, and the season's musicals were forced to price their top ticket at $9.90. As a result, **Baker Street** (16 February 1965, Broadway) achieved a record gross of $103,000 for a holiday week in which it played an extra matinee. Incessant increases in costs, admissions, and grosses soon made comparative figures meaningless. *Baker Street* drew a large attendance early in its run because the popular Sherlock Holmes legend was sumptuously and imaginatively mounted and superbly performed. However, it was the seventh new book musical in a row with a disappointing libretto and, worse, a thin, colorless score. Jerome Coopersmith used three of Conan Doyle's stories— "The Adventure of the Empty House," "A Scandal in Bohemia," and "The Final Problem"—with a free hand that distressed many Baker Street Irregulars. After Holmes (Fritz Weaver) helps the musical star Irene Adler (Inga Swenson) retrieve some letters, he discovers she has become infatuated with him. She intrudes into his desperate attempt to prevent Moriarty (Martin Gabel) from stealing Queen Victoria's jewels during the Diamond Jubilee. Goodness and celibacy triumph. The production's most discussed scene was the Diamond Jubilee parade, cleverly depicted by Bil Baird's marionettes.

Weaver and Gabel temporarily abandoned their more serious acting careers to give delightfully melodramatic performances.

A tacky recreation of the stripper shows of the Minsky era was moved uptown after playing several years off-Broadway. At its new home **This Was Burlesque,** with the former burlesque queen Ann Corio as headliner, added 124 performances to its record.

The only other musical, aside from *Fiddler on the Roof,* with any real merit this season was **Do I Hear a Waltz?** (18 March 1965, 46th St.). It was singularly fitting that what was meritorious in the show derived from the pen of Richard Rodgers, the composer who twenty-two years before had given this era its first durable masterpiece. That the show ultimately was set down in the record books as a failure was attributable to its unpleasant story and an inexplicably slack, draggy production. Arthur Laurents reworked the libretto from his own successful play *The Time of the Cuckoo.* Its heroine was Leona Samish (Elizabeth Allen), a lonely, naïve, but rather grasping and greedy American woman. She is a spinster, convinced that when the right man comes along the air around him will sing a waltz. On vacation in Venice she visits the shop of Renato di Rossi (Sergio Franchi). Leona is captivated by his good looks and glib charm. She accepts his offer of a date, but breaks it when she learns he is married. However, when he presents her with a bejeweled necklace she falls completely under his spell. Of course, Renato is simply a cynical, calculating Casanova. Leona discovers that Renato has not paid for the necklace and that she must pay for it herself. Her disillusion is complete when she learns that Renato has been given a commission on the purchase price. Only the title song, a refreshingly sweeping waltz, sung by Leona, entered the canon of Rodgers' standards. The rest of the music, while not especially memorable, was thoughtful and effective. With Stephen Sondheim's competent lyrics, the songs ranged from the introspective "Moon In My Window," in which the principal female characters—Leona, Signora Fioria—examine their ideas of romance, to the humorous "This Week Americans," in which Signora Fioria (Carol Bruce) recounts the cyclical trials of a *pensione* keeper, to the expected easy musical comedy gaiety of "Perfectly Lovely Couple." With no star of the caliber of Shirley Booth or Katharine Hepburn (who had played the original stage and film Leonas) on which to focus interest and with general disappointment in the offering itself, *Do I Hear a Waltz?* ran only 220 performances,

the shortest run accorded a Rodgers work during the era.

On 1 April, **Maurice Chevalier at 77** presented the indefatigable star in another one-man show for a thirty-one-performance run. Two weeks later the London musical hit **Half a Sixpence** (25 April 1965, Broadhurst) arrived with the English teenagers' delight, Tommy Steele, heading the cast. This musical version of H. G. Wells's *Kipps* pleased New York as much as it had the West End, settling in for a long stay.

One oddball attraction started off May. **Ken Murray's Hollywood** (10 May 1965, Golden) was a self-indulgent solo show by the well-known producer and comedian, filled with his reminiscences and home movies. A pianist accompanied the films and sometimes the commentary.

May's two more traditional musicals brought the season and the era to a close. **Flora, the Red Menace** (11 May 1965, Alvin), the last American book musical of the act, reverted to the increasingly voguish thirties for its background. This musical version of Lester Atwell's novel *Love Is Just Around the Corner* was dramatized by George Abbott and Robert Russell, and set to John Kander's music and Fred Ebb's lyrics. The story told how sweet, accepting Flora, a would-be fashion designer just out of school, is persuaded by her boyfriend, Harry Toukarian (Bob Dishy), to join the Communist Party. Harry is a stammerer, determined to cure his impediment by speaking with a mouth filled with pebbles. Flora almost loses him to the voluptuous Comrade Charlotte (Cathryn Damon). All the Communists succeed in doing is to stage a pretentious ballet, "The Tree of Life." Flora and the U.S. survive. The show was another in the depressingly drab chain of new works, and it ran largely on the strength of Liza Minnelli's likable portrayal of the title role. Miss Minnelli was the daughter of Vincente Minnelli, the distinguished stage and screen director, and of Judy Garland, onetime Hollywood musical star. An off-Broadway revival of *Best Foot Forward* had shown that Miss Minnelli had a persona all her own, and *Flora, the Red Menace* confirmed it.

Anthony Newley and Leslie Bricusse created a sequel to *Stop The World!—I Want To Get Off* and entitled it **The Roar of the Greasepaint—The Smell of the Crowd** (16 May 1965, Shubert). Like its predecessor, it was an allegory, in this case a confrontation of the "haves" represented by Sir (Cyril Ritchard) and the "have nots" in the person of Cocky (Newley). At times it was hard to distinguish between the two since almost all the costumes were ragged; Cocky and Sir made their first entrance dressed like the leading figures in *Waiting for Godot*. As in the earlier work, a single, skeletonized set served to represent the world. The show had two good tunes, Cocky's "Who Can I Turn To? (When Nobody Needs Me)," a ballad reminiscent of the earlier "What Kind Of Fool Am I?," and Cocky and Sir's sprightly "A Wonderful Day Like Today," which achieved general acceptance only after the show closed. The show struck many as too close a rewrite of the first Bricusse and Newley work. Its run, as a result, was curtailed. The show had been given to New York before London, but after the disappointing New York run no London mounting materialized.

Intermission

Exhaustion, 1965–1969

The years covered in this chapter were unhappy ones for both the United States and the American Musical Theatre. A controversial, escalating war in Asia led to domestic turmoil. Rioters burned and looted American cities. A generation of youngsters called themselves "flower children" and advocated "LOVE," but their loving all too often proved to be free, promiscuous love, while their ragamuffin dress and their lengthy, unkempt hairstyles (even for the boys) betrayed their fundamental rebelliousness and disorderliness. At the 1968 Democratic Convention in Chicago, their uncompromisingly obstructive behavior provoked Mayor Daley to send in his police, who acted less like disciplined law officers and more like vicious storm troopers. Both protesters and the "Establishment" received black eyes, figuratively and literally. Many attributed the Republican victory in the fall at least in part to the public's sickened response to the melees it had watched on television newscasts. How the Republican victors misused their victory became tragically clear a few years later. It would have been remarkable had the lyric

stage been able to ignore and override these upheavals, but for several seasons the American Musical Theatre had been manifesting unmistakable signs of exhaustion. Beset by the collapse of so much order and decorum, it, too, fell apart.

Merely getting to the theatre became something of an ordeal. New York's aging playhouses were clustered together in an area fast growing sleazy and occasionally dangerous. Honky-tonk bars and shops vending pornography crowded into the Times Square district. Derelicts, female and male prostitutes, and muggers pestered and sometimes molested playgoers. For those still hoping to have a night on the town, the slow but steady disappearance of nightclubs shortened such evenings appreciably. All that was left was dinner and a show.

But dinner and a show were beginning to cost a bundle. Inflation, fueled by the Vietnam War (and later, even more so by the oil cartel), created havoc on both sides of the footlights. Few theatregoes were old enough to remember that from the Civil War to World War I ticket prices held steady at a top of

$1.50, or, at most, $2.00. But many could attest to the relative stability that prevailed from the twenties to the early fifties, always acknowledging the drop in sales that reflected hard times during the Depression. Now a $6.00 top gave way to $7.20, which quickly shot up above the $10.00 level and gave every indication of rising to astronomical heights in the foreseeable future. Of necessity the theatre grew increasingly elitist, depending to no small extent on the expense-account trade. To compensate for escalating costs producers started to reduce the ranks of the chorus drastically and to cut down on the lavishness of scenery—skeletonized and basic unit sets appeared more frequently.

Largely because of economic pressures the theatre offered less assurance of regular employment. The day when, if she needed it or wanted it, a Lillian Russell or a Marilyn Miller or an Ethel Merman could be certain of a new show every season was gone, seemingly forever. Within a few seasons, the last of the musical theatre's first ladies would slip quietly into a not entirely voluntary retirement. There simply would be no more ready-at-hand vehicles for Gwen Verdon or Chita Rivera, while Angela Lansbury, who came to the musical stage rather late but who gave great promise of becoming an active queen mother of that stage, found a safe haven in television midway into the next act. Following their departures no successor loomed in the wings. Miss Lansbury's eventual berth underscored one major reason: Except for a fortunate few, Broadway's financial rewards, for all its inflated ticket prices and salaries, were meager compared with television's or film's. As a result a phenomenon that had been a nuisance since sound films and the Depression swelled into a plague. Brilliant young talent would appear, be hailed as a bright hope for tomorrow, and by that tomorrow be in Hollywood never to return. Witness, to name one striking example, Barbra Streisand. At least, a television or film star, especially if her career seemed in danger of fading, might attempt to revitalize it by starring for a time on Broadway or taking a musical on the road. But no great star made a point of reappearing regularly.

Partly as cause, partly as effect, fewer and fewer genuinely good musicals premiered, while many of the better offerings seemed wistfully derivative.

Aesthetically, one major development away from Broadway vitally affected the American Musical Theatre and, to a degree, suggested how senescent and out of touch it had become. With the arrival of the British singing group the Beatles in 1964, rock music exploded across the land, driving every other musical sound into panicky retreat. Broadway's older, traditional composers were thrown for a loss, and many never again were heard from. Those who remained more or less active found that their newer efforts were not awarded the constant replaying on records or radio that their older songs had been given, though here the fault lay partly in an incontestable falling-off of memorably melodic invention. As far as memorable melodies went, the American Musical Theatre suddenly had grown less memorable and less captivatingly musical. With few exceptions, audiences rarely left new musicals singing their music.

In healthier days, Broadway had responded quickly and fruitfully to new musical idioms, brilliantly appropriating ragtime and jazz to its own purposes. By the time swing entered the picture an older musical theatre, catering in some measure to an aging audience, was less willing or less able to respond. In its own defense it retorted that swing's repetitive, percussive mannerisms were essentially untheatrical and unmelodic. It was a legitimate argument, up to a point. Actually, when the first softer stirrings of rock were heard, way back in the late 1940s, Broadway quickly attempted to incorporate it. "Rock, Rock, Rock" was one of the musical delights of *As the Girls Go* in 1948. But once rock and roll established itself as the dominant popular musical style, it hurried on to a more metallic, throbbing form, often bellicose and almost always deafening.

Inevitably, Broadway had to make some response. Its initial stabs, most notably with *Hair* and *Your Own Thing*, were in many ways satisfying and hopeful. But rock quickly grew more assertive, and not just in its sound. Many of the leading rock groups composed their own songs and were reluctant to sing anything else, particularly if songs did not originate with fellow rock performers or composers. The youngsters who ran away with the field also seemed to have little knowledge of or interest in musical theatre. Of course, as rock music spread out pervasively across the land, Broadway composers and lyricists had to adopt or adapt bits and pieces of its style: the insistent rhythms and newer modulations of its music, the disheartening banality of its lyrics. Orchestrators added electronic instruments to pit bands, in part to allow for smaller and therefore less costly orchestras.

And that probably also helped promote one of rock's most identifiable signatures: its employment of ubiquitous miking and blaring amplification.

The louder the better, rock enthusiasts insisted. But miking and amplification not only grossly distort natural sounds, they also inject a confusing element of misdirection, since the sound no longer seems to emanate directly from the singers or the instruments. However acceptable this may be in rock concerts, usually held in vast arenas or stadiums, it has a stupefyingly pernicious effect in comparatively small legitimate theatres. To blame rock solely for a practice that quickly spread in traditional playhouses would be unfair. As we have seen, miking was first tried and dropped in the 1940s. It was revived in the 1950s. (Some students claim that Richard Rodgers first demanded it so that audiences at larger touring houses could hear the words to the songs for *South Pacific*; others state that the producers of *My Fair Lady* and *Jamaica* reintroduced it when they realized that Rex Harrison or Lena Horne could not project their songs properly. No one offers irrefutable proof, so blame is unassignable.) But by the end of this intermission virtually all musicals were miked and amplified.

Yet even when Broadway could be perceived to be down in the dumps, it persisted in slogging on. Now and then a beguiling bit of entertainment or something a mite more adventuresome but still highly enjoyable snapped the pervasive blues and allowed Broadway to smile for a while. Yet decline and despair dug deep into Broadway's very marrow. While the act that followed this short intermission saw the emergence of an exciting, daring new talent, found reason to rejoice in a batch of revivals and retrospectives, and ultimately succumbed to the blandishments of some importations that elbowed aside virtually all competition, there could be no gainsaying that the American Musical Theatre was in trouble.

1965–1966

Statistics for the very first season of this intermission hint at the malaise that pervaded the period. Although twenty-eight musicals presented themselves for Broadway's approval, twelve of these were revivals mounted by either the New York City Center Light Opera Company or the Music Theatre of Lincoln Center. Of the remaining sixteen lyric works, importations accounted for four, including one revival. A number of the new American book shows, as well as several importations, seemed determined efforts to capitalize on earlier successes.

The City Center had both its productions on the boards before Lincoln Center unveiled its two summer offerings. As was their wont both houses played safe by bringing back recent popular hits. The City Center offered *South Pacific* (7 April 1949) with Ray Middleton as de Becque on 2 June 1965 and *The Music Man* (19 December 1957) with Bert Parks in the title role on 16 June, while the Music Theatre followed with *Kismet* (3 December 1953), in which Alfred Drake recreated his original role, on 22 June, and *Carousel* (19 April 1945), also featuring its original male lead, John Raitt, on 10 August. David Merrick contributed to the flood of revivals by returning *Oliver!* to the New York stage for eight weeks beginning 2 August. Before the first new musical of the season appeared the New York City Opera gave theatregoers and opera lovers a chance to reevaluate Menotti's *The Saint of Bleecker Street* when the company added it to its repertory on 29 September. (Its fall season also included the increasingly inevitable *Die Fledermaus* and *The Merry Widow*.) Two more operas originally done as Broadway shows were included in its spring season: *Street Scene* on 24 February and *The Consul* on 17 March.

Pickwick (4 October 1965, 46th St.) was a West End adaptation of Dickens's material, clearly designed to follow in *Oliver!*'s lucrative footsteps. In London it had met with some modest success; in New York, where, like *Oliver!*, it was sponsored by David Merrick it was a quick failure.

An even quicker failure, **Drat! The Cat!** (10 October 1965, Martin Beck), survived a single week. In spirit the musical was not a little unlike the lyric mock-melodramas the Krimskys had offered at their American Music Hall in the thirties. Its libretto told of the love affair that blossoms between Bob Purefoy (Elliot Gould), a distressingly inept policeman, and Alice Van Guilder (Lesley Ann Warren), a kooky, criminal-minded heiress. In one respect Purefoy is a kindred soul to Alice, since both have easy berths in life thanks to their fathers. Purefoy's father was a Chief of Detectives. Unfortunately the drolleries in conception were not quite so amusing in the glare of the spotlights.

The World of Charles Aznavour (14 October 1965, Ambassador) allowed the popular French singer a month-long chance to serenade his devotees with his one-man show.

One of the most eagerly awaited musicals of the season, **On a Clear Day You Can See Forever** (17 October 1965, Hellinger) had at first been announced as *I Picked a Daisy* and promised to offer the fruits of a newly established collaboration of two of the American Musical Theatre's greatest talents, Alan Jay Lerner and Richard Rodgers. But a few months of working together convinced the pair that their habits and theories were too disparate. Lerner retained the rights to the story and joined with composer Burton Lane to create the piece. Lane's score was theatrically effective, and in its title song (sung by the romantic leads) had one superior number that has survived long after the show played its final performance. As always, Lerner created literate dialogue for an imaginative story. But as he so often had before, he failed to tie it all together in a completely viable libretto. To some extent Lerner's problem may have derived from the fact that his was the only libretto of the season not based on an earlier work. In this instance, however, his problem may have been exacerbated by his trying to go too far with his theme of extrasensory perception, allowing his heroine to predict the future as well as to recall a past existence. Although he tied the past and the future together adroitly at the end, he asked his audience in the interim to look both ways at once. Dr. Mark Bruckner (John Cullum), attempting to demonstrate hypnosis to a class at his family's clinic, finds he has unwittingly hypnotized not his intended subject but a highly susceptible young lady, Daisy Gamble (Barbara Harris). When the class leaves, Daisy begs the doctor to cure her addiction to smoking, an addiction which threatens to hinder her prospects for marrying Warren Smith (William Daniels). Bruckner agrees to work with her, although it is not her addiction that intrigues him. He quickly establishes that she is gifted with extrasensory perception—she knows when a phone is about to ring or where Bruckner has misplaced his keys. She makes plants grow by talking to them. Equally curious is her insistence that she remembers another life as Melinda Wells, a spunky eighteenth-century wench. Almost against his will Bruckner discovers himself accepting Daisy's stories—and falling in love with her. Although it means missing an interview with Warren's prospective employers, Daisy accompanies Bruckner to the Frick Museum and then on a boat ride, "On The S.S. Bernard Cohn." At subsequent meetings in his office Mark grows increasingly fascinated by Daisy's adventures as Melinda and seems to become even more enamored of the uninhibited Melinda than of Daisy. Melinda marries a painter and, when she learns how unfaithful her husband is, runs away to America on a ship named the

Trelawney. But Mark's budding infatuation is jolted when his stolid brother Conrad (Michael Lewis)—who has "been an analyst so long, he invades privacy instinctively"—comes across the tape Mark has made of his session with Daisy and warns him he will cause the clinic to become a laughingstock. When Mark's materials are published, he loses his job. But a rich Greek appears offering Mark almost limitless resources to pursue his study. To Mark's distress Daisy has played one of his tapes, one on which he muses, "Poor sweet nothing little Daisy. It's not your fault you're not Melinda." Hurt, Daisy walks out of his life. Trusting her ESP will hear his pleas, Mark cries, "Come Back To Me." She hears and heeds, but only to tell him she has a plane ticket for California. At the airport she has a premonition the plane will meet with an accident. When the announcer advises the name of the plane is the *Trelawney*, memories of her drowning in a shipwreck flood back. She cannot explain them, but understands she and Mark will work out the riddle together. Faulty as it was, the show ran 280 performances, sparked by Barbara Harris's wide-eyed, captivating Daisy. A later road tour proved disappointing.

November's first two shows also achieved runs that a half-century or so before would probably have assured them a respectable profit, but in the befuddled theatrical economy of their own day placed them on the wrong side of the ledger. **The Zulu and the Zayda** (10 November 1965, Cort) had a book by Howard da Silva and Felix Leon, based on a Dan Jacobson story, and music by Harold Rome. Some critics viewed it as a straight play with songs, but Rome's eleven musical numbers (plus reprises and orchestral passages) suggest it was indeed a musical. The absence of dancing—surprising, given the possibilities of its African setting—may have promoted some doubts. But the show's Africa is not the colorful, throbbing jungle of some earlier shows. For the most part the action unfolds in a Jewish suburb of Johannesburg, where the Grossman family hires a towering Zulu called Paulus to be a companion for their grandfather. (*Zayda* is Yiddish for grandfather.) The principal attraction of the evening was the clowning of the diminutive, sad-eyed Menasha Skulnik, long a favorite downtown in the Yiddish theatres and for a few seasons before *The Zulu and the Zayda* equally popular with Broadway audiences. He kept the show alive until April.

Three nights after Skulnik opened, one of the leading ladies of the American stage, Julie Harris, cast her lot with the musical theatre. It proved an unhappy decision. Her musical, **Skyscraper** (13 November 1965, Lunt-Fontanne), was a lyric version of Elmer Rice's 1945 hit, *Dream Girl*. Peter Stone adapted the text, while Sammy Cahn wrote words to James Van Heusen's music. Broadway's once infallible team of Feuer and Martin produced the evening. Looking back in his autobiography, Cahn terms the production "One devastating experience." He is proud of his lyrics for "Everybody Has A Right To Be Wrong" (sung in the show by Peter L. Marshall), and the song did in fact meet with some popularity. The book faithfully retained Rice's basic story of Georgina Allerton, who spends most of her waking hours in Walter Mitty–like dreams of fame, fortune, and romance, but added a contemporary touch by placing her in an old brownstone surrounded by modern high-rise buildings and menaced by developers. Much of Georgina's dreaming centers around her assistant at her antique shop, Roger Somerhill (Charles Nelson Reilly), whom she envisages in such romantic guises as a secret agent and a toreador. Roger proves treacherous, conspiring with the developers who would demolish her house. By the end of the evening she has at least come down to earth enough to agree to marry Timothy Bushman (Marshall), a young architect, and the two arrange to save her home and shop. Two witty Michael Kidd dances had fun at the expense of flirting construction workers and Georgina's ideas of a lady's honor. Robert Randolph's scenery strikingly juxtaposed Georgina's warm rooms against an imposing, impersonal skyline. Miss Harris's stylish acting, Reilly's hilariously unctuous obnoxiousness, and "twofers" (cheap tickets, two for the price of one) allowed *Skyscraper* to run out the season.

The season's biggest hit opened on 22 November without much fanfare at a temporary theatre that had been erected on the New York University campus to house the ill-fated repertory company that later played briefly at Lincoln Center. **Man of La Mancha** was a musical version of Cervantes's *Don Quixote* that had tried out at the Goodspeed Opera House in Connecticut. Although it had no advance sale to speak of, generally excellent reviews and favorable word of mouth from audiences that no longer demanded the well-mannered niceties of an earlier era soon made it the "hottest" ticket in town. In Dale Wasserman's adaptation, with lyrics by Joe Darion and music by Mitch Leigh, Cervantes's masterpiece became a hard-driving, often rough-talking, frequently compassionate lyric drama. The show made few concession to theatergoers, playing out its entire story in one basic set and without intermission. The dancing, especially one brutal "Abduction" ballet, was as violent and unyielding as much of the dialogue and lyrics. Wasserman employed a frame device, beginning the evening with the imprisonment of Cervantes and his servant. In reading his tale to his fellow prisoners, the Spaniard is transformed into Don Quixote and his servant becomes Sancho. According to Quixote, "the wild winds of fortune will carry onward,/Oh whithersoever they blow." They blow him, fittingly, to a windmill, although in the Don's eyes the mill is a fearsome ogre. He can bring himself to admit he has tilted at a windmill only by claiming an enchanter had magically reshaped the fiend. Not until a lord of a castle dubs him a knight will he be able to destroy the enchanter. Quixote's addled mind allows a dilapidating roadside inn to become a suitable castle and the innkeeper its lord. Even Aldonza, the inn's sluttish serving girl, is elevated to "Sweet Lady [and] fair virgin." Going still further, the Don rechristens her Dulcinea and apostrophizes, "[T]hy name is like a prayer an angle whispers." He confesses to the baffled girl that his mission in life is "To dream the impossible dream … To reach the unreachable star." No sooner has the obliging innkeeper dubbed Quixote Knight of the Woeful Countenance than the new knight's mettle is severely tested. Rough muleteers attack and abduct Aldonza. For a moment, Cervantes becomes himself again as the Inquisition enters to remove one of his fellow prisoners. As the Don, he stumbles into a gypsy encampment, where he recovers the much bedraggled Aldonza, refusing to heed her pleas to accept her for what she is. To a fanfare of trumpets a warrior, the Knight of the Mirrors, appears and jousts with Quixote. In the warrior's mirrors the Don sees his own reflection and is soon brought to realize he is "A madman dressed for a masquerade!" The warrior reveals himself to be Dr. Carrasco, sent to Cervantes to rid him of his delusions. He succeeds all too well. Even Aldonza, insisting she is Dulcinea and begging the virtually lifeless man to continue his impossible dream, cannot get an encouraging response. The Inquisition arrives to lead Cervantes away, as his fellow prisoners exhort him "To live with your heart striving upward." Leigh's music played as important a part in the show's success as Wasserman's book. The score was in a totally modern idiom. The chromatic progressions of "The Impossible Dream" (called in the program "The Quest") were instantly appealing, and the song became an enormously popular hit. Indeed, it could be considered the last major hit to emerge from Broadway before rock and roll overwhelmed the nation. Of course, its hymn-like tune played over heavy chords did suggest a certain rock quality. "Dulcinea" and the title song also received significant replaying outside the theatre. The original cast included a number of fine singing actors: Richard Kiley was Cervantes (who sang both hit songs); Joan Diener, Aldonza; Ray Middleton, the Innkeeper; and Robert Rounseville, a priest. In one curious bit of casting Sancho was performed by Irving Jacobson, a refugee from the moribund Yiddish theatre. In its Village auditorium and later at an uptown house Man of La Mancha compiled 2,328 performances. Its touring and international companies thrived as well.

Robert Wright and George Forrest, who had embellished their book and lyrics to Song of Norway (21 August 1944) with Grieg's music and their book and lyrics for Kismet (3 December 1953) with Borodin's melodies, turned to Rachmaninoff for their tunes in Anya (29 November 1965, Ziegfeld), their adaptation of Marcelle Maurette and Guy Bolton's popular Anastasia. The story once again seemed to support the claim of the young lady who appeared mysteriously in Berlin in 1925 professing to be the sole surviving member of Czar Nicholas's supposedly slaughtered family. In a sizzling encounter in the second act Anya convinces the Dowager Empress she is the real Anastasia. The play had been lush hokum; the musical seemed elaborate ho-hum. A fine cast included Constance Towers and Lillian Gish in the pivotal roles as well as Lawrence Brooks, Irra Petina, and John Michael King in important singing parts. Poor attendance closed the show after two weeks. When it closed, the finest musical theatre New York had known closed with it. Joseph Urban's gorgeous, spacious Ziegfeld was demolished shortly after the departure of its last tenant.

An embarrassingly bad attempt to put Marjorie Kinnan Rawlings's once-popular novel The Yearling (10 December 1965, Alvin) on the boards met with almost instant disaster. The stage was simply no place to tell a story in which much of the action revolves around a fawn. Jody Baxter's attachment to his yearling and the understanding of life his yearling's death gives Jody might seem moving, if mawkish, on the printed page or even on the screen, but it proved to be one form of realism the stage could not handle. Three performances was the extent of The Yearling's run.

La Grosse Valise (14 December 1965, 54th St.) ran twice as long, compiling a total of seven performances. Its brief stay was obviously disappointing, since this Robert Dhery contrivance (with music by Gerard Calvi) had been touted as a sequel to Dhery's La Plume de Ma Tante and had enjoyed some Paris acclaim. The show was a departure from the earlier work in several ways. It had a thin plotline about an enormous trunk that is opened at customs and out of which pours a parade of songs and sketches. But the trunk was little more than a mute compère, and the show, despite its claim to having a book, was a revue. A more meaningful change was the inclusion of a number of songs that suggested they wanted a separate life outside the theatre. The suggestion was underscored by Harold Rome's creating English lyrics for them. In La Plume de Ma Tante, the musical numbers had been an integral, unextractable part of the show.

A revival of Oklahoma! (31 March 1943) with John Davidson and Susan Watson began a three-week run at the City Center the night after La Grosse Valise opened. The revival was the last lyric offering of the year. The first new musical of 1966 didn't arrive until late January, but in many respects it was worth waiting for. Sweet Charity (29 January 1966, Palace) was a song-and-dance version of Fellini's film Nights of Cabiria, with a pronounced emphasis on the dancing half. Although the popular playwright Neil Simon transferred the work to the stage and reset the story in New York, and although Dorothy Fields and Cy Coleman created lyrics and music that were soon causing coins to be fed into jukeboxes, the principal attractions of the evening were the dancing of Gwen Verdon and the staging of her choreographer-husband, Bob Fosse. Fosse's stylized clustered posturings soon became something of a trademark. In Simon's version Charity is a warm-hearted, unlucky dance hostess at the honky-tonk Fandango Ballroom. A lonely walk in Central Park costs her a purse and a dunking in the lake. She latches on to a famous Italian movie star (James Luisi), whose date has left him in a huff, but, when he takes her to his apartment and she joyously dances with his top hat and cane, his contrite date reappears, so Charity is relegated to a closet while the other two make love. At a YMHA lecture series she meets an accountant named Oscar (John McMartin). They are stranded together in an elevator, where she learns he is claustrophobic, and later stranded in mid-air on a Coney Island amusement ride, where he discovers she is acrophobic. She lies about her job, pretending she works in a bank. But Oscar confesses he had known her real employment all along. Although he insists her past will not interfere with his kind feelings about her, he finally admits marriage would be impossible. The show ends with Charity again alone on a park bench.

Some critics were surprised by the amount of sentimentality in Simon's book and by the lack of the consistently sharp comedy his straight plays presented. Reviewers were often even more critical of the score, which seemed to them lackluster on first hearing. The public disagreed, and within a short time both "Big Spender" and "Baby, Dream Your Dream" were being whistled and sung everywhere. Curiously neither of these songs was performed in the show by Miss Verdon; Helen Gallagher and Thelma Oliver, playing Charity's sister hostesses, introduced the pair. *Sweet Charity* brought with it an additional blessing to Broadway by capturing the historic Palace Theatre for the legitimate fold. Once the shrine of vaudeville and long given over to films, it was completely refurbished and, to a small extent, compensated for the loss of the Ziegfeld.

A white African revue called **Wait a Minim!** (7 March 1966, Golden) and relying heavily on folk material and folk instruments, not always from Africa, began a long run, repeating a success it had enjoyed in its homeland and in London. On those few occasions when they discarded folk material, the eight cast members took light-hearted digs at their homeland's racial policies.

Although Duke Ellington was one of the most respected and successful of the nation's jazz musicians, good luck had always eluded him when he attempted something for the Broadway stage. Nothing changed with **Pousse-Café** (18 March 1966, 46th St.). While the skillful Jerome Weidman adapted the classic 1930 film *The Blue Angel* for the stage, and while the equally skillful Lilo and Theodore Bikel recreated the parts Marlene Dietrich and Emil Jannings had played, the show folded after a humiliating three performances. Weidman moved the story of the small-town professor ruined by his infatuation for a minor nightclub performer to 1920 New Orleans. Neither Ellington nor Weidman seemed to care that only one show set in modern New Orleans had ever succeeded, and that show—*Louisiana Purchase* (28 May 1940)—made little attempt to capitalize on the town's colorful atmosphere.

As it did every so often, Broadway put aside its pretensions and looked to the comic strips for musical inspiration. Some critics thought **It's a Bird ... It's a Plane ... It's SUPERMAN** (29 March 1966, Alvin) better-than-average foolery. A small

cult formed; but the public at large did not accept its judgment, and *SUPERMAN* was dealt a knockout blow by the summer heat. The story would have done the strip proud. Underneath his everyday business clothes mild-mannered newspaperman Clark Kent (Bob Holiday) wears the flashy tights, snug-fitting shirt with the big S on the chest, and cape that reveal he is Superman, child of another planet sent to Earth when that planet was destroyed. Kent generally effects his clothes change in any convenient telephone booth. He works with pretty Lois Lane (Patricia Marand), who dreams of being loved by Superman, never for a moment suspecting he is typing away at the next desk. For the moment Superman's nemesis is a mad scientist, Dr. Sedgwick (Michael O'Sullivan). Sedgwick is embittered because he has never received a Nobel Prize. He invites Superman to the dedication of a physics hall he has obsequiously named for the hero. When the strongman is helplessly occupied supporting a speaker's collapsed platform, Sedgwick blows up Metropolis's city hall. Although Superman is reviled in the papers, Sedgwick wants more than to humble him. He wants Superman dead. He lures him into a supposed death trap in a power station by kidnapping Lois. But in "Bow! Bam! Zonk!" Superman assails Sedgwick and frees Lois. Sedgwick inadvertently electrocutes himself. Lois's love for the hero now knows no bounds, but it is doomed to remain unrequited. A deadly missile is heading toward Metropolis, and with his "Up, up and away!" Superman flies off to intercept it. Invisible wiring allowed Superman to fly high above the stage; but no mechanism could make the show soar into the hit column. The failure of the show left its songwriters, Lee Adams and Charles Strouse, still looking for a successor to their *Bye Bye Birdie* (14 April 1960).

On 20 April the New York City Light Opera Company launched a Frank Loesser festival at the City Center. Three of the four openings fell in the current season: *How to Succeed in Business Without Really Trying* (14 October 1964) with Billy DeWolfe as Biggley and *The Most Happy Fella* (3 May 1956) with Art Lund again singing Joe, followed on 11 May by *Where's Charley?* (11 October 1948) with the small part of Donna Lucia D'Alvadorez played by the former Metropolitan Opera prima donna Eleanor Steber.

Richard Llewellyn's old novel *How Green Was My Valley* was dusted off and theatricalized as **A Time for Singing** (21 May 1966, Broadway). Given its Welsh setting it should have occasioned some fine choral singing—and it did. But the music the singers were given was drab and did little to enhance the grim story of the Morgan family's tribulations during accidents and union agitation in their mining town. The show was another of the season's quick flops, leaving after forty-one showings.

Mame (24 May 1966, Winter Garden), on the other hand, ran and ran, compiling 1,508 performances in New York. It would have been surprising if it hadn't, for Patrick Dennis's irrepressible auntie had made cash registers jingle happily as a novel, a film, and stage play. Jerome Lawrence and Robert E. Lee, who had made the long-run stage adaptation, fashioned the book, and Jerry Herman, whose *Hello, Dolly!* was still packing them in on 44th Street, composed the score. If the show left critics and audiences generally content, it also left many with a sense of *déjà vu* or perhaps *déjà entendu*. The story and even some of the lines had become familiar, but more to the point Mame Dennis (Angela Lansbury) was a sister under the skin to Dolly Gallagher Levi, and Herman seemed to be consciously trying to rewrite some of his old songs to fit new molds. The title song had much the same lilt as his earlier title song and repeated the heroine's name just as incessantly. Its tone was harder and a little more driving than the sunny, affectionate "Hello, Dolly!," but the difference was one of degree not kind. A number of the other tunes possessed a desperate, martial gaiety that seemed a determined effort to invest the evening with life. But if there was at once something secondhand and second-rate about the score it nevertheless worked effectively in the theatre, especially in the splashy, professional production.

Miss Lansbury's Mame was interrupted in the middle of a chic cocktail party by the arrival of her orphaned ten-year-old nephew, Patrick Dennis (Frankie Michaels), and his timid, prayerful chaperone, Agnes Gooch (Jane Connell). All Mame can think to do is advise him to "circulate." But when the guests have gone, Mame settles down to plan her young ward's education. Over the protestations of a guardian from the bank she enrolls the boy in a progressive school where children spend part of the day naked. With time the two become close, so close Patrick considers Mame "My Best Girl," although Agnes remains as part of the household. But the year is 1929, and the stock market crash leaves Mame without a cent. A job as manicurist leads to a romance with a rich young Southerner (Charles Braswell). His family is snobbish and conspires to break up the affair, but when she actually catches the fox in a hunt, they have no choice but to salute and welcome "Mame." Years pass. Mame's husband has died, and soon she is again ensconced in a luxurious New York apartment. Patrick (now older and played by Jerry Lanning) is courting a light-headed socialite, Gloria Upson (Diane Walker). Mame decides to put an end to the romance because she rightly concludes Gloria is the wrong girl for Patrick. But she also admits she doesn't really want to lose Patrick, a confession she painfully reveals in "If He Walked Into My Life." She scares away the Upson clan with her plan to build a home to house unwed mothers next door to their property. Still Patrick is of a marriageable age and disposition, so before long he has wed Pegeen Ryan (Diane Coupe). More time passes, Patrick and Pegeen bring their ten-year-old son Michael to Mame, and Mame offers to take him with her around the world. They agree, provided she brings Michael back for the beginning of school on Labor Day. Mame accepts the condition, privately assuring Michael Labor Day is sometime in November. Mame's most hilarious moment came in a parody of an old-time musical comedy number. Since "The Man In The Moon" is a miss, Mame squirms uncomfortably on a gigantic new moon, finally slipping and wrecking the scene. If Miss Lansbury's performance was pivotal, she was handsomely abetted by the hoarse drolleries of Beatrice Arthur as her fairweather friend, Vera. In a backbiting duet, "Bosom Buddies," they stopped the show, especially when Vera assured Mame that she didn't seem old, merely somewhere between "forty and death."

The season's last offering was a revival on 31 May of *Annie Get Your Gun* (16 May 1946) by the Music Theatre of Lincoln Center. Because its original star, Ethel Merman, was playing Annie Oakley again twenty-one years after she created the part, some wags referred to the show as "Granny Get Your Gun," but even in the vastness of the New York State Theatre Miss Merman had no problem projecting her songs or her personality. Irving Berlin showed his faith in her by giving her a new song, "Old Fashioned Wedding," a contrapuntal number on the order of "You're Just In Love" and "Simple Melody." The book was also slightly revised to make Miss Merman the absolute cynosure by omitting an unimportant secondary love story. With the love story went the lovers' song "Who Do You Love, I Hope." So successful was the revival, if not the new song, that it was taken on a brief tour when *Show*

Boat was due and in the next season brought back to a regular Broadway house.

1966–1967

The season opened with the customary City Center and Lincoln Center revivals. *Guys and Dolls* (24 November 1950) arrived on 8 June to complete the Frank Loesser festival the 55th Street house had inaugurated at the end of the preceding session. Vivian Blaine was back to recreate her classic Adelaide, while Hugh O'Brian played Sky. *Show Boat* (27 December 1927) sailed into the New York State Theatre on 19 July. Kern and Hammerstein's masterpiece was attractively mounted and splendidly cast. David Wayne was Cap'n Andy; Barbara Cook, Magnolia; Stephen Douglass, Ravenal; William Warfield, Joe; and Constance Towers, Julie. *Show Boat* played until 10 September when it was taken on the road, where it had disappointing grosses despite good notices.

September's lone musical entry was **A Hand Is on the Gate** (21 September 1966, Longacre), an assemblage of African-American poetry and folk song performed by a small cast that included Josephine Premice, James Earl Jones, and Cicely Tyson. A modest enterprise, it met with a modest reception, surviving two and a half weeks.

The New York City Opera made a bow to Broadway when it again inserted *The Consul* into its repertory on 6 October. But the season's first more or less traditional musical did not arrive until October, and in this case it was decidedly less traditional than most. In fact, **The Apple Tree** (18 October 1966, Shubert) was three one-act pieces presented together as a complete evening. Mark Twain's *The Diary of Adam and Eve* provided the inspiration for the first act. Only three characters appear: a somewhat nervous, obsessive Adam (Alan Alda), a carefree, tactile Eve (Barbara Harris), and the Snake (Larry Blyden), who destroys the couple's bliss by persuading Eve to eat "the rich ripe round red rosy apples." Life outside Eden transforms Adam into a quietly desperate wage-earner and Eve into a resigned housewife. The second act used Frank R. Stockton's famous short story, *The Lady or the Tiger?*, as its source. Probably only a handful in the audience remembered this same story had provided the frame for De Wolf Hopper's full-length musicalization way back in 1888. In the new retelling King Arik (Marc Jordan) catches his war hero, Captain Sanjar (Alda), kissing Princess Barbara (Miss Harris) and

sentences him to open one of two doors. A hungry tiger lurks behind one; a beautiful woman whom he must marry awaits him behind the other. His beloved Barbara signals which door he should open. The curtain falls as Stockton's story concluded, without showing which choice Barbara made. The final playlet, based on Jules Feiffer's *Passionella*, finds a little chimney sweep, Ella (Miss Harris), dreaming she has become the famous and glamorous movie star of the title. Her Passionella bears a startling physical resemblance to Hollywood sex symbol Marilyn Monroe. (Passionella's career is relived in a giant montage of old footage and stills.) In her dream she marries the black-leather-jacketed, hippie rock sensation Flip (Alda); she awakes to reality and settles for scruffy little George L. Brown (Alda). Jerry Bock and Sheldon Harnick departed from their practice of only writing songs to create (originally with Jerome Coopersmith) the book (or booklets) for the evening. Their work had an admirably consistent style and tone, but not enough punch to revive the tired businessman; nevertheless the show ran out the season.

Neither of the other two October entries was quite in the Broadway mainstream. A Swedish "marionette" version of *The Threepenny Opera* recorded thirteen performances at the Billy Rose. The marionettes were not the expected puppets but actors performing behind cutout figures. Swedish gave way to French four nights later when a one-man show entitled **Gilbert Bécaud on Broadway** raised its curtain. Monsieur Bécaud spent nineteen performances serenading ticket holders with popular French songs. Still a third alien language was heard on the Broadway stage when **Let's Sing Yiddish** led off the parade of November musicals. Using Yiddish folksongs and folktales, the evening was essentially a revue with its first half set in an old-world shtetl and its second act in America. The appeal of Yiddish theatre had long since waned, but enough was left to allow the musical to compile 107 performances.

On 15 November another language foreign to many Americans graced the musical stage: the king's English. The D'Oyly Carte began a limited and not too enriching stay at the City Center, giving *The Pirates of Penzance, The Mikado, Ruddigore, H. M. S. Pinafore,* and *Patience.*

The next evening **The Apparition Theater of Prague** opened. A combination of pantomime, ballet, and drama, it depended for effect largely on black-garbed performers moving against black backdrops and working objects covered with luminous paint. The same night saw yet another foreign musical offering premiere. *Les Ballets Africains* was a collection of native dances from French-influenced areas of Africa. The Czechs entertained New York for twenty-one showings, the Africans for eighty-five.

Not until late November did a musical at once original and traditional open in New York. For being both comfortably daring and derivative it was rewarded with the longest run of the season. **Cabaret** (20 November 1966, Broadhurst) was a lyric version of John Van Druten's hit of fifteen years before, *I Am a Camera*, itself a dramatization of earlier Christopher Isherwood stories. Its book was by Joe Masteroff, its lyrics by Fred Ebb, and its music by John Kander. Because it was set in the heyday of the Weill–Brecht collaboration and because its story had something of the epic-drama undercurrents of that team's pieces, the authors and producer-director more than once mimicked the musical styles, orchestrations, and staging techniques associated with *The Threepenny Opera* or *The Rise and Fall of the City of Mahagonny*. The relationship of *Cabaret* to these earlier works was underscored by the presence in the original cast of Lotte Lenya (Weill's wife and the original Jenny) in the important role of the landlady, Frau Schneider. But the Weill–Brecht masterpieces were neither slavishly copied nor parodied. *Cabaret*'s creators were solid contemporary craftsmen, attuned to the requirements of the musical theatre of their day and able to fulfill those requirements handsomely.

The curtain is up as the audience enters. A stylized set suggests a sleazy cabaret, the Kit Kat Klub, against a larger background of jazz-age Berlin. A spotlight reveals a heavily made-up Master of Ceremonies (Joel Grey)—white face, rouged cheeks, heavy lashes, and cupid-bow lips—who sings a tinny "Willkommen" to his customers in three languages. On a train heading toward this same Berlin, Cliff Bradshaw (Bert Convy), a fledgling American writer, encounters a pleasant young German, Ernst Ludwig (Edward Winter). Ludwig seems to be engaged in some sort of smuggling, and Cliff, a little amused by the whole thing, helps him through customs. The grateful Ernst promises to become Cliff's friend and help open doors for him. Cliff takes a room at Frau Schneider's. The good lady professes to have once been rich and adored. The fates have not been especially kind to her, but she shrugs them off with "So What?" She lives only for the moment, and at this moment another

boarder, a Jew named Herr Schultz (Jack Gilford), seems to be on the verge of proposing marriage to her. Cliff visits the Kit Kat Klub, where he meets an English entertainer, Sally Bowles (Jill Haworth). Sally begins to visit Cliff in his room. He is quickly taken by her forlorn charm, finding her "Perfectly Marvelous." Sally's view of life is wholly carpe diem. She insists, "Why should I wake up? This dream is going so well." But the dream has not long to run. Ernst visits Cliff asking him to aid with further smuggling. By now it is clear that Ernst is a Nazi and that the money he keeps bringing in illegally is to aid the Nazi coffers. Cliff demurs. But Ernst does not leave without warning Frau Schneider not to wed Schultz: "He is not a German." A rock thrown through the rooming-house window convinces the landlady of the sad truth behind the young Nazi's threat. Cliff begs Sally to leave Germany with him. Instead, she returns to the Kit Kat Klub. Cliff follows her, and in an argument there with Ernst he is badly beaten by Ernst's henchmen. Sally continues to sing to the club's patrons, telling them life is a "Cabaret" and inviting each and every "old chum" to come to the cabaret. When Cliff learns that Sally has had an abortion, paying for it with her fur coat, he walks out of her life. Alone on the train heading out of Germany, he begins to write his reminiscences. The Master of Ceremonies appears again, and in three languages wishes the audience good-bye.

Although inevitably there was a mixing of contemporary sounds with sounds of the show's era, *Cabaret* had a generally consistent, evocative sense of time and place. It poignantly portrayed the seediness and forced gaiety of Berlin nightlife as the Nazi menace grew. Not even intermission was allowed to break the spell. With the curtain remaining up, the Kit Kat Klub's all-girl band played jazzily until the action resumed. Grey had the evening's best notices. His appearances were far more numerous than the brief summary of the show suggests; he appeared in all the scenes at the Kit Kat Klub, singing several numbers with the chorus line. But as so often happens with scenes set in nightclubs, the songs had little relevance to the main action other than to underscore the era's tinselly, unwholesome attempts at escape. In *Cabaret*'s case these nightclub songs were among the weaker numbers in the show, put across largely because of fine staging and Grey's chilly brilliance. Audiences by now had become inured to the realistic librettos of the modern American Musical Theatre. *Cabaret* ran 1,165 performances in New York and toured successfully, although it was one of the rare modern Broadway hits that London failed to take to its heart.

One not insignificant reason for *Cabaret's* immediate popularity was the relative emptiness of the musicals that followed it. Within a month three more new book musicals appeared. In all three instances the main attraction of the evening was appealing performers. The shows met with varying degrees of success—and failure. The first to arrive was **Walking Happy** (26 November 1966, Lunt-Fontanne), a musical version of Harold Brighouse's *Hobson's Choice*. Hobson in this case was not the legendary English liveryman but Maggie Hobson (Louise Troy), daughter of a Lancashire shoemaker. To her father's consternation Maggie falls in love with his meek, bungling apprentice, Will Mossop (Norman Wisdom). In short order she makes Will into a fine shoemaker as well as a husband. The score for the evening was by James Van Heusen with lyrics by Sammy Cahn. The two had provided the songs for the preceding season's *Skyscraper* (13 November 1965). Their material for *Walking Happy* represented a decline from even *Skyscraper's* modest attainments. For most theatregoers the principal inducement to line up at the box office was to watch the antics of the pint-sized English comic Norman Wisdom. Unfortunately, he was not well known enough to help the show survive more than twenty weeks. The show's closing brought to an unhappy end the once astonishingly successful New York career of its producers, Feuer and Martin.

An even more amazingly successful producing career was slowly winding down when David Merrick escorted in **I Do! I Do!** (5 December 1966, 46th St.). The show was a musical version of Jan de Hartog's *The Fourposter*, a two-character comedy that had originally opened on Broadway a few weeks before the premiere of *I Am a Camera, Cabaret's* source. Once again the bedroom was its sole setting and a husband and wife its only characters. The play begins just before the turn of the century with the wedding of Michael and Agnes, and then follows the couple through the joys and tribulations of fifty years of married life. The joys include the births of their children, celebrated in "My Cup Runneth Over," while tribulations come to a head just before the first-act curtain when Michael reveals he has had an extramarital affair. He staunchly proclaims it is "A Well Known Fact" that middle-aged men are especially attractive to many women. Furious and hurt, Agnes dons an extravagantly feathered hat and announces she will turn herself

into a sexually stimulating creature everyone will call "Flaming Agnes." At loggerheads, the two agree "The Honeymoon Is Over." But affection and good sense prevail. The marriage continues on its inexorable road until old age forces Michael and Agnes to give up their large house. Another young couple are taking their place, so just before they depart they leave a bottle of champagne on the bed, covering the bottle with a pillow on which has been inscribed GOD IS LOVE.

Inevitably the musicalization of so intimate a play led to additional theatricalization, but Harvey Schmidt and Tom Jones never let their changes vulgarize the material. Unfortunately, their good taste was not matched by any telling inspiration. Nothing from the work achieved the popularity of their material for *The Fantasticks* (3 May 1960). *I Do! I Do!'s* run of over a year was attributable to the appeal of its two stars, Mary Martin and Robert Preston, and to Gower Champion's lively staging. Typical of Champion's inventiveness was the dance he gave Preston to accompany "I Love My Wife." Something between a soft-shoe and tap routine, Preston performed it barefoot, in a dressing gown, with top hat and cane.

Ten nights later **A Joyful Noise** (15 December 1966, Hellinger) began a brief stay. Based on Borden Deal's novel *The Insolent Breed*, it recounted the courtship of Jenny Lee (Susan Watson) by the wandering minstrel, Shade Motley (John Raitt). Shade is run out of little Macedonia, Tennessee, by Jenny Lee's father, but he moves on to become a success at Nashville's Grand Ole Opry. The prospect of a rich, settled life in Nashville holds little interest for Shade. His love for Jenny Lee and his wanderlust bring him back to Macedonia. Obviously the show's music relied heavily on the popular country-and-western folk music styles of the day. But the newly created "folk" songs offered nothing memorable, and the show folded after a mere twelve performances. Raitt must have watched with a certain bittersweet curiosity the revival of *Carousel* (19 April 1945) that opened at the City Center the same evening *A Joyful Noise* opened. Raitt, of course, had been *Carousel's* original Billy Bigelow. The revival outran Raitt's new vehicle by a week.

Donald Swann, playing the piano, and Michael Flanders, reciting from his wheelchair, returned two nights after Christmas with their second two-man show, **At the Drop of Another Hat** (27 December 1966, Booth). It suffered the fate of most sequels, falling far short of the vogue of the original. But it was by no means a failure. The Englishmen regaled audiences until early April of 1967.

Oddly it was almost April before another musical arrived. **Sherry!** (28 March 1967, Alvin) was a musical version of Kaufman and Hart's 1939 hit *The Man Who Came to Dinner*. As he had twenty-seven years before, Sheridan Whiteside (Clive Revill) finds himself confined after a fall in the Mesalia, Ohio, home of the comfortably bourgeois Stanleys. He proceeds to disrupt the household with his imperious ways until his hosts soon pray for his early departure. Catastrophically, the adaptation was put into relatively inexperienced hands. The show's weaknesses were aggravated by cast problems during the tryout. The show New York finally saw was anything but the riotously festive romp the straight-play version had been. *Sherry!* struggled along for nine weeks before throwing in the towel.

April was a remarkably busy month. **Hello, Solly!**, a Yiddish-English vaudeville, began the parade on the 4th. No one seriously confused its title with the musical at the St. James, and David Merrick, *Dolly's* producer, didn't even attempt to get some free publicity with a prestaged hassle. The new piece ran sixty-eight performances at Henry Miller's lovely theatre (shortly to be converted to a pornographic movie house) and left quietly.

The City Center offered a spring season of three revivals, beginning with *Finian's Rainbow* (10 January 1947) with Nancy Dussault as Sharon on 5 April. *The Sound of Music* (16 November 1959), featuring Bob Wright and Constance Towers, followed three weeks later, and *Wonderful Town* (25 February 1953), starring Elaine Stritch, brought up the rear on 14 May.

Aesthetically and commercially, Broadway musicalizations of Hollywood films had rarely proved satisfying, but this disappointing history refused to discourage new attempts. In one respect **Illya Darling** (11 April 1967, Hellinger) seemed to stand a better chance to bridge the forms successfully than had most earlier efforts, for the show was a lyric stage version of *Never on Sunday*, with a libretto by the same man, Jules Dassin, who had created the piece for the screen and with its charismatic star, Melina Mercouri, repeating her movie role. Illya is a prostitute, working the waterfront in modern Piraeus. She is an open-handed and open-hearted girl who plies her trade only from Monday through Saturday, leaving Sunday open to entertain friends and customers lavishly at her own expense. Her carefree life is disrupted by the arrival of an American tourist,

a teacher named, curiously, Homer Thrace (Orson Bean). He determines to make a good woman of Illya. For a while he appears to succeed. He gets her to abandon her old ways and gives her instruction in the liberal arts. Happy with the change he has wrought, he even tries to convert Illya's fellow prostitutes. He ends by antagonizing them and by making Illya realize how unnaturally constrained her new existence is. She gratefully reverts to her old ways, and Homer, coming to understand that she was a good woman before he met her, returns home wiser if not happier.

The music for the show was by Manos Hadjidakis, a Greek whose exile from Greece had made him something of a *cause célèbre*. Hadjidakis had written the score for the motion picture, and the popularity of its title song played no small part in the film's success. His new score was often zestful, but never outstandingly memorable. *Illya* inevitably suffered from limitations the stage imposed on the free flow of the film script. Although Oliver Smith's scenery moved back and forth between Illya's apartment, the Acropolis, tavernas, and shipyards in Piraeus, it could not capture the sun-splashed, sea-washed abandon of the film. David Ewen gives a telling example of a scene that could not be transferred to the stage in which Illya, wearing a revealing bathing suit, goes for a swim in the harbor, prompting scores of sailors and fishermen to jump in after her. The show was most successful in its intimate moments, notably when Illya teaches an innocent American sailor the facts of life in "Love, Love, Love." Thanks largely to Miss Mercouri's presence, the show was able to run, with some forcing, for 318 performances.

April's last offering was the only new book musical of the season to have a libretto not based on an earlier work. But **Hallelujah, Baby!** (26 April 1967, Martin Beck) (exclamation points were the rage of the season) did not resort to a carefully plotted, crescendoing story. Instead it employed the device used some years before in *Love Life*, a chronicle extending over a number of years in which the principals, nonetheless, never age. In this case the principals are Georgina (Leslie Uggams), a twenty-five-year-old black woman; her black boyfriend, Clem (Robert Hooks); and her white lover, Harvey (Allen Case). After a brief introduction in which Georgina explains the nature of the evening, the setting hurtles back to the turn of the century. Georgina, made by her mother to clean the floor of their simple home, sings longingly of "My Own Morning." When she discovers Clem has lost their wedding money in a crap game, she leaves for New York to earn her way in show business. She scores a quick success in a 1920 cabaret. When the Depression hits, Georgina finds herself in a breadline with only the paltry sums doled out by the Federal Theatre to sustain her hope. World War II brings recovery, and Georgina goes to work in a cheap nightclub near an army base. By the fifties she is a major nightclub star. Her success with the white world alienates Clem, who has embraced the civil rights movement. But in the sixties, Georgina contrives a happy ending, rousingly assuring everyone "Now's The Time."

The evening had a solidly crafted score by Jule Styne and lyrics by Comden and Green. Though the music was essentially contemporary, Styne was careful to suggest the correct patterns and flavor of each period the show passed through. Curiously, the show was at its best recreating the black-inspired jazz of the twenties. Georgina sang and the appropriately named Tip and Tap (Winston De Witt Hemsley and Alan Weeks) danced to the infectious beat of "Feet Do Yo' Stuff." Unfortunately, Arthur Laurents's book could not make up its mind whether it wanted to be an entertainment or a political tract. His preachings on racism worked against the entertainment of the rest of the show. Happily, Miss Uggams's charm made the show palatable and kept it on stage for nine months.

The season concluded with a third Yiddish musical, **Sing Israel Sing** (11 May 1967, Atkinson), built around a joyous kibbutz wedding. The musical's appeal was limited, and it closed after two weeks so that it could be translated into English in hopes of finding a larger audience.

In this season of librettos that were more chronicles than tightly knit plots, the most successful of the off-Broadway shows fell in with the vogue. **You're a Good Man, Charlie Brown** (7 March 1967, 80 St. Marks) was populated with youngsters from Charles M. Schulz's adored comic strip Peanuts. With becoming and sensible modesty this low-budget show chronicled a very limited time span—one day in the life of Charlie (Gary Burghoff) and his friends. All the well-known figures were present: Charlie, of course, Lucy (Reva Rose), Linus (Bob Balaban), Schroeder (Skip Hinnant), and even the dog Snoopy (Bill Hinnant). The vignettes depicting them followed no real pattern, seeming almost as haphazard as their childish world. After an opening paean to Charlie ("You could be King./If only you weren't so wishywashy)," Lucy dreams of being a queen and bossing the world ("Queen Lucy");

Linus sings of his need for his security blanket ("My Blanket And Me"); Snoopy plans to capture the Red Baron; a baseball game (where Charlie's teammates sing a rousing "T.E.A.M.") degenerates into a poll gauging Lucy's popularity. In the end the youngsters and the dog each give his idea of what true happiness is, with Charlie Brown concluding "Happiness" is "anyone and anything that's loved by you." Clark Gesner wrote both the libretto and the songs. Although nothing from the evening enjoyed a vogue outside the theatre, the show itself repeated something of the phenomenal success of the comic strip. Road companies were set up to tour regular-size legitimate theaters (one ran a year at the Wilbur in Boston), while the New York contingent tallied 1,597 showings.

1967–1968

The parade of mediocrities continued. One new revue and eleven new book shows presented themselves for New York's evaluation. Almost without exception they received low grades. The single runaway hit of the season, *Hair*, began promisingly downtown, caught on uptown because of sensational publicity accorded a nude scene, and ultimately settled down to a long run when its superb score received wide play. Yet for all its deserved success, it was far from flawless. Among the other musical offerings only *George M!* managed a full year's stay. It survived largely on the appeal of its turn-of-the-century Cohan melodies and, to a lesser extent, the performance of Joel Grey in the title role. Star performances were the only explanation for the season's two other relatively long runs. All in all, a sad year for the American Musical Theatre—uptown. But *Hair* was not alone in providing off-Broadway with exciting new ideas for the lyric stage. Throughout the season, small, out-of-the-way houses raised their curtains on innovative, satisfying musicals that put the big time to shame.

The season began with the promised English translation of *Sing Israel Sing*. The new language infused no new life into the show. One additional week was all it could garner.

The Music Theatre of Lincoln Center revived *South Pacific* (7 April 1949) with Florence Henderson and the Metropolitan Opera's Giorgio Tozzi on 12 June and ran it until 9 September for a total of 104 performances. Ominously, inflationary costs had prompted the dropping of a two-show season.

When *Sweet Charity* ended its stay at the Palace, the great old flagship of vaudeville spent the summer months, while waiting for its next legitimate offering, hosting a number of contemporary vaudeville bills. The *Best Plays* volume for the year lists them as revues—and indeed they were little different from the one-man shows that recently had played standard auditoriums. But vaudeville at the Palace, if only for sentimental reasons, stands somewhat apart. For the record, headliners included Judy Garland, Eddie Fisher, and Buddy Hackett. Marlene Dietrich competed with them across Times Square at the Lunt-Fontanne.

While Broadway bided its time, off-Broadway came alive. The mushrooming protest against the Vietnam War was the theme of **Now Is the Time for All Good Men** (26 September 1967, de Lys), a musical that occupied the same stage so long given over to *The Threepenny Opera*. The new work followed the downfall of a popular young teacher, Mike Butler (David Cryer), after the small, conservative town of Bloomdale, Indiana, discovers he has been imprisoned for refusing to fight. The show was perhaps more preachy than entertaining, but Greenwich Village proved far more sympathetic to its outlook than Bloomdale might have, so the show ran to 31 December. In a few weeks *Hair*, preaching much the same message, would elicit a more enthusiastic response.

Broadway had no interest in preaching, but its very first major musical offering suggested it had little ability to entertain either. Nunnally Johnson, so long successful in Hollywood, adapted his daughter Nora's novel *The World of Henry Orient* first into a film and then into a stage musical, calling the latter **Henry, Sweet Henry** (23 October 1967, Palace), with music by Bob Merrill and with Don Ameche as star. The sweet Henry of the title is an unattached man-about-town who finds his footsteps dogged by a lonesome, neglected, infatuated teenager, Valerie Boyd (Robin Wilson). For the ten weeks the show survived some of the biggest applause was awarded to Alice Playten, who clowned her way through the evening as a second teenager, the brattish Kafritz.

Over a month elapsed before another major mounting appeared uptown. But off-Broadway was bursting with energy and song. *Hair* was unveiled for a limited run on 29 October at the New York Shakespeare Festival's Public Theatre. It received generally favorable notices, and theatregoers responded in sufficient numbers to move it to a second small off-Broadway house until the end of January. By that

time demand for seats had reached the point where a run in a larger uptown Broadway house was called for. The show was closed, expanded, and revised. It will be treated more fully under its Broadway opening.

In Circles (5 November 1967, Cherry Lane) was an offbeat revue based on Gertrude Stein material and with music by Al Carmines. One critic described it as "A complex arrangement of word, song and dance effects, each one conceived as describing its own circles." Carmines became one of the most praised and sought-after of off-Broadway composers, but unlike so many of his associates he never earned the affection of the public at large nor succeeded uptown. He did, however, prosper handsomely with the new show, which ran out the season.

World turmoil and the decline of theatrical creativity sent many benumbed and bored playgoers in search of the joys and certainties of the good old days, even if they were the good old days of the Depression. Since Hollywood was not given to burlesquing its old movies, off Broadway took it upon itself to do the job. The first of several musical plays kidding screen musicals of the thirties attacked one of the most obvious targets, Shirley Temple. **Curley McDimple** (22 November 1967, Wheeler) spent the evening spoofing the inanities of the child star's films so well it compiled a run of 931 performances before New York would let it go. Bayn Johnson was Curley.

When Broadway finally got around to unveiling its second major new musical of the season, it did at least offer something of a rarity—a show based on an "original idea." Regrettably its setting, the world of Wall Street, and its title, **How Now, Dow Jones** (7 December 1967, Lunt-Fontanne), seemed suspiciously close to *How to Succeed in Business Without Really Trying* (14 October 1961). Even more regrettably, it wasn't a particularly well-written piece. The original idea, however, was the sort that had propped up many a show in a less demanding day. Charley (Anthony Roberts), a young man trying to succeed, has promised to marry his girl, Kate (Marilyn Mason), who works on Wall Street, just as soon as the Dow Jones average hits 1,000. Kate issues a report showing the figure has been reached, and it takes all of the second act to put things back in order. The show ran out the season, thanks in no small part to the determination of producer David Merrick.

The City Center gave New Yorkers a pleasant holiday gift with a low-priced revival of *Brigadoon*

(13 March 1947), with Bill Hayes and Russell Nype, that opened on 13 December and closed New Year's Eve. From 25 April to 19 May the Center mounted a repertory of Gilbert and Sullivan works that included *The Pirates of Penzance, H. M. S. Pinafore, The Mikado, The Yeomen of the Guard,* and *Patience.* Later the house closed the year by offering a revival of *The King and I,* with Constance Towers again Anna. The show had been revived four years earlier at Lincoln Center. Yet, though the City Center was soon to have no competition, it remained steadfastly in the rut of reviving the biggest hits of recent years. This repetition, as much as inflation, was soon to bring its quarter-of-a-century history to an end.

One more play with music appeared before 1967 went on its way. But **How to Be a Jewish Mother** (28 December 1967, Hudson) was no more a full-fledged musical than was its first cousin, *The Zulu and the Zayda* (10 November 1965). It was a two-character comedy, a series of sketches in which a middle-aged Jewish mother and a slightly baffled African American interact. Five songs were interspersed. It was also, in any case, a quick flop, leaving two fine performers, Molly Picon and Godfrey Cambridge, at liberty again.

The differences and similarities between the first off-Broadway show of 1968 and the first uptown production were revealing. In a sad, curious way the similarities loomed larger in the long run. Both followed the now almost universal practice of deriving their material from an old show. Both relied heavily for effect on the use of filmed projections. And saddest of all, but again typical of the modern American musical, both failed to produce a single song inventive and melodic enough to survive the show. But the off-Broadway show, like *Hair* before it, brought the latest musical sound, rock and roll, to the American Musical Theatre, while the big uptown production embraced, however feebly, more traditional idioms. Equally significant, the little show on the edge of Greenwich Village, using minimal sets and employing unknown performers, depended often on trenchant, relevant wit, while the mammoth mounting just off Times Square required stars to gloss over deficiencies.

The off-Broadway musical, **Your Own Thing** (13 January 1968, Orpheum), arrived first. A lyric adaptation of Shakespeare's *Twelfth Night,* it adroitly welded Shakespeare's story and some of his dialogue with the latest in teenage speech and rock music. In this retelling the action transpires in "Manhattan Island, Illyria," where Orson (Tom Ligon) is a theatrical agent and Olivia (Marcia Rodd) the operator of a discotheque. The confusion between Viola and her brother Sebastian seemed more understandable than it probably had been at anytime since Elizabethan days because of the long hair teenage boys were wearing during this period. In the show Viola (Leland Palmer) and Sebastian (Rusty Thacker), both rock singers who have been separated and have lost all their music in a shipwreck, coincidentally apply to the same agent when they seek work. Viola, informed that Orson requires a male singer for a rock group, dresses as a boy and calls herself Charlie. When Orson sends Charlie with a love letter to Olivia, the familiar complications ensue. In the end Viola is engaged to Orson and Sebastian to Olivia. Sebastian is not at all disturbed by Olivia's being a good ten years older than he. As he and his rock group, the Apocalypse, enjoin their listeners, "Do your own thing—or die." The use of photographs with voiced comments was one of the highlights of the production, brilliantly blending Shakespeare and pertinent contemporary asides. The very first slide showed Everett Dirksen, a Senate leader and flowery orator, while a voice not unlike his read the opening of *Twelfth Night*—"If music be the food of love, play on!"—only to add, "I can't remember if that's Marlowe or Bacon." Queen Elizabeth, Humphrey Bogart, Michelangelo's Sistine God, and John Wayne have a hilarious discourse, with Wayne lamenting he can no longer tell boys from girls because of the long hair. At the very end of the show, the Sistine God calls out to Jesus, and, when Christ responds, "Yes, Father?" God inquires, "When are you going to get your hair cut?" The show ran 933 performances at its small downtown house, but like *You're a Good Man, Charlie Brown,* road companies were sent out to play regular legitimate theatres. The companies established contemporary records on several of their stands.

The uptown show was **The Happy Time** (18 January 1968, Broadway), a musical rendering of Samuel Taylor's 1950 hit of the same name, which itself was based on a book by Robert L. Fontaine. It was another David Merrick production which ran as long as it did because of the producer's heavy publicity and timely forcing. Merrick was not aided by his authors, playwright N. Richard Nash and the songwriters of *Cabaret* (20 November 1966), composer John Kander and lyricist Fred Ebb. Their work was solid but uninspired. The story recorded the growing up and coming of age of young Bibi Bonnard (Mike Rupert) in the bosom of his loving, eccentric French-Canadian family. Because Robert Goulet and David Wayne were the stars, there was some change of emphasis from the straight play, but there was no change in its warm, affectionate tone. Goulet portrayed a footloose photographer whose recollections shaped the plot, while Wayne was the baffled but understanding paterfamilias. In a red top hat, Wayne stopped the show recounting his feats as a ladies' man in "The Life Of The Party." Gower Champion furthered the action with clever filmed sequences. In an urgent quest for novelty to mask a lack of quality, gimmicks such as eschewing an overture appeared. But they neither helped nor hindered the evening.

A small-scale "cabaret revue," with just four performers, devoted entirely to the songs and commentary of one man opened 22 January at the Village Gate. It was not the sort of entertainment one would expect to enjoy a long life, but the Belgian Jacques Brel had gathered about him so loyal, persuasive a cult that by the time **Jacques Brel Is Alive and Well and Living in Paris** closed it had run up an astounding 1,847 performances, making it the third longest engagement in off-Broadway history. The adoration accorded Brel is hinted at in the title. For at the time, when some theologians were asking, "Is God dead?" others were replying that God was alive and well in various locations. Mort Shuman helped adapt it and starred, but Ellie Stone was the performer everyone remembered.

On 27 January **Darling of the Day** (27 January 1968, Abbott) premiered. Taking as its source a somewhat unlikely prospect for musicalization, Arnold Bennett's *Buried Alive*, it retold in song and dance the courtship by mail of Alice Challice, widow of the valet of the famous artist Priam Farll, by none other than Farll himself. He stoops to conquer, assuming the identity of a valet. The book was originally credited to Nunnally Johnson, who had perhaps hoped to erase the demerit he received on his return to Broadway earlier in the season for *Henry, Sweet Henry*. But his latest adaptation proved even less stageworthy than his former. By the time *Darling of the Day* reached Broadway, his name had been dropped from the credits and the authorship of the book was left for the audiences to guess at. Composer Jule Styne and lyricist E. Y. Harburg allowed their names to remain on the program, although nothing they offered caught the public's fancy. By common consent the highlight of the evening was the desperate-faced, captivating clowning of the English comedienne Patricia Routledge as Alice. The popular screen actor Vincent Price was her leading man.

In the fourteen years that had passed since the original *House of Flowers* (30 December 1954) closed, persistent stories had blamed the show's failure on changes made during its Philadelphia tryout. Saint-Subber, the producer of the ill-fated venture, apparently agreed and retained enough faith in the Harold Arlen–Truman Capote work to chance a revival. Unfortunately, since the new production on 28 January was to be at the tiny off-Broadway Theatre de Lys, the evocative, lavishly praised Oliver Messel sets were not recreated. Five new songs were added. The show was coolly received and quickly closed, leaving unanswered whether the first mounting, before tinkering, had been as good as its boosters believed.

Steve Lawrence and his wife, Eydie Gorme, were still sufficiently potent drawing cards to let producers ignore Lawrence's unprofessional behavior during the stay of *What Makes Sammy Run?* (27 February 1964) and create a new vehicle for the couple, **Golden Rainbow** (4 February 1968, Shubert). Arnold Schulman's play of several seasons back, *A Hole in the Head*, was selected for adaptation. Moving the action from Miami to Las Vegas allowed for splashier, noisier production numbers, but the basic story remained. Larry Davis is a widower with two passions in life: his down-at-the-heels hotel and his young son, Ally (Scott Jacoby). But Larry stands to lose both. The hotel may be taken from him if he cannot meet a mortgage payment; his son may be given over to his sister-in-law, who has claimed Ally is not being given a wholesome upbringing. Much of Judy's vehement moralizing masks her love for her brother-in-law. Her real feelings are revealed in the course of the evening, and by curtain time she has given Larry the money he needs for the mortgage and accepted his proposal of marriage. Ernest Kinoy's libretto was workmanlike though it sacrificed some depth by concentrating on the stars. At least one of the songs for which Walter Marks wrote both words and music, "I've Got To Be Me," met with popular acclaim. The show ran just short of one year.

Two foreign offerings followed. **The Grand Music Hall of Israel** began a sixty-four-performance stay early in February, while *Les Ballets Africains* returned toward the end of the month to give fifty-five additional performances.

March's lone entry was a lyric version of John Steinbeck's novel *East of Eden*, retitled confidently

Here's Where I Belong (3 March 1968, Rose). New Yorkers didn't agree, and the piece closed ignominiously after just one showing. The authors were largely untried in the Broadway arena. Although they wisely attempted to cut down to workable size Steinbeck's vast romantic canvas of California farm country during World War I, concentrating on the father-and-son relationship between Adam Trask (Paul Rogers) and young Caleb (Walter McGinn), the material proved intractable in their inexperienced hands.

A number of other relatively inexperienced hands had only slightly better luck with **The Education of H*Y*M*A*N* K*A*P*L*A*N** (4 April 1968, Alvin), a musical version of Leo Rosten's collections of short stories. Set in New York on the Lower East Side across the country from *Here's Where I Belong*'s locale, but in almost the same era—the years immediately after World War I—the scenes depicted the eager efforts of a band of Jewish immigrants to make themselves at home in their new world. But again craftsmanship was wanting, and the appeal of Jewish themes was becoming a bit overexploited. Despite Tom Bosley's attractive performance as Hyman, the tailor, the new show lasted a mere three and a half weeks.

But the appeal of George M. Cohan and his songs of a happier Broadway was evident in long lines at the box office even before **George M!** (10 April 1968, Palace) opened. A loosely thrown-together biography of the great song-and-dance man, with a comparatviely small cast that found itself playing a number of roles, it nevertheless was at once reasonably faithful and, when Cohan's songs were being sung, enthrallingly entertaining. Unlike the film biography of Cohan, *George M!* had no qualms about portraying his first marriage. It moved from his early vaudeville to his initially cool reception, his triumph, and his sad disillusionment late in life. Unlike James Cagney, Joel Grey made no attempt to mimic Cohan's mannerisms. Though the *Times* saluted his performance as "sharp as a whiplash," dissenters missed Cohan's warmth. Cohan might have been better honored by an honest revival of one of his masterpieces, but with little competition around the public asked no questions, so *George M!* ran over a year.

The third and final new musical in April was **I'm Solomon** (23 April 1968, Hellinger), another Jewish theme by more inexperienced authors. It ran seven performances. There were a few departures in the show. For one, the setting was biblical, and, two, the authors, apparently aware of their own inadequacies, allowed interpolations—a policy virtually extinct in the American Musical Theatre. One number had lyrics by Erich Segal, a young scholar who went on to write the best-selling novel *Love Story*. The plot employed a folk motif as old as the musical setting—the look-alike commoner who substitutes for his king. In this case the commoner was Yoni (Dick Shawn), a cobbler in ancient Jerusalem whose resemblance to King Solomon (Shawn) allows the monarch to leave his throne and move among his people. Sadly, the show's failure deprived the theatergoers of a chance to savor Rouben Ter-Arutunian's scenery that poetically mixed Eastern with anachronistic Art Nouveau motifs.

The expanded, revised **Hair** reopened uptown at the Biltmore on 29 April. In every respect—commercial, historic, aesthetic—it was far and away the most important musical offering of the season, possibly of the era. And yet, inexplicably, it was in some ways a tragic failure. The book uptown first-nighters saw and the book played by the road companies and, in general, by the overseas editions was a decimated version of the already relatively plotless story told earlier downtown. Rambling, almost formless, if it had a central figure at all it was probably Claude (James Rado), a long-haired, sometimes bewildered rebel against what his hippie culture termed "the Establishment." Brooklyn bred, he romantically lies that he comes from Manchester, England—perhaps mistaking it as the home of the greatest of all rock groups, the Beatles. He billets himself in the small apartment shared by his friend Berger (Gerome Ragni) and Berger's girl, Sheila (Lynn Kellogg). His own girl, Jeannie (Sally Eaton), is pregnant with someone else's child. Problems of racial inequality, drugs, homosexuality, poverty, and free love rear their heads, often without motivation or connection with the plot, but long enough to allow strongly worded protests in song. Claude's pivotal dilemma is whether or not to burn his draft card and join the growing draft evasion movement. Puzzlingly, he elects to accept the Establishment's rules, allowing himself to be drafted. He is killed, and his friends gather to mourn his useless, unnecessary death.

At a time when tightly knit librettos were often propping up disappointing, unmelodic, or pretentious scores, the book for *Hair* represented a startling reversion to an older approach to musical theatre. It did follow the pattern of its day by offering some very imaginative, impressive staging. Indeed, staging was coming to outclass even librettos as the mainstay of the modern musical—a phenomenon in itself a reversion to the still earlier musical theatre of *The Black Crook* (12 September 1866) and the Kiralfys. Tom O'Horgan, called in to restage the production for uptown, filled the evening with theatric pyrotechnics. The show's most notorious scene placed a number of nude men and women at the front of the stage during the first-act finale. Flickering, relatively dim lights ensured that the scene was more sensational than revealing. At one point cast members dressed as policemen rushed down the aisles from the back of the house scaring more gullible patrons by announcing they were raiding the show. But the telling strength of *Hair* was its score—rich in melody and, more important, finally working a thoroughly contemporary musical sound into the Broadway mainstream. *Bye Bye Birdie* (14 April 1960) had employed some rock-and-roll sounds to tell a story in which a rock-and-roll star figured prominently, but its delightful score was, for the most part, doggedly traditional. *Hair* accepted no such compromise. From beginning to end Galt MacDermot's music and Gerome Ragni and James Rado's lyrics—all much expanded for the uptown version—utilized nothing but the chromatics, rhythms, and word patterns of the new form. Somehow, though, MacDermot's strong, memorable melodies imposed themselves over the incessant throbbings of rock orchestration, and even Ragni and Rado's lyrics, while a far cry from the polished rhymes of Broadway's masters, avoided pitfalls presented by the often languid, monotonous, and expository words to most songs in the style. The sweet, soft optimism of "Good Morning Starshine" and the more exulting hopefulness of "Aquarius" quickly attained universal recognition. In the show the irrelevant non sequiturs of "Frank Mills," in which an otherwise unimportant character named Crissy (Shelley Plimpton) stoically accepts the ups and downs of her teenage passion, were a nightly show-stopper. If the songs' lyrics seemed a bit odd and uncomfortable, it was because in this instance MacDermot had wryly set prose to music. The tremendous popularity of the show's music ultimately outweighed the scandal of the nude scene in accounting for the evening's success. For many staid, older playgoers in the audience *Hair* allowed a brief, vicarious participation in the protest movements of the sixties. *Hair* ran a total of 1,844 performances in its uptown and downtown engagements, three less than *Jacques Brel*. But there was of course no comparison. *Hair* played a large, regular theatre

for all but the first three months of its life, and its numerous companies across the country and in foreign theatrical capitals generally played in the best houses. (Still it is noteworthy that the four longest-running musicals of the season were off-Broadway creations.)

In a very important sense, though, *Hair* was a failure, for it failed to usher in a new era in the American Musical Theatre. Though rock continued to dominate popular song for years to come, it played little further part on the Broadway musical scene. The contrast in this respect between *Hair* and, say, *Watch Your Step!* (8 December 1914)—which also suffered from a weak "book, if any"—or *Lady, Be Good!* (1 December 1924), is saddening. The fault cannot be laid at the feet of the new sound, however unthearical, unmelodic, and uninteresting it often seems. The authors of *Hair* proved this need not be the case. But, as with swing, Broadway had apparently grown too old and decrepit to embrace youthful forms.

Since Leonard Sillman was no longer the producer, but merely the director, some perverse Broadway politicking included his name in the official title of **Leonard Sillman's New Faces of 1968** (2 May 1968, Booth). The revue kidded everything from Greek tragedy (in "Hullabaloo at Thebes") to saccharine beauty pageants (in "Missed America"). The evening was not well received, and none of the new faces went on to become familiar faces on Broadway as had several performers in earlier editions. This edition was the last of the series, though there were promises every season or two of another until Sillman's death.

1968–1969

During the first months of the new season the American Musical Theatre seemed to be sinking deeper into the preceding season's mire. The escalation of the Vietnam War, the shock of President Johnson's decision not to run again, and the ensuing election campaign between Richard Nixon and Hubert Humphrey offered Americans more gripping if less diverting occupation. Not until the middle of November, just after the election, did Broadway come to life. In retrospect some of the excitement and success seems as much a reaction to months of mediocrity as witness to any genuine overriding merit.

The summer months and early fall were rife with revivals. June saw mountings of *My Fair Lady* (15 March 1956) with Fritz Weaver and Inga Swenson at the City Center and *West Side Story* (26 September 1957) at the New York State. The Lerner and Loewe masterpiece recorded an additional two and a half weeks, while the Laurents-Sondheim-Bernstein opus ran until September. In December the City Center revived *Carnival* (13 April 1961), with tiny Pierre Olaf recreating his poignant role.

Noël Coward's Sweet Potato (29 September 1968, Barrymore), a revue anthologizing some of Coward's best material, chalked up forty-four showings in two slightly separated engagements.

October was busy although not especially fruitful. In the first week of the month Marlene Dietrich and Gilbert Bécaud brought back their one-man programs, the quasi-legendary Miss Dietrich far outrunning M. Bécaud.

A Yiddish-English musical, **The Megilla of Itzik Manger,** arrived from Israel and pleased a specialized audience for two months at the small John Golden Theatre. The musical took the biblical story of Esther and transplanted it in a European shtetl.

The season's first original American musical was neither very original nor 100 percent Yankee, being a musical version of George Bernard Shaw's *Caesar and Cleopatra.* Rechristened **Her First Roman** (20 October 1968, Lunt-Fontanne), it had book, lyrics, and music by Ervin Drake, another relatively inexperienced hand. Richard Kiley moved over from playing Don Quixote to portray Caesar, while the young, black Leslie Uggams impersonated Cleopatra. As in Shaw's comedy, the sometimes naïve, sometimes wily queen has a brief one-sided romance with the great emperor and in the end must accept his promise to send her a handsome young soldier named Marc Antony. If the producers were hoping the great Shaw would provide the basis for another *My Fair Lady* (15 March 1956), their hopes were quickly dashed. *Her First Roman* folded after two weeks.

A second new musical by unknowns, **Maggie Flynn** (23 October 1968, ANTA), fared only a little better. Its story reflected the same racial ecumenism as its casting and the casting of *Her First Roman.* Set at the time of the Civil War draft riots, when Irish protesters lynched blacks and destroyed property, it followed its heroine's attempts to save her orphanage and its youthful Negro wards. She not only succeeds, she finds time for romance with a fellow Irishman, Phineas (Jack Cassidy). Thanks largely to the presence of the popular actress Shirley Jones in the title role, *Maggie Flynn* survived for ten weeks despite its mediocrity.

October closed with a financially disappointing visit by the D'Oyly Carte, offering New Yorkers

H. M. S. Pinafore, Patience, The Mikado, The Pirates of Penzance, and *Iolanthe.*

The first long run of the season began just after campaign politics were set aside. A musical version of Nikos Kazantzakis's magnificently rich, vital novel *Zorba the Greek*—a novel which had already been translated into a popular motion picture— **Zorba** (17 November 1968, Imperial) represented the efforts of librettist Joseph Stein, lyricist Fred Ebb, and composer John Kander. Because they were professionals in a musical theatre increasingly trafficking in tyros, they devised a solidly crafted work that retained much of the original's juices. That their work was not their best was glossed over in a colorful, lively production, mounted and staged by Harold Prince. Boris Aronson's sets often relied heavily on black and white, so that a stylized green tree stood out dramatically. A Greek-like chorus led by Lorraine Serabian performed much the same function that the compère had performed in the team's *Cabaret,* and performed it with almost as much style and success. Added to this was Herschel Bernardi's dynamic performance in the title role. His life-embracing Zorba persuades young Nikos (John Cunningham) to reopen a mine he has inherited, but Zorba recklessly squanders the money Nikos has given him to purchase mine equipment. Nikos's sweetheart is murdered in a family vendetta. Neither failure nor tragedy daunts Zorba. He insists the only way to enjoy life is to accept whatever it offers. Though no song hit emerged, the "production values" were sufficient to allow the show to run nine months.

Promises, Promises (1 December 1968, Shubert), an even better and more successful musical, compiled a run of 1,281 showings. This time the source was a popular movie, *The Apartment.* Once again top professionals provided the adaptation. Broadway's most successful playwright, Neil Simon, created the book, and Hal David put words to Burt Bacharach's thoroughly contemporary music. Bacharach was the best known of the younger generation of songwriters, although he was a comparative stranger to Broadway. Simon remained faithful to the original Billy Wilder and I.A.L. Diamond story of Chuck Baxter (Jerry Orbach), a young executive who hopes to speed his rise to the top of the corporate ladder by lending the key to his bachelor's apartment to his bosses. When Fran Kubelik (Jill O'Hara), one of the young women brought to his digs, attempts suicide there, Chuck finds he must bring her to her senses in more ways than one. Naturally, romance follows. He succeeds with the help of a wisecracking Jewish doctor who luckily rents the neighboring apartment. *Variety* praised Orbach as "superb," describing his interpretation as "half slickie, half schlemiel, but always endearing—especially in a funny series of audience asides Simon has created for him." Bacharach's score contained at least two songs that enjoyed an immediate popular vogue, the title number, sung by Chuck just before the finale, and Fran and Chuck's "I'll Never Fall In Love Again."

The two big Broadway musicals were followed by the major off-Broadway success of the season, **Dames at Sea** (20 December 1968, Bouwerie Lane). A spoof of old Ruby Keeler and Dick Powell movies, it had begun life some years before as a short cabaret sketch, and by the time it reached the Bouwerie Lane had been stretched into a two-hour entertainment with a cast of six and an orchestra of three. To make its twitting obvious it called its heroine, a tap dancer from Utah, Ruby (Bernadette Peters), and its hero, a song-writing sailor, Dick (David Christmas); Ruby gets a part in a Broadway musical with a nautical theme. Its star, Mona (Tamara Long), wangles an opening night on a battleship. Mona also tries to wangle Dick's songs away from him and Dick himself away from Ruby. But when she gets seasick on opening night, Ruby takes over, becomes a star, and captures Dick permanently. The evening was filled with thirtyish touches: umbrellas opening and shutting in musical numbers, tap dances that moved up and down steps, and dialogue such as "your name is gonna go up in lights." Like *Curley McDimple* the preceding season, *Dames at Sea* was the sort of travesty Hollywood might better have done about itself had it been willing. As it was, the musical proved the only major lyric piece of interest in an off-Broadway season that was a marked comedown from the year before. It achieved a run of 575 performances.

A member of Actors Equity from the age of nine, **BERNADETTE PETERS** (née Lazzara) was born 28 February 1948 in Ozone Park, New York. She made her Broadway debut at ten in *The Most Happy Fella* at the New York City Center. Featured off-Broadway roles in *The Penny Friend* (1966) and *Curley McDimple* (1967) followed, leading to the roles of Josie Cohan (opposite Joel Grey) in *George M!* and Ruby in *Dames at Sea* (both 1968).

The year 1969 began on a dismal note. **The Fig Leaves Are Falling** opened at the Broadhurst on 2 January and closed on 4 January. During its half week it recounted the problems in Harry and Lillian Stone's marriage brought about by Harry's flirtation with his secretary, Pookie (Jenny O'Hara). Even the performances of Barry Nelson as Harry and the fine singing comedienne Dorothy Loudon as Lillian were to no avail.

The critics, if not the public, found themselves happier with January's second musical, **Celebration** (22 January 1969, Ambassador). Written by Tom Jones and Harvey Schmidt, who had created off-Broadway's long-running *The Fantasticks* (3 May 1960), it was an allegorical parable. Its narrator-hobo-confidence man, Potemkin (Keith Charles), falls in with Orphan (Michael Glenn-Smith), a young boy who has fled from an institutional home as it was about to be demolished, taking with him a stained glass "Eye of God." Orphan is seeking to recreate the garden he so loved at his orphanage. Together Potemkin and Orphan attend Rich's New Year's Eve party. Rich (Ted Thurston) laments that he was once young, innocent, and happy, but that now he is bitter, impotent, and surrounded by artificiality. Both Rich and Orphan fall in love with Angel (Susan Watson), a girl longing to be somebody, who has been hired to entertain at the party. Somehow Orphan obtains his garden and there seduces Angel before Rich's eyes. Before the vengeful Rich can retaliate, Potemkin initiates a ritual battle between winter and summer in which Rich is destroyed. The sun shines on the young victors as Potemkin sings, "Every day—Make a celebration." The production had only the four principals, a small chorus of masked "revelers," and an even smaller on-stage orchestra of percussion and strings, but it could not draw enough attendance to run beyond fourteen weeks.

January's last musical was a show that had been produced successfully in Atlanta. It revolved around Lester Maddox, the Georgia restaurant owner who attained national prominence when he used an ax handle to keep blacks out of his establishment and who later was elected governor of the state. **Red, White and Maddox** (26 January 1969, Cort) took Maddox (Jay Garner) on to the presidency of the United States and allowed him virtually to destroy the nation. The satire seemed funnier closer to home. New Yorkers could not foresee that in a number such as "The Impeachment Waltz" the spoof was touching on an issue that would later become a national tragedy. *Red, White and Maddox* survived only forty-one performances on Broadway.

Still another disappointment was the London hit **Canterbury Tales** (3 February 1969, O'Neill). Its New York run of 121 showings fell far short of its long West End stay, despite a fine cast led by Martyn Green, Hermione Baddeley, and George Rose. Chaucer's pilgrims became characters in the four bawdy stories retold: "The Miller's Tale," "The Steward's Tale," "The Merchant's Tale," and "The Wife of Bath's Tale." Curiously, another musicalization of Chaucer had opened off-Broadway the preceding week. **Get Thee to Canterbury** (25 January 1969, Sheridan Square) fared even more poorly, closing after twenty showings.

A fourth interesting failure was **Dear World** (6 February 1969, Hellinger), a lyric version of Giraudoux's *The Madwoman of Chaillot.* Countess Aurelia (Angela Lansbury), the Madwoman of Chaillot and her cronies—the Madwoman of Montmartre (Jane Connell) and the Madwoman of the Flea Market (Carmen Matthews)—confound the saner rich men and help the course of true love. Jerry Herman's title song repeated the title as often and effectively as he had the titles of *Hello, Dolly!* (16 January 1964) and *Mame* (24 May 1966), although the song failed to catch on. Neither Herman, librettists Jerome Lawrence and Robert E. Lee, nor Miss Lansbury could recapture the peculiar magic of the 1948 production. *Dear World* departed after 132 performances.

1776 (16 March 1969, 46th St.) was the season's second major success. Its tremendous success, indeed, its very success, came as a surprise to much of Broadway's smart money. Its librettist, Peter Stone, had been represented on Broadway only by his work on two failures, *Kean* (21 November 1961) and *Skyscraper* (13 November 1965). Its composer, Sherman Edwards, had never been heard from before. Even more dubious than the work's virtually unknown authors was its subject, the great debate leading to the signing of the Declaration of Independence. What the doubters overlooked was that a great debate is always good theatre. Luckily, Edwards and Stone approached the problem with intelligence and integrity. They eschewed all the standard formulas for easy entertainment. There were no toe-tapping melodies or high-kicking choruses. The one tune that bordered on being a love song was kept at arm's length by lyrics such as "Soon, madame, we shall walk in Cupid's grove together."

The evening's most poignant moment came when a bedraggled young courier interrupted the convention to describe the ardors of war in "Momma, Look Sharp." To build dramatic tension there was no intermission. Adams (William Daniels), Franklin (Howard da Silva), Jefferson (Ken Howard), and the other founding fathers came alive in the give-and-take of its arguments. At the end the delegates stepped up one by one to sign the Declaration, slowly fading behind a projection of the document while the Liberty Bell tolled. For many, Daniels's stiff-necked but appealing Adams was the evening's hero. The reward for high-mindedness was a run of 1,217 performances, just sixty-four less than that of the more obviously commercial *Promises, Promises.*

The rest of the season ran downhill. Three of the four remaining shows stayed less than a week, the fourth hardly much longer. Two nights after *1776* premiered, Ray Bolger returned to Broadway in a picaresque musical called **Come Summer** (18 March 1969, Lunt-Fontanne). Set in the Connecticut River valley in 1840, it followed Phineas Sharp, a peddler, and his young friend, Jude Schribner (David Cryer), on their peregrinations. Though Agnes de Mille choreographed a poetic lovers' idyll and a stirring loggers' dance, and Bolger had a show-stopping routine in "Feather In My Shoe," dancing aside, the evening had little to offer.

The same week saw the one-performance run of a pretentious musical version of Melville's *Billy Budd* entitled simply **Billy** (22 March 1969, Rose). Like *1776*, it was performed without intermission. But lacking that work's merits, it seemed all the more tedious for the lack of a breather.

A third show to be performed without intermission was **Trumpets of the Lord** (29 April 1969, Atkinson). An anthology of sermons and hymns tied together in a supposed black revival meeting, the musical had enjoyed some success off-Broadway in 1963–1964. It had clearly exhausted its appeal there, for it could eke out only a single week uptown although it had enjoyed a notable pre-Broadway success at Ford's Theatre in Washington.

The season's last show was a strange hodgepodge of a musical, based on a Spanish zarzuela, *La Verbena de la Paloma.* Although its title was **Fiesta in Madrid** (28 May 1969, City Center), it was done in Spanish, leaving anyone not fluent in the language to guess at the details of an apothecary's fling with two young ladies. So peculiar an offering done so late in the year was foredoomed.

of modern musical stages. Act Four brought these early efforts to prolific fruition. Act Five introduced a new totality and a sometimes too conscious artfulness into the musical theatre. Act Six, which, like the two preceding acts, can be divided into two scenes, boasted no such incontestable unity. In spite of the appalling amount of dross, three, possibly four styles of modern musical theatre dominated the act.

That questionable "fourth" style is not actually a style, but rather is a reflection of the way Broadway musicals came to be created in this period. First of all, it is a reflection of the paucity of fine composers active in the theatre. With the exception of Stephen Sondheim, who will be discussed in the next paragraph, Cy Coleman, hard-luck Charles Strouse, and possibly Jerry Herman, Broadway no longer had melodists willing or able to supply it with a sustained, memorable parade of scores. The musical theatre's towering master, Richard Rodgers, died at the end of this act's first scene. Arthur Schwartz, Harold Arlen, Frederick Loewe, and Irving Berlin, all long out of the picture, died in 1984, 1986, 1988, and 1989, respectively. A still very young Jerry Bock withdrew from the arena as the new act opened, while an older Jule Styne seemed to have retired quietly midway in the act. Harold Rome, who expressed eagerness to write more musicals, was not granted opportunities. As a result Broadway relied more on its librettists, lyricists, and directors. One leading lyricist-librettist, Alan Jay Lerner, said during this time that a good book made a show a hit, while a great score allowed the show to live on. Unfortunately, even Lerner, who died in 1986, hit a fallow period before his death. Since he was not alone in encountering creative difficulties, directors became especially important. Hal Prince became the guru of the "concept musical," in which a directorial subtext was woven into a musical's fabric and colored its mounting. Thus, according to Broadway scuttlebutt, the grim picture of the industrial revolution that added a special dimension to the original production of *Sweeney Todd* was Prince's, not Sondheim's, contribution to the evening. More intriguing, choreographers took over directorial as well as dance chores to impose their stamp on modern musicals. Distinguished director-choreographers such as Gower Champion, Bob Fosse, Michael Bennett, and Tommy Tune were notably significant, sometimes assuming dictatorial creative control—originating the very ideas for their musicals and molding their entire development. No fewer than four books have appeared detailing the genesis and growth of *A Chorus Line* under

Bennett's authoritarian hand. Their work was fresh, theatrically brilliant, and, for a time, ongoing. But Champion died in 1980, Bennett and Fosse in 1987. Moreover, splendid as their work was, it largely died with them. Scores and texts can be published, but the inspiration that a great director brings to a production, the careful nuances of pacing and movement, cannot readily be handed down.

The most fascinatingly intellectualized of all Broadway musicals have been those of Stephen Sondheim. They are essentially *sui generis*. No one has been able to imitate them successfully. Sondheim's songs often take repeated hearings to appreciate fully and to like. They and the books of his collaborators offered precious little escapism. The shows' characters confronted unpleasant choices, then frequently lamented the roads they didn't take. Life, as these shows saw it, was awash in bittersweet ambivalence, with the emphasis on the bitter. Some critics have accused Sondheim of being misanthropic, a charge he has denied passionately. But whether in response to these charges or for other reasons, his later works have been perceived as a mite sunnier, perhaps providing a fragile optimism. In production, all adhered to the modern penchant for spectacle (the act's most important, retrogressive trait). In Sondheim's shows spectacle served as a frame for emotional studies which ultimately, if indirectly, commented on contemporary social problems.

The second group of shows (considering Sondheim's and not the directors' as the first) were old-fashioned in their quest for pure escapism. The period's revivals and retrospectives suggested all was not happy in the modern theatre. Of course, revivals from every bygone period should be a part of any vigorous theatre's agenda. But audiences came away from *No, No, Nanette; Irene;* and *Me and My Girl* transported into a giddier world and often ruing that more such diversions weren't common fare. Retrospectives are a slightly different matter. The number of such skit-less revues, chock full of delicious old tunes, attested in another way to the demise of great songwriting on Broadway. Broadway in these years also saw one oddity, a new old show, *My One and Only*, which, by the time it reached New York, had hung a new story on an old, augmented score.

The blockbusters of the act's second scene—and what blockbusters they were, commercially if not artistically!—were retrogressive in that they were importations, mostly from England. In this respect they harked back to Act One, when so many outstanding hits came from overseas. Two were by

Andrew Lloyd Webber, who earlier had enjoyed big, though not such humongous, successes with *Jesus Christ Superstar, Evita,* and *Joseph and the Amazing Technicolor Dreamcoat. Les Misérables* also came by way of London, but it was the work of Frenchmen, suggesting that perhaps the home of nineteenth-century opéra bouffe might also be able to provide entertainments for a show-starved Manhattan. Several of these shows began life as recordings. This, plus the rock influences they displayed, might have served as excuses for the miking and amplification employed when they were brought on stage. A large number of these musicals were sung-through, pop operas (really operettas) that surpassed even operettas and comic operas of yore in the extent of the musical numbers. In another respect many reversed the order seen in Sondheim shows by focusing on social problems and demonstrating the emotional responses only secondarily.

If a majority of these shows glossed over textual weaknesses with spectacle, that spectacle differed from nineteenth-century spectacle in important ways. Gone were the elaborately painted settings (regularly whisked into the flies or pulled into the wings to create an applauded "transformation scene"), gone were casts of a hundred or more, and gone were rank upon rank of gorgeous girls in eye-popping costumes. Rather the new spectacles were architecturally and electronically conceived, relying on movable towers and bridges, frequently loaded with electric lights and other apparatus, on turntables, and on what Hollywood terms "special effects" (witness candelabras rising out of the misty waters of the Paris sewers in *The Phantom of the Opera*). Casts shrank to a handful of players, and show girls all but disappeared.

And the theatre grew more and more expensive. Sometimes cruelly so. Top ticket prices for musicals rose to $55.00 (in the late summer of 1990 one incoming musical bruited to be contemplating a $100 top for the choicest seats). But given the national inflation and the even more preposterous inflation of costs on Broadway, where new musicals were now purported to be regularly budgeted in the upper seven figures, the cost of the best orchestra seats was not out of line. Indeed, it may be perceived as a comparative bargain. What ran amok and became totally out of hand was the cost of balcony seats (although "balcony" had turned into a dirty word, so balconies were now considered mezzanines). For many decades the cost of the cheapest seat in a Broadway theatre was pegged at

one-sixth, or one-fourth, or, at very worst, one-third of the top price. Thus, way back when ticket prices went no higher than $1.50 or $2.00 (and admittedly that's very far back—before World War I), the least expensive seats could be purchased for fifty cents and occasionally for less. At a time not that long ago, right after World War II, when many musicals commanded a $6.00 top, the upper reaches of the theatre were available for $1.00 or $1.50. But by 1990 a $55.00 top was often paired with a bottom price of $32.50 or $37.50. The healthy spread, which allowed students and those with small incomes to attend plays regularly, vanished. The counter argument was that "half price" tickets generally were available at the TKTS booth in Times Square. But buying tickets in this manner subjected would-be playgoers to the indignity not only of having to wait in a long line that often snaked its way circuitously around the block but also meant that they must be buffeted by rain, snow, winds, summer heat, or winter freezes. The relative comfort of a box office lobby was cynically denied them. Furthermore, those ticket-buyers who purchased their tickets at full price at the box office not infrequently discovered that they were sitting next to someone who paid far less, and sometimes that the purchasers of cut-price tickets were in better seats than theirs. No wonder so many once loyal playgoers deserted the theatre. In discouraging young playgoers from easy access to reasonably priced balcony seats the theatre was also failing to develop a new generation of theatregoers to replace old-timers dying off.

Demographics, as mentioned earlier, also played a part in affecting attendance. Large areas of New York and those cities which once served as major tryout or touring centers were no longer populated by the white theatregoers who had only a short ride (by car or in public transportation) to downtown playhouses. Huge sections of cities once home to the Irish and Jews, who for years constituted a disproportionate number of the theatregoing public, were now home to newcomers. Several seasons witnessed a happy surge in the number of black musicals, and these were patronized in turn by an impressively growing coterie of black theatregoers. But professionals complained privately that these same blacks rarely attended nonblack shows. For people who had settled in the suburbs, going to the theatre entailed traversing a greater distance, often through areas they once lived in and which they now perceived to be distressingly down-at-heel or even dangerous.

For all these reasons and others—ballooning prices, changing demographics, the comparative cheapness of film-house admissions, and the misconceived notion that television is a truly "free" entertainment—attending the theatre was less and less a casual affair, a pleasant chance to while away an evening or an afternoon. It became more of a special occasion or event. With this in mind, theatregoers were less willing to risk wasting their money on musicals of dubious merit. The "modest" hit became a rarity. Most musicals that did not open to generally laudatory reviews quickly posted closing notices—frequently folding as soon as dismissive criticisms appeared. Few that attempted to buck criticism (all too often that of a city's lone major surviving paper) faced an uphill struggle. As a result, the hits ran longer and in some cases turned into the blockbusters already mentioned. Although figures for total grosses rose annually they rose because of increasing ticket prices. Attendance moved up and down within a limited range. It was not a healthy situation. But for the time it was all we had. Lovers of the best our musical theatre can offer could only sit and wait—and hope.

SCENE ONE

Startlingly New, Delightfully Old, 1969–1981

1969–1970

A lone, appalling statistic betrays the ghastliness of the 1969–1970 season: Half of the new musicals—seven out of fourteen—ran a week or less. Three of these each closed after their opening nights. Of the remaining seven none was a runaway success, and two longer runs were attributable to the attractions' stars. Out of all the songs from all the shows, at best a single number—the title song of *Applause*—gave any promise of becoming a standard. Of course, Sondheim's songs for *Company* occupied a niche of their own.

Oklahoma! (31 March 1943) was revived by the Music Theatre of Lincoln Center on 23 June and ran until September with Bruce Yarnell as Curley and the *Wizard of Oz* witch Margaret Hamilton as Aunt Eller. This marked the sixth major revival of the work since its original production closed. Most of the revivals were produced at City Center or the Music Theatre. With Richard Rodgers and the New York

Opera coming to an amicable parting of the ways, *Oklahoma!* marked the end of the Lincoln Center series and, with the City Center having suspended its program, the end of over a quarter of a century of popular-priced revivals. It was gratifyingly appropriate that *Oklahoma!*, which inaugurated the great era whose works filled these revival bills, should consciously or otherwise have been selected to write "finis" to them.

Nothing further called the critics from the comfort of their firesides until 2 October when **The New Music Hall of Israel**, a revised version of the imported vaudeville that had played the Palace in 1968, returned for a two-month stay.

Three more weeks went by before the first new musical of the season appeared. **Jimmy** (23 October 1969, Winter Garden) was a lyric biography of New York's colorful mayor Jimmy Walker. Its untried authors based their work on Gene Fowler's *Beau James*, although material on Walker was easily accessible. They may have understood a pitfall ignored by a number of hands who, before and after, thought lives of famous figures automatically translate into good theatre. History that is fondly remembered or that comes alive on the printed page does not necessarily answer the requirements of dramatic structure. Oddly enough, Walker's life probably did. His meteoric rise and tragic fall set against a Charlestoning, gaudy jazz age seems almost a natural. However, the authors lacked the ability or know-how to handle the story. They wisely confined their libretto to the seven most vital years in the mayor's life, 1925–1931, framing the evening in Walker's embittered departure for Europe. Moreover, they peopled their cast with reincarnations of such celebrities at Eddie Dowling, Texas Guinan, Izzy and Moe, and, of course, Walker's mistress and eventual second wife, Betty Compton. A popular nightclub comedian, Frank Gorshin, was enlisted to portray the Mayor. The entertainment fell far short of becoming another *Fiorello!* (23 November 1959), surviving a mere eighty-four showings.

A figure as controversial to his contemporaries as Walker had been to the twenties provided the sole reason for possibly attending **Buck White** (2 December 1969, Abbott). Muhammad Ali (né Cassius Clay) was the champion (former) heavyweight prizefighter of the day. He chose to challenge Broadway in a musical version of *Big Time Buck White*, a play which described the turmoil that ensues when its militant black titular hero arrives to address the Beautiful Allelujah Days Society. All the action takes place at the society's meeting hall. Ali and the show, another by relatively inexperienced writers, went down for the count of seven performances.

The successful conversion of *Lili*, a film played to a background of a touring French circus, into *Carnival* may have prompted the first of the season's one-performance fiascos. As its name reveals, **La Strada** (14 December 1969, Lunt-Fontanne) was a musicalization of Fellini's popular motion picture, retelling the bittersweet romance of Gelsomina (Bernadette Peters) and Mario (Larry Kert) as their troupe wanders across lower Italy. The songs were by Lionel Bart, who, as far as Broadway was concerned, had written nothing but *Oliver!*

Coco (18 December 1969, Hellinger) fared much better. What its fate might have been but for the presence of Katharine Hepburn in the title role is unpleasant to contemplate. Like *Jimmy*, this slightly romanticized biography of the great fashion designer Gabrielle "Coco" Chanel was framed in a high point of Miss Chanel's life, her attempted comeback after World War II. But unlike *Jimmy*, the frame was expanded and actually embodied what insubstantial plot there was. Coco's comeback seems thwarted when the French press hands her scathing notices, but Americans from "Ohrbach's, Bloomingdale's, Best and Saks" save the day. A trite subplot injected a love interest between one of Coco's protégées and a young man. Alan Jay Lerner provided the book and lyrics, with his rhymes outshining his libretto as usual. The songs were by André Previn, a well-known young composer and conductor. They were undistinguished. Neither Chanel nor her associates were called upon to create the costumes; Cecil Beaton was enlisted for the chore. His dresses and gowns were as disappointing as the show itself. His gowns seemed far too feminine to suggest Chanel's elegant, slightly masculine lines. The show's obvious prop remained Miss Hepburn, who was on stage virtually from beginning to end, coasting through on her unique glamour. Ewen has perspicaciously compared the show to *Roberta*, another musical whose background is the world of high fashion. His conclusion is that *Coco* had all of *Roberta's* drawbacks and nothing to equal its enchanting Jerome Kern score. In dollars and cents the musical's record reveals what was happening to Broadway. The show cost close to a million dollars to mount (Paramount Pictures absorbed most of the charges); it could gross $128,000 a week with a break-even

mark of $80,000 (Miss Hepburn alone is reputed to have received $15,000 per). Although it ran 332 performances, it failed to recoup its investment.

January, like November, brought no new musicals. The two that arrived in February were among the season's disasters, but before they premiered the popular French singing star Charles Aznavour came in with a one-man program of song, offered in English as well as French. Both **Gantry** (14 February 1970, Abbott) and **Georgy** (26 February 1970, Winter Garden) were by inexperienced hands. *Elmer Gantry*, Sinclair Lewis's tale of a hypocritical, opportunistic, hard-drinking revival preacher (Robert Shaw) and his relationship with the evangelistic Sister Sharon (Rita Moreno) provided the source of the former. Lewis's powerful diatribe seemed more watery than boozy on stage; it folded after one performance. *Georgy* lasted half a week. Based on the novel and the well-liked movie *Georgy Girl*, the evening recreated the love and adventures of an independent-minded young Londoner (Dilys Watling). Her principal heartthrob is a man old enough to be her father, James Leamington (Stephen Elliot).

The abrupt closings of these shows, along with musicals such as *La Strada*, demonstrated the desperation that was masking both a lack of creativity and an absence of any new striking style to pursue. In general the public refused to sit through musicalizations of old novels never meant to be abridged into two-and-a-half-hours' traffic on a stage or of recent movies more at home on the less constricted screen. Yet the failures, as the records show, did little to discourage more of the same.

The Best Plays described Sam Shepard's **Operation Sidewinder** (12 March 1970, Vivian Beaumont) as "a grab-bag of episodes about a deadly military device in the form of a large mechanical rattlesnake." Hopi symbolism and scenes of violence were sprinkled through the evening, as were all or parts of twelve songs, two of them credited to Shepard himself. Nonetheless, the annual, in its categorizing of the season's offerings, listed the work, rightly, under "plays" rather than "musicals."

Operation Sidewinder aside, March was the busiest month of the season, bringing with it five more traditional new musicals. The first and the last were the most successful. Ossie Davis, aided by Philip Rose and Peter Udell, turned his 1961 comedy, *Purlie Victorious*, into a libretto for which Gary Geld wrote some appropriately light-hearted music. The flashback frame device so voguish during the year was again employed to recount the young preacher Purlie's return to his home in southern Georgia bent on improving the lot of his fellow blacks. His plans are opposed by the redneck Ol' Cap'n (John Heffernan), but Cap'n's son, Charlie (C. David Colson) has more liberal views and helps the minister. Purlie also wins the hand of Lutiebelle (Melba Moore). Much of the hilarious humor of **Purlie** (15 March 1970, Broadway) came at the expense of bigotry—such as the dismayed Cap'n's complaint that a college education only teaches students to mispronounce "nigger" as if it were spelled "negro." Funny as the show was, it was even better when it was rousing, and it was rousing from its opening revival hymn, "Walk Him Up The Stairs," to the hymn's reprise at the close. Purlie (Cleavon Little) added to the festivities singing "New Fangled Preacher Man," a gospel song set over "a series of rocking rhythmic breaks." The attractive, seemingly shy Miss Moore lit up the stage singing of her feelings for Purlie in "I Got Love." *Purlie* was such good fun it racked up 686 performances and toured successfully.

Growing outrage at the waste and stupidity of the Vietnam War was given vent in **Blood Red Roses** (22 March 1970, Golden), a plotless musical that chose to mask its fury by setting its action during the Crimean War. Queen Victoria, Prince Albert, Florence Nightingale, and Lord Raglan were all recalled from the past. But vitriolic assaults and a lack of inspiration prevented the evening from being in the least entertaining. It was removed from the stage after its initial showing.

Figures from the past were evoked again in **Minnie's Boys** (26 March 1970, Imperial), a musical biography of the young Marx Brothers and their famed mother. Once again nostalgia and sentimentality were no substitute for theatrical craftsmanship or inspiration. Although Groucho's son, Arthur, had a hand in the book, the evening was put together by still another contingent of tyros. The antics of the Marx Brothers themselves might have saved it by making it so zany no one would have noticed its flaws. Sadly the great clowns were either dead or too old to play themselves as young men. The young men who did, notably Lewis J. Stadlen as Groucho, avoided recreating the famous old Marx Brothers routines, settling instead for more impressionistic impersonations. Stadlen had one uproarious scene in which he substituted for Chico while still performing his own bit as Groucho. Shelley Winters played the loving, if pushy, Minnie. The show survived a slightly forced run of ten weeks.

But yet more experienced hands also could come a cropper. Leonard Spigelgass, Jule Styne, and Sammy Cahn learned this as they watched **Look to the Lilies** (29 March 1970, Lunt-Fontanne) succumb after twenty-five showings. Their musical was based on William E. Barrett's novel *Lilies of the Field*, which had been already used as the source of a popular motion picture. It told a tale of racial ecumenism in which Homer, a vagrant, hostile African-American, is persuaded by some New Mexican nuns to build them a chapel. The chapel built, he moves on. In his autobiography, Cahn placed much of the blame for the show's failure on the evening's Homer, Al Freeman, Jr., who Cahn believed couldn't act or sing. Not even Shirley Booth as the Mother Superior could overcome the problems his miscasting produced. Cahn admits his astonishment that he and Styne created "a show without one successful song coming out of it," but suggests "I, Yes, Me! That's Who!" might someday be given a second chance. He adds, "I'm especially proud of that song." The song was the very last number in the show and had to express the love which had developed between the Mother Superior and Homer.

Applause (30 March 1970, Palace), the season's biggest hit, was March's last offering. In the manner of so many shows of recent years, it was a lyric redaction of a successful film, the famous Bette Davis vehicle *All About Eve*, and in the manner of so many of the current season's shows it employed a flashback frame device. At the Tony Awards Margo Channing (Lauren Bacall), the preceding year's winner, presents the trophy to Eve Harrington (Penny Fuller). In the flashback a star-struck, unknown young Eve appears at the stage door of the theatre where Margo is playing, and before Margo realizes what she is doing the actress has all but adopted the youngster. Eve mimics Margo's every action and in no time has insinuated her way into the affection of all the people who are important in Margo's life. The wife of Margo's favorite playwright even arranges to strand the star in the country so that Eve, who has become Margo's understudy, can go on. The playwright himself, Buzz (Brandon Maggart), decides to write his next work for Eve. By the end of the evening Margo has accepted a proposal of marriage from her director, Bill Sampson (Len Cariou), the only one of her friends who has remained steadfastly loyal, and she has also accepted retirement. The solidly crafted libretto by Comden and Green sizzled with taut, bitchy give-and-takes. When Margo begins to suspect Buzz's affection for Eve, she charges her own performances have covered up his weak playwriting:

Buzz: You empty-headed, conceited bass fiddle! You're just a body and a voice! Don't ever forget—I'm the brain!
Margo: Till the autopsy, there's no proof!

Charles Strouse set Lee Adams's words to music and in the title song (sung by Bonnie Franklin as a bar waitress) came up with the most successful tune to emerge from a Broadway show during the season. Ron Fields, who served both as director and choreographer, kept the action sizzling, especially during a giddy scene in which Margo joins patrons at a gay bar in feeling punchy and bleary, "But Alive." Lauren Bacall's electric cavorting gave the show its biggest boost, propelling it to a run of 896 performances.

Hopes ran high for April's first musical, a lyric rendering of William Alfred's five-year-old blank verse drama, *Hogan's Goat*. Alfred himself helped with both the libretto and the lyrics, while Mitch Leigh, who composed the score for *Man of La Mancha* (22 November 1965), created the songs. The principals included some of Broadway's finest talents: Robert Weede, Helen Gallagher, Tommy Rail, and Joan Diener. Like *Man of La Mancha*, the new musical, **Cry for Us All** (8 April 1970, Broadhurst), was performed without intermission. It relentlessly followed the destruction of the promising political career of Matt Stanton (Steve Arlen) by Mayor Quinn (Weede). When Quinn reveals that Matt has hidden the facts of his first marriage, the argument that follows leads to the accidental death of his second wife, Kathleen (Miss Diener). The strength of the original play eluded the adapters, and the show closed after nine performances.

A revival of Sandy Wilson's spoof, *The Boy Friend*, began a disappointing run at the Ambassador on 14 April. Eight nights later **Park** (22 April 1970, Golden), a musical that had first seen the light of day at an experimental theatre in Baltimore, was delivered to New York for inspection. It was intimate, but pretentious, and New York didn't take to it. For five performances a young couple (Don Scardino and Joan Hackett) and an older couple (David Brooks and Julie Wilson) met in a park and talked out their problems.

The only musical of the season other than *Applause* to close with a profit was its last, **Company** (26 April 1970, Alvin). It was in some respects an oddball piece, as innovative as commercial Broadway was likely to get without tripping over itself. George

Furth's book had no plot. It was a chronicle whose action was framed by several birthdays in the life of its protagonist, a New York bachelor named Robert (Dean Jones), Bobby to his friends. His friends are blasé, jaded New Yorkers, one of whom, Joanne (Elaine Stritch), insists, "It's not the gift, it's the cost that counts." Bobby's visits to supposedly happily married couples prove disenchanting. At Harry and Sarah's, Bobby realizes that Harry (Charles Kimbrough) is an alcoholic and Sarah (Barbara Barrie) has become hostile and sniping. Bobby's married male friends insist marriage pulls one's emotions in two directions at once and that they are forever "Sorry-Grateful." At Peter and Susan's, Bobby discovers the seemingly blissful pair (John Cunningham and Merle Louise) have decided to get a divorce. David (George Coe) and Jenny (Teri Ralston) despair of keeping up with a younger crowd. Bobby escapes into a daydream about his girlfriends, only to hear them complain, "You Could Drive A Person Crazy." His men friends reassure him, "Have I Got A Girl For You!," and Bobby himself is certain "Someone Is Waiting." But Bobby's evenings with Marta (Pamela Myers), a kooky left-wing intellectual, and April (Susan Browning), an airline stewardess, suggest neither is the someone. At Bobby's next birthday he and his friends celebrate the joys of being "Side By Side By Side" and ask each other, "What Would We Do Without You?" Another year passes, bringing more meetings and more disillusionments, such as a slightly tipsy Joanne's toast to her bored fellow matrons, "The Ladies Who Lunch." When Bobby's next birthday rolls around, his friends arrange a surprise party—but Bobby never appears. A little reluctantly Bobby has decided to go his way alone. A single skeletonized set served on its various levels to house whatever byplay was transpiring. Stephen Sondheim created the songs. His melodies were intelligent and musicianly but, in the unfortunate pattern of the day, not demandingly memorable. His lyrics, however, were the high point of the evening, again confirming that he alone— possibly with Lerner at his best—was keeping alive the literate, brittle tradition of the old masters. One of his songs, "The Ladies Who Lunch," with which Miss Stritch won rounds of applause, remains for many playgoers their fondest memory of the show. Michael Bennett's novel choreography for "Side By Side By Side" took old-fashioned straw hats and canes and made "the hats slash the air and the canes slap the floor to stress the harshness of what is being stomped out."

The off-Broadway season produced nothing that promised to be any more memorable or enduring than the shows which raised their curtains in the big houses near Times Square. But in one respect there was a distinct, noteworthy difference. The majority of off-Broadway musicals gave forth with an unmistakably contemporary sound: rock. Despite the success of *Hair*, Broadway, with rare exceptions, was determinedly avoiding the idiom. But in the smaller houses *The Last Sweet Days of Isaac*, *The Me Nobody Knows* (to be discussed when it reaches Broadway in the next season), *Salvation*, *Mod Donna*, and others sang to the melodies and rhythms of the sound. In *The Best Plays of 1969–1970* Otis L. Guernsey devoted an entire chapter to excerpts from the lyrics of these shows, insisting, "The Rock Lyric is a literary form developed in this decade; as different from the June-moon cadences of our rose-colored memory as the Beatles from the Lombardo brothers." Of course he is correct about the difference, however unfair his adjective "rose-colored" and his recalling the Lombardos may be. Regrettably, he makes no attempt to define the new style. Rock lyrics tend to be prosey, quietly preachy, and given to folklorish repetitiveness. For those accustomed to the brilliance and precision of Cole Porter, Lorenz Hart, and Ira Gershwin they take some getting used to. One example Guernsey quotes from **Salvation** (24 September 1969, Jan Hus), a song called "In Between," runs:

> *You, I wanted you, in the mornin' and over again*
> *You, I wanted you, in the evenin' and over again*
> *And in between, and in between and in between*
> *I wanted all of your friends!*

A few regular off-Broadway composers, especially Al Carmines, stuck more closely to older traditions.

Off-Broadway shows tended to be more loosely constructed, with plots, when they had them, that defiantly rejected a boy-meets-girl formula. For example, **Sambo** (12 December 1969, Public), "a black opera with white spots," was essentially an accounting of black alienation from white society seen through the eyes of characters perverted from children's fairy tales, such as Untogether Cinderella and Jack Homey. **Mod Donna** (24 April 1970, Public) was a four-character piece in which a bored couple agree to exchange partners (while a chorus comments on the women's liberation movement and sexual exploitation). The treatment was a far remove from the light-hearted or elegant handling

similar stories had received in, say, *So Long, Letty* (23 October 1916) or *Apple Blossoms* (7 October 1919). *Salvation* was a revue principally satirizing the religious and moral extremes of the day. **The Last Sweet Days of Isaac** (26 January 1970, East Side) imprisoned a young boy and girl first in a stalled elevator, then in a jail. Even Carmines's **Promenade** (4 June 1969, Promenade), with a book by Maria Irene Fornes, spent the night mischievously seeing the world through the eyes of two prisoners, 105 and 106. The most successful off-Broadway musical was a revue called **Oh, Calcutta!**, its title a fanciful Anglicization of some French scatology. It was devised by the English drama critic Kenneth Tynan, and its contributors, besides Tynan himself, included Samuel Beckett, Jules Feiffer, and John Lennon (of the Beatles). Their material was at best lackluster. But from 17 June on the show packed the Eden Theatre (not long since the Phoenix) because so much of the piece was performed completely in the nude. What must have been the reaction of the ghosts of chorus girls in *The Black Crook* (12 September 1866), who had played just a few blocks away?

1970–1971

One discouraging season followed another. Statistically, the count of new musicals dropped still further. Eliminating revivals, moves uptown from off-Broadway, and Yiddish-tune shows that arrived in the fall, only nine new lyric pieces were unveiled. (By stretching definitions *Variety* was able to list a total of seventeen.) A number of shows, *Paul Sills' Story Theater*, for one, were straight plays interlarded with songs.

With both vaudeville and traditional revue dead, their components sometimes reappeared in isolated and extended offerings. An example was **Bob and Ray: The Two and Only** (24 September 1970; Golden). A decade or so earlier, Bob Elliott and Ray Goulding had gained national fame as Bert and Harry Piel in the Piel's beer commercials. Now they offered playgoers a whole evening of imaginary interviews with such hilariously inventive characters as the Komodo Dragon Expert, Chester Hasbrouck Frisbie, Dr. Mu, and Good Professor Groggins.

The potent Jewish influence on Broadway which stemmed from extensive, loyal patronage manifested itself conspicuously at the beginning of the season. The first new musical arrived nearly six months after the last musical premiere and celebrated the rise of the most important Jewish family of the modern era, The Rothschilds (19 October 1970, Lunt-Fontanne). Based on Frederic Morton's popular account of the clan, Sherman Yellen's book followed the fortunes of the family from their humble German beginnings to their powerful influence at the Congress of Vienna. Son Nathan (Paul Hecht) was sent to London and given the requisite love interest in the second act. The Rothschilds's songs were by Jerry Bock and Sheldon Harnick, who together had been responsible for the songs in Fiddler on the Roof (22 September 1964), still running at the time their new show premiered. The new melodies lacked the fiber and melodic inspiration of their earlier material; not a single hit emerged. For many the high spot of the evening was the performance of Keene Curtis, impersonating several of the historic figures who crossed the Rothschilds' paths, from Prince William at the beginning of the show to Metternich at the end. But Hal Linden as Meyer Rothschild was equally fine, walking away at the end of the season with a Tony Award. Advance interest and lack of stiff competition enabled the musical to run out the season.

Light, Lively and Yiddish, a Yiddish musical with an English-speaking compère, and **The President's Daughter,** which mixed English and Yiddish dialogue, followed in late October and early November. Both found limited markets.

Probably the most eagerly awaited musical of the season was **Two by Two** (10 November 1970, Imperial). As it had in The Rothschilds, Jewish lore provided its story. But in this instance the material was of somewhat more universal appeal, since the evening was a recounting of the Old Testament's legend of Noah. Peter Stone's book leaned heavily on Clifford Odets's The Flowering Peach, which Menasha Skulnik had starred in during the 1954–955 season. Expectations ran high for two reasons. First, the new show's score was by Richard Rodgers. Second, the musical was to bring Danny Kaye back to Broadway after several decades' absence. Stone, who had written the solidly competent book for 1776 (16 March 1969), wrote a reasonably serviceable libretto for the new piece. It discovered the pious Noah obeying God's commandments in a world increasingly remote from God. Noah cannot even impart his piety to his sons and their wives. Their father's pleas to build an ark to ride out the coming flood are met with derision. Noah finally succeeds in building the boat and gets his family and the world's animals on board before the rain begins. Noah's rescue

deepens his religious convictions. That his God would stop to create and save so small a living thing as a tiny bird fills the old man with wonder. Regrettably, Rodgers's score, like the book, was no more than serviceable. Martin Charnin wrote the lyrics for the songs, the best of which was supposed to be "I Do Not Know A Day I Did Not Love You." It remained for Kaye to sustain the evening, and he did, in a way that infuriated Rodgers. Shortly after the opening Kaye tore a ligament in his leg. Once out of the hospital he returned to perform in a wheelchair or on crutches. Disregarding the text and staging, he turned Two by Two into what Rodgers disgustedly termed "one-by-one vaudeville." His antics probably saved the show, which he kept going for just short of a year and which closed with a small profit.

In the preceding May an unusual musical had opened off-Broadway. **The Me Nobody Knows** (18 December 1970, Hayes) took its lyrics and dialogue from the writing of underprivileged schoolchildren in the greater New York City area. Though the adapters necessarily revised substantial portions of the material, they left four poems untouched: "Fugue For Four Girls," "Rejoice," "The Horse," and "War Babies." Essentially a revue singing a song of sociological significance, it possessed a fetching blend of worldliness and naïveté that aided its young performers in compiling a record of 586 performances.

The long-run hit of 1953, The Teahouse of the August Moon, was the source of **Lovely Ladies, Kind Gentlemen** (28 December 1970, Majestic), which appeared after an extended transcontinental tour. The evening again recounted the stratagems employed by the wily Sakini (Kenneth Nelson) to build a teahouse for his fellow Okinawans during the American occupation. Sakini had the sometimes helpless sympathy of young Captain Fisby (Ron Husmann) as both took on the doltish, befuddled old army man, Colonel Purdy (David Burns). At one point the almost completed teahouse has to be taken down. But by the end of the night it sits serenely in its Japanese garden. If Sakini was a latter-day Sultan of Sulu, his show was not. Musicalized, as were so many of the shows of the period, by generally untried or uninspired hands, it sat lumberingly on the stage. After two weeks the teahouse was dismantled for good.

On 12 January 1971, the Ritz Theatre, for years given over to radio and television, returned to the legitimate fold with "a rock opera," **Soon.** Its story followed an ambitious rock group in its climb to the top. Early success and drive bring them quickly to

New York, but club dates and recording sessions show them some ugly aspects of the professional musical world, and they soon take to the road again. The show itself never took to the road. It folded after three showings, leaving the small, old Ritz seeking a new tenant.

Broadway's huge Jewish market was tapped again when **Ari** (15 January 1971, Hellinger), a musical version of Leon Uris's Zionist novel *Exodus*, premiered. Uris himself adapted the book and wrote the lyrics. Walt Smith composed the melodies. Both men were novices on the Broadway musical scene, and their labors were inept. David Cryer played Ari Ben Canaan, whose attempt to lead a band of Jewish refugees out of Cyprus and into Palestine was withdrawn after nineteen representations.

A revival of *No, No, Nanette* (16 September 1925) proved the biggest hit of the year, even before it opened at the 46th Street on 19 January. When the show went into rehearsals, songs not in the original were added and a substantially revised book was in hand. By some curious theatrical chemistry the interpolated songs disappeared during the tryouts, and the score first-nighters heard was, with a few discreet omissions, the same that had delighted first-nighters of forty-six years before. Though much of the dialogue was rewritten and some of the steeliest barbs inexplicably removed, the story hewed close to the original. Its carefree spirit, if not its cynical letter, was faithfully retained. Ruby Keller, Patsy Kelly, and choreographer Busby Berkeley made much-heralded returns to the stage. Miss Keeler, Jack Gilford, Helen Gallagher, Bobby Van, and a large, frenetically tapping chorus made this revival a dancing show such as Broadway hadn't thrilled to in years. Night after night the beloved old songs stopped the proceedings and elicited repeated encores. In this version "I Want To Be Happy" was sung by Jimmy (Gilford) and Nanette (Susan Watson), then rousingly danced by Mrs. Smith (Miss Keeler) and the chorus. Tom (Roger Rathburn) and Nanette once more embraced in "Tea For Two."

Nostalgia par excellence, the New York company rolled up 861 performances, far outrunning the original New York stay. Road companies thrived, although by and large their runs fell far short of runs the original's touring troupes enjoyed in the same cities. Yet, significantly, the show's great songs enjoyed no similar revival on the airways. Aging theatregoers might walk out of the theatre humming them, but rock and roll was virtually all radio and television wanted.

A week after this glorious bit of past nonsense regaled Broadway, the rage of off-Broadway, *Oh, Calcutta!*, moved uptown to the Belasco to continue its stay—nudes and all.

Neither February nor March brought any musicals, but a comparatively busy April began with the season's most interesting new musical, **Follies** (4 April 1971, Winter Garden). In one sense *Follies*, by hinting at the lavishness and tunefulness of the great old annuals, catered to the same craving for nostalgia that *No, No, Nanette* attempted to appease. But its very lack of prodigal opulence and endearingly memorable songs suggested how irretrievably far away that bygone theatre now was. *Follies's* loose, essentially plotless structure and its intelligent, if necessarily superficial, introspection suggested the inadequacy of contemporary alternatives. Although the show was highly praised and had a reasonably long, if slightly forced, run, it wound up in the red, and a projected road tour collapsed after several weeks. The show's initial $800,000 cost precluded a return on investment (none of Ziegfeld's far more opulent *Follies* ever cost even $300,000). The demolition of the Ziegfeld possibly suggested the story, which takes place in a partially torn-down theatre. A reunion of old-timers who had starred or played in the old "Weismann Follies" is in progress. Weismann, unlike Ziegfeld, was portrayed as still alive, and his shows were not said to go back as far as the real Follies, but the analogy was unmistakable. Most of the glittering figures have not aged well, nor have their late years been especially successful. The principal couples are Sally and Buddy Plummer (Dorothy Collins and Gene Nelson) and Phyllis and Ben Stone (Alexis Smith and John McMartin). Sally had loved Ben in their younger days. The reunion revives the old passions, but Ben had run away from Sally before and runs away again. The show was presented without intermission. Throughout the story "memory-figures" appeared in the background. (At least one real Ziegfeld favorite—Ethel Shutta—played a brief scene.) Often these "memory-figures" were merely gorgeously costumed chorus girls parading out of the past. Just as often they were youthful versions of the old-timers. Sally and Ben's memory-figures (Marti Rolph and Kurt Peterson), for example, reappear to relive their old heartbreaks as the older Sally and Ben attempt to handle rekindled ardors. Playwright James Goldman created the literate book that looked on unblinkingly as illusions were destroyed, and Stephen Sondheim did the songs. Sondheim's tunes were frequently gentle parodies of melodies that had graced long-gone shows, but his lyrics had the expected Sondheim brilliance, a brilliance lyrics from the old annuals rarely approached. One girl, describing the years that followed her Follies glamour, rhymed "Abie's Irish Rose" with "Dionne-babies, Major Bowes."

In a season turning desperately to the joys of another era, a revival of Paul Green and Kurt Weill's bleak musical tract *Johnny Johnson* (19 November 1936) was singularly ill-timed. Its first performance on 11 April was its last.

Sadly, a gay, harmless romp whose title recalled the advertisements for shows of Nanette's and Ziegfeld's days, **70, Girls, 70** (15 April 1971, Broadhurst), didn't survive much longer, less than five weeks. The show had been beset with problems on the road; its leading male comic, David Burns, died during the tryout. But its innocent tale of denizens from an old folks' home who set out to rob the rich and feed the poor was brought to life by a fine cast that included Mildred Natwick, Lillian Roth, Hans Conried, and Joey Faye.

A musical version of *Frank Merriwell's School Days* entitled **Frank Merriwell; or, Honor Challenged** (24 April 1971, Longacre) fared less well, running no longer than *Johnny Johnson*. The scenes were treated as chapters and given chapter headings such as "The Blow of a Coward," "Terror at the Junction," and "Death by Dynamite." It was a cute idea, but as close as its neophyte authors came to attractive innovation.

Earl of Ruston (7 May 1971, Rose) was the season's final musical. Only the third major show to employ rock, it met with the fate attending most rock shows uptown—complete failure. Again much of the problem stemmed from its authors' lack of experience. The librettists and lyricists, C. C. Courtney and Regan Courtney, claimed the story was a threnody for their cousin, Earl Woods, who spent most of his life in mental institutions. Both Courtneys played Earl during the voguishly intermissionless evening.

After Broadway closed up shop for the season, off-Broadway offered what proved to be its major achievement for the year. **Godspell** was a musical based on the Gospel according to St. Matthew, with a book by John-Michael Tebelak and songs by Stephen Schwartz. Originally performed at Café La Mama, the celebrated off-off-Broadway house, it moved to the Cherry Lane on 17 May and then uptown. It ran into 1977. A small cast costumed in Raggedy Ann style reinterpreted the Bible story

in consciously naïve, simplistic terms, singing and dancing to the strains of a minuscule orchestra. Schwartz's contemporary revival songs were typified by "Day by Day," introduced by Robin Lamont and company.

> **STEPHEN SCHWARTZ** was born in New York City on 6 March 1948. He began to study piano at the age of seven, and later majored in drama at Carnegie Tech. His first work on Broadway was the theme song for the 1969 play *Butterflies Are Free*. Young Schwartz also collaborated with Leonard Bernstein on the lyrics for Bernstein's *Mass*.

1971–1972

In one sense this was the most interesting, promising season since the end of the last great act. Three of its biggest hits sang out loudly and uncompromisingly in rock terms, suggesting that Broadway would finally manipulate the latest musical rage to its own advantage. Of the three long runs with rock scores, only *Jesus Christ Superstar*'s music had any strong appeal outside the theatre, while both *Jesus Christ Superstar* and *Grease* betrayed the formless librettos endemic among rock musicals. *Grease* also demonstrated that Broadway was embracing the "latest musical rage" when the rage was about to wane, for *Grease*'s songs reflected the rock-and-roll sounds of twenty years earlier at the time the idiom was first taking hold across the country. To this extent *Grease* fell in curiously with the "nostalgia craze" making one of its periodic reappearances. The preceding season's revival of *No, No, Nanette* had fueled the craze. *Grease* allowed a younger generation to recapture the sounds and joys of its youth. The season also saw a number of revivals that might have seemed part of this same need to recall the past. Significantly, at least one of the old shows brought back to life had never elicited affection in the first place. Its revival suggested rather that Broadway could on occasion exercise a surprising sense of responsibility.

A revival of a show too new to elicit twinges of nostalgia opened the season. *You're a Good Man, Charlie Brown* (7 March 1967) arrived at the tiny Golden Theatre on 1 June and ran out the month.

No further lyric pieces appeared until **Jesus Christ Superstar** (12 October 1971, Hellinger) exploded in a circus of gaudy color and amplified sound. Originally a wildly successful rock LP album, written and recorded in England, it recounted the last seven days of Jesus in contemporary terms. Tom O'Horgan, the pyrotechnical young director made famous by *Hair*, was responsible for bringing it very much alive on stage. Alone of the season's shows its music attained national popularity, though actually the music was well known long before the piece went into rehearsal. The uncanny blending of rock sound with revivalist fervor made Andrew Lloyd Webber's melody for the chorus's title song a momentary anthem, while Tim Rice's thoughtful lyrics, coupled with a second memorable Webber tune, helped spread the appeal of "I Don't Know How To Love Him," sung in the show by Mary Magdalene (Yvonne Elliman). *Jesus Christ Superstar* ran out the season, although complaints of irreverence and anti-Semitism were leveled at the show.

A second show to run out the year and into the next arrived eight nights later. Like *Jesus Christ Superstar*, **Ain't Supposed to Die a Natural Death** (20 October 1971, Barrymore) had been a recording before it became a show and, like *Superstar*, it was more chronicle than plot. Indeed it lacked even the thread of biblical narrative that tied Webber and Rice's work together. Its author, Melvin Van Peebles, was, like Webber and Rice, new to Broadway. A black bursting with things to say and the need to say them, he was to be heard from again later in the season. Although Peebles subtitled these vignettes of lower-class black life "Tunes from Blackness," he gave more emphasis to his words than to his melodies, insisting the lyrics be spoken rather than sung, so that their meaning would project more clearly. The show's nineteen numbers mirrored all sides of African-American life: yowling, griping, and defiance on the one hand, optimism and warmth on the other. Unfortunately, hostility prevailed. The show was framed in hatred. Its opening number, "Just Don't Make No Sense" (sung by Arthur French), complained, "Everybody be getting in the race to keep me in my place"; its last number found a harridan (Minnie Gentry) hoping to "Put A Curse On You." In its all-black cast, a policeman wore a white mask.

Having appealed to Christians and blacks in its first two fall offerings, Broadway almost inevitably turned to its large Jewish constituency, providing an Israeli revue, **To Live Another Summer, To Pass Another Winter**. Its small cast entertained at the Helen Hayes (normally given over to straight plays) until March. A second Israeli show, **Only Fools Are Sad,** was a November entry, running like its compatriot until March.

October's final offering was a lavish revival of Comden-Green-Bernstein's World War II hit, *On the Town* (28 December 1944). If the show had lost something of its timeliness, it lost nothing of its style and wit. Regrettably, its producers, although they were more intelligent and responsible than most of the breed merchandising revivals for Broadway, could not come up with performers to equal the originals—Nancy Walker, Sono Osato, or Comden and Green themselves. A second-rate cast deprived the show of the necessary élan and the ability to click. *On the Town* closed after seventy-three showings, a major disappointment.

November's only new American musical was **The Grass Harp** (2 November 1971, Beck), a lyric version of Truman Capote's novel. Capote's own dramatization had failed in 1952, and this musical version by two inexperienced hands was an even quicker failure twenty years later, running a mere week. As she had in the book and in the play, Dolly Talbo (Barbara Cook) takes to life in a tree-house to escape from the world and especially from what she believes are attempts by her sister to commercialize a dropsy cure. The show was yet one more musical falling in with the practice of omitting intermissions.

The play critics later proclaimed the best musical of the season, **Two Gentlemen of Verona** (1 December 1971, St. James), had originally been performed in the summer at Joseph Papp's outdoor New York Shakespeare Festival in Central Park. It was played now in a regular theatre on a brightly colored multilevel skeleton set with the theatre's rear wall painted "a luminous Mediterranean blue, a Botticelli blue, stolen from the sky behind Venus being born." In this modern-day lyrical rendering, Milan and Verona came to have a distinctly Puerto Rican tinge, not unlike *Romeo and Juliet* turned into *West Side Story* (26 September 1957). In this tale of a fickle gentleman who turns on both his friend and sweetheart, Raul Julia played the undependable Proteus. Galt MacDermot's music was good, although nowhere near as melodic nor as popular as his masterful *Hair* score. John Guare and Mel Shapiro did the book, and Guare alone composed the lyrics. His lyrics were often simplistic, one line merely repeating the word "love" nine times. Disgracefully, the repetitious, innocuous "love" gave way to unabashedly scatological lines. The show, for all its offensive passages, finally caught on, after meeting initial resistance from patrons, who resented a $15.00 top for much the same show that had been given free months earlier. During its run, however, *Two Gentlemen of Verona* exposed the lamentable state of musical production and talent on Broadway when a performance had to be canceled as a result of a breakdown of its amplification system. Singing in "live" Broadway shows was rarely fully "live" anymore.

More newcomers tried their hand at a Broadway musical and failed with **Wild and Wonderful** (7 December 1971, Lyceum). Though the show had an up-to-the-minute theme, telling of the CIA's attempt to infiltrate the youth movement, its ineptness was even more telling. Its first performance was its last.

Tom O'Horgan was director for the second time in the season when **Inner City** (14 December 1971, Barrymore) raised its curtain. The evening was based on Eve Merriam's book *The Inner City Mother Goose* and fell in with the social protest so rampant on the musical stage. To music by Helen Miller, the cast sang Miss Merriam's muckraking parodies of beloved old nursery rhymes. "Three Blind Mice," for example, became "You'll Find Mice." Subtitled "A Street Cantata," the show, essentially a revue, ran three months.

The last musical of 1971 originated in Canada and enjoyed a modest London run before tackling Broadway. **Anne of Green Gables** was a musicalization of L. M. Montgomery's novel, brought to the City Center on 21 December for a two-week run. New Yorkers rejected its old-fashioned sentimentality, and no one pleaded for an extended engagement.

The Sign in Sidney Brustein's Window (26 January 1972, Longacre), Lorraine Hansberry's 1964 play about a foolish but unquenchable do-gooder, was partially musicalized for this revival. The seven numbers were sung by a chorus to comment on the plot's turns.

Grease (14 February 1972, Eden) opened off-Broadway. Public response was so immediate and so enthusiastic that by the summer the musical was playing at the Broadhurst, a regular Times Square house. Like so many of the season's lyric works, *Grease* sang in rock and roll, but its sounds harked back to early days of the idiom as a group of youngsters gather for a high school reunion and relive the joys and pains of adolescence in the fifties. In those seemingly halcyon days Danny Zuko (Barry Bostwick),

a member of the "Burger Palace Boys"—a greaser (slicked-hair) gang at Rydell High—loves Sandy Dumbrowski (Carole Demas), an innocent who has transferred from Immaculata. When Danny refuses to conform to her prim idea of behavior, she dons tight jeans, adopts a bouffant hair-do, and stoops to conquer. As she does, she also gives a would-be rival, Betty Rizzo (Adrienne Barbeau), her comeuppance. In the first act Betty had taunted her with "Look At Me, I'm Sandra Dee." Sandy's swinging second-act reprise puts Betty in her place. The fads of the fifties were all made fun of: pajama parties, singers such as Elvis Presley and Fabian, and a wriggling dance called the Hully Gully. For the most part, *Grease* was another loosely constructed chronicle. Affectionate and funny, if not memorably melodic, it soon sent out profitable road companies and was produced overseas. Before its New York troupe packed its bags, it had chalked up a new long-run record of 3,388 performances. However, its moment in the spotlight as champ was brief.

March brought in two shows: a new musical and a revival of a not too old hit. Both failed. The new work was based on journalist Joe McGinness's successful study of commercialization in national elections, **The Selling of the President** (22 March 1972, Shubert). Although the title was retained, the history of President Nixon's bid for a second term was fictionalized. The scandal-beset incumbent was replaced by an imaginary Senator George W. Mason (Pat Hingle), and his campaign controlled not by issues but by public relations men and television executives. It seemed a bitter, almost true-to-life expansion of a spoof Jules Munshin had done years before in *Bless You All* (14 December 1950). As had become so commonplace in a distressed Broadway, the writing was in the hands of optimistic, but untested, tyros. The job, if it could have been done successfully at all, was botched; *The Selling of the President* closed after five showings.

But a revival of *A Funny Thing Happened on the Way to the Forum* (8 May 1962) seemed to have everything going for it. Its original co-librettist and director, Burt Shevelove, was back in his old stand, and Stephen Sondheim added new numbers to freshen his still fresh score. Fine clowns such as Phil Silvers, Lew Parker, and Larry Blyden were on hand to dish out the merriment. But despite good notices, the public refused to line up at the box office, and the show folded with the summer.

Another array of fine talent had better luck with inferior material in **Sugar** (9 April 1972, Majestic).

David Merrick, no longer as active as he once was, produced this stage version of the popular film *Some Like It Hot.* The book was adapted by Peter Stone—of *1776* (16 March 1969)—while Jule Styne put melodies to Bob Merrill's lyrics. Stone's libretto adhered closely enough to the original story of two musicians of the Prohibition era who witness a gang slaying and are forced to disguise themselves as members of an all-girl orchestra to avoid being silenced. One of the men's disguises is so successful he must spend the evening warding off the advances of an old lecher. The freedom of movement afforded by films was lacking and, as had happened with earlier translations of film farces to the musical stage, much of the wild zaniness was lost. Still, Cyril Ritchard and Robert Morse were such capital comedians they often made audiences forget the show's inadequacies. Elaine Joyce played Sugar Kane, a candied variant of Marilyn Monroe's role in the original film. Sparked by Ritchard's and Morse's performances as the old man and the "girl" of his dreams, the show stayed on the boards all through the season and well into the next.

That's Entertainment (14 April 1972, Edison) proved far less entertaining. An anthology of song hits by Howard Dietz and Arthur Schwartz performed by a small cast, it was withdrawn after four performances.

April's next offering was a revival of Maxwell Anderson and Kurt Weill's *Lost in the Stars* (30 October 1949). Since the original production had been at best a *succès d'estime*, its resurrection could not seriously be considered part of the nostalgia craze. The new production, mounted initially for the Kennedy Center in Washington, confirmed the judgments of nearly a quarter of a century earlier. With Brock Peters singing the minister, *Lost in the Stars* remained a melodic, richly textured, but fatally static piece. Years before, Broadway's theatrical columnist Walter Winchell had said something to the effect that it is difficult to revive an old hit, impossible to revive an old flop. The musical's thirty-nine performances recalled and underscored his sentiment.

Lost in the Stars had a racially mixed cast, performing the work of two white men. A sort of revue by a black and sung entirely by blacks arrived the next night. Micki Grant's Don't Bother Me, I Can't Cope (19 April 1972, Playhouse) often put new lyrics to familiar old melodies to sing its songs of black men's attitudes to a world they don't own. Less strident and more infectiously rhythmic than some

other black musicals of the season, it proved popular both in New York and on the road.

Four musicals arrived in May, a surprising figure considering the lateness of the season and the number of musicals that had already found audiences. All four failed. Different Times (1 May 1972, ANTA) was another loosely structured chronicle spread over sixty-five years from 1905 to 1970, depicting the problems engendered by changing mores and the influx of foreign blood into American families. Entirely written and directed by Michael Brown, it found few takers and left after three weeks.

The religious bent evidenced in musicals during this time reappeared when Hard Job Being God (15 May 1972, Edison) attempted to follow in the footsteps of *Godspell* and *Jesus Christ Superstar.* Although it used the same rock sound as its predecessors, it concentrated its attention on the Old Testament (and the Apocrypha) rather than the New Testament. Its small cast, with the exception of the actor who portrayed God (Tom Martel), assumed several roles in a history that ranged from Sarah and Abraham through Moses and David to Susanna. The musical lacked the professional know-how of the earlier hits and folded after six showings.

The night after *Hard Job Being God* opened, Melvin Van Peebles had his second musical of the season ready. Peebles, in fact, produced and directed Don't Play Us Cheap! (16 May 1972, Barrymore) as well as putting it all on paper. His simple plot had two bungling demons—Trinity (Joe Keyes, Jr.) and David (Avon Long)—attempt to throw monkey wrenches into an uninhibited Harlem party. They get their comeuppance. The show was less hostile than Peebles's *Ain't Supposed to Die a Natural Death*, but the market for musicals in general and black musicals in particular was momentarily satiated. *Don't Play Us Cheap* struggled into the hot weather before surrendering.

Heathen (21 May 1972, Rose), the season's last musical, chalked up a single performance. Not quite a chronicle, it juxtaposed the world of 1819 with that of 1972. A young nineteenth-century missionary, the Reverend Jonathan Beacon (Russ Thacker), sets out from Boston to convert heathen Hawaiians. A latter-day Jonathan seems more secular but finds religion in his own way.

1972–1973

Broadway groped aimlessly and flailed helplessly all season long. There seemed to be little the musical theater would not resort to in an attempt to revitalize itself, to find a new style, and, perhaps, to begin a new era. At one time or another during the theatrical year the lyric stage housed *commedia dell'arte*, rock, a faithless revival of a half-century-old musical comedy filled with juicy old songs, a tasteful attempt to write a modern operetta disappointing only for its juiceless new melodies, formless librettos ineptly derived from original ideas, and well-plotted librettos ineptly adapted from other works. Often, directors showed more daring and imagination than writers. Three shows earned themselves long runs, though only one—*A Little Night Music*—earned it solely on its own merits.

The season began with two revivals. *Man of La Mancha* opened at the Vivian Beaumont Theatre in Lincoln Center on 22 June with Richard Kiley again in the title part and remained until the Center's repertory company was ready to resume its operations at the end of October. Nothing else appeared until 15 September, when *Jacques Brel Is Alive and Well and Living in Paris* was brought in for a limited engagement.

Two importations were among the early October offerings. Each played a week at the Palace. The first was an Israeli army revue, **From Israel with Love;** the second, a Maori revue that had enjoyed a successful run in its native New Zealand, **Pacific Paradise.** Sandwiched between these two foreign offerings was the first new musical of the season, **Dude** (9 October 1972, Broadway), subtitled *The Highway Life. Dude* was created by two of the young writers of *Hair*, Gerome Ragni and Galt MacDermot. Ragni's libretto was even more incohesive, some said incoherent, than his material for *Hair*. It took Dude, first as a boy (Ralph Carter), later as a man (Nat Morris), into all parts of the cosmos, as well as into all parts of the specially reconstructed Broadway Theatre, in his search for religious and secular truths. Ragni peopled his cast with such oddball characters as #33, Mother Earth, Bread, Esso, Texaco, Noname, World War Too, and the Theater Wings. The show made it sorely obvious that Ragni was not going to sit down and learn the art of theatrical construction. Unfortunately for him, MacDermot's rock score, lacking the melody and appeal of his earlier music for *Hair*, could do nothing to save the evening. Nor could the show's stager, Tom O'Horgan, for all his free employment of the whole auditorium, devise anything as notorious as his former nude scene to win the musical some sensational publicity. The show closed after sixteen performances. The shock

of *Dude's* failure—after such high hopes—no doubt dampened Broadway's infatuation with rock and youth culture.

Three nights after *Dude* opened, another musical with a similar theme appeared. **Hurry, Harry** (12 October 1972, Ritz) kept its hero, Harrison Fairchild IV (Samuel D. Ratcliffe), earth-bound and confined within the proscenium arch, but sent him, between frequent visits to his psychiatrist, as far afield as Greece and Africa, in search of many of the same truths Dude was seeking. Written by unknowns and denied the ballyhoo that preceded *Dude's* premiere, *Hurry, Harry* survived a mere two performances. The alliterative lilt of the show's title, so reminiscent of titles of a long-gone day, underlined how far librettos had strayed from the era when they hoped only to entertain.

Revues followed the trend as well. **Mother Earth** (19 October 1972, Belasco) spent an entire evening pleading in songs and sketches for an understanding of ecological necessities and for an end to our exploitation of our resources. Not many people wanted to be preached to, so the revue closed after twelve showings.

Pippin (23 October 1972, Imperial), with a libretto by Roger O. Hirson and songs by *Godspell's* Stephen Schwartz, was the biggest hit of the season and October's last new musical. Oddly enough it employed much the same story both *Dude* and *Hurry, Harry* had used. Quests for "identity" were, as a popular expression of the day went, "in." The show also employed the increasingly popular device of playing without an intermission. But *Pippin* departed from the contemporary settings the other musicals had, turning instead to the times of Charlemagne. Charlemagne's son Pepin, respelled Pippin (John Rubinstein), looks for meaning in a succession of scenes, whose titles reveal the direction in which the boy has turned: War, The Flesh, Revolution. Nothing satisfies, and Pippin settles for a life of indolent ease. If there was a connection between weak plots and more or less unhappy endings no one stopped to consider it. Even the merely competent writing was glossed over by the clever, stylized staging choreographed by Bob Fosse. His cast was transformed into a collection of *commedia dell'arte* clowns cavorting in whatever manner the mood of the moment demanded. Performing honors went to Ben Vereen as a compère capable of playing both God and the Devil. Assisted by what has become acknowledged as one of the most astute television advertising campaigns, *Pippin*, despite its essential emptiness, ran and ran.

A young composer, Peter Link, heard his music played for first-nighters at two shows which opened one evening apart in November. This apparent streak of good fortune soured a bit when the first show, the New York Shakespeare Festival's *Much Ado About Nothing*, for which he wrote only incidental numbers, proved one of the hits of the season, while **Lysistrata** (13 November 1972, Atkinson), for which he created a more traditional Broadway score, folded after a single week. Not even the presence of Melina Mercouri in the title role helped. Three more flops followed in fast succession.

Oscar Wilde's self-destructive life was musicalized as **Dear Oscar** (16 November 1972, Playhouse). Unhesitatingly depicting even his homosexual leanings, it found no ready audience and left after five showings. On the very night it closed, **Ambassador** (19 November 1972, Lunt-Fontanne), a lyric adaptation of Henry James's *The Ambassadors*, offered itself for inspection. Its American authors, unable to get a hearing, had produced the musical first in London where it had a short run. Its New York run was even shorter: nineteen performances. The show was lavishly mounted, with Howard Keel portraying Lambert Strether, a proper New England lawyer sent to Paris on business, where he falls in love with Marie de Vionnet. The popular French actress Danielle Darrieux played Marie.

On the 28th the new Uris Theatre opened with a musical that boasted the second Galt MacDermot score of the season, **Via Galactica**. Set a thousand years in the future—2972—in a world destructive of individuality, it narrated the adventurous expedition of Gabriel Finn (Raul Julia) and his girl, Omaha (Virginia Vestoff), to set up a "New Jerusalem" in another solar system. As he had in *The Rothschilds* (19 October 1970), Keene Curtis almost stole the show, this time as the intellectual, disembodied head of Dr. Isaacs, wheeling around in a heart-lung machine. Like O'Horgan with *Dude*, Peter Hall ignored the boundaries imposed by the proscenium, flying spaceships out over the audience. A trampoline-covered stage allowed performers to bounce up and down to simulate weightlessness. Yet the show's possibilities were never successfully realized; it folded after one week, and the new Uris embarked on what for several years seemed to be a luckless career.

The procession of failures continued into January. **Tricks** (8 January 1973, Alvin), a musical version of Molière's *Les Fourberies de Scapin*, bedecked itself in *commedia dell'arte* finery and presented René Auberjonois in the leading role. The show had met with acclaim and some success at the Actors Theatre in Louisville and the Arena Stage in Washington, but New York would have none of it. It was gone after one week.

February's first musical also closed on the wrong side of the ledger. Nonetheless, **Shelter** (6 February 1973, Golden) had the small consolation of running a full month (at least double the run of any other flop that had opened during the season) and of garnering favorable or respectful reviews from a number of leading critics. The show had book and lyrics by Gretchen Cryer and music by Nancy Ford, two artists who had earned good reputations for themselves off-Broadway. Its story dared to suggested that boy–girl relationships were still of interest, even though it framed its hero's love-life in a decidedly offbeat narrative and setting. Michael (Terry Kiser) is a young man who writes television commercials and lives in a television studio with a talking computer named Arthur ("talked" by an unseen Tony Wells). Arthur follows his roommate's amours with interest, helping or hindering as he sees fit, especially when a young lady named Maud (Marcia Rodd) comes along. A second young lady who entered the picture had the unlikely name of Wednesday November (Susan Browning). Much the best part of the evening may have been Tony Walton's stunningly conceived single set, a television studio whose ambience was constantly changed by various pictures projected against its walls.

Just when the season was beginning to look hopeless, **A Little Night Music** raised its curtain. This musical version of Ingmar Bergman's film *Smiles of a Summer Night* opened 25 February at the Shubert to general critical cheering. Its old-world elegance led several of the cheering critics to label it an operetta, and Stephen Sondheim's waltz-filled score seemed to confirm the judgment. Yet Bergman's tale, as retold by Hugh Wheeler, interwove a series of love stories that were the essence of worldly cynicism, bathing them in warm, deceptively sentimental glows. True operetta had always been doggedly sentimental, however cynical its veneer. Set in the eerie, romantic light of a turn-of-the-century Swedish summer, *A Little Night Music* concerned itself primarily with the attempt of middle-aged Fredrik Egerman (Len Cariou) to free himself from an unwise, unconsummated second marriage to a girl his son's age. Fredrik finds he is falling in love with his former mistress,

Desirée (Glynis Johns), the beautiful actress daughter of old Mme. Armfeldt (Hermione Gingold), who herself had enjoyed memorable "Liaisons" in her younger days. Desirée's present lover, Count Carl-Magnus (Laurence Guittard), suspecting Fredrik's intentions, sends his wife to indiscreetly make the young Mme. Egerman (Victoria Mallory) aware of them. A candlelit dinner party at Mme. Armfeldt's brings matters to a head. Fredrik's son, Henrik (Mark Lambert), elopes with his stepmother, the count returns to his wife, and Fredrik has Desirée all to himself. Having rearranged the latest liaisons, Mme. Armfeldt dies unobserved in her chair. As in all of Sondheim's works, his lyrics outshone his music. However, for the first time since *A Funny Thing Happened on the Way to the Forum* (8 May 1962), Sondheim did create one melody that enjoyed wide and instant popular appeal. After a not entirely satisfactory meeting with Fredrik in her room, Desirée covers her real emotions by suggesting they "Send In The Clowns." Gorgeously mounted in the subtly tinted, free-flowing sets of Boris Aronson, the show ran 600 performances. Its touring companies and international companies prospered as well. The production was another feather in the cap of Harold Prince who, with *Fiddler on the Roof* (22 September 1964), *Cabaret* (October 20 1966), and all the recent Sondheim shows, had replaced David Merrick as the major producer in the American Musical Theatre. Prince went one step further than most of his predecessors, staging his own productions.

Hugh Wheeler, in collaboration with Joseph Stein, had a second book ready for the first of March's two musicals on the 13th. The show was, ostensibly, a revival of *Irene* (18 November 1919), but it was a revival that demonstrated little faith in the value of the original. Not only was a new book created for the evening, but most of the original numbers were discarded and replaced by either other old songs or by entirely new tunes. The new libretto managed to salvage the names of the original principals and thoughtfully retained the basic Cinderella motif—a motif the original *Irene* had helped make the dominant theme of the early twenties musicals. Once again Irene O'Dare, now a poor little Irish piano-tuner, is called to the home of the rich Marshalls, falls in love with handsome Donald Marshall (Monte Markham), and, aided by a male dress designer who trades under the name of Madame Lucy (George S. Irving), wins Donald over the objections of both families. The old songs added to the show included "They Go Wild, Simply Wild, Over Me" (with lyrics

by *Irene's* original lyricist, Joseph McCarthy, and music by Fred Fisher) and "You Made Me Love You" (McCarthy/James Monaco). Audiences out for pure entertainment and unbothered by historical accuracy applauded them as much as they did "Alice Blue Gown." Ignoring the suggestions of intimacy in the original, the show was gaudily mounted and vigorously staged by Gower Champion. Its latter-day Irene, Debbie Reynolds, crooned her songs into a microphone, projecting a flavor far different from the soaring soprano of Edith Day and her followers. To justify her costarring billing, Patsy Kelly clowned broadly in the expanded role of Mrs. O'Dare. The show surpassed the run of the original, dancing merrily on at the new Minskoff for two years. But it left Broadway under a cloud when its accounting practices prevented it from showing a profit after so lengthy a stay.

The best of the season's more traditional non-innovative lyric works was **Seesaw** (18 March 1973, Uris), March's other musical. The show was adapted by Michael Bennett from William Gibson's two-character comedy, *Two for the Seesaw*, which Henry Fonda and Anne Bancroft had played so memorably in 1958. The demands of musical comedy necessitated some expansion in the cast of characters, but Bennett wisely kept them peripheral and, as a result, managed to convey much of the original's intimacy. Of the sixteen numbers in the show, the two principals fail to appear only in three and had nine of thirteen remaining songs to themselves. Oddly, although all of Cy Coleman's music was easy on the ears and Dorothy Fields's lyrics were skillful, if a bit tougher than was her wont, the writers gave the evening's single show-stopper, "It's Not Where You Start," to a minor character and the dancers. Tommy Tune sang this most patently old-fashioned of the evening's melodies while dancing with an avalanche of multi-colored balloons. Ken Howard played Jerry Ryan, the young but mature Midwest attorney whose brief romance with the volatile, gesticulating Manhattanite, Gittel Mosca (Michele Lee), occupied the evening. In the end, the two go their separate ways. *Seesaw*, with numerous cast changes, ran out the season and into the next. But its run was slightly forced, and it never returned its initial investment.

Three musicals, opening six days apart in the middle of May, brought the season to a close. None succeeded. The best of the lot was indubitably **Cyrano** (13 May 1973, Palace), which the popular English novelist Anthony Burgess adapted from the

Rostand play and for which he provided lyrics. Much of the strength of the evening came from a bravura performance by the Canadian actor Christopher Plummer. But the score was weak, and, as Victor Herbert and his associates had learned three-quarters of a century before, *Cyrano de Bergerac* seemingly defies musicalization.

A revue called **Nash at Nine** (17 May 1972, Hayes) was devoted, appropriately, to the verse of Ogden Nash. Set to music by Milton Rosenstock, one of Broadway's leading conductors, and performed without intermission by a small cast that included the distinguished actor E. G. Marshall, it learned to its dismay that although Nash's admirers were legion few of them would pay to sit through an evening of nothing but his rhymes.

The season ended as it began, with a young man searching for his "identity." Walter Smith (Don Murray) is not a little unlike Walter Mitty. He works as dutifully as he can for Mr. Baggett (Mort Marshall) of Baggett Nitrates, but he is given to uncontrollable dreaming. The big dream of the evening finds him as the star of an imaginary musical comedy singing his heart out to a young lady called The Dancing Melody (Bonnie Walter). A clever idea, **Smith** (19 May 1973, Eden) was executed with some charm, but not enough. The dream was shattered for good after two weeks.

Off-Broadway had a generally dull season. But the successful **Oh, Coward!** (4 October 1972, New) and the not quite so successful **Berlin to Broadway with Kurt Weill** (1 October 1972, de Lys) presented homages to leading composers in a form of musical montage Broadway would quickly emulate.

1973–1974

The American Musical Theatre had become barren. To fill the empty playhouses, producers rushed in one-man and one-woman shows, montages, and revivals. In desperation a great film was translated, songs and all, onto the stage. Almost nothing worked. For the first time in years, no musical was awarded a place in the *Best Plays* series.

No shows appeared throughout the height of the summer. The season opened on 5 September at the Uris, ominously, with a low-budget revival of *The Desert Song* (30 November 1926). Some of the minor numbers, especially the comic numbers, were given new lyrics, and the setting was advanced inexplicably into the voguish thirties. The reception was anything but cordial, although, significantly, the

skimpy production itself was attacked as much as or more than was the idea of reviving an old-style operetta. The Red Shadow (David Cryer) and his Riffs rode off after two weeks.

A month and a half elapsed before another musical appeared. When the first new lyric work of the season finally did appear it was warmly welcomed and quickly settled down to become one of the two major hits of the theatrical year. **Raisin** (18 October 1973, 46th St.) was a musical version of Lorraine Hansberry's 1959 success, *A Raisin in the Sun*, depicting the efforts of the Younger clan to leave their ghetto existence behind them. Widowed Lena Younger (Virginia Capers) is the matriarch of the group. She hopes to put her daughter, Beneatha (Deborah Allen), through medical school; to help her married son, Walter (Joe Morton), buy a liquor store; and to move her family to a better home. Walter's would-be partner absconds with all their savings, but Lena at least contrives to buy a home in a better neighborhood. Like most of the period's musicals, *Raisin* was created by names that were meaningless to most Broadway theatregoers, but librettists Charlotte Zaltzberg and Robert Nemiroff (Nemiroff was also the show's producer), lyricist Robert Brittan, and composer Judd Woldin provided material that came to life effectively in the theatre—especially in Donald McKayle's sizzling African dance number—even if it was not particularly memorable after the final curtain.

Molly (1 November 1973, Alvin) was based on the once popular radio series *The Goldbergs*, a series that had long since been made into a moderately successful play, *Me and Molly*, for the show's original star, Gertrude Berg. Miss Berg was dead, and Kaye Ballard assumed the principal role. Set in the fashionable thirties, *Molly* watched its heroine help her family and friends through the rigors of the Depression. Although Miss Ballard was a skilled comedienne, there was something ersatz about her Yiddish warmth. Indeed there was more of 1973 Broadway than of the 1933 Bronx about the whole evening. The show closed after sixty-eight performances, probably allowing the Goldberg family to rest peacefully hereafter in radio history.

Perhaps no other show of this period demonstrated the dire plight of the American Musical Theatre as cruelly as **Gigi** (13 November 1973, Uris). For *Gigi* was simply Lerner and Loewe's enchanting film musical lifted off the screen and set down a little uncomfortably on a legitimate stage. The show originated in California with Edwin Lester's Los

Angeles and San Francisco Light Opera Company. In years past the group had been responsible for some unusual made-to-order presentations such as *Song of Norway* (21 August 1944) and *Gypsy Lady* (17 September 1946). But even though all these works used older material, material often not initially conceived for the stage, they were assembled with a discernible iota of creativity. The translation of *Gigi* from film script to play script was mere hack work. Lester was careful to give his show a sumptuous mounting, and he was thoughtful in his casting. Alfred Drake, Daniel Massey, Agnes Moorehead, and a newcomer, Karin Wolfe, played the pivotal roles. For want of competition the show was able to run three months.

Good Evening (14 November 1973, Plymouth), a two-man revue by and with half of the team responsible for *Beyond the Fringe*, was imported on 14 November. Peter Cook and Dudley Moore's civilized nonsense, called *Beyond the Fridge* in London, ran out the season.

By contrast, **Bette Midler at the Palace** (3 December 1973, Palace) was essentially a one-woman entertainment which lingered for only nineteen performances.

A revival of *The Pajama Game* (13 May 1954) was notable for the return of George Abbott as stager nearly twenty years later, but also the color-blind casting of Cab Calloway and Barbara McNair. Despite this up-to-the-minute thinking, a majority of critics reviewing the 9 December opening at the Lunt-Fontanne deemed the show sadly "dated."

The City Center Acting Company included one musical in its repertory, Gay's *Beggar's Opera*, which is offered at the Billy Rose on the 22nd.

New Year's Eve brought **An Evening with Josephine Baker** into the Palace for a one-week stay. Although she was surrounded by an array of competent music hall talent, Miss Baker was indeed the whole evening, even if to some her glamour and material (much of which she had offered in her 1964 appearance) were more than a bit frayed.

Up the street at the Winter Garden a much younger lady raised the curtain on her one-woman show six nights later, 6 January 1974. **Liza**, of course, was Liza Minnelli. Assisted by four youthful dancers and by some new material Fred Ebb and John Kander designed around her talents, she delighted her fans for twenty-three showings.

Lorelei (27 January 1974, Palace) was almost a one-woman show. Without Carol Channing it would have been nothing. The musical illustrated almost as poignantly as *Gigi* the exhausted state of the musical theatre. The show's subtitle, *Gentlemen Still Prefer Blondes*, betrayed its genesis, for the show was a collection of the best scenes and songs from the 1949 musical, framed by a prologue and epilogue in which an aging, widowed, but wealthy Lorelei Lee Esmond elaborated on her past. For the show Jule Styne wrote several new songs to lyrics by Comden and Green. None approached the popularity of the original's best numbers. Like *Gigi*, *Lorelei* had no stiff competition. As a result, she ran out the season.

Only one musical arrived in February, called **Rainbow Jones** (13 February 1974, Music Box); it survived for a single performance. The young lady of the title (played by Ruby Pearson) spent most of her day in Central Park cavorting with fantasy animals such as Leona (Peggy Hagen Lampery) and C. A. Fox (G. I. Robbins).

March was busier and happier, although it got off to an unpromising start with a six-character musical, entitled fittingly **Sextet** (3 March 1974, Bijou). Following the growing trend, the show was performed without intermission. Played entirely in a single apartment setting, it dissected the heterosexual and homosexual longings of four boys and two girls. All its "trendiness" wasn't enough. The musical was withdrawn after nine showings.

A gaudy, stomping evocation of the era of boogie-woogie and jitterbugging, **Over Here** (6 March 1974, Shubert) trucked in next, bringing with it as stars the two surviving of the original three Andrews Sisters. Played out on a single basic set that simulated the late art-deco stage frames often employed by the big bands, it told a simple story of two singers, Pauline and Paulette de Paul (Maxene and Patty Andrews), embarking on a trip to entertain soldiers during World War II and searching for a third voice to fill out their act. They also find themselves searching for a German spy in their midst. The spy turns out to be the very girl they have hired to make a threesome, Mitzi (Janie Sell). She is unmasked by her all too thorough German indoctrination. Asked to sing the second chorus of "The Star Spangled Banner," she knows all the words—something no true-blooded American can claim. The show's music and orchestrations unerringly captured the sounds and textures of the swing era, but the songs were therefore too consciously out of date to receive any play away from the theatre. The show ran a year on Broadway, closing when the Andrews Sisters and the producers could not come to terms on a contract for a tour.

The most surprising and the biggest hit of the year first saw the light of day in Brooklyn as part of that borough's Chelsea Theater Center program. It moved to Manhattan on 10 March. A number of well-known Broadway hands assisted in turning the revival of Bernstein's *Candide* (1 December 1956) into a success that must have gone far to heal the hurts the earlier production's failure had inflicted. Hugh Wheeler's new book at once tightened and liberated the tale (for example, Pangloss was minimized). Lewis J. Stadlen, who played Pangloss, also undertook several other roles; Mark Baker was Candide, and Maureen Brennan, Cunegonde. If their singing fell below the original's standards, their lively acting compensated. Bernstein's orchestrations were also cut down. Ignited by Harold Prince's electrifying staging, *Candide* exploded all over the house. In this respect, the producers were fortunate that the old barn of a theatre, the Broadway, had been done over the preceding year to meet the same expansive requirements of *Dude* (9 October 1972). Some spectators could even sit in specially constructed "bleachers." Stephen Sondheim contributed new lyrics, and some previously unused ones by the late John Latouche were employed. All in all, everything combined to make *Candide* a rousing triumph and earn for it a place in the permanent repertory.

The rest of the season was downhill. April brought in two montages and a one-man show. The montages arrived first, five nights apart. Alan Jay Lerner's "cavalcade of American music" from 1895 to the present, called without much imagination **Music! Music!** (11 April 1974, City Center), was unveiled at the City Center. It covered a range of styles and composers from ragtime to rock. No doubt some confusion was created when Sammy Cahn opened his revue and called it **Words and Music** (16 April 1974, Golden). The words were all by Cahn, and the music by various songsmiths he had worked with for the past forty years. Since Hollywod had been kinder to him than Broadway, much of the material he and three young assistants performed came out of films. The evening proved the popular adage that "less is more," and Cahn's limited selection played into the summer, while Lerner's extensive potpourri was gone after thirty-seven representations.

Sammy, a one-man show for Sammy Davis, Jr. (actually assisted by a handful of other artists), played the troubled Uris for two weeks beginning 23 April.

An unusual setting and subject—eleventh-century Japan and its Samurai warriors—were not sufficient novelty to save **Ride the Winds** (16 May 1974, Bijou), a musical written entirely by John Driver. It lasted a mere three showings.

Just before the calendar brought the season to a halt, an offbeat, appealing little musical show appeared at the Cort. **The Magic Show** (28 May 1974. Cort) had a book by Bob Randall and songs by Stephen Schwartz. Schwartz, with the scores for *Godspell* (17 May 1971) and *Pippin* (23 October 1972) already to his credit, demonstrated a propensity for choosing such oddball works. As always, his music was pleasant, lively, and forgettable. The book, which told how a fading New Jersey nightclub, the Passaic Top Hat, saves itself from insolvency by hiring a magic act, was merely an excuse on which to hang the spectacular illusions. Its small cast, small orchestra, and single set kept its running costs low so that this intermissionless entertainment—eminently suitable for children—prospered for 1,920 performances.

1974–1975

Two smash hits were the sole commercial bright spots of the new season, yet both succeeded despite often unenthusiastic notices. Their popularity had to be attributed to something other than genuine artistic merit. Except for the profits enjoyed by these two shows—*The Wiz* and *Shenandoah*—and for one revival brought back for a limited stay, the season was a washout.

But before the season proper got under way, the New York City Opera's fall season listed *Mikado* and *Fledermaus* on its schedule (and, in the spring, *The Consul*).

On Broadway proper, a fine revival came first, on 23 September at the Winter Garden. Seeing *Gypsy* (21 May 1959) fifteen years after the original opening night led most critics to rejoice that the musical remained "Still Mysteriously Perfect Theatre." Wisely, the revival remained absolutely faithful to the text, while not attempting to mimic slavishly the original mounting. Both the production and the performances tended to be warmer than the first, yet, in sum, equally valid. Angela Lansbury, who had played Ethel Merman's role in London, recreated her more humane interpretation of Rose. If she seemed at first glance too young and beautiful to be believable, her thoughtful acting and stylish, energetic rendering of the songs quickly won over skeptics. *Gypsy* delighted again for 120 performances.

Whenever Broadway has sought to have fun at the expense of silent movies, it has fallen flat on its face. **Mack & Mabel** (6 October 1974, Majestic) proved no exception. Old-timers probably guessed even before the curtain rose that Mack (Robert Preston) was Mack Sennett and Mabel (Bernadette Peters) Mabel Normand. In Michael Stewart's book Mabel is swooped from her job in a delicatessen and made a star by the great director. But Mabel wants more than stardom; she wants Mack's love. When Mack remains too preoccupied with his films to notice, Mabel takes to drugs and hits the skids. While Preston's forthright Mack and Miss Peters's wide-eyed, waif-like Mabel were both appealing, Gower Champion's imaginative staging frequently stole the show. Champion resorted to films, as he had in *The Happy Time* (18 January 1968), for *Mack and Mabel*, offering a montage of silent film comedy that to many was the high point of the evening. He had bathing beauties slide down a giant, multi-colored corkscrew and, in keeping with the popular pretense that prosceniums had disappeared, swung Mack out over the audience on a camera dolly. Jerry Herman's music was lively, but not memorable. For all its happier moments, the show could not sustain its festive gaiety, folding after eight weeks.

October also saw a rash of star turns, with Charles Aznavour, Andy Williams and Michel Legrand, Tony Bennett and Lena Horne, and Anthony Newley and Henry Mancini all making appearances at traditional Broadway houses. Only the Bennett–Horne combination ran for more than two weeks.

Some years back in *Show Girl* (12 January 1961), Carol Channing had mocked the lugubrious propensities of modern musicals, singing songs such as "This Is A Darned Fine Funeral" and "Love Is A Sickness." A "play with music" that was a one-performance flop suggested there were no lengths the new musical would not go to in its search for suffering. **Mourning Pictures** (10 November 1974, Lyceum) spent the evening with a young poet (Kathryn Walker) as she watched her mother (Leora Dana) die of cancer.

A stager as imaginative as Gower Champion, Tom O'Horgan was responsible for what life **Sgt. Pepper's Lonely Hearts Club Band on the Road** (17 November 1974, Beacon) displayed. His heroine (Kay Cole) made her first appearance singing from the audience; his other performers threw multicolored Frisbees at patrons. O'Horgan and Robin Wagner derived their entertainment from a popular Beatles album, adding seventeen additional McCartney and Lennon songs to fill out the evening. A thread of plot watched Billy Shears (Ted Neeley)

sell his soul to become a rock star. Only at the end, when Sgt. Pepper (David Patrick Kelly) appears as a sort of *deus ex machina* and destroys a pair of silver eyeglasses Billy has been wearing, does Billy give promise of reaching his goal. The show was offered at a large, converted film house far uptown from the theatre heartland. It ran just one performance more than *Mack & Mabel*.

Two revivals followed. On 20 December, at the new Circle in the Square, Ted Mann brought back *Where's Charley?* (11 October 1948). Its new Charley, Raul Julia, was far closer to college age than Bolger had been, even if he was not as lithe and supple as the great dancer. Faithfully resuscitated, and with a redeeming sense of style, the musical played out a limited engagement of seventy-six performances.

No such sense of style, or anything else redeeming, graced a tasteless revival of *Good News* (6 September 1927) on 23 December at the St. James. This wonderful, melodic glimpse of 1927 collegiate shenanigans was not even allowed to retain its roaring twenties setting, but instead was moved up to the fadingly voguish thirties. Two relatively minor roles were expanded for its stars, two long-unheard-from movie favorites, Alice Faye and John Payne. DeSylva, Brown, and Henderson songs from other shows, or from their Hollywood and Tin Pan Alley output, were inserted to enhance a score that needed no enhancing. The producers played safe by touring the show for months around the country and by giving weeks of previews in New York before allowing the critics in. During the previews Payne withdrew and was replaced by Gene Nelson. Once the critics reported their findings, the revival was doomed. It closed sixteen performances later.

The season's two smash hits arrived two nights apart at the beginning of January 1975. **The Wiz** (5 January 1975, Majestic) was an all-black recreation of *The Wizard of Oz*, far more faithful to the original (and to the story millions knew from the film version) than was Fred Stone and Dave Montgomery's 1903 vehicle. Once again a tornado blew little Dorothy (Stephanie Mills) from her home to the wonderful land of Oz. Only after she helps a Scarecrow (Hinton Battle), the Tinman (Tiger Haynes), and a cowardly Lion (Ted Ross) achieve their ambitions does she return to Earth. The new book and score were adequate, even if some critics complained the latter was "vastly overamplified." At least one song from Charlie Smalls's "soul"-tinged score, "Ease On Down The Road," enjoyed some popularity. The show's clever production was its strong point. Costumes and sets both were eye-catching and witty. The witches' flowing, brightly painted dresses and weird headpieces suggested extravagant Ziegfeld costumes gone amok. The wizard's balloon had a gondola made of old iron stoves and musical instruments, while one of its three balloons looked like a monstrous electric light-bulb. In a ballet, the tornado was personified by a dancer (Evelyn Thomas) in long, slender clouds of dark drapes.

Production was anything but the strong point of **Shenandoah** (7 January 1975, Alvin). Its scenery was dismissed as "drab and unimaginative," while its staging was condemned as "undistinguished." Indeed, its book, based on a James Stewart movie of the same name, and its music were little better. The story recounted the attempts of the Anderson family to stay clear of the Civil War's bloody turmoil. Only when the family's youngest son (Joseph Shapiro) is kidnapped by Union soldiers do Charlie Anderson (John Cullum) and his older boys get fighting mad. *Shenandoah* had been preceded by some glowing reports. Critical reception in New York was anything but ecstatic, though Cullum's solemn, strong-voiced performance received general praise, and the show got off to a slow start. Word soon spread that for all its faults the show was wholesome and sentimental. Aided by cut-rate tickets, it kept its head above water. In time momentum told. Although it rarely played to capacity, it rarely had a losing week. It was even able to send out a road company.

Between these two hits, one intermissionless oddity premiered. Set in a mental ward, where a greedy, fame-obsessed black poet and playwright reviews his tormented life just before he dies, **Black Picture Show** (6 January 1975, Vivian Beaumont) contained a sizable musical program. This did not prevent *Best Plays* and many critics from categorizing it as a "play."

A leader in the "pop art" field, Andy Warhol, produced January's last musical, **Man on the Moon** (29 January 1975, Little), a work with book, music, and lyrics by John Phillips, a former member of a popular singing group. His story told how Dr. Bomb (Harlan S. Foss) sends his brother and sister-in-law to establish a hotel on Canis Major. Later he launches a bomb that will hurl the moon at the hotel. Somehow in all this nonsense an astronaut (Eric Lang) finds time to fall in love with Bomb's niece (Genevieve Waite). Curiously, Warhol did not design the show's sets, which were dreary. In his bitingly witty review for the *Times*, Clive Barnes insisted the best part of the evening was watching the "beautiful people" walk in late. Although the musical played the

smallest theatre remaining on Broadway, Barnes snidely noted that Lang "sings with a strong microphone." The critic cried longingly, "Bring back 'Via Galactica!'" Warhol quickly withdrew his mistake.

A revue written by and starring a popular singer of country rock, Harry Chapin, was February's only entrant. The songs, mostly with a radical bent, belonged to what one critic described as the "somebody done somebody wrong" school. There were no skits. A revolving geodesic bandstand and the use of closed circuit television brought some novelty to the staging, but the songs' restricted appeal confined the run of **The Night That Made America Famous** (26 February 1975, Barrymore) to just over one month.

Goodtime Charley (3 March 1975, Palace) propelled audiences back to the fifteenth century and retold the effect of Joan of Arc (Ann Reinking) on the young Dauphin (Joel Grey). The show and the production were a collection of contradictions that ultimately proved self-defeating, taking the evening off the boards after three months. The book could not make up its mind whether it wanted to be flippant or serious. Despite its title and its star, Grey, Charley was not its pivotal figure; Joan was. Even its assets worked against the show in some way. For example, Rouben Ter-Arutunian designed an attractive basic set, a semicircle of steps backed with Romanesque pillars and arches. Unfortunately, the set took up so much space it cramped the action and, especially, the dances.

Having already witnessed musicals about a woman dying of cancer and a saint burned at the stake, Broadway was probably not too surprised when a musical appeared treating the My Lai incident, in which American soldiers had massacred innocent Vietnamese. The trial of the officer in charge, Lt. William L. Calley, had made headlines for weeks. In a rock opera, devoid of spoken dialogue and laced with relentless dancing, the **Lieutenant** (9 March 1975, Lyceum) was not named Calley, but the identification was unmistakable. The show proffered the argument that American militarism, not the officer (Eddie Mekka), must shoulder the real blame. The Prosecutor (Burt Rodriguez) summed up the author's sentiments in "The Conscience Of A Nation." Wartime massacres proved no more palatable to theatregoers than cancer or martyrdom, so *Lieutenant* folded after nine showings.

The next night the musical stage progressed from massacres to monsters. **The Rocky Horror Show** (10 March 1975, Belasco) originally opened unheralded in London at a dilapidated cinema house that reinforced the very atmosphere for which the evening strove. The show was a travesty of old horror movies, centering on a character named Frank N. Furter (Tim Curry), a creature with a baritone voice and black lips, dressed as a transvestite in fishnet tights. The work's author, Richard O'Brien, took part in the performance under the name Ritz O'Brien, impersonating a hunchbacked butler, Riff-Raff. The entertainment was presented in cabaret style, without intermission. In order to create the proper ambience, the Belasco was drastically remodeled, even to having boxes removed. In doing so the theatre owners apparently destroyed some Everett Shinn murals and permanently defaced one of America's unique auditoriums. They probably never retrieved the costs of their remodeling, for *The Rocky Horror Show* couldn't survive a full month.

For years Buster Davis had been a prominent conductor and orchestrator for Broadway musicals. When he at last attempted to write an entire evening on his own, he came a cropper with a five-performance flop called **Doctor Jazz** (19 March 1975, Winter Garden). Davis's book followed the rise of a young man (Bobby Van) from his days as a hustler for New Orleans prostitutes to his realization of his dream to be a jazz trumpeter. Although Davis supplemented his own score with songs by Eubie Blake, King Oliver, and Harry Von Tilzer, the evening failed to catch fire or evoke a proper sense of period. Even Raoul Pène du Bois's art-deco scenery was out of place in a story purporting to unfold between 1917 and 1925. While Van did some fine tap-dancing that included an interesting slide-walking step, his talents were never fully utilized.

A kooky revue centering upon the talents of Bette Midler, **Clams on the Half Shell** (17 April 1975. Minskoff), depended largely on her popularity to see it through its eighty-eight performances. It was really a concert, presented in the guise of a cabaret and heavily amplified. Lionel Hampton assisted.

A second song revue came in a month later. **Rodgers and Hart** (13 May 1975, Hayes) employed twelve young performers to sing ninety-eight of the team's songs in whole or in part. Romantic numbers monopolized the first half; satiric, the second. The pastiche found enough of an audience to run until mid-August.

1975–1976

In reviewing the original-cast recordings for the season's first two shows—the season's two biggest

hits—the *Times* headed its notice, "Musicals to Be Seen, Not Heard." As the season progressed, this sad truism had to be applied to every new lyric work that premiered. Theatregoers could on occasion walk out whistling memorable melodies, but only if they had been attending one of the season's revivals or pastiches—or, just possibly, if they had sat through a fascinating work Broadway was enjoying for the first time but that had been written nearly seventy years before. Good mounting, clever staging, and superb dancing accounted for much of the season's excitement.

Chicago (3 June 1975, 46th St.), a musicalization of Maurine Dallas Watkins's 1926 hit of the same name, began the season on an upbeat note. The adaptation by Bob Fosse and Fred Ebb, with music by John Kander and lyrics by Ebb, remained faithful to the original tale of Roxy Hart (Gwen Verdon), who kills her lover, enjoys the notoriety, but is relieved to be acquitted thanks to the hanky-panky of her shyster lawyer (Jerry Orbach). In her freedom she forms a nightclub act with another released murderess (Chita Rivera). Although "And All That Jazz" became rather popular and still is heard at times, the songs were commonplace, the music and singing annoyingly amplified, the lyrics and dialogue often more than impolite. On the other hand, Fosse's staging was taut; his cakewalks, Charlestons (the show retained its 1926 setting), and soft-shoes vivacious and identifiably angular. Tony Walton employed a basic art-deco unit set, flanked by translucent columns depicting vaudeville and other long-gone greats, and with an onstage band performing from a platform in the rear. Suggestions of vaudeville were furthered by songs that recalled two-a-day favorites. For example, Roxy's trusting husband (Barney Martin) complains he is a transparent "Mister Cellophane" in a song clearly patterned after Bert Williams's "Nobody." Julian Eltinge and Bert Savoy were evoked when a newspaperwoman called Mary Sunshine (M. O'Haughey), a lady with a soaring soprano voice, was revealed to be a man. One especially impressive feat was Fosse's ingenious use of a very small chorus, made to seem larger than it was. Choruses were getting smaller each year.

The next show to open used no chorus at all, since all the principals were young hopefuls auditioning for **A Chorus Line** (25 July 1975, Shubert). Originally mounted the preceding 15 April at Joseph Papp's New York Shakespeare Festival, the musical was conceived by its director and choreographer, Michael Bennett. Its book was by James

Kirkwood and Nicholas Dante; its songs had music by Marvin Hamlisch and lyrics by Edward Kleban. The work, performed without intermission, without any real scenery (except a mirrored rear wall), and with the entire cast in work clothes, described how a choreographer, Zach (Robert LuPone), selects his chorus of eight from seventeen applicants not merely by watching the youngsters dance but by having each recite his or her history. Sagas of neurosis, frustration, homosexuality, and hope follow. The most painful for Zach is the plea of his former mistress, Cassie (Donna McKechnie), who had held more important parts, only to lose ground when she couldn't act. She is determined to dance, even if she has to be just another chorus girl. After Zach makes his choices, the entire cast in satiny top hats and dress clothes—the only major costume change of the evening—strut in a high-kicking finale, "One." The musical's lone standard love ballad, "What I Did For Love," enjoyed some replaying away from the theatre. Although no small number of playgoers objected to A Chorus Line's taxing them with its characters' whining about personal problems, the show's unquestionable integrity helped it grab almost every award within reach. It moved on to establish a new long-run record for Broadway, closing only after an astonishing fifteen years, or 6,137 performances. The show marked the apogee of Bennett's tragically meteoric career.

Aside from the New York City Opera's Fledermaus and Pinafore, no more musicals appeared until the fall.

MICHAEL BENNETT (DiFiglia) was born on 8 April 1943 (though some suggest the year was actually 1941) in Buffalo. From his childhood on, his doting mother encouraged his flair for theatricals and dancing. He made his Broadway debut in 1961, serving as a chorus boy in Subways Are for Sleeping. By 1966 he was awarded his first choreographic assignment with A Joyful Noise. The show failed, but more successful assignments followed with such musicals as Promises, Promises; Company; and Follies.

John Houseman's touring troupe, the Acting Company, opened its repertory season on 7 October with a new musical, The Robber Bridegroom. While it stayed only two weeks, its reception was so encouraging it returned in the next season for an unlimited run (and will be taken up in detail at that time).

In 1953 Menasha Skulnik had left the fading Yiddish theatre and delighted Broadway with his lovable antics in a comedy about the clothing industry, The Fifth Season. He played a harassed partner whose associate prefers watching beautiful models to watching the business. On 12 October the Eden, an off-Broadway house in the heart of Times Square, raised its curtain on a musicalized version, partly in English, partly in Yiddish, produced by Jewish Nostalgic Production, Inc. The original title was retained. Joseph Buloff assumed Skulnik's old role, but he was given only one song to sing. Even so, the offering proved attractive enough to run until the end of January at the small house.

The next musical was something of a curiosity, and something of a marvel. Scott Joplin had written his ragtime opera, Treemonisha (21 October 1975, Palace), in 1907 but was never able to see it beyond a run-through. In the intervening years, his orchestrations were lost. The mid-seventies revival of ragtime and especially of Joplin's rag "The Entertainer" prompted Gunther Schuller to study old ragtime orchestrations in the Red Back Book and recreate an approximation of Joplin's intentions. It began as a production of the Houston Grand Opera, conducted by Schuller, and later toured briefly before reaching Broadway. Designer Franco Colavecchia mixed African voodoo and Southern rural motifs with warm, vibrant colors, and choreographer Louis Johnson moved from joyous swinging and jumping dances in "Goin' Around" and "Aunt Dinah Has Blowed De Horn" to fantastically conceived animals cavorting in a ballet, "The Frolic Of The Bears," to a stately, classic rag at the end in "A Real Slow Drag." A fine cast of black singing actors brought Joplin's simple story irresistibly to life. A childless couple, Ned (Willard White) and Monisha (Betty Allen and Lorna Myers, alternating), find a baby under a tree, and so name it Treemonisha (Carmen Balthrop or Kathleen Battle). They persuade white people to educate her. The opera begins when Treemonisha is eighteen. A voodoo conjurer, Zodzetrick (Ben Harney), abducts her to stop her from enlightening her neighbors. A friend, Remus (Curtis Rayam), disguised as a scarecrow, leads her rescuers. Once free, she forgives the kidnapper, and her neighbors elect her to lead them. Excellent as the production and performance were, Joplin's superb melodic gifts outshone them. Moving from the touching pathos of Monisha's "I Want To See My Child," to a quartet of cotton-pickers' "We Will Rest Awhile" to the exuberant dance numbers, they gave Broadway its most rewarding score of the season. The show, brought in for a limited engagement, played eight weeks, but no further tour followed, ostensibly because the physical production was too cumbersome for most road theatres to handle.

Another long-gone black entertainer figured prominently in the next musical to open on Broadway. The accurately titled piece was essentially a two-woman show, and one of those women was dead. **Me and Bessie** (22 October 1975, Ambassador) offered Linda Hopkins narrating the tragic history of Bessie Smith and singing the songs Miss Smith made famous. When the Ambassador Theatre proved much too large for so intimate an evening, *Me and Bessie* was moved to the smaller Edison, another off-Broadway house in the Times Square area. There it settled in comfortably for a long run.

A third black company arrived at the Minskoff on 6 November, with a revival of *Hello, Dolly!* (16 January 1964) starring Pearl Bailey, supported by Billy Daniels as Horace. Miss Bailey and her troupe added another fifty-one performances to the show's Broadway record.

One week later an all-star cast (Lillian Gish, Tammy Grimes, Larry Kert, John Raitt, Cyril Ritchard, Patrice Munsel, and Dick Shawn) presented a potpourri claiming to demonstrate the development of the American musical. Whether tunes such as "Sweet Betsy From Pike," "Skip To My Lou," or "Mademoiselle From Armentiers" were ever sung in legitimate musicals was moot, while assigning songs from operettas of the 1920s and 1930s to "Early Broadway" suggested either ignorance or disdain of the American Musical Theatre. Apparently theatergoers weren't interested in so careless a hodgepodge, so **A Musical Jubilee** (13 November 1975, St. James) was withdrawn after ninety-two showings.

Boccaccio (24 November 1975, Edison), an inept attempt to translate the more bawdy moments of *The Decameron* to the musical stage, folded after a single week.

One of the joys of an earlier Broadway, *Very Good Eddie* (23 December 1915) was revived at the Booth on 21 December. The production had originated at the Goodspeed Opera House in East Haddam, Connecticut. Although the revival was tasteless and insensitive, so good was the original and so barren was the competition that the show ran out the season. Much of Jerome Kern's original score was discarded. In its stead songs from other Kern shows were added, including "Hot Dog," from as late as 1922. Worse, the material was not even played straight, but rather was mocked in a style fashionably known as "camp."

Home Sweet Homer (4 January 1976, Palace) came in after a ten-month tour that relied on the lure of Yul Brynner to overcome scathing notices. When Broadway's critics proved just as damning, the show's first New York performance was also its last. Acted out on a single dark-hued set, the work was an intermissionless and interminable retelling of *The Odyssey* with Brynner as Odysseus, Joan Diener as Penelope, and Russ Thacker as Telemachus.

Several of the musical theatre's giants promised new works during the season. Stephen Sondheim's appeared first. **Pacific Overtures** (11 January 1976, Winter Garden) was daring and innovative—too daring, innovative, and untheatrical for many. Sondheim and his librettist, John Weidman, attempted to portray Commodore Perry's opening of Japan from a Japanese viewpoint. The entire cast was Asian—even the Americans were played by Asians. (All the players took several roles.) At first the Japanese are frightened and reluctant, but at the very end the scene switches to twentieth-century Japan, and the American intrusion is seen as justification for Japan's expansionist policies. Sondheim used not only Oriental instruments to convey his moods, but poetry highly suggestive of Japanese haiku. The mounting drew strongly on the Japanese Kabuki theatre. Boris Aronson's poetic sets had a distinctly Oriental tinge. He designed Perry's ship to resemble a dragon as much as a vessel. Accordingly, the "Americans" used makeup that suggested they were not only foreign, but possibly fearful monsters. The show made no concession to the tired businessman, so its run was modest and its profits nil.

A free rock adaptation of *Hamlet*—**Rockabye Hamlet** (17 February 1976, Minskoff)—sometimes went to Shakespeare for its dialogue and occasional lyrics in songs such as "That It Should Come To This" and "Tis Pity, Tis True," but more often was content to employ contemporary jargon in its speech and in songs on the order of "He Got It In The Ear," "Have I Got A Girl For You," and "The Rosencrantz And Guildenstern Boogie." Even so resourceful a director as Gower Champion couldn't find a way to make the mixture palatable. The show folded after a single week.

An all-black revue attempted much the same retrospective of a bygone Harlem that *A Musical Jubilee* had tried for our lyric stage. Some of the songs in **Bubbling Brown Sugar** (2 March 1976, ANTA) were new, but the evening's best moments came when it sang its older songs and did its older dances, notably when Vernon Washington recalled Bill Robinson's brand of tapping and when Avon Long sang Bert Williams's "Nobody." The great Harlem nightspots, the Savoy Theatre, and Lenox Avenue all provided backgrounds for fondly remembered melodies by Fats Waller, Duke Ellington, Shelton Brooks, Maceo Pinkard, and Eubie Blake. The show ran out the season and through the next.

A twentieth-anniversary remounting of *My Fair Lady* (15 March 1956) faithfully recreated not only Oliver Smith's sumptuous settings and Cecil Beaton's beautiful gowns, but also Moss Hart's staging and Hanya Holm's choreography. With Ian Richardson as Higgins and Christine Andreas as Eliza, the work opened at the St. James on the 25th and played on for nearly a year.

Two more offbeat entertainments followed, five nights apart. **Monty Python Live!** (14 April 1976, City Center) was a "multimedia" frolic featuring many regulars from the BBC's uproarious, lunatic-fringe series *Monty Python's Flying Circus.*

On the 19th at the Palace, Shirley MacLaine, assisted by a chorus of three men and two girls, brought in her one-woman show for two weeks. Between bits of dancing and monologues written for her by Fred Ebb, Miss MacLaine sang songs from as far back as *Madame Sherry*'s "Every Little Movement" to *Sweet Charity*'s "Big Spender." The production was brought back for an additional stand later at season's end.

Richard Rodgers suffered one of his most embarrassing failures when his **Rex** (25 April 1976, Lunt-Fontanne) closed after just forty-one performances. Rodgers himself was not at fault. His score was attractive, and the show's demise probably deprived "No Song More Pleasing" of a place in his canon. Sheldon Harnick's lyrics were also pleasant. Unfortunately, Sherman Yellen's book was unwieldy, dealing with Henry VIII and his wives in the first act, and in the second with Henry's love--hate relationship to his daughter Elizabeth (played by Penny Fuller, who also played a wife in the first act). The mercurial English actor Nicol Williamson portrayed Henry.

An at times delightful bit of fluff, **So Long, 174th Street** (27 April 1976, Harkness) was probably booked too far uptown at the out-of-the-way

Harkness to have a chance to find an audience. The show itself was second-rate, but its flaws were frequently glossed over by the clowning of Robert Morse and George S. Irving. Morse brought his perennial boyish charm to the role of a young man in the Depression whose parents want him to be a pharmacist but who dreams of being a great star. The show was cleverly framed, beginning as he is interviewed in a dressing room just before he is to receive an honor and ending as he walks up the podium to deliver his thanks for being elected pharmacist of the year. In between, his dreams allow him to dance with a hat and cane in a big production number of the title song and allow his butler (Irving) a hilarious, if smutty, song suggesting the young star is busy making love to every glamour girl in Hollywood.

Joseph Papp's venturesome New York Shakespeare Festival brought back Bertolt Brecht and Kurt Weill's *Threepenny Opera*, decked out in late Victorian costumes and settings, and using a new, scatological translation by Ralph Manheim and John Willett that purported to be closer to Brecht's original than Blitzstein's fine reworking. With Raul Julia as Mack the Knife, the revival, which opened at the Vivian Beaumont on 1 May, quickly found a receptive audience and ran for months.

If Sondheim and Rodgers met with bad luck during the season, their lot was fortunate compared to Leonard Bernstein and Alan Jay Lerner's. Their **1600 Pennsylvania Avenue** (4 May 1976, Hellinger) was a one-week fiasco. It took a servant's-eye view of the White House from Washington to Teddy Roosevelt. Handsome Ken Howard played all the Presidents, the fine English comedienne with the desperate smile, Patricia Routledge, played all the First Ladies, and Gilbert Price played an apparently eternal butler. The show turned "The Star Spangled Banner" into a minuet and the post--Civil War boom into "The Robber Baron Minstrel Parade." But Lerner's continuing inability to write well-constructed librettos from original ideas undermined the entertainment.

England's D'Oyly Carte had found its visits increasingly short and less profitable. When it returned the night after *1600 Pennsylvania Avenue*'s premiere, it confined its visit to less than three weeks and performed only the most popular, sure-fire works: *The Mikado, The Pirates of Penzance,* and *H. M. S. Pinafore.* The response was not overwhelming.

A small, charming, unpretentious musical ended the season. A group of novices used a story much like Agatha Christie's *Ten Little Indians* to create a comical musical mystery about ten people marooned on an island estate, Rancour's Retreat, and murdered one by one. One of the characters was the appropriately named Miss Tweed, a combination of Miss Christie and her Miss Marple. Played by the hefty English music hall favorite Tessie O'Shea, she helped underscore the show's debt in "I Owe It All (To Agatha Christie)." Even the somber, cumbersome Victorian furniture was as witty as it was murderous. Sadly, audiences couldn't be corralled, so **Something's Afoot** (27 May 1976, Lyceum) departed when summer came.

1976–1977

This was a season of revivals rather than revival. Broadway had seen over half the musicals offered to it before, while one "new" show had actually premiered in Berlin nearly fifty years earlier.

June offered two attractions: **An Evening with Diana Ross** (14 June 1976, Palace) and a revival of *Pal Joey* at the Circle in the Square on the 27th. Ross was supported by three more girl singers and three male mimes. A few older songs, such as "The Lady Is A Tramp" and "My Man," were mixed in with more recent pop tunes.

An obscene, sex-obsessed off-Broadway cabaret show, **Let My People Come** (7 July 1976, Morosco) was rushed uptown. Both off-Broadway and on, the show discouraged critics from reviewing it, and it was condemned by the League of New York Theatres and Producers. Despite or perhaps because of this it survived for 102 playings.

By coincidence, Salvation Army dolls and their shady guys framed the principal season. *Guys and Dolls* (24 November 1950), with an all-black cast, braved the hot weather to open on 22 July at the Broadway. If this version smacked more of Harlem than of Brooklyn, Queens, or the seedier sections of white Manhattan, it nonetheless had style, gusto, and a gratifying faithfulness to the original. Adelaide (Norma Donaldson), Nathan (Robert Guillaume), Sarah (Ernestine Jackson), and Sky (James Randolph) replayed their adventures well into the season. The revival prompted Clive Barnes of the *Times* to note that the great songs of the old shows were "the element that keeps [them] alive." All through the year only the old shows really sent audiences away singing.

In its fall and spring seasons the New York City Opera raised its curtain on several classics: *H. M. S.*

Pinafore, Die Fledermaus, La Belle Hélène, The Saint of Bleecker Street, and *The Pirates of Penzance.*

Going Up (25 December 1917) was another oldie—a virtually forgotten one—filled with buoyant, humble melodies. The revival originated at the Goodspeed Opera House in East Haddam, Connecticut, and came to the Golden on 19 September. If Goodspeed had a tradition of bravely resuscitating obscure past hits, it also had a tradition of presenting them faithlessly and tastelessly. *Going Up* was no exception. The book was altered, songs written for other shows interpolated, and the entire mounting, even what were meant to be its tender moments, played for laughs. For all its faults, the second-string critic the *Times* sent to review the show could still quite rightly find it full of charm. But the revival had more charm than staying power.

Debbie Reynolds brought a vaudeville into the Minskoff briefly, while the nudist revue *Oh, Calcutta!* was revived at the Edison.

Porgy and Bess (10 October 1935) was actually more than a revival. The version unveiled at the Uris on 25 September was Broadway's first chance to hear virtually the complete score Gershwin wrote, including such generally omitted passages as the extended opening and "The Buzzard Song" in its proper place. The production had originated with the Houston Grand Opera Company as its contribution to the nation's bicentennial celebration. As they often had in earlier revivals, several singers alternated in each of the principal roles. For opening night Porgy was sung by Donnie Ray Albert and Bess by Clamma Dale.

The National Folk Theatre of Ireland sailed over with **Siamsa** (27 September 1976, Palace), a compilation of dances, songs, fiddling, and other Celtic diversions. It ran one week.

A handful of New Yorkers had seen **The Robber Bridegroom** (9 October 1976, Biltmore) when it visited Broadway a year earlier as part of the repertory of John Houseman's band, the Acting Company. Based on a novella by Eudora Welty, the musical had book and lyrics by Alfred Uhry and music by Robert Waldman. Its story followed the picaresque adventures of Jamie Lockhart (Barry Bostwick) after he is separated from his beloved through the machinations of her wicked stepmother. Folksy and light, if not insistently memorable, the show played through most of the season.

Miking and amplification allowed some weak-voiced crooners to appear at large, legitimate venues. Thus, the most famous of all crooners ventured an appearance in **Bing Crosby on Broadway** (7 December 1976, Uris). Crosby was assisted by Rosemary Clooney, a gaggle of younger Crosbys, Joe Buskin and his quartet, and an on-stage band, the Billy Byers Orchestra. Reversing Diana Ross's balance, the older star emphasized older songs from "Where The Blue Of The Night (Meets The Gold Of The Day)" onward. The troupe performed for a week and a half.

A show from which much had been expected closed immediately after it opened. With Richard Adler and Will Holt writing the songs, George Abbott attempted to turn Shakespeare's *Twelfth Night* into much the same sort of romp he had created out of *A Comedy of Errors, The Boys from Syracuse* (23 November 1938). That a number of relatively unknown hands had done the job superbly eight years before in *Your Own Thing* (13 January 1968) failed to daunt the eighty-nine-year-old Abbott. Unlike *The Boys from Syracuse*, which employed only a single line from Shakespeare, **Music Is** (20 December 1976, St. James) leaned frequently on the original text, much more than had *Your Own Thing*. But the 1968 production had brought to its adaptation a point of view, a deliciously irreverent two-faced stance that allowed it to josh the very story it was following. Somehow *Music Is* lost itself shunting between two worlds. Its high moments came fitfully. Sebastian (Joel Higgins) and Olivia (Sherry Mathis) had one pleasant song, "Please Be Human," while Malvolio (Christopher Hewitt) had his day with "I Am It." Choreographer Patricia Birch offered a splendid *galop* for her Offenbachian first-act finale.

An adaptation of the Gospel according to St. Matthew, presented with black revival-meeting fervor, **Your Arms Too Short to Box with God** (22 December 1976, Lyceum) set feet stomping and hands clapping. Amusingly, this show, which had been created for the Spoleto Festival, sent enthusiastic critics back to the very words they had used to salute the happy black musicals of half a century before: "the best singing and dancing on Broadway," "rollicks with contagious high spirits." Vinnette Carroll, Micki Grant, and Alex Bradford—all associates in *Don't Bother Me, I Can't Cope* (19 April 1972)—shaped the evening, which included William Hardy, Jr., a remarkable baritone capable of soaring above "the highest register ordinarily associated with the most adventurous male voice."

Fiddler on the Roof (22 September 1964) returned on 28 December with Zero Mostel once again its Tevye. The stay at the Winter Garden was announced as limited, though the limits were set not by attendance but by Mostel's willingness to remain with the show. His willingness lasted through the spring.

In an odd, sad way, the black shows of the twenties were again recalled by **Ipi-Tombi** (11 January 1977, Harkness). Though the show had been a major hit in London, this collection of South African native dances was coolly received by New York critics and hounded by left-wing pickets. It struggled on for a brief time before calling it quits. Shortly after it closed the Harkness was sold for demolition or conversion. In recent years the out-of-the-way house had served unsuccessfully as a dance auditorium and legitimate theatre. Before that it had been a television studio and a grind movie house. But in the twenties, as the Colonial Theatre, it had been used for lesser vaudeville and legitimate attractions, including black shows held unworthy of Times Square.

Eighteen years had passed since New Yorkers were first invited to *A Party with Betty Comden and Adolph Green* (23 December 1958). The two were "at home" again, accompanied only by a pianist, on 10 February at the Morosco. Singing lyrics they set to Jule Styne's or Leonard Bernstein's or Cy Coleman's music, they delighted their loyal admirers. That these admirers were fewer in number than they had a right to hope was revealed when they moved their entertainment to the smaller Little Theatre and shortly thereafter sent the last of their guests home.

Three hits arrived over a six-night span in mid-April. **Side by Side by Sondheim** (18 April 1977, Music Box) was a low-budget (cast of four) anthology of Stephen Sondheim's songs. Curiously, the show had originated in London. As a slightly premature retrospective, it confirmed Sondheim's brilliance as a lyricist; Clive Barnes in the *Times* went further, asserting the show proved he was "the master lyricist of American popular music." But even Barnes had to make excuses for Sondheim's failings as a melodist. Still, his word wizardry was intriguing enough to make the evening worthwhile.

Barnes began his review for **I Love My Wife** (17 April 1977, Barrymore) noting that Broadway was bound to get around to wife-swapping, since Hollywood had done it years ago. Barnes was clearly too young to remember Broadway got there first, with *So Long, Letty* (23 October 1916). The small cast was abetted by a small on-stage orchestra. The musicians—dressed as devils, or in pajamas—acted as a sort of modern-day Greek chorus might, commenting flippantly on the liaisons, which, by the by, never got very far. Barnes and most other critics singled out lanky Lenny Baker as the best of the straying spouses. Baker's Alvin employs every conceivable delaying tactic—needing ages to undress, painstakingly folding every garment, then insisting on finishing off a banana cream pie. Michael Stewart wrote the book and lyrics to Cy Coleman's music, the best of which was probably the lively "Hey There, Good Times" and the title song. By now Coleman was increasingly perceived as the most prolific and consistently successful Broadway composer of his day.

> CY COLEMAN was born Seymour Kaufman in New York on 14 July 1929. He gave concerts as a child prodigy, then studied at New York's High School of Music and Art and at the New York College of Music. His interest in jazz led him to become a nightclub pianist. In 1953 he interpolated a song into *John Murray Anderson's Almanac*, but he did not hit the big time until *Wildcat* in 1960.

The season's biggest hit was the last of April's trio, **Annie** (21 April 1977, Alvin). Based on the once-famous comic strip *Little Orphan Annie*, the musical sent its waif (Andrea McArdle) from an orphanage run by the comically villainous Miss Hannigan (Dorothy Loudon) into the arms of the fabulously rich, totally bald Daddy Warbucks (Reid Shelton). Under his aegis Annie gets to meet Franklin D. Roosevelt and even has J. Edgar Hoover enlisted to help find her real parents. When the FBI discovers her parents are dead, Annie is adopted by Warbucks. He and Annie share all their adventures with her loyal dog, Sandy. "Tomorrow," Annie's paean of hope for the future, became the last Broadway show song for several seasons to enjoy widespread appeal. Otherwise Charles Strouse's music (to lyrics by Martin Charnin) was pleasant but not exceptional. Peter Gennaro had fun allowing a small band of ragged waifs to strut and kick as if they were in the long line of Radio City Music Hall Rockettes, whom Gennaro still supervised at the time. The popularity of its hit song and the show's appeal to the proverbial

"children of all ages" helped it to run for a whopping 2,377 performances. Road companies also enjoyed lengthy runs.

> CHARLES STROUSE was born in New York on 7 June 1928 and studied not only at the Eastman School of Music but also with Nadia Boulanger and Aaron Copland. Before writing music for off-Broadway revues, he served as rehearsal pianist for several shows. Success came with his score for *Bye Bye Birdie* in 1960. A musician's musician, his music has not always appealed to the public. Moreover, he frequently has had the misfortune of composing fine scores for books that doomed the entertainment.

A sumptuous revival of Rodgers and Hammerstein's *The King and I* (29 March 1951) on 2 May at the Uris brought Yul Brynner back to recreate the role of the king. Constance Towers played his Anna. At a time when musicals were generally unmelodic, often formless, and frequently preachy or scatological, the revival was poignantly hailed as a "Reminder of [a] Golden Age." The public responded in such numbers that, even in the record-breaking heat of July, *The King and I* played to 98 percent capacity.

From an even earlier, perhaps more golden age came a musical New York had never really seen before, Kurt Weill and Bertolt Brecht's **Happy End** (7 May 1977, Beck). With its tale of underworld guys and Salvation Army dolls, it was originally written for Berlin in 1929, at almost a halfway point between the time New York first saw *The Belle of New York* (28 September 1897) and the Broadway premiere of *Guys and Dolls* (24 November 1950). Brecht's Salvation Army lass is Hallelujah Lil (Meryl Streep). When she capitulates to the charms of the murderous Bill Cracker (Bob Gunton), she is stripped of her uniform. She reforms Cracker and his gang in time to put her uniform back on before the final curtain. The show, in Michael Feingold's translation, had originated at the Chelsea in Brooklyn. Despite critical kudos and superior Weill melodies such as "Surabaya Johnny" and "The Bilbao Song," theatregoers stayed away, so *Happy End* ended its run unhappily with the coming of warm weather.

Two oddities deserve passing mention. **Toller Cranston's Ice Show** (19 May 1977, Palace), with the Canadian skater heading the company, unveiled a variety of beautiful numbers, ranging from ballet to tango to rock and roll. It ran two weeks. At the Winter Garden something called **Beatlemania** played weeks and weeks of previews without, apparently, ever opening officially. The entertainment surrounded four young men impersonating the rock stars with "slides, film, and video projects, read-outs from a giant ticker tape and a great many lights."

1977–1978

Like the preceding season, 1977–1978 was one of revivals rather than revival. Certainly the early months offered little more than a parade of old faces. On 4 August, *Hair* (29 April 1968) returned to the Biltmore and added another 108 performances to its record. *Man of La Mancha* (22 November 1965) came into the Palace on 15 September for a limited stay as part of a national tour. It chalked up 124 performances. October's revival was Victor Borge in his popular one-man show, *Comedy in Music*. Borge added much fresh material to his evening, but *Hair* and *Man of La Mancha* were presented with a large degree of fidelity to their originals (with Richard Kiley again in his starring role). Here and there, critics suggested these book shows had lost something of their old luster—a criticism also voiced when *Jesus Christ Superstar* (12 October 1971) appeared at the Longacre on 23 November. But carping critics were in the minority. Still, *Superstar* failed to find the hoped-for audience and was withdrawn after ninety-six showings.

The New York City Opera also gave lovers of older musicals some treats, in the fall presenting *Die Fledermaus* and *The Pirates of Penzance*, and in the spring, besides the Strauss, *The Merry Widow* and *The Saint of Bleecker Street*.

Another "superstar" had arrived in October with the first original musical of the season. **The Act** (29 October 1977, Majestic) was created solely as a vehicle for Liza Minnelli. John Kander and Fred Ebb, who had written material for her earlier, did the songs, while George Furth developed the thinnest of books. Miss Minnelli played Michelle Craig, a once-important film star whose career collapses after she loses her husband. She determines to make a comeback with a nightclub act for Las Vegas. Little enthusiasm was shown for the book or lyrics, but there was general rejoicing over Miss Minnelli's skills as an entertainer. However, the rejoicing was soon soured when it was learned Miss Minnelli had prerecorded some of her songs and was merely mouthing them on stage. Walter Kerr led the protests with an article in the *Times* headed, "A Theatre Critic Gets That 'Synching' Feeling." The disclosures brought out in the open a growing displeasure with the abuse—indeed, with the very use—of amplification in what was supposedly "live" theatre. Proponents insisted that today's audiences, lulled by films and television, no longer had an ear for naturally voiced singing and dialogue. Still, for the first time in years, in review after review of musicals that followed, complaints were expressed about the unnatural sounds emanating from loudspeakers on the proscenium. Most theatregoers would probably be surprised to learn that the battle had first been joined thirty-seven years before when Richard Watts, Jr., and Brooks Atkinson had bewailed Earl Carroll's use of microphones in his last *Vanities* (13 January 1940). Miss Minnelli aggravated matters later in the run when she insisted even mouthing songs was too arduous for the customary eight performances a week. Tantrums, fainting spells, and dramatic exits were the stock-in-trade of early prima donnas such as Lillian Russell or Delia Fox, but these ladies had at least performed in a theatre that required muscle and vocal cords.

The next musical to arrive, **On the Twentieth Century** (19 February 1978, St. James), tried to be a good old-fashioned musical comedy. It was lavishly mounted, star-studded, blessed with a solid, funny story, and offered songs that, for this day and age, could be considered slightly arioso. Based on *Twentieth Century*, an old play by Ben Hecht and Charles MacArthur, and remembered by most theatregoers for the film version with John Barrymore and Carole Lombard, it told another tale of a theatrical has-been desperately seeking a comeback. In this case the has-been is the flamboyant producer Oscar Jaffe (John Cullum), and key to his resurrection is his former star and mistress, Lily Garland (Madeline Kahn). His attempts to woo her back while they travel by train cross-country are sometimes interrupted by a zany religious fanatic (Imogene Coca). Betty Comden and Adolph Green devised the book and lyrics, and Cy Coleman the music. But for many the star of the evening was Robin Wagner's "brilliantly effective" recreation of the famous old train. *Variety* began its notice, "It's ominous when an audience leaves a musical whistling the scenery." Still, for all its faults, the evening was rattling good fun.

If the audiences that left whistling the scenery were not always capacity, they were close to it for a long while.

By the standards of the time, March was busy. Four musicals appeared: three new and one old. Actually the first of the "new" musicals was an old friend in disguise. **Timbuktu** (1 March 1978, Hellinger) was merely *Kismet* (3 December 1953) revised to meet the requirements of its all-black cast. New songs, often based on African folk music rather than on Borodin, were added to give some tonal verisimilitude to the change of venue from Baghdad to the half-legendary African watering spot. Geoffrey Holder's costumes and Tony Straiges's sets had a Ziegfeldian opulence. Eartha Kitt, Melba Moore, and Gilbert Price were starred. Though all three were capital performers, none had Alfred Drake's commanding theatrical presence. One result was that some critics felt the show lacked a certain backbone. As with *On the Twentieth Century*, however, the show's attractions helped minimize its shortcomings, and *Timbuktu* did good, though not sellout, business.

Four nights later New Yorkers once again had a chance to say *Hello, Dolly!* (16 January 1964). With Carol Channing returned to head the fun at the Lunt-Fontanne, the show, which had enjoyed a profitable pre-Broadway tour, settled in for a run.

March's next entry underscored the importance of choreographers to contemporary Broadway. The musical was the brainchild of Bob Fosse and was devoted entirely to **Dancin'** (27 March 1978, Broadhurst). There was no story, nor any dialogue or new songs as Broadway normally understood them. Instead, sixteen talented hoofers danced in a variety of styles to music "from Bach through John Philip Sousa and George M. Cohan to Johnny Mercer and Cat Stevens." Without a story or lavish sets to hang the dances on, some critics felt the dances failed to provide a totally satisfactory evening. Other critics were ecstatic. At least in its early weeks the show seemed to attract hordes of playgoers willing to decide for themselves. They decided they liked it. So did New York's many foreign visitors, who wanted to enjoy a Broadway show but who spoke little or no English. For them the musical presented no obstacles, only pleasurable escape. As a result, *Dancin'* ran for 1,774 performances.

If complaints about amplification were growing, Broadway's reception of the next musical stood to revive an even older complaint, namely that Broadway critics often killed shows the road loved.

A History of the American Film (30 March 1978 ANTA) had been mounted at several important regional theatres, generally to resounding acclaim. The evening was a series of vignettes spoofing famous films and film stars from the silent era to the present. Christopher Durang wrote the book and lyrics to Mel Marvin's score. What many American cities had viewed as stylish drollery, New York rejected as a crass, humorless hodgepodge. It was just this sort of reaction that inspired Richard Adler to attempt to found a hospitable base for new musicals in North Carolina. Adler had not had a New York success since *Damn Yankees* (5 May 1955), although a number of distinguished critics, led by Richard Coe of the *Washington Post*, praised his later works, especially *Music Is* (20 December 1976).

A collection of songs by Fats Waller provided the meat for an entire evening named after his most famous song, **Ain't Misbehavin'** (9 May 1978, Longacre). A small cast presented at least two songs which have long been credited to Jimmy McHugh, but which the producers have announced Waller actually wrote and sold the rights to: "I Can't Give You Anything But Love" and "Sunny Side Of The Street."

The next night brought the premiere of **Angel** (10 May 1978, Minskoff). To music by Gary Geld, Peter Udell and Ketti Frings provided a libretto adapted from Frings's prizewinning stage version of Thomas Wolfe's *Look Homeward, Angel*. The bittersweet saga of Eugene Gant's adolescence in North Carolina, of his soured-on-life father and his dreamy mother, was recreated in homey, sentimental terms. Since so many of the people behind the scenes had been responsible for *Shenandoah* (7 January 1975), Broadway had some advance inkling of the musical's tenor. The initial pre-opening advertisement confirmed this, reprinting Kevin Kelly's notice, from the Boston *Sunday Globe*, that underscored *Angel*'s kinship to the earlier show.

Like *A Chorus Line* (25 July 1975), **Runaways** (13 May 1978, Plymouth) began life in one of Joseph Papp's off-Broadway auditoriums. And like *A Chorus Line*, it was essentially a chamber musical allowing a collection of people to come forward with their histories and personal problems. Conceived and written by Elizabeth Swados, the evening recounted the often humorous, often harrowing experiences of children who have run away from home. Daringly, Swados employed several real runaways in her cast. As a result, the *Times* found one of the pleasures of the production "its rough edges and its freshness" and also hailed "a lowdown travesty of punk rock" called "Where Are Those People Who Did 'Hair'?" *Variety* also singled out the song. The trade paper may have also given this sort of show an official label when it tagged it a "musical collage."

May's fourth musical was **Working** (14 May 1978, 46th Street), a lyric version of Studs Terkel's slices of lower-class life. A group effort to an even greater extent than many musicals, its advertisements listed songs by six writers, including Micki Grant, Mary Rodgers, and Stephen Schwartz.

Two oddball musicals were also seen during the season. A Russian importation called **Estrada** played a brief stand at the Majestic in September, while a glorified rock concert, not unlike the preceding season's *Beatlemania*, ran for a few weeks at the Palace. Just as the earlier show had concentrated on the music of the group its title celebrated, the new piece honored a famous rock figure, insisting in its title, **Elvis the Legend Lives.**

1978–1979

In contrast to the two preceding seasons, 1978–1979 was not awash in revivals, although two of the homemade ones were of uncommon interest. Nevertheless, the past was omnipresent throughout the theatrical year in one dramatic guise or another. On much rarer occasions, the season was also fresh and vital, daringly extending the boundaries of popular musical theatre. But old or new, stale or original, comfortable or shocking, it was a busy season. Musicals almost outnumbered nonmusicals. *Variety* listed twenty of the year's thirty-seven productions as lyrical offerings of some sort.

The season's very first offering provided an exciting example of how the old and the new might be dovetailed. **The American Dance Machine** (14 June 1978, Century) was more than a musical. It was an idea that grew into a permanent company, and all of it was the brainchild of a spunky, imaginative and dedicated choreographer, Lee Theodore. Her idea was to keep alive—and joyously kicking—the best dances from bygone Broadway shows. This time around, her program culled routines from more than a dozen shows, ranging, alphabetically, from *The Boy Friend* to *Walking Happy*. There were some problems. Neither records nor survivors were on hand to detail dance numbers from older shows, thereby depriving the entertainment of a certain breadth. The dances, of necessity, had to be taken out of their original context, thereby sometimes depriving them

of a certain meaningfulness, and their creators and earliest interpreters were not available or willing to participate in their original roles, thus depriving the dances of a certain authenticity and strength. For all that, the evening was as delightful as it was instructive. The show ran six months, toured, and was revived several times.

> **TOMMY TUNE** was born in Wichita Falls, Texas, on 28 February 1939. He made his Broadway debut as a chorus boy in 1965, and first called real attention to himself in *Seesaw* in 1973. But with *Whorehouse* he proved that he was more than a lanky, pleasant-looking, if slightly epicene performer and revealed major skills as a choreographer and director.

A raunchy ranch, whose chicks made some feathers fly, was the subject of **The Best Little Whorehouse in Texas** (19 June 1978, 46th St.). The musical, with book by Larry L. King and Peter Masterson and songs by Carol Hall, had opened off-Broadway in April and had been such an immediate hit that it was hurried uptown. Its story retold the sad saga of a much-loved brothel, shut down after some self-serving television do-gooders singled it out for their hypocritical censure. The chief villain was the greasily handsome Melvin P. Thorpe (Clint Allmon), who smirks and glowers at the camera while sporting a bouffant blond wig and dressed in red, white, and blue (with nothing less than the stars and stripes for a tie). The lady of the evening (should we call her madam?) was Mona Stangley (Carlin Glynn). Caught in the middle was a foul-mouthed, fun-loving sheriff with a heart of gold, Ed Earl Dodd (Henderson Forsythe). The multi-leveled unit set made the house look anything but homey, the costumes were tacky, the country-style music hardly memorable. But Tommy Tune, who co-directed and choreographed, imparted his singular, always engaging pizzazz to the evening. Some hackles were raised when the producers took out ads featuring only the title's most eye-catching word. All in all, the musical was harmless fun, despite its title. But that title no doubt helped it achieve an astounding run of 1,576 performances.

In a sense, an even longer run was approaching its end when the D'Oyly Carte began a brief visit to the New York State Theatre on 17 July. Its repertory consisted of *Iolanthe, The Mikado, H. M. S. Pinafore*, and *The Pirates of Penzance*. By this time the company was living not on its reputation, which had plunged shamefully and deservedly, but on its name. Within a very few seasons even that name would belong solely to history. In its final years the company's casts were mediocre and its stagings painfully hidebound. Its management had apparently forgotten that its founder, Richard D'Oyly Carte, had not confined himself to producing Gilbert and Sullivan. Had the company injected some fresh air into its membership, its productions, and its repertory (like, say, Vienna's *Volksoper*) it might have not only survived but possibly flourished. The Savoyards were followed at the same huge house on 3 August by a ho-hum revival of *Stop the World—I Want to Get Off* (3 October 1962), with the energetic Sammy Davis, Jr., as Littlechap.

Critics and first-nighters trekked back to the New York State Theatre—the city's most beautiful opera house—for yet another revival. Only on this occasion it was the New York City Opera which was opening its season with an operetta that by rights belonged in Broadway's domain. And thereby hangs a tale.

European-style operetta has been out of fashion for more than half a century. Its fall from grace began in the late twenties, when a surfeit of mostly mediocre examples turned many playgoers and more critics sour on the form. (Playgoers remained far more receptive than critics, making such operettas as *My Maryland* and *The New Moon* long-run successes despite numerous scathing reviews.) At first, objections focused primarily on the very nature of such works—their often preposterous plots, their sometimes Graustarkian settings, the seeming obsolescence of their florid melodies and equally florid dialogue. But in the 1930s two other assaults were launched. One tied the basic form to Austria and Germany and thus, resorting to guilt by association, with the Nazi movement. Many of the critics who seemed to see red at such a horrible connection were happier to see a different sort of red elsewhere. To them operetta, wallowing in royalty, gilded palaces, sumptuous costumes, and sweet waltzes, was a betrayal of the "working class" they so admired. Within a few years new operettas were almost as scarce as hens' teeth. No one could ever again legitimately claim to be surfeited with

second-rate examples. And, of course, by the mid-1940s Nazism had been crushed. Yet such was the pervasive, scarring effect of the assault that when Rodgers and Hammerstein infused new life into the genre they were careful to emphasize from the start their new American settings and their increased reliance on American musical idioms. Moreover, they assiduously refused to admit their shows were operettas, instead noisily insisting that they were something new and wonderful known as "musical plays." Hardly a voice was raised to point out that for decades operettas often had been termed musical plays. The new name, however, allowed critics and others to adopt a convenient double standard. New American works in Rodgers and Hammerstein's splendid tradition (always with a nod to Kern and Hammerstein's *Show Boat*) could be lauded to the skies while anything smacking of merry widows, vagabond kings, or student princes was excoriated. No wonder so few revivals dared brave Broadway.

So the New York City Opera was most definitely entitled to plaudits for attempting to resurrect *Naughty Marietta* (7 November 1910) on 4 September. (The troupe also brought back *The Merry Widow* and *Street Scene*.) Unfortunately, as far as Herbert's operetta was concerned, the company did not have the courage of its convictions—or else those convictions had been battered and compromised by decades of singularly mean, often unwarranted disdain. A "new book and additional lyrics" were no real improvement on Rida Johnson Young's sturdy, if now slightly musty, original. (Would the company ever think to rewrite even the stodgiest librettos of the operas in its repertory?) Equally horrifying, Victor Herbert's great score was cavalierly tampered with. For no good reason a song was brought over from his failed *Prince Ananais*, and the shrewdly developed order of the songs in the original (see pp. 304–305) was sent helter-skelter. For example, the operetta's great hit, "Ah, Sweet Mystery Of Life," was not sung in its entirety in the 1910 production until the very end of the evening, although snatches of it were played and sung to build up suspense (and it was played in the entr'acte). In the new version, it was offered in full in a senseless, dreamlike prologue.

A newspaper strike mercifully deprived less knowledgeable, susceptible readers of notices at first. Later, when the *Times*—New York City's only surviving major newspaper, other than tabloids—got around to reviewing this and subsequent revivals at the opera house, it rarely missed the chance to hurl daggers at the genre in general. The idea of a supposedly impartial paper sending critics who knowingly share the same prejudice against operettas to expostulate on them was not lost on more balanced, temperate theatregoers, who rued the demise of a more competitive, independent heyday.

Eubie! (20 September 1978, Ambassador) featured a different order of old songs, the rag- and jazz-based melodies of ninety-five-year-old Eubie Blake. In recent years Blake had reemerged from obscurity to become a beguiling raconteur on television. Most of his music remained steadfastly forgotten, with only "I'm Just Wild About Harry" and "Memories Of You" retaining their precarious hold on popularity. If most of his songs were, as *Variety* noted, "basically routine," they were brought to life with all the colorful razzmatazz that an economically pinched Broadway would allow, although some tastelessly contemporary orchestrations and that ubiquitous modern outrage, amplification, often hampered an appreciation of their delicacy. Still, there was enough to appreciate and enjoy to allow *Eubie!* a year's run.

Gorey Stories (30 October 1978, Booth), some of Edward Gorey's modern gothic tales, set to music by David Aldrich, opened and closed on the same night.

A not-all-that-old French film was the source of King of Hearts (22 October 1978, Minskoff), which told of a group of inmates of a French insane asylum caught between German and American troops in World War II. By the evening's end the inmates appeared to be the only truly sane people, and even the warring soldiers had decided to hole up permanently and peacefully in the institution. An elaborate turntable moved the action from a bordello to a circus and even to a cathedral roof. A largely undistinguished affair, the musical was able to survive only until early December.

Much had been expected of Platinum (12 November 1978, Hellinger). This musical dealing with a fading screen actress who attempts to make a comeback as a rock singer starred Alexis Smith, a faded screen star who had displayed glittering possibilities for Broadway stardom in earlier appearances. Her glitter—gold or platinum—was in no way tarnished; but the musical itself was dross. A single set representing a studio (and which one critic compared to an airplane hangar) and atrocious amplification (which the same critic insisted "puts [performers] behind thick plate glass and for all their volume, they no longer reach us") only made matters worse. Miss Smith won gasps when she appeared in beautiful, drapey gowns and later in

tight leather pants, but for all her allure she could not keep her vehicle going beyond its thirty-third performance.

Anticipation was even greater for Ballroom (14 December 1978, Majestic), the first new musical to emanate from Michael Bennett's fertile talent since *A Chorus Line.* He worked with a book by Jerome Kass, which the librettist had derived from his own highly praised television drama *Queen of the Stardust Ballroom.* The music was by Billy Goldenberger and the lyrics by Alan and Marilyn Bergman. Kass's story centered on a lonely widow, Bea Asher (Dorothy Loudon), who finds escape and solace by becoming part of a group of middle-aged regulars at a dance hall. She falls in love there with Al Rossi (Vincent Gardenia), and by the time she is elected the group's annual queen she has come to terms with the shocking revelation that he is married. Kass tried to emphasize the sweet in this bittersweet saga by not killing off Bea at the end, as he had in the original version. And Bennett enlivened the evening with a variety of dances, ranging from sedate waltzes and fox-trots to a modern hustle. Sadly, neither the sweetening nor the enlivening was more than serviceable. Moreover, the seemingly inevitable comparisons with *A Chorus Line* made *Ballroom* look to be even more disappointing than it might have otherwise. A hefty advance sale allowed the musical to chalk up a run of just over three months.

On the 19th (John Curry's) Ice Dancing, which had played two weeks in late November at the Felt Forum, reopened at the Minskoff. The Olympic star and his company employed music from classical and modern composers to skate all manner of classical and modern dances. Curry's show added thirty-seven more performances to its record during its Minskoff run.

That was thirty-six performances more than A Broadway Musical (21 December 1978, Lunt-Fontanne) could record. Officially, this star-crossed musical played one performance, but contemporary practice does not take official count of New York previews that long since have supplanted the New Haven–Boston–Philadelphia tryouts of yesteryear. Embellished with songs by Charles Strouse and Lee Adams, William F. Brown's book described how a crass Broadway producer attempts to turn "The Final Point," a black playwright's provocative look at basketball, into a charming song-and-dance entertainment called "Sneakers." The only song singled out by critics was a comic number about the she-dragons who once arranged theatre parties, "Yenta Power."

Another instance of players who in bygone times would have been part of a vaudeville or revue bill now arriving with an entire evening of their own material was **Monteith and Rand** (2 January 1979, Booth). This attractive young couple, John Monteith and Suzanne Rand, regaled audiences with two-people sketches and solo characterizations, some prepared in advance, some improvised on the spot. They lingered into March.

Many old-timers affectionately recalled Louis Calhern and Oscar Karlweis cavorting together as an anti-Semitic Polish army officer and a sly, resourceful Jew forced to flee Nazism together in *Jacobowsky and the Colonel* in 1944. It seemed a natural for a musicalization. Indeed, it had become an opera, presented in Germany in the 1960s. That didn't work, nor did a more light-hearted, light-headed Broadway lyric version known as **The Grand Tour** (11 January 1979, Palace). Not even Joel Grey's droll performance as Jacobowsky, and Jerry Herman's lively, melodic, if not truly memorable songs could nudge the troubled show across the border to success.

Nor could controversy, heavy television advertising, and much forcing turn **Saravà** (11 January 1979, Hellinger) into a money-maker. N. Richard Nash did its book and lyrics, Mitch Leigh its music. The controversy started with the non-opening. The musical began its previews on 11 January, with the official opening announced for the end of the month. But an obvious need for repairs, coupled with surprisingly good houses attracted by both its advertising and pleased word of mouth, prompted its producers subsequently to announce so many delays that newspapers simply picked their own dates to attend and review the show. Those reviews ranged from sharp dismissals to virtual raves. The show was based on Jorge Amado's best-selling *Dona Flor and Her Two Husbands*, which had been made into a successful Brazilian film, and which recounted the dilemma of the beautiful, oversexed widow (Tovah Feldshuh) whose second marriage to the nondescript Teo (Michael Ingram) is bedeviled by the insistent return of her handsome first husband's ghost (P. J. Benjamin), anxious for a few more fiery nights between the sheets. For the briefest time there seemed to be a chance that the show might catch on, but eventually, at season's end, like Flor, it had to give up the ghost.

By contrast, **They're Playing Our Song** (11 February 1979, Imperial) ran and ran, until it had compiled 1,082 performances. The reasons for its long-run success were probably not its delightful, solid book by Neil Simon nor its competent if undistinguished songs by composer Marvin Hamlisch and lyricist Carole Bayer Sager (although the title number enjoyed a limited popularity), but rather its capitulation to Broadway's insane contemporary economics. The show had only two principals and a chorus (which portrayed the principals' alter egos) so tiny (six) that it could have fit snugly onto a conductor's podium. Simon's plot reportedly was inspired by the on-again, off-again romance of his songwriting associates. His principals were a young composer, Vernon Gersch (Robert Klein), and a young lyricist, Sonia Walsk (Lucie Arnaz). They embark on a professional collaboration which shortly evolves into a romantic one. Its course is anything but smooth, what with Sonia's former lover calling at odd hours and Vernon's car breaking down on a trip to Long Island, forcing them to sleep in a strange house. In the end they go separate ways, albeit not without a vague promise to join up again someday.

Whoopee! (4 December 1928) was what disc jockeys might call a golden oldie, with the exclamation point added for a 1979 touch. Except for the late *Banjo Eyes* (25 December 1941), the original production had served as Eddie Cantor's last major Broadway vehicle. Cantor was long gone, and with him went some of the show's special sparkle. (The Ziegfeld touch was also missing.) Nevertheless, the revival was given a colorful production that retained much of the original's verve and good, innocent fun. Charles Repole essayed the Cantor role with great charm. Purists lamented the capricious tampering with Walter Donaldson's fine score—the cutting of "Come West, Little Girl, Come West" and the addition of Donaldson songs not written for the original version. But first-nighters at the ANTA on 14 February and other patrons during the revival's six-month stand probably weren't aware of the changes and couldn't have cared less. On the road the show starred Imogene Coca, which may have disturbed the libretto's not very fragile balance. The production had originated at Connecticut's Goodspeed Opera House and once again attested to that theatre's brave willingness to explore a neglected past.

Bravery of another sort was demonstrated at what became the season's most discussed musical, **Sweeney Todd, the Demon Barber of Fleet Street** (1 March 1979, Uris). Stephen Sondheim supplied the music and lyrics; Hugh Wheeler the book, which was based on Christopher Bond's 1973 drama *Sweeney Todd*, which in turn was derived from George Dibdin Pitt's old favorite, his 1847 melodrama *The String* *of Pearls*. When the embittered Sweeney Todd (Len Cariou) is set free from an unjust imprisonment, he returns to London and again sets up as a barber. He slits the throats of his customers, including the venal judge who imprisoned him, and turns over the bodies to his friend Mrs. Lovett (Angela Lansbury), who bakes them into pies. However, when he discovers he has inadvertently murdered his long-lost wife, his mind snaps completely and he shoves Mrs. Lovett into her own oven. A young boy whom Mrs. Lovett had befriended then kills Todd. The gruesomeness of the subject was accentuated both by some graphic staging, which depicted the slittings, and by the gloomy settings, which grippingly caught the sootiness and impersonal cruelty of London in the Industrial Revolution. It was further underscored by some of Sondheim's most brutal lyrics, especially those that allowed Todd to spew out his envenomed view of mankind. At the same time, Sondheim balanced these with exquisitely tender and haunting melodic pieces such as "Johanna" and "Not While I'm Around" and with what may be the most deliciously funny song written about cannibalism, "A Little Priest." In this last-named, Todd and Mrs. Lovett debate the relative tenderness and tastiness of various professional men (once they are baked into her pies). Cariou's performance, if somewhat narrowly conceived, offered a vivid portrait of a determined, hate-filled figure. Miss Lansbury ranged more widely, finding both comedy and pathos in her character's amoral innocence, albeit at times she edged dangerously close to caricature. Hobe Morrison, *Variety's* remarkably astute critic, who probably had his finger on Broadway's pulse more tellingly than any of his colleagues, wrote, "Most show-goers will either revel in the Stephen Sondheim–Hugh Wheeler musical or loathe it."

Sondheim was later to state at a conference that modern musicals should be abrasive, and not the comforting pabulum they once were. Many who loathed the show were seen walking out on it. Others remained to give it one of those standing ovations becoming all too common and meaningless on Broadway and to hail it as a masterpiece. Both sides were right. Certainly the musical—it was almost an opera—was Sondheim's most fully realized work, in its perceptions, its abiding sense of tone and style, its musicianship and its brilliance of rhyme. But in its story, and his consistent, unrelenting approach to that story, it was also his most off-putting. Yet a superb musical such as *Sweeney Todd* has to be welcomed occasionally as a thoughtful, variant experiment. The show played a year on Broadway, but a later tour was apparently not as profitable as the producers had hoped, if it was profitable at all.

The controversy over the work did not die quickly, as so many theatrical spats do, and gives promise of remaining heated, or at least biased, so long at the musical is produced. When the original stars handed over their parts to replacements (George Hearn and Dorothy Loudon), *Variety's* follow-up review concluded adamantly that *Sweeney Todd* was "an overinflated treatment of a small folk myth, an operatic approach to a story that doesn't need it. It asks for but doesn't earn intellectual respectability." A 1985 Baltimore mounting provoked Scott Fosdick, the bright young critic of the *News American* there, to insist: "Sondheim's extravagantly acclaimed Broadway opera is nothing but stuff and musical nonsense to my opinionated eye and ear. If you ask me, Sondheim fans—and theater lobbies are lousy with them—tend to be slippery pedants. If you say you find the man's tunes dull and lifeless, they say that he's aiming for a higher art. Then if you start arguing the demerits of Sondheim as opera, they'll rejoin, 'Of course, you must realize, he's writing for musical theatre.'"

HAROLD PRINCE was born in New York on 30 January 1928. After studying at the University of Pennsylvania, he served as a stage manager, then was co-producer of several important Broadway musicals, beginning with *The Pajama Game* in 1954. He struck out on his own as producer and finally began directing his own productions. His intellectual approach to staging gave rise to the term "concept musical."

ANGELA LANSBURY was born in London on 16 October 1925 and came to Broadway after a long career in films. Her initial stage appearances were in straight plays. Her first role in a musical was in Stephen Sondheim's failed *Anyone Can Whistle* in 1964. Although Hollywood most often cast the attractive redhead in bitchy roles, on Broadway she demonstrated a remarkable versatility, ranging from farce to drama.

For both Hal Prince, the show's director, and Miss Lansbury the musical marked high points in their careers.

Spokesong; or, The Common Wheel (15 March 1979, Circle in the Square) was an odd, borderline case—a dramatic play set against current and older turmoils in Ireland. It was laced with songs, which had music by Jimmy Kennedy, of "Red Sails In The Sunset" fame, and lyrics by the playwright Stewart Parker.

By coincidence, another somewhat similar play followed close on its heels. **Zoot Suit** (25 March 1979, Winter Garden), which dealt with perceived persecution of Chicanos in Los Angeles, had been a major, long-run success there. It used original new songs as well as recordings of contemporary popular favorites to heighten its coloring and tensions. New Yorkers wouldn't buy.

Nor would they buy a charmingly old-fashioned musical that seemed to have wandered on stage a quarter-century too late. **Carmelina** (8 April 1979, St. James), which was based on the film *Buona Sera, Mrs. Campbell*, had a book by Alan Jay Lerner and Joseph Stein, lyrics by Lerner, and music by Burton Lane. Its plot recounted how Carmelina (Georgia Brown), telling all her Italian neighbors she is a war widow, has actually been milking three gull-ible ex-GIs for child support. When the three, each unaware of the others, return to Carmelina's Italian village for a reunion, her lucrative scheme is exposed. But then Carmelina knows she can always say "yes" to her persistent suitor, the local café proprietor, Vittorio Bruno (Cesare Siepi). Otis L. Guernsey Jr., who agreed that *Carmelina* deserved a better fate, described it accurately as "a snugly, predictably, even tritely entertaining piece," adding "for which there is a place on the Broadway agenda." Alas, the latter clause is no longer true. Broadway will not make room for such pleasantries. The show went down to defeat after two weeks, taking with it "One More Walk Around The Garden," Lane's captivating Italianate trio, turned into a show-stopper by the three gulled GIs. One of the GIs was played by John Michael King, who had introduced "On The Street Where You Live" in *My Fair Lady* and was the son of the great 1920s musical star Dennis King.

My Old Friends (12 April 1979, 22 Steps) had been playing since mid-January at an off-Broadway house before moving to a theatre that was situated in the Broadway area but really was still off-Broadway in size and approach. It dealt with life in a retirement home. Whatever its virtues, it could not prevail on playgoers—young or old—to purchase tickets, so soon departed.

The Utter Glory of Morrisey Hall (13 May 1979, Hellinger) could not depart soon enough, even if it gave only one official performance on Broadway. It provided the sort of embarrassment a struggling musical theatre did not need. *Variety* stated that it was the season's "nadir"; the *Times*, after desperately trying to find some virtues in it, finally impaled it as "a mess." Rumor had bruited that it was originally to have been a musical version of the pop-ular English film *Belles of St. Trinian's*, and, though its story of wacky carryings-on at a bizarre girls' school in England certainly echoed that hilarious film, the echoes were faint and unfunny and, appar-ently for legal reasons, the connection was strenu-ously denied. Celeste Holm suffered from being miscast as the daffy headmistress, a role played so unforgettably by Alastair Sim in the movie on which the show was not based.

Peter Allen: Up in One (23 May 1979, Biltmore) was, to nobody's surprise, a one-man show starring Peter Allen. Essentially a nightclub act, its songs ranged from "Dixie," "Just A Gigolo," and "Harlem On My Mind" to new ones written expressly for the star. One was clearly its governing number, so it ran one week.

The season's last major show was its saddest, for it turned out to offer the final new Richard Rodgers score Broadway was ever to hear. **I Remember Mama** (31 May 1979, Majestic) was based on the 1944 play of the same name—an even more likely candidate for musicalization than *Jacobowsky and the Colonel*, and no one was a more logical choice to do its score than Rodgers. Its story, set in turn-of-the-century San Francisco, cast a roseate spotlight on a determined mother who raises a family in the face of heartbreaking odds. At one point she disguises her-self as a scrubwoman to visit her little daughter, who is quarantined in the hospital. Yet just about every-thing that could go wrong did go wrong. Perhaps the most serious problem was the grotesque miscast-ing of Liv Ullmann. Anyone remembering Mady Christians or Charlotte Greenwood (who headed the road company) or Irene Dunne (of the film version) had to blanch watching this new Mama, who was not only patently too young and beauti-ful, but conveyed nothing of the warmth, wisdom, or selfless dedication her predecessors had broad-cast across the footlights. Nor could George Hearn do much with the colorless role of Papa. Probably George S. Irving fared best in the juicy part of Uncle

Chris, winning encores with "It's Going To Be Good To Be Gone." But Irving is a consummate modern-day musical comic, and his success suggests he or his role was out of step with the more sweetly sentimental humor of much of the show. All the players had to buck the fact that the new production, both in its Philadelphia tryout and on Broadway, played in huge theatres which militated against a requisite intimacy. (The 1944 original had played the tiny Music Box.) Worse, amplification distorted any surviving wisps of intimacy, making these supposedly endearing flesh-and-blood figures impersonally, ridiculously tinny. A leaden book was no help; nor were pedestrian lyrics (mostly by Martin Charnin). Rodgers's score was not among his best, but it had several melodies, such as "Ev'ry Day" and "You Could Not Please Me More," which might have found a place in his canon in happier times and with happier rhymes. The musical's troubles on the road—an additional lyricist, a new director, a new choreographer—had become so public that its fate was probably sealed long before it opened to disheartened notices. It struggled until the beginning of September and, when it closed, became Rodgers's first show in more than thirty years not to have an original-cast album, although many from the cast did reassemble to make a recording half a dozen years later. Whatever *I Remember Mama* deserved, Rodgers deserved better.

Meanwhile over on Sixth Avenue the Radio City Music Hall continued its on-again, off-again attempt to resuscitate the heyday of the old Hippodrome's brainless spectacles. Its salute to Gotham, **A New York Summer,** which opened on 31 May and ran until October, was at heart an expanded version of the eye-filling shows (complete with thirty-six Rockettes) that the house long had featured between films.

1979–1980

By *Variety*'s count, the new season was even busier than the last. It was also a slightly happier one, although nothing as original and probing as *Sweeney Todd* appeared. (Which may have been one reason the season was happier.) Once again, echoes of the past resounded to give the season many of its liveliest, most memorable moments.

A double-decker off-Broadway establishment hit the jackpot twice during the season with small-scaled revues on show-business themes. **Scrambled**

Feet (11 June 1979, Village Gate Upstairs) looked at the contemporary scene in such numbers as "Theatre-Party-Ladies," "Love In The Wings," and "Advice To Producers," all performed by a bright-eyed young cast composed of two men, two women, and a duck. Later in the season **One Mo' Time** (22 October 1979, Village Gate Downstairs) examined black vaudeville in 1920s New Orleans. Culling its material from the past, the show was even more successful. *Scrambled Feet* ran for 831 performances, while *One Mo' Time* had to be repeated 1,372 times and eventually sent a road company out to first-class touring houses.

One of the increasingly numerous one-man shows was **Bruce Forsythe on Broadway** (12 June 1979, Winter Garden). The entertainer sang some standard songs and offered imitations and monologues. Broadway was not especially entertained, so the show folded after five performances.

The season proceeded unassumingly enough with a one-woman show, **The Madwoman of Central Park West** (13 June 1979, 22 Steps). The one woman, the self-proclaimed madwoman, was Phyllis Newman, a.k.a. Mrs. Adolph Green, and her stories and songs all purported to be a sort of comic and melodic autobiography, retailing the vicissitudes of raising children and a brilliant husband in a swank apartment high above the city. Since Mrs. Green had some show business connections, her show's credits included such names as Arthur Laurents, Leonard Bernstein, Kander and Ebb, Bock and Harnick, Betty Comden, and the man some playgoers may have thought was Miss Comden's husband, Miss Newman's husband. Something of an inner-circle entertainment, it spanned the summer heat.

The Cinderella Era, which dominated Broadway musicals in the early 1920s, was evoked amid multi-colored strobe lights and blaring, pulsating modern music in **Got Tu Go Disco** (25 June 1979, Minskoff). Its shopgirl heroine, Cassette (Irene Cara), is persuaded to attend a trendy discotheque, is dressed up in a borrowed gown, and at the dance wins a contest with her dreamboat, Billy (Patrick Jude). Overwhelmed, she flees and is sought out for the expected happy ending. The contemporary psychedelic lighting played on mirrored, multi-level settings. Film clippings attempted to provide comments on the action. But nothing worked. The show folded after one week.

Whether **Broadway Opry '79** (27 July 1979, St. James) was a legitimate musical or merely a country-music concert in a legitimate theatre is moot. Most critics thought it was the latter. Most playgoers didn't think anything at all, for they came in such sparse numbers that the entertainment closed abruptly in mid-week.

Opera houses sometimes had to do Broadway's work for it. On 30 July the Metropolitan presented Tom Stoppard and André Previn's curious London success **Every Good Boy Deserves Favour**, a political allegory in which a lunatic attempts to control a great orchestra. And indeed a full orchestra was utilized—something Broadway could not afford. The show's engagement was limited to eight performances. Later the Met staged *The Rise and Fall of the City of Mahagonny*, while the New York City Opera again presented *Naughty Marietta, The Merry Widow*, and *Street Scene*.

A dismal, economically pinched black version of *Alice in Wonderland*, entitled **But Never Jam Today** (21 July 1979, Longacre), eked out a week's stand. Its small cast often doubled, tripled, or quadrupled in brass.

Television's zany Gilda Radner defied the heat for seven weeks to offer what was essentially another one-woman show, **Live from New York** (2 August 1979, Winter Garden). She cavorted as RoseAnne Roseannadanna and other characters she had popularized on *Saturday Night Live*. Don Novello, the outlandish Father Guido Sarducci on the same program, headed a small supporting roster.

The season began in earnest, if that's the right word for it, with a high-flying revival of *Peter Pan* (20 October 1954) at the Lunt-Fontanne on 6 September. Sandy Duncan and George Rose were no Mary Martin and Cyril Ritchard, but then Mary Martin and Cyril Ritchard were not Miss Duncan and Mr. Rose. A certain rococo elegance and arch style were missing now, but in its place was a more joyous boisterousness. Children who weren't born in 1954 weren't bothered by the change. They applauded as wildly as ever to bring Tinkerbell back from death's door, and the revival far outran the run of the original, spanning the season and playing well into the next for 551 performances.

The three musicals which followed, though all new, all looked back nostalgically or cynically at an unrestorable past. The first of the new shows also reinforced the harsh drift of a musical theatre less beguilingly musical or refreshingly comic. The previous season Hal Prince had staged a work about a deranged barber who slit his customers' throats

and turned over their bodies to his lady friend to bake into pies. Now he gave his attention to a Latin American dictator and the streetwalker he makes his wife. Her rise to power is commented on, somewhat anachronistically, by a Communist terrorist. **Evita** (25 September 1979, Broadway) was Andrew Lloyd Webber and Tim Rice's hugely successful retelling of the Perón story, as seen through the eyes of Che Guevara. Perón was played by Bob Gunton, Evita by Patti LuPone, and Che by Mandy Patinkin. Miss LuPone had the evening's most popular song, "Don't Cry For Me, Argentina." But the real star of the show was probably Prince, who cleverly turned his chorus into placard-waving *descamisados*, booted troopers, or whatever other group was necessary to give the illusion of action to a singularly undramatic recounting of a dramatic story. Further distractions were supplied by such increasingly tired devices as film clips (the show opened with a film being interrupted to announce Evita's death) and stagehands switching settings in full view of the audience. A mediocre musical turned into superior theatre, it held audiences for 1,567 performances.

MANDY (Mandel Bruce) PATINKIN was born 30 November 1952 in Chicago, Illinois, to a conservative Jewish family. After training at The Juilliard School in 1979 he was cast in his breakthrough role as Che in *Evita*, a role that used his distinctive tenor voice to powerful effect.

Blessed with a great belting voice, PATTI LUPONE was born 21 April 1949 in Northport, New York. As both a graduate of The Juilliard School's first class and a founding member of John Houseman's The Acting Company, LuPone mastered a classical repertoire at an early age. Her early musical theatre roles included Lucy Lockit in *The Beggar's Opera* and Rosamund in *The Robber Bridegroom*, for which she received a Tony nomination in 1976.

The 1940's Radio Hour (7 October 1979, St. James) said almost everything that had to be said in its title. Its you've-heard-this-one-before story centered on a Hit Parade–like program from radio's heyday. Among the many off-mike problems besetting the program are a hard-drinking crooner and the possible loss of a sponsor. The show's music was not new, featuring instead the non-Broadway pop songs of that long-gone day. For three months "Chattanooga Choo Choo," "Ain't She Sweet," "That Old Black Magic," and other old favorites set feet tapping and sent audiences out humming.

The next night Sugar Babies (8 October 1979, Hellinger) romped in. And what a romp it was, with a paunchy, graying Mickey Rooney and a still shapely Ann Miller cavorting through routines and songs from Minsky's glory years. This affectionate salute to the best of burlesque was the brainchild of Ralph Allen, a professor who need never again waste his time in the musty, poor-paying halls of academia. Double takes, double entendres, pratfalls, fright wigs, bumps and grinds, and stripteases were combined in an irresistible entertainment whose slickness and glitter Minsky might have envied. For those who might take umbrage at such shenanigans there was also an amusing, old-fashioned dog act. There was no teary song pleading for audiences not to cry for Minsky. There was no need for it. Audiences were too busy having the sort of totally escapist good time that the musical theatre was providing all too rarely. Rooney and Miss Miller regaled Broadway for 1,208 performances, then packed them in on the road until mid-1986. Curiously, a second company, with Broadway's Carol Charming and Robert Morse as stars, failed and had to be withdrawn.

A beautiful and unmiked revival of The Most Happy Fella (3 May 1956) came into the Majestic on 11 October, with Metropolitan Opera basso Giorgio Tozzi in the lead. It won critical praise, but regrettably could not lure many playgoers. After a mere fifty-two playings it was gone.

The Radio City Music Hall offered four more of its gargantuan spectacles during the season. The first was Snow White and the Seven Dwarfs on 18 October. It was derived from the famed Disney film, and its run was interrupted to allow for the mounting of The Magnificent Christmas Spectacular, beginning on 25 November. It's Spring, on 18 March, offered the traditional Easter pageant and the Vienna Choir Boys. On 8 May the house brought out A Rockette Spectacular. This production starred Ginger Rogers, remembered by some as the lesser half of filmdom's Astaire and Rogers partnership. Neither age nor the theatre's cavernous vastness was especially kind to her. The Rockettes remained the real attraction, something Miss Rogers acknowledged by departing after a few weeks.

A trio of performers performed the intermissionless A Kurt Weill Cabaret (5 November 1979, Bijou) for nine weeks. The show came to town after a long tour to the delight of Weill's many New York admirers.

Strider (November 21, 79, Hayes) had been so well received off-Broadway that it was finally brought uptown, where it added 241 performances to its record. The Russian play, based on a Tolstoy story and sprinkled with songs, told of a horse (Gerald Hiken) who is perceived as a symbol of all underdogs.

King of Schnorrers (28 November 1979, Playhouse), a musicalization of a work by Israel Zang-will, was set colorfully in late eighteenth-century London but told a timeless Jewish folktale, a bit reminiscent of Kismet, centering on a leader of beggars, his daughter, and her lover. The Playhouse was one of several small, essentially off-Broadway–type theatres in the Broadway area. Small as it was, it could not keep the king on his throne for more than two months.

Variety reviewed Bette! Divine Madness (5 December 1979, Majestic) in its nightclub section. Although it was branded a one-woman show, its star, the frazzle-haired Bette Midler, shared the stage with an unusually large supporting group, including an eleven-piece band. To some extent it was almost a vaudeville show, albeit dominated by its star who demanded early on: "Show some respect. I'm a screen goddess now, in the great tradition of Shirley Temple, Zasu Pitts and Miss Piggy."

A pleasing, faithful revival of Oklahoma! (31 March 1943) came into the Palace on 13 December. Director William Hammerstein's fine cast was headed by Laurence Guittard as Curly, Christine Andreas as Laurey, Martin Vidnovic as Jud, Christine Ebersole as Ado Annie, and Harry Groener as Will (along with old-timer Mary Wickes as Aunt Eller). All of these youngsters seemed to be of the sort who thirty or more years earlier might have gone on to long careers and possibly even stardom on our musical stages. But our cruelly constricted lyric theatre was not to afford them many chances. Not only were there fewer musicals (especially of Oklahoma!'s ilk), but another problem continued to rear its head. The musical was greeted as warmly as The Most Happy

Fella had been and ran for nine months, yet there was a feeling that this run, too, was disappointing. One reason may have been that playgoers, reading between the lines and sometimes the lines themselves in morning-after notices, had become aware critics were starting to complain of a creakiness in the books of such musical plays. The charge leveled against the old shows which these later "musical plays" had swept from the stage, that the music was wonderful but the libretto flawed, was slowly but ineluctably being turned against them. The problem, of course, was not so much an artistic one as a generational one. Each age must condemn the not very distant past and allow the next age to reconsider it, if it chooses.

Earlier the season had seen a failed black musicalization of *Alice in Wonderland*. The year was ushered out with **Comin' Uptown** (20 December 1979, Winter Garden), which attempted to reset *A Christmas Carol* in Harlem. The new version centered on Scrooge (Gregory Hines), a heartless slum landlord, and shoved aside Dickens's other characters. Hines's roof-raising dances were not enough to sustain the show.

In passing it should be noted that two versions of Victor Herbert's great children's treat, *Babes in Toyland*, played New York during the season. Both were heavily revised. One was seen off-Broadway; the larger mounting was performed at the Felt Forum for two weeks beginning 21 December.

The failure of *Comin' Uptown* might have provided an anticlimactic ending to the year, had not Richard Rodgers died on 30 December. Although such great composers as Irving Berlin and Arthur Schwartz survived, they were distressingly inactive. Rodgers had remained productive to the last and, along with Victor Herbert and Jerome Kern, represented a triumvirate and succession that had glorified and expanded the American musical theatre for more than three-quarters of a century. (Had he lived longer, Gershwin might have claimed a place in that select group.) The great era of musical theatre to which Rodgers had contributed so much no doubt ended more than a decade earlier, but his death wrote an unquestionable finish to the age.

Another borderline theatre, the Rialto, played host on 12 February to 1980's first musical, an insipid revival of *Canterbury Tales* (3 February 1969), which survived for two weeks.

A better revival followed when *West Side Story* (26 September 1957) appeared at the Minskoff on 14 February. Yet its reception furthered the notion

that critics were changing their perceptions of once-pedestaled musical plays. For example, Walter Kerr in the *Times* exclaimed his surprise at finding the show to be growing "more innocent" with the years and his becoming aware of its "airiness and playfulness." He also said the most apparent parallels to *Romeo and Juliet* "seem pat and synthetic. Worse, they rob us of the emotions we ought to feel." But under the direction of choreographer Jerome Robbins, the show retained much of its vitality and added another 333 performances to its record. Perhaps historians will see some significance in the fact that none of the three great musical plays revived during the season ran nearly as long as the totally escapist, light-hearted *Peter Pan*—the only revival to surpass its initial run.

Nine evenings later the New York City Opera once more revived *Die Fledermaus*, while on 20 March the company delighted Kurt Weill admirers by bringing out his more serious, rarely done **Silverlake.**

Unlike the giants of the past, such as the late Richard Rodgers, the creators and interpreters of modern popular music seem to have had little or no theatregoing in their upbringing, and therein may be a partial explanation of why most musicals employing the newer idioms have seemed so often inept. **Reggae** (27 March 1980, Biltmore) may be an example. Reggae, of course, is the rhythmic, black Jamaican soul music. In the musical, Faith (Sheryl Lee Ralph) returns home to Jamaica after becoming a popular singer in the United States. She takes up again with her old lover, Esau (Philip Michael Thomas), but since he has become a marijuana grower they are soon involved with gangsters. Helpful Rastafarians contribute to a happy ending. One critic, taken aback by the numerous names credited with the book and songs, concluded this was a musical written by a committee. The scenery was scant and unattractive, although Raoul Pène du Bois's color-splashed costumes and Eric Turner's stringy wigs gave the proceedings a picturesque quality. But not for long. Reggae enthusiasts were no more theatregoers than were the music's creators and performers.

Happy New Year (27 April 1980, Morosco) took Philip Barry's *Holiday*, which told of a young man who decides to have his fun now and worry about the consequences later, and paired it with old Cole Porter standards such as "Night And Day" and "You Do Something To Me." The result was a dreary, short-lived hodgepodge that demonstrated the absence of knowing, creative, and original talent in our lyric theatre.

On paper, **Barnum** (30 April 1980, St. James) probably wasn't any better. Mark Bramble's slim story line contrasted the legendary Barnum (Jim Dale) with his down-to-earth wife, Chairy (Glenn Close), and suggested a possible liaison with Jenny Lind (Marianne Tatum). Cy Coleman's score (to lyrics by Michael Stewart) was lively as all getout but had no sticking power. What made the evening was the gaudy production and Dale's bravura performance. David Mitchell's brightly hued circus spilled out beyond the proscenium. Even the pit band was regularly dispersed everywhere but where you might look for it. Dale—gauntly handsome and much too young to look like Barnum—played the clown, rode a unicycle, walked a tightrope, performed magic acts, and made the audience his friend for life. Diverting theatre rather than a contribution to our lyric literature, the show ran two years.

So far the season's new musical hits had gone for their material to the Argentina of a generation ago, the sleazy burlesque houses of a slightly earlier day, and the tinselly world of a nineteenth-century showman. The season's last new musical success went west, to Hollywood, in that fabled town's halcyon days and nights. **A Day in Hollywood/A Night in the Ukraine** (1 May 1980, Golden) was an intimate English revue that looked with wry humor on American film figures and their eccentricities. The first act supposedly took place in the lobby of Grauman's Chinese Theatre. Among its barbed moments were "Famous Feet," a dance routine that offered nods to everyone from Astaire and Rogers to Mickey and Minnie Mouse, and "Doin' The Production Code," which shredded the puritanism of Will Hays's heyday. The second act purported to be a Russian play as the Marx Brothers might have filmed it. Interestingly, Harpo was impersonated by an actress, Priscilla Lopez. Apart from some minor Jerry Herman additions, the evening relied on well-loved standards from bygone films and, most important of all, on Tommy Tune's uncanny theatrical savvy to whip the entertainment into shape. The revue ran over a year.

Black Broadway (4 May 1980, Town Hall) was "a concert musical" filled with an all-black cast who saluted the great black composers and performers of yesteryear. Many of the numbers had been heard in *Ain't Misbehavin'* (9 May 1978) and *Eubie!* (11 January 1979), but no matter. They were wonderful, and the singers, who concertized for twenty-five

performances, put them across with a special élan and fervor.

Musical Chairs (14 May 1980, Rialto) was another off-Broadway musical done, geographically at least, on Broadway. It supposedly took place in the auditorium of an old church which had been converted to theatrical use and told of a playwright's attempt at a comeback Two weeks, and it was gone.

Blackstone (19 May 1980, Majestic), an evening of sleight-of-hand and other more spectacular magic tricks, was performed by a troupe headed by Harry Blackstone, the not-yet-famous magician son of a famous magician father.

The season closed with a one-man show, **Billy Bishop Goes to War** (29 May 1980, Morosco), in which Eric Peterson, who helped write the show with composer John Gray, enacted not only the WWI ace but officers, several ladies, and even King George V. Gray played the accompanying melodies and sometimes commented on the action. In the *Best Plays*, Otis L. Guernsey asked, "[I]s it a play, is it musical, is it a virtuoso specialty act?" When push came to shove, he classified it as a play. Peterson's performance was masterful, but Broadway wouldn't buy, so after a week and a half it was hustled off-Broadway, where it ran nearly ten more weeks.

1980–1981

Once again, it was a busy season for musicals. And once again, most of the biggest hits turned to old shows, old songs, or simply the general appeal of bygone days for inspiration. At the same time, the public and often the critics turned increasingly cold shoulders to revivals of gems from the post-*Oklahoma!* era. An alarmingly unquenchable inflation also played havoc. It discouraged producers from gambling on new shows and new talents and prompted them, frequently to their eventual dismay, to fall back on the apparent safety of old favorites. It meant staggering losses when a show failed, and it precipitated the closing of doubtful entries. Economics no longer allowed a show to stand up and fight. A disheartening number of shows—musicals and straight plays—threw in the towel after a single performance.

June, a month when tourists traditionally pile into New York, was amazingly active, suggesting that producers were looking on musicals as hot-weather entertainment, much as they had at the turn of the century before the days of air conditioning.

The month's parade was led by *Your Arms Too Short to Box with God* (22 December 1976), which opened at the Ambassador on the 2nd and ran until mid-October. Some of the show's songs had been written by Micki Grant, who was responsible for the book, lyrics, and music of the next entry, **It's So Nice to Be Civilized** (3 June 1980, Martin Beck), an ironic title considering the show was set in a black ghetto and most of its characters inhabited Sweetbitter Street. A rambling, disjointed libretto tried to tell several stories at once, including the attempt of a white social worker to get gang members to help paint a mural. Tepid reviews and no known stars compelled *Civilized* to close in its first week.

Dick Van Dyke headed the revival of *The Music Man* (19 December 1957) that came into the City Center for a limited engagement on 5 June. Since there was no hue and cry to hold the show over, it played out its scheduled stand and left.

Fearless Frank (15 June 1980, Princess) was basically another off-Broadway musical housed in a second-class theatre in the Broadway area. (The theatre had been called the 22 Steps the previous year and long ago had been the Latin Quarter nightclub.) The fearless hero of the title was Frank Harris, the notorious roué and litterateur, who died in 1931. His biography, ostensibly dictated to his secretary in Nice, was relived in a series of music hall vignettes. The musical had been done in London without much success. In New York it lasted a week and a half, despite the *Times* praising it for "one of the wittiest books of the season."

Manhattan Showboat (30 June 1980, Radio City Music Hall) gave patrons a glittering survey of American show business, with scenes depicting such aspects as the circus, nightclubs, vaudeville, and Broadway musicals. The huge, revolving stage, the gigantic sets, and the high-kicking Rockettes all added to the fun.

As he had in the original, Richard Burton dominated the revival of *Camelot* (3 December 1960), which began a limited stay at the vast New York State Theatre on 8 July.

The generally sorry state of creativity in the American Musical Theatre was nowhere better illustrated than in the year's biggest hit, **42nd Street** (25 August 1980, Winter Garden), a theatricalization of the 1933 classic Warner Bros. film. The story of an untested hoofer (Wanda Richert) shoved into overnight stardom by a desperate producer (Jerry Orbach) after his bitchy leading lady (Tammy Grimes) breaks her ankle was retained

and performed with tongue only slightly in cheek. Many of Harry Warren's original songs were also retained, and they were supplemented not by new numbers but by Warren tunes from other films. The resulting array of welcome old standards included "Lullaby Of Broadway," "About A Quarter To Nine," "Shuffle Off To Buffalo," "We're In The Money," and, of course, the title song. A chorus larger than Broadway had seen in ages set hearts pounding with its rhythmically tapping feet. If the result was superb modern-day entertainment, it could not hide the fact that 42nd Street had abandoned live musicals half a century before and that not only Broadway, but Hollywood as well, no longer churned out such captivating, melodic inanities. An additional, very special pall was cast on the opening night when producer David Merrick interrupted the curtain calls to disclose that the show's director and choreographer, Gower Champion, had died that same day.

On 29 August the New York City Opera once more shamed commercial Broadway by reviving the sort of Ruritanian operetta that Broadway shuns. Its selection was Romberg's most popular work, *The Student Prince* (2 December 1924), and it gave operetta loyalists a rare chance to hear such glorious bits of romantic hokum as "Serenade," "Deep In My Heart, Dear," and the "Drinking Song." The following month the troupe resurrected *Die Fledermaus* and, in October, *Silverlake*.

If the star-crossed love affair of a student prince and a beer garden waitress was no longer Broadway's idea of a viable subject for musicalization, Daniel Keyes's novel *Flowers for Algernon* was. Its story told how scientists, buoyed by upgrading the IQ of a mouse named Algernon, attempt the same experiment on a brain-damaged bakery worker named Charlie (P. J. Benjamin). Unfortunately, **Charlie and Algernon** (14 September 1980, Hayes) was more preachy and pontificating than diverting, and Charles Strouse's lively but not top-drawer score was little help. According to one critic the mouse, uncredited on the playbill, performed "a mean little soft shoe." But that didn't help either. The musical compiled seventeen showings.

The growing disfavor into which the great post-*Oklahoma!* musicals were falling could be read in the morning-after reviews of a revival of *Brigadoon* (13 March 1947) at the Majestic on 16 October. *Variety* began its notice by observing, "An outstanding element... is its melodic richness," while the *Times* complained that the story's "unwieldy elements" were not "artfully integrated" and "must labor under the dated, elaborate conventions of old-fashioned musicals." *Variety* went on to call the book "solid," and nowhere was the criticism severe, but as in some of the previous season's criticisms the notion that these once highly vaunted books were becoming rickety with age and that the shows' ultimate strength was in their great music was promising to take hold much as it long since had in all too many faddists' perceptions of 1920s and 1930s musicals. Possibly as a result of this reined-in reception the revival went into the annals with a disappointing run of 133 performances. Its excellent cast included Meg Bussert as Fiona and Martin Vidnovic, who had won praise the preceding season as Jud in *Oklahoma!*, as Tommy.

Banjo Dancing (21 October 1980, Century) was a one-man show in which Stephen Wade joked and told stories along with playing his banjo. Produced in one more of those small off-Broadway–like theatres in the heart of the playhouse district (this theatre had once been Billy Rose's Diamond Horseshoe), it survived a month. Wade found a happier reception in small theatres and boîtes out of town.

An utterly enchanting evening of nostalgia, with a minuscule cast of six, **Tintypes** (23 October 1980, Golden) had won acclaim in regional theatres and in an off-Broadway mounting before moving to the big time. It framed its seemingly irresistible mélange of songs, almost all from the century's first decade, in the slightest story (sketch might be better) of immigrants arriving in America. The songs included Cohan's "The Yankee Doodle Boy," Sousa's "El Capitan's Song," Herbert's "Toyland," and the 1918 hit "Smiles." Oddly, the public resisted, and the musical had a somewhat forced run of just under three months.

One reason for the public's resistance and for the reception accorded some subsequent retrospectives was the subtle editorial twisting of some of the notices, as typified by the influential *Times*. Suggesting that for all its charming virtues the show lacked a certain pizzazz, Frank Rich concluded his first paragraph, "The pre-1914 years were a time for sweet Scott Joplin ragtime and sparklers; hot Fats Waller jazz and fireworks were still waiting in the wings." In the pre-1914 years of which Rich writes so glibly, Scott Joplin (represented by three songs in the show) was known only to a small coterie. The music which enjoyed widespread popularity in mainstream America came from the pens of Herbert, Sousa, Cohan, Joe Howard, Carrie Jacobs Bond, and their competitors. Similarly, without minimizing the black wellsprings of jazz, Waller was not perceived as the best or quintessential exponent in the 1920s. How about Gershwin, for example?

These warped perceptions may have had a small hand in the dismissive notices accorded **Perfectly Frank** (30 November 1980, Hayes), a retrospective tribute to Frank Loesser. But the show, in this case, was its own worst enemy. To begin with, Loesser, the most musicianly witty of contemporary composers, may be the hardest to take out of context. Something is often lost. "I Believe In You" becomes a lesser (no pun) love song when not sung by the hero to himself in front of a mirror. There was also something lackluster and unimaginative about both casting and staging. *Perfectly Frank* was an imperfect tribute that lasted little more than a fortnight.

But it was infinitely superior to the lamentable **Onward Victoria** (14 December 1980, Beck), whose opening and closing nights were one and the same. The musical purported to detail the escapades of a famous nineteenth-century feminist, Victoria Woodhull (Jill Eikenberry). Indicative of its material was a lyric sung by the censoring Anthony Comstock (Jim Jansen), who equates *Oedipus Rex* with "perverted sex," and who goes on to assure his listeners, "I knew it was a shabby drama/When I heard what that king did to his momma."

By contrast, only inconsolable purists refused to enjoy a revival of *The Pirates of Penzance* (31 December 1879), which Joseph Papp's New York Shakespeare Festival had first presented in Central Park the preceding July and which was moved to Broadway at the Uris Theatre on 8 January 1981. What purists bewailed was the replacement of Sullivan's masterful orchestrations by new ones with a pronounced contemporary sound, the tampering with Sullivan's score, including material from other shows, the use of mikes and amplification by singers who couldn't sing without them, and a jettisoning of the cobwebby D'Oyly Carte staging traditions. Frederic and Mabel were assigned to two rock stars, Rex Smith and Linda Ronstadt. George Rose was lauded for his Maj. General Stanley and stopped the show with "I Am The Very Model of A Modern Major General." But the evening's star was Kevin Kline as the Pirate King. He proved an accomplished enough singer and a superbly acrobatic clown, infusing the role with a zip and zing it almost assuredly never before had. During its 772-performance run on Broadway and successful road trips the comic opera no doubt provided many playgoers with the jolliest possible introduction to Gilbert and Sullivan, as well as teaching them the source of "Hail, Hail, The Gang's All Here."

A truly oddball offering, **Shakespeare's Cabaret** (21 January 1981, Bijou) was a six-singer, ninety-minute-long, intermissionless potpourri of Bardic rhymes, not all of which were presented precisely as Shakespeare had written them. They pleased an esoteric coterie for more than a month.

The 5 O'Clock Girl (10 October 1927), singing such Kalmar and Ruby songs as "Thinking Of You," but singing nothing with social significance, was a sitting duck for Broadway's critics when it floated into the Helen Hayes on 28 January. To make matters worse, Goodspeed, where the revival had originated, pursued its usual practice of tinkering and camping. After two weeks, the young lady packed her bags and left.

Some more old songs were heard in the show *Piaf*, a theatrical biography of the famed French singer, but this often obscene piece was actually a straight play, not a musical.

And still additional old material was heard in a revival of *Jacques Brel Is Alive and Well and Living in Paris* (22 January 1968), which started a brief stay at Town Hall on 19 February.

Sophisticated Ladies (1 March 1981, Lunt-Fontanne) did for Duke Ellington what *Perfectly Frank* had failed to do for Loesser. Some of the reasons were obvious. Most of Loesser's great songs were written for Broadway shows and were such an integral part of those shows that they lost a little in isolation. On the other hand, Ellington's efforts for Broadway were failures; his best songs were unattached gems; and he wrote when tempos were different and were as often as not slanted toward a dancing audience. That danceability, set against a splashy lavishness (compared with *Perfectly Frank*'s rather pallid and staid intimacy), gave the new retrospective a singular theatricality. No wonder, then, that Gregory Hines's high stepping stole the spotlight and brought down the house. Once again, however unwittingly, reviews harked back to critics' response to black shows of the twenties and early thirties: "It's primarily a dance presentation," *Variety* suggested. But the lively dances, the glitter (at one point a large illuminated COTTON CLUB sign dropped from the flies), and the frequently familiar melodies lured playgoers for nearly two years.

The idea to **Bring Back Birdie** (5 May 1981, Beck) was an egregious miscalculation. All too many playgoers remembered *Bye Bye Birdie* (14 April 1960) with special delight, so it was a hard act to follow, and the creators of the original simply couldn't recreate the good-humored glee and embraceable melodies that lit up the older work. The new story recounted how Albert (now portrayed by an apparently bored and zestless Donald O'Connor) and Rose (once again Chita Rivera) try, twenty years after the events depicted before, to bring back Conrad Birdie for a guest appearance on a Grammy Awards show. Recalling the pigeonholed telephoning teenagers of the 1960 show, the creators tried to come up with a similar gimmick by moving gigantic television sets back and forth, up and down, during the evening. After four performances (plus thirty-one previews), Birdie went back to oblivion.

Another large, illuminated sign, this one proclaiming NEW YORK, was part of the spectacle of **America** (13 March 1981, Radio City Music Hall). So were the Rockettes kicking their heels to "Stars And Stripes Forever." There was a Mardi Gras parade as only Radio City could recreate it, a sketch in which the figures in Grant Wood's *American Gothic* debate whether they are posing in "Io-way" or "Io-wuh," and, shades of Ziegfeld, an elaborate lobster costume to salute Maine.

Broadway Follies (15 March 1981, Nederlander) seemed to be a hastily assembled vaudeville designed to relight the stage of an out-of-the-way, hard-to-book theatre. A juggler, pantomimists, a music hall belter, and others constituted the lackluster bill, which beat the hastiest of retreats following the first performance.

Lauren Bacall was unmistakably the **Woman of the Year** (29 March 1981, Palace) in Broadway's musicalization of a Tracy–Hepburn classic. Peter Stone wrote the book, Kander and Ebb the songs. In the original boy-meets-girl or man-meets-woman yarn the heroine was a haughty intellectual, the hero a down-to-earth sports writer. In the updating Tess Harding (Miss Bacall) is an internationally famous television hostess and her vis-à-vis a cartoonist (Harry Guardino). For the most part the musical was a triumph of professionalism over real talent. Miss Bacall carried the evening almost single-handedly, although she had tremendous help when she and Marilyn Cooper, who played a dowdy housewife, stopped the show just before the final curtain by each insisting that "The Grass Is Always Greener" on the other's side of the fence. The show compiled 770 performances and suggested that critics may not have fully appreciated its essential strengths, for when Miss Bacall vacated her part Raquel Welch took over and acquitted herself handsomely.

Aah Oui Genty! (9 April 1981, O'Neill) was a French "marionette revue by and with the Compagnie Philippe Genty," proffering complete marionettes, marottes (dummy's heads), hand puppets, and black-light effects. It stayed for only twenty-nine performances.

Critics came down hard on **Copperfield** (13 April 1981, ANTA). The musical was so ineptly and hopelessly written that even so skilled and dependable a comedian as George S. Irving could do nothing with the authors' version of Micawber. The show struggled along for a losing two weeks.

A revival of *Can-Can* (7 May 1953) couldn't run even half that long when it was offered at the Minskoff on 30 April. On paper it should have fared better. A stellar cast, sometimes probably better than the original, included Zizi Jeanmaire (dancing to Roland Petit's choreography), Ron Husmann, David Brooks, and Swen Swenson (although Pamela Sousa could not hope to match the incomparable Gwen Verdon). Once again, however, the musical belonged to an era being stubbornly reevaluated by pontificators whose favorite denunciation seems to be "dated." The *Times* dug up its tired charge about a "creaky libretto," while *Variety* began, "Even the greatest composers are at the mercy of librettists." (Librettist Abe Burrows, by the way, was credited with revising his original text.)

Can-Can's producers may have taken a little heart from the fact that its five-performance run was four more than achieved by **The Moony Shapiro Songbook** (3 May 1981, Morosco). The show was a dismally misfiring spoof of those musical retrospectives (such as *Perfectly Frank* and *Sophisticated Ladies*) popping up on and off Broadway. Hailed in London, it fell flat in New York.

Inacent Black (6 May 1981, Biltmore), a play with songs, described how an angel (Melba Moore) shows up to assist a troubled black family from Long Island. It bombed.

Not so **Lena Home: The Lady and Her Music** (12 May 1981, Nederlander). Essentially a one-woman show, it received some of the most wildly enthusiastic and unmerited raves of any musical in years. Miss Home was a great beauty with an unusually velvety and precise delivery, always a visual and auditory treat in films. But she really had no place on a Broadway stage, clinging to a mike and insistently amplified, in what was little more than an expanded nightclub act. Later, she added insult to injury by going on the road with the show and often playing in mammoth old film houses, thus depriving playgoers

not only of the sound of her natural voice but of the physical, visual intimacy so much a part of the best live theatre. No matter. She dazzled critics and audiences alike singing such standbys as "Stormy Weather" and "The Lady Is A Tramp," throwing in bits of autobiography between numbers. She remained in town for nine months, then went on tour. It was an upbeat ending to an uneven season on Broadway.

But off-Broadway had one more surprise in store. Taking a look at a subject that was still largely a no-no in uptown musicals, William Finn's **March of the Falsettos** (20 May 1981, Playwrights Horizons) told how a nice Jewish father, Marvin (Michael Rupert), decides he is a homosexual, leaves his wife, Trina (Alison Fraser), and his son, Jason (James Kushner), and takes up with a lover, Whizzer Brown (Stephen Bogardus). By evening's end, Trina and Marvin's psychiatrist, Mendel (Chip Zien), are a pair. With no spoken dialogue and no intermission, the musical quickly became the darling of a raffish set that often condemns Broadway and inflates the value of almost anything that smacks of off-Broadway.

SCENE TWO

A Musical Trade Imbalance, 1981–1995

1981–1982

The American Musical Theatre offered little in this new season to generate the sort of electric excitement it had so often in the past. The number of productions slipped; so did their quality. An exceptional percentage of arriving musicals were revivals, and not one of these scored a resounding success.

Four (or five) revivals got the season under way. The first was *This Was Burlesque* (16 March 1965), which opened at the Princess on 23 June. Ann Corio again headed the cast, but now she had to compete with Mickey Rooney and Ann Miller, who were packing them in with the far snazzier *Sugar Babies* just a short walk away. So Miss Corio, her strippers, and her comics took their final bow less than a month later.

Fiddler on the Roof (22 September 1964), which had first reached Broadway during the same season in which *This Was Burlesque* moved there from downtown, was brought in for a seven-week stand at the oversized New York State Theatre on 9 July.

It had spent months touring the country. Herschel Bernardi, one of Zero Mostel's many replacements during the original long run, was Tevye. Maria Karnilova recreated her part of Golde, Boris Aronson recreated his pastel-tinted sets, and Tom Abbott "reproduced" Jerome Robbins's dances. Warmly received, the operetta did good business, but not enough to command an extended run.

Also arriving on the heels of a cross-country tour was *My Fair Lady* (15 March 1956), with seventy-three-year-old Rex Harrison and ninety-two-year-old Cathleen Nesbitt once more as the reptilian Higgins and his compassionate mother. And once again settings, costumes, and dances were all designed to recall the original production. A bit of theatrical legend almost came to pass on opening night, only to fall apart anticlimactically. The actress slated to play Eliza was indisposed and her understudy went on—to merely polite applause. The musical opened on 18 August at the Uris, a barn of a legitimate theatre. Booked for a twelve-week stand, it stayed a few weeks more—adding another 119 performances to the musical's record.

On 4 September the New York City Opera enlivened its season with an unlikely revival, *Song of Norway* (21 August 1944). Even when it was first presented the operetta represented a triumph of brilliant production and magnificent singing over hack writing and adaptation. But Grieg's melodies were lovely and not inappropriate for an opera house. Of course, the faddist and the doctrinaire among critics were driven up the wall. The company had opened the season by remounting *The Student Prince*, and the *Times* began its review by noting, "[T]he operetta [as a genre] is as dead as the era that gave it birth." The critic went on to characterize this genre as a pastiche of "cloying tonality, lacrhymose tunes and cardboard nostalgia." The paper sent another critic to review *Song of Norway*, and he said much the same thing, leading some readers to wonder whether the *Times* reviewing staff was hired with the idea of reflecting disparate points of view or was simply cloned. The late-summer repertory also included *Die Fledermaus*.

An Evening with Dave Allen (20 September 1981, Booth) had the BBC favorite presenting his comic monologues and a few ditties. But not for long.

A dreary rock musical, **Marlowe** (21 October 1981, Rialto), didn't further the cause of its genre. Purportedly a lyrical biography of the famous playwright, its small cast, dressed in tacky costumes

and framed in tacky scenery, enacted such bits as Marlowe getting stoned on marijuana with Shakespeare and Burbage.

Years ago, between the golden era of operetta and the dross age of rock musical, Rodgers and Hart wrote a captivating musical comedy based on Shakespeare's *Comedy of Errors*. They named their version *The Boys from Syracuse* (23 November 1938). Critics saw **Oh, Brother!** (10 November 1981, ANTA) as a rehashing of Shakespeare's saga, this time without Rodgers and Hart's gaiety, charm, wit, and melody. The plot was reset in the contemporary, troubled Middle East, and one twin was white while the other was black.

A good measure of sanity and beauty was restored to our musical stage when *Camelot* (3 December 1960) came in from the road on 15 November at the Winter Garden. This was the same production that had played New York the preceding season, except that Richard Harris had replaced the ailing Richard Burton as King Arthur. The *Times*'s principal critic, Frank Rich, took Burton's absence as an excuse to attack the show itself. He fell back on the old argument that the music was lovely, but… . *Variety*'s critic echoed his sentiments. In *Camelot*'s case, the flaws of the book were apparent from the start, yet Rich's and *Variety*'s criticism here suggests rather the continuing reevaluation and downgrading of the classical musical plays of the 1940s, 1950s, and 1960s. The revival lingered six weeks, to disappointing business, and eventually returned to the more welcoming road.

For some time rumors had been circulating that Stephen Sondheim was going to show scoffing detractors that he could write a good old-fashioned type of musical comedy, without any of his abrasive misanthropy or daring artistic invention. **Merrily We Roll Along** (16 November 1981, Alvin) wasn't that show. Based on the famous 1934 play of Kaufman and Hart, it told the sad tale of how success spoiled Franklin Shepard (Jim Walton) and told it with a reverse chronology that begins with rich, smug Shepard giving the 1980 commencement address at his alma mater, Lake Forest Academy, and ends with his graduation from the school twenty-five years before. In the meanwhile he has walked out on his wife, betrayed his friends, and scuttled all his early idealism in his ruthless climb to the top. The mounting was a disaster. A penny-pinching production, composed largely of platforms and metal scaffolding, and a cast of inexperienced youngsters spotlighted the work's shortcomings. The show was withdrawn after an inglorious sixteen playings, but subsequent regional productions have suggested that, with some rewriting, the musical, especially its superb, insinuatingly catchy Sondheim songs, merits serious reconsideration.

The next night brought in another dud, one that had fewer artistic ambitions but nonetheless reached out a bit for its subject matter. That theme was the struggle of Jackie Robinson (David Alan Grier) to break into white-monopolized baseball. Dull, even when it was not preachy, **The First** (17 November 1981, Beck) went to bat a mere thirty-seven times.

If African Americans took a long time to break into baseball's major leagues, they long since had found that talent could get them to the top in show business, especially since so much modern American music has black roots. **Dreamgirls** (20 December 1981, Imperial) had music by Henry Krieger and book and lyrics by Tom Eyen. Eyen's tale was supposedly derived from the real saga of a famous black singing group, the Supremes. The musical's black youngsters have virtually scaled the heights when their manager, Curtis Taylor, Jr. (Ben Harney), tells one of the trio, Effie (Jennifer Holliday), who has been his mistress, that she lacks the class to push the group over the top. He also tells her he has a new girl. Effie goes on to achieve a personal success. As with so many modern musicals, the text was not the thing. The work had been developed by director-choreographer Michael Bennett, who heightened the show's strongest moments and covered its weaker ones by brilliant staging. Bennett relied cleverly on huge banks of lights, moved on high-rising towers and long bridges, to create stunning effects. And Jennifer Holliday stopped the show cold just before the first-act curtain when, on learning Taylor's decision, she sang "And I Am Telling You I'm Not Going." *Dreamgirls* ran nearly four years.

On 15 January 1982, a cabaret revue called **Forbidden Broadway** opened with a tiny cast at Palsson's Supper Club. The revue was the work of Gerard Alessandrini. A sometimes sophomoric, sometimes overlong affair, it was for the most part a right-on-the-button, hilarious send-up of Broadway, its writers, directors, and stars. "Hello, Carol!," sung to the tune of "Hello, Dolly!," had fun at the expense of Broadway's original, once-and-possibly-future Dolly, Carol Channing. Mary Martin, Stephen Sondheim, and any number of musical theatre celebrities came under Alessandrini's cutting knife. By the following fall, the show was elevated to the status of an off-Broadway production and continued on and on, regularly inserting fresh material.

Little Me (17 November 1962) had once served as Sid Caesar's last Broadway vehicle, and the great clown had turned it into a lunatic field day by impersonating all the major male figures. A revival, which minced into the Eugene O'Neill on 21 January and shuffled out dispiritedly one month later, attempted to portion out his roles to two actors. James Coco and Victor Garber were experienced comedians, but they were not clowns of the old Caesar school. With so many belly laughs gone, the show had to rely on its often funny Neil Simon book, its often memorable Cy Coleman score, and its Peter Gennaro choreography. They were good, but obviously not enough.

A one-month dud, **The Curse of an Aching Heart** (25 January 1982, Little) related the saga of twenty years in the life of a Brooklyn girl (Faye Dunaway). Ignoring its few musical interludes, most commentators saw it as a straight play.

Although Andrew Lloyd Webber and Tim Rice's **Joseph and the Amazing Technicolor Dreamcoat** (27 January 1982, Royale) had been produced in Brooklyn in late 1976 and had subsequently been seen around the country, it reached Broadway only on the strength of a successful off-Broadway mounting the previous November. To many people's surprise, this retelling of the biblical legend chalked up a run of 747 performances before it was through.

Another surprise success was **Pump Boys and Dinettes** (4 February 1982, Princess), which also began life off-Broadway, then moved to an off-Broadway–type house in the heart of the theatre district. There was no real story to this nondescript six-character (four boys, two dinettes) concert, which one critic nevertheless managed to characterize as "gas jockeys and diner waitresses singing to each other across the highway, in an assortment of country music styles and moods." Perhaps because it was contemporary and unassuming, perhaps because its ticket prices were less than those of the first-class houses in the neighborhood, it compiled a run of 573 performances.

After a long tour in which several players took the leading role, a revival of George M. Cohan's *Little Johnny Jones* (7 November 1904) danced into the Alvin on 21 March, with television's little Donny Osmond as star. It danced for only a single showing (not counting the traditionally uncounted previews). Blame for the fiasco is hard to place. Since much of the original score is apparently lost without any hope of rediscovery, songs from other Cohan shows had to be added. Wisely the producers avoided turning it into a Cohan hit parade, settling instead for obscure songs that fit into the story, more or less; sometimes the story was changed slightly to accommodate them. But then the story itself was drastically rewritten, with what amounted to all of Cohan's last act (set in San Francisco) winding up in the disposal. The sets and costumes, which seemed so attractive when Goodspeed first mounted the revival, struck many as tired and threadbare. The staging, as so often happens at Goodspeed, verged on the campy. And the cast, even the well-intentioned star, lacked the requisite flair. But for all those drawbacks, the production had enough charm to more than hint at what delightful theatre the musical must have been three-quarters of a century before.

That was just a year or so prior to the opening of the now long gone Hippodrome, but playgoers could also get some idea of the elephantine extravaganzas presented there by buying tickets to **Encore** (26 March 1982, Radio City Music Hall), which was offered as the theatre's "Golden Jubilee Spectacular." Each scene centered on a famous song, from "The Lord's Prayer," "Kamenoi Ostrow," "Rhapsody In Blue," and Ravel's "Bolero," to Broadway show stoppers. And then, of course, there were the Rockettes.

An odd, not unlikable musical that was a cross between musical comedy and revue—tilting toward the latter—arrived with the dissuasive title **Is There Life After High School?** (7 May 1982, Barrymore). No cast member (there were only nine) played a single part, but instead each represented an assortment of old grads looking back, mostly with affection, on their high school days. Three of the men, for example, recalled the effect of a six-pack in "Beer," while the whole company, echoing and enlarging upon the memorable march in *The Music Man*, remembered the school marching band in "Thousands Of Trumpets." A week and a half was enough to prove the show didn't have sufficient life for Broadway, but it seemed a natural for regional and dinner theatres.

If nine performers could act out a musical with a straggling title, it required some two dozen singers and dancers to breathe vitality into **Nine** (9 May 1982, 46th St.). A musical version of Fellini's film 8½, with an Arthur Kopit book and Maury Yeston songs, it examined the plight of an Italian film director, Guido Contini (Raul Julia), who is both creatively and emotionally exhausted. He looks to recruit his resources by analyzing his relationships with the women in his life, most importantly his mother (Taina Elg); Saraghina (Kathi Moss), who introduced him to sex; his producer, Liliane LaFleur (Liliane Montevecchi); his unhappy wife, Luisa (Karen Akers); and his mistress, Carla (Anita Morris). By curtain time he has worked out his problems. Typical of Tommy Tune's highly praised staging was a black-stockinged Miss Morris suggestively dancing alone all the while her dance simulated a couple's lovemaking. Indeed, unsubtle eroticism was a keynote of the evening and probably explained much of this overrated musical's appeal, which kept it on the boards in New York for almost two full years.

Another musical about school days and saddled with an elongated, questioning title was **Do Black Patent Leather Shoes Really Reflect Up?** (27 May 1982, Alvin). The show had been a tremendous success in several regional theatres, one reason why Broadway's more brahmin chauvinists may have turned up their noses. Its light-hearted, occasionally mildly off-color story took Eddie Ryan (Russ Thacker) and Becky Bakowski (Maureen Moore) through their parochial school days, finally showing the way to true love. But the plot was secondary. The musical's main aim was to twit the rigidities of Catholic schooling. It did so without much wit but with a great amount of affection and hearty good nature. The show ran less than a week in New York but continued to delight audiences around the country.

1982–1983

While the number of musicals held steady, the American lyric stage brought forth almost nothing that was fresh and exciting in this latest session. England provided the only new musical to send critics reaching for their more glowing adjectives and to prompt playgoers to line up at the box office. The two American-made musicals to turn a profit ran back to the 1920s and 1930s for their material. Yet the musical theatre was not faring as miserably as its nonsinging competition. At the beginning of June, *Variety* noted that the closing of Katharine Hepburn's tour in *West Side Waltz* meant that for the first time in memory not a single straight play was on the road. The trade sheet called this "the culmination of a trend that has been developing for several years as Broadway musicals have come to dominate the road almost exclusively."

On Broadway, June was busy but unsatisfying. The first two presentations appeared in the small, off-Broadway–like theatres nestled in between the larger first-class houses. **Blues in the Night** (2 June 1982, Rialto) was set in a shabby Chicago hotel were three nameless women told about their troubled lives by singing their way through a repertory of classic blues songs. A piano-playing saloon singer spelled the ladies. Leslie Uggams was the best-known of the performers in what was little more than an elaborate concert. It ran 53 performances.

Cleavage (23 June 1982, Playhouse) had a larger cast (nine) but ran far fewer performances (one). In its brief life it warbled about the ups and downs of love with such songs as "Believe In Me, Or I'll Be Leavin' You."

Broadway proper's first offering of the season also managed only a single official performance, and though its players were assigned character names, it, too, was little more than a glorified concert. **Play Me a Country Song** (27 June 1982, Virginia) employed a thin line about an all-night party at a truck stop to play country songs for Broadway.

Seven Brides for Seven Brothers (8 July 1982, Alvin) dragged a magnificent, wide-open, scenically gorgeous MGM musical onto a constricting Broadway stage. No doubt the success of the last season's *42nd Street* had been an incentive, with the failure of the earlier *Gigi* (14 November 1973) forgotten or waved aside. Designed as a touring production, this story of a band of rowdy brothers who kidnap unwilling brides and are eventually tamed by the girls was decried as shabbily mounted and unexceptionally cast. New York gave it a mere five showings.

For years a fine old theatre, the Hudson, had been out of the legitimate fold. Now, under an assumed name, it returned briefly and unhappily to Broadway's ranks. Its tenant was **Manhattan Rhythm** (21 July 1982, Savoy), an undistinguished dance revue conceived by and featuring John Devlin. Dances were offered to music from various epochs—jazz era, big band era, rock and roll, country and western—in roughly chronological order. Subsequently, the house again disappeared from standard listings, devoting itself to industrial shows and award ceremonies.

Matters were brighter and a mite grislier off-Broadway, where **Little Shop of Horrors** (27 July 1982, Orpheum) opened, having already delighted patrons off-off-Broadway. The little shop was actually a florist shop; the horror was innocent-sounding Audrey II, a plant which displays an alarming capacity to eat everything in sight, including the shop's customers, as it grows and grows. Audrey, looking ever so much like a goosepimpled dolphin crossed with an octopus and a crab, was manipulated by a puppeteer and given voice by another player. A delicious send-up of then voguish horror films, the show was soon gobbling up awards and luring suspecting patrons.

The New York City Opera brought in three revivals during its fall season: *The Merry Widow* on 7 September, *Candide* on 13 October, and, most adventurously, *The Grand Duchess of Gérolstein* on the 23rd.

On 9 September *Your Arms Too Short to Box with God* (22 December 1976) came into the Alvin for yet another New York stand and stayed nine weeks.

Much was hoped for, and nothing fulfilled, in **A Doll's Life** (23 September 1982, Hellinger). Three of Broadway's most successful practitioners—Betty Comden, Adolph Green, and Harold Prince—combined with the far less successful Larry Grossman to explore what might have happened after the neurotic, thieving Nora slammed the door on her family and respectability in Ibsen's *A Doll's House*. Their retelling began with a contemporary rehearsal of Ibsen's play but soon moved back in time. An uncertain, humorless libretto depicted Nora as leading the life of an 1880ish woman's libber. Obviously uninspired by all this, Prince fell back on a bag of his much-used directorial tricks—such as cast and chorus members watching and commenting on the action from a bridge high above the stage. After five performances the musical was given a merciful funeral.

Even more was hoped for from **Cats** (7 October 1982, Winter Garden), and this time the hopes were not dashed. The musical was Andrew Lloyd Webber's lyrical resetting of T. S. Eliot's *Old Possum's Book of Practical Cats* (with a small amount of additional material, mostly by director Trevor Nunn). All the characters were larger-than-life cats and the setting was a larger-than-life dump or junkyard. An all but invisible plot centered on the selection of one cat to ascend to heaven to be reborn. Among the candidates are a past-her-prime beauty, Grizabella (Betty Buckley), the aging actor Gus (Stephen Hanan), and the criminal Macavity (Kenneth Ard). By the time Grizabella sings the evening's heart-tugging hit, "Memory," there can be no doubt who will be selected, and, sure enough, she is lifted skyward in a blaze of illumination on a smoke-spewing tire.

Most critics agreed that the show was not a great musical. Frank Rich of the *Times* put his finger on the main reason for its success when he noted it "transports the audience into a complete fantasy world that could only exist in the theater and yet, these days, rarely does." Some playgoers, responding to the bruited rumor that Webber had conceived the work originally as a chamber musical, felt it might well have been even more beguiling without the overblown production, the admittedly knock-out gimmickry, and the insultingly blaring amplification. Perhaps someday a revival may risk that sort of staging. The show was advertised as "now and forever." Around the time of this writing it was announced that this longest-running production in Broadway history would close, after eighteen years and 7,397 performances. It did close, after 7,485 performances.

Rock 'n' Roll! The First 5,000 Years (24 October 1982, St. James) received upbeat notices but could not attract playgoers, suggesting that theatre was not a habit with the rock-and-roll generation. The show opened with an actor resembling Little Richard casting aside a Frank Sinatra recording and launching into a rendition of "Tutti Frutti." Thereafter, against a continuing background of historic film clips, entertainers brought back songs associated with Elvis Presley, the Beatles, the Rolling Stones, and a host of other rock-and-roll favorites, generally hewing close to the original sound and mimicking the performers' physical eccentricities. After just nine performances the rocking and rolling ceased abruptly.

Herman Van Veen: All of Him (8 December 1982, Ambassador) billed its Dutch star as a "singer, violinist, mime, composer, poet, children's book author, playwright, essayist, clown and entertainer, and one of Europe's most renowned musical theatre performers." To Americans, who found little humor in his regularly throwing rice at them, he seemed as talentless as he was cocky.

Just days after the show opened, *U.S. News and World Report* featured an article headlined "The 'Last Hurrah' for Old Broadway?" and offering a discouraging picture of the once-Great White Way. A month later, before the next musical arrived, the *Times* ran a front-page article pointing out that at midpoint the theatre season was in the worst slump in a decade. Things would get gloomier still in succeeding seasons.

A little cheer and forgetfulness came in the guise of a magic show, **Merlin** (13 February 1983, Hellinger), which in turn was disguised as a Broadway musical. The plot had Merlin (Doug Henning) battling a treacherous queen (Chita Rivera). The versatile Miss Rivera was given nothing to do, and Henning was so bad an actor that Merlin was never convincing. But Henning was a good magician, so for six months children of all ages could gape and delight at his tricks.

Almost everyone liked the revival of *On Your Toes* (11 April 1936), which danced into the Virginia on 6 March—almost everybody, that is, except Frank Rich, whose *Times* review was so gratuitously vicious and smart-alecky as to leave Broadway stunned. It was rumored that cast members and other theatrical folk were seen sporting buttons advocating "Get Rich Quick." The monopolistic *Times* has such a stranglehold on how the arts are perceived in New York that for a time the show's future was in doubt. But word of mouth eventually rushed to its aid, and while the musical did not do land-office business nor, apparently, quite turn a profit, it did manage a 505-performance run, longer than the original. The show restored Hans Spialek's 1936 orchestrations, and its scenery had an incontestable period charm. Donald Saddler restaged Balanchine's famous ballets with gusto and style. Moreover, the cast was superior, especially Natalia Makarova as the ballerina and George S. Irving as the unhappy Russian. A road company, with Leslie Caron in the lead, had to close after one month because of injuries the star sustained. This superb, thoughtful revival deserved a better history.

Only a two-week stand by Charles Aznavour in his one-man show entitled, appropriately, **Aznavour** (14 March 1983, Lunt-Fontanne) came between *On Your Toes* and several more revivals.

The first was a necessarily inflated and amplified revival of *Porgy and Bess* (10 October 1935) at the vast Radio City Music Hall on 7 April. Most reviewers thought the production, which offered the complete, three-hour version, was as fine as one could get in such depersonalizing space. It chalked up forty-five performances.

Show Boat (27 December 1927) was brought into the smaller, but still barnlike Uris on 24 April in a production first staged at the Houston Grand Opera. In some ways it was more a scholar's production than a playgoer's. Attempts were made to restore some of the original Robert Russell Bennett orchestrations and numbers that had been traditionally deleted in revivals, and a few of the sets attempted to recreate an idea of Joseph Urban's originals. But the company was small, too many of the sets and costumes looked like leftovers from a second-rate touring outfit, and the supposed opera singers had to be miked. Donald O'Connor made an interesting Cap'n Andy and brought down the house with a second-act tap dance that no doubt was not in the original. Sourly received in New York, the *Cotton Blossom* weighed anchor after less than six weeks.

The season's last hit began life as a projected revival of the 1927 Gershwin musical *Funny Face*. But some strange things happened on the way to the first night. The original story was dropped, and put in its place was a yarn about an American, Capt. Billy Buck Chandler (Tommy Tune), who is determined to be the first man to fly solo from the United States to Paris, and his distracting love affair with an English Channel swimmer, Edith Herbert (Twiggy). Also discarded was much of Gershwin's *Funny Face* score, although "'S Wonderful," "He Loves And She Loves," "High Hat," "Funny Face," and one other song were retained. Filling the gaps were other Gershwin show songs, such as "Strike Up The Band!" And then there was a new title—taken from that fifth song salvaged from the original— **My One and Only** (1 May 1983, St. James). With Tune not only costarring but co-choreographing, the dancing vied with the beloved old melodies as the evening's high points, although some playgoers were surprised that all the chorus boys were black. However, they gave credence to a wild dance routine set in a Harlem chapel to the music of "Kickin' The Clouds Away." Tune did not seem to fit so macho a hero, but when he danced no one cared. Twiggy could not act, sing, or dance, but she had an irresistible stage presence that offered some compensation. Gaudy settings underscored the gay 1920ish mood, and the show ran for two years.

Although **The Flying Karamazov Brothers** (10 May 1983, Ritz) brandished names like Dmitri, Alyosha, and Smerdyakov, wags were quick to point out that they were not brothers, Karamazovs, or flyers. What did fly were cleavers, sickles, musical instruments, and burning torches—for the five performers were jugglers who interspersed their juggling with a little comedy and music. They really belonged on a vaudeville bill, but vaudeville was dead. They had to be content with a five-week run.

The season ended not with a bang, but a bomb. **Dance a Little Closer** (11 May 1983, Minskoff)—a one-performance fiasco—was Alan Jay Lerner and Charles Strouse's musicalization of Robert E. Sherwood's *Idiot's Delight*. Once again a seedy song-and-dance man, Harry Aikens (Len Cariou), meets up with an old flame, Cynthia Brookfield-Bailey (Liz Robertson), in an Austrian border hotel just as the world awaits another war, and the pair rekindle their old fires. Only now it is World War III that everyone awaits. To indicate how updated his book was Lerner made Cynthia the mistress of a diplomat, Dr. Josef Winkler (George Rose), whom everyone took for Henry Kissinger. Most reviewers applauded Strouse's melodies and Lerner's elegant lyrics, but the praise stopped there. Oddities included an ice-skating number by two supposed homosexuals. The show was ploddingly heavy (Lerner had almost never been a satisfying librettist) and, in spite of its title, never actually got up and danced.

1983–1984

The new season was largely defined by two disparate hits—one near the beginning and one near the end. Both of these shows gave Broadway some cause for jubilation. Many of the shows that opened in between sparked lively discussions, but few had runs that amounted to anything or even gave their backers hope for a return on investment. And runs and profits are what really count on Broadway.

Five-Six-Seven-Eight... Dance! (15 June 1983, Radio City Music Hall) was an extravaganza mounted primarily as a showcase for fey Sandy Duncan. She performed along with her not-much-larger husband, Don Correia (who even had a whole scene to himself, called unimaginatively "5-6-7-8... Husband!"), clownish Bill Irwin (who tried to audition for the Rockettes while the band played "Tea For Two"), and Marge Champion. To the delight of her many fans, Miss Duncan flew through her "I'm Flying" number from *Peter Pan*. To the delight of Radio City regulars, the Rockettes were also back (no place could be found for them in the last season's *Porgy and Bess*). Family fun, the show ran until early September.

July and August belonged to Jerry Herman, even if July brought a whopping disappointment. A faithful revival of *Mame* (24 May 1966), which was trotted out in the wide-open spaces of the Gershwin (né Uris) on the 24th, with the original star (Angela Lansbury), many of the original supporting players, the original orchestrations, and recreations of the original scenery, costumes, and dances, was treated by the critical fraternity as an archaeological exercise. In short, its reception offered yet one more instance of the recently vaunted past being dismissed as dated. Since the old type of theatregoing loyalist, who went regularly to the theatre come hell, high water, or a Brooks Atkinson pan, for the most part had died or found more vital interests elsewhere, the reviews doomed the show. Auntie Mame stopped opening new windows after forty-one tries.

In a happy turnabout, Herman's newest offering, **La Cage aux Folles** (21 August 1983, Palace), was the season's biggest musical hit. With its high-kicking chorus, its instantly hummable songs, and its emphasis on laughs, the show was an unabashed throwback to the more carefree musicals of yore (a point Herman underlined months later when accepting a Tony Award). Yet its theme and story were both of an order that until recently no musical comedy would have dared dwell on. When they pulled off their wigs the chorines proved to be boys. Of course, homosexuals had fluttered across musical stages for decades, but only as passing comic figures, and their sexual preferences remained unmentioned. The silence had been broken in recent years, as witnessed by off-Broadway's *March of the Falsettos* (20 May 1981) and the two admittedly gay men singing "Why Can't The World Go And Leave Us Alone?" on Broadway in the last season's *Dance a Little Closer*. The two gay men in *La Cage aux Folles* feel much the same way, although their lives are complicated by the fact that one of them had a brief heterosexual liaison years before, and out of that came a son who has grown up and now wants to marry. The men are Georges (Gene Barry), proprietor of the nightclub which gives the show its name, and his lover of twenty years, Albin (George Hearn), the club's leading female impersonator. Their need to gain the approval of the son's prospective father-in-law, a crusader against homosexuals, provided the evening with its most poignant and most hilarious moments. Equally touching were Albin's prima-donna fears of the ravages of age. A pastel-colored St. Tropez and glittery nightclub scenes (with outlandishly gaudy drag costumes) provided a wonderfully evocative background. Among the more likable Herman songs were Albin's pleading "I Am What I Am" (sung heartbreakingly at the end of the first act after Georges demands that Albin disappear before the interview with the future father-in-law), the lively "The Best Of Times," and two more romantic numbers assigned to Georges, "Song On The Sand" and "Look Over There." The clever libretto by Harvey Fierstein, best known for his play about gay men, *Torch Song Trilogy*, was taken from the popular French film. If the musical pulled many of its punches, it succeeded in pleasing not merely more hardened Broadway regulars but even little old ladies from Dubuque and, just possibly, anti-homosexual evangelists from Cornpone, Alabama.

On 29 September, before the next musical arrived, *A Chorus Line* gave its 3,389th performance and thus became the longest-running show in Broadway history up to that time. Its astonishing long run was as much a comment on the decline of Broadway and the Broadway musical as it was on the show's incontestable excellence. The show was not a product of either the melodic heyday of the 1920s and 1930s or of the more studiously crafted and ambitious (or pretentious) works that followed in the wake of *Oklahoma!* and which kept appearing with awesome regularity until the mid-1960s. Its score was modest, its book unflinching in its willingness to be unpleasant; it had no scenery or costumes to speak of, and a small cast by the standards of yesteryear. Moreover, in a country whose population continued to explode it had relatively little telling competition on a shrinking Broadway.

The New York City Opera's fall season offered two holdovers from last year: *The Merry Widow* and *Candide*.

A revival of *Zorba* (17 November 1968), resoundingly successful on the road, was made welcome in New York when it raised its curtain at the Broadway on 16 October. Its star was Anthony Quinn, who had starred in the fine film version of the novel on which the musical was based. His presence no doubt accounted for much of the good box office, since Broadway and the road increasingly were offering productions, more often than not revivals, which featured a major if fading film star. The star's fame drew audiences who were not experienced playgoers and who saw theatregoing not as a habit but as a special occasion.

Another group coming more and more into the theatre was blacks, although their patronage was reserved primarily for shows by, about, or with blacks. One such show may have been **Amen Corner** (10 November 1983, Nederlander), a musicalization of James Baldwin's play. Its story of a woman pastor at a Harlem storefront church, who decides her ministry is preventing her from realizing her opportunities as a mother and wife, was filled with rousing gospel music. Unfortunately, the uplifting songs underscored how flaccid the rest of the play was. The show sang its last less than a month later.

An interesting, offbeat experiment was **La Tragedie de Carmen** (17 November 1983, Beaumont), in which Peter Brook, working with

Jean-Claude Carrière and Marius Constant, stripped Bizet's *Carmen* down to an eighty-minute, chorusless, intermissionless retelling of passionate intensity. The work was accomplished by a fifteen-piece orchestra. By going back to Mérimée's original, Brook and Carrière were able to insert some additional action not found in Meilhac and Halévy's libretto. For example, Carmen's husband was brought in and was murdered by Don José, and the bloodied body of Escamillo, gored to death by a bull, was borne on stage. A large backlog of performers took turns singing the principal roles. Late in the run an English translation by Sheldon Harnick was performed on alternate nights. In one version or the other, the musical ran through April.

Two short-lived, intermissionless productions mounted off the beaten path are listed in the *Best Plays* Broadway record, so will be mentioned here. In **Haarlem Nocturne** (18 November 1984, Latin Quarter) five performers capered in both songs and sketches, while a little later in the season **Streetheat** (27 January 1985, 54th St. Theatre Cabaret) professed to relate "a modern-day dream story of New York City's "now" culture."

Marilyn (20 November 1983, Minskoff) was a two-week dud. Like all too many recent Broadway musicals, its long list of credits suggested it was written by committee, and a committee totally devoid of theatrical know-how at that. Half a century ago a musical entitled *Marilyn* might have been about Marilyn Miller, the blond, Dresden-china doll who had been Broadway's musical comedy queen. But by 1983 she was largely forgotten and Marilyn could only mean Marilyn Monroe. However, this inept new musical made a hash of rehashing her biography. A trio of singers, labeled "Destiny," sauntered in and out of the action. Just prior to the final number, which occurred shortly before the emotionally troubled star might have committed suicide, a group of chorus boys came on stage in pink plumbers' costumes to salute her as "Miss Bubbles."

Critics had fun tearing apart *Marilyn*, but they obviously did not enjoy having to spank **Doonesbury** (21 November 1983, Biltmore), which *Variety* noted had "wit but not bite." Garry Trudeau took his characters from his famous comic strip, providing them with several threads of plot rather than a single story. There was Doonesbury (Ralph Bruneau) trying to get up enough nerve to ask J. J. (Kate Burton) to marry him, and the spaced-out Zonker (Albert Macklin) worrying whether his nutty Uncle Duke (Gary Beach) will bulldoze his

dorm and replace it with a condominium. Even set to the overrated Elizabeth Swados's dreary music (played by a four-piece, onstage band with synthesizer), this was the sort of show that might have carved a snug niche in a more economically sane Broadway. As it was, it struggled along for three months. Perhaps an afterlife still awaits it in school and regional productions.

Baby (4 December 1983, Ethel Barrymore) did better, running out the season and giving hints of developing into a cult show. Its book was by Sybille Pearson, its lyrics by Richard Maltby, Jr., and music by David Shire. This determinedly intimate musical had no real plot, but focused instead on three couples and how each deals with the woman's pregnancy—or lack of it. One couple is a pair of unmarried undergraduates, and another is approaching middle age and expecting the arrival of a late-in-life accident, while the final pair are battling to overcome apparent infertility. Not exactly your old boy-meets-girl story, but no new musical during the season was built around this once ubiquitous motif. Swirling curtains provided much of the scenery, while slides repeatedly projecting images of a developing fetus provided proof this was not romantic fluff. One of the couples was played by Catherine Cox and Martin Vidnovic, two superior performers who received enthusiastic notices in whatever show they played, but who, like so many other fine young performers, could not carve out a major career in our shrunken, transmuted musical theatre.

Peg (14 December 1983, Lunt-Fontanne) was a one-woman show, a self-pitying self-portrait starring Peggy Lee, a singing favorite of yesteryear. Many of the songs were new and written to describe her abused childhood, her husband's boozing, and all her other personal problems. Most of her old favorites were saved for late in the show, by which time numbers of discouraged playgoers had walked out. The show opened on Wednesday and closed on Saturday.

There was a time when the theatre offered African Americans virtually their only route to fame and fortune. Some measure of how the black condition has so greatly improved could be seen in the story of **The Tap Dance Kid** (21 December 1983, Broadhurst). Little Willie (Alfonso Ribeiro) has a room filled with pictures of Fred Astaire and Bill Robinson, and dreams of following, almost literally, in their scintillating footsteps. But his successful lawyer father (Samuel E. Wright) will not hear of such absurd, demeaning daydreams. He insists,

"We didn't get off the plantation until we stopped dancing and started doing." Luckily Willie's Uncle Dipsey (Hinton Battle), a dancer-choreographer, disagrees. He encourages the boy and finally wins over to his side his sister, Willie's mother (Hattie Winston), who had once been a dancer herself. Indeed, so had Willie's grandfather, Daddy Bates (Alan Weeks), who returns from the grave to join in encouraging the boy by doing some of his old dances. One show-stopping number, "Fabulous Feet," had Battle and the chorus tapping away—in sneakers. The show, loosely based on Louise Fitzhugh's novel *Nobody's Family Is Going to Change*, got off to a slow start, but soon proved to be what *Variety* had branded it from the beginning, an audience show. It ran a year and a half.

The multi-talented Chita Rivera and the talentless (at least on stage) Liza Minnelli were the stars of **The Rink** (9 February 1984, Beck), the Terrence McNally–John Kander–Fred Ebb musical about a mother and her estranged daughter fighting over the disposal of a family-owned skating rink. Flashbacks indicated how the estrangement arose, but the women are reconciled in time for the final curtain. A small supporting cast reappeared in numerous roles. Inevitably, choreographer Graciela Daniele got some of the cast on roller skates, for one of the few enlivening moments of the evening. Peter Larkin's setting depicted the decaying rink alongside an amusement park roller coaster. Critics normally as poles apart as John Simon of *New York* magazine and Michael Feingold of the *Village Voice* pointed out how unworthy Miss Minnelli was to have her name in lights on Broadway (Simon even suffers a nervous collapse thinking about her nose), yet *The Rink* offered another instance of how Hollywood names could lure a certain breed of playgoer, while dedicated, more talented stage performers could not. The show was able to hold its head above water financially until Miss Minnelli left with the onset of summer heat. Without her—though the superior Miss Rivera remained—the box office fell to a point where the show could no longer continue.

The Human Comedy (5 April 1984, Royale) was so warmly received when it premiered at one of Joseph Papp's downtown showcases that it was hurried uptown. With a libretto (all lyrics, no spoken dialogue) by William Dumaresq and music by Galt MacDermot, it was a musicalization of William Saroyan's World War II opus and was performed by a large cast in colorless period costumes and with little scenery except for chairs and some props. Its loose, expansive story centered on a widowed mother (Bonnie Koloc) and her sons, one of whom goes off to die in the war. MacDermot's music encompassed the whole range of American musical idiom, and Dumaresq's libretto never pandered or cheapened, but Broadway audiences, seeking gaudier entertainment elsewhere, demurred, so the show was withdrawn after less than two weeks.

The season's second *Merry Widow*, this time sung in German by the Vienna Volksoper, was part of that famed company's repertory presented to Americans at the State beginning on 10 April. *Die Fledermaus* and *Czardas Princess* comprised the remaining two offerings.

The Gershwin Theatre became a glorified nightclub when the hour-and-a-half-long Las Vegas entertainment **Shirley MacLaine on Broadway** (19 April 1984, Gershwin) came in for a limited engagement. Although she was assisted by four dancers and a small onstage orchestra, the star's singing and clowning were the only attraction during her five-and-a-half-week stand.

A revival of *Oliver!* (6 January 1963), with Ron Moody, the original London Fagin, in the cast, opened at the Mark Hellinger on 29 April. Finding few takers, the show departed after seventeen performances.

Sunday in the Park with George (2 May 1984, Booth), the season's last new musical, soon enlisted a vociferous cheering section, led noticeably by the *Times*, which ran so many boosting followups that *Variety* published a special story on them. Bernadette Peters and Mandy Patinkin were the leads in the musical with Stephen Sondheim songs and a James Lapine book. Of course, any musical with Sondheim songs is a Sondheim musical. He unquestionably determines the drift and tone of his shows. And this time he had a surprise in store for his legions of admirers. The wholesale, unyielding despair, misanthropy, and emotional flagellation of all his recent works were discarded in favor of an often sentimental warmth and a tentative optimism, with only enough of his former negativism to remind you that this was Sondheim speaking about a real world. The play's two acts told two separate but clearly connected stories. The first act, set in Paris a hundred years ago, dealt with Georges Seurat's struggle to finish *A Sunday Afternoon on the Island of La Grande Jatte* and, in a stunning piece of staging, concluded with the characters on stage falling into place to replicate the now famous masterpiece. The second act, set in the present, spotlighted another

George, this time the painter's great-grandson, who is a modernist sculptor. He, too, must battle in isolation to achieve his own artistic statement. Yet despite glowing performances by Miss Peters (as Seurat's mistress, Dot, and as Seurat's daughter and the younger George's grandmother, Marie) and by Patinkin as both artists, the characters flickered to life only on rare occasions. Even so, a song such as "Children And Art," Marie's apostrophe to her long-gone mother, could be heartrending. But Sondheim was examining ideas, not characters. As a result, alongside Sondheim's advocates, there would always be detractors who would agree with *Variety* that "dispassionate respect rather than enjoyment is likely to be the predominant reaction." Such controversy no doubt stimulated ticket sales, so *Sunday in the Park with George* ran a year and a half, but it was then withdrawn as too risky for the road.

A revival of *The Wiz* (5 January 1975) blew into the Lunt-Fontanne on 24 May to write "finis" to the season.

1984–1985

The 1984–1985 season may well go down in history as Broadway's worst. In numbers, new productions sank to what can safely be called an all-time low. (*Variety's* count was thirty-one, although *Best Plays* listed thirty-five, which it saw as up one from the 1983–1984 season.) Not since British redcoats abandoned New York at the end of the Revolution two hundred years earlier had so few plays been mounted in first-class theatres. Of course, in the late 1780s New York had only one first-class house, used the same scenery from one play to the next, and usually gave no more than two or three representations of each work—but New York was a little smaller then.

Almost inevitably the musical stage reflected the stage at large. The new season witnessed the number of musicals plummet along with a drop in the number of straight plays. Distressingly the drop in numbers was accompanied by a dismaying drop in quality.

Gotta Getaway! (13 June 1984, Radio City Music Hall) continued the giant theatre's tradition of unwittingly echoing the extravaganzas presented decades earlier when the Hippodrome flourished down the street. Show after show there took its goggle-eyed patrons on tours of the world, and that is just what this new one did. Audiences were transported to old Peking, to a tropical island in the midst of a wild voodoo ceremony, to under the sea, and to the Statue of Liberty, where the Rockettes danced while also holding torches aloft.

Once again in its summer–fall season, the New York City Opera returned *The Merry Widow* and *Candide* to its stage, and on 11 October added Sondheim's *Sweeney Todd*.

In contrast to the show at the Music Hall the first musical to appear in the new season at a regular, if off-Broadway, legitimate theatre was small scale, even for today's much-cut-down Broadway. In **Quilters** (25 September 1984, Lawrence), a patchwork collection of songs, monologues, and sketches was enacted by a woman and six girls, said to be her daughters. Essentially what they sang and narrated was a paean to American womanhood. The show had enjoyed widespread popularity in regional theatres and continued to do so, even after Broadway audiences rejected it.

They also rejected a lavish revival of Friml's *The Three Musketeers* (13 March 1928), an operetta which the *Times*, maintaining its decades-old assault on the genre, dismissed as little more than "a routine English Christmas pantomime" and no better than "Broadway's 1983 kiddies show, 'Merlin.'" The revival opened at the Broadway on 11 November. This time the criticism had some justification, for the production, while gorgeous to look at, was hokey (a character made an entrance riding a horse through the auditorium and up onto the stage), and the singing was miked and amplified (outrageous virtually anytime and unconscionable in a Broadway operetta). In another shameful and tasteless practice, songs such as "Only A Rose" were brought over from the composer's other works.

Puccini's **La Bohème** (29 November 1984, Public) didn't fare much better than Friml's operetta had. It was presented in English by Joseph Papp, with the leading roles assumed by pop singers (including Linda Ronstadt) and with a twelve-piece band beneath them. Quite possibly Papp envisioned another refreshing *Pirates*. It didn't work out that way, and there was no call to move the mounting to Broadway.

Doug Henning and His World of Magic (11 December 1984, Lunt-Fontanne) delivered what its title promised, thereby pleasing playgoers, including many children, seeking holiday fare.

The season's biggest hit was a revival of *The King and I* (29 March 1951), which came into the Broadway Theatre on 7 January. The star was an ailing Yul Brynner, the original, then-unstarred

King. He had been raking in the *bahts* and filling his royal coffers on a prolonged, exceptionally successful tour, and his New York engagement (closing as he played the role for the 4,625th time) was advertised as his farewell. His fans packed the huge Broadway for weeks. Interestingly, a newspaper article which appeared during the run noted that those fans were again not necessarily regular theatregoers, but rather people who made a visit to the show a special occasion. Mary Beth Peil played the role first performed thirty-three years before by Gertrude Lawrence. Miss Lawrence had died during the run of the original production; Brynner died shortly after this revival closed.

A musicalization of the lives of **Harrigan 'n Hart** (31 January 1985, Longacre) might have seemed like a natural for Broadway. Unfortunately, Broadway delighted in being increasingly unnatural, so librettist Michael Stewart, along with making any number of other mistakes, attempted to imply some homosexual bond between the famous partners. Harry Groener was stuck with a cloyingly goody-goody interpretation of Harrigan, while Mark Hamill had neither the Adonis-like appearance nor raffish charisma Hart was said to have. The show's most dramatic moment came when Hart's ambitious wife, Gerta Granville (Christine Ebersole), malevolently brings about a rupture in the two men's relationship. Although the score intermingled new songs (with Max Showalter music and Peter Walker lyrics) with a grab-bag of long-forgotten Braham–Harrigan favorites, it did nothing to help the situation. It was good to hear the likes of "Maggie Murphy's Home" sung again on a New York stage, but not good enough to justify an otherwise unavailing evening.

If Harrigan and Hart were the darlings of Broadway in the 1880s, Ellie Greenwich had been an admired creator of "girl-group" music in the 1960s. Now she herself appeared as "Ellie Greenwich (1980s)" in **Leader of the Pack** (8 April 1985, Ambassador), an amorphous musical that set out to tell of her life as "Ellie Greenwich (1960s)" (Dinah Manoff) with her collaborator-husband of the time, Jeff Barry (Patrick Cassidy), and use these purported biographical snippets as an excuse to resing her old songs. Crotchety critics, obviously not hippie children of the sixties, complained that the decibel level of the amplification was ear-splitting. For a brief time, the public seemed willing to ignore such cavils and defy the critics, and it looked as if the show would catch on. However, before long

attendance faded, and the musical went the way of most of the season.

When *Take Me Along* (22 October 1959) first appeared on Broadway it was dominated by the larger-than-life performances of Jackie Gleason and Walter Pidgeon, especially the former. The Goodspeed-originated revival which came into the Martin Beck on 14 April had no stars and also had some new songs by the show's composer, Bob Merrill, but what it had most of was a homey charm, good taste, and credibility. Such assets were small change to a Broadway where overblown multi-million-dollar musicals were the rage. If one does not count previews, then the revival's opening night was also its only night.

But even overblown, multi-million-dollar musicals could bomb, as Hal Prince and his associates learned to their chagrin when **Grind** (16 April 1985, Hellinger) premiered. The musical revolved (literally) around a racially mixed burlesque house in a seedy area of 1933 Chicago. Its politically didactic story depicted racial tensions within the theatre, where blacks and whites work together all the while being carefully segregated. The culmination is a theatrically convenient race riot outside the theatre at the same time the burlesque show inside is featuring a harmless song and dance, with the hatred and violence overwhelming the tacky escapism. Clarke Dunham's Reginald Marsh–like setting turned to reveal the cheap, garish façade and marquee of the theatre, the stage and ugly, labyrinthine wings, and the cramped, unwashed dressing rooms. Ben Vereen was the supple song-and-dance man; Leilani Jones the resolute girl determined to use her stripping to escape from the ghetto; Tim Nolan a hate-filled stooge; and, best of all, Stubby Kaye as the fading clown.

The musical prompted an interesting attack by John Podhoretz in the Washington *Times*, even if the attack, coming when the musical theatre was at a nadir, was something like hitting a man when he's down. And in this instance the attack was leveled as much at one man—Hal Prince—as it was at the whole modern school of musicals in which Prince and his erstwhile associate, Stephen Sondheim, loom so large. Opening by accusing Prince of "art-slaughter," Podhoretz reached back to suggest that "the musical took a crucial, and in retrospect suicidal, step into the realm of social commentary" with *West Side Story* and that Prince and Sondheim, with the "concept musical," actually created "an anti-musical, a self-destructive form in which characters were taken to task and made fun of for doing things like bursting into song." He concluded that a grating ugliness had replaced the sweet, memorable melodies, the care-chasing fun, and the winning attractiveness of the musicals of old. Podhoretz was clearly a member of a large, if largely silent, minority—and possibly a majority—of playgoers or potential playgoers alienated by much of the modern American theatre. He might also have attacked the ubiquitous amplification and the resigned acceptance of it by responsibility-shirking critics or, just as readily, lambasted papers which incessantly derided apolitical genres such as operetta and promoted propagandizing plays all the while displaying the most obscene capitalistic greed in the increase of their advertising rates (up 300 percent at one major daily while inflation accounted for only 60 percent).

Perhaps because so little was expected of it, **Big River** (25 April 1985, O'Neill) provided playgoers and critics, desperate for a passable musical, with an unexpectedly pleasant evening in the theatre. Since this was a musicalization of Mark Twain's *Huckleberry Finn*, the big river was the Mississippi, and its painted recreation, sinuous and silvery in the moonlight, by designer Heidi Landesman not only elicited a storm of applause but evoked memories of the artfully painted panoramas that graced the stages of Mark Twain's own era. Country-music composer Roger Miller supplied melodies that caught the evening's gentle, bucolic spirit, even if they did not promise to keep on rolling after the show had closed. Daniel H. Jenkins and Ron Richardson made a likable Huck and Jim, although both were patently too old for their roles. (Of course, in Huck's day, thanks to dimmer lighting, many an aged actor got away with playing a young man.) René Auberjonois and Bob Gunton, two fine actors who have never really had the chance to live up to their early promise, gave capital performances as the Duke and the King. In a better season, Broadway might well have passed up *Big River*, but the musical theatre's paucity of truly meritorious new works allowed the show's minor but palpable enough charms to be savored.

1985–1986

The new season was better than the previous one, but that wasn't saying much. Broadway had nowhere to go but up, and it barely made it.

An off-Broadway revival of *Dames at Sea* (20 December 1968) began the season pleasantly enough at the Lamb's Theatre on 12 June. But the need to hark back theatrically was indicative of much to come.

In fact, the musical theatre not only rummaged through its own attic, but once again attempted to put old, beloved films on stage. After many delays and more rumors of desperate doctoring, **Singin' in the Rain** (2 July 1985, Gershwin) launched the season on Broadway. With Gene Kelly, Debbie Reynolds, and Donald O'Connor as stars, this spoof of filmdom's painful transition from silents to talkies had quickly become a classic Hollywood musical. Comden and Green, who had written the screenplay, made the adaptation. The show had done exceptionally well in London, where it had opened two years earlier. For New York, a much ballyhooed avant-garde choreographer, Twyla Tharp, was called in to direct and choreograph. Her work left many playgoers wondering what all the ballyhoo was about. The cast comprised largely unknowns, none of whom had the irresistible glamour of their Hollywood counterparts. *Singin' in the Rain* ran out the season without making a profit.

Reaching back still further, the New York City Opera offered another in its series of revivals of old operettas, this time including *The Mikado* and *The Merry Widow*. The series was certainly ill-advised, since the house is much too large to do proper justice to these often neglected favorites. Yet Broadway, where they belong, won't touch them anymore. One reason is Broadway's fear of the *Times*, which for decades has conducted a relentlessly vicious, smug campaign against operetta. The paper had its vitriol ready when *The Student Prince* (2 December 1924) was brought back on 7 July: "If you're a sucker for sentiment," it suggested with snide condescension, "'The Student Prince' is clearly for you." This sort of attack, apparently the *Times's* theatrically correct equivalent of the "political correctness" infesting so many of our campuses, continued with dauntless consistency and persistency in the following months and seasons.

In October the *Times* berated the New York City Opera for mounting *Kismet*, and in March, although the newspaper once had hailed *Brigadoon* as a fine departure from Graustarkian operetta, it assailed the company's revival with its ever-ready daggers, snarling that it "drips with a sentimentality" and "comes saddled with a clumsy subplot." (A few weeks earlier the *Times's* first-string critic gratuitously got his knife into one of our best 1930s musical comedies, *On Your Toes*, by noting that a New York City Ballet staging of "Slaughter on Tenth Avenue" was "joyously rescued from the dreary book." Never mind that he had been slapped for his earlier attempt to sabotage the fine 1983 revival of the show!) True, during the 1986–1987 season the paper acknowledged that "the overture had scarcely begun when the audience broke out to welcome the return of heartwarming melodies" in *The New Moon* and added it was "definitely a viable operetta," only to compensate for such unwonted largess by panning the mounting. But it hurriedly reverted to its old stance to bash a relatively modern masterpiece, *South Pacific*, as "awkwardly archaic." When *The Student Prince* came back in the next season, the paper, seemingly tired of attacking operetta as operetta, took a new, more perverse tack, pontificating that "As a drama ... 'Student Prince' is insufferable."

During the 1987–1988 season its assault on *The Merry Widow* was more openly political: "In the politics of the performing arts, the City Opera has always negotiated between an adventurous left wing and a conservative status quo. This production leans hard to the right side of the company's constituency, with a ... production meant more to soothe than to uplift." Words such as "adventurous" and "uplift" were giveaways, although the critic missed a golden opportunity to employ "reactionary," since many playgoers, reacting to the lack of delightful bits of escapist fluff and beguiling melodies, naturally want to retreat from a not very satisfying status quo to a rosier past. A few weeks later the paper corrected its earlier slip by sniffing, "More than anything else, 'The New Moon' confirms that by the late 1920s, operetta was a genre destined to die." Signaling that even newer works soon would be accorded similar treatment, the critic compared Romberg's work to *Les Misérables*, branding the newer hit "impossibly sententious and overblown." That bygone musical comedies were also open to the *Times*'s disdain was shown when a 1989 revival of *The Pajama Game* was assailed for its "archaic" music and text. Not even Bernstein's *Candide* was spared, a reviewer bemoaning, "Bernstein's score ... could hardly have been inspired by the book now housing it," moving on to condemn the work as a "tacky, cartoonish, soulless show," and concluding it became "boring." Of course, this fascinating musical has had book troubles from the beginning; nonetheless, the *Times*'s perpetual attack on the books of musical revivals suggests a lack of understanding of the whole musical theatre genre and hurts our theatre's efforts to keep alive legitimate (in both senses of the word) attempts to sustain a full slate of theatrical offerings.

An August article in *Variety* noted another major reason for problems Broadway had been confronting and would continue to confront. In the ten years since 1975, prices on goods in general had gone up 60 percent. But the *Times*'s advertising rates had jumped 300 percent and union benefits 600 percent. The trade sheet estimated that tickets could have cost a third less if increases had merely doubled that of the national inflation average.

For the moment, Andrew Lloyd Webber could do no wrong, even when he offered Broadway almost nothing, as he did in **Song and Dance** (18 September 1985, Royale). His first act presented a song cycle (with words by Don Black and Richard Maltby, Jr.) warbled by the pathetic Emma (Bernadette Peters), "a girl who lets men take advantage." Act II found Christopher d'Amboise and eight other dancers leaping and pirouetting to music Webber adapted from classical sources. Even in the face of many very cool notices, the show ran out the season and then some.

The New York City Opera tried again with *Kismet* (3 December 1953) on 4 October. Since *Variety* does not list opera houses, its reception at the box office cannot be readily determined.

One surprise success was **Tango Argentino** (9 October 1985, Hellinger), which came all the way from Buenos Aires, by way of Paris, to offer a full evening of traditional tango dancing.

A group of Italian theatrical troupes performed at the Vivian Beaumont during October as part of an Italian Cultural Month. Two of their bills were musicals, each of which gave a pair of performances. **La Gatta Cenerentola,** opening on the 19th, was based on an old fable; **Pipino il Breve,** which came in on the 25th, had life-sized puppets recounting the marriage of France's King Pippin to Berta of Hungary.

Two flops followed. The first was **Mayor** (23 October 1985, Latin Quarter), a musicalized version of feisty Mayor Koch's memoirs. Charles Strouse provided the music, and Lenny Wolpe played His Honor, but it all had seemed more attractive in the tighter confines of the cabaret where it originated some months before.

"They don't come much worse," *Variety* bewailed of **The News** (7 November 1985, Hayes). This rock musical, all but completely sung (with mikes in hand in Broadway's tiniest house), told of an editor seeking to expose a mad sex-killer, unaware his daughter is about to date the man. *The News* shut down after half a week.

The huge Radio City Music Hall maintained its Hippodrome tradition when it revived its annual *Magnificent Christmas Spectacular* on 15 November. Among this year's best numbers were "A Teddy Bear's Dream," with thirty-two life-sized pandas, koalas, and more old-fashioned cuddlies cavorting to Tchaikovsky's music, and the Rockettes in a precision "Parade Of The Wooden Soldiers."

The season's longest run on Broadway—608 performances—would eventually be tallied by **The Mystery of Edwin Drood** (2 December 1985, Imperial), which moved to Broadway after winning plaudits at the New York Shakespeare Festival in Central Park. Musicalized Dickens, it took the form of a play-within-a-play, a tacky English touring troupe at Greater Dorping-on-Sea presenting the local yokels with its highly emotive version. The troupe was presided over by a waspish chairman (George Rose) and included Betty Buckley and Cleo Laine. The play's main novelty occurred near its end when the chairman came to the front of the stage and cajoled the real rather than the imagined audience to vote for its choice of the culprit. The cast then adjusted the rest of the entertainment to fall in line with the audience's choice. The show, with book, lyrics, and music by Rupert Holmes, was clever and cute, but not truly top-notch.

Neither was **Nunsense** (12 December 1985, Cherry Lane), for which another loner, Dan Goggin, supplied book, lyrics, and music. But, at least in terms of performances, the show far outran even *Drood*. It went on for 3,672 performances— the second longest run in off-Broadway history (at the time of its closing). Licensed companies in other cities also chalked up remarkable stands. Of course, the musical played very small houses. It didn't need any more room to act out its saga of five lovable nuns putting on an often unintentionally funny variety show at their Hoboken school to pay for the burial of all their other sisters, who have died of food poisoning after eating in the school's cafeteria.

A not very distant past was saluted by Dorothy Loudon, Chita Rivera, Leslie Uggams, and supporting performers in **Jerry's Girls** (18 December 1985, St. James), which offered a frequently glitzy, sometimes campy retrospective of Jerry Herman's Broadway songs. The revue even included material from *La Cage aux Folles*, then still playing at the Palace—only in a turnabout, this all-girl cast dressed up as men.

The season's second four-performance flop was **Wind in the Willows** (20 December 1985,

Nederlander), a musicalization of Kenneth Grahame's long-popular children's book. His anthropomorphic story centered on a scapegrace Toad (Nathan Lane), a nature-loving Rat (David Carroll), and, most of all, a Mole (Vicki Lewis) determined to live a better life aboveground. Critics let this one down gently, suggesting it might do better in intimate playhouses catering to children.

NATHAN (Joseph) LANE was born in Jersey City, New Jersey, on 3 February 1956. Upon discovering that his name was already taken by another member of Actors Equity, he decided to go by Nathan Lane, a tribute to *Guys and Dolls'* Nathan Detroit. His Broadway debut opposite George C. Scott in Noël Coward's *Present Laughter* brought him acclaim and garnered him the role of Prince Fergus alongside Doug Henning and Chita Rivera in *Merlin*.

The Robert Klein Show (20 December 1985, Circle in the Square) was a one-man show with four performers, the three others being singers (two girls, one boy) who helped spell the star between his stand-up comedy routines that took a jaundiced view of matters of the day. Two weeks sufficed.

Another of Broadway's Jerrys was the inspiration for the short-lived **Jerome Kern Goes to Hollywood** (23 January 1986, Ritz). This glorified concert, which included many of Kern's Broadway songs (though they were subsequently sung in films), had started life in a minuscule London venue, where it was well received. Something essential apparently was lost when it transferred to a larger (but still small) Broadway house. Best received among its four singers was seventy-seven-year-old Elisabeth Welch. Off-Broadway also remembered the composer with **Ladies and Gentlemen, Jerome Kern** (10 June 1985, Clurman). Other applauded lookbacks included **Williams and Walker** (9 March 1986, American Place), which recalled two great black entertainers, and **Beehive** (30 March 1986, Top of the Gate), an extremely successful resurrection of the songs and singers of the sixties.

A larger-scale, all-black retrospective, **Uptown...It's Hot** (16 February 1986, Lunt-Fontanne), failed to find a welcome. With Maurice Hines featured in some of his dazzling dance routines, the revue ran through a wide range of black or black-influenced music from the jazz era (it quirkily placed some 1920s hits in its opening section, supposedly devoted to the thirties) to the rap of the eighties. But for some reason the show rarely caught fire.

Brigadoon (13 March 1947) enjoyed a New York City Opera revival on 1 March.

The season's last two shows were the work of Bob Fosse—his first work for Broadway in some years, and, as it turned out, his last. **Big Deal** (10 April 1986, Broadway) was a musical version of the film *Big Deal on Madonna Street*. It depicted small-time hoods planning and bungling a robbery. Fosse himself reset it in a predominantly black world of 1930s Chicago and used selected period songs for the score. Critics found the result "ponderous and cheerless." Only a jitterbug number, "Beat Me Daddy Eight To The Bar," with its boogie-woogie dance, roused most playgoers.

The season ended much in the way it began, with a revival. *Sweet Charity* (29 January 1966) starred a popular black entertainer, Debbie Allen.

1986–1987

The new season was much busier than the preceding one, yet for all its exertions brought forth only two indisputable, if distinctly different, hits (both from overseas).

The two earliest entrants were not musicals, but were filled with the sort of material that revues and vaudeville once had trafficked in so joyously. *Mummenschanz* (24 June 1986, Hayes) was an evening of Swiss pantomime. Broadway had welcomed it before, in 1977, and welcomed it again. **Robert Klein on Broadway** (25 June 1986, Nederlander) was a solo evening of stand-up comedy (sort of a cut-down version of the previous season's *The Robert Klein Show*), offered for only two performances that were taped for later showing on TV.

Many felt that off-Broadway put its best foot forward virtually at the start of its season with **Olympus on My Mind** (25 July 1986, Lamb's), which, like *Out of This World* (21 December 1950), had fun with the Amphitryon legend. Since its original run it has developed into something of a cult favorite.

The real season began bleakly enough with another in the ongoing vogue for longing looks at an irretrievable past. **Honky Tonk Nights** (7 August 1986, Biltmore) struggled vainly—for four performances—to recreate the spirit of black vaudeville,

with the players retailing their woes directly to the audience. Its "pastiche songs and bewhiskered comedy sketches" fell flat.

The next entry was a revival of sorts—"of sorts" since Broadway never had seen the show before. **Me and My Girl** (10 August 1986, Marquis), which served to introduce Broadway's newest theatre, had been Lupino Lane's popular West End vehicle during World War II. Its book and lyrics had been the work of L. Arthur Rose and Douglas Furber; Noel Gay had composed the music. A wildly successful 1985 London revival had refurbished the book (with great taste and fidelity) and added Gay songs from other sources. It had also skyrocketed to celebrity Robert Lindsay, a fine actor whom London previously had praised for his Hamlet. What New York now saw was a musical asplash with color, sumptuous sets and costumes, and some of the best broad comedy bits in years. Its plot unfolded the ludicrous happenings which arise after a cockney layabout inherits an earldom. Gay's contagiously hummable musical numbers were capped by the title song and "The Lambeth Walk." For the latter, the cast left the stage and danced in the aisles, with Lindsay's Bill Snibson even cajoling ladies of the audience to join him in the dance. A brilliant supporting cast was led by Jane Connell as a snooty grande dame and George S. Irving as a more understanding nobleman. Yet the show remained Lindsay's. Grabbing gold watches and ladies' fleshy breasts or tangling with regal robes, he singlehandedly restored a seemingly lost Bobby Clark tradition to Broadway. And he made the show's intentionally corny lines seem masterful. Asked by one haughty lady, "Do you know my daughter, May?" he acknowledged that he didn't, but thanked her for the hint.

Charles Strouse's fine score (with Stephen Schwartz's lyrics) and equally fine singing by opera's Teresa Stratas could not overcome the burden of Joseph Stein's leaden book for **Rags** (21 August 1986, Hellinger). The musical depicted the obstacles thrown in the path of a Jewish immigrant from the time she lands at Ellis Island through her early days on the Lower East Side.

The New Moon (19 September 1928) opened at the New York State Theatre on the 26th.

A rash of failures followed. **Rowan Atkinson at the Atkinson** (14 October 1986, Atkinson) was another instance of a comedian (this one English) stretching material that would have been better in a revue or a vaudeville turn.

In **Raggedy Ann** (16 October 1986, Nederlander), with a book by Broadway playwright William Gibson and songs by TV's Joe Raposo, a little girl (Lisa Rieffel) is transported to a never-never land where good, represented by Raggedy Ann (Ivy Austin), tussles with the forces of evil for her soul. The show earlier had played Moscow as part of an exchange program.

Flamenco Puro (19 October 1986, Hellinger) offered an evening of Spanish gypsy song and dance.

The hero of **Into the Light** (22 October 1986, Neil Simon) is a scientist (Dean Jones) so determined to establish the truth or bogusness of the Shroud of Turin that he neglects his love-starved son (Danny Gerard) until just before the final curtain. The stage glittered with laser lights and high-tech graphic projections, nuns jitterbugged, and lyrics ran to the order of "science without data/will not get you from alpha to beta."

There were not-dissimilar black-light effects in **A Little Like Magic** (26 October 1986, Lyceum), an all-puppet musical which traveled down from Canada. Bits included a spoof of a dying swan ballet, an extended, "terrifying" version of "The Sorcerer's Apprentice," and puppet images of well-known entertainers such as Liza Minnelli and Liberace.

L'Chaim—To Life! (5 November 1986, Town Hall) was a Yiddish-English revue, which even flew to Buenos Aires for some Yiddish-Latin numbers.

An $8 million advance sale awaited the annual *Magnificent Christmas Spectacular* that opened at Radio City Music Hall on the 14th. Along with the expected "Living Nativity" and "Parade Of The Wooden Soldiers" was a scene at an ice-skating rink and row after row of Rockettes in shortened Santa costumes.

Oh Coward!, done off-Broadway in 1972, brought its Noël Coward potpourri to the Helen Hayes on the 17th.

Smile (24 November 1986, Lunt-Fontanne), with music by Marvin Hamlisch, was a musical version of a popular film. In transition much of the charm and bite of this tale of a high school beauty contest was lost. Bright, pastelish sets and costumes were among the show's more memorable virtues.

The World According to Me! (22 December 1986, Atkinson) was another full evening of stand-up comedy, this time offered by an amusingly abrasive, very New Yorkish Jackie Mason. Once again the best of it was revue material looking for a revue. Broadway loved it anyway.

The Stratford Festival from Canada offered its superb, freshly thought-out version of *The Mikado* (19 August 1885), playing two engagements, first at the City Center, beginning 13 January 1987, and then, in answer to continuing demand, at the Virginia, beginning 2 April. Eric Donkin's deliriously incisive Ko-Ko sparked an excellent cast. The mounting, done without plaguey amplification, had gorgeous settings—a fan that opened to fill the rear of the stage, a giant moon, poetically twisted trees—which allowed for pictures that suggested Ziegfeldian beauty and opulence.

Stardust (19 February 1987, Biltmore) employed the increasingly tired device of a lecturing narrator and a handful of singers to present an evening of songs with Mitchell Parish lyrics. Besides "Star Dust" the program included such old standards as "Stars Fell On Alabama," "Sophisticated Lady," and "Volare."

On 2 March the New York City Opera raised its curtain on a revival of *South Pacific* (7 April 1949), with Susan Bigelow and the Met's Justino Diaz in the leading roles.

The season's biggest hit was the behemoth, pretentious, and outrageously amplified **Les Misérables** (12 March 1987, Broadway). A musicalized version of Victor Hugo's novel, whose original French libretto was the work of Alain Boublil and Jean-Marc Natel to a score by Claude-Michel Schönberg and for which Boublil, Schönberg, Herbert Kretzmer, and James Fenton supplied an English text, it enjoyed an $11 million advance and even before it opened became the latest blockbuster musical to be perceived as a Broadway "event" rather than a casual entertainment. Colm Wilkinson was spotlighted as the idealistic Jean Valjean; Terrence Mann, the fanatical Javert; Randy Graff, the pathetic Famine; Judy Kuhn and David Bryant, the beset lovers. John Napier's remarkable settings featured a pair of towers which "dip, slide and interlock to form the student rebels' barricade," while David Hershey's equally imaginative lighting gave a special menace to the sewers through which Valjean must escape. Choosing among Schönberg's melodic output, critics praised "I Dreamed A Dream," "On My Own," and "Empty Chairs At Empty Tables." For all its multiple virtues and astonishing success, the question remains: Is *Les Misérables* that good? While most Broadway critics cheered, at least one—Howard Kissel of the *Daily News*—thought not, seeing the evening primarily as spectacle and dismissing the music as "drivel—singsong, repetitious and emotionally dead."

And then there was Andrew Lloyd Webber's latest, **Starlight Express** (15 March 1987, Gershwin). The production was the most expensive on Broadway up to its time, $8 million, ran 761 performances, and appears not to have paid off its investment. No cats this time. Instead, all the performers (on roller skates and in absurdly futuristic costumes) were trains, dashing back and forth on tiers of ramps, bridges, and catwalks. What passed for a plot recounted the fight of an eager young steam engine (Greg Mowry) to foil the machinations of a gangsterish diesel (Robert Torti).

The season's last two shows demonstrated how little Broadway is willing or able to do for its best performers. The first, a double bill consisting of **The Regard of Flight** and **The Clown Bagatelles** (12 April 1987, Beaumont), displayed the art of Bill Irwin, who might have been a modern-day Bobby Clark or Bert Lahr given the proper shows. It had been done in 1982 off-Broadway. **Barbara Cook: A Concert for the Theatre** (15 April 1987, Ambassador) featured one of Broadway's most beguiling leading ladies of a few years back in a solo show. Sadly, she sang almost none of the songs she had sung on Broadway, relying instead on a wide range of standards. Just as sadly, she employed a hand mike to project in the relatively small house. Live theatre ain't what it used to be. In fact, it ain't truly live anymore.

1987–1988

It was another busy season, towered over once again by another importation. And what did American writers offer their own audiences? Precious little. Only two new native works had appreciable merit, although both were nearly drowned out by the thundering ballyhoo accorded London's latest contribution. Revivals of earlier Broadway hits provided some small compensation.

A few of those revivals ushered in the season, with *Dreamgirls* (20 December 1981) embarking on a five-month return at the Ambassador on 28 June.

The New York City Opera remounted two Romberg works during its summer season— *The Student Prince* (2 December 1924) on 7 July and *The Desert Song* (30 November 1926) on 25 August—along with *Sweeney Todd* on 29 July and *Die Fledermaus* on 26 September.

The season's first novelty was **Roza** (1 October 1987, Royale), which told how a Polish concentration camp survivor (Georgia Brown) moves to Paris and befriends the dregs of the city's society. According to Frank Rich, the show was "shrouded in cigar-smoke hues that attempt to belie the material's sentimentality and advertise a thematic gravity ... [and was played out in] a tilted, topsy-turvy heap of distorted rooms and twisted stairways."

With the classic revue form and vaudeville long dead, Broadway continued to present full-evening entertainments by artists who might have flourished in those bygone forms. The latest was a one-man show, **Mort Sahl on Broadway** (11 October 1987, Simon).

Four performances were all that **Late Nite Comic** (15 October 1987, Ritz) could muster. Walloped by *Variety* as "staggeringly dreadful," it related the love-life and professional clawing of a pickup dancer and a would-be comic. Its songs and dances were dismissed as "adequate for a Rotary Club amateur production."

The season's most successful revival was *Anything Goes* (24 November 1934) at the Vivian Beaumont on the 19th. As is too often the case, Broadway lacked faith in the original material, so a new book by Timothy Crouse (Russel's son) and John Weidman was employed. It may not have been the real goods, but it was singularly entertaining and reasonably faithful. One basic setting showed a couple of decks of a ship, with the orchestra ensconced on the upper deck and the lower deck revolving to allow for scene changes. Patti LuPone was starred in the Ethel Merman part. She came across as cold and cheap, and with her unyielding nasal delivery managed to make some of Porter's best-known lyrics unintelligible. The cramped stage allowed for only minimal dancing. Yet for all the production's faults, the old show was so good it remained capital entertainment.

Cabaret (20 November 1966), with Joel Grey recreating his brilliant performance as a painted, scabrous master of ceremonies, arrived at the Imperial on the 22nd and ran out the season.

South Africa gave us a protest musical, **Sarafina!** (25 October 1987, Newhouse), in which black high school students put on a play attacking apartheid and praising Nelson Mandela, the leader of the rebellious ANC. Exhilarating *mbaaanga* music enlivened the performance. An enthusiastic reception prompted a move to Broadway, where the musical enjoyed a long run.

Don't Get God Started (29 October 1987, Longacre) might have been called an evangelical revue, with sermonizing sketches and gospel songs interwoven. It ran eleven weeks.

There rarely is a middle ground with a Stephen Sondheim musical. Most audiences either love it or hate it. **Into the Woods** (5 November 1987, Beck), for which James Lapine supplied the book, was no exception. While beloved fairy-tale characters come to life on stage, this was really not a children's musical. A childless baker (Chip Zien) and his wife (Joanna Gleason), hexed by a wicked if funny witch (Bernadette Peters), go off into an enchanted woods in hopes of counteracting the hex. There they meet Cinderella (Kim Crosby), her Prince (Robert Westenberg), Little Red Riding Hood (Danielle Ferland), the Wolf (also Westenberg), Rapunzel (Pamela Winslow), and similar figures. By the end of Act I everything seems to be happily resolved. But a murderous presence looms in the woods, and in the second act death, tragedy, and grim resolution prevail. Among the better-received songs were the comic "Agony" and the soulful "No One Is Alone." Magnificent picture-book sets and costumes included a woods with trees that soared into the flies as well as ominous-looking undergrowth.

Off-Broadway welcomed **Oil City Symphony** (5 November 1987, Circle-in-the-Square Downtown) that same evening. Four high school graduates form a band to present a concert in honor of a favorite teacher. Their backwater, locked-in-the-fifties music-making and their droll comments were in marked contrast to the more strident pronouncements of the black students in *Sarafina!*, but equally good theatre.

Red, white, and blue flags a-waving and songs set to music by John Philip Sousa gave **Teddy and Alice** (12 November 1987, Minskoff) some better moments. But all in all this recreation of Teddy Roosevelt (Len Cariou), his daughter Alice (Nancy Hume), and Alice's romance with Nick Longworth (Ron Raines) was a badly botched, often embarrassing affair.

The Magnificent Christmas Spectacular delighted both loyalists and first-timers when it made its annual return to Radio City Music Hall on the following night.

Those engagingly comic magicians, *Penn and Teller*, who had offered their full evening of magic off Broadway in April of 1985 and had run a year and a half, then came to the Ritz on 1 December. Penn was the garrulous one, Teller his silent crony.

Andrew Lloyd Webber's **The Phantom of the Opera** (26 January 1988, Majestic) was the season's runaway hit. Its story of a disfigured, masked, murderous madman (Michael Crawford) who haunts the Paris Opera and kidnaps a rising prima donna (Sarah Brightman) was well known to oldsters, especially those familiar with Lon Chaney's incomparable silent film based on Gaston Leroux's novel. This version played down the more horrific and terrifying aspects of previous versions and even tacked on a happier ending. What made the evening so spellbinding was its brilliant spectacle. There was the grand staircase of the Opera House filled with revelers at a costume ball, a cloud-swept view of nighttime Paris seen from the Opera House's roof, and the misty, candle-lit waterways of the Paris sewers. Dark, forbidding colors dominated, occasionally punctuated by a screaming bit of bright red or a defiant white. Webber's music—the work was sung through—was pleasant, particularly his seductive "The Music Of The Night." With a $16.5 million advance and lots of money notices, the operetta and its road companies turned away disappointed playgoers for years on end.

A second religious musical, **The Gospel at Colonus** (24 March 1988, Lunt-Fontanne), received generally good reviews but found only modest-sized audiences for its translation of Sophocles' drama into an evening of black evangelical fervor.

Nor did a Brazilian revue of native song and dance, **Oba Oba** (29 March 1988, Ambassador), fare well at the box office.

An unpublished writer (Michael Rupert), who has disappeared for four months, returns to his squalid apartment and reads his **Mail** (14 April 1988, Music Box). As he reads, the writers, whether dunners, bulk-mail advertisers, his agent, or his sweetheart, come alive to act out the missives. A revolving set and garish costumes were no help.

Michael Feinstein in Concert (19 April 1988, Lyceum) was an evening filled with the popular young pianist playing and singing well-known songs.

Chess (28 April 1988, Imperial), with lyrics by Tim Rice and music by members of Sweden's ABBA rock group, had been a smash hit in London, although some Americans who saw it there came away offended at its virulently anti-Yankee tilt. A toned-down book was supplied by Richard Nelson for the Broadway production. The basic story was retained. It detailed the rivalry between a tantrum-throwing, nasty American chess champion (David Carroll) and his better-behaved Russian opponent (Phillip Casnoff). Before long they are also rivals for the hand of a Hungarian refugee (Judy Kuhn), who starts out loving the American but leaves him for the Russian. Sliding, drab towers and a revolve provided some of the spectacle that Broadway has increasingly substituted for quality material. However, *Chess* did produce two songs that won some acceptance outside the theatre: the love duet, "I Know Him So Well," and "One Night In Bangkok" (the latter a cue for a tour of the city's sleazy nightspots). But even these were damaged in the theatre by what one critic condemned as "shrilly" overamplifying.

Grotesquely loud amplification—in Broadway's tiniest house—also marred the pleasures of **Romance, Romance** (1 May 1988, Hayes), a double bill of unexceptional but beguiling little musicals. **The Little Comedy** was based on an Arthur Schnitzler piece in which rich lovers pretend to be of a lower social class in order to forward their courtship. **Summer Share,** based on Jean Renard's *Pain de Ménage,* told of two married couples who contemplate switching spouses. Four singers comprised the entire cast. But, oh! that amplification!

The season closed with an unmitigated disaster, the Royal Shakespeare Company's transatlantic bomb, **Carrie** (12 May 1988, Virginia). This musical version of a Stephen King horror novel featured high school brats slaughtering pigs (while stereophonic speakers screeched out the animals' death cries and red disco lights flashed), a fanatically religious mother (Betty Buckley) stabbing her daughter, and the same little girl—the titular Carrie (Linzi Hateley)—revenging herself on her contemptuous, contemptible classmates by using her supernatural powers to roast them alive at a prom. This misbegotten affair left after just five performances. Aftershocks reverberated even in England.

There were more pleasant aftershocks at season's end when Broadway grosses were reported to have risen 21 percent to a whopping $253 million. Theatre moguls credited the rash of hit musicals—especially such foreign spectacles as *Cats, Les Mis, Me and My Girl,* and *Phantom*—for the increase, ignoring the fact that a new $50.00 top for musicals meant more money but not necessarily more playgoers. About the same time Broadway also celebrated Irving Berlin's one hundredth birthday, taking wistful cognizance of his feeling that Broadway no longer welcomed his kind of music or his kind of musical. Broadway had not seen a new Berlin show in more than a quarter of a century—and never would again.

1988–1989

When it was all over, *Variety* summed up the new season in a single, damning word—abysmal. New offerings were so scarce and so meretricious that red-faced Tony Award officials announced that the categories for best book and best score of a musical would be omitted at the 1989 prize fest. Only four new book musicals premiered, and one of those was actually at an off-Broadway–style house which just happened to be located on Broadway. In another article, *Variety* observed: "The fadeaway of book musicals is a legit phenomenon whose complex causes include the reluctance of established playwrights to subjugate their creative autonomy to the collaborative process, the astronomical cost of fully developed narrative musicals and the corresponding reluctance of financing sources to encourage them… the perceived impatience of younger theatregoers with the "slow" development of storylines and uncertainty among writers and producers as to what constitutes a satisfying plot in today's musical theater." Unstated, but clearly hinted at, was the assault by some of the most widely promulgated of New York's few remaining critics on many forms of lighter or older entertainments. More and more angry articles had begun to appear assailing the often most slashing of these reviewers, the *Times's* Frank Rich, who had earned himself the dubious title of "the Butcher of Broadway."

The New York City Opera brought back *The Merry Widow* (21 October 1907) on 6 July, *The New Moon* (19 September 1928) on the 19th, and *Naughty Marietta* (7 November 1910) on 30 August.

After the Lehar revival at the New York State Opera House, **Canciones de Mi Padre** (12 July 1988, Minskoff) offered Broadway an evening of traditional Mexican songs, dances, and instrumentals with Linda Ronstadt and a fine mariachi band headlining. One critic bewailed that the dancers' feet were hidden from view by sound equipment and footlights.

A revival of *Ain't Misbehavin'* (9 May 1978) at the Ambassador on 15 August happily reunited its small original cast. The entertainment ran until mid-January. On 5 October, *Michael Feinstein in Concert* (19 April 1988) relit the Booth for a much shorter stand.

A fourth concert-cum-Broadway-musical was **Kenny Loggins on Broadway** (1 November 1988, Simon), with its singer-composer star performing in various modes, from folk to rock, accompanied by a small onstage band that sometimes helped with the singing, too.

Radio City Music Hall dropped the word "Magnificent" from its annual *Christmas Spectacular,* which opened this year on 11 November, but all the traditional delights were still there, in all their traditional magnificence.

To suggest that the scenery stole the show at **Legs Diamond** (26 December 1988, Hellinger) was to insult the scenery. The show wasn't worth stealing. Rumors to that effect had abounded through two months of tortured previews. The musical recounted the rise of a second-rate nitery hoofer to power in Prohibition's murderous world of bootlegging, and his ultimate downfall. Peter Allen, himself from the niteries, not only starred but wrote the songs. Harvey Fierstein and Charles Suppon contributed the dreadful excuse for a book. Allen had no charisma to project across the footlights and was no great shakes as a singer, dancer, or comedian. Even his smile grew fatiguing. But there was that scenery! The musical began when a proscenium-filling electric sign, advertising the show's title, lit up the house—and Allen made his first appearance from between the huge letters. The settings then moved from a prison to Penn Station to the streets and boîtes of 1920s Manhattan, with appropriately garish costumes for the hapless cast.

The same era was brought to life in the next entry. Although **Black and Blue** (26 January 1989, Minskof F) had African-American performers belting and stepping to famous and not-so-famous blues and jazz numbers of the twenties and thirties, it was not an American show. The producers of *Tango Argentino* and *Flamenco Puro* had offered it first to Paris, where it had been a hit. In a sense it was a throwback to such bygone shows as *Blackbirds of 1928*, with drapery (and sophisticated modern lighting) instead of spectacle providing frames for its personable, zesty entertainers. Besides the lighting, bows to modernity included dispensing with skits, and often outrageously blaring amplification. When the show's choreography won the season's Tony Award, it reminded many older theatregoers that black shows of the twenties and thirties usually were perceived primarily as dancing shows.

Rodney Dangerfield on Broadway (2 February 1989, Hellinger) was a one-man show starring the TV and nightclub comic famous for jokingly complaining he gets "no respect." He tickled playgoers' funnybones for a single week.

The season's most eagerly awaited show was **Jerome Robbins' Broadway** (26 February 1989, Imperial), and while it proved to be a hit, it did not become the blockbuster its producers (the Shubert organization) had hoped it would be. Plans for a road company were dropped early on. Yet one more in Broadway's long line of retrospectives—which serve to underline the ongoing paucity of great new shows—the musical offered an evening of Robbins's dances, culled from many of the most memorable hits he choreographed. These included the sailors' fancy-free dancing from *On the Town* (28 December 1944), the menacing rumbles of *West Side Story* (26 September 1957), the hilarious "Mack Sennett Ballet" (here renamed for the song that preceded and underscored it, "On A Sunday By The Sea") from *High Button Shoes* (9 October 1947), and the tediously overlong "The Small House of Uncle Thomas" from *The King and I* (29 March 1951). Some of the numbers seemed a little less gripping when taken out of context. However, one number had never been seen in context by most playgoers. "Mr. Monotony" had been dropped during the tryouts of two Irving Berlin shows.

Just before *Jerome Robbins' Broadway* closed in September of 1990, newspapers, a trade sheet, and a theatre magazine all carried articles comparing its fate with that of *Black and Blue*, which had opened with small expectations but was still playing profitably. They revealed that while the Robbins musical regularly outgrossed its competitor, Broadway's vicious economics doomed it. It had been capitalized at $8 million (and still would be $4 million in the red when it closed), and cost approximately $424,000 a week to run, while *Black and Blue*, which had been capitalized at a "mere" $5.5 million, could break even at $280,000 a week. To put Broadway's ghastly economics in perspective, the closing show's manager noted that when he had managed *Fade Out—Fade In* (26 May 1964) twenty-five years earlier, that musical had a weekly net of just $40,000. Parenthetically, he might have added that twenty years before *Fade Out—Fade In, Oklahoma!* made a handsome weekly profit on a capacity take of $35,000!

Robbins had served as co-director, but not choreographer, for the original production of *The Pajama Game* (13 May 1954), which the New York City Opera brought back on 4 March. So unabashed a musical comedy was an odd choice for the company, which wisely enlisted such Broadway stalwarts as Judy Kaye and Richard Muenz for the leads. An old hit was a new hit all over again.

Conversely, an old flop became a new flop when it finally found a home on the Great White Way. **Chu Chem** (17 March 1989, Ritz) had originally been dropped—the whole show—during its tryouts way back in 1966 in Philadelphia. Nearly a quarter of a century later a small-scale off-off-Broadway retrial was so favorably received that the production was hustled to a main-stem theatre. The story was set in fourteenth-century China, where three Jews come seeking a lost tribe of Israel that supposedly had settled there ages ago. The local prince (Kevin Gray) falls in love with the Jewess (Emily Zacharias), but she will not have him unless he brings about the feminist reforms she demands. The sets were simple; their colors, along with those of the costumes, surprisingly restrained. But in one delightful departure from Broadway's lowering norms, the singers seem not to have been miked or amplified. You heard honest-to-goodness voices coming from singers who were positioned just where their voices suggested they would be.

Broadway moved from medieval China to turn-of-the-century Kansas when the Radio City Music Hall succumbed to the vogue for translating films to the stage. Turn-of-the-century Kansas could only mean **The Wizard of Oz** (22 March 1989), but resorting to a more modern horror, the dialogue and music were prerecorded, with the players merely lip-synching.

Another modern horror—Broadway critics refusing to allow themselves or their readers to be entertained—may have been exemplified by the failure of **Welcome to the Club** (13 April 1989, Music Box). The musical, with a book by A. E. Hotchner, music by Cy Coleman, and lyrics by the two men, was set entirely in a prison ward reserved for men (and one wild woman) who have refused to pay their alimony. At previews audiences laughed long and loud at the humor and applauded the songs heartily. But after the largely thumbs-down reviews appeared, no one seemed to find the show very enjoyable, so it was withdrawn a week and a half later.

Such short runs, plus the dearth of replacements, meant theatre owners had to look elsewhere for bookings. Once again a house in danger of a long period of shuttering turned over its stage to a pop concert: **Barry Manilow at the Gershwin** (18 April 1989).

Yet for all the difficulties regular Broadway houses experienced filling their stages, new houses were still opening. The Criterion Center Stage Right was a small off-Broadway–style house which had been carved out of a former movie theatre that had been built on the site of several long-gone playhouses. For a brief time it served as home to **Starmites** (27 April 1989), a small rock musical which told how a

timid young girl, Eleanor (Liz Larsen), addicted to comic books, is magically whisked away to outer space. There she, a hunk named Spacepunk (Brian Lane Green), and his four buddies, The Starmites, battle to save the universe. Among the people who cross her path are a towering goddess (Sharon McNight), who looks suspiciously like Mommy, and the goddess's kooky daughter, who astonishingly resembles Eleanor (and who was also played by Miss Larsen).

Ghetto (April 30, 89, Circle in the Square) was an Israeli play, which had also been done in Germany and England, and which told of a Jewish theatrical band performing in the Vilna ghetto during the Nazi occupation. It had some songs, but essentially was a straight play.

The season closed with **Largely New York** (1 May 1989, St. James). It wasn't a musical, although it played a house that customarily hosted big musicals. Instead it was a generally silent evening of pantomime headed by the ineffable Bill Irwin, who cavorted as an innocent confronting life's romances and difficulties. Ingenious sight gags and amusing props added to the fun. But the gnawing thought remains that on a healthier—and, okay, more old-fashioned—Broadway, Irwin would have attracted far vaster audiences in knock-about musical vehicles.

1989–1990

After the disastrous 1988–1989 season the Broadway musical theatre almost had to improve—and it did. The new season was busier and more rewarding, although once again no truly superior work emerged.

As they had the preceding year, revivals mounted by the New York City Opera at the New York State Theatre launched the festivities. Included in this year's repertory were three productions audiences had applauded before: *The Mikado, The Merry Widow*, and *The Desert Song*. Departing from such older favorites, on 18 July the company gave New Yorkers a fresh mounting of Leonard Bernstein's brilliant modern-day operetta, *Candide* (1 December 1956).

In marked contrast to such operettas requiring huge casts and tons of scenery were the one-man shows so common recently on a money-strapped Broadway. As often as not they were given unimaginative, slightly pretentious titles such as *Whatshisname at the Suchandsuch Theatre* or *Youknowwho in Concert*. Broadway's first offering adopted the latter form, but with an amusing stinger added: **Mandy**

Patinkin in Concert: Dress Casual (25 July 1989, Hayes). Accompanied only by a pianist, the young actor and singer presented an evening of varied songs, ranging from "When The Red, Red Robin Comes Bob, Bob Bobbin' Along" to Sondheim's "No More." Early on, he warned audiences that if he didn't sing a song to his own satisfaction, he'd repeat it to get it right.

A lackluster revival of *Shenandoah* (7 January 1975), with John Cullum again in the lead, came into the Virginia on 8 August, but stayed only a brief time.

A revival of *Sweeney Todd* (1 March 1979) received a more vociferous welcome from the critics when it was played out at the Circle in the Square on 14 September. The theatre itself was strung with clothesline on which were hung tattered garments bathed in orange and red glows, and its walls became the walls of London's nineteenth-century tenements, with yellow lights burning behind dirty windowpanes. The smallness of the house and the closeness of its thrust stage gave the work, starring a chalky-faced Bob Gunton as Todd and Beth Fowler as a good-humored Mrs. Lovett, a singular intimacy and immediacy. One critic observed, "With the great increase in drug-related crime and violence on our city streets, the metaphor of cannibalism in the play and the terrifying events on stage do not seem nearly as remote as we once thought them to be." For whatever reason, attendance, at first encouraging, soon fell off, and the show's run was disappointing.

Broadway turned thumbs down on **Dangerous Games** (19 October 1989, Nederlander), an evening of two danced musicals, conceived and choreographed by Graciela Daniele. The first, **Tango,** was set in the 1930s in an Argentine brothel, where a pair of brothers fight over a girl, while the second, **Orfeo,** was set in the supposed contemporary hell of Argentina under its rightist soldiers.

Sid Caesar & Company: Does Anybody Know What I'm Talking About? (1 November 1989, Golden) was an almost old-style revue, offering as it did a few new songs along with its comedy (but with no old-time spectacle). At heart, however, it was a one-man show. Caesar was in excellent form, especially as a cocky, double-talking polymath, giving his preposterous version of Einstein's theory, then careening through the reading of a romantic novel "in guttural German, hand-waving Italian and barked Japanese." But somehow great clowns have always seemed funnier committing their comic mayhem against a background of scenic opulence and relieved now and then by major musical numbers. This skimpy mounting skimped along for just five showings. Beloved old comics are beloved for only so long.

The latest beloved film to see the footlights was **Meet Me in St. Louis** (2 November 1989, Gershwin), and it enjoyed a season-long, if forced, run despite a critical drubbing. A competent cast and eye-filling scenery, including a sumptuous ballroom and a cute little trolley (for "The Trolley Song," naturally), no doubt helped.

But rock star Sting and the talented British director John Dexter could do nothing for *The Threepenny Opera* (13 April 1933), a drab, leaden revival that began a short run at the Lunt-Fontanne on 5 November.

A new musical fared no better. **The Prince of Central Park** (9 November 1989, Belasco) told what follows after a middle-aged jogger (Jo Anne Worley), whose husband has left her for a younger woman and whose daughter has gone on to a career, encounters a twelve-year-old runaway (Richard Blake) in a tree house in the park. Critics noted that the show's soft-rock score was "insistently cheery even when muggers are singing about ripping off little old ladies." Audiences could also note that on many nights (well, not that many, since the show had a brief stay) the turntable wouldn't turn properly.

Radio City Music Hall relit on the 10th for its annual *Christmas Spectacular*. This edition began when a spoof of the "Nutcracker" ballet, so popular in its classic form at this season with dance troupes around the country, was interrupted by the arrival of Ebenezer Scrooge. In short order all the extravaganza's standard characters, from the Wise Men to its wooden soldiers, made their appearances. The beautiful but cavernous theatre also played host to two other entertainments. An all-girl Japanese revue, **Takarazuka,** which offered Japanese songs and dances, and Japanese interpretations of material from Broadway musicals, had come in for a week beginning 25 October. Later in the season the **Easter Extravaganza** played a short stand starting on 11 April. No problems here.

But there were problems at **Grand Hotel** (12 November 1989, Beck). Playgoers entering the house saw on its stage what looked like a shiny erector-set construction, supposedly representing two floors of a posh Berlin hostelry. Columns (gilded and glassed) divided the floors into smaller, constricting compartments. The upper level housed the orchestra. The action all took place on the lower level, which served for any part of the hotel where incidents happened to be unfolding. Old-timers and late-night TV addicts were already familiar with the story that MGM had filmed from Vicki Baum's novel. Central to this footlight version were a fading ballerina (Liliane Montevecchi), a suave but impoverished and unscrupulous aristocrat (David Carroll), a dying Jew (Michael Jeter) out for one last fling, and a wild young girl (Jane Krakowski). Rumors abounded during previews that Luther Davis's book and Robert Wright and George Forrest's songs were unsatisfactory. Maury Weston was called in for new songs, and the book, too, was redone. The changes were really not any better. What made the show so memorable, for those who found it worthwhile in the first place, was Tommy Tune's staging, with the cast weaving around the pillars or marching softly in unison. The show did not come truly alive until almost the last few minutes, when the dying Jew kicked up his heels in a vigorous Charleston. Broadway has had its cult shows, and this production of *Grand Hotel* certainly had its own cult. Others will be content to let the film remain the classic version.

Yet Broadway has developed its own classics, even if faddist, self-inflating critics constantly play musical chairs with the list. One which for the time being seems to hold a secure place in the game is *Gypsy* (21 May 1959). Still amazingly fresh after a prolonged cross-country tour, this latest revival settled into the St. James on 16 November, with Tyne Daly, a television celebrity, in the lead. Greeted by virtually universal huzzahs, the revival ran out the season and continued through much of the next. It ran for 582 performances (with one brief hiatus).

Victor Borge's Holiday Show on Broadway (5 December 1989, Atkinson) allowed the beloved pianistic comedian to again delight his followers with his sometimes sly, sometimes outrageous humor and playing.

City of Angels (11 December 1989, Virginia) is unlikely to ever be considered a classic, but it was the first novelty of the season to make an incontestable hit with both critics and audiences. Larry Gelbart's amusing enough book juxtaposed the real-life problems of Stine (Gregg Edelman), a screenwriter, with those of Stone (James Naughton), the detective he writes about in a film. Somehow all the other people the writer must deal with in the real world find their celluloid counterparts. Settings (sometimes separate, sometimes side by side) showed that real world in gaudy Hollywood colors, the film sequences (never actually films) largely in blacks, whites, and grays. Cy Coleman and lyricist David

Zippel supplied pleasant songs, although none gave promise of becoming a standard. For all its many delights, there was something off-putting about the musical, which seemed to be entertaining playgoers while at the same time keeping them at arm's length. You could like *City of Angels*; you couldn't "love" it.

You couldn't love **Junon and Avos—The Hope** (7 January 1990, City Center) either, and it was hard to like, too. For one, it was sung-through in Russian and Russian-accented Spanish (with a tuxedoed English-speaking narrator at the side of the stage sometimes giving a hint of what was happening). Nor were its songs outstanding. It was, however, lavishly mounted and excellently choreographed. Its story supposedly was true and recalled how a Russian count sailed to 1806 California in search of trade, fell in love with the daughter of the Spanish governor, sailed away after promising to marry her, and died before he could return. The girl became a nun. Junon and Avos were not the lovers; they were the count's ships.

Practically from the day of its premiere, *The Sound of Music* (16 November 1959) has had numerous critical detractors and hordes of play-going admirers. The divisiveness remained when Debby Boone headed the cast of the New York City Opera's production on 8 March.

Oba Oba '90 (15 March 1990, Marquis) was a new edition of the Brazilian folk revue Broadway had seen during the 1987–1988 season. Once again, Broadway wasn't bowled over.

For many, the season's last major musical was its most eagerly awaited. Yet for many of those who held such high expectations, Andrew Lloyd Webber's **Aspects of Love** (8 April 1990, Broadhurst) proved a disappointment. Others, perhaps not expecting so much, found this latest sung-through "pop opera" more accessible and feeling than his recent hits. A young Englishman (Michael Ball), a French actress (Ann Crumb), the Englishman's playboy uncle (Kevin Colson), a young bisexual Italian artist (Kathleen Rowe McAllen), and the actress's daughter (Danielle Du Clos) seem to be forever changing romantic partners. Maria Bjornson's overly elaborate sets, for all their faults, captured tellingly many glimpses of Europe just after World War II. In England several of the songs had earned widespread popularity. Not so in America, even though one critic noted, "We hear 'Love Changes Everything'—a repetitive insistent tune—endlessly. (At first I tried to clock its reoccurrences: After the initial hearing at 8:08 it reappeared at 8:25, then at 8:37. By 8:20

we had heard the second take-home tune, 'Seeing Is Believing,' which was reprised by 8:30.) I wish the 'C' train came this often."

Truly Blessed (22 April 1990, Longacre) was a small-cast affair, mixing old songs and some new gospel-like melodies to recount the life and art of Mahalia Jackson (Queen Esther Marrow). It had a brief run.

So did **A Change in the Heir** (29 April 1990, Edison). It was set in a mythical kingdom where claimants for the throne are raised as members of the opposite sex to their real one. Even the all-too-neglected, charming Judy Blazer could not save this one.

A frightening glimpse of where the musical theatre might be heading was evidenced during the season in a news report from Toronto. *Les Misérables* was presented at the SkyDome "before a record-breaking 52,011 people ... . Fans sitting in the upper SkyDome levels could barely distinguish the musicians dressed in black. But the JumboTron videoscreen and four smaller screens zoomed in on the actors' faces so tightly that tears and spit were visible." Live theatre?

1990–1991

Live theatre, certainly live (although miked and amplified) musical theatre, fared no better in the new season than it had the year before. Indeed, the quality of its novelties dropped perceptibly.

Even before Broadway began belatedly welcoming new offerings, the New York City Opera's late-summer repertory dusted off Sondheim's *A Little Night Music* (25 February 1973) and Weill's *Street Scene* (9 January 1947). (In October the company's programs once again included *The Mikado*.) And Michael Feinstein came back in his glorified evening of cocktail-lounge music at the Golden on 2 October. Similarly, **Jackie Mason: Brand New** (17 October 1990, Neil Simon) gave this Borscht Circuit revue comedian, now without a Borscht Circuit or a revue, a third chance to regale New Yawkas with his Yiddish-American humor. (Much later in the season, **Penn & Teller: The Refrigerator Tour** (3 April 1991, Eugene O'Neill) allowed these hilariously funny magicians, also deprived of two-a-day and revue stages, their third opportunity to mystify and tickle audiences. However, their return engagement was less successful than Mason's. Mike-clinging Judy Garland's mike-clinging daughter entertained her admirers briefly in **Liza Minnelli: Stepping Out**

at **Radio City** (23 April 1991), then for a longer return the following January.

One very oddball attraction came—and left hurriedly—before more typical novelties appeared. **Bugs Bunny on Broadway** (4 October 1990, Gershwin) was a mixed-media mélange of cartoons and humans, rock and roll on the one hand and Wagner and Liszt on the other. Broadway wouldn't buy.

The first new musical that traditionalists would recognize as such was **Once on This Island** (18 October 1990, Booth). Based on Rosa Guy's novel *My Love, My Love* and with music by Stephen Flaherty and book and lyrics by Lynn Ahrens, this black entertainment was set in the French Antilles and told how Ti Moune (La Chanze) nurses the mulatto aristocrat Daniel (Jerry Dixon) back to health after an automobile accident. To assure his love she bargains away her soul to Papa Ge (Eric Riley), the demon of death. But instead of walking off with Daniel she is turned into a tree. The show had initially been offered off-Broadway before moving uptown. Insubstantial albeit beguiling, the musical ran out the season.

A second black cast generated sparks in David Merrick's revival of the old Gershwin musical *Oh, Kay!* (1 November 1926), with its story reset in modern-day Harlem. But the sparks did not ignite a fire, so the show was quickly withdrawn. Merrick tried to bring it back again in the spring only to have it fold during previews.

Buddy: The Buddy Holly Story (4 November 1990, Shubert) was essentially a concert of the long-dead American rock star's music, interwoven with snatches of his life. A huge hit in England, it received a cool reception here and had a somewhat forced run of seven months with Paul Hipp as Holly.

Those Were the Days (7 November 1990, Edison) was a revue singing songs mostly from the Yiddish theatre's heyday.

Two nights later the Radio City Music Hall's *Christmas Spectacular* began its annual stand. Included were the Rockettes dancing in precision as beardless, short-skirted Santa Clauses and a compact version of *A Christmas Carol* that sported flying ghosts.

Another revival was *Fiddler on the Roof* (22 September 1964), which came into the Gershwin on the 18th, with the Israeli star Topol as Tevye. Inevitably, at least one faddist critic saw the work as "just a little musty." Playgoers didn't agree or didn't care, so the musical ran until mid-June.

The season's major disaster, **Shogun: The Musical** (20 November 1990, Marquis), was taken from James Clavell's best-selling novel. John Driver provided the book and lyrics, and Paul Chihara the music. As the evening began, lightning burst across the black- and gold-lacquered screen that served as a show curtain. The screen parted to reveal a ship foundering in a storm. Later in this saga of a ship-wrecked Occidental sea captain (Philip Casnoff), his romance with the beautiful Lady Mariko (June Angela), and his battles with the tyrannical over-lord Toranga (Francis Ruivivar) and other Japanese nobles, an earthquake threatened to swallow up the cast. But gorgeous costumes and scenery and attention-grabbing effects could not compensate for three hours of tedium. Clavell is said to have poured his own money into keeping the show running, but even he had to throw in the towel after nine weeks.

Something called **An Evening with Harry Connick, Jr., and His Orchestra** (23 November 1990, Lunt-Fontanne) appeared and disappeared quickly. It was little more than a concert of swing-era music, performed by a tiny "big band."

As another Christmas treat, Cathy Rigby flew across the stage in *Peter Pan* (20 October 1954), which began a limited engagement at the Lunt-Fontanne on 13 December.

In 1930 Langston Hughes and Zora Neale Hurston wrote a comedy about the turmoil unleashed in a small Florida town by Jim and Dave pursuing Daisy. **Mule Bone** (14 February 1991, Barrymore), however, did not reach Broadway until more than sixty years later, by which time it was "embellished with several musical numbers" accompanied by a four-player band. Even *Best Plays* was at something of a loss over what to consider this bor-derline affair. In its annual summary of productions it listed it under "plays" rather than "musicals," but elsewhere branded it a "musical play." In any case, New York wasn't interested for long.

Off-Broadway's most satisfying entry during the season was **And the World Goes' Round** (18 March 1991, Westside), the latest example of the long-on-going fashion for retrospectives. This time, five tal-ented youngsters, abetted by adept and imaginative staging, fetchingly sang an eveningful of Kander and Ebb songs.

No show of the season engendered more con-troversy or more publicity than **Miss Saigon** (11 April 1991, Broadway). Actors' Equity tried to pre-vent the male lead from the original London com-pany from playing on the grounds that he was not an Oriental. Never mind that one of the union's loudest bellyachers had herself played the Oriental Mother Courage a few seasons back. Whether the controversy was staged or not, editorialists in news-papers and on the airwaves soon took up producer Cameron Mackintosh's cause. After all, this sort of nonsense not only prevented a producer from hiring whomever he judged the best available performer but smacked of reverse racism. Mackintosh nois-ily canceled the opening, but then reconsidered when the abashed union had to retreat. The big question became whether the show, resetting the *Madama Butterfly* story in Vietnam at the time of the American withdrawal, was worth all the fuss. The *Daily News* headlined its review "Viet Numb!" and the *Post*, "Amiss in 'Saigon.' " Jonathan Pryce, whose casting as the pimp had provoked the brouhaha, won high praise, and Lea Salonga as the Butterfly-ish Kim was also applauded. Then, of course, there was the spectacular scene in which a two-seater heli-copter, with three glaring searchlights in its under-belly, descended behind an ashen scrim. Panicky soldiers pack into it, but the overloaded craft takes off anyway. The musical was the work of some of the men who had created *Les Misérables*: Claude-Michel Schönberg for the music, Alain Boublil and Schönberg for the book, and Boublil along with the American Richard Maltby, Jr., for the lyrics. The huge advance sale, the publicity, and a dearth of first-rate shows helped the musical run for many years. (Months after the show opened, the *New Yorker*, in one of its weekly thumbnail follow-ups of Broadway shows, wrote merely, "Oh, the horror! The horror!") As of this writing, a closing has been announced: New Year's Eve 2001.

There was also controversy over **The Secret Garden** (25 April 1991, St. James), which com-poser Lucy Simon and lyricist-librettist Marsha Norman took from Frances Hodgson Burnett's novel. But the controversy was quiet and digni-fied, with many playgoers arguing that the musical was lifeless and boring, and just as many seeing it as gentle and charming. In a setting described vari-ously as a "rococo... pop-up period toy-theater" and "a cornucopia of Victorian doll-house imagery," the orphaned Mary Lennox (Daisy Eagan) comes to live with her secretive, moody Yorkshire uncle (Mandy Patinkin), who maintains a carefully locked, possi-bly magical garden once cultivated by his late wife. Eerily lit ghosts from the little girl's and the uncle's pasts wander through the action. They disappear after the two rid themselves of their obsession with what is gone forever. Despite divided reactions, the musical ran more than 700 performances, without, apparently, recouping its original costs.

Three nights later at the Marquis, Tyne Daly returned for a rerun of her revival of *Gypsy*.

The last of the season's new Broadway novelties was **The Will Rogers Follies** (1 May 1991, Palace). Considering its stifling mediocrity, it was a surprising, and in at least one respect well-deserved, success. Some of the musical theatre's best surviving creators were in at its birth: Cy Coleman doing the music, Peter Stone the book, Betty Comden and Adolph Green the lyrics, and Tommy Tune the dances. None did themselves proud in this small-cast, episodic retelling of the life of the comedian (Keith Carradine)—with Wiley Post (Paul Ukena, Jr.) rising regularly from his seat in a box to beg Rogers to go flying with him. Where the show excelled was in its ability to recreate the beauty and mass effect of Ziegfeld's heyday, using only a dozen and a half gorgeous chorus girls and imaginative costumes that turned the girls into horned steers, gems, red-white-and-blue political dollies, or simply beautifully befeathered young ladies. It says something that, apart from the girls and their costumes, the runaway hit of the show was the comic cavorting of six dogs billed as Brackney's Madcap Mutts. Aided by some cleverly publicized replacements, especially financier Donald Trump's celebrated friend and eventual wife, Maria Maples, the musical compiled just short of 1,000 performances.

1991–1992

Although by the numbers the new season might have been looked at as busier than many recent ones, it was low on originality. Virtually every musical to appear was either a revival or a new compilation of old materials. Further, the novelties seemed reluctant to retail anything but show business yarns—or at least something closely allied to show business.

In what was emerging as a new pattern, a revival by the New York City Opera at its really-too-large-for-Broadway-musicals Lincoln Center home launched the season. It did so on 4 September with one of the more logical selections for its oversized auditorium, Frank Loesser's gorgeously melodic mélange of opera, operetta, and musical comedy, *The Most Happy Fella* (3 May 1956). Curiously, Broadway, which had not seen a revival of the musical in eleven years, would see two this season. Louis Quilico sang Tony.

Before Broadway got going, off-Broadway applauded what proved to be its longest-running hit of the season, **Return to the Forbidden Planet** (13 October 1991, Variety Arts), a London hit that mixed a spoof of old science-fiction films with a plot suggested by Shakespeare's *The Tempest* and employed a hodgepodge rock-and-roll score to give the proceedings a beat.

Europe was also the source of Broadway's first novelty, **André Heller's Wonderhouse** (20 October 1991, Broadhurst). As a surprise for his wife (Patty Maloney) on her seventieth birthday, a man (Billy Barty) rents an abandoned theatre and presents a show consisting of old-time vaudeville turns. These include a whiteface clown, a man who cuts papers into fantastic designs, a magician, an Amazon lady whistler, and a pair of aging, comically klutzy dancers. *Variety* correctly predicted that New Yorkers would not buy this "low-key celebration of innocence."

The New York City Opera's second revival, on 7 November, was Lerner and Loewe's *Brigadoon* (13 March 1947). The cast was unexceptional.

Just over a week later, on the 15th, the Radio City Music Hall brought out its annual *Christmas Spectacular*, with its lavish depiction of the Nativity, an ice-skating scene, and the Rockettes in a series of routines, including "The Parade of the Wooden Soldiers."

On the 27th Cathy Rigby returned for a brief engagement at the Minskoff in the *Peter Pan* with which she had delighted youngsters the year before.

Catskills on Broadway (5 December 1991, Lunt-Fontanne) was a largely musicless revue devoted to four Borscht Circuit–style comedians, Freddie Roman, Dick Capri, Marilyn Michaels, and Mal Z. Lawrence. It kept its large-musical-size house laughing and crowded throughout the season and well into the next.

Then came **Nick & Nora** (8 December 1991, Marquis), which librettist-director Arthur Laurents, composer Charles Strouse, and lyricist Richard Maltby, Jr., had taken from the beloved old *Thin Man* films, themselves taken from Dashiell Hammett's writings. The show had been promised for months and months, was noisily postponed on several occasions, then went through a rumor-filled nine weeks of full-priced previews. If that was not sufficient to scare away playgoers, critics pounced on lines and song titles from the show to hurl back at it. One critic observed, ""You may think there's no point to this story" sings Nick Charles at one point, and I thought, you've hit the nail on the head"; another remarked, "It's a bit near the knuckle that the best number is called 'Let's Go Home.'" That pointless story Nick (Barry Bostwick) spoke about told of his and Nora's visit to friends in Hollywood. When a producer's mistress (Faith Prince) is murdered, Nora (Joanna Gleason) takes charge of solving it and does, even if the corpse must come to life several times to help reconstruct events. Fetishism, sadism, drug addiction, feminism, and lesbianism all lurked on the fringes of the plot (and would return with a vengeance in later shows). The skimpy production threw in the towel one week after the notices appeared. Interestingly, on 2 December, just before *Nick & Nora* opened, the American Jewish Theatre revived another Strouse flop, *Rags* (21 August 1986). Critics reviewing the offering lamented what a fine Strouse score had been lost in the play's failure, and subsequently used it to whip the composer for his latest, lackluster effort.

The season's second revival of *The Most Happy Fella* stood in marked contrast to its first. It opened at the intimate Booth on 13 February and used only two pianos to accompany the players. Most critics felt the mounting accorded a singular and unexpected directness and warmth to Loesser's sometimes overblown work, even though many found the cast nothing to write paragraphs about. Playgoers were not quite so enthusiastic, but enough of them came to let the revival run seven months.

At Vienna's Volksoper and Budapest's Favorosi, revivals are often tinkered with, on occasion heavily. The public explanation has been that the works have become "dated," but privately it is acknowledged that the real reason is to extend the copyright and allow the tinkerers an ongoing share of royalties. For years the notoriously greedy, bitchy Leonore Gershwin and her lazy, reclusive husband, Ira, whom she seems to have dominated, made headlines in an effort to retain their income. Furthermore, they appear to have despised the men who created librettos for the Gershwin shows, so, while fighting to protect their own interests, they cavalierly threw out their collaborators' efforts and brought in new writers. One instance resulted in *My One and Only* (1 May 1983). A second was **Crazy for You** (19 February 1992, Shubert), which once had been *Girl Crazy* (14 January 1930). The best of the Gershwins' great songs from the original were retained, and those that were discarded were replaced by songs from other shows and films, including "Someone To Watch Over Me," "They Can't Take That Away From Me," and "Slap That Bass." Guy Bolton and

Jack McGowan's delightful story of a playboy who heads west to escape girls and runs right into their arms was replaced by Ken Ludwig's equally workable tale of a man who finds love and success when he attempts to save an old theatre. Besides the memorable melodies and the laugh-rich book, the best thing about the show was Susan Stroman's stage-filling dances, with dancers even cavorting on the roofs of a western mining town in the first-act finale. What did come in for criticism was the strangely inept casting, with the *Times*'s David Richards confessing, "It may be the first Broadway musical that left me eager to catch the replacement cast." Ignoring such shortcomings, the public packed the theatre. The musical ran until January 1996, chalking up 1,622 playings.

SUSAN STROMAN was born 17 October 1954 in Wilmington, Delaware. Her parents encouraged her early interest in music and dance, enrolling her in dance class when she was five. Her first professional job was in *Hit the Deck* at Goodspeed Opera House in 1977, followed by a featured role as Leslie in *Whoopee!* on Broadway in 1979. Forsaking performing for staging, "Stro," as she is known to her friends, honed her craft first as an assistant director, then assistant choreographer, choreographer, director of summer stock theatre, industrials and club acts, and, eventually, choreographer for the Vineyard Theatre's revised *Flora, the Red Menace* in 1984. From there she moved to the New York City Opera, off-Broadway, and, before long, big-budget Broadway productions.

In the days of the original *Girl Crazy*, producers had usually brought in their shows early, hoping for a season-long run before the summer heat killed business. Now, with the prestigious Tony Awards coming in late spring and with theatres air-conditioned, shows come in late, trusting an award will propel them through the hot weather and allow them to run through the following season. Thus, nine musicals premiered in April of 1992. The first was a London hit, **Five Guys Named Moe** (8 April

1992, Eugene O'Neill), ostensibly a retrospective of a heretofore deservedly forgotten black American composer, saxophonist, and orchestra leader. The man was Louis Jordan, whose immortal numbers include "Is You Is Or Is You Ain't My Baby?" In an era of political correctness, when things black must be extolled even at the expense of superior white achievements, Broadway's leftish critics failed to observe a salient irony: What made the show a delight was the same thing that had overcome the sometimes ingrained bigotry of old critics: the lively dancing and the good-natured pleasure the entertainers took in their own performing. And going back even before the early black revues of the 1920s, this revue had a thin plot—in which Big Moe, Little Moe, No Moe, Eat Moe, and Four-Eyed Moe seemingly jump out of a radio to attempt to distract a young man upset with an unhappy love life.

On the 10th, the Radio City Music Hall's *Easter Show* restored its famed pageant "The Glory of Easter," which had been performed annually from 1933 to 1979. Other sections had the Rockettes dancing a tribute to the Gershwins and mingling with a brilliant laser display. The finale was called "Rainbow Follies."

One of Broadway's most delightful and best-loved musicals, *Guys and Dolls* (24 November 1950), was given a superior revival at the Martin Beck on the 14th. It was a colorful mounting that emphasized comedy at the expense of romance. Thus, the hits of the evening were pudgy Nathan Lane's shticky Nathan Detroit and the hilariously economical Adelaide of Faith Prince (the lively corpse of *Nick & Nora*). Peter Gallagher and Josie de Guzman were Sky Masterson and Sarah Brown. Tony Walton's garishly vulgar settings had a humor of their own. Aided by the production's, Prince's, and Walton's winning Tonys, the show was the first of three April arrivals to run through the summer and all of the next season. In fact, this *Guys and Dolls* became the longest-running revival in Broadway history at a regular house (the second, *Oh, Calcutta!* played a minuscule venue), albeit its 1,144 performances fell just short of the original's 1,200.

Metro (16 April 1992, Minskoff) was supposedly a long-running hit in Warsaw, but its American version, performed by young Polish players attempting to speak English, survived only a week and a half. The kids have been rejected at an audition, so have invaded a subway station to display their talents. There were laser and black light effects, and a show curtain that may have been trying to make some wry political statement, since it seemed to be an iron curtain.

A week and a half was also all that Broadway would give to **The High Rollers Social and Pleasure Club** (21 April 1992, Helen Hayes), a nightclub revue set in New Orleans during Mardi Gras and featuring some songs of its on-stage bandleader, Allen Toussaint. Not unexpectedly, it concluded with a song not by Toussaint, "When The Saints Go Marchin' In."

Gypsy Passion (22 April 1992, Town Hall) was a flamenco entertainment held together loosely by the tale of a gypsy group visiting Seville and the love affair of two young gypsies. Although it stayed only two weeks, it proved enough of a draw to be brought back in the next season.

Of course Spain was also the setting for a revival at the Marquis on the 24th of *Man of La Mancha* (22 November 1965), with Raul Julia in the title role. Greeted by divided notices, the production struggled along until killed by the summer's heat.

Two big hits, both running more than a year, closed out the season. The first to arrive was **Jelly's Last Jam** (26 April 1992, Virginia), which was set in "The Jungle Inn—a lowdown club somewhere's 'tween heaven 'n' hell." There Jelly Roll Morton, on the last day of his life, examines that life and the music it brought forth. Morton was perhaps more deserving of a retrospective than Jordan, though his music was not all that much better, if it was better at all. Moreover, to please the politically correct crowd, Morton's life was seen in no small measure as a battle against whites or white-imposed perceptions. The musical begins when a Death figure, here called the Chimney Man (Keith David), insists on reviewing the dying man's past. Jelly Roll is obviously not a nice man, abrasive and selfish, and ultimately unable to cope when his style goes out of fashion. Three gals in black dresses, the Hunnies, come in and out of the action like an ancient Greek chorus, at one point singing their feelings to Jelly and his girl as the pair attempt to make love. Happily, the producers hired one of Broadway's most electrifying and amiable dancers, Gregory Hines, to play the lead. He and a brilliant chorus of black dancers often stopped the show with their pulsating routines. More than one critic subscribed to Jeffrey Sweet's subsequent assessment in the *Best Plays*, where he called it "an exciting if unfulfilled evening."

Nor was **Falsettos** (29 April 1992, John Golden) all that new, since it was created largely by combining two of William Finn's earlier, off-Broadway musicals, *March of the Falsettos* (20 May 1981) and *Falsettoland* (28 June 1990). So once again Marvin (Michael Rupert) leaves his wife for a gay love affair with Whizzer (Stephen Bogardus), only to have Whizzer come down with AIDS. Not only was male homosexuality in evidence, but lesbianism as well. But with so few modern musicals offering boy-meets-girl, playgoers after some degree of diversion lit on this one, which at least had the saving grace of being frequently amusing in its observations.

1992–1993

The seasons followed one another without much perceptible change. The number of musical productions remained essentially the same. So did their nature. New musicals continued to lack the abundant, memorable melodies of older ones. Many, perhaps most, dealt with subjects that would scarcely have been touched on years ago. Remarkable technical mounting often replaced quality writing as the shows' noteworthy feature. And this new technology regularly included unnatural, sometimes shrill and deafening, amplification.

Once again the New York City Opera brought in the season's first musical. In one probably meaningless change, the group's two revivals were the season's only major resurrections. The initial offering was *110 in the Shade* (24 October 1963), which opened at the New York State Theatre on 18 July. Richard Muenz and Karen Ziemba had the leads.

Anna Karenina (26 August 1992, Circle in the Square), a musicalization of Tolstoy's novel about an unhappily married woman whose refusal to accept her era's proprieties drives her to suicide received a critical slating, struggled bravely for a little over a month, then disappeared.

Some observers considered **The Music of Andrew Lloyd Webber** (22 September 1992, Radio City Music Hall) merely the latest in Broadway's ongoing line of retrospectives. Others looked on it as a concert. Michael Crawford headed the cast. (Not dissimilarly, **Tommy Tune Tonite!** [28 December 1992, Gershwin] was deemed, by many of those who saw it in its ten-performance stand, another in the recent line of glorified one-man shows.)

Oba Oba 93 (1 October 1992, Marquis) was an updated version of a Brazilian revue first done on Broadway in March of 1988. The "93" in its title was too optimistic, for the show folded in mid-November.

The New York City Opera's second revival was Marc Blitzstein's *Regina* (31 October 1949). When this arioso version of Lillian Hellman's *The Little Foxes* was first done on Broadway, some commentators suggested it belonged rightly in an opera repertory. Since then, the New York City Opera had presented it twice, in 1953 and 1958, before this return.

The Radio City Music Hall's annual *Christmas Spectacular* arrived on 13 November, little altered from the previous season's edition. Four nights later, last season's *Gypsy Passion* also returned, this time to the Plymouth, where it lingered until the beginning of January.

3 from Brooklyn (19 November 1992, Helen Hayes) was a small-cast revue that professed to offer a cabbie's-eye view of his home turf. Adrienne Tolsch shone with her comedy about everyday Jewish life in the borough.

In **The Sheik of Avenue B** (27 November 1992, Town Hall) the cast represented 1932 radio performers on the Blue Network's *Town Hall Tonight* show. The first act was supposedly the early broadcast of the entertainment, while the second act described the audience warm-up and the later, repeat broadcast. The players recounted memories of Jewish life in their younger days and sang obscure songs ranging from Charles K. Harris's 1899 "A Rabbi's Daughter" to Billy Rose and Fred Fisher's 1927 "Yiddisha Charleston." The musical had only a limited appeal.

Broadcasting—this time the television genre—also served as the background for **My Favorite Year** (10 December 1992, Vivian Beaumont), taken from a 1982 film of the same name. Benjy Stone (Evan Pappas), a Brooklyn-born comedy writer on the wildly popular TV series starring King Kaiser [read Sid Caesar] (Tom Mardirosian), discovers he is to chaperon the program's guest star, Hollywood's great swashbuckler, Alan Swann (Tim Curry), around town. Since Swann is Benjy's ideal, imagine his shock when he learns that Swann is a mean drunkard and Benjy's real duty is to keep him sober and nice. Benjy decides to take him home to Mother (Lainie Kazan). He's given a big welcome there, but afterwards not much happens.

Not much really happened in **Fool Moon** (25 February 1993, Richard Rodgers) either, but then the show, being largely pantomime, had no plot. Fortunately its two mute clowns were mild, childlike Bill Irwin and mischievous, pugnacious David Shiner. Shiner made his first entrance from the auditorium, lumbering over startled members of the audience. Later some playgoers were brought on stage to help in a silent movie spoof and a scene about romance in a restaurant. At one point Irwin and Shiner shot back and forth across the stage like "horizontal bungee jumpers"; at another they disappeared into the flies riding on a crescent moon. An on-stage yokel band called the Red Clay Ramblers provided lively accompaniments. The show ran through the summer, but for all its hilarity the sad thought remains that in a healthier theatrical era such fine clowns would be provided with full-blown, major vehicles year in, year out.

For many playgoers, the most eagerly awaited novelty of the season was **The Goodbye Girl** (4 March 1993, Marquis), which Neil Simon adapted from his own film of the same title. David Zippel put words to Marvin Hamlisch's tunes. None of the writers was in particularly good form, so it remained for the show's two stars, the lovingly vulnerable Bernadette Peters and TV's leprechaunish Martin Short, to carry the evening. They did it with élan. Peters was Paula, a young dancer whose lover has walked out on her and rented their apartment to a stranger. That stranger proves to be Elliot, an actor. The pair dislike each other at once, but for economy's sake agree to room together. As everyone knew would happen, by 10:40 (earlier curtains have long since meant shows no longer end at eleven) the couple found themselves in love. Critic after critic pointed out a change in the story that Simon made to accommodate political correctness, although none of these essentially leftish critics made any attempt to extend his remarks into a generalized comment on the price paid for pandering to such lunacy. In the original, Elliot was told by a wacko director to play Shakespeare's Richard III as if the king were a homosexual. Thanks to its stars the show ran, with some forcing, until the hot weather.

Without any stars, **The Song of Jacob Zulu** (24 March 1993, Plymouth) managed to last for just under eight weeks. It told of a young black boy (K. Todd Freeman) caught between loyalty to his deeply rooted African family and his fight for independence. A nine-member group called Ladysmith Black Mambazo sang, a cappella, both original and traditional material by way of comment on the story.

Once again April was busy, beginning on the 2nd with Radio City Music Hall's annual *Easter Show*, basically unchanged from the previous season.

Ain't Broadway Grand (18 April 1993, Lunt-Fontanne) related a fictional story about once

very real people. Its central figure was the famous producer Mike Todd (Mike Burstyn). Todd has decided to produce a truly artistic, meritorious show called *Of the People*, but by the time he turns it into a success he has had to make it the same sort of raucous girlie show playgoers expect from him. Others restored to life included Bobby Clark, Gypsy Rose Lee, and Joan Blondell. But neither the quick nor the returned-from-the-dead could save this noisy mess with tinny tunes by Mitch Leigh, a dull book by Thomas Meehan and Lee Adams, and disappointing Adams lyrics. (One wonders if Adams and Charles Strouse might join up again to recreate some of their old magic.)

The next two shows both turned out to be hits despite some off-putting notices. Perhaps not surprisingly, given recent theatrical history, both came from England. **The Who's Tommy** (22 April 1993, St. James) had begun life as a recording, like so many not too distant English hits. It was the work of a rock group called The Who and especially of the band's composer, Peter Townshend. Subsequently the piece was given concert performances (including at the Metropolitan Opera House in 1970) and was even made into a 1975 film. As a child, Tommy, watching in a mirror, sees his father kill his mother's lover. The boy is traumatized and left deaf, dumb, and blind. Despite these handicaps he somehow becomes a pinball wizard. Attempts by various people to restore his health, including a prostitute who offers to spend the night with him, all fail. Not until Tommy is eighteen and his mother smashes the mirror in which he witnessed the killing do his faculties return. His admirers desert him, but he still has his family. The story itself seems the kind that would be dissuasive to many playgoers, and difficulties were aggravated by Tommy's having to be played at different ages by three different performers. But Des McAnuff's production was chock full of technological wizardry: all manner of amazing lighting effects; the rear of the stage occupied by twenty-seven huge screens on which were projected more startling, often explosive, effects; a gigantic pinball machine rising from the stage to twist, turn, and ultimately blow up; and finally, the whole auditorium seemingly converted into the inside of a pinball machine. The musical ran a little more than two years.

Willy Russell's **Blood Brothers** (25 April 1993, Music Box) also told an unpleasant story. Twins separated at birth are raised in totally different environments, one in the slums by his own mother, the other by wealthy adoptive parents. When their lives cross in later years the result is personal tragedy. The show received numerous negative notices, struggled along, and was almost ready to close until the producer was inspired to recast it with popular young American singers, David and Shaun Cassidy, in the leads. Their names helped turn business around and allowed the musical to run for two years.

Nothing saved **Tango Pasión** (28 April 1993, Longacre). An Argentine cast used the setting of a Buenos Aires bar and a series of tangos to comment on life there over a fifty-year period.

"Finally! A Broadway musical about torture and male bonding in a banana republic prison cell." Thus Howard Kissel of the *Daily News* opened his review of **Kiss of the Spider Woman** (3 May 1993, Broadhurst), a musical which librettist Terrence McNally, composer John Kander, lyricist Fred Ebb, and director Harold Prince had fashioned from a novel by Manuel Puig that later had been made into a controversial film. Molina (Brent Carver), a confessed homosexual, and Valentin (Anthony Crivello), a revolutionary, are cellmates. Since Valentin hates homosexuals, he draws a white chalk line across the floor of the cell and warns Molina not to overstep it. So Molina takes refuge in dreams about a film star (Chita Rivera) who once played a vampirish lady whose kisses were fatal. Despite their differences the men slowly become friends, even lovers. When he is released Molina agrees to attempt to get a message to Valentin's co-conspirators, but he is caught and tortured, although he refuses to give away Valentin's secret. He is shot, but seemingly comes alive long enough to dance a tango with the Spider Woman. Despite the show's grim story and often foul language, most critics found much to praise, especially in Prince's staging and the vital performances of the sixtyish Rivera and the young Carver. They were more divided over the book and even less satisfied with the songs. Edith Oliver of the *New Yorker*, who liked the show and even admitted to crying at it (as she had earlier at *The Goodbye Girl*), added another complaint: "[T]he music was so overamplified that I missed more than I heard." For all the unfavorable comments, the musical ran for 906 performances, six more than *The Who's Tommy*.

Off-Broadway was not particularly exciting during this session. A twenty-fifth-anniversary revival of *Jacques Brel Is Alive and Well and Living in Paris* came in to the Village Gate on 18 October and stayed around until February. A musical featuring the writings of long-dead Allan Sherman, who regularly put hilarious new, customarily New York–or Jewish-oriented lyrics to old melodies, was framed in a loose story of life in a Florida retirement community and was called **Hello Muddah, Hello Fadduh** (5 December 1992, Circle in the Square Downtown). (The title song employed the famous melody from Ponchielli's "Dance of the Hours"; "Sarah Jackman" once had been "Frère Jacques.") Aided immeasurably by Tovah Feldshuh as a potpourri of Jewish types, the entertainment ran from late autumn into the hot weather. Manhattan Theatre Club subscribers were about the only playgoers to see the highly praised and, of course, artistically correct **Sondheim—Putting It Together** at the group's City Center Theatre on 1 April. Not all that original in putting together a grab bag of Sondheim songs, it was certainly laudable for bringing back Julie Andrews after decades away from the theatre.

1993–1994

Only five musical novelties chanced Broadway during the season. Four of these were commercial failures, and the lone hit—a smash hit at that—was merely a transposition to the stage of a popular animated film. Yet thanks to a slew of revivals, several of them excellent, the season was not unsatisfying.

A revival of Jerry Bock, Sheldon Harnick, and Joe Masteroff's intimate musical gem, *She Loves Me* (23 May 1963), launched the parade on 10 June at the Roundabout Theatre Company's Criterion Center Stage Right with Judy Kuhn, Boyd Gaines, and Howard McGillin in the principal roles. Among the few additions to this essentially faithful reconstruction were choreographer Rob Marshall's charming dances for the café patrons and shop customers. "It will take you back," Edwin Wilson wrote of the show in the Wall *Street Journal*, "to an era when music and the bittersweet pleasure of romance were captured unashamedly in lilting melodies and witty, intelligent lyrics." Playgoers concurred, so the mounting was hurried into a regular Broadway house for an extended run.

Less happily, a tacky revival of *Camelot* (3 December 1960) opened at the Gershwin on 21 June with Robert Goulet, the show's original Lancelot, now playing King Arthur. Sourly received, it lingered only until early August.

On 17 August, the New York City Opera restored *The Student Prince* (2 December 1924) to its repertory for a handful of performances, and on 12 September it brought out *The Mikado* (19 August 1885) for a week's playing. Then, on 9 November, the company presented a novelty that was not really all that new. Rodgers and Hammerstein's **Cinderella** had first been seen by millions of Americans on television on 23 March 1957. Subsequently a revised version was also televised, and equally tampered-with live stagings popped up all across the country. The new version added tasteless, anachronistic jokes by Steve Allen and was further altered by director-choreographer Robert Johanson. Swelling the original score were several songs that had been dropped from other Rodgers and Hammerstein shows. The production stayed on for two weeks.

Far more welcome was a revival of Andrew Lloyd Webber's *Joseph and the Amazing Technicolor Dreamcoat* (27 January 1982) at the Minskoff on 10 November. Despite some critical carpings, it ran out the season.

Of necessity shorter-lived, the sixty-first annual edition of the *Radio City Christmas Spectacular* raised its curtain on the 12th and played to crowded houses until 8 January, once more offering its version of Dickens's *A Christmas Carol*, the long-limbed, high-kicking Rockettes in "The Parade of the Wooden Soldiers," and the stage-filling "Living Nativity."

Having succeeded so handsomely with its *She Loves Me*, the Roundabout Theatre Company essayed a Rodgers and Hammerstein retrospective, **A Grand Night for Singing** (17 November 1993, Criterion Center Stage Right). Three men and two women ran through a potpourri of the team's show, film, and television songs. They sang them for a month and a half.

The season's first genuine novelty was a Dutch affair, the latest attempt to put songs to Rostand's great classic. **Cyrano, the Musical** (21 November 1993. Neil Simon), with music by Ad Van Dijk, and book and lyrics by Koen Van Dijk, and translations credited to Peter Reeves and Sheldon Harnick, featured Bill Van Dijk in the title role. The scenery, often rising out of the floor or dropping from the flies in full view of the audience, was eye-popping. The special effects, such as the glaring, deafening battle explosions, were awesome. And the costumes were beautiful. But the musical itself was mediocre and set its Dutch producer back $12 million by the time he threw in the towel after a forced run of 137 performances.

Several critics pounced on the strange, unromantic scenery employed in the latest revival of *My Fair Lady* (15 March 1956), at the Virginia on 9 December, noting, for example, that Higgins's

study was furnished in one corner with a towering "phrenological head" (twelve feet high, a commentator estimated) and elsewhere with a "gargantuan upstage Rube Goldberg contraption" in lieu of his traditional phonographic equipment. Nor were aisle-sitters all that happy about the cast headed by Richard Chamberlain as Higgins (albeit they did have praise for Julian Holloway in the Doolittle role his father had created). But the show has been a favorite of the playgoing public from the start, and this return—following an extended tour—added twenty-one more weeks to its credit.

By contrast, the dying old year's last novelty could manage only half a week. **The Red Shoes** (16 December 1993, Gershwin) was a staged musicalization of the famous 1948 film. Once again, the heroine (Margaret Illmann) hopes to become a great ballerina, but her emotions are pulled in opposite ways by the ballet company's head (Steve Barton), who would control every aspect of her private life, and a more selfless, sensitive young composer (Hugh Panaro). Her dilemma drives the girl to suicide. Reviewers praised Illmann's dancing (she was a member of the Canadian National Ballet) and Lar Lubovitch's dances, as well as the sometimes sumptuous scenery. But they were unhappy with Jule Styne's score—his last before his death—with Marsha Norman's book, and with her and Paul Stryker's lyrics.

A depressing sign of Broadway's condition, not a single show of any sort opened in a first-class house between the premiere of *The Red Shoes* and the hugely successful revival, ten weeks later, of *Damn Yankees* (5 May 1955) at the Marquis on 3 March. The show was a lavish, largely faithful reconstruction, with an excellent cast that nonetheless could not erase memories of Gwen Verdon and Ray Walston. Applegate (Victor Garber) was handed a lion's share of the changes. Thus, his office in a Senate basement featured a large picture of Joe McCarthy, his list of great lovers in history mentioned J. Edgar Hoover and Clyde Tolson, his pyrotechnics included blowing up a cat, and he, not Joe (Jarrod Emick), sang the "Two Lost Souls" duet with Lola (Bebe Neuwirth). At the end of 1994, the musical closed temporarily, only to reopen the following March with Hollywood comedian Jerry Lewis starred as Applegate. After the New York run finally ended in August, Lewis took the show out for an extended national tour and, eventually, to London.

Another fine revival came in three weeks later. But, oddly enough, this remounting of Rodgers and

Hammerstein's too rarely seen *Carousel* (19 April 1945) at the Vivian Beaumont on the 24th came over from England, where it had originally been done by none other than the Royal National Theatre. Aided by designer Bob Crowley's evocative settings, director Nicholas Hytner's breakaway staging added an unexpected freshness to the piece. Placing the story quickly in its social context, the curtain rose on eight mill girls working beneath a mammoth, luminous clock. Their long, hard workday over, they rush out to meet their boat-building menfolk, and only then move on to the amusement park. Later, Julie (Sally Murphy) and Billy (Michael Hayden) talk, standing on what seems like the curve of the earth, watched over solely by a humongous golden moon. Some critics complained that Julie's unstinting loyalty to Billy—and he was made to seem less pleasant in this mounting—remained hard to accept. But the revival still enjoyed a good run (337 performances), albeit it could not approach the popularity of Rodgers and Hammerstein's other masterpieces.

On the 27th, the Radio City Music Hall brought out its annual *Radio City Easter Show*, featuring the spectacular "Glory of Easter" pageant, which has been a feature of the entertainment since 1933, as well as the Rockettes in a salute to Gershwin and a laser number called "Dancing in the Dark," and ending with a rainbow finale.

Said to have cost a record $12 million to produce, the Walt Disney company's stage version of its highly popular animated film **Beauty and the Beast** (18 April 1994, Palace) was received with unqualified rapture by the youngsters for whom it was intended and with some very modified rapture by considerably older professional critics. The story, itself taken from a beloved fairy tale, remained the same. A prince (Terrence Mann) has been turned into a grotesque beast by a woman angry that he refused to shelter her from a storm. The curse will last until a pretty girl finds him and falls in love with him. And, sure enough, the lovely Belle (Susan Egan) comes to his castle, is at first repelled by his ugliness, but in time comes to love him, so her kiss transforms him back to a handsome young man. Of course, to fill out the two and a half hours expected for a stage show, additional songs were added to those composer Alan Menken and his late lyricist, Howard Ashman, had created. Tim Rice served as Menken's wordsmith on the new numbers. But what really mattered were the Disneyesque tricks: cancan-ing knives and forks, a soft-shoeing candelabrum, a somersaulting carpet, and—most of all—a beast turned into a

prince in midair amid clouds of smoke and flashing, rainbow-hued lights. (In another depressing indication of the decline of truly live theatre, it was announced that the musical's sound budget—in good measure for miking and amplification—was a record $1.5 million of the show's $12 million cost.)

Curiously, although it was as much a contrast with *Beauty and the Beast* as possible, the new Stephen Sondheim–James Lapine intermissionless musical, **Passion** (9 May 1994, Plymouth), was seen by several critics as a more human recounting of the same basic story, this time with a homely woman as the beast and a young soldier as the beauty. The work was based on Ettore Scola's Italian film *Passione d'Amore*, itself taken from I. U. Tarchetti's novel *Fosca*. The musical begins in nineteenth-century Italy with two nude lovers in bed. They are a beautiful married woman, Clara (Marin Mazzie), and a dashing officer, Giorgio (Jere Shea), who is not her husband. But their idyll is seemingly shattered by Giorgio's being transferred to another post. There he meets the homely, love-starved Fosca (Donna Murphy). She falls in love with him and pursues him, even though he tells her he still loves Clara. Indeed, he still contrives to see Clara, although she will not abandon her husband for fear of losing her child. In time Giorgio is forced to fight a duel with Fosca's cousin, his colonel (Gregg Edelman). He seriously wounds the colonel. But Fosca has made herself sick over her relationship with Giorgio, and, after the duel, Giorgio himself has a nervous breakdown. On his recovery, he learns that Fosca has died. He cries out, "Your love will live in me." The *Times*'s David Richards called the work "an unalloyed love story, one that wants to penetrate the heart's deepest mysteries," only to suggest "the enterprise never quite pays off." The musical had a not unreasonable run of 280 performances, sustained largely by Sondheim's determined loyalists.

The next evening brought in a sequel to a once popular musical and it met with the usual fate of sequels. **The Best Little Whorehouse Goes Public** (10 May 1994, Lunt-Fontanne), obviously a follow-up to *The Best Little Whorehouse in Texas* (19 June 1978), was a two-week dud. This time around one Senator A. Harry Hardast (Ronn Carroll) determines to close a Las Vegas brothel called Stallion Fields. Never mind that the IRS has put Mona Stangley (Dee Hoty), once of the Lone Star State's Chicken Ranch, in charge, hoping that her professional know-how will help it recover $26 million in back taxes. But then the senator is so ignorant that he confuses "nolo contendere" with "incognito," both of which he believes are Spanish. In one scene, pudgy, balding men in nothing but bathrobes and socks push about large, television-set-like boxes, each with a sexy girl inside, and end up seemingly having sex with the boxes.

Tommy Tune, who co-directed and co-choreographed *The Best Little Whorehouse Goes Public*, was also one of the producers of the revival of *Grease* (14 February 1972), which closed out the season the next evening at the Eugene O'Neill. Some critics assailed the mounting's aggressive vulgarity, including a huge collage of images recalling the fifties but "done up in Day-Glo pinks and greens and oranges, which are the colors of another decade, and, in any case, tire your eyes out before the show is half over." Still, welcomed by enough other critics and public alike, the show settled in for a very long run.

Off-Broadway's musical season was lackluster. Probably the most eagerly anticipated of its new offerings was **Annie Warbucks** (9 August 1993, Variety Arts), which composer Charles Strouse, lyricist Martin Charnin and librettist Thomas Meehan created as a sequel to *Annie* (21 April 1977), In this continuation Daddy Warbucks (Harve Presnell) has sixty days in which to marry or else lose his right to adopt Annie (Kathryn Zaremba). The musical lingered for six months.

1994–1995

What a dismayingly unproductive, yet not totally unsatisfying season the new theatrical year was! Only five musicals were mounted at traditional, first-class Broadway houses. Three of these were revivals, a fourth was a retrospective of works by two 1950–1960ish songwriters, and only the fifth was a genuine novelty with a real book and fresh music. But that show came from England. Clearly the American Musical Theatre remained in the doldrums.

Before Broadway became active, off-Broadway offered playgoers three musicals that enjoyed long runs. All three focused on minorities. Clarence Cuthbertson and George Broderick's **Faith Journey** (21 July 1994, Lamb's) framed its theme of the burgeoning civil rights movement of the late fifties and early sixties in the story of Paul, minister at the Second Street Baptist Church, who at first is reluctant to support the protests, but eventually comes to join them, all the while he struggles over his feelings for two women. The story was larded with such defiant hymns as "By Any Means Necessary" and "Ain't

Gonna Let Nobody Turn Me 'Round." A long list of writers had a hand in That's Life (1 August 1994, Playhouse 91), a revue that looked on with tolerant amusement at Jews trying to preserve their heritage yet adapt in a Christian-dominated, inflation-beset America. Among the song titles were "We All Could Be Jewish If We Tried A Little Harder," "The Geshrunken Meshuggena Rag," and "Bei Mir Bist Du Rap."

For the second time in recent seasons Jelly Roll Morton served as inspiration for a semibiographical musical, this time an essentially one-man show written and performed by Vernel Bagneris and called, simply, **Jelly Roll!** (9 August 1994, 47th St.). A Norwegian ragtime-and-jazz pianist abetted the star.

"Just Keeps Rollin' Along," "It's Still Rollin' Along," and similar headlines welcomed Broadway's umpteenth revival of *Show Boat* (27 December 1927), which sailed into the Gershwin on 2 October. Yet in many ways it was a strange mounting. Unlike earlier productions, this one came from Canada. Moreover, its radio advertisements, with a deep, distinctly black voice plugging the show as songs associated with blacks in the musical were played in the background, suggested that this would be a determinedly politically correct version. Director Hal Prince, with all too typical New Yorkish bravado, made some cavalier changes not only in the libretto but in the musical program as well, thus adding songs from the 1936 film version and assigning "Why Do I Love You?" to Parthy (Elaine Stritch) to sing to the infant Kim instead of keeping it as a sadly and hollowly optimistic duet for the lovers just before Ravenal (Mark Jacoby) deserts Magnolia (Rebecca Luker). To his credit, Prince made the principals more rounded and therefore in some ways more interesting than previous directors had, adding, for example, an intriguing complexity to Parthy's formerly one-note, battle-axe personality. Sumptuously mounted, brought to life with real vigor, and subsequently awarded a lion's share of the season's Tonys, the show quickly settled in to what became *Show Boat*'s longest American run—949 performances. (Later in the season, Prince brought out an off-Broadway musicalization of an Ingmar Bergman screenplay as **The Petrified Prince** [18 December 1994, Public]. Set in a nineteenth-century Ruritania, it followed the saga of an emotionally disturbed, mute prince who finds his voice and the wherewithal to defeat his enemies thanks to a "heart-of-gold." The show was handed dismissive notices, so quickly disappeared.)

One of the great delights and surprise successes off-Broadway not long ago had been Dan Goggin's *Nunsense*, which went on to establish one of off-Broadway's lengthiest runs—3,672 performances. An offshoot, Goggin's **Nunsense 2: The Sequel** (21 October 1994, Douglas Fairbanks), was not nearly so fresh and charming, so suffered the fate of many follow-ups. It lingered only four months, or 149 playings, during which the same disaster-prone sisters of the original planned a second benefit. One of its segments was a pop quiz with the winner receiving a St. Christopher's medal. But the sisters' endeavors do not run smoothly, especially after a rival religious order insists it was the rightful winner of a Publishers Clearinghouse Sweepstakes, which the nuns are sure they have won.

The New York City Opera continued to include onetime Broadway hits in its repertory, even though its house was much too large for such shows and though it could not enlist ideal Broadway-style players for many of the roles. In the fall, on 8 November, the troupe brought out *Wonderful Town*; in early spring, on 26 March, *The Merry Widow* was revived.

As it had now for so many years, the Radio City Music Hall remounted two sumptuous and traditional offerings, filled with huge casts, stunning scenery that moved, often as the audience watched, on huge mechanical stages, and the ever-popular precision line, the Rockettes. The *Radio City Christmas Spectacular* began a 193-performance stand on 11 November. The less-in-demand *Radio City Easter Show*, presented for only twenty-four performances at the 6,000-seat house, raised its curtain on 8 April.

The season's lone book-show novelty was Andrew Lloyd Webber's London smash **Sunset Boulevard** (17 November 1994, Minskoff), a theatrical musicalization of the famous 1950 Billy Wilder–Gloria Swanson film classic. Don Black and Christopher Hampton provided the book and lyrics, and Glenn Close—"whitened face, black and gold robes, clinging talons"—assumed Swanson's role of Norma Desmond, a long-neglected silent screen star determined to make a comeback. When she has an argument with and is disappointed in her love for the young writer (Alan Campbell) she has taken on to help her, she shoots him. Her sometime director and husband and now loyal butler (George Hearn), pretending to be a director shooting her comeback film, tricks her into surrendering. John Napier's eye-popping settings included a swimming pool, with the writer's dead, floating body seen from pool's

bottom at the start of the show, and the grotesquely ornate Desmond living room, sporting a mammoth organ beneath a huge, curling motion-picture-palace staircase. Critics divided on the show itself ("[I]t's so bad, it might be hugely enjoyable, if you enjoy kitsch"; "the best musical since 'Gypsy'"), but most applauded Close, especially for not overdoing the camp. In part because there was nothing else new to see, the public came in droves. Yet although the show ran two and a half years, it failed to pay back its investment (either in New York or London), causing headline-making financial problems for Lloyd Webber's production company.

A choice instance of descendants of bygone vaudeville and revue evenings having to contrive a full night's entertainment in legitimate playhouses was **The Flying Karamazov Brothers Do the Impossible!** (20 November 1994, Helen Hayes). At one point these amusing acrobats and jugglers offered to juggle any three objects the audience might send up to the stage, provided they weighed not less than an ounce and not more than ten pounds and were no bigger than a breadbox. Only one arrival at Madison Square Garden came between the Karamazovs and another group of performers who earlier might have been confined to two-a-day and revue stages. An intermissionless **Comedy Tonight** (18 December 1994, Lunt-Fontanne) featured four stand-up comedians—Joy Behar, Michael Davis, Dorothy Loudon, and Mort Sahl—backed by a small combo. The acrobats lingered nearly two months at their tiny house; the comics just one week at their much bigger auditorium.

Down at the Garden, in the large, curiously wedge-shaped, low-ceilinged auditorium that had once been the Felt Forum but had now been rechristened the Paramount, playgoers could watch a lavish (reputedly $12 million), ninety-minute, intermissionless version of **A Christmas Carol**, starting on 1 December. This version had a book by Mike Ockrent and Lynn Ahrens, lyrics by Ahrens, and music by Alan Menken, as well as a line of tap dancers (pretending at one point to be fruit) and a horse. It also moved the action for little apparent reason from Dickens's 1840s to the 1880s. Actually playgoers could choose from three versions of the famous story during the season, for it was also being retold as part of the Radio City extravaganza and later in the month was offered as a one-man show by Patrick Stewart at a regular Broadway house.

Shortly after the Dickens piece closed at the Paramount, the same theatre brought in a touring revival of *Jesus Christ Superstar* on 17 January. Indifferently received, it moved out after just sixteen performances.

The City Center, which once had given playgoers fully staged revivals or return engagements at bargain prices, beginning on 16 February brought out **Encores! Great American Musicals in Concert,** proffering three bygone song-and-dance entertainments, each for four performances. The selection really did not probe all that adventurously or all that far back. Still, it gave some musical theatre buffs who had never seen the originals or wanted to relive their earlier visits opportunities to enjoy *Call Me Madam, Out of This World*, and the far more frequently staged *Pal Joey.*

March was the season's busiest month, to some extent because Broadway offerings wanted to raise their curtains in time to win Tony nominations. Leading the parade was a smallish (nine singers, seven musicians) retrospective, **Smokey Joe's Café** (2 March 1995, Virginia), replaying the music of the not quite immortal Jerry Leiber and Mike Stoller, whose rock-and-rollish ditties were popularized in the fifties and sixties by the likes of Elvis Presley. Among the resurrected numbers were "Fools Fall In Love" and "Hound Dog." Some critics suggested the show might have been more suitable for an intimate nightclub, but the lack of competition and its low budget helped it prosper strongly right through several seasons, not closing until it had achieved 2,036 performances.

Off-Broadway presented a not dissimilar entertainment, this time with some of the performers doubling in brass as both singers and musicians. And it, too, ran into the following season. **Swingtime Canteen** (14 March 1995, Blue Angel) used a thin plot about five girls on a World War II USO tour of Europe to sing popular melodies of the period.

However much they may have disagreed on the costumes and high-tech scenery in "powder blue, mustard yellow, avocado green, St. Joseph's Aspirin for Children orange," most critics adored the revival of *How to Succeed in Business Without Really Trying*

(14 October 1961), which lit up the stage at the Richard Rodgers on the 23rd. They were particularly happy with Matthew Broderick's J. Pierrepont Finch—a role for which he quickly garnered a Tony. Somewhat forlornly, *Variety* observed his performance could "make a musical-theater star of Broderick, as the original did for Robert Morse, if we actually had a musical theater, or a Broadway, anymore." (In fairness, look how downhill most of Morse's subsequent career was.) Kudos were also handed out to choreographer Wayne Cilento and to the long-retired but still-admired CBS anchorman Walter Cronkite, whose recorded voice broadcast the pronouncements of the how-to book's author.

No such enthusiasm or long run greeted the season's final revival, *Gentlemen Prefer Blondes*. Without the ineffable Carol Channing and with a "summerstock spareness of look" that underscored its origins at Connecticut's Goodspeed Opera House, the musical comedy lasted for only three weeks after opening at the Lyceum on 10 April.

Despite its relatively long run (by older standards, at least), the failure of *Sunset Boulevard* to become a blockbuster or even to close in the black seems to have signaled the end of the brief hegemony of London musical giants and of French-written (if London- and not Paris-mounted) ones. In retrospect their numbers were remarkably few and the men principally behind them fewer still. Composer Andrew Lloyd Webber came first, and when he joined forces with the young London producer Cameron Mackintosh to bring out *Cats*, the short heyday of these foreign works was truly launched. The pair followed with *The Phantom of the Opera*, and then, after they split, Mackintosh brought out the works of a French team, *Les Misérables* and *Miss Saigon*. The phenomenal runs of these shows were abetted by exceptional publicity, or merchandising, if you prefer, and by frequent lack of major competition. Their long runs alone would accord them a stellar place in American Musical Theatre, but in the long run, long runs do not necessarily guarantee long afterlives. Only time will tell.

Intermission

Technological Spectacles, Retrospectives, and Revivals, 1995–2000

Just what will happen to the American Musical Theatre in coming years is not clear. Certainly no unmistakable pattern from 1995 to 2000 emerged in the several seasons since the last of the imported blockbusters. Each season brought in at least one smash hit, but each show was markedly different. Yet neither *Rent* nor *Titanic* did anything to restore the cheery, memorably tuneful boy-meets-girl musical to the stage, while the sunnier *Lion King* was essentially a magnificently imaginative spectacle. For one reason or another, a few shows such as *Jekyll and Hyde* and *The Scarlet Pimpernel* defied critics and enjoyed surprising stands. But in no small measure revivals kept Broadway glowing with excitement—witness *The King and I, A Funny Thing Happened on the Way to the Forum, Chicago,* and *Cabaret,* to name a few.

1995–1996

The new season demonstrated little or no improvement over the last one. There were five original, more or less traditional, book musicals; three all-singing-and-dancing revues; a handful of solo and specialty shows; and, most satisfying for many playgoers, several splendid revivals.

An aging comedian, Red Buttons, opened the season with his one-man show, **Buttons on Broadway** (8 June 1995, Ambassador), filled with his nightclub-circuit stand-up comedy and trite, comic ditties. He stayed around for one month.

"Why do I keep coming back to this forgotten village?" is a cry heard throughout the eighty-minute-long, intermissionless **Chronicle of a Death Foretold** (15 June 1995, Plymouth), which Graciela Daniele and Jim Lewis adapted from a Gabriel García Márquez novel and for which Bob Telson wrote the music. The inhabitants of the village, somewhere in Latin America, look the other way as the vengeful brothers of a young bride (Saundra Santiago) set out to slaughter the nattily white-suited man (George de la Peña) who may have deflowered her before her wedding—or then again, may not have. Inspired by African and Latin (especially tango) forms, Daniele's dances were performed before a cracked bluish wall decorated with bird symbols and a dislocated door. The show closed the same night as Buttons's.

At the New York City Opera, the company again resurrected *The Mikado* as part of its repertory, beginning on 23 September, and again in the spring on 23 March.

Sooner or later all once-idolized musicals are seen to have book trouble. That fate befell *Company* (26 April 1970) when it was revived at the Roundabout on 5 October, with Boyd Gaines in the lead. More than one critic suggested that the best way to enjoy the show's treats was merely to listen to the original-cast recording. Two months, and the entertainment was gone.

Patti LuPone on Broadway (12 October 1995, Walter Kerr) had to be content with a month and a half, during which time the star serenaded her loyalists with a range of standard songs, some of which, such as "Don't Cry For Me, Argentina," she herself had introduced them to.

A week later, on the 19th at the Lunt-Fontanne, an older and bigger musical comedy favorite, the seemingly ageless Carol Charming, returned in her seemingly umpteenth revival of *Hello, Dolly!*, chalking up an additional 118 performances.

Instead of devoting itself to a potpourri of songs by some long-gone composer, **Swinging on a Star** (22 October 1995, Music Box) concentrated on the lyrics of one wordsmith—Johnny Burke. Since Burke, who died way back in 1964, worked primarily in Hollywood, film songs dominated the evening. They included "Pennies From Heaven" (music, Arthur Johnson), "Personality," and the title song (both with music by Jimmy Van Heusen). A series of contrived little thematic sketches, with appropriate backgrounds, set the stage for each medley. At least one reviewer lamented the need to mike singers in so small a house.

More Hollywood songs were heard in the young season's most ballyhooed and awaited extravaganza, Blake Edwards's theatricalization of his film **Victor/Victoria** (25 October 1995, Marquis). Since the original composer, Henry Mancini, had died, the score was filled out with new melodies by Frank Wildhorn. Leslie Bricusse wrote the lyrics. For theatregoers the real excitement of the evening was promised by the return to Broadway footlights of the long absent Julie Andrews. Andrews played Victoria Grant, a young English singer down and out in 1930s Paris. She is taken on by an older homosexual (Tony Roberts), who persuades her to pretend she is a boy performing as a female impersonator. The ploy works, except that Victoria is pursued by a dashing American gangster (Michael Nouri) who sees through it. Settings included various bits of Paris, most spectacularly a simultaneous view of posh neighboring duplex apartments. By opening night the musical had reputedly cost $8.5 million and enjoyed a $15 million advance. Unfortunately, word of problems had cropped up during the show's extended tryout. Broadway's morning-after and subsequent notices were little help. Thus, *Variety* concluded, "Though Andrews, Roberts and company are doing their damnedest up there to make 'Victor/Victoria' sing, it never does. It's just no fun at all." Despite all the critical headshaking, Andrews and her eventual replacements were able to lure playgoers to the huge theatre into the 1997–1998 season for 734 performances.

Four nights later meek, polite Bill Irwin and aggressive David Shiner were welcomed back in their joyous mélange of mime, stunts, and sketches, *Fool Moon*, at the Ambassador. They were abetted in their antics by the Spike Jones–like Red Clay Ramblers. Although the company lingered for two months, one once again wished the clowns could be let loose to play havoc with the sort of girlie extravaganza that Bobby Clark or Bert Lahr or the Marx Brothers once cavorted in so riotously.

The annual *Radio City Christmas Spectacular* returned on 8 November and played through 7 January, but in that two-month period packed the 6,000-seat auditorium for 189 performances. (Under normal circumstances a show reaches its two hundredth performance after six months. Considering, then, that your largest regular Broadway house seats no more than 2,000, the figure means that the two-month run is the equivalent of a year-and-a-half sellout on Broadway.) All the beloved Nativity pageantry, the high-kicking Rockettes, and Santa Claus were back to delight young and old alike. On 6 April the house brought back its annual, this one with the Easter pageant, the Rockettes, and, instead of Santa Claus, capering rabbits. It gave twenty-seven performances.

With vaudeville and revue dead, for the umpteenth time in recent decades a performer who might have found a more enduring, congenial home there was forced to expand his turn into a full evening on Broadway. On the same day that Radio City unfurled its latest edition of its Christmas pageant, an intermissionless one-man show listed variously as **The Many Voices of Danny Gans** and **Danny Gans** on Broadway came into the Neil Simon. Gans, who was reputed to be able to mimic 200 different speakers, was assisted by a small combo whose members also sang now and then.

Two other Christmas revivals were offered playgoers. At the New York State Theatre the New York City Opera brought back Rodgers and Hammerstein's *Cinderella* on the 9th for twelve performances. Among theatrical celebrities who assumed major or minor roles for the occasion were Sally Ann Howes (Fairy Godmother), Jean Stapleton (Stepmother), Jane Powell (Queen), and George S. Irving (King).

Similarly, the Madison Square Garden Theatre restored *A Christmas Carol* on the 20th, keeping it going for eighty-eight playings.

An Irish dance ensemble that had been delighting the British Isles came in with their collection of folklike song and stepping, **Riverdance—The Show** (13 March 1996, Radio City Music Hall), garnered a storm of applause for eight performances, then moved on to the hinterlands.

Far more New Yawk centered was the latest evening of Jackie Mason's very acid, very Jewish humor, **Love Thy Neighbor** (24 March 1996, Booth), still another instance of a great comedian with no revue to house his wit making a whole, musicless evening of fun on his own. New Yawkas and New Yawkophiles kept it going for more than seven months.

Conversely, **State Fair** (27 March 1996, Music Box) had been touring the American hinterlands for some time before braving Broadway. A theatricalization of the twice-made Rodgers and Hammerstein film musical, it added to such classics as "It Might As Well Be Spring" and "It's A Grand Night For Singing," songs from other R&H works to swell the score, and enlisted such no longer young stage and screen favorites as John Davidson, Kathryn Crosby, Andrea McArdle, and Donna McKechnie. Eerily, its producers' masthead boasted two once-luminous, long-silent names—David Merrick and the Theatre Guild. But that didn't stop the bitchier, more faddist critics from dismissing it as "flat, gooey, white-bread" or "seriously uninspired." Other reviewers, perhaps aware of how approving audiences on the road had been, equivocated a bit. Thus Clive Barnes observed in the *Post*, "I enjoyed myself, as I think will everyone who can welcome a modestly produced musical where 'the corn is as high as an elephant's eye.'" Playgoers who elected to judge for themselves this saga of the Frake family as they head off for the 1946 Iowa State Fair, where Papa (Davidson) will enter his prize pig and Mama (Crosby) her pickles and mincemeat (the latter soon overspiked with booze), kept the show on the boards through the summer.

More Rodgers and Hammerstein followed, and this time was passionately embraced by both aisle-sitters and the public. Under the direction of Englishman Christopher Renshaw, this production of *The King and I* had begun life in Australia. It opened at the Neil Simon on 11 April. Arriving first-nighters were greeted by a facade covered with pomegranate elephants and murals of gilded dancers. Once inside the auditorium they saw that even the boxes were decorated "as if they were part of an Eastern temple." The curtain rose on a bustling, incense-imbued dockside scene, which several commentators suggested was more like something out of *Miss Saigon* than like their recollection of the original. The rest of the $5.5 million production was equally lavish and compelling. Donna Murphy made an at-first prim and prissy but ultimately captivating Anna, while the patently boyish Lou Diamond Phillips, with shaved temples and the rest of his hair topknotted, added a peculiar generational tug to the story. The revival chalked up 807 performances.

Just as the second Rodgers and Hammerstein entry was made more welcome than the first, so with the second Sondheim revival. But not as unreservedly. For some felt that Nathan Lane, the star of Jerry Zaks's revival of *A Funny Thing Happened on the Way to the Forum*, which romped into the St. James on the 18th, while a brilliant comedian, was no Zero Mostel. Nor were his fellow clowns quite as experienced or adept as their predecessors. Still, the consensus was that everything fell together for an uproarious enough evening. Like *The King and I*, this revival settled in for a long run of 715 performances. (No one seems to have remarked that the revivals had switched the berths of their originals, although, of course, in those bygone days the Neil Simon was called the Alvin.)

Initially mounted downtown at the Public Theater in November, **Bring in 'da Noise, Bring in 'da Funk** (25 April 1996, Ambassador) was the brainchild of director-producer George C. Wolfe and twenty-two-year-old choreographer Savion Glover. Reg E. Gaines provided the book; Daryl Waters, the music. The show attempted to offer a history of blacks in America largely through the medium of tap. At the start, a performer recited the names of slave ships while Glover did a dirge-like shuffle across the stage. Later bits of history were sometimes projected on a screen at the rear. One item offered was that certain slaveowners banned the use of drums, prompting the blacks to employ their feet all the more for both communication and rhythm. Later the dancers became cogs in a heartless piece of machinery. Then, blacks of various backgrounds tried to hail a cab in New York. A few critics caviled at the "merciless" drubbing given beloved old-timer Bill Robinson, because his art was so apolitical. Still, the musical provided the third song-and-dance smash hit in a row and chalked up 1,523 performances.

The next entry was no smash hit. In fact, when **Big** (28 April 1996, Shubert) threw in the towel after a six-month run, it reportedly had lost all of its $10.3 million investment, and then some—making it possibly the costliest flop to date in Broadway history. There had been great expectations to start with, in part because, like two other of the season's musicals, it represented a staged version of a popular film. Its adapters included John Weidman for the book, David Shire for the music, Richard Maltby, Jr., for lyrics, Mike Ockrent for direction, and Susan Stroman for choreography. Once again soon-to-be-thirteen John Baskin (Patrick Lewis) is granted his wish to see what it will be like to be a grown man. As Big Josh (Daniel Jenkins) he runs off to New York. There he finds work at a toy factory, whose boss (Jon Cypher) complains that the company can no longer come up with blockbusters because its designers all have MBAs instead of imagination. A trip to FAO Schwarz allows Josh to join a batch of youngsters stomping out "Chopsticks" on a gigantic keyboard. Josh is subsequently pursued by a predatory marketing director (Crista Moore) and even loses his virginity before complications prompt him to return to being his thirteen-year-old self. Unfortunately the writing and staging, albeit pleasant, were uninspired. Perhaps most memorable were Robin Wagner's settings for a carnival with a roller coaster, the Port Authority bus terminal, and a restaurant that some felt looked like Tavern on the Green.

Rent (29 April 1996, Nederlander), the season's final musical, blending soft rock, rap-pop, and a touch of gospel, quickly became its most talked about and most garlanded. It was the work of a largely unknown thirty-five-year-old, Jonathan Larson, who died unexpectedly of an aortic aneurism the day before the show's off-off-Broadway opening in January. His youthful death contributed no end to the talk and, some cynics hinted, to the subsequent garlanding. Those honors included the Pulitzer Prize even before it moved up to Broadway. Its story was a modern-day retelling, removed to a New York tenement, of the Murger novel of bohemian life that had inspired the operas of Leoncavallo and, more famously, Puccini. Mimi (Daphne Rubin-Vega) is now an HIV-infected drug addict who ekes out a living performing at an S-and-M club. Rudolfo has become Roger (Adam Pascal), also HIV-infected, a composer who hopes to write one great "song to leave behind" before he dies. They meet, as before, when Mimi comes to find a light for her candle, since the electricity in the building has gone off. The story unfolds, often with many of the old familiar complications, between two Christmas Eves. But Mimi does not die, and the ending seems to imply that Mimi and Roger will both prove survivors. They agree to go on without regret, living as if there is "no day but today." Larson injected other once taboo subjects into the retelling, including muggings, mixed-race romances, and lesbianism. The setting was variously described as "like a pile of junk," "garbage-style scenery," and "a tangled slash of urban detritus that threatened to burst through the roof… with elements reaching out into the house." Costumes were "grungy" and "hip." To add to the atmosphere, the theatre itself, long dark, was not refurbished and seemed "mildly dilapidated." With its hit song, "Seasons of Love," quickly taking to the air, the show packed them in.

1996–1997

Although the season certainly had its rewarding moments, for the most part it was disappointing. Adjectives such as "lackluster" and "uninspired" were sprinkled liberally throughout postseason assessments. However, in one respect it was a pleasant surprise, for it was far busier than most recent sessions. Nearly a dozen and a half song-and-dance entertainments, some new, some old, some mixed, vied for attention by Broadway playgoers.

But off-Broadway provided the season's first hits. Joe DiPietro and Jimmy Roberts's good, old-fashioned revue (with both songs and sketches), **I Love You, You're Perfect, Now Change** (1 August 1996, Westside) led the parade. It allowed four youngsters to examine the joys and problems of good, old-fashioned heterosexual love and marriage, from the opening "Cantata For A First Date" through the title-song finale. As one commentator observed, "the show struck a chord with audiences so deluged with gay themes they're relieved to be reminded that ninety percent of the time men still date women."

A second songs-and-skits revue, with a slightly larger cast—five—also had a lengthy run, in this case one day more than two years. **When Pigs Fly** (14 August 1996, Douglas Fairbanks) joked and sang about the difficulties encountered in modern-day America, using the frame device of putting on a show.

With **Forbidden Broadway Strikes Back** (17 October 1996, Triad) Gerard Alessandrini gave four performers a chance to cavort in his latest spoof of Broadway. It added another 850 playings to his delightful series' astonishing, ongoing record.

On Broadway itself, much of what was old came first. If one ignores the late-summer presentations of *Four Saints in Three Acts* and *H. M. S. Pinafore* by the New York City Opera, then the season began so late that its first offering was actually the annual *Radio City Christmas Spectacular*, which began a two-month stand at the Music Hall on 7 November. As usual the attraction featured its magnificent Nativity pageant and the high-kicking, precision Rockettes. Some new Christmas songs by writers not unknown to Broadway also embellished the show.

The New York City Opera, announcing it was dropping its decades-long practice of including time-honored Broadway musical comedies and operettas in its repertory, bowed out on 13 November with a "listless" revival of Lerner and Loewe's magical 1947 triumph, *Brigadoon*. The auditorium had always been too vast for the relative intimacy of traditional Broadway shows, and mixing Broadway and more specialized opera performers rarely came off with any panache. Faddism prevented the company from venturing more than occasionally into the realm of Graustarckian operetta, a genre it might have done proud by, even if New York's still more faddist critics would have reacted sourly. (Later in the season the company did restore *The Mikado*, on 8 March.)

But Broadway could revive its best not-so-oldies with real panache, as the remounting of Kander and Ebb's 1975 smash, *Chicago*, proved the next evening. It was a smash hit all over again. The production had initially been performed the previous spring as part of the Encore! series of semidecorated concert revivals. (Its other revivals were *One Touch of Venus* and *DuBarry Was a Lady*.) Enthusiastically embraced, it was brought to the big time at the Richard Rodgers on the 14th. A number of reviewers used virtually identical expressions to comment on the "stripped-to-the-bare-bones," "stripped-down-to-basics" approach, but agreed that in this instance "less can be more." Black chairs and ladders, some glittering

curtains, and frequently skimpy, periodless black formal wear accounted for scenery and costumes. A star-packed cast included Ann Reinking (who recreated much of Bob Fosse's original choreography for the evening) as Roxie, Bebe Neuwirth as Velma, James Naughton as the cynical lawyer, Flynn, and Joel Grey as Roxie's put-upon husband. An onstage thirteen-piece jazz orchestra accompanied them.

A handful of devoted theatregoers had seen *Juan Darién* when it was played off-off-Broadway in 1988. Now it was selected to reopen the refurbished Vivian Beaumont on 24 November. Julie Taymor, working with several collaborators, conceived the ninety-minute show, wrote the book (based on a tale by Horacio Quiroga), designed the phantasmagoric costumes and scenery, and staged the revival. Her co-librettist, Elliot Goldenthal, wrote the music and original lyrics, basing his songs on Latin American folk and liturgical material. A woman (Andrea Frierson Toney), whose baby has died in a plague, adopts a jaguar cub, whose mother has been killed by hunters. She raises it so lovingly that it becomes a seemingly human boy, Juan Darién (boy soprano Daniel Hodd). But after the mother dies, Juan is taken under the wing of a cruel circus master (Martin Santangelo), who alerts villagers to the boy's origins. The villagers torture the child and leave him for dead. He is rescued by jaguars and so returns to the wild. Taymor utilized a variety of techniques "ranging from Bunraku and shadow puppets to actors wearing out-sized masks." And many of her effects were startling and beautiful. A dollhouse-size church, aglow from within, crumbles as the jungle encroaches; the top of a child's head opens to disclose a lush blossom. Critics admired the staging, but some questioned how audiences, particularly youngsters, would react. The piece played out its limited engagement.

For a third year running *A Christmas Carol* came in to the Madison Square Garden Theatre to divert children of all ages. Even before they entered the main auditorium, first-nighters on the 26th were regaled in the lobby by carolers and jugglers. When the lights went out and the show began, a new Scrooge in the person of Tony Randall headed the carryings-on. Some aisle-sitters carped that the score seemed weaker with each repetition, that the peculiarly wide-bodied, low-ceilinged stage played havoc with sight lines, and that the miking and amplifying was uncommonly atrocious ("Tiny Tim, for instance, sings a whole refrain before you realize he is standing on the second floor of the Cratchit house").

Nor did the next revival evoke much joy. The header for Clive Barnes's review in the *Post* read: "This lumpy 'Mattress' has no spring." It referred, of course, to the remounting of the 1959 musical *Once upon a Mattress*, which had helped Carol Burnett rocket to fame, and which now starred the young and much prettier Sarah Jessica Parker when it lit up the stage of the Broadhurst on 19 December. Barnes's colleagues largely concurred with his dismissal, seeing the work itself as "underimagined," the star, who had only the smallest gift for comedy, as "miscast," and the essentially humorless staging as "misbegotten." What kudos they could bestow went to John Lee Beatty's cartoonish sets and Jane Greenwood's luridly pastel costumes. Pre-opening ballyhoo and Parker's celebrity helped the attraction linger until spring.

Mid-February saw the first of the latest Encore! series of concert-revivals, *Sweet Adeline*. In subsequent months the group brought back *Promises, Promises* and *The Boys from Syracuse*.

Its title, **Mandy Patinkin in Concert** (1 March 1997, Lyceum), said everything that had to be said about this latest one-man show, which closed after seventeen recitals.

The season's first "new" show, **Play On!** (20 March 1997, Atkinson), was not truly that new. All its songs were culled from Duke Ellington's catalogue and included such standards as "Don't Get Around Much Anymore" and "Mood Indigo." Its book was Cheryl L. West's updating of *Twelfth Night* to Harlem in the 1940s. Vy (Cheryl Freeman), a young black songwriter, arrives there hoping to hit paydirt. She is told that if she wants to go places in the business and win the affection of a more established composer, Duke (Carl Anderson), she must pose as a man. Duke himself is in love with a nightclub singer, Liv (Tonya Pinkins), who is managed by the glib Rev [read Malvolio] (Lawrence Hamilton). Many reviewers, in what have become for them stereotypical reviews of black shows, complained the characters were stereotypes and, going further back to notices from the twenties onwards, saw the entertainment as "stronger on pep than polish" or "very conventionally high-spirited and bojangles." The musical departed after a short struggle.

Nor was a revival of *Annie* (21 April 1977), which lumbered into the Martin Beck on the 26th, made welcome. A notable black perfomer, Nell Carter, was miscast and starred as the villainous Miss Hannigan, in an otherwise largely white and tacky production.

Two nights later the annual *Radio City Spring Spectacular* began a two-week stand with the Rockettes once again the featured attraction. (In between its two annuals the Music Hall briefly offered a touring, imported Irish dance show, **Lord of the Dance**, beginning on 4 March.)

Like *Play On!*, **Dream** (3 April 1997, Royale), which began April's parade of musicals, was chock full of famous oldies. Only this time they were not by one composer, but rather by a single lyricist—Johnny Mercer. Among the men whose music he set words to were Harold Arlen, Hoagy Carmichael, and Jerome Kern. Their still-beloved hits included "Blues In The Night," "You Were Never Lovelier," and "That Old Black Magic." For a value-for-money two-and-a-half hours Lesley Ann Warren, a well-aged Margaret Whiting, jazz guitarist John Pizzarelli, and some young dancers reminded theatregoers of forty-four incomparable songs. Unfortunately, the low-budget setting and costumes were seen as dreary, and the staging and choreography as insipid, while a few kitschy touches, such as two huge Oscar statues marching across the stage, brought embarrassed giggles. For all that, the show did find a small public.

Five more musicals—they hoped to be the season's main contenders—premiered in seven nights' time. (In what may be a telling comment on the modern musical's drift, not one of the four novelties in this group had a happily-ever-after ending.) Broadway wags and smart money were prepared to laugh up their sleeves at a song-and-dancer dealing with the sinking of the **Titanic** (23 April 1997, Lunt-Fontanne). The year's most expensive mounting, at $10 million it cost more than the great ship had—although, of course, that takes no account of eight and a half decades of inflation. When initial previews had to be delayed because the ship wouldn't sink, the snickering became increasingly audible. And word of mouth was almost entirely negative. Then, following hectic backstage rewriting, the morning-after notices featured such headers as "Can't Stop That Sinking Feeling" and "'Titanic' Takes a Dive." However, the *Times*'s Ben Brantley, maintaining a middle course, observed that the show "doesn't sink. Unfortunately, that is also probably the most exciting thing that can be said about it." Interestingly, the *Post*, below Clive Barnes's pan, offered opinions by five first-nighters, apparently selected at random. Four of the five were highly favorable, while the fifth's only complaint was the poor score. Slowly, but seemingly ineluctably, laudatory comments began to be whispered about. A short while later, the *New Yorker*'s critic, having had additional time to consider her judgment, concluded: "[L]ittle by little you realize that you are in the presence of a genuine addition to the American musical theatre." Later still, in early June, after the Tony jurists had their opportunity to compare it with its rivals, *Titanic* walked off with most of the major Tony Awards. By autumn long lines at the box office had turned the show into Broadway's top grosser—pulling in more than $700,000 a week. A touring company was announced. Yet the ending was not all that happy. Two years later the show closed after a little more than 800 performances—a great run by older standards but not all that spectacular in the *fin-de-siècle* era of seemingly endless runs. Moreover, the show had not fully recouped its costs. Still, with a cut-down production starting out on the road and with foreign rights and revenues in the offing, the producers continued to feel the musical might someday show a profit.

The first act of Peter Stone's book, following the vessel's departure, showed glimpses of life aboard ship through cutouts in what apparently was meant to represent the ship's black hull: the owners and officers pursuing their own selfish ends on the bridge (White Star owner Ismay [David Garrison] recklessly urging more and more speed); the bejeweled first-class passengers (the doomed Strauses [Larry Keith and Alma Cuervo] still affectionately devoted in their twilight years); the fun-loving second-class voyagers; and the lowly third-class occupants. At the end of the first act the hull flies up and a model of the ship is seen crossing the stage, exiting into the wings. A crash is heard. The second act depicts the slow listing of the ship, then the angled deck goes dark. When the lights come up survivors, wrapped in blankets, tell the audience what happened. Several critics recorded that the most effective moment of the sinking occurred when a wheeled cart rolled on its own across the Grand Salon. In the style of many recent Broadway pop operas, the show was virtually sung through. Whether any of Maury Yeston's songs—so regularly hymn-or anthem-like—prove take-away hits remains to be seen.

More was expected from Kander and Ebb's latest, **Steel Pier** (24 April 1997, Richard Rodgers), but the consensus was the entertainment disappointed. "Life's a party; why don't you come to the Steel Pier," a lyric proclaimed, prompting one reviewer to remark, "Audiences are almost dared not to add

a silent 'ol' chum.'" Yet in some ways the new show seemed closer to the team's *Chicago* than its *Cabaret*. The year is 1933 and dance marathons are the rage. At a big one at Atlantic City's Steel Pier, where the prize is $2,000 and a chance at stardom, Rita (Karen Ziemba) suddenly finds herself partnerless, so the slick-haired, oily-tongued, manipulative master of ceremonies, Mick Hamilton (Gregory Harrison), who, unbeknownst to the other contestants, is secretly married to Rita, enlists a handsome stunt pilot, Bill Kelly (Daniel MacDonald), to support her. Mick does not know that Bill has recently been killed in a crash but has miraculously been granted a three-week reprieve. (The musical starts with the sound of a plane crash, then Bill rising to his feet, helped by white-clad ghostly or angelic dancers.) Of course, love blossoms between Rita and Bill, and Mick is shown to be a craven bully. In the end, the white figures come to reclaim Bill, so Rita packs her bag and heads out to find a better life somewhere else. Although Tony Walton's glittery, carnivalish setting won applause, and Debra Monk stopped the show with a "bump-and-grind tribute to promiscuity," "Everybody's Girl," in which she longed to be a modern-day Carmen, the hit of the evening was Susan Stroman's brilliant and variegated choreography. She had—à la *Flying Down to Rio*—chorines romping on plane wings; the fox-trots, rhumbas, and Susie Q's of the period; and even found langorous grace in the couples' moments of exhaustion. Yet of all the later April openings, *Steel Pier* was the first to throw in the towel, closing in June.

Recordings of Cy Coleman's songs for **The Life** (26 April 1997, Barrymore) had been in circulation for some years, and, indeed, the show had been given a workshop production in 1990, so Broadway regulars had some idea of what to expect. Nonetheless, as with all the month's offerings, the show's notices were for the most part letdowns. In this instance a number of commentators rued that Coleman and his collaborators, lyricist Ira Gasman and David Newman, who helped the others on the book, resurrected the sleazy world of black prostitution in Times Square just when the area was being cleaned up. Queen (Pamela Isaacs) gives all her earnings to her pimp and lover, Fleetwood (Kevin Ramsey), to help support his cocaine habit. She has even taken the rap for him and served time as a result. She does so because she feels certain that she is Fleetwood's one-and-only. But then a small-time grifter, Jojo (Sam Harris), persuades Fleetwood to take on additional girls. At the Port Authority bus station he enlists a seemingly innocent blonde, Mary (Bellamy Young), who turns out not to be innocent at all. Upset, Queen leaves and falls in with the malevolent Memphis (Chuck Cooper). Things go downhill from there. All this was played out against a background of Robin Wagner's brick-wall and neon settings. The show ran for 465 performances, yet closed $7 million in the red.

As with The Life, many in the first-night audience for composer Frank Wildhorn and librettist-lyricist Leslie Bricusse's **Jekyll and Hyde** (28 April 1997, Plymouth) were familiar with the songs and perhaps in a few cases with the pop opera itself. For the production had been touring for several years, two CDs of its score had been released and sold 250,000 copies, and several numbers had gone on to international fame. Aisle-sitters referred to the musical as a cult show. So generally dismissive notices didn't really matter. When the wicked directors of St. Jude's Hospital refuse to allow Dr. Jekyll (Robert Cuccioli) a laboratory, he performs his experiments in private, soon unwittingly creating his own evil half, Hyde. As Hyde he sets about murdering everyone who stands in his way, even slaughtering the prostitute (Linda Eder) Jekyll has taken a liking to. Fog-filled, blood-red settings underscored the action. Cuccioli performed Jekyll with his shoulder-length hair pulled neatly back in a ponytail, but allowed the hair to go wild as Hyde. His big anthem was "This Is The Moment," in which he hopes "all the dreaming, scheming and screaming become one." The song has reportedly been sung at the Olympics, the Miss America Pageant, and the 1996 Democratic Convention. But reviewers felt Eder had better numbers—"A New Life" and "Someone Like You." They predicted a bright future for her and her Streisand-like delivery (albeit one reviewer noted she needed "echo-chamber assistance").

April's last entry was Hal Prince's latest revival of Candide (1 December 1956), which he brought into the Gershwin on the 29th. The critics split sharply on the result, many hailing it for its emphasis on humor and its accordingly appropriate, visually dazzling settings. Other lamented the acrobatic and chromatic excesses at the expense of the music. To these naysayers much of the comedy was intrusive and ho-hum, and the settings vulgarly gaudy. For those who did admire the mounting, Clarke Dunham's colorful "wooden cutouts, carnival midway banners, party lights and circus wagons turn the stage into a traveling freak show of the 18th century." And

there were kudos for Jason Danieley's Candide and Harolyn Blackwell's Cunegonde.

For many the real attraction of the ninety-minute **The Wizard of Oz** (15 May 1997, Madison Square Garden Theatre), which Robert Johanson and John Kane had adapted from the beloved MGM film and which had been tried out at the Paper Mill Playhouse some years back, was the presence in the cast as the Wicked Witch of television's gross vulgarian Roseanne. She was no Margaret Hamilton, and she was panned: "amateurish," "strident and mechanical," "screeching." Nor were the settings applauded. The tornado was seen as "a flapping bolt of cloth," and Munchkinland as "milk bottles decorated with bathroom tiles" or "wooden cutouts of milk bottle vases." Advance sales allowed the show to do well in its limited stand.

In many ways the season's most eagerly awaited premiere came last—on 18 May. On stage was a concert version of a work-in-progress musical by Alan Menken and Tim Rice, **King David.** Even allowing that the work probably was to be rewritten, reviewers nonetheless gave it a determined thumbs-down. Ben Brantley suggested the choice of such a weak piece may have been intentional, for the real interest of the evening was that after sixty years the magnificent New Amsterdam Theatre, once the flagship of a busy 42nd Street and now restored for a reported $36 million, was again back in the legitimate fold. There were raves all around for the restoration. It was as loving and as reasonably faithful as possible—although what had reputedly been a gentlemen's smoking room had become in these fume-free days a general lobby. And it was announced that the house's first major attraction, in the fall, would be a stage version of Disney's animated film The Lion King. (Disney owns the house.) What all this betokens is hard to guess. Old-timers, of whom there are fewer and fewer with each passing year, might remember when the playhouse was host to many editions of the Ziegfeld Follies, to Marilyn Miller in Jerome Kern's Sally, and to Fred and Adele Astaire in the Schwartz–Dietz revue The Band Wagon. Time will tell. But at least for the present it offers the slim hope that a cleaned-up Times Square and 42nd Street will once more be vital parts of Theatreland.

1997–1998

June brought in one success, **Forever Tango** (19 June 1997, Walter Kerr), the latest in a parade of mountings devoted to the great Argentine dance. Not the surprise *Tango Argentino* (9 October 1985) had been, but far lustier and skillful than *Tango Pasión* (28 April 1993), its seductive pizzazz beguiled customers for more than a year.

A South African musical, **Umabatha: The Zulu Macbeth,** which had already been seen off-Broadway, was brought into the New York State Theatre for seven performances beginning on 21 July. Its title gave a fair idea of what was seen on stage.

Midsummer welcomed the season's first more traditional song-and-dance entertainment on 14 August at the Roundabout. A superb revival of *1776* (6 March 1969), it featured Brent Spiner as a forceful John Adams and Pat Hingle as a wise, avuncular Ben Franklin. The musical was so heartily greeted that it moved to a full-size Broadway house after its initial engagement at the more intimate venue was completed.

Having already housed a South African production, the New York State Theatre also briefly offered its stage to a Korean extravaganza, **The Last Empress.** Performed in Korean by a largely Korean cast, it purported to tell the true story of the assassination of the Korean empress by the Japanese early in the century. The incident has been the source of ongoing Korean–Japanese hatred. The work, initially mounted on 15 August for twelve playings, was returned at the beginning of the next season for twenty-four more performances.

The season's first major novelty, **Side Show** (16 October 1997, Richard Rodgers), prompted several reviewers to expound on what they perceived to be the general plight of the modern lyric stage. Leaping on the new attraction's title, Howard Kissel of the *Daily News* observed, "The musical theater, once in the center ring of American culture, is increasingly a side show." And he saw the new work as a perfect example of why, dismissing it as "earnest, visually arresting but hollow... a musical for musical-theater enthusiasts." The *Wall Street Journal*'s Donald Lyons concluded his notice by branding the effort "an archetypically mediocre musical of the 1990s." To some extent the *Times*'s Ben Brantley was right on the button when he suggested: "[T]his musical seems guaranteed to divide its audience into violent tribes of admirers and detractors." Thus, the amiable Clive Barnes urged his readers in the *Post* not to pass it by.

The show was based on the real-life saga of the Hilton girls, Siamese twins who won a modicum of renown as performers in vaudeville and an early talking film. The work's opening lyrics, quoted by

critic after critic, set the tone: "Come look at the freaks; come gape at the geeks; only pennies for peeks." Daisy (Emily Skinner) and Violet (Alice Ripley) Hilton are joined at the hip. Fortunately, they are blond beauties with some singing ability. Aided by two young men, whose interest in them may be suspect, they leave a freak show and head for more legitimate outlets. The men are a fledgling songwriter, Buddy Foster (Hugh Panaro), and a two-a-day scout, Terry Connor (Jeff McCarthy). Quiet Violet dreams of a husband and a home; the more demanding Daisy, of fame. So in no small measure their fate is sealed. The only one who truly loves them is Jake (Norm Lewis), a black man who has been impersonating a cannibal king. Of course, given the social mores of the time nothing can come of his affection. In the end, the girls head off to Hollywood. (In actuality, after their one film failed, Daisy and Violet closed out their days as employees in a southern supermarket.) The performers won a round of genuine applause, although the most excited kudos were lavished on designer Robin Wagner's mood-setting, rearrangeable bleachers. Bill Russell's book (he also did the lyrics) earned fewer encomiums, but did garner praise for raising "intriguing issues about prejudice, identity and the nature of love." Reviewers seemed more divided about Henry Krieger's score. Several scenes spoofing the lavish settings of the era were show-stoppers, especially a King Tut number complete with crocodiles, swan-shaped harps, and chorus boys decked out in pharaonic getups.

Brantley might well have prophesied that opinions about the season's next musical, **Triumph of Love** (23 October 1997, Royale), would be as disparate as those that greeted *Side Show*. He himself condemned its "crude, anything-for-a-laugh avidity," assailing in particular its "sophomoric lewdness," while his fellow aisle-sitter Jeffrey Lyons rued that "the soufflé obstinately refuses to rise." Conversely, the *Daily News*'s new critic, Fintan O'Toole, spoke for the show's many admirers when he welcomed it as "animated, colorful, fast and very funny," with "the charm of a fairy tale and the knockabout humor of a slightly bawdy romp." Librettist James Magruder, lyricist Susan Birkenhead, and composer Jeffrey Stock based their offering on Pierre de Marivaux's eighteenth-century comedy. In ancient Greece two anti-romantic philosophers, the bald, whitish-faced Hermocrates (F. Murray Abraham) and the tight-laced, bespectacled Hesione (Betty Buckley), have been carefully indoctrinating their handsome young student, Agis (Christopher Sieber). The hoydenish Princess Léonide (Susan Egan) invades their purple-and-green topiary garden, ultimately wins Agis's heart, and discovers he is the true heir to her throne. However, before that happy ending, she dons several disguises, including one as a boy, to teach Hesione and Hermocrates the basic and urgent pull of real love. Despite its supposed classical scenery, costumes and setting placed the action squarely in Marivaux's time. By general agreement, the highlight of the evening was Buckley's singing of "Serenity," in which she confesses that the disguised Léonide has awakened in her long repressed sentiments that used to tug "at my heart like hungry birds."

Off Broadway sprang to life with an amusing revue by myriad hands, **Secrets Every Smart Traveler Should Know** (30 October 1997, Triad), in which six entertainers regaled audiences with comic slants on voyagers' tribulations such as Ugly Americans, missing baggage, and Montezuma's revenge. One show-stopping number, "Customs," had a would-be smuggler itemize all the contraband he hopes to sneak in. The show ran two seasons and into a third.

On 7 November the annual *Radio City Christmas Spectacular* began a two-month stand at the Music Hall. (Aside from a brief late-September return of *Riverdance*, this was the only major stage attraction at the huge house this season.)

There was little disagreement about **The Scarlet Pimpernel** (9 November 1997, Minskoff), a supposedly $10 million musicalization of Baroness Orczy's 1905 swashbuckling novel. Reviewers were virtually unanimous in slating it. "A dispirited, dispiriting evening," "leaves us not entertained, not even campily pained, but numb," and "a camped-up version of an already campy burlesque of history" were some of the damning verdicts. Frank Wildhorn's score was waved away as "pulpy pop," "synthetic, characterless and so instantly unmemorable that even the repeats have a wilted freshness to them." Nan Knighton's book and lyrics were characterized as "wooden." The staging was seen as "a series of ornately costumed tableaux for which the cardinal rule appears to have been: don't just do something, stand there." Douglas Sills received the evening's best notices as Percy Blakeney, a disguised English aristocrat who attempts to save Frenchmen from the guillotine during the Revolution, albeit many complained his foppish moments were overdone. Christine Andreas as his possibly disloyal, blackmailed wife, Marguerite, was slapped on the wrist for "her apparent Edith Piaf impersonation." As the blackmailing villain of the piece, Chauvelin, who covets Marguerite for himself, Terrence Mann performed with "his eyelids at half mast, his voice at a languorous murmur and his face in a glazed, couldn't-care-less expression"—a far cry from his rendition of earlier miscreants in *Les Misérables* and *Beauty and the Beast*. Despite drubbings, the show ran and ran, not always to crowded houses, then, in the fall of 1998, was rewritten, largely recast (except for Sills), and restaged. It closed for only a week for final rehearsals, then reopened for public and critical inspection. Once again the critics pooh-poohed the affair. It shuttered a second time at the end of May 1999, reopened the following September, and finally closed for good, having played 772 performances without recouping its costs.

The season's most eagerly anticipated opening followed, when **The Lion King** (13 November 1997, New Amsterdam) raised its curtain. After years of much ballyhoo, the lovingly restored New Amsterdam Theatre welcomed its first regular attraction. The Walt Disney Company both produced the show (based on an earlier Disney animation) and resurrected the famous playhouse—thus accelerating the revival of 42nd Street. No more appropriate conjunction of show and theatre could be imagined, for from its opening in 1903 until its conversion to films in the 1930s the gorgeous, baroque New Amsterdam had played host to most of Ziegfeld's legendarily opulent *Follies* as well as other celebrated extravaganzas. The musical began as an exotic call is heard piercing the midnight-blue African sky. A luminous paper sun rises to light up the scene, and golden giraffes (costumed actors on stilts) gambol across the stage. Down the theatre's aisles come a whole colorful safari of other animals—additional players in masks, some on stilts, and some wearing tails. Later, even the grasslands and bushes of the African veldt are given life by performers: thus the grasses sit up, disclosing they are balanced on the heads of natives. Again, beautifully stylized animals romp in and out among the carriers. All this eye-popping staging was the work of the young Julie Taymor, who, along with Richard Hudson, also served as designer.

In Roger Allers and Irene Mecchi's book, an evil uncle, Scar (John Vickery), murders the lion king, Mufasa (Samuel E. Wright), and foists the blame on Simba (Scott Irby-Ranniar), the young heir-apparent. The boy takes to the forest, comes to realize his uncle's treachery, and sets about reclaiming his throne. Subsequent effects included one in which the face of the dead Mufasa is reformed into a starry mask. "Seen purely as visual tapestry, there is simply nothing else like it," Ben Brantley concluded of the entire spectacle.

He and his co-reviewers were not quite so enthusiastic about the show's other aspects. Many critics complained that the show was too long (two hours and forty minutes) and sometimes dragged. Most were indifferent to the choreography. Nor were they all that thrilled with the Elton John and Tim Rice songs—taken from the film and supplemented by a handful of new numbers. "For a musical," Clive Barnes lamented, "this music takes a back seat." (In fairness, it should be remembered that few enduring numbers came from Ziegfeld's twenty-one editions of his *Follies*, although the New Amsterdam also played host to such melody-packed and often sumptuous triumphs as *The Merry Widow* [21 October 1907], *Sally* [21 December 1920], and *The Band Wagon* [3 June 1931].) Still, whatever its flaws, the mounting, rumored to have cost nearly $15 million, would be around for many years.

Once again, the Theatre at Madison Square Garden revived its annual *A Christmas Carol*, this time on 23 November. For the latest edition, Hal Linden and Roddy McDowall alternated as Scrooge. Linden was seen as the more menacing of the two; McDowall, the more sniveling.

A mostly black cast of eight, often clinging to microphones in a tiny venue, sang, jumped, and slithered during a retrospective revue of pop and rhythm-and-blues tunes from the sixties and seventies, **Street Corner Symphony** (24 November 1997, Atkinson). The ninety-minute entertainment had the smallest of plots, showing kids gathering under a Gainesville, Florida, streetlight to rehearse material they might be asked to perform at a local playhouse. Reviewers felt the tackily mounted evening belonged more properly in a nightclub.

The next new offering, **Ragtime** (18 January 1998, Ford), a theatricalization of E. L. Doctorow's novel, was unveiled in a "new" playhouse. Actually the auditorium, pretentiously labeled the Ford Center for the Performing Arts, was built on the site of two of 42nd Street's once major theatres, the Lyric and the Apollo, and used vestiges of both buildings in its construction. The $10 million entertainment came to Broadway after longish runs in Toronto and Los Angeles. As expected in a contemporary musical, its scenery and costumes were splendid. Its action was framed in the concourse of the old Penn Station and featured colorful slide projections of places such as Orchard Street, Union Square, and Harlem as seen under the El. There were also cleverly simulated fireworks. Three groups were highlighted in the story: a family of love-starved, well-to-do New Rochelle Wasps, known expressionistically only as Mother (Marin Mazzie), Father (Mark Jacoby), etc.; a fresh-off-the-boat Jewish immigrant, Tateh (Peter Friedman), and his shy, nameless daughter (Lea Michele); and a black honky-tonk pianist, Coalhouse Walker, Jr. (Brian Stokes Mitchell), and his pregnant girlfriend, Sarah (Audra McDonald). Naturally, their paths intermingle, and both blacks are murdered by violent bigots before an otherwise happy ending. Not all critics approved of Terrence McNally's book. One complained that it carried dangerously pervasive political correctness to extremes, showing the Wasps as bad, the Jews as better, and the blacks as best—"a Marxist cartoon." Nor did all the reviewers relish composer Stephen Flaherty and lyricist Lynn Ahrens's songs, bewailing "some functional music and murky lyrics" or "a numbing succession of open-throated anthems." Still, the attraction seemed a crowd-pleaser, although one wag referred to the new theatre and its premiere attraction as Hydrox to the Disney theatre and show's Oreo. The musical ran for 861 playings.

An even more controversial musical followed, **The Capeman** (29 January 1998, Marquis), an $11 million sung-through recounting of the history of a real-life young Puerto Rican killer. The celebrated songwriter and singer Paul Simon conceived the evening, for which he and Derek Walcott wrote book and lyrics. The central figure was Sal Agron (played at different ages by Evan Jay Newman, Marc Anthony, and Ruben Blades). As a youngster he is berated by nuns for bed-wetting and abandoned by his father. In New York his stepfather is so abusive that the teen is driven to join a vicious gang. Wearing his signature cape, he kills a pair of white boys in 1959. The murder makes headlines. Sal is sentenced to prison, where he teaches himself to read and turns to poetry and philosophy. He is finally released in 1979, but dies seven years later just before his forty-third birthday. Many were offended by the seeming glorification of a murderer. Others, more neutral on that matter, deplored the lack of depth and flair in the story's retelling. Simon's songs won considerable praise from several aisle-sitters, and he was defiantly aggressive about the drubbing the rest of the show received. The musical folded in late March, with newspapers broadcasting that its $11 million loss made it the most costly failure in theatrical history. (But see similar claims for *Cyrano* and *Big*.)

Beginning again in February, Encore! offered three concert-revivals. This season's list permitted rehearings for *Strike Up the Band, Li'l Abner,* and *St. Louis Woman.*

Conversely, a revival of one of the biggest money-makers in American Musical Theatre history followed with the arrival at the Martin Beck on 12 March of Rodgers and Hammerstein's *The Sound of Music* (16 November 1959). Critics had not been bowled over when they first reviewed the operetta thirty-nine years earlier, and they were, if anything, less enchanted this time. They complained variously about the "hokey, tepid book," the lack of "vocal power," or the "slightly cheesy-looking" settings. But to a man they recognized that despite their reservations the show had become one of the best-loved of musicals, so predicted it once again would please vast numbers of young and old playgoers. Several songs Rodgers wrote alone for the movie version after Hammerstein's death were included, but failed to add anything to the evening. The leading role, made memorable originally by Mary Martin on stage and Julie Andrews in the film, was assumed by Rebecca Luker. The operetta ran to good houses until late June 1999, for a total of 540 performances, yet reportedly still closed in the red.

A second revival, on the 19th at what had once been the small, charming Henry Miller Theatre, received compelling reviews. The old auditorium had been converted into a 512-seat nightclub to house Sam Mendes's "darkly revisionist," "wondrously sleazy," "heavily angst-ridden" interpretation of Kander and Ebb's *Cabaret* (20 November 1966). Mendes' directorial changes—he had staged the work a few seasons before in London—all seemed designed to bring out the horrific immediacy of the Nazi era. Thus, Alan Cummings's androgynous Emcee was more patently malignant, displaying red and blue eye shadow, sequins on his nipples, suspenders on his crotch, and even, when he dropped his pants, a swastika tattooed on his backside. Similarly, Natasha Richardson as Sally turned the title song "(formerly an anthem of hedonism) into a tragic dirge, a descent into despair."

The successful revival of old favorites (albeit with a marked darkening of tone) and the diverse fate of the year's novelties prompted a late-season reassessment of the state of the American Musical Theatre by Vincent Canby in the *Times*, a reassessment far more extensive and probing than those proffered at the season's start. In bold print, the article asked, "Where is the joyous spirit that musicals had in an earlier age?" and ruefully concluded that "the Broadway musical is no further along now than it was last September or 10 years ago" and that the best of the revivals "force us to recognize what the American musical lost as it grew up and became more sober-sided."

Two Broadway rehashes of well-liked Hollywood films wrote "finis" to the season. In both instances the critical consensus was "Go see the film." At the St. James, the attraction on 27 April was **High Society,** Cole Porter's cinematic redaction of Philip Barry's popular comedy *The Philadelphia Story.* Arthur Kopit provided a new book, now set not on the Main Line but at Oyster Bay, and additional Porter songs, not in the film, were snatched from other shows of his. Still, the aisle-sitters found the romp flat, prompting yet another dismayed reviewer to rue that "musicals aren't what they used to be."

At the Theatre at Madison Square Garden the offering on 6 May was *The Wizard of Oz,* which the house had offered last season. Some of this year's casting seemed more inspired—with seventy-seven-year-old Mickey Rooney as a showman–con-man Wizard and, most especially, seventy-one-year-old Eartha Kitt, she of the delicious purring growl, as the Wicked Witch. Kitt was even given a jitterbug number that had been cut from the film. Sixteen-year-old Jessica Grové was Dorothy. As usual at the Garden, playgoers found the lobby cluttered with hawkers and "theme park" memorabilia.

1998–1999

The season's opener was **An Evening with Jerry Herman** (28 July 1998, Booth), a retrospective featuring the bantam, tuxedoed composer at the piano (assisted by a bass player), with a hyperactive, tuxedoed Lee Roy Reams and a more reserved, bespangled Florence Lacey to sing along. Production values were minimal, primarily lighting changes and "faintly cheesy" lightbulb-fringed drops simulating marquees announcing Herman's shows. The entertainment had already been seen in a nightclub version and heard on a CD. Criticisms ranged from "a fundamentally fun show" to "makes up in heart and verve what it may lack in sophistication and variety" to "numbingly mediocre." The public wouldn't buy it, so its run was short.

Swan Lake (5 October 1998, Neil Simon) was an updated British rendering of Tchaikovsky's classic ballet, as conceived and choreographed by Matthew Bourne. Among the most striking alterations was a line of male swans, one of whom seduces the Prince. Although Bourne and the show's publicists proclaimed that no homosexual context should be read into this (and many of the better critics agreed), a disproportionate number of gay men comprised the attraction's audiences. A hit in London, in Los Angeles, and on TV, the entertainment did excellent business during its limited stand.

Mamaloshen (13 October 1998, Belasco), a one-man show, featured Mandy Patinkin (accompanied by a pianist and a violinist) in a concert of Yiddish songs and, like Herman's entertainment, had been seen previously in a nightclub. In truth, although many of the songs were traditional Jewish standbys, some were surprisingly intriguing Yiddish versions of such favorites as "Over The Rainbow," "Maria" (from *West Side Story*), and even "White Christmas." After another limited stand, Patinkin took his show on the road.

Aznavour on Broadway (21 October 1998, Marquis) was the title of Charles Aznavour's latest brief Manhattan visit. Short, lean, and now silver-haired, the popular French singer sang his program, much of which he had written himself, half in his native language and half in English. He was assisted by a small band and two other vocalists. His numbers were varied, but at least one commentator felt he was still at his best "as he wanders between speech and song as if down a darkened, rain-slick Paris street, trailing cigarette smoke and regret."

The season's first full-scale musical was **Footloose** (22 October 1998, Richard Rodgers). Based on a 1984 movie of the same name, its book was by Dean Pitchford (who had written the original screenplay) and Walter Bobbie; its songs, with Pitchford lyrics, by various hands but mostly by Tom Snow. As the earlier version had, the live one told how young Ren McCormick (Jeremy Kushnier) from Chicago arrives in a stolid backwater and tries to get his fellow youngsters up and dancing, despite an ordinance prohibiting it. Seems the town's minister (Stephen Lee Anderson) had pushed through the measure after losing a son in a drunk-driving accident following a dance. Matters grow complicated when Ren falls in love with the cleric's daughter, Ariel (Jennifer Laura Thompson). Inevitably, since this is a song-and-dance show, the minister sees the error of his ways. Dances, performed in the skimpiest of sets, employed "skate boards, shopping carts, waitresses on roller skates, motorcycles on tiny wheels and

kids who jump around a lot at gym." Critics turned thumbs firmly down on all of it, albeit the *Post's* Clive Barnes noted that, having the same producers who defied reviews to turn *Titanic* into a smash, the show just possibly might also become a hit.

At the Radio City Music Hall the annual *Christmas Spectacular* arrived on 5 November, featuring as always the great Nativity pageant and the high-kicking, precision Rockettes. Not long after the show closed in early January, the great old house also shuttered—for a prolonged refurbishing. So there would be no Easter offering this year.

A rash of revivals began when *Little Me* (17 November 1962) skipped in on the 12th at the Criterion with a TV favorite, tiny Martin Short, assuming all the roles that Sid Caesar once had clowned through. Highly divided reviews depended largely on the particular critic's reaction to the star. The entertainment ran for 101 performances.

On the 17th at the Marquis two great, mostly mum clowns, Bill Irwin and David Shiner, brought back their *Fool Moon*. Typical of the nonsense was their first appearance, with Shiner rudely trying to obtain a seat in the audience and the silent Irwin, walking on with a microphone that won't work, becoming entangled first in the mike's cord and then in the curtain, which abruptly lifts him on high. Once again the Red Clay Ramblers provided musical accompaniment during the limited stand.

Variety and the three major New York dailies gave *On the Town* (28 December 1944) more or less gentle thumbs down when it reappeared on the 21st at the Gershwin. Considering the importance of dance to the musical, the *Times's* Ben Brantley's assessment, "an aura of exertion that is only rarely translated into the effervescence that is the lifeblood of both cities and musicals," suggested the seriousness of the problem. Nor was the comedy in good hands. Those who recalled sly, brilliantly hilarious Nancy Walker could only cringe watching a loud, gross vulgarian, Lea DeLaria, attempt her old role. (In fairness, several critics thought her among the best things in the revival.) Playgoers stayed away, so the show closed quickly.

And once again *Peter Pan* (20 October 1954) delighted children and their sometimes reluctant parents when it flew into the Marquis on the 23rd with Cathy Rigby in the title role. There were some complaints from older playgoers and critics about the ghastly miking and amplification, and also some regrets that nobody in the cast could match the splendors of the original stars.

A character in *School for Scandal* remarks that one cannot be witty without at least a little malice. But when does malice take over and destroy real wit? That question was raised by **I'm Still Here … Damn It!** (5 November 1998, Booth), a one-woman show starring Sandra Bernhard. "This is foul-mouthed comedy as an extreme sport," one critic bewailed. On a set described variously as "a fancy Moroccan restaurant" and "a Turkish bordello," Bernhard appeared in a sluttishly scanty black shift and proceeded to denigrate myriad celebrities, tell some stories, and, backed by a small band, sing a few songs, all the while clinging to a microphone in one of Broadway's tiniest venues.

The misleadingly titled **Parade** (17 December 1998, Vivian Beaumont) had a book by Pultizer Prize-winning Alfred Uhry, best known for his stories of Southern Jews, and songs by newcomer Jason Robert Brown. Uhry's tale recounted a dark moment in American history, when a Jewish New Yorker, Leo Frank (Brent Carver), working in Georgia in 1913, was falsely accused of murdering a young girl, found guilty in a patently unfair trial, and eventually lynched. Considering the ghastly subject, it was not surprising that the musical was brought to life by Hal Prince, one of Broadway's leading fun-busters. Gnarled branches of a huge tree filled much of the stage, so the rest of the scenery was sparse. And much of the music, as had become the case in recent Broadway shows, was anthem-like. Critics divided sharply on the show, with assessments ranging from "earnest downer… about as compelling as watching herring shot in a barrel" through mixed notices (including barbs that the audience was clearly regaled by a dancing lynch mob) to such raves (the majority verdict) as "a soaring musical experience, a show that reaches for the stars and shines just as bright." Theatregoers sided with the naysayers, forcing the musical to shutter after a little more than two months.

Fosse (14 January 1999, Broadhurst) recreated many of the best, sexually fueled dance numbers from old Bob Fosse shows and films. Perhaps because they were taken out of context, or perhaps because the choreographer was no longer alive to restage them himself (Ann Reinking and Chet Walker did that job), many critics felt the evening lacked Fosse's special pizzazz. Still others wished "it would never stop." In dismal testimony to how mediocre this season's musicals were, the show, with no new music, no new dances, and no book, at season's end was awarded the Tony for the year's best new musical.

Another dance revue, **Dein Perry's Steel City** (26 January 1999, Radio City Music Hall), was allowed to occupy the huge house for a few nights before the building was given over to its planned renovation. *Variety* suggested this "massively scaled, hydraulically hyperactive" affair was designed for football stadiums and the raucous crowds that fill them for rock concerts (or, the paper might have added, demolition derbies). Numbers had dancers tapping and stomping over, in, and even under a pair of automobiles.

Most reviewers gave a "Crayola crayon–bright" revival of *You're a Good Man, Charlie Brown* (7 March 1967) a gentle spanking when it opened on 4 February at the Ambassador: "more two-dimensional than the comic strip"; "sadly shrunken in a Times Square theater." In a politically correct, multicultural mounting, Schroeder was played by a black and Linus by an Oriental. And Charlie was given a "curly-topped… helium-voiced" sister, Sally, who was played by the show-stealing Kristin Chenoweth. Sally and Schroeder were each assigned one of the two new songs, written not by Clark Gesner but by Andrew Lippa. The show lingered into June.

Encore!, as was becoming its custom, launched its season of concert-revivals in February, this year bringing out *Babes in Arms, Ziegfeld Follies of 1936*, and *Do Re Mi*.

Yet another politically correct revival tore any critical consensus to shreds. "A show with a distinct identity crisis… a show that wants to wow us with old-style panache even as its stylistic frame seems to argue that that isn't enough," wailed *Variety*, while the *Times* rued the "acrid smog" of a "misconceived revival." That revival, which raised its curtain at the Marquis on 4 March, was none other than Irving Berlin's beloved *Annie Get Your Gun* (16 May 1946). Peter Stone wrote the reconstructed book, which eliminated such ethnically and sexually "offensive" songs as "I'm An Indian, Too" and "I'm A Bad, Bad Man," at the same time that it redrew many of the characterizations. However, the tabloids rushed to the show's defense, the *Daily News*'s banner reading "Peters scores bull's-eye with 'Annie'" and the *Post*'s announcing, "'Annie Get Your Gun' is on target." However, Bernadette Peters, as Annie Oakley, walked off with a fistful of largely laudatory notices and helped pack the theatre for many months.

Band in Berlin (7 March 1999, Helen Hayes) was an oddity. Five male singers and one male pianist, known in the contemporary cabaret world as the Hudson Shad, assumed the roles of a similar singing group, the Comedian Harmonists, popular in Germany during the 1920s and early 1930s, until the Nazis put an end to them because several of the members were Jewish. Their ninety-minute concert was coupled with projections and some faked documentary film. But the story and the concert never fully came to life.

Still more old material recalled the often sad plight of poor black vaudevillians at the time that so many white vaudevillians were flourishing. In **Rollin' on the T.O.B.A.** (Theater Owners' Booking Association), performers resuscitated some black vaudeville comedy and sang and danced to the music of Eubie Blake, Duke Ellington, Fats Waller, and, in one curious instance, Charles Gounod. A hit off-Broadway, it was moved into the old Henry Miller's (now called the Kit Kat Klub at Henry Miller's) on 24 March.

Still another short-lived attempt to resurrect the past came with **Marlene** (11 April 1999, Cort). Pam Gems, who had written better received stage biographies of Edith Piaf and English painter Stanley Spencer, this time displeased New Yorkers, although the show had been playing internationally for several seasons. Sitting in a dressing room near the end of her career, Marlene Dietrich (Sian Phillips) reminisces about high points in her often newsworthy life. Then she heads on stage to give her audience a thirty-minute concert of her best-known songs. Critics singled out "Lili Marlene" and not "Falling In Love Again" as the standout number.

Even shorter-lived than *Marlene* was another retrospective, this one devoted to **The Gershwins' Fascinating Rhythm** (21 April 1999, Longacre). A ninety-minute, small-cast, intermissionless compilation of twenty-seven George and Ira classics, it was slammed by reviewers for "its desperately funkified arrangements." "The overall goal," Donald Lyons lamented in the *Post*, "seems to be to dumb down the Gershwins and render them accessible to patrons of MTV." Tacky settings and costumes were no help.

Having twice successfully defied critical onslaughts with *Jekyll and Hyde* and *The Scarlet Pimpernel*, composer Frank Wildhorn tried again with **The Civil War** (22 April 1999, St. James). He collaborated with Gregory Boyd and Jack Murphy on the book and lyrics. Actually there was precious little book (or at least no plot to speak of). Instead, in a loose chronology it offered quick glimpses of slave anguish, interrupted romances, Frederick Douglass, and the supposed voice of Abraham Lincoln. All this was played out against a background of minimalist

scenery. Essentially, then, the show was largely a succession of typical Wildhorn songs, pleasant, but undistinguished and derivative. *Variety*, bewailing the show's "easy pieties and bombastic tone," concluded: "In just over two hours, Wildhorn and his collaborators manage to thoroughly trivialize a sizeable chunk of American history." And once again grotesque amplification was condemned: "The show seems to want to make up in aural amplification what it lacks in textual depth. The Battle of Bull Run couldn't have been louder than experiencing this musical from row G in the orchestra." When, in early June, it failed to win a sought-after Tony, the show abruptly closed.

Trivializing a terrible American tragedy, dumbing down the Gershwins, and tampering with Irving Berlin's masterpiece in order to pander to political correctness give more than a small hint of why the Broadway musical had fallen on such dire times. About the only topics treated with proper respect and flair by the leftists who dominated the American stage were blacks and black music. Thus, even though it offered nothing truly new, **It Ain't Nothin' But the Blues** (24 April 1999, Vivian Beaumont) was embraced by aisle-sitters as the season's most satisfactory song-and-dance offering. The show had started life in several widely separated regional theatres and then played briefly at the New Victory on 42nd Street before being rushed uptown to Lincoln Center. Beginning with a few chants from an unspoiled Africa, it moved quickly to southern slave quarters and, as the blues became accepted, to a northern big city. The cast of seven was mostly black, but did include a lanky white banjo player.

1999–2000

At a time of endemic and noisy political correctness, the season's first opening underscored an interesting point. Virtually from the day when black shows were allowed to entertain white audiences critics singled out the ardor of black performers while more often than not deprecating the quality of the material they performed. A South African work, **Kat and the Kings** (19 August 1999, Cort), coming a hundred years after the first black musical played a white house, found this generation of reviewers holding to the old line. True, such patently racial salutes as "risible dental displays" and "high stepping" gave way to more generalized kudos—"sensational," "delightfully buoyant," and "exhaustingly eager" (this last employed by at least two critics)—but the tenor was the same. The story and songs the players offered were not unlike last season's *Band in Berlin*, only instead of Jews in Nazi Germany the actors represented "colored" singers in South Africa. A frame device had an aging shoeshine man recall how he and his young friends began their rise as a popular vocal group, only to be quashed by local racial laws. A somewhat forced run kept the show going until the beginning of January.

A new dance musical, **Contact** (7 October 1999, Newhouse), actually proved to be three short pieces, with storylines conceived by John Weidman and choreographed by Susan Stroman. The first piece, *Swinging*, brought to life Fragonard's famous painting "The Swing," but managed to inject some delightfully risqué notions and motions into the seemingly innocent, bucolic work. Here a lovely peeress and her hunky, but sullen servant played out the tryst. In *Did You Move?* the repressed wife of a small-time gangster, eating with him in a cheap Italian restaurant, indulges in some Walter Mitty–ish reveries whenever her husband gets up to help himself to the buffet. The chief dancelet of the night sported the same moniker as the whole evening. Boyd Gaines portrayed a jaded, suicidal TV director whose bungled attempt at killing himself provokes a wild dream of a visit to a swinging nightclub where he is, at least for a time, revitalized by the seductive stepping of a gorgeous young girl (Deborah Yates). There was no live music, but pre-recorded background music ranged from Bizet to Benny Goodman. Virtually unanimous critical raves prompted playgoers to besiege the box office, so the show was eventually moved to a larger auditorium in the Lincoln Center complex.

Dame Edna: The Royal Tour (17 October 1999, Booth) featured the sort of solo performer who in bygone days would have been accorded sketches in a revue or a Julian Eltinge–type of specialty plot. Barry Humphries, an Australian, in fact has a repertory of hilarious (and occasionally touching) characters whom he has been depicting for decades now all over the English-speaking world. However, for his Broadway debut, Humphries concentrated on his most famous creation, the brazenly outspoken Dame Edna Everage. One critic described her as a "garish hybrid of Margaret Thatcher (hair and ego) and Liberace (wardrobe and ego)." Typical of her barbed wit was her assurance that as a foreigner she could enjoy "diplomatic immunity for being politically incorrect," and that she could freely say things Americans could no longer say in public.

Critics were as virtually unanimous about **Saturday Night Fever** (21 October 1999, Minskoff), a stage adaptation of the 1977 film, as they had been about *Contact*, except this time they were all thumbs down. The story about a young paint salesman who can only escape self-awareness of his own mediocrity by dancing at a disco on weekends was retained, and so, the critics lamented, was everything else— even to the dialogue, the songs, the dancing, the recreated scenery and costumes. True, the performers were new, but they couldn't hold a candle to the originals. Since the box office had taken in somewhere between sixteen and twenty million dollars before opening night, there was a good chance that the production might catch on with at least enough elements of the modern theatregoing public to become a hit. And, in fact, boom times saw it was still running at season's end.

James Joyce's The Dead (28 October 1999, Playwrights Horizon) was probably even more offbeat than *Contact*. Based on Joyce's famous short story in *Dubliners*, it had a book by Richard Nelson, folklorish music by Shaun Davey, lyrics by Nelson and Davey, and recounted one annual Christmas dinner given by two aging aunts (Sally Ann Howes and Marni Nixon) and their niece (Emily Skinner) for family and friends. These visitors, in what several aisle-sitters branded a "Chekhovian" musical, included an amiable tippler (Stephen Spinella), his nose-in-the-air mother (Paddy Croft), an operatic tenor (John Kelly), the aunts' nephew Gabriel (Christopher Walken)—who served as a sort of narrator—and Gabriel's wife, Gretta (Blair Brown). Precious little happens, except that Gabriel learns that years ago a young man had died of unrequited love for Gretta and he recognizes that he himself is incapable of such deep devotion. Despite some reservations, especially about Walken's cold performance, critics welcomed the work. In short order it was hustled into the Belasco, where it ran until spring.

On 4 November the Radio City Music Hall raised its curtain on its annual *Christmas Spectacular*, replete as always with a magnificent Nativity scene, the high-kicking, precision Rockettes, a joyous glimpse of Santa's busy workshop, and other treats for the eye, the ear, and the soul, if not for the mind.

Most reviewers looked favorably on a revival of *Tango Argentino* (9 October 1985) when it arrived for a limited stand at the Gershwin on 17 November, but they were even more enthusiastic about a brilliant and surprisingly faithful revival of *Kiss Me, Kate* (30 December 1948) at the Martin Beck the next night. They waved away their own quibbles about the slightness of Sam and Bella Spewack's book to gleefully garland both the great Cole Porter score and the superb cast, headed by Marin Mazzie and Brian Stokes Mitchell. (In a sign of the times, no major commentator mentioned that Mitchell was a light-skinned African American.) Perhaps inevitably, there was some minor tinkering—a few new jokes, the unnecessary addition of "From This Moment On," and, equally baffling, new orchestrations replacing Robert Russell Bennett's great originals. (Is this because singers, in these miked and amplified days, can no longer project over a full-bodied orchestra, or were there some economic reasons?) Still, it was wunderbar, as one critic observed, to be "transported back to the days when the Broadway musical was a land of easygoing enchantment."

Certainly in recent decades, no one has ever accused Stephen Sondheim of providing audiences with easygoing enchantment. But to allow the droll, affectionate Carol Burnett and four fine supporting singers to offer a Sondheim potpourri in *Putting It Together* (21 November 1999, Ethel Barrymore)—a reworking of a revue presented off-Broadway with Julie Andrews in 1993—had its own rewards. Critics applauded the star and, in large measure, the songwriter. Yet, Donald Lyons of the *Post* concluded his notice with a comparison that many readers must have embraced: "The Broadway revivals of 'Kiss Me, Kate' and of this within days are too tempting to ignore. Both Porter and Sondheim are clever wordsmiths adept at expressing disillusion and sexual bitterness, but Porter doesn't linger there. His constant message (and it's one he earned the right to preach) is: Cheer up, be brave and bright. Sondheim's self-pitying sourness only seems more grown-up; it's actually shallow and callow."

The parade of revivals continued with the annual return of *A Christmas Carol* for its seasonal engagement at the Theatre at Madison Square Garden on 30 November. Tony Roberts was a more amiable Scrooge than most earlier ones.

There was virtual unanimity in the critical paeans for Audra McDonald, who assumed the title role in **Marie Christine** (2 December 1999, Vivian Beaumont), Michael John LaChiusa's resetting of the Medea legend in 1894 New Orleans and Chicago. A majority of critics panned LaChiusa's libretto—"a bore," one called it—but divided vigorously on the merits of his music. Anthony Crivello portrayed Marie's white lover, Dante—the author's recreation of Jason.

Sondheim's frequently fascinating self-pity was answered by some less imaginative, more treacly self-pitying when an over-fifty Liza Minnelli assured loyal audiences, "I'm making a comeback" on opening night of her one-woman (plus six male singer-dancers) show, **Minnelli on Minnelli** (8 December 1999, Palace). She framed the show as a tribute to her father, projected all sorts of pictures of mommy and daddy (and baby Liza), and sang many of the songs associated with the Minnellis. (Mommy, of course, was Judy Garland. But several reviewers noted Liza never mentioned Judy by name.) *Variety* suggested that the show was "as much support group as it [was] a concert." However, Minnelli's admirers could not have cared less.

Swing! (9 December 1999, St. James), an evening devoted to the music and hip-tossing, high-bouncing dances of the big band era, proved irresistible to aisle-sitters: "... could hardly be more exuberant or fun. It's a sure winner," one ended his joyous salute. Of course, there were brief excursions into the Latin and country dancing of the day as well. In one number a man unable to sleep because of his neighbor's drumming goes into a lively tap routine and is quickly joined by hoofers bedecked in pink, purple, and red pajamas. However, the musical, while running out the season, proved a surprisingly disappointing draw.

The year (and, for many who can't count correctly, the century and the millennium) ended with Jackie Mason again hilariously lambasting everything dear and sacred in his latest one-man show, **Much Ado About Everything** (30 December 1999, Golden). Typical of his barbs was his analysis of George W. Bush, the son of a former president and now himself a White House candidate. According to the "chubby Jewish leprechaun" of a comedian, the younger Bush is "brilliant, unless you ask him a question."

That Encore! would present its three concert-revivals starting in February had become a tradition. This season was no exception. Its trio of offerings was *On a Clear Day You Can See Forever, Tenderloin,* and *Wonderful Town.*

For the second time this season, a Sondheim musical offered itself for theatregoers' consideration. Only on this occasion it was not a potpourri of older material, but rather the first New York outing (at an off-Broadway house) of a 1954 opus by the then-unknown creator. **Saturday Night** (17 February 2000, Second Stage) told of the leader of some rough-and-tumble Brooklyn youngsters who dreams of living the high life in 1929 Manhattan, takes the wrong roads to achieve his aim, but for whom everything ends happily. No one seemed to care for Julius J. Epstein's lackluster book, but Sondheim's somewhat more traditional melodies than his later ones and, most of all, his brilliant lyrics won kudos everywhere.

The late 1920s was also the era of **The Wild Party** (24 February 2000, City Center Stage 1), which the respected Manhattan Theater Club rushed into one of its venues in order to beat another version announced for Broadway in the spring. Both versions admitted to being based on Joseph Moncure March's poem. The story recounts the ill-fated rivalry of two vaudevillians and lovers, Burrs and Queenie, with Quenie's best-friend, Kate, and her new boyfriend, Mr. Black. The pairs swap partners which results in a brawl and Burrs' death. The initial version had music and libretto by Andrew Lippa. Critic after critic, recalling how the once original and occasionally shocking stories and stagings of *Chicago* and *Cabaret* had stunned some in their day, nonetheless thought the new show reduced matters to a largely unattractive, unnecessary degeneracy. Possibly because some glamorous figures took leading roles, the second version, which settled into the Virginia on 13 April with songs by Michael John LaChiusa and a book by LaChiusa and George C. Wolfe, garnered a much better reception. The first couple, a pair of mediocre vaudevillians, was played by Mandy Patinkin and Toni Collette, a film starlet. The seemingly ageless, embraceable Eartha Kitt was the heroine's friend. The male intruder was now merely named Black and was portrayed by Yancy Arias as a "bargain basement Valentino." Some other changes had Patinkin not in a clown's makeup, but in Jolson-like blackface, and he is murdered by his woman's new lover.

Reviewers could not even agree on the running time of the unappealingly titled **Squonk** (29 February 2000, Helen Hayes), a small-cast transplant from Pittsburgh and an East Village boîte. It was clocked, variously, at seventy, eighty, or ninety minutes. Subtitled **BigSmörgasbord-WünderWerk**, this multimedia, hippyish, intellectualized Olsen and Johnson blended "a little puppetry with scrap heap statuary and video" to examine "the body and the things it eats and fears." At one point a playgoer was brought on stage and X-rayed to suggest he had swallowed a clarinet. A majority of critics found the whole affair indigestible, but several graciously admitted that many theatregoers might deem it palatable.

On 7 March the New York City Opera restored *Porgy and Bess* to its repertory. The revival was welcomed, albeit with varying reservations.

Riverdance on Broadway (16 March 2000, Gershwin) ·was a souped-up version of the earlier *Riverdance* (13 March 1996), which had played a few years before at the Radio City Music Hall as part of a wildly successful worldwide tour. In its latest incarnation it offered not only the Irish dancing that had filled the former mounting but a Moscow Folk Ballet, African songs and choreography, flamenco routines, and much else in what one exhausted critic called "a global goulash."

Nearly half a century earlier, Verdi's *Aida* had been reset during the Civil War for a brief Broadway run as *My Darlin' Aida* (27 October 1952). Whatever might have been said against it, at least it retained much of the opera's most important asset, Verdi's score. The **Aida** (23 March 2000, Palace) which now lumbered in didn't even do that, instead jettisoning Verdi's beloved music for the pallid melodies of rock pianist Elton John, set to lyrics by Tim Rice. The new book, by Linda Woolverton, Robert Falls, and David Henry Hwang, opened and closed in the Egyptian room of a modern museum, in between transporting museum visitors to the ancient world where the heroine (Heather Headley) and Radames (Adam Pascal) play out their destinies in terms of modern, politically correct angst. Headley received far and away the best notices, but many aisle-sitters also spotlighted Sherie Rene Scott's Amneris, portrayed as a consummate clothes horse, and her show-stopping "My Strongest Suit" ("I would rather wear a barrel than conservative apparel"). The *Times*, noting that the musical was produced by one of the Disney's organization's many branches, advised its readers, "Wait for the cartoon."

Forty-four professional ballroom dancers offered New Yorkers "a high-energy, heart-pounding display" of their art when **Burn the Floor** waltzed, tangoed, rhumbaed, and jitter-bugged into the Radio City Music Hall for three performances beginning 5 April.

Critics slammed a grungy "T-Shirts and Leather" revival of *Jesus Christ Superstar* (12 October 1971), when it arrived at the Ford Center on 16 April, at the same time taking the opportunity to reject the show itself. Jeffrey Lyons closed his review, "It was cheap in 1971, and it's even worse now."

Julie Taymor's visually imaginative mounting of Carlo Gozzi's **The Green Bird** (18 April 2000, Cort) was translated by Albert Bermel and Ted Emery and had music by Elliot Goldenthal. The story recounted the adventures of a pair of youngsters who have been raised by peasants after their wicked grandmother has cheated them of their inheritance. Most reviewers found the plot and music ho-hum, but saluted Taymor's brilliant effects: "Big, shiny McIntosh-like apples split open to reveal platinum-blond sirens," a statue of a nude goddess "melts into animation," while the beautiful bird of the title is shown guarded by "a pyramid of chattering skulls."

The season's last musical was the first major New York revival of Meredith Willson's beloved *The Music Man* (19 December 1957). Its arrival at the Neil Simon on 27 April led to some perhaps not so surprising judgments. Certainly not for the first time, critics deemed an old favorite still strong musically but increasingly creaky in its book. It has been a decades-old cry. In this instance, according to at least one commentator, there may have been a special reason for the problem. Susan Stroman is currently Broadway's most imaginative and exciting choreographer, but her direction of this show's book and the show's casting suggest she may be willing to sacrifice other elements of a show simply to call attention to her dances. For example, the revival's Harold Hill, the relatively untried and unknown Craig Bierko, was more than competent, but never as irresistible as Robert Preston. Indeed, possibly the sole member of the cast to compare to the original was Rebecca Luker, and even in her case the "overzealous amplification" left open the question of whether her Marian the librarian was equal to Barbara Cook's. Still, reviews were so embracing that the show almost certainly will enjoy a long run.

All in all, it was, considering the day and age, a very good season. Shortly before they wrote "finis" to the year, papers were already extolling "another championship season," "a critic-proof cash bonanza," and noting "producers are all singing, all dancing, as box office heads for a huge finale." So, at least financially, the news was good.

But what of quality? It would be hard to dispute the fact that there were fewer and fewer takeaway songs coming from Broadway. No doubt this was partly because they no longer received the replaying they once did on radio and television, which meant people were unable to readily familiarize themselves with them as they once could. But, at least for many older theatregoers, including several knowledgeable aisle-sitters who have been quoted, much of the lightness and fun had gone from both the songs and librettos. Creators of our new musicals appeared to take themselves far too seriously. As has been said, musical comedy is neither as delightfully musical nor as comic as it used to be. Old-style operetta is long gone, as are slapdash topical revues and gorgeous girlie shows. (In the case of revues, their modern-day descendants are the dutiful musical retrospectives given various composers and lyricists.) What's left? The musical play! A more or less pretentious moniker that seems to cover virtually the entire range of modern musical theatre. Some of them have been magnificent (and are, in fact, merely Americanized, new-styled operetta. Only don't tell that to the shade of Oscar Hammerstein II, who helped create several of the greatest.) But all too many have been leaden soporifics, keeping audiences awake only by their outrageous miking and amplification.

That brings us to one final point. We have been railing against these horrors for many years now (and quoting critics who have shared our dismay). Yet, in truth, there should be nothing wrong with miking and amplifying shows. After all, theatrical costumes and scenery and lighting are quite unnatural. And we accept them uncomplainingly when they are well done. Ah, there's the rub! Well done! On Broadway and on the American road they seem never to be well done. Yet that needn't be the case. Some American opera houses have been subtly miked and amplified for years. The auditoriums at London's Royal National Theatre have recently been fitted out with amazing skill, so that if, say, you attended a performance there of *Lady in the Dark*, knowing full well the sound had been played with, you were nonetheless almost never aware of the tinkering, and on the few transient occasions when you were, it could easily be overlooked. The answer would seem to be to build these amplification systems carefully into the auditoriums. The problem would seem to be that theatre owners refuse to be burdened with the expense, leaving it for producers to jerry-build systems externally for each show.

Act Seven

The Twenty-First Century, 2000–2010

The end of the twentieth century and the start of the new millennium welcomed some subtle changes to the art and commerce of musical theatre. While annual combined attendance to Broadway plays and musicals remained largely flat at just above or below 12 million for the 2000–2010 decade, the previous decade witnessed a strong increase from 7,314,000 to 11,937,000, as measured by the Broadway League Inc. (formerly the League of American Theatre Producers) and reported to *Variety*. Similarly, the number of new musicals presented on Broadway fluctuated from six to thirteen throughout the first decade of the twenty-first century, averaging about ten, as in the past two seasons. Musical revivals numbered between three and six per season. Keeping pace with inflation the average ticket price on Broadway rose from $55.75 in 2000–2001 to $85.56 in 2009–2010.

What *has* changed are the four themes introduced in the preface: (1) the global dominance of the American musical and its expansion into previously unexplored, un-exploited territories and cultures, (2) an increased synergy between musical theatre, film, and television, (3) the decline of the traditional book musical with an original score, and the concomitant rise of pre-existing pop music wed to revue-like biographical narratives, or retro-fitted to new stories, and (4) the emergence of institutions and organizations dedicated to creating new musicals (the National Alliance for Musical Theatre, New York Musical Theatre Festival, and various Fringe Festivals) or preserving those of the past (Encores in New York, Reprise in Los Angeles), joining long-standing institutions such as the Goodspeed Opera House in East Haddam, Connecticut, and the York Theatre in New York City. Additionally, the revolution of the Internet and related technologies has expedited the flow of information about musicals; it has also afforded unexpected efficiencies in the technical production and marketing of musical theatre.

As of 2010, the annual Broadway gross is in excess of $1 billion (combined with road business of nearly $650 million), leaving no doubt about the economic impact of this art form/industry.

Movies Hit Broadway, 2000–2005

2000–2001

The season got off to a late start with **The Full Monty** (26 October 2000, Eugene O'Neill), an adaptation of the popular 1997 British film about a group of unemployed steelworkers who decide to strip to raise money. Transposed from the film's Sheffield, UK to Buffalo, New York, Terrence McNally's broadly comic book mined the humor and pathos of the original story. Newcomer David Yazbek composed a nimble pop score that made some liken him to a modern-day Frank Loesser; Jack O'Brien directed with his customary skill and authority; and dancer-turned-choreographer Jerry Mitchell found his break-out opportunity to transpose his provocative dances from the Broadway Bares fundraisers to a full-fledged Broadway musical. Patrick Wilson starred as Jerry Lukowski, who plotted the scheme with help from his buddy Ryan Burkhart (John Ellison Conlee) and four desperate recruits played by Jason Danieley, André De Shields, Romain Frugé and Marcus Neville. In the role of their on-stage pianist, Kathleen Freeman wisecracked with tough gal, seen-it-all-before charm. Emily Skinner, Annie Golden, Patti Perkins and Lisa Datz shared dubious honor playing neglected wives and girlfriends. Critics generally admired *Monty*'s achievements, even if the scruffy appeal of the original film was somewhat diluted by its stage adaptation, and audiences supported it for an almost two-year run.

Broadway diva Patti LuPone brought her solo show **Patti LuPone: Matters of the Heart** to the Vivian Beaumont (13 November 2000) for a brief series of Sunday and Monday night performances. **Borscht Belt Buffet on Broadway** (24 October 2000, Town Hall) offered a modest revue of Catskills humor on the concert stage for two weeks. The Theatre at Madison Square Garden opened the seventh annual season of its musical *A Christmas Carol* (24 November 2000) for family audiences, with Frank Langella as Scrooge.

A twenty-fifth anniversary Broadway revival of Richard O'Brien's *The Rocky Horror Show* (10 March 1975) was probably inevitable, given the worldwide success and international cult status of the stage musical and 1975 film. Borrowing freely from the proven film iconography and numerous stage revivals from around the world, this *Rocky Horror* (15 November 2000, Circle in the Square) determined to dispel the curse of the initial production's Broadway failure. Abetted by a first-rate cast—Tom Hewitt as transvestite Frank 'N' Furter, Jarrod Emick and Alice Ripley as naifs Brad and Janet, and supporting characters played by Raúl Esparza, rocker Joan Jett, *Rent* veteran Daphne Rubin-Vega, Lea DeLaria, and television talk-show legend Dick Cavett—director Chris Ashley and choreographer Jerry Mitchell successfully aped the film's well-known songs and silly plot. David Rockwell's imaginative and playful thrust scenic design allowed the director to stage the musical with a portion of the audience seated among the actors, facilitating participation and, often, hysteria more typical of a rock concert than a Broadway musical. In an effort to simulate the film's cult midnight showings, the show's producers sold "Audience Participation Kits" for $10, allowing viewers to pelt the actors and sing along. Even if *Rocky Horror* no longer shocked audiences with its science-fiction, glam-rock, sexually ambiguous trappings, the evening functioned as a reunion for those who knew and loved the film. *Rocky* yelled, screamed and strutted for just over a year.

With an eye on the family musical market otherwise dominated by Disney, **Seussical** (30 November 2000, Richard Rodgers) arrived following a calamitous pre-Broadway tryout. Dr. Seuss' famously subversive children's illustrated books (*The Cat in the Hat, How the Grinch Stole Christmas*, etc.) had been reading staples for more than fifty years, so a stage musical adaptation seemed a brilliant idea. *Seussical* had reportedly been a delight in its bare bones workshop form, but the sheer weight of its $10.5 million production, with elaborate costumes, pop-up sets and visual effects, overwhelmed its gently whimsical story. Songwriters Lynn Ahrens (lyrics) and Stephen Flaherty (music) conceived the book with an assist from Eric Idle of Monty Python fame; director Frank Galati had previously served Ahrens and Flaherty well with their epic musical *Ragtime*. Much of the score had the right playful touch ("Oh, the Thinks You Can Think!," "Horton Hears a Who," "Amayzing Mayzie"). But Seuss' irreverent, nonsensical humor and his absurdist visual adventures did not marry well with the demands for a coherent musical theatre plot. Emblematic of the show's difficulty was its casting. While the gifted mime David Shiner may have borne a physical resemblance to the lanky Cat in the Hat, his singing voice was unappealing, and no ordinary mortal could hope to match the bizzareness of Seuss' original creation. Kevin Chamberlin was oddly touching as Horton the Elephant, but the theatrical characterizations of Gertrude McFuzz, Mayzie LaBird, the Sour Kangaroo, the Wickersham Brothers, and the denizens of Whoville were generally shrill and desperate to please. *Seussical*, even with the re-casting of Rosie O'Donnell as the Cat in the Hat in the middle of its run, eked out a disappointing six-month engagement.

As an antidote to the puerile joys of *Seussical* and the contemporary excesses of *The Full Monty* and *Rocky Horror*, a new musical adaptation of Charlotte Brontë's **Jane Eyre** (10 December 2000, Brooks Atkinson) brought gothic romance and traditional storytelling back to the Broadway stage. Reviewers and playgoers divided evenly as to the show's merits. John Caird (book, co-director, co-lyricist) applied his narrative skills—proven during past triumphs *Les Misérables* and *Nicholas Nickleby*—to the plot, but the brooding, interior emotions of Brontë proved more difficult to dramatize and stage than the larger-than-life passions of Hugo and Dickens. Paul Gordon's middling score recalled other superior romantic musical theatre scores, with its stream-of-consciousness ballads, Euro-pop melodramatics and earnest, preachy lyrics. John Napier's constantly revolving turntable and projections attempted to compensate with constant movement for the long, familiar narrative. If Marla Schaffel was much prettier than any Jane ought to be, and James Barbour's Rochester predictably heroic, they seldom generated genuine romantic heat on the stage. The haste to tell the full story reduced *Jane Eyre* to romance novel dimensions and denied the production depth of focus that would have rendered the famous story truly moving. With no Tony wins, *Jane Eyre* closed its doors after seven months.

Encores' eighth annual season of classic musicals at New York City Center spanned four decades with *A Connecticut Yankee* (3 November 1927), *Bloomer Girl* (5 October 1944) and *Hair* (29 April 1968). Opening the season on 8 February 2001, Rodgers & Hart's adaptation of Mark Twain's novel *A Connecticut Yankee in King Arthur's Court* hadn't visited Broadway since its 1943 revival, the version presented here. The time travel farce, with a sixth-century plot trapped in a mid-twentieth century vernacular, proved mostly lame ("Meet me at the moat," or "Tell thou that to the Marines!"). Notwithstanding a fine cast (Judith Blazer, Christine Ebersole, Steven Sutcliffe) the R&H standards were the evening's best rewards. Equally neglected in recent years, *Bloomer Girl's* (revived 22 March 2001) Civil War-era tale of incipient feminism now plays as rather quaint.

Arlen and Harburg's memorable score ("Right as the Rain," "The Eagle and Me," "Evelina") received a welcome airing, but neither the principals—Kate Jennings Grant (Evelina), Michael Park (her suitor Jeff Calhoun), Philip Bosco and Kathleen Chalfant—nor Brad Rouse's direction or Rob Ashford's choreography, could make a compelling case for a full-scale revival. Familiar to most and far from neglected, *Hair* was a controversial choice for an Encores revival on 3 May 2001; perhaps its anti-war, free-love, casual-drug-use and down-town-Hippie aesthetic would seem tame or dated some thirty-three years later. Kathleen Marshall's affectionate staging reminded all of the potency of Galt MacDermott, Gerome Ragni and James Rado's score, arguably the first great rock musical, and the last Broadway musical to invade the pop charts several times over. Luther Creek's doomed Claude, Tom Plotkin's Berger, Idina Menzel's Sheila, Kevin Cahoon's Woof, and Michael McElroy's Hud made for a youthful tribe, but some critics felt that Marshall's production recreated hippiedom as "just another show-biz style" rather than capturing the show's true spirit of protest and rage.

The first Broadway musical opening of the new year, **A Class Act** (9 November 2000, Manhattan Theatre Club; 11 March 2001, Ambassador) was a posthumous biography of composer and lyricist Ed Kleban, best known as the unsung lyricist of *A Chorus Line*. With a book lovingly assembled by Linda Kline (Kleban's life partner) and Lonny Price (director), the musical illustrated the frustrations of toiling backstage in the world of musical theatre. Opening with Kleban's memorial service as a dramatic portal to the exploration of his life, Kleban was revealed as an imperfect, frustrated, yet talented soul. Price, artistic director of Musical Theatre Works, shepherded this unique project through its development at MTW, to an off-Broadway berth at Manhattan Theatre Club, and finally a Broadway transfer. *A Class Act* would have us believe that Kleban's loss was our tragedy, and his best songs, "The Next Best Thing to Love," "Better" and "Under Separate Cover" make that case. In spite of a top-notch cast including Price himself, Nancy Anderson, Donna Bullock, Randy Graff, Sara Ramirez, Jeff Blumenkrantz, and David Hibbard, *A Class Act* never quite succeeded in escaping its limitations as mere insider theatre folklore, or else the biography of a tiresome, unfulfilled person. Despite a devoted, loyal fan base, *A Class Act* closed before summer.

The most eagerly awaited musical of the season was Mel Brooks's stage transposition of his own movie, **The Producers** (19 April 2001, St. James). The ferocious 1967 film satire of two conniving crooks, the bully theatre producer Max Bialystock and his timid accountant Leo Bloom, had long been a cult film favorite. The premise was both riotous and caustic: Bialystock and Bloom oversell interests in a surefire failure of a musical, *Springtime for Hitler*, only to watch it become a phenomenal success. Although Brooks had once toiled in early 1950s television and written the books to two forgotten Broadway musicals, *Shinbone Alley* and *All American*, he had since achieved widespread fame and success in the 1970-1980s as the producer-director of a series of film farces: his first, *The Producers*, followed by *Blazing Saddles*, *Young Frankenstein*, *History of the World: Part 1* and *Spaceballs*, to name but a few. In plotting his return to the stage, he assembled a formidable production team: co-librettist Thomas Meehan (*Annie*), director-choreographer Susan Stroman (*Contact*), scenic designer Robin Wagner, and costume designer William Ivey Long. An aggressive consortium of producers was likewise assembled, in order to raise the $10.5 million that would go into the production. Nathan Lane and Matthew Broderick accepted the unenviable task of dispelling indelible filmgoer memories of Zero Mostel as Bialystock and Gene Wilder as Bloom. With an extravagance seldom seen since the days of Ziegfeld, Brooks produced a dizzying musical farce that began with loud laughs, assumed gale-force speed and intensity, and never let up until the final curtain. As in all his films, Brooks dispensed with political correctness, leaving no satiric victim unscathed: blacks, homosexuals, Jews, Nazis, octogenarians with walkers, busty dumb blondes, nebbishes, and everyone else suffered equal comic abuse. Liberal use was made of every known four letter word, as well as some creative new ones.

The Producers met with all but unanimous critical acclaim. No one remarked upon Brooks' mediocre skills as a pastiche composer, perhaps because the top-notch orchestrations, and musical and vocal arrangements concealed the thinness of the material. Maybe that was Brooks' very intent. His raucous vaudeville ditties mimicked seemingly every musical from the 1950s and 1960s. Stroman's imaginative and excessive staging hammered the numbers home. Everyone delighted in spotting quotes or references to Broadway icons, such as Ziegfeld ("Springtime for Hitler"), *42nd Street* ("You're going out there a silly

hysterical queen and you're coming back a great big passing-for-straight Broadway star!"), Sondheim's *Follies* ("Little Old Lady Land"), "Ol' Man River" ("Oh, I debits all duh mornin'" in "I Wanna Be a Producer"). All the musical numbers reiterated their thinly veiled subtexts with scant narrative surprise: "Keep It Gay" (the homosexual tribute), "When You Got It, Flaunt It" (big breasts), "In Old Bavaria" (faux Nazi sentiment), "Along Came Bialy" (libidinous old ladies), "We Can Do It" (the buddy song), "I Wanna Be a Producer" (show-biz tap dance), "Haben Sie Gehoert Das Deutsche Band?" (German oompah band). Brooks' touch only faltered when faced with a narrative challenge, in the shapeless rant for Bialystock, "Betrayed."

Success later became a curse for *The Producers*. In response to the unprecedented demand for tickets, its producers reintroduced the practice of selling "premium seats," marketed as the best seats in the house and priced from $250-500. However welcome the attempt to reclaim revenues for the production that had previously been siphoned off to speculators, the premium cost became a problem once the stars departed or were out sick or on vacation. Other shows followed suit, but a consumer backlash developed—it became assumed that productions now routinely withheld all choice seats from public sale. *The Producers* retained its premium appeal as long as Lane and Broderick were in the cast or once they resumed their roles after several years away, but the over six-year run proved somewhat shorter than expected, given the initial critical hysteria.

Three spring musical revivals competed head-to-head for the awards sweepstakes. *Follies* (4 April 1971) was Roundabout Theatre Company's ambitious attempt to strip Stephen Sondheim and James Goldman's legendary musical of its sumptuous trappings, and reduce it to gritty, backstage realism. Opening 5 April 2001 at the Belasco, the architects of this misguided production were English play director Matthew Warchus and choreographer Kathleen Marshall. Among the four principals, Judith Ivey and Blythe Danner had no musical experience whatsoever, while Gregory Harrison and Treat Williams had but one or two musicals to their credit. If the emphasis on the text was intended as a "book- or actor-centered approach," the result was musically compromised, dramatically tedious and visually dull. In a nod to traditional *Follies* casting, the supporting cast was a show biz who's who: Polly Bergen, Marge Champion, Donald Saddler, Joan Roberts, Carol Woods, Jane White, and Betty

Garrett. This new, mostly unloved *Follies* departed in three months.

Bells Are Ringing (29 November 1956) had not seen a Broadway revival in almost fifty years when it arrived 12 April 2001 at the Plymouth. Comedienne Faith Prince possessed the irrepressible comic gifts and requisite warmth to bring the story of Ella and the Susanswerphone Answering Service back to Broadway. Marc Kudisch assumed the part of her love interest Jeff Moss, while Tina Landau directed and Jeff Calhoun choreographed. The majority of viewers found the romantic hijinks of *Bells Are Ringing* too old-fashioned and regrettably silly.

42nd Street (25 August 1980), Gower Champion's affectionate valentine to the 1930s cinematic musical spectacles of Busby Berkeley, had not been absent long from Broadway, and some imagined this return might be too soon after the previous incarnation's close twelve years prior. This lavish re-mounting (2 May 2001, Ford Center) saw Champion's work faithfully re-directed by its surviving librettist Mark Bramble and re-choreographed by Randy Skinner, Champion's assistant on the original. Once disparaged by David Merrick as mere "lead-ins and cross-overs," Bramble made minor revisions to his and Michael Stewart's book, including a newly ambiguous ending and a more romantic Julian Marsh, played by Michael Cumptsy. The composite Harry Warren-Al Dubin score, with nine interpolations borrowed freely from seven other Berkeley film-musicals, was further tweaked by the addition of "I Only Have Eyes for You" for Christine Ebersole (Dorothy Brock) and "With Plenty of Money and You" for Kate Levering (Peggy Sawyer) and a chorus of men. With a singing/dancing ensemble of twenty-eight, *42nd Street* celebrated old-fashioned Broadway showmanship at its best. A few critics, notably Ben Brantley in The New York *Times*, carped that the production lacked any real spark of imagination, instead relying heavily on clichés and a distant sense of spectacle. Brantley complained that the revival "has the thrice-watered-down feeling of a pastiche of a pastiche." But for most Broadway audiences, this *42nd Street* was good enough for a three-year run, proving that famous line from the show, "the most glorious words in the English language" are musical comedy.

Apart from *A Class Act* and *Urinetown*, which transferred to Broadway the following season, off-Broadway produced few significant new musicals this season. **Bat Boy: The Musical** (20 March 2001, Union Square) spun a *Rocky Horror/Little Shop of Horrors*-style gothic rock musical from a simple tabloid news story about a boy raised as a bat in a cave. **Love, Janis** (22 April 2001), a loose bio-musical on the life of Janis Joplin, offered a conventional rock music anthology revue for an almost two-year run at the Village.

2001–2002

Following the terrorist assault on the World Trade Center's twin towers the morning of 11 September, Broadway's 2001–2002 season got off to a precipitous and shaky, but ultimately defiant start with two musical smash hits, *Urinetown* and *Mamma Mia!* All Broadway productions shut down for two nights, and *Urinetown* opened bravely one week later than originally scheduled. First glimpsed at the New York Fringe Festival in August 1999, followed by a spring 2001 Off-Broadway tryout, **Urinetown** (20 September 2001, Henry Miller's) was a mock Brecht-Weill-Blitzstein musical comedy by newcomers Gregg Kotis (book, lyrics) and Mark Hollmann (music, lyrics) in which the corporate forces of evil deny access to public urinals for all the ordinary folks of Urinetown. This political fable satirized leftist agit-prop, musical comedy cliché, good vs. evil, and film noir conventions with a sophomoric zest that everyone found refreshing. Its themes (innocent people suffering at the invisible hand of evil, victims thrown from skyscrapers, Malthusian concepts of a man-made apocalypse, the arrogance of privilege) resonated strongly and proved strangely prescient in the days following 9/11. *Urinetown* won many fans for its scrappy production, helmed by John Rando (direction) and John Carrafa (choreography). Its cast included Broadway veterans John Cullum (as evil Caldwell B. Cladwell), Jeff McCarthy (Officer Lockstock), Nancy Opel (Penelope Pennywise), Hunter Foster (hero Bobby Strong), and newcomers Spencer Kayden and Jennifer Laura Thompson. *Urinetown* prospered for two-and-a-half years.

Mamma Mia! (18 October 2001, Winter Garden) arrived one month later with the imprimatur of its London blockbuster success. Using the pre-existing music catalogue of Swedish pop group ABBA, a trio of women, Catherine Johnson (book writer), Phyllida Lloyd (director) and Judy Craymer (producer) cobbled together the story of expatriate British mother Donna Sheridan (Louise Pitre) and her teenage daughter, Sophie (Tina Maddigan), who live peacefully on a Greek island. Without telling her mother, Sophie invites all three men who could be her biological father to her impending wedding. Donna's best friends Tanya (Karen Mason) and Rosie (Judy Kaye) arrive too, and the revelations and reversals play out to a predictably joyous finale. Even if the book owed much to the film *Buona Sera, Mrs. Campbell* (1968), its musical adaptation *Carmelina*, and the Willy Russell play *Shirley Valentine*, the loose sitcom plot nonetheless served as an amiable framework on which to hang twenty or more hit pop songs the audience was happy to recognize and hum along to ("Dancing Queen," "Take a Chance on Me," "Winner Takes It All"). No matter that the majority of drama critics scoffed at the sloppy dramaturgy, the shoe-horned song cues, and the over-amplified score. *Mamma Mia!* captured the giddy sense of optimism Broadway theatergoers sought in the wake of 9/11. It continues to run more than ten years after its original UK premiere in London, New York, and capitals around the world, has spawned the highest-grossing film musical ever (2008; directed by Phyllida Lloyd), and proved to the skeptical ABBA songwriters, whose *Chess* had flopped on Broadway in 1988, that an unlikely hit musical could be spun from their back catalogue.

Much was expected of **Thou Shalt Not** (25 October 2001, Plymouth), for which pop songwriter Harry Connick, Jr., wrote the songs, librettist David Thompson updated Emile Zola's novel *Thérèse Raquin,* and director-choreographer Susan Stroman offered a fluid staging. This Lincoln Center Theater production ultimately met with universal pans and limped through its scheduled three-month run. Thérèse (Kate Levering) and her husband Camille (Norbert Leo Butz) are both jazz musicians in a post-World War II New Orleans jazz club run by his mother, Mme. Raquin (Debra Monk). Thérèse falls for her husband's friend Laurent Leclaire (Craig Bierko), just back from the war, and together they plot Camille's murder. With the exception of Butz's solo "Tugboat," most of Connick's jazz score proved resolutely untheatrical, and Thompson's book never captured the steamy, sordid excitement of the story. If Stroman's staging captured the aura of New Orleans' ninth ward, it lacked theatrical weight and relevance to the ill-conceived story. Strangely, Butz survived his role as an on-stage corpse to receive the production's best notices.

By Jeeves (28 October 2001, Helen Hayes) represented the culmination of a determined twenty-seven-year effort by Andrew Lloyd Webber and the distinguished British playwright Alan Ayckbourn to fashion a pocket-sized musical from P. G. Wodehouse's beloved Jeeves stories. Their earlier adaptation, simply titled *Jeeves*, had failed at Her Majesty's Theatre, London, in 1974, but this more modest version enjoyed a moderate success in London in 1996. Further revised first for Canadian audiences, then for playgoers in Washington, D.C. Pittsburgh, Los Angeles, and finally at the Goodspeed Opera House in Connecticut, *By Jeeves* opened on Broadway with a cast of thirteen and an orchestra of six. The helpless, hapless, yet wealthy Bertie Wooster (John Scherer) is forever reprieved by his resourceful valet Jeeves (Martin Jarvis) from multiple social calamities suffered only by the British idle rich. The particular whimsies of the nonsensical plot and madcap songs mattered less than did beloved Wodehouse characters with names like Stiffy Byng, Honoria Glossop, Bingo Little, Gussie Fink-Nottle, Harold "Stinker" Pinker, and Cyrus Budge III. Critics divided evenly on the show's merits, but the theatre-going public showed scant interest, and *By Jeeves* departed in eleven weeks.

Among the season's holiday offerings and limited runs, Madison Square Garden presented its eighth annual outing of Alan Menken's musical *A Christmas Carol* (27 November 2001), with Tim Curry as Scrooge. Gilbert & Sullivan were well represented in New York City Opera's repertory with *The Mikado* (15 September 2001, New York State), while the New York Gilbert & Sullivan Players celebrated their traditional two-week season at the start of the new year with *H. M. S. Pinafore, The Pirates of Penzance* and another *Mikado*. Lincoln Center Theater presented Barbara Cook in a solo program of **Mostly Sondheim** (14 January 2002, Vivian Beaumont) for a series of Sunday/Monday night performances.

As if Barbara Cook weren't enough of a reminder of Broadway's Golden Age, two legendary ladies of Broadway opened limited runs of solo shows to admiring audiences: **Beatrice Arthur on Broadway: Just Between Friends** (17 February 2002, Booth) and **Elaine Stritch at Liberty** (21 February 2002, Neil Simon). Beloved for her deadpan comic timing in Broadway comedies and in television's long-running *Maude* and *The Golden Girls*, Bea Arthur was accompanied by pianist Billy Goldenberg in songs from *Mame* (in which she appeared as Vera Charles opposite Angela Lansbury in 1966), *Gypsy*, *Threepenny Opera* (reprising her off-Broadway 1954 role as Lucy Brown), and Goldenberg's own *Ballroom*. But it was the comedy and career anecdotes, not her limited singing range, in which her performance excelled. Stritch's evening, a transfer from off-Broadway's Public Theatre (7 November 2001) in response to critical raves, was a more ambitious yet personal stroll through Broadway's literature of drama, comedy and musicals. *At Liberty* was devised by Stritch with an assist from *New Yorker* theatre critic John Lahr and the firm directorial hand of George C. Wolfe. Stritch regaled her audiences with stories of the early Actors Studio, Marlon Brando, Rock Hudson, Noël Coward, Ethel Merman, and Stephen Sondheim, and with songs from *Angel in the Wings, Goldilocks, Sail Away!,* and *Company.* At age seventy-six, clad in black tights and a loose-fitting white shirt, Stritch strutted and sang her way through an ambitious two and three-quarters hours of Broadway folklore, gossip, personal reminiscences, and nineteen songs, before taking her show on the road to London and to posterity on DVD. One last Broadway diva, Liza Minnelli, made an ill-conceived comeback with her sloppily assembled one-woman musical revue, **Liza's Back...** (31 May 2002, Beacon), which played a one-week engagement to her loyal cadre of fans.

Off-Broadway's long-running revue *One Mo' Time* (22 October 1979) attempted a Broadway revival on 6 March 2002 at the Longacre, but expired after three weeks. Its original creator, director, and star, Vernel Bagneris, returned in his original capacity as Papa Du, accompanied by three talented singers of jazz standards, blues and torchy double-entendre ditties, Roz Ryan, B. J. Crosby, and Rosalind Brown. Set in 1926 in the mythical New Orleans' Lyric Theatre for all-black audiences, this *One Mo' Time* lacked the smoky, crowded-café-table-with-drinks intimacy of the Village Gate original. The distance and formality of the proscenium staging muted its gritty impact, inviting unwelcome comparison to other more stylish Broadway revues such as *Black and Blue, Sophisticated Ladies, Eubie* and *Ain't Misbehavin'.* Though it won moderately favorable notices, the public showed no interest.

Sweet Smell of Success (14 March 2002, Martin Beck) was expected to be the great new American musical of the season, but came up short. The gifted John Guare adapted Ernest Lehman and Clifford Odets' film noir tale of New York hard-hitting newspaper columnist J. J. Hunsecker (John Lithgow), inspired by Walter Winchell, with music by Marvin Hamlisch and lyrics by Craig Carnelia. Hunsecker's young protégé Sidney Falco (Brian D'Arcy James) learns all about the dark side of newspaper reporting at the feet of his master. Hunsecker's half-sister Susan (Kelli O'Hara) enlists Falco's help in concealing her romance with talentless jazz musician Dallas (Jack Noseworthy), while Falco falls in love with her himself. But Falco's desperation to succeed proves a Faustian bargain when Hunsecker's possessiveness and machinations bring both men down at the musical's close. Nothwithstanding the A-list talents deployed, the musical adaptation muted the brilliance of the screen original. Not only were the writing and direction faulted, but some felt the indisputably likable Lithgow was miscast as the Machiavellian Hunsecker, despite his inspired and determined efforts. Nicholas Hytner, new executive director of London's Royal National Theatre, and Christopher Wheeldon, young resident choreographer of the New York City Ballet, offered ambitious staging. Hamlisch composed arguably the most sophisticated, textured score of his career, capturing New York's tough, jazz-inflected showbiz nightlife of the 1950s. Perhaps the darkness of *Sweet Smell's* story was ill-timed for a New York struggling to recover its balance in the wake of 9/11. Winning only a single Tony, for Lithgow's Hunsecker, *Sweet Smell* was gone before summer.

Much more to Broadway's liking, with its welcome optimism and patriotism, was the revival of Rodgers and Hammerstein's *Oklahoma!* (31 March 1943). Under the revelatory direction of Trevor Nunn, and with all new choreography by Susan Stroman to supplant the iconic original by Agnes de Mille, this production (21 March 2002, Gershwin) originated in London some four years earlier on the sprawling thrust stage of the Royal National Theatre's Olivier Theatre. Because producer Cameron Mackintosh's efforts to transfer the London company intact had been denied by Actors Equity, this revival retained only its Laurey (Josephina Gabrielle) and Jud Fry (Shuler Hensley). Its re-staging and re-casting for American audiences on the Gershwin's wide proscenium somehow dimmed the magic; one reviewer claimed that the mystery and fluidity of the London production had inexplicably evaporated. Patrick Wilson won the plum lead role of Curly, and Andrea Martin essayed the comedic role of Aunt Eller. Some transatlantic viewers preferred the UK production, with Hugh Jackman's pre-Hollywood star turn as Curly and Maureen Lipman's stern-faced Aunt Eller, performances which had been captured for all to see on home DVD. Nonetheless, Trevor Nunn's direction succeeded in taking a serious succeeded in taking a at the psychological motivations of the principal Curley-Laurey-Jud love triangle and proved innovative in other ways. Whereas Laurey had always been double-cast with a dancer "dream Laurey" for her ballet, Nunn and Stroman cast one dancer/actress (Gabrielle) in the part. Hensley's dark, brooding and complex Jud Fry made a compelling rival for Laurey's hand and won him a Tony Award for Best Supporting Actor in a Musical. Leave it to an English director to show Broadway how to stage this most American of musicals. *Oklahoma!* thrived for a year.

Encores, New York City Center's concert stagings of seldom-seen American musicals, celebrated its ninth season with *Carnival* (13 April 1961), *Golden Boy* (20 October 1964), and *The Pajama Game* (13 May 1954) at the New York City Center. *Carnival* (reappearing 21 February 2002) was exceptionally well-cast with soon-to-be Hollywood star Anne Hathaway as Lili, Brian Stokes Mitchell as Paul, Douglas Sills as Marco the Magnificent, and Debbie Gravitte as his codependent Rosalie. Jim Henson's company custom-designed Muppets for the puppet characters who talk to Lili. This feather-weight confection was imaginatively staged and choreographed by Kathleen Marshall, winning kudos as well for Michael Stewart's book and Bob Merrill's score. Arriving 21 March 2002, Walter Bobbie's staging of *Golden Boy* celebrated the strengths of the score and, free of the superstar casting of a Sammy Davis, Jr., revealed the weaknesses of its book. Alfonso Ribeiro, best remembered for his adolescent leap to stardom in *The Tap Dance Kid*, played Joe Wellington opposite Anastasia Barzee's Lorna Moon. Where once the contemporary shock of *Golden Boy*'s interracial love mirrored Sammy Davis's own personal life, the book's melodramatic twists proved less compelling thirty-eight years later. Encores closed its season with an amiable staging of *The Pajama Game* on 3 May 2002, starring Karen Ziemba and Brent Barrett and directed by John Rando.

In a rare exploration of neglected American operetta, the New York City Opera mounted the first ever revival of John Philip Sousa's **The Glass Blowers, or the American Maid** (16 April 2002, NewYork State), which had been staged two summers earlier at Glimmerglass. Written in 1909 and produced on Broadway for a mere two weeks as *The American Maid* (3 March 1913, Broadway), Leonard Liebling's libretto, restored by Jerrold Fisher and William Martin, satirized American jingoism, organized labor, self-made millionaires and social-climbing. More than a mere composer of the marches for which he is remembered today, Sousa crafted richly melodic score that aspired to a musical sophistication and complexity far superior to the prevailing Tin Pan Alley ditties and pseudo-operatic romances

of pre-World War I Broadway scores. Christopher Alden's stylish production was defeated only by the dismal acoustics of the vast New York State Theatre, a house twice as large as that for which the original was intended.

Thoroughly Modern Millie (18 April 2002, Marquis) proved to be the season's totally unexpected hit and Tony Award-winner for Best Musical. Re-thought and re-drawn top to bottom from a much-maligned 1967 film vehicle for Julie Andrews, this "new" Broadway musical retained only two numbers (the title song and "Jimmy") and a few vestiges of the plot from the original, while carpentering a determinedly old-fashioned, well-paced production replete with melody, gags, tap dancing, art deco spectacle, and boy-meets-girl sentiment. The plot had little suspense and plenty of hijinks: small-town dreamer Millie comes to big, bad New York in search of a wealthy husband, only to fall for a paperclip salesman. Sutton Foster fearlessly assumed the title role of Milly Dillmount, which she was originally hired to understudy and for which she won stardom and a Tony Award for Best Actress in a Musical. The scene-stealing night-club singer Muzzy Van Hossmere, originally conceived for Carol Channing on film but now reenvisioned as a faux Cotton Club-type star, was played by Sheryl Lee Ralph. Harriet Harris chewed the scenery as Mrs. Meers—once indelibly defined by Beatrice Lillie—a boarding house proprietor with a side business in sex slavery. Gavin Creel and Marc Kudisch assumed the dutiful roles of male suitors Jimmy Smith and Trevor Graydon. Michael Mayer offered a confident, brash traditional musical comedy staging, abetted by Rob Ashford's "peppy" choreography. Dick Scanlan wrote the new book in conjunction with the original screenplay's author, Richard Morris. Typical of the show's camp sense of humor were Mrs. Meers' two Chinese henchmen, whose song "Muquin" turned out to be Al Jolson's popular standard "Mammy" in Chinese with malaprop supertitles. Jeanine Tesori composed a pleasant faux-1920s musical comedy score of nine new songs to Scanlan's lyrics, with interpolations from Victor Herbert, Sir Arthur Sullivan, Walter Donaldson, and Tschaikovsky's "Nutcracker Suite." Despite less than rave reviews, *Millie* thrived for more than two years.

A late season revival of Sondheim & Lapine's *Into the Woods* (5 November 1987) snatched the Best Musical Revival Tony from the expected clutches of *Oklahoma!* Opening 30 April 2002 at the Broadhurst, reviewers and theatregoers welcomed director Lapine's revisitation of his musical synthesis of the Brothers Grimm stories, displaying a newfound appreciation for its fairytale world turned upside down. The intimacy of the Broadhurst, a simpler storybook set design, excellent casting and a familiarity with the score won this classic musical many new admirers. Its authors took the opportunity to modify their work in minor, subtle ways: they added a duet ("Our Little World") for the Witch and Rapunzel and shifted the dramatic focus from the Baker and his wife (Stephen DeRosa and Kerry O'Malley) to Cinderella (Laura Benanti) and her princes (Greg Edelman and Christopher Sieber). Milky-White, the cow, previously a cut-out on wheels, was now played by a live actor, Chad Kimball. The nominal starring role of the witch was played by Vanessa Williams, less enigmatically than the role's originator, Bernadette Peters. Most reviewers found this revival sunnier and more playful than the 1987 original, that is, more "family-friendly." *Variety* found its "intermittent silliness... more memorable than its murky musings on the pains and perils of maturity." But the sheer density and complexity of the narrative, and its profoundly sophisticated and adult musical score, ultimately limited its popularity to an eight month run.

Off-Broadway introduced three notable musicals. **tick... tick... boom!** (13 June 2001, Jane Street) opened as a posthumous gift from Jonathan Larson (creator of *Rent*), assembled by David Auburn from autobiographical materials about a young writer struggling to make his life in Manhattan work. It marked an auspicious career break for male lead Raúl Esparza as Jonathan, with Jerry Dixon as his best friend and Amy Spanger as the woman in their lives. Jason Robert Brown, who had written the much-admired *Parade* in 1998, offered an autobiographical account of a marriage in meltdown, **The Last Five Years** (3 March 2002, Minetta Lane), told both backwards and forwards. Norbert Leo Butz and Sherie Rene Scott were the unhappy/happy couple. *tick... tick... boom!* lasted six months, and *The Last Five Years* expired after two months, but both have since prospered in regional and international productions. In spite of critical ridicule from mostly male reviewers, **Menopause: The Musical** (4 April 2002, Theatre Four) found a captive female audience for a four-year run, followed by dozens of regional and international productions. Author Jeanie Linders created schematic roles (Power Woman, Earth Mother, Soap Star, Iowa Housewife) for a revusical of "women's issues," attaching parody lyrics to recognizable pop songs of the 1960s and 1970s.

In sum, the 2001-2002 season, although lacking in innovation and reliant upon recognizable film titles, and proven shows and stars, represented a brave recovery for an industry seriously wounded.

2002–2003

Broadway's season began with a most unorthodox revival, a fully staged Japanese-language production of Stephen Sondheim and John Weidman's *Pacific Overtures* (11 January 1976). Presented for a week's limited run (9 July 2002) by the Lincoln Center Festival in Avery Fisher Hall, a concert venue typically used for classical music, Amon Miyamoto's imaginative New National Theatre of Tokyo staging was recreated with an all-Japanese cast; English-language supertitles were introduced for American audiences. Miyamoto discreetly added a few women to the all-male cast, yet retained men as the Shogun's mother and the operator of the Kanagawa brothel. Sondheim's music was reorchestrated from twenty-four to seven instruments, affording it a brittle, Eastern sound. Miyamoto's staging discarded Harold Prince's original Kabuki touches, and instead embraced stylistic devices of classic Noh drama, with its use of masks and of men playing both male and female roles. Some missed the splendors of Florence Klotz's costumes and Boris Aronson's sets, with their elaborate paper dragons. But Emi Wada's costumes were wonderfully bizarre, with Commodore Perry as a scarecrow on stilts and Americans as hairy devils. Rumi Matsui's wooden temple set, on the other hand, used simple sliding screens to focus attention on the actors and the text. Linguistic barriers melted for theatregoers mostly familiar with the work, and the hard-working cast was stunned by American audiences' exuberant response, which contrasted sharply with the typical reserve of Japanese theatregoers. The theatrical apotheosis of the evening came with the unfurling of a giant American flag across the Hall's ceiling to mark the arrival of Commodore Perry and the subsequent Lion Dance; this upstaged even Act II's revisionist staging of "Next," with its newly added references to the atomic bombings of Hiroshima and Nagasaki. The dramatic irony of a Japanese production of an American musical about the discovery of Japan became a Rashomon-like theatrical prism, us watching them watching us. It was a multicultural musical theatre puzzle that Sondheim, Weidman, and Prince probably could never have imagined.

The season's musical blockbuster **Hairspray** (15 August 2002, Neil Simon) was greeted by unanimous critical huzzahs. This musical adaptation of John Waters' 1988 cult film, with its gently subversive book by Mark O'Donnell and Thomas Meehan and a retro 1960s pop score by Marc Shaiman and Scott Wittman, told the Cinderella story of a chubby girl from Baltimore, Tracy Turnblad (Marissa Jaret Winokur), who beats the odds to win the teenage boy of her dreams. The vehicle for her quest is Corny Collins' (Clarke Thorell) local pop music television show starring the heartthrob of her unrequited affection, Link Larkin (Matthew Morrison). Collins's show (loosely patterned after Dick Clark's *American Bandstand*) excludes not only blacks, but also fat girls like Tracy. The fun of the story stems from Tracy's efforts to turn the tables on the dark forces of prejudice, exemplified by Velma Von Tussle (Linda Hart) and her perfectly blond daughter Amber (Laura Bell Bundy), with the help of her pal Penny Pingleton (Kerry Butler) and her mom Prudy Pingleton (Jackie Hoffman, doubling as a gym teacher and matron). Sharing star billing with Tracy was her mother Edna Turnblad, played with restrained comic brilliance by Harvey Fierstein in drag; Dick Latessa offered a sweet cameo as Tracy's dad, Wilbur. Tracy's instinctively democratic impulses invite collaboration with the black kids, led by Seaweed (Corey Reynolds) and his mom Motormouth Maybelle (Mary Bond Davis). Jack O'Brien's stylish, fast-paced direction, Jerry Mitchell's propulsive choreography of 1960s dance crazes, David Rockwell's gloriously garish pink, orange, and purple cartoon sets, and William Ivey Long's extravagant costumes combined to turn *Hairspray* into a rousing entertainment. Shaiman and Wittman's score deftly captured the pop rhythm & blues (pre-Beatles) sound of 1962, with its rousing opening "Good Morning, Baltimore," the infectious "You Can't Stop the Beat," and a brief traditional soft-shoe duet for Wilbur and Edna, "Timeless to Me." *Hairspray* was also the first of many twenty-first century musicals to articulate the theme of girl empowerment, which attracted a huge new demographic to Broadway musical comedy. *Hairspray* ran for six and a half years, became a worldwide success in more than a dozen languages, and spawned a 2007 film remake.

Inspired in part by the enthusiastic response to the 1997 Encores revival, Roundabout Theatre offered its own revised adaptation of Rodgers & Hart's *The Boys from Syracuse* (23 November 1938) for a limited run, 18 August 2002 at the American Airlines Theatre. But Nicky Silvers' new book, Scott Ellis' direction, Rob Ashford's choreography, and Don Sebesky's new orchestrations afforded a mostly joyless evening. The two Antipholuses (Jonathan Dokuchitz and Tom Hewitt) and Dromios (Lee Wilkof and Chip Zien) were besotted with and mistaken by their respective women played by Lauren Mitchell, Erin Dilly, and Toni DiBuono (Georgia Engel made an unbilled cameo during the finale), but none could bring *The Boys from Syracuse* to comic life. In order to "sex up" the book, Silver inserted a chorus of Courtesans led by Jackée Harry, and assigned the chorines two Rodgers & Hart songs ("A Lady Must Live" from *America's Sweetheart* and "You Took Advantage of Me" from *Present Arms*). Typical of this production's misjudgement, the surefire trio "Sing for Your Supper" was expanded into a generic production number with courtesans and chorus. This revival suggested that perhaps George Abbott and Rodgers & Hart really knew best—even the Encores staging had been wise not to stray far from the original.

A similar fate greeted the long-aborning revision of Rodgers & Hammerstein's *Flower Drum Song* (1 December 1958), which arrived 17 October 2002 at the Virginia for a four-month run. Joseph Fields and Oscar Hammerstein's original book typified a uniquely outdated 1950s perception of race and Asian assimilation into mainstream American culture. Playwright David Henry Hwang, best known for his play *M. Butterfly* and the book to Disney's *Aida*, was commissioned to leave the show in its general historical period (now 1960, from the early 1950s in the original) and preserve the original score, but bring C. Y. Lee's original story into contemporary focus. The clash of the older and younger generations was retained and sharpened; for example, Hwang made the hero Ta (José Llana) disparaging of his father Wang's (Randall Duk Kim) love of traditional Peking opera. Mei-Lei (Lea Salonga) was less dewy-eyed and more assured as a newcomer from mainland China, while Linda Low (Sandra Allen) and Madam Liang (Jodi Long) exemplified different styles of assimilation, through show biz and corporate entrepreneurism, respectively. The new book satisfied few—for instance, Wang's sudden abandonment of his lifelong career in Chinese opera was less than plausible. Robert Longbottom's exceptionally cinematic staging and Robin Wagner's stunning stage design were major assets to a fascinating and controversial evening's entertainment.

Amour (20 October 2002, Music Box) was a translation by English playwright/director Jeremy Sams of a French musical, *Le Passe-Muraille*, with a through-sung score by Michel Legrand and book by Didier van Cauwelaert. Set in Paris in 1950, *Amour* told the mystical story of a young man, Dusoleil (Malcolm Gets), whose unrequited love for the beautiful Isabelle (Melissa Errico) enables him to walk through walls. Once his love is consummated, this inexplicable supernatural talent evaporates. This tender, fragile fable offered American theatregoers much charm and enchantment, but for many critics the story was inconsequential and slight. Perhaps something was "lost in translation" from the original. Although Gets and Errico were personable and appealing, the evening was never compelling; the ensemble of painter, policeman, whore, doctor, and prosecutor were little more than the usual French clichés. Legrand's musical idiom, so effective in his film *The Umbrellas of Cherbourg*, offered neither highs nor lows, but a seamless flow of music that became sameness. James Lapine's staging and Scott Pask's scenic design managed such technical feats as characters appearing to walk through walls, but the evening seldom managed to be anything more than merely pleasant. Much to the dismay of its champion and producer, Gerald Schoenfeld, *Amour* expired after two weeks.

L'Étoile, an 1877 French opera bouffe by Emanuel Chabrier, seen before in New York profoundly altered as *The Merry Monarch* (18 August 1890), was given a new English language presentation by the New York City Opera in repertoire (22 October 2002, New York State). *Amour*'s Jeremy Sams provided the translation, George Manahan conducted, and Mark Lamos, whose production had originated with New York's upstate Glimmerglass Opera, directed. Stylish casting and singing made for a delightful evening, although the director's coarse touch somewhat marred what was otherwise a gossamer entertainment.

Movin' Out (24 October 2002, Richard Rodgers) was conceived by its director/choreographer Twyla Tharp as a modern dance homage to pop songwriter Billy Joel. A virtuoso company of Tharp dancers performed to a compilation score performed by Joel-soundalike Michael Cavanaugh. Tharp devised a dramatic premise for the songs in which three buddies from Long Island, Eddie (John Selya), Tony (Keith Roberts) and James (Benjamin B. Bowman) all depart for the Vietnam War. Once James dies and the war ends, Eddie and Tony return

shattered; *Movin' Out* charts their personal and emotional odysseys, and ultimate reconciliation with the women in their lives, Brenda (Elizabeth Parkinson) and Judy (Ashley Tuttle). The sheer athleticism and poetry of Tharp's choreography took Broadway dance to previously unseen heights. Much of the audience fascination stemmed from the skill with which Tharp reimagined well-known Joel songs: "Shameless" became a pas de deux for Roberts and Parkinson, "Goodnight Saigon" a tour de force for John Selya, and "She's Got a Way." Even if *Movin' Out* was ·an untraditional musical entertainment, most critics and audiences responded with enthusiasm through its three-year run.

Russell Simmons' Def Poetry Jam (14 November 2002, Longacre) was a transfer to stage from television's HBO of a unique cultural hybrid phenomenon, a poetry "slam," in which nine contemporary poets try to top each other in a spontaneous performance competition. On stage it resembled a hip-hop/rap revue, with poetry creating its own music, matching verbal excitement with aural intensity in a mixture of solo and group recitations. Although never a capacity draw in its six-month run, *Def Poetry Jam* attracted a young, hip audience to the theatre, redefined modern poetry as theatre, won a Tony Award as the season's best Special Event, and toured nationally and internationally.

Comedian Jackie Mason offered his latest one-man comic riff, Prune Danish (22 October 2002, Royale) for a disappointing five-week run. Among the holiday offerings, Mandy Patinkin Celebrating Sondheim (2 December 2002) was a marathon of thirty-five Sondheim songs performed in one act with Paul Ford at the piano, performed on *Urinetown*'s dark nights at Henry Miller's. Madison Square Garden's traditional Christmas musical *A Christmas Carol* (1 December 1994) made its ninth annual appearance 5 December, with F. Murray Abraham starring as Scrooge.

Man of La Mancha (22 November 1965) reappeared in its first New York revival (5 December 2002, Martin Beck) without the original famed Albert Marre/Jack Cole staging and Howard Bay set design. Brian Stokes Mitchell starred as the weary poet and sage Cervantes who imagines himself to be the knight Don Quixote. Mary Elizabeth Mastrantonio assumed the double mantle of courtesan Aldonza and muse Dulcinea. Ernie Sabella as the dutiful Sancho followed his master to his fate. British director Jonathan Kent directed this controversial restaging with new costume and scenic design by

Paul Brown. Instead of the show's traditional empty stage, Brown's staging included a prison or pit surrounded by high walls and a drawbridge. Critics and audiences divided evenly as to the revival's merits, and Mitchell and company tilted at windmills for nine months.

La Bohème, Australian stage and film director Baz Luhrmann's acclaimed staging of Puccini's opera, was presented to New York audiences (8 December 2002, Broadway) as an ambitious musical theatre spectacle with rotating casts of three Mimis, three Rudolphos, two Musettas, and two Marcellos. On the one hand, an open-ended commercial engagement of the opera mounted as though it were a Broadway musical must be considered a success; it ran seven months. Without altering the music, Luhrmann reset the story in the 1950s, sped up the staging, cut two intermissions, cast youthful and talented singers, and adorned the production with hip super-titles (e.g. "Hang out with us"). Luhrmann's frequent set-design collaborator, Catherine Martin, used giant black-and-white photographs as well as bold flashes of color, such as a brilliant illuminated red sign advertising "L'Amour." Subtlety was abandoned for youthful chic. On the other hand, its producers and the public anticipated a lengthier run, given La Bohème's iconic status, its affiliation with the long-running Rent (which shares La Bohème's plot), and Luhrmann's high cinematic profile, success with the property on the Australian stage, and unabashed rebranding of Bohème as a youth-appeal show.

The following night, critical knives were drawn for Dance of the Vampires (9 December 2002, Minskoff), an American adaptation of the German success Tanz der Vampire, by Michael Kunze (book, lyrics) and Jim Steinman (music), itself a retelling of the 1967 Roman Polanski film The Fearless Vampire Killers. Shorn of its stylish Gothic European staging, Dance of the Vampires was reconceived for American tastes by its producers, original authors, and American bookwriter David Ives as a campy parody of itself. Despite seven weeks of previews to heal this muddled concept, and the substantial commercial draw of the original Phantom of the Opera, Michael Crawford (Count von Kroplock), Dance of the Vampires was critically lambasted. Who can forget the sight of jolly Alpine villagers extolling the virtues of garlic or Crawford persuading us that "Death Is Such an Odd Thing"? Vampires lasted seven weeks, no longer than it spent in previews.

Imaginary Friends (12 December 2002, Ethel Barrymore) was more of a play with music—six songs precisely—than a full-scale musical. Author Nora Ephron (Sleepless in Seattle, When Harry Met Sally...) created a fictional version of the celebrated rivalry between two tempestuous women authors, Lillian Hellman (Swoosie Kurtz) and Mary McCarthy (Cherry Jones), drawing on their own work. Harry Groener multitasked as all of the assorted men in their lives, be it husband, lover, father, friend, media gadfly, literary agent or publisher (Dashiell Hammett, Philip Rahv, James T. Farrell, Stephen Spender, Uncle Myers, Dick Cavett, and Max Hellman, respectively). Precisely why Ephron, her producers, and director Jack O'Brien believed this non-musical subject demanded six songs was unclear from the realized production. The pleasant, incidental score by Marvin Hamlisch and Craig Carnelia added a heightened sense of unreality, but little depth, to what was otherwise an amusing sling-fest of bitchery. These two literary lions departed after two months.

For its tenth season, New York City Center's Encores revived three neglected musicals with surprising results: House of Flowers (30 December 1954), The New Moon (19 September 1928), and No Strings (15 March 1962). A legend and a mystery since its original Broadway staging by Peter Brook and a brief Off-Broadway revival in 1968, House of Flowers has defied all efforts at its resurrection. This concert staging (13 February 2003) by Encores' artistic director-in-residence Kathleen Marshall, with a revised book by young African American playwright Kirsten Childs—whose Off-Broadway musical The Bubbly Black Girl Sheds her Skin won notice—failed to lift the curse. The fanciful tale of the rivalry between Madame Fleur (Tonya Pinkins), Madame Tango (Armelia McQueen) and their respective brothels never simmered to a boil; neither did the predicament of the youthful Ottilie (Nikki M. James). The appeal of the original Truman Capote short story, accompanied onstage by a much-admired Harold Arlen-Capote score, was rendered crass in this staging. Encores' first true operetta revival, The New Moon, was greeted with initial skepticism upon announcement, then unexpected critical glee when it opened on 27 March 2003. David Ives slimmed the book without sacrificing its story, its humor or romance, and Chicago-based director Gary Griffin did an able job of staging this swashbuckling romance seldom seen but for a New York City Opera production in 1988. Seasoned opera baritone Rodney Gilfry assumed the mantle of hero Robert Mission, and Christiane Noll sang his beloved Marianne. Burke Moses was Mission's incompetent rival, Captain Georges Duval, while the supporting servants Julie and Alexander were played by Lauren Ward and Peter Benson. Romberg and Hammerstein's score sounded thrilling, compensating for the melodramatic absurdities of the book. Playgoers roared with delight at Robert Mission's prescient remark: "A man may love his country, monsieur, and forswear its rulers." A bittersweet interracial romance by Richard Rodgers and Samuel Taylor, *No Strings* (returning 8 May 2003) had not been seen in more than forty years, and it was hoped that Encores could restore its place in the musical theatre repertoire with just a slight reworking of its book. David Ives again tidied the book; Ann Reinking directed and choreographed. Alas, Taylor's work emerged as tepid and witless, and its perception of interracial romance as shallow and insensitive, even for its moment in 1962. Rodgers' lyrics proved more workmanlike than notable, and Reinking's staging offered little revelation or joy. There was no discernible passion or romantic chemistry between the two leads, David Jordan (James Naughton) and Barbara Woodruff (Maya Days), leaving the audience to wonder what all the fuss or regret was about. The supporting cast of major Broadway talents (Len Cariou, Penny Fuller, Marc Kudisch, Emily Skinner) only highlighted the emptiness of the story.

Urban Cowboy (27 March 2003, Broadhurst) was an attempt to musicalize the popular 1980 John Travolta film, with a book written by Aaron Lathan, co-author of the original screenplay, and Philip Oesterman. Augmenting the three songs retained from the film ("Could I Have This Dance," "Lookin' for Love," "The Devil Went Down to Georgia") were nearly a dozen more specific to the plot by Jason Robert Brown, Bob Stillman, and Jeff Blumenkrantz. Even the best of the new (Brown's "That's How Texas Was Born" and "It Don't Get Better Than This," Blumenkrantz' "All Because of You") couldn't measure up to the country & western standards they evoked. Matt Cavanaugh assumed the thankless task of recreating Travolta's famous role as Bud, and Jenn Colella played his girl Sissy, originated by Debra Winger. Sally Mayes and Leo Burmeister offered comic relief as Aunt Corene and Uncle Bob. Despite ambitious direction from Lonny Price, audiences and critics thought a musical *Urban Cowboy* was a lousy idea, and the horse left the stable after eight weeks.

The New York City Opera revived its staging by Scott Ellis of Stephen Sondheim and Hugh Wheeler's classic *A Little Night Music* (25 February 1973) for eleven performances in repertory beginning 11 March. In spite of star-studded Broadway casting in all but one principal role (opera star Kristin Huxhold as child bride Anne Egerman), the vast spaces of the New York State Theatre diminished whatever joys could be found in this chamber operetta. Jeremy Irons and Juliet Stevenson as Fredrik Egerman and Desirée Armfeldt were virtuoso actors but middling singers; they were supported by Broadway pros Marc Kudisch (Count Carl-Magnus), Michelle Pawk (his wife Charlotte), Danny Gurwin (Fredrik's son Henrik), and Jessica Boevers (Petra, the maid).

Two major revivals vied for honors in the spring dash toward the Tony nominations: *Nine* (9 May 1982) and *Gypsy* (21 May 1959). Under the auspices of Roundabout Theatre, *Nine*, opening 10 April 2003 at the Eugene O'Neill, featured film star Antonio Banderas in his singing and Broadway stage debut. David Leveaux, better known as a stager of opera and classical plays, directed, with choreography by Jonathan Butterell. Difficult as it was to dispel the memory of Tommy Tune's original staging, with its imaginative use of chairs as props and set, Lawrence Miller's all-white set, and William Ivey Long's extravagant costumes, this revival of *Nine* reaffirmed the exceptional splendor of the show's stage conception and Maury Yeston score. Banderas may have lacked the expected operatic vocal range, but he delivered the requisite Latin machismo and charisma with astonishing skill and focus. Surrounded by a dazzling array of women, Banderas' Guido Contini resisted the entreaties of his wife Luisa (Mary Stuart Masterson), actress protégé Claudia (Laura Benanti), mistress Carla (Jane Krakowski, who won a Tony for the role), mother (Mary Beth Peil), first seducer (Myra Lucretia Taylor) and producer (Chita Rivera), among others. Notwithstanding some muddy staging, *Nine* won the Best Musical Revival Tony over its rivals, and prospered for eight months, longer than its scheduled run. *Gypsy*, opening 1 May 2003 at the Shubert with the improbable casting of the infinitely talented and appealing Bernadette Peters as embittered stage mother Rose, attempted a revisionist look at a well-known, much-loved and often revived musical. English stage and film director Sam Mendes, constrained by the original Jerome Robbins choreography—effectively recreated by Jerry Mitchell—delivered a darker yet sweeter Rose in Peters. Many argued she was truly miscast. Her performance was nonetheless brave, honest, vocally unprecedented, and always interesting, even if she was never the monster that Ethel Merman, Angela Lansbury, or Tyne Daly had been before her. John Dossett played her loyal, loving Herbie. This *Gypsy* defied the odds to run thirteen months.

A surprise transfer to Broadway after a limited winter run at the New Victory, **A Year with Frog and Toad** (13 April 2003, Cort) was the Children's Theatre Company of Minneapolis' musical adaptation of the children's book series by Arnold Lobel. Brothers Willie (book and lyrics) and Richard Reale (music) wrote the work, which evoked a spare *Wind in the Willows*-like tale of anthropomorphic friends Frog (Jay Goede) and Toad (Mark Linn-Baker). Despite modest critical approval and even a Tony nomination for Best Musical in a weak season, *Frog and Toad* could never quite shake its public perception as kiddie fare, and folded after a forced run of two months. **The Look of Love** (4 May 2003, Studio 54) was not the first effort to assemble a revue from the oeuvre of pop songwriters Burt Bacharach (music) and Hal David (lyrics). Both an off-Broadway revue, *Back to Bacharach and David* (25 March 1993, Club 53), and a regional theatre tryout, *What the World Needs Now* (2 April 1999, Old Globe, San Diego), had aspired and failed, and now bookwriter David Thompson, director Scott Ellis, choreographer Ann Reinking, and musical arranger David Loud conspired to get it right the third time around. Unfortunately, none of the elements—concept, staging or casting—pleased anyone, and *The Look of Love* suffered every nasty epithet ever tossed at the ridiculed genre of "jukebox musical." Distinctive Broadway talents Liz Callaway, Capathia Jenkins, Jonathan Dokuchitz, Eugene Fleming, Desmond Richardson, and Janine LaManna struggled to create any particular impression. Favorite songs such as "Alfie," "What's New Pussycat?," "One Less Bell to Answer," "Raindrops Keep Falling on My Head," "What the World Needs Now," "Do You Know the Way to San Jose?," and "This Guy's in Love with You" were dismissed as vapid, dull, and overly familiar. The revue expired quietly at the close of its Roundabout Theatre subscription run.

Off-Broadway musicals endured a sparse year, artistically and financially, leaving it to non-profit and subsidized venues to deliver experimental or new works from unknown writers. Lincoln Center Theater offered **A Man of No Importance** (10 October 2002, Newhouse), a stage adaptation of the 1994 British film by Terrence McNally (book),

Stephen Flaherty (music) and Lynn Ahrens (lyrics). It told the modest story of Alfie Byrne (Roger Rees), a theatre-obsessed bus driver in Dublin in 1964, whose homosexuality is revealed through his participation in amateur theatrical productions. After the epic scale of their *Ragtime*, McNally-Ahrens-Flaherty attempted a smaller, more intimate tale, which disappointed most critics with its inconsequentiality. **Tommy Tune: White Tie & Tails** (18 December, Little Shubert) marked not only the inauguration of a new Off-Broadway musical house from the Shuberts, but also an eagerly awaited return to the stage of a popular star. That both failed came as an unexpected surprise to all; Tune has since returned to directing, seldom performing now except for limited concert tours. The Little Shubert proved too expensive to book, and remains most often dark. **Avenue Q** (19 March 2003, Vineyard), an intimate, innovative, and very funny musical comedy combining puppets, video, and live actors, was a total surprise hit. It transferred to Broadway four months later (see 2003/4 season). **Zanna Don't!** (20 March 2003, John Houseman) imagined a parallel universe where homosexuality was the norm and straight men and women were a minority. Its clever book and score by Tim Acito and Alexander Dinelaris and fast-paced staging by Devanand Janki won many admirers, but *Zanna* couldn't survive the summer. Many industry observers were left to ponder whether Off-Broadway musicals could survive commercial runs at all, and indeed in seasons to come, many a small musical chose to gamble on Broadway, rather than wither in neglect Off-Broadway.

The 2002–2003 season sauntered to a close with a limited two-week run of TV political pundit Bill Maher in **Bill Maher: Victory Begins at Home**, really a stand-up monologuist testing the cross-over boundaries between television and stage (5 May 2003, Virginia). Overall, this very average Broadway season was dominated by competent revivals and two giant hits—*Hairspray* and *Movin' Out*—cobbled together from pop culture, but included little of serious consequence or enduring artistic merit.

2003–2004

The 2003–2004 Broadway season began with a pair of late July openings originating from non-profit auspices. Roundabout presented a limited engagement revival of *Big River: The Adventures of Huckleberry Finn* (25 April 1985, revival 24 July 2003 at the American Airlines) which originated as a co-production between California's Deaf West Theatre and Los Angeles' Mark Taper Forum. Under Jeff Calhoun's skillful staging, the production was simultaneously sung and performed in American Sign Language, with several of the principal roles (Silas; Miss Watson; Joanna Wilkes; Huck Finn, played by Tyrone Giordano) performed by non-speaking actors. Michael McElroy and Michael Arden as Jim and Tom Sawyer, respectively, both signed and spoke their roles. The wonder of rediscovering Twain's familiar classic was in the production's dynamic new approach to old-fashioned storytelling. This imaginative staging concept won *Big River* a new generation of admirers.

Avenue Q (31 July 2003, John Golden) boasted a team of unknown actors, writers, director, and designers, as well as a raft of rave reviews from its spring off-Broadway launch at the Vineyard. Could a small-scale, sophomoric musical comedy, recognizable as an adult-themed send-up of television's popular *Sesame Street*, open during the dog days of summer and find enduring success on Broadway? More rave reviews, capacity houses, and a multi-year run proved that *Avenue Q* was a true surprise and a refreshingly original work. Jeff Whitty's book, Robert Lopez and Jeff Marx's score, and Rick Lyons' puppets depicted the everyday lives of the residents of Avenue Q, a fictional, but Queens-like, outer-borough of New York City. *Avenue Q* looked like a very risky theatrical endeavor at first glance: (1) its principal singer-actors needed to be equally skilled puppeteers, (2) its flat, cartoon set looked like that of a children's television show, (3) the production required a complex and expensive mix of live action, song and video, and (4) its use of puppets ran the risk of discouraging its intended adult audience. But the skillful quality of the writing, performances, and direction combined to present an imaginative and charming musical comedy. Its book took on political correctness with a brashness that would make Mel Brooks proud. Its perky score had much of the edgy, sing-song charm of television's foul-mouthed *South Park*, with titles like "It Sucks to Be Me," "The Internet is for Porn," and "Everyone's a Little Bit Racist." In the season's end Tony Award sweepstakes, *Avenue Q* played the David to *Wicked*'s Goliath, and stole the Best Musical award.

One of Off-Broadway's most popular and longest running musicals, *Little Shop of Horrors* (22 July 1982) made its much-anticipated Broadway debut on 2 October 2003 at the Virginia. The pulp-fiction story of Audrey II, the hungry plant that devours Seymour, Audrey, Mushnik, and many other denizens of Skid Row, had by now assumed a camp classic status; its audience, like that of *The Rocky Horror Show*, knew every plot twist, if not every song. Veteran musical comedy stager Jerry Zaks (last revivals of *Guys and Dolls* and *A Funny Thing Happened on the Way to the Forum*) rescued the production from its troubled Florida tryout, re-cast all but one of its leads, and brought in a stylish, flashy, and entertaining production. Hunter Foster, the hero of *Urinetown*, assumed the role of Seymour, and Kerry Butler, late of *Hairspray*, played the archetypal dumb blond, Audrey. Douglas Sills more than quadrupled as Orin the mad dentist, Bernstein, Luce, Snip, and everyone else. All but a handful of critics greeted *Little Shop* with glee, content that the scruffy charm of the original off-Broadway production had not been lost. But a few lone dissenters carped that the $10 million revival had succumbed to glitz ("genus Mackintoshia, species superspectacularii"), and that the bargain basement wonders of Roger Corman's 1960 film and the subversive, dirty, and dangerous edges of the original musical had been polished to a high gloss. This *Little Shop* prospered modestly for eleven months, but never became the super smash everyone had hoped and many had expected.

A multimedia revue, **Sinatra—His Voice, His World, His Way** (15 October 2003, Radio City Music Hall), plagued by technical mishaps, played a one-week stint, combining authentic archival film and television footage, enhanced Sinatra studio vocals, singers, dancers (the Rockettes), and a live forty-piece orchestra. With guitarist John Pizzarelli as host, the evening was an amiable stroll through Sinatra iconography and greatest hits. An oversize Sinatra loomed onscreen above the tiny performers below. Unsurprisingly, the voice on screen upstaged the actors on stage, in spite of director Des McAnuff's imaginative efforts to reconcile the disparate elements.

The late Peter Allen, Australian pop superstar, fared somewhat better with his musical biography **The Boy from Oz** (16 October 2003, Imperial), which became a smash hit because of the charisma of its lead, Hugh Jackman. *The Boy from Oz* had originated in Australia in 1998, with Todd McKenney as its lead and a book by the late playwright Nick Enright. Because local-boy-turned-international-star Peter Allen is not the household name in America that he is in Australia, American playwright Martin Sherman revised the book for American consumption. Most critics dismissed Sherman's book as mere show business clichés, with which twenty-one of Peter Allen's songs (including five from his musical *Legs Diamond*) were skillfully interpolated with mixed results. Some songs from Allen's catalogue ("When I Get My Name in Lights," "Everything Old Is New Again," "I Go to Rio," "The Best That You Can Do ([Theme from Arthur]") lent themselves well to the presentational demands of the script. Conversely, out-of-context ballads were less persuasive when reassigned to book-driven moments for characters like Judy Garland, Liza Minnelli, and Allen's dead lover, Greg Connell. Jackman's unflinching, fearless, and joyously uninhibited performance galloped over the hackneyed book, undistinguished staging by Philip William McKinley and Joey McKneely, and mediocre sets and costumes from the usually infallible Robin Wagner and William Ivey Long. This Jackman vehicle built to a capacity draw over its eleven-month run, as long as its star was willing to stay. Jackman later toured Australia in an arena-style restaging, a personal triumph.

Based on Gregory Maguire's best-selling 1995 prequel to L. Frank Baum's *The Wizard of Oz*, **Wicked** (30 October 2003, Gershwin) opened to mixed reviews but swiftly built into a massive, international hit. Winnie Holzman's adaptation slimmed Maguire's dense, sodden plot about two rival young witches, the candy pink and white do-gooder Glinda (Kristin Chenoweth), and the green-fleshed, idealistic, and misunderstood Elphaba (Idina Menzel). *Wicked*'s book, which functioned as a back-story and apology for *The Wizard of Oz*'s unfairly maligned Wicked Witch of the West, was saddled with political symbolism of freedom vs. fascism, sermons on the battle between good and evil, a multitude of extraneous characters, and the requisite over-amplified power ballads of simulated dramatic depth. Its enduring popularity and distinction lie in its vision of a world dominated and defined by its women; the men, on the other hand, are all inconsequential or weak, whether the elfin Boq (Christopher Fitzgerald), the witches' nominal love interest Fiyero (Norbert Leo Butz), Doctor Dillamond (William Youmans), or the ineffectual Wizard himself (Joel Grey). The $14 million production budget was reflected in the lavish sets and large cast of thirty. Among the Stephen Schwartz songs to emerge from the score with any enduring impact were "Defying Gravity" (Act I finale), "What Is This Feeling?" (the witches' duet of mutual love and loathing), "Popular" (Glinda's philosophy), and their Act II duet of reconciliation, "For Good." After

years of capacity business, *Wicked*'s enduring appeal can be attributed to the legend of Oz and a fascination with all things Oz, its empowerment of women, and its traditional Broadway offering of big-budget family entertainment.

Pop icon Boy George's autobiographical musical **Taboo** enjoyed a modest fifteen-month London run before it opened on Broadway 13 November 2003 at the Plymouth. Set in London's dance clubs of the 1980s, *Taboo* recounted Boy George's (Euan Morton) emergence as a young, openly gay singer-songwriter, contrasted with the decline and death from AIDS of performance artist Leigh Bowery (played by George O'Dowd, the real Boy George), as narrated by nightclub owner Philip Sallon (Raúl Esparza). English director and co-conceiver Christopher Renshaw, book author Mark Davies (whose work was revised for American audiences by Charles Busch), choreographer Mark Dendy, and designers Tim Goodchild, Mike Nicholls, and Bobby Pearce captured the louche excesses and extravagantly tacky milieu of the 1980s British rock scene. Boy George's score consisted of new songs plus some older pop music chestnuts from his catalogue, including "Karma Chameleon" and "Do You Really Want to Hurt Me?" Producer Rosie O'Donnell optioned the modest, tatty English production, revised and inflated to $10-million Broadway proportions. While a distracted O'Donnell defended herself in court in an unrelated lawsuit, *Taboo* struggled through three weeks of turbulent previews, and opened to reviews ranging from mixed to negative. Although admired by some for the bravery of its subject, *Taboo*'s book offered a muddled story divided between Boy George and Leigh Bowery and filled with bitchery, pathos, and too many ballads. Despite O'Donnell's unwavering support, *Taboo* collapsed after three months.

Broadway's favorite joke-meister Jackie Mason attempted a musical revue variation upon his traditional solo show format, **Laughing Room Only** (19 November 2003, Brooks Atkinson). Despite help from five supporting, willing farceurs, Jackie Mason's patter seemed as fresh as a stale bagel; Dough Katsaros' forgettable songs didn't help. Unlike the full-season runs of Mason's six previous Broadway outings, *Laughing Room Only* suffered universal pans and departed after two weeks.

Wonderful Town (25 February 1953) had been so warmly received on the occasion of its Encores! revival almost four years earlier that Roger Berlind and *Chicago* producers Barry and Fran Weissler elected to re-mount, and in part re-cast, that production for an open run at the Martin Beck (23 November 2003). Once again, Donna Murphy thrilled and dazzled critics and audiences with her droll Ruth Sherwood, while Jennifer Westfeldt, star and co-author of the film *Kissing Jessica Stein* (2001, directed by Charles Herman-Wurmfeld), made her Broadway debut as sister Eileen. Kathleen Marshall directed and choreographed Encores-style, with the upstage orchestra under the bright, brassy direction of Rob Fisher. During its run, the Martin Beck Theatre was posthumously renamed the Hirschfeld, after beloved *New York Times* caricaturist Al Hirschfeld. With Brooke Shields assuming the lead role at the start of its second year, this *Wonderful Town* ran happily amuck for fifteen months, only forty-six performances fewer than the original Rosalind Russell 1953 smash.

Among the family-friendly holiday offerings, Madison Square Garden presented its tenth annual *A Christmas Carol* (1 December 1994), with Jim Dale as Scrooge, giving forty-seven performances in twenty-four days from 4 December.

Never Gonna Dance (4 December 2003, Broadhurst) represented a good-faith effort to create a new stage musical from the Fred Astaire/Ginger Rogers/Jerome Kern 1936 film *Swing Time*. Jeffrey Hatcher authored the stage adaptation, while director Michael Greif and choreographer Jerry Mitchell attempted to recapture the effortless charm and terpsichorean feats of the original. Unknown but "brave, likable young dancers" Noah Racey and Nancy Lemonager stepped into Astaire and Rogers' shoes as Lucky Garnett and Penny Carroll. Karen Ziemba outshown nominal star Lemonager as her sidekick Mabel, while Peter Gerety won laughs as Alfred G. Morgenthal, a stockbroker down on his luck. But Hatcher's book flattened its principals into ordinary archetypes, and the talented supporting cast (Ron Orbach, Peter Bartlett, David Pittu, Eugene Fleming, Deidre Goodwin) struggled to illuminate minor characters who were mere clichés. Genuine dramatic conflict was missing from the story of Lucky's attempts to lose his fiancée's affections in order to replace them with Penny's. Lemonager and especially Racey were capable dancers but not quite stars. The art deco glamour of 1930s Manhattan appeared merely ordinary or ersatz in Robin Wagner's sets. Mitchell's choreography seldom conveyed anything meaningful—many of the production numbers would have routinely fit into *42nd Street* or any other period musical set

in Manhattan. Five standards from Jerome Kern's original film score ("Pick Yourself Up," "The Way You Look Tonight," "Waltz in Swing Time," "A Fine Romance," "Never Gonna Dance") were augmented by twelve additional Kern titles, of which four were truly unknown. The overwhelmingly mixed notices condemned *Never Gonna Dance* to an eleven-week run.

Gilbert & Sullivan were well represented this season, with *The Mikado* returning to the New York City Opera repertory for the first time since 2001, and the New York Gilbert & Sullivan Players offering modest revivals of *Iolanthe*, *H. M. S. Pinafore* and *The Mikado* at the New York City Center for a two-week January season from 9 January 2004.

Encores' tenth annual season at New York City Center offered New Yorkers one Gershwin rarity, *Pardon My English* (20 January 1933), sandwiched between two well-known titles, *Can-Can* (7 May 1953) and *Bye Bye Birdie* (14 April 1960). *Can-Can* has always been admired for its Cole Porter score ("I Love Paris" and "C'est Magnifique" among others) and derided for its Abe Burrows book, a cheesy American smirk masquerading as French sensuality. A perfect candidate for Encores treatment, *Can-Can* opened 13 February 2004 with a slimmed libretto. Director Lonny Price and star Patti LuPone (Pistache) emphasized *Can-Can*'s strengths and diminished its weaknesses. Decked out in brilliant reds and ample décolletage, LuPone commanded the stage like a fire truck responding to seven alarms. *The New York Times* noted the "newly burnished suppleness" to her once strident voice and "a refreshing delicacy" to her comic timing. Charlotte d'Amboise assumed the delectable dance lead originally played by Gwen Verdon, Claudine, while *Can-Can*'s colorless male roles fell to Michael Nouri (Aristede), Reg Rogers (Boris), Paul Schoeffler (Hilaire), and Eli Wallach (Paul Barriere).

Undoubtedly the most obscure title ever presented in Encores' history, *Pardon My English*'s incomprehensibly silly book centers on a British secret agent (Brian d'Arcy James) who suffers amnesia when hit on the head, and finds himself transported to Dresden. Prohibition is the satiric target, and in a last gasp of pre-Nazi-era humor, Germans are depicted as clumsy, beer-drinking fools. Under the playfully giddy direction of Gary Griffin, Herbert Fields' and Morrie Ryskind's original book was reconstituted from extant scraps by Encores!' ever-resourceful resident comic genius, David Ives. *Pardon My English*, which opened

25 March 2004, afforded audiences the opportunity to hear some Gershwin chestnuts ("Isn't It a Pity?," "My Cousin in Milwaukee," and "The Lorelei") and many wonderful unknowns ("I've Got to be There," "Freud and Jung and Adler") in their intended dramatic contexts and with their original orchestrations. Emily Skinner channeled Ethel Merman and Marlene Dietrich as the robust Polish-accented diva Gita, Jennifer Laura Thompson charmed as the ingénue heroine Frieda, and Rob Bartlett struggled to be funny as Commissioner Bauer. Encores!' season closer on 6 May was a safe choice, Strouse & Adams' *Bye Bye Birdie*, which had oddly escaped any previous Broadway revival despite a 1963 film, popular Tommy Tune sixteen-month national tour in 1991–1992, and 1995 television adaptation. Jerry Zaks directed, Casey Nicholaw choreographed, and Rob Fisher conducted this bright, breezy, faithful, and fun revival. Broadway's favorite virtuosic dancer-comedienne Karen Ziemba (Rosie) assumed a role once tailored to Chita Rivera, and the ever-appealing Daniel Jenkins, of *Big River* and *Big*, took on the Dick Van Dyke role (Albert). Broadway stalwarts filled supporting roles: Encores!' director of *Chicago*, Walter Bobbie (Harry MacAfee), Doris Roberts of stage and television (Mae Peterson), Jessica Grové (Kim MacAfee), and Victoria Clark (Doris MacAfee). What was missing from the enjoyable candy-floss production was any sense that rock 'n' roll was dangerous or in any way subversive. Bob Gaynor's performance as Conrad Birdie, dubbed "just a low grade earthquake" by *The New York Times*, did nothing to help matters. With no momentum for a Broadway transfer, *Birdie* would have to wait five more years for its next New York appearance.

Fiddler on the Roof (22 September 1964) had always been produced on Broadway with Jerome Robbins' direction and choreography and Boris Aronson's sets faithfully recreated. This new revival, opening 26 February 2004 at the Minskoff, with staging by British director David Leveaux, promised a fresh, if inevitably controversial, approach, notwithstanding Jonathan Buttrell's restaging of Robbins' choreography. Tom Pye's unit set consisted of a bare wooden stage without walls, with a row of feeble birch trees on the horizon; a twenty-six-piece orchestra was placed not in the pit, but upstage left. Its Tevye (Alfred Molina) wasn't Jewish, but a gifted English classical stage and film actor of Spanish-Italian descent; he was succeeded by openly gay actor and writer Harvey Fierstein,

opposite Rosie O'Donnell as his wife Golde. What emerged from all these risks, revisions, and changes (even a new song, "Topsy Turvy," was added for Yente, the matchmaker, by reunited musical team Jerry Bock and Sheldon Harnick) was an affirmation of *Fiddler on the Roof*'s enduring stature as a work of classic musical theatre. Some critics complained that this *Fiddler*'s rough edges had been smoothed or sanitized, that the Jewish culture and customs (for instance, separation of the sexes) were more musical comedy than authentic—for instance, *The New York Times*' Ben Brantley titled his review "A Cozy Little McShtetl." This new, if not improved, *Fiddler* prospered for almost two years.

Assassins (27 January 1991), Stephen Sondheim and John Weidman's off-Broadway *success d'estime*, returned in Roundabout Theatre Company's full-scale production for a twelve-week Broadway run at Studio 54 on 22 April 2004. Originally scheduled for the 2001–2002 season, then postponed after 9/11, Joe Mantello directed this musical exploration of the psyches and psychoses of nine presidential assassins. Sondheim and Weidman probed in dialogue and song the tormented minds of these frustrated, misunderstood or disenfranchised souls driven to extreme acts of violence. Imaginatively designed by Robert Brill as if set in a third-rate carnival, and impressively cast with top Broadway talent, *Assassins* proved difficult to like but easier to admire. James Barbour (Leon Czolgosz, William McKinley's assassin), Alexander Gemignani (John Hinckley, Ronald Reagan's would-be killer), Denis O'Hare (Charles Guiteau, James Garfield's assassin), Jeffrey Kuhn (Giuseppe Zangara, Franklin Delano Roosevelt's attempted assassin), Mario Cantone (Samuel Byck, Richard Nixon's failed killer), Mary Catherine Garrison (Squeaky Fromme, Gerald Ford's would-be killer), Becky Ann Baker (Sara Jane Moore, another attempted Ford assassin), Michael Cerveris (John Wilkes Booth), and Neil Patrick Harris (Lee Harvey Oswald) all presented monstrously unhappy, deranged people with shocking, acerbic clarity. Tying these protagonists together were Marc Kudisch (Playground Proprietor) and Neil Patrick Harris (doubling as Balladeer). Sondheim and Weidman drew thematic parallels and contrasts between their principals in the seductive, toe-tapping "Everybody Has the Right to be Happy." The mournful 1960s pop ballad "Unworthy of Your Love" explored the have-nots' eerie obsession with celebrity. Transcending the revue-like structure, Weidman's single scary, if not altogether persuasive, dramatic conceit placed the ghost of Booth at the Dallas Book Depository, urging an uncertain Oswald to pull the trigger on Kennedy, so that Oswald may live on in infamy rather than obscurity. At the end of the evening, if Sondheim and Weidman's insights were predatory speculations about people best forgotten, *Assassins* succeeded in making its viewers thoroughly uncomfortable. Controversial yet exciting and rewarding for many critics (twelve favorable, three mixed, and three negative reviews), the very repugnance of its subject kept *Assassins* from achieving a longer popular run.

Bombay Dreams (29 April 2004, Broadway) brought the conventions of India's Bollywood film musical spectaculars to the Broadway stage via London's West End, where it originated under the aegis of Andrew Lloyd Webber for a two-year run. Its book, by Meera Syal, told a traditional tale of an Indian boy, Akaash (Manu Narayan), from the slums of Bombay, whose dream of starring in a Bollywood film miraculously comes true. Typically, he ultimately wins the heart of his true love Priya (Anisha Nagarajan) despite the machinations of his scheming film costar Rani (Ayesha Dharker). He also defeats his rival Vikram (Deep Katdare) and the forces of corporate greed who would demolish his ancestral neighborhood for profit. India's best-known pop composer, A. R. Rahman, delivered a catchy, tuneful score of ballads and dance novelties, culminating in the spectacular filming scene, "Shakalaka Baby." Don Black's insipid lyrics, however, added little, and director Steven Pimlott and choreographer Anthony Van Laast reproduced their London staging without inspiration. This Bollywood fable of improbable coincidences was adorned with the requisite clichés of the genre: the hyper-athletic hero, duels to the death, hero's loving mother (cookbook author Madhur Jaffrey), all-knowing eunuch, eruption of water fountains at climactic moments, and the nonstop visual spectacle of Indian music and dance. Notwithstanding American "improvements" to the book by Thomas Meehan and an uncredited assist on the lyrics by David Yazbek, American critics disparaged the show as synthetic, bland and uncompelling ("A Bollywood of bubblegum," "Coloring by the Numbers," "Amazing, technicolor...dud?"), *Bombay Dreams* enjoyed a forced run and moderate commercial success for eight months.

Caroline, or Change (2 May 2004, Eugene O'Neill) proved to be the most ambitious musical of the season, transferring to Broadway following a two-month off-Broadway run at the Public Theater.

Tony Kushner, the much-lauded author of the epic play *Angels in America*, attempted his first musical, the finished libretto for which was assigned to Jeanine Tesori for a musical score. Drawn from his own experiences growing up Jewish in America's racially divided South during the turmoil of the mid-1960s, Kushner's story told of the contentious relationship between an eight-year-old boy, Noah Gellman (Harrison Chad), and the household's African-American maid Caroline Thibodeaux (Tonya Pinkins). Noah turns to Caroline because of the remoteness of his widowed father, Stuart Gellman (David Costabile), and his new stepmother, Rose Stopnick Gellman (Veanne Cox). Conflict flares when Rose punishes Noah for leaving spare change in his pocket by telling Caroline to take whatever he leaves there, until, calamitously, a $20 bill goes missing. These domestic crises made for an unlikely musical play, but Kushner's prolific imagination probed his characters' emotions and flaws in mostly free verse, through-sung style. Tesori provided an eclectic pastiche score ranging from Motown to Mozart, encompassing traditional Broadway, rock 'n' roll, children's songs, and rhythm and blues; nonetheless, many viewers found the score bland and inconsistent. Director George C. Wolfe elicited complex, tender performances from his cast, but both critics and audiences were sharply divided as to the production's merits. Anika Noni Rose won the Tony for Best Supporting Actress in a Musical for her role as Emmie, Caroline's rebel daughter. Propelled to Broadway on the strength of Kushner's reputation and raves from the toughest critics, Ben Brantley (*New York Times*) and John Heilpern (*New York Observer*) during its off-Broadway run, *Caroline, or Change* struggled bravely to win a broader audience during its four-month run.

Rounding out the spring revivals, New York City Opera brought back its popular Hal Prince staging of Stephen Sondheim's *Sweeney Todd: The Demon Barber of Fleet Street* (1 March 1979) for eleven performances beginning 9 March 2004. London's reigning diva Elaine Paige played Mrs. Lovett, while Timothy Nolan and Mark Delevan alternated as Sweeney Todd. The New York Philharmonic offered four performances of Leonard Bernstein's *Candide* (1 December 1956) at Avery Fisher Hall. Lonny Price's semi-staged production placed the orchestra (under the direction of Marin Alsop) in the center of the stage, surrounded by Voltaire's characters and their wild adventures. A starry combination of Broadway and opera talents enlightened and entertained: Kristin Chenoweth (Cunegonde), Paul Groves (Candide), Sir Thomas Allen (Pangloss), Patti LuPone (Old Woman), Jeff Blumenkrantz (Maximilian), and Janine LaManna (Paquette). Price's inventive direction maintained an animated pace, but his updated references and interpolated jokes were deemed crude and vulgar for Philharmonic tastes. *Candide*'s original Cunegonde offered her own one-woman revue, **Barbara Cook's Broadway** (28 March 2004, Vivian Beaumont), a tour of Broadway's best in American popular song from 1923–1974, through several dark nights at the Lincoln Center venue.

Off-Broadway musicals posted merely an average year; apart from the Broadway transfer of the aforementioned *Caroline, or Change*, only four shows achieved substantial runs. As a follow-up to their long-running success, *I Love You! You're Perfect! Now Change*, authors Joe DiPietro and Jimmy Roberts wrote a formulaic sequel about marital relationships, **The Thing About Men** (27 August 2003, Promenade), which had nothing to say that hadn't been said better before; despite that, the public rallied for a seven-month run. Another five-character musical, **The Musical of Musicals—The Musical!** (16 December 2003, York), prospered far longer in three engagements with its exhaustive self-parody of the musical comedy idiom. Eric Rockwell (music) and Joanne Bogart (lyrics) told the same archetypal musical comedy plot in five contrasting styles: Rodgers & Hammerstein, Stephen Sondheim, Jerry Herman, Andrew Lloyd Webber, and Kander & Ebb. **Fame on 42nd Street** (7 November 2003, Little Shubert) revisited the *Fame* franchise already exhausted by the television series and 1980 feature film. Its youthful, high-energy cast sang predictably of their hopes and dreams for eight months in spite of tepid reviews. **Toxic Audio in Loudmouth** (18 April 2004, John Houseman) exploited five a cappella voices in imitation of musical instruments; the gimmick wore thin after seven months. In conclusion, the 2003–2004 Broadway season was both prosperous and inventive, a healthy recovery for the Broadway musical.

2004–2005

Lincoln Center Theater opened its season with **The Frogs** (22 July 2004, Vivian Beaumont), previously adapted from Aristophanes in 1974 by Burt Shevelove and Stephen Sondheim for a one-week run, originally performed by the Yale Repertory Theatre in their university swimming pool. This revision by actor Nathan Lane as a vehicle for himself, with Susan Stroman as director-choreographer, eschewed the aquatics, added six songs, and expanded the undergraduate novelty to a full evening's entertainment. As in the time of Aristophanes (405 BC), Shevelove (1974) and now Lane (2004), the state is plagued by war and poor leadership. Dionysus (Lane), god of both wine and drama, travels with his aide Xanthias (Roger Bart) to Hades in search of a playwright who can solve the world's problems. With the help of the boatman Charon (John Bynum), Herakles (Burke Moses), and an effete Pluto (Peter Bartlett), Dionysus pits the intellect of George Bernard Shaw (Daniel Davis) against the sentiments of Shakespeare (Michael Siberry). Sondheim's consummate skill and wit promised an erudite score, but there was little reason why a trip to hell or a debate between Shaw and Shakespeare should sing; nor did they. Stroman deployed animated Greek statues, a chorus of busty babes, frogs bungee-jumping, imaginative otherworldly sets by Giles Cadle, indeed every trick in the book to make *The Frogs* fun. But neither the comic ripostes of Lane and Bart, the staging wizardry of Stroman, the ample resources of Lincoln Center Theater, nor the melodic gifts of Sondheim could make *The Frogs* succeed as a popular entertainment. This evening of shtick masquerading as classical theatre played out its scheduled three-month run.

Luis Bravo's dance revue *Forever Tango* (19 June 1997) returned to the Shubert (24 July 2004) for a fifteen-week summer run, having toured the world for a seven-year interim. Even if this modest staging (fourteen dancers, twelve musicians onstage) of virtuosic couples seldom matched the elegant intensity of 1985's *Tango Argentino*, it nonetheless afforded an enjoyable summer entertainment.

Dracula, the Musical (19 August 2004, Belasco) marked the first of many musical theatre nadirs this season. With nary a credit to the story's original author Bram Stoker, Christopher Hampton and Don Black wrote the deadpan book and lyrics, Frank Wildhorn composed the pop-opera score, and Des McAnuff directed at a frantic pace. All of the requisite clichés of Transylvania Victoriana—the obligatory flying on wires, blood-sucking vampires, insipid female victims, bodice ripping, and horror movie sound effects—were dutifully exploited and unimaginatively attached to a lame storyline fitted out with forgettable power ballads. Black's lyrics were worse than what he had written for *Bombay Dreams*: "The fear and the desire, I was on fire, the ground moved as we kissed, I wish I could stay in the mist." Another gem: "We don't have to go down that road, we don't have to shoulder that great load." Tom Hewitt, having survived a year as Frank 'N' Furter in *The Rocky Horror Show*, played the eponymous hero, while two of Broadway's finest ingénues, Melissa Errico and Kelli O'Hara, were his victims Mina Murray and Lucy Westenra. Critics were unanimous in their contempt, finding this *Dracula* more boring than fun to laugh at, unlike *Dance of the Vampires*. Headlines such as "It sucks!," "Fresh kill on Broadway," "The Bat Awakens, Stretches, Yawns" had a withering effect on the box office. Its producers, Dodger Productions and Joop van den Ende, mistakenly supposing their product had international prospects, kept *Dracula* open for a forced run of four months.

Brooklyn, the Musical (21 October 2004,. Plymouth) suffered a similarly contemptuous reception from the reviewers ("Jump off the bridge," "A catastrophe of naïveté," and "Fuhgeddaboudit"), but eked out an eight-month run because of its talented cast of five principals and a vocal ensemble of three, low operating costs and a scruffy underdog advertising campaign. Set in a slum corner underneath the Brooklyn Bridge, the set and costumes were a catalogue of recycled plastic, metal and detritus; its cast members all doubled as "City Weeds." First-time authors Mark Shoenfeld and Barri McPherson told a tale of a French orphan named Brooklyn (Eden Espinosa) in search of her biological father Taylor (Kevin Anderson); Brooklyn's mother Faith (Karen Olivo) hanged herself, leaving the child with a sole clue, a lullaby. With the help of a magical Streetsinger (Cleavant Derricks), Brooklyn finds her Vietnam-veteran father, with whom she reunites tearfully, and predictably, after a climactic singing competition where she proves her talent. This less-than-plausible fable of one-dimensional dramaturgy afforded no more than a pretext for forgettable pop ballads of "unearned emotional peaks." Among the quoted lyrics: "Sometimes with our tears we can water roses," "There's a story behind those empty eyes that no one wants to know," and "When you change someone's life, you change your own." That such bromidic sentiments found an audience was due to the appeal of the cast, whose careers survived *Brooklyn*.

Laugh Whore (24 October 2004, Cort) was not so much a musical revue as Mario Cantone's one-man stand-up comedy routine fitted out with seven original and parody songs, assorted interpolations and spontaneous impersonations. Cantone, best known for his sidekick role on TV's *Sex and the City*, wrote the songs with the help of actor Jerry Dixon and songwriter Harold Lubin; *Laugh Whore* was nominally staged by *Wicked* director Joe Mantello. Cantone targeted his ferociously comic and aggressively gay assaults at familiar female cultural icons such as Judy Garland, Liza Minnelli, Cher, and Tina Turner, even at one point crossing over to Michael Jackson. He offered a blistering account of his Italian-American adolescence in Newton, Massachusetts, playing all members of his extended family. Each night Cantone, decked out in a feather boa, serenaded a helpless volunteer from the audience with Bert Kalmar and Harry Ruby's "Nevertheless." In closing, Cantone invited his audience to suggest the names of famous women who never lived to perform Eve Ensler's celebrated off-Broadway show *The Vagina Monologues*. With rapid-fire precision, Cantone improvised his own hypothetical, foul-mouthed responses. The critical response to *Laugh Whore* was remarkably positive, but the show's limited appeal was sufficient for no more than its scheduled two-month run and its planned filming by producer Showtime Networks, for later cable broadcast.

Joining Cantone later in Broadway's solo show format were Whoopi Goldberg, Billy Crystal, Eve Ensler, Jackie Mason, and not least, Australia's **Dame Edna: Back with a Vengeance!** (12 November 2004, Music Box). Barry Humphries, creator of the unique Edna Everage persona, returned to Broadway after an absence of five years in this musical comedy revue of his own devising, backed by an ensemble of four "Ednaettes" and his on-stage pianist, Wayne Barker. Act I conformed to previous expectations, with Dame Edna's celebration of her own celebrity (she is "a glittering gigastar"), dismayed accounts of her dysfunctional children Kenny and Valmay ("my children come last"), and generous insults directed at a willing audience. Dame Edna dispensed sexual advice to couples ("just ask yourself, what would Edna do") and examined the psychic properties of audience members' shoes, whose size, shape and fetid smells provoked contagious laughter. Act II staggered somewhat from an unwieldy improvised playlet about Edna's childhood, acted lamely by audience volunteers under Edna's coaching. But Humphries' fearless assault on middle-class mediocrity and banalities, spontaneous verbal sparring, and traditional finale in which Edna invited the audience to sway gladiolas in unison ("grab life by the shaft") never failed to delight a loyal public. Critical raves allowed *Edna* to run for four months.

Absent the ubiquitous *A Christmas Carol* as family musical entertainment for the first time in ten years, New York City Opera returned its production of Rodgers & Hammerstein's **Cinderella** (9 November 1993) to its repertory for thirteen performances starting 12 November 2004 at the New York State. Broadway choreographer Baayork Lee restaged the production with an eye for spectacle, with exuberant choreography and the interpolation of starry Broadway and television name casting; Gerald Steichen conducted. Whereas the original 1957 television premiere focused its attention on Julie Andrews' Cinderella, this production's sweet Cinderella, Sarah Uriarte Berry, and her Prince, Christopher Sieber, were upstaged by the supporting cast. Downtown's drag diva John Epperson made his City Opera debut as the Wicked Stepmother, joined at the hip by her conniving daughters, Lea DeLaria and Ana Gasteyer. Television's Renée Taylor and Dick Van Patten provided benign support as the Queen and King. The New York Gilbert & Sullivan Players brought back their traditional staging of *The Mikado* for two weeks from 7 January 2005 at New York City Center.

Inspired by the surprise success of Amon Miyamoto's Japanese-language revival of *Pacific Overtures* (11 January 1976) in summer 2002 for Lincoln Center's summer festival, Roundabout Theatre Company invited him to stage it in English (2 December 2004, Studio 54). Miyamoto retained Rumi Matsui as designer of sets and masks, but hired a different costume designer, Junko Koshino. The rest of his production team were decidedly Broadway professionals: Paul Gemignani (conductor), Jonathan Tunick (reduced orchestrations for seven), Brian MacDevitt (lighting), and Dan Moses Schreier (sound). The majority of New York critics and audiences found Miyamoto's staging less satisfactory than his earlier effort; this version had an uneasy mix of Japanese Noh techniques wedded to broad Broadway musical comedy staging and coarse humor. Perhaps Miyamoto's affection in Japan for traditional American musical comedy accounted for his "flashy," "kitschy," and "hideous" choices.

This confluence of styles, which purported to show us both the conflicting Japanese and American perceptions of Commodore Perry's arrival in Japan and their aftermath, seldom jelled into a cohesive whole. B. D. Wong, best known for his lead in the play *M. Butterfly*, assumed the role of the Reciter, but was found lacking in authority or gravitas compared to the original, Mako, in 1976. Paolo Montalbán was the fisherman, Manjiro, resistant to the West, and Michael K. Lee was the samurai Kayama who grows increasingly more western in his habits and thinking. Two veterans from the 1976 production returned: Sab Shimono, formerly Manjiro, now the authoritarian Lord Abe, and Alvin Y. F. Ing, who recreated his distinctive role as the Shogun's evil mother. Even if this was not a *Pacific Overtures* for the ages, Sondheim enthusiasts welcomed the rare opportunity to witness a full staging during its scheduled two-month run.

The very antithesis of *Pacific Overtures*, Jerry Herman's musical comedy *La Cage aux Folles* (21 August 1983) was revived under the direction of champ farceur Jerry Zaks, with choreography by Jerry Mitchell. This *La Cage*, revived 9 December 2004 at the Marquis, had as its Georges dramatic actor but musical theatre neophyte Daniel Davis, while its Albin was Gary Beach, veteran Broadway gypsy turned star. Whereas in 1983, George Hearn's Albin was the emotional core and strength of the show opposite Gene Barry's agreeable Georges, the weight of this revival shifted to Davis' portrayal of Georges alongside Beach's flighty and temperamental Albin. *La Cage* was no longer radical or groundbreaking as musical comedy; its book structure, if respectably old-fashioned twenty-one years ago, was now clumsy and mechanical. The sentiments of Herman's lyrics were now tame where once they had been bold. Popular culture's embrace of gay characters in film (for instance, as in *The Birdcage*, a 1996 film remake of *La Cage*), theatre (Harvey Fierstein's *Torchsong Trilogy*, Tony Kushner's *Angels in America*) and television (*Will and Grace*) was now ubiquitous and commonplace. The mixed reviews faulted Zaks' ordinary direction but admired Mitchell's dynamic choreography. Notwithstanding a Tony win for Best Revival of a Musical, this enjoyable middlebrow entertainment never quite built to capacity, and business waned after seven months. Late in the run a personal dispute between Davis and the rest of the company and producers depleted what momentum the production had and created a slew of bad publicity. Broadway legend Robert Goulet took over Davis' role in mid-April, but his star power kept the show going for only two additional months.

Finally, a new musical arrived in January. **Little Women** (23 January 2005, Virginia), Louisa May Alcott's roman à clef, had been dramatized as a play, film, and even television musical, but never before as a Broadway musical. Long aborning in development, its producers jettisoned one unknown songwriting team for another, Jason Howland (music) and Mindi Dickstein (lyrics), attached to the same book by Allan Knee, whose play version for children's theatre had once been commissioned by Theatreworks USA. Under the direction of Susan H. Schulman, who had helmed the last *Sound of Music* (1997) and *The Secret Garden*, this *Little Women* was greeted with critical dismay—it was deemed competent but uninspired. Knee's book emphasized Jo March's aspirations to become a writer with two lengthy fantasy sequences, while dutifully enumerating the novel's famous plot points with telegraphic speed and minimal depth. Howland's music and Dickstein's lyrics were disparaged as "brisk, sprightly and forgettable," and "weak, generic, and when it's not unnoticeable, boring." The production's greatest asset was its Jo, Sutton Foster, once again the plucky heroine as she had been in *Thoroughly Modern Millie*. Supported by her adoring mother Marmee (Maureen McGovern), her erstwhile suitor Professor Bhaer (John Hickok), and the closest of her sisters, Beth (Megan McGinnis), Foster's Jo March almost made a musical out of the stock theatrical clichés of ambition, determination and drive. Bereft of Tony nominations, *Little Women* departed after four months.

One more nail in the coffin for the derided genre of jukebox musical, **Good Vibrations** (2 February 2005, Eugene O'Neill) was culled from the music catalog of the Beach Boys, whose Top 40 pop hits dominated the airwaves in the early 1960s. Playwright Richard Dresser imagined a comic strip plot (bad boy uses good girl's car to take him and his buddies to California) studded with thirty-two pop songs, all penned by Brian Wilson and the Beach Boys. John Carrafa, choreographer of the recent *Into the Woods* revival, *Urinetown*, and *Dance of the Vampires*, both directed and choreographed. Ben Brantley, critic for *The New York Times*, declined to mention individual cast members by name, out of pity for their predicament; he deplored the "catchy" songs "borrowed and mutilated" for the occasion. Perhaps lead producers Dodger Theatricals

and Joop van den Ende, inspired by the success of *Mamma Mia!*, thought they could cash in on the pop songbook craze with a facile, undiscriminating public. It didn't work: *Good Vibrations* ended its run after twelve weeks.

Encores' annual triptych of neglected musicals opened with *A Tree Grows in Brooklyn* (19 April 1951), followed with *Purlie* (15 March 1970), and closing with *The Apple Tree* (18 October 1966) at New York City Center. *A Tree Grows in Brooklyn* (10 February 2005) had long enjoyed a loyal following among musical theatre enthusiasts, and Encores offered theatregoers a rare opportunity to hear the score performed with its original orchestrations, the first production to do so in more than fifty years. As in the flawed original, Emily Skinner's Cissy dominated the storyline about two star-crossed lovers, Johnny Nolan (Jason Danieley) and Katie (Sally Murphy). Nancy Anderson and John Ellison Conlee offered effective support as neighbors. David Ives' skillful concert adaptation could not conceal the wan writing, in spite of capable performances and a winning score. Gary Griffin directed with a firm and sensitive hand, and Rob Fisher conducted with his customary "warmth and verve." *Purlie* (31 March 2005), had been equally neglected for the past thirty years, undoubtedly because its comic assault on white racism has become dated since its musical (1970) and dramatic (1961) debuts. If original playwright Ossie Davis' intent was "to point a mocking finger at racial segregation and laugh it out of existence," director Sheldon Epps proved unable to whip this twenty-first-century audience into sustained glee. Television's Blair Underwood boasted a handsome stage presence and charisma, but somehow lacked the revivalist zeal Purlie Victorious demands. Anika Noni Rose, Tony winner for the previous season's *Caroline, or Change*, captured much of Lutiebelle's quiet charm, but failed to raise the roof with her signature "I Got Love." Lillias White offered steely vocal support as Missy, and John Cullum effortlessly captured the villainy of Ol' Cap'n Cotchipee. *The Apple Tree* (12 May 2005; directed by Gary Griffin) had long been discarded, having been considered a vehicle for its original star, Barbara Harris. Perhaps Kristin Chenoweth was attracted to *The Apple Tree* as she had been to Harris' previous triumph, *On a Clear Day* (1965; Encores 2000), because the triptych of Eve, Princess Barbára and Ella/Passionella in *The Apple Tree* fit Chenoweth's talents to a T. Malcolm Gets was her romantic partner as Adam, Captain Sanjar, and Flip, the Prince Charming. Michael Cerveris was her temptation as the Snake and the narrator in *The Lady or the Tiger* and *Passionella* tales. Despite its smart casting, *The Apple Tree*'s charms were mostly with Miss Chenoweth, who did not disappoint.

The first bona fide new musical hit of the season arrived 3 March 2005 at the Imperial with **Dirty Rotten Scoundrels**, adapted from the successful 1988 film starring Michael Caine and Steve Martin as two conmen on the make on the French Riviera. The *Full Monty* team, composer/lyricist David Yazbek, director Jack O'Brien, and choreographer Jerry Mitchell, reunited to create a brash, brazen, and occasionally bawdy tale of mayhem; Jeffrey Lane penned the funny book. Suave swindler Lawrence Jameson (John Lithgow) discovers a scrappy young interloper, Freddy Benson (Norbert Leo Butz) attempting to con guileless, wealthy women into relinquishing their money and jewels. Divorcée Muriel Eubanks (Joanna Gleason), young American oil heiress Jolene Oaks (Sara Gettelfinger), and American "soap queen" Christine Colgate (Sherie Rene Scott) become their quarries, while Andre Thibault (Gregory Jbara) is a French policeman on the take. O'Brien knew well that speed is key for such a comic roller coaster ride, but the rapid-fire premise afforded scant opportunity for Mitchell's choreographic expression. David Rockwell designed handsome if archetypal Riviera resort sets that came apart and reassembled to match the comic pace. All of this would have been for naught were it not for the production's two greatest strengths: Norbert Leo Butz's breakthrough star performance and Yazbek's incomparably clever lyrics. Butz imagines the riches awaiting him in "Great Big Stuff": "Oh give me a home where the centerfolds roam, Guccione on the phone, he got a party going on, / And Hef'll have me over to play some naked Twister, Blotto in the Grotto, with a Playmate and her sister." Butz's desperation, fearless physical comedy, and peerless timing set the tone and pace for the evening's entertainment and won him a Tony Award for Best Actor in a Musical. If Yazbek's music was seldom as memorable as his lyrics, it supported his virtuosic rhymes. Consider Muriel's self-examination: "My prince goes off to war and once again I'm royally screwed; perhaps a Xanax and a half will brighten up my mood." Or Jolene's affection for her home state Oklahoma: "And we'll motor into Tulsa for the weeken', through the windows of the pick-up we'll be peekin.' Not a tree or a Jew, to block the lovely view. There's a racetrack and a zoo, and Oral Roberts U."

Lithgow struggled gamely to keep up, serving as a comparable straight man to Butz's lunacy. Late in the run Lithgow was succeeded by Jonathan Pryce, who proved more comfortable with Jameson's unscrupulous character. *Scoundrels* romped through an eighteen-month run.

The season's blockbuster musical success, **Monty Python's Spamalot** (17 March 2005, Shubert), a sophomoric feast of comic silliness, arrived two weeks later under the direction of Mike Nichols. With book and lyrics "lovingly ripped off from" the 1975 film *Monty Python and the Holy Grail* co-written by Eric Idle, one-sixth of the original Python team, the musical adaptation dutifully recreated many of the beloved gags, stunts, and set-pieces Python fans expected, such as killer rabbits, flying cows, squeals of "Ni!," flatulence, and fractured French. But the narrative demands of musical theatre forced some unwelcome coherence upon the anarchy of the original and introduced some extraneous satiric targets, such as musical comedy itself, over-sung Andrew Lloyd Webber ballads, Jews in New York theatre audiences, etc. John Du Prez and Idle composed some agreeably forgettable pastiche songs. Even if the music and comedic interpolations proved lame beside the film's hysterical, iconic origins, *Spamalot* won many new fans, including men who otherwise might have cared little for musical comedy. Tim Curry played the absent-minded King Arthur alongside television stars Hank Azaria (Sir Lancelot) and *Frasier*'s David Hyde Pierce (Sir Robin). Christopher Sieber played Sir Galahad, and Sara Ramirez was the full-voiced, big-breasted Lady of the Lake. The goofy Knights of Spamalot roamed Broadway for almost four years.

Inevitably with time, Elvis Presley, anathema to Broadway in the 1950s, a satiric target in *Bye Bye Birdie* in 1960, and an impersonation in *Elvis: The Legend Lives!* in 1978, would ultimately arrive in a new Broadway musical, **All Shook Up** (24 March 2005, Palace). Playwright/lyricist Joe DiPietro crafted a jukebox musical using the back catalogue of hit Presley songs, set in 1955 in "a Midwest town no one ever heard of." Cheyenne Jackson made his star-turn debut as Chad, an imitation Presley bad-boy motorcylist from nowheresville who sweeps small-town sweetheart Natalie Haller (Jenn Gambatese) off her feet. Not much dramatic tension there, as the story's outcome was inevitable from the start, as were cartoon-like obstacles from the local sheriff, mayor, parents, and rival boyfriends. Despite competent direction from Chris Ashley and energetic choreography from Ken Roberson and Sergio Trujillo, the show had no threat of sex, danger to the social order, or anything else that might elicit a thrill. The toothless *All Shook Up* eked out a six-month run, then took to the road.

Amidst the sea of musical comedy silliness, **The Light in the Piazza** (18 April 2005, Vivian Beaumont) reminded Broadway audiences that musical theatre could tell a complex, serious story of emotional surprise and still manage to entertain. *Piazza* was jointly developed by Lincoln Center Theater, Chicago's Goodman Theatre and Seattle's Intiman Theatre, with book by Craig Lucas drawn from Elizabeth Spencer's 1960 novella. Adam Guettel, famously dogged by his pedigree as Richard Rodgers' grandson, penned music and lyrics. A startlingly beautiful work, *Piazza* told the story of an American mother and daughter, Margaret and Clara Johnson (Victoria Clark and Kelli O'Hara), traveling in Italy in the 1950s. Unknown to the Italians and indeed to the audience until her mother confides her story, Clara's adolescence was retarded by a horseback riding accident at age ten. Her sudden and mutual infatuation with Fabrizio Naccarelli leads to an unpredictably swift marriage. The musical's narrative strength arose from its articulate contrasts between, and expression of, Italian and American cultures and misunderstandings, and from Margaret Johnson's ambivalence in both protecting and securing a future for her daughter. Bartlett Sher's incisive and sensitive direction helped a gifted cast bring this remarkable story to theatrical life. Victoria Clark triumphed in the role of her career as Margaret, battling her husband, daughter, and Clara's suitor and his family, to a sublime realization and fulfillment of her role as a mother. Her solo, "Dividing Day," offered a shattering view of Johnson's empty marriage. Matthew Morrison was especially effective as the lover Fabrizio, with demanding arias in Italian and appealingly clumsy English. O'Hara's Clara deftly met the challenge of appearing not too smart, yet beautiful in the flush of young love, in a role easily ten years younger than she. Guettel's score was musically sophisticated, complex, witty, romantic, evocative of 1950s Italy, and brilliantly wedded to character in both English and idiomatic Italian. *The Light in the Piazza* prospered happily for 504 performances over fifteen months, followed by a short tour.

The family musical spectacle **Chitty Chitty Bang Bang** (28 April 2005, Hilton) arrived on the heels of its success at the London Palladium. Based on Ian Fleming's novel for children about the eponymous flying car, *Chitty Chitty Bang Bang* became a film musical in 1968 under Albert "Cubby" Broccoli, producer of all of Fleming's James Bond films. This stage production was Broccoli's dream, as fulfilled by his widow Dana Broccoli. Its score by Richard M. and Robert B. Sherman followed in the style of their score for Disney's *Mary Poppins*. The title song, with its audience singalong accompanied by the debut of the flying car, was admittedly catchy, but the rest of the score was pleasantly forgettable. Jeremy Sams adapted the film's screenplay for the stage, and Adrian Noble and Gillian Lynne directed and choreographed this lavish extravaganza whose car upstaged the best imaginable cast, with Raúl Esparza as the car's hapless, sweet mechanic, Caractacus Potts; Erin Dilly as his romantic partner, Truly Scrumptious; and Philip Bosco as Grandpa Potts. The forces of evil were immensely entertaining: Baron and Baroness Bombast (Marc Kudisch, Jan Maxwell), their wicked underlings Goran and Boris (Chip Zien, Robert Sella), and the fearsome Childcatcher (Kevin Cahoon). American audiences were less enchanted by *CCBB* than their London counterparts, indicating that a mighty fortune may have been squandered on an inconsequential property. *Chitty* departed at year-end after eight months and a sizable loss.

The 25th Annual Putnam County Spelling Bee (2 May 2005, Circle in the Square) proved to be an unexpected delight in its Broadway transfer following its off-Broadway premiere (7 February 2005, Second Stage). Initially conceived by Rebecca Feldman with a book by Rachel Sheinkin and music and lyrics by William Finn, *Spelling Bee* was precisely what its title suggests, the final round of a middle school spelling contest featuring six nerdy children—played by Deborah S. Craig, Jesse Tyler Ferguson, Dan Fogler, Celia Keenan-Bolger, José Llana, and Sarah Saltzberg—each of whom is wildly and endearingly eccentric. They are supervised by a former champion (Lisa Howard), the school vice-principal (Jay Reiss), and the school "comfort counselor" (Derrick Baskin). James Lapine directed with a sensitivity to two chronic theatre hazards, what Charles Isherwood in *The New York Times* named as "audience participation, and the usually ghastly conceit of adult actors playing kids." Designer Beowulf Borrit transposed the instantly recognizable high school gymnasium set from its Second Stage proscenium arch to Circle in the Square's thrust stage, creating an illusion of greater intimacy and proximity. Sheinkin's book built both suspense and humor with its demands that contestants spell words like "cystitis", "strabismus," and "crepuscule." When offered a word's use in a sentence, we and the contestants are told: "Billy, put down that phylactery. We're Episcopalian." The audience participation swelled the ranks of contestants beyond six and afforded the sport of watching willing victims lose. Finn's witty lyrics far exceeded the serviceable melodies provided them. *Spelling Bee* held its contests for 1,136 performances, nearly three years.

Sweet Charity (29 January 1966), last seen on Broadway in 1986, was revived as a vehicle for Christina Applegate, former star of television's *Married...With Children*. In its Chicago tryout, Applegate broke her foot, causing the production to close down and nearly be abandoned. Like Charity Hope Valentine herself, the indefatigable Applegate vowed to open the show, in a backstage saga that became its own Broadway tabloid folklore. Could she dance the virtuoso role, or would understudy Charlotte d'Amboise open the show? *Sweet Charity* (4 May 2005, Al Hirschfeld) ultimately sneaked in under the wire on the last day of the season's Tony Award eligibility. Producers Barry and Fran Weissler, whose revival of *Chicago* with Bob Fosse-style choreography had proven a long-run phenomenon, imagined Fosse's *Sweet Charity*, with *Chicago* stager Walter Bobbie and Wayne Cilento reworking Fosse's choreography, would repeat *Chicago*'s success. But there the similarities ended. Remarkable though Applegate's recovery was, *Sweet Charity* is an exhausting tour de force for one virtuoso singer-dancer-actress, whereas *Chicago* generously distributes its singing and dancing chores among its principals and ensemble. Applegate was fine in the role, but fell short of being a sensation, and the show itself felt somewhat tired and old-fashioned. Denis O'Hare excelled as the eccentric Oscar Lindquist, Charity's hopeless beau, yet the rest of the production was deemed only mildly enjoyable by critics. This *Sweet Charity* lasted eight months.

Brian Stokes Mitchell, one of Broadway's new crop of leading men, assembled a solo show with the help of playwright Charles Randolph Wright under the title **Love/Life, A Life in Song** (15 May 2005, Vivian Beaumont). Lincoln Center presented Mitchell on a series of dark Sunday and Monday nights concurrent with the run of *The Light in the Piazza*. Featuring an assortment of romantic ballads, Broadway standards and American popular songs, Mitchell's performance satisfied his loyal supporters, even if he appeared altogether too pleased with himself. New York City Opera brought back its popular revival of *Candide* (1 December 1956) for ten performances in March in repertory, at the same time that the eternally touring *Riverdance* (13 March 1996) returned to Radio City Music Hall for a tenth-anniversary, one-week engagement. One other Broadway staple, Jackie Mason, returned for his eighth consecutive outing, **Jackie Mason: Freshly Squeezed** (23 March 2005, Helen Hayes); audiences howled for six months.

Off-Broadway musicals in 2004-2005 were few but surprisingly interesting. After a brief holiday debut at the New Victory in 1999 to laudatory reviews and an international tour, *Shockheaded Peter* returned 22 February 2005 to the Little Shubert. This musical adaptation of Heinrich Hoffmann's nineteenth-century German classic *Struwwelpeter* told several macabre, cautionary tales about unruly children; Phelim McDermott and Julian Crouch directed. Its dimly lit, Victorian toy theatre set, supported by the eerie falsetto voice of Martin Jacques and music of the Tiger Lillies, conjured up an enchantingly bizarre and wicked world. Despite critical raves, *Shockheaded Peter* never found its cult audience after three months. Following an autumn launch at the New York Musical Theatre Festival (NYMF), **Altar Boyz** (1 March 2005, Dodger Stages) offered a parody of a Christian boy band in a countdown to save souls. Kevin Del Aguila provided the funny book, and Gary Adler and Michael Patrick's score displayed a variety of recognizable boy-band musical tropes. Its exuberant cast of five parodied an easy target for five years, and *Altar Boyz* has since been seen throughout the country and world. **Dessa Rose** (21 March 2005, Mitzi E. Newhouse) represented an over-ambitious attempt to musicalize Shirley Anne Williams' story of an unlikely friendship between a female ex-slave and a white woman during the 1840s. Lynn Ahrens' cumbersome book alternated between flashback and narration, and Stephen Flaherty's pleasant pastiche score never scaled the emotional heights and depths it aspired to. Its gifted principals, LaChanze and Rachel York, were required to play their younger and older selves interchangeably. This Lincoln Center Theater production played out its subscription engagement, now swiftly forgotten. In summary, after a poor start in the fall, Broadway musical theatre recovered its pace in the spring for a better than average season.

SCENE TWO

Pop Music Takes Over the Musical, 2005–2010

2005–2006

Broadway's summer began with **The Blonde in the Thunderbird** (17 July 2005, Brooks Atkinson), a solo confessional revue of the life and career of television star Suzanne Somers. Devised and directed by veteran Hollywood writers Ken and Mitzie Welch from the performer's memoirs *Keeping Secrets* and *After the Fall*, *Thunderbird* consisted of Somers deconstructing her crafted dumb blond persona, perfected on the ABC sitcom *Three's Company*, and subsequent diet, work-out and home shopping programs. This dubious exercise in self-fascination was leavened with a mix of Broadway ("Take Back Your Mink," "If You Knew Susie," "Fifty Percent," "She Loves Me") and Hollywood ("Pick Yourself Up," "If I Only Had a Brain") standards whose lyrics were revised by the Welches. They also penned five undistinguished "special material" songs to round out the ninety-five-minute running time. If Somers imagined that a theatrical entertainment could be packaged from her battles with low self-esteem, teenage pregnancy, alcoholism, parental abuse, and divorce, she and husband/producer Alan Hamel were mistaken. This odd entertainment fled town in one week.

The life and music of the Beatles' John **Lennon** (14 August 2005, Broadhurst) were celebrated and eulogized in this revue created and directed by Don Scardino "with the permission of" Lennon's widow, Yoko Ono. Whereas the longevity of Lennon's compositions need scarcely be questioned, the unfortunate concept and production choices condemned this production to a six-week run. Lennon was portrayed by not one but all nine cast members in a misguided attempt to prove he was a sort of Everyman, or perhaps all things to all people. By contrast, Yoko Ono was played by just one actress, Julie Danao-Salkin. Imagine a John Lennon musical with almost no Beatles songs. Two previously unpublished John Lennon songs were included, "India, India" and "I Don't Want to Lose You." Will Chase bore the closest vocal and physical resemblance to Lennon, who was otherwise portrayed by Chuck Cooper, Terrence Mann, and Chad Kimball, among others. The cast were forced to compete with live footage of the real John Lennon. In Act II Lennon's post-Beatles legacy became the production's focus,

overwhelming the production with sentiment and deification. However touching the authentic video of Lennon and Yoko Ono performing "Imagine" at the evening's end, *Lennon* itself proved resolutely untheatrical and unsatisfying.

Latinologues (13 October 2005, Helen Hayes) consisted of revue sketches for its cast of three men and one woman. Performed in English with vulgar asides in Spanish, the evening offered mostly ethnic stereotypes, made palatable only by the talented cast, Eugenio Derbez, Rick Najera (also the author), René Lavan and Shirley A. Rumierk. Nominally directed by Cheech Marin of comedy duo *Cheech & Chong*, *Latinologues* stayed on Broadway for three months as an interlude during a national tour.

In My Life (20 October 2005, Music Box) was an original musical with book, music, lyrics, and direction by Joseph Brooks, composer of the ubiquitous 1977 hit ballad "You Light Up My Life." Its irrational story followed J. T. (Christopher J. Hanke), a jingle writer and likable fellow with Tourette's syndrome, who falls in love at first sight with the cute, compulsive Jenny (Jessica Boevers) at a New York City diner. J. T.'s headaches reveal that he has a brain tumor, leading J. T.'s dead mom (Roberta Gumbel) and baby sister (Chiara Navarra), God (Michael J. Farina) and gay angel Winston (David Turner) all to argue and sing about how strange life is, how "Life Turns on a Dime," why this story should be an opera. From thus utterly insipid, incoherent nonsense comes the inevitable happy ending. Brooks himself produced this vanity project for sixty-one performances and twenty-three previews, at a reported cost of $7.2 million.

Stephen Sondheim and Hugh Wheeler's *Sweeney Todd, the Demon Barber of Fleet Street* (1 March 1979), seldom absent from the opera house or New York stages, returned 3 November 2005 to the Eugene O'Neill in a stylized, minimalist production from British director John Doyle. Born of the economic and spatial limitations of the Watermill Theatre in Newbury, UK, where it originated, its cast of ten played all the roles and constituted the entire orchestra. What might at first glance have appeared to be a dubious gimmick or unwelcome distraction proved extraordinarily fascinating and gripping to watch. Sweeney (Michael Cerveris) played a lyric guitar, Mrs. Lovett (Patti LuPone) a grotesquely comic tuba and a triangle, Judge Turpin (Mark Jacoby) a trumpet, Johanna (Lauren Molina) a cello, the Beadle (Alexander Gemignani) both keyboard and flute, etc. Amazingly Donna Lynne Champlin played rival male barber Pirelli, doubling on accordion, keyboard and flute. The empty, raked stage design and simple costume design by Doyle, abetted by the shrewdly atmospheric lighting by Richard G. Jones, conjured the familiar locations of nineteenth-century London with simple chairs, props, a small coffin, and buckets of stage blood, generously spattered. A few viewers missed the splendors of the original's twenty-seven-piece orchestra and the epic scale of Harold Prince's original staging, but most theatergoers delighted in this new *Sweeney Todd* as a Victorian "penny dreadful." *Sweeney* lasted ten months, then took to the road.

Jersey Boys (6 November 2005, August Wilson) told the story of Frank Valli and the Four Seasons, using their famous 1960s pop-song catalogue to chart their rise from obscurity to international fame. However derisive the term "jukebox musical" may have been with previous efforts to bring to Broadway the Beatles, Buddy Holly, ABBA, Lieber & Stoller, Elvis Presley, and the Beach Boys, *Jersey Boys* finally got it right and the critics all raved. *Jersey Boys* told a conventional rags-to-riches tale about a couple of kids, Frankie Valli (John Lloyd Young), Tommy DeVito (Christian Hoff), Nick Massi (J. Robert Spencer) and Bob Gaudio (Daniel Reichard), who struggle with sudden success, girls, drugs, booze, and the usual setbacks. Women were relegated to minor roles as wives and girlfriends. After some rough starts, Valli's unusual falsetto voice gels with those of his buddies to create the Four Seasons; Gaudio's gift to create a songwriter, matched with music producer and lyricist Bob Crewe (Peter Gregus), yields such smash hits as "Sherry," "Big Girls Don't Cry," "Walk Like a Man," "Rag Doll" and "Can't Take My Eyes Off You." Director Des McAnuff and bookwriters Marshall Brickman and Rick Elice maintained a tight narrative pace, allowing the songs to stand as performance pieces. *Jersey Boys* took the season's Tony Award for Best Musical, traveled happily across the United States, and performed well in Britain, Australia, and Canada where the music was less known. Five years later it is still a capacity draw.

The Woman in White (17 November 2005, Marquis) heralded an ambitious new musical from über-composer Andrew Lloyd Webber. Based on the 1860 mystery thriller by Wilkie Collins, *The Woman in White* had already proven a success in London's West End, where it ran for nineteen months. Playwright Charlotte Jones, with lyrics by David Zippel, told a complex, twisted tale of murder, ghostly secrets, betrayal and concealed identities. Two half-sisters, Marian Halcombe

(Maria Friedman) and Laura Fairlie (Jill Paice), are equally attracted to handsome art instructor Walter Hartright (Adam Brazier) at their wealthy estate Limmeridge House. Laura's wicked suitor, Sir Percival Glyde (Ron Bohmer), in collusion with Count Fosco (Michael Ball), has imprisoned the eponymous, ghostly Anne Catherick (Angela Christian), declared her insane and seized her fortune. Laura's uncanny resemblance to Anne precipitates a round of revelations and reversals whereby Glyde and Fosco's perfidy is uncovered and lovers are reunited. Webber's lush, melodic score was drenched with melodramatic sentiment ("I Believe My Heart," "Evermore Without You") for the romantic triangle, while Marian's solo "All for Laura" best captured the conflicted loyalties of sisterly love. Count Fosco provided welcome comic relief in two of the show's better songs, "A Gift for Living Well" and "You Can Get Away with Anything," the last performed with a live white mouse. *The Woman in White* was saddled with William Dudley's computer-generated scenic projections of a multitude of Victorian household interiors and exteriors. Its camera's eye zoomed and swooped across the landscape at a dizzying, disorienting pace at odds with the intense, methodical drama unfolding; additionally, the principals often appeared as bleached-out silhouettes against the projections. Following mixed reviews, *The Woman in White* ran for fifteen weeks, ultimately collapsing in mid-winter.

A touring company of *Peter Pan* (20 October 1955) arrived at the Theater at Madison Square Garden on 30 November 2005 for a month of holiday performances. At age fifty-three, former gymnast Cathy Rigby became a boyish Peter Pan, and James Clow played her nemesis, Captain Hook. Glen Casale directed this revival produced by Rigby and her husband Tom McCoy.

The Color Purple (1 December 2005, Broadway) offered a faithful, sentimental musical adaptation of Alice Walker's Pulitzer Prize-winning novel (1982) and the Warner Bros. film directed by Stephen Spielberg (1985). In Marsha Norman's book, the sheer narrative density of events surrounding Celie's (LaChanze) emotional awakening at times diminished the dramatic power viewers recalled from the novel and film. Pop songwriters Brenda Russell, Allee Willis, and Stephen Bray contributed an agreeable mélange of rhythm and blues, gospel, blues, and soul that was easy on the ear, if seldom distinctive. *The Color Purple* was however blessed with an audience familiar with its story, loyal to producer

Oprah Winfrey (also the star of the film), and awed by LaChanze's compelling, heartbreaking performance as Celie. Her enduring love for her sister Nettie enables her to survive rape at age fourteen, the removal of her children at birth, and her brutal subjugation by men. Few of the other characters proved notable, although the formidable Sofia (Felicia P. Fields) and independent Shug Avery (Elizabeth Withers-Mendes) tried hard. Despite a moving closing song, Celie's "*I'm Here*," *Purple* never achieved the emotional resonance it had on the printred page or on film. Nevertheless, the production prospered for almost two and a half years.

Chita Rivera: The Dancer's Life (11 December 2005, Gerald Schoenfeld) presented its star and a supporting cast of ten in an affectionate biographical scrapbook of Rivera's career since 1952. At age seventy-two, Rivera still commanded the stage with a physical grace and intensity few women of any age could match. Unfortunately, this stage vehicle was seldom equal to her talents. Terrence McNally's sketchy book traced her childhood ("Dancing on the Kitchen Table"), early ballet classes, and gypsy stage life in productions from *Call Me Madam* to *Mr. Wonderful*, her breakthrough to stardom in *West Side Story* in 1957, and personal successes in *Bye Bye Birdie, Sweet Charity, Chicago*, and *The Rink*. A more generic Act Two addressed the grueling audition process, the men in her life, the choreographers she worked with, more from her later shows including *Kiss of the Spider Woman*, and ultimately a Kennedy Center honor in 2002. Though no one expected Rivera to dance as she did in her prime, director Graciela Daniele graciously included the defining choreography of Jack Cole, Peter Gennaro, Bob Fosse, and Jerome Robbins. Of the new songs commissioned from Lynn Ahrens and Stephen Flaherty for the occasion, only "A Woman the World Has Never Seen" proved up to par. Welcomed though Chita was, *The Dancer's Life* never found a wide audience during its nine weeks on Broadway.

The Pajama Game (13 May 1954) was revived by Roundabout Theater Company (23 February 2006, American Airlines) as a vehicle for pop star crooner Harry Connick Jr., who played pajama-factory superintendent Sid Sorokin in his Broadway musical debut. Kathleen Marshall's traditional staging, combined with the production's shrewd casting, delivered a smash package that could have happily run a year or three, had not Connick had to leave after four months for other recording and performance commitments. His rival for control at the Sleep-Tite Pajama Factory, Babe Williams, was played by

Kelli O'Hara, the dewy-eyed heroine of *The Light in the Piazza* and *Sweet Smell of Success*. Highlights included a galvanic "There Once Was a Man," staged with what one critic termed the gusto of an Elvis Presley–Ann-Margret number and "Hernando's Hideaway," reconceived with Connick at the keyboard and Megan Lawrence playing comic foil as Gladys. In addition to some minor revisions to the book by Peter Ackerman, three songs were restored to the score, "The World Around Us" (a solo for Sid), "If You Win, You Lose" (for Babe), and "The Three of Us" for a droll Michael McKean as Hines. Even if Marshall's choreography never quite matched Bob Fosse's for wit and sensuality, her *Pajama Game* captured the 1950s with infectious glee.

The country-western songs of Johnny Cash, widely popularized in the 2005 film *Walk the Line*, arrived on Broadway as the jukebox revue **Ring of Fire** (12 March 2006, Ethel Barrymore). Conceived by its lead producer William Meade for a cast of six and a band of eight, *Ring of Fire* was directed by Richard Maltby, Jr., forever known as the principal architect of the first and arguably best jukebox revue ever, *Ain't Misbehavin'*. Wisely eschewing a chronological biography, Maltby and Meade chose a thematic structure encompassing not only songs written by Cash, but also Cash's cover versions of songs by other composers. Opening with the despairing "Hurt," recorded by Cash at the end of his career, *Ring of Fire* progressed from youthful idealism to the hard life of a working musician, concluding with repentance and spiritual forgiveness. Absent were the rough edges of drug addiction, alcoholism, and divorce, replaced by anodyne, cheerful singers, strutting cowboys, cute novelty songs ("Egg Suckin' Dog," "Flushed from the Bathroom of Your Heart") and a total lack of narrative urgency. Individual performers occasionally shone (Jarrod Emick with "Look at Them Beans," Lari White's "I Still Miss Someone"), but Johnny Cash's true man-in-black essence was never fully captured in *Ring of Fire*, which departed after seven weeks.

Bertolt Brecht and Kurt Weill's *The Threepenny Opera* (13 April 1933) returned in a much-anticipated adaptation by Wallace Shawn (book, lyrics) and Scott Elliott (direction) that proved a surprise disaster for its producer, Roundabout Theatre Company (20 April 2006, Studio 54). Only the composer's original orchestration for ten sparkled amidst Shawn's witless and crude lyrics. Whereas the original 1928 Berlin production effectively confronted its bourgeois audience with its own hypocrisies, Shawn and Elliott merely assaulted this audience with excessive nudity, profanity, neon, leather, cocaine, and a cross-dressing Lucy Brown. The numbingly tedious evening wallowed in self-conscious, artificial depravity without ever creating any genuinely plausible menace or dramatic tension. Alan Cumming's Macheath lacked the authority of his Emcee in Roundabout's hit *Cabaret*. Without any towering presence, Macheath's women, criminal rivals, and his own gang of petty thieves became a cacophonous gaggle of hangers-on. An otherwise gifted cast (Jim Dale and Ana Gasteyer as Mr. and Mrs. Peachum, rock diva Cyndi Lauper as Jenny, singer Nellie McKay as Polly Peachum, and Christopher Innvar as Tiger Brown) appeared lost in the confusion. Supported only by Roundabout subscribers and the morbidly curious, *Threepenny* ran for its allotted ten weeks.

Lestat (25 April 2006, Palace) marked an unfortunate attempt by Warner Bros. Theater Ventures to musicalize Anne Rice's immensely popular novels collectively known as "The Vampire Chronicles." Its book by Linda Woolverton telescoped the eighteenth-century adventures of the vampire Lestat (Hugh Panaro). Lestat's mother Gabrielle (Carolee Carmello), his adopted ten-year old daughter Claudia (Allison Fischer), widower Louis (Jim Stanek), and the truly evil Armand (Drew Sarich) were thinly dramatized characters whose actors struggled to enliven with depth and meaning. This oddly homoerotic melodrama was heavy with plot exposition, leaden pop ballads by Elton John and Bernie Taupin, and risible dialogue ("I will never find solace! She was my solace! She stood between me and the abyss!"). Fans of the Rice novels may have recognized fleeting and familiar elements, but the narrative flow was bewildering to newcomers. Director Matt Wolf, who had collaborated with Woolverton on Disney's *Beauty and the Beast*, was unable to create any genuine dramatic excitement with the story he was given. *Lestat*, the third vampire musical to fail in four years, closed its doors after a six-week run.

Yet another formulaic adaptation of a film (1998) into a musical, **The Wedding Singer** (27 April 2006, Al Hirschfeld) told the story of Robbie Hart (Stephen Lynch), a sweet loser from Ridgefield, New Jersey. How this hapless, nice guy wins the sweet waitress Julia Sullivan (Laura Benanti) he yearns for is standard-issue Hollywood romantic comedy. Rita Gardner, an ingénue forty-six years ago in *The Fantasticks*, played a foul-mouthed,

rapping grandma. The comic talents of the film's Adam Sandler and dewy-eyed Drew Barrymore had proven the principal draw for movie audiences. On Broadway, newcomers Matthew Sklar (music), Chad Beguelin (book, lyrics), and Tim Herlihy (original screenplay, book) attempted the same magic with middling results, retaining the film's only two original songs ("Somebody Kill Me," "Grow Old with You"). Director John Rando kept the story moving at warp speed, abetted by Rob Ashford's choreographic quotes from the 1980s songs "Material Girl," "Thriller," and "Flashdance." Next to the season's conspicuous failures of *Lennon, In My Life, Ring of Fire, Threepenny Opera, Lestat,* and *Hot Feet,* the amiable if ordinary charms of *The Wedding Singer* allowed it to run almost nine months.

Hot Feet (30 April 2006, Hilton) married the plot of Michael Powell and Emeric Pressburger's film classic *The Red Shoes* (1948) to the rhythm & blues catalogue of band Earth, Wind & Fire. Conceived, directed, and choreographed by Maurice Hines as a dance musical in the vernacular of the free-form "krumping" style of street dance, as well as hip-hop and ballet, *Hot Feet* told the story of seventeen-year-old Kalimba (Vivian Nixon) from the Bronx, who is lured by choreographer Anthony (Michael Balderrama) and wicked impresario Victor Serpentine (Keith David). Cast as the star of Anthony's titular ballet, Kalimba dances to her death in this cliché-ridden, Faustian tale of good and evil. Despite six new songs by EW&F's Maurice White, mostly for the heroine's mother (Anne Duquesnay), the jukebox score proved ill-suited for telling the story. Heru Ptah's sketchy, silly premise recalled better Hollywood pop musical films like *Saturday Night Fever, Staying Alive,* or *Footloose,* while the poor acting suggested that cast members were chosen exclusively for their dance talents. In spite of unanimous critical drubbing, producer Transamerica kept *Hot Feet* on the boards for twelve weeks.

A dark-horse surprise musical comedy hit from Toronto by way of Los Angeles, **The Drowsy Chaperone** (1 May 2006, Marquis) was an affectionate homage to the musical comedies of the 1920s and those who love them too much. To charmingly derivative music and lyrics by Lisa Lambert and Greg Morrison, Bob Martin and Don McKellar's egregiously silly book invited the audience into a darkened apartment occupied by a Man in Chair (Bob Martin, again): "I hate theater. Well, it's so disappointing isn't it? Once upon a time you could depend upon Cole Porter or the Gershwins to surprise us with a story and a few good songs. Now it's 'Please, Elton John, must we continue this charade?'" His passion for obscure musical comedies of the 1920s spring to life in his imagination before our eyes with a scratchy recording of the long forgotten confection, "The Drowsy Chaperone." Even if the nonsense that followed seldom matched the charms of *The Boy Friend,* or the revival of *No, No Nanette,* Sutton Foster as a Broadway glamour-girl, Beth Leavel as the eponymous drunken vamp, and Danny Burstein as a ludicrous Latin lover led the small cast through one hundred minutes of enjoyable musical comedy fun. Notable moments included Foster's show-stopper "Show-Off," Leavel's "As We Stumble Along," and Georgia Engel and Edward Hibbert's "Love Is Always Lovely in the End." David Gallo's clever set allowed a shabby apartment to morph into art deco splendor in an instant, while Casey Nicholaw's direction and choreography sustained the merriment of the show's slight conceit. *Drowsy* prospered for nineteen months.

Disney Theatricals continued its animated-film-to-stage formula with **Tarzan** (10 May 2006, Richard Rodgers), based on the 1912 novel *Tarzan of the Apes* by Edgar Rice Burroughs and the Disney movie (1999) with songs by Phil Collins. With its ambitious director Bob Crowley also responsible for set and costume design, *Tarzan's* visual concept was principally an empty stage with iridescent green jungle vines, on whose foliage swing Tarzan and the wild creatures of the ensemble. The show opened with an impressive shipwreck and the killing of the hero's parents by a hungry leopard. The orphan boy is adopted by gorillas, then meets his true love Jane and a visiting group of British botanists. Aside from eye-popping feats of bungee jumping from aerial designer Pichón Baldinu and muscular choreography from Merle Tankard, this earthbound *Tarzan* seldom matched the visual imagination of the animated film on which it was based. David Henry Hwang's doggedly wordy book plumbed the traditional Disney family-based themes of father–son rivalry, young love, motherly devotion, and growth from boyhood to manhood. Collins doubled the film's five songs; both new songs and old were equally forgettable. *American Idol* contestant Josh Strickland assumed the title role with feral, masculine authority, but Jenn Gambatese (Jane Porter) and Tim Jerome (Professor Porter) struggled with inconsistent British accents and stupid dialogue. As Tarzan's adoptive ape-father Kerchak, Shuler Hensley was confined to grunting in his

fur suit; Chester Gregory II played Terk, Tarzan's wise-cracking sidekick—another Disney cliché. Merle Dandridge as the adoptive mother Kala had the best song, "You'll Be in My Heart." *Tarzan* hung around for fourteen months.

The season's parade of revivals began early with the New York City Opera production of Gilbert & Sullivan's *Patience, or Bunthorne's Bride* directed with excessive silliness by Tazewell Thompson, in co-production with Glimmerglass Opera (10 September 2005, NY State). London's visiting heart-throb Michael Ball was Bunthorne, Kevin Burdette sang well as Grosvenor, and Timothy Nolen was Calverley. New York Gilbert & Sullivan Players' *H. M. S. Pinafore* and *The Mikado* made repertory stops at City Center in early January. *The Most Happy Fella* (3 May 1956) arrived in early spring for two weeks in repertory at NYC Opera (4 March 2006) in a faithful if unremarkable staging by Philip William McKinley. Paul Sorvino failed to measure up vocally as Tony, but Lisa Vroman and Ivan Hernandez excelled as the lovers Rosabella and Joe.

The Encores season at New York City Center presented two popular titles, *Kismet* (3 December 1953) and *Of Thee I Sing* (26 December 1931), as well as the lesser-known Kander & Ebb musical *70, Girls, 70* (15 April 1971). Lonny Price staged *Kismet* (9 February 2006) with a light comic touch befitting its absurd story, in which Baghdad is the world's gayest playground and its hero jokes of torture and death. Its Hajj was Brian Stokes Mitchell, and Marin Mazzie romped as the vixenish Lalume. Next up, *70, Girls, 70* (30 March 2006) was staged by Kathleen Marshall with deluxe ensemble casting: Olympia Dukakis in her first musical (Ida), Anita Gillette (Eunice), Charlotte Rae (Sadie), Mary Jo Catlett (Fritzi), Carole Cook (Gert), Bob Dishy (Walter), George S. Irving (Harry), and Carleton Carpenter (McIlhenny), among others. Even if the direction, vocals and plotting were shaky, the concert staging instilled a great affection for its able, tireless geriatric cast.

The Gershwins' *Of Thee I Sing* (11 May 2006) hardly qualifies as neglected, but John Rando's giddy concert staging offered a rare chance to hear the score in its original orchestration. Kaufman and Ryskind's book proved surprisingly timely for the twenty-first century, with its president under threat of impeachment, international provocation from the French, a chief executive's improper relations with a woman, and Supreme Court controversy. Victor Garber was the bewildered president John P. Wintergreen, Jennifer Laura Thompson his faithful wife Mary, and Jenny Powers a sultry Diana Devereaux. Perhaps the biggest surprise was the inspired casting of Jefferson Mays as the hapless, forgotten vice president Alexander Throttlebottom. Whereas *Of Thee I Sing* was not well-served by its revival in 1952, this production was warmly welcomed back in 2006.

Off-Broadway produced several notable musicals in an otherwise lean year. A spring hit (*Grey Gardens*, 7 March 2006, Playwrights Horizons) transferred to Broadway in the fall, and will be discussed at length in the following season. Michael John LaChiusa wrote libretto and music for two ambitious through-sung musicals, **See What I Wanna See** (30 October 2005, Public) and **Bernarda Alba** (6 March 2006, Mitzi E. Newhouse), for limited runs. In the latter, based on the famed 1936 Federico García Lorca play, Phylicia Rashad headed a cast of ten women as they suffered through emotional meltdown. While LaChiusa's constant music blunted the impact of Lorca's tragedy, it heightened the former show's dramatic tension, inherent in the Japanese *Rashomon* stories of Ryunosuke Akutagawa. Set in both ancient Japan and contemporary New York, *See What I Wanna See* told a pair of contrasting tales, R. Shomon and Gloryday, with a cast of Marc Kudisch, Idina Menzel and Mary Testa. A welcome revival of *Jacques Brel Is Alive and Well and Living in Paris* (22 January 1968) delivered a year's run at the Zipper beginning 27 March. In summary, an exhilarating year for revivals was matched by a mediocre season for new Broadway musicals, reprieved only by *Jersey Boys, The Color Purple The Drowsy Chaperone*, and the surprise transfer of *Grey Gardens*.

2006–2007

Two modest comedy revues lit up Broadway in late summer. Downtown hip came uptown for a limited four-week run with **Kiki & Herb: Alive on Broadway** (15 August 2006, Helen Hayes), wherein Kiki (Justin Bond), accompanied by Herb (Kenny Mellman), sent up every mediocre, self-pitying lounge singer with snappy, anecdotal banter punctuated by songs like The Cure's "Let's Go to Bed" and the Scissor Sisters' "Take Your Mama Out." Such political incorrectness and drag queen clichés appealed strongly to the loyal if limited audience who didn't get enough of Kiki & Herb during their Farewell Concert at Carnegie Hall in 2004. (Bond and Mellman had performed the act since the early 1990s.) **Martin Short: Fame Becomes Me** (17 August 2006, Bernard B. Jacobs) appealed to precisely the opposite crowd, those who longed for a wholesome, old-fashioned musical comedy revue, albeit one that resembled television's *Saturday Night Live* or *SCTV*, where Short got his start. Conceived principally as a showcase for its star, the loosely autobiographical book attempted to satirize the public obsession with celebrity. Returning as the sycophantic interviewer Jiminy Glick of the mock late-night television show *Primetime with Jiminy Glick*, Short "interviewed" Judy Garland, Ellen DeGeneres, Celine Dion, Britney Spears, Joan Rivers, Liza Minnelli, Tommy Tune, and Bob Fosse, all played by members of the small supporting cast. Despite some enjoyable songs from *Hairspray*'s Scott Wittman and Marc Shaiman, *Fame Becomes Me* was desperate to entertain and only sporadically amusing, and closed by the year's end.

A feast of musical revivals began with *A Chorus Line* (25 July 1975), whose original co-stager, Bob Avian, directed, while Baayork Lee (the show's original Connie Wong) lovingly restaged Michael Bennett's definitive choreography. This first Broadway revival since the original closed sixteen years prior revealed choreography as fresh as the day it was created. The book, on the other hand, with its descent into self-scrutiny and anxiety about the brevity of a dancer's career, now played awkwardly. A cast of exemplary dancers, especially Charlotte d'Amboise as Cassie, Deidre Goodwin (Sheila), Jason Tam (Paul), Michael Beresse (Zach), and Jessica Lee Goldyn (Val) recreated much of the original excitement. What was missing was the original cast's visceral connection to the characters, which the actors had helped create during a series of workshops, based on their own experiences. Nonetheless this *Chorus Line* (5 October 2006, Gerald Schoenfeld) won a new generation of admirers, ran nearly two years and toured profitably long after.

The Times They Are A-Changin' (26 October 2006, Brooks Atkinson) was dancer and choreographer Twyla Tharp's theatrical staging of Bob Dylan's song catalogue, built around a father, Captain Ahrab (Thom Sesma), and son Coyote's (Michael Arden) competing affection for a circus runaway, Cleo (Lisa Brescia). The Oedipal rivalry was never dramatically compelling, and Dylan's introspective songs remained steadfastly untheatrical as they were retrofitted into the story. His signature social and political insights remained extraneous to the narrative—as well as seemingly unsuitable for standard choreography—with pop classics such as "Mr. Tambourine

Man" falling strangely flat. Cleo's solo "Everything is Broken" brought the action to a complete halt. Faced with a unanimous drubbing, the show closed after just a month.

Grey Gardens (2 November 2006, Walter Kerr), a transfer from Playwrights Horizons the previous spring, set to music the famous 1975 Maysles brothers' documentary about the decline and descent into madness of Edith Bouvier Beale and her daughter, Little Edie, in New York's upscale East Hampton. Bookwriter Doug Wright, composer Scott Frankel, and lyricist Michael Korie took an unlikely subject for musicalization and crafted an intimate musical built around the eccentricities of human character. Whereas Act II hewed closely to the original film set in the mid-1970s, the show's authors wrote an all-new Act I exploring the root causes of the Beales' tragedy, when mother and daughter were the doyennes of Long Island society at the start of World War II. The production inventively used the same cast in different roles in each act. Christine Ebersole scored a personal triumph as the mother Edith Bouvier Beale in Act I, then as her daughter Little Edie thirty years later in Act II. Erin Davie played the teenage heiress Little Edie in Act I, while Mary Louise Wilson assumed the part of the aging, delusional, often bedridden mother in Act. A capable supporting cast also played dual roles, including John McMartin as the disapproving grandfather in Act I and Norman Vincent Peale in Act II, and Matt Cavanaugh as prospective suitor Joseph Kennedy, Jr., in Act I and a local handyman in Act II. Ebersole excelled in several memorable songs, among them a Noël Coward pastiche, "Will You?," the climactic "Another Winter in a Summer Town," and most memorably the Act II opener, "The Revolutionary Costume for Today." Mary Louise Wilson was at her most memorable (other, arguably, than when she wasn't eating cat food,) in her solo "The Cake I Had." If the jolly pastiche of Act I never quite matched the emotional desolation of Act II, Michael Greif's tender direction delivered a compelling evening's theatre. *Grey Gardens* was elitist, not mass-market entertainment; its appeal wilted after nine months.

Dr. Seuss' How the Grinch Stole Christmas (8 November 2006, Hilton) was a seventy-minute holiday confection performed eleven times weekly for family audiences. Based on Dr. Seuss's (a.k.a. Theodore Geisel) children's book and borrowing the 1966 animated film's most beloved song, "You're a Mean One, Mr. Grinch" (by Seuss and composer

Albert Hague), the story told of the tiny denizens of Whoville, from whom the wicked green Grinch (Patrick Page) plans to steal Christmas. As narrated by the Grinch's dog Max (John Cullum as the older Max, Rusty Ross as the younger), Christmas is inevitably saved and the Scrooge-like Grinch reformed. Timothy Mason's workmanlike book and lyrics and new music by Mel Marvin added little to the merriment. Matt August directed this production, which had originally been conceived and staged by Jack O'Brien as an annual event for San Diego's Old Globe Theatre. Families flocked for the scheduled nine weeks.

Les Misérables (12 March 1987) returned to Broadway after a three-year absence in a scaled-down revival by its original creators and producer. Whatever this production (9 November 2006, Broadhurst) may have gained in intimacy compared to its previous berth at the larger Broadway Theatre, it suffered from indifferent casting, a slimming of the narrative to "Cliff's Notes" basics, and a loss of epic grandeur and tragedy. The requisite components were still present, but scored less impact. As Jean Valjean, Alexander Gemignani sang well, but lacked the necessary age and life experience of his ordeal, while an infinitely likable Norm Lewis regrettably did not possess the evil obsessiveness his Javert demanded. Daphne Rubin-Vega appeared too contemporary as the short-lived Fantine. Celia Keenan-Bolger was moving as Eponine and Aaron Lazaar rallied his partisans effectively as Enroljas. The popular *Les Mis* stayed for a year, then resumed touring.

Mary Poppins (16 November 2006, New Amsterdam), a London import and co-production from Disney Theatricals and producer Cameron Mackintosh, brought the 1964 Disney film and stories by P. L. Travers to the musical stage. Set in London circa 1900, the stage adaptation by Julian Fellowes dutifully followed everyone's favorite nanny, Mary Poppins (Ashley Brown), into the puritanical home of the Banks family, where she wreaks havoc and restores love to all. Bert, the jolly dustman, was performed by expert dancer Gavin Lee, whose authentic English accent was a welcome improvement upon Dick Van Dyke's original. Daniel Jenkins and Rebecca Luker were appropriately formal as parents George and Winifred Banks, and their two children, played by a rotating cast of child actors, were happily more mischievous and less saccharine than expected. The famous Richard B. Sherman–Robert B. Sherman score was retained ("Chim Chim Cher-ee," "Supercalifragilisticexpialidocious,"

"Let's Go Fly a Kite," "Step in Time," "A Spoonful of Sugar") and augmented by several mostly competent new interpolations ("Anything Can Happen," "Practically Perfect," "Brimstone and Treacle," and the tepid "Temper, Temper") by George Stiles and Anthony Drewe. Although the production, directed by Richard Eyre and Matthew Bourne and choreographed by Bourne and Stephen Mear, had been substantially tightened and brightened since its London debut in 2004, *Mary Poppins* still felt methodically calculated and carpentered. Other than a clever tap dance around the proscenium by Bert, the production seldom displayed much in the way of spontaneity or wit. Nonetheless, *Mary Poppins* kept family audiences entertained for more than four years.

Unquestionably the most inspired revival of the season, John Doyle's unorthodox staging of Stephen Sondheim and George Furth's *Company* (26 April 1970) provoked both admiration and controversy. Influenced by the staging concept and success of the recent revival of *Sweeney Todd*, the entire cast of *Company* doubled as its orchestra. Following a run at Cincinnati's Playhouse in the Park, this very different *Company* opened 29 November 2006 at the Ethel Barrymore for a 247-performance run. Each cast member's emotions, temperament, and inner thoughts gained immeasurable expressiveness and nuance. As *Variety*'s critic suggested, "trumpets and flutes begin to seem as logical an accessory for these sophisticates as a handbag, cigarette or cocktail." When Raúl Esparza as Bobby finally sits at the piano for the first time to sing "Being Alive" haltingly, Doyle's theatrical conceit paid handsome dividends. Esparza captured Bobby's brooding sadness and confusion, while Barbara Walsh, as Joanne, was charismatically brittle, man-hungry and desperate. The rest of the cast defined themselves vividly as individuals and adeptly made tangible the show's sexual ambiguities. The only excision from the original was the virtuoso dance solo, "Tick Tock." Despite its modest run, this *Company* was taped for broadcast and preserved on home video.

A tired touring edition of *Annie* (21 April 1977) arrived for four weeks at the Theater at Madison Square Garden (6 December 2006). Although faithfully restaged by its original director, Martin Charnin, with the same sets and costumes, the show's freshness faded into forced cheerfulness. Conrad John Schuck, a veteran Daddy Warbucks, delivered a solid performance, and newcomer Marissa O'Donnell charmed as the little orphan

with pluck and a big voice. Only Kathie Lee Gifford disappointed as a coarse and hammy Miss Hannigan. *The Apple Tree* (18 October 1966) had won many plaudits in its 2005 Encores staging, especially for its star Kristin Chenoweth (Eve/Princess Barbará/ Ella-Passionella). Roundabout Theatre Company generously gave *The Apple Tree* a fuller staging (17 December 2006, Studio 54) for a twelve-week run. Brian D'Arcy James replaced Malcolm Gets as Adam/Sanjar/Flip-Prince Charming, and Marc Kudisch returned as the Snake/Balladeer/Narrator. Gary Griffin, Andy Blankenbuehler, and Rob Fisher repeated their Encores duties as director, choreographer, and conductor. Alas, the very slightness of *The Apple Tree*'s charms became all the more apparent with a full production.

The winter's bounty of revivals included New York Gilbert & Sullivan Players' return to City Center with not only *The Yeomen of the Guard* and *The Mikado*, but also the first appearance in more than a century of Arthur Sullivan and Basil Hood's *The Rose of Persia* (6 September 1900). Its very modest staging offered a welcome look at an obscure work. The New York City Opera revived *The Pirates of Penzance* for two weeks beginning 3 March 2007 with Broadway interlopers Marc Kudisch as the Pirate King and Mark Jacoby as Major General Stanley. Lillian Groag's sluggish staging and the New York State Theatre's obstinate acoustics did G&S no favors.

High Fidelity (7 December 2006, Imperial) took Nick Hornby's admired 1995 novel set in Britain and its 2000 film version reset in Chicago and transposed them to a sorry used-record shop in Brooklyn called Championship Vinyl. The show's clumsy book by David Lindsay-Abaire, pseudo-jukebox music by Tom Kitt, and lyrics by Amanda Green flattened this tale of losers into blandness. Ron (Will Chase), the shop's owner, excels in the arcane details of backlist rock 'n' roll but cannot sustain a relationship with his longtime lover, Laura (Jenn Colella). The crazy denizens of the record shop offer minor distractions, but Jay Klaitz as Barry was not able to match the wild, career-making behavior of his screen predecessor, Jack Black. However appealing the score's best songs, such as Will's "Desert Island Top 5 Breakups," the show's very premise begged for recognizable interpolations from the Beatles, the Rolling Stones, the Kinks, Aretha Franklin, Bruce Springsteen, or the Sex Pistols, with which any new music could not compete. Faced with indifferent to hostile reviews, *High Fidelity* faded in two weeks.

Spring Awakening (10 December 2006, Eugene O'Neill), a contemporary rock adaptation of Frank Wedekind's 1891 classic play, an incendiary assault on the German school system, had been a surprise off-Broadway hit for the Atlantic Theatre Company in June. A critics' favorite, its free-form book and lyrics by Steven Sater and hip rock score by Duncan Sheik proved an exhilarating and odd marriage of bitter source material wedded to propulsive staging by Michael Mayer and uniquely stylized, modern dance choreography for non-dancers from Bill T. Jones. The "awakening" of the title refers to the characters' coming of age, and primarily of their sexual maturation. Thwarted by adults, all of the German youth are misunderstood, in particular its three central protagonists, Wendla (Lea Michele), Melchior (John Gallagher Jr.), and their suicidal best friend, Moritz (Jonathan Groff). The youthful, immensely talented cast brought the story's tragedy to vivid life. Standouts in the score were Wendla's inquiry about pregnancy, "Mama Who Bore Me," the students' "The Bitch of Living," and Moritz's parents lament, "Left Behind." Its closing anthem, "The Song of Purple Summer," offered some solace to musical-theatre audiences, even if it betrayed the final bleakness of Wedekind's original. *Spring Awakening* ran for more than two years, although many hoped it would run longer and join *Rent* as a youthful musical theatre classic.

Encores' season of musical revivals in concert at New York City Center began with Stephen Sondheim and William Goldman's seminal work, *Follies* (4 April 1970). As if to banish the sorry distaste of Roundabout's recent revival on the cheap, Casey Nicholaw's elegant concert staging demonstrated how much more can be accomplished with astute casting, a sure directorial focus, and the glorious sound of a full orchestration. This revival's (9 February 2007) Ben and Phyllis Stone were Victor Garber and Donna Murphy, whose icy marriage is the show's emotional center; its Buddy and Sally Plummer, a former hoofer-jokester and his psychologically fragile wife, were Michael McGrath and Victoria Clark. As with many New York musical supporting casts, this one was a celebrity roll call of yesterday—it was a thrill to rediscover Jo Anne Worley (a giddy Stella Deems), Christine Baranski (a young Carlotta Campion), Yvonne Constant (an authentic Solange LaFitte), Mimi Hines (a dynamite Hattie Walker), and the Metropolitan Opera's Lucine Amara (as the aging operetta doyenne Heidi Schiller). Encores' next offering, *Face the Music*

(17 February 1932), constituted an astonishing feat of restoration in Irving Berlin and Moss Hart's revusical of depression-era corruption and comic foolery. Blessed with Irving Berlin's charming score and a tighter book revised by David Ives, this *Face the Music* (30 March 2007) allowed champion farceurs Judy Kaye (as Mrs. Myrtle Meshbesher, dripping with diamonds), Lee Wilkof (her husband, the most crooked cop ever to hit show business), and Walter Bobbie (down-on-his-luck producer Hal Reisman) to cavort across the stage. Its purposefully awful musical-within-a-musical *Rhinestones of 1932* recalled Mel Brooks' later farce *The Producers* with uncanny similarity. Encores' final offering of the season, **Stairway to Paradise** (11 May 2007), was not a revival but a composite revue of songs and sketches loosely assembled from 1907–1957, the dates of the first and last Ziegfeld Follies. Its songs by a who's-who of authors, composers and lyricists (such as Irving Berlin, Cole Porter, and Rodgers and Hart) were assembled by Jack Viertel and capably directed by Jerry Zaks. As talented as its cast was (Kristin Chenoweth, Kevin Chamberlin, Christopher Fitzgerald, Ruthie Henshall, Capathia Jenkins), none could match the larger-than-life personalities (Fannie Brice, Ethel Waters, Al Jolson, Jimmy Durante) for whom these songs and sketches were first custom-tailored. Laudable as was the attempt to revive the vanished species of the elaborate musical Broadway revue, *Stairway to Paradise* reaffirmed that audience tastes have indeed consigned most revue to television. Nonetheless it was a genuine pleasure to hear Irving Berlin's "Suppertime," Dietz & Schwartz's "Triplets" and "Dancing in the Dark," Gorney & E. H. Harburg's "Brother, Can You Spare a Dime," Blake & Razaf's "My Handy Man," and many others with a full orchestra.

Curtains (22 March 2007, Hirschfeld) arrived on Broadway following a gestation period of nearly twenty years, three years after the death of its lyricist Fred Ebb. Originally conceived by Peter Stone, its book was now by Rupert Holmes, who assisted composer John Kander with additional lyrics. Both a murder mystery musical comedy and an homage to the brash and silly musicals of the 1950s, *Curtains* took place in 1959 onstage at the Boston tryout of a musical called *Robbin' Hood of the Old West*. Its much-loathed leading lady is murdered before our eyes on opening night, and detective Lieutenant Frank Cioffi (David Hyde Pierce) solves the crime Agatha Christie-style by investigating the many probable suspects, both within and outside the company.

This willfully silly story was populated by a host of colorful theatricals: crass producer Carmen Bernstein (Debra Monk), composer and lyricist, once a couple, now separated (Jason Danieley and Karen Ziemba), swishy English director Christopher Belling (Edward Hibbert), the sweet ingénue (Jill Paice). Although staged by Scott Ellis and choreographed by Rob Ashford with great enthusiasm, pace, and style, the sheer burden of so much narrative seldom permitted the production to levitate with joy. The strained effort showed, and at times it seemed as though you really *were* watching a mediocre musical from 1959. Nonetheless *Curtains* was great fun for those who wanted an old-fashioned musical, and it delighted crowds for 511 performances.

The Pirate Queen (5 April 2007, Hilton) promised epic romance and adventure on a grand scale from the authors of *Les Misérables* (Alain Boublil and Claude-Michel Schonberg), director of *Ragtime* (Frank Galati), and producers of *Riverdance*. Based on Morgan Llywelyn's 1986 novel *Grania: She King of the Irish Seas*, *The Pirate Queen* delivered stock melodramatic characters, music derivative of *Les Misérables*, and predictable *Riverdance*-style choreography. What on paper looked like a brilliant marriage of talents emerged as a giant animated cartoon of dashing pirates and storms at sea, with a generic plot about plucky heroine Grania (Stephanie J. Block) defending her Irish homeland from a steely, humorless Queen Elizabeth I of England (Linda Balgord). Forced by duty into a loveless marriage with Donal (Marcus Chait), Grania forgoes true love with her soul-mate Tiernan (Hadley Frasier). However satisfying the final showdown between Grania and Elizabeth, it was too little, too late. Weak dramaturgy and the production's thirty-five musical numbers and twenty-five scenes exhausted the audience's patience and elicited unanimous pans from the critics. *The Pirate Queen* closed after eleven weeks and a month of previews.

Legally Blonde (29 April 2007, Palace) transposed the hit 2001 Hollywood comedy to the stage with tireless energy and a jolly dose of girl empowerment in blinding pink. Heather Hach's book, adapted from the MGM screenplay and 2001 novel by Amanda Brown, was paired with a score by husband-and-wife team Laurence O'Keefe and Nell Benjamin. The dizzying pace was established in its opening number "Omigod You Guys." At her college graduation, heroine Elle Woods (Laura Bell Bundy) is dumped by her intended beau, Warner

Huntington III (Richard H Blake). Unwilling to accept defeat, Elle follows him to Harvard Law School, where her meteoric and wildly implausible rise overtakes the worthless Warner. Elle earns the professional esteem of law professor Callahan (Michael Rupert) in a tumultuous court case where she exposes the true murderer in song, "There! Right There!" Rupert had the show's best song, "Blood in the Water," which illustrated the ruthlessness of the legal profession. Elle inevitably finds true love in her loyal chum Emmett Forrest (Christian Borle). This delightfully silly confection was kept afloat by the nonstop callisthenic staging of Jerry Mitchell, heretofore choreographer of *Hairspray, Dirty Rotten Soundrels,* and the last *La Cage aux Folles.* Serious critics and the Tony-nominating committee dismissed *Legally Blonde* as fluff, but the show prospered for a sixteen-month run, a precedent-breaking live telecast on MTV, a successful national tour, and London debut in 2010.

LoveMusik (3 May 2007) was an ambitious attempt by director Harold Prince and playwright Alfred Uhry to fashion a serious biographical musical around the life and music of husband and wife Kurt Weill (Michael Cerveris) and Lotte Lenya (Donna Murphy). As presented by the Manhattan Theatre Club, *LoveMusik* depicted this irreconcilable couple in a regrettably tedious, yet lovingly faithful, production. Perhaps *LoveMusik* was hampered by the weight of the true story of Weill's early fame in Germany: his unlikely romance with Lenya; their inconsistent marriage, flight to France, and emigration to the United States; Weill's Broadway successes and early death at fifty; and finally Lenya's long and loving sponsorship of Weill's oeuvre. Illustrating their odyssey were twenty-nine often fascinating musical numbers, some familiar, many obscure, which mitigated the otherwise static evening. Cerveris was touching as the meek, geeky composer, while Murphy's Lenya was an eccentric caricature of impulsive, smoky, defensive swagger. Emblematic of the evening's imaginative reuse of songs was "That's Him" from *One Touch of Venus*, originally a woman's ode to her man, here repositioned as Weill's bitter reflection on Lenya's adultery. Critics and audiences were respectful, and *LoveMusik* played out it subscription run of eight weeks plus previews.

A long-awaited revival of Schmidt and Jones' *110 in the Shade* (24 October 1963) materialized to close the season on 9 May 2007 at Roundabout Theatre Company's Studio 54. Lonny Price provided sensitive direction for this musical rainmaker story, but the imbalance in casting prevented the production from realizing its true potential. Despite her formidable acting technique, Audra MacDonald, as the spinster Lizzie Curry, was such a radiant, electrifying presence that it was difficult to accept her as plain and loveless; her transformation into a woman fully capable of love was nonetheless moving. The two men vying for her affection were longtime admirer and town sheriff File (Christopher Innvar) and the itinerant conman and professed rainmaker, Starbuck (Steve Kazee). However appealing the brooding Innvar and cocky Kazee, neither burned as brightly as their costar. John Cullum and Bobby Steggert registered strongly in small roles as Lizzie's father and little brother. One previously cut song, "Evening Star," was added for Starbuck. *110* extended its subscription run for a total of ninety-five performances.

Off-Broadway posted a modest year. *The Fantasticks* (3 May 1960), absent for little more than four years, returned to a new uptown berth at the Snapple Theatre Center on 23 August 2006. Librettist Tom Jones faithfully restaged Word Baker's original work and performed as the Old Actor under the alias of Thomas Bruce. Led by talented newcomer Santino Fontana (Matt) and Broadway veterans Burke Moses (Narrator), Leo Burmeister (Hucklebee), and Martin Vidnovic (Bellomy), *The Fantasticks* settled into its new home indefinitely. A pocket-sized musical farce for two manic singer-actors, **Gutenberg! The Musical!** (3 December 2006, 59E59) was written by Steve Brown and Anthony King. Its nonsensical plot about the tiny German town Gutenberg and a mad monk was but a pretext for the nonstop antics of Christopher Fitzgerald and Jeremy Shamos, who performed triple duty in multiple disguises. The season's other two breakout hits, *In the Heights* (8 February 2007, 37 Arts) and *Passing Strange* (14 May 2007, Public), transferred to Broadway for the following season, and will be addressed at length below. In sum, this was a prosperous season of welcome variety and many surprises.

2007–2008

Xanadu (10 July 2007, Helen Hayes) was the improbable adaptation of a universally derided movie musical failure, the 1980 film starring Olivia Newton-John. The musical benefited from a popular film soundtrack by Jeff Lynne and John Farrar that yielded disco classics "I'm Alive," "Magic," "Dancin'" and "Suddenly." Other jukebox interpolations included "Evil Woman" and "Have You Ever Been Mellow?." Comic playwright Douglas Carter Beane encouraged audiences to laugh at the very foolishness of its story, while director Chris Ashley and choreographer Dan Knechtges turned the tiny stage of the Helen Hayes into a creative asset, filling the stage with the full cast and orchestra and putting roller skates on the busy principal actors. The plot was truly laughable: a Greek goddess-muse named Clio (Kerry Butler) descends to earth in disguise as the mortal Kira, a simple Australian girl on roller blades. In Venice Beach, California, she meets the struggling artist Sonny (Cheyenne Jackson), whose greatest hope is to re-open an abandoned roller-rink named Xanadu. Once Kira falls in love with the mortal Sonny, her two jealous sisters (Jackie Hoffman, Mary Testa) and Zeus (Tony Roberts, doubling as the owner of the roller rink) intercede. *Xanadu*, with its intimacy and refusal to take itself seriously, was the antithesis of the season's musical goliath, Mel Brooks' *Young Frankenstein*. Greeted with unexpected critical hosannas, *Xanadu* surprised naysayers by running for sixteen months.

City Center's Encores series initiated a new summer program (augmenting its winter schedule) with a three-week production of *Gypsy* (21 May 1959) staged by its librettist, Arthur Laurents. Starring Patti LuPone as Rose, this revival (14 July 2007) was later re-mounted for an open run 27 March 2008 at the St. James on Broadway. Known for having played many roles originated by Ethel Merman (Reno Sweeney in *Anything Goes*, Annie Oakley in *Annie Get Your Gun*), LuPone gave Rose a defiant interpretation all her own, abetted by Laurents, whose muscular, unsentimental staging refocused attention on the brilliance of the book. Jerome Robbins' definitive musical blocking was faithfully recreated by Bonnie Walker, but this revival was emphatically Laurents' vision, not Robbins', sometimes at the expense of perfunctory musical numbers. LuPone was helped immeasurably by her two co-stars, Laura Benanti as wallflower-turned-stripper Gypsy Rose Lee and Boyd Gaines as Herbie, who delivered powerhouse performances of equal stature to LuPone's. For those who derided the recent Roses of Bernadette Peters and Tyne Daly, here was a definitive revival of *Gypsy* for the ages.

Another revival of a popular title, *Grease* (14 February 1972, revived 19 August 2007, Brooks Atkinson) received slash-and-burn reviews from the critics but prospered for fifteen months on the strength of its title and the novelty of its casting method: leads Max Crumm (Danny Zuko) and Laura Osnes (Sandy Dumbrowski) were chosen by a voting public during NBC's reality television show *Grease: You're the One That I Want*. Crumm and Osnes, both competent performers, grew immeasurably during the run. Kathleen Marshall's slick direction and choreography could not conceal the formulaic, mercenary inspiration for the revival, which attracted happy tourists for the duration of its run.

Young Frankenstein (8 November 2007, Hilton) faced the insurmountable obstacle of matching or exceeding Mel Brooks's previous screen-to-stage triumph, the smash hit *The Producers*. The perceived arrogance of its producers (Brooks and Robert F. X. Sillerman) with regard to the show's $135-plus ticket pricing and availability inspired nasty preview gossip from the public, press and theatregoers, a liability from which it never recovered during its forced fourteen-month run. Using *The Producers* as a template, the same creative team—Brooks, director Susan Stroman, and co-bookwriter Thomas Meehan, and even the same set, costume, lighting, and sound designers, orchestrator, music director, and music supervisor—applied a replicated formula to Brooks and Gene Wilder's 1974 film farce, *Young Frankenstein*, but the story proved less suited to musicalization. The serious, young New York doctor Frederick Frankenstein (Roger Bart), heir to the family castle in Transylvania, returns to claim his inheritance and stumbles upon his uncle's machinery. Abandoning his stuffy fiancée Elizabeth (Megan Mullally) back in New York, the young doctor, helped by his buxom blonde assistant Inga (Sutton Foster), grim housekeeper Frau Blucher (Andrea Martin), and the hunchback Igor (Christopher Fitzgerald), bring The Monster (Shuler Hensley) back to life. The apex of both the original film and the stage version was the absurdist interpolation of Irving Berlin's standard, "Puttin' on the Ritz," performed by Dr. Frankenstein and a grunting Monster as a tap dance extravaganza for the ages. Only two new musical numbers came close to matching that brilliance, "Roll in the Hay," sung by Inga from the back of a horse-drawn cart, and Act II's "Deep Love," Elizabeth's carnal embrace of the Monster. The rest of the evening proved that unlimited money, resource, and talent do not automatically equal success. The showbiz and backstage setting of *The Producers* had invited song and dance, but turning *Young Frankenstein* into

a musical was a stretch—one that ultimately did not work.

The following night, the previous season's family Christmas offering, *Dr. Seuss' How the Grinch Stole Christmas* (8 November 2006) returned for a ten-week season to the St. James Theatre.

Disney's latest entry in the screen-to-stage sweepstakes was The Little Mermaid (10 January 2008, Lunt-Fontanne), adapted from its popular 1989 animated film by the late Howard Ashman and Alan Menken. Doug Wright (author of *Grey Gardens* and *I Am My Own Wife*) adapted John Musker and Ron Clements' screenplay, and Glenn Slater wrote new lyrics to augment the six songs retained from film, of which Ariel's ballad "Part of Your World," the calypso "Under the Sea," wicked Ursula's "Poor Unfortunate Souls" and crustacean Sebastian's "Kiss the Girl" had become well-known worldwide. Loosely based on a short story by Hans Christian Andersen, *The Little Mermaid*'s heroine, Ariel (Sierra Boggess), is not content with her life underwater, preferring "The World Above." When Prince Eric (Sean Palmer) is tossed overboard, Ariel saves his life; they promptly fall in love. The evil sea witch Ursula (Sherie Rene Scott), eager to avenge her brother (and Ariel's father) King Triton (Norm Lewis), persuades Ariel to surrender her voice to become a mortal for three days, promising Ariel that she can become mortal forever if she can win a kiss from Prince Eric. Ursula's plot is inevitably thwarted and Ariel gets her voice back, captures the prince and wins her father's blessing. Under the stage direction of Francesca Zambello, *The Little Mermaid* was a very busy, noisy, intensely colorful family-friendly entertainment of no particular distinction. The most difficult creative challenge was for set designer George Tsypin to create an underwater style that could match the visual excitement of the animated film—hence the use of much plastic and plexiglass to symbolize wetness, and lighting by Natasha Katz to replicate the shimmers and translucence of water. Costume designer Tatiana Noginova employed wheel-heeled footwear so that Stephen Mears' choreography could distinguish between walking, floating, and swimming. *The Little Mermaid* delighted audiences for twenty months, reportedly just shy of full recoupment. As with most Disney titles, a long, happy ancillary life (including a national tour) suggests that *The Little Mermaid* will likely be immortal.

Carnegie Hall was the unorthodox venue for a London import, Jerry Springer: The Opera (29 January 2008) seeking a wider acceptance and a fuller staging than the glorified concert version presented for two nights. Its book and lyrics by Stewart Lee and Richard Thomas, who also composed its score (which was not really that of an opera), took the recognizable form of Jerry Springer's lurid television talk show in Act I, at the end of which Springer is murdered. In hell in Act II, Springer encounters God, Jesus, Mary, and the Devil. The production's irreverence, crude characters and casually explicit language made *Jerry Springer: The Opera* a hit at the National Theatre in London, though it was a comparably modest success in its West End transfer. Its subsequent telecast on the BBC provoked thousands of complaints from viewers, proving what Springer himself could argue, that notoriety becomes success. In the New York production, staged by *Avenue Q*'s Jason Moore, Springer was played by veteran actor and Hollywood star Harvey Keitel, who lacked the youthful energy and iconoclastic spirit of the London production's lead (Michael Brandon) and the real Jerry Springer. David Bedella repeated his Laurence Olivier Award-winning turn as the Devil. What good fun there was in *Jerry Springer* stemmed from the dysfunctional thrill of hearing scatological language set to verismo, Handel-mimicking music, although the book slipped into repetitiveness in Act II. *Jerry Springer: The Opera* has yet to find a widespread American audience.

Encores' season opened with the seldom-revived Tony Award-winner for Best Musical, *Applause* (30 March 1970), offered a rare sighting of Marc Blitzstein's much-lamented failure *Juno* (9 March 1959), and closed with the revival adaptation of *No, No, Nanette* (19 January 1971; original production 11 March 1925). Under the perfunctory direction and choreography of Kathleen Marshall, *Applause* no longer delighted as it had almost forty years prior. Christine Ebersole was stage diva Margo Channing and Erin Davie her youthful nemesis Eve Harrington. Michael Park assumed the role of the man in Margo's life, Bill Sampson. Betty Comden and Adolph Green's update of the classic 1950 film *All About Eve* was no improvement on the original, and the score by Charles Strouse and Lee Adams was not as memorable as their other work. On the other hand, *Juno* (27 March 2008) afforded a rare opportunity to reexamine a celebrated failure. Director Garry Hynes, a skilled interpreter of Irish culture (particularly the plays of Martin McDonagh) brought a deep and instinctive understanding to this musical adaptation of the 1924 play *Juno and the Paycock* by Sean O'Casey. Despite premium casting of Victoria

Clark as Juno, this revival plodded and never got off the ground. Conrad John Schuck had the bluster but seldom the pathos of "Captain" Jack Boyle; Dermot Crowley clowned as his drinking buddy, "Joxer" Daly. Celia Keenan-Bolger (Mary Boyle) was profoundly moving as the jilted daughter, especially during the gem "I Wish It So." It was Marc Blitzstein's glorious score, heard for the first time in almost fifty years in its original orchestration, that thrilled the ear. The season's closer was a proven crowd-pleaser, *No, No, Nanette* (8 May 2008), and Walter Bobbie's exuberant staging, supported by Randy Skinner's tap-happy choreography, was a total joy. *Nanette* is nothing but a confection, yet shorn of its spectacular Busby Berkeley direction, one wondered whether this production could soar. Fortunately, fortuitously smart casting helped. Sandy Duncan was as beguiling a Sue Smith as was the 1971 revival's Ruby Keeler, and Charles Kimbrough was delightful as her oft-befuddled husband. Beth Leavel and Michael Berresse danced up a storm as Lucille and Billy Early. The young lovers, Nanette (Mara Davi) and Tom (Shonn Wiley) imbued themselves with as much charm as their roles permitted. The genuine fun in *Nanette*'s silliness was welcome proof that old-fashioned musical comedy could still work for a modern audience.

Pulitzer Prize-winner *Sunday in the Park with George* (2 May 1984) returned to Broadway in its first full-scale revival, courtesy of London's Menier Chocolate Factory, where it had scored a major success. Under the sure, sensitive hand of director Sam Buntrock, Stephen Sondheim and James Lapine's *Sunday in the Park with George* opened 21 February 2008 at the Roundabout Theatre's Studio 54 for a five-month run. Essential to the revival's success were its charismatic two leads from London, Daniel Evans as pointillist painter Georges Seurat and Jenna Russell as his suffering model and mistress Dot. Equally significant was the design team, with sets and costumes by David Farley and the remarkable light projections by Timothy Bird and the Knifedge Creative Network. The digital image technology used throughout enhanced the show's dramatic themes of the artist's work in progress and the artist in isolation, a substantive improvement over the 1984 original. This was especially true in the 1980s-set Act II—whereas the modern art sequence "Chromolume #7" had been almost risible in the original production, its digital realization finally permitted Act II's dramatic arc to land with emotional precision.

Passing Strange (28 February 2008, Belasco), an unlikely off-Broadway export, was a musical *bildungsroman*, a coming-of-age story by the African-American guitarist Stew (with additional music by Heidi Rodewald), who both narrates and presides over this genre-defying musical evening. Stew's younger self, identified only as Youth (Daniel Breaker) starta as an unremarkable middle-class kid in suburban Los Angeles, refuses his mother's (Eisa Davis) entreaties to attend church, formed his own garage band, flees to Amsterdam, and experiments with drugs, sex, and rock 'n' roll, thereby discovering his own identity. The sheer self-absorption of this intimate, personal narrative could have proven tiresome were it not for Stew's wry, self-deprecating skill with the story and a supporting cast of infinite talent and imagination. Among the standouts were Colman Domingo as Mr. Franklin, the gay choir director who offers Youth his first joint, and Rebecca Naomi Jones, and De'Adre Aziza, who attempt to teach Youth about sex and love. Staged with blinding lights on a mostly empty stage more reminiscent of a rock concert than a musical, *Passing Strange* won fervent admirers in the press and public, and a bushel of Tony nominations, but struggled to find an audience in its four months. Spike Lee filmed the stage musical for his *Passing Strange: The Movie* (2009), which assured the production's future life.

No less autobiographical, **In the Heights** (9 March 2008, Richard Rodgers) was conceived with music and lyrics by Lin-Manuel Miranda as a celebration of the Latino culture of his childhood neighborhood, Washington Heights, in northern Manhattan. With a book by Quiara Alegría Hudes, direction by newcomer Thomas Kail, and choreography by Andy Blankenbuehler, *In the Heights* was a critical success off-Broadway in February 2007; despite a tepid initial response from the public, its determined producers, Kevin McCollum, Jeffrey Seller and Jill Furman, tightened the project over the a five-month off-Broadway run. This unlikeliest of Broadway transfers received a royal welcome from the critics, won the Tony for Best Musical, and ran for more than two years. *In the Heights* at heart was a surprisingly traditional, sentimental soap opera of very satisfying proportions. It starred Miranda as Usnavi, the unprepossessing owner of a small bodega dispensing café con leche and kindness to all the local customers. His surrogate grandmother Abuela Claudia (Olga Merediz) worries about Usnavi's future, while his cousin Sonny (Robin de Jesús) eagerly awaits his own future and the exploits

he hopes it includes. The gypsy-cab company next door is run by Camila and Kevin Rosario (Priscilla Lopez and Carlos Gomez), whose daughter Nina (Mandy Gonzalez) has had a rough first year at Stanford University. Other locals include Benny (Christopher Jackson), the top dispatcher at the Rosarios' cab company and admirer of Nina; Daniela (Andréa Burns), the leader of the beauty-parlor gossip clique; and Vanessa (Karen Olivo), Usnavi's love interest, who dreams of escaping the neighborhood. An unexpected power failure at the end of Act I results in confusion and upheaval for this cast of eccentric characters. Passions run high, secrets are revealed, and an unexpected death and serendipitous lottery ticket teach all a lesson about love and family by the final curtain. The ensemble numbers (particularly Usnavi's opening title song, with its clever use of rap music) and dancing outshone the ballads, but Nina and Benny's "When the Sun Goes Down" and Nina's "Everything I Know" stood out. First conceived by its author while still a student at Wesleyan University, *In the Heights* was a valentine to Miranda's neighborhood and a good-faith effort to undermine negative ethnic stereotypes.

A full-scale Broadway revival had long eluded Rodgers and Hammerstein's *South Pacific* (7 April 1949), apart from a summer Lincoln Center engagement in 1967, several short City Center revivals in the 1950s and 1960s, and an unremarkable New York City Opera staging in 1987. Consequently, Lincoln Center Theatre's revival (3 April 2008) at the Vivian Beaumont faced overwhelming expectations. On the basis of his fine work on *The Light in the Piazza*, Bartlett Sher was selected to direct, and he chose *Piazza*'s ingénue, Kelli O'Hara, as his Nellie Forbush. As Forbush, O'Hara radiated American brashness, vitality, and provincialism, yielding, by the end of the production, to a deeper understanding of the embattled world she inhabits in the South Pacific during World War II. A great mystery surrounded the casting of Paulo Szot, a Polish-Brazilian baritone opera singer unknown to the theatre community, in the role of Emile de Becque, famously created by bass Ezio Pinza. Szot's musical theatre debut created a sensation. His renditions of "Some Enchanted Evening" and "This Nearly Was Mine" brought a particular freshness to widely known, oft-interpreted songs. Matthew Morrison was compelling as the doomed Lieutenant Cable, Danny Burstein brought fresh glee to Luther Billis' hijinks, and Loretta Ables Sayre gave Bloody Mary integrity and charm in a role often played for laughs. Sher's direction reflected a deep respect for the text, free from new-age directorial spin or musical comedy cliché. Among its many virtues was the use, indeed display, of the full orchestra revealed during the overture, as the thrust stage briefly receded. In an era of ever-dwindling orchestra size, the luxurious sound of thirty instruments was unique and welcome. In a rarity among revivals, there was scant revision of the text, other than a few lines of Nellie's that implied racism and the restoration of a cut song, "My Girl Back Home," for Cable and Nellie. The unsentimental toughness of Sher's staging exposed the ugliness of American racism and xenophobia much as Hammerstein had intended, and was particularly timely, as America was then debating the candidacy of Barack Obama as a potential president. This new *South Pacific* opened to ecstatic notices and ran for one thousand performances.

A serious contender in a season of frothy, silly new musicals, **A Catered Affair** (17 April 2008, Walter Kerr) was a well-meaning disappointment. Adapted from a television drama by Paddy Chayefsky and a 1956 movie with a screenplay by Gore Vidal, and with a book by Harvey Fierstein and score by John Bucchino, *A Catered Affair* probed the private lives and disappointments of the Hurley household in the Bronx in 1953. The Hurleys have just returned from a Washington, D.C. memorial service for their son killed in Korea. Aggie Hurley (Faith Prince) wants her daughter Janey (Leslie Kritzer) to have a traditional wedding with all the trappings, as one last gasp of happiness before Janey's marriage inevitably settles into dullness. Patriarch Tom Hurley (Tom Wopat) has a once-in-a-lifetime opportunity to buy out his partners in his taxi business, but would have to use the same scarce funds Aggie would need for the wedding, as well as money for their son's death benefit. Uncle Winston (Fierstein), a confirmed bachelor, narrates the tale with uncertain detachment and humor, his very participation or existence challenged. Janey's fiancé, Ralph (Matt Cavenaugh), just wants to escape with Janey as soon as possible. Here was an unglamorous musical about a family of wounded souls and the intimacy of love and marriage. John Doyle's minimalist direction shed all brash musical comedy conventions in a modest, sensitive production. Alas, what all hoped would be a profoundly moving story often proved merely sad, small, and ordinary. Its songs, however touching and intelligent, mostly vanished quickly after being heard. The best were "One White Dress," in which mother and daughter select a wedding dress, "Don't Ever Stop

Saying I Love You" for the engaged couple, and Tom's eloquent self-defense "I Stayed." With mixed reviews and without a Tony nomination for Best Musical, *A Catered Affair* lingered bravely for three months.

Edging out *A Catered Affair* in Tony nomination sweepstakes for Best Musical, Best Book, and Best Original Score for a Musical was **Cry-Baby** (24 April 2008, Marquis), a musical adaptation of the 1990 cult John Waters film. The *Hairspray* team of Mark O'Donnell and Thomas Meehan set their tale in Baltimore once again, this time in 1954. Good girl Allison Vernon-Williams (Elizabeth Stanley) falls for bad boy Wade "Cry-Baby" Walker (James Snyder, in the role originated by Johnny Depp), and bubblegum pop surrenders to sex and rock 'n' roll. Allison's mother (Harriet Harris) and square fiancé (Christopher J. Hanke) try to stop Allison to no avail. The rockabilly, doo-wop score penned by David Javerbaum and Adam Schlesinger was alternately subversive, insipid, or derivative of its 1950s era without ever being truly memorable. Songs such as "The Anti-Polio Picnic" and jokes about iron lungs and dirty communism were seldom as funny as intended. "You Can't Beat the System" was uninspired, an obvious imitation of *Hairspray*'s superior "You Can't Stop the Beat." Snyder and his prison buddies scored the show's best dance number with "Jailyard Jubilee," thrillingly staged by Rob Ashford with license plates as tap shoes. But *Cry-Baby*, under Mark Brokaw's frenetic direction, registered mostly as a generic parody of teenage delinquent movies; bereft of Tony wins, it closed after two months.

A sudden late season arrival courtesy of Arlington, Virginia's Signature Theatre was **Glory Days** (6 May 2008, Circle in the Square). A youthful first effort by James Gardiner (book) and Nick Blaemire (music, lyrics), *Glory Days*, directed by Eric Schaeffer, told the story of a reunion of four high-school buddies one year post-graduation. No longer as close as they once were, each struggles to reconcile their differences and find some common ground. Will (Steven Booth) is their ringleader, Skip (Adam Halpin) the most intellectually mature and thoughtful. A rift emerges between Jack (Jesse JP Johnson), who realizes he is gay, and the intolerant Andy (Andrew C. Call) who would prefer not to know about his friend's revelation. Set amidst the bleachers of the football field, *Glory Days* evoked those painful days of adolescence with musical numbers that were heart-felt, pleasant pop rock, but seldom indelible. Though the show was unanimously panned by critics, it came as a shock to many when *Glory Days* folded on opening night; perhaps had it opened off-Broadway it might have won a more sympathetic audience.

Rounding out the season's revivals were a return engagement of New York City Opera's staple production of Leonard Bernstein and Hugh Wheeler's version of *Candide* (10 March 1974) in the Harold Prince staging, which first appeared in the City Opera repertory 13 October 1982, and again in 1983, 1984, 1986, 1989 and 2005. As restaged by Arthur Masella and conducted by George Manahan, this *Candide* (8 April 2008, New York State) has always been welcomed by New York audiences. Its titular hero was Daniel Reichard, on leave from *Jersey Boys*, with Lauren Worsham and Lielle Berman alternating as Cunegonde. Richard Kind was a droll Voltaire/Pangloss, and Judith Blazer won big laughs as the Old Lady, especially during "I Am Easily Assimilated." Alan Jay Lerner and Frederick Loewe's *Camelot* (3 December 1960) received a concert staging by Lonny Price, as presented by the New York Philharmonic in Avery Fisher Hall for five performances on 7 May 2008. Gabriel Byrne was remarkably uncertain and un-musical as King Arthur, alongside the vocally and dramatically impressive opera star Nathan Gunn as Lancelot. Marin Mazzie had charm and beauty as muse Guenevere, and Christopher Lloyd milked what humor he could from a tiresome King Pellinore. Price's inconsistent direction offered jarring contemporary lapses in taste alongside the medieval setting and text, especially with Bobby Steggert's punk version of the villainous Mordred. Whatever pleasure could be derived from hearing Loewe's score played by the Philharmonic was marred by the direction and Byrne's performance, alas recorded and televised for all to see. In sum, this was a *Camelot* best forgotten.

Off-Broadway musicals celebrated an exemplary season of creativity. **Gone Missing** (24 June 2007, Barrow Street) was a collaborative work between composer Michael Friedman and innovative theatre troupe The Civilians, whose interviews were edited and directed by artistic director Steve Cosson. More a high-concept musical than a revue, *Gone Missing* documented what happens when everyday items are lost by New Yorkers—that is, they "go missing." On a bare stage, a cast of six men and women in gray suits conjured up endless stories of surprise and delight, through song. With multiple extensions, *Gone Missing* stayed for six months. **Celia** (26 September 2007, New World Stages) celebrated the life of the late Latin music diva Celia Cruz, presented on alternate nights in Spanish and English. Xiomara

Laugart sang Cruz's songs, as recalled through the eyes of her loving husband, for a full season of 269 performances. **The Glorious Ones** (5 November 2007, Mitzi E. Newhouse) attempted to capture the rowdy humor of a commedia dell'arte troupe in Italy during the sixteenth century. Based on a 1974 novel by Francine Prose, its witless book and lyrics by Lynn Ahrens were paired with colorless, generic music by Stephen Flaherty. Under the direction and choreography of Graciela Daniele, a talented cast including Marc Kudisch (Flaminio Scala), Natalie Venetia Belcon (Columbina), David Patrick Kelly (Pantalone), and John Kassir (Dottore) desperately clowned around to no avail for the scheduled six weeks under Lincoln Center Theatre auspices.

Make Me a Song (12 November 2007, New World Stages), a revue of William Finn's musical theatre catalogue, received warm reviews but failed to draw audiences after seven weeks. An import from Chicago, **Adding Machine** (26 February 2008, Minetta Lane) heralded the arrival of new talents Joshua Schmidt (music, libretto) and Jason Loewith (libretto), David Cromer (director). Adapted from Elmer Rice's 1923 play, the musical was a grim account of the ordinary Mr. Zero (Joel Hatch) who, unexpectedly fired after twenty-five years of loyal service and replaced by an adding machine, takes vengeance and murders his boss. This bracing, discomforting musical charts Mr. Zero's adventures through an afterlife in the Elysian Fields. With the aid of Takeshi Kata's haunting sets, Cromer created a gloomy, sinister world and a fanciful, warped afterlife. Despite the strange subject matter as the basis for a musical, *Adding Machine* garnered a storm of critical acclaim and ran for five months. Last but not least, *Next to Normal* (13 February 13 2008, Second Stage) was a challenging contemporary musical about a family whose mother is bipolar. An encouraging critical response to its limited two-month run attracted a commercial transfer to Broadway in the 2008–2009 season, where it will discussed at greater length.

The 2007–2008 season was notable for its experimentation and the emergence of talented new writers, as well as several exemplary revivals with both imagination and taste.

2008–2009

More of a Las Vegas circus musical spectacular than a Broadway show, the touring **Cirque Dreams: Jungle Fantasy** (26 June 2008, Broadway) arrived in time to lure in summer visitors to New York. Created and directed by Neil Goldberg, artistic director of performance company Cirque Productions, *Cirque Dreams* introduced its nominal hero the Adventurer (Marcello Balestracci) who visits the jungle by day (Act I) and night (Act II), the latter a spectacle of day-glow colors illuminated by black light. There he encounters butterflies, bees, zebras, giraffes, and immense flowers populated by a host of contortionists, trapeze artists, musclemen, jugglers, and illusionists. Whereas its visuals were enjoyable, *Cirque Dreams* was diminished by treacly, generic songs written and sung by Mother Nature (Jill Diane Winters, also the production's musical director). *Cirque Dreams* stayed the scheduled two months, then departed for the road billed "direct from Broadway."

Newcomers Jeff Bowen (music and lyrics) and Hunter Bell (book) hastily wrote the short musical [title of show] (17 July 2008, Lyceum) about the process of trying to write an as-yet-untitled musical for submission to the New York Musical Theatre Festival, where it was first performed in September 2004. By way of further development at the Eugene O'Neill Theatre Center (2005) and two engagements at the Vineyard Theatre (2006), this "little show that could" starring Bowen and Bell as themselves, along with Heidi Blickenstaff and Susan Blackwell, arrived on Broadway for a summer run. Despite encouraging notices and a loyal following of insider theatre fans, [title of show] lasted for only a three-month run. Bell, Bowen, Blickenstaff, and Blackwell were very funny, effusively conveying their desperate wish to be "Part of It All." However, the very premise of the show was best served by its off and off-off-Broadway venues; the magisterial splendor of the Lyceum revealed all too clearly the thinness of the show's make-it-up-as-we-go-along premise. Self-absorption can be fun in small doses, but a full evening of it proved tiresome.

The husband-and-wife team of Ron Sharpe and Barbra Russell first met onstage playing Marius and Cosette in the Broadway production of *Les Misérables*, and eventually decided to produce their own literary musical set in post-revolutionary France, **A Tale of Two Cities** (18 September 2008, Al Hirschfeld). With nineteen co-producers, this musical adaptation of Charles Dickens' classic 1859 novel, with book, music and lyrics by Jill Santoriello, was suspiciously derivative of *Les Misérables*, but lacked that production's skill and imagination. Upon his release from the Bastille in Paris after a seventeen-year imprisonment, Dr. Alexandre Manette (Gregg Edelman) and his daughter Lucie (Brandi Burkhardt) return to England, where Lucie weds French nobleman Charles Darnay (Aaron Lazar). Back in Paris during the Reign of Terror, Darnay's romantic rival Sydney Carton (James Barbour) sacrifices his own life so that Lucie and Charles may be reunited. Santoriello's rambling, unfocused book and generic pop ballads defeated whatever artistry director-choreographer Warren Carlyle and the capable cast attempted to achieve. Revolving turntables, barricades, swordfights, wenches and drunkards at the tavern, the threat of the guillotine, disguises, revelations and betrayals notwithstanding, *A Tale of Two Cities* folded after sixty performances.

If Disney's *High School Musical* franchise could attract a whole new generation to musical theatre via television and film, then why couldn't Jason Robert Brown's **13** (5 October 2008, Bernard B. Jacobs)? Here was an original story about teenagers, as performed by teenagers, both in its cast and the onstage band. Brown's music and lyrics were wed to Dan Elish and Robert Horn's book about Evan (Graham Phillips), a thirteen-year-old New Yorker whose parents' divorce relocates him and his mom to small-town Appleton, Indiana. Evan discovers that he is a fish out of water, and fears that no one will show up to his bar mitzvah. He befriends neighbor Patrice (Allie Trimm) and wheelchair-bound Archie (Aaron Simon Gross), but gets teased by cool skater Brett (Eric M. Nelsen) and his cheerleader girlfriend, Kendra (Delaney Moro). Growing pains and adolescent battles for acceptance were predictably resolved by final curtain. By any measure, the young cast was impressively talented and engaging; Jeremy Sams' direction and Christopher Gattelli's choreography captured their youthful energy. The score's best were the trio "If That's What It Is" and the bad guys' quartet "Bad Bad News," but too many songs were fraught with message, such as "Becoming a Man" or "Brand New You." Despite some agreeable reviews, *13* never caught on with its target audience or the traditional theatre-going demographic, who likely considered it to be just "kid stuff." *13* departed in three months.

London's smash hit **Billy Elliot: The Musical** (13 November 2008, Imperial) approached its New York run warily. Despite the worldwide success of the 2000 film on which the musical was based, apprehensions abounded that New York audiences would not be partial to the characters' thick Northeast

English accents, dancing kids in tutus, or conflicts centered around the bitter 1984–1985 coalminers' strike and the divisive politics of Margaret Thatcher. Against the wishes of his family, and indeed his community's traditional expectations, Billy Elliot (David Alvarez/Kiril Kulish/Trent Kowalik) discovers at an early age his predilection and talent for dance. Helped only by his garrulous dance teacher Mrs. Wilkinson (Haydn Gwynne) and his mother's ghost (Leah Hocking), Billy gradually wins the support of his father (Gregory Jbara), grandmother (Carole Shelley) and finally his brother Tony (Santino Fontana). Elton John composed his best score yet for theatre with an eye and ear for character development and story, set against a book and lyrics by Lee Hall, derived from his screenplay. Stephen Daldry's visceral direction heightened the drama and suspense, and Peter Darling's choreography embraced rigorous displays of ballet, contemporary popular dance styles, and Stomp-style percussive tap, turning dance into the lingua franca for Billy's trajectory to success. Billy's solo "Electricity" and the full company's "Solidarity" were high points, upstaged perhaps by Billy's soaring solo dance with his older self (Stephen Hanna) to close Act I. Billy Elliot was greeted warmly by New York critics and audiences, won ten Tony Awards, including Best Musical and Best Actor in a Musical for its alternating trio of Billys, and has lasted through a multi-year run.

The season's musical revivals began early with Damn Yankees (5 May 1955) in an Encores staging for a three-week summer season 5 July 2008 at New York City Center. Unlike the 1994 production of a revised version of the show, here was an opportunity to revisit Damn Yankees as it had been written, with the original Don Walker orchestrations. Sean Hayes, featured star from television's Will & Grace, made his New York stage debut as Applegate/The Devil, to great acclaim. Jane Krakowski, an eyeful as Lola, and Cheyenne Jackson, playing gullible Joe Hardy, were just as warmly received. Excellent support from Randy Graff as long-suffering wife Meg Boyd and Megan Lawrence as the irrepressible Gloria Thorpe rounded out a company that director John Rando whipped into tip-top musical comedy form. Mary MacLeod faithfully replicated Bob Fosse's original choreography. The regular Encores fall series resumed with On the Town (28 December 1944), again under the direction of John Rando, on 19 November. After a deplorable critical response to 1971 and 1998 stagings, it was a true pleasure to encounter a near-perfect On the Town. With the

exception of Jerome Robbins' original choreography to "New York, New York," "Times Square Ballet," and "Ya Got Me," dances were newly choreographed by Warren Carlisle, to surprisingly warm notices. The three sailors, Ozzie, Chip, and Gabey (Christian Borle, Justin Bohon, Tony Yazbek), were all well cast. The three women, Ivy Smith, Hildy Esterhazy, and Claire de Loone, whom the men encounter during their twenty-four-hour Manhattan adventure, were Jessica Lee Goldyn, Leslie Kritzer, and Jennifer Laura Thompson. In two small cameos, Andrea Martin was hysterical as Madame Dilly and Michael Cumpsty made memorable the otherwise forgettable Judge Pitkin W. Bridgework. This On the Town was a fitting ninetieth birthday gift to Leonard Bernstein.

It was not a revival, but **White Christmas** (23 November 2008, Marquis), with music by Irving Berlin, could well have been. Purposefully staged by Walter Bobbie as if it were a 1950s musical, with an excellent dance ensemble of eighteen guided by the skillful eye of Randy Skinner, this sentimental stage remake of the 1954 film was designed to be easy family entertainment for the winter holidays. With a book by David Ives and Paul Blake, White Christmas had been polished and pruned through more than a dozen licensed regional theatre productions since its world premiere at the St. Louis Municipal Opera in 2000. The plot revolved around two show-business buddies, Bob Wallace and Phil Davis (Stephen Bogardus and Jeffery Denman, in roles originated in the film by Bing Crosby and Danny Kaye), who attempt to charm their way into the hearts of sisters Betty and Judy Haynes (Kerry O'Malley, Meredith Patterson). With its big, old-fashioned painted backdrops by Anna Louizos and a handful of Irving Berlin standards taken from his back catalogue to augment the film score, White Christmas charmed theatergoers with its believable time warp experience. Apart from the requisite "White Christmas," with snow falling on the audience, other interpolated pleasures included "Falling Out of Love Can Be Fun" from the 1949 musical Miss Liberty, the Rockette-style production number "I Love a Piano," and "Blue Skies" as an Act I finale. Despite divergent notices, this well-oiled crowd pleaser played to excellent business for six weeks, longer than its scheduled run.

Liza Minnelli staged a Broadway comeback in a nostalgic revue fittingly titled **Liza's at the Palace...!** (3 December 2008). Backed by a twelve-piece orchestra, Liza sang a mix of old favorites heavy with Kander & Ebb ("My Own Best Friend," "Cabaret," "And the World Goes 'Round," "New York,

New York") as well as some less well-known numbers (a moving "What Makes a Man?" by Charles Aznavour and Styne–Comden-Green's "If" from *Two on the Aisle*). Act II was largely devoted to the memory of Minnelli's godmother, vocal arranger, composer, singer, and author Kay Thompson, whose club act Minnelli attempted to recreate. Signature special material by Thompson such as "Hello, Hello," "Jubilee Time," and "I Love a Violin" eluded Minnelli's grasp, as did such chestnuts as "Basin Street Blues" and the Gershwins' "Clap Yo' Hands," and "Liza." Generous as was this gesture, Minnelli's performance pleased her loyal fans but won few new admirers during its month-long run.

Shrek The Musical (14 December 2008, Broadway) marked the Broadway debut of film studio Dreamworks as a creative producer of Broadway musical family fare, a territory long dominated by Disney. Based on their 2001 animated film adapted from the 1990 book by William Steig, *Shrek*'s titular character, played by Brian d'Arcy James, is a green lump of an ogre who prefers to live alone in the swamp. When evil Lord Farquaad's (Christopher Sieber) edict sends all the fairy-tale creatures into Shrek's swamp, Shrek determines to abandon his solitary life to save his new neighbors. Joined by his stalwart Donkey (Daniel Breaker), Shrek embarks on an odyssey that leads him to the feisty Princess Fiona (Sutton Foster), trapped for life in a remote castle. Following multiple misunderstandings and Farquaad's thwarted wedding to Fiona, Shrek kisses Fiona, thereby lifting her lifelong curse, only to discover that she too is a green ogress. They live happily ever after. Because most audiences knew the Shrek story well, the creators' challenge was to adapt familiar characters and dramatic situations into a logistically practicable stage production. David Lindsay-Abaire's book and lyrics charmingly navigated the comic twists and turns of this fairy tale for children and adults, and Jeanine Tesori provided a varied Broadway score. Act I's best songs were Shrek's defining "Big Bright Beautiful World" and "Who I'd Be," and Fiona's "I Know It's Today," during which she waits for the perfect prince of her dreams. Act II opened strongly with Fiona's "Morning Person," her flatulence duet with Shrek, "I Think I Got You Beat," and the comic staging of "The Ballad of Farquaad." Midway through the run, Neil Diamond's "I'm a Believer" was interpolated for a sing-along finale, to give audience members a song they already knew. Critical response was mixed to favorable, admiring of the talented cast and lavish

production design by Tim Hatley, and less so for the book and score. *Shrek* managed to run little more than a year without recouping its massive capitalization, but a national tour and international productions were scheduled to follow.

Rodgers & Hart's classic *Pal Joey* (25 December 1940) had long been overdue for a Broadway revival, hopes for such having been stoked by an Encores revival in 1995 and several regional productions. Roundabout delivered its new *Pal Joey* 18 December 2010 at Studio 54; seventy years later lightning did not strike as it had in 1940 and 1952. The cast was not to blame: Stockard Channing (steely socialite Vera), Matthew Risch (the heel Joey, an overnight understudy takeover), and Martha Plimpton (displaying brash confidence in her musical theatre debut in the role of Gladys Bump) were all stellar. Although director Joe Mantello delivered a tough, cynical, worldly production high on grit, it was comparably low on fun and charm. Graciela Daniele's ordinary choreography added little to the sleazy nightclub numbers and gave Joey little of distinction to do. Don Sebesky's sketchy new orchestrations, played by an orchestra divided into two balcony boxes, disassembled Rodgers' smooth, jazzy score. Playwright Richard Greenberg skillfully revised O'Hara's original book, retaining its vinegary tone while adding wit of his own. Joey and good girl Linda's (Jenny Fellner) relationship got an added boost from the interpolation of "Are You My Love?" (from the 1936 film *Dancing Pirate*) and Linda's trustful "I Still Believe in You" (from the 1930 musical *Simple Simon*); Joey's defiant but bruised "I'm Talkin' to My Pal" was restored to *Pal Joey*'s closing scene. These improvements were not enough to bring *Pal Joey* to an enduring new life like that of its thematic cousin *Chicago*; Roundabout's *Pal Joey* played just its ten weeks plus previews.

Encores' concert-staged revival of *Music in the Air* (8 November 1932) breathed welcome life into this long neglected Jerome Kern-Oscar Hammerstein II operetta, opening 5 February 2009 for a scheduled run of five performances. Under the direction of Gary Griffin, the show's charming homage to a bucolic, benign pre-Nazi Bavaria and Munich—and its playful evocation of backstage theatre clichés—proved much more fun than audiences expected. Kristin Chenoweth played Frieda Hatzfeld, the capricious prima donna, and Douglas Sills hammed shamelessly as her captive playwright, Bruno Mahler. As the sweet if colorless ingénue, Sierra Bogess was Sieglinde Lessing, courted by the young schoolmaster Karl Reder (Ryan Silverman). Kern's robust command of melody and the glorious Robert Russell Bennett orchestrations proved the evening's highlights.

The Story of My Life (19 February 2009, Booth), a modest two-person character study originating in Toronto, arrived for a week's stay on Broadway; perhaps had it opened off-Broadway it might have received a warmer welcome. On the occasion of a memorial service for the life of Alvin Kelby (Malcolm Gets), his best friend Thomas Weaver (Will Chase) recalls their childhood friendship and gradual parting, with Alvin staying behind in their hometown and Tom moving away and enjoying a prosperous writing career, the success of which Tom attributes to his best friend's gift for words—Tom appropriated Alvin's life without credit. Richard Maltby, Jr., directed with a sure hand, preventing the story, told in epistolary form, from sinking into maudlin sentimentality. Both actors could not have been bettered in their roles, while Neil Bartram's pleasant music and lyrics and Brian Hill's book reminded us of the ordinariness rather than the universality of the characters. The best songs were Alvin's recollection of his first grade teacher, "Mrs. Remington," and Tom's story of "The Butterfly," inspired by Alvin. Here was a sensitive, insightful musical—a rebuke to Times Square glitz—but at a top price of $110, a highly improbable candidate for Broadway success.

Frank Loesser's classic Guys and Dolls (24 November 1950) has seldom been absent from Broadway for long, the last hugely successful production having closed fourteen years before this latest revival. Director Des McAnuff, a high flyer since the success of Jersey Boys, thought he had just the right recipe for a fast-paced revival for the twenty-first century 1 March 2009 at the Nederlander. Writer and newspaperman Damon Runyon himself, on whose stories the musical was based, opened the show, but the interpolation of his character added little. With state-of-the-art digital video design from Dustin O'Neill and scenic design by Robert Brill, McAnuff's production raced from Times Square to the Biltmore Garage to the local Salvation Army office in seconds; even Sergio Trujillo's fast-paced choreography could not keep up. Alas, "chemistry," that elusive quality that Sarah Brown (Kate Jennings Bryan) and Sky Masterson (Craig Bierko) speak of, was precisely what this production's casting lacked. Neither the pairing of irrepressible liar Nathan Detroit (Oliver Platt) and his long-term squeeze

Adelaide (Lauren Graham), nor that of Sarah Brown and Sky Masterson was ever plausible, or truly entertaining. This Guys and Dolls ricocheted across the stage with force and panache, but little feeling or conviction. The memory of superior revivals hobbled this production, which was pummeled by the critics and lasted little more than three months.

On the other hand, a revival of West Side Story (26 September 1957) felt long overdue. With original librettist Arthur Laurents now serving as director at age ninety-one, and Jerome Robbins' iconic choreography recreated by Joey McKneely, this production was eagerly awaited. Much attention was given to Laurents' belief that the Sharks and their girlfriends would speak Spanish among themselves, only occasionally lapsing into English when it suited the situation. Armed with this revisionist approach not possible in 1957, Laurents, in collaboration with Stephen Sondheim, invited In the Heights's Lin-Manuel Miranda to fashion plausible Spanish dialogue and lyrics for particular scenes and songs. "I Feel Pretty" became "Me Siento Hermosa" and "A Boy Like That" became "Un Hombre Así." Although Laurents and the producers assumed that many theatregoers knew or could figure out what was being said or sung, the changes were partially rescinded after five months, possibly because of the confusion they caused. That elusive casting "chemistry" that plagued the Guys and Dolls revival was fully present in this West Side Story, which opened 19 March 2009 at the Palace. A twenty-one-year-old unknown from Buenos Aires, Josefina Scaglione, gave a touching, beautifully sung Maria. Many viewers felt Matt Cavenaugh was miscast as Tony—that he was too old and self-assured and lacked the right vocal timbre. A memorable Anita is a prerequisite to any West Side, and Karen Olivo's commanding presence and fiery temper rightly won her a Tony Award for Best Featured Actress in a Musical. Laurents made a number of other questionable changes. "Somewhere," originally sung offstage by someone simply listed as "a girl," was now sung onstage by a boy soprano in the role of Kiddo. The Nightmare was excised from the Somewhere Ballet, thereby removing the dramatic impetus for Tony and Maria's initial consummation of their love. At the close of the show, Tony's lifeless body, once movingly carried both by Jets and Sharks, was now removed only by the Jets. Though a popular success, West Side Story and Arthur Laurents were largely overlooked in the year-end awards, perhaps because this version was seldom as truly moving as Robbins' original.

The feast of revivals continued unabated with Encores' *Finian's Rainbow* (10 January 1947), whose felicitous casting and production by director-choreographer Warren Carlyle descended upon New York's City Center on 26 March 2009 to much unanticipated acclaim. After a failed tryout in 1999, it was widely assumed that Harburg and Saidy's book for *Finian's* was too old-fashioned, unwieldy, and, worst of all, politically incorrect. But Harburg's liberal conscience was a generation ahead of the curve, and the Encores revival showed *Finian's Rainbow* to be a timeless classic. A unique and simple solution was found to the problem of Senator Billboard Rawkins (Philip Bosco, Ruben Santiago-Hudson as counterpart Billboard) turning from white to black to white: use two actors, instead of blackface. Tony Award-winning dramatic actor Jim Norton accorded Finian McLonergan an eloquence and integrity seldom found in the role. Kate Baldwin, a stunning redhead with a silken voice, was an ideal match as his daughter Sharon. Cheyenne Jackson had the ideal cockiness and swagger for the part of Woody Mahoney, Rainbow Valley's landowner, while Jeremy Bobb was the very model of a leprechaun, channeling a Jim Carrey-esque mischief. Rob Berman's effective conducting brought Burton Lane's score to vivid life. Such was the enthusiasm it generated that plans were made to bring *Finian's Rainbow* back to Broadway the following season for an open run.

Hair (27 April 1968), the quintessential American rock musical, made a triumphant return to Broadway on 31 March 2009 at the Al Hirschfeld Theatre, direct from a summer run at the Delacorte Theatre in Central Park. The unanimity of the critical acclaim for Diane Paulus' inspired revival was all the more satisfying because *Hair* had always been a hit only with the public, and was often dismissed as a cultural phenomenon by the critics. Making little or no attempt to update the script, Paulus presented *Hair* with utmost fidelity to the spirit of the text, its music and lyrics, free of condescension or twenty-first century revisionism. Gavin Creel played Claude, rebel turned Army enlistee and leader of the tribe. Will Swenson captured Berger's reckless, wandering spirit with feral abandon. No mere nostalgia trip, in this revival Paulus, choreographer Karole Armitage, and their company captured the essential spirit of the youth of 1968. In the Tony Award sweepstakes for Best Revival of a Musical, *Hair* scored an upset win over its rival *West Side Story*, and recouped its $5.76-million investment in a record five months.

A national tour of *The Wizard of Oz* made a two-week stop at the WaMu Theatre at Madison Square Garden from 26 March 2009. Typical of the production's carbon copy aesthetic, its Dorothy Gale was notable primarily for sounding like Judy Garland.

Rock of Ages (7 April 2009, Brooks Atkinson) was an unabashed jukebox musical cobbled together from the 1980s hits of Styx, Pat Benatar, Twisted Sister, Poison, Asia, and more. Greeted warmly upon its off-Broadway debut 1 October 2008 at New World Stages, *Rock of Ages* told a time-worn tale of Sherrie (Amy Spanger), a small-town Kansas would-be actress who arrives at the Bourbon Club on Los Angeles' Sunset Strip, where she falls for aspiring rock star Drew (Constantine Maroulis). James Carpinello played Stacee, the rival for Sherrie's affection, who scores with Bon Jovi's "Wanted Dead of Alive." Few would have imagined that "Can't Fight This Feeling" (originally by REO Speedwagon) or "Don't Stop Believing" (Journey) would find a second life in a book musical, yet Chris D'Arienzo's book, though slight, was efficient, self-mocking, and delivered its song cues with a keen sense of fun. Kristin Hanggi's direction, Kelly Devine's choreography, and the grungy unit set by Beowulf Borrit captured the big-haired, hard-drinking, hard-smoking, drug-filled days of 1980s rock music. This crowd pleaser prospered with a long theatrical life.

Next to Normal (15 April 2009, Booth) was a modest six-person rock musical about a suburban family attempting to deal with a mother's chronic depression. Substantially re-tooled since its 2008 premiere at the off-Broadway Second Stage Theatre via Washington, D.C.'s Arena Stage, *Next to Normal* won many admirers for its willingness to confront bipolar disorder in musical theatre terms, simultaneously challenging and entertaining its audience. Its book and lyrics by Brian Yorkey and score by Tom Kitt were awarded the Pulitzer Prize in spring 2010 for, according to the Pulitzer committee, "having expanded the scope of subject matter for musicals." Alice Ripley played Diana, the mother in question, in a gripping performance of acute emotional pain and confusion. Diana is tormented by the presence of her late son Gabe (Aaron Tveit), more real to her than her husband or daughter. Her suffering husband Dan (J. Robert Spencer) exhibits enormous resilience and patience, and her daughter Natalie (Jennifer Damiano) finds refuge from her family with boyfriend Henry (Adam Chanler-Berat). Louis Hobson played two doctors, Madden and Fine (pun intended). Among the standout songs were Diana's "I Miss the Mountains," a lament for the highs and lows she feels without medication, and Gabe's insistence to his mother "I'm Alive." Dan's overly optimistic hope that Diana will recover ("A Light in the Dark") closed Act I. *Next to Normal*, that rarity among musicals, an original work not based on a film, a small musical among Broadway behemoths, ran for more than a year, recouped, and embarked on a national tour, giving hope that adventurous musical-theatre writing could still thrive.

9 to 5: The Musical (30 April 2009, Marquis) was supposed to be a sure thing. A brash musical comedy based on the hit 1980 film *Nine to Five*, about three women taking charge of their office lives, *9 to 5: The Musical* was fitted out with country & western songs by Dolly Parton. Patricia Resnik adapted the book from her own screenplay co-authored with Colin Higgins. Joe Mantello directed with comedic speed and finesse, and Andy Blankenbuehler provided energetic, sexy choreography. At the offices of Consolidated Industries, longtime employee Violet Newstead (Allison Janney) greets newcomer Judy Bernly (Stephanie J. Block) and warns her to steer clear of lecherous boss Franklin Hart, Jr. (Marc Kudisch), who has eyes for his buxom blonde secretary Doralee Rhodes (Megan Hilty, in the role originated by Dolly Parton in the film). How these three girls kidnap Hart, truss him in his own home, and exact their revenge is the fun of *9 to 5*. In Hart's absence, the three reform Consolidated and uncover further evidence of Hart's misdeeds. In a double-cross finale, Hart wins praise from his boss for his management of the company, but is then dispatched to Bolivia to run a subsidiary and is never heard from again. This cartoon of corporate skullduggery and girl power at the office may have been fresh fun in 1980, but had grown stale by 2009. *The New York Times* objected to its "lewd slapstick" and cheesy sitcom jokes. Few of Parton's songs were deemed memorable; perhaps best was "Backwoods Barbie" for Hilty. Empty-handed at the Tonys and snubbed by critics who preferred *Rock of Ages*, *9 to 5* played less than four months.

Off-Broadway had an unexceptional season. Two hit shows regrouped for Broadway transfer the following season, and will be discussed at length below: *Fela!* (4 September 2008, 37 Arts) and *Everyday Rapture* (3 May 2009, Second Stage). **The Marvelous Wonderettes** (14 September 2008, Westside Arts) was an anodyne compilation of girl group songs, set in Act I at the Springfield High School prom in 1958, and at its tenth year reunion in Act II. The book by Roger Bean told of petty rivalries, predictable betrayals, and confrontations, echoed in four-part harmony songs as well as solos, duets and trios. Audiences flocked for 545 performances. *The Marvelous Wonderettes* will no doubt plague many a community theatre in years to come. Its antithesis, Stephen Sondheim and John Weidman's long-aborning musical **Road Show** (18 November 2008, Newman), previously known as *Wise Guys* and then *Bounce*, finally received its full New York premiere, courtesy of the Public Theater, running for two months. Using a simple unit set of his own design, British director John Doyle, long the conceptual architect of production economy, employed a fifteen-member cast to tell a sweeping epic of the rivalry of two brothers in America from 1896 to 1933. *Road Show* chronicled the adventures of huckster Wilson Mizner (Michael Cerveris) and dreamer Addison Mizner (Alexander Gemignani) in Alaska, their independent travels around the world, and their final collaboration in Boca Raton. The complexity of the fraternal relationship, its frustrations and betrayals made for fascinating and rewarding musical theatre, nothing less than you would expect from its authors. That it failed to find a longer life and wider acceptance was a profound disappointment to all. But Sondheim's musicals have, over time, often proved more resilient and enduring than the works of lesser mortals, and *Road Show* will no doubt return to the stage in future iterations.

2009–2010

Encores' summer series of seldom-seen musical revivals launched the season early with *The Wiz* (5 January 1975). Directed and choreographed by the same team (Thomas Kail, Andy Blankenbuehler) responsible for *In the Heights*, this high-spirited, crowd-pleasing revival incorporated elements of hip-hop and break dance into its musical numbers. The production eschewed big sets for bold swatches of color and inventively brought the orchestra onstage during the opening scene's tornado. Pop star Ashanti, as Dorothy, looked uncomfortable in the dialogue scenes for which she had little skill; similarly, Orlando Jones lacked the requisite presence for The Wizard who rules Oz without any genuine authority. Only Broadway veteran LaChanze exhibited a thrilling command of the stage in her opening song as Aunt Em, "The Feeling We Once Had," and as Glinda with the closing "Believe in Yourself." Although William F. Brown's topical book was updated with contemporary gags and Charlie Smalls' infectious disco and pop score sounded great in its full orchestration, *The Wiz* (opening 18 June 2009), never a critics' favorite, was largely dismissed by the press as a mess. Nonetheless audiences cheered for its limited three-week run.

Given the immense popularity of such television dance shows as *Dancing with the Stars* and *So You Think You Can Dance*, its live progenitor **Burn the Floor** (2 August 2009, Longacre) was long overdue for a Broadway engagement, having toured thirty countries in ten years. Conceived and directed by Jason Gilkison, this showcase of Latin and ballroom dance featured eighteen athletic dancers and two vocalists in a fast-paced variety program of virtuosic choreography ranging from traditional waltz to jive, paso doble, swing, foxtrot, Lindy Hop, quickstep, cha-cha, rumba, mambo and salsa. *Burn the Floor* extended its initial run to five months. Another dance musical, **Tanguera** (7 October 2009, New York City Center), imported its entire cast from Buenos Aires for a two-week run. Billed disingenuously as the "first tango musical ever," *Tanguera* told its love-triangle narrative primarily through Mora Godoy's choreography. Giselle (Rocío de Los Santos), a young French immigrant arriving in Buenos Aires at the beginning of the twentieth century, is torn between Gaudencio (Oscar Martínez Pey), her older patron and gangster, and Lorenzo (Esteban Domenichini), a handsome young dock-worker. The principals dance, but do not sing, in Diego Romay's archetypal story. The four Spanish-language songs with English supertitles were allotted to actress Marianella; legendary tango dancer María Nieves had a delicious cameo as a brothel madam.

Roundabout Theatre Company debuted its newly reconstructed venue on 43rd Street with *Bye Bye Birdie* (14 April 1960, Henry Miller's Theatre), only seen in New York in an Encores concert staging in 2004. As directed and choreographed by Robert Longbottom, this staple musical comedy of "American middle-brow culture meets rock 'n' roll" was stubbornly miscast and its production ill-conceived. John Stamos played the frustrated talent promoter Albert Peterson, embodied so memorably by Dick Van Dyke on stage and in the 1963 film, as a charmless nerd, uncomfortable in his own skin, or for that matter, this musical. What did his long-suffering secretary Rose ever see in him? Gina Gershon's Rose was slick but lacked definable character; if the role of Rose was conceived for a dancer (Chita Rivera in the original stage musical),

Gershon looked mostly lost. Above-the-title billing was accorded to Bill Irwin in the cartoonish role of heroine Kim's father, Mr. McAfee, but his clowning overplayed whatever humor the role actually had to the point of tiresomeness. Jayne Houdyshell scored the most laughs as Albert's domineering mother, while the gifted Dee Hoty was under-utilized as Kim's mom. Allie Trimm was genuinely sweet as the teenage Kim, but heartthrob Conrad Birdie, as played by wholesome Nolan Gerard Funk, posed no real threat to the impressionable youth of suburban America. Although Andrew Jackness's sets were engineered to move quickly to keep the action moving, they had a visual ordinariness matched by insipid pastel costumes from Gregg Barnes. The director's smartest choice was to cast real youths, rather than adults playing half their age, as the teenagers of Sweet Apple, making the ensemble dance numbers one of the production's few satisfactions. Unwilling to trust the light comedy material for what it is, Longbottom and his cast pushed too hard for laughs. Whatever pleasures Charles Strouse and Lee Adams' score had to offer were sacrificed in perfunctory vocals, despite sparkling, all-new orchestrations from Jonathan Tunick. This joyless *Birdie* was excoriated by the critics, and coasted through a four-month run on its Roundabout subscriber base.

Memphis (19 October 2009, Shubert) was the first of two musicals this season to celebrate the early days of rock music. Set in early-1950s Memphis, Tennessee, the musical's unlikely hero is a white boy, Huey Calhoun (Chad Kimball), whose tireless advocacy of black rhythm and blues rescues him from unemployment and propels him on a great adventure in love and fame. Huey's foolishness gets him in trouble with both whites and African Americans, including nightclub owner Delray (J. Bernard Calloway), whose sister Felicia (Montego Glover) is the gifted singer Huey falls for. The guileless Huey just wants everyone to get along and share a love of rock 'n' roll—his rejoinder to every situation is a cheerful "Hockadoo!" Once Huey is the town's top disc jockey, it is but a short step to putting rock music on television, first locally in Memphis, then nationally. Huey's televised interracial kiss with Felicia creates a riot and precipitates their break-up ("Ain't Nothin' But a Kiss"). Years later, after Felicia becomes a renowned star, they enjoy a bittersweet reunion ("Steal Your Rock 'n' Roll"). *Memphis* offered few original surprises in its rags-to-riches story, with predictable melodramas, setbacks, and inevitable heartbreak and success.

Director Christopher Ashley maintained an electric pace and constant visual excitement that hardly gave the audience a slack moment to consider the illogic of the book. Sergio Trujillo's energetic choreography replicated many of the dance crazes of the 1950s. David Bryan penned music and lyrics; Joe DiPietro (*I Love You, You're Perfect, Now Change* and *All Shook Up*) collaborated on lyrics and wrote the book. None of the new songs were as memorable as the 1950s rhythm-and-blues standards by the Platters, Elvis Presley, Chuck Berry, James Brown, and Fats Domino they were meant to evoke, but in true musical-theatre form, the score did advance the plot and illuminate character with intelligent, if not exactly brilliant, lyrics. In sum, *Memphis* was a terrific production of a mediocre musical; at season's end, *Memphis* won Tony awards for Best Musical, Book, Score, and Orchestration.

As an encore to its Encores staging the preceding spring, *Finian's Rainbow* (10 January 1947) transferred to Broadway for an open run at the St. James Theatre on 29 October. Shedding the obligatory scripts in hand from its Encores production, director Warren Carlyle polished his company to a vivid sheen. Such was the spell of the show's tuneful music, exceptionally witty lyrics, cleverly political book and outstanding cast that *Finian's Rainbow* again received mostly rave notices. All of the originally cast principals returned, other than a new Senator Billboard Rawkins (David Schramm), and "Bill" Rawkins (Chuck Cooper). Arthur Perlman was credited with "book adaptation" whereby the black-white-black Rawkins characterization was further refined to contemporary tastes, yet kept fully true to the spirit of lyricist and co-bookwriter Yip Harburg's intent of promoting racial integration. The musical's subtle post-war message of American hope and harmony proved surprisingly resonant in 2009 with a newly-elected African-American president, while the show's jokes about banks, easy credit, rural poverty, and cronyism could not have been more topical. Despite ringing endorsements, *Finian's* played to half houses for only twelve weeks.

Propelled by loud acclaim at Washington, D.C.'s Kennedy Center the preceding spring, *Ragtime* (18 January 1998) returned to Broadway's Neil Simon Theatre in a taut, focused, and slim revival on 15 November. Marcia Milgrom Dodge's incisive direction and effective choreography presented this musical epic with stylish, fascinating clarity for its two acts and eighteen scenes. The talented principals in this revival could hardly match the over-sized star turns of the original Coalhouse Walker, Brian Stokes Mitchell, or Sarah, Audra MacDonald. But this *Ragtime* strangely benefitted from a warm sense of ensemble, so that the expansive tapestry of the story did not become unbalanced. Quentin Earl Darrington's piano-player Coalhouse Walker Jr. admirably won the heart of the audience early on, and Stephanie Umoh's Sarah, Coalhouse's lover, was enchanting from her first entrance. Christiane Noll was potent as the moral conscience of a liberal America in her caring, loving performance as Mother, while Ron Bohmer was stalwart if scarcely believable in the underwritten role of Father. As Mother's Younger Brother, Bobby Steggert delivered a compelling performance playing a radical committed to helping Coalhouse Walker. The rich sound of James Moore's orchestra of twenty-eight was a thrill and a rarity, when so many Broadway orchestras are half that size. Despite complimentary reviews, the box office never ignited for this *Ragtime*, which left in eight weeks.

A plethora of revivals continued with a return eight-week engagement of last year's *White Christmas* (23 November 2008) at the Marquis from 13 November. Recast entirely with top if not starry talent, its Bob Wallace/Bing Crosby was a lanky, agreeable James Clow, and its Phil Davis/Danny Kaye was the warm-hearted dancer Tony Yazbek. The icy Betty Haynes/Rosemary Clooney role was played by gorgeous songstress Melissa Errico, and adorable ingénue Mara Davi was her sister Judy Haynes/Vera Ellen. The cumulative effect of these cast changes was mostly indistinguishable, suggesting that this musical was durable if not the most inventive. The first show of Encores' new season was the Gershwins' *Girl Crazy* (14 October 1930) in its first New York revival ever under the direction of Jerry Zaks. This production afforded a fascinating comparison with 1992's *Crazy for You*, a revision of *Girl Crazy*, which ran for four years and spawned productions around the world. Rob Fisher conducted Robert Russell Bennett's glorious period orchestrations, Warren Carlyle (*Finian's Rainbow*) choreographed new dances, and David Ives tidied up Guy Bolton and Jack MacGowan's rambling book. Chris Diamantopoulos was riotously funny and charming as east-coaster Danny Churchill chasing cowgirl Molly Gray (Becki Newton, Diamantopoulos' wife). Diamantopoulos was the real thing, a triple threat actor-singer-dancer, but as adorable as Newton looked, her charm never crossed the footlights. Wayne Knight struggled to make sense or fun of the ethnic stereotype of a Jewish cabbie stranded in Custerville, Arizona. Ana Gasteyer and Marc Kudisch chewed the scenery as cartoonish Frisco Kate Follicle and her husband Slick. *Girl Crazy* was a typical Encores musical—it was a show with a great score that could not support a full-scale staged revival as a commercial venture.

Far from a traditional Broadway musical in narrative structure, musical style, dramatic idiom or dance form, *Fela!* (23 November 2009, Eugene O'Neill) was a startlingly original, radical work of dance theatre. Conceived by choreographer Bill T. Jones (*Spring Awakening*), librettist Jim Lewis (*Chronicle of a Death Foretold*), and producer Stephen Hendel, *Fela!* is a musical hagiography of Nigeria's famed Afrobeat composer, performer, and political activist Fela Anikulapo-Kuti (1938–1997). First presented in August 2008 for two months off-Broadway at 37 Arts, *Fela!* arrived on Broadway to near unanimous critical acclaim. The performance was nominally Fela's final concert at the Shrine, a nightclub in his private compound in Lagos, Nigeria, in the summer of 1978. The dramatic conceit allowed Fela to tell us about his rise and fall, his evolution as a musician, and his political rage at Nigerian generals and politicians, who he describes as suppressors of democracy and dissent, squanderers of Nigeria's natural resources, and tyrants against the marginalized, helpless and poor. None of Fela's original songs and rudimentary lyrics were ever intended to tell a theatrical story, so their staging attempted to compensate for the lack of a coherent libretto. Much of the fascination of *Fela!* as a Broadway entertainment stemmed from its selective use of Fela Kuti's music and persona to create a reverential biography of Fela, the myth. *Fela!* was lucky to have two charismatic, yet very different, actors (Sahr Ngaujah, Kevin Mambo) alternated in the demanding title role. The production invited the audience to celebrate Fela's cult of personality through full participation, by shouting back in response, dancing in their seats, singing along, or applauding frequently. Bill T. Jones assembled an exceptionally talented ensemble of dancers and singers to introduce, or better yet seduce, Broadway audiences unfamiliar with Fela Kuti and the Afrobeat musical style.

Eagerly anticipated for being Catherine Zeta-Jones' Broadway stage debut and Angela Lansbury's surprise return to musical theatre, Trevor Nunn's revival of Stephen Sondheim and Hugh Wheeler's classic *A Little Night Music* (25 February 1973) was a major disappointment. The revival opened for a limited run 13 December 2009 at the Walter Kerr Theatre to mixed reviews. Initially conceived for the small Menier Chocolate Factory in London, this intimate staging proved vulgar and coarse, with not a single moment of human insight, charm, or wit to the text or score. Nunn's stage direction, the lame choreography by Lynn Page, and the production's thin orchestrations offered little reward and were hardly compensated by the starriness of the cast. The gracious, extraordinarily beautiful Catherine Zeta-Jones was miscast and unconvincing as dramatic stage actress Desirée Armfeldt. Her singing was uneven, perfunctory, and flat. Alexander Hanson as her suitor Fredrik Egerman was indifferent and dull, seldom seeming like a man inspired by his true love. The indomitable Angela Lansbury as Madame Armfeldt, on the other hand, costumed in white finery like her demented Countess Aurelia in Jerry Herman's *Dear World* (1969), elicited laughs, insight, and warmth with a simple word or gesture. Ramona Mallory as child-bride Anne Egerman possessed an exquisite singing voice, but her acting was embarrassing, her lyrical delivery mechanical. Aaron Lazar was clumsy and wooden as Count Carl-Magnus Malcolm, and Erin Davie made a woeful, petty Countess Charlotte Malcolm, missing every opportunity for humor and cynicism in the text and lyrics. Only her bitterness remained. Despite the production's sorry reviews, the audience was filled to capacity, except when the stars were absent. In a definite trend on Broadway, success has become increasingly closely linked to the celebrity of the faces in a cast—audiences happily spent $130 to see Zeta-Jones, whereas critically acclaimed productions of *Ragtime* and *Finian's Rainbow* failed without celebrity tie-ins. Once the Tony-award-winning Zeta-Jones and Lansbury departed, *Night Music* was luxuriously recast for the summer with Bernadette Peters and Elaine Stritch.

The New York Gilbert & Sullivan Players resumed their annual tenancy of New York City Center for two weeks beginning 8 January 2010 with the usual suspects, *The Mikado*, *The Pirates of Penzance*, *H. M. S. Pinafore*, and the less frequently seen *Ruddigore*. The mid-winter offering from Encores was Harold Rome and S. N. Behrman's *Fanny* (4 November 1954), as directed by Marc Bruni and conducted by Rob Berman. This lush romantic musical in the Rodgers & Hammerstein idiom was well-served by trusting hands. George Hearn was a satisfactory César, lacking only Ezio Pinza's deep bass voice. Fred Applegate's Panisse captured the lonely soul longing for a wife and son with aplomb. James Snyder and Elena Shaddow did as much with the thinly-drawn lovers Marius and Fanny as could be expected from David Ives' truncated text. The glory of Harold Rome's most ambitious score proved the evening's biggest treat during *Fanny*'s five performances from 4 February 2010. *Riverdance* (13 March 1996) returned for one week at Radio City Music Hall in what was billed as its farewell tour on 17 March 2010. Emmanuel Chabrier's *L'Étoile* (22 October 2002) was revived for six performances at the New York City Opera from 18 March 2010, performed felicitously in its original French for the first time, not in English as it had been eight years before. Alain Gauthier restaged Mark Lamos' handsome production, with Emmanuel Plasson conducting. Jennifer Zetlan and Julie Boulianne were the lovers Laoula and Lazuli.

Dame Edna Everage, the famous Australian housewife-turned-superstar invented and embodied by Barry Humphries, and Michael Feinstein, foremost champion of the great American songbook, shared the Henry Miller's Theatre stage in **All About Me** (13 March 2010, Henry Miller's), an ill-conceived revue staged by Casey Nicholaw. Humphries and Feinstein devised and developed the show, assisted by Lizzie Spender and Terrence Flannery, while Rob Bowman conducted a brassy onstage band. Fans of Dame Edna expected the usual banter and insults directed at members of the audience, the massacre of songs old and new ("Ol' Man River" and "The Dingo Ate My Baby"), parade of extravagant costumes, and outrageous claims (for instance, that Edna is George Gershwin's illegitimate daughter). Edna won big laughs sprawled across the piano, unable to get down. Michael Feinstein, having starred on Broadway in his own solo shows in 1988 and 1990, appeared less comfortable as straight man to Dame Edna's shenanigans. At his best, in homage to Sinatra, Feinstein offered his own swinging "The Lady is a Tramp." His heartfelt renditions of Gershwin's "Strike Up the Band," Rodgers & Hart's "My Romance," or a one-minute medley of Rodgers & Hammerstein's *Oklahoma!* belonged elsewhere, perhaps in his own intimate nightclub setting, Feinstein's at the Regency. The evening's lame conceit was that both Dame Edna and Feinstein think *All About Me* is his or her solo star turn, supported by two different playbills. The shared stage proved a misfire, and *All About Me* was gone in twenty performances.

In **Come Fly Away** (25 March 2010), Twyla Tharp choreographed a glossy homage to the voice,

persona and style of Frank Sinatra. No ordinary Broadway dancers, her remarkable company were the Olympic athletes of modern dance, exhilarating to watch. The production was set inside an unspecified New York nightclub with an onstage orchestra of nineteen. The conflicting tempers and emotions of the four couples were wordlessly illustrated in dance. If Tharp's "concept and book" lacked any dramatic tension, it was the distinctive personalities of the dancers and their virtuoso dance vocabulary that retained viewer interest for two hours and through two acts. Keith Roberts and Karine Plantadit smoldered but ended up "Just Friends" in "Summer Wind," "That's Life" and "One for My Baby." Charlie Neshyba-Hodges and Laura Mead were the waiter and new girl in town; their comic flirtation played out in "Moonlight Becomes You," "Let's Fall in Love," "Pick Yourself Up," and "My Funny Valentine," among others. Tharp designated Matthew Stockwell Dibble and Rika Okamoto as "the rebound couple that has a one-night affair." They sparked in "Yes Sir, That's My Baby" and "Wave." John Selya and Holley Farmer were the "it" couple whose affair intensifies through "I've Got a Crush on You," "Witchcraft," and "Teach Me Tonight." These four couples were supported by a dance ensemble of six and vocalist Hilary Gardner, whose solos and occasional duets with a pre-recorded Sinatra varied the sound palate. Russ Kassoff conducted a brassy orchestra to compliment the recorded Sinatra tracks.

A six-month national tour of **The 101 Dalmatians Musical** (7 April 2010, The Theater at Madison Square Garden), sponsored by Purina Dog Chow, came to an abrupt end after its two weeks in New York. The show's book by B. T. McNicholl, based on the 1956 novel by Dodie Smith, was unfortunately infantile, tedious, and over-long, with ballads and mindless production numbers by McNicholl and Styx composer Dennis DeYoung. The talent roster— Jerry Zaks as director, Warren Carlyle as choreographer, Sara Gettelfinger as Cruella De Vil, and James Ludwig as lead dog Pongo—inspired high expectations that went thoroughly unfulfilled. Robert Morgan's costumes put all adult characters on stilts so that, along with Heidi Ettinger's oversized sets, the children's ensemble of puppies appeared in plausible perspective.

In conjunction with Stephen Sondheim's eightieth birthday, Encores scheduled his most celebrated failure, *Anyone Can Whistle* (4 April 1964), as its final show of the season on 8 April 2010. Blessed with excellent casting, this *Whistle,* imaginatively directed and choreographed by Casey Nicholaw, exceeded all expectations by winning the best reviews the show has ever seen. Donna Murphy played town mayor extraordinaire Cora Hoover Hooper with a brashness that channeled both Kay Thompson and Angela Lansbury. Nurse Fay Apple was radiantly, passionately played by Sutton Foster, in a role that showcased her many talents better than the last five musicals she had starred in. As J. Bowden Hapgood, Raúl Esparza's brisk oscillation between sanity and insanity was a pleasure to behold. Edward Hibbert, Jeff Blumenkrantz, and John Ellison Conlee were hilarious as Cora's yes-men and sidekicks. David Ives' concert adaptation of Arthur Laurents' eccentric book sacrificed little in what will long be remembered as a definitive *Anyone Can Whistle*.

Inspired by the macabre yet humorous cartoons of Charles Addams, **The Addams Family** (8 April 2010, Lunt-Fontanne) was a sporadically satisfying, largely uneven old-fashioned musical comedy. This eccentric clan is beloved and well-known to generations of Americans, having first appeared as cartoons (1933–1988), then in a television series (1964–1966) and two feature films (1991, 1993). Light-hearted morbidity is their natural state. The Addams Family—Gomez Adams (Nathan Lane), wife Morticia (Bebe Neuwirth), teenage daughter Wednesday (Krysta Rodriguez), son Pugsley (Adam Riegler), Uncle Fester (Kevin Chamberlin) and Grandma (Jackie Hoffman)—inhabit a joyously derelict, once lavish mansion overlooking New York City's Central Park, accompanied by their silent, looming butler Lurch (Zachary James), a giant squid in the basement, a hand in a box named "Thing," and a loose head covered in long hair known as "It." Once the overture started with the famous theme by Vic Mizzy borrowed from the television series, a willing audience snapped its fingers in happy collusion. Alas, for want of a good idea, bookwriters Marshall Brickman and Rick Elice (*Jersey Boys*) resorted to the over-familiar plot device of a disastrous first meeting with prospective in-laws. Once the musical's premise is swiftly disclosed and sung about ("One Normal Night"), the fun abates, and the evening became a series of gags, special effects, sentimental ballads (by Andrew Lippa), and tiresome, forgettable musical numbers choreographed by Sergio Trujillo. Uncle Fester's profession of his love for the moon, "The Moon and Me," the fun yet extraneous pseudo-1930s quartet "Let's Not Talk About Anything Else But Love," and "Tango de

Amor," a dance showcase for Bebe Neuwirth, were the production's best numbers. Phelim McDermott and Julian Crouch, who conceived *Shockheaded Peter* for the musical stage, jointly shared credit for production design and direction, but when *The Addams Family* foundered in its Chicago tryout, McDermott and Crouch were shelved, and show-doctor Jerry Zaks was invited as "creative consultant" to hammer the musical into shape. When *The Addams Family* worked at all, it was because of Lane's skillful comic presence as Gomez, Neuwirth's charm as Morticia, and Chamberlin's inspired lunacy as Uncle Fester, who ultimately departs for his beloved moon with a rocket strapped to his back. The audience's collective affection for these characters enabled *The Addams Family* to run at capacity business despite terrible reviews.

Million Dollar Quartet (11 April 2010, Nederlander) was an archetype of jukebox musicals, a mythical re-imagining of one fabled afternoon, December 4, 1956, when Elvis Presley (Eddie Clendening), Carl Perkins (Robert Britton Lyons), Jerry Lee Lewis (Levi Kreis), and Johnny Cash (Lance Guest) jammed together at the Sun Records studio in Memphis, presided over by Sun Records owner Sam Phillips (Hunter Foster). Colin Escott and Floyd Mutrux's book played fast and loose with the true story, inserting a girlfriend for Presley (Elizabeth Stanley as Dyanne), and allowing each singer to perform some of his greatest hits by final curtain. For rock 'n' roll fanatics, this moment in musical history may have resonated, but as musical theatre it was little more than sloppy opportunism—a pop concert. Under Eric Schaeffer's direction, the singers gave plausible impersonations. Most compelling of the four was Kreis as bad boy Jerry Lee Lewis, adeptly mimicking Lewis' wild physicality and devil-may-care attack on the piano during "Great Balls of Fire" and "Whole Lotta Shakin' Goin' On." Lyons was the least-known, Carl Perkins, whose early numbers "Matchbox" and "Who Do You Love?" impressed. As Presley, Clendening had the early looks, the cool, and sound right, but lacked any sense of danger or the visceral excitement that would capture the imagination of all of America. His early numbers, "Memories Are Made of This" and "That's All Right," were winning enough, but it was only in his final solo, "Hound Dog," that this Presley took charge. Laidback and seemingly disinterested, Guest had a nice Johnny Cash-like sound, but looked twenty years older than his pals, and lacked the intensity of Joaquin

Phoenix's compelling performance as Cash in the 2005 film biography *Walk the Line*.

La Cage Aux Folles (21 August 1983) returned unexpectedly to Broadway (18 April 2010, Longacre) after an absence of five years, propelled by its London success at the Menier Chocolate Factory as directed by Terry Johnson on 18 April 2010 at the Longacre. Retaining his design team (Tim Shortall, scenery; Matthew Wright, costumes; Nick Richings, lighting) and production team (Lynne Page, choreography; Jason Carr, music supervision, orchestrations, dance arrangements), Johnson recruited a top-notch American cast to support Douglas Hodge, playing the role of Albin as he had in London. Trained as a classical actor, Hodge delivered a deeply etched, complex portrait of a loving gay man as performer, husband, and father that was at once profoundly moving and riotously funny. Kelsey Grammer, as Albin's partner Georges, displayed surprising self-assurance and grace. Robin de Jesús was a spontaneously silly Jacob, flamboyantly Latin in a role traditionally played by an African American man. A. J. Shively and Elena Shaddow acquitted themselves with dignity in the otherwise insipid roles of Georges' son Jean-Michel and fiancée Anne. As Anne's parents, Veanne Cox and Fred Applegate shone despite the modesty of their roles, while Christine Andreas sparkled in the small role of Jacqueline. The spatial and economic constraints of the Menier Chocolate Factory inspired a tatty, run-down scenic design compared to what has traditionally been a flashy French Riviera setting. The legendary drag performing troupe Les Cagelles, a mere six compared to the original twelve, was even more brazen and coarse than usual, and Lynne Page's witty choreography managed to surprise where drag cliché had become predictable. Nominated for ten Tony Awards, this *La Cage Aux Folles* was a hit, winning Tonys for Best Revival, Director, and Best Actor (for Hodge).

From a 2004 rock album of thirteen songs that sold five million units domestically and fourteen million worldwide came a theatrical staging of California punk band Green Day's **American Idiot** (20 April 2010, St. James). Unquestionably the most innovative new musical of the season, it remains to be seen whether *American Idiot* will endure as a major work of musical theatre by attracting new and younger audiences, or whether it is merely a loud, angry anthem of limited appeal. Green Day's original album contained a tiny thread of a story

centered around two figures, Jesus of Suburbia and St. Jimmy. Stage director Michael Mayer joined with Green Day's Billie Jo Armstrong to fashion a sketchy narrative about three disaffected youths, Johnny (a riveting John Gallagher Jr.), Will (Michael Esper) and Tunny (Stark Sands) from Jingletown, USA, set in the "recent past." Disgusted with their humdrum suburban existence and lack of prospects, and contemptuous of the Bush government's misinformation and the media's complicit emptiness, Johnny, Will, and Tunny lashed out in the opening number about how each refuses to end up an "American Idiot." Becoming just that seems their destiny, and the audience witnesses their progressive descent into personal hell. Nominally the spiritual center of the show, Johnny moves to the big city, falls in love with Whatsername (Rebecca Naomi Jones), then succumbs to the temptations offered by drug-dealer St. Jimmy (Tony Vincent). Tunny accompanies Johnny at first, then impulsively joins the United States Army, where he swiftly loses a leg in Iraq. Will never leaves home; once he discovers that his girlfriend Heather is pregnant, he just sits in front of his television getting high. In "We're Coming Home Again," the three friends reunite back home a year later. If the slight story was predictable, director Michael Mayer, choreographer Steven Hoggett, scenic designer Christine Jones, and the eight-piece band supervised by Tom Kitt delivered a fast-paced ninety-minute production of non-stop propulsive energy. Jones' set was a clutter of forty-three video screens with a jumble of posters scattered seemingly at random amongst the musicians. Hoggett propelled his principals and ensemble about the stage with a thrashing punk sensibility. In the most visually arresting sequence, a bed-ridden Tunny dreams of the "Extraordinary Girl" (Christina Sajous) with whom he dances suspended above his hospital bed, his leg intact. All of this disparate energy was harnessed to showcase the songs that many in the audience knew by heart. Apart from the thirteen original songs, several others were interpolated from Green Day's 2009 album *21ˢᵗ Century Breakdown*. Other standouts in the score were "Boulevard of Broken Dreams" for Johnny, Tunny, and Whatsername, and the patriotic "Are We the Waiting?" To the credit of sound designer Brian Ronan, the lyrics were always audible despite the ear-splitting volume.

As if Stephen Sondheim had not been fêted enough for his eightieth birthday, James Lapine conceived and directed a new revue, **Sondheim on**

Sondheim (22 April 2010, Studio 54), with a cast of eight principals and Sondheim himself on a state-of-the-art video screen video. An enjoyable evening's entertainment with few surprises for musical theatre enthusiasts, the revue mostly resembled a public television biography special. Barbara Cook, Vanessa Williams, Tom Wopat, and Norma Lewis constituted the two mature couples, and the four young adults were Leslie Kritzer, Euan Morton, Eric Mackey, and Matthew Scott. Some selections worked well, such as Cook's "Send in the Clowns" and "Loving You," Morton's "Franklin Sheppard, Inc.," Mackey's "The Wedding is Off," and the young quartet's "Opening Doors." Other songs did not suit their performers' talents: "You Could Drive a Person Crazy" proved a peculiar duet for Wopat and Cook, and Wopat struggled with "Finishing the Hat." Williams fared little better with "Ah, But Underneath" and "Smile, Girls." Sondheim composed one new song for the occasion, "God," a self-mocking ensemble inspired by a 1994 *New York* Magazine cover story asking, "Is Sondheim God?" Beowulf Borrit's rotating platform afforded multiple scenic configuration but was upstaged by Peter Flaherty's extraordinary video-projection design, that lit a series of blocks, which broke up and reassembled in startling shapes and configurations. Ultimately it was Sondheim himself, his narration and comments, filmed mostly at his home, who upstaged the performers. The skimpy orchestrations by Michael Starobin frequently reminded the listener of superior performances heard elsewhere. *Sondheim on Sondheim* received cordial reviews, and with an extension played a two-month subscription run.

The unexpected inspiration for the season's revival of *Promises, Promises* (1 December 1968) was the wildly popular television series *Mad Men*, with its bright, chic 1960s Manhattan corporate setting. Under the efficient direction and choreography of Rob Ashford, the appeal of this revival, originally based on the 1960 film *The Apartment*, was its star casting, of Sean Hayes (television's *Will & Grace*) and Kristin Chenoweth (*Wicked, You're a Good Man, Charlie Brown*). Hayes won instant audience loyalty with his opening number, during which he charmed and confided in the audience like a musical theatre veteran. Whereas in the original production Chenoweth's role, Fran Kubelik, was an emotional victim, book-writer Neil Simon tweaked the role for his female star and added two songs from the pop catalogue of Burt Bacharach (music) and Hal

David (lyrics). The first, an extraneous "I Say a Little Prayer," allowed Fran to kibbitz with her fellow secretaries about her secret relationship with boss J. D. Sheldrake (Tony Goldwyn). The second, the ballad "A House Is Not a Home," now closed Act I and accompanied Fran's realization that her relationship with Sheldrake is finished. The resourceful and resilient Chenoweth was simply unable to play a frail victim, but her irrepressible comic skills and charm still delighted her loyal fans. Few could argue that as floozy barfly Marge Macdougall, Katie Finneran stole the show during her brief fifteen minutes, winning a Best Supporting Tony award. In his eagerness not to imitate Michael Bennett's famous original staging, Ashford's own ideas seldom measured up. In Ashford's hands, the overture was wildly over-staged using the entire company, leaving the subsequent "Grapes of Roth" and "Turkey Lurkey Time" as underwhelming afterthoughts. The four executives desperate to use Chuck's apartment for their romantic assignations were no longer as funny as they had been in 1968,. Nonetheless, *Promises* was enjoyable mainstream entertainment, and a big hit all over again despite gripes from the critics.

The last, and perhaps least, of the musical season was **Everyday Rapture** (29 April 2010, American Airlines), Roundabout Theatre Company's last-minute substitution for a cancelled subscription play, and a transfer from Second Stage's off-Broadway season from 3 May 2009. Conceived by Dick Scanlan and Sherie Rene Scott as a musical autobiography for Scott, and directed by Michael Mayer, *Everyday Rapture* was little more than an overblown cabaret act lost on a Broadway stage. Scott is immensely talented, as her previous stints on and Off-Broadway have amply demonstrated. The description of her childhood in a Mennonite community in Topeka, Kansas was touching, while the threat of eternal damnation for any lapse or variation in proscribed behavior was especially forbidding. Scott's Rumspringa, the adolescent's twelve-month break from faith and austerity, lead her to break faith with her past completely and find her way to New York, have an affair with a magician, get an abortion and start a show business career. Musical numbers, none of which lingered in the mind, were arranged and orchestrated by Tom Kitt and generously interspersed throughout the narrative. As back-up, Scott was supported by two loud-voiced girls billed as the "Mennonettes." She frequently reconsidered the advice given her by a rabbi and written on two scraps of paper: "I am a speck of dust" and "The world was created for me." Such dime-store philosophizing was a discredit to her substantial performing talent;. *Everyday Rapture* played its two-month subscription season.

Off-Broadway posted an adventurous season, but enduring work did not materialize until **Yank!** (25 February 2010, York), a new musical about a gay serviceman in World War II, by two brothers, David (book, lyrics) and Joseph Zellnik (music, arrangements). Told as a flashback, *Yank!* recounted the emotional odyssey of a raw recruit, Stu (Bobby Steggert), whose enduring love for Mitch (Ivan Hernandez) survived the war, only to be dashed by Mitch's lack of courage at war's end. Nancy Anderson assumed all female roles in a series of quick changes. The Zellnik brothers purposefully styled their musical in a traditional Rodgers & Hammerstein 1940s-1950s idiom, which they deemed more effective and subversive than a confrontational show. Under Igor Goldin's direction, *Yank!* received excellent reviews and extended for two months. Whether it finds a future life beyond off-Broadway remains to be seen.

Before his death in 2004, lyricist Fred Ebb had nearly completed work on **The Scottsboro Boys** (10 March 2010, Vineyard), an ambitious musical created with Ebb's lifelong collaborator John Kander, their frequent bookwriter David Thompson, and virtuoso stager Susan Stroman. Its true story from 1931 of nine African-American men falsely accused of rape by two white prostitutes played out in the tabloid press and national imagination for almost a decade, a symbol of American injustice. Kander & Ebb and their collaborators elected to use the archaic, now disgraced, idiom of a minstrel show to tell their story. Stroman was equal to this challenge, using an empty stage and more than a dozen chairs to conjure up multiple locations, including a train, jail cell, and courtroom. *The Scottsboro Boys* subverted the minstrel show concept by using its mostly black cast to play not only the victims, but also the conniving prostitutes, sheriffs, and some well-meaning but patronizing attorneys and judges. *The Scottsboro Boys* opened with the company promising us "a night of merriment, of laughter, songs and jokes," then segued to the nine boys hitching a train ride with an infectious "Commencing in Chattanooga." Once unfairly charged with rape, Haywood Patterson (Brandon Victor Dixon) emerged as their spokesman, the most articulate and principled of the group. John Cullum, the sole white member of the cast, doubled as Interlocutor, an ineffective Judge and the

Governor of Alabama. The evening's end packed a triple punch: (1) Haywood's "You Can't Do Me," a devastating refusal to capitulate, (2) the title song telling in shocking blackface, what happened to each of the nine, and (3) a final chilling visual tableau some thirty years later of Rosa Parks taking her seat at the front of a bus, marking a symbolic end to racial segregation. The cumulative weight of that distinctive Kander & Ebb trademark cynicism as found in *Cabaret*'s emcee, *Chicago*'s Velma Kelly and Roxie Hart, and *Kiss of the Spiderwoman*'s Molina was expressed in *The Scottsboro Boys*, which may yet take its place alongside its creators' better-known musical triumphs.

Bloody Bloody Andrew Jackson (6 April 2010, Public) took America's fabled seventh president Andrew Jackson (1767-1845) as its inspiration for a reckless adventure in rewriting history, "emo" rock style—that is, through "emotional" punk rock,. In the hands of playwright and director Alex Timbers and songwriter Michael Friedman, Andrew Jackson (Benjamin Walker) was re-imagined as an impetuous twenty-something rock heartthrob with a disregard for authority, an eye for girls, and a quick shot with a rifle. When he loses an election, he whines, "It's really unfair, and frankly it's starting to get on my nerves." Walker delivered a charismatic performance with nonchalant über-confidence, dressed in black jeans, a tight white shirt, boots, and a pistol, and sometimes caked with blood. His adversaries, disciples and henchmen doubled as musicians or band vocalists. For all the anarchy, contemporary idioms, and spontaneous frenzy, *Bloody Bloody Andrew Jackson* remained strangely faithful to the details of Jackson's life and spurious arrogance, yet embodied much of the idealism of youth overthrowing any traditional regime. From the rousing opening anthem "Populism, Yea, Yea," the audience was thrust from 1824 to the present and back. Much of Timbers's staging captured the spontaneous energy of a fraternity house initiation ritual, deadpan silliness, and an eagerness to shock. But what was so unexpected was the erudition of the lyrics. A fall 2010 Broadway transfer beckoned.

At decade's close, it is startling to find musical theatre assuming new forms, embracing new music styles far removed from the traditional music theatre of Rodgers & Hammerstein, Stephen Sondheim, Andrew Lloyd Webber, and Kander & Ebb. The use of existing pop music, re-tooled and retro-fitted to a narrative for which it was never intended, is now commonly accepted practice. Once derided as jukebox musicals, pasticcios, or whatever pejorative name you choose, new Broadway and off-Broadway productions have re-appropriated popular music for theatrical use in inventive ways. *All* idioms of music are now welcomed, so long as the dramaturgy, production and cast talent meet the challenge. Any season that can produce dynamic new work such as *Fela!, Memphis, American Idiot, The Scottsboro Boys, Yank!,* and *Bloody Bloody Andrew Jackson,* as well as memorable revivals of *Ragtime, Finian's Rainbow, La Cage Aux Folles,* and *Anyone Can Whistle* augurs well for the future of the American musical.

Indexes

There are four indexes. The first lists all the musicals mentioned in this book, except certain operas performed in repertory with lighter pieces. The second is a supplementary index listing sources (plays, books, etc.) on which these musicals are based, unless the name of the musical and its source are the same. The third index lists songs from these musicals, if they are mentioned in the text. The fourth index is a listing of major persons associated with the musicals. We have attempted to list all authors mentioned in the book, but actors, choreographers, set designers, etc., have generally been listed only if they appear at least three times in the text.

Shows

Ba-ta-clan, 28
Baba, **42,** 48
Babes and the Baron, The, **253**
Babes in Arms, **559,** 564, 576, 596, 824
Babes in the Wood, The; or, Who Killed Cock Robin?,
    45, **45,** 63, **122,** 280
Babes in Toyland, **228,** 233, 251, 510, 522
Babette, **230**
Babiole, **62**
Baby, **782**
Bachelor Belles, The, **307**
Back to Bacharach and David, 844
Bad Boy and His Teddy Bears, The, **281**
Bad Habits of 1926, **465**
Bagels and Yox, **642**
Baggage Check, A, **182**
Bajour, **703**
Baker Street, **703**
Bal Nègre, **615**
Balkan Princess,The, **309–310**
Ballet Ballads, **623**
Ballet Girl, The, **181**
Ballet of Niagara, 305
Ballets Africans, Les, 716
Ballroom, **762,** 836
Ballyhoo of 1930, **522**
Ballyhoo of 1932, **534**
Bamboche, **692**
Bamboola, **507**
Band Box Follies, The, **482**
Band in Berlin, 826
Band Wagon, The, **524,** 525, 533, 534, 818, 821
Banjo Dancing, 772
Banjo Eyes, **586,** 587, 686, 763
Bankers and Brokers, **249,** 265, 281
Barbara Cook: A Concert for the Theatre, **791**
Barbara Cook's Broadway, **850**
Barbe Bleue, **26,** 34, 41
Barber of Seville, The, 15, 593
Bare Facts of 1926, **468**
Bare Facts of 1927, **481**
Barefoot Boy with Cheek, **618**
Barnum, **770**
Baron Trenck, **322**
Baroness Fiddlesticks, The, **241**
Barrier, The, **636**
Barry Manilow at the Gershwin, **795**
Barry of Ballymore, **309**
Basoche, The, **142**
Bat Boy: The Musical, **835**
Bathing Girl, The, **160,** 162
Battling Buttler, **433**
Bavards, Les, **27**

Be Yourself, **446**
Beast in Me, The, **694–695**
Beat the Band, **592**
Beatlemania, **758,** 760
Beatrice Arthur on Broadway: Just Between Friends,
    836
Beautiful Galatea, The, 73–74
Beautiful Star, **129**
Beauty and the Beast, **807,** 820
Beauty Doctor, The, **250**
Beauty Shop, The, **232, 343**
Beauty Spot, The, **290,** 294
Beehive, **788**
Beg, Borrow or Steal, **678**
Beggar Student, The, **80,** 87, 88, 102, 334
Beggar's Holiday, **615**
Beggars off Horseback, 440
Beggar's Opera, The, 2, 94, 460, 493, 539, 665, 767
Begum, The, **105,** 117, 160, 338
Belle Hélène, La, **26,** 190, 755
Belle of Avenue A, The, **250**
Belle of Bohemia, The, **199**
Belle of Bond Street, The, **342**
Belle of Bridgeport, The, **200**
Belle of Brittany. The, **298**
Belle of Broadway, The, **210,** 279
Belle of London Town, The, **268**
Belle of Mayfair, The, **267**
Belle of New York, The, **178,** 180, 181, 193, 757
Belle of Newport, The, **231**
Belle of the Barbers' Ball, The, 286
Belle of the West, The, **252**
Belle Paree, La, **311,** 320
Belles of the Kitchen, The, 33, 66, 76
Bellman, **103**
Bells Are Ringing, **663,** 835
Belmont Varieties, **535**
Ben Franklin in Paris, **702**
Berlin to Broadway with Kurt Weill, **746**
Bernarda Alba, **862**
Best Foot Forward, **585,** 618, 704
Best Little Whorehouse Goes Public, The, **807,** 808
Best Little Whorehouse in Texas, The, **760**
Betsy, **320**
Bette! Divine Madness, **768**
Bette Midler at the Palace, **747**
Better 'Ole, The, **386,** 511
Better Times, **424,** 425
Betty, 534
Betty Be Good, **400**
Betty Lee, **451,** 511
Between the Devil, **566,** 568
Beyond the Fringe, **692**

Boys from Syracuse, The, **571,** 572, 577, 775, 816, 840
Brand New City Directory, The, **144**
Brass Monkey, A, **109**
Bravo Giovanni, **691**
Brazilian, The, **117,** 118
Breaking into Society, **250**
Brian Boru, **171**
Bric-A-Brac, **54, 114**
Bridal Trap, The, 98
Bride Elect, The, **183,** 186
Brigadoon, 102, **617,** 634, 665, 682, 691, 693, 703,
    720–721, 771, 786, 789, 800, 815
Brigands, Les, **31,** 113, 115
Bright Eyes, **301,** 302
Bright Lights of 1944, **598**
Bring Back Birdie, **773**
Bring in 'da Noise, Bring in 'da Funk, **813**
Bringing Up Father, **453**
Bringing Up Father at the Seashore, 453
Bringing Up Father in Ireland, 453
Bringing Up Father on Broadway, 453
Broadway and Buttermilk, **366**
Broadway Brevities of 1920, **404**
Broadway Follies, **773**
Broadway Honeymoon, **336**
Broadway Jones, 335, 498
Broadway Musical, A, **762**
Broadway Nights, **508**
Broadway Opry '79, **766**
Broadway Sho-Window, **556**
Broadway to Tokio, **196**
Broadway Whirl, The, **411**
Broken Idol, A, **296,** 299
Brook, The, **52,** 58, 64
Brooklyn, the Musical, **851**
Brown Buddies, **519**
Brownies, The, **155,** 505
Brown's in Town, **191**
Bruce Forsythe on Broadway, **766**
Bubbling Brown Sugar, **754**
Bubbly Black Girl Sheds Her Skin, The, 842
Buck White, **732**
Buddies, **394,** 410, 415
Buddy: The Buddy Holly Story, **798**
Bugs Bunny on Broadway, **798**
Bunch and Judy, The, **428**
Bunch of Keys, A, **77,** 84
Bunk of 1926, **464**
Bunthorne's Bride, 861
Bunty, Bulls and Strings, 321
Bunty Pulls the Strings, 321, 325
Burgomaster, The, **202**
Burn the Floor, **828,** 879

Buster Brown, **245**
Busy Izzie (The Mazuma Man), **223,** 277
Busy Izzy's Boodle, **283**
But Never Jam Today, **767**
Butterflies Are Free, 739
Buttons, **52**
Buttons on Broadway, **811**
Buttrio Square, **645,** 670
Buy-it-Dear, 'Tis Made of Cashmere, **10**
Buzz-Buzz, 473
Buzzin' Around, **401**
By Jeeves, **836**
By Jupiter, 588
By King's Command, **153**
By the Beautiful Sea, **650**
By the Sad Sea Waves, **191**
By the Way, **463**
Bye, Bye, Barbara, **443**
Bye, Bye Bonnie, **476**
Bye Bye Birdie, **678,** 689, 713, 724, 757, 847, 848,
    854, 859, 879

Cabalgata, **630**
Cabaret, 649, **716,** 717, 721, 745, 791, 811, 817, 822,
    860, 886
Cabin in the Sky, **580,** 581
Cad, the Tomboy, **78**
Cadet Girl, The, **198**
Cadets, 118
Cadi, The, **127**
Café Crown, **699**
Cage aux Folles, La, **781,** 852, 866, 884, 887
Caliph, The, **167**
Call Me Madam, **635,** 636, 664, 668, 691, 859
Call Me Mister, **612,** 613, 651
Calling All Stars, **548**
Camaralazman and Badoura, 23
Cambridge Circus, **702**
Camelot, **681,** 682, 685, 771, 805, 872
Camille, 333, 414
Can-Can, **646,** 647, 655, 668, 672, 691, 774, 847
Canard á Trois Becs, Le, 41
Canary, The, **386,** 387
Canary Cottage, **369,** 372
Canciones de Mi Padre, **793**
Candide (1933), **540**
Candide (1956), **663,** 748, 849, 856
Candide (1974), 872
Candide (1982), 778
Candide (1984), 784
Candide (1987–1988), 787
Candide (1989–1990), 795

Candle Light, 568
Candy, **139,** 140
Candy Kid, The, **279**
Candy Shop, The, **294**
Cannibal King, The, 274
Capeman, The, **821**
Capitan, El, 72, 138, 159, 165, 166, 220
Captain Cook, **176**
Captain Jinks of the Horse Marines, 456, **457,** 458
Captain Karl, **131**
Captain Mishler, **84**
Captain Rufus, **275**
Captain Thérèse, **133**
Carib Song, **609**
Caribbean Carnival, **620**
Carl, the Fiddler, 33, **33–34,** 45
Carmelina, **765**
Carmen, 74, 106, 357, 782
Carmen; or, Soldiers and Seville-ians, **62**
Carmen Jones, **601,** 604, 612, 661
Carmen up to Date, 134–135
Carnival, **683,** 684, 725, 733, 838
Carnival in Flanders, **648**
Caroline, **429**
Caroline, or Change, **849**
Carousel, 556, 606, 651, 666, 709, 717, 807
Carrie, **793**
Casino Girl, The, **197,** 199, 212, 368
Castles in Spain, **66**
Castles in the Air, **117, 469,** 470
Cat and the Fiddle, The, **281, 528,** 530, 536,
    542, 694
Catch a Star!, **657,** 660
Catch of the Season, The, **248, 364**
Catered Affair, A, **871**
Catherine, **190**
Cats, **778,** 793
Catskills on Broadway, **800**
Cavalleria Rusticana, 177
Caviar, **544**
Celebrated Hard Case, A, 44
Celebration, **726**
Celia, **872**
Celibacy, 88
Cendrillon, 22
Cents Vierges, Les, **35**
Century Girl, The, **367,** 368, 377
Century Revue, The, **402**
Chamberlain Brown's Scrap Book, **533**
Champagne, Sec, **541,** 593
Change in the Heir, A, **798**
Change Your Luck, **516**
Chanson d'Amour, 417

Chanson de Fortunio, La, **27**
Chaperones, The, **212,** 279
Chaperons, The, **212**
Charity Begins at Home, **59**
Charity Girl, The, **327**
Charlatan, The, **186,** 187
Charlie and Algernon, **771**
Charlie's Aunt, 586
Charlot's Revue of 1924, **436,** 454
Charlot's Revue of 1926, **461**
Chatter, 91, 92
Chauve Souris, **420,** 423, 426, 442, 448, 451, 456,
    477, 546, 671
Chauve Souris 1943, **597**
Check 44; or, Tobogganing, **106**
Checkers, 399
Chee-Chee, 495, **497,** 501, 514, 595, 607
Cheek, **78**
Cheep, 436, 473
Cheer Up, 374
Cherry Blossoms, 389, **478**
Chess, **792,** 793
Chicago, 649, **750,** 811, 815, 817, 856, 859, 886
Chieftain, The, 161
Chiffon Girl, The, **437**
Child of Fortune, The, **133,** 134
Children in the Wood, The, 38
Children of the Ghetto, 311
Chilpéric, **39**
Chimes of Normandy, The, 55, 64, 70, 72, 84, 525
Chin-Chin, **348,** 349, 352, 359, 361, 375, 405
China Doll, A, **241**
China Rose, **452**
Chinese Honeymoon, A, **212,** 214, 234, 315
Ching Chow High; or, A Cracked Piece of
    China, **28**
Chita Rivera: The Dancer's Life, **859**
Chitty Chitty Bang Bang, **855**
Chocolate Dandies, The, **444,** 452
Chocolate Soldier, The, 271, 297, 419, 510, 525, 544,
    590, 617
Chorus Line, A, 730, **750,** 752, 759, 762, 862
Chow Chow; or, A Tale of Pekin, **34,** 216–217, 218,
    224
Chris and the Wonderful Lamp, **196**
Christine, **679**
Christmas Carol, A (1979), 769
Christmas Carol, A (1990), 798, 806
Christmas Carol, A (1994), **808,** 841, 847
Christmas Carol, A (1996), 813, 815
Christmas Carol, A (1997–1998), 821
Christmas Carol, A (1999), 827
Christmas Carol, A (2000), 832

Christmas Carol, A (2001), 836
Christmas Pantomime Rehearsal, A, 97
Christmas Spectacular (Radio City), 803, 806, 808, 815, 820, 826. *See also* Magnificent Christmas Spectacular, The
Chronicle of a Death Foretold, **811,** 881
Chu Chem, **794**
Chu Chin Chow, 372, 376
Chuckles of 1922, 427
Cigale, La, **129,** 141
Cinderella, 15, 23, **23,** 63, **131, 806,** 813, **852**
Cinderella at School, **65,** 72, 77, 151
Cinderella on Broadway, **401,** 405
Cinders, 430
Cingalee, The, **239**
Circus Day, **207**
Circus Girl, The, 308
Circus in Town, A, **103**
Circus Princess, The, **478**
Cirque Dreams: Jungle Fantasy, **872–873**
City Chap, The, **460,** 472, 480
City Directory, The, **116,** 121
City of Angels, **797**
Civil War, The, **825**
Clair de Lune, 446
Clams on the Half Shell, **750**
Class Act, A, **833,** 835
Claude Duval, **71**
Claudius Nero, **121**
Cleavage, **778**
Clinging Vine, The, **428,** 433
Clio, 91, 92
Cloches de Corneville, Les, 80, 474. *See also* Chimes of Normandy, The
Clorindy; or, The Origin of the Cake Walk, **185**
Clover, **113**
Clown Bagatelles, The, **791**
Co-optimists, The, 491
Coarse Hair, The, 105
Coat Tales, 375
Coco, **733**
Cocoanuts, The, **462,** 602
Codfish Aristocracy, **215**
Coeur et la Main, Le, 77
Cohan and Harris Minstrels, The, **286, 296**
Cohan Revue of 1916, The, **362**
Cohan Revue of 1918, The, **379**
Colleen Bawn, The, 17, 27
College Widow, The, 292, 374
Color Purple, The, **858,** 862
Come Along, 389, **389**
Come Fly Away, **882**
Come Out of the Kitchen, 448

Come Summer, **727**
Come to Bohemia, **364**
Comedy in Music, **648,** 758
Comedy in Music Opus 2, **702**
Comedy Tonight, **808**
Comic Annual, **8**
Comic Supplement, The, 442
Comin' Thro' the Rye, **256**
Comin' Uptown, **769**
Common Clay, 475
Company, 732, **735,** 752, 812, 837, 864
Comte Obligado, **504**
Con-Curers, The, **183**
Concert Varieties, **608,** 609
Connecticut Yankee, A, 480, **486,** 493, 511, 600, 833
Conquering Hero, The, **683,** 684
Conquerors, The, 183
Constant Couple, The, 2
Consul, The, **634,** 645, 675, 690, 709, 715, 748
Contact, **826**
Contented Woman, A, **172**
Continental Varieties (1934), **546**
Continental Varieties (1936), **554**
Contrabandista, The, 71
Contrast, The, 3, 5
Conversation Piece, **546**
Cook's Tour at Koster and Bial's, A, **184**
Copper and Brass, **668**
Copperfield, **774**
Coralline; or, Sir Rupert The Reckless, 28
Cordelia's Aspirations, 57, 65, **80,** 90, 102, 105, 142
Corsair, The, **104,** 110
Corsican Brothers & Co. The; or, What London Laughs At, 87
Cosmo Varieties, 535
Cotton Field Frolics, 188
Count Me In, **592**
Count of Luxembourg, The, 331, 339, 510, 545
Countess Du Barry, 77
Countess Maritza, 394, **470**
Country Girl, A, **216,** 313
Country Sport, A, **147**
Courted into Court, **172**
Courtin' Time, **641**
Cousin Lucy, **358,** 362
Cowboy Girl, The, **261**
Cox and Box, **51,** 546, 601, 621
Cradle Will Rock, The, 568, 573, 573, 621, 675
Cranks, **663**
Crazy for You, **801,** 880
Crazy Quilt, 529
Crazy with the Heat, **583**
Crinoline Girl, The, **342**

Dolores, **107**
Don Caesar, **97**
Don Quixote (DeKoven), 127
Donagh, The, 123
Donna Juanita, **67**, 69, 74
Donnybrook!, **101, 684**
Donovans, The, **40**
Don't Bother Me, I Can't Cope, **742**, 756
Don't Get God Started, **791**
Don't Play Us Cheap!, **742**
Doonesbury, **782**
Dora Bella etc. and the Dyed Hair, **29**
Dorcas, **172**
Doris, 112
Dorothy, 92, **105**, 160
Double Dublin, **696**
Doug Henning and His World of Magic, **783**
Dove of Peace, The, **328**
Dovetta, **112**, 148
Down on the Suwanee River, **164**
Down the Pike, **240**
Dr. Seuss' How the Grinch Stole Christmas, **863**, 868
Dr. Syntax, **151**
Dracula, the Musical, **850**
Dragon de Villars, Le, **27**
Dramatic Review for 1868, The, **27**
Drat! The Cat!, **709**
Dream City, 264, **264**, 267
Dream Girl, 426, 443, 475, 711
Dream with Music, **602**
Dreamgirls, **776**, 791
Dreams (1880), 70, 86
Dreams; or, Fun in a Photographic Gallery, **61**
Dreigroschenoper, Die. *See* Threepenny Opera, The
Dress Parade, The, **225**
Drowsy Chaperone, The, **860, 862**
Drum Major, The, **115**
DuBarry, The, 536
DuBarry Was a Lady, **577**, 579, 581, 815
Duchess, The, **317**, 426, 534
Duchess of Dantzic, The, **245**
Dude, **743**, 748
Dude, The, 84
Duffy's Blunders, **156**
Duke of Duluth, The, **249**

Earl and the Girl, The, **252**
Earl Carrol Vanities, The (1923), **432**
Earl Carrol Vanities, The (1925), **456, 462**
Earl Carrol Vanities, The (1928), **495**
Earl Carrol Vanities, The (1931), **526**
Earl Carrol Vanities, The (1932), **535**

Earl Carrol Vanities, The (1940), **535, 578**
Earl Carroll's Sketch Book, **507,** 509, 515
Earl of Ruston, **739**
Early to Bed, **597,** 602, 619
Earthquake, The, 305
East Wind, **528**
Easter Extravaganza, **796**
Easter Show (Radio City), 802, 804, 807, 808
Easy Dawson, 248
Eccentricities of Davy Crockett, The, 623
Echo, The, **303,** 356
Ed Wynn Carnival, The, **398–399**
Eddie Fisher at the Winter Garden, **691**
Edgewood Folks, 61
Education of H*Y*M*A*N K*A*P*L*A*N,
   The, **723**
Edwin and Angelina, 7
Eight Bells, **126**
Eileen, **370–371,** 372
Eileen Asthore, **266**
Elaine Stritch at Liberty, **836,** 837
Electric Light, **53**
Elfins and Mermaids, **67**
Elixir of Love, The, 106
Elopers, The, **343**
Elsie, 430
Elsie Janis and Her Gang, **396, 420,** 423, 452
Elves, The, 23
Elvis: The Legend Lives, **760,** 854
Elysium, **134**
Emerald Isle, The, **215**
Emigrant Train, The; or, Go West!, 59
Emigration to America, 103
Enchanted Isle, **483**
Enchantment, **53**
Enchantress, The (Balfe opera), **16**
Enchantress, The (Herbert), **317,** 320
Encore, **777**
Encores! Great American Musicals in
   Concert, **810**
English Daisy, An, 232, 237
Erminie, 91, **97,** 98, 100, 104, 106, 112, 114, 120, 139,
   145, 152–153, 172, 184, 193, 228, 230, 408
Errand Boy, The, **239**
Estrada, **760**
Estrella, **81**
Eternal Road, The, 557
Eubie!, **762,** 770, 837
Evangeline, 31, 36, **38,** 44, 48, 57, 61, 68, 87, 93, 112,
   119, 127, 139, 166, 237
Evening with Beatrice Lillie, An, **644,** 689
Evening with Dave Allen, An, **775**
Evening with Diana Ross, An, **755**

Hurly-Burly, **186,** 196, 325
Hurry, Harry, **743**
Husband (?), The, **275**
Hustler, The, **131**

I Can Get It for You Wholesale, **690,** 698
I Do! I Do!, **717**
I Feel Wonderful, 685
I Had a Ball, **703**
I Love My Wife, **756**
I Love You, You're Perfect, Now Change, **814,** 850,
    880
I Married an Angel, **567,** 568, 569, 599
I Remember Mama, **765,** 766
Ice Dancing (John Curry's), **762**
Icetime of 1946, **614**
Icetime of 1948, **618**
I'd Rather Be Right, **563,** 564
Idea,The, 149
Idol's Eye, The, **179,** 195
If I Were You, **141,** 458
If the Shoe Fits, **615,** 616
I'll Say She Is!, **438,** 462
Ill Treated Il Trovatore, 59, 63
Illustrators' Show, The, **554,** 600
Illya Darling, **718**
I'm Solomon, **723**
I'm Still Here ... Damn It!, **824**
Imaginary Friends, **842**
In Atlantic City, **186**
In Circles, **720**
In Dahomey, **222,** 223, 258
In Gay New York, **166,** 183
In Gay Paree, **191,** 195
In Gayest Manhattan; or, Around New York in Ninety
    Minutes, **174**
In Gotham, **187**
In Hayti, **296**
In Honor Bound, 97
In Mexico, **171**
In My Life, **857,** 860
In New York Town, **251**
In Newport, 244
In Old Madrid, 178
In Posterland, **217,** 218
In the Heights, 867, **870,** 876, 878
In Town, 153, **177**
Inacent Black, **774**
Indiana, **101**
Indigo, **126**
Influence; or, True Love Never Runs Smooth. See
    Arctic; or, The North Pole Expedition

Inner City, **741**
Innocent Eyes, **439**
Inside U.S.A., **622**
International Cup, The, **305**
International Revue, The, **514**
International Soiree, **670**
Into the Light, **790**
Into the Woods, **792,** 853
Investigation, **86,** 99
Invisible Prince, The, 23
Iolanthe, **74,** 75, 76, 77, 79, 102, 122, 134, 334, 354,
    458, 465, 483, 525, 544, 601, 621, 645, 658, 685,
    692, 703, 725, 761, 847
Iole, **340**
Ipi-Tombi, **756**
Irene, **395,** 396, 401, 407, 417, 418, 427, 428, 677,
    730, 745
Irish Artist, The, **154,** 161
Irish Gentleman, An, **180**
Irish Immigrant, The, 17
Irish Minstrel, The, 108, 110, 123, 165
Irishman's Love, An, **122**
Irma La Douce, **680,** 689
Is There Life After High School?, **777**
Isham's Octoroons, **194**
Island of Jewels, **14**
Isle o' Dreams, The, **332**
Isle of Bong Bong, The, **246**
Isle of Champagne, The, **140,** 141, 146, 184
Isle of Gold, The, **175**
Isle of Spice, The, **226,** 231, **235,** 236, 238, 258
It Ain't Nothin' But the Blues, **825**
It Happened in Nordland, **242,** 263, 298, 543
It Happens on Ice, **580**
It's a Bird...It's a Plane...It's SUPERMAN, **713**
It's So Nice to Be Civilized, **771**
It's Up to You, **409**
It's Up to You, John Henry, **251**
Ivy Leaf, The, **95**
Ixion; or, The Man at the Wheel, **27, 34,** 109

Jacinta, **156**
Jack and Gill (pantomime), 23
Jack and Gill Went Up the Hill, 22
Jack and Jill, **430,** 467
Jack and the Beanstalk, 25, **171,** 173, **529**
Jack Harkaway at Sea, 37
Jack-in-the-Box, **94**
Jack o' Lantern, **375,** 405, 416
Jack Sheppard, **94,** 152
Jackie Mason: Brand New, **798**
Jackie Mason: Freshly Squeezed, **856**

Jackpot, **601**
Jack's Romance, **353**
Jacqueline, 139
Jacques Brel is Alive and Well and Living in Paris, **722,**
    724, 743, 773, 805, 862
Jamaica, **668,** 709
James Joyce's The Dead, **826**
Jane Eyre, **833**
Jane O'Day of Broadway, 366
Japan at Night, 214
Jeanne, Jeanette et Jeanneton, 104
Jekyll and Hyde, 811, **818,** 825
Jelly Roll!, **808**
Jelly's Last Jam, **802**
Jennie, **695**
Jerome Kern Goes to Hollywood, **788**
Jerome Robbins' Broadway, **794**
Jerry Springer: The Opera, **868–869**
Jerry's Girls, **788**
Jersey Boys, **858,** 862, 872, 876
Jersey Lily, The, **227, 234**
Jesus Christ Superstar, 731, 739, **740,** 742, 758, 810,
    828
Jewel of Asia, The, **221**
Jim Crow in London, 12
Jim Jam Jems, **405**
Jimmie, **402,** 403, 407
Jimmy, **732,** 733
John Henry, **578**
John Murray Anderson's Almanac, **648,** 757
Johnny Johnson, **557,** 558, 739
Johnny on the Spot, **191**
Jolie Parfumeuse, La, **39**
Jolly Bachelors, The, **71, 299,** 300
Jolly Baron, A, **249**
Jolly Musketeer, The, **189,** 190, 193
Jolly Surprise, A, **133**
Jollyanna, 641
Jonica, 515, **515,** 532
Joseph and His Brothers, 103
Joseph and the Amazing Technicolor Dreamcoat, 731,
    776, 806
Josephine Sold by Her Sisters, **99**
Jotham Valley, **639**
Jour et la Nuit, Le, 70
Joyce Grenfell Requests the Pleasure, **658**
Joyful Noise, A, **717,** 752
Juan Darién, 815
Jubilee, **552**
Judy, **477**
Judy Forgot, **306**
Jumbles, **52**
Jumbo, 555

Jumbo, the Trick Elephant, **72**
Jumping Jupiter, **310**
June Days, **456**
June Love, **409**
Juno, **673,** 869
Junon and Avos—The Hope, **797**
Jupiter, **133**
Just a Joke, **258**
Just a Minute, 395, **498**
Just Because, **421**
Just Fancy, **486**

Kafoozelum, **247**
Kajanka, **115**
Karl, the Peddler, **131**
Kat and the Kings, **825**
Kate Kip Buyer, **189**
Katherine Dunham and Her Company, **658**
Katie Did, **310**
Katinka, **360,** 385
Katja, **472**
Katzenjammer Kids, The, **201**
Kean, **687,** 727
Keep 'Em Laughing, **587**
Keep It Clean, **507**
Keep Kool's, **440**
Keep Moving, **545**
Keep Off the Grass, **579**
Keep Shufflin', **492,** 507
Kelly, **703**
Kelly, John T., **103**
Ken Murray's Hollywood, **704**
Kenilworth, 35, **100**
Kenny Loggins on Broadway, **793**
Kerry Gow, The, 123
Khédive, The, **126,** 129
Kid, The, **139**
Kid Boots, **436**
Kiki, 366, 381
Kiki and Herb: Alive on Broadway, **862**
Kilpatrick's Old Time Minstrels, **515**
Kindergarden, The, **89**
King and I, The, 118, **639,** 661, 671, 672, 676, 679,
    695, 700, 721, 757, 794, 811, 813
King Casey, **279**
King Charming, **10,** 11
King Cole II, **112**
King David, **818**
King Dodo, **211,** 415
King Highball, **215**
King Kaliko, **134**
King Maker, The, **284**

Love Call, The, 427, **485**, 489
Love Cure, The, **296**
Love Dreams, **418**
Love in a Mist, 495
Love in a Village, 15
Love in ye Days of Charles ye Second, 91
Love Letter, The, **417**
Love Life, **624, 718**
Love/Life, A Life in Song, **856**
Love Mill, The, **380**, 381
Love o' Mike, **369**, 372
Love Song, The, **452**
Love Thy Neighbor, **813**
Lovely Ladies, Kind Gentlemen, **737**
Lovely Lady, **490**
LoveMusik, **866**
Lovers and Lunatics, **258**
Love's Lottery, **237**
Low and Behold, 544
Lower Berth Thirteen, **306**
Luana, **518**, 528
Lucia di Lammermoor, 64, 68
Luckee Girl, **496**
Lucky, **477**
Lucky Break, A, 480
Lucky Dog, A, **265**
Lunatics and Lovers, **225**
Lustige Witwe, Die, 278
Lute Song, **611**, 673
Lysistrata, 683, **744**

M. Butterfly, 840, 852
Macbeth (G. L. Fox travesty), 166
Mack and Mabel, **749**
Macushla, **321**
Mad Bargain, A, **142**
Madam Moselle, **343**
Madam Piper, **83, 84**, 112
Madame Angot's Daughter, 57
Madame du Hurry, 206
Madame L'Achiduc, **39, 41**
Madame Sans Gêne, 159
Madame Sherry, **304**, 305, 312, 315, 340, 403, 471, 484, 754
Madame Troubadour, **306**
Madcap, The, **491**
Madcap Duchess, The, **339**
Madcap Princess, A, **236**
Madeleine; or, The Magic Kiss, **157**
Madelon, **106**
Madge Smith, Attorney, **201**
Madwoman of Central Park West, The, **766**

Magdalena, **624**
Maggie, **646**
Maggie Flynn, **725**
Maggie the Midget, **107**
Magic Flute, The, 29
Magic Knight, The, **264**
Magic Melody, The, 409, 557
Magic Melody, The (Offenbach), 196, **395**
Magic Pills, 25
Magic Ring, The, **433**
Magic Show, The, **748**
Magic Slipper, The, **53**, 59
Magnificent Christmas Spectacular, The, **768**, 788, 790, 792
Magnolia Lady, The, **448**
Maid and the Millionaire, The, **272**
Maid and the Moonshiner, The, **99**, 101, 178
Maid and the Mummy, The, **235**
Maid as Mistress, The, 602
Maid in America, **353**
Maid Marian, **209**
Maid of Athens, The, **342**
Maid of Belleville, The, **98**
Maid of Plymouth, The, 148, 161
Maid of the Mountains, The, **384**
Mail, **792**
Major, The, **67**, 70, 90
Major Barbara, 362
Make a Wish, **640**
Make It Snappy, **422**, 482
Make Me a Song, **872**
Make Mine Manhattan, **621**, 622, 651, 693
Mamaloshen, **823**
Mama's Baby Boy, **323**
Mame, **714**, 727, 780
Mamelle Sallie, 281
Mamma Mia!, **835**
Mam'selle Awkins, **197**
Mam'selle Napoleon, **231**
Mamselle Sallie, **266**
Mam'zelle, **88**
Mamzelle Champagne, **260**, 272
Mam'zelle Nitouche, 195
Man from China, The, **234**
Man from Cook's, The, **322**
Man from Mars, The, 206
Man from Now, The, **262**, 265
Man in the Moon, A, **693**
Man in the Moon, The, **192**
Man of La Mancha, **711**, 712, 735, 743, 758, 802, 841
Man of No Importance, A, **844**
Man Who Owns Broadway, The, **297**

Molly O', **364**
Monks of Malabar, The, **198**
Monsieur Beaucaire, **396**, 446
Monsieur Landry, **27**
Monte Carlo, 183, **183**
Monte Cristo, Jr., 110, 119, **389**
Monteith and Rand, **763**
Monty Python Live!, **754**
Monty Python's Spamalot, **854**
Moonlight, **437**
Moonshine, **251**
Moony Shapiro Songbook, The, **774**
Mordecai Lyons, **75**
Morning, Noon and Night, **289**
Morris Gest's Midnight Whirl, **397**
Mort Sahl on Broadway, **791**
Most Happy Fella, The, 661, 673, 713, 726, 768–769, 800, 801, 861
Mostly Sondheim, **836**
Mother Earth, **743**
Mother Goose, **172, 193, 230,** 231
Mother Goose Party, The, **84**
Mother Hubbard; or, Harlequin Little Bo-Peep, 28
Motor Girl, The, **295**
Mountebanks, The, 141, **141**
Mourning Pictures, **749**
Mousquetaires au Convent, Les, 69
Movin' Out, **841,** 844
Mr. Blarney from Ireland, **256**
Mr. Bluebeard, **221,** 234, 292
Mr. Coney's Isle, **203**
Mr. Hamlet of Broadway, **292, 364**
Mr. Lode of Koal, **298**
Mr. Mix of Wickham, **237**
Mr. Pickwick, **220**
Mr. Popple of Ippleton, 354
Mr. President, 362, **691,** 692
Mr. Strauss Goes to Boston, 609
Mr. Wix of Wickham, 374
Mr. Wonderful, **660,** 859
Mrs. Black is Back, **240**
Mrs. Delaney of Newport, **229**
Mrs. Mac, the Mayor, **241**
Mrs. O'Brien, Esq, **140**
Mrs. Partington, 118
Mrs. Patterson, **653**
Much Ado About Everything, **827**
Much Ado About the Merchant of Venice, **27**
Muddy Day, The, **78**
Muldoon's Picnic, **69**
Mule Bone, **799**
Mulligan Guards' Ball, The, **48,** 49, 65, 79, 140
Mulligan Guards' Chowder, The, 53, 63

Mulligan Guards' Christmas, The, **55,** 56
Mulligan Guards' Nominee, The, **63,** 79
Mulligan Guards' Picnic, The, **47,** 48, 60
Mulligan Guards' Surprise, The, **57,** 80–81, 89
Mulligans' Silver Wedding, The, **65,** 81
Mummenschanz, 789
Mum's the Word, **581**
Murder at the Vanities, **540,** 541, 543
Murder in the Old Red Barn, **555**
Murphy's Wedding, 59
Murray Anderson's Almanac, **508**
Music Box Revue 1921–1922, The, **416, 512**
Music Box Revue 1922–1923, The, **426**
Music Box Revue 1923–1924, The, **433**
Music Box Revue 1924–1925, The, **450**
Music Hath Charms, 549, **549**
Music in May, **505**
Music in My Heart, **619**
Music in the Air, **536,** 642, 694, 875
Music Is, **756,** 759
Music Man, The, 666, **669,** 681, 695, 709, 771, 777, 829
Music! Music!, **748**
Music of Andrew Lloyd Webber, The, **803**
Musical Chairs, **770**
Musical Jubilee, A, **753,** 754
Musical of Musicals—The Musical, The, **850**
Musketeers, The, 77, 90
Musquitoe, The, 10
Mutt and Jeff, **319**
Mutt and Jeff in Mexico, 319
My Aunt Bridget, **101**
My Boys, **181**
My Cinderella Girl, **301**
My Darlin' Aida, **645,** 828
My Dear Public, 598, **598**
My Fair Lady, **658,** 659, 660, 665, 681, 682, 699, 709, 725, 754, 765, 775
My Favorite Year, **803**
My Friend from Dixie, 338
My Friend from India, 310
My Friend from Kentucky, 338
My Girl, **448**
My Golden Girl, **397,** 398
My Lady, **203**
My Lady Molly, **232**
My Lady's Glove, **373,** 377
My Lady's Maid, **263**
My Little Friend, **334**
My Magnolia, **468**
My Maryland, 480, **483** 761
My Milliner's Bill, 97
My Old Friends, **765**

My One and Only, 730, **780**, 801
My Princess, **485**
My Romance, **625**
My Son Dan, 166
My Sweetheart, **74,** 123
My Tom-Boy Girl, **247**
My Uncle Barbassou, 134
Myles Aroon, **111,** 123, 279
Mysteries and Miseries of New York, The, **9**
Mystery Moon, **517,** 619
Mystery of Edwin Drood, The, **788**
Mystic Isle, The; or The Law of Averages, **100**

Nadjy, **107,** 111
Naiad Queen, The, **14**
Namiko-San, **480**
Nancy Brown, **221–222**
Nancy Hanks, The, **182**
Nanon, **91**
Nash at Nine, **746**
Natja, **452**
Natural Gas, **107**
Nature, **177,** 178
Naughty Cinderella, **461**
Naughty Marietta, 271, 302, **307,** 444,
    460, 465, 477, 510, 525, 677, 761,
    767, 793
Naughty Naught ('00), **559,** 563, **571,** 614
Naughty Riquette, **470**
Nearly a Hero, **283**
Ned Wayburn's Gambols, **503**
Needs Must; or The Ballad Singers, **4**
Nell Go In, **200**
Nell Gwynn, **88**
Nellie Bly, **611**
Neptune's Daughter, **267**
Nervous Set, The, **674**
Never Gonna Dance, **847**
Never Homes, The, **318,** 469
New Boys and Girls, The, **133**
New Chauve Souris, **528**
New Faces (1934), **544,** 549
New Faces (1936), **556**
New Faces (1942), **593**
New Faces (1952), **643,** 669
New Faces (1956), 662, **662**
New Faces (1962), **689**
New Fritz, Our Cousin German, The, **45,** 47
New Girl in Town, **665,** 672
New Hellzapoppin, The, **569**
New Moon, The, 495, **496,** 510, 528, 602, 761, 787,
    789, 793, 842

New Music Hall of Israel, The, **732**
New Parlor Match, A, 87
New Pins and Needles, 565
New Priorities of 1943, **591**
New York Summer, A, 766
New Yorkers, The, **207,** 208, **477, 521,** 522, 523, 641,
    646
Newcomers, The, **432,** 544
Newlyweds and Their Baby, The, **293**
Newport; or, The Swimmer, the Singer, and the
    Cypher, **54**
News, The, 787
Next President, The, **670**
Next to Normal, 872, **877,** 878
Next Year, 163
Nia-For-Li-Ca; or, The Halls of Montezuma, **45**
Nic Nax of 1926, **469**
Nicholas Nickleby, 833
Nick and Nora, **800,** 801, 802
Nifties of 1923, **433**
Night at the Circus, A, **132,** 144, 171
Night Boat, The, **398,** 401
Night Clerk, The, **162**
Night in New York, A, **172**
Night in Paris, A, **463**
Night in Rome, A, 23
Night in Spain, A, **378, 479**
Night in Venice, A, **83, 506**
Night Music, 881
Night of Love, **583**
Night of the Fourth, The, **203**
Night That Made America Famous, The, **750**
Night with the Pierrots, 321
Nightcap, 685
Nightingale, The, **475**
Nikki, **527**
Nina Rosa, **518**
Nine, 777, 843
9:15 Revue, **514**
9 to 5: The Musical, 878
1940!; or, Crummles in Search of Novelty, **10**
1940's Radio Hour, The, 768
1942, **143**
1999, **180**
Ninety in the Shade, **353**
Niniche, 93, 207
No, No, Nanette, 435, 436, **457,** 458, 459, 485, 651,
    677, 730, 738, 739, 861, 869
No for an Answer, **583**
No Other Girl, **443**
No Strings, **689,** 842, 843
Noble Rogue, A, **509**
Nobody Home, **354,** 356, 360, 361, 400

Two Gay Benedicts, 84
Two Gentlemen of Verona, **740, 741**
Two Is Company, **358**
Two Islands, **277**
Two Little Brides, **323**
Two Little Girls in Blue, **409,** 410, 429
Two on the Aisle, **641,** 642, 875
Two Roses, The, **241**
Two's Company, **645,** 669
Tyrolean, The, **129**
Tzigane, The, **158**

U and I, **123**
Umabatha: The Zulu Macbeth, **819**
Umpire, The, **253,** 270
Uncle Célestin, **132**
Uncle Sam, **82**
Uncle Tom's Cabin (as musical), 13, 26, 72, 221, 467,
    639
Under Many Flags, **325**
Under the Counter, **619**
Under the Gaslight, 87
Under the Red Globe, **174**
Unsinkable Molly Brown, The, **681**
Up and Down Broadway, **303**
Up in Central Park, 554, 604, **606,** 615, 625
Up in the Clouds, **419**
Up She Goes, 427
Ups-a-Daisy, **498**
Upside Down, **107**
Uptown...It's Hot, **788–789**
Urban Cowboy, **843**
Urinetown, **835,** 841, 845, 853
Utopia, Ltd., 149
Utter Glory of Morrisey Hall, The, **765**

Vagabond King, The, **460, 461,** 492, 549, 597
Vagina Dialogues, The, 851
Valerie; or, The Treasured Tokens, **52**
Vamp, The, **658,** 670
Vanderbilt Cup, The, **256,** 280, 295
Vanderbilt Revue, The, **520**
Vanities of 1923, **432**
Vanities of 1926, **469**
Vanities of 1927, **476**
Vanities of 1940, 758
Velvet Lady, The, **388**
Venetian Glass Nephew, The, **523**
Venetian Romance, A, **234,** 244
Venice Preserved, 2
Venus, **72**

Vera Violetta, **319,** 321
Véronique, **251**
Very Good Eddie, **360,** 361, 364, 370, 379, 753
Very Little Faust and More Marguerite, 177
Very Warm for May, **576,** 577, 579
Via Galactica, **744**
Vicar of Bray, The, **74**
Vice Admiral, The, **134**
Viceroy, The, **197**
Victor, the Bluestocking, **106**
Victor Borge's Holiday Show on Broadway, **797**
Victor/Victoria, **812**
Vie Parisienne, La, **27,** 41, 82, 83, 604, 698
Vienna Life, **203**
Viking, The, **157**
Vintage '60, **680**
Virginia, **562**
Virginia; or, Ringing the Changes, 76
Virginia Mummy, The, 12
Virginia Unmasked, 2
Vision of the Sun, The, **15**
Viva O'Brien, **585**
Vivian's Papas, 226
Vogelhändler, Der, 129
Vogues of 1924, **437**
Voyage en Chine, Le, **39**
Voyage en Suisse, Le, **67**
Voyage of Susette, The, **147**
Voyagers in Southern Seas, **66**

Waddy Googan, **109**
Wager, The, **51,** 52
Wait a Minim!, **713**
Wake Up and Dream, **512**
Walk a Little Faster, **537**
Walk with Music, **579**
Walking Happy, **717,** 760
Wall Street Girl, The, **323**
Waltz Dream, A, **282**
Waltzes from Vienna, 546
Wanderer, The, **247**
Wang, **123,** 139, 140, 151, 234, 315
Wanted, 1000 Milliners, 23
Wanted, a Partner, **82**
War Bubbles, **184**
Wars of the World, **348**
Wartime Wedding, A, 171
Watch Your Step!, **351,** 356, 359, 636, 724
Water Queen, The, **111,** 113
Way Down South, 135
We, Us and Co. at Mud Springs, **88,** 95
Weary Willie Walker, **210**

Sources

Songs

Blue Ocean Blues, 493
Blue Room, The, 464, 501
Blue Shadows, 495
Blue Skies, 874
Blues In The Night, 514, 816
Body And Soul, 520
Bolero, 526, 777
Bongo On The Congo, 438
Bonnie Banks, 573
Bonnie Little Johnnie, 191
Bonus Blues, The, 420
Boogy-Woogy, 581
Boom Tir-ra Tir-ra, 123. *See also* Ta-Ra-Ra-Boom-
    Dee-Ay
Bosom Buddies, 714
Boston Beguine, The, 583, 644
Bow! Bam! Zonk!, 713
Bowery, The, 130, 131, 148
Boy Like That, A, 876
Boy! What Love Has Done To Me!, 519
Brand New You, 873
Break It Up, 592
Br'er Rabbit, 598
Bride Elect March, The, 183–184
Brimstone and Treacle, 864
Bring Along The Camera, 310
Brooklyn, U.S.A., 606
Brooklyn Cantata, 587
Brother, Can You Spare A Dime?, 508, 535, 865
Brown October Ale, 128
Brush Up Your Shakespeare, 627
Bubble, Bubble, 58
Budweiser's A Friend Of Mine, 272
Buggy Riding, 406
Bull Dog, 364
Bulls And Bears, 249
Bully Song, The, 161
Bum Won, The, 677
Bungalow in Quogue, 375
Bushel And A Peck, A, 637
But-After The Ball Was Over, 383
But Alive, 735
But In The Morning, No, 577
But Not For Me, 519
Butterfly, The, 304, 876
Button Up Your Overcoat, 503
Buy A Bond, 382
Buy Yourself A Balloon, 558
Buzzard Song, The, 755
By Any Means Necessary, 808
By Myself, 566
By The Light Of The Silvery Moon, 296

By The Mississinewah, 594
By The Saskatchewan, 310, 311
By The Sycamore Tree, 226
Bye, Bye, Baby, 633
Bye And Bye, 458
Bye Bye Dear Old Broadway, 272
Bye Bye Dreamy Eyes, 279

Cab Song, 609
Cabaret, 716, 874
Cake I Had, The, 863
Cake Walk Strut, The, 481
California, Here I Come, 418, 452
Call Of The South, 450
Camptown Races, 13
Can't Fight This Feeling, 877
Can't Help Lovin' Dat Man, 489
Can't Take My Eyes Off You, 858
Can't We Be Friends?, 506
Can't You Hear Our Country Calling?, 372
Cantata For A First Date, 814
Capitan's Song, El, 166, 772
Caprice Viennois, 604
Captain Hook's Waltz, 652
Caresses, 407
Carlotta, 601
Carolina In The Morning, 426
Castle Of Dreams, 396
Catherine The Great, 575
Cats On Our Back Fence, The, 96
Celeste Aida, 645
C'est Magnifique, 647
Chansonette, 434
Chaperone, The, 131
Chaplin Walk, The, 355
Chappies Of The Day, 245
Charleston, The, 434
Charleston Blues, The, 76
Chattanooga Choo Choo, 768
Cheerful Little Earful, 521
Chestnutty Language Of Lovers, The, 209
Chick! Chick! Chick!, 406
Children And Art, 784
Chim Chim Cheree, 864
Chinatown, My Chinatown, 303
Chinese-American Rag, 398
Chinese Honeymoon, A, 349
Chinky China Charleston, 460
Chloe, 381
Chop Stick Rag, 321
Chough And Crow, 11

Keep The Home Fires Burning, 506
Keep The Love Lamps Burning In The Windows Of
　　Your Eyes, 400
Kickin' The Clouds Away, 453, 780
Kids, 679
Kiss In The Dark, A, 426
Kiss Me, Kate, 627
Kiss Me Again, 254
Kiss Me To Sleep, 201
Kiss of Love, The, 157
Kiss the Girl, 868
Kiss Waltz, The, 310, 311
Kohala Welcome, 493
Kosher Kleagle, 469

Ladies Who Lunch, The, 735
Ladies Who Sing With The Band, The, 597
Lady Is A Tramp, The, 559, 755, 774, 882
Lady Is A WAC, The, 592
Lady Of The Evening, 426
Lambeth Walk, The, 789
Lambs' March, The, 72
Lamplight, 544
Land Of Broken Dreams, 478
Land Of Long Ago, The, 451
Land Of My Own Romance, The, 317
Land Where The Good Songs Go, The, 377
Lardy Dah, 61
Last Part Of Every Party, The, 396
Last Round-Up, The, 543
Latins Know How, 579
Lazy Afternoon, 650
Leader Of Vanity Fair, The, 216
Leap From The Earth To The Sky, A, 148
Learn To Smile, 417
Left All Alone Again Blues, 398
Left Behind, 865
Legalize My Name, 612
Legend Of The Frogs, The, 166
Legend Of The Pearls, The, 416
Legs, Legs, Legs, 507
Lesson in Flirtation, A, 205
Let Me Entertain You, 674
Let Me Live And Die in Dixie, 308
Let Me Match My Private Life With Yours, 535
Let Us March Along, 72
Let's Be Buddies, 581
Let's Comb Beaches, 592
Let's Do It, 498
Let's Fall in Love, 882
Let's Fly Away, 522
Let's Go Around The Town, 351

Let's Go Back To The Waltz, 691, 692
Let's Go Fly a Kite, 864
Let's Go Home, 801
Let's Go to Bed, 861
Let's Have Another Cup of Coffee, 531, 532
Let's Make Love, 291
Let's Not Talk About Love, 585
Let's Swing It, 550
Let's Take An Old-Fashioned Walk, 630
Liaisons, 745
Lida Rose, 669
Life Does A Man A Favor, 670
Life Is Just A Bowl Of Cherries, 532
Life Of The Party, The, 722
Life Turns on a Dime, 857
Life Was Pie For The Pioneer, 580
Lili Marlene, 825
Limehouse Blues, 436
Listen To Me, 415
Listen To The Mocking Bird, 217
Lit'l Gal, 274
Little Bungalow, A, 462
Little Daughter Nell, 146
Little Fish In A Big Pond, A, 630
Little Girl At Home, A, 328
Little Girl Blue, 553
Little Girl From Little Rock, A, 633
Little Girls Goodbye, 394
Little Green Snake, 676
Little Gypsy Maid, The, 211
Little House In Soho, A, 490
Little Jack Frost, 591
Little Jazz Bird, 449
Little Joint With A Juke Box, A, 585
Little Love, A Little Kiss, A, 335
Little Mary Sunshine, 676
Little Miss Victory Jones, 592
Little Old Lady, 558
Little Priest, A, 764
Little Red Riding Hood, 435
Little Skipper From Heaven Above, A, 557
Little Things (Meant So Much To Me), 638
Little Tin Box, 677
Little Tune, Go Away, 385
Little White House (At The End Of Honeymoon
　　Lane), The, 471
Little Widow Dunn, The, 53, 58
Live And Die In Dixieland, 359
Living Nativity, 790
Liza, 508, 875
Lizzie Borden, 644
Loads Of Love, 689
Locked Out After Nine, 60

Marie Cahill's Arab Love Song, 290
Marie From Sunny Italy, 351
Marriage Type Love, 647
Marry The Man Today, 637
Marrying For Love, 635
Marvelous Millers, 321
Mary Kelly's Beau, 60
Mary's A Grand Old Name, 254, 255
Mascot Of The Troop, The, 254
Massa's In De Cold Cold Ground, 13
Matchbox, 883
Matchmaker, Matchmaker, 701
Maxim's, 278
May Tells All, 576
McNally's Row Of Flats, 76
Me Siento Hermosa, 876
Meat And Potatoes, 692
Meet Me At The Garden Gate, 45
Mein Lieber Schwan, 264
Meine Kleine Akrobat, 534
Memories Are Made of This, 883
Memories Of You, 520, 762
Memory, 778
Memory Lane, 437
Memphis Blues, The, 466
Merry Widow Waltz, The, 278
Message of Spring, The, 241
Message Of The Red, Red Rose, The, 288
Message Of The Violet, The, 223, 288
Mexiconga, The, 575
Mighty Dollar, The, 266
Mighty Lak A Rose, 387
Miller's Tale, The, 726
Mimi Jazz, 405
Minstrel Parade, The, 351
Miss Hannah From Savannah, 200
Miss Marmelstein, 690
Missionary Man, A, 218
Mister And Missus Fitch, 537
Mister Cellophane, 750
Mister Dooley, 214, 234
Mister Johnson Turn Me Loose, 173
Mister Moon-Man Turn Off Your Light, 312
Mister Snow, 607
Moanin' Low, 506
Modiste, The, 568
Molly Dear, It's You I'm After, 347
Molly O!, 127
Molly O'Halleron, 364
Mon Homme. *See* My Man
Monkey Doodle, 335
Monkey Doodle-Doo, The, 462
Monkey In The Mango Tree, 668

Moon Am Shinin', 451
Moon-Faced, Starry-Eyed, 616
Moon Shines On The Moonshine, The, 404
Moon Song, 380
Moonbeams, 263
Moonlight Bay, 342
Moonlight Becomes You, 882
Moonlight Kisses, 433
More I Can Not Wish You, 637
More I See Of Others, Dear, The Better I Like You,
    The, 350
More Than You Know, 510
Moritat, 649
Most Beautiful Girl In The World, The, 553
Most Expensive Statue In The World, The, 630
Most Gentlemen Don't Like Love, 571
Mother, 483
Mother Machree, 309, 332
Mothers O'Men, 503
Mountain Greenery, 466
Mountain High—Valley Low, 612
Mounties, The, 445, 485
Moving Day In Jungle Town, 296
Mr. Dooley, 212
Mr. Gallagher and Mr. Shean, 422
Mr. Tambourine Man, 863
Mr. Washington, Uncle George, 634
Mrs. Remington, 876
Much More, 679
Mulligan's Promises, 63
Music Goes Round and Round, The, 555
Music Of Home, The, 678
Music Of The Night, The, 790
Mutual Admiration Society, 664
My Arab Complex, 549
My Baby-Talk Lady!, 383
My Baby's Arms, 391
My Beautiful Lady, 311, 327
My Best Girl, 714
My Best Love, 840
My Blanket And Me, 719
My Blue Heaven, 482
My Boy And I, 435, 457
My Broncho Boy, 256
My Coal Black Mammy, 426
My Cousin In Milwaukee, 538, 848
My Cretonne Girl, 432
My Cup Runneth Over, 717
My Darling, 535
My Darling, My Darling, 625
My Favorite Things, 676
My First True Love, 238
My Funny Valentine, 559, 882

My Gal's A High Born Lady, 484
My Girl Back Home, 871
My Handy Man, 865
My Heart Beats For You, 418
My Heart Belongs To Daddy, 571
My Heart Is Unemployed, 569
My Heart Stood Still, 486
My Heart's Delight, 180
My Hero, 297
My Hometown, 698
My Honeysuckle Baby, 291
My Honeysuckle Girl, 218
My Hula Maid, 355
My Illinois, 246
My Irish Girl, 269
My Irish Molly O!, 260, 364
My Land, My Flag, 358
My Landlady, 327
My Last Affair, 544, 556
My Little Gypsy Maid, 218
My Little Side Door, 83
My Lonesome Little Louisiana, 251
My Lord And Master, 639
My Lucky Star, 503
My Mammy, 381
My Man, 414, 420, 425, 435, 554, 755
My One And Only, 487
My Own Best Friend, 874
My Own Morning, 718
My Own United States, 218
My Pajama Beauty, 209
My Paradise, 360
My Paramount-Publix-Roxy Rose, 545
My Pretty Rosebud, 249
My Romance, 553
My Rose Of Spain, 479
My Rose Of The Ghetto, 316
My Sambo, 212
My Scarecrow Coon, 250
My Ship, 584
My Song, 527
My Sunny Tennessee, 408
My Sword And I, 492
My Tiger Lily, 196
My Time Of Day, 637
My Wild Irish Rose, 190

Namely You, 663
Name's La Guardia, The, 677
Nancy Brown, 210, 214
Napoleon, 668
Naughty, Naughty Nancy, 677

Naughty Men, The, 20
Near To You, 657
'Neath The Old Cherry Tree, 280
'Neath The Southern Moon, 307
Nellie Kelly, I Love You, 428
Neopolitan Love Song, 358
Nesting Time In Flatbush, 369, 370
Nestle By My Side, 269
Never Gonna Dance, 847
Never Never Land, 652
Never Take The Horseshoe From The Door, 53
Never Too Late For Love, 653
Nevermore, 451
New Ashmolean Marching Society And Students'
    Conservatory Band, The, 625
New Fangled Preacher Man, 734
New-Fangled Tango, A, 664
New Life, A, 818
New Sun In The Sky, 525
New York, New York, 606, 874–875
Next, 839
Next Best Thing To Love, The, 833
Nigger With A White Spot On His Face, 164
Night And Day, 537, 769
Night Was Made For Love, The, 528
Nightcap, A, 63
Nightingale, The Moon And I, The, 608
No More, 796
No One'll Ever Love You (Like You Do), 671
No Other Love, 647
No Song More Pleasing, 754
Nobody, 750
Nobody But You, 390
Nobody Home Cake Walk, 355
Nobody Makes A Pass At Me, 565
Nobody Told Me, 689
Nobody Wants Me, 469
Nobody's Heart, 588
Nora Malone, 301
Not As Good As Last Year, 495
Not For All The Rice In China, 541
Not While I'm Around, 764
Not Yet, 379
Nothin' For Nothin', 634
Nothing At All, 656
Now's The Time, 719

Ocarina, The, 635
Odle-De-O, 491
Of Thee I Sing, 529
Off The Record, 564
Oh, Baby, 476

Parade Night, 558
Parade Of The Wooden Soldiers, The, 420, 425, 597, 790, 800, 806
Parasols On Parade, 526
Paris Is A Paradise For Coons, 311, 523
Paris Loves Lovers, 655
Parlez-moi d'Amour, 546
Part of Your World, 868
Party's Over, The, 663
Peek-A-Boo, 127
Peg O' My Heart, 335
Pennies From Heaven, 812
People, 698, 699
People Will Say We're In Love, 595
Percolatin', 516
Perfect Evening, A, 673
Perfectly Lovely Couple, 704
Personality, 812
Pick-Pocket Tango, 672
Pick Yourself Up, 847, 857, 882
Pie, 435
Pigtails And Freckles, 692
Pinky Panky Poo, 216
Pitcher Of Beer, The, 56
Plain We Live, 654
Plant You Now, Dig You Later, 582
Play Gypsies—Dance Gypsies, 470
Playland, 266
Play's The Thing, The, 157
Please Be Human, 756
Plenty of Money and You, 835
Poker Love, 266
Police Report, A, 8
Politics And Poker, 677
Polly Wolly Doodle, 13
Poor Butterfly, 358, 366
Poor Porgy, 553
Poor Unfortunate Souls, 868
Poppy Smoke, 537
Poppyland, 397
Populism, Yea, Yea, 886
Porcelain Maid, 426
Pore Jud Is Daid, 595
Practically Perfect, 864
Pretty Baby, 359
Pretty Girl (The Earl Carroll Vanities), 495
Pretty Girl, A (Wang), 123
Pretty Girl Is Like A Melody, A, 391
Pretty Little Maid Of Zanzibar, 250
Princess Zenobia, The, 568
Prisoner's Song, The, 478
Prohibition Blues, 388
Promenade Walk, The, 456

Pullman Porter's Ball, The, 206
Puritan Prance, The, 316
Purity Brigade, The, 179
Push De Button, 668
Push Dem Clouds Away, 131
Pussy Foot, The, 671
Put A Curse On You, 740
Put On A Happy Face, 679
Put On Your Old Grey Bonnet, 342, 631
Put Your Arms Around Me Honey, 305
Puttin' On The Ritz, 868
Puzzlement, A, 639

Queen Lucy, 719
Queen Of The Track, The, 218
Quest, The, 711
Quiet Game of Bridge, A, 520
Quiet Girl, A, 646

Race Track Girls, The, 182
Racing Blues, 400
Racing Game, 287
Rackety Coo, 360
Rag Doll, 858
Rag Time Liz, 187
Ragtime Chinaman, 221
Ragtime Sextet, 322
Ragtime Temple Bells, 349
Rain In Spain, The, 659
Rainbow Girl, The, 377
Raindrops Keep Falling on My Head, 844
Rangers' Song, The, 477
Raunchy, 696
Real American Folk Song, The, 386
Real Slow Drag, A, 752
Rebecca Of Sunnybrook Farm, 335
Red, White, And Blue, 286
Red, Whites And Blues, 587
Red Hot Chicago, 515
Red Peppers, 558
Red Sails In The Sunset, 553, 765
Red Sky, 267
Remember The Face Of Your Driver, 500
Remembering You, 456
Rememb'ring, 451
Rendezvous Time In Paree, 574
Rest Room Rose, 524
Reuben And Cynthia, 130, 131, 148, 198
Revolutionary Costume for Today, The, 863
Rhapsody in Blue, 475, 573, 777
Rhode Island Is Famous For You, 622

Sighing, Ah Sighing, 72, 166
Silver Moon, 483
Silver Threads Among The Gold, 631
Simple Joys Of Maidenhood, The, 682
Simple Melody, 351, 400, 636
Since The Days Of Grandmama, 328–329
Sing For Your Supper, 572
Sing Me A Song With Social Significance, 564
Sir Frog And Mistress Toad, 218
Siren's Song, 374
Sister Mary Has The Measles, 199
Sister Susie's Sewing Shirts For Soliders, 348
Sit Down, You're Rocking The Boat, 637
Sixteen Going On Seventeen, 676
Size Thirteen Collar, 361
Skidmore Masquerade, The, 63
Skids Are On Review, The, 56
Skids Are Out Today, 53, 55
Skids Are Out Tonight, 63
Skip To My Lou, 753
Slaughter On Tenth Avenue, 555, 652
Slave Of Love, The, 444
Sleepin' Bee, A, 654
Small Town Girl, The, 379, 400
Small World, 674, 675
Smile Girls, 885
Smile She Means For You, The, 304
Smiles, 304
Smiling Isle, The, 219
Smoke Gets in Your Eyes, 543
Smoke Rings, 419
Smokin' Reefers, 534, 537
Snow Baby, The, 184
Snowball Sammy, 240
So Am I, 449, 450
So Far, 620
So Long Mary, 254, 255
So What?, 716
Social Director, 644
Soft Lights And Sweet Music, 531
Softly, As In A Morning Sunrise, 497
Soldier Need Not Fear, A, 156
Some Day, 459
Some Enchanted Evening, 628, 629, 870
Some Little Bug Is Going To Find You, 359
Some People, 674
Some Sort Of Somebody, 360, 361
Some Things Are Better Left Unsaid, 164
Some Wonderful Sort Of Someone, 386
Somebody, Somewhere, 661
Somebody Else, 476
Somebody Loves Me, 442, 449
Someday When Dreams Come True, 269

Someone Is Waiting, 735
Someone Like You, 818
Something Seems Tingle-Ingleing, 340, 429
Something Sort Of Grandish, 616, 641
Something To Remember You By, 520
Something Wonderful, 639
Something You Never Had Before, 688
Something's Coming, 667
Sometimes I'm Happy, 479
Somewhere, 667, 876
Song Is You, The, 536
Song of India, 477
Song of Purple Summer, The, 865
Song Of The Navy, 286
Song Of The Strollers, The, 205
Song Of The Vulgar Boatman, 491
Song Of The Woodman, 558
Song On The Sand, 781
Soon It's Gonna Rain, 679
Sophisticated Lady, 790
Sorry—Grateful, 735
Soul-Saving Sadie, 543
Sousa Melodies, 363
South America Take It Away!, 613
South American Way, The, 574
South Fifth Avenue, 65
South Sea Isles, 414
Spanish Shawl, A, 479
Spoonful of Sugar, A, 864
Spring In Vienna, 564
Spring Is Here, 568
Springtime Cometh, The, 641
St. Louis Blues, 466, 524
Standing On The Corner, 661
Star Dust, 558, 790
Star Spangled Banner, The, 184, 343, 372, 747, 754
Stars Fell On Alabama, 790
Stay Well, 631
Stay With The Happy People, 635
Staying Young, 676
Steal Your Rock 'n' Roll, 879
Steam Heat, 651, 657
Steam Is On The Beam, The, 592
Stop Dat Rag, 299
Stormy Weather, 514, 774
Stouthearted Men, 497
Strange Music, 603
Stranger In Paradise, 648
Straw Hat in The Rain, 549
Streets Of New York, The, 263, 264
Streets of Paris, The, 574
Strenuous, 250
Strike Out McCracken, 216

People

Aarons, Alex A., 462, 493, 538
Aarons, Alfred E., 187, 197, 199, 206, 241, 306
Abarbanell, Lina, 267, 304, 366, 471, 512, 521, 597
ABBA, 836, 858
Abbott, Bud, 574
Abbott, Emma, 64, 68
Abbott, George, 555–556, 571, 586, 592, 621, 624–625, 640, 650, 656, 662, 665, 677, 681, 704, 747, 840
Abeles, Edward, 299, 379
Aberni, Luis, 471
Aborn, Milton, 143, 540
Abraham, David, 296
Abraham, F. Murray, 819
Abrahams, Maurice, 338
Acito, Tim, 844
Ackerman, Peter, 859
Adahm, J., 114
Adair, Yvonne, 626, 632
Adam, Robert, 248
Adams, Edith, 646, 662
Adams, Frank R., 241, 246, 248, 253, 269, 272, 283, 284, 287, 293, 299, 301, 345, 427, 592, 593, 690
Adams, Franklin P., 504
Adams, Ida M., 310
Adams, Joe, 668
Adams, Lee, 661, 702, 713, 762, 804, 869, 879
Adams, Margaret, 552
Adams, Maude, 109
Adams, Nick, 249
Adamson, Harold, 586, 626
Addams, Charles, 643, 883
Addinsell, Richard, 670
Ade, George, 220, 226, 238, 292, 299, 374
Adelman, Charles, 248
Adler, Else, 359, 409
Adler, Gary, 856
Adler, Hyman, 533
Adler, Larry, 534, 579
Adler, Richard, 651, 687, 756, 759

Adolfi, Gustav, 73
Adrian, Max, 663
Ager, Milton, 492, 508
Agnew, Claresse, 180
Agron, Sal, 821
Ahrens, Lynn, 809, 821, 832, 844, 856, 859, 872
Aimée, Marie, 34, 45, 51, 53, 80, 100
Ainsworth, Edith, 117
Akers, Karen, 777
Akst, Harry, 436, 549
Akutagawa, Ryunosuke, 862
Alberghetti, Anna Maria, 684
Albert, Donie Ray, 755
Albert, Eddie, 572, 630
Albert, Ernest, 376
Albertson, Jack, 582
Albini, Felix, 322
Alda, Alan, 715
Alda, Robert, 636, 637
Alden, Christopher, 838
Alden, John, 148
Aldrich, Charles T., 348
Aldrich, David, 762
Aleichem, Sholom, 701
Alexander, Rod, 634
Alfino, Edward, 319
Alfred, William, 735
Ali, George, 227
Ali, Muhammad (Cassius Clay), 732
Allen, Beatrice, 375, 455
Allen, Betty, 752
Allen, Dave, 775
Allen, Deborah, 746, 789
Allen, Elizabeth, 704
Allen, Fred, 437, 506, 520, 535, 632
Allen, Harry, 62, 449
Allen, Joseph, 513
Allen, Lester, 414, 431, 443, 512
Allen, Louise, 380, 388
Allen, Peter, 765, 794, 845, 846
Allen, Sandra, 840

Allen, Sir Thomas, 850
Allen, Steve, 693, 806
Allen, Walter, 162
Allen, Woody, 679
Allesandrini, Gerald, 815
Allmon, Clint, 760
Allup, Rebecca, 106
Alt, Natalie, 336, 378
Altman, Ruth, 518
Alton, Robert, 555
Alvarez, Anita, 616
Alvarez, David, 874
Amado, Jorge, 763
Amara, Lucine, 865
Ameche, Don, 655, 671, 683, 720
Ames, Florence, 433, 541
Ames, Florenz, 429
Ames, Percy, 265
Ames, Winthrop, 465, 483, 546
Amsterdam, Morey, 623
Amundsen, Monte, 673
Anders, Glenn, 566
Andersen, Hans Christian, 427
Anderson, Carl, 816
Anderson, George, 273, 317, 354, 375
Anderson, Hans Christian, 868
Anderson, John Murray, 391, 450, 544, 549, 554
Anderson, Kevin, 851
Anderson, Leroy, 670
Anderson, Marian, 565
Anderson, Maxwell, 570, 631, 742
Anderson, Nancy, 833, 853, 886
Anderson, Percy, 187
Anderson, Stephan Lee, 823
Anderson, Will R., 287, 389
Andes, Keith, 646, 682
Andreas, Christine, 754, 768, 884
Andrews, A. G., 158
Andrews, Billy, 506
Andrews, Julie, 651, 652, 658, 660, 676, 682, 812, 827, 852
Andrews, Maxene, 747
Andrews, Patty, 747
Angela, June, 799
Angelus, Muriel, 572, 586, 597
Anikulapo-Kuti, Fela, 881
Anstey, F., 599
Anthony, Marc, 821
Anthony, Norman, 534
Applegate, Christina, 856
Applegate, Fred, 881, 884
Arcade, Franklin, 360

Archer, Belle, 89
Archer, Harry, 432, 448, 459, 498
Archer, Isabelle, 122
Archer, Will, 216
Archie, Will, 318
Archmere, Ollie, 131
Ard, Kenneth, 778
Ardelli, Roberto, 471
Arden, Eve, 554, 577, 585
Arden, Michael, 845, 862
Arden, Victor, 505
Arias, Yancy, 828
Arkin, Alan, 685
Arkin, Ted, 582
Arlen, Harold, 514, 517, 523, 535, 544, 558, 565, 591, 603, 668, 678, 722, 730, 735, 816, 833, 842
Arliss, George, 298
Armand, J. C., 64
Armin, Walter, 571
Armitage, Karole, 877
Armont, Paul, 421
Armstrong, Billie Jo, 884
Armstrong, Louis, 507, 577, 649, 697
Armstrong, Paul, 451
Armstrong, W. M., 161, 197
Armus, Sidney, 644
Arnaz, Desi, 576
Arnaz, Lucie, 763
Arne, Michael, 1
Arno, Peter, 508, 529
Arnold, Ion, 111
Aronson, Boris, 604, 725, 839, 848
Aronson, Rudolf, 75, 79, 90, 142, 402
Arren, Charlotte, 550
Arthur, Art, 622
Arthur, Beatrice, 655, 701, 836
Arthur, Jean, 634
Arthur, Lee, 250, 384
Arthur, Paul, 97
Arthur, Robert Alan, 687, 688
Asaf, George, 368
Ash, Samuel, 360, 392, 486
Ashford, Rob, 833, 838, 840, 860, 866, 871
Ashley, Chris, 832, 867, 879–880
Ashley, Minnie, 195
Ashman, Howard, 807, 868
Ashton, Tony, 1
Asia (rock music group), 877
Astaire, Adele and/or Fred, 378, 394, 417, 420–421, 428, 449, 450, 487, 521, 525, 537, 768, 818, 847
Astaire, Lilyan, 535
Astrova, Marie, 419

Atchison-Ely, Edgar, 290
Atherton, Alice, 34, 44, 58, 61, 84
Atkinson, Brooks, 465, 506, 521, 527, 541, 543, 566, 575, 576, 578, 583, 649, 758, 781
Atteridge, Harold, 291, 301, 303, 395, 401, 443, 452, 466, 479, 493, 504, 527
Atwell, Lester, 704
Atwell, Roy, 359, 387
Auberjonois, René, 744, 786
Auburn, David, 839
Auburn, Jayne, 449
Audran, Edmond, 64, 66, 67, 68, 87, 98, 101, 129, 141, 179
Auer, Mischa, 587
Auerbach, Arnold, 622
Augarde, Adrienne, 292
August, Matt, 863
Aumont, Jean Pierre, 693
Auracher, Harry, 321
Austen, Jane, 673
Austin, Ivy, 790
Averill, Perry, 146
Axelrod, George, 623
Ayckbourn, Alan, 836
Ayer, Nat D., 303
Ayers, Lemuel, 594, 638
Ayre, Charlotte, 491
Azaria, Hank, 854
Aznavour, Charles, 733, 749, 779, 823

Babcock, Theodore, 202
Bacall, Lauren, 734, 735, 773
Bach, J. S., 759
Bacharach, Burt, 844, 885
Backus, Charles, 79
Baddeley, Hermione, 727
Baer, Abel, 478
Bagby, George, 504
Bagg, Helen, 303
Bagley, Ben, 655
Bagneris, Vernel, 808, 837
Bailey, Frankie, 321
Bailey, Pearl, 638, 654, 698, 753
Bailey, Robin, 695
Bainter, Fay, 382
Baird, Bil and Cora, 640, 693, 703
Baird, Steward, 340
Baird, Stewart, 350, 375
Bairnsfather, Bruce, 386
Baker, Becky Ann, 8, 848
Baker, Benny, 585, 601
Baker, Charles D., 72
Baker, David, 668, 680

Baker, Edythe, 408, 463
Baker, Emily, 55
Baker, Josephine, 411, 541, 698, 747
Baker, Kenny, 599
Baker, Mabella, 183
Baker, Phil, 403, 433, 456, 516, 524, 549, 587
Baker, R. Melville, 209, 236
Baker, Word, 867
Baker, Thomas, 20
Balaban, Bob, 719
Balanchine, George, 555, 568, 579, 581, 587, 599, 600, 779
Balderrama, Michael, 860
Baldinu, Pichón, 860
Baldwin, Kate, 877
Baldwin, Tallmadge, 159
Baldwin, Winnie, 453
Balestracci, Marcello, 873
Balfe, Louise, 112
Balfe, Michael William, 16, 29, 78
Balgord, Linda, 866
Balieff, Nikita, 420, 528, 546
Ball, Ernest R., 350
Ball, Lucille, 682
Ball, Michael, 796, 858, 861
Ball, Ernest R., 332
Ballard, Kaye, 650, 693, 695, 746
Balsam, Martin, 692
Balthrop, Carmen, 752
Bancroft, Anne, 745
Banderas, Antonio, 843
Banker, Betsy, 112
Bankhead, Tallulah, 664
Banks, Leslie, 631
Baral, Robert, 391, 398, 425, 431
Baranski, Christine, 865
Barbaretto, Burrell, 310, 340
Barbeau, Adrienne, 741
Barber, Joyce, 493
Barbour, James, 833, 848, 873
Barclay, Don, 461
Barker, Edith, 203
Barker, George Washinton, 268
Barker, Jack, 457, 462
Barker, John, 485, 503, 525
Barker, Richard, 92, 108, 110, 116, 119, 133, 134, 152, 164, 167, 168, 187, 189
Barnabee, Henry Clay, 58, 62, 128, 144, 147, 155, 165, 171, 174, 180, 197, 209, 216
Barnard, Charles, 51
Barnes, Clive, 755, 756, 816, 819, 823
Barnes, Gregg, 879
Barnes, Howard, 594

Boyd, Joe, 454
Boyd, Meg, 874
Boyer, Lucienne, 546
Boyle, Jack, 673
Boyle, John, 503
Bozardt, Victor, 475
Bracken, Eddie, 665, 678
Bradbury, Jessie, 328
Bradbury, Lane, 674
Bradfield, W. Louis, 153, 177
Bradford, Alex, 756
Bradford, Roark, 578
Bradley, M., 69
Bradshaw, Charles, 249
Brady, Diamond Jim, 541
Brady, Scott, 673
Brady, William A., 236, 247, 323, 354
Bragiotti, S. Herbert, 502
Braham, David, 27, 39, 40, 48, 49, 53, 56, 57, 60, 63,
   67, 69, 73, 75, 78, 79, 81, 86, 94, 95, 97, 106, 109,
   110, 120, 122, 140, 146, 156, 166, 189, 785
Braham, John, 52, 97, 104
Braham, Leonora, 56, 62
Bramble, Mark, 770, 835
Brand, John, 66, 99, 105, 139
Brandon, Michael, 869
Brandt, Sophie, 284
Branson, Philip, 70
Brantley, Ben, 818, 819, 823, 835, 848, 849
Braswell, Charles, 714
Bratton, John W., 200, 207, 229, 234, 248
Bravo, Luis, 850
Bray, Stephen, 858
Brazier, Adam, 858
Breaker, Daniel, 870, 875
Breau, Louis, 405
Brecht, Bertolt, 539, 540, 649, 665, 716, 754, 757,
   835, 859
Breedon, Arnold, 65
Breen, Grace, 371
Breitenbach, Robert, 120, 134, 144, 170
Breitenfeld, Emil, 380
Brel, Jacques, 722
Brennan, Eileen, 676, 677, 695, 697
Brennan, J. Keirn, 518
Brennan, Jay, 425
Brent, Romney, 454, 465, 506
Brescia, Lisa, 862
Brewster, Pat, 605
Brian, Donald, 254, 278–279, 337, 347, 362, 377, 384,
   394, 395, 419, 427, 525, 544, 577
Brian, Mary, 579
Brice, Elizabeth, 283, 295, 309, 322, 401

Brice, Fanny, 302, 303, 312, 333, 364, 372, 377, 414,
   420, 425, 434, 450, 504, 507, 521, 524, 543, 554,
   555, 593, 698, 699, 865
Brickman, Marshall, 858, 883
Bricusse, Leslie, 704, 812, 818
Briggs, Bowness, 152
Brighouse, Harold, 717
Brightman, Sarah, 792
Brill, Robert, 848, 876
Brinkley, Grace, 515, 530
Brinkworth, W. H., 34
Briquet, Jean, 336, 342
Brisson, Carl, 557
Bristow, George, 16
Brittan, Robert, 746
Britten, Benjamin, 626, 638
Britton, Pamela, 617
Broadhurst, George, 222, 250, 275, 305, 384
Broadhurst, Miss, 6
Broccoli, Albert "Cubby," 855
Brock, Dorothy, 835
Brock, Jerry, 669
Brockbank, Harrison, 302, 333, 385, 393
Brocolini, Signor, 82
Broderick, George, 110, 155, 808
Broderick, Helen, 433, 474, 511, 525, 535, 541
Broderick, Matthew, 810, 834
Broderick, William, 140
Brodie, Steve, 158
Brokaw, Mark, 871
Bromberg, J. Edward, 615
Bronson, Edna, 227
Brook, Peter, 781–782
Brooke, Tyler, 397
Brookfield, Charles, 142, 167
Brooks, David, 603, 617, 774
Brooks, Joseph, 857
Brooks, Lawrence, 603, 625
Brooks, Matty, 580, 622
Brooks, Mel, 665, 689, 834, 865, 867, 868
Brooks, Shelton, 424, 754
Broones, Martin, 478
Broske, Octavia, 326
Brotherson, Eric, 598, 632
Brougham, John, 9, 11, 14, 27, 35, 43, 103, 150
Broun, Heywood, 381, 427, 447, 526
Brown and Watts, 416
Brown, Agnes Caine, 268, 274
Brown, Anne, 587
Brown, Ashley, 863
Brown, Bill, 488
Brown, Blair, 826
Brown, Calvin, 495

Carrington, Katherine, 536
Carroll, Albert, 439, 479, 494, 506, 516, 535, 604
Carroll, David, 788, 792, 796
Carroll, Diahann, 654, 689
Carroll, Earl, 335, 367, 380, 432, 436, 446, 456, 460,
    462, 469, 476, 481, 488, 495, 504, 507, 517, 526,
    533, 540, 541, 550, 562, 578, 644, 758
Carroll, Harry, 343, 348, 381, 395, 401
Carroll, Jane, 459
Carroll, Jean, 581
Carroll, June, 643
Carroll, Leo G., 568
Carroll, Marie, 370
Carroll, Richard F., 117, 155, 159, 183, 184
Carroll, Robert, 619
Carroll, Ronn, 807
Carroll, Vinnette, 756
Carson, Doris, 555
Carson, Jack, 643
Carson, Jeannie, 679
Carson, Mindy, 665, 669
Carter, Frank, 393
Carter, Jack, 660
Carter, Leslie, 129
Carter, Lincoln J., 281
Carter, Nell, 816
Carter, Terry, 687
Cartlett, Walter, 478
Carus, Emma, 201, 204, 214, 319
Carver, Brent, 805, 824
Caryll, Earl, 421
Caryll, Ivan, 161, 172, 175, 186, 206, 208, 228, 245,
    252, 261, 265, 269, 270, 287, 302, 304, 308, 310,
    312, 326, 349, 375, 376, 385, 386, 405, 491
Casale, Glen, 858
Case, Allen, 673, 718
Cash, Johnny, 859
Casnoff, Phillip, 792, 799
Cassavant, Louis, 200, 375, 483
Cassidy, David, 805
Cassidy, Jack, 623, 644, 653, 662, 665, 694, 700, 725
Cassidy, Patrick, 785
Cassidy, Shaun, 805
Castle, Irene, 328, 332, 351, 364, 377
Castle, Vernon, 262, 294, 299, 300, 328, 332
Castle, William, 95
Castleton, Kate, 94
Castling, Harry, 347
Casto, Jean, 582, 606
Cather, Willa, 346
Catlett, Mary Jo, 697, 861
Catlett, Walter, 381, 407, 449, 500
Cato, Minto, 520

Cauble, Rebekah, 461
Cavanaugh, Alice, 440
Cavanaugh, Evelyn, 429, 464
Cavanaugh, Matt, 843, 863
Cavanaugh, Michael, 841
Cavenaugh, Matt, 871, 876
Cavett, Dick, 832, 842
Cawthorn, Joseph, 177, 181, 188, 193, 231, 250, 259,
    260, 289, 290, 296, 308, 328, 347, 362, 375, 386,
    406, 420, 459
Ceeley, Leonard, 485, 518
Celeste, Marie, 176, 193
Cellier, Alfred, 59, 62, 92, 105, 112, 141, 160
Cerbi, Mamie, 110
Cerveris, Michael, 848, 854, 857, 866, 878
Chabrier, Emile, 119
Chabrier, Emmanuel, 882
Chad, Harrison, 849
Chadwick, George W., 151
Chait, Marcus, 866
Chalfant, Kathleen, 833
Chamberlain, Ida Hoyt, 483
Chamberlain, Kevin, 832, 865
Chamberlain, Peggy, 494
Chamberlain, Richard, 806
Chamberlin, Kevin, 883
Chambers, Howard, 309
Chambers, Kitty, 320
Chambers, Robert W., 340
Champion, Gower, 574, 587, 592, 623, 626, 640, 684,
    717, 722, 730, 745, 749, 753, 771, 835
Champion, Marge, 780, 834
Champlin, Donna Lynne, 857
Chanel, Gabrielle "Coco," 733
Chang, Phil, 486
Chanler-Berat, Adam, 877
Channing, Carol, 626, 632, 633, 658, 683, 697, 747,
    749, 759, 768, 776, 810, 812, 838
Channing, Stockard, 876
Chapin, Frederick, 212, 235, 247
Chapin, Harry, 750
Chaplin, Sydney, 663, 688, 698
Chapman, Blanche, 219
Chapman, Ed, 53
Chapman, John, 623
Chapman, William, 678
Charig, Phil, 485, 503, 520, 527, 602, 657
Charlap, Mark (Moose), 652, 683
Charles, Keith, 726
Charlot, André, 436
Charnin, Martin, 737, 757, 808, 864
Chartock, S. M., 631, 645
Chartok, S. M., 544

Chase, Ilka, 548, 579
Chase, Will, 857, 864, 876
Chassaigne, Francis, 83, 107, 117
Chatelaine, Stella, 343
Chatrian Alexandre, 142
Chatteron Jack, 156
Chatterton, Ruth, 448
Chaucer, Geoffrey, 727
Chayefsky, Paddy, 871
Chenowith, Kristin, 824, 846, 850, 853, 864, 865, 875, 885
Cher, 851
Chesney, Jack, 625
Chester Hale Girls, 486, 488, 490, 493, 501, 502, 506
Chester, Alfred, 506
Chevalier, Maurice, 515, 617, 622, 658, 693
Chiari, Walter, 688
Chihara, Paul, 799
Childs, Jeanette, 312
Childs, Nathaniel, 58, 61
Chilvers, Hugh, 195, 404
Chilvers, Thomas, 189
Ching, William, 620
Chisholm, Robert, 488, 509, 568, 570, 574, 578
Chivers, Hugh, 189–190
Chivot, Henri, 168
Chizzola, C. A., 39, 41
Chodorov, Jerome, 633, 646, 649
Chopin, Frederic, 382, 496, 609
Christian, Angela, 858
Christians, Mady, 765
Christie, Agatha, 755
Christie, Audrey, 567, 568
Christie, Jennie, 83
Christmas, David, 726
Christy, George, 13, 21, 24
Church, Sandra, 674
Churchill, Stuart, 591
Chute, B. J., 678
Ciannelli, Edouard, 397
Ciceri, Charles, S, 6–7
Cilento, Wayne, 810, 856
Claire, Helen, 586
Claire, Ina, 319, 347, 356, 357, 364, 379
Clancy, Venie, 48
Clark and McCullough, 392, 426, 450, 470, 529, 549. *See also* Clark, Bobby; McCullough, Paul
Clark, Alexander, 154, 197, 214, 224, 235, 559
Clark, Bobby, 337, 392, 427, 470, 513, 529, 537, 555, 574, 590, 592, 601, 611, 617, 625, 626, 641, 657, 789, 791, 804, 812. *See also* Clark and McCullough
Clark, Edward, 369, 400, 403
Clark, Eugene, 50

Clark, Harry, 644
Clark, Hilda, 161, 181
Clark, Kenneth, 301
Clark, Marguerite, 220, 250, 290, 300
Clark, Victoria, 848, 855, 869
Clark, Wilfred, 502
Clarke, Eugene, 57, 62
Clarke, Gordon, 574
Clarke, Grant, 338, 414
Clarke, John Sleeper, 16–17, 492
Clarke, Richard, 116
Clary, Robert, 643
Clary, Wilton, 636
Clavell, James, 799
Clay, Frederic, 56, 59, 80
Clay, Lilly, 88
Clayton, Bessie, 131, 192, 198, 202, 206, 267, 277, 282
Clayton, Gilbert, 220
Clayton, Jan, 606, 611, 661
Cleary, Michael, 521, 559
Clement, Ada, 232
Clements, Dudley, 513, 529, 546
Clements, Ron, 868
Clendening, Eddie, 883
Cleveland Minstrels, 120, 168
Cleveland, Phyllis, 453, 460
Clifford, Billy S., 249
Clifford, Kathleen, 278
Cline, Maggie, 171
Clooney, Rosemary, 756, 880
Close, Glenn, 770, 809
Clow, James, 858
Clyde, June, 566
Coast, John, 451
Cobb, George L., 340
Cobb, Will, 232, 267, 272, 282
Coca, Imogene, 516, 526, 544, 549, 567, 576, 583, 608, 758
Cochran, Charles, 414
Cochrane, June, 487
Coco, James, 776
Coe, George, 735
Coe, Isabelle, 154
Coedès, Auguste, 72
Coffin, Hayden, 134, 141
Coghlan, Charles F., 43
Cohah, Nellie, 223
Cohan, George M., 48, 203, 204, 206, 213, 223–224, 231, 239, 240, 254–255, 257, 258, 259, 270, 280, 281, 284, 286, 289, 297, 308, 310, 317–318, 322, 325, 338, 345, 350, 351, 352, 353, 362, 371, 379, 387, 389, 392, 404, 406, 408, 416, 417, 428, 440,

448, 471, 475, 484, 497–498, 513, 564, 593, 723,
759, 772, 776, 777
Cohan, Jerry, 48, 204, 223, 239, 257, 318
Cohan, Josephine, 236
Cohan, Josie, 204, 223
Cohan, Nellie, 204, 318
Cohen, Alexander, 587
Cohen, Frieda Pauline, 224
Colavecchia, Franco, 752
Cole and Johnson, 222, 231, 240, 251, 274, 294, 410.
See also Cole, Bob; Johnson, James Weldon
Cole, Bob, 183, 200, 214, 243, 294
Cole, Jack, 587, 596, 602, 633, 859
Cole, Kay, 749
Colella, Jenn, 864
Coleman, Cy, 682, 692, 712, 730, 745, 756, 757, 770,
776, 795, 796, 800, 817
Coleman, Emil, 590
Coleman, Lillian, 223
Coleman, Warren, 552
Collette, Toni, 828
Collier, Constance, 506
Collier, WIlliam, 116, 118, 181, 321, 352, 362, 404,
416–417, 433, 463, 479
Collins, 3, 322
Collins, Charles, 513, 559, 560
Collins, Dorothy, 738
Collins, Gene, 488
Collins, José, 320, 335, 343, 350, 384
Collins, Lottie, 320
Collins, Madeline, 452
Collins, Phil, 860
Collins, Russell, 558, 634
Collins, Sam, 236
Collins, Wilke, 858
Collyer, Dan, 100, 106, 146, 166, 187
Colson, C. David, 734
Colson, Kevin, 796
Colton, John, 429
Colville, Samuel, 53
Comden, Betty, 605, 611, 646, 662, 663, 670, 683,
719, 734, 740, 758, 766, 778, 786, 800, 869
Compton, Betty, 460, 469, 487, 499, 512, 732
Comstock, Ray, 283, 353, 376, 396, 404, 437
Conkey, Thomas, 337, 384
Conlee, John Ellison, 832, 853, 883
Conley, William, 286
Connell, Dora, 80
Connell, Edward, 57
Connell, Greg, 846
Connell, Jane, 714, 727
Connelly, Marc, 366, 427, 431, 446, 518, 524
Connelly, Marcus C., 333, 358

Connick, Harry, Jr., 799, 836, 859
Conor, Harry, 130, 178, 202, 212, 225, 308, 321, 352
Conquest, George, 60
Conrad, Con, 437, 451, 465
Conried, Hans, 647, 739
Conried, Heinrich, 272
Conroy, John, 236
Constant, Yvonne, 865
Convy, Bert, 695, 701, 716
Conway, Curt, 587
Conway, Shirl, 654
Cook, Barbara, 640, 641, 648, 651, 664, 669, 679, 688,
694, 715, 740, 829, 836, 885
Cook, Carole, 861
Cook, Furneaux, 56
Cook, James F., 292
Cook, Joe, 432, 446, 518, 541, 580
Cook, Joe, Jr., 591
Cook, John, 56
Cook, Olga, 394, 417
Cook, Peter, 747
Cook, Will Marion, 185, 207, 211, 222, 259, 283,
302, 359
Cookson, Peter, 646
Cooper, Chcuk, 818, 857, 880
Cooper, Harry, 338
Cooper, Marilyn, 667, 690, 773
Cooper, Melville, 552, 597, 606, 634, 640
Coopersmith, Jerome, 715
Coote, Robert, 659, 682
Coots, J. Fred, 447, 456, 461, 463, 466, 486, 511
Copeland, Virginia, 654
Copland, Aaron, 757
Coppin, Grace, 563
Coppini, Ettore, 80
Corbett, James J., 376
Corbett, Leonora, 615
Cordon, Juliette, 155
Corio, Ann, 774
Corliss, E. W., 182, 196, 210
Corman, Roger, 845
Cornell, Katherine, 483
Correia, Don, 780
Corsini, Beppo, 395
Cort, John, 358, 369, 430, 452
Corthell, Herbert, 395
Corts, John, 405
Corwey, Irwin, 593
Costa, David, 20
Costabile, David, 849
Costello, Lou, 574, 575
Costigan, Hames, 695
Cotlow, Marilyn, 618

Cotton, R. F., 176
Cottrelly, Mathilde, 75, 83, 89, 90, 91, 98, 99, 102, 105, 107, 113, 180, 205
Coupe, Diane, 714
Courtland, Jerome, 640, 641
Courtleigh, William, 262
Courtneidge, Cicely, 463
Courtney, C. C. and Regan, 739
Courtney, Inez, 505
Courtney, Maud, 203
Covarrubias, Miguel, 454
Coward, Noël, 507, 508, 510, 521, 524, 525, 541, 546, 558, 572, 591, 612–613, 622, 685, 699, 725, 788, 863
Cowl, Jane, 364, 591
Cowles, Eugene, 128, 148, 165, 174, 188, 195, 230, 262, 323
Cox, Catherine, 782
Cox, Elvia, 151
Cox, Hazel, 302, 359
Cox, Louise, 381
Cox, Veanne, 849, 884
Cox, Wally, 633
Coyne, Joseph, 201, 208, 247, 259, 279
Craig, David, 668
Craig, Deborah S., 855
Crandal, Nelson, 668
Crane, W. H., 37, 42
Cranko, John, 663
Cranston, Toller, 758
Craske, Edith, 115
Crater, Allene, 181, 263, 299
Crater, Bertha, 263
Craven, Frank, 399, 427
Crawford, Cheryl, 587
Crawford, Clifton, 203, 207, 231, 260, 285, 319, 326, 354, 359, 368, 457
Crawford, James C., 232
Crawford, Kathryn, 522
Crawford, Michael, 792, 803, 842
Craymer, Judy, 835
Creamer, Henry S., 280, 359, 399, 423, 492
Creek, Luther, 833
Creel, Gavin, 838, 877
Cremieux, H., 35
Crivello, Anthony, 805, 827
Croffut,W. A., 62
Croft, Paddy, 826
Croker, Richard, 194
Cronkite, Walter, 810
Crook, John, 165
Crooker, Earle, 554
Cropper, Roy, 533

Crosby, B. J., 837
Crosby, Bing, 636, 756, 874, 880
Crosby, Gary, 636
Crosby, Kathryn, 813
Crosby, Kim, 792
Crosby, Wagner, 247
Cross, Richard, 671
Cross, Wellington, 457
Crossy, J. S., 56, 57
Crothers, Rachel, 350
Crouch, Julian, 856, 883
Crouse, Russel, 523, 547, 556, 565, 635, 662, 664, 691
Crouse, Timothy, 791
Crowley, Ann, 641
Crowley, Bob, 807, 860
Crowley, Dermot, 869
Crowninshield, Frank, 346
Crozier, Eric, 638
Crumb, Ann, 796
Crumit, Frank, 400, 403, 415, 433
Crumm, Max, 868
Cruz, Celia, 872
Cryer, David, 720, 727, 738, 746
Cryer, Gretchen, 744
Crystal, Billy, 851
Cuccioli, Robert, 818
Cuervo, Alma, 817
Cullington, William, 145
Cullum, John, 710, 750, 758, 796, 835, 863, 867, 886
Cummings, Alan, 860
Cummings, Vicki, 529, 559, 592
Cumpsty, Michael, 874
Cunningham, Arthur, 186, 483
Cunningham, Cecil, 332, 338, 342, 348
Cunningham, Davis, 653
Cunningham, John, 725, 735
Cure, The (rock music group), 862
Currie, William H., 173
Curry, John, 762
Curry, Tim, 751, 803, 836
Curtis, Keene, 737, 744
Curtis, M. B., 164
Curtis, Willard, 259, 285
Cushing, Catherine Chisholm, 385, 399
Cushman, Charlotte, 39, 174
Cuthbertson,Clarence, 808
Cutler, Ben, 563
Cutty, Thomas, 247
Cuvillier, Charles, 349, 366
Cypher, Jon, 814
Czibulka, 112

d'Amboise, Charlotte, 847, 856, 862
d'Amboise, Christopher, 787
d'Ancourt, Grenet, 349
D'Arcy James, Brian, 837, 864, 875
d'Arcy James, Brian, 847
D'Arienzo, Chris, 877
D'Arle, Yvonne, 470
D'Armond, Frank, 546
D'Armond, Isabel, 287
D'Arville, Camille, 107, 144, 148, 157, 158, 170
d'Ennery, Adolphe, 67
d'Orsay, Lawrence, 291
D'Oyly Carte, Richard, 59, 65, 68, 74, 92, 96, 102,
    108, 116, 149, 546, 556, 564, 572, 580, 621, 639,
    645, 680, 692, 703, 715, 754, 761, 772
da Silva, Howard, 567, 594, 677, 710, 727
Dabney, Ford T., 355, 481
Daboll, W. S., 97–98, 106
Dafora, Asadata, 544
Dahl, Magda, 282
Dahm-Peterson, Adolph, 165
Dailey, Dan, 559
Dailey, Peter F., 142, 147, 170, 177, 186, 190, 192,
    200, 235, 243, 252, 262, 282, 321
Dalberg, Camile, 394
Dale, Alan, 376, 414
Dale, Clamma, 755
Dale, Glen, 437, 475
Dale, Jim, 770, 847, 860
Dallas, J. J., 149
Daly, Arnold, 432
Daly, Augustin, 34, 35, 36, 54, 57, 72, 88, 352
Daly, Dan, 141, 151, 159, 162, 164, 176, 179, 193,
    198, 202, 207, 251
Daly, Lucy, 150
Daly, Tyne, 796, 800, 844, 867
Daly, Vinie, 234
Daly, Wilder, 130, 322
Damiano, Jennifer, 877
Damita, Lily, 511
Damon, Cathryn, 704
Damrosch, Walter, 328
Dana, Leora, 749
Danao-Salkin, Julie, 857
Dance, George, 212
Dandridge, Merle, 861
Dandy, Jess, 288
Danforth, Will, 179
Daniele, Graciela, 783, 796, 811–812, 859, 872, 876
Danieley, Jason, 832, 853, 866
Daniels, Billy, 753
Daniels, Danny, 616
Daniels, David, 654

Daniels, Eleanor, 390
Daniels, Frank, 52, 84, 162, 179, 195, 209, 228, 242,
    246–247, 265
Daniels, William, 710, 727
Danilova, Alexandra, 670
Danner, Blythe, 834
Darcy, Maurice, 179
Dare, Ada, 179
Dare, Violet, 298
Darell, Frederick, 99
Darewski, Herman, 386, 398
Darion, Joe, 665, 711
Darling, Edward A., 71, 102
Darling, Jean, 606
Darnton, Charles, 385
Darrington, Earl, 880
Dassin, Jules, 718
Datz, Lisa, 832
Dauvray, Helen, 157
Davenport, E. L., 50
Davenport, Eva, 134, 178, 233, 317
Davenport, Fanny, 107
Davenport, Harry, 122, 145, 179, 191, 207, 214
Davey, Shaun, 826
Davi, Mara, 869, 880
David, Frank, 104
David, Hal, 844, 885
David, Keith, 802, 860
David, Mack, 697
David, Worton, 347, 355
Davidge, W., 50
Davidson, Dore, 79, 228
Davidson, John, 698, 712, 813
Davidson, W. B., 409
Davie, Erin, 863, 869, 881
Davies, Brian, 690
Davies, E. D., 35, 36
Davies, Mark, 846
Davin, Collin, 285
Davis, Benny, 371, 507
Davis, Bessie McCoy, 377, 392, 397
Davis, Bette, 645, 734
Davis, Buster, 751
Davis, Charles L., 109
Davis, Collin, 241
Davis, Daniel, 850, 852
Davis, Eddie, 580, 602, 656
Davis, Henry, 552
Davis, Ivan L., 178
Davis, Jessie Bartlett, 128, 144, 148, 155, 165,
    171, 174
Davis, Luther, 796
Davis, Maria, 308

Diaz, Justino, 790
Dibble, Matthew Stockwell, 882
Dibdin, Charles, 1
DiBuono, Toni, 840
Dickens, Charles, 873
Dickey, Annamary, 604, 620
Dickson, Charles, 164, 181, 191, 284, 301
Dickson, Dorothy, 379, 380, 389, 399
Dickson, Sherman, 562
Diener, Joan, 623, 712, 735, 753
Dietrich, Marlene, 96, 673, 713, 720, 725,
    825, 848
Dietz, Henry, 157, 447
Dietz, Howard, 432, 447, 473, 479, 504, 505, 506,
    514, 518, 520, 524, 534, 548, 551, 566, 579, 601,
    604, 622, 688, 695, 696, 742, 865
Dill, Max M., 282
Dilley, Dorothy, 465, 488
Dillingham, Charles, 229, 254, 264, 299, 320, 328,
    358, 366, 367, 374, 375, 377, 386, 398, 399, 417,
    425, 433, 435, 452, 459, 460, 477, 484, 513, 515,
    517, 525, 531, 544
Dillon, Ben T., 282
Dillon, Richard H., 145
Dilly, Erin, 840, 855
Dinelaris, Alexander, 844
Dingeon, Helen, 111
Dion, Celine, 862
DiPietro, Joe, 814, 850, 854, 880
Dishy, Bob, 704, 861
Ditmar, Edward A., 188–189
Ditrichstein, Leo, 164, 340, 379
Dix, Beulah Marie, 443
Dixen and Doyle, 376
Dixey, Henry E., 44, 47, 58, 63, 77, 80, 81, 86, 87, 105,
    110, 115, 118, 119, 134, 149–150, 166, 170, 175,
    184, 193, 202, 237, 376
Dixon, Adele, 566
Dixon, Brandon Victor, 886
Dixon, Harland, 361, 386, 418
Dixon, Jerry, 839, 851
Dixon, Lee, 594
Dixon, Mort, 521
Doane, Frank, 209, 217, 290
Dockstader, Lew, 69, 100, 106, 107, 110, 118,
    154–155, 209, 231, 238, 256, 267, 323, 422
Doctorow, E. L., 821
Dodge, Jerry, 697
Dodge, Marcia Milgrom, 880
Doherty, Lindy, 642
Dokuchitz, Jonathan, 840, 844
Dolan, Junior, 555
Dolan, Robert Emmett, 516, 632, 698

Dolaro, Selina, 68, 80
Dolin, Anton, 514, 604
Dolin, Gerald, 551
Dolly Sisters, 312, 322, 341, 382, 446
Domenichini, Esteban, 879
Domingo, Colman, 870
Domino, Fats, 880
Donaghey, Frederick, 316, 325
Donahue, Jack, 401, 424, 446, 459, 503, 511
Donaldson, Arthur, 201, 223
Donaldson, John, 559
Donaldson, Norma, 755
Donaldson, Walter, 367, 381, 426, 463, 482, 501,
    763, 838
Donaro, Selina, 64
Donizetti, Gaetano, 23, 29, 90
Donkin, Eric, 790
Donnelly, Dorothy, 417, 450, 463, 485
Donnelly, H. Grattan, 121, 152
Donnelly, Henry V., 99, 148, 171, 256
Donnelly, John, 84
Donovan, Warde, 615
Dooley, Johnny, 388, 401
Dooley, Ray, 371, 383, 391, 392, 401, 414, 433, 442,
    468, 484, 495, 549
Doran, Dick, 600
Doremus, Mrs. C., 125
Doro, Marie, 261
Dorsey, Jimmy, 527
Dossert, Frank, 302
Dossett, John, 844
Douglas, Larry, 639
Douglas, Melvyn, 673
Douglass, Charles Noel, 2, 268
Douglass, Frederick, 825
Douglass, Margaret, 603
Douglass, Stephen, 640, 650, 656, 668,
    696, 715
Dovey, Alice, 298, 300, 310, 354, 360
Dowling, Eddie, 428, 471, 484, 549, 624, 732
Dowling, Jean, 425
Downs, Johnny, 610, 622
Doyle, Arthur Conan, 703
Doyle, J. W., 453
Doyle, James, 376, 386
Doyle, John, 857, 858, 864, 871, 878
Drake, Alfred, 559, 568, 572, 576, 578, 594, 596, 605,
    615, 621, 626, 634, 641, 648, 687, 698, 709,
    747, 759
Drake, Ervin, 698, 725
Draper, Paul, 587, 593, 656, 695
Dresser, Louise, 188, 262, 368
Dressier, Marie, 188, 204, 329, 408

Dressler, Marie, 134, 146, 164, 165, 192, 202, 204, 209, 215, 238, 239, 256, 300, 429
Drew, Charles H., 84
Drew, Georgiana, 43
Drew, John, 39, 209
Drewe, Anthony, 864
Dreyfuss, Henry, 539
Driver, John, 799
Drouet, Robert, 333
Du Bois, Raoul Pène, 549, 576, 577, 581, 624
Du Clos, Danielle, 796
Du Fre Houston, Ethel, 337
du Maurier, George, 158
Du Prez, John, 854
Dubin, Al, 461, 605, 835
Duchene, Marie, 307
Dudley, S. H., 312
Duff, J. C., 64, 83, 88, 92, 114, 122
Duff, Jimmy, 64, 77
Duffy, Henry, 600
Duffy, Jimmy, 507
Dukakis, Olympia, 861
Duke, Vernon, 472, 516, 520, 535, 537, 538, 543, 549, 554, 558, 580, 586, 587, 601, 604, 645, 661
Dulo, Jane, 610
Dumaresq, William, 783
Dumas, Alexandre, 492, 687
Dumbrille, Douglass R., 492
Dumke, Ralph, 588
Dumont, Margaret, 499
Dunaway, Faye, 776
Dunbar, Errol, 230
Dunbar, Marion, 158
Dunbar, Paul Laurence, 185, 222, 274, 350
Dunbar, R. N., 111
Duncan Sisters, 384, 451
Duncan, Doris, 440
Duncan, Isadora, 168, 304
Duncan, Sandy, 767, 780, 869
Duncan, Todd, 552, 581, 587, 631
Duncan, W. C., 310
Duncan, William Cary, 399, 510
Dundy, Elmer S., 246
Dunham, Clarke, 818
Dunham, Katherine, 581, 598, 607, 609, 615, 620, 634, 692
Dunlap, William, 5, 6
Dunn, Allan, 259
Dunn, Arthur, 224
Dunn, Emma, 415
Dunn, James, 581
Dunn, Mrs. Julia E., 40
Dunn, Ralph, 681

Dunne, Charlotte, 765
Dunne, Irene, 460, 490, 496
Dupree, Frank, 134
Dupree, Minnie, 127
Dupuis, Marie, 279
Duquesnay, Anne, 860
Durand, A., 170
Durand, Edward, 288, 360
Durang, Christopher, 759
Durante, Jimmy, 508, 519, 522, 539, 553, 556, 557, 572, 573, 579, 865
Duru, Alfred, 168
Dussault, Nancy, 683, 703, 718
Duval, Franca, 671
Dylan, Bob, 862
Dyllyn, Bernard, 157

Eagan, Daisy, 799
Eager, Edward, 602, 635
Eagle, Jeanne, 604
Earle, Virginia, 159, 164, 197, 207, 232
Easton, L., 157
Eaton, Doris, 496
Eaton, Mary, 394, 422, 434, 436, 478, 485
Eaton, Paul, 108
Eaton, Sally, 723
Ebb, Fred, 680, 704, 716, 721, 725, 747, 751, 754, 758, 766, 783, 799, 805, 815, 817, 822, 850, 861, 865, 874, 886
Ebersole, Christine, 768, 785, 833, 835, 863, 869
Ebert, Franz, 120, 139, 153, 170
Ebony Steppers, 498
Ebsen, Buddy, 534, 575
Ebsen, Vilma, 534
Eburne, Maude, 386–387
Eckstein, Ernest, 121
Edelman, Gregg, 796, 807, 839, 873
Eden, Anthony, 565
Eder, Linda, 818
Edmond, Grace, 326
Edna, Dame, 851–852
Edouin, Mrs., 45
Edouin, Willie, 44, 52, 58, 61, 70, 77, 84, 201
Edson, Eddy, 279
Edwardes, George, 110, 153, 162, 177, 340
Edwards, Alan, 449, 473, 484, 499
Edwards, Blake, 812
Edwards, Cliff "Ukelele Ike," 459
Edwards, Gus, 232, 245, 247, 260, 262, 267, 272, 556, 593
Edwards, Julian, 134, 142, 147, 165, 171, 175, 189, 196, 218, 237, 260, 268, 284

Ewell, Tom, 623
Ewen, David, 409, 465, 718
Ewing, Max, 479
Eyen, Tom, 776
Eyre, Richard, 864
Eysler, Edmund, 296, 320, 357
Eythe, William, 626, 634
Eyton, Frank, 520

Fabares, Nanette. See Fabray, Nanette
Fabian, William, 292
Fabray, Nanette, 582, 585, 601, 619, 624, 633, 634, 640, 692
Fabris, Amanda, 171
Fagan, Barney, 120
Fagan, Joan, 684
Fain, Sammy, 527, 567, 569, 573, 580, 586, 615, 633, 656, 702
Fairbanks Twins, 408, 409
Fairbanks, Douglas, 245
Fairbanks, Madeleine, 488
Fairbanks, Marion, 447
Fairchild, Edgar, 477
Fairlamb, Remington, 52
Fairleigh, Harry, 233, 279
Falconer, Helen, 349
Fall, Leo, 297, 306, 336
Fallon, Eva, 307, 342, 358, 388
Falls, Robert, 828
Fannie, H. B., 83
Farina, Michael J., 857
Farkas, Karl, 609
Farleigh, Harry, 278
Farley, David, 869
Farmer, Holley, 882
Farnie, H. B., 27, 29, 101
Farnum, Dustin, 190
Farrar, Geraldine, 321, 387
Farrar, John, 867
Farrell, Alice, 309
Farrell, Anthony Brady, 632, 633
Farrell, Charles, 657
Farrell, James T., 842
Faust, Lotta, 203, 207, 268
Favor, Edward M., 121
Fay, Elfie, 234, 250
Fay, Frank, 379, 405, 423, 432, 488, 540, 573, 598
Fay, Hugh, 69, 114
Faye, Alice, 749
Faye, Joey, 614, 619, 739
Fears, Peggy, 442, 468, 478
Feiffer, Jules, 715, 736

Feingold, Michael, 783
Feinstein, Michael, 882
Feldman, Rebecca, 855
Feldshuh, Tovah, 763
Felix, Hugo, 399, 403, 438
Fellini, Federico, 712
Fellner, Jenny, 876
Fellows, Edith, 619
Fender, Harry, 381
Fenton, James, 790
Fenton, Mabel, 148, 259, 282
Ferber, Edna, 678
Ferguson, Jesse Tyler, 855
Ferland, Danielle, 792
Fernandez, Bijou, 564
Ferrer, Jose, 696
Fetter, Ted, 558, 563, 570
Feuer, Cy, 672, 686, 711, 717
Field, Kate, 59
Fielding, May, 66
Fields, Benny, 493, 603
Fields, Dorothy, 458, 493, 514, 520, 526, 527, 573, 601, 606, 613, 633, 640, 650, 672, 712
Fields, Felicia P., 859
Fields, Gracie, 588
Fields, Herbert, 458, 464, 475, 478, 486, 494, 497, 502, 538, 577, 581, 593, 606, 613, 633, 649, 672, 847
Fields, Joe, 249, 330, 646, 671, 840
Fields, Lew, 167, 242, 262, 277, 287, 298, 300, 309, 318, 319, 334–335, 338, 364, 377, 382, 402, 408, 411, 458, 464, 472, 478, 502, 520
Fields, Ron, 735
Fields, W. C., 249, 263, 356, 372, 383, 401, 414, 424, 432, 442, 495, 518, 522, 534, 645
Fierstein, Harvey, 794, 840, 848, 852, 871
Figman, Max, 134, 142, 169, 274, 458, 497, 521
Figman, Oscar, 379
Finck, Herman, 347
Fine, Sylvia, 576, 585
Fink, Henry, 327
Finn, William, 774, 802–803, 855, 872
Finneran, Katie, 885
Fischer, Alice, 234, 282
Fischer, Allison, 860
Fischer, Clifford C., 587, 591
Fischer, Harry, 63
Fish, Marguerite, 110
Fisher, Alice, 256
Fisher, Eddie, 693, 720
Fisher, Fred, 745
Fisher, Harry, 47, 49, 69, 78, 81, 94, 122, 294, 320
Fisher, Irving, 386, 407

Freeman, Cheryl, 816
Freeman, H. Lawrence, 257
Freeman, K. Todd, 804
Freeman, Kathleen, 832
Freeman, Max, 104, 115, 121
French, Arthur, 740
French, Henri, 260
Fretwell, Elbert, 342
Frey, Hugo, 343
Friedlander, William, 404
Friedlander, William B., 453
Friedman, Charles, 569
Friedman, Maria, 858
Friedman, Michael, 872, 886
Friedman, Peter, 821
Friend, Cliff, 510
Friganza, Trixie, 134, 238, 304, 324
Friml, Rudolf, 330, 331, 335, 344, 354, 360, 366, 369,
    377, 385, 386, 394, 409, 410, 413, 414, 419, 420,
    429, 430, 434, 444, 445, 458, 459, 460, 468, 472,
    488, 489, 492, 514, 518, 528, 548, 549, 590,
    695, 784
Frings, Ketti, 759
Frisco, Joe, 495
Frohman, Charles, 129, 141, 142, 237, 265, 275,
    288, 347
Froman, Jane, 543, 579
Frost, Robert, 346
Frothingham, George, 62, 128, 323
Frugé, Romain, 832
Frye, Dwight, 437
Fuller, Loie, 99, 102, 104, 110, 131
Fuller, Molly, 169
Fuller, Penny, 734, 754, 843
Fulton, A.K., 94
Fulton, Maud, 294
Funk, Nolan Gerard, 879
Furman, Jill, 870
Furst, William, 106, 129, 138, 146, 152, 159, 160, 182
Furth, George, 735, 758, 864
Furth, Seymour, 272
Fyffe, Will, 535
Fyleman, Rose, 524

Gabel, Martin, 703
Gabriel, Gilbert, 526, 539
Gabriel, Max, 184, 245
Gabrielle, Josephina, 837
Gaillard, Francis, 111
Gaines, Boyd, 805, 812, 826, 867
Gaines, Muriel, 614
Gaines, Reg E., 813

Gaines, Sam, 338
Gaites, Joseph M., 191
Galati, Frank, 832, 866
Gallagher and Shean, 289, 438, 448, 650
Gallagher, Edward, 323
Gallagher, Helen, 640, 645, 656, 665,
    713, 735, 738
Gallagher, John, Jr., 865, 884
Gallagher, Peter, 802
Gallagher, Skeet, 460, 478
Gallaudet, John, 523
Gallo, David, 860
Galloway, Katherine, 364
Galton, Blanche, 50
Gambatese, Jean, 854, 861
Ganne, M. Louis, 305
Gannon, Kim, 641
Gantvoort, Carl, 340, 387
Garber, Victor, 776, 806, 861
Garbo, Greta, 534
García Márquez, Gabriel, 811
Garde, Betty, 594
Gardenia, Vincent, 762
Gardiner, James, 871
Gardiner, Reginald, 551, 558, 644, 699
Gardner, Hillary, 882
Gardner, Jack, 280, 297, 304
Gardner, Rita, 679, 688, 860
Garland, Judy, 198, 704, 720, 827, 846, 851,
    862, 877
Garland, Robert, 610
Garner, Jay, 726
Garr, Eddie, 539
Garrar, Geraldine, 364
Garrett, Betty, 587, 592, 601, 613, 678, 834
Garrick, Helena Collier, 321
Garrick, John, 531
Garrison, David, 817
Garrison, Mary Catherine, 848
Garson, Marion, 265
Garvie, Edward, 235, 388
Gasman, Ira, 817
Gasteyer, Ana, 852, 860, 881
Gateson, Marjorie, 403, 408, 421, 429, 437, 650
Gattelli, Christopher, 873
Gaunt, Percy, 129, 130, 158, 173
Gauthier, Alain, 882
Gautier, Dick, 678
Gaxton, William, 486, 511, 530, 531, 541, 547, 556,
    571, 579, 587–588, 596, 608, 611, 643
Gay, John, 2, 95, 539
Gay, Noel, 789
Gayler, Charles, 30, 33–34

Gaylor, Bobby, 220
Gaylor, Robert, 134
Gaynes, George, 634, 638, 646
Gaynor, Bob, 848
Gaynor, Janet, 657
Gaze, Leslie, 294
Gear, Luella, 491, 498, 537, 544, 555, 565, 574, 583, 592
Gebest, Charles, 343
Gee, Lottie, 444
Geer, Will, 567
Gehrue, Mayme, 200
Geisel, Theodore (Dr. Seuss), 863
Gelbart, Larry, 683, 690, 796
Geld, Gary, 733, 759
Gemignani, Alexander, 848, 857, 863, 878
Gems, Pam, 825
Genée, Adelaide, 57, 64, 282, 298, 307
Gennaro, Peter, 757, 776, 859
Gensler, Lewis, 426, 446, 452, 457, 470, 498, 523, 534
Gentry, Minnie, 740
George, Yvonne, 425
Gerard, Danny, 790
Gerard, E., 171
Gerber, Alex, 402
Gerety, Peter, 847
German, Edward, 226, 279
Gerrard, Alfred, 388, 406
Gerrish, Sylvia, 104, 110
Gershon, Gina, 879
Gershwin, George, 357, 365, 381, 388, 390, 397, 399, 400, 404, 414, 421, 428, 432, 436, 469, 473, 475, 491, 508, 512, 513, 531, 538, 542, 551, 552, 553, 561, 584, 590, 607, 780, 801
Gershwin, Ira, 297, 380, 403, 442, 446, 450, 453, 461, 463, 469, 490–491, 500, 508, 512, 516, 521, 526, 542, 544, 554, 564, 599, 606, 615, 736
Gesner, Clark, 719, 824
Gest, Morris, 396, 404, 437
Gets, Malcolm, 864, 876
Gettelfinger, Sara, 854, 882
Geva, Tamara, 534, 555, 652
Ghostley, Alice, 644, 662, 695
Gibbs, Wolcott, 583
Gibson Girls, 579
Gibson, Charles Dana, 225
Gibson, Virginia, 664
Gibson, William, 702, 745, 790
Gideon, Melville, 491
Gielgud, John, 558
Gifford, Julia, 218
Gifford, Kathie Lee, 864

Gilbert and Sullivan, 46, 51, 53, 68, 71, 74, 76, 82, 87, 90, 92, 102, 105, 110, 116, 121, 122, 149, 166, 188, 247, 342, 354, 356, 375, 451, 453, 479, 513, 524, 531, 546, 551, 564, 570, 572, 580, 608, 631, 645, 658, 698, 703, 721, 761, 772–773, 836, 847, 852, 861, 864. *See also* Gilbert, W. S.
Gilbert, Billy, 617, 645
Gilbert, Fred, 140
Gilbert, Jean, 502
Gilbert, Mrs., 66
Gilbert, W. S., 42, 50, 56, 59, 113, 141, 161, 312, 442, 455
Gilbert, Willie, 686
Gilfoil, Harry, 207
Gilford, Jack, 582, 633, 690–691, 716, 738
Gilkison, Jason, 879
Gill, William, 52, 60, 86, 88, 97, 119, 141, 145, 181, 241
Gillespie, Arthur, 343
Gillette, Anita, 690, 692, 703, 861
Gillette, Priscilla, 632, 638, 650
Gillette, William, 177, 395
Gillingwater, Claude, 254, 299
Gilman, Lotta, 126
Gilman, Mabel, 191, 193, 197
Gilman, Mabelle, 217
Gilpin, Charles, 275
Gilroy, Mamie, 197
Gimbel, Norman, 683
Gingold, Hermione, 648, 649, 673, 679, 745
Giordano, Tyrone, 845
Girard, Kate, 79
Giraud, Harry, 274
Giraudoux, Jean, 638
Giroux, Maude, 114
Gish, Lillian, 712, 753
Givot, George, 601
Glaser, Lulu, 132, 145, 152, 168, 184, 187, 201, 204, 208, 236, 249, 282, 288, 308
Gleason, Helen, 559, 583, 590
Gleason, Jackie, 602, 612, 628, 675, 676, 785
Gleason, James, 480, 491
Gleason, Joanna, 792, 801, 854
Gleckler, Robert, 511
Glendinning, Ernest, 333, 415, 444
Glenn, Julius, 338
Glenn, Vivian, 453
Glenn-Smith, Michael, 726
Glick, Sammy, 698
Glickman, William, 654, 669
Glover, Amelia, 144, 149
Glover, Marie, 70
Glover, Montego, 879

Glover, Savion, 813
Glyn, Elinor, 494
Glynn, Carlin, 760
Goddard, Paulette, 468
Godfrey, Arthur, 612
Godfrey, Bertram, 201
Godfrey, Dorothy, 381
Godfrey, Thomas, 3
Godoy, Marie, 171
Godoy, Mora, 879
Goede, Jay, 844
Goetz, E. Ray, 259, 269, 272, 357, 364, 372, 379, 398, 411, 432
Goetzl, Anselm, 389
Goff, Jerry, 513
Goggin, Dan, 809
Goldberg, Neil, 873
Goldberg, Rube, 508, 518, 806
Goldberg, Whoopi, 851
Golden, Annie, 832
Golden, Grace, 117, 140, 160
Golden, John, 202, 233, 246, 277, 293, 303, 322, 349, 366, 367
Golden, Richard, 261
Goldenberg, Billy, 836
Goldenberger, Billy, 762
Goldenthal, Elliot, 815, 829
Goldie, Beatrice, 157
Goldin, Igor, 886
Goldman, James and/or William, 688, 738
Goldman, William, 865
Goldner, Charles, 649
Goldoni, Carlo, 634
Goldsmith, Oliver, 241
Goldsworthy, John, 363, 375, 515
Goldwyn, Sam, 502
Goldwyn, Tony, 885
Goldyn, Jessica Lee, 862, 874
Gomer, Selma, 120
Gomez, Carlos, 870
Gon, Jeni Le, 558
Gonzalez, Mandy, 870
Goodchild, Tim, 846
Goode, Jack, 614
Goodman, Al, 401, 411, 470
Goodman, Benny, 519, 526, 550, 577, 604, 826
Goodman, Dody, 655
Goodrich, E. T., 25
Goodrich, Frances, 527
Goodwin, Deidre, 847, 862
Goodwin, Gloria, 369

Goodwin, J. Cheever, 38, 39, 46, 65, 84, 112, 118, 121, 123, 143, 151, 152, 157, 158, 160, 169, 174, 182, 192, 197, 198, 208, 215
Goodwin, Nat (N. C.), 44, 54, 93–94, 99, 102, 106, 247
Gordon, Alice, 305
Gordon, Amy, 71, 81
Gordon, Bert, 580
Gordon, Kitty, 295, 296, 306, 311, 317
Gordon, Lady Duff, 364
Gordon, Mack, 525, 532, 534
Gordon, Max, 520, 535, 542, 546, 576, 606, 608, 615
Gordon, Paul, 833
Gordon, Waxey, 532, 539
Gorenflo, Marie, 56
Gorey, Edward, 762
Gorme, Eydie, 722
Gorney, Jay, 446, 464, 479, 480, 507, 517, 535, 582, 631, 865
Gorshin, Frank, 732
Gorski, Virginia, 621
Gottschalk, Frederick, 231
Gottschalk, Louis F., 333
Gould, Berni, 592
Gould, Elliot, 690, 709
Gould, Morton, 611, 633
Gould, Walter, 76
Gould, William, 201, 234
Goulding, Ray, 736
Goulet, Robert, 682, 722, 805, 852–853
Gounod, Charles, 825
Gourlay, John, 83
Grable, Betty, 577
Grady, Thomas J., 122
Graff, Randy, 790, 833, 874
Grafton, Gloria, 553
Graham, Frederick, 387
Graham, Harry, 452
Graham, Irvin, 556, 591
Graham, John, 513
Graham, Lauren, 876
Graham, Lillian, 312
Graham, Martha, 433
Graham, R. E., 53, 66, 74, 82, 90, 96, 110, 189, 201, 234, 349
Graham, Ronald, 562, 572, 577, 587, 588, 602, 643
Graham, William, 301, 676
Grainger, Porter, 454, 518, 519
Gramm, Donald, 650
Grammer, Kelsey, 884
Granger, Farley, 673, 679
Granger, Maud, 43
Granger, Michael, 701
Grant, Bert, 401

Grant, Cary, 510
Grant, Frances, 402
Grant, John B., 100
Grant, Kate Jennings, 833
Grant, Mary, 609
Grant, Micki, 756, 760
Grant, Sidney, 324
Grant, Sydney, 296, 440
Granville, Bernard, 316, 327, 341, 343, 348, 356, 357,
 364, 395, 397, 420, 430, 432, 470
Granville, Gertie, 69
Grapewin, Charles, 247
Grau, Maurice, 27, 39, 41, 53, 62, 69, 73, 80, 87,
 92, 104
Graver, Leonard, 78, 83
Gravitte, Debbie, 838
Gray, Alexander, 453
Gray, Dolores, 604, 641, 648, 673
Gray, Gilda, 391, 411, 422
Gray, Helen, 542
Gray, John, 770
Gray, Kevin, 795
Gray, Maude, 334
Gray, Roger, 469
Gray, Timothy, 699
Gray, William, 47, 56, 63
Greanin, Leon, 597
Greaza, Walter N., 560
Green Day, 884
Green, Adolph, 605, 611, 646, 662, 663, 670, 683,
 719, 734, 740, 758, 766, 778, 786, 800, 869
Green, Amanda, 864
Green, Brian Lane, 795
Green, Denis, 627
Green, James, 562
Green, Johnny, 520, 529, 540, 592
Green, Marion, 448
Green, Martyn, 645, 662, 727
Green, Mitzi, 559, 579, 592, 611
Green, Paul, 557, 739
Green, Schuyler, 355
Green, Stanley, 374, 517, 537, 558
Green, Sylvan, 553
Green, Thomas Evans, 165
Greenbank, Percy, 347
Greenberg, Richard, 876
Greene, Clay M., 106, 116, 120, 147, 148, 152, 191, 197
Greene, Frank, 444
Greene, Marion, 396
Greene, Schuyler, 361, 386
Greener, Dorothy, 639, 655
Greenleaf, Augusta, 263
Greensfelder, J. S., 161

Greenstreet, Sydney, 491
Greenwich, Ellie, 785
Greenwood, Barrett, 409, 428
Greenwood, Charlotte, 324, 335, 371, 421, 426, 447,
 478, 481, 507, 638, 765
Greenwood, Jane, 816
Greenwood, Letitia, 367
Greger, Stanley, 692
Gregory, Chester, II, 861
Gregory, Dick, 691
Gregory, Gilbert, 289
Gregory, Paul, 488, 501
Gregus, Peter, 858
Greif, Michael, 863
Grenfell, Joyce, 658, 670
Greville, Jessie, 54
Grey, Clifford, 461, 491, 492
Grey, Frank, 464, 488
Grey, Joel, 661, 716, 719, 723, 750, 763, 791,
 815, 846
Grey, Minerva, 397
Greybrooke, Ethel, 112
Gribble, Harry, 382
Grief, Michael, 847
Grieg, Edvard, 603, 712, 775
Grier, David Alan, 776
Griffies, Ethel, 630
Griffin, Gary, 847, 853, 876
Griffith, Andy, 673
Grimaldi, Lorrie, 360
Grimes, Tammy, 661, 681, 699, 753, 771
Grisel, Louis R., 254
Griswold, Gertrude, 102
Groag, Lillian, 864
Groener, Harry, 768, 785
Grofé, Ferde, 573
Groff, Jonathan, 865
Groody, Louise, 384, 398, 418, 435, 457, 478
Gross, Aaron Simon, 873
Grossman, Larry, 778
Grossmith, George, Jr., 162, 236, 265, 288, 519
Grossmith, Lawrence, 262, 354, 369
Grové, Jessica, 848
Groves, Charles, 61
Groves, Paul, 850
Grubb, Lillian, 86, 106
Guardino, Harry, 699, 773
Guare, John, 740, 837
Guernsey, Otis L., 736, 770
Guernsey, Otis L., Jr., 765
Guest, Lance, 883
Guétary, Georges, 633
Guillaume, Robert, 755

Guillemand, Marcel, 310
Guinan, Texas, 732
Guitard, Laurence, 768
Guitry, Sacha, 474
Guittard, Laurence, 745
Gumbel, Roberta, 857
Gunn, Nathan, 872
Gunning, Louise, 220, 268, 289, 310, 312, 333
Gunter, A. C., 77, 133
Gunther, John, 622
Gunton, Bob, 757, 767, 786, 796
Gurwin, Danny, 843
Guthrie, Tyrone, 670, 680
Gwynne, Haydn, 874

Haakon, Paul, 551, 566
Haas, Dolly, 673
Haas, Hugo, 624
Hackett, Albert, 527
Hackett, Buddy, 703, 720
Hackett, Joan, 735
Hadjidakis, Manos, 718
Hadley, Henry, 222
Hagan, Clyde, 544
Haggard, H. Rider, 106
Haggin, Ben Ali, 372, 401
Hague, Albert, 654, 672, 676
Hahn, Reynaldo, 474
Hajos, Karl, 452
Hajos, Mitzi, 337, 341, 363
Hale, Chester, 573
Hale, Helen, 263
Haley Sisters, 371
Haley, Jack, 503, 537, 578, 591, 622
Hall, Adelaide, 494, 519
Hall, Bettina, 528, 547, 574
Hall, Glenn, 339
Hall, Josephine, 199, 202, 206, 225
Hall, Juanita, 628, 654
Hall, Natalie, 515, 531, 536, 549, 570
Hall, Owen, 153, 228
Hall, Pauline, 72, 88, 91, 93, 97, 106, 115, 139
Hall, Peter, 744
Hall, Thurston, 349, 368
Hall, W. D., 257
Hallam, Clyde, 649
Hallam, Henry, 110
Hallam, Mr. & Mrs. Lewis, 2, 5, 6
Hallen, Fred, 149, 197
Halliday, Robert, 474, 496, 519, 549, 556
Hallor, Edith, 374
Halperin, Nan, 432

Halpin, Adam, 871
Halton, Marie, 117
Hamel, Alan, 857
Hamilton, Caroline, 128
Hamilton, Harry, 62
Hamilton, James, 464
Hamilton, Laura, 346
Hamilton, Lawrence, 816
Hamilton, Margaret, 732, 818
Hamilton, Nancy, 544, 572, 578, 592, 612
Hamilton, William, 105
Hamlin, Fred R., 228, 242
Hamlisch, Marvin, 752, 763, 790, 804, 837, 842
Hammerstein, Arthur, 129, 144, 165, 375, 402, 433, 445, 463, 472, 488, 502, 509, 517, 522, 525
Hammerstein, Oscar, 170, 177, 184, 224, 272, 330, 402, 407, 601, 671, 676, 684
Hammerstein, Oscar, II, 397, 402, 424, 426, 429, 459, 472, 489, 496, 500, 509, 523, 526, 528, 536, 553, 576, 586, 594, 680, 829, 876
Hammerstein, Oscar, IV, 485
Hammerstein, Reginald, 488, 509
Hammerstein, William, 768
Hammett, Dashiell, 800, 842
Hammond, Percy, 298, 414, 437, 462
Hampton, Alf M., 109, 114, 116
Hampton, Christopher, 809, 850
Hampton, Hope, 485
Hampton, Lionel, 751
Hampton, Stewart, 499
Hanan, Stephen, 778
Handers, Thomas, 379
Haney, Carol, 650, 651
Haney, Felix, 259
Hanggi, Kristin, 877
Hanke, Christopher, 857, 871
Hanley, Ellen, 618, 677
Hanley, James, 414, 442, 468, 471, 484, 549
Hanlon Family, 88
Hanlon, Toma, 119
Hanlon-Lees Family, 67
Hanna, Stephen, 874
Hansberry, Lorraine, 741, 746
Hansen, William, 617
Hanson, Alexander, 881
Harbach, Otto, 285, 301, 304, 312, 314–315, 331, 369, 377, 407, 435, 457, 459, 465, 472, 474, 477, 488, 496, 518, 528, 542, 543, 557
Harburg, E. Y. (Yip), 507, 508, 516, 517, 520, 534, 535, 543, 544, 558, 565, 580, 603, 607, 616, 668, 683, 722, 833, 865, 877, 880
Harcourt, William K., 291
Harding, Miss, 6

Harding, Warren Gamaliel, 407

Hardy, William, Jr., 756

Hare, Ernest, 303

Harkrider, John, 490, 493

Harlan, Otis, 133, 164, 186, 196, 201, 202, 256, 264, 320

Harling, Franke, 472

Harney, Ben, 138, 173, 752, 776

Harnick, Sheldon M., 644, 655, 669, 677, 680, 681, 693, 694, 701, 715, 737, 754, 766, 782, 805, 806, 848

Harold, Donald, 149

Harold, Lizzie, 44

Harrigan and Braham, 39, 785

Harrigan and Hart, 28, 36, 39, 40, 42, 43, 44, 46, 47, 53, 60, 67, 69, 73, 79, 86, 88, 90

Harrigan, Edward Green, 46–47, 63, 65, 107, 109, 110, 111, 120, 143, 145, 147, 148, 149, 189, 276, 332

Harrigan, James, 263

Harrigan, Ned, 33, 44, 45, 53, 56, 57, 58, 60, 63, 65, 75, 76, 78, 79, 81, 82, 83, 86, 89, 90, 94, 100, 104, 105, 106, 112, 122, 125, 131, 140, 144, 145–146, 156, 166, 280

Harrington, Joseph, 201

Harris, Barbara, 685, 710, 715, 853

Harris, Charles K., 130, 148, 239, 286, 489, 803

Harris, Harriet, 838, 871

Harris, Julie, 710

Harris, Marion, 476

Harris, Neil Patrick, 848

Harris, Richard, 775

Harris, Sam, 286, 350, 400, 416, 450, 531, 541, 817

Harris, Winifred, 425

Harrison, Alfred, 372

Harrison, Alice, 66

Harrison, Gregory, 817, 834

Harrison, Lee, 243

Harrison, Louis, 44, 47, 58, 66, 83, 140, 146, 159, 164, 176, 192, 201, 204, 209, 289

Harrison, Rex, 658, 659, 660, 709, 775

Harrold, Orville, 307

Harrold, Patti, 429

Harry, Jackée, 840

Harsh, Howard, 378

Hart, Albert, 183, 259

Hart, Anthony (Tony), 33, 44, 47, 48, 49, 56, 57, 63, 65, 67, 74, 75, 76, 78, 81, 83, 86, 89, 95, 99, 100, 103, 104, 140, 189, 276, 332, 391, 457

Hart, Blossom, 593

Hart, Gussie, 166

Hart, Joe, 149, 260

Hart, Joseph, 209–210, 236

Hart, Larry, 571

Hart, Laura, 840

Hart, Linda, 840

Hart, Lorenz, 297, 391, 402, 442, 455, 464, 506, 599, 601, 736

Hart, Margie, 592

Hart, Moss, 513, 515, 532, 541, 552, 569, 578, 596, 601, 604, 622, 630, 660, 682, 718, 754, 775, 865

Hart, Roxie, 886

Hart, Teddy, 571

Hart, Vivian, 476, 512

Hartman, Ferris, 119, 126, 192, 305, 500

Hartman, Grace, 587, 621, 628, 634

Hartman, Paul, 534, 587, 621, 628, 634, 643

Hartsell, Harold, 112, 312

Hartung, Elsa, 224

Harvey, Clarence, 260

Harvey, James Clarence, 303, 390

Haskell, Jack, 692

Hassell, George, 369, 399, 470, 502

Hastings, Alice, 53

Hatch, Joel, 872

Hately, Linzi, 793

Hatfield, Lansing, 574, 604

Hathaway, Anne, 838

Hatley, Tim, 876

Hatton, Anne Julia, 4

Hauerbach, Otto. See Harbach, Otto

Hauser, Franklin, 549

Haverly, J. H., 14, 63, 69, 78, 82, 214

Havoc, June, 601, 604

Hawkins, Iris, 340

Hawkins, John F., 487

Hawkins, Walter S., 182

Haworth, Jill, 716

Hawtrey, Charles, 97

Hay, Mary, 435, 459, 500

Hayakawa, Sessue, 480

Hayden, Michael, 807

Hayden, Susan, 421

Haydn, Richard, 578

Hayes, Bill, 647, 721

Hayes, Catherine, 332

Hayes, Helen, 298–299, 300, 318, 773, 790

Hayes, Peter Lind, 624

Hayes, Richard, 674, 695

Hayes, Sean, 885

Haynes, John, 510

Haynes, Tiger, 749

Hays, William Shakespeare, 13

Hayward, Leland, 674

Hazelton, W. B., 53

Hazzard, Jack, 390

Hazzard, John E., 303, 317, 361, 367, 398, 415, 421, 425, 435, 465

Headley, Heather, 828
Healey, Eunice, 549
Healey, Mary, 614
Healy, Betty, 479, 506
Healy, Dan, 496
Healy, Ted, 479, 506, 523, 524
Hearn, George, 765, 781, 809, 852, 881
Hearst, William Randolph, 608
Heartz, H. L., 209, 210, 233, 294
Heatherton, Ray, 559
Hecht, Ben, 553, 604, 645, 758
Hecht, Paul, 737
Heckart, Eileen, 688
Hedley, Charles, 515
Heege, Gus, 158
Heffernan, John, 734
Hein, Silvio, 251–252, 262, 301, 336, 343, 348, 349,
   359, 375, 379, 398, 399, 422
Helburn, Theresa, 563
Held, Anna, 170, 191, 195, 207, 231, 238, 266, 272,
   291, 302, 308, 340, 368, 541
Hellinger, Mark, 532
Hellman, Lillian, 632, 662, 803
Hellman, Max, 842
Hellmesberger, Joseph, 125
Helton, Percy, 488
Hendel, Stephen, 881
Henderson, David, 104, 110, 116, 192, 211, 221,
   456, 483
Henderson, Florence, 648, 653, 696, 719
Henderson, Isabel, 544
Henderson, Jack, 287, 310
Henderson, Ray, 357, 405, 425, 467, 484, 495, 498,
   499, 503, 515, 527, 532, 539, 547, 549, 554, 596
Hendricks, John, 362
Hengler, Flo, 299
Hengler, Mae, 299
Henning, Doug, 779, 788
Hennings, Dora, 80
Henshall, Ruthie, 865
Henshaw, J. E., 192, 298
Hensley, Shuler, 837, 861, 868
Henson, Jim, 838
Hepburn, Katherine, 544, 588, 704, 733, 777
Herbert, Edith, 780
Herbert, Evelyn, 461, 483, 496, 519, 539, 544
Herbert, Joseph, 146, 158, 184, 188, 269, 289
Herbert, Joseph, Jr., 303
Herbert, Victor, 151, 155–156, 162, 169, 174, 175,
   179, 180, 187, 190, 193, 195, 196, 211, 213, 228,
   230, 242, 247, 249, 251, 253, 262, 265, 270, 287,
   290, 291, 298, 302, 307, 316–317, 327, 328, 330,
   335, 336, 339, 344, 350, 358, 366, 368, 371, 372,

377, 388, 397, 401, 404, 407, 414, 426, 442, 443,
   452, 476, 514, 614, 617, 695, 746, 761, 769, 838
Herendeen, Frederick, 343, 553, 559
Herford, Oliver, 303
Herlie, Eileen, 675, 689
Herlihy, Tim, 860
Herman, Al, 416
Herman, Jerry, 679, 685–686, 697, 714, 727, 730, 749,
   763, 770, 780, 788, 850
Hernandez, Ivavn, 861, 886
Herne, James A., 133
Heron, Edward, 292
Herring, Fanny, 22
Hershey, David, 790
Hertz, Henrik, 147
Hervé (Florimond Roger), 27, 31, 39, 195
Herz, Ralph, 268, 276, 282, 301, 304, 327, 341, 343,
   389, 397
Hess Sisters, 311
Heuberger, Richard, 321
Hewitt, Christopher, 756
Hewitt, James, 4, 5, 6
Hewitt, Tom, 832, 840, 851
Hewlett, James, 11
Heyman, Edward, 520, 540
Heyward, Dorothy, 515
Heyward, DuBose, 551
Heywood, Donald, 481, 518, 548, 558
Hibbard, David, 833
Hibbard, Edna, 380
Hibbert, Edward, 860, 866, 883
Hickman, Alfred, 261
Hicks, Seymour, 162
Higgins, Colin, 878
Higgins, Joel, 756
Hiken, Gerald, 768
Hildegarde, 593
Hill, Annabelle, 626
Hill, Arthur, 702
Hill, Billy, 543
Hill, Brian, 876
Hill, Harold, 829
Hill, J. Leubrie, 338, 339
Hilliam, B. C., 410
Hilliard, Bob, 645
Hilliard, Harry, 342
Hills, Florence, 396
Hilton, James, 662
Hilty, Megan, 878
Hines, Elisabeth, 409, 417, 428
Hines, Elizabeth, 443
Hines, Gregory, 769, 773, 802
Hines, Maurice, 860

Hines, Mimi, 865
Hingle, Pat, 741, 819
Hinnant, Bill, 719
Hinnant, Skip, 719
Hirsch, Louis, 295, 306, 320, 322, 335, 357, 364, 377,
  383, 387, 403, 413, 417, 425, 451
Hirschfield, Al, 847
Hirschfield, Harry, 526
Hirschfield, Max, 172, 242
Hirson, Roger O., 743
Hitchcock, Raymond, 133, 162, 173, 196, 200, 202,
  204, 211, 233, 274, 294, 297, 319, 343, 367, 371,
  377, 379, 393, 406, 414, 423, 447, 486
Hitchcock,Raymond, 188
Hite, Mabel, 284, 312
Hoban, Stella, 322, 326
Hobart, George V., 175, 199, 200, 201, 202, 207, 209,
  210, 227, 236, 240, 246, 251, 256, 269, 282, 290,
  294, 296, 298, 301, 316, 349, 405
Hobson, Louis, 877
Hocking, Leah, 874
Hoctor, Harriet, 535
Hodd, Daniel, 815
Hodge, Douglas, 884
Hodges, Joy, 513, 611
Hodgkinson Mr. & Mrs. John, 4, 5, 6, 7
Hodson, Georgina, 10
Hoey, Evelyn, 511, 537
Hoey, William, 88, 140, 156
Hoff, Christian, 858
Hoff, Edwin W., 144, 148, 177
Hoffman, Aaron, 236, 281–282, 443
Hoffman, Bern, 662
Hoffman, Gertrude, 240, 244, 266, 463
Hoffman, Jackie, 840, 867, 883
Hoffman, Max, 244, 276, 509
Hogan, Ernest, 185, 257, 280
Hoggett, Steven, 884
Hoist, Edward, 180
Holbrook, Alice, 184
Holbrook, Florence, 253, 301, 325
Holcomb, William, 244
Holder, Geoffrey, 698, 759
Holgate, Ronald, 690
Holiday, Billie, 622
Holiday, Bob, 713
Hollaender, Victor, 302
Holland, G., 11
Holliday, Jennifer, 776
Holliday, Judy, 663, 694
Hollins, Hilda, 233
Hollins, Mabel, 233
Hollins, Maud, 189

Hollis, John, 166
Hollman, Mark, 835
Holloway, Julian, 806
Holloway, Stanley, 659, 680
Holloway, Sterling, 454, 516
Holly, Buddy, 858
Holm, Celeste, 594, 596, 603, 765
Holm, Hanya, 754
Holm, John Cecil, 586
Holman, Libby, 479, 480, 500, 501, 503, 506, 520,
  548, 568, 652
Holmes, Rayley, 396
Holmes, Rupert, 788, 865
Holmes, Taylor, 332, 421, 471, 547
Holmes, Violet, 191
Holofcener, Larry, 660
Holst, Edward, 103
Holt, Will, 756
Holtz, Lou, 522, 549, 587, 603
Holzman, Winnie, 846
Home, C. Morton, 308
Home, Lena, 573, 774
Home, William, 602
Honey, George, 171
Hong, Arabella, 672
Hood, Basil, 864
Hooker, Brian, 459, 549
Hooks, Robert, 718
Hope, Anthony, 461
Hope, Bob, 498, 534, 542, 547, 554, 556, 557
Hopkins, Arthur, 471
Hopkins, Linda, 753
Hopkins, Miriam, 432
Hopkinson, Francis, 3
Hopper, Charles, 140
Hopper, Edna Wallace, 165, 185, 196, 262, 280, 310
Hopper, Edward, 443
Hopper, Hedda, 608
Hopwood, Avery, 386, 440
Horan, Edward, 544
Horgan, Patrick, 672
Horn, Robert, 873
Hornby, Nick, 864
Horne, Lena, 668, 709, 749
Horner, Harry, 585
Horton, Robert, 696
Horwitt, Arnold B., 621, 622, 654, 676
Horwitz, Charles, 215
Hoschna, Karl, 252, 285, 301, 303, 312, 323, 344, 345
Hosmer, Alice, 51, 59
Hosmer, Lucius, 268
Hotchner, A. E., 795
Hoty, Dee, 807

Houdyshell, Jayne, 879
Hough, Will M., 241, 246, 248, 253, 269, 272, 283, 284, 287, 293, 299, 301, 325, 345, 404, 592, 593
Houseman, John, 566, 574, 752
Houston, Dorothy, 504
Houston, George, 504, 523, 549
Howard Brothers, 341, 426, 495, 575
Howard, Bronson, 54
Howard, Esther, 453
Howard, Eugene, 324, 367, 408, 510, 527, 534, 554
Howard, George, 115
Howard, Joe, 218, 221, 241, 246, 248, 253, 260, 269, 272, 273, 283–284, 287, 293, 299, 301, 306, 312, 331, 336, 343, 345, 395, 592, 593, 684, 772
Howard, John, 645
Howard, Joseph E., 208
Howard, Ken, 727, 745, 754
Howard, Leslie, 568
Howard, Lisa, 855
Howard, Sidney, 611
Howard, Tom, 433, 523, 544
Howard, Willie, 324, 367, 408, 452, 510, 519, 527, 534, 554, 575, 583, 587, 598, 623
Howell, Lottice, 471
Howes, Bobby, 679
Howes, Sally Ann, 687, 691, 693, 698, 813, 826
Howland, Jobyna, 202, 324, 381
Howland, Olin, 396
Howson, Emma, 35
Howson, John, 62, 64, 75, 78, 83
Hoyer, Roy, 435, 501
Hoyt, Charles H., 77, 78, 84, 87, 97, 99, 104, 109, 121, 129, 145, 154, 163, 164, 168, 169, 173, 178, 186, 215, 243, 367, 386
Hoyt, Dee, 879
Hoyt, Henry E., 158
Hubbard, Elbert, 340
Hubbell, Raymond, 224, 245, 257, 262, 266, 281, 288, 294, 299, 312, 318, 319, 335, 354, 358, 366, 372, 374, 382, 396, 441, 442, 499
Hudes, Quiara Alegría, 870
Hudson, Richard, 820
Hughes, Charles Evans, 364
Hughes, Langston, 615, 636, 666, 696, 799
Hughes, Leila, 342
Hughes, Rupert, 215, 380
Hulburt, Jack, 463
Hull, Warren, 483, 492
Hume, Nancy, 792
Humphries, Barry, 851, 882
Hundley, John, 502, 505
Hunt, Ida Brooks, 287, 297
Hunter, Eddie, 430

Hunter, Glenn, 505
Hunter, Harry, 48
Hunting, Dorothy, 237
Hupfeld, Herman, 524, 527, 535, 540, 558
Hurlbut, Gladys, 578
Hurley, Laurel, 650
Hurney, John, 574
Hurnside, R. H., 261
Hurston, Zora Neale, 799
Hurok, Sol, 533, 598
Husmann, Ron, 681, 689, 737, 774
Huston, Philip, 571
Huston, Walter, 570
Hutchinson, Edward, 220
Hutton, Betty, 578
Huxhold, Kristin, 843
Hwang, David Henry, 828, 860
Hyams, Joe, 336
Hyams, John, 206, 234, 315, 346
Hyde-White, Wilfred, 619
Hydes, Watty, 172
Hyman, Ed, 535
Hynes, Garry, 869
Hyson, Carl, 399
Hytner, Nicholas, 807

Idle, Eric, 832, 854
Illmann, Margaret, 806
Ing, Alvin, 355, 852
Ingram, Michael, 763
Ingram, Rex, 581
Innvar, Christopher, 860, 867
Intropidi, Josie, 316, 343
Intropodi, Ethel, 491
Irby-Ranniar, Scott, 820
Irons, Jeremy, 843
Irving, George S., 632, 665, 691, 745, 754, 765–766, 779, 789, 813, 861
Irving, Henry, 82, 84, 86, 90, 166
Irwin, Bill, 780, 791, 795, 803–804, 823, 879
Irwin, Flora, 170
Irwin, May, 64, 127, 133, 142, 147, 161, 173, 180, 189, 195, 200, 201, 240
Irwin, Will, 549, 550, 586, 611
Isaacs, Pamela, 817
Isham, Edwin, 162
Isherwood, Charles, 855
Itzel, Adam Jr., 93–94
Ives, Burl, 591, 605, 650
Ives, David, 843, 847, 865, 874, 880, 882, 883
Ivey, Judith, 834

Jackman, Hugh, 837, 845, 846
Jackson, Arthur, 390
Jackson, Cheyenne, 867, 874, 877
Jackson, Christopher, 870
Jackson, Ernestine, 755
Jackson, Ethel, 197, 204, 266, 278, 323
Jackson, Frederick, 388
Jackson, Joseph, 116
Jackson, Tony, 359
Jacobi, Lou, 700
Jacobi, Victor, 337, 375, 394, 407, 413, 417, 418
Jacobson, Dan, 710
Jacobson, Irving, 712
Jacoby, Mark, 808, 821, 857, 864
Jacoby, Scott, 722
Jacques, Martin, 856
Jacquet, H. Maurice, 521
Jaeger, Bertha, 170
Jaffe, Joe, 504
Jakobowski, Edward, 97, 114, 153, 155
James, Harry, 173
James, Henry, 744
James, Millie, 456
James, Olga, 660
James, Paul, 506, 514, 518
James, Ray, 676
James, Zachary, 883
Jane, Mary, 453
Janis, Elsie, 256, 277, 292, 328, 361, 367, 452, 573
Janki, Devanand, 844
Janney, Allison, 878
Janney, Russell, 549
Jannings, Emil, 713
Jansen, Jim, 772
Jansen, Marie, 74, 77, 108, 113, 119, 132, 146, 182
Janssen, Werner, 418, 429, 469
January, Lois, 575
Janvier, Emma, 367
Jardon, Dorothy, 305, 320, 338
Jarnac, Dorothy, 624
Jarno, George, 308
Jarrett, Art, 579
Jarvis, Martin, 836
Jarvis, Sidney, 318
Javerbaum, David, 871
Jbara, Gregory, 874
Jeanette, Gertrude, 631
Jeanmaire, Zizi, 649, 659, 703, 774
Jefferson, Joseph, 6, 19, 21, 118
Jeffreys, Anne, 615, 625, 643
Jenkins, Allen, 593
Jenkins, Capathia, 844, 865

Jenkins, Daniel H., 786, 814, 848, 863
Jenkins, George, 597, 683
Jenkins, Steve, 434, 492
Jennings, John W., 116
Jeritza, Maria, 549
Jerman, Jerry, 881
Jerome, Ben, 231, 236, 248, 266, 305, 316, 326, 336, 485
Jerome, Jerome K., 377
Jerome, Tim, 861
Jerome, William, 212, 227, 229, 249, 250, 252, 272, 327
Jessel, George, 430, 521, 585, 586, 591, 593
Jessop, George H., 88, 89, 111
Jesús, Robin de, 870
Jeter, Michael, 796
Jett, Joan, 832
Jewell, Clara Alene, 180
Jines, Henry, 562
Joel, Billy, 841
Johanson, Robert, 806, 818
John, Elton, 821, 828, 860, 874
Johns, Brooke, 443
Johns, Glynis, 745
Johns,Brooke, 434
Johnson, Albert, 525, 544, 548
Johnson, Alice, 155, 190
Johnson, Arte, 655
Johnson, Arthur, 812
Johnson, Bayn, 720
Johnson, Billy, 183, 185, 593, 611. *See also* Cole and Johnson
Johnson, Carroll, 115, 131
Johnson, Catherine, 835
Johnson, Christine, 607
Johnson, Edward, 282, 582
Johnson, Ethel, 263
Johnson, Fred, 454
Johnson, Hall, 411
Johnson, Haven, 544, 556
Johnson, Howard, 405
Johnson, J. Rosamond, 200, 243, 294, 298, 527, 552, 581, 587
Johnson, James Weldon, 183, 198, 200
Johnson, Jesse JP, 871
Johnson, Jimmy, 492
Johnson, John, 6
Johnson, Louis, 752
Johnson, Nunnally, 526, 615, 720
Johnson, Orrin, 418
Johnson, Rosamund, 183
Johnson, Susan, 661, 672, 684
Johnson, Terry, 884
Johnston, Alice, 116

Johnston, Fannie, 148, 201
Johnston, Johnny, 640
Johnstone, Justine, 357, 361
Johnstone, Tom and Will B., 419, 438, 460
Johnstone, Will B., 389
Jolson, Al, 198, 311, 320, 322, 323, 333, 342, 348, 363, 388–389, 418, 438, 451, 452, 467, 474, 508, 523, 524, 525, 551, 580, 618, 838, 865
Jonay, Roberta, 620
Jones, Allan, 544, 590, 601
Jones, Anne, 673
Jones, Bill T., 865, 881
Jones, Charlotte, 858
Jones, Cherry, 842
Jones, Christine, 884
Jones, Dean, 735, 790
Jones, E. Forrest, 134
Jones, James Earl, 715
Jones, John Price, 418, 435, 461, 478, 482, 503
Jones, Leilani, 785
Jones, Nellie, 49
Jones, Rebecca Naomi, 870, 884
Jones, Richard G., 858
Jones, Robert Edmond, 574
Jones, Shirley, 665, 725
Jones, Sidney, 164, 195, 199, 232, 347
Jones, Stephen, 457, 480
Jones, Sydney, 153
Jones, T. C., 662, 666, 668
Jones, Tom, 679, 696, 726, 867
Jones, Walter, 143, 192, 203, 279, 282, 380
Jongeyans George. See Gaynes, George
Jonson, Ben, 698
Joplin, Janis, 835
Joplin, Scott, 346, 752, 772
Joray, Peter, 510
Jordan, Joe, 257, 275, 302, 519, 527
Jordan, Louis, 802
Jordan, Marc, 715
Joseph, Carl, 120
Journey, 877
Joyce, Carol, 460
Joyce, Laura, 64, 66, 75, 78
Jude, Patrick, 766
Judels, Charles, 354, 406
Judge, Jack, 348
Judic, Anna, 92
Julia, Raul, 740, 744, 749, 754, 777, 802
June, Roma, 385

Kahn, Gus, 359, 383, 418, 426, 465
Kahn, Madeline, 758

Kahn, Otto, 494
Kahn, Roger Wolfe, 494, 500, 514
Kail, Thomas, 870, 878
Kalhurst, Eric, 498
Kalich, Jacob, 592
Kalisz, Armand, 382
Kalman, Emmerich, 335, 341, 365, 368, 375, 426, 470, 478, 488, 609
Kalmar, Bert, 401, 408, 431, 443, 470, 477, 486, 490, 496, 512, 585, 851
Kander, John, 688–689, 704, 716, 721, 725, 758, 766, 783, 799, 805, 815, 817, 822, 850, 861, 865, 874, 886
Kane, Gail, 321
Kane, Helen, 479, 496, 540
Kane, John, 818
Kane, Lida, 477
Kanin, Garson, 682
Kappeler, Alfred, 312, 319
Karl, Tom, 62, 128
Karloff, Boris, 634
Karlweis, Dorothy, 593
Karlweis, Oscar, 763
Karnilova, Maria, 674, 701
Kassir, John, 872
Kassoff, Russ, 882
Kata, Takeshi, 872
Katdare, Deep, 849
Katscher, Robert, 524
Katz, Natasha, 868
Kaufman, George S., 427, 431, 446, 462, 499, 506, 512, 513, 524, 529, 531, 532, 541, 569, 604, 615, 643, 655, 718, 775
Kaufman, S. Jay, 440
Kayden, Spencer, 835
Kaye, Danny, 576, 584, 585, 645, 693, 737, 874, 880
Kaye, Judy, 794, 836, 865
Kaye, Stubby, 637, 663, 785
Kazan, Lainie, 803
Kazantzakis, Nilos, 725
Kazee, Steve, 867
Kean, Jane, 597, 656
Keane, Doris, 439
Keane, George, 617
Keane, Robert Emmett, 371
Kearns, Allen, 389, 432, 453, 462, 475, 487, 494, 502, 519
Keel, Howard, 678, 744
Keeler, Marion, 488
Keeler, Ruby, 478, 508, 666, 869
Keenan-Bolger, Celia, 855, 863, 869
Keene, Dick, 484
Keene, Laura, 14
Keene, Richard, 463

Klein, Manuel, 246, 253, 267, 291, 305, 315, 319, 325, 336, 340, 358, 409
Klein, Paul, 680
Klein, Robert, 763
Kleinsinger, George, 665
Kline, Kevin, 772
Kline, Linda, 833
Klotz, Florence, 839
Klugman, Jack, 674
Knapp, Dorothy, 462, 504
Knechtge, Dan, 867
Knight, Frederick, 284
Knight, George S., 43, 44, 90
Knight, June, 537, 552
Knight, Percival, 367, 386, 393
Knight, Wayne, 880
Knighton, Nan, 820
Knilling, Anthony, 493
Knoblock, Edward, 648
Kober, Arthur, 644
Koch, Edward, 787
Koehler, Ted, 514, 535, 547
Kolb, C. William, 282
Kollmar, Richard, 570, 576, 597, 602
Koloc, Bonnie, 783
Kopit, Arthur, 777, 822
Korie, Michael, 863
Korngold, Erich Wolfgang, 593, 602
Koshino, Junko, 852
Kosta, Tessa, 376, 389, 399, 410, 419, 429, 449, 453, 463, 510
Koster, Tessa, 466
Kowalik, Trent, 874
Krakowski, Jane, 796, 843, 874
Krause, Fritz, 144
Kreis, Levi, 883
Kreisler, Fritz, 393, 394, 404, 417, 604
Kretzmer, Herbert, 790
Krieger, Henry, 776, 819
Krimsky Brothers, 559, 571, 709
Kritzer, Leslie, 871, 874, 885
Kronenberger, Louis, 610
Kruger, Jacques, 44, 61, 83, 86, 95, 108, 121, 149, 173
Krupa, Gene, 519
Kudisch, Marc, 835, 838, 843, 848, 855, 862, 864, 872, 878, 881
Kuhn, Jeffrey, 848
Kuhn, Judy, 790, 792, 805
Kuhn, Walter, 480
Kulish, Kiril, 874
Kummer, Clare, 321
Kunneke, Edward, 452, 461
Kunze, Michael, 842

Kurton, Peggy, 418
Kurtz, Swoosie, 842
Kushner, James, 774
Kushnier, Jeremy, 823
Kussell, Daniel, 496

La Maire, Rufus, 456
La Mar, Albert, 207
La Redd, Cora, 505
La Rue, Grace, 266, 306, 371, 493
La Shelle, Kirk, 196
La Verre, Madelon, 402
LaChanze, 856, 858–859, 878
Lachaume, Aimee, 204, 207
LaChiusa, Michael John, 827, 828, 862
Lacombe, Paul, 104
Lacy, Harry, 66
Lacy, Rophino, 15
Ladd, Hank, 591, 628
Ladysmith Black Mambazo, 804
Lahr, Bert, 499, 515, 519, 532, 535, 536, 544, 554, 558, 577, 604, 641, 676, 791, 812
Laine, Cleo, 788
Lake, Harriette, 523, 527
Lalor, Frank, 210, 232, 310, 340, 349, 361, 366
LaManna, Janine, 844, 850
Lamas, Fernando, 664
Lamb, Frank E., 88
Lambert, Lisa, 860
Lambert, Mark, 745
Lambert, Maude, 208, 218, 300, 320
Lamont, Jennie, 332
Lamont, Robin, 739
Lamos, Mark, 882
Lampery, Peggy Hagen, 747
Lamson, Albert, 312
Landau, Tina, 835
Landers, Alfred C., 167
Landis, Carole, 605
Lane, Burton, 517, 520, 524, 535, 580, 605, 616, 625, 765, 877
Lane, Gloria, 634, 653
Lane, Nathan, 813, 834, 850, 883
Lane, William Henry (Master Juba), 13
Lang, Andrew, 563
Lang, Charles F., 57, 82
Lang, Eric, 750
Lang, Gertrude, 483, 486
Lang, Harold, 612, 622, 626, 640, 662, 664
Lang, Peter, 128, 168, 429
Langdon, Margaret, 639
Langella, Frank, 832

Mabley, Jackie "Moms," 577
MacArthur, Charles, 553, 758
Macaulay, Joseph, 481, 485, 492, 518
MacConnell, Harry T., 199
MacDermott, Galt, 724, 740, 743, 744, 783, 833
MacDevitt, Brian, 852
MacDonald, Audra, 867, 880
MacDonald, Ballard, 302, 325, 401, 482
MacDonald, Christie, 145, 183, 192, 196, 198, 200,
    208, 232, 238, 257, 267, 282, 300, 308, 336,
    337, 399
MacDonald, Daniel, 817
MacDonald, Donald, 348, 380, 430
MacDonald, Jeannette, 425, 491, 501, 503
MacDonald, W. H., 128, 143, 148, 155, 165, 171,
    174, 216
MacDonald, W. M., 209
MacDonough, Glen, 146, 169, 187, 189, 196, 200,
    207, 251, 287, 294, 298, 299, 354, 382
MacDonough, Harry, 103, 139, 154, 176, 189, 334
Macdonough, Harry, 120
MacFarlane, George, 290, 342, 427
MacGowan, Jack, 880
MacGowan, Kenneth, 402
MacGowran, Jack, 673
MacGrath, Leueen, 655
Mack, Andrew, 133, 180, 193, 300, 302, 447
Mack, Annie, 44, 49, 56, 63, 67, 75
Mack, Cecil, 211, 262, 524
Mack, Edward, 145
Mack, Russell, 448
Mack, W. F., 149
Mackay, Ellin, 467
Mackay, John A., 78, 90
Macke, James B., 156
MacKenzie, Alice, 512
Mackey, Eric, 885
Mackie, Florence, 348
MacKintosh, Cameron, 799, 810, 837, 863
Macklin, Albert, 782
MacLaine, Shirley, 754
MacLeod, Mary, 874
MacNeil, Patricia, 634
MacNichol, Lizzie, 155, 159, 188
MacRae, Gordon, 612
MacRae, Sheila, 703
MacWatters, Virginia, 609
Madden, Edward, 282, 320
Madden, Jeanne, 570
Maentz, Clara, 260
Maffitt, James S., 36, 41, 57, 64, 79
Maggart, Brandon, 734
Magruder, James, 819

Maguire, Gregory, 846
Maher, Bill, 844
Mahn, H. B., 69
Mahoney, Will, 443, 488, 507, 526, 656
Mahoney, Woody, 877
Maida, Edith, 325
Majeroni, George, 278
Majilton, Frank, 80
Makarova, Natalia, 779
Malbin, Elaine, 645
Malcolm-Smith, George, 610
Maley, Denman, 294
Maley, Stephen, 309
Malina, Luba, 609
Mallory, Ramona, 881
Mallory, Victoria, 745
Maloney, Patty, 800
Maltby, Richard, Jr., 782, 787, 799, 800, 814, 859
Mamoulian, Rouben, 604, 633
Manahan, George, 872
Mancini, Henry, 749, 812
Mandel, Frank, 349, 398, 402, 407, 417, 437, 457,
    474, 496, 528, 553
Mandeville, William C., 219
Manheim, Ralph, 754
Manilow, Barry, 795
Mankiewicz, Herman, 440
Mann, Louis, 159, 227, 268
Mann, Terrence, 790, 807, 820, 857
Manners, J. Hartley, 295
Manning, Irene, 611
Manning, James H., 203, 254
Manoff, Dinah, 785
Manola, Marion, 103, 109, 117, 141, 142
Mansfield, Richard, 166, 229, 450
Mantello, Joe, 848, 851, 878
Mantle, Burns, 151, 260, 390, 420, 427, 431, 432, 472,
    480, 494, 536, 550
Manville, Lorraine, 438
Maple, Audrey, 330, 377, 449
Marais, Joseph, 614
Marand, Patricia, 644, 713
Marbe, Fay, 388
Marble, Scott, 100, 101, 111
Marbury, Elizabeth, 354, 379, 414, 495
March, Fredric, 458
March, Joseph Moncure, 828
Mardirosian, Tom, 803
Maretzek, Max, 42
Marie, Paola, 53
Marin, Cheech, 857
Marion, George, Jr., 378, 592, 597, 602, 609, 615
Marker, Preshy, 690

Markey, Enid, 468, 568
Markham, Monte, 745
Markham, Pauline, 34, 66, 82
Markoe, Peter, 4
Markova, Alicia, 604
Marks, Edward B., 294
Marks, Gerald, 598, 622
Marks, Maurice, 491
Marks, Walter, 722
Marlowe, Gloria, 654
Marlowe, James C., 281
Marlowe, Mary, 453
Maroulis, Constantine, 877
Marquis, Don, 662, 665
Mars, Antony, 331
Mars, Leo, 254
Marsden, Fred, 77, 78, 108
Marsh, Howard, 403, 417, 450, 478, 489, 490, 521, 524, 533, 536
Marsh, Reginald, 425, 432
Marshall, "Red," 592
Marshall, Armina, 633
Marshall, Austin, 513
Marshall, Boyd, 407
Marshall, E. G., 746
Marshall, Everett, 527, 539, 549, 596
Marshall, Harry B., 210
Marshall, Henry I., 322
Marshall, James R., 419
Marshall, Kathleen, 833, 834, 838, 859, 861, 868, 869
Marshall, Mort, 746
Marshall, Peter L., 711
Marston, Richard, 168
Martel, Tom, 742
Martin, Andrea, 837, 868, 874
Martin, Barney, 751
Martin, Bob, 860
Martin, Catherine, 842
Martin, David, 666
Martin, Dolores, 643
Martin, Ernest, 672, 686, 711, 717
Martin, Hugh, 621, 640, 699
Martin, John, 7
Martin, Mary, 571, 599, 611, 613, 628, 629, 652, 673, 676, 695, 717, 767, 776, 822
Martin, Norman L., 680
Martin, Steve, 854
Martin, Theodore, 319
Martin, Virginia, 686, 693
Martin, William, 838
Martindell, Edward, 238, 274, 307, 353
Martinetti, Ignacio, 116, 199, 284
Martínez Pey, Oscar, 879

Martinot, Sadie, 91
Martyn, Kathlene, 449
Martz, Mattie, 235
Marvenga, Ilse, 423, 451, 510, 533
Marvin, Mel, 759, 863
Marx Brothers, 289, 438–439, 462, 499, 518, 593, 734, 770, 812
Marx, Adolph (Harpo). *See* Marx Brothers
Marx, Herbert (Zeppo). *See* Marx Brothers
Marx, Jeff, 845
Marx, Julius (Groucho). *See* Marx Brothers
Marx, Leonard (Chico). *See* Marx Brothers
Marx, Milton (Gummo). *See* Marx Brothers
Mason, Hilda, 171
Mason, Jackie, 790, 813, 827, 841, 846, 851
Mason, Karen, 836
Mason, Marilyn, 720
Mason, Pauline, 471
Massey, Blanche, 153
Massey, Daniel, 694, 747
Massey, Ilona, 596
Massi, Bernice, 698
Massine, Leonide, 512
Masteroff, Joe, 694, 716, 805
Masterson, Mary Stuart, 843
Masterson, Peter, 760
Mastin, Will, 660
Mathews, Charles, 8
Mathis, Sherry, 756
Matteson, Ruth, 572, 609
Matthau, Walter, 656
Matthews, Carmen, 727
Matthews, Inez, 631
Matthews, J. Sherrie, 173, 191, 203
Matthews, Jessie, 512, 587
Matthews, Roger, 410
Mattson, Eric, 607
Mature, Victor, 584
Maughan, Dora, 519
Maurel, Mrs. Victor, 426
Maurette, Marcelle, 712
Maxwell, Arthur, 605, 647
Maxwell, Jan, 855
Maxwell, Vera, 312
May, Edna, 179, 202, 236, 272
Mayehoff, Eddie, 604, 608
Mayer, Edwin Justus, 606
Mayer, Michael, 865, 884, 885
Mayes, Sally, 843
Mayfair, Mitzi, 558
Mayfied, Julian, 631
Mayfield, Cleo, 357, 398
Mayhew, Stella, 241, 299, 311, 322, 479

McQueen, Armelia, 842
McQueen, Butterfly, 577
McVeigh, Bridget, 125
McVey, John, 278
Mead, Laura, 882
Meade, Ada, 384
Meade, William, 859
Meader, George, 528
Meakins, Charles, 338
Mears, Stephen, 864, 868
Medford, Kay, 678
Medina, Louisa, 14
Meehan, Thomas, 804, 808, 834, 840, 849, 868, 871
Meek, Donald, 394, 531
Mehan, Dodd, 523
Meiser, Edith, 465
Mekka, Eddie, 750
Melmoth, Mrs., 6
Melnotte, R., 33
Melville, Allan, 649
Melville, Emilie, 70
Melville, George D., 115
Mendes, Sam, 843
Mendum, Georgie Drew, 287
Menken, Alan, 807, 818, 836, 868
Menotti, Gian Carlo, 618, 634, 635, 653, 654, 709
Menzel, Idina, 833, 846, 862
Mercer, Frances, 593
Mercer, Johnny, 516, 535, 573, 579, 632, 663, 678,
    759, 816
Mercer, Ruby, 557, 590
Mercouri, Melina, 718, 744
Meredith, Burgess, 633
Meredith, Morley, 679
Merediz, Olga, 870
Mérimée, Prosper, 782
Merkyl, Wilmuth, 337, 350
Merlin, Joanna, 701
Merman, Ethel, 519, 527, 537, 547, 548, 556, 557,
    572, 573, 577, 581, 593, 594, 604, 613, 635, 674,
    697–698, 708, 714, 748, 844, 848, 867
Merola, Gaetano, 307
Merriam, Eve, 741
Merrick, David, 653, 668, 671, 673, 674, 680, 682, 683,
    688, 690, 696, 709, 721, 742, 745, 771, 813, 835
Merrill, Blanche, 401
Merrill, Bob, 665, 675, 683, 742, 785, 838
Merrill, Gary, 591
Merville, Lena, 118
Messager, André, 142, 396
Messel, Oliver, 654, 722
Mestayer, W. A., 38, 47, 55, 88, 106, 111, 122, 133
Metaxa, George, 528, 548

Methot, Mayo, 510
Meyer, George W., 363
Meyer, Joseph, 418, 461, 486, 494, 503, 515
Meyerberg, Michael, 611
Meyerowitz, Jan, 636
Meyers, Henry, 496
Meyers, Louise, 400
Michaels, Frankie, 714
Michaels, Marilyn, 800
Michaels, Robert, 426
Michele, Lea, 821, 865
Michelena, Kate, 195
Michelena, Vera, 234, 261, 279, 282, 306, 343,
    377, 418
Michener, Dean, 650
Michener, James A., 628
Middleton, Ray, 529, 542, 570, 575, 613, 624, 709, 712
Midler, Bette, 751, 768
Mielziner, Jo, 537, 576, 607, 609, 639
Migenes, Julia, 701
Milan, Madeline, 132
Milburn, Mary, 401, 463
Miles, Carlotta, 438
Millar Gertie, 70
Millard, Marie, 159
Miller, Alice Duer, 448, 456, 542
Miller, Ann, 575, 768, 774
Miller, Flourney, 275, 280, 359, 410, 434, 492, 520,
    529, 538, 588, 643
Miller, Fred, 121
Miller, Fred, Jr., 151
Miller, Glenn, 519, 526
Miller, Henry, 142, 350, 718, 825
Miller, Irving C., 416
Miller, Joe, 276, 381, 405
Miller, John, 354
Miller, Lawrence, 843
Miller, Marilyn, 343, 355, 367, 379, 383, 391, 399,
    407, 408, 422, 434, 459, 466, 519, 521, 541, 555,
    556, 623, 708, 782, 818
Miller, Midge, 477, 507
Miller, Roger, 786
Miller, Susan, 592
Miller, Wynne, 681
Millership, Florrie, 406
Millöcker, Karl, 77, 87, 90, 91, 98, 120, 133, 134
Mills, Arthur, 379
Mills, Bertha, 276
Mills, Eva, 50
Mills, Florence, 411, 424, 447–448
Mills, Frederick, 52
Mills, Harry, 142
Mills, Kerry, 316

Morrison, Greg, 860
Morrison, Matthew, 840
Morrissey, Will, 401, 432, 477, 507, 605
Morrow, Doretta, 639, 648
Morrow, Karen, 703
Morse, Henry Woolson, 65, 103, 119, 151, 169
Morse, Robert, 670, 673, 675, 686, 742, 754, 768, 810
Morse, Theodore, 282
Morse, Woolson, 112
Mortimer, James, 24
Morton, Clara, 250
Morton, Dorothy, 162, 168, 192
Morton, Euan, 846, 885
Morton, Frederic, 737
Morton, Hugh, 172, 176, 178, 179, 181, 185
Morton, Joe, 746
Morton, Kate, 250
Morton, Paul, 250
Morton, Sam, 250
Moses, Burke, 850, 867
Mosier, Enid, 654
Moss, Arnold, 580
Moss, Kathi, 777
Mostel, Zero, 587, 608, 690, 701, 756, 775
Mostyn, Hallen, 158
Moten, Edna, 529
Motzan, Otto, 355
Moulan, Frank, 188, 219, 220, 269, 300, 341, 354,
    377, 403, 415, 421, 524
Mowry, Greg, 791
Muenz, Richard, 794, 803
Mullaly, Megan, 868
Mullaly, W. S., 116
Mulle, Tiny Ida, 89
Mundy, James, 658
Mundy, John, 635
Mundy, Meg, 612
Munro, Bill, 392
Munsel, Patrice, 753
Munshin, Jules, 638, 683, 688
Munson, Ona, 473, 484, 498
Mura, Corinna, 601
Murphy, C. W., 347, 355
Murphy, Donna, 807, 813, 847, 866, 883
Murphy, George, 526
Murphy, Jack, 825
Murphy, Joseph, 123
Murphy, Mark, 99, 125
Murphy, Owen, 446, 492
Murphy, Sally, 807, 853
Murphy, Stanley, 322
Murphy, Tim, 109, 121
Murray, Don, 746

Murray, Elizabeth, 304, 305, 323, 331, 352, 484
Murray, J. Harold, 452, 457, 470, 477, 528, 549
Murray, Ken, 550, 631
Murray, Mae, 356
Murray, Thomas, 99
Murray, Wynn, 559, 572, 587
Musker, John, 868
Mutrux, Floyd, 883
Myers, Annie, 109, 118
Myers, Henry, 683
Myers, Lorna, 752
Myers, Pamela, 735
Myers, Richard, 500, 516, 529, 535, 540
Myers, Sammy, 452
Myers, Uncle, 842
Myrtil, Odette, 437, 470, 496, 528

Nagarajan, Anisha, 849
Nagel, Conrad, 642
Nagle, E. F., 145
Naismith, Laurence, 695
Najera, Rick, 857
Nance, Clarence, 499
Nani, Mlle., 80
Napier, John, 809
Nash, John, 80
Nash, N. Richard, 682, 696, 721
Nash, Ogden, 599, 645, 746
Natel, Jean-Marc, 790
Natwick, Mildred, 739
Naudain, May, 277, 360
Naughton, James, 796, 815, 843
Navarra, Chiara, 857
Naylor, H., 33
Nazzaro, Nat, 469
Neeley, Ted, 749
Neff, Hildegarde, 655
Neill, Edward, Jr., 512
Neilson, Alice, 152
Neilson, Francis, 156
Nell, Edward, Jr., 497
Nelsen, Eric M., 873
Nelson, Barry, 726
Nelson, Gene, 626, 738, 749
Nelson, Kenneth, 641, 679, 737
Nelson, Richard, 792, 826
Nemiroff, Robert, 746
Nesbitt, Cathleen, 660, 775
Neshyba-Hodges, Charlie, 882
Neuendorff, Adolph, 94
Neuwirth, Bebe, 806, 815, 883
Neville, Marcus, 832

Parson, George, 280
Parsons, Louella, 608
Parton, Dolly, 878
Pascal, Adam, 814, 828
Pascal, Milton, 602
Pasch, Reginald, 416
Pastor, Tony, 40, 46, 50, 60, 64, 68, 72, 73, 84, 88, 94,
  114, 118, 191
Patinkin, Mandy, 767, 783, 795–796, 799,
  823, 828
Paton, Alan, 631
Patrick, Michael, 856
Patricola, Tom, 431, 443, 455, 495
Patterson, Dick, 700
Patterson, Meredith, 874
Patterson, W. C., 284
Paul, Betty, 646
Paulding, Frederick, 301
Paulton, Edward, 343, 405
Paulton, Harry, 97, 105, 107, 114, 172
Paulus, Diane, 877
Pavek, Janet, 679
Pavlova, Anna, 366
Pawk, Michelle, 843
Payn, Graham, 622
Payne, John, 749
Payton, Lew, 444
Peacock, Bertram, 417, 474
Peakes, J. C., 35
Peale, Norman Vincent, 863
Pearce, Alice, 593, 623
Pearce, Bobby, 846
Pearl, Jack, 463, 487, 504, 514, 525
Pearson, Molly, 570
Pearson, Ruby, 747
Pearson, Sybille, 782
Peck, Raymond, 218, 221, 223, 469
Peck, Sam, 359, 410, 434, 492, 529
Peil, Mary Beth, 785, 843
Pelhan, R. W., 12
Pellaton, Albert, 342
Pendleton, Austin, 701
Pène du Bois, Raoul, 751, 769
Pennington, Ann, 335, 343, 356, 383, 390, 400, 414,
  423, 434, 442, 443, 466, 495, 522, 527, 575, 596
Pennington, Bill, 438
Pennington, May, 438
Percival, Walter, 254, 282, 284, 289, 322
Perelman, S. J., 524, 537, 599
Perkins, Anthony, 678
Perkins, Carl, 883
Perkins, Carrie E., 232, 268
Perkins, Kenneth, 619

Perkins, Patti, 832
Perkins, Ray, 493
Perlet, Herman, 197
Perlman, Arthur, 880
Perot, Cynthia, 396
Perrin, Sam, 610
Perry, Irene, 90
Perugini, Don Giovanni, 75, 98, 102, 156, 197
Peters, Bernadette, 726, 749, 783, 784, 787, 792, 804,
  824, 839, 843, 867, 881
Peters, Brock, 742
Peters, W. F., 253, 291, 301, 334
Peterson, Eric, 770
Peterson, Kurt, 738
Petina, Irra, 603, 624, 653, 664, 712
Petit, Charles, 497
Petit, Roland, 774
Petrass, Sari, 366
Pettigue, Amy, 625
Peyton, Dave, 238
Philip, Adolph, 405
Philip, William E., 174
Philipp, Adolph, 149, 336, 342
Phillip, William E., 171
Phillips, Adelaide, 58, 62
Phillips, Graham, 873
Phillips, John, 750
Phillips, Lou Diamond, 813
Phoenix, Joacquin, 884
Phyllis, Norah, 116
Piaf, Edith, 620, 633, 825
Pickens, Jane, 632, 642
Pickert, Rolly, 559
Picon, Molly, 592, 685, 721
Pidgeon, Walter, 675, 785
Pidgin, Charles F., 52
Pierce, Betty, 409
Pierce, David Hyde, 854, 865
Pilcer, Harry, 281, 298, 320, 333
Pinero, Arthur Wing, 240
Pinkard, Maceo, 428, 754
Pinkins, Tonya, 816, 842, 849
Pinza, Ezio, 628, 653, 870, 881
Pitchford, Dean, 823
Pitkin, Robert, 340, 359, 374, 616
Pitkin, Walter, 544
Pitou, Augustus, 532
Pitt, George Dibdin, 763
Pitts, Zazu, 768
Pittu, David, 847
Pixley, Annie, 77, 133, 141
Pixley, Frank, 202, 211, 223, 241, 269, 288, 289,
  292, 329

Pizzarelli, John, 816, 845
Planché, James Robinson, 9–11, 10
Planquette, Robert, 74, 120, 133, 144, 309
Plant, Mark, 552
Plantadit, Karine, 882
Plasson, Emmanuel, 882
Platt, Oliver, 876
Platters, The, 880
Pleininger, Carl, 170
Plimpton, Martha, 876
Plimpton, Shelley, 724
Plotkin, Tom, 833
Plummer, Buddy and Sally, 865
Plummer, Christopher, 746
Plunkett, Charles, 119
Poison (rock music group), 877
Pokrass, Samuel, 543
Polanski, Roman, 842
Poleri, David, 653
Polk, Gordon, 664
Pollack, Lew, 411
Pollard, Michael J., 678
Pollock, Channing, 337, 414
Pollock, Frank, 183, 297, 328, 363
Ponazecki, Joe, 701
Poppen, Detmar, 267, 419, 492, 525, 590
Porcasi, Paul, 403
Porter, Cole, 297, 357, 359, 363–364, 394, 397, 442,
    446, 491, 511, 512, 522, 524, 537, 548, 552, 556,
    561, 569, 571, 577, 581, 582, 593, 594, 599, 601,
    604, 613, 626, 638, 647, 655, 702, 736, 769, 822,
    827, 847, 865
Post, Lilly, 75
Post, W. H., 459, 488
Poston, Tom, 683
Potter, Paul M., 116, 164, 183
Pounds, Courtice, 92, 102, 104, 106
Powell, Dawn, 587
Powell, Eleanor, 491, 515, 519, 551
Powell, Felix, 368
Powell, Jane, 813
Powell, Michael, 860
Power, Tyrone, 141, 376
Powers, James T., 36, 61, 77, 84, 97, 98, 104, 106, 108,
    115, 122, 142, 164, 170, 175, 186, 199, 206, 221,
    226, 232, 266, 323
Powers, Marie, 618, 634
Powers, Tom, 370, 418
Pratt, S. G., 80
Premice, Josephine, 715
Presley, Elvis, 779, 810, 854, 858, 859, 880, 883
Presnell, Harve, 681, 808
Pressburger, Emeric, 860

Preston, J., 82
Preston, Robert, 669, 702, 717, 749, 829
Previn, André, 516, 733, 767
Price, Adelaide, 8
Price, Georgie, 401, 593
Price, Gilbert, 754
Price, Lonny, 833, 847, 861, 867, 872
Price, Mark, 186
Priest, Janet, 235, 288
Primrose and West Minstrels, 120, 154
Primus, Pearl, 620
Prince, Faith, 801, 802, 835, 871
Prince, Hal, 765, 767, 785, 808, 818, 824, 849
Prince, Harold, 745, 764, 778, 805, 839, 858, 866
Printemps, Yvonne, 474
Prior, Allan, 488, 500, 510
Prior, Lulu, 33
Proctor, Warren, 452
Prose, Francine, 872
Prouty, Jed, 350
Prowse, Juliet, 691
Prud'homme, Cameron, 665
Pruette, William, 147, 148, 155, 212, 236, 254, 261,
    317, 334
Pryce, Jonathan, 799
Pryce, Leontyne, 646
Ptah, Heru, 860
Puccini, Giacomo, 607
Puck, Eva, 433, 464
Puck, Harry, 460, 491
Puerner, Charles, 102, 129, 134
Puig, Manuel, 805
Purcell, Charles, 373, 388, 389, 395, 402, 408, 458,
    475, 477, 525, 540, 544
Purviance, Roy, 316
Pye, Tom, 848

Quayle, Q. Q., 522
Quilico, Louis, 800
Quillan, Joe, 586, 611
Quine, Richard, 576
Quinlan, Gertrude, 309
Quinn, Anthony, 781
Quiroga, Horacio, 815

Racey, Noah, 847
Rachmaninoff, Serge, 712
Radcliffe, James, 99, 122
Radner, Gildner, 767
Rado, James, 723, 724, 833
Rae, Charlotte, 661, 861

Raft, George, 460, 481
Ragland, Oscar, 375, 405, 435
Ragni, Gerome, 723, 724, 743, 833
Rahn, Muriel, 601
Rahv, Philip, 842
Rail, Tommy, 685, 735
Raines, Ron, 792
Rainger, Ralph, 506
Raitt, John, 606, 607, 624, 643, 648, 650, 709, 717, 753
Rall, Tommy, 673
Ralph Readers Girls, 493
Ralph, Julia, 255
Ralph, Sheryl Lee, 769, 838
Ralston, Teri, 735
Ramirez, Sara, 833, 854
Ramsey, Alice, 338
Ramsey, Kevin, 817
Rand, Suzanne, 763
Randall, Bob, 748
Randall, Carl, 356, 379, 470, 491, 524, 531, 583, 585
Randall, Tony, 670, 815
Rando, John, 835, 838, 860, 861, 874
Randolph, Clemence, 429
Randolph, Eva, 119
Randolph, James, 755
Randolph, William, 194
Ranken, Frederick, 196, 221, 222, 230, 250, 253, 267
Rankin, Phyllis, 193
Ransome, John A., 54, 223
Raposo, Joe, 790
Rasch, Albertina, 455, 477, 478, 485, 493, 508, 511, 520, 532, 535, 580, 609
Rascoe, Burton, 596
Rasely, George, 574
Rashad, Phylicia, 862
Ratcliffe, Samuel D., 743
Rathburn, Roger, 738
Ratliff, Joseph, 277, 294
Rawlings, Marjorie Kinnan, 712
Rawlston, Zelma, 348
Ray, Emma, 279
Ray, James, 279
Ray, Johnny, 182, 240
Rayam, Curtis, 752
Raye, Martha, 580
Raymond and Mars, 152
Raymond, Frederick, Jr., 403
Raymond, Helen, 360
Raymond, J. F., 57
Raymond, Maud, 259, 301
Raymond, Ray, 388, 408, 421
Raymond, William, 291, 298
Raynaud, Charles, 112

Rayworth, Rita, 608
Razaf, Andy, 492, 507, 520, 865
Read, Mary, 514, 553
Reale, Richard and Willie, 844
Reals, Grace, 157
Reardon, John, 683
Reddie, Milton, 562, 567
Redding, Eugene, 210
Redfield, Billy, 618, 638
Redford, Dave, 363
Redmond, Helen, 179
Redpath, Olive, 193
Redway, Eddie, 253
Reece, R., 44
Reed, Charlie, 116
Reed, Florence, 376, 379
Reed, Napoleon, 643
Reed, Paul, 686
Rees, Roger, 844
Reese, David, 323
Reeves, Peter, 806
Reeves-Smith, H., 546
Regan, Walter, 395, 429, 430
Regay, Pearl, 444
Rehan, Ada, 57, 64, 66, 174
Reichard, Daniel, 858, 872
Reichner, Bickely, 556
Reid, Hal, 237, 280
Reid, Margaret, 148
Reiff, Antoine, Jr., 25–26
Reiffarth, Jennie, 86, 176
Reilly, Charles Nelson, 127, 686, 697, 711
Reimherr, George, 452
Reiner, Fritz, 574
Reinhard, John, 304
Reinhardt, Gottfried, 593
Reinhardt, Heinrich, 308, 334
Reinhardt, Max, 321, 450, 494, 593, 602
Reinking, Ann, 750, 815, 824, 843, 844
Reisner, C. Francis, 371
Reiss, Jay, 855
Remick, Lee, 699
Renard, Jean, 793
Renaud, Andre, 535
Rennie, J. H., 55
Renshaw, Christopher, 813, 846
Renwick, Charles, 110
Resnik, Patricia, 878
Revel, Harry, 527, 532, 610
Revill, Clive, 693, 718
Reynolds, Corey, 840
Reynolds, Debbie, 745, 755, 786
Reynolds, Genevieve, 82

Reynolds, Herbert, 355, 361, 369
Reynolds, James, 398, 403, 414, 433, 434, 450, 459, 549
Rhodes, Eric, 537
Rhodes, Erik, 647
Rhodes, Harrison, 362, 478
Rhodes, Lila, 318
Rhodes, Robert, 509
Riano, Rene, 416
Ribeiro, Alfonso, 782, 838
Ricard, Amy, 228
Ricci, Bertha, 83, 98, 104, 106, 110, 121, 131, 145
Rice, Anne, 860
Rice, Edward E., 39, 46, 50, 52, 58, 61, 65, 68, 73, 74, 81, 86, 89, 90, 104, 118, 143, 163, 172, 178, 181, 183, 185, 210, 237
Rice, Elmer, 615, 872
Rice, Fanny, 120, 152
Rice, Gitz, 410, 469
Rice, John C., 173
Rice, T. D., 11–12
Rice, Tim, 740, 807, 818, 821, 828
Rich, Frank, 772, 775, 779, 791
Rich, Helen, 405
Rich, Irene, 625
Rich, Lizzie, 47
Richards, Donald, 616
Richards, George, 97, 145, 181, 226
Richards, Regina, 389
Richardson, Desmond, 844
Richardson, Ian, 754
Richardson, Jane, 396, 404
Richardson, Natasha, 822
Richardson, Ron, 786
Richert, Wanda, 771
Richings, Caroline, 23, 31
Richings, Nick, 884
Richings-Bernard, Caroline, 29
Richman, Arthur, 461
Richman, Harry, 466, 495, 514, 525, 536, 547, 591
Ricketts, Thomas, 181
Rickey, Sam, 47
Ridge, Frank, 368
Ridges, Stanley, 435, 503
Rieffel, Lisa, 790
Riegler, Adam, 883
Riesenfeld, Hugo, 400
Rigaud, George, 609
Rigby, Cathy, 799, 800, 823, 858
Riggs, Ralph, 335, 594
Riggs, T. Lawrason, 363
Rigl, Betty, 20
Rigl, Emily, 43
Rille, Laurent De, 62

Rimsky-Korsakov, Nicholas, 508
Rinehart, Mary Roberts, 386
Ring, Blanche, 214, 217, 221, 225, 227, 242, 247, 250, 251, 259, 260, 277, 282, 294, 301, 323, 342, 364, 366, 411, 502, 513, 519, 567
Ringold, George, 43
Ripley, Alice, 819, 832, 877
Ripple, Pacie, 496
Risch, Matthew, 876
Rising, W. S., 81, 82, 89, 96, 112
Ritchard, Cyril, 652, 683, 704, 742, 753, 767
Ritchie, Adele, 152, 196, 198, 204, 208, 212, 232, 245, 259, 269
Ritter, Thelma, 665
Ritz Brothers, 460
Rivera, Chita, 655, 667, 668, 678, 679, 703, 708, 751, 773, 779, 788, 805, 843, 848, 859, 879
Rivers, Joan, 862
Rives, Amelie, 495
Robbins, G. I., 747
Robbins, Jerome, 576, 605, 619, 621, 639, 652, 666, 702, 769, 775, 794, 843, 848, 859, 867, 874, 876
Robeldo, Julian, 416
Roberti, Lyda, 522, 542
Roberts, Anthony, 720, 812, 827, 867
Roberts, Ben, 601, 602
Roberts, C. Luckyeth, 468
Roberts, Doris, 848
Roberts, Dorothy, 582
Roberts, Jimmy, 814, 850
Roberts, Joan, 594, 609, 610, 834
Roberts, Keith, 882
Roberts, Lee S., 383
Roberts, R. A., 154
Roberts, Roy, 648
Robertson, Guy, 424, 429, 463, 490, 496, 509, 518, 544, 567
Robertson, Ken, 855
Robertson, Liz, 780
Robeson, Paul, 533, 574, 578
Robin, Leo, 486
Robinson, Anna, 178
Robinson, Bartlett, 559
Robinson, Bill, 236, 494, 507, 519, 573, 608, 754, 814
Robinson, Carl, 542
Robinson, Clarence, 454
Robinson, E. A., 346
Robinson, Earl, 574, 653
Robinson, Peter, 142
Robson, Stuart, 66
Robyn, Alfred G., 156, 274, 332
Rockefeller, John D., 272, 541
Rockwell, David, 832, 840, 854

Ruby, Ellalee, 482
Ruby, Harry, 401, 408, 431, 443, 470, 477, 486, 490,
    496, 499, 512, 585, 851
Ruge, William, 115
Ruggiero, Gabrielle, 654
Ruggles, Charles, 470, 500–501
Ruivivar, Francis, 799
Rumierk, Shirley, 857
Rumshinsky, Joseph, 592
Runyon, Damon, 636, 876
Rupert, Michael, 792, 803, 866
Rupert, Mike, 721, 774
Rushmore, Vivian, 319
Rushworth, Frank, 188, 209, 231, 245, 288
Russell Market Girls, 498
Russell, Anna, 648
Russell, Brenda, 858
Russell, Gilbert, 608, 614
Russell, Jack, 650
Russell, James, 207
Russell, Jenna, 869
Russell, John, 207
Russell, Lillian, 64, 68, 73, 75, 78, 79, 90, 95, 99, 105,
    107, 116, 120, 125, 129, 141, 142, 144, 146, 149,
    154, 155, 156, 157, 158, 165, 166, 172, 173, 175,
    190, 193, 194, 197, 198, 206, 216, 237, 242, 321,
    422, 541, 708, 758
Russell, Robert, 675, 704
Russell, Rosalind, 646, 847
Russell, Sol Smith, 60, 102
Russell, Willy, 804
Russo, Dan, 418
Rutherford, Jack, 501
Rutledge, Margaret, 282
Ryan, Robert, 692
Ryan, Roz, 837
Ryan, Sue, 596, 606
Ryley, J. H., 56, 65, 68, 71, 72, 74, 82, 90, 110
Ryley, Phil H., 261, 266, 310
Ryskind, Morrie, 462, 469, 479, 499, 513, 521, 523,
    530, 541, 579, 643, 847, 861

Sabel, Josephine, 484
Sablon, Jean, 574
Saddler, Donald, 779, 834
Sadler, Josie, 116, 226
Sager, Carole Bayer, 763
Sahl, Mort, 670, 791, 809
Saidy, Fred, 668, 683, 877
Sajous, Christina, 884
Sale, Chic, 371, 389, 456

Sallert, Ulla, 702
Salonga, Lea, 799
Salsbury Troubadours, 106
Salsbury, Nat, 40, 73, 82, 102
Salt, Waldo, 653
Saltzberg, Sarah, 855
Sams, Jeremy, 855, 873
Samuels, Arthur, 432
Samuels, Walter G., 503
San Francisco Minstrels, 110
San Juan, Olga, 642
Sanchez, Jamie, 667
Sand, George, 496
Sanderson, Julia, 245, 261, 275, 292, 315, 332, 347,
    362, 375, 386, 406, 415
Sands, Dorothy, 439, 479, 494, 506
Sands, Stark, 884
Sanford, H. L., 309
Sangalli, Rita, 20
Santangelo, Martin, 815
Santiago, Saundra, 811
Santiago-Hudson, Ruben, 877
Santley, Fred, 409, 455, 488
Santley, Joseph, 302, 306, 361, 367, 384, 387, 406,
    433, 461, 472, 478, 486
Santoriello, Jill, 873
Sardou, Victorien, 100, 107, 245
Sargeant, Mary, 560
Sarich, Drew, 860
Sarnoff, Dorothy, 593, 624, 645
Saroyan, William, 783
Sartre, Jean-Paul, 687
Sater, Steven, 865
Saunders, John Monk, 527
Saunders, Lanna, 685
Savage, Henry, 296, 428
Savo, Jimmy, 437, 517, 550, 571, 581, 592
Savoy, Bert, 377, 403, 433, 662, 666, 751
Sawyer, Ivy, 367, 384, 387, 406, 461, 478, 486
Sawyer, Peggy, 835
Saxe, Templar, 219, 232, 234, 266
Saxon, Marie, 460, 470, 498
Sayers, Henry J., 139
Sayre, Loretta Ables, 870
Sayre, Theodore, 56
Scaglione, Josefina, 876
Scanlan, Dick, 838, 885
Scanlan, W. J., 73, 97, 108, 115, 123, 127, 154
Scanlan, Walter, 371, 388, 397
Scardino, Don, 735
Schackleton, Robert, 617
Schaeffer, Eric, 871

Shea, Jere, 807
Shean, Al, 223, 242, 289, 323, 358, 401, 510, 536. *See also* Gallagher and Shean
Sheehan, John J., 208
Sheehan, Lester, 341
Sheik, Duncan, 865
Sheinkin, Rachel, 855
Sheldon, Edward, 356, 475, 625
Sheldon, Sidney, 601, 602, 672
Shelley, Carole, 874
Shelley, Frances, 512
Shelley, Joshua, 621
Shelly, Joshua, 634
Shelton, James, 544, 576, 653
Shelton, Reid, 757
Shelvey, Matt, 567
Shephard, Sam, 733
Sher, Bartlett, 870
Sheridan, John F., 140
Sherman, Allan, 805
Sherman, Charles, 645
Sherman, Hiram, 569, 581, 645
Sherman, Martin, 845–846
Sherman, Richard B., 863–864
Sherman, Richard M., 855
Sherman, Robert B., 855, 863–864
Sherman, Shirley, 464
Sherwood, Robert, 630, 693, 780
Sherwood, Ruth, 847
Shevelove, Burt, 690, 741, 850
Shields, Brooke, 847
Shields, Ren, 214, 232, 260
Shields, William, 1
Shiner, David, 803–804, 812, 823, 832
Shipman, Helen, 437, 455
Shipman, Samuel, 619
Shipp, J. A., 258, 298
Shipps, J. A., 222
Shire, David, 782, 814
Shirley, Florence, 379, 393
Shively, A. J., 884
Shoenfeld, Mark, 851
Short, Hassard, 426, 447, 525, 532, 542, 621
Short, Martin, 804, 823
Shortall, Tim, 884
Showalter, Max, 785
Shriner, Herb, 622
Shubert Brothers (Sam Lee and/or J. J.), 257, 328, 368, 379, 381, 399, 425, 432, 443, 452, 456, 460, 461, 470, 481, 483, 485, 501, 505, 506, 510, 517, 522, 523, 527, 554, 566, 579, 583, 591, 606, 625, 844
Shubert, J. J., 243–244, 373

Shubert, Lee, 243–244, 369, 579
Shubert, Sam S., 212, 215, 243–244
Shulman, Max, 618, 628
Shuman, Mort, 722
Shutta, Ethel, 426, 442, 501, 598, 738
Shy, Gus, 483
Sidney, George, 283
Sieber, Christopher, 820, 839, 852, 854, 875
Siegel, Arthur, 643, 644
Siepi, Cesare, 691, 765
Sillerman, Robert F. X., 868
Sillman, Leonard, 432, 479, 544, 549, 583, 593, 666, 724
Sills, Doug, 820, 838, 845, 875
Silveira, Mary, 523
Silverman, Albert, 550
Silverman, Ryan, 876
Silvers, Louis, 418
Silvers, Nicky, 840
Silvers, Phil, 619, 682–683, 741
Silvers, Sid, 456, 479, 522, 537
Sim, Alastair, 765
Simmons, Bartlett, 495
Simms, Hilda, 696
Simon, Danny and Neil, 657
Simon, John, 783
Simon, Louis, 437, 453, 476
Simon, Louise, 385
Simon, Lucy, 799
Simon, Neil, 692, 712, 725, 776, 804, 813, 885
Simon, Paul, 821
Simon, Simone, 579
Simons, Seymour B., 386
Sims, G. R., 80
Simson, Alfred, 449
Sinatra, Frank, 609, 779, 882
Sinclair, Arthur, 553
Singer, Marion, 58, 123
Singer, Mort, 253, 283
Sirmay, Albert, 513
Sissle, Noble, 410, 444, 538, 588
Skelly, Hal, 384, 398, 401, 451, 539
Skinner, Emily, 819, 826, 832, 848, 853
Skinner, Randy, 835, 869, 874
Sklar, Matthew, 860
Skulnik, Menasha, 737, 752
Slater, Glenn, 868
Slaughter, Walter, 178
Slavin, John, 164, 176, 190, 204, 207, 266, 281, 299, 302
Slayter, Marcus, 533
Slezak, Walter, 522, 536, 553, 568, 653
Sloan, Mike, 668

Streep, Meryl, 757
Streisand, Barbra, 679, 690, 698, 699, 708
Strickland, Josh, 861
Stritch, Elaine, 621, 671, 685, 718, 735, 808, 881
Stroheim, Eric von, 553
Stroman, Susan, 801, 814, 817, 826, 834, 837, 850, 868, 886
Stromberg, John, 168, 192, 194, 198, 216, 227, 321
Strong, D. A., 21
Strouse, Charles, 661, 689, 690, 702, 713, 730, 735, 757, 762, 771, 780, 787, 789, 800, 801, 804, 808, 869, 879
Stryker, Muriel, 434
Stuart, Leslie, 217, 236, 308, 320
Stuart, Ruby, 112
Stuart, Virginia, 298
Sturges, Charles, 109
Sturges, Preston, 640, 648, 683
Sturgis, James A., 127
Styne, Jule, 620, 625, 633, 635, 645, 652, 662, 663, 670, 674, 675, 683, 688, 698, 700, 722, 730, 734, 756, 806
Styx (rock music group), 877, 882
Sullivan, Arthur, 42, 56, 71, 133, 161, 198, 215, 239, 838, 864. *See also* Gilbert and Sullivan
Sullivan, Brian, 615
Sullivan, Ed, 588
Sullivan, Henry, 508
Sullivan, James E., 296
Sullivan, Jo, 651, 661, 683
Sullivan, John Maurice, 460
Sullivan, Lee, 579, 617
Sullivan, Mark, 123
Sullivan, N. J., 203
Sumac, Yma, 640
Summerville, Amelia, 81, 86, 93, 104, 121, 159, 171, 197, 201, 204, 209
Sunday, Billy, 371
Sundgaard, Arnold, 604
Sunshine, Marion, 361
Suppé, Franz von, 51, 59, 67, 88, 109, 113
Suppon, Charles, 794
Suratt, Valeska, 267, 277, 312
Suskind, Milton, 460
Sutcliffe, Steven, 833
Sutherland, Evelyn Greenleaf, 443
Suzuki, Pat, 671
Swados, Elizabeth, 759, 782
Swain, Carrie, 72, 94
Swan, Mark E., 278
Swann, Donald, 670, 675, 717
Swanson, Gloria, 809
Sweatnam, Willis, 144, 190

Sweet, Jeffrey, 802
Swenson, Inga, 696, 703, 724
Swenson, Swen, 774
Swenson, Will, 877
Swerling, Jo, 636
Swift, Kay, 506, 514, 518, 550
Swinburne, Ann, 339
Sydenham, George, 309
Sydney, Ethel, 162
Sykes, Jerome, 140, 176, 181, 190, 196, 200, 219
Sykes, Olive Logan, 54
Sylva, Marguerite, 176, 178, 204, 318
Sylvia and Richard, 562

Tabain, Bal, 283
Tabbert, William, 628, 653
Taber, Richard, 321
Taiz, Lillian, 505
Talbot, Howard, 212, 300, 388
Talbot, Hugh, 56, 183
Talby, Kate, 116, 149
Taliaferro, Edith, 405
Tallman, George L., 229, 259
Talva, Galina, 635
Tam, Jason, 862
Tamara, 567
Tamaris, Helen, 606
Tanguay, Eva, 203, 212, 251, 296, 448
Tankard, Merle, 860
Tannehill, Frank Jr., 83, 114, 182
Tanner, Cora S., 82
Tanner, James T., 177, 181, 347
Tarazona Brothers, 376
Tarbox, Russell, 521
Tarchetti, I. Umazzie., 807
Tarkington, Booth, 396, 463, 641
Tatum, Marianne, 770
Tauber, Richard, 614
Taupin, Bernie, 860
Tavor, Edward M., 279
Taylor, Bert Leston, 205
Taylor, Billy, 502
Taylor, Deems, 303
Taylor, Dwight, 638
Taylor, Eva, 480
Taylor, Jane, 448, 480
Taylor, Laurette, 438, 439, 695
Taylor, Mary, 8
Taylor, Myra Lucretia, 843
Taylor, Raynor, 4
Taylor, Renée, 852
Taylor, Samuel, 688, 843

Watts, Richard, Jr., 505, 578, 591, 758
Wayburn, Ned (Edward), 191, 207, 226, 299, 335, 358, 364
Wayne, Blanche, 278
Wayne, Charles, 214
Wayne, David, 616, 715, 722
Wayne, Paula, 702
Weathersby, Eliza, 44
Weaver, Fritz, 703, 724
Weaver, H. A., Jr., 94
Webb, Clifton, 369, 388, 397, 459, 490, 500, 505, 506, 534, 536, 541, 553, 568
Webb, Edward, 125
Webber, Andrew Lloyd. See Lloyd Webber, Andrew
Webber, Florence, 402
Weber and Fields, 167, 170, 174, 175, 177, 180, 183, 186, 187, 189, 190, 193, 194, 196, 198, 199, 205, 208, 209, 215, 216, 227, 231, 238, 250, 255–256, 286, 321, 352, 353, 404, 444, 504. *See also* Fields, Lew; Weber, Joe
Weber, Joe, 167, 242, 264, 277
Weber, Lisa, 34
Webster, Lizzie, 48
Wedekind, Frank, 865
Weede, Robert, 661, 685, 735
Weeks, Ada Mae, 388, 405
Weeks, Alan, 783
Wehlen, Emmy, 310, 322
Weidman, Charles, 535, 540
Weidman, Jerome, 677, 681, 690, 713
Weidman, John, 753, 791, 814, 826, 839, 848, 878
Weil, Oscar, 113, 171
Weill, Kurt, 539, 540, 557, 570, 584, 599, 606, 616, 624, 631, 649, 665, 716, 739, 742, 754, 757, 768, 769, 835, 859, 866
Weinstock, Jack, 686
Weiss, George, 660
Weissler, Barry and Fran, 846–847, 856
Welch, Ben, 402
Welch, Eilisabeth, 788
Welch, Ken and Mitzie, 857
Welch, Raquel, 773
Welchman, Harry, 461
Welford, Nancy, 430, 478, 492
Welles, Orson, 566, 593, 608, 613
Wellington, Joe, 838
Wells, H. G., 704
Wells, John, 510
Wells, Julia Elizabeth. *See* Andrews, Julie
Wells, Tony, 744
Welsh, Ben, 235
Welsh, Joe, 289
Welsh, Scott, 326, 405

Wendel, Elmarie, 677
Wendling, Pete, 363
Wenrich, Percy, 409, 422, 469, 517
Wentworth, Estelle, 232
Wescott, Marcy, 572, 576
Wessell, Vivian, 369
West, Cheryl L., 816
West, Mae, 322–323, 385, 425, 494, 577
West, Paul, 229, 234, 248, 272
West, Willie, 135
Westenberg, Robert, 792
Westfeldt, Jennifer, 847
Westford, Owen, 172
Westley, John, 280
Weston, Al H., 227
Weston, Maury, 796
Weston, Ruth, 557
Weyman, Stanley, 174
Whalen, Edw. G., 119
Wheat, Laurence, 280
Wheaton, Anna, 324, 348, 370, 399, 408
Whedon, John, 632
Wheelan, Arthur, 160
Wheeler, Bert, 477, 591, 598
Wheeler, Hugh, 744, 763, 843, 857, 872, 881
Wheeler, Van Rensselaer, 168, 189, 208, 212, 242
Wheeler, A. C., 102
Whelan, Alfred C., 167, 179
Whiffen, Thomas, 50, 486
Whipper, Leigh, 516
Whistler, Edna, 342
Whit-Lock, Billy, 12
White, Edwin, 181
White, Frances, 371, 383, 402, 421, 476
White, George, 356–357, 400, 455, 484, 515, 526, 536, 539
White, Jane, 673, 834
White, Lari, 859
White, Maurice, 860
White, Miles, 607
White, Olive, 190
White, R. C., 125
White, Ruth, 482
White, Sammy, 367, 433, 464
White, Stanford, 194, 286
White, T. H., 681
White, Willard, 752
Whitehall, Josephine, 339
Whitehead, Ralph, 481
Whiteman, Paul, 424, 432, 434, 478, 553
Whitemore, Henry, 462
Whiting, Jack, 460, 485, 490, 498, 511, 523, 536, 549, 566, 577, 579, 580, 592, 645, 650

Whiting, Margaret, 816
Whiting, Richard, 363, 389, 390, 391
Whitman, Frank, 311
Whitman, Scott, 862
Whitney, Howard, 241
Whitney, Myron, 58, 62
Whitney, Race, 284
Whittell, Josephine, 400
Whitty, Jeff, 845
Who, The (rock music group), 804
Wickes, Mary, 601
Widman, Anneliese, 670
Wilbur, Richard, 664
Wild, John, 43, 56, 79, 81, 83, 94, 100, 111, 118,
    131, 146
Wild, Jonathan, 99
Wilde, Oscar, 68, 340, 425, 479, 508, 744
Wilder, Alec, 337, 347, 429, 449, 501, 522, 688
Wilder, Billy, 131, 809
Wilder, Gene, 834, 868
Wilder, Thornton, 670, 697
Wildhorn, Frank, 812, 818, 820, 825, 850
Wiley, Shonn, 869
Wilke, Hubert, 81, 103, 105, 111, 113, 118, 120, 140,
    155, 158, 205, 245
Wilkes, Joanna, 845
Wilkfof, Lee, 840
Wilkinson, A., 71
Wilkinson, Colm, 790
Wilkof, Lee, 865
Willard, John, 360
Willett, John, 754
Williams, Andy, 749
Williams, Bert, 169, 170, 195, 199–200, 222, 256,
    258, 298, 302, 312, 314, 327, 343, 349, 364, 372,
    391, 404, 434, 754
Williams, Clarence, 480
Williams, Derek, 552
Williams, Egbert, 222
Williams, Frances, 466, 495, 510, 522, 527, 544,
    575, 598
Williams, Frank, 257
Williams, Fritz, 294, 319
Williams, Gus, 84, 94, 123
Williams, Harry, 250, 264, 268, 291, 296, 348
Williams, Hattie, 247, 261, 288, 325, 336
Williams, Hope, 522, 539
Williams, Hugh, 553
Williams, Jesse, 77
Williams, Shirley Ann, 856
Williams, Tennessee, 656, 657
Williams, Treat, 834
Williams, Vanessa, 839, 885

Williams, W. R., 261
Williams, William, 497, 528
Williamson, Nicol, 754
Willis, Allee, 858
Willis-Hepner, Louise, 181
Wills, Nat M., 180, 226, 249–250, 265
Willson, Meredith, 669, 681, 695, 829
Wilner, Max, 395
Wilson, A. H., 157
Wilson, Dooley, 580, 603
Wilson, Dorothy, 453
Wilson, Edwin, 337, 805
Wilson, Francis, 38, 60, 75, 89, 93, 95, 98, 106, 113,
    118, 124, 132, 138, 145, 152, 168, 178, 180, 184,
    193, 208, 228, 408, 551
Wilson, Hansford, 387
Wilson, John P., 184
Wilson, Knox, 202
Wilson, Lloyd, 129
Wilson, Mary Louise, 863
Wilson, Patricia, 677
Wilson, Patrick, 832, 837
Wilson, Robin, 720
Wilson, Sandy, 735
Wilson, Speedy, 506
Wimperis, Arthur, 347
Winchell, Walter, 516, 569, 593, 742, 837
Winfrey, Oprah, 858
Wing, Ted, 402
Winger, Debra, 843
Wink, Frederick, 117
Winninger, Charles, 379, 394, 411, 457, 474, 485, 489,
    548, 642
Winokur, Marissa Jaret, 840
Winslow, Herbert Hall, 108, 125,
    188, 268, 4553
Winslow, Pamela, 792
Winston, Hattie, 783
Winston, Jeannie, 51, 59, 63, 67, 71
Winter, Edward, 716
Winters, Jill Diane, 873
Winters, Laurence, 650
Winters, Shelley, 734
Winwood, Estelle, 422
Wisdom, Norman, 717
Wise, Clark, 113
Wise, Thomas, 275, 475
Witchie, Kathryn, 335
Withee, Mabel, 408, 462
Withers-Mendes, Elizabeth, 859
Witmark, Isadore, 212, 286, 324, 358, 379, 389
Witmark, Julius, 141
Wittman, Scott, 840

Wodehouse, P. G., 367, 368, 370, 374, 385, 387, 396, 407, 437, 472, 475, 490–491, 492, 524, 547, 568, 571, 599, 836
Woldin, Judd, 746
Wolf, Matt, 860
Wolfe, George C., 813, 828, 849
Wolfe, Jacque, 578
Wolfe, Karin, 747
Wolfe, Thomas, 759
Wolpe, Lenny, 787
Wong, B. D., 852
Wood, Cyrus, 373, 456
Wood, Douglas J., 373
Wood, Mrs. John, 35
Wood, Mrs. Joseph, 15
Wood, Peggy, 373, 394, 420, 438, 541
Wood, William B., 144
Woodruff, Henry, 293
Woods, Carol, 834
Woodward, Edward, 699
Wooley, Mark, 249
Woolf, Benjamin Edward, 22–23, 54, 62, 66, 157
Woolf, Edgar Allan, 260, 380, 384, 400, 409
Woolf, Walter, 394, 399, 402, 410, 426, 430, 470, 502, 539, 553
Woollcott, Alexander, 399, 414, 420, 462
Woolley, Monty, 555, 570
Woolsey, Robert, 409, 477
Woolverton, Linda, 828, 860
Wopat, Tom, 871, 885
Worley, Jo Anne, 796, 865
Worrell Sisters, 26
Worrell, Sophie, 42
Worsham, Lauren, 872
Worth, Billie, 641
Worth, Sidney, 158
Wray, Fay, 527
Wright, Bob, 718
Wright, Charles Randloph, 856
Wright, Doug, 863, 868
Wright, Fred, Jr., 310
Wright, Huntley, 275
Wright, Martha, 619
Wright, Matthew, 884
Wright, Robert, 624, 648, 653, 665, 687, 703, 712, 796
Wright, Samuel E., 782, 820
Wrightson, Earl, 602, 606
Wycherly, William, 563
Wyckoff, Evelyn, 587
Wyler, Gretchen, 655
Wylie, Elinor, 523
Wynn, Bessie, 220, 301, 330

Wynn, Ed, 306, 343, 356, 376, 385, 398–399, 419, 447, 484, 514, 518, 528, 529, 565, 566, 580, 590
Wynn, Keenan, 572, 578
Wynn, Nan, 604

Yarnell, Bruce, 732
Yates, Deborah, 826
Yazbek, David, 832, 849
Yazbek, Tony, 874
Yeamans, Annie, 33, 44, 49, 53, 56, 57, 63, 79, 81, 83, 86, 94, 100, 101, 109, 122, 146, 235, 276
Yeamans, Jennie, 106, 107, 121, 139, 162, 197
Yellen, Jack, 340, 492, 522, 554, 575, 586
Yellen, Sherman, 737, 754
Yeston, Maury, 777, 817, 843
Yohe, May, 201
York, Rachel, 856
Yorke, Alice, 285, 328
Yorke, Gus, 249
Yorkey, Brian, 877
Youmans, Vincent, 409–410, 429, 435, 436, 474, 478, 479, 500, 506, 510, 514, 521, 531, 537
Youmans, William, 846
Young, Bellamy, 818
Young, George, 604
Young, Halfred, 483
Young, Joe, 363, 381, 519
Young, John E., 310, 339, 397
Young, John Lloyd, 858
Young, Ralph, 672
Young, Rida Johnson, 300, 309, 321, 373, 385, 443, 761
Young, Roland, 394
Young, Victor, 540, 635
Young, Waldemar, 284
Young, William, 141
Youngman, Henny, 591
Yvain, Maurice, 414, 435, 496

Zabelle, Flora, 233, 274, 293, 321
Zacharias, Emily, 795
Zaks, Jerry, 813, 845, 848, 852, 865, 880, 882
Zaltzberg, Charlotte, 746
Zamecnik, J. S., 309
Zaremba, Kathryn, 808
Zell and Genée, 91
Zella, Gertrude, 123
Zeller, Carl, 129
Zellnik, David, 886
Zellnik, Joseph, 886
Zender, Marguerite, 397, 509